DICTIONARY OF WOMEN WORLDWIDE:

25,000 Women through the Ages

DICTIONARY OF WOMEN WORLDWIDE:

25,000 Women through the Ages

Volume 3
INDICES

Anne Commire, Editor
Deborah Klezmer, Associate Editor

YORKIN PUBLICATIONS

THOMSON GALE

Detroit • New York • San Francisco • New Haven, Conn. • Waterville, Maine • London • Munich

THOMSON
GALE

Dictionary of Women Worldwide: 25,000 Women through the Ages

Yorkin Publications Staff
Anne Commire, *Editor*
Deborah Klezmer, *Associate Editor*
Eileen O'Pasek, *Editorial Assistant*
Chetna Chopra, Jennifer Jue-Steuck, Bronwyn Law-Viljoen, Catherine Powers, Elizabeth Renaud, Andy Smith, Mary Staub, *Contributors*

Project Editor
Margaret Mazurkiewicz

Editorial Support Services
Emmanuel T. Barrido, Luann Brennan

Rights Acquisitions Management
Jackie Jones, Kim Smilay

Imaging
Lezlie Light, Christine O'Bryan

Composition
Evi Seoud

Product Design
Jennifer Wahi

Manufacturing
Rita Wimberley

For more information, contact
Thomson Gale
27500 Drake Rd.
Farmington Hills, MI 48331-3535
Or you can visit our Internet site at
http://www.gale.com

LIBRARY OF CONGRESS CATALOGING-IN-PUBLICATION DATA

Dictionary of women worldwide : 25,000 women through the ages / Anne Commire, editor ; Deborah Klezmer, associate editor.
p. cm.
Includes bibliographical references.
ISBN 0-7876-7585-7 (set hardcover : alk. paper) –
ISBN 0-7876-7676-4 (vol 1 : alk. paper) –
ISBN 0-7876-7677-2 (vol 2 : alk. paper) –
ISBN 1-4144-1861-2 (vol 3 : alk. paper)
1. Women–Biography–Dictionaries.
I. Commire, Anne. II. Klezmer, Deborah.

CT3202.D53 2006
920.72–dc22 2006008290

British Library Cataloguing-in-Publication Data
A catalogue record for this book is available from the British Library

This title is also available as an e-book
ISBN 0-7876-9394-4
Contact your Thompson Gale sales representative for ordering information.

Printed in the United States of America
10 9 8 7 6 5 4 3 2

CONTENTS

Volume 1

Contents v

Introduction. vii

Genealogical Charts xi

MAIN ENTRIES A-L 1-1176

Volume 2

Contents v

Introduction. vii

MAIN ENTRIES M-Z. 1177-2068

Volume 3

Contents v

Introduction. vii

Era Index 2069–2188

Geographic Index. 2189–2335

Occupational Index 2337–2572

INTRODUCTION

The idea for *Dictionary of Women Worldwide* (*DWW*) began while we were editing the 17-volume set of reference books entitled *Women in World History* (*WIWH*). While frequently turning to dictionaries for help, we were startled by the paucity of women included. In one oft-used biographical dictionary under 5% were women. Other biographical dictionaries had the same or less. It soon became clear that as long as women's entries had to compete with each other for the small percentage of pages set aside for them in traditional dictionaries, these sources were nearly useless to readers looking for a more balanced view of history.

And did those women included in conventional biographical dictionaries get short shrift? Let us approximate the ways. In one recent edition, Abigail Adams was allotted around 25 words, Rosa Bonheur, Empress Theodora, Hypatia, Charlotte Corday, Aspasia, Berthe Morisot, Anna Comnena, between 30 and 40, Mary Cassatt, Dorothea Dix and Anne Boleyn, around 50, Teresa of Avila, 75, and Rosa Luxemburg, 80. As for the men: Halsford Mackinder was allotted around 80 words, Charles Parry, Vincas Kreve and August Kotzebue, over 100, Gebhard Blucher, over 200, Charles I, over 400, Oliver Cromwell, over 600, and Napoleon, over 900. Richard Milhous Nixon, well over 400, was a great deal longer than Indira Gandhi, around 100, Empress Maria Theresa, around 125, Catherine II the Great, around 150, Queen Victoria, around 250, and Elizabeth I, 350.

Dictionary of Women Worldwide is a single source for researching women of any time period and any field of endeavor. It can answer a question quickly, saving users an afternoon slog on the Internet. Since the advent of the Web, conventional wisdom would have us believe that the women in *DWW* can be found quickly and easily in cyberspace. Would that were true; it would certainly have made our job easier. To make the most of the Internet, name variations, correct spellings, dates and personal information are vital. Being multilingual also helps. As well, the Internet has a kind of now-you-see-it-now-you-don't quality. Sites that were there yesterday, loaded with information, vanish like vapor. (Remember those in-depth personal accounts of athletes for the Sydney Olympics? Gone now.) "The average lifespan of a Web page today is 100 days," noted Brewster Kahle of the Internet Archive in San Francisco in 2003. Our goal was to produce a work that would allow the user to verify facts, answer ready reference questions, and begin to research a woman in less time than it takes to log on.

Because of the subject matter, the entries for *DWW* had to be longer than those found in a standard dictionary. For women, the personal is indeed the political. Who the king married is not traditionally required; who the queen married is. In an entry for Eleanor Dulles, listing her brother is essential. In an entry for John Foster Dulles, listing his sister is annoyingly optional. Names of husbands are also important; these are names that the women often went by in public and private life (e.g., Mrs. John Drew). More often than not, after time-consuming sleuthing, we only found a death date for an entrant after uncovering one or all of her married names. We also came across numerous duplicate entries in other biographical dictionaries, women who were listed under two different names, because without personal information it was impossible to see the duplication.

Realizing the influence that such name variations have had in fracturing women's historical identities was one of the greatest lessons we learned while editing *Women in World History.* The genealogical charts we produced for that work are also included in this volume for reasons best explained in the following excerpt from the introduction of *WIWH.* The excerpt addresses two of the most difficult challenges involved in an undertaking like *Dictionary of Women Worldwide:* sorting out and cross-referencing the myriad names given to historical women and naming the nameless.

Throughout the ages, fathers and sons have been scrupulously documented in historical records; for mothers and daughters, birth and death dates are often unknown and approximated. Many cultures do not even count daughters as children. The king's daughter was often treated with the same indifference as the daughter of a tavern owner. But, like certain Soviet leaders who made an art form of airbrushing discredited colleagues from the photographic record, history has occasionally left in a hand or an elbow by mistake. We encountered one historic tome that solemnly noted: "Ariadne was a 5th-century Byzantine empress and daughter of the childless Leo I." Leo had no sons. Records of Eliza Lynch, a major figure in the cultural and political development of Paraguay, scrupulously list her children with dictator Francisco Solano López: "Jan (b. 1855); Enrique (b. 1858); Federico (b. 1860); Carlos (b. 1861); Leopoldo (b. 1862); Miguel (b. 1866); and three daughters, names unknown."

For expediency, historians have eliminated what they perceive to be the secondary storyline. When a woman is known to exist historically, she has often been the casualty of streamlining. The secret to good writing is brevity. "The Holy Roman emperor Otto I arranged a marriage for his son Otto II to a Byzantine empress" is much more readable than "Empress Adelaide of Burgundy and Holy Roman emperor Otto I arranged a marriage for their son Otto II to Theophano, a Byzantine empress."

In the world's text, women have been relegated to common nouns (the queen, the princess, the sister of Charles IV, the duchess of Carlisle) and possessive pronouns ("and his daughter," "and his mother," "and his wife"). In many accounts that chronicle the early years of the 20th century, this phrase appears: "The 1914 assassination of Archduke Franz Ferdinand and his wife led directly to World War I." (Worse, in most reports Archduchess Sophie Chotek's death goes unmentioned; Franz Ferdinand dies alone.) Michael Collins storms the barricade during the Easter rising, and Michael Collins is named; Constance Markievicz and Winifred Carney storm the same barricade, and they are referred to as "two women activists." The often-used phrase "Einstein and his wife" (he had two) evokes an image of a disheveled genius and a drab, faceless woman when, in fact, Mileva Einstein-Marić did the computations for his theory of relativity.

We were determined not to leave a mother, wife, duchess or daughter unturned. Take Ingeborg. Our morning would start simply enough; then we would read: "After his marriage at Amiens, on August 14, 1193, Philip II Augustus, king of France, took a sudden aversion to his 18-year-old Danish bride and sought a divorce." Well, there it was. Obviously, by her marriage to Philip II Augustus, the Danish bride was a queen of France, but who was she? From one source, we learned that she was on good terms with the ensuing French kings; from another, that she lived peacefully, gaining a reputation for kindness. From a third, that she died highly esteemed but, as in the previous sources, nameless, either in 1237 or 1238. Within an hour, we had her name: Ingeborg. By mid-morning, we learned that Ingeborg was the daughter of Waldemar I the Great, king of Denmark. No mother mentioned. Now we had a nameless Danish queen, and a barely named French one.

To give complete and accurate information on Ingeborg, we needed her mother, but while pouring through Palle Lauring's *A History of Denmark,* we read in passing that Philip Augustus "had threatened to cast off his first wife." Another ball in the air. Now we had a nameless Danish queen, one barely named daughter, and an unnamed first wife. By noon, we had uncovered Isabella, first wife of Philip and daughter of Baldwin V, count of Hainault. No mother mentioned. Unfortunately, we had also uncovered a third wife, known only as the mother of Philip Hurepel. Now we had the aforementioned twosome, a newly named first wife, and an unknown third. By mid-afternoon, we gleaned that the mother of Philip Hurepel was named Agnes; she was also the mother of the nonessential Marie. By late afternoon, we had a headache. The results of our day's exploration can be found under the names Agnes of Meran (d. 1201), Ingeborg (c. 1176-1237/38), Isabella of Hainault (1170-1190), and Marie of France (1198-c. 1223). As far as we were able to ascertain, Ingeborg's mother was either Sophie of Russia or Richezza of Poland. No one knows for sure. These were not idle chases. Often the woman off-handedly referred to as the "queen-regent" or "queen mother" turned out to be someone of major import, like Catherine de Medici or Eleanor of Aquitaine. A towering stack of books would eventually straighten out these problems, but the quantity needed will not be found in a small library collection.

The majority of the time, when we did find the woman for whom we were looking, she didn't have one name; she had five or six. Unlike most men whose various names have been sifted down over time to one or two, Holy Roman Empress Agnes of Poitou strolls through the history books as Agnes of Aquitaine, Agnes of Guienne, Agnes of Bavaria, or Agnes of Germany. The dowager empress of China, in her various transliterations, is known as Cixi or Tz'u-hsi, Tse-Hi, Tsu-Hsi, Tze Hsi, Tzu Hsi, Tsze Hsi An, Yehonala, Xiaoqin Xian Huanghou, Xi Taihou, Nala Taihou, Lao Fuoye, or Imperial Concubine Yi. Running down these names easily added years to the project, but we had no choice. Otherwise, the same woman would be scattered throughout our series as Yolande of Brienne on page 29, Jolanta on page 403, and Isabella II of Jerusalem on page 1602.

Name changes that accompany marriage added to the difficulty. Women from outside Russia took on Russian names when they married tsars; one minute they're Sophia Augusta Frederika, princess of Anhalt-Zerbst, the next minute they're Catherine II the Great. East Germany's Christa Rothenburger won the Olympic gold medal in speedskating in 1984. In 1992, she won the silver medal as Christa Luding. In some books, Alice Guy Blache can be found under B; in others, Alice Guy-Blache is found under G. Then there's the longtime bugbear: Mrs. John D. Rockefeller. Which one? Mrs. John D. the 1st, the 3rd, or junior? So often, the dreaded, "the philanthropist, Mrs. Reid," stopped us cold. Is that Mrs. Ogden Mills Reid or Mrs. Whitelaw Reid?

We were not alone in our exasperation. "How are you listing Etta Palm?," queried one of our French historians about an assignment: "As *Palm, Etta Aelders? Palm Aelders, Etta?* or Palm d'Aelders, Etta? My best sources call her Etta Palm d'Aelders, but I'll put her under Palm because she's more widely known to English audiences as Etta Palm. Whew! You'd think there would be more uniformity in these matters."

Researching the lives of Roman women in Republican times was also daunting. Free Roman men had three or four names: the praenomen or given name, the nomen or family name, and sometimes the cognomen or distinguishing name: thus, Gaius Julius Caesar. The women, however, were given only one name, the feminine form of the family name. That is why the daughters of Julius Caesar and his sister are all named Julia. Only Julia. Historians have taken to qualifiers like Julia Minor and Julia Major, but it has not solved the problem. Five of the Julias can be found in *Women in World History* [and *Dictionary of Women Worldwide*], as well as all eight Cleopatras (Cleopatra VII is the famous one), five Arsinoes, seven sisters Bonaparte, seven Beatrice d'Estes, numerous Euphrosynes, Eurydices, Eudocias, Theopanos, Theodoras, Zoes, Faustinas, and Flavias, many Sforzas and Viscontis, and all 35 women named Medici.

Eventually, we picked up speed. With the material we had accumulated, we could begin to answer our own questions more readily and find the women more quickly. Out of necessity, we were using Women in *World History* as a primary reference source, long before it was completed.

We were also using our charts. Women are rarely included on existing genealogies. A Chinese journalist recalled being handed a copy of her family tree which stretched back 3,000 years. "Not one woman was included on the tree," she noted, "not a mother, a sister, a daughter, a wife." For expediency, women have been left off charts which, while following the male line, are difficult enough to read without adding a cadre of women. When women do appear because of their regal status, usually only their sons are noted on the ancestral line below. In one case, a son was included who had died at age six, while his surviving sister, who had become queen of a neighboring country, was missing.

Determined to come up with an easy-to-use cast list, we set about giving one name to each woman on the world stage as she made her entrances and exits throughout the series. In order to do this, we needed to make our own charts, settle on a name for the subject, and add dates if known. Without identifying dates, five Margarets of Austria all look alike. Thought was given to imposing a rational system on the names, but problems outweighed the advantages. One commonly used data base made a stab at it by changing all Catherines to Katherine. Thus, they had Katherine the Great. Whenever possible, we have tried to use the name by which the subject has been most clearly identified in historical contexts. In so doing, the inconsistencies arise. A Spanish historian might call a queen Isabella; an English historian might call the same queen Elizabeth; a French and German historian, Elisabeth; a Russian historian, Elizaveta.

If the women were difficult for us to locate without knowing the exact name used, we knew the task would be even more difficult for our readers. For this reason, we offer many avenues to find the women sought: by the charts, by indexing, by cross-referencing of collective name variants (*Rejcka. Variant of Ryksa.*), by cross-referencing of name variations within the entries (*Gonzaga, Eleanor [1534-1594].* See Eleanora of Austria.), and by cross-referencing of titles (Pembroke, countess of. See Clifford Anne [1590-1676].).

We began to rely so heavily on our genealogical charts—all 85 of them—that we decided to put them in the front of Volume I [in both *WIWH* and *DWW*], alphabetized by country. If a woman is bolded on the chart, she appears in her own entry under the name given. Sometimes her sketch will just be personal data, but as Rutger's Kay Vandergrift notes: "The first step for those who are the 'others' in traditional history is to prove their very existence."

We envisioned a series heavily focused on international women, many of whom were enormously important, even revered in their own countries, though seldom known in the United States. Most books in the U.S. cover only American women; by so doing, they isolate women's accomplishments to the last 200 years and neglect about 3,000 years of women's history. An international emphasis, however, did not prove easy. Since much of the information and many of the primary sources we needed for our research were not available in

English, we asked professors to undertake translations. More than 300 contributors, from over 20 nations, participated in the *WIWH* project [and their contributions are reflected in *DWW*].

Readers will inevitably find omissions and inequities in length. We invite suggestions for inclusion in every area from our readers. We have also spent years checking our facts. Nonetheless, because women have been ignored historically, the record is replete with inaccuracies which have been given widespread circulation. Thus, there will be errors in these volumes. We welcome suggestions and corrections.

Anne Commire
Deborah Klezmer

ERA INDEX

32nd Century BCE
Mer-neith (fl. c. 3100 BCE)
Neithotep (fl. c. 3100 BCE)

31st Century BCE
Inanna (fl. c. 3000 BCE)

27th Century BCE
Hetepheres I (fl. c. 2630 BCE)
Khamerernebty I (fl. c. 2600 BCE)
Khamerernebty II (fl. c. 2600 BCE)

26th Century BCE
Iti (c. 2563–2424 BCE)
Khentkawes (fl. c. 2510 BCE)

25th Century BCE
Iti (c. 2563–2424 BCE)

24th Century BCE
Enheduanna (fl. 2300 BCE)

21st Century BCE
Kerenhappuch (fl. 2000 BCE)
Keziah (fl. 2000 BCE)

18th Century BCE
Dinah (fl. 1730 BCE)
Rebekah (fl. around 18th c. BCE)

17th Century BCE
Sobek-neferu (fl. 1680–1674 BCE)

16th Century BCE
Ahhotep (r. 1570–1546 BCE)
Ahmose-Nefertari (c. 1570–1535 BCE)
Hatshepsut (c. 1515–1468 BCE)
Leah (fl. c. 1500 BCE)
Maachah (fl. 1575 BCE)
Rachel (fl. c. 1500 BCE)
Thermuthis (fl. 1500 BCE)

15th Century BCE
Mutemwia (fl. 1420–1411 BCE)
Tiy (c. 1400–1340 BCE)

14th Century BCE
Miriam the Prophet (fl. c. 13th or 14th c. BCE)
Mutnedjmet (c. 1360–1326 BCE)
Nefertiti (c. 1375–1336 BCE)
Tiy (c. 1400–1340 BCE)

13th Century BCE
Akhat-milki (fl. 1265 BCE)
Cassandra (possibly fl. around 1200 BCE)
Delilah (1200–1000 BCE?)
Miriam the Prophet (fl. c. 13th or 14th c. BCE)
Nefertari (c. 1295–1256 BCE)
Tauseret (c. 1220–1188 BCE)

12th Century BCE
Deborah (fl. 12th c. BCE)
Jael (fl. c. 1125 BCE)
Messene (fl. early 12th c. BCE)
Naomi (fl. 1100 BCE)
Orpah (fl. 1100 BCE)
Rahab (fl. 1100 BCE)
Ruth (fl. 1100 BCE)
Tamar (fl. 1100 BCE)
Tauseret (c. 1220–1188 BCE)

11th Century BCE
Abigail (fl. 1000 BCE)
Abigail (fl. 1010 BCE)
Abishag of Shunem (fl. 1000 BCE)
Abital (fl. 1000 BCE)
Ahinoam (fl. 1020 BCE)
Ahinoam of Jezreel (fl. 1000 BCE)
Bathsheba (fl. 1010–975 BCE)
Delilah (1200–1000 BCE?)
Eglah (fl. 1000 BCE)
Fu Hao (fl. 1040 BCE)
Haggith (fl. 1000 BCE)
Hannah (fl. 11th c. BCE)
Maacah (fl. 1000 BCE)
Tamar (fl. 1000 BCE)

10th Century BCE
Abihail (fl. 970 BCE)
Bashemath (fl. 900 BCE)
Bathsheba (fl. 1010–975 BCE)
Maacah (fl. 931 BCE)
Naamah (fl. 900 BCE)
Sheba, Queen of (fl. 10th c. BCE)

9th Century BCE
Athaliah (r. 842–836 BCE)
Dido (fl. 800 BCE)
Jezebel (d. 884 BCE)
Larentia, Acca (fl. 9th, 8th, or 7th c. BCE)

8th Century BCE
Larentia, Acca (fl. 9th, 8th, or 7th c. BCE)
Sammuramat (fl. 8th c. BCE)

7th Century BCE
Erinna (fl. 7th c. BCE)
Larentia, Acca (fl. 9th, 8th, or 7th c. BCE)
Nehushta (fl. 610 BCE)
Nitocris (c. 660–584 BCE)
Nitocris (fl. 6th c. BCE)
Tanaquil (fl. late 7th–early 6th BCE)

6th Century BCE
Agariste (fl. 515 BCE–490 BCE)
Ambapali (fl. c. 540 BCE)
Arignote (fl. 6th c. BCE)
Artemisia I (c. 520–? BCE)
Atossa (c. 545–c. 470s BCE)
Cassandane (fl. 500s BCE)
Cleobulina of Rhodes (fl. 570 BCE)
Cloelia (c. 508 BCE)
Damo (fl. 6th c. BCE)
Judith (fl. early 6th c. BCE)
Lucretia (?–510 BCE)
Mahapajapati (fl. 570 BCE)
Maya (d. around 563 BCE)
Megalostrata (fl. 6 BCE)
Myia (fl. 6th c. BCE)
Nitocris (c. 660–584 BCE)
Panthea (?–c. 545 BCE)
Pheretima (fl. 6th c. BCE)
Rhodopis (fl. 6th c. BCE)
Sappho (c. 612–c. 557 BCE)
Susanna (fl. 6th c. BCE)
Tamiris (fl. 550–530 BCE)
Tanaquil (fl. late 7th–early 6th BCE)
Telesilla (fl. 6th or 5th c. BCE)
Theano (fl. 6th c. BCE)
Tullia (fl. 535 BCE)
Veturia (late 6th c.–mid–5th c. BCE)
Volumnia (late 6th c.–mid–5th c. BCE)
Yasodhara (fl. 547 BCE)

5th Century BCE
Agariste (fl. 515 BCE–490 BCE)
Aspasia of Miletus (c. 464 BCE–c. 420 BCE)
Aspasia the Younger (fl. 415–370 BCE)
Corinna (fl. 5th or 3rd c. BCE)
Diotima of Mantinea (fl. 400s BCE)
Esther (fl. 475 BCE)
Eurydice (c. 410–350s BCE)
Lais (fl. 425 BCE)
Myrtis (fl. early 5th c. BCE)
Parysatis I (fl. 440–385 BCE)
Phintys of Sparta (fl. c. 400 BCE)
Praxilla (fl. 450 BCE)
Statira I (c. 425–? BCE)
Telesilla (fl. 6th or 5th c. BCE)
Theano II (fl. 5th c. BCE)
Vashti (fl. 5th c. BCE)
Veturia (late 6th c.–mid–5th c. BCE)
Volumnia (late 6th c.–mid–5th c. BCE)
Xanthippe (c. 435 BCE–?)

4th Century BCE
Ada (c. 380–c. 323 BCE)
Aesara of Lucania (fl. 400s–300s BCE)
Agnodice (fl. 4th c. BCE)
Apama (c. 290 BCE–?)
Apama (fl. 324 BCE)
Arete of Cyrene (fl. 4th c. BCE)
Arsinoe (fl. 4th c. BCE)
Arsinoe II Philadelphus (c. 316–270 BCE)
Artemisia II (c. 395–351 BCE)
Aspasia the Younger (fl. 415–370 BCE)
Audata (fl. 358 BCE)
Axiothea of Phlius (fl. 4th c. BCE)
Cleopatra (b. 354 BCE)
Cynisca (fl. 396–392 BCE)
Cynnane (c. 357–322 BCE)
Eurydice (c. 337–317 BCE)
Eurydice (c. 410–350s BCE)
Eurydice (fl. 321 BCE)
Helena (fl. after 333 BCE)
Hipparchia (fl. 300s BCE)
Lais (fl. 385 BCE)
Lasthenia of Mantinea (fl. 4 BCE)
Lysandra (fl. 300 BCE)
Moero (fl. 4th–3rd BCE)
Moschine (fl. 4 BCE)
Nicaea (fl. 300 BCE)
Nicarete of Megara (fl. 300 BCE)
Nicesipolis (d. around 345 BCE)
Nossis of Locri (fl. 300 BCE)
Olympias (c. 371–316 BCE)
Parysatis II (c. 350–323 BCE)
Phila I (fl. c. 320 BCE)
Phila II (c. 300 BCE–?)
Philinna (c. 380–after c. 356 BCE)
Phryne (c. 365–c. 295 BCE)
Ptolemais (c. 315 BCE–?)
Roxana (fl. 350 BCE)
Roxane (c. 345–310 BCE)

Statira II (c. 360–331 BCE)
Statira III (fl. 324 BCE)
Stratonice I (c. 319–254 BCE)
Thais (fl. 331 BCE)
Thalestris (fl. 334 BCE)
Theoxena (fl. 315 BCE)
Thessalonike (c. 345–297 BCE)
Timoclea (c. 370–? BCE)

3rd Century BCE
Anyte of Tegea (fl. 3rd c. BCE)
Apama (fl. 245 BCE)
Arsinoe I (d. 247 BCE)
Arsinoe III (fl. c. 250–210/05 BCE)
Arsinoe II Philadelphus (c. 316–270 BCE)
Berenice I (c. 345 BCE–c. 275 BCE)
Berenice II of Cyrene (c. 273–221 BCE)
Berenice Syra (c. 280–246 BCE)
Bilistiche (fl. 268–264 BCE)
Calypso (fl. c. 200 BCE)
Claudia Quinta (fl. 220–206 BCE)
Cleopatra I (c. 210–176 BCE)
Hedyle (fl. 3rd century BCE)
Irene (fl. 200 BCE?)
Keturah (fl. 3rd, 2nd, or 1st c. BCE)
Laodice I (c. 285–c. 236 BCE)
Laodice II (fl. 250 BCE)
Laodice III (fl. 200 BCE)
Leontium (fl. 300–250 BCE)
Melissa (fl. around 3 BCE)
Moero (fl. 4th–3rd BCE)
Perictione (fl. 400 BCE)
Sarah (fl. 3rd, 2nd, or 1st c. BCE)
Sophonisba (c. 225–203 BCE)
Stratonice I (c. 319–254 BCE)
Stratonice II (c. 285–228 BCE)
Stratonice III (fl. 250 BCE)
Teuta (c. 260–after 228 BCE)
Timarete (fl. 3rd c. BCE)

2nd Century BCE
Aemilia (fl. 195 BCE)
Aurelia (c. 120 BCE–54 BCE)
Cleopatra Berenice III (c. 115–80 BCE)
Cleopatra I (c. 210–176 BCE)
Cleopatra II (c. 183–116 BCE)
Cleopatra III (c. 155–101 BCE)
Cleopatra IV (c. 135–112 BCE)
Cleopatra Selene (c. 130–69 BCE)
Cleopatra Thea (c. 165–121 BCE)
Cleopatra Tryphaena (d. after 112 BCE)
Cornelia (c. 100–68 BCE)
Cornelia (c. 195–c. 115 BCE)
Hagar (fl. 3rd, 2nd, or 1st c. BCE)
Julia Minor (c. 100–51 BCE)
Keturah (fl. 3rd, 2nd, or 1st c. BCE)
Laelia (fl. 2nd c. BCE)
Laodice (fl. 129 BCE)
Livia (fl. 100 BCE)
Lü Hou (r. 195–180 BCE)
Marcia (fl. 100 BCE)
Merab (fl. 1000 BCE)
Michal (fl. 1000 BCE)
Parthenis (fl. 2nd c. BCE)
Rhodogune (fl. 2nd c. BCE)
Sarah (fl. 3rd, 2nd, or 1st c. BCE)
Sempronia (c. 168 BCE–?)
Sempronia (fl. 2nd–1st c. BCE)
Servilia I (fl. 100 BCE)
Servilia II (c. 100–after 42 BCE)

1st Century BCE
Agrippina the Elder (c. 14 BCE–33 CE)
Alexandra (d. 27 BCE)
Alexandra (r. 76–67 BCE)
Amanishakhete (r. c. 41–12 BCE)
Antistia (fl. 80 BCE)
Antonia Major (39 BCE–?)
Antonia Minor (36 BCE–37 CE)
Anula (r. 47–42 BCE)
Arsinoe IV (d. 41 BCE)
Atia the Elder (c. 80 BCE–?)
Ban Jieyu (c. 48–c. 6 BCE)
Berenice (c. 35 BCE–?)
Berenice IV (fl. 79–55 BCE)
Calpurnia (c. 70 BCE–?)
Cleopatra (fl. 1st c. BCE)
Cleopatra Berenice III (c. 115–80 BCE)
Cleopatra Selene (c. 130–69 BCE)
Cleopatra VII (69–30 BCE)
Cleopatra V Selene (c. 40 BCE–?)
Cleopatra V Tryphaena (c. 95–c. 57 BCE)
Clodia (c. 60 BCE–?)
Clodia (c. 94–post 45 BCE)
Cornelia (c. 100–68 BCE)
Cornelia (c. 75–after 48 BCE)
Cornelia (fl. 1st c. BCE)
Cypros (fl. 28 CE)
Cyprus (c. 90 BCE–?)
Domitia Lepida (c. 19 BCE–?)
Fausta, Cornelia (b. 88 BCE)
Fulvia (c. 85/80–40 BCE)
Hagar (fl. 3rd, 2nd, or 1st c. BCE)
Herodias (c. 14 BCE–after 40 CE)
Hortensia (fl. 1st c. BCE)
Iaia (fl. c. 100 BCE)
Julia (c. 18 BCE–28 CE)
Julia (39 BCE–14 CE)
Julia (d. 54 BCE)
Julia (d. 68 BCE)
Julia Maior (fl. 1st. c. BCE)
Julia Minor (c. 100–51 BCE)
Junia I (fl. 1st c. BCE)
Junia II (fl. 1st c. BCE)
Junia III (fl. 1st c. BCE)
Keturah (fl. 3rd, 2nd, or 1st c. BCE)
Lais (fl. 1st c. BCE)
Livia Drusilla (58 BCE–29 CE)
Livilla (c. 14/11 BCE–c. 31 CE)
Malthace (fl. 40 BCE)
Marcella the Elder (fl. 25 BCE)
Marcella the Younger (fl. 20 BCE)
Mariamne the Hasmonian (c. 60–c. 29 BCE)
Mary the Virgin (20 BCE–40 CE)
Mucia (fl. 80 BCE)
Octavia (c. 69–11)
Pompeia (fl. 60 BCE)
Pompeia (c. 87 BCE–?)
Pomponia (fl. 25 BCE)
Portia (c. 70–43 BCE)
Portia (fl. 80 BCE)
Salome (c. 65 BCE–10 CE)
Sarah (fl. 3rd, 2nd, or 1st c. BCE)
Scribonia (c. 75 BCE–after 16 CE)
Sempronia (fl. 2nd–1st c. BCE)
Sulpicia I (fl. 1st c. BCE)
Terentia (fl. 69–45 BCE)
Tullia (c. 79–45 BCE)
Wang Zhaojun (52 BCE–18 CE)

1st Century
Acte (fl. 55–69)
Agrippina the Elder (c. 14 BCE–33 CE)
Agrippina the Younger (15–59)
Anastasia (fl. 54–68)
Anne (fl. 1st c.)
Antonia Major (39 BCE–?)
Arria Major (d. 42)
Ban Zhao (c. 45–c. 120)
Basilissa (fl. 54–68)
Berenice (28–after 80)
Boudica (26/30–60)
Cartimandua (fl. 43–69)
Claudia (fl. 26–36)
Claudia Antonia (27–66
Domitia Longina (fl. 80s)
Domitia Paulina I (fl. 76)
Domitia Paulina II (fl. 80–100)
Dorcas (fl. 37)
Drusilla (15–38)
Drusilla (c. 37–c. 41 CE)
Drusilla (38–79 CE)
Elizabeth (fl. 1st c.)
Eponina (40–78)
Fannia (fl. mid–1st c.)
Flavia Domitilla (c. 60–96)
Flavia Domitilla (fl. 39)
Flavia Domitilla (fl. 60)
Julia (39 BCE–14 CE)
Julia (c. 18 BCE–28 CE)
Julia Livilla (c. 16 –after 38)
Junia Claudilla (fl. 32)
Justina (d. 64)
Livia Orestilla (fl. 32)
Livilla (c. 14/11 BCE–c. 31 CE)
Locusta (fl. 54)
Lollia Paulina (fl. 38–39)
Lydia (fl. 53)
Mariamne (fl. 1st c.)
Martha and Mary of Bethany (fl. early 1st c.)
Mary Magdalene (fl. early 1st c.)
Mary the Jewess (fl. 1st, 2nd or 3rd c.)
Mary the Virgin (20 BCE–40 CE)
Messalina, Statilia (fl. 66–68)
Messalina, Valeria (c. 23–48)
Milonia Caesonia (d. 41)
Octavia (39–62 CE)
Olympias (fl. 1st c.)
Paetina (fl. 30)
Pamphila (fl. 1st c.)
Phoebe of Cenchreae (fl. 1st c.)
Plautia Urgulanilla (fl. 25)
Poppaea Sabina (d. 47)
Poppaea Sabina (d. 65 CE)
Priscilla (fl. 1st c.)
Rupilia Faustina (fl. 90)
Sabina (88–136)
Salome II (fl. 1st c.)
Salome III (c. 15 –?)
Sapphira (fl. 1st c.)
Scholastica (c. 480–543)
Sivali (d. 93)
Sulpicia II (fl. 1st c.)
Thecla (fl. 1st c. CE)
Thusnelda (fl. 1st c. CE)
Trung Sisters (d. 43 CE)
Ulpia Marciana (fl. 98–117 CE)
Veronica (fl. 1st c.?)
Vespasia Polla (fl. 50)
Vipsania Agrippina (?–20)

2nd Century
Aurelia Fadilla (d. before 138)
Balbilla (fl. 130)
Ban Zhao (c. 45–c. 120)
Beruriah (fl. 2nd c.)
Blandina (d. 177)
Bruttia Crispina (d. 185)
Cai Yan (c. 162–239)
Cecilia (c. 154–c. 207)
Cornificia (b. 160)
Deng (r. 105–121)
Domitia Faustina (b. 147)
Fadilla (b. 159)
Faustina I (c. 90–141)
Faustina II (130–175)
Faustina III (b. 151)
Felicitas (d. 203)
Felicitas of Rome (d. 162?)
Julia Domna (c. 170–217)
Julia Maesa (c. 170–224)
Julia Mamaea (c. 190–235)
Lucilla (b. 150)
Marcia (fl. 177–192)
Mary the Jewess (fl. 1st, 2nd or 3rd c.)
Matidia I (d. 119)
Matidia II (fl. 110)
Perpetua (181–203)
Philaenis (fl. 2nd c.)
Plotina (d. 122)
Sabina (88–136)
Sophia (fl. early 2nd c.)
Timoxena (fl. 2nd c.)
Vibia Aurelia Sabina (b. 166)

3rd Century
Agatha (d. 251)
Anastasia (d. 304)
Barbara (fl. 3rd c.)
Ba Trieu (225–248)
Cai Yan (c. 162–239)
Cecilia (c. 154–c. 207)
Columba of Sens (d. 274?)
Constantia (c. 293–?)
Eugenia (d. around 258)

Eulalia (290–304)
Eusebia of Bergamo (fl. 3rd c.)
Eutropia (fl. 270–300)
Faith (290–303)
Felicitas (d. 203)
Helena (c. 255–329)
Himiko (fl. 3rd c.)
Jingū (c. 201–269)
Julia Domna (c. 170–217)
Julia Maesa (c. 170–224)
Julia Mamaea (c. 190–235)
Julia Paula (fl. 220)
Julia Soaemias (d. 222)
Margaret of Antioch (c. 255–c. 275)
Mary the Jewess (fl. 1st, 2nd or 3rd c.)
Minervina (fl. 290–307)
Perpetua (181–203)
Regina (d. around 251)
Salonina (r. 254–268)
Theodora (fl. 3rd c.)
Ursula (fl. 3rd or 5th c.)
Victoria (d. around 253)
Wei Shuo (272–349)
Zenobia (r. 267–272)

4th Century

Aemilia Hilaria (fl. 350)
Afra (fl. c. 304)
Agape of Thessalonica (d. 304)
Agnes (d. possibly c. 304)
Albia Domnica (fl. 4th c.)
Anastasia (d. 304)
Anthusa (c. 324/334–?)
Asclepignia (c. 375–?)
Bibiana (d. 363)
Catherine of Alexandria (?–305)
Charito (fl. 300s)
Chionia (d. 304)
Constantina (c. 321–c. 354)
Egeria (fl. 4th c.)
Emmelia of Cappadocia (fl. 300s)
Eulalia (290–304)
Eusebia of Macedonia (fl. 300)
Eustochium (c. 368–c. 419)
Eutropia (fl. 270–300)
Eutropia (fl. 330s)
Fabiola (d. 399)
Faith (290–303)
Fausta (d. 324)
Faustina of Antioch (fl. 300s)
Flaccilla (c. 355–386)
Galla (fl. 320)
Galla (c. 365–394)
Helena (c. 320–?)
Hilaria (fl. 304)
Hypatia (c. 375–415)
Irene (d. 304)
Irene of Spain (fl. 300s)
Juliana of Nicomedia (d. about 305)
Julitta of Caesarea (d. about 305)
Justina (d. 304)
Justina (fl. 350–370)
Lea (d. about 383)
Leocadia (d. about 303)
Lucy (d. 303)
Macrina (327–379)
Marcella of Rome (c. 325–410)
Marcellina (fl. 4th c.)
Mavia (c. 350–c. 430)
Melania the Elder (c. 350–c. 410)
Melania the Younger (c. 385–439)
Monica (331–387)
Nonna (c. 305–c. 374)
Olympias (c. 365–408)
Paula (347–404)
Pharandzem (c. 320–c. 364)
Proba (fl. 4th c.)
Pulcheria (c. 376–385)
Severa, Marina (fl. 4th c.)
Sosipatra (fl. 4th c.)
Su Hui (fl. 4th c.)
Theodora (d. 304)
Wei Shuo (272–349)

5th Century

Amalaberga (fl. 400s)
Ariadne (fl. 457–515)
Audofleda (c. 470–?)
Basine (fl. 428)
Basine (fl. 465)
Bridget (c. 453–c. 524)
Clotilda (470–545)
Eudocia (c. 400–460)
Eudocia of Byzantium (d. 404)
Euphrasia of Constantinople (d. around 412)
Eustochium (c. 368–c. 419)
Flaccilla (d. 431)
Geneviève (c. 422–512)
Guinevere (d. 470 or 542)
Honoria (c. 420–?)
Hua Mu-Lan (fl. 5th c.)
Ildico (fl. 453)
Licinia Eudoxia (422–before 490)
Mary of Egypt (d. 430)
Mavia (c. 350–c. 430)
Melania the Elder (c. 350–c. 410)
Melania the Younger (c. 385–439)
Olympias (c. 365–408)
Paula (347–404)
Placidia (fl. 440s)
Placidia, Galla (c. 390–450)
Pulcheria (c. 398–453)
Serena (d. 410)
Ursula (fl. 3rd or 5th c.)
Verina (fl. 437–483)
Vigilantia (c. 485–?)

6th Century

Amalasuntha (c. 498–535)
Amina (died c. 576)
Anastasia (fl. 500s)
Anastasia the Patrician (d. 567)
Arabia (fl. 570)
Aregunde (fl. 6th c.)
Audovera (d. 580)
Bertha of Avenay (fl. 6th c.)
Brunhilda (c. 533–613)
Chrodielde (fl. 590)
Chunsina (fl. 6th c.)
Clotilda (470–545)
Clotsinda (fl. 6th c.)
Comitona (fl. 500s)
Constantina (fl. 582–602)
Deoteria (fl. 535)
Dode (b. 586)
Faileuba (fl. 586–587)
Fredegund (c. 547–597)
Galswintha (d. around 568)
Geneviève (c. 422–512)
Georgia (d. 6th c.)
Guinevere (d. 470 or 542)
Guntheuca (fl. 525)
Helaria (fl. 6th c.)
Ingoberge (519–589)
Ingunde (fl. 517)
Ino-Anastasia (fl. 575–582)
Ita of Ireland (d. 570)
Khadijah (c. 555–619)
Khansa (c. 575–c. 645)
Khirniq (fl. late 6th c.)
Lupicinia-Euphemia (d. 523)
Modthryth (fl. 520)
Modwenna (d. 518)
Monegunde (fl. 6th c.)
Ninnoc (fl. 6th c.)
Radegund of Poitiers (518–587)
Riguntha (fl. 580s)
Sophia (c. 525–after 600)
Suavegotta (fl. 504)
Suiko (554–628)
Theodelinda (568–628)
Theodora (c. 500–548)
Vigilantia (c. 485–?)
Vuldetrade (fl. 550)
Vultrogotha (fl. 558)
Wuldetrada of the Lombards (fl. 6th c.)

7th Century

A'ishah bint Abi Bakr (c. 613–678)
A'ishah bint Talhah (fl. 7th c.)
Aldegund (c. 630–684)
Aldetrude (fl. 7th c)
Alphaida (c. 654–c. 714)
Amalia (d. 690)
Anastasia (fl. 600s)
Anstrude of Laon (fl. 7th c.)
Austrebertha (635–704)
Balthild (c. 630–c. 680)
Begga (613–698)
Begga of Egremont (fl. 7th c.)
Beretrude (d. 620)
Bertha of Kent (c. 565–c. 616)
Bertille (d. 705/713)
Bilchilde (d. 675)
Cendrith (fl. 680s)
Clotilde (d. 691)
Constantina (fl. 582–602)
Cuneswith (fl. 7th c.)
Cyneburg of Gloucester (c. 660–710)
Cyneburg of Mercia (fl. 655)
Cynewise (fl. 7th c.)
Dympna (fl. 650)
Eanfleda (626–?)
Ebba (c. 610–c. 683)
Edburga of Bicester (d. 650)
Edith of Aylesbury (fl. 7th c.)
Elfthrith (fl. 7th c.)
Elthelthrith (630–679)
Emma (fl. 600s)
Engyth (fl. 7th c.)
Ermenburga (fl. late 600s)
Ethelberga of Northumbria (d. 647)
Ethelburga (d. 665)
Ethelburga (d. 676?)
Fabia-Eudocia (fl. 600s)
Fara (d. 667)
Fatimah (605/11–632/33)
Fausta (fl. 600s)
Florentina (d. 7th c.)
Folcheid (fl. 7th c.)
Gemmei (c. 661–721)
Genshō (680–748)
Gertrude of Nivelles (626–659)
Gregoria-Anastasia (fl. 640s)
Hafsah (fl. 7th c.)
Hereswitha (d. around 690)
Hilda of Whitby (614–680)
Himnechildis (r. 662–675)
Hind bint 'Utba (d. 610)
Ida of Nivelles (597–652)
Irene of Santarem (fl. 7th c.)
Jitō (645–702)
Juwairiyah (fl. 627)
Kahina (r. 695–703)
Khadijah (c. 555–619)
Khansa (c. 575–c. 645)
Kōgyoku-Saimei (594–661)
Lathgertha (b. around 665)
Layla al-Akhyaliyya (fl. 650–660)
Leontia (fl. 602–610)
Liadan (fl. 7th c.)
Libussa (c. 680–738)
Madelberte (fl. 7th c.)
Maimunah bint al-Harith (fl. 7th c.)
Martina (fl. 600s)
Maryam the Egyptian (fl. 7th c.)
Matilda (fl. 680s)
Mildred (d. 700?)
Modesta of Trier (d. about 680)
Nanthilde (610–642)
Odilia (fl. 620)
Orthryth of Mercia (fl. 7th c.)
Osith (died c. 700)
Ostrith (d. 697)
Plectrudis (fl. 665–717)
Ragnetrude (fl. 630)
'Raihanah bint Zaid (fl. 7th c.)
Ramlah (fl. 7th c.)
Saewara (fl. 630)
Safiyah (fl. 7th c.)
Salaberga of Laon (d. around 665)
Sawdah bint Zama (fl. 7th c.)
Sexburga (d. around 699)
Sigolena of Albi (fl. 7th c.)
Sophia (c. 525–after 600)
Tanaquille (d. 696)

Theodelinda (568–628)
Umm Ruman (fl. 7th c.)
Umm Salamah (fl. 7th c.)
Wandru (c. 628–688)
Wencheng (c. 620–680)
Withburga (fl. 7th c.)
Wulfetrud of Nivelles (fl. 7th c.)
Wu Zetian (624–705)
Xoc, Lady (c. 660–c. 720)
Zaynab bint Jahsh (c. 590–c. 640)

8th Century
Abassa (fl. 8th c.)
Adela (d. 735)
Alphaida (c. 654–c. 714)
Austrebertha (635–704)
Azza al-Maila (fl. c. 707)
Basilissa (d. 780)
Bertha (719–783)
Bertha (779–after 823)
Bertha of Blangy (d. 725)
Bertha of Toulouse (fl. late 700s)
Berthgyth (fl. 8th c.)
Bertille (d. 705/713)
Chiltrud (fl. 700s)
Chrotrud (d. 724)
Cyneburg of Gloucester (c. 660–710)
Cynethryth (fl. 736–796)
Cyniburg (fl. 8th c.)
Dananir al Barmakiyya (fl. late 8th c.)
Desiderata (d. 773)
Eadburgh (c. 773–after 802)
Edburga (d. 751)
Edonne (fl. 8th c.)
Elflaed (d. 714)
Ermengarde (c. 778–818)
Ermenilda (d. around 700)
Ethelburg (fl. 722)
Eudocia (fl. 700s)
Fastrada (d. 794)
Frideswide (d. 735?)
Gemmei (c. 661–721)
Geneviève de Brabant (fl. 8th c.)
Genshō (680–748)
Gerberge of the Lombards (fl. mid–700s)
Gisela (c. 753–807)
Gisela of Chelles (781–814)
Gudula of Brussels (d. 712?)
Guntrud of Bavaria (fl. 715)
Habbaba (d. 724)
Herlind of Maasryck (fl. 8th c.)
Hilda of Hartlepool (fl. 8th c.)
Hildegarde of Swabia (c. 757–783)
Hildeletha (fl. 700)
Hiltrude of Liessies (d. late 700s)
Himiltrude (fl. 700s)
Hygeburg (fl. 8th c.)
Irene (fl. 700s)
Irene of Athens (c. 752–803)
Irene of the Khazars (d. 750?)
Irmina (d. 716)
Jitō (645–702)
Khaizaran (d. 790)
Kōken-Shōtoku (718–770)
Libussa (c. 680–738)
Lioba (700–779)
Maria (fl. 700s)
Maria of Amnia (fl. 782)
Martel, Adeloga (fl. 775)
Milburg (d. 722?)
Mildgyth (fl. early 700s)
Mildred (d. 700?)
Mutayyam al-Hashimiyya (fl. 8th c.)
Plectrudis (fl. 665–717)
Rabi'a (c. 714–801)
Regintrud (fl. 8th c.)
Reinhild (fl. 8th c.)
Rotrude (c. 778–after 839)
Sunnichild (d. 741)
Thecla (c. 775–c. 823)
Theoctista (c. 740–c. 802)
Theodora of the Khazars (fl. 700s)
Theodota (c. 775–early 800s)
Theodrada (b. between 783 and 794)
Theudesinda (fl. 700)
Valasca (fl. 738)
Walpurgis (c. 710–777)
Wanda of Poland (fl. 730)
Werburga (d. 700?)
Wu Zetian (624–705)
Xoc, Lady (c. 660–c. 720)
Xue Tao (c. 760–c. 832)

9th Century
Adelaide (c. 794–after 852)
Adelaide (fl. 860s)
Adelaide Judith (fl. 879)
Anan (fl. 9th c.)
Anastasia (fl. 800s)
Anastasia (d. about 860)
Ansgard (fl. 863)
Asa (c. 800–c. 850)
Barca-Theodosia (fl. 800s)
Beatrice of Vermandois (880–931)
Bertha (779–after 823)
Bertha of Avenay (c. 830–c. 852)
Bid'a (856–915)
Columba of Cordova (d. 853)
Cunegunde (fl. 800s)
Dhuoda of Septimania (fl. 820–843)
Eadburgh (c. 773–after 802)
Eadburh (fl. 9th century)
Edith (d. 871)
Elfwyn (c. 882–?)
Elswitha (d. 902)
Emma of Bavaria (d. 876)
Engelberga (c. 840–890)
Engelberga of Aquitaine (877–917)
Ermengarde (c. 778–818)
Ermengarde of Provence (fl. 876)
Ermentrude (d. 869)
Etheldreda (d. around 840)
Ethelflaed (869–918)
Ethelgeofu (d. around 896)
Ethelswyth (c. 843–889)
Eudocia Decapolita (fl. 800s)
Eudocia Ingerina (fl. 800s)
Euphrosyne (c. 790–840)
Fadl (d. around 870)
Farida (c. 830–?)
Fergusa (fl. 800s)
Flora of Cordova (d. 851)
Gerberga (d. 896)
Gisela (c. 753–807)
Gisela (c. 819–c. 874)
Gisela of Chelles (781–814)
Gormflaith (c. 870–925)
Hathumoda (d. 874)
Hildegard (c. 802–841)
Hildegarde of Bavaria (c. 840–?)
Hiltrude (fl. 800s)
Inan (fl. c. 800)
Irene of Athens (c. 752–803)
Irfan (fl. mid–800s)
Irmengard (c. 800–851)
Irmentrude (d. 820)
Ise (877–940)
Jehosheba (fl. 9th c.)
Joan (d. 858)
Judith of Bavaria (802–843)
Kassia (c. 800/810–before 867)
Litwinde (fl. 850)
Liutgard (d. 885)
Luitgarde (d. 800)
Mahbuba (fl. 9th c.)
Maria of Cordova (d. 851)
Maria of Macedonia (d. around 864)
Martel, Judith (c. 844–?)
Matilda of Saxony (c. 892–968)
Milh al-Attara (fl. 840s)
Oda of Bavaria (fl. 890s)
Olga (c. 890–969)
Ono no Komachi (c. 830–?)
Onshi (872–907)
Oraib (797–890)
Osburga (?–c. 855)
Poppa of Normandy (fl. 880)
Prokopia (fl. 800s)
Pulcheria (fl. 800s)
Rabi'a (c. 714–801)
Redburga (fl. 825)
Regina (fl. 9th c.)
Richilde (d. 894)
Ringart (fl. 822–825)
Rothild (c. 871–c. 928)
Rothilde (fl. 840)
Rotrud (800–841)
Rotrude (c. 778–after 839)
Shariyya (b. around 815)
Tetberga (fl. 9th c.)
Thecla (c. 775–c. 823)
Thecla (c. 823–c. 870)
Theoctista (c. 740–c. 802)
Theodorade (fl. 9th c.)
Theodora of Rome (c. 875–c. 925)
Theodora the Blessed (c. 810–c. 860)
Theodota (c. 775–early 800s)
Theodrada (b. between 783 and 794)
Theophano (c. 866–c. 897)
Theophano of Athens (fl. 800s)
Thyra (d. 940)
Ubaida (fl. c. 830)
Ulayya (fl. 800s)
Waldrada (fl. 9th c.)
Wulfthryth (fl. 860s)
Xue Tao (c. 760–c. 832)
Zoë Zautzina (c. 870–c. 899)
Zubeida (d. 831)

10th Century
Adela (fl. 900s)
Adelaide of Anjou (fl. 10th c.)
Adelaide of Burgundy (931–999)
Adelaide of Poitou (c. 950–c. 1004)
Adelaide of Quedlinburg (977–1045)
Adele of Normandy (c. 917–c. 962)
Agnes of Aquitaine (c. 995–1068)
Anna of Byzantium (963–1011)
Anna of Byzantium (fl. 901)
Arsinde (fl. 934–957)
Astrid of the Obotrites (c. 979–?)
Beatrice of Vermandois (880–931)
Bertha-Eudocia the Frank (fl. 900s)
Bertha of Swabia (fl. 900s)
Christine of Gandersheim (d. 919)
Constance of Arles (c. 980–1032)
Cunigunde of France (c. 900–?)
Cunigunde of Swabia (fl. 900s)
Dobravy of Bohemia (d. 977)
Drahomira of Bohemia (d. after 932)
Ecgwynn (d. around 901)
Edburga (d. 960)
Edflaed (c. 900–?)
Edgifu (902–951)
Edgifu (c. 917–?)
Edgifu (d. 968)
Edgitha (c. 912–946)
Edhild (d. 946)
Edith (d. 937)
Edith (c. 961–984)
Edla (fl. 900s)
Elfgifu (c. 914–?)
Elfgifu (d. 944)
Elfgifu (d. 959)
Elfgifu (c. 963–1002)
Elflaed (c. 905–c. 963)
Elflaed (d. 920)
Elfthrith (d. 929)
Elswitha (d. 902)
Emma of Burgundy (d. 939)
Emma of Italy (948–after 990)
Emma of Paris (d. 968)
Emnilde (fl. 986)
Engelberga of Aquitaine (877–917)
Ethelflaed (869–918)
Ethelflaed (d. 962)
Ethelflaed (d. after 975)
Ethelflaeda (c. 963–c. 1016)
Ethelflaeda (fl. 900s)
Eudocia (b. 978)
Eudocia Baiane (d. 902)
Frederona (d. 917)
Gerberga (r. 959–1001)
Gerberga of Saxony (c. 910–969)
Gerloc (d. 963)
Geyra (fl. 980s)
Gisela Martel (d. 919)
Gisela of Bavaria (c. 975–1033)

Gorka (fl. 920s)
Gormflaith (c. 870–925)
Gormflaith of Ireland (fl. 980–1015)
Gyrid (fl. 950s)
Hatheburg (fl. 906)
Hedwig (d. 903)
Hedwig (c. 915–965)
Hedwig of Eberhard (930–992)
Helena Lekapena (c. 920–961)
Helena of Alypia (fl. 980s)
Hemma of Bohemia (c. 930–c. 1005)
Hetha (fl. 10th c.)
Hrotsvitha of Gandersheim (c. 935–1001)
Ida of Swabia (d. 986)
Irene of Constantinople (d. around 921)
Izumi Shikibu (c. 975–c. 1027)
Judith (fl. 10th c.)
Judith of Bavaria (c. 925–987)
Judith of Fiuli (fl. 910–925)
Judith of Hungary (fl. late 900s)
Laura (fl. 10th c.)
Leodegundia (fl. 10th c.)
Liutgard of Saxony (d. 953)
Ludmila (859–920)
Marozia Crescentii (885–938)
Matilda Martel (943–c. 982)
Matilda of Essen (949–1011)
Matilda of Quedlinburg (c. 953–999)
Matilda of Saxony (c. 892–968)
Matilda of Saxony (978–1025)
Michitsuna no haha (c. 936–995)
Murasaki Shikibu (c. 973–c. 1015)
Oda (806–913)
Oda of Germany and North Marck (fl. 900s)
Olga (c. 890–969)
Predeslava of Hungary (fl. 960)
Pribyslava (fl. 10th c.)
Richilde of Autun (d. around 910)
Rinshi (fl. 900s)
Rothild (c. 871–c. 928)
Sadako (r. 976–1001)
Sarolta (fl. 900s)
Sei Shōnagon (c. 965–?)
Shoshi (fl. 990–1010)
Sigrid the Haughty (d. before 1013)
Sophia of Gandersheim (c. 975–1039)
Theodora (fl. early 900s)
Theodora (fl. late 900s)
Theodora of Rome (c. 875–c. 925)
Theodora the Younger (c. 900–c. 950)
Theophano (c. 940–?)
Thora (fl. 900s)
Thyra (d. 940)
Thyra of Denmark (d. 1000)
Uma no Naishi (fl. 10th c.)
Viborada (d. 925)
Wulfthryth (c. 945–1000)
Zoë Carbopsina (c. 890–920)
Zoë Porphyrogenita (980–1050)

11th Century

Adela Capet (c. 1010–1079)
Adelaide of Hungary (d. 1062)
Adelaide of Kiev (c. 1070–1109)
Adelaide of Maurienne (1092–1154)
Adelaide of Poitou (c. 950–c. 1004)
Adelaide of Quedlinburg (977–1045)
Adelaide of Rheinfelden (c. 1065–?)
Adela of Blois (1062–c. 1137)
Adele (r. 1017–1031)
Adelicia (1029–1090)
Adeliza (d. 1066?)
Agatha (fl. 1060)
Agatha of Hungary (c. 1025–?)
Agnes of Aquitaine (c. 995–1068)
Agnes of Poitou (1024–1077)
Agnes of Poitou (1052–1078)
Akazome Emon (d. 1027)
Alice of Normandy (fl. 1017–1037)
Anastasia of Russia (c. 1023–after 1074)
Anna of Byzantium (963–1011)
Anne of Kiev (1024–1066)
A Nong (c. 1005–1055)
Arlette (fl. c. 1010)
Asmā (c. 1028–1084)
Astrid of the Obotrites (c. 979–?)
Aubrey of Buonalbergo (fl. 1000s)
Beatrice of Lorraine (c. 1020–1076)
Bertha of Burgundy (964–1024)
Bertha of Burgundy (d. 1097)
Bertha of Chartres (d. 1084)
Bertha of Holland (1055–1094)
Bertha of Savoy (1051–1087)
Bethoc (fl. 1000)
Bethoc (fl. 11th c.)
Bodil of Norway (fl. 1090s)
Casilda (d. about 1007)
Catherine of Bulgaria (fl. 1050)
Cecilia (c. 1059–1126)
Christina (fl. 1086)
Christina of Markyate (1096–1160)
Constance (c. 1066–1090)
Constance of Arles (c. 980–1032)
Constance of Burgundy (1046–c. 1093)
Corbert, Sybilla (fl. 11th century)
Cunigunde (d. 1040?)
Daini no Sanmi (999–after 1078)
Diaz, Jimena (fl. 1074–1100)
Doada (fl. 990–1005)
Doda (fl. 1040)
Donata (fl. 11th century)
Eadgyth Swanneshals (c. 1012–?)
Ealdgyth (fl. 1016)
Edith (c. 1025–1075)
Edith (fl. 1009)
Edith (fl. 1040)
Edith (fl. 1063)
Eleanor of Normandy (fl. 1000s)
Elfgifu (c. 963–1002)
Elfgifu (c. 997–?)
Elfgifu of Northampton (c. 1000–1044)
Elflaed (fl. 1030)
Elfthrith (c. 945–1002)
Elgiva (fl. 1020)
Elizabeth of Kiev (fl. 1045)
Elvira (1038–1101)
Elvira (fl. 1080s)
Elvira Gonzalez of Galicia (d. 1022)
Emma (fl. 1080s)
Emma of Norfolk (d. 1100)
Emma of Normandy (c. 985–1052)
Emma of Werden (d. around 1050)
Ermengarde of Anjou (1018–1076)
Ermengarde of Carcassonne (d. 1070)
Ermentrude de Roucy (d. 1005)
Este, Cunegunda d' (c. 1012–1055)
Estefania of Barcelona (fl. 1038)
Estrith (fl. 1017–1032)
Ethelreda (fl. 1090)
Eudocia Macrembolitissa (1021–1096)
Fredesendis (fl. 1000)
Fredesendis (fl. 1050)
Gerberga (r. 959–1001)
Gersenda (fl. 1000)
Gertrude of Saxony (fl. 1070)
Gilberga (d. 1054)
Gisela of Bavaria (c. 975–1033)
Gisela of Burgundy (d. 1006)
Gisela of Swabia (d. 1043)
Gladys (fl. 1075)
Godgifu (c. 1010–c. 1049)
Godiva (c. 1040–1080)
Gormflaith of Ireland (fl. 980–1015)
Griselda (fl. 11th c.)
Gruaidh (fl. 11 c.)
Gruoch (fl. 1020–1054)
Gundred (d. 1085)
Gunhild (c. 1020–1038)
Gunhilda of Denmark (d. 1002)
Gunhilda of Poland (d. around 1015)
Gunhild of Norway (d. 1054)
Gunnor of Denmark (d. 1031)
Gyde (fl. 1054)
Gyseth (fl. 1070)
Gytha (fl. 1022–1042)
Hawise of Brittany (d. 1072)
Hawise of Normandy (d. 1034)
Helen of Hungary (fl. mid–1000s)
Helia de Semur (fl. 1020–1046)
Hildegarde de Beaugency (fl. 1080)
Hildegarde of Swabia (fl. 1050)
Hildegard of Burgundy (1050–after 1104)
Hrotsvitha of Gandersheim (c. 935–1001)
Ida of Lorraine (1040–1113)
Imagi of Luxemburg (c. 1000–1057)
Ingebiorge (fl. 1045–1068)
Ingeborg of Sweden (fl. 1070)
Ingigerd Haraldsdottir (fl. 1075)
Ingigerd Olafsdottir (c. 1001–1050)
Ingirid (fl. 1067)
Irene Ducas (c. 1066–1133)
Irene of Byzantium (d. 1067)
Isabel of Urgel (fl. 1065)
Izumi Shikibu (c. 975–c. 1027)
Judith of Flanders (1032–1094)
Judith of Normandy (c. 1054–after 1086)
Judith of Rennes (c. 982–1018)
Lucy of Scotland (d. 1090)
Ma-gcig Lab-sgron (c. 1055–c. 1149)
Margaret (fl. 1000s)
Margaret, St. (c. 1046–1093)
Maria (fl. 995–1025)
Maria Comnena (fl. 1090s)
Maria of Alania (fl. 1070–1081)
Maria of Kiev (d. 1087)
Marie of Bulgaria (c. 1046–?)
Marie of Salerno (fl. 1000s)
Matilda of Essen (949–1011)
Matilda of Flanders (c. 1031–1083)
Matilda of Germany (d. before 1044)
Matilda of Saxony (978–1025)
Matilda of Scotland (1080–1118)
Matilda of Tuscany (1046–1115)
Maud of Normandy (d. 1017)
Munia Elvira (995–1067)
Muñoz, Jimena (c. 1065–1128)
Murasaki Shikibu (c. 973–c. 1015)
Muriella (fl. 1000)
Nesta Tewdr (fl. 1090)
Oda (fl. 1000)
Oda of Lorraine (fl. mid–1000)
Ogive of Luxemburg (d. 1030)
Papia of Envermeu (fl. 1020)
Philippa de Rouergue (c. 1074–1118)
Placencia (fl. 1068)
Richesa of Lorraine (d. 1067)
Richesa of Poland (fl. 1030–1040)
Richilde (1034–1086)
Sadako (r. 976–1001)
Sancha de Aybar (fl. 11th c.)
Sancha of Aragon (d. 1073)
Sancha of Leon (1013–1067)
Sarashina (c. 1008–1060)
Sarolta (fl. 1000s)
Shoshi (fl. 990–1010)
Sibylle of Burgundy (1065–1102)
Sichelgaita of Salerno (1040–1090)
Sigrid the Haughty (d. before 1013)
Sophia of Gandersheim (c. 975–1039)
Sophie of Hungary (d. 1095)
Synadene of Byzantium (c. 1050–?)
Teresa of Aragon (1037–?)
Teresa of Castile (c. 1080–1130)
Theodora Comnena (fl. 1080s)
Theodora Ducas (fl. 11th c.)
Theodora Porphyrogenita (c. 989–1056)
Thyra (d. 1018)
Trotula (c. 1040s–1097)
Ulfhild of Denmark (d. before 1070)
Urraca (1033–1101)
Urraca (c. 1079–1126)
Urraca of Aragon (fl. 11th c.)
Uta of Passau (fl. 11th c.)
Wallada (fl. 11th c.)
Wolfida of Saxony (c. 1075–1126)
Wulfhild (fl. 11th c.)
Wulfthryth (c. 945–1000)
Zaida (d. 1107)
Zoe Ducas (fl. 11th c.)
Zoë Porphyrogenita (980–1050)

12th Century

Adelaide de Condet (fl. 12th c.)
Adelaide of Kiev (c. 1070–1109)
Adelaide of Maurienne (1092–1154)
Adelaide of Montserrat (fl. 1100)
Adelaide of Savona (d. 1118)
Adelaide of Vohburg (fl. 1140s)

Era Index

Adela of Blois (1062–c. 1137)
Adela of Meissen (fl. 1100s)
Adele of Champagne (1145–1206)
Adelicia de Warrenne (d. 1178)
Adelicia of Louvain (c. 1102–1151)
Aelith de Poitiers (c. 1123–?)
Aénor of Châtellerault (d. 1130)
Agatha of Lorraine (fl. 1100s)
Agnes-Anne of France (b. 1171)
Agnes de Nevers (r. 1181–1192)
Agnes de Poitiers (fl. 1135)
Agnes of Austria (fl. 1100s)
Agnes of Courtenay (1136–1186)
Agnes of Germany (1074–1143)
Agnes of Looss (fl. 1150–1175)
Agnes of Poland (1137–after 1181)
Agnes of Saarbrucken (fl. 1130)
Alais (fl. 12th c.)
Alais of France (1160–?)
Alamanda of France (fl. late 12th c.)
Aldrude (fl. 1172)
Alice (1150–c. 1197)
Alice of Jerusalem (c. 1106–?)
Alisia of Antioch (fl. 1100s)
Alix of Vergy (d. after 1218)
Almucs de Castelnau (fl. 12th c.)
Angharad (d. 1162)
Anna Comnena (1083–1153/55)
Anna Dalassena (c. 1025–1105)
Anna of Cumin (d. 1111)
Anne of Chatillon-Antioche (c. 1155–c. 1185)
Arwa (1052–1137)
Astrid (fl. 1100s)
Aubigny, Agatha d' (fl. 1100s)
Ava of Melk (d. 1127)
Avisa of Gloucester (c. 1167–1217)
Barbara of Byzantium (d. 1125)
Beatrice (fl. c. 1100s)
Beatrice of Rethel (fl. 1150s)
Beatrice of Upper Burgundy (1145–1184)
Beatrix of Lens (d. around 1216)
Beaumont, Hawise (d. 1197)
Beaumont, Isabel (c. 1104–d. after 1172)
Berengaria of Castile (1180–1246)
Berengaria of Castile (b. around 1199)
Berengaria of Navarre (c. 1163–c. 1230)
Berengaria of Provence (1108–1149)
Bertha-Irene of Sulzbach (d. 1161)
Bertha of Biburg (d. 1151)
Bertha of Brittany (d. 1163)
Bertrada of Evreux (fl. 1170s)
Bertrada of Montfort (d. after 1117)
Blanche of Navarre (d. 1158)
Bona of Pisa (c. 1156–1207)
Cecilia (c. 1059–1126)
Cecilia of France (fl. 1100s)
Christina of Markyate (1096–1160)
Christina of Sweden (d. 1122)
Christina Stigsdottir (fl. 1160s)
Christina the Astonishing (c. 1150–c. 1224)
Clare, Isabel de (c. 1174–1220)
Clemence of Barking (fl. 12th c.)
Clementia (d. 1133)
Clementina of Zahringen (fl. 1150s)
Clifford, Rosamund (c. 1145–1176)
Constance (fl. 1100)
Constance Capet (c. 1128–1176)
Constance of Antioch (1128–1164)
Constance of Brittany (1161–1201)
Constance of Castile (d. 1160)
Constance of France (fl. 1100s)
Constance of Sicily (1154–1198)
Constance of Toulouse (fl. 12th century)
Costanza (1182–1202)
de Dia, Beatrice (c. 1160–1212)
Devorgilla (1109–1193)
Diaz, Jimena (fl. 1074–1100)
Douce I (d. 1190)
Douce of Aragon (1160–1198)
Dunkeld, Ada (c. 1145–1206)
Eleanor of Aquitaine (1122–1204)
Eleanor of Castile (1162–1214)
Elizabeth of Schönau (c. 1129–1164)
Elvira (d. 1135)
Emma de Gatinais (fl. 1150–1170)
Emma of Norfolk (d. 1100)
Ermengarde of Anjou (d. 1147)
Ermengarde of Narbonne (c. 1120–c. 1194)
Ermentrude (d. 1126)
Eschiva of Ibelin (fl. late 1100s)
Eudocia Comnena (fl. 1100)
Eudocia of Byzantium (fl. 1181)
Euphemia (fl. 1100s)
Euphemia of Kiev (d. 1139)
Euphrosine (d. 1102)
Euphrosyne of Kiev (fl. 1130–1180)
FitzGilbert, Constance (fl. 12th c.)
Fitzhammon, Amabel (d. 1157)
Frithpoll, Margaret (d. 1130)
Garsenda (1170–c. 1257)
Gertrude of Flanders (d. 1117)
Gertrude of Meissen (d. 1117)
Gertrude of Poland (d. 1107)
Gertrude of Saxony (1115–1143)
Gertrude of Saxony (c. 1155–1196)
Gertrude of Sulzbach (d. 1146)
Gertrude of Swabia (c. 1104–1191)
Gisela of Burgundy (fl. 1100s)
Gladys (fl. 1100s)
Guda (fl. late 12th c.)
Guidosalvi, Sancia (fl. early 12th c.)
Gunnhild (fl. 1150s)
Gwenllian of Wales (fl. 1137)
Hawise (d. after 1135)
Hawise of Salisbury (fl. 12th c.)
Haye, Nicolaa de la (1160–1218)
Hedwig of Silesia (1174–1243)
Helen (fl. 1100s)
Helena of Serbia (fl. 1100s)
Heloise (c. 1100–1163)
Helvidis (fl. 1136)
Herrad of Hohenberg (c. 1130–1195)
Hersende of Champagne (fl. 12th c.)
Hildegard of Bingen (1098–1179)
Hildegard of Burgundy (1050–after 1104)
Hildegund (d. 1188)
Hodierna (fl. 1100s)
Hodierna of Jerusalem (c. 1115–after 1162)
Hōjo Masako (1157–1225)
Hombelina (1092–1141)
Ida of Austria (d. 1101?)
Ida of Lorraine (1040–1113)
Ida of Lower Lorraine (d. 1162)
Ida of Namur (fl. 12th c.)
Ida Plantagenet (fl. 1175)
Ide d'Alsace (c. 1161–1216)
Ingeborg (c. 1176–1237/38)
Ingeborg of Russia (fl. 1118–1131)
Irene (fl. late 1100s)
Irene Angela of Byzantium (d. 1208)
Irene Ducas (c. 1066–1133)
Irene of Kiev (fl. 1122)
Isabel (fl. 1183)
Isabel de Warrenne (c. 1137–1203)
Isabella (b. 1180)
Isabella of Hainault (1170–1190)
Isabel of Beaumont (fl. 1150)
Isabel of Vermandois (d. before 1147)
Iselda, Lady (fl. 12th c.)
Iseut de Capio (1140–?)
Ivetta of Huy (1158–1228)
Joanna of Sicily (1165–1199)
Joan of Montferrat (d. 1127)
Jolanta (fl. 1100s)
Joveta of Jerusalem (1120–?)
Judith of Bavaria (fl. 1120s)
Jutta of Sponheim (d. 1136)
Kristina (fl. 1150)
Li Qingzhao (1083–c. 1151)
Lombarda (b. 1190)
Lucy de Blois (d. 1120)
Ludmilla of Bohemia (fl. 1100s)
Lutgardis (fl. 1139)
Ma-gcig Lab-sgron (c. 1055–c. 1149)
Malmfrid of Russia (fl. 1100s)
Mama-Ocllo (fl. around 12th c.)
Marared (fl. 1173)
Mareri, Filippa (c. 1190–1236)
Margarethe of Västergötland (fl. 1100)
Margaret-Mary of Hungary (c. 1177–?)
Margaret of Alsace (c. 1135–1194)
Margaret of France (1158–1198)
Margaret of Geneva (fl. late 1100s–early 1200s)
Margaret of Huntingdon (c. 1140–1201)
Margaret of Limburg (d. 1172)
Margaret of Navarre (fl. 1154–1172)
Margaret of Turenne (fl. 12th c.)
Marguerite de Brabant (c. 1192–?)
Marguerite de l'Aigle (d. 1141)
Maria Comnena (fl. 1100s)
Maria de Ventadour (b. 1165)
Maria of Byzantium (fl. 12th c.)
Maria of Kiev (d. 1146)
Maria of Montpellier (1181–1213)
Marie de Champagne (1145–1198)
Marie de France (c. 1140–1200)
Marie of Antioch (d. 1183)
Marie of Boulogne (d. 1182)
Marie of Champagne (c. 1180–1203)
Marie of Kiev (d. 1179)
Mary of Atholl (d. 1116)
Mary of Oignies (1177–1213)
Mathilde de Mayenne (fl. 12th c.)
Matilda (fl. 1100s)
Matilda, Empress (1102–1167)
Matilda de Blois (d. 1120)
Matilda of Anjou (1107–1154)
Matilda of Boulogne (c. 1103–1152)
Matilda of Château-du-Loir (fl. 12th c.)
Matilda of England (1156–1189)
Matilda of Maurienne (c. 1125–1157)
Matilda of Northumberland (c. 1074–1131)
Matilda of Portugal (c. 1149–1173)
Matilda of Scotland (1080–1118)
Matilda of Tuscany (1046–1115)
Matilde of Vienne (d. after 1145)
Maud Carinthia (c. 1105–1160)
Maude of Alsace (1163–c. 1210)
Maude of Chester (1171–1233)
Mechtild of Driessen (d. 1160)
Melisande (1105–1161)
Melisande (fl. 1100)
Morphia of Melitene (fl. 1085–1120)
Muñoz, Jimena (c. 1065–1128)
Percy, Agnes (fl. 1120s)
Perez, Gontrada (fl. 1100s)
Petronilla (1135–1174)
Philippa de Rouergue (c. 1074–1118)
Philippa of Antioch (fl. 1100s)
Preslava of Russia (fl. 1100)
Priska-Irene of Hungary (c. 1085–1133)
Ragnhild (fl. 1100s)
Richensia of Nordheim (1095–1141)
Richilde (d. 1100)
Richizza of Poland (1116–1185)
Ryksa of Poland (d. 1185)
Salomea (d. 1144)
Sancha (c. 1178–1229)
Sancha of Castile and Leon (1164–1208)
Sancha of Castile and Leon (d. 1179)
Shizuka Gozen (fl. 12th c.)
Sibylla (1160–1190)
Sibylle of Burgundy (1065–1102)
Sibylle of Burgundy (1126–1150)
Sophia of Zahringen (fl. 12th c.)
Sophie of Russia (c. 1140–1198)
Stade, Richardis von (d. 1152)
Susan of Powys (fl. 1100s)
Sybilla (d. 1122)
Sybilla of Anjou (1112–1165)
Sybil of Conversano (d. 1103)
Talvace, Adela (d. 1174)
Tamara (1160–1212)
Tangwystl (fl. 1180–1210)
Teresa of Castile (c. 1080–1130)
Teresa of Portugal (1157–1218)
Theodora Comnena (1145–after 1183)
Theodora Comnena (fl. 1140)
Theresa Henriques (c. 1176–1250)
Thora (fl. 1100s)
Thora Johnsdottir (fl. 1000s)
Tibors (b. around 1130)
Tomoe Gozen (fl. c. 12th c.)
Trava, Teresa Fernandez de (fl. 1170)
Ulfhild (fl. 1112)
Urraca (1033–1101)
Urraca (c. 1079–1126)
Urraca (c. 1096–c. 1130)

Urraca of Castile (d. 1179)
Urraca of Portugal (c. 1151–1188)
Zaida (d. 1107)
Zbyslawa (fl. 1100)

13th Century

Adelaide of Burgundy (d. 1273)
Adelaide of Schaerbeck (d. 1250)
Adele of Champagne (1145–1206)
Agnes Capet (1260–1327)
Agnes de Dampierre (1237–1288)
Agnes of Assisi (1207–1232)
Agnes of Austria (1281–1364)
Agnes of Beaujeu (d. 1231)
Agnes of Bohemia (1205–1282)
Agnes of Bohemia (1269–1297)
Agnes of Bourbon (d. 1287)
Agnes of Habsburg (c. 1257–1322)
Agnes of Huntingdonshire (fl. 13th c.)
Agnes of Jouarre (fl. early 13th c.)
Agnes of Meran (d. 1201)
Agnes of Monte Pulciano (1274–1317)
Agnes of Quedlinburg (1184–1203)
Agnes of Saxony (fl. 1200s)
Alice (1201–1221)
Alice (1280–1291)
Alice de Courtenay (d. 1211)
Alice le Brun (d. 1255)
Alice of Champagne (fl. 1200s)
Alix of Vergy (d. after 1218)
Alix of Vergy (r. 1248–c. 1290)
Amicie de Courtenay (d. 1275)
Angela of Foligno (1249–1309)
Angharad (fl. 13th c.)
Anna Angelina (d. 1210?)
Anna of Bohemia (fl. 1230s)
Anna of Hohenberg (c. 1230–1281)
Anna of Hungary (d. around 1284)
Anna of Hungary (fl. 1244)
Anna of Silesia (fl. 1200s)
Anna Paleologina-Cantacuzene (fl. 1270–1313)
Anne of York (fl. 13th c.)
Avelina de Forz (1259–1274)
Avisa of Gloucester (c. 1167–1217)
Balliol, Ada (fl. 1256)
Balliol, Cecily (d. before 1273)
Balliol, Eleanor (fl. 1230)
Balliol, Margaret (c. 1255–?)
Beatrice (1242–1275)
Beatrice of Anjou (d. 1275)
Beatrice of Castile and Leon (1242–1303)
Beatrice of Kent (d. after 1280)
Beatrice of Nazareth (c. 1200–1268)
Beatrice of Provence (d. 1267)
Beatrice of Savoy (fl. 1240s)
Beatrice of Savoy (d. 1268)
Beatrice of Swabia (1198–1235)
Beatrice Portinari (c. 1265–1290)
Beatrix de Bourgogne (1257–1310)
Beatrix of Lens (d. around 1216)
Beauchamp, Isabel (fl. 1285)
Benedicta of Assisi (d. 1260)
Berengaria (1194–1221)
Berengaria of Castile (1180–1246)
Berengaria of Navarre (c. 1163–c. 1230)
Bertha of Marbais (d. 1247)
Blanche of Artois (c. 1247–1302)
Blanche of Castile (1188–1252)
Blanche of France (1253–1321)
Blanche of France (c. 1266–1305)
Blanche of Navarre (d. 1229)
Blanche of Navarre (fl. 1239)
Bohun, Maud (fl. 1240s)
Bohun, Maud (fl. 1275)
Branca (c. 1192–1240)
Branca (1259–1321)
Braose, Annora de (d. 1241)
Braose, Eleanor de (fl. 1250s)
Braose, Eve de (fl. 1220s)
Braose, Isabel de (d. 1248?)
Braose, Loretta de (d. 1266)
Braose, Maud de (d. 1211)
Bruce, Isabel (c. 1278–1358)
Castelloza, Na (fl. early 13th c.)
Catherine de Courtenay (d. 1307)
Catherine of Habsburg (c. 1254–1282)
Chabi (fl. 13th c.)
Christian (d. 1246)
Christian de Plessetis (c. 1250–?)
Christina the Astonishing (c. 1150–c. 1224)
Clare, Amicia de (1220–1283)
Clare, Isabel de (1226–1254)
Clare, Isabel de (c. 1174–1220)
Clare, Margaret de (1249–1313)
Clare, Margaret de (fl. 1280–1322)
Clare of Assisi (c. 1194–1253)
Claricia of Augsburg (fl. 1220)
Clementia of Habsburg (d. 1293)
Constance-Anna of Hohenstaufen (fl. 13th century)
Constance of Aragon (d. 1222)
Constance of Aragon (d. 1283)
Constance of Brittany (1161–1201)
Constance of Hungary (d. 1240)
Constance of Sicily (d. 1302)
Costanza (1182–1202)
Cunegunde (1234–1292)
Cunigunde of Hohenstaufen (fl. 1215–1230)
Cunigunde of Hungary (d. 1285)
Dagmar of Bohemia (d. 1212)
Dessilava (fl. 1197–1207)
Devorgilla (d. 1290)
Donatella (fl. 1271)
Dunkeld, Ada (c. 1145–1206)
Dunkeld, Ada (c. 1195–after 1241)
Ebner, Christine (1277–1355)
Ebner, Margarethe (1291–1351)
Eleanor, the Maid of Brittany (1184–1241)
Eleanor de Warrenne (c. 1250–?)
Eleanor of Aquitaine (1122–1204)
Eleanor of Castile (1202–1244)
Eleanor of Castile (1241–1290)
Eleanor of Montfort (1215–1275)
Eleanor of Montfort (1252–1282)
Eleanor of Provence (c. 1222–1291)
Eleanor Plantagenet (1264–1297)
Elizabeth of Bavaria (fl. 1200s)
Elizabeth of Brabant (1243–1261)
Elizabeth of Courtenay (d. 1205)
Elizabeth of Hungary (1207–1231)
Elizabeth of Hungary (fl. 1250s)
Elizabeth of Kumania (c. 1242–?)
Elizabeth of Poland (fl. 1298–1305)
Elizabeth of Portugal (1271–1336)
Elizabeth of Sicily (fl. 1200s)
Elizabeth of Silesia (fl. 1257)
Elizabeth of Tyrol (c. 1262–1313)
Ellen of Wales (d. 1253)
Ermengarde of Beaumont (d. 1234)
Ermesind of Luxemburg (d. 1247)
Ermesind of Luxemburg (fl. 1200)
Eschiva of Ibelin (r. 1282–c. 1284)
Este, Beata Beatrice I d' (d. 1226)
Este, Beata Beatrice II d' (d. 1262)
Este, Beatrice d' (d. 1245)
Este, Beatrice d' (fl. 1290s)
Este, Costanza d' (fl. 1200s)
Este, Giovanna d' (fl. 1240s)
Este, Giovanna d' (fl. 1280s)
Este, Mambilia d' (fl. 1200s)
Eudocia (c. 1260–?)
Eudocia Angelina (fl. 1204)
Eulogia Paleologina (fl. 1200s)
Euphrosyne (d. 1203)
Euphrosyne (fl. 1200s)
Euphrosyne of Opole (d. 1293)
Falconieri, Juliana (1270–1341)
Falkestein, Beatrice von (c. 1253–1277)
Fitzalan, Alice (fl. 1285)
Fitzalan, Maud (fl. 1200s)
Fitzrobert, Amicia (d. 1225)
Francesca da Rimini (d. 1285?)
Furneria of Mirepoix (fl. 13th c.)
Garcia, Sancha (fl. 1230)
Garsenda (1170–c. 1257)
Gertrude of Andrechs-Meran (c. 1185–1213)
Gertrude of Hackeborne (1232–1292)
Gertrude of Metz (d. 1225)
Gertrude the Great (1256–1302)
Gladys the Black (d. 1251)
Guan Daosheng (1262–1319)
Guglielma of Milan (d. 1282)
Guillelma de Rosers (fl. 1240–1260)
Guirande de Lavaur (d. 1211)
Guzman, Mayor de (d. 1262)
Hadewijch (fl. 13th c.)
Haye, Nicolaa de la (1160–1218)
Hedwig of Habsburg (d. 1286)
Helen (fl. 1275)
Helena of Epirus (fl. 1250s)
Helen Asen of Bulgaria (d. 1255?)
Helene of Brunswick-Luneburg (d. 1273)
Helen of Denmark (d. 1233)
Hersende of France (fl. 1250)
Hōjo Masako (1157–1225)
Humilitas of Faenza (1226–1310)
Ida de Macon (d. 1224)
Ida of Louvain (d. 1260)
Ida of Nivelles (d. 1232)
Ide d'Alsace (c. 1161–1216)
Inga (fl. 1204)
Ingeborg (c. 1176–1237/38)
Ingeborg (d. 1254)
Ingeborg of Denmark (d. 1287)
Iolande of Hungary (1215–1251)
Irene Angela of Byzantium (d. 1208)
Irene Lascaris (d. around 1270)
Irene Lascaris (fl. 1222–1235)
Irene Paleologina (fl. 1279–1280)
Irmingard of Zelle (c. 1200–1260)
Isabel (fl. 1225)
Isabel de Warrenne (c. 1137–1203)
Isabel de Warrenne (b. 1253)
Isabel de Warrenne (d. 1282)
Isabella (1206–1251)
Isabella (d. 1282)
Isabella Capet (fl. 1250)
Isabella de Redvers (1237–1293)
Isabella I of Jerusalem (d. 1205)
Isabella of Angoulême (1186–1246)
Isabella of Aragon (1243–1271)
Isabella of Cyprus (fl. 1230s)
Isabella of Cyprus (fl. 1250s)
Isabella of England (1214–1241)
Isabella of Mar (d. 1296)
Isabelle (1225–1270)
Ivetta of Huy (1158–1228)
Jacoba di Settesoli (d. about 1273)
Jeanne de Chatillon (d. 1292)
Joan (1210–1238)
Joan de Clare (c. 1268–after 1322)
Joan de Quinci (d. 1283)
Joan de Vere (fl. 1280s)
Joan I of Navarre (1273–1305)
Joanna of Ponthieu (d. 1251)
Joanna of Ponthieu (d. 1279)
Joan of Acre (1272–1307)
Joan of England (d. 1237)
Joan of Toulouse (d. 1271)
Johanna of Flanders (c. 1200–1244)
Judith (1271–1297)
Juliana of Cornillon (1192–1258)
Jutta (d. 1284)
Jutta of Saxony (d. around 1267)
Kanga (fl. 1220)
Kassi (1241–?)
Katherine (fl. 13th c.)
Katherine Plantagenet (1253–1257)
Lacey, Maud (fl. 1230–1250)
Lacy, Alice (1281–1348)
Laurette de St. Valery (fl. 1200)
Lecavella, Mabilia (fl. 1206)
Leonora of Savoy (fl. 1200)
Leonor of Portugal (1211–1231)
Lissiardi, Sibille (fl. 13th c.)
Lucia (r. 1288–1289)
Lucia of Rugia (fl. 1220)
Lucienne of Segni (r. around 1252–1258)
Ludgarda (fl. 1200s)
Lutgard (1182–1246)
Mabel of Bury St. Edmunds (fl. 1230)
Mafalda (c. 1197–1257)
Mahaut (c. 1270–1329)
Mahaut de Courtenay (d. 1257)
Mahaut I (r. 1215–1242)
Mahaut II de Dampierre (1234–1266)
Mahaut of Burgundy (d. 1202)
Malgorzata (fl. 1290s)
Margaret (1240–1275)

Margaret (1275–1318)
Margaret (d. 1209)
Margaret (d. 1228)
Margaret (d. 1270)
Margaret (d. 1275)
Margaret, Maid of Norway (c. 1283–1290)
Margaret Capet (d. 1271)
Margaret de Burgh (c. 1193–1259)
Margaret de Burgh (c. 1226–1243)
Margaret de Foix (d. 1258)
Margaret le Brun (d. 1283)
Margaret of Anjou (c. 1272–1299)
Margaret of Antioch-Lusignan (fl. 1283–1291)
Margaret of Austria (fl. 1200s)
Margaret of Babenberg (fl. 1252)
Margaret of Cortona (1247–1297)
Margaret of Flanders (1202–1280)
Margaret of Flanders (d. 1285)
Margaret of Geneva (fl. late 1100s–early 1200s)
Margaret of Germany (1237–1270)
Margaret of Hungary (1242–1270)
Margaret of Huntingdon (c. 1140–1201)
Margaret of Norway (1261–1283)
Margaret of Pomerania (d. 1282)
Margaret of Provence (1221–1295)
Marguerite (r. 1218–1230)
Marguerite de Bourgogne (1250–1308)
Marguerite de Brabant (c. 1192–?)
Maria (fl. 1200s)
Maria Lascaris (fl. 1234–1242)
Maria of Montpellier (1181–1213)
Maria Paleologina (fl. 1271–1279)
Marie (fl. 13th c.)
Marie de Chatillon (r. 1230–1241)
Marie de Courtenay (fl. 1215)
Marie of Brabant (fl. 1250)
Marie of Brabant (c. 1260–1321)
Marie of Champagne (c. 1180–1203)
Marie of France (1198–c. 1223)
Marie of Lusignan (d. 1260)
Marie of Montferrat (d. 1212)
Marie of Swabia (c. 1201–1235)
Marjorie of Carrick (c. 1254–1292)
Marjory (d. 1244)
Marjory (fl. 13th c.)
Marshall, Isabel (1200–1240)
Marshall, Maud (d. 1248)
Marshall, Sybilla (fl. 1230)
Martha of Denmark (c. 1272–1341)
Mary (1278–1332)
Mary de Coucy (c. 1220–c. 1260)
Mary of Antioch (d. 1277)
Mary of Brabant (c. 1191–c. 1260)
Mary of Oignies (1177–1213)
Matilda (d. 1252)
Matilda de Dammartin (d. 1258)
Matilda of Brandenburg (d. 1261)
Matilda of Habsburg (1251–1304)
Matilda of Nassau (fl. 1285–1310)
Maude of Brabant (1224–1288)
Maude of Chester (1171–1233)
Maud of Lusignan (d. 1241)
Maud of Mandeville (d. 1236)
Mechtild of Hackeborne (1241–1298)
Mechtild of Holstein (d. 1288)
Mechtild of Magdeburg (c. 1207–c. 1282)
Melisande (fl. 1200s)
Mencia de Haro (d. 1270)
Mercuriade of Salerno (fl. 1200)
Montanaria (fl. 1272)
Montfort, Amicia (fl. 1208)
Mortimer, Isabel (fl. 1267)
Mortimer, Margaret (d. around 1296)
Mortimer, Maud (c. 1229–1301)
Odette de Pougy (fl. 1266)
Patiniere, Agnes (fl. 1286)
Perez, Maria (fl. 13th c.)
Philippa de Dreux (d. 1240)
Philippa of Foix (fl. 13th c.)
Philippa of Lesser Armenia (fl. 1200s)
Pisano, Nicola (fl. 1278)
Plaisance of Antioch (d. 1261)
Ponthiey, Adelaide (fl. 1248)
Razia (1211–1240)
Richeza Eriksdottir (fl. 1200s)
Richiza (fl. 1251)
Richizza of Denmark (d. 1220)
Rose of Viterbo (1235–1252)
Rusudani (b. 1195)
Ryksa (fl. 1288)
Ryksa of Poland (1288–1335)
Salome of Hungary (1201–c. 1270)
Sancha of Castile and Leon (1164–1208)
Sancha of Provence (c. 1225–1261)
Scholastica of Champagne (d. 1219)
Segrave, Margaret (c. 1280–?)
Senena (fl. 1200s)
Shajar al-Durr (d. 1259)
Sibylla of Armenia (fl. 1200s)
Sophia (fl. 1211)
Sophia of Denmark (1217–1248)
Sophia of Thuringia (1224–1284)
Sophie (fl. 1200s)
Sophie of Denmark (d. 1286)
Sophie Valdemarsdottir (d. 1241)
Steinbach, Sabina von (fl. 13th c.)
Tamara (1160–1212)
Tangwystl (fl. 1180–1210)
Teresa of Portugal (1157–1218)
Theodora Ducas (fl. 1200s)
Theodora Paleologina (fl. 1200s)
Theodosia (fl. 1220)
Theresa Henriques (c. 1176–1250)
Thomasse (fl. 1292)
Urraca of Castile (c. 1186–1220)
Yolanda of Gnesen (d. 1299)
Yolande de Coucy (d. 1222)
Yolande de Courtenay (d. 1233)
Yolande de Dreux (1212–1248)
Yolande de Dreux (d. 1238)
Yolande de Dreux (d. 1272)
Yolande of Aragon (d. 1300)
Yolande of Brienne (1212–1228)
Yolande of Burgundy (1248–1280)
Yolande of Courtenay (d. 1219)
Zabel (b. around 1210)
Zita of Lucca (1218–1275)

14th Century

Adasse (fl. 1348)
Adelheid of Holstein (fl. 1314)
Agnes Capet (1260–1327)
Agnes of Austria (1281–1364)
Agnes of Brandenburg (d. 1304)
Agnes of Habsburg (c. 1257–1322)
Aldona of Lithuania (d. 1339)
Alice de Joinville (fl. 14th c.)
Almeida, Brites de (fl. 1385)
Angela of Foligno (1249–1309)
Anna Anachoutlou (r. 1341–1342)
Anna of Bohemia (fl. 1318)
Anna of Habsburg (d. 1327)
Anna of Schweidnitz (c. 1340–?)
Anna of the Palatinate (fl. 1300s)
Anna Paleologina (d. 1340)
Anna Paleologina-Cantacuzene (fl. 1270–1313)
Anna von Munzingen (fl. 1327)
Anne of Bohemia (1366–1394)
Anne of Savoy (c. 1320–1353)
Armentières, Péronelle d' (fl. 14th c.)
Audley, Alice (d. 1374)
Audley, Margaret (fl. 1340s)
Badlesmere, Elizabeth (fl. 1315–1342)
Badlesmere, Maud (d. 1366)
Balliol, Margaret (fl. 1300s)
Barre, Margot de la (d. 1390)
Beatrice of Brandenburg (1360–1414)
Beatrice of Castile and Leon (1242–1303)
Beatrice of Castile and Leon (1293–1359)
Beatrice of Portugal (1372–after 1409)
Beatrice of Portugal (c. 1347–1381)
Beatrice of Silesia (fl. 1300s)
Beatrice of Wittelsbach (1344–1359)
Beatrix de Bourgogne (1257–1310)
Beaufort, Joan (c. 1379–1440)
Beaumont, Isabel (d. 1368)
Blanche of Boulogne (1326–1360)
Blanche of Bourbon (c. 1338–1361)
Blanche of Burgundy (1288–1348)
Blanche of Burgundy (1296–1326)
Blanche of Dreux (c. 1396–c. 1418)
Blanche of France (c. 1266–1305)
Blanche of France (1328–1392)
Blanche of Lancaster (1341–1369)
Blanche of Namur (d. 1363)
Blanche of Naples (d. 1310)
Blanche of Navarre (1331–1398)
Blanche of Rossi (d. 1237)
Blanche of Savoy (c. 1337–?)
Blanche of Valois (c. 1316–?)
Bocchi, Dorotea (fl. 1390–1430)
Bohun, Alianore (d. 1313)
Bohun, Eleanor (fl. 1327–1340)
Bohun, Eleanor (1366–1399)
Bona of Bohemia (1315–1349)
Boneta, Prous (d. 1323)
Bridget of Sweden (1303–1373)
Brigue, Jehenne de (d. 1391)
Bruce, Christian (d. 1356)
Bruce, Margaret (c. 1286–?)
Bruce, Margaret (1296–1316)
Bruce, Margaret (d. 1346)
Bruce, Mary (fl. 1290–1316)
Bruce, Matilda (c. 1285–c. 1326)
Bruce, Matilda (d. 1353)
Cardny, Marion (fl. 1300s)
Castro, Inez de (c. 1320–1355)
Catherine de Courtenay (d. 1307)
Catherine of Burgundy (1378–1425)
Catherine of Gorizia (fl. late 1300s)
Catherine of Lancaster (1372–1418)
Catherine of Siena (1347–1380)
Catherine of Sweden (c. 1330–1381)
Catherine of Tarento (fl. early 1300s)
Catherine of Vendôme (r. 1374–1412)
Chaworth, Maud (1282–c. 1322)
Christine de Pizan (c. 1363–c. 1431)
Clare, Eleanor de (1292–1337)
Clare, Elizabeth de (1295–1360)
Clare, Margaret de (fl. 1280–1322)
Clare, Margaret de (c. 1293–1342)
Clemence of Hungary (1293–1328)
Colette (1381–1447)
Comyn, Alice (fl. 1318)
Constance (c. 1374–1416)
Constance of Aragon (d. 1327)
Constance of Aragon (c. 1350–?)
Constance of Castile (1323–1345)
Constance of Castile (1354–1394)
Constance of Portugal (1290–1313)
Constance of Sicily (d. 1302)
Courtenay, Margaret (fl. 1330)
Cunegunde (d. 1357)
Cunegunde (d. after 1370)
Cunigunde of Bohemia (d. 1321)
d'Andrea, Novella (d. 1333)
de Almania, Jacqueline Felicia (fl. 1322)
de la Cerda, Blanche (c. 1311–1347)
della Scala, Beatrice (1340–1384)
Droiturière, Marion la (d. 1390)
Drummond, Annabella (1350–1401)
Drummond, Margaret (d. 1375)
Dunbar, Agnes (1312–1369)
Dunbar, Christine (c. 1350–?)
Ebner, Christine (1277–1355)
Ebner, Margarethe (1291–1351)
Eleanor d'Arborea (c. 1360–c. 1404)
Eleanor of Albuquerque (1374–1435)
Eleanor of Aragon (1358–1382)
Eleanor of Castile (1307–1359)
Eleanor of Portugal (1328–1348)
Eleanor of Sicily (d. 1375)
Eleanor of Woodstock (1318–1355)
Eleanor Plantagenet (c. 1318–1372)
Eleonore of Savoy (d. 1324)
Elizabeth de Burgh (d. 1327)
Elizabeth de Burgh (1332–1363)
Elizabeth of Bohemia (1292–1339)
Elizabeth of Bohemia (1358–1373)
Elizabeth of Bosnia (d. 1339)
Elizabeth of Bosnia (c. 1345–1387)
Elizabeth of Gorlitz (c. 1380–c. 1444)
Elizabeth of Habsburg (1293–1352)
Elizabeth of Holstein (fl. 1329)
Elizabeth of Lancaster (1364–1425)
Elizabeth of Poland (fl. 1298–1305)
Elizabeth of Poland (1305–1380)
Elizabeth of Poland (d. 1361)

Elizabeth of Pomerania (1347–1393)
Elizabeth of Portugal (1271–1336)
Elizabeth of Sicily (d. 1349)
Elizabeth of Tyrol (c. 1262–1313)
Elizabeth Plantagenet (1282–1316)
Elizabeth the Good (1386–1420)
Este, Alda d' (1333–1381)
Este, Alda d' (fl. 1300s)
Este, Beatrice d' (fl. 1300s)
Este, Beatrice d' (d. 1334)
Este, Beatrice d' (fl. 1350s)
Este, Elisa d' (?–1329)
Este, Giacoma d' (fl. 1300)
Este, Giacoma d' (fl. 1300s)
Este, Giovanna d' (fl. 1300s)
Este, Isotta d' (fl. 1300s)
Este, Lippa d'
Este, Verde d' (fl. 1300s)
Euphemia (1317–after 1336)
Euphemia of Pomerania (d. 1330)
Euphemia of Rugen (d. 1312)
Falconieri, Juliana (1270–1341)
Ferrers, Anne (d. 1342)
Fitzalan, Alice (d. around 1338)
Fitzalan, Alice (1352–1416)
Fitzalan, Elizabeth (d. 1385)
Fitzalan, Joan (fl. 1325)
Foix, Janine-Marie de (fl. 1377)
Gattilusi, Eugenia (fl. late 1390s)
Gauhar Shad (c. 1378–1459)
Gertrude of Ostend (d. 1358)
Gertrude the Great (1256–1302)
Gilette of Narbonne (fl. 1300)
Giliani, Allessandra (1307–1326)
Glendower, Margaret (fl. late 1300s)
Gonzaga, Margherita (d. 1399)
Graham, Margaret (d. 1380)
Grandison, Katharine (fl. 1305–1340)
Guan Daosheng (1262–1319)
Guzman, Leonora de (1310–1351)
Hayles, Alice (d. after 1326)
Hedwig of Holstein (d. 1325)
Helena Cantacuzene (fl. 1340s)
Helvig of Denmark (fl. 1350s)
Helwig of Prague (fl. 14th c.)
Holland, Alianor (c. 1373–1405)
Holland, Joan (c. 1356–1384)
Holland, Joan (c. 1380–1434)
Hotot, Agnes (fl. 14th c.)
Humilitas of Faenza (1226–1310)
Ingeborg (c. 1300–c. 1360)
Ingeborg (d. 1319)
Ingeborg (1347–1370)
Irene (fl. 1310)
Irene Asen (fl. 1300s)
Irene of Brunswick (fl. 1300s)
Irene of Montferrat (fl. 1300)
Irmengard of Oettingen (fl. 14th c.)
Isaac, Joan (fl. 1300s)
Isabeau of Bavaria (1371–1435)
Isabel de Limoges (1283–1328)
Isabella (1332–1382)
Isabella of Aragon (c. 1300–1330)
Isabella of Buchan (fl. 1290–1310)
Isabella of France (1296–1358)
Isabelle of Cornwall (fl. 14th c.)
Isabelle of France (1349–1372)
Isabelle of Savoy (d. 1383)
Isabel of Castile (1355–1392)
Isabel of Fife (c. 1332–1389)
Isabel Plantagenet (c. 1317–c. 1347)
Jadwiga (1374–1399)
Jadwiga of Glogow (fl. late 1300s)
Jane of France (1343–1373)
Jeanne de Belleville (fl. 1343)
Jeanne de Bourbon (1338–1378)
Jeanne de Castile (r. 1366–1374)
Jeanne de Montfort (c. 1310–c. 1376)
Jeanne de Penthièvre (c. 1320–1384)
Jeanne I (d. 1346)
Jeanne II (r. 1346–1355)
Jeanne II of Burgundy (1308–1347)
Jeanne I of Burgundy (c. 1291–1330)
Jeanne of Burgundy (1293–1348)
Jeanne of Burgundy (1344–1360)
Jeanne of Chalon (1300–1333)
Jeanne of Valois (c. 1294–1342)
Jeanne of Valois (c. 1304–?)
Joan (1384–1400)
Joan de Clare (c. 1268–after 1322)
Joan II of Navarre (1309–1349)
Joan I of Navarre (1273–1305)
Joanna (1333–1348)
Joanna II of Naples (1374–1435)
Joanna I of Naples (1326–1382)
Joanna of Brabant (1322–1406)
Joanna of Castile (1339–1381)
Joanna of Navarre (c. 1370–1437)
Joan of Acre (1272–1307)
Joan of Evreux (d. 1370)
Joan of Hainault (c. 1310–?)
Joan of Kent (1328–1385)
Joan of the Tower (1321–1362)
Joan Plantagenet (c. 1312–c. 1345)
Johanna of Bavaria (c. 1373–1410)
Johanna of Pfirt (1300–1351)
Julianna du Guesdin (fl. 1370)
Julianna of Ruthenia (fl. 1377)
Julian of Norwich (c. 1342–c. 1416)
Katharina von Gebweiler (fl. c. 1340)
Katherine of Holland (d. 1401)
Katherine of Sutton (d. 1376)
Keith, Margaret (fl. 1395)
Kempe, Margery (c. 1373–after 1438)
Krystyna Rokiczanska (fl. 1300s)
Kyteler, Alice (fl. 1324)
Lacy, Alice (1281–1348)
Lal Ded (b. 1355)
Lambertini, Imelda (1320–1333)
Langmann, Adelheid (d. 1375)
Latimer, Elizabeth (d. 1395)
Leitch, Moira (fl. late 1300s)
Lenore of Sicily (1289–1341)
Leonora Telles (c. 1350–1386)
Lidwina of Schiedam (1380–1433)
López de Córdoba, Leonor (1362–1412)
Lorenzo, Teresa (fl. 1358)
Macruari, Amy (fl. 1300s)
Mahaut (c. 1270–1329)
Mahaut de Chatillon (d. 1358)
Maillé, Jeanne-Marie de (1331–1414)
Manny, Anne (b. 1355)
Margaret (1275–1318)
Margaret (c. 1320–1400)
Margaret (1346–1361)
Margaret Christofsdottir (c. 1305–1340)
Margaret de Burgh (d. 1303)
Margarethe (1370–c. 1400)
Margaret I of Denmark (1353–1412)
Margaret Maultasch (1318–1369)
Margaret of Artois (d. 1382)
Margaret of Attenduli (1375–?)
Margaret of Brabant (d. 1311)
Margaret of Brabant (1323–1368)
Margaret of Burgundy (1290–1315)
Margaret of Burgundy (c. 1376–1441)
Margaret of Corigliano (fl. 14th c.)
Margaret of Flanders (1350–1405)
Margaret of France (c. 1282–1318)
Margaret of Hainault (d. 1342)
Margaret of Holland (d. 1356)
Margaret of Kent (1327–before 1352)
Margaret of Naples (fl. late 1300s)
Margaret of Ypres (fl. 1322)
Margaret Wake of Liddell (c. 1299–1349)
Marguerite de Bourgogne (1250–1308)
Marguerite de Thouars (r. 1365–1377)
Maria Cantacuzene (fl. 1300s)
Maria dei Conti d'Aquino (fl. 1300s)
Maria de Molina (d. 1321)
Maria-Kyratza Asen (fl. late 1300s)
Maria of Aragon (fl. 1311)
Maria of Armenia (fl. 1300)
Maria of Hungary (1371–1395)
Maria of Navarre (fl. 1340)
Maria of Portugal (1313–1357)
Marie de Bourbon (fl. 1350s)
Marie de Padilla (1335–1361)
Marie de St. Pol (1304–1377)
Marie of Brabant (c. 1260–1321)
Marie of Evreux (d. 1335)
Marie of France (1344–1404)
Marie of Guelders (1325–1399)
Marie of Guise (d. 1404)
Marie of Hainault (fl. 1300)
Marie of Hungary (d. 1323)
Marie of Mecklenburg (fl. 1380)
Marie of Naples (fl. 1300s)
Marie of Valois (fl. 14th c.)
Marr, Margaret (d. after 1384)
Martha of Denmark (c. 1272–1341)
Mary (1278–1332)
Mary (1344–1362)
Mary de Bohun (1369–1394)
Mary de Coucy (fl. 1370)
Mary de Monthermer (1298–after 1371)
Mary of Luxemburg (1305–1323)
Marzia (fl. 1357)
Matilda de Burgh (d. 1315)
Matilda of Bavaria (fl. 1300s)
Matilda of Guelders (d. 1380)
Matilda of Habsburg (1251–1304)
Matilda of Narbonne (d. after 1348)
Matilda of Nassau (fl. 1285–1310)
Maud Plantagenet (c. 1310–c. 1377)
Maud Plantagenet (1335–1362)
Mayfreda de Pirovano (d. 1300)
Merete Ulfsdatter (fl. 1320–1370)
Michelina of Pesaro (1300–1356)
Mohun, Elizabeth (fl. 14th c.)
Mohun, Joan (fl. 14th c.)
Montacute, Joan (fl. 1300s)
Montacute, Maud (fl. 1380s)
Montacute, Philippa (fl. 1352)
Monthermer, Margaret (fl. 1350)
Mortimer, Agnes (fl. 1347)
Mortimer, Beatrice (d. 1383)
Mortimer, Catherine (c. 1313–1369)
Mortimer, Catherine (d. before 1413)
Mortimer, Joan (fl. 1300)
Mortimer, Maud (c. 1229–1301)
Mortimer, Philippa (1355–1382)
Mortimer, Philippa (1375–1401)
Mowbray, Isabel (fl. late 1300s)
Muir, Elizabeth (d. before 1355)
Neville, Margaret (d. 1372)
Neville, Margaret (c. 1377–c. 1424)
Novella (d. 1333)
Noves, Laure de (1308–1348)
Oignt, Marguerite d' (d. 1310)
Percy, Elizabeth (1371–1417)
Percy, Mary (1320–1362)
Perrers, Alice (d. 1400)
Philippa de Coucy (fl. 1300s)
Philippa of Hainault (1314–1369)
Philippa of Lancaster (c. 1359–1415)
Philippine of Luxemburg (d. 1311)
Ponten, Clare van der (fl. 14th c.)
Porete, Marguerite (d. 1310)
Richilde (fl. 1300s)
Robine, Marie (d. 1399)
Romano, Francesca (fl. 1321)
Ross, Euphemia (d. 1387)
Rouet, Philippa (c. 1348–c. 1387)
Ruilly, Macette de (d. 1391)
Russell, Margery (d. around 1380)
Ryksa of Poland (1288–1335)
Sadeler, Agnes (fl. 1386)
Sarah of Görlitz (fl. 1388)
Sarah of St. Gilles (fl. 1326)
Sati Beg (c. 1300–after 1342)
Segrave, Anne (d. around 1377)
Segrave, Elizabeth (1338–1399)
Sophia of Malines (d. 1329)
Sophie of Lithuania (1370–1453)
Stafford, Margaret (d. 1396)
Stafford, Philippa (d. before 1386)
Stagel, Elsbeth (c. 1300–c. 1366)
Stewart, Egidia (d. after 1388)
Stewart, Egidia (fl. 14th c.)
Stewart, Elizabeth (fl. 1300s)
Stewart, Euphemia (c. 1375–1415)
Stewart, Isabel (fl. 1390–1410)
Stewart, Katherine (d. after 1394)
Stewart, Margaret (fl. 1350)
Stewart, Margaret (fl. 14th c.)
Telles, Maria (d. 1379)
Teresa d'Entenza (fl. 1319)

Theodora Cantacuzene (fl. 14th c.)
Theodora Paleologina (fl. 14th c.)
Ufford, Margaret de (fl. 14th c.)
Vega, Elvira de la (fl. late 1300s)
Vere, Margaret de (fl. 14th c.)
Vere, Maud de (fl. 1360s)
Virdimura of Sicily (fl. 1376)
Visconti, Agnes (c. 1365–1391)
Visconti, Catherine (c. 1360–1404)
Visconti, Thaddaea (d. 1381)
Visconti, Valentina (1366–1408)
Visconti, Violet (c. 1353–1386)
Visconti, Virida (c. 1354–1414)
Wollerin, Cecilie (d. 1341)
Yolande de Bar (fl. 14th c.)
Yolande de Dreux (d. 1323)
Yolande of Aragon (1379–1442)
Yolande of Aragon (fl. 14th c.)

15th Century

Agnes of Burgundy (d. 1476)
Alice de Bryene (d. 1435)
Almada, Filipa de (fl. 15th c.)
Amboise, Francise d' (1427–1485)
Amlingyn, Katherine (fl. late-15th c.)
Anacáona (fl. 1492)
Anastaise (fl. 1400)
Angela of Brescia (1474–1540)
Anna of Brunswick (fl. 1400s)
Anna of Moscow (1393–1417)
Anna of Savoy (1455–1480)
Anna of Saxony (1420–1462)
Anne de la Tour (d. 1512)
Anne of Austria (1432–1462)
Anne of Beaujeu (c. 1460–1522)
Anne of Brittany (c. 1477–1514)
Anne of Lusignan (b. before 1430)
Anne of Saxony (1437–1512)
Anne of Warwick (1456–1485)
Anne Plantagenet (1383–1438)
Anne Plantagenet (1439–1476)
Anne Valois (c. 1405–1432)
Antonia (1456–1491)
Barbara of Brandenburg (1422–1481)
Barbara of Cilli (fl. 1390–1410)
Barbara of Poland (1478–1534)
Barbara of Saxe-Wittenberg (c. 1405–1465)
Beatrice of Beja (1430–1506)
Beatrice of Brandenburg (1360–1414)
Beatrice of Naples (1457–1508)
Beatrice of Portugal (1372–after 1409)
Beatrice of Portugal (d. 1439)
Beatrix da Silva (1424–1490)
Beauchamp, Anne (1426–1492)
Beauchamp, Eleanor (1408–1468)
Beauchamp, Elizabeth (fl. 1400s)
Beauchamp, Elizabeth (fl. 1420)
Beauchamp, Elizabeth (d. around 1480)
Beauchamp, Margaret (d. 1482)
Beaufort, Eleanor (d. 1501)
Beaufort, Joan (c. 1379–1440)
Beaufort, Joan (c. 1410–1445)
Beaufort, Margaret (c. 1407–?)
Beaufort, Margaret (1443–1509)
Beaufort, Margaret (d. 1474)
Benci, Ginevra de' (b. 1457)
Berkeley, Elizabeth (fl. 1390–1410)
Bernauer, Agnes (d. 1435)
Berners, Juliana (c. 1388–?)
Bertken, Sister (c. 1427–1514)
Blanche (c. 1392–1409)
Blanche of Dreux (c. 1396–c. 1418)
Blanche of Navarre (1385–1441)
Blanche of Navarre (1424–1464)
Bocchi, Dorotea (fl. 1390–1430)
Bonne of Armagnac (d. 1415)
Bonne of Artois (d. 1425)
Bonville, Cecily (1460–1530)
Borgia, Lucrezia (1480–1519)
Bourchier, Anne (c. 1417–1474)
Boyd, Mary (fl. 1487)
Brézé, Charlotte de (c. 1444/49–?)
Cartagena, Teresa de (c. 1420–1470)
Catalina (1403–1439)
Catherine (c. 1420–1493)
Catherine de Foix (c. 1470–1517)
Catherine de France (1428–1446)
Catherine of Achaea (d. 1465)
Catherine of Bologna (1413–1463)
Catherine of Bourbon (d. 1469)
Catherine of Brittany (1428–c. 1476)
Catherine of Burgundy (1378–1425)
Catherine of Cleves (1417–1479)
Catherine of Genoa (1447–1510)
Catherine of Lancaster (1372–1418)
Catherine of Pomerania (d. 1426)
Catherine of Saxony (1421–1476)
Catherine of Valois (1401–1437)
Catherine of Vendôme (r. 1374–1412)
Cattanei, Vannozza (1442–1518)
Cecilia (1469–1507)
Cely, Margery (fl. late 15th c.)
Cereta, Laura, of Brescia (1469–1499)
Charlotte of Lusignan (1442–1487)
Charlotte of Savoy (c. 1442–1483)
Chaucer, Alice (fl. 1400s)
Christina of Saxony (1461–1521)
Christine de Pizan (c. 1363–c. 1431)
Churchill, Sarah Jennings (1660–1744)
Cimburca of Masovia (c. 1396–1429)
Claude des Armoises (fl. 1400s)
Claudine (1451–1514)
Clifford, Maud (d. 1446)
Cobham, Eleanor (d. 1452)
Colette (1381–1447)
Colonna, Catherine (d. around 1440)
Columba of Rieti (1467–1501)
Constance (c. 1374–1416)
Cornaro, Caterina (1454–1510)
Cunegunde (1465–1520)
Dandolo, Giovanna (fl. 1457)
David, Catherine (fl. 15th c.)
del Giocondo, Lisa (1474–?)
del Maino, Agnes (fl. 1420s)
Despenser, Elizabeth (d. 1408)
Despenser, Isabel (1400–1439)
Dorothea of Brandenburg (1430–1495)
Dorothea of Brandenburg (1446–1519)
Douglas, Elizabeth (d. before 1451)
Douglas, Margaret (b. around 1427)
Douglas, Marjory (d. 1420)
Drummond, Annabella (1350–1401)
Drummond, Margaret (c. 1472–1502)
Dunbar, Christine (c. 1350–?)
Eleanor d'Arborea (c. 1360–c. 1404)
Eleanor of Albuquerque (1374–1435)
Eleanor of Navarre (1425–1479)
Eleanor of Portugal (1434–1467)
Eleanor of Portugal (1458–1525)
Eleanor Trastamara (d. 1415)
Elizabeth of Bavaria-Landshut (1383–1442)
Elizabeth of Gorlitz (c. 1380–c. 1444)
Elizabeth of Hungary (c. 1430–1505)
Elizabeth of Lancaster (1364–1425)
Elizabeth of Luxemburg (1409–1442)
Elizabeth of Nevers (fl. 1460)
Este, Beatrice d' (1427–1497)
Este, Beatrice d' (1475–1497)
Este, Bianca Maria d' (1440–1506)
Este, Gigliola d'
Este, Ginevra d' (1414–1440)
Este, Isabella d' (1474–1539)
Este, Isotta d' (1425–1456)
Este, Lucia d' (1419–1437)
Este, Lucrezia d' (d. 1516/18)
Este, Lucrezia d'
Este, Margherita d' (d. 1452)
Este, Parisina d' (fl. 1400)
Este, Pizzocara d' (fl. 1400s)
Este, Ricciarda d'
Este, Taddea d' (1365–1404)
Eudoxia of Moscow (1483–1513)
Eustochia (1444–1469)
Eyck, Margaretha van (fl. 1420s–1430s)
Farnese, Giulia (1474–1518?)
Fedele, Cassandra Fidelis (1465–1558)
Ferrers, Elizabeth (1392–1434)
Ferrers, Mary (d. 1457)
Filleul, Jeanne (1424–1498)
Firenze, Francesca da (fl. 15th c.)
Fitzalan, Alice (1352–1416)
Fitzalan, Amy (fl. 1440)
Fitzalan, Elizabeth (fl. 1408–1417)
Fitzalan, Elizabeth (d. 1425)
Fitzalan, Joan (d. 1419)
Fitzalan, Margaret (b. around 1388)
Fitzhugh, Anne (fl. 1466)
Foix, Anne de (fl. 1480–1500)
Frances of Rome (1384–1440)
Fugger, Barbara Baesinger (d. 1497)
Galindo, Beatriz (1475–1534)
Gattilusi, Caterina (fl. 1440)
Gauhar Shad (c. 1378–1459)
Gonzaga, Barbara (1455–1505)
Gonzaga, Cecilia (1426–1451)
Gonzaga, Cecilia (1451–1472)
Gonzaga, Chiara (1465–1505)
Gonzaga, Dorotea (1449–1462)
Gonzaga, Margherita (1418–1439)
Gonzaga, Paola (1393–1453)
Gonzaga, Paola (1463–1497)
Graham, Euphemia (d. 1469)
Greenaway, Margaret (fl. 15th c.)
Grumbach, Argula von (1492–after 1563)
Guillemete du Luys (fl. 1479)
Hachette, Jeanne (c. 1454–?)
Hamilton, Elizabeth (c. 1480–?)
Hankford, Anne (1431–1485)
Harcourt, Johanna (d. 1488)
Hatzler, Clara (fl. 1452)
Haynes, Margery (fl. 15th c.)
Hedvig (d. 1436)
Helena Dragas (fl. 1400)
Helene of Moscow (1474–1513)
Helen Paleologina (c. 1415–1458)
Herbert, Katherine (c. 1471–?)
Hill, Joan (fl. 1460)
Holland, Alianor (c. 1373–1405)
Holland, Anne (fl. 1440–1462)
Holland, Anne (d. 1474)
Holland, Constance (1387–1437)
Holland, Eleanor (c. 1385–?)
Holland, Elizabeth (c. 1383–?)
Holland, Joan (c. 1380–1434)
Holland, Margaret (1385–1429)
Hoo, Anne (c. 1425–1484)
Howard, Catherine (fl. 1450)
Howard, Catherine (d. 1452)
Howard, Catherine (d. after 1478)
Howard, Elizabeth (c. 1410–1475)
Howard, Margaret (fl. 1450)
Hoya, Katherina von (d. around 1470)
Hull, Eleanor (fl. 15th c.)
Ingoldsthorp, Isabel (fl. 15th c.)
Ippolita (1446–1484)
Isabeau of Bavaria (1371–1435)
Isabel (1386–1402)
Isabel (1409–1484)
Isabel (d. 1457?)
Isabel de Clermont (d. 1465)
Isabella (r. 1398–1412)
Isabella I (1451–1504)
Isabella of Asturias (1471–1498)
Isabella of Braganza (1402–1465)
Isabella of Braganza (1459–1521)
Isabella of Naples (1470–1524)
Isabella of Portugal (1397–1471)
Isabella of Valois (1389–c. 1410)
Isabel la Paloma (1432–1455)
Isabelle of Bourbon (d. 1465)
Isabelle of Lorraine (1410–1453)
Isabel of Aragon (1409–1443)
Isabel of Portugal (1428–1496)
Jacqueline of Hainault (1401–1436)
Jacquetta of Luxemburg (c. 1416–1472)
Jeanne de France (c. 1464–1505)
Jeanne de Laval (d. 1498)
Jeanne de Sarmaize (fl. 1456)
Jeanne des Armoises (fl. 1438)
Jeanne of Bourbon (1434–1482)
Jeanne of Bourbon (d. 1493)
Jeanne of Lorraine (1458–1480)
Joan (1384–1400)
Joanna (1452–1490)
Joanna Enriquez (1425–1468)
Joanna II of Naples (1374–1435)
Joanna of Aragon (1454–1517)
Joanna of Brabant (1322–1406)

Joanna of Naples (1478–1518)
Joanna of Navarre (c. 1370–1437)
Joanna of Portugal (1439–1475)
Joan of Arc (c. 1412–1431)
Joan Valois (1391–1433)
Johanna of Bavaria (c. 1373–1410)
Jolanthe of Lorraine (d. 1500)
Juana la Beltraneja (1462–1530)
Juana la Loca (1479–1555)
Judith of Bavaria (fl. 1390s–1400)
Katherine of Holland (d. 1401)
Katherine Plantagenet (1479–1527)
Keith, Muriel (d. 1449)
Kempe, Margery (c. 1373–after 1438)
Kirkeby, Elizabeth (fl. 1482)
Kottanner, Helene (fl. 1440)
Landriani, Lucrezia (fl. 1450s)
Langton, Jane (fl. 15th c.)
Leonora of Aragon (1405–1445)
Leonora of Aragon (1450–1493)
Leslie, Euphemia (d. after 1424)
Leslie, Mary (d. 1429)
Lisle, Honora Grenville (c. 1495–1566)
Longabarba, Bona (fl. 15th c.)
Louise of Savoy (1476–1531)
Lucia of Narni (1476–1544)
Lucy, Elizabeth (fl. 1460s)
Madeleine of France (1443–1486)
Maillé, Jeanne-Marie de (1331–1414)
Malatesta, Anna (fl. 15th c.)
Malatesta, Battista da Montefeltro (1383–1450)
Margaret (c. 1320–1400)
Margaret (1395–1447)
Margaret del Balzo (fl. 15th c.)
Margaret de Rohan (1397–1428)
Margaret de Rohan (fl. 1449)
Margarethe (1370–c. 1400)
Margaret I of Denmark (1353–1412)
Margaret of Anjou (1429–1482)
Margaret of Baden (d. 1457)
Margaret of Bavaria (fl. 1390–1410)
Margaret of Bavaria (d. 1424)
Margaret of Bavaria (1445–1479)
Margaret of Bourbon (d. 1483)
Margaret of Brandenburg (c. 1450–1489)
Margaret of Burgundy (c. 1376–1441)
Margaret of Burgundy (d. 1441)
Margaret of Cleves (fl. early 1400s)
Margaret of Denmark (1456–1486)
Margaret of Flanders (1350–1405)
Margaret of Lorraine (1463–1521)
Margaret of Savoy (d. 1483)
Margaret of Saxony (c. 1416–1486)
Margaret of Saxony (1449–1501)
Margaret of Saxony (1469–1528)
Margaret of Scotland (1424–1445)
Margaret of York (1446–1503)
Marguerite de Bressieux (d. 1450)
Marguerite de Foix (fl. 1456–1477)
Marguerite of Orleans (d. 1466)
Maria of Aragon (1403–1445)
Maria of Aragon (fl. 1440)
Maria of Castile (1401–1458)
Maria of Savoy (fl. 1400s)
Maria of Sicily (d. 1402)
Maria of Trebizond (d. 1439)
Maria of Tver (c. 1440–1467)
Marie (1393–1438)
Marie de Bourbon (fl. 1440s)
Marie of Anjou (1404–1463)
Marie of Cleves (1426–1486)
Marie of Dreux (1391–1446)
Marie of France (1344–1404)
Marie of Guise (d. 1404)
Marie of Orleans (d. 1493)
Marietta (fl. 1430s)
Mary of Burgundy (c. 1400–1463)
Mary of Burgundy (d. 1428)
Mary of Burgundy (1457–1482)
Mary of Guelders (d. 1405)
Mary of Guelders (1433–1463)
Mary Plantagenet (1467–1482)
Medea (d. 1440)
Medici, Bianca de (fl. late 1400s)
Medici, Clarice de (c. 1453–1487)
Medici, Contessina de (fl. 1400–1460)
Medici, Contessina de (fl. 15th c.)
Medici, Ginevra de (fl. 1450–1460)
Medici, Ginevra de (fl. 15th c.)
Medici, Laudomia de (fl. 1460s)
Medici, Lucrezia de (1425–1482)
Medici, Lucrezia de (b. around 1480)
Medici, Luisa de (fl. 15th c.)
Medici, Maria de (fl. late 1400s)
Medici, Nannina de (fl. 15th c.)
Medici, Piccarda de (fl. 15th c.)
Medici, Semiramide de (fl. 1480s)
Mendoza, Ana de (fl. late 1400s)
Michelle Valois (1394–1422)
Mihri Khatun (fl. 15/16th c.)
Mila, Adriana (fl. 1469–1502)
Mohun, Philippa (d. 1431)
Montacute, Alice (c. 1406–1463)
Montacute, Anne (d. 1457)
Montacute, Margaret (fl. 1400s)
Montefeltro, Elisabetta (1471–1526)
Montefeltro, Elisabetta (fl. 15th c.)
Montefeltro, Giovanna (fl. 15th c.)
Montgomery, Margaret (fl. 1438)
More, Alice (c. 1472–1545)
More, Jane Colt (c. 1488–1511)
Mortimer, Anne (1390–1411)
Mortimer, Catherine (d. before 1413)
Mortimer, Eleanor (c. 1395–1418)
Mortimer, Philippa (1375–1401)
Mowbray, Anne (1472–1481)
Mowbray, Margaret (fl. 1400)
Neville, Alice (fl. 1480s)
Neville, Anne (d. 1480)
Neville, Catherine (c. 1397–1483)
Neville, Catherine (fl. 1460)
Neville, Cecily (1415–1495)
Neville, Cecily (fl. 1480s)
Neville, Eleanor (c. 1413–1472)
Neville, Eleanor (fl. 1480s)
Neville, Isabel (1451–1476)
Neville, Joan (fl. 1468)
Neville, Joan (fl. 1480s)
Neville, Lucy (fl. 15th c.)
Neville, Margaret (c. 1377–c. 1424)
Neville, Margaret (b. 1466)
Nogarola, Isotta (c. 1416–1466)
Ormani, Maria (fl. 1453)
Paston, Agnes (c. 1405–1479)
Paston, Margaret (1423–1484)
Percy, Anne (fl. 1470s)
Percy, Elizabeth (1371–1417)
Percy, Elizabeth (d. 1437)
Percy, Katherine (b. 1423)
Perestrello-Moniz, Filippa (d. 1483)
Perez, Inez (fl. 1400)
Philippa (1394–1430)
Philippa of Lancaster (c. 1359–1415)
Pieronne of Brittany (d. 1430)
Pirckheimer, Caritas (1467–1532)
Pole, Elizabeth de la (1444–1503)
Pole, Margaret (1473–1541)
Poynings, Eleanor (d. 1483)
Radegonde (d. 1445)
Renée de Bourbon (fl. 1477)
Rita of Cascia (1381–1457)
Rodiani, Onorata (d. 1452)
Roos, Margaret (fl. 1420)
Rose of Burford (fl. 15th c.)
Ross, Euphemia (d. after 1394)
Sancha of Aragon (1478–1506)
Sanuti, Nicolosa (fl. 1453)
Savorgnan, Maria (fl. 1500)
Scepens, Elizabeth (fl. 1476)
Sforza, Anna (1473–1497)
Sforza, Battista (1446–1472)
Sforza, Bianca Maria (1472–1510)
Sforza, Bianca Simonetta (fl. 15th c.)
Sforza, Cammilla (fl. 15th c.)
Sforza, Caterina (c. 1462–1509)
Sforza, Chiara (b. around 1464)
Sforza, Costanza (fl. 1445)
Sforza, Ginevra (1440–1507)
Sforza, Ippolita (fl. 15th c.)
Sforza, Maddalena (1472–1490)
Sforza, Polissena (fl. 15th c.)
Sforza, Seraphina (1434–1478)
Shipton, Mother (1488–1561)
Shore, Jane (c. 1445–c. 1527)
Sinclair, Catherine (fl. 1475)
Sinclair, Eleanor (d. 1518)
Sophia of Bavaria (fl. 1390s–1400s)
Sophia of Byzantium (1448–1503)
Sophia of Kiev (fl. 1420s)
Sophie of Montferrat (fl. 15th c.)
Sophie of Poland (1464–1512)
Sorel, Agnes (1422–1450)
Stafford, Anne (c. 1400–1432)
Stafford, Anne (d. 1472)
Stafford, Catherine (d. 1419)
Stafford, Catherine (d. 1476)
Stafford, Constance (d. 1474)
Stewart, Annabella (d. after 1471)
Stewart, Anne (fl. 1515)
Stewart, Beatrice (d. around 1424)
Stewart, Eleanor (1427–1496)
Stewart, Elizabeth (c. 1390–?)
Stewart, Elizabeth (d. before 1411)
Stewart, Euphemia (c. 1375–1415)
Stewart, Isabel (fl. 1390–1410)
Stewart, Isabel (d. 1494)
Stewart, Jean (d. after 1404)
Stewart, Jean (d. 1486)
Stewart, Joan (fl. 15th c.)
Stewart, Margaret (d. before 1456)
Stewart, Margaret (fl. 1460–1520)
Stewart, Marjorie (d. after 1417)
Stewart, Marjory (d. before 1432)
Stewart, Mary (d. 1465)
Stewart, Mary (d. 1458)
Strozzi, Alessandra (1406–1469)
Strozzi, Marietta Palla (fl. 1468)
Swynford, Catherine (c. 1350–1403)
Talbot, Anne (d. 1440)
Talbot, Elizabeth (d. 1487)
Talbot, Elizabeth (d. around 1506)
Teresa de Cartagena (fl. 1400)
Theodosia of Moscow (1475–1501)
Tocco, Magdalena-Theodora (fl. mid–1400s)
Tylney, Agnes (1476–1545)
Tylney, Elizabeth (d. 1497)
Vespucci, Simonetta (d. 1476)
Villena, Isabel de (1430–1490)
Visconti, Bianca Maria (1423–1470)
Visconti, Catherine (c. 1360–1404)
Visconti, Elizabeth (d. 1432)
Visconti, Valentina (1366–1408)
Visconti, Virida (c. 1354–1414)
Woodville, Anne (b. around 1458)
Woodville, Elizabeth (1437–1492)
Woodville, Jacquetta (fl. 15th c.)
Woodville, Katherine (c. 1442–1512)
Woodville, Margaret (fl. 1450s)
Woodville, Mary (c. 1443–c. 1480)
Wychingham, Elizabeth (fl. 15th c.)
Yolande of Aragon (1379–1442)
Yolande of France (1434–1478)
Yolande of Vaudemont (1428–1483)

16th Century

Abrabanel, Benvenida (d. 1560)
Acarie, Barbe (1566–1618)
Accoramboni, Vittoria (c. 1557–1585)
Agnes of Barby (1540–1569)
Agnes of Hesse (1527–1555)
Aissa Koli (1497–1504)
Aleotti, Raffaella (c. 1570–c. 1646)
Aleotti, Vittoria (c. 1573–c. 1620)
Ambree, Mary (fl. 1584)
Amelia of Cleves (1517–1586)
Amelia of Denmark (1580–1639)
Amina (c. 1533–c. 1598)
Anastasia Romanova (d. 1560)
Andreini, Isabella (1562–1604)
Anger, Jane (fl. c. 1580)
Anguissola, Anna Maria (c. 1545–?)
Anguissola, Elena (c. 1525–after 1584)
Anguissola, Europa (c. 1542–?)
Anguissola, Sofonisba (1532–1625)
Anna Catherina of Brandenburg (1575–1612)
Anna Jagello (1523–1596)
Anna Maria of the Palatinate (1561–1589)
Anna of Bohemia and Hungary (1503–1547)

Anna of Brandenburg (1487–1514)
Anna of Brandenburg (1507–1567)
Anna of Brunswick (1528–1590)
Anna of Denmark (1532–1585)
Anna of Egmont (1533–1558)
Anna of Prussia (1576–1625)
Anna of Saxony (1544–1577)
Anna of Styria (1573–1598)
Anna Sophia of Prussia (1527–1591)
Anne de la Tour (c. 1496–1524)
Anne de la Tour (d. 1512)
Anne Marie of Brunswick (1532–1568)
Anne of Austria (c. 1550–1580)
Anne of Beaujeu (c. 1460–1522)
Anne of Brittany (c. 1477–1514)
Anne of Cleves (1515–1557)
Anne of Denmark (1574–1619)
Anne of Ferrara (1531–1607)
Antoinette of Bourbon (1494–1583)
Aragona, Tullia d' (1510–1556)
Arden, Alice (1516–1551)
Ascham, Margaret Howe (c. 1535–1590)
Askew, Anne (c. 1521–1546)
Assandra, Caterina (fl. 1580–1609)
Aubespine, Madeleine de l' (1546–1596)
Audley, Margaret (d. 1564)
Bacon, Anne Cooke (1528–1610)
Bagenal, Mabel (c. 1571–1595)
Balfour, Alison (d. 1596)
Barbara Radziwell (1520–1551)
Barbara Zapolya (fl. 1500)
Barton, Elizabeth (c. 1506–1534)
Basset, Mary Roper (fl. 1544–1572)
Bathory, Elizabeth (1560–1614)
Beatrice of Beja (1430–1506)
Beatrice of Cenci (1577–1599)
Beatrice of Naples (1457–1508)
Beatrice of Portugal (1504–1538)
Beaufort, Eleanor (d. 1501)
Benincasa, Ursula (1547–1618)
Bertie, Catharine (1519–1580)
Bertken, Sister (c. 1427–1514)
Bethune, Elizabeth (fl. 16th c.)
Bijns, Anna (1493/94–1575)
Blount, Elizabeth (c. 1502–c. 1540)
Bocher, Joan (d. 1550)
Boleyn, Anne (c. 1507–1536)
Boleyn, Mary (d. 1543)
Bona of Savoy (c. 1450–c. 1505)
Bonville, Cecily (1460–1530)
Bora, Katharina von (1499–1550)
Borgia, Lucrezia (1480–1519)
Bourchier, Anne (1512–1571)
Bourgeois, Louise (1563–1636)
Brahe, Sophia (1556–1643)
Brandon, Anne (d. 1557)
Brandon, Eleanor (c. 1520–1547)
Brandon, Frances (1517–1559)
Braunschweig-Lüneburg, Elisabeth von (1519–1558)
Briet, Marguerite de (c. 1510–c. 1550)
Browne, Anne (d. 1511)
Bullinger, Anna (c. 1504–1564)
Cappello, Bianca (1548–1587)
Carey, Catherine (1529–1569)
Carey, Elizabeth (before 1558–c. 1617)
Carey, Elizabeth (1576–1635)
Carmichael, Elizabeth (fl. 1530s)
Caro Mallén de Soto, Ana (c. 1590–1650)
Carvajal, Luisa de (1568–1614)
Cary, Elizabeth (1586–1639)
Castro, Públia Hortênsia de (1548–1595)
Casulana, Maddalena (c. 1540–1583)
Catherine (1507–1578)
Catherine de Clermont (fl. 16th c.)
Catherine de Foix (c. 1470–1517)
Catherine Jagello (1525–1583)
Catherine of Aragon (1485–1536)
Catherine of Bourbon (c. 1555–1604)
Catherine of Brunswick-Wolfenbuttel (1488–1563)
Catherine of Cleves (fl. 1550s)
Catherine of Custrin (1549–1602)
Catherine of Guise (1552–c. 1594)
Catherine of Habsburg (1533–1572)
Catherine of Pomerania (d. 1526)
Catherine of Portugal (1540–1614)
Catherine of Ricci (c. 1522–1589)
Catherine of Spain (1567–1597)
Cattanei, Vannozza (1442–1518)
Cavendish, Elizabeth (d. 1582)
Cecil, Anne (1556–1589)
Cecil, Mildred Cooke (1526–1589)
Cecilia (1469–1507)
Chand Bibi (1550–1599)
Chantal, Jeanne de (1572–1641)
Charlotte (1516–1524)
Charlotte of Bourbon (d. 1582)
Charlotte of Vendôme (fl. 15th c.)
Châteaubriant, Comtesse de (c. 1490–1537)
Chinchon, Ana, countess of (1576–1639)
Christina of Denmark (1521–1590)
Christina of Holstein-Gottorp (1573–1625)
Christina of Saxony (1461–1521)
Christine of Hesse (1543–1604)
Christine of Lorraine (c. 1571–1637)
Christine of Saxony (1505–1549)
Churchill, Sarah Jennings (1660–1744)
Cibò, Caterina (fl. 1533)
Claude de France (1499–1524)
Claude de France (1547–1575)
Clermont, Claude-Catherine de (1545–1603)
Clifford, Margaret (c. 1560–1616)
Clifford, Margaret (d. 1596)
Clinton, Elizabeth Knevet (c. 1574–c. 1630)
Clitherow, Margaret (1556–1586)
Coignard, Gabrielle de (c. 1550–1586)
Coligny, Louise de (1555–1620)
Colonna, Vittoria (c. 1490–1547)
Columba of Rieti (1467–1501)
Colville, Elizabeth (c. 1571–1600s)
Cornaro, Caterina (1454–1510)
Courtenay, Gertrude (c. 1504–1558)
Cunegunde (1465–1520)
Dacre, Elizabeth (b. before 1566)
Dacre, Marie (1563–1578)
Danvers, Magdalene (1561–1627)
Dare, Virginia (b. 1587)
Davies, Eleanor (1590–1652)
Delaye, Marguerite (fl. 1569)
Diane de France (1538–1619)
Diane de Poitiers (1499–1566)
Dianti, Laura (fl. 1527)
Digby, Lettice (c. 1588–1658)
Dobo, Katica (fl. 1552)
Dorothea of Brandenburg (1446–1519)
Dorothea of Denmark (1520–1580)
Dorothea of Denmark (1528–1575)
Dorothea of Saxe-Lauenburg (1511–1571)
Dorothea of Saxony (1563–1587)
Dorothea Oldenburg (1504–1547)
Dorothy of Denmark (1546–1617)
Douglas, Margaret (1515–1578)
Dowriche, Anne (before 1560–after 1613)
Duci, Filippa (fl. 16th c.)
du Guillet, Pernette (c. 1520–1545)
Durgawati (d. 1564)
Dyveke (c. 1491–1517)
Eleanor of Portugal (1498–1558)
Eleonora of Austria (1534–1594)
Eleonore Hohenzollern (1583–1607)
Elisabeth of Habsburg (1501–1526)
Elisabeth of Habsburg (1554–1592)
Elizabeth I (1533–1603)
Elizabeth of Anhalt (1563–1607)
Elizabeth of Bohemia (1596–1662)
Elizabeth of Brandenburg (1510–1558)
Elizabeth of Denmark (1485–1555)
Elizabeth of Denmark (1524–1586)
Elizabeth of Denmark (1573–1626)
Elizabeth of Habsburg (d. 1545)
Elizabeth of Hungary (c. 1430–1505)
Elizabeth of Valois (1545–1568)
Elizabeth of Wittelsbach (1540–1594)
Elizabeth of York (1466–1503)
Elphinstone, Eupheme (fl. 1500s)
Emilia of Orange (1569–1629)
Enríquez de Guzmán, Feliciana (c. 1580–1640)
Entragues, Henriette d' (1579–1633)
Erskine, Margaret (fl. 1530s)
Este, Bianca Maria d' (1440–1506)
Este, Eleonora d' (1515–1575)
Este, Eleonora d' (1537–1581)
Este, Elisabetta d' (fl. 1500)
Este, Isabella d' (1474–1539)
Este, Lucrezia d' (d. 1516/18)
Este, Lucrezia d' (1535–1598)
Este, Virginia d' (b. 1573?)
Estienne, Nicole d' (c. 1544–c. 1596)
Estrées, Angélique, d' (fl. 16th c.)
Estrées, Diane, d' (b. 1572)
Estrées, Françoise Babou de la Bourdaisière, Dame d' (fl. 16th c.)
Estrées, Gabrielle d' (1573–1599)
Étampes, Anne de Pisseleu d'Heilly, Duchesse d' (1508–c. 1580)
Eudoxia Jaroslavovna (1534–1581)
Farnese, Giulia (1474–1518?)
Fedele, Cassandra Fidelis (1465–1558)
Fiennes, Anne (d. 1595)
Fingerin, Agnes (d. 1515)
Fitton, Mary (c. 1578–1647)
Fitzalan, Katherine (b. around 1520)
Fitzalan, Katherine (fl. 1530s)
Fitzalan, Mary (d. 1557)
Fitzgerald, Elizabeth (c. 1528–1589)
Fitzgerald, Katherine (c. 1500–1604)
Fitzroy, Mary (c. 1519–1557)
Fleming, Jane (fl. 1550s)
Flemming, Mary (fl. 1540s)
Flore, Jeanne (fl. early 16th c.)
Foix, Anne de (fl. 1480–1500)
Foix, Germaine de (1488–1538)
Fontana, Lavinia (1552–1614)
Fornari, Maria Victoria (1562–1617)
Franco, Veronica (1546–1591)
Galigaï, Leonora (c. 1570–1617)
Galindo, Beatriz (1475–1534)
Galizia, Fede (1578–1630)
Gambara, Veronica (1485–1550)
Gheenst, Johanna van der (fl. 16th c.)
Ghisi, Diana (c. 1530–1590)
Glinskaia, Anna (d. 1553)
Glinski, Elena (c. 1506–1538)
Godunova, Xenia (1582–1622)
Gonzaga, Anna (1585–1618)
Gonzaga, Anna Caterina (1566–1621)
Gonzaga, Antonia (d. 1538)
Gonzaga, Barbara (1455–1505)
Gonzaga, Chiara (1465–1505)
Gonzaga, Eleonora (1493–1543)
Gonzaga, Ippolita (1503–1570)
Gonzaga, Ippolita (1535–1563)
Gonzaga, Isabella (1537–1579)
Gonzaga, Isabella (d. 1559)
Gonzaga, Margherita (1510–1566)
Gonzaga, Margherita (1561–1628)
Gonzaga, Margherita (1564–1618)
Gonzaga, Paola (1508–1569)
Gournay, Marie le Jars de (1565–1645)
Grey, Catherine (c. 1540–1568)
Grey, Elizabeth (fl. 1482–1530)
Grey, Elizabeth (1505–1526)
Grey, Lady Jane (1537–1554)
Grey, Mary (1545–1578)
Grumbach, Argula von (1492–after 1563)
Grymeston, Elizabeth Bernye (d. 1603)
Guicciardini, Isabella (fl. 16th c.)
Guillard, Charlotte (d. 1556)
Gülabahar (fl. 1521)
Gulbadan (c. 1522–1603)
Guzman, Eleonore de (d. 1512)
Hafsa (d. 1534)
Hastings, Anne (c. 1487–?)
Hastings, Anne (d. after 1506)
Hathaway, Anne (1556–1623)
Hatice (fl. 1500–1536)
Hedwig of Poland (1513–1573)
Helene of Moldavia (d. 1505)
Helene of Moscow (1474–1513)
Hemessen, Caterina van (c. 1528–c. 1587)
Henrietta of Cleves (r. 1564–1601)
Herbert, Mary (1561–1621)
Heymair, Magdalena (c. 1545–after 1586)
Hoby, Margaret (1571–1633)
Howard, Anne (1475–1511)
Howard, Anne (d. 1559)
Howard, Catherine (1520/22–1542)
Howard, Catherine (d. 1548)
Howard, Catherine (d. 1596)

Howard, Dorothy (fl. 1500)
Howard, Elizabeth (1494–1558)
Howard, Elizabeth (?–1538)
Howard, Elizabeth (d. 1534)
Howard, Isabel (fl. 1500s)
Howard, Jane (d. 1593)
Howard, Joyce (fl. 1500s)
Howard, Margaret (fl. 1500s)
Howard, Mary (fl. 1500s)
Howard, Muriel (d. 1512)
Hoyers, Anna Ovena (1584–1655)
Hungerford, Agnes (d. 1524)
Inglis, Esther (1571–1624)
Isabella Clara Eugenia of Austria (1566–1633)
Isabella del Balzo (d. 1533)
Isabella I (1451–1504)
Isabella of Braganza (1459–1521)
Isabella of Braganza (c. 1512–1576)
Isabella of Naples (1470–1524)
Isabella of Poland (1519–1559)
Isabella of Portugal (1503–1539)
Jane of Bourbon-Vendome (d. 1511)
Jeanne d'Albret (1528–1572)
Jeanne de Lestonac (1556–1640)
Joana de Mendoza (d. 1580)
Joanna of Aragon (1454–1517)
Joanna of Austria (1535–1573)
Joanna of Austria (1546–1578)
Joanna of Naples (1478–1518)
Jocelin, Elizabeth (1596–1622)
Jodha Bai (d. 1613)
Jolanthe of Lorraine (d. 1500)
Juana la Beltraneja (1462–1530)
Juana la Loca (1479–1555)
Juliane of Nassau-Dillenburg (1546–1588)
Juliane of Stolberg-Wernigrode (1506–1580)
Katarina of Saxe-Lüneburg (1513–1535)
Katarina Stenbock (1536–1621)
Katherine Plantagenet (1479–1527)
Killigrew, Catherine (c. 1530–1583)
Knollys, Lettice (c. 1541–1634)
Kösem (1589–1651)
Labé, Louise (c. 1523–1566)
Lemp, Rebecca (d. 1590)
Leyburne, Elizabeth (d. 1567)
Line, Anne (d. 1601)
Lisle, Honora Grenville (c. 1495–1566)
Locke, Anne Vaughan (c. 1530–c. 1590)
Louisa Juliana (1576–1644)
Louise de Brézé (fl. 1555)
Louise de Montmorency (fl. 1498–1525)
Louise of Lorraine (1554–1601)
Louise of Savoy (1476–1531)
Loynes, Antoinette de (fl. 16th c.)
Loynes, Camille de (fl. 16th c.)
Lucia of Narni (1476–1544)
Lumley, Joanna (c. 1537–1576)
Maansdatter, Katherine (1550–1612)
MacDonald, Finula (fl. 1569–1592)
Madeleine de la Tour d'Auvergne (1501–1519)
Madeleine de Saint-Nectaire (fl. 1575)
Madeleine of France (1520–1537)
Magdalena (1532–1590)
Magdalena (fl. late 1500s)
Magdalene of Saxony (1507–1534)
Malatesta (fl. 1504–1505)
Malinche (c. 1500–1531)
Mansenée, Desle la (c. 1502–1529)
Margareta Leijonhufvud (1514–1551)
Margaret of Angoulême (1492–1549)
Margaret of Austria (1480–1530)
Margaret of Austria (c. 1577–1611)
Margaret of Lorraine (1463–1521)
Margaret of Parma (1522–1586)
Margaret of Savoy (1523–1574)
Margaret of Saxony (1449–1501)
Margaret of Saxony (1469–1528)
Margaret of Valois (1553–1615)
Margaret of Vendôme (fl. 16th c.)
Margaret of York (1446–1503)
Margaret Tudor (1489–1541)
Marguerite of Lorraine (c. 1561–?)
Maria Anna of Bavaria (1574–1616)
Maria de Portugal (1521–1577)
Maria Eleanora (1550–1608)
Mariana of Jesus (1565–1624)
Maria of Castile (1482–1517)
Maria of Circassia (d. 1569)
Maria of Julich-Berg (fl. 1515)
Maria of Portugal (1538–1577)
Marie de Brabant (c. 1530–c. 1600)
Marie of Austria (1528–1603)
Marie of Brandenburg-Kulmbach (1519–1567)
Marie of Luxemburg (d. 1546)
Marie of Luxemburg (fl. 16th c.)
Marquets, Anne de (1533–1588)
Martelli, Camilla (fl. 1570s)
Martha the Nun (1560–1631)
Martin, Dorcas Eglestone (fl. 16th c.)
Mary (1531–1581)
Mary I (1516–1558)
Mary Magdalen of Pazzi (1566–1607)
Mary of Bavaria (1551–1608)
Mary of Guise (1515–1560)
Mary of Hungary (1505–1558)
Mary of Portugal (1527–1545)
Mary Stuart (1542–1587)
Mary Tudor (1496–1533)
Medici, Alfonsina de (d. 1520)
Medici, Catherine de (1519–1589)
Medici, Clarice de (1493–1528)
Medici, Eleonora de (1522–1562)
Medici, Eleonora de (1556–1576)
Medici, Eleonora de (1567–1611)
Medici, Isabella de (1542–1576)
Medici, Laudomia de (fl. 1530s)
Medici, Lucrezia de (c. 1544–1561)
Medici, Maddalena de (d. 1519)
Medici, Maria Soderini de (fl. 16th c.)
Medici, Marie de (c. 1573–1642)
Mendoza, Ana de (1540–1592)
Mihri Khatun (fl. 15/16th c.)
Mihrimah (1522–1575)
Mildmay, Grace (1553–1620)
Mira Bai (1498–1547)
Miremont, Jacqueline de (fl. 16th c.)
Mniszek, Marina (c. 1588–1614)
Molesworth, Martha (1577–1646)
Molza, Tarquinia (1542–1617)
Montefeltro, Elisabetta (1471–1526)
Morata, Fulvia Olympia (1526–1555)
More, Agnes (1591–1656)
More, Alice (c. 1472–1545)
More, Gertrude (1606–1633)
More, Jane Colt (c. 1488–1511)
Nasi, Gracia Mendes (1510–1569)
Neville, Jane (d. 1538)
Neville, Margaret (d. 1506)
Njinga (c. 1580s–1663)
Nurbanu (1525–1583)
Nur Jahan (1577–1645)
Odaldi, Annalena (1572–1638)
O'Malley, Grace (c. 1530–1603)
Orsini, Belleza (d. 1528)
Padilla, Maria Pacheco (c. 1496–1531)
Paletzi, Juliane (d. 1569)
Parker, Jane (d. 1542?)
Parr, Anne (d. 1552)
Parr, Catherine (1512–1548)
Parr, Maud Greene (1495–1529)
Parthenay, Anne de (fl. 16th c.)
Percy, Eleanor (d. 1530)
Philiberta of Savoy (c. 1498–1524)
Philippa of Guelders (d. 1547)
Pico, Caterina (d. 1501)
Pirckheimer, Caritas (1467–1532)
Pole, Elizabeth de la (1444–1503)
Pole, Ursula (d. 1570)
Pozzo, Modesta (1555–1592)
Renée of France (1510–1575)
Renée of Montpensier (fl. 1500s)
Rich, Penelope (c. 1562–1607)
Robsart, Amy (c. 1532–1560)
Roches, Catherine des (1542–1587)
Roches, Madeleine des (1520–1587)
Romanov, Anna (fl. 1550)
Romanov, Euphamia (fl. 1550)
Romanov, Martha (fl. 1550)
Romieu, Marie de (c. 1545–c. 1590)
Roper, Margaret More (1505–1544)
Rossi, Properzia de (c. 1490–1530)
Rothelin, Jacqueline de Rohan, Marquise de (c. 1520–1587)
Rovere, Giulia della (fl. 16th c.)
Roxelana (c. 1504–1558)
Russell, Elizabeth (1540–1609)
Sabine of Bavaria (1492–1564)
Sabine of Brandenburg-Ansbach (1529–1575)
Sabuco, Oliva de Nantes Barrera (1562–1625)
Safiye (d. 1603)
Sah (fl. 1500s)
Salviati, Elena (fl. early 1500s)
Salviati, Maria (1499–1543)
Sampson, Agnes (d. 1591)
Savorgnan, Maria (fl. 1500)
Seymour, Anne (c. 1532–1587)
Seymour, Jane (c. 1509–1537)
Seymour, Jane (1541–1560)
Seymour, Margaret (c. 1533–?)
Sforza, Angela (fl. 1500s)
Sforza, Bianca Maria (1472–1510)
Sforza, Bona (1493–1557)
Sforza, Caterina (c. 1462–1509)
Sforza, Ginevra (1440–1507)
Sforza, Ginevra Tiepolo (fl. 16th c.)
Shaw, Elizabeth (fl. 1500s)
Shipton, Mother (1488–1561)
Shirley, Elizabeth (c. 1568–1641)
Shore, Jane (c. 1445–c. 1527)
Sibylle Elizabeth of Wurttemberg (1584–1606)
Sibylle of Anhalt (1564–1614)
Sigea, Luisa (c. 1531–1560)
Sigurana, Caterina (fl. 1543)
Sinclair, Eleanor (d. 1518)
Sobakin, Marta (d. 1571)
Solomonia (fl. 16th c.)
Sophia (fl. 1500s)
Sophia of Byzantium (1448–1503)
Sophia of Mecklenburg (1508–1541)
Sophia of Mecklenburg (1557–1631)
Sophia of Pomerania (1498–1568)
Sophie of Brandenburg (1568–1622)
Sophie of Holstein-Gottorp (1569–1634)
Sophie of Liegnitz (1525–1546)
Sophie of Poland (1464–1512)
Sourdis, Isabelle de (fl. 16th c.)
Stafford, Catherine (fl. 1530)
Stafford, Elizabeth (1494–1558)
Stafford, Elizabeth (d. 1532)
Stampa, Gaspara (1523–1554)
Stanhope, Anne (1497–1587)
Stanley, Margaret (fl. 16th c.)
Stewart, Anne (fl. 1515)
Stewart, Elizabeth (fl. 1578)
Stewart, Elizabeth (fl. 16th c.)
Stewart, Margaret (fl. 1460–1520)
Stuart, Arabella (1575–1615)
Suzanne of Bavaria (1502–1543)
Suzanne of Bourbon (1491–1521)
Sybilla of Brandenburg (fl. 1500)
Sybilla of Cleves (1514–1554)
Talbot, Elizabeth (d. around 1506)
Talbot, Elizabeth (1518–1608)
Tavernier, Nicole (fl. 1594)
Tecuichpo (d. 1551)
Teerlinc, Levina (c. 1520–1576)
Teresa of Avila (1515–1582)
Theodosia of Moscow (1475–1501)
Trussel, Elizabeth (1496–1527)
Turner, Anne (1576–1615)
Turunku Bakwa (fl. 1530s)
Tyler, Margaret (d. 1595)
Tylney, Agnes (1476–1545)
Ursula of Brandenburg (1488–1510)
Vassiltschikov, Anna (16th c.)
Vere, Frances de (d. 1577)
Wa Shi (1498–1560)
Wentworth, Margaret (d. 1550)
Whitney, Isabella (fl. 1567–1575)
Willums, Sigbrit (fl. 1507–1523)
Woodville, Katherine (c. 1442–1512)
Wotton, Margaret (fl. 16th c.)
Young, Elizabeth (fl. 1558)
Zell, Katharina Schütz (c. 1497–1562)
Zuzoric, Cvijeta (c. 1555–1600)
Zwingli, Anna Reinhard (1487–c. 1538)

17th Century

Abarca, Maria Francisca de (fl. 1640–1656)
Acarie, Barbe (1566–1618)
Acevedo, Angela de (d. 1644)
Adams, Mary (d. 1702)
Agreda, Sor María de (1602–1665)
Alacoque, Marguerite Marie (1647–1690)
Albertina Agnes (d. 1696)
Alcoforado, Mariana (1640–1723)
Alden, Priscilla (c. 1602–c. 1685)
Aleotti, Raffaella (c. 1570–c. 1646)
Aleotti, Vittoria (c. 1573–c. 1620)
Alexander, Mary (1693–1760)
Alleine, Theodosia (fl. 17th c.)
Allen, Hannah Archer (fl. 1680s)
Amarilis (fl. 17th c.)
Amelia of Denmark (1580–1639)
Amelia of Solms (1602–1675)
Andreini, Isabella (1562–1604)
Anguissola, Sofonisba (1532–1625)
Anna Constancia (1619–1651)
Anna Sophia of Denmark (1647–1717)
Anne (1665–1714)
Anne-Eleanor of Hesse-Darmstadt (1601–1659)
Anne Henriette Louise (1647–1723)
Anne-Marie d'Bourbon-Orleans (1669–1728)
Anne of Austria (1601–1666)
Anne of Denmark (1574–1619)
Anne of Ferrara (1531–1607)
Anne of Velasquez (1585–1607)
Ariadne (fl. 1696)
Armitage, Goody (fl. 1643)
Arnauld, Angélique (1624–1684)
Arnauld, Jacqueline Marie (1591–1661)
Arnauld, Jeanne Catherine (1593–1671)
Arundel, Ann (1557–1630)
Arundel, Anne (d. 1642)
Arundel, Blanche (1583–1649)
Ascarelli, Devora (fl. 1601)
Assandra, Caterina (fl. 1580–1609)
Astell, Mary (1666–1731)
Augusta Maria of Holstein-Gottorp (1649–1728)
Aulnoy, Marie Catherine, Countess d' (c. 1650–1705)
Awashonks (fl. mid–late 17th c.)
Bacon, Anne Cooke (1528–1610)
Baillie, Grizel (1665–1746)
Baird, Frances (d. 1708)
Bankes, Mary (1598–1661)
Barber, Mary (c. 1690–1757)
Barker, Jane (1652–1732)
Baroni, Leonora (1611–1670)
Barry, Elizabeth (1658–1713)
Basile, Adriana (c. 1590–c. 1640)
Bathory, Elizabeth (1560–1614)
Baume, Madame de la (fl. 17th c.)
Bavent, Madeleine (fl. 1642)
Bazincourt, Mlle Thomas de (fl. 18th c.)
Beale, Mary (1632–1699)
Beatrice, Dona (c. 1684–1706)
Beaumont, Agnes (1652–1720)
Beaumont, Mary (d. 1632)
Behn, Aphra (1640?–1689)
Bejart, Armande (c. 1642–1700)
Bejart, Geneviève (c. 1622–1675)
Bejart, Madeleine (1618–1672)
Bembo, Antonia (1643–1715)
Bendish, Bridget (c. 1650–1726)
Benizelos, Philothey (fl. 1650)
Bentley, Catherine (fl. 1635)
Berkeley, Frances (1634–after 1695)
Bernard, Catherine (1662–1712)
Biddle, Hester (1629–1696)
Blaugdone, Barbara (c. 1609–1705)
Boothby, Frances (fl. 1669)
Bourgeois, Louise (1563–1636)
Bourgeoys, Marguerite (1620–1700)
Bourignon, Antoinette (1616–1680)
Bowers, Bathsheba (c. 1672–1718)
Bracegirdle, Anne (1671–1748)
Bradstreet, Anne (1612–1672)
Brahe, Sophia (1556–1643)
Branch, Elizabeth (1673–1740)
Braunschweig-Lüneburg, Sibylle Ursula von (1629–1671)
Braunschweig-Lüneburg, Sophie Elisabeth von (1613–1676)
Brent, Margaret (c. 1601–1671)
Brézé, Claire-Clémence de Maillé de (1628–1694)
Brinvilliers, Marie de (1630–1676)
Buffet, Marguerite (d. 1680)
Burnet, Elizabeth (1661–1709)
Burras, Anne (fl. 1609)
Caccini, Francesca (1587–c. 1626)
Caesar, Mary (1677–1741)
Cairns, Elizabeth (1685–1714)
Cantofoli, Ginevra (1618–1672)
Carey, Elizabeth (before 1558–c. 1617)
Carey, Elizabeth (1576–1635)
Carey, Mary (c. 1610–c. 1680)
Caro Mallén de Soto, Ana (c. 1590–1650)
Carriera, Rosalba (1675–1757)
Carvajal, Luisa de (1568–1614)
Carvajal, Mariana de (c. 1620–1680)
Cary, Anne (1615–1671)
Cary, Elizabeth (1586–1639)
Cary, Lucy (1619–1650)
Cary, Mary (c. 1621–after 1653)
Casalina, Lucia (1677–1762)
Castillo y Guevara, Francisca Josefa del (1671–1742)
Catherine (1584–1638)
Catherine of Bourbon (c. 1555–1604)
Catherine of Braganza (1638–1705)
Catherine of Custrin (1549–1602)
Catherine of Lorraine (fl. 1600s)
Cavanagh, Kit (1667–1739)
Cavendish, Christiana (1595–1675)
Cavendish, Elizabeth (1626–1663)
Cavendish, Jane (1621–1669)
Cavendish, Margaret (1623–1673)
Caylus, Marthe M. (1673–1729)
Cecil, Anne (d. 1637)
Cecil, Elizabeth (1619–1689)
Cecil, Georgiana (1827–1899)
Cecilia Renata of Austria (1611–1644)
Cellier, Elizabeth (fl. 1679)
Çentlivre, Susanna (c. 1669–1723)
Černínová z Harasova, Zuzana (1601–1654)
Champmesle, Marie (c. 1642–1698)
Chandler, Mary (1687–1745)
Chantal, Jeanne de (1572–1641)
Charlotte Amalia of Hesse (1650–1714)
Charlotte de Montmorency (1594–1650)
Charlotte Elizabeth of Bavaria (1652–1722)
Charlotte of Hesse (1627–1687)
Chéron, Elisabeth-Sophie (1648–1711)
Chidley, Katherine (fl. 1641)
Chinchon, Ana, countess of (1576–1639)
Chivers, Elizabeth (1682–1712)
Cho (1809–1890)
Christina Casimir (fl. 1640–1660)
Christina of Holstein-Gottorp (1573–1625)
Christina of Sweden (1626–1689)
Christine of Baden-Durlach (1645–1705)
Christine of France (1606–1663)
Christine of Hesse (1543–1604)
Christine of Lorraine (c. 1571–1637)
Chudleigh, Mary Lee (1656–1710)
Churchill, Arabella (1648–1714)
Churchill, Deborah (1677–1708)
Claudia Felicitas (fl. 17th c.)
Clifford, Anne (1590–1676)
Clifford, Margaret (c. 1560–1616)
Clinton, Elizabeth Knevet (c. 1574–c. 1630)
Cockburn, Catharine Trotter (1679–1749)
Coit, Mehetabel Chandler (1673–1758)
Coligny, Henriette de (1618–1683)
Coligny, Louise de (1555–1620)
Collier, Mary (c. 1690–c. 1762)
Collins, Ann (fl. mid–17th c.)
Colville, Elizabeth (c. 1571–1600s)
Constance de Cezelli (d. 1617)
Constance of Styria (1588–1631)
Cornaro Piscopia, Elena Lucretia (1646–1684)
Cotton, Priscilla (d. 1664)
Coventry, Anne (1673–1763)
Cowper, Mary (1685–1724)
Cromwell, Bridget (1624–c. 1660)
Cromwell, Elizabeth (1598–1665)
Cromwell, Mary (1636–1712)
Cunigunde Sobieska (fl. 1690s)
Cunitz, Maria (1610–1664)
Cunningham, Ann (d. 1647)
Dacier, Anne (1654–1720)
Danvers, Magdalene (1561–1627)
Davies, Eleanor (1590–1652)
Davies, Moll (fl. 1673)
Davy, Sarah (c. 1639–1670)
Davys, Mary (1674–1731)
de Ayala, Josefa (1630–1684)
Delanoue, Jeanne (1666–1736)
Delorme, Marion (c. 1613–1650)
Demandols de la Palud, Madeleine (fl. 17th century)
des Anges, Jeanne (fl. 1632)
Deshayes, Catherine (d. 1680)
Deshoulières, Antoinette (1638–1694)
Desmier, Eleanor (1639–1722)
Devereux, Frances (d. 1674)
Diane de France (1538–1619)
Digby, Lettice (c. 1588–1658)
Dixon, Margaret (1670–1753)
Dolgorukova, Marie (d. 1625)
Dorothea Hedwig of Brunswick-Wolfenbuttel (1587–1609)
Dorothy of Denmark (1546–1617)
Downing, Lucy Winthrop (c. 1600–1679)
Dowriche, Anne (before 1560–after 1613)
Drake, Elizabeth (fl. 1625–1656)
Drake, Judith (fl. 1696)
Dumée, Jeanne (fl. 1680)
du Noyer, Anne-Marguérite Petit (1663–1719)
Dustin, Hannah (1657–c. 1736)
Du Verger, Susan (before 1625–after 1657)
Dyer, Mary Barrett (c. 1591–1660)
Egerton, Sarah Fyge (c. 1670–1723)
Egual, Maria (1698–1735)
Eleanor Habsburg (1653–1697)
Eleanor of Pfalz-Neuburg (1655–1720)
Eleanor of Saxe-Eisenach (1662–1696)
Eleonore Hohenzollern (1583–1607)
Elizabeth Amalia of Hesse (1635–1709)
Elizabeth-Charlotte (1676–1744)
Elizabeth Charlotte of the Palatinate (fl. 1620)
Elizabeth de Bourbon (1614–1664)
Elizabeth Henrietta of Hesse-Cassel (1661–1683)
Elizabeth I (1533–1603)
Elizabeth of Anhalt (1563–1607)
Elizabeth of Bohemia (1596–1662)
Elizabeth of Bohemia (1618–1680)
Elizabeth of Brunswick-Wolfenbuttel (1593–1650)
Elizabeth of Denmark (1573–1626)
Elizabeth Sophie of Saxe-Altenburg (1619–1680)
Elizabeth Stuart (1635–1650)
Elizabeth Valois (1602–1644)
Emilia of Orange (1569–1629)
Engelbretsdatter, Dorothe (1634–1716)
Enríquez de Guzmán, Feliciana (c. 1580–1640)
Entragues, Henriette d' (1579–1633)
Ephelia (fl. 1660s–1680s)
Épine, Margherita de l' (c. 1683–1746)
Erauso, Catalina de (1592–1635)
Erskine, Mary (1629–1707)
Estaugh, Elizabeth Haddon (1680–1762)
Este, Catherine d' (fl. 1700)
Eudoxia Streshnev (1608–1645)
Evelyn, Mary (1665–1685)
Fanshawe, Anne (1625–1680)
Fell, Margaret (1614–1702)
Fernig, Théophile de (c. 1779–c. 1818)
Fetti, Lucrina (fl. 1614–1651)
Fiennes, Celia (1662–1741)
Finch, Anne (1631–1679)
Finch, Anne (1661–1720)
Fisher, Margaret (b. 1689)
Fisher, Mary (c. 1623–1698)
Fiske, Sarah Symmes (1652–1692)
Fitton, Mary (c. 1578–1647)
Fitzgerald, Katherine (c. 1500–1604)
Fitzroy, Charlotte (1664–1717)
Fontaine, Mlle de la (1655–1738)
Fontana, Lavinia (1552–1614)
Fontanges, Duchesse de (1661–1681)
Fornari, Maria Victoria (1562–1617)
Françoise d'Orleans (fl. 1650)
Françoise-Marie de Bourbon (1677–1749)
Franklin, Ann (1696–1763)
Frederica Amalie (1649–1704)
French, Mary (fl. 1703)
Frith, Mary (c. 1584–1659)

Fuchs, Anna Rupertina (1657–1722)
Galigaï, Leonora (c. 1570–1617)
Galilei, Maria Celeste (1600–1634)
Galizia, Fede (1578–1630)
Garzoni, Giovanna (1600–1670)
Geddes, Janet (fl. 1637)
Gentileschi, Artemisia (1593–c. 1653)
Gethin, Grace Norton (1676–1697)
Glover, Elizabeth Harris (d. 1643)
Glückel of Hameln (1646–1724)
Godunova, Irene (d. 1603)
Godunova, Xenia (1582–1622)
Gonzaga, Anna (1585–1618)
Gonzaga, Anna Caterina (1566–1621)
Gonzaga, Anne de (1616–1684)
Gonzaga, Eleonora I (1598–1655)
Gonzaga, Eleonora II (1628–1686)
Gonzaga, Isabella (fl. 1600s)
Gonzaga, Margherita (1561–1628)
Gonzaga, Margherita (1564–1618)
Gonzaga, Margherita (1591–1632)
Gonzaga, Maria (1609–1660)
Goodhue, Sarah Whipple (1641–1681)
Goose, Elizabeth (1665–1757)
Gournay, Marie le Jars de (1565–1645)
Graffigny, Françoise de (1695–1758)
Grange, Rachel (1682–1745)
Greiffenberg, Catharina Regina von (1633–1694)
Grey, Elizabeth (1581–1651)
Griffin, Jane (1680–1720)
Grignan, Françoise-Marguerite de Sévigné, Countess de (1646–1705)
Grushevski, Agraphia (1662–1681)
Grymeston, Elizabeth Bernye (d. 1603)
Guette, Catherine de la (1613–1676)
Guyon, Jeanne Marie Bouviéres de la Mothe (1648–1717)
Gwynn, Nell (1650–1687)
Hadice Turhan (1627–1683)
Halkett, Anne (1622–1699)
Hamilton, Anne (1636–1716)
Hamilton, Elizabeth (1641–1708)
Hamilton, Mary (1613–1638)
Hammon, Mary (c. 1633–?)
Hanson, Elizabeth Meader (1684–1737)
Harley, Brilliana (c. 1600–1643)
Hastings, Elizabeth (1682–1739)
Hathaway, Anne (1556–1623)
Hay, Lucy (1599–1660)
Hayden, Anna Tompson (1648–after 1720)
Hedwig of Denmark (1581–1641)
Hedwig of Holstein-Gottorp (1636–1715)
Hedwig Wittelsbach (fl. late 1600s)
Henrietta Anne (1644–1670)
Henrietta Catherine of Nassau (1637–1708)
Henrietta Maria (1609–1669)
Henrietta Maria (1626–1651)
Henrietta of Savoy (c. 1630–?)
Herbert, Lucy (1669–1744)
Herbert, Mary (1561–1621)
Hoby, Margaret (1571–1633)
Holland, Catherine (1637–1720)
Hopton, Susanna Harvey (1627–1708)
Hoskens, Jane Fenn (1694–c. 1750)
Housden, Jane (d. 1714)
Howard, Catherine (d. 1672)
Howard, Frances (1593–1632)
Hoyers, Anna Ovena (1584–1655)
Huber, Marie (1695–1753)
Hume, Anna (fl. 1644)
Hume, Elizabeth (c. 1599–1633)
Hutchinson, Anne (1591–1643)
Hutchinson, Lucy (1620–post 1675)
Hyde, Anne (1638–1671)
Inglis, Esther (1571–1624)
Isabella Clara Eugenia of Austria (1566–1633)
Jacquet de la Guerre, Elisabeth-Claude (c. 1666–1729)
Jahanara (1614–1681)
James, Elinor (c. 1645–1719)
Jans, Annetje (c. 1605–1663)
Jeanne de Lestonac (1556–1640)
Joanna of Portugal (1636–1653)
Jocelin, Elizabeth (1596–1622)
Jodha Bai (d. 1613)
Johanna Elizabeth of Baden-Durlach (1651–1680)
Johnson, Esther (1681–1728)
Johnston, Henrietta (c. 1670–1728)
Juana Inés de la Cruz (1651–1695)
Katarina Stenbock (1536–1621)
Kéroüalle, Louise de (1649–1734)
Kielmansegge, Sophia Charlotte von (1673–1725)
Killigrew, Anne (1660–1685)
Killigrew, Elizabeth (c. 1622–?)
Kincaid, Jean (1579–1600)
King, Anne (1621–after 1684)
Kirch, Maria Winkelmann (1670–1720)
Kirkhoven, Catherine (d. 1667)
Knight, Sarah Kemble (1666–1727)
Knipp, Mrs. (fl. 1670)
Knollys, Elizabeth (c. 1586–1658)
Knollys, Lettice (c. 1541–1634)
Knyvett, Catherine (d. 1633)
Königsmark, Aurora von (1662–1728)
Kuntsch, Margaretha Susanna von (1651–1716)
La Fayette, Marie-Madeleine de (1634–1693)
La Force, Charlotte-Rose de Caumont de (1650–1724)
La Gratiosa (d. 1659)
Lalla Rookh (fl. 1600s)
Lambert, Anne Thérèse de Marguenat de Courcelles, Marquise de (1647–1733)
Lane, Jane (d. 1689)
La Roche, Guilhem (1644–1710)
La Sablière, Marguerite de (1640–1693)
La Vallière, Louise de (1644–1710)
Lead, Jane Ward (1623–1704)
Le Camus, Madame (fl. 17th c.)
Leigh, Dorothy Kempe (fl. 1616)
Lenclos, Ninon de (1623–1705)
Leonarda, Isabella (1620–1704)
Leyster, Judith (1609–1660)
L'Héritier, Marie-Jeanne (1664–1734)
Lisle, Alice (c. 1614–1685)
Livingston, Alida Schuyler (1656–1727)
Longueville, Anne Geneviève, Duchesse de (1619–1679)
Louisa (1622–1709)
Louisa Henrietta of Orange (1627–1667)
Louisa Juliana (1576–1644)
Louise (1692–1712)
Louise Dorothea of Brandenburg (1680–1705)
Louise Marie de Gonzague (1611–1667)
Louise of Lorraine (1554–1601)
Louise of Mecklenburg-Gustrow (1667–1721)
Luisa de Guzman (1613–1666)
Lussan, Marguerite de (1682–1758)
Maansdatter, Katherine (1550–1612)
MacLeod, Mary (c. 1615–c. 1706)
Madeleine of Anhalt-Zerbst (1679–1740)
Magdalena Sybilla (1587–1659)
Magdalena Sybilla (1617–1668)
Magdalena Sybilla of Holstein-Gottorp (1631–1719)
Magdalene of Brandenburg (1582–1616)
Magdalene of Oldenburg (1585–1657)
Magnus (d. 1676)
Maintenon, Françoise d'Aubigné, Marquise de (1635–1719)
Makin, Bathsua (1608–1675)
Man, Judith (fl. 1640s)
Mance, Jeanne (1606–1673)
Mancini, Hortense (1646–1699)
Mancini, Laure (1635–1657)
Mancini, Marie (1640–1715)
Mancini, Marie-Anne (1649–1714)
Mancini, Olympia (c. 1639–1708)
Mandame, Mary (fl. 1639)
Manley, Mary de la Rivière (1663–1724)
Manmati (d. 1619)
Maratti Zappi, Faustina (c. 1680–1745)
Margaret of Austria (c. 1577–1611)
Margaret of Parma (b. 1612)
Margaret of Savoy (fl. 1609–1612)
Margaret of Valois (1553–1615)
Margaret Theresa of Spain (1651–1673)
Marguerite Louise of Orleans (c. 1645–1721)
Marguerite of Lorraine (fl. 1632)
Maria Anna of Austria (c. 1634–1696)
Maria Anna of Bavaria (1574–1616)
Maria Anna of Bavaria (1610–1665)
Maria Anna of Bavaria (1660–1690)
Maria Anna of Neuberg (1667–1740)
Maria Anna of Spain (1606–1646)
Maria Antonia (1669–1692)
Maria do Céu (1658–1753)
Maria Eleanora (1550–1608)
Maria Eleonora of Brandenburg (1599–1655)
Maria Elisabeth (1680–1741)
Maria Leopoldine (1632–1649)
Maria Magdalena of Austria (1589–1631)
Mariana de Paredes (1618–1645)
Maria Nagaia (d. 1612)
Mariana of Jesus (1565–1624)
Maria of Austria (1584–1649)
Maria Skuratova (d. 1605)
Maria Sophia of Neuberg (1666–1699)
Maria Teresa of Spain (1638–1683)
Marie-Anne de la Trémouille (c. 1642–1722)
Marie Casimir (1641–1716)
Marie de Bourbon (1606–1627)
Marie de Brabant (c. 1530–c. 1600)
Marie de l'Incarnation (1599–1672)
Marie Elizabeth of Saxony (1610–1684)
Marie Françoise of Savoy (1646–1683)
Marie Louise d'Orleans (1662–1689)
Marie of Austria (1528–1603)
Marie of Mecklenburg-Gustrow (1659–1701)
Marillac, Louise de (1591–1660)
Mariscotti, Hyacintha (d. 1640)
Marpha (1664–1716)
Martha the Nun (1560–1631)
Martinozzi, Anne-Marie (1637–1672)
Martinozzi, Laura (fl. 1658)
Mary II (1662–1694)
Mary Magdalen of Pazzi (1566–1607)
Mary of Bavaria (1551–1608)
Mary of Modena (1658–1718)
Mary of Orange (1631–1660)
Mary Tudor (1673–1726)
Masham, Abigail (1670–1734)
Masham, Damaris (1658–1708)
Mason, Elizabeth (d. 1712)
Massimi, Petronilla Paolini (1663–1726)
Maupin, d'Aubigny (c. 1670–1707)
Mavrokordatou, Alexandra (1605–1684)
Maxwell, Winifred (1672–1749)
Medici, Anna de (1616–?)
Medici, Anna Maria Luisa de (1667–1743)
Medici, Caterina de (1593–1629)
Medici, Claudia de (1604–1648)
Medici, Eleonora de (1567–1611)
Medici, Eleonora de (1591–1617)
Medici, Eleonora de (fl. 1690)
Medici, Maddalena de (1600–1633)
Medici, Maria Cristina de (1610–1632)
Medici, Marie de (c. 1573–1642)
Medici, Vittoria de (d. 1694)
Meisho (1624–1696)
Meneses, Juana Josefa de (1651–1709)
Merian, Maria Sybilla (1647–1717)
Meurdrac, Marie (fl. 17th c.)
Mignot, Claudine Françoise (c. 1617–1711)
Mildmay, Grace (1553–1620)
Miloslavskaia, Maria (1626–1669)
Miramion, Madame de (1629–1696)
Mniszek, Marina (c. 1588–1614)
Moders, Mary (1643–1673)
Moillon, Louise (1610–1696)
Molesworth, Martha (1577–1646)
Molza, Tarquinia (1542–1617)
Monck, Mary (c. 1678–1715)
Montagu, Lady Mary Wortley (1689–1762)
Montespan, Françoise, Marquise de (1640–1707)
Montour, Isabelle (1667–c. 1750)
Montpensier, Anne Marie Louise d'Orléans, Duchesse de (1627–1693)
Moody, Deborah (c. 1583–c. 1659)
More, Agnes (1591–1656)
More, Gertrude (1606–1633)
More, Mary (d. 1713/15)
Morozova, Theodosia (d. 1675)
Moth, Sophie Amalie (fl. 1670s)
Motteville, Françoise Bertaut de (c. 1621–1689)
Mumtaz Mahal (c. 1592–1631)
Munda, Constantia (fl. early 17th c.)
Munk, Kirsten (1598–1658)
Murat, Henriette Julie de (1670–1716)
Murray, Elizabeth (1626–1698)

Musi, Maria Maddalena (1669–1751)
Myddelton, Jane (1645–1692)
Narishkina, Natalya (1651–1694)
Nemours, Marie d'Orleans, duchess de (c. 1625–1707)
Neufvic, Madame de (fl. 17th c.)
Nicole of Lorraine (c. 1608–1657)
Njinga (c. 1580s–1663)
Norman, Goodwife (fl. mid–17th c.)
Norton, Frances (1640–1731)
Nur Jahan (1577–1645)
Nurse, Rebecca (1621–1692)
Nuthead, Dinah (fl. 1696)
Odaldi, Annalena (1572–1638)
O'Donnell, Mary Stuart (fl. early 1600s)
Oldfield, Anne (1683–1730)
O'Malley, Grace (c. 1530–1603)
Oosterwyck, Maria van (1630–1693)
Osborne, Dorothy (1627–1695)
Owen, Jane (fl. 1617–1634)
Pakington, Dorothy (d. 1679)
Palmer, Anne (1661–1722)
Palmer, Barbara (1672–1737)
Parr, Susanna (fl. 1659)
Parthenay, Catherine de (1554–1631)
Pascal, Gilberte (1620–1687)
Pascal, Jacqueline (1625–1661)
Peeters, Clara (1594–after 1657)
Pegge, Catherine (fl. 1657)
Penn, Gulielma Springett (1644–1694)
Penn, Hannah (1671–1726)
Pepys, Elizabeth (1640–1669)
Percy, Elizabeth (1667–1722)
Périer, Marguerite (c. 1645–?)
Philips, Katherine (1631–1664)
Philipse, Margaret Hardenbrook (d. 1690)
Pix, Mary Griffith (1666–1709)
Pocahontas (c. 1596–1617)
Poisson, Madeleine-Angelique (1684–1770)
Polwhele, Elizabeth (fl. mid–to–late 17th c.)
Poole, Elizabeth (fl. 1648)
Prévost, Françoise (1680–1741)
Rambouillet, Catherine de Vivonne, Marquise de (1588–1665)
Ranfaing, Élizabeth of (d. 1649)
Renzi, Anna (c. 1620–1660)
Rich, Mary (1625–1678)
Rich, Penelope (c. 1562–1607)
Rochechouart, Gabrielle de (1645–1704)
Rohan-Montbazon, Marie de (1600–1679)
Roldán, Luisa (1656–1704)
Romanov, Anna (1632–1692)
Romanov, Irina (fl. 1601)
Romanov, Irina (1627–1679)
Romanov, Natalya (1674–1716)
Romanov, Sophie (1634–1676)
Rosa, Anella de (1613–1649)
Rose of Lima (1586–1617)
Rowe, Elizabeth Singer (1674–1737)
Rowlandson, Mary (c. 1635–after 1682)
Russell, Elizabeth (1540–1609)
Russell, Lucy (c. 1581–1627)
Russell, Rachel (1636–1723)
Ruysch, Rachel (1664–1750)
Sablé, Madeleine de Souvré, Marquise de (c. 1599–1678)
Sabuco, Oliva de Nantes Barrera (1562–1625)
Saenger von Mossau, Renata (1680–1749)
Safiye (d. 1603)
Salete, Mme de (fl. 1600)
Saltykova, Praskovya (1664–1723)
San Félix, Sor Marcela de (1605–1688)
Schrader, Catharina Geertuida (1656–1745)
Schulenburg, Ehrengard Melusina von der (1667–1743)
Schwarz, Sybilla (1621–1638)
Scott, Anne (1651–1731)
Scudéry, Madeleine de (1607–1701)
Scudéry, Marie-Madeleine du Moncel de Montinvall de (1627–1711)
Sedley, Catharine (1657–1717)
Sévigné, Marie de (1626–1696)
Sexburga (c. 627–673)
Seymour, Frances (d. 1679)
Seymour, Jane (d. 1679)
Seymour, Mary (d. 1673)
Sharp, Jane (fl. 1671)
Shirley, Elizabeth (c. 1568–1641)
Sibylle Elizabeth of Wurttemberg (1584–1606)
Sibylle of Anhalt (1564–1614)
Sibylle of Brunswick-Luneburg (1584–1652)
Sidney, Dorothy (1617–1684)
Sirani, Elizabetta (1638–1665)
Smith, Margaret (fl. 1660)
Somerset, Anne (1631–1662)
Somerset, Elizabeth (fl. 1650)
Somerset, Henrietta (1669–1715)
Sophia (1630–1714)
Sophia Alekseyevna (1657–1704)
Sophia Carlotte (1673–1725)
Sophia Dorothea of Brunswick-Celle (1666–1726)
Sophia Dorothea of Brunswick-Lüneburg-Hanover (1687–1757)
Sophia of Mecklenburg (1557–1631)
Sophie Amalie of Brunswick-Lüneberg (1628–1685)
Sophie Charlotte of Hanover (1668–1705)
Sophie Hedwig (1677–1735)
Sophie Louise of Mecklenburg (1685–1735)
Sophie of Brandenburg (1568–1622)
Sophie of Holstein-Gottorp (1569–1634)
Sophie of Solms-Laubach (1594–1651)
Souza e Mello, Beatriz de (c. 1650–1700)
Spara, Hieronyma (d. 1659)
Speght, Rachel (1597–c. 1630)
Staal de Launay, Madame de (1684–1750)
Stanley, Charlotte (1599–1664)
Starbuck, Mary Coffyn (1644/45–1717)
Steevens, Grissell (1653–1746)
Stella, Claudine Bousonnet (1636–1697)
Stockfleth, Maria Katharina (c. 1633–1692)
Strozzi, Barbara (1619–1664)
Stuart, Arabella (1575–1615)
Stuart, Elizabeth (d. 1673)
Stuart, Frances (1647–1702)
Subligny, Marie-Thérèse Perdou de (1666–1736)
Sullam, Sara Coppia (1590–1641)
Sutcliffe, Alice (c. 1600–?)
Talbot, Elizabeth (1518–1608)
Talbot, Mary (d. 1632)
Tarabotti, Arcangela (1604–1652)
Taylor, Elizabeth (d. 1708)
Tekakwitha, Kateri (1656–1680)
Thimelby, Gertrude Aston (c. 1617–1668)
Thomas, Alice (fl. 1670s)
Thomas, Elizabeth (1675–1731)
Thornton, Alice (1626–c. 1707)
Tipper, Elizabeth (fl. late 17th c.)
Tofana (1653–1723)
Trapnel, Anna (fl. 1642–1661)
Traske, Mary (fl. 1660)
Tripp, Grace (1691–1710)
Turner, Anne (1576–1615)
Turner, Jane (before 1640–after 1660)
Ulfeldt, Leonora Christina (1621–1698)
Ulrica Eleanora of Denmark (1656–1693)
Van Cortlandt, Annettje Lockermans (c. 1620–after 1665)
Van Rensselaer, Maria Van Cortlandt (1645–c. 1688)
van Schurmann, Anna Maria (1607–1678)
Vaux, Anne (fl. 1605–1635)
Verbruggen, Susanna (c. 1667–1703)
Vercheres, Madeleine de (1678–1747)
Vicente, Paula (1519–1576)
Vieregg, Elizabeth Helene (fl. 17th c.)
Villedieu, Catherine des Jardins, Mme de (c. 1640–1683)
Villiers, Anne (d. 1688)
Villiers, Barbara (c. 1641–1709)
Villiers, Barbara (d. 1708)
Villiers, Elizabeth (c. 1657–1733)
Villiers, Frances (c. 1633–1677)
Villiers, Susan (fl. 17th c.)
Violante do Céu (1601–1693)
Waller, Anne (c. 1603–1662)
Walsingham, Frances (d. 1631)
Walter, Lucy (c. 1630–1658)
Ward, Mary (1586–1645)
Wardlaw, Elizabeth (1677–1727)
Waser, Anna (1678–1714)
Weamys, Anna (fl. 1650s)
Wentworth, Henrietta Maria (c. 1657–1686)
Wesley, Susanna (1669–1742)
Weston, Elizabeth Jane (1582–1612)
Wetamoo (c. 1650–1676)
Wharton, Anne (1659–1685)
Wilhelmina of Brunswick (1673–1742)
Wilhelmine (1650–1706)
Winthrop, Margaret (c. 1591–1647)
Woolley, Hannah (1623–1677)
Wriothesly, Elizabeth (d. 1690)
Wroth, Mary (c. 1587–c. 1651)
Zayas y Sotomayor, María de (1590–c. 1650)
Zeb-un-Nissa (1639–1702)
Zeidler, Susanna Elisabeth (1657–1706)
Ziegler, Christiane Mariane von (1695–1760)
Zrinska, Ana Katarina (1625–1673)
Zrinyi, Ilona (1643–1703)

18th Century

Abington, Frances (1737–1815)
Abrams, Harriett (c. 1758–c. 1822)
Abrantès, Laure d' (1784–1838)
Acland, Lady Harriet (1750–1815)
Adam, Jean (1710–1765)
Adams, Abigail (1744–1818)
Adams, Abigail (1765–1813)
Adams, Hannah (1755–1831)
Adams, Louisa Catherine (1775–1852)
Adams, Mary (d. 1702)
Adams, Susan Boylston (d. 1797)
Adams, Susanna Boylston (1769–1828)
Adelaide (1777–1847)
Adelaide, Madame (1732–1800)
Adler, Lydia (1704–?)
Agnesi, Maria Gaetana (1718–1799)
Agnesi, Maria Teresa (1720–1795)
Ahlefeld, Charlotte von (1781–1849)
Aisse (c. 1694–1733)
Aitken, Jane (1764–1832)
Albertina of Baden-Durlach (1682–1755)
Albertine (1753–1829)
Albrecht, Sophie (1757–1840)
Albrizzi, Isabella Teotochi, Contessa d' (1770–1836)
Alcock, Mary (1742–1798)
Alcoforado, Mariana (1640–1723)
Alexander, Mary (1693–1760)
Alexandra Pavlovna (1783–1801)
Allard, Marie (1742–1802)
Almy, Mary Gould (1735–1808)
Alorna, Marquesa de (1750–c. 1839)
Amalie of Hesse-Darmstadt (1754–1832)
Ambler, Mary Cary (fl. 1700s)
Amelia (1783–1810)
Amelia of Anhalt-Dessau (1666–1726)
Amelia Sophia (1711–1786)
Amory, Katherine (1731–1777)
Anna Amalia of Prussia (1723–1787)
Anna Amalia of Saxe-Weimar (1739–1807)
Anna Ivanovna (1693–1740)
Anna Leopoldovna (1718–1746)
Anna Petrovna (1757–1758)
Anna Sophia of Denmark (1647–1717)
Anna Victoria of Savoy (fl. 18th c.)
Anne (1665–1714)
Anne (1709–1759)
Anne Henriette Louise (1647–1723)
Anne-Marie d'Bourbon-Orleans (1669–1728)
Anne Petrovna (1708–1728)
Antoinette Saxe-Coburg (1779–1824)
Antonini, Theresa (1785–1809)
Archambault, Mademoiselle (c. 1724–?)
Arnould, Sophie (1740–1802)
Arnstein, Fanny von (1758–1818)
Ashbridge, Elizabeth (1713–1755)
Astell, Mary (1666–1731)
Astor, Sarah Todd (1761–1832)
Aubin, Penelope (c. 1685–1731)
Augusta Guelph (1737–1813)
Augusta Maria of Baden-Baden (1704–1726)
Augusta Maria of Holstein-Gottorp (1649–1728)
Augusta of Brunswick-Wolfenbuttel (1764–1788)
Augusta of Reuss-Ebersdorf (1757–1831)
Augusta of Saxe-Gotha (1719–1772)
Aulnoy, Marie Catherine, Countess d' (c. 1650–1705)
Austen, Jane (1775–1817)
Auzou, Pauline Desmarquets (1775–1835)
Azurduy de Padilla, Juana (1781–1862)
Baader, Amalie (b. 1763)

Babois, Marguerite-Victoire (1760–1839)
Baccelli, Giovanna (c. 1753–1801)
Bach, Anna Magdalena (1701–1760)
Bach, Maria Barbara (d. 1720)
Bache, Sarah (1743–1808)
Baddeley, Sophia (1745–1786)
Bailey, Abigail Abbott (1746–1815)
Bailey, Ann (1742–1825)
Bailey, Anna Warner (1758–1851)
Baillie, Grizel (1665–1746)
Baillie, Joanna (1762–1851)
Baker, Sarah (1736–1816)
Ball, Frances (1794–1861)
Ballard, Martha Moore (1735–1812)
Bandettini, Teresa (1763–1837)
Banks, Sarah Sophia (1744–1818)
Banti, Brigitta (c. 1756–1806)
Barat, Madeleine Sophie (1779–1865)
Barbauld, Anna Letitia (1743–1825)
Barber, Mary (c. 1690–1757)
Barbier, Marie-Anne (c. 1670–1742)
Baret, Jeanne (1740–after 1795)
Barker, Jane (1652–1732)
Barnard, Hannah Jenkins (d. 1825)
Barry, Ann Street (1734–1801)
Barry, Elizabeth (1658–1713)
Bartlett, Mary (d. 1789)
Basseporte, Magdalene (?–c. 1780)
Bassi, Laura (1711–1778)
Bastidas, Micaela (1745–1781)
Bateman, Hester (1709–1794)
Bateman, Mary (1768–1809)
Bawr, Alexandrine de (1773–1860)
Bayne, Margaret (1798–1835)
Beatrice, Dona (c. 1684–1706)
Beauharnais, Fanny de (1737–1813)
Beaumer, Madame de (d. 1766)
Beaumont, Agnes (1652–1720)
Beauvau, Marie Charlotte (1729–1807)
Beccary, Madame (fl. 18th c.)
Becker, Christiane (1778–1797)
Beddingfield, Ann (1742–1763)
Bekker, Elizabeth (1738–1804)
Bellamy, George Anne (1727–1788)
Belloc, Louise (1796–1881)
Belot, Madame (1719–1804)
Béltran, Manuela (fl. 18th c.)
Bembo, Antonia (1643–1715)
Benc, Adriana Gabrieli del (c. 1755–1799)
Benett, Etheldred (1776–1845)
Benger, Elizabeth (1778–1827)
Benislawska, Konstancja (1747–1806)
Bennett, Anna Maria (c. 1750–1808)
Benoist, Françoise-Albine (1724–1809)
Benoist, Marie (1768–1826)
Bentinck, Margaret (1714–1785)
Bergalli, Luisa (1703–1779)
Berlepsch, Emilie von (1755–1830)
Bernard, Catherine (1662–1712)
Bernhardi, Sophie (1775–1833)
Berry, Mary (1763–1852)
Bertaud, Marie Rosalie (c. 1700–?)
Bethune, Joanne (1770–1860)
Bias, Fanny (1789–1825)
Biehl, Charlotta Dorothea (1731–1788)
Biheron, Marie-Catherine (1719–1786)
Billington, Elizabeth (c. 1765/68–1818)
Bingham, Anne Willing (1764–1801)
Blachford, Theodosia (1745–1817)
Blackburne, Anna (1726–1793)
Blamire, Susanna (1747–1794)
Blanchard, Madeleine Sophie (1778–1819)
Bland, Maria Theresa (1769–1838)
Blandy, Mary (1719–1752)
Blaugdone, Barbara (c. 1609–1705)
Bleecker, Ann Eliza (1752–1783)
Blount, Martha (1690–1762)
Blower, Elizabeth (1763–after 1816)
Bocage, Marie-Anne Le Page du (1710–1802)
Bocanegra, Gertrudis (1765–1817)
Bodin de Boismortier, Suzanne (c. 1722–?)
Boivin, Marie Anne (1773–1847)
Boizot, Marie (1748–?)
Bonaparte, Alexandrine Jouberthon (1778–1855)
Bonaparte, Christine (1773–1800)
Bonaparte, Elisa (1777–1820)
Bonaparte, Elizabeth Patterson (1785–1879)
Bonaparte, Julie Clary (1771–1845)
Bonaparte, Letizia (1750–1836)
Bonaparte, Pauline (1780–1825)
Bonhote, Elizabeth (1744–1818)
Bonney, Anne (1700–?)
Bordoni, Faustina (c. 1700–1781)
Borja, Ana de (c. 1640–1706)
Boscawen, Fanny (1719–1805)
Bouboulina, Laskarina (1771–1825)
Boufflers, Madeleine-Angelique, Duchesse de (1707–1787)
Boufflers, Marie (1706–1747)
Boufflers-Rouvrel, Marie Charlotte Hippolyte, Countess de (1724–c. 1800)
Bouliar, Marie Geneviève (1762–1825)
Bourdic-Viot, Marie-Henriette Payad d'Estang de (1746–1802)
Bourette, Charlotte Rouyer (1714–1784)
Bowers, Bathsheba (c. 1672–1718)
Bowne, Eliza Southgate (1783–1809)
Boyd, Elizabeth (fl. 1727–1745)
Bošković, Anica (1714–1804)
Bracegirdle, Anne (1671–1748)
Brachmann, Louise (1777–1822)
Bradford, Cornelia Smith (d. 1755)
Branch, Elizabeth (1673–1740)
Brant, Molly (c. 1736–1796)
Brewster, Martha Wadsworth (fl. 1725–1757)
Briche, Adelaide de la (1755–1844)
Brion, Friederike Elisabeth (1752–1813)
Broadingham, Elizabeth (d. 1776)
Brohon, Jacqueline-Aimée (1731–1778)
Brooke, Charlotte (1740–1793)
Brooke, Frances (1724–1789)
Brooks, Maria Gowen (c. 1794–1845)
Brown, Anna (1747–1810)
Brown, Elizabeth (1753–1812)
Browne, Maria da Felicidade do Couto (c. 1797–1861)
Brownrigg, Elizabeth (1720–1767)
Brûlon, Angélique (1772–1859)
Brun, Friederike (1765–1835)
Brun, Marie-Marguerite de Maison-Forte (1713–1794)
Brunton, Mary (1778–1818)
Bryant, Mary (1765–?)
Buchan, Elspeth (1738–1791)
Buff, Charlotte (1753–1828)
Bui Thi Xuan (d. 1771)
Bulfinch, Hannah Apthorp (1768–1841)
Bunina, Anna Petrovna (1774–1829)
Burnet, Elizabeth (1661–1709)
Burney, Fanny (1752–1840)
Burney, Sarah Harriet (1772–1844)
Burr, Esther Edwards (1732–1758)
Burr, Theodosia (1783–1813)
Bury, Charlotte (1775–1861)
Butchill, Elizabeth (1758–1780)
Butler, Eleanor (c. 1738–1829)
Butterworth, Mary Peck (1686–1775)
Buxton, Mary Ann (c. 1795–1888)
Byrd, Mary Willing (1740–1814)
Cadière, Catherine (b. 1709)
Cadogan, Sarah (1706–1751)
Caesar, Mary (1677–1741)
Cairns, Elizabeth (1685–1714)
Calderwood, Margaret (1715–1774)
Callender, Hannah (1737–1801)
Calvillo, María del Carmen (1765–1856)
Camargo, Marie-Anne Cupis de (1710–1770)
Campan, Jeanne Louise Henriette (1752–1822)
Campanini, Barbara (1721–1799)
Candeille, Julie (1767–1834)
Candler, Ann (1740–1814)
Capet, Gabrielle (1761–1817)
Carlota Joaquina (1775–1830)
Caroline Elizabeth (1713–1757)
Caroline Matilda (1751–1775)
Caroline of Ansbach (1683–1737)
Caroline of Birkenfeld-Zweibrucken (1721–1774)
Caroline of Brunswick (1768–1821)
Caroline of Hesse-Darmstadt (1746–1821)
Caroline of Nassau (fl. 1730s)
Caroline of Nassau-Usingen (1762–1823)
Caroline of Orange (1743–1787)
Caroline of Parma (1770–1804)
Carrelet de Marron, Marie-Anne (1725–1778)
Carriera, Rosalba (1675–1757)
Carson, Ann (d. 1824)
Carter, Elizabeth (1717–1806)
Casalina, Lucia (1677–1762)
Castillo y Guevara, Francisca Josefa del (1671–1742)
Catalani, Angelica (1780–1849)
Catchpole, Margaret (1762–1819)
Catherine Charlotte of Hildburghausen (1787–1847)
Catherine I (1684–1727)
Catherine II the Great (1729–1796)
Catherine of Mecklenburg-Schwerin (1692–1733)
Catley, Ann (1745–1789)
Caulier, Madeleine (d. 1712)
Caulkins, Frances Manwaring (1795–1869)
Cavalieri, Caterina (1760–1801)
Cavanagh, Kit (1667–1739)
Cave, Jane (c. 1754–1813)
Cavendish, Elizabeth (1759–1824)
Cavendish, Georgiana (1757–1806)
Cavendish, Henrietta (d. 1755)
Cavendish-Bentinck, Elizabeth (1735–1825)
Cayetana, Maria del Pilar Teresa (1762–1802)
Caylus, Marthe M. (1673–1729)
Centlivre, Susanna (c. 1669–1723)
Chambers, Charlotte (d. 1821)
Chamblit, Rebekah (d. 1733)
Champagneux, Madame (1781–1858)
Chandler, Mary (1687–1745)
Chapman, Anne Maria (1791–1855)
Chapone, Hester (1727–1801)
Charke, Charlotte Cibber (1713–1760)
Charlotte (1769–1818)
Charlotte-Aglae (1700–1761)
Charlotte Amalia of Hesse (1650–1714)
Charlotte Amalie (1706–1782)
Charlotte Augusta Matilda (1766–1828)
Charlotte Elizabeth of Bavaria (1652–1722)
Charlotte of Brunswick-Wolfenbüttel (1694–1715)
Charlotte of Hesse-Darmstadt (1755–1785)
Charlotte of Mecklenburg-Strelitz (1744–1818)
Charlotte of Oldenburg (1759–1818)
Charpentier, Constance Marie (1767–1841)
Charriere, Isabelle de (1740–1805)
Chastenay, Victorine de (1771–1855)
Châteauroux, Marie Anne de Mailly-Nesle, Duchesse de (1717–1744)
Châtelet, Émilie du (1706–1749)
Chen Duansheng (1751–1796)
Chéron, Elisabeth-Sophie (1648–1711)
Chézy, Helmina von (1783–1856)
Chivers, Elizabeth (1682–1712)
Christine of Baden-Durlach (1645–1705)
Christine of Bourbon (1779–1849)
Chudleigh, Elizabeth (1720–1788)
Chudleigh, Mary Lee (1656–1710)
Churchill, Anne (1684–1716)
Churchill, Arabella (1648–1714)
Churchill, Deborah (1677–1708)
Churchill, Henrietta (1681–1733)
Churchill, Mary (1689–1751)
Cibber, Susannah (1714–1766)
Clairon, Mlle (1723–1802)
Clara (1697–1744)
Clarke, Mary Anne (c. 1776–1852)
Clicquot, Mme (1777–1866)
Clive, Kitty (1711–1785)
Clive, Margaret (1735–1817)
Cobbold, Elizabeth (c. 1764–1824)
Cockburn, Alicia (1713–1794)
Cockburn, Catharine Trotter (1679–1749)
Coicy, Madame de (fl. 18th c.)
Coit, Mehetabel Chandler (1673–1758)
Coke, Jane Elizabeth (1777–1863)
Colden, Jane (1724–1766)
Colleville, Anne-Hyacinthe de Saint-Léger de (1761–1824)
Collier, Jane (1710–c. 1754)
Collier, Jeanie (c. 1791–1861)
Collier, Mary (c. 1690–c. 1762)
Collot, Marie-Anne (1748–1821)
Collyer, Mary (d. 1763)
Condorcet, Sophie Marie Louise, Marquise de (1764–1822)
Contat, Louise (1760–1813)

Contat, Marie (1769–1846)
Cooper, Elizabeth (fl. 1737)
Cooper, Mary Wright (1714–1778)
Corbin, Lucidor (fl. 18th c.)
Corbin, Margaret Cochran (1751–c. 1800)
Corday, Charlotte (1768–1793)
Cornelys, Theresa (1723–1797)
Cosson de La Cressonière, Charlotte Cathérine (1740–1813)
Cosway, Maria (1759–1838)
Cottin, Sophie (1770–1807)
Coulon, Anne-Jacqueline (fl. 18th c.)
Courtauld, Louisa (1729–1807)
Coventry, Anne (1673–1763)
Cowles, Julia (1785–1803)
Cowley, Hannah (1743–1809)
Cowper, Mary (1685–1724)
Cranch, Elizabeth (1743–1811)
Cranch, Mary Smith (1741–1811)
Craven, Elizabeth (1750–1828)
Crawford, Jane Todd (1763–1842)
Crequy, Renée Caroline de Froulay, Marquise de (1714–1803)
Crespé, Marie-Madeleine (1760–1796)
Crocker, Hannah Mather (1752–1829)
Cromwell, Mary (1636–1712)
Crouch, Anna Maria (1763–1805)
Cunningham, Letitia (fl. 1783)
Custis, Eleanor "Nellie" Calvert (fl. 1775)
Custis, Eleanor "Nelly" Parke (1779–1852)
Cuzzoni, Francesca (c. 1698–1770)
Czartoryska, Isabella (1746–1835)
Dacier, Anne (1654–1720)
Dacre, Barbarina (1768–1854)
Dacre, Charlotte (c. 1772–1825)
Dagoe, Hannah (d. 1763)
d'Albert, Marie-Madeleine Bonafous (fl. 18th c.)
Dalibard, Françoise-Thérèse Aumerle de Saint-Phalier (d. 1757)
Dalrymple, Grace (1758–1823)
Damer, Anne Seymour (1748–1828)
d'Angeville, Henriette (1795–1871)
Danilova, Maria (1793–1810)
Danton, Gabrielle (d. 1793)
Danton, Louise (1777–1856)
Danzi, Maria Margarethe (1768–1800)
d'Arconville, Geneviève (1720–1805)
Darragh, Lydia Barrington (1729–1789)
Dashkova, Ekaterina (1744–1810)
Davys, Mary (1674–1731)
Dawson, Nancy (c. 1735–1767)
Deffand, Marie Anne de Vichy-Chamrond, Marquise du (1697–1780)
Deken, Aagje (1741–1804)
Delany, Mary Granville (1700–1788)
De Mist, Augusta (1783–1832)
Denis, Louise (c. 1710–1790)
Dennie, Abigail (1715–1745)
Denny, Arbella (1707–1792)
de Rivery, Aimee Dubucq (c. 1762–1817)
Desgarcins, Magdeleine Marie (1769–1797)
Désirée (1777–1860)
Desmares, Christine (1682–1753)
Desmier, Eleanor (1639–1722)
Desmoulins, Lucile (1771–1794)
Dewees, Mary Coburn (fl. 1787–1788)
Dickinson, Frances (1755–1830)
Diver, Jenny (1700–1740)
Dixon, Margaret (1670–1753)
Dolgorukaia, Natalia Borisovna (1714–1771)
Dorion, Marie (c. 1790–1850)
Dorval, Marie (1798–1849)
Douvillier, Suzanne (1778–1826)
Drake, Frances Denny (1797–1875)
Draper, Margaret (d. around 1800)
Drinker, Elizabeth Sandwith (1734–1807)
du Barry, Jeanne Bécu, Comtesse (1743–1793)
Duchesne, Rose Philippine (1769–1852)
Du Coudray, Angélique (1712–1789)
Dudley, Dorothy (fl. 1775)
Duff, Mary Ann Dyke (1794–1857)
Dufrénoy, Adelaïde de (1765–1825)
Dumesnil, Marie Françoise (1713–1803)
Duncombe, Susanna (1725–1812)
Dunlap, Jane (fl. 1771)
Dunlop, Eliza Hamilton (1796–1880)
du Noyer, Anne-Marguérite Petit (1663–1719)
Duparc, Françoise (1726–1778)
Durand, Catherine (d. 1736)
Duras, Claire de (1777–1828)
Dustin, Hannah (1657–c. 1736)
Dutton, Anne (fl. 1743)
Edgeworth, Maria (1768–1849)
Edwards, Sarah Pierpont (1710–1758)
Egerton, Sarah Fyge (c. 1670–1723)
Egual, Maria (1698–1735)
Ehrmann, Marianne (1755–1795)
Eleanor of Pfalz-Neuburg (1655–1720)
Elie de Beaumont, Anne Louise (1730–1783)
Élisabeth, Madame (1764–1794)
Elizabeth (1770–1840)
Elizabeth Amalia of Hesse (1635–1709)
Elizabeth Caroline (1740–1759)
Elizabeth-Charlotte (1676–1744)
Elizabeth Christina of Brunswick-Wolfenbuttel (1691–1750)
Elizabeth Christina of Brunswick-Wolfenbuttel (1715–1797)
Elizabeth Frederike of Bayreuth (fl. 1750)
Elizabeth of Austria (1743–1808)
Elizabeth of Lorraine (1711–1741)
Elizabeth of Saxe-Hildburghausen (1713–1761)
Elizabeth of Wurttemberg (1767–1790)
Elizabeth Petrovna (1709–1762)
Elliott, Charlotte (1789–1871)
Elphinstone, Hester Maria (1764–1857)
Elstob, Elizabeth (1683–1756)
Emerson, Mary Moody (1774–1863)
Emmerich, Anna Katharina (1774–1824)
Engel, Regula (1761–1853)
Engelbretsdatter, Dorothe (1634–1716)
Engelhard, Magdalene Philippine (1756–1831)
Épinay, Louise-Florence-Pétronille, Madame la Live d' (1726–1783)
Épine, Margherita de l' (c. 1683–1746)
Eppes, Maria Jefferson (1778–1804)
Erskine, Mary (1629–1707)
Erxleben, Dorothea (1715–1762)
Estaugh, Elizabeth Haddon (1680–1762)
Eudoxia Lopukhina (1669–1731)
Fagnan, Marie-Antoinette (d. 1770)
Falconbridge, Anna Maria (fl. 1790–1794)
Falconnet, Françoise-Cécile de Chaumont (1738–1819)
Fanshawe, Catherine Maria (1765–1834)
Farnese, Elizabeth (1692–1766)
Farrar, Cynthia (1795–1862)
Farrar, Eliza Rotch (1791–1870)
Farren, Elizabeth (c. 1759–1829)
Faugeres, Margaretta V. (1771–1801)
Fauques, Marianne-Agnès Pillement, Dame de (1721–1773)
Favart, Marie (1727–1772)
Fay, Eliza (1756–1816)
Fel, Marie (1713–1794)
Fell, Margaret (1614–1702)
Fenno, Jenny (c. 1765–?)
Fenton, Lavinia (1708–1760)
Fenwick, Eliza (1766–1840)
Ferguson, Elizabeth Graeme (1737–1801)
Fermor, Arabella (d. 1738)
Fermor, Henrietta Louisa (d. 1761)
Fernig, Félicité de (c. 1776–after 1831)
Fernig, Théophile de (c. 1779–c. 1818)
Fielding, Sarah (1710–1768)
Fiennes, Celia (1662–1741)
Figueur, Thérèse (1774–1861)
Finch, Anne (1661–1720)
Fischer, Caroline Auguste (1764–1834)
Fisher, Margaret (b. 1689)
Fisher, Sarah Logan (1751–1796)
Fitnat-Khanim (c. 1725–1780)
Fitzgerald, Pamela (1773–1831)
Fitzhenry, Mrs. (d. 1790?)
Fitzherbert, Maria Anne (1756–1837)
Fitzroy, Charlotte (1664–1717)
Fitzroy, Isabel (1726–1782)
Follen, Eliza (1787–1860)
Fontaine, Mlle de la (1655–1738)
Fontaines, Marie-Louise-Charlotte de Pelard de Givry, Comtesse de (1660–1730)
Fontette de Sommery, Mademoiselle (fl. 18th c.)
Foster, Hannah Webster (1758–1840)
Fouqué, Karoline Freifrau de la Motte (1774–1831)
Fourqueux, Madame de (fl. 18th c.)
Fox, Elizabeth Vassall (1770–1845)
Fragonard, Marie Anne (1745–c. 1823)
Françoise-Marie de Bourbon (1677–1749)
Frankland, Agnes (1726–1783)
Franklin, Ann (1696–1763)
Franks, Rebecca (c. 1760–1823)
Frederica Amalie (1649–1704)
Frederica Louise (1715–1784)
Frederica Louise (1770–1819)
Frederica of Hesse (1751–1805)
Frederica of Hesse-Darmstadt (1752–1782)
Frederica of Mecklenburg-Strelitz (1778–1841)
Frederica of Prussia (1767–1820)
Frederica Wilhelmina of Prussia (1774–1837)
French, Mary (fl. 1703)
Friederike of Hesse-Cassel (1722–1787)
Frietschie, Barbara (1766–1862)
Frohberg, Regina (1783–1850)
Frölich, Henriette (1768–1833)
Fry, Elizabeth (1780–1845)
Fuchs, Anna Rupertina (1657–1722)
Fulhame, Elizabeth (fl. 1780)
Fuller, Anne (fl. late 18th c.)
Fuller, Elizabeth (1775–1856)
Fumelh, Madame de (fl. 18th c.)
Gabrielli, Caterina (1730–1796)
Gacon-Dufour, Marie Armande Jeanne (1753–c. 1835)
Galitzin, Amalie von (1748–1806)
Galli, Caterina (c. 1723–1804)
Galloway, Grace Growden (d. 1782)
Gardie, Anna (c. 1760–1798)
Gay, Sophie (1776–1852)
Genlis, Stéphanie-Félicité, Comtesse de (1746–1830)
Geoffrin, Marie Thérèse (1699–1777)
Gérard, Marguerite (1761–1837)
Germain, Sophie (1776–1831)
Glasse, Hannah (1708–1770)
Glinska, Teofila (c. 1765–1799)
Glover, Julia (1779–1850)
Glückel of Hameln (1646–1724)
Goddard, Mary Katherine (1738–1816)
Goddard, Sarah Updike (c. 1700–1770)
Godin des Odonais, Isabel (1728–d. after 1773)
Goethe, Cornelia (c. 1751–c. 1778)
Goethe, Elisabeth (1730–1808)
Goose, Elizabeth (1665–1757)
Go-Sakuramachi (1740–1814)
Gottsched, Luise Adelgunde (1713–1762)
Gouges, Olympe de (1748–1793)
Graffigny, Françoise de (1695–1758)
Graham, Isabella (1742–1814)
Grange, Rachel (1682–1745)
Grant, Anne (1755–1838)
Gratz, Rebecca (1781–1869)
Green, Anne Catherine (c. 1720–1775)
Greene, Catharine Littlefield (1755–1814)
Greene, Catharine Ray (d. 1794)
Grétry, Lucile (1772–1790)
Grierson, Constantia (c. 1706–c. 1732)
Grieve, Elizabeth Harriet (1735–?)
Griffin, Jane (1680–1720)
Griffith, Elizabeth (c. 1720–1793)
Griffiths, Ann (1776–1805)
Griffitts, Hannah (1727–1817)
Grignan, Françoise-Marguerite de Sévigné, Countess de (1646–1705)
Grubb, Sarah Lynes (1773–1842)
Grubb, Sarah Tuke (1756–1790)
Guérin, Mother Theodore (1798–1856)
Guibert, Elisabeth (1725–1788)
Guibert, Louise-Alexandrine, Comtesse de (d. 1826)
Guimard, Marie Madeleine (1743–1816)
Guizot, Pauline (1773–1827)
Gunning, Elizabeth (1734–1790)
Gunning, Elizabeth (1769–1823)
Gunning, Maria (1733–1760)
Gunning, Susannah Minifie (c. 1740–1800)
Gutridge, Molly (fl. 1778)
Guyon, Jeanne Marie Bouviéres de la Mothe (1648–1717)
Gyllembourg-Ehrensvärd, Thomasine (1773–1856)
Hack, Maria (1777–1844)

Hallam, Mrs. Lewis (?–1774)
Hamilton, Anne (1636–1716)
Hamilton, Anne (1766–1846)
Hamilton, Catherine (1738–1782)
Hamilton, Elizabeth (1641–1708)
Hamilton, Elizabeth (1758–1816)
Hamilton, Elizabeth Schuyler (1757–c. 1854)
Hamilton, Emma (1765–1815)
Hamilton, Mary (1705–?)
Hamilton, Mary (1739–1816)
Hands, Elizabeth (fl. 1789)
Hanke, Henriette (1785–1862)
Hanson, Elizabeth Meader (1684–1737)
Hanway, Mary Ann (c. 1755–c. 1823)
Harel, Marie (fl. 1790)
Harlowe, Sarah (1765–1852)
Harris, Phoebe (1755–1786)
Harrison, Anna Symmes (1775–1864)
Hart, Julia Catherine (1796–1867)
Hart, Nancy (c. 1735–1830)
Hastings, Elizabeth (1682–1739)
Hastings, Selina (1707–1791)
Hausset, Nicole Colleson du (1713–1801)
Hawkins, Laetitia Matilda (1759–1835)
Hayden, Anna Tompson (1648–after 1720)
Hayden, Esther Allen (c. 1713–1758)
Hayes, Catherine (1690–1726)
Hays, Mary (1760–1843)
Haywood, Eliza (c. 1693–1756)
Heaton, Hannah Cook (1721–1794)
Hébert, Madame (d. 1794)
Heck, Barbara Ruckle (1734–1804)
Hedwig of Holstein-Gottorp (1636–1715)
Hedwig Sophia (1681–1708)
Heinel, Anna (1753–1808)
Heinemann, Barbara (1795–1883)
Helena Pavlovna (1784–1803)
Helvétius, Madame (1719–1800)
Hemings, Sally (1773–1835)
Hendel, Henriette (1772–1849)
Henrietta Catherine of Nassau (1637–1708)
Henrietta of Nassau-Weilburg (1780–1857)
Henriette (1727–1752)
Herbert, Lucy (1669–1744)
Herschel, Caroline (1750–1848)
Hervey, Elizabeth (c. 1748–c. 1820)
Hervey, Mary (1700–1768)
Herz, Henriette (1764–1847)
Hicks, Elizabeth (1705–1716)
Hicks, Mary (d. 1716)
Hill, Frances Mulligan (1799–1884)
Hill, Hannah, Jr (1703–1714)
Hill, Patty Smith (1868–1946)
Hinematioro (d. 1823)
Hippisley, E. (fl. 1741–1766)
Hippisley, Jane (d. 1791)
Hodgkins, Sarah Perkins (c. 1750–1803)
Holland, Catherine (1637–1720)
Holyoke, Mary Vial (1737–1802)
Hong, Lady (1735–1850)
Hopton, Susanna Harvey (1627–1708)
Horne, Janet (d. 1727)
Horton, Ann (1743–1808)
Horton, Christiana (c. 1696–c. 1756)
Hoskens, Jane Fenn (1694–c. 1750)
Houdetot, Sophie, Comtesse d' (1730–1813)
Housden, Jane (d. 1714)
Howard, Henrietta (1688–1767)
Ho Xuan Huong (fl. late 18th c.)
Huber, Marie (1695–1753)
Huber, Therese (1764–1829)
Hume, Sophia Wigington (1702–1774)
Huntington, Anne Huntington (d. 1790)
Hutchinson, Amy (1733–1750)
Hyde, Catherine (1701–1777)
Hyde, Jane (d. 1725)
Inchbald, Elizabeth (1753–1821)
Inman, Elizabeth Murray (c. 1724–1785)
Isabel (1772–1827)
Isabella of Parma (1741–1763)
Istomina, Avdotia (1799–1848)
Jackson, Rachel Donelson (1767–1828)
Jacquet de la Guerre, Elisabeth-Claude (c. 1666–1729)
Jagemann, Karoline (1777–1848)
James, Elinor (c. 1645–1719)
Jeanne of Nemours (1644–1724)
Jefferson, Martha (1748–1782)
Jeffries, Elizabeth (d. 1752)
Jemison, Mary (1742–1833)
Jennings, Frances (d. 1730)
Jodin, Mademoiselle (fl. 18th c.)
Johanna Elizabeth of Holstein-Gottorp (1712–1760)
Johnson, Esther (1681–1728)
Johnson, Susannah Willard (1729–1810)
Johnston, Henrietta (c. 1670–1728)
Johnstone, Isobel (1781–1857)
Jones, Rebecca (1739–1818)
Jordan, Dora (1761–1816)
Josephine (1763–1814)
Josephine of Lorraine (1753–1757)
Julie (fl. 1770)
Jumel, Eliza Bowen (1775–1865)
Kaahumanu (1777–1832)
Kapiolani (c. 1781–1841)
Karatza, Rallou (1778–1830)
Karsch, Anna Luise (1722–1791)
Kauffmann, Angelica (1741–1807)
Kemble, Eliza (1761–1836)
Kemble, Elizabeth (c. 1763–1841)
Kemble, Maria Theresa (1774–1838)
Kemble, Priscilla (1756–1845)
Kemp, Charlotte (1790–1860)
Kennett, Margaret Brett (fl. 1723–1725)
Keopuolani (c. 1778–1823)
Kéroüalle, Louise de (1649–1734)
Kielmansegge, Sophia Charlotte von (1673–1725)
Kinnan, Mary (1763–1848)
Kirch, Maria Winkelmann (1670–1720)
Kirchgessner, Marianne (1769–1808)
Knight, Ellis Cornelia (1758–1837)
Knight, Mary (1749–1788)
Knight, Sarah Kemble (1666–1727)
Königsmark, Aurora von (1662–1728)
Krüdener, Julie de (1764–1824)
Kuntsch, Margaretha Susanna von (1651–1716)
Labille-Guiard, Adelaide (1749–1803)
Lachapelle, Marie (1769–1821)
Lacombe, Claire (1765–?)
Lafayette, Marie Adrienne de (1760–1807)
Lafite, Marie-Elisabeth Bouée de (c. 1750–1794)
La Force, Charlotte-Rose de Caumont de (1650–1724)
Lagrave, Comtesse de (1770–1820)
La Guesnerie, Charlotte Charbonnier de (1710–1785)
Laisse, Madame de (fl. 18th c.)
Lalande, Amélie Lefrançais de (fl. 1790)
Lalaurie, Delphine (c. 1790–?)
Lama, Giulia (c. 1685–c. 1753)
Lamb, Mary Anne (1764–1847)
Lamballe, Marie Thérèse Louise of Savoy-Carignano, Princesse de (1749–1792)
Lambert, Anne Thérèse de Marguenat de Courcelles, Marquise de (1647–1733)
La Motte, Jeanne de Valois, countess de (1756–1791)
Lange, Aloysia (c. 1761–1839)
Lange, Anne Françoise Elizabeth (1772–1816)
Lany, Louise-Madeleine (1733–1777)
La Roche, Guilhem (1644–1710)
La Roche, Sophie von (1730–1807)
La Rochejacquelein, Marie Louise Victoire, marquise de (1772–1857)
La Tour du Pin, Henriette de (1770–1853)
La Vallière, Louise de (1644–1710)
Lavoisier, Marie (1758–1836)
Leach, Christiana (fl. 1765–1796)
Lead, Jane Ward (1623–1704)
Leadbetter, Mary (1758–1826)
Leapor, Mary (1722–1746)
Lebrun, Franziska (1756–1791)
Lecompte, Eugenie Anna (c. 1798–c. 1850)
Lecouvreur, Adrienne (1690–1730)
Ledoux, Jeanne Philiberte (1767–1840)
Lee, Ann (1736–1784)
Lee, Hannah Farnham (1780–1865)
Lee, Harriet (1757–1851)
Lee, Jarena (1783–c. 1849)
Lee, Lucinda (fl. 1787)
Lee, Sophia (1750–1824)
Lefanu, Alicia (1753–1817)
Lefanu, Elizabeth (1758–1837)
Lefebvre, Catherine (c. 1764–after 1820)
Le Givre de Richebourg, Madame (1710–1780)
Lemoine, Marie Victoire (1754–1820)
Lenclos, Ninon de (1623–1705)
Lenngren, Anna Maria (1754–1817)
Lennox, Caroline (1723–1774)
Lennox, Charlotte (1720–1804)
Lennox, Emily (1731–1814)
Lennox, Louisa (1743–1821)
Lennox, Sarah (1745–1826)
Le Noir, Elizabeth Anne (c. 1755–1841)
Lenormand, Marie Anne Adélaïde (1772–1843)
Léon, Pauline (1758–?)
Leonarda, Isabella (1620–1704)
Lepaute, Hortense (1723–1788)
Le Prince de Beaumont, Marie (1711–1780)
Lespinasse, Julie de (1732–1776)
Leveson-Gower, Elizabeth (1765–1839)
Levesque, Louise Cavelier (1703–1743)
Lewson, Jane (c. 1700–1816)
Lézardière, Pauline de (1754–1835)
Lezay Marnezia, Charlotte Antoinette de Bressy, Marquise de (c. 1705–1785)
L'Héritier, Marie-Jeanne (1664–1734)
Liang Desheng (1771–1847)
Lichtenau, Countess von (1753–1820)
Lightfoot, Hannah (fl. 1768)
Lindsay, Anne (1750–1825)
Linley, Elizabeth (1754–1792)
Linley, Maria (1763–1784)
Linley, Mary (1758–1787)
Lisiewska, Anna (1721–1782)
Lisiewska, Rosina (1716–1783)
Litchfield, Harriett (1777–1854)
Little, Janet (1759–1813)
Livingston, Alida Schuyler (1656–1727)
Livingston, Anne Shippen (1763–1841)
Logan, Deborah Norris (1761–1839)
Logan, Martha (1704–1779)
Louisa (1622–1709)
Louisa Amelia (1773–1802)
Louisa Anne (1749–1768)
Louisa Christina of Bavaria (fl. 1726)
Louisa Henrietta de Conti (1726–1759)
Louisa Ulrica of Prussia (1720–1782)
Louise (1692–1712)
Louise-Adelaide (1698–1743)
Louise Adelaide de Bourbon (1757–1824)
Louise Augusta (1771–1843)
Louise-Diana (1716–1736)
Louise Dorothea of Brandenburg (1680–1705)
Louise-Elisabeth de Bourbon Condé (1693–1775)
Louise Elizabeth (1709–1750)
Louise Elizabeth (1727–1759)
Louise Marie (1737–1787)
Louise Marie of Bourbon (1753–1821)
Louise of Brunswick-Wolfenbuttel (1722–1780)
Louise of Denmark (1750–1831)
Louise of England (1724–1751)
Louise of Hesse-Cassel (1688–1765)
Louise of Hohenlohe-Langenburg (1763–1837)
Louise of Mecklenburg-Gustrow (1667–1721)
Louise of Prussia (1776–1810)
Louise of Saxe-Gotha (1756–1808)
Louise of Saxe-Hilburghausen (1726–1756)
Louise of Stolberg-Gedern (1752–1824)
Lubert, Mlle de (c. 1710–c. 1779)
Ludington, Sybil (1761–1839)
Lussan, Marguerite de (1682–1758)
Macarthur, Elizabeth (1767–1850)
Macaulay, Catharine (1731–1791)
Macdonald, Flora (1722–1790)
Maclehose, Agnes (1759–1841)
MacLeod, Mary (c. 1615–c. 1706)
Macquarie, Elizabeth (1778–1835)
Mactier, Susie (1854–1936)
Maddalena of Canossa (1774–1833)
Madeleine of Anhalt-Zerbst (1679–1740)
Madison, Dolley Payne (1768–1849)
Magdalena Sybilla of Holstein-Gottorp (1631–1719)
Maher, Mary Cecilia (1799–1878)
Mailly, Louise Julie de Mailly-Nesle, Comtesse de (1710–1751)
Maintenon, Françoise d'Aubigné, Marquise de (1635–1719)
Malcolm, Sarah (c. 1710–1733)
Mancini, Marie (1640–1715)

Mancini, Marie-Anne (1649–1714)
Mancini, Olympia (c. 1639–1708)
Manigault, Ann Ashby (1703–1782)
Manley, Mary de la Rivière (1663–1724)
Manzolini, Anna Morandi (1716–1774)
Mar, Frances, Countess of (1690–1761)
Mara, Gertrud (1749–1833)
Maratti Zappi, Faustina (c. 1680–1745)
Marcet, Jane (1769–1858)
Marguerite Louise of Orleans (c. 1645–1721)
Maria Amalia (1724–1730)
Maria Amalia (1746–1804)
Maria Amalia of Saxony (1724–1760)
Maria Ana Victoria (1718–1781)
Maria Anna (1718–1744)
Maria Anna of Neuberg (1667–1740)
Maria Antonia of Austria (1683–1754)
Maria Antonia of Austria (1724–1780)
Maria Antonia of Naples (1784–1806)
Maria Antonia of Spain (1729–1785)
Maria Augusta of Thurn and Taxis (1706–1756)
Maria Barbara of Braganza (1711–1758)
Maria Beatrice of Modena (1750–1829)
Maria Carolina (1752–1814)
Maria Charlotte of Sardinia (c. 1761–c. 1786)
Maria Christina (1742–1798)
Maria Christina of Saxony (1779–1851)
Maria Clementina of Austria (1777–1801)
Maria Elisabeth (1680–1741)
Maria Francisca of Sulzbach (fl. 18th c.)
Maria I of Braganza (1734–1816)
Maria Josepha of Bavaria (1739–1767)
Maria Juliana of Brunswick (1729–1796)
Maria Leopoldina (1776–1848)
Maria Louisa of Spain (1745–1792)
Maria Luisa Teresa of Parma (1751–1819)
Maria Magdalena (1689–1743)
Mariana Victoria (1768–1788)
Maria Teresa of Austria (1773–1832)
Maria Teresa of Naples (1772–1807)
Maria Teresa of Savoy (1756–1805)
Maria Theresa of Austria (1717–1780)
Maria Theresa of Spain (1726–1746)
Marie Adelaide of Savoy (1685–1712)
Marie-Anne de la Trémouille (c. 1642–1722)
Marie Antoinette (1755–1793)
Marie Casimir (1641–1716)
Marie Clotilde (1759–1802)
Marie Clotilde (d. 1794)
Marie de Bourbon (fl. 18th c.)
Marie Josepha (1699–1757)
Marie Josephe of Saxony (1731–1767)
Marie Leczinska (1703–1768)
Marie Louise (1695–1719)
Marie Louise Albertine of Leiningen-Heidesheim (1729–1818)
Marie Louise d'Orleans (1750–1822)
Marie Louise of Savoy (1688–1714)
Marie of Mecklenburg-Gustrow (1659–1701)
Marie Sophie of Hesse-Cassel (1767–1852)
Marie Thérèse Charlotte (1778–1851)
Marpha (1664–1716)
Mars, Ann Françoise (1779–1847)
Marsh-Caldwell, Anne (1791–1874)
Martinez, Marianne (1744–1812)
Mary (1718–1794)
Mary (1776–1857)
Mary-Elizabeth of Padua (1782–1808)
Mary of Hesse-Cassel (1723–1772)
Mary of Modena (1658–1718)
Mary Tudor (1673–1726)
Masham, Abigail (1670–1734)
Masham, Damaris (1658–1708)
Mason, Elizabeth (d. 1712)
Massimi, Petronilla Paolini (1663–1726)
Masters, Sybilla (d. 1720)
Mathews, Ann Teresa (1732–1800)
Mattocks, Isabella (1746–1826)
Mauduit, Louise (1784–1862)
Maupin, d'Aubigny (c. 1670–1707)
Maxwell, Mary (fl. 1715)
Maxwell, Winifred (1672–1749)
Mayer, Constance (c. 1778–1821)
McAuley, Catherine (1778–1841)
McCauley, Mary Ludwig Hays (1754–1832)
McCracken, Mary Ann (1770–1866)
McCrea, Jane (c. 1752–1777)
McKain, Douglas Mary (1789–1873)
McLeod, Mrs. (d. 1727)
McTier, Martha (c. 1743–1837)
Mecom, Jane Franklin (1712–1794)
Medici, Anna Maria de (d. 1741)
Medici, Anna Maria Luisa de (1667–1743)
Medici, Violante Beatrice de (d. 1731)
Meeke, Mary (d. 1816)
Mellon, Harriot (c. 1777–1837)
Melmoth, Charlotte (1749–1823)
Mendelssohn, Dorothea (1764–1839)
Mendelssohn, Henriette (1768–1831)
Mendenhall, Dorothy Reed (1874–1964)
Meneses, Juana Josefa de (1651–1709)
Menetewab (c. 1720–1770)
Merard de Saint-Just, Anne-Jeanne-Félicité d'Ormoy (1765–1830)
Mereau-Brentano, Sophie (1770–1806)
Merian, Maria Sybilla (1647–1717)
Merken, Lucretia Wilhelmina van (1721–1789)
Merry, Ann Brunton (1769–1808)
Mignot, Claudine Françoise (c. 1617–1711)
Miller, Anna Riggs (1741–1781)
Miremont, Anne d'Aubourg de La Bove, Comtesse de (1735–1811)
Mitford, Mary Russell (1787–1855)
Mixer, Elizabeth (fl. 1707–1720)
Mmanthatisi (c. 1780–c. 1836)
Monbart, Marie-Joséphine de Lescun (1758–1800)
Monck, Mary (c. 1678–1715)
Monckton, Mary (1746–1840)
Monnet, Marie Moreau (1752–1798)
Monroe, Elizabeth (1768–1830)
Monroe, Eliza Kortright (1786–1840)
Mons, Anna (d. 1714)
Montagu, Elizabeth (1720–1800)
Montagu, Lady Mary Wortley (1689–1762)
Montanclos, Marie-Emilie Maryon de (1736–1812)
Montansier, Marguerite (1730–1820)
Montespan, Françoise, Marquise de (1640–1707)
Montesson, Charlotte Jeanne Béraud de la Haye de Riou, marquise de (1737–1805)
Montolieu, Pauline (1751–1832)
Montour, Isabelle (1667–c. 1750)
Moody, Elizabeth (1737–1814)
Moore, Jane Elizabeth (1738–?)
Moorhead, Sarah Parsons (fl. 1741–1742)
More, Hannah (1745–1833)
More, Mary (d. 1713/15)
Morency, Barbe-Suzanne-Aimable Giroux de (1770–?)
Morgan, Sydney (1780–1859)
Morris, Margaret Hill (1737–1816)
Moser, Mary (1744–1819)
Mott, Lucretia (1793–1880)
Mozart, Constanze (1762–1842)
Mozart, Maria Anna (1751–1829)
Mulally, Teresa (1728–1803)
Murat, Henriette Julie de (1670–1716)
Murray, Judith Sargent (1751–1820)
Musgrove, Mary (c. 1690–c. 1763)
Musi, Maria Maddalena (1669–1751)
Nagle, Nano (1718–1784)
Nairne, Carolina (1766–1845)
Nandi (c. 1760s–1827)
Nanny (fl. 1730s)
Nanye'hi (1738–1822)
Natalie of Hesse-Darmstadt (1755–1776)
Naubert, Christiane Benedikte (1756–1819)
Necker, Suzanne (1739–1794)
Necker de Saussure, Albertine (1766–1841)
Needham, Elizabeth (d. 1731)
Nelson, Frances Herbert (1761–1831)
Nemours, Marie d'Orleans, duchess de (c. 1625–1707)
Neuber, Caroline (1697–1760)
Nicholson, Margaret (c. 1750–c. 1828)
Nihell, Elizabeth (1723–after 1772)
Nikola, Helene Knez (1765–1842)
Nisbet, Mary (1778–1855)
Noailles, Anne Claude Laurence, duchesse de (d. 1793)
Norton, Frances (1640–1731)
O'Connell, Eileen (c. 1743–c. 1800)
Ogilvie, Catherine (1746–?)
O'Keeffe, Adelaide (1776–c. 1855)
Oldfield, Anne (1683–1730)
O'Murphy, Marie-Louise (1737–1814)
Opie, Amelia (1769–1853)
Ortíz de Dominguez, Josefa (c. 1768–1829)
Osborn, Sarah (1714–1796)
Pagan, Isobel (c. 1742–1821)
Pallerini, Antonia (1790–1870)
Palli, Angelica (1798–1875)
Palm, Etta Aelders (1743–1799)
Palmer, Anne (1661–1722)
Palmer, Barbara (1672–1737)
Palmer, Mary (1716–1794)
Paradis, Maria Theresia von (1759–1824)
Parker, Mary Ann (fl. 1795)
Parrish, Anne (1760–1800)
Parsons, Eliza (c. 1748–1811)
Peabody, Elizabeth Palmer (1778–1853)
Peacock, Lucy (fl. 1785–1816)
Pelham, Mary Singleton Copley (c. 1710–1789)
Penn, Hannah (1671–1726)
Pentreath, Dolly (1685–1777)
Percy, Elizabeth (1667–1722)
Percy, Elizabeth (d. 1704)
Percy, Elizabeth (1716–1776)
Pérez, Eulalia Arrila de (c. 1773–c. 1878)
Perkins, Elizabeth Peck (c. 1735–1807)
Phelps, Elizabeth Porter (1747–1817)
Philippa-Elizabeth (1714–1734)
Philippine Charlotte (1716–1801)
Pichler, Karoline (1769–1843)
Pierce, Sarah (1767–1852)
Pilkington, Laetitia (c. 1708–1750)
Pilkington, Mary (1766–1839)
Pimentel, Eleonora (c. 1768–1799)
Pinckney, Eliza Lucas (1722–1793)
Pinney, Eunice Griswold (1770–1849)
Piozzi, Hester Lynch (1741–1821)
Pix, Mary Griffith (1666–1709)
Pledge, Sarah (d. 1752)
Plisson, Marie-Prudence (1727–1788)
Poe, Elizabeth (c. 1787–1811)
Poisson, Madeleine-Angelique (1684–1770)
Pokou (c. 1700–c. 1760)
Polier, Marie-Elizabeth (1742–1817)
Polignac, Yolande Martine Gabrielle de (1749–1793)
Pompadour, Jeanne-Antoinette Poisson, Duchesse de (1721–1764)
Ponsonby, Sarah (1755–1831)
Pope, Jane (1742–1818)
Porter, Anna Maria (1780–1832)
Porter, Jane (1776–1850)
Porter, Mary (d. 1765)
Porter, Sarah (fl. 1791)
Post, Lydia Minturn (fl. 1776–1783)
Poulain, Mme (c. 1750–c. 1800)
Prévost, Françoise (1680–1741)
Prie, Jeanne Agnes Berthelot de Pléneuf, Marquise de (1698–1727)
Prince, Lucy Terry (c. 1730–1821)
Prince, Nancy Gardner (1799–?)
Prior, Margaret (1773–1842)
Pritchard, Hannah (1711–1768)
Puisieux, Madeleine de (1720–1798)
Radcliffe, Ann (1764–1823)
Radcliffe, Charlotte Maria (d. 1755)
Radcliffe, Mary Ann (c. 1746–after 1810)
Radziwill, Francisca (1705–1753)
Ramsay, Martha Laurens (1759–1811)
Randolph, Martha Jefferson (1775–1836)
Rask, Gertrud (fl. 1721)
Raucourt, Mlle (1756–1815)
Rawle, Anna (c. 1757–1828)
Ray, Martha (d. 1779)
Read, Deborah (1707–1774)
Read, Mary (1680–1721)
Récamier, Juliette (1777–1849)
Recke, Elisa von der (1754–1833)
Reed, Esther De Berdt (1746–1780)
Reeve, Clara (1729–1807)
Reibey, Mary (1777–1855)
Reichardt, Louise (1779–1826)
Rémusat, Claire, comtesse de (1780–1821)
Renneville, Sophie de (1772–1822)
Reventlow, Anne Sophie (1693–1743)
Riccoboni, Marie-Jeanne (1713–1792)

Rich, Elizabeth (fl. 1710)
Rind, Clementina (c. 1740–1774)
Robert, Marie-Anne de Roumier (1705–1771)
Robert-Kéralio, Louise (1758–1821)
Roberts, Mary (1788–1864)
Robespierre, Charlotte (1760–1840)
Robinson, Anastasia (c. 1692–1755)
Robinson, Mary (1758–1800)
Robinson, Therese Albertine Louise von Jakob (1797–1870)
Roche, Regina Maria (c. 1764–1845)
Roland, Madame (1754–1793)
Roldán, Luisa (1656–1704)
Romanov, Natalya (1674–1716)
Ross, Betsy (1752–1836)
Ross, Marie-Henriette LeJeune (1762–1860)
Roulstone, Elizabeth (fl. 1804)
Rowe, Elizabeth Singer (1674–1737)
Rowson, Susanna (1762–1824)
Royall, Anne (1769–1854)
Rush, Rebecca (1779–1850)
Russell, Rachel (1636–1723)
Ruysch, Rachel (1664–1750)
Sacajawea (c. 1787–c. 1812 or 1884)
Saenger von Mossau, Renata (1680–1749)
Saint-Chamond, Claire-Marie Mazarelli, Marquise de La Vieuville de (1731–?)
Sallé, Marie (1707–1756)
Salm-Dyck, Constance de (1767–1845)
Saltykova, Praskovya (1664–1723)
Sampson, Deborah (1760–1827)
Sanders, Elizabeth Elkins (1762–1851)
Saunderson, Mary (d. 1712)
Savignac, Alida de (1790–1847)
Schaw, Janet (d. around 1801)
Schlegel-Schelling, Caroline (1763–1809)
Schopenhauer, Johanna (1766–1838)
Schrader, Catharina Geertuida (1656–1745)
Schulenburg, Ehrengard Melusina von der (1667–1743)
Schuyler, Catherine Van Rensselaer (1734–1803)
Scott, Anne (1651–1731)
Scott, Mary (1751–1793)
Scott, Sarah (1723–1795)
Scudéry, Madeleine de (1607–1701)
Scudéry, Marie-Madeleine du Moncel de Montinvall de (1627–1711)
Secord, Laura (1775–1868)
Sedgwick, Catharine (1789–1867)
Sedley, Catharine (1657–1717)
Ségur, Sophie Rostopchine, Comtesse de (1799–1874)
Serres, Olivia (1772–1834)
Sessions, Patty Bartlett (1795–1892)
Seward, Anna (1742–1809)
Seymour, Frances Thynne (1699–1754)
Sheridan, Caroline Henrietta Callander (1779–1851)
Sheridan, Frances (1724–1766)
Sherwood, Mary Martha (1775–1851)
Shippen, Peggy (1760–1804)
Siddons, Harriet (1783–1844)
Siddons, Sarah (1755–1831)
Siebold, Charlotte Heidenreich von (1788–1859)
Siebold, Josepha von (1771–1849)
Silang, Gabriela (1731–1763)
Silva e Orta, Teresa M. da (c. 1711–1793)
Slocum, Frances (1773–1847)
Smith, Anna Young (1756–1780)
Smith, Charlotte (1749–1806)
Smith, Elizabeth "Betsy" (1750–1815)
Smith, Elizabeth Quincy (1721–1775)
Smith, Eunice (1757–1823)
Smith, Margaret Bayard (1778–1844)
Snell, Hannah (1723–1792)
Sobieski, Clementina (1702–1735)
Somerset, Henrietta (1669–1715)
Somerset, Henrietta (d. 1726)
Somerville, Mary Fairfax (1780–1872)
Sophia (1630–1714)
Sophia Alekseyevna (1657–1704)
Sophia Carlotte (1673–1725)
Sophia Dorothea of Brandenburg (1736–1798)
Sophia Dorothea of Brunswick-Celle (1666–1726)
Sophia Dorothea of Brunswick-Lüneburg-Hanover (1687–1757)
Sophia Dorothea of Wurttemberg (1759–1828)
Sophia Matilda (1773–1844)
Sophia Matilda (1777–1848)
Sophia of Bayreuth (1700–1770)
Sophia of Denmark (1746–1813)
Sophia of Mecklenburg (1758–1794)
Sophie (1734–1782)
Sophie Caroline (1737–1817)
Sophie Charlotte of Hanover (1668–1705)
Sophie Louise of Mecklenburg (1685–1735)
Southcott, Joanna (1750–1814)
Southey, Caroline Anne (1786–1854)
Souza-Botelho, Adélaïde Filleul, marquise of (1761–1836)
Souza e Mello, Beatriz de (c. 1650–1700)
Spencer, Barbara (d. 1721)
Spencer, Henrietta Frances (1761–1821)
Staal de Launay, Madame de (1684–1750)
Staël, Germaine de (1766–1817)
Stanhope, Hester (1776–1839)
Starbuck, Mary Coffyn (1644/45–1717)
Steele, Anne (1717–1778)
Steevens, Grissell (1653–1746)
Stein, Charlotte von (1742–1827)
Stephanie de Beauharnais (1789–1860)
Stepney, Catherine (1785–1845)
Stewart-Mackenzie, Maria (1783–1862)
Stockton, Annis Boudinot (1736–1801)
Stoneman, Abigail (c. 1740–?)
Storace, Nancy (1765–1817)
Stuart, Frances (1647–1702)
Stuart, Louisa (1757–1851)
Subligny, Marie-Thérèse Perdou de (1666–1736)
Taft, Lydia (c. 1711–1778)
Takács, Eva (1779–1845)
Talbot, Catherine (1721–1770)
Talbot, Mary Anne (1778–1808)
Tallien, Thérésa (1773–1835)
Tarnow, Fanny (1779–1862)
Taylor, Ann (1782–1866)
Taylor, Ann Martin (1757–1830)
Taylor, Jane (1783–1824)
Taylor, Margaret Smith (1788–1852)
Tencin, Claudine Alexandrine Guérin de (1685–1749)
Tenney, Tabitha Gilman (1762–1837)
Teresa, Mother (c. 1766–1846)
Théot, Catherine (d. 1794)
Theresa (1767–1827)
Théroigne de Méricourt, Anne-Josèphe (1762–1817)
Thomas, Elizabeth (1675–1731)
Thompson, Sarah (1774–1852)
Thornton, Alice (1626–c. 1707)
Timothy, Ann (c. 1727–1792)
Timothy, Elizabeth (d. 1757)
Todi, Luiza Rosa (1753–1833)
Tofana (1653–1723)
Tofts, Catherine (c. 1685–1756)
Tone, Matilda (c. 1769–1849)
Tonna, Charlotte Elizabeth (1790–1846)
Toro, Maria Teresa (d. 1803)
Trench, Melesina (1768–1827)
Trimmer, Sarah (1741–1810)
Tripp, Grace (1691–1710)
Trollope, Frances Milton (c. 1779–1863)
Turell, Jane (1708–1735)
Turner, Elizabeth (1774–1846)
Tussaud, Marie (1761–1850)
Tzavella, Moscho (1760–1803)
Udham Bai (fl. 1748–1754)
Ulrica Eleanora (1688–1741)
Unzer, Johanne Charlotte (1725–1782)
Ursinus, Sophie (1760–1836)
Vallayer-Coster, Anne (1744–1818)
Vandenhoeck, Anna (1709–1787)
Vardill, Anna Jane (1781–1852)
Varnhagen, Rahel (1771–1833)
Veigel, Eva-Maria (1724–1822)
Verbruggen, Susanna (c. 1667–1703)
Vercheres, Madeleine de (1678–1747)
Vere, Diana de (d. 1742)
Vesey, Elizabeth (c. 1715–1791)
Vestris, Thérèse (1726–1808)
Victoire, Madame (1733–1799)
Vigée-Le Brun, Elisabeth (1755–1842)
Villegas, Micaela (1748–1819)
Villeneuve, Gabrielle-Suzanne de (c. 1695–1755)
Villers, Mme (fl. late 18th c.)
Villiers, Barbara (c. 1641–1709)
Villiers, Barbara (d. 1708)
Villiers, Elizabeth (c. 1657–1733)
Vintimille, Pauline Félicité, Marquise de (1712–1741)
Wakefield, Priscilla (1751–1832)
Walewska, Marie (1786–1817)
Walker, Helen (1710–1791)
Walkinshaw, Clementina (c. 1726–1802)
Wallmoden, Amalie Sophie Marianne (1704–1765)
Walpole, Maria (1736–1807)
Warder, Ann Head (1758–1829)
Wardlaw, Elizabeth (1677–1727)
Warren, Caroline Matilda (1785–1844)
Warren, Mercy Otis (1728–1814)
Waser, Anna (1678–1714)
Washington, Martha (1731–1802)
Watteville, Benigna von (1725–1789)
Wenham, Jane (d. 1730)
Wesley, Emilia (1692–1771)
Wesley, Martha (1706–1791)
Wesley, Mehetabel (1697–1750)
Wesley, Susanna (1669–1742)
West, Elizabeth (fl. early 18th c.)
West, Jane (1758–1852)
Wheatley, Phillis (c. 1752–1784)
Wilhelmina (1709–1758)
Wilhelmina of Brunswick (1673–1742)
Wilhelmina of Prussia (1751–1820)
Wilhelmine (1650–1706)
Wilhelmine (1747–1820)
Wilhelmine of Baden (1788–1836)
Wilhelmine of Darmstadt (1765–1796)
Wilkinson, Jemima (1752–1819)
Williams, Ann (d. 1753)
Williams, Anna (1706–1783)
Williams, Helen Maria (1762–1827)
Williams, Marianne (1793–1879)
Wilmot, Olivia (d. 1774)
Wilson, Elizabeth (d. 1786)
Wilson, Harriette (1786–1855)
Wilson, Helen Ann (1793/94–1871)
Wilson, Sarah (1750–?)
Winslow, Anna Green (1759–1779)
Wiseman, Jane (fl. 17th c.)
Wister, Sarah (1761–1804)
Wobeser, Caroline von (1769–1807)
Woffington, Peg (c. 1714–1760)
Wollstonecraft, Mary (1759–1797)
Wolzogen, Karoline von (1763–1847)
Wood, Sally Sayward Barrell Keating (1759–1855)
Wordsworth, Dorothy (1771–1855)
Wright, Lucy (1760–1821)
Wright, Patience Lovell (1725–1786)
Wright, Susanna (1697–1784)
Yates, Mary Ann (1728–1787)
Yearsley, Ann (1752–1806)
Young, Cecilia (c. 1711–1789)
Young, Esther (1717–1795)
Young, Isabella (d. 1795)
Youville, Marie Marguerite d' (1701–1771)
Zane, Betty (c. 1766–c. 1831)
Zaunemann, Sidonia Hedwig (1714–1740)
Zeb-un-Nissa (1639–1702)
Zenger, Anna Catharina (c. 1704–1751)
Ziegler, Christiane Mariane von (1695–1760)
Zrinyi, Ilona (1643–1703)
Zwanziger, Anna (1760–1811)

19th Century

Abbott, Bessie (d. 1937)
Abbott, Edith (1876–1957)
Abbott, Elenore Plaisted (1873–1935)
Abbott, Emma (1850–1891)
Abbott, Evelyn (1843–1901)
Abbott, Grace (1878–1939)
Abbott, Mary Martha (1823–1898)
Abbott, Maude (1869–1940)
Abbott, Merriel (c. 1893–1977)
Abbott, Mother (1846–1934)
Abel, Annie Heloise (1873–1947)
Abel, Theodora (1899–1998)
Aberdeen, Ishbel Maria Gordon, Lady (1857–1939)
Abington, Frances (1737–1815)
Abraham, Caroline Harriet (1809–1877)
Abraham, Constance Palgrave (1864–1942)

Abrams, Harriett (c. 1758–c. 1822)
Abrantès, Laure d' (1784–1838)
Achurch, Janet (1864–1916)
Ackerman, Paula (1893–1989)
Ackermann, Louise Victorine (1813–1890)
Ackté, Aino (1876–1944)
Acland, Lady Harriet (1750–1815)
Acosta de Samper, Soledad (1833–1913)
Acton, Eliza (1799–1859)
Adam, Juliette la Messine (1836–1936)
Adams, Abigail (1744–1818)
Adams, Abigail (1765–1813)
Adams, Abigail Brooks (1808–1889)
Adams, Annette (1877–1956)
Adams, Clover (1843–1885)
Adams, Evangeline Smith (1873–1932)
Adams, Hannah (1755–1831)
Adams, Harriet Chalmers (1875–1937)
Adams, Louisa Catherine (1775–1852)
Adams, Maude (1872–1953)
Adams, Sarah Flower (1805–1848)
Adams, Susanna Boylston (1769–1828)
Adamson, Catherine (1868–1925)
Addams, Jane (1860–1935)
Addison, Agnes (c. 1841–1903)
Addison, Laura (d. 1852)
Adelaide (1777–1847)
Adelaide (1821–1899)
Adelaide (c. 1884–1959)
Adelaide, Madame (1732–1800)
Adelaide of Hohenlohe-Langenburg (1835–1900)
Adelaide of Saxe-Meiningen (1792–1849)
Adelaide of Schaumburg (1875–1971)
Adelgunde of Bavaria (1823–1914)
Adelheid (1831–1909)
Adler, Emma (1858–1935)
Adler, Sara (1858–1953)
Adlerstrahle, Maertha (1868–1956)
Afua Koba (fl. 1834–1884)
Agassiz, Elizabeth Cary (1822–1907)
Agnes, Lore (1876–1953)
Agostina (1788–1857)
Agoult, Marie d' (1805–1876)
Aguilar, Grace (1816–1847)
Agustini, Delmira (1886–1914)
Ahern, Lizzie (1877–1969)
Ahern, Mary Eileen (1860–1938)
Ahlefeld, Charlotte von (1781–1849)
Aikenhead, Mary (1787–1858)
Aikens, Charlotte (c. 1868–1949)
Aikin, Lucy (1781–1864)
Ainianos, Aganice (1838–1892)
Aitken, Jane (1764–1832)
Aitken, Jessie (1867–1934)
Akeley, Delia J. (1875–1970)
Akeley, Mary Jobe (1878–1966)
Akselrod, Liubo (1868–1946)
Alabaster, Ann O'Connor (1842–1915)
Albani, Emma (c. 1847–1930)
Albert, Caterina (1869–1966)
Albert, Octavia V.R. (1853–c. 1899)
Albertazzi, Emma (1813–1847)
Alberti, Sophie (1826–1892)
Albertine (1753–1829)
Albertine (1797–1838)
Alboni, Marietta (1823–1894)
Albrecht, Sophie (1757–1840)
Albrizzi, Isabella Teotochi, Contessa d' (1770–1836)
Alcock, Nora (1874–1972)
Alcott, Anna Bronson (1831–1893)
Alcott, Louisa May (1832–1888)
Alcott, May (1840–1879)
Alda, Frances (1879–1952)
Alden, Cynthia Westover (1862–1931)
Alden, Isabella (1841–1930)
Aldis, Mary (1872–1949)
Aldrich-Blake, Louisa (1865–1925)
Alençon, Emilienne d' (fl. late 1800s)
Alexander, Annie Montague (1867–1949)
Alexander, Cecil Frances (1818–1895)
Alexander, Claire (1898–1927)
Alexander, Francesca (1837–1917)
Alexander, Jessie (1876–1962)
Alexandra Feodorovna (1872–1918)
Alexandra Nikolaevna (1825–1844)
Alexandra of Denmark (1844–1925)
Alexandra of Oldenburg (1838–1900)
Alexandra of Saxe-Altenburg (1830–1911)
Alexandra Oldenburg (1870–1891)
Alexandra Pavlovna (1783–1801)
Alexandra Saxe-Coburg (1878–1942)
Alexandrina of Baden (1820–1904)
Alexandrina of Mecklenburg-Schwerin (1879–1952)
Alexandrine of Prussia (1803–1892)
Alford, Marianne Margaret (1817–1888)
Aliberty, Soteria (1847–1929)
Alice Maud Mary (1843–1878)
Alicia of Parma (1849–1935)
Aliye, Fatima (1862–1936)
Allard, Marie (1742–1802)
Allart, Hortense (1801–1879)
Allen, Elizabeth Chase (1832–1911)
Allen, Frances S. (1854–1941)
Allen, Mary E. (1858–1941)
Allen, Mary Sophia (1878–1964)
Allen, Sadie (c. 1868–?)
Allen, Susan Westford (c. 1865–1944)
Allen, Viola (1867–1948)
Allingham, Helen Patterson (1848–1926)
Almeida, Julia Lopes de (1862–1934)
Almy, Mary Gould (1735–1808)
Alorna, Marquesa de (1750–c. 1839)
Amália, Narcisa (1852–1924)
Amalia of Bavaria (1801–1877)
Amalie (1818–1875)
Amalie Auguste (1788–1851)
Amalie of Saxe-Coburg-Gotha (1848–1894)
Amalie of Saxony (1794–1870)
Amazon Army of Dahomey (1818–1892)
Ambrosius, Johanna (b. 1854)
Amelia (1783–1810)
Amelia of Leuchtenburg (1812–1873)
Amelia of Wurttemberg (1799–1848)
Ames, Blanche (1878–1969)
Ames, Eleanor Maria (1830–1908)
Ames, Fanny Baker (1840–1931)
Ames, Mary Clemmer (1831–1884)
Amohau, Merekotia (1898–1978)
Amparo Ruiz de Burton, Maria (1832–1895)
Anagnos, Julia (1844–1886)
Anastasia Petrovitch-Njegos (1868–1935)
Anastasia Romanova (1860–1922)
Ancelot, Marguerite (1792–1875)
Ancher, Anna (1859–1935)
Andersen, Catherine Ann (1870–1957)
Anderson, Bella (1864–?)
Anderson, Caroline Still (1848–1919)
Anderson, Elizabeth Garrett (1836–1917)
Anderson, Elizabeth Milbank (1850–1921)
Anderson, Ellen Alice (1882–1978)
Anderson, Isabel Perkins (1876–1948)
Anderson, Lucy (1797–1878)
Anderson, Mary (1859–1940)
Anderson, Mary (1872–1964)
Anderson, Mary Patricia (1887–1966)
Anderson, Maybanke (1845–1927)
Anderson, Sophie (1823–1903)
Anderson-Ivantzova, Elizabeth (c. 1893–1973)
Andreas-Salomé, Lou (1861–1937)
Andree, Elfrida (1841–1929)
Andreeva, Maria Fedorovna (1868–1953)
Andrews, Eliza Frances (1840–1931)
Andrews, Elsie Euphemia (1888–1948)
Andrews, Fannie Fern (1867–1950)
Andrews, Jane (1833–1887)
Andrews, Mary Raymond (1860–1936)
Andreyanova, Yelena Ivanovna (1816–1857)
Angell, Helen Cordelia (1847–1884)
Angers, Félicité (1845–1924)
Angiolini, Giuseppina (c. 1800–?)
Anglin, Margaret (1876–1958)
Angwin, Maria L. (1849–1898)
Anichkova, Anna (1868–1935)
Anker, Nini Roll (1873–1942)
Annabelle (1878–1961)
Anna Juliana of Saxe-Coburg-Saalfeld (1781–1860)
Anna Maria of Saxony (1836–1859)
Anna Pavlovna (1795–1865)
Anneke, Mathilde Franziska (1817–1884)
Annenkova-Bernár, Nina Pávlovna (1859/64–1933)
Anning, Mary (1799–1847)
Ansell, Mary (1877–1899)
Anstice, Sophia (1849–1926)
Anthony, Bessie (1880–1912)
Anthony, Katharine Susan (1877–1965)
Anthony, Susan B. (1820–1906)
Antoinette Saxe-Coburg (1779–1824)
Antonia (1858–1883)
Antonia of Portugal (1845–1913)
Antonini, Theresa (1785–1809)
Appleton, Honor C. (1879–1951)
Aquino, Melchora (1812–1919)
Arber, Agnes (1879–1960)
Arbuthnot, May Hill (1884–1969)
Archer-Gilligan, Amy (1869–1928)
Arden, Elizabeth (1878–1966)
Arenal, Concepción (1820–1893)
Ari, Carina (1897–1970)
Armand, Inessa (1874–1920)
Armer, Laura Adams (1874–1963)
Armitage, Ella (1841–1931)
Armitage, Rachelina Hepburn (1873–1955)
Armour, Rebecca (1846–1891)
Armstrong, Margaret Neilson (1867–1944)
Arndt, Hermina (1885–1926)
Arnim, Bettine von (1785–1859)
Arnim, Elizabeth von (1866–1941)
Arnould, Sophie (1740–1802)
Arnould-Plessy, Jeanne (1819–1897)
Arnstein, Fanny von (1758–1818)
Arthur, Ellen Herndon (1837–1880)
Arthur, Julia (1869–1950)
Artôt, Désirée (1835–1907)
Artyukhina, Aleksandra (1889–1969)
Arvelo Larriva, Enriqueta (1886–1963)
Ashwell, Lena (1872–1957)
Askew, Sarah B. (c. 1863–1942)
Asquith, Margot Tennant (1864–1945)
Assing, Ludmilla (1821–1880)
Assing, Ottilie (1819–1884)
Astafieva, Serafima (1876–1934)
Aston, Luise (1814–1871)
Astor, Augusta (fl. 1820s–1890s)
Astor, Caroline Schermerhorn (1830–1908)
Astor, Nancy Witcher (1879–1964)
Astor, Sarah Todd (1761–1832)
Atherton, Gertrude (1857–1948)
Atkins, Anna (1797–1871)
Atkins, Mary (1819–1882)
Atkinson, Eleanor (1863–1942)
Atkinson, Eudora Clark (1831–?)
Atkinson, Jane Maria (1824–1914)
Atkinson, Juliette P. (1873–1944)
Atkinson, Lily May (1866–1921)
Atkinson, Louisa (1834–1872)
Attwell, Mabel Lucie (1879–1964)
Atwater, Helen (1876–1947)
Aubert, Constance (1803–?)
Aubert, Mary Joseph (1835–1926)
Audouard, Olympe (1830–1890)
Audoux, Marguerite (1863–1937)
Augarde, Adrienne (d. 1913)
Augarde, Amy (1868–1959)
Augarde, Louise (1863–1909)
Augusta, Mlle (1806–1901)
Augusta Guelph (1737–1813)
Augusta Guelph (1768–1840)
Augusta Guelph (1822–1916)
Augusta of Hesse-Cassel (1797–1889)
Augusta of Reuss-Ebersdorf (1757–1831)
Augusta of Saxe-Weimar (1811–1890)
Augusta of Tuscany (1825–1864)
Augusta of Wurttemberg (1826–1898)
Aurora of San Donato (1873–1904)
Aus der Ohe, Adele (1864–1937)
Austen, Alice (1866–1952)
Austen, Jane (1775–1817)
Austen, Winifred (1876–1964)
Austin, Jane Goodwin (1831–1894)
Austin, Mary Hunter (1868–1934)
Austin, Sarah (1793–1867)
Austral, Florence (1894–1968)
Auzou, Pauline Desmarquets (1775–1835)
Avery, Martha (1851–1929)
Avery, Rachel G. (1858–1919)
Aves, Isabel Annie (1887–1938)
Avilova, Lidya (c. 1864–1943)
Avril, Jane (1868–1943)

Ayer, Harriet Hubbard (1849–1903)
Ayres, Anne (1816–1896)
Ayrton, Hertha Marks (1854–1923)
Ayscough, Florence (1875/78–1942)
Azurduy de Padilla, Juana (1781–1862)
Babcock, Maud May (1867–1954)
Babcock, Winnifred (1875–1954)
Baber, Esther Mary (1871–1956)
Babois, Marguerite-Victoire (1760–1839)
Baccelli, Giovanna (c. 1753–1801)
Bache, Sarah (1743–1808)
Bacheracht, Therese von (1804–1852)
Bacinetti-Florenzi, Marianna (1802–1870)
Backer, Harriet (1845–1932)
Backer-Grondahl, Agathe (1847–1907)
Baclanova, Olga (1899–1974)
Bacon, Albion Fellows (1865–1933)
Bacon, Alice Mabel (1858–1918)
Bacon, Delia Salter (1811–1859)
Bacon, Gertrude (1874–1949)
Bacon, Josephine Dodge (1876–1961)
Bacon, Peggy (1895–1987)
Badarzewski-Baranowska, Tekla (1834–1861)
Baden-Powell, Agnes (1858–1945)
Baden-Powell, Olave (1889–1977)
Badger, Charlotte (fl. 1806–1808)
Bagley, Amelia (1870–1956)
Bagley, Sarah (b. 1806)
Bagnold, Enid (1889–1981)
Bagryana, Elisaveta (1893–1991)
Bagshaw, Elizabeth (1881–1982)
Bailey, Abigail Abbott (1746–1815)
Bailey, Ann (1742–1825)
Bailey, Anna Warner (1758–1851)
Bailey, Carolyn Sherwin (1875–1961)
Bailey, Florence (1863–1948)
Bailey, Frankie (1859–1953)
Bailey, Hannah Johnston (1839–1923)
Bailey, Mary (1890–1960)
Bailey, Temple (c. 1869–1953)
Baillie, Grisell (1822–1921)
Baillie, Joanna (1762–1851)
Bain, Wilhelmina Sherriff (1848–1944)
Baird, Dorothea (1875–1933)
Bai Wei (1894–1987)
Bajer, Matilde (1840–1934)
Baker, Florence von Sass (1841–1916)
Baker, Harriette Newell (1815–1893)
Baker, Isabel Noeline (1878–1958)
Baker, Kate (1861–1953)
Baker, Louisa Alice (1856–1926)
Baker, Mary Ann (1834–1905)
Baker, Nina Brown (1888–1957)
Baker, S. Josephine (1873–1945)
Baker, Sarah (1736–1816)
Baker McLaglan, Eleanor Southey (1879–1969)
Balabanoff, Angelica (1878–1965)
Balachova, Alexandra (1887–1905)
Balch, Emily Greene (1867–1961)
Baldina, Alexandra Maria (1885–1977)
Baldwin, Charlotte Fowler (1805–1873)
Baldwin, Faith (1893–1978)
Baldwin, Maria Louise (1856–1922)
Balfour, Betty (1867–1942)
Balfour, Clara Lucas (1808–1878)
Balfour, Frances (1858–1931)
Ball, Anne Elizabeth (1808–1872)
Ball, Frances (1794–1861)
Ballard, Martha Moore (1735–1812)
Ballestrem, Eufemia von (1859–1941)
Ballinger, Margaret (1894–1980)
Ballou, Germaine (b. 1899)
Bambace, Angela (1898–1975)
Banahan, Mary Gertrude (1855/56?–1932)
Bancroft, Jessie (1867–1952)
Bancroft, Lady (1839–1921)
Bandettini, Teresa (1763–1837)
Bang, Nina (1866–1928)
Banks, Isabella (1821–1897)
Banks, Sarah Sophia (1744–1818)
Banky, Vilma (1898–1991)
Bannerman, Helen (1862–1946)
Bannerman, Jane (c. 1835–1923)
Banning, Margaret Culkin (1891–1982)
Banti, Brigitta (c. 1756–1806)
Bara, Theda (1885–1955)
Barakat, Hidiya Afifi (1898–1969)
Barandas, Ana Eurídice Eufrosina de (1806–1856)
Baranovskaya, Vera (c. 1870–1935)
Barat, Madeleine Sophie (1779–1865)
Barbauld, Anna Letitia (1743–1825)
Barber, Fanny (c. 1864–1952)
Barber, Margaret Fairless (1869–1901)
Barberi, Maria (1880–?)
Barbi, Alice (1862–1948)
Barbier, Adèle Euphrasie (1829–1893)
Barbosa, Pilar (1898–1997)
Barcelo, Gertrudis (c. 1820–1852)
Barclay, Florence Louisa (1862–1921)
Barine, Arvède (1840–1908)
Barker, Cicely Mary (1895–1973)
Barker, M.C. (1879–1963)
Barker, Ma (1872–1935)
Barker, Mary Anne (1831–1911)
Barlow, Billie (1862–1937)
Barlow, Hannah (1851–1916)
Barlow, Jane (c. 1857–1917)
Barnard, Hannah Jenkins (d. 1825)
Barnard, Kate (1875–1930)
Barnard, Marjorie (1897–1987)
Barnes, Charlotte Mary Sanford (1818–1863)
Barnes, Djuna (1892–1982)
Barnes, Margaret Ayer (1886–1967)
Barnes, Mary Downing (1850–1898)
Barnes, Zadel (1841–1917)
Barnett, Henrietta (1851–1936)
Barney, Alice Pike (1857–1931)
Barney, Natalie Clifford (1876–1972)
Barney, Nora (1883–1971)
Barnicoat, Constance Alice (1872–1922)
Barns, Cornelia Baxter (1888–1941)
Barnum, Gertrude (1866–1948)
Baron, Devorah (1887–1956)
Baron, Emilie (c. 1834–1852)
Barr, Amelia Huddleston (1831–1919)
Barra, Emma de la (1861–1947)
Barraud, Sarah Maria (c. 1823–1895)
Barrer, Nina Agatha Rosamond (1879–1965)
Barrett, Janie Porter (1865–1948)
Barrett, Kate Waller (1857–1925)
Barringer, Emily Dunning (1876–1961)
Barrington, Margaret (1896–1982)
Barriscale, Bessie (1884–1965)
Barron, Hannah Ward (1829–1898)
Barron, Jennie Loitman (1891–1969)
Barrow, Frances Elizabeth (1822–1894)
Barrows, Isabel Hayes (1845–1913)
Barry, Ann Street (1734–1801)
Barry, Iris (1895–1969)
Barry, Leonora M. (1849–1930)
Barry, Mary Ann (1855–1874)
Barrymore, Ethel (1879–1959)
Bartelme, Mary (1866–1954)
Bartet, Jeanne Julia (1854–1941)
Barth, Beatrice Mary (1877–1966)
Bartholomew, Ann Sheppard (1811–1891)
Bartlett, Adelaide (c. 1856–?)
Bartolini-Badelli, Giustina (fl. 1840)
Barton, Clara (1821–1912)
Barton, Dora (1884–1966)
Barton, Emma (1872–1938)
Barykova, Anna Pavlovna (1839–1893)
Basch, Anamarija (1893–after 1945)
Bascom, Florence (1862–1945)
Basham, Maud Ruby (1879–1963)
Bashkirtseff, Marie (1859–1884)
Bass, Charlotta Spears (1880–1969)
Bass, Mary Elizabeth (1876–1956)
Bassett, Ann (1878–1956)
Basten, Alice (1876–1955)
Bate, Dorothea (1879–1951)
Bateham, Josephine (1829–1901)
Bateman, Jessie (1877–1940)
Bateman, Kate (1842–1917)
Bateman, Mary (1768–1809)
Bates, Blanche (1873–1941)
Bates, Charlotte Fiske (1838–1916)
Bates, Clara Doty (1838–1895)
Bates, Daisy May (1859–1951)
Bates, Harriet Leonora (1856–1886)
Bates, Katherine Lee (1859–1929)
Bates, Mary (1861–1954)
Bates, Sophia Ann (1817–1899)
Bateson, Mary (1865–1906)
Bathildis of Schaumburg-Lippe (1873–1962)
Batson, Flora (1864–1906)
Batson, Henrietta M. (1859–1943)
Batterham, Mary Rose (c. 1870–1927)
Bauchens, Anne (1881–1967)
Bauer, Helene (1871–1942)
Bauer, Karoline (1807–1877)
Bauer, Klara (1836–1876)
Baughan, Blanche Edith (1870–1958)
Baum, Marie (1874–1964)
Baum, Vicki (1888–1960)
Baume, Rosetta Lulah (1871–1934)
Bäumer, Gertrud (1873–1954)
Baur, Clara (1835–1912)
Bawr, Alexandrine de (1773–1860)
Baxter, Millicent Amiel (1888–1984)
Bayer, Adèle (1814–1892)
Bayes, Nora (1880–1928)
Baylis, Lilian (1874–1937)
Bayliss, Blanche (fl. 1894)
Bayly, Ada Ellen (1857–1903)
Bayne, Beverly (1894–1982)
Bayne, Margaret (1798–1835)
Baynton, Barbara (1857–1929)
Ba_ar, Sukufe Nihal (1896–1973)
Beach, Amy Cheney (1867–1944)
Beale, Dorothea (1831–1906)
Beals, Jessie Tarbox (1870–1942)
Bear-Crawford, Annette (1853–1899)
Beard, Mary (1876–1946)
Beard, Mary Ritter (1876–1958)
Beatrice (1857–1944)
Beatty, May (1880–1945)
Beaugrand, Léontine (1842–1925)
Beauharnais, Fanny de (1737–1813)
Beaumont, Muriel (1881–1957)
Beauvain d'Althenheim, Gabrielle (1814–1886)
Beaux, Cecilia (1855–1942)
Beck, Elizabeth Louisa (c. 1862–1931)
Beck, Sophie (1858–?)
Becker, Lydia (1827–1890)
Becker, Marie Alexander (1877–194?)
Becker, May Lamberton (1873–1958)
Beckwith, Martha Warren (1871–1959)
Bedell, Harriet M. (1875–1969)
Beecher, Catharine (1800–1878)
Beere, Estelle Girda (1875–1959)
Beers, Ethel Lynn (1827–1879)
Beeton, Isabella Mary (1836–1865)
Beland, Lucy (1871–1941)
Belgioso, Cristina (1808–1871)
Bell, Elizabeth Viola (1897–1990)
Bell, Gertrude (1868–1926)
Bell, Jane (1873–1959)
Bell, Laura (1829–1894)
Bell, Lilian (1867–1929)
Bell, Mabel Hubbard (1857–1923)
Bell, Margaret Brenda (1891–1979)
Bell, Muriel Emma (1898–1974)
Bella, Antoinetta (b. 1863)
Bellamy, Elizabeth (1845–1940)
Bellamy, Elizabeth Whitfield (1839–1900)
Belleville-Oury, Anna Caroline de (1808–1880)
Bellincioni, Gemma (1864–1950)
Belloc, Louise (1796–1881)
Belloc-Lowndes, Marie (1868–1947)
Belmont, Alva Smith (1853–1933)
Belot, Madame (1719–1804)
Bender, Kate (1849–?)
Benedictsson, Victoria (1850–1888)
Benett, Etheldred (1776–1845)
Benger, Elizabeth (1778–1827)
Beniczky-Bajza, Helene (1840–1905)
Benislawska, Konstancja (1747–1806)
Benjamin, Ethel Rebecca (1875–1943)
Bennett, Agnes Elizabeth Lloyd (1872–1960)
Bennett, Alice (1851–1925)
Bennett, Anna Maria (c. 1750–1808)
Bennett, Belle Harris (1852–1922)
Bennett, Louie (1870–1956)
Bennett, Mary Jane (c. 1816–1885)
Bennett, Mary Katharine (1864–1950)
Benois, Nadia (1896–1975)
Benoist, Françoise-Albine (1724–1809)

Benoist, Marie (1768–1826)
Benson, Gertrude (1886–1964)
Bentham, Ethel (1861–1931)
Bentley, Irene (d. 1940)
Ben-Yehuda, Hemda (1873–1951)
Ben-Yusuf, Zaida (fl. 1897–1907)
Berenson, Mary (1864–1944)
Berens-Totenohl, Josefa (1891–1969)
Beretta, Caterina (1839–1911)
Bergen, Nella (1873–1919)
Bergere, Valerie (1872–1938)
Beringer, Esmé (1875–1972)
Berlepsch, Emilie von (1755–1830)
Bernadette of Lourdes (1844–1879)
Bernal, Emilia (1884–1964)
Bernhardi, Sophie (1775–1833)
Bernhardt, Sarah (1844–1923)
Berry, Harriet Morehead (1877–1940)
Berry, Martha McChesney (1866–1942)
Berry, Mary (1763–1852)
Bertin, Louise Angélique (1805–1877)
Bertrana, Aurora (1899–1974)
Besant, Annie (1847–1933)
Beskow, Elsa (1874–1953)
Best, Mary Ellen (1809–1891)
Betham-Edwards, Matilda (1836–1919)
Bethell, Mary Ursula (1874–1945)
Bethell, Thyra Talvase (1882–1972)
Bethune, Joanne (1770–1860)
Bethune, Louise Blanchard (1856–1913)
Bethune, Mary McLeod (1875–1955)
Betjeman, Agnes Muir (1885–1964)
Betts, Ethel Franklin (1878–?)
Beutler, Margarete (1876–1949)
Bevier, Isabel (1860–1942)
Bevington, L.S. (1845–1895)
Bews, Mary Ellen (1856–1945)
Beynon, Francis Marion (1884–1951)
Bias, Fanny (1789–1825)
Bibby, Mary Ann (c. 1832–1910)
Bichovsky, Elisheva (1888–1949)
Bickerdyke, Mary Ann (1817–1901)
Bicknell, Jessie (1871–1956)
Bidder, Marion Greenwood (1862–1932)
Bigot de Morogues, Marie (1786–1820)
Bigottini, Emilie (1784–1858)
Bilansky, Ann (1820–1860)
Billington, Elizabeth (c. 1765/68–1818)
Billington-Greig, Teresa (1877–1964)
Bingham, Amelia (1869–1927)
Bingham, Sybil Moseley (1792–1848)
Birchfield, Constance Alice (1898–1994)
Birch-Pfeiffer, Charlotte (1800–1868)
Birney, Alice McLellan (1858–1907)
Birtles, Mary (1859–1943)
Bishop, Ann (1899–1990)
Bishop, Ann Rivière (1810–1884)
Bishop, Bernice Pauahi (1831–1884)
Bishop, Harriet E. (1817–1883)
Bishop, Isabella (1831–1904)
Bismarck, Johanna von (1824–1894)
Bissell, Emily (1861–1948)
Bittenbender, Ada Matilda (1848–1925)
Bjarklind, Unnur Benediktsdóttir (1881–1946)
Bjelke-Petersen, Marie (1874–1969)
Blachford, Theodosia (1745–1817)
Black, Clementina (1854–1922)
Black, Helen McKenzie (1896–1963)
Black, Martha Louise (1866–1957)
Black, Winifred Sweet (1863–1936)
Blackburn, Helen (1842–1903)
Blackburn, Jemima (1823–1909)
Blackburn, Jessy (1894–1995)
Blackburn, Kathleen (1892–1968)
Blackett, Annie Maude (1889–1956)
Blackie, Jeannetta Margaret (1864–1955)
Blackwell, Alice Stone (1857–1950)
Blackwell, Elizabeth (1821–1910)
Blackwell, Ellen Wright (1864–1952)
Blackwell, Emily (1826–1910)
Blackwood, Beatrice (1889–1975)
Blackwood, Hariot (c. 1845–1891)
Blackwood, Helen Selina (1807–1867)
Blagg, Mary Adela (1858–1944)
Blahetka, Marie Leopoldine (1811–1887)
Blaine, Anita McCormick (1866–1954)
Blair, Catherine (1872–1946)
Blair, Emily Newell (1877–1951)
Blake, Lillie Devereux (1833–1913)
Blaker, Eliza Ann (1854–1926)
Blanc, Marie-Thérèse (1840–1907)
Blanchard, Madeleine Sophie (1778–1819)
Blanche, Ada (1862–1953)
Blanchecotte, Augustine-Malvina (1830–1895)
Blanche of Bourbon (1868–1949)
Bland, Lilian (1878–1971)
Bland, Maria Theresa (1769–1838)
Blangy, Hermine (c. 1820–c. 1865)
Blankenburg, Lucretia L. (1845–1937)
Blatch, Harriot Stanton (1856–1940)
Blavatsky, Helena (1831–1891)
Blaze de Bury, Rose (?–1894)
Bleibtreu, Hedwig (1868–1958)
Bleschke, Johanna (1894–1936)
Blessington, Marguerite, Countess of (1789–1849)
Blind, Mathilde (1841–1896)
Bliss, Anna (1843–1925)
Bliss, Lillie (1864–1931)
Bliss, Mary Elizabeth (1824–1909)
Bliss, Mildred Barnes (1879–1969)
Bloede, Gertrude (1845–1905)
Blomfield, Dorothy (1858–1932)
Bloodworth, Rhoda Alice (1889–1980)
Bloomer, Amelia Jenks (1818–1894)
Bloor, Ella Reeve (1862–1951)
Blow, Susan Elizabeth (1843–1916)
Blower, Elizabeth (1763–after 1816)
Bluffstein, Sophie (1854–1891)
Blunt, Anne (1837–1917)
Blunt, Katharine (1876–1954)
Bluwstein, Rachel (1890–1931)
Boardman, Mabel (1860–1946)
Bocage, Marie-Anne Le Page du (1710–1802)
Bocanegra, Gertrudis (1765–1817)
Bock, Amy Maud (1859–1943)
Bodenwieser, Gertrud (1886–1959)
Bodichon, Barbara (1827–1891)
Bodkin, Maud (1875–1967)
Bodley, Rachel (1831–1888)
Bogle, Helen McDermott (1871–?)
Bogle, Sarah C.N. (1870–1932)
Böhlau, Helene (1859–1940)
Böhl von Faber, Cecilia (1796–1877)
Bohm-Schuch, Clara (1879–1936)
Bohuszewiczowna, Maria (1865–1887)
Boit, Elizabeth Eaton (1849–1932)
Boivin, Marie Anne (1773–1847)
Bollmann, Minna (1876–1935)
Bol Poel, Martha (1877–1956)
Bolte, Amely (1811–1891)
Bolton, Mildred Mary (1886–1943)
Bolton, Sarah Knowles (1841–1916)
Bolton, Sarah T. (1814–1893)
Bonacci Brunamonti, Maria Alinda (1841–1903)
Bonaparte, Alexandrine Jouberthon (1778–1855)
Bonaparte, Carolina (1782–1839)
Bonaparte, Christine (1773–1800)
Bonaparte, Elisa (1777–1820)
Bond, Carrie Jacobs (1862–1946)
Bond, Elizabeth Powell (1841–1926)
Bondfield, Margaret (1873–1953)
Bonfanti, Marietta (1845–1921)
Bonheur, Juliette (1830–1891)
Bonheur, Rosa (1822–1899)
Bonhote, Elizabeth (1744–1818)
Boninsegna, Celestina (1877–1947)
Bonmartini, Linda (1873–?)
Bonner, Marita (1899–1971)
Bonner, Sherwood (1849–1883)
Bonnevie, Kristine (1872–1948)
Bonney, Mary Lucinda (1816–1900)
Bonnin, Gertrude Simmons (1876–1938)
Bonstelle, Jessie (1871–1932)
Boole, Ella (1858–1952)
Booth, Agnes (1843–1910)
Booth, Angela Elizabeth (1869–1954)
Booth, Catherine (1829–1890)
Booth, Ellen Scripps (1863–1948)
Booth, Evangeline (1865–1950)
Booth, Evelyn Mary (1897–1988)
Booth, Mary Louise (1831–1889)
Booth, Maud Ballington (1865–1948)
Booth, Sarah (1793–1867)
Booth-Tucker, Emma Moss (1860–1903)
Borchardt, Selma Munter (1895–1968)
Borden, Lizzie (1860–1927)
Borgese Freschi, Maria (1881–1947)
Borgström, Hilda (1871–1953)
Bormann, Maria Benedita Câmara de (1853–1895)
Boronat, Olimpia (1867–1934)
Borrero, Dulce María (1883–1945)
Borrero, Juana (1877–1896)
Borrowman, Agnes (1881–1955)
Boscawen, Fanny (1719–1805)
Boschek, Anna (1874–1957)
Boschetti, Amina (1836–1881)
Bose, Abala (1865–1951)
Bosse, Harriet (1878–1961)
Boswell, Annabella (1826–1916)
Botkin, Cordelia (c. 1854–1910)
Botta, Anne C.L. (1815–1891)
Bottome, Margaret McDonald (1827–1906)
Bouboulina, Laskarina (1771–1825)
Boucherett, Jessie (1825–1905)
Boucicault, Nina (1867–1950)
Boughton, Alice (1866–1943)
Bouliar, Marie Geneviève (1762–1825)
Bourdic-Viot, Marie-Henriette Payad d'Estang de (1746–1802)
Bouvet, Marguerite (1865–1915)
Bouvier, Jeanne (1865–1964)
Bowell, Harriet (1829–1884)
Bowen, Gretta (1880–1981)
Bowen, Louise (1859–1953)
Bowers, Elizabeth Crocker (1830–1895)
Bowles, Eva del Vakia (1875–1943)
Bowman, Nellie (1878–?)
Bowne, Eliza Southgate (1783–1809)
Boyce, Ann (c. 1827–1914)
Boyce, Neith (1872–1951)
Boyd, Belle (1844–1900)
Boy-Ed, Ida (1852–1928)
Boyle, Eleanor Vere (1825–1916)
Boyle, Helen (1869–1957)
Boys-Smith, Winifred Lily (1865–1939)
Bozzacchi, Giuseppina (1853–1870)
Bošković, Anica (1714–1804)
Brace, Julia (1806–1884)
Bracetti, Mariana (1840–c. 1904)
Brachmann, Louise (1777–1822)
Brachvogel, Carry (1864–1942)
Brackett, Anna Callender (1836–1911)
Bracquemond, Marie (1840–1916)
Braddon, Mary Elizabeth (1835–1915)
Bradford, Cornelia Foster (1847–1935)
Bradley, Amy Morris (1823–1904)
Bradley, Katharine Harris (1846–1914)
Bradley, Lydia Moss (1816–1908)
Bradshaw, Maria (1801–1862)
Bradwell, Myra (1831–1894)
Brady, Mary (1821–1864)
Braham, Leonora (1853–1931)
Braithwaite, Lilian (1873–1948)
Bramwell-Booth, Catherine (1883–1987)
Branch, Anna Hempstead (1875–1937)
Branch, Mary Lydia Bolles (1840–1922)
Brandegee, Mary Katharine (1844–1920)
Brandt, Marianne (1842–1921)
Braslau, Sophie (1888–1935)
Brassey, Anna (1839–1887)
Braun, Lily (1865–1916)
Bravo, Florence (1845–1878)
Bray, Anna Eliza (1790–1883)
Brazil, Angela (1868–1947)
Bré, Ruth (1862–1911)
Breckinridge, Madeline McDowell (1872–1920)
Breckinridge, Margaret E. (d. 1864)
Breckinridge, Sophonisba Preston (1866–1948)
Brécourt, Jeanne (b. 1837)
Breden, Christiane von (1839–1901)
Bregendahl, Marie (1867–1940)
Brehm, Marie Caroline (1859–1926)
Brema, Marie (1856–1925)
Bremer, Edith (1885–1964)
Bremer, Fredrika (1801–1865)
Brenchley, Winifred (1883–1953)
Brennan, Anna Teresa (1879–1962)
Brent-Dyer, Elinor M. (1894–1969)

Breshkovsky, Catherine (1844–1934)
Breslau, Louise (1857–1927)
Brewer, Lucy (fl. 1812)
Brewster, Anne Hampton (1818–1892)
Brianza, Carlotta (1862–1930)
Briche, Adelaide de la (1755–1844)
Bridges, Fidelia (1834–1923)
Bridgman, Eliza Jane (1805–1871)
Bridgman, Laura (1829–1889)
Briggs, Emily Edson (1830–1910)
Briggs, Margaret Jane (1892–1961)
Brigham, Emma Frances (1855–1881)
Brigham, Mary Ann (1829–1889)
Bright, Dora Estella (1863–1951)
Bright, Mary Golding (1857–1945)
Brightwen, Eliza (1830–1906)
Brigman, Anne W. (1869–1950)
Brion, Friederike Elisabeth (1752–1813)
Bristow, Lily (fl. 1890s)
Britton, Elizabeth Knight (1858–1934)
Brlić-Mažuranić, Ivana (1874–1938)
Broadwick, Tiny (1893–1978)
Brohan, Augustine Suzanne (1807–1887)
Brohan, Émilie Madeleine (1833–1900)
Brohan, Josephine Félicité Augustine (1824–1893)
Bromhall, Margaret Ann (1890–1967)
Bronsart, Ingeborg von (1840–1913)
Brontë, Anne (1820–1849)
Brontë, Charlotte (1816–1855)
Brontë, Emily (1818–1848)
Brooke, Cynthia (1875–1949)
Brooke, Evelyn Gertrude (1879–1962)
Brooks, Harriet (1876–1933)
Brooks, Maria Gowen (c. 1794–1845)
Brooks, Romaine (1874–1970)
Broom, Christina (1863–1939)
Broomall, Anna (1847–1931)
Brotherton, Alice Williams (1848–1930)
Brough, Fanny Whiteside (1854–1914)
Brough, Mary (1863–1934)
Broughton, Phyllis (1862–1926)
Broughton, Rhoda (1840–1920)
Brovar, Anna Iakovlevna (1887–1917)
Brown, Abbie Farwell (1871–1927)
Brown, Alice (1856–1948)
Brown, Alice Van Vechten (1862–1949)
Brown, Anna (1747–1810)
Brown, Charlotte (c. 1795–1855)
Brown, Charlotte (1846–1904)
Brown, Charlotte Emerson (1838–1895)
Brown, Charlotte Hawkins (c. 1883–1961)
Brown, Edith Mary (1864–1956)
Brown, Eliza (d. 1896)
Brown, Elizabeth (1753–1812)
Brown, Hallie Quinn (c. 1845–1949)
Brown, Jessie (1892–1985)
Brown, Lucy (fl. 1895)
Brown, Margaret A. (1867–?)
Brown, Martha McClellan (1838–1916)
Brown, Molly (1867–1932)
Brown, Olympia (1835–1926)
Brown Blackwell, Antoinette (1825–1921)
Browne, Augusta (1820–1882)
Browne, Frances (1816–1879)
Browne, Harriet Louisa (1829–1906)
Browne, Maria da Felicidade do Couto (c. 1797–1861)
Browne, Sidney Jane (1850–1941)
Brownell, Kady (b. 1842)
Browning, Elizabeth Barrett (1806–1861)
Brownscombe, Jennie Augusta (1850–1936)
Brownson, Josephine (1880–1942)
Bruce, Catherine Wolfe (1816–1900)
Bruce, Mary Grant (1878–1958)
Brück, Christa-Anita (1899–?)
Bruggen, Carry van (1881–1932)
Brugnoli, Amalia (c. 1808–?)
Brûlon, Angélique (1772–1859)
Brun, Friederike (1765–1835)
Brunet, Marta (1897–1967)
Brunschvicg, Cécile (1877–1946)
Brunton, Louisa (c. 1785–1860)
Brunton, Mary (1778–1818)
Bryan, Anna E. (1858–1901)
Bryan, Mary Edwards (1838–1913)
Bryant, Alice Gertrude (c. 1862–1942)
Bryant, Sophie (1850–1922)
Buchan, Anna (1878–1948)
Buchanan, Dorothy (1899–1985)
Buchanan, Margaret (1864–1940)
Büchner, Luise (1821–1877)
Buckel, C. Annette (1833–1912)
Buckingham, Rosetta (c. 1843–1864)
Buckland, Jessie Lillian (1878–1939)
Buckland, Mary Morland (d. 1857)
Buckman, Rosina (1881–1948)
Budzynska-Tylicka, Justyna (1876–1936)
Buff, Charlotte (1753–1828)
Buffalo-Calf-Road-Woman (fl. 1876)
Bulfinch, Hannah Apthorp (1768–1841)
Bulich, Vera Sergeevna (1898–1954)
Bullette, Julia (d. 1867)
Bullock, Margaret (1845–1903)
Bullowa, Emilie (1869–1942)
Bülow, Frieda von (1857–1909)
Bülow, Margarete von (1860–1884)
Bulstrode, Emily Mary (1867–1959)
Bulstrode, Jane Helena (1862–1946)
Bulwer-Lytton, Rosina, Lady (1802–1882)
Bunbury, Selina (1802–1882)
Bunge de Gálvez, Delfina (1881–1952)
Bunina, Anna Petrovna (1774–1829)
Bunzel, Ruth (1898–1990)
Burchenal, Elizabeth (1876–1959)
Burdekin, Katharine (1896–1963)
Burdett-Coutts, Angela (1814–1906)
Burdock, Mary Ann (1805–1835)
Burgess, Georgina Jane (c. 1839–1904)
Burgos Seguí, Carmen de (1867–1932)
Burkholder, Mabel (1881–1973)
Burleigh, Celia C. (1826–1875)
Burlin, Natalie Curtis (1875–1921)
Burn, Margaret Gordon (1825–1918)
Burnand, Lily (1865–?)
Burnett, Frances Hodgson (1849–1924)
Burney, Fanny (1752–1840)
Burney, Sarah Harriet (1772–1844)
Burns, Lucy (1879–1966)
Burns, Violet Alberta Jessie (1893–1972)
Burr, Theodosia (1783–1813)
Burroughs, Nannie Helen (c. 1878–1961)
Burton, Annie L. (fl. 19th c.)
Burton, Isabel (1831–1896)
Bury, Charlotte (1775–1861)
Busby, Amy (c. 1872–1957)
Busoni, Anna (1833–1909)
Buss, Frances Mary (1827–1894)
Butler, Eleanor (c. 1738–1829)
Butler, Elizabeth Thompson (1846–1933)
Butler, Grace Ellen (1886–1862)
Butler, Helen May (1867–1957)
Butler, Ida (1868–1949)
Butler, Josephine (1828–1906)
Butler, Margaret Mary (1883–1947)
Butler, Mother Marie Joseph (1860–1940)
Butler, Selena Sloan (1872–1964)
Butsova, Hilda (1896–1976)
Butt, Clara (1872–1936)
Butters, Mary (fl. 1839)
Button, Isabel (1863–1921)
Buxton, Mary Ann (c. 1795–1888)
Byers, Margaret (1832–1912)
Byrd, Mary Willing (1740–1814)
Byron, Kitty (c. 1879–?)
Bögli, Lina (1858–1941)
Cabello de Carbonera, Mercedes (1845–1909)
Cabete, Adelaide (1867–1935)
Cable, Mildred (1878–1952)
Cabot, Dolce Ann (1862–1943)
Cabrini, Frances Xavier (1850–1917)
Cadbury, Dorothy Adlington (1892–1987)
Cadbury, Geraldine Southall (1865–1941)
Cadden, Mamie (c. 1894–1959)
Cady, H. Emilie (1848–1941)
Caffyn, Kathleen (1853–1926)
Cahill, Mabel E. (1863–?)
Cahill, Marie (1870–1933)
Caird, Mona Alison (1858–1932)
Calderón de la Barca, Frances (1804–1882)
Caldwell, Anne (1876–1936)
Caldwell, Marianne (1866–1933)
Caldwell, Mary Gwendolin (1863–1909)
Calkins, Mary Whiton (1863–1930)
Callahan, Sophia Alice (1868–1894)
Callcott, Maria (1785–1842)
Callen, Maude (1899–1990)
Callender, Hannah (1737–1801)
Calvé, Emma (1858–1942)
Calvert, Louie (c. 1893–1926)
Calvillo, María del Carmen (1765–1856)
Cama, Bhikaiji (1861–1936)
Cambridge, Ada (1844–1926)
Cameron, Agnes Deans (1863–1912)
Cameron, Bessy (c. 1851–1895)
Cameron, Donaldina (1869–1968)
Cameron, Julia Margaret (1815–1879)
Cameron, Kate (1874–1965)
Cameron, Lucy Lyttleton (1781–1858)
Cameron, Robina Thomson (1892–1971)
Campan, Jeanne Louise Henriette (1752–1822)
Campbell, Grace MacLennan (1895–1963)
Campbell, Helen Stuart (1839–1918)
Campbell, Lady Colin (1857–1911)
Campbell, Mary (1877–1954)
Campbell, Mrs. Patrick (1865–1940)
Campbell, Persia (1898–1974)
Candeille, Julie (1767–1834)
Candler, Ann (1740–1814)
Candy, Alice (1888–1977)
Cannary, Martha Jane (1852–1903)
Cannon, Annie Jump (1863–1941)
Cannon, Harriet Starr (1823–1896)
Cannon, Ida (1877–1960)
Cano, María (1887–1967)
Cansino, Elisa (b. 1895)
Canth, Minna (1844–1897)
Canty, Mary Agnes (1879–1950)
Capet, Gabrielle (1761–1817)
Cappiani, Luisa (1835—?)
Caradus, Elizabeth (1832–1912)
Caraway, Hattie Wyatt (1878–1950)
Cardale, Effie (1873–1960)
Cardell-Oliver, Florence (1876–1965)
Carey, Ida Harriet (1891–1982)
Carey, Miriam E. (1858–1937)
Carey, Rosa Nouchette (1840–1909)
Carlén, Emilia (1807–1892)
Carlén, Rosa (1836–1883)
Carlota (1840–1927)
Carlota Joaquina (1775–1830)
Carlyle, Jane Welsh (1801–1866)
Carmichael, Amy (1867–1971)
Carnachan, Blanche Eleanor (1871–1954)
Carnegie, Louise Whitfield (1857–1946)
Caro, Margaret (1848–1938)
Caro, Pauline (1835–1901)
Caroline (1793–1812)
Caroline (1793–1881)
Caroline Amelia of Augustenburg (1796–1881)
Caroline Augusta of Bavaria (1792–1873)
Caroline Louise of Saxe-Weimar (1786–1816)
Caroline Matilda of Schleswig Holstein (1860–1932)
Caroline of Austria (1801–1832)
Caroline of Baden (1776–1841)
Caroline of Bourbon (1822–1869)
Caroline of Brunswick (1768–1821)
Caroline of Hesse-Darmstadt (1746–1821)
Caroline of Mecklenburg-Strelitz (1821–1876)
Caroline of Naples (1798–1870)
Caroline of Nassau-Usingen (1762–1823)
Caroline of Parma (1770–1804)
Caroline of Saxony (1833–1907)
Caroline of Sicily (1820–1861)
Carothers, E. Eleanor (1882–1957)
Carpenter, Mary (1807–1877)
Carr, Emily (1871–1945)
Carran, Catherine (1842–1935)
Carr-Cook, Madge (1856–1933)
Carrel, Felicite (fl. 1860s)
Carreño, Teresa (1853–1917)
Carroll, Anna Ella (1815–1894)
Carroll, Heni Materoa (1852/56?–1930)
Carse, Matilda Bradley (1835–1917)
Carson, Ann (d. 1824)
Carswell, Catherine (1879–1946)
Carter, Elizabeth (1717–1806)
Carter, Eunice Hunton (1899–1970)
Carter, Mrs. Leslie (1862–1937)

Carter, Una Isabel (1890–1954)
Cartwright, Julia (1851–1924)
Carus, Emma (1879–1927)
Carvajal, María Isabel (1888–1949)
Carver, Louise (1869–1956)
Cary, Alice (1820–1871)
Cary, Annie Louise (1841–1921)
Cary, Elisabeth Luther (1867–1936)
Cary, Mary Ann Shadd (1823–1893)
Cary, Phoebe (1824–1871)
Case, Adelaide (1887–1948)
Casely-Hayford, Adelaide (1868–1960)
Cashman, Nellie (1844–1925)
Cassatt, Mary (1844–1926)
Cassie, Alice Mary (1887–1963)
Castiglione, Virginie, Countess de (1837–1899)
Castle, Amy (1880–?)
Castro, Rosalía de (1837–1885)
Caswell, Maude (c. 1880–?)
Catalani, Angelica (1780–1849)
Catargi, Marie (fl. 1850s)
Catchpole, Margaret (1762–1819)
Cather, Willa (1873–1947)
Catherine Frederica of Wurttemberg (1821–1898)
Catherine of Russia (1788–1819)
Catherine of Wurttemberg (1783–1835)
Catherine Romanov (1878–1959)
Catherwood, Mary Hartwell (1847–1902)
Catt, Carrie Chapman (1859–1947)
Cauer, Minna (1841–1922)
Caulkins, Frances Manwaring (1795–1869)
Cavalieri, Caterina (1760–1801)
Cavalieri, Lina (1874–1944)
Cavallazzi, Malvina (c. 1852–1924)
Cave, Jane (c. 1754–1813)
Cavell, Edith (1865–1915)
Cavendish, Ada (1839–1895)
Cavendish, Elizabeth (1759–1824)
Cavendish, Georgiana (1757–1806)
Cavendish, Georgiana (1783–1858)
Cavendish, Lucy Caroline (1841–1925)
Cavendish-Bentinck, Elizabeth (1735–1825)
Cavendish-Bentinck, Nina (c. 1860–?)
Cayla, Comtesse du (1785–1852)
Cayvan, Georgia (1857–1906)
Cazneau, Jane McManus (1807–1878)
Cecilia of Baden (1839–1891)
Celeste, Madame (1811–1882)
Cerri, Cecilie (1872–1931)
Cerrito, Fanny (1817–1909)
Chabrillan, Céleste de (1824–1909)
Chace, Elizabeth Buffum (1806–1899)
Chace, Marian (1896–1970)
Chadwick, Cassie L. (1859–1907)
Chambefort, Marie (fl. 1850)
Chambers, Charlotte (d. 1821)
Chaminade, Cécile (1857–1944)
Chandler, Elizabeth Margaret (1807–1834)
Chanler, Margaret (b. 1862)
Chapin, Augusta (1836–1905)
Chapin, Sallie F. (c. 1830–1896)
Chapman, Anne Maria (1791–1855)
Chapman, Caroline (c. 1818–1876)
Chapman, Edythe (1863–1948)
Chapman, Maria (1806–1885)
Chapman, Pansy (1892–1973)
Chapman, Sylvia (1896–1995)
Chapman, Vera (1898–1996)
Chapone, Hester (1727–1801)
Chard-Williams, Ada (c. 1876–1900)
Charisse, Calliope (c. 1880–1946)
Charles, Elizabeth (1828–1896)
Charles, Lallie (1869–1919)
Charlesworth, Maria (1819–1880)
Charlotte (1769–1818)
Charlotte Augusta (1796–1817)
Charlotte Augusta Matilda (1766–1828)
Charlotte Frederica of Mecklenburg-Schwerin (1784–1840)
Charlotte of Mecklenburg-Strelitz (1744–1818)
Charlotte of Prussia (1798–1860)
Charlotte of Saxe-Meiningen (1860–1919)
Charlotte Oldenburg (1789–1864)
Charpentier, Constance Marie (1767–1841)
Charriere, Isabelle de (1740–1805)
Charteris, Catherine Morice (1835–1918)
Chartroule, Marie-Amélie (1848–1912)
Chase, Agnes Meara (1869–1963)
Chase, Edna Woolman (1877–1957)
Chastenay, Victorine de (1771–1855)
Chauvin, Jeanne (1862–1926)
Chazal, Aline-Marie (1825–1869)
Cheeseman, Clara (1852–1943)
Cheesman, Lucy Evelyn (1881–1969)
Chemis, Annie (1862–1939)
Cheney, Ednah Dow (1824–1904)
Chéri, Rose (1824–1861)
Cherrington, Te Paea (c. 1877–1937)
Cherry, Addie (c. 1859–1942)
Cherry, Effie (d. 1944)
Chesebrough, Caroline (1825–1873)
Chesnut, Mary Boykin (1823–1886)
Chevalier, Caroline (c. 1832–1917)
Chevigné, Laure de (1860–1936)
Chézy, Helmina von (1783–1856)
Chica, Elena (1828–1888)
Chichester, Sophia (1795–1847)
Chick, Harriette (1875–1977)
Child, Lydia Maria (1802–1880)
Ching Shih (fl. 1807–1810)
Chinn, May Edward (1896–1980)
Chisholm, Caroline (1808–1877)
Chitty, Letitia (1897–1982)
Chiumina, Olga Nikolaevna (1865–1909)
Choiseul-Meuse, Félicité de (fl. 19th c.)
Cholmondeley, Mary (1859–1925)
Chona, Maria (1845–1936)
Chopin, Kate (1850–1904)
Chotek, Sophie (1868–1914)
Christaller, Helene (1872–1953)
Christina of Sardinia (1812–1836)
Churchill, Fanny (1822–1899)
Churchill, Jennie Jerome (1854–1921)
Churchill, May (1876–1929)
Churilova, L.A. (1875–1937)
Cialente, Fausta (1898–1994)
Ci'an (1837–1881)
Cinti-Damoreau, Laure (1801–1863)
Ciocca, Giovanna (c. 1825–?)
Cixi (1835–1908)
Claflin, Tennessee (1846–1923)
Clairmont, Claire (1798–1879)
Clairon, Mlle (1723–1802)
Clapp, Cornelia Maria (1849–1934)
Clapp, Louise (1819–1906)
Clare, Ada (1836–1874)
Clark, Catherine Anthony (1892–1977)
Clark, Cora Maris (1885–1967)
Clark, Hilda (1881–1955)
Clark, Kate Emma (1847–1926)
Clark, Nancy Talbot (1825–1901)
Clarke, Grace Julian (1865–1938)
Clarke, Helen (c. 1897–?)
Clarke, Helen Archibald (1860–1926)
Clarke, Julia (d. 1912)
Clarke, Mary Anne (c. 1776–1852)
Clarke, Mary Bayard (1827–1886)
Clarke, Mary Cowden (1809–1898)
Clarke, Mary Frances (1803–1887)
Clarke, Mary Goulden (d. 1910)
Clarke, Rebecca (1886–1979)
Clarke, Rebecca Sophia (1833–1906)
Clarke, Sarah Jones (1840–1929)
Claudel, Camille (1864–1943)
Clauss-Szárvady, Wilhelmina (1834–1907)
Claxton, Kate (1848–1924)
Clay, Laura (1849–1941)
Clay, Virginia Tunstall (1825–1915)
Claypole, Edith Jane (1870–1915)
Clayton, S. Lillian (1876–1930)
Cleaves, Margaret (1848–1917)
Clementine of Austria (1798–1881)
Clementine of Belgium (1872–1955)
Clementine of Orleans (1817–1907)
Clement-Scott, Margaret (fl. 19th c.)
Clerke, Agnes Mary (1842–1907)
Clerke, Ellen Mary (1840–1906)
Cleveland, Emeline Horton (1829–1878)
Cleveland, Frances Folsom (1864–1947)
Cleveland, Rose Elizabeth (b. 1846)
Cleveland, Ruth (1891–1904)
Clicquot, Mme (1777–1866)
Cliff, Clarice (1899–1972)
Cline, Genevieve (1879–1959)
Cline, Maggie (1857–1934)
Clisby, Harriet (1830–1931)
Clive, Caroline (1801–1873)
Clotilde of Savoy (1843–1911)
Clotilde of Saxe-Coburg-Gotha (1846–1927)
Clough, Jemima (1820–1892)
Coad, Nellie (1883–1974)
Coates, Florence Nicholson (1850–1927)
Cobbe, Frances Power (1822–1904)
Cobbold, Elizabeth (c. 1764–1824)
Coghlan, Rose (1852–1932)
Cohan, Josephine (1876–1916)
Cohen, Harriet (1895–1967)
Cohen, Myra (1892–1959)
Coignet, Clarisse (1823–?)
Coke, Jane Elizabeth (1777–1863)
Colaço, Branca de Gonta (1880–1944)
Colbran, Isabella (1785–1845)
Colby, Clara Bewick (1846–1916)
Colclough, Mary Ann (1836–1885)
Colcord, Joanna Carver (1882–1960)
Cole, Anna Russell (1846–1926)
Cole, Rebecca J. (1846–1922)
Coleman, Alice Merriam (1858–1936)
Coleman, Ann Raney Thomas (1810–1897)
Coleman, Kit (1864–1915)
Colenso, Elizabeth (1821–1904)
Coleridge, Mary Elizabeth (1861–1907)
Coleridge, Sara (1802–1852)
Colet, Louise (1810–1876)
Colette (1873–1954)
Collet, Clara (1860–1948)
Collett, Camilla (1813–1895)
Colleville, Anne-Hyacinthe de Saint-Léger de (1761–1824)
Collier, Constance (1878–1955)
Collier, Edith (1885–1964)
Collier, Jane Annie (1869–1955)
Collier, Jeanie (c. 1791–1861)
Collins, Ellen (1828–1912)
Collins, Jennie (1828–1887)
Collins, Lottie (c. 1866–1910)
Collot, Marie-Anne (1748–1821)
Colman, Julia (1828–1909)
Colter, Mary Elizabeth (1869–1949)
Colton, Elizabeth Avery (1872–1924)
Colton, Mary (1822–1898)
Colvin, Brenda (1897–1981)
Coman, Katharine (1857–1915)
Comfort, Anna Manning (1845–1931)
Compton, Katherine (1853–1928)
Compton, Virginia (1853–1940)
Comstock, Ada Louise (1876–1973)
Comstock, Anna Botsford (1854–1930)
Comstock, Elizabeth Leslie (1815–1891)
Comstock, Nanette (1873–1942)
Conant, Hannah Chaplin (1809–1865)
Conboy, Sara McLaughlin (1870–1928)
Concannon, Helena (1878–1952)
Condorcet, Sophie Marie Louise, Marquise de (1764–1822)
Cone, Claribel (1864–1929)
Cone, Etta (1870–1949)
Cones, Nancy Ford (1869–1962)
Connelly, Cornelia (1809–1879)
Connon, Helen (c. 1859–1903)
Cons, Emma (1838–1912)
Constance Jones, E.E. (1848–1922)
Contat, Louise (1760–1813)
Contat, Marie (1769–1846)
Converse, Harriet Maxwell (1836–1903)
Cook, Edith Maud (d. 1910)
Cook, Eliza (1818–1889)
Cook, Freda Mary (1896–1990)
Cooke, Anna Rice (1853–1934)
Cooke, Flora (1864–1953)
Cooke, Rose Terry (1827–1892)
Coolbrith, Ina Donna (1841–1928)
Coolidge, Elizabeth Sprague (1863–1953)
Coolidge, Grace Goodhue (1879–1957)
Cooper, Anna J. (c. 1858–1964)
Cooper, Edith Emma (1862–1913)
Cooper, Sarah Ingersoll (1835–1896)
Cooper, Susan Fenimore (1813–1894)

Coory, Shirefie (c. 1864–1950)
Cope, Mother Marianne (1838–1918)
Coppin, Fanny Jackson (1837–1913)
Coquillard-Albrier, Albertine (c. 1810–1846)
Corbaux, Fanny (1812–1883)
Corbett, Marie (1859–1932)
Corbett-Ashby, Margery (1882–1981)
Corbin, Hazel (1894–1988)
Corelli, Marie (1855–1924)
Cornford, Frances Crofts (1886–1960)
Cornwallis, C.F. (1786–1858)
Coronado, Carolina (1820–1911)
Correa, Deolinda (fl. 1830)
Corson, Juliet (1841–1897)
Cortines, Júlia (1868–1948)
Cory, Annie Sophie (1868–1952)
Cossey, Alice Eleanor (1879–1970)
Cossgrove, Selina (1849–1929)
Cosson de La Cressonière, Charlotte Cathérine (1740–1813)
Costa, Emília de Sousa (1877–1957)
Costello, Louisa Stuart (1799–1870)
Cosway, Maria (1759–1838)
Cotten, Sallie Southall (1846–1929)
Cottin, Sophie (1770–1807)
Cotton, Mary Ann (1822–1873)
Cottrell, Violet May (1887–1971)
Couchman, Elizabeth (1876–1982)
Coudreau, Octavie (c. 1870–c. 1910)
Courtauld, Katherine (1856–1935)
Courtauld, Louisa (1729–1807)
Courths-Mahler, Hedwig (1867–1950)
Courtney, Kathleen (1878–1974)
Cousins, Margaret (1878–1954)
Couvreur, Jessie (1848–1897)
Couzins, Phoebe Wilson (1842–1913)
Cowan, Edith (1861–1932)
Cowie, Bessie Lee (1860–1950)
Cowie, Eliza Jane (1835–1902)
Cowie, Helen Stephen (1875–1956)
Cowles, Anna Roosevelt (1855–1931)
Cowles, Betsey Mix (1810–1876)
Cowles, Julia (1785–1803)
Cowley, Hannah (1743–1809)
Cox, Hazel (b. 1887)
Cox, Louise H.K. (1865–1945)
Cox, Ray (b. 1880)
Coyle, Grace Longwell (1892–1962)
Crabtree, Lotta (1847–1924)
Cradock, Mrs. H.C. (1863–1941)
Craft, Ellen (1826–c. 1891)
Craig, Edith (1869–1947)
Craig, May (1888–1975)
Craig, Minnie D. (1883–1965)
Craighill, Margaret (1898–1977)
Craigie, Pearl Mary Teresa (1867–1906)
Craik, Dinah Maria Mulock (1826–1887)
Cranch, Elizabeth (1743–1811)
Cranch, Mary Smith (1741–1811)
Crandall, Ella Phillips (1871–1938)
Crandall, Prudence (1803–1890)
Crane, Caroline Bartlett (1858–1935)
Cranston, Kate (1850–1934)
Crapsey, Adelaide (1878–1914)
Craske, Margaret (1892–1990)
Cratty, Mabel (1868–1928)
Craven, Elizabeth (1750–1828)
Craven, Pauline (1808–1891)
Crawford, Jane Todd (1763–1842)
Crawford, Louise Macartney (1790–1858)
Crequy, Renée Caroline de Froulay, Marquise de (1714–1803)
Crews, Laura Hope (1879–1942)
Cripps, Sarah Ann (c. 1821–1892)
Crisi, Maria (1892–1953)
Crocker, Hannah Mather (1752–1829)
Crocker, Lucretia (1829–1886)
Croizette, Sophie Alexandrine (1847–1901)
Croker, Bithia May (c. 1849–1920)
Croly, Jane Cunningham (1829–1901)
Crosby, Elizabeth (1888–1983)
Crosby, Fanny (1820–1915)
Crosman, Henrietta (1861–1944)
Crossley, Ada Jemima (1871–1929)
Crothers, Rachel (1878–1958)
Crouch, Anna Maria (1763–1805)
Crowdy, Rachel (1884–1964)
Crowe, Catherine Anne (c. 1800–1876)
Crowe, Ellen (c. 1845–1930)
Cruickshank, Margaret Barnet (1873–1918)
Crumpler, Rebecca Lee (1831–1895)
Cruvelli, Sofia (1826–1907)
Cryer, Sarah (1848–1929)
Cucchi, Claudine (1834–1913)
Cuddie, Mary (1823–1889)
Cullis, Winifred Clara (1875–1956)
Cumming, Kate (c. 1828–1909)
Cummings, Alma (b. 1890)
Cummings, Marian (c. 1892–1984)
Cummins, Maria Susanna (1827–1866)
Cunard, Maud (1872–1948)
Cunningham, Ann Pamela (1816–1875)
Cunnington, Eveline Willert (1849–1916)
Curie, Marie (1867–1934)
Currie, Ethel Dobbie (1898–1963)
Currie, Mary Montgomerie (1843–1905)
Curtis, Kathleen Maisey (1892–1994)
Curzon, Mary Leiter (1870–1906)
Curzon, Sarah Anne (1833–1898)
Cusack, Margaret Anne (1832–1899)
Cushier, Elizabeth (1837–1932)
Cushman, Charlotte Saunders (1816–1876)
Cushman, Pauline (1833–1893)
Cushman, Vera (1876–1946)
Cust, Aleen (1868–1937)
Custance, Olive (1874–1944)
Custer, Elizabeth Bacon (1842–1933)
Custis, Eleanor "Nelly" Parke (1779–1852)
Cutler, Hannah Conant (1815–1896)
Cutler, Kate (1870–1955)
Czartoryska, Isabella (1746–1835)
Dacre, Barbarina (1768–1854)
Dacre, Charlotte (c. 1772–1825)
Daisy, Princess (1873–1943)
Dal, Ingerid (1895–1985)
Daldy, Amey (c. 1829–1920)
Dale, Margaret (1876–1972)
D'Alessandri-Valdine, Blanche (c. 1862–1948)
Dall, Caroline Wells (1822–1912)
Dalrymple, Learmonth White (1827–1906)
Daly, Mary (c. 1861–1901)
Daly, Mary Agnes
Damer, Anne Seymour (1748–1828)
d'Angeville, Henriette (1795–1871)
Daniel, Annie Sturges (1858–1944)
Daniels, Mabel Wheeler (1878–1971)
Danilova, Maria (1793–1810)
Danzi, Maria Margarethe (1768–1800)
Darclée, Hariclea (1860–1939)
d'Arconville, Geneviève (1720–1805)
D'Arcy, Ella (c. 1856–1937)
Dargan, Olive Tilford (1869–1968)
Darling, Flora (1840–1910)
Darling, Grace (1815–1842)
Darling, May (1887–1971)
Darrow, Anna (1876–1959)
Daryush, Elizabeth (1887–1977)
Dashkova, Ekaterina (1744–1810)
Dat So La Lee (c. 1835–1925)
Daubié, Julie-Victoire (1824–1874)
Daudet, Julia (1844–1940)
Dauthendey, Elisabeth (1854–1943)
Davenport, Fanny (1850–1898)
David, Caroline Edgeworth (1856–1951)
David-Neel, Alexandra (1868–1969)
Davidson, Lucretia Maria (1808–1825)
Davidson, Margaret Miller (1823–1838)
Davies, Emily (1830–1921)
Davies, Fanny (1861–1934)
Davies, Margaret Llewelyn (1861–1944)
Davis, Alice Brown (1852–1935)
Davis, Frances Elliott (1882–1965)
Davis, Katharine Bement (1860–1935)
Davis, Mary E.P. (c. 1840–1924)
Davis, Mary Fenn (1824–1886)
Davis, Mollie Moore (1844–1909)
Davis, Paulina Wright (1813–1876)
Davis, Rebecca Harding (1831–1910)
Davis, Varina Howell (1826–1906)
Davison, Emily (1872–1913)
Dawbin, Annie Maria (1816–1905)
Dawson, Mary Elizabeth (1833–1924)
Deamer, Dulcie (1890–1972)
Dean, Dora (c. 1872–1950)
Dean, Jennie (1852–1913)
Dean, Julia (1830–1868)
Dean, Margie (1896–1918)
Dean, Williamina (1844–1895)
Deans, Jane (1823–1911)
De Brémont, Anna (1864–1922)
Decker, Sarah Platt (1852–1912)
de Cleyre, Voltairine (1866–1912)
De Graffenried, Clare (1849–1921)
Dejanović, Draga (1843–1870)
Déjazet, Pauline-Virginie (1797–1875)
Deken, Aagje (1741–1804)
Deland, Margaret (1857–1945)
Delano, Jane Arminda (1862–1919)
de Lara, Adelina (1872–1961)
de la Roche, Mazo (1879–1961)
Delarue-Mardrus, Lucie (1880–1945)
Deledda, Grazia (1871–1936)
Delille, Henriette (1813–1862)
Dell'Era, Antoinetta (1861–?)
Delroy, Irene (1898–?)
Delta, Penelope (1871–1941)
de Lussan, Zélie (1861–1949)
Démar, Claire (1800–1833)
Demel, Anna (1872–1956)
De Mist, Augusta (1783–1832)
Demorest, Ellen Curtis (1824–1898)
DeMorgan, Evelyn (1850–1919)
Dempsey, Sister Mary Joseph (1856–1939)
Denison, Flora MacDonald (1867–1921)
Denison, Mary Andrews (1826–1911)
Denman, Gertrude (1884–1954)
Dennett, Mary Ware (1872–1947)
Densmore, Frances (1867–1957)
Dent, Edith (1863–1948)
Denton, Mary Florence (1857–1947)
Deraismes, Maria (1828–1894)
de Rivery, Aimee Dubucq (c. 1762–1817)
Dermoût, Maria (1888–1962)
Deroin, Jeanne-Françoise (1805–1894)
D'Erzell, Catalina (1897–1937)
Desbordes-Valmore, Marceline (1785–1859)
Descard, Maria (1847–1927)
Desclée, Aimée Olympe (1836–1874)
Désirée (1777–1860)
Despard, Charlotte (1844–1939)
Desprès, Suzanne (1875–1951)
Dessoff, Margarethe (1874–1944)
De Swirska, Tamara (c. 1890–?)
Deutsch, Babette (1895–1982)
DeVoe, Emma Smith (1848–1927)
de Voie, Bessie (b. around 1888)
Dewey, Alice Chipman (1858–1927)
De Witt, Lydia (1859–1928)
de Wolfe, Elsie (1865–1950)
Dexter, Caroline (1819–1884)
Diakonova, Elizaveta (1874–1902)
Diamond, Ann (c. 1827–1881)
Diaz, Abby (1821–1904)
Dickey, Sarah (1838–1904)
Dickin, Maria (1870–1951)
Dickinson, Anna E. (1842–1932)
Dickinson, Emily (1830–1886)
Dickinson, Frances (1755–1830)
Dickson, Amanda America (1849–1893)
Dickson, Mary Bernard (c. 1810–1895)
Dieulafoy, Jane (1851–1916)
Digby el Mesrab, Jane (1807–1881)
Diggs, Annie LePorte (1848–1916)
Dilke, Emily (1840–1904)
Diller, Angela (1877–1968)
Dillwyn, Amy (1845–1935)
Dimock, Susan (1847–1875)
Di Murska, Ilma (1836–1889)
Dinwiddie, Emily (1879–1949)
Disraeli, Mary Anne (1792–1872)
Dittmar, Louise (1807–1884)
Dix, Dorothea Lynde (1802–1887)
Dixie, Florence (1857–1905)
Dixon Jones, Mary Amanda (1828–1908)
Dmitrieff, Elizabeth (1851–1910)
Dmitrieva, Elizaveta Ivanovna (1887–1928)
Dmitrieva, Valentina (1859–1948)
Dobson, Emily (1842–1934)

Dock, Lavinia L. (1858–1956)
Dodge, Eva F. (1896–1990)
Dodge, Grace Hoadley (1856–1914)
Dodge, Josephine (1855–1928)
Dodge, Mary Abigail (1833–1896)
Dodge, Mary Mapes (1831–1905)
Dohan, Edith Hall (1877–1943)
Dohm, Hedwig (1831–1919)
Dolgorukaia, Alexandra (1836–c. 1914)
Dolgorukova, Ekaterina (1847–1922)
Dolley, Sarah Adamson (1829–1909)
Domenech i Escate de Canellas, Maria (1877–1952)
Don, Rachel (1866–1941)
Donahue, Margaret (c. 1893–1978)
Donald, Janet (c. 1819–1892)
Donaldson, Viva (1893–1970)
Doner, Kitty (1895–1988)
Donlon, Mary H. (1894–1977)
Donnelly, Dorothy (1880–1928)
Donnelly, Lucy (1870–1948)
Doo, Unui (1873/75?–1940)
D'Or, Henrietta (1844–1886)
Doraldina (c. 1893–c. 1925)
Doremus, Sarah Platt (1802–1877)
Dorion, Marie (c. 1790–1850)
D'Orme, Aileen (1877–1939)
Dorothea, Princess of Lieven (1785–1857)
Dorr, Julia Caroline (1825–1913)
Dorr, Rheta Childe (1866–1948)
Dorsey, Sarah Anne (1829–1879)
Dorsey, Susan Miller (1857–1946)
Dorval, Marie (1798–1849)
Dostalova, Leopolda (1879–1972)
Doubrovska, Felia (1896–1981)
Doudet, Célestine (b. 1817)
Dougall, Lily (1858–1923)
Dougherty, Ellen (c. 1843–1919)
Dougherty, Sarah (c. 1817–1898)
Douglas, Adèle Cutts (1835–1899)
Douglas, Amanda Minnie (1831–1916)
Douglass, Helen Pitts (1838–1903)
Douglass, Sarah Mapps (1806–1882)
Douvillier, Suzanne (1778–1826)
Downey, June Etta (1875–1932)
Downie, Dorothy G. (1894–1960)
Dracopoulou, Theony (1883–1968)
Draga (1867–1903)
Drake, Frances Denny (1797–1875)
Drane, Augusta Theodosia (1823–1894)
Dransfeld, Hedwig (1871–1925)
Draper, Helen (1871–1951)
Draper, Mary Anna Palmer (1839–1914)
Drayton, Grace Gebbie (1877–1936)
Dreier, Katherine Sophie (1877–1952)
Dreier, Mary Elisabeth (1875–1963)
Dressler, Marie (1869–1934)
Drew, Georgiana Emma (1854–1893)
Drew, Louisa Lane (1820–1897)
Drexel, Mary Katharine (1858–1955)
Drinker, Catherine Ann (1841–1922)
Drinker, Elizabeth Sandwith (1734–1807)
Drinker, Ernesta (1852–1939)
Drinkwater, Jennie M. (1841–1900)
Droste-Hülshoff, Annette von (1797–1848)
Drouet, Juliette (1806–1883)
Drummond, Dolores (1834–1926)
Drummond, Flora (1869–1949)
Druse, Roxana (1846–1889)
Duchêne, Gabrielle (1870–1954)
Duchesne, Rose Philippine (1769–1852)
Duckering, Florence West (1869–1951)
Duclaux, Agnes Mary F. (1856–1944)
Du Faur, Emmeline Freda (1882–1935)
Duff, Mary Ann Dyke (1794–1857)
Duff-Gordon, Lucie (1821–1869)
Dufrénoy, Adelaïde de (1765–1825)
Dugdale, Henrietta (1826–1918)
Duggan, Eileen May (1894–1972)
Duley, Margaret (1894–1968)
Dumesnil, Marie Françoise (1713–1803)
Dumilâtre, Adèle (1821–1909)
Dummer, Ethel Sturges (1866–1954)
Dumolard, Marie (1816–?)
Dunbar, Flanders (1902–1959)
Dunbar-Nelson, Alice (1875–1935)
Duncan, Elizabeth (c. 1874–1948)
Duncan, Irma (1897–1978)
Duncan, Isadora (1878–1927)
Duncan, Maria Teresa (1895–1987)
Duncan, Sara Jeanette (1861–1922)
Duncombe, Susanna (1725–1812)
Dunedin, Maudie (c. 1888–1937)
Dunham, Ethel Collins (1883–1969)
Duniway, Abigail Scott (1834–1915)
Dunlop, Eliza Hamilton (1796–1880)
Dunscombe, Adaliza (1867–1943)
Dupree, Minnie (1873–1947)
Dupuy, Eliza Ann (1814–1881)
Durand, Marguerite (1864–1936)
Duras, Claire de (1777–1828)
Durgan, Bridget (c. 1845–1867)
Durham, Mary Edith (1863–1944)
Düringsfeld, Ida von (1815–1876)
Durocher, Marie (1809–1893)
Durova, Nadezhda (1783–1866)
Duse, Eleonora (1858–1924)
Dutt, Toru (1856–1877)
Duvernay, Pauline (1813–1894)
Dux, Emilienne (b. 1874)
Dwyer, Ada (1863–1952)
Dybwad, Johanne (1867–1950)
Dyer, Amelia Elizabeth (1839–1896)
Dyke, Eunice (1883–1969)
Dyson, Elizabeth Geertruida (1897–1951)
Eakins, Susan Hannah (1851–1938)
Eales, Nellie B. (1889–1989)
Eames, Emma (1865–1952)
Earle, Alice Morse (1851–1911)
Earle, Virginia (1875–1937)
Eastlake, Elizabeth (1809–1893)
Eastman, Annis Ford (1852–1910)
Eastman, Crystal (1881–1928)
Eastman, Elaine Goodale (1863–1953)
Eastman, Linda A. (1867–1963)
Eastwood, Alice (1859–1953)
Eaton, Edith (1865–1914)
Eaton, Peggy (c. 1799–1879)
Eaves, Elsie (1898–1983)
Eberhardt, Isabelle (1877–1904)
Eberle, Abastenia St. Leger (1878–1942)
Ebner-Eschenbach, Marie (1830–1916)
Eckerson, Sophia H. (d. 1954)
Eckhardt-Gramatté, S.C. (1899–1974)
Eckstorm, Fannie Pearson Hardy (1865–1946)
Eddy, Mary Baker (1821–1910)
Eden, Emily (1797–1869)
Edger, Kate (1857–1935)
Edgeworth, Maria (1768–1849)
Edgren, Anne Charlotte (1849–1892)
Edmonds, Emma (1841–1898)
Edmunds, Christiana (1835–1907)
Edson, Katherine Philips (1870–1933)
Eduardova, Eugenia (1882–1980)
Edvina, Louise (1878–1948)
Edwards, Amelia B. (1831–1892)
Edwards, Henrietta Muir (1849–1933)
Egorova, Lyubov (1880–1972)
Eibenschütz-Dernbourg, Ilona (1872–1967)
Eigenmann, Rosa Smith (1858–1947)
Einstein, Hannah Bachman (1862–1929)
Einstein-Marić, Mileva (1875–1948)
Eise, Ida Gertrude (1891–1978)
Elder, Kate (fl. 1881)
Eleanora of Reuss (1860–1917)
Eleanor of Solms-Hohensolms-Lich (1871–1937)
Elena of Montenegro (1873–1952)
Elgar, Alice (1848–1920)
Elgood, Cornelia (1874–1960)
Elisa, Henriqueta (1843–1885)
Elisabeth of Saxe-Altenburg (1826–1896)
Elizabeth (1770–1840)
Elizabeth (1831–1903)
Elizabeth (fl. 1850s)
Elizabeth Hohenzollern (1815–1885)
Elizabeth Maria of Thurn and Taxis (1860–1881)
Elizabeth of Anhalt-Dessau (1857–1933)
Elizabeth of Austria (1743–1808)
Elizabeth of Baden (1779–1826)
Elizabeth of Bavaria (1801–1873)
Elizabeth of Bavaria (1837–1898)
Elizabeth of Bavaria (1876–1965)
Elizabeth of Brunswick (1746–1840)
Elizabeth of Savoy-Carignan (1800–1856)
Elizabeth of Saxony (1830–1912)
Elizabeth of the Trinity (1880–1906)
Elizabeth of Wied (1843–1916)
Elizabeth of Wurttemberg (1802–1864)
Ella (1864–1918)
Ellen, Mary Ann (1897–1949)
Ellet, Elizabeth (c. 1812–1877)
Elliott, Charlotte (1789–1871)
Elliott, Gertrude (1874–1950)
Elliott, Harriet Wiseman (1884–1947)
Elliott, Maud Howe (1854–1948)
Elliott, Maxine (1868–1940)
Elliott, Sarah Barnwell (1848–1928)
Ellis, Ellen (1829–1895)
Ellis, Mina A. (1870–1956)
Ellis, Sarah Stickney (c. 1799–1872)
Ellis-Fermor, Una Mary (1894–1958)
Elliston, Daisy (b. 1894)
Elmendorf, Theresa West (1855–1932)
Elphinstone, Hester Maria (1764–1857)
Elphinstone, Margaret Mercer (1788–1867)
Elseeta (1883–1903)
Elsie, Lily (1886–1962)
Elsom, Sarah Ann (1867–1962)
Elssler, Fanny (1810–1884)
Elssler, Thérèse (1808–1878)
Emerson, Ellen Russell (1837–1907)
Emerson, Ellen Tucker (1811–1831)
Emerson, Ellen Tucker (1839–1909)
Emerson, Lidian Jackson (1802–1892)
Emerson, Mary Moody (1774–1863)
Emery, Pollie (1875–1958)
Emery, Winifred (1862–1924)
Emma (1836–1885)
Emmerich, Anna Katharina (1774–1824)
Emmons, Chansonetta Stanley (1858–1937)
Engel, Regula (1761–1853)
Èngelgardt, Sofia Vladimirovna (1828–1894)
Engelhard, Magdalene Philippine (1756–1831)
England, Maud Russell (1863–1956)
Eppes, Maria Jefferson (1778–1804)
Erickson, Hilda (1859–1968)
Eristavi-Xostaria, Anastasia (1868–1951)
Ermolova, Mariia (1853–1928)
Eschstruth, Nataly von (1860–1939)
Espina, Concha (1869–1955)
Espinosa, Judith (1877–1949)
Espinosa, Mimi (1893–1936)
Essipova, Annette (1851–1914)
Eugénie (1826–1920)
Eugenie (1830–1889)
Eugénie Hortense (1808–1847)
Eulalia (1864–1958)
Evans, Alice Catherine (1881–1975)
Evans, Ann (c. 1836–1916)
Evans, Elizabeth Glendower (1856–1937)
Evans, Mary Anne (1819–1880)
Evans, Matilda Arabella (1872–1935)
Everleigh, Aida (1864–1960)
Everleigh, Minna (1866–1948)
Ewing, Juliana Horatia (1841–1885)
Fabbri, Flora (c. 1807–c. 1857)
Fabish, Agnes (1873–1947)
Fachiri, Adila (1886–1962)
Fairbrother, Sydney (1872–1941)
Fairfax, Marion (1875–1979)
Faithfull, Emily (1835–1895)
Falcon, Marie Cornélie (1814–1897)
Falconer, Martha Platt (1862–1941)
Falconnet, Françoise-Cécile de Chaumont (1738–1819)
Fanshawe, Catherine Maria (1765–1834)
Farley, Harriet (1813–1907)
Farmer, Fannie Merritt (1857–1915)
Farnham, Eliza W. (1815–1864)
Farningham, Marianne (1834–1909)
Farnsworth, Emma J. (1860–1952)
Farrand, Beatrix Jones (1872–1959)
Farrar, Cynthia (1795–1862)
Farrar, Eliza Rotch (1791–1870)
Farren, Elizabeth (c. 1759–1829)
Farren, Nellie (1848–1904)
Farrenc, Louise (1804–1875)
Fassett, Cornelia (1831–1898)
Fatima, Djemille (c. 1890–1921)

Faucit, Helena Saville (1817–1898)
Faugeres, Margaretta V. (1771–1801)
Faulkner, Ruawahine Irihapeti (?–1855)
Faust, Lotta (1880–1910)
Favart, Marie (b. 1833)
Favre, Julie Velten (1834–1896)
Fawcett, Millicent Garrett (1847–1929)
Fawcett, Philippa (1868–1948)
Fay, Amy (1844–1928)
Fay, Eliza (1756–1816)
Fearn, Anne Walter (1865–1939)
Fedde, Sister Elizabeth (1850–1921)
Federova, Sophia (1879–1963)
Fedorovitch, Sophie (1893–1953)
Félix, Lia (b. 1830)
Felton, Rebecca Latimer (1835–1930)
Fenayrou, Gabrielle (b. 1850)
Fenning, Elizabeth (1792–1815)
Fenwick, Eliza (1766–1840)
Fenwick, Ethel Gordon (1857–1947)
Feodore of Hohenlohe-Langenburg (1866–1932)
Feodore of Leiningen (1807–1872)
Ferguson, Abbie Park (1837–1919)
Ferguson, Elizabeth Graeme (1737–1801)
Ferguson, Margaret Clay (1863–1951)
Ferguson, Miriam A. (1875–1961)
Fergusson, Elizabeth (1867–1930)
Fern, Fanny (1811–1872)
Ferner, Ellen Elizabeth (1869–1930)
Fernig, Félicité de (c. 1776–after 1831)
Ferrais, Amalia (1830–1904)
Ferrari, Carlotta (1837–1907)
Ferrari, Gabrielle (1851–1921)
Ferrers, Helen (1869–1943
Ferrier, Susan Edmonstone (1782–1854)
Ferrin, Mary Upton (1810–1881)
Feuchères, Sophie, Baronne de (c. 1795–1841)
Fewings, Eliza Anne (1857–1940)
Fickert, Auguste (1855–1910)
Field, Ethel Maude (1882–1967)
Field, Kate (1838–1896)
Fields, Annie Adams (1834–1915)
Fields, Mary (c. 1832–1914)
Figner, Vera (1852–1942)
Figueur, Thérèse (1774–1861)
Filippi, Rosina (1866–1930)
Filkins, Grace (c. 1865–1962)
Fillmore, Abigail Powers (1798–1853)
Fillmore, Myrtle Page (1845–1931)
Filosofova, Anna (1837–1912)
Finley, Martha (1828–1909)
Finnie, Jessie (c. 1821–?)
Fiocre, Eugénie (1845–1908)
Fischer, Caroline Auguste (1764–1834)
Fish, Marian (1853–1915)
Fisher, Clara (1811–1898)
Fisher, Dorothy Canfield (1879–1958)
Fiske, Fidelia (1816–1864)
Fiske, Minnie Maddern (1865–1932)
Fitzclarence, Amelia (1807–1858)
Fitzgerald, Eugenia Tucker (c. 1834–1928)
Fitzgerald, Pamela (1773–1831)
FitzGibbon, Hanorah Philomena (1889–1979)
Fitzherbert, Maria Anne (1756–1837)
Fitzjames, Louise (b. 1809)
Fitzwilliam, Fanny Elizabeth (1801–1854)
Flanagan, Sinéad (1878–1975)
Fleming, Margaret (1803–1811)
Fleming, May Agnes (1840–1880)
Fleming, Williamina Paton (1857–1911)
Fletcher, Alice Cunningham (1838–1923)
Flikke, Julia Otteson (1879–1965)
Flöge, Emilie (1874–1952)
Florence, Malvina Pray (1830–1906)
Florence, Mary Sargant (1857–1954)
Florentino, Leona (1849–1884)
Flower, Eliza (1803–1846)
Flower, Lucy (1837–1921)
Fogerty, Elsie (1865–1945)
Foley, Edna (1878–1943)
Foley, Margaret (c. 1827–1877)
Folger, Emily (1858–1936)
Follansbee, Elizabeth A. (1839–1917)
Follen, Eliza (1787–1860)
Follett, Mary Parker (1868–1933)
Foltz, Clara (1849–1934)
Foot, Katherine (c. 1852–?)
Foote, Maria (c. 1797–1867)
Foote, Mary Hallock (1847–1938)
Forbes, Margaret (c. 1807–1877)
Force, Julia (1860–?)
Force, Juliana (1876–1948)
Ford, Isabella O. (1855–1924)
Forman, Ada (b. around 1895)
Fornaroli, Cia (1888–1954)
Fornia, Rita (1878–1922)
Forsh, Olga (1873–1961)
Förster-Nietzsche, Elisabeth (1846–1935)
Forten, Margaretta (1808–1875)
Fortesque-Brickdale, Eleanor (1872–1945)
Fortune, Mary (fl. 1866–1910)
Foster, Emily Sophia (1842–1897)
Foster, Hannah Webster (1758–1840)
Foster, J. Ellen (1840–1910)
Fothergill, Jessie (1851–1891)
Fountaine, Margaret (1862–1940)
Fouqué, Karoline Freifrau de la Motte (1774–1831)
Fowle, Elida Rumsey (1842–1919)
Fowler, Lydia Folger (1822–1879)
Fox, Caroline (1819–1871)
Fox, Charlotte Milligan (1864–1916)
Fox, Della (1870–1913)
Fox, Elizabeth Vassall (1770–1845)
Fox, Kate (c. 1839–1892)
Fox, Leah (c. 1818–1890)
Fox, Margaret (c. 1833–1893)
Fox, Mary (b. 1817)
Fragonard, Marie Anne (1745–c. 1823)
Frame, Alice (1878–1941)
Frampton, Eleanor (1896–1973)
Francey, Henriette (b. around 1859)
Franchi, Anna (1866–1954)
Francis, Catherine Augusta (1836–1916)
Francis, Milly (c. 1802–1848)
Francisca of Portugal (1800–1834)
Francisca of Portugal (1824–1898)
François, Louise von (1817–1893)
Françoise d'Orleans (1844–1925)
Frank, Rosaline Margaret (1864–1954)
Franklin, Eleanor (1795–1825)
Franklin, Jane (1792–1875)
Franklin, Martha Minerva (1870–1968)
Franklin, Miles (1879–1954)
Franks, Rebecca (c. 1760–1823)
Fraser, Annie Isabel (1868–1939)
Fraser, Eliza (c. 1798–1858)
Fraser, Isabella (1857–1932)
Fraser, Janet (1883–1945)
Fraser, Margaret (1866–1951)
Fraser, Mary Crawford (1851–1922)
Fraser, Mary Isabel (1863–1942)
Frazier, Maude (1881–1963)
Frederica Dorothea of Baden (1781–1826)
Frederica Louise (1770–1819)
Frederica of Hesse (1751–1805)
Frederica of Mecklenburg-Strelitz (1778–1841)
Frederica Wilhelmina of Prussia (1774–1837)
Frederick, Christine (1883–1970)
Fredericka of Hanover (1848–1926)
Freeman, Alice (1857–1936)
Freeman, Caroline (c. 1855–1914)
Freeman, Emma B. (1880–1927)
Freeman, Mary E. Wilkins (1852–1930)
Freer, Agnes Rand (1878–1972)
Frémont, Jessie Benton (1824–1902)
Fremstad, Olive (1871–1951)
French, Alice (1850–1934)
French, Annie (1872–1965)
French, Evangeline (1869–1960)
French, Francesca (1871–1960)
Freundlich, Emmy (1878–1948)
Freytag-Loringhoven, Elsa von (1875–1927)
Friedberg, Berta (1864–1944)
Frietschie, Barbara (1766–1862)
Frohberg, Regina (1783–1850)
Frölich, Henriette (1768–1833)
Froman, Margareta (1890–1970)
Fromm-Reichmann, Frieda (1889–1957)
Frost, Constance Helen (c. 1862–1920)
Fry, Elizabeth (1780–1845)
Fry, Laura Ann (1857–1943)
Fry, Margery (1874–1958)
Führer, Charlotte (1834–1907)
Fukuda, Hideko (1865–1927)
Fuld, Carrie (1864–1944)
Fullam, Augusta Fairfield (1876–1914)
Fuller, Elizabeth (1775–1856)
Fuller, Ida (1874–1975)
Fuller, Loïe (1862–1928)
Fuller, Lucia Fairchild (1870–1924)
Fuller, Margaret (1810–1850)
Fuller, Meta Warrick (1877–1968)
Fuller, Minnie Rutherford (1868–1946)
Fuller, Sarah (1836–1927)
Fullerton, Georgiana Charlotte (1812–1885)
Fullerton, Mary Eliza (1868–1946)
Fulton, Catherine (1829–1919)
Fulton, Mary Hannah (1854–1927)
Fuocco, Sofia (1830–1916)
Furbish, Kate (1834–1931)
Furley, Matilda (1813–1899)
Furse, Katharine (1875–1952)
Furuhjelm, Annie (1854–1937)
Gabain, Ethel Leontine (1883–1950)
Gacon-Dufour, Marie Armande Jeanne (1753–c. 1835)
Gadski, Johanna (1872–1932)
Gage, Frances D. (1808–1884)
Gage, Matilda Joslyn (1826–1898)
Gage, Susanna Phelps (1857–1915)
Gagneur, Louise (1832–1902)
Gagneur, Marguerite (1857–1945)
Gaines, Irene McCoy (1892–1964)
Gaines, Myra Clark (1805–1885)
Gale, Zona (1874–1938)
Galitzin, Amalie von (1748–1806)
Gallagher, Kitty (fl. mid-19th c.)
Galli, Caterina (c. 1723–1804)
Galli, Rosina (1896–1940)
Galli-Marié, Célestine (1840–1905)
Gan, Elena Andreevna (1814–1842)
Gantt, Rosa (1875–1935)
Garborg, Hulda (1862–1934)
Gardener, Helen Hamilton (1853–1925)
Gardiner, Kate (1885–1974)
Gardiner, Lisa (c. 1896–1958)
Gard'ner, Elizabeth Anne (1858–1926)
Gardner, Helen (1878–1946)
Gardner, Isabella Stewart (1840–1924)
Gardner, Margaret (1844–1929)
Gardner, Maria Louisa (1879–1968)
Gardner, Mary Sewall (1871–1961)
Garfield, Lucretia (1832–1918)
Garfield, Viola (1899–1983)
Garibaldi, Anita (c. 1821–1849)
Garlick, Eunice Harriett (1883–1951)
Garmson, Aileen (c. 1861–1951)
Garnet, Sarah (1831–1911)
Garnett, Constance (1862–1946)
Garrett, Emma (c. 1846–1893)
Garrett, Mary Elizabeth (1854–1915)
Garrett, Mary Smith (1839–1925)
Garrison, Lucy McKim (1842–1877)
Gaskell, Elizabeth (1810–1865)
Gatty, Margaret (1809–1873)
Gault, Alma Elizabeth (1891–1981)
Gaunt, Mary (1861–1942)
Gautier, Judith (1845–1917)
Gaxton, Madeline (1897–1990)
Gay, Sophie (1776–1852)
Geddes, Annabella Mary (1864–1955)
Gee, Dolly (1897–1978)
Geister, Janet M. (1885–1964)
Geistinger, Marie (1833–1903)
Gelfman, Gesia (d. 1882)
Gellhorn, Edna (1878–1970)
Geltzer, Ykaterina (1876–1962)
Genée, Adeline (1878–1970)
Géniat, Marcelle (1879–1959)
Genlis, Stéphanie-Félicité, Comtesse de (1746–1830)
Genth, Lillian (1876–1953)
George, Elizabeth (c. 1814–1902)
George, Grace (1879–1961)
Georges, Marguerite J. (c. 1787–1867)
Gérard, Marguerite (1761–1837)
Gerdt, Elizaveta (1891–1975)
Gérin-Lajoie, Marie (1867–1945)
Germain, Sophie (1776–1831)

Gerould, Katharine (1879–1944)
Gersten, Berta (c. 1896–1972)
Gerster, Etelka (1855–1920)
Gertsyk, Adelaida (1874–1925)
Gestefeld, Ursula Newell (1845–1921)
Giaconi, Luisa (1870–1908)
Gibb, Helen (1838–1914)
Gibbons, Abby Hopper (1801–1893)
Gibbs, Mary Elizabeth (1836–1920)
Gibbs, May (1877–1969)
Gibson, Emily Patricia (1863/64?–1947)
Gibson, Helena Fannie (1868–1938)
Gibson, Irene Langhorne (1873–1956)
Gibson, Mary Victoria (1864–1929)
Gilbert, Anne (1821–1904)
Gilbert, Linda (1847–1895)
Gilder, Jeannette Leonard (1849–1916)
Gildersleeve, Virginia Crocheron (1877–1965)
Gill, Mary Gabriel (1837–1905)
Gill, Zillah Smith (1859–1937)
Gillespie, Mabel (1877–1923)
Gillespie, Mother Angela (1824–1887)
Gillett, Emma (1852–1927)
Gillies, Janet (1864–1947)
Gilman, Caroline Howard (1794–1888)
Gilman, Charlotte Perkins (1860–1935)
Gilman, Elisabeth (1867–1950)
Gilmer, Elizabeth May (1880–1960)
Gilmer, Elizabeth Meriwether (1861–1951)
Gilmore, Mary (1865–1962)
Gilmour, Christina (c. 1824–c. 1911)
Ginner, Ruby (c. 1886–1978)
Ginzburg, Evgenia (1896–1980)
Gippius, Zinaida (1869–1945)
Girardin, Delphine (1804–1855)
Giriat, Madame (b. 1866)
Gisela (1856–1932)
Gittos, Marianne (1830–1908)
Glaser, Lulu (1874–1958)
Glasgow, Ellen (1873–1945)
Glaspell, Susan (1876–1948)
Glass, Bonnie (b. around 1895)
Gleason, Kate (1865–1933)
Gleason, Rachel Brooks (1820–1905)
Gleditsch, Ellen (1879–1968)
Gleichen, Feodora (1861–1922)
Glen, Esther (1881–1940)
Glenn, Mary Willcox (1869–1940)
Glinka, Avdotia Pavlovna (1795–1863)
Glover, Amelia (c. 1873–?)
Glover, Julia (1779–1850)
Glümer, Claire von (1825–1906)
Glyn, Elinor (1864–1943)
Goddard, Arabella (1836–1922)
Goddard, Mary Katherine (1738–1816)
Goddard, Victorine (1844–1935)
Godley, Charlotte (1821–1907)
Goegg, Marie (1826–1899)
Goethe, Elisabeth (1730–1808)
Goldfrank, Esther S. (1896–1997)
Goldman, Emma (1869–1940)
Goldmark, Josephine (1877–1950)
Goldstein, Vida (1869–1949)
Goldthwaite, Anne Wilson (1869–1944)
Golubkina, Anna (1864–1927)
Gómez de Avellaneda, Gertrudis (1814–1873)
Gonne, Maud (1866–1953)
Gonzaga, Chiquinha (1847–1935)
Gonzalès, Eva (1849–1883)
Goodrich, Annie Warburton (1866–1954)
Goodridge, Sarah (1788–1853)
Goodson, Katharine (1872–1958)
Goodwin, Bridget (c. 1802/27–1899)
Goold, Maria Vere (1877–1908)
Gordon, Anna Adams (1853–1931)
Gordon, Annie Elizabeth (1873–1951)
Gordon, Doris Clifton (1890–1956)
Gordon, Dorothy (1889–1970)
Gordon, Eliza (1877–1938)
Gordon, Jean Margaret (1865–1931)
Gordon, Kate M. (1861–1932)
Gordon, Laura de Force (1838–1907)
Gordon-Baille, Mary Ann (1857–?)
Gordon-Cumming, Eka (1837–1924)
Gore, Catherine (1799–1861)
Gore-Booth, Eva (1870–1926)
Gorriti, Juana Manuela (1816–1892)
Go-Sakuramachi (1740–1814)
Gosse, Sylvia (1881–1968)
Gottfried, Gesina Margaretha (d. 1828)
Goudvis, Bertha (1876–1966)
Gouel, Eva (d. 1915)
Gougar, Helen (1843–1907)
Goulue, La (1869–1929)
Gourd, Emilie (1879–1946)
Graham, Isabella (1742–1814)
Graham, Rose (1879–1974)
Graham, Shirley (1896–1977)
Grahn, Lucile (1819–1907)
Grajales, Mariana (1808–1893)
Gramatica, Emma (1875–1965)
Gramatica, Irma (1873–1962)
Gramont, Elizabeth de (fl. 1875–1935)
Grandval, Marie Felicia (1830–1907)
Granger, Josie (1853–1934)
Grant, Anne (1755–1838)
Grant, Julia (1826–1902)
Grant, Zilpah (1794–1874)
Grantzow, Adele (1845–1877)
Gratz, Rebecca (1781–1869)
Gray, Eileen (1878–1976)
Gray, Teresa Corinna Ubertis (1877–1964)
Greatorex, Eliza (1820–1897)
Greaves, Mary Ann (1834–1897)
Greeley-Smith, Nixola (1880–1919)
Green, Anna Katharine (1846–1935)
Green, Elizabeth Shippen (1871–1954)
Green, Hetty (1834–1916)
Green, Mary Anne Everett (1818–1895)
Greenaway, Kate (1846–1901)
Greene, Belle da Costa (1883–1950)
Greene, Catharine Littlefield (1755–1814)
Greene, Cordelia A. (1831–1905)
Greene, Sarah Pratt (1856–1935)
Greenfield, Elizabeth Taylor (c. 1819–1876)
Greenhow, Rose O'Neal (c. 1817–1864)
Greenwell, Dora (1821–1882)
Greenwood, Ellen Sarah (1837–1917)
Greenwood, Sarah (c. 1809–1889)
Greet, Clare (1871–1939)
Gregg, Christina (c. 1814–1882)
Gregory, Augusta (1852–1932)
Grenfell, Helen L. (b. 1868)
Gréville, Alice (1842–1903)
Greville, Frances Evelyn (1861–1938)
Grew, Mary A. (1813–1896)
Grey, Elizabeth (d. 1818)
Grey, Elizabeth (d. 1822)
Grey, Katherine (1873–1950)
Grey, Maria Georgina (1816–1906)
Grieg, Nina (1845–1935)
Griffin, Elsie Mary (1884–1968)
Griffing, Josephine White (1814–1872)
Griffith, Emily (c. 1880–1947)
Griffiths, Ann (1776–1805)
Griffitts, Hannah (1727–1817)
Grillet, Louise Hortense (1865–1952)
Grimké, Angelina E. (1805–1879)
Grimké, Charlotte L. Forten (1837–1914)
Grimké, Sarah Moore (1792–1873)
Grimshaw, Beatrice (c. 1870–1953)
Grinder, Martha (1815–1866)
Grisi, Carlotta (1819–1899)
Grisi, Giuditta (1805–1840)
Grisi, Giulia (1811–1869)
Grogger, Paula (1892–1984)
Gromova, Vera (1891–1973)
Grossmann, Edith Searle (1863–1931)
Grote, Harriet (1792–1878)
Grotell, Maija (1899–1973)
Grubb, Sarah Lynes (1773–1842)
Gruenberg, Sidonie (1881–1974)
Guacci, Giuseppina (1807–1848)
Guard, Elizabeth (1814–1870)
Guérin, Eugénie de (1805–1848)
Guérin, Mother Theodore (1798–1856)
Guerrero, Maria (1867–1928)
Guest, Lady Charlotte (1812–1895)
Guggenheim, Florence Shloss (1863–1944)
Guggenheim, Irene (1868–1954)
Guggenheim, Olga H. (1877–1970)
Guibert, Louise-Alexandrine, Comtesse de (d. 1826)
Guiccioli, Teresa (c. 1801–1873)
Guilbert, Yvette (1865–1944)
Guimarães Peixoto Bretas, Ana Lins do (1889–1985)
Guimard, Marie Madeleine (1743–1816)
Guiney, Louise Imogen (1861–1920)
Guizot, Pauline (1773–1827)
Gulbranson, Ellen (1863–1947)
Gulick, Alice Gordon (1847–1903)
Gulick, Charlotte Vetter (1865–1928)
Gullen, Augusta Stowe (1857–1943)
Gulliver, Julia Henrietta (1856–1940)
Günderrode, Karoline von (1780–1806)
Gunn, Elizabeth Catherine (1879–1963)
Gunn, Jeannie (1870–1961)
Gunness, Belle (1860–c. 1908)
Gunning, Elizabeth (1769–1823)
Gunning, Susannah Minifie (c. 1740–1800)
Gunther, Erna (1896–1982)
Gurevich, Liubov (1866–1940)
Gurney, Eliza (1801–1881)
Gurney, Nella Hooper (1838–1887)
Guro, Elena (1877–1913)
Gutheil-Schoder, Marie (1874–1935)
Guthrie, Mary Jane (1895–1975)
Gutiérrez de Mendoza, Juana Belén (1875–1942)
Guy-Blaché, Alice (1875–1968)
Guy-Stéphan, Marie (1818–1873)
Gyllembourg-Ehrensvärd, Thomasine (1773–1856)
Hack, Maria (1777–1844)
Hackley, E. Azalia Smith (1867–1922)
Hading, Jane (1859–1933)
Hagan, Ellen (1873–1958)
Hagman, Lucina (1853–1946)
Hahn, Dorothy (1876–1950)
Hahn-Hahn, Ida, Countess von (1805–1880)
Haig, Emma (1898–1939)
Haines, Helen (1872–1961)
Hainisch, Marianne (1839–1936)
Halcombe, Edith Stanway (1844–1903)
Haldane, Elizabeth S. (1862–1937)
Hale, Ellen Day (1855–1940)
Hale, Louise Closser (1872–1933)
Hale, Lucretia Peabody (1820–1900)
Hale, Maria Selina (1864–1951)
Hale, Ruth (1886–1934)
Hale, Sarah Josepha (1788–1879)
Hale, Sarah Preston (1796–1866)
Hale, Susan (1833–1910)
Haley, Margaret A. (1861–1939)
Hall, Anna Maria (1800–1881)
Hall, Anne (1792–1863)
Hall, Augusta (1802–1896)
Hall, Elsie (1877–1976)
Hall, Emma Amelia (1837–1884)
Hall, Rosetta Sherwood (1865–1951)
Hallowell, Anna (1831–1905)
Hames, Mary (1827–1919)
Hamilton, Alice (1869–1970)
Hamilton, Cicely (1872–1952)
Hamilton, Edith (1867–1963)
Hamilton, Elizabeth (1758–1816)
Hamilton, Elizabeth Jane (1805–1897)
Hamilton, Elizabeth Schuyler (1757–c. 1854)
Hamilton, Emma (1765–1815)
Hamilton, Gordon (1892–1967)
Hamilton, Mary (1739–1816)
Hamm, Margherita (1867–1907)
Hanaford, Phebe Ann (1829–1921)
Hanan, Susanna (1870–1970)
Hanbury, Elizabeth (1793–1901)
Hancock, Cornelia (1840–1927)
Handel-Mazzetti, Enrica von (1871–1955)
Hani, Motoko (1873–1957)
Hanim, Leyla (1850–1936)
Hanim, Nigar (1862–1918)
Hanke, Henriette (1785–1862)
Hanks, Nancy (1783–1818)
Hanscom, Adelaide (1876–1932)
Hanska, Éveline, Countess (1801–1882)
Hansteen, Aasta (1824–1908)
Hanway, Mary Ann (c. 1755–c. 1823)
Hapgood, Isabel (1850–1928)
Hardey, Mary Aloysia (1809–1886)
Harding, Florence K. (1860–1924)
Hardy, Anna Eliza (1839–1934)
Harford, Lesbia (1891–1927)

Harkness, Anna M. Richardson (1837–1926)
Harkness, Mary Stillman (1874–1950)
Harlowe, Sarah (1765–1852)
Harned, Virginia (1872–1946)
Harper, Frances E.W. (1825–1911)
Harper, Ida Husted (1851–1931)
Harraden, Beatrice (1864–1936)
Harriman, Mary (1851–1932)
Harris, Charlotte (1819–?)
Harris, Corra May (1869–1935)
Harris, Emily Cumming (c. 1836–1925)
Harris, Jane Elizabeth (c. 1852–1942)
Harris, Mary Belle (1874–1957)
Harrison, Anna Symmes (1775–1864)
Harrison, Caroline Scott (1832–1892)
Harrison, Constance Cary (1843–1920)
Harrison, Elizabeth (1849–1927)
Harrison, Jane Ellen (1850–1928)
Harrison, Jane Irwin (1804–1846)
Harrison, Marguerite (1879–1967)
Harrison, Mary Scott Dimmick (1858–1948)
Harrison, Susie Frances (1859–1935)
Harrold, Agnes (c. 1830–1903)
Harry, Myriam (1869–1958)
Harsant, Florence Marie (1891–1994)
Hart, Alice (fl. late–19th c.)
Hart, Flo (c. 1896–1960)
Hart, Julia Catherine (1796–1867)
Hart, Nancy (c. 1735–1830)
Hart, Nancy (c. 1846–1902)
Hart, Pearl (c. 1875–c. 1924)
Haruko (1850–1914)
Hasbrouck, Lydia Sayer (1827–1910)
Haselden, Frances Isabella (c. 1841–1936)
Haslam, Anna (1829–1922)
Hasselqvist, Jenny (1894–1978)
Hastings, Caroline (1841–1922)
Hastings, Flora (1806–1839)
Hatcher, Orie Latham (1868–1946)
Hatton, Marion (1835–1905)
Haughery, Margaret Gaffney (1813–1882)
Hauk, Minnie (1851–1929)
Hauke, Julie von (1825–1895)
Hausset, Nicole Colleson du (1713–1801)
Havemeyer, Louisine (1855–1929)
Haven, Emily Bradley Neal (1827–1863)
Havergal, Frances Ridley (1836–1879)
Haviland, Laura S. (1808–1898)
Hawarden, Clementina (1822–1865)
Hawes, Harriet Boyd (1871–1945)
Hawkins, Laetitia Matilda (1759–1835)
Hawkins, Mary (1875–1950)
Hawthorne, Margaret Jane Scott (1869–1958)
Hawthorne, Sophia Peabody (1809–1871)
Hay, Mary Garrett (1857–1928)
Hayden, Mary (1862–1942)
Hayden, Mother Mary Bridget (1814–1890)
Hayden, Sophia (1868–1953)
Haydon, Ethel (1878–1954)
Hayes, Catherine (1825–1861)
Hayes, Lucy Webb (1831–1889)
Haygood, Laura Askew (1845–1900)
Hays, Mary (1760–1843)
Hazard, Caroline (1856–1945)
Hazeltine, Mary (1868–1949)
Hazrat Mahal (c. 1820–1879)
Heap, Sarah (1870–1960)
Hearst, Phoebe A. (1842–1919)
Heath, Sophie (1896–1939)
Hebard, Grace Raymond (1861–1936)
Heberle, Thérèse (1806–1840)
Heck, Barbara Ruckle (1734–1804)
Hector, Annie French (1825–1902)
Heer, Anna (1863–1918)
Hegan, Eliza Parks (1861–1917)
Hei, Akenehi (1877/78?–1910)
Heiberg, Johanne Luise (1812–1890)
Heinel, Anna (1753–1808)
Heinemann, Barbara (1795–1883)
Held, Anna (c. 1865–1918)
Helena (1846–1923)
Helena Pavlovna (1784–1803)
Helena Victoria (1870–1948)
Helene Louise of Mecklenburg-Schwerin (1814–1858)
Helene of Bavaria (1834–1890)
Helene of Wurttemberg (1807–1873)
Helen of Nassau (1831–1888)
Hellaby, Amy Maria (1864–1955)
Helmer, Bessie Bradwell (1858–1927)
Hemans, Felicia D. (1793–1835)
Hemenway, Abby (1828–1890)
Hemenway, Mary Porter Tileston (1820–1894)
Hemings, Sally (1773–1835)
Hendel, Henriette (1772–1849)
Henderson, Alice Corbin (1881–1949)
Henderson, Virginia (1897–1996)
Hengler, Flora (c. 1887–1965)
Hengler, May (c. 1884–1952)
Henmyer, Annie W. (1827–1900)
Henning, Rachel (1826–1914)
Hennings, Betty (1850–1939)
Hennings, Emmy (1885–1948)
Henningsen, Agnes (1868–1962)
Henrietta Adrienne (1792–1864)
Henrietta of Belgium (1870–1948)
Henrietta of Nassau-Weilburg (1780–1857)
Henrotin, Ellen Martin (1847–1922)
Henry, Alice (1857–1943)
Henry, Annie (1879–1971)
Henrys, Catherine (c. 1805–1855)
Hensel, Luise (1798–1876)
Hentz, Caroline Lee (1800–1856)
Herangi, Te Kirihaehae Te Puea (1883–1952)
Herbelin, Jeanne Mathilde (1820–1904)
Herford, Beatrice (c. 1868–1952)
Héricourt, Jenny Poinsard (1809–1875)
Hermine of Waldeck and Pyrmont (1827–1910)
Herne, Chrystal (1882–1950)
Herne, Katharine Corcoran (1857–1943)
Heron, Matilda (1830–1877)
Herrera Garrido, Francisca (1869–1950)
Herrick, Christine Terhune (1859–1944)
Herrick, Hermione Ruth (1889–1983)
Herron, Carrie Rand (1867–1914)
Herschel, Caroline (1750–1848)
Hervey, Elizabeth (c. 1748–c. 1820)
Herwegh, Emma (1817–1904)
Herz, Henriette (1764–1847)
Heslop, Mary Kingdon (1885–1955)
Hesse, Fanny Angelina (1850–1934)
Hesselgren, Kerstin (1872–1962)
Hetherington, Jessie Isabel (1882–1971)
Hetley, Georgina Burne (1832–1898)
Hewett, Ellen Anne (1843–1926)
Hewett, Mary Elizabeth Grenside (1857–1892)
Hewins, Caroline Maria (1846–1926)
Hewlett, Hilda Beatrice (1864–1943)
He Xiangning (1879–1972)
Heyking, Elisabeth von (1861–1925)
Heyman, Katherine Ruth (1877–1944)
Hibbard, Hope (1893–1988)
Hickey, Emily Henrietta (1845–1924)
Hickey, Mary St. Domitille (1882–1958)
Hicks, Adelaide (1845–1930)
Hicks, Amie (c. 1839–1917)
Higgins, Sarah (1830–1923)
Higuchi, Ichiyo (1872–1896)
Hikapuhi (1860/71?–1934)
Hildegarde of Bavaria (1825–1864)
Hill, Emily (1847–1930)
Hill, Frances Mulligan (1799–1884)
Hill, Grace Livingston (1865–1947)
Hill, Mabel (1872–1956)
Hill, Octavia (1838–1912)
Hill, Patty Smith (1868–1946)
Hillern, Wilhelmine von (1836–1916)
Hind, Cora (1861–1942)
Hine-i-paketia (fl. 1850–1870)
Hine-i-turama (c. 1818–1864)
Hinematioro (d. 1823)
Hinerangi, Sophia (c. 1830–1911)
Hinkle, Beatrice M. (1874–1953)
Hirsch, Rachel (1870–1953)
Hirst, Grace (1805–1901)
Hobhouse, Emily (1860–1926)
Hobhouse, Violet (1864–1902)
Hobson, Elizabeth Christophers (1831–1912)
Hodder, Jessie Donaldson (1867–1931)
Hodge, Annie Mabel (1862–1938)
Hodges, Faustina Hasse (1822–1895)
Hodgkins, Frances (1869–1947)
Hodgkins, Sarah Perkins (c. 1750–1803)
Hodgson, Elizabeth (1814–1877)
Hodson, Henrietta (1841–1910)
Hoey, Jane M. (1892–1968)
Hofmann, Elise (1889–1955)
Hogan, Aileen I. (1899–1981)
Hoge, Jane (1811–1890)
Hohenhausen, Elizabeth (1789–1857)
Holden, Edith B. (1871–1920)
Holden, Effie M. (b. 1867)
Holden, Evelyn (1877–c. 1969)
Holden, Violet (b. 1873)
Holford, Alice Hannah (1867–1966)
Hollar, Constance (1881–1945)
Holley, Marietta (1836–1926)
Holley, Mary Austin (1784–1846)
Holley, Sallie (1818–1893)
Holmès, Augusta (1847–1903)
Holmes, Julia Archibald (1838–1887)
Holmes, Mary Jane (1825–1907)
Holst, Clara (1868–1935)
Holt, Winifred (1870–1945)
Holyoke, Mary Vial (1737–1802)
Homan, Gertrude (1880–1951)
Homer, Louise (1871–1947)
Hong, Lady (1735–1850)
Honner, Maria (1812–1870)
Hood, Mary (c. 1822–1902)
Hoodless, Adelaide (1857–1910)
Hooker, Isabella Beecher (1822–1907)
Hooper, Ellen Sturgis (1812–1848)
Hooper, Jessie Jack (1865–1935)
Hooper, Kate Challis (1894–1982)
Hoover, Lou Henry (1874–1944)
Hopekirk, Helen (1856–1945)
Hopkins, Ellice (1836–1904)
Hopkins, Emma Curtis (1853–1925)
Hopkins, Juliet (1818–1890)
Hopkins, Pauline E. (1859–1930)
Hopper, Edna Wallace (1864–1959)
Horniman, Annie (1860–1937)
Horrell, Elizabeth (1826–1913)
Horsley, Alice Woodward (1871–1957)
Hortense de Beauharnais (1783–1837)
Horton, Ann (1743–1808)
Hosmer, Harriet (1830–1908)
Hossain, Rokeya Sakhawat (1880–1932)
Houdetot, Sophie, Comtesse d' (1730–1813)
Houston, Lucy (1858–1936)
Houston, Margaret Lea (1819–1867)
Howard, Ada Lydia (1829–1907)
Howard, Blanche Willis (1847–1898)
Howard, Caroline Cadette (1821–?)
Howard, Catherine (d. 1874)
Howard, Cordelia (1848–1941)
Howard, Elizabeth Ann (1823–1865)
Howard, Rosalind Frances (1845–1921)
Howe, Julia Ward (1819–1910)
Howe, Lois (c. 1864–1964)
Howes, Edith Annie (1872–1954)
Howie, Fanny Rose (1868–1916)
Howitt, Mary (1799–1888)
Howland, Emily (1827–1929)
Howland, Jobyna (1880–1936)
Howley, Calasanctius (1848–1933)
How-Martyn, Edith (1875–1954)
Hoyt, Mary F. (1858–1958)
Huber, Therese (1764–1829)
Huch, Ricarda (1864–1947)
Huggins, Margaret (1848–1915)
Hughan, Jessie (1875–1955)
Hug-Hellmuth, Hermine (1871–1924)
Hughes, Adella (1869–1950)
Hughes, Annie (1869–1954)
Hugo, Adèle (1830–1915)
Hugonnay, Vilma (1847–1922)
Hull, Eleanor Henrietta (1860–1935)
Hull, Hannah (1872–1958)
Hull, Helen Rose (1888–1971)
Humphrey, Edith (1875–1977)
Hungerford, Margaret Wolfe (c. 1855–1897)
Hunt, Frances Irwin (1890–1981)
Hunt, Harriot Kezia (1805–1875)
Hunt, Mary Hanchett (1830–1906)
Hunt, Violet (1866–1942)
Huntington, Anna Hyatt (1876–1973)

Huntington, Emily (1841–1909)
Hunton, Addie D. Waites (1875–1943)
Hurd-Mead, Kate Campbell (1867–1941)
Hurdon, Elizabeth (1868–1941)
Hurd-Wood, Kathleen Gertrude (1886–1965)
Huson, Florence (1857–1915)
Hutchins, Grace (1885–1969)
Hutchinson, Abigail (1829–1892)
Hutchinson, Amy Hadfield (1874–1971)
Hutchinson, Amy May (1888–1985)
Hutchison, Isobel Wylie (1899–1982)
Hyde, Ida (1857–1945)
Hyslop, Beatrice Fry (1899–1973)
Iams, Lucy (1855–1924)
Icaza, Carmen de (1899–1979)
Ickes, Anna Thompson (1873–1935)
Ida of Saxe-Coburg-Meiningen (1794–1852)
Ida of Schaumburg-Lippe (1852–1891)
Ihrer, Emma (1857–1911)
Illington, Marie (d. 1927)
Imlay, Fanny (1794–1816)
Immerwahr, Clara (1870–1915)
Inchbald, Elizabeth (1753–1821)
Inescort, Elaine (c. 1877–1964)
Ingeborg of Denmark (1878–1958)
Ingelow, Jean (1820–1897)
Ingham, Mary Hall (1866–1937)
Inglis, Elsie Maud (1864–1917)
Inglis, Helen Clyde (1867–1945)
Innes, Catherine Lucy (1839/40–1900)
Innes, Mary Jane (1852–1941)
Invernizio, Carolina (1858–1916)
Iordanidou, Maria (1897–1989)
Ipatescu, Ana (1805–1855)
Irene, Sister (1823–1896)
Irene of Hesse-Darmstadt (1866–1953)
Irvine, Jean Kennedy (c. 1877–1962)
Irvine-Smith, Fanny Louise (1878–1948)
Irving, Ethel (1869–1963)
Irving, Isabel (1871–1944)
Irving, Margaret (1898–1988)
Irwin, Agnes (1841–1914)
Irwin, Elisabeth (1880–1942)
Irwin, Flo (born c. 1860)
Irwin, May (1862–1938)
Isaacs, Edith (1878–1956)
Isaacs, Susan (1885–1948)
Isabel (1772–1827)
Isabella II (1830–1904)
Isabella of Croy-Dulmen (1856–1931)
Isabella of Orleans (1878–1961)
Isabel Maria (1801–1876)
Isabel of Brazil (1846–1921)
Isitt, Kathleen (1876–?)
Isom, Mary Frances (1865–1920)
Istomina, Avdotia (1799–1848)
Jackson, Ann Fletcher (1833–1903)
Jackson, Helen Hunt (1830–1885)
Jackson, Julia (fl. 19th c.)
Jackson, Mary Jane (b. 1836)
Jackson, Mercy B. (1802–1877)
Jackson, Rachel Donelson (1767–1828)
Jackson, Rebecca Cox (1795–1871)
Jackson, Sarah Elizabeth (1858–1946)
Jaclard, Anna (1843–1887)
Jacobi, Mary Putnam (1842–1906)
Jacobs, Aletta (1854–1929)
Jacobs, Frances Wisebart (1843–1892)
Jacobs, Harriet A. (1813–1897)
Jacobs, Pattie Ruffner (1875–1935)
Jacobsen, Inger Kathrine (1867–1939)
Jacobson, Ethel May (1877–1965)
Jaczynowska, Katarzyna (1875–1920)
Jagemann, Karoline (1777–1848)
Jagiello, Appolonia (1825–1866)
Jalandoni, Magdalena (1891–1978)
Jambrišak, Marija (1847–1937)
James, Alice (1848–1892)
James, Alice Gibbens (1849–1922)
James, Annie Isabella (1884–1965)
James, Mary Walsh (1810–1882)
James, Zerelda (c. 1824–1911)
Jameson, Anna Brownell (1794–1860)
Jamet, Marie (1820–1893)
Jamison, Cecilia V. (1837–1909)
Janauschek, Fanny (1829–1904)
Janitschek, Maria (1859–1927)
Janny, Amélia (1838–1914)
Janotha, Natalia (1856–1932)
Januaria (1822–1901)
Japha, Louise (1826–1889)
Jarnević, Dragojla (1812–1875)
Jarrell, Ira (1896–1973)
Jarrett, Mary Cromwell (1877–1961)
Jarvis, Anna M. (1864–1948)
Jarvis, Lucy (1919—)
Jay, Harriett (1863–1932)
Jean, Sally Lucas (1878–1971)
Jeanes, Anna Thomas (1822–1907)
Jeanneret, Marie (d. 1884)
Jebb, Eglantyne (1876–1928)
Jeffreys, Ellen Penelope (1827–1904)
Jegado, HélÒne (1803–1851)
Jekyll, Gertrude (1843–1932)
Jellicoe, Anne (1823–1880)
Jemison, Mary (1742–1833)
Jenckes, Virginia Ellis (1877–1975)
Jenkins, Helen Hartley (1860–1934)
Jensen, Thit (1876–1957)
Jentzer, Emma R.H. (c. 1883–1972)
Jermy, Louie (1864–1934)
Jerrold, Mary (1877–1955)
Jervey, Caroline Howard (1823–1877)
Jesenská, Ružena (1863–1940)
Jesus, Gregoria de (1875–1943)
Jewett, Sarah Orne (1849–1909)
Jewsbury, Geraldine (1812–1880)
Jewsbury, Maria Jane (1800–1833)
Jex-Blake, Sophia (1840–1912)
Joel, Grace Jane (1865–1924)
Johansson, Anna (1860–1917)
Johansson, Ronny (b. 1891)
John, Gwen (1876–1939)
Johns, Ethel (1879–1968)
Johnson, Adelaide (1859–1955)
Johnson, E. Pauline (1861–1913)
Johnson, Eliza McCardle (1810–1876)
Johnson, Ellen Cheney (1829–1899)
Johnson, Georgia Douglas (1877–1966)
Johnson, Halle (1864–1901)
Johnson, Helen Kendrick (1844–1917)
Johnson, Susannah Willard (1729–1810)
Johnston, Amy Isabella (1872–1908)
Johnston, Annie Fellows (1863–1931)
Johnston, Frances Benjamin (1864–1952)
Johnston, Mary (1870–1936)
Johnstone, Isobel (1781–1857)
Jones, Amanda Theodosia (1835–1914)
Jones, Jane Elizabeth (1813–1896)
Jones, Mary Harris (1830–1930)
Jones, Rebecca (1739–1818)
Jones, Sissieretta (1869–1933)
Jones, Sybil (1808–1873)
Jordan, Dora (1761–1816)
Jordan, Elizabeth Garver (1865–1947)
Joseph, Mother (1823–1902)
Josephine (1763–1814)
Josephine Beauharnais (1807–1876)
Josephine of Baden (1813–1900)
Josephine of Belgium (1872–1958)
Joshi, Anandibai (1865–1887)
Jotuni, Maria (1880–1943)
Juarez, Margarita (1826–1871)
Juch, Emma (1860–1939)
Juchacz, Marie (1879–1956)
Judson, Ann Hasseltine (1789–1826)
Judson, Emily Chubbuck (1817–1854)
Judson, Sarah Boardman (1803–1845)
Jugan, Jeanne (1792–1879)
Júlia, Francisca (1871–1920)
Jull, Roberta (1872–1961)
Jumel, Eliza Bowen (1775–1865)
Jury, Te Aitu-o-te-rangi (c. 1820–1854)
Jutta of Mecklenburg-Strelitz (1880–1946)
Kaahumanu (1777–1832)
Kaaro, Ani (fl. 1885–1901)
Kaffka, Margit (1880–1918)
Kahn, Florence (1878–1951)
Kahn, Florence Prag (1866–1948)
Kahutia, Riperata (c. 1838–1887)
Kairi, Evanthia (1797–1866)
Kaiser, Isabella (1866–1925)
Kaiulani (1875–1899)
Kalama (c. 1820–1870)
Kalich, Bertha (1874–1939)
Kamamalu (c. 1803–1824)
Kamamalu, Victoria (1838–1866)
Kander, Lizzie Black (1858–1940)
Kane, Amy Grace (1879–1979)
Kapiolani (1834–1899)
Kapiolani (c. 1781–1841)
Kapule, Deborah (c. 1798–1853)
Karalli, Vera (1889–1972)
Karinska, Barbara (1886–1983)
Karr, Carme (1865–1943)
Kartini (1879–1904)
Käsebier, Gertrude (1852–1934)
Kauffmann, Angelica (1741–1807)
Kaur, Rajkumari Amrit (1889–1964)
Kaus, Gina (1894–1985)
Kautsky, Luise (1864–1944)
Kautsky, Minna (1837–1912)
Kavanagh, Julia (1824–1877)
Kaye-Smith, Sheila (1887–1956)
Kazantzaki, Galateia (1886–1962)
Kean, Ellen (1805–1880)
Kearney, Belle (1863–1939)
Keckley, Elizabeth (c. 1824–1907)
Keeley, Mary Anne (c. 1806–1899)
Keen, Dora (1871–1963)
Keene, Laura (c. 1826–1873)
Kehajia, Kalliopi (1839–1905)
Kehew, Mary Morton (1859–1918)
Keith, Marcia (1859–1950)
Kellas, Eliza (1864–1943)
Keller, Helen (1880–1968)
Keller, Nettie Florence (1875–1974)
Kelley, Abby (1810–1887)
Kelley, Edith Summers (1884–1956)
Kelley, Florence (1859–1932)
Kellogg, Clara Louise (1842–1916)
Kellogg, Louise Phelps (1862–1942)
Kellor, Frances Alice (1873–1952)
Kells, Isabella (1861–1938)
Kelly, Annie Elizabeth (1877–1946)
Kelly, Ethel (1875–1949)
Kelly, Fanny Wiggins (1845–1904)
Kelly, Florence Finch (1858–1939)
Kelly, Kate (1862–1898)
Kelsey, Lavinia Jane (1856–1948)
Kelso, Elizabeth (1889–1967)
Kemble, Adelaide (1814–1879)
Kemble, Eliza (1761–1836)
Kemble, Elizabeth (c. 1763–1841)
Kemble, Fanny (1809–1893)
Kemble, Maria Theresa (1774–1838)
Kemble, Priscilla (1756–1845)
Kemp, Charlotte (1790–1860)
Kempfer, Hannah Jensen (1880–1943)
Kendal, Madge (1849–1935)
Kendall, Marie Hartig (1854–1943)
Kendrick, Pearl L. (1890–1980)
Kennedy, Kate (1827–1890)
Kennedy-Fraser, Marjorie (1857–1930)
Kenney, Annie (1879–1953)
Kenny, Alice Annie (1875–1960)
Kenny, Elizabeth (1880–1952)
Kent, Constance (1844–?)
Kent, Thelma Rene (1899–1946)
Kenworthy, Marion E. (c. 1891–1980)
Keppel, Alice (1869–1947)
Kerr, Sophie (1880–1965)
Key, Ellen (1849–1926)
Khanim, Leyla (d. 1847/48)
Khvoshchinskaia, Nadezhda (1824–1889)
Khvoshchinskaia, Sofia (1828–1865)
Kidder, Kathryn (1867–1939)
Kieler, Laura (1849–1932)
Kielland, Kitty L. (1843–1914)
Kies, Mary Dixon (fl. 19th c.)
Kilgore, Carrie B. (1838–1908)
Kimball, Martha G. (1840–1894)
Kinau (c. 1805–1839)
King, Grace Elizabeth (c. 1852–1932)
King, Helen Dean (1869–1955)
King, Henrietta Chamberlain (1832–1925)
King, Isabel Grace Mackenzie (1843–1917)
King, Jessie Marion (1875–1949)

King, Lida Shaw (1868–1932)
King, Louisa Yeomans (1863–1948)
King, Martha (1802/03–1897)
King, Mazie (b. around 1880)
King, Mollie (1885–1981)
King, Nellie (1895–1935)
Kingsbury, Susan (1870–1949)
Kingsford, Anna (1846–1888)
Kingsley, Elizabeth (1871–1957)
Kingsley, Mary H. (1862–1900)
Kingsley, Mary St. Leger (1852–1931)
Kinkel, Johanna (1810–1858)
Kinnaird, Mary Jane (1816–1888)
Kinnan, Mary (1763–1848)
Kinney, Dita Hopkins (1854–1921)
Kinzie, Juliette Magill (1806–1870)
Kirby, Mary Kostka (1863–1952)
Kirchgessner, Marianne (1769–1808)
Kirk, Cybele Ethel (1870–1957)
Kirkaldy, Jane Willis (c. 1869–1932)
Kirkland, Caroline Matilda (1801–1864)
Kirpishchikova, Anna (1848–1927)
Kirschner, Lola (1854–1934)
Kishida, Toshiko (1863–1901)
Kissling, Margaret (1808–1891)
Kitson, Theo A.R. (1871–1932)
Klafsky, Katharina (1855–1896)
Kleeberg, Clotilde (1866–1909)
Klimek, Tillie (1865–1936)
Klumpke, Anna Elizabeth (1856–1942)
Klumpke, Augusta (1859–1927)
Klumpke, Dorothea (1861–1942)
Knight, Ellis Cornelia (1758–1837)
Knight, Laura (1877–1970)
Knight, Margaret (1838–1914)
Knipper-Chekova, Olga (1870–1959)
Knopf, Eleanora Bliss (1883–1974)
Knorr, Frances (1868–1894)
Knowlton, Helen Mary (1832–1918)
Knox, Elizabeth (1899–1963)
Knox, Isa (1831–1903)
Knox, Rose Markward (1857–1950)
Kobiakova, Aleksandra (1823–1892)
Kobrynska, Natalia Ivanovna (1855–1920)
Kobylianska, Olha (1863–1942)
Kohary, Antoinette (1797–1862)
Kohut, Rebekah (1864–1951)
Koidula, Lydia (1843–1886)
Kokoro-Barrett, Hiria (1870–1943)
Kolb, Annette (1870–1967)
Kolb, ThérÒse (1856–1935)
Kollontai, Alexandra (1872–1952)
Kollwitz, Käthe (1867–1945)
Komarova, Varvara (1862–1942)
Komissarzhevskaya, Vera (1864–1910)
König, Alma Johanna (1887–c. 1942)
Konopnicka, Maria (1842–1910)
Korolewicz-Waydowa, Janina (1875–1955)
Korty, Sonia (1892–1955)
Köstler, Marie (1879–1965)
Koszutska, Maria (1876–1939)
Kotopoúli, Maríka (1887–1954)
Kovalevskaya, Sophia (1850–1891)
Kovalskaia, Elizaveta (1851–1943)
Krandievskaya, Anastasiia (1865–1938)
Krandievskaya, Natalia (1888–1963)
Krasnohorska, Eliska (1847–1926)
Kraus-Boelté, Maria (1836–1918)
Krebs-Brenning, Marie (1851–1900)
Kremnitz, Marie (1852–1916)
Krestovskaya, Maria V. (1862–1910)
Krieger, Victorina (b. 1896)
Kroeber, Theodora (1897–1979)
Kroeger, Alice (1864–1909)
Krog, Gina (1847–1916)
Kronold, Selma (1861–1920)
Krüdener, Julie de (1764–1824)
Krupskaya, Nadezhda (1869–1939)
Kruscениski, Salomea (1873–1952)
Krusenstjerna, Agnes von (1894–1940)
Kryszak, Mary Olszewski (1875–1945)
Kryzhanovskaia, Vera Ivanovna (1861–1924)
Kshesinskaia, Matilda (1872–1971)
Kugler, Anna Sarah (1856–1930)
Kuliscioff, Anna (c. 1854–1925)
Kulman, Elisabeth (1808–1825)
Kuroda, Chika (1884–1968)
Kurz, Isolde (1853–1944)
Kurz, Selma (1874–1933)
Kuznetsova, Maria (1880–1966)
Kwast, Frieda Hodapp (1880–1949)
Kyrk, Hazel (1886–1957)
La Belle Marie (c. 1882–1935)
LaBelle Oceana (c. 1835–?)
Labille-Guiard, Adelaide (1749–1803)
Labotsibeni Gwamile laMdluli (c. 1858–1925)
Labouré, Catherine (1806–1875)
Lachapelle, Marie (1769–1821)
Lachman, Thérèse (1819–1884)
Lacore, Suzanne (1875–1975)
Lacoste, Catherine
Lacy, Harriette Deborah (1807–1874)
Ladd, Anna Coleman (1878–1939)
Ladd, Kate Macy (1863–1945)
Ladd-Franklin, Christine (1847–1930)
Lafarge, Marie (1816–1852)
Lafayette, Marie Adrienne de (1760–1807)
La Flesche, Susan (1865–1915)
La Flesche, Susette (1854–1902)
La Follette, Belle Case (1859–1931)
LaForge, Margaret Getchell (1841–1880)
Lagerlöf, Selma (1858–1940)
La Grange, Anna de (1825–1905)
La Hye, Louise (1810–1838)
Laidlaw, Harriet Burton (1873–1949)
Laird, Carobeth (1895–1983)
Lakey, Alice (1857–1935)
Lakshmibai (c. 1835–1858)
Lamas, Maria (1893–1983)
Lamb, Caroline (1785–1828)
Lamb, Emily (d. 1869)
Lamb, Martha J.R. (1826–1893)
Lamb, Mary Anne (1764–1847)
Lamorlière, Rosalie (fl. 1793–1837)
Lancaster-Wallis, Ellen (1856–?)
Landes, Bertha Knight (1868–1943)
Landon, Letitia Elizabeth (1802–1838)
Landowska, Wanda (1877–1959)
Landseer, Jessica (1810–1880)
Lane, Gertrude B. (1874–1941)
Lane, Grace (1876–1956)
Lane, Harriet (1830–1903)
Laney, Lucy Craft (1854–1933)
Lang, Josephine (1815–1880)
Lang, Leonora (1851–1933)
Lang, Margaret Ruthven (1867–1972)
Lang, Marie (1858–1934)
Lange, Aloysia (c. 1761–1839)
Lange, Anne Françoise Elizabeth (1772–1816)
Lange, Elizabeth Clovis (1784–1882)
Lange, Helene (1848–1930)
Langner, Ilse (1899–1987)
Langtry, Lillie (1853–1929)
Lanner, Katti (1829–1908)
Lanvin, Jeanne (1867–1946)
La Palme, Béatrice (1878–1921)
Lapauze, Jeanne (1860–1920)
Lappo-Danilevskaia, N.A. (c. 1875–1951)
Larcom, Lucy (1824–1893)
Larkin, Delia (1878–1949)
La Roche, Sophie von (1730–1807)
La Rochejacquelein, Marie Louise Victoire, marquise de (1772–1857)
Larpent, Anna Margaretta (fl. 1815–1830)
Lask, Berta (1878–1967)
Laskaridou, Aikaterini (1842–1916)
Lasker-Schüler, Else (1869–1945)
Lathrop, Julia Clifford (1858–1932)
Lathrop, Rose Hawthorne (1851–1926)
Latimer, Elizabeth W. (1822–1904)
La Tour du Pin, Henriette de (1770–1853)
Lauber, Cécile (1887–1981)
Laughlin, Clara E. (1873–1941)
Laughlin, Gail (1868–1952)
Laurel, Kay (1890–1927)
Laurier, Zoé (1841–1921)
Lavallière, Eve (c. 1866–1929)
Lavater-Sloman, Mary (1891–1980)
Laveau, Marie (1801–1881)
Laveau, Marie (1827–1897)
La Verne, Lucille (1869–1945)
Lavoisier, Marie (1758–1836)
Law, Alice Easton (1870–1942)
Law, Mary Blythe (1873–1955)
Law, Sallie Chapman (1805–1894)
Lawless, Emily (1845–1913)
Lawrence, Susan (1871–1947)
Laws, Annie (1855–1927)
Lawson, Louisa (1848–1920)
Lawson, Roberta Campbell (1878–1940)
Lazarus, Emma (1849–1887)
Leach, Abby (1855–1918)
Leadbetter, Mary (1758–1826)
Leahy, Mary Gonzaga (1870–1958)
Leakey, Caroline Woolmer (1827–1881)
Lease, Mary Elizabeth (1853–1933)
Leavitt, Henrietta Swan (1868–1921)
Leavitt, Mary (1830–1912)
Le Beau, Luise Adolpha (1850–1927)
Leblanc, Georgette (c. 1875–1941)
Le Blond, Elizabeth (1861–1934)
Lebour, Marie (1877–1971)
Leclercq, Carlotta (c. 1840–1893)
Leclercq, Rose (c. 1845–1899)
Lecompte, Eugenie Anna (c. 1798–c. 1850)
Ledoux, Jeanne Philiberte (1767–1840)
Lee, Agnes (1841–1873)
Lee, Anne Carter (1839–1862)
Lee, Hannah Farnham (1780–1865)
Lee, Harriet (1757–1851)
Lee, Ida (1865–1943)
Lee, Jarena (1783–c. 1849)
Lee, Jennie (c. 1846–1930)
Lee, Mary (1821–1909)
Lee, Mary Ann (1823–1899)
Lee, Mary Custis (c. 1808–1873)
Lee, Mary Custis (1835–1918)
Lee, Mary Isabella (1871–1939)
Lee, Mildred Childe (1846–1905)
Lee, Muna (1895–1965)
Lee, Sarah (1791–1856)
Lee, Sophia (1750–1824)
Leete, Harriet L. (c. 1875–1927)
Lefanu, Alicia (1753–1817)
Lefanu, Alicia (c. 1795–c. 1826)
Lefanu, Elizabeth (1758–1837)
Lefebvre, Catherine (c. 1764–after 1820)
Le Fort, Gertrud von (1876–1971)
Legat, Nadine (c. 1895–?)
Legh, Alice (1855–1948)
Legnani, Pierina (1863–1923)
Lehmann, Adelaide (c. 1830–1851)
Lehmann, Lilli (1848–1929)
Lehmann, Liza (1862–1918)
Lehmann, Lotte (1888–1976)
Leigh, Augusta (1784–1851)
Leigh, Frances Butler (1838–1910)
Lemel, Nathalie (1827–1921)
Lemmon, Sarah Plummer (1836–1923)
Lemoine, Angélina (1843–?)
Lemoine, Marie Victoire (1754–1820)
Lemon, Margaretta Louisa (1860–1953)
Lender, Marcelle (fl. 1890–1914)
Lenngren, Anna Maria (1754–1817)
Lennox, Charlotte (1720–1804)
Lennox, Louisa (1743–1821)
Le Noir, Elizabeth Anne (c. 1755–1841)
Lenormand, Marie Anne Adélaïde (1772–1843)
Léo, André (1832–1900)
Léon, Léonie (1838–1906)
Leonowens, Anna (c. 1831–1914)
Leontias, Sappho (1832–1900)
Leopoldina of Austria (1797–1826)
Leopoldine (1837–1903)
Leprohon, Rosanna (1832–1879)
Lermontova, Julia (1846–1919)
Leroux, Pauline (1809–1891)
Leslie, Amy (1855–1939)
Leslie, Annie (1869–1948)
Leslie, Eliza (1787–1858)
Leslie, May Sybil (1887–1937)
Leslie, Miriam Folline Squier (1836–1914)
L'Esperance, Elise Strang (c. 1879–1959)
Lessore, Thérèse (1884–1945)
Leverson, Ada (1862–1933)
Le Vert, Octavia Walton (1811–1877)
Leveson-Gower, Elizabeth (1765–1839)
Leveson-Gower, Harriet (1785–1862)

Leveson-Gower, Harriet Elizabeth Georgiana (1806–1868)
Levey, Ethel (1880–1955)
Levy, Amy (1861–1889)
Levy, Florence Nightingale (1870–1947)
Lewald, Fanny (1811–1889)
Lewis, Agnes Smith (1843–1926)
Lewis, Edmonia (c. 1845–c. 1909)
Lewis, Estelle Anna (1824–1880)
Lewis, Ethelreda (1875–1946)
Lewis, Graceanna (1821–1912)
Lewis, Ida (1842–1911)
Lewis, Margaret Reed (1881–1970)
Lewson, Jane (c. 1700–1816)
Leyel, Hilda (1880–1957)
Lézardière, Pauline de (1754–1835)
Lhevinne, Rosina (1880–1976)
Liang Desheng (1771–1847)
Libbey, Laura Jean (1862–1925)
Lichnowsky, Mechthilde (1879–1958)
Lichtenau, Countess von (1753–1820)
Liddell, Alice (1852–1934)
Liebling, Estelle (1880–1970)
Liliuokalani (1838–1917)
Lincoln, Mary Johnson (1844–1921)
Lincoln, Mary Todd (1818–1882)
Lind, Jenny (1820–1887)
Lind, Letty (1862–1923)
Lindsay, Anne (1750–1825)
Linskill, Mary (1840–1891)
Linton, Eliza Lynn (1822–1898)
Lipman, Clara (1869–1952)
Lipperini, Guendalina (c. 1862–1914)
Lippincott, Sara Clarke (1823–1904)
Lipsius, Marie (1837–1927)
Lisa, Mary Manuel (1782–1869)
Lister, Anne (1791–1840)
Litchfield, Harriett (1777–1854)
Litten, Irmgard (1879–1953)
Little, Janet (1759–1813)
Littledale, Clara (1891–1956)
Littlefield, Caroline (c. 1882–1957)
Litton, Marie (1847–1884)
Litvinov, Ivy (1889–1977)
Liubatovich, Olga (1853–1917)
Liubatovich, Vera (1855–1907)
Livermore, Harriet (1788–1868)
Livermore, Mary A. (1820–1905)
Livingston, Anne Shippen (1763–1841)
Livingston, Nora G.E. (1848–1927)
Livingstone, Mary Moffatt (1820–1862)
Livry, Emma (1842–1863)
Lizars, Kathleen MacFarlane (d. 1931)
Lloyd, Alice (1873–1949)
Lloyd, Alice (1876–1962)
Lloyd, Marie (1870–1922)
Locke, Bessie (1865–1952)
Lockrey, Sarah Hunt (1863–1929)
Lockwood, Belva Ann (1830–1917)
Loeb, Sophie Irene (1876–1929)
Loftus, Cissie (1876–1943)
Loftus, Kitty (1867–1927)
Loftus, Marie (1857–1940)
Logan, Deborah Norris (1761–1839)
Logan, Laura R. (1879–1974)
Logan, Mary Cunningham (1838–1923)
Logan, Olive (1839–1909)
Lohman, Ann Trow (1812–1878)
Loisinger, Joanna (1865–1951)
Lokelani, Princess Lei (c. 1898–1921)
Lo Keong, Matilda (c. 1854–1915)
Lokhvitskaia, Mirra (1869–1905)
Long, Marguerite (1874–1966)
Longfellow, Frances Appleton (1819–1861)
Longfield, Cynthia (1896–1991)
Longman, Evelyn Beatrice (1874–1954)
Longshore, Hannah E. (1819–1901)
Longstaff, Mary Jane (c. 1855–1935)
Longworth, Maria Theresa (c. 1832–1881)
Loos, Cécile Ines (1883–1959)
Lord, Lucy Takiora (c. 1842–1893)
Lorimer, Margaret (1866–1954)
Lothrop, Alice (1870–1920)
Lothrop, Harriet (1844–1924)
Loudon, Jane Webb (1807–1858)
Louisa Amelia (1773–1802)
Louisa Carlotta of Naples (1804–1844)
Louise (1808–1870)
Louise (1848–1939)
Louise Adelaide de Bourbon (1757–1824)
Louise Augusta (1771–1843)
Louise Caroline (1875–1906)
Louise Charlotte of Mecklenburg-Schwerin (1779–1801)
Louise d'Orléans (1812–1850)
Louise Margaret of Prussia (1860–1917)
Louise Marie of Bourbon (1753–1821)
Louise of Baden (1811–1854)
Louise of Baden (1838–1923)
Louise of Belgium (1858–1924)
Louise of Bourbon-Berry (1819–1864)
Louise of Denmark (1750–1831)
Louise of Hesse-Cassel (1789–1867)
Louise of Hesse-Cassel (1817–1898)
Louise of Hesse-Darmstadt (d. 1830)
Louise of Hohenlohe-Langenburg (1763–1837)
Louise of Parma (1802–1857)
Louise of Prussia (1776–1810)
Louise of Saxe-Gotha (1756–1808)
Louise of Saxe-Gotha-Altenburg (1800–1831)
Louise of Stolberg-Gedern (1752–1824)
Louise of Sweden (1851–1926)
Louise of the Netherlands (1828–1871)
Louise Victoria (1867–1931)
Love, Mabel (1874–1953)
Love, Ripeka Wharawhara (1882–1953)
Lovejoy, Esther Pohl (1869–1967)
Lovelace, Ada Byron, Countess of (1815–1852)
Loveling, Virginie (1836–1923)
Lovell, Ann (1803/11–1869)
Lovell, Maria Anne (1803–1877)
Lovell-Smith, Rata Alice (1894–1969)
Loveman, Amy (1881–1955)
Loveridge, Emily Lemoine (1860–1941)
Low, Caroline Sarah (1876–1934)
Low, Juliette Gordon (1860–1927)
Low, Mary Fairchild (1858–1946)
Lowell, Amy (1874–1925)
Lowell, Josephine Shaw (1843–1905)
Lowell, Maria White (1821–1853)
Lowe-Porter, Helen (1876–1963)
Lowry, Edith (1897–1970)
Lozier, Clemence S. (1813–1888)
Lucas, Margaret Bright (1818–1890)
Lucca, Pauline (1841–1908)
Lüders, Marie-Elizabeth (1888–1966)
Ludington, Sybil (1761–1839)
Ludovica (1808–1892)
Luhan, Mabel Dodge (1879–1962)
Luisa Fernanda (1832–1897)
Luke, Jemima (1813–1906)
Lukens, Rebecca (1794–1854)
Lukhmanova, N.A. (1840–1907)
Lukom, Elena (1891–1968)
Lundberg, Emma (1881–1954)
Lundequist, Gerda (1871–1959)
Lupita, Madre (1878–1963)
Lusk, Grace (1878–1938)
Lütken, Hulda (1896–1947)
Luxemburg, Rosa (1870–1919)
Luxford, Nola (1895–1994)
Lu Yin (1899–1934)
Lyell, Mary Horner (1808–1873)
Lyman, Mary Ely (1887–1975)
Lynch, Eliza (1835–1886)
Lynch, Margaret (fl. 1867–1868)
Lynn, Kathleen (1874–1955)
Lyon, Genevieve (c. 1893–1916)
Lyon, Mary (1797–1849)
Lyons, Sophie (1848–1924)
Lyttelton, Edith (1865–1948)
Lytton, Constance (1869–1923)
Lytton, Emily (1874–1964)
Maas-Fjetterstrom, Marta (1873–1941)
Maass, Clara (1876–1901)
Macandrew, Jennie (1866–1949)
Macarthur, Elizabeth (1767–1850)
Macarthur, Mary Reid (1880–1921)
Macarthur-Onslow, Elizabeth (1840–1911)
MacDonald, Christie (1875–1962)
MacDonald, Elizabeth Roberts (1864–1922)
MacDonald, Frances (1874–1921)
Macdonald, Georgiana (1840–1920)
Macdonald, Isabella (1809–1857)
Macdonald, Susan Agnes (1836–1920)
MacDowell, Marian (1857–1956)
MacFall, Frances E. (1854–1943)
Macfarlane, Edith Mary (1871–1948)
MacGill, Helen Gregory (1871–1947)
MacGregor, Esther Miller (1874–1961)
Machado, Gilka (1893–1980)
Machar, Agnes Maule (1837–1927)
Mack, Louise (1874–1935)
Mack, Nila (1891–1953)
Mackay, Catherine Julia (1864–1944)
Mackay, Elizabeth (c. 1845–1897)
Mackay, Elizabeth Ann Louisa (1843–1908)
Mackay, Jessie (1864–1938)
Mackay, Maria Jane (1844–1933)
Mackellar, Dorothea (1885–1968)
MacKenzie, Jane (1825–1893)
Mackenzie, Jean Kenyon (1874–1936)
MacKillop, Mary Helen (1842–1909)
MacKinnon, Joanna (1878–1966)
Mackintosh, Margaret (1865–1933)
Maclean, Hester (1859–1932)
Maclean, Ida Smedley (1877–1944)
MacLean, Vida (1881–1970)
Maclehose, Agnes (1759–1841)
MacLeish, Martha Hillard (1856–1947)
Macleod, Charlotte (1852–1950)
MacManus, Anna Johnston (1866–1902)
Macmillan, Chrystal (1871–1937)
MacMurchy, Helen (1862–1953)
MacMurchy, Marjory (1869–1938)
Macomber, Mary Lizzie (1861–1916)
Macphail, Katherine Stewart (1888–1974)
Macpherson, Margaret Louisa (1895–1974)
Macquarie, Elizabeth (1778–1835)
MacRobert, Rachel (1884–1954)
Mactier, Susie (1854–1936)
Macurdy, Grace Harriet (1866–1946)
Macy, Anne Sullivan (1866–1936)
Maddalena of Canossa (1774–1833)
Madison, Dolley Payne (1768–1849)
Magdalen women (c. 1820s–early 1970s)
Magee, Martha Maria (d. 1846)
Mageras, Georgia Lathouris (1867–1950)
Magoffin, Susan Shelby (1827–c. 1855)
Magruder, Julia (1854–1907)
Maher, Mary Cecilia (1799–1878)
Mahler, Alma (1879–1964)
Mahoney, Mary Eliza (1845–1926)
Mahony, Marion (1871–1961)
Mahupuku, Maata (1890–1952)
Maihi, Rehutai (1895–1967)
Mairet, Ethel (1872–1952)
Maitland, Agnes Catherine (1850–1906)
Major, Ethel Lillie (1890–1934)
Malcolm, Emilie Monson (1829/30–1905)
Mallinger, Mathilde (1847–1920)
Mallon, Mary (1867–1938)
Malone, Annie Turnbo (1869–1957)
Maltby, Margaret E. (1860–1944)
Mamoshina, Glafira Adolfovna (c. 1870–1942)
Mancini, Evelina (1849–1896)
Mancini, Laura (1823–1869)
Mander, Jane (1877–1949)
Mangakahia, Meri Te Tai (1868–1920)
Mann, Ida (1893–1983)
Mann, Mary Peabody (1806–1887)
Mannering, Mary (1876–1953)
Mannes, Clara Damrosch (1869–1948)
Manning, Anne (1807–1879)
Manning, Leah (1886–1977)
Manning, Maria (c. 1821–1849)
Manning, Marie (c. 1873–1945)
Mannoury d'Ectot, Madame de (fl. 1880)
Mansel, Lucy (c. 1830–1915)
Mansfield, Arabella (1846–1911)
Mansfield, Portia (1887–1979)
Mansilla de García, Eduarda (1838–1892)
Mara, Gertrud (1749–1833)
Marble, Mary (d. 1965)
Marbury, Elisabeth (1856–1933)
Marcet, Jane (1769–1858)
Marchant, Bessie (1862–1941)
Marchant, Maria Élise Allman (1869–1919)

Marchenko, Anastasiia Iakovlevna (1830–1880)
Marchesi, Blanche (1863–1940)
Marchesi, Mathilde (1821–1913)
Margaret Beatrice (1872–1954)
Margaret Clementine (1870–1955)
Margaret of Parma (1847–1893)
Margaret of Savoy (1851–1926)
Margaret of Saxony (1840–1858)
Margaret Sophie (1870–1902)
Marghieri, Clotilde (1897–1981)
Maria Amalia (1746–1804)
Maria Amalia (1782–1866)
Maria Anna of Portugal (1843–1884)
Maria Anna of Savoy (1803–1884)
Maria Anna of Saxony (1795–1865)
Maria Anna of Saxony (1799–1832)
Maria Annunziata (1843–1871)
Maria Annunziata (1876–1961)
Maria Antonia of Naples (1784–1806)
Maria Antonia of Portugal (1862–1959)
Maria Antonia of Sicily (1814–1898)
Maria Beatrice of Modena (1750–1829)
Maria Beatrice of Modena (1824–1906)
Maria Beatrice of Sardinia (1792–1840)
Maria Carolina (1752–1814)
Maria Christina of Austria (1858–1929)
Maria Christina of Saxony (1779–1851)
Maria Clementina of Austria (1777–1801)
Maria Cristina I of Naples (1806–1878)
Maria Cristina of Sicily (1877–1947)
Maria dal Pozzo (fl. 19th c.)
Maria de Fonte (fl. 1846)
Maria de la Paz (1862–1946)
Maria de las Mercedes (1860–1878)
Maria de las Mercedes (1880–1904)
Maria Dorothea of Austria (1867–1932)
Maria Gabriele of Bavaria (1878–1912)
Maria Henrietta of Austria (1836–1902)
Maria II da Gloria (1819–1853)
Maria Immaculata (1878–1968)
Maria Immaculata of Sicily (1844–1899)
Maria I of Braganza (1734–1816)
Maria Isabel Francisca (1851–1931)
Maria Isabella (1834–1901)
Maria Isabella (1848–1919)
Maria Isabel of Portugal (1797–1818)
Maria Josepha of Portugal (1857–1943)
Maria Josepha of Saxony (1803–1829)
Maria Josepha of Saxony (1867–1944)
Maria Leopoldina (1776–1848)
Maria Ludovica (1798–1857)
Maria Ludovica (1845–1917)
Maria Ludovica of Modena (1787–1816)
Maria Luisa of Etruria (1782–1824)
Maria Luisa Teresa of Parma (1751–1819)
Maria Nikolaevna (1819–1876)
Marianne of the Netherlands (1810–1883)
Maria of Bavaria (1805–1877)
Maria of Bavaria (1872–1954)
Maria of Mecklenburg-Schwerin (1854–1920)
Maria of Prussia (1825–1889)
Maria of Waldeck (1857–1882)
Maria of Wurttemberg (1797–1855)
Maria Pia (1847–1911)
Maria Sophia Amalia (1841–1925)
Maria Teresa of Austria (1773–1832)
Maria Teresa of Este (1849–1919)
Maria Teresa of Naples (1772–1807)
Maria Teresa of Savoy (1756–1805)
Maria Theresa of Portugal (1855–1944)
Maria Theresa of Tuscany (1801–1855)
Marie (1876–1940)
Marie Adelaide of Austria (1822–1855)
Marie Alexandrovna (1853–1920)
Marie-Amelie of Orleans (1865–1951)
Marie-Anne of Braganza (1861–1942)
Marie Clotilde (1759–1802)
Marie d'Orleans (1813–1839)
Marie Feodorovna (1847–1928)
Marie Isabella of Spain (1789–1848)
Marie Josephine of Savoy (d. 1810)
Marie Laetitia (1866–1890)
Marie Louise (1872–1956)
Marie Louise (1879–1948)
Marie Louise Albertine of Leiningen-Heidesheim (1729–1818)
Marie Louise d'Orleans (1750–1822)
Marie Louise of Austria (1791–1847)
Marie Louise of Parma (1870–1899)
Marie of Baden (1817–1888)
Marie of Hesse-Darmstadt (1824–1880)
Marie of Hohenzollern-Sigmaringen (1845–1912)
Marie of Nassau (1841–1910)
Marie of Rumania (1875–1938)
Marie of Saxe-Weimar-Eisenach (1808–1877)
Marie Pavlovna (1786–1859)
Marie Sophie of Hesse-Cassel (1767–1852)
Marie Thérèse Charlotte (1778–1851)
Marie-Thérèse de Soubiran (1834–1889)
Marie Therese of Bourbon (fl. 19th c.)
Marie Valerie (1868–1924)
Marín del Solar, Mercedes (1804–1866)
Marinetti, Benedetta Cappa (1897–1977)
Markham, Pauline (d. 1919)
Markham, Violet Rosa (1872–1959)
Markievicz, Constance (1868–1927)
Marlatt, Abby L. (1869–1943)
Marlitt, Eugenie (1825–1887)
Marlowe, Julia (1866–1950)
MarniÒre, Jeanne (1854–1910)
Marot, Helen (1865–1940)
Marothy-Soltesova, Elena (1855–1939)
Marryat, Florence (1837–1899)
Mars, Ann Françoise (1779–1847)
Marsden, Kate (1859–1931)
Marshall, Clara (1847–1931)
Marshall, Sheina (1896–1977)
Marsh-Caldwell, Anne (1791–1874)
Martel de Janville, Comtesse de (1850–1932)
Märten, Lu (1879–1970)
Martin, Anne Henrietta (1875–1951)
Martin, C.E.M. (1847–1937)
Martin, Emma (1812–1851)
Martin, Georgia (1866–1946)
Martin, Hannah (1830–1903)
Martin, Lillien Jane (1851–1943)
Martin, Maria (1796–1863)
Martin, Mary Ann (1817–1884)
Martin, Mary Letitia (1815–1850)
Martin, Violet (1862–1915)
Martindale, Hilda (1875–1952)
Martineau, Harriet (1802–1876)
Martinez, Marianne (1744–1812)
Martínez Sierra, María de la O (1874–1974)
Martin-Spencer, Lilly (1822–1902)
Marwedel, Emma (1818–1893)
Marx, Jenny von Westphalen (1814–1881)
Marx, Laura (1845–1911)
Marx-Aveling, Eleanor (1855–1898)
Mary (1776–1857)
Mary Adelaide (1833–1897)
Mary-Elizabeth of Padua (1782–1808)
Mary of Baden (1834–1899)
Mary of Battenberg (1852–1923)
Mary of Hanover (1849–1904)
Mary of Hesse-Cassel (1796–1880)
Mary of Hesse-Homburg (1785–1846)
Mary of Saxe-Altenburg (1818–1907)
Mary of Teck (1867–1953)
Mary of Wurttemberg (1799–1860)
Masaryk, Alice Garrigue (1879–1966)
Masaryk, Charlotte Garrigue (1850–1923)
Mason, Biddy (1818–1891)
Masset, Louise (c. 1863–1900)
Massey, Christina Allan (1863–1932)
Massy, Annie (1867–1931)
Matamoros, Mercedes (1851–1906)
Matenga, Huria (1840/42–1909)
Materna, Amalie (1844–1918)
Mathers, Helen (1853–1920)
Matheson, Elizabeth (1866–1958)
Mathew, Sarah Louise (c. 1805–1890)
Mathews, Ann Teresa (1732–1800)
Mathieson, Catherine (1818–1883)
Mathilde of Bavaria (1843–1925)
Matilda (1813–1862)
Matthews, Victoria Earle (1861–1907)
Matthison, Edith (1875–1955)
Mattocks, Isabella (1746–1826)
Matto de Turner, Clorinda (1854–1909)
Maude, Sibylla Emily (1862–1935)
Mauduit, Louise (1784–1862)
Maunder, Annie Russell (1868–1947)
Mauri, Rosita (1856–1923)
Maury, Antonia (1866–1952)
Maury, Carlotta (1874–1938)
Mavrogenous, Manto (d. 1848)
Maxwell, Alice Heron (1860–1949)
Maxwell, Anna Caroline (1851–1929)
Maxwell, Kate (fl. 1886)
May, Abby W. (1829–1888)
May, Edna (1875–1948)
May, Isabella (1850–1926)
Maybrick, Florence Elizabeth (c. 1853–1941)
Mayer, Constance (c. 1778–1821)
Mayer, Emilie (1821–1883)
Mayhew, Kate (1853–1944)
Mayne, Ethel Colburn (1865–1941)
Mayo, Katherine (1867–1940)
Mayo, Margaret (1882–1951)
Mayo, Mary Anne (1845–1903)
Mayo, Sara Tew (1869–1930)
Mayor, Flora M. (1872–1932)
Mayreder, Rosa (1858–1938)
Maywood, Augusta (1825–1876)
McAllister, Anne Hunter (1892–1983)
McAuley, Catherine (1778–1841)
McBeth, Susan Law (1830–1893)
McCarthy, Lillah (1875–1960)
McCarthy, Mary Ann Recknall (1866–1933)
McCarthy, Maud (1858–1949)
McClung, Nellie L. (1873–1951)
McCord, Louisa S. (1810–1879)
McCormick, Anne O'Hare (1880–1954)
McCormick, Edith Rockefeller (1872–1932)
McCormick, Katharine Dexter (1875–1967)
McCormick, Katherine Medill (d. 1932)
McCormick, Nettie Fowler (1835–1923)
McCormick, Ruth Hanna (1880–1944)
McCoubrey, Margaret (1880–1955)
McCoy, Bessie (1888–1931)
McCracken, Elizabeth (c. 1865–1944)
McCracken, Mary Ann (1770–1866)
McCrackin, Josephine Clifford (1838–1920)
McCrae, Georgiana Huntly (1804–1890)
McCreery, Maria (1883–1938)
McCulloch, Catharine (1862–1945)
McDonald, Agnes (1829–1906)
McDonald, Hedwick Wilhelmina (1893–1959)
McDowell, Anne E. (1826–1901)
McDowell, Mary Eliza (1854–1936)
McElroy, Mary Arthur (d. 1916)
McFarland, Beulah (c. 1898–1964)
McGee, Anita Newcomb (1864–1940)
McGroarty, Sister Julia (1827–1901)
McHugh, Fanny (1861–1943)
McIlwraith, Jean Newton (1859–1938)
McIntosh, Caroline C. (1813–1881)
McIntosh, Madge (1875–1950)
McIntosh, Maria (1803–1878)
McIntyre, Molly (c. 1886–1952)
McKain, Douglas Mary (1789–1873)
McKane, Alice Woodby (1865–1948)
McKenzie, Margaret (c. 1837–1925)
McKim, Ann (d. 1875)
McKinley, Ida Saxton (1847–1907)
McKinney, Louise (1868–1931)
McLachlan, Laurentia (1866–1953)
McLaren, Agnes (1837–1913)
McLaren, Louise Leonard (1885–1968)
McLaughlin, M. Louise (1847–1939)
McLean, Mary Hancock (1861–1930)
McLean, Mary Jane (1866–1949)
McMain, Eleanor Laura (1866–1934)
McMaster, Elizabeth Jennet (1847–1903)
McMillan, Margaret (1860–1931)
McMillan, Rachel (1859–1917)
McNaught, Rose (1893–1978)
McNeill, Florence Marian (1885–1973)
McQueen, Mary (1860–1945)
McTier, Martha (c. 1743–1837)
McVicar, Annie (1862–1954)
Mead, Elizabeth Storrs (1832–1917)
Mead, Lucia Ames (1856–1936)
Mears, Helen Farnsworth (1872–1916)
Mechlin, Leila (1874–1949)
Meech, Matilda (c. 1825–1907)
Meeke, Mary (d. 1816)

Mehlig, Anna (1846–1928)
Mei (d. 1875)
Mei-Figner, Medea (1859–1952)
Meitner, Lise (1878–1968)
Melba, Nellie (1861–1931)
Melbourne, Elizabeth (d. 1818)
Mellanby, May (1882–1978)
Mellish, Edith Mary (1861–1922)
Mellon, Harriot (c. 1777–1837)
Mellon, Sarah Jane (1824–1909)
Melmoth, Charlotte (1749–1823)
Melnotte, Violet (1856–1935)
Meloney, Marie (1878–1943)
Melpomene (fl. 1896)
Melville, Eliza Ellen (1882–1946)
Melville, Rose (1873–1946)
Mendelssohn, Dorothea (1764–1839)
Mendelssohn, Henriette (1768–1831)
Mendelssohn-Hensel, Fanny (1805–1847)
Mendenhall, Dorothy Reed (1874–1964)
Menken, Adah Isaacs (1835–1868)
Menten, Maude (1879–1960)
Menter, Sophie (1846–1918)
Menzelli, Elisabetta (c. 1860–c. 1929)
Menzelli, Lola (c. 1898–1951)
Merard de Saint-Just, Anne-Jeanne-Félicité d'Ormoy (1765–1830)
Mercé, Antonia (c. 1886–1936)
Mercier, Euphrasie (1823–?)
Mercoeur, Elisa (1809–1835)
Mereau-Brentano, Sophie (1770–1806)
Meredith, Louisa Anne (1812–1895)
Mergler, Marie Josepha (1851–1901)
Mérode, Cléo de (c. 1875–1966)
Merrick, Caroline (1825–1908)
Merrick, Myra King (1825–1899)
Merrill, Mary (1853–1924)
Merritt, Anna Lea (1844–1930)
Merry, Ann Brunton (1769–1808)
Metcalfe, Augusta Corson (1881–1971)
Metzger, HélOne (1889–1944)
Mew, Charlotte (1869–1928)
Mexia, Ynes (1870–1938)
Meyer, Annie Nathan (1867–1951)
Meyer, Lucy (1849–1922)
Meyer, Olga (1889–1972)
Meynell, Alice (1847–1922)
Meynell, Alicia (fl. 1804–1805)
Meysenburg, Malwida von (1816–1903)
Michael, Julia Warner (b. 1879)
Michaëlis, Karin (1872–1950)
Michel, Louise (1830–1905)
Miegel, Agnes (1879–1964)
Migliaccio, Lucia (1770–1826)
Mihi-ki-te-kapua (?–1872/80)
Mikhaylova, Maria (1866–1943)
Milbanke, Anne (1792–1860)
Milder-Hauptmann, Anna (1785–1838)
Milena (1847–1923)
Militsyna, Elizaveta Mitrofanovna (1869–1930)
Militza of Montenegro (1866–1951)
Millar, Annie Cleland (1855–1939)
Millar, Gertie (1879–1952)
Miller, Alice Duer (1874–1942)
Miller, Annie Jenness (b. 1859)
Miller, Elizabeth Smith (1822–1911)
Miller, Emily Huntington (1833–1913)
Miller, Emma Guffey (1874–1970)
Miller, Florence Fenwick (1854–1935)
Miller, Olive Thorne (1831–1918)
Milligan, Alice (1866–1953)
Millman, Bird (1895–1940)
Mills, Susan Tolman (1825–1912)
Milne, Mary Jane (1840–1921)
Min (1851–1895)
Minchin, Alice Ethel (1889–1966)
Miner, Myrtilla (1815–1864)
Miner, Sarah Luella (1861–1935)
Minijima, Kiyo (1833–1919)
Mink, Paule (1839–1901)
Minnigerode, Lucy (1871–1935)
Minoka-Hill, Rosa (1876–1952)
Minor, Virginia L. (1824–1894)
Miolan-Carvalho, Marie (1827–1895)
Mirabeau, Comtesse de (1827–1914)
Miremont, Anne d'Aubourg de La Bove, Comtesse de (1735–1811)
Misme, Jane (1865–1935)
Mistinguett (1875–1956)
Mitchel, Jenny (1820–1899)
Mitchell, Hannah (1871–1956)
Mitchell, Lucy (1845–1888)
Mitchell, Lucy Sprague (1878–1967)
Mitchell, Margaret J. (1832–1918)
Mitchell, Maria (1818–1889)
Mitchell, Marion (1876–1955)
Mitford, Mary Russell (1787–1855)
M'Lachlan, Jessie (c. 1834–1899)
Mmanthatisi (c. 1780–c. 1836)
Modersohn-Becker, Paula (1876–1907)
Modjeska, Helena (1840–1909)
Moffatt, Mary Smith (1795–1870)
Mohl, Mary (1793–1883)
Moïse, Penina (1797–1880)
Molesworth, Mary Louisa (1839–1921)
Molloy, Georgiana (1805–1842)
Monckton, Mary (1746–1840)
Moncrieff, Pérrine (1893–1979)
Monk, Maria (1816–1849)
Monkman, Phyllis (1892–1976)
Monod, Sarah (1836–1912)
Monroe, Elizabeth (1768–1830)
Monroe, Eliza Kortright (1786–1840)
Monroe, Harriet (1860–1936)
Monroe, Maria Hester (1803–1850)
Monserdà de Macía, Dolors (1845–1919)
Montagu, Elizabeth (1720–1800)
Montalba, Clara (1842–1929)
Montalba, Henrietta Skerrett (1856–1893)
Montanclos, Marie-Emilie Maryon de (1736–1812)
Montansier, Marguerite (1730–1820)
Montesson, Charlotte Jeanne Béraud de la Haye de Riou, marquise de (1737–1805)
Montessori, Maria (1870–1952)
Montez, Lola (1818–1861)
Montgomery, Helen Barrett (1861–1934)
Montgomery, Lucy Maud (1874–1942)
Montgomery, Mary (fl. 1891–1914)
Montolieu, Pauline (1751–1832)
Montoriol i Puig, Carme (1893–1966)
Montvid, A.S. (b. 1845)
Moodie, Geraldine (1853–1945)
Moodie, Susanna (1803–1885)
Moody, Agnes Claypole (1870–1954)
Moody, Elizabeth (1737–1814)
Moody, Emma Revell (1842–1903)
Moon, Lorna (1886–1930)
Moon, Lottie (1840–1912)
Mooney, Julie (1888–1915)
Moore, Anne Carroll (1871–1961)
Moore, Aubertine Woodward (1841–1929)
Moore, Clara (1824–1899)
Moore, Decima (1871–1964)
Moore, Elisabeth H. (1876–1959)
Moore, Eva (1870–1955)
Moore, Julia A. (1847–1920)
Moore, Maggie (1847–1929)
Moore, Mary Emelia (1869–1951)
Moran, Mary Nimmo (1842–1899)
More, Hannah (1745–1833)
Moreau de Justo, Alicia (1885–1986)
Moreno, Marguerite (1871–1948)
Morete, Maraea (1844–1907)
Morgan, Anna (1851–1936)
Morgan, Anne (1873–1952)
Morgan, Frances Louisa (1845–1924)
Morgan, Jane Norton Grew (1868–1925)
Morgan, Julia (1872–1957)
Morgan, Mary Kimball (1861–1948)
Morgan, Sydney (1780–1859)
Morgenstern, Lina B. (1830–1909)
Morison, Harriet (1862–1925)
Morisot, Berthe (1841–1895)
Morlacchi, Guiseppina (1836–1886)
Morpurgo, Rachel (1790–1871)
Morris, Clara (1847–1925)
Morris, Esther Hobart (1814–1902)
Morris, Jane Burden (1839–1914)
Morris, Margaret (1890–1981)
Morris, Margaret Hill (1737–1816)
Morris, May (1862–1938)
Morrison, Annie Christina (1870–1953)
Morrow, Elizabeth Cutter (1873–1955)
Mortimer, Mary (1816–1877)
Morton, Katherine E. (1885–1968)
Morton, Martha (1865–1925)
Morton, Rosalie Slaughter (1876–1968)
Moser, Mary (1744–1819)
Moses, Anna "Grandma" (1860–1961)
Mosher, Clelia Duel (1863–1940)
Mosher, Eliza Maria (1846–1928)
Moskowitz, Belle (1877–1933)
Mosolova, Vera (1875–1949)
Moss, Emma Sadler (1898–1970)
Moss, Marjorie (c. 1895–1935)
Mossetti, Carlotta (1890–?)
Moten, Lucy Ellen (1851–1933)
Moulton, Louise Chandler (1835–1908)
Moutza-Martinengou, Elisavet (1801–1832)
Mowatt, Anna Cora (1819–1870)
Mozart, Constanze (1762–1842)
Mozart, Maria Anna (1751–1829)
Mozzoni, Anna Maria (1837–1920)
Mudge, Isadore (1875–1957)
Muir, Willa (1890–1970)
Muir-Wood, Helen (1895–1968)
Mulally, Teresa (1728–1803)
Mulholland, Rosa (1841–1921)
Mullany, Kate (1845–1906)
Müller, Clara (1860–1905)
Müller, Mary Ann (c. 1819–1902)
Mulvany, Sybil Mary (1899–1983)
Mumford, Mary Bassett (1842–1935)
Munck, Ebba (1858–1946)
Mundt, Klara Müller (1814–1873)
Münter, Gabriele (1877–1962)
Murfree, Mary N. (1850–1922)
Murphy, Emily (1868–1933)
Murray, Anna Maria (1808–1899)
Murray, Judith Sargent (1751–1820)
Murray, Lilian (1871–1960)
Murray, Margaret (1863–1963)
Murrell, Christine (1874–1933)
Murtfeldt, Mary (1848–1913)
Mussey, Ellen Spencer (1850–1936)
Myers, Caroline Clark (c. 1888–1980)
Myers, Phoebe (1866–1947)
Myrtel, Hera (1868–?)
Naden, Constance Caroline Woodhill (1858–1889)
Nagródskaia, Evdokiia (1866–1930)
Nahienaena (c. 1815–1836)
Naidu, Sarojini (1879–1949)
Nampeyo (c. 1860–1942)
Nandi (c. 1760s–1827)
Nansen, Betty (1873–1943)
Nanye'hi (1738–1822)
Nassif, Malak Hifni (1886–1918)
Natalie, Mlle (c. 1895–1922)
Nathalia Keshko (1859–1941)
Nathan, Maud (1862–1946)
Nathoy, Lalu (1853–1933)
Nation, Carry (1846–1911)
Naubert, Christiane Benedikte (1756–1819)
Nawfal, Hind (fl. 1890s)
Nazáreva, Kapitolina Valerianovna (1847–1900)
Nazimova, Alla (1879–1945)
Necker de Saussure, Albertine (1766–1841)
Needham, Dorothy (1896–1987)
Negri, Ada (1870–1945)
Negron Muñoz, Mercedes (1895–1973)
Neill, Elizabeth Grace (1846–1926)
Neilson, Adelaide (1846–1880)
Neilson, Julia Emilie (1868–1957)
Neilson, Nellie (1873–1947)
Nelidova, Lydia (1863–1929)
Nelson, Frances Herbert (1761–1831)
Nemcová, Bozena (c. 1817–1862)
Nenadovich, Persida (1813–1873)
Neruda, Wilma (c. 1838–1911)
Nesbit, Edith (1858–1924)
Nestor, Agnes (1880–1948)
Nethersole, Olga (1863–1951)
Neumann, Theresa (1898–1962)
Nevada, Emma (1859–1940)
Nevill, Dorothy Fanny (1826–1913)
Newbigin, Marion I. (1869–1934)
Newcomb, Ethel (1875–1959)

Newcomb, Josephine L. (1816–1901)
Newell, Harriet Atwood (1793–1812)
Newell, Susan (1893–1923)
Newman, Angelia L. (1837 1910)
Newman, Julia St. Clair (1818–?)
Newman, Mehetabel (c. 1822–1908)
Newport, Matilda (c. 1795–1837)
Newsom, Ella King (1838–1919)
Newton, Lily (1893–1981)
Newton, Wharetutu Anne (fl. 1827–1870)
Ney, Elisabet (1833–1907)
Nezhdanova, Antonina (1873–1950)
Nga-kahu-whero (fl. 1800–1836)
Ngata, Arihia Kane (1879–1929)
Niboyet, Eugénie (1797–1883)
Nicholls, Marjory Lydia (1890–1930)
Nicholls, Rhoda Holmes (1854–1930)
Nichols, Clarina (1810–1885)
Nichols, Etta Grigsby (1897–1994)
Nichols, Mary Gove (1810–1884)
Nichols, Minerva Parker (1861–1949)
Nicholson, Eliza Jane (1849–1896)
Nicholson, Margaret (c. 1750–c. 1828)
Nicol, Helen Lyster (1854–1932)
Nicolson, Adela Florence (1865–1904)
Nielsen, Alice (c. 1870–1943)
Nielsen, Augusta (1822–1902)
Niese, Charlotte (1854–1935)
Niese, Hansi (1875–1934)
Nightingale, Florence (1820–1910)
Ni Guizhen (c. 1869–1931)
Nikambe, Shevantibai M. (b. 1865)
Nikola, Helene Knez (1765–1842)
Nikolaeva, Klavdiia (1893–1944)
Niles, Blair (1880–1959)
Nillson, Carlotta (c. 1878–1951)
Nilsson, Christine (1843–1921)
Niniwa-i-te-rangi (1854–1929)
Nisbet, Mary (1778–1855)
Nisbett, Louisa Cranstoun (1812–1858)
Nissen, Erika (1845–1903)
Nivedita, Sister (1867–1911)
Noailles, Anna de (1876 1933)
Noblet, Lise (1801–1852)
Nogami, Yaeko (1885–1985)
Nongqause (c. 1840–c. 1900)
Nonteta Bungu (c. 1875–1935)
Nordi, Cleo (b. 1899)
Nordica, Lillian (1857–1914)
Norgate, Kate (1853–1935)
Noronha, Joana de (fl. c. 1850)
North, Marianne (1830–1890)
Northcroft, Hilda Margaret (1882–1951)
Norton, Alice Peloubet (1860–1928)
Norton, Caroline (1808–1877)
Norton, Mary T. (1875–1959)
Nourse, Elizabeth (1859–1938)
Nováková, Teréza (1853–1912)
Novello, Clara (1818–1908)
Novello-Davies, Clara (1861–1943)
Nowland, Mary Josepha (1863–1935)
Noyes, Clara Dutton (1869–1936)
Nunneley, Kathleen Mary (1872–1956)
Nurpeissova, Dina (1861–1955)
Nutt, Emma M. (c. 1849–1926)
Nuttall, Zelia (1857–1933)
Nutting, Mary Adelaide (1858–1948)
Oakley, Annie (1860–1926)
Oakley, Violet (1874–1961)
Oatman, Olive Ann (c. 1838–1903)
O'Connell, Mary (1814–1897)
O'Connell, Sarah (c. 1822–1870)
O'Day, Caroline (1869–1943)
O'Doherty, Mary Anne (1826–1910)
O'Donnell, Ann (c. 1857–1934)
Oelschlagel, Charlotte (c. 1899–after 1948)
Ogilvie, Catherine (1746–?)
Ogilvie Farquharson, Marian (1846–1912)
Ogilvie Gordon, Maria M. (1864–1939)
O'Hagan, Mary (1823–1876)
O'Hanlon, Virginia (c. 1899–1971)
O'Hare, Kate Richards (1876–1948)
O'Keeffe, Adelaide (1776–c. 1855)
Okwei of Osomari (1872–1943)
Olberg, Oda (1872–1955)
Oldenburg, Mary (1865–1909)
Oldfield, Pearl Peden (1876–1962)
Olga, Princess Paley (1865–1929)
Olga Alexandrovna (1882–1960)
Olga Constantinovna (1851–1926)
Olga Iurevskaya (1873–1925)
Olga of Russia (1822–1892)
Oliphant, Margaret (1828–1897)
Olivier, Edith (c. 1879–1948)
Olsson, Hagar (1893–1978)
O'Malley, Mary Dolling (1889–1974)
O'Meara, Kathleen (1839–1888)
O'Murphy, Marie-Louise (1737–1814)
O'Neale, Lila M. (1886–1948)
O'Neill, Eliza (1791–1872)
O'Neill, Rose Cecil (1874–1944)
Onians, Edith (1866–1955)
Opie, Amelia (1769–1853)
Orchard, Sadie (c. 1853–1943)
Orczy, Emma (1865–1947)
O'Reilly, Leonora (1870–1927)
Orelli, Susanna (1845–1939)
Orgeni, Aglaja (1841–1926)
Ormerod, Eleanor A. (1828–1901)
Ortíz de Dominguez, Josefa (c. 1768–1829)
Orvieto, Laura (1876–1953)
Orzeszkowa, Eliza (1841–1910)
Osborn, Daisy (1888–1957)
Osborn, Emily Mary (1834–c. 1885)
Osborne, Fanny (1852–1934)
Osborne, Mary D. (1875–1946)
Osborne, Susan M. (1858–1918)
Osburn, Lucy (1835–1891)
Osgood, Frances (1811–1850)
O'Shea, Katherine (1845–1921)
Osorio, Ana de Castro (1872–1935)
Ostler, Emma Brignell (c. 1848–1922)
O'Sullivan, Mary Kenney (1864–1943)
Otero, Caroline (1868–1965)
Ottendorfer, Anna Uhl (1815 1884)
Otto-Peters, Luise (1819–1895)
Ouspenskaya, Maria (1876–1949)
Ovington, Mary White (1865–1951)
Owens-Adair, Bethenia (1840–1926)
Paalzow, Henriette (1788–1847)
Paca (1825–1860)
Pachler-Koschak, Marie (1792 1855)
Packard, Elizabeth (1816–1897)
Packard, Sophia B. (1824–1891)
Pagan, Isobel (c. 1742–1821)
Page, Gertrude (1873–1922)
Paget, Mary (1865–1919)
Paget, Muriel (1876–1938)
Paget, Nielsine (1858–1932)
Paget, Rosalind (1855–1948)
Paget, Violet (1856–1935)
Pagliero, Camilia (1859–1925)
Palencia, Isabel de (1878–c. 1950)
Palladino, Emma (c. 1860–1922)
Palladino, Eusapia (1854–1918)
Pallerini, Antonia (1790–1870)
Palli, Angelica (1798–1875)
Palmer, Alice Freeman (1855–1902)
Palmer, Alice May (1886–1977)
Palmer, Bertha Honoré (1849–1918)
Palmer, Elizabeth Mary (1832–1897)
Palmer, Frances Flora (1812–1876)
Palmer, Lizzie Merrill (1838–1916)
Palmer, Phoebe Worrall (1807–1874)
Palmer, Sophia French (1853–1920)
Panaeva, Avdotia (c. 1819–1893)
Panagiotatou, Angeliki (1878–1954)
Pankhurst, Christabel (1880–1958)
Pankhurst, Emmeline (1858–1928)
Pankhurst, Sylvia (1882–1960)
Paoli, Betty (1814–1894)
Papadat-Bengescu, Hortensia (1876–1955)
Papadopoulou, Alexandra (1867–1906)
Papakura, Makereti (1873–1930)
Pappenheim, Bertha (1859–1936)
Paradis, Maria Theresia von (1759–1824)
Paradis, Marie (fl. 1808)
Parata, Katherine Te Rongokahira (1873–1939)
Pardo Bazán, Emilia (1852–1921)
Pardoe, Julia (1804–1862)
Parepa-Rosa, Euphrosyne (1836–1874)
Park, Maud Wood (1871–1955)
Parker, Agnes Miller (1895–1980)
Parker, Catherine Langloh (c. 1856–1940)
Parker, Cynthia Ann (c. 1827–c. 1864)
Parker, Julia O'Connor (1890–1972)
Parker, Valeria Hopkins (1879–1959)
Parkes, Bessie Rayner (1829–1925)
Parkhurst, Charlotte (d. 1879)
Parkhurst, Helen (1887–1973)
Parkinson, Alice May (1889–1949)
Parlby, Irene (1868–1965)
Parloa, Maria (1843–1909)
Parnell, Anna (1852–1911)
Parr, Harriet (1828–1900)
Parren, Kalliroe (1861–1940)
Parrish, Celestia (1853–1918)
Parsons, Eliza (c. 1748–1811)
Parsons, Elizabeth (1846–1924)
Parsons, Elsie Clews (1875–1941)
Parsons, Emily Elizabeth (1824–1880)
Parsons, Mary (1813–1885)
Partridge, Margaret (b. 1891)
Pasta, Giuditta (1797–1865)
Patch, Edith (1876–1954)
Paterson, Ada Gertrude (1880–1937)
Paterson, Emma (1848–1886)
Patey, Janet Monach (1842 1894)
Patrick, Mary Mills (1850–1940)
Patten, Mary Ann (1837–1861)
Patterson, Hannah (1879–1937)
Patterson, Martha Johnson (1828–1901)
Patterson, Mary Jane (1840–1894)
Patterson, Nan (c. 1882–?)
Patti, Adelina (1843–1919)
Pattison, Dorothy W. (1832–1878)
Paul, Annette (1863–1952)
Pauline of Saxe Weimar (1852–1904)
Pauline of Wurttemberg (1800–1873)
Pauline of Wurttemberg (1810–1856)
Pauline of Wurttemberg (1877–1965)
Pavlova, Karolina (1807–1893)
Payne, Sylvia (1880–1974)
Peabody, Elizabeth Palmer (1778–1853)
Peabody, Elizabeth Palmer (1804–1894)
Peabody, Josephine Preston (1874–1922)
Peacock, Lucy (fl. 1785–1816)
Peabody, Lucy (1861–1949)
Peacocke, Isabel Maud (1881–1973)
Peake, Mary S. (1823–1862)
Peale, Anna Claypoole (1791–1878)
Peale, Margaretta Angelica (1795–1882)
Peale, Sarah Miriam (1800–1885)
Pearcey, Mary Eleanor (1866–1890)
Pearl, Cora (c. 1837–1886)
Pearson, Issette (fl. 1893)
Peary, Josephine (1863–1955)
Pechey-Phipson, Edith (1845–1908)
Peck, Annie Smith (1850–1935)
Peck, Ellen (1829–1915)
Peebles, Florence (1874–1956)
Peete, Louise (1883–1947)
Peixotto, Jessica (1864–1941)
Pelletier, Henriette (c. 1864–1961)
Pelletier, Madeleine (1874–1939)
Pember, Phoebe Yates (1823–1913)
Pendleton, Ellen Fitz (1864–1936)
Pengelly, Edna (1874–1959)
Penkinson, Sophie (fl. late 1890s)
Pennell, Elizabeth Robins (1855–1936)
Pennington, Mary Engle (1872–1952)
Percoto, Caterina (1812–1887)
Pérez, Eulalia Arrila de (c. 1773–c. 1878)
Perkins, Elizabeth Peck (c. 1735–1807)
Perkins, Frances (1880–1965)
Perkins, Lucy Fitch (1865–1937)
Perovskaya, Sonia (1853–1881)
Perrin, Ethel (1871–1962)
Perry, Lilla Cabot (c. 1848–1933)
Pestana, Alice (1860–1929)
Peter, Sarah Worthington (1800–1877)
Peterkin, Julia (1880–1961)
Petersen, Alicia O'Shea (1862–1923)
Petherick, Mary (fl. 1887)
Pethick-Lawrence, Emmeline (1867–1954)
Petipa, Marie (1836–1882)
Petipa, Marie (1857–1930)
Petre, Maude (1863–1942)

Petrie, Hilda (1871–1957)
Pettit, Katherine (1868–1936)
Pfeiffer, Anna Ursula (1813–1863)
Pfeiffer, Emily Jane (1827–1890)
Pfeiffer, Ida (1797–1858)
Phelps, Almira Lincoln (1793–1884)
Phelps, Elizabeth Porter (1747–1817)
Phelps, Elizabeth Wooster Stuart (1815–1852)
Philippine Charlotte (1716–1801)
Phillipps, Adelaide (1833–1882)
Phillips, Harriet Newton (1819–1901)
Phillips, Marion (1881–1932)
Phillpotts, Bertha Surtees (1877–1932)
Phule, Savitribai (1831–1897)
Pia of Sicily (1849–1882)
Pichler, Karoline (1769–1843)
Pichler, Magdalena (1881–1920)
Pickens, Lucy (1832–1899)
Pickersgill, Mary (1776–1857)
Pierangeli, Rina Faccio (1876–1960)
Pierce, Jane Means (1806–1863)
Pierce, Sarah (1767–1852)
Pigeon, Anna (fl. 1860s)
Pigeon, Ellen (fl. 1860s)
Pike, Mary (1824–1908)
Pilgrim, Ada (1867–1965)
Pilkington, Mary (1766–1839)
Pinchot, Cornelia (1881–1960)
Pinepine Te Rika (1857/58–1954)
Pinkham, Lydia E. (1819–1883)
Pinney, Eunice Griswold (1770–1849)
Piozzi, Hester Lynch (1741–1821)
Piper, Leonora E. (1859–1950)
Pirrie, Margaret Montgomery (1857–1935)
Pitini-Morera, Hariata Whakatau (1871/72?–1938)
Pitt, Marie E.J. (1869–1948)
Place, Etta (fl. 1896–1905)
Place, Martha (1848–1899)
Plaminkova, Frantiska (1875–1942)
Plater, Emilja (1806–1831)
Plato, Ann (c. 1820–?)
Platts-Mills, Daisy Elizabeth (1868–1956)
Player, Mary Josephine (c. 1857–1924)
Pleasant, Mary Ellen (c. 1814–1904)
Plessis, Alphonsine (1824–1847)
Pleyel, Maria Felicite (1811–1875)
Ploennies, Luise von (1803–1872)
Plummer, Mary Wright (1856–1916)
Pockels, Agnes (1862–1935)
Poe, Elizabeth (c. 1787–1811)
Poe, Virginia Clemm (1822–1847)
Poliakova, Elena (1884–1972)
Polier, Marie-Elizabeth (1742–1817)
Polk, Sarah Childress (1803–1891)
Polson, Florence Ada Mary Lamb (1877–1941)
Polyblank, Ellen Albertina (1840–1930)
Pomare, Hariata (fl. 1863–1864)
Pompilj, Vittoria Aganoor (1855–1910)
Ponsonby, Sarah (1755–1831)
Ponthon, Louise de (d. 1821)
Pool, Judith Graham (1919–1975)
Pool, Maria Louise (1841–1898)
Pope, Jane (1742–1818)
Pope, Maria Sophia (1818–1909)
Popp, Adelheid (1869–1939)
Porn, Hanna (1860–1913)
Portapovitch, Anna Knapton (1890–1974)
Porter, Anna Maria (1780–1832)
Porter, Annie (1880–1963)
Porter, Charlotte Endymion (1857–1942)
Porter, Eleanor H. (1868–1920)
Porter, Elizabeth Kerr (1894–1989)
Porter, Eliza Chappell (1807–1888)
Porter, Helen Kemp (1899–1987)
Porter, Jane (1776–1850)
Porter, Mary Winearls (1886–1980)
Porter, Sarah (1791–1862)
Porter, Sarah (1813–1900)
Post, Emily (1872–1960)
Potonié-Pierre, Eugénie (1844–1898)
Potter, Beatrix (1866–1943)
Potter, Cora (1857–1936)
Potter, Electa (1790–1854)
Potts, Mary Florence (c. 1853–?)
Pougy, Liane de (1866–c. 1940)
Pounder, Cheryl
Powell, Louise Mathilde (1871–1943)
Powell, Mary Sadler (1854/55?–1946)
Powell, Maud (1867–1920)
Powers, Harriet (1837–1911)
Poyntz, Juliet Stuart (1886–c. 1937)
Praed, Rosa (1851–1935)
Praeger, Sophia Rosamund (1867–1954)
Prang, Mary D. Hicks (1836–1927)
Pratt, Anna Beach (1867–1932)
Pratt, Anne (1806–1893)
Pratt, Ruth (1877–1965)
Preissova, Gabriela (1862–1946)
Prentiss, Elizabeth Payson (1818–1878)
Preobrazhenska, Olga (1871–1962)
Preradovic, Paula von (1887–1951)
Preshaw, Jane (1839–1926)
Preston, Ann (1813–1872)
Preston, Margaret Junkin (1820–1897)
Preston, Margaret Rose (c. 1875–1963)
Preston, May Wilson (1873–1949)
Price, Ellen (1878–1968)
Price, Juliette (1831–1906)
Prince, Lucy Terry (c. 1730–1821)
Prince, Mary (c. 1788–after 1833)
Pringle, Elizabeth Allston (1845–1921)
Prior, Margaret (1773–1842)
Procter, Adelaide (1825–1864)
Prosperi, Carola (1883–1975)
Prout, Mary Ann (1801–1884)
Pryor, Sara Agnes (1830–1912)
Przybyszewska, Dagny Juel (1867–1901)
Pudney, Elizabeth Allen (1894–1976)
Pudney, Elizabeth Jane (1862–1938)
Pugh, Sarah (1800–1884)
Puhiwahine Te Rangi-hirawea, Rihi (d. 1906)
Pulling, Mary Etheldred (1871–1951)
Pulman, Elizabeth (1836–1900)
Purcell, Samuelene (1898–1982)
Purser, Sarah (1848–1943)
Purvis, Harriet Forten (1810–1875)
Purvis, Sarah Forten (c. 1811–c. 1898)
Pusich, Antónia Gertrudes (1805–1883)
Putnam, Alice Whiting (1841–1919)
Putnam, Bertha Haven (1872–1960)
Putnam, Emily James (1865–1944)
Putnam, Helen (1857–1951)
Putnam, Mary T.S. (1810–1898)
Pye, Edith (1876–1965)
Qiu Jin (c. 1875–1907)
Qualter, Tot (1894–1974)
Quinton, Amelia S. (1833–1926)
Quinton, Cornelia B. Sage (1876–1936)
Raab, Esther (1894–1981)
Rachel (1821–1858)
Radcliffe, Ann (1764–1823)
Radcliffe, Mary Ann (c. 1746–after 1810)
Raeburn, Agnes Middleton (1872–1955)
Rafanelli, Leda (1880–1971)
Raiche, Bessica (c. 1874–1932)
Raisin, Catherine (1855–1945)
Ralfe, Catherine Hester (c. 1831–1912)
Ralph, Margaret (c. 1822–1913)
Ramabai, Pandita (1858–1922)
Rama Rau, Dhanvanthi (1893–1987)
Ramée, Louise de la (1839–1908)
Ramsay, Martha Laurens (1759–1811)
Ranavalona I (1792–1861)
Ranavalona II (1829–1883)
Ranavalona III (1861–1917)
Rand, Caroline Amanda (1828–1905)
Rand, Ellen (1875–1941)
Randall, Amelia Mary (1844–1930)
Randolph, Martha Jefferson (1775–1836)
Randolph, Virginia (1874–1958)
Rasmussen, Louise Christine (1815–1874)
Rathbone, Eleanor (1872–1946)
Rathbone, Hannah Mary (1798–1878)
Rathbone, Josephine Adams (1864–1941)
Rathbun, Mary Jane (1860–1943)
Ratner, Anna (c. 1892–1967)
Rattray, Lizzie Frost (1855–1931)
Raucourt, Mlle (1756–1815)
Ravera, Camilla (1889–1988)
Ray, Charlotte E. (1850–1911)
Ray, H. Cordelia (c. 1849–1916)
Rayner, M.C. (c. 1894–1948)
Ream, Vinnie (1847–1914)
Récamier, Juliette (1777–1849)
Recke, Elisa von der (1754–1833)
Reed, Mary (1854–1943)
Reed, Myrtle (1874–1911)
Rees, Annie Lee (1864–1949)
Rees, Rosemary (c. 1876–1963)
Reese, Lizette Woodworth (1856–1935)
Reeve, Clara (1729–1807)
Reeve, Elsie (1885–1927)
Reeves, Magdalene Stuart (1865–1953)
Regan, Agnes (1869–1943)
Rehan, Ada (1857–1916)
Reibey, Mary (1777–1855)
Reichardt, Louise (1779–1826)
Reid, Elisabeth Mills (1858–1931)
Reignolds, Catherine Mary (1836–1911)
Reinhardt, Aurelia Henry (1877–1948)
Reis, Maria Firmina dos (1825–1917)
Réjane, Gabrielle (1857–1920)
Remond, Sarah Parker (1826–1894)
Rémusat, Claire, comtesse de (1780–1821)
Rendall, Martha (d. 1909)
Renneville, Sophie de (1772–1822)
Rentoul, Annie Isobel (c. 1855–1928)
Repplier, Agnes (1855–1950)
Rere-o-maki (d. 1868)
Resvoll, Thekla (1871–1948)
Resvoll-Holmsen, Hanna (1873–1943)
Retter, Hannah (1839–1940)
Reuter, Gabriele (1859–1941)
Reventlow, Franziska von (1871–1918)
Reybaud, Fanny (1802–1871)
Reymond, Claire (c. 1868–?)
Reynolds, Belle (fl. 1860s)
Reynolds, Myra (1853–1936)
Reynolds, Rachel Selina (1838–1928)
Rhodes, Mary (c. 1782–1853)
Richards, Ellen Swallow (1842–1911)
Richards, Laura E. (1850–1943)
Richards, Linda (1841–1930)
Richardson, Dorothy (1873–1957)
Richardson, Effie Newbigging (1849/50?–1928)
Richardson, Henry Handel (1870–1946)
Richardson, Katy (1864–1927)
Richman, Julia (1855–1912)
Richmond, Dorothy Kate (1861–1935)
Richmond, Mary E. (1861–1928)
Richmond, Mary Elizabeth (1853–1949)
Richter, Elise (1865–1943)
Richter, Emma (1888–1956)
Ricker, Marilla (1840–1920)
Rickert, Edith (1871–1938)
Rickett, Mary Ellen (1861–1925)
Riddell, Charlotte (1832–1906)
Rider-Kelsey, Corinne (1877–1947)
Ridge, Lola (1873–1941)
Riepp, Mother Benedicta (1825–1862)
Rikiriki, Atareta Kawana Ropiha Mere (c. 1855–1926)
Rinehart, Mary Roberts (1876–1958)
Ripley, Martha Rogers (1843–1912)
Ripley, Sarah Alden (1793–1867)
Ripley, Sophia (1803–1861)
Ristori, Adelaide (1822–1906)
Ritchie, Anne Isabella (1837–1919)
Ritchie, Harriet Maria (1818–1907)
Rittenhouse, Jessie Belle (1869–1948)
Rivé-King, Julie (1854–1937)
Rives, Amélie (1863–1945)
Riwai, Kiti Karaka (1870–1927)
Robb, Isabel Hampton (1860–1910)
Robb, Mary Anne (1829–1912)
Robbins, Jane Elizabeth (1860–1946)
Robert-Angelini, Enif (1886–1976)
Robert-Kéralio, Louise (1758–1821)
Roberts, Florence (1871–1927)
Roberts, Lydia (1879–1965)
Roberts, Mary (1788–1864)
Roberts, Mary Louise (1886–1968)
Roberts, Mary May (1877–1959)
Robertson, Agnes (1833–1916)
Robertson, Alice Mary (1854–1931)
Robertson, Ann (1825–1922)
Robertson, Ann Worcester (1826–1905)
Robertson, Margaret Murray (1823–1897)
Robertson, Muriel (1883–1973)

Robespierre, Charlotte (1760–1840)
Robins, Denise Naomi (1897–1985)
Robins, Elizabeth (1862–1952)
Robins, Margaret Dreier (1868–1945)
Robinson, Harriet Hanson (1825–1911)
Robinson, Henrietta (1816–1905)
Robinson, Jane Bancroft (1847–1932)
Robinson, Mary (d. 1837)
Robinson, Sarah Jane (d. 1905)
Robinson, Therese Albertine Louise von Jakob (1797–1870)
Robscheit-Robbins, Frieda (1888–1973)
Robson, May (1858–1942)
Roche, Regina Maria (c. 1764–1845)
Rochester, Anna (1880–1966)
Rockefeller, Abby Aldrich (1874–1948)
Rockefeller, Laura Spelman (1839–1915)
Rodgers, Elizabeth Flynn (1847–1939)
Rodríguez de Tió, Lola (1843–1924)
Roebling, Emily (1844–1903)
Rogers, Clara Kathleen (1844–1931)
Rogers, Elizabeth Ann (1829–1921)
Rogers, Grace Rainey (1867–1943)
Rogers, Harriet B. (1834–1919)
Roland, Pauline (1805–1852)
Roland Holst, Henriëtte (1869–1952)
Rolleston, Elizabeth Mary (1845–1940)
Rollett, Hilda (1873–1970)
Romanov, Catherine (1827–1894)
Romanov, Elizabeth (1826–1845)
Romein-Verschoor, Annie (1895–1978)
Rongonui, Kahupake (1868/69?–1947)
Ronner-Knip, Henriette (1821–1909)
Rood, Florence (1873–1944)
Rooke, Irene (c. 1878–1958)
Rooney, Josie (b. 1892)
Rooney, Julia (b. 1893)
Roosevelt, Alice Lee (1861–1884)
Roosevelt, Anna Hall (1863–1892)
Roosevelt, Edith Kermit Carow (1861–1948)
Roosevelt, Sara Delano (1854–1941)
Rorer, Sarah Tyson (1849–1937)
Rorke, Kate (1866–1945)
Ros, Amanda (1860–1939)
Rosas, Encarnación de (1795–1838)
Rosati, Carolina (1826–1905)
Rose, Ernestine (1810–1892)
Roshanara (1849–1926)
Ross, Betsy (1752–1836)
Ross, Charlotte Whitehead (1843–1916)
Ross, Forrestina Elizabeth (1860–1936)
Ross, Frances Jane (1869–1950)
Ross, Marie-Henriette LeJeune (1762–1860)
Ross, Nellie Tayloe (1876–1977)
Rossetti, Christina (1830–1894)
Rossetti, Maria Francesca (1827–1876)
Rostopchina, Evdokiya (1811–1858)
Rothmann, Maria Elisabeth (1875–1975)
Rothschild, Constance de (1843–1931)
Rothschild, Mathilde de (1874–1926)
Roulstone, Elizabeth (fl. 1804)
Rousanne, Mme (1894–1958)
Roussel, Nelly (1878–1922)
Rout, Ettie Annie (1877–1936)
Rowan, Ellis (1848–1922)
Rowson, Susanna (1762–1824)
Royall, Anne (1769–1854)
Royce, Sarah (1819–1891)
Roy de Clotte le Barillier, Berthe (1868–1927)
Royde-Smith, Naomi Gwladys (c. 1880–1964)
Royer, Clémence (1830–1902)
Roys-Gavitt, Elmina M. (1828–1898)
Rozanova, Olga (1886–1918)
Rubinstein, Helena (1870–1965)
Rubinstein, Ida (1880–1960)
Ruck, Berta (1878–1978)
Rudel-Zeynek, Olga (1871–1948)
Rudman, Annie (1844–1928)
Rüegg, Annelise (1879–1934)
Ruffin, Josephine St. Pierre (1842–1924)
Runcie, Constance Faunt Le Roy (1836–1911)
Runciman, Jane Elizabeth (1873–1950)
Runeberg, Fredrika (1807–1879)
Rush, Rebecca (1779–1850)
Russell, Alys Smith (1866–1951)
Russell, Annie (1864–1936)
Russell, Lillian (1861–1922)
Russell, Mary du Caurroy (1865–1937)
Russell, Mother Mary Baptist (1829–1898)
Rute, Mme de (1831–1902)
Rutherford, Frances Armstrong (1842–1922)
Rutherford, Mildred (1851–1928)
Rutledge, Ann (1813–1835)
Ryan, Catherine O'Connell (1865–1936)
Rye, Maria Susan (1829–1903)
Rymill, Mary Ann (c. 1817–1897)
Saarinen, Loja (1879–1968)
Sabin, Ellen (1850–1949)
Sabin, Florence (1871–1953)
Sacajawea (c. 1787–c. 1812 or 1884)
Sacchetto, Rita (1879–1959)
Sach, Amelia (1873–1902)
Sacher, Anna (1859–1930)
Sadlier, Mary Anne (1820–1903)
Sáenz, Manuela (1797–1856)
Safford, Mary Jane (1834–1891)
Sage, Margaret Olivia (1828–1918)
Saint Mars, Gabrielle de (1804–1872)
Sakharoff, Clotilde (1892–1974)
Salavarrieta, Pola (1795–1817)
Sale, Florentia (c. 1790–1853)
Salhias de Tournemire, Elizaveta (1815–1892)
Salis-Marschlins, Meta (1855–1929)
Salm-Dyck, Constance de (1767–1845)
Salmon, Lucy Maynard (1853–1927)
Salmond, Sarah (1864–1956)
Salm-Salm, Agnes, Princess (1840–1912)
Salomon, Alice (1872–1948)
Salter, Susanna Medora (1860–1961)
Salverson, Laura Goodman (1890–1970)
Salvini-Donatelli, Fanny (c. 1815–1891)
Salvioni, Guglierma (1842–?)
Samoilova, Konkordiya (1876–1921)
Sampson, Deborah (1760–1827)
Sampson, Kathleen (1892–1980)
Sand, George (1804–1876)
Sanders, Elizabeth Elkins (1762–1851)
Sanderson, Sybil (1865–1903)
Sandes, Flora (1876–1956)
Sanford, Maria Louise (1836–1920)
Sangalli, Rita (1849–1909)
Sanger, Alice B.
Sangster, Margaret (1838–1912)
Sankovskaya, Yekaterina (c. 1816–1878)
Sansay, Leonora (fl. 1807–1823)
Sargant, Ethel (1863–1918)
Sargeant, N.C. (fl. 1895)
Sartain, Emily (1841–1927)
Sass, Marie Constance (1834–1907)
Satthianadhan, Krupabai (1862–1894)
Saunders, Edith (1865–1945)
Saunders, Marshall (1861–1947)
Savell, Edith Alma Eileen (1883–1970)
Savić-Rebac, Anica (1892–1935)
Savignac, Alida de (1790–1847)
Sawyer, Caroline M. Fisher (1812–1894)
Say, Lucy Sistare (1801–1885)
Sayer, Ettie (1875–1923)
Sayers, Peig (1873–1958)
Scales, Helen Flora Victoria (1887–1975)
Scanlan, Nelle (1882–1968)
Scarborough, Dorothy (1878–1935)
Scharlieb, Mary Ann (1845–1930)
Schaumann, Ruth (1899–1975)
Scheff, Fritzi (1879–1954)
Schirmacher, Käthe (1859–1930)
Schlegel-Schelling, Caroline (1763–1809)
Schlesinger, Therese (1863–1940)
Schmahl, Jeanne (1846–1916)
Schmidt, Auguste (1833–1902)
Schnackenberg, Annie Jane (1835–1905)
Schneider, Hortense (1833–1920)
Schoff, Hannah Kent (1853–1940)
Schofield, Martha (1839–1916)
Schollar, Ludmilla (c. 1888–1978)
Schoolcraft, Jane Johnston (1800–1841)
Schopenhauer, Adele (1797–1849)
Schopenhauer, Johanna (1766–1838)
Schratt, Katharina (1853–1940)
Schreiber, Adele (1872–1957)
Schreiner, Olive (1855–1920)
Schrieck, Louise van der (1813–1886)
Schröder-Devrient, Wilhelmine (1804–1860)
Schroeder, Bertha (1872–1953)
Schumann, Clara (1819–1896)
Schumann, Elisabeth (1885–1952)
Schumann-Heink, Ernestine (1861–1936)
Schurz, Margarethe Meyer (1833–1876)
Schuster, Norah (1892–1991)
Schuyler, Catherine Van Rensselaer (1734–1803)
Schuyler, Louisa Lee (1837–1926)
Schwarzwald, Eugenie (1872–1940)
Schwerin, Jeanette (1852–1899)
Schwimmer, Rosika (1877–1948)
Scidmore, Eliza Ruhamah (1856–1928)
Scott, Charlotte Angas (1858–1931)
Scott, Evelyn (1893–1963)
Scott, Jessie Ann (1883–1959)
Scott, Mary Edith (1888–1979)
Scott, Rose (1847–1925)
Scott-Maxwell, Florida (1883–1979)
Scriabin, Vera (1875–1920)
Scripps, Ellen Browning (1836–1932)
Scudder, Ida (1870–1960)
Scudder, Janet (1869–1940)
Scudder, Vida (1861–1954)
Seacole, Mary Jane (c. 1805–1881)
Seager, Esther (c. 1835–1911)
Seaman, Elizabeth Cochrane (1864–1922)
Secord, Laura (1775–1868)
Sedgwick, Anne Douglas (1873–1935)
Sedgwick, Catharine (1789–1867)
Sedova, Julia (1880–1969)
Ségalas, Anais (1814–1895)
Ségur, Sophie Rostopchine, Comtesse de (1799–1874)
Seidel, Amalie (1876–1952)
Seifullina, Lydia (1889–1954)
Sekulić, Isadora (1877–1958)
Sellers, Kathryn (1870–1939)
Sembrich, Marcella (1858–1935)
Semenova, Ekaterina (1786–1849)
Semple, Ellen Churchill (1863–1932)
Semple, Letitia Tyler (1821–1907)
Serao, Matilde (1856–1927)
Sergeant, Adeline (1851–1904)
Serres, Olivia (1772–1834)
Sert, Misia (1872–1950)
Sessions, Kate O. (1857–1940)
Sessions, Patty Bartlett (1795–1892)
Seton, Elizabeth Ann (1774–1821)
Seton, Grace Gallatin (1872–1959)
Severance, Caroline M. (1820–1914)
Séverine (1855–1929)
Seville, Carolina Ada (1874–1955)
Sewall, Lucy Ellen (1837–1890)
Sewall, May Wright (1844–1920)
Seward, Anna (1742–1809)
Sewell, Anna (1820–1878)
Sewell, Elizabeth Missing (1815–1906)
Sewell, Mary Wright (1797–1884)
Sexton, Elsie Wilkins (1868–1959)
Seymour, Georgiana (d. 1884)
Seymour, Mary F. (1846–1893)
Seymour, May Davenport (d. 1967)
Shaarawi, Huda (1879–1947)
Shabanova, Anna (1848–1932)
Shabelska, Maria (1898–1980)
Shafer, Helen Almira (1839–1894)
Shannon, Effie (1867–1954)
Shapir, Olga (1850–1916)
Sharp, Katharine Lucinda (1865–1914)
Shattuck, Lydia (1822–1889)
Shaw, Anna Howard (1847–1919)
Shaw, Flora (1852–1929)
Shaw, Flora Madeline (1864–1927)
Shaw, Mary G. (1854–1929)
Shaw, Pauline Agassiz (1841–1917)
Shayle George, Frances (c. 1827–1890)
Shchepkina-Kupernik, Tatiana (1874–1952)
Sheahan, Marion (1892–1994)
Sheehy-Skeffington, Hanna (1877–1946)
Sheepshanks, Mary (1872–1958)
Sheldon, May French (1847–1936)
Shelley, Mary (1797–1851)
Shepard, Helen Miller (1868–1938)
Shepherd, Mary (c. 1780–1847)
Sheppard, Kate (1847–1934)

Sheremetskaia, Natalia (1880–1952)
Sheridan, Caroline Henrietta Callander (1779–1851)
Sherman, Lydia (d. 1878)
Sherman, Mary Belle (1862–1935)
Sherwin, Belle (1868–1955)
Sherwood, Katharine Margaret (1841–1914)
Sherwood, Mary (1856–1935)
Sherwood, Mary Elizabeth (1826–1903)
Sherwood, Mary Martha (1775–1851)
Sherwood, Maud Winifred (1880–1956)
Shinn, Millicent Washburn (1858–1940)
Shipp, Ellis Reynolds (1847–1939)
Shippen, Peggy (1760–1804)
Shirreff, Emily (1814–1897)
Shkapskaia, Mariia (1891–1952)
Shochat, Manya (1878–1961)
Shore, Henrietta (1880–1963)
Shortt, Elizabeth Smith (1859–1949)
Shtern, Lina (1878–1968)
Shuler, Nettie Rogers (1862–1939)
Siddal, Elizabeth (1829–1862)
Siddons, Harriet (1783–1844)
Siddons, Sarah (1755–1831)
Sidgwick, Eleonora Mildred (1845–1936)
Siebold, Charlotte Heidenreich von (1788–1859)
Siebold, Josepha von (1771–1849)
Siedeberg, Emily Hancock (1873–1968)
Siems, Margarethe (1879–1952)
Sieveking, Amalie (1794–1859)
Sievwright, Margaret Home (1844–1905)
Sigerson, Dora (1866–1918)
Sigerson, Hester (d. 1898)
Sigourney, Lydia H. (1791–1865)
Sill, Anna Peck (1816–1889)
Sillanpää, Miina (1866–1952)
Simcox, Edith (1844–1901)
Simkhovitch, Mary (1867–1951)
Simms, Florence (1873–1923)
Simonovich-Efimova, Nina (1877–1948)
Simpson, Mary Elizabeth (1865–1948)
Simpson-Serven, Ida (c. 1850s–c. 1896)
Sinclair, Catherine (1780–1864)
Sinclair, Catherine (1817–1891)
Sinclair, Elizabeth McHutcheson (1800–1892)
Sinclair, May (1863–1946)
Sinden, Topsy (1878–1951)
Singer, Winnaretta (1865–1943)
Sinués, Maria del Pilar (1835–1893)
Siteman, Isabella Flora (c. 1842–1919)
Sitterly, Charlotte Moore (1898–1990)
Skinner, Constance Lindsay (1877–1939)
Skinner, Mollie (1876–1955)
Skobtsova, Maria (1891–1945)
Skram, Amalie (1846–1905)
Skrine, Agnes (c. 1865–1955)
Slagle, Eleanor Clarke (1871–1942)
Slancikova, Bozena (1867–1951)
Slater, Frances Charlotte (1892–1947)
Slavikova, Ludmila (1890–1943)
Slessor, Mary (1848–1915)
Slocum, Frances (1773–1847)
Slosson, Annie Trumbull (1838–1926)
Slutskaya, Vera (1874–1917)
Slye, Maud (1869–1954)
Small, Mary Elizabeth (1812/13–1908)
Smedley, Menella Bute (c. 1820–1877)
Smellie, Elizabeth Lawrie (1884–1968)
Smirnova, Sofia (1852–1921)
Smith, Abby (1797–1878)
Smith, Amanda Berry (1837–1915)
Smith, Annie Lorrain (1854–1937)
Smith, Bathsheba (1822–1910)
Smith, Charlotte (1749–1806)
Smith, Elizabeth "Betsy" (1750–1815)
Smith, Elizabeth Oakes (1806–1893)
Smith, Eliza Roxey Snow (1804–1887)
Smith, Emma Hale (1804–1879)
Smith, Erminnie A. Platt (1836–1886)
Smith, Eunice (1757–1823)
Smith, Frances Hagell (1877–1948)
Smith, Grace Cossington (1892–1984)
Smith, Hannah Whitall (1832–1911)
Smith, Helen Hay (1873–1918)
Smith, Jessie Willcox (1863–1935)
Smith, Julia (1792–1886)
Smith, Lucy Masey (1861–1936)
Smith, Madeleine Hamilton (1835–1928)
Smith, Margaret Bayard (1778–1844)
Smith, Mary Ellen (1861–1933)
Smith, Nora Archibald (1859?–1934)
Smith, Sophia (1796–1870)
Smith, Virginia Thrall (1836–1903)
Smith, Zilpha Drew (1851–1926)
Smithson, Harriet Constance (1800–1854)
Smyth, Ethel (1858–1944)
Smythe, Emily Anne (c. 1845–1887)
Snelling, Lilian (1879–1972)
Snively, Mary Agnes (1847–1933)
Snow, Sarah Ellen Oliver (1864–1939)
Sohier, Elizabeth Putnam (1847–1926)
Sokhanskaia, Nadezhda (1823–1884)
Sokolova, Eugenia (1850–1925)
Soljak, Miriam Bridelia (1879–1971)
Solomon, Hannah Greenebaum (1858–1942)
Solov'eva, Poliksena (1867–1924)
Somerset, Isabella (1851–1921)
Somerville, E. (1858–1949)
Somerville, Mary Fairfax (1780–1872)
Somerville, Nellie Nugent (1863–1952)
Sontag, Henriette (c. 1803–1854)
Sophia (1868–1927)
Sophia Dorothea of Wurttemberg (1759–1828)
Sophia Matilda (1773–1844)
Sophia Matilda (1777–1848)
Sophia of Denmark (1746–1813)
Sophia of Nassau (1824–1897)
Sophia of Nassau (1836–1913)
Sophia of Sweden (1801–1865)
Sophia of Wurttemberg (1818–1877)
Sophie Caroline (1737–1817)
Sophie Charlotte of Oldenburg (1879–1964)
Sophie of Bavaria (1805–1872)
Sophie of Bayern (1847–1897)
Sophie of Prussia (1870–1932)
Sorabji, Cornelia (1866–1954)
Sorma, Agnes (1862–1927)
Soule, Caroline White (1824–1903)
Southcott, Joanna (1750–1814)
Southey, Caroline Anne (1786–1854)
Southworth, E.D.E.N. (1819–1899)
Souza, Auta de (1876–1901)
Souza-Botelho, Adélaïde Filleul, marquise of (1761–1836)
Sowerby, Millicent (1878–1967)
Spalding, Catherine (1793–1858)
Spalding, Eliza (1807–1851)
Spence, Catherine (1825–1910)
Spencer, Anna (1851–1931)
Spencer, Cornelia Phillips (1825–1908)
Spencer, Henrietta Frances (1761–1821)
Spencer, Lilly Martin (1822–1902)
Spencer Smith, Joan (1891–1965)
Speraz, Beatrice (1843–1923)
Sperrey, Eleanor Catherine (1862–1893)
Speyer, Ellin Prince (1849–1921)
Speyer, Leonora (1872–1956)
Spinelli, Evelita Juanita (1889–1941)
Spofford, Grace Harriet (1887–1974)
Spofford, Harriet Prescott (1835–1921)
Sponer, Hertha (1895–1968)
Spong, Hilda (1875–1955)
Spottiswoode, Alicia Ann (1810–1900)
Sprague, Kate Chase (1840–1899)
Spurgeon, Caroline F.E. (1869–1942)
Spyri, Emily Kempin (1853–1901)
Spyri, Johanna (1827–1901)
Squires, Catharine (1843–1912)
Squires, Helena E. (1879–1959)
St. Clair, Sallie (1842–1867)
St. Denis, Ruth (1877–1968)
St. John, Florence (1854–1912)
Stace, Helen McRae (1850–1926)
Staël, Germaine de (1766–1817)
Stanford, Jane (1828–1905)
Stanhope, Hester (1776–1839)
Stanislavski, Maria Lilina (b. around 1870)
Stanton, Elizabeth Cady (1815–1902)
Stanwood, Cordelia (1865–1958)
Starkie, Enid (1897–1970)
Starr, Belle (1848–1889)
Starr, Eliza Allen (1824–1901)
Starr, Ellen Gates (1859–1940)
Stasova, Elena (1873–1966)
Stasova, Nadezhda (1822–1895)
Statham, Edith May (1853–1951)
Staveley, Dulcie (1898–1995)
Stearns, Lutie (1866–1943)
Stebbins, Emma (1815–1882)
Steel, Dorothy (1884–1965)
Steel, Flora Annie (1847–1929)
Steiff, Margarete (1847–1909)
Stein, Charlotte von (1742–1827)
Stein, Gertrude (1874–1946)
Stephanie (1837–1859)
Stephanie de Beauharnais (1789–1860)
Stephanie of Belgium (1864–1945)
Stephansen, Elizabeth (1872–1961)
Stephen, Julia Prinsep (1846–1895)
Stephens, Alice Barber (1858–1932)
Stephens, Ann S. (1810–1886)
Stephens, Catherine (1794–1882)
Stephens, Kate (1853–1938)
Stepney, Catherine (1785–1845)
Stern, Frances (1873–1947)
Stetson, Augusta (1842–1928)
Stettheimer, Florine (1871–1944)
Stevens, Alzina (1849–1900)
Stevens, Georgia Lydia (1870–1946)
Stevens, Lillian (1844–1914)
Stevens, Nettie Maria (1861–1912)
Stevenson, Fanny (1840–1914)
Stevenson, Margaret Beveridge (1865–1941)
Stevenson, Matilda (1849–1915)
Stevenson, Sarah Hackett (1841–1909)
Stevenson, Sara Yorke (1847–1921)
Steward, Susan McKinney (1847–1918)
Stewart, Adela Blanche (1846–1910)
Stewart, Catherine Campbell (1881–1957)
Stewart, Cora Wilson (1875–1958)
Stewart, Eliza Daniel (1816–1908)
Stewart, Frances Ann (1840–1916)
Stewart, Isabel Maitland (1878–1963)
Stewart, Maria W. (1803–1879)
Stewart, Mary Downie (1876–1957)
Stewart, Nellie (1858–1931)
Stewart-Mackenzie, Maria (1783–1862)
Stewart-Murray, Katharine (1874–1960)
Stewart-Richardson, Lady Constance (1883–1932)
Stimson, Julia (1881–1948)
Stinson, Marjorie (1894–1975)
Stirling, Mary Anne (1815–1895)
Stirling, Mihi Kotukutuku (1870–1956)
Stockert-Meynert, Dora von (1870–1947)
Stockley, Cynthia (1872–1936)
Stöcklin, Franziska (1894–1931)
Stockton, Annis Boudinot (1736–1801)
Stockton, Betsey (c. 1798–1865)
Stoddard, Cora Frances (1872–1936)
Stoddard, Elizabeth Drew (1823–1902)
Stoddart, Margaret Olrog (1865–1934)
Stoeckel, Ellen Battell (1851–1939)
Stoecker, Helene (1869–1943)
Stojadinović-Srpkinja, Milica (1830–1878)
Stokes, Caroline Phelps (1854–1909)
Stokes, Olivia Phelps (1847–1927)
Stokes, Rose Pastor (1879–1933)
Stolitsa, Liubov (1884–1934)
Stolz, Teresa (1834–1902)
Stone, Constance (1856–1902)
Stone, Hannah (1893–1941)
Stone, Lucinda Hinsdale (1814–1900)
Stone, Lucy (1818–1893)
Stoneman, Bertha (1866–1943)
Stopa, Wanda (1899–1925)
Stopes, Marie (1880–1958)
Stopford Green, Alice (1847–1929)
Storace, Nancy (1765–1817)
Storchio, Rosina (1876–1945)
Storer, Maria (1849–1932)
Stothard, Sarah Sophia (1825/26–1901)
Stout, Anna Paterson (1858–1931)
Stover, Mary Johnson (1832–1883)
Stowe, Emily Howard (1831–1903)
Stowe, Harriet Beecher (1811–1896)
Strachey, Pippa (1872–1968)
Strachey, Ray (1887–1940)
Stratton, Helen (fl. 1891–1925)
Stratton-Porter, Gene (1863–1924)

Straus, Ida (1849–1912)
Strauss, Sara Milford (1896–1979)
Strauss und Torney, Lulu von (1873–1956)
Strepponi, Giuseppina (1815–1897)
Stretton, Hesba (1832–1911)
Strickland, Agnes (1796–1874)
Stritt, Marie (1856–1928)
Strong, Ann Monroe Gilchrist (1875–1957)
Strong, Harriet (1844–1929)
Stuart, Bathia Howie (1893–1987)
Stuart, Jane (1812–1888)
Stuart, Louisa (1757–1851)
Stuart, Miranda (c. 1795–1865)
Stuart, Ruth McEnery (c. 1849–1917)
Stuart, Wilhelmina Magdalene (1895–1985)
Stuart Wortley, Emmeline (1806–1855)
Sucher, Rosa (1847–1927)
Suckling, Sophia Lois (1893–1990)
Suisted, Laura Jane (1840–1903)
Sullivan, Mary Quinn (1877–1939)
Surratt, Mary E. (c. 1820–1865)
Surville, Laure (1800–1871)
Suslova, Nadezhda (1845–1916)
Sutherland, Mary (1893–1955)
Sutherland, Mary Ann (1864–1948)
Sutherland, Selina Murray McDonald (1839–1909)
Sutliffe, Irene H. (1850–1936)
Suttner, Bertha von (1843–1914)
Svetla, Caroline (1830–1899)
Swain, Clara A. (1834–1910)
Swainson, Mary Anne (c. 1833–1897)
Swanwick, Anna (1813–1899)
Swanwick, Helena (1864–1939)
Swartz, Maud O'Farrell (1879–1937)
Swetchine, Anne Sophie (1782–1857)
Swett, Jane (b. 1805)
Swift, Anne (1829/35–?)
Swift, Delia (fl. 1850s)
Swisshelm, Jane Grey (1815–1884)
Szold, Henrietta (1860–1945)
Szumowska, Antoinette (1868–1938)
Szymanowska, Maria Agata (1789–1831)
Taft, Helen Herron (1861–1943)
Taglioni, Louisa (1823–1893)
Taglioni, Maria (1804–1884)
Taglioni, Marie (1833–1891)
Taiaroa, Tini Kerei (c. 1846–1934)
Takács, Eva (1779–1845)
Talbert, Mary Morris (1866–1923)
Talbot, Marion (1858–1948)
Talbot, Mary Anne (1778–1808)
Talcott, Eliza (1836–1911)
Tallien, Thérésa (1773–1835)
Talma, Madame (1771–1860)
Tamairangi (fl. 1820–1828)
Tammes, Tine (1871–1947)
Tanguay, Eva (1878–1947)
Tanner, Ilona (1895–1955)
Tappan, Caroline Sturgis (1819–1888)
Tappan, Eva March (1854–1930)
Tapsell, Ngatai Tohi Te Ururangi (1844–1928)
Tarbell, Ida (1857–1944)
Tarnow, Fanny (1779–1862)
Tarnowska, Maria (1878–1923)
Tarsouli, Athena (1884–1974)
Tasker, Marianne Allen (1852–1911)
Tastu, Amable (1798–1885)
Tautari, Mary (d. 1906)
Tautphoeus, Baroness von (1807–1893)
Taylor, Ann (1782–1866)
Taylor, Anna Edson (c. 1858–c. 1921)
Taylor, Annie Royle (1855–c. 1920)
Taylor, Ann Martin (1757–1830)
Taylor, Elizabeth Best (1868–1941)
Taylor, Eva (1879–1966)
Taylor, Florence M. (1879–1969)
Taylor, Harriet (1807–1858)
Taylor, Helen (1831–1907)
Taylor, Jane (1783–1824)
Taylor, Janet (1804–1870)
Taylor, Knox (1814–1835)
Taylor, Laurette (1884–1946)
Taylor, Louisa Jane (1846–1883)
Taylor, Lucy Hobbs (1833–1910)
Taylor, Margaret Smith (1788–1852)
Taylor, Mary (1817–1893)
Taylor, Mary (1898–1984)
Taylor, Sophia Louisa (1847–1903)
Taylor, Susie King (1848–1912)
Taymuriyya, 'A'isha 'Ismat al- (1840–1902)
Taytu (c. 1850–1918)
Tecson, Trinidad (1848–1928)
Teffi, N.A. (1872–1952)
Te Kahuhiapo, Rahera (1820s?–1910)
Te Kakapi, Ripeka Wharawhara-i-te-rangi (?–1880)
Te Kiri Karamu, Heni (1840–1933)
Teleki, Blanka (1806–1862)
Tempest, Florence (c. 1891–?)
Tempest, Marie (1864–1942)
Templeton, Fay (1865–1939)
Tenetahi, Rahui Te Kiri (d. 1913)
Tennant, Margaret Mary (1869–1946)
Tenney, Tabitha Gilman (1762–1837)
Tennyson, Emily (1813–1896)
Te Paea Tiaho (1820s?–1875)
Te Pikinga (c. 1800–after 1868)
Teplova, Nadezhda Sergeevna (1814–1848)
Te Rangi-i-paia II (fl. 1818–1829)
Te Rau-o-te-rangi, Kahe (?–c. 1871)
Teresa, Mother (c. 1766–1846)
Teresa Cristina of Bourbon (1822–1889)
Teresa of Portugal (1793–1874)
Terhune, Mary Virginia (1830–1922)
Ternan, Frances Eleanor (c. 1803–1873)
Ternina, Milka (1863–1941)
Te Rohu (fl. 1820–1850)
Terrell, Mary Church (1863–1954)
Terriss, Ellaline (1871–1971)
Terry, Ellen (1847–1928)
Terry, Kate (1844–1924)
Terry, Marion (1852–1930)
Terry-Lewis, Mabel (1872–1957)
Tesky, Adeline Margaret (c. 1850–1924)
Te Taiawatea Rangitukehu, Maata (1848/49?–1929)
Tetrazzini, Eva (1862–1938)
Tetrazzini, Luisa (1871–1940)
Te Whaiti, Kaihau Te Rangikakapi Maikara (1863–1937)
Te Wherowhero, Piupiu (1886/87?–1937)
Thaxter, Celia Laighton (1835–1894)
Theodelinde (1814–1857)
Theodoropoulou, Avra (1880–1963)
Theresa of Austria (1816–1867)
Theresa of Liechtenstein (1850–1938)
Theresa of Savoy (1803–1879)
Theresa of Saxe-Altenburg (1836–1914)
Theresa of Saxony (1792–1854)
Therese of Bourbon (1817–1886)
Thérèse of Lisieux (1873–1897)
Therese of Nassau (1815–1871)
Théroigne de Méricourt, Anne-Josèphe (1762–1817)
Thoburn, Isabella (1840–1901)
Thomas, Agnes (fl. 1878–1926)
Thomas, Edith Matilda (1854–1925)
Thomas, Lillian Beynon (1874–1961)
Thomas, M. Carey (1857–1935)
Thomas, Mary Myers (1816–1888)
Thompson, Annie E. (1845–1913)
Thompson, Blanche Edith (1874–1963)
Thompson, Edith (c. 1894–1923)
Thompson, Eliza (1816–1905)
Thompson, Elizabeth Rowell (1821–1899)
Thompson, Eloise Bibb (1878–1928)
Thompson, Flora (1876–1947)
Thompson, Gertrude Hickman (1877–1950)
Thompson, Lydia (1836–1908)
Thompson, Marion Beatrice (1877–1964)
Thompson, Mary Harris (1829–1895)
Thompson, Sarah (1774–1852)
Thoms, Adah B. (c. 1863–1943)
Thomson, Jane (1858–1944)
Thoresen, Cecilie (1858–1911)
Thorne, Florence (1877–1973)
Thorne, Harriet V.S. (1843–1926)
Thorpe, Rose Hartwick (1850–1939)
Thurber, Jeannette (1850–1946)
Thursby, Emma (1845–1931)
Thurston, Katherine (1875–1911)
Thurston, Lucy (1795–1876)
Thurston, Mabel (1869–1960)
Thurston, Matilda (1875–1958)
Thygeson, Sylvie Thompson (1868–1975)
Thyra Oldenburg (1853–1933)
Ticknor, Anna Eliot (1823–1896)
Tiernan, Frances Fisher (1846–1920)
Tietjens, Therese (1831–1877)
Tighe, Mary (1772–1810)
Tilbury, Zeffie (1863–1950)
Tilley, Vesta (1864–1952)
Tilton, Elizabeth (1834–c. 1896)
Timanoff, Vera (1855–1942)
Tinayre, Marcelle (c. 1870–1948)
Tinayre, Marguerite (1831–?)
Tingley, Katherine (1847–1929)
Tinné, Alexandrine (1839–1869)
Tinsley, Annie Turner (1808–1885)
Titus, Shirley Carew (1892–1967)
Tod, Isabella (1836–1896)
Todd, Mabel Loomis (1858–1932)
Todd, Margaret G. (1859–1918)
Todd, Marion Marsh (1841–post 1913)
Todi, Luiza Rosa (1753–1833)
Toklas, Alice B. (1877–1967)
Tolstoy, Sonya (1844–1919)
Tomaszewicz-Dobrska, Anna (1854–1918)
Tompkins, Sally Louisa (1833–1916)
Tone, Matilda (c. 1769–1849)
Tonna, Charlotte Elizabeth (1790–1846)
Topeora, Rangi Kuini Wikitoria (?–1865/73)
Toppan, Jane (1854–1938)
Torlesse, Elizabeth Henrietta (1835/36–1922)
Toro, Maria Teresa (d. 1803)
Torrezão, Guiomar (1844–1898)
Torriani, Maria Antonietta (1840–1920)
Tosatti, Barbara Maria (1891–1934)
Toselli, Louisa (1870–1947)
Tourtel, Mary (1874–1948)
Towne, Laura Matilda (1825–1901)
Tracy, Martha (1876–1942)
Tracy, Mona Innis (1892–1959)
Traill, Catherine Parr (1802–1899)
Trapani, Antonia von (b. 1851)
Trask, Kate Nichols (1853–1922)
Treble, Lillian M. (1854–1909)
Tree, Maud Holt (1858–1937)
Trefilova, Vera (1875–1943)
Trench, Melesina (1768–1827)
Trimmer, Sarah (1741–1810)
Tripe, Mary Elizabeth (1870–1939)
Tristan, Flora (1803–1844)
Troll-Borostyani, Irma von (1847–1912)
Trollope, Frances Milton (c. 1779–1863)
Trollope, Theodosia (1825–1865)
Trotter, Mildred (1899–1991)
Trouhanova, Natalia (1885–1956)
Troup, Augusta Lewis (c. 1848–1920)
Trout, Jenny Kidd (1841–1921)
Truax, Sarah (1877–1958)
Trubnikova, Mariia (1835–1897)
Truganini (1812–1876)
Truth, Sojourner (c. 1797–1883)
Tsebrikova, M.K. (1835–1917)
Tubbs, Alice (1851–1930)
Tubman, Harriet (1821–1913)
Tucker, Charlotte Maria (1821–1893)
Tuckwell, Gertrude (1861–1951)
Tupper, Frances (1826–1912)
Turikatuku (d. 1827)
Turnbull, Julia Anne (1822–1887)
Turner, Elizabeth (1774–1846)
Turner, Eliza Sproat (1826–1903)
Turner, Ethel (1872–1958)
Turner, Florence E. (c. 1888–1946)
Turner, Mary (d. 1918)
Tusap, Srbuhi (1841–1901)
Tussaud, Marie (1761–1850)
Tuthill, Louisa Huggins (1799–1879)
Tutwiler, Julia Strudwick (1841–1916)
Twining, Louisa (1820–1912)
Tyler, Adeline Blanchard (1805–1875)
Tyler, Alice S. (1859–1944)
Tyler, Julia Gardiner (1820–1889)
Tyler, Letitia (1790–1842)
Tyler, Odette (1869–1936)
Tyler, Priscilla Cooper (1816–1889)
Tynan, Katharine (1861–1931)
Tzavella, Moscho (1760–1803)

Ueland, Clara Hampson (1860–1927)
Uhl, Frida (1872–1943)
Ukrainka, Lesya (1871–1913)
Ullmann, Regina (1884–1961)
Underhill, Evelyn (1875–1941)
Underhill, Ruth Murray (1883–1984)
Underwood, Lillias (1851–1921)
Unger, Caroline (1803–1877)
Upton, Harriet Taylor (1853–1945)
Ursinus, Sophie (1760–1836)
Urso, Camilla (1842–1902)
Uzès, Anne, Duchesse d' (1847–1933)
Vachell, Eleanor (1879–1948)
Vaganova, Agrippina (1879–1951)
Valadon, Suzanne (1865–1938)
Valentine, Lila (1865–1921)
Valentine, Winifred Annie (1886–1968)
Valette, Aline (1850–1899)
Vallayer-Coster, Anne (1744–1818)
Vallette, Marguerite (1860–1953)
Valli, Valli (1882–1927)
Van Blarcom, Carolyn (1879–1960)
Vanbrugh, Irene (1872–1949)
Vanbrugh, Violet (1867–1942)
Van Buren, Adeline (1894–1949)
Van Buren, Angelica (1816–1878)
Van Buren, Augusta
Van Buren, Hannah Hoes (1783–1819)
Van Chu-Lin (1893/94?–1946)
Van Cott, Margaret (1830–1914)
Vandamm, Florence (1883–1966)
Van Deman, Esther (1862–1937)
Vanderbilt, Alice Gwynne (1845–1934)
Vanderbilt, Consuelo (1877–1964)
Vanderbilt, Maria (1821–1896)
Vanderbilt, Sophia Johnson (1797–1868)
Vane-Tempest, Frances Anne Emily (d. 1865)
Vane-Tempest-Stewart, Edith (1878–1949)
Vane-Tempest-Stewart, Theresa (1856–1919)
Van Grippenberg, Alexandra (1859–1913)
Van Hoosen, Bertha (1863–1952)
Van Lew, Elizabeth (1818–1900)
Van Rensselaer, Mariana (1851–1934)
Van Rensselaer, Martha (1864–1932)
Vansittart, Henrietta (1840–1883)
Vansova, Terezia (1857–1942)
Van Valkenburgh, Elizabeth (1799–1846)
Van Vorst, Marie Louise (1867–1936)
Van Zandt, Marie (1858–1919)
Vardill, Anna Jane (1781–1852)
Varnhagen, Rahel (1771–1833)
Vasconcellos, Karoline Michaëlis de (1851–1925)
Vassar, Queenie (1870–1960)
Vaughan, Janet (1899–1993)
Vaughan, Kate (c. 1852–1903)
Vautrin, Minnie (1886–1941)
Vaux, Clotilde de (1815–1846)
Vaz de Carvalho, Maria Amália (1847–1921)
Vazem, Ekaterina (1848–1937)
Vaz Ferreira, María Eugenia (1875–1924)
Veigel, Eva-Maria (1724–1822)
Velásquez, Loreta (1842–1897)
Veley, Margaret (1843–1887)
Vengerova, Zinaida (1867–1941)
Ventós i Cullell, Palmira (1862–1917)
Vera Constantinovna (1854–1912)
Verbitskaia, Anastasiia (1861–1928)
Verne, Mathilde (1865–1936)
Verney, Margaret Maria (1844–1930)
Vérone, Maria (1874–1938)
Vertua Gentile, Anna (1850–1927)
Veselitskaia, Lidiia Ivanovna (1857–1936)
Veselkova-Kil'shtet, M.G. (1861–1931)
Vestris, Lucia (1797–1856)
Vestris, Thérèse (1726–1808)
Vetsera, Marie (1871–1889)
Vezin, Jane Elizabeth (1827–1902)
Viardot, Louise (1841–1918)
Viardot, Pauline (1821–1910)
Vicario, Leona (1789–1842)
Victor, Frances (1826–1902)
Victor, Metta (1831–1885)
Victoria (1819–1901)
Victoria (1866–1929)
Victoria (1868–1935)
Victoria Adelaide (1840–1901)
Victoria Melita of Saxe-Coburg (1876–1936)
Victoria of Baden (1862–1930)
Victoria of Coburg (1786–1861)
Victoria of Hesse-Darmstadt (1863–1950)
Victoria of Mecklenburg-Strelitz (1878–1948)
Victoria of Saxe-Coburg (1822–1857)
Vidal, Mary Theresa (1815–1869 or 1873)
Viebig, Clara (1860–1952)
Vigée-Le Brun, Elisabeth (1755–1842)
Vilinska, Mariya (1834–1907)
Villard, Fanny Garrison (1844–1928)
Villers, Mme (fl. late 18th c.)
Villiers, Margaret Elizabeth Child- (1849–1945)
Villinger, Hermine (1849–1917)
Vincent, Mary Ann (1818–1887)
Vincent, Mother (1819–1892)
Vincent, Ruth (1877–1955)
Viola, Emilia Ferretti (1844–1929)
Vionnet, Madeleine (1876–1975)
Vitelli, Annie (c. 1837–?)
Vitorino, Virginia (1897–1967)
Vivanti, Annie (1868–1942)
Vivien, Renée (1877–1909)
Vögtlin, Marie (1845–1916)
Voigt-Diederichs, Helene (1875–1961)
Voilquin, Suzanne (1801–1877)
Vokes, May (d. 1957)
Volkonskaya, Maria (1805–1863)
Von Ertmann, Dorothea (1781–1849)
von Essen, Siri (1850–1912)
von Haynau, Edith (1884–1978)
von Meck, Nadezhda (1831–1894)
Vonnoh, Bessie Potter (1872–1955)
Vorse, Mary Heaton (1874–1966)
Voynich, Ethel (1864–1960)
Wagner, Cosima (1837–1930)
Wagner, Johanna (1826–1894)
Wagner, Minna (c. 1800–1866)
Waitaoro (c. 1848–1929)
Waite, Catherine (1829–1913)
Waitohi (?–1839)
Wakefield, Priscilla (1751–1832)
Wald, Lillian D. (1867–1940)
Waldegrave, Frances (1821–1879)
Waldmann, Maria (1842–1920)
Walewska, Marie (1786–1817)
Walford, Lucy (1845–1915)
Walker, Ada Overton (1870–1914)
Walker, Charlotte (1876–1958)
Walker, Edyth (1867–1950)
Walker, Ethel (1861–1951)
Walker, Lucy (1836–1916)
Walker, Madame C.J. (1867–1919)
Walker, Maggie Lena (1867–1934)
Walker, Mary Broadfoot (c. 1888–1974)
Walker, Mary Edwards (1832–1919)
Walkinshaw, Clementina (c. 1726–1802)
Wallace, Nellie (1870–1948)
Wallace, Zerelda G. (1817–1901)
Waller, Florence (1862–1912)
Wallis, Mary Ann Lake (1821–1910)
Wallis, Ruth Sawtell (1895–1978)
Wallwork, Elizabeth (1883–1969)
Walpole, Maria (1736–1807)
Walter, Cornelia Wells (1813–1898)
Walters, Catherine (1839–1920)
Walton, Florence (1891–1981)
Walworth, Ellen Hardin (1832–1915)
Warburg, Agnes (1872–1953)
Ward, Anne (c. 1825–1896)
Ward, Catharine Barnes (1851–1913)
Ward, Dorothy (1890–1987)
Ward, Elizabeth Stuart Phelps (1844–1911)
Ward, Geneviève (1838–1922)
Ward, Harriet (1808–c. 1860)
Ward, Henrietta (1832–1924)
Ward, Hortense (1872–1944)
Ward, Ida Caroline (1880–1949)
Ward, Maisie (1889–1975)
Ward, Mary (1827–1869)
Ward, Mrs. Humphry (1851–1920)
Warder, Ann Head (1758–1829)
Waring, Anna Letitia (1823–1910)
Warington, Katherine (1897–1993)
Warner, Anna Bartlett (1827–1915)
Warner, Estella Ford (1891–1974)
Warner, Susan Bogert (1819–1885)
Warren, Caroline Matilda (1785–1844)
Warren, Lavinia (1841–1919)
Warren, Mercy Otis (1728–1814)
Waser, Maria (1878–1939)
Washburn, Margaret Floy (1871–1939)
Washington, Josephine (1861–1949)
Washington, Margaret Murray (c. 1861–1925)
Washington, Martha (1731–1802)
Washington, Olivia Davidson (1854–1889)
Watkins, Gladys Elinor (1884–1939)
Watson, Edith (1861–1943)
Watson, Ellen (1861–1889)
Watson, Rosamund (1860–1911)
Watts Russell, Elizabeth Rose Rebecca (1833/34–1905)
Way, Amanda M. (1828–1914)
Weaver, Harriet Shaw (1876–1961)
Webb, Beatrice (1858–1943)
Webb, Catherine (1859–1947)
Webb, Elida (1895–1975)
Webb, Mary (1881–1927)
Weber, Helene (1881–1962)
Weber, Helene Marie (b. 1824)
Weber, Jeanne (1875–1910)
Webster, Augusta (1837–1894)
Webster, Clara Vestris (1821–1844)
Webster, Jean (1876–1916)
Webster, Kate (1849–1879)
Webster, Mary Morison (1894–1980)
Weed, Ella (1853–1894)
Weeks-Shaw, Clara S. (1857–1940)
Weir, Irene (1862–1944)
Weiss, Jeanne Daniloff (1868–1891)
Weiss, Josephine (1805–1852)
Welch, Georgiana (1792–1879)
Weldon, Barbara (1829/30–1882)
Wells, Ada (1863–1933)
Wells, Alice Stebbins (1873–1957)
Wells, Carolyn (1862–1942)
Wells, Charlotte Fowler (1814–1901)
Wells, Emmeline B. (1828–1921)
Wells, Kate Gannett (1838–1911)
Wells, Marguerite Milton (1872–1959)
Wells, Mary Ann (c. 1895–1971)
Wells-Barnett, Ida (1862–1931)
Welsh, Lilian (1858–1938)
Wendt, Julia Bracken (1871–1942)
Wenger, Lisa (1858–1941)
Wentscher, Dora (1883–1964)
Wentworth, Cecile de (c. 1853–1933)
Werbezirk, Gisela (1875–1956)
West, Jane (1758–1852)
Westbrook, Harriet (1795–1816)
Westley, Helen (1875–1942)
Weston, Agnes (1840–1918)
Weston, Jessie Edith (1867–1944)
Weston, Jessie Laidlay (1850–1928)
Wetherald, Ethelwyn (1857–1940)
Wetherill, Louisa Wade (1877–1945)
Wharton, Anne Hollingsworth (1845–1928)
Wharton, Edith (1862–1937)
Wheeler, Anna Doyle (1785–c. 1850)
Wheeler, Candace (1827–1923)
Wheeler, Ruth (1877–1948)
Wheelock, Lucy (1857–1946)
Whiffin, Blanche (1845–1936)
Whitaker, Mabel (1884–1976)
Whitcher, Frances Miriam Berry (1811–1852)
White, Alma Bridwell (1862–1946)
White, Anna (1831–1910)
White, Eartha M. (1876–1974)
White, Edna Noble (1879–1954)
White, Eliza Orne (1856–1947)
White, Ellen Gould (1827–1915)
White, Emily Louisa Merielina (1839–1936)
White, Helen Magill (1853–1944)
White, Margaret (c. 1888–1977)
White, Maude Valerie (1855–1937)
Whiteside, Jane (1855–1875)
Whiting, Lilian (1847–1942)
Whiting, Sarah F. (1847–1927)
Whitman, Narcissa (1808–1847)
Whitman, Sarah Helen (1803–1878)
Whitney, Adeline Dutton (1824–1906)
Whitney, Anne (1821–1915)

Whitney, Charlotte Anita (1867–1955)
Whitney, Gertrude Vanderbilt (1875–1942)
Whitney, Helen Hay (1876–1944)
Whitney, Mary Watson (1847–1921)
Whittelsey, Abigail Goodrich (1788–1858)
Whitty, May (1865–1948)
Wickham, Anna (1883–1947)
Widdemer, Margaret (1884–1978)
Wied, Martina (1882–1957)
Wieniawska, Irene Regine (1880–1932)
Wiggin, Kate Douglas (1856–1923)
Wiggins, Myra Albert (1869–1956)
Wijnberg, Rosalie (1887–1973)
Wilcox, Ella Wheeler (1850–1919)
Wilcox, Elsie Hart (1879–1954)
Wilde, Jane (1821–1896)
Wilder, Laura Ingalls (1867–1957)
Wildermuth, Ottilie (1817–1877)
Wilding, Cora (1888–1982)
Wilhelmina (1880–1962)
Wilhelmina of Prussia (1751–1820)
Wilhelmine (1747–1820)
Wilhelmine (1808–1891)
Wilhelmine of Baden (1788–1836)
Wilkinson, Jemima (1752–1819)
Willard, Emma Hart (1787–1870)
Willard, Frances E. (1839–1898)
Williams, Anna Maria (1839–1929)
Williams, Anna Wessels (1863–1954)
Williams, Eileen Hope (1884–1958)
Williams, Elizabeth Sprague (1869–1922)
Williams, Ethel (1863–1948)
Williams, Fannie Barrier (1855–1944)
Williams, Hattie (1872–1942)
Williams, Helen Maria (1762–1827)
Williams, Ivy (1877–1966)
Williams, Jane (c. 1801–1896)
Williams, Marianne (1793–1879)
Williams, Matilda Alice (1875–1973)
Williams, Sarah (1841–1868)
Williamson, Jessie Marguerite (c. 1855–1937)
Willing, Jennie Fowler (1834–1916)
Willits, Mary (1855–1902)
Willmott, Ellen (c. 1859–1934)
Wilman, Maria (1867–1957)
Wilson, Anne Glenny (1848–1930)
Wilson, Augusta Evans (1835–1909)
Wilson, Catherine (1842–1862)
Wilson, Charlotte (1854–1944)
Wilson, Edith Bolling (1872–1961)
Wilson, Ellen Axson (1860–1914)
Wilson, Fanny (1874–1958)
Wilson, Fiammetta Worthington (1864–1920)
Wilson, Harriet E. Adams (c. 1827–c. 1870)
Wilson, Harriette (1786–1855)
Wilson, Helen Ann (1793/94–1871)
Wilson, Helen Mary (1869–1957)
Winch, Hope (1895–1944)
Windeyer, Mary (1836–1912)
Winkworth, Catherine (1827–1878)
Winkworth, Susanna (1820–1884)
Winlock, Anna (1857–1904)
Winnemucca, Sarah (1844–1891)
Winser, Beatrice (1869–1947)
Winter, Alice Ames (1865–1944)
Winter, John Strange (1856–1911)
Wise, Louise Waterman (1874–1947)
Wiseman, Hilda Alexandra (1894–1982)
Wister, Sarah (1761–1804)
Wister, Sarah Butler (1835–1908)
Withington, Alfreda (1860–1951)
Withington, Eliza (1825–1877)
Witt, Henriette de (1829–1908)
Wittenmyer, Annie Turner (1827–1900)
Wittpenn, Caroline Stevens Alexander (1859–1932)
Wobeser, Caroline von (1769–1807)
Wohlers, Eliza (c. 1812–1891)
Wolfe, Catharine L. (1828–1887)
Wolfenstein, Martha (1869–1905)
Wollstein, Martha (1868–1939)
Wolstenholme-Elmy, Elizabeth (1834–1913)
Wolter, Charlotte (1834–1897)
Wolzogen, Karoline von (1763–1847)
Wood, Daisey (1877–?)
Wood, Edith Elmer (1871–1945)
Wood, Ellen Price (1814–1887)
Wood, Florence (c. 1854–1954)
Wood, Mary Elizabeth (1861–1931)
Wood, Matilda (1831–1915)
Wood, Sally Sayward Barrell Keating (1759–1855)
Wood, Susan (1836–1880)
Woodbridge, Louise Deshong (1848–1925)
Woodbury, Helen Sumner (1876–1933)
Woodhull, Victoria (1838–1927)
Woodrow, Nancy Mann Waddel (c. 1866–1935)
Woods, Katharine Pearson (1853–1923)
Woolley, Helen (1874–1947)
Woolley, Mary E. (1863–1947)
Woolman, Mary Schenck (1860–1940)
Woolsey, Abby Howland (1828–1893)
Woolsey, Georgeanna Muirson (1833–1906)
Woolsey, Jane Stuart (1830–1891)
Woolson, Abba Goold (1838–1921)
Woolson, Constance Fenimore (1840–1894)
Wootten, Bayard (1875–1959)
Wordsworth, Dorothy (1771–1855)
Wordsworth, Elizabeth (1840–1932)
Wörishöffer, Sophie (1838–1890)
Workman, Fanny (1859–1925)
Wormeley, Katharine Prescott (1830–1908)
Worms, Pamela Lee (d. 1852)
Wrede, Mathilda (1864–1928)
Wright, Frances (1795–1852)
Wright, Haidée (1868–1943)
Wright, Laura Maria (1809–1886)
Wright, Lucy (1760–1821)
Wright, Mabel Osgood (1859–1934)
Wright, Maginel (1881–1966)
Wright, Martha Coffin (1806–1875)
Wright, Sophie Bell (1866–1912)
Wyllie, Kate (d. 1913)
Wyndham, Mary (1861–1931)
Wynekoop, Alice (1870–1952)
Wyse Power, Jennie (1858–1941)
Xenia Alexandrovna (1876–1960)
Yaa Akyaa (c. 1837–c. 1921)
Yaa Asantewaa (c. 1850–1921)
Yakunchikova, Maria (1870–1901)
Yale, Caroline A. (1848–1933)
Yamada, Waka (1879–1956)
Yáñez, María Flora (1898–1982)
Yarros, Rachelle (1869–1946)
Yasui, Kono (1880–1971)
Yates, Elizabeth (1799–1860)
Yates, Elizabeth (c. 1844–1918)
Yates, Ngawini (1852/53?–1910)
Yavorska, Lydia (1869–1921)
Yaw, Ellen Beach (1868–1947)
Yearsley, Ann (1752–1806)
Yeats, Elizabeth (1868–1940)
Yeats, Lily (1866–1949)
Yeomans, Amelia (1842–1913)
Yessayan, Zabel (1878–1943)
Yohé, May (1869–1938)
Yoko (c. 1849–1906)
Yonge, Charlotte Mary (1823–1901)
Yosano, Akiko (1878–1942)
Yoshiko (1834–1907)
Yoshioka, Yayoi (1871–1959)
Young, Ann Eliza (b. 1844)
Young, Anne Sewell (1871–1961)
Young, E.H. (1880–1949)
Young, Ella (1867–1951)
Young, Ella Flagg (1845–1918)
Young, Grace Chisholm (1868–1944)
Young, Mary Sophie (1872–1919)
Young, Rida Johnson (1869–1926)
Young, Rose Maud (1865–1947)
Younger, Maud (1870–1936)
Younghusband, Adela Mary (1878–1969)
Zabriskie, Louise (1887–1957)
Zagorka, Maria Jurić (1873–1957)
Zakrzewska, Marie (1829–1902)
Zambelli, Carlotta (1875–1968)
Zamudio, Adela (1854–1928)
Zane, Betty (c. 1766–c. 1831)
Zanfretta, Francesca (1862–1952)
Zanfretta, Marietta (c. 1837–1898)
Zapolska, Gabriela (1857–1921)
Zasulich, Vera (1849–1919)
Zauditu (1876–1930)
Zeisler, Fannie Bloomfield (1863–1927)
Zelle, Margaretha (1876–1917)
Zeller, Eva (1923—)
Zetkin, Clara (1857–1933)
Zhadovskaia, Iuliia Valerianovna (1824–1883)
Zhukova, Maria (1804–1855)
Zillman, Bertha (d. 1893)
Zimbalist, Mary Louise Curtis (1876–1970)
Zimmermann, Agnes (1847–1925)
Zinóveva-Annibal, Lidiia Dmitrievna (1866–1907)
Zintkala Nuni (c. 1890–c. 1919)
Zitz, Kathinka (1801–1877)
Żmichowska, Narcyza (1819–1876)
Zorka of Montenegro (1864–1890)
Zuccari, Anna Radius (1846–1918)
Zucchi, Virginia (1849–1930)
Zur Mühlen, Hermynia (1883–1951)
Zwanziger, Anna (1760–1811)

20th Century

Aadland, Beverly (1943—)
Aakesson, Birgit (1908–2001)
Aaliyah (1979–2001)
Aarones, Ann Kristin (1973—)
Aarons, Ruth Hughes (1918–1980)
Aaronsohn, Sarah (1890–1917)
Abady, Josephine (c. 1950–2002)
Abaijah, Josephine (1942—)
Abakanowicz, Magdalena (1930—)
Abarbanell, Lina (1879–1963)
Abarca, Lydia (1951—)
Abassova, Tamilla (1982—)
Abayomi, Oyinkansola (1897–1990)
Abba, Marta (1900–1988)
Abbe, Kathryn (1919—)
Abbéma, Louise (1858–1927)
Abbott, Berenice (1898–1991)
Abbott, Bessie (d. 1937)
Abbott, Diahnne (1945—)
Abbott, Diane (1953—)
Abbott, Edith (1876–1957)
Abbott, Elenore Plaisted (1873–1935)
Abbott, Emma (1850–1891)
Abbott, Evelyn (1843–1901)
Abbott, Grace (1878–1939)
Abbott, Lorraine (1937—)
Abbott, Margaret (1878–1955)
Abbott, Maude (1869–1940)
Abbott, Merriel (c. 1893–1977)
Abbott, Mother (1846–1934)
Abboud, Simonne (c. 1930—)
Abdallah, Nia (1984—)
Abdel-Aziz, Malak (1923—)
Abdellah, Faye Glenn (1919—)
Abdel Rahman, Aisha (1913–1998)
Abdo, Reema (1963—)
Abegg, Elisabeth (1882–1974)
Abel, Annie Heloise (1873–1947)
Abel, Hazel (1888–1966)
Abel, Irene (1953—)
Abel, Theodora (1899–1998)
Abercrombie, M.L.J. (1909–1984)
Aberdeen, Ishbel Maria Gordon, Lady (1857–1939)
Abernethy, Moira (1939—)
Abiertas, Josepha (1894–1929)
Abraham, Constance Palgrave (1864–1942)
Abrahamowitsch, Ruth (1907–1974)
Abrahams, Doris Cole (1925—)
Abrahams, Ottilie Grete (1937—)
Abramova, Anastasia (1902—)
Abramova, Nelli (1940—)
Abrashitova, Elena (1974—)
Abrosimova, Svetlana (1980—)
Abzug, Bella (1920–1998)
Ace, Jane (1905–1974)
Acedo, Carmen (1975—)
Acheson, Anne Crawford (1882–1962)
Acheson, Carrie (1934—)
Achkina, Rita (fl. 1968)
Achurch, Janet (1864–1916)
Acker, Jean (1893–1978)
Acker, Kathy (1943–1997)
Ackerman, Val (1959—)
Ackermann, Rosemarie (1952—)
Ackland, Valentine (1906–1969)
Ackté, Aino (1876–1944)
Acosta de Samper, Soledad (1833–1913)

Acquanetta (1921–2004)
Acuña, Dora (fl. 1940s)
Adair, Jean (1872–1953)
Adair, Virginia Hamilton (1913–2004)
Adam, Juliette la Messine (1836–1936)
Adam, Madge (1912–2001)
Adamek, Donna (1957—)
Adamova, Adela (1927—)
Adams, Adrienne (1906–2002)
Adams, Alice (1926–1999)
Adams, Annette (1877–1956)
Adams, Carolyn (1943—)
Adams, Charity (1917–2002)
Adams, Claire (1898–1978)
Adams, Clara (born c. 1899)
Adams, Constance (1874–1960)
Adams, Diana (1927–1993)
Adams, Dorothy (1900–1988)
Adams, Edie (1927—)
Adams, Evangeline Smith (1873–1932)
Adams, Fae Margaret (1918—)
Adams, Glenda (1939—)
Adams, Harriet Chalmers (1875–1937)
Adams, Harriet Stratemeyer (c. 1893–1982)
Adams, Ida (c. 1888–1960)
Adams, Irene (1947—)
Adams, Jane (1921—)
Adams, Julie (1926—)
Adams, Kathryn (1893–1959)
Adams, Léonie Fuller (1899–1988)
Adams, Lynn (c. 1958—)
Adams, Mary Grace (1898–1984)
Adams, Maude (1872–1953)
Adams, Millicent (1942—)
Adams, Miriam (1907—)
Adams, Nancy M. (1926—)
Adams, Sharon Sites (c. 1930—)
Adams, Truda (1890–1958)
Adam Smith, Janet (1905–1999)
Adam-Smith, Patsy (1924–2001)
Adamson, Catherine (1868–1925)
Adamson, Joy (1910–1980)
Adato, Perry Miller
Adcock, Fleur (1934—)
Addams, Dawn (1930–1985)
Addams, Jane (1860–1935)
Addison, Agnes (c. 1841–1903)
Addison, Carlotta (1849–1914)
Addor, Ady (c. 1935—)
Adelaide (c. 1884–1959)
Adelaide of Hohenlohe-Langenburg (1835–1900)
Adelaide of Saxe-Meiningen (1891–1971)
Adelaide of Schaumburg (1875–1971)
Adelgunde of Bavaria (1823–1914)
Adelheid (1831–1909)
Adie, Kate (1945—)
Adivar, Halide Edib (c. 1884–1964)
Adler, Alexandra (1901–2001)
Adler, C.S. (1932—)
Adler, Celia (1890–1979)
Adler, Emma (1858–1935)
Adler, Frances (d. 1964)
Adler, Julia (1897–1995)
Adler, Margarete (1896–?)
Adler, Polly (1899–1962)
Adler, Renata (1938—)
Adler, Sara (1858–1953)
Adler, Stella (1902–1993)
Adler, Valentine (1898–1942)
Adlerstrahle, Maertha (1868–1956)
Adnan, Etel (1925—)
Adolf, Helen (1895–1998)
Adorée, Renée (1898–1933)
Adret, Françoise (1920—)
Adrian, Iris (1912–1994)
Adrienne, Jean (b. 1905)
Aebi, Tania (1966—)
Afolabi, Bisi
Afrasiloaia, Felicia (1954—)
Agache, Lavinia (1966—)
Agaoglu, Adalet (1929—)
Agar, Eileen (1899–1991)
Agassiz, Elizabeth Cary (1822–1907)
Agate, May (1892–1960)
Aghdashloo, Shohreh (1952—)
Agnelli, Susanna (1922—)
Agnes, Lore (1876–1953)
Agoglia, Esmeralda (1926—)
Agsteribbe, Estella (1909–1943)
Aguero, Taimaris (1977—)
Aguirre, Mirta (1912—)
Agustini, Delmira (1886–1914)
Ahearn, Theresa (1951–2000)
Ahern, Catherine Ita (1915—)
Ahern, Kathy (1949–1996)
Ahern, Lizzie (1877–1969)
Ahern, Mary Eileen (1860–1938
Ahern, Nuala (1949—)
Ahlander, Thecla (1855–1925)
Ahlberg, Janet (1944–1994)
Ahlers, Anny (1906–1933)
Ahmad, Fathiyya (c. 1898–1975)
Ahmann-Leighton, Crissy (1970—)
Ahmanson, Caroline (1918–2005)
Ahrenholz, Brigitte (1952—)
Ahrens, Marlene (1933—)
Ahrweiler, Hélène (1916—)
Aicega, Magdalena (1973—)
Aichinger, Ilse (1921—)
Aidoo, Ama Ata (1942—)
Aihara, Toshiko (1939—)
Aiken, Joan (1924–2004)
Aiken, Kimberly (c. 1975—)
Aikens, Charlotte (c. 1868–1949)
Aimée, Anouk (1932—)
Ainardi, Sylviane H. (1947—)
Aindili, Eirini (1983—)
Ainsworth, Ruth (1908–1984)
Airy, Anna (1882–1964)
Aitchison, Helen (1881–?)
Aitken, Janet Gladys (1908–1988)
Aitken, Jessie (1867–1934)
Aitkin, Yvonne (1911—)
Ajakaiye, Deborah Enilo (c. 1940—)
Ajunwa, Chioma (1970—)
Ajzenberg-Selove, Fay (1926—)
Aked, Muriel (1887–1955)
Akeley, Delia J. (1875–1970)
Akeley, Mary Jobe (1878–1966)
Akerman, Chantal (1950—)
Akers, Dolly Smith (1901–1986)
Akers, Michelle (1966—)
Akesson, Sonja (1926–1977)
Akhaminova, Yelena (1961—)
Akhatova, Albina (1976—)
Akhmadulina, Bella (1937—)
Akhmatova, Anna (1889–1966)
Akhmerova, Leylya (1957—)
Akhurst, Daphne (1903–1933)
Akimoto, Matsuyo (1911—)
Akin, Gülten (1933—)
Akin, Susan (c. 1964—)
Akins, Zoe (1886–1958)
Akiyoshi, Toshiko (1929—)
Akobia, Marina (1975—)
Akselrod, Liubo (1868–1946)
Aksyonova-Shapovalova, Lyudmila (1947—)
Alabaster, Ann O'Connor (1842–1915)
Alain, Marie-Claire (1926—)
Alakija, Aduke (1921—)
Alarie, Pierrette (1921—)
Alba, Nanina (1915–1968)
Albanese, Licia (1913—)
Albanesi, Meggie (1899–1923)
Albani, Emma (c. 1847–1930)
Alberghetti, Anna Maria (1936—)
Albers, Anni (1899–1994)
Albert, Caterina (1869–1966)
Albertine, Viv (1955—)
Albertson, Lillian (1881–1962)
Albertson, Mabel (1901–1982)
Albin-Guillot, Laure (c. 1880–1962)
Albrecht, Angele (1942—)
Albrecht, Bertie (?–1943)
Albrecht, Sylvia (1962—)
Albrecht-Loretan, Brigitte (1970—)
Albright, Lola (1925—)
Albright, Madeleine (1937—)
Albright, Tenley (1935—)
Alcantara, Dolores Jimenez (1909–1999)
Alcock, Nora (1874–1972)
Alcock, Vivien (1924–2003)
Alcorta, Gloria (1915—)
Alcott, Amy (1956—)
Alda, Frances (1879–1952)
Aldecoa, Josefina R. (1926—)
Alden, Cynthia Westover (1862–1931)
Alden, Hortense (1903–1999)
Alden, Isabella (1841–1930)
Alden, Mary (1883–1946)
Aldis, Dorothy (1896–1966)
Aldis, Mary (1872–1949)
Aldous, Lucette (1938—)
Aldredge, Theoni V. (1932—)
Aldrich, Anne Reeve (1866–1892)
Aldrich, Bess Streeter (1881–1954)
Aldrich-Blake, Louisa (1865–1925)
Aleandro, Norma (1936—)
Alegría, Claribel (1924—)
Aleksandrovna, Vera (1895–1966)
Alekseeva, Lidiya (1909—)
Alekseyeva, Galina (1946—)
Alekseyeva-Kreft, Galina (1950—)
Alenikoff, Frances (1920—)
Alexander, Annie Montague (1867–1949)
Alexander, Buffy (c. 1977—)
Alexander, Claire (1898–1927)
Alexander, Dorothy (1904–1986)
Alexander, Florence (1904–1993)
Alexander, Francesca (1837–1917)
Alexander, Hattie (1901–1968)
Alexander, Jane (1939—)
Alexander, Janet (d. 1961)
Alexander, Jessie (1876–1962)
Alexander, Julie (1938–2003)
Alexander, Katherine (1898–1981)
Alexander, Leni (1924—)
Alexander, Lisa (1968—)
Alexander, Lucy Maclay (fl. 1950s)
Alexander, Muriel (1898–1975)
Alexander, Sadie (1898–1989)
Alexander, Wendy
Alexandra (1921–1993)
Alexandra Feodorovna (1872–1918)
Alexandra Guelph (1882–1963)
Alexandra of Denmark (1844–1925)
Alexandra of Kent (1936—)
Alexandra of Oldenburg (1838–1900)
Alexandra of Saxe-Altenburg (1830–1911)
Alexandra Saxe-Coburg (1878–1942)
Alexandra Victoria (1891–1959)
Alexandra Victoria of Schleswig-Holstein (1887–1957)
Alexandrina of Baden (1820–1904)
Alexandrina of Mecklenburg-Schwerin (1879–1952)
Alexiou, Elli (1894–1988)
Alf, Fé (c. 1910—)
Alfeyeva, Lidiya (1946—)
Alfon, Estrella (1917–1982)
Algeranova, Claudie (1924—)
Ali, Aruna Asaf (c. 1909–1996)
Aliberty, Soteria (1847–1929)
Alice of Athlone (1883–1981)
Alice of Battenberg (1885–1969)
Aliger, Margarita Iosifovna (1915–1992)
Aline Sitoe (c. 1920–1944)
Aliye, Fatima (1862–1936)
Ali-Zadeh, Franghiz (1947—)
Alkhateeb, Sharifa (1946–2004)
Allagulova, Yulia
Allan, Elizabeth (1908–1990)
Allan, Maude (1883–1956)
Allan-Shetter, Liz (1947—)
Allbritton, Louise (1920–1979)
Allbut, Barbara (1940—)
Allbut, Phyllis (1942—)
Allen, Adrianne (1907–1993)
Allen, Betty (1936—)
Allen, Betty Molesworth (1913–2002)
Allen, Charlotte Vale (1941—)
Allen, Debbie (1950—)
Allen, Dede (1923—)
Allen, Elizabeth Chase (1832–1911)
Allen, Florence Ellinwood (1884–1966)
Allen, Frances S. (1854–1941)
Allen, Gracie (1902–1964)
Allen, Jay Presson (1922–2006)
Allen, Kate (1974—)

Allen, Katherine (1970—)
Allen, Margaret (1906–1949)
Allen, Mary E. (1858–1941)
Allen, Maryon (1925—)
Allen, Mary Sophia (1878–1964)
Allen, Monique (1971—)
Allen, Pamela Kay (1934—)
Allen, Paula Gunn (1939—)
Allen, Rita (d. 1968)
Allen, Rosalie (1924–2003)
Allen, Sandra (1978—)
Allen, Sarita (1954—)
Allen, Susan Westford (c. 1865–1944)
Allen, Tori (1988—)
Allen, Vera (1897–1987)
Allen, Viola (1867–1948)
Allenby, Kate (1974—)
Allenby, Peggy (1905–1967)
Allende, Isabel (1942—)
Allfrey, Phyllis Shand (1915–1986)
Allgood, Sara (1883–1950)
Alliluyeva, Svetlana (1926—)
Alliluyeva-Stalin, Nadezhda (1901–1932)
Allingham, Helen Patterson (1848–1926)
Allingham, Margery (1904–1966)
Allison, Fran (1907–1989)
Allison, May (1890–1989)
Allitt, Beverley Gail (1969—)
Allred, Gloria (1941—)
Allucci, Carmela (1970—)
Allwyn, Astrid (1905–1978)
Allyson, June (1917—)
Almedingen, E.M. (1898–1971)
Almeida, Julia Lopes de (1862–1934)
Almeida Garrett, Teresa (1953—)
Almog, Ruth (1936—)
Almon, Baylee (1994–1995)
Almond, Linda (1881–1987)
Almy, Millie (1915–2001)
Aloni, Shulamit (1931—)
Alonso, Alicia (1921—)
Alonso, Dora (1910–2001)
Alós, Concha (1922—)
Alozie, Glory (1977—)
Alpar, Gitta (1900–1991)
Alshammar, Therese (1977—)
Alsop, Susan Mary (d. 2004)
Alston, Barbara (1945—)
Altwegg, Jeanette (1930—)
Aluli, Irmgard (c. 1912–2001)
Alupei, Angela (1972—)
Alvarado, Elvia (1938—)
Alvares, Ana (1965—)
Alvarez, Anita (1920—)
Alvarez, Carmen (c. 1936—)
Alvarez, Lili de (1905—)
Alvarez de Toledo, Luisa Isabel (1936—)
Alvarez Rios, Maria (1919—)
Alves Lima, Daniela (1984—)
Amachree, Mactabene (1978—)
Amália, Narcisa (1852–1924)
Amanar, Simona (1979—)
Amanpour, Christiane (1958—)
Amantova, Ingrida
Amathila, Libertine Appolus (1940—)
Amati, Olga (1924—)
Amato, Serena (1974—)
Amaya, Carmen (1913–1963)
Ambrose, Alice (1906–2001)
Ambrosetti, Bianca (1914–1929)
Ambrosie, Christie (1976—)
Ameling, Elly (1938—)
America^3 Team (1995—)
Ames, Adrienne (1907–1947)
Ames, Blanche (1878–1969)
Ames, Fanny Baker (1840–1931)
Ames, Frances (1920–2002)
Ames, Jessie Daniel (1883–1972)
Ames, Rosemary (1906–1988)
Amico, Leah (1974—)
Amiel, Josette (1930—)
Amin, Adibah (1936—)
Amini-Hudson, Johari (1935—)
Ammers-Küller, Johanna van (1884–1966)
Amohau, Merekotia (1898–1978)
Amoore, Judith Pollock (1940—)
Amor, Guadalupe (1920—)
Amos, Tori (1963—)
Amosova, Zinaida (fl. 1976)
Amphlett, Christina (c. 1960—)
Amrane, Djamila (1939—)
Amritanandamayi, Mata (1953—)
Amrouche, Fadhma Mansour (1882–1967)
Amrouche, Marie-Louise (1913–1976)
Amundrud, Gail (1957—)
Anable, Gloria Hollister (1903–1988)
Anagnostaki, Loula (1940—)
Ananko, Tatyana (1984—)
Anastasi, Anne (1908–2001)
Anastasia (1901–1918)
Anastasia Petrovitch-Njegos (1868–1935)
Anastasovski, Svetlana (1961—)
Ancher, Anna (1859–1935)
Anchutina, Leda (1915–1989)
Anckarsvard, Karin (1915–1969)
Ancker-Johnson, Betsy (1927—)
Andam, Aba A. Bentil (c. 1960—)
Anders, Beth (1951—)
Anders, Luana (1938–1996)
Anders, Merry (1932—)
Andersen, Anja Jul (1969—)
Andersen, Astrid Hjertenaes (1915–1985)
Andersen, Camilla (1973—)
Andersen, Catherine Ann (1870–1957)
Andersen, Dorothy Hansine (1901–1963)
Andersen, Greta (1927—)
Andersen, Kjerstin (1958—)
Andersen, Kristine (1976—)
Andersen, Lale (1905–1972)
Andersen, Linda (1969—)
Andersen, Lisa (1969—)
Andersen, Roxanne (1912–2002)
Andersen-Scheiss, Gabriela (1945—)
Anderson, Anna (1902–1984)
Anderson, Anne (1874–1930)
Anderson, Barbara (1926—)
Anderson, Beth (1950—)
Anderson, Bette B. (c. 1929—)
Anderson, Caroline Still (1848–1919)
Anderson, Chamelle (1981—)
Anderson, Claire (1895–1964)
Anderson, Claire (fl. 1940s)
Anderson, Doris (1921—)
Anderson, Elda E. (1899–1961)
Anderson, Elizabeth Garrett (1836–1917)
Anderson, Elizabeth Milbank (1850–1921)
Anderson, Ellen Alice (1882–1978)
Anderson, Erica (1914–1976)
Anderson, Ernestine (1928—)
Anderson, Ethel Mason (1883–1958)
Anderson, Eugenie Moore (1909–1997)
Anderson, Evelyn (1907–1994)
Anderson, Evelyn N. (1909–1977)
Anderson, Isabel Perkins (1876–1948)
Anderson, Ivie (1904–1949)
Anderson, Janet (1949—)
Anderson, Janet (1956—)
Anderson, Jessica (1916—)
Anderson, Jodi (1957—)
Anderson, Judith (1898–1992)
Anderson, Katherine (1944—)
Anderson, Laurie (1947—)
Anderson, Lea (1959—)
Anderson, Margaret (1900–1997)
Anderson, Margaret Carolyn (1886–1973)
Anderson, Marian (1897–1993)
Anderson, Mary (1859–1940)
Anderson, Mary (1872–1964)
Anderson, Mary Patricia (1887–1966)
Anderson, Maybanke (1845–1927)
Anderson, Mignon (1892–1983)
Anderson, Regina M. (1900–1993)
Anderson, Robin (1948–2002)
Anderson-Ivantzova, Elizabeth (c. 1893–1973)
Anderson-Scott, Carol (1935–2003)
Andersson, Agneta (1961—)
Andersson, Bibi (1935—)
Andersson, Gerd (1932—)
Andersson, Harriet (1932—)
Anderton, Elizabeth (1938—)
Andics, Erzsebet (1902–1986)
Anding, Carola (1960—)
Andjaparidze, Veriko (1900–1987)
Ando, Misako (1971—)
Andra, Fern (1893–1974)
Andrade, Leny (1943—)
Andre, Gwili (1908–1959)
André, Valerie (1922—)
Andreae, Felicity (1914—)
Andreas-Salomé, Lou (1861–1937)
Andreassen, Gunn Margit (1973—)
Andree, Elfrida (1841–1929)
Andreeva, Maria Fedorovna (1868–1953)
Andreeva-Babakhan, Anna Misaakovna (1923—)
Andresen, Sophia de Mello Breyner (1919–2004)
Andress, Ursula (1936—)
Andreu, Blanca (1959—)
Andrew, Janice (1943—)
Andrews, Ann (1890–1986)
Andrews, Barbara (c. 1934–1978)
Andrews, Doris (1920–2003)
Andrews, Elizabeth Bullock (1911–2002)
Andrews, Eliza Frances (1840–1931)
Andrews, Elsie Euphemia (1888–1948)
Andrews, Fannie Fern (1867–1950)
Andrews, Julie (1935—)
Andrews, LaVerne (1911–1967)
Andrews, Lois (1924–1968)
Andrews, Mary Raymond (1860–1936)
Andrews, Maxene (1916–1995)
Andrews, Michelle (1971—)
Andrews, Nancy (1924–1989)
Andrews, Patti (1918—)
Andrews, Theresa (1962—)
Andreyuk, Yelena (1958—)
Andriesse, Emmy (1914–1953)
Andrus, Ethel Percy (1884–1967)
Andujar, Claudia (1931—)
Angel, Albalucía (1939—)
Angel, Heather (1909–1986)
Angeli, Pier (1932–1971)
Angelica, Mother (1923—)
Angelilli, Roberta (1965—)
Angelopoulos-Daskalaki, Gianna (1955—)
Angelou, Maya (1928—)
Angelus, Muriel (1909–2004)
Angerer, Nadine (1978—)
Angers, Félicité (1845–1924)
Anghelaki-Rooke, Katerina (1939—)
Anglada, Maria Angels (1930–1999)
Anglin, Margaret (1876–1958)
Anguissola, Lucia (c. 1536–1565)
Angus, Dorothy (1891–1979)
Angus, Rita (1908–1970)
Angyal, Eva (1955—)
Anichkova, Anna (1868–1935)
Anikeeva, Ekaterina (1965—)
Anisimova, Natalya (1960—)
Anisimova, Nina (1909—)
Anisimova, Tatyana (1949—)
Anisimova, Vera (1952—)
Anissina, Marina (1975—)
Anitas, Herta (1967—)
Anke, Hannelore (1957—)
Anker, Nini Roll (1873–1942)
Anker-Doedens, Alida van der (1922—)
Ankers, Evelyn (1918–1985)
Annabella (1909–1996)
Annabelle (1878–1961)
Anna Maria Theresa (1879–1961)
Annan, Alyson (1973—)
Anne, Princess (1950—)
Anne-Marie Oldenburg (1946—)
Annenkova, Julia (c. 1898–c. 1938)
Anne of Bourbon-Parma (1923—)
Annis, Francesca (1944—)
Ann-Margret (1941—)
Anno, Noriko (1976—)
An Sang-Mi
Anscombe, G.E.M. (1919–2001)
Anselmi, Tina (1927—)
Anson, Laura (1892–1968)
Anstei, Olga Nikolaevna (1912–1985)
Anstice, Sophia (1849–1926)
Antal, Dana (1977—)
Antarjanam, Lalitambika (1909–1987)
Anthony, Bessie (1880–1912)
Anthony, Katharine Susan (1877–1965)

Anthony, Mary (c. 1920—)
Anthony, Susan B. (1820–1906)
Anthony, Susan B., II (1916–1991)
Antin, Mary (1881–1949)
Antoinette of Luxemburg (1899–1954)
Antolin, Jeanette (1981—)
Antonakakis, Suzana (1935—)
Antonelli, Laura (1941—)
Antonia of Portugal (1845–1913)
Antoniska, Mariela (1975—)
Antonova, Elena (1974–)
Antonova, Yelena (1952—)
Antony, Hilda (1896–?)
Antrim, Angela (1911–1984)
Anttila, S. Inkeri (1916—)
Antyukh, Natalia (1981—)
Anzaldúa, Gloria E. (1942–2004)
An Zhongxin (Fl. 1996)
Aoki, Mayumi (1953—)
Aoki, Tsuru (1892–1961)
Aoki, Yayoi (1927—)
Aouchal, Leila (1937—)
Apel, Katrin (1973—)
Apgar, Virginia (1909–1974)
Apinée, Irena (c. 1930—)
Aposteanu, Angelica (1954—)
Apostol, Chira (1960—)
Apostoloy, Electra (1911–1944)
Appel, Anna (1888–1963)
Appel, Gabriele (1958—)
Appeldoorn, Tessa (1973—)
Applebee, Constance (1873–1981)
Appleby, Dorothy (1906–1990)
Appleton, Honor C. (1879–1951)
Appleton, Jean (1911–2003)
Appleyard, Beatrice (1918–1994)
Apponyi, Geraldine (1915–2002)
Apréleva, Elena Ivanovna (1846–1923)
Aptheker, Bettina (1944—)
Aquash, Anna Mae (1945–1976)
Aquino, Corazon (1933—)
Aquino, Melchora (1812–1919)
Arad, Yael (1967—)
Aragon, Jesusita (1908—)
Arakida, Yuko (1954—)
Arango, Débora (1907—)
Aranyi, Jelly d' (1895–1966)
Araujo, Alexandra (1972—)
Araúz, Blanca (d. 1933)
Araz, Nezihe (1922—)
Arba-Puscatu, Rodica (1962—)
Arbatova, Mia (c. 1910—)
Arbenina, Stella (1885–1976)
Arber, Agnes (1879–1960)
Arbus, Diane (1923–1971)
Arbuthnot, May Hill (1884–1969)
Arbutina, Andjelija (1967—)
Arcain, Janeth (1969—)
Arceo, Liwayway (1924—)
Archer, Caroline Lilian (1922–1978)
Archer, Maria (1905–1982)
Archer, Robyn (1948—)
Archer, Violet Balestreri (1913–2000)
Archer-Gilligan, Amy (1869–1928)
Arden, Daphne (1941—)
Arden, Elizabeth (1878–1966)
Arden, Eve (1907–1990)
Arden, Toni (fl. 1950s)
Arderiu, Clementina (1899–1976)
Ardzhannikova, Lyudmila (1958—)
Arenal, Julie (1942—)
Arendsee, Martha (1885–1953)
Arendt, Gisela (1918–1969)
Arendt, Hannah (1906–1975)
Aresty, Esther B. (1908–2000)
Aretz, Isabel (1909—)
Argerich, Martha (1941—)
Argiriadou, Chryssoula (1901–1998)
Argyle, Pearl (1910–1947)
Ari, Carina (1897–1970)
Arimori, Yuko (1966—)
Ariyoshi, Sawako (1931–1984)
Arkhipova, Anna (1973—)
Arletty (1898–1992)
Arlington, Lizzie (1876–1917)
Arliss, Florence (1871–1950)
Armand, Inessa (1874–1920)
Armasescu, Mihaela (1963—)
Armatrading, Joan (1947—)
Armbrust, Barbara (1963—)
Armbrust, Roma (1927–2003)
Armen, Kay (1920—)
Armen, Margaret (1921–2003)
Armer, Laura Adams (1874–1963)
Armitage, Ella (1841–1931)
Armitage, Heather (1933—)
Armitage, Karole (1954—)
Armitage, Pauline
Armitage, Rachelina Hepburn (1873–1955)
Armour, Mary Nicol Neill (1902–2000)
Armour, Toby (1936—)
Armstead, Izora (1942–2004)
Armstrong, Anne L. (1927—)
Armstrong, Debbie (1963—)
Armstrong, Eileen (1894–1981)
Armstrong, Gillian (1950—)
Armstrong, Hilary (1945—)
Armstrong, Jenny (1970—)
Armstrong, Lil Hardin (1898–1971)
Armstrong, Margaret Neilson (1867–1944)
Armstrong, Penny (1946—)
Armstrong-Jones, Sarah (1964—)
Arnaud, Yvonne (1892–1958)
Arndt, Hermina (1885–1926)
Arndt, Judith (1976—)
Arne, Sigrid (1894–1973)
Arnell, Amy (1919—)
Arnesen, Liv (1953—)
Arnim, Elizabeth von (1866–1941)
Arnold, Becky (1936—)
Arnold, Bené (1953—)
Arnold, Dorothy (1917–1984)
Arnold, Emmy (1884–1980)
Arnold, Eve (1913—)
Arnold, June (1926–1982)
Arnold, Mary Beth (1981—)
Arnothy, Christine (1930—)
Arnoul, Françoise (1931—)
Arnow, Harriette Simpson (1908–1986)
Arnst, Bobbe (1903–1980)
Arnstein, Margaret (1904–1972)
Arol, Victoria Yar (1948—)
Aron, Geraldine (1941—)
Arova, Sonia (1927–2001)
Arquimbau, Rosa Maria (1910—)
Arron, Christine (1973—)
Arrondo, Ines (1977—)
Arroyo, Gloria Macapagal (1947—)
Arroyo, Martina (1935—)
Arsenault, Samantha (1981—)
Arsiennieva, Natalia (1903—)
Artamonova, Evguenia (1975—)
Arteshina, Olga (1982—)
Arthur, Bea (1923—)
Arthur, Charthel (1946—)
Arthur, Daphne (1925—)
Arthur, Jean (1900–1991)
Arthur, Julia (1869–1950)
Artôt, Désirée (1835–1907)
Artyukhina, Aleksandra (1889–1969)
Arundale, Sybil (1882–1965)
Arvanitaki, Angélique (1901–1983)
Arvelo Larriva, Enriqueta (1886–1963)
Arvidson, Linda (1884–1949)
Arzhannikova, Tatiana (1964—)
Arzner, Dorothy (1897–1979)
Asakawa, Hitomi (1948)
Asakawa, Takako (1938—)
Asanova, Dinara (1942–1985)
Asensio, Manola (1946—)
Ash, Maie (b. 1888)
Ash, Mary Kay (1918–2001)
Ashbrook, Jean (1934—)
Ashcraft, Juanita (1921—2000)
Ashcroft, Peggy (1907–1991)
Asher, Elise (c. 1912–2004)
Asherson, Renée (1915—)
Ashford, Daisy (1881–1972)
Ashford, Evelyn (1957—)
Ashley, Elizabeth (1939—)
Ashley, Laura (1925–1985)
Ashley, Merrill (1950—)
Ashley, Pauline (1932–2003)
Ashrawi, Hanan (1946—)
Ashton, Helen (1891–1958)
Ashton-Warner, Sylvia (1908–1984)
Ashumova, Irada (1958—)
Ashur, Radwa (1946—)
Ashwell, Lena (1872–1957)
Ashworth, Jeanne (1938—)
Asilian, Dimitra (1972—)
Askew, Sarah B. (c. 1863–1942)
Asp, Anna (1946—)
Aspinall, Nan Jane (fl. 1911)
Asquith, Cynthia (1887–1960)
Asquith, Margot Tennant (1864–1945)
Asquith, Ruby (c. 1910—)
Asselin, Marie-Claude
Ast, Pat (1941–2001)
Astafei, Galina (1968—)
Astafieva, Serafima (1876–1934)
Astaire, Adele (1898–1981)
Astakhova, Polina (1936—)
Astley, Thea (1925–2004)
Astor, Brooke (b. 1902)
Astor, Caroline Schermerhorn (1830–1908)
Astor, Gertrude (1887–1977)
Astor, Madeleine Talmadge (c. 1893–1940)
Astor, Mary (1906–1987)
Astor, Nancy Witcher (1879–1964)
Astorga, Nora (1949–1988)
Astrid of Sweden (1905–1935)
Astrologes, Maria (1951—)
Astrup, Heidi (1972—)
Aszkielowiczowna, Halina (1947—)
Atencia, Maria Victoria (1931—)
Atherton, Candy (1955—)
Atherton, Gertrude (1857–1948)
Atkins, Babs (1917–2004)
Atkins, Charlotte (1950—)
Atkins, Eileen (1934—)
Atkins, Evelyn (c. 1910–1997)
Atkins, Gillian (1963—)
Atkins, Susan (1948—)
Atkins, Vera (c. 1908–2000)
Atkinson, Eleanor (1863–1942)
Atkinson, Jane Maria (1824–1914)
Atkinson, Juliette P. (1873–1944)
Atkinson, Lily May (1866–1921)
Atkinson, Ti-Grace (1939—)
Atlas, Consuelo (1944–1979)
Atler, Vanessa (1982—)
Attar, Samar (1940—)
Attwell, Mabel Lucie (1879–1964)
Attwood, Julie Maree (1957—)
Attwooll, Elspeth (1943—)
Atwater, Edith (1911–1986)
Atwater, Helen (1876–1947)
Atwell, Winifred (1914–1983)
Atwood, Donna (c. 1923—)
Atwood, Margaret (1939—)
Atwood, Susan (1953—)
Aubert, Mary Joseph (1835–1926)
Aubrac, Lucie (1912—)
Aubrey, Madge (1902–1970)
Aubry, Cécile (1928—)
Auch, Susan (1966—)
Audina, Mia (1979—)
Audley, Maxine (1923–1992)
Audoux, Marguerite (1863–1937)
Audran, Stéphane (1932—)
Audry, Jacqueline (1908–1977)
Auel, Jean (1936—)
Auer, Johanna (1950—)
Auer, Judith (1905–1944)
Auerbach, Beatrice Fox (1887–1968)
Auerbach, Charlotte (1899–1994)
Auerbach, Edith (1903—)
Auerbach, Ellen (1906–2004)
Auerswald, Ingrid (1957—)
Aufles, Inger
Augarde, Adrienne (d. 1913)
Augarde, Amy (1868–1959)
Augspurg, Anita (1857–1943)
August, Bonnie (1947–2003)
Augusta, Mlle (1806–1901)
Augusta Guelph (1822–1916)
Augustat, Elise (1889–1940)

Augusta Victoria (1890–1966)
Augustesen, Susanne (1956—)
Augustine, Rose (1910–2003)
Aulenti, Gae (1927—)
Ault, Marie (1870–1951)
Aung San Suu Kyi (1945—)
Aunli, Berit
Auriol, Jacqueline (1917–2000)
Auroi, Danielle (1944—)
Aury, Dominique (1907–1998)
Aus der Ohe, Adele (1864–1937)
Ausländer, Rose (1901–1988)
Aussem, Cilly (1909–1963)
Austen, Alice (1866–1952)
Austen, Winifred (1876–1964)
Austin, Debbie (1948—)
Austin, Debra (1955—)
Austin, Lovie (1887–1972)
Austin, Margaret (1933—)
Austin, Mary Hunter (1868–1934)
Austin, Tracy (1962—)
Austral, Florence (1894–1968)
Avedon, Barbara Hammer (1930–1994)
Averina, Tatiana (1950–2001)
Averkova, Oksana (1970—)
Avery, Martha (1851–1929)
Avery, Mary Ellen (1927—)
Avery, Rachel G. (1858–1919)
Aves, Isabel Annie (1887–1938)
Avilés Perea, María Antonia
Avilova, Lidya (c. 1864–1943)
Avison, Margaret (1918—)
Av-Paul, Annette (1944—)
Avril, Jane (1868–1943)
Avril, Suzanne (fl. 1920s)
Awiakta (1936—)
Awolowo, Hannah (1915—)
Axioti, Melpo (1906–1973)
Axton, Estelle (1918–2004)
Axton, Mae Boren (1914–1997)
Axum, Donna (c. 1924—)
Ay, Evelyn (c. 1934—)
Ayer, Harriet Hubbard (1849–1903)
Ayling, Sue (1945–2003)
Aylward, Gladys (1902–1970)
Aymar, Luciana (1977—)
Ayres, Agnes (1896–1940)
Ayres, Mary Andrews (fl. 1970s)
Ayres, Ruby Mildred (1883–1955)
Ayrton, Hertha Marks (1854–1923)
Ayscough, Florence (1875/78–1942)
Ayton, Sarah (1980—)
Ayuso González, María del Pilar (1942—)
Ayverdi, Samiha (1906–1993)
Azarova, Elena (1973—)
Aznavourian, Karina (1974—)
Azon, Sandra (1973—)
Azzi, Jennifer (1968—)
Bâ, Mariama (1929–1981)
Baard, Francina (1901–1997)
Baarova, Lida (1914–2000)
Baas-Kaiser, Christina (1938—)
Babakova, Inga (1967—)
Babanina, Svetlana (1943—)
Babanova, Maria (b. 1900)
Babashoff, Shirley (1957—)
Babbin, Jacqueline (1921–2001)
Babb-Sprague, Kristen (1968—)
Babcock, Maud May (1867–1954)
Babcock, Winnifred (1875–1954)
Baber, Esther Mary (1871–1956)
Babilenska, Gertruda (1902–1997)
Babilonia, Tai (1959—)
Bacall, Lauren (1924—)
Bacewicz, Grazyna (1909–1969)
Bach, Maria (1896–1978)
Bachauer, Gina (1913–1976)
Bachmann, Ingeborg (1926–1973)
Bachmann, Tina (1978—)
Bachor, Isabell (1983—)
Bachrach, Elise Wald (1899–1940)
Backander, Helge (1891–1958)
Backer, Harriet (1845–1932)
Backer-Grondahl, Agathe (1847–1907)
Backhouse, Elizabeth (b. 1917)
Baclanova, Olga (1899–1974)
Bacon, Albion Fellows (1865–1933)
Bacon, Alice Mabel (1858–1918)
Bacon, Faith (1909–1956)
Bacon, Gertrude (1874–1949)
Bacon, Josephine Dodge (1876–1961)
Bacon, Mabel (fl. 1910)
Bacon, Mary (1948–1991)
Bacon, Peggy (1895–1987)
Baddeley, Angela (1904–1976)
Baddeley, Hermione (1906–1986)
Badea, Ioana (1964—)
Badea, Laura (1970—)
Baden-Powell, Agnes (1858–1945)
Baden-Powell, Olave (1889–1977)
Badgley, Helen (1908–1977)
Badham, Mary (1952—)
Badorek, Gabriele (1952—)
Badulina, Svetlana (1960—)
Baels, Liliane (1916–2002)
Baez, Joan (1941—)
Bage, Freda (1883–1970)
Bagley, Amelia (1870–1956)
Bagnold, Enid (1889–1981)
Bagnold, Lisbeth (1947—)
Bagryana, Elisaveta (1893–1991)
Bagryantseva, Yelizaveta (1920—)
Bagshaw, Elizabeth (1881–1982)
Bahmann, Angelika (1952—)
Bahrke, Shannon (1980—)
Bahr-Mildenburg, Anna (1872–1947)
Baier, Anke (1972—)
Bai Fengxi (1934—)
Baikauskaite, Laimute (1956—)
Baik Myung-Sun (1956—)
Bailes, Margaret Johnson (1951—)
Bailey, Aleen (1980—)
Bailey, Angela (1962—)
Bailey, Barbara Vernon (1910–2003)
Bailey, Carolyn Sherwin (1875–1961)
Bailey, Chris (1972—)
Bailey, Elizabeth (1938—)
Bailey, Florence (1863–1948)
Bailey, Frankie (1859–1953)
Bailey, Hannah Johnston (1839–1923)
Bailey, Mary (1890–1960)
Bailey, Mildred (1903–1951)
Bailey, Pearl (1918–1990)
Bailey, Temple (c. 1869–1953)
Bailin, Gladys (1930—)
Baillie, Grisell (1822–1921)
Baillie, Isobel (1895–1983)
Baillie, Jackie (1964—)
Bain, Wilhelmina Sherriff (1848–1944)
Bainbridge, Beryl (1933—)
Bainter, Fay (1891–1968)
Baird, Cora (c. 1912–1967)
Baird, Dorothea (1875–1933)
Baird, Irene (1901–1981)
Baird, Leah (1883–1971)
Baird, Vera (1951—)
Baitova, Svetlana (1972—)
Baiul, Oksana (1977—)
Bai Wei (1894–1987)
Bajer, Matilde (1840–1934)
Bajkusa, Vesna (1970—)
Bakanic, Ladislava (1924—)
Baker, Anita (1958—)
Baker, Augusta (1911–1998)
Baker, Belle (1893–1957)
Baker, Bonnie (b. 1917)
Baker, Carlee (1978—)
Baker, Carroll (1931—)
Baker, Diane (1938—)
Baker, Dorothy (1907–1968)
Baker, Elizabeth (d. 1962)
Baker, Ella (1903–1986)
Baker, Elsie (1909–2003)
Baker, Florence von Sass (1841–1916)
Baker, Irene Bailey (1901–1994)
Baker, Iris (b. 1901)
Baker, Isabel Noeline (1878–1958)
Baker, Janet (1933—)
Baker, Josephine (1906–1975)
Baker, Kate (1861–1953)
Baker, Kathy (1961—)
Baker, Laurie (1976—)
Baker, LaVern (1929–1997)
Baker, Louisa Alice (1856–1926)
Baker, Mary Ann (1834–1905)
Baker, Nina Brown (1888–1957)
Baker, S. Josephine (1873–1945)
Baker McLaglan, Eleanor Southey (1879–1969)
Bakken, Jill (1977—)
Bakogianni, Niki (1968—)
Bakova, Ani (1957—)
Balabanoff, Angelica (1878–1965)
Balabanova, Hanna (1969—)
Balachova, Alexandra (1887–1905)
Balas, Iolanda (1936—)
Balazs, Erzsebet (1920—)
Balch, Emily Greene (1867–1961)
Baldina, Alexandra Maria (1885–1977)
Baldo, Marta
Baldus, Brita Pia (1965—)
Baldwin, Ethel Frances (1879–1967)
Baldwin, Faith (1893–1978)
Baldwin, Maria Louise (1856–1922)
Baldwin, Ruth Ann (fl. 1915–1921)
Baldwin, Sally (1940–2003)
Baldycheva, Nina
Balfour, Betty (1867–1942)
Balfour, Betty (1903–1979)
Balfour, Eve (1898–1990)
Balfour, Frances (1858–1931)
Balfour, Jean (1927—)
Balfour, Katharine (c. 1921–1990)
Balin, Ina (1937–1990)
Balin, Mireille (1911–1968)
Balkanska, Mimi (b. 1902)
Ball, Catherine (1951—)
Ball, Lucille (1911–1989)
Ball, Suzan (1933–1950)
Ballanger, Felicia (1971—)
Ballantyne, Sara (c. 1964—)
Ballard, Florence (1943–1976)
Ballard, Kaye (1926—)
Ballard, Lucinda (1906–1993)
Ballesteros, Mercedes (1913–1995)
Ballestrem, Eufemia von (1859–1941)
Ballin, Mabel (1887–1958)
Ballinger, Margaret (1894–1980)
Balliser, Helen (fl. 1914)
Ballon, Ellen (1898–1969)
Ballou, Esther Williamson (1915–1973)
Ballou, Germaine (b. 1899)
Balogh, Beatrix (1974—)
Balogh, Suzanne (1973—)
Balthasar, Ramona (1964—)
Baly, Monica E. (1914–1998)
Balzer, Karin (1938—)
Bambace, Angela (1898–1975)
Bambara, Toni Cade (1939–1995)
Bampton, Rose (1907—)
Ban, Oana (1986—)
Banahan, Mary Gertrude (1855/56?–1932)
Bancroft, Ann (1955—)
Bancroft, Anne (1931–2005)
Bancroft, Jessie (1867–1952)
Bancroft, Lady (1839–1921)
Bandaranaike, Sirimavo (1916–2000)
Bandler, Faith (1918—)
Bang, Nina (1866–1928)
Bang, Soo-Hyun (1972—)
Baniszewski, Gertrude Wright (1929–1990)
Bankhead, Tallulah (1902–1968)
Banks, Lynne Reid (1929—)
Banks, Margaret (1924—)
Banky, Vilma (1898–1991)
Bannerjee, Karuna (1919–2001)
Bannerman, Helen (1862–1946)
Bannerman, Jane (c. 1835–1923)
Bannerman, Kay (1919–1991)
Bannerman, Margaret (1896–1976)
Banning, Margaret Culkin (1891–1982)
Bannon, Ann (1932—)
Banotti, Mary (1939—)
Bañuelos, Romana Acosta (1925—)
Banus, Maria (1914–1999)
Bara, Theda (1885–1955)
Barakat, Hidiya Afifi (1898–1969)
Baraksanova, Irina (1969—)
Baranova, Elena (1972—)

Baranova, Lyubov
Baranovskaya, Vera (c. 1870–1935)
Baranskaya, Natalia (b. 1908)
Baraquio, Angela Perez (1976—)
Barascu, Aurica (1974—)
Barbara, Agatha (1923–2002)
Barber, Fanny (c. 1864–1952)
Barber, Mary (1911–1965)
Barbi, Alice (1862–1948)
Barbieri, Fedora (1919–2003)
Barbieri, Margaret (1947—)
Barbosa, Pilar (1898–1997)
Barbour, Joyce (1901–1977)
Barbulova-Kelbecheva, Siyka (1951—)
Barclay, Florence Louisa (1862–1921)
Barclay-Smith, Phyllis (1903–1980)
Bard, Mary (1904–1970)
Bardach, Georgina (1983—)
Bardet, Anne-Lise (1974—)
Bardin, Madeleine (c. 1920—)
Bardotte, Brigitte (1934—)
Bardwell, Leland (1928—)
Barea Cobos, Maria (1966—)
Barel, Olesya (1960—)
Barfoot, Joan (1946—)
Bari, Judi (1949–1997)
Bari, Lynn (1913–1989)
Bari, Nina K. (1901–1961)
Bari, Tania (1936—)
Barine, Arvède (1840–1908)
Barkentin, Marjorie (c. 1891–1974)
Barker, A.L. (1918–2002)
Barker, Cicely Mary (1895–1973)
Barker, Florence (b. 1908)
Barker, Francine (1947—)
Barker, Kylene (c. 1956—)
Barker, M.C. (1879–1963)
Barker, Ma (1872–1935)
Barker, Mary Anne (1831–1911)
Barkley, Jane Hadley (1911–1964)
Barkman, Jane (1951—)
Barkova, Anna Aleksandrovna (1901–1976)
Barlois, Valerie (1969—)
Barlow, Billie (1862–1937)
Barlow, Hannah (1851–1916)
Barlow, Jane (c. 1857–1917)
Barnard, Kate (1875–1930)
Barnard, Marjorie (1897–1987)
Barnes, Binnie (1903–1998)
Barnes, Debra Dene (c. 1947—)
Barnes, Djuna (1892–1982)
Barnes, Jhane (1954—)
Barnes, Josephine (1912–1999)
Barnes, Kirsten (1968—)
Barnes, Margaret Ayer (1886–1967)
Barnes, Monica (1936—)
Barnes, Pancho (1901–1975)
Barnes, Winifred (1894–1935)
Barnett, Henrietta (1851–1936)
Barnett, Pamela (1944—)
Barney, Alice Pike (1857–1931)
Barney, Elvira Dolores (c. 1905–c. 1936)
Barney, Natalie Clifford (1876–1972)
Barney, Nora (1883–1971)
Barnicoat, Constance Alice (1872–1922)
Barns, Cornelia Baxter (1888–1941)
Barns-Graham, Wilhelmina (1912–2004)
Barnum, Gertrude (1866–1948)
Barnwell, Barbara Olive (c. 1919–c. 1977)
Baron, Devorah (1887–1956)
Baron, Mietje (1908–1948)
Barone, Marian E. (1924–1996)
Baronova, Irina (1919—)
Barot, Madeleine (1909–1995)
Barr, Amelia Huddleston (1831–1919)
Barr, Beth (1971—)
Barr, Margaret Scolari (1901–1987)
Barra, Emma de la (1861–1947)
Barraine, Elsa (1910–1999)
Barrault, Marie-Christine (1944—)
Barre, Alexandra (1958—)
Barreno, Maria Isabel (1939—)
Barrer, Nina Agatha Rosamond (1879–1965)
Barret, Dorothy (1917–1987)
Barrett, Edith (1906–1977)
Barrett, Janie Porter (1865–1948)
Barrett, Kate Waller (1857–1925)
Barrett, Minnette (1880–1964)
Barrett, Rona (1934—)
Barrett, Rose Tyler (b. 1889)
Barrie, Elaine (1915–2003)
Barrie, Mona (1909–1964)
Barrie, Wendy (1912–1978)
Barrientos, Maria (1884–1946)
Barringer, Emily Dunning (1876–1961)
Barrington, Margaret (1896–1982)
Barrio Gutierrez, Sonia (1969—)
Barrios de Chúngara, Domitila (1937—)
Barriscale, Bessie (1884–1965)
Barron, Gayle (c. 1947—)
Barron, Jennie Loitman (1891–1969)
Barros, Leila (1971—)
Barros, Lorena (d. 1976)
Barros, Zoila (1976—)
Barroso, Maria Aliçe (1926—)
Barrow, Nita (1916–1995)
Barrows, Isabel Hayes (1845–1913)
Barry, Bonny (1960—)
Barry, Deidre (1972—)
Barry, Elaine (d. 1948)
Barry, Iris (1895–1969)
Barry, Leonora M. (1849–1930)
Barry, Myra (1957—)
Barrymore, Diana (1921–1960)
Barrymore, Ethel (1879–1959)
Barskaya, Margarita A. (1903–1938)
Barstow, Edith (1907–1960)
Barsukova, Yulia (1978—)
Bartel, Jean (c. 1924—)
Bartelme, Mary (1866–1954)
Bartels, Tineke (1951—)
Bartet, Jeanne Julia (1854–1941)
Barth, Beatrice Mary (1877–1966)
Bartholomew, Susan (1969—)
Bartkowicz, Peaches (1949—)
Bartlett, Ethel (1896–1978)
Bartok, Ditta Pasztory (1902–1982)
Bartok, Eva (1926–1998)
Barton, Clara (1821–1912)
Barton, Donna (c. 1967—)
Barton, Dora (1884–1966)
Barton, Emma (1872–1938)
Barton, Glenys (1944—)
Barton, Jane (1851–1938)
Barton, Mary (d. 1970)
Barton, Pam (1917–1943)
Bartosik, Alison (1983—)
Barwirth, Anita (1918—)
Baryard, Malin (1975—)
Barysheva, Olga (1954—)
Basch, Anamarija (1893–after 1945)
Bascom, Florence (1862–1945)
Basford, Kathleen (1916–1998)
Basham, Maud Ruby (1879–1963)
Bashir, Marie (1930—)
Basich, Tina (1969—)
Basquette, Lina (1907–1995)
Bass, Charlotta Spears (1880–1969)
Bass, Mary Elizabeth (1876–1956)
Bassett, Angela (1958—)
Bassett, Ann (1878–1956)
Bassey, Shirley (1937—)
Basten, Alice (1876–1955)
Bastos, Regina (1960—)
Batchelor, Joy (1914–1991)
Batchelor, Mary (1927—)
Bate, Dorothea (1879–1951)
Bateham, Josephine (1829–1901)
Bateman, Jessie (1877–1940)
Bateman, Kate (1842–1917)
Bates, Barbara (1925–1969)
Bates, Blanche (1873–1941)
Bates, Daisy Lee (1914–1999)
Bates, Daisy May (1859–1951)
Bates, Elizabeth (1947–2003)
Bates, Florence (1888–1954)
Bates, Katherine Lee (1859–1929)
Bates, Kathy (1948—)
Bates, Mary (1861–1954)
Bates, Ruby (1913–1976)
Bates, Vietta M. (1922–1972)
Bateson, Mary (1865–1906)
Bathildis of Schaumburg-Lippe (1873–1962)
Batkovic, Suzy (1980—)
Bat-Miriam, Yocheved (1901–1980)
Batsiushka, Hanna (1981—)
Batson, Flora (1864–1906)
Batson, Henrietta M. (1859–1943)
Battaglia, Letizia (1935—)
Battelle, Ann (1968—)
Batten, Guin (1967—)
Batten, Jean Gardner (1909–1982)
Batten, Kim (1969—)
Batten, Miriam (1964—)
Batten, Mollie (1905–1985)
Batterham, Mary Rose (c. 1870–1927)
Battle, Kathleen (1948—)
Batyrchina, Jana (1979—)
Bau, Sabine (1969—)
Bauchens, Anne (1881–1967)
Baudisch-Wittke, Gudrun (1907–1982)
Bauer, Alice (1927–2002)
Bauer, Catherine Krouse (1905–1964)
Bauer, Charita (1922–1985)
Bauer, Helene (1871–1942)
Bauer, Margaret (1927—)
Bauer, Marion (1887–1955)
Bauer, Sybil (1903–1927)
Bauer, Veronika (1979—)
Bauer, Viola (1976—)
Bauerschmidt, Maritta (1950—)
Bauersmith, Paula (1909–1987)
Baugh, Laura (1955—)
Baughan, Blanche Edith (1870–1958)
Bauld, Alison (1944—)
Baum, Marianne (1912–1942)
Baum, Marie (1874–1964)
Baum, Vicki (1888–1960)
Bauma, Herma (1915–2003)
Baumann, Edith (1909–1973)
Baume, Rosetta Lulah (1871–1934)
Baumer, Daniela
Bäumer, Gertrud (1873–1954)
Baumgartner, Ann (c. 1923—)
Baur, Clara (1835–1912)
Baur, Margrit (1937—)
Bausch, Pina (1940—)
Baverel, Myriam (1981—)
Bavier, Frances (1902–1989)
Bawden, Nina (1925—)
Baxley, Barbara (1923–1990)
Baxter, Anne (1923–1985)
Baxter, Jane (1909–1996)
Baxter, Millicent Amiel (1888–1984)
Bay, Josephine Perfect (1900–1962)
Ba Yan (1962—)
Bayard, Sylviane (1957—)
Bayer, Johanna (1915–2000)
Bayes, Nora (1880–1928)
Baylis, Lilian (1874–1937)
Baylis, Meredith (1929–2002)
Baylis, Nadine (1940—)
Bayliss, Lisa (1966—)
Bayly, Ada Ellen (1857–1903)
Bayne, Beverly (1894–1982)
Baynes, Deserie (1960—)
Baynes, Pauline (1922—)
Baynton, Barbara (1857–1929)
Bazanova, Marina (1962—)
Bazhanova, Svetlana (1972—)
Bazin, Janine (1923–2003)
Bazon-Chelariu, Adriana (1963—)
Ba_ar, Sukufe Nihal (1896–1973)
Beach, Amy Cheney (1867–1944)
Beach, Cyprian (1893–1951)
Beach, Holly (b. 1884)
Beach, Sylvia (1887–1962)
Beachley, Layne (1972—)
Beale, Dorothea (1831–1906)
Beals, Jessie Tarbox (1870–1942)
Beaman, Hana (1982—)
Beames, Adrienne
Bean, Janet Beveridge (1964—)
Beard, Amanda (1981—)
Beard, Betsy (1961—)
Beard, Mary (1876–1946)
Beard, Mary Ritter (1876–1958)
Bearden, Bessye (1888–1943)

Bearnish, Geraldine (1885–1972)
Beat, Janet Eveline (1937—)
Beath, Betty (1932—)
Beatrice (1857–1944)
Beatrice of Saxe-Coburg (1884–1966)
Beatrix (b. 1938)
Beatriz of Spain (1909–2002)
Beattie, Ann (1947—)
Beattie, Mollie (1947–1996)
Beatty, Bessie (1886–1947)
Beatty, May (1880–1945)
Beatty, Patricia (1936—)
Beaudet, Louise (1861–1947)
Beaugrand, Léontine (1842–1925)
Beaumont, Diana (1909–1964)
Beaumont, Florence (c. 1912–1967)
Beaumont, Lyne (1978—)
Beaumont, Muriel (1881–1957)
Beauprey, Jeanne (1961—)
Beauregard, Robin (1979—)
Beauvoir, Simone de (1908–1986)
Beaux, Cecilia (1855–1942)
Beavers, Louise (1902–1962)
Bébel-Gisler, Dany (1935–2003)
Bechard, Kelly (1978—)
Becher, Hilla (1934—)
Becher, Lilly (1901–1976)
Bechke, Elena (1966—)
Bechtel, Louise Seaman (1894–1985)
Bechtereva, Natalia (1924—)
Becirspahic, Mirsada (1957—)
Beck, Audrey P. (1931–1983)
Beck, Beatrix (1914—)
Beck, Elizabeth Louisa (c. 1862–1931)
Beck, Emily Morison (1915–2004)
Beck, Martha (c. 1921–1951)
Beck, Sophie (1858–?)
Becker, Britta (1973—)
Becker, Carolyn (1958—)
Becker, Ellen (1960—)
Becker, Jillian (1932—)
Becker, Marie Alexander (1877–194?)
Becker, May Lamberton (1873–1958)
Becker, Sabine (1959—)
Becker-Dey, Courtenay (1965—)
Becker Pinkston, Elizabeth (1903–1989)
Becker-Steiner, Marion (1950—)
Beckett, Margaret (1943—)
Beckett, Mary (1926—)
Beckham, Victoria (1974—)
Beckmann, Gudrun (1955—)
Beckman-Shcherbina, Elena (1881–1951)
Beckwith, Martha Warren (1871–1959)
Beclea-Szekely, Violeta (1965—)
Bedard, Myriam (1969—)
Beddington, Rosa (1956–2001)
Bede, Shelda (1973—)
Bedell, Harriet M. (1875–1969)
Bedells, Phyllis (1893–1985)
Bederkhan, Leila (b. around 1903)
Bedford, B.J. (1972—)
Bedford, Barbara (1903–1981)
Bedford, Marie (1907—)
Bedford, Sybille (1911–2006)
Bedregal, Yolanda (1916–1999)
Beeby, Doris (1894–1948)
Beech, Olive Ann (1903–1993)
Beecher, Janet (1884–1955)
Beechman, Laurie (c. 1955–1998)
Beeman, Ruth Coates (1925—)
Beer, Patricia (1919–1999)
Beere, Estelle Girda (1875–1959)
Beere, Thekla (1901–1991)
Beese, Lotte (1903–1988)
Begard, Isabelle (1960—)
Begg, Anne (1955—)
Beglin, Elizabeth (1957—)
Beglyakova, Irina (1933—)
Begtrup, Bodil (1903–1987)
Begue, Laetitia (1980—)
Behar, Adriana (1969—)
Behle, Petra (1969—)
Behmer-Vater, Anke (1961—)
Behrendt, Kerstin (1967—)
Behrendt-Hampe, Jutta (1960—)
Behrens, Hildegard (1937—)
Beier, Roswitha (1956—)
Beig, Maria (1920—)
Beimler-Herker, Centa (1909—)
Beinhorn, Elly (1907—)
Beiser, Trude (1927—)
Bejarano, Esther (1924—)
Bekatorou, Sofia (1977—)
Bekesi, Ilona (1953—)
Bekkevold, Kristin (1977—)
Belan, Tatyana (1982—)
Beland, Lucy (1871–1941)
Belbin, Tracey (1967—)
Belfiore, Liliana (1952—)
Belfrage, Sally (1936–1994)
Bel Geddes, Barbara (1922–2005)
Belikova, Anastasia (1979—)
Belishova, Liri (1923—)
Belita (1923–2005)
Bell, Eileen (1943—)
Bell, Elizabeth Viola (1897–1990)
Bell, Florence (1909—)
Bell, Gertrude (1868–1926)
Bell, Jane (1873–1959)
Bell, Lilian (1867–1929)
Bell, Lynette (1947—)
Bell, Maggie (1945—)
Bell, Margaret Brenda (1891–1979)
Bell, Marie (1900–1985)
Bell, Marilyn (1937—)
Bell, Marion (1919–1997)
Bell, Mary (c. 1957—)
Bell, Mary Hayley (1911–2005)
Bell, Muriel Emma (1898–1974)
Bell, Nora Kizer (1941–2004)
Bell, Peggy Kirk (1921—)
Bell, Regla (1971—)
Bell, Teresa Z. (1966—)
Bell, Vanessa (1879–1961)
Bell, Vera (1906—)
Bella, Antoinetta (b. 1863)
Bellamy, Elizabeth (1845–1940)
Bellamy, Madge (1899–1990)
Bellanca, Dorothy (1894–1946)
Belle, Anne (1935–2003)
Belle, Regina (1963—)
Bellew, Kyrle (1887–1948)
Bellil, Samira (1972–2004)
Bellincioni, Gemma (1864–1950)
Belloc-Lowndes, Marie (1868–1947)
Bellon, Denise (1902–1999)
Bellonci, Maria (1902–1986)
Bellutti, Antonella (1968—)
Belmondo, Stefania (1969—)
Belmont, Alva Smith (1853–1933)
Belmont, Eleanor Robson (1879–1979)
Belmore, Bertha (1882–1953)
Beloff, Nora (1919–1997)
Beloff-Chain, Anne (1921–1991)
Beloglazova, Galina (1967—)
Belote, Melissa (1956—)
Belova, Elena (1965—)
Belova, Irina (1968—)
Belova, Irina (1980—)
Belova-Novikova, Yelena (1947—)
Beltran, Daima (1972—)
Beltran, Lola (1932–1996)
Beluguina, Olesia (1984—)
Bemberg, Maria Luisa (1922–1995)
Benaderet, Bea (1906–1968)
Benario, Olga (1908–1942)
Benatar, Pat (1953—)
Benchley, Belle (1882–1973)
Bender, Kate (1849–?)
Benedict, Ruth (1887–1948)
Benedikte (1944—)
Benerito, Ruth (1916—)
Benesh, Joan (1920—)
Benet, Laura (1884–1979)
Benetton, Guiliana (1935—)
Bengtsson, Birgitta (1965—)
Ben Haddou, Halima (fl. 1980s)
Ben-Haim, Marylise (1928–2001)
Benham, Dorothy (c. 1956—)
Benham, Gertrude (1867–1938)
Benhassi, Hasna (1978—)
Benida, Nouria (1970—)
Benitez-Rexach, Lucienne (1905–1968)
Benjamin, Ethel Rebecca (1875–1943)
Benjamin, Hilde (1902–1989)
Benko, Lindsay (1976—)
Bennedsen, Dorte (1938—)
Bennett, Agnes Elizabeth Lloyd (1872–1960)
Bennett, Alice (1851–1925)
Bennett, Alma (1889–1958)
Bennett, Barbara (1906–1958)
Bennett, Belle (1891–1932)
Bennett, Belle Harris (1852–1922)
Bennett, Brooke (1980—)
Bennett, Constance (1904–1965)
Bennett, Eileen (1920—)
Bennett, Enid (1893–1969)
Bennett, Estelle (1944—)
Bennett, Evelyn (b. 1905)
Bennett, Gwendolyn B. (1902–1981)
Bennett, Isadora (d. 1980)
Bennett, Isobel (b. 1909)
Bennett, Jill (1931–1990)
Bennett, Joan (1910–1990)
Bennett, Louie (1870–1956)
Bennett, Louise Simone (1919—)
Bennett, Marjorie (1896–1982)
Bennett, Mary Katharine (1864–1950)
Bennett, Mary Montgomerie (1881–1961)
Bennett, Mavis (1900–1990)
Bennett, Olga (1947—)
Bennett, Patricia (1947—)
Bennett, Wilda (1894–1967)
Benninga, Carina (1962—)
Bennion, Lianne (1972—)
Benois, Nadia (1896–1975)
Benson, Gertrude (1886–1964)
Benson, Linda (c. 1944—)
Benson, Mary (1919–2000)
Benson, Mildred (1905–2002)
Benson, Rita Romilly (1900–1980)
Benson, Sally (1900–1972)
Benson, Stella (1892–1933)
Bent, Buena (c. 1890–1957)
Bentham, Ethel (1861–1931)
Bentley, Elizabeth Turrill (1908–1963)
Bentley, Gladys (1907–1960)
Bentley, Helen Delich (1923—)
Bentley, Irene (1904–1965)
Bentley, Irene (d. 1940)
Bentley, Muriel (1917–1999)
Bentley, Phyllis (1894–1977)
Bentley, Ursula (1945–2004)
Bentum, Cornelia van (1965—)
Ben-Yehuda, Hemda (1873–1951)
Ben-Yusuf, Zaida (fl. 1897–1907)
Benzell, Mimi (1922–1970)
Benzoni, Juliette (1920—)
Ben Zvi, Rachel Yanait (1886–1979)
Beranger, Clara (1886–1956)
Berber, Anita (1899–1928)
Berberian, Cathy (1925–1983)
Berberova, Lalka (1965—)
Berberova, Nina (1901–1993)
Berbie, Jane (1931—)
Berendt, Rachel (d. 1957)
Berenguer, Amanda (1924—)
Berenson, Berry (1948–2001)
Berenson, Marisa (1946—)
Berenson, Mary (1864–1944)
Berenson, Senda (1868–1954)
Berens-Totenohl, Josefa (1891–1969)
Berès, Pervenche (1957—)
Beresford, Anne (1919—)
Beresford-Howe, Constance (1922—)
Beretta, Caterina (1839–1911)
Berezhnaya, Elena (1977—)
Berg, Aina (b. 1902)
Berg, Gertrude (1899–1966)
Berg, Helene (b. 1906)
Berg, Jacomina van den (1909—)
Berg, Laura (1975—)
Berg, Leila (1917—)
Berg, Patty (1918—)
Berganza, Teresa (1934—)
Bergen, Candice (1946—)
Bergen, Larisa (1949—)
Bergen, Nella (1873–1919)

Bergen, Polly (1929—)
Berger, Erna (1900–1990)
Berger, Maria (1956—)
Berger, Nicole (1934–1967)
Berger, Senta (1941—)
Bergere, Ouida (1885–1974)
Bergere, Valerie (1872–1938)
Bergeron, Marian (1918–2002)
Berggolts, Olga (1910–1975)
Berggren, Evy (1934—)
Berghaus, Ruth (1927–1996)
Berghmans, Ingrid (1961—)
Bergman, Ingrid (1915–1982)
Bergman, Marilyn (1929—)
Bergmann-Pohl, Sabine (1946—)
Bergner, Elisabeth (1897–1986)
Bergqvist, Kajsa (1976—)
Bergroth, Kersti (1886–1975)
Bergsma, Deanne (1941—)
Beri, Beth (c. 1904—)
Beringer, Aimée Daniell (1856–1936)
Beringer, Esmé (1875–1972)
Beringer, Vera (1879–1964)
Beriosova, Svetlana (1932–1998)
Berk, Lotte (1913–2003)
Berke, Dorothea (c. 1900—)
Berksoy, Semiha (1910–2004)
Berman, Sara Mae (1936—)
Bernal, Emilia (1884–1964)
Bernard, Dorothy (1890–1955)
Bernard, Jessie (1903–1996)
Bernard, Karen (1948—)
Bernardino, Minerva (1907–1998)
Bernays, Marie (1883–1939)
Berndt, Catherine Webb (1918–1994)
Bernhard, Ruth (1905—)
Bernhardt, Sarah (1844–1923)
Bernier, Sylvie (1964—)
Berning, Susie Maxwell (1941—)
Bernson, Kathryn (1950—)
Bernstein, Aline (1882–1955)
Bernstein, Hilda (1915—)
Bernstein, Sylvia (1915–2003)
Bernstein, Theresa Ferber (1890–2002)
Berry, Halle (1966—)
Berry, Harriet Morehead (1877–1940)
Berry, Martha McChesney (1866–1942)
Berthod, Madeleine (1931—)
Berthod, Sylviane (1977—)
Bertini, Francesca (1888–1985)
Bertolaccini, Silvia (1959—)
Bertolini, Livia (fl. 1920s–1930s)
Bertram, Elsie (1912–2003)
Bertrana, Aurora (1899–1974)
Bertsch, Marguerite (1889–1967)
Bervoets, Marguerite (1914–1944)
Besant, Annie (1847–1933)
Beseliene, Vida (1956—)
Besfamilnaya, Nadezhda (1950—)
Beskow, Elsa (1874–1953)
Besnyö, Eva (1910–2003)
Bessa-Luís, Agustina (1922—)
Besserer, Eugénie (1868–1934)
Bessmertnova, Natalia (1941—)
Besson, Colette (1946—)
Bessonova, Anna (1984—)
Best, Edna (1900–1974)
Bestemianova, Natalia (1960—)
Betancourt, Ingrid (1961—)
Betbeze, Yolande (1930—)
Betham-Edwards, Matilda (1836–1919)
Bethânia, Maria (1946—)
Bethell, Mary Ursula (1874–1945)
Bethell, Thyra Talvase (1882–1972)
Bethune, Louise Blanchard (1856–1913)
Bethune, Mary McLeod (1875–1955)
Betker, Jan (c. 1960—)
Bettis, Valerie (1919–1982)
Betjeman, Agnes Muir (1885–1964)
Betts, Anna Whelan (1873–1959)
Betts, Doris (1932—)
Betts, Ethel Franklin (1878–?)
Betz, Pauline (1919—)
Beumer, Catharina (1947—)
Beutler, Maja (1936—)
Beutler, Margarete (1876–1949)
Bevans, Philippa (1913–1968)
Bevier, Isabel (1860–1942)
Bevilacqua, Alma (1910–1988)
Bewley, Lois (c. 1936—)
Bews, Mary Ellen (1856–1945)
Bey, Hannelore (1941—)
Beyer, Helga (1920–1942)
Beyermann, Ina (1967—)
Beynon, Francis Marion (1884–1951)
Bhandari, Mannu (1931—)
Bhardwaj, Mohini (1978—)
Bhatia, June (1919—)
Bhreathnach, Naimh (1945—)
Bhutto, Benazir (1953—)
Bhutto, Nusrat (1929—)
Bianchedi, Diana (1969—)
Bianchini, Angela (1921—)
Bianco, Margery Williams (1881–1944)
Bianco, Pamela (1906–1994)
Bianco, Suzannah (1973—)
Bibby, Mary Ann (c. 1832–1910)
Bibesco, Elizabeth (1897–1943)
Bibesco, Marthe Lucie (1887–1973)
Bible, Frances L. (1919–2001)
Bicherova, Olga (1966—)
Bichovsky, Elisheva (1888–1949)
Bichyk, Yuliya (1983—)
Bicknell, Jessie (1871–1956)
Bidaud, Laurence (1968—)
Bidder, Anna McClean (1903–2001)
Bidder, Marion Greenwood (1862–1932)
Bidiouane, Nouzha (1969—)
Bidstrup, Jane (c. 1956—)
Bidstrup, Lene (1966—)
Biebl, Heidi (1941—)
Biechi, Anni (1940—)
Biehl, Amy (1967–1993)
Bielenberg, Christabel (1909–2003)
Biermann, Aenne (1898–1933)
Biesenthal, Laryssa (1971—)
Bigelow, Kathryn (1951—)
Biggs, Rosemary (1912–2001)
Bikcin, Hamide (1978—)
Bileck, Pamela (1968—)
Billington, Adeline (1825–1917)
Billington, Francelia (1895–1934)
Billington-Greig, Teresa (1877–1964)
Biltauere, Astra (1944—)
Bimolt, Klena (1945—)
Binchy, Maeve (1940—)
Binder, Aranka (1966—)
Bing, Ilse (1899–1998)
Bingham, Amelia (1869–1927)
Bingham, Henrietta (1901–1968)
Bingham, Millicent Todd (1880–1968)
Binkiene, Sofija (1902–1984)
Binney, Constance (1896–1989)
Binns, Hilda May (1945—)
Binnuna, Khanatta (1940—)
Binoche, Juliette (1964—)
Bins, Patrícia (1930—)
Biracree, Thelma (1904–1997)
Birch, Gina (1956—)
Birch, Patricia (c. 1930—)
Birchfield, Constance Alice (1898–1994)
Bird, Billie (1908–2002)
Bird, Bonnie (1914–1995)
Bird, Dorothy (c. 1913—)
Bird, Lorraine
Bird, Nancy (1915—)
Bird, Sue (1980—)
Birdsong, Cindy (1939—)
Birell, Tala (1907–1958)
Biret, Idil (1941—)
Birgitta of Sweden (1937—)
Birkett, Viva (1887–1934)
Birney, Alice McLellan (1858–1907)
Birtles, Mary (1859–1943)
Biryukova, Alexandra (1929—)
Bischof, Martina (1957—)
Bischoff, Ilse (1903–1976)
Bischoff, Sabine (1958—)
Bishop, Ann (1899–1990)
Bishop, Cath (1971—)
Bishop, Claire Huchet (1898–1993)
Bishop, Elizabeth (1911–1979)
Bishop, Georgianna M. (1878–1971)
Bishop, Hazel (1906–1998)
Bishop, Isabel (1902–1988)
Bishop, Isabella (1831–1904)
Bishop, Julie (1914–2001)
Bishop, Kate (b. 1847)
Bishop, Kelly (1944—)
Bisland, Elizabeth (1863–1929)
Bissell, Emily (1861–1948)
Bittenbender, Ada Matilda (1848–1925)
Bi Wenjing (1981—)
Bjarklind, Unnur Benediktsdóttir (1881–1946)
Bjedov, Djurdica (1947—)
Bjedov, Mira (1955—)
Bjelke-Petersen, Marie (1874–1969)
Bjerkrheim, Susann Goksoer (1970—)
Bjerregaard, Ritt (1941—)
Bjoergen, Marit (1900—)
Bjork (1965—)
Björk, Anita (1923—)
Bjorkland, Penny (1941—)
Bjørn, Dinna (1947—)
Bjornson, Maria (1949–2002)
Black, Cilla (1943—)
Black, Clementina (1854–1922)
Black, Elinor F.E. (1905–1982)
Black, Helen McKenzie (1896–1963)
Black, Marilyn (1944—)
Black, Martha Louise (1866–1957)
Black, Shirley Temple (1928—)
Black, Winifred Sweet (1863–1936)
Blackadder, Elizabeth (1931—)
Blackburn, Doris Amelia (1889–1970)
Blackburn, Helen (1842–1903)
Blackburn, Jemima (1823–1909)
Blackburn, Jessy (1894–1995)
Blackburn, Kathleen (1892–1968)
Blackburn, Molly (c. 1931–1985)
Blackett, Annie Maude (1889–1956)
Blackham, Dorothy Isabel (1896–1975)
Blackie, Jeannetta Margaret (1864–1955)
Blackler, Betty (1929—)
Blackman, Honor (1926—)
Blackman, Liz (1949—)
Blackstone, Tessa (1942—)
Blackwell, Alice Stone (1857–1950)
Blackwell, Elizabeth (1821–1910)
Blackwell, Ellen Wright (1864–1952)
Blackwell, Emily (1826–1910)
Blackwood, Beatrice (1889–1975)
Blackwood, Margaret (1909–1986)
Blagg, Mary Adela (1858–1944)
Blagoeva, Stella Dimitrova (1887–1954)
Blagoeva, Yordanka (1947—)
Blahoski, Alana (1974—)
Blaine, Anita McCormick (1866–1954)
Blaine, Vivian (1921–1995)
Blair, Betsy (1923—)
Blair, Bonnie (1964—)
Blair, Catherine (1872–1946)
Blair, Cherie (1954—)
Blair, Emily Newell (1877–1951)
Blair, Janet (1921—)
Blair, Mary (c. 1895–1947)
Blair, Pamela (1949—)
Blais, Marie-Claire (1939—)
Blake, Amanda (1929–1989)
Blake, Lillie Devereux (1833–1913)
Blaker, Eliza Ann (1854–1926)
Blalock, Jane (1945—)
Blanc, Isabelle (1975—)
Blanc, Marie-Thérèse (1840–1907)
Blanca, Nida (1936–2001)
Blancard, Jacqueline (1909—)
Blanchard, Mari (1927–1970)
Blanchard, Theresa Weld (1893–1978)
Blanche, Ada (1862–1953)
Blanche, Marie (1893—)
Blanche of Bourbon (1868–1949)
Blanchfield, Florence (1884–1971)
Blanchi, Elisa (1987—)
Blanco, Kathleen (1942—)
Bland, Harriet (1915–1991)
Bland, Lilian (1878–1971)
Blandick, Clara (1880–1962)
Blane, Sally (1910–1997)

Blank, Carla (c. 1940—)
Blankenburg, Lucretia L. (1845–1937)
Blankers-Koen, Fanny (1918–2004)
Blasberg, Claudia (1975—)
Blasco Soto, Miriam (1963—)
Blatch, Harriot Stanton (1856–1940)
Blatter, Barbara (1970—)
Blayney, May (1875–1953)
Blazejowski, Carol (1957—)
Blazkova, Milada (1958—)
Blears, Hazel Anne (1956—)
Blecher, Miriam (1912–1979)
Bleeker, Caroline Emilie (1897–1985)
Bleibtreu, Hedwig (1868–1958)
Bleibtrey, Ethelda M. (1902–1978)
Bleiler, Gretchen (1981—)
Bleschke, Johanna (1894–1936)
Bley, Carla (1938—)
Blige, Mary J. (1971—)
Bligh, Anna Maria
Blinks, Susan (1957—)
Bliss, Anna (1843–1925)
Bliss, Catherine (1908–1989)
Bliss, Lillie (1864–1931)
Bliss, Mary Elizabeth (1824–1909)
Bliss, Mildred Barnes (1879–1969)
Blitch, Iris Faircloth (1912–1993)
Bloch, Suzanne (1907–2002)
Blodgett, Katharine Burr (1898–1979)
Blomberg, Vanja (1929—)
Blomfield, Dorothy (1858–1932)
Blondal, Patricia (1926–1959)
Blondeau, Barbara (1938–1974)
Blondell, Joan (1906–1979)
Bloodworth, Rhoda Alice (1889–1980)
Bloom, Claire (1931—)
Bloom, Ursula (1893–1984)
Bloom, Verna (1939—)
Bloor, Ella Reeve (1862–1951)
Blow, Susan Elizabeth (1843–1916)
Blue, Rita Hassan (c. 1905–1973)
Blum, Arlene (1945—)
Blum, Klara (1904–1971)
Blume, Judy (1938—)
Blumental, Felicja (1908–1991)
Blunt, Anne (1837–1917)
Blunt, Katharine (1876–1954)
Bluwstein, Rachel (1890–1931)
Blyth, Ann (1928—)
Blythe, Betty (1893–1972)
Blythe, Coralie (1880–1928)
Blyton, Enid (1897–1968)
Board, Lillian (1948–1970)
Boardman, Diane (c. 1950—)
Boardman, Eleanor (1898–1991)
Boardman, Mabel (1860–1946)
Bobath, Berta (1907–1991)
Bobeica, Iulia (1967—)
Bober, Phyllis (1920–2002)
Bobis, Ildiko (1945—)
Bobkova, Hana (1929—)
Boboc, Loredana (1984—)
Bobrova, Natalia (1978—)
Bocharova, Nina (1924—)
Bochatay, Fernande (1946—)
Bochina, Natalya (1962—)
Bock, Amy Maud (1859–1943)
Bodard, Mag (1916—)
Boddie, Barbara White (1940—)
Boden, Margaret (1936—)
Bodendorf, Carla (1953—)
Bodenwieser, Gertrud (1886–1959)
Bodet, Stéphanie (1976—)
Bodkin, Maud (1875–1967)
Bodziak, Ericleia (1969—)
Boe, Anette
Boedding-Eckhoff, Inge (1947—)
Boehm, Annett (1980—)
Boehm, Helen F. (b. early 1920s)
Boehm, Mary Louise (1924–2002)
Boekhorst, Josephine (1957—)
Boenisch, Yvonne (1980—)
Boesler, Martina (1957—)
Boesler, Petra (1955—)
Bofill, Angela (1954—)
Bogan, Louise (1897–1970)
Bogan, Lucille (1897–1948)
Bogdanova, Krasimira (1949—)
Bogdanova, Svetlana (1964—)
Bogdanova, Yuliya (1964—)
Bogen, Erna (1906—)
Boggs, Lindy (1916—)
Boginskaya, Svetlana (1973—)
Bogle, Helen McDermott (1871–?)
Bogle, Sarah C.N. (1870–1932)
Boglioli, Wendy (1955—)
Bogomolova, Ludmilla (1932—)
Bogoraz, Larisa (c. 1930–2004)
Bogoslovskaya, Olga (1964—)
Böhlau, Helene (1859–1940)
Bohley, Bärbel (1945—)
Bohm-Schuch, Clara (1879–1936)
Bohr, Margrethe (1890–1984)
Boiardi, Helen (1905–1995)
Boissevain, Inez M. (1886–1916)
Boissevain, Mia (1878–1959)
Boit, Elizabeth Eaton (1849–1932)
Bokel, Claudia (1973—)
Boland, Bridget (1904–1988)
Boland, Eavan (1944—)
Boland, Mary (1880–1965)
Boland, Veronica Grace (1899–1982)
Bolden, Jeanette (1960—)
Bolduc, Marie (1894–1941)
Bolen, Lin (1941—)
Boley, May (1881–1963)
Bolger, Deirdre (1938—)
Bolhuis-Eysvogel, Marjolein (1961—)
Bolkan, Florinda (1941—)
Bolland, Adrienne (1895–1975)
Bollinger, Anne (c. 1923–1962)
Bollmann, Minna (1876–1935)
Bol Poel, Martha (1877–1956)
Bolt, Carol (1941–2000)
Bolton, Frances Payne (1885–1977)
Bolton, Ruthie (1967—)
Bolton, Sarah Knowles (1841–1916)
Bombal, María Luisa (1910–1980)
Bombeck, Erma (1927–1996)
Bompard, Gabrielle (1869–?)
Bonacci Brunamonti, Maria Alinda (1841–1903)
Bonafini, Hebe de (1928—)
Bonaly, Surya (1973—)
Bonanni, Laudomia (1907–2002)
Bonaparte, Marie (1882–1962)
Boncheva, Rumeliana (1957—)
Bond, Carrie Jacobs (1862–1946)
Bond, Elizabeth Powell (1841–1926)
Bond, Jessie (1853–1942)
Bond, Lilian (1908–1991)
Bond, Mary (1939—)
Bond, Sheila (1928—)
Bond, Sudie (1928–1984)
Bond, Victoria (1950—)
Bondar, Elena (1958—)
Bondar, Roberta (1945—)
Bondarenko, Olga (1960—)
Bondfield, Margaret (1873–1953)
Bondi, Beulah (1892–1981)
Bonds, Margaret (1913–1972)
Bonds, Rosie (1944—)
Bonfanti, Marietta (1845–1921)
Bonfils, Helen (c. 1890–1972)
Bonham-Carter, Violet (1887–1969)
Bonhoeffer, Emmi (1905–1991)
Bonino, Emma (1948—)
Boninsegna, Celestina (1877–1947)
Bonita, Maria (c. 1908–1938)
Bonmartini, Linda (1873–?)
Bonner, Antoinette (1892–1920)
Bonner, Beth (1952–1998)
Bonner, Elena (1923—)
Bonner, Isabel (1907–1955)
Bonner, Margerie (1905–1988)
Bonner, Marita (1899–1971)
Bonner, Mary (1885–1935)
Bonner, Priscilla (1899–1996)
Bonnevie, Kristine (1872–1948)
Bonnevie, Margarete Ottilie (1884–1970)
Bonney, Linda (1949—)
Bonney, Lores (1897–1994)
Bonney, Mary Lucinda (1816–1900)
Bonney, Thérèse (1894–1978)
Bonnin, Gertrude Simmons (1876–1938)
Bono, Mary (1961—)
Bonoff, Karla (1952—)
Bonstelle, Jessie (1871–1932)
Bontas, Cristina (1973—)
Bontecou, Lee (1931—)
Bontje, Ellen (1958—)
Boogerd-Quaak, Johanna L.A. (1944—)
Boogert, Kristie (1973—)
Booij, Minke (1977—)
Boole, Ella (1858–1952)
Boom, Christel (1927–2004)
Boomgaardt, Ageeth (1972—)
Boone, Debby (1956—)
Boorapolchai, Yaowapa (1984—)
Booth, Adrian (1918—)
Booth, Agnes (1843–1910)
Booth, Angela Elizabeth (1869–1954)
Booth, Edwina (1904–1991)
Booth, Ellen Scripps (1863–1948)
Booth, Evangeline (1865–1950)
Booth, Evelyn Mary (1897–1988)
Booth, Jane Bastanchury (1948—)
Booth, Karin (1919–1992)
Booth, Margaret (1898–2002)
Booth, Maud Ballington (1865–1948)
Booth, Shirley (1907–1992)
Boothby, Dora (1881–1970)
Boothroyd, Betty (1929—)
Booth-Tucker, Emma Moss (1860–1903)
Borboni, Paola (1900–1995)
Borchardt, Selma Munter (1895–1968)
Borchers, Cornell (1925—)
Borchert, Katrin (1969—)
Borchmann, Anke (1954—)
Borckink, Annie (1951—)
Borda, Deborah (1949—)
Borden, Amanda (1977—)
Borden, Laura (1862–1940)
Borden, Lizzie (1860–1927)
Borden, Olive (1906–1947)
Borders, Ila (1975—)
Bordes, Armonia (1945—)
Bordoni, Irene (1895–1953)
Borelli, LaVerne (1909—)
Borg, Anita (1949–2003)
Borg, Dorothy (1901–1993)
Borg, Veda Ann (1915–1973)
Borgese Freschi, Maria (1881–1947)
Borgström, Hilda (1871–1953)
Bori, Lucrezia (1887–1960)
Boring, Alice Middleton (1883–1955)
Boris, Ruthanna (1918—)
Borisova, Verka (1955—)
Borkh, Inge (1917—)
Bormann, Gerda (1909–1946)
Borne, Bonita (1952—)
Börner, Jacqueline (1965—)
Boron, Kathrin (1969—)
Boronat, Olimpia (1867–1934)
Boros, Ferike (1880–1951)
Borozna, Lyudmila (1954—)
Borregaard Otzen, Christina (1975—)
Borrel, Andrée (1919–1944)
Borrero, Dulce María (1883–1945)
Borrowman, Agnes (1881–1955)
Borst-Eilers, Els (1932—)
Bortolozzi, Francesca (1968—)
Borysenko, Nataliya (1975—)
Borzenkova, Galina (1964—)
Bos, Alida van den (1902—)
Bosakova-Vechtova, Eva (1931–1991)
Bosboom-Toussaint, Anna (1812–1886)
Bosch, Aurora (c. 1940—)
Bosch, Edith (1980—)
Boschek, Anna (1874–1957)
Bosco, María Angélica (1917—)
Bosco, Monique (1927—)
Bose, Abala (1865–1951)
Bosé, Lucia (1931—)
Boserup, Esther (1910–1999)
Bosone, Reva Beck (1895–1983)
Bosse, Harriet (1878–1961)
Bosshardt, Alida M. (1913—)
Bosshart, Dominique (1977—)

Boston, Lucy Maria (1892–1990)
Bosurgi, Silvia (1979—)
Boswell, Annabella (1826–1916)
Boswell, Cathy (1962—)
Boswell, Connee (1907–1976)
Bota, Kinga (1977—)
Botchkareva, Evguenia
Botchkareva, Maria (1889–?)
Botelho, Fernanda (1926—)
Botha, Wendy (1965—)
Botkin, Cordelia (c. 1854–1910)
Botsford, Beth (1981—)
Botterill, Jennifer (1979—)
Bottome, Margaret McDonald (1827–1906)
Bottome, Phyllis (1884–1963)
Bottomley, Virginia (1948—)
Bottzau, Tina (1971—)
Botwinska, Adela (b. 1904)
Boucher, Denise (1935—)
Boucherett, Jessie (1825–1905)
Boucicault, Nina (1867–1950)
Boudin, Kathy (1943—)
Boudjenah, Yasmine (1970—)
Boudrias, Christine (1972—)
Boughton, Alice (1866–1943)
Bouhired, Djamila (1937—)
Boulanger, Lili (1893–1918)
Boulanger, Nadia (1887–1979)
Boulaz, Loulou (1912—)
Boulmerka, Hassiba (1968—)
Boulter, Rosalyn (1916–1997)
Boulton, Agnes (1893–1968)
Bouman, Kea (1903–1998)
Boumediene-Thiery, Alima (1956—)
Boupacha, Djamila (1942—)
Bourassa, Jocelyn (1947—)
Bourgeois, Louise (b. 1911)
Bourin, Jeanne (1922–2004)
Bourke-White, Margaret (1904–1971)
Boutilier, Joy (1939—)
Bouvet, Marguerite (1865–1915)
Bouvier, Jeanne (1865–1964)
Bouvier, Léone (c. 1929—)
Bovasso, Julie (1930–1991)
Bove, Joan (1901–2001)
Boveri, Margret (1900–1975)
Bovt, Violette (1927—)
Bovy, Berthe (1887–1977)
Bow, Clara (1904–1965)
Bowden, Pamela (1925–2003)
Bowden, Sally (c. 1948—)
Bowen, Catherine Drinker (1897–1973)
Bowen, Elizabeth (1899–1973)
Bowen, Gretta (1880–1981)
Bowen, Louise (1859–1953)
Bower, Alberta (1922—)
Bower, Beverly (d. 2002)
Bower, Carol (1956—)
Bowers, Lally (1917–1984)
Bowes, Alice (c. 1890–1969)
Bowles, Eva del Vakia (1875–1943)
Bowles, Jane (1917–1973)
Bowman, Deborah (1963—)
Bowman, Nellie (b. 1878)
Bowman, Patricia (1904–1999)
Bowring, Eva Kelly (1892–1985)
Box, Betty E. (1915–1999)
Box, Muriel (1905–1991)
Boxer, Barbara (1940—)
Boxx, Gillian (1973—)
Boxx, Shannon (1977—)
Boyack, Sarah (1961—)
Boyarskikh, Claudia (1939—)
Boyce, Ann (c. 1827–1914)
Boyce, Johanna (1954—)
Boyce, Neith (1872–1951)
Boyd, Anne (1946—)
Boyd, Carla (1975—)
Boyd, Eva (1945–2003)
Boyd, Liona (1950—)
Boyd, Louise Arner (1887–1972)
Boyd, Megan (1915–2001)
Boyd, Susan (1949–2004)
Boye, Karin (1900–1941)
Boy-Ed, Ida (1852–1928)
Boylan, Mary (1913–1984)
Boyle, Darian (c. 1968—)
Boyle, Desley (1948—)
Boyle, Eleanor Vere (1825–1916)
Boyle, Helen (1869–1957)
Boyle, Kay (1902–1992)
Boyle, Raelene (1951—)
Boylen, Christilot (1947—)
Boyne, Eva Leonard (1886–1960)
Boys, Beverly (1951—)
Boys-Smith, Winifred Lily (1865–1939)
Bozhurina, Tsvetana (1952—)
Bozyk, Reizl (1914–1993)
Bozzino, Tina (fl. 1920s–30s)
Brabants, Jeanne (1920—)
Bracetti, Mariana (1840–c. 1904)
Brachvogel, Carry (1864–1942)
Brackeen, JoAnne (1938—)
Brackett, Anna Callender (1836–1911)
Brackett, Leigh (1915–1978)
Bracquemond, Marie (1840–1916)
Braddock, Bessie (1899–1970)
Braddon, Mary Elizabeth (1835–1915)
Braden, Anne (1924–2006)
Bradford, Barbara Taylor (1933—)
Bradford, Cornelia Foster (1847–1935)
Bradley, Amber (1980—)
Bradley, Amy Morris (1823–1904)
Bradley, Grace (1913—)
Bradley, Jenny
Bradley, Katharine Harris (1846–1914)
Bradley, Lillian Trimble (1875–?)
Bradley, Lisa (1941—)
Bradley, Lydia Moss (1816–1908)
Bradley, Marion Zimmer (1930–1999)
Bradley, Pat (1951—)
Bradna, Olympe (1920—)
Brady, Alice (1892–1939)
Brady, Mildred Edie (1906–1965)
Brady, Veronica (1890–1964)
Brae, June (1917–2000)
Braga, Maria Ondina (1932–2003)
Braga, Sonia (1950—)
Braggiotti, Berthe (c. 1900–c. 1925)
Braggiotti, Francesca (1902–1998)
Braggiotti, Gloria (c. 1905—)
Bragina, Lyudmila (1943—)
Braham, Leonora (1853–1931)
Brain, Marilyn (1959—)
Braithwaite, Lilian (1873–1948)
Brakewell, Jeanette (1974—)
Bramlett, Bonnie (1944—)
Bramley, Jenny Rosenthal (1910–1997)
Bramwell-Booth, Catherine (1883–1987)
Branch, Anna Hempstead (1875–1937)
Branch, Mary Lydia Bolles (1840–1922)
Brancourt, Karen (1962—)
Brand, Colette
Brand, Esther (1924—)
Brand, Mona (1915—)
Brand, Phoebe (1907–2004)
Brand, Sybil (c. 1899–2004)
Brandão, Fiama Hasse Pais (1938—)
Brandebusemeyer, Nicole (1974—)
Brandegee, Mary Katharine (1844–1920)
Brandès, Marthe (1862–1930)
Brandes-Brilleslijper, Janny (c. 1918–2003)
Brandstrom, Elsa (1888–1948)
Brandt, Marianne (1842–1921)
Brandt, Marianne (1893–1983)
Brandt, Muriel (1909–1981)
Brandy (1979—)
Branham, Sara Elizabeth (1888–1962)
Branigan, Laura (1957–2004)
Branitzka, Nathalie (1905–1977)
Brankin, Rhona
Branscombe, Gena (1881–1977)
Brant, Beth (1941—)
Brantenberg, Gerd (1941—)
Branzell, Karin (1891–1974)
Braslau, Sophie (1888–1935)
Brasseur, Isabelle (1970—)
Braumueller, Ellen (1910—)
Braun, Carol Mosely (1947—)
Braun, E. Lucy (1889–1971)
Braun, Eva (1912–1945)
Braun, Johanna (1929—)
Braun, Lily (1865–1916)
Braun, Maria-Johanna (1911–1982)
Braun, Sabine (1965—)
Braun-Vogelstein, Julie (1883–1971)
Braxton, Toni (1967—)
Brayley, Sally (1937—)
Brayton, Lily (1876–1953)
Brazil, Angela (1868–1947)
Bré, Ruth (1862–1911)
Breamer, Sylvia (1897–1943)
Breckinridge, Madeline McDowell (1872–1920)
Breckinridge, Mary (1881–1965)
Breckinridge, Mary Marvin (1905–2002)
Breckinridge, Sophonisba Preston (1866–1948)
Bredael, Annelies (1965—)
Bredahl, Charlotte (1957—)
Breden, Christiane von (1839–1901)
Breen, Nellie (c. 1898–1986)
Breer, Murle MacKenzie (1939—)
Bregendahl, Marie (1867–1940)
Brehm, Marie Caroline (1859–1926)
Breiken, Dagmar (1963—)
Brejchová, Hana (c. 1943—)
Brejchová, Jana (1940—)
Brema, Marie (1856–1925)
Bremer, Edith (1885–1964)
Bremer, Lucille (1923–1996)
Bremner, Janice (1974—)
Brenchley, Winifred (1883–1953)
Brendel, Daniela (1973—)
Brennan, Anna Teresa (1879–1962)
Brennan, Eileen (1935—)
Brennan, Fanny (1921–2001)
Brennan, Maire (1952—)
Brenner, Dori (1946–2000)
Brenner, Veronica (1974—)
Brent, Evelyn (1899–1975)
Brent-Dyer, Elinor M. (1894–1969)
Breshkovsky, Catherine (1844–1934)
Brésil, Marguerite (1880–1923)
Breslau, Louise (1857–1927)
Breslauer, Marianne (1909–2001)
Breuer, Grit (1972—)
Breuer-Dukat, Renate (1939—)
Brewer, Margaret A. (1930—)
Brewer, Teresa (1931—)
Brewster, Barbara (1918–2005)
Brewster, Elizabeth (1922—)
Brewster, Gloria (1918–1996)
Brexner, Edeltraud (1927—)
Breyer, Hiltrud (1957—)
Brezhneva, Galina (1929—)
Brezhneva, Viktoriya (1908–1995)
Brian, Mary (1906–2002)
Briand, Anne (1968—)
Brianza, Carlotta (1862–1930)
Brice, Carol (1918–1985)
Brice, Elizabeth (c. 1885–1965)
Brice, Fanny (1891–1951)
Brickell, Edie (1966—)
Brico, Antonia (1902–1989)
Bridger, Bub (1924—)
Bridges, Alice (1916—)
Bridges, Fidelia (1834–1923)
Bridges, Ruby (c. 1954—)
Brienese, Karin (1969—)
Briercliffe, Nellie (1889–1966)
Briggs, Emily Edson (1830–1910)
Briggs, Karen (1963—)
Briggs, Margaret Jane (1892–1961)
Bright, Dora Estella (1863–1951)
Bright, Mary (1954–2002)
Bright, Mary Golding (1857–1945)
Brightman, Sarah (1960—)
Brightwen, Eliza (1830–1906)
Brigitha, Enith Salle (1955—)
Brigman, Anne W. (1869–1950)
Brill, Debbie (1953—)
Brill, Patti (1923–1963)
Brink, Carol Ryrie (1895–1981)
Brinker, Nancy G. (1946—)
Brinkley, Christie (1953—)
Brinsmead, Hesba Fay (1922–2003)
Brion, Hélène (1882–1962)
Briscoe, Lottie (1870–1950)
Brisco-Hooks, Valerie (1960—)

Brissac, Virginia (1883–1979)
Brisson, Therese (1966—)
Britain, Radie (1897–1994)
Britt, May (1933—)
Brittain, Vera (1893–1970)
Britton, Alison (1948—)
Britton, Barbara (1919–1980)
Britton, Elizabeth Knight (1858–1934)
Britton, Hutin (1876–1965)
Britton, Nan (1896–1991)
Britton, Pamela (1923–1974)
Britton, Rosa María (1936—)
Britz, Jerilyn (1943—)
Brlić-Mažuranić, Ivana (1874–1938)
Broad, Molly Corbett (c. 1941—)
Broadwick, Tiny (1893–1978)
Broccoli, Dana (1922–2004)
Brock, Karena (1942—)
Brockovich, Erin (1960—)
Brockwell, Gladys (1894–1929)
Brodbeck, May (1917–1983)
Brodber, Erna (1936—)
Broder, Jane (d. 1977)
Broderick, Helen (1890–1959)
Brodsgaard, Karen (1978—)
Brogan, Michelle (1973—)
Brogden, Cindy (1957—)
Brogden, Gwendoline (1891–?)
Brøgger, Suzanne (1944—)
Bromhall, Margaret Ann (1890–1967)
Bromley, Dorothy Dunbar (1896–1986)
Bron, Eleanor (1934—)
Brondello, Sandy (1968—)
Broner, E.M. (1930—)
Bronhill, June (1929–2005)
Broniewska, Janina (1904–1981)
Bronner, Augusta Fox (1881–1966)
Bronsart, Ingeborg von (1840–1913)
Bronskaya, Eugenia (1882–1953)
Bronson, Betty (1906–1971)
Bronson, Lillian (1902–1995)
Brook, Helen (1907–1997)
Brooke, Annette (1947—)
Brooke, Cynthia (1875–1949)
Brooke, Evelyn Gertrude (1879–1962)
Brooke, Hillary (1914–1999)
Brooke-Rose, Christine (1923—)
Brookner, Anita (1928—)
Brooks, Angie (1928—)
Brooks, Charlotte (1918—)
Brooks, Dolores (1946—)
Brooks, Geraldine (1925–1977)
Brooks, Gwendolyn (1917–2000)
Brooks, Hadda (1916–2002)
Brooks, Harriet (1876–1933)
Brooks, Lela (b. 1908)
Brooks, Louise (1906–1985)
Brooks, Matilda M. (1888–1981)
Brooks, Pauline (1912–1967)
Brooks, Phyllis (1914–1995)
Brooks, Romaine (1874–1970)
Brookshaw, Dorothy (1912—)
Broom, Christina (1863–1939)
Broomall, Anna (1847–1931)
Brophy, Brigid (1929–1995)
Broquedis, Marguerite (1893–1983)
Brossard, Nicole (1943—)
Brothers, Joyce (1928—)
Brotherton, Alice Williams (1848–1930)
Brough, Fanny Whiteside (1854–1914)
Brough, Louise (1923—)
Brough, Mary (1863–1934)
Broughton, Rhoda (1840–1920)
Brouletova, Lioubov
Brouquier, Veronique (1957—)
Brousse, Amy (1910–1963)
Brouwenstijn, Gré (1915–1999)
Brouwer, Bertha (1930—)
Brovar, Anna Iakovlevna (1887–1917)
Brown, Abbie Farwell (1871–1927)
Brown, Ada (1889–1950)
Brown, Alice (1856–1948)
Brown, Alice Regina (1960—)
Brown, Alice Van Vechten (1862–1949)
Brown, Audrey (b. 1913)
Brown, Audrey Alexandra (1904–1998)
Brown, Beverly (1941–2002)
Brown, Carol Page (1953—)
Brown, Carolyn (1927—)
Brown, Charlotte (1846–1904)
Brown, Charlotte Hawkins (c. 1883–1961)
Brown, Cindy (1965—)
Brown, Cleo (1905–1995)
Brown, Dorothy L. (1919–2004)
Brown, Earlene Dennis (1935—)
Brown, Edith Mary (1864–1956)
Brown, Elaine (1943—)
Brown, Foxy (1979—)
Brown, Georgia (1933–1992)
Brown, Hallie Quinn (c. 1845–1949)
Brown, Helen Gurley (1922—)
Brown, Hilary (1952—)
Brown, Iona (1941–2004)
Brown, Jessica (c. 1900–?)
Brown, Jessie (1892–1985)
Brown, Joanne (1972—)
Brown, Josephine (1892–1976)
Brown, Judi (1961—)
Brown, Karen (1955—)
Brown, Karen (1963—)
Brown, Katie (1982—)
Brown, Kay (1903–1995)
Brown, Leah (1975—)
Brown, Linda (1943—)
Brown, Marcia (1918—)
Brown, Margaret Elizabeth (1918—)
Brown, Margaret Wise (1910–1952)
Brown, Martha McClellan (1838–1916)
Brown, Mary Jane (1917–1997)
Brown, Melanie (1975—)
Brown, Minnijean (1942—)
Brown, Molly (1867–1932)
Brown, Olympia (1835–1926)
Brown, Pamela (1917–1975)
Brown, Rachel Fuller (1898–1980)
Brown, Rita Mae (1944—)
Brown, Rosel George (1926–1967)
Brown, Rosellen (1939—)
Brown, Rosemary (1916–2001)
Brown, Rosemary (1930—)
Brown, Ruth (1928—)
Brown, Tina (1953—)
Brown, Trisha (1936—)
Brown, Vanessa (1928–1999)
Brown, Vera Scantlebury (1889–1946)
Brown, Vida (1922—)
Brown, Virginia Mae (1923–1991)
Brownbill, Kay
Brown Blackwell, Antoinette (1825–1921)
Browne, Coral (1913–1991)
Browne, Harriet Louisa (1829–1906)
Browne, Helen Edith (1911–1987)
Browne, Irene (1896–1965)
Browne, Kathleen Anne (b. 1878)
Browne, Leslie (1958—)
Browne, Marjorie (1910–1990)
Browne, Mary K. (1891–1971)
Browne, Rosalind Bengelsdorf (1916–1979)
Browne, Sidney Jane (1850–1941)
Browner, Carol M. (1956—)
Browning, Angela (1946—)
Brown-Miller, Lisa (1966—)
Brownscombe, Jennie Augusta (1850–1936)
Brownson, Josephine (1880–1942)
Brownstein, Carrie (1974—)
Broxon, Mildred Downey (1944—)
Bruce, Betty (1920–1974)
Bruce, Catherine Wolfe (1816–1900)
Bruce, Ethel (1879–1967)
Bruce, Kate (1858–1946)
Bruce, Mary Grant (1878–1958)
Bruce, Tonie Edgar (1892–1966)
Bruce, Virginia (1910–1982)
Bruce, Wendy (1973—)
Brück, Christa-Anita (1899–?)
Brückner, Christine (1921–1996)
Brues, Alice (1913—)
Bruggen, Carry van (1881–1932)
Brugha, Caitlin (1879–1959)
Bruha, Antonia (1915—)
Brühne, Vera (1910—)
Brüll, Ilse (1925–1942)
Brunauer, Esther C. (1901–1959)
Brundage, Jennifer (1973—)
Brune, Adrienne (b. 1892)
Brune, Gabrielle (b. 1912)
Brunet, Caroline (1969—)
Brunet, Marta (1897–1967)
Brunet, Roberta (1965—)
Brüning, Elfriede (1910—)
Brunner, Josefine (1909–1943)
Brunner, Melitta (1907—)
Brunner, Ursula (1941—)
Bruno, Gioia Carmen (1965—)
Brunschvicg, Cécile (1877–1946)
Brunswick, Ruth Mack (1897–1946)
Bruntland, Gro Harlem (1939—)
Brunton, Dorothy (1893–1977)
Brusnikina, Olga (1978—)
Brusselmans, Anne (c. 1905—)
Brustein, Norma (c. 1929–1979)
Brutsaert, Elke (1968—)
Bryan, Anna E. (1858–1901)
Bryan, Jane (1918—)
Bryan, Mary Edwards (1838–1913)
Bryant, Alice Gertrude (c. 1862–1942)
Bryant, Bonnie (1943—)
Bryant, Charlotte (c. 1902–1936)
Bryant, Deborah (c. 1946—)
Bryant, Dorothy (1930—)
Bryant, Felice (1925–2003)
Bryant, Hazel (1939–1983)
Bryant, Lane (1879–1951)
Bryant, Louise (1885–1936)
Bryant, Millicent (1878–1927)
Bryant, Rosalyn (1956—)
Bryant, Sophie (1850–1922)
Bryceland, Yvonne (1926–1992)
Bryk, Rut (1916–1999)
Bryn, Alexia (1889–1983)
Bryner, Vera (d. 1967)
Bryson, Bernarda (1903–2004)
Brystygierowa, Julia (1902–1980)
Bryunina, Mira (1951—)
Bryzgina, Olga (1963—)
Buber-Neumann, Margarete (1901–1989)
Bubley, Esther (1921–1998)
Buchan, Anna (1878–1948)
Buchanan, Dorothy (1899–1985)
Buchanan, Isobel Wilson (1954—)
Buchanan, Margaret (1864–1940)
Buchanan, Vera Daerr (1902–1955)
Buchner, Annemarie
Buck, Carrie (d. 1983)
Buck, Heather (1926—)
Buck, Karen (1958—)
Buck, Kitty (1907–2001)
Buck, Linda B. (1947—)
Buck, Pearl S. (1892–1973)
Buckel, C. Annette (1833–1912)
Buckland, Jessie Lillian (1878–1939)
Buckman, Rosina (1881–1948)
Bucur, Florica (1959—)
Budapest, Z. (1940—)
Budberg, Moura (1892–1974)
Budd, Zola (1966—)
Budke, Mary Anne (1953—)
Budzynska-Tylicka, Justyna (1876–1936)
Buehrmann, Elizabeth (1886–1954)
Buell, Marjorie Henderson (1905–1993)
Bueno, Maria (1939—)
Buerger, Erna (1909–1958)
Bufalino, Brenda (1937—)
Bufanu, Valeria (1946—)
Buferd, Marilyn (1925–1990)
Buffington, Adele (1900–1973)
Buford-Bailey, Tonja (1970—)
Bugarinovic, Melanija (1905–1986)
Bugbee, Emma (1888–1981)
Buggy, Regina (1959—)
Buglisi, Jacqulyn (1951—)
Bugrimova, Irina (1910–2001)
Bühler, Charlotte (1893–1974)
Buhr-Weigelt, Liane (1956—)
Buitenweg, Kathalijne Maria (1970—)
Bujdoso, Agota (1943—)
Bujold, Geneviève (1942—)
Bukharina, Galina (1945—)

Bukovec, Brigita (1970—)
Bularda-Homeghi, Olga (1958—)
Bülbring, Edith (1903–1990)
Bulbulia, Katharine (1943—)
Buldakova, Lyudmila (1938—)
Bulich, Vera Sergeevna (1898–1954)
Buller, Annie (1896–1973)
Bullett, Vicky (1967—)
Bullin, Katharina (1959—)
Bullowa, Emilie (1869–1942)
Bullrich, Silvina (1915–1990)
Bullwinkel, Vivian (1915–2000)
Bulnes, Esmée (1900–1986)
Bülow, Frieda von (1857–1909)
Bulstrode, Emily Mary (1867–1959)
Bulstrode, Jane Helena (1862–1946)
Bumbry, Grace (1937—)
Bunatyants, Elen (1970—)
Bunge de Gálvez, Delfina (1881–1952)
Bunke, Tamara (1937–1967)
Bunker, Carol Laise (1918–1991)
Bunting, Mary Ingraham (1910–1998)
Bunton, Emma (1976—)
Bunzel, Ruth (1898–1990)
Burani, Michelette (1882–1957)
Burbidge, Margaret (1919—)
Burchenal, Elizabeth (1876–1959)
Burcica, Constanta (1971—)
Burda, Lyubov (1953—)
Burdekin, Katharine (1896–1963)
Burdett-Coutts, Angela (1814–1906)
Burdeyna, Nataliya (1974—)
Buresova, Charlotte (1904–1984)
Burfeindt, Betty (1945—)
Burford, Anne Gorsuch (1942–2004)
Burford, Barbara (1944—)
Burger, Fritzi
Burger, Hildegard (1905–1943)
Burgess, Annie (1969—)
Burgess, Dorothy (1907–1961)
Burgess, Georgina Jane (c. 1839–1904)
Burgess, Renate (1910–1988)
Burgess, Yvonne (1936—)
Burgher, Michelle (1977—)
Burgin, Annie Mona (1903–1985)
Burgos Seguí, Carmen de (1867–1932)
Burjan, Hildegard (1883–1933)
Burka, Ellen Petra (1921—)
Burka, Petra (1946—)
Burka, Sylvia (1954—)
Burkart, Claudia (1980—)
Burkart, Erika (1922—)
Burke, Barbara (1917—)
Burke, Billie (1885–1970)
Burke, Frances (c. 1921—)
Burke, Georgia (1880–1986)
Burke, Joan T. (1929—)
Burke, Kathleen (1913–1980)
Burke, Lynn (1943—)
Burke, Patricia (1917–2003)
Burke, Sarah (1982—)
Burke, Selma Hortense (1900–1995)
Burke, Yvonne Brathwaite (1932—)
Burkholder, Mabel (1881–1973)
Burlet, Delphyne (1966—)
Burlin, Natalie Curtis (1875–1921)
Burmystrova, Ganna (1977—)
Burn, Margaret Gordon (1825–1918)
Burnand, Lily (1865–?)
Burne, Nancy (1912–1954)
Burnell, Jocelyn Bell (1943—)
Burnett, Carol (1933—)
Burnett, Frances Hodgson (1849–1924)
Burnett, Hallie Southgate (1908–1991)
Burnford, Sheila (1918–1984)
Burnham, Viola (1930–2003)
Burns, Lauren (1974—)
Burns, Lindsay
Burns, Louise (1949—)
Burns, Lucy (1879–1966)
Burns, Violet Alberta Jessie (1893–1972)
Burnside, Cara-Beth (1968—)
Burosch, Hannelore (1947—)
Burr, Leslie (1956—)
Burr, Marilyn (1933—)
Burrell, Daisy (b. 1893)
Burridge, Pam (1965—)
Burroughs, Margaret Taylor (1917—)
Burroughs, Nannie Helen (c. 1878–1961)
Burrows, Eva (1929—)
Burrows-Fontaine, Evan (1898–1984)
Bursac, Marija (1921–1943)
Burstyn, Ellen (1932—)
Burt, Laura (1872–1952)
Burton, Beryl (1937–1996)
Burton, Denise (1956—)
Burton, Joan (1949—)
Burton, Pearlie (1904–1993)
Burton, Sala (1925–1987)
Burton, Virginia Lee (1909–1968)
Buryakina, Olga (1958—)
Busch, Mae (1891–1946)
Busch, Sabine (1962—)
Buschschulte, Antje (1978—)
Bush, Barbara (1924—)
Bush, Dorothy V. (1916–1991)
Bush, Frances Cleveland (d. 1967)
Bush, Kate (1958—)
Bush, Laura (1946—)
Bush, Lesley (1947—)
Bush, Noreen (1905–1977)
Bush, Pauline (1886–1969)
Bushfield, Vera Cahalan (1889–1976)
Busley, Jessie (1869–1950)
Bussman, Gabriele (1959—)
Busta, Christine (1914–1987)
Bustos, Crystl (1977—)
Butala, Sharon (1940—)
Butcher, Rosemary (1947—)
Butcher, Susan (1954—)
Bute, Mary Ellen (1906–1983)
Buter, Yvonne (1959—)
Butler, Eleanor (c. 1915–1997)
Butler, Elizabeth Beardsley (c. 1885–1911)
Butler, Elizabeth Thompson (1846–1933)
Butler, Helen May (1867–1957)
Butler, Ida (1868–1949)
Butler, Josephine (1828–1906)
Butler, Margaret Mary (1883–1947)
Butler, Mother Marie Joseph (1860–1940)
Butler, Octavia E. (1947—)
Butler, Selena Sloan (1872–1964)
Butler-Sloss, Elizabeth (1933—)
Butsova, Hilda (1896–1976)
Butt, Clara (1872–1936)
Buttfield, Nancy (1912—)
Button, Isabel (1863–1921)
Buttrose, Ita (1942—)
Butts, Mary (1890–1937)
Butuzova, Natalya (1954—)
Butyrskaya, Maria (1972—)
Buzonas, Gail Johnson (1954—)
Buzunova, Natalya (1958—)
Byars, Betsy (1928—)
Byatt, A.S. (1936—)
Bye, Karyn (1971—)
Byers, Margaret (1832–1912)
Byington, Spring (1886–1971)
Bykova, Natalya (1958—)
Bykova, Tamara (1958—)
Bylund, Ingamay (1949—)
Byon Kyung-Ja (1956—)
Byrne, Jane (1934—)
Byron, Beverly Butcher (1932—)
Byron, Katharine Edgar (1903–1976)
Byron, Kathleen (1922—)
Byron, Kitty (c. 1879–?)
Byron, Marion (1911–1985)
Bystrova, Galina (1934—)
Bögli, Lina (1858–1941)
Caballé, Montserrat (1933—)
Cabanillas, Nuria (1980—)
Cabello de Carbonera, Mercedes (1845–1909)
Cabete, Adelaide (1867–1935)
Cable, Mildred (1878–1952)
Cabot, Dolce Ann (1862–1943)
Cabot, Susan (1927–1986)
Cabrera, Lydia (1899–1991)
Cabrini, Frances Xavier (1850–1917)
Cacchi, Paola (1945—)
Caccialanza, Gisella (1914–1998)
Cáceres, Esther de (1903–1971)
Cachat, Beth (1951—)
Cadbury, Dorothy Adlington (1892–1987)
Cadbury, Geraldine Southall (1865–1941)
Cadbury, Rachel (b. 1894)
Cadden, Mamie (c. 1894–1959)
Cadell, Jean (1884–1967)
Cadilla de Martínez, Maria (1886–1951)
Caduff, Sylvia (1937—)
Cady, H. Emilie (1848–1941)
Caesar, Doris Porter (1892–1971)
Caffyn, Kathleen (1853–1926)
Cagney, Frances (1901–1994)
Cagney, Jeanne (1919–1984)
Cahan, Cora (1940—)
Cahill, Lily (1885–1955)
Cahill, Mabel E. (1863–?)
Cahill, Marie (1870–1933)
Cahun, Claude (1894–1954)
Cai Chang (1900–1990)
Cai Huijue
Caillaux, Henriette (?–1943)
Caird, Maureen (1951—)
Caird, Mona Alison (1858–1932)
Cajal, Rosa María (1920—)
Calamai, Clara (1915–1998)
Caldeira, Hilma (1972—)
Calder, Liz (1938—)
Calderón, Sila M. (1942—)
Calderon Diaz, Rosir (1984—)
Calderone, Mary Steichen (1904–1998)
Calderon Martinez, Mercedes (1965—)
Caldicott, Helen (1938—)
Caldwell, Anne (1876–1936)
Caldwell, Marianne (1866–1933)
Caldwell, Mary Gwendolin (1863–1909)
Caldwell, Sarah (1924–2006)
Caldwell, Taylor (1900–1985)
Caldwell, Zoë (1933—)
Calhoun, Alice (1900–1966)
Calhoun, Marge (fl. 1950s)
Calisher, Hortense (b. 1911)
Calkins, Mary Whiton (1863–1930)
Callaghan, Audrey (1915–2005)
Callas, Maria (1923–1977)
Callen, Maude (1899–1990)
Callender, Beverley (1956—)
Callender, Marie (1907–1995)
Callender, Sheila (1914–2004)
Callens, Els (1970—)
Calligaris, Novella (1954—)
Callil, Carmen (1938—)
Callison, Carole Jo (1938—)
Calloway, Blanche (1902–1973)
Callwood, June (1924—)
Calthrop, Gladys E. (1894–1980)
Calton, Patsy (1948–2005)
Calub, Dyana (1975—)
Calvé, Emma (1858–1942)
Calvert, Catherine (1890–1971)
Calvert, Lilian (1909–2000)
Calvert, Mrs. Charles (1837–1921)
Calvert, Patricia (1906–1978)
Calvert, Phyllis (1915–2002)
Calvet, Corinne (1921–2001)
Calvo de Aguilar, Isabel (1916—)
Calypso Rose (1940—)
Calzada, Alba (1945—)
Cam, Helen M. (1885–1968)
Cama, Bhikaiji (1861–1936)
Camber, Irene (1926—)
Cambridge, Ada (1844–1926)
Cameron, Agnes Deans (1863–1912)
Cameron, Donaldina (1869–1968)
Cameron, Dorothy (d. 1958)
Cameron, Eleanor (1912–1996)
Cameron, Hilda (b. 1912)
Cameron, Julia (c. 1947—)
Cameron, Kate (1874–1965)
Cameron, Michelle (1962—)
Cameron, Robina Thomson (1892–1971)
Cameron, Violet (1862–1919)
Cammermeyer, Margarethe (1942—)
Campanelli, Pauline (1943–2001)
Campbell, Anne (1940—)
Campbell, Beatrice (1922–1979)
Campbell, Cassie (1973—)

Campbell, Charlotte C. (1914–1993)
Campbell, Edith (d. 1945)
Campbell, Grace MacLennan (1895–1963)
Campbell, Helen Stuart (1839–1918)
Campbell, Jeannette (1916–2003)
Campbell, Judy (1916–2004)
Campbell, Juliet (1970—)
Campbell, Kate (1899–1986)
Campbell, Kim (1947—)
Campbell, Lady Colin (1857–1911)
Campbell, Lady Colin (1949—)
Campbell, Lady Jeanne (1928—)
Campbell, Laurel (1902–1971)
Campbell, Louise (1911–1997)
Campbell, Maria (1940—)
Campbell, Mary (1877–1954)
Campbell, Mary Katherine (1905–1990)
Campbell, Maude B. (c. 1908–?)
Campbell, Meg (1937—)
Campbell, Mrs. Patrick (1865–1940)
Campbell, Naomi (1970—)
Campbell, Persia (1898–1974)
Campbell, Stella Tanner (b. 1886)
Campbell, Veronica (1982—)
Campbell, Violet (1892–1970)
Campion, Jane (1954—)
Camplin, Alisa (1974—)
Campoamor, Clara (1888–1972)
Camps, Miriam (1916–1994)
Canal, Marguerite (1890–1978)
Canale, Gianna Maria (1927—)
Canary, Christa (1962—)
Candy, Alice (1888–1977)
Canfield, Ella Jean (1918—)
Canins, Maria (1949—)
Cannary, Martha Jane (1852–1903)
Cannon, Annie Jump (1863–1941)
Cannon, Dyan (1937—)
Cannon, Ida (1877–1960)
Cano, María (1887–1967)
Canova, Judy (1916–1983)
Cansino, Elisa (b. 1895)
Canter-Lund, Hilda M. (1922—)
Canto, Estela (1919–1994)
Cantrell, Lana (1943—)
Canty, Mary Agnes (1879–1950)
Cao Mianying
Capécia, Mayotte (1928–1953)
Capellmann, Nadine (1965—)
Capers, Virginia (1925–2004)
Caperton, Harriette (c. 1913—)
Capes, Lee (1961—)
Capes, Michelle (1966—)
Capmany Farnes, Maria Aurèlia (1918—)
Caponi, Donna (1945—)
Cappiello, Rosa (1942—)
Capps, Lois (1938—)
Capriati, Jennifer (1976—)
Caprice, June (1899–1936)
Capucine (1931–1990)
Carabella, Flora (1926–1999)
Carabillo, Toni (1926–1997)
Caradus, Elizabeth (1832–1912)
Caramagno, Denise (1961—)
Caraway, Hattie Wyatt (1878–1950)
Carbon, Sally (1967—)
Cardale, Effie (1873–1960)
Cardell-Oliver, Florence (1876–1965)
Carden, Joan (1937—)
Cárdenas, Nancy (1934–1994)
Cardinal, Marie (1929–2001)
Cardinale, Claudia (1939—)
Cardus, Ana (1943—)
Carère, Christine (1930—)
Carew, Edith Mary (1868–?)
Carew, Mary (1913–2002)
Carew, Ora (1893–1955)
Carey, Eva (fl. 1921)
Carey, Ida Harriet (1891–1982)
Carey, Mariah (1970—)
Carey, Miriam E. (1858–1937)
Carey, Olive (1896–1988)
Carey, Rosa Nouchette (1840–1909)
Carhart, Georgiana (d. 1959)
Carles, Emilie (1900–1979)
Carleton, Claire (1913–1979)
Carlier, Madeleine (c. 1876–?)
Carlin, Cynthia (d. 1973)
Carline, Nancy (1909–2004)
Carlisle, Alexandra (1886–1936)
Carlisle, Belinda (1958—)
Carlisle, Kitty (b. 1910)
Carlisle, Mary (b. 1912)
Carlotti, Marie-Arlette (1952—)
Carlsen, Agnete (1971—)
Carlson, Carolyn (1943—)
Carlson, Gretchen (c. 1966—)
Carlson, Violet (d. 1997)
Carlstedt, Lily (1926—)
Carmen, Jewel (1897–1984)
Carmichael, Amy (1867–1971)
Carmona, Adriana (1972—)
Carnachan, Blanche Eleanor (1871–1954)
Carne, Judy (1939—)
Carnegie, Caroline (1934—)
Carnegie, Hattie (1886–1956)
Carnegie, Louise Whitfield (1857–1946)
Carnegie, Maud (1893–1945)
Carner, JoAnne (1939—)
Carnes, Kim (1945—)
Carney, Kate (1870–1950)
Carney, Winifred (1887–1943)
Caro, Margaret (1848–1938)
Caro, Pauline (1835–1901)
Carol, Martine (1922–1967)
Carol, Sue (1906–1982)
Caroline Matilda of Denmark (1912–1995)
Caroline Matilda of Schleswig-Holstein (1860–1932)
Caroline of Monaco (1957—)
Caroline of Saxony (1833–1907)
Caron, Christine (1948—)
Caron, Leslie (1931—)
Caron, Margaret Pettibone (b. around 1904)
Carosio, Margherita (1908–2005)
Carothers, E. Eleanor (1882–1957)
Carpadios, Marissa (1977—)
Carpenter, Constance (1904–1992)
Carpenter, Iris (b. 1906)
Carpenter, Karen (1950–1983)
Carpenter, Marion (1920–2002)
Carpenter, Mary Chapin (1958—)
Carpenter, Maud (d. 1967)
Carpenter, Thelma (1922–1997)
Carpenter Phinney, Connie (1957—)
Carpinteri, Laura (b. 1910)
Carr, Ann (1958—)
Carr, Catherine (1954—)
Carr, Emily (1871–1945)
Carr, Emma Perry (1880–1972)
Carr, Mary (1874–1973)
Carr, Vikki (1941—)
Carran, Catherine (1842–1935)
Carranza, María Mercedes (1945–2003)
Carr-Boyd, Ann (1938—)
Carr-Cook, Madge (1856–1933)
Carré, Mathilde (1908–c. 1970)
Carrel, Dany (1935—)
Carreño, Teresa (1853–1917)
Carrigan, Sara (1980—)
Carrighar, Sally (1898–1985)
Carrilho, Maria (1943—)
Carrillo de la Paz, Nancy (1986—)
Carrington, Dora (1893–1932)
Carrington, Ethel (1889–1962)
Carrington, Joanna (1931–2003)
Carrington, Leonora (1917—)
Carroll, Dee (1925–1980)
Carroll, Diahann (1935—)
Carroll, Gladys Hasty (1904–1999)
Carroll, Heni Materoa (1852/56?–1930)
Carroll, Madeleine (1906–1987)
Carroll, Nancy (1903–1965)
Carroll, Vinnette (1922–2002)
Carruthers, Kitty (1962—)
Carse, Matilda Bradley (1835–1917)
Carson, Gladys (b. 1903)
Carson, Joan (1935—)
Carson, Julia (1938—)
Carson, Rachel (1907–1964)
Carson, Violet (1898–1983)
Carstensen-Nathansen, Fritze (1925—)
Carswell, Catherine (1879–1946)
Carte, Bridget D'Oyly (1908–1985)
Carten, Audrey (b. 1900)
Carter, Amy (1967—)
Carter, Angela (1940–1992)
Carter, Anita (1933–1999)
Carter, Ann Shaw (1922—)
Carter, Betty (1929–1998)
Carter, Carlene (1955—)
Carter, Eunice Hunton (1899–1970)
Carter, Helen (1927–1998)
Carter, Helena (1923–2000)
Carter, Janis (1913–1994)
Carter, Jeanette (1923–2006)
Carter, Maybelle (1909–1978)
Carter, Mrs. Leslie (1862–1937)
Carter, Nell (1894–1965)
Carter, Nell (1948–2003)
Carter, Rosalynn (1927—)
Carter, Sarah (1898–1979)
Carter, Una Isabel (1890–1954)
Cartier, Diana (1939—)
Cartland, Barbara (1901–2000)
Cartlidge, Katrin (1961–2002)
Carton, Pauline (1884–1974)
Cartwright, Julia (1851–1924)
Cartwright, Mary L. (1900–1998)
Cartwright, Peggy (1912–2001)
Carus, Emma (1879–1927)
Carus-Wilson, Eleanora Mary (1897–1977)
Carvajal, María Isabel (1888–1949)
Carvajal Rivera, Magaly Esther (1968—)
Carvalho, Dinora de (1905—)
Carvalho, Maria Judite de (1921–1998)
Carven (b. 1909)
Carver, Kathryn (1899–1947)
Carver, Louise (1869–1956)
Carver, Lynne (1909–1955)
Carver, Tina (c. 1923–1982)
Carver-Dias, Claire (1977—)
Cary, Annie Louise (1841–1921)
Cary, Elisabeth Luther (1867–1936)
Casadesus, Gaby (1901–1999)
Casagrande, Anna (1958—)
Casals, Rosemary (1948—)
Casanova, Danielle (1909–1943)
Casares, Maria (1922–1996)
Casaretto, Caroline (1978—)
Case, Adelaide (1887–1948)
Caselotti, Adriana (1916–1997)
Casely-Hayford, Adelaide (1868–1960)
Casely-Hayford, Gladys (1904–1950)
Casey, Maie (1892–1983)
Casgrain, Thérèse (1896–1981)
Cash, June Carter (1929–2003)
Cash, Kellye (c. 1965—)
Cash, Rosalind (1938–1995)
Cash, Rosanne (1955—)
Cash, Swin (1979—)
Cashin, Bonnie (1915–2000)
Cashman, Karen
Cashman, Mel (1891–1979)
Cashman, Nellie (1844–1925)
Caslaru, Beatrice (1975—)
Caslavska, Vera (1942—)
Cason, Barbara (1928–1990)
Caspary, Vera (1899–1987)
Cass, Peggy (1924–1999)
Cassab, Judy (1920—)
Cassatt, Mary (1844–1926)
Cassian, Nina (1924—)
Cassidy, Eileen (1932–1995)
Cassidy, Sheila (1937—)
Cassie, Alice Mary (1887–1963)
Cassie Cooper, Vivienne (1926—)
Casson, Ann (1915–1990)
Casson, Margaret MacDonald (1913–1999)
Casson, Mary (b. 1914)
Castellanos, Rosario (1925–1974)
Castenschiold, Thora (1882–1979)
Castle, Amy (1880–?)
Castle, Barbara (1910–2002)
Castle, Irene (c. 1893–1969)
Castle, Naomi (1974—)
Castle, Peggie (1926–1973)
Castles, Amy (1880–1951)
Castro, Fernanda de (1900–1994)

Castro Alves, Diná Silveira de (1911–1983)
Castroviejo, Concha (1915–1995)
Caswell, Maude (c. 1880–?)
Catchings, Tamika (1979—)
Cather, Willa (1873–1947)
Catherwood, Ethel (1910–1987)
Catherwood, Mary Hartwell (1847–1902)
Catlett, Elizabeth (b. 1915)
Cato, Nancy (1917–2000)
Caton-Thompson, Gertrude (1888–1985)
Catt, Carrie Chapman (1859–1947)
Catterson, Pat (1946—)
Catuna, Anuta (1968—)
Cauer, Minna (1841–1922)
Caulfield, Joan (1922–1921)
Caulkins, Tracy (1963—)
Caullery, Isabelle (1955—)
Cauquil, Chantal (1949—)
Cavagnoud, Regine (1970–2001)
Cavalieri, Lina (1874–1944)
Cavallazzi, Malvina (c. 1852–1924)
Cavalleri, Silvia (1972—)
Cavani, Liliana (1933—)
Cavell, Edith (1865–1915)
Cavendish, Lucy Caroline (1841–1925)
Cawley, Shirley (1932—)
Cayetana Fitz-James Stuart y Silva, Maria del Rosario (1926—)
Cayvan, Georgia (1857–1906)
Ceausescu, Elena (1916–1989)
Cebotari, Maria (1910–1949)
Ceccarelli, Daniela (1975—)
Cecchi D'Amico, Suso (1914—)
Cecil, Sylvia (1906–1983)
Cecilia of Mecklenburg-Schwerin (1886–1954)
Cederna, Camilla (1921–1997)
Cederqvist, Jane (1945—)
Cederschiöld, Charlotte (1944—)
Celli, Faith (1888–1942)
Centeno, Yvette (1940—)
Ceplak, Jolanda (1976—)
Cerdeira Morterero, Carmen (1958—)
Cermakova, Jirina (1944—)
Cerri, Cecilie (1872–1931)
Cerrito, Fanny (1817–1909)
Cervera, Luisa (1964—)
César, Ana Cristina (1952–1983)
Cesari, Welleda (1920—)
Cha, Theresa Hak Kyung (1951–1982)
Chabot, Maria (1913–2001)
Chabrillan, Céleste de (1824–1909)
Chace, Marian (1896–1970)
Chacel, Rosa (1898–1994)
Chachkova, Lioubov (1977—)
Chacón, Dulce (1954–2003)
Chacón Nardi, Rafaela (1926–2001)
Chadimova, Alena (1931—)
Chadwick, Cassie L. (1859–1907)
Chadwick, Florence (1918–1995)
Chadwick, Helen (1953–1996)
Chadwick, Helene (1897–1940)
Chaffee, Suzy (1946—)
Chai, Ling (1966—)
Chaibi, Aïcha
Chaikina, Liza (d. 1941)
Cha Jae-Kyung (1971—)
Chalker, Lynda (1942—)
Chalmers, Angela (1963—)
Chamberlain, Ann Marie (1935—)
Chamberlain, Lindy (1948—)
Chambers, Anne Cox (1919—)
Chambers, Dorothea Lambert (1878–1960)
Chambers, Norah (1905–1989)
Chamie, Tatiana (d. 1953)
Chaminade, Cécile (1857–1944)
Chamorro, Violeta (1929—)
Champagne, Andrée (1939—)
Champion, Marge (1919—)
Champlin, Jane (1917–1943)
Chan, Erin (1979—)
Chancellor, Joyce (1906—)
Chand, Meira (1942—)
Chandler, Dorothy Buffum (1901–1997)
Chandler, Helen (1906–1965)
Chandler, Janet (1915–1994)
Chandler, Jennifer (1959—)
Chandler, Michelle
Chanel, Coco (1883–1971)
Chaney, Frances (1915–2004)
Chang, Diana (1934—)
Chang, Eileen (1920–1995)
Chang, Iris (1968–2004)
Chang Eun-Jung (1970—)
Chang Hee-Sook (1955—)
Channing, Carol (1921—)
Channing, Stockard (1944—)
Chao Na
Chapelle, Dickey (1919–1972)
Chapin, Anne Morrison (1892–1967)
Chapin, Augusta (1836–1905)
Chaplin, Geraldine (1944—)
Chaplin, Lita Grey (1908–1995)
Chaplin, Oona O'Neill (1925–1991)
Chapman, Edythe (1863–1948)
Chapman, Marguerite (1918–1999)
Chapman, Merilyn (1962—)
Chapman, Pansy (1892–1973)
Chapman, Susan (1962—)
Chapman, Sylvia (1896–1995)
Chapman, Tracy (1964—)
Chapman, Vera (1898–1996)
Chapman, Yvonne (1940—)
Chardonnet, Michele (1956—)
Chard-Williams, Ada (c. 1876–1900)
Charest, Isabelle (1971—)
Charisse, Calliope (c. 1880–1946)
Charisse, Cyd (1921—)
Charles, Daedra (1969—)
Charles, Eugenia (1919–2005)
Charles, Lallie (1869–1919)
Charles, Suzette (1963—)
Charleson, Mary (1890–1961)
Charlotte (1896–1985)
Charlotte of Saxe-Meiningen (1860–1919)
Charnas, Suzy McKee (1939—)
Charrat, Janine (1924—)
Charteris, Catherine Morice (1835–1918)
Charteris, Violet (1888–1971)
Chartrand, Isabelle (1978—)
Chartroule, Marie-Amélie (1848–1912)
Charvatova, Olga (1962—)
Chase, Agnes Meara (1869–1963)
Chase, Alison Becker (c. 1948—)
Chase, Arline (1900–1926)
Chase, Barrie (1933—)
Chase, Edna Woolman (1877–1957)
Chase, Elizabeth (1950—)
Chase, Ilka (1905–1978)
Chase, Lucia (1897–1986)
Chase, Martha (1927–2003)
Chase, Mary Coyle (1907–1981)
Chase, Mary Ellen (1887–1973)
Chase, Pauline (1885–1962)
Chasen, Maude (1904–2001)
Chase-Riboud, Barbara (1936—)
Chast, Roz (1954—)
Chastain, Brandi (1968—)
Chatterton, Ruth (1893–1961)
Chattopadhyaya, Kamaladevi (1903–1988)
Chatwin, Margaret (c. 1881–1937)
Chatziioannou, Ioanna (1973—)
Chauncy, Nan (1900–1970)
Chausson, Anne-Caroline (1977—)
Chauvet, Marie (1916–1973)
Chauvin, Jeanne (1862–1926)
Chauviré, Yvette (1917—)
Chavez-Thompson, Linda (1944—)
Chawaf, Chantal (1943—)
Chawla, Kalpana (1961–2003)
Chebukina, Yelena (1965—)
Chedid, Andrée (1921—)
Cheeseborough, Chandra (1959—)
Cheeseman, Clara (1852–1943)
Cheeseman, Gwen (1951—)
Cheeseman, Sylvia (1929—)
Cheesman, Lucy Evelyn (1881–1969)
Chelgren, Pamela (c. 1949—)
Chemis, Annie (1862–1939)
Chen, Joan (1961—)
Chen, Joyce (1918–1994)
Chen, Lu (1976—)
Chen, Si-Lan (1909—)
Chenal-Minuzzo, Giuliana (1931—)
Chenchik, Taisiya (1936—)
Chen Cuiting (1971—)
Cheney, Dorothy Bundy (1916—)
Cheney, Ednah Dow (1824–1904)
Cheney, Leona Pressler (1904–1982)
Cheney, Lynne (1941—)
Chen Hong (1968—)
Chen Hong
Chen Jieru (fl. 1920)
Chen Jing (1968—)
Chen Jing (1975—)
Chen Jingrong (1917–1989)
Chen Li Ju (1981—)
Chen Muhua (c. 1940—)
Chennault, Anna (1923—)
Chenoweth, Helen (1938—)
Chen Ruiqing (1932—)
Chen Ruoxi (1938—)
Chen Shih Hsin (1978—)
Chen Tiejun (1904–1928)
Chen Xiaomin (1977—)
Chen Yan (1981—)
Chen Yanqing (1979—)
Chen Yongyan (1962—)
Chen Yuefang (1963—)
Chen Yueling (1968—)
Chen Yufeng
Chen Zhen (1963—)
Chen Zhong (1982—)
Chen Zihe (1968—)
Chen Zongying (1902–2003)
Chepchumba, Joyce (1970—)
Chepeleva, Anna (1984—)
Cher (1946—)
Cheremisina, Nina (1946—)
Cherevatova, Olena (1970—)
Cherkasova, Marina
Cherkasova, Valentina (1958—)
Chernyshova, Lyudmila (1952—)
Chernyshova, Nadezhda (1951—)
Cherrill, Virginia (1908–1996)
Cherrington, Te Paea (c. 1877–1937)
Cherry, Addie (c. 1859–1942)
Cherry, Effie (d. 1944)
Cherry, Frances (1937—)
Cherry, Helen (1915–2001)
Cherry, Neneh (1963—)
Cherryh, C.J. (1942—)
Chervinskaya, Lidiya Davydovna (1907–1988)
Cheryazova, Lina (1968—)
Chesimard, Joanne (1948—)
Chesler, Phyllis (1940—)
Chester, Betty (1895–1943)
Cheung, Katherine (1904–2003)
Chevalier, Caroline (c. 1832–1917)
Chevenix, Helen (1886–1963)
Chevigné, Laure de (1860–1936)
Chewikar, Princess (1876–1947)
Chiang, Faina (1916–2004)
Chiappa, Imelda (1966—)
Chiaureli, Sofiko (1937—)
Chiba, Ginko (1938—)
Chibesakunda, Lombe Phyllis (1944—)
Chicago, Judy (1939—)
Chichibu Setsuko (1909–1995)
Chick, Harriette (1875–1977)
Chick, Sandra (1947—)
Chiepe, Gaositwe (c. 1924—)
Chiesa, Laura (1971—)
Chifley, Elizabeth (1886–1962)
Chilcott, Susan (1963–2003)
Child, Joan (1921—)
Child, Julia (1912–2004)
Childers, Naomi (1892–1964)
Childress, Alice (1916–1994)
Childs, Lucinda (1940—)
Chilver, Sally (1914—)
Chin, Tsai (1937—)
Ching, Laura Blears (c. 1951—)
Chinn, May Edward (1896–1980)
Chirac, Bernadette (1933—)
Chiriaeff, Ludmilla (1924–1996)
Chirwa, Vera (1933—)
Chisholm, Janet (1929–2004)
Chisholm, Linda (1957—)

Chisholm, Melanie (1974—)
Chisholm, Shirley (1924–2005)
Chi Shu-Ju (c. 1983—)
Chitnis, Leela (1909–2003)
Chitty, Letitia (1897–1982)
Chiumina, Olga Nikolaevna (1865–1909)
Chivás, Silvia (1954—)
Chizhova, Nadezhda (1945—)
Chladek, Dana (1963—)
Chmielnicka, Lidia (1939—)
Choate, Mrs. Allison (b. 1910)
Choate, Pearl (1907–1983)
Cho Eun-Hee (1972—)
Cho Eun-Jung
Choi, Sook Nyul (1937—)
Choi Aei-Young (1959—)
Choi Choon-Ok (1965—)
Choi Eun-Kyung (1984—)
Choi Eun-Kyung
Choi Im-Jeong (1981—)
Choi Kyung-Hee (1966—)
Choi Min-Kyung
Choi Mi-Soon
Chojnowska-Liskiewicz, Krystyna (1937—)
Cho Ki-Hyang (1963—)
Cholmondeley, Mary (1859–1925)
Cho Min-Sun
Choms, Wladyslawa Laryssa (1891–1966)
Chona, Maria (1845–1936)
Chopin, Kate (1850–1904)
Chopra, Joyce (1938—)
Choquet-Bruhat, Yvonne (1923—)
Chotek, Sophie (1868–1914)
Chouteau, Yvonne (1929—)
Chow, Amy (1978—)
Chow, Tina (1950–1992)
Chowdhury, Eulie (1923—)
Choy, Elizabeth (b. 1910)
Cho Youn-Jeong (1969—)
Chrétien, Aline (1936—)
Christaller, Helene (1872–1953)
Christensen, Inger (1935—)
Christian, Linda (1923—)
Christian, Meg (1946—)
Christians, Mady (1900–1951)
Christie, Agatha (1890–1976)
Christie, Dorothy (b. 1896)
Christie, Julie (1941—)
Christie, Susan (c. 1969—)
Christina Bernadotte (b. 1943)
Christine, Virginia (1920–1996)
Christine of Hesse-Cassel (1933—)
Christman, Elisabeth (1881–1975)
Christodoulou, Evangelia
Christoffersen, Birte (1924—)
Christofi, Styllou (c. 1900–1954)
Christopher, Patricia (c. 1934—)
Christy, Barrett (1971—)
Christy, June (1925–1990)
Chryssa (1933—)
Chtyrenko, Olga
Chu, Julie (1982—)
Chudina, Alexandra (1923–1990)
Chugtai, Ismat (1915–1991)
Chukanova, Olga (1980—)
Chukovskaya, Lidiya (1907–1996)
Chulabhorn, Princess (1957—)
Chung, Connie (1946—)
Chung, Kyung-Wha (1948—)
Chung, Myung-wha (1944—)
Chung Eun-Kyung (1965—)
Chung Sang-Hyun (1963—)
Chung So-Young (1967—)
Chunikhovskaya, Irina (1968—)
Chun Lee-Kyung (c. 1976—)
Church, Ellen (c. 1905–1965)
Church, Esmé (1893–1972)
Church, Marguerite Stitt (1892–1990)
Churchill, Caryl (1938—)
Churchill, Clementine (1885–1977)
Churchill, Diana (1913–1994)
Churchill, Diana Spencer (1909–1963)
Churchill, Jennie Jerome (1854–1921)
Churchill, Marguerite (1909–2000)
Churchill, Mary (1922—)
Churchill, May (1876–1929)
Churchill, Sarah (1914–1982)
Churilova, L.A. (1875–1937)
Chusovitina, Oksana (1975—)
Chute, B.J. (1913–1987)
Chute, Carolyn (1947—)
Chute, Marchette (1909–1994)
Chytilova, Vera (1929—)
Cialente, Fausta (1898–1994)
Ciano, Edda (1910–1995)
Cicciolina (1951—)
Cicierska, Margaret
Cicot, Christine (1964—)
Cieply-Wieczorkowna, Teresa (1937—)
Cigna, Gina (1900–2001)
Cilento, Diane (1933—)
Cilento, Phyllis (1894–1987)
Çiller, Tansu (1946—)
Cintrón, Conchita (1922—)
Cioncan, Maria (1977—)
Cisneros, Eleonora de (1878–1934)
Cisneros, Evelyn (1958—)
Cisneros, Sandra (1954—)
Cisse, Jeanne-Martin (1926—)
Cistjakova, Galina (1962—)
Cixi (1835–1908)
Cixous, Hélène (1938—)
Claflin, Tennessee (1846–1923)
Claiborne, Liz (1929—)
Claire, Helen (1911–1974)
Claire, Ina (1892–1985)
Clampitt, Amy (1920–1994)
Clapham, Diana (1957—)
Clapp, Cornelia Maria (1849–1934)
Clapp, Louise (1819–1906)
Clapp, Margaret (1910–1974)
Clare, Mary (1894–1970)
Clark, Barbara Lynne (1958—)
Clark, Catherine Anthony (1892–1977)
Clark, Cheryl (1950—)
Clark, Cora Maris (1885–1967)
Clark, Eleanor (1913–1996)
Clark, Eugenie (1922—)
Clark, Georgia Neese (1900–1995)
Clark, Helen (1954—)
Clark, Helen Elizabeth (1950—)
Clark, Hilda (1881–1955)
Clark, Joan (1934—)
Clark, Karen (1972—)
Clark, Kate Emma (1847–1926)
Clark, Kelly (1983—)
Clark, Laurel (1961–2003)
Clark, Lesley Ann (1948—)
Clark, Liddy (1953—)
Clark, Lynda (1949—)
Clark, Mamo (1914–1986)
Clark, Marguerite (1883–1940)
Clark, Marjorie (b. 1909)
Clark, Mary Ellen (1962—)
Clark, Mary Higgins (1929—)
Clark, Mattie Moss (1925–1994)
Clark, Nancy Talbot (1825–1901)
Clark, Peggy (c. 1916–1996)
Clark, Petula (1932—)
Clark, Sally (1958–)
Clark, Septima Poinsette (1898–1987)
Clarke, Betty Ross (1896–1947)
Clarke, Edith (1883–1959)
Clarke, Eldece (1965—)
Clarke, Gillian (1937—)
Clarke, Grace Julian (1865–1938)
Clarke, Helen (c. 1897–?)
Clarke, Helen Archibald (1860–1926)
Clarke, Julia (d. 1912)
Clarke, Kathleen (1878–1972)
Clarke, Mae (1907–1992)
Clarke, Martha (1944—)
Clarke, Mary (1924—)
Clarke, Mary Goulden (d. 1910)
Clarke, Maura (1931—)
Clarke, Patricia Hannah (1919—)
Clarke, Rebecca (1886–1979)
Clarke, Rebecca Sophia (1833–1906)
Clarke, Sarah Jones (1840–1929)
Clarke, Shirley (1925–1997)
Clark Sisters (fl. 1940s)
Claster, Nancy (1915–1997)
Claudel, Camille (1864–1943)
Claudel, Véronique (1966—)
Claus, Hildrun (1939—)
Clausen, Stefanie (1900–1981)
Clauss-Szárvady, Wilhelmina (1834–1907)
Claxton, Kate (1848–1924)
Clay, Laura (1849–1941)
Clay, Theresa (1911–1995)
Clay, Virginia Tunstall (1825–1915)
Clayburgh, Alma (d. 1958)
Clayden, Pauline (1922—)
Claypole, Edith Jane (1870–1915)
Clayton, Barbara (1922—)
Clayton, Bessie (c. 1878–1948)
Clayton, Ethel (1882–1966)
Clayton, Eva M. (1934—)
Clayton, Jan (1917–1983)
Clayton, Marguerite (1891–1968)
Clayton, S. Lillian (1876–1930)
Cleare, Ivy (1948—)
Cleary, Beverly (1916—)
Cleaves, Jessica (1948—)
Cleaves, Margaret (1848–1917)
Cleland, Tammy (1975—)
Clément, Catherine (1939—)
Clement, Elspeth (1956—)
Clementine of Orleans (1817–1907)
Clement-Scott, Margaret (fl. 19th c.)
Clerke, Agnes Mary (1842–1907)
Clerke, Ellen Mary (1840–1906)
Cleveland, Frances Folsom (1864–1947)
Cleveland, Ruth (1891–1904)
Clidat, France (1932—)
Cliff, Clarice (1899–1972)
Cliff, Leslie (1955—)
Cliff, Michelle (1946—)
Cliff, Theresa (1978—)
Clifford, Betsy (1953—)
Clifford, Camille (1885–1970)
Clifford, Kathleen (1887–1962)
Clifford, Mrs. W.K. (1846–1929)
Clifford, Ruth (1900–1998)
Clift, Charmian (1923–1969)
Clift, Martha (fl. 1930s)
Clifton, Lucille (1936—)
Clignet, Marion (1964—)
Clijsters, Kim (1983—)
Cline, Aleisha (1970—)
Cline, Genevieve (1879–1959)
Cline, Maggie (1857–1934)
Cline, Patsy (1932–1963)
Clinton, Chelsea (1980—)
Clinton, Hillary Rodham (1947—)
Clisby, Harriet (1830–1931)
Cloete, Hestrie (1978—)
Clooney, Rosemary (1928–2002)
Close, Glenn (1947—)
Clotilde of Saxe-Coburg-Gotha (1846–1927)
Cloutier, Suzanne (1927–2003)
Clouzot, Vera (1921–1960)
Clubb, Elizabeth (1922—)
Clune, Deirdre (1959—)
Cluysenaar, Anne (1936—)
Clwyd, Ann (1937—)
Clyde, June (1909–1987)
Clymer, Eleanor (1906–2001)
Coachman, Alice (1923—)
Coad, Nellie (1883–1974)
Coakes, Marion (1947—)
Coates, Anne V. (1925—)
Coates, Dorothy Love (1928–2002)
Coates, Florence Nicholson (1850–1927)
Coates, Gloria (1938—)
Coatsworth, Elizabeth (1893–1986)
Cobb, Jerrie (1931—)
Cobb, Jewell Plummer (1924—)
Cobbe, Frances Power (1822–1904)
Cobbold, Hermione (1905–2004)
Cobbs, Janet (1967—)
Coberger, Annelise (1971—)
Cobian, Miguelina (1941—)
Cobos, Antonia (c. 1920—)
Coburn, Doris (fl. 1970s)
Coburn-Carroll, Cindy (fl. 1980s)
Coca, Imogene (1909–2001)
Cocéa, Alice (1899–1970)

Cochelea, Veronica (1965—)
Cochran, Angela (1965—)
Cochran, Barbara (1951—)
Cochran, Jacqueline (1906–1980)
Cochran, Linda (1953—)
Cochran, Marilyn (1950—)
Cockburn, Karen (1980—)
Cockburn, Patricia (1914–1989)
Cockerill, Kay (1964—)
Codina, Iverna (1918—)
Coe, Dawn (1960—)
Coe, Sue (1951—)
Coetzer, Amanda (1971—)
Coffee, Lenore (1896–1984)
Coffey, Ann (1946—)
Coghen Alberdingk, Mercedes (1962—)
Coghlan, Gertrude (1876–1952)
Coghlan, Rose (1852–1932)
Cohan, Georgette (b. 1900)
Cohan, Helen F. (1910–1996)
Cohan, Josephine (1876–1916)
Cohen, Harriet (1895–1967)
Cohen, Lona (1913–1993)
Cohen, Myra (1892–1959)
Cohen, Rose (1880–1925)
Cohen, Shula (fl. 1960s)
Cohen, Tiffany (1966—)
Cohen, Ze'eva (1940—)
Cohn, Fannia (c. 1885–1962)
Cohn, Marianne (1921–1944)
Coimbra, Erika (1980—)
Coit, Margaret L. (1919–2003)
Cojocaru, Christiana (1962—)
Coke, Alexandra (1891–1984)
Colaço, Branca de Gonta (1880–1944)
Colander-Richardson, LaTasha (1976—)
Colban, Marie (1814–1884)
Colbert, Claudette (1903–1996)
Colborn, Theodora (1927—)
Colby, Christine (c. 1950—)
Colby, Clara Bewick (1846–1916)
Colcord, Joanna Carver (1882–1960)
Cole, Anna Russell (1846–1926)
Cole, Edith (1870–1927)
Cole, Johnnetta B. (1936—)
Cole, Kay (1948—)
Cole, Margaret (1893–1980)
Cole, Mary (c. 1913—)
Cole, Natalie (1950—)
Cole, Paula (1968—)
Cole, Rebecca J. (1846–1922)
Colegate, Isabel (1931—)
Colella, Lynn (1950—)
Coleman, Alice Merriam (1858–1936)
Coleman, Bessie (1892–1926)
Coleman, Corrine Grad (1927–2004)
Coleman, Fanny (1840–1919)
Coleman, Georgia (1912–1940)
Coleman, Kit (1864–1915)
Coleman, Mary (1914–2001)
Coleman, Mary Sue (1943—)
Coleman, Nancy (1912–2000)
Colenso, Elizabeth (1821–1904)
Coleridge, Ethel (1883–1976)
Coleridge, Georgina (1916–2003)
Coleridge, Mary Elizabeth (1861–1907)
Coleridge-Taylor, Avril (1903–1998)
Coles, Joyce (b, around 1904)
Colette (1873–1954)
Coley, Doris (1941–2000)
Colin, Jean (1905–1989)
Colledge, Cecilia (1920—)
Collet, Clara (1860–1948)
Colley, Anne (1951—)
Colliard, Renée (fl. 1950s)
Collier, Constance (1878–1955)
Collier, Edith (1885–1964)
Collier, Jane Annie (1869–1955)
Collier, Jeanne (1946—)
Collier, Lesley (1947—)
Collier, Lois (1919–1999)
Collier, Patience (1910–1987)
Collinge, Patricia (1892–1974)
Collingwood, Elizabeth (1924—)
Collino, Maria (1947—)
Collins, Addie Mae (d. 1963)
Collins, Anne (1951—)
Collins, Barbara-Rose (1939—)
Collins, Cardiss (1931—)
Collins, Christine (1969—)
Collins, Cora Sue (1927—)
Collins, Diana (1917–2003)
Collins, Dorothy (1926–1994)
Collins, Eileen (1956—)
Collins, Ellen (1828–1912)
Collins, Gail (1945—)
Collins, Jackie (1937—)
Collins, Janet (1917–2003)
Collins, Joan (1933—)
Collins, José (1887–1958)
Collins, Kathleen (1942–1988)
Collins, Lottie (c. 1866–1910)
Collins, Martha Layne (1936—)
Collins, Marva (1936—)
Collins, Pauline (1940—)
Collins-O'Driscoll, Margaret (1878–1945)
Collyer, June (1907–1968)
Colman, Julia (1828–1909)
Colombetti, Bruna (1936—)
Colon, Maria (1958—)
Colonia, Regina Célia (1940—)
Colqhoun, Alva (1942—)
Colquhoun, Ithell (1906–1988)
Colt, Ethel Barrymore (1912–1977)
Colter, Mary Elizabeth (1869–1949)
Colton, Elizabeth Avery (1872–1924)
Coltrane, Alice (1937—)
Colum, Mary Gunning (1884–1957)
Columbo, Patricia (1957—)
Colville, Meg (1918–2004)
Colvin, Brenda (1897–1981)
Colvin, Shawn (1956—)
Colwell, Rita R. (1934—)
Colwin, Laurie (1944–1992)
Colyer, Evelyn (1902–1930)
Coman, Katharine (1857–1915)
Coman, Otilia (1942—)
Comaneci, Nadia (1961—)
Comberti, Micaela (1952–2003)
Comden, Betty (1915—)
Comfort, Anna Manning (1845–1931)
Comingore, Dorothy (1913–1971)
Commins, Kathleen (1909–2003)
Compagnoni, Deborah (1970—)
Compson, Betty (1897–1974)
Compton, Betty (1907–1944)
Compton, Fay (1894–1978)
Compton, Katherine (1853–1928)
Compton, Madge (c. 1892–1970)
Compton, Viola (1886–1971)
Compton-Burnett, Ivy (1884–1969)
Comstock, Ada Louise (1876–1973)
Comstock, Anna Botsford (1854–1930)
Comstock, Nanette (1873–1942)
Conboy, Sara McLaughlin (1870–1928)
Concannon, Helena (1878–1952)
Conceicao, Janina (1972—)
Conde, Carmen (1907–1996)
Conde, Felisa (c. 1920—)
Condé, Maryse (1937—)
Cone, Carin (1940—)
Cone, Claribel (1864–1929)
Cone, Etta (1870–1949)
Cones, Nancy Ford (1869–1962)
Cong Xued (1963—)
Conklin, Peggy (1902–2003)
Conley, Peggy (1947—)
Conley, Sandra (1943—)
Conn, Elenor (fl. 1980s)
Conn, Shena
Connally, Nellie (1919—)
Connelly, Ana Paula (1972—)
Conner, Nadine (1907–2003)
Connolly, Maureen (1934–1969)
Connolly-O'Brien, Nora (1893–1981)
Connon, Helen (c. 1859–1903)
Connor, Chris (1927—)
Conrad, Karen (1919–1976)
Conrad-Martius, Hedwig (1888–1966)
Conradt, Jody (1941—)
Conran, Shirley (1932—)
Cons, Emma (1838–1912)
Constance Jones, E.E. (1848–1922)
Constantin, Mariana (1960—)
Constantin-Buhaev, Agafia (1955—)
Constantinescu, Mariana (1956—)
Consuelo, Beatriz (c. 1930—)
Content, Marjorie (1895–1984)
Conti, Francesca (1972—)
Conti, Italia (1874–1946)
Contreras, Gloria (1934—)
Converse, Harriet Maxwell (1836–1903)
Conway, Jill Ker (1934—)
Conway, Verona (1910–1986)
Coo, Eva (d. 1935)
Cook, Allison (1972—)
Cook, Barbara (1927—)
Cook, Beryl (1926—)
Cook, Cordelia E. (1919–1996)
Cook, Edith Maud (d. 1910)
Cook, Freda Mary (1896–1990)
Cook, Judith (1933–2004)
Cook, Mary (1863–1950)
Cook, Myrtle (1902–1985)
Cook, Natalie (1975—)
Cook, Sheri (1953—)
Cook, Stephanie (1972—)
Cooke, Anna Rice (1853–1934)
Cooke, Emma
Cooke, Flora (1864–1953)
Cooke, Hope (1940—)
Cookson, Catherine (1906–1998)
Coolbrith, Ina Donna (1841–1928)
Coolidge, Elizabeth Sprague (1863–1953)
Coolidge, Grace Goodhue (1879–1957)
Coolidge, Martha (1946—)
Coolidge, Priscilla
Coolidge, Rita (1944—)
Coomber, Alex (1973—)
Coombs, Claire (1974—)
Coombs, Patricia (1926—)
Cooney, Barbara (1917–2000)
Cooney, Cecelia (1904–1969)
Cooney, Joan Ganz (1929—)
Cooper, Anna J. (c. 1858–1964)
Cooper, Bette (c. 1920—)
Cooper, Charlotte (1871–1966)
Cooper, Christin (1961—)
Cooper, Cynthia (1964—)
Cooper, Diana Duff (1892–1986)
Cooper, Dulcie (1903–1981)
Cooper, Edith Emma (1862–1913)
Cooper, Edna Mae (1900–1986)
Cooper, Eileen (1953—)
Cooper, Gladys (1888–1971)
Cooper, J. California (1940s—)
Cooper, Jacqui (1973—)
Cooper, Jessie (1914–1993)
Cooper, Jilly (1937—)
Cooper, Kim (1965—)
Cooper, Lillian Kemble (1891–1977)
Cooper, Margaret Joyce (b. 1909)
Cooper, Miriam (1891–1976)
Cooper, Susie (1902–1995)
Cooper, Violet Kemble (1886–1961)
Cooper, Whina (1895–1994)
Cooper, Yvette (1969—)
Cooper-Flynn, Beverley (1966—)
Coory, Shirefie (c. 1864–1950)
Cope, Mother Marianne (1838–1918)
Copeland, Lillian (1904–1964)
Copeland-Durham, Emily (1984—)
Copley, Clara (d. 1949)
Copley, Helen (1922–2004)
Coppi, Hilde (1909–1943)
Coppin, Fanny Jackson (1837–1913)
Copps, Sheila (1952—)
Corban-Banovici, Sofia (1956—)
Corbett, Leonora (1908–1960)
Corbett, Marie (1859–1932)
Corbett-Ashby, Margery (1882–1981)
Corbey, Dorette (1957—)
Corbin, Hazel (1894–1988)
Corbin, Virginia Lee (1910–1942)
Corby, Ellen (1911–1998)
Corda, Maria (1898–1975)
Corday, Mara (1930—)
Corday, Rita (1920–1992)

Cordelier, Jeanne (1944—)
Cordell, Cathleen (1915–1997)
Cordua, Beatrice (1943—)
Corelli, Marie (1855–1924)
Cori, Gerty T. (1896–1957)
Corio, Ann (1914–1999)
Corkle, Francesca (1952—)
Cormier, Lucia M. (1909–1993)
Cornelisen, Ann (1926–2003)
Cornelius, Kathy (1932—)
Cornell, Katharine (1893–1974)
Cornell, Sheila (1962—)
Cornescou, Irina Soltanovna (1916—)
Cornet, Lynda (1962—)
Cornett, Leanza (1971—)
Cornfield, Ellen (1948—)
Cornford, Frances Crofts (1886–1960)
Cornish, Mary (c. 1899–?)
Cornwall, Anne (1897–1980)
Coronado, Carolina (1820–1911)
Corradi, Doris (1922—)
Correia, Hélia (1939—)
Correia, Natália (1923–1993)
Corri, Adrienne (1930—)
Corridon, Marie (1930—)
Corrigan, Mairead (1944—)
Corrock, Susan (1951—)
Corson, Marilyn (1954—)
Corston, Jean (1942—)
Cortesa, Valentina (1924—)
Cortez, Jayne (1936—)
Corti, Maria (1915–2002)
Cortin, Hélène (1972—)
Cortines, Júlia (1868–1948)
Cory, Annie Sophie (1868–1952)
Cosby, Camille (1945—)
Cosgrave, Niamh (1964—)
Cossey, Alice Eleanor (1879–1970)
Cossgrove, Selina (1849–1929)
Cossotto, Fiorenza (1935—)
Costa, Marlenis (1973—)
Costa, Renata (1986—)
Costello, Dolores (1905–1979)
Costello, Eileen (1870–1962)
Costello, Helene (1903–1957)
Costian, Daniela (1965—)
Costie, Candace (1963—)
Cotera, Martha (1938—)
Cothran, Shirley (c. 1953—)
Cotrubas, Ileana (1939—)
Cottee, Kay (1954—)
Cotten, Elizabeth (c. 1893–1987)
Cotten, Sallie Southall (1846–1929)
Cottenjé, Mireille (1933—)
Cotton, Lucy (c. 1891–1948)
Cottrell, Dorothy (1902–1957)
Cottrell, Violet May (1887–1971)
Couchman, Elizabeth (1876–1982)
Coudreau, Octavie (c. 1870–c. 1910)
Coughlan, Angela (1952—)
Coughlan, Mary (1965—)
Coughlin, Natalie (1982—)
Coughlin, Paula A. (c. 1961—)
Coulson, Juanita (1933—)
Coulter, Jean
Coulton, Mary Rose (1906–2002)
Courau, Clotilde (1969—)
Courcel, Nicole (1930—)
Couric, Katie (1957—)
Cournoyea, Nellie J. (1940—)
Court, Hazel (1926—)
Court, Margaret Smith (1942—)
Courtauld, Katherine (1856–1935)
Courtenay-Latimer, Marjorie (1907–2004)
Courths-Mahler, Hedwig (1867–1950)
Courtneidge, Cicely (1893–1980)
Courtneidge, Rosaline (1903–1926)
Courtney, Annie
Courtney, Inez (1908–1975)
Courtney, Kathleen (1878–1974)
Courtney, Patricia (c. 1932–2003)
Cousins, Margaret (1878–1954)
Coutinho, Sônia (1939—)
Couzins, Phoebe Wilson (1842–1913)
Couzyn, Jeni (1942—)
Covell, Phyllis (1895–1982)
Coventry, Kirsty (1983—)
Coventry, Pamela (d. 1939)
Cowan, Edith (1861–1932)
Cowan, Ruth (1901–1993)
Cowart, Juanita (1944—)
Cowen, Donna (c. 1950—)
Cowie, Bessie Lee (1860–1950)
Cowie, Eliza Jane (1835–1902)
Cowie, Helen Stephen (1875–1956)
Cowie, Laura (1892–1969)
Cowl, Jane (1883–1950)
Cowles, Anna Roosevelt (1855–1931)
Cowles, Fleur (1910—)
Cowles, Virginia (1912–1983)
Cowley, Gillian (1955—)
Cowley, Joy (1936—)
Cowsill, Barbara (1929–1985)
Cowsill, Susan (1960—)
Cox, Alison (1979—)
Cox, Annemarie (1966—)
Cox, Crystal (1979—)
Cox, Gertrude Mary (1900–1978)
Cox, Hazel (b. 1887)
Cox, Ida (1896–1967)
Cox, Lynne (1957—)
Cox, Margaret (1963—)
Cox, Ray (b. 1880)
Coyle, Grace Longwell (1892–1962)
Coyle, Rose (1914–1988)
Coyne, Colleen (1971—)
Crabtree, Lotta (1847–1924)
Craciunescu, Florenta (1955—)
Cradock, Fanny (1909–1994)
Cradock, Mrs. H.C. (1863–1941)
Crafter, Jane (1955—)
Craig, Betty (1957—)
Craig, Christine (1943—)
Craig, Edith (1869–1947)
Craig, Edith (1907–1979)
Craig, Helen (1912–1986)
Craig, Jenny (1932—)
Craig, Judy (1946—)
Craig, May (1888–1975)
Craig, May (1889–1972)
Craig, Minnie D. (1883–1965)
Craig, Molly (c. 1917–2004)
Craig, Nell (1891–1965)
Craig, Sandra (1942—)
Craighill, Margaret (1898–1977)
Craigie, Cathie (1954—)
Craigie, Pearl Mary Teresa (1867–1906)
Crain, Jeanne (1925–2003)
Crandall, Ella Phillips (1871–1938)
Crane, Caroline Bartlett (1858–1935)
Crane, Eva (1911—)
Crane, Norma (1928–1973)
Cranston, Kate (1850–1934)
Cranz, Christl (1914–2004)
Crapp, Lorraine J. (1938—)
Crapsey, Adelaide (1878–1914)
Craske, Margaret (1892–1990)
Cratty, Mabel (1868–1928)
Craven, Margaret (1901–1980)
Crawford, Cheryl (1902–1986)
Crawford, Cindy (1966—)
Crawford, Fiona (1977—)
Crawford, Jean Ashley (1939—)
Crawford, Joan (1906–1977)
Crawford, Mimi (d. 1966)
Crawford, Ruth (1901–1953)
Crawford, Shannon (1963—)
Crawford Rogert, Yunaika (1982—)
Creed, Clifford Anne (1938—)
Creider, Jane Tapsubei (c. 1940s—)
Creighton, Mary Frances (1899–1936)
Cremer, Erika (1900–1996)
Crespin, Régine (1927—)
Cresson, Edith (1934—)
Crews, Laura Hope (1879–1942)
Crimmins, Alice (1941—)
Cripps, Isobel (1891–1979)
Crisi, Maria (1892–1953)
Crisler, Lois (1897–1971)
Crispell, Marilyn (1947—)
Crist, Judith (1922—)
Cristina (1965—)
Cristina, Ines (b. 1875)
Critchfield, Lee (c. 1909—)
Crochet, Evelyne (1934—)
Crocker, Fay (1914—)
Crocker, Mary Lou (1944—)
Crockett, Jean A. (1919–1998)
Crockett, Rita Louise (1957—)
Crocombe, Marjorie Tuainekore (fl. 1970s)
Croft, June (1963—)
Croft, Peta-Kaye (1972—)
Croker, Bithia May (c. 1849–1920)
Croker, Norma (1934—)
Croll, Tina (1943—)
Crooks, Charmaine (1961—)
Cropley, Eileen (1932—)
Cropper, Hilary (1941–2004)
Crosby, Caresse (1892–1970)
Crosby, Elizabeth (1888–1983)
Crosby, Fanny (1820–1915)
Crosman, Henrietta (1861–1944)
Cross, Jessica (b. 1909)
Cross, Joan (1900–1993)
Cross, Zora (1890–1964)
Cross-Battle, Tara (1968—)
Crossley, Ada Jemima (1871–1929)
Crosson, Marvel (1904–1929)
Croteau, Julie (1970—)
Crothers, Rachel (1878–1958)
Crow, Sheryl (1962—)
Crow, Tamara (1977—)
Crow Dog, Mary (1953—)
Crowdy, Rachel (1884–1964)
Crowe, Ellen (c. 1845–1930)
Crowe, Sylvia (1901–1997)
Crowley, Honor Mary (1903–1966)
Crowley, Pat (1929—)
Crowley, Rosemary (1938—)
Crozier, Catharine (1914–2003)
Crudgington, Carolyn (1968—)
Cruft, Catherine Holway (1927—)
Cruickshank, Margaret Barnet (1873–1918)
Crump, Diane (1949—)
Crusat, Paulina (1900–1981)
Cruso, Thalassa (1908–1997)
Crutchley, Rosalie (1921–1997)
Cruvelli, Sofia (1826–1907)
Cruz, Celia (1924–2003)
Cryer, Ann (1939—)
Cryer, Gretchen (1935—)
Cryer, Sarah (1848–1929)
Csák, Ibolya (b. 1915)
Csaszar, Monika (1954—)
Csikne-Horvath, Klara (1947—)
Csillik, Margit (b. 1914)
Csisztu, Zsuzsa (1970—)
Csizmazia, Kim (c. 1968—)
Cucchi, Claudine (1834–1913)
Cuderman, Alenka (1961—)
Cudone, Carolyn (1918—)
Cui Yongmei (1969—)
Cullberg, Birgit (1908–1999)
Cullen, Betsy (1938—)
Cullis, Winifred Clara (1875–1956)
Cumba Jay, Yumileidi (1975—)
Cumming, Adelaide Hawley (1905–1998)
Cumming, Dorothy (1899–1983)
Cumming, Kate (c. 1828–1909)
Cumming, Ruth (c. 1904–1967)
Cummings, Alma (b. 1890)
Cummings, Blondell (c. 1948—)
Cummings, Constance (1910–2005)
Cummings, Edith (1899–1984)
Cummings, Ruth (1894–1984)
Cummings, Vicki (1913–1969)
Cummins, Peggy (1925—)
Cunard, Grace (c. 1891–1967)
Cunard, Maud (1872–1948)
Cunard, Nancy (1896–1965)
Cunha, Marcia Regina (1969—)
Cunliffe, Stella (1917—)
Cunningham, Agnes (1909–2004)
Cunningham, Elizabeth Anne
Cunningham, Imogen (1883–1976)
Cunningham, Minnie Fisher (1882–1964)
Cunningham, Roseanna (1951—)
Cunningham, Sarah (1918–1986)

Cunnington, Eveline Willert (1849–1916)
Cuoco, Joyce (1953—)
Curie, Ève (b. 1904)
Curie, Marie (1867–1934)
Curless, Ann (1965—)
Curley, Wilma (1937—)
Curran, Margaret (c. 1962—)
Currie, Cherie (1959—)
Currie, Edwina (1946—)
Currie, Ethel Dobbie (1898–1963)
Currie, Mary Montgomerie (1843–1905)
Currier, Ruth (1926—)
Curry, Denise (1959—)
Curry, Jenny (1984—)
Curtin, Elsie (1890–1975)
Curtis, Ann (1926—)
Curtis, Charlotte (1928–1987)
Curtis, Doris Malkin (1914–1991)
Curtis, Harriot (1881–1974)
Curtis, Jamie Lee (1958—)
Curtis, Kathleen Maisey (1892–1994)
Curtis, Peggy (1883–1965)
Curtis-Thomas, Claire (1958—)
Curtright, Jorja (1923–1985)
Curzon, Grace Hinds (1878–1958)
Curzon, Irene (1896–1966)
Curzon, Mary Leiter (1870–1906)
Cusack, Dymphna (1902–1981)
Cushier, Elizabeth (1837–1932)
Cushing, Catherine Chisholm (1874–1952)
Cushing, Justine B. (b. 1918)
Cushman, Vera (1876–1946)
Cussons, Sheila (1922–2004)
Cust, Aleen (1868–1937)
Custance, Olive (1874–1944)
Custer, Elizabeth Bacon (1842–1933)
Cuthbert, Betty (1938—)
Cuthbert, Juliet (1964—)
Cutina, Laura (1968—)
Cutler, Kate (1870–1955)
Cutler, Robyn (1948—)
Cutrone, Angela
Cutter, Kiki (1951—)
Cutts, Patricia (1926–1974)
Czajkowska, Krystyna (1936—)
Czekalla, Barbara (1951—)
Czerny-Stefanska, Halina (1922–2001)
Czigany, Kinga (1952—)
Czobel, Lisa (1906–1992)
Czopek, Agnieszka (1964—)
Dabrowska, Maria (1889–1965)
Daché, Lilly (1898–1989)
Dafoe, Frances (1929—)
Dafovska, Ekaterina (1976—)
Dagmar (1921–2001)
Dagover, Lil (1897–1980)
Dahl, Arlene (1924—)
Dahl, Aslaug
Dahlbeck, Eva (1920—)
Dahle, Gunn-Rita (1973—)
Dahle, Mona (1970—)
Dahlmo, Marianne
Dahl-Wolfe, Louise (1895–1989)
Dahne, Heike (1961—)
Dahne, Sabine (1950—)
Dai, Ailian (1916–2006)
Daigle, Sylvie (1962—)
Dai Houying (1938–1996)
Dainton, Marie (1881–1938)
Dai Qing (1941—)
Daisy, Princess (1873–1943)
Dakides, Tara (1975—)
Dal, Ingerid (1895–1985)
Daldy, Amey (c. 1829–1920)
Dale, Daphne (1931–1982)
Dale, Esther (1885–1961)
Dale, Kathleen (1895–1984)
Dale, Margaret (1876–1972)
Dale, Margaret (1922—)
Dale, Virginia (1917–1994)
D'Alessandri-Valdine, Blanche (c. 1862–1948)
Daley, Cass (1915–1975)
Dali, Gala (1894–1982)
Dalida (1933–1987)
Dall, Caroline Wells (1822–1912)
Dallas, Ruth (1919—)
Dallmann, Petra (1978—)
Dal Monte, Toti (1893–1975)
d'Alpuget, Blanche (1944—)
Dalrymple, Jean (1910–1998)
Dalrymple, Learmonth White (1827–1906)
Dalton, Doris (1910–1984)
Dalton, Dorothy (1893–1972)
Dalton, Dorothy (1922–1973)
Dalton, Judy Tegart (fl. 1960s–1970s)
Dalton, Katharina (1916–2004)
Daly, Mary (1928—)
Daly, Mary (c. 1861–1901)
Daly, Tyne (1946—)
Dalyell, Elsie (1881–1948)
Dalziel, Lianne (1960—)
Damian, Georgeta (1976—)
Damião, Elisa Maria (1946—)
Damita, Lili (1901–1994)
Damon, Cathryn (1930–1987)
Dampierre, Emmanuela del (b. 1913)
Dan, Aurora (1955—)
Dana, Leora (1923–1983)
Dana, Marie Louise (c. 1876–1946)
Dana, Viola (1897–1987)
Danco, Suzanne (1911–2000)
Dando, Jill (1961–1999)
Dando, Suzanne (1961—)
Dandridge, Dorothy (1923–1965)
Dane, Clemence (1888–1965)
Dangalakova-Bogomilova, Tanya (1964—)
Danias, Starr (1949—)
Daniel, Annie Sturges (1858–1944)
Daniel, Beth (1956—)
Daniel, Ellie (1950—)
Daniele, Graciela (1939—)
Danieli, Cecilia (1943—)
Daniels, Bebe (1901–1971)
Daniels, Isabelle Frances (1937—)
Daniels, Mabel Wheeler (1878–1971)
Daniels, Martha Catalina (d. 2002)
Daniels, Maxine (1930–2003)
Daniels, Sarah (1957—)
Danilova, Alexandra (1903–1997)
Danilova, Olga (1970—)
Danilova, Pelageya (1918—)
Daninthe, Sarah (1980—)
Dann, Mary (d. 2005)
Danner, Blythe (1943—)
Danner, Margaret (1910–1984)
D'Antuono, Eleanor (1939—)
Dantzscher, Jamie (1982—)
Dänzer, Frieda
Danziger, Paula (1944–2004)
Daong Khin Khin Lay (1913—)
Darby, Eileen (1916–2004)
Darc, Mireille (1938—)
Darcel, Denise (1925—)
Darclée, Hariclea (1860–1939)
D'Arcy, Ella (c. 1856–1937)
D'Arcy, Margaretta (1934—)
Dare, Phyllis (1890–1975)
Dare, Zena (1887–1975)
Dargan, Olive Tilford (1869–1968)
Dark, Eleanor (1901–1985)
Darling, Flora (1840–1910)
Darling, May (1887–1971)
Darlington, Jennie (c. 1925—)
Darmond, Grace (1898–1963)
Darnell, Linda (1921–1965)
d'Arnell, Nydia (d. 1970)
Darragh, Miss (d. 1917)
Darras, Danielle (1943—)
Darré, Jeanne-Marie (1905–1999)
Darrieux, Danielle (1917—)
Darrow, Anna (1876–1959)
Darsonval, Lycette (1912–1996)
Darton, Patience (1911–1996)
Darvas, Julia (c. 1919—)
Darvas, Lili (1902–1974)
Darvi, Bella (1927–1971)
Darwell, Jane (1879–1967)
Darwitz, Natalie (1982—)
Daryush, Elizabeth (1887–1977)
Das, Kamala (1934—)
Dash, Julie (1952—)
Dash, Sarah (1945—)
Dashwood, Elizabeth Monica (1890–1943)
Dasic-Kitic, Svetlana (1960—)
Da Silva, Ana (1949—)
da Silva, Benedita (1942—)
da Silva, Fabiola (1979—)
Dassault, Madeleine (1901–1992)
Dat So La Lee (c. 1835–1925)
Datta, Naomi (1922—)
Daubechies, Ingrid (1954—)
Daudet, Julia (1844–1940)
Daugaard, Line (1978—)
d'Aulaire, Ingri (1904–1980)
Daumier, Sophie (1934–2004)
Dauniene, Tamara (1951—)
Daunt, Yvonne (b. around 1900)
Dauser, Sue (1888–1972)
Dauthendey, Elisabeth (1854–1943)
Davenport, Gwen (1909–2002)
Davenport, Lindsay (1976—)
Davenport, Marcia (1903–1996)
Daves, Joan (1919–1997)
Davey, Constance (1882–1963)
Davey, Nuna (1902–1977)
Davey, Valerie (1940—)
David, Caroline Edgeworth (1856–1951)
David, Elizabeth (1913–1992)
David, Ilisaine Karen (1977—)
David-Neel, Alexandra (1868–1969)
Davidovich, Bella (1928—)
Davidow, Ruth (1911–1999)
Davidson, Mary Frances (1902–1986)
Davidson, Robyn (1950—)
Davies, Betty (1935—)
Davies, Betty Ann (1910–1955)
Davies, Caryn (1982—)
Davies, Dorothy Ida (1899–1987)
Davies, Elizabeth Valerie (b. 1912)
Davies, Emily (1830–1921)
Davies, Fanny (1861–1934)
Davies, Gwendoline (1882–1951)
Davies, Judy Joy (1928—)
Davies, Laura (1963—)
Davies, Lilian May (1915—)
Davies, Lillian (1895–1932)
Davies, Margaret (1884–1963)
Davies, Margaret (1914–1982)
Davies, Margaret Llewelyn (1861–1944)
Davies, Marion (1897–1961)
Davies, Patricia (1956—)
Davies, Sharron (1962—)
Davies, Siobhan (1950—)
Davies, Sonja (1923–2005)
Davis, Adelle (1904–1974)
Davis, Alice Brown (1852–1935)
Davis, Angela (1944—)
Davis, Bette (1908–1989)
Davis, Clarissa (1967—)
Davis, Dorothy Hilliard (1917–1994)
Davis, Fay (1872–1945)
Davis, Frances Elliott (1882–1965)
Davis, Gail (1925–1997)
Davis, Gladys (b. 1893)
Davis, Heather (1974—)
Davis, Hilda (1905–2001)
Davis, Jessica (1978—)
Davis, Joan (1907–1961)
Davis, Judy (1955—)
Davis, Katharine Bement (1860–1935)
Davis, Marguerite (1889–1980)
Davis, Mary E.P. (c. 1840–1924)
Davis, Mary
Davis, Mollie Moore (1844–1909)
Davis, Pa Tepaeru Ariki (1923–1990)
Davis, Rebecca Harding (1831–1910)
Davis, Skeeter (1931–2004)
Davis, Theresa (1950—)
Davis, Varina Howell (1826–1906)
Davison, Emily (1872–1913)
Davis-Thompson, Pauline (1966—)
d'Avril, Yola (1907–1984)
Davy, Nadia (1980—)
Davydenko, Tamara
Davydova, Anastasia (1983—)
Davydova, Yelena (1961—)
Daw, Evelyn (1912–1970)
Daw, Marjorie (1902–1979)

Dawbin, Annie Maria (1816–1905)
Dawes, Dominique (1976—)
Dawes, Eva (1912—)
Dawidowicz, Lucy (1915–1990)
Daw Khin Myo Chit (1915–2003)
Daw Mi Mi Khaing (1916–1990)
Dawn, Dolly (1916–2002)
Dawn, Hazel (1891–1988)
Dawn, Isabel (1905–1966)
Daw San San (1944–1990)
Dawson, Alice Madge (c. 1980–2003)
Dawson, Mary Elizabeth (1833–1924)
Day, Alice (1905–1995)
Day, Doris (1924—)
Day, Dorothy (1897–1980)
Day, Edith (1896–1971)
Day, Frances (1907–1984)
Day, Josette (1914–1978)
Day, Laraine (1917—)
Day, Marceline (1907–2000)
Daydé, Liane (1932—)
Daykarhanova, Tamara (1889–1980)
Dazie, Mademoiselle (1882–1952)
D'Costa, Jean (1937—)
Deacon, Susan
de Acosta, Mercedes (1893–1968)
Deakin, Pattie (1863–1934)
de Alonso, Carmen (1909—)
Deamer, Dulcie (1890–1972)
Dean, Brenda (1943—)
Dean, Dora (c. 1872–1950)
Dean, Janet (1949—)
Dean, Jennie (1852–1913)
Dean, Julia (1878–1952)
Dean, Laura (1945—)
Dean, Margie (1896–1918)
Dean, Priscilla (1896–1987)
Dean, Vera Micheles (1903–1972)
Dean, Williamina (1844–1895)
Deane, Doris (1900–1974)
Deane, Helen Wendler (1917–1966)
De Angeli, Marguerite (1889–1987)
De Angelo, Ana Marie (1955—)
Deans, Jane (1823–1911)
Deardurff, Deena (1957—)
Dearie, Blossom (1926—)
de Banzie, Brenda (1915–1981)
de Bary, Amy-Catherine (1944—)
Debeche, Jamila (1925—)
de Belo, Roseli (1969—)
Debenham, Cicely (1891–1955)
Debernard, Danielle (1954—)
Debertshäuser, Monika
de Bettignies, Louise (d. 1918)
de Beus, Bernadette de (1958—)
de Blois, Natalie (1921—)
Debo, Angie (1890–1988)
de Bray, Yvonne (1889–1954)
De Brémont, Anna (1864–1922)
de Bruijn, Chantal (1976—)
de Bruijn, Inge (1973—)
de Brún, Bairbre (1954—)
de Brunhoff, Cécile (1903–2003)
De Burgh, Aimée (d. 1946)
de Burgos, Julia (1914–1953)
Debyasuvan, Boonlua Kunjara (1911–1982)
DeCamp, Rosemary (1910–2001)
De Carlo, Yvonne (1922—)
De Casalis, Jeanne (1897–1966)
DeCastro, Peggy (1921–2004)
De Cespedes, Alba (1911–1997)
Decker, Sarah Platt (1852–1912)
de Cleyre, Voltairine (1866–1912)
DeCosta, Sara (1977—)
Dedieu, Virginie (1979—)
Dee, Frances (1907–2004)
Dee, Ruby (1923—)
Dee, Sandra (1942–2005)
Deelstra, Atje (1938—)
Deer, Ada (1935—)
Deering, Olive (1918–1986)
Deevy, Teresa (1894–1963)
Defar, Meseret (1983—)
DeFranco, Marisa (1955—)
DeFranco, Merlina (1957—)
DeFrantz, Anita (1952—)
DeGaetani, Jan (1933–1989)
de Galard, Geneviève (1925—)
de Gaulle, Geneviève (1921–2002)
de Gaulle, Yvonne (1900–1979)
DeGeneres, Ellen (1958—)
De Graffenried, Clare (1849–1921)
De Groen, Alma (1941—)
Degutiene, Irena (1949—)
de Haan, Annemiek (1981—)
DeHaven, Flora (1883–1950)
DeHaven, Gloria (1924—)
de Havilland, Olivia (1916—)
de Heij, Stella
Dehner, Dorothy (1901–1994)
de Hoyos, Angela (1940—)
de Ibáñez, Sara (1909–1971)
Deininger, Beate (1962—)
Deiters, Julie (1975—)
De Jong, Bettie (1933—)
de Jong, Dola (1911–2003)
de Jong, Reggie (1964—)
de Jongh, Andree (1916—)
Dekanova, Vlasta (1909–1974)
De Keersmaeker, Anne Teresa (1960—)
de Keyser, Ethel (1926–2004)
De Keyser, Véronique (1945—)
Dekker, Inge (1985—)
Dekkers, Hurnet (1974—)
de Klerk, Marike (1937–2001)
de Kok, Irene (1963—)
de Kooning, Elaine Fried (1918–1989)
De La Bije, Willy (1934—)
De La Guerra, Alejandra (1968—)
de Laguna, Frederica (1906–2004)
de Laguna, Frederica (b. around 1874)
de Laguna, Grace Mead (1878–1978)
De La Haye, Ina (1906–1972)
De La Motte, Marguerite (1902–1950)
Deland, Margaret (1857–1945)
Delander, Lois (1911–1985)
Delaney, Shelagh (1939—)
Delano, Jane Arminda (1862–1919)
Delany, Annie Elizabeth (1891–1995)
Delany, Maureen (d. 1961)
Delany, Sarah Louise (1889–1999)
de la Pasture, Mrs. Henry (d. 1945)
De Lappe, Gemze (1922—)
de Lara, Adelina (1872–1961)
de la Roche, Mazo (1879–1961)
Delarue-Mardrus, Lucie (1880–1945)
Delarverié, Stormé (1922—)
Delaunay, Sonia (1885–1979)
De Lauretis, Teresa (1938—)
DeLauro, Rosa L. (1943—)
De Lavallade, Carmen (1931—)
DeLay, Dorothy (1917–2002)
Delbo, Charlotte (1913–1985)
De Leath, Vaughan (1900–1943)
Deledda, Grazia (1871–1936)
de Leeuw, Dianne
Delehanty, Megan (1968—)
De Leporte, Rita (c. 1910—)
de Levie, Elka (1905–1979)
Delf, Juliet (d. 1962)
Deli, Rita (c. 1972—)
De Lima, Clara Rosa (1923—)
Della Casa, Lisa (1919—)
Delle Grazie, Marie Eugenie (1864–1931)
Dell'Era, Antoinetta (1861–?)
Delmar, Viña (1903–1990)
Deloria, Ella (1888–1971)
Delphy, Christine (1941—)
Del Rio, Dolores (1905–1983)
Delroy, Irene (1898–?)
Delta, Penelope (1871–1941)
Deltcheva, Ina (1977–)
De Luce, Virginia (1921–1997)
de Lussan, Zélie (1861–1949)
Del Vando, Amapola (1910–1988)
Delysia, Alice (1889–1979)
Delza, Elizabeth (c. 1903—)
De Marco, Renée (c. 1913—)
De Marco, Sally (1921—)
DeMarinis, Anne
De Mattei, Susan (1962—)
Dembo, Tamara (1902–1993)
Demel, Anna (1872–1956)
De Melker, Daisy Louisa (1886–1932)
de Mello, Theresa (1913–1997)
DeMent, Iris (1961—)
Dementieva, Elena (1981—)
Dementyeva, Yelizaveta (1928—)
Demers, Anık (1972—)
Demessieux, Jeanne (1921–1968)
de Mille, Agnes (1905–1993)
De Mille, Beatrice (1853–1923)
De Mille, Katherine (1911–1995)
Demina, Svetlana (c. 1960—)
Deming, Dorothy (1893–1972)
Demireva, Bojanka (1969—)
Demleitner, Elisabeth
Demongeot, Mylène (1936—)
DeMorgan, Evelyn (1850–1919)
Dempsey, Sister Mary Joseph (1856–1939)
Dempster, Carol (1901–1991)
Dench, Judy (1934—)
Dench, Patricia (1932—)
Dendeberova, Yelena (1969—)
Denenberg, Gail (1947—)
Deneuve, Catherine (1943—)
Deng Yaping (1973—)
Deng Yingchao (1903–1992)
Deng Yuzhi (1900–1996)
Denham, Isolde (1920—)
Denis, María (1916–2004)
Denis, Michaela (1914–2003)
Denison, Flora MacDonald (1867–1921)
Denison, Mary Andrews (1826–1911)
Deniz, Leslie (1962—)
Denman, Gertrude (1884–1954)
Dennett, Mary Ware (1872–1947)
Dennis, Clare (1916–1971)
Dennis, Sandy (1937–1992)
Dennison, Jo-Carroll (c. 1924—)
Denny, Sandy (1947–1978)
Densen-Gerber, Judianne (1934–2003)
Densmore, Frances (1867–1957)
Dent, Edith (1863–1948)
Denton, Jean (1935–2001)
Denton, Mary Florence (1857–1947)
Denton, Sandy (1969—)
de Passe, Suzanne (1946—)
de Paula, Monica Angelica (1978—)
De Putti, Lya (1899–1932)
Derckx, Annemiek (1954—)
Deren, Maya (1908–1961)
De Reuck, Colleen (1964—)
De Reyes, Consuelo (1893–1948)
Derickson, Uli (1944–2005)
deRiel, Emily (1974—)
De Rivoyre, Christine (1921—)
Derman, Vergie (1942—)
Dermendzhieva, Vanya (1952—)
Dermoût, Maria (1888–1962)
Dernesch, Helga (1939—)
Deroche, Elise-Raymonde (1886–1919)
de Roever, Lisanne (1979—)
de Rover, Jolanda (1963—)
Derricotte, Juliette (1897–1931)
De Rue, Carmen (1908–1986)
de Ruiter, Wietske
Dervis, Suat (1905–1972)
Deryugina, Natalya (1971—)
D'Erzell, Catalina (1897–1937)
Derzhinskaya, Zeniya (1889–1951)
Desai, Anita (1937—)
De Sarnez, Marielle (1951—)
Descamps, Marie-Hélène (1938—)
Descard, Maria (1847–1927)
Deseo, Suzanne (1913–2003)
Desforges, Jean Catherine (1929—)
Desha (1892–1965)
DeShannon, Jackie (1944—)
Deshpande, Shashi (1938—)
Desiree Bernadotte (1938—)
Deslys, Gaby (1884–1920)
Desmond, Astra (1893–1973)
Desmond, Eileen (1932—)
Desmond, Florence (1905–1993)
Desmond, Lucy (b. 1889)
De Sousa, May (1887–1948)
de Sousa, Noémia (1926—)

Despard, Charlotte (1844–1939)
Despotovic, Vesna (1961—)
Desprès, Suzanne (1875–1951)
Dessaur, C.I. (1931–2002)
Dessoff, Margarethe (1874–1944)
De Stefani, Livia (1913—)
Destinn, Emmy (1878–1930)
Destivelle, Catherine (1960—)
De Swirska, Tamara (c. 1890–?)
Dettweiler, Helen (1914–1990)
Deutsch, Babette (1895–1982)
Deutsch, Helen (1906–1992)
Deutsch, Helene (1884–1982)
Deutscher, Tamara (1913–1990)
Deutschkron, Inge (1922—)
de Valera, Sile (1954—)
de Valois, Ninette (1898–2001)
Devanny, Jean (1894–1962)
de Varona, Donna (1947—)
Devers, Gail (1966—)
Devetzi, Hrysopiyi (1975—)
De Veyrac, Christine (1959—)
de Veyrinas, Françoise (1943—)
Devi, Ashapurna (1909–1995)
Devi, Mahasveta (1926—)
Devi, Maitreyi (1914–1990)
De Vito, Gioconda (1907–1994)
DeVoe, Emma Smith (1848–1927)
de Voie, Bessie (b. around 1888)
Devold, Kristin Krohn (1961—)
Devore, Dorothy (1899–1976)
Devoy, Susan (1964—)
de Vries, Dorien (1965—)
Devyatova, Tatyana (1949—)
Dewar, Phyllis (1915–1961)
Dewe, Colleen (1930–1993)
Dewey, Alice Chipman (1858–1927)
Dewhurst, Colleen (1924–1991)
De Witt, Lydia (1859–1928)
de Wolfe, Elsie (1865–1950)
Dewson, Molly (1874–1962)
D'haen, Christine (1923—)
Diachenko, Nada (1946—)
Diaconescu, Camelia (1963—)
Diakonova, Elizaveta (1874–1902)
Diallo, Nafissatou (1941–1982)
Diamant, Anita (1917–1996)
Diamond, Selma (1920–1985)
Diana (1961–1997)
Dianda, Hilda (1925—)
Dias, Virna (1971—)
Diaz, Abby (1821–1904)
Diaz, Eileen (1979—)
Diaz, Mary F. (c. 1962–2004)
Diaz-Balart, Mirta (c. 1928—)
Díaz Lozano, Argentina (1912–1999)
Dibaba, Ejigayehu (1982—)
Dibaba, Tirunesh (1985—)
Di Bona, Linda (1946—)
Di Centa, Manuela (1963—)
Dick, Evelyn (1922—)
Dick, Gladys (1881–1963)
Dickason, Gladys (1903–1971)
Dickens, Helen Octavia (1909–2001)
Dickens, Monica (1915–1992)
Dickenscheid, Tanja (1969—)
Dicker-Brandeis, Friedl (1898–1944)
Dickerson, Nancy (1927–1997)
Dickey, Nancy Wilson (1950—)
Dickey, Sarah (1838–1904)
Dickin, Maria (1870–1951)
Dickinson, Angie (1931—)
Dickinson, Anna E. (1842–1932)
Dickinson, Judy (1950—)
Dickson, Anne (1928—)
Dickson, Barbara (1947—)
Dickson, Dorothy (1893–1995)
Dickson, Gloria (1916–1945)
Dickson, Joan (1921–1994)
Didion, Joan (1934—)
Diduck, Judy (1966—)
Diebold, Laure (1915–1964)
Diefenbaker, Edna Mae (1901–1951)
Diefenbaker, Olive (1902–1976)
Diemer, Emma Lou (1927—)
Dienelt, Kerry (1969—)
Diers, Ines (1963—)
Dietrich, Marlene (1901–1992)
Dieulafoy, Jane (1851–1916)
Díez González, Rosa M. (1952—)
DiFranco, Ani (1970—)
Diggs, Annie LePorte (1848–1916)
Diggs, Irene (1906—)
di Giacomo, Marina (1976—)
Digre, Berit (1967—)
Dijkstra, Sjoukje (1942—)
Dilke, Emily (1840–1904)
Dill, Mary Lou (1948—)
Dillard, Annie (1945—)
Diller, Angela (1877–1968)
Diller, Phyllis (1917—)
Dilley, Dorothy (b. around 1907)
Dillon, Diane (1933—)
Dillon, Melinda (1939—)
Dillwyn, Amy (1845–1935)
di Lorenzo, Tina (1872–1930)
Dilova, Diana (1952—)
di Mario, Tania (1979—)
Dimitrova, Blaga (1922—)
Dimitrova, Ghena (1941–2005)
Dimitrova, Rositsa (1955—)
Dimitrova, Tanya (1957—)
Dinescu, Violeta (1953—)
Dinesen, Isak (1885–1962)
Dingeldein, Margaret (1980—)
Ding Ling (1904–1985)
Ding Meiyuan (1979—)
Ding Ning (1924—)
Dinnerstein, Dorothy (1923–1992)
Dinsdale, Shirley (c. 1928–1999)
Dinwiddie, Emily (1879–1949)
Diogo, Luisa (1958—)
Dion, Céline (1968—)
Dionne, Annette (1934—)
Dionne, Cécile (1934—)
Dionne, Deidra (1982—)
Dionne, Émilie (1934–1954)
Dionne, Marie (1934–1970)
Dionne, Yvonne (1934–2001)
Diosdado, Ana (1938—)
Di Prima, Diane (1934—)
Dirie, Waris (1967—)
Dirkmaat, Megan (1976—)
Di Robilant, Daisy, Countess (fl. 1922–1933)
Disl, Ursula (1970—)
Disney, Lillian (1899–1997)
Dissard, Marie Louise (b. 1880)
Ditchburn, Ann (c. 1950—)
Ditlevsen, Tove (1917–1976)
Ditzel, Nana (1923–2005)
Dix, Beulah Marie (1876–1970)
Dix, Dorothy (1892–1970)
Dixie, Florence (1857–1905)
Dixon, Adele (1908–1992)
Dixon, Diane (1964—)
Dixon, Jean (1896–1981)
Dixon, Jeane (1918–1997)
Dixon, Medina (1962—)
Dixon, Reather (1945—)
Dixon, Tina (1976—)
Dixon, Victoria (1959—)
Dixon Jones, Mary Amanda (1828–1908)
Dizhur, Bella (b. 1906)
Djukica, Slavic (1960—)
Djuraskovic, Vera (1949—)
Djurica, Mirjana (1961—)
Djurkovic, Zorica (1957—)
Dlugoszewski, Lucia (1925–2000)
Dluzewska, Malgorzata (1958—)
Dmitrieff, Elizabeth (1851–1910)
Dmitrieva, Elizaveta Ivanovna (1887–1928)
Dmitrieva, Valentina (1859–1948)
Dobbins, Georgia (1944–1980)
Doberschuetz-Mey, Gerlinde (1964—)
Dobesova, Bozena (1914—)
Doble, Frances (1902–1969)
Dobmeier, Annette (1968—)
Dobratz, Erin (1982—)
Dobre, Aurelia (1972—)
Dobre-Balan, Anisoara (1966—)
Dobritoiu, Elena (1957—)
Dobson, Deborah (c. 1950—)
Dobson, Emily (1842–1934)
Dobson, Louise (1972—)
Dobson, Rosemary (1920—)
Dobson, Ruth (1918–1989)
Dock, Lavinia L. (1858–1956)
Dod, Charlotte (1871–1960)
Doda, Carol
Dodd, Claire (1908–1973)
Dodd, Lynley Stuart (1941—)
Dodge, Eva F. (1896–1990)
Dodge, Grace Hoadley (1856–1914)
Dodge, Josephine (1855–1928)
Dodge, Mary Mapes (1831–1905)
Doerdelmann, Sylvia (1970—)
Doering, Jane (c. 1922—)
Doerr, Harriet (1910–2002)
Doerries, Jana (1975—)
Dogonadze, Anna (1973—)
Dohan, Edith Hall (1877–1943)
Dohm, Hedwig (1831–1919)
Dohnal, Darcie
Dohrn, Bernardine (1942—)
Doi, Takako (1928—)
Dokic, Jelena (1983—)
Dole, Elizabeth Hanford (1936—)
Dolgopolova, Elena (1980—)
Dolgorukaia, Alexandra (1836–c. 1914)
Dolgorukova, Ekaterina (1847–1922)
Dolley, Sarah Adamson (1829–1909)
Dolly, Jenny (1892–1941)
Dolly, Rosie (1892–1970)
Dolma, Pachen (c. 1933–2002)
Dolores (c. 1890–1975)
Dolson, Mildred (1918—)
Doman, Amanda (1977—)
Domanska, Janina (1912–1995)
Dombeck, Carola (1960—)
Domenech i Escate de Canellas, Maria (1877–1952)
Domergue, Faith (1924–1999)
Domin, Hilde (1909–2006)
Dominguez, María Alicia (1908—)
Domitien, Elisabeth (1926—)
Don, Rachel (1866–1941)
Donadio, Candida (1929–2001)
Donahue, Hessie (fl. 1892—)
Donahue, Margaret (c. 1893–1978)
Donalda, Pauline (1882–1970)
Donaldson, Margaret Caldwell (1926—)
Donaldson, Mary (1921–2003)
Donaldson, Mary (1972—)
Donaldson, Norma (1928–1994)
Donaldson, Viva (1893–1970)
Donath, Ursula (1931—)
Donchenko, Natalya (1932—)
Donegan, Dorothy (1922–1998)
Doner, Kitty (1895–1988)
Donescu, Anghelache (1945—)
Dong Fangxiao (1983—)
Donguzashvili, Tea (1976—)
Dönhoff, Marion, Countess (1909–2002)
DonHowe, Gwyda (1933–1988)
Donisthorpe, G. Sheila (1898–1946)
Donkova, Yordanka (1961—)
Donlon, Mary H. (1894–1977)
Donnell, Jeff (1921–1988)
Donnelly, Dorothy (1880–1928)
Donnelly, Euphrasia (b. 1906)
Donnelly, Geraldine (1965—)
Donnelly, Lucy (1870–1948)
Donnelly, Patricia (c. 1920—)
Donnelly, Ruth (1896–1982)
Donner, Vyvyan (1895–1965)
Donners, Wilhelmina (1974—)
Donohoe, Shelagh (1965—)
Donovan, Anne (1961—)
Donovan, Carrie (1928–2001)
Donovan, Jean (1953—)
Donska, Maria (1912–1996)
Donusz, Eva (1967—)
Dony, Christina Mayne (1910–1995)
Doo, Unui (1873/75?–1940)
Doolittle, Hilda (1886–1961)
Dorado Gomez, Natalia (1967—)
Doraldina (c. 1893–c. 1925)
Doran, Ann (1911–2000)
Dorfmann, Ania (1899–1984)

Dorfmeister, Michaela (1973—)
Dorio, Gabriella (1957—)
Dorléac, Françoise (1942–1967)
Dorman, Loretta (1963—)
Dorman, Sonya (1924—)
D'Orme, Aileen (1877–1939)
Dormer, Daisy (1889–1947)
Dormon, Carrie (1888–1971)
Dorn, Erna (1912–1953)
Dornemann, Luise (1901–1992)
Dornik, Polona (1962—)
Doro, Marie (1882–1956)
Dorodnova, Oksana (1974—)
Dorothea of Bavaria (1920—)
Dorr, Julia Caroline (1825–1913)
Dorr, Rheta Childe (1866–1948)
Dörre, Katrin (1961—)
Dörrie, Doris (1955—)
Dors, Diana (1931–1984)
D'Orsay, Fifi (1904–1983)
Dorsey, Susan Miller (1857–1946)
Dorziat, Gabrielle (1886–1979)
Doscher, Doris (1882–1970)
Doss, Nannie (1905–1965)
dos Santos, Andreia (1977—)
dos Santos, Cintia (1975—)
dos Santos Augusto, Rosana (1982—)
Dostalova, Leopolda (1879–1972)
Dostoevsky, Anna (1846–1918)
D'Ottavio, Frazia (1985—)
Doubrovska, Felia (1896–1981)
Doucet, Catherine (1875–1958)
Dougall, Lily (1858–1923)
Dougherty, Ellen (c. 1843–1919)
Doughty, Sue (1948—)
Douglas, Amanda Minnie (1831–1916)
Douglas, Ann (b. 1901)
Douglas, Emily Taft (1899–1994)
Douglas, Helen Gahagan (1900–1980)
Douglas, Helyn (c. 1945—)
Douglas, Lizzie (1897–1973)
Douglas, Marjory Stoneman (1890–1998)
Douglas, Mary Tew (1921—)
Douglas, Sandra (1967—)
Douglass, Anna Murray (1813–1882)
Douglass, Margaret (d. 1949)
Dove, Billie (1900–1997)
Dove, Rita (1952—)
Dovey, Alice (1884–1969)
Dovzan, Alenka (1976—)
Dow, Peggy (1928—)
Dowd, Nancy (1944—)
Dowdall, Jane (1899–1974)
Dowding, Angela (1919—)
Dowling, Constance (1920–1969)
Dowling, Doris (1921–2004)
Dowling, Joan (1928–1954)
Downey, June Etta (1875–1932)
Downie, Dorothy G. (1894–1960)
Downie, Mary Alice (1934—)
Downing, Virginia (1904–1996)
Downs, Cathy (1924–1976)
Downs, Deirdre (c. 1980—)
Doyle, Avril (1949—)
Doyle, Patricia (d. 1975)
Drabble, Margaret (1939—)
Dracopoulou, Theony (1883–1968)
Draga (1867–1903)
Dragila, Stacy (1971—)
Dragoicheva, Tsola (1893–1993)
Dragonette, Jessica (1900–1980)
Drake, Betsy (1923—)
Drake, Dona (1914–1989)
Drake, Fabia (1904–1990)
Drake, Frances (1908–2000)
Drake-Brockman, Henrietta (1901–1968)
Dransfeld, Hedwig (1871–1925)
Draper, Dorothy (1888–1969)
Draper, Elisabeth (1900–1993)
Draper, Helen (1871–1951)
Draper, Mary Anna Palmer (1839–1914)
Draper, Ruth (1884–1956)
Draves, Victoria (1924—)
Drayton, Grace Gebbie (1877–1936)
Dreaver, Mary (1887–1964)
Drechsler, Heike (1964—)
Dreier, Katherine Sophie (1877–1952)
Dreier, Mary Elisabeth (1875–1963)
Dreifuss, Ruth (1940—)
Dresdel, Sonia (1909–1976)
Dressel, Vally (1893—)
Dresser, Louise (1878–1965)
Dressler, Marie (1869–1934)
Drevjana, Alena (1969—)
Drew, Ellen (1914–2003)
Drew, Jane (1911–1996)
Drew, Lucille (1890–1925)
Drew-Baker, Kathleen M. (1901–1957)
Drewery, Corinne (1959—)
Drewitz, Ingeborg (1923–1986)
Drexel, Constance (1894–1956)
Drexel, Mary Katharine (1858–1955)
Drexel, Wiltrud (1950—)
Dreyfuss, Anne (1957—)
Drif, Zohra (1941—)
Drinker, Catherine Ann (1841–1922)
Drinkwater, Jennie M. (1841–1900)
Driscoll, Clara (1881–1945)
Driscoll, Jean (1966—)
Driver, Senta (1942—)
Drljaca, Radmila (1959—)
Drolet, Marie-Eve (1982—)
Drolet, Nancy (1973—)
Dronke, Minnie Maria (1904–1987)
Dronova, Nina
Drouin, Candice (1976—)
Drower, E.S. (1879–1972)
Drower, Margaret S. (c. 1913—)
Drown, Julia (1962—)
Dru, Joanne (1923–1996)
Drummond, Dolores (1834–1926)
Drummond, Flora (1869–1949)
Dryburgh, Margaret (1890–1945)
Drylie, Patricia (c. 1928–1993)
Duane, Diane (1952—)
du Bief, Jacqueline
Du Bois, Cora (1903–1991)
Dubois, Marie (1937—)
Du Boulay, Christine (c. 1923—)
Dubuisson, Pauline (1926—)
Duby-Blom, Gertrude (1901–1993)
Duchêne, Gabrielle (1870–1954)
Duchesnay, Isabelle (1973—)
Duchkova, Milena (1952—)
Duckering, Florence West (1869–1951)
Duckworth, Marilyn (1935—)
Duclaux, Agnes Mary F. (1856–1944)
Duczynska, Ilona (1897–1978)
Dudarova, Veronika (1916—)
Duder, Tessa (1940—)
Dudeva, Diana (1968—)
Dudinskaya, Natalya (1912–2003)
Dudleston, Penny (1952—)
Dudley, Doris (1917–1985)
Dudley, Jane (1912–2001)
Dudley Ward, Penelope (1914–1982)
Dudnik, Olesia (1974—)
Duenkel, Ginny (1947—)
Duerk, Alene B. (1920—)
Du Faur, Emmeline Freda (1882–1935)
Duff Gordon, Lucy (1862–1935)
Duffy, Martha (c. 1936–1997)
Duffy, Maureen (1933—)
du Fresne, Yvonne (1929—)
Dugdale, Henrietta (1826–1918)
Duggan, Eileen May (1894–1972)
Duggan, Keltie (1970—)
Dührkop Dührkop, Bárbara (1945—)
Duigan, Suzanne Lawless (1924–1993)
Dukakis, Olympia (1931—)
Duke, Doris (1912–1993)
Duke, Patty (1946—)
Dulac, Germaine (1882–1942)
Duley, Margaret (1894–1968)
Dullemen, Inez van (1925—)
Dulles, Eleanor Lansing (1895–1996)
du Maurier, Daphne (1907–1989)
Dumbadze, Nina (1919–1983)
Dumcheva, Antonina (1958—)
Dumilâtre, Adèle (1821–1909)
Dumitrache, Maria Magdalena (1977—)
Dumitrescu, Roxana (1967—)
Dumitrescu-Doletti, Joanna (1902–1963)
Dumitru, Viorica (1946—)
Dumm, Edwina (1893–1990)
Dummer, Ethel Sturges (1866–1954)
Dumont, Brigitte (1944—)
Dumont, Margaret (1889–1965)
Duna, Steffi (1910–1992)
Dunavska, Adriana (1970—)
Dunaway, Faye (1941—)
Dunbar, Diane
Dunbar, Dixie (1915–1991)
Dunbar, Flanders (1902–1959)
Dunbar-Nelson, Alice (1875–1935)
Dunca, Rodica (1965—)
Duncan, Elizabeth (c. 1874–1948)
Duncan, Irma (1897–1978)
Duncan, Isadora (1878–1927)
Duncan, Lois (1934—)
Duncan, Maria Teresa (1895–1987)
Duncan, Mary (1895–1993)
Duncan, Rosetta (1890–1959)
Duncan, Sandy (1946—)
Duncan, Sandy Frances (1942—)
Duncan, Sara Jeanette (1861–1922)
Duncan, Sheena (1932—)
Duncan, Vivian (1902–1986)
Dunedin, Maudie (c. 1888–1937)
Dunfield, Sonya Klopfer (c. 1936—)
Dunham, Ethel Collins (1883–1969)
Dunham, Katherine (1909–2006)
Dünhaupt, Angelika
Duniway, Abigail Scott (1834–1915)
Dunkle, Nancy (1955—)
Dunlap, Ericka (1982—)
Dunlop, Florence (c. 1896–1963)
Dunn, Barbara (c. 1910—)
Dunn, Emma (1875–1966)
Dunn, Gertrude (c. 1932–2004)
Dunn, Josephine (1906–1983)
Dunn, Loula Friend (1896–1977)
Dunn, Natalie (1956—)
Dunn, Nell (1936—)
Dunn, Shannon (1972—)
Dunn, Tricia (1974—)
Dunn, Velma (1918—)
Dunne, Irene (1898–1990)
Dunne, Jean Gilligan (1951—)
Dunnett, Dorothy (1923–2001)
Dunnock, Mildred (1900–1991)
Dunscombe, Adaliza (1867–1943)
Dunwoody, Gwyneth (1930—)
Duplitzer, Imke (1975—)
Du Pont, Patricia (1894–1973)
du Pré, Jacqueline (1945–1987)
Dupree, Minnie (1873–1947)
Duprez, June (1918–1984)
Dupuis, Lori (1972—)
Dupureur, Maryvonne (1937—)
Durack, Fanny (1889–1956)
Durack, Mary (1913–1994)
Durand, Lucile (1930—)
Durand, Marguerite (1864–1936)
Durant, Ariel (1898–1981)
Duranti, Francesca (1935—)
Duras, Marguerite (1914–1996)
Durbin, Deanna (1921—)
Durfee, Minta (1897–1975)
Durham, Dianne (1968—)
Durham, Mary Edith (1863–1944)
Durieux, Tilla (1880–1971)
Durr, Françoise (1942—)
Duse, Eleonora (1858–1924)
Dusserre, Michelle (1968—)
Dutrieu, Hélène (1877–1961)
Duval, Helen (1916—)
Duvholt, Kristine (1974—)
Dux, Emilienne (b. 1874)
Duxbury, Elspeth (1909–1967)
Duyster, Willemijn
Dvorak, Ann (1912–1979)
Dwan, Dorothy (1907–1981)
Dworkin, Andrea (1946–2005)
Dwyer, Ada (1863–1952)
Dwyer, Doriot Anthony (1922—)
Dwyer, Florence Price (1902–1976)
Dyachenko, Tatyana (1960—)

Dybendahl Hartz, Trude (1966—)
Dybkjaer, Lone (1940—)
Dybwad, Johanne (1867–1950)
Dyk, Ruth (1901–2000)
Dyke, Eunice (1883–1969)
Dylewska, Izabella (1968—)
Dynalix, Paulette (1917—)
Dyroen-Lancer, Becky (1971—)
Dyson, Elizabeth Geertruida (1897–1951)
Dzerzhinska, Sofia (1882–1968)
Dzhandzhgava, Tatyana (1964—)
Dzhigalova, Lyudmila (1962—)
Dzhugeli, Medeya (1925—)
Dzieciol, Iwona (1975—)
Dziouba, Irina
Eadie, Helen
Eady, Dorothy (1904–1981)
Eagels, Jeanne (1894–1929)
Eagle, Angela (1961—)
Eagle, Maria (1961—)
Eakins, Susan Hannah (1851–1938)
Eales, Nellie B. (1889–1989)
Eames, Clare (1896–1930)
Eames, Emma (1865–1952)
Eames, Ray (1912–1988)
Eames, Virginia (1889–1971)
Eardley, Joan (1921–1963)
Earhart, Amelia (1897–1937)
Earle, Alice Morse (1851–1911)
Earle, Virginia (1875–1937)
Early, Penny Ann (c. 1946—)
Eastlake-Smith, Gladys (1883–1941)
Eastman, Annis Ford (1852–1910)
Eastman, Carole (1934–2004)
Eastman, Crystal (1881–1928)
Eastman, Elaine Goodale (1863–1953)
Eastman, Linda A. (1867–1963)
Easton, Florence (1882–1955)
Easton, Sheena (1959—)
Eastwood, Alice (1859–1953)
Eaton, Edith (1865–1914)
Eaton, Mary (1901–1948)
Eaton, Pearl (1898–1958)
Eaton, Shirley (1937—)
Eaubonne, Françoise d' (1920–2005)
Eaves, Elsie (1898–1983)
Ebadi, Shirin (1947—)
Eberhardt, Isabelle (1877–1904)
Eberhart, Mignon G. (1899–1996)
Eberle, Abastenia St. Leger (1878–1942)
Eberle, Emilia (1964—)
Eberle, Verena (1950—)
Ebert, Henrietta (1954—)
Ebert, Joyce (1933–1997)
Ebner-Eschenbach, Marie (1830–1916)
Ebnoether, Luzia (1971—)
Ebsen, Vilma (1911—)
Ebtekar, Massoumeh (1960—)
Eburne, Maude (1875–1960)
Eccles, Janet (1895–1966)
Eccles, Mary Hyde (1912–2003)
Echerer, Raina A. Mercedes (1963—)
Echols, Sheila Ann (1964—)
Eckart, Jean (1921–1993)
Eckbauer-Baumann, Edith (1949—)
Eckerson, Sophia H. (d. 1954)
Eckert, Cynthia (1965—)
Eckford, Elizabeth (1942—)
Eckhardt-Gramatté, S.C. (1899–1974)
Eckstorm, Fannie Pearson Hardy (1865–1946)
Eddy, Bernice (b. 1903)
Eddy, Helen Jerome (1897–1990)
Eddy, Mary Baker (1821–1910)
Edebone, Peta (1969—)
Edelman, Marian Wright (1939—)
Eden, Barbara (1934—)
Eden, Clarissa (1920—)
Eder, Elfriede (1970—)
Ederle, Gertrude (1905–2003)
Edgell, Zee (1941—)
Edger, Kate (1857–1935)
Edginton, May (1883–1957)
Edinger, Tilly (1897–1967)
Ediss, Connie (1871–1934)
Edmond, Lauris (1924–2000)
Edmond, Wendy (1946—)
Edmonton Grads (1915–1940)
Edmunds, Elizabeth M. (c. 1941—)
Edson, Katherine Philips (1870–1933)
Edstrom, Sonja
Eduardova, Eugenia (1882–1980)
Edvina, Louise (1878–1948)
Edwards, Edna Park (c. 1895–1967)
Edwards, Gloria (1944–1988)
Edwards, Henrietta Muir (1849–1933)
Edwards, India (1895–1990)
Edwards, Margaret (1939—)
Edwards, Penny (1928–1998)
Edwards, Teresa (1964—)
Edwards, Torri (1977—)
Edwards, Tracey (1962—)
Efflatoun, Inji (1923–1989)
Eftedal, Siri (1966—)
Ega, Françoise (1920–1976)
Egami, Ayano
Egami, Yumi (1957—)
Egerszegi, Krisztina (1974—)
Egervári, Márti (1956—)
Eggar, Samantha (1938—)
Egger, Sabine (1977—)
Eggerth, Marta (1912—)
Egnot, Leslie (1963—)
Egorova, Lyubov (1880–1972)
Egorova, Lyubov (1966—)
Egresi, Vilma (1936–1979)
Egri, Susanna (1926—)
Ehre, Ida (1900–1989)
Ehrenreich, Barbara (1941—)
Ehret, Gloria (1941—)
Ehrhardt, Anneliese (1950—)
Ehrlich, Aline (1928–1991)
Ehrlich, Ida Lublenski (d. 1986)
Eibenschütz-Dernbourg, Ilona (1872–1967)
Eichenberger, Sabine
Eife, Andrea (1956—)
Eigenmann, Rosa Smith (1858–1947)
Eijs, Irene (1966—)
Eilber, Janet (1951—)
Eilberg, Amy (1954—)
Eilers, Sally (1908–1978)
Eilika of Oldenburg (1928—)
Eilika of Oldenburg (1972—)
Einoder-Straube, Thea (1951—)
Einstein, Hannah Bachman (1862–1929)
Einstein-Marić, Mileva (1875–1948)
Eise, Ida Gertrude (1891–1978)
Eisemann-Schier, Ruth (c. 1942—)
Eisenberg, Mary Jane (1951—)
Eisenblätter, Charlotte (1903–1944)
Eisenhower, Mamie (1896–1979)
Eisenschneider, Elvira (1924–c. 1944)
Eisenstein, Judith (1909–1996)
Eisenstein, Phyllis (1946—)
Eisinger, Irene (1903–1994)
Eisler, Charlotte (1894–1970)
Eisner, Lotte (1896–1983)
Ekberg, Anita (1931—)
Ekman, Kirsten (1933—)
Elder, Anne (1918–1976)
Elder, Dorothy-Grace
Elder, Ruth (1902–1977)
Elders, Joycelyn (1933—)
Eldershaw, Flora (1897–1956)
Eldred, Pam (c. 1948—)
Eldridge, Florence (1901–1988)
Eleanora of Reuss (1860–1917)
Eleanor of Solms-Hohensolms-Lich (1871–1937)
Elejarde, Marlene (1950–1989)
Elena (1963—)
Elena of Montenegro (1873–1952)
Elg, Taina (1931—)
Elgar, Alice (1848–1920)
Elgin, Suzette Haden (1936—)
Elgood, Cornelia (1874–1960)
Elias, Rosalind (1930—)
Eliasson, Marthe (1969—)
Eline, Grace (1898—)
Eline, Marie (1902–1981)
Elion, Gertrude B. (1918–1999)
Eliot, Martha May (1891–1978)
Eliot, Vivienne (1889–1947)
Elisabeth (1894–1956)
Elizabeth (1831–1903)
Elizabeth Bowes-Lyon (1900–2002)
Elizabeth II (1926—)
Elizabeth of Anhalt-Dessau (1857–1933)
Elizabeth of Baden (1779–1826)
Elizabeth of Bavaria (1876–1965)
Elizabeth of Saxony (1830–1912)
Elizabeth of the Trinity (1880–1906)
Elizabeth of Thurn and Taxis (1903–1976)
Elizabeth of Wied (1843–1916)
Elizabeth of Yugoslavia (1936—)
Elizabeth Oldenburg (1904–1955)
Elizabeth von Habsburg (1883–1963)
Ella (1864–1918)
Ellen, Mary Ann (1897–1949)
Ellerbee, Linda (1944—)
Ellerman, Winifred (1894–1983)
Ellinaki, Georgia (1974—)
Elliot, Cass (1941–1974)
Elliott, Cheri (1970—)
Elliott, Gertrude (1874–1950)
Elliott, Harriet Wiseman (1884–1947)
Elliott, Madge (1896–1955)
Elliott, Maud Howe (1854–1948)
Elliott, Maxine (1868–1940)
Elliott, Missy (1971—)
Elliott, Sarah Barnwell (1848–1928)
Ellis, Betty (c. 1941—)
Ellis, Edith (c. 1874–1960)
Ellis, Evelyn (1894–1958)
Ellis, Florence Hawley (1906–1991)
Ellis, Kathleen (1946—)
Ellis, Lucille (c. 1915—)
Ellis, Mary (1897–2003)
Ellis, Mina A. (1870–1956)
Ellis, Patricia (1916–1970)
Ellis, Ruth (1927–1955)
Ellis, Terry (1966—)
Ellis-Fermor, Una Mary (1894–1958)
Elliston, Daisy (b. 1894)
Ellman, Louise (1945—)
Ellmann, Barbara (1950—)
Elmendorf, Theresa West (1855–1932)
El Moutawakel, Nawal (1962—)
Elms, Lauris (1931—)
El Saadawi, Nawal (1931—)
Elseeta (1883–1903)
Elsener, Patricia (1929—)
Elsie, Lily (1886–1962)
Elsner, Gisela (1937–1992)
Elsom, Isobel (1893–1981)
Elsom, Sarah Ann (1867–1962)
Elste, Meta (1921—)
Eluard, Nusch (1906–1946)
Elvin, Violetta (1925—)
Emecheta, Buchi (1944—)
Emerald, Connie (1891–1959)
Emerson, Ellen Russell (1837–1907)
Emerson, Faye (1917–1983)
Emerson, Gladys Anderson (1903–1984)
Emerson, Gloria (1929–2004)
Emerson, Hope (1897–1960)
Emery, Katherine (1906–1980)
Emery, Pollie (1875–1958)
Emery, Winifred (1862–1924)
Emhart, Maria (1901–1981)
Emirzyan, Sirvard (1966—)
Emma of Waldeck (1858–1934)
Emmelmann-Siemon, Kirsten (1961—)
Emmet, Katherine (c. 1882–1960)
Emmett, Dorothy Mary (b. 1904)
Emmons, Chansonetta Stanley (1858–1937)
Emms, Gail (1977—)
Emoto, Yuko (1972—)
Emshwiller, Carol (1921—)
Ena (1887–1969)
Enchi, Fumiko (1905–1986)
Ender, Kornelia (1958—)
Enderlein, Ortrun (1943–)
Endicott, Lori (1967—)
Ener, Güner (1935—)
Engdahl, Sylvia (1933—)
Engel, Marian (1933–1985)
Engelhard, Jane (1917–2004)
Engel-Kramer, Ingrid (1943—)
Engelmann, Helene

Enger, Babben
England, Lynndie (1982—)
England, Maud Russell (1863–1956)
Englehorn, Shirley (1940—)
English, Ada (c. 1878–1944)
English, Sarah (1955—)
Engquist, Ludmila (1964—)
Enoki, Miswo (1939—)
Enright, Elizabeth (1909–1968)
Ensing, Riemke (1939—)
Ensler, Eve (1953—)
Entenmann, Martha (1906–1996)
Enters, Angna (1907–1989)
Enthoven, Gabrielle (1868–1950)
Entwhistle, Peg (1908–1932)
Enya (1961—)
Ephron, Nora (1941—)
Ephron, Phoebe (1914–1971)
Epple, Irene (1957—)
Epple, Maria (1959—)
Epstein, Charlotte (1884–1938)
Epstein, Marie (c. 1899–1995)
Epstein, Selma (1927—)
Erbesfield, Robyn (1963—)
Erbil, Leyla (1931—)
Ercic, Emilija (1962—)
Erdman, Jean (1917—)
Erdmann, Susi-Lisa (1968—)
Erdos, Eva
Eremia, Alexandra (1987—)
Erickson, Hilda (1859–1968)
Ericsson, Ingela (1968—)
Eriksen, Ann (1971—)
Eriksen, Gunn (1956—)
Eriksen, Hanne (1960—)
Erikson, Joan (c. 1902–1997)
Eriksson, Agneta (1965—)
Eriksson, Anna-Lisa
Eriksson, Marianne (1952—)
Eristavi-Xostaria, Anastasia (1868–1951)
Ermakova, Anastasia (1983—)
Ermakova, Oxana (1973—)
Ermolaeva, Galina
Ermoleva, Zinaida (1898–1974)
Ermolova, Mariia (1853–1928)
Ernaux, Annie (1940—)
Ernst, Kitty (1926—)
Ernsting-Krienke, Nadine (1974—)
Errath, Christine (1956—)
Ertl, Martina (1973—)
Esau, Katherine (1898–1997)
Escher, Gitta (1957—)
Eschstruth, Nataly von (1860–1939)
Escoffery, Gloria (1923–2002)
Escot, Pozzi (1933—)
Escott, Cicely Margaret (1908–1977)
Escovedo, Sheila (1957—)
Eshkol, Noa (1927—)
Eskenazi, Roza (c. 1900–1980)
Esmat (d. 1995)
Esmond, Annie (1873–1945)
Esmond, Jill (1908–1990)
Espanca, Florbela (1894–1930)
Esperanza, Maria (1928–2004)
Espert, Nuria (1935—)
Espeseth, Gro (1972—)
Espina, Concha (1869–1955)
Espín de Castro, Vilma (1934—)
Espinosa, Judith (1877–1949)
Espinosa, Mimi (1893–1936)
Esquivel, Laura (1950—)
Essen, Viola (1926–1969)
Esser, Roswitha (1941—)
Esserman, Carol (c. 1945—)
Essipova, Annette (1851–1914)
Estefan, Gloria (1957—)
Estes, Ellen (1978—)
Esteve-Coll, Elizabeth (1938—)
Estópinal, Renee (1949—)
Estrela Moura, Elaine (1982—)
Estrich, Susan R. (1952—)
Etcherelli, Claire (1934—)
Etheridge, Melissa (1961—)
Ethridge, Mary Camille (1964—)
Etting, Ruth (1896–1978)
Eugénie (1826–1920)
Eustis, Dorothy (1886–1946)
Evan, Blanche (1909–1982)
Evangelista, Linda (1965—)
Evans, Alice Catherine (1881–1975)
Evans, Ann (c. 1836–1916)
Evans, Edith (1888–1976)
Evans, Elizabeth Glendower (1856–1937)
Evans, Janet (1971—)
Evans, Jillian (1959—)
Evans, Joan (1934—)
Evans, Kathy (1948–2003)
Evans, Madge (1909–1981)
Evans, Mari (1923—)
Evans, Matilda Arabella (1872–1935)
Evans, Minnie (1892–1987)
Evans, Nancy (1915–2000)
Evans, Renee (1908–1971)
Evatt, Elizabeth (1933—)
Evdokimova, Eva (1948—)
Evdokimova, Irina (1978—)
Evelyn, Judith (1913–1967)
Everest, Barbara (1890–1968)
Everett, Betty (1939–2001)
Everett, Eva (1942—)
Everleigh, Aida (1864–1960)
Everleigh, Minna (1866–1948)
Everlund, Gurli (1902–1985)
Evers, Meike (1977—)
Evers-Swindell, Caroline (1978—)
Evers-Swindell, Georgina (1978—)
Evers-Williams, Myrlie (1933—)
Evert, Chris (1954—)
Everts, Sabine (1961—)
Ewing, Annabelle (1960—)
Ewing, Margaret (1945–2006)
Ewing, Winnie (1929—)
Exene (1956—)
Exner, Judith Campbell (d. 1999)
Exter, Alexandra (1882–1949)
Eybers, Elisabeth (1915—)
Eyles, Joan M. (1907–1986)
Eyles, Leonora (1889–1960)
Eymers, Truus (1903–1988)
Eyton, Bessie (1890–1965)
Ezekiel, Denise Tourover (1903–1980)
Ezhova, Ljudmilla (1982—)
Ezzell, Cheryl (c. 1979—)
Faber, Beryl (d. 1912)
Fabian, Dora (1901–1935)
Fabian, Françoise (1932—)
Fabiani, Linda (1956—)
Fabiola (1928—)
Fabish, Agnes (1873–1947)
Fabray, Nanette (1920—)
Fachiri, Adila (1886–1962)
Fadden, Ilma (d. 1987)
Fadeyeva, Mariya (1958—)
Fadia (1943–2002)
Fadiman, Annalee (1916–2002)
Faggs, Mae (1932—)
Fagin, Claire (1926—)
Fahmy, Marguérite Laurent (b. around 1900)
Fahnrich, Gabriele (1968—)
Fainlight, Ruth (1931—)
Fair, Elinor (1902–1957)
Fair, Lorrie (1978—)
Fairbairn, Joyce (1939—)
Fairbairns, Zöe (1948—)
Fairbanks, Madeline (1900–1989)
Fairbanks, Marion (1900–1973)
Fairbrother, Nicola (1970—)
Fairbrother, Sydney (1872–1941)
Fairclough, Ellen (1905–2004)
Faire, Virginia Brown (1904–1980)
Fairfax, Lettice (1876–1948)
Fairfax, Marion (1875–1979)
Fairhurst, Sue
Fairuz (1935—)
Faithfull, Marianne (1946—)
Faiz, Alys (1914–2003)
Fajardo, Demisse (1964—)
Falca, Marinella (1986—)
Falck, Hildegard (1949—)
Falcón, Lidia (1935—)
Falconer, Martha Platt (1862–1941)
Falconetti, Renée (1892–1946)
Faletic, Dana (1977—)
Falk, Ria
Falkenburg, Jinx (1919–2003)
Falkender, Marcia (1932—)
Falkenhayn, Benita von (d. 1935)
Fallaci, Oriana (1930—)
Fallis, Barbara (1924–1980)
Fallon, Trisha (1972—)
Fältskog, Agnetha (1950—)
Famose, Annie (1944—)
Fanthorpe, U.A. (1929—)
Fan Yunjie (1972—)
Farber, Viola (1931–1998)
Farebrother, Violet (1888–1969)
Farenthold, Frances "Sissy" (1926—)
Farial (1938—)
Farida (1921–1988)
Farina, Mimi (1945–2001)
Farjeon, Annabel (1919—)
Farjeon, Eleanor (1881–1965)
Farkas, Agnes (1973—)
Farkas, Andrea (c. 1969—)
Farkas, Ruth L. (1906–1996)
Farley, Harriet (1813–1907)
Farmborough, Florence (1887–1978)
Farmer, Beverley (1941—)
Farmer, Fannie Merritt (1857–1915)
Farmer, Frances (1913–1970)
Farmer, Virginia (1898–1988)
Farmer-Patrick, Sandra (1962—)
Farnadi, Edith (1921–1973)
Farningham, Marianne (1834–1909)
Farnsworth, Emma J. (1860–1952)
Farquhar, Marilyn (1928—)
Farr, Wanda K. (1895–1983)
Farrally, Betty (1915–1989)
Farrand, Beatrix Jones (1872–1959)
Farrar, Geraldine (1882–1967)
Farrar, Gwen (1899–1944)
Farrar, Margaret (1897–1984)
Farrell, Eileen (1920–2002)
Farrell, Glenda (1904–1971)
Farrell, Peggy (1920—)
Farrell, Renita (1972—)
Farrell, Suzanne (1945—)
Farren, Nellie (1848–1904)
Farrer, Margaret (1914–1997)
Farrés, Carmen (1931–1976)
Farrokhzad, Forugh (1935–1967)
Farron, Julia (1922—)
Farrow, Mia (1945—)
Fassbaender, Brigitte (1939—)
Fassie, Brenda (1964–2004)
Fatima, Djemille (c. 1890–1921)
Faulk, Mary Lena (1926–1995)
Fauntz, Jane (1910–1989)
Fauset, Crystal Bird (1893–1965)
Fauset, Jessie Redmon (1882–1961)
Faust, Lotta (1880–1910)
Faut, Jean (1925—)
Favart, Edmée (1886–1941)
Favor, Suzy (1968—)
Fawcett, Joy (1968—)
Fawcett, Maisie (1902–1988)
Fawcett, Marion (1886–1957)
Fawcett, Millicent Garrett (1847–1929)
Fawcett, Philippa (1868–1948)
Fawzia (1921—)
Fawzia (1940–2005)
Fay, Amy (1844–1928)
Fay, Vivien (b. around 1908)
Faye, Alice (1912–1998)
Faye, Julia (1893–1966)
Fazan, Eleanor (1930—)
Fazekas, Mrs. Julius (d. 1929)
Fazenda, Louise (1895–1962)
Fazlic, Jasna (1970—)
Fealy, Maude (1883–1971)
Fearn, Anne Walter (1865–1939)
Fedde, Sister Elizabeth (1850–1921)
Federova, Nina (1958—)
Federova, Sophia (1879–1963)
Fedicheva, Kaleria (1936—)
Fedorovitch, Sophie (1893–1953)
Fedotkina, Svetlana (1967—)
Fedotova, Irina (1975—)

Feeney, Carol (1964—)
Feher, Anna (1921—)
Feigenheimer, Irene (1946—)
Feinstein, Dianne (1933—)
Feinstein, Elaine (1930—)
Feklistova, Maria (1976—)
Feldman, Andrea (1948–1972)
Feldman, Gladys (1891–1974)
Felice, Cynthia (1942—)
Felix, Allyson (1985—)
Felix, Maria (1914–2002)
Felix, Sylviane (1977—)
Felke, Petra (1959—)
Fell, Honor (1900–1986)
Fellows, Edith (1923—)
Felton, Rebecca Latimer (1835–1930)
Felton, Verna (1890–1966)
Fénelon, Fania (1918–1983)
Feng, Amy (1969—)
Feng Keng (1907–1931)
Feng Kun (1978—)
Feng Yuanjun (1900–1974)
Fenley, Molissa (1954—)
Fennell, Nuala (1935—)
Fenwick, Ethel Gordon (1857–1947)
Fenwick, Irene (1887–1936)
Fenwick, Millicent (1910–1992)
Feodore of Hohenlohe-Langenburg (1866–1932)
Feofanova, Svetlana (1980—)
Ferber, Edna (1885–1968)
Ferdinand, Marie (1978—)
Fergerson, Mable (1955—)
Ferguson, Abbie Park (1837–1919)
Ferguson, Cathy Jean (1948—)
Ferguson, Debbie (1976—)
Ferguson, Dottie (1923–2003)
Ferguson, Elsie (1883–1961)
Ferguson, Helen (1901–1977)
Ferguson, Margaret Clay (1863–1951)
Ferguson, Miriam A. (1875–1961)
Ferguson, Patricia (1958—)
Ferguson, Sarah (1959—)
Fergusson, Elizabeth (1867–1930)
Fergusson, Mary (1914–1997)
Fergusson, Muriel McQueen (1899–1997)
Ferland, Barbara (1919—)
Fernandez, Adriana (1971—)
Fernandez, Alina (1956—)
Fernandez, Ana Ivis (1973—)
Fernandez, Bijou (1877–1961)
Fernandez, Gigi (1964—)
Fernandez, Isabel (1972—)
Fernandez, Lisa (1971—)
Fernandez, Mary Joe (1971—)
Fernandez, Mrs. E.L. (1852–1909)
Fernández Ochoa, Blanca (1963—)
Fernando, Gilda Cordero (1930—)
Fernando, Sylvia (1904–1983)
Ferneck, Christine (1969—)
Ferner, Ellen Elizabeth (1869–1930)
Ferragamo, Fiamma (1941–1998)
Ferrais, Amalia (1830–1904)
Ferrari, Gabrielle (1851–1921)
Ferrari, Maria Paz (1973—)
Ferraris, Jan (1947—)
Ferraro, Geraldine (1935—)
Ferré, Rosario (1938—)
Ferreira, Anne (1961—)
Ferrell, Barbara (1947—)
Ferrer, Concepció (1938—)
Ferrero, Anna-Maria (1931—)
Ferrers, Helen (1869–1943
Ferrer Salat, Beatriz (1966—)
Ferri, Olga (1928—)
Ferrier, Kathleen (1912–1953)
Ferris, Elizabeth (1940—)
Ferris, Michelle (1976—)
Feryabnikova, Nelli (1949—)
Fetzer, Brigitte (1956—)
Feuillère, Edwige (1907–1998)
Feury, Peggy (1924–1985)
Fewings, Eliza Anne (1857–1940)
Fiacconi, Franca (1965—)
Fiamengo, Marya (1926—)
Fibingerova, Helena (1949—)
Fichandler, Zelda (1924—)
Fichtel, Anja (1968—)
Fick, Sigrid (1887–1979)
Fickert, Auguste (1855–1910)
Fiebig, Cora (c. 1934—)
Fiebiger, Christel (1946—)
Fiedler, Bobbi (1937—)
Fiedler, Ellen (1958—)
Field, Betty (1918–1973)
Field, Ethel Maude (1882–1967)
Field, Jessie (1881–1971)
Field, Mary (1896–c. 1968)
Field, Pattie H. (b. around 1902)
Field, Rachel Lyman (1894–1942)
Field, Sally (1946—)
Field, Sara Bard (1882–1974)
Field, Shirley Anne (1936—)
Field, Sylvia (1901–1998)
Field, Virginia (1917–1992)
Fields, Crystal (1969—)
Fields, Debbi (1956—)
Fields, Dorothy (1904–1974)
Fields, Evelyn J.
Fields, Gracie (1898–1979)
Fields, Julia (1938—)
Fields, Mary (c. 1832–1914)
Fields, Verna (1918–1982)
Fiennes, Virginia (1947–2004)
Fifield, Elaine (1930–1999)
Figes, Eva (1932—)
Figini, Michela (1966—)
Figner, Vera (1852–1942)
Figueiredo, Ilda (1948—)
Figueras-Dotti, Marta (1957—)
Figueroa, Ana (1907–1970)
Figues de Saint Marie, Solenne (1979—)
Figuli, Margita (1909–1995)
Fikotová, Olga (1932—)
Filatova, Maria (1961—)
Filipova, Nadya (1959—)
Filipović, Zlata (1981—)
Filippi, Rosina (1866–1930)
Filkins, Grace (c. 1865–1962)
Fillmore, Myrtle Page (1845–1931)
Filosofova, Anna (1837–1912)
Finas, Lucette (1921—)
Finch, Flora (1867–1940)
Finch, Jennie (1980—)
Finch, Jennifer (1966—)
Findlay, Ruth (1904–1949)
Fine, Perle (1908–1988)
Fine, Sylvia (1913–1991)
Fine, Vivian (1913–2000)
Fingerhut, Arden (1945–1994)
Fini, Leonor (1908–1996)
Finley, Martha (1828–1909)
Finnbogadóttir, Vigdís (1930—)
Finn-Burrell, Michelle (1965—)
Finneran, Sharon (1946—)
Finney, Joan (1925–2001)
Finnie, Linda (1952—)
Finnigan, Joan (1925—)
Fiocre, Eugénie (1845–1908)
Fiorenza, Elisabeth Schuessler (1938—)
Firestone, Shulamith (1945—)
Fireva, Tatyana (1982—)
Firsova, Elena Olegovna (1950—)
First, Ruth (1925–1982)
Fischer, Alice (1869–1947)
Fischer, Ann (1919–1971)
Fischer, Annie (1914–1995)
Fischer, Birgit (1962—)
Fischer, Greta (1909–1988)
Fischer, Margarita (1886–1975)
Fischer, Mary Ann (1933—)
Fischer, Ruth (1895–1961)
Fish, Jennifer (1949—)
Fish, Maree (1963—)
Fish, Marian (1853–1915)
Fisher, Aileen (19096–2002)
Fisher, Allison (1968—)
Fisher, Anna L. (1949—)
Fisher, Cicely Corbett (1885–1959)
Fisher, Doris (1915–2003)
Fisher, Doris
Fisher, Dorothy Canfield (1879–1958)
Fisher, M.F.K. (1908–1992)
Fisher, Margaret (c. 1874–1958)
Fisher, Mary (c. 1946—)
Fisher, Nellie (1920–1994)
Fisher, Sarah (1980—)
Fisk, Sari
Fiske, Minnie Maddern (1865–1932)
Fitschen, Doris (1968—)
Fittko, Lisa (1909–2005)
Fitton, Doris (1897–1985)
Fitzgerald, Benita (1961—)
FitzGerald, Eithne (1950—)
Fitzgerald, Ella (1917–1996)
Fitzgerald, Eugenia Tucker (c. 1834–1928)
Fitzgerald, Frances (1950—)
Fitzgerald, Frances Scott (1921–1986)
Fitzgerald, Geraldine (1913–2005)
Fitzgerald, Lillian (d. 1947)
Fitzgerald, Penelope (1916–2000)
Fitzgerald, Zelda (1900–1948)
Fitz-Gibbon, Bernice (c. 1895–1982)
FitzGibbon, Hanorah Philomena (1889–1979)
Fitzhugh, Louise (1928–1974)
Fitzjames, Natalie (b. 1819)
Fitzsimons, Lorna (1967—)
Flachmeier, Laurie (1959—)
Flack, Roberta (1937—)
Flagg, Elise (1951—)
Flagg, Fannie (1941—)
Flagstad, Kirsten (1895–1962)
Flaherty, Frances Hubbard (c. 1886–1972)
Flaherty, Mary (1953—)
Flanagan, Hallie (1889–1969)
Flanagan, Jeanne (1957—)
Flanagan, Sinéad (1878–1975)
Flanner, Janet (1892–1978)
Flannery, Judy (1939–1997)
Flautre, Hélène (1958—)
Fleeson, Doris (1901–1970)
Fleischer, Ottilie (1911—)
Fleischmann, Torrance (1949—)
Fleischmann, Trude (1895–1990)
Fleisser, Marieluise (1901–1974)
Fleming, Alice (1882–1952)
Fleming, Amalia (1912–1986)
Fleming, Nancy (c. 1941—)
Fleming, Peggy (1948—)
Fleming, Renée (1959—)
Fleming, Rhonda (1922—)
Fleming, Williamina Paton (1857–1911)
Flemming, Marialiese (1933—)
Flesch, Colette (1937—)
Flessel, Laura (1971—)
Fletcher, Alice Cunningham (1838–1923)
Fletcher, Caroline (1906—)
Fletcher, Chris (1955—)
Fletcher, Jennie (1890–1968)
Fletcher, Louise (1934—)
Fletcher, Maria (c. 1942—)
Fleury, Catherine (1966—)
Flexner, Anne Crawford (1874–1955)
Flexner, Jennie M. (1882–1944)
Flikke, Julia Otteson (1879–1965)
Flindt, Vivi (1943—)
Flint, Caroline (1961—)
Flint, Elizabeth (b. 1909)
Flint, Helen (1898–1967)
Flintoff, Debra (1960—)
Flöge, Emilie (1874–1952)
Flon, Suzanne (1918–2005)
Flood, Debbie (1980—)
Florea, Rodica (1983—)
Florence, Malvina Pray (1830–1906)
Florence, Mary Sargant (1857–1954)
Flores, Lola (1924–1995)
Florey, Margaret (1904–1994)
Florman, Marianne (1964—)
Flory, Regine (1894–1926)
Flosadottir, Vala (1978—)
Flower, Lucy (1837–1921)
Flowers, Bess (1898–1984)
Flowers, Tairia (1981—)
Flowers, Vonetta (1973—)
Flowerton, Consuelo (1900–1965)
Flügge-Lotz, Irmgard (1903–1974)
Flynn, Elizabeth Gurley (1890–1964)
Flynn, Jeannie

Foch, Nina (1924—)
Fogerty, Elsie (1865–1945)
Fokina, Vera (1886–1958)
Fokke, Annemieke (1967—)
Foley, Edna (1878–1943)
Foley, Martha (c. 1897–1977)
Folger, Emily (1858–1936)
Follansbee, Elizabeth A. (1839–1917)
Follas, Selina
Follett, Barbara (1942—)
Follett, Mary Parker (1868–1933)
Follett, Rosemary (1948—)
Foltova, Vlasta (1913—)
Foltz, Clara (1849–1934)
Fonaroff, Nina (1914–2003)
Fonda, Jane (1937—)
Fontaine, Joan (1917—)
Fontaine, Lillian (1886–1975)
Fontana, Giovanna (1915–2004)
Fontanne, Lynn (1887–1983)
Fonteyn, Karen (1969—)
Fonteyn, Margot (1919–1991)
Fontyn, Jacqueline (1930—)
Foot, Katherine (c. 1852–?)
Foot, Philippa (1920—)
Foote, Mary Hallock (1847–1938)
Forbes, Brenda (1909–1996)
Forbes, Esther (1891–1967)
Forbes, Mary (1880–1974)
Forbes, Mary Elizabeth (1879–1964)
Forbes, Rosita (1893–1967)
Forbes-Robertson, Beatrice (1883–1967)
Forbes-Robertson, Jean (1905–1962)
Forbes-Sempill, Elizabeth (1912–1965)
Force, Juliana (1876–1948)
Ford, Atina (c. 1972—)
Ford, Betty (1918—)
Ford, Eileen (1922—)
Ford, Harriet (c. 1863–1949)
Ford, Isabella O. (1855–1924)
Ford, Ita (1940—)
Ford, Judith (c. 1950—)
Ford, Lita (1958—)
Ford, Mary (1924–1977)
Ford, Michelle Jan (1962—)
Ford, Patricia (1921—)
Ford, Penny (1964—)
Ford, Susan (1957—)
Forde, Eugenie (1879–1940)
Forde, Florrie (1876–1940)
Forde, Leneen (1935—)
Forde, Vera (1894–1967)
Forde, Victoria (1896–1964)
Forder, Annemarie (1978—)
Fordham, Julia (1962—)
Forgan, Liz (1944—)
Forkel, Karen (1970—)
Forman, Ada (b. around 1895)
Formby, Margaret (1929–2003)
Fórmica, Mercedes (1916—)
Fornalska, Malgorzata (1902–1944)
Fornaroli, Cia (1888–1954)
Fornia, Rita (1878–1922)
Forrest, Ann (1895–1985)
Forrest, Helen (1918–1999)
Forrest, Sally (1928—)
Forsberg, Magdalena (1967—)
Forsh, Olga (1873–1961)
Forster, Margaret (1938—)
Förster-Nietzsche, Elisabeth (1846–1935)
Forster-Pieloth, Kerstin (1965—)
Fort, Cornelia (1919–1943)
Fort, Syvilla (c. 1917–1975)
Fortescue, May (1862–1950)
Fortesque-Brickdale, Eleanor (1872–1945)
Forti, Simone (c. 1935—)
Fortuyn-Leenmans, Margaretha Droogleever (1909–1998)
Fosburgh, Minnie Astor (1906–1978)
Fossey, Dian (1932–1985)
Foster, Diane (1928—)
Foster, Dianne (1928—)
Foster, Frances (1924–1997)
Foster, Gae (b. 1903)
Foster, Gloria (1933–2001)
Foster, J. Ellen (1840–1910)
Foster, Jacqueline (1947—)
Foster, Jodie (1962—)
Foster, Lillian (d. 1949)
Foster, Margot (1958—)
Foster, Marie (1917–2003)
Foster, Susanna (1924—)
Fothergill, Dorothy (1945—)
Foudy, Julie (1971—)
Fountaine, Margaret (1862–1940)
Fourtou, Janelly (1939—)
Fout, Nina (1959—)
Fowke, Edith (1913–1996)
Fowle, Elida Rumsey (1842–1919)
Fowler, Marjorie (1920–2003)
Fowler, Tillie (1942–2005)
Fox, Beryl (1931—)
Fox, Carol (1926–1981)
Fox, Catherine (1977—)
Fox, Charlotte Milligan (1864–1916)
Fox, Della (1870–1913)
Fox, Dorothy (b. around 1914)
Fox, Francine (1949—)
Fox, Jackie (1959—)
Fox, Joanne (1979—)
Fox, Mildred (1971—)
Fox, Paula (1923—)
Fox, Ruby (1945—)
Fox, Sidney (1910–1942)
Fox-Jerusalmi, Myriam (1961—)
Foy, Madeline (1903–1988)
Foy, Mary (1901–1987)
Foyle, Christina (d. 1999)
Fracci, Carla (1936—)
Fradon, Ramona (1926—)
Fraenkel, Naomi (1920—)
Fraga, Kely (1974—)
Frahm, Pernille (1954—)
Fraisse, Geneviève (1948—)
Fraley, Ingrid (1949—)
Frame, Alice (1878–1941)
Frame, Janet (1924–2004)
Frampton, Eleanor (1896–1973)
Franca, Celia (1921—)
France, Ruth (1913–1968)
Franchi, Anna (1866–1954)
Francia, Mirka (1975—)
Francine, Anne (1917–1999)
Francis, Anne (1930—)
Francis, Arlene (1908–2001)
Francis, Catherine Augusta (1836–1916)
Francis, Clare (1946—)
Francis, Connie (1938—)
Francis, Eve (1886–1980)
Francis, Kay (1899–1968)
Francisco, Betty (1900–1950)
Franco, Carmen Polo de (1902–1988)
Francois, Elma (1897–1944)
Françoise d'Orleans (1844–1925)
Françoise of Guise (1902–1953)
Frandl, Josefine
Frank, Anne (1929–1945)
Frank, Antje (1968—)
Frank, Dottie (1941—)
Frank, Jacqueline (1980—)
Frank, Margot (1926–1945)
Frank, Mary K. (1911–1988)
Frank, Nance (1949—)
Frank, Rosaline Margaret (1864–1954)
Frankau, Pamela (1908–1967)
Franken, Rose (c. 1895–1988)
Frankenthaler, Helen (1928—)
Frankeva, Antoaneta (1971—)
Franklin, Alberta (1896–1976)
Franklin, Aretha (1942—)
Franklin, Erma (1938–2002)
Franklin, Irene (1876–1941)
Franklin, Martha Minerva (1870–1968)
Franklin, Miles (1879–1954)
Franklin, Rosalind (1920–1958)
Franklin, Shirley (1945—)
Franklyn, Beth (c. 1873–1956)
Franklyn, Lidije (1922—)
Franks, Lucinda (1946—)
Frantz, Virginia Kneeland (1896–1967)
Frasca, Mary (d. 1973)
Fraser, Agnes (1877–1968)
Fraser, Alexa Stirling (1897–1977)
Fraser, Annie Isabel (1868–1939)
Fraser, Antonia (1932—)
Fraser, Dawn (1937—)
Fraser, Elizabeth (1963—)
Fraser, Gretchen (1919–1994)
Fraser, Isabella (1857–1932)
Fraser, Janet (1883–1945)
Fraser, Margaret (1866–1951)
Fraser, Mary Crawford (1851–1922)
Fraser, Mary Isabel (1863–1942)
Fraser, Roslin (1927–1997)
Fraser, Shelagh (1922–2000)
Fraser, Susan (1966—)
Fraser, Sylvia (1935—)
Fraser, Tamie (1936—)
Fraser, Wendy (1963—)
Frassoni, Monica (1963—)
Fratellini, Annie (1932–1997)
Fratianne, Linda (1960—)
Frazee, Jane (1918–1985)
Frazier, Maude (1881–1963)
Frechette, Sylvie (1967—)
Frederick, Christine (1883–1970)
Frederick, Lynne (1954–1994)
Frederick, Marcia (1963—)
Frederick, Pauline (1881–1938)
Frederick, Pauline (1908–1990)
Fredericka (1917–1981)
Fredericka of Hanover (1848–1926)
Fredriksson, Marie (1958—)
Freed, Amanda (1979—)
Freedman, Nancy (1920—)
Freeman, Alice (1857–1936)
Freeman, Caroline (c. 1855–1914)
Freeman, Cathy (1973—)
Freeman, Emma B. (1880–1927)
Freeman, Gillian (1929—)
Freeman, Joan (1918–1998)
Freeman, Kathleen (1919–2001)
Freeman, Lucy (1916–2004)
Freeman, Mary E. Wilkins (1852–1930)
Freeman, Mavis (1907—)
Freeman, Mavis (1918—)
Freeman, Michele
Freeman, Mona (1926—)
Freeman, Muriel (1897—)
Freeman, Ruth B. (1906–1982)
Freer, Agnes Rand (1878–1972)
Frei, Tanya (1972—)
Freier, Recha (1892–1984)
Freist, Greta (1904–1993)
Fremantle, Anne (1909–2002)
Frémont, Jessie Benton (1824–1902)
Fremstad, Olive (1871–1951)
French, Alice (1850–1934)
French, Annie (1872–1965)
French, Dawn (1957—)
French, Evangeline (1869–1960)
French, Francesca (1871–1960)
French, Heather (1974—)
French, Marilyn (1929—)
French, Michelle (1977—)
French, Ruth (b. 1906)
French, Valerie (1932–1990)
Freni, Mirella (1935—)
Frenkel-Brunswik, Else (1908–1958)
Fretter, Vera (1905–1992)
Freud, Anna (1895–1982)
Freund, Gisèle (1912–2000)
Freundlich, Emmy (1878–1948)
Freytag-Loringhoven, Elsa von (1875–1927)
Fricioiu, Maria (1960—)
Fricker, Brenda (1945—)
Friday, Dallas J. (1986—)
Friday, Nancy (1937—)
Friebus, Florida (1909–1988)
Friedan, Betty (1921–2006)
Friedberg, Berta (1864–1944)
Friedl, Ernestine (1920—)
Friedman, Elizebeth (d. 1980)
Friedman, Esther Pauline (1918–2002)
Friedman, Pauline Esther (1918—)
Friedne-Banfalvi, Klara (1931—)
Friedrich, Heike (1970—)
Friend, Charlotte (1921–1987)

Friesinger, Anni (1977—)
Friganza, Trixie (1870–1955)
Frigerio, Marta Lía (1925–1985)
Frings, Ketti (1909–1981)
Frink, Elisabeth (1930–1993)
Frintu, Rodica (1960—)
Fris, Maria (1932–1961)
Frischmann, Justine (1969—)
Frischmuth, Barbara (1941—)
Frissell, Toni (1907–1988)
Frizzell, Mary (1913–1972)
Frizzell, Mildred (1911—)
Froehlich, Silvia (1959—)
Froelian, Isolde (1908–1957)
Froeseth, Hege (1969—)
Frolova, Inna (1965—)
Frolova, Lyudmila (1953—)
Frolova, Nina (1948—)
Frolova, Tatiana (1967—)
Froman, Jane (1907–1980)
Froman, Margareta (1890–1970)
Fromm, Erika (1909–2003)
Frommater, Uta (1948—)
Fromme, Lynette (1948—)
Fromm-Reichmann, Frieda (1889–1957)
Frost, Constance Helen (c. 1862–1920)
Frost, Phyllis (1917–2004)
Frost, Winifred (1902–1979)
Frostic, Gwen (1906–2001)
Fruelund, Katrine (1978—)
Frustol, Tone Gunn (1975—)
Fry, Laura Ann (1857–1943)
Fry, Margery (1874–1958)
Fry, Shirley (1927—)
Frye, Mary E. (1905–2004)
Fubuki, Koshiji (1924–1980)
Fuchs, Ruth (1946—)
Fuerstner, Fiona (1936—)
Fuertes, Gloria (1917–1998)
Fugard, Sheila (1932—)
Führer, Charlotte (1834–1907)
Fuhrmann, Barbel (1940—)
Fujii, Raika (1974—)
Fujii, Yumiko (c. 1972—)
Fujiki, Mayuko (1975—)
Fujimaru, Michiyo (1979—)
Fujimoto, Yuko (1943—)
Fukuda, Hideko (1865–1927)
Fukunaka, Sachiko (1946—)
Fuld, Carrie (1864–1944)
Fullam, Augusta Fairfield (1876–1914)
Fullana, Margarita (1972—)
Fuller, Amy (1968—)
Fuller, Frances (1907–1980)
Fuller, Ida (1874–1975)
Fuller, Loïe (1862–1928)
Fuller, Lucia Fairchild (1870–1924)
Fuller, Mary (1888–1973)
Fuller, Meta Warrick (1877–1968)
Fuller, Minnie Rutherford (1868–1946)
Fuller, Rosalinde (1901–1982)
Fuller, Sarah (1836–1927)
Fullerton, Mary Eliza (1868–1946)
Fulton, Catherine (1829–1919)
Fulton, Margaret Barr (1900–1989)
Fulton, Mary Hannah (1854–1927)
Fulton, Maude (1881–1950)
Fu Mingxia (1978—)
Fung, Lori (1963—)
Funicello, Annette (1942—)
Funk, Wally (1939—)
Funkenhauser, Zita-Eva (1966—)
Funnell, Pippa (1968—)
Fuocco, Sofia (1830–1916)
Furbish, Kate (1834–1931)
Furlong, Monica (1930–2003)
Furman, Bess (1894–1969)
Furneaux, Yvonne (1928—)
Furness, Betty (1916–1994)
Furness, Vera (1921–2002)
Furse, Judith (1912–1974)
Furse, Katharine (1875–1952)
Furse, Margaret (1911–1974)
Furtado, Juliana (1967—)
Furtsch, Evelyn (1911—)
Furtseva, Ekaterina (1910–1974)
Furuhjelm, Annie (1854–1937)
Furukawa, Makiko (1947—)
Fürüzan (1935—)
Fusar-Poli, Barbara (1972—)
Fuss, Sonja (1978—)
Fussenegger, Gertrud (1912—)
Fu Yuehua (c. 1947—)
Fynes, Sevatheda (1974—)
Fyodorova, Olga (1983—)
Gaal, Franciska (1904–1972)
Gabain, Ethel Leontine (1883–1950)
Gabarra, Carin (1965—)
Gabellanes Marieta, Nagore (1973—)
Gabl, Gertrud (1948–1976)
Gabor, Eva (1919–1995)
Gabor, Georgeta (1962—)
Gabor, Jolie (1894–1997)
Gabor, Magda (1914–1997)
Gabor, Zsa Zsa (1917—)
Gabriel Koether, Rosemarie (1956—)
Gacioch, Rose (1915–2004)
Gadski, Johanna (1872–1932)
Gafencu, Liliana (1975—)
Gág, Wanda (1893–1946)
Gage, Susanna Phelps (1857–1915)
Gagneur, Louise (1832–1902)
Gagneur, Marguerite (1857–1945)
Gaidinliu, Rani (1915–1993)
Gaigerova, Varvara Andrianovna (1903–1944)
Gaines, Chryste (1970—)
Gaines, Irene McCoy (1892–1964)
Gal, Jenny (1969—)
Gal, Jessica (1971—)
Galdikas, Biruté (1948—)
Gale, Tristan (1980—)
Gale, Zona (1874–1938)
Galeana, Benita (1904–1995)
Galgóczi, Erzsébet (1930–1989)
Galieva, Roza (1977—)
Galindo de Topete, Hermila (1896–1954)
Galkina, Lioubov (1973—)
Gallagher, Ann (1967—)
Gallagher, Helen (1926—)
Gallagher, Kim (1964–2002)
Gallagher, Rosie (1970–2003)
Galland, Bertha (1876–1932)
Gallant, Mavis (1922—)
Gallardo, Miriam (1968—)
Gallardo, Sara (1931–1988)
Gallatin, Alberta (c. 1861–1948)
Galli, Rosina (1896–1940)
Galli-Curci, Amelita (1882–1963)
Gallina, Juliane (1970—)
Galloway, Louise (d. 1949)
Galushka, Vera (1945—)
Galvão, Patricia (1910–1962)
Galvarriato, Eulalia (1905–1997)
Galvin, Sheila (1914–1983)
Gam, Rita (1928—)
Gambarelli, Maria (1900–1990)
Gambaro, Griselda (1928—)
Gambero, Anabel (1972—)
Gamin, Judith (1930—)
Gamova, Ekaterina (1980—)
Gamson, Annabelle (1928—)
Gándara, Carmen (1900–1977)
Gandhi, Indira (1917–1984)
Gandhi, Kasturba (1869–1944)
Gandhi, Sonia (1946—)
Gandolfi, Annapia (1964—)
Gandy, Kim A. (c. 1954—)
Gánina, Maja (1927—)
Ganser, Marge (c. 1948–1996)
Ganser, Mary Ann (c. 1948–1971)
Gansky-Sachse, Diana (1963—)
Gant, Phyllis (1922—)
Gantt, Rosa (1875–1935)
Gao E (1962—)
Gao Feng (1982—)
Gao Hong (1967—)
Gao Jing (1975—)
Gao Jun (1969—)
Gao Ling (1979—)
Gao Min (1970—)
Gao Xiumin (1963—)
Gao Yaojie (c. 1927—)
Gapchenko, Emma (1938—)
Garapick, Nancy (1961—)
Garatti-Saville, Eleanor (1909—)
Garaud, Marie-Françoise (1934—)
Garayeva, Yuliya
Garbo, Greta (1905–1990)
Garborg, Hulda (1862–1934)
Garbousova, Raya (1909–1997)
Garbrecht-Enfeldt, Monique (1968—)
Garceau, Catherine (1978—)
Garcia, Agustina Soledad (1981—)
García, Marta (c. 1945—)
Garcia, Rosa (1964—)
García Marruz, Fina (1923—)
Garcia-O'Brien, Tanya (c. 1973—)
García-Orcoyen Tormo, Cristina (1948—)
Garde, Betty (1905–1989)
Gardella, Tess (1897–1950)
Garden, Mary (1874–1967)
Gardener, Helen Hamilton (1853–1925)
Gardiner, Antoinette (1941—)
Gardiner, Kate (1885–1974)
Gardiner, Lisa (c. 1896–1958)
Gardiner, Margaret (1904–2005)
Gardiner, Muriel (1901–1985)
Gardner, Ava (1922–1990)
Gard'ner, Elizabeth Anne (1858–1926)
Gardner, Frances (1913–1989)
Gardner, Helen (1878–1946)
Gardner, Helen (1884–1968)
Gardner, Helen Louise (1908–1986)
Gardner, Isabella (1915–1981)
Gardner, Isabella Stewart (1840–1924)
Gardner, Janet (1962—)
Gardner, Julia Anna (1882–1960)
Gardner, Kay (1941–2002)
Gardner, Margaret (1844–1929)
Gardner, Maria Louisa (1879–1968)
Gardner, Mary Sewall (1871–1961)
Gardner, Maureen (1928–1974)
Gardner, Suzi (1960—)
Gare, Nene (1919–1994)
Gareau, France (1967—)
Gareau, Jacqueline (1953—)
Garefrekes, Kerstin (1979—)
Garfield, Lucretia (1832–1918)
Garfield, Viola (1899–1983)
Garg, Mridula (1938—)
Garilhe, Renee (1923—)
Garisch-Culmberger, Renate (1939—)
Garland, Judy (1922–1969)
Garlick, Eunice Harriett (1883–1951)
Garmson, Aileen (c. 1861–1951)
Garner, Helen (1942—)
Garner, Peggy Ann (1931–1984)
Garner, Sarah (1971—)
Garnet, Sarah (1831–1911)
Garnett, Constance (1862–1946)
Garon, Pauline (1900–1965)
Garrett, Betty (1919—)
Garrett, Mary Elizabeth (1854–1915)
Garrett, Mary Smith (1839–1925)
Garrett, Maureen (1922—)
Garrison, Mabel (1886–1963)
Garrison, Zina (1963—)
Garro, Elena (1916–1998)
Garrod, Dorothy A. (1892–1969)
Garson, Greer (1904–1996)
Garth, Midi (1920—)
Garufi, Bianca (1920—)
Garvey, Amy Jacques (1896–1973)
Garvie, Sheila (fl. 1960s)
Gaskell, Sonia (1904–1974)
Gaskin, Ina May (1940—)
Gasteazoro, Ana (1950–1993)
Gatehouse, Eleanor Wright (1886–1973)
Gates, Eleanor (1871–1951)
Gates, Nancy (1926—)
Gates, Ruth (1886–1966)
Gateson, Marjorie (1891–1977)
Gathers, Helen (1943—)
Gato, Idalmis (1971—)
Gattinoni, Fernanda (1906–2002)
Gaudin-Latrille, Brigitte (1958—)
Gaudron, Mary Genevieve (1943—)
Gaugel, Heide-Elke (1959—)

Gaughin, Lorraine (1924–1974)
Gault, Alma Elizabeth (1891–1981)
Gaunt, Mary (1861–1942)
Gauntier, Gene (1885–1966)
Gauthier, Eva (1885–1958)
Gauthier, Xavière (1942—)
Gautier, Felisa Rincón de (1897–1994)
Gautier, Judith (1845–1917)
Gavriljuk, Nina (1965—)
Gaxton, Madeline (1897–1990)
Gay, Maisie (1883–1945)
Gayatri Devi (1919—)
Gayatri Devi (c. 1897–1995)
Gayle, Crystal (1951—)
Gaynor, Gloria (1949—)
Gaynor, Janet (1906–1984)
Gaynor, Mitzi (1930—)
Gaytan, Andrea
Gear, Luella (1897–1980)
Gebara, Ivone (1944—)
Gebhardt, Evelyne (1954—)
Ge Cuilin (1930—)
Geczi, Erika (1959—)
Geddes, Annabella Mary (1864–1955)
Geddes, Jane (1960—)
Geddes, Wilhelmina (1887–1955)
Gee, Dolly (1897–1978)
Gee, Helen (1919–2004)
Geer, Charlotte (1957—)
Ge Fei (1975—)
Geijssen, Carolina (1947—)
Geiringer, Hilda (1893–1973)
Geise, Sugar (1909–1988)
Geisler, Ilse
Geissler, Ines (1963—)
Geister, Janet M. (1885–1964)
Gelisio, Deborah (1976—)
Geller, Margaret Joan (1947—)
Gellhorn, Edna (1878–1970)
Gellhorn, Martha (1908–1998)
Gelman, Polina (1919—)
Geltzer, Ykaterina (1876–1962)
Gems, Pam (1925—)
Genauss, Carsta (1959—)
Gencer, Leyla (1924—)
Genée, Adeline (1878–1970)
Genenger, Martha (1911—)
Geneviève (1920–2004)
Genhart, Cecile Staub (1898–1983)
Géniat, Marcelle (1879–1959)
Genovese, Kitty (1935–1964)
Genth, Lillian (1876–1953)
Gentile-Cordiale, Edera (1920–1993)
Gentle, Alice (1889–1958)
Gentry, Bobbie (1944—)
Gentry, Eva (c. 1920—)
Gentzel, Inga (1908–1991)
Geoghegan-Quinn, Máire (1950—)
Georgatou, Maria (c. 1983—)
George, Carolyn (1927—)
George, Elizabeth (c. 1814–1902)
George, Gladys (1900–1954)
George, Grace (1879–1961)
George, Maude (1888–1963)
George, Maureen (1955—)
George, Muriel (1883–1965)
George, Phyllis (1949—)
George, Zelma Watson (1904–1994)
Georgescu, Elena (1964—)
Georgi, Yvonne (1903–1975)
Georgieva, Anka (1959—)
Georgieva, Magdalena (1962—)
Georgieva, Maya (1955—)
Georgieva-Panayotovna, Kapka (1951—)
Geppi-Aikens, Diane (c. 1963–2003)
Geraghty, Agnes (1906–1974)
Geraghty, Carmelita (1901–1966)
Gerasimenok, Irina (1970—)
Gerdt, Elizaveta (1891–1975)
Gerg, Hilde (1975—)
Gerhardt, Elena (1883–1961)
Gerhardt, Ida (1905–1997)
Gérin-Lajoie, Marie (1867–1945)
Gerlits, Irina (1966—)
Germaine, Diane (1944—)
Germanova, Silviya (1961—)
Gerould, Katharine (1879–1944)
Gersão, Teolinda (1940—)
Gerschau, Kerstin (1958—)
Gersten, Berta (c. 1896–1972)
Gerster, Etelka (1855–1920)
Gert, Valeska (1900–1978)
Gertsyk, Adelaida (1874–1925)
Gesheva-Tsvetkova, Vanya (1960—)
Gessner, Adrienne (1896–1987)
Gestefeld, Ursula Newell (1845–1921)
Gestring, Marjorie (1922–1992)
Geva, Tamara (1906–1997)
Geweniger, Ute (1964—)
Ge Yang (1916—)
Ghalem, Nadia (1941—)
Ghilardotti, Fiorella (1946—)
Giacobbe, Maria (1928—)
Giaconi, Luisa (1870–1908)
Giannini, Dusolina (1900–1986)
Gianoni, Lavinia (1911—)
Gianulias, Nikki (1959—)
Giavotti, Luigina (1916–1976)
Gibault, Claire (1945—)
Gibb, Helen (1838–1914)
Gibb, Roberta (1942—)
Gibbons, E. Joan (1902–1988)
Gibbons, Stella (1902–1989)
Gibbs, Georgia (1920—)
Gibbs, Lois (1946—)
Gibbs, Mary Elizabeth (1836–1920)
Gibbs, May (1877–1969)
Gibbs, Pearl (1901–1983)
Gibson, Althea (1927–2003)
Gibson, Catherine (1931—)
Gibson, Cheryl (1959—)
Gibson, Deborah (1970—)
Gibson, Dorothy (1889–1946)
Gibson, Emily Patricia (1863/64?–1947)
Gibson, Helen (1892–1977)
Gibson, Helena Fannie (1868–1938)
Gibson, Irene Langhorne (1873–1956)
Gibson, Mary Victoria (1864–1929)
Gibson, Michelle (1969—)
Gibson, Perla Siedle (d. 1971)
Gibson, Wynne (1903–1987)
Giddens, Rebecca (1977—)
Gideon, Miriam (1906–1996)
Gidley, Sandra (1957—)
Gielgud, Maina (1945—)
Gies, Miep (b. 1909)
Gifford, Frances (1920–1994)
Gigli, Elena (1985—)
Gilbert, Anne (1821–1904)
Gilbert, Jody (1916–1979)
Gilbert, Katherine Everett (1886–1952)
Gilbert, Mercedes (1894–1952)
Gilbert, Ronnie (1926—)
Gilbert, Ruth (1917—)
Gilbert, Ruth (d. 1993)
Gilbert, Sandra M. (1936—)
Gilberto, Astrud (1940—)
Gilbreth, Lillian Moller (1878–1972)
Gilchrist, Connie (1901–1985)
Gilchrist, Ellen (1935—)
Gilder, Jeannette Leonard (1849–1916)
Gilder, Virginia (1958—)
Gildernew, Michelle (1970—)
Gildersleeve, Virginia Crocheron (1877–1965)
Gilks, Gillian (1959—)
Gill, Mary Gabriel (1837–1905)
Gill, Neena (1956—)
Gill, Zillah Smith (1859–1937)
Gillan, Cheryl (1952—)
Gillars, Mildred E. (1900–1988)
Gillespie, Mabel (1877–1923)
Gillett, Emma (1852–1927)
Gillette, Genevieve (1898–1986)
Gilliatt, Penelope (1932–1993)
Gillies, Janet (1864–1947)
Gillig, Marie-Hélène (1946—)
Gilligan, Carol (1936—)
Gilliland, Helen (1897–1942)
Gillmor, Frances (1903–1993)
Gillmore, Margalo (1897–1986)
Gillmore, Ruth (d. 1976)
Gillom, Jennifer (1964—)
Gillon, Karen (1967—)
Gilman, Charlotte Perkins (1860–1935)
Gilman, Elisabeth (1867–1950)
Gilmer, Elizabeth May (1880–1960)
Gilmer, Elizabeth Meriwether (1861–1951)
Gilmore, Mary (1865–1962)
Gilmore, Rebecca
Gilmore, Virginia (1919–1986)
Gilmour, Sally (1921–2004)
Gilot, Françoise (1922—)
Gilpin, Laura (1891–1979)
Gilroy, Beryl (1924–2001)
Gilroy, Linda (1949—)
Gilyazova, Nailiya (1953—)
Gil Young-Ah (1970—)
Gimbutas, Marija (1921–1994)
Gimenez, Estela
Gineste, Marie-Rose (1911—)
Gingold, Hermione (1897–1987)
Ginner, Ruby (c. 1886–1978)
Ginsburg, Mirra (1909–2000)
Ginsburg, Ruth Bader (1933—)
Ginzburg, Evgenia (1896–1980)
Ginzburg, Lidiia (1902–1990)
Ginzburg, Natalia (1916–1991)
Giordani, Claudia (1955—)
Giorgi, Virginia (1914—)
Giovanna of Italy (1907–2000)
Giovanni, Nikki (1943—)
Giove, Missy (1972—)
Gippius, Zinaida (1869–1945)
Gipps, Ruth (1921—)
Girard, Patricia (1968—)
Girardot, Annie (1931—)
Giriat, Madame (b. 1866)
Giroud, Françoise (1916–2003)
Gisbert Carbonell de Mesa, Teresa (1926—)
Gisela (1856–1932)
Gish, Dorothy (1898–1968)
Gish, Lillian (1893–1993)
Gísladóttir, Sólrún
Gisolf, Carolina (1910—)
Gisolo, Margaret (1914–2003)
Gitana, Gertie (1887–1957)
Gitelman, Claudia (1938—)
Gittos, Marianne (1830–1908)
Giuranna, Barbara (1902–1998)
Giurca, Elena (1946—)
Givney, Kathryn (1896–1978)
Glabe, Karen (1942—)
Gladisheva, Svetlana (1971—)
Gladney, Edna (1886–1961)
Gladstone, Catherine (1812–1900)
Glantz, Margo (1930—)
Glanville-Hicks, Peggy (1912–1990)
Glase, Anne-Karin (1954—)
Glaser, Elizabeth (1947–1994)
Glaser, Lulu (1874–1958)
Glaser, Pease (1961—)
Glasgow, Ellen (1873–1945)
Glaspell, Susan (1876–1948)
Glass, Bonnie (b. around 1895)
Glass, Joanna (1936—)
Glass, Julie (1979—)
Glatskikh, Olga (1989—)
Glaum, Louise (1894–1970)
Glazkova, Anna (1981—)
Gleason, Kate (1865–1933)
Gleason, Lucile (1886–1947)
Gleason, Rachel Brooks (1820–1905)
Gleditsch, Ellen (1879–1968)
Gleichen, Feodora (1861–1922)
Glen, Esther (1881–1940)
Glenn, Alice (1927—)
Glenn, Laura (1945—)
Glenn, Mary Willcox (1869–1940)
Glennie, Evelyn (1965—)
Gless, Sharon (1943—)
Glockshuber, Margot
Glover, Amelia (c. 1873–?)
Glover, Jane Allison (1949—)
Glubokova, Lidiya (1953—)
Gluck (1895–1978)
Gluck, Alma (1884–1938)
Glück, Louise (1943—)
Gluck, Rena (1933—)

Glueck, Eleanor Touroff (1898–1972)
Glümer, Claire von (1825–1906)
Glushchenko, Tatyana (1956—)
Glutting, Charlotte E. (1910–1996)
Glyn, Elinor (1864–1943)
Glynne, Mary (1895–1954)
Gnauck, Maxi (1964—)
Go, Shizuko (1929—)
Goddard, Arabella (1836–1922)
Goddard, Paulette (1905–1990)
Goddard, Victorine (1844–1935)
Godden, Rumer (1907–1998)
Godina, Elena (1977—)
Godley, Charlotte (1821–1907)
Godman, Trish (1939—)
Godowsky, Dagmar (1897–1975)
Godwin, Gail (1937—)
Goebbels, Magda (d. 1945)
Goebel, Barbara (1943—)
Goering, Emmy (1893–1973)
Goermann, Monica (1964—)
Goetschl, Renate (1975—)
Goetz, Janina (1981—)
Goetze, Vicki (1972—)
Goffin, Cora (1902–2004)
Gogean, Gina (1977—)
Goggans, Lalla (1906–1987)
Gogoberidze, Lana (1928—)
Gogova, Tanya (1950—)
Göhr, Marlies (1958—)
Goitschel, Christine (1944—)
Goitschel, Marielle (1945—)
Goksoer, Susann (1970—)
Golcheva, Nadka (1952—)
Golda, Natalie (1981—)
Goldberg, Lea (1911–1970)
Goldberg, Rose (d. 1966)
Goldberg, Whoopi (1949—)
Golden, Diana (1963–2001)
Goldfrank, Esther S. (1896–1997)
Goldie, Annabel (1950—)
Goldman, Emma (1869–1940)
Goldman, Hetty (1881–1972)
Goldman-Rakic, Patricia S. (1937–2003)
Goldmark, Josephine (1877–1950)
Goldobina, Tatiana (1975—)
Goldring, Winifred (1888–1971)
Goldsmith, Grace Arabell (1904–1975)
Goldstein, Jennie (1896–1960)
Goldstein, Vida (1869–1949)
Goldthwaite, Anne Wilson (1869–1944)
Golea, Eugenia (1969—)
Golic, Sladjana (1960—)
Golimowska, Maria (1932—)
Goll, Claire (1891–1977)
Gollner, Nana (1919–1980)
Golovkina, Sofia (1915–2004)
Golubkina, Anna (1864–1927)
Golubnichaya, Mariya (1924—)
Gombell, Minna (1892–1973)
Gomez, Elena (1985—)
Gomez, Sara (1943–1974)
Gomez-Acebo, Margaret (fl. 20th c.)
Gomis, Anna (1973—)
Gommers, Maria (1939—)
Goncalves, Lilian Cristina (1979—)
Goncalves, Olga (1937—)
Goncharenko, Svetlana (1971—)
Goncharova, Natalia (1881–1962)
Goncharova, Natalia (1988—)
Gong Zhichao (1977—)
Gonne, Maud (1866–1953)
Gonobobleva, Tatyana Pavlovna (1948—)
Gonzaga, Chiquinha (1847–1935)
González, Beatriz (1938—)
González Álvarez, Laura (1941—)
Gonzalez Laguillo, Maria (1961—)
Gonzalez Morales, Driulys (1973—)
Gonzalez Oliva, Mariana (1976—)
Goodall, Jane (1934—)
Goodbody, Buzz (1946–1975)
Goodenough, Florence Laura (1886–1959)
Goodman, Ellen (1941—)
Goodman, Shirley (1936–2005)
Goodrich, Annie Warburton (1866–1954)
Goodrich, Edna (1883–1971)
Goodrich, Frances (1891–1984)
Goodson, Katharine (1872–1958)
Goodson, Sadie (c. 1900—)
Goodwin, Doris Kearns (1943—)
Goodwin, Michelle (1966—)
Goolagong Cawley, Evonne (1951—)
Goold, Maria Vere (1877–1908)
Goossens, Marie (1894–1991)
Goossens, Sidonie (1899–2004)
Gorb, Tatyana (1965—)
Gorbacheva, Raisa (1932–1999)
Gorbanevskaya, Natalya Yevgenevna (1936—)
Gorbyatkova, Nelli (1958–1981)
Gorchakova, Yelena (1933—)
Gordeeva, Ekaterina (1971—)
Gordimer, Nadine (1923—)
Gordon, Anna Adams (1853–1931)
Gordon, Annie Elizabeth (1873–1951)
Gordon, Bridgette (1967—)
Gordon, Caroline (1895–1981)
Gordon, Doris Clifton (1890–1956)
Gordon, Dorothy (1889–1970)
Gordon, Eliza (1877–1938)
Gordon, Gale Ann (1943—)
Gordon, Hannah (1941—)
Gordon, Helen (1934—)
Gordon, Isabella (1901–1988)
Gordon, Jean (1918—)
Gordon, Jean Margaret (1865–1931)
Gordon, Julia Swayne (1878–1933)
Gordon, Kate M. (1861–1932)
Gordon, Kim (1953—)
Gordon, Kitty (1878–1974)
Gordon, Laura de Force (1838–1907)
Gordon, Mary (1882–1963)
Gordon, Noele (1923–1985)
Gordon, Ruth (1896–1985)
Gordon, Vera (1886–1948)
Gordon-Cumming, Eka (1837–1924)
Gordon-Lazareff, Hélène (1909–1988)
Gordon-Watson, Mary (1948—)
Gore, Altovise (1935—)
Gore, Leslie (1946—)
Gore-Booth, Eva (1870–1926)
Gorecka, Halina (1938—)
Goretzki, Viola (1956—)
Gorham, Kathleen (1932–1983)
Goring, Sonia (1940—)
Gorman, Margaret (1905–1995)
Gorman, Miki (1935—)
Gormé, Eydie (1931—)
Gorokhova, Galina (1938—)
Gorokhovskaya, Mariya (1921—)
Gorr, Rita (1926—)
Gorris, Marleen (1948—)
Gorton, Bettina (c. 1916–1983)
Goslar, Hannah (1928—)
Goslar, Lotte (1907–1997)
Goss, Olga May (1916–1994)
Gosse, Christine (1964—)
Gosse, Sylvia (1881–1968)
Gossick, Sue (1947—)
Gossweiler, Marianne (1943—)
Gotlieb, Phyllis (1926—)
Götte, Jeannette (1979—)
Gottschlich, Stefanie (1978—)
Gotz, Daniela (1987—)
Gouault-Haston, Laurence
Goudal, Jetta (1891–1985)
Goudge, Elizabeth (1900–1984)
Goudvis, Bertha (1876–1966)
Gouel, Eva (d. 1915)
Gougar, Helen (1843–1907)
Goulandris, Niki (1925—)
Gould, Beatrice Blackmar (c. 1899–1989)
Gould, Lois (1932–2002)
Gould, Sandra (1916–1999)
Gould, Shane (1956—)
Goulding, Valerie (1918–2003)
Goulet-Nadon, Amelie (1983—)
Goulue, La (1869–1929)
Gourd, Emilie (1879–1946)
Govorova, Olena (1973—)
Govrin, Gloria (1942—)
Gower, Pauline (1910–1947)
Gowing, Margaret (1921–1998)
Goyette, Cynthia (1946—)
Goyette, Danielle (1966—)
Goyshchik-Nasanova, Tatyana (1952—)
Grable, Betty (1916–1973)
Grabowski, Halina (1928–2003)
Grabowski, Petra (1952—)
Grace, Patricia (1937—)
Gracen, Elizabeth (1960—)
Gradante, Anna-Maria (1976—)
Graf, Steffi (1969—)
Graf, Stephanie (1973—)
Grafton, Sue (1940)
Graham, Barbara Wood (1923–1955)
Graham, Bette Nesmith (1924–1980)
Graham, Georgia (1900–1988)
Graham, Katharine (1917–2001)
Graham, Kim (1971—)
Graham, Martha (1894–1991)
Graham, Rose (1879–1974)
Graham, Sheila (1904–1988)
Graham, Shirley (1896–1977)
Grahame, Christine (1944—)
Grahame, Gloria (1924–1981)
Grahame, Margot (1911–1982)
Grahame Johnstone, Anne (1928–1998)
Grahame Johnstone, Janet (1928–1979)
Graham-Fenton, Lorraine (1973—)
Grahn, Judy (1940—)
Grahn, Lucile (1819–1907)
Grainger, Katherine (1975—)
Gramatica, Emma (1875–1965)
Gramatica, Irma (1873–1962)
Gramcko, Ida (1924–1994)
Gramont, Elizabeth de (fl. 1875–1935)
Granahan, Kathryn E. (1894–1979)
Granata, Maria (1921—)
Granato, Cammi (1971—)
Grancharova, Zoya (1966—)
Grandin, Ethel (1894–1988)
Grandval, Marie Felicia (1830–1907)
Grandy, Maria (1937–1998)
Granger, Josie (1853–1934)
Granger, Michele (1970—)
Granholm, Jennifer M. (1959—)
Grann, Phyllis (1937—)
Grant, Amy (1960—)
Grant, Ann (1955—)
Grant, Jane (1895–1972)
Grant, Julia (1826–1902)
Grant, Kathryn (1933—)
Grant, Lee (1927—)
Grant, Pauline (1915—)
Grant, Rhoda (1963—)
Grant, Valentine (1881–1949)
Grant Duff, Shiela (1913–2004)
Granville, Bonita (1923–1988)
Granville, Christine (1915–1952)
Granville, Louise (1895–1968)
Granville-Barker, Helen (d. 1950)
Grasegger, Käthe
Grasso, Ella (1919–1981)
Gratcheva, Tatiana (1973—)
Grau, Shirley Ann (1929—)
Gravenstijn, Deborah (1974—)
Graves, Beryl (1915–2003)
Graves, Carie (1953—)
Graves, Clotilde Inez Mary (1863–1932)
Graves, Nancy (1940–1995)
Gray, Coleen (1922—)
Gray, Dolores (1924–2002)
Gray, Dulcie (1919—)
Gray, Eileen (1878–1976)
Gray, Eve (1900–1983)
Gray, Gilda (1901–1959)
Gray, Hanna Holborn (1930—)
Gray, Macy (1970—)
Gray, Nadia (1923–1994)
Gray, Nicolete (1911–1997)
Gray, Oriel (1920–2003)
Gray, Sally (1916—)
Gray, Teresa Corinna Ubertis (1877–1964)
Grayson, Betty Evans (1925–1979)
Grayson, Kathryn (1922—)
Gréco, Juliette (1926—)
Gredal, Eva (1927–1995)
Greeley-Smith, Nixola (1880–1919)

Green, Anna Katharine (1846–1935)
Green, Constance McLaughlin (1897–1975)
Green, Debbie (1958—)
Green, Debora (c. 1951—)
Green, Dorothy (1886–1961)
Green, Dorothy (1892–1963)
Green, Dorothy (1915–1991)
Green, Edith Starrett (1910–1987)
Green, Elizabeth Shippen (1871–1954)
Green, Grace Winifred (1907–1976)
Green, Hetty (1834–1916)
Green, Janet (1914–1993)
Green, Lucinda (1953—)
Green, Mitzi (1920–1969)
Green, Tammie (1959—)
Green, Vera Mae (1928–1982)
Greenbaum, Dorothea Schwarcz (1893–1986)
Greene, Angela (1879—)
Greene, Angela (1921–1978)
Greene, Belle da Costa (1883–1950)
Greene, Cordelia A. (1831–1905)
Greene, Gertrude Glass (1904–1956)
Greene, Nancy (1943—)
Greene, Sarah Pratt (1856–1935)
Greener, Dorothy (1917–1971)
Greenfield, Meg (1930–1999)
Greenhough, Dorothy (1875–1965)
Greenway, Isabella Selmes (1886–1953)
Greenwood, Charlotte (1890–1978)
Greenwood, Edith
Greenwood, Ellen Sarah (1837–1917)
Greenwood, Joan (1921–1987)
Greenwood, Marion (1909–1980)
Greer, Germaine (1939—)
Greer, Jane (1924–2001)
Greet, Clare (1871–1939)
Greeves, Marion Janet (1894–1979)
Greevy, Bernadette (1939—)
Gregg, Virginia (1916–1986)
Grego, Melania (1973—)
Grégoire, Colette Anna (1931–1966)
Gregor, Nora (1901–1949)
Gregory, Augusta (1852–1932)
Gregory, Cynthia (1946—)
Greig, Margaret (1922–1999)
Greig, Marion (1954—)
Greiner Petter-Memm, Simone (1967—)
Grenard, Lizz (1965—)
Grenfell, Joyce (1910–1979)
Grès, Alix (1910–1993)
Grese, Irma (1923–1945)
Gress, Elsa (1919–1989)
Gresser, Gisela (1906–2000)
Gréville, Alice (1842–1903)
Greville, Frances Evelyn (1861–1938)
Greville, Julia (1979—)
Grew, Mary (1902–1971)
Grey, Beryl (1927—)
Grey, Denise (1896–1996)
Grey, Jane (1883–1944)
Grey, Katherine (1873–1950)
Grey, Maria Georgina (1816–1906)
Grey, Nan (1918–1993)
Grey, Virginia (1917–2004)
Grey-Gardner, Robyn (1964—)
Grieg, Nina (1845–1935)
Grier, Pam (1949—)
Grierson, Mary (1912—)
Griffies, Ethel (1878–1975)
Griffin, Eleanore (1904–1995)
Griffin, Ellen (1918–1986)
Griffin, Elsie Mary (1884–1968)
Griffith, Corinne (1894–1979)
Griffith, Emily (c. 1880–1947)
Griffith, Nanci (1953—)
Griffith, Phyllis (c. 1922—)
Griffith, Yolanda (1970—)
Griffiths, Jane (1954—)
Griffiths, Martha Wright (1912–2003)
Grigg, Mary (1897–1971)
Grigoras, Anca (1957—)
Grigoras, Cristina (1966—)
Grigorescu, Claudia (1968—)
Grigorieva, Tatiana (1975—)
Grigson, Jane (1928–1990)
Grillet, Louise Hortense (1865–1952)
Grillo, Gabriela (1952—)
Grillo, Joann (1939–1999)
Grimes, Tammy (1934—)
Grimké, Angelina Weld (1880–1958)
Grimké, Charlotte L. Forten (1837–1914)
Grimm, Cherry Barbara (1930–2002)
Grimshaw, Beatrice (c. 1870–1953)
Grinberg, Maria (1908–1979)
Grings, Inka (1978—)
Grinham, Judith (1939—)
Grini, Kjersti (1971—)
Gripe, Maria (1923—)
Griscom, Frances C. (1880–1973)
Grishchenkova, Alla (1961—)
Grishina, Oksana (1968—)
Grishuk, Pasha (1972—)
Griswold, Denny (1908–2001)
Gritsi-Milliex, Tatiana (1920—)
Grizodubova, Valentina (1910–1993)
Groener, Lissy (1954—)
Groenewold, Renate (1976—)
Groes, Lis (1910–1074)
Groesbeek, Maria (1937–1970)
Grogger, Paula (1892–1984)
Gromova, Lyudmila (1942—)
Gromova, Maria (1984—)
Gromova, Vera (1891–1973)
Gronbek, Maja (1971—)
Grönfeldt Bergman, Lisbeth (1948—)
Groody, Louise (1897–1961)
Groot, Chantal (1982—)
Grosheva, Yelena (1979—)
Groshkova, Tatiana (1973—)
Grossetête, Françoise (1946—)
Grossfeld, Muriel Davis (1941—)
Grossinger, Jennie (1892–1972)
Grossman, Edith (1936—)
Grossman, Haika (1919–1996)
Grossmann, Edith Searle (1863–1931)
Grossmann, Judith (1931—)
Grotell, Maija (1899–1973)
Grothaus, Gisela (1955—)
Groult, Benoîte (1921—)
Groult, Flora (1925—)
Grové, Henriette (1922—)
Groza, Maria (1918—)
Grozdeva, Maria (1972—)
Grozdeva, Svetlana (1959—)
Gruber, Lilo (1915–1992)
Gruber, Ruth (1911—)
Gruberová, Edita (1946—)
Gruchala, Sylwia (1981—)
Grudneva, Yelena (1974—)
Gruenberg, Sidonie (1881–1974)
Grumbach, Doris (1918—)
Grundig, Lea (1906–1977)
Grunert, Martina (1949—)
Gsovsky, Tatiana (1901–1993)
Guan Weizhen (1964—)
Guay, Lucie (1958—)
Gubaidulina, Sofia (1931—)
Gude, Franziska (1976—)
Gudereit, Marcia (c. 1966—)
Gudz, Lyudmila (1969—)
Gudzineviciute, Daina (1965—)
Gueden, Hilde (1915–1988)
Gueiler Tejada, Lydia (1921—)
Guellouz, Souad (1937—)
Guenther, Sarah (1983—)
Gueorguieva, Diliana (1965—)
Guerin, Veronica (1960–1996)
Guerra Cabrera, Patricia (1965—)
Guerrero, Maria (1867–1928)
Guerrero Mendez, Belem (1974—)
Guest, C.Z. (1920–2003)
Guest, Irene (1900–1979)
Guevara, Ana (1977—)
Gufler, Edith (1962—)
Guggenheim, Florence Shloss (1863–1944)
Guggenheim, Irene (1868–1954)
Guggenheim, Olga H. (1877–1970)
Guggenheim, Peggy (1898–1979)
Guggenheimer, Minnie (1882–1966)
Guglielminetti, Amalia (1881–1941)
Guibal, Brigitte (1971—)
Guidacci, Margherita (1921–1992)
Guidi, Rachele (1891–1979)
Guido, Beatriz (1924—)
Guidry, Carlette (1969—)
Guiducci, Armanda (1923–1992)
Guigova, Maria (1947—)
Guilbert, Yvette (1865–1944)
Guild, Nancy (1925–1999)
Guillemot, Agnès (1931—)
Guilló, Magdalena (1940—)
Guimarães, Elina (1904–1991)
Guimarães Peixoto Bretas, Ana Lins do (1889–1985)
Guinan, Texas (1884–1933)
Guiney, Louise Imogen (1861–1920)
Guinness, Heather (1910—)
Guion, Connie M. (1882–1971)
Guisewite, Cathy (1950—)
Gu Jun (1975—)
Gulacsy, Maria (1941—)
Gulbrandsen, Ragnhild (1977—)
Gulbrandsen, Solveig (1981—)
Gulbranson, Ellen (1863–1947)
Gulick, Alice Gordon (1847–1903)
Gulick, Charlotte Vetter (1865–1928)
Gulla, Alejandra (1977—)
Gullen, Augusta Stowe (1857–1943)
Gulliver, Julia Henrietta (1856–1940)
Gulyasne-Koeteles, Erzsebet (1924—)
Gummel-Helmboldt, Margitte (1941—)
Gund, Agnes (1938—)
Gunda, Saida (1959—)
Gundersen, Trude (1977—)
Gunn, Elizabeth Catherine (1879–1963)
Gunn, Jeannie (1870–1961)
Gunnarsson, Martine (1927—)
Gunnarsson, Susanne (1963—)
Gunnell, Sally (1966—)
Gunness, Belle (1860–c. 1908)
Gunning, Louise (1879–1960)
Gunther, Erna (1896–1982)
Guo Dandan (1977—)
Guo Jingjing (1981—)
Guo Yue (1988—)
Guppy, Eileen M. (1903–1980)
Guraieb Kuri, Rosa (1931—)
Gurendez, Lorena (1981—)
Gurevich, Liubov (1866–1940)
Gureyeva, Lyudmila (1943—)
Gurie, Sigrid (1911–1969)
Gurina, Elena
Gurney, Hilda (1943—)
Gurney, Rachel (1920–2001)
Guro, Elena (1877–1913)
Gurova, Elena (1972—)
Gurr, Donna Marie (1955—)
Guryeva, Yelena (1958—)
Gusakova, Maria
Gusenbauer, Ilona (1947—)
Guseva, Elina (1964—)
Guseva, Klara (1937—)
Gushterova, Vangelia (1911–1996)
Gustafson, Elisabet (1964—)
Gustafsson, Tina (1962—)
Gustafsson, Toini (1938—)
Gustavo, Roseli (1971—)
Gustavson, Linda (1949—)
Gusterson, Bridgette (1973—)
Gustilina, Diana (1974—)
Gutheil-Schoder, Marie (1874–1935)
Guthke, Karin (1956—)
Guthrie, Janet (1938—)
Guthrie, Mary Jane (1895–1975)
Gutiérrez-Cortines, Cristina (1939—)
Gutiérrez de Mendoza, Juana Belén (1875–1942)
Gutsu, Tatyana (1976—)
Gutteridge, Helena Rose (1879–1960)
Gu Xiaoli (1971—)
Guy, Rosa (1925—)
Guy-Blaché, Alice (1875–1968)
Guy-Quint, Catherine (1949—)
Guzenko, Olga (1956—)
Gwynne, Anne (1918–2003)
Gwynne-Vaughan, Helen (1879–1967)
Gyarmati, Andrea (1954—)
Gyarmati, Olga (1924—)
Gyenge, Valeria (1933—)
Gylling, Jane (1902–1961)

Gynt, Greta (1916–2000)
Gyring, Elizabeth (1906–1970)
Gyulai-Drimba, Ileana (1946—)
Gyurova, Ginka (1954—)
Gyurova, Krasimira (1953—)
Haacker, Kathrin (1967—)
Haas, Christl (1943–2001)
Haas, Dolly (1910–1994)
Haas, Monique (1906–1987)
Haase, Helga (1934–1989)
Haase, Mandy (1982—)
Habets, Marie-Louise (1905–1986)
Hablützel-Bürki, Gianna (1969—)
Hachin-Trinquet, Pascale (1958—)
Hacker, Marilyn (1942—)
Hackett, Jeanette (c. 1898–1979)
Hackett, Joan (1942–1983)
Hackley, E. Azalia Smith (1867–1922)
Hadarean, Vanda (1976—)
Hadding, Annette (1975—)
Haddon, Eileen (1921–2003)
Haden, Sara (1897–1981)
Hadid, Zaha (1950—)
Hading, Jane (1859–1933)
Haebler, Ingrid (1926—)
Haesaert, Clara (1924—)
Haesebrouck, Ann (1963—)
Haffenden, Elizabeth (1906–1976)
Hagan, Ellen (1873–1958)
Hagen, Birgit (1957—)
Hagen, Jean (1923–1977)
Hagen, Nina (1955—)
Hagen, Uta (1919–2004)
Hagenbaumer, Eva (1967—)
Hagerup, Inger (1905–1985)
Hagge, Marlene Bauer (1934—)
Hagiwara, Yoko (1920—)
Haglund, Maria (1972—)
Hagman, Lucina (1853–1946)
Hagn, Johanna
Hagood, Margaret (1907–1963)
Hahn, Anna Marie (1906–1938)
Hahn, Birgit (1958—)
Hahn, Dorothy (1876–1950)
Hahn, Emily (1905–1997)
Hahn, Helene B. (c. 1940—)
Haig, Emma (1898–1939)
Haigneré, Claudie (1957—)
Haines, Helen (1872–1961)
Haines, Janine (1945–2004)
Hainisch, Marianne (1839–1936)
Haislett, Nicole (1972—)
Hajkova, Jirina (1954—)
Hakanson, Ulla (1937—)
Halamová, Masa (1908–1995)
Halbsguth, Ruth (1916—)
Halcombe, Edith Stanway (1844–1903)
Haldane, Charlotte (1894–1969)
Haldane, Elizabeth S. (1862–1937)
Hale, Barbara (1921—)
Hale, Binnie (1899–1984)
Hale, Clara (1905–1992)
Hale, Ellen Day (1855–1940)
Hale, Georgia (1905–1985)
Hale, Lilian Westcott (1881–1963)
Hale, Louise Closser (1872–1933)
Hale, Lucretia Peabody (1820–1900)
Hale, Mamie O. (1911–c. 1968)
Hale, Maria Selina (1864–1951)
Hale, Nancy (1908–1988)
Hale, Ruth (1886–1934)
Hale, Sue Sally (1937–2003)
Hale, Susan (1833–1910)
Hale, Una (1922–2005)
Haley, Margaret A. (1861–1939)
Halicka, Antonina (1908–1973)
Halim, Tahiya (1919–2003)
Halimi, Gisèle (1927—)
Halkia, Fani (1979—)
Hall, Adelaide (1904–1993)
Hall, Cara Vincent (1922—)
Hall, Elisa (1900–1982)
Hall, Ella (1896–1982)
Hall, Elsie (1877–1976)
Hall, Evelyne (1909–1993)
Hall, Geraldine (1905–1970)
Hall, Grayson (1923–1985)
Hall, Juanita (1901–1968)
Hall, Katie Beatrice (1938—)
Hall, Kaye (1951—)
Hall, Lydia E. (1906–1969)
Hall, Natalie (1904–1994)
Hall, Radclyffe (1880–1943)
Hall, Rosetta Sherwood (1865–1951)
Hall, Theodora Clemens (1902–1980)
Hallaren, Mary A. (1907–2005)
Halliday, Margaret (1956—)
Halliwell, Geri (1972—)
Hallowell, Anna (1831–1905)
Halls, Ethel May (1882–1967)
Halonen, Tarja (1943—)
Halpert, Edith Gregor (c. 1900–1970)
Halprin, Ann (1920—)
Halstead, Nellie (1910–1991)
Haltvik, Trine (1965—)
Hama, Keiko (1947—)
Hamaguchi, Kyoko (1978—)
Hamann, Conny (1969—)
Hambrook, Sharon (1963—)
Hamer, Fannie Lou (1917–1977)
Hamill, Dorothy (1956—)
Hamilton, Alice (1869–1970)
Hamilton, Carrie (1963–2002)
Hamilton, Cicely (1872–1952)
Hamilton, Edith (1867–1963)
Hamilton, Gordon (1892–1967)
Hamilton, Margaret (1902–1985)
Hamilton, Mary (1882–1966)
Hamilton, Nancy (1908–1985)
Hamilton, Tara (1982—)
Hamilton, Virginia (1936–2002)
Hamlett, Dilys (1928–2002)
Hamlin, Shelley (1949—)
Hamm, Margherita (1867–1907)
Hamm, Mia (1972—)
Hammarberg, Gretchen
Hammerer, Resi (1925—)
Hammerstein, Dorothy (1899–1987)
Hammerstein, Elaine (1897–1948)
Hammond, Blodwen (1908–1973)
Hammond, Dorothy (c. 1876–1950)
Hammond, Joan (1912–1996)
Hammond, Kathleen (1951—)
Hammond, Kay (1909–1980)
Hammond, Virginia (1893–1972)
Hamnett, Katherine (1952—)
Hamnett, Nina (1890–1956)
Hamper, Geneviève (c. 1889–1971)
Hampshire, Margaret (1918–2004)
Hampshire, Susan (1938—)
Hampton, Hope (1897–1982)
Hampton, Mabel (1902–1989)
Han, Suyin (1917—)
Hanafin, Mary (1959—)
Hanaford, Phebe Ann (1829–1921)
Han Aili (1937—)
Hanan, Susanna (1870–1970)
Hanau, Marthe (c. 1884–1935)
Hanbury, Elizabeth (1793–1901)
Hancock, Cornelia (1840–1927)
Hancock, Florence (1893–1974)
Hancock, Joy (1898–1986)
Handa, Yuriko (1940—)
Handayani, Lilies (1965—)
Handel-Mazzetti, Enrica von (1871–1955)
Handl, Irene (1901–1987)
Handler, Ruth (1916–2002)
Handzlic, Jean (d. 1963)
Handzová, Viera (1931–1997)
Hanel, Birgitte (1954—)
Haney, Carol (1924–1964)
Han Hwa-Soo (1963—)
Han Hyun-Sook (1970—)
Hani, Motoko (1873–1957)
Hanim, Latife (1898–1975)
Hanim, Leyla (1850–1936)
Hanisch, Cornelia (1952—)
Hanka, Erika (1905–1958)
Hanke, Suzanne (1948—)
Han Keum-Sil (1968—)
Hankin, Simone
Hanks, Jane Richardson (b. 1908)
Hanks, Nancy (1927–1983)
Hanna, Carmel (1946—)
Hannam, Edith (1878–1951)
Hannan, Cora (c. 1912—)
Hannen, Lynley (1964—)
Hannon, Camilla (1936—)
Han Ok-Kyung (1965—)
Han Pil-Hwa (1942—)
Hanrahan, Barbara (1939–1991)
Hansberry, Lorraine (1930–1965)
Hanscom, Adelaide (1876–1932)
Hansen, Anja (1973—)
Hansen, Christina Roslyng (1978—)
Hansen, Jacqueline A. (c. 1949—)
Hansen, Juanita (1895–1961)
Hansen, Julia Butler (1907–1988)
Hansen, Pia (1965—)
Hansen, Trine
Hanshaw, Annette (1910–1985)
Hanson, Beverly (1924—)
Hanson, Brooke (1978—)
Hanson, Gladys (1883–1973)
Hanson, Jean (1919–1973)
Hanson, Luise V. (1913–2003)
Hanson, Marla (c. 1962—)
Hanson-Dyer, Louise (1884–1962)
Hansteen, Aasta (1824–1908)
Hansteen, Kirsten (1903–1974)
Han Sun-Hee (1973—)
Han Xue (1981—)
Han Yaqin (1963—)
Hapgood, Isabel (1850–1928)
Happe-Krey, Ursula (1926—)
Hara, Kazuko (1935—)
Hara, Setsuko (1920—)
Harada, Saho (1982—)
Harada, Yasuko (1928—)
Haralamow, Ingrid
Harand, Irene (1900–1975)
Harareet, Haya (1931—)
Harari, Manya (1905–1969)
Haraszty, Eszter (1920–1994)
Hard, Darlene (1936—)
Hardcastle, Sarah (1969—)
Harden, Cecil Murray (1894–1984)
Hardie, Kelly (1969—)
Harding, Ann (1902–1981)
Harding, Florence K. (1860–1924)
Harding, Jan (1925—)
Harding, Phyllis (b. 1907)
Harding, Tanya (1972—)
Harding, Tonya (1970—)
Hardwick, Elizabeth (1916—)
Hardy, Anna Eliza (1839–1934)
Hardy, Barbara (1924—)
Hardy, Catherine (1930—)
Hareven, Shulamit (1930–2003)
Harford, Lesbia (1891–1927)
Hargreaves, Alison (1962–1995)
Haringa, Ingrid (1964—)
Harjo, Joy (1951—)
Harkness, Anna M. Richardson (1837–1926)
Harkness, Georgia (1891–1974)
Harkness, Mary Stillman (1874–1950)
Harkness, Rebekah (1915–1982)
Harland, Georgina (1978—)
Harley, Katherine (1881–1961)
Harlow, Jean (1911–1937)
Harman, Harriet (1950—)
Harman, Katie Marie (c. 1980—)
Harnack, Mildred (1902–1943)
Harned, Virginia (1872–1946)
Harney, Mary (1953—)
Harold, Erika (c. 1980—)
Harper, Frances E.W. (1825–1911)
Harper, Ida Husted (1851–1931)
Harper, Valerie (1940—)
Harraden, Beatrice (1864–1936)
Harrigan, Lori (1970—)
Harrigan, Nedda (1899–1989)
Harriman, Florence Jaffray (1870–1967)
Harriman, Mary (1851–1932)
Harriman, Pamela (1920–1997)
Harrington, Penny (c. 1943—)
Harris, Addie (1940–1982)
Harris, Barbara (1930—)

Harris, Barbara (1935—)
Harris, Barbara (1945—)
Harris, Christie (1907–2002)
Harris, Claire (1937—)
Harris, Corra May (1869–1935)
Harris, Dionna (1968—)
Harris, Edna Mae (1910–1997)
Harris, Emily Cumming (c. 1836–1925)
Harris, Emmylou (1947—)
Harris, Jackie
Harris, Jane Elizabeth (c. 1852–1942)
Harris, Joan (1920—)
Harris, Julie (1921—)
Harris, Julie (1925—)
Harris, Lois (1940—)
Harris, Lusia Mae (1955—)
Harris, Marjorie Silliman (1890–1976)
Harris, Mary Belle (1874–1957)
Harris, Mildred (1901–1944)
Harris, Patricia Roberts (1924–1985)
Harris, Renee (1885–1969)
Harris, Rosemary (1927—)
Harris, Sylvia (d. 1966)
Harrison, Barbara Grizzuti (1934–2002)
Harrison, Beatrice (1892–1965)
Harrison, Constance Cary (1843–1920)
Harrison, Elizabeth (1849–1927)
Harrison, Hazel (1883–1969)
Harrison, Jane Ellen (1850–1928)
Harrison, Joan (1935—)
Harrison, Joan (c. 1908–1994)
Harrison, June (1925–1974)
Harrison, Kathleen (1892–1995)
Harrison, Marguerite (1879–1967)
Harrison, Mary Scott Dimmick (1858–1948)
Harrison, May (1891–1959)
Harrison, Ruth (1911–1974)
Harrison, Susie Frances (1859–1935)
Harrold, Agnes (c. 1830–1903)
Harrop, Loretta (1975—)
Harrower, Elizabeth (1928—)
Harrower, Kristi (1975—)
Harry, Deborah (1945—)
Harry, Myriam (1869–1958)
Harsant, Florence Marie (1891–1994)
Harshaw, Margaret (1909–1997)
Harstick, Sara (1981—)
Hart, Annie (d. 1947)
Hart, Dolores (1938—)
Hart, Doris (1925—)
Hart, Flo (c. 1896–1960)
Hart, Jane (1920—)
Hart, Judith (1924—)
Hart, Margie (1916—)
Hart, Nancy (c. 1846–1902)
Hart, Pearl (c. 1875–c. 1924)
Harte, Betty (c. 1882–1965)
Hartel, Lis (1921—)
Hartigan, Anne Le Marquand (1931—)
Hartigan, Grace (1922—)
Hartlaub, Geno (1915—)
Hartley, Blythe (1982—)
Hartley, Donna-Marie (1955—)
Hartley, Margaret
Hartley, Mariette (1940—)
Hartman, Elizabeth (1941–1987)
Hartman, Grace (1907–1955)
Hartmann, Ingrid (1930—)
Hartwig, Julia (1921—)
Haruko (1850–1914)
Harup, Karen-Margrete (1924—)
Harvey, Antje (1967—)
Harvey, Ethel Browne (1885–1965)
Harvey, Georgette (c. 1882–1952)
Harvey, Leisha (1947—)
Harvey, Lilian (1906–1968)
Harvey, Mary (1965—)
Harvey, P.J. (1969—)
Harvie Anderson, Betty (1913–1979)
Harwood, Elizabeth (1938–1990)
Harwood, Gwen (1920–1995)
Harzendorf, Christiane (1967—)
Hasbrouck, Lydia Sayer (1827–1910)
Hase, Dagmar (1969—)
Hasegawa, Itsuko (1941—)
Hasegawa, Tomoko (1963—)
Haselbach, Anna Elisabeth (1942—)
Haselden, Frances Isabella (c. 1841–1936)
Hasenjager-Robb, Daphne (1929—)
Hashemi, Faezeh (1963—)
Hashiguchi, Miho (1977—)
Hashimi, Aquila al- (1953–2003)
Hashimoto, Seiko (1964—)
Hashman, Judy (1935—)
Haskil, Clara (1895–1960)
Haslam, Anna (1829–1922)
Haslam, Juliet (1969—)
Hasler, Marie (1945—)
Haslett, Caroline (1895–1957)
Hasoutra (1906–1978)
Hassall, Joan (1906–1988)
Hassan, Margaret (1944–2004)
Hasse, Ute (1963—)
Hasselqvist, Jenny (1894–1978)
Hasso, Signe (1910–2002)
Hastings, Caroline (1841–1922)
Hastings, Denise (1958—)
Haszard, Rhona (1901–1931)
Hatch, Annia (1978—)
Hatcher, Orie Latham (1868–1946)
Hatfield, Juliana (1967—)
Hathaway, Sibyl (1884–1974)
Hatherly, Ana Maria (1929—)
Hato, Ana Matawhaura (1907–1953)
Hattestad, Stine Lise
Hattestad, Trine (1966—)
Hatton, Fanny (c. 1870–1939)
Hatton, Marion (1835–1905)
Hattori, Michiko (1968—)
Hatvany, Lili (1890–1967)
Hatz, Elizabeth (1952—)
Hatzimichali, Angeliki (1895–1956)
Haug, Jutta D. (1951—)
Haugen, Tone (1964—)
Haugenes, Margunn (1970—)
Hauk, Minnie (1851–1929)
Hauková, Jiřina (1919—)
Hauptmann, Anna (1898–1994)
Haushofer, Marlen (1920–1970)
Hautala, Heidi Anneli (1955—)
Hautval, Adelaide (1906–1988)
Havel, Olga (1933–1996)
Havemeyer, Louisine (1855–1929)
Haver, June (1926–2005)
Haver, Phyllis (1899–1960)
Havoc, June (1916—)
Hawco, Sherry (d. 1991)
Hawes, Elizabeth (1903–1971)
Hawes, Harriet Boyd (1871–1945)
Hawke, Hazel (1929—)
Hawker, Lilian E. (1908–1991)
Hawkes, Jacquetta (1910–1996)
Hawkes, Rechelle (1967—)
Hawkes, Sharlene (c. 1964—)
Hawkins, Mary (1875–1950)
Hawkins, Mary Ann (1919–1993)
Hawkins, Paula Fickes (1927—)
Hawley, Christine (1949—)
Hawley, Wanda (1895–1963)
Hawn, Goldie (1945—)
Haworth, Cheryl (1983—)
Hawthorne, Margaret Jane Scott (1869–1958)
Hawtrey, Marjory (1900–1952)
Hay, Elizabeth Dexter (1927—)
Hay, Jean Emily (1903–1984)
Hay, Mary (1901–1957)
Hay, Mary Garrett (1857–1928)
Hay, Vanessa Briscoe (1955—)
Hayashi, Fumiko (1903–1951)
Hayashi, Kyoko (1930—)
Haycraft, Anna Margaret (1932–2005)
Haydée, Marcia (1939—)
Hayden, Mary (1862–1942)
Hayden, Melissa (1923—)
Hayden, Sophia (1868–1953)
Haydon, Julie (1910–1994)
Haye, Helen (1874–1957)
Hayek, Salma (1966—)
Hayes, Allison (1930–1977)
Hayes, Helen (1900–1993)
Hayes, Joanna (1976—)
Hayes, Maggie (1916–1977)
Hayes, Nevada (1885–1941)
Hayes, Patricia (1909–1998)
Hayes, Patty (1955—)
Haygood, Laura Askew (1845–1900)
Hayman, Lillian (1922–1994)
Haynes, Elizabeth Ross (1883–1953)
Haynie, Sandra B. (1943—)
Hayward, Lillie (1891–1978)
Hayward, Susan (1917–1975)
Haywood, Claire (c. 1916–1978)
Hayworth, Rita (1918–1987)
Haza, Ofra (1957–2001)
Hazan, Adeline (1956—)
Hazard, Caroline (1856–1945)
Hazeltine, Mary (1868–1949)
Hazen, Elizabeth Lee (1883–1975)
Hazlett, Olive C. (1890–1974)
Hazzard, Shirley (1931—)
Head, Bessie (1937–1986)
Head, Edith (1897–1981)
Heady, Bonnie (1912–1953)
Heal, Sylvia (1942—)
Healey, Eunice (c. 1920—)
Healy, Pamela (1963—)
Heaney, Geraldine (1967—)
Heap, Jane (1887–1964)
Heap, Sarah (1870–1960)
Hearnshaw, Susan (1961—)
Hearst, Catherine Campbell (1917–1998)
Hearst, Millicent (1882–1974)
Hearst, Patricia Campbell (1954—)
Hearst, Phoebe A. (1842–1919)
Heath, Clarita (c. 1916–2003)
Heath, Sophie (1896–1939)
Heaton, Anne (1930—)
Hebard, Grace Raymond (1861–1936)
Hébert, Anne (1916–2000)
Hecher, Traudl (1943—)
Heckart, Eileen (1919–2001)
Hecker, Genevieve (1884–1960)
Heckler, Margaret M. (1931—)
Heckscher, Grete (1901–1987)
Hedberg, Doris (1936—)
Heddle, Kathleen (1965—)
Hederman, Carmencita (1939—)
Hedgepeth, Whitney L. (1971—)
Hedkvist Petersen, Ewa (1952—)
Hedman, Martha (1883–1974)
Hedren, Tippi (1931—)
Hedrick, Heather (c. 1972—)
Heemskerk, Marianne (1944—)
Heemstra, Ella van (1900–1984)
Heenan, Frances (1910–1956)
Heenan, Katie (1985—)
Heer, Anna (1863–1918)
Heffernan, Fallon (1986—)
Hefford, Jayna (1977—)
Heflin, Alma (fl. 1930s)
Hegamin, Lucille (1894–1970)
Hegan, Eliza Parks (1861–1917)
Heggtveit, Anne (1939—)
Hegh, Hanne (1960—)
Hei, Akenehi (1877/78?–1910)
Heiberg, Marianne (1945–2004)
Heidemann, Britta (1982—)
Heiden, Beth (1959—)
Height, Dorothy (1912—)
Heijting-Schuhmacher, Irma (1925—)
Heikel, Karin Alice (1901–1944)
Heilbron, Rose (1914–2005)
Heilbrun, Carolyn Gold (1926–2003)
Heill, Claudia (1982—)
Heim, Andrea (1961—)
Heine, Jutta (1940—)
Heinecke, Birgit (1957—)
Heinrich, Christina (1949—)
Heinrichs, April (1964—)
Heiss-Jenkins, Carol (1940—)
Heitzer, Regine (fl. 1960s)
He Jianping (1963—)
He Jun (1969—)
Helakh, Natallia (1978—)
Helburn, Theresa (1887–1959)
Held, Anna (c. 1865–1918)
Heldman, Gladys (1922–2003)
Heldman, Julie (1945—)

Heldy, Fanny (1888–1973)
Helen (b. 1950)
Helena (1846–1923)
Helena of Russia (1882–1957)
Helena Victoria (1870–1948)
Helene (1903–1924)
Helen of Greece (1896–1982)
Helen of Schleswig-Holstein (1888–1962)
Helen of Waldeck and Pyrmont (1861–1922)
Helen of Waldeck and Pyrmont (1899–1948)
He Liping
Hellaby, Amy Maria (1864–1955)
Hellemans, Greet (1959—)
Hellemans, Nicolette (1961—)
Helliwell, Ethel (c. 1905—)
Hellman, Lillian (1905–1984)
Hellmann, Angelika (1954—)
Hellmann-Opitz, Martina (1960—)
Helm, Brigitte (1908–1996)
Helm, June (1924—)
Helmer, Bessie Bradwell (1858–1927)
Helmond, Katherine (1934—)
Helmrich, Dorothy (1889–1984)
Helser, Brenda (1926—)
Helten, Inge (1950—)
Heming, Violet (1895–1981)
Hemingway, Margaux (1955–1996)
Hemingway, Marie (c. 1893–1939)
Hemingway, Mariel (1961—)
Hemmings, Deon (1968—)
Hempel, Claudia (1958—)
Hempel, Frieda (1885–1955)
Hemsley, Estelle (1887–1968)
Hendel, Yehudit (1926—)
Henderlite, Rachel (1905–1991)
Henderson, Alice Corbin (1881–1949)
Henderson, Christina Kirk (1861–1953)
Henderson, Danielle (1977—)
Henderson, Jo (1934–1988)
Henderson, Mary (1919–2004)
Henderson, Monique (1983—)
Henderson, Stella (1871–1962)
Henderson, Virginia (1897–1996)
Henderson, Zenna (1917–1983)
Hendl, Susan (1949—)
Hendrawati, Agung (1975—)
Hendriks, Irene (1958—)
Hendrix, Brunhilde (1938—)
Hendrix, Wanda (1928–1981)
Hendryx, Nona (1945—)
Hengler, Flora (c. 1887–1965)
Hengler, May (c. 1884–1952)
Henie, Sonja (1912–1969)
Henin-Hardenne, Justine (1982—)
Henke, Jana (1973—)
Henkel, Andrea (1977—)
Henkel, Manuela (1974—)
Henkel-Redetzky, Heike (1964—)
Henley, Beth (1952—)
Henmyer, Annie W. (1827–1900)
Hennagan, Monique (1976—)
Henne, Jan (1947—)
Henneberg, Jill
Henneberger, Barbi (d. 1964)
Henneken, Thamar (1979—)
Henning, Anne (1955—)
Henning, Eva (1920—)
Henning, Rachel (1826–1914)
Henning-Jensen, Astrid (1914–2002)
Hennings, Betty (1850–1939)
Hennings, Emmy (1885–1948)
Henningsen, Agnes (1868–1962)
Hennock, Frieda B. (1904–1960)
Henri, Florence (1895–1982)
Henrich, Christy (1973–1994)
Henrietta of Belgium (1870–1948)
Henriksen, Henriette (1970—)
Henrion, Daphne Hardy (1917–2003)
Henriot-Schweitzer, Nicole (1925–2001)
Henrotin, Ellen Martin (1847–1922)
Henry, Alice (1857–1943)
Henry, Annie (1879–1971)
Henry, Charlotte (1913–1980)
Henry, Gale (1893–1972)
Henry, Jodie (1983—)
Henry, Lea (1961—)
Henry, Marguerite (1902–1997)
Henry, Mary E.F. (1940—)
Henson, Lisa (1960—)
Hentschel, Franziska (1970—)
Hepburn, Audrey (1929–1993)
Hepburn, Katharine (1907–2003)
Hepworth, Barbara (1903–1975)
He Qi (1973—)
Herangi, Te Kirihaehae Te Puea (1883–1952)
Herbelin, Jeanne Mathilde (1820–1904)
Herber, Maxi (1920—)
Herbert, Jocelyn (1917–2003)
Herbst, Christine (1957—)
Herbst, Josephine (1892–1969)
Hercus, Ann (1942—)
Heredia, Isabel (1963—)
Herford, Beatrice (c. 1868–1952)
Heritage, Doris Brown (1942—)
Herlie, Eileen (1919—)
Herman, Barbara (c. 1952—)
Herman, Robin (c. 1952—)
Hermange, Marie-Thérèse (1947—)
Hermes, Gertrude (1901–1983)
Hermine of Reuss (1887–1947)
Hermine of Waldeck and Pyrmont (1827–1910)
Hermodsson, Elisabet Hermine (1927—)
Hermon, Sylvia (1955—)
Hernandez, Amelia (c. 1930—)
Hernandez, Angela (c. 1949—)
Hernández, Luisa Josefina (1928—)
Hernández, Maria (1896–1986)
Hernandez, Maria de la Paz (1977—)
Herne, Chrystal (1882–1950)
Herne, Katharine Corcoran (1857–1943)
Herranz García, Maria Esther (1969—)
Herrera Garrido, Francisca (1869–1950)
Herrick, Christine Terhune (1859–1944)
Herrick, Elinore Morehouse (1895–1964)
Herrick, Genevieve Forbes (1894–1962)
Herrick, Hermione Ruth (1889–1983)
Herrmann, Liselotte (1909–1938)
Herron, Carrie Rand (1867–1914)
Herron, Cindy (1965—)
Hersch, Jeanne (1910–2000)
Herscher, Sylvia (1913–2004)
Herschmann, Nicole (1975—)
Hertha of Ysenburg and Budingen (1883–1972)
Hervey, Irene (1910–1998)
Herwegh, Emma (1817–1904)
Herzberg, Judith (1934—)
Herzeleide (1918–1989)
Heseltine, Mary J. (1910–2002)
Heslop, Mary Kingdon (1885–1955)
Hess, Erika (1962—)
Hess, Myra (1890–1965)
Hess, Sabine (1958—)
Hesse, Eva (1936–1970)
Hesse, Fanny Angelina (1850–1934)
Hesse-Bukowska, Barbara (1930—)
Hesselgren, Kerstin (1872–1962)
Hessling, Catherine (1899–1979)
Hetherington, Jessie Isabel (1882–1971)
Hewett, Dorothy (1923–2002)
Hewett, Ellen Anne (1843–1926)
Hewins, Caroline Maria (1846–1926)
Hewitt, Patricia (1948—)
He Xiangning (1879–1972)
He Yanwen (1966—)
Heyer, Georgette (1902–1974)
Heyhoe-Flint, Rachael (1939—)
He Ying (1977—)
Heyking, Elisabeth von (1861–1925)
Heylen, Ilse (1977—)
Heyman, Katherine Ruth (1877–1944)
Heymann, Lida (1867–1943)
Heymans, Emilie (1981—)
Heyns, Penny (1974—)
Heyward, Dorothy (1890–1961)
Heywood, Anne (1932—)
Heywood, Joan (1923—)
He Zizhen (fl. 1930s)
Hibbard, Edna (c. 1895–1942)
Hibbard, Hope (1893–1988)
Hibbert, Eleanor (1906–1993)
Hickey, Eileen (1886–1960)
Hickey, Emily Henrietta (1845–1924)
Hickey, Mary St. Domitille (1882–1958)
Hickling, Grace (1908–1986)
Hickman, Libbie (1965—)
Hickok, Lorena A. (1893–1968)
Hicks, Adelaide (1845–1930)
Hicks, Amie (c. 1839–1917)
Hicks, Betty (1920—)
Hicks, Betty Seymour (1904—)
Hicks, Helen (1911–1974)
Hicks, Louise Day (1916–2003)
Hicks, Sheila (1934—)
Hickson, Joan (1906–1998)
Hidalgo, Elvira de (1892–1980)
Hidari, Sachiko (1930–2001)
Hieden-Sommer, Helga (1934—)
Hier, Ethel Glenn (1889–1971)
Hieronymi, Ruth (1947—)
Hietamies, Mirja
Higgins, Marguerite (1920–1966)
Higgins, Pam (1945—)
Higgins, Rosalyn (1937—)
Higgins, Sarah (1830–1923)
Higgins, Yvette (1978—)
Highsmith, Patricia (1921–1995)
Hightower, Rosella (1920—)
Higson, Allison (1973—)
Higuchi, Chako (1945—)
Hikage, Atsuko (1954—)
Hikapuhi (1860/71?–1934)
Hildebrand, Sara (1979—)
Hilgertova, Stepanka (1968—)
Hill, Anita (1956—)
Hill, Betty (1919–2004)
Hill, Cindy (1948—)
Hill, Debra (1950–2005)
Hill, Dorothy (1907–1997)
Hill, Emily (1847–1930)
Hill, Ernestine (1899–1972)
Hill, Grace Livingston (1865–1947)
Hill, Jo (1963—)
Hill, Lauryn (1975—)
Hill, Lynn (1961—)
Hill, Mabel (1872–1956)
Hill, Martha (1900–1995)
Hill, Octavia (1838–1912)
Hill, Opal S. (1892–1981)
Hill, Susan (1942—)
Hill, Thelma (1925–1977)
Hill, Virginia (1907–1967)
Hill, Virginia (1916–1966)
Hillas, Lorraine (1961—)
Hillen, Francisca (1959—)
Hiller, Wendy (1912–2003)
Hillern, Wilhelmine von (1836–1916)
Hillesum, Etty (1914–1943)
Hilliard, Harriet (1909–1994)
Hilliard, Patricia (1916–2001)
Hillis, Margaret (1921—)
Hill-Lowe, Beatrice
Hillman, Bessie (1889–1970)
Hills, Carla (1934—)
Hills, Tina S. (1921—)
Hillyard, Blanche Bingley (1864–1938)
Hilmo, Elisabeth (1976—)
Hilst, Hilda (1930—)
Hilsz, Maryse (1903–1946)
Hind, Cora (1861–1942)
Hinderas, Natalie (1927–1987)
Hindley, Myra (1942–2002)
Hindmarch, Gladys (1940—)
Hindmarsh, Mary (1921–2000)
Hindorff, Silvia (1961—)
Hineira, Arapera (1932—)
Hinerangi, Sophia (c. 1830–1911)
Hines, Elizabeth (1899–1971)
Hingis, Martina (1980—)
Hingst, Ariane (1979—)
Hinkle, Beatrice M. (1874–1953)
Hinkson, Mary (1930—)
Hinson, Lois E. (1926—)
Hinzmann, Gabriele (1947—)
Hipp, Jutta (1925–2003)
Hiratsuka, Raichō (1886–1971)
Hird, Judith (c. 1946—)
Hird, Thora (1911–2003)
Hiro, Norie (1965—)

Hirose, Miyoko (1959—)
Hirsch, Mary (c. 1913—)
Hirsch, Rachel (1870–1953)
Hirst, Grace (1805–1901)
Hiscock, Eileen (1909—)
Hite, Shere (1943—)
Hitomi, Kinue (1908–1931)
Hoban, Lillian (1925–1998)
Hobart, Rose (1906–2000)
Hobby, Gladys Lounsbury (1910–1993)
Hobby, Oveta Culp (1905–1995)
Hobhouse, Emily (1860–1926)
Hobson, Elizabeth Christophers (1831–1912)
Hobson, Laura Z. (1900–1986)
Hobson, Valerie (1917–1998)
Höch, Hannah (1889–1978)
Hochleitner, Dorothea
Hockaday, Margaret (1907–1992)
Hockfield, Susan (1951—)
Hoctor, Harriet (1905–1977)
Hodder, Jessie Donaldson (1867–1931)
Hodge, Annie Mabel (1862–1938)
Hodge, Margaret (1944—)
Hodges, Joy (1914–2003)
Hodgkin, Dorothy (1910–1994)
Hodgkins, Frances (1869–1947)
Hodgskin, Natalie (1976—)
Hodgson, Tasha (1974—)
Hodrova, Daniela (1946—)
Hodson, Henrietta (1841–1910)
Hoefly, Ethel Ann (1919–2003)
Hoey, Iris (1885–1979)
Hoey, Jane M. (1892–1968)
Hoey, Kate (1946—)
Hofer, Evelyn (1922—)
Hoff, Karen (1921—)
Hoff, Magdalene (1940—)
Hoff, Ursula (1909–2005)
Hoff, Vanda (b. around 1900)
Hoffleit, E. Dorrit (1907—)
Hoffman, Abby (1947—)
Hoffman, Alice (1952—)
Hoffman, Anette (1971—)
Hoffman, Claire Giannini (1904–1997)
Hoffman, Joyce (c. 1948—)
Hoffman, Malvina (1885–1966)
Hoffmann, Beata
Hoffmann, Gertrude (1871–1966)
Hoffmann, Melanie (1974—)
Hoffmeister, Gunhild (1944—)
Hofmann, Adele (d. 2001)
Hofmann, Elise (1889–1955)
Hofmo, Gunvor (1921–1995)
Hogan, Aileen I. (1899–1981)
Hogan, Brigid (1932—)
Hogan, Linda (1947—)
Hogg, Ima (1882–1975)
Hogg, Sarah (1946—)
Hogg, Wendy (1956—)
Hogness, Hanne (1967—)
Hogshead, Nancy (1962—)
Hohn, Annette (1966—)
Hokinson, Helen E. (1893–1949)
Holden, Edith B. (1871–1920)
Holden, Evelyn (1877–c. 1969)
Holden, Fay (1893–1973)
Holden, Gloria (1908–1991)
Holden, Helene (1935—)
Holden, Joan (1939—)
Holden, Mari (1971—)
Holden, Molly (1927–1981)
Holdmann, Anni (1900–1960)
Holdsclaw, Chamique (1977—)
Holford, Alice Hannah (1867–1966)
Holford, Ingrid (1920—)
Holiday, Billie (c. 1915–1959)
Holladay, Wilhelmina Cole (1922—)
Holland, Agnieszka (1948—)
Holland, Annie (1965—)
Holland, Cecelia (1943—)
Holland, Dulcie Sybil (1913—)
Holland, Mary (1935–2004)
Holland, Tara Dawn (c. 1972—)
Hollar, Constance (1881–1945)
Holley, Marietta (1836–1926)
Holliday, Jennifer (1960—)
Holliday, Jenny (1964—)
Holliday, Judy (1921–1965)
Hollingsworth, Margaret (1940—)
Hollingworth, Leta Stetter (1886–1939)
Hollins, Marion B. (1892–1944)
Hollinshead, Ariel (1929—)
Holloway, Sue (1955—)
Holly, J. Hunter (1932–1982)
Holm, Celeste (1919—)
Holm, Dörthe (c. 1973—)
Holm, Eleanor (1913–2004)
Holm, Hanya (1888–1992)
Holm, Jeanne (1921—)
Holman, Dorothy (1883–?)
Holman, Libby (1904–1971)
Holmer, Ulrike (1967—)
Holmes, Anna-Marie (1943—)
Holmès, Augusta (1847–1903)
Holmes, Helen (1892–1950)
Holmes, Kelly (1970—)
Holmes, Mary Jane (1825–1907)
Holsboer, Noor (1967—)
Holst, Clara (1868–1935)
Holst, Imogen (1907–1984)
Holt, Jennifer (1920–1997)
Holt, Marjorie Sewell (1920—)
Holt, Stella (d. 1967)
Holt, Winifred (1870–1945)
Holt, Zara (1909–1989)
Holtby, Winifred (1898–1935)
Holter, Harriet (1922–1997)
Holtrop-van Gelder, Betty (1866–1962)
Holtzman, Elizabeth (1941—)
Holtzmann, Fanny (1895–1980)
Holum, Dianne (1951—)
Holum, Kirsten (c. 1981—)
Holzner, Ulrike
Homaira (1916–2002)
Homer, Louise (1871–1947)
Hommes, Nienke (1977—)
Hommola, Ute (1952—)
Honan, Cathy (1951—)
Honan, Tras (1930—)
Honcharova, Iryna (1974—)
Hone, Evie (1894–1955)
Honecker, Margot (1927—)
Honeyball, Mary (1952—)
Honeyman, Nan Wood (1881–1970)
Honeyman, Susie
Hong Ch-Ok (1970—)
Hong Jeong-Ho (1974—)
Honningen, Mette (1944—)
Honsova, Zdeka (1927–1994)
Hoobler, Icie Macy (1892–1984)
Hood, Darla (1931–1979)
Hood, Mary (c. 1822–1902)
Hoodless, Adelaide (1857–1910)
Hooker, Evelyn (1907–1996)
Hooker, Isabella Beecher (1822–1907)
Hooper, Jessie Jack (1865–1935)
Hooper, Kate Challis (1894–1982)
Hooper, Kate
Hoover, H.M. (1935—)
Hoover, Katherine (1937—)
Hoover, Lou Henry (1874–1944)
Hopekirk, Helen (1856–1945)
Hopkins, Ellice (1836–1904)
Hopkins, Emma Curtis (1853–1925)
Hopkins, Miriam (1902–1972)
Hopkins, Pauline E. (1859–1930)
Hopkins, Thelma (1936—)
Hoppe, Marianne (1909–2002)
Hopper, Edna Wallace (1864–1959)
Hopper, Grace Murray (1906–1992)
Hopper, Hedda (1885–1966)
Hopper, Victoria (1909—)
Hore, Kerry (1981—)
Horn, Camilla (1903–1996)
Horn, Miriam Burns (1904–1951)
Horna, Kati (1912–2000)
Horne, Alice Merrill (1868–1948)
Horne, Katharyn (1932—)
Horne, Lena (1917—)
Horne, Marilyn (1929—)
Horne, Myrtle (1892–1969)
Horneber, Petra (1965—)
Hörner, Silke (1965—)
Horney, Brigitte (1911–1988)
Horney, Karen (1885–1952)
Hornig-Miseler, Carola (1962—)
Horniman, Annie (1860–1937)
Horny, Katherine (1969—)
Horovitz, Frances (1938–1983)
Horrell, Elizabeth (1826–1913)
Horsbrugh, Florence (1889–1969)
Horsley, Alice Woodward (1871–1957)
Horstmann, Dorothy M. (1911–2001)
Horta, Maria Teresa (1937—)
Horton, Gladys (1944—)
Horton, Mildred McAfee (1900–1994)
Horvat-Florea, Elena (1958—)
Horvath, Julia (1924–1947)
Horwich, Frances (1908–2001)
Hosain, Attia (1913–1998)
Hoskins, Olive (1882–1975)
Hosmer, Harriet (1830–1908)
Hospital, Janette Turner (1942—)
Hossain, Rokeya Sakhawat (1880–1932)
Hotchkiss, Avis (fl. 1915)
Hotchkiss, Effie (fl. 1915)
Houghton, Edith (1912—)
Houghton, Frances (1980—)
Hould-Marchand, Valérie (1980—)
Hoult, Norah (1898–1984)
Housden, Nina (1916—)
Houston, Cissy (1933—)
Houston, Lucy (1858–1936)
Houston, Thelma (1946—)
Houston, Whitney (1963—)
Houter, Marleen (1961—)
Hou Yuzhu (1963—)
Hovland, Ingeborg (1969—)
Howard, Ada Lydia (1829–1907)
Howard, Cordelia (1848–1941)
Howard, Denean (1964—)
Howard, Elizabeth Jane (1923—)
Howard, Esther (1892–1965)
Howard, Frances (1903–1976)
Howard, Jane (1934–1996)
Howard, Janette (1944—)
Howard, Jean (1910–2000)
Howard, Jessica (1984—)
Howard, Kathleen (1879–1956)
Howard, Kathy (c. 1961—)
Howard, Mabel (1893–1972)
Howard, Rosalind Frances (1845–1921)
Howard, Sherri (1962—)
Howatch, Susan (1940—)
Howe, Fanny (1942—)
Howe, Julia Ward (1819–1910)
Howe, Lois (c. 1864–1964)
Howe, Susan (1937—)
Howe, Tina (1937—)
Howell, Alice (1888–1961)
Howell, Lida (1859–1939)
Howell, Mary (1932–1998)
Howes, Barbara (1914–1996)
Howes, Dulcie (1908–1993)
Howes, Edith Annie (1872–1954)
Howes, Mary (1941—)
Howes, Sally Ann (1930—)
Howey, Kate Louise (1973—)
Howie, Fanny Rose (1868–1916)
Howland, Emily (1827–1929)
Howland, Jobyna (1880–1936)
Howley, Calasanctius (1848–1933)
How-Martyn, Edith (1875–1954)
Hoxha, Nexhmije (1920—)
Hoy, Bettina (1962—)
Hoyer, Dore (1911–1967)
Hoyt, Beatrix (1880–1963)
Hoyt, Julia (c. 1897–1955)
Hoyt, Mary F. (1858–1958)
Hoyte-Smith, Joslyn Y. (1954—)
Hrebrinova, Anna (1908—)
Hruba, Berta (1946—)
Huang Hua (1969—)
Huang Mandan (1983—)
Huang Nanyan (1977—)
Huang Qingyun (1920—)
Huang Qun (1969—)
Huang Shanshan (1986—)

Huang Sui (1982—)
Huang Xiaomin (1970—)
Huang Zhihong (1965—)
Huang Zongying (1925—)
Hubackova, Ida (1954—)
Hubbard, Ruth (1924—)
Huber, Andrea (1975—)
Huber, Gusti (1914–1993)
Huch, Ricarda (1864–1947)
Huck, Winnifred Sprague Mason (1882–1936)
Hucles, Angela (1978—)
Hu Die (1908–1989)
Hudson, Martha (1939—)
Hudson, Nikki (1976—)
Hudson, Rochelle (1916–1972)
Hudson, Winson (1916–2004)
Huebler, Anna (1885–1976)
Huebner, Robin (1961—)
Huelsenbeck, Sarina (1962—)
Huerta, Dolores (1930—)
Huff, Louise (1895–1973)
Hufstedler, Shirley Mount (1925—)
Huggett, Susan (1954—)
Huggins, Margaret (1848–1915)
Hughan, Jessie (1875–1955)
Hug-Hellmuth, Hermine (1871–1924)
Hughes, Adelaide (1884–1960)
Hughes, Adella (1869–1950)
Hughes, Annie (1869–1954)
Hughes, Beverley (1950—)
Hughes, Clara (1972—)
Hughes, Edna (1916—)
Hughes, Janis (1958—)
Hughes, Joanna (1977—)
Hughes, Karen (1956—)
Hughes, Kathleen (1928—)
Hughes, Mary (1874–1958)
Hughes, Mary Beth (1919–1995)
Hughes, Monica (1925–2003)
Hughes, Sarah (1985—)
Hughes, Sarah T. (1896–1985)
Hughes, Wendy (1950—)
Hugo, Adèle (1830–1915)
Hugonnay, Vilma (1847–1922)
Huh Soon-Young (1975—)
Huh Young-Sook (1975—)
Hulette, Gladys (1896–1991)
Hull, Eleanor Henrietta (1860–1935)
Hull, Hannah (1872–1958)
Hull, Helen Rose (1888–1971)
Hull, Josephine (1886–1957)
Hull, Peggy (1889–1967)
Hulme, Juliet Marion (1938—)
Hulme, Kathryn (1900–1981)
Hulme, Keri (1947—)
Hulten, Vivi-Anne (1911–2003)
Humble, Joan (1951—)
Hume, Benita (1906–1967)
Hummel, Berta (1909–1946)
Hummert, Anne (1905–1996)
Humphrey, Doris (1895–1958)
Humphrey, Edith (1875–1977)
Humphrey, Muriel (1912–1998)
Humphrey, Terin (1986—)
Humphries, Carmel (1909–1986)
Hundvin, Mia (1977—)
Hunger, Daniela (1972—)
Hunt, Eva (1934–1980)
Hunt, Frances Irwin (1890–1981)
Hunt, Helen (1963—)
Hunt, Marsha (1917—)
Hunt, Martita (1900–1969)
Hunt, Mary Hanchett (1830–1906)
Hunt, Violet (1866–1942)
Hunte, Heather (1959—)
Hunter, Alberta (1895–1984)
Hunter, Clementine (1886–1988)
Hunter, Holly (1958—)
Hunter, Kim (1922–2002)
Hunter, Kristin (1931—)
Hunter, Mollie (1922—)
Hunter, Rita (1933–2001)
Hunter-Gault, Charlayne (1942—)
Huntington, Anna Hyatt (1876–1973)
Huntington, Emily (1841–1909)
Huntley, Joni (1956—)
Hunton, Addie D. Waites (1875–1943)
Hunyady, Emese (1966—)
Hupalo, Katherine (1890–1974)
Huppert, Isabelle (1953—)
Hurd, Dorothy Campbell (1883–1945)
Hurd, Edith Thacher (1910–1997)
Hurd, Gale Anne (1955—)
Hurd-Mead, Kate Campbell (1867–1941)
Hurdon, Elizabeth (1868–1941)
Hurd-Wood, Kathleen Gertrude (1886–1965)
Hurlock, Madeline (1899–1989)
Hurmuzachi, Georgeta (1936—)
Hurst, Fannie (1889–1968)
Hurst, Margery (1913–1989)
Hurston, Zora Neale (c. 1891–1960)
Hurtis, Muriel (1979—)
Huson, Florence (1857–1915)
Hussey, Gemma (1938—)
Hussey, Ruth (1911–2005)
Husted, Marjorie Child (c. 1892–1986)
Hustede, Heike (1946—)
Huston, Anjelica (1951—)
Hutchins, Colleen Kay (c. 1927—)
Hutchins, Grace (1885–1969)
Hutchinson, Amy Hadfield (1874–1971)
Hutchinson, Amy May (1888–1985)
Hutchinson, Jeanette (1951—)
Hutchinson, Josephine (1903–1998)
Hutchinson, Pamela (1958—)
Hutchinson, Sheila (1953—)
Hutchinson, Wanda (1951—)
Hutchison, Isobel Wylie (1899–1982)
Hutchison, Kay Bailey (1943—)
Hutchison, Muriel (1915–1975)
Hutson, Jean (1914–1998)
Hutton, Barbara (1912–1979)
Hutton, Betty (1921—)
Hutton, Ina Ray (1916–1984)
Hutton, Lauren (1943—)
Huttunen, Eevi (1922—)
Huxley, Elspeth (1907–1997)
Huxley, Julia Arnold (1862–1908)
Huxley, Juliette (1896–1994)
Huxtable, Ada Louise (1921—)
Hu Yadong (1968—)
Hveger, Ragnhild (1920—)
Hwang Hae-Young (1966—)
Hwang He-Suk (1945—)
Hwang Keum-Sook (1963—)
Hwang Kyung-Sun (1978—)
Hwang Ok-Sil (c. 1972—)
Hyams, Leila (1905–1977)
Hyde, Ida (1857–1945)
Hyde, Miriam Beatrice (1913–2005)
Hyder, Qurratulain (1927—)
Hyer, Martha (1924—)
Hykova, Lenka (1985—)
Hyland, Diana (1936–1977)
Hyland, Frances (1927–2004)
Hylton, Jane (1927–1979)
Hyman, Dorothy (1941—)
Hyman, Flo (1954–1986)
Hyman, Libbie Henrietta (1888–1969)
Hyman, Misty (1979—)
Hyman, Phyllis (1949–1995)
Hyman, Prudence (1914–1995)
Hyman, Trina Schart (1939–2004)
Hynde, Chrissie (1951—)
Hyslop, Beatrice Fry (1899–1973)
Hyslop, Fiona (1964—)
Hyson, Dorothy (1914–1996)
Hyun Jung-Hwa (1969—)
Hyun Sook-Hee
Hyytianen, Eija
Iams, Lucy (1855–1924)
Ian, Janis (1951—)
Ibarbourou, Juana de (1895–1979)
Ibarra de Piedra, Rosario (1927—)
Ibárruri, Dolores (1895–1989)
Icaza, Carmen de (1899–1979)
Ichikawa, Fusae (1893–1981)
Ichino, Yoko (c. 1954—)
Icho, Chiharu (1981—)
Icho, Kaori (1984—)
Ichtchenko, Natalia (1986—)
Ickes, Anna Thompson (1873–1935)
Idar, Jovita (1885–1946)
Ide, Letitia (1909–1993)
Idehen, Faith (1973—)
Idem, Josefa (1964—)
Idlibi, 'Ulfah al- (1912—)
Iffat (1916–2000)
Ifill, Gwen (1955—)
Igaly, Diana (1965—)
Ighodaro, Irene (1916–1995)
Ignat, Doina (1968—)
Ignatova, Lilia (1965—)
Ihrer, Emma (1857–1911)
Iida, Takako (1946—)
Iivari, Ulpu (1948—)
Ikeda, Hiroko
Ikeda, Keiko (1933—)
Iko, Momoko (1940—)
Ileana (1909–1991)
Iles, Katica (1946—)
Ilienko, Natalia (1967—)
Ilieva, Valentina (1962—)
Ilieva, Zhaneta (1984—)
Iliuta, Ana (1958—)
Illington, Margaret (1881–1934)
Illington, Marie (d. 1927)
Ily, Nicole (1932—)
Ilyenkova, Irina (1980—)
Ilyina, Vera (1974—)
Ilyina-Kolesnikova, Nadezhda (1949—)
Imaleyene, Fatime-Zohra (1936—)
Imison, Rachel (1978—)
Immerwahr, Clara (1870–1915)
Impekoven, Niddy (1904–2002)
Ina Maria of Bassewitz-Levitzow (1888–1973)
Inber, Vera (1890–1972)
Inescort, Elaine (c. 1877–1964)
Inescort, Frieda (1900–1976)
Ingalls, Laura H. (c. 1900–c. 1988)
Ingeborg of Denmark (1878–1958)
Ingham, Mary Hall (1866–1937)
Inglesby, Mona (1918—)
Inglis, Elsie Maud (1864–1917)
Inglis, Helen Clyde (1867–1945)
Ingraham, Mary Shotwell (1887–1981)
Ingram, Sheila Rena (1957—)
Ingrid of Sweden (1910–2000)
Ingstad, Anne-Stine (c. 1918–1997)
Inkster, Juli (1960—)
Inman, Florence (1890–1986)
Innes, Mary Jane (1852–1941)
Inness, Jean (1900–1978)
Inoue, Setsuko (1946—)
Intropodi, Ethel (d. 1946)
Inui, Emi (1983—)
Invernizio, Carolina (1858–1916)
Inyama, Rosemary (b. 1903)
Inzhuvatova, Galina (1952—)
Ionescu, Atanasia (1935—)
Ionescu, Nastasia (1954—)
Ionescu, Valeria (1960—)
Ionita, Raluca (1976—)
Iordanidou, Maria (1897–1989)
Iotti, Nilde (1920–1999)
Iouchkova, Angelina
Iovan, Sonia (1935—)
Ireland, Jill (1936–1990)
Ireland, Patricia (1945—)
Iremonger, Lucille (c. 1916–1989?)
Irene (1901–1962)
Irene (1904–1974)
Irene (1942—)
Irene (1953—)
Irene Emma (1939—)
Irene of Hesse-Darmstadt (1866–1953)
Ireys, Alice (1911–2000)
Irigaray, Luce (1930—)
Irina (1895–1970)
Irma of Hohenlohe-Langenburg (1902–1986)
Irvine, Jean Kennedy (c. 1877–1962)
Irvine-Smith, Fanny Louise (1878–1948)
Irving, Ethel (1869–1963)
Irving, Isabel (1871–1944)
Irving, Margaret (1898–1988)
Irwin, Agnes (1841–1914)
Irwin, Elisabeth (1880–1942)
Irwin, Estelle Mae (1923—)

Irwin, Inez Haynes (1873–1970)
Irwin, May (1862–1938)
Isaacs, Edith (1878–1956)
Isaacs, Stella (1894–1971)
Isaacs, Susan (1885–1948)
Isabella II (1830–1904)
Isabella of Croy-Dulmen (1856–1931)
Isabella of Guise (1900–1983)
Isabella of Orleans (1878–1961)
Isabella of Orleans (1911–2003)
Isakova, Maria (1918—)
Isaksen, Lone (1941—)
Isarescu, Andreea (1984—)
Ishida, Kyoko (1960—)
Ishigaki, Rin (1920—)
Ishikawa, Taeko (c. 1976—)
Ishmouratova, Svetlana (1972—)
Ishoy, Cynthia (1952—)
Isinbayeva, Yelena (1982—)
Isler, Jennifer (1963—)
Isler Béguin, Marie Anne (1956—)
Isobe, Sata (1944—)
Isoda, Yoko
Isom, Mary Frances (1865–1920)
Issaia, Nana (1934—)
Issakova, Natalia
Istomina, Anna (1925—)
Itkina, Maria (1932—)
Ito, Kazue (1977—)
Ito, Midori (1969—)
Iturbi, Amparo (1898–1969)
Ivan, Paula (1963—)
Ivan, Rosalind (1880–1959)
Ivanova, Borislava (1966—)
Ivanova, Ioulia
Ivanova, Kira (c. 1963–2001)
Ivanova, Natalia (c. 1971—)
Ivanova, Natalya (1981—)
Ivanova, Olimpiada (1970—)
Ivanova, Svetlana (1974—)
Ivanova-Kalinina, Lidiya (1937—)
Ivanovskaia, Praskovia (1853–1935)
Ivey, Jean Eichelberger (1923—)
Ivins, Molly (c. 1944—)
Ivinskaya, Olga (1912–1995)
Ivinskaya, Tatyana (1958—)
Ivogün, Maria (1891–1987)
Ivosev, Aleksandra (1974—)
Iwabuchi, Yumi (1979—)
Iwahara, Toyoko (1945—)
Iwasaki, Kyoko (1978—)
Iyall, Debora (1954—)
Izquierdo, Lilia (1967—)
Izquierdo Rojo, Maria (1946—)
Izzard, Molly (1919–2004)
Jaapies, Mieke (1943—)
Jaatteenmaki, Anneli (1955—)
Jabavu, Noni (1919—)
Jaburkova, Jozka (d. 1944)
Jackman, Mary (1943—)
Jackson, Alice (1887–1974)
Jackson, Anne (1926—)
Jackson, Ann Fletcher (1833–1903)
Jackson, Caroline F. (1946—)
Jackson, Cordell (1923–2004)
Jackson, Ethel (1877–1957)
Jackson, Freda (1909–1990)
Jackson, Glenda (1936—)
Jackson, Grace (1961—)
Jackson, Helen (1939—)
Jackson, Janet (1966—)
Jackson, Lauren (1981—)
Jackson, Mahalia (1911–1972)
Jackson, Marjorie (1931—)
Jackson, Mary Percy (1904–2000)
Jackson, Nell (1929–1988)
Jackson, Rowena (1926—)
Jackson, Sarah Elizabeth (1858–1946)
Jackson, Shirley (1916–1965)
Jackson, Shirley Ann (1946—)
Jackson, Sylvia (c. 1951—)
Jackson, Tammy (1962—)
Jackson, Trina (1977—)
Jackson, Wanda (1937—)
Jacob, Naomi Ellington (1889–1964)
Jacob, Rosamund (1888–1960)
Jacobellis, Lindsey (1985—)
Jacobi, Lotte (1896–1990)
Jacobi, Mary Putnam (1842–1906)
Jacobini, Maria (1890–1944)
Jacobs, Aletta (1854–1929)
Jacobs, Helen Hull (1908–1997)
Jacobs, Pattie Ruffner (1875–1935)
Jacobs, Simmone (1966—)
Jacobsen, Else (1911–1965)
Jacobsen, Inger Kathrine (1867–1939)
Jacobsen, Josephine (1908–2003)
Jacobson, Ethel May (1877–1965)
Jacobson, Helen (d. 1974)
Jacobson, Henrietta (1906–1988)
Jacobson, Louise (1924–1943)
Jacobson, Sada (1983—)
Jacobsson, Ulla (1929–1982)
Jacot, Michele (1952—)
Jacques, Hattie (1922–1980)
Jacquin, Lisa (1962—)
Jaczynowska, Katarzyna (1875–1920)
Jagan, Janet (1920—)
Jagger, Amy
Jahl, Evelin (1956—)
Jahn, Sabine (1953—)
Jahoda, Marie (1907–2001)
Jahren, Anne
Jakobsdóttir, Svava (1930—)
Jakobsson, Ludowika (1884–1968)
Jakubowska, Krystyna (1942—)
Jakubowska, Wanda (1907–1998)
Jalandoni, Magdalena (1891–1978)
Jambrišak, Marija (1847–1937)
James, Alice Gibbens (1849–1922)
James, Annie Isabella (1884–1965)
James, Cheryl (1964—)
James, Claire (1920–1986)
James, Esther Marion Pretoria (1900–1990)
James, Etta (1938—)
James, Florence (1902–1993)
James, Hilda (b. 1904)
James, Naomi (1949—)
James, P.D. (1920—)
James, Susan Gail (1953—)
James, Zerelda (c. 1824–1911)
Jameson, Betty (1919—)
Jameson, Helen (1963—)
Jameson, Joyce (1932–1987)
Jameson, Storm (1891–1986)
Jamieson, Cathy (1956—)
Jamieson, Margaret (1953—)
Jamieson, Penny (1942—)
Jamison, Cecilia V. (1837–1909)
Jamison, Judith (1943—)
Janauschek, Fanny (1829–1904)
Janés, Clara (1940—)
Janeway, Elizabeth (1913–2005)
Jang Hye Ock
Jang Ji-Won (1979—)
Jang Mi-Ran (1983—)
Jang Ok-Rim (1948—)
Jang Ri-Ra (1969—)
Jang So-Hee (1978—)
Jang Yong-Ho
Janicke, Marina (1954—)
Janics, Natasa (1982—)
Janis, Elsie (1889–1956)
Janiszewska, Barbara (1936—)
Janitschek, Maria (1859–1927)
Janko, Eva (1945—)
Jankovic, Ljubinka (1958—)
Janny, Amélia (1838–1914)
Janosi, Zsuzsanna (1963—)
Janosine-Ducza, Aniko (1942—)
Janotha, Natalia (1856–1932)
Janowitz, Gundula (1937—)
Jansen, Elly (1929—)
Jansen, Linda
Jansson, Tove (1914–2001)
Januaria (1822–1901)
Janz, Karen (1952—)
Jarboro, Caterina (1908–1986)
Jardin, Anne (1959—)
Jarratt, Jan (1958—)
Jarrell, Ira (1896–1973)
Jarrett, Mary Cromwell (1877–1961)
Jarvela, Satu
Jarvis, Anna M. (1864–1948)
Jarvis, Lilian (1931—)
Jarvis, Lucy (1919—)
Jaschke, Martina (1960—)
Jasontek, Rebecca (1975—)
Jaunzeme, Ineze (1932—)
Jay, Harriett (1863–1932)
Jay, Isabel (1879–1927)
Jayakar, Pupul (1915–1999)
Jayasinghe, Susanthika (1975—)
Jeakins, Dorothy (1914–1995)
Jean, Gloria (1926—)
Jean, Sally Lucas (1878–1971)
Jeanes, Anna Thomas (1822–1907)
Jeanmaire, Zizi (1924—)
Jeans, Constance (b. 1899)
Jeans, Isabel (1891–1985)
Jeans, Ursula (1906–1973)
Jebb, Eglantyne (1876–1928)
Jedrzejczak, Otylia (1983—)
Jefferis, Barbara (1917–2004)
Jeffrey, Mildred (1910–2004)
Jeffrey, Rhi (1986—)
Jeffreys, Anne (1923—)
Jeffreys, Ellen Penelope (1827–1904)
Jeffreys, Ellis (1872–1943)
Jeffs, Doreen (d. 1965)
Jeggle, Elisabeth (1947—)
Jehan, Noor (1926–2000)
Jekyll, Gertrude (1843–1932)
Jelicich, Dorothy (1928—)
Jelinek, Elfriede (1946—)
Jellett, Mainie (1897–1944)
Jellicoe, Ann (1927—)
Jelsma, Clara Mitsuko (1931—)
Jemison, Alice Lee (1901–1964)
Jemison, Mae (1956—)
Jenckes, Virginia Ellis (1877–1975)
Jenkin, Penelope M. (1902–1994)
Jenkins, Helen Hartley (1860–1934)
Jenner, Andrea (1891–1985)
Jenner, Ann (1944—)
Jenner, Caryl (1917—)
Jennings, Elizabeth Joan (1926–2001)
Jennings, Gertrude E. (d. 1958)
Jennings, Lynn (1960—)
Jens, Salome (1935—)
Jensen, Anne Elisabet (1951—)
Jensen, Anne Grethe (1951—)
Jensen, Bjorg Eva (1960—)
Jensen, Christine Boe (1975—)
Jensen, Dorte (1972—)
Jensen, Thit (1876–1957)
Jensen, Trine (1980—)
Jenssen, Elois (1922–2004)
Jentsch, Martina (1968—)
Jentzer, Emma R.H. (c. 1883–1972)
Jeong Hyoi-Soon (1964—)
Jeong Myung-Hee (1964—)
Jeon Young-Sun
Jepson, Helen (1904–1997)
Jeremic, Slavica (1957—)
Jergens, Adele (1917–2002)
Jeriova, Kvetoslava (1956—)
Jeritza, Maria (1887–1982)
Jermy, Louie (1864–1934)
Jerome, Helen (b. 1883)
Jerome, Rowena (1889–?)
Jerrold, Mary (1877–1955)
Jesenská, Milena (1896–1945)
Jesenská, Ružena (1863–1940)
Jesionowska, Celina (1933—)
Jespersen, Helle (1968—)
Jesse, Fryniwyd Tennyson (1888–1958)
Jessel, Patricia (1929–1968)
Jessen, Ruth (1936—)
Jessup, Marion (b. 1897)
Jessye, Eva (1895–1992)
Jesús, Carolina Maria de (c. 1913–1977)
Jesus, Clementina de (1902–1987)
Jesus, Gregoria de (1875–1943)
Jett, Joan (1958—)
Jeung Soon-Bok (1960—)
Jewell, Isabel (1907–1972)
Jewell, Lynne (1959—)

Era Index

Jewell, Wanda (1954—)
Jewett, Sarah Orne (1849–1909)
Jex-Blake, Sophia (1840–1912)
Jezek, Linda (1960—)
Jhabvala, Ruth Prawer (1927—)
Jiagge, Annie (1918–1996)
Jiang Cuihua
Jiang Qing (1914–1991)
Jiang Ying (1963—)
Jiang Yonghua (1973—)
Jiao Zhimin (1963—)
Jiles, Pamela (1955—)
Ji Liya (1981—)
Jillana (1934—)
Jimbo, Rei
Jiménez, Soledad (1874–1966)
Jimenez Mendivil, Soraya (1977—)
Jin Deok San
Jinnah, Fatima (1893–1967)
Jin Won-Sim (1965—)
Jiricna, Eva (1939—)
Jochmann, Rosa (1901–1994)
Joel, Grace Jane (1865–1924)
Joenpelto, Eeva (1921–2004)
Joens, Karin (1953—)
Johann, Zita (1904–1993)
Johansen, Aud (1930—)
Johansen, Hanna (1939—)
Johanson, Margareta (1895–1978)
Johansson, Anna (1860–1917)
Johansson, Irma
Johansson, Ronny (b. 1891)
Jo Hea-Jung (1953—)
John, Gwen (1876–1939)
John, Rosamund (1913–1998)
Jöhncke, Louise (1976—)
John-Paetz-Moebius, Sabine (1957—)
Johns, Ethel (1879–1968)
Johns, Glynis (1923—)
Johns, Helen (1914—)
Johnsen, Vibeke (1968—)
Johnson, Adelaide (1859–1955)
Johnson, Amy (1903–1941)
Johnson, Brandy (1973—)
Johnson, Celia (1908–1982)
Johnson, Chris (1958—)
Johnson, Courtney (1974—)
Johnson, E. Pauline (1861–1913)
Johnson, Eleanor Murdoch (1892–1987)
Johnson, Ella (1923–2004)
Johnson, Emma (1980—)
Johnson, Georgia Douglas (1877–1966)
Johnson, Halle (1864–1901)
Johnson, Helene (1906–1995)
Johnson, Helen Kendrick (1844–1917)
Johnson, Jenna (1967—)
Johnson, Josephine Winslow (1910–1990)
Johnson, Julie (1903–1973)
Johnson, Kate (1978—)
Johnson, Kathryn (1967—)
Johnson, Kathy (1959—)
Johnson, Katie (1878–1957)
Johnson, Kay (1904–1975)
Johnson, Lady Bird (1912—)
Johnson, Luci Baines (1947—)
Johnson, Lynda Bird (1944—)
Johnson, Melanie (1955—)
Johnson, Nancy (1935—)
Johnson, Nicole (c. 1974—)
Johnson, Opha Mae (c. 1899—)
Johnson, Osa (1894–1953)
Johnson, Pamela Hansford (1912–1981)
Johnson, Phyllis (1886–1967)
Johnson, Rita (1912–1965)
Johnson, Shannon (1974—)
Johnson, Sheryl (1957—)
Johnson, Sunny (1953–1984)
Johnson, Tish (1962—)
Johnson, Virginia E. (1925—)
Johnston, Amy Isabella (1872–1908)
Johnston, Annie Fellows (1863–1931)
Johnston, Carol (1958—)
Johnston, Frances Benjamin (1864–1952)
Johnston, Jennifer (1930—)
Johnston, Jill (1929—)
Johnston, Julanne (1900–1988)
Johnston, Margaret (1917–2002)
Johnston, Mary (1870–1936)
Johnston, Rita Margaret (1935—)
Johnstone, Anna Hill (1913–1992)
Johnstone, Ann Casey (1921—)
Johnstone, Hilda Lorne (b. 1902)
Johnstone, Justine (1895–1982)
Johnston-Forbes, Cathy (1963—)
Jokielowa, Dorota (1934–1993)
Jolas, Betsy (1926—)
Jolas, Maria (1893–1987)
Joliot-Curie, Irène (1897–1956)
Jolley, Elizabeth (1923—)
Jolly, Allison (1956—)
Joly, Andrée (1901–1993)
Jonas, Maryla (1911–1959)
Jonas, Regina (1902–1944)
Jones, Amanda Theodosia (1835–1914)
Jones, Anissa (1958–1976)
Jones, Ann Haydon (1938—)
Jones, Barbara (1937—)
Jones, Brenda (1936—)
Jones, Caroline R. (1942–2001)
Jones, Carolyn (1929–1983)
Jones, Carolyn (1969—)
Jones, Elizabeth (c. 1935—)
Jones, Elizabeth Marina (1926—)
Jones, Esther (1969—)
Jones, Etta (1928–2001)
Jones, Grace (1952—)
Jones, Gwyneth (1936—)
Jones, Hazel (1896–1974)
Jones, Helen (1954—)
Jones, Jennifer (1919—)
Jones, Leisel (1985—)
Jones, Linda (1944–1972)
Jones, Lois M. (1934–2000)
Jones, Loïs Mailou (1905–1998)
Jones, Lynne (1951—)
Jones, Marcia (1941—)
Jones, Margo (1911–1955)
Jones, Marilyn (1940—)
Jones, Marion (1879–1965)
Jones, Marion (1975—)
Jones, Marion Patrick (1934—)
Jones, Mary Harris (1830–1930)
Jones, Maxine (1966—)
Jones, Michellie (1969—)
Jones, Patricia (1930—)
Jones, Shirley (1934—)
Jones, Sissieretta (1869–1933)
Jones, Steffi (1972—)
Jones, Susan (1952—)
Jong, Erica (1942—)
Jonker, Ingrid (1933–1965)
Jonrowe, DeeDee (1953—)
Jonsson, Magdalena (1969—)
Joo Min-Jin (1983—)
Joplin, Janis (1943–1970)
Jordan, Barbara (1936–1996)
Jordan, Dorothy (1906–1988)
Jordan, Elizabeth Garver (1865–1947)
Jordan, June (1936–2002)
Jordan, Marian (1896–1961)
Jordan, Sara Murray (1884–1959)
Jordan, Sheila (1928—)
Jordan, Vi (d. 1982)
Jorgensen, Janel (1971—)
Jorgensen, Rikke Horlykke (1976—)
Jorgensen, Silje (1977—)
Jorge Pádua, Maria Tereza (1943—)
Joseph, Helen (1905–1992)
Joseph, Jenefer (1932—)
Joseph, Mother (1823–1902)
Josephine-Charlotte of Belgium (1927—)
Josephine of Baden (1813–1900)
Josephine of Belgium (1872–1958)
Josephson, Karen (1964—)
Josephson, Sarah (1964—)
Joshua, Joan O. (1912–1993)
Josland, Claudie (1946—)
Jossinet, Frederique (1975—)
Jotuni, Maria (1880–1943)
Joubert, Elsa (1922—)
Joudry, Patricia (1921–2000)
Jowell, Tessa (1947—)
Joy, Génèviève (1919—)
Joy, Leatrice (1893–1985)
Joyce, Alice (1889–1955)
Joyce, Brenda (1915—)
Joyce, Eileen (1908–1991)
Joyce, Joan (1940—)
Joyce, Kara Lynn (1985—)
Joyce, Lucia (1907–1982)
Joyce, Nora (1884–1951)
Joyce, Peggy Hopkins (1893–1957)
Joyce, Rebecca
Joyeux, Odette (1914–2000)
Joyner, Florence Griffith (1959–1998)
Joyner, Marjorie Stewart (1896–1994)
Joyner-Kersee, Jackie (1962—)
Jozwiakowska, Jaroslawa (1937—)
Juch, Emma (1860–1939)
Juchacz, Marie (1879–1956)
Judd, Ashley (1968—)
Judd, Isabel
Judd, Naomi (1946—)
Judd, Winnie Ruth (1905–1998)
Judd, Wynonna (1964—)
Judge, Arline (1912–1974)
Juhaszne-Nagy, Katalin (1932—)
Júlia, Francisca (1871–1920)
Juliana (1909–2004)
Julin-Mauroy, Magda (1894–1990)
Jull, Roberta (1872–1961)
Jumper, Betty Mae (1923—)
June (1901–c. 1984)
Jung, Lovieanne (1980—)
Junge, Traudel (1920–2002)
Junger, Esther (c. 1915—)
Jung Jae-Eun (c. 1981—)
Jungjohann, Caren (1970—)
Jungmann, Elisabeth (d. 1959)
Jung Soo-Nok (1955—)
Jung Sung-Sook
Jung Sun Yong
Junker, Helen (1905—)
Junker, Karin (1940—)
Jurado, Alicia (1915—)
Jurado, Jeanette (1966—)
Jurado, Katy (1924–2002)
Jurca, Branca (1914–1999)
Jurinac, Sena (1921—)
Jurney, Dorothy Misener (1909–2002)
Jurrilëns, Henny (1949—)
Justin, Enid (1894–1990)
Jutta of Mecklenburg-Strelitz (1880–1946)
Juvonen, Helvi (1919–1959)
Kaaro, Ani (fl. 1885–1901)
Kabaeva, Alina (1983—)
Kaberry, Phyllis (1910–1977)
Kabos, Ilona (1893–1973)
Kaciusyte, Lina (1963—)
Kadaré, Elena (1943—)
Kadlecova, Jirina (1948—)
Kael, Pauline (1919–2001)
Kaesling, Dagmar (1947—)
Kaffka, Margit (1880–1918)
Kagabu, Yoko (1960—)
Kagan, Elena (1960—)
Kahana-Carmon, Amalia (1930—)
Kahlo, Frida (1907–1954)
Kahn, Florence (1878–1951)
Kahn, Florence Prag (1866–1948)
Kahn, Lilly (c. 1898–1978)
Kahn, Madeline (1942–1999)
Kai, Una (1928—)
Kain, Karen (1951—)
Kaiser, Isabella (1866–1925)
Kaiser, Natasha (1967—)
Kaisheva, Rumyana (1955—)
Kajiwara, Mari (1952—)
Kajosmaa, Marjatta
Kalama, Thelma (1931–1999)
K'alandadze, Ana (1924—)
Kalediene, Birute (1934—)
Kalich, Bertha (1874–1939)
Kalimbet, Irina (1968—)
Kalinchuk, Yekaterina (1922—)
Kalinina, Ganna (1979—)
Kalinina, Irina (1959—)
Kalinina, Natalia (1973—)

Kaliska, Elena (1972—)
Kallen, Kitty (1922—)
Kallen, Lucille (1922–1999)
Kallies, Monika (1956—)
Kallir, Lilian (1931–2004)
Kalmus, Natalie (1878–1965)
Kalmykova, Maria (1978—)
Kalocsai, Margit (b. 1909)
Kalvak, Helen (1901–1984)
Kamal, Sufia (1911–1999)
Kamali, Norma (1945—)
Kameaim, Wandee (1978—)
Kamenshek, Dorothy (1925—)
Kaminska, Ida (1899–1980)
Kaminskaite, Leonora (1951–1986)
Kammerling, Anna-Karin (1980—)
Kanaga, Consuelo (1894–1978)
Kanahele, Helen Lake (1916–1976)
Kanakaole, Edith K. (1913–1979)
Kander, Lizzie Black (1858–1940)
Kane, Amy Grace (1879–1979)
Kane, Gail (1887–1966)
Kane, Helen (1903–1966)
Kane, Marjorie (1909–1992)
Kane, Sarah (1971–1999)
Kanesaka, Katsuko (1954—)
Kang Cho-Hyun (1982—)
Kang Jae-Won (1965—)
Kang Keqing (1911–1992)
Kang Ok-Sun (1946—)
Kania-Enke, Karin (1961—)
Kanin, Fay (1917—)
Kankus, Roberta A. (1953—)
Kann, Edith (1907–1987)
Kanner-Rosenthal, Hedwig (1882–1959)
Kantor, Aniko
Kantûrkova, Eva (1930—)
Kanwar, Roop (c. 1969–1987)
Kapheim, Ramona (1958—)
Kaplan, Fanya (1883–1918)
Kaplan, Nelly (1931—)
Kapralova, Vitezslava (1915–1940)
Kaptur, Marcy (1946—)
Kar, Ida (1908–1970)
Karadjordjevic, Helen (1884–1962)
Karagianni, Eftychia (1973—)
Karalli, Vera (1889–1972)
Karamanou, Anna (1947—)
Karan, Donna (1948—)
Karasyova, Olga (1949—)
Karavaeva, Irina (1975—)
Karina, Anna (1940—)
Karioka, Tahiya (c. 1921–1999)
Karle, Isabella (1921—)
Karlen, Maud (1932—)
Karlova, Larisa (1958—)
Karlsson, Eva (1961—)
Karlstadt, Liesl (1892–1960)
Karnilova, Maria (1920–2001)
Karodia, Farida (1942—)
Karpati-Karcsics, Iren (1927—)
Karpatkin, Rhoda Hendrick (1930—)
Karpenko, Viktoria (1984—)
Karpinski, Stephanie (1912–2005)
Karpova, Elena (1980—)
Karr, Carme (1865–1943)
Karres, Sylvia (1976—)
Karsavina, Tamara (1885–1978)
Karstens, Gerda (1903–1988)
Kartini (1879–1904)
Karyami, Zacharoula (1983—)
Kasabian, Linda (1949—)
Kasaeva, Zarema (1987—)
Kasai, Masae (1933—)
Kasatkina, Natalia (1934—)
Kaschnitz, Marie Luise (1901–1974)
Kaschube, Ilse (1953—)
Käsebier, Gertrude (1852–1934)
Kashfi, Anna (1934—)
Kasilag, Lucrecia R. (1918—)
Kasparkova, Sarka (1971—)
Kassebaum, Nancy Landon (1932—)
Kasten, Barbara (1936—)
Kastl, Sonja (1929—)
Kastor, Deena (1973—)
Katia (1977—)
Kato, Kiyomi (1953—)
Katusheva, Marita (1938—)
Katz, Lillian (1927—)
Katznelson, Shulamit (1919–1999)
Katznelson-Shazar, Rachel (1888–1975)
Kaufer, Evelyn (1953—)
Kaufman, Beatrice (1894–1945)
Kaufmann, Sylvia-Yvonne (1955—)
Kaun, Elfriede (1914—)
Kauppi, Piia-Noora (1975—)
Kaur, Rajkumari Amrit (1889–1964)
Kaus, Gina (1894–1985)
Kauschke, Katrin (1971—)
Kautsky, Luise (1864–1944)
Kautsky, Minna (1837–1912)
Kavan, Anna (1901–1968)
Kawabe, Miho (1974—)
Kawaguchi, Yoriko (1941—)
Kawakubo, Rei (1942—)
Kawamoto, Evelyn (1933—)
Kawasaki, Ayumi (1984—)
Kawase, Akiko (1971—)
Kawashima, Naoko (1981—)
Kawashima, Yoshiko (1906–1947)
Kay, Beatrice (1907–1986)
Kaye, M.M. (1908–2004)
Kaye, Nora (1920–1987)
Kaye-Smith, Sheila (1887–1956)
Kazakova, Oksana (1975—)
Kazankina, Tatyana (1951—)
Kazantzaki, Eleni (1903–2004)
Kazantzaki, Galateia (1886–1962)
Kazantzis, Judith (1940—)
Kazel, Dorothy (1931—)
Keall, Judy (1942—)
Kean, Betty (1915–1986)
Kean, Jane (1924—)
Keane, Doris (1881–1945)
Keane, Fiorella (1930–1976)
Keane, Molly (1904–1996)
Kearney, Belle (1863–1939)
Kearney, Miriam (1959—)
Kearns-MacWhinney, Linda (1888–1951)
Keating, Annita (1949—)
Keaton, Diane (1946—)
Keaveney, Cecilia (1968—)
Keckley, Elizabeth (c. 1824–1907)
Kedrova, Lila (1918–2000)
Kee, Elizabeth (1895–1975)
Keeble, Sally (1951—)
Keech, Margaret Majella
Keefe, Zena (1896–1977)
Keeler, Christine (1942—)
Keeler, Kathryn (1956—)
Keeler, Ruby (1909–1993)
Keen, Ann (1948—)
Keene, Constance (1921–2005)
Keesing, Nancy (1923–1993)
Kefala, Antigone (1935—)
Kehajia, Kalliopi (1839–1905)
Kehew, Mary Morton (1859–1918)
Keil, Birgit (1944—)
Kéita, Aoua (1912–1979)
Keith, Agnes Newton (1901–1982)
Keith, Marcia (1859–1950)
Keith, Vicki (1959—)
Kékessy, Andrea
Kelemen, Marta (1954—)
Kelesidou, Anastasia (1972—)
Keleti, Ágnes (1921—)
Kelety, Julia (d. 1972)
Kellar, Becky (1975—)
Kellas, Eliza (1864–1943)
Keller, Evelyn Fox (1936—)
Keller, Helen (1880–1968)
Keller, Natascha (1977—)
Keller, Nettie Florence (1875–1974)
Kellerman, Annette (1886–1975)
Kellerman, Sally (1936—)
Kelley, Beverly Gwinn (c. 1952—)
Kelley, Edith Summers (1884–1956)
Kelley, Florence (1859–1932)
Kellner, Rosa (1910—)
Kellogg, Clara Louise (1842–1916)
Kellogg, Louise Phelps (1862–1942)
Kellor, Frances Alice (1873–1952)
Kells, Isabella (1861–1938)
Kelly, Annie Elizabeth (1877–1946)
Kelly, Dorothy (1894–1966)
Kelly, Edna Flannery (1906–1997)
Kelly, Emily (d. 1922)
Kelly, Ethel (1875–1949)
Kelly, Fanny Wiggins (1845–1904)
Kelly, Florence Finch (1858–1939)
Kelly, Grace (1928–1982)
Kelly, Gwen (1922—)
Kelly, Isabel (1906–1983)
Kelly, Jo Ann (1944–1990)
Kelly, Judy (1913–1991)
Kelly, Kathryn Thorne (1904–1998?)
Kelly, Kitty (1902–1968)
Kelly, Leontine (1920—)
Kelly, Maeve (1930—)
Kelly, Margaret (1910–2004)
Kelly, Margaret (1956—)
Kelly, Mary (1952—)
Kelly, Nancy (1921–1995)
Kelly, Patsy (1910–1981)
Kelly, Paula (1939—)
Kelly, Pearl (1894–1983)
Kelly, Petra (1947–1992)
Kelly, Ruth (1968—)
Kelsall, Karen (1962—)
Kelsey, Frances O. (1914—)
Kelsey, Lavinia Jane (1856–1948)
Kelso, Elizabeth (1889–1967)
Kelton, Pert (1907–1968)
Kemmer, Heike (1962—)
Kemner, Caren (1965—)
Kemp, Jennifer (1955—)
Kempfer, Hannah Jensen (1880–1943)
Kempner, Patty (1942—)
Kempson, Rachel (1910–2003)
Kemp-Welch, Joan (1906–1999)
Kendal, Felicity (1946—)
Kendal, Madge (1849–1935)
Kendall, Barbara Anne (1967—)
Kendall, Kay (1926–1959)
Kendall, Marie Hartig (1854–1943)
Kendrick, Pearl L. (1890–1980)
Kennard, Gaby (1944—)
Kennard, Olga (1924—)
Kennedy, Adrienne (1931—)
Kennedy, Courtney (1979—)
Kennedy, Ethel (1928—)
Kennedy, Florynce (1916–2000)
Kennedy, Geraldine (1951—)
Kennedy, Helena (1950—)
Kennedy, Jacqueline (1929–1994)
Kennedy, Jane (1958—)
Kennedy, Joan (1936—)
Kennedy, Karol (1932–2004)
Kennedy, Kathleen (1920–1948)
Kennedy, Kathleen (1954—)
Kennedy, Louise St. John (1950—)
Kennedy, Madge (1890–1987)
Kennedy, Margaret (1896–1967)
Kennedy, Margaret L. (b. 1892)
Kennedy, Merna (1908–1944)
Kennedy, Rose Fitzgerald (1890–1995)
Kennedy, Rosemary (1918–2005)
Kennedy, Suzanne (c. 1955—)
Kennedy-Fraser, Marjorie (1857–1930)
Kennelly, Barbara (1936—)
Kennelly, Keala (1978—)
Kenney, Annie (1879–1953)
Kennibrew, Dee Dee (1945—)
Kenny, Alice Annie (1875–1960)
Kenny, Elizabeth (1880–1952)
Kent, Allegra (1937—)
Kent, Barbara (b. 1906)
Kent, Constance (1844–?)
Kent, Jean (1921—)
Kent, Leslie (1981—)
Kent, Linda (1946—)
Kent, Thelma Rene (1899–1946)
Kent, Victoria (1898–1987)
Kenworthy, Marion E. (c. 1891–1980)
Kenyatta, Margaret (1928—)
Kenyon, Doris (1897–1979)
Kenyon, Dorothy (1888–1972)
Kenyon, Kathleen (1906–1978)

Keogh, Helen (1951—)
Keohane, Nannerl (1940—)
Keppel, Alice (1869–1947)
Keppelhoff-Wiechert, Hedwig (1939—)
Kerima (1925—)
Kermer, Romy (1956—)
Kernohan, Liz (1939–2004)
Kerr, Anita (1927—)
Kerr, Deborah (1921—)
Kerr, Jane (1968—)
Kerr, Jean (1923–2003)
Kerr, Sophie (1880–1965)
Kerrigan, Nancy (1969—)
Ker-Seymer, Barbara (b. 1905)
Kershaw, Willette (1890–1960)
Kersten, Dagmar (1970—)
Kertesz, Aliz (1935—)
Kery, Aniko (1956—)
Kessler, Margot (1948—)
Kessler, Romi (1963—)
Kéthly, Anna (1889–1976)
Keun, Irmgard (1905–1982)
Keur, Dorothy (1904–1989)
Kevlian, Valentina (1980—)
Key, Ellen (1849–1926)
Ke Yan (1929—)
Keyes, Evelyn (1919—)
Keys, Martha Elizabeth (1930—)
Kezhova, Eleonora (1985—)
Kezine-Pethoe, Zsuzsanna (1945—)
Khabarova, Irina (1966—)
Khalifa, Sahar (1941—)
Kham, Alina (1959—)
Khambatta, Persis (1950–1998)
Khan, Begum Liaquat Ali (1905–1990)
Khan, Chaka (1953—)
Khan, Noor Inayat (1914–1944)
Khasyanova, Elvira (1981—)
Khieu Ponnary (1920–2003)
Khloptseva, Yelena (1960—)
Khnykina, Nadezhda (1933–1994)
Khodotovich, Ekaterina (1972—)
Khoklova, Olga (d. 1955)
Kholodnya, Vera (1893–1919)
Khomiakova, Valeriia (d. 1942)
Khorkina, Svetlana (1979—)
Khote, Durga (c. 1905–1991)
Khouri, Callie (1957—)
Khristova, Ivanka (1941—)
Khristova, Tsvetanka (1962—)
Khudashova, Yelena (1965—)
Khudorozhkina, Irina (1968—)
Khuri, Colette (1937—)
Kiaerskou, Lotte (1975—)
Kibbee, Lois (1922–1993)
Kidd, Margaret Henderson (1900–1989)
Kidder, Kathryn (1867–1939)
Kidder, Margot (1948—)
Kiddle, Margaret (1914–1958)
Kidman, Fiona (1940—)
Kidman, Nicole (1967—)
Kidson, Elsa Beatrice (1905–1979)
Kiehl, Marina (1965—)
Kielan, Urszula (1960—)
Kielgass, Kerstin (1969—)
Kielland, Kitty L. (1843–1914)
Kiengsiri, Kanha (1911—)
Kiermayer, Susanne (1968—)
Kiesl, Theresia (1963—)
Kight-Wingard, Lenore (1911–2000)
Kikuko, Princess (d. 2004)
Kilborn, Pam (1939—)
Kilbourn, Annelisa (1967–2002)
Kilbourne, Andrea (1980—)
Kilgallen, Dorothy (1913–1965)
Kilgore, Carrie B. (1838–1908)
Kilius, Marika (1943—)
Killingbeck, Molly (1959—)
Killough, Lee (1942—)
Kilmury, Diana (1948—)
Kilpi, Eeva (1928—)
Kim, Nelli (1957—)
Kim, Ronyoung (1926–1987)
Kimball, Judy (1938—)
Kim Bo-Ram
Kim Cha-Youn (1981—)
Kim Cheong-Shim (1976—)
Kim Choon-Rye (1966—)
Kimenye, Barbara (1940—)
Kim Eun-Mi (1975—)
Kim Eun-Sook (1963—)
Kim Gwang Suk (c. 1976—)
Kim Hwa-Sook (1971—)
Kim Hwa-Soon (1962—)
Kim Hyang-Mi (1979—)
Kim Hyun-Mi (1967—)
Kim Hyun-Ok (1974—)
Ki Mi-Sook (1967—)
Kim Jeong-Mi (1975—)
Kim Jin-Ho (1961—)
Kim Jo-Sun
Kim Jum-Sook (c. 1968—)
Kim Kyung-Ah (1977—)
Kim Kyung-Soon (1965—)
Kim Kyung-Wook
Kim Mi-Hyun (1977—)
Kim Mi-Jung (1971—)
Kim Mi-Sim (1970—)
Kim Mi-Sook (1962—)
Kim Mi-Sun (1964—)
Kim Moo-Kyo
Kim Myong-Soon (1964—)
Kim Myong-Suk (1947—)
Kim Myung-Ok
Kim Nam-Soon
Kim Ok-Hwa (1958—)
Kim Rang (1974—)
Kim Ryang-Hee
Kim So-Hee
Kim Soon-Duk (1967—)
Kim Soo-Nyung (1971—)
Kim Su-Dae (1942—)
Kimura, Saeko (1963—)
Kim Yeun-Ja (1943—)
Kim Young-Hee (1963—)
Kim Young-Sook (1965—)
Kim Yun-Mi
Kim Zung-Bok (1945—)
Kincaid, Jamaica (1949—)
Kinch, Myra (1904–1981)
King, Alberta Williams (1903–1974)
King, Andrea (1919–2003)
King, Anita (1891–1963)
King, Annette (1947—)
King, Betsy (1955—)
King, Billie Jean (1943—)
King, Carole (1942—)
King, Carol Weiss (1895–1952)
King, Coretta Scott (1927–2006)
King, Dottie (c. 1896–1923)
King, Eleanor (1906–1991)
King, Ellen (b. 1909)
King, Grace Elizabeth (c. 1852–1932)
King, Helen Dean (1869–1955)
King, Henrietta Chamberlain (1832–1925)
King, Isabel Grace Mackenzie (1843–1917)
King, Jane (d. 1971)
King, Jessie Marion (1875–1949)
King, Joyce (1921—)
King, Katie (1975—)
King, Lida Shaw (1868–1932)
King, Louisa Yeomans (1863–1948)
King, Mabel (1932–1999)
King, Mary (1961—)
King, Mazie (b. around 1880)
King, Micki (1944—)
King, Mollie (1885–1981)
King, Nellie (1895–1935)
King, Oona (1967—)
King, Rebecca (c. 1950—)
Kingsbury, Susan (1870–1949)
Kingsley, Dorothy (1909–1997)
Kingsley, Elizabeth (1871–1957)
Kingsley, Mary H. (1862–1900)
Kingsley, Mary St. Leger (1852–1931)
Kingsley, Susan (1946–1984)
Kingsolver, Barbara (1955—)
Kingston, Maxine Hong (1940—)
Kingston, Winifred (1894–1967)
Kinigi, Sylvie (1953—)
Kinney, Dita Hopkins (1854–1921)
Kinnock, Glenys (1944—)
Kinoshita, Alicia (1967—)
Kinsella, Kathleen (d. 1961)
Kinshofer, Christa (1961—)
Kint, Cor (d. 2002)
Kiplagat, Lornah (1974—)
Kipling, Charlotte (1919–1992)
Kippin, Vicky (1942—)
Kiraly Picot, Hajnalka (1971—)
Kira of Leiningen (b. 1930)
Kira of Russia (1909–1967)
Kirby, Dorothy (1920—)
Kirby, Mary Kostka (1863–1952)
Kirchwey, Freda (1893–1976)
Kirichenko, Olga (1976—)
Kirk, Cybele Ethel (1870–1957)
Kirk, Jenny (1945—)
Kirk, Phyllis (1926—)
Kirkaldy, Jane Willis (c. 1869–1932)
Kirkbride, Julie (1960—)
Kirkland, Gelsey (1952—)
Kirkland, Johnna (1950—)
Kirkland, Muriel (1903–1971)
Kirkland-Casgrain, Marie-Claire (1924—)
Kirkpatrick, Helen (1909–1997)
Kirkpatrick, Jeane (1926—)
Kirkus, Virginia (1893–1980)
Kirkwhite, Iris (c. 1900–1975)
Kirkwood, Julieta (1936–1985)
Kirkwood, Pat (1921—)
Kirner, Joan (1938—)
Kirouac, Martha Wilkinson (1948—)
Kirpishchikova, Anna (1848–1927)
Kirsch, Sarah (1935—)
Kirschner, Lola (1854–1934)
Kirsova, Helene (1910–1962)
Kirst, Jutta (1954—)
Kirsten, Dorothy (1910–1992)
Kirvesniemi, Marja-Liisa (1955—)
Kisabaka, Linda (1969—)
Kische, Marion (1958—)
Kiselyova, Larisa (1970—)
Kishida, Toshiko (1863–1901)
Kisseleva, Maria (1974—)
Kitao, Kanako (1982—)
Kitchell, Iva (1908–1983)
Kite, Jessie
Kitson, Theo A.R. (1871–1932)
Kitt, Eartha (1928—)
Kittelsen, Grete Prytz (1917—)
Kittrell, Flemmie (1904–1980)
Kitzinger, Sheila (1929—)
Kizer, Carolyn (1925—)
Kjaergaard, Tonje (1975—)
Kjeldaas, Stine Brun (1975—)
Klamt, Ewa (1950—)
Klapezynski, Ulrike (1953—)
Klarsfeld, Beate (1939—)
Klass, Christa (1951—)
Klassen, Cindy (1979—)
Klata, Katarzyna (1972—)
Kleber, Ina (1964—)
Klecker, Denise (1972—)
Kleeberg, Clotilde (1866–1909)
Kleegman, Sophia (1901–1971)
Kleiberne-Kontsek, Jolan (1939—)
Klein, Anne (1923–1974)
Klein, Helga (1931—)
Klein, Kit (1910–1985)
Klein, Melanie (1882–1960)
Klein, Robin (1936—)
Kleine, Megan (1974—)
Kleinert, Nadine (1975—)
Klepfisz, Irena (1941—)
Klier, Cornelia (1957—)
Klier-Schaller, Johanna (1952—)
Klimek, Tillie (1865–1936)
Klimova, Marina (1966—)
Klimova, Natalya (1951—)
Klimova, Rita (1931–1993)
Klimovica-Drevina, Inta (1951—)
Klobukowska, Ewa (1946—)
Klochkova, Yana (1982—)
Klochneva, Olga (1968—)
Klotz, Ulrike (1970—)
Kluft, Carolina (1983—)
Klug, Annette (1969—)

Kluge, Anja (1964—)
Klumpke, Anna Elizabeth (1856–1942)
Klumpke, Augusta (1859–1927)
Klumpke, Dorothea (1861–1942)
Knab, Ursula (1929–1989)
Knacke, Christiane (1962—)
Knape, Ulrika (1955—)
Knapp, Evalyn (1908–1981)
Knef, Hildegard (1925–2002)
Knight, Gladys (1944—)
Knight, June (1913–1987)
Knight, Laura (1877–1970)
Knight, Margaret (1838–1914)
Knight, Shirley (1936—)
Knighton, Margaret (1955—)
Knipper-Chekova, Olga (1870–1959)
Knol, Monique (1964—)
Knoll, Florence Schust (1917—)
Knopf, Blanche (1894–1966)
Knopf, Eleanora Bliss (1883–1974)
Knowles, Beyoncé (1981—)
Knowlton, Helen Mary (1832–1918)
Knox, Debbie (1968—)
Knox, Elizabeth (1899–1963)
Knox, Elyse (1917—)
Knox, Isa (1831–1903)
Knox, Rose Markward (1857–1950)
Knudsen, Monica (1975—)
Knudsen, Peggy (1923–1980)
Knuth, Maria (d. 1954)
Knutson, Coya Gjesdal (1912–1996)
Knyazeva, Olga (1954—)
Koban, Rita (1965—)
Kobart, Ruth (1924–2002)
Kobayashi, Yoshimi (c. 1968—)
Kober, Alice Elizabeth (1906–1950)
Kobrynska, Natalia Ivanovna (1855–1920)
Kobylianska, Olha (1863–1942)
Koch, Beate (1967—)
Koch, Ilse (1906–1967)
Koch, Marianne (1930—)
Koch, Marita (1957—)
Koch, Martina (1959—)
Kochergina-Makarets, Tatyana (1956—)
Kochetkova, Dina (1977—)
Kock, Karin (1891–1976)
Kocsis, Erzsebet
Koea, Shonagh (1939—)
Koeck, Brigitte
Koefoed, Charlotte (1957—)
Koehler, Christa (1951—)
Koehler, Gisela (1931—)
Koehler, Kathe (1913—)
Koenig, Rita
Koepke-Knetsch, Christiane (1956—)
Koeppen, Kerstin (1967—)
Koering, Dorothea (1880–1945)
Koesun, Ruth Ann (1928—)
Kogan, Claude (1919–1959)
Kogawa, Joy (1935—)
Ko Gi-Hyun (1986—)
Kohde-Kilsch, Claudia (1963—)
Kohl, Hannelore (1933–2001)
Köhler-Richter, Emmy (1918—)
Kohner, Kathy (1941—)
Kohner, Susan (1936—)
Kohut, Rebekah (1864–1951)
Kojevnikova, Elizaveta
Kojima, Yukiyo (1945—)
Kok, Ada (1947—)
Kokeny, Beatrix
Kokoro-Barrett, Hiria (1870–1943)
Kola, Pamela
Kolar-Merdan, Jasna (1956—)
Kolb, Annette (1870–1967)
Kolb, Barbara (1939—)
Kolb, Claudia (1949—)
Kolb, Thérèse (1856–1935)
Kolesnikova, Anastasia (1984—)
Kolesnikova, Vera (1968—)
Koleva, Elizabeth (1972—)
Koleva, Maria
Kolkova, Olga (1955—)
Kolling, Janne (1968—)
Kollontai, Alexandra (1872–1952)
Kollwitz, Käthe (1867–1945)
Kolmar, Gertrud (1894–1943)
Kolokoltseva, Berta (1937—)
Kolpakova, Irina (1933—)
Kolpakova, Tatyana (1959—)
Kolstad, Eva (1918–1998)
Koltunova, Julia (1989—)
Komarova, Stanislava (1986—)
Komarova, Varvara (1862–1942)
Komarovsky, Mirra (1906–1999)
Komen, Susan G. (1944–1980)
Komisarz, Rachel (1976—)
Komisova, Vera (1953—)
Komissarzhevskaya, Vera (1864–1910)
Komnenovic, Jelica (1960—)
Kondakova, Yelena (c. 1955—)
Kondo, Masako (1941—)
Kondrashina, Anna (1955—)
Kondratieva, Marina (1934—)
Kondratyeva, Lyudmila (1958—)
Koner, Pauline (1912–2001)
Konetzni, Anny (1902–1968)
Konetzni, Hilde (1905–1980)
Konga, Pauline (c. 1971—)
Konie, Gwendoline (1938—)
König, Alma Johanna (1887–c. 1942)
Königsdorf, Helga (1938—)
Konihowski, Diane Jones (1951—)
Kono, Taeko (1926—)
Konopacka, Halina (1900–1989)
Konopnicka, Maria (1842–1910)
Konoukh, Sofia (1980—)
Konrads, Ilsa (1944—)
Konstam, Phyllis (1907–1976)
Konyayeva, Nadezhda (1931—)
Konzett, Ursula (1959—)
Koolen, Nicole (1972—)
Koontz, Elizabeth (1919–1989)
Kopsky, Doris
Koptagel, Yuksel (1931—)
Korbut, Olga (1955—)
Korchinska, Maria (1895–1979)
Kordaczukowna, Danuta (1939–1988)
Koren, Katja (1975—)
Korhola, Eija-Riitta Anneli (1959—)
Korholz, Laurel (1970—)
Korjus, Miliza (1900–1980)
Korn, Alison (1970—)
Kornman, Mary (1915–1973)
Korolchik, Yanina (1976—)
Koroleva, Maria (1974—)
Korolewicz-Waydowa, Janina (1875–1955)
Korshunova, Tatyana (1956—)
Korsmo, Lisbeth (1948—)
Korstin, Ilona (1980—)
Korty, Sonia (1892–1955)
Korukovets, Alexandra (1976—)
Korytova, Svetlana (1968—)
Koscianska, Czeslawa (1959—)
Koscina, Sylva (1933–1994)
Koseki, Shiori (c. 1972—)
Kosenkova, Klavdiya (1949—)
Koshel, Antonina (1954—)
Koshevaya, Marina (1960—)
Kosmodemyanskaya, Zoya (1923–1941)
Kossak, Zofia (1890–1968)
Kossamak (1904–1975)
Kosta, Tessa (1893–1981)
Kostadinova, Stefka (1965—)
Kostelic, Janica (1982—)
Koster, Barbel (1957—)
Kostevych, Olena (1985—)
Kostina, Oksana (1972–1993)
Köstler, Marie (1879–1965)
Kostner, Isolde (1975—)
Kostrzewa, Ute (1961—)
Kosuge, Mari (1975—)
Koszutska, Maria (1876–1939)
Kotani, Mikako (1966—)
Köth, Erika (1925–1989)
Kotlyarova, Olga (1976—)
Kotopoúli, Maríka (1887–1954)
Kotova, Tatyana (1976—)
Kotowna-Walowa, Natalia (1938—)
Koujela, Olga (1985—)
Koukleva, Galina (1972—)
Kournikova, Anna (1981—)
Koutouzova, Natalia (1975—)
Kouza, Loujaya M.
Kouzina, Svetlana (1975—)
Kovach, Nora (1931—)
Kovacs, Agnes (1981—)
Kovacs, Edit (1954—)
Kovacs, Katalin (1976—)
Kovacsne-Nyari, Magdolna (1921—)
Kovalova, Marie (1927—)
Kovalskaia, Elizaveta (1851–1943)
Kovalyova, Anna (1983—)
Kovpan, Valentina (1950—)
Kowal, Kristy (1978—)
Kowalski, Kerstin (1976—)
Kowalski, Manja (1976—)
Kown Soo-Hyun
Kozakova, Olga (1951—)
Kozlova, Anna (1972—)
Koznick, Kristina (1975—)
Kozompoli, Stavroula (1974—)
Kozyr, Valentina (1950—)
Kozyreva, Lyubov (1956—)
Krachevskaya-Dolzhenko, Svetlana (1944—)
Kraft, Karen (1969—)
Krainik, Ardis (1929–1997)
Krajcirova, Maria (1948—)
Kraker, Steffi (1960—)
Kralickova, Jarmila (1944—)
Krall, Diana (1964—)
Krall, Hanna (1937—)
Kramer, Leonie (1924—)
Krandievskaya, Anastasiia (1865–1938)
Krandievskaya, Natalia (1888–1963)
Krandievskaya, Natalia (1923—)
Krantz, Judith (1928—)
Krasner, Lee (1908–1984)
Krasnikova, Natella (1953—)
Krasnohorska, Eliska (1847–1926)
Krasnomovets, Olesya (1979—)
Krasnova, Vera (1950—)
Krasovska, Olena (1976—)
Krasovskaya, Vera (d. 1999)
Krassovska, Nathalie (1918–2005)
Kratochvilova, Jarmila (1951—)
Kratsa-Tsagaropoulou, Rodi (1953—)
Kraus, Alanna (1977—)
Kraus, Angelika (1950—)
Kraus, Greta (1907–1998)
Kraus, Lili (1903–1986)
Kraus-Boelté, Maria (1836–1918)
Krause, Barbara (1959—)
Krause, Christiane (1950—)
Krause, Roswitha (1949—)
Krause, Sigrun
Kraushaar, Silke (1970—)
Krauss, Alison (1971—)
Krauss, Gertrud (1903–1977)
Krauss, Kathe (1906–1970)
Kravets, Inessa (1966—)
Kraynova, Tatyana (1967—)
Krebs, Nathalie (1895–1978)
Krebs-Brenning, Marie (1851–1900)
Krehl, Constanze Angela (1956—)
Kreiner, Kathy (1954—)
Kremer, Mitzi (1968—)
Kremnitz, Marie (1852–1916)
Krenwinkel, Patricia (1947—)
Krepkina, Vera (1933—)
Kreps, Juanita (1921—)
Krestovskaya, Maria V. (1862–1910)
Kretschman, Kelly (1979—)
Kretzschmar, Waltraud (1948—)
Krieger, Victorina (b. 1896)
Kriel, Marianne
Krim, Mathilde (1926—)
Kringen, Goril (1972—)
Kripalani, Sucheta (1908–1974)
Kristeva, Julia (1941—)
Kristiansen, Ingrid (1956—)
Kristolova, Anka (1955—)
Krivelyova, Svetlana (1969—)
Krivochei, Elena
Krivosheyeva, Olga (1961—)
Krizova, Jirina (1948—)
Kroc, Joan (1928–2003)
Kroeber, Theodora (1897–1979)

Kroeger, Alice (1864–1909)
Krog, Gina (1847–1916)
Krokhina, Lyudmila (1954—)
Kronauer, Brigitte (1940—)
Kronberger, Lily
Kronberger, Petra (1969—)
Krone, Julie (1963—)
Kroniger, Annegret (1952—)
Kronold, Selma (1861–1920)
Krueger, Katrin (1959—)
Krueger, Luise (1915—)
Krug, Barbara (1956—)
Kruger, Alma (1868–1960)
Kruger, Barbara (1945—)
Kruglova, Larisa (1972—)
Kruglova, Yelena (1962—)
Krull, Germaine (1897–1985)
Krupowa, Krystyna (1939—)
Krupp, Bertha (1886–1957)
Krupskaya, Nadezhda (1869–1939)
Krusceniski, Salomea (1873–1952)
Kruse, Pamela (1950—)
Krusenstjerna, Agnes von (1894–1940)
Krutova, Ninel (1926—)
Krutzler, Eszter (1981—)
Kryczka, Kelly (1961—)
Krylova, Anjelika (1973—)
Krylova, Lidiya (1951—)
Kryszak, Mary Olszewski (1875–1945)
Kryuchkova, Maria (1988—)
Kryzhanovskaia, Vera Ivanovna (1861–1924)
Krzesinska, Elzbieta (1934—)
Kshesinskaia, Matilda (1872–1971)
Ksiazkiewicz, Malgorzata (1967—)
Kubickova-Posnerova, Jana (1945—)
Kübler-Ross, Elisabeth (1926–2004)
Kuchinskaya, Natalia (1949—)
Kuckhoff, Greta (1902–1981)
Kuczinski, Ruth (1907–2000)
Kuderikova, Marie (1921–1943)
Kudreva, Natalya (1942—)
Kuehn, Anke (1981—)
Kuehne, Kelli (1977—)
Kuehne, Rita (1947—)
Kuehnemund, Jan (1961—)
Kuehn-Lohs, Gabriele (1957—)
Kuenzel, Claudia (1978—)
Kueper, Ursula (1937—)
Kugler, Anna Sarah (1856–1930)
Kuhlman, Kathryn (1907–1976)
Kuhn, Irene Corbally (1898–1995)
Kuhn, Maggie (1905–1995)
Kuhnt, Irina (1968—)
Kuipers, Ellen
Kui Yuanyuan (1981—)
Kukuck, Felicitas (1914–2001)
Kulakova, Galina (1942—)
Kulcsar, Anita (1976—)
Kulcsar, Ilse (1902–1973)
Kulesza, Kasia (1976—)
Kulikowski, Theresa (1980—)
Kuliscioff, Anna (c. 1854–1925)
Kulp, Nancy (1921–1991)
Kumaratunga, Chandrika Bandaranaike (1945—)
Kumbernuss, Astrid (1970—)
Kumin, Maxine (1925—)
Kummer, Clare (1873–1958)
Kumysh, Marina (1964—)
Kuncewicz, Maria (1899–1989)
Kunin, Madeleine (1933—)
Kunisch, Kornelia (1959—)
Kunke, Steffi (1908–1942)
Kuntz, Florence (1969—)
Kuo Yi-Hang (1975—)
Kuper, Hilda B. (1911–1992)
Kupets, Courtney (1986—)
Kupfernagel, Hanka (1964—)
Küppers, Anneliese (1929—)
Kuragina, Olga (1959—)
Kurahashi, Yumiko (1935—)
Kurbakova, Tatiana (1986—)
Kurbatova-Gruycheva, Stoyanka (1955—)
Kurgapkina, Ninel (1929—)
Kurishima, Sumiko (1902–1987)
Kurkova, Katerina (1983—)
Kuroda, Chika (1884–1968)
Kuroyanagi, Tetsuko (1933—)
Kursinski, Anne (1959—)
Kurth, Andrea (1957—)
Kurtz, Carmen (1911–1999)
Kurvyakova, Raisa (1945—)
Kurys, Diane (1948—)
Kurys, Sophie (1925—)
Kuryshko-Nagirnaya, Yekatarina (1949—)
Kurz, Isolde (1853–1944)
Kurz, Selma (1874–1933)
Kusakabe, Kie
Kuscsik, Nina (c. 1940—)
Kushida Fuki (1899–2001)
Kushner, Natalya (1954—)
Kusner, Kathy (1940—)
Kutkaite, Dalia (1965—)
Kuzenkova, Olga (1970—)
Kuznetsova, Evgenia (1980—)
Kuznetsova, Maria (1880–1966)
Kuznetsova, Svetlana (1985—)
Kuzwayo, Ellen (1914–2006)
Kvapilova, Hana (1860–1907)
Kvesic, Kornelija (1964—)
Kvitland, Bente (1974—)
Kvrivichvili, Khatuna (1974—)
Kwadzniewska, Maria (1913—)
Kwag Hye-Jeong (1975—)
Kwan, Michelle (1980—)
Kwan, Nancy (1939—)
Kwast, Frieda Hodapp (1880–1949)
Kwon Chang Sook
Kyasht, Lydia (1885–1959)
Kyburz, Rosemary (1944—)
Kye Sun-Hui (1979—)
Kyo, Machiko (1924—)
Kyrk, Hazel (1886–1957)
Kyselicova, Alena (1957—)
Laage, Barbara (1920–1988)
La Badie, Florence (1888–1917)
Labakova, Jana (1966—)
La Barbara, Joan (1947—)
Labbé, Denise (1926—)
LaBelle, Patti (1944—)
La Belle Marie (c. 1882–1935)
Laborde Duanes, Yurisel (1979—)
Labotsibeni Gwamile laMdluli (c. 1858–1925)
Labrada Diaz, Yanelis Yuliet (1981—)
Laby, Jean (1915—)
Lacey, Janet (1903–1988)
Lacey, Venus (1967—)
Lachmann, Karen (1916–1962)
Lacis, Asja (1891–1979)
Lackie, Ethel (1907–1979)
Lacore, Suzanne (1875–1975)
Lacoste, Catherine (1945—)
Lacrosil, Michèle (1915—)
Lacuesta, Natalie (1981—)
Ladd, Anna Coleman (1878–1939)
Ladd, Diane (1932—)
Ladd, Kate Macy (1863–1945)
Ladde, Cornelia (1915—)
Ladd-Franklin, Christine (1847–1930)
Ladewig, Marion (1914—)
LaDuke, Winona (1959—)
Ladynina, Marina (1908–2003)
Laemmle, Carla (b. 1909)
Laerkesen, Anna (1942—)
Laffitte, María (1902–1986)
La Flesche, Susan (1865–1915)
La Flesche, Susette (1854–1902)
La Follette, Belle Case (1859–1931)
La Follette, Fola (1882–1970)
Lafon, Madeleine (1924–1967)
Lafont, Bernadette (1938—)
Laforet, Carmen (1921–2004)
Lagerberg, Catherina (1941—)
Lagerlöf, Selma (1858–1940)
Lagorio, Gina (1930—)
La Grange, Anna de (1825–1905)
Laguiller, Arlette (1940—)
Lahodova, Jana (1957—)
Laidlaw, Harriet Burton (1873–1949)
Laine, Cleo (1927—)
Laine, Doris (1959—)
Laing, Eleanor (1958—)
Laing, Elizabeth (1959—)
Laird, Carobeth (1895–1983)
Lait, Jacqui (1947—)
Lai Yawen (1970—)
Lake, Alice (1895–1967)
Lake, Florence (1904–1980)
Lake, Veronica (1919–1973)
Lakey, Alice (1857–1935)
Lakic, Mara (1963—)
Lakine-Toth Harsanyi, Katalin (1948—)
Lakwena, Alice (1960—)
Lalive, Caroline (1979—)
Lalumiere, Catherine (1935—)
La Lupe (1939–1992)
Lamarca, Tania (1980—)
Lamarque, Libertad (1908–2000)
La Marr, Barbara (c. 1896–1926)
Lamarr, Hedy (1913–2000)
Lamas, Maria (1893–1983)
Lambert, Adelaide (1907–1996)
Lambert, Betty (1933–1983)
Lambert, Jean (1950—)
Lambert, Margaret Bergmann (1914—)
Lambert, Nathalie (1963—)
Lambine, Janna (c. 1951—)
Lambrino, Jeanne (1898–1953)
Lamburn, Richmal Crompton (1890–1969)
La Meri (1899–1988)
Lamon, Sophie (1985—)
Lamont, Johann (1957—)
La Montagne-Beauregard, Blanche (1899–1960)
Lamour, Dorothy (1914–1996)
Lampert, Rachel (1948—)
Lampert, Zohra (1937—)
Lampkin, Daisy (1883–1965)
Lamy, Jennifer (1949—)
Lancaster, Nancy (1897–1994)
Lancefield, Rebecca Craighill (1895–1981)
Lanchester, Elsa (1902–1986)
Lancien, Nathalie (1970—)
Landau, Klavdia Gustavovna (1922–1990)
Landells, Suzanne (1964—)
Lander, Louisa (1826–1923)
Lander, Margot (1910–1961)
Lander, Toni (1931–1985)
Landes, Bertha Knight (1868–1943)
Landes, Ruth (1908–1991)
Landeta, Matilde (1910–1999)
Landgraf, Sigrid (1959—)
Landi, Elissa (1904–1948)
Landin, Hope (1893–1973)
Landis, Carole (1919–1948)
Landis, Jessie Royce (1904–1972)
Landon, Margaret (1903–1993)
Landowska, Wanda (1877–1959)
Landry, Jackie (1940–1997)
Lane, Elizabeth (1905–1988)
Lane, Gertrude B. (1874–1941)
Lane, Grace (1876–1956)
Lane, Harriet (1830–1903)
Lane, Lola (1909–1981)
Lane, Maryon (1931—)
Lane, Pinkie Gordon (1925—)
Lane, Priscilla (1917–1995)
Lane, Rosemary (1914–1974)
Lane, Rose Wilder (1886–1968)
Laney, Lucy Craft (1854–1933)
Lang, June (1915—)
Lang, K.D. (1961—)
Lang, Leonora (1851–1933)
Lang, Margaret Ruthven (1867–1972)
Lang, Maria (1948—)
Lang, Marie (1858–1934)
Lang, Raven (1942—)
Lang-Beck, Ivana (1912–1983)
Langbein, Martha (1941—)
Lange, Dorothea (1895–1965)
Lange, Helene (1848–1930)
Lange, Hope (1931–2003)
Lange, Jessica (1949—)
Lange, Marita (1943—)
Lange, Norah (1906–1972)
Langenhagen, Brigitte (1939—)
Langer, Lucyna (1956—)
Langer, Susanne Knauth (1895–1985)
Langford, Bonnie (1964—)
Langford, Frances (1914–2005)

Langgässer, Elisabeth (1899–1950)
Langley, Eve (1908–1974)
Langley, Katherine (1888–1948)
Langley, Neva (c. 1934—)
Langner, Ilse (1899–1987)
Lang Ping (1960—)
Langtry, Lillie (1853–1929)
Lannaman, Sonia M. (1956—)
Lanner, Katti (1829–1908)
Lannoy, Micheline
Lanphier, Fay (1906–1959)
Lansbury, Angela (1925—)
Lansing, Joi (1928–1972)
Lansing, Sherry (1944—)
Lantratov, Vera (1947—)
Lanvin, Jeanne (1867–1946)
Lao Lishi (1987—)
La Palme, Béatrice (1878–1921)
Lapauze, Jeanne (1860–1920)
Lapid, Shulamit (1934—)
Lapitskaya, Natalya (1962—)
LaPlanche, Rosemary (1923–1979)
La Plante, Laura (1904–1996)
La Plante, Lynda (1946—)
Lapp, Bernice (1917—)
Lappo-Danilevskaia, N.A. (c. 1875–1951)
Lara, Georgia (1980—)
Laredo, Ruth (1937–2005)
Larkin, Delia (1878–1949)
La Rochefoucauld, Edmée, Duchesse de (1895–1991)
La Roe, Else K. (1900–1970)
La Roy, Rita (1907–1993)
Larrieu, Francie (1952—)
Larrimore, Francine (1898–1975)
Larrocha, Alicia de (1923—)
Lars, Claudia (1899–1974)
Larsen, Christine (1967—)
Larsen, Gerd (1920–2001)
Larsen, Nella (1891–1964)
Larsen, Tonje (1975—)
Larson, Nicolette (1952–1997)
Larson-Mason, Christine (1956—)
LaRue, Florence (1944—)
La Rue, Grace (1880–1956)
Lascelles, Ernita (1890–1972)
Lascelles, Patricia (1926—)
Laschenova, Natalia (1973—)
Laser, Christine (1951—)
Lashko, Irina (1973—)
Lask, Berta (1878–1967)
Laskaridou, Aikaterini (1842–1916)
Lasker, Mary (1900–1994)
Lasker-Schüler, Else (1869–1945)
Laski, Marghanita (1915–1988)
Laskine, Lily (1893–1988)
Lasovskaya, Inna (1969—)
Lasser, Louise (1939—)
Lassig, Rosemary (1941—)
La Sylphe (c. 1900—)
Latamblet Daudinot, Norka (1962—)
Lathan-Brehmer, Christina (1958—)
Lathbury, Kathleen Culhane (1900–1993)
Lathrop, Julia Clifford (1858–1932)
Lathrop, Rose Hawthorne (1851–1926)
Latif, Badri (1977—)
Latimer, Elizabeth W. (1822–1904)
Latimer, Sally (1910—)
Latta, Victoria (1951—)
Latynina, Larissa (1934—)
Latzsch, Heike (1973—)
Lau, Jutta (1955—)
Lauber, Cécile (1887–1981)
Lauder, Estée (1908–2004)
Lauer, Bonnie (1951—)
Lauer, Hilde (1943—)
Laughlin, Clara E. (1873–1941)
Laughlin, Gail (1868–1952)
Laumann, Daniele (1961—)
Laumann, Silken (1964—)
Lauper, Cyndi (1953—)
Laurel, Kay (1890–1927)
Laurence, Margaret (1926–1987)
Laurencin, Marie (1883–1956)
Laurie, Piper (1932—)
Laurien, Hanna-Renate (1928—)
Laurier, Zoé (1841–1921)
Laurijsen, Martha (1954—)
Lauristin, Marju (1940—)
Lauritsen, Susanne (1967—)
Laval, Josée (c. 1906—1990)
Lavallière, Eve (c. 1866–1929)
Lavant, Christine (1915–1973)
Lavarch, Linda (1958—)
Lavater-Sloman, Mary (1891–1980)
Lavell, Carol (1943—)
Lavenson, Alma (1897–1989)
Laverick, Elise (1975—)
Laverick, Elizabeth (1925—)
La Verne, Lucille (1869–1945)
Laverty, Maura (1907–1966)
Lavi, Daliah (1940—)
Lavin, Mary (1912–1996)
LaVine, Jacqueline (1929—)
LaVoe, Spivy (1906–1971)
Lavric, Florica (1962—)
Lavrinenko, Natalya
Lavrova, Natalia (1984—)
Lavrsen, Helena (c. 1963—)
Law, Alice Easton (1870–1942)
Law, Kelley (1966—)
Law, Leslie (1965—)
Law, Mary Blythe (1873–1955)
Law, Ruth (1887–1970)
Lawanson, Ruth (1963—)
Lawford, Patricia Kennedy (1924—)
Lawless, Emily (1845–1913)
Lawlor, Patsy (1933–1998)
Lawrance, Jody (1930–1986)
Lawrence, Andrea Mead (1932—)
Lawrence, Carmen Mary (1948—)
Lawrence, Carol (1932—)
Lawrence, Chiara (1975—)
Lawrence, Daisy Gordon (c. 1900—)
Lawrence, Eleanor (1936–2001)
Lawrence, Elizabeth (1904–1985)
Lawrence, Florence (1886–1938)
Lawrence, Frieda (1879–1956)
Lawrence, Gertrude (1898–1952)
Lawrence, Jackie (1948—)
Lawrence, Janice (1962—)
Lawrence, Margaret (1889–1929)
Lawrence, Marjorie (1908–1979)
Lawrence, Mary Wells (1928—)
Lawrence, Pauline (1900–1971)
Lawrence, Susan (1871–1947)
Lawrence, Tayna (1975—)
Lawrence, Viola (1894–1973)
Lawrenson, Helen (1907–1982)
Lawrie, Jean Grant (1914—)
Laws, Annie (1855–1927)
Lawson, Joan (1907–2002)
Lawson, Louisa (1848–1920)
Lawson, Mary (1910–1941)
Lawson, Priscilla (1914–1958)
Lawson, Roberta Campbell (1878–1940)
Lawson, Winifred (1892–1961)
Lawyer, April (1975—)
Lay, Marion (1948—)
Laybourne, Geraldine (1947—)
Laybourne, Roxie (1910–2003)
Laye, Evelyn (1900–1996)
Lazakovich, Tamara (1954—)
Lazar, Elisabeta (1950—)
Lazarová, Katarina (1914—)
Lazuk, Maria (1983—)
Lazutina, Larissa (1965—)
Lazzari, Carolina (c. 1889–1946)
Leach, Abby (1855–1918)
Leachman, Cloris (1926—)
Leacock, Eleanor Burke (1922–1987)
Leahy, Mary Gonzaga (1870–1958)
Leakey, Mary Nicol (1913–1996)
Leander, Zarah (1907–1981)
Lear, Evelyn (1926—)
Lear, Frances (1923–1996)
Lease, Mary Elizabeth (1853–1933)
Leatherwood, Lillie (1964—)
Leaver, Henrietta (c. 1916–1993)
Leavis, Q.D. (1906–1981)
Leavitt, Henrietta Swan (1868–1921)
Leavitt, Mary (1830–1912)
Le Beau, Luise Adolpha (1850–1927)
Lebedeva, Natalya (1949—)
Lebedeva, Sarra (1892–1967)
Lebedeva, Tatyana (1976—)
Leblanc, Georgette (c. 1875–1941)
Le Blond, Elizabeth (1861–1934)
Lebour, Marie (1877–1971)
Lebron, Lolita (1919—)
Lebrun, Céline (1976—)
Lecheva, Vesela (1964—)
Lechner, Erica
Leclerc, Annie (1940—)
Leclerc, Ginette (1912–1992)
Le Clercq, Tanaquil (1929–2000)
Lederer, Gretchen (1891–1955)
Ledermann, Alexandra (1969—)
Ledovskaya, Tatyana (1966—)
Leduc, Violette (1907–1972)
Ledwigowa, Jozefa (1935—)
Lee, Alma (1912–1990)
Lee, Anna (1913–2004)
Lee, Auriol (1880–1941)
Lee, Barbara (1946—)
Lee, Barbara (1947–1992)
Lee, Belinda (1935–1961)
Lee, Beverly (1941—)
Lee, Brenda (1944—)
Lee, Dixie (1911–1952)
Lee, Gina (1943–2002)
Lee, Gwen (1904–1961)
Lee, Gypsy Rose (1914–1970)
Lee, Harper (1926—)
Lee, Ida (1865–1943)
Lee, Jane (c. 1912–1957)
Lee, Jennie (1848–1925)
Lee, Jennie (1904–1988)
Lee, Jennie (c. 1846–1930)
Lee, Lila (1901–1973)
Lee, Mary (1821–1909)
Lee, Mary Custis (1835–1918)
Lee, Mary Isabella (1871–1939)
Lee, Mildred Childe (1846–1905)
Lee, Muna (1895–1965)
Lee, Peggy (1920–2002)
Lee, Rose Hum (1904–1964)
Lee, Ruth (1895–1975)
Lee, Sondra (1930—)
Lee, Susan (1966—)
Lee, Tanith (1947—)
Lee, Virginia (1965—)
Lee Bo-Na (1981—)
Leech, Faith (1941—)
Leech, Margaret (1893–1974)
Leeds, Andrea (1913–1984)
Lee Eun-Kyung (1972—)
Lee Eun Kyung
Lee Eun-Sil (1976—)
Lee Eun-Young
Lee-Gartner, Kerrin (1966—)
Lee Gong-Joo (1980—)
Lee Ho-Youn (1971—)
Lee Hyung-Sook (1964—)
Lee Ji-Young
Lee Ki-Soon (1966—)
Lee Kyung-Won (1980—)
Lee Lai-shan (1970—)
Lee Long, Rosa
Lee Mi-Ja (1963—)
Leeming, Marjorie (1903–1987)
Lee Mi-Young (1969—)
Lees, Sue (1941–2003)
Lee Sang-Eun (1975—)
Lee Smith, Jenny (1948—)
Lee Soon-Bok (1950—)
Lee Soon-Ei (1965—)
Lee Soo-Nok (1955—)
Lee Sung-Jin (1985—)
Lee Sun-Hee
Leete, Harriet L. (c. 1875–1927)
Lee Young-Ja (1964—)
Lefanu, Nicola (1947—)
Lefaucheux, Marie-Helene (1904–1964)
Lefebvre, Janou (1945—)
Le Fort, Gertrud von (1876–1971)
Le Gallienne, Eva (1899–1991)
Leganger, Cecilie (1975—)
Le Garrec, Evelyne

Legat, Nadine (c. 1895–?)
Legh, Alice (1855–1948)
Leginska, Ethel (1886–1970)
Legnani, Pierina (1863–1923)
LeGon, Jeni (1916—)
Legrand, Lise (1976—)
Le Guin, Ursula K. (1929—)
Lehane, Jan (1941—)
Lehmann, Beatrix (1903–1979)
Lehmann, Christa (1922—)
Lehmann, Heike (1962—)
Lehmann, Helma (1953—)
Lehmann, Inge (1888–1993)
Lehmann, Lilli (1848–1929)
Lehmann, Lotte (1888–1976)
Lehmann, Rosamond (1901–1990)
Lehmann, Sonja (1979—)
Lehn, Unni (1977—)
Lehr, Anna (1890–1974)
Lehtonen, Mirja (1942—)
Leibovitz, Annie (1949—)
Leichter, Käthe (1895–1942)
Leider, Frida (1888–1975)
Leigh, Adèle (1928–2004)
Leigh, Carolyn (1926–1983)
Leigh, Frances Butler (1838–1910)
Leigh, Janet (1927–2004)
Leigh, Vivien (1913–1967)
Leighton, Clare (1899–1989)
Leighton, Dorothea (1908–1989)
Leighton, Margaret (1922–1976)
Lei Li
Leistenschneider, Nicole (1967—)
Leitch, Cecil (1891–1977)
Leitzel, Lillian (1892–1931)
Lejeune, C.A. (1897–1973)
Lejeune, Elisabeth (1963—)
Le Jingyi (1975—)
Leland, Sara (1941—)
Lelas, Zana (1970—)
Lelkesne-Tomann, Rozalia (1950—)
Le Mair, H. Willebeek (1889–1966)
Lemass, Eileen (1932—)
Le May Doan, Catriona (1970—)
Lemel, Nathalie (1827–1921)
Lemhenyine-Tass, Olga (1929—)
Lemlich, Clara (1888–1982)
Lemmon, Sarah Plummer (1836–1923)
Lemnitz, Tiana (1897–1994)
Lemoine-Luccioni, Eugénie (1912—)
Lemon, Margaretta Louisa (1860–1953)
Lempereur, Ingrid (1969—)
Lempicka, Tamara de (1898–1980)
Lemsine, Aicha (1942—)
Lenczyk, Grace (1927—)
Lender, Marcelle (fl. 1890–1914)
Lendorff, Gertrud (1900–1986)
Leng, Virginia (1955—)
L'Engle, Madeleine (1918—)
Lenglen, Suzanne (1899–1938)
Lenihan, Winifred (1898–1964)
Lennart, Isobel (1915–1971)
Lennox, Annie (1954—)
Lennox, Avril (1956—)
LeNoire, Rosetta (1911–2002)
Lenski, Lois (1893–1974)
Lenton, Lisbeth (1985—)
Lenya, Lotte (1898–1981)
Lenz, Consetta (1918–1980)
Léo, André (1832–1900)
Léon, Léonie (1838–1906)
León, Maria Teresa (1903–1988)
Leonard, Carol L. (1950—)
Leonard, Marion (1881–1956)
Leonardi Cortesi, Natascia (1971—)
Leonardos, Stela (1923—)
Leone, Giuseppina (1934—)
Leonhardt, Carolin (1984—)
Leonida (b. 1914)
Leonida, Florica (1987—)
Leonova, Aleksandra (1964—)
Leonowens, Anna (c. 1831–1914)
Leontias, Sappho (1832–1900)
Leontovich, Eugénie (1894–1993)
Leontyeva, Galina (1941—)
Lepadatu, Viorica (1971—)
Lepennec, Emilie (1987—)
Lepeshinskaya, Olga (1916—)
LePoole, Alexandra (1959—)
Leporska, Zoya (1918–1996)
Lermontova, Julia (1846–1919)
Lermontova, Nadezhda Vladimirovna (1885–1921)
Lerner, Gerda (1920—)
Lerwill, Sheila (1928—)
LeShan, Eda J. (1922–2002)
Lesik, Vera (1910–1975)
Leskova, Tatiana (1922—)
Leslie, Amy (1855–1939)
Leslie, Annie (1869–1948)
Leslie, Bethel (1929–1999)
Leslie, Gladys (1899–1976)
Leslie, Joan (1925—)
Leslie, Lisa (1972—)
Leslie, May Sybil (1887–1937)
Leslie, Miriam Folline Squier (1836–1914)
Lesovaya, Tatyana (1956—)
L'Esperance, Elise Strang (c. 1879–1959)
Lesser, Patricia (1933—)
Lessing, Doris (1919—)
Lessore, Thérèse (1884–1945)
Lester, Joyce (1958—)
LeSueur, Emily Porter (1972—)
Le Sueur, Frances (1919–1995)
Le Sueur, Meridel (1900–1996)
Letham, Isobel (1899–1995)
Letourneau, Fanny (1979—)
Leu, Evelyne (1976—)
Leusteanu, Elena (1935—)
Leverson, Ada (1862–1933)
Leverton, Irene (1924—)
Levertov, Denise (1923–1997)
Levey, Ethel (1880–1955)
Levi, Natalia (1901–1972)
Levien, Sonya (1888–1960)
Levi-Montalcini, Rita (b. 1909)
Levina, Ioulia (1973—)
Levine, Lena (1903–1965)
Levinson, Luisa Mercedes (1909–1988)
Levinson, Tamara (1976—)
Leviska, Helvi Lemmiki (1902–1982)
Levison, Mary (1923—)
Levitt, Helen (1913—)
Levy, Chandra (1977–2001)
Levy, Florence Nightingale (1870–1947)
Levy, Jerre (1938—)
Levy, Julia (1934—)
Lew, Bird (c. 1966—)
Lewin, Jeannette
Lewis, Abby (1910–1997)
Lewis, Agnes Smith (1843–1926)
Lewis, Bertha (1887–1931)
Lewis, Bobo (1926–1998)
Lewis, Cathy (1916–1968)
Lewis, Charlotte (1955—)
Lewis, Denise (1972—)
Lewis, Edmonia (c. 1845–c. 1909)
Lewis, Edna (1916–2006)
Lewis, Elma (1921–2004)
Lewis, Ethelreda (1875–1946)
Lewis, Flora (1922–2002)
Lewis, Graceanna (1821–1912)
Lewis, Hayley (1974—)
Lewis, Ida (1842–1911)
Lewis, Loida (c. 1943—)
Lewis, Margaret Reed (1881–1970)
Lewis, Shari (1933–1998)
Lewis, Vera (1873–1956)
Lewisohn, Alice (1883–1972)
Lewisohn, Irene (1892–1944)
Lewitzky, Bella (1915–2004)
Lewsley, Patricia (1957—)
Leyel, Hilda (1880–1957)
Leyman, Ann-Britt (1922—)
Lhevinne, Rosina (1880–1976)
Li, Florence Tim Oi (1907–1992)
Liang Qin
Liang Yan (1961—)
Libbey, Laura Jean (1862–1925)
Liberáki, Margaríta (1919—)
Li Bun-Hui (1968—)
Lichnowsky, Mechthilde (1879–1958)
Lichtenberg, Jacqueline (1942—)
Li Chunxiu (1969—)
Lid, Hilde Synnove
Liddell, Alice (1852–1934)
Liddell, Helen (1950—)
Lidman, Sara (1923–2004)
Li Dongmei (1969—)
Lidova, Irene (1907–2002)
Lidstone, Dorothy (1938—)
Li Du (1982—)
Li Duihong (1970—)
Lieberman-Cline, Nancy (1958—)
Liebes, Dorothy (1897–1972)
Liebhart, Gertrude (1928—)
Liebling, Estelle (1880–1970)
Liebrecht, Savyon (1948—)
Li Feng-Ying (1975—)
Lightner, A.M. (1904–1988)
Lightner, Candy (1946—)
Lightner, Winnie (1899–1971)
Lignell, Kristen (c. 1965—)
Lignot, Myriam (1975—)
Li Guojun (1966—)
Li Huifen (1963—)
Li Huixin (1937—)
Li Ji (1986—)
Li Ju (1976—)
Likimani, Muthoni (c. 1940—)
Li Lan (1961—)
Liley, Tammy (1965—)
Li Lingjuan (1966—)
Liliuokalani (1838–1917)
Lil' Kim (1975—)
Lillak, Tiina (1961—)
Lillie, Beatrice (1894–1989)
Lilly, Gweneth (1920–2004)
Lilly, Kristine (1971—)
Lima, Ricarda (1979—)
Limbau, Mariana (1977—)
Li Meisu (1959—)
Lim Jeong-Sook
Lim Kye-Sook (1964—)
Lim Mi-Kyung (1967—)
Lim O-Kyung (1971—)
Limpert, Marianne (1972—)
Lin, Hazel (1913–1986)
Lin, Maya (1959—)
Lin, Tai-yi (1926—)
Li Na
Li Na (1984—)
Lincoln, Abbey (1930—)
Lincoln, Mary Johnson (1844–1921)
Lind, Joan (1952—)
Lind, Letty (1862–1923)
Lind, Nathalie (1918–1999)
Lindahl, Margaretha (c. 1971—)
Lindberg, Karin (1929—)
Lindbergh, Anne Morrow (1906–2001)
Lindblom, Gunnel (1931—)
Lindfors, Viveca (1920–1995)
Lindgren, Astrid (1907–2002)
Lindgren, Marie
Lindh, Anna (1957–2003)
Lindh, Hilary (1969—)
Lindley, Audra (1918–1997)
Lindner, Dorte
Lindner, Helga (1951—)
Lindner, Herta (1920–1943)
Lindo, Olga (1899–1968)
Lindsay, Gillian Anne (1973—)
Lindsay, Margaret (1910–1981)
Lindsey, Estelle Lawton (1868–1955)
Lindstrom, Pia (1938—)
Lingens-Reiner, Ella (1908–2002)
Ling Jie (1982—)
Lingle, Linda (1953—)
Lingnau, Corinna (1960—)
Lingor, Renate (1975—)
Ling Shuhua (1904–1990)
Lin Haiyin (1918–2001)
Linichuk, Natalia
Lin Li (1970—)
Linn, Bambi (1926—)
Lin Qiaozhi (1901–1983)
Lin Sang (1977—)
Linse, Cornelia (1959—)
Linsenhoff, Ann-Kathrin (1960—)

Linsenhoff, Liselott (1927—)
Linssen-Vaessen, Marie-Louise (1928–1993)
Lin Weining (1979—)
Lin Yanfen (1971—)
Liosi, Kyriaki (1979—)
Lipa, Elisabeta (1964—)
Lipinski, Tara (1982—)
Lipka, Juliane (c. 1860–c. 1929)
Lipkin, Jean (1926—)
Lipkovskay, Natalia (1979—)
Lipkowska, Lydia (1882–1958)
Lipman, Clara (1869–1952)
Lipman, Maureen (1946—)
Lipperini, Guendalina (c. 1862–1914)
Lippincott, Sara Clarke (1823–1904)
Lipsius, Marie (1837–1927)
Lipson, Edna (1914–1996)
Lipson-Gruzen, Berenice (1925–1998)
Li Qing (1972—)
Li Ronghua (1956—)
Lisboa, Henriquetta (1904–1985)
Lisboa, Irene (1892–1958)
Li Shan (1980—)
Li Shufang (1979—)
Li Shuxian (1924–1997)
Lisi, Virna (1936—)
Liskova, Hana (1952—)
Lisnianskaya, Inna (1928—)
Lisovskaya, Natalya (1962—)
Lispector, Clarice (1920–1977)
Lissaman, Elizabeth Hazel (1901–1991)
Lister, Moira (1923—)
Lister, Sandra (1961—)
Liston, Melba (1926—)
Lita-Vatasoiu, Emilia (1933—)
Litchfield, Jessie (1883–1956)
Li Ting (1980—)
Li Ting (1987—)
Litoshenko, Mariya (1949—)
Litten, Irmgard (1879–1953)
Little, Ann (1891–1984)
Little, Jean (1932—)
Little, Sally (1951—)
Little, Tawny (c. 1957—)
Littledale, Clara (1891–1956)
Littlefield, Caroline (c. 1882–1957)
Littlefield, Catherine (1904–1951)
Littlefield, Dorothie (c. 1908–1953)
Littlefield, Nancy (c. 1929—)
Littlewood, Joan (1914–2002)
Litvinov, Ivy (1889–1977)
Litvyak, Lidiya (1921–1943)
Litz, Katharine (c. 1918–1978)
Liu, Nienling (1934—)
Liu Ailing (1967—)
Liubatovich, Olga (1853–1917)
Liubatovich, Vera (1855–1907)
Liu Chunhong (1985—)
Liu Jun (1969—)
Liu Limin (1976—)
Liu Liping (1958—)
Liu Qing (1964—)
Liu Wei
Liu Xia (1979—)
Liu Xiaoning (1975—)
Liu Xuan (1979—)
Liu Xuqing (1968—)
Liu Yaju
Liu Yanan (1980—)
Liu Ying (1974—)
Liu Yumei (1961—)
Liu Yuxiang (1975—)
Liu Zhen (1930—)
Liuzzo, Viola (1925–1965)
Livbjerg, Signe (1980—)
Lively, Penelope (1933—)
Livermore, Mary A. (1820–1905)
Livesay, Dorothy (1909–1996)
Livingston, Margaret (1896–1984)
Livingston, Nora G.E. (1848–1927)
Livingstone, Marilyn (1952—)
Li Xiaoqin (1961—)
Li Xin (1969—)
Li Yan (1976—)
Li Yanjun (1963—)
Li Yan
Li Yueming (1968—)
Li Yuqin (d. 2001)
Lizars, Kathleen MacFarlane (d. 1931)
Li Zhongyun (1967—)
Li Zhuo (1981—)
Ljungdahl, Carina (1960—)
Llanes, Tara (1976—)
Lloret, Maria Isabel (1971—)
Lloyd, Alice (1873–1949)
Lloyd, Alice (1876–1962)
Lloyd, Andrea (1965—)
Lloyd, Doris (1896–1968)
Lloyd, Dorothy Jordan (1889–1946)
Lloyd, Gweneth (1901–1993)
Lloyd, Marie (1870–1922)
Lloyd, Marilyn Laird (1929—)
Lloyd, Maude (1908–2004)
Lloyd, Rosie (b. 1879)
Lloyd-Davies, Vanessa (1960–2005)
Lloyd George, Frances Stevenson (1888–1972)
Lloyd George, Margaret (1866–1941)
Lloyd George, Megan (1902–1966)
Loaies, Ionela (1979—)
Lobacheva, Irina (1973—)
Lobanova, Natalya (1947—)
Lobatch, Marina (1970—)
Lobazniuk, Ekaterina (1983—)
Lobo, Rebecca (1973—)
Lobova, Nina (1957—)
Lochhead, Liz (1947—)
Lock, Jane (1954—)
Locke, Bessie (1865–1952)
Locke, Elsie (1912–2001)
Locke, Katherine (1910–1995)
Locke, Sumner (1881–1917)
Lockhart, June (1925—)
Lockhart, Kathleen (1894–1978)
Lockrey, Sarah Hunt (1863–1929)
Lockwood, Annea F. (1939—)
Lockwood, Belva Ann (1830–1917)
Lockwood, Margaret (1916–1990)
Loden, Barbara (1932–1980)
Lodhi, Maleeha (c. 1953—)
Loeb, Sophie Irene (1876–1929)
Loebinger, Lotte (1905–1999)
Loewe, Gabriele (1958—)
Loftus, Cissie (1876–1943)
Loftus, Marie (1857–1940)
Logan, Ella (1913–1969)
Logan, Jacqueline (1901–1983)
Logan, Laura R. (1879–1974)
Logan, Mary Cunningham (1838–1923)
Logan, Olive (1839–1909)
Logan, Onnie Lee (c. 1910–1995)
Loghin, Mihaela (1952—)
Logic, Lora (c. 1961—)
Loginova, Lidiya (1951—)
Logounova, Tatiana (1980—)
Logue, Jenny (c. 1982—)
Logvinenko, Marina (1961—)
Lohmar, Leni (1914—)
Löhr, Marie (1890–1975)
Loisinger, Joanna (1865–1951)
Lokelani, Princess Lei (c. 1898–1921)
Lo Keong, Matilda (c. 1854–1915)
Lokhvitskaia, Mirra (1869–1905)
Lollobrigida, Gina (1927—)
Lomba, Marisabel
Lombard, Carole (1908–1942)
Lombardi, Lella (1941–1992)
London, Julie (1926–2000)
Long, Catherine Small (1924—)
Long, Jill Lynette (1952—)
Long, Kathleen (1896–1968)
Long, Marguerite (1874–1966)
Long, Tania (1913–1998)
Longfield, Cynthia (1896–1991)
Longford, Elizabeth (1906–2002)
Longhi, Lucia Lopresti (1895–1985)
Longman, Evelyn Beatrice (1874–1954)
Longman, Irene Maud (1877–1964)
Longo, Jeannie (1958—)
Longshore, Hannah E. (1819–1901)
Longstaff, Mary Jane (c. 1855–1935)
Longworth, Alice Roosevelt (1884–1980)
Lonsbrough, Anita (1941—)
Lonsdale, Kathleen (1903–1971)
Lonzi-Ragno, Antonella (1940—)
Looney, Shelley (1972—)
Loos, Anita (1893–1981)
Loos, Cécile Ines (1883–1959)
Lopes, Katia (1973—)
Lopes, Lisa (1971–2002)
Lopez, Encarnación (1898–1945)
Lopez, Nancy (1957—)
Lopokova, Lydia (c. 1892–1981)
Lopukhova, Evgenia (1884–1941)
Loraine, Violet (1886–1956)
Lorcia, Suzanne (1902–1999)
Lord, Bette Bao (1938—)
Lord, Marjorie (1918—)
Lord, Pauline (1890–1950)
Lorde, Athena (1915–1973)
Lorde, Audre (1934–1992)
Loren, Sophia (1934—)
Lorengar, Pilar (1928—)
Lorentzen, Ingeborg (1957—)
Lorentzen, Ragnhild (1968—)
Lorenz, Ericka (1981—)
Lorimer, Margaret (1866–1954)
Loriod, Yvonne (1924–2001)
Lorne, Marion (1888–1968)
Loroupe, Tegla (1973—)
Lorraine, Emily (c. 1878–1944)
Lorraine, Louise (1901–1981)
Lorrayne, Vyvyan (1939—)
Lortel, Lucille (1902–1999)
Losaberidze, Ketevan (1949—)
Los Angeles, Victoria de (1923–2005)
Losch, Claudia (1960—)
Losch, Tilly (1903–1975)
Lothrop, Alice (1870–1920)
Lothrop, Harriet (1844–1924)
Lotsey, Nancy (c. 1955—)
Lott, Elsie S. (fl. 1940s)
Lotz, Ingrid (1934—)
Loudon, Dorothy (1933–2003)
Loudov, Ivana (1941—)
Loughlin, Anne (1894–1979)
Loughran, Beatrix (1896–1975)
Louise (1848–1939)
Louise, Anita (1915–1970)
Louise, Ruth Harriet (1906–1944)
Louise, Tina (1934—)
Louise Caroline (1875–1906)
Louise Margaret of Prussia (1860–1917)
Louise Mountbatten (1889–1965)
Louise of Baden (1838–1923)
Louise of Belgium (1858–1924)
Louise of Orleans (1882–1952)
Louise of Sweden (1851–1926)
Louw, Anna M. (1913–2003)
Love, Barbara (1941—)
Love, Bessie (1898–1986)
Love, Darlene (1938—)
Love, Mabel (1874–1953)
Love, Nancy (1914–1976)
Love, Ripeka Wharawhara (1882–1953)
Love, Susan (1948—)
Løveid, Cecilie (1951—)
Lovejoy, Esther Pohl (1869–1967)
Lovelace, Linda (1952–2002)
Lovelace, Maud Hart (1892–1980)
Loveless, Lea (1971—)
Loveling, Virginie (1836–1923)
Lovell-Smith, Rata Alice (1894–1969)
Lovely, Louise (1895–1980)
Loveman, Amy (1881–1955)
Loveridge, Emily Lemoine (1860–1941)
Lovin, Fita (1951—)
Low, Bet (1924—)
Low, Caroline Sarah (1876–1934)
Low, Juliette Gordon (1860–1927)
Low, Mary Fairchild (1858–1946)
Lowe, Sara (1984—)
Lowell, Amy (1874–1925)
Lowell, Josephine Shaw (1843–1905)
Lowe-McConnell, Rosemary (1921—)
Löwenstein, Helga Maria zu (1910–2004)
Lowe-Porter, Helen (1876–1963)
Lowey, Nita M. (1937—)
Lowney, Shannon (1969–1994)

Lowry, Edith (1897–1970)
Lowry, Judith (1890–1976)
Lowry, Lois (1937—)
Lowry-Corry, Dorothy (1885–1967)
Lowther, Patricia Louise (1935–1975)
Lowy, Dora (1977—)
Loy, Mina (1882–1966)
Loy, Myrna (1905–1993)
Loy, Rosetta (1931—)
Loynaz, Dulce María (1902–1997)
Luahine, Iolani (1915–1978)
Lualdi, Antonella (1931—)
Luan Jujie (1958—)
Lubetkin, Zivia (1914–1978)
Lubic, Ruth Watson (1927—)
Lu Bin (1977—)
Lubin, Germaine (1890–1979)
Lucas, Caroline (1960—)
Lucas, Joy (1917—)
Luce, Claire (1903–1989)
Luce, Clare Boothe (1903–1987)
Luce, Lila (1899–1999)
Luchaire, Corinne (1921–1950)
Lucia (1908–2001)
Lucia, Sister (1907–2005)
Lucic, Mirjana (1982—)
Lucid, Shannon (1943—)
Luckett, LeToya (1981—)
Luckner, Gertrud (1900–1995)
Lucy, Autherine Juanita (1929—)
Lüders, Marie-Elizabeth (1888–1966)
Ludford, Sarah (1951—)
Ludington, Nancy
Ludwig, Christa (1924—)
Ludwig, Paula (1900–1974)
Luettge, Johanna (1936—)
Luft, Lia (1938—)
Luhan, Mabel Dodge (1879–1962)
Lu Huali (1972—)
Luis, Alejandrina (1967—)
Lukanina, Ninel (1937—)
Luke, Jemima (1813–1906)
Luke, Theresa (1967—)
Lukhmanova, N.A. (1840–1907)
Lukkarinen, Marjut (1966—)
Lukom, Elena (1891–1968)
Lu Li (1976—)
Lulling, Astrid (1929—)
Lulu (1948—)
Lumley, Joanna (1946—)
Luna, Rosa (1937–1993)
Luna Castellano, Diadenis
Lundberg, Emma (1881–1954)
Lunde, Vibeke (1921–1962)
Lundeberg, Helen (1908–1999)
Lundequist, Gerda (1871–1959)
Lung, Noemi Ildiko (1968—)
Lunn, Janet (1928—)
Luo Shu (1903–1938)
Luo Wei (1983—)
Luo Xuejuan (1984—)
Lupescu, Elena (c. 1896–1977)
Lupetey Cobas, Yurieleidys (1981—)
Lupino, Ida (1914–1995)
Lupino, Natalina (1963—)
Lupita, Madre (1878–1963)
Lurie, Alison (1926—)
Lurie, Nancy O. (1924—)
Lurz, Dagmar (1959—)
Lusarreta, Pilar de (1914–1967)
Lusk, Georgia Lee (1893–1971)
Lusk, Grace (1878–1938)
Lussac, Elodie (1979—)
Lussu, Joyce Salvadori (1912–1988)
Lutayeva-Berzina, Valentina (1956—)
Lütken, Hulda (1896–1947)
Lutyens, Elisabeth (1906–1983)
Lutyens, Mary (1908–1999)
Lutz, Berta (1894–1976)
Lutze, Manuela (1974—)
Lux, Amelie (1977—)
Luxemburg, Rosa (1870–1919)
Luxford, Nola (1895–1994)
Lu Yin (1899–1934)
Luz, Helen (1972—)
Luz, Silvia (1975—)
Lwin, Annabella (1965—)
Lyall, Katharine C. (1941—)
Lyapina, Nataliya (1976—)
Lyapina, Oksana (1980—)
Lyell, Lottie (1890–1925)
Lyles, Anjette (1917–1977)
Lyman, Mary Ely (1887–1975)
Lympany, Moura (1916–2005)
Lynch, Celia (1908–1989)
Lynch, Kathleen (1953—)
Lynch, Laura (1958—)
Lyngstad, Frida (1945—)
Lynn, Barbara (1942—)
Lynn, Diana (1926–1971)
Lynn, Elizabeth A. (1946—)
Lynn, Janet (1953—)
Lynn, Kathleen (1874–1955)
Lynn, Loretta (1935—)
Lynn, Sharon (1901–1963)
Lynn, Vera (1917—)
Lynne, Elizabeth (1948—)
Lynne, Gillian (1926—)
Lyon, Annabelle (c. 1915—)
Lyon, Genevieve (c. 1893–1916)
Lyon, Mary Frances (1925—)
Lyons, Beatrice (1930—)
Lyons, Enid (1897–1981)
Lyons, Sophie (1848–1924)
Lysenko, Tatiana (1975—)
Lytle, Nancy A. (1924–1987)
Lyttelton, Edith (1865–1948)
Lyttelton, Edith Joan (1873–1945)
Lytton, Constance (1869–1923)
Lytton, Emily (1874–1964)
Lyubimova, Nadezhda (1959—)
Lyukhina, Tamara (1939—)
Maakal, Jenny (1913—)
Maar, Dora (1907–1997)
Maas, Annelies (1960—)
Maas-Fjetterstrom, Marta (1873–1941)
Maass, Clara (1876–1901)
Maathai, Wangari (1940—)
Määttä, Pirkko (1959—)
Mabley, Jackie (1894–1975)
Macandrew, Jennie (1866–1949)
Macardle, Dorothy (1889–1958)
MacArthur, Ellen (1976—)
MacArthur, Mary (1930–1949)
Macarthur, Mary Reid (1880–1921)
Macarthur-Onslow, Elizabeth (1840–1911)
Macaulay, Rose (1881–1958)
MacColl, Kirsty (1959–2000)
MacDonald, Barbara K. (1957—)
MacDonald, Betty (1908–1958)
MacDonald, Blossom (1895–1978)
MacDonald, Christie (1875–1962)
MacDonald, Elaine (1943—)
MacDonald, Elizabeth Roberts (1864–1922)
MacDonald, Fiona (1974—)
MacDonald, Frances (1874–1921)
Macdonald, Georgiana (1840–1920)
MacDonald, Irene (1933–2002)
MacDonald, Jeanette (1903–1965)
MacDonald, Katherine (1881–1956)
Macdonald, Linsey (1964—)
MacDonald, Margaret (c. 1907–1956)
MacDonald, Margo (c. 1948—)
MacDonald, Noel (1915—)
MacEwen, Gwendolyn (1941–1987)
MacFadden, Gertrude (c. 1900–1967)
MacFall, Frances E. (1854–1943)
Macfarlane, Edith Mary (1871–1948)
MacGibbon, Harriet (1905–1987)
MacGill, Elsie (d. 1980)
MacGill, Helen Gregory (1871–1947)
MacGill, Moyna (1895–1975)
MacGillavry, Carolina H. (1904–1993)
Macgoye, Marjorie Oludhe (1928—)
MacGrath, Leueen (1914–1992)
MacGraw, Ali (1938—)
MacGregor, Esther Miller (1874–1961)
MacGregor, Sue (1941—)
Machado, Gilka (1893–1980)
Machado, Luz (1916–1999)
Machar, Agnes Maule (1837–1927)
Machel, Graca (1946—)
Machnow, Emy (1897–1974)
Maciel Mota, Miraildes (1978—)
MacInnes, Helen (1907–1985)
MacIver, Loren (1909–1998)
Mack, Helen (1913–1986)
Mack, Louise (1874–1935)
Mack, Marion (1902–1989)
Mack, Nila (1891–1953)
Mackaill, Dorothy (1903–1990)
Mackay, Catherine Julia (1864–1944)
Mackay, Elizabeth Ann Louisa (1843–1908)
Mackay, Jessie (1864–1938)
Mackay, Maria Jane (1844–1933)
Mackay, Nancy (1929—)
Mackellar, Dorothea (1885–1968)
Mackenzie, Ada (1891–1973)
MacKenzie, Gisele (1927–2003)
Mackenzie, Jean Kenyon (1874–1936)
Mackenzie, Midge (1938–2004)
Mackin, Catherine (1939–1982)
MacKinlay, Jean Sterling (1882–1958)
Mackinnon, Catherine A. (1946—)
MacKinnon, Joanna (1878–1966)
Mackintosh, Margaret (1865–1933)
Macklin, Madge (1893–1962)
MacLaine, Shirley (1934—)
MacLaren, Mary (1896–1985)
Maclean, Hester (1859–1932)
Maclean, Ida Smedley (1877–1944)
Maclean, Kate (1958—)
MacLean, Katherine (1925—)
MacLean, Vida (1881–1970)
MacLeish, Martha Hillard (1856–1947)
Macleod, Charlotte (1852–1950)
Macleod, Jaime (1976—)
MacLeod, Juana-Luisa (1898–1919)
MacLeod, Sheila (1939—)
MacMahon, Aline (1899–1991)
MacManus, Anna Johnston (1866–1902)
Macmillan, Chrystal (1871–1937)
Macmillan, Maureen (1943—)
MacMillan, Shannon (1974—)
MacMurchy, Helen (1862–1953)
MacMurchy, Marjory (1869–1938)
Macnaghten, Anne (1908–2002)
Macnamara, Jean (1899–1968)
Macomber, Mary Lizzie (1861–1916)
Maconachie, Bessie
Maconchy, Elizabeth (1907–1994)
Macoviciuc, Camelia (1968—)
Macphail, Agnes (1890–1954)
Macphail, Katherine Stewart (1888–1974)
Macpherson, Jay (1931—)
Macpherson, Jeanie (1887–1946)
Macpherson, Margaret Louisa (1895–1974)
MacPherson, Michelle (1966—)
Macpherson, Wendy (1968—)
MacRobert, Rachel (1884–1954)
MacSwiney, Mary (1872–1942)
Mactaggart, Fiona (1953—)
Mactier, Kate (1975—)
Macurdy, Grace Harriet (1866–1946)
Macy, Anne Sullivan (1866–1936)
Macy, Gertrude (1904–1983)
Macy, Robin Lynn (1958—)
Madar, Olga (1915–1996)
Madary, Ilona (1916—)
Madden, Beezie (1963—)
Maddern, Merle (1887–1984)
Maddox, Rose (1925–1998)
Madeleine (b. 1982)
Madeleva, Sister Mary (1887–1964)
Madgett, Naomi Long (1923—)
Madikizela-Mandela, Winnie (1934—)
Madina, Stefka (1963—)
Madison, Cleo (1883–1964)
Madison, Helene (1913–1970)
Madonna (1958—)
Madsen, Gitte (1969—)
Maeda, Echiko (1952—)
Maehata, Hideko (1914–1995)
Maes, Nelly (1941—)
Mafalda of Hesse (1902–1944)
Maffett, Debra Sue (c. 1957—)
Magafan, Ethel (1916–1993)
Magafan, Jenne (1916–1952)

Magdalen women (c. 1820s–early 1970s)
Magee, Joni (1941—)
Magee, Samantha (1983—)
Mager, Manuela (1962—)
Mageras, Georgia Lathouris (1867–1950)
Magers, Rose (1960—)
Magnani, Anna (1908–1973)
Magnes, Frances (1919—)
Magnussen, Karen (1952—)
Magogo ka Dinizulu, Constance (1900–1984)
Magoni, Paoletta (1964—)
Magruder, Julia (1854–1907)
Maher, Kim (1971—)
Maher, Robyn (1959—)
Mahler, Alma (1879–1964)
Mahon, Alice (1937—)
Mahoney, Mary Eliza (1845–1926)
Mahony, Marion (1871–1961)
Mahringer, Erika (1924—)
Mahupuku, Maata (1890–1952)
Mahy, Margaret (1936—)
Maier, Ulrike (1967–1994)
Maiga-Ka, Aminata (1940—)
Maihi, Rehutai (1895–1967)
Maij-Weggen, Hanja (1943—)
Maillart, Ella (1903–1997)
Maillet, Antonine (1929—)
Main, Marjorie (1890–1975)
Maines, Natalie (1974—)
Maiques Dern, Ana (1967—)
Mairet, Ethel (1872–1952)
Maitland, Agnes Catherine (1850–1906)
Maitland, Clover (1972—)
Maiztegui, Laura
Majerová, Marie (1882–1967)
Majoli, Iva (1977—)
Major, Clare Tree (d. 1954)
Major, Ethel Lillie (1890–1934)
Major, Maeghan (1984—)
Majstorovic, Biljana (1959—)
Makarova, Elena (1951—)
Makarova, Inna (1928—)
Makarova, Natalia (1940—)
Makarova, Tamara (1907–1997)
Makaryeva, Nadiezhda (1925—)
Makaveeva, Petkana (1952—)
Makeba, Miriam (1932—)
Makemson, Maud Worcester (1891–1977)
Makhina, Antonina (1958—)
Makhubu, Lydia (1937—)
Makogonova, Irina (1959—)
Makray, Katalin (1945—)
Maksimovic, Desanka (1898–1993)
Ma Kum-Ja (1955—)
Malabarba, Germana (1913–2002)
Malaga, Natalia (1964—)
Malaika, Nazik al- (1923–1992)
Malaika, Salma al- (1908–1953)
Malakhovskaya, Natalia (1947—)
Malato, Giusy (1971—)
Malchugina-Mikheyeva, Galina (1962—)
Malcolm, Emilie Monson (1829/30–1905)
Malcomson, Ruth (1906–1988)
Male, Carolyn Therese (1966—)
Maleeva, Magdalena (1975—)
Maleeva, Manuela (1967—)
Maletzki, Doris (1952—)
Malibran, Maria (1808–1836)
Malina, Judith (1926—)
Malinovska, Valentina
Malison, Joyce (c. 1935—)
Mallaber, Judy (1951—)
Malleson, Joan (1900–1956)
Malleswari, Karnam (1975—)
Mallet-Joris, Françoise (1930—)
Mallinger, Mathilde (1847–1920)
Malliori, Minerva Melpomeni (1952—)
Mallon, Mary (1867–1938)
Mallon, Meg (1963—)
Mallory, Boots (1913–1958)
Mallory, Molla (1884–1959)
Malmström, Cecilia (1968—)
Malo, Gina (1909–1963)
Malone, Annie Turnbo (1869–1957)
Malone, Bernie (1948—)
Malone, Dorothy (1925—)
Malone, Maicel (1969—)
Maloney, Kristen (1981—)
Maloney, Lucia (c. 1950–1978)
Malpede, Karen (1945—)
Malraux, Clara (c. 1897–1982)
Maltby, Margaret E. (1860–1944)
Malukhina, Anna (1958—)
Malyon, Eily (1879–1961)
Mamlok, Ursula (1928—)
Mamoshina, Glafira Adolfovna (c. 1870–1942)
Manaudou, Laure (1986—)
Mana-Zucca (1887–1981)
Manchester, Melissa (1951—)
Mandel, Maria (1912–1948)
Mandel, Miriam (1930–1982)
Mandelstam, Nadezhda (1899–1980)
Mander, Jane (1877–1949)
Mandrell, Barbara (1948—)
Mang, Veronique (1984—)
Mangakahia, Meri Te Tai (1868–1920)
Mangano, Silvana (1930–1989)
Mangeshkar, Lata (1929—)
Mangolte, Babette (c. 1945—)
Manicom, Jacqueline (1938–1976)
Manina, Tamara (1934—)
Maniourova, Gouzel (1978—)
Manjani, Miréla (1976—)
Mankiller, Wilma (1945—)
Mankin, Helen Douglas (1894–1956)
Mankova, Svetlana (1962—)
Manley, Dorothy (1927—)
Manley, Effa (1900–1981)
Manley, Elizabeth (1965—)
Mann, Aimee (1960—)
Mann, Carol (1941—)
Mann, Elisabeth (1918–2002)
Mann, Erika (1905–1969)
Mann, Erika (1950—)
Mann, Ida (1893–1983)
Mann, Shelley (1937—)
Manner, Eeva-Liisa (1921–1995)
Mannering, Mary (1876–1953)
Manners, Martha (1924–1977)
Mannes, Clara Damrosch (1869–1948)
Mannes, Marya (1904–1990)
Mannheim, Lucie (1899–1976)
Mannin, Ethel (1900–1984)
Manning, Irene (1912–2004)
Manning, Katharine (1904–1974)
Manning, Leah (1886–1977)
Manning, Madeline (1948—)
Manning, Marie (c. 1873–1945)
Manning, Mary (1906–1999)
Manning, Olivia (1908–1980)
Manoliu, Lia (1932–1998)
Manos, Aspasia (1896–1972)
Manrique Perez, Silvia (1973—)
Mansel, Lucy (c. 1830–1915)
Mansfield, Arabella (1846–1911)
Mansfield, Jayne (1933–1967)
Mansfield, Katherine (1888–1923)
Mansfield, Martha (1899–1923)
Mansfield, Portia (1887–1979)
Mansour, Agnes Mary (c. 1931–2004)
Mansour, Joyce (1928–1987)
Mantle, Winifred Langford (1911–1983)
Manton, Irene (1904–1988)
Manton, Sidnie (1902–1979)
Manus, Rosa (1881–1942)
Manzini, Gianna (1896–1974)
Manès, Gina (1893–1989)
Mao Fumei (1892–?)
Mar, Sabrina (1970—)
Mara, Adele (1923—)
Maracci, Carmelita (1911–1988)
Maracineanu, Roxana (1975—)
Maragall Verge, Elisabeth (1970—)
Maraini, Dacia (1936—)
Marangoni, Clara (1915—)
Maranhão, Heloísa (1925—)
Marble, Alice (1913–1990)
Marble, Mary (d. 1965)
Marbury, Elisabeth (1856–1933)
Marcari Oliva, Hortencia (1959—)
March, Eve (1910–1974)
March, Susana (1918–1991)
Marchal, Arlette (1902–1984)
Marchand, Collette (1925—)
Marchand, Corinne (1937—)
Marchand, Nancy (1928–2000)
Marchant, Bessie (1862–1941)
Marchant, Maria Elise Allman (1869–1919)
Marchesi, Blanche (1863–1940)
Marchesi, Mathilde (1821–1913)
Marcos, Imelda (1929—)
Marcus, Adele (1905–1995)
Marcus, Marie (1914–2003)
Marcus, Ruth Barcan (1921—)
Marden, Adrienne (1909–1978)
Marden, Anne (1958—)
Mareckova, Eva (1964—)
Marek, Martha Lowenstein (1904–1938)
Maretskaya, Vera (1906–1978)
Margalot, Mercedes (1975—)
Margaret (1912–1993)
Margaret (1949—)
Margaret Beatrice (1872–1954)
Margaret Bernadotte (1934—)
Margaret Clementine (1870–1955)
Margaretha of Sweden (1899–1977)
Margaret of Baden (1932—)
Margaret of Connaught (1882–1920)
Margaret of Savoy (1851–1926)
Margaret Rose (1930–2002)
Margaret Sophie (1870–1902)
Margarita Maria (1939—)
Marghieri, Clotilde (1897–1981)
Margo (1918–1985)
Margolin, Janet (1943–1993)
Margrethe II (1940—)
Margriet Francisca (1943—)
Margulis, Lynn (1938—)
Maria Annunziata (1876–1961)
Maria Antonia of Portugal (1862–1959)
Maria Beatrice of Modena (1824–1906)
Maria Christina (1947—)
Maria Christina of Austria (1858–1929)
Maria Cristina (1911–1996)
Maria Cristina of Sicily (1877–1947)
Maria da Gloria (1946—)
Maria de la Esperanza (1914—)
Maria de la Paz (1862–1946)
Maria de las Mercedes (1880–1904)
Maria de las Mercedes (1910–2000)
Maria del Pilar (1936—)
Maria Dorothea of Austria (1867–1932)
Maria Gabriele of Bavaria (1878–1912)
Maria Henrietta of Austria (1836–1902)
Maria Immaculata (1878–1968)
Maria Isabel Francisca (1851–1931)
Maria Isabella (1834–1901)
Maria Isabella (1848–1919)
Maria Josepha of Portugal (1857–1943)
Maria Josepha of Saxony (1867–1944)
Maria Ludovica (1845–1917)
Mariani, Felice (1954—)
Maria of Mecklenburg-Schwerin (1854–1920)
Maria of Savoy (1914—)
Maria Pia (1847–1911)
Maria Sophia Amalia (1841–1925)
Maria Teresa (1882–1912)
Maria Teresa of Este (1849–1919)
Maria Theresa of Portugal (1855–1944)
Maria Theresa of Wurttemberg (1934—)
Maric, Ljubica (1909–2003)
Marie (1876–1940)
Marie (1899–1918)
Marie (1900–1961)
Marie, Teena (1956—)
Marie Adelaide of Luxemburg (1894–1924)
Marie Alexandra of Baden (1902–1944)
Marie Alexandrovna (1853–1920)
Marie-Amelie of Orleans (1865–1951)
Marie-Anne of Braganza (1861–1942)
Marie-Cecile Hohenzollern (1942—)
Marie Feodorovna (1847–1928)
Marie-Ileana (1933–1959)
Marie José of Belgium (1906–2001)
Marie Louise (1872–1956)
Marie Louise (1879–1948)
Marie Louise of Bulgaria (1933—)
Marie Melita of Hohenlohe-Langenburg (1899–1967)

Era Index

Marie of Anhalt (1898–1983)
Marie of Hohenzollern-Sigmaringen (1845–1912)
Marie of Nassau (1841–1910)
Marie of Rumania (1875–1938)
Marie of Russia (1907–1951)
Marie Pavlovna (1890–1958)
Marin, Gladys (1941–2005)
Marin, Maguy (1951—)
Marina of Greece (1906–1968)
Marinescu, Alexandra (1981—)
Marinescu-Borcanea, Tecla (1960—)
Marinetti, Benedetta Cappa (1897–1977)
Marinoff, Fania (1890–1971)
Marinova, Mila (1974—)
Marinova, Tereza (1977—)
Marinova, Zornitsa (1987—)
Mario, Queena (1896–1951)
Marion, Frances (1888–1973)
Maris, Mona (1903–1991)
Marisol (1930—)
Maritain, Raïssa (1883–1960)
Maritza, Sari (1910–1987)
Mark, Mary Ellen (1940—)
Marken, Jeanne (1895–1976)
Markey, Enid (1891–1981)
Markham, Beryl (1902–1986)
Markham, Pauline (d. 1919)
Markievicz, Constance (1868–1927)
Marko, Jadwiga (1939—)
Markova, Alicia (1910–2004)
Markova, Olga
Markova, Olga (c. 1969—)
Markova, Olga (1974—)
Markovic, Mirjana (1942—)
Markovic, Vera (1931—)
Marks, Rita (c. 1908–1976)
Markus, Erzsebet (1969—)
Markushevska, Galyna (1976—)
Marlatt, Abby (1916—)
Marlatt, Abby L. (1869–1943)
Marley, Cedella (1967—)
Marley, Rita (1946—)
Marlowe, Julia (1866–1950)
Marlowe, June (1903–1984)
Marlowe, Missy (1971—)
Marlowe, Nora (1915–1977)
Marly, Florence (1918–1978)
Marmein, Irene (1894–1972)
Marmein, Miriam (1897–1970)
Marmein, Phyllis (1908–1994)
Marmont, Louise (1967—)
Marnière, Jeanne (1854–1910)
Maron, Monika (1941—)
Maroney, Susan Jean (1974—)
Maros, Magda (1951—)
Marosi, Paula (1936—)
Marot, Helen (1865–1940)
Marothy-Soltesova, Elena (1855–1939)
Marquardt, Melissa (1983—)
Marquet, Mary (1895–1979)
Marquis, Gail (1956—)
Marr, Sally (1906–1997)
Marrack, Philippa (1945—)
Marriott, Alice Sheets (1907–2000)
Marriott, Anne (1913–1997)
Marron, Eugenie (1899–1999)
Marsden, Karen (1962—)
Marsden, Kate (1859–1931)
Marsh, Jean (1934—)
Marsh, Joan (1913–2000)
Marsh, Mae (1895–1968)
Marsh, Marian (1913—)
Marsh, Ngaio (1895–1982)
Marshall, Brenda (1915–1992)
Marshall, Catherine (1914–1983)
Marshall, Clara (1847–1931)
Marshall, Joyce (1913—)
Marshall, Kirstie (1969—)
Marshall, Lois (1924–1997)
Marshall, Margaret (1949—)
Marshall, Niní (1903–1996)
Marshall, Paule Burke (1929—)
Marshall, Penny (1942—)
Marshall, Sheina (1896–1977)
Marshall, Susan (1958—)
Marshall, Trudy (1922–2004)
Marsman, Margot (1932—)
Marson, Aileen (1912–1939)
Marson, Una (1905–1965)
Martel de Janville, Comtesse de (1850–1932)
Märten, Lu (1879–1970)
Marten Garcia, Maritza (1963—)
Martens, Camille (1976—)
Martens, Maria (1955—)
Martensson, Agneta (1961—)
Martha de Freitas (1958—)
Martha of Sweden (1901–1954)
Martin, Agnes (1912–2004)
Martin, Anne Henrietta (1875–1951)
Martin, C.E.M. (1847–1937)
Martin, Camilla (1974—)
Martin, Claire (1914—)
Martin, Gael (1956—)
Martin, Georgia (1866–1946)
Martin, Hannah (1830–1903)
Martin, Helen (1909–2000)
Martin, LaVonna (1966—)
Martin, Lillien Jane (1851–1943)
Martin, Lynn (1939—)
Martin, Marianne (1961—)
Martin, Marion (1908–1985)
Martin, Mary (1907–1969)
Martin, Mary (1913–1990)
Martin, Millicent (1934—)
Martin, Mother Mary (1892–1975)
Martin, Patricia J. (1928—)
Martin, Rhona (1966—)
Martin, Sara (1884–1955)
Martin, Violet (1862–1915)
Martin, Vivian (1893–1987)
Martindale, Hilda (1875–1952)
Martinelli, Elsa (1932—)
Martinez, Conchita (1972—)
Martinez, Estibaliz
Martinez, Maria Montoya (1887–1980)
Martinez, Vilma (1943—)
Martinez Adlun, Maybelis (1977—)
Martínez Sierra, Maria de la O (1874–1974)
Martín Gaite, Carmen (1925—)
Martino, Angel (1967—)
Martinod, Marie (c. 1984—)
Martinsen, Bente (1972—)
Martinson, Moa (1890–1964)
Martin-Spencer, Lilly (1822–1902)
Martinsson, Barbro
Marucha (1944–1991)
Maruoka, Hideko (1903–1990)
Marwick, Tricia (1953—)
Marx, Laura (1845–1911)
Marx, Susan Fleming (1908–2002)
Mary (1897–1965)
Mary (b. 1964)
Mary of Battenberg (1852–1923)
Mary of Hanover (1849–1904)
Mary of Saxe-Altenburg (1818–1907)
Mary of Teck (1867–1953)
Marzouk, Zahia (1906–1988)
Masakayan, Liz (1964—)
Masako (1963—)
Masaryk, Alice Garrigue (1879–1966)
Masaryk, Charlotte Garrigue (1850–1923)
Masina, Giulietta (1920–1994)
Mašiotene, Ona (1883–1949)
Maskell, Virginia (1936–1968)
Maskova, Hana (1949–1972)
Maslakova-Zharkova, Lyudmila (1952—)
Maslow, Sophie (1911—)
Masnada, Florence (1968—)
Mason, Alice Trumbull (1904–1971)
Mason, Ann (c. 1898–1948)
Mason, Bobbie Ann (1940—)
Mason, Lisa (1982—)
Mason, Lucy Randolph (1882–1959)
Mason, Marge (1918–1974)
Mason, Marsha (1942—)
Mason, Monica (1941—)
Mason, Pamela (1918–1996)
Mason, Shirley (1900–1979)
Mason-Brown, Michele (1939—)
Masotta, Paula Karina (1972—)
Massari, Lea (1933—)
Massary, Fritzi (1882–1969)
Massee, May (1881–1966)
Massen, Osa (1916–2006)
Masseroni, Daniela (1985—)
Masset, Louise (c. 1863–1900)
Massevitch, Alla G. (1918—)
Massey, Christina Allan (1863–1932)
Massey, Debbie (1950—)
Massey, Edith (1918–1984)
Massey, Ilona (1910–1974)
Massingham, Dorothy (1889–1933)
Massy, Annie (1867–1931)
Massy-Beresford, Monica (1894–1945)
Mastenbroek, Rie (1919–2003)
Master, Edith (1932—)
Masterkova, Svetlana (1968—)
Masters, Margaret (1934—)
Masters, Olga (1919–1986)
Maston, June (1928—)
Masubuchi, Mariko (1980—)
Mataira, Katarina Te Heikoko (1932—)
Matalin, Mary (1953—)
Matamoros, Mercedes (1851–1906)
Matefi, Eszter
Matenga, Huria (1840/42–1909)
Matera, Barbara (1929–2001)
Materna, Amalie (1844–1918)
Matevusheva, Svitlana (1981—)
Mathé, Carmen (1938—)
Mather, Margrethe (c. 1885–1952)
Mathers, Helen (1853–1920)
Matheson, Elizabeth (1866–1958)
Mathews, Carmen (1914–1995)
Mathews, Marlene (1934—)
Mathews, Vera Laughton (1888–1959)
Mathieu, Simone (1908–1980)
Mathieu, Susie
Mathieu, Véronique (1955—)
Mathilda (1925–1997)
Mathilde (1820–1904)
Mathilde of Bavaria (1843–1925)
Mathilde of Belgium (1973—)
Mathis, June (1892–1927)
Mathison, Melissa (1950—)
Matijass, Julia (1973—)
Matikainen, Marjo (1965—)
Matilda of Leiningen (b. 1936)
Matiyevskaya, Yelena (1961—)
Matouskova-Sinova, Matylda (1933—)
Matova, Nonka (1954—)
Matsuda, Noriko (1952—)
Matsui, Yayori (1934–2002)
Matsumoto, Naomi (1968—)
Matsumura, Katsumi (1944—)
Matsumura, Yoshiko (1941—)
Matsutani, Miyoko (1926—)
Matteson, Ruth (1909–1975)
Matthews, Burnita S. (1894–1988)
Matthews, Donna (1971—)
Matthews, Janet (1965—)
Matthews, Jessie (1907–1981)
Matthews, Kelly (1982—)
Matthews, Margaret (1935—)
Matthews, Victoria (1954—)
Matthews, Victoria Earle (1861–1907)
Matthiasdottir, Louisa (1917–2000)
Matthijsse, Margriet (1977—)
Matthison, Edith (1875–1955)
Matto de Turner, Clorinda (1854–1909)
Mattox, Martha (1879–1933)
Matuscsakne-Ronay, Ildiko (1946—)
Matute, Ana Maria (1926—)
Matveyeva, Novella Niklayevna (1934—)
Matyas, Auguszta
Matz, Evelyn (1955—)
Matzenauer, Margaret (1881–1963)
Matzinger, Polly (1947—)
Maud (1869–1938)
Maude, Caitlín (1941–1982)
Maude, Margery (1889–1979)
Maude, Sibylla Emily (1862–1935)
Mauer, Renata (1969—)
Mauermayer, Gisela (1913–1995)
Maule, Annabel (1922—)
Maunder, Annie Russell (1868–1947)
Maunder, Maria (1972—)
Maura, Carmen (1945—)

Mauresmo, Amelie (1979—)
Maurey, Nicole (1925—)
Mauri, Rosita (1856–1923)
Maurice, Mary (1844–1918)
Maurizio, Anna (1900–1993)
Maury, Antonia (1866–1952)
Maury, Carlotta (1874–1938)
Ma Xiangjun (1964—)
Maximova, Ekaterina (1939—)
Maxtone Graham, Joyce (1901–1953)
Maxwell, Alice Heron (1860–1949)
Maxwell, Anna Caroline (1851–1929)
Maxwell, Constantia (1886–1962)
Maxwell, Elsa (1883–1963)
Maxwell, Lois (1927—)
Maxwell, Marilyn (1921–1972)
Maxwell, Vera (1901–1995)
Maxwell, Vera (c. 1892–1950)
Maxwell-Pierson, Stephanie (1964—)
May, Catherine Dean (1914–2004)
May, Doris (1902–1984)
May, Edna (1875–1948)
May, Elaine (1932—)
May, Fiona (1969—)
May, Geraldine (1895–1997)
May, Gisela (1924—)
May, Isabella (1850–1926)
May, Misty (1977—)
May, Pamela (1917–2005)
May, Theresa (1956—)
May, Valerie (c. 1915/16—)
Ma Yanhong (1963—)
Mayawati (1956—)
Maybrick, Florence Elizabeth (c. 1853–1941)
Mayer, Bronwyn
Mayer, Diana K. (c. 1947—)
Mayer, Helene (1910–1953)
Mayer, Jacquelyn (c. 1942—)
Mayer, Maria Goeppert (1906–1972)
Mayfair, Mitzi (1914–1976)
Mayhar, Ardath (1930—)
Mayhew, Kate (1853–1944)
Ma Ying
Maynard, Mary (c. 1938—)
Mayne, Ethel Colburn (1865–1941)
Maynor, Dorothy (1910–1996)
Mayo, Katherine (1867–1940)
Mayo, Margaret (1882–1951)
Mayo, Mary Anne (1845–1903)
Mayo, Sara Tew (1869–1930)
Mayo, Virginia (1920–2005)
Mayor, Flora M. (1872–1932)
Mayreder, Rosa (1858–1938)
Mayröcker, Friederike (1924—)
Mazeas, Jacqueline (1920—)
Mazina, Maria (1964—)
Maziy, Svetlana (1968—)
Mbango Etone, Françoise (1976—)
Mbogo, Jael (1939—)
McAleese, Mary (1951—)
McAliskey, Bernadette Devlin (1947—)
McAliskey, Roisin (1971—)
McAllister, Anne Hunter (1892–1983)
McAllister, Susie (1947—)
McAlpine, Rachel (1940—)
McAuliffe, Christa (1948–1986)
McAuliffe-Ennis, Helena (1951—)
McAvan, Linda (1962—)
McAvoy, May (1901–1984)
McBean, Marnie (1968—)
McBride, Mary Margaret (1899–1976)
McBride, Patricia (1942—)
McCafferty, Chris (1945—)
McCaffrey, Anne (1926—)
McCambridge, Mercedes (1916–2004)
McCardell, Claire (1905–1958)
McCarthy, Arlene (1960—)
McCarthy, Carolyn (1944—)
McCarthy, Kathryn O'Loughlin (1894–1952)
McCarthy, Lillah (1875–1960)
McCarthy, Mary (1912–1989)
McCarthy, Mary Ann Recknall (1866–1933)
McCarthy, Maud (1858–1949)
McCarthy, Patricia (1911–1943)
McCarthy, Peggy (1956—)
McCartney, Linda (1941–1998)
McCarty, Mary (1923–1980)
McCarty, Patti (1921–1985)
McCauley, Diane (1946—)
McClain, Katrina (1965—)
McClellan, Catharine (1921—)
McClements, Lyn (1951—)
McClendon, Rosalie (1884–1936)
McClendon, Sarah (1910–2003)
McClintock, Barbara (1902–1992)
McClung, Nellie L. (1873–1951)
McColgan-Lynch, Elizabeth (1964—)
McCollum, Ruby (1915—)
McComas, Carroll (1886–1962)
McCombs, Elizabeth Reid (1873–1935)
McConnell, Lulu (1882–1962)
McConnell, Suzanne (1966—)
McCoo, Marilyn (1943—)
McCool, Courtney (1988—)
McCord, Joan (1930–2004)
McCorkle, Susannah (1946–2001)
McCormack, Katheryn (1974—)
McCormack, Patty (1945—)
McCormick, Anne O'Hare (1880–1954)
McCormick, Edith Rockefeller (1872–1932)
McCormick, Katharine Dexter (1875–1967)
McCormick, Katherine Medill (d. 1932)
McCormick, Kelly (1960—)
McCormick, Nettie Fowler (1835–1923)
McCormick, Patricia (1930—)
McCormick, Ruth Hanna (1880–1944)
McCoubrey, Margaret (1880–1955)
McCoy, Bessie (1888–1931)
McCoy, Elizabeth (1903–1978)
McCoy, Gertrude (1890–1967)
McCoy, Iola Fuller (1906–1993)
McCracken, Elizabeth (c. 1865–1944)
McCracken, Esther Helen (1902–1971)
McCracken, Joan (1922–1961)
McCrackin, Josephine Clifford (1838–1920)
McCray, Nikki (1971—)
McCreery, Maria (1883–1938)
McCue, Lillian de la Torre Bueno (1902–1993)
McCullers, Carson (1917–1967)
McCulloch, Catharine (1862–1945)
McCullough, Colleen (1937—)
McCully, Emily Arnold (1939—)
McCusker, Joan (c. 1966—)
McCusker, Marilyn Wehrle (1944–1979)
McCutcheon, Floretta (1888–1967)
McDaniel, Hattie (1895–1952)
McDaniel, Mildred (1933–2004)
McDermid, Heather (1968—)
McDermid, Sally (1965—)
McDermid, Val (1955—)
McDevitt, Ruth (1895–1976)
McDonagh, Isobel (1899–1982)
McDonagh, Paulette (1901–1978)
McDonagh, Phyllis (1900–1978)
McDonagh, Siobhain (1960—)
McDonald, Agnes (1829–1906)
McDonald, Audra (1970—)
McDonald, Beverly (1970—)
McDonald, Deborah (1954—)
McDonald, Gabrielle Kirk (1942—)
McDonald, Grace (1918–1999)
McDonald, Hedwick Wilhelmina (1893–1959)
McDonald, Julie (1970—)
McDonald, Marie (1923–1965)
McDormand, Frances (1957—)
McDougall, Adelaide (1909–2000)
McDowell, Anne E. (1826–1901)
McDowell, Claire (1877–1966)
McDowell, Mary Eliza (1854–1936)
McElderry, Margaret K. (1912—)
McElmury, Audrey (1943—)
McElroy, Mary Arthur (d. 1916)
McEntire, Reba (1955—)
McEwan, Geraldine (1932—)
McEwen, Anne (c. 1903–1967)
McFall, Lauren (1980—)
McFalls, Jennifer (1971—)
McFarland, Beulah (c. 1898–1964)
McFarland, Irene (fl. 1925)
McFarlane, Elaine (1942—)
McFarlane, Tracey (1966—)
McGahey, Kathleen (1960—)
McGee, Anita Newcomb (1864–1940)
McGee, Pamela (1962—)
McGehee, Helen (1921—)
McGennis, Marian (1953—)
McGhee, Carla (1968—)
McGill, Linda (1945—)
McGinley, Phyllis (1905–1978)
McGrath, Kathleen (1952–2002)
McGraw, Eloise Jarvis (1915–2000)
McGregor, Yvonne (1961—)
McGrory, Mary (1918–2004)
McGugan, Irene (1952—)
McGuinness, Catherine (1934—)
McGuinness, Norah (1901–1980)
McGuire, Anne (1949—)
McGuire, Dorothy (1916–2001)
McGuire, Edith (1944—)
McGuire, Kathryn (1903–1978)
McGuire, Phyllis (1931—)
McHugh, Fanny (1861–1943)
McIlwraith, Jean Newton (1859–1938)
McIntire, Barbara (1935—)
McIntosh, Anne (1954—)
McIntosh, Gail (1955—)
McIntosh, Lyndsay (1955—)
McIntosh, Madge (1875–1950)
McIntosh, Millicent Carey (1898–2001)
McIntyre, Elizabeth (1965—)
McIntyre, Leila (1882–1953)
McIntyre, Molly (c. 1886–1952)
McIntyre, Vonda N. (1948—)
McIsaac, Shona (1960—)
McKane, Alice Woodby (1865–1948)
McKane, Kitty (1896–1992)
McKay, Heather (1941—)
McKean, Olive (1915—)
McKechin, Ann (1961—)
McKechnie, Donna (1940—)
McKechnie, Sheila (1948–2004)
McKee, Maria (1964—)
McKenna, Lesley (1974—)
McKenna, Marthe (1893–1969)
McKenna, Patricia (1957—)
McKenna, Rollie (1918–2003)
McKenna, Rosemary (1941—)
McKenna, Siobhan (1922–1986)
McKenna, Virginia (1931—)
McKenney, Ruth (1911–1972)
McKenzie, Ella (1911–1987)
McKenzie, Eva B. (1889–1967)
McKenzie, Grace (b. 1903)
McKenzie, Ida Mae (1911–1986)
McKenzie, Jean (1901–1964)
McKenzie, Julia (1941—)
McKenzie, Margaret (c. 1837–1925)
McKiernan, Catherina (1969—)
McKillop, Patricia (1956—)
McKillop, Peggy (1909–1998)
McKim, Josephine (1910—)
McKinley, Ida Saxton (1847–1907)
McKinney, Cynthia (1955—)
McKinney, Louise (1868–1931)
McKinney, Nina Mae (c. 1912–1967)
McKinney, Tamara (1962—)
McKinnon, Betty (1924—)
McKisack, May (1900–1981)
McKnight, Kim
McKnight, Marian (c. 1937—)
McLachlan, Laurentia (1866–1953)
McLachlan, Sarah (1968—)
McLachlin, Beverley (1943—)
McLaren, Agnes (1837–1913)
McLaren, Anne Laura (1927—)
McLaren, Louise Leonard (1885–1968)
McLauchlan, Joy (1948—)
McLaughlin, Audrey (1936—)
McLaughlin, Florence (1916—)
McLaughlin, M. Louise (1847–1939)
McLaughlin-Gill, Frances (1919—)
McLean, Alice (1886–1968)
McLean, Barbara (1903–1996)
McLean, Evalyn Walsh (1886–1947)
McLean, Kathryn (1909–1966)
McLean, Mary Hancock (1861–1930)
McLean, Mary Jane (1866–1949)
McLennan, Margo (1938–2004)

McLeod, Catherine (1921–1997)
McLeod, Fiona (1957—)
McLeod, Mary Adelia (1938—)
McLerie, Allyn Ann (1926—)
McLish, Rachel (1958—)
MC Lyte (1971—)
McMahon, Brigitte (1967—)
McMahon, Sonia (1932—)
McMain, Eleanor Laura (1866–1934)
McMann, Sara (1980—)
McManus, Liz (1947—)
McMaster, Elizabeth Jennet (1847–1903)
McMein, Neysa (1888–1949)
McMillan, Clara Gooding (1894–1976)
McMillan, Ethel (1904–1987)
McMillan, Kathy (1957—)
McMillan, Margaret (1860–1931)
McMillan, Rachel (1859–1917)
McMillan, Terry (1951—)
McMordie, Julia (1860–1942)
McMurry, Lillian Shedd (1921–1999)
McNabb, Dinah
McNair, Denise (d. 1963)
McNair, Winifred (1877–1954)
McNally, Eryl Margaret (1942—)
McNally, Karen Cook (1940—)
McNamara, Julianne (1966—)
McNamara, Maggie (1928–1978)
McNaught, Lesley (1966—)
McNaught, Rose (1893–1978)
McNeil, Claudia (1917–1993)
McNeil, Florence (1937—)
McNeil, Loretta T. (1907–1988)
McNeill, Florence Marian (1885–1973)
McNeill, Janet (1907–1994)
McNeill, Pauline (c. 1967—)
McNulty, Faith (1918–2005)
McPartland, Marian (1920—)
McPaul, Louise (1969—)
McPeak, Holly (1969—)
McPherson, Aimee Semple (1890–1944)
McPherson, Heather (1942—)
McQueen, Mary (1860–1945)
McQueen, Thelma (1911–1995)
McQuillan, Rachel (1971—)
McRae, Carmen (1920–1994)
McRae, Francine (1969—)
McTeer, Maureen (1952—)
McVicar, Annie (1862–1954)
McVie, Christine (1943—)
McWhinney, Madeline H. (1922—)
McWhinnie, Mary Alice (1922–1980)
McWilliams, Jackie (1964—)
McWilliams, Monica (1954—)
Mead, Elizabeth Storrs (1832–1917)
Mead, Lucia Ames (1856–1936)
Mead, Lynda Lee (c. 1939—)
Mead, Margaret (1901–1978)
Mead, Sylvia Earle (1935—)
Meadows, Audrey (1922–1996)
Meadows, Jayne (1920—)
Meagher, Aileen (1910–1987)
Meagher, Mary T. (1964—)
Meaker, Marijane (1927—)
Mealing, Philomena (1912–2002)
Means, Jacqueline (1936—)
Means, Marianne (1934—)
Meany, Helen (1904–1991)
Meares, Anna (1983—)
Mearig, Kim (1963—)
Mears, Elizabeth (1900–1988)
Mears, Helen Farnsworth (1872–1916)
Mechlin, Leila (1874–1949)
Mechtel, Angelika (1943–2000)
Medalen, Linda (1965—)
Medford, Kay (1914–1980)
Medicine, Beatrice A. (1923—)
Medina, Patricia (1919—)
Medio, Dolores (1914–1996)
Medveczky, Krisztina (1958—)
Mee, Margaret (1909–1988)
Meech, Matilda (c. 1825–1907)
Meena (1956–1987)
Meer, Fatima (1928—)
Mees, Helga (1937—)
Meeuwsen, Terry (1949—)
Meftakhetdinova, Zemfira (1963—)
Megyerine-Pacsai, Marta (1952—)
Mehl, Gabriele (1967—)
Mehlig, Anna (1846–1928)
Mehta, Hansa (1897–1995)
Mei-Figner, Medea (1859–1952)
Meighen, Isabel J. (1883–1985)
Meignan, Laetitia (1960—)
Meigs, Cornelia Lynde (1884–1973)
Meijer, Elien (1970—)
Meili, Launi (1963—)
Meinert, Maren (1973—)
Meinhof, Ulrike (1934–1972)
Meir, Golda (1898–1978)
Meireles, Cecília (1901–1964)
Meiselas, Susan (1948—)
Meiser, Edith (1898–1993)
Meissner, Katrin (1973—)
Meissnitzer, Alexandra (1973—)
Meitner, Lise (1878–1968)
Mekeel, Joyce (1931—)
Mekshilo, Eudokia
Meksz, Aniko (1965—)
Melba, Nellie (1861–1931)
Melendez, Jolinda (1954—)
Melendez Rodriguez, Urbia
Melidoni, Aniopi (1977—)
Melien, Lori (1972—)
Melikova, Genia (c. 1930–2004)
Melinte, Doina (1956—)
Melissanthi (c. 1907–c. 1991)
Mell, Marisa (1939–1992)
Mellanby, Helen (1911–2001)
Mellanby, May (1882–1978)
Meller, Raquel (1888–1962)
Mellgren, Dagny (1978—)
Mellish, Edith Mary (1861–1922)
Mellon, Gwen Grant (1911–2000)
Mellon, Sarah Jane (1824–1909)
Mellor, Fleur (1936—)
Melnik, Faina (1945—)
Melnik, Olga (1974—)
Melnikova, Antonina (1958—)
Melnikova, Elena
Meloney, Marie (1878–1943)
Melville, Eliza Ellen (1882–1946)
Melville, June (1915–1970)
Melville, Rose (1873–1946)
Memmel, Chellsie (1988—)
Menchik, Vera (1906–1944)
Menchú, Rigoberta (1959—)
Menco, Sara (1920—)
Menczer, Pauline (1970—)
Mendelenyine-Agoston, Judit (1937—)
Mendels, Josepha (1902–1995)
Mendes, Jonna (1979—)
Méndez, Josefina (c. 1940—)
Mendoza, Amalia (1923–2001)
Mendoza, Jessica (1980—)
Mendoza, Lydia (1916—)
Menebhi, Saïda (1952–1977)
Menen (1899–1962)
Menendez, Osleidys (1979—)
Meneres, Maria Alberta (1930—)
Menis, Argentina (1948—)
Menken, Helen (1901–1966)
Menken, Marie (1909–1970)
Menken-Schaudt, Carol (1957—)
Mensing, Barbara (1960—)
Menten, Maude (1879–1960)
Menter, Sophie (1846–1918)
Menuhin, Diana (1912–2003)
Menuhin, Hephzibah (1920–1981)
Menuhin, Marutha (1896–1996)
Menuhin, Yaltah (1921–2001)
Menzelli, Elisabetta (c. 1860–c. 1929)
Menzelli, Lola (c. 1898–1951)
Menzies, Pattie (1899–1995)
Menzies, Trixie Te Arama (1936—)
Merande, Doro (1892–1975)
Mercé, Antonia (c. 1886–1936)
Mercer, Beryl (1882–1939)
Mercer, Frances (1915–2000)
Mercer, Jacque (1931–1982)
Mercer, Mabel (1900–1983)
Merchant, Natalie (1963—)
Merchant, Vivien (1929–1983)
Mercier, Margaret (1937—)
Mercouri, Melina (1923–1994)
Meredith, Gwen (b. 1907)
Meredith, Iris (1915–1980)
Meredyth, Bess (1890–1969)
Mergler, Marie Josepha (1851–1901)
Meriluoto, Paivi (1952—)
Meriwether, Lee Ann (1935—)
Meriwether, Louise (1923—)
Merk, Larisa (1971—)
Merkel, Angela (1954—)
Merkel, Una (1903–1986)
Merle, Carole (1964—)
Merleni, Irini (1982—)
Merman, Ethel (1912–1984)
Mermet, Karine (1974—)
Mermey, Fayvelle (1916–1977)
Mernissi, Fatima (1940—)
Mero, Yolanda (1887–1963)
Mérode, Cléo de (c. 1875–1966)
Merrall, Mary (1890–1973)
Merrell, Mary (1938—)
Merret, Faustine (1978—)
Merriam, Charlotte (1906–1972)
Merrick, Caroline (1825–1908)
Merrick, Myra King (1825–1899)
Merril, Judith (1923–1997)
Merrill, Beth (1892–1986)
Merrill, Dina (1925—)
Merrill, Gretchen (1925–1965)
Merrill, Jan (1956—)
Merrill, Mary (1853–1924)
Merriman, Nan (1920—)
Merritt, Anna Lea (1844–1930)
Merritt, Kim (c. 1955—)
Merritt, Theresa (1924–1998)
Merron, Gillian (1959—)
Merry, Katharine (1974—)
Mersereau, Violet (1892–1975)
Merten, Lauri (1960—)
Merz, Sue (1972—)
Mesa Luaces, Liana (1977—)
Meseke, Marilyn (1916–2001)
Meshcheryakova, Natalya (1972—)
Meskhi, Leila (1968—)
Messenger, Margaret (1948—)
Messenger-Harris, Beverly (1947—)
Messerer, Sulamith (1908–2004)
Messick, Dale (1906–2005)
Messmer, Magali (1971—)
Messner, Pat (1954—)
Mesta, Perle (1889–1975)
Mestre, Audrey (1974–2002)
Meszaros, Erika (1966—)
Meszaros, Gabriella (b. 1913)
Mészáros, Márta (1931—)
Metalious, Grace (1924–1964)
Metcalf, Harriet (1958—)
Metcalfe, Alexandra (1903–1995)
Metcalfe, Augusta Corson (1881–1971)
Metella, Malia (1982—)
Metheny, Linda (1948—)
Methot, Mayo (1904–1951)
Metodieva, Penka (1950—)
Metraux, Rhoda (1914–2003)
Metschuck, Caren (1963—)
Mette-Marit (1973—)
Metz, Karin (1956—)
Metzger, Hélène (1889–1944)
Mew, Charlotte (1869–1928)
Mexia, Ynes (1870–1938)
Meyen, Janna (1977—)
Meyer, Agnes (1887–1970)
Meyer, Annie Nathan (1867–1951)
Meyer, Antoinette
Meyer, Debbie (1952—)
Meyer, Elana (1966—)
Meyer, Gertrud (1914—)
Meyer, Helen (1907–2003)
Meyer, Joyce (1943—)
Meyer, Lucy (1849–1922)
Meyer, Olga (1889–1972)
Meyerhoff, Jane (1924–2004)
Meyers, Ann (1955—)
Meyers, Jan (1928—)

Meyers, Mary (1946—)
Meyfarth, Ulrike (1956—)
Meygret, Anne (1965—)
Meynell, Alice (1847–1922)
Meynell, Viola (1886–1956)
Meyner, Helen Stevenson (1929–1997)
Meysel, Inge (1910–2004)
Meysenburg, Malwida von (1816–1903)
Mhac An tSaoi, Máire (1922—)
Michael, Gertrude (1910–1965)
Michael, Julia Warner (b. 1879)
Michaelis, Hanny (1922—)
Michaëlis, Karin (1872–1950)
Michaelis, Liane (1953—)
Michael of Kent (1945—)
Michel, Louise (1830–1905)
Michelena, Beatriz (1890–1942)
Micheler, Elisabeth (1966—)
Michelman, Kate (1942—)
Michiko (1934—)
Mickelson, Anna (1980—)
Mickler, Ingrid (1942—)
Micsa, Maria (1953—)
Midler, Bette (1945—)
Midori (1971—)
Midthun, Kristin (1961—)
Miegel, Agnes (1879–1964)
Mieth, Hansel (1909–1998)
Miftakhutdinova, Diana (1973—)
Miguélez Ramos, Rosa (1953—)
Mihaly, Aneta (1957—)
Mikey, Fanny (1931—)
Mikhaylova, Angelina (1960—)
Mikhaylova, Maria (1866–1943)
Mikhaylova, Snezhana (1954—)
Mikhaylovskaya, Lyudmila (1937—)
Mikkelsen, Henriette Roende (1980—)
Mikkelsplass, Marit (1965—)
Mikulich, Alena (1977—)
Mikulski, Barbara (1936—)
Milani, Milena (1922—)
Milanov, Zinka (1906–1989)
Milashkina, Tamara Andreyevna (1934—)
Milbrett, Tiffeny (1972—)
Milch, Klara (1891—)
Milchina, Lolita
Mildmay, Audrey (1900–1953)
Milena (1847–1923)
Miles, Jearl (1966—)
Miles, Lizzie (1895–1963)
Miles, Sarah (1941—)
Miles, Sylvia (1932—)
Miles, Vera (1929—)
Miley, Marion (c. 1914–1941)
Militsyna, Elizaveta Mitrofanovna (1869–1930)
Militza of Montenegro (1866–1951)
Millar, Annie Cleland (1855–1939)
Millar, Gertie (1879–1952)
Millar, Margaret (1915–1994)
Millard, Evelyn (1869–1941)
Millard, Ursula (b. 1901)
Millay, Edna St. Vincent (1892–1950)
Millay, Norma (d. 1986)
Miller, Alice (1923—)
Miller, Alice (1956—)
Miller, Alice Duer (1874–1942)
Miller, Anita (1951—)
Miller, Ann (1919–2004)
Miller, Bebe (1950—)
Miller, Bertha Mahony (1882–1969)
Miller, Caroline (1903–1992)
Miller, Cheryl (1964—)
Miller, Colleen (1932—)
Miller, Dorothy Canning (1904–2003)
Miller, Elizabeth Smith (1822–1911)
Miller, Emily Huntington (1833–1913)
Miller, Emma Guffey (1874–1970)
Miller, Florence Fenwick (1854–1935)
Miller, Freda (c. 1910–1960)
Miller, Frieda S. (1889–1973)
Miller, Gail
Miller, Inger (1972—)
Miller, Jane (1945—)
Miller, Jessie Maude (1910–1972)
Miller, Jo-Ann (1958—)
Miller, Joyce D. (1928—)
Miller, Katrina (1975—)
Miller, Lee (1907–1977)
Miller, Lucille (1930—)
Miller, Marilyn (1898–1936)
Miller, Olive Thorne (1831–1918)
Miller, Patricia (1927—)
Miller, Patsy Ruth (1904–1995)
Miller, Ruth (1919–1969)
Miller, Shannon (1977—)
Miller, Sharon Kay (1941—)
Miller, Susanne (1915—)
Miller, Tammy (1967—)
Millet, Cleusa (c. 1931–1998)
Millett, Kate (1934—)
Millican, Arthenia J. Bates (1920—)
Milligan, Alice (1866–1953)
Millikin, Kerry
Millin, Sarah (1888–1968)
Millington, Jean (1949—)
Millington, June (1950—)
Millis, Nancy (1922—)
Millman, Bird (1895–1940)
Mills, Alice (1986—)
Mills, Amy (c. 1949—)
Mills, Barbara (1940—)
Mills, Eleanor (1888–1922)
Mills, Florence (1895–1927)
Mills, Hayley (1946—)
Mills, Lorna H. (1916–1998)
Mills, Mary (1940—)
Mills, Melissa (1973—)
Mills, Phoebe (1972—)
Mills, Stephanie (1957—)
Mills, Susan Tolman (1825–1912)
Milne, Leslie (1956—)
Milne, Mary Jane (1840–1921)
Milner, Brenda Atkinson (1918—)
Milner, Marion (1900–1998)
Milo, Sandra (1935—)
Milolevic, Vesna (1955—)
Milosavljeric, Ljubinka (1917—)
Milosevic, Bojana (1965—)
Milosovici, Lavinia (1976—)
Milton, DeLisha (1974—)
Milton, Gladys (1924–1999)
Min, Anchee (1957—)
Minaicheva, Galina (1929—)
Minamoto, Sumika (1979—)
Minchin, Alice Ethel (1889–1966)
Minea-Sorohan, Anisoara (1963—)
Miner, Dorothy (1904–1973)
Miner, Jan (1917–2004)
Miner, Sarah Luella (1861–1935)
Mineyeva, Olga (1952—)
Min Hye-Sook (1970—)
Minijima, Kiyo (1833–1919)
Mink, Patsy (1927–2002)
Mink, Paule (1839–1901)
Minkh, Irina (1964—)
Minnelli, Liza (1946—)
Minner, Ruth Ann (1935—)
Minnert, Sandra (1973—)
Minnigerode, Lucy (1871–1935)
Minoka-Hill, Rosa (1876–1952)
Minter, Mary Miles (1902–1984)
Minton, Yvonne (1938—)
Minus, Rene (1943—)
Miou-Miou (1950—)
Mir, Isabelle (1949—)
Mirabal de González, Patria (1924–1960)
Mirabal de Guzmán, María Teresa (1936–1960)
Mirabal de Tavárez, Minerva (1927–1960)
Mirabeau, Comtesse de (1827–1914)
Mirabella, Erin (1978—)
Miramova, Elena (c. 1905—)
Miranda, Carmen (1909–1955)
Miranda, Isa (1909–1982)
Miranda, Patricia (1979—)
Mireille (1906–1996)
Miró, Pilar (1940–1997)
Miroshina, Yelena (1974—)
Mirren, Helen (1945—)
Misakova, Miloslava (1922—)
Misevich, Vera (1945—)
Mishak, Valentina (1942—)
Mishenina, Galina (1950—)
Mishina, Masumi (1982—)
Mishkowsky, Zelda Shneurson (1914–1984)
Mishkutenok, Natalia (1970—)
Misme, Jane (1865–1935)
Misnik, Alla (1967—)
Mistinguett (1875–1956)
Mistral, Gabriela (1889–1957)
Mitchell, Abbie (1884–1960)
Mitchell, Elizabeth (1966—)
Mitchell, Elyne (1913–2002)
Mitchell, Gladys (1901–1983)
Mitchell, Hannah (1871–1956)
Mitchell, Jackie (1912–1987)
Mitchell, Joan (1926–1992)
Mitchell, Joni (1943—)
Mitchell, Juliet (1934—)
Mitchell, Lucy Sprague (1878–1967)
Mitchell, Margaret (1900–1949)
Mitchell, Margaret J. (1832–1918)
Mitchell, Marion (1876–1955)
Mitchell, Martha (1918–1976)
Mitchell, Michelle (1962—)
Mitchell, Nikole
Mitchell, Olivia (1947—)
Mitchell, Rhea (1890–1957)
Mitchell, Roma (1913–2000)
Mitchell, Ruth (c. 1888–1969)
Mitchell, Yvonne (1925–1979)
Mitchell-Taverner, Claire (1970—)
Mitchison, Naomi (1897–1999)
Mitchison, Rosalind (1919–2002)
Mitford, Deborah (1920—)
Mitford, Diana (1910–2003)
Mitford, Jessica (1917–1996)
Mitford, Nancy (1904–1973)
Mitford, Unity (1914–1948)
Mitic, Vukica (1953—)
Mitova, Silvia (1976—)
Mitryuk, Natalya (1959—)
Mitsuya, Yuko (1958—)
Mittermaier, Rosi (1950—)
Mittermayer, Tatjana (1964—)
Mitterrand, Danielle (1924—)
Mitts, Heather (1978—)
Miura, Ayako (1922–1999)
Miura, Hanako (1975—)
Miura, Tamaki (1884–1946)
Miyajima, Keiko (1965—)
Miyamoto, Emiko (1937—)
Miyao, Tomiko (1926—)
Mizoguchi, Noriko (1971—)
Mizuta, Tamae (1929—)
Mladova, Milada (c. 1918—)
Mlakar, Pia (1908–2000)
Mlakar, Veronika (1935—)
Mleczko, A.J. (1975—)
Mnouchkine, Ariane (1938—)
Mntwana, Ida (1903–1960)
Mobley, Mamie Till (1921–2003)
Mobley, Mary Ann (1939—)
Mocanu, Diana (1984—)
Moceanu, Dominique (1981—)
Mochizuki, Noriko (1967—)
Mock, Jerrie (1925—)
Model, Lisette (1901–1983)
Modersohn-Becker, Paula (1876–1907)
Modeva, Mariyka (1954—)
Modjeska, Helena (1840–1909)
Mödl, Martha (1912–2001)
Modotti, Tina (1896–1942)
Moe, Karen (1952—)
Moehring, Anke (1969—)
Moeller-Gladisch, Silke (1964—)
Moen-Guidon, Anita (1967—)
Moffat, Gwen (1924—)
Moffatt, Laura (1954—)
Moffo, Anna (1932–2006)
Mofford, Rose (1922—)
Moggridge, Jackie (1922–2004)
Moholy, Lucia (1894–1989)
Moholy-Nagy, Sibyl (1903–1971)
Mohr, Nicholasa (1935—)
Mo Huilan (1979—)
Moir, Margaret (1941—)
Moisant, Matilde (c. 1877–1964)
Moiseeva, Irina (1955—)

Moiseiwitsch, Tanya (1914–2003)
Molander, Karin (1889–1978)
Molesworth, Mary Louisa (1839–1921)
Molik, Alicia (1981—)
Molinari, Susan (1958—)
Molin-Kongsgard, Anne (1977—)
Mollenhauer, Paula (1908–1988)
Moller, Lorraine (1955—)
Møllerup, Mette (1931—)
Molloy, Cate (1955—)
Molnar, Andrea (1975—)
Molnarne-Bodo, Andrea (1934—)
Molony, Helena (1884–1967)
Molton, Flora (1908–1990)
Moncrieff, Gladys (1892–1976)
Moncrieff, Pérrine (1893–1979)
Moneymaker, Kelly (1965—)
Mongella, Gertrude (1945—)
Monica (1980—)
Monk, Meredith (1942—)
Monkman, Phyllis (1892–1976)
Monnier, Adrienne (c. 1892–1955)
Monnot, Marguerite (1903–1961)
Monod, Sarah (1836–1912)
Monplaisir, Emma (1918—)
Monroe, Harriet (1860–1936)
Monroe, Jessica (1966—)
Monroe, Marilyn (1926–1962)
Monserdà de Macía, Dolors (1845–1919)
Montagu, Elizabeth (1909–2002)
Montagu, Helen (1928–2004)
Montagu-Douglas-Scott, Alice (1901–2004)
Montalba, Clara (1842–1929)
Montana, Patsy (1909–1996)
Monte, Hilda (1914–1945)
Montealegre, Felicia (d. 1978)
Montemayor, Alice Dickerson (1902–1989)
Montesi, Wilma (1932–1953)
Montessori, Maria (1870–1952)
Montez, Maria (1918–1951)
Montfort, Elizabeth (1954—)
Montgomery, Charlotte (1958—)
Montgomery, Elizabeth (1933–1995)
Montgomery, Goodee (1906–1978)
Montgomery, Helen Barrett (1861–1934)
Montgomery, Lucy Maud (1874–1942)
Montgomery, Mary (fl. 1891–1914)
Montgomery, Peggy (1917—)
Montiel, Sarita (1928—)
Montiero, June (1946—)
Montillet, Carole (1973—)
Montminy, Anne (1975—)
Montoriol i Puig, Carme (1893–1966)
Montrelay, Michèle
Montseny, Federica (1905–1994)
Montvid, A.S. (b. 1845)
Moodie, Geraldine (1853–1945)
Moody, Agnes Claypole (1870–1954)
Moody, Anne (1940—)
Moody, Emma Revell (1842–1903)
Moody, Heather (1973—)
Moon, Lorna (1886–1930)
Moon, Lottie (1840–1912)
Mooney, Julie (1888–1915)
Mooney, Mary (1958—)
Mooney, Ria (1904–1973)
Moon Hyang-Ja (1972—)
Moon Kyeong-Ha (1980—)
Moon Kyung-Ja (1965—)
Moon Pil-Hee (1982—)
Moore, Ann (1950—)
Moore, Anne Carroll (1871–1961)
Moore, Aubertine Woodward (1841–1929)
Moore, Audley (1898–1997)
Moore, C.L. (1911–1987)
Moore, Cleo (1928–1973)
Moore, Colleen (1900–1988)
Moore, Constance (1919–2005)
Moore, Decima (1871–1964)
Moore, Elisabeth H. (1876–1959)
Moore, Ellie Durall (1940—)
Moore, Eva (1870–1955)
Moore, Grace (1898–1947)
Moore, Ida (1882–1964)
Moore, Isabella (1894–1975)
Moore, Jessie (1865–1910)
Moore, Juanita (1922—)
Moore, Julia A. (1847–1920)
Moore, Lilian (1909–2004)
Moore, Lillian (1911–1967)
Moore, Maggie (1847–1929)
Moore, Marianne (1887–1972)
Moore, Mary Emelia (1869–1951)
Moore, Mary Tyler (1936—)
Moore, Sara Jane (1930—)
Moore, Terry (1929—)
Moorehead, Agnes (1900–1974)
Moosdorf, Johanna (1911–2000)
Mora, Constancia de la (1906–1950)
Morace, Carolina (1964—)
Morales, Hilda (1946—)
Moran, Dolores (1924–1982)
Moran, Gussie (1923—)
Moran, Lois (1907–1990)
Moran, Margaret (1955—)
Moran, Patsy (1903–1968)
Moran, Peggy (1918–2002)
Moran, Polly (1884–1952)
Morandini, Giuliana (1938—)
Morani, Alma Dea (1907–2001)
Morante, Elsa (1912–1985)
Moras, Karen (1954—)
Morath, Inge (1923–2002)
Moravcova, Martina (1976—)
Morawetz, Cathleen Synge (1923—)
Mordecai, Pamela (1942—)
Mørdre, Berit
Moreau, Janet (1927—)
Moreau, Jeanne (1928—)
Moreau, Mady (1928—)
Moreau de Justo, Alicia (1885–1986)
Moreira de Melo, Fatima (1978—)
Morella, Constance A. (1931—)
Moreman, Marjorie
Moreno, Luisa (1906–1992)
Moreno, Marguerite (1871–1948)
Moreno, Patricia (1988—)
Moreno, Rita (1931—)
Moreno, Virginia R. (1925—)
Moreno, Yipsi (1980—)
Morerod, Lise-Marie (1956—)
Moressee-Pichot, Sophie (1962—)
Morete, Maraea (1844–1907)
Moreton, Ursula (1903–1973)
Morett, Charlene (1957—)
Morgan, Agnes Fay (1884–1968)
Morgan, Anna (1851–1936)
Morgan, Anne (1873–1952)
Morgan, Ann Haven (1882–1966)
Morgan, Barbara (1900–1992)
Morgan, Claudia (1912–1974)
Morgan, Eluned (1967—)
Morgan, Frances Louisa (1845–1924)
Morgan, Helen (1900–1941)
Morgan, Helen (1966—)
Morgan, Jane (1924—)
Morgan, Jane Norton Grew (1868–1925)
Morgan, Jaye P. (1931—)
Morgan, Joan (1905–2004)
Morgan, Julia (1872–1957)
Morgan, Julie (1944—)
Morgan, Marion (c. 1887–1971)
Morgan, Mary Kimball (1861–1948)
Morgan, Maud (1903–1999)
Morgan, Michèle (1920—)
Morgan, Robin (1941—)
Morgan, Sally (1951—)
Morgan, Sandra (1942—)
Morgantini, Luisa (1940—)
Morgenstern, Lina B. (1830–1909)
Morgner, Irmtraud (1933–1990)
Mori, Mari (1903–1987)
Morico, Lucia (1975—)
Morin, Micheline (fl. 1930s)
Morin, Nea (1906–1986)
Morini, Erica (1904–1995)
Morio, Maiko (1967—)
Morisaki, Kazue (1927—)
Morishita, Yoko (1948—)
Morison, Harriet (1862–1925)
Morison, Patricia (1914—)
Morissette, Alanis (1974—)
Morita, Kimie (1958—)
Morits, Yunna (1937—)
Morkis, Dorothy (1942—)
Morlay, Gaby (1893–1964)
Morley, Karen (1905–2003)
Morley, Ruth (1925–1991)
Moroder, Karin (1974—)
Morozova, Natalia (1973—)
Morrell, Ottoline (1873–1938)
Morrice, Jane (1954—)
Morris, Anita (1943–1994)
Morris, Betty (1948—)
Morris, Clara (1847–1925)
Morris, Estelle (1952—)
Morris, Esther Hobart (1814–1902)
Morris, Jan (1926—)
Morris, Jane Burden (1839–1914)
Morris, Janet E. (1946—)
Morris, Jenny (1972—)
Morris, Margaret (1890–1981)
Morris, Mary (1895–1970)
Morris, Mary (1915–1988)
Morris, May (1862–1938)
Morris, Pamela (1906–2002)
Morrison, Adrienne (1889–1940)
Morrison, Ann (1916–1978)
Morrison, Annie Christina (1870–1953)
Morrison, Melissa (1971—)
Morrison, Toni (1931—)
Morrow, Doretta (1927–1968)
Morrow, Elizabeth Cutter (1873–1955)
Morrow, Simmone (1976—)
Morrow, Suzanne
Morse, Ella Mae (1925–1999)
Morskova, Natalya (1966—)
Mortensen, Karin (1977—)
Mortimer, Angela (1932—)
Mortimer, Dorothy (1898–1950)
Mortimer, Penelope (1918–1999)
Morton, Azie Taylor (c. 1936–2003)
Morton, Clara (c. 1882–1948)
Morton, Katherine E. (1885–1968)
Morton, Lucy (1898–1980)
Morton, Margaret (1968—)
Morton, Martha (1865–1925)
Morton, Rosalie Slaughter (1876–1968)
Moscoso, Mireya (1946—)
Moser, Ana (1968—)
Moser, Christina (1960—)
Moses, Anna "Grandma" (1860–1961)
Mosheim, Grete (1905–1986)
Mosher, Clelia Duel (1863–1940)
Mosher, Eliza Maria (1846–1928)
Moskalenko, Larisa (1963—)
Moskowitz, Belle (1877–1933)
Mosley, Cynthia (1898–1933)
Mosley, Tracey (1973—)
Mosolova, Vera (1875–1949)
Mosquera Mena, Mabel (1969—)
Mosquini, Marie (1899–1983)
Moss, Cynthia (1940—)
Moss, Emma Sadler (1898–1970)
Moss, Kate (1974—)
Moss, Marjorie (c. 1895–1935)
Mossetti, Carlotta (1890–?)
Mostel, Kate (1918–1986)
Mostepanova, Olga (1968—)
Moszumanska-Nazar, Krystyna (1924—)
Mota, Rosa (1958—)
Moten, Etta (1901–2004)
Moten, Lucy Ellen (1851–1933)
Motley, Constance Baker (1921–2005)
Motos Iceta, Teresa (1963—)
Motoyoshi, Miwako (1960—)
Motte, Claire (1937—)
Moulton, Barbara (1915–1997)
Moulton, Louise Chandler (1835–1908)
Mounsey, Tara (1978—)
Mounsey, Yvonne (c. 1921—)
Mountbatten, Edwina Ashley (1901–1960)
Mountbatten, Irene (1890–1956)
Mountbatten, Pamela (1929—)
Mountbatten, Patricia (1924—)
Mountford, Kali (1954—)
Mourning Dove (c. 1888–1936)
Mouskouri, Nana (1934—)

Movsessian, Vicki (1972—)
Mowatt, Judy (1952—)
Mowbray, Alison (1971—)
Mowlam, Mo (1949–2005)
Moyd, Pauline
Moyer, Diane (1958—)
Moyes, Patricia (1923–2000)
Moyet, Alison (1961—)
Moylan, Mary-Ellen (1926—)
Moynihan, Mary (c. 1903–?)
Moynihan-Cronin, Breeda (1953—)
Mozzoni, Anna Maria (1837–1920)
M'rabet, Fadéla (1935—)
Mroczkiewicz, Magdalena (1979—)
Mucke, Manuela (1975—)
Muckelt, Ethel (c. 1900—)
Mudge, Isadore (1875–1957)
Muehe, Lotte (1910–1981)
Mueller, Claudia (1974—)
Mueller, Gabi
Mueller, Irina (1951—)
Mueller, Kerstin (1969—)
Mueller, Leah Poulos (1951—)
Mueller, Martina (1980—)
Mueller, Petra (1965—)
Mueller, Romy (1958—)
Mueller, Silke (1978—)
Mueller, Susanne (1972—)
Muellerova, Milena (1923—)
Muenzer, Lori-Ann (1966—)
Mugabe, Sally (1932–1992)
Mugo, Micere Githae (1942—)
Mugosa, Ljiljana (1962—)
Mugosa, Svetlana (1964—)
Muir, Esther (1903–1995)
Muir, Florabel (1889–1970)
Muir, Helen (1920–2005)
Muir, Jean (1911–1996)
Muir, Jean (1928–1995)
Muir, Willa (1890–1970)
Muir-Wood, Helen (1895–1968)
Muis, Marianne (1968—)
Muis, Mildred (1968—)
Mujanovic, Razija (1967—)
Mujuru, Joyce (1955—)
Mukai, Chiaki (1952—)
Mukhacheva, Lubov
Mukherjee, Bharati (1938—)
Mukhina, Elena (1960—)
Mukhina, Vera (1889–1953)
Mukoda, Kuniko (1929–1981)
Mulder, Eefke (1977—)
Mulder, Elisabeth (1904–1987)
Muldowney, Shirley (1940—)
Mulenga, Alice (1924–1978)
Mulford, Wendy (1941—)
Mulholland, Clara (d. 1934)
Mulholland, Rosa (1841–1921)
Mulkerns, Val (1925—)
Mulkey, Kim (1962—)
Mullany, Kate (1845–1906)
Mullen, Barbara (1914–1979)
Müller, Anna-Maria (1949—)
Müller, Clara (1860–1905)
Müller, Emilia Franziska (1951—)
Muller, Gertrude (1887–1954)
Muller, Jennifer (1949—)
Müller, Mary Ann (c. 1819–1902)
Müller, Renate (1907–1937)
Müller, Rosemarie (1949—)
Muller-Schwarze, Christine
Mulligan, Mary (1960—)
Mullinix, Siri (1978—)
Mullins, Aimee (c. 1973—)
Mulroney, Mila (1953—)
Mulvany, Josephine (1901–1967)
Mulvany, Sybil Mary (1899–1983)
Mumford, Mary Bassett (1842–1935)
Mummhardt, Christine (1951—)
Münchow, Kirsten (1977—)
Munck, Ebba (1858–1946)
Mundinger, Mary O. (1937—)
Mundt, Kristina (1966—)
Munkhbayar, Dorzhsuren (1969—)
Munn, Meg (1959—)
Munoz Carrazana, Aniara (1980—)
Munoz Martinez, Almudena (1968—)
Munro, Alice (1931—)
Munro, Janet (1934–1972)
Munro, Mimi (1952—)
Munro, Thalia (1982—)
Munsel, Patrice (1925—)
Munson, Audrey (1891–1996)
Munson, Ona (1894–1955)
Münter, Gabriele (1877–1962)
Munz, Diana (1982—)
Muradyan, Nina (1954—)
Murat, Princess Eugène (1878–1936)
Muratova, Kira (1934—)
Muratova, Sofiya (1929—)
Murdaugh, Angela (1940—)
Murden, Tori (1963—)
Murdoch, Iris (1919–1999)
Murdoch, Nina (1890–1976)
Murdock, Margaret (1942—)
Murfin, Jane (1893–1955)
Murfree, Mary N. (1850–1922)
Muria, Anna (1904–2002)
Murie, Margaret (1902–2003)
Murnaghan, Sheelagh (1924–1993)
Murphy, Brianne (1933–2003)
Murphy, Dervla (1931—)
Murphy, Edna (1899–1974)
Murphy, Emily (1868–1933)
Murphy, Janice (1942—)
Murphy, Lizzie (1894–1964)
Murphy, Mary (1931—)
Murphy, Sara (1883–1975)
Murray, Anne (1945—)
Murray, Elaine (1954—)
Murray, Elizabeth (1871–1946)
Murray, Elizabeth (1940—)
Murray, Katherine (1894–1974)
Murray, Kathleen (d. 1969)
Murray, Kathryn (1906–1999)
Murray, Lilian (1871–1960)
Murray, Mae (1885–1965)
Murray, Margaret (1863–1963)
Murray, Patty (1950—)
Murray, Pauli (1910–1985)
Murray, Rosemary (1913–2004)
Murray, Ruby (1935–1996)
Murray, Yvonne (1964—)
Murrell, Christine (1874–1933)
Murrell, Hilda (c. 1906–1984)
Murtfeldt, Mary (1848–1913)
Murzina, Elena (1984—)
Musa, Gilda (1926–1999)
Muscardini, Cristiana (1948—)
Musgrave, Thea (1928—)
Musidora (1884–1957)
Musser, Tharon (1925—)
Mussey, Ellen Spencer (1850–1936)
Mussolini, Alessandra (1962—)
Mustonen, Kaija (1941—)
Musumeci, Maddalena (1976—)
Mutafchieva, Vera P. (1929—)
Mutola, Maria (1972—)
Muzio, Christine (1951—)
Muzio, Claudia (1889–1936)
Mvungi, Martha
Myburgh, Jeanette (1940—)
Myburgh, Natalie (1940—)
Mydans, Shelley (1915–2002)
Myers, Carmel (1899–1980)
Myers, Caroline Clark (c. 1888–1980)
Myers, Dee Dee (1961—)
Myers, Paula Jean (1934—)
Myers, Phoebe (1866–1947)
Myers, Viola (1928—)
Myerson, Bess (1924—)
Myklebust, Merete (1973—)
Myles, Lynda (1947—)
Myller, Riita (1956—)
Mylonaki, Anthoula (1984—)
Myoung Bok-Hee (1979—)
Myrdal, Alva (1902–1986)
Myrmael, Marit
Myrtel, Hera (b. 1868)
Myrtil, Odette (1898–1978)
Myskina, Anastasia (1981—)
Mystakidou, Elisavet (1977—)
Nadejda Michaelovna (1896–1963)
Nadejda of Bulgaria (1899–1958)
Nadezhdina, Nadezhda (1908–1979)
Nadig, Marie-Thérèse (1954—)
Nadja (c. 1900–1945)
Nagako (1903–2000)
Nagejkina, Svetlana (1965—)
Nagel, Anne (1915–1966)
Nagródskaia, Evdokiia (1866–1930)
Nagy, Aniko
Nagy, Annamaria (1982—)
Nagy, Ilona (1951—)
Nagy, Marianna (1957—)
Nagy, Marianna
Nagy, Timea (1970—)
Nagy, Zsuzsanna (1951—)
Naheed, Kishwar (1940—)
Naidu, Sarojini (1879–1949)
Naimushina, Elena (1964—)
Nair, Mira (1957—)
Naito, Emi (1979—)
Nakada, Kumi (1965—)
Nakajima, Riho (1978—)
Nakamura, Kiharu (1913–2004)
Nakamura, Mai (1979—)
Nakamura, Reiko (1982—)
Nakamura, Taniko (1943—)
Nakanishi, Yuko (1981—)
Nakao, Miki (1978—)
Nakatindi, Princess (c. 1943—)
Nakic, Danira (1969—)
Nákou, Lilika (1903–1989)
Nakova, Dolores (1957—)
Naldi, Nita (1897–1961)
Nalkowska, Zofia (1884–1954)
Nall, Anita (1976—)
Namakelua, Alice K. (1892–1987)
Namba, Yasuko (1949–1996)
Nam Eun-Young (1970—)
Namjoshi, Suniti (1941—)
Nampeyo (c. 1860–1942)
Nansen, Betty (1873–1943)
Napier, Geills (1937—)
Napierkowska, Stacia (1886–1945)
Napoletano, Pasqualina (1949—)
Napolitano, Johnette (1957—)
Napolski, Nancy (1974—)
Naranjo, Carmen (1928—)
Nariman (1934–2005)
Nascimento Pinheiro, Graziele (1981—)
Nash, Diane (1938—)
Nash, Florence (1888–1950)
Nash, June (1911–1979)
Nash, Mary (1885–1976)
Nashar, Beryl (1923—)
Nasralla, Emily (1931—)
Nasrin, Taslima (1962—)
Nasser, Tahia (1923—)
Nassif, Anna (1933—)
Nassif, Malak Hifni (1886–1918)
Nat, Marie-José (1940—)
Natalie, Mlle (c. 1895–1922)
Nathalia Keshko (1859–1941)
Nathan, Maud (1862–1946)
Nathaniel, Cathy (1949—)
Nathhorst, Louise (1955—)
Nathoy, Lalu (1853–1933)
Nation, Carry (1846–1911)
Nattrass, Susan (1950—)
Natwick, Mildred (1908–1994)
Naudé, Adèle (1910–1981)
Navratilova, Martina (1956—)
Nayar, Sushila (1914–2001)
Naylor, Genevieve (1915–1989)
Naylor, Gloria (1950—)
Naylor, Phyllis Reynolds (1933—)
Nazaré, Maria Escolástica Da Conceição (1894–1986)
Nazarova, Natalya (1979—)
Nazarova, Olga (1955—)
Nazarova-Bagryantseva, Irina (1957—)
Nazimova, Alla (1879–1945)
Nazli (1894–1978)
Ndereba, Catherine (1972—)
Neagle, Anna (1904–1986)
Neal, Patricia (1926—)
Neall, Gail (1955—)

Era Index

Nealy, Frances (1918–1997)
Near, Holly (1949—)
Nearing, Helen (1904–1995)
Neary, Colleen (1952—)
Neary, Patricia (1942—)
Necula, Veronica (1967—)
Neculai, Viorica (1967—)
Neculita, Maria (1974—)
Nedreaas, Torborg (1906–1987)
Needham, Dorothy (1896–1987)
Neel, Alice (1900–1984)
Neelissen, Catharina (1961—)
Nef, Sonja (1972—)
Negri, Ada (1870–1945)
Negri, Pola (1894–1987)
Negrone, Carina (1911—)
Negron Muñoz, Mercedes (1895–1973)
Neher, Carola (1900–1942)
Nehru, Kamala (1899–1936)
Nehua, Katerina (1903–1948)
Neill, Elizabeth Grace (1846–1926)
Neilson, Julia Emilie (1868–1957)
Neilson, Nellie (1873–1947)
Neilson, Sandy (1956—)
Neilson-Terry, Phyllis (1892–1977)
Neimke, Kathrin (1966—)
Neisser, Kersten (1956—)
Nelidova, Lydia (1863–1929)
Nelis, Mary (1935—)
Nelken, Margarita (1896–1968)
Nelly (1899–1998)
Nelson, Beryce Ann (1947—)
Nelson, Cindy (1955—)
Nelson, Clara Meleka (1901–1979)
Nelson, Diane (1958—)
Nelson, Jodie (1976—)
Nelson, Marjorie (1937—)
Nelson, Maud (1881–1944)
Nelson, Ruth (1905–1992)
Nelson, Tracy (1944—)
Nelson-Carr, Lindy (1952—)
Nelsova, Zara (1917–2002)
Nemashkalo, Yelena (1963—)
Nemchinova, Vera (1899–1984)
Nemenoff, Genia (1905–1989)
Nemes Nagy, Agnes (1922–1991)
Nemeth, Angela (1946—)
Nemeth, Erzsebet (1953—)
Nemeth, Helga (1973—)
Neneniene-Casaitite, Aldona (1949—)
Nerina, Nadia (1927—)
Neris, Salomeja (1904–1945)
Nerius, Steffi (1972—)
Neruda, Wilma (c. 1838–1911)
Nesbit, Edith (1858–1924)
Nesbit, Evelyn (1884–1967)
Nesbitt, Cathleen (1888–1982)
Nesbitt, Miriam (1873–1954)
Nesbitt, Stephanie (1985—)
Nessim, Barbara (1939—)
Nesterenko, Yuliya (1979—)
Nestle, Joan (1940—)
Nestor, Agnes (1880–1948)
Netessova, Maria (1983—)
Nethersole, Olga (1863–1951)
Netter, Mildrette (1948—)
Nettleton, Lois (1929—)
Neubauer-Ruebsam, Dagmar (1962—)
Neuberger, Maurine B. (1906–2000)
Neufeld, Elizabeth F. (1928—)
Neuffer, Elizabeth (1956–2003)
Neuffer, Judy (1949—)
Neumann, Annett (1970—)
Neumann, Hanna (1914–1971)
Neumann, Liselotte (1966—)
Neumann, Theresa (1898–1962)
Neumann, Vera (1907–1993)
Neumannova, Katerina (1973—)
Neunast, Daniela (1966—)
Neuner, Angelika (1969—)
Neuner, Doris (1970—)
Nevada, Emma (1859–1940)
Nevada, Mignon (1885–1970)
Nevejean, Yvonne (1900–1987)
Nevelson, Louise (1899–1988)
Neves, Claudia (1975—)
Neveu, Ginette (1919–1949)
Nevill, Dorothy Fanny (1826–1913)
Nevill, Mary (1961—)
Neville, Phoebe (1941—)
Neville-Jones, Pauline (1939—)
Newall, Sybil (1854–1929)
Newberry, Barbara (1910—)
Newbery, Chantelle (1977—)
Newbigin, Marion I. (1869–1934)
Newby-Fraser, Paula (1962—)
Newcomb, Ethel (1875–1959)
Newcomb, Mary (1893–1966)
Newell, Susan (1893–1923)
Newhouse, Alice (1924–2004)
Newhouse, Caroline H. (1910–2003)
Newlin, Dika (1923—)
Newman, Angelia L. (1837–1910)
Newman, Frances (1883–1928)
Newman, Mehetabel (c. 1822–1908)
Newman, Nanette (1934—)
Newman, Pauline (1887–1986)
Newmar, Julie (1935—)
Newsom, Carol (1946–2003)
Newsom, Ella King (1838–1919)
Newton, Joy (1913–1996)
Newton, Juice (1952—)
Newton, Lily (1893–1981)
Newton-John, Olivia (1948—)
Newton Turner, Helen (1908–1995)
Ney, Elisabet (1833–1907)
Ney, Elly (1882–1968)
Ney, Marie (1895–1981)
Neykova, Rumyana (1973—)
Nezhdanova, Antonina (1873–1950)
Ngata, Arihia Kane (1879–1929)
Ngcobo, Lauretta (1932—)
Ngoyi, Lilian (1911–1980)
Nguyen Thi Dinh (1920–1992)
Nhiwatiwa, Naomi (1940—)
Nhu, Madame (1924—)
Nian Yun (c. 1983—)
Nice, Margaret Morse (1883–1974)
Nichiforov, Maria (1951—)
Nicholas, Alison (1962—)
Nicholas, Charlotte (fl. 1915)
Nicholas, Cindy (1957—)
Nicholls, Mandy (1968—)
Nicholls, Marjory Lydia (1890–1930)
Nicholls, Rhoda Holmes (1854–1930)
Nichols, Anne (1891–1966)
Nichols, Barbara (1929–1976)
Nichols, Dandy (1907–1986)
Nichols, Etta Grigsby (1897–1994)
Nichols, Minerva Parker (1861–1949)
Nichols, Ruth (1901–1960)
Nicholson, Emma (1941—)
Nicholson, Nora (1889–1973)
Nicholson, Winifred (1893–1981)
Nichtern, Claire (c. 1921–1994)
Ni Chuilleanáin, Eiléan (1942—)
Nickerson, Camille (1884–1982)
Nicks, Stevie (1948—)
Nico (1938–1988)
Nicol, Helen Lyster (1854–1932)
Nicoll, Ashley (1963—)
Nicolson, Adela Florence (1865–1904)
Niculescu-Margarit, Elena (1936—)
Nidetch, Jean (1923—)
Ni Dhomhnaill, Nuala (1952—)
Niebler, Angelika (1963—)
Niedecker, Lorine (1903–1970)
Niederkirchner, Käte (1909–1944)
Niedernhuber, Barbara (1974—)
Niehaus, Jutta (1964—)
Nieh Hualing (1925—)
Nielsen, Alice (c. 1870–1943)
Nielsen, Anja (1975—)
Nielsen, Asta (1881–1972)
Nielsen, Augusta (1822–1902)
Nielsen, Jerri (1953—)
Nielsen, Lone Smidt (1961—)
Nielsson, Susanne (1960—)
Nieman, Nancy (1933—)
Niemann, Gunda (1966—)
Niemczykowa, Barbara (1943—)
Nienhuys, Janna
Niepce, Janine (1921—)
Niese, Charlotte (1854–1935)
Niese, Hansi (1875–1934)
Niesen, Gertrude (1910–1975)
Nieuwenhuizen, Anneloes (1963—)
Niggli, Josefina (1910–1983)
Nigh, Jane (1925–1993)
Nightingale, Florence (1820–1910)
Ni Guizhen (c. 1869–1931)
Nijinska, Bronislava (1891–1972)
Nijinska, Romola (1891–1978)
Nikishina, Svetlana (1958—)
Nikitina, Alice (1909–1978)
Nikolaeva, Klavdiia (1893–1944)
Nikolaeva, Olga (1972—)
Nikolayeva, Margarita (1935—)
Nikolayeva, Tatiana (1924–1993)
Nikolayeva, Yelena (1966—)
Nikonova, Valentina (1952—)
Nikoultchina, Irina (1974—)
Nikulina, Marina (1963—)
Niles, Blair (1880–1959)
Niles, Mary Ann (1938–1987)
Nillson, Carlotta (c. 1878–1951)
Nilsen, Elin (1968—)
Nilsen, Jeanette (1972—)
Nilsmark, Catrin (1967—)
Nilsson, Anna Q. (1889–1974)
Nilsson, Birgit (1918–2005)
Nilsson, Christine (1843–1921)
Nilsson, Karin (b. 1904)
Nimmanhemin, M.L. Bupha Kunjara (1905–1963)
Nin, Anais (1903–1977)
Niniwa-i-te-rangi (1854–1929)
Ninova, Violeta (1963—)
Niogret, Corinne (1972—)
Nisima, Maureen (1981—)
Nissen, Greta (1906–1988)
Niu Jianfeng (1981—)
Nivedita, Sister (1867–1911)
Nixon, Agnes (1927—)
Nixon, Joan Lowery (1927–2003)
Nixon, Julie (1948—)
Nixon, Marion (1904–1983)
Nixon, Marni (1929—)
Nixon, Pat (1912–1993)
Nixon, Tricia (1946—)
Njau, Rebeka (1932—)
Nkrumah, Fathia (c. 1931—)
Noach, Ilse (1908–1998)
Noack, Angelika (1952—)
Noack, Marianne (1951—)
Noailles, Anna de (1876–1933)
Noailles, Marie-Laure de (1902–1970)
Noall, Patricia (1970—)
Noble, Cheryl (1956—)
Noble, Cindy (1958—)
Noble, Mary (1911–2002)
Nóbrega, Isabel da (1925—)
Noce, Teresa (1900–1980)
Noddack, Ida (1896–1978)
Nöel, Magali (1932—)
Noemi, Lea (1883–1973)
Noergaard, Louise Bager (1982—)
Noether, Emmy (1882–1935)
Nogami, Yaeko (1885–1985)
Noguchi, Constance Tom (1948—)
Noguchi, Mizuki (1978—)
Nolan, Jeanette (1911–1998)
Nolan, Kathleen (1933—)
Nolan, Mae Ella (1886–1973)
Nolan, Rachel (1974—)
Nollen, Maike (1977—)
Nong Qunhua (1966—)
Noonan, Peggy (1950—)
Noor al-Hussein (1951—)
Nord, Kathleen (1965—)
Nordby, Bente (1974—)
Norden, Christine (1924–1988)
Nordheim, Helena (1903–1943)
Nordi, Cleo (b. 1899)
Nordica, Lillian (1857–1914)
Nordin, Hjoerdis (1932—)
Nordstrom, Ursula (1910–1988)
Norelius, Kristine (1956—)
Norelius, Martha (1908–1955)

Noren, Svea (1895–1985)
Norgate, Kate (1853–1935)
Noris, Assia (1912–1998)
Norman, Decima (1909–1983)
Norman, Dorothy (1905–1997)
Norman, Jessye (1945—)
Norman, Maidie (1912–1998)
Norman, Marsha (1947—)
Normand, Kirstin (1974—)
Normand, Mabel (1892–1930)
Normanton, Helena (1883–1957)
Norodom Monineath Sihanouk (1936—)
Norrell, Catherine Dorris (1901–1981)
Norris, Kathleen (1880–1966)
North, Sheree (1933–2005)
Northcroft, Hilda Margaret (1882–1951)
Norton, Alice Peloubet (1860–1928)
Norton, Andre (1912–2005)
Norton, Eleanor Holmes (1937—)
Norton, Mary (1903–1992)
Norton, Mary T. (1875–1959)
Noskova, Luiza (1968—)
Noskowiak, Sonya (1900–1975)
Nöstlinger, Christine (1936—)
Notari, Elvira (1875–1946)
Nothnagel, Anke (1966—)
Nott, Andrea (1982—)
Nott, Kathleen (1909–1999)
Nott, Tara (1972—)
Nourse, Elizabeth (1859–1938)
Novaës, Guiomar (1895–1979)
Novak, Eva (1898–1988)
Novak, Eva (1930—)
Novak, Helga (1935—)
Novak, Ilona (1925—)
Novak, Jane (1896–1990)
Novak, Kim (1933—)
Novak, Nina (1927—)
Nováková, Teréza (1853–1912)
Novarra-Reber, Sue (1955—)
Novello, Antonia (1944—)
Novello, Clara (1818–1908)
Novello-Davies, Clara (1861–1943)
Novokshchenova, Olga (1974—)
Novotna, Jana (1968—)
Novotna, Jarmila (1907–1994)
Nowak, Cecile (1967—)
Nowicka, Joanna (1966—)
Nowland, Mary Josepha (1863–1935)
Noyes, Blanche (1900–1981)
Noyes, Clara Dutton (1869–1936)
Noziere, Violette (1915–1966)
Nugent, Andrea (1968—)
Nunes, Natália (1921—)
Nunn, Glynis (1960—)
Nunneley, Kathleen Mary (1872–1956)
Nurpeissova, Dina (1861–1955)
Nurutdinova, Liliya (1963—)
Nussbaum, Karen (1950—)
Nüsslein-Volhard, Christiane (1942—)
Nuthall, Betty (1911–1983)
Nutt, Emma M. (c. 1849–1926)
Nuttall, Zelia (1857–1933)
Nutting, Mary Adelaide (1858–1948)
Nuveman, Stacey (1978—)
Nuyen, France (1939—)
Nwapa, Flora (1931–1993)
Nyad, Diana (1949—)
Nyberg, Katarina (1965—)
Nybraaten, Inger-Helene (1960—)
Nyembe, Dorothy (1930–1998)
Nymark Andersen, Nina (1972—)
Nyro, Laura (1947–1997)
Nystrom, Karen (1969—)
Nzimiro, Mary (1898–1993)
Oakar, Mary Rose (1940—)
Oakley, Ann (1944—)
Oakley, Annie (1860–1926)
Oakley, Laura (1880–1957)
Oakley, Violet (1874–1961)
Oancia, Ecaterina (1954—)
Oates, Joyce Carol (1938—)
Oatman, Olive Ann (c. 1838–1903)
Oba, Minako (1930—)
Oberg, Margo (1953—)
Oberheuser, Herta (1911–1978)
Oberhoffner, Ute
Oberon, Merle (1911–1979)
O'Brien, Catherine (1881–1963)
O'Brien, Edna (1930—)
O'Brien, Kate (1897–1974)
O'Brien, Margaret (1937—)
O'Brien, Miriam (1898–1976)
O'Brien, Virginia (1896–1987)
O'Brien, Virginia (1919–2001)
O'Brien-Moore, Erin (1902–1979)
O'Callaghan, Kathleen (1888–1961)
Ocampo, Silvina (1903–1993)
Ocampo, Victoria (1890–1979)
Ocampo-Friedmann, Roseli (1937—)
O'Carroll, Maureen (1913–1984)
O'Casey, Eileen (1900–1995)
Ochichi, Isabella (1979—)
Ochoa, Elisa
Ochoa, Ellen (1958—)
Ochs, Debra (1966—)
Ocloo, Esther (1919–2002)
O'Connell, Helen (1920–1993)
O'Connell, Patricia (d. 1975)
O'Connor, Colleen
O'Connor, Ellen (1857–1933)
O'Connor, Flannery (1925–1964)
O'Connor, Karen (1958—)
O'Connor, Kathleen (1935—)
O'Connor, Mary Anne (1953—)
O'Connor, Sandra Day (1930—)
O'Connor, Sinéad (1966—)
O'Connor, Una (1880–1959)
Oda, Cheko
Odaga, Asenath (1938—)
Odaka, Emiko (1962—)
O'Day, Anita (1919—)
O'Day, Caroline (1869–1943)
O'Day, Molly (1911–1998)
Oddon, Yvonne (1902–1982)
Odebrecht, Viola (1983—)
Oden, Elaina (1967—)
Oden, Kimberley (1964—)
Odena, Lina (1911–1936)
Odetta (1930—)
Odhnoff, Camilla (1923—)
Odinokova-Berezhnaya, Lyubov (1955—)
Odio Benito, Elizabeth (1939—)
Odoevtseva, Irina (c. 1895–1990)
O'Doherty, Eileen (b. 1891)
O'Doherty, Mary Anne (1826–1910)
O'Doherty, Mignon (1890–1961)
O'Donnell, Ann (c. 1857–1934)
O'Donnell, Cathy (1923–1970)
O'Donnell, Liz (1956—)
O'Donnell, May (1906–2004)
O'Donnell, Phyllis (1937—)
O'Donnell, Rosie (1962—)
Odozi Obodo, Madam (1909–1995)
O'Driscoll, Martha (1922–1998)
Oelkers-Caragioff, Olga (1887–1969)
Oelschlagel, Charlotte (c. 1899–after 1948)
Oertli, Brigitte (1962—)
Oestvold, Line (1978—)
O'Faolain, Julia (1932—)
O'Faolain, Nuala (1940—)
O'Farrell, Bernadette (1924–1999)
O'Farrill, Raisa (1972—)
Ogbeifo, Ruth (1967—)
Ogier, Bulle (1939—)
Ogilvie Farquharson, Marian (1846–1912)
Ogilvie Gordon, Maria M. (1864–1939)
Ogiyenko, Valentina (1965—)
Ognjenovic, Mirjana (1953—)
Ogot, Grace (1930—)
O'Grady, Diane (1967—)
Ogunkoya, Falilat (1969—)
O'Hagan, Dara (1964—)
O'Hair, Madalyn Murray (1919–1995)
O'Hanlon, Virginia (c. 1899–1971)
O'Hara, Mary (1885–1980)
O'Hara, Maureen (1920—)
O'Hara, Shirley (1910–1979)
O'Hara, Shirley (1924–2002)
Ohara, Tomie (b. 1912)
O'Hare, Kate Richards (1876–1948)
Oh Kyo-Moon
Ohlson, Agnes K. (1902–1991)
Ohr, Martine (1964—)
Ohsako, Tatsuko (1952—)
Oh Seung-Shin
Oh Sung-Ok (1972—)
Ohta, Tomoko (1933—)
Oh Yong-Ran (1972—)
Oikonomopoulou, Aikaterini (1978—)
Oinuma, Sumie (1946—)
Okamoto, Ayako (1951—)
Okamoto, Mariko (1951—)
Okamoto, Yoriko (1971—)
Okayo, Margaret (1976—)
Okazaki, Tomomi (1971—)
O'Keeffe, Georgia (1887–1986)
O'Kelley, Mattie Lou (c. 1908–1997)
Okin, Susan Moller (1946–2004)
Okino, Betty (1975—)
Okorokova, Antonina (1941—)
Okoye, Ifeoma
Okuno, Fumiko (1972—)
Okwei of Osomari (1872–1943)
Olah, Susanna (d. around 1929)
Olaru, Maria (1982—)
Olberg, Oda (1872–1955)
Oldenburg, Astrid (1932—)
Oldenburg, Cecily (1911–1937)
Oldenburg, Margaret (1895–1992)
Oldenburg, Margaret (1905–1981)
Oldenburg, Martha (1971—)
Oldenburg, Mary (1865–1909)
Oldenburg, Ragnhild (1930—)
Oldfather, Irene (1954—)
Oldfield, Pearl Peden (1876–1962)
Olds, Elizabeth (1896–1991)
Olenewa, Maria (1893–1965)
Olga (1884–1958)
Olga (1895–1918)
Olga, Princess Paley (1865–1929)
Olga Alexandrovna (1882–1960)
Olga Constantinovna (1851–1926)
Olga Iurevskaya (1873–1925)
Olga Oldenburg (1903–1981)
Olin, Lena (1955—)
Oliphant, Betty (1918–2004)
Oliveira, Alessandra (1973—)
Oliveira, Elisangela (1978—)
Oliveira, Marli de (1935—)
Oliveira, Walewska (1979—)
Oliver, Edith (1913–1998)
Oliver, Edna May (1883–1942)
Oliver, Mary (1935—)
Oliver, Susan (1937–1990)
Oliver, Thelma (1941—)
Olivero, Magda (b. 1910)
Oliveros, Pauline (1932—)
Olivette, Nina (c. 1908–1971)
Olive Vancells, Nuria (1968—)
Olivier, Edith (c. 1879–1948)
Olivier, Fernande (1884–1966)
Olizarenko, Nadezhda (1953—)
Olliwier, Eva (1904–1955)
Olmsted, Barbara (1959—)
Olmsted, Gertrude (1897–1975)
Olmsted, Mildred Scott (1890–1990)
Olney, Violet (1911—)
Olrich, April (1931—)
Olsen, Tillie (c. 1912—)
Olsen, Zoe Ann (1931—)
Olson, Leslee (1978—)
Olson, Nancy (1928—)
Olsson, Anna (1964—)
Olsson, Hagar (1893–1978)
Olteanu, Ioana (1966—)
Olunina, Alevtina (1930—)
O'Malley, Grania (1885–1973)
O'Malley, Mary Dolling (1889–1974)
Oman, Julia Trevelyan (1930–2003)
Ombres, Rossana (1931—)
O'Meara, Kathleen (1960—)
Omelenchuk, Jeanne (1931—)
Omelianchik, Oksana (1970—)
Omens, Estelle (1928–1983)
Omilade, Navina (1981—)
Omlie, Phoebe Fairgrave (1902–1975)
Onassis, Christina (1950–1988)

Ondieki, Lisa (1960—)
Ondra, Anny (1902–1987)
O'Neal, Christine (1949—)
O'Neal, Tatum (1963—)
O'Neal, Zelma (1903–1989)
O'Neale, Lila M. (1886–1948)
O'Neil, Barbara (1909–1980)
O'Neil, Kitty (1947—)
O'Neil, Nance (1874–1965)
O'Neil, Nancy (1911–1995)
O'Neil, Peggy (1898–1960)
O'Neil, Sally (1908–1968)
O'Neill, Carlotta (1888–1970)
O'Neill, Maire (1885–1952)
O'Neill, Rose Cecil (1874–1944)
O'Neill, Susie (1973—)
Oneto, Vanina (1973—)
Onians, Edith (1866–1955)
Onishi, Junko (1974—)
Ono, Kiyoko (1936—)
Ono, Yoko (1933—)
Onodi, Henrietta (1974—)
Onoprienko, Galina (1963—)
Onyali, Mary (1968—)
Onyango, Grace (1934—)
Oomen-Ruijten, Ria G.H.C. (1950—)
Opara, Charity (1972—)
Opara-Thompson, Christy (1971—)
Opdyke, Irene (1918–2003)
Opie, Iona (1923—)
Oppelt, Britta (1978—)
Oppenheim, Méret (1913–1985)
Oppenheimer, Jane Marion (1911–1996)
Oppens, Ursula (1944—)
Orantes, Ana (c. 1937–1997)
Orbell, Margaret (1934—)
Orchard, Sadie (c. 1853–1943)
Orcutt, Edith (c. 1918–1973)
Orcutt, Maureen (b. 1907)
Orczy, Emma (1865–1947)
Ordonówna, Hanka (1904–1950)
Ordway, Katharine (1899–1979)
O'Regan, Katherine (1946—)
O'Reilly, Heather (1985—)
O'Reilly, Leonora (1870–1927)
Orelli, Susanna (1845–1939)
Oremans, Miriam (1972—)
Organ, Diana (1952—)
Orgeni, Aglaja (1841–1926)
Orkin, Ruth (1921–1985)
Orlando, Mariane (1934—)
Orlova, Liubov (1902–1975)
Ormerod, Eleanor A. (1828–1901)
Oros, Rozalia (1963—)
O'Rourke, Heather (1975–1988)
O'Rourke, Mary (1937—)
Orphee, Elvira (1930—)
Orr, Alice Greenough (1902–1995)
Orr, Kay (1939—)
Orr, Vickie (1967—)
Ortese, Anna Maria (1914–1998)
Ortiz, Cristina (1950—)
Ortiz, Letizia (1972—)
Ortiz Calvo, Tania (1965—)
Ortiz Charro, Yahima (1981—)
Orton, Beth (1970—)
Ortrud of Schleswig-Holstein-Sonderburg-Glucksburg (1925—)
Orvieto, Laura (1876–1953)
Orwig, Bernice (1976—)
Orzeszkowa, Eliza (1841–1910)
Osadchaya, Liliya (1953—)
Osato, Sono (1919–1953)
Osborn, Daisy (1888–1957)
Osborne, Estelle Massey (1901–1981)
Osborne, Fanny (1852–1934)
Osborne, Joan (1962—)
Osborne, Margaret (1918—)
Osborne, Marie (1911—)
Osborne, Mary (1921–1992)
Osborne, Mary D. (1875–1946)
Osborne, Sandra (1956—)
Osborne, Vivienne (1896–1961)
Osburn, Ruth (1912–1994)
Osgerby, Ann (1963—)
O'Shea, Katherine (1845–1921)
O'Shea, Tessie (1913–1995)
Osiier, Ellen (1890–1962)
Osipenko, Alla (1932—)
Osipenko, Polina (1907–1939)
Osipova, Irina (1981—)
Osipowich, Albina (1911–1964)
Oslin, K.T. (1941—)
Osmanoglu, Gevheri (1904–1980)
Osmond, Marie (1959—)
Osório, Ana de Castro (1872–1935)
Osserman, Wendy (1942—)
O'Steen, Shyril (1960—)
Osten, Maria (1908–1942)
Ostenso, Martha (1900–1963)
Ostergaard, Solveig (1939—)
Osterman, Catherine (1983—)
Ostermeyer, Micheline (1922–2001)
Ostler, Emma Brignell (c. 1848–1922)
Ostriche, Muriel (1896–1989)
Ostromecka, Krystyna (1948—)
O'Sullivan, Jan (1950—)
O'Sullivan, Keala (1950—)
O'Sullivan, Mairan D. (1919–1987)
O'Sullivan, Mary Kenney (1864–1943)
O'Sullivan, Maureen (1911–1998)
O'Sullivan, Sonia (1969—)
Oswald, Marina (1941—)
Oswalda, Ossi (1897–1948)
Osygus, Simone (1968—)
Osypenko, Inna (1982—)
Otake, Eiko (1952—)
Otani, Sachiko (1965—)
Otero, Caroline (1868–1965)
O'Toole, Barbara (1960—)
O'Toole, Maureen (1961—)
Otsetova, Svetlana (1950—)
Ott, Mirjam (1972—)
Ott, Patricia (1960—)
Ottenberg, Nettie Podell (1887–1982)
Ottenbrite, Anne (1966—)
Ottesen-Jensen, Elise (1886–1973)
Ottey, Merlene (1960—)
Otto, Kristin (1966—)
Otto, Louise (1896—)
Otto, Sylke (1969—)
Otto-Crepin, Margit (1945—)
Otway-Ruthven, Jocelyn (1909–1989)
Ouden, Willemijntje den (1918–1997)
Ouellette, Caroline (1979—)
Oughton, Diana (1942–1970)
Oughton, Winifred (1890–1964)
Ou Jingbai
Oulehlova, Lenka (1973—)
Ouspenskaya, Maria (1876–1949)
Ousset, Cécile (1936—)
Outhwaite, Ida Rentoul (1888–1960)
Ovari, Eva (1961—)
Ovchinnikova, Elena (1982—)
Ovechkina, Nadezhda (1958—)
Ovechkina, Tatyana (1950—)
Overbeck, Carla (1969—)
Overlach, Helene (1894–1983)
Oversloot, Maria (1914—)
Ovington, Mary White (1865–1951)
Ovtchinnikova, Elena (1965—)
Owen, Catherine Dale (1900–1965)
Owen, Laurence (1945–1961)
Owen, Maribel (1941–1961)
Owen, Maribel Vinson (1911–1961)
Owen, Nora (1945—)
Owen, Seena (1894–1966)
Owens, Claire Myers (1896–1983)
Owens, Evelyn P. (1931—)
Owens, Patricia (1925–2000)
Owens, Shirley (1941—)
Owens-Adair, Bethenia (1840–1926)
Owings, Margaret Wentworth (1913–1999)
Ozegovic, Sanja (1959—)
Ozick, Cynthia (1928—)
Ozolina, Elvira (1939—)
Paasche, Maria (1909–2000)
Pacari, Nina (1961—)
Paciotti, Elena Ornella (1941—)
Pack, Doris (1942—)
Packer, Ann E. (1942—)
Packer, Joy (1905–1977)
Padar, Ildiko (1970—)
Paddleford, Clementine (1900–1967)
Padovani, Lea (1920–1991)
Paduraru, Maria (1970—)
Paek Myong-Suk (1954—)
Paemel, Monika van (1945—)
Paerson, Anja (1981—)
Pagava, Ethery (1932—)
Page, Annette (1952—)
Page, Dorothy G. (1921–1989)
Page, Estelle Lawson (1907–1983)
Page, Ethel (c. 1875–1958)
Page, Evelyn (1899–1987)
Page, Gale (1913–1983)
Page, Geneviève (1930—)
Page, Geraldine (1924–1987)
Page, Gertrude (1873–1922)
Page, LaWanda (1920–2002)
Page, P.K. (1916—)
Page, Patti (1927—)
Page, Ruth (1899–1991)
Paget, Debra (1933—)
Paget, Dorothy (1905–1960)
Paget, Mary (1865–1919)
Paget, Muriel (1876–1938)
Paget, Nielsine (1858–1932)
Paget, Rosalind (1855–1948)
Paget, Violet (1856–1935)
Paglia, Camille (1947—)
Pagliero, Camilia (1859–1925)
Pagliughi, Lina (1907–1980)
Pahlavi, Ashraf (1919—)
Pahlavi, Farah (1938—)
Pahlavi, Soraya (1932–2001)
Paige, Elaine (1948—)
Paige, Janis (1922—)
Paige, Jean (1895–1990)
Paige, Mabel (1879–1954)
Painter, Eleanor (1890–1947)
Paisley, Eileen (1934—)
Pak, Se Ri (1977—)
Pakhalina, Yulia (1977—)
Pakhmutova, Alexandra (1929—)
Pakholchik, Olena (1964—)
Pakhomova, Ludmila (d. 1986)
Palacios, Lucila (1902–1994)
Palchikova, Irina (1959—)
Palcy, Euzhan (1957—)
Palencia, Isabel de (1878–c. 1950)
Paley, Babe (1915–1978)
Paley, Grace (1922)
Palfi, Marion (1907–1978)
Palfrey, Sarah (1912–1996)
Palfyova, Matylda (1912–1944)
Palinger, Katalin (1978—)
Paliyska, Diana (1966—)
Pall, Olga (1947—)
Palladino, Emma (c. 1860–1922)
Palladino, Eusapia (1854–1918)
Palli, Anne-Marie (1955—)
Palmer, Alice Freeman (1855–1902)
Palmer, Alice May (1886–1977)
Palmer, Bertha Honoré (1849–1918)
Palmer, Helen (1917–1979)
Palmer, Leland (1940—)
Palmer, Lilli (1914–1986)
Palmer, Lillian (b. 1913)
Palmer, Lizzie Merrill (1838–1916)
Palmer, Maria (1917–1981)
Palmer, Nettie (1885–1964)
Palmer, Sandra (1941—)
Palmer, Sophia French (1853–1920)
Palmolive (1955—)
Paltrow, Gwyneth (1972—)
Palucca, Gret (1902–1993)
Pàmies, Teresa (1919—)
Pampanini, Silvana (1925—)
Panagiotatou, Angeliki (1878–1954)
Panchuk, Lyudmila (1956—)
Pandit, Vijaya Lakshmi (1900–1990)
Panfil, Wanda (1959—)
Pang Jiaying (1985—)
Pankhurst, Adela (1885–1961)
Pankhurst, Christabel (1880–1958)
Pankhurst, Emmeline (1858–1928)
Pankhurst, Sylvia (1882–1960)

Pankina, Aleksandra
Panov, Galina (1949—)
Panova, Bianca (1970—)
Panova, Vera (1905–1973)
Pantazi, Charikleia (1985—)
Pantelimon, Oana (1972—)
Panter-Downes, Mollie (1906–1997)
Pantoja, Antonia (1922–2002)
Panton, Catherine (1955—)
Pan Wenli (1969—)
Paola (1937—)
Papadat-Bengescu, Hortensia (1876–1955)
Papadopoulou, Alexandra (1867–1906)
Papakura, Makereti (1873–1930)
Papariga, Alexandra (1945—)
Papas, Irene (1926—)
Pappenheim, Bertha (1859–1936)
Papuc, Ioana (1984—)
Parain-Vial, Jeanne (b. 1912)
Paramygina, Svetlana (1965—)
Paraskevin-Young, Connie (1961—)
Parata, Katherine Te Rongokahira (1873–1939)
Pardo Bazán, Emilia (1852–1921)
Parek, Lagle (1941—)
Paretsky, Sara (1947—)
Pargeter, Edith (c. 1913–1995)
Parish, Sister (1910–1994)
Parisien, Julie (1971—)
Park, Grace (1979—)
Park, Ida May (1879–1954)
Park, Maud Wood (1871–1955)
Park, Merle (1937—)
Park, Rosemary (1907–2004)
Park, Ruth (1923—)
Park Chan-Sook (1959—)
Parke, Mary (1908–1989)
Parker, Agnes Miller (1895–1980)
Parker, Bonnie (1910–1934)
Parker, Bridget (1939—)
Parker, Catherine Langloh (c. 1856–1940)
Parker, Cecilia (1905–1993)
Parker, Claire (1906–1981)
Parker, Dehra (1882–1963)
Parker, Denise (1973—)
Parker, Dorothy (1893–1967)
Parker, Eleanor (1922—)
Parker, Jean (1915–2005)
Parker, Julia O'Connor (1890–1972)
Parker, Lottie Blair (c. 1858–1937)
Parker, Madeleine (c. 1909–1936)
Parker, Pat (1944–1989)
Parker, Pauline Yvonne (1938—)
Parker, Suzy (1932–1932)
Parker, Valeria Hopkins (1879–1959)
Parker-Bowles, Camilla (1947—)
Parkes, Bessie Rayner (1829–1925)
Park Hae-Jung
Parkhomchuk, Irina (1965—)
Parkhurst, Helen (1887–1973)
Park Hye-Won (1983—)
Parkinson, Alice May (1889–1949)
Parkinson, Georgina (1938—)
Park Jeong-Lim (1970—)
Park Kap-Sook (1970—)
Park Mi-Kum (1955—)
Parks, Hildy (1926–2004)
Parks, Rosa (1913—)
Parks, Suzan-Lori (1963—)
Park Soon-Ja (1966—)
Park Sung-Hyun (1983—)
Parlby, Irene (1868–1965)
Parlo, Dita (1906–1971)
Parloa, Maria (1843–1909)
Parlow, Cindy (1978—)
Parlow, Kathleen (1890–1963)
Parnell, Anna (1852–1911)
Parnis, Mollie (1905–1992)
Parnok, Sophia (1885–1933)
Parra, Teresa de la (1889–1936)
Parra, Violeta (1917–1967)
Parren, Kalliroe (1861–1940)
Parrish, Anne (1888–1957)
Parrish, Celestia (1853–1918)
Parrish, Helen (1922–1959)
Parritt, Barbara (1944—)
Parsley, Lea Ann (1968—)
Parsons, Betty Pierson (1900–1982)
Parsons, Elizabeth (1846–1924)
Parsons, Elsie Clews (1875–1941)
Parsons, Estelle (1927—)
Parsons, Harriet (1906–1983)
Parsons, Louella (1881–1972)
Parsons, Nancie (1904–1968)
Parton, Dolly (1946—)
Parton, Mabel (b. 1881)
Partridge, Frances (1900–2004)
Partridge, Kathleen (1963—)
Partridge, Margaret (b. 1891)
Parturier, Françoise (1919—)
Parun, Vesna (1922—)
Paruzzi, Gabriella (1969—)
Parviainen, Katri (1914–2002)
Pasca, Mirela (1975—)
Pascal, Amy (1959—)
Pascal, Christine (1953–1996)
Pascalina, Sister (1894–1983)
Pascal-Trouillot, Ertha (1943—)
Pascual, Carolina (1976—)
Pascu-Ene-Dersidan, Ana (1944—)
Pashley, Anne (1935—)
Pasini, Claudia (1939—)
Paskuy, Eva (1948—)
Pasokha, Anna (1949—)
Pasternak, Josephine (1900–1993)
Pastor, Claudia (1971—)
Pastuszka, Aneta (1978—)
Patch, Edith (1876–1954)
Paterson, Ada Gertrude (1880–1937)
Paterson, Isabel (c. 1886–1961)
Paterson, Jennifer (1928–1999)
Paterson, Pat (1911–1978)
Patil, Smita (1955–1986)
Patmore, Sharon (1963—)
Paton Walsh, Jill (1937—)
Patoulidou, Paraskevi (1965—)
Patrascoiu, Aneta (1957—)
Patrick, Dorothy (1921–1987)
Patrick, Gail (1911–1980)
Patrick, Mary Mills (1850–1940)
Patrick, Ruth (1907—)
Patrie, Béatrice (1957—)
Patten, Dorothy (1905–1975)
Patten, Luana (1938–1996)
Patten, Marguerite (1915—)
Patterson, Alicia (1906–1963)
Patterson, Audrey (1926–1996)
Patterson, Carly (1988—)
Patterson, Eleanor Medill (1881–1948)
Patterson, Elizabeth (1874–1966)
Patterson, Elizabeth J. (1939—)
Patterson, Francine (1947—)
Patterson, Hannah (1879–1937)
Patterson, Marie (1934—)
Patterson, Martha Johnson (1828–1901)
Patterson, Nan (c. 1882–?)
Patton, Frances Gray (1906–2000)
Pauca, Simona (1969—)
Pauker, Ana (c. 1893–1960)
Paul, Alice (1885–1977)
Paul, Annette (1863–1952)
Paul, Joanna (1945–2003)
Pauley, Jane (1950—)
Paul-Foulds, June (1934—)
Pauli, Hertha (1909–1973)
Pauline of Saxe-Weimar (1852–1904)
Pauline of Wurttemberg (1877–1965)
Paulsen, Marit (1939—)
Paulu, Blanka (1954—)
Pausin, Ilse (1919—)
Pavan, Marisa (1932—)
Pavicevic, Zorica (1956—)
Pavlina, Yevgenia (1979—)
Pavlova, Anna (1881–1931)
Pavlova, Anna (1987—)
Pavlova, Nadezhda (1956—)
Pavlovich, Yaroslava
Pavlow, Muriel (1921—)
Pawlik, Eva (1927–1983)
Pawlikowska, Maria (1891–1945)
Paxinou, Katina (1900–1973)
Payne, Ethel (1911–1991)
Payne, Freda (1945—)
Payne, Katy (1937—)
Payne, Marita (1960—)
Payne, Nicola (1960—)
Payne, Nicolle (1976—)
Payne, Sylvia (1880–1974)
Payne, Thelma (1896–1988)
Payne, Virginia (1908–1977)
Payne-Gaposchkin, Cecilia (1900–1979)
Payson, Joan Whitney (1903–1975)
Payson, Sandra (c. 1926–2004)
Payton, Barbara (1927–1967)
Payton, Carolyn Robertson (1925–2001)
Paz Paredes, Margarita (1922–1980)
Pazyun, Mariya (1953—)
Peabody, Josephine Preston (1874–1922)
Peabody, Lucy (1861–1949)
Peacocke, Isabel Maud (1881–1973)
Peake, Felicity (1913–2002)
Peale, Ruth Stafford (b. 1906)
Pearce, Alice (1913–1966)
Pearce, Caroline (1925—)
Pearce, Christie (1975—)
Pearce, Jean (1921—)
Pearce, Louise (1885–1959)
Pearce, May (1915–1981)
Pearce, Morna (1932—)
Pearce, Philippa (1920—)
Pearce, Vera (1896–1966)
Pearl, Minnie (1912–1996)
Pearsall, Phyllis (1906–1996)
Pearse, Margaret (1857–1932)
Pearse, Margaret Mary (1878–1968)
Pearson, Landon Carter (1930—)
Pearson, Maryon (1901–1989)
Pearson, Michele (1962—)
Pearson, Molly (d. 1959)
Pearson, Virginia (1886–1958)
Peary, Josephine (1863–1955)
Pease, Heather (1975—)
Peattie, Cathy (c. 1956—)
Pechenkina, Natalya (1946—)
Pecherskaya, Svetlana (1968—)
Pechey-Phipson, Edith (1845–1908)
Pechstein, Claudia (1972—)
Pechstein, Heidi (1944—)
Peck, Annie Smith (1850–1935)
Peck, Ellen (1829–1915)
Peden, Irene (1925—)
Pedersen, Elaine (1936–2000)
Pedersen, Helga (1911–1980)
Pedersen, Hilde G. (1964—)
Pedersen, Lena (1940—)
Pedersen, Share (1963—)
Pedersen, Solveig
Pedersen, Susan (1953—)
Pedretti, Erica (1930—)
Peebles, Ann (1947—)
Peebles, Florence (1874–1956)
Peek, Alison (1969—)
Peete, Louise (1883–1947)
Peijs, Karla M.H. (1944—)
Peixotto, Jessica (1864–1941)
Pejacevic, Dora (1885–1923)
Pekic, Sofija (1953—)
Pekli, Maria (1972—)
Pelen, Perrine (1960—)
Peleshenko, Larisa (1964—)
Pelish, Thelma (1926–1983)
Pellegrini, Federica (1988—)
Pellegrino, Aline (1982—)
Pelletier, Annie (1973—)
Pelletier, Henriette (c. 1864–1961)
Pelletier, Madeleine (1874–1939)
Pellicer, Pina (1935–1964)
Pelosi, Nancy (1940—)
Pels, Auguste van (1900–1945)
Pember, Phoebe Yates (1823–1913)
Peña, Tonita (1893–1949)
Pendleton, Ellen Fitz (1864–1936)
Penes, Mihaela (1947—)
Penfold, Merimeri (1924—)
Pengelly, Edna (1874–1959)
Peng Ping (1967—)
Penicheiro, Ticha (1974—)
Pennell, Elizabeth Robins (1855–1936)
Penney, Jennifer (1946—)

Pennington, Ann (1892–1971)
Pennington, Mary Engle (1872–1952)
Pennington, Winifred (1915—)
Penninx, Nelleke (1971—)
Pennison, Marleen (1951—)
Penson, Lillian Margery (1896–1963)
Pentland, Barbara (1912–2000)
Pepa, Mari (1913–2004)
Peplau, Hildegard E. (1909–1999)
Pepper, Beverly (1924—)
Pepper, Dottie D. (1965—)
Peppler, Mary Jo (1944—)
Pequegnot, Laure (1975—)
Peratrovich, Elizabeth Wanamaker (1911–1958)
Perazic, Jasmina (1960—)
Perchina, Irina (1978—)
Percy, Eileen (1899–1973)
Percy, Karen (1966—)
Perec, Marie-Jose (1968—)
Pereira, Irene Rice (1902–1971)
Pereira, Jacqueline (1964—)
Pereira da Silva, Kelly (1985—)
Pereira Ribeiro, Tania (1974—)
Perey, Marguerite (1909–1975)
Pereyaslavec, Valentina (1907–1998)
Perez del Solar, Gabriela (1968—)
Perham, Linda (1947—)
Perham, Margery (1895–1982)
Peri Rossi, Cristina (1941—)
Peris-Kneebone, Nova (1971—)
Perkins, Frances (1880–1965)
Perkins, Lucy Fitch (1865–1937)
Perkins, Millie (1938—)
Perkins, Susan (c. 1954—)
Perkucin, Gordana (1962—)
Perón, Eva (1919–1952)
Perón, Isabel (1931—)
Perreau, Gigi (1941—)
Perreault, Annie (1971—)
Perriand, Charlotte (1903–1999)
Perrier, Glorianne (1929—)
Perrin, Ethel (1871–1962)
Perrone, Elisabetta (1968—)
Perrot, Kim (c. 1967–1999)
Perry, Antoinette (1888–1946)
Perry, Elaine (1921–1986)
Perry, Eleanor (1915–1981)
Perry, Frances (1907–1993)
Perry, Julia (1924–1979)
Perry, Katherine (1897–1983)
Perry, Lilla Cabot (c. 1848–1933)
Perry, Margaret (1913—)
Perry, Nanceen (1977—)
Perry, Ruth (1939—)
Perry, Wanda (1917–1985)
Persson, Elisabeth (1964—)
Pert, Candace B. (1946—)
Perversi, Luigina (1914–1983)
Pery, Angela Olivia (1897–1981)
Pery, Sylvia (1935—)
Pesotta, Rose (1896–1965)
Pestana, Alice (1860–1929)
Petacci, Clara (1912–1945)
Peter, Birgit (1964—)
Peterkin, Julia (1880–1961)
Peters, Bernadette (1948—)
Peters, Jean (1926–2000)
Peters, Kristina (1968—)
Peters, Mary (1939—)
Peters, Roberta (1930—)
Peters, Roumania (1917–2003)
Peters, Susan (1921–1952)
Petersen, Alicia O'Shea (1862–1923)
Petersen-Kallensee, Marga (1919—)
Petersmann, Cerstin (1964—)
Peterson, Amy (1971—)
Peterson, Ann (1947—)
Peterson, Esther (1906–1997)
Peterson, Marjorie (1906–1974)
Peterson, Mary (1927—)
Peterson, Sylvia (1946—)
Pethick-Lawrence, Emmeline (1867–1954)
Petipa, Marie (1857–1930)
Petit, Magdalena (1900–1968)
Petkova, Ognyana (1964—)
Petkova-Vergova, Mariya (1950—)
Petrass, Sari (1890–1930)
Petre, Maude (1863–1942)
Petri, Heather (1978—)
Petrickova, Kvetoslava (1952—)
Petrie, Haylea (1969—)
Petrie, Hilda (1871–1957)
Petrik, Larissa (1949—)
Petrova, Ioulia (1979—)
Petrova, Ludmila (1968—)
Petrova, Maria (1975—)
Petrova, Olena (1972—)
Petrova, Olga (1886–1977)
Petrova, Tatiana (1973—)
Petrova, Yelena (1966—)
Petrovschi, Oana (1986—)
Petrovýkh, Mariia (1908–1979)
Petrucci, Roxy (1962—)
Petrunova, Silva (1956—)
Petruseva, Natalia (1955—)
Petrushevskaya, Ludmilla (1938—)
Petry, Ann (1908–1997)
Petry, Lucile (1902–1999)
Pettersen, Brit
Pettersen, Karin (1964—)
Pettersen, Marianne (1975—)
Pettersson, Ann-Sofi (1932—)
Pettersson, Goeta (1926—)
Pettersson, Wivan (1904–1976)
Pettis, Bridget (1971—)
Pettis, Shirley Neil (1924—)
Pettit, Katherine (1868–1936)
Petty, Mary (1899–1976)
Petushkova, Yelena (1940—)
Petzold, Barbara (1955—)
Peyton, Kim (1957–1986)
Pezzo, Paola (1969—)
Pfeffer, Anna (1945—)
Pfeiffer, Jane Cahill (1932—)
Pfeiffer, Michelle (1957—)
Pflueger, Joan (1931—)
Pflug, Monika (1954—)
Pfohl, Cornelia (1971—)
Pfost, Gracie (1906–1965)
Phagan, Mary (c. 1899–1913)
Phair, Liz (1967—)
Phalle, Niki de Saint (1930–2002)
Phelps, Jaycie (1979—)
Philbin, Eva (1914—)
Philbin, Mary (1903–1993)
Philippart, Nathalie (c. 1926—)
Philips, Mary (1901–1975)
Phillips, Anita Frances
Phillips, Brenda (1958—)
Phillips, Chynna (1968—)
Phillips, Clara (1899—)
Phillips, Dorothy (1889–1980)
Phillips, Esther (1935–1984)
Phillips, Frances L. (1896–1986)
Phillips, Harriet Newton (1819–1901)
Phillips, Irna (1901–1973)
Phillips, Julia (1944–2002)
Phillips, Karen (1966—)
Phillips, Kristie (1972—)
Phillips, Lena Madesin (1881–1955)
Phillips, Margaret (1923–1984)
Phillips, Marion (1881–1932)
Phillips, Michelle (1944—)
Phillips, Siân (1934—)
Phillips, Zara (1981—)
Phillpotts, Adelaide (1896–c. 1995)
Phillpotts, Bertha Surtees (1877–1932)
Phipps, Sally (1909–1978)
Phipson, Joan (1912–2003)
Phoolan Devi (1963–2001)
Phranc (1957—)
Phuc, Kim (c. 1963—)
Piaf, Edith (1915–1963)
Picasso, Paloma (1949—)
Piccinini, Amelia (1917–1979)
Pichler, Magdalena (1881–1920)
Pickens, Helen (1910—)
Pickens, Jane (1908–1992)
Pickens, Patti (1914–1995)
Pickerill, Cecily Mary Wise (1903–1988)
Pickett, Fuchsia T. (1918–2004)
Pickford, Lottie (1895–1936)
Pickford, Mary (1893–1979)
Pickford, Mary (1902–2002)
Picking, Anne (1958—)
Pickles, Edith Carrie
Pickthall, Marjorie (1883–1922)
Picon, Molly (1898–1992)
Pielen, Silke (1955—)
Pielke, Christiane (1963—)
Pienkowska, Alina (1952–2002)
Pierangeli, Rina Faccio (1876–1960)
Pierantozzi, Emanuela (1968—)
Pierce, Joanne E. (c. 1941—)
Pierce, Judith (1930–2003)
Pierce, Mary (1975—)
Piercy, Marge (1936—)
Piestewa, Lori Ann (1980–2003)
Pigniczki, Krisztina (1975—)
Pi Hongyan (1979—)
Pike, Mary (1824–1908)
Pike, Mervyn (1918–2004)
Pilcher, Rosamunde (1924—)
Pilejczyk, Helena (1931—)
Pilgrim, Ada (1867–1965)
Pilley, Dorothy (1893–1986)
Pimnacova, Bohumila (1947—)
Pinayeva-Khvedosyuk, Lyudmila (1936—)
Pinchot, Cornelia (1881–1960)
Pinepine Te Rika (1857/58–1954)
Pinigina-Kulchunova, Mariya (1958—)
Pino, Rosario (d. 1933)
Piñon, Nélida (1937—)
Pintasilgo, Maria de Lurdes (1930–2004)
Pinto, Adriana (1978—)
Pious, Minerva (1903–1979)
Piper, Carly (1983—)
Piper, Cherie (1981—)
Piper, Leonora E. (1859–1950)
Piper, Myfanwy (1911–1997)
Pipota, Constanta (1971—)
Pippig, Uta (1965—)
Pires, Maria-Joao (1944—)
Pires Tavares, Sandra (1973—)
Pirie, Antoinette (1905–1991)
Pirrie, Margaret Montgomery (1857–1935)
Pisani, Sandra (1959—)
Pisareva, Mariya (1934—)
Piscator, Maria Ley (1899–1999)
Piserchia, Doris (1928—)
Piseth Pilika (1965–1999)
Pisier, Marie-France (1944—)
Piskun, Elena (1978—)
Piszczek, Renata (1969—)
Pitini-Morera, Hariata Whakatau (1871/72?–1938)
Pitman, Jenny (1946—)
Pitoëff, Ludmilla (1896–1951)
Pitot, Genevieve (c. 1920—)
Pitou, Penny (1938—)
Pitseolak (c. 1900–1983)
Pitt, Marie E.J. (1869–1948)
Pitter, Ruth (1897–1992)
Pitt-Rivers, Rosalind (1907–1990)
Pitts, ZaSu (1898–1963)
Pivovarova, Olga (1956—)
Pizarnik, Alejandra (1936–1972)
Pizzavini, Diana (1911–1989)
Pizzey, Erin (1939—)
Plá, Josefina (1909–1999)
Plá, Mirta (1940–2003)
Place, Etta (fl. 1896–1905)
Place, Marcella (1959—)
Plachyne-Korondi, Margit (1932—)
Plaetzer, Kjersti (1972—)
Plaminkova, Frantiska (1875–1942)
Planck-Szabó, Herma (1902–1986)
Planinc, Milka (1924—)
Plath, Sylvia (1932–1963)
Platt, Louise (1915–2003)
Platt of Writtle, Baroness (1923—)
Platts-Mills, Daisy Elizabeth (1868–1956)
Platz, Elizabeth
Plavsic, Biljana (1930—)
Player, Mary Josephine (c. 1857–1924)
Player, Willa B. (1909–2003)
Playfair, Judy (1953—)
Pleasant, Mary Ellen (c. 1814–1904)
Pleijel, Agneta (1940—)

Plesca, Aurora (1963—)
Pleshette, Suzanne (1937—)
Plesman, Suzanne
Plewinski, Catherine (1968—)
Plisetskaya, Maya (1925—)
Ploch, Jutta (1960—)
Plooij-Van Gorsel, Elly (1947—)
Plotnikova, Elena (1978—)
Plowright, Joan (1929—)
Plummer, Mary Wright (1856–1916)
Pockels, Agnes (1862–1935)
Podestà, Rossana (1934—)
Podhanyiova, Viera (1960—)
Podkopayeva, Lilia (1978—)
Poehlsen, Paula (1913—)
Poelvoorde, Rita (1951—)
Poetzl, Ine (1976—)
Poewe, Sarah (1983—)
Pogosheva-Safonova, Tamara (1946—)
Pohlers, Conny (1978—)
Poinso-Chapuis, Germaine (1901–1981)
Pointer, Anita (1948—)
Pointer, Bonnie (1950—)
Pointer, June (1954–2006)
Pointer, Ruth (1946—)
Poiree, Liv Grete (1974—)
Poirot, Catherine (1963—)
Polaire (1879–1939)
Polak, Anna (1906–1943)
Polcz, Alaine (1921—)
Poleska, Anne (1980—)
Poletti, Syria (1919–1991)
Poley, Viola (1955—)
Polgar, Judit (1976—)
Poliakoff, Olga (c. 1935—)
Poliakova, Elena (1884–1972)
Poli Bortone, Adriana (1943—)
Polidouri, Maria (1902–1930)
Polis, Carol
Polit, Cornelia (1963—)
Polite, Carlene Hatcher (1932—)
Polkunen, Sirkka (1927—)
Poll, Claudia (1972—)
Poll, Sylvia (1970—)
Pollack, Andrea (1961—)
Pollak, Anna (1912–1996)
Pollak, Burglinde (1951—)
Pollard, Marjorie (1899–1982)
Pollard, Velma (1937—)
Pollatou, Anna (1983—)
Pollitzer, Anita (1894–1975)
Pollock, Jessie
Pollock, Nancy (1905–1979)
Pollock, Sharon (1936—)
Polokova, Iveta (1970—)
Polozkova, Alëna (1979—)
Polsak, Udomporn (1981—)
Polson, Florence Ada Mary Lamb (1877–1941)
Polyblank, Ellen Albertina (1840–1930)
Pomoshchnikova, Natalya (1965—)
Pompeia, Núria (1938—)
Pompilj, Vittoria Aganoor (1855–1910)
Poniatowska, Elena (1932—)
Ponomareva-Romashkova, Nina (1929—)
Ponor, Catalina (1987—)
Pons, Lily (1898–1976)
Ponselle, Carmela (1892–1977)
Ponselle, Rosa (1897–1981)
Pontes, Sister Dulce Lopes (1914–1992)
Pontois, Noëlla (1943—)
Pontoppidan, Clara (1883–1975)
Ponyaeva, Tatyana (1946—)
Poole, Monica (1921–2003)
Pooley, Violet (1886–1965)
Poor, Anne (1918–2002)
Popa, Celestina (1970—)
Popa, Eugenia (1973—)
Pope, Maria Sophia (1818–1909)
Popescu, Marioara (1962—)
Popkova, Vera (1943—)
Poplavskaja, Kristina (1972—)
Popova, Diana (1976—)
Popova, Liubov (1889–1924)
Popova, Nina (1922—)
Popova, Valentina (1972—)
Popova-Aleksandrova, Larisa (1957—)
Popovici, Elise (1921—)
Popp, Adelheid (1869–1939)
Popp, Lucia (1939–1993)
Poppler, Jericho (1951—)
Poradnik-Bobrus, Lyudmila (1946—)
Poreceanu, Uta (1936—)
Porn, Hanna (1860–1913)
Portal, Magda (1903–1989)
Portal, Marta (1930—)
Portapovitch, Anna Knapton (1890–1974)
Porten, Henny (1888–1960)
Porter, Annie (1880–1963)
Porter, Charlotte Endymion (1857–1942)
Porter, Dorothy Germain (1924—)
Porter, Eleanor H. (1868–1920)
Porter, Elizabeth Kerr (1894–1989)
Porter, Gladys M. (1894–1967)
Porter, Gwendoline (c. 1909—)
Porter, Helen Kemp (1899–1987)
Porter, Jean (1924—)
Porter, Katherine Anne (1890–1980)
Porter, Marguerite (c. 1956—)
Porter, Mary Bea (1949—)
Porter, Mary Winearls (1886–1980)
Porter, Natalia (1980—)
Porter, Nyree Dawn (1936–2001)
Porter, Stacey (1982—)
Porter, Sylvia (1913–1991)
Portillo, Lourdes
Portillo-Trambley, Estela (1936–1999)
Pörtner, Margit (c. 1973—)
Portnoy, Ethel (1927–2004)
Portwich, Ramona (1967—)
Porzecowna, Elzbieta (1945—)
Pos, Alette (1962—)
Posevina, Elena (1986—)
Possekel, Elvira (1953—)
Post, Emily (1872–1960)
Post, Marjorie Merriweather (1887–1973)
Post, Sandra (1948—)
Postell, Ashley (1986—)
Postel-Vinay, Anise (1928—)
Postlewait, Kathy (1949—)
Poston, Elizabeth (1905–1987)
Potachova, Olga (1976—)
Potec, Camelia Alina (1982—)
Poto, Alicia (1978—)
Potorac, Gabriela (1973—)
Potter, Beatrix (1866–1943)
Potter, Cora (1857–1936)
Potter, Cynthia (1950—)
Potter, Maureen (1925–2004)
Potter, Sally (1949—)
Pottharst, Kerri-Ann (1965—)
Pottinger, Judith (1956—)
Pötzsch, Anett (1961—)
Pought, Emma (1942—)
Pought, Jannie (1944–1980)
Pougy, Liane de (1866–c. 1940)
Pound, Louise (1872–1958)
Pounder, Cheryl (1976—)
Pounder, Cheryl
Powdermaker, Hortense (1896–1970)
Powell, Dawn (1897–1965)
Powell, Dilys (1901–1995)
Powell, Eleanor (1910–1982)
Powell, Jane (1929—)
Powell, Katrina (1972—)
Powell, Kristy (1980—)
Powell, Lisa (1970—)
Powell, Louise Mathilde (1871–1943)
Powell, Mary Sadler (1854/55?–1946)
Powell, Maud (1867–1920)
Powell, Sandy (1960—)
Powell, Susan (c. 1959—)
Power, Eileen (1889–1940)
Power, Laurel Jean (1953—)
Powers, Georgia Davis (1923—)
Powers, Harriet (1837–1911)
Powers, Leona (1896–1970)
Powers, Mala (1931—)
Powers, Marie (1902–1973)
Poynton, Dorothy (1915—)
Poyntz, Juliet Stuart (1886–c. 1937)
Poysti, Toini K.
Pozzi, Antonia (1912–1938)
Pracht, Eva-Maria (1937—)
Prado, Adélia (1936—)
Praed, Rosa (1851–1935)
Praeger, Sophia Rosamund (1867–1954)
Prang, Mary D. Hicks (1836–1927)
Pratt, Anna Beach (1867–1932)
Pratt, Daria (1861–1938)
Pratt, Dolly (1955—)
Pratt, Eliza Jane (1902–1981)
Preis, Ellen (1912—)
Preisser, Cherry (1918–1964)
Preisser, June (1920–1984)
Preissova, Gabriela (1862–1946)
Prejean, Helen (1939—)
Premice, Josephine (1926–2001)
Premont, Marie-Hélene (1977—)
Prendergast, Sharon Marley (1964—)
Prentice, Bridget (1952—)
Prentice, Jo Ann (1933—)
Prentiss, Paula (1939—)
Preobrazhenska, Olga (1871–1962)
Preobrazhenskaya, Nina (1956—)
Preradovic, Paula von (1887–1951)
Presacan, Claudia (1979—)
Preshaw, Jane (1839–1926)
Presle, Micheline (1922—)
Press, Irina (1939—)
Press, Tamara (1939—)
Presti, Ida (1924–1967)
Preston, Margaret Rose (c. 1875–1963)
Preston, May Wilson (1873–1949)
Pretinha (1975—)
Prets, Christa (1947—)
Pretty, Arline (1885–1978)
Preuss, Phyllis (1939—)
Prevost, Hélène
Prevost, Marie (1895–1937)
Prewitt, Cheryl (c. 1957—)
Price, Ellen (1878–1968)
Price, Eugenia (1916–1996)
Price, Florence B. (1888–1953)
Price, Hayley
Price, Juliette (1831–1906)
Price, Kate (1872–1943)
Price, Leontyne (1927—)
Price, Margaret (1941—)
Price, Nancy (1880–1970)
Price, Roberta MacAdams (1881–1959)
Prichard, Katharine Susannah (1883–1969)
Prickett, Maudie (1914–1976)
Priemer, Petra (1961—)
Priesand, Sally Jane (1946—)
Priest, Ivy Baker (1905–1975)
Priestner, Cathy (1958—)
Primarolo, Dawn (1954—)
Primo de Rivera, Pilar (1913–1991)
Primrose-Smith, Elizabeth (c. 1948—)
Primus, Pearl (1919–1994)
Pringle, Aileen (1895–1989)
Pringle, Elizabeth Allston (1845–1921)
Pringle, Mia Lilly (1920–1983)
Prinsloo, Christine (1952—)
Printemps, Yvonne (1894–1977)
Prinz, Birgit (1977—)
Prior, Maddy (1947—)
Prishchepa, Nadezhda (1956—)
Pritam, Amrita (1919–2005)
Privalova, Irina (1968—)
Probert, Michelle (1960—)
Procopé, Ulla (1921–1968)
Produnova, Elena (1980—)
Proeber, Martina (1963—)
Proell-Moser, Annemarie (1953—)
Prokasheva, Lyudmila (1969—)
Prokhorova, Yelena (1978—)
Prokoff, Sandra (1975—)
Prokop, Liese (1941—)
Prophet, Elizabeth (1890–1960)
Prophet, Elizabeth Clare (1940—)
Prorochenko-Burakova, Tatyana (1952—)
Proskouriakoff, Tatiana (1909–1985)
Prosperi, Carola (1883–1975)
Protopopov, Ludmila (1935—)
Prou, Suzanne (1920–1995)
Proulx, E. Annie (1935—)
Prouty, Olive Higgins (1882–1974)

Providokhina-Fyodorenko, Tatyana (1953—)
Provine, Dorothy (1937—)
Provis, Nicole (1969—)
Prowse, Juliet (1936–1996)
Prozumenshchykova, Galina (1948—)
Prudskova, Valentina (1938—)
Prunskiene, Kazimiera (1943—)
Pryakhina, Svetlana (1970—)
Przybyszewska, Stanislawa (1901–1935)
Ptaschkina, Nelly (1903–1920)
Ptujec, Jasna (1959—)
Puck, Eva (1892–1979)
Pudney, Elizabeth Allen (1894–1976)
Pudney, Elizabeth Jane (1862–1938)
Pueschel, Karin (1958—)
Pufe, Margitta (1952—)
Pugacheva, Alla (1949—)
Pugh, Madelyn (c. 1921—)
Pugovskaya, Olga (1942—)
Puhiwahine Te Rangi-hirawea, Rihi (d. 1906)
Pühringer, Uta Barbara (1943—)
Puica, Maricica (1950—)
Pukui, Mary Kawena (1895–1986)
Pulling, Mary Etheldred (1871–1951)
Pulman, Elizabeth (1836–1900)
Pulver, Lilo (1929—)
Pulz, Penny (1953—)
Pung, Jackie (1921—)
Purcell, Irene (1902–1972)
Purcell, Samuelene (1898–1982)
Purser, Sarah (1848–1943)
Purviance, Edna (1894–1958)
Pustovit, Antonina (1955—)
Pusula, Senja (1941—)
Putli Bai (1929–1958)
Putnam, Alice Whiting (1841–1919)
Putnam, Bertha Haven (1872–1960)
Putnam, Emily James (1865–1944)
Putnam, Helen (1857–1951)
Putzer, Karen (1978—)
Puzhevich, Olga (1983—)
Pye, Edith (1876–1965)
Pyke, Margaret (1893–1966)
Pyleva, Olga (1975—)
Pym, Barbara (1913–1980)
Pyritz, Dana (1970—)
Qian Hong (1971—)
Qian Zhengying (1923—)
Qiao Hong (1968—)
Qiao Yunping
Qin Dongya (1978—)
Qin Yiyuan
Qiong Yao (1938—)
Qiu Chen (1963—)
Qiu Jin (c. 1875–1907)
Qualter, Tot (1894–1974)
Quance, Kristine (1975—)
Quann, Megan (1984—)
Quant, Mary (1934—)
Quaranta, Isabella (1892–1975)
Quaranta, Letizia (1892–1974)
Quaranta, Lidia (1891–1928)
Quaretti, Lea (1912–1981)
Quass, Margaret (1926–2003)
Quatro, Suzi (1950—)
Queen Latifah (1970—)
Queeny, Mary (1913–2003)
Queirós, Raquel de (1910–2003)
Queizán, María Xosé (1938—)
Queler, Eve (1936—)
Quesada, Violetta (1947—)
Questel, Mae (1908–1998)
Questiaux, Nicole (1931—)
Quik, Martijntje (1973—)
Quill, Máirin (1940—)
Quimby, Edith (1891–1982)
Quimby, Harriet (1875–1912)
Quin, Ann (1936–1973)
Quin, Joyce (1944—)
Quindlen, Anna (1953—)
Quinlan, Karen Ann (1954–1985)
Quinn, Helen (1943—)
Quinn, Jane Bryant (1939—)
Quinn, Mary Ann (c. 1928—)
Quintanal, Maria (1969—)
Quintero Alvarez, Ioamnet (1972—)
Quinton, Amelia S. (1833–1926)
Quinton, Carol (1936—)
Quinton, Cornelia B. Sage (1876–1936)
Quiroga, Elena (1919–1995)
Quirot, Ana (1963—)
Quist, Anne Marie (1957—)
Quisthoudt-Rowohl, Godelieve (1947—)
Qu Yunxia (1972—)
Qvist, Trine (c. 1967—)
Raab, Esther (1894–1981)
Rabasova, Jana (1933—)
Rabbani, Ruhiyyih (1910–2000)
Rabin, Leah (1928–2000)
Rablen, Eva (1905—)
Racine, Jean (1978—)
Racinet, Delphine (1973—)
Radanova, Evgenia (1977—)
Radchenko, Olena (1973—)
Radcliffe, Charlotte (b. 1903)
Radcliffe, Nora (1946—)
Radcliffe, Paula (1973—)
Radi, Nuha al- (1941–2004)
Radke, Lina (1903–1983)
Radkova, Kostadinka (1962—)
Radner, Gilda (1946–1989)
Radochla, Birgit (1945—)
Radovic, Vesna (1950—)
Radu, Elena (1975—)
Raducan, Andreea (1983—)
Radulovic, Bojana (c. 1973—)
Radyonska, Tanya (1924—)
Radzevich, Nadezhda (1953—)
Raeburn, Agnes Middleton (1872–1955)
Raeva, Iliana (1963—)
Rafael, Sylvia (1938–2005)
Rafanelli, Leda (1880–1971)
Rafferty, Frances (1922–2004)
Rafko, Kaye Lani (c. 1963—)
Ragghianti, Marie (1942—)
Ragusa, Cinzia (1977—)
Rahn, Muriel (1911–1961)
Rahon, Alice (1904–1987)
Rai, Pamela (1966—)
Raiche, Bessica (c. 1874–1932)
Raikh, Zinaida (1894–1939)
Raine, Kathleen (1908–2003)
Rainer, Luise (1910—)
Rainer, Yvonne (1934—)
Raines, Ella (1920–1988)
Rainey, Barbara Allen (1948–1982)
Rainey, Ma (1886–1939)
Rainier, Priaulx (1903–1986)
Raisa, Rosa (1893–1963)
Raisin, Catherine (1855–1945)
Raitt, Bonnie (1949—)
Rajalakshmi, R. (1926—)
Rajnai, Klara (1953—)
Rakels, Heidi (1968—)
Rakhmatulina, Oxana (1976—)
Rakoczy, Helena (1921—)
Rakusz, Eva (1961—)
Ra Kyung-Min (1976—)
Ralenkova, Anelia (1963—)
Ralfe, Catherine Hester (c. 1831–1912)
Ralov, Kirsten (1922–1999)
Ralph, Jessie (1864–1944)
Ralph, Margaret (c. 1822–1913)
Ralston, Esther (1902–1994)
Ralston, Jobyna (1900–1967)
Ralston, Vera Hruba (1921–2003)
Ramabai, Pandita (1858–1922)
Rama Rau, Dhanvanthi (1893–1987)
Rama Rau, Santha (1923—)
Rambeau, Marjorie (1889–1970)
Rambert, Marie (1888–1982)
Rambova, Natacha (1897–1966)
Rame, Franca (1929—)
Ramée, Louise de la (1839–1908)
Ramenofsky, Marilyn (1946—)
Ramey, Nancy (1940—)
Ramey, Venus (c. 1925—)
Ramirez, Maria Teresa (1953—)
Ramirez, Sara Estela (1881–1910)
Ramirez Hechevarria, Daymi (1983—)
Ramirez Merino, Virginia (1964—)
Ramo, Roberta Cooper (1942—)
Ramondino, Fabrizia (1936—)
Ramoskiene, Genovaite (1945—)
Ramphele, Mamphela (1947—)
Rampling, Charlotte (1945—)
Ramsay, Alison (1959—)
Ramsay, Patricia (1886–1974)
Ramseier, Doris (1939—)
Ramsey, Alice Huyler (1886–1983)
Ramsey, Alicia (1864–1933)
Ramsey, Anne (1929–1988)
Ramsey, Elizabeth M. (1906–1993)
Ramsey, Sue (1970—)
Ramsland, Sarah Katherine (1882–1964)
Ran, Shulamit (1949—)
Ranavalona III (1861–1917)
Rand, Ayn (1905–1982)
Rand, Caroline Amanda (1828–1905)
Rand, Ellen (1875–1941)
Rand, Gertrude (1886–1970)
Rand, Mary (1940—)
Rand, Sally (1904–1979)
Randall, Amelia Mary (1844–1930)
Randall, Claire (1919—)
Randall, Marta (1948—)
Randall, Martha (1948—)
Randolph, Amanda (1896–1967)
Randolph, Barbara (d. 2002)
Randolph, Elsie (1904–1982)
Randolph, Isabel (1889–1973)
Randolph, Lillian (1898–1980)
Randolph, Virginia (1874–1958)
Randzio-Plath, Christa (1940—)
Ranguelova, Kristina (1985—)
Rania (1970—)
Rankin, Annabelle (1908–1986)
Rankin, Janice (1972—)
Rankin, Jeannette (1880–1973)
Rankin, Judy (1945—)
Rankin, Nell (1924–2005)
Ransome-Kuti, Funmilayo (1900–1978)
Rantala, Lene (1968—)
Rantanen, Heli Orvokki (1970—)
Rantanen, Siiri (1924—)
Rapoport, Lydia (1923–1971)
Rapp, Anita (1977—)
Rapp, Susan (1965—)
Rasch, Albertina (1896–1967)
Raschhofer, Daniela (1960—)
Rashad, Phylicia (1948—)
Rashid, Saleha Abdul (1939—)
Raskin, Judith (1928–1984)
Raskina, Yulia (1982—)
Raskova, Marina (1912–1943)
Rasmussen, Bodil Steen (1957—)
Rasp, Renate (1935—)
Rastvorova, Valentina (1933—)
Ratana, Iriaka (1905–1981)
Ratcliffe, Jane (1917–1999)
Rāteb, Aisha (1928—)
Ratebzad, Anahita (1931—)
Rathbone, Eleanor (1872–1946)
Rathbone, Josephine Adams (1864–1941)
Rathbun, Mary Jane (1860–1943)
Rathebe, Dolly (1928–2004)
Rathgeber, Lisa (1961—)
Ratia, Armi (1912–1979)
Ratner, Anna (c. 1892–1967)
Rattenbury, Alma (c. 1904–1935)
Rattray, Lizzie Frost (1855–1931)
Ratushinskaya, Irina (1954—)
Raubal, Geli (c. 1908–1931)
Ravan, Genya (1942—)
Ravenscroft, Gladys (1888–1960)
Ravera, Camilla (1889–1988)
Raverat, Gwen (1885–1957)
Ravikovitch, Dahlia (1936—)
Rawlings, Marjorie Kinnan (1896–1953)
Rawlinson, Gloria (1918–1995)
Rawls, Betsy (1928—)
Rawls, Katherine (1918–1982)
Ray, Charlotte E. (1850–1911)
Ray, Dixy Lee (1914–1994)
Ray, Elise (1982—)
Ray, H. Cordelia (c. 1849–1916)
Ray, René (1911–1993)
Raye, Martha (1916–1994)

Rayet, Jacqueline (1932—)
Rayhel, Oxana (1977—)
Raymond, Eleanor (1887–1989)
Raymond, Helen (c. 1885–1965)
Raymond, Lisa (1973—)
Raymond, Paula (1923–2003)
Rayner, M.C. (c. 1894–1948)
Razumova, Natalya (1961—)
Read, Cari (1970—)
Read, Imelda Mary (1939—)
Reagan, Maureen (1941–2001)
Reagan, Nancy (1921—)
Reals, Gail (c. 1937—)
Ream, Vinnie (1847–1914)
Rebay, Hilla (1890–1967)
Rebuck, Gail (1950—)
Reddick, Cat (1982—)
Reddon, Lesley (1970—)
Reddy, Helen (1941—)
Redgrave, Lynn (1943—)
Redgrave, Vanessa (1937—)
Redmond, Bridget Mary (1905–1952)
Redondo Jiménez, Encarnación (1944—)
Redpath, Anne (1895–1965)
Redpath, Christine (1951—)
Redpath, Jean (1937—)
Reece, Gabrielle (1970—)
Reece, Louise Goff (1898–1970)
Reed, Alma (1889–1966)
Reed, Donna (1921–1986)
Reed, Florence (1883–1967)
Reed, Janet (1916–2000)
Reed, Kit (1932—)
Reed, Mary (1854–1943)
Reed, Myrtle (1874–1911)
Reed, Rowena (1900–1988)
Reel, Chi Cheng (1944—)
Rees, Annie Lee (1864–1949)
Rees, Gwendolen (1906–1994)
Rees, Rosemary (c. 1876–1963)
Reese, Della (1931—)
Reese, Gail (1946—)
Reese, Lizette Woodworth (1856–1935)
Reeve, Elsie (1885–1927)
Reeves, Connie (1901–2003)
Reeves, Helen (1980—)
Reeves, Magdalene Stuart (1865–1953)
Reeves, Martha (1941—)
Regan, Agnes (1869–1943)
Regan, Sylvia (1908–2003)
Reger, Janet (1935–2005)
Regina, Elis (1945–1982)
Regnell, Lisa (1887–1979)
Rego, Paula (1935—)
Regoczy, Krisztina
Rehan, Ada (1857–1916)
Rehn, Elisabeth (1935—)
Rehor, Grete (1910–1987)
Reich, Lilly (1885–1947)
Reichard, Gladys (1893–1955)
Reiche, Maria (1903–1998)
Reichert, Ossi
Reichova, Alena (1933—)
Reid, Beryl (1918–1996)
Reid, Charlotte Thompson (b. 1913)
Reid, Clarice D. (1931—)
Reid, Dorothy Davenport (1895–1977)
Reid, Elisabeth Mills (1858–1931)
Reid, Florence (c. 1870–1950)
Reid, Frances (b. 1913)
Reid, Helen Rogers (1882–1970)
Reid, Kate (1930–1993)
Reid, Margaret (1935—)
Reid, Maria (1895–1979)
Reid, Rose Marie (1906–1978)
Reignolds, Catherine Mary (1836–1911)
Reik, Haviva (1914–1944)
Reilly, Dianne (1969—)
Reiman, Elise (c. 1910—)
Reimann, Brigitte (1933–1973)
Reimer, Daniela (1982—)
Reinders, Agnes (1913–1993)
Reineck, Heidemarie (1952—)
Reiner, Ethel Linder (d. 1971)
Reinhardt, Aurelia Henry (1877–1948)
Reinhardt, Sybille (1957—)
Reinig, Christa (1926—)
Reiniger, Lotte (1899–1981)
Reinisch, Rica (1965—)
Reinking, Ann (1949—)
Reinshagen, Gerlind (1926—)
Reis, Maria Firmina dos (1825–1917)
Reischauer, Haru (c. 1915–1998)
Reisenberg, Nadia (1904–1983)
Reisner, Larissa (1895–1926)
Reiter, Frances (1904–1977)
Reitsch, Hanna (1912–1979)
Reitz, Dana (1948—)
Réjane, Gabrielle (1857–1920)
Rekha (1954—)
Reljin, Milena (1967—)
Remey, Ethel (1895–1979)
Remick, Lee (1935–1991)
Remington, Barbara (1936—)
Remler, Emily (1957–1990)
Renard, Rosita (1894–1949)
Renaud, Madeleine (1903–1994)
Renault, Mary (1905–1983)
Rendall, Martha (d. 1909)
Rendell, Ruth (1930—)
Rendle, Sharon (1966—)
Rendschmidt, Elsa (1886–1969)
Renée (1926—)
Renger, Annemarie (1919—)
Renk, Silke (1967—)
Rennie, Rhoda
Reno, Janet (1938—)
Renoth, Heidi Maria (1978—)
Rensch, Katharina (1964—)
Rentoul, Annie Isobel (c. 1855–1928)
Rentoul, Annie Rattray (1882–1978)
Repko, Elena (1975—)
Repplier, Agnes (1855–1950)
Reschke, Karin (1940—)
Resino, Carmen (1941—)
Resnik, Judith (1949–1986)
Resnik, Muriel (c. 1917–1995)
Resnik, Regina (1922—)
Respighi, Elsa (1894–1996)
Restituta, Sister (1894–1943)
Restoux, Marie-Claire (1968—)
Restrepo, Ximena (1969—)
Resvoll, Thekla (1871–1948)
Resvoll-Holmsen, Hanna (1873–1943)
Rethberg, Elisabeth (1894–1976)
Retter, Hannah (1839–1940)
Retton, Mary Lou (1968—)
Reuteler, Fabienne (1979—)
Reuter, Gabriele (1859–1941)
Reve Jimenez, Odalis (1970—)
Reventlow, Franziska von (1871–1918)
Revere, Anne (1903–1990)
Revier, Dorothy (1904–1993)
Reville, Alma (1899–1982)
Revsin, Leslie (1944–2004)
Rexach, Sylvia (1922–1961)
Rey, Margret (1906–1996)
Reynolds, Adeline DeWalt (1862–1961)
Reynolds, Debbie (1932—)
Reynolds, Jane (c. 1897—)
Reynolds, Malvina (1900–1978)
Reynolds, Marjorie (1917–1997)
Reynolds, Mary (c. 1890–1974)
Reynolds, Myra (1853–1936)
Reynolds, Rachel Selina (1838–1928)
Reynolds, Vera (1899–1962)
Reza, Yasmina (1959—)
Rezkova, Miloslava (1950—)
Reztsova, Anfisa (1964—)
Rheaume, Manon (1972—)
Rhind, Ethel (c. 1879–1952)
Rhode, Kim (1979—)
Rhodes, Betty (c. 1935–1987)
Rhodes, Billie (1894–1988)
Rhodes, Zandra (1940—)
Rhondda, Margaret (1883–1958)
Rhys, Jean (1890–1979)
Rhys-Jones, Sophie (1965—)
Riabouchinska, Tatiana (1917–2000)
Riale, Karen (c. 1949—)
Riano, Renie (1899–1971)
Ribeiro, Fernanda (1969—)
Ribeiro Cabral, Juliana (1981—)
Ricard, Marthe (1889–1982)
Ricarda, Ana (c. 1925—)
Ricci, Nina (1883–1970)
Rice, Alice Hegan (1870–1942)
Rice, Anne (1941—)
Rice, Bridget Mary (1885–1967)
Rice, Condoleezza (1954—)
Rice, Florence (1907–1974)
Rice, Joan (1930–1997)
Rice-Davies, Mandy (1944—)
Rich, Adrienne (1929—)
Rich, Irene (1891–1988)
Rich, Louise Dickinson (1903–1991)
Richards, Ann (1917—)
Richards, Ann Willis (1933—)
Richards, Audrey Isabel (1899–1984)
Richards, Beah (1920–2000)
Richards, Ellen Swallow (1842–1911)
Richards, Julie Burns (1970—)
Richards, Laura E. (1850–1943)
Richards, Linda (1841–1930)
Richards, Renée (1934—)
Richards, Sandie (1968—)
Richards, Sanya (1985—)
Richards, Shelah (1903–1985)
Richardson, Dorothy (1873–1957)
Richardson, Dot (1961—)
Richardson, Effie Newbigging (1849/50?–1928)
Richardson, Gloria (1922—)
Richardson, Henry Handel (1870–1946)
Richardson, Jillian (1965—)
Richardson, Katy (1864–1927)
Richardson, Luba Lyons (1949—)
Richardson, Michelle (1969—)
Richardson, Miranda (1958—)
Richardson, Nicole (1970—)
Richardson, Ruth (1950—)
Richey, Helen (1910–1947)
Richier, Germaine (1904–1959)
Richman, Julia (1855–1912)
Richmond, Dorothy Kate (1861–1935)
Richmond, Mary E. (1861–1928)
Richmond, Mary Elizabeth (1853–1949)
Richter, Annegret (1950—)
Richter, Elise (1865–1943)
Richter, Emma (1888–1956)
Richter, Gisela (1882–1972)
Richter, Ilona (1953—)
Richter, Kristina (1946—)
Richter, Marga (1926—)
Richter, Simona Marcela (1972—)
Richter, Ulrike (1959—)
Ri Chun-Ok (1947—)
Ricker, Maelle (1978—)
Ricker, Marilla (1840–1920)
Rickert, Edith (1871–1938)
Ricketson, Gail (1953—)
Rickett, Mary Ellen (1861–1925)
Rickon, Kelly (1959—)
Ricna, Hana (1968—)
Riddell, Charlotte (1832–1906)
Riddles, Libby (1956—)
Ride, Sally (1951—)
Rider-Kelsey, Corinne (1877–1947)
Ridge, Lola (1873–1941)
Ridge, Therese (1941—)
Ridgley, Cleo (1893–1962)
Ridgway, Rozanne Lejeanne (1935—)
Riding, Laura (1901–1991)
Ridler, Anne (1912–2001)
Ridruejo, Mónica (1963—)
Rie, Lucie (1902–1995)
Riedel, Petra (1964—)
Riefenstahl, Leni (1902–2003)
Ries, Frédérique (1959—)
Rifaat, Alifa (1930–1996)
Rigby, Cathy (1952—)
Rigg, Diana (1938—)
Riggin, Aileen (1906–2002)
Riggs, Katherine Witchie (d. 1967)
Riihivuori, Hilkka (1952—)
Riise, Hege (1969—)
Riise-Arndt, Eva (1919—)
Riis-Jorgensen, Karin (1952—)
Rijker, Lucia (1967—)

Rikiriki, Atareta Kawana Ropiha Mere (c. 1855–1926)
Riley, Bridget (1931—)
Riley, Corinne Boyd (1893–1979)
Riley, Dawn (1964—)
Riley, Jeannie C. (1945—)
Riley, Mary Velasquez (1908–1987)
Riley, Polly Ann (1926–2002)
Riley, Ruth (1979—)
Riley, Samantha (1972—)
Rimington, Stella (1935—)
Rimoldi, Jorgelina (1972—)
Rinaldi, Angela (c. 1916—)
Rinehart, Mary Roberts (1876–1958)
Ring, Blanche (1877–1961)
Ring, Frances (1882–1951)
Ringgold, Faith (1934—)
Ringwood, Gwen Pharis (1910–1984)
Rinker, Laurie (1962—)
Rinne, Fanny (1980—)
Rinser, Luise (1911–2002)
Riperton, Minnie (1947–1979)
Ripley, Martha Rogers (1843–1912)
Rippin, Jane Deeter (1882–1953)
Risdon, Elisabeth (1887–1958)
Ri Song Hui (1978—)
Ristori, Adelaide (1822–1906)
Ritchie, Anne Isabella (1837–1919)
Ritchie, Harriet Maria (1818–1907)
Ritchie, Jean (1922—)
Ritchie, Sharon Kay (c. 1937—)
Rittenhouse, Jessie Belle (1869–1948)
Ritter, Erika (1948—)
Ritter, Louise (1958—)
Ritter, Thelma (1905–1969)
Riva, Emmanuelle (1927—)
Riva, Maria (1924—)
Rivé-King, Julie (1854–1937)
Rivera, Chita (1933—)
Rives, Amélie (1863–1945)
Riwai, Kiti Karaka (1870–1927)
Rizea, Elisabeta (1912–2003)
Rizk, Amina (1910–2003)
Rizzo, Patti (1960—)
Rizzotti, Jennifer (1974—)
Roache, Viola (1885–1961)
Roba, Fatuma (1973—)
Robb, Isabel Hampton (1860–1910)
Robb, Mary Anne (1829–1912)
Robbiani, Heidi (1950—)
Robbins, Gale (1921–1980)
Robbins, Jane Elizabeth (1860–1946)
Robbins, Kelly (1969—)
Roberson, LaTavia (1981—)
Robert-Angelini, Enif (1886–1976)
Roberti, Lyda (1906–1938)
Roberts, Cokie (1943—)
Roberts, Doris (1929—)
Roberts, Edith (1899–1935)
Roberts, Eirlys (b. 1911)
Roberts, Elisa Mary (1970—)
Roberts, Elizabeth Madox (1881–1941)
Roberts, Flora (c. 1921–1998)
Roberts, Florence (1861–1940)
Roberts, Florence (1871–1927)
Roberts, Julia (1967—)
Roberts, Kate (1891–1985)
Roberts, Lydia (1879–1965)
Roberts, Lynne (1919–1978)
Roberts, Marguerite (1905–1989)
Roberts, Mary Louise (1886–1968)
Roberts, Mary May (1877–1959)
Roberts, Patricia (1955—)
Roberts, Rachel (1927–1980)
Roberts, Robin (1960—)
Roberts, Sheila (1937—)
Roberts, Sue (1948—)
Roberts, Susan (1939—)
Roberts, Tiffany (1977—)
Robertson, Agnes (1833–1916)
Robertson, Alice Mary (1854–1931)
Robertson, Ann (1825–1922)
Robertson, Ann Worcester (1826–1905)
Robertson, Brenda May (1929—)
Robertson, Carol (d. 1963)
Robertson, E. Arnot (1903–1961)
Robertson, Grace (1930—)
Robertson, Heather (1942—)
Robertson, Jeannie (1908–1975)
Robertson, Muriel (1883–1973)
Robertson, Shirley (1968—)
Robertson, Sonia (1947—)
Robeson, Eslanda Goode (1896–1965)
Robin, Dany (1927–1995)
Robin, Mado (1918–1960)
Robins, Denise Naomi (1897–1985)
Robins, Elizabeth (1862–1952)
Robins, Margaret Dreier (1868–1945)
Robinson, Betty (1911–1997)
Robinson, Cynthia (1946—)
Robinson, Dawn (1968—)
Robinson, Dot (1912–1999)
Robinson, Emma (1971—)
Robinson, Fiona (1969—)
Robinson, Gertrude (1890–1962)
Robinson, Harriet Hanson (1825–1911)
Robinson, Henrietta (1816–1905)
Robinson, Iris (1949—)
Robinson, Jane Bancroft (1847–1932)
Robinson, Jo Ann (1911–1992)
Robinson, Joan Violet (1903–1983)
Robinson, Julia B. (1919–1985)
Robinson, Kathleen (1901–1983)
Robinson, Madeleine (1916–2004)
Robinson, Madeleine (b. 1908)
Robinson, Mary (1944—)
Robinson, Moushaumi (1981—)
Robinson, Ruby Doris Smith (1942–1967)
Robinson, Sarah Jane (d. 1905)
Robinson, Shawna (1964—)
Robinson, Vicki Sue (1954–2000)
Robison, Emily (1972—)
Robison, Paula (1941—)
Robison, Shona (1966—)
Robscheit-Robbins, Frieda (1888–1973)
Robson, Flora (1902–1984)
Robson, May (1858–1942)
Robu, Doina (1967—)
Roc, Patricia (1915–2003)
Roch, Madeleine (1884–1930)
Rochat, Laurence (1979—)
Rochat-Moser, Franziska (1966–2002)
Roche, Barbara (1954—)
Roche, Danni (1970—)
Roche, Josephine (1886–1976)
Roche, Maggie (1951—)
Roche, Melanie (1970—)
Roche, Suzzy (1956—)
Roche, Terre (1953—)
Rochefort, Christiane (1917–1998)
Rochester, Anna (1880–1966)
Rocheva, Nina
Rockefeller, Abby Aldrich (1874–1948)
Rockefeller, Blanchette Hooker (1909–1992)
Rockefeller, Laura Spelman (1839–1915)
Rockefeller, Margaret (1915–1996)
Rockefeller, Margaretta (1926—)
Rockefeller, Martha Baird (1895–1971)
Rockefeller, Mary Todhunter (1907–1999)
Rockmore, Clara (1911–1998)
Roddick, Anita (1942—)
Rode, Lizzie (1933—)
Rodewald, Marion (1976—)
Rodgers, Brid (1935—)
Rodgers, Elizabeth Flynn (1847–1939)
Rodin, Judith (1944—)
Rodnina, Irina (1949—)
Rodoreda, Mercè (1909–1983)
Rodrigues, Amalia (1921–1999)
Rodrigues, Karin (1971—)
Rodrigues, Monica (1967—)
Rodríguez, Ana (1938—)
Rodriguez, Estelita (1928–1966)
Rodríguez, Evangelina (1879–1947)
Rodriguez, Jennifer (1976—)
Rodriguez, Judith (1936—)
Rodriguez, Zhandra (1947—)
Rodríguez de Tió, Lola (1843–1924)
Rodríguez Ramos, María (1963—)
Rodriguez Suarez, Maria (1957—)
Rodriguez Villanueva, Estela (1967—)
Roe, Allison (1957—)
Roe, Marion (1936—)
Roebling, Emily (1844–1903)
Roebling, Mary G. (1906–1994)
Roenstroem, Eva (1932—)
Roering, Gun (1930—)
Roether, Sabine (1957—)
Roethlisberger, Nadia (1972—)
Roffe, Diann (1967—)
Roffeis, Karla (1958—)
Rogachyova, Lyudmila (1966—)
Rogatis, Teresa de (1893–1979)
Rogers, Annette (b. 1913)
Rogers, Clara Kathleen (1844–1931)
Rogers, Dale Evans (1912–2001)
Rogers, Edith MacTavish (1876–1947)
Rogers, Edith Nourse (1881–1960)
Rogers, Elizabeth Ann (1829–1921)
Rogers, Ginger (1911–1995)
Rogers, Grace Rainey (1867–1943)
Rogers, Jean (1916–1991)
Rogers, Martha E. (1914–1994)
Rogers, Mother Mary Joseph (1882–1955)
Rogge, Florence (b. 1904)
Rognoni, Cecilia (1976—)
Rogowska, Anna (1981—)
Rogozhina, Lyudmila (1959—)
Rohde, Brigitte (1954—)
Rohde, Lisa (1955—)
Rohde, Ruth Bryan Owen (1885–1954)
Rohländer, Uta (1969—)
Rojcewicz, Susan (1953—)
Roje, Ana (1909—)
Rökk, Marika (1913–2004)
Rokne, Marianne (1978—)
Roland, Betty (1903–1996)
Roland, Ruth (1892–1937)
Roland Holst, Henriëtte (1869–1952)
Roldan Reyna, Pilar (1944—)
Roles, Barbara
Roley, Susan Lynn (c. 1947—)
Rolle, Esther (1920–1998)
Rolleston, Elizabeth Mary (1845–1940)
Rollett, Hilda (1873–1970)
Rollins, Charlemae Hill (1897–1979)
Rolton, Gillian (1956—)
Rom, Dagmar (1928—)
Romack, Barbara (1932—)
Romagnoli, Diana (1977—)
Roman, Ruth (1922–1999)
Romance, Viviane (1909–1991)
Romano, Lalla (1906–2001)
Romanova, Maria (1886–1954)
Romanova, Yelena (1963—)
Romary, Janice-Lee (1927—)
Romasko, Olga (1968—)
Romay, Fulgencia (1944—)
Rombauer, Irma S. (1877–1962)
Rome, Esther (1945–1995)
Romein-Verschoor, Annie (1895–1978)
Romero, Rebecca (1980—)
Rongonui, Kahupake (1868/69?–1947)
Ronne, Edith (1919—)
Ronner-Knip, Henriette (1821–1909)
Ronstadt, Linda (1946—)
Ronzhina, Olena (1970—)
Rood, Florence (1873–1944)
Rooke, Daphne (1914—)
Rooke, Irene (c. 1878–1958)
Rooney, Giaan (1982—)
Rooney, Josie (b. 1892)
Rooney, Julia (b. 1893)
Roope, Clover (1937—)
Roosevelt, Edith Kermit Carow (1861–1948)
Roosevelt, Eleanor (1884–1962)
Roosevelt, Ethel Carow (1891–1977)
Roosevelt, Sara Delano (1854–1941)
Roper, Marion
Roque, Jacqueline (d. 1986)
Rorer, Sarah Tyson (1849–1937)
Rork, Ann (1908–1988)
Rorke, Kate (1866–1945)
Rorke, Mary (1858–1938)
Ros, Amanda (1860–1939)
Rosa (1906–1983)
Rosati, Carolina (1826–1905)
Rosay, Françoise (1891–1974)
Rosazza, Joan (1935—)

Rosca, Ninotchka (1941—)
Rosca-Racila, Valeria (1957—)
Rosé, Alma (1906–1944)
Rose, Helen (1904–1985)
Rose, Kay (1922–2002)
Rose, Margo (1903–1997)
Rose, Merri (1955—)
Rose, Sylvia (1962—)
Roseanne (1952—)
Rosenbaum, Hedwig
Rosenberg, Anna M. (1902–1983)
Rosenberg, Ethel (1915–1953)
Rosenberg, Grete (1896–1979)
Rosendahl, Heidemarie (1947—)
Rosenfeld, Fanny (1905–1969)
Rosenqvist, Susanne (1967—)
Rosenthal, Ida Cohen (1886–1973)
Rosenthal, Jean (1912–1969)
Rosenthal, Jody (1962—)
Roshanara (1849–1926)
Roshchina, Nadezhda (1954—)
Roshchina, Tatyana (1941—)
Roslavleva, Natalia (1907–1977)
Ros-Lehtinen, Ileana (1952—)
Rosman, Alice Grant (1887–1961)
Ross, Annie (1930—)
Ross, Charlotte Whitehead (1843–1916)
Ross, Diana (1944—)
Ross, Forrestina Elizabeth (1860–1936)
Ross, Frances Jane (1869–1950)
Ross, Hilda (1883–1959)
Ross, Ishbel (1895–1975)
Ross, Ishobel (1890–1965)
Ross, Lillian (1926—)
Ross, Nellie Tayloe (1876–1977)
Ross, Shirley (1909–1975)
Ross-Craig, Stella (1906—)
Rosselli, Amelia (1930–1996)
Rosser, Celia E. (1930—)
Rossi Drago, Eleonora (1925—)
Rossner, Petra (1966—)
Rost, Christina (1952—)
Rostock, Marlies
Rostova, Anna (1950—)
Rosu, Monica (1987—)
Roth, Ann (1931—)
Roth, Hella (1963—)
Roth, Lillian (1910–1980)
Roth-Behrendt, Dagmar (1953—)
Rothe, Mechtild (1947—)
Rothenberger, Anneliese (1924—)
Rothenberger, Gonnelien
Rothenburger-Luding, Christa (1959—)
Rothhammer, Keena (1957—)
Rothlein, Arlene (1939–1976)
Rothman, Stephanie (1936—)
Rothmann, Maria Elisabeth (1875–1975)
Rothschild, Constance de (1843–1931)
Rothschild, Jeanne de (1908–2003)
Rothschild, Judith (1921–1993)
Rothschild, Mathilde de (1874–1926)
Rothschild, Miriam (1908–2005)
Rothwell, Evelyn (b. 1911)
Rottenberg, Silke (1972—)
Rotter, Emilia
Roudenko, Lubov (1915—)
Roudy, Yvette (1929—)
Roug, Kristine (1975—)
Roukema, Margaret (1929—)
Roumpesi, Antigoni (1983—)
Round, Dorothy (1908–1982)
Rountree, Martha (1911–1999)
Roure, Martine (1948—)
Rourke, Constance (1885–1941)
Rousanne, Mme (1894–1958)
Roussel, Nelly (1878–1922)
Rout, Ettie Annie (1877–1936)
Routledge, Patricia (1929—)
Roux, Aline (1935—)
Rover, Constance (1910–2005)
Rowan, Ellis (1848–1922)
Rowbotham, Sheila (1943—)
Rowe, Marilyn (1946—)
Rowell, Mary (1958—)
Rowland, Kelly (1981—)
Rowlands, Gena (1934—)
Rowling, J.K. (1965—)
Roxon, Lillian (1932–1973)
Roy, Arundhati (1961—)
Roy, Gabrielle (1909–1983)
Roy, Julie (c. 1938—)
Roy de Clotte le Barillier, Berthe (1868–1927)
Royden, A. Maude (1876–1956)
Royde-Smith, Naomi Gwladys (c. 1880–1964)
Royer, Clémence (1830–1902)
Royle, Selena (1904–1983)
Rozanova, Olga (1886–1918)
Rozeanu, Angelica (1921–2006)
Rozeira de Souza Silva, Cristiane (1985—)
Rozengolts-Levina, Eva (1898–1975)
Rozgon, Nadezhda (1952—)
Rozhanskaya, Mariam (1928—)
Rozsnyoi, Katalin (1942—)
Ruano Pascual, Virginia (1973—)
Rubens, Alma (1897–1931)
Rubens, Bernice (1928–2004)
Rubenstein, Blanche (c. 1897–1969)
Rubin, Barbara Jo (1949—)
Rubin, Chandra (1976—)
Rubin, Vera (1911–1985)
Rubin, Vera Cooper (1928—)
Rubinstein, Helena (1870–1965)
Rubinstein, Ida (1880–1960)
Rubinstein, Mala (1905–1999)
Rubinstein, Renate (1929–1990)
Rublevska, Jelena (1976—)
Ruby, Karine (1978—)
Ruck, Berta (1878–1978)
Rücker, Anja (1972—)
Rudasne-Antal, Marta (1937—)
Ruddins, Kimberly (1963—)
Ruddock, Joan (1943—)
Rudel-Zeynek, Olga (1871–1948)
Rudishauser, Corrie (1973—)
Rudkin, Margaret (1897–1967)
Rudkovskaya, Yelena (1973—)
Rudman, Annie (1844–1928)
Rudner, Sara (1944—)
Rudolph, Renate (1949—)
Rudolph, Wilma (1940–1994)
Rudovskaya, Lyubov (1950—)
Rue, Rosemary (1928–2004)
Rueckes, Anette (1951—)
Rueda, Eva (1971—)
Rüegg, Annelise (1879–1934)
Ruegg, Yvonne
Ruehn, Melita (1965—)
Ruether, Rosemary (1936—)
Ruffin, Josephine St. Pierre (1842–1924)
Ruggiero, Angela (1980—)
Rühle, Heide (1948—)
Rührold, Ute
Ruick, Barbara (1930–1974)
Ruiz, Brunhilda (1936—)
Ruiz, Rosie (c. 1954—)
Ruiz, Tracie (1963—)
Ruiz, Yumilka (1978—)
Rukavishnikova, Olga (1955—)
Rukeyser, Muriel (1913–1980)
Rule, Jane (1931—)
Rule, Janice (1931–2003)
Rule, Margaret (1928—)
Rulon, Kelly (1984—)
Rumbewas, Raema Lisa (1980—)
Rumbold, Freda (1913—)
Rumsey, Mary Harriman (1881–1934)
Runcie, Constance Faunt Le Roy (1836–1911)
Runciman, Jane Elizabeth (1873–1950)
Rund, Cathleen (1977—)
Runge, Erika (1939—)
Ruoppa, Eeva (1932—)
Rupshiene, Angele (1952—)
Rusanova, Lyubov (1954—)
Rush, Barbara (1927—)
Rush, Cathy
Rusnachenko, Natalya (1969—)
Russ, Joanna (1937—)
Russell, Alys Smith (1866–1951)
Russell, Anna (b. 1911)
Russell, Annie (1864–1936)
Russell, Christine (1945—)
Russell, Dora (1894–1986)
Russell, Dora Isella (1925—)
Russell, Dorothy Stuart (1895–1983)
Russell, Elizabeth S. (1913—)
Russell, Ernestine (1938—)
Russell, Francia (1938—)
Russell, Gail (1924–1961)
Russell, Jane (1921—)
Russell, Jane Anne (1911–1967)
Russell, Kathleen
Russell, Lillian (1861–1922)
Russell, Mary du Caurroy (1865–1937)
Russell, Rosalind (1908–1976)
Russo, Marine (1980—)
Rustamova, Zebinisso (1955—)
Rute, Mme de (1831–1902)
Rutherford, Ann (1917—)
Rutherford, Frances Armstrong (1842–1922)
Rutherford, Margaret (1892–1972)
Rutherford, Mildred (1851–1928)
Ruth-Rolland, J.M. (1937–1995)
Rutkiewicz, Wanda (1943—)
Rutkowska, Jadwiga (1934—)
Rutledge, Margaret Fane (1914–2004)
Rutschow, Katrin (1975—)
Ruttner-Kolisko, Agnes (1911–1991)
Ruuska, Sylvia (1942—)
Ru Zhijuan (1925—)
Ruzicka, Marla (1976–2005)
Ruzickova, Hana (1941–1981)
Ruzickova, Vera (1928—)
Ruzina, Yelena (1964—)
Ryabchinskaya, Yuliya (1947–1973)
Ryan, Anne (1889–1954)
Ryan, Catherine O'Connell (1865–1936)
Ryan, Elizabeth (1891–1979)
Ryan, Fran (1916–2000)
Ryan, Irene (1902–1973)
Ryan, Joan (1955—)
Ryan, Kathleen (1922–1985)
Ryan, Mary (1885–1948)
Ryan, Mary Bridget (1898–1981)
Ryan, Meg (1961—)
Ryan, Peggy (1924–2004)
Ryan, Sarah (1977—)
Ryan, Sheila (1921–1975)
Rybicka, Anna (1977—)
Ryder, Sue (1923–2000)
Rye, Daphne (1916—)
Rye, Maria Susan (1829–1903)
Rylova, Tamara (1931—)
Ryman, Brenda (1922–1983)
Ryom Chun-Ja (1942—)
Ryon, Luann (1953—)
Rysanek, Leonie (1926–1998)
Ryskal, Inna (1944—)
Rytova, Galina (1975—)
Ryu Ji-Hae (1976—)
Ryum, Ulla (1937—)
Ryzhova, Antonina (1934—)
Saad, Siti binti (c. 1880–1950)
Saadi, Elvira (1952—)
Saalfeld, Romy (1960—)
Saariaho, Kaija (1952—)
Saarinen, Aline (1914–1972)
Saarinen, Loja (1879–1968)
Sabaite, Nijole (1950—)
Sabalsajaray, Nibuya (1951–1974)
Sabatini, Gabriela (1970—)
Sabin, Ellen (1850–1949)
Sabin, Florence (1871–1953)
Sabin, Pauline Morton (1887–1955)
Saburova, Irina (1907–1979)
Sacalici, Elena (1937—)
Sacchetto, Rita (1879–1959)
Sach, Amelia (1873–1902)
Sachenbacher, Evi (1980—)
Sacher, Anna (1859–1930)
Sachs, Nelly (1891–1970)
Sackville-West, Vita (1892–1962)
Sadako (1885–1951)
Sadat, Jehan (1933—)
Sade (1959—)
Sadlier, Mary Anne (1820–1903)
Sadova, Natalya (1972—)
Sadovnycha, Olena (1967—)
Sadovskaya, Tatyana (1966—)

Saenz-Alonso, Mercedes (1916–2000)
Saettem, Birgitte (1978—)
Sáez, Irene (1961—)
Safier, Gloria (d. 1985)
Safina, Yuliya (1950—)
Safronova, Natalia (1979—)
Saga, Michiko (1934—)
Sagan, Françoise (1935–2004)
Sagan, Leontine (1889–1974)
Sage, Kay (1898–1963)
Sage, Margaret Olivia (1828–1918)
Sager, Ruth (1918–1997)
Sagine-Ujlakine-Rejto, Ildiko (1937—)
Sagstuen, Tonje (1971—)
Sahgal, Nayantara (1927—)
Saiki, Patricia Fukuda (1930—)
Saiman, Nurfitriyana (1962—)
Saimo, Sylvi (1914–2004)
Saint, Dora Jessie (1913—)
Saint, Eva Marie (1924—)
Saint-Cyr, Renée (1904–2004)
Sainte-Marie, Buffy (1941—)
Saint-Laurent, Jeanne (1887–1966)
Sais, Marin (1890–1971)
Saito, Haruka (1970—)
Sakai, Hiroko (1978—)
Sakamoto, Naoko (1985—)
Sakaue, Yoko (1968—)
Sakharoff, Clotilde (1892–1974)
Sakickiene, Birute (1968—)
Sakovitsne-Domolky, Lidia (1936—)
Salapatyska, Stella (1979—)
Salazar Blanco, Iridia (1982—)
Sale, Jamie (1977—)
Sale, Virginia (1899–1992)
Salerno-Sonnenberg, Nadja (1961—)
Salikhova, Roza (1944—)
Salisachs, Mercedes (1916—)
Salis-Marschlins, Meta (1855–1929)
Salminen, Sally (1906–1976)
Salmon, Lucy Maynard (1853–1927)
Salmond, Sarah (1864–1956)
Salmonova, Lyda (1889–1968)
Salmons, Josephine (b. 1904)
Salm-Salm, Agnes, Princess (1840–1912)
Salomon, Alice (1872–1948)
Salomon, Charlotte (1917–1943)
Salote Topou III (1900–1965)
Salsberg, Germain Merle (1950—)
Salt, Barbara (1904–1975)
Salter, Susanna Medora (1860–1961)
Salukvadze, Nino (1969—)
Salumae, Erika (1962—)
Salverson, Laura Goodman (1890–1970)
Salzgeber, Ulla (1958—)
Samaroff, Olga (1882–1948)
Samman, Ghada al- (1942—)
Samoilova, Konkordiya (1876–1921)
Samoilova, Tatania (1934—)
Samolenko, Tatyana (1961—)
Samotesova, Lyudmila (1939—)
Sampson, Edith S. (1901–1979)
Sampson, Kathleen (1892–1980)
Sampson, Teddy (1898–1970)
Sampter, Jessie (1883–1938)
Sams, Doris (1927—)
Samuel Ramos, Adriana (1966—)
Samuelson, Joan Benoit (1957—)
Samusenko-Petrenko, Tatyana (1938—)
Sanchez, Carol Lee (1934—)
Sanchez, Celia (1920–1980)
Sanchez, Linda T. (1969—)
Sanchez, Loretta (1960—)
Sanchez, Sonia (1934—)
Sanchez Salfran, Marta (1973—)
Sanchez Vicario, Arantxa (1971—)
Sand, Inge (1928–1974)
Sand, Monique (1944—)
Sanda, Dominique (1948—)
Sandahl, Ingrid (1924—)
Sandars, Nancy K. (1914—)
Sandaune, Brit (1972—)
Sandbaek, Ulla Margrethe (1943—)
Sandberg-Fries, Yvonne (1950—)
Sandel, Cora (1880–1974)
Sandelin, Lucy Giovinco (c. 1958—)
Sandeno, Kaitlin (1983—)
Sander, Anne Quast (1937—)
Sander, Helke (1937—)
Sander, Jil (1943—)
Sander, Maria (1924—)
Sanders, Annemarie (1958—)
Sanders, Dorothy Lucie (1903–1987)
Sanders, Marlene (1931—)
Sanders, Summer (1972—)
Sanders, Tonya (1968—)
Sanders-Brahms, Helma (1940—)
Sanderson, Julia (1887–1975)
Sanderson, Sybil (1865–1903)
Sanderson, Tessa (1956—)
Sanders-Ten Holte, Maria Johanna (1941—)
Sandes, Flora (1876–1956)
Sandie, Shelley (1969—)
Sandig, Marita (1958—)
Sandorne-Nagy, Margit (1921—)
Sandoz, Mari (1896–1966)
Sands, Diana (1934–1973)
Sands, Dorothy (1893–1980)
Sandve, Monica (1973—)
Sanford, Isabel (1917–2004)
Sanford, Katherine (1915—)
Sanford, Maria Louise (1836–1920)
Sangalli, Rita (1849–1909)
Sanger, Margaret (1879–1966)
Sanger, Ruth Ann (1918–2001)
Sang Lan (1981—)
Sanglard, Ana Flavia (1970—)
Sangster, Margaret (1838–1912)
Sang Xue (1984—)
San Juan, Olga (1927—)
Sankova, Galina (b. 1904)
Sansom, Odette (1912–1995)
Sansome, Eva (1906–?)
Sanson, Yvonne (1926—)
Santamaría, Haydée (1922–1980)
Santiglia, Peggy (1944—)
Santolalla, Irene Silva de (1902–1992)
Santoni, Elisa (1987—)
Santos, Adriana (1971—)
Santos, Kelly (1979—)
Santos Arrascaeta, Beatriz (1947—)
Sanvitale, Francesca (1928—)
Sapenter, Debra (1952—)
Sapp, Carolyn (1967—)
Sappington, Margo (1947—)
Sarabhai, Anusyabehn (1885–1972)
Saralegui, Cristina (1948—)
Sarandon, Susan (1946—)
Saranti, Galateia (1920—)
Sarfatti, Margherita (1880–1961)
Sargant, Ethel (1863–1918)
Sargent, Pamela (1948—)
Sargsian, Inessa (1972—)
Sarraute, Nathalie (1900–1999)
Sarrazin, Albertine (1937–1967)
Sarry, Christine (1946—)
Sarstadt, Marian (1942—)
Sartain, Emily (1841–1927)
Sarton, May (1912–1995)
Sartori, Amalia (1947—)
Saruhashi, Katsuko (1920—)
Sarycheva, Tatyana (1949—)
Sasaki, Setsuko (1944—)
Sass, Marie Constance (1834–1907)
Sata, Ineko (1904–1998)
Sato, Aiko (1923—)
Sato, Liane (1964—)
Sato, Rie (1980—)
Sato, Yuka (1973—)
Sato, Yuki (1980—)
Satoya, Tae (c. 1977—)
Sattin, Rebecca (1980—)
Saubert, Jean
Sauca, Lucia (1963—)
Saunders, Cicely (1918–2005)
Saunders, Doris (1921—)
Saunders, Edith (1865–1945)
Saunders, Jackie (1892–1954)
Saunders, Jennifer (1958—)
Saunders, Marshall (1861–1947)
Saunders, Vivien (1946—)
Sauquillo Pérez Del Arco, Francisca (1943—)
Sauvage, Louise (1973—)
Sauvé, Jeanne (1922–1993)
Savage, Augusta (1892–1962)
Savary, Olga (1933—)
Savell, Edith Alma Eileen (1883–1970)
Savelyeva, Tatyana (1947—)
Savery, Jill (1972—)
Savic, Rada (1961—)
Savić-Rebac, Anica (1892–1935)
Saville, Jane (1974—)
Saville, Kathleen (1956—)
Savina, Nina (1915–1965)
Savitch, Jessica (1947–1983)
Savitskaya, Galina (1961—)
Savitskaya, Svetlana (1948—)
Savkina, Larisa (1955—)
Savolainen, Jaana (1964—)
Savon Carmenate, Amarilys (1974—)
Saw, Ruth (1901–1983)
Sawachi, Hisae (1930—)
Sawako Noma (c. 1944—)
Sawyer, Ivy (1898–1999)
Sawyer, Laura (1885–1970)
Sawyer, Ruth (1880–1970)
Saxe, Susan (1947—)
Saxon, Marie (1904–1941)
Sayao, Bidu (1902–1999)
Sayer, Ettie (1875–1923)
Sayers, Dorothy L. (1893–1957)
Sayers, Peig (1873–1958)
Sayre, Nora (1932–2001)
Sayres, Aurelie (1977—)
Sazanovich, Natalya (1973—)
Sazonenkova, Elena (1973—)
Sbarbati, Luciana (1946—)
Scala, Gia (1934–1972)
Scales, Helen Flora Victoria (1887–1975)
Scales, Jessie Sleet (fl. 1900)
Scales, Prunella (1932—)
Scallon, Dana Rosemary (1950—)
Scanlan, Nelle (1882–1968)
Scanlon, Mary (1947—)
Scapin, Ylenia (1975—)
Scarborough, Dorothy (1878–1935)
Scarlat, Roxana (1975—)
Schacherer-Elek, Ilona (1907–1988)
Schaefer, Laurel Lea (c. 1949—)
Schaeffer, Rebecca (1967–1989)
Schaeffer, Wendy (c. 1975—)
Schafer, Natalie (1900–1991)
Schaffer, Ine (1923—)
Schaffner, Anne-Marie (1945—)
Schaft, Hannie (1920–1945)
Schanne, Margrethe (1921—)
Scharff-Goldhaber, Gertrude (1911–1998)
Scharlieb, Mary Ann (1845–1930)
Scharrer, Berta (1906–1995)
Scharrer, Irene (1888–1971)
Schary, Hope Skillman (1908–1981)
Schau, Virginia M. (1915–1989)
Schaumann, Ruth (1899–1975)
Scheele, Karin (1968—)
Scheepstra, Maartje (1980—)
Scheff, Fritzi (1879–1954)
Scheiblich, Christine (1954—)
Schekeryk, Melanie (1947—)
Schell, Maria (1926–2005)
Schenk, Franziska (1974—)
Schenk, Lynn (1945—)
Schennikova, Angelika (1969—)
Scherbak, Barb (1958—)
Scherberger-Weiss, Rosemarie (1935—)
Scherchen, Tona (1938—)
Schiaffino, Rosanna (1938—)
Schiaparelli, Elsa (1890–1973)
Schieferdecker, Bettina (1968—)
Schierhuber, Agnes (1946—)
Schifano, Helen (1922—)
Schiff, Dorothy (1903–1989)
Schiffer, Claudia (1970—)
Schiffman, Suzanne (1929–2001)
Schileru, Dacia W.
Schindler, Emilie (1909–2001)
Schirmacher, Käthe (1859–1930)
Schjoldager, Mette (1977—)
Schlafly, Phyllis (1924—)

Schlamme, Martha (1922–1985)
Schlegel, Elfi (1964—)
Schleicher, Ursula (1933—)
Schlein, Miriam (1926–2004)
Schleper, Sarah (1979—)
Schlesinger, Therese (1863–1940)
Schley, Gabriela (1964—)
Schlicht, Svenja (1967—)
Schlösinger, Rose (1907–1943)
Schlossberg, Caroline Kennedy (1957—)
Schlotfeldt, Rozella M. (b. 1914—)
Schlueter-Schmidt, Karin (1937—)
Schlunegger, Hedy (1923–2003)
Schmahl, Jeanne (1846–1916)
Schmeisser, Richarda (1954—)
Schmich, Mary Teresa (1954—)
Schmid, Adelheid (1938—)
Schmid, Susanne (1960—)
Schmidgall, Jenny (1979—)
Schmidt, Auguste (1833–1902)
Schmidt, Carmela (1962—)
Schmidt, Cerstin
Schmidt, Helene (1906–1985)
Schmidt, Ingrid (1945—)
Schmidt, Kathryn (1953—)
Schmidt, Magdalena (1949—)
Schmidt, Martina (1960—)
Schmidt, Rikke (1975—)
Schmidt, Sybille (1967—)
Schmidt, Veronika
Schmirler, Sandra (1963–2000)
Schmitt, Christine (1953—)
Schmitt, Julie (b. 1913)
Schmitt, Sandra (c. 1982–2000)
Schmitz, Ingeborg (1922—)
Schmuck, Christa
Schmuck, Uta (1949—)
Schnackenberg, Annie Jane (1835–1905)
Schneider, Angela (1959—)
Schneider, Claudine (1947—)
Schneider, Magda (1909–1996)
Schneider, Petra (1963—)
Schneider, Romy (1938–1982)
Schneider, Vreni (1964—)
Schneiderman, Rose (1882–1972)
Schneyder, Nathalie (1968—)
Schnitzer, Henriette (1891–1979)
Schoenberg, Bessie (1906–1997)
Schoenfield, Dana (1953—)
Schoenrock, Sybille (1964—)
Schoff, Hannah Kent (1853–1940)
Schofield, Martha (1839–1916)
Scholl, Inge (c. 1917–1998)
Scholl, Sophie (1921–1943)
Schollar, Ludmilla (c. 1888–1978)
Scholtz-Klink, Gertrud (1902–1999)
Scholz, Anke (1978—)
Scholz, Lilly
Schön, Elizabeth (1921–2001)
Schöne, Andrea Mitscherlich (1961—)
Schonthal, Ruth (1924—)
Schooling, Elizabeth (1919—)
Schoonmaker, Thelma (1940—)
Schöpf, Regina
Schopman, Janneke (1977—)
Schörling, Inger (1946—)
Schoultz, Solveig von (1907–1996)
Schou Nilsen, Laila (1919–1998)
Schrader, Hilde (1910–1966)
Schramm, Beate (1966—)
Schramm, Bernardina Adriana (1900–1987)
Schratt, Katharina (1853–1940)
Schreiber, Adele (1872–1957)
Schreiner, Olive (1855–1920)
Schriber, Margrit (1939—)
Schroeder, Bertha (1872–1953)
Schroeder, Ilka (1978—)
Schroeder, Louise (1887–1957)
Schroeder, Patricia (1940—)
Schroedter, Elisabeth (1959—)
Schröer-Lehmann, Beatrix (1963—)
Schroeter, Martina (1960—)
Schroth, Clara (1920—)
Schroth, Frances (b. 1893)
Schuba, Beatrix (1951—)
Schubert, Helga (1940—)
Schuck, Anett (1970—)
Schuler, Carolyn (1943—)
Schuler, Laura (1970—)
Schulter-Mattler, Heike (1958—)
Schultz, Annette (1957—)
Schultz, Sigrid (1893–1980)
Schulze, Sabina (1972—)
Schulze-Boysen, Libertas (1913–1942)
Schumacher, Elisabeth (1904–1942)
Schumacher, Sandra (1966—)
Schumann, Elisabeth (1885–1952)
Schumann, Margit (1952—)
Schumann-Heink, Ernestine (1861–1936)
Schuster, Norah (1892–1991)
Schuster, Susanne (1963—)
Schut, Johanna (1944—)
Schütte-Lihotzky, Margarete (1897–2000)
Schutting, Julian (1937—)
Schuttpelz, Barbara (1956—)
Schütz, Birgit (1958—)
Schütz, Helga (1937—)
Schuyler, Louisa Lee (1837–1926)
Schuyler, Philippa Duke (1931–1967)
Schwandt, Rhonda (1963—)
Schwartz, Anna Jacobson (1915—)
Schwarz, Elisabeth (1936—)
Schwarz, Solange (1910–2000)
Schwarz, Vera (1888–1964)
Schwarz-Bart, Simone (1938—)
Schwarzenbach, Annemarie (1908–1942)
Schwarzhaupt, Elisabeth (1901–1986)
Schwarzkopf, Elisabeth (1915—)
Schwarzwald, Eugenie (1872–1940)
Schwede, Bianka (1953—)
Schwen, Missy (1972—)
Schwerzmann, Ingeburg (1967—)
Schwikert, Tasha (1984—)
Schwimmer, Rosika (1877–1948)
Scidmore, Eliza Ruhamah (1856–1928)
Scieri, Antoinette (fl. 1920s)
Sciocchetti, Marina (1954—)
Sciolti, Gabriella (1974—)
Sciutti, Graziella (1927–2001)
Scott, Ann London (1929–1975)
Scott, Barbara Ann (1929—)
Scott, Beckie (1970—)
Scott, Blanche (1885–1970)
Scott, Charlotte Angas (1858–1931)
Scott, Christine Margaret (1946—)
Scott, Desley Carleton (1943—)
Scott, Elizabeth Whitworth (1898–1972)
Scott, Esther Mae (1893–1979)
Scott, Evelyn (1893–1963)
Scott, Hazel (1920–1981)
Scott, Ivy (1886–1947)
Scott, Janette (1938—)
Scott, Jessie Ann (1883–1959)
Scott, Lizabeth (1922—)
Scott, Margaret (1875–1938)
Scott, Margaret (1922—)
Scott, Margaretta (1912–2005)
Scott, Martha (1914–2003)
Scott, Mary Edith (1888–1979)
Scott, Rose (1847–1925)
Scott, Rosie (1948—)
Scott, Ruby Payne (1912–1981)
Scott, Sheila (1927–1988)
Scott, Sherry (c. 1948—)
Scott, Shirley (1934–2002)
Scott-Brown, Denise (1931—)
Scott-Maxwell, Florida (1883–1979)
Scotto, Renata (1933—)
Scott-Pomales, Catherine
Scovell, E.J. (1907–1999)
Scriabin, Vera (1875–1920)
Scripps, Ellen Browning (1836–1932)
Scrivener, Christiane (1925—)
Scrivens, Jean (1935—)
Scudamore, Margaret (1884–1958)
Scudder, Ida (1870–1960)
Scudder, Janet (1869–1940)
Scudder, Laura Clough (1881–1959)
Scudder, Vida (1861–1954)
Scullin, Sarah (1880–1962)
Scurry, Briana (1971—)
Seager, Esther (c. 1835–1911)
Seaman, Elizabeth Cochrane (1864–1922)
Sears, Eleanora (1881–1968)
Sears, Mary (1905–1997)
Sears, Mary (1939—)
Sears, Zelda (1873–1935)
Seastrand, Andrea (1941—)
Seaton, Anna (1964—)
Sebastian, Dorothy (1903–1957)
Sebastiani, Sylvia (1916–2003)
Sebbar, Leila (1941—)
Seberg, Jean (1938–1979)
Seda, Dori (1951–1988)
Sedakova, Olga (c. 1972—)
Seddon, Margaret (1872–1968)
Seddon, Rhea (1947—)
Sedgwick, Anne Douglas (1873–1935)
Sedgwick, Edie (1943–1971)
Sedgwick, Josie (1898–1973)
Sedlackova, Jaroslava (1946—)
Sedova, Julia (1880–1969)
Seefried, Irmgard (1919–1988)
Seeger, Peggy (1935—)
Seeley, Blossom (1891–1974)
Segal, Vivienne (1897–1992)
Seghers, Anna (1900–1983)
Segun, Mabel (1930—)
Sehmisch, Elke (1955—)
Seibert, Florence B. (1897–1991)
Seick, Karin (1961—)
Seid, Ruth (1913–1995)
Seidel, Amalie (1876–1952)
Seidel, Ina (1885–1974)
Seidel, Martie (1969—)
Seidelman, Susan (1952—)
Seidl, Lea (1895–1987)
Seidler, Helga (1949—)
Seifullina, Lydia (1889–1954)
Seigneuret, Michele (1934—)
Seizinger, Katja (1972—)
Sekaric, Jasna (1965—)
Sekulić, Isadora (1877–1958)
Selbach, Johanna (1918—)
Selbert, Elisabeth (1896–1986)
Selby, Sarah (1905–1980)
Selena (1971–1995)
Seles, Monica (1973—)
Selezneva, Larisa (1963—)
Sell, Janie (1941—)
Sellars, Elizabeth (1923—)
Sellers, Kathryn (1870–1939)
Sellick, Phyllis (b. 1911)
Selva, Blanche (1884–1942)
Selznick, Irene Mayer (1910–1990)
Sembrich, Marcella (1858–1935)
Semjonova, Uljana (1952—)
Semple, Ellen Churchill (1863–1932)
Semykina, Tetyana (1973—)
Semyonova, Marina (b. 1908)
Semyonova, Olga (1964—)
Semyonova, Svetlana (1958—)
Sender, Toni (1888–1964)
Sendler, Irena (b. 1910)
Senesh, Hannah (1921–1944)
Senff, Dina (1920—)
Senior, Olive (1941—)
Sensini, Alessandra (1970—)
Senyurt, Hulya (1973—)
September, Dulcie (1935–1988)
Serao, Matilde (1856–1927)
Serbezova, Mariana (1959—)
Serdyuk, Kateryna
Serebrianskaya, Yekaterina (1977—)
Serebryakova, Zinaida (1884–1967)
Seredina, Antonina (1930—)
Sergava, Katharine (1910–2005)
Sergeant, Adeline (1851–1904)
Serlenga, Nikki (1978—)
Seroczynska, Elwira (1931—)
Serota, Beatrice (1919–2002)
Serrahima, Nuria (1937—)
Serrano, Eugenia (1918—)
Serrano, Lupe (1930—)
Serreau, Coline (1947—)
Serreau, Geneviève (1915–1981)
Sert, Misia (1872–1950)
Servoss, Mary (1881–1968)

Sessions, Almira (1888–1974)
Sessions, Kate O. (1857–1940)
Seth, Reidun (1966—)
Seton, Grace Gallatin (1872–1959)
Setouchi, Jakucho (1922—)
Seufert, Christina (1957—)
Sevens, Elizabeth (1949—)
Severance, Caroline M. (1820–1914)
Séverine (1855–1929)
Severn, Margaret (1901–1997)
Severson, Kim (1973—)
Sevilla, Carmen (1930—)
Seville, Carolina Ada (1874–1955)
Sevostyanova, Nadezhda (1953—)
Sewall, May Wright (1844–1920)
Sewell, Edna (1881–1967)
Sewell, Elizabeth Missing (1815–1906)
Sexton, Anne (1928–1974)
Sexton, Elsie Wilkins (1868–1959)
Sey, Jennifer (1969—)
Seyfert, Gabriele (1948—)
Seyler, Athene (1889–1990)
Seymour, Anne (1909–1988)
Seymour, Clarine (1898–1920)
Seymour, Ethel (1881–1963)
Seymour, Jane (1951—)
Seymour, Jane (c. 1898–1956)
Seymour, Lynn (1939—)
Seymour, May Davenport (d. 1967)
Seyrig, Delphine (1932–1990)
Shaarawi, Huda (1879–1947)
Shabanova, Anna (1848–1932)
Shabanova, Rafiga (1943—)
Shabazz, Betty (1936–1997)
Shabelska, Maria (1898–1980)
Shaffer, Alexandra (1976—)
Shafik, Doria (1908–1975)
Shaginian, Marietta (1888–1982)
Shaheen, Jeanne (1947—)
Shain, Eva (1917–1999)
Shakhovskaya, Eugenie M. (1889–?)
Shakhovskaya, Zinaida (1906–2001)
Shakira (1977—)
Shalala, Donna (1941—)
Shalamova, Elena (1982—)
Shaler, Eleanor (1900–1989)
Shamray-Rudko, Galina (1931—)
Shane, Mary Driscoll (c. 1949—)
Shange, Ntozake (1948—)
Shannon, Effie (1867–1954)
Shannon, Peggy (1907–1941)
Shanté, Roxanne (1970—)
Shan Ying (1978—)
Shapir, Olga (1850–1916)
Shapiro, Betty Kronman (1907–1989)
Shaposhnikova, Natalia (1961—)
Sharaff, Irene (1910–1993)
Sharapova, Maria (1987—)
Sharman, Helen (1963—)
Sharmay, Lyubov (1956—)
Sharp, Katharine Lucinda (1865–1914)
Sharp, Margery (1905–1991)
Sharp, Susie M. (1907–1996)
Shaver, Dorothy (1897–1959)
Shaw, Anna Howard (1847–1919)
Shaw, Elizabeth (1920–1992)
Shaw, Fiona (1958—)
Shaw, Flora (1852–1929)
Shaw, Flora Madeline (1864–1927)
Shaw, Helen (1913–1985)
Shaw, Mary G. (1854–1929)
Shaw, Pauline Agassiz (1841–1917)
Shaw, Reta (1912–1982)
Shaw, Susan (1929–1978)
Shaw, Victoria (1935–1988)
Shaw, Wini (1910–1982)
Shawlee, Joan (1926–1987)
Shaykh, Hanan al- (1945—)
Shayne, Tamara (1902–1983)
Shchegoleva, Tatiana (1982—)
Shchelkanova, Tatyana (1937—)
Shchepkina-Kupernik, Tatiana (1874–1952)
Shchetinina, Lyudmila (1951—)
Sheahan, Marion (1892–1994)
Shealey, Courtney (c. 1978—)
Shearer, Janet (1958—)
Shearer, Jill (1936—)
Shearer, Moira (1926–2006)
Shearer, Norma (1900–1983)
Sheehan, Margaret Flavin (d. 1969)
Sheehan, Patty (1956—)
Sheehy, Kathy (1970—)
Sheehy-Skeffington, Hanna (1877–1946)
Sheen, Gillian (1928—)
Sheepshanks, Mary (1872–1958)
Sheina, Svetlana (1918–2005)
Sheldon, Joan Mary (1943—)
Sheldon, May French (1847–1936)
Shelest, Alla (1919–1998)
Shelley, Barbara (1933—)
Shelton, Karen (1957—)
Shen Rong (1935—)
Shepard, Helen Miller (1868–1938)
Shepard, Mary (1909–2000)
Shepardson, Mary Thygeson (1906–1997)
Shephard, Gillian (1940—)
Shepherd, Cybill (1949—)
Shepherd, Dolly (d. 1983)
Shepherd, Karen (1940—)
Shepherd-Barron, Dorothy (1897–1953)
Shepitko, Larissa (1938–1979)
Shepley, Ruth (1892–1951)
Sheppard, Kate (1847–1934)
Sher, Lisa (1969—)
Sheremeta, Liubov (1980—)
Sheremetskaia, Natalia (1880–1952)
Sheridan, Ann (1915–1967)
Sheridan, Clare (1885–1970)
Sheridan, Dinah (1920—)
Sheridan, Margaret (1889–1958)
Sherif, Carolyn Wood (1922–1982)
Sherk, Cathy (1950—)
Sherkat, Shahla (c. 1956—)
Sherlock, Sheila (1918–2001)
Sherman, Mary Belle (1862–1935)
Sherman, Yvonne (1930–2005)
Sherman-Kauf, Patti (1963—)
Sherwin, Belle (1868–1955)
Sherwood, Katharine Margaret (1841–1914)
Sherwood, Mary (1856–1935)
Sherwood, Mary Elizabeth (1826–1903)
Sherwood, Maud Winifred (1880–1956)
Sherwood, Sheila (1945—)
Sheshenina, Marina (1985—)
Shevchenko, Elena (1971—)
Shevchenko, Lyudmyla (1975—)
Shevtsova, Lyudmila (1934—)
Shewchuk, Tammy Lee (1977—)
Shibaki, Yoshiko (b. 1914)
Shibata, Ai (1982—)
Shibuki, Ayano (1941—)
Shields, Carol (1935–2003)
Shields, Ella (1879–1952)
Shields, Margaret (1941—)
Shields, Susan (1952—)
Shige, Yumiko (1965—)
Shigeko (1925–1961)
Shi Guihong
Shikolenko, Natalya (1964—)
Shiley, Jean (1911–1998)
Shilling, Beatrice (1909–1990)
Shilova, Irina (1960—)
Shimakage, Seiko (1949—)
Shimanskaya, Vera (1981—)
Shim Eun-Jung (1971—)
Shindle, Kate (1979—)
Shinn, Millicent Washburn (1858–1940)
Shinoda, Miho (1972—)
Shinozaki, Yoko (1945—)
Shiokawa, Michiko (1951—)
Shiono, Nanami (1937—)
Shipley, Debra (1957—)
Shipley, Jenny (1952—)
Shipley, Ruth B. (1885–1966)
Shipman, Nell (1892–1970)
Shipp, Ellis Reynolds (1847–1939)
Shirai, Takako (1952—)
Shirley, Anne (1917–1993)
Shirley, Dorothy (1939—)
Shishigina, Olga (1968—)
Shishikura, Kunie (1946—)
Shishova, Albina (1966—)
Shishova, Lyudmila (1940—)
Shiubhlaigh, Maire Nic (1884–1958)
Shive, Natalya (1963—)
Shkapskaia, Mariia (1891–1952)
Shkurnova, Olga (1962—)
Shmonina, Marina (1965—)
Shochat, Manya (1878–1961)
Shockley, Ann Allen (1925—)
Shockley, Marian (1911–1981)
Shoemaker, Ann (1891–1978)
Shoemaker, Carolyn (1929—)
Shon Mi-Na (1964—)
Shopp, BeBe (1930—)
Shore, Dinah (1917–1994)
Shore, Henrietta (1880–1963)
Shorina, Anna (1982—)
Short, Clare (1946—)
Short, Elizabeth (1925–1947)
Short, Florence (1889–1946)
Short, Gertrude (1902–1968)
Shortall, Róisín (1954—)
Shorten, Monica (1923–1993)
Shortt, Elizabeth Smith (1859–1949)
Shouaa, Ghada (1972—)
Shouse, Kay (1896–1994)
Showalter, Elaine (1941—)
Shrimpton, Jean (1942—)
Shriver, Eunice Kennedy (1921—)
Shriver, Maria (1955—)
Shriver, Pam (1962—)
Shtarkelova, Margarita (1951—)
Shtereva, Nikolina (1955—)
Shtern, Lina (1878–1968)
Shub, Esther (1894–1959)
Shubina, Lyudmila (1948—)
Shubina, Mariya (1930—)
Shubina, Yelena (1974—)
Shui Qingxia (1976—)
Shuler, Nettie Rogers (1862–1939)
Shulman, Alix Kates (1932—)
Shurr, Gertrude (c. 1920—)
Shushunova, Elena (1969—)
Shutta, Ethel (1896–1976)
Shuvayeva, Nadezhda (1952—)
Shvaybovich, Yelena (1966—)
Shvyganova, Tatyana (1960—)
Shynkarenko, Tetyana (1978—)
Sibley, Antoinette (1939—)
Sideri, Cornelia (1938—)
Sidgwick, Eleonora Mildred (1845–1936)
Sidhwa, Bapsi (1938—)
Sidney, Sylvia (1910–1999)
Sidorenko, Tatyana (1966—)
Sidorova, Evgenyia (c. 1935—)
Sidorova, Tatyana (1936—)
Sidorova-Burochkina, Valentina (1954—)
Siebert, Gloria (1964—)
Siebert, Muriel (1932—)
Siech, Birte (1967—)
Siedeberg, Emily Hancock (1873–1968)
Siefert, Silvia (1953—)
Siegelaar, Sarah (1981—)
Siegl, Siegrun (1954—)
Siems, Margarethe (1879–1952)
Sierens, Gayle (1954—)
Siering, Lauri (1957—)
Sierra, Stella (1917–1997)
Sievwright, Margaret Home (1844–1905)
Sigerson, Dora (1866–1918)
Signoret, Simone (1921–1985)
Sigurdsen, Gertrud (1923—)
Sikakane, Joyce Nomafa (1943—)
Sikolova, Helena (1949—)
Sikveland, Annette (1972—)
Silai, Ileana (1941—)
Silhanova, Olga (1920–1986)
Silinga, Annie (1910–1983)
Silivas, Daniela (1970—)
Silko, Leslie Marmon (1948—)
Silkwood, Karen (1946–1974)
Sillanpää, Miina (1866–1952)
Silliman, Lynn (1959—)
Sills, Beverly (1929—)
Silva, Clara (1905–1976)
Silva, Jackie (1962—)
Silva, Maria Angelica (1966—)

Silva, Paula (1962—)
Silva, Raquel (1978—)
Silva Vila, María Inés (1926—)
Silver, Joan Micklin (1935—)
Silvia Sommerlath (1943—)
Sim, Sheila (1922—)
Simagina, Irina (1982—)
Simaite, Ona (1899–1970)
Simcox, Edith (1844–1901)
Simeoni, Sara (1953—)
Simionato, Giulietta (1910—)
Simkhovitch, Mary (1867–1951)
Simkins, Modjeska M. (1899–1992)
Simmons, Coralie (1977—)
Simmons, Erin (1976—)
Simmons, Jean (1929—)
Simmons, Ruth J. (1945—)
Simmons-Carrasco, Heather (1970—)
Simms, Florence (1873–1923)
Simms, Ginny (1915–1994)
Simms, Hilda (1920–1994)
Simon, Carly (1945—)
Simon, Kate (1912–1990)
Simon, Lidia (1973—)
Simon, Simone (1910–2005)
Simone, Kirsten (1934—)
Simone, Madame (1877–1985)
Simone, Nina (1933–2003)
Simonetto de Portela, Noemi (1926—)
Simonis, Anita (1926—)
Simonovich-Efimova, Nina (1877–1948)
Simons, Ann (1980—)
Simons, Beverly (1938—)
Simons, Nancy (1938—)
Simons de Ridder, Alexandra (1963—)
Simpson, Adele (1903–1995)
Simpson, Carole (1940—)
Simpson, Edna Oakes (1891–1984)
Simpson, Fiona (1965—)
Simpson, Helen (1897–1940)
Simpson, Janet (1944—)
Simpson, Juliene (1953—)
Simpson, Mary Elizabeth (1865–1948)
Simpson, Mary Michael (1925—)
Simpson, Nicole Brown (1959–1994)
Simpson, Sherone (1984—)
Simpson, Valerie (1946—)
Sims, Joan (1930–2001)
Sims, Naomi (1948—)
Sinatra, Nancy (1940—)
Sinclair, Betty (1907–1983)
Sinclair, Madge (1938–1995)
Sinclair, May (1863–1946)
Sinden, Topsy (1878–1951)
Singer, Eleanor (1903–1999)
Singer, Heike (1964—)
Singer, Margaret (1921–2003)
Singer, Winnaretta (1865–1943)
Singleton, Penny (1908–2003)
Singstad, Karin (1958—)
Sinko, Andrea (1967—)
Sinn, Pearl (1967—)
Sinnige, Clarinda (1973—)
Sintenis, Renée (1888–1965)
Sipilä, Helvi (1915—)
Sipprell, Clara (1885–1975)
Sirch, Cornelia (1966—)
Sirikit (1932—)
Sirota, Beate (1923—)
Sirridge, Marjorie S. (1921—)
Sissi (1967—)
Sisulu, Albertina (1918—)
Siteman, Isabella Flora (c. 1842–1919)
Sithole-Niang, Idah (1957—)
Siti, Beata (c. 1974—)
Sitterly, Charlotte Moore (1898–1990)
Sitwell, Edith (1887–1964)
Siukalo, Ganna (1976—)
Sivkova, Anna (1982—)
Sixsmith, Jane (1967—)
Sizova, Alla (1939—)
Sjöberg, Johanna (1978—)
Sjoeqvist, Laura (1903–1964)
Skachko-Pakhovskaya, Tatyana (1954—)
Skakun, Nataliya (1981—)
Skala, Lilia (1896–1994)
Skaldina, Oksana (1972—)
Skerlatova, Girgina (1954—)
Skillman, Melanie (1954—)
Skinner, Constance Lindsay (1877–1939)
Skinner, Cornelia Otis (1901–1979)
Skinner, Julie (1968—)
Skinner, Mollie (1876–1955)
Skipworth, Alison (1863–1952)
Skirving, Angie (1981—)
Skjelbreid, Ann-Elen (1971—)
Sklenickova, Miroslava (1951—)
Skoblikova, Lydia (1939—)
Skobtsova, Maria (1891–1945)
Sköld, Berit (1939—)
Skolimowska, Kamila (1982—)
Skorik, Irene (1928—)
Skoronel, Vera (1909–1932)
Skotvoll, Annette (1968—)
Skov, Rikke (1980—)
Skrabatun, Valentina (1958—)
Skram, Amalie (1846–1905)
Skrbkova, Milada (1897–1965)
Skrine, Agnes (c. 1865–1955)
Skujyte, Austra (1979—)
Slagle, Eleanor Clarke (1871–1942)
Slamet, Winarni Binti (1975—)
Slancikova, Bozena (1867–1951)
Slaney, Mary Decker (1958—)
Slater, Frances Charlotte (1892–1947)
Slaton, Danielle (1980—)
Slatter, Kate (1971—)
Slaughter, Lenora S. (1906–2000)
Slaughter, Louise M. (1929—)
Slavcheva, Evladiya (1962—)
Slavenska, Mia (1914–2000)
Slavikova, Ludmila (1890–1943)
Sledge, Debra (1955—)
Sledge, Joni (1957—)
Sledge, Kathy (1959—)
Sledge, Kim (1958—)
Sleeper, Martha (1907–1983)
Slenczynska, Ruth (1925—)
Slesarenko, Yelena (1982—)
Slesinger, Tess (1905–1945)
Slessor, Mary (1848–1915)
Slick, Grace (1939—)
Sliwkowa, Maria (1935—)
Slizowska, Barbara (1938—)
Sloan, Susan (1958—)
Slosson, Annie Trumbull (1838–1926)
Slowe, Lucy Diggs (1885–1937)
Slupianek, Ilona (1956—)
Slutskaya, Irina (1979—)
Slutskaya, Vera (1874–1917)
Sly, Wendy (1959—)
Slye, Maud (1869–1954)
Slyusareva, Olga (1969—)
Smabers, Hanneke (1973—)
Smabers, Minke (1979—)
Small, Kim (1965—)
Small, Mary Elizabeth (1812/13–1908)
Small, Sami Jo (1976—)
Smallwood, Norma (c. 1908–1966)
Smallwood-Cook, Kathryn (1960—)
Smart, Elizabeth (1913–1986)
Smart, Pamela Wojas (1967—)
Smeal, Eleanor (1939—)
Smedley, Agnes (1892–1950)
Smellie, Elizabeth Lawrie (1884–1968)
Smendzianka, Regina (1924—)
Smet, Miet (1943—)
Smetanina, Raisa (1929—)
Smidova, Lenka (1975—)
Smieton, Mary (1902–2005)
Smiley, Jane (1949—)
Smirnova, Irina (1968—)
Smirnova, Ludmila (1949—)
Smirnova, Sofia (1852–1921)
Smirnow, Zoya (fl. 1914)
Smit, Gretha (1976—)
Smith, Ada (1894–1984)
Smith, Ada
Smith, Alexis (1921–1993)
Smith, Amanda Berry (1837–1915)
Smith, Angela (1959—)
Smith, Anna Deavere (1950—)
Smith, Annette
Smith, Annie Lorrain (1854–1937)
Smith, Arlene (1941—)
Smith, Bathsheba (1822–1910)
Smith, Bessie (1894–1937)
Smith, Betty (1896–1972)
Smith, Bev (1960—)
Smith, Bill (1886–1975)
Smith, Caroline (1906—)
Smith, Chloethiel Woodard (1910–1992)
Smith, Christine Anne (1946—)
Smith, Clara (1894–1935)
Smith, Delia (1941—)
Smith, Dodie (1896–1990)
Smith, Donalda (d. 1998)
Smith, Elaine (1963—)
Smith, Ethel (1907–1979)
Smith, Evelyn E. (1922–2000)
Smith, Fiona (1973—)
Smith, Frances Hagell (1877–1948)
Smith, Geraldine (1961—)
Smith, Gina (1957—)
Smith, Grace Cossington (1892–1984)
Smith, Hannah Whitall (1832–1911)
Smith, Hazel Brannon (1914–1994)
Smith, Helen Hay (1873–1918)
Smith, Hilda
Smith, Jacqui (1962—)
Smith, Jean Kennedy (1928—)
Smith, Jessie Willcox (1863–1935)
Smith, Julia Frances (1911–1989)
Smith, Julie (1968—)
Smith, Kate (1907–1986)
Smith, Katie (1974—)
Smith, Keely (1932—)
Smith, Kendra (1960—)
Smith, Lillian (1897–1966)
Smith, Liz (1923—)
Smith, Lucy Masey (1861–1936)
Smith, Mabel (1924–1972)
Smith, Maggie (1934—)
Smith, Mamie (1883–1946)
Smith, Margaret (1961—)
Smith, Margaret Charles (b. 1906)
Smith, Margaret Chase (1897–1995)
Smith, Marilynn (1929—)
Smith, Mary Ellen (1861–1933)
Smith, Mary Louise (1914–1997)
Smith, Michele (1967—)
Smith, Michelle (1969—)
Smith, Muriel Burrell (1923–1985)
Smith, Nora Archibald (1859?–1934)
Smith, Patti (1946—)
Smith, Pauline (1882–1959)
Smith, Phylis (1965—)
Smith, Queenie (1898–1978)
Smith, Rebecca (1959—)
Smith, Robyn (1942—)
Smith, Ronetta (1980—)
Smith, Samantha (1972–1985)
Smith, Sammi (1943–2005)
Smith, Shannon (1961—)
Smith, Shawntel (1971—)
Smith, Stevie (1902–1971)
Smith, Tricia (1957—)
Smith, Trixie (1895–1943)
Smith, Virginia Dodd (1911–2006)
Smith, Virginia Thrall (1836–1903)
Smith, Wiffi (1936—)
Smith, Willie Mae Ford (1904–1994)
Smith, Zilpha Drew (1851–1926)
Smither, Elizabeth (1941—)
Smith-Rosenberg, Carroll
Smithson, Alison (1928–1993)
Smoleyeva, Nina (1948—)
Smoller, Dorothy (c. 1901–1926)
Smosarska, Jadwiga (1898–1971)
Smucker, Barbara (1915–2003)
Smulders, Marlies (1982—)
Smurova, Elena (1973—)
Smylie, Elizabeth (1963—)
Smyth, Donna (1943—)
Smyth, Ethel (1858–1944)
Smyth, Patty (1957—)
Smythe, Pat (1928–1996)
Snell, Belinda (1981—)

Snelling, Lilian (1879–1972)
Snep-Balan, Doina Liliana (1963—)
Snite, Betsy (1938–1984)
Snively, Mary Agnes (1847–1933)
Snoeks, Jiske (1978—)
Snow, Helen Foster (1907–1997)
Snow, Marguerite (1889–1958)
Snow, Phoebe (1952—)
Snow, Sarah Ellen Oliver (1864–1939)
Snow, Valaida (c. 1903–1956)
Snowden, Leigh (1929–1982)
Snowe, Olympia J. (1947—)
Snyder, Alice D. (1887–1943)
Snyder, Ruth (1893–1928)
Snytina, Natalia (1971—)
Sobotka, Ruth (1925–1967)
Sobral, Leila (1974—)
Sobral, Marta (1964—)
Sobrero, Kate (1976—)
Sobti, Krishna (1925—)
Söderbaum, Kristina (1912—)
Södergran, Edith (1892–1923)
Söderström, Elisabeth (1927—)
Söderström, Marit (1962—)
Sofola, Zulu (1935–1995)
Sofronie, Daniela (1988—)
Sofronova, Antonina (1892–1966)
Sohier, Elizabeth Putnam (1847–1926)
Sohnemann, Kate (1913—)
Sohonie, Kamala (1911—)
Soia, Elena (1981—)
Sokolova, Elena (1980—)
Sokolova, Elena
Sokolova, Eugenia (1850–1925)
Sokolova, Lydia (1896–1974)
Sokolova, Lyubov (1921–2001)
Sokolova-Kulichkova, Natalya (1949—)
Sokolow, Anna (1910–2000)
Sokolowska, Beata (1974—)
Solano, Solita (1888–1975)
Soleil, Germaine (1913–1996)
Soler, Yolanda
Solinas Donghi, Beatrice (1923—)
Soljak, Miriam Bridelia (1879–1971)
Sollmann, Melitta
Solntseva, Yulia (1901–1989)
Sologne, Madeleine (1912–1995)
Solomon, Hannah Greenebaum (1858–1942)
Solov'eva, Poliksena (1867–1924)
Solovova, Olga (1953—)
Somer, Hilde (1922–1979)
Somers, Armonía (1914–1994)
Somerset, Isabella (1851–1921)
Somerville, E. (1858–1949)
Somerville, Nellie Nugent (1863–1952)
Sommer, Renate (1958—)
Somogi, Judith (1937–1988)
Sondergaard, Gale (1899–1985)
Song Ailing (1890–1973)
Song Ji-Hyun (1969—)
Song Meiling (1897–2003)
Song Nina (1980—)
Song Qingling (1893–1981)
Song Xiaobo (1958—)
Sonja (1937—)
Sono, Ayako (1931—)
Sontag, Susan (1933–2004)
Soper, Eileen Louise (1900–1989)
Sophia (1868–1927)
Sophia (1957—)
Sophia of Greece (1938—)
Sophia of Greece (b. 1914)
Sophia of Nassau (1836–1913)
Sophie Charlotte of Oldenburg (1879–1964)
Sophie of Nassau (1902–1941)
Sophie of Prussia (1870–1932)
Sorabji, Cornelia (1866–1954)
Soray, Turkan (1945—)
Sorel, Cécile (1873–1966)
Sorel, Claudette (1930—)
Sorel, Felicia (1904–1972)
Sorensen, Inge (1924—)
Sorensen, Jette Hejli (1961—)
Sorensen, Patsy (1952—)
Sorenson, Carol (1942—)
Sorenstam, Annika (1970—)
Sorenstam, Charlotta (1973—)
Sorgdrager, Winnie (1948—)
Sorgers, Jana (1967—)
Soriano, Elena (1917–1996)
Sorkin, Naomi (1948—)
Sørlie, Else-Marthe (1978—)
Sorma, Agnes (1862–1927)
Sornosa Martínez, María (1949—)
Sorokina, Anna (1976—)
Sorokina, Nina (1942—)
Sosa, Mercedes (1935—)
Sostorics, Colleen (1979—)
Sothern, Ann (1909–2001)
Sothern, Georgia (1912–1981)
Sotherton, Kelly (1976—)
Sotiriou, Dido (1909–2004)
Sotnikova, Yuliya (1970—)
Souez, Ina (1903–1992)
Soule, Caroline White (1824–1903)
Soundarya (1972–2004)
Southern, Eileen Jackson (1920–2002)
Southern, Jeri (1926–1991)
Southworth, Helen (1956—)
Souza, Auta de (1876–1901)
Souza, Helia (1970—)
Sovetnikova, Galina (1955—)
Sowerby, Githa (1876–1970)
Sowerby, Millicent (1878–1967)
Sow Fall, Aminata (1941—)
Soyer, Ida (1909–1970)
Soysal, Sevgi (1936–1976)
Spacek, Sissy (1949—)
Spafford, Belle Smith (1895–1982)
Spagnuolo, Filomena (1903–1987)
Spain, Elsie (1879–1970)
Spain, Fay (1932–1983)
Spain, Jayne (1927—)
Spark, Muriel (1918–2006)
Sparks, Donita (1963—)
Spaziani, Maria Luisa (1924—)
Speare, Elizabeth George (1908–1994)
Spears, Britney (1981—)
Spector, Ronnie (1943—)
Speirs, Annie (1889–1926)
Spellman, Gladys Noon (1918–1988)
Spelman, Caroline (1958—)
Spence, Catherine (1825–1910)
Spence, Judith (1957—)
Spencer, Anna (1851–1931)
Spencer, Anne (1882–1975)
Spencer, Cornelia Phillips (1825–1908)
Spencer, Dorothy (b. 1909)
Spencer, Elizabeth (1921—)
Spencer, Jane (1957—)
Spencer, Lilly Martin (1822–1902)
Spencer, Sarah (1955—)
Spencer Bower, Olivia (1905–1982)
Spencer Smith, Joan (1891–1965)
Spender, Dale (1943—)
Speraz, Beatrice (1843–1923)
Sperber, Sylvia (1965—)
Sperling, Hilde (1908–1981)
Spessivtzeva, Olga (1895–1980)
Spewack, Bella (1899–1990)
Speyer, Ellin Prince (1849–1921)
Speyer, Leonora (1872–1956)
Spheeris, Penelope (1945—)
Spiel, Hilde (1911–1990)
Spies, Daisy (1905–2000)
Spillane, Joan (1943—)
Spinelli, Evelita Juanita (1889–1941)
Spira, Camilla (1906–1997)
Spira, Steffie (1908–1995)
Spircu, Doina (1970—)
Spiridonova, Maria (1884–1941)
Spitz, Sabine (1971—)
Spivak, Gayatri Chakravorty (1942—)
Spivey, Victoria (1906–1976)
Spofford, Grace Harriet (1887–1974)
Spofford, Harriet Prescott (1835–1921)
Spolin, Viola (1906–1994)
Sponer, Hertha (1895–1968)
Spong, Hilda (1875–1955)
Spooner, Cecil (1875–1953)
Spooner, Edna May (1873–1953)
Spooner, Molly (1914–1997)
Sporn, Rachael (1968—)
Spottiswoode, Alicia Ann (1810–1900)
Springfield, Dusty (1939–1999)
Spry, Constance (1886–1960)
Spurgeon, Caroline F.E. (1869–1942)
Spurgin, Patricia (1965—)
Spuzich, Sandra (1937—)
Spyri, Emily Kempin (1853–1901)
Spyri, Johanna (1827–1901)
Squire, Rachel (1954–2006)
Squires, Catharine (1843–1912)
Squires, Helena E. (1879–1959)
Sramkova, Iveta (1963—)
Sri, Indriyani (1978—)
Srncova, Bozena (1925—)
St. Clair, Lydia (1898–1970)
St. Clair, Stephanie (fl. 1920s–30s)
St. Clair, Yvonne (1914–1971)
St. Denis, Ruth (1877–1968)
St. Denis, Teddie (b. 1909)
St. George, Katharine (1894–1983)
St. James, Lyn (1947—)
St. John, Florence (1854–1912)
St. Johns, Adela Rogers (1894–1988)
St. Louis, France (1959—)
St. Pierre, Kim (1978—)
Stabenow, Debbie (1950—)
Stace, Helen McRae (1850–1926)
Stacey, Kim (1980—)
Stachow, Danuta (1934—)
Stachowski, Amber (1983—)
Stack, Chelle (1973—)
Stacker, Brenann (1987—)
Stacy, Hollis (1954—)
Stad-de Jong, Xenia (1922—)
Stafford, Jean (1915–1979)
Stafford, Jo (1920—)
Stahl, Lesley (1941—)
Stahl, Rose (1870–1955)
Stahl-Iencic, Ecaterina (1946—)
Staiculescu, Doina (1967—)
Staley, Dawn (1970—)
Stallmaier, Veronika (1966—)
Stalman, Ria (1951—)
Stammers, Kay (1914–2005)
Stamp Taylor, Edith (1904–1946)
Stanciu, Anisoara (1962—)
Stanford, Jane (1828–1905)
Stang, Dorothy (1931–2005)
Stanley, Kim (1925–2001)
Stanley, Louise (1883–1954)
Stanley, Martha M. (1867–1950)
Stanley, Mary (1919–1980)
Stanley, Winifred Claire (1909–1996)
Stansfield, Lisa (1966—)
Stanton, Elizabeth Cady (1815–1902)
Stanulet, Mihaela (1966—)
Stanwood, Cordelia (1865–1958)
Stanwyck, Barbara (1907–1990)
Staples, Cleo (1934—)
Staples, Mavis (1940—)
Staples, Yvonne (1939—)
Stapleton, Maureen (1925–2006)
Stapleton, Ruth Carter (1929–1983)
Starbird, Kate (1975—)
Stark, Freya (1893–1993)
Starke, Pauline (1900–1977)
Starke, Ute (1939—)
Starkey, Phyllis (1947—)
Starkie, Enid (1897–1970)
Starovoitova, Galina (1946–1998)
Starr, Ellen Gates (1859–1940)
Starr, Frances Grant (1886–1973)
Starr, Kay (1922—)
Starr, Muriel (1888–1950)
Starre, Katie (1971—)
Stasova, Elena (1873–1966)
Stasyuk, Natalia (1969—)
Statham, Edith May (1853–1951)
Stauffenberg, Litta von (c. 1905–1945)
Stauffer, Brenda (1961—)
Stauner, Gabriele (1948—)
Staupers, Mabel (1890–1989)
Staveley, Dulcie (1898–1995)
Staver, Julie (1952—)
Staw, Sala (d. 1972)

Stead, Christina (1902–1983)
Stearns, Lutie (1866–1943)
Stearns, Sally (c. 1915—)
Stebbing, L. Susan (1885–1943)
Steber, Eleanor (1914–1990)
Stecher, Renate (1950—)
Steding, Katy (1967—)
Stedman, Myrtle (1885–1938)
Steed, Gitel P. (1914–1977)
Steel, Dawn (1946–1997)
Steel, Dorothy (1884–1965)
Steel, Flora Annie (1847–1929)
Steele, Alison (c. 1937–1995)
Steele, Barbara (1937—)
Steele, Danielle (1947—)
Steele, Joyce
Steele, Micki (1954—)
Steenberghe, Florentine (1967—)
Steer, Irene (1889–1947)
Stefan, Maria (1954—)
Stefan, Verena (1947—)
Stefanek, Gertrud (1959—)
Steffin, Christel (1940—)
Stegemann, Kerstin (1977—)
Steggall, Zali (1974—)
Steiff, Margarete (1847–1909)
Stein, Edith (1891–1942)
Stein, Gertrude (1874–1946)
Stein, Marion (1926—)
Steinbach, Angela (1955—)
Steinbach, Sabine (1952—)
Steinbeck, Janet (1951—)
Steindorf, Ute (1957—)
Steinem, Gloria (1934—)
Steinseifer, Carrie (1968—)
Steinwachs, Ginka (1942—)
Stellmach, Manuela (1970—)
Stelma, Jacoba (1907—)
Steloff, Frances (1887–1989)
Sten, Anna (1908–1993)
Stenina, Valentina (1936—)
Stenzel, Ursula (1945—)
Stepan, Mary Louise (1935—)
Stepanova, Maria (1979—)
Stepanova, Varvara (1894–1958)
Stepanskaya, Galina (1949—)
Stephanie of Belgium (1864–1945)
Stephanie of Monaco (1965—)
Stephansen, Elizabeth (1872–1961)
Stephens, Alice Barber (1858–1932)
Stephens, Frances (1924–1978)
Stephens, Helen (1918–1994)
Stephens, Kate (1853–1938)
Stephenson, Elsie (1916–1967)
Stephenson, Jan (1951—)
Stephenson, Marjory (1885–1948)
Stepnik, Ayelen (1975—)
Sterbinszky, Amalia (1950—)
Sterkel, Jill (1961—)
Sterling, Jan (1921–2004)
Stern, Catherine Brieger (1894–1973)
Stern, Edith Rosenwald (1895–1980)
Stern, Elizabeth (1915–1980)
Stern, Frances (1873–1947)
Stern, G.B. (1890–1973)
Stern, Irma (1894–1966)
Sternhagen, Frances (1930—)
Stetsenko, Tatyana (1957—)
Stetson, Augusta (1842–1928)
Stetson, Helen (1887–1982)
Stettheimer, Florine (1871–1944)
Steuer, Anni (b. 1913)
Steurer, Florence (1949—)
Stevens, Connie (1938—)
Stevens, Emily (1882–1928)
Stevens, Georgia Lydia (1870–1946)
Stevens, Inger (1934–1970)
Stevens, Julie (1916–1984)
Stevens, K.T. (1919–1994)
Stevens, Lillian (1844–1914)
Stevens, May (1924—)
Stevens, Nettie Maria (1861–1912)
Stevens, Risë (1913—)
Stevens, Rochelle (1966—)
Stevens, Stella (1936—)
Stevenson, Anne (1933—)
Stevenson, Fanny (1840–1914)
Stevenson, Greta Barbara (1911–1990)
Stevenson, Juliet (1956—)
Stevenson, Margaret Beveridge (1865–1941)
Stevenson, Matilda (1849–1915)
Stevenson, Nicole (1971—)
Stevenson, Rona (1911–1988)
Stevenson, Sarah Hackett (1841–1909)
Stevenson, Sara Yorke (1847–1921)
Steward, Natalie (1943—)
Steward, Susan McKinney (1847–1918)
Stewart, Adela Blanche (1846–1910)
Stewart, Alexandra (1939—)
Stewart, Alice (1906–2002)
Stewart, Anastasia (1883–1923)
Stewart, Anita (1895–1961)
Stewart, Catherine Campbell (1881–1957)
Stewart, Cora Wilson (1875–1958)
Stewart, Elaine (1929—)
Stewart, Eliza Daniel (1816–1908)
Stewart, Ellen (c. 1920—)
Stewart, Frances Ann (1840–1916)
Stewart, Isabel Maitland (1878–1963)
Stewart, Jean (1930—)
Stewart, Katherine (c. 1861–1949)
Stewart, Martha (1941—)
Stewart, Mary (1916—)
Stewart, Mary Downie (1876–1957)
Stewart, Nellie (1858–1931)
Stewart, Olga Margaret (1920–1998)
Stewart, Sarah (1906–1976)
Stewart, Sarah (1911—)
Stewart, Sophie (1908–1977)
Stewart-Murray, Katharine (1874–1960)
Stewart-Richardson, Lady Constance (1883–1932)
Stich-Randall, Teresa (1927—)
Sticker, Josephine (1894—)
Stickles, Terri Lee (1946—)
Stickney, Dorothy (1896–1998)
Stiefl, Regina (1966—)
Stignani, Ebe (1903–1975)
Stihler, Catherine (1973—)
Still, Megan (1972—)
Stimson, Julia (1881–1948)
Stindt, Hermine (1888–1974)
Stinson, Katherine (1891–1977)
Stinson, Marjorie (1894–1975)
Stirling, Mihi Kotukutuku (1870–1956)
Stives, Karen (1950—)
Stjernstedt, Rosemary (1912–1998)
Stöbe, Ilse (1911–1942)
Stobs, Shirley (1942—)
Stockbauer, Hannah (1982—)
Stockenström, Wilma (1933—)
Stockert-Meynert, Dora von (1870–1947)
Stockley, Cynthia (1872–1936)
Stöcklin, Franziska (1894–1931)
Stocks, Mary Danvers (1891–1975)
Stoddard, Cora Frances (1872–1936)
Stoddard, Elizabeth Drew (1823–1902)
Stoddart, Margaret Olrog (1865–1934)
Stoeckel, Ellen Battell (1851–1939)
Stoecker, Helene (1869–1943)
Stoecklin, Stephane (1969—)
Stoere, Heidi (1973—)
Stoeva, Vasilka (1940—)
Stokes, Caroline Phelps (1854–1909)
Stokes, Olivia Phelps (1847–1927)
Stokes, Rose Pastor (1879–1933)
Stokes, Shelly (1967—)
Stoler, Shirley (1929–1999)
Stolitsa, Liubov (1884–1934)
Stolk, Gloria (1918–1979)
Stolz, Teresa (1834–1902)
Stone, Barbara Gwendoline (1962—)
Stone, Beth (1940—)
Stone, Carol (1915—)
Stone, Constance (1856–1902)
Stone, Dorothy (1905–1974)
Stone, Grace Zaring (1896–1991)
Stone, Hannah (1893–1941)
Stone, Nikki (1971—)
Stone, Paula (1912–1997)
Stone, Rosie (1945—)
Stone, Ruth (1915—)
Stone, Sharon (1958—)
Stone, Toni (1921–1996)
Stonehouse, Ruth (1892–1941)
Stoneman, Bertha (1866–1943)
Stones, Margaret (1920—)
Stopes, Marie (1880–1958)
Stopford Green, Alice (1847–1929)
Storchio, Rosina (1876–1945)
Storczer, Beata (1969—)
Storer, Maria (1849–1932)
Storey, Edith (1892–1955)
Storm, Gale (1922—)
Storm, Lesley (1898–1975)
Storni, Alfonsina (1892–1938)
Story, Gertrude (1929—)
Stothard, Sarah Sophia (1825/26–1901)
Stouder, Sharon (1948—)
Stout, Anna Paterson (1858–1931)
Stout, Juanita Kidd (1919–1998)
Stoute, Jennifer (1965—)
Stovbchataya, Ludmila (1974—)
Stove, Betty (1945—)
Stover-Irwin, Juno (1928—)
Stowe, Emily Howard (1831–1903)
Stowell, Belinda (1971—)
Stoyanova, Boriana (1968—)
Stoyanova, Mariya (1947—)
Stoyanova, Penka (1950—)
Stoyanova, Radka (1964—)
Strachey, Pippa (1872–1968)
Strachey, Ray (1887–1940)
Stradner, Rose (1913–1958)
Straight, Beatrice (1914–2001)
Straker, Karen (1964—)
Strandberg, Britt
Strang, Ruth (1895–1971)
Strange, Michael (1890–1950)
Strasberg, Paula (1911–1966)
Strasberg, Susan (1938–1999)
Stratas, Teresa (1938—)
Stratton, Dorothy (b. 1899)
Stratton, Helen (fl. 1891–1925)
Stratton Porter, Gene (1863–1924)
Strauch, Annegret (1968—)
Straus, Ida (1849–1912)
Strauss, Astrid (1968—)
Strauss, Jennifer (1933—)
Strauss, Sara Milford (1896–1979)
Strauss und Torney, Lulu von (1873–1956)
Strazheva, Olga (1972—)
Streatfeild, Noel (1895–1986)
Streb, Elizabeth (1950—)
Streb, Marla (1965—)
Strecen-Maseikaite, Sigita (1958—)
Streep, Meryl (1949—)
Street, Jessie (1889–1970)
Street, Picabo (1971—)
Streeter, Alison (1964—)
Streeter, Ruth Cheney (1895–1990)
Streich, Rita (1920–1987)
Streidt, Ellen (1952—)
Streisand, Barbra (1942—)
Streit, Marlene Stewart (1934—)
Strengell, Marianne (1909–1998)
Stretton, Hesba (1832–1911)
Strickland, Mabel (1899–1988)
Strickland, Shirley (1925–2004)
Strike, Hilda (1910–1989)
Stringer, C. Vivian (1948—)
Stringfield, Bessie B. (1912–1993)
Stritch, Elaine (1925—)
Stritt, Marie (1856–1928)
Stroescu, Silvia (1985—)
Stroganova, Nina (1919—)
Strong, Anna Louise (1885–1970)
Strong, Ann Monroe Gilchrist (1875–1957)
Strong, Eithne (1923–1999)
Strong, Harriet (1844–1929)
Strong, Judy (1960—)
Strong, Lori (1972—)
Strong, Shirley (1958—)
Strossen, Nadine (1950—)
Stroyeva, Vera (b. 1903)
Strozzi, Kay (1899–1996)
Struchkova, Raissa (1925–2005)
Strug, Kerri (1977—)
Strunnikova, Natalya (1964—)

Struppert, Barbel (1950—)
Struthers, Karen Lee (1963—)
Stuart, Aimée (c. 1885–1981)
Stuart, Bathia Howie (1893–1987)
Stuart, Gisela (1955—)
Stuart, Gloria (1909—)
Stuart, Mary (1926–2002)
Stuart, Ruth McEnery (c. 1849–1917)
Stuart, Wilhelmina Magdalene (1895–1985)
Stubnick, Christa (1933—)
Stückelberger, Christine (1947—)
Studneva, Marina (1959—)
Stukalava, Tatsiana (1975—)
Stunyo, Jeanne (1936—)
Sturgeon, Nicola (1970—)
Sturgis, Katharine Boucot (1903–1987)
Sturm, J.C. (1927—)
Sturrup, Chandra (1971—)
Styopina, Viktoriya (1976—)
Styrene, Poly (c. 1962—)
Suarez, Paola (1976—)
Subbulakshmi, M.S. (1916–2004)
Sube, Karola (1964—)
Sucher, Rosa (1847–1927)
Suchocka, Hanna (1946—)
Suckling, Sophia Lois (1893–1990)
Suckow, Ruth (1892–1960)
Sudduth, Jill (1971—)
Sudlow, Joan (1892–1970)
Sudre, Margie (1943—)
Suess, Birgit (1962—)
Suesse, Dana (1909–1987)
Sugawara, Noriko (1972—)
Sugawara, Risa (1977—)
Suggia, Guilhermina (1888–1950)
Suggs, Louise (1923—)
Sugimoto, Sonoko (1925—)
Sugiyama, Kayoko (1961—)
Suharto, Siti (1923–1996)
Suh Hyo-Sun (1966—)
Suh Kwang-Mi (1965—)
Su Hsueh-lin (1897–1999)
Su Huijuan (1964—)
Suihkonen, Liisa (1943—)
Suisted, Laura Jane (1840–1903)
Sui Xinmei
Sukarnoputri, Megawati (1947—)
Suk Eun-Mi (1976—)
Sukharnova, Olga (1955—)
Suk Min-Hee (1968—)
Sukova, Helena (1965—)
Sukova, Vera (1931–1982)
Sulka, Elaine (1933–1994)
Sullavan, Margaret (1911–1960)
Sullerot, Evelyne (1924—)
Sullivan, Carryn (1955—)
Sullivan, Cynthia Jan (1937—)
Sullivan, Jean (1923–2003)
Sullivan, Kathryn (1951—)
Sullivan, Leonor Kretzer (1902–1988)
Sullivan, Mary Quinn (1877–1939)
Sullivan, Maxine (1911–1987)
Sulner, Hanna (1917–1999)
Sulzberger, I.O. (1892–1990)
Sumac, Yma (1927—)
Sumako, Matsui (1886–1919)
Sumii, Sue (1902–1997)
Summer, Donna (1948—)
Summers, Essie (1912–1998)
Summers, Leonora (1897–1976)
Summers, Merna (1933—)
Summersby, Kay (1908–1975)
Summerskill, Edith (1901–1980)
Summerton, Laura (1983—)
Summitt, Pat (1952—)
Sumner, Jessie (1898–1994)
Sumners, Rosalynn (1964—)
Sumnikova, Irina (1964—)
Sundal, Heidi (1962—)
Sun Dandan
Sundby, Siren (1982—)
Sunderland, Nan (1898–1973)
Sundhage, Pia (1960—)
Sundstrom, Becky (1976—)
Sundstrom, Shana (1973—)
Sunesen, Gitte (1971—)
Sun Fuming (1974—)
Sung Jung-A (1965—)
Sung Kyung-Hwa (1965—)
Sun Jin (1980—)
Sunn, Rell (1951–1998)
Sunohara, Vicky (1970—)
Sun Qingmei
Sunshine, Marion (1894–1963)
Suntaque, Andreia (1977—)
Sun Tian Tian (1981—)
Sun Wen (1973—)
Sun Xiulan (1961—)
Sun Yue (1973—)
Supervia, Conchita (1895–1936)
Suplicy, Marta (c. 1946—)
Suraiya (1929–2004)
Suranova-Kucmanova, Eva (1946—)
Suruagy, Sandra (1963—)
Susann, Jacqueline (1921–1974)
Susanti, Susi (1971—)
Susanu, Viorica (1975—)
Suslova, Nadezhda (1845–1916)
Sussiek, Christine (1960—)
Süssmuth, Rita (1937—)
Suta, Khassaraporn (1971—)
Sutcliff, Rosemary (1920–1992)
Sutherland, Efua (1924–1996)
Sutherland, Joan (1926—)
Sutherland, Lucy Stuart (1903–1980)
Sutherland, Margaret (1897–1984)
Sutherland, Margaret (1941—)
Sutherland, Mary (1893–1955)
Sutherland, Mary Ann (1864–1948)
Sutherland, Selina Murray McDonald (1839–1909)
Sutliffe, Irene H. (1850–1936)
Sutter, Linda (1941–1995)
Suttner, Bertha von (1843–1914)
Sutton, Carol (1933–1985)
Sutton, Eve (1906—)
Sutton, May (1887–1975)
Suzman, Helen (1917—)
Suzman, Janet (1939—)
Suzuki, Emiko (1981—)
Svedberg, Ruth (1903–2004)
Svedova-Schoenova, Lydmila (1936—)
Svendsen, Cathrine (1967—)
Svensson, Tina (1970—)
Svet, Mateja (1968—)
Svetlova, Marina (1922—)
Svilova, Elizaveta (1900–1975)
Svobodova, Gabriela (1953—)
Svobodova, Martina (1983—)
Svolou, Maria (d. 1976)
Svubova, Dagmar
Swaab, Ninna (1940—)
Swagerty, Jane (1951—)
Swail, Julie (1972—)
Swain, Clara A. (1834–1910)
Swank, Hilary (1974—)
Swann, Caroline Burke (d. 1964)
Swanson, Gloria (1897–1983)
Swanson, Pipsan Saarinen (1905–1979)
Swanwick, Helena (1864–1939)
Swarthout, Gladys (1904–1969)
Swartz, Maud O'Farrell (1879–1937)
Sweet, Blanche (1895–1986)
Sweet, Rachel (1963—)
Swenson, May (1913–1989)
Swiebel, Joke (1941—)
Swift, Jane M. (1965—)
Swinburne, Nora (1902–2000)
Swindler, Mary Hamilton (1884–1967)
Switzer, Kathy (1947—)
Switzer, Mary E. (1900–1971)
Swoopes, Sheryl (1971—)
Sybilla of Saxe-Coburg-Gotha (1908–1972)
Sydor, Alison (1966—)
Syers, Madge Cave (1881–1917)
Sykes, Bobbi (1943—)
Sykorova, Marie (1952—)
Sylvie (1883–1970)
Sylwan, Kari (1959—)
Syms, Nancy Roth (1939—)
Syms, Sylvia (1916–1992)
Syms, Sylvia (1934—)
Szabo, Ecaterina (1966—)
Szabo, Gabriela (1975—)
Szabó, Magda (1917—)
Szabo, Reka (1967—)
Szabo, Szilvia (1978—)
Szabo, Tünde (1974—)
Szabo, Violette (1921–1945)
Szabo-Orban, Olga (1938—)
Szalay Horvathne, Gyongyi
Szanto, Anna
Szczepanska, Aneta (1972—)
Szczerbinska-Krolowa, Lidia (1935—)
Szczesniewska, Zofia (1943–1988)
Szekely, Eva (1927—)
Szekelyne-Marvalics, Gyorgyi (1924—)
Szenes, Katalin (b. 1899)
Szewczyk, Barbara (1970—)
Szewinska, Irena (1946—)
Szilagyi, Katalin
Szocs, Zsuzsanna (1962—)
Szoke, Katalin (1935—)
Szold, Henrietta (1860–1943)
Szolnoki, Maria (1947—)
Szönyi, Erzsebet (1924—)
Szumigalski, Anne (1922–1999)
Szumowska, Antoinette (1868–1938)
Szwajger, Adina Blady (1917–1993)
Szydlowska, Irena (1928–1983)
Szymborska, Wislawa (1923—)
Taba, Hilda (1902–1967)
Tabakova, Maja (1978—)
Tabakova, Yuliya (1980—)
Tabankin, Margery Ann (c. 1948—)
Tabei, Junko (1939—)
Taber, Gladys (1899–1980)
Tabouis, Geneviève (1892–1985)
Tachibana, Miya (1974—)
Tae, Satoya (1976—)
Taeuber, Irene Barnes (1906–1974)
Tafoya, Margaret (1904–2001)
Taft, Helen Herron (1861–1943)
Taft, Jessie (1882–1960)
Taggard, Genevieve (1894–1948)
Taggart, Edith Ashover (1909–1997)
Taggart, Michele (1970—)
Tagliabue, Elena (1977—)
Tagliaferro, Magda (1893–1986)
Tagwerker, Andrea
Taiaroa, Tini Kerei (c. 1846–1934)
Tailleferre, Germaine (1892–1983)
Taillon, Jacinthe (1977—)
Tait, Agnes (c. 1897–1981)
Tait, Dorothy (1905–1972)
Tajima, Yasuko (1981—)
Tajolmolouk (1896–1981)
Takagi, Tokuko Nagai (1891–1919)
Takahashi, Kaori (1974—)
Takahashi, Naoko (1972—)
Takahashi, Takako (1932—)
Takalo, Helena (1947—)
Takamine, Hideko (1924—)
Takayama, Aki (1970—)
Takayama, Juri (1976—)
Takayama, Suzue (1946—)
Takayanagi, Shoko (1954—)
Takeda, Miho (1976—)
Takei, Kei (1946—)
Takenishi, Hiroko (1929—)
Talalayeva, Lyubov (1953—)
Talanova, Nadejda (1967—)
Talavera, Tracee (1966—)
Talbert, Mary Morris (1866–1923)
Talbot, Marion (1858–1948)
Talbot, Nadine (1913–2003)
Talbott, Gloria (1931–2000)
Talcott, Eliza (1836–1911)
Taleva, Ivelina (1979—)
Taliaferro, Edith (1893–1958)
Taliaferro, Mabel (1887–1979)
Tallchief, Maria (1925—)
Tallchief, Marjorie (1927—)
Talley, Marion (1906–1983)
Talley, Nedra (1946—)
Talma, Louise (1906–1996)
Talmadge, Constance (1897–1973)
Talmadge, Natalie (1897–1969)
Talmadge, Norma (1893–1957)

Talvo, Tyyne (b. 1919)
Talysheva-Tregub, Tatyana (1937—)
Tamara (1907–1943)
Tamiris, Helen (1902–1966)
Tammes, Tine (1871–1947)
Tamoto, Hiroko (c. 1974—)
Tamura, Ryoko (1975—)
Tan, Amy (1952—)
Tanabe, Seiko (1928—)
Tanabe, Yoko (1966—)
Tanaka, Junko (1973—)
Tanaka, Kinuyo (1907–1977)
Tanaka, Masami (1979—)
Tanaka, Miyako (1967—)
Tanaka, Satoko (1942—)
Tanase, Anca (1968—)
Tancheva, Galina (1987—)
Tancheva, Vladislava (1987—)
Tanderup, Anne Dorthe (1972—)
Tandy, Jessica (1909–1994)
Tanger, Helen (1978—)
Tangeraas, Trine (1971—)
Tang Gonghong (1979—)
Tang Jiuhong (1969—)
Tang Lin (1975—)
Tangney, Dorothy (1911–1985)
Tanguay, Eva (1878–1947)
Tang Yongshu
Tanida, Kuniko (1939—)
Tanimoto, Ayumi (1981—)
Tannenbaum, Jane Belo (1904–1968)
Tanner, Clara Lee (1905–1997)
Tanner, Elaine (1951—)
Tanner, Ilona (1895–1955)
Tanner, Marion (1891–1985)
Tanner, Vera (b. 1906)
Tanning, Dorothea (b. 1910)
Tan Xue (1984—)
Tanzini, Luisa (b. 1914)
Tao Hua
Tao Luna (1974—)
Taormina, Sheila (1969—)
Tapley, Rose (1881–1956)
Tappan, Eva March (1854–1930)
Tappin, Ashley T. (1974—)
Tapsell, Ngatai Tohi Te Ururangi (1844–1928)
Tarabini, Patricia (1968—)
Tarakanova, Nelli (1954—)
Taran, Ruslana (1970—)
Taranina, Viktoria
Taran-Iordache, Maricica Titie (1962—)
Tarasova, Alla (1898–1973)
Tarbell, Ida (1857–1944)
Tarnowska, Maria (1878–1923)
Taro, Gerda (1910–1937)
Tarpley, Lindsay (1983—)
Tarrant, Margaret (1888–1959)
Tarry, Ellen (b. 1906)
Tarsouli, Athena (1884–1974)
Taschau, Hannelies (1937—)
Tashman, Lilyan (1899–1934)
Tasker, Marianne Allen (1852–1911)
Tate, Mavis (1893–1947)
Tate, Phyllis (1911–1987)
Tate, Sharon (1943–1969)
Tateno, Chiyori (1970—)
Tatham, Reidun (1978—)
Tatiana (1897–1918)
Tatsumi, Juri (1979—)
Tattersall, Philippa (c. 1975—)
Tauber, Ulrike (1958—)
Tauber-Arp, Sophie (1889–1943)
Taurasi, Diana (1982—)
Tauskey, Mary Anne (1955—)
Taussig, Helen Brooke (1898–1986)
Tautari, Mary (d. 1906)
Tavares, Salette (1922–1994)
Taverner, Sonia (1936—)
Taylan, Nurcan (1983—)
Taylor, Alma (1895–1974)
Taylor, Angella (1958—)
Taylor, Ann (1947—)
Taylor, Anna Edson (c. 1858–c. 1921)
Taylor, Annie Royle (1855–c. 1920)
Taylor, Betty (1916–1977)
Taylor, Brenda (1934—)
Taylor, Brenda (1962—)
Taylor, Dari (1944—)
Taylor, Elizabeth (1912–1975)
Taylor, Elizabeth (1932—)
Taylor, Elizabeth Best (1868–1941)
Taylor, Estelle (1894–1958)
Taylor, Eva (1879–1966)
Taylor, Eva (1895–1977)
Taylor, Florence M. (1879–1969)
Taylor, Helen (1831–1907)
Taylor, June (1917–2004)
Taylor, Kamala (1924–2004)
Taylor, Koko (1935—)
Taylor, Laurette (1884–1946)
Taylor, Lily Ross (1886–1969)
Taylor, Lucy Hobbs (1833–1910)
Taylor, Mary (1898–1984)
Taylor, Megan (1920–1993)
Taylor, Melanie Smith (1949—)
Taylor, Penny (1981—)
Taylor, Rachael (1976—)
Taylor, Renée (1933—)
Taylor, Ruth (1908–1984)
Taylor, Sophia Louisa (1847–1903)
Taylor, Stella (1929–2003)
Taylor, Susie King (1848–1912)
Taylor, Valerie (1902–1988)
Taylor, Valerie (1935—)
Taylor-Quinn, Madeleine (1951—)
Taylor-Smith, Shelley (1961—)
Taymor, Julie (1952—)
Taymuriyya, 'A'isha 'Ismat al- (1840–1902)
Taytu (c. 1850–1918)
Tchachina, Irina (1982—)
Tchepalova, Julija (1976—)
Tcherina, Ludmilla (1924–2004)
Tcherkassky, Marianna (1955—)
Tchernicheva, Lubov (1890–1976)
Teale, Nellie (1900–1993)
Teasdale, Sara (1884–1933)
Teasdale, Verree (1904–1987)
Tebaldi, Renata (1922–2004)
Tebenikhina, Irina (1978—)
Tecson, Trinidad (1848–1928)
Teer, Barbara Ann (1937—)
Teeters, Nancy Hays (1930—)
Teeuwen, Josepha (1974—)
Teffi, N.A. (1872–1952)
Teitel, Carol (1923–1986)
Te Kahuhiapo, Rahera (1820s?–1910)
Te Kanawa, Kiri (1944—)
Te Kiri Karamu, Heni (1840–1933)
Telalkowska, Wanda (1905–1986)
Telkes, Maria (1900–1995)
Tell, Alma (1892–1937)
Tell, Olive (1894–1951)
Telleria Goni, Maider (1973—)
Telles, Lygia Fagundes (1923—)
Tellez, Dora Maria (1957—)
Tellez Palacio, Dulce M. (1983—)
Telva, Marion (1897–1962)
Temes, Judit (1930—)
Tempest, Florence (c. 1891–?)
Tempest, Marie (1864–1942)
Templeton, Fay (1865–1939)
Templeton, Olive (1883–1979)
Templeton, Rini (1935–1986)
Tenagneworq (1913–2003)
ten Boom, Corrie (1892–1983)
ten Elsen, Eva-Maria (1937—)
Tenetahi, Rahui Te Kiri (d. 1913)
Teng, Teresa (1953–1995)
Tennant, Eleanor (1895–1974)
Tennant, Emma (1937—)
Tennant, Kylie (1912–1988)
Tennant, Margaret Mary (1869–1946)
Tennant, Veronica (1946—)
Tennent, Madge Cook (1889–1972)
Tennet, Elizabeth
Tennille, Toni (1943—)
Terabust, Elisabetta (1946—)
Terán, Ana Enriqueta (1919—)
Te Rangimarie, Puna Himene (fl. 1908–1911)
ter Beek, Carin (1970—)
Teresa, Mother (1910–1997)
Tereshchuk-Antipova, Tetiana (1969—)
Tereshkova, Valentina (1937—)
Tergit, Gabrielle (1894–1982)
Terhune, Mary Virginia (1830–1922)
Termeulen, Johanna (1929–2001)
Ternina, Milka (1863–1941)
Terpstra, Erica (1943—)
Terrell, Mary Church (1863–1954)
Terrell, Tammi (1946–1970)
Terris, Norma (1904–1989)
Terriss, Ellaline (1871–1971)
Terrón i Cusí, Anna (1962—)
Terry, Alice (1899–1987)
Terry, Beatrice (b. 1890)
Terry, Ellen (1847–1928)
Terry, Hazel (1918–1974)
Terry, Kate (1844–1924)
Terry, Marion (1852–1930)
Terry, Megan (1932—)
Terry, Minnie (b. 1882)
Terry, Olive (1884—)
Terry-Lewis, Mabel (1872–1957)
Terwillegar, Erica (1963—)
Teryoshina, Yelena (1959—)
Terzian, Alicia (1938—)
Teske, Charlotte (1949—)
Teske, Rachel (1972—)
Tesky, Adeline Margaret (c. 1850–1924)
Teslenko, Olga (1981—)
Tess, Giulia (1889–1976)
Te Taiawatea Rangitukehu, Maata (1848/49?–1929)
Teter, Hannah (1987—)
Tetrazzini, Eva
(1862–1938)
Tetrazzini, Luisa (1871–1940)
Tetzel, Joan (1921–1977)
Tetzner, Gerti (1936—)
Teuscher, Cristina (1978—)
Te Whaiti, Kaihau Te Rangikakapi Maikara
(1863–1937)
Te Wherowhero, Piupiu (1886/87?–1937)
Tewkesbury, Joan (1936—)
Texidor, Greville (1902–1964)
Tey, Josephine (1896–1952)
Teyte, Maggie (1888–1976)
Thaden, Louise (1905–1979)
Thane, Elswyth (1900–1984)
Thánou, Ekateríni (1975—)
Thant, Mme (1900–1989)
Tharp, Twyla (1941—)
Tharpe, Rosetta (1915–1973)
Thatcher, Margaret (1925—)
Thatcher, Molly Day (d. 1963)
Thate, Carole (1971—)
Thaxter, Phyllis (1921—)
Theato, Diemut R. (1937—)
Thebom, Blanche (b. 1918)
Theilade, Nini (b. 1915)
Themans-Simons, Judikje (1904–1943)
Theodora Oldenburg (1906–1969)
Theodorescu, Monica (1963—)
Theodoropoulou, Avra (1880–1963)
Théoret, France (1942—)
Theorin, Maj Britt (1932—)
Theresa of Liechtenstein (1850–1938)
Theresa of Saxe-Altenburg (1836–1914)
Thesmar, Ghislaine (1943—)
Theuerkauff-Vorbrich, Gudrun (1937—)
Theurer, Elisabeth (1956—)
Thiam, Awa (1936—)
Thielemann, Ursula (1958—)
Thieme, Jana (1970—)
Thien, Margot (1971—)
Thiess, Ursula (1924—)
Thigpen, Lynne (1948–2003)
Thimig, Helene (1889–1974)
Thimm-Finger, Ute (1958—)
Thirkell, Angela (1890–1961)
Thoburn, Isabella (1840–1901)
Thom, Linda (1943—)
Thomas, Agnes (fl. 1878–1926)
Thomas, Alma (1891–1978)
Thomas, Audrey (1935—)
Thomas, Caitlin (1913–1994)
Thomas, Carla (1942—)
Thomas, Clara (1919—)
Thomas, Debi (1967—)

Thomas, Edith Matilda (1854–1925)
Thomas, Edna (1885–1974)
Thomas, Elean (1947–2004)
Thomas, Helen (1920—)
Thomas, Joyce Carol (1938—)
Thomas, Lera Millard (1900–1993)
Thomas, Lillian Beynon (1874–1961)
Thomas, M. Carey (1857–1935)
Thomas, Marlo (1937—)
Thomas, Mary (1932–1997)
Thomas, Mary (1946—)
Thomas, Olive (1884–1920)
Thomas, Petria (1975—)
Thomas, Rozonda (1971—)
Thomaschinski, Simone (1970—)
Thomas-Mauro, Nicole (1951—)
Thompson, Blanche Edith (1874–1963)
Thompson, Carol Semple (1948—)
Thompson, Clara (1893–1958)
Thompson, Donielle (1981—)
Thompson, Dorothy (1893–1961)
Thompson, Edith (c. 1894–1923)
Thompson, Eliza (1816–1905)
Thompson, Eloise Bibb (1878–1928)
Thompson, Emma (1959—)
Thompson, Era Bell (1906–1986)
Thompson, Flora (1876–1947)
Thompson, Freda (1906–1980)
Thompson, Gertrude Hickman (1877–1950)
Thompson, Helen (1908–1974)
Thompson, Jennie (1981—)
Thompson, Jenny (1973—)
Thompson, Joanne (1965—)
Thompson, Kay (1908–1998)
Thompson, Lesley (1959—)
Thompson, Linda (1948—)
Thompson, Louise (1901–1999)
Thompson, Lydia (1836–1908)
Thompson, Marion Beatrice (1877–1964)
Thompson, May (d. 1978)
Thompson, Ruth (1887–1970)
Thompson, Sada (1929—)
Thompson, Sylvia (1902–1968)
Thompson, Tina (1975—)
Thoms, Adah B. (c. 1863–1943)
Thomsen, Camilla Ingemann (1974—)
Thomson, Elaine (1957—)
Thomson, Jane (1858–1944)
Thomson, Kirsten (1983—)
Thomson, Muriel (1954—)
Thongsuk, Pawina (1979—)
Thorborg, Kerstin (1896–1970)
Thorburn, June (1930–1967)
Thoresen, Cecilie (1858–1911)
Thorn, Robyn (1945—)
Thorn, Tracey (1962—)
Thorndike, Eileen (1891–1954)
Thorndike, Sybil (1882–1976)
Thorne, Florence (1877–1973)
Thorne, Harriet V.S. (1843–1926)
Thorning-Schmidt, Helle (1966—)
Thornton, Kathryn (1952—)
Thornton, Willie Mae (1926–1984)
Thorogood, Alfreda (1942—)
Thorpe, Rose Hartwick (1850–1939)
Thors, Astrid (1957—)
Thorsness, Kristen (1960—)
Thorup, Kirsten (1942—)
Thost, Nicola (1977—)
Thrower, Norma (1936—)
Thuemer, Petra (1961—)
Thuemmler-Pawlak, Doerte (1971—)
Thuerig, Karin (1972—)
Thulin, Ingrid (1926–2004)
Thun, Kjersti (1974—)
Thurber, Jeannette (1850–1946)
Thurman, Karen L. (1951—)
Thurman, Sue (1903–1996)
Thurman, Tracey
Thurman, Uma (1970—)
Thurner, Helene
Thursby, Emma (1845–1931)
Thurston, Katherine (1875–1911)
Thurston, Mabel (1869–1960)
Thurston, Matilda (1875–1958)
Thygeson, Sylvie Thompson (1868–1975)
Thyra of Denmark (1880–1945)
Thyra Oldenburg (1853–1933)
Thyssen, Marianne L.P. (1956—)
Tibbetts, Margaret Joy (1919—)
Tiburzi, Bonnie (1948—)
Ticho, Anna (1894–1980)
Tichtchenko, Elizaveta (1975—)
Tickey, Bertha (1925—)
Tidd, Rachel (1984—)
Tidwell-Lucas, Gypsy (c. 1975—)
Tiedemann, Charlotte (1919–1979)
Tiempo, Edith L. (1919—)
Tiernan, Frances Fisher (1846–1920)
Tierney, Gene (1920–1991)
Tietjens, Eunice (1884–1944)
Tietz, Marion (1952—)
Tiffany (1971—)
Tighe, Mary (1772–1810)
Tighe, Virginia (1923–1995)
Tiit, Cecilia (1962—)
Tikhonina, Tamara (1934—)
Tikhonova, Tamara (1964—)
Tikkanen, Märta (1935—)
Tilberis, Liz (1947–1999)
Tilbury, Zeffie (1863–1950)
Tilghman, Shirley M. (1946—)
Tiller, Nadja (1929—)
Tilley, Vesta (1864–1952)
Tillion, Germaine (b. 1907)
Tilly, Dorothy (1883–1970)
Tilton, Martha (1915—)
Timanoff, Vera (1855–1942)
Timmer, Marianne (1974—)
Timms, Michelle (1965—)
Timms, Sally (1959—)
Timochenko, Alexandra (1972—)
Timoshkina-Sherstyuk, Natalya (1952—)
Tinayre, Marcelle (c. 1870–1948)
Tindall, Gillian (1938—)
Tingley, Katherine (1847–1929)
Tinsley, Pauline (1928—)
Tiourina, Elena (1971—)
Tipo, Maria (1931—)
Tipper, Constance (1894–1995)
Tipton, Billy (1914–1989)
Tirikatene-Sullivan, Whetu (1932—)
Tirlea-Manolache, Ionela (1976—)
Tissot, Alice (1895–1971)
Titcume, Natalie (1975—)
Titheradge, Madge (1887–1961)
Titlic, Ana (1952—)
Tito, Jovanka Broz (1924—)
Titova, Ludmila (1962—)
Titus, Shirley Carew (1892–1967)
Tizard, Catherine (1931—)
Tizard, Judith (1956—)
Tjoerhom, Linda (1979—)
Tjugum, Heidi (1973—)
Tkachenko, Marina (1965—)
Tkachenko, Nadezhda (1948—)
Tkacikova-Tacova, Adolfina (1939—)
Tlali, Miriam (1933—)
Tobey, Beatrice (d. 1993)
Tobin, Genevieve (1899–1995)
Tobin, Vivian (1902–2002)
Tochenova, Klavdiya (1921—)
Todd, Ann (1909–1993)
Todd, Ann (1931—)
Todd, E.L. (fl. early 1900s)
Todd, Mabel Loomis (1858–1932)
Todd, Margaret G. (1859–1918)
Todd, Marion Marsh (1841–post 1913)
Todd, Olga Taussky (1906–1995)
Todd, Thelma (1905–1935)
Todorova, Rita (1958—)
Todten, Jaqueline (1954—)
Toguri, Iva (1916—)
Tokareva, Viktoria (1937—)
Toklas, Alice B. (1877–1967)
Tokoun, Elena (1974—)
Tolkacheva, Irina (1982—)
Tolkounova, Irina (1971—)
Tolstaya, Tatyana (1951—)
Tolstoy, Alexandra (1884–1979)
Tolstoy, Sonya (1844–1919)
Toma, Sanda (1956—)
Toma, Sanda (1970—)
Tomashova, Tatyana (1975—)
Tomaszewicz-Dobrska, Anna (1854–1918)
Tombleson, Esmé (1917—)
Tomioka, Taeko (1937—)
Tomlin, Lily (1939—)
Tompkins, Sally Louisa (1833–1916)
Tone, Lel (c. 1971—)
Tonelli, Annalena (1943–2003)
Tonge, Jenny (1941—)
Tonkovic, Marija (1959—)
Tonolli, Livia (1909–1985)
Toor, Frances (1890–1956)
Tooth, Liane (1962—)
Topham, Mirabel (d. 1980)
Toppan, Jane (1854–1938)
Topperwein, Elizabeth "Plinky" (c. 1886–1945)
Topping, Jenny (1980—)
Tordasi Schwarczenberger, Ildiko (1951—)
Toren, Marta (1926–1957)
Torgersson, Therese (1976—)
Torlesse, Elizabeth Henrietta (1835/36–1922)
Tornikidu, Yelena (1965—)
Torrealva, Gina (1961—)
Torrence, Gwen (1965—)
Torres, Dara (1967—)
Torres, Lolita (1930–2002)
Torres, Raquel (1908–1987)
Torres, Regla (1975—)
Torres, Vanessa (1986—)
Torres, Xohana (1931—)
Torres Marques, Helena (1941—)
Torriani, Maria Antonietta (1840–1920)
Torvill, Jayne (1957—)
Tosatti, Barbara Maria (1891–1934)
Toselli, Louisa (1870–1947)
Tostevin, Lola Lemire (1937—)
Toth, Beatrix
Toth, Judit (b. 1906)
Toth, Noemi (1976—)
Toth Harsanyi, Borbala (1946—)
Tothne-Kovacs, Annamaria (1945—)
Totschnig, Brigitte (1954—)
Toumanova, Tamara (1919–1996)
Toumine, Nesta (c. 1912–1995)
Touray, Josephine (1979—)
Tourel, Jennie (1899–1973)
Tourischeva, Ludmila (1952—)
Tourky, Loudy (1979—)
Tourtel, Mary (1874–1948)
Tousek, Yvonne (1980—)
Toussaint, Cheryl (1952—)
Touw, Daphne (1970—)
Tovstogan, Yevgeniya (1965—)
Tower, Joan (1938—)
Towers, Julie (1976—)
Towle, Charlotte (1896–1966)
Towle, Katherine (1898–1986)
Towne, Laura Matilda (1825–1901)
Townsend, Cathy (1937—)
Townsend, Sue (1946—)
Toxopeus, Jacqueline (1968—)
Toye, Wendy (1917—)
Toyen (1902–1980)
Traa, Kari (1974—)
Traba, Marta (1930–1983)
Tracy, Honor (1913–1989)
Tracy, Martha (1876–1942)
Tracy, Mona Innis (1892–1959)
Tracy, Paula (1939—)
Trailine, Helen (1928—)
Trandenkova-Krivosheva, Marina (1967—)
Tran Hieu Ngan (1974—)
Trasca, Marioara (1962—)
Trask, Kate Nichols (1853–1922)
Traubel, Helen (1899–1972)
Traurig, Christine (1957—)
Travell, Janet G. (1901–1997)
Travers, Linden (1913–2001)
Travers, Mary (1936—)
Travers, P.L. (1906–1996)
Travers, Susan (1909–2003)
Traversa, Lucia (1965—)
Traverse, Madlaine (1875–1964)
Treble, Lillian M. (1854–1909)
Tree, Dolly (1899–1962)

Tree, Dorothy (1906–1992)
Tree, Marietta (1917–1991)
Tree, Maud Holt (1858–1937)
Tree, Viola (1884–1938)
Treen, Mary (1907–1989)
Trefilova, Vera (1875–1943)
Trefusis, Violet (1894–1972)
Tregunno, Jane (1962—)
Treiber, Birgit (1960—)
Tremain, Rose (1943—)
Trentini, Emma (1878–1959)
Trettel, Lidia (1973—)
Trevor, Claire (1909–2000)
Trevor-Jones, Mabel (fl. 1904–1921)
Trewavas, Ethelwynn (1900–1992)
Trier Mørch, Dea (1941—)
Trigère, Pauline (1912–2002)
Trilling, Diana (1905–1996)
Trillini, Giovanna (1970—)
Trinquet, Veronique (1956—)
Trintignant, Nadine (1934—)
Triolet, Elsa (1896–1970)
Tripe, Mary Elizabeth (1870–1939)
Trisler, Joyce (1934–1979)
Trocmé, Magda (1901–1996)
Troes, Olga (1914—)
Trofimova-Gopova, Nina (1953—)
Troll-Borostyani, Irma von (1847–1912)
Tronconi, Carolina (b. 1913)
Trotman, Julia (1968—)
Trotsky, Natalia Ivanovna (1882–1962)
Trotter, Deedee (1982—)
Trotter, Mildred (1899–1991)
Trotter, Virginia Yapp (1921–1998)
Trotzig, Birgitta (1929—)
Trouhanova, Natalia (1885–1956)
Troup, Augusta Lewis (c. 1848–1920)
Trout, Jenny Kidd (1841–1921)
Troy, Doris (1937–2004)
Troy, Louise (1933–1994)
Troyanos, Tatiana (1938–1993)
Truax, Sarah (1877–1958)
Trudeau, Margaret (1948—)
Trueman, Paula (1900–1994)
Truitt, Anne (1921–2004)
Truman, Bess (1885–1982)
Truman, Margaret (1924—)
Trunnelle, Mabel (1879–1981)
Trusca, Gabriela (1957—)
Tryon, Amy (1970—)
Tsagarayeva, Larisa (1958—)
Tsahai Haile Selassie (1919–1942)
Tsang, Tasha (1970—)
Tschechowa, Olga (1897–1980)
Tschitschko, Helene (1908–1992)
Tsebrikova, M.K. (1835–1917)
Tserbe-Nessina, Valentyna (1969—)
Tsirkova, Svetlana (1945—)
Tsotadze, Liana (1961—)
Tsoulfa, Emilia (1973—)
Tsoumeleka, Athanasia (1982—)
Tsukada, Maki (1982—)
Tsukasa, Yoko (1934—)
Tsumura, Setsuko (1928—)
Tsunoda, Fusako (1914—)
Tsuper, Alla (c. 1980—)
Tsushima, Yuko (1947—)
Tsvetaeva, Marina (1892–1941)
Tsygitsa, Olena (1975—)
Tsyhuleva, Oksana
Tsylinskaya, Natallia (1975—)
Tubbs, Alice (1851–1930)
Tubman, Harriet (1821–1913)
Tuchman, Barbara (1912–1989)
Tucker, C. DeLores (1927–2005)
Tucker, Corin (1972—)
Tucker, Sophie (1884–1966)
Tucker, Tanya (1958—)
Tuckwell, Gertrude (1861–1951)
Tudoran, Ioana (1948—)
Tudor-Hart, Edith (1908–1978)
Tueni, Nadia (1935–1983)
Tueting, Sarah (1976—)
Tufan-Guzganu, Elisabeta (1964—)
Tufnell, Meriel (1948–2002)
Tufty, Esther Van Wagoner (1896–1986)
Tugurlan, Mirela (1980—)
Tula, María Teresa (1951—)
Tullis, Julie (1939–1986)
Tully, Alice (1902–1993)
Tully, Mary Jean Crenshaw (1925–2003)
Tulu, Derartu (1969—)
Tumiati, Lucia (1926—)
Tuomaite, Vitalija (1964—)
Tuqan, Fadwa (1917–2003)
Turchina, Zinaida (1946—)
Tureck, Rosalyn (1914–2003)
Turisini, Valentina (1969—)
Turlington, Christy (1969—)
Turnbull, Wendy (1952—)
Turner, Cathy (1962—)
Turner, Debbye (1966—)
Turner, Dumitrita (1964—)
Turner, Eliza Sproat (1826–1903)
Turner, Ethel (1872–1958)
Turner, Eva (1892–1990)
Turner, Florence E. (c. 1888–1946)
Turner, Kathleen (1954—)
Turner, Kim (1961—)
Turner, Lana (1921–1995)
Turner, Lesley (1942—)
Turner, Mary (d. 1918)
Turner, Sherri (1956—)
Turner, Tina (1938—)
Turner-Warwick, Margaret (1924—)
Turpie, Marion (d. 1967)
Tuschak, Katalin (1959—)
Tusquets, Esther (1936—)
Tutin, Dorothy (1930–2001)
Tuttle, Lurene (1906–1986)
Tutwiler, Julia Strudwick (1841–1916)
Tuve, Rosemond (1903–1964)
Tuyaa, Nyam-Osoryn (1958—)
Twain, Shania (1965—)
Tweedie, Jill (1936–1993)
Tweedy, Hilda (b. 1911)
Twelvetrees, Helen (1908–1958)
Twigg, Rebecca (1963—)
Twiggy (1946—)
Twining, Louisa (1820–1912)
Tyabji, Kamila (1918–2004)
Ty Casper, Linda (1931—)
Tyler, Alice S. (1859–1944)
Tyler, Anne (1941—)
Tyler, Danielle (1974—)
Tyler, Dorothy J. (1920—)
Tyler, Judy (1933–1957)
Tyler, Odette (1869–1936)
Tyler-Sharman, Lucy (1965—)
Tymoshenko, Yulia (1960—)
Tynan, Katharine (1861–1931)
Tynan, Kathleen (1937–1995)
Tyshkevich, Tamara (1931—)
Tyson, Cicely (1933—)
Tyurina, Lyubov (1943—)
Tyus, Wyomia (1945—)
Uca, Feleknas (1976—)
Uchida, Christine (1952—)
Uchida, Mitsuko (1948—)
Uchida, Yoshiko (1921–1992)
Ucok, Bahriye (d. 1990)
Udaltsova, Nadezhda (1885–1961)
Ueland, Clara Hampson (1860–1927)
Ueno, Chizuko (1948—)
Ueno, Masae (1979—)
Ueno, Yukiko (1982—)
Uga, Elisa (1968—)
Uggams, Leslie (1943—)
Uhl, Frida (1872–1943)
Uhlig, Petra (1954—)
Ukrainka, Lesya (1871–1913)
Ulanova, Galina (1910–1998)
Ulasi, Adaora Lily (1932—)
Ulion, Gretchen (1972—)
Ullman, Tracey (1959—)
Ullmann, Liv (1939—)
Ullmann, Regina (1884–1961)
Ullrich, Kay (1943—)
Ullrich, Luise (1911–1985)
Ulmann, Doris (1882–1934)
Ulmer, Sarah (1976—)
Ulric, Lenore (1892–1970)
Ulyanova, Marie (1878–1937)
Umanets, Nina (1956—)
Umeh, Stella (1975—)
Umeki, Miyoshi (1929—)
Um Kalthum (c. 1898–1975)
Under, Marie (1883–1980)
Underhill, Evelyn (1875–1941)
Underhill, Ruth Murray (1883–1984)
Underwood, Agness Wilson (1902–1984)
Underwood, Lillias (1851–1921)
Undset, Sigrid (1882–1949)
Unger, Gladys B. (c. 1885–1940)
Unger, Mary Ann (1945–1998)
Ungureanu, Corina (1980—)
Ungureanu, Teodora (1960—)
Uno, Chiyo (1897–1996)
Unsoeld, Jolene (1931—)
Up, Ari (1962—)
Uphoff, Nicole (1967—)
Upton, Harriet Taylor (1853–1945)
Upton, Mary (1946—)
Urbaniak, Dorota (1972—)
Urbanova, Marta (1960—)
Urbanovich, Galina (1917—)
Ure, Mary (1933–1975)
Urecal, Minerva (1894–1966)
Uribe, Cenaida (1964—)
Urrutia, Maria Isabel (1965—)
Urselmann, Wiltrud (1942—)
Urso, Camilla (1842–1902)
Ursuleac, Viorica (1894–1985)
Ushakova, Irina (1954—)
Usova, Maia (1964—)
Ustinova, Natalya (1944—)
Ustrowski, Betina (1976—)
Ustvolskaya, Galina (1919—)
Ustyuzhanina, Tatyana (1965—)
Utley, Freda (1898–1977)
Utondu, Beatrice (1969—)
Utsugi, Reika (1963—)
Uttley, Alison (1884–1976)
Uvarov, Olga (1910–2001)
Uwilingiyimana, Agathe (1953–1994)
Uzès, Anne, Duchesse d' (1847–1933)
Vaa, Aslaug (1889–1965)
Vaandrager, Wiljon (1957—)
Vaccaro, Brenda (1939—)
Vaccaroni, Dorina (1963—)
Vachell, Eleanor (1879–1948)
Vachetta, Roseline (1951—)
Vadaszne-Vanya, Maria (1950—)
Vadkerti-Gavorníková, Lydia (1932–1999)
Vaganova, Agrippina (1879–1951)
Vague, Vera (1906–1974)
Vail, Myrtle (1888–1978)
Vakalo, Eleni (1921—)
Valadon, Suzanne (1865–1938)
Välbe, Elena (1968—)
Valdes, Carmen (1954—)
Valenciano Martínez-Orozco, María Elena (1960—)
Valentí, Helena (1940—)
Valentina (1899–1989)
Valentine, Grace (1884–1964)
Valentine, Lila (1865–1921)
Valentine, Winifred Annie (1886–1968)
Valenzuela, Luisa (1938—)
Valerie, Joan (1911–1983)
Valeyeva, Natalya (1969—)
Valla, Trebisonda (1916—)
Valle, Inger-Louise (1921—)
Valle Silva, Luisa del (1896–1962)
Vallette, Marguerite (1860–1953)
Valli, Alida (1921–2006)
Valli, Valli (1882–1927)
Valli, Virginia (1895–1968)
Vallier, Hélène (1932–1988)
Vallin, Ninon (1886–1961)
Valova, Elena (1963—)
Van Almsick, Franziska (1978—)
van Baalen, Coby (1957—)
Van Blarcom, Carolyn (1879–1960)
Van Brempt, Kathleen (1969—)
Vanbrugh, Irene (1872–1949)
Vanbrugh, Prudence (1902—)
Vanbrugh, Violet (1867–1942)
Van Buren, Adeline (1894–1949)

Van Buren, Augusta
Van Buren, Hannah Hoes (1783–1819)
Van Buren, Mabel (1878–1947)
VanCaspel, Venita (1922—)
Vance, Danitra (1954–1994)
Vance, Nina (1914–1980)
Vance, Norma (1927–1956)
Vance, Vivian (1909–1979)
Van Chu-Lin (1893/94?–1946)
Van Cleve, Edith (1894–1985)
Van Cott, Margaret (1830–1914)
Vancurova, Vera (1932—)
Vandamm, Florence (1883–1966)
Vandecaveye, Gella (1973—)
van de Kieft, Fleur (1973—)
Van Deman, Esther (1862–1937)
Van Deman, Irene (1889–1961)
van den Boogaard, Dillianne (1974—)
van den Burg, Ieke (1952—)
Vandenhende, Severine (1974—)
Vanderbeck, Florence (1884–1935)
van der Ben, Helena (1964—)
Vanderbilt, Alice Gwynne (1845–1934)
Vanderbilt, Amy (1908–1974)
Vanderbilt, Consuelo (1877–1964)
Vanderbilt, Gertrude (1880–1960)
Vanderbilt, Gladys Moore (1886–1965)
Vanderbilt, Gloria (1924—)
Van Derbur, Marilyn (c. 1937—)
Vanderburg, Helen (1959—)
van der Goes, Frederica
van der Kade-Koudijs, Gerda (1923—)
Van der Kamp, Anna (1972—)
van Der Kolk, Kirsten (1975—)
Van der Mark, Christine (1917–1969)
van der Plaats, Adriana (1971—)
Vanderpool, Sylvia (1936—)
van der Vaart, Macha (1972—)
van der Vegt, Anna (1903–1983)
van der Wielen, Suzan (1971—)
van der Wildt, Paulina (1944—)
van Deurs, Brigitte (1946—)
Van de Vate, Nancy (1930—)
Van Dishoeck, Pieta (1972—)
van Doorn, Marieke (1960—)
Van Doren, Irita (1891–1966)
Van Doren, Mamie (1931—)
Van Dover, Cindy (1954—)
van Drogenbroek, Marieke (1964—)
Van Duyn, Mona (1921–2004)
Van Dyke, Vonda Kay (c. 1944—)
Van Dyken, Amy (1973—)
Vane, Daphne (1918–1966)
Vane-Tempest-Stewart, Edith (1878–1949)
Vane-Tempest-Stewart, Theresa (1856–1919)
van Ettekoven, Harriet (1961—)
van Eupen, Marit (1969—)
Van Fleet, Jo (1919–1996)
van Geenhuizen, Miek (1981—)
Vangelovska, Stojna (1965—)
Van Gennip, Yvonne (1964—)
Van Gordon, Cyrena (1896–1964)
Van Grippenberg, Alexandra (1859–1913)
van Grunsven, Anky (1968—)
Vangsaae, Mona (1920–1983)
Van Hamel, Martine (1945—)
van Heyningen, Ruth (1917—)
Van Hoosen, Bertha (1863–1952)
Van Houten, Leslie (1949—)
van Kessel, Lieve (1977—)
Van Kleeck, Mary Abby (1883–1972)
Van Lancker, Anne E.M. (1954—)
van Langen, Ellen (1966—)
van Manen, Aletta (1958—)
van Moorsel, Leontien (1970—)
Vann, Jesse Matthews (c. 1890–1967)
Van Nes, Eeke (1969—)
Vano, Donna (c. 1955—)
van Praagh, Peggy (1910–1990)
Van Randwijk, Petronella (1905–1978)
Van Rensselaer, Mariana (1851–1934)
Van Rensselaer, Martha (1864–1932)
van Rijn, Wilma (1971—)
van Rooijen, Manon (1982—)
van Roost, Dominique (1973—)
van Rumpt, Annemarieke (1980—)
van Rumt, Hendrika (b. 1897)
Van Runkle, Theadora (1940—)
Vansova, Terezia (1857–1942)
van Staveren, Petra (1966—)
van Stockum, Hilda (b. 1908)
Van Studdiford, Grace (1873–1927)
Van Upp, Virginia (1902–1970)
van Velsen, Wilma (1964—)
van Vliet, Petronella (1926—)
van Voorn, Koosje (1935—)
Van Vorst, Marie Louise (1867–1936)
Van Waters, Miriam (1887–1974)
van Weerdenburg, Wilhelmina (1946—)
Van Wie, Virginia (1909–1997)
Van Zandt, Marie (1858–1919)
Vanzetta, Bice (1961—)
Varady, Julia (1941—)
Varcoe, Helen (b. 1907)
Varda, Agnes (1928—)
Varden, Evelyn (1893–1958)
Varden, Norma (1898–1989)
Vare, Glenna Collett (1903–1989)
Varganova, Svetlana (1964—)
Vargas, Chavela (1919—)
Vargas, Virginia (1945—)
Várnay, Astrid (1918—)
Varo, Remedios (1906–1963)
Varsi, Diane (1937–1992)
Vartio, Marja-Liisa (1924–1966)
Vasarhelyi Weckinger, Edit (1923—)
Vasco, María (1975—)
Vasconcellos, Karoline Michaëlis de (1851–1925)
Vaseva, Lilyana (1955—)
Vasey, Jessie (1897–1966)
Vasilchenko, Olga (1956—)
Vasilevskaia, Elena (1978—)
Vasilieva, Yulia (1978—)
Vasilkova, Elvira (1962—)
Vassar, Queenie (1870–1960)
Vassilieva, Ekaterina (1976—)
Vassioukova, Olga (1980—)
Vatachka, Vjara (1980—)
Vaucher, Yvette (1929—)
Vaughan, Gladys (d. 1987)
Vaughan, Hilda (1892–1985)
Vaughan, Janet (1899–1993)
Vaughan, Kate (c. 1852–1903)
Vaughan, Sarah (1924–1990)
Vaughn, Hilda (1898–1957)
Vaught, Wilma L. (1930—)
Vaussard, Christiane (1923—)
Vautier, Catherine (1902–1989)
Vautrin, Minnie (1886–1941)
Vaytsekhovskaya, Yelena (1958—)
Vaz de Carvalho, Maria Amália (1847–1921)
Vaz Dias, Selma (1911–1977)
Vazem, Ekaterina (1848–1937)
Vaz Ferreira, María Eugenia (1875–1924)
Veazie, Carol (1895–1984)
Vecheslova, Tatiana (1910–1991)
Vecsei, Eva (1930—)
Védrès, Nicole (1911–1965)
Veenstra, Myrna (1975—)
Vega, Ana Lydia (1946—)
Vega, Suzanne (1959—)
Veil, Simone (1927—)
Vejjabul, Pierra (b. 1909)
Velarde, Pablita (1918—)
Velãsquez, Lucila (1928—)
Velazquez, Consuelo (1916–2005)
Veldhuis, Marleen (1979—)
Velez, Lisa (1967—)
Velez, Lupe (1908–1944)
Velho da Costa, Maria (1938—)
Velichkovskaia, Tamara Antonovna (1908–1990)
Velinova, Iskra (1953—)
Venable, Evelyn (1913–1993)
Venciené, Vida
Venema, Anneke (1971—)
Vengerova, Isabelle (1877–1956)
Vengerova, Zinaida (1867–1941)
Ventós i Cullell, Palmira (1862–1917)
Ventre, Fran (1941—)
Venttsel, Elena Sergeevna (1907–2002)
Venturella, Michelle (1973—)
Venturini, Fernanda (1970—)
Venturini, Tisha (1973—)
Venuta, Benay (1911–1995)
Vera Constantinovna (1854–1912)
Vera-Ellen (1920–1981)
Veranes, Sibelis (1974—)
Verbeek, Tonya (1977—)
Verbitskaia, Anastasiia (1861–1928)
Vercesi, Ines (1916–1997)
Verchinina, Nina (1910–1995)
Verdecia, Legna (1972—)
Verdon, Gwen (1925–2000)
Verdugo, Elena (1926—)
Verdy, Violette (1931—)
Vered, Ilana (1939—)
Veres-Ioja, Viorica (1962—)
Verey, Rosemary (1918–2001)
Vergelyuk, Maryna (1978—)
Vermirovska, Zdena (1913—)
Verne, Kaaren (1918–1967)
Verne, Mathilde (1865–1936)
Verney, Margaret Maria (1844–1930)
Vernizzi, Laura (1985—)
Vernon, Anne (1924—)
Vernon, Barbara (1916–1978)
Vernon, Mabel (1883–1975)
Vérone, Maria (1874–1938)
Verrett, Shirley (1931—)
Versois, Odile (1930–1980)
Verstappen, Annemarie (1965—)
Vertua Gentile, Anna (1850–1927)
Vesaas, Halldis Moren (1907–1995)
Veselitskaia, Lidiia Ivanovna (1857–1936)
Veselkova-Kil'shtet, M.G. (1861–1931)
Vessel, Anne Marie (1949—)
Vestergaard, Mette (1975—)
Vestly, Anne-Cath (1920—)
Vestoff, Floria (1920–1963)
Vetrovska, Marie (1912–1987)
Veysberg, Yuliya (1878–1942)
Vezin, Jane Elizabeth (1827–1902)
Vezzali, Valentina (1974—)
Via Dufresne, Begona (1971—)
Via Dufresne, Natalia (1973—)
Viardot, Louise (1841–1918)
Viardot, Pauline (1821–1910)
Vicent, Tania (1976—)
Vickers, Janeene (1968—)
Vickers, Martha (1925–1971)
Vickery, Joyce (1908–1979)
Vicol, Maria (1935—)
Victor, Lucia (1912–1986)
Victor, Wilma (1919–1987)
Victoria (1819–1901)
Victoria (1866–1929)
Victoria (1868–1935)
Victoria (1977—)
Victoria Adelaide of Schleswig-Holstein (1885–1970)
Victoria Louise (1892–1980)
Victoria Melita of Saxe-Coburg (1876–1936)
Victoria of Baden (1862–1930)
Victoria of Hesse-Darmstadt (1863–1950)
Victoria of Mecklenburg-Strelitz (1878–1948)
Vidal, Doriane (1976—)
Vidal, Ginette (b. 1931)
Vidali, Lynn (1952—)
Vidar, Jorunn (1918—)
Vidor, Florence (1895–1977)
Viebig, Clara (1860–1952)
Viehoff, Valerie (1976—)
Vieira, Maruja (1922—)
Vieira da Silva, Maria Elena (1908–1992)
Vierdag, Maria (b. 1905)
Viertel, Salka (1889–1978)
Viganò, Renata (1900–1976)
Vik, Bjørg (1935—)
Vike-Freiberga, Vaira (1937—)
Vilagos, Penny (1963—)
Vilagos, Vicky (1963—)
Vilariño, Idea (1920—)
Vilinska, Mariya (1834–1907)
Villa, Brenda (1980—)
Villameur, Lise (1905–2004)
Villard, Fanny Garrison (1844–1928)
Villarino, María de (1905–1994)
Villiers, Margaret Elizabeth Child- (1849–1945)
Villiers, Theresa (1968—)

Villinger, Hermine (1849–1917)
Vilmorin, Louise de (1902–1969)
Vince, Marion Lloyd (1906–1969)
Vincent, Madge (b. 1884)
Vincent, Marjorie (c. 1965—)
Vincent, Ruth (1877–1955)
Vinge, Joan D. (1948—)
Vining, Elizabeth Gray (1902–1999)
Vinson, Helen (1907–1999)
Viola, Emilia Ferretti (1844–1929)
Vionnet, Madeleine (1876–1975)
Viscopoleanu, Viorica (1939—)
Vise, Hollie (1987—)
Vishnevskaya, Galina (1926—)
Viski, Erzsebet (1980—)
Visnjic, Biserka (1953—)
Visser, Adriana (1961—)
Vitorino, Virginia (1897–1967)
Vitrichenko, Elena (1976—)
Vittadini, Rita (1914–2000)
Vitti, Monica (1931—)
Vivanti, Annie (1868–1942)
Vivian, Ruth (c. 1883–1949)
Vivien, Renée (1877–1909)
Vlachos, Helen (1911–1995)
Vlady, Marina (1938—)
Vlasova, Yulia
Vlasto, Didi (1903–1985)
Vlasto, Dominique (1946—)
Vlieghuis, Kirsten (1976—)
Vodopyanova, Natalia (1981—)
Voelker, Sabine (1973—)
Voelkner, Iris (1960—)
Vogel, Dorothy (1935—)
Vogel, Renate (1955—)
Vögtlin, Marie (1845–1916)
Voigt, Angela (1951—)
Voigt, Franka (1963—)
Voigt-Diederichs, Helene (1875–1961)
Voinea, Camelia (1970—)
Voit, Eszter (1916—)
Vojinovic, Zorica (1958—)
Vokes, May (d. 1957)
Volchek, Natalya
Volchetskaya, Yelena (1943—)
Volk, Helen (1954—)
Völker, Sandra (1974—)
Volkova, Vera (1904–1975)
Volkova, Yelena (1960—)
Vollertsen, Julie (1959—)
Vollmar, Jocelyn (1925—)
Vollmer, Dana (1987—)
Vollmer, Lula (d. 1955)
Volpi, Giulia (1970—)
von Aroldingen, Karin (1941—)
Von Bremen, Wilhelmina (1909–1976)
von Busing, Fritzi (c. 1884–1948)
von Furstenberg, Diane (1946—)
von Harbou, Thea (1888–1954)
von Haynau, Edith (1884–1978)
von Moltke, Freya (b. 1911)
von Nagel, Ida (1917–1971)
Von Nagy, Käthe (1909–1973)
Vonnoh, Bessie Potter (1872–1955)
von Richthofen, Else (1874–1973)
Von Rosen, Elsa Marianne (1924—)
von Rosen, Maud (1925—)
von Saltza, Chris (1944—)
Von Seck-Nothnagel, Anke (1966—)
Von Stade, Frederica (1945—)
Von Trapp, Maria (1905–1987)
Von Trotta, Margarethe (1942—)
von Weiler, Sophie (1958—)
von Wiegand, Charmion (1896–1993)
Voorbij, Aartje (1940—)
Vorlova, Slavka (1894–1973)
Voronina, Zinaida (1947—)
Voros, Zsuzsanna (1977—)
Vorse, Mary Heaton (1874–1966)
Voskes, Elles (1964—)
Voskuijl, Bep (d. 1983)
Voss, Christina (1952—)
Voutilainen, Katrina (1975—)
Voynich, Ethel (1864–1960)
Voznesenskaya, Julia (1940—)
Vrba, Elisabeth (1942—)
Vreeland, Diana (1903–1989)
Vronsky, Vitya (1909–1992)
Vrugt, Johanna Petronella (1905–1960)
Vucanovich, Barbara F. (1921—)
Vukojicic, Paola (1974—)
Vuyk, Beb (1905–1991)
Vymazalova, Lenka (1959—)
Vyroubova, Nina (1921—)
Vyuzhanina, Galina (1952—)
Waara, Jennie (1975—)
Waard, Elly de (1940—)
Wachtel, Christine (1965—)
Wachter, Anita (1967—)
Waciuma, Charity (1936—)
Waddell, Helen (1889–1965)
Waddingham, Dorothea (1899–1936)
Waddington, Miriam (1917–2004)
Waddles, Charleszetta (1912–2001)
Waddy, Charis (1909–2004)
Waddy, Harriet (1904–1999)
Wade, Margaret (1912–1995)
Wade, Virginia (1945—)
Wademant, Annette (1928—)
Wagner, Allison (1977—)
Wagner, Aly (1980—)
Wagner, Barbara (1938—)
Wagner, Catherina (1919—)
Wagner, Cosima (1837–1930)
Wägner, Elin (1882–1949)
Wagner, Friedelind (1918–1991)
Wagner, Katrin (1977—)
Wagner, Sandra (1969—)
Wagner, Winifred (1897–1980)
Wagner-Stange, Ute (1966—)
Wagstaff, Elizabeth (1974—)
Wainwright, Helen (1906—)
Waitaoro (c. 1848–1929)
Waite, Catherine (1829–1913)
Waitz, Grete (1953—)
Wajs, Jadwiga (1912–1990)
Wakeling, Gwen (1901–1982)
Wakoski, Diane (1937—)
Walcamp, Marie (1894–1936)
Walcott, Mary Morris (1860–1940)
Wald, Florence (1917—)
Wald, Lillian D. (1867–1940)
Wald, Patricia McGowan (1928—)
Waldo, Carolyn (1964—)
Waldo, Ruth Fanshaw (1885–1975)
Waldorf, Wilella (c. 1900–1946)
Walentynowicz, Anna (1929—)
Wales, Ethel (1878–1952)
Waleska, Peggy (1980—)
Walford, Lucy (1845–1915)
Walker, Ada Overton (1870–1914)
Walker, A'Lelia (1885–1931)
Walker, Alice (1944—)
Walker, Barbara Jo (1926–2000)
Walker, Betty (1928–1982)
Walker, Charlotte (1876–1958)
Walker, Colleen (1956—)
Walker, Edyth (1867–1950)
Walker, Ethel (1861–1951)
Walker, Helen (1920–1968)
Walker, June (1900–1966)
Walker, Kath (1920–1993)
Walker, Laura (1970—)
Walker, Lillian (1887–1975)
Walker, Lucy (1836–1916)
Walker, Madame C.J. (1867–1919)
Walker, Maggie Lena (1867–1934)
Walker, Margaret (1915–1998)
Walker, Mary Broadfoot (c. 1888–1974)
Walker, Mary Edwards (1832–1919)
Walker, Michelle (1952—)
Walker, Nancy (1922–1992)
Walker, Nella (1880–1971)
Walker, Olene S. (1930—)
Walker, Polly (b. 1908)
Walkowiak, Daniela (1935—)
Wall, Geraldine (1912–1970)
Wall, Lyndsay (1985—)
Wallace, Bronwen (1945–1989)
Wallace, Jean (1923–1990)
Wallace, Lila Acheson (1889–1984)
Wallace, Lucille (1898–1977)
Wallace, Mary (1959—)
Wallace, Nellie (1870–1948)
Wallace, Regina (1886–1978)
Wallace, Sippie (1898–1986)
Wallace, Zerelda G. (1817–1901)
Wallach, Yonah (1944–1985)
Wallenda, Helen (1910–1996)
Waller, Florence (1862–1912)
Waller, Judith Cary (1889–1973)
Walley, Joan (1949—)
Wallis, Diana (1954—)
Wallis, Mary Ann Lake (1821–1910)
Wallis, Ruth Sawtell (1895–1978)
Wallis, Shani (1933—)
Walliser, Maria (1963—)
Wallmann, Margarethe (1901–1922)
Wallwork, Elizabeth (1883–1969)
Waln, Nora (1895–1964)
Walsh, Kay (1914–2005)
Walsh, Kerri (1978—)
Walsh, Loretta (1898–c. 1988)
Walsh, María Elena (1930—)
Walsh, Mary (1929–1976)
Walsh, Stella (1911–1980)
Walter, Annika (1975—)
Walter, Louisa (1978—)
Walter, Martina (1963—)
Walter, Silja (1919—)
Walter-Martin, Steffi (1962—)
Walters, Barbara (1929—)
Walters, Bernice R. (1912–1975)
Walters, Catherine (1839–1920)
Walters, Julie (1950—)
Walters, Lisa (1960—)
Walton, Angie (1966—)
Walton, Dorothy (1908—)
Walton, Florence (1891–1981)
Walworth, Ellen Hardin (1832–1915)
Wambach, Abby (1980—)
Wambaugh, Sarah (1882–1955)
Wami, Gete (1974—)
Wander, Maxie (1933–1977)
Wandor, Michelene (1940—)
Wang, Vera (1949—)
Wang Chengyi (1983—)
Wang Chunlu (1978—)
Wang Fang (1967—)
Wang Guangmei (1922—)
Wang Hee-Kyung (1970—)
Wang Hong (1965—)
Wang Huifeng (1968—)
Wang Jun (1963—)
Wang Junxia (1973—)
Wang Lihong (1970—)
Wang Lina (1978—)
Wang Linwei (1956—)
Wang Liping (1973—)
Wang Liping (1976—)
Wang Mingxing (1961—)
Wang Nan (1978—)
Wang Xianbo
Wang Xiaohong (1968—)
Wang Xiaozhu (1973—)
Wang Xu (1985—)
Wang Yajun (1962—)
Wang Yan (1971—)
Wang Yi (1973—)
Wang Ying
Wang Ziling (1972—)
Warburg, Agnes (1872–1953)
Ward, Barbara (1914–1981)
Ward, Catharine Barnes (1851–1913)
Ward, Claire (1972—)
Ward, Clara Mae (1924–1973)
Ward, Dorothy (1890–1987)
Ward, Elizabeth Stuart Phelps (1844–1911)
Ward, Fannie (1865–1952)
Ward, Geneviève (1838–1922)
Ward, Henrietta (1832–1924)
Ward, Hortense (1872–1944)
Ward, Ida Caroline (1880–1949)
Ward, Irene (1895–1980)
Ward, Maisie (1889–1975)
Ward, Mrs. Humphry (1851–1920)
Ward, Natalie (1975—)
Ward, Polly (1908–1987)

Ward, Winifred Louise (1884–1975)
Wardhani, Kusuma (1964—)
Warfield, Irene (c. 1896–1961)
Waring, Anna Letitia (1823–1910)
Waring, Laura Wheeler (1887–1948)
Waring, Margaret (1887–1968)
Waring, Marilyn (1952—)
Warington, Katherine (1897–1993)
Warmond, Ellen (1930—)
Warmus, Carolyn (1964—)
Warner, Anna Bartlett (1827–1915)
Warner, Anne (1954—)
Warner, Anne Marie (1945—)
Warner, Bonny (1962—)
Warner, Deborah (1959—)
Warner, Estella Ford (1891–1974)
Warner, Gloria (c. 1914–1934)
Warner, Marina (1946—)
Warner, Sylvia Townsend (1893–1978)
Warnes, Jennifer (1947—)
Warnicke, Heike (1966—)
Warnock, Mary (1924—)
Warren, Althea (1886–1958)
Warren, Elinor Remick (1900–1991)
Warren, Lavinia (1841–1919)
Warrick, Ruth (1915–2005)
Wartenberg, Christiane (1956—)
Warwick, Dionne (1940—)
Warwick, Lyn (1946—)
Waser, Maria (1878–1939)
Wash, Martha
Washam, Jo Ann (1950—)
Washbourne, Mona (1903–1988)
Washburn, Margaret Floy (1871–1939)
Washburn, Mary (1907–1994)
Washington, Bennetta (1918–1991)
Washington, Dinah (1924–1963)
Washington, Fredi (1903–1994)
Washington, Josephine (1861–1949)
Washington, Margaret Murray (c. 1861–1925)
Washington, Ora (1899–1971)
Washington, Sarah Spencer (1889–?)
Wasilewska, Wanda (1905–1964)
Wasserstein, Wendy (1950–2006)
Watanabe, Yoko (1953–2004)
Waters, Alice (1944—)
Waters, Ethel (1896–1977)
Waters, Maxine (1938—)
Watkins, Gladys Elinor (1884–1939)
Watkins, Linda (1908–1976)
Watkins, Margaret (1884–1969)
Watkins, Tionne (1970—)
Watkins, Yoko Kawashima (1933—)
Watkinson, Angela (1941—)
Watley, Jody (1959—)
Watley, Natasha (1981—)
Watson, Ada (1859–1921)
Watson, Debbie (1965—)
Watson, Edith (1861–1943)
Watson, Janet Vida (1923–1985)
Watson, Jean (1933—)
Watson, Jill (1963—)
Watson, Linda (1955—)
Watson, Lucile (1879–1962)
Watson, Lynette (1952—)
Watson, Maud (b. 1864)
Watson, Pokey (1950—)
Watson, Rosamund (1860–1911)
Watson, Sheila (1909–1998)
Watt, Kathryn (1964—)
Wattleton, Faye (1943—)
Watts, Heather (1953—)
Watts, Helen (1927—)
Watts Russell, Elizabeth Rose Rebecca (1833/34–1905)
Wauneka, Annie Dodge (1910–1997)
Way, Amanda M. (1828–1914)
Wayburn, Peggy (1917–2002)
Wayne, Carol (1942–1985)
Wayte, Mary (1965—)
Weatherspoon, Teresa (1965—)
Weaver, Harriet Shaw (1876–1961)
Weaver, Marjorie (1913–1994)
Weaver, Sigourney (1949—)
Webb, Beatrice (1858–1943)
Webb, Catherine (1859–1947)
Webb, Electra Havemeyer (1888–1960)
Webb, Elida (1895–1975)
Webb, Karrie (1974—)
Webb, Laura (1941–2001)
Webb, Mary (1881–1927)
Webb, Phyllis (1927—)
Webb, Sarah (1977—)
Webb, Sharon (1936—)
Webb, Violet (1915—)
Weber, Christiane (1962—)
Weber, Helene (1881–1962)
Weber, Jeanne (1875–1910)
Weber, Jutta (1954—)
Weber, Lois (1881–1939)
Weber, Regina (1963—)
Weber-Koszto, Monika (1966—)
Webster, Jean (1876–1916)
Webster, Margaret (1905–1972)
Webster, Mary McCallum (1906–1985)
Webster, Mary Morison (1894–1980)
Weddington, Sarah R. (1945—)
Wedemeyer, Maria von (c. 1924–1977)
Wedgwood, C.V. (1910–1997)
Wedgwood, Camilla H. (1901–1955)
Weed, Ethel (1906–1975)
Weekes, Liz (1971—)
Weeks, Ada May (1898–1978)
Weeks, Dorothy (1893–1990)
Weeks, Marion (1886–1968)
Weeks-Shaw, Clara S. (1857–1940)
Wegman, Froukje (1979—)
Wegner, Gudrun (1955—)
Wehr-Hásler, Sábine (1967—)
Wehselau, Mariechen (1906–1992)
Weidenbach, Lisa Larsen (c. 1962—)
Weidler, Virginia (1926–1968)
Weiermann-Lietz, Andrea (1958—)
Weigang, Birte (1968—)
Weigel, Helene (1900–1971)
Weigl, Vally (1889–1982)
Wei Haiying
Wei Junyi (1917–2002)
Weil, Simone (1909–1943)
Weiler, Barbara (1946—)
Weinberg, Wendy (1958—)
Weinbrecht, Donna (1965—)
Weingarten, Violet (1915–1976)
Wei Ning (1982—)
Weinstein, Hannah (1911–1984)
Weinzweig, Helen (1915—)
Wei Qiang
Weir, Amanda (1986—)
Weir, Irene (1862–1944)
Weir, Judith (1954—)
Weir, Molly (1910–2004)
Weis, Jessica McCullough (1901–1963)
Weisberger, Barbara (c. 1926—)
Weishoff, Paula (1962—)
Weiss, Alta (1889–1964)
Weiss, Bianca (1968—)
Weiss, Gisela (1943—)
Weiss, Janet (1965—)
Weiss, Liz
Weiss, Louise (1893–1983)
Weiss, Mary
Weissensteiner, Gerda (1969—)
Weissman, Dora (1881–1974)
Weizmann, Vera (1881–1966)
Welch, Ann (1917–2002)
Welch, Barbara (c. 1904–1986)
Welch, Elisabeth (1904–2003)
Welch, Priscilla (1944—)
Welch, Raquel (1940—)
Weld, Tuesday (1943—)
Weldon, Fay (1931—)
Welitsch, Ljuba (1913–1996)
Welles, Gwen (1951–1993)
Wellesley, Dorothy (1889–1956)
Wellman, Emily Ann (d. 1946)
Wells, Ada (1863–1933)
Wells, Alice (1927–1987)
Wells, Alice Stebbins (1873–1957)
Wells, Carolyn (1862–1942)
Wells, Catherine (d. 1927)
Wells, Charlotte Fowler (1814–1901)
Wells, Doreen (1937—)
Wells, Emmeline B. (1828–1921)
Wells, Fay Gillis (1908–2002)
Wells, Kate Gannett (1838–1911)
Wells, Kitty (b. 1919)
Wells, Marguerite Milton (1872–1959)
Wells, Mary (1943–1992)
Wells, Mary Ann (c. 1895–1971)
Wells, Melissa Foelsch (1932—)
Wells-Barnett, Ida (1862–1931)
Welsh, Jane (1905–2001)
Welsh, Lilian (1858–1938)
Welter, Ariadna (1930–1998)
Weltfish, Gene (1902–1980)
Welty, Eudora (1909–2001)
Wendell, Krissy (1981—)
Wendl, Ingrid (1940—)
Wendt, Julia Bracken (1871–1942)
Wenger, Lisa (1858–1941)
Wen Jieruo (1927—)
Wen Lirong (1969—)
Wentscher, Dora (1883–1964)
Wentworth, Cecile de (c. 1853–1933)
Wen Xiaoyu (1938—)
Wenzel, Hanni (1951—)
Wenzel, Kirsten (1961—)
Wenzel-Perillo, Brigitta (1949—)
Werbezirk, Gisela (1875–1956)
Werbrouck, Ulla (1972—)
Were, Miriam (1940—)
Werlein, Elizebeth Thomas (1883–1946)
Werner, Ilse (1918—)
Werner, Marianne (1924—)
Werremeier, Stefani (1968—)
Werth, Isabell (1969—)
Wertmüller, Lina (1928—)
Wesley, Cynthia (d. 1963)
Wesley, Mary (1912–2002)
Wessel, Helene (1898–1969)
Wessel-Kirchels, Ute (1953—)
Wessely, Paula (1907–2000)
West, Claire (1893–1980)
West, Dorothy (1907–1998)
West, Dottie (1932–1991)
West, Elizabeth (1927–1962)
West, Jessamyn (1902–1984)
West, Mae (1893–1980)
West, Rebecca (1892–1983)
West, Rosemary (1953—)
West, Sandy (1960—)
West, Vera (1900–1947)
West, Winifred (1881–1971)
Westcott, Helen (1928–1998)
Westendorf, Anke (1954—)
Westerhof, Marieke (1974—)
Westermann, Liesel (1944—)
Westley, Helen (1875–1942)
Westman, Nydia (1902–1970)
Weston, Agnes (1840–1918)
Weston, Cecil (1889–1976)
Weston, Jessie Edith (1867–1944)
Weston, Jessie Laidlay (1850–1928)
Weston, Ruth (1906–1955)
Westover, Winifred (1899–1978)
Westphal, Heidi (1959—)
Westwood, Vivienne (1941—)
Wetherald, Ethelwyn (1857–1940)
Wethered, Joyce (1901–1997)
Wetherill, Louisa Wade (1877–1945)
Wetmore, Joan (1911–1989)
Wetzko, Gabriele (1954—)
Wexler, Nancy (1945—)
Weygand, Hannelore (1924—)
Weymouth, Tina (1950—)
Whalen, Sara (1976—)
Wharton, Anne Hollingsworth (1845–1928)
Wharton, Edith (1862–1937)
Wheatcroft, Georgina (1965—)
Wheaton, Anne (1892–1977)
Wheeldon, Alice (fl. 1917)
Wheeler, Anna Pell (1883–1966)
Wheeler, Candace (1827–1923)
Wheeler, Lucile (1935—)
Wheeler, Ruth (1877–1948)
Wheelock, Lucy (1857–1946)
Whelan, Arleen (1916–1993)
Whelan, Cyprienne Gabel (d. 1985)

Whiffin, Blanche (1845–1936)
Whipple, Mary (1980—)
Whitaker, Mabel (1884–1976)
Whitbread, Fatima (1961—)
White, Alice (1904–1983)
White, Alma Bridwell (1862–1946)
White, Amy (1968—)
White, Anna (1831–1910)
White, Anna Lois (1903–1984)
White, Antonia (1899–1980)
White, Carol (1942–1991)
White, Chrissie (1894–1989)
White, Donna (1954—)
White, Eartha M. (1876–1974)
White, Edna Noble (1879–1954)
White, Eliza Orne (1856–1947)
White, Ellen Gould (1827–1915)
White, Emily Louisa Merielina (1839–1936)
White, Frances (1896–1969)
White, Helen C. (1896–1967)
White, Helen Magill (1853–1944)
White, Isabella (1894–1972)
White, Karyn (1965—)
White, Katharine S. (1892–1977)
White, Margaret (c. 1888–1977)
White, Marilyn Elaine (1944—)
White, Maude Valerie (1855–1937)
White, Morgan (1983—)
White, Oona (1922–2005)
White, Pearl (1889–1938)
White, Ruth (1914–1969)
White, Sandra (1951—)
White, Sue Shelton (1887–1943)
White, Willye B. (1939—)
Whitefield, Karen (1970—)
Whitehouse, Davina (1912–2002)
Whitelaw, Billie (1932—)
Whitestone, Heather (c. 1973—)
Whitfield, Beverly (1954–1996)
Whiting, Lilian (1847–1942)
Whiting, Margaret (1924—)
Whiting, Sarah F. (1847–1927)
Whitlam, Margaret (1919—)
Whitman, Christine Todd (1946—)
Whitmire, Kathy (1946—)
Whitney, Adeline Dutton (1824–1906)
Whitney, Anne (1821–1915)
Whitney, Betsey Cushing Roosevelt (1908–1998)
Whitney, Charlotte Anita (1867–1955)
Whitney, Dorothy Payne (1887–1968)
Whitney, Eleanore (1917—)
Whitney, Flora Payne (1897–1986)
Whitney, Gertrude Vanderbilt (1875–1942)
Whitney, Helen Hay (1876–1944)
Whitney, Mary Watson (1847–1921)
Whitney, Phyllis A. (b. 1903)
Whitney, Ruth (1928–1999)
Whittier, Polly (1877–1946)
Whittle, Jenny (1973—)
Whitton, Charlotte (1896–1975)
Whitty, May (1865–1948)
Whitworth, Kathy (1939—)
Whyte, Edna Gardner (1902–1992)
Whyte, Kathleen (1909–1996)
Whyte, Sandra (1970—)
Wiberg, Pernilla (1970—)
Wichfeld-Muus, Varinka (1922–2002)
Wichman, Sharon (1952—)
Wickenheiser, Hayley (1978—)
Wickes, Mary (1916–1995)
Wickham, Anna (1883–1947)
Wickwire, Nancy (1925–1974)
Widdecombe, Ann (1947—)
Widdemer, Margaret (1884–1978)
Widdowson, Elsie (1906–2000)
Wideman, Lydia (1920—)
Widnall, Sheila (1938—)
Wiechowna, Wanda (1946—)
Wieck, Dorothea (1908–1986)
Wied, Martina (1882–1957)
Wiegmann, Bettina (1971—)
Wieland, Joyce (1931–1998)
Wielema, Geertje (1934—)
Wieniawska, Irene Regine (1880–1932)
Wiesenthal, Grete (1885–1970)
Wiesman, Linden (1975—)
Wifstrand, Naima (1890–1968)
Wiggin, Kate Douglas (1856–1923)
Wiggins, Myra Albert (1869–1956)
Wightman, Hazel Hotchkiss (1886–1974)
Wigman, Mary (1886–1973)
Wijenaike, Punyakanthi (1935—)
Wijnberg, Rosalie (1887–1973)
Wijsmuller-Meijer, Truus (c. 1896–1978)
Wilber, Doreen (1930—)
Wilberforce, Octavia (1888–1963)
Wilcox, Ella Wheeler (1850–1919)
Wilcox, Elsie Hart (1879–1954)
Wilcox, Lisa (1966—)
Wild, Anke (1967—)
Wild, Eleonora (1969—)
Wild, Ute (1965—)
Wilde, Fran (1948—)
Wilden, Rita (1947—)
Wilder, Laura Ingalls (1867–1957)
Wilding, Cora (1888–1982)
Wilding, Dorothy (1893–1976)
Wiley, Lee (1915–1975)
Wiley, Mildred (1901–2000)
Wilhelm, Anja (1968—)
Wilhelm, Kate (1928—)
Wilhelm, Kati (1976—)
Wilhelmina (1880–1962)
Wilke, Marina (1958—)
Wilker, Gertrud (1924–1984)
Wilkes, Debbi (c. 1947—)
Wilkins, Brooke (1974—)
Wilkinson, Anne (1910–1961)
Wilkinson, Ellen (1891–1947)
Wilkinson, Iris (1906–1939)
Wilkinson, Laura (1977—)
Wilkinson, Marguerite Ogden (1883–1928)
Willard, Mary (1941—)
Willcox, Sheila (1936—)
Willebrandt, Mabel Walker (1889–1963)
Willeford, Mary B. (1900–1941)
Williams, Anna Maria (1839–1929)
Williams, Anna Wessels (1863–1954)
Williams, Betty (1943—)
Williams, Betty (1944—)
Williams, Camilla (1922—)
Williams, Cara (1925—)
Williams, Christa (1978—)
Williams, Cicely (1893–1992)
Williams, Clara (1888–1928)
Williams, Deniece (1951—)
Williams, Eileen Hope (1884–1958)
Williams, Elizabeth Sprague (1869–1922)
Williams, Esther (1923—)
Williams, Ethel (1863–1948)
Williams, Fannie Barrier (1855–1944)
Williams, Frances (1903–1959)
Williams, Grace (1906–1977)
Williams, Hattie (1872–1942)
Williams, Hope (1897–1990)
Williams, Ivy (1877–1966)
Williams, Jody (1950—)
Williams, Kathlyn (1888–1960)
Williams, Lauryn (1983—)
Williams, Lavinia (1916–1989)
Williams, Lucinda (1937—)
Williams, Lucinda (1953—)
Williams, Lynn (1960—)
Williams, Marion (1927–1994)
Williams, Mary Lou (1910–1981)
Williams, Mary Wilhelmine (1878–1944)
Williams, Matilda Alice (1875–1973)
Williams, Michelle (1980—)
Williams, Natalie (1970—)
Williams, Novlene (1982—)
Williams, Serena (1981—)
Williams, Sherley Anne (1944–1999)
Williams, Shirley (1930—)
Williams, Tonique (1976—)
Williams, Vanessa (1963—)
Williams, Venus (1980—)
Williams, Victoria (1958—)
Williams, Wendy Lian (1967—)
Williams, Wendy O. (1951–1998)
Williams, Yvette (1929—)
Williamson, Alison (1971—)
Williamson, Audrey (1926—)
Williamson, Jessie Marguerite (c. 1855–1937)
Williamson, Sarah Eileen (1974—)
Willing, Jennie Fowler (1834–1916)
Willis, Connie (1945—)
Willis, Frances (1899–1983)
Willits, Mary (1855–1902)
Willmott, Ellen (c. 1859–1934)
Willoughby, Frances L. (c. 1906–1984)
Wills, Helen Newington (1905–1998)
Willson, Rini Zarova (d. 1966)
Willumsen, Dorrit (1940—)
Wilman, Maria (1867–1957)
Wilson, Anne Glenny (1848–1930)
Wilson, Augusta Evans (1835–1909)
Wilson, Bertha (1923—)
Wilson, Cairine (1885–1962)
Wilson, Carnie (1968—)
Wilson, Charlotte (1854–1944)
Wilson, Deborah (1955—)
Wilson, Edith (1896–1981)
Wilson, Edith Bolling (1872–1961)
Wilson, Ellen Axson (1860–1914)
Wilson, Enid (b. 1910)
Wilson, Ethel (1888–1980)
Wilson, Ethel (d. 1980)
Wilson, Fanny (1874–1958)
Wilson, Fiammetta Worthington (1864–1920)
Wilson, Heather (1960—)
Wilson, Helen Mary (1869–1957)
Wilson, Jean (1910–1933)
Wilson, Kini (1872–1962)
Wilson, Lois (1894–1988)
Wilson, Margaret Bush (1919—)
Wilson, Margaret W. (1882–1973)
Wilson, Margery (1896–1986)
Wilson, Marie (1916–1972)
Wilson, Marilyn (1943—)
Wilson, Mary (1916—)
Wilson, Mary (1944—)
Wilson, Monica Hunter (1908–1982)
Wilson, Nancy (1937—)
Wilson, Naomi (1940—)
Wilson, Peggy (1934—)
Wilson, Romer (1891–1930)
Wilson, Ruth (1919–2001)
Wilson, Sallie (1932—)
Wilson, Staci (1976—)
Wilson, Stacy (1965—)
Wilson, Tracy
Wilson, Wendy (1969—)
Wiman, Anna Deere (1924–1963)
Wimbersky, Petra (1982—)
Winant, Ethel (1922–2003)
Winch, Hope (1895–1944)
Winch, Joan
Winckless, Sarah (1973—)
Windeyer, Mary (1836–1912)
Windsor, Claire (1897–1972)
Windsor, Marie (1919–2000)
Windsor, Wallis Warfield, duchess of (1895–1986)
Wine-Banks, Jill (1943—)
Winfrey, Oprah (1954—)
Wing, Toby (1915–2001)
Winger, Debra (1955—)
Wingo, Effiegene Locke (1883–1962)
Winkel, Kornelia (1944—)
Winn, Anona (1907–1994)
Winser, Beatrice (1869–1947)
Winsloe, Christa (1888–1944)
Winslow, Ola Elizabeth (c. 1885–1977)
Winsor, Kathleen (1919–2003)
Winter, Alice Ames (1865–1944)
Winter, Ethel (1924—)
Winter, Joanne (1924—)
Winter, John Strange (1856–1911)
Winter, Liane (1942—)
Winterbach, Ingrid (1948—)
Winters, Marian (1924–1978)
Winters, Shelley (1920–2006)
Winterton, Ann (1941—)
Winterton, Rosie (1958—)
Winton, Jane (1905–1959)
Wintour, Anna (1949—)
Winwood, Estelle (1883–1984)
Wiratthaworn, Aree (1980—)
Wise, Brownie (1913–1992)

Wise, Louise Waterman (1874–1947)
Wiseman, Hilda Alexandra (1894–1982)
Wiskemann, Elizabeth Meta (1899–1971)
Wister, Sarah Butler (1835–1908)
Withee, Mabel (d. 1952)
Witherington, Pearl (1914—)
Withers, Googie (1917—)
Withers, Jane (1926—)
Witherspoon, Cora (1890–1957)
Withington, Alfreda (1860–1951)
Witt, Henriette de (1829–1908)
Witt, Katarina (1965—)
Wittig, Monique (1935–2003)
Wittpenn, Caroline Stevens Alexander (1859–1932)
Witty, Chris (1975—)
Witziers-Timmer, Jeanette (1923–2005)
Wöckel-Eckert, Bärbel (1955—)
Wodars, Sigrun (1965—)
Woerishoffer, Carola (1885–1911)
Woetzel, Mandy (1973—)
Wohmann, Gabriele (1932—)
Woizikowska, Sonia (1919—)
Wolcott, Marion Post (1910–1990)
Wolf, Christa (1929—)
Wolf, Hazel (1898–2000)
Wolf, Kate (1942–1986)
Wolf, Sigrid (1964—)
Wolfenstein, Martha (1869–1905)
Wolff, Helen (1906–1994)
Wolff, Ingrid (1964—)
Wolff, Victoria (1903–1992)
Wolfson, Theresa (1897–1972)
Wollschlaeger, Susanne (1967—)
Wollstein, Martha (1868–1939)
Wolstenholme-Elmy, Elizabeth (1834–1913)
Wolters, Kara (1975—)
Wong, Anna May (1907–1961)
Wong, Betty Ann (1938—)
Wong, Jade Snow (1919–2006)
Wong-Staal, Flossie (1946—)
Won Hye-Kyung
Wood, Anna (1966—)
Wood, Audrey (1905–1985)
Wood, Audrey (1908–1998)
Wood, Beatrice (1893–1998)
Wood, Carolyn (1945—)
Wood, Daisey (1877–?)
Wood, Edith Elmer (1871–1945)
Wood, Evelyn (1909–1995)
Wood, Florence (c. 1854–1954)
Wood, Marjorie (1882–1955)
Wood, Mary Elizabeth (1861–1931)
Wood, Matilda (1831–1915)
Wood, Natalie (1938–1981)
Wood, Peggy (1892–1978)
Wood, Thelma (1901–1970)
Wood, Yvonne (b. 1914)
Woodard, Lynette (1959—)
Woodbridge, Louise Deshong (1848–1925)
Woodbridge, Margaret (1902—)
Woodbury, Clare (c. 1880–1949)
Woodbury, Helen Sumner (1876–1933)
Woodbury, Joan (1915–1989)
Woodgate, Margaret (1935—)
Woodham-Smith, Cecil (1896–1977)
Woodhead, Cynthia (1964—)
Woodhouse, Danielle
Woodhouse, Margaret Chase Going (1890–1984)
Woodhull, Victoria (1838–1927)
Woodley, Erin (1972—)
Woodrow, Nancy Mann Waddel (c. 1866–1935)
Woods, Doris
Woods, Katharine Pearson (1853–1923)
Woods, Taryn (1975—)
Woodsmall, Ruth F. (1883–1963)
Woodstra, Susan (1957—)
Woodward, Danielle (1965—)
Woodward, Ellen Sullivan (1887–1971)
Woodward, Joanne (1930—)
Woo Hyun-Jung
Woolf, Virginia (1882–1941)
Woolley, Helen (1874–1947)
Woolley, Mary E. (1863–1947)
Woolliams, Anne (1926–1999)
Woolman, Mary Schenck (1860–1940)
Woolsey, Georgeanna Muirson (1833–1906)
Woolsey, Lynn C. (1937—)
Woolsey, Sarah Chauncey (1835–1905)
Woolson, Abba Goold (1838–1921)
Woo Sun-Hee (1978—)
Wootten, Bayard (1875–1959)
Wootton, Barbara (1897–1988)
Wordsworth, Elizabeth (1840–1932)
Worhel, Esther (1975—)
Workman, Fanny (1859–1925)
Wormeley, Katharine Prescott (1830–1908)
Wormington, H. Marie (1914–1994)
Worsley, Katherine (1933—)
Worth, Irene (1916–2002)
Worthington, Kay (1959—)
Wray, Fay (1907–2004)
Wrede, Mathilda (1864–1928)
Wright, Belinda (1927—)
Wright, Betty (1953—)
Wright, Camille (1955—)
Wright, Cobina (1887–1970)
Wright, Cobina Jr. (1921—)
Wright, Dana (1959—)
Wright, Haidée (1868–1943)
Wright, Helen (1914–1997)
Wright, Helena (1887–1982)
Wright, Jane Cooke (1919—)
Wright, Judith (1915–2000)
Wright, L.R. (1939–2001)
Wright, Mabel Osgood (1859–1934)
Wright, Maginel (1881–1966)
Wright, Mary Clabaugh (1917–1970)
Wright, Mickey (1935—)
Wright, Muriel Hazel (1889–1975)
Wright, Patricia (1945—)
Wright, Rebecca (1942—)
Wright, Sarah Elizabeth (1928—)
Wright, Sophie Bell (1866–1912)
Wright, Syreeta (1946–2004)
Wright, Teresa (1918–2005)
Wrightson, Patricia (1921—)
Wrinch, Dorothy (1894–1976)
Wrobel, Agata (1981—)
Wu, Chien-Shiung (1912–1997)
Wu Dan (1968—)
Wu Hui Ju (1982—)
Wujak, Brigitte (1955—)
Wu Jiani (1966—)
Wu Lanying (d. 1929)
Wulz, Wanda (1903–1984)
Wu Minxia (1985—)
Wunderlich, Claudia (1956—)
Wunderlich, Frieda (1884–1965)
Wunderlich, Magdalena (1952—)
Wunderlich, Pia (1975—)
Wunderlich, Tina (1977—)
Wuolijoki, Hella (1886–1954)
Wuornos, Aileen (1956–2002)
Wurdemann, Audrey Mary (1911–1960)
Wu Wenying (1932—)
Wu Xiaoxuan (1958—)
Wu Xingjiang (1957—)
Wu Yi (1938—)
Wu Yongmei (1975—)
Wyatt, Jane (1911—)
Wyatt, Rachel (1929—)
Wyborn, Kerry (1977—)
Wycherly, Margaret (1881–1956)
Wyeth, Henriette (1907–1997)
Wyland, Wendy (1964–2003)
Wylie, Elinor (1885–1928)
Wylie, Ida A.R. (1885–1959)
Wylie, Wilhelmina (1892–1984)
Wyllie, Kate (d. 1913)
Wyludda, Ilke (1969—)
Wyman, Jane (1914—)
Wymore, Patrice (1926—)
Wyndham, Mary (1861–1931)
Wynekoop, Alice (1870–1952)
Wynette, Tammy (1942–1998)
Wynter, Dana (1927—)
Wynter, Sylvia (1928—)
Wynyard, Diana (1906–1964)
Wyse Power, Jennie (1858–1941)
Wysoczanska, Barbara (1949—)
Xenia Alexandrovna (1876–1960)
Xian Dongmei (1975—)
Xiang Jingyu (1895–1928)
Xiao Hong (1911–1942)
Xiaojiao Sun (1984—)
Xie Huilin (1975—)
Xie Wanying (1900–1999)
Xie Xide (1921–2000)
Xing Huina (1984—)
Xirinacs, Olga (1936—)
Xiu Lijuan (1957—)
Xue Shen (1978—)
Xu Jian
Xu Nannan (1979—)
Xu Yanmei (1971—)
Xu Yanwei (1984—)
Yaa Akyaa (c. 1837–c. 1921)
Yaa Asantewaa (c. 1850–1921)
Yabe, Sayaka
Yakko, Sada (d. 1946)
Yakovleva, Olga (1963—)
Yakunchikova, Maria (1870–1901)
Yale, Caroline A. (1848–1933)
Yalow, Rosalyn (1921—)
Yamada, Eri (1984—)
Yamada, Isuzu (1917—)
Yamada, Mitsuye (1923—)
Yamada, Miyo (c. 1976—)
Yamada, Waka (1879–1956)
Yamaguchi, Kristi (1971—)
Yamaji, Noriko (1970—)
Yamamoto, Hiromi (1970—)
Yamamoto, Michiko (1936—)
Yamamoto, Noriko (1945—)
Yamauchi, Wakako (1924—)
Yamazaki, Tomoko (1931—)
Yamazaki, Toyoko (1924—)
Yamazaki, Yaeko (1950—)
Yampolsky, Mariana (1925–2002)
Yanaranop, Sukanya (1931—)
Yáñez, María Flora (1898–1982)
Yan Fang
Yang Bo (1973—)
Yang Hao (1980—)
Yang Jiang (b. 1911)
Yang Shaoqi
Yang Wei (1979—)
Yang Wenyi (1972—)
Yang Xia (1977—)
Yang Xiao (1964—)
Yang Xiaojun (1963—)
Yang Xilan (1961—)
Yang Yang (1976—)
Yang Yang (1977—)
Yang Ying (1977—)
Yang Young-Ja (1964—)
Yang Yu (1985—)
Yang Yun (c. 1984—)
Yanjmaa, Sühbaataryn (1893–1962)
Yano, Hiromi (1955—)
Yanovych, Iryna (1976—)
Yao Fen (1967—)
Yarborough, Sara (1950—)
Yarbro, Chelsea Quinn (1942—)
Yard, Molly (1912–2005)
Yarde, Margaret (1878–1944)
Yarros, Rachelle (1869–1946)
Yasui, Kono (1880–1971)
Yatchenko, Irina (1965—)
Yates, Elizabeth (c. 1844–1918)
Yates, Frances Amelia (1899–1981)
Yates, Ngawini (1852/53?–1910)
Yatsenko, Olena (1977—)
Yavorska, Lydia (1869–1921)
Yaw, Ellen Beach (1868–1947)
Yazova, Yana (1912–1974)
Yeager, Jeana (1952—)
Yearwood, Trisha (1964—)
Yeats, Elizabeth (1868–1940)
Yeats, Lily (1866–1949)
Yegorova, Irina (1940—)
Yegorova, Lyudmila (1931—)
Yegorova, Valentina (1964—)
Ye Jiayin (1924—)
Yelesina, Yelena (1970—)
Yembakhtova, Tatyana (1956—)
Yener, Aslihan (1946—)
Yeo Kab-Soon (1974—)

Yeomans, Amelia (1842–1913)
Ye Qiaobo (1964—)
Yermolayeva, Galina (1948—)
Yeroshina, Radya
Yessayan, Zabel (1878–1943)
Yevkova, Olga (1965—)
Yevonde (1893–1975)
Ye Wenling (1942—)
Ye Zhaoying (1974—)
Yezierska, Anzia (c. 1881–1970)
Yin Jian (1978—)
Ylla (1911–1955)
Yohé, May (1869–1938)
Yoko (c. 1849–1906)
Yokosawa, Yuki (1980—)
Yokoyama, Juri (1955—)
Yolanda Margherita of Italy (1901–1986)
Yoneda, Yuko (1979—)
Yonge, Charlotte Mary (1823–1901)
Yoon Byung-Soon (1963—)
Yoon Hye-Young
Yoon Soo-Kyung (1964—)
Yoon Young-Sook (1971—)
Yordanova, Reni (1953—)
Yordanova, Todorka (1956—)
Yordanova, Zdravka (1950—)
Yorgova, Diana (1942—)
Yorgova, Diana Vassilleva (1971—)
York, Susannah (1941—)
Yorkin, Nicole (1958—)
Yorkin, Peg (1927—)
Yosano, Akiko (1878–1942)
Yoshida, Mariko (1954—)
Yoshida, Saori (1982—)
Yoshida, Setsuko (1942—)
Yoshioka, Yayoi (1871–1959)
You Jae-Sook
Young, Anne Sewell (1871–1961)
Young, Clara Kimball (1890–1960)
Young, Dannette (1964—)
Young, E.H. (1880–1949)
Young, Ella (1867–1951)
Young, Ella Flagg (1845–1918)
Young, Grace Chisholm (1868–1944)
Young, Janet (1926–2002)
Young, Loretta (1913–2000)
Young, Marguerite (1908–1995)
Young, Mary Marsden (1880–1971)
Young, Mary Sophie (1872–1919)
Young, Rida Johnson (1869–1926)
Young, Rose Maud (1865–1947)
Young, Sheila (1950—)
Young, Wanda (1944—)
Younger, Maud (1870–1936)
Younghusband, Adela Mary (1878–1969)
Younghusband, Eileen Louise (1902–1981)
Youngs, Elaine (1970—)
Yourcenar, Marguerite (1903–1987)
Youshkevitch, Nina (c. 1921–1998)
Youskevitch, Maria (c. 1946—)
Yow, Kay (1942—)
Yuan, Tina (c. 1950—)
Yuan Hua (1974—)
Yuan Jing (b. 1914)
Yuan Shu Chi (1984—)
Yuasa, Toshiko (1909–1980)
Yudina, Maria (1899–1970)
Yu Hongqi
Yu Jung-Hye (1954—)
Yu Kyung-Hwa (1953—)
Yu Lihua (1932—)
Yu Manzhen (fl. 1900)
Yun Mi-Jin (1983—)
Yun Young-Nae (1952—)
Yurchenko, Natalia (1965—)
Yurchenya, Marina (1959—)
Yuric, Dragica (1963—)
Yuriko (b. 1920)
Yurina, Esfir (1923—)
Yurka, Blanche (1887–1974)
Yurkina, Olga (1976—)
Yusova, Zoya (1948—)
Yusuf, Fatima (1971—)
Yu Sun-Bok (1970—)
Yva (1900–1942)
Zabar, Lillian (1905–1995)
Zabelina, Aleksandra (1937—)
Zabell, Theresa (1965—)
Zabelle, Flora (1880–1968)
Zabirova, Zulfia (1973—)
Zabolotnaia, Natalia (1985—)
Zaboluyeva, Svetlana (1966—)
Zabriskie, Louise (1887–1957)
Zachrisson, Vendela (1978—)
Zachry, Caroline B. (1894–1945)
Zaczkiewicz, Claudia (1962—)
Zagoni-Predescu, Marlena (1951—)
Zagorka, Maria Jurić (1873–1957)
Zagunis, Mariel (1985—)
Zaharias, Babe Didrikson (1911–1956)
Zahourek, Berta (1896–1967)
Zakarias, Maria (1952—)
Zakharova, Galina (1947—)
Zakharova, Nadezhda (1945—)
Zakharova, Olga (1973—)
Zakharova, Stella (1963—)
Zakharova, Svetlana (1970—)
Zakharova, Tatyana (1951—)
Zakrzewska, Marie (1829–1902)
Zalaffi, Margherita (1966—)
Zalaine-Koevi, Maria (1923—)
Zaleska, Katherine (1919—)
Zamba, Frieda (1965—)
Zambelli, Carlotta (1875–1968)
Zambrano, María (1904–1991)
Zamolodchikova, Elena (1982—)
Zamora, Daisy (1950—)
Zamudio, Adela (1854–1928)
Zanchi, Manuela (1977—)
Zanfretta, Francesca (1862–1952)
Zange-Schönbrunn, Gabi (1961—)
Zani, Giselda (1909–1975)
Zanotto, Kendra (1981—)
Zapata Olivella, Delia (1926–2001)
Zapolska, Gabriela (1857–1921)
Zardoya, Concha (1914–2004)
Zaripova, Amina (1976—)
Zasipkina, Maria (1985—)
Zaslavskaya, Tatyana (1924—)
Zaspa, Larysa (1971—)
Zasulich, Vera (1849–1919)
Zasulskaya, Natalya (1969—)
Zatopek, Dana (1922—)
Zaturenska, Marya Alexandrovna (1902–1982)
Zauditu (1876–1930)
Zayak, Elaine (1965—)
Zayyat, Latifa al- (1923—)
Zazdravnykh, Valentina (1954—)
Zeghers, Margriet (1954—)
Zehrt, Monika (1952—)
Zei, Alki (1925—)
Zeidler, Judith (1968—)
Zeisel, Eva (b. 1906)
Zeisler, Fannie Bloomfield (1863–1927)
Zelepukina, Svetlana (1980—)
Zelikovich Dumcheva, Antonina (1958—)
Zelinová, Hana (b. 1914)
Zelle, Margaretha (1876–1917)
Zeller, Eva (1923—)
Zellner, Martina (1974—)
Zemina, Kathryn (1968—)
Zeng Xiaoying (1929—)
Zenz, Therese (1932—)
Zetkin, Clara (1857–1933)
Zetterling, Mai (1925–1994)
Zetterlund, Monica (1937–2005)
Zetterlund, Yoko (1969—)
Zguriška, Zuska (1900–1984)
Zhang Chunfang
Zhang Di (1968—)
Zhang Hui (1959—)
Zhang Jie (1937—)
Zhang Jiewen (1981—)
Zhang Juanjuan (1981—)
Zhang Meihong (1963—)
Zhang Na (1980—)
Zhang Nan (1986—)
Zhang Ning (1975—)
Zhang Ouying (1975—)
Zhang Peijun (1958—)
Zhang Ping (1982—)
Zhang Rongfang (1957—)
Zhang Ruifang (1918—)
Zhang Shan (1968—)
Zhang Xianghua (1968—)
Zhang Xiaodong (1964—)
Zhang Xiuyun (1976—)
Zhang Yali (1964—)
Zhang Yanmei
Zhang Yining (1981—)
Zhang Yuehong (1975—)
Zhang Yueqin (1960—)
Zhan Shuping (1964—)
Zhao Kun (1973—)
Zhao Lihong (1972—)
Zhao Luorui (b. 1912)
Zhao Ruirui (1981—)
Zhao Yufen (1948—)
Zheng Dongmei (1967—)
Zheng Haixia (1967—)
Zheng Meizhu (1962—)
Zheng Min (1920—)
Zhirko, Yelena (1968—)
Zhirova, Marina (1963—)
Zhivanevskaya, Nina (1977—)
Zhivkova, Lyudmila (1942–1981)
Zhong Honglian
Zhou Jihong (1965—)
Zhou Mi (1979—)
Zhou Ping (1968—)
Zhou Qiurui (1967—)
Zhou Shouying (1969—)
Zhou Suhong (1979—)
Zhou Xiaolan (1957—)
Zhou Xiuhua (1966—)
Zhuang Xiaoyan (1969—)
Zhuang Yong (1972—)
Zhu Juefeng (1964—)
Zhuk, Tatiana
Zhulina, Valentina (1953—)
Zhu Ling (1957—)
Zhupina, Olena (1973—)
Zhupiyeva, Yelena (1960—)
Zhurova, Svetlana (1972—)
Zhu Yingwen (1981—)
Zhu Yunying (1978—)
Zia, Khaleda (1946—)
Zide, Rochelle (1938—)
Ziegelmeyer, Nikki (c. 1975—)
Ziegler, Anne (1910–2003)
Ziganshina, Natalia (1985—)
Zilber, Irina (c. 1980—)
Ziliute, Diana (1976—)
Zilporite, Laima (1967—)
Zimbalist, Mary Louise Curtis (1876–1970)
Zimetbaum, Mala (1920–1944)
Zimmerman, Mary Beth (1960—)
Zimmerman, Suzanne (1925—)
Zimmermann, Agnes (1847–1925)
Zimmermann, Edith
Zimmermann, Gerda (1927—)
Zimmermann, Heidi (1946—)
Zimmermann, Kathrin (1966—)
Zimmermann-Weber, Annemarie (1940—)
Zindler, Petra (1966—)
Zinkeisen, Doris (1898–1991)
Zinn, Elfi (1953—)
Zinner, Hedda (1902–1990)
Zinóveva-Annibal, Lidiia Dmitrievna (1866–1907)
Zintkala Nuni (c. 1890–c. 1919)
Zipprodt, Patricia (1925–1999)
Zirimu, Elvania Namukwaya (1938–1979)
Zirzow, Carola (1954—)
Zissener, Sabine (1970—)
Zita of Parma (1892–1989)
Ziyada, Mayy (1886–1941)
Zlatin, Sabina (1907–1996)
Zmeskal, Kim (1976—)
Znak, Marina (1961—)
Zobelt, Roswietha (1954—)
Zober, Hannelore (1946—)
Zoch, Jacqueline (1949—)
Zoff, Marianne (1893–1984)
Zographou, Lili
Zolner, Urska (1982—)
Zolotow, Charlotte (b. 1915)
Zong Pu (1928—)
Zorach, Marguerite Thompson (1887–1968)

Zorba, Myrsini (1949—)
Zorina, Vera (1917–2003)
Zorlutuna, Halidé Nusret (1901–1984)
Zozula, Vera
Zrihen, Olga (1953—)
Zsak, Marcela (1956—)
Zscherpe, Iris (1967—)
Zsembery, Tamasne (1967—)
Zubareva, Olga (1958—)
Zubko, Yelena (1953—)
Zuccari, Anna Radius (1846–1918)
Zucchi, Virginia (1849–1930)
Zuchold, Erika (1947—)
Zurek, Natasza (1978—)
Zur Mühlen, Hermynia (1883–1951)
Zürn, Unica (1916–1970)
Zvereva, Ellina (1960—)
Zvereva, Natasha (1971—)
Zwehl, Julia (1976—)
Zwi, Rose (1928—)
Zwicky, Fay (1933—)
Zwiers, Claudia
Zwilich, Ellen Taaffe (1939—)
Zwink, Tara (1973—)
Zybina, Galina (1931—)
Zykina, Olesya (1980—)
Zyuskova, Nina (1952—)

GEOGRAPHIC INDEX

AFGHANISTAN

Central Asian republic
Part of Persian Empire (c. 500 BCE)
Conquered by Alexander the Great (4th c. BCE)
Part of Seleucid Empire (323 BCE)
Ruled by Kushan Empire (2nd–3rd c. CE)
Ruled by Sassanid, Mongol, and Turkish Empires (4th–5th c.)
Ruled by Persian Empire (6th c.)
Islam introduced (7th c.)
Islamic Era (10th–12th c.)
Invaded by Genghis Khan (13th c.)
Ruled by Tammerlane (14th–15th c.)
Ruled by Moghul dynasty (16th c.)
Southern Afghanistan ruled by Persia (18th c.)
Mujahideen established (1978)
U.S.S.R. invasion (1979)
Ruled by Taliban (1992–2001)

Gauhar Shad (c. 1378–1459)
Homaira (1916–2002)
Meena (1956–1987)
Ratebzad, Anahita (1931—)

AFRICAN-AMERICAN

Abbott, Diahnne (1945—)
Adams, Carolyn (1943—)
Adams, Charity (1917–2002)
Alba, Nanina (1915–1968)
Albert, Octavia V.R. (1853–c. 1899)
Alexander, Sadie (1898–1989)
Allen, Debbie (1950—)
Anderson, Caroline Still (1848–1919)
Anderson, Chantelle (1981—)
Anderson, Evelyn (1907–1994)
Anderson, Ivie (1904–1949)
Anderson, Katherine (1944—)
Anderson, Marian (1897–1993)
Anderson, Regina M. (1900–1993)
Angelou, Maya (1928—)
Armstead, Izora (1942–2004)
Armstrong, Lil Hardin (1898–1971)
Arroyo, Martina (1935—)
Bailes, Margaret Johnson (1951—)
Bailey, Pearl (1918–1990)
Baker, Josephine (1906–1975)
Baker, LaVern (1929–1997)
Baldwin, Maria Louise (1856–1922)
Ballard, Florence (1943–1976)
Bambara, Toni Cade (1939–1995)
Barrett, Janie Porter (1865–1948)
Bass, Charlotta Spears (1880–1969)
Bassett, Angela (1958—)
Bates, Daisy Lee (1914–1999)
Batson, Flora (1864–1906)
Batten, Kim (1969—)
Battle, Kathleen (1948—)
Bearden, Bessye (1888–1943)
Beavers, Louise (1902–1962)
Bennett, Gwendolyn B. (1902–1981)
Bentley, Gladys (1907–1960)
Berry, Halle (1966—)
Bethune, Mary McLeod (1875–1955)
Birdsong, Cindy (1939—)
Bogan, Lucille (1897–1948)
Bolden, Jeanette (1960—)
Bolton, Ruthie (1967—)
Bolton-Holifield, Ruthie (1967—)
Bonds, Margaret (1913–1972)
Bonds, Rosie (1944—)
Bonner, Marita (1899–1971)
Boswell, Cathy (1962—)
Bowles, Eva del Vakia (1875–1943)
Braun, Carol Mosely (1947—)
Brice, Carol (1918–1985)
Bridges, Ruby (c. 1954—)
Brisco-Hooks, Valerie (1960—)
Brooks, Gwendolyn (1917–2000)
Brown, Alice Regina (1960—)
Brown, Charlotte Hawkins (c. 1883–1961)
Brown, Cindy (1965—)
Brown, Dorothy L. (1919–2004)
Brown, Elaine (1943—)
Brown, Hallie Quinn (c. 1845–1949)
Brown, Karen (1955—)
Brown, Linda (1943—)
Brown, Minnijean (1942—)
Brown, Ruth (1928—)
Bryant, Hazel (1939–1983)
Bryant, Rosalyn (1956—)
Bullett, Vicky (1967—)
Bumbry, Grace (1937—)
Burke, Georgia (1880–1986)
Burke, Selma Hortense (1900–1995)
Burke, Yvonne Brathwaite (1932—)
Burroughs, Margaret Taylor (1917—)
Burroughs, Nannie Helen (c. 1878–1961)
Burton, Annie L. (fl. 19th c.)
Butler, Octavia E. (1947—)
Butler, Selena Sloan (1872–1964)
Callen, Maude (1899–1990)
Capers, Virginia (1925–2004)
Carpenter, Thelma (1922–1997)
Carroll, Diahann (1935—)
Carroll, Vinnette (1922–2002)
Carson, Julia (1938—)
Carter, Eunice Hunton (1899–1970)
Carter, Nell (1948–2003)
Cash, Rosalind (1938–1995)
Cash, Swin (1979—)
Catchings, Tamika (1979—)
Catlett, Elizabeth (b. 1915)
Chapman, Tracy (1964—)
Charles, Suzette (1963—)
Chase-Riboud, Barbara (1936—)
Cheeseborough, Chandra (1959—)
Chesimard, Joanne (1948—)
Childress, Alice (1916–1994)
Chinn, May Edward (1896–1980)
Chisholm, Shirley (1924–2005)
Clark, Septima Poinsette (1898–1987)
Clayton, Eva M. (1934—)
Cleaves, Jessica (1948—)
Clifton, Lucille (1936—)
Coachman, Alice (1923—)
Coates, Dorothy Love (1928–2002)
Cobb, Jewell Plummer (1924—)
Colander-Richardson, LaTasha (1976—)
Cole, Johnnetta B. (1936—)
Cole, Natalie (1950—)
Cole, Rebecca J. (1846–1922)
Coleman, Bessie (1892–1926)
Coley, Doris (1941–2000)
Collins, Addie Mae (d. 1963)
Collins, Barbara-Rose (1939—)
Collins, Janet (1917–2003)
Collins, Kathleen (1942–1988)
Collins, Marva (1936—)
Cooper, J. California (1940s—)
Coppin, Fanny Jackson (1837–1913)
Cortez, Jayne (1936—)
Cosby, Camille (1945—)
Cotten, Elizabeth (c. 1893–1987)
Cowart, Juanita (1944—)
Craft, Ellen (1826–c. 1891)
Crumpler, Rebecca Lee (1831–1895)
Dandridge, Dorothy (1923–1965)
Daniels, Isabelle Frances (1937—)
Danner, Margaret (1910–1984)
Dash, Julie (1952—)
Davis, Angela (1944—)
Davis, Clarissa (1967—)
Davis, Frances Elliott (1882–1965)
Davis, Hilda (1905–2001)
Davis, Mary
Dawes, Dominique (1976—)
Dean, Dora (c. 1872–1950)
Dean, Jennie (1852–1913)
Dee, Ruby (1923—)
DeFrantz, Anita (1952—)
Delany, Annie Elizabeth (1891–1995)
Delany, Sarah Louise (1889–1999)
Delarverié, Stormé (1922—)
Delille, Henriette (1813–1862)
Derricotte, Juliette (1897–1931)
Dickens, Helen Octavia (1909–2001)
Diggs, Irene (1906—)
Dixon, Diane (1964—)
Dobbins, Georgia (1944–1980)
Donaldson, Norma (1928–1994)
Douglass, Anna Murray (1813–1882)
Douglass, Sarah Mapps (1806–1882)
Dove, Rita (1952—)
Dunbar-Nelson, Alice (1875–1935)
Dunham, Katherine (1909–2006)
Dunlap, Ericka (1982—)
Durham, Dianne (1968—)
Echols, Sheila Ann (1964—)
Eckford, Elizabeth (1942—)
Edwards, Gloria (1944–1988)
Edwards, Teresa (1964—)
Edwards, Torri (1977—)
Elders, Joycelyn (1933—)
Ellis, Evelyn (1894–1958)
Evans, Mari (1923—)
Evans, Matilda Arabella (1872–1935)
Evans, Minnie (1892–1987)
Evers-Williams, Myrlie (1933—)
Faggs, Mae (1932—)
Fauset, Crystal Bird (1893–1965)
Ferdinand, Marie (1978—)
Fergerson, Mable (1955—)
Ferrell, Barbara (1947—)
Fields, Evelyn J.

Fields, Julia (1938—)
Fields, Mary (c. 1832–1914)
Fitzgerald, Benita (1961—)
Fitzgerald, Ella (1917–1996)
Flack, Roberta (1937—)
Flowers, Vonetta (1973—)
Ford, Penny (1964—)
Forten, Margaretta (1808–1875)
Foster, Frances (1924–1997)
Foster, Gloria (1933–2001)
Franklin, Aretha (1942—)
Franklin, Erma (1938–2002)
Franklin, Martha Minerva (1870–1968)
Franklin, Shirley (1945—)
Gaines, Chryste (1970—)
Gaines, Irene McCoy (1892–1964)
Garrison, Zina (1963—)
Garvey, Amy Jacques (1896–1973)
Gaynor, Gloria (1949—)
George, Zelma Watson (1904–1994)
Gibson, Althea (1927—)
Gibson, Althea (1927–2003)
Gilbert, Mercedes (1894–1952)
Gillom, Jennifer (1964—)
Goldberg, Whoopi (1949—)
Goodman, Shirley (1936–2005)
Goodson, Sadie (c. 1900—)
Graham, Shirley (1896–1977)
Gray, Macy (1970—)
Green, Vera Mae (1928–1982)
Greenfield, Elizabeth Taylor (c. 1819–1876)
Grier, Pam (1949—)
Grimké, Angelina Weld (1880–1958)
Grimké, Charlotte L. Forten (1837–1914)
Hackley, E. Azalia Smith (1867–1922)
Hale, Mamie O. (1911–c. 1968)
Hall, Adelaide (1904–1993)
Hall, Juanita (1901–1968)
Hamer, Fannie Lou (1917–1977)
Hamilton, Virginia (1936–2002)
Hampton, Mabel (1902–1989)
Hansberry, Lorraine (1930–1965)
Hardy, Catherine (1930—)
Harris, Addie (1940–1982)
Harris, Barbara (1930—)
Harris, Barbara (1945—)
Harris, Edna Mae (1910–1997)
Harris, Lusia Mae (1955—)
Harris, Patricia Roberts (1924–1985)
Harrison, Hazel (1883–1969)
Harvey, Georgette (c. 1882–1952)
Hayman, Lillian (1922–1994)
Haynes, Elizabeth Ross (1883–1953)
Hegamin, Lucille (1894–1970)
Hemings, Sally (1773–1835)
Hemsley, Estelle (1887–1968)
Hendryx, Nona (1945—)
Hennagan, Monique (1976—)
Hill, Lauryn (1975—)
Hinderas, Natalie (1927–1987)
Holdsclaw, Chamique (1977—)
Holiday, Billie (c. 1915–1959)
Holliday, Jennifer (1960—)
Hopkins, Pauline E. (1859–1930)
Horne, Lena (1917—)
Horton, Gladys (1944—)
Houston, Cissy (1933—)
Houston, Thelma (1946—)
Houston, Whitney (1963—)
Howard, Denean (1964—)
Howard, Sherri (1962—)
Hudson, Martha (1939—)
Hudson, Winson (1916–2004)
Hunter, Alberta (1895–1984)
Hunter, Clementine (1886–1988)
Hunter, Kristin (1931—)
Hunter-Gault, Charlayne (1942—)
Hunton, Addie D. Waites (1875–1943)
Hurston, Zora Neale (c. 1891–1960)
Hyman, Flo (1954–1986)
Hyman, Phyllis (1949–1995)
Ingram, Sheila Rena (1957—)
Jackson, Janet (1966—)
Jackson, Nell (1929–1988)
Jackson, Rebecca Cox (1795–1871)
Jackson, Shirley Ann (1946—)
Jackson, Tammy (1962—)
Jacobs, Harriet A. (1813–1897)
James, Etta (1938—)
Jamison, Judith (1943—)
Jarboro, Caterina (1908–1986)
Jemison, Mae (1956—)
Jessye, Eva (1895–1992)
Jiles, Pamela (1955—)
Johnson, Ella (1923–2004)
Johnson, Halle (1864–1901)
Johnson, Shannon (1974—)
Jones, Barbara (1937—)
Jones, Caroline R. (1942–2001)
Jones, Etta (1928–2001)
Jones, Linda (1944–1972)
Jones, Loïs Mailou (1905–1998)
Jones, Marion (1975—)
Jones, Sissieretta (1869–1933)
Jordan, June (1936–2002)
Joyner, Florence Griffith (1959–1998)
Joyner, Marjorie Stewart (1896–1994)
Joyner-Kersee, Jackie (1962—)
Kanaga, Consuelo (1894–1978)
Keckley, Elizabeth (c. 1824–1907)
Kelly, Leontine (1920—)
Kennedy, Adrienne (1931—)
Kennedy, Florynce (1916–2000)
Khan, Chaka (1953—)
King, Alberta Williams (1903–1974)
King, Coretta Scott (1927–2006)
King, Mabel (1932–1999)
Kitt, Eartha (1928—)
Kittrell, Flemmie (1904–1980)
Knight, Gladys (1944—)
Knowles, Beyoncé (1981—)
Koontz, Elizabeth (1919–1989)
LaBelle, Patti (1944—)
Lacey, Venus (1967—)
Lampkin, Daisy (1883–1965)
Lane, Pinkie Gordon (1925—)
Laney, Lucy Craft (1854–1933)
Lange, Elizabeth Clovis (1784–1882)
Larsen, Nella (1891–1964)
Lawrence, Janice (1962—)
Leatherwood, Lillie (1964—)
Lee, Barbara (1946—)
Lee, Barbara (1947–1992)
Lee, Beverly (1941—)
Lee, Jarena (1783–c. 1849)
LeGon, Jeni (1916—)
LeNoire, Rosetta (1911–2002)
Leslie, Lisa (1972—)
Lewis, Charlotte (1955—)
Lewis, Edmonia (c. 1845–c. 1909)
Lewis, Edna (1916–2006)
Lewis, Elma (1921–2004)
Logan, Onnie Lee (c. 1910–1995)
Lopes, Lisa (1971–2002)
Lorde, Audre (1934–1992)
Love, Barbara (1941—)
Lucy, Autherine Juanita (1929—)
Madgett, Naomi Long (1923—)
Magers, Rose (1960—)
Mahoney, Mary Eliza (1845–1926)
Malone, Annie Turnbo (1869–1957)
Malone, Maicel (1969—)
Marquis, Gail (1956—)
Marshall, Paule Burke (1929—)
Martin, Helen (1909–2000)
Martin, LaVonna (1966—)
Martin, Sara (1884–1955)
Matthews, Margaret (1935—)
Matthews, Victoria Earle (1861–1907)
McCollum, Ruby (1915—)
McCray, Nikki (1971—)
McDaniel, Hattie (1895–1952)
McDaniel, Mildred (1933–2004)
McDonald, Audra (1970—)
McDonald, Gabrielle Kirk (1942—)
McGee, Pamela (1962—)
McGhee, Carla (1968—)
McGuire, Edith (1944—)
McKane, Alice Woodby (1865–1948)
McKinney, Cynthia (1955—)
McKinney, Nina Mae (c. 1912–1967)
MC Lyte (1971—)
McMillan, Kathy (1957—)
McMillan, Terry (1951—)
McNeil, Claudia (1917–1993)
McQueen, Thelma (1911–1995)
Meriwether, Louise (1923—)
Merritt, Theresa (1924–1998)
Miles, Jearl (1966—)
Miller, Cheryl (1964—)
Miller, Inger (1972—)
Millican, Arthenia J. Bates (1920—)
Mills, Stephanie (1957—)
Milton, DeLisha (1974—)
Milton, Gladys (1924–1999)
Miner, Myrtilla (1815–1864)
Mitchell, Abbie (1884–1960)
Mobley, Mamie Till (1921–2003)
Monica (1980—)
Montiero, June (1946—)
Moody, Anne (1940—)
Moore, Audley (1898–1997)
Moore, Juanita (1922—)
Morrison, Melissa (1971—)
Morrison, Toni (1931—)
Morton, Azie Taylor (c. 1936–2003)
Motley, Constance Baker (1921–2005)
Murray, Pauli (1910–1985)
Nash, Diane (1938—)
Naylor, Gloria (1950—)
Nealy, Frances (1918–1997)
Netter, Mildrette (1948—)
Nickerson, Camille (1884–1982)
Norman, Jessye (1945—)
Norman, Maidie (1912–1998)
Norton, Eleanor Holmes (1937—)
Osborne, Estelle Massey (1901–1981)
Page, LaWanda (1920–2002)
Parker, Pat (1944–1989)
Parks, Rosa (1913—)
Parks, Suzan-Lori (1963—)
Parritt, Barbara (1944—)
Patterson, Audrey (1926–1996)
Patterson, Mary Jane (1840–1894)
Patterson-Tyler, Audrey (1926–1996)
Payne, Ethel (1911–1991)
Payton, Carolyn Robertson (1925–2001)
Peake, Mary S. (1823–1862)
Perrot, Kim (c. 1967–1999)
Perry, Julia (1924–1979)
Perry, Nanceen (1977—)
Peters, Roumania (1917–2003)
Petry, Ann (1908–1997)
Pettis, Bridget (1971—)
Plato, Ann (c. 1820–?)
Player, Willa B. (1909–2003)
Pleasant, Mary Ellen (c. 1814–1904)
Pointer, Anita (1948—)

Pointer, Bonnie (1950—)
Pointer, June (1954—)
Pointer, Ruth (1946—)
Pointer Sisters (1973—)
Polite, Carlene Hatcher (1932—)
Powers, Georgia Davis (1923—)
Powers, Harriet (1837–1911)
Price, Florence B. (1888–1953)
Price, Leontyne (1927—)
Primus, Pearl (1919–1994)
Prince, Lucy Terry (c. 1730–1821)
Prophet, Elizabeth (1890–1960)
Prout, Mary Ann (1801–1884)
Purvis, Harriet Forten (1810–1875)
Purvis, Sarah Forten (c. 1811–c. 1898)
Queen Latifah (1970—)
Rahn, Muriel (1911–1961)
Rainey, Ma (1886–1939)
Randolph, Amanda (1896–1967)
Randolph, Barbara (d. 2002)
Randolph, Lillian (1898–1980)
Randolph, Virginia (1874–1958)
Rashad, Phylicia (1948—)
Ray, Charlotte E. (1850–1911)
Ray, H. Cordelia (c. 1849–1916)
Reese, Della (1931—)
Reeves, Martha (1941—)
Reid, Clarice D. (1931—)
Remond, Sarah Parker (1826–1894)
Rice, Condoleezza (1954—)
Richards, Beah (1920–2000)
Richardson, Gloria (1922—)
Ringgold, Faith (1934—)
Riperton, Minnie (1947–1979)
Roberts, Patricia (1955—)
Roberts, Robin (1960—)
Robeson, Eslanda Goode (1896–1965)
Robinson, Cynthia (1946—)
Robinson, Jo Ann (1911–1992)
Robinson, Ruby Doris Smith (1942–1967)
Robinson, Vicki Sue (1954–2000)
Rolle, Esther (1920–1998)
Rollins, Charlemae Hill (1897–1979)
Ross, Diana (1944—)
Rubin, Chandra (1976—)
Rudolph, Wilma (1940–1994)
Ruffin, Josephine St. Pierre (1842–1924)
Sampson, Edith S. (1901–1979)
Sanchez, Sonia (1934—)
Sands, Diana (1934–1973)
Sanford, Isabel (1917–2004)
Sapenter, Debra (1952—)
Saunders, Doris (1921—)
Savage, Augusta (1892–1962)
Scales, Jessie Sleet (fl. 1900)
Schuyler, Philippa Duke (1931–1967)
Scott, Esther Mae (1893–1979)
Scott, Hazel (1920–1981)
Scott, Shirley (1934–2002)
Scurry, Briana (1971—)
Shabazz, Betty (1936–1997)
Shange, Ntozake (1948—)
Shockley, Ann Allen (1925—)
Simkins, Modjeska M. (1899–1992)
Simmons, Ruth J. (1945—)
Simms, Hilda (1920–1994)
Simone, Nina (1933–2003)
Simpson, Carole (1940—)
Sims, Naomi (1948—)
Slowe, Lucy Diggs (1885–1937)
Smith, Ada (1894–1984)
Smith, Amanda Berry (1837–1915)
Smith, Anna Deavere (1950—)
Smith, Bessie (1894–1937)
Smith, Clara (1894–1935)
Smith, Mabel (1924–1972)
Smith, Mamie (1883–1946)
Smith, Margaret Charles (b. 1906)
Smith, Muriel Burrell (1923–1985)
Smith, Willie Mae Ford (1904–1994)
Snow, Valaida (c. 1903–1956)
Southern, Eileen Jackson (1920–2002)
Spencer, Anne (1882–1975)
Spivey, Victoria (1906–1976)
St. Clair, Stephanie (fl. 1920s–30s)
Staples, Cleo (1934—)
Staples, Mavis (1940—)
Staples, Yvonne (1939—)
Staupers, Mabel (1890–1989)
Steward, Susan McKinney (1847–1918)
Stewart, Ellen (c. 1920—)
Stewart, Maria W. (1803–1879)
Stockton, Betsey (c. 1798–1865)
Stone, Toni (1921–1996)
Stringfield, Bessie B. (1912–1993)
Sullivan, Maxine (1911–1987)
Supremes, The (1964–1977)
Swoopes, Sheryl (1971—)
Talbert, Mary Morris (1866–1923)
Tarry, Ellen (b. 1906)
Taylor, Eva (1895–1977)
Taylor, Susie King (1848–1912)
Teer, Barbara Ann (1937—)
Terrell, Mary Church (1863–1954)
Tharpe, Rosetta (1915–1973)
Thigpen, Lynne (1948–2003)
Thomas, Alma (1891–1978)
Thomas, Carla (1942—)
Thomas, Debi (1967—)
Thomas, Edna (1885–1974)
Thomas, Joyce Carol (1938—)
Thompson, Eloise Bibb (1878–1928)
Thompson, Era Bell (1906–1986)
Thompson, Louise (1901–1999)
Thompson, Tina (1975—)
Thoms, Adah B. (c. 1863–1943)
Thornton, Willie Mae (1926–1984)
Thurman, Sue (1903–1996)
Torrence, Gwen (1965—)
Toussaint, Cheryl (1952—)
Troy, Doris (1937–2004)
Truth, Sojourner (c. 1797–1883)
Tubman, Harriet (1821–1913)
Tucker, C. DeLores (1927–2005)
Turner, Debbye (1966—)
Turner, Kim (1961—)
Turner, Mary (d. 1918)
Turner, Tina (1938—)
Tyson, Cicely (1933—)
Tyus, Wyomia (1945—)
Uggams, Leslie (1943—)
Vance, Danitra (1954–1994)
Vanderpool, Sylvia (1936—)
Vann, Jesse Matthews (c. 1890–1967)
Vaughan, Sarah (1924–1990)
Verrett, Shirley (1931—)
Vincent, Marjorie (c. 1965—)
Waddles, Charleszetta (1912–2001)
Waddy, Harriet (1904–1999)
Walker, Ada Overton (1870–1914)
Walker, Madame C.J. (1867–1919)
Walker, Maggie Lena (1867–1934)
Walker, Margaret (1915–1998)
Wallace, Sippie (1898–1986)
Ward, Clara Mae (1924–1973)
Waring, Laura Wheeler (1887–1948)
Warwick, Dionne (1940—)
Washington, Dinah (1924–1963)
Washington, Fredi (1903–1994)
Washington, Josephine (1861–1949)
Washington, Margaret Murray (c. 1861–1925)
Washington, Olivia Davidson (1854–1889)
Washington, Ora (1899–1971)
Washington, Sarah Spencer (1889–?)
Waters, Ethel (1896–1977)
Wattleton, Faye (1943—)
Weatherspoon, Teresa (1965—)
Webb, Elida (1895–1975)
Welch, Elisabeth (1904–2003)
Wells, Mary (1943–1992)
Wells-Barnett, Ida (1862–1931)
West, Dorothy (1907–1998)
Wheatley, Phillis (c. 1752–1784)
White, Eartha M. (1876–1974)
White, Karyn (1965—)
White, Marilyn Elaine (1944—)
White, Willye B. (1939—)
Williams, Camilla (1922—)
Williams, Fannie Barrier (1855–1944)
Williams, Lavinia (1916–1989)
Williams, Lucinda (1937—)
Williams, Marion (1927–1994)
Williams, Mary Lou (1910–1981)
Williams, Serena (1981—)
Williams, Sherley Anne (1944–1999)
Williams, Vanessa (1963—)
Williams, Venus (1980—)
Wilson, Edith (1896–1981)
Wilson, Harriet E. Adams (c. 1827–c. 1870)
Wilson, Margaret Bush (1919—)
Wilson, Mary (1944—)
Wilson, Nancy (1937—)
Winfrey, Oprah (1954—)
Woodard, Lynette (1959—)
Wright, Jane Cooke (1919—)
Wright, Sarah Elizabeth (1928—)
Wright, Syreeta (1946–2004)
Young, Wanda (1944—)

ALBANIA

Ancient country of the East Caucasus
Comprised Illyria and Epirus
Ruled by Roman Empire (8th–4th c. CE)
Ruled by Goths (4th and 5th c.)
Ruled by Eastern Empire (6th–13th c.)
Ruled by Serbia (7th c.)
Partially annexed to Bulgaria (11th c.)
Ruled by Ottoman Empire (15th–20th c.)
Achieved independence (1912)
Ruled by Serbia (1913)
Achieved independence (1917)
Became a republic (1925–1928)
Ruled by monarchy (1928–1939)
Ruled by Italy (1939)
Ruled by Greece (1941)
Occupied by Nazi Germany (1941)
Achieved independence (1944)
Became People's Republic (1946)

Apponyi, Geraldine (1915–2002)
Belishova, Liri (1923—)
Hoxha, Nexhmije (1920—)
Kadaré, Elena (1943—)
Manjani, Miréla (1976—)
Teresa, Mother (1910–1997)

ALBANY

Ancient kingdom in mid-eastern Scotland
See Scotland.

ALBERSTROFF

City in Moselle, France
See France.

ALENÁON

Medieval territory of France
See France.

ALGERIA

North African republic
Conquered by Vandals (5th c.)
Ruled by Byzantine Empire (6th c.)
Islam introduced (7th–8th c.)
Ruled by Fatimid dynasty (10th c.)
Ruled by Spain (15th c.)
Ruled by Ottoman Empire (16th c.)
Ruled by France (18th–19th c.)
Achieved independence (1962)
See also Numidia.

Amrane, Djamila (1939—)
Amrouche, Fadhma Mansour (1882–1967)
Amrouche, Marie-Louise (1913–1976)
Aouchal, Leila (1937—)
Arnoul, Françoise (1931—)
Bellil, Samira (1972–2004)
Ben-Halim, Maryse (1920–2001)
Benida, Nouria (1970—)
Bouhired, Djamila (1937—)
Boulmerka, Hassiba (1968—)
Boupacha, Djamila (1942—)
Debeche, Jamila (1925—)
Destivelle, Catherine (1960—)
Drif, Zohra (1941—)
Fabian, Françoise (1932—)
Fratellini, Annie (1932–1997)
French, Evangeline (1869–1960)
Ghalem, Nadia (1941—)
Grégoire, Colette Anna (1931–1966)
Imaleyene, Fatime-Zohra (1936—)
Kerima (1925—)
Lemsine, Aicha (1942—)
Monica (331–387)
M'rabet, Fadéla (1935—)
Polaire (1879–1939)
Sebbar, Leila (1941—)
Weiss, Jeanne Daniloff (1868–1891)

ALGONQUIN

Native North American northeast indigenous group

Pocahontas (c. 1596–1617)

ALPES MARITIMES

French department
See France.

AMERICA, COLONIAL

Dare, Virginia (b. 1587)
Dustin, Hannah (1657–c. 1736)
Pelham, Mary Singleton Copley (c. 1710–1789)
Penn, Gulielma Springett (1644–1694)
Penn, Hannah (1671–1726)
Philipse, Margaret Hardenbrook (d. 1690)
Reed, Esther De Berdt (1746–1780)
Rowlandson, Mary (c. 1635–after 1682)
Royall, Anne (1769–1854)
Timothy, Ann (c. 1727–1792)
Timothy, Elizabeth (d. 1757)
Van Cortlandt, Annettje Lockermans (c. 1620–after 1665)
Van Rensselaer, Maria Van Cortlandt (1645–c. 1688)
Warren, Mercy Otis (1728–1814)
Winthrop, Margaret (c. 1591–1647)
Wright, Susanna (1697–1784)

ANATOLIA

See Asia Minor.

ANGOLA

Former Portuguese West Africa

Njinga (c. 1580s–1663)

ANHALT

Former German state
Part of Magdeburg and Halle districts in eastern Germany
See Germany.

ANJOU

Historical region in northwest France
Fiefdom established by Capetian kings (10th–11th c.)
Acquired Touraine (1044), and Maine (1110)
Ruled by England (12th c.)
Returned to France (1204)
Inherited by Charles of Naples and Sicily (1246)
Became a duchy (1297)
Annexed to French crown (1480)
See France.

ANSBACH

Prussian principality
See Prussia.

ANTIOCH

Syrian principality (11th c.)
See Asia Minor.

APACHE

Native North American southwest indigenous group

Riley, Mary Velasquez (1908–1987)

APULIA

Region in southeast Italy
Settled by Apulians (4th c. BCE)
Part of Roman Empire with Calabria (3rd c. BCE)
Conquered by Lombards (7th c.)
Ruled by Byzantine Empire (9th c.)
Became county after Norman conquest (1042)
Became a duchy (1059)
United with Kingdom of the Two Sicilies (1130)
Invaded by papal forces (13th c.)
See Italy.

AQUITAINE

Historical region of southwest France
Became duchy after Frankish conquest (6th c.)
Became subkingdom under Charlemagne (8th c.)
Reunited to French crown (9th c.)
Became powerful feudal duchy (10th–11th c.)
Passed to English Plantagenets (12th c.)
See England.
See France.

ARABIAN PENINSULA

Southwestern Asian peninsula
Center of Minaean and Sabaean kingdoms (11th c. BCE)
Invaed by Assyrians, Hebrews, and Romans (before 6th c. CE)
Under Persian rule (6th c.)
Consolidated under Mohammed (7th c.)
Ruled by Karmathians (10th c.)
Ruled by Mamelukes (before 16th c.)
Ruled by Ottoman Empire (16th c.)
Ruled by Wahabi Empire (19th c.)
Consolidated (1932)
See also Saudi Arabia.

Abassa (fl. 8th c.)
A'ishah bint Abi Bakr (c. 613–678)
A'ishah bint Talhah (fl. 7th c.)
Anan (fl. 9th c.)
Azza al-Maila (fl. c. 707)
Bid'a (856–915)
Dananir al Barmakiyya (fl. late 8th c.)
Fadl (d. around 870)
Farida (c. 830–?)
Fatimah (605/11–632/33)
Habbaba (d. 724)
Hafsah (fl. 7th c.)
Hind bint 'Utba (d. 610)
Inan (fl. c. 800)
Irfan (fl. mid–800s)
Juwairiyah (fl. 627)
Khadijah (c. 555–619)
Khaizaran (d. 790)
Khansa (c. 575–c. 645)
Layla al-Akhyaliyya (fl. 650–660)
Mahbuba (fl. 9th c.)
Maryam the Egyptian (fl. 7th c.)
Milh al-Attara (fl. 840s)
Mutayyam al-Hashimiyya (fl. 8th c.)
Oraib (797–890)
'Raihanah bint Zaid (fl. 7th c.)
Ramlah (fl. 7th c.)
Safiyah
Sawdah bint Zama
Shariyya (b. around 815)
Sheba, Queen of (fl. 10th c. BCE)
Ubaida (fl. c. 830)
Ulayya (fl. 800s)
Um Kalthum (c. 1898–1975)
Umm Ruman (fl. 7th c.)
Umm Salamah (fl. 7th c.)
Zaynab bint Jahsh (c. 590–c. 640)
Zubeida (d. 831)

ARAGON

Conquered by Visigoths (5th c.)
Conquered by Moors (8th c.)
Became independent kingdom (11th c.)
Ruled Navarre and Saragossa (11th–12th c.)
United with Catalonia and Barcelona (12th c.)
Briefly held Kingdom of the Two Sicilies (13th c.)
Obtained Sardinia and Corsica (13th c.)
Conquered Naples (15th c.)
United with Castile (15th c.)
See also Spain.

Agnes de Poitiers (fl. 1135)
Maria of Montpellier (1181–1213)
Maria of Navarre (fl. 1340)
Petronilla (1135–1174)
Philippa de Rouergue (c. 1074–1118)
Sancha of Aragon (d. 1073)
Sancha of Castile and Leon (1164–1208)
Teresa d'Entenza (fl. 1319)
Teresa of Aragon (1037–?)
Urraca (c. 1096–c. 1130)
Urraca of Aragon (fl. 11th c.)
Yolande de Bar

ARGENTEUIL

City in Val-d'Oise department of northern France
See France.

ARGENTINA

South American federal republic
Discovered by Spain (16th c.)
Included in viceroyalty of La Plata (18th c.)
Gained independence from Spain (19th c.)

Adamova, Adela (1927—)
Agar, Eileen (1899–1991)
Agoglia, Esmeralda (1926—)
Aicega, Magdalena (1973—)
Alcorta, Gloria (1915—)
Aleandro, Norma (1936—)
Amato, Serena (1974—)
Anderson, Anne (1874–1930)
Antoniska, Mariela (1975—)
Aretz, Isabel (1909—)
Argerich, Martha (1941—)
Arrondo, Ines (1977—)
Aymar, Luciana (1977—)
Azurduy de Padilla, Juana (1781–1862)
Bardach, Georgina (1983—)
Barra, Emma de la (1861–1947)
Belfiore, Liliana (1952—)

Bemberg, Maria Luisa (1922–1995)
Bertolaccini, Silvia (1959—)
Bonafini, Hebe de (1928—)
Bosco, María Angélica (1917—)
Bullrich, Silvina (1915–1990)
Bulnes, Esmée (1900–1986)
Bunge de Gálvez, Delfina (1881–1952)
Bunke, Tamara (1937–1967)
Burkart, Claudia (1980—)
Campbell, Jeannette (1916–2003)
Canto, Estela (1919–1994)
Codina, Iverna (1918—)
Correa, Deolinda (fl. 1830)
Daniele, Graciela (1939—)
Denis, María (1916–2004)
Dianda, Hilda (1925—)
di Giacomo, Marina (1976—)
Dominguez, María Alicia (1908—)
Ferrari, Maria Paz (1973—)
Ferri, Olga (1928—)
Fini, Leonor (1908–1996)
Frigerio, Marta Lía (1925–1985)
Gallardo, Sara (1931–1988)
Gambaro, Griselda (1928—)
Gambero, Anabel (1972—)
Gándara, Carmen (1900–1977)
Garcia, Agustina Soledad (1981—)
Gonzalez Oliva, Mariana (1976—)
Gorriti, Juana Manuela (1816–1892)
Granata, Maria (1921—)
Guido, Beatriz (1924—)
Gulla, Alejandra (1977—)
Hernandez, Maria de la Paz (1977—)
Jurado, Alicia (1915—)
Kaplan, Nelly (1931—)
Lamarque, Libertad (1908–2000)
Lange, Norah (1906–1972)
Levinson, Luisa Mercedes (1909–1988)
Lopez, Encarnación (1898–1945)
Lusarreta, Pilar de (1914–1967)
Maiztegui, Laura
Mansilla de García, Eduarda (1838–1892)
Margalot, Mercedes (1975—)
Maris, Mona (1903–1991)
Marshall, Niní (1903–1996)
Masotta, Paula Karina (1972—)
Mercé, Antonia (c. 1886–1936)
Mikey, Fanny (1931—)
Moreau de Justo, Alicia (1885–1986)
Noronha, Joana de (fl. c. 1850)
Ocampo, Silvina (1903–1993)
Ocampo, Victoria (1890–1979)
Olberg, Oda (1872–1955)
Oneto, Vanina (1973—)
Orphee, Elvira (1930—)
Perón, Eva (1919–1952)
Perón, Isabel (1931—)
Pizarnik, Alejandra (1936–1972)
Poletti, Syria (1919–1991)
Rimoldi, Jorgelina (1972—)
Rognoni, Cecilia (1976—)
Rosas, Encarnación de (1795–1838)
Russo, Marine (1980—)
Sabatini, Gabriela (1970—)
Shabelska, Maria (1898–1980)
Simonetto de Portela, Noemi (1926—)
Sosa, Mercedes (1935—)
Stepnik, Ayelen (1975—)
Storni, Alfonsina (1892–1938)
Suarez, Paola (1976—)
Tarabini, Patricia (1968—)
Terzian, Alicia (1938—)
Torres, Lolita (1930–2002)
Traba, Marta (1930–1983)
Valenzuela, Luisa (1938—)
Villarino, María de (1905–1994)
Vukojicic, Paola (1974—)
Walsh, María Elena (1930—)

ARGOS

Ancient city-state in northeastern Greece
Joined with Corinth, Mantinea, and Elis against Sparta (5th c. BCE)
Joined with Corinth, Athens, and Thebes in Corinthian War (4th c. BCE)
Captured by Franks and held in fief to Athens (13th c.)
Ruled by Byzantine Empire (13th–15th c.)
Ruled by Ottoman Empire (15th–19th c.)
Destroyed (1825)
See Greece.

ARMENIA

Ancient country in western Asia
Equivalent to Kingdom of Van (13th–9th c. BCE)
Ruled by Media (7th–6th c. BCE)
Ruled by Persia (6th–4th c. BCE)
Reunited with Artaxata (1st c. BCE)
Ruled by Persian and Roman Empires (3rd–7th c.)
Ruled by Ottoman Empire (16th c.)
Ruled by Russia (19th c.)
Country divided into Turkish Armenia and Armenian Soviet Socialist Republic (20th c.)
Achieved independence (1991)

Aznavourian, Karina (1974—)
Pharandzem (c. 320–c. 364)
Philippa of Lesser Armenia (fl. 1200s)
Sibylla of Armenia (fl. 1200s)
Tusap, Srbuhi (1841–1901)
Yessayan, Zabel (1878–1943)
Zabel (b. around 1210)

ARMENIA, LESSER

Ancient country and region in southeast Asia Minor
Called Cilicia and conquered by Cyrus
Became satrapy of Persian Empire
Conquered by Alexander the Great (4th c. BCE)
Conquered by Pompey and made a Roman province (1st c. BCE)
Invaded by Arabs (8th c.)
Became an independent Armenian principality (11th c.)
Became kingdom (12th c.)
Conquered by Turks (15th c.)
See Armenia.
See Turkey.

ARRAN

Island in Bute county in Firth of Clyde off coast of Scotland
See Scotland.

ARTOIS

Historical region in northern France
See France.

ARUNDEL

Borough of West Sussex, England
See England.

ASHANTI KINGDOM

See Ghana.

ASIA MINOR

Western Asian peninsula
Kingdom of Hittites (20th–13th c. BCE)
Ruled by Greece (11th c. BCE)
Ruled by Lydia (7th–6th c. BCE)
Ruled by Persia (6th–4th c. BCE)
Conquered by Alexander of Macedon (4th c. BCE)
Divided into small kingdoms (Pergamum, Cappadocia, Bithynia, and Pontus)
Ruled by Roman Empire (2nd c. BCE)
Ruled by Byzantine Empire (4th–6th c.)
Invaded by Arabs (7th c.)
Ruled by Seljuk Empire as Anatolia, Sultanate of Rum (11th c.)
Crusades established Latin empires of Nicaea and Trebizond
Invaded by Mongols (13th c.)
Ruled by Ottoman Empire (14th–15th c.)

Ada (c. 380–c. 323 BCE)
Alice of Jerusalem (c. 1106–?)
Anne of Chatillon-Antioche (c. 1155–c. 1185)
Apama (c. 290 BCE–?)
Apama (fl. 245 BCE)
Artemisia I (c. 520–? BCE)
Artemisia II (c. 395–351 BCE)
Berenice Syra (c. 280–246 BCE)
Cassandra (possibly fl. around 1200 BCE)
Cecilia of France (fl. 1100s)
Constance of Antioch (1128–1164)
Constance of France (fl. 1100s)
Hatice (fl. 1500–1536)
Helen Asen of Bulgaria (d. 1255?)
Maria-Kyratza Asen (fl. late 1300s)
Melisande (fl. 1200s)
Nonna (c. 305–c. 374)
Pelagia
Phila II (c. 300 BCE–?)
Philippa of Antioch (fl. 1100s)
Philippa of Lesser Armenia (fl. 1200s)
Sosipatra (fl. 4th c.)
Stratonice I (c. 319–254 BCE)
Stratonice II (c. 285–228 BCE)
Stratonice III (fl. 250 BCE)
Thecla (fl. 1st c.)
Tocco, Magdalena-Theodora (fl. mid-1400s)

ASSINIBOINE

Native North American Great Plains indigenous group

Akers, Dolly Smith (1902—)

ASSYRIA

Ancient empire in western Asia
Probable origins in Sumerian Ashur (c. 28th c. BCE)
Ruled by Babylonia (c. 20th–19th c. BCE)
Conquered Israel, Damascus, Babylon, and Samaria (8th c. BCE)
Ruled by Roman Empire (7th c. CE)
Part of Caliphate (7th c. CE)

Sammuramat (fl. 8th c. BCE)

ATHENS

Ancient city-state of Greece
Included territory of Attica
Abolished hereditary kingship (7th c. BCE)
Became a democracy (6th c. BCE)
Defeated Persia (5th c. BCE)
Allied to Thessaly, Achaea, Argos, Samos, Chinos, Naxos, and Cyclades (5th c. BCE)
Defeated after Second Peloponnesian War (5th c. BCE)
Allied against Sparta (4th c. BCE)
Ruled by Macedonian Empire (4th c. BCE)
See Greece.

ATHOLL

District in north Perth county, Scotland
See Scotland.

AUSTRALIA

Independent state in Southern hemisphere
First sighted by the Spanish
Explored by the Dutch and named New Holland (17th c.)
Claimed by Britain and named New South Wales (18th c.)
Rapid development after gold rush (1851)
Called Australia (19th c.)
Became commonwealth (1901)
See also Australian aborigine.

Abbott, Mother (1846–1934)
Adams, Glenda (1939—)
Adam-Smith, Patsy (1924–2001)
Adamson, Catherine (1868–1925)
Ahern, Lizzie (1877–1969)
Aitkin, Yvonne (1911—)
Akhurst, Daphne (1903–1933)
Aldous, Lucette (1938—)
Allen, Kate (1974—)
Allen, Katherine (1970—)
Allen, Monique (1971—)
Allen, Sandra (1978—)
Amoore, Judith Pollock (1940—)
Amphlett, Christina (c. 1960—)
Anderson, Ethel Mason (1883–1958)
Anderson, Jessica (1916—)
Anderson, Judith (1898–1992)
Anderson, Maybanke (1845–1927)
Anderson, Robin (1948–2002)
Andrew, Janice (1943—)
Andrews, Michelle (1971—)
Annan, Alyson (1973—)
Appleton, Jean (1911–2003)
Archer, Caroline Lilian (1922–1978)
Archer, Robyn (1948—)
Armstrong, Gillian (1950—)
Armstrong, Jenny (1970—)
Astley, Thea (1925–2004)
Atkinson, Louisa (1834–1872)
Attwood, Julie Maree (1957—)
Austral, Florence (1894–1968)
Backhouse, Elizabeth (b. 1917)
Bage, Freda (1883–1970)
Baker, Mary Ann (1834–1905)
Balogh, Suzanne (1973—)
Banahan, Mary Gertrude (1855/56?–1932)
Bandler, Faith (1918—)
Barnard, Marjorie (1897–1987)
Barrie, Mona (1909–1964)
Barron, Hannah Ward (1829–1898)
Barry, Bonny (1960—)
Barton, Jane (1851–1938)
Bashir, Marie (1930—)
Batkovic, Suzy (1980—)
Bauld, Alison (1944—)
Baynes, Deserie (1960—)
Baynton, Barbara (1857–1929)
Beachley, Layne (1972—)
Beames, Adrienne
Bear-Crawford, Annette (1853–1899)
Beath, Betty (1932—)
Beeby, Doris (1894–1948)
Belbin, Tracey (1967—)
Bell, Jane (1873–1959)
Bell, Lynette (1947—)
Bennett, Agnes Elizabeth Lloyd (1872–1960)
Bennett, Enid (1893–1969)
Bennett, Isobel (b. 1909)
Bennett, Marjorie (1896–1982)
Bennett, Mary Montgomerie (1881–1961)
Berndt, Catherine Webb (1918–1994)
Bird, Lorraine
Bird, Nancy (1915—)
Bjelke-Petersen, Marie (1874–1969)
Black, Marilyn (1944—)
Blackburn, Doris Amelia (1889–1970)
Blackwood, Margaret (1909–1986)
Bligh, Anna Maria
Bock, Amy Maud (1859–1943)
Bodenwieser, Gertrud (1886–1959)
Bonney, Lores (1897–1994)
Booth, Agnes (1843–1910)
Booth, Angela Elizabeth (1869–1954)
Boswell, Annabella (1826–1916)
Botha, Wendy (1965—)
Bowman, Deborah (1963—)
Boyce, Ann (c. 1827–1914)
Boyd, Anne (1946—)
Boyd, Carla (1975—)
Boyle, Desley (1948—)
Boyle, Raelene (1951—)
Bradley, Amber (1980—)
Brancourt, Karen (1962—)
Brand, Mona (1915—)
Breamer, Sylvia (1897–1943)
Brennan, Anna Teresa (1879–1962)
Briggs, Margaret Jane (1892–1961)
Brinsmead, Hesba Fay (1922–2003)
Brogan, Michelle (1973—)
Brondello, Sandy (1968—)
Bronhill, June (1929–2005)
Brooke, Cynthia (1875–1949)
Brown, Eliza (d. 1896)
Brown, Joanne (1972—)
Brown, Vera Scantlebury (1889–1946)
Brownbill, Kay
Browne, Coral (1913–1991)
Bruce, Ethel (1879–1967)
Bruce, Mary Grant (1878–1958)
Brune, Adrienne (b. 1892)
Brunton, Dorothy (1893–1977)
Bryant, Millicent (1878–1927)
Buchanan, Isobel Wilson (1954—)
Buckingham, Rosetta (c. 1843–1864)
Bullwinkel, Vivian (1915–2000)
Burgess, Annie (1969—)
Burn, Margaret Gordon (1825–1918)
Burns, Lauren (1974—)
Burr, Marilyn (1933—)
Burridge, Pam (1965—)
Burrows, Eva (1929—)
Busch, Mae (1891–1946)
Buttfield, Nancy (1912—)
Buttrose, Ita (1942—)
Caird, Maureen (1951—)
Caldwell, Zoë (1933—)
Callil, Carmen (1938—)
Calub, Dyana (1975—)
Cambridge, Ada (1844–1926)
Cameron, Bessy (c. 1851–1895)
Campbell, Kate (1899–1986)
Campbell, Persia (1898–1974)
Campion, Jane (1954—)
Camplin, Alisa (1974—)
Cantrell, Lana (1943—)
Canty, Mary Agnes (1879–1950)
Capes, Lee (1961—)
Capes, Michelle (1966—)
Cappiello, Rosa (1942—)
Carbon, Sally (1967—)
Cardell-Oliver, Florence (1876–1965)
Carden, Joan (1937—)
Carpadios, Marissa (1977—)
Carr-Boyd, Ann (1938—)
Carrigan, Sara (1980—)
Casey, Maie (1892–1983)
Cashman, Mel (1891–1979)
Cassab, Judy (1920—)
Cassidy, Sheila (1937—)
Castle, Naomi (1974—)
Castles, Amy (1880–1951)
Catchpole, Margaret (1762–1819)
Cato, Nancy (1917–2000)
Chamberlain, Lindy (1948—)
Chandler, Michelle
Chapman, Susan (1962—)
Chapman, Yvonne (1940—)
Chauncy, Nan (1900–1970)
Chifley, Elizabeth (1886–1962)
Child, Joan (1921—)
Cilento, Diane (1933—)
Cilento, Phyllis (1894–1987)
Clark, Kate Emma (1847–1926)
Clark, Lesley Ann (1948—)
Clark, Liddy (1953—)
Clement, Elspeth (1956—)
Clift, Charmian (1923–1969)
Clisby, Harriet (1830–1931)
Colqhoun, Alva (1942—)
Colton, Mary (1822–1898)
Commins, Kathleen (1909–2003)
Connon, Helen (c. 1859–1903)
Conway, Jill Ker (1934—)
Cook, Allison (1972—)
Cook, Mary (1863–1950)
Cook, Natalie (1975—)
Cooper, Dulcie (1903–1981)
Cooper, Jacqui (1973—)
Cooper, Jessie (1914–1993)
Cooper, Kim (1965—)
Coory, Shirefie (c. 1864–1950)
Costian, Daniela (1965—)
Cottee, Kay (1954—)
Cottrell, Dorothy (1902–1957)
Couchman, Elizabeth (1876–1982)
Coulton, Mary Rose (1906–2002)
Court, Margaret Smith (1942—)
Couvreur, Jessie (1848–1897)
Cowan, Edith (1861–1932)
Cowie, Bessie Lee (1860–1950)
Crafter, Jane (1955—)
Craig, Molly (c. 1917–2004)
Craig, Sandra (1942—)
Crapp, Lorraine J. (1938—)
Crawford, Fiona (1977—)
Croft, Peta-Kaye (1972—)
Croker, Norma (1934—)
Cross, Zora (1890–1964)
Crossley, Ada Jemima (1871–1929)
Crowley, Rosemary (1938—)
Crudgington, Carolyn (1968—)
Cumming, Dorothy (1899–1983)
Cunningham, Elizabeth Anne
Curtin, Elsie (1890–1975)
Curzon, Grace Hinds
Cusack, Dymphna (1902–1981)
Cuthbert, Betty (1938—)
d'Alpuget, Blanche (1944—)
Dalton, Judy Tegart (fl. 1960s–1970s)
Dalyell, Elsie (1881–1948)
Dark, Eleanor (1901–1985)
Davey, Constance (1882–1963)
David, Caroline Edgeworth (1856–1951)
Davidson, Robyn (1950—)
Davies, Judy Joy (1928—)
Davis, Judy (1955—)
Dawbin, Annie Maria (1816–1905)
Dawson, Alice Madge (c. 1980–2003)
Deakin, Pattie (1863–1934)
Deamer, Dulcie (1890–1972)
De Groen, Alma (1941—)
Dench, Patricia (1932—)
Denman, Gertrude (1884–1954)
Dennis, Clare (1916–1971)
Deseo, Suzanne (1913–2003)
Devanny, Jean (1894–1962)
Dexter, Caroline (1819–1884)
Dienelt, Kerry (1969—)
Dobson, Emily (1842–1934)
Dobson, Louise (1972—)
Dobson, Rosemary (1920—)
Dobson, Ruth (1918–1989)
Doman, Amanda (1977—)
Donaldson, Mary (1972—)
Dorman, Loretta (1963—)
Drake-Brockman, Henrietta (1901–1968)
Drummond, Dolores (1834–1926)
Du Faur, Emmeline Freda (1882–1935)

Dugdale, Henrietta (1826–1918)
Duigan, Suzanne Lawless (1924–1993)
Dunlop, Eliza Hamilton (1796–1880)
Durack, Fanny (1889–1956)
Durack, Mary (1913–1994)
Edebone, Peta (1969—)
Edmond, Wendy (1946—)
Elder, Anne (1918–1976)
Eldershaw, Flora (1897–1956)
Elliott, Madge (1896–1955)
Elms, Lauris (1931—)
Evatt, Elizabeth (1933—)
Fadden, Ilma (d. 1987)
Fairhurst, Sue
Faletic, Dana (1977—)
Fallon, Trisha (1972—)
Farmer, Beverley (1941—)
Farrell, Renita (1972—)
Fawcett, Maisie (1902–1988)
Ferris, Michelle (1976—)
Fewings, Eliza Anne (1857–1940)
Fifield, Elaine (1930–1999)
Fish, Maree (1963—)
Fisher, Margaret (c. 1874–1958)
Fitton, Doris (1897–1985)
Flintoff, Debra (1960—)
Follas, Selina
Follett, Rosemary (1948—)
Ford, Michelle Jan (1962—)
Forde, Florrie (1876–1940)
Forde, Leneen (1935—)
Forde, Vera (1894–1967)
Forder, Annemarie (1978—)
Fortune, Mary (fl. 1866–1910)
Foster, Margot (1958—)
Fox, Joanne (1979—)
Francis, Catherine Augusta (1836–1916)
Franklin, Miles (1879–1954)
Fraser, Dawn (1937—)
Fraser, Eliza (c. 1798–1858)
Fraser, Tamie (1936—)
Freeman, Cathy (1973—)
Freeman, Joan (1918–1998)
Freeman, Mavis (1907—)
Frost, Phyllis (1917–2004)
Fullerton, Mary Eliza (1868–1946)
Gallagher, Kitty (fl. mid-19th c.)
Gamin, Judith (1930—)
Gant, Phyllis (1922—)
Gare, Nene (1919–1994)
Garmson, Aileen (c. 1861–1951)
Garner, Helen (1942—)
Gatehouse, Eleanor Wright (1886–1973)
Gaudron, Mary Genevieve (1943—)
Gaunt, Mary (1861–1942)
Gibbs, May (1877–1969)
Gill, Mary Gabriel (1837–1905)
Gilmore, Mary (1865–1962)
Gilmore, Rebecca
Gilmour, Sally (1921–2004)
Glanville-Hicks, Peggy (1912–1990)
Goldstein, Vida (1869–1949)
Goodwin, Bridget (c. 1802/27–1899)
Goolagong Cawley, Evonne (1951—)
Gordon, Annie Elizabeth (1873–1951)
Gordon, Doris Clifton (1890–1956)
Gorham, Kathleen (1932–1983)
Gorton, Bettina (c. 1916–1983)
Goss, Olga May (1916–1994)
Gould, Shane (1956—)
Granville, Louise (1895–1968)
Gray, Oriel (1920–2003)
Green, Dorothy (1915–1991)
Greer, Germaine (1939—)
Greville, Julia (1979—)
Grey-Gardner, Robyn (1964—)
Grigorieva, Tatiana (1975—)
Grimm, Cherry Barbara (1930–2002)
Grossmann, Edith Searle (1863–1931)
Guard, Elizabeth (1814–1870)
Gunn, Jeannie (1870–1961)
Gusterson, Bridgette (1973—)
Haines, Janine (1945–2004)
Hale, Una (1922–2005)
Hall, Elsie (1877–1976)
Halliday, Margaret (1956—)
Hammond, Joan (1912–1996)
Hankin, Simone
Hannan, Cora (c. 1912—)
Hanrahan, Barbara (1939–1991)
Hanson, Brooke (1978—)
Hanson-Dyer, Louise (1884–1962)
Hardie, Kelly (1969—)
Harding, Tanya (1972—)
Harford, Lesbia (1891–1927)
Harrop, Loretta (1975—)
Harrower, Elizabeth (1928—)
Harrower, Kristi (1975—)
Harvey, Leisha (1947—)
Harwood, Gwen (1920–1995)
Haslam, Juliet (1969—)
Hawke, Hazel (1929—)
Hawkes, Rechelle (1967—)
Hay, Jean Emily (1903–1984)
Haydon, Ethel (1878–1954)
Hazzard, Shirley (1931—)
Helmrich, Dorothy (1889–1984)
Henderson, Stella (1871–1962)
Henning, Rachel (1826–1914)
Henry, Alice (1857–1943)
Henry, Jodie (1983—)
Henrys, Catherine (c. 1805–1855)
Heseltine, Mary J. (1910–2002)
Hetherington, Jessie Isabel (1882–1971)
Hewett, Dorothy (1923–2002)
Higgins, Yvette (1978—)
Hill, Dorothy (1907–1997)
Hill, Ernestine (1899–1972)
Hill, Jo (1963—)
Hillas, Lorraine (1961—)
Hindmarsh, Mary (1921–2000)
Hodgskin, Natalie (1976—)
Hoff, Ursula (1909–2005)
Holland, Dulcie Sybil (1913—)
Holliday, Jenny (1964—)
Holt, Zara (1909–1989)
Hooper, Kate
Hore, Kerry (1981—)
Hospital, Janette Turner (1942—)
Howard, Janette (1944—)
Howley, Calasanctius (1848–1933)
Hudson, Nikki (1976—)
Hughes, Joanna (1977—)
Hughes, Mary (1874–1958)
Hughes, Wendy (1950—)
Hyde, Miriam Beatrice (1913–2005)
Imison, Rachel (1978—)
Jackson, Alice (1887–1974)
Jackson, Lauren (1981—)
Jackson, Marjorie (1931—)
James, Florence (1902–1993)
Jarratt, Jan (1958—)
Jefferis, Barbara (1917–2004)
Jenner, Andrea (1891–1985)
Johnson, Emma (1980—)
Johnston, Margaret (1917–2002)
Jolley, Elizabeth (1923—)
Jones, Brenda (1936—)
Jones, Leisel (1985—)
Jones, Marilyn (1940—)
Jones, Michellie (1969—)
Jordan, Vi (d. 1982)
Joyce, Eileen (1908–1991)
Joyce, Rebecca
Jull, Roberta (1872–1961)
Kaberry, Phyllis (1910–1977)
Keating, Annita (1949—)
Keech, Margaret Majella
Keesing, Nancy (1923–1993)
Kefala, Antigone (1935—)
Kellerman, Annette (1886–1975)
Kelly, Ethel (1875–1949)
Kelly, Gwen (1922—)
Kelly, Judy (1913–1991)
Kelly, Kate (1862–1898)
Kelly, Pearl (1894–1983)
Kennard, Gaby (1944—)
Kennedy, Louise St. John (1950—)
Kenny, Elizabeth (1880–1952)
Kernohan, Liz (1939–2004)
Kiddle, Margaret (1914–1958)
Kidman, Nicole (1967—)
Kilborn, Pam (1939—)
King, Joyce (1921—)
Kippin, Vicky (1942—)
Kirby, Mary Kostka (1863–1952)
Kirner, Joan (1938—)
Kirsova, Helene (1910–1962)
Klein, Robin (1936—)
Knorr, Frances (1868–1894)
Konrads, Ilsa (1944—)
Kramer, Leonie (1924—)
Kyburz, Rosemary (1944—)
Laby, Jean (1915—)
Lamy, Jennifer (1949—)
Landells, Suzanne (1964—)
Langley, Eve (1908–1974)
Lascelles, Patricia (1926—)
Lashko, Irina (1973—)
Lassig, Rosemary (1941—)
Lavarch, Linda (1958—)
Lawrence, Carmen Mary (1948—)
Lawrence, Marjorie (1908–1979)
Lawson, Louisa (1848–1920)
Leakey, Caroline Woolmer (1827–1881)
Lee, Alma (1912–1990)
Lee, Ida (1865–1943)
Lee, Mary (1821–1909)
Lee, Susan (1966—)
Lee, Virginia (1965—)
Leech, Faith (1941—)
Lee Long, Rosa
Lehane, Jan (1941—)
Lenton, Lisbeth (1985—)
Lester, Joyce (1958—)
Letham, Isobel (1899–1995)
Lewis, Hayley (1974—)
Litchfield, Jessie (1883–1956)
Lock, Jane (1954—)
Locke, Sumner (1881–1917)
Löhr, Marie (1890–1975)
Longman, Irene Maud (1877–1964)
Lovely, Louise (1895–1980)
Lyell, Lottie (1890–1925)
Lyons, Beatrice (1930—)
Lyons, Enid (1897–1981)
Macarthur, Elizabeth (1767–1850)
Macarthur-Onslow, Elizabeth (1840–1911)
Mack, Louise (1874–1935)
Mackay, Catherine Julia (1864–1944)
Mackay, Maria Jane (1844–1933)
Mackellar, Dorothea (1885–1968)
MacKillop, Mary Helen (1842–1909)
Maclean, Hester (1859–1932)
Macnamara, Jean (1899–1968)
Mactier, Kate (1975—)
Maher, Robyn (1959—)
Maitland, Clover (1972—)

Male, Carolyn Therese (1966—)
Maroney, Susan Jean (1974—)
Marsden, Karen (1962—)
Marshall, Kirstie (1969—)
Martin, C.E.M. (1847–1937)
Martin, Gael (1956—)
Mason-Brown, Michele (1939—)
Massey, Christina Allan (1863–1932)
Masters, Margaret (1934—)
Masters, Olga (1919–1986)
Maston, June (1928—)
Mathews, Marlene (1934—)
Maxwell, Alice Heron (1860–1949)
May, Valerie (c. 1915/16—)
Mayer, Bronwyn
McCarthy, Maud (1858–1949)
McCauley, Diane (1946—)
McClements, Lyn (1951—)
McCrae, Georgiana Huntly (1804–1890)
McCullough, Colleen (1937—)
McDermid, Sally (1965—)
McDonagh, Isobel (1899–1982)
McDonagh, Paulette (1901–1978)
McDonagh, Phyllis (1900–1978)
McDonald, Julie (1970—)
McEwen, Anne (c. 1903–1967)
McGill, Linda (1945—)
McKay, Heather (1941—)
McKillop, Peggy (1909–1998)
McKinnon, Betty (1924—)
McLennan, Margo (1938–2004)
McMahon, Sonia (1932—)
McPaul, Louise (1969—)
McQueen, Mary (1860–1945)
McQuillan, Rachel (1971—)
McRae, Francine (1969—)
Mealing, Philomena (1912–2002)
Meares, Anna (1983—)
Melba, Nellie (1861–1931)
Mellor, Fleur (1936—)
Menczer, Pauline (1970—)
Menzies, Pattie (1899–1995)
Meredith, Gwen (b. 1907)
Meredith, Louisa Anne (1812–1895)
Miller, Gail
Miller, Jessie Maude (1910–1972)
Miller, Jo-Ann (1958—)
Miller, Katrina (1975—)
Millis, Nancy (1922—)
Mills, Alice (1986—)
Mills, Melissa (1973—)
Minton, Yvonne (1938—)
Mitchell, Elyne (1913–2002)
Mitchell, Roma (1913–2000)
Mitchell-Taverner, Claire (1970—)
Molik, Alicia (1981—)
Molloy, Cate (1955—)
Molloy, Georgiana (1805–1842)
Moncrieff, Gladys (1892–1976)
Montagu, Helen (1928–2004)
Moore, Maggie (1847–1929)
Moras, Karen (1954—)
Morgan, Sally (1951—)
Morgan, Sandra (1942—)
Morris, Jenny (1972—)
Morrow, Simmone (1976—)
Mosley, Tracey (1973—)
Murdoch, Nina (1890–1976)
Murphy, Janice (1942—)
Murray, Anna Maria (1808–1899)
Nashar, Beryl (1923—)
Neall, Gail (1955—)
Nelson, Beryce Ann (1947—)
Nelson, Marjorie (1937—)
Nelson-Carr, Lindy (1952—)
Newbery, Chantelle (1977—)
Newton-John, Olivia (1948—)
Newton Turner, Helen (1908–1995)
Nolan, Rachel (1974—)
Norman, Decima (1909–1983)
Nowland, Mary Josepha (1863–1935)
Nunn, Glynis (1960—)
O'Doherty, Mignon (1890–1961)
O'Donnell, Phyllis (1937—)
Ondieki, Lisa (1960—)
O'Neil, Nancy (1911–1995)
O'Neill, Susie (1973—)
Onians, Edith (1866–1955)
Ostler, Emma Brignell (c. 1848–1922)
Outhwaite, Ida Rentoul (1888–1960)
Page, Ethel (c. 1875–1958)
Palmer, Helen (1917–1979)
Palmer, Nettie (1885–1964)
Park, Ruth (1923—)
Parker, Catherine Langloh (c. 1856–1940)
Partridge, Kathleen (1963—)
Patmore, Sharon (1963—)
Paul, Annette (1863–1952)
Pearce, Caroline (1925—)
Pearce, Jean (1921—)
Pearce, May (1915–1981)
Pearce, Morna (1932—)
Pearce, Vera (1896–1966)
Pearce Sisters (fl. 1936–1956)
Pearson, Michele (1962—)
Peek, Alison (1969—)
Pekli, Maria (1972—)
Pereira, Jacqueline (1964—)
Peris-Kneebone, Nova (1971—)
Petersen, Alicia O'Shea (1862–1923)
Petrie, Haylea (1969—)
Phillips, Anita Frances
Phillips, Karen (1966—)
Phipson, Joan (1912–2003)
Pisani, Sandra (1959—)
Pitt, Marie E.J. (1869–1948)
Platts-Mills, Daisy Elizabeth (1868–1956)
Playfair, Judy (1953—)
Polson, Florence Ada Mary Lamb (1877–1941)
Porter, Natalia (1980—)
Porter, Stacey (1982—)
Poto, Alicia (1978—)
Pottharst, Kerri-Ann (1965—)
Powell, Katrina (1972—)
Powell, Lisa (1970—)
Power, Laurel Jean (1953—)
Praed, Rosa (1851–1935)
Pratt, Dolly (1955—)
Preshaw, Jane (1839–1926)
Preston, Margaret Rose (c. 1875–1963)
Prichard, Katharine Susannah (1883–1969)
Provis, Nicole (1969—)
Pulz, Penny (1953—)
Quinn, Helen (1943—)
Rankin, Annabelle (1908–1986)
Reddy, Helen (1941—)
Rees, Annie Lee (1864–1949)
Reeve, Elsie (1885–1927)
Reeves, Magdalene Stuart (1865–1953)
Reibey, Mary (1777–1855)
Reid, Florence (c. 1870–1950)
Reid, Margaret (1935—)
Reilly, Dianne (1969—)
Rendall, Martha (d. 1909)
Rentoul, Annie Isobel (c. 1855–1928)
Rentoul, Annie Rattray (1882–1978)
Retter, Hannah (1839–1940)
Reynolds, Rachel Selina (1838–1928)
Richards, Ann (1917—)
Richardson, Henry Handel (1870–1946)
Richardson, Nicole (1970—)
Riley, Samantha (1972—)
Roberts, Elisa Mary (1970—)
Robinson, Dot (1912–1999)
Robinson, Fiona (1969—)
Robinson, Kathleen (1901–1983)
Robson, May (1858–1942)
Roche, Danni (1970—)
Roche, Melanie (1970—)
Rodriguez, Judith (1936—)
Roland, Betty (1903–1996)
Rolton, Gillian (1956—)
Rooke, Daphne (1914—)
Rooney, Giaan (1982—)
Rose, Merri (1955—)
Rosman, Alice Grant (1887–1961)
Rosser, Celia E. (1930—)
Rout, Ettie Annie (1877–1936)
Rowan, Ellis (1848–1922)
Rowe, Marilyn (1946—)
Roxon, Lillian (1932–1973)
Ryan, Sarah (1977—)
Sanders, Dorothy Lucie (1903–1987)
Sandie, Shelley (1969—)
Sanger, Ruth Ann (1918–2001)
Sattin, Rebecca (1980—)
Sauvage, Louise (1973—)
Saville, Jane (1974—)
Schaeffer, Wendy (c. 1975—)
Schroeder, Bertha (1872–1953)
Scott, Christine Margaret (1946—)
Scott, Desley Carleton (1943—)
Scott, Ivy (1886–1947)
Scott, Margaret (1922—)
Scott, Rose (1847–1925)
Scott, Ruby Payne (1912–1981)
Scullin, Sarah (1880–1962)
Shaw, Victoria (1935–1988)
Shearer, Jill (1936—)
Sheldon, Joan Mary (1943—)
Sherwood, Maud Winifred (1880–1956)
Simpson, Fiona (1965—)
Simpson, Helen (1897–1940)
Skinner, Mollie (1876–1955)
Skirving, Angie (1981—)
Slatter, Kate (1971—)
Small, Kim (1965—)
Small, Mary Elizabeth (1812/13–1908)
Smith, Bill (1886–1975)
Smith, Christine Anne (1946—)
Smith, Grace Cossington (1892–1984)
Smylie, Elizabeth (1963—)
Snell, Belinda (1981—)
Soper, Eileen Louise (1900–1989)
Spence, Catherine (1825–1910)
Spence, Judith (1957—)
Spender, Dale (1943—)
Sperrey, Eleanor Catherine (1862–1893)
Sporn, Rachael (1968—)
Starr, Muriel (1888–1950)
Starre, Katie (1971—)
Stead, Christina (1902–1983)
Steele, Joyce
Steggall, Zali (1974—)
Steinbeck, Janet (1951—)
Stephenson, Jan (1951—)
Stevenson, Nicole (1971—)
Stewart, Frances Ann (1840–1916)
Stewart, Nellie (1858–1931)
Still, Megan (1972—)
Stone, Barbara Gwendoline (1962—)
Stone, Constance (1856–1902)
Stones, Margaret (1920—)
Stowell, Belinda (1971—)
Strauss, Jennifer (1933—)
Street, Jessie (1889–1970)
Strickland, Shirley (1925–2004)

Struthers, Karen Lee (1963—)
Suckling, Sophia Lois (1893–1990)
Sullivan, Carryn (1955—)
Summerton, Laura (1983—)
Sutherland, Joan (1926—)
Sutherland, Lucy Stuart (1903–1980)
Sutherland, Margaret (1897–1984)
Sutherland, Margaret (1941—)
Sutherland, Selina Murray McDonald (1839–1909)
Sykes, Bobbi (1943—)
Tangney, Dorothy (1911–1985)
Taylor, Florence M. (1879–1969)
Taylor, Penny (1981—)
Taylor, Rachael (1976—)
Taylor, Valerie (1935—)
Taylor-Smith, Shelley (1961—)
Tennant, Kylie (1912–1988)
Teske, Rachel (1972—)
Texidor, Greville (1902–1964)
Thomas, Petria (1975—)
Thompson, Freda (1906–1980)
Thomson, Kirsten (1983—)
Thorn, Robyn (1945—)
Thrower, Norma (1936—)
Timms, Michelle (1965—)
Titcume, Natalie (1975—)
Titheradge, Madge (1887–1961)
Tooth, Liane (1962—)
Tourky, Loudy (1979—)
Towers, Julie (1976—)
Tracy, Mona Innis (1892–1959)
Travers, P.L. (1906–1996)
Trevor-Jones, Mabel (fl. 1904–1921)
Truganini (1812–1876)
Turnbull, Wendy (1952—)
Turner, Ethel (1872–1958)
Turner, Lesley (1942—)
Tyler-Sharman, Lucy (1965—)
Vasey, Jessie (1897–1966)
Vernon, Barbara (1916–1978)
Vickery, Joyce (1908–1979)
Vidal, Mary Theresa (1815–1869 or 1873)
Vincent, Mother (1819–1892)
Vitelli, Annie (c. 1837–?)
Waddy, Charis (1909–2004)
Walker, Kath (1920–1993)
Ward, Natalie (1975—)
Warner, Anne Marie (1945—)
Warwick, Lyn (1946—)
Watson, Ada (1859–1921)
Watson, Debbie (1965—)
Watson, Lynette (1952—)
Watt, Kathryn (1964—)
Webb, Karrie (1974—)
Weekes, Liz (1971—)
West, Winifred (1881–1971)
Wetmore, Joan (1911–1989)
Whitfield, Beverly (1954–1996)
Whitlam, Margaret (1919—)
Whittle, Jenny (1973—)
Wilkins, Brooke (1974—)
Williams, Matilda Alice (1875–1973)
Wilson, Anne Glenny (1848–1930)
Wilson, Marilyn (1943—)
Wilson, Naomi (1940—)
Windeyer, Mary (1836–1912)
Winn, Anona (1907–1994)
Wiseman, Hilda Alexandra (1894–1982)
Wood, Anna (1966—)
Wood, Susan (1836–1880)
Woodgate, Margaret (1935—)
Woodhouse, Danielle
Woods, Taryn (1975—)
Woodward, Danielle (1965—)
Wright, Judith (1915–2000)
Wrightson, Patricia (1921—)
Wyborn, Kerry (1977—)
Wylie, Ida A.R. (1885–1959)
Wylie, Wilhelmina (1892–1984)
Wylie, Wilhelmina (b. 1892)
Yurina, Esfir (1923—)
Zwi, Rose (1928—)
Zwicky, Fay (1933—)

AUSTRALIAN ABORIGINE

Archer, Caroline Lilian (1922–1978)
Bandler, Faith (1918—)
Cameron, Bessy (c. 1851–1895)
Freeman, Cathy (1973—)
Goolagong Cawley, Evonne (1951—)
Morgan, Sally (1951—)
Peris-Kneebone, Nova (1971—)
Sykes, Bobbi (1943—)
Walker, Kath (1920–1993)

AUSTRASIA

Eastern part of Kingdom of the Franks (6th c.)
Kingdom with Neustria (6th c.)
Ceased to exist in Frankish Empire (c. 8th c.)
See also Franks, Kingdom of the.

Bilchilde (d. 675)
Brunhilda (c. 533–613)
Deoteria (fl. 535)
Faileuba (fl. 586–587)
Gerberge of the Lombards (fl. mid–700s)
Himnechildis (r. 662–675)
Matilda (fl. 680s)
Nanthilde (610–642)
Plectrudis (fl. 665–717)
Ragnetrude (fl. 630)
Suavegotta (fl. 504)
Theudesinda (fl. 700)
Vuldetrade (fl. 550)
Wulfetrud of Nivelles

AUSTRIA

Central European republic
Conquered by Rome (1st c. BCE)
Invaded by Huns (5th c.)
Settled by Slovenes as Kingdom of Avars (6th c.)
Established as East Mark by Charlemagne (8th c.)
Part of Holy Roman Empire (10th c.)
Became independent duchy under Habsburgs (12th c.)
Claimed by Bohemia (13th c.)
Ruled by Spain (16th c.)
Ruled Slavonia, Transylvania, and most of Hungary (17th c.)
Ruled Spanish Netherlands, Sardinia, and Naples (18th c.)
Became Austrian Empire (19th c.)
Defeated by Prussia (19th c.)
Incorporated into German Reich (1938–1945)
Reestablished as Republic (1945)
Occupied by U.S., U.S.S.R., Great Britain, and France (1945–1955)
Declared neutral state (1955)
See also Germany.
See also Prussia.

Adamson, Joy (1910–1980)
Adler, Emma (1858–1935)
Adler, Margarete (1896–?)
Adler, Valentine (1898–1942)
Adolf, Helen (b. 1895)
Agnes of Austria (1281–1364)
Agnes of Austria (fl. 1100s)
Agnes of Bohemia (1269–1297)
Aichinger, Ilse (1921—)
Alexandra Guelph (1882–1963)
Alexandra Pavlovna (1783–1801)
Anderson, Erica (1914–1976)
Anna of Styria (1573–1598)
Anne of Austria (1432–1462)
Anne of Austria (c. 1550–1580)
Arnstein, Fanny von (1758–1818)
Auer, Johanna (1950—)
Augusta of Tuscany (1825–1864)
Bach, Maria (1896–1978)
Bachmann, Ingeborg (1926–1973)
Bahr-Mildenburg, Anna (1872–1947)
Baudisch-Wittke, Gudrun (1907–1982)
Bauer, Helene (1871–1942)
Bauer, Margaret (1927—)
Bauma, Herma (1915–2003)
Bayer, Johanna (1915–2000)
Beatrice of Brandenburg (1360–1414)
Beiser, Trude (1927—)
Berger, Maria (1956—)
Berger, Senta (1941—)
Bergner, Elisabeth (1897–1986)
Blahetka, Marie Leopoldine (1811–1887)
Bleibtreu, Hedwig (1868–1958)
Bodenwieser, Gertrud (1886–1959)
Boschek, Anna (1874–1957)
Bosco, Monique (1927—)
Brandt, Marianne (1842–1921)
Breden, Christiane von (1839–1901)
Brexner, Edeltraud (1927—)
Brown, Vanessa (1928–1999)
Bruha, Antonia (1915—)
Brüll, Ilse (1925–1942)
Brunner, Josefine (1909–1943)
Brunner, Melitta (1907—)
Bühler, Charlotte (1893–1974)
Burger, Fritzi
Burger, Hildegard (1905–1943)
Burjan, Hildegard (1883–1933)
Busta, Christine (1914–1987)
Cappiani, Luisa (b. 1835)
Carnegie, Hattie (1886–1956)
Caroline of Austria (1801–1832)
Catherine (c. 1420–1493)
Catherine of Burgundy (1378–1425)
Cavalieri, Caterina (1760–1801)
Cerri, Cecilie (1872–1931)
Chotek, Sophie (1868–1914)
Christians, Mady (1900–1951)
Cimburca of Masovia (c. 1396–1429)
Clotilde of Saxe-Coburg-Gotha (1846–1927)
Cremer, Erika (1900–1996)
Delle Grazie, Marie Eugenie (1864–1931)
Demel, Anna (1872–1956)
Dernesch, Helga (1939—)
Dessoff, Margarethe (1874–1944)
Dicker-Brandeis, Friedl (1898–1944)
D'Or, Henrietta (1844–1886)
Dorfmeister, Michaela (1973—)
Drexel, Wiltrud (1950—)
Duczynska, Ilona (1897–1978)
Ebner-Eschenbach, Marie (1830–1916)
Echerer, Raina A. Mercedes (1963—)
Eder, Elfriede (1970—)
Egger, Sabine (1977—)
Ehre, Ida (1900–1989)
Eisinger, Irene (1903–1994)
Eisler, Charlotte (1894–1970)
Elizabeth (1831–1903)
Elizabeth (fl. 1850s)
Elizabeth of Bavaria (1837–1898)
Elizabeth of Bohemia (1358–1373)
Elisabeth of Habsburg (1554–1592)
Elizabeth of Luxemburg (1409–1442)
Elizabeth of Savoy-Carignan (1800–1856)
Elizabeth von Habsburg (1883–1963)
Elssler, Fanny (1810–1884)
Elssler, Thérèse (1808–1878)
Emhart, Maria (1901–1981)
Engelmann, Helene

Geographic Index

Fickert, Auguste (1855–1910)
Fittko, Lisa (1909–2005)
Flemming, Marialiese (1933—)
Flöge, Emilie (1874–1952)
Frandl, Josefine
Freist, Greta (1904–1993)
Frenkel-Brunswik, Else (1908–1958)
Freud, Anna (1895–1982)
Freundlich, Emmy (1878–1948)
Frischmuth, Barbara (1941—)
Fussenegger, Gertrud (1912—)
Gabl, Gertrud (1948–1976)
Geistinger, Marie (1833–1903)
Gessner, Adrienne (1896–1987)
Gies, Miep (b. 1909)
Gisela (1856–1932)
Goetschl, Renate (1975—)
Gonzaga, Anna Caterina (1566–1621)
Graf, Stephanie (1973—)
Gregor, Nora (1901–1949)
Greiffenberg, Catharina Regina von (1633–1694)
Grogger, Paula (1892–1984)
Gueden, Hilde (1915–1988)
Gusenbauer, Ilona (1947—)
Gyring, Elizabeth (1906–1970)
Haas, Christl (1943–2001)
Haebler, Ingrid (1926—)
Hainisch, Marianne (1839–1936)
Hammerer, Resi (1925—)
Handel-Mazzetti, Enrica von (1871–1955)
Hanka, Erika (1905–1958)
Harand, Irene (1900–1975)
Haselbach, Anna Elisabeth (1942—)
Haushofer, Marlen (1920–1970)
Heberle, Thérèse (1806–1840)
Hecher, Traudl (1943—)
Heill, Claudia (1982—)
Heitzer, Regine (fl. 1960s)
Hieden-Sommer, Helga (1934—)
Hildegarde of Bavaria (1825–1864)
Hochleitner, Dorothea
Hofmann, Elise (1889–1955)
Huber, Gusti (1914–1993)
Hug-Hellmuth, Hermine (1871–1924)
Hunyady, Emese (1966—)
Ida of Austria (d. 1101?)
Ileana (1909–1991)
Jacquetta of Luxemburg (c. 1416–1472)
Jahoda, Marie (1907–2001)
Janitschek, Maria (1859–1927)
Janko, Eva (1945—)
Jelinek, Elfriede (1946—)
Joanna of Austria (1535–1573)
Joanna of Austria (1546–1578)
Jochmann, Rosa (1901–1994)
Johanna of Bavaria (c. 1373–1410)
Johanna of Pfirt (1300–1351)
Kallir, Lilian (1931–2004)
Kann, Edith (1907–1987)
Kaus, Gina (1894–1985)
Kautsky, Luise (1864–1944)
Kautsky, Minna (1837–1912)
Kiesl, Theresia (1963—)
Klein, Melanie (1882–1960)
Koeck, Brigitte
Konetzni, Anny (1902–1968)
Konetzni, Hilde (1905–1980)
König, Alma Johanna (1887–c. 1942)
Köstler, Marie (1879–1965)
Kottanner, Helene (fl. 1440)
Kraus, Greta (1907–1998)
Krauss, Gertrud (1903–1977)
Kronberger, Petra (1969—)
Kulcsar, Ilse (1902–1973)
Kunke, Steffi (1908–1942)
Kurz, Selma (1874–1933)
Lamarr, Hedy (1913–2000)
Landi, Elissa (1904–1948)
Lang, Marie (1858–1934)
Lanner, Katti (1829–1908)
Lavant, Christine (1915–1973)
Leichter, Käthe (1895–1942)
Lenya, Lotte (1898–1981)
Liebhart, Gertrude (1928—)
Lingens-Reiner, Ella (1908–2002)
Losch, Tilly (1903–1975)
Lucca, Pauline (1841–1908)
Mahler, Alma (1879–1964)
Mahringer, Erika (1924—)
Maier, Ulrike (1967–1994)
Mandel, Maria (1912–1948)
Marek, Martha Lowenstein (1904–1938)
Margaret (1395–1447)
Margaret of Austria (c. 1577–1611)
Margaret of Babenberg (fl. 1252)
Margaret Sophie (1870–1902)
Maria Amalia (1724–1730)
Maria Anna (1718–1744)
Maria Anna of Savoy (1803–1884)
Maria Annunziata (1843–1871)
Maria Annunziata (1876–1961)
Maria Christina (1742–1798)
Maria Cristina of Sicily (1877–1947)
Maria Immaculata of Sicily (1844–1899)
Maria Josepha of Bavaria (1739–1767)
Maria Josepha of Saxony (1867–1944)
Maria Louisa of Spain (1745–1792)
Maria Ludovica of Modena (1787–1816)
Maria Magdalena (1689–1743)
Maria of Austria (1584–1649)
Maria of Wurttemberg (1797–1855)
Maria Theresa of Portugal (1855–1944)
Marie Antoinette (1755–1793)
Marie-Ileana (1933–1959)
Marie of Austria (1528–1603)
Marie Valerie (1868–1924)
Martinez, Marianne (1744–1812)
Massary, Fritzi (1882–1969)
Materna, Amalie (1844–1918)
Mayreder, Rosa (1858–1938)
Mayröcker, Friederike (1924—)
Meissnitzer, Alexandra (1973—)
Meitner, Lise (1878–1968)
Milch, Klara (1891—)
Milder-Hauptmann, Anna (1785–1838)
Model, Lisette (1901–1983)
Monte, Hilda (1914–1945)
Morath, Inge (1923–2002)
Morini, Erica (1904–1995)
Morley, Ruth (1925–1991)
Morpurgo, Rachel (1790–1871)
Mozart, Maria Anna (1751–1829)
Neuner, Angelika (1969—)
Neuner, Doris (1970—)
Niese, Hansi (1875–1934)
Noach, Ilse (1908–1998)
Nöstlinger, Christine (1936—)
Pachler-Koschak, Marie (1792–1855)
Pagliero, Camilia (1859–1925)
Pall, Olga (1947—)
Palmer, Maria (1917–1981)
Paoli, Betty (1814–1894)
Paradis, Maria Theresia von (1759–1824)
Pauli, Hertha (1909–1973)
Pausin, Ilse (1919—)
Pawlik, Eva (1927–1983)
Pfeiffer, Ida (1797–1858)
Pichler, Karoline (1769–1843)
Piscator, Maria Ley (1899–1999)
Planck-Szabó, Herma (1902–1986)
Pockels, Agnes (1862–1935)
Poetzl, Ine (1976—)
Popp, Adelheid (1869–1939)
Preis, Ellen (1912—)
Preradovic, Paula von (1887–1951)
Prets, Christa (1947—)
Pringle, Mia Lilly (1920–1983)
Proell-Moser, Annemarie (1953—)
Prokop, Liese (1941—)
Pühringer, Uta Barbara (1943—)
Rainer, Luise (1910—)
Rapoport, Lydia (1923–1971)
Rasch, Albertina (1896–1967)
Raschhofer, Daniela (1960—)
Rehor, Grete (1910–1987)
Restituta, Sister (1894–1943)
Richter, Elise (1865–1943)
Rie, Lucie (1902–1995)
Rom, Dagmar (1928—)
Rosa (1906–1983)
Rosé, Alma (1906–1944)
Rudel-Zeynek, Olga (1871–1948)
Ruttner-Kolisko, Agnes (1911–1991)
Rysanek, Leonie (1926–1998)
Sacher, Anna (1859–1930)
Schaffer, Ine (1923—)
Scheele, Karin (1968—)
Scheff, Fritzi (1879–1954)
Schell, Maria (1926–2005)
Schierhuber, Agnes (1946—)
Schlamme, Martha (1922–1985)
Schlesinger, Therese (1863–1940)
Schneider, Romy (1938–1982)
Scholz, Lilly
Schöpf, Regina
Schratt, Katharina (1853–1940)
Schreiber, Adele (1872–1957)
Schuba, Beatrix (1951—)
Schütte-Lihotzky, Margarete (1897–2000)
Schutting, Julian (1937—)
Schwarz, Elisabeth (1936—)
Schwarz, Vera (1888–1964)
Schwarzwald, Eugenie (1872–1940)
Seidel, Amalie (1876–1952)
Seidl, Lea (1895–1987)
Sirota, Beate (1923—)
Skala, Lilia (1896–1994)
Sobotka, Ruth (1925–1967)
Somer, Hilde (1922–1979)
Sophie of Bavaria (1805–1872)
Spiel, Hilde (1911–1990)
Spira, Steffie (1908–1995)
Stallmaier, Veronika (1966—)
Stein, Marion (1926—)
Steinbach, Sabina von (fl. 13th c.)
Stenzel, Ursula (1945—)
Stewart, Eleanor (1427–1496)
Sticker, Josephine (1894—)
Stockert-Meynert, Dora von (1870–1947)
Stradner, Rose (1913–1958)
Suttner, Bertha von (1843–1914)
Tagwerker, Andrea
Theurer, Elisabeth (1956—)
Thimig, Helene (1889–1974)
Thurner, Helene
Ticho, Anna (1894–1980)
Tiller, Nadja (1929—)
Todd, Olga Taussky (1906–1995)
Toselli, Louisa (1870–1947)
Totschnig, Brigitte (1954—)
Troll-Borostyani, Irma von (1847–1912)
Tschitschko, Helene (1908–1992)
Tudor-Hart, Edith (1908–1978)
Uhl, Frida (1872–1943)
Ullrich, Luise (1911–1985)
Unger, Caroline (1803–1877)
Uta of Passau (fl. 11th c.)

Vetsera, Marie (1871–1889)
Visconti, Virida (c. 1354–1414)
Von Ertmann, Dorothea (1781–1849)
Von Trapp, Maria (1905–1987)
Wachter, Anita (1967—)
Waldmann, Maria (1842–1920)
Wander, Maxie (1933–1977)
Weigel, Helene (1900–1971)
Weigl, Vally (1889–1982)
Weiss, Josephine (1805–1852)
Wendl, Ingrid (1940—)
Werbezirk, Gisela (1875–1956)
Wessely, Paula (1907–2000)
Wied, Martina (1882–1957)
Wiesenthal, Grete (1885–1970)
Wilhelmina of Brunswick (1673–1742)
Wolf, Sigrid (1964—)
Wolter, Charlotte (1834–1897)
Ylla (1911–1955)
Zahourek, Berta (1896–1967)
Zeisler, Fannie Bloomfield (1863–1927)
Zimmermann, Edith
Zimmermann, Heidi (1946—)
Zita of Parma (1892–1989)
Zoff, Marianne (1893–1984)
Zur Mühlen, Hermynia (1883–1951)

AUSTRIA-HUNGARY

Former monarchy in central Europe
Restored partial Hungarian autonomy over Austria, Hungary, and Czechoslovakia, Bukovina and Transylvania in Romania, part of Yugoslavia, Galicia in Poland, and part of Italy (1867)
Administered Turkish provinces of Bosnia and Herzegovina (1908)
Issued ultimatum to Serbia after assassination of Archduke Francis Ferdinand, leading to World War I (1914)
See Austria.
See Hungary.

AUVERGNE

Historical region of south-central France
Defeated by Visigoths (5th c.)
Conquered by Clovis (6th c.)
Part of Aquitaine (6th–7th c.)
Became countship (8th c.)
Divided into four lordships (14th c.)
Passed to Bourbons (15th c.)
Passed to France (16th c.)
See France.

AXUM

Ethiopian region
See Ethiopia.

AZERBAIJAN

Former province of northwest Iran and U.S.S.R.
Near East independent state
Ruled by Macedonians and Persians (before 7th c.)
Part of Byzantine Empire (7th c.)
Ruled by Arabs (7th c.)
Ruled by Seljuks (11th c.)
Ruled by Mongols (13th–15th c.)
Annexed by Russia (19th c.)
Part of the Transcaucasian Republic (1917–1918)
Became Azerbaijan Soviet Socialist Republic (1922)
Became independent state (1991)

Ali-Zadeh, Franghiz (1947—)
Arsiennieva, Natalia (1903—)
Ashumova, Irada (1958—)
Meftakhetdinova, Zemfira (1963—)

AZTEC EMPIRE

Central Mexican civilization

Tecuichpo (d. 1551)

BABYLONIA

City-kingdom (21st–18th c. BCE)
Conquered Mesopotamia (20th c. BCE)
Ruled by Kassite Dynasty (18th–12th c. BCE)
Rules by Elamite Dynasty (12th–8th c. BCE)
Ruled by Assyria (8th–7th c. BCE)
Ruled by Persia (6th–4th c. BCE)
See also Iran.

Enheduanna (fl. 2300 BCE)
Inanna (fl. c. 3000 BCE)
Nitocris (fl. 6th c. BCE)
Panthea (?–c. 545 BCE)

BACTRIA

Ancient country of southwest Asia
Part of Persian Empire (6th c. BCE)
Conquered by Alexander the Great (4th c. BCE)
Ruled by Seleucid Empire (4th c. BCE)
Kingdom destroyed by invasions (2nd c. BCE)

Apama (fl. 324 BCE)
Roxane (c. 345–310 BCE)

BADEN

Former German state
Became electorate (1803)
Became grand duchy (1805)
Supported Austria against Prussia (1866)
Joined German Empire (1871)
Proclaimed a republic (1918)
Southern part became state of West Germany (1949)
Northern part incorporated in Württemberg-Baden (1951)
See Germany.

BAHAMAS

Clarke, Eldece (1965—)
Davis-Thompson, Pauline (1966—)
Ferguson, Debbie (1976—)
Fynes, Sevatheda (1974—)
Michael, Julia Warner (b. 1879)
Sturrup, Chandra (1971—)
Williams, Tonique (1976—)

BANGLADESH

Former East Pakistan
Part of Bengal
See also India.

Nasrin, Taslima (1962—)

BAR

Historic town in Podolia, a Lithuania possession (16th c.)
Held briefly by Poland (16th c.)
Held by Turkey (17th c.)
Part of Russia in First Partition of Poland (1793)
See Russia.

BARBADOS

Probably discovered by Portugal (16th c.)
Became colony of England (17th c.)
Warred with England, France, and Spain (17th–18th c.)
Member of West Indies Federation (1958–1962)
Achieved independence (1966)

Barrow, Nita (1916–1995)

BARI

Province of Apulia, Italy
Dominated by Goths, Greeks, Saracens, Byzantines, Normans, Germans, and Venetians
Part of Kingdom of Naples (16th c.)
See Italy.

BASRA

City in Iraq
See Iraq.

BAVARIA

Conquered by Rome (1st c. BCE)
Part of Kingdom of the Franks (6th c.)
Became a duchy in Holy Roman Empire (c. 10th c.)
Bavarian East Mark became duchy of Austria (11th c.)
Awarded to House of Wittelsbach (12th c.)
Divided into Upper and Lower Bavaria (13th c.)
Became electorate (17th c.)
United with Palatinate (18th c.)
Joined Austria in war against Prussia (19th c.)
Joined North German Confederation and German Empire (19th c.)
Became a republic (1918); abolished by National Socialist Regime (1933)
Occupied by U.S. (1945); adopted new constitution (1946)

Adelgunde of Bavaria (1823–1914)
Agnes of Looss (fl. 1150–1175)
Agnes of Poitou (1024–1077)
Agnes of Saxony (fl. 1200s)
Amalia of Bavaria (1801–1877)
Amalie Auguste (1788–1851)
Amalie of Saxe-Coburg-Gotha (1848–1894)
Anna of Brunswick (1528–1590)
Anna of Brunswick (fl. 1400s)
Anna of Silesia (fl. 1200s)
Catherine of Cleves (fl. 1550s)
Cunigunde Sobieska (fl. 1690s)
Elizabeth of Silesia (fl. 1257)
Folcheid (fl. 7th c.)
Gisela of Burgundy (d. 1006)
Guntrud of Bavaria (fl. 715)
Hedwig of Silesia (1174–1243)
Margaret of Cleves (fl. early 1400s)
Maria Anna of Bavaria (1610–1665)
Maria Antonia (1669–1692)
Maria Francisca of Sulzbach (fl. 18th c.)
Maria Gabriele of Bavaria (1878–1912)
Maria of Prussia (1825–1889)
Maria Sophia Amalia (1841–1925)
Maria Teresa of Este (1849–1919)
Matilda of Bavaria (fl. 1300s)
Oda of Bavaria (fl. 890s)
Pichler, Magdalena (1881–1920)
Regintrud (fl. 8th c.)
Sophia of Bavaria (fl. 1390s–1400s)
Sophie of Bavaria (1805–1872)
Sophie of Bayern (1847–1897)
Sunnichild (d. 741)
Suzanne of Bavaria (1502–1543)
Theresa of Saxony (1792–1854)
Visconti, Elizabeth (d. 1432)
Visconti, Thaddaea (d. 1381)
Wilhelmine of Darmstadt (1765–1796)
Wolfida of Saxony (c. 1075–1126)
Wuldetrada of the Lombards
Zwanziger, Anna (1760–1811)

BAYREUTH

City in West Germany
Founded (1194)
Ruled by Prussia (1791)
Taken by Napoleon (1806)
Became part of Bavaria (1810)
See Bavaria.
See Germany.
See Prussia.

BEAUJEU

City in Burgundy, France
See France.

BEDFORD

Borough of Bedfordshire in southeastern central England
See England.

Geographic Index

BEIRA

Former province of Portugal
See Portugal.

BELARUS

Became Polotsk after breakup of Kiev (11th c.)
Became Grand Duchy of Lithuania (13th c.)
United with Poland in a confederation (14th c.)
Became territory of Belorussia after partitions of Russia, Prussia, and Austria (18th c.)
Became Belorusian National Republic (1918)
Became Belorussian Soviet Socialist Republic (1919)
Western Belorussia absorbed by Poland; central part remained Belorussian S.S.R.; eastern part became part of Russia (1921)
Belorussian S.S.R. incorporated into the Soviet Union (1933)
Became independent Belarus (1991)
See also Poland.
See also Russia.

Ananko, Tatyana (1984—)
Arbatova, Mia (c. 1910—)
Arsiennieva, Natalia (1903—)
Arzhannikova, Tatiana (1964—)
Baitova, Svetlana (1972—)
Batsiushka, Hanna (1981—)
Belan, Tatyana (1982—)
Bichyk, Yuliya (1983—)
Boginskaya, Svetlana (1973—)
Davydenko, Tamara
Glazkova, Anna (1981—)
Helakh, Natallia (1978—)
Ilyenkova, Irina (1980—)
Khodotovich, Ekaterina (1972—)
Korolchik, Yanina (1976—)
Lavrinenko, Natalya
Lazakovich, Tamara (1954—)
Lazuk, Maria (1983—)
Mikulich, Alena (1977—)
Milchina, Lolita
Mishkutenok, Natalia (1970—)
Nesterenko, Yuliya (1979—)
Pankina, Aleksandra
Paramygina, Svetlana (1965—)
Pavlina, Yevgenia (1979—)
Pavlovich, Yaroslava
Petrik, Larissa (1949—)
Piskun, Elena (1978—)
Polozkova, Alëna (1979—)
Puzhevich, Olga (1983—)
Raskina, Yulia (1982—)
Sazanovich, Natalya (1973—)
Skrabatun, Valentina (1958—)
Stasyuk, Natalia (1969—)
Stukalava, Tatsiana (1975—)
Tsuper, Alla (c. 1980—)
Tsylinskaya, Natallia (1975—)
Volchek, Natalya
Yatchenko, Irina (1965—)
Yurkina, Olga (1976—)
Znak, Marina (1961—)
Zvereva, Ellina (1960—)
Zvereva, Natasha (1971—)

BELGIAN CONGO

See Congo.

BELGICA

Ancient country in Northeast Gallia
One of five administrative areas of Gaul
See Belgium.

BELGIUM

Roman province of Belgica (1st c. BCE)
Part of Carolingian kingdom of Lotharingia
Duchy of Flanders became dependency of France
Attached to medieval empire as duchy of Lower Lorraine
Broke into territories of the Netherlands (15th c.)
United into Burgundy, ruled by the Habsburgs (15th c.)
Ruled by Spanish Habsburgs (16th c.)
Territories lost to Spain and France (17th c.)
Territories reunited to Holland as independent kingdom of the Netherlands (19th c.)
Invaded by Germany (1914)
Occupied by Nazi Germany (1940)
Liberated by Allies (1944)

Adelaide of Schaerbeck (d. 1250)
Adelicia of Louvain (c. 1102–1151)
Akerman, Chantal (1950—)
Aldegund (c. 630–684)
Antoinette of Luxemburg (1899–1954)
Artôt, Désirée (1835–1907)
Astrid of Sweden (1905–1935)
Baels, Liliane (1916–2002)
Beatrice of Nazareth (c. 1200–1268)
Beck, Beatrix (1914—)
Becker, Marie Alexander (1877–194?)
Begga (613–698)
Berghmans, Ingrid (1961—)
Bervoets, Marguerite (1914–1944)
Bol Poel, Martha (1877–1956)
Bovy, Berthe (1887–1977)
Brabants, Jeanne (1920—)
Bredael, Annelies (1965—)
Callens, Els (1970—)
Carlota (1840–1927)
Claiborne, Liz (1929—)
Clementine of Belgium (1872–1955)
Clijsters, Kim (1983—)
Coombs, Claire (1974—)
Cornescou, Irina Soltanovna (1916—)
Danco, Suzanne (1911–2000)
Daubechies, Ingrid (1954—)
de Jongh, Andree (1916—)
De Keersmaeker, Anne Teresa (1960—)
De Keyser, Véronique (1945—)
D'Or, Henrietta (1844–1886)
Dutrieu, Hélène (1877–1961)
Elizabeth of Bavaria (1876–1965)
Ermesind of Luxemburg (d. 1247)
Fabiola (1928—)
Fontyn, Jacqueline (1930—)
Francis, Eve (1886–1980)
Frassoni, Monica (1963—)
French, Francesca (1871–1960)
Gollner, Nana (1919–1980)
Gorr, Rita (1926—)
Gudula of Brussels (d. 712?)
Haesebrouck, Ann (1963—)
Heldy, Fanny (1888–1973)
Henin-Hardenne, Justine (1982—)
Henrietta of Belgium (1870–1948)
Herlind of Maasryck (fl. 8th c.)
Heylen, Ilse (1977—)
Heymans, Emilie (1981—)
Ida of Nivelles (d. 1232)
Ivetta of Huy (1158–1228)
Josephine-Charlotte of Belgium (1927—)
Josephine of Belgium (1872–1958)
Lannoy, Micheline
Lecompte, Eugenie Anna (c. 1798–c. 1850)
Lempereur, Ingrid (1969—)
Lomba, Marisabel
Louise d'Orléans (1812–1850)
Louise of Belgium (1858–1924)
Loveling, Virginie (1836–1923)
Maes, Nelly (1941—)
Mallet-Joris, Françoise (1930—)
Margaret of Austria (1480–1530)
Maria Henrietta of Austria (1836–1902)
Marlowe, Missy (1971—)
Mary of Oignies (1177–1213)
Mathilde of Belgium (1973—)
McKenna, Marthe (1893–1969)
Nevejean, Yvonne (1900–1987)
Paemel, Monika van (1945—)
Paola (1937—)
Poelvoorde, Rita (1951—)
Rakels, Heidi (1968—)
Richilde (1034–1086)
Ries, Frédérique (1959—)
Sass, Marie Constance (1834–1907)
Scepens, Elizabeth (fl. 1476)
Simons, Ann (1980—)
Smet, Miet (1943—)
Sophia of Malines (d. 1329)
Sorensen, Patsy (1952—)
Stephanie of Belgium (1864–1945)
Thyssen, Marianne L.P. (1956—)
Van Brempt, Kathleen (1969—)
Vandecaveye, Gella (1973—)
Van Lancker, Anne E.M. (1954—)
van Roost, Dominique (1973—)
von Furstenberg, Diane (1946—)
Wademant, Annette (1928—)
Wandru (c. 628–688)
Werbrouck, Ulla (1972—)
Wulfetrud of Nivelles
Zrihen, Olga (1953—)

BENGAL

Ancient Hindu region and former province of northeast British India
Center of Maurya and Gupta Empires (3rd c.)
Conquered by Afghans (12th c.)
Taken from Afghans by Moguls (16th c.)
Calcutta founded by the English (17th c.)
Made autonomous province (20th c.)
Divided into East Bengal (Bangladesh) and West Bengal, part of India (1947)
See India.

BENIN

Formerly part of Upper Guinea, West Africa
Name given by French to their territory on Guinea coast
See Dahomey.

BERMUDA

British colony of c. 300 islands in western North Atlantic Ocean
Visited by Spanish (16th c.)
Colonized by English (17th c.)
Adopted constitution (1968)

Prince, Mary (c. 1788–after 1833)

BIBLICAL WORLD, WOMEN OF

Abigail (fl. 1000 BCE)
Abigail (fl. 1010 BCE)
Abihail (fl. 970 BCE)
Abishag of Shunem (fl. 1000 BCE)
Abital (fl. 1000 BCE)
Adah
Agape of Thessalonica (d. 304)
Asenath
Bashemath (fl. 900 BCE)
Bathsheba (fl. 1010–975 BCE)
Berenice (c. 35 BCE–?)
Bilhah
Chionia of Thessalonica (d. 304)
Claudia (fl. 26–36)
Cypros (fl. 28)
Cyprus (c. 90 BCE–?)
Deborah (fl. 12th c. BCE)
Delilah (1200–1000 BCE?)
Dinah (fl. 1730 BCE)
Dorcas (fl. 37)

Eglah (fl. 1000 BCE)
Elisheba
Elizabeth (fl. 1st c.)
Esther (fl. 475 BCE)
Eunice
Eve
Hagar (fl. 3rd, 2nd, or 1st c. BCE)
Haggith (fl. 1000 BCE)
Hannah (fl. 11th c. BCE)
Huldah
Irene of Thessalonica (d. 304)
Iscah
Jael (fl. c. 1125 BCE)
Jecholiah
Jedidah
Jehudijah
Jemima
Jerusha
Jezebel (d. 884 BCE)
Joanna
Jochebed
Judith (fl. early 6th c. BCE)
Keturah (fl. 3rd, 2nd, or 1st c. BCE)
Keziah (fl. 2000 BCE)
Lois
Lo-Ruhamah
Lydia (fl. 53)
Maacah (fl. 931 BCE)
Maachah (fl. 1575 BCE)
Mahlah
Malthace (fl. 40 BCE)
Mariamne (fl. 1st c.)
Mariamne the Hasmonian (c. 60–c. 29 BCE)
Martha of Bethany (fl. early 1st c.)
Mary Magdalene (fl. early 1st c.)
Mary of Bethany (fl. early 1st c.)
Mary of Cleophas
Mary of Jerusalem
Mary the Virgin (20 BCE–40 CE)
Mehetabel
Merab (fl. 1000 BCE)
Meshullemeth
Michal (fl. 1000 BCE)
Milcah
Miriam
Miriam the Prophet (fl. c. 13th or 14th c. BCE)
Naamah (fl. 900 BCE)
Naamah
Naarah
Naomi (fl. 1100 BCE)
Nehushta (fl. 610 BCE)
Noadiah
Noah
Orpah (fl. 1100 BCE)
Peninnah
Persis
Rahab (fl. 1100 BCE)
Rhoda
Rizpah
Ruth (fl. 1100 BCE)
Salome (fl. 65–20 BCE)
Salome II (fl. 1st c.)
Salome III (c. 15–?)
Sambethe
Sapphira (fl. 1st c.)
Sarah (fl. 3rd, 2nd, or 1st c. BCE)
Susanna (fl. 6th c. BCE)
Syntyche
Syro-Phoenician
Tamar (fl. 1000 BCE)
Tamar (fl. 1100 BCE)
Tirzah
Zilpah
Zipporah

BITHYNIA

Ancient country in northwest Asia Minor
Settled by Thracians
Nicomedia founded (264 BCE)
Became Roman province (74 BCE)
Divided into two parts under Byzantine Empire
See Asia Minor.

BLOIS

City in Loir-et-Cher department of northern central France
See France.

BOEOTIA

District and ancient republic in eastern central Greece
Inhabited by Aeolians from Thessaly
Boeotian League formed (c. 600–550 BCE)
Forced to join Delian League (457 BCE)
Defeated Athenians (424 BCE)
Dominated Greece (371 BCE)
See Greece.

BOHEMIA

Settled by Slavic people (5th c.)
Part of Kingdom of Moravia (c. 10th c.)
Became electorate in Holy Roman Empire (12th c.)
Ruled by Austria (16th–20th c.)
Part of German protectorate of Bohemia and Moravia (1939)
Became province of Czechoslovakia (1945)
Became part of Czech Soviet Republic (1968)
See also Czechoslovakia.
See also Germany.

Adelaide of Hungary (d. 1062)
Agnes of Bohemia (1205–1282)
Agnes of Bohemia (1269–1297)
Anna of Bohemia (fl. 1230s)
Anna of Bohemia (fl. 1318)
Anna of Bohemia and Hungary (1503–1547)
Anne of Bohemia (1366–1394)
Barbara of Cilli (fl. 1390–1410)
Bona of Bohemia (1315–1349)
Černínová z Harasova, Zuzana (1601–1654)
Constance of Hungary (d. 1240)
Cunigunde of Bohemia (d. 1321)
Cunigunde of Hohenstaufen (fl. 1215–1230)
Cunigunde of Hungary (d. 1285)
Drahomira of Bohemia (d. after 932)
Elizabeth of Bohemia (1292–1339)
Elizabeth of Bohemia (1596–1662)
Elizabeth of Poland (fl. 1298–1305)
Foix, Anne de (fl. 1480–1500)
Gonzaga, Eleonora I (1598–1655)
Gonzaga, Eleonora II (1628–1686)
Hemma of Bohemia (c. 930–c. 1005)
Judith (1271–1297)
Libussa (c. 680–738)
Ludmila (859–920)
Madeleine of France (1443–1486)
Margaret of Babenberg (fl. 1252)
Maria Anna of Bavaria (1574–1616)
Maria Anna of Spain (1606–1646)
Maria Leopoldine (1632–1649)
Maria Magdalena (1689–1743)
Maria of Hungary (1371–1395)
Pribyslava (fl. 10th c.)
Rosenbaum, Hedwig
Ryksa of Poland (1288–1335)
Sophia of Bavaria (fl. 1390s–1400s)
Stolz, Teresa (1834–1902)
Valasca (fl. 738)

BOLIVIA

Barrios de Chúngara, Domitila (1937—)
Bedregal, Yolanda (1916–1999)
Gisbert Carbonell de Mesa, Teresa (1926—)
Gueiler Tejada, Lydia (1921—)
Zamudio, Adela (1854–1928)

BOLOGNA

Province of Emilia-Romagna in northern Italy
Made Roman military colony (192 BCE)
Ruled briefly by Lombards (12th c.)
Ruled by Bentivoglio and Visconti families (15th c.)
Incorporated into States of the Church (16th c.)
Occupied by France (18th c.)
Occupied by Austria (19th c.)
Annexed to Kingdom of Italy (1860)
Controlled by Germany (1943–1945)
See Italy.

BOSNIA

Part of the Roman Empire (1st–4th c. CE)
Settled by Slavs, who formed several counties and duchies (7th c.)
Ruled by Croatia (10th c.)
Ruled by Kings of Hungary (11th–12th c.)
Gained independence (13th c.)
Conquered by Ottoman Turks (15th c)
Bosnia-Herzegovina annexed to Austria-Hungary (1908)
Serbia's ruler crowned King of the Serbs, Croats, and Slovenes, of Yugoslavia (1918)
Bosnia-Herzegovina fell to Croatia and was ruled by Fascist Italy (1941)
Bosnia-Herzegovina restored pre-1918 borders, becoming one of six constituent republics, including Serbia, Croatia, Montenegro, Macedonia, and Slovenia (1970s)
Bosnia-Herzegovina declares its independence (1992)

Filipović, Zlata (1981—)
Jurinac, Sena (1921—)

BOTSWANA

Occupied by Britain as Bechuanaland (19th–20th c.)
Became independent republic (1966)

Chiepe, Gaositwe (c. 1924—)
Head, Bessie (1937–1986)

BOULOGNE

City in Pas-de-Calais department of northern France
Inhabitants massacred by Normans (882)
Taken by England (1544)
Sold back to France (1550) and demolished (1553)
Region used by Napoleon in preparation of attack on England (1803–1805)
Taken by Germany (1940)
See France.

BOURBON

One of Mascarene Islands in Indian Ocean
Discovered and colonized by France as Isle de Bourbon (16th c.)
Occupied by Britain (18th c.)
Became territory of France (1946)
Also called Réunion
See France.

BRABANT

Former duchy of the Netherlands
Settled by the Franks (5th c.)
Included in Kingdom of Lotharingia (9th c.)
Included in duchy of Lower Lorraine (10th c.)
Became independent duchy (12th c.)
Passed to House of Burgundy (1430)
Inherited by Habsburgs (1477)
Awarded to United Provinces (17th c.)
Southern section remained part of Spanish Netherlands, later Austrian Netherlands (17th c.)
United under French rule (1794–1814)
Included in Kingdom of Netherlands (1815–1830)
See Netherlands.

BRACCIANO

Town north of Rome, Italy
See Italy.

BRAGANZA

District in northeast Portugal
See Portugal.

BRANDENBURG

Early Prussian province
Germanic inhabitants replaced by Slavic Wends
Conquered by Albert the Bear, margrave of Brandenburg (12th c.)
Became province of Prussia (14th c.)
Warred against Poland and Sweden (15th–16th c.)
Became leading power as Brandenburg-Prussia (17th c.)
Elector became King of Prussia (18th c.)
Eastern section became part of Poland (1945)
Western section became part of East Germany (1945)
See Germany.
See Poland.
See Prussia.

BRAZIL

Discovered by Spain and awarded to Portugal (15th c.)
Settled briefly by France and Holland (16th c.)
Became part of United Kingdom of Portugal, Brazil, and Algarve (19th c.)
Allied with Argentina and Uruguay against Paraguay (19th c.)
Proclaimed independence (1822)
Became United States of Brazil (1891)

Addor, Ady (c. 1935—)
Almeida, Julia Lopes de (1862–1934)
Alvares, Ana (1965—)
Alves Lima, Daniela (1984—)
Amália, Narcisa (1852–1924)
Amelia of Leuchtenburg (1812–1873)
Andrade, Leny (1943—)
Andujar, Claudia (1931—)
Araujo, Alexandra (1972—)
Arcain, Janeth (1969—)
Bambace, Angela (1898–1975)
Barandas, Ana Eurídice Eufrosina de (1806–1856)
Barros, Leila (1971—)
Barroso, Maria Alice (1926—)
Bede, Shelda (1973—)
Behar, Adriana (1969—)
Bethânia, Maria (1946—)
Bins, Patrícia (1930—)
Bodziak, Ericleia (1969—)
Bolkan, Florinda (1941—)
Bonita, Maria (c. 1908–1938)
Bormann, Maria Benedita Câmara de (1853–1895)
Braga, Sonia (1950—)
Bueno, Maria (1939—)
Caldeira, Hilma (1972—)
Carvalho, Dinora de (1905—)
Castro Alves, Diná Silveira de (1911–1983)
César, Ana Cristina (1952–1983)
Clouzot, Vera (1921–1960)
Coimbra, Erika (1980—)
Colonia, Regina Célia (1940—)
Conceicao, Janina (1972—)
Connelly, Ana Paula (1972—)
Consuelo, Beatriz (c. 1930—)
Cortines, Júlia (1868–1948)
Costa, Renata (1986—)
Coutinho, Sônia (1939—)
Cunha, Marcia Regina (1969—)
da Silva, Benedita (1942—)
da Silva, Fabiola (1979—)
David, Ilisaine Karen (1977—)
de Belo, Roseli (1969—)
de Paula, Monica Angelica (1978—)
Dias, Virna (1971—)
dos Santos, Andreia (1977—)
dos Santos, Cintia (1975—)
dos Santos Augusto, Rosana (1982—)
Durocher, Marie (1809–1893)
Estrela Moura, Elaine (1982—)
Fraga, Kely (1974—)
Francisca of Portugal (1824–1898)
Galvão, Patricia (1910–1962)
Garibaldi, Anita (c. 1821–1849)
Gebara, Ivone (1944—)
Gilberto, Astrud (1940—)
Goncalves, Lilian Cristina (1979—)
Gonzaga, Chiquinha (1847–1935)
Grossmann, Judith (1931—)
Guimarães Peixoto Bretas, Ana Lins do (1889–1985)
Gustavo, Roseli (1971—)
Haydée, Marcia (1939—)
Hilst, Hilda (1930—)
Isabel of Brazil (1846–1921)
Januaria (1822–1901)
Jesús, Carolina Maria de (c. 1913–1977)
Jesus, Clementina de (1902–1987)
Jorge Pádua, Maria Tereza (1943—)
Júlia, Francisca (1871–1920)
Katia (1977—)
Leonardos, Stela (1923—)
Leopoldina of Austria (1797–1826)
Lima, Ricarda (1979—)
Lisboa, Henriquetta (1904–1985)
Lispector, Clarice (1920–1977)
Lopes, Katia (1973—)
Lorentzen, Ragnhild (1968—)
Luft, Lia (1938—)
Lutz, Berta (1894–1976)
Luz, Helen (1972—)
Luz, Silvia (1975—)
Machado, Gilka (1893–1980)
Maciel Mota, Miraildes (1978—)
Maranhão, Heloísa (1925—)
Marcari Oliva, Hortencia (1959—)
Meireles, Cecília (1901–1964)
Millet, Cleusa (c. 1931–1998)
Miranda, Carmen (1909–1955)
Moser, Ana (1968—)
Nascimento Pinheiro, Graziele (1981—)
Nazaré, Maria Escolástica Da Conceição (1894–1986)
Neves, Claudia (1975—)
Noronha, Joana de (fl. c. 1850)
Novaës, Guiomar (1895–1979)
Oliveira, Alessandra (1973—)
Oliveira, Elisangela (1978—)
Oliveira, Marli de (1935—)
Oliveira, Walewska (1979—)
Ortiz, Cristina (1950—)
Pastor, Claudia (1971—)
Pellegrino, Aline (1982—)
Pereira da Silva, Kelly (1985—)
Pereira Ribeiro, Tania (1974—)
Piñon, Nélida (1937—)
Pinto, Adriana (1978—)
Pires Tavares, Sandra (1973—)
Pontes, Sister Dulce Lopes (1914–1992)
Prado, Adélia (1936—)
Queirós, Raquel de (1910–2003)
Regina, Elis (1945–1982)
Reis, Maria Firmina dos (1825–1917)
Ribeiro Cabral, Juliana (1981—)
Rodrigues, Karin (1971—)
Rodrigues, Monica (1967—)
Rozeira de Souza Silva, Cristiane (1985—)
Samuel Ramos, Adriana (1966—)
Sanglard, Ana Flavia (1970—)
Santos, Adriana (1971—)
Santos, Kelly (1979—)
Savary, Olga (1933—)
Sayao, Bidu (1902–1999)
Silva, Jackie (1962—)
Silva, Maria Angelica (1966—)
Silva, Paula (1962—)
Silva, Raquel (1978—)
Silva e Orta, Teresa M. da (c. 1711–1793)
Sissi (1967—)
Sobral, Leila (1974—)
Sobral, Marta (1964—)
Souza, Auta de (1876–1901)
Souza, Helia (1970—)
Stang, Dorothy (1931–2005)
Suntaque, Andreia (1977—)
Suplicy, Marta (c. 1946—)
Suruagy, Sandra (1963—)
Tagliaferro, Magda (1893–1986)
Telles, Lygia Fagundes (1923—)
Teresa Cristina of Bourbon (1822–1889)
Venturini, Fernanda (1970—)

BRITISH GUIANA

See Guyana.

BRITTANY

Historic peninsular region of northwest France
Occupied by Celts driven from southwest England by Anglo-Saxon invasions (5th–6th c.)
Subdued by Merovingian and Carolingian kingdoms (10th c.)
Geoffrey I of Rennes became duke of Brittany (10th c.)
Became fief of England (12th c.)
Claimed as vassal state by France (13th c.)
Became a province of France until Revolution (17th–18th c.)
See England.
See France.

BRUNSWICK

Former state of Germany
Founded (9th c.)
Member of Hanseatic League (13th c.)
Member of Schmalkaldic League (17th c.)
Passed to dukes of Brunswick-Wolfenbütel (18th c.)
Duchy of Brunswick annexed to Kingdom of Westphalia (19th c.)
Incorporated into Lower Saxoxy, West Germany (1945)
See Germany.

BUCKINGHAM

Borough of Buckinghamshire in southeast central England
See England.

BULGARIA

Formerly Moesia and Thrace
Invaded by Bulgars (6th c.)
Invaded by Russians and Byzantines (10th c.)
Part of Byzantine Empire (11th–12th c.)
Part of Ottoman Empire (13th c.)
Joined with Macedonia as principality (1877)
Macedonia returned to Turkey (1878)
Warred with Serbia and reconciled with Russia (1896)
Declared independence from Turkey (1908)
Invaded by Nazi Germany (1941)
Invaded by U.S.S.R. (1944)
Abolished monarchy and became a people's republic (1946)
Participated with Soviet Union in occupation of Czechoslovakia (1968)

Amalie of Saxe-Coburg-Gotha (1848–1894)
Arova, Sonia (1927–2001)
Bagryana, Elisaveta (1893–1991)
Bakova, Ani (1957—)
Balkanska, Mimi (b. 1902)
Barbulova-Kelbecheva, Siyka (1951—)
Berberova, Lalka (1965—)
Blagoeva, Stella Dimitrova (1887–1954)
Blagoeva, Yordanka (1947—)

Bogdanova, Krasimira (1949—)
Boncheva, Rumeliana (1957—)
Borisova, Verka (1955—)
Bozhurina, Tsvetana (1952—)
Dafovska, Ekaterina (1976—)
Dangalakova-Bogomilova, Tanya (1964—)
Deltcheva, Ina (1977–)
Demireva, Bojanka (1969—)
Dermendzhieva, Vanya (1952—)
Dessilava (fl. 1197–1207)
Dilova, Diana (1952—)
Dimitrova, Blaga (1922—)
Dimitrova, Ghena (1941–2005)
Dimitrova, Rositsa (1955—)
Dimitrova, Tanya (1957—)
Donkova, Yordanka (1961—)
Dragoicheva, Tsola (1893–1993)
Dudeva, Diana (1968—)
Dunavska, Adriana (1970—)
Eleanora of Reuss (1860–1917)
Filipova, Nadya (1959—)
Frankeva, Antoaneta (1971—)
Georgieva, Anka (1959—)
Georgieva, Magdalena (1962—)
Georgieva, Maya (1955—)
Georgieva-Panayotovna, Kapka (1951—)
Germanova, Silviya (1961—)
Gesheva-Tsvetkova, Vanya (1960—)
Giovanna of Italy (1907—)
Giovanna of Italy (1907–2000)
Gogova, Tanya (1950—)
Golcheva, Nadka (1952—)
Gomez-Acebo, Margaret
Grancharova, Zoya (1966—)
Grozdeva, Maria (1972—)
Gueorguieva, Diliana (1965—)
Guigova, Maria (1947—)
Gushterova, Vangelia (1911–1996)
Gyurova, Ginka (1954—)
Gyurova, Krasimira (1953—)
Helen Asen of Bulgaria (d. 1255?)
Ignatova, Lilia (1965—)
Ilieva, Valentina (1962—)
Ilieva, Zhaneta (1984—)
Irene Lascaris (d. around 1270)
Irene Paleologina (fl. 1279–1280)
Ivanova, Borislava (1966—)
Kaisheva, Rumyana (1955—)
Kevlian, Valentina (1980—)
Kezhova, Eleonora (1985—)
Khristova, Ivanka (1941—)
Khristova, Tsvetanka (1962—)
Koleva, Maria
Kostadinova, Stefka (1965—)
Kristeva, Julia (1941—)
Kristolova, Anka (1955—)
Kurbatova-Gruycheva, Stoyanka (1955—)
Lecheva, Vesela (1964—)
Loisinger, Joanna (1865–1951)
Madina, Stefka (1963—)
Makaveeva, Petkana (1952—)
Maleeva, Magdalena (1975—)
Maleeva, Manuela (1967—)
Maria Paleologina (fl. 1271–1279)
Marie Louise of Bulgaria (1933—)
Marie Louise of Parma (1870–1899)
Marie of Bulgaria (c. 1046–?)
Marinova, Tereza (1977—)
Marinova, Zornitsa (1987—)
Matova, Nonka (1954—)
Metodieva, Penka (1950—)
Mikhaylova, Angelina (1960—)
Mikhaylova, Snezhana (1954—)
Miller, Susanne (1915—)
Mitova, Silvia (1976—)
Modeva, Mariyka (1954—)
Mutafchieva, Vera P. (1929—)
Nadejda of Bulgaria (1899–1958)
Nakova, Dolores (1957—)
Neykova, Rumyana (1973—)
Nicaea (fl. 300 BCE)
Nikoultchina, Irina (1974—)
Ninova, Violeta (1963—)
Otsetova, Svetlana (1950—)
Paliyska, Diana (1966—)
Panova, Bianca (1970—)
Petkova, Ognyana (1964—)
Petkova-Vergova, Mariya (1950—)
Petrova, Maria (1975—)
Petrunova, Silva (1956—)
Radanova, Evgenia (1977—)
Radkova, Kostadinka (1962—)
Raeva, Iliana (1963—)
Ralenkova, Anelia (1963—)
Ranguelova, Kristina (1985—)
Rhodopis (fl. 6th c. BCE)
Roudenko, Lubov (1915—)
Salapatyska, Stella (1979—)
Serbezova, Mariana (1959—)
Shtarkelova, Margarita (1951—)
Shtereva, Nikolina (1955—)
Skerlatova, Girgina (1954—)
Slavcheva, Evladiya (1962—)
Stoeva, Vasilka (1940—)
Stoyanova, Boriana (1968—)
Stoyanova, Mariya (1947—)
Stoyanova, Penka (1950—)
Stoyanova, Radka (1964—)
Tabakova, Maja (1978—)
Taleva, Ivelina (1979—)
Tancheva, Galina (1987—)
Tancheva, Vladislava (1987—)
Todorova, Rita (1958—)
Vaseva, Lilyana (1955—)
Vatachka, Vjara (1980—)
Velinova, Iskra (1953—)
Welitsch, Ljuba (1913–1996)
Yazova, Yana (1912–1974)
Yordanova, Reni (1953—)
Yordanova, Todorka (1956—)
Yordanova, Zdravka (1950—)
Yorgova, Diana (1942—)
Yorgova, Diana Vassilleva (1971—)
Zhivkova, Lyudmila (1942–1981)

BURGUNDY

Founded by Burgundians (5th c.)
Conquered by Merovingians and became part of Frankish Empire (6th c.)
Divided into Lower (Provence) and Upper (Arles) Burgundy (9th c.)
Duchy of Burgundy formed (9th c.)
Became part of Holy Roman Empire as Kingdom of Burgundy (11th c.)
Annexed to France until Revolution (18th c.)
See France.

BURMA

Southeast Asian republic
Inhabited by Mongols (3rd c.)
United under Pagan dynasty overthrown by Mongols (13th c.)
Modern Burmese state founded (18th c.)
Warred with Britain, which retained Rangoon (19th c.)
Upper Burma formed, including Mandalay (19th c.)
Became province of British India; made crown colony (1937)
Invaded by Japan (1942)
Achieved independence (1947)

Aung San Suu Kyi (1945—)
Daong Khin Khin Lay (1913—)
Daw Khin Myo Chit (1915–2003)
Daw Mi Mi Khaing (1916–1990)
Daw San San (1944–1990)
Lwin, Annabella (1965—)
Mountbatten, Edwina Ashley (1901–1960)
Mountbatten, Pamela (1929—)
Mountbatten, Patricia (1924—)
Thant, Mme (1900–1989)

BURUNDI

Kinigi, Sylvie (1953—)

BUTE

Island off coast of Scotland
See Scotland.

BYZANTINE EMPIRE

Under Theodosian Dynasty as Eastern Roman Empire (395–450)
Under Thracian Dynasty (450–518)
Under Justinian Dynasty (518–610)
Attacked by Persians, Arabs, and Bulgars (7th–10th c.)
Under Heraclian Dynasty (610–717)
Under Isaurian Dynasty (717–820)
Under Amorian Dynasty (820–867)
Under Macedonian Dynasty, comprising South Balkans, Greece, Asia Minor, and Southern Italy (867–1059)
Under Ducas Dynasty (1059–1081)
Under Comnenus Dynasty (1081–1185)
Under Angelus Dynasty (1185–1204)
Empire divided into Latin Empire, Greek empires of Trebizond and Nicaea, and Venetian and Greek holdings (1204)
Under Latin Emperors (1204–1261)
Under Lascaris Dynasty as Empire of Nicaea (1206–1262)
Under Palaeologus Dynasty (1261–1453)
Constantinople captured by Turks (1453)

Agnes-Anne of France (b. 1171)
Albia Domnica (fl. 4th c.)
Albia Domnica
Anastasia (fl. 500s)
Anastasia (fl. 600s)
Anastasia (fl. 800s)
Anastasia the Patrician (d. 567)
Anna Anachoutlou (r. 1341–1342)
Anna Angelina (d. 1210?)
Anna Comnena (1083–1153/55)
Anna Dalassena (c. 1025–1105)
Anna of Byzantium (963–1011)
Anna of Byzantium (fl. 901)
Anna of Hungary (d. around 1284)
Anna of Saxony (1420–1462)
Anna Paleologina (d. 1340)
Anna Paleologina-Cantacuzene (fl. 1270–1313)
Anne of Savoy (c. 1320–1353)
Arabia (fl. 570)
Ariadne (fl. 457–515)
Barca-Theodosia (fl. 800s)
Berengaria of Castile (b. around 1199)
Bertha-Eudocia the Frank (fl. 900s)
Bertha-Irene of Sulzbach (d. 1161)
Catherine of Achaea (d. 1465)
Catherine of Bulgaria (fl. 1050)
Catherine of Tarento (fl. early 1300s)
Charito (fl. 300s)
Comitona (fl. 500s)
Constance-Anna of Hohenstaufen (fl. 13th century)
Constance-Anna of Hohenstaufen
Constantina (fl. 582–602)
Emmelia of Cappadocia (fl. 300s)
Eudocia (b. 978)
Eudocia (c. 1260–?)
Eudocia (fl. 700s)
Eudocia Angelina (fl. 1204)

Eudocia Baiane (d. 902)
Eudocia Comnena (fl. 1100)
Eudocia Decapolita (fl. 800s)
Eudocia Ingerina (fl. 800s)
Eudocia Macrembolitissa (1021–1096)
Eudocia of Byzantium (d. 404)
Eudocia of Byzantium (fl. 1181)
Eulogia Paleologina (fl. 1200s)
Euphrosyne (c. 790–840)
Euphrosyne (d. 1203)
Euphrosyne (fl. 1200s)
Eusebia of Macedonia (fl. 300)
Fabia-Eudocia (fl. 600s)
Fausta (d. 324)
Fausta (fl. 600s)
Faustina of Antioch (fl. 300s)
Galla (fl. 320)
Gregoria-Anastasia (fl. 640s)
Helena (c. 320–?)
Helena Cantacuzene (fl. 1340s)
Helena Dragas (fl. 1400)
Helena Lekapena (c. 920–961)
Helena of Alypia (fl. 980s)
Ino-Anastasia (fl. 575–582)
Irene (fl. 700s)
Irene (fl. late 1100s)
Irene Asen (fl. 1300s)
Irene Ducas (c. 1066–1133)
Irene Lascaris (fl. 1222–1235)
Irene of Athens (c. 752–803)
Irene of Brunswick (fl. 1300s)
Irene of Byzantium (d. 1067)
Irene of Constantinople (d. around 921)
Irene of Montferrat (fl. 1300)
Irene of the Khazars (d. 750?)
Kassia (c. 800/810–before 867)
Leontia (fl. 602–610)
Lupicinia-Euphemia (d. 523)
Macrina (327–379)
Maria (fl. 1200s)
Maria (fl. 700s)
Maria Cantacuzene (fl. 1300s)
Maria Comnena (fl. 1090s)
Maria of Alania (fl. 1070–1081)
Maria of Amnia (fl. 782)
Maria of Armenia (fl. 1300)
Maria of Trebizond (d. 1439)
Marie de Courtenay (fl. 1215)
Marie of Antioch (d. 1183)
Martina (fl. 600s)
Moero (fl. 4th–3rd BCE)
Olympias (c. 365–408)
Priska-Irene of Hungary (c. 1085–1133)
Prokopia (fl. 800s)
Pulcheria (c. 398–453)
Sophia (c. 525–after 600)
Sophie of Montferrat (fl. 15th c.)
Synadene of Byzantium (c. 1050–?)
Thecla (c. 775–c. 823)
Thecla (c. 823–c. 870)
Theoctista (c. 740–c. 802)
Theodora (c. 500–548)
Theodora (fl. early 900s)
Theodora (fl. late 900s)
Theodora Cantacuzene (fl. 14th c.)
Theodora Comnena (fl. 1080s)
Theodora Comnena (fl. 1140)
Theodora Comnena (1145–after 1183)
Theodora Ducas (fl. 11th c.)
Theodora Ducas (fl. 1200s)
Theodora of the Khazars (fl. 700s)
Theodora Paleologina (fl. 1200s)
Theodora Paleologina (fl. 14th c.)
Theodora Porphyrogenita (c. 989–1056)
Theodora the Blessed (c. 810–c. 860)
Theodota (c. 775–early 800s)
Theophano (c. 866–c. 897)
Theophano (c. 940–?)
Theophano of Athens (fl. 800s)
Verina (fl. 437–483)
Vigilantia (c. 485–?)
Yolande of Courtenay (d. 1219)
Zoë Carbopsina (c. 890–920)
Zoe Ducas
Zoë Porphyrogenita (980–1050)
Zoë Zautzina (c. 870–c. 899)

CAITHNESS

County in northern Scotland
See Scotland.

CAMBODIA

Founded (c. 5th c.)
Ruled by Khmer Empire (11th c.)
Became province of Annam or Siam (13th–17th c.)
Became vassal of Siam (1844)
Became French protectorate (1863)
Lost Battambang to Thailand (1941)
Gained independence (1954)
Abolished monarchy (1970)

Khieu Ponnary (1920–2003)
Kossamak (1904–1975)
Mei (d. 1875)
Norodom Monineath Sihanouk (1936—)
Piseth Pilika (1965–1999)

CAMBRIDGE

Borough of Cambridgeshire in eastern England
See England.

CAMEROON

Mbango Etone, Françoise (1976—)

CANAAN

Ancient name of portion of Palestine now occupied by Israel and Lebanon
Settled probably by Amorites and Hittites (c. 33rd–22nd c. BCE)
Hebrews subdued pre-Israelite race returning from Egypt (c. 13th c. BCE)
Also referred to as province of Egyptian empire in western Asia
See Israel.
See Jordan.
See Lebanon.
See Palestine.
See Syria.

CANADA

Discovered by Norsemen (c. 11th c.)
Portions colonized by France (17th c.)
Portions claimed by England (18th c.)
Boundaries with U.S. settled (18th–20th c.)
Dominion of Canada established (1867)
Partnership with Britain (1931)

Abbott, Mary Martha (1823–1898)
Abbott, Maude (1869–1940)
Abdo, Reema (1963—)
Adair, Jean (1872–1953)
Adams, Claire (1898–1978)
Aikens, Charlotte (c. 1868–1949)
Alarie, Pierrette (1921—)
Albani, Emma (c. 1847–1930)
Alexander, Buffy (c. 1977—)
Alexander, Jessie (1876–1962)
Alexander, Lisa (1968—)
Allan, Maude (1883–1956)
Allen, Charlotte Vale (1941—)
Amundrud, Gail (1957—)
Andersen, Roxanne (1912–2002)
Anderson, Doris (1921—)
Angers, Félicité (1845–1924)
Anglin, Margaret (1876–1958)
Angwin, Maria L. (1849–1898)
Antal, Dana (1977—)
Apinée, Irena (c. 1930—)
Aquash, Anna Mae (1945–1976)
Archer, Violet Balestreri (1913–2000)
Armbrust, Barbara (1963—)
Armour, Rebecca (1846–1891)
Arthur, Julia (1869–1950)
Asselin, Marie-Claude
Atwood, Margaret (1939—)
Auch, Susan (1966—)
Avison, Margaret (1918—)
Av-Paul, Annette (1944—)
Babcock, Winnifred (1875–1954)
Bagshaw, Elizabeth (1881–1982)
Bailey, Angela (1962—)
Baird, Irene (1901–1981)
Ballon, Ellen (1898–1969)
Banks, Margaret (1924—)
Bannerman, Margaret (1896–1976)
Barfoot, Joan (1946—)
Barnes, Kirsten (1968—)
Barre, Alexandra (1958—)
Bauer, Veronika (1979—)
Beals, Jessie Tarbox (1870–1942)
Beatty, Patricia (1936—)
Beaudet, Louise (1861–1947)
Beaumont, Lyne (1978—)
Bechard, Kelly (1978—)
Beck, Elizabeth Louisa (c. 1862–1931)
Bedard, Myriam (1969—)
Bell, Florence (1909—)
Bell, Marilyn (1937—)
Beresford-Howe, Constance (1922—)
Bernier, Sylvie (1964—)
Betker, Jan (c. 1960—)
Beynon, Francis Marion (1884–1951)
Bhatia, June (1919—)
Biesenthal, Laryssa (1971—)
Binns, Hilda May (1945—)
Bird, Dorothy (c. 1913—)
Birtles, Mary (1859–1943)
Black, Elinor F.E. (1905–1982)
Black, Martha Louise (1866–1957)
Blais, Marie-Claire (1939—)
Blondal, Patricia (1926–1959)
Bolduc, Marie (1894–1941)
Bolt, Carol (1941–2000)
Bondar, Roberta (1945—)
Borden, Laura (1862–1940)
Bosco, Monique (1927—)
Bosshart, Dominique (1977—)
Botterill, Jennifer (1979—)
Boucher, Denise (1935—)
Boudrias, Christine (1972—)
Bourassa, Jocelyn (1947—)
Bowell, Harriet (1829–1884)
Boyd, Liona (1950—)
Boylen, Christilot (1947—)
Boys, Beverly (1951—)
Brain, Marilyn (1959—)
Branscombe, Gena (1881–1977)
Brasseur, Isabelle (1970—)
Brayley, Sally (1937—)
Bremner, Janice (1974—)
Brenner, Veronica (1974—)
Brewster, Elizabeth (1922—)
Brill, Debbie (1953—)
Brisson, Therese (1966—)
Brooks, Harriet (1876–1933)
Brooks, Lela (b. 1908)
Brookshaw, Dorothy (1912—)
Brossard, Nicole (1943—)
Brown, Audrey Alexandra (1904–1998)
Brown, Margaret A. (1867–?)

Brown, Rosemary (1930—)
Brunet, Caroline (1969—)
Bujold, Geneviève (1942—)
Buller, Annie (1896–1973)
Burka, Ellen Petra (1921—)
Burka, Petra (1946—)
Burka, Sylvia (1954—)
Burke, Sarah (1982—)
Burkholder, Mabel (1881–1973)
Burnford, Sheila (1918–1984)
Butala, Sharon (1940—)
Callwood, June (1924—)
Cameron, Agnes Deans (1863–1912)
Cameron, Eleanor (1912–1996)
Cameron, Hilda (b. 1912)
Cameron, Michelle (1962—)
Campbell, Cassie (1973—)
Campbell, Grace MacLennan (1895–1963)
Campbell, Kim (1947—)
Campbell, Maria (1940—)
Canadian Women's National Ice Hockey Team (1998)
Canfield, Ella Jean (1918—)
Carr, Emily (1871–1945)
Cartwright, Peggy (1912–2001)
Carver-Dias, Claire (1977—)
Casgrain, Thérèse (1896–1981)
Catherwood, Ethel (1910–1987)
Chadwick, Cassie L. (1859–1907)
Chalmers, Angela (1963—)
Champagne, Andrée (1939—)
Chan, Erin (1979—)
Charest, Isabelle (1971—)
Chartrand, Isabelle (1978—)
Chiriaeff, Ludmilla (1924–1996)
Chrétien, Aline (1936—)
Clark, Barbara Lynne (1958—)
Clark, Catherine Anthony (1892–1977)
Clark, Joan (1934—)
Clark, Karen (1972—)
Cliff, Leslie (1955—)
Clifford, Betsy (1953—)
Cline, Aleisha (1970—)
Cloutier, Suzanne (1927–2003)
Cockburn, Karen (1980—)
Coe, Dawn (1960—)
Coleman, Kit (1864–1915)
Collins, Dorothy (1926–1994)
Conway, Jill Ker (1934—)
Coo, Eva (d. 1935)
Cook, Myrtle (1902–1985)
Cook, Sheri (1953—)
Copps, Sheila (1952—)
Corbin, Hazel (1894–1988)
Corson, Marilyn (1954—)
Coughlan, Angela (1952—)
Cournoyea, Nellie J. (1940—)
Craig, Betty (1957—)
Crawford, Shannon (1963—)
Creider, Jane Tapsubei (c. 1940s—)
Crooks, Charmaine (1961—)
Csizmazia, Kim (c. 1968—)
Curzon, Sarah Anne (1833–1898)
Cutrone, Angela
Dafoe, Frances (1929—)
Daigle, Sylvie (1962—)
Darmond, Grace (1898–1963)
Davis, Heather (1974—)
Davis, Mary E.P. (c. 1840–1924)
Dawes, Eva (1912—)
De Carlo, Yvonne (1922—)
DeFranco, Marisa (1955—)
DeFranco, Merlina (1957—)
de la Roche, Mazo (1879–1961)
Delehanty, Megan (1968—)
Demers, Anik (1972—)
De Mille, Katherine (1911–1995)
Denison, Flora MacDonald (1867–1921)
Dewar, Phyllis (1915–1961)
Dewhurst, Colleen (1924–1991)
Diamond, Selma (1920–1985)
Dick, Evelyn (1922—)
Diduck, Judy (1966—)
Diefenbaker, Edna Mae (1901–1951)
Diefenbaker, Olive (1902–1976)
Dion, Céline (1968—)
Dionne, Annette (1934—)
Dionne, Cécile (1934—)
Dionne, Deidra (1982—)
Dionne, Émilie (1934–1954)
Dionne, Marie (1934–1970)
Dionne, Yvonne (1934–2001)
Dionne Quintuplets
Ditchburn, Ann (c. 1950—)
Doble, Frances (1902–1969)
Dolson, Mildred (1918—)
Donalda, Pauline (1882–1970)
Donnelly, Geraldine (1965—)
D'Orsay, Fifi (1904–1983)
Dougall, Lily (1858–1923)
Dougherty, Sarah (c. 1817–1898)
Downie, Mary Alice (1934—)
Drolet, Marie-Eve (1982—)
Drolet, Nancy (1973—)
Drouin, Candice (1976—)
Drylie, Patricia (c. 1928–1993)
Duchesnay, Isabelle (1973—)
Duggan, Keltie (1970—)
Duley, Margaret (1894–1968)
Duncan, Sandy Frances (1942—)
Duncan, Sara Jeanette (1861–1922)
Dunfield, Sonya Klopfer (c. 1936—)
Dunlop, Florence (c. 1896–1963)
Dupuis, Lori (1972—)
Durand, Lucile (1930—)
Durbin, Deanna (1921—)
Dyke, Eunice (1883–1969)
Easton, Florence (1882–1955)
Eastwood, Alice (1859–1953)
Eaton, Edith (1865–1914)
Eburne, Maude (1875–1960)
Eckhardt-Gramatté, S.C. (1899–1974)
Edmonds, Emma (1841–1898)
Edmonton Grads (1915–1940)
Edvina, Louise (1878–1948)
Edwards, Henrietta Muir (1849–1933)
Ellis, Mina A. (1870–1956)
Engel, Marian (1933–1985)
Erikson, Joan (c. 1902–1997)
Evangelista, Linda (1965—)
Fairbairn, Joyce (1939—)
Fairclough, Ellen (1905–2004)
Farrally, Betty (1915–1989)
Ferguson, Dottie (1923–2003)
Fergusson, Muriel McQueen (1899–1997)
Fiamengo, Marya (1926—)
Finnigan, Joan (1925—)
Firestone, Shulamith (1945—)
Fleming, May Agnes (1840–1880)
Fonteyn, Karen (1969—)
Ford, Atina (c. 1972—)
Forde, Leneen (1935—)
Fortune, Mary (fl. 1866–1910)
Foster, Diane (1928—)
Foster, Dianne (1928—)
Fowke, Edith (1913–1996)
Fox, Beryl (1931—)
Fox, Kate (c. 1839–1892)
Fox, Leah (c. 1818–1890)
Fox, Margaret (c. 1833–1893)
Fraser, Sylvia (1935—)
Frechette, Sylvie (1967—)
Freeman, Alice (1857–1936)
Frizzell, Mary (1913–1972)
Frizzell, Mildred (1911—)
Führer, Charlotte (1834–1907)
Fung, Lori (1963—)
Gallant, Mavis (1922—)
Garapick, Nancy (1961—)
Garceau, Catherine (1978—)
Gareau, France (1967—)
Gareau, Jacqueline (1953—)
Garon, Pauline (1900–1965)
Gauthier, Eva (1885–1958)
Gérin-Lajoie, Marie (1867–1945)
Ghalem, Nadia (1941—)
Gibson, Cheryl (1959—)
Glass, Joanna (1936—)
Goermann, Monica (1964—)
Gordon, Jean (1918—)
Gotlieb, Phyllis (1926—)
Goulet-Nadon, Amelie (1983—)
Goyette, Danielle (1966—)
Granholm, Jennifer M. (1959—)
Greene, Nancy (1943—)
Guay, Lucie (1958—)
Gudereit, Marcia (c. 1966—)
Gullen, Augusta Stowe (1857–1943)
Gurr, Donna Marie (1955—)
Gutteridge, Helena Rose (1879–1960)
Hall, Rosetta Sherwood (1865–1951)
Hambrook, Sharon (1963—)
Hamilton, Elizabeth Jane (1805–1897)
Hamm, Margherita (1867–1907)
Harris, Christie (1907–2002)
Harris, Claire (1937—)
Harrison, Susie Frances (1859–1935)
Harrold, Agnes (c. 1830–1903)
Hart, Julia Catherine (1796–1867)
Hart, Pearl (c. 1875–c. 1924)
Hartley, Blythe (1982—)
Hashman, Judy (1935—)
Haviland, Laura S. (1808–1898)
Hawco, Sherry (d. 1991)
Hawkins, Mary (1875–1950)
Hayden, Melissa (1923—)
Heaney, Geraldine (1967—)
Hébert, Anne (1916–2000)
Heddle, Kathleen (1965—)
Hefford, Jayna (1977—)
Hegan, Eliza Parks (1861–1917)
Heggtveit, Anne (1939—)
Heymans, Emilie (1981—)
Higson, Allison (1973—)
Hind, Cora (1861–1942)
Hindmarch, Gladys (1940—)
Hoffman, Abby (1947—)
Hogan, Aileen I. (1899–1981)
Hogg, Wendy (1956—)
Holden, Helene (1935—)
Hollingsworth, Margaret (1940—)
Holloway, Sue (1955—)
Holmes, Anna-Marie (1943—)
Hoodless, Adelaide (1857–1910)
Hopper, Victoria (1909—)
Hospital, Janette Turner (1942—)
Hould-Marchand, Valérie (1980—)
Howard, Kathleen (1879–1956)
Howes, Mary (1941—)
Hughes, Clara (1972—)
Hughes, Monica (1925–2003)
Hyland, Frances (1927–2004)
Inman, Florence (1890–1986)
Irwin, Flo (born c. 1860)
Irwin, May (1862–1938)
Ishoy, Cynthia (1952—)
Istomina, Anna (1925—)
Jackson, Mary Percy (1904–2000)

James, Susan Gail (1953—)
Jamison, Cecilia V. (1837–1909)
Jardin, Anne (1959—)
Jarvis, Lilian (1931—)
Johns, Ethel (1879–1968)
Johnston, Carol (1958—)
Johnston, Rita Margaret (1935—)
Jones, Patricia (1930—)
Joseph, Mother (1823–1902)
Joudry, Patricia (1921–2000)
Kain, Karen (1951—)
Kalvak, Helen (1901–1984)
Karodia, Farida (1942—)
Kedrova, Lila (1918–2000)
Keith, Vicki (1959—)
Kellar, Becky (1975—)
Kelley, Edith Summers (1884–1956)
Kelly, Ethel (1875–1949)
Kelsall, Karen (1962—)
Kelsey, Frances O. (1914—)
Kent, Barbara (b. 1906)
Kerr, Jane (1968—)
Kidder, Margot (1948—)
Killingbeck, Molly (1959—)
Kilmury, Diana (1948—)
King, Isabel Grace Mackenzie (1843–1917)
Kirkland-Casgrain, Marie-Claire (1924—)
Klassen, Cindy (1979—)
Kogawa, Joy (1935—)
Konihowski, Diane Jones (1951—)
Korn, Alison (1970—)
Krall, Diana (1964—)
Kraus, Alanna (1977—)
Kraus, Greta (1907–1998)
Kreiner, Kathy (1954—)
Kryczka, Kelly (1961—)
Kulesza, Kasia (1976—)
Lambert, Betty (1933–1983)
Lambert, Nathalie (1963—)
La Montagne-Beauregard, Blanche (1899–1960)
Lang, K.D. (1961—)
La Palme, Béatrice (1878–1921)
La Roy, Rita (1907–1993)
Larsen, Christine (1967—)
Laumann, Daniele (1961—)
Laumann, Silken (1964—)
Laurence, Margaret (1926–1987)
Laurier, Zoé (1841–1921)
Law, Kelley (1966—)
Lawrence, Florence (1886–1938)
Lay, Marion (1948—)
Lee-Gartner, Kerrin (1966—)
Leeming, Marjorie (1903–1987)
LeGon, Jeni (1916—)
Le May Doan, Catriona (1970—)
Leprohon, Rosanna (1832–1879)
Lesik, Vera (1910–1975)
Letourneau, Fanny (1979—)
Levy, Julia (1934—)
Li, Florence Tim Oi (1907–1992)
Lidstone, Dorothy (1938—)
Lillie, Beatrice (1894–1989)
Limpert, Marianne (1972—)
Little, Jean (1932—)
Livesay, Dorothy (1909–1996)
Livingston, Nora G.E. (1848–1927)
Lizars, Kathleen MacFarlane (d. 1931)
Lloyd, Gweneth (1901–1993)
Logan, Laura R. (1879–1974)
Long, Tania (1913–1998)
Lowther, Patricia Louise (1935–1975)
Luke, Theresa (1967—)
Lunn, Janet (1928—)
MacDonald, Elizabeth Roberts (1864–1922)
MacDonald, Irene (1933–2002)
Macdonald, Isabella (1809–1857)
MacDonald, Noel (1915—)
Macdonald, Susan Agnes (1836–1920)
MacEwen, Gwendolyn (1941–1987)
MacGill, Elsie (d. 1980)
MacGill, Helen Gregory (1871–1947)
MacGregor, Esther Miller (1874–1961)
Machar, Agnes Maule (1837–1927)
Mackay, Nancy (1929—)
Mackenzie, Ada (1891–1973)
MacKenzie, Gisele (1927–2003)
MacKenzie, Jane (1825–1893)
Macleod, Charlotte (1852–1950)
MacMurchy, Helen (1862–1953)
MacMurchy, Marjory (1869–1938)
Macphail, Agnes (1890–1954)
Macpherson, Jay (1931—)
MacPherson, Michelle (1966—)
Magnussen, Karen (1952—)
Maillet, Antonine (1929—)
Mance, Jeanne (1606–1673)
Mandel, Miriam (1930–1982)
Manley, Elizabeth (1965—)
Mann, Elisabeth (1918–2002)
Marriott, Anne (1913–1997)
Marshall, Joyce (1913—)
Marshall, Lois (1924–1997)
Martens, Camille (1976—)
Martin, Agnes (1912–2004)
Martin, Claire (1914—)
Matheson, Elizabeth (1866–1958)
Matthews, Janet (1965—)
Matthews, Victoria (1954—)
Maunder, Maria (1972—)
Maxwell, Lois (1927—)
McBean, Marnie (1968—)
McClung, Nellie L. (1873–1951)
McCormack, Katheryn (1974—)
McCormack, Kathy
McCusker, Joan (c. 1966—)
McDermid, Heather (1968—)
McDougall, Adelaide (1909–2000)
McIlwraith, Jean Newton (1859–1938)
McKinney, Louise (1868–1931)
McLachlan, Sarah (1968—)
McLachlin, Beverley (1943—)
McLaughlin, Audrey (1936—)
McLerie, Allyn Ann (1926—)
McManus, Liz (1947—)
McMaster, Elizabeth Jennet (1847–1903)
McNeil, Florence (1937—)
McPherson, Aimee Semple (1890–1944)
McTeer, Maureen (1952—)
Meagher, Aileen (1910–1987)
Meighen, Isabel J. (1883–1985)
Melien, Lori (1972—)
Mellanby, Helen (1911–2001)
Menten, Maude (1879–1960)
Mercier, Margaret (1937—)
Messner, Pat (1954—)
Millar, Margaret (1915–1994)
Milner, Brenda Atkinson (1918—)
Mitchell, Joni (1943—)
Monk, Maria (1816–1849)
Monroe, Jessica (1966—)
Montgomery, Lucy Maud (1874–1942)
Montminy, Anne (1975—)
Montreal Massacre (1989)
Moodie, Geraldine (1853–1945)
Moodie, Susanna (1803–1885)
Morissette, Alanis (1974—)
Morrow, Suzanne
Moyd, Pauline
Muenzer, Lori-Ann (1966—)
Mulroney, Mila (1953—)
Munro, Alice (1931—)
Murphy, Emily (1868–1933)
Murray, Anne (1945—)
Myers, Viola (1928—)
Napier, Geills (1937—)
Nattrass, Susan (1950—)
Nelson, Diane (1958—)
Nelsova, Zara (1917–2002)
Nesbitt, Stephanie (1985—)
Nicholas, Cindy (1957—)
Nicoll, Ashley (1963—)
Noall, Patricia (1970—)
Noble, Cheryl (1956—)
Normand, Kirstin (1974—)
Nugent, Andrea (1968—)
Nutting, Mary Adelaide (1858–1948)
Nystrom, Karen (1969—)
O'Grady, Diane (1967—)
Oliphant, Betty (1918–2004)
Olmsted, Barbara (1959—)
Ostenso, Martha (1900–1963)
Ottenbrite, Anne (1966—)
Ouellette, Caroline (1979—)
Owens, Patricia (1925–2000)
Page, P.K. (1916—)
Palmer, Lillian (b. 1913)
Parisien, Julie (1971—)
Parker, Cecilia (1905–1993)
Parlby, Irene (1868–1965)
Parlow, Kathleen (1890–1963)
Paterson, Isabel (c. 1886–1961)
Patrick, Dorothy (1921–1987)
Payne, Marita (1960—)
Pearson, Landon Carter (1930—)
Pearson, Maryon (1901–1989)
Pedersen, Lena (1940—)
Pelletier, Annie (1973—)
Pelletier, Henriette (c. 1864–1961)
Pengelly, Edna (1874–1959)
Penney, Jennifer (1946—)
Pentland, Barbara (1912–2000)
Percy, Karen (1966—)
Perreault, Annie (1971—)
Pickford, Mary (1893–1979)
Pickthall, Marjorie (1883–1922)
Pierce, Mary (1975—)
Piper, Cherie (1981—)
Pollock, Sharon (1936—)
Pooley, Violet (1886–1965)
Porter, Gladys M. (1894–1967)
Post, Sandra (1948—)
Pounder, Cheryl (1976—)
Pracht, Eva-Maria (1937—)
Premont, Marie-Hélene (1977—)
Prevost, Marie (1895–1937)
Price, Roberta MacAdams (1881–1959)
Priestner, Cathy (1958—)
Radyonska, Tanya (1924—)
Rai, Pamela (1966—)
Ramsland, Sarah Katherine (1882–1964)
Read, Cari (1970—)
Reddon, Lesley (1970—)
Reid, Kate (1930–1993)
Reid, Rose Marie (1906–1978)
Remington, Barbara (1936—)
Rheaume, Manon (1972—)
Richardson, Jillian (1965—)
Richardson, Luba Lyons (1949—)
Ricker, Maelle (1978—)
Ringwood, Gwen Pharis (1910–1984)
Ritter, Erika (1948—)
Robb, Isabel Hampton (1860–1910)
Robertson, Brenda May (1929—)
Robertson, Heather (1942—)
Robertson, Margaret Murray (1823–1897)
Robinson, Emma (1971—)
Rogers, Edith MacTavish (1876–1947)

Rosenfeld, Fanny (1905–1969)
Ross, Charlotte Whitehead (1843–1916)
Ross, Marie-Henriette LeJeune (1762–1860)
Roy, Gabrielle (1909–1983)
Rule, Jane (1931—)
Russell, Anna (b. 1911)
Russell, Ernestine (1938—)
Rutherford, Ann (1917—)
Rutledge, Margaret Fane (1914–2004)
Sadlier, Mary Anne (1820–1903)
Saint-Laurent, Jeanne (1887–1966)
Sale, Jamie (1977—)
Salsberg, Germain Merle (1950—)
Salverson, Laura Goodman (1890–1970)
Saunders, Marshall (1861–1947)
Sauvé, Jeanne (1922–1993)
Scales, Jessie Sleet (fl. 1900)
Scherbak, Barb (1958—)
Schlegel, Elfi (1964—)
Schmirler, Sandra (1963–2000)
Schneider, Angela (1959—)
Schuler, Laura (1970—)
Scott, Barbara Ann (1929—)
Scott, Beckie (1970—)
Secord, Laura (1775–1868)
Senior, Olive (1941—)
Seymour, Jane (c. 1898–1956)
Seymour, Lynn (1939—)
Shaw, Flora Madeline (1864–1927)
Shearer, Norma (1900–1983)
Sherk, Cathy (1950—)
Shewchuk, Tammy Lee (1977—)
Shields, Carol (1935–2003)
Shipman, Nell (1892–1970)
Shore, Henrietta (1880–1963)
Shortt, Elizabeth Smith (1859–1949)
Simmons, Erin (1976—)
Simons, Beverly (1938—)
Sipprell, Clara (1885–1975)
Skinner, Constance Lindsay (1877–1939)
Skinner, Julie (1968—)
Sloan, Susan (1958—)
Small, Sami Jo (1976—)
Smart, Elizabeth (1913–1986)
Smellie, Elizabeth Lawrie (1884–1968)
Smith, Alexis (1921–1993)
Smith, Bev (1960—)
Smith, Donalda (d. 1998)
Smith, Ethel (1907–1979)
Smith, Fiona (1973—)
Smith, Gina (1957—)
Smith, Mary Ellen (1861–1933)
Smith, Rebecca (1959—)
Smith, Shannon (1961—)
Smith, Tricia (1957—)
Smucker, Barbara (1915–2003)
Smyth, Donna (1943—)
Snively, Mary Agnes (1847–1933)
Sostorics, Colleen (1979—)
Squires, Helena E. (1879–1959)
St. Louis, France (1959—)
St. Pierre, Kim (1978—)
Stahl, Rose (1870–1955)
Starr, Muriel (1888–1950)
Stern, Elizabeth (1915–1980)
Stewart, Alexandra (1939—)
Stewart, Isabel Maitland (1878–1963)
Stewart, Olga Margaret (1920–1998)
Story, Gertrude (1929—)
Stowe, Emily Howard (1831–1903)
Stratas, Teresa (1938—)
Streit, Marlene Stewart (1934—)
Strike, Hilda (1910–1989)
Strong, Lori (1972—)
Summers, Merna (1933—)
Sunohara, Vicky (1970—)
Sydor, Alison (1966—)
Szumigalski, Anne (1922–1999)
Taillon, Jacinthe (1977—)
Tanguay, Eva (1878–1947)
Tanner, Elaine (1951—)
Tatham, Reidun (1978—)
Taverner, Sonia (1936—)
Taylor, Angella (1958—)
Taylor, Betty (1916–1977)
Taylor, Brenda (1962—)
Teasdale, Sara (1884–1933)
Tennant, Veronica (1946—)
Tesky, Adeline Margaret (c. 1850–1924)
Théoret, France (1942—)
Thom, Linda (1943—)
Thomas, Audrey (1935—)
Thomas, Clara (1919—)
Thomas, Lillian Beynon (1874–1961)
Thompson, Annie E. (1845–1913)
Thompson, Lesley (1959—)
Tilghman, Shirley M. (1946—)
Tostevin, Lola Lemire (1937—)
Tousek, Yvonne (1980—)
Townsend, Cathy (1937—)
Traill, Catherine Parr (1802–1899)
Treble, Lillian M. (1854–1909)
Tregunno, Jane (1962—)
Trout, Jenny Kidd (1841–1921)
Trudeau, Margaret (1948—)
Tsang, Tasha (1970—)
Tupper, Frances (1826–1912)
Twain, Shania (1965—)
Umeh, Stella (1975—)
Urbaniak, Dorota (1972—)
Van Deman, Irene (1889–1961)
Vanderburg, Helen (1959—)
Van der Kamp, Anna (1972—)
Van der Mark, Christine (1917–1969)
Veazie, Carol (1895–1984)
Vecsei, Eva (1930—)
Verbeek, Tonya (1977—)
Vercheres, Madeleine de (1678–1747)
Vicent, Tania (1976—)
Vilagos, Penny (1963—)
Vilagos, Vicky (1963—)
Waddington, Miriam (1917–2004)
Wagner, Barbara (1938—)
Waldo, Carolyn (1964—)
Wallace, Bronwen (1945–1989)
Wallace, Lila Acheson (1889–1984)
Walters, Lisa (1960—)
Walton, Dorothy (1908—)
Watson, Lucile (1879–1962)
Watson, Sheila (1909–1998)
Webb, Phyllis (1927—)
Weinzweig, Helen (1915—)
Wetherald, Ethelwyn (1857–1940)
Wheatcroft, Georgina (1965—)
Wheeler, Lucile (1935—)
White, Oona (1922–2005)
Whitton, Charlotte (1896–1975)
Wickenheiser, Hayley (1978—)
Wieland, Joyce (1931–1998)
Wilkes, Debbi (c. 1947—)
Wilkinson, Anne (1910–1961)
Wilkinson, Marguerite Ogden (1883–1928)
Williams, Lynn (1960—)
Willing, Jennie Fowler (1834–1916)
Wilson, Bertha (1923—)
Wilson, Cairine (1885–1962)
Wilson, Ethel (1888–1980)
Wilson, Jean (1910–1933)
Wilson, Ruth (1919–2001)
Wilson, Stacy (1965—)
Wilson, Tracy
Wolf, Hazel (1898–2000)
Woodley, Erin (1972—)
Worthington, Kay (1959—)
Wray, Fay (1907—)
Wright, Dana (1959—)
Wright, L.R. (1939–2001)
Wyatt, Rachel (1929—)
Ye Jiayin (1924—)
Yeomans, Amelia (1842–1913)
Youville, Marie Marguerite d' (1701–1771)
Zurek, Natasza (1978—)

CANADIAN FIRST NATIONS INDIGENOUS WOMEN

Aquash, Anna Mae (1945–1976)
Johnson, E. Pauline (1861–1913)
Pitseolak (c. 1900–1983)
Sainte-Marie, Buffy (1941—)
Tekakwitha, Kateri (1656–1680)

CAPPADOCIA

District of eastern Asia Minor
Former satrapy of Persian Empire
Became semi-independent kingdom and a separate dynasty (c. 255 BCE)
Became Roman province (1st c. CE)
See Asia Minor.

CARIA

Ancient division of southwest Asia Minor
Settled by Doric and Ionic colonies
Ruled by independent king Mausolus (c. 4th c. BCE)
Taken from Persia by Alexander (4th c. BCE)
Incorporated in Roman province of Asia (129 BCE)
See Asia Minor.

CARIBBEAN

See West Indies.

CARINTHIA

Southern Austrian state
Originally inhabited by Celts
Part of Roman province of Noricum
Invaded by Germans and Slovens
Part of Bavaria, belonged to Carolingian Empire (8th c.)
Became separate duchy (10th c.)
Passed to Habsburgs (14th c.)
Became Austrian crownland (1849)
Southern portion taken by Yugoslavia (1920)
See Austria.

CARISBROOKE

Village and parish in Isle of Wight, southern England
See England.

CARTHAGE

Ancient city and state in North Africa
Founded by colonists from Kingdom of Tyre (8th c. BCE)
Conquered West Africa, Sicily, and Sardinia (5th c. BCE)
Engaged in Punic Wars with Rome (3rd c. BCE)
Destroyed following Third Punic War (2nd c. BCE)
Site of colony founded by Caesar (1st c. BCE)
Captured by Vandals (5th c.)
Part of Byzantine Empire (6th c.)
Lost to Arabs (7th c.)

Kahina (r. 695–703)
Sophonisba (c. 225–203 BCE)

CASAMANCE

Region in West Africa (now Senegal)
See Senegal.

CASERTA

Province of Campania, Italy
See Italy.

Geographic Index

CASSEL

City in West Germany, founded (before 10th c.)
Captured by France; aided Britain in war against America (18th c.)
Capital of Kingdom of Westphalia (19th c.)
See Germany.

CASTILE

Region in, and ancient kingdom of Spain
Originally extension of Kingdom of León (10th c.)
United with Navarre (1029)
United with León (1037)
Conquered Moorish kingdoms (11th–13th c.)
United with Aragon (1479)
See Spain.

CELLE

City in Saxony, West Germany
See Germany.

CENTRAL AFRICAN REPUBLIC

Capital city of Bangui established by France (1889)
United with Chad to form French colony of Ubangi-Shari-Chad (1906)
Became part of French Equitorial Africa (1910)
Separated from Chad (1920)
Became republic within French Community (1958)
Achieved independence (1960)

Domitien, Elisabeth (1926—)
Ruth-Rolland, J.M. (1937–1995)

CEYLON

Center of Buddhist civilization (3rd c. BCE)
Settled by the Portuguese (1505)
Settled by the Dutch (1658)
Settled by the British (1796)
Colonized by Britain (1833)
Achieved independence (1948)
Known as Sri Lanka (1972)

Anula (r. 47–42 BCE)
Bandaranaike, Sirimavo (1916–2000)
Fernando, Sylvia (1904–1983)
Kumaratunga, Chandrika Bandaranaike (1945—)
Sivali (d. 93)

CHAMBORD

Village in Loir-et-Cher department of France
See France.

CHAMPAGNE

Region of northeastern France
See France.

CHANNEL ISLANDS

Hewett, Ellen Anne (1843–1926)

CHARTRES

City in Eure-et-Loir department of France
See France.

CHATILLON

Commune in Hauts-de-Seine department of France
See France.

CHEROKEE

Native North American Southeast indigenous group

Jemison, Alice Lee (1901–1964)
Mankiller, Wilma (1945—)
Nanye'hi (1738–1822)
Smallwood, Norma (c. 1908–1966)

CHEYENNE

Native North American Great Plains indigenous group

Buffalo-Calf-Road-Woman (fl. 1876)

CHICANA

See Mexican-American.

CHICKASAW

Hogan, Linda (1947—)

CHILE

Republic in southwest South America
North settled by the Inca (15th c.)
Invaded by Spain (16th c.)
Gained independence (1818)

Ahrens, Marlene (1933—)
Alexander, Leni (1924—)
Allende, Isabel (1942—)
Antony, Hilda (1896–?)
Bombal, María Luisa (1910–1980)
Brunet, Marta (1897–1967)
Cassidy, Sheila (1937—)
Cintrón, Conchita (1922—)
de Alonso, Carmen (1909—)
Falkenburg, Jinx (1919–2003)
Figueroa, Ana (1907–1970)
Gaboimilla
Kirkwood, Julieta (1936–1985)
Marin, Gladys (1941–2005)
Marín del Solar, Mercedes (1804–1866)
Mistral, Gabriela (1889–1957)
Parra, Violeta (1917–1967)
Petit, Magdalena (1900–1968)
Poliakova, Elena (1884–1972)
Renard, Rosita (1894–1949)
Vargas, Virginia (1945—)
Yáñez, María Flora (1898–1982)

CHINA

Ruled by Chou Dynasty (12th–3rd c. BCE)
Divided into warring feudal states (8th–3rd c. BCE)
Ruled by Han Dynasty (202 BCE–220 CE)
Reconquered Annam and Canton; took northern Korea
Buddhism introduced (1st c. CE)
Split into kingdoms of Han, Wu, and Wei (3rd c.)
Christianity and Islam introduced (7th–10th c.)
Ruled by Sung Dynasty (960–1127)
Ruled by Southern Sungs (1127–1280)
Ruled by Mongol Dynasty (1260–1368)
Ming Dynasty established (1368–1644)
Under Manchu Dynasty, Chinese Empire included Manchuria, Mongolia, Tibet, and Turkistan; and claims to Korea, Annam, Siam, Burma and Nepal (17th c.)
Lost Hong Kong, Korea, Taiwan, and Pescadores (1895)
Manchu Dynasty overthrown and Chinese Republic established (1922)

A Nong (c. 1005–1055)
An Zhongxin (Fl. 1996)
Bai Fengxi (1934—)
Bai Wei (1894–1987)
Ban Jieyu (c. 48–c. 6 BCE)
Ban Zhao (c. 45–c. 120)
Ba Yan (1962—)
Bi Wenjing (1981—)
Bridgman, Eliza Jane (1805–1871)
Cai Chang (1900–1990)
Cai Huijue
Cai Yan (c. 162–239)
Cao Mianying
Carmona, Adriana (1972—)
Chabi (fl. 13th c.)
Chai, Ling (1966—)
Chang, Eileen (1920–1995)
Chao Na
Chen, Joan (1961—)
Chen, Joyce (1918–1994)
Chen, Lu (1976—)
Chen, Si-Lan (1909—)
Chen Cuiting (1971—)
Chen Duansheng (1751–1796)
Chen Hong (1968—)
Chen Jieru (fl. 1920)
Chen Jing (1968—)
Chen Jing (1975—)
Chen Jingrong (1917–1989)
Chen Li Ju (1981—)
Chen Lu (1976—)
Chen Muhua (c. 1940—)
Chennault, Anna (1923—)
Chen Ruiqing (1932—)
Chen Shih Hsin (1978—)
Chen Tiejun (1904–1928)
Chen Xiaomin (1977—)
Chen Yan (1981—)
Chen Yanqing (1979—)
Chen Yongyan (1962—)
Chen Yuefang (1963—)
Chen Yueling (1968—)
Chen Yufeng
Chen Zhen (1963—)
Chen Zhong (1982—)
Chen Zihe (1968—)
Chen Zongying (1902–2003)
Cheung, Katherine (1904–2003)
Chin, Tsai (1937—)
Ching Shih (fl. 1807–1810)
Chi Shu-Ju (c. 1983—)
Ci'an (1837–1881)
Cixi (1835–1908)
Cong Xued (1963—)
Cui Yongmei (1969—)
Dai, Ailian (1916–2006)
Dai Houying (1938–1996)
Dai Qing (1941—)
Deng (r. 105–121)
Deng Yaping (1973—)
Deng Yingchao (1903–1992)
Deng Yuzhi (1900–1996)
Ding Ling (1904–1985)
Ding Meiyuan (1979—)
Ding Ning (1924—)
Dong Fangxiao (1983—)
Doo, Unui (1873/75?–1940)
Eames, Emma (1865–1952)
Fan Yunjie (1972—)
Fearn, Anne Walter (1865–1939)
Feng, Amy (1969—)
Feng Keng (1907–1931)
Feng Kun (1978—)
Feng Yuanjun (1900–1974)
Frame, Alice (1878–1941)
Fu Hao (fl. 1040 BCE)
Fulton, Mary Hannah (1854–1927)
Fu Mingxia (1978—)
Fu Yuehua (c. 1947—)
Gao E (1962—)
Gao Feng (1982—)
Gao Hong (1967—)
Gao Jing (1975—)
Gao Jun (1969—)
Gao Ling (1979—)
Gao Min (1970—)
Gao Xiumin (1963—)
Gao Yaojie (c. 1927—)
Ge Cuilin (1930—)
Ge Fei (1975—)
Ge Yang (1916—)
Gong Zhichao (1977—)
Guan Daosheng (1262–1319)
Guan Weizhen (1964—)
Gu Jun (1975—)
Guo Dandan (1977—)

Guo Jingjing (1981—)
Guo Yue (1988—)
Gu Xiaoli (1971—)
Han, Suyin (1917—)
Han Aili (1937—)
Han Suyin (1917—)
Han Xue (1981—)
Han Yaqin (1963—)
He Jianping (1963—)
He Jun (1969—)
He Liping
He Qi (1973—)
He Xiangning (1879–1972)
He Yanwen (1966—)
He Ying (1977—)
He Zizhen (fl. 1930s)
Himiko (fl. 3rd c.)
Hou Yuzhu (1963—)
Hua Mu-Lan (fl. 5th c.)
Huang Hua (1969—)
Huang Mandan (1983—)
Huang Nanyan (1977—)
Huang Qingyun (1920—)
Huang Qun (1969—)
Huang Shanshan (1986—)
Huang Sui (1982—)
Huang Xiaomin (1970—)
Huang Zhihong (1965—)
Huang Zongying (1925—)
Hu Die (1908–1989)
Hu Yadong (1968—)
James, Annie Isabella (1884–1965)
Jiang Cuihua
Jiang Qing (1914–1991)
Jiang Ying (1963—)
Jiang Yonghua (1973—)
Jiao Zhimin (1963—)
Ji Liya (1981—)
Kang Keqing (1911–1992)
Kawashima, Yoshiko (1906–1947)
Ke Yan (1929—)
Kui Yuanyuan (1981—)
Kuo Yi-Hang (1975—)
Lai Yawen (1970—)
Lang Ping (1960—)
Lao Lishi (1987—)
Lee, Rose Hum (1904–1964)
Lee Lai-shan (1970—)
Lei Li
Le Jingyi (1975—)
Li, Florence Tim Oi (1907–1992)
Liang Desheng (1771–1847)
Liang Qin
Liang Yan (1961—)
Li Chunxiu (1969—)
Li Dongmei (1969—)
Li Du (1982—)
Li Duihong (1970—)
Li Feng-Ying (1975—)
Li Guojun (1966—)
Li Huifen (1963—)
Li Huixin (1937—)
Li Ji (1986—)
Li Ju (1976—)
Li Lan (1961—)
Li Lingjuan (1966—)
Li Meisu (1959—)
Lin, Hazel (1913–1986)
Lin, Tai-yi (1926—)
Li Na (1984—)
Ling Jie (1982—)
Ling Shuhua (1904–1990)
Lin Haiyin (1918–2001)
Lin Li (1970—)
Lin Qiaozhi (1901–1983)
Lin Sang (1977—)
Lin Weining (1979—)
Lin Yanfen (1971—)
Li Qing (1972—)
Li Qingzhao (1083–c. 1151)
Li Ronghua (1956—)
Li Shan (1980—)
Li Shufang (1979—)
Li Shuxian (1924–1997)
Li Ting (1980—)
Li Ting (1987—)
Liu, Nienling (1934—)
Liu Ailing (1967—)
Liu Chunhong (1985—)
Liu Jun (1969—)
Liu Limin (1976—)
Liu Liping (1958—)
Liu Qing (1964—)
Liu Wei
Liu Xia (1979—)
Liu Xiaoning (1975—)
Liu Xuan (1979—)
Liu Xuqing (1968—)
Liu Yaju
Liu Yanan (1980—)
Liu Ying (1974—)
Liu Yumei (1961—)
Liu Yuxiang (1975—)
Liu Zhen (1930—)
Li Xiaoqin (1961—)
Li Xin (1969—)
Li Yan (1976—)
Li Yanjun (1963—)
Li Yueming (1968—)
Li Yuqin (d. 2001)
Li Zhongyun (1967—)
Li Zhuo (1981—)
Lo Keong, Matilda (c. 1854–1915)
Lord, Bette Bao (1938—)
Luan Jujie (1958—)
Lu Bin (1977—)
Lü Hou (r. 195–180 BCE)
Lu Huali (1972—)
Lu Li (1976—)
Luo Shu (1903–1938)
Luo Wei (1983—)
Luo Xuejuan (1984—)
Lu Yin (1899–1934)
Mao Fumei (1892–?)
Ma Xiangjun (1964—)
Ma Yanhong (1963—)
Ma Ying
Mellish, Edith Mary (1861–1922)
Min, Anchee (1957—)
Mo Huilan (1979—)
Nathoy, Lalu (1853–1933)
Nian Yun (c. 1983—)
Nieh Hualing (1925—)
Niu Jianfeng (1981—)
Nong Qunhua (1966—)
Ou Jingbai
Pang Jiaying (1985—)
Pan Wenli (1969—)
Peng Ping (1967—)
Pi Hongyan (1979—)
Qian Hong (1971—)
Qian Zhengying (1923—)
Qiao Hong (1968—)
Qiao Yunping
Qin Dongya (1978—)
Qin Yiyuan
Qiu Chen (1963—)
Qiu Jin (c. 1875–1907)
Qu Yunxia (1972—)
Ru Zhijuan (1925—)
Sang Lan (1981—)
Sang Xue (1984—)
Scherchen, Tona (1938—)
Shan Ying (1978—)
Shen Rong (1935—)
Shi Guihong
Shui Qingxia (1976—)
Song Meiling (1897–2003)
Song Nina (1980—)
Song Qingling (1893–1981)
Song Sisters
Song Xiaobo (1958—)
Su Hsueh-lin (1897–1999)
Su Hui (fl. 4th c.)
Su Huijuan (1964—)
Sui Xinmei
Sun Dandan
Sun Fuming (1974—)
Sun Jin (1980—)
Sun Qingmei
Sun Tian Tian (1981—)
Sun Wen (1973—)
Sun Xiulan (1961—)
Sun Yue (1973—)
Tang Gonghong (1979—)
Tang Jiuhong (1969—)
Tang Lin (1975—)
Tang Yongshu
Tan Xue (1984—)
Tao Hua
Tao Luna (1974—)
Van Chu-Lin (1893/94?–1946)
Wang Chengyi (1983—)
Wang Chunlu (1978—)
Wang Fang (1967—)
Wang Guangmei (1922—)
Wang Hong (1965—)
Wang Huifeng (1968—)
Wang Jun (1963—)
Wang Junxia (1973—)
Wang Lihong (1970—)
Wang Lina (1978—)
Wang Linwei (1956—)
Wang Liping (1973—)
Wang Liping (1976—)
Wang Mingxing (1961—)
Wang Nan (1978—)
Wang Xianbo
Wang Xiaohong (1968—)
Wang Xiaozhu (1973—)
Wang Xu (1985—)
Wang Yajun (1962—)
Wang Yan (1971—)
Wang Yi (1973—)
Wang Ying
Wang Zhaojun (52 BCE–18 CE)
Wang Ziling (1972—)
Wa Shi (1498–1560)
Wei Haiying
Wei Junyi (1917–2002)
Wei Ning (1982—)
Wei Qiang
Wei Shuo (272–349)
Wencheng (c. 620–680)
Wen Jieruo (1927—)
Wen Lirong (1969—)
Wen Xiaoyu (1938—)
Wong, Anna May (1907–1961)
Wong, Jade Snow (1919—)
Wu, Chien-Shiung (1912–1997)
Wu Dan (1968—)
Wu Hui Ju (1982—)
Wu Jiani (1966—)
Wu Lanying (d. 1929)
Wu Minxia (1985—)
Wu Wenying (1932—)
Wu Xiaoxuan (1958—)
Wu Xingjiang (1957—)

Wu Yi (1938—)
Wu Yongmei (1975—)
Wu Zetian (624–705)
Xian Dongmei (1975—)
Xiang Jingyü (1895–1928)
Xiao Hong (1911–1942)
Xiaojiao Sun (1984—)
Xie Huilin (1975—)
Xie Wanying (1900–1999)
Xie Xide (1921–2000)
Xing Huina (1984—)
Xiu Lijuan (1957—)
Xue Shen (1978—)
Xue Tao (c. 760–c. 832)
Xu Jian
Xu Nannan (1979—)
Xu Yanmei (1971—)
Xu Yanwei (1984—)
Yan Fang
Yang Bo (1973—)
Yang Hao (1980—)
Yang Jiang (b. 1911)
Yang Shaoqi
Yang Wei (1979—)
Yang Wenyi (1972—)
Yang Xia (1977—)
Yang Xiao (1964—)
Yang Xiaojun (1963—)
Yang Xilan (1961—)
Yang Yang (1976—)
Yang Yang (1977—)
Yang Ying (1977—)
Yang Yu (1985—)
Yang Yun (c. 1984—)
Yao Fen (1967—)
Ye Jiayin (1924—)
Ye Qiaobo (1964—)
Ye Wenling (1942—)
Ye Zhaoying (1974—)
Yin Jian (1978—)
Yoshiko Kawashima (1906–1948)
Yuan, Tina (c. 1950—)
Yuan Hua (1974—)
Yuan Jing (b. 1914)
Yuan Shu Chi (1984—)
Yu Hongqi
Yu Lihua (1932—)
Yu Manzhen (fl. 1900)
Zeng Xiaoying (1929—)
Zhang Chunfang
Zhang Di (1968—)
Zhang Hui (1959—)
Zhang Jie (1937—)
Zhang Jiewen (1981—)
Zhang Juanjuan (1981—)
Zhang Meihong (1963—)
Zhang Na (1980—)
Zhang Nan (1986—)
Zhang Ning (1975—)
Zhang Ouying (1975—)
Zhang Peijun (1958—)
Zhang Ping (1982—)
Zhang Rongfang (1957—)
Zhang Ruifang (1918—)
Zhang Shan (1968—)
Zhang Xianghua (1968—)
Zhang Xiaodong (1964—)
Zhang Xiuyun (1976—)
Zhang Yali (1964—)
Zhang Yanmei
Zhang Yining (1981—)
Zhang Yuehong (1975—)
Zhang Yueqin (1960—)
Zhan Shuping (1964—)
Zhao Kun (1973—)
Zhao Lihong (1972—)
Zhao Luorui (b. 1912)
Zhao Ruirui (1981—)
Zhao Yufen (1948—)
Zheng Dongmei (1967—)
Zheng Haixia (1967—)
Zheng Meizhu (1962—)
Zheng Min (1920—)
Zhong Honglian
Zhou Jihong (1965—)
Zhou Mi (1979—)
Zhou Ping (1968—)
Zhou Qiurui (1967—)
Zhou Shouying (1969—)
Zhou Suhong (1979—)
Zhou Xiaolan (1957—)
Zhou Xiuhua (1966—)
Zhuang Xiaoyan (1969—)
Zhuang Yong (1972—)
Zhu Juefeng (1964—)
Zhu Ling (1957—)
Zhu Yingwen (1981—)
Zhu Yunying (1978—)
Zong Pu (1928—)

CHOCTAW

Native North American Southeast indigenous group

Victor, Wilma (1919–1987)
Wright, Muriel Hazel (1889–1975)

CLEVELAND

District in North Riding, Yorkshire, England

See England.

CLEVES

Old duchy of Germany
Passed to elector of Brandenburg and to Prussia (17th c.)
Passed to France (1805)
Reverted to Prussia (1814)
Occupied by Belgians (1925)

See Germany.
See Prussia.

COBURG

City in Bavaria, West Germany
Passed to Ernestine line of dukes of Saxony (1485)
Seat of dukes of Coburg and residence of dukes of Saxe-Coburg-Gotha
Capital of Saxe-Coburg (1735)
Became part of Bavaria (1920)

See Bavaria.
See Germany.

COLOMBIA

Claimed by Spain (16th c.)
Made separate viceroyalty of New Granada (18th c.)
Achieved independence from Spain (1819)
Lost Venezuela and Ecuador (1830)
Reorganized into Grenadine Confederation (1858)
Reorganized into United States of Colombia (1863)
Reorganized with Panama into Republic of Colombia (1886)
Lost Panama (1903)
Settled border disputes with Ecuador, Venezuela, Brazil, and Peru (1919–1934)
Joined Andean Group (1969)

Acosta de Samper, Soledad (1833–1913)
Angel, Albalucía (1939—)
Arango, Débora (1907—)
Béltran, Manuela (fl. 18th c.)
Betancourt, Ingrid (1961—)
Cano, María (1887–1967)
Carranza, María Mercedes (1945–2003)
Castillo y Guevara, Francisca Josefa del (1671–1742)
Daniels, Martha Catalina (d. 2002)
González, Beatriz (1938—)
Mikey, Fanny (1931—)
Mosquera Mena, Mabel (1969—)
Portal, Marta (1930—)
Restrepo, Ximena (1969—)
Salavarrieta, Pola (1795–1817)
Shakira (1977—)
Urrutia, Maria Isabel (1965—)
Vieira, Maruja (1922—)
Zapata Olivella, Delia (1926–2001)

CONGO

Republic in Equatorial Africa
Became a territory of French Equatorial Africa (1910)
Became republic within French community (1958)
Achieved independence (1960)

Beatrice, Dona (c. 1684–1706)

CONSTANTINOPLE (NOW ISTANBUL)

Province of Turkey
Founded by Greeks as Byzantium (7th c. BCE)
Name changed to Constantinople (330 CE)
Capital of Byzantine Empire

See Byzantine Empire.

COOK ISLANDS

Group of 15 islands in South Pacific Ocean
Discovered by Captain Cook (1773)
Became British protectorate (1888)
Became part of New Zealand (1901)

See New Zealand.

CORNWALL

Former county in southwest England
Became a duchy (1337)

See England.

CORSICA

French Island in Mediterranean Sea

See France.

COSTA RICA

Carvajal, María Isabel (1888–1949)
Montealegre, Felicia (d. 1978)
Naranjo, Carmen (1928—)
Odio Benito, Elizabeth (1939—)
Poll, Claudia (1972—)
Poll, Sylvia (1970—)
Vargas, Chavela (1919—)

COURLAND

Former Russian territory on East Baltic coast
A duchy inhabited by Lettish people and Cours (13th c.)
Conquered by Teutonic Knights
Given to Poland and Lithuania
Became Polish duchy (1561)
Came under Russian rule (1737)
Became part of Latvia (1918)

See Latvia.
See Poland.
See Russia.

CREE

Canadian First Nations indigenous group

McDougall, Adelaide (1909–2000)
Sainte-Marie, Buffy (1941—)

CREEK

Native North American Southeast indigenous group

Francis, Milly (c. 1802–1848)
Musgrove, Mary (c. 1690–c. 1763)

CRIMEA

Subdivision of Ukrainian S.S.R. and U.S.S.R.

Cimmerian inhabitants expelled by Scythians (7th c. BCE)
West coast settled by Greeks (6th c. BCE)
Seat of Greek kingdom of Cimmerian Bosporus (5th c.)
Invaded by Goths, Huns, and Khazars, who held Crimea in Russian kingdom (7th–10th c.)
Part of Byzantine Empire (until c. 1000)
Belonged to Khanate of Golden Horde (13th c.)
Tatar khanate overthrown by Ottoman Turks (15th c.)
Incorporated by Russia (1783)
Proclaimed independent Crimean Republic (1918)
Republic liquidated (1945)
See Russia.

CROATIA

Inhabited by Croats (7th c.)
Became a kingdom (10th c.)
Ruled by Hungary (1091–1526)
Ruled by Turkey (1526–1809)
Ruled by France; became part of Napoleon's Illyrian Provinces (1809–1813)
Ruled by Austria-Hungary (1813–1918)
United to establish kingdom of Serbs, Croats, and Slovenes (1918)
Croatia and Slavonia became Savaska and united with Primorje to form Croatia (1941)
Becomes federative republic (1946)
Proclaims independence (1991)

Bošković, Anica (1714–1804)
Brlič-Mažuranić, Ivana (1874–1938)
Di Murska, Ilma (1836–1889)
Hanka, Erika (1905–1958)
Helen of Hungary (fl. mid-1000s)
Jambrišak, Marija (1847–1937)
Jarnević, Dragojla (1812–1875)
Kostelic, Janica (1982—)
Majoli, Iva (1977—)
Mallinger, Mathilde (1847–1920)
Milanov, Zinka (1906–1989)
Parun, Vesna (1922—)
Pejacevic, Dora (1885–1923)
Planinc, Milka (1924—)
Ternina, Milka (1863–1941)
Tito, Jovanka Broz (1924—)
Zagorka (1873–1957)
Zrinska, Ana Katarina (1625–1673)
Zuzoric, Cvijeta (c. 1555–1600)

CROTONA

Commune in Cantanzaro province in southern Italy
See Italy.

CUBA

Island in Greater Antilles, West Indies
Discovered by Columbus and claimed by Spain (1492)
Havana captured by Britain (1762–1763)
United States entered Spanish-American War following Cuban revolts (1898)
Became protectorate of United States (1901)
Established as a republic (1902)
Proclaimed a Communist state (1959)

Aguero, Taimaris (1977—)
Aguirre, Mirta (1912—)
Alonso, Alicia (1921—)
Alonso, Dora (1910–2001)
Alvarez Rios, Maria (1919—)
Barros, Zoila (1976—)
Bell, Regla (1971—)
Beltran, Daima (1972—)
Bernal, Emilia (1884–1964)
Borrero, Dulce María (1883–1945)
Borrero, Juana (1877–1896)
Bosch, Aurora (c. 1940—)
Cabrera, Lydia (1899–1991)
Calderon Diaz, Rosir (1984—)
Calderon Martinez, Mercedes (1965—)
Carrillo de la Paz, Nancy (1986—)
Carvajal Rivera, Magaly Esther (1968—)
Chacón Nardi, Rafaela (1926–2001)
Chivás, Silvia (1954—)
Cobian, Miguelina (1941—)
Colon, Maria (1958—)
Costa, Marlenis (1973—)
Crawford Rogert, Yunaika (1982—)
Cruz, Celia (1924–2003)
Cumba Jay, Yumileidi (1975—)
Diaz-Balart, Mirta (c. 1928—)
Elejarde, Marlene (1950–1989)
Espín de Castro, Vilma (1934—)
Fernandez, Alina (1956—)
Fernandez, Ana Ivis (1973—)
Francia, Mirka (1975—)
García, Marta (c. 1945—)
García Marruz, Fina (1923—)
Gato, Idalmis (1971—)
Gomez, Sara (1943–1974)
Gonzalez Morales, Driulys (1973—)
Grajales, Mariana (1808–1893)
Hatch, Annia (1978—)
Izquierdo, Lilia (1967—)
Laborde Duanes, Yurisel (1979—)
Labrada Diaz, Yanelis Yuliet (1981—)
La Lupe (1939–1992)
Latamblet Daudinot, Norka (1962—)
Loynaz, Dulce María (1902–1997)
Luis, Alejandrina (1967—)
Luna Castellano, Diadenis
Lupetey Cobas, Yurieleidys (1981—)
Marley, Rita (1946—)
Marten Garcia, Maritza (1963—)
Martinez Adlun, Maybelis (1977—)
Marucha (1944–1991)
Matamoros, Mercedes (1851–1906)
Melendez Rodriguez, Urbia
Méndez, Josefina (c. 1940—)
Menendez, Osleidys (1979—)
Mesa Luaces, Liana (1977—)
Moreno, Yipsi (1980—)
Munoz Carrazana, Aniara (1980—)
O'Farrill, Raisa (1972—)
Ortiz Calvo, Tania (1965—)
Ortiz Charro, Yahima (1981—)
Plá, Mirta (1940–2003)
Quesada, Violetta (1947—)
Quintero Alvarez, Ioamnet (1972—)
Quirot, Ana (1963—)
Ramirez Hechevarria, Daymi (1983—)
Reve Jimenez, Odalis (1970—)
Rodríguez, Ana (1938—)
Rodriguez, Estelita (1928–1966)
Rodriguez Villanueva, Estela (1967—)
Romay, Fulgencia (1944—)
Ruiz, Rosie (c. 1954—)
Ruiz, Yumilka (1978—)
Sanchez, Celia (1920–1980)
Sanchez Salfran, Marta (1973—)
Santamaría, Haydée (1922–1980)
Saralegui, Cristina (1948—)
Savon Carmenate, Amarilys (1974—)
Tellez Palacio, Dulce M. (1983—)
Torres, Regla (1975—)
Valdes, Carmen (1954—)
Velásquez, Loreta (1842–1897)
Veranes, Sibelis (1974—)
Verdecia, Legna (1972—)

CYPRUS

Island republic in Mediterranean Sea
Colonized by ancient Greeks
Ruled by Assyrian, Persian, Ptolemaic, and Byzantine Empires (until 7th c.)
Captured by Saracens (7th–10th c.)
Captured by England (12th c.)
Ruled by Lusignan dynasty (12th–15th c.)
Ruled by Turkey (16th–19th c.)
Became British crown colony (1925–1960)
Achieved independence (1960)

Alice of Champagne (fl. 1200s)
Anastasia (fl. 500s)
Anne of Lusignan (b. before 1430)
Charlotte of Lusignan (1442–1487)
Christofi, Styllou (c. 1900–1954)
Comitona (fl. 500s)
Cornaro, Caterina (1454–1510)
Helen Paleologina (c. 1415–1458)
Isabella (d. 1282)
Isabella of Cyprus (fl. 1250s)
Medea (d. 1440)
Plaisance of Antioch (d. 1261)

CYRENE

Ancient city in North Africa
Settled by the Greeks (6th c. BCE)
Ruled by Ptolemies (4th c. BCE)
Became Roman province with Crete (1st c. BCE)

Pheretima (fl. 6th c. BCE)

CZECHOSLOVAKIA

Inhabited by Slavic tribes (6th c.)
Czech tribes of Moravia helped destroy Avar Empire (c. 796)
Magyar invasion ended unity of Czech and Slovak tribes (c. 907)
Ruled by Habsburgs (17th c.)
Republic formed by Czechs and Slovaks from Austria-Hungary (1918)
Sudetenland annexed to Germany; Teschen to Poland; Ruthenia to Hungary (1938)
Declared independence (1939)
Remainder of Czech state became German protectorate of Bohemia and Moravia (1939–1945)
Came under Soviet domination (1948)
Bohemia and Moravia became Czech Republic; Slovakia became Slovak Republic (1992)

Adela of Meissen (fl. 1100s)
Agnes of Bohemia (1205–1282)
Agnes of Bohemia (1269–1297)
Albright, Madeleine (1937—)
Blazkova, Milada (1958—)
Bobkova, Hana (1929—)
Bosakova-Vechtova, Eva (1931–1991)
Buresova, Charlotte (1904–1984)
Caslavska, Vera (1942—)
Çermakova, Jirina (1944—)
Černínová z Harasova, Zuzana (1601–1654)
Chadimova, Alena (1931—)
Charvatova, Olga (1962—)
Chytilova, Vera (1929—)
Clauss-Szárvady, Wilhelmina (1834–1907)
Dekanova, Vlasta (1909–1974)
Derickson, Uli (1944–2005)
Destinn, Emmy (1878–1930)
Dobesova, Bozena (1914—)
Dostalova, Leopolda (1879–1972)
Drevjana, Alena (1969—)
Duchkova, Milena (1952—)
Fibingerova, Helena (1949—)
Fikotová, Olga (1932—)
Fischer, Greta (1909–1988)
Foltova, Vlasta (1913—)
Gruberová, Edita (1946—)
Hajkova, Jirina (1954—)
Halamová, Masa (1908–1995)
Handzová, Viera (1931–1997)
Hauková, Jiřina (1919—)
Havel, Olga (1933–1996)
Hilgertova, Stepanka (1968—)
Hodrova, Daniela (1946—)
Honsova, Zdeka (1927–1994)
Hrebrinova, Anna (1908—)
Hruba, Berta (1946—)

Hubackova, Ida (1954—)
Hykova, Lenka (1985—)
Jaburkova, Jozka (d. 1944)
Janauschek, Fanny (1829–1904)
Jeriova, Kvetoslava (1956—)
Jeritza, Maria (1887–1982)
Jesenská, Milena (1896–1945)
Jesenská, Ružena (1863–1940)
Jiricna, Eva (1939—)
Kadlecova, Jirina (1948—)
Kaliska, Elena (1972—)
Kantûrkova, Eva (1930—)
Kapralova, Vitezslava (1915–1940)
Kasparkova, Sarka (1971—)
Kirschner, Lola (1854–1934)
Klimova, Rita (1931–1993)
Kovalova, Marie (1927—)
Krajcirova, Maria (1948—)
Kralickova, Jarmila (1944—)
Krasnohorska, Eliska (1847–1926)
Kratochvilova, Jarmila (1951—)
Krizova, Jirina (1948—)
Kubickova-Posnerova, Jana (1945—)
Kuderikova, Marie (1921–1943)
Kurkova, Katerina (1983—)
Kvapilova, Hana (1860–1907)
Kyselicova, Alena (1957—)
Labakova, Jana (1966—)
Lahodova, Jana (1957—)
Lazarová, Katarina (1914—)
Lindner, Herta (1920–1943)
Liskova, Hana (1952—)
Loudov, Ivana (1941—)
Majerová, Marie (1882–1967)
Mareckova, Eva (1964—)
Marly, Florence (1918–1978)
Marothy-Soltesova, Elena (1855–1939)
Masaryk, Alice Garrigue (1879–1966)
Maskova, Hana (1949–1972)
Matouskova-Sinova, Matylda (1933—)
Menchik, Vera (1906–1944)
Michael of Kent (1945—)
Misakova, Miloslava (1922—)
Moholy, Lucia (1894–1989)
Muellerova, Milena (1923—)
Navratilova, Martina (1956—)
Nemcová, Bozena (c. 1817–1862)
Neruda, Wilma (c. 1838–1911)
Neumannova, Katerina (1973—)
Nováková, Teréza (1853–1912)
Novotna, Jana (1968—)
Novotna, Jarmila (1907–1994)
Oulehlova, Lenka (1973—)
Palfyova, Matylda (1912–1944)
Paulu, Blanka (1954—)
Petrickova, Kvetoslava (1952—)
Pimnacova, Bohumila (1947—)
Plaminkova, Frantiska (1875–1942)
Podhanyiova, Viera (1960—)
Polokova, Iveta (1970—)
Popp, Lucia (1939–1993)
Preissova, Gabriela (1862–1946)
Rabasova, Jana (1933—)
Reichova, Alena (1933—)
Reik, Haviva (1914–1944)
Rezkova, Miloslava (1950—)
Ricna, Hana (1968—)
Ruzickova, Hana (1941–1981)
Ruzickova, Vera (1928—)
Schindler, Emilie (1909–2001)
Schumann-Heink, Ernestine (1861–1936)
Sedlackova, Jaroslava (1946—)
Sikolova, Helena (1949—)
Silhanova, Olga (1920–1986)
Sklenickova, Miroslava (1951—)
Skrbkova, Milada (1897–1965)
Slavikova, Ludmila (1890–1943)
Smidova, Lenka (1975—)
Sramkova, Iveta (1963—)
Srncova, Bozena (1925—)
Sukova, Helena (1965—)
Sukova, Vera (1931–1982)
Suranova-Kucmanova, Eva (1946—)
Svedova-Schoenova, Lydmila (1936—)
Svetla, Caroline (1830–1899)
Svobodova, Gabriela (1953—)
Svubova, Dagmar
Sykorova, Marie (1952—)
Ticho, Anna (1894–1980)
Tkacikova-Tacova, Adolfina (1939—)
Toyen (1902–1980)
Urbanova, Marta (1960—)
Vancurova, Vera (1932—)
Vermirovska, Zdena (1913—)
Vetrovska, Marie (1912–1987)
Vorlova, Slavka (1894–1973)
Vymazalova, Lenka (1959—)
Zatopek, Dana (1922—)
Zguriška, Zuska (1900–1984)

CZECH REPUBLIC

Brejchová, Hana (c. 1943—)
Brejchová, Jana (1940—)
Ralston, Vera Hruba (1921–2003)
Salmonova, Lyda (1889–1968)

DAHOMEY

Republic in West Africa
Became French colony (1894)
Achieved independence (1960)
Changed name to Benin (1976)

Amazon Army of Dahomey (1818–1892)

DARMSTADT

City in Hesse, West Germany
See Germany.

DENMARK

Kingdom in northwest Europe
Settled by Danes (6th c.)
Raided England, France, and Low Countries (8th–10th c.)
Empired included Schleswig, southern Sweden, and England (1014), and Norway and Copenhagen (1018–1035)
Expansion under Waldenmar dynasty (14th c.)
Scandinavia united under Oldenburg monarchy (15th–19th c.)
Warred with independent Sweden and lost power and territory (17th c.)
Norway and Helgoland ceded (1814)
Duchies of Schleswig and Holstein lost in war with Austria and Prussia (1864)
Sold Danish West Indies (Virgin Islands) to United States (1917)
Iceland became a sovereign state in union with Denmark (1918–1944)
Awarded East Greenland (1931)
Occupied by Nazi Germany (1940–1945)
Adopted new constitution (1946)

Adelaide of Hohenlohe-Langenburg (1835–1900)
Adelheid of Holstein (fl. 1314)
Agnes of Brandenburg (d. 1304)
Alexandra of Denmark (1844–1925)
Alexandrina of Mecklenburg-Schwerin (1879–1952)
Alice of Battenberg (1885–1969)
Amelia of Denmark (1580–1639)
Ancher, Anna (1859–1935)
Andersen, Anja Jul (1969—)
Andersen, Camilla (1973—)
Andersen, Greta (1927—)
Andersen, Kristine (1976—)
Andre, Gwili (1908–1959)
Anna Catherina of Brandenburg (1575–1612)
Anna of Brandenburg (1487–1514)
Anna of Denmark (1532–1585)
Anna Sophia of Denmark (1647–1717)
Anne-Marie Oldenburg (1946—)
Anne of Denmark (1574–1619)
Astrup, Heidi (1972—)
Augusta of Schleswig-Holstein (1858–1921)
Augustesen, Susanne (1956—)
Bajer, Matilde (1840–1934)
Bang, Nina (1866–1928)
Begtrup, Bodil (1903–1987)
Benedikte (1944—)
Bennedsen, Dorte (1938—)
Berengaria (1194–1221)
Bidstrup, Jane (c. 1956—)
Bidstrup, Lene (1966—)
Biehl, Charlotta Dorothea (1731–1788)
Bjelke-Petersen, Marie (1874–1969)
Bjerregaard, Ritt (1941—)
Bjørn, Dinna (1947—)
Bodil of Norway (fl. 1090s)
Bohr, Margrethe (1890–1984)
Borregaard Otzen, Christina (1975—)
Boserup, Esther (1910–1999)
Bottzau, Tina (1971—)
Brahe, Sophia (1556–1643)
Bregendahl, Marie (1867–1940)
Brodsgaard, Karen (1978—)
Brøgger, Suzanne (1944—)
Carlstedt, Lily (1926—)
Caroline (1793–1881)
Caroline Amelia of Augustenburg (1796–1881)
Caroline Matilda (1751–1775)
Caroline Matilda of Denmark (1912–1995)
Carstensen-Nathansen, Fritze (1925—)
Castenschiold, Thora (1882–1979)
Catherine of Pomerania (d. 1426)
Charlotte Amalia of Hesse (1650–1714)
Charlotte Amalie (1706–1782)
Charlotte Oldenburg (1789–1864)
Christensen, Inger (1935—)
Christina of Saxony (1461–1521)
Christoffersen, Birte (1924—)
Clausen, Stefanie (1900–1981)
Dagmar of Bohemia (d. 1212)
Daugaard, Line (1978—)
Dinesen, Isak (1885–1962)
Ditlevsen, Tove (1917–1976)
Ditzel, Nana (1923–2005)
Donaldson, Mary (1972—)
Dorothea of Brandenburg (1430–1495)
Dorothea of Denmark (1520–1580)
Dorothea of Denmark (1528–1575)
Dorothea of Saxe-Lauenburg (1511–1571)
Dorothy of Denmark (1546–1617)
Dybkjaer, Lone (1940—)
Dyveke (c. 1491–1517)
Elisabeth of Habsburg (1501–1526)
Elizabeth of Holstein (fl. 1329)
Eriksen, Hanne (1960—)
Estrith (fl. 1017–1032)
Euphemia of Pomerania (d. 1330)
Flindt, Vivi (1943—)
Florman, Marianne (1964—)
Forrest, Ann (1895–1985)
Frahm, Pernille (1954—)
Frederica Amalie (1649–1704)
Freytag-Loringhoven, Elsa von (1875–1927)
Frithpoll, Margaret (d. 1130)
Fruelund, Katrine (1978—)
Genée, Adeline (1878–1970)

Gertrude of Saxony (c. 1155–1196)
Giacobbe, Maria (1928—)
Grahn, Lucile (1819–1907)
Gredal, Eva (1927–1995)
Gress, Elsa (1919–1989)
Groes, Lis (1910–1074)
Gronbek, Maja (1971—)
Gunhilda of Denmark (d. 1002)
Gunhild of Norway (d. 1054)
Gyde (fl. 1054)
Gyllembourg-Ehrensvärd, Thomasine (1773–1856)
Gyrid (fl. 950s)
Gytha (fl. 1022–1042)
Hamann, Conny (1969—)
Hanel, Birgitte (1954—)
Hansen, Anja (1973—)
Hansen, Christina Roslyng (1978—)
Hansen, Trine
Hartel, Lis (1921—)
Harup, Karen-Margrete (1924—)
Heckscher, Grete (1901–1987)
Hedwig of Denmark (1581–1641)
Heemstra, Ella van (1900–1984)
Heiberg, Johanne Luise (1812–1890)
Helvig of Denmark (fl. 1350s)
Henning-Jensen, Astrid (1914–2002)
Hennings, Betty (1850–1939)
Henningsen, Agnes (1868–1962)
Hetha (fl. 10th c.)
Hoff, Karen (1921—)
Hoffman, Anette (1971—)
Holm, Dörthe (c. 1973—)
Honningen, Mette (1944—)
Hveger, Ragnhild (1920—)
Ingeborg (1347–1370)
Ingeborg (d. 1319)
Ingeborg of Russia (fl. 1118–1131)
Ingrid of Sweden (1910–2000)
Isaksen, Lone (1941—)
Jacobsen, Else (1911–1965)
Jacobsen, Inger Kathrine (1867–1939)
Jensen, Anne Elisabet (1951—)
Jensen, Anne Grethe (1951—)
Jensen, Dorte (1972—)
Jensen, Thit (1876–1957)
Jensen, Trine (1980—)
Jespersen, Helle (1968—)
Jorgensen, Rikke Horlykke (1976—)
Jutta (d. 1284)
Karina, Anna (1940—)
Karstens, Gerda (1903–1988)
Kiaerskou, Lotte (1975—)
Kinoshita, Alicia (1967—)
Kirsova, Helene (1910–1962)
Kjaergaard, Tonje (1975—)
Koefoed, Charlotte (1957—)
Kolling, Janne (1968—)
Krebs, Nathalie (1895–1978)
Lachmann, Karen (1916–1962)
Laerkesen, Anna (1942—)
Lander, Margot (1910–1961)
Lander, Toni (1931–1985)
Lathgertha (b. around 665)
Lauritsen, Susanne (1967—)
Lavrsen, Helena (c. 1963—)
Lehmann, Inge (1888–1993)
Leitzel, Lillian (1892–1931)
Leonor of Portugal (1211–1231)
Lind, Nathalie (1918–1999)
Livbjerg, Signe (1980—)
Louise of Denmark (1750–1831)
Louise of England (1724–1751)
Louise of Hesse-Cassel (1688–1765)
Louise of Mecklenburg-Gustrow (1667–1721)
Louise of Saxe-Hilburghausen (1726–1756)
Louise of Sweden (1851–1926)
Lütken, Hulda (1896–1947)
Madsen, Gitte (1969—)
Magdalena Sybilla (1617–1668)
Malinovska, Valentina
Malmfrid of Russia (fl. 1100s)
Margaret Christofsdottir (c. 1305–1340)
Margarethe of Västergötland (fl. 1100)
Margaret I of Denmark (1353–1412)
Margaret of Pomerania (d. 1282)
Margrethe II (1940—)
Maria Juliana of Brunswick (1729–1796)
Marie of Mecklenburg (fl. 1380)
Marie Sophie of Hesse-Cassel (1767–1852)
Martin, Camilla (1974—)
Massen, Osa (1916–2006)
Massy-Beresford, Monica (1894–1945)
Mechtild of Holstein (d. 1288)
Michaëlis, Karin (1872–1950)
Mikkelsen, Henriette Roende (1980—)
Møllerup, Mette (1931—)
Mortensen, Karin (1977—)
Moth, Sophie Amalie (fl. 1670s)
Munk, Kirsten (1598–1658)
Nansen, Betty (1873–1943)
Nielsen, Anja (1975—)
Nielsen, Asta (1881–1972)
Nielsen, Augusta (1822–1902)
Nielsen, Lone Smidt (1961—)
Nielsson, Susanne (1960—)
Noergaard, Louise Bager (1982—)
Oldenburg, Mary (1865–1909)
Ortrud of Schleswig-Holstein-Sonderburg-Glucksburg (1925—)
Osiier, Ellen (1890–1962)
Ostergaard, Solveig (1939—)
Paget, Nielsine (1858–1932)
Pedersen, Helga (1911–1980)
Philippa (1394–1430)
Pontoppidan, Clara (1883–1975)
Pörtner, Margit (c. 1973—)
Price, Ellen (1878–1968)
Price, Juliette (1831–1906)
Qvist, Trine (c. 1967—)
Ragnhild (fl. 1100s)
Ralov, Kirsten (1922–1999)
Rantala, Lene (1968—)
Rask, Gertrud (fl. 1721)
Rasmussen, Bodil Steen (1957—)
Rasmussen, Louise Christine (1815–1874)
Reventlow, Anne Sophie (1693–1743)
Richilde (fl. 1300s)
Riise-Arndt, Eva (1919—)
Riis-Jorgensen, Karin (1952—)
Rode, Lizzie (1933—)
Roug, Kristine (1975—)
Ryum, Ulla (1937—)
Sand, Inge (1928–1974)
Sandbaek, Ulla Margrethe (1943—)
Schanne, Margrethe (1921—)
Schjoldager, Mette (1977—)
Schmidt, Rikke (1975—)
Sigrid the Haughty (d. before 1013)
Simone, Kirsten (1934—)
Skov, Rikke (1980—)
Sophia of Bayreuth (1700–1770)
Sophia of Denmark (1217–1248)
Sophia of Denmark (1746–1813)
Sophia of Mecklenburg (1557–1631)
Sophia of Mecklenburg (1758–1794)
Sophia of Pomerania (1498–1568)
Sophie Amalie of Brunswick-Lüneberg (1628–1685)
Sophie Hedwig (1677–1735)
Sophie of Denmark (d. 1286)
Sophie of Russia (c. 1140–1198)
Sorensen, Inge (1924—)
Sorensen, Jette Hejli (1961—)
Stroganova, Nina (1919—)
Sunesen, Gitte (1971—)
Tanderup, Anne Dorthe (1972—)
Theilade, Nini (b. 1915)
Thomsen, Camilla Ingemann (1974—)
Thora (fl. 900s)
Thorning-Schmidt, Helle (1966—)
Thorup, Kirsten (1942—)
Thyra (d. 940)
Thyra of Denmark (1880–1945)
Thyra of Denmark (d. 1000)
Thyra Oldenburg (1853–1933)
Touray, Josephine (1979—)
Trier Mørch, Dea (1941—)
Ulfeldt, Leonora Christina (1621–1698)
Ulfhild (fl. 1112)
Ulfhild of Denmark (d. before 1070)
van Deurs,Brigitte (1946—)
Vangsaae, Mona (1920–1983)
Vessel, Anne Marie (1949—)
Vestergaard, Mette (1975—)
Victoria Adelaide of Schleswig-Holstein (1885–1970)
Vieregg, Elizabeth Helene (fl. 17th c.)
Wichfeld-Muus, Varinka (1922–2002)
Wilhelmine (1808–1891)
Willums, Sigbrit (fl. 1507–1523)
Willumsen, Dorrit (1940—)

DERBY

County borough of Derbyshire in north central England

See England.

DESSAU

City in Halle district of East Germany

See Germany.

DIOLA

West African indigenous group

Aline Sitoe (c. 1920–1944)

DOMINICA

Island republic in the West Indies
Discovered by Columbus (1493)
Granted to Earl of Carlisle; left in Carib possession (until 18th c.)
Settled by the French but taken by the English (1759)
Recaptured by France (1778); restored to Britain (1783)
Incorporated with Leeward Island (1833)
Administered by Windward Island (1940)
Achieved independence (1978)

Allfrey, Phyllis Shand (1915–1986)
Bernardino, Minerva (1907–1998)
Charles, Eugenia (1919–2005)
Gardie, Anna (c. 1760–1798)
Mirabal de González, Patria (1924–1960)
Mirabal de Guzmán, María Teresa (1936–1960)
Mirabal de Tavárez, Minerva (1927–1960)
Rodríguez, Evangelina (1879–1947)

DOMINICAN REPUBLIC

DeCastro, Peggy (1921–2004)

DORCHESTER

Borough of Dorsetshire in southern England

See England.

DOUGLAS

Town in Island of Man, England

See England.

DUNSTER

Medieval town in Somerset, England
See England.

DURLACH

Town in northwest Baden-Würtemberg district of West Germany
See Germany.

DYSART

Former burgh in county of Fife, Scotland
See Scotland.

EAST ANGLIA

Ancient division of England
Probably settled by the Angles
Emerged as a kingdom in Anglo-Saxon Heptarchy
Absorbed by Mercia (7th–8th c.)
Became a Danish territory (9th c.)
Conquered by Wessex (10th c.)
See England.

EAST INDIES

Collective name for India, Indochina, and Malay Archipelago
See Indonesia.

EAST PAKISTAN

See Bengal.

EBOLI

Commune in Salerno province, Campania, southern Italy
See Italy.

ECUADOR

Republic in northwest South America
Ancient name was Quito
Conquered by Peru before conquered by Spanish (16th c.)
Won independence from Spain (1822)
Seceded from Great Colombia to become Ecuador (1830)

Mariana de Paredes (1618–1645)
Pacari, Nina (1961—)
Sáenz, Manuela (1797–1856)

EGYPT

Republic in northeast Africa with Sinai Peninsula in Asia
Old Kingdom under Thinite Dynasty; united Upper and Lower Egypt (3400 BCE)
Under Memphite Dynasty (2900 BCE)
Middle Kingdom under Heracleopolitan Dynasties (2445 BCE)
Under Theban Dynasty (2160 BCE)
Under Hyksos Dynasties (1788 BCE)
New Kingdom under Diospolite Dynasties (1580 BCE)
Under Tanite Dynasty (1090 BCE)
Under Bubastite Dynasty (945 BCE)
Under Saite Dynasty (718 BCE)
Under Ethiopian Dynasty (712 BCE)
Under Saite Dynasty (663 BCE)
Under Persia (523 BCE)
Under Greece (323 BCE)
Under Tulunid Dynasty (868 CE)
Under Ikhshidites (935 CE)
Under Ayyubid Dynasty (1171)
Under Turkey (1805)
Under Great Britain (1879)
United with Syria (1958)
As United Arab Republic (1961)
As Arab Republic of Egypt (1970)

Abdel-Aziz, Malak (1923—)
Abdel Rahman, Aisha (1913–1998)
Ahhotep (r. 1570–1546 BCE)
Ahmad, Fathiyya (c. 1898–1975)
Ahmose-Nefertari (c. 1570–1535 BCE)
Arsinoe (fl. 4th c. BCE)
Arsinoe I (d. 247 BCE)
Arsinoe III (fl. c. 250–210/05 BCE)
Arsinoe II Philadelphus (c. 316–270 BCE)
Arsinoe IV (d. 41 BCE)
Asenath
Ashur, Radwa (1946—)
Badi'a Masabnik
Barakat, Hidiya Afifi (1898–1969)
Berenice I (c. 345 BCE–c. 275 BCE)
Berenice II of Cyrene (c. 273–221 BCE)
Berenice IV (fl. 79–55 BCE)
Bilistiche (fl. 268–264 BCE)
Catherine of Alexandria (?–305)
Chedid, Andrée (1921—)
Chewikar, Princess (1876–1947)
Cleopatra (fl. 1st c. BCE)
Cleopatra Berenice III (c. 115–80 BCE)
Cleopatra I (c. 210–176 BCE)
Cleopatra II (c. 183–116 BCE)
Cleopatra III (c. 155–101 BCE)
Cleopatra IV (c. 135–112 BCE)
Cleopatra Selene (c. 130–69 BCE)
Cleopatra VII (69–30 BCE)
Cleopatra V Tryphaena (c. 95–c. 57 BCE)
Dalida (1933–1987)
Eady, Dorothy (1904–1981)
Efflatoun, Inji (1923–1989)
Egyptian Feminism (1800–1980)
Egyptian Singers and Entrepreneurs (fl. 1920s)
El Saadawi, Nawal (1931—)
Fadia (1943–2002)
Farial (1938—)
Farida (1921–1988)
Fathiyya Ahmad (c. 1898–1975)
Fawzia (1921—)
Fawzia (1940–2005)
Hagar (fl. 3rd, 2nd, or 1st c. BCE)
Halim, Tahiya (1919–2003)
Hatshepsut (c. 1515–1468 BCE)
Heslop, Mary Kingdon (1885–1955)
Hetepheres I (fl. c. 2630 BCE)
Hypatia (c. 375–415)
Iti (c. 2563–2424 BCE)
Khamerernebty I (fl. c. 2600 BCE)
Khamerernebty II (fl. c. 2600 BCE)
Khentkawes (fl. c. 2510 BCE)
Mahdiyya, Munira al- (c. 1895–1965)
Marson, Aileen (1912–1939)
Marzouk, Zahia (1906–1988)
Mer-neith (fl. c. 3100 BCE)
Miriam the Prophet (fl. c. 13th or 14th c. BCE)
Mutemwia (fl. 1420–1411 BCE)
Mutnedjmet (c. 1360–1326 BCE)
Na'ima al-Masriyya
Nariman (1934–2005)
Nasser, Tahia (1923—)
Nassif, Malak Hifni (1886–1918)
Nawfal, Hind (fl. 1890s)
Nazli (1894–1978)
Nefertari (c. 1295–1256 BCE)
Nefertiti (c. 1375–1336 BCE)
Neithotep (fl. c. 3100 BCE)
Nitocris (c. 660–584 BCE)
Nkrumah, Fathia (c. 1931—)
Phantasia
Ptolemais (c. 315 BCE–?)
Queeny, Mary (1913–2003)
Rāteb, Aisha (1928—)
Reuter, Gabriele (1859–1941)
Rifaat, Alifa (1930–1996)
Rizk, Amina (1910–2003)
Sadat, Jehan (1933—)
Shaarawi, Huda (1879–1947)
Shafik, Doria (1908–1975)
Shajar al-Durr (d. 1259)
Sobek-neferu (fl. 1680–1674 BCE)
Tauseret (c. 1220–1188 BCE)
Theodora (d. 304)
Thermuthis (fl. 1500 BCE)
Tiy (c. 1400–1340 BCE)
Zayyat, Latifa al- (1923—)

EJISU

Region in Ghana
See Ghana.

EL SALVADOR

Republic in Central America
Discovered by Alvarado (1523)
Gained independence from Spain (1821)
Gained independence from Mexico (1823)
Member of United Provinces of Central America (1823–1839)
Adopted new constitution (1962)

Gasteazoro, Ana (1950–1993)
Lars, Claudia (1899–1974)
Tula, María Teresa (1951—)

ELY

District in Cambridgeshire in eastern England
See England.

ENGLAND

Under Danish rule (1016–1042)
Under Saxon rule (1042–1066)
Under House of Normandy (1066–1135)
Under House of Blois (1135–1154)
Under House of Anjou, later Plantagenet (1154–1399)
Under House of Lancaster (1399–1461)
Under House of York (1461–1470)
Restored to House of Lancaster (1471)
Restored to House of York (1471–1485)
Under House of Tudor (1485–1603)
Under House of Stuart (1603–1649)
As commonwealth of England (1653–1659)
Under House of Stuart (1660–1688)
Under Houses of Orange and Stuart (1689–1702)
Under House of Stuart (1702–1714)
Under House of Hanover (1714–1901)
Under Houses of Saxe-Coburg-Gotha (1901–1910)
Under House of Windsor (1910—)

Abbott, Diane (1953—)
Abbott, Evelyn (1843–1901)
Abel, Annie Heloise (1873–1947)
Abercrombie, M.L.J. (1909–1984)
Aberdeen, Ishbel Maria Gordon, Lady (1857–1939)
Abington, Frances (1737–1815)
Abraham, Caroline Harriet (1809–1877)
Abraham, Constance Palgrave (1864–1942)
Abrahams, Doris Cole (1925—)
Abrams, Harriett (c. 1758–c. 1822)
Achurch, Janet (1864–1916)
Ackland, Valentine (1906–1969)
Acland, Lady Harriet (1750–1815)
Acton, Eliza (1799–1859)
Adam, Madge (1912–2001)
Adams, Mary (d. 1702)
Adams, Mary Grace (1898–1984)
Adams, Miriam (1907—)
Adams, Sarah Flower (1805–1848)
Adams, Truda (1890–1958)
Adcock, Fleur (1934—)
Addams, Dawn (1930–1985)
Addison, Carlotta (1849–1914)
Addison, Laura (d. 1852)
Adelaide de Condet (fl. 12th c.)
Adelaide of Saxe-Meiningen (1792–1849)

Adela of Blois (1062–c. 1137)
Adelicia de Warrenne (d. 1178)
Adelicia of Louvain (c. 1102–1151)
Adie, Kate (1945—)
Adler, Lydia (1704–?)
Adrienne, Jean (b. 1905)
Agar, Eileen (1899–1991)
Agate, May (1892–1960)
Agatha (fl. 1060)
Agatha of Hungary (c. 1025–?)
Agnes of Huntingdonshire (fl. 13th c.)
Aguilar, Grace (1816–1847)
Ahlberg, Janet (1944–1994)
Aiken, Joan (1924–2004)
Aikin, Lucy (1781–1864)
Ainsworth, Ruth (1908–1984)
Airy, Anna (1882–1964)
Aitchison, Helen (1881–?)
Aitken, Janet Gladys (1908–1988)
Aked, Muriel (1887–1955)
Alabaster, Ann O'Connor (1842–1915)
Albanesi, Meggie (1899–1923)
Albertazzi, Emma (1813–1847)
Albertine, Viv (1955—)
Alcock, Mary (1742–1798)
Alcock, Vivien (1924–2003)
Aldous, Lucette (1938—)
Aldrich-Blake, Louisa (1865–1925)
Alexander, Janet (d. 1961)
Alexander, Julie (1938–2003)
Alexandra of Denmark (1844–1925)
Alexandra of Kent (1936—)
Alexandra Victoria (1891–1959)
Alexandrina of Baden (1820–1904)
Alford, Marianne Margaret (1817–1888)
Algeranova, Claudie (1924—)
Alice (1201–1221)
Alice (1280–1291)
Alice de Bryene (d. 1435)
Alice de Joinville (fl. 14th c.)
Alice le Brun (d. 1255)
Alice Maud Mary (1843–1878)
Alice of Athlone (1883–1981)
Alice of Battenberg (1885–1969)
Allan, Elizabeth (1908–1990)
Alleine, Theodosia (fl. 17th c.)
Allen, Adrianne (1907–1993)
Allen, Hannah Archer (fl. 1680s)
Allen, Margaret (1906–1949)
Allen, Mary Sophia (1878–1964)
Allenby, Kate (1974—)
Allingham, Helen Patterson (1848–1926)
Allingham, Margery (1904–1966)
Allitt, Beverley Gail (1969—)
Altwegg, Jeanette (1930—)
Amanpour, Christiane (1958—)
Amelia (1783–1810)
Amelia of Cleves (1517–1586)
Amelia Sophia (1711–1786)
Anderson, Elizabeth Garrett (1836–1917)
Anderson, Janet (1949—)
Anderson, Lea (1959—)
Anderson, Lucy (1797–1878)
Anderson, Margaret (1900–1997)
Anderson, Sophie (1823–1903)
Anderton, Elizabeth (1938—)
Andreae, Felicity (1914—)
Andrews, Julie (1935—)
Angel, Heather (1909–1986)
Angell, Helen Cordelia (1847–1884)
Angelus, Muriel (b. 1909)
Anger, Jane (fl. c. 1580)
Ankers, Evelyn (1918–1985)
Anne (1665–1714)
Anne (1709–1759)
Anne, Princess (1950—)
Anne of Bohemia (1366–1394)
Anne of Cleves (1515–1557)
Anne of Warwick (1456–1485)
Anne of York (fl. 13th c.)
Anne Plantagenet (1383–1438)
Anne Plantagenet (1439–1476)
Anne Valois (c. 1405–1432)
Anning, Mary (1799–1847)
Annis, Francesca (1944—)
Anscombe, G.E.M. (1919–2001)
Ansell, Mary (1877–1899)
Anstice, Sophia (1849–1926)
Antony, Hilda (1896–?)
Applebee, Constance (1873–1981)
Appleton, Honor C. (1879–1951)
Appleyard, Beatrice (1918–1994)
Arbenina, Stella (1885–1976)
Arber, Agnes (1879–1960)
Arden, Alice (1516–1551)
Argyle, Pearl (1910–1947)
Ariadne (fl. 1696)
Arliss, Florence (1871–1950)
Armatrading, Joan (1947—)
Armitage, Ella (1841–1931)
Armstrong, Eileen (1894–1981)
Armstrong, Hilary (1945—)
Armstrong-Jones, Sarah (1964—)
Arnaud, Yvonne (1892–1958)
Arnim, Elizabeth von (1866–1941)
Arthur, Daphne (1925—)
Arundale, Sybil (1882–1965)
Arundel, Ann (1557–1630)
Arundel, Anne (d. 1642)
Arundel, Blanche (1583–1649)
Ascham, Margaret Howe (c. 1535–1590)
Ash, Maie (b. 1888)
Ashbridge, Elizabeth (1713–1755)
Ashcroft, Peggy (1907–1991)
Asherson, Renée (1915—)
Ashford, Daisy (1881–1972)
Ashley, Pauline (1932–2003)
Ashton, Helen (1891–1958)
Ashwell, Lena (1872–1957)
Askew, Anne (c. 1521–1546)
Asquith, Cynthia (1887–1960)
Astell, Mary (1666–1731)
Astor, Nancy Witcher (1879–1964)
Atherton, Candy (1955—)
Atkins, Anna (1797–1871)
Atkins, Babs (1917–2004)
Atkins, Charlotte (1950—)
Atkins, Eileen (1934—)
Atkins, Evelyn (c. 1910–1997)
Atkins, Vera (c. 1908–2000)
Atkinson, Jane Maria (1824–1914)
Attwell, Mabel Lucie (1879–1964)
Aubigny, Agatha d' (fl. 1100s)
Aubin, Penelope (c. 1685–1731)
Aubrey, Madge (1902–1970)
Audley, Alice (d. 1374)
Audley, Margaret (d. 1564)
Audley, Margaret (fl. 1340s)
Audley, Maxine (1923–1992)
Augarde, Adrienne (d. 1913)
Augarde, Amy (1868–1959)
Augarde, Louise (1863–1909)
Augusta Guelph (1768–1840)
Augusta of Hesse-Cassel (1797–1889)
Ault, Marie (1870–1951)
Austen, Jane (1775–1817)
Austen, Winifred (1876–1964)
Austin, Sarah (1793–1867)
Avelina de Forz (1259–1274)
Avisa of Gloucester (c. 1167–1217)
Ayling, Sue (1945–2003)
Aylward, Gladys (1902–1970)
Ayres, Anne (1816–1896)
Ayres, Ruby Mildred (1883–1955)
Ayton, Sarah (1980—)
Bacon, Anne Cooke (1528–1610)
Bacon, Gertrude (1874–1949)
Baddeley, Angela (1904–1976)
Baddeley, Hermione (1906–1986)
Baddeley, Sophia (1745–1786)
Baden-Powell, Agnes (1858–1945)
Baden-Powell, Olave (1889–1977)
Badger, Charlotte (fl. 1806–1808)
Badlesmere, Elizabeth (fl. 1315–1342)
Badlesmere, Maud (d. 1366)
Bagnold, Enid (1889–1981)
Bailey, Ann (1742–1825)
Bailey, Barbara Vernon (1910–2003)
Bailey, Mary (1890–1960)
Baillie, Joanna (1762–1851)
Bainbridge, Beryl (1933—)
Baird, Dorothea (1875–1933)
Baird, Frances (d. 1708)
Baird, Vera (1951—)
Baker, Elizabeth (d. 1962)
Baker, Elsie (1909–2003)
Baker, Florence von Sass (1841–1916)
Baker, Iris (b. 1901)
Baker, Janet (1933—)
Baker, Louisa Alice (1856–1926)
Baker, Sarah (1736–1816)
Baldwin, Sally (1940–2003)
Balfour, Betty (1867–1942)
Balfour, Betty (1903–1979)
Balfour, Clara Lucas (1808–1878)
Balfour, Eve (1898–1990)
Balfour, Frances (1858–1931)
Baly, Monica E. (1914–1998)
Bancroft, Lady (1839–1921)
Bankes, Mary (1598–1661)
Banks, Isabella (1821–1897)
Banks, Lynne Reid (1929—)
Banks, Sarah Sophia (1744–1818)
Bannerman, Kay (1919–1991)
Barbauld, Anna Letitia (1743–1825)
Barber, Margaret Fairless (1869–1901)
Barber, Mary (1911–1965)
Barbieri, Margaret (1947—)
Barbour, Joyce (1901–1977)
Barclay, Florence Louisa (1862–1921)
Barclay-Smith, Phyllis (1903–1980)
Barker, A.L. (1918–2002)
Barker, Cicely Mary (1895–1973)
Barker, Florence (b. 1908)
Barker, Jane (1652–1732)
Barlow, Billie (1862–1937)
Barlow, Hannah (1851–1916)
Barnes, Binnie (1903–1998)
Barnes, Josephine (1912–1999)
Barnes, Winifred (1894–1935)
Barnett, Henrietta (1851–1936)
Barney, Elvira Dolores (c. 1905–c. 1936)
Barney, Nora (1883–1971)
Barraud, Sarah Maria (c. 1823–1895)
Barrie, Mona (1909–1964)
Barrie, Wendy (1912–1978)
Barry, Elizabeth (1658–1713)
Barry, Iris (1895–1969)
Barry, Mary Ann (1855–1874)
Barth, Beatrice Mary (1877–1966)
Bartholomew, Ann Sheppard (1811–1891)
Bartlett, Adelaide (c. 1856–?)
Bartlett, Ethel (1896–1978)
Barton, Dora (1884–1966)
Barton, Elizabeth (c. 1506–1534)
Barton, Emma (1872–1938)
Barton, Glenys (1944—)
Barton, Mary (d. 1970)

Barton, Pam (1917–1943)
Basford, Kathleen (1916–1998)
Basham, Maud Ruby (1879–1963)
Basset, Mary Roper (fl. 1544–1572)
Batchelor, Joy (1914–1991)
Bate, Dorothea (1879–1951)
Bateman, Hester (1709–1794)
Bateman, Jessie (1877–1940)
Bateman, Mary (1768–1809)
Bates, Sophia Ann (1817–1899)
Bateson, Mary (1865–1906)
Batson, Henrietta M. (1859–1943)
Batten, Guin (1967—)
Batten, Miriam (1964—)
Batten, Mollie (1905–1985)
Baughan, Blanche Edith (1870–1958)
Bawden, Nina (1925—)
Baxter, Jane (1909–1996)
Baylis, Lilian (1874–1937)
Baylis, Nadine (1940—)
Bayliss, Lisa (1966—)
Bayly, Ada Ellen (1857–1903)
Baynes, Pauline (1922—)
Beale, Dorothea (1831–1906)
Beale, Mary (1632–1699)
Bearnish, Geraldine (1885–1972)
Beat, Janet Eveline (1937—)
Beatrice (1242–1275)
Beatrice (1857–1944)
Beatrice of Kent (d. after 1280)
Beatrice of Portugal (d. 1439)
Beatrice of Saxe-Coburg (1884–1966)
Beauchamp, Anne (1426–1492)
Beauchamp, Eleanor (1408–1468)
Beauchamp, Elizabeth (fl. 1400s)
Beauchamp, Elizabeth (fl. 1420)
Beauchamp, Elizabeth (d. around 1480)
Beauchamp, Isabel (fl. 1285)
Beauchamp, Margaret (d. 1482)
Beaufort, Eleanor (d. 1501)
Beaufort, Joan (c. 1379–1440)
Beaufort, Margaret (c. 1407–?)
Beaufort, Margaret (1443–1509)
Beaufort, Margaret (d. 1474)
Beaumont, Agnes (1652–1720)
Beaumont, Diana (1909–1964)
Beaumont, Hawise (d. 1197)
Beaumont, Isabel (c. 1104–d. after 1172)
Beaumont, Isabel (d. 1368)
Beaumont, Mary (d. 1632)
Beaumont, Muriel (1881–1957)
Becker, Jillian (1932—)
Beckett, Margaret (1943—)
Beckham, Victoria (1974—)
Beddingfield, Ann (1742–1763)
Beddington, Rosa (1956–2001)
Bedells, Phyllis (1893–1985)
Bedford, Sybille (b. 1911)
Beer, Patricia (1919–1999)
Beeton, Isabella Mary (1836–1865)
Begg, Anne (1955—)
Behn, Aphra (1640?–1689)
Belita (1923–2005)
Bell, Gertrude (1868–1926)
Bell, Mary (c. 1957—)
Bell, Mary Hayley (1911–2005)
Bell, Vanessa (1879–1961)
Bellamy, Elizabeth (1845–1940)
Bellew, Kyrle (1887–1948)
Belmont, Eleanor Robson (1879–1979)
Belmore, Bertha (1882–1953)
Beloff, Nora (1919–1997)
Beloff-Chain, Anne (1921–1991)
Bendish, Bridget (c. 1650–1726)
Benesh, Joan (1920—)
Benett, Etheldred (1776–1845)
Benger, Elizabeth (1778–1827)
Benham, Gertrude (1867–1938)
Benjamin, Ethel Rebecca (1875–1943)
Bennett, Agnes Elizabeth Lloyd (1872–1960)
Bennett, Anna Maria (c. 1750–1808)
Bennett, Eileen (1920—)
Bennett, Jill (1931–1990)
Bennett, Mary Jane (c. 1816–1885)
Bennett, Mary Montgomerie (1881–1961)
Bennett, Mavis (1900–1990)
Benois, Nadia (1896–1975)
Benson, Gertrude (1886–1964)
Benson, Mary (1919–2000)
Benson, Stella (1892–1933)
Bent, Buena (c. 1890–1957)
Bentham, Ethel (1861–1931)
Bentinck, Margaret (1714–1785)
Bentley, Catherine (fl. 1635)
Bentley, Phyllis (1894–1977)
Bentley, Ursula (1945–2004)
Ben-Yusuf, Zaida (fl. 1897–1907)
Berendt, Rachel (d. 1957)
Berengaria of Navarre (c. 1163–c. 1230)
Beresford, Anne (1919—)
Berg, Leila (1917—)
Bergner, Elisabeth (1897–1986)
Bergsma, Deanne (1941—)
Beringer, Aimée Daniell (1856–1936)
Beringer, Esmé (1875–1972)
Beringer, Vera (1879–1964)
Beriosova, Svetlana (1932–1998)
Berk, Lotte (1913–2003)
Berkeley, Elizabeth (fl. 1390–1410)
Berners, Juliana (c. 1388–?)
Berry, Mary (1763–1852)
Bertha of Kent (c. 565–c. 616)
Berthgyth (fl. 8th c.)
Bertie, Catharine (1519–1580)
Bertram, Elsie (1912–2003)
Besant, Annie (1847–1933)
Best, Edna (1900–1974)
Best, Mary Ellen (1809–1891)
Bevans, Philippa (1913–1968)
Bevington, L.S. (1845–1895)
Bianco, Margery Williams (1881–1944)
Bianco, Pamela (1906–1994)
Bibby, Mary Ann (c. 1832–1910)
Bibesco, Elizabeth (1897–1943)
Bidder, Anna McClean (1903–2001)
Bidder, Marion Greenwood (1862–1932)
Biddle, Hester (1629–1696)
Bielenberg, Christabel (1909–2003)
Biggs, Rosemary (1912–2001)
Billington, Adeline (1825–1917)
Billington, Elizabeth (c. 1765/68–1818)
Billington-Greig, Teresa (1877–1964)
Birch, Gina (1956—)
Birchfield, Constance Alice (1898–1994)
Birkett, Viva (1887–1934)
Bishop, Ann (1899–1990)
Bishop, Ann Rivière (1810–1884)
Bishop, Cath (1971—)
Bishop, Isabella (1831–1904)
Bishop, Kate (b. 1847)
Bjornson, Maria (1949–2002)
Black, Cilla (1943—)
Black, Clementina (1854–1922)
Blackburn, Jessy (1894–1995)
Blackburn, Kathleen (1892–1968)
Blackburne, Anna (1726–1793)
Blackett, Annie Maude (1889–1956)
Blackie, Jeannetta Margaret (1864–1955)
Blackler, Betty (1929—)
Blackman, Honor (1926—)
Blackman, Liz (1949—)
Blackstone, Tessa (1942—)
Blackwell, Elizabeth (1821–1910)
Blackwell, Ellen Wright (1864–1952)
Blackwell, Emily (1826–1910)
Blackwood, Beatrice (1889–1975)
Blagg, Mary Adela (1858–1944)
Blair, Cherie (1954—)
Blamire, Susanna (1747–1794)
Blanche, Ada (1862–1953)
Blanche, Marie (1893—)
Blanche of Artois (c. 1247–1302)
Blanche of Lancaster (1341–1369)
Bland, Maria Theresa (1769–1838)
Blandy, Mary (1719–1752)
Blaugdone, Barbara (c. 1609–1705)
Blayney, May (1875–1953)
Blears, Hazel Anne (1956—)
Blind, Mathilde (1841–1896)
Bliss, Catherine (1908–1989)
Blomfield, Dorothy (1858–1932)
Bloodworth, Rhoda Alice (1889–1980)
Bloom, Claire (1931—)
Bloom, Ursula (1893–1984)
Blount, Elizabeth (c. 1502–c. 1540)
Blount, Martha (1690–1762)
Blower, Elizabeth (1763–after 1816)
Blunt, Anne (1837–1917)
Blythe, Coralie (1880–1928)
Blyton, Enid (1897–1968)
Board, Lillian (1948–1970)
Bobath, Berta (1907–1991)
Bocher, Joan (d. 1550)
Boden, Margaret (1936—)
Bodichon, Barbara (1827–1891)
Bodkin, Maud (1875–1967)
Bohun, Alianore (d. 1313)
Bohun, Eleanor (1366–1399)
Bohun, Eleanor (fl. 1327–1340)
Bohun, Maud (fl. 1240s)
Bohun, Maud (fl. 1275)
Boland, Bridget (1904–1988)
Boleyn, Anne (c. 1507–1536)
Boleyn, Mary (d. 1543)
Bond, Jessie (1853–1942)
Bond, Lilian (1908–1991)
Bondfield, Margaret (1873–1953)
Bonham-Carter, Violet (1887–1969)
Bonhote, Elizabeth (1744–1818)
Bonney, Anne (1700–?)
Bonville, Cecily (1460–1530)
Booth, Catherine (1829–1890)
Booth, Evangeline (1865–1950)
Booth, Sarah (1793–1867)
Boothby, Dora (1881–1970)
Boothby, Frances (fl. 1669)
Boothroyd, Betty (1929—)
Borrowman, Agnes (1881–1955)
Boscawen, Fanny (1719–1805)
Boston, Lucy Maria (1892–1990)
Bottome, Phyllis (1884–1963)
Boucherett, Jessie (1825–1905)
Boucicault, Nina (1867–1950)
Boudica (26/30–60)
Boulter, Rosalyn (1916–1997)
Boulton, Agnes (1893–1968)
Bourchier, Anne (1512–1571)
Bourchier, Anne (c. 1417–1474)
Bowden, Pamela (1925–2003)
Bowers, Lally (1917–1984)
Bowes, Alice (c. 1890–1969)
Bowman, Nellie (b. 1878)
Box, Muriel (1905–1991)
Boyd, Elizabeth (fl. 1727–1745)
Boyle, Eleanor Vere (1825–1916)
Boyle, Helen (1869–1957)
Boyne, Eva Leonard (1886–1960)
Boys-Smith, Winifred Lily (1865–1939)

Bracegirdle, Anne (1671–1748)
Braddock, Bessie (1899–1970)
Braddon, Mary Elizabeth (1835–1915)
Bradford, Barbara Taylor (1933—)
Bradley, Katharine Harris (1846–1914)
Bradshaw, Maria (1801–1862)
Brady, Veronica (1890–1964)
Brae, June (1917–2000)
Braham, Leonora (1853–1931)
Braithwaite, Lilian (1873–1948)
Brakewell, Jeanette (1974—)
Bramwell-Booth, Catherine (1883–1987)
Branch, Elizabeth (1673–1740)
Brandon, Anne (d. 1557)
Brandon, Eleanor (c. 1520–1547)
Brandon, Frances (1517–1559)
Braose, Annora de (d. 1241)
Braose, Eleanor de (fl. 1250s)
Braose, Eve de (fl. 1220s)
Braose, Loretta de (d. 1266)
Braose, Maud de (d. 1211)
Brassey, Anna (1839–1887)
Bravo, Florence (1845–1878)
Bray, Anna Eliza (1790–1883)
Brayley, Sally (1937—)
Brayton, Lily (1876–1953)
Brazil, Angela (1868–1947)
Brema, Marie (1856–1925)
Brenchley, Winifred (1883–1953)
Brent-Dyer, Elinor M. (1894–1969)
Briercliffe, Nellie (1889–1966)
Briggs, Karen (1963—)
Bright, Dora Estella (1863–1951)
Bright, Mary Golding (1857–1945)
Brightman, Sarah (1960—)
Brightwen, Eliza (1830–1906)
Bristow, Lily (fl. 1890s)
Brittain, Vera (1893–1970)
Britton, Alison (1948—)
Britton, Hutin (1876–1965)
Broadingham, Elizabeth (d. 1776)
Brogden, Gwendoline (1891–?)
Bromhall, Margaret Ann (1890–1967)
Bron, Eleanor (1934—)
Brontë, Anne (1820–1849)
Brontë, Charlotte (1816–1855)
Brontë, Emily (1818–1848)
Brontë Sisters
Brook, Helen (1907–1997)
Brooke, Annette (1947—)
Brooke, Frances (1724–1789)
Brooke-Rose, Christine (1923—)
Brookner, Anita (1928—)
Broom, Christina (1863–1939)
Brough, Fanny Whiteside (1854–1914)
Brough, Mary (1863–1934)
Broughton, Phyllis (1862–1926)
Brown, Audrey (b. 1913)
Brown, Charlotte (c. 1795–1855)
Brown, Edith Mary (1864–1956)
Brown, Georgia (1933–1992)
Brown, Iona (1941–2004)
Brown, Karen (1963—)
Brown, Margaret Elizabeth (1918—)
Brown, Melanie (1975—)
Brown, Pamela (1917–1975)
Brown, Rosemary (1916–2001)
Brown, Tina (1953—)
Browne, Anne (d. 1511)
Browne, Helen Edith (1911–1987)
Browne, Irene (1896–1965)
Browne, Marjorie (1910–1990)
Browning, Angela (1946—)
Browning, Elizabeth Barrett (1806–1861)
Brownrigg, Elizabeth (1720–1767)
Brune, Adrienne (b. 1892)
Brune, Gabrielle (b. 1912)
Brunton, Dorothy (1893–1977)
Brunton, Louisa (c. 1785–1860)
Brusselsmans, Anne
Bryant, Charlotte (c. 1902–1936)
Bryant, Mary (1765–?)
Buchanan, Dorothy (1899–1985)
Buchanan, Margaret (1864–1940)
Buck, Heather (1926—)
Buck, Karen (1958—)
Buckland, Mary Morland (d. 1857)
Bülbring, Edith (1903–1990)
Bullette, Julia (d. 1867)
Bulnes, Esmée (1900–1986)
Bulstrode, Emily Mary (1867–1959)
Bulstrode, Jane Helena (1862–1946)
Bulwer-Lytton, Rosina, Lady (1802–1882)
Bunton, Emma (1976—)
Burbidge, Margaret (1919—)
Burdekin, Katharine (1896–1963)
Burdett-Coutts, Angela (1814–1906)
Burdock, Mary Ann (1805–1835)
Burford, Barbara (1944—)
Burke, Barbara (1917—)
Burke, Patricia (1917–2003)
Burnand, Lily (1865–?)
Burne, Nancy (1912–1954)
Burnet, Elizabeth (1661–1709)
Burnett, Frances Hodgson (1849–1924)
Burney, Fanny (1752–1840)
Burney, Sarah Harriet (1772–1844)
Burr, Marilyn (1933—)
Burrell, Daisy (b. 1893)
Burt, Laura (1872–1952)
Burton, Beryl (1937–1996)
Burton, Denise (1956—)
Burton, Isabel (1831–1896)
Bury, Charlotte (1775–1861)
Bush, Noreen (1905–1977)
Buss, Frances Mary (1827–1894)
Butcher, Rosemary (1947—)
Butchill, Elizabeth (1758–1780)
Butler, Elizabeth Thompson (1846–1933)
Butler-Sloss, Elizabeth (1933—)
Butsova, Hilda (1896–1976)
Butt, Clara (1872–1936)
Buxton, Mary Ann (c. 1795–1888)
Byatt, A.S. (1936—)
Byron, Kathleen (1922—)
Byron, Kitty (c. 1879–?)
Cable, Mildred (1878–1952)
Cadbury, Dorothy Adlington (1892–1987)
Cadbury, Geraldine Southall (1865–1941)
Cadbury, Rachel (b. 1894)
Cadogan, Sarah (1706–1751)
Caesar, Mary (1677–1741)
Caird, Mona Alison (1858–1932)
Calder, Liz (1938—)
Caldwell, Marianne (1866–1933)
Caldwell, Taylor (1900–1985)
Callaghan, Audrey (1915–2005)
Callcott, Maria (1785–1842)
Callender, Beverley (1956—)
Callender, Sheila (1914–2004)
Calthrop, Gladys E. (1894–1980)
Calton, Patsy (1948–2005)
Calvert, Louie (c. 1893–1926)
Calvert, Mrs. Charles (1837–1921)
Calvert, Patricia (1906–1978)
Calvert, Phyllis (1915–2002)
Cam, Helen M. (1885–1968)
Cameron, Julia Margaret (1815–1879)
Cameron, Lucy Lyttleton (1781–1858)
Cameron, Violet (1862–1919)
Campbell, Anne (1940—)
Campbell, Judy (1916–2004)
Campbell, Lady Colin (1857–1911)
Campbell, Lady Colin (1949—)
Campbell, Lady Jeanne (1928—)
Campbell, Mary (1877–1954)
Campbell, Mrs. Patrick (1865–1940)
Campbell, Naomi (1970—)
Campbell, Stella Tanner (b. 1886)
Campbell, Violet (1892–1970)
Candler, Ann (1740–1814)
Canter-Lund, Hilda M. (1922—)
Carew, Edith Mary (1868–?)
Carey, Catherine (1529–1569)
Carey, Elizabeth (1576–1635)
Carey, Elizabeth (before 1558–c. 1617)
Carey, Mary (c. 1610–c. 1680)
Carey, Rosa Nouchette (1840–1909)
Carline, Nancy (1909–2004)
Carlisle, Alexandra (1886–1936)
Carne, Judy (1939—)
Carnegie, Maud (1893–1945)
Carney, Kate (1870–1950)
Caroline of Ansbach (1683–1737)
Caroline of Brunswick (1768–1821)
Carpenter, Constance (1904–1992)
Carpenter, Iris (b. 1906)
Carpenter, Mary (1807–1877)
Carpenter, Maud (d. 1967)
Carr-Cook, Madge (1856–1933)
Carrington, Dora (1893–1932)
Carrington, Ethel (1889–1962)
Carrington, Joanna (1931–2003)
Carrington, Leonora (1917—)
Carroll, Madeleine (1906–1987)
Carson, Gladys (b. 1903)
Carson, Violet (1898–1983)
Carswell, Catherine (1879–1946)
Carte, Bridget D'Oyly (1908–1985)
Carten, Audrey (b. 1900)
Carter, Angela (1940–1992)
Carter, Elizabeth (1717–1806)
Carter, Nell (1894–1965)
Cartland, Barbara (1901–2000)
Cartlidge, Katrin (1961–2002)
Cartwright, Julia (1851–1924)
Cartwright, Mary L. (1900–1998)
Carus-Wilson, Eleanora Mary (1897–1977)
Cary, Anne (1615–1671)
Cary, Elizabeth (1586–1639)
Cary, Lucy (1619–1650)
Cary, Mary (c. 1621–after 1653)
Cassidy, Sheila (1937—)
Casson, Ann (1915–1990)
Casson, Mary (b. 1914)
Castle, Barbara (1910–2002)
Catchpole, Margaret (1762–1819)
Catherine of Aragon (1485–1536)
Catherine of Braganza (1638–1705)
Catherine of Brittany (1428–c. 1476)
Catherine of Valois (1401–1437)
Catley, Ann (1745–1789)
Caton-Thompson, Gertrude (1888–1985)
Cavallazzi, Malvina (c. 1852–1924)
Cavanagh, Kit (1667–1739)
Cavell, Edith (1865–1915)
Cavendish, Ada (1839–1895)
Cavendish, Christiana (1595–1675)
Cavendish, Elizabeth (d. 1582)
Cavendish, Elizabeth (1626–1663)
Cavendish, Elizabeth (1759–1824)
Cavendish, Georgiana (1757–1806)
Cavendish, Georgiana (1783–1858)
Cavendish, Henrietta (d. 1755)
Cavendish, Jane (1621–1669)
Cavendish, Lucy Caroline (1841–1925)
Cavendish, Margaret (1623–1673)
Cavendish-Bentinck, Elizabeth (1735–1825)

Cavendish-Bentinck, Nina (c. 1860–?)
Cawley, Shirley (1932—)
Cecil, Anne (1556–1589)
Cecil, Anne (d. 1637)
Cecil, Georgiana (1827–1899)
Cecil, Mildred Cooke (1526–1589)
Cecil, Sylvia (1906–1983)
Cecilia (1469–1507)
Celli, Faith (1888–1942)
Cellier, Elizabeth (fl. 1679)
Cely, Margery (fl. late 15th c.)
Cendrith (fl. 680s)
Centlivre, Susanna (c. 1669–1723)
Cerri, Cecilie (1872–1931)
Chadwick, Helen (1953–1996)
Chalker, Lynda (1942—)
Chambers, Dorothea Lambert (1878–1960)
Chand, Meira (1942—)
Chandler, Mary (1687–1745)
Chapman, Anne Maria (1791–1855)
Chapman, Caroline (c. 1818–1876)
Chapman, Vera (1898–1996)
Chapone, Hester (1727–1801)
Chard-Williams, Ada (c. 1876–1900)
Charke, Charlotte Cibber (1713–1760)
Charles, Elizabeth (1828–1896)
Charles, Lallie (1869–1919)
Charlesworth, Maria (1819–1880)
Charlotte Augusta Matilda (1766–1828)
Charlotte of Mecklenburg-Strelitz (1744–1818)
Charteris, Violet (1888–1971)
Chase, Pauline (1885–1962)
Chatwin, Margaret (c. 1881–1937)
Chaucer, Alice (fl. 1400s)
Chaworth, Maud (1282–c. 1322)
Cheeseman, Sylvia (1929—)
Cheesman, Lucy Evelyn (1881–1969)
Cherry, Helen (1915–2001)
Cherry, Neneh (1963—)
Chester, Betty (1895–1943)
Chevalier, Caroline (c. 1832–1917)
Chichester, Sophia (1795–1847)
Chick, Harriette (1875–1977)
Chidley, Katherine (fl. 1641)
Chilcott, Susan (1963–2003)
Chilver, Sally (1914—)
Chisholm, Caroline (1808–1877)
Chisholm, Janet (1929–2004)
Chisholm, Melanie (1974—)
Chitty, Letitia (1897–1982)
Chivers, Elizabeth (1682–1712)
Cholmondeley, Mary (1859–1925)
Christian de Plessetis (c. 1250–?)
Christie, Agatha (1890–1976)
Christie, Dorothy (b. 1896)
Christie, Julie (1941—)
Christina (fl. 1086)
Christina of Markyate (1096–1160)
Chudleigh, Elizabeth (1720–1788)
Chudleigh, Mary Lee (1656–1710)
Church, Esmé (1893–1972)
Churchill, Anne (1684–1716)
Churchill, Arabella (1648–1714)
Churchill, Caryl (1938—)
Churchill, Clementine (1885–1977)
Churchill, Deborah (1677–1708)
Churchill, Diana (1913–1994)
Churchill, Diana Spencer (1909–1963)
Churchill, Fanny (1822–1899)
Churchill, Henrietta (1681–1733)
Churchill, Mary (1689–1751)
Churchill, Mary (1922—)
Churchill, Sarah (1914–1982)
Churchill, Sarah Jennings (1660–1744)
Cibber, Susannah (1714–1766)
Cilento, Diane (1933—)
Clairmont, Claire (1798–1879)
Clapham, Diana (1957—)
Clare, Amicia de (1220–1283)
Clare, Eleanor de (1292–1337)
Clare, Elizabeth de (1295–1360)
Clare, Isabel de (c. 1174–1220)
Clare, Margaret de (1249–1313)
Clare, Margaret de (fl. 1280–1322)
Clare, Margaret de (c. 1293–1342)
Clare, Mary (1894–1970)
Clark, Catherine Anthony (1892–1977)
Clark, Helen (1954—)
Clark, Hilda (1881–1955)
Clark, Kate Emma (1847–1926)
Clark, Lynda (1949—)
Clark, Petula (1932—)
Clarke, Mary Anne (c. 1776–1852)
Clarke, Mary Cowden (1809–1898)
Clarke, Mary Goulden (d. 1910)
Clarke, Rebecca (1886–1979)
Clay, Theresa (1911–1995)
Clayden, Pauline (1922—)
Claypole, Edith Jane (1870–1915)
Clayton, Barbara (1922—)
Clemence of Barking (fl. 12th c.)
Clement-Scott, Margaret (fl. 19th c.)
Cliff, Clarice (1899–1972)
Clifford, Anne (1590–1676)
Clifford, Camille (1885–1970)
Clifford, Margaret (c. 1560–1616)
Clifford, Margaret (d. 1596)
Clifford, Maud (d. 1446)
Clifford, Mrs. W.K. (1846–1929)
Clifford, Rosamund (c. 1145–1176)
Clisby, Harriet (1830–1931)
Clitherow, Margaret (1556–1586)
Clive, Caroline (1801–1873)
Clive, Kitty (1711–1785)
Clive, Margaret (1735–1817)
Clough, Jemima (1820–1892)
Clubb, Elizabeth (1922—)
Clwyd, Ann (1937—)
Coad, Nellie (1883–1974)
Coakes, Marion (1947—)
Coates, Anne V. (1925—)
Cobbold, Elizabeth (c. 1764–1824)
Cobbold, Hermione (1905–2004)
Cobham, Eleanor (d. 1452)
Coe, Sue (1951—)
Coffey, Ann (1946—)
Coghlan, Rose (1852–1932)
Cohen, Harriet (1895–1967)
Coke, Alexandra (1891–1984)
Coke, Jane Elizabeth (1777–1863)
Colclough, Mary Ann (1836–1885)
Cole, Edith (1870–1927)
Cole, Margaret (1893–1980)
Colegate, Isabel (1931—)
Coleman, Ann Raney Thomas (1810–1897)
Coleman, Fanny (1840–1919)
Coleridge, Ethel (1883–1976)
Coleridge, Mary Elizabeth (1861–1907)
Coleridge, Sara (1802–1852)
Coleridge-Taylor, Avril (1903–1998)
Colin, Jean (1905–1989)
Colledge, Cecilia (1920—)
Collet, Clara (1860–1948)
Collier, Constance (1878–1955)
Collier, Jane (1710–c. 1754)
Collier, Lesley (1947—)
Collier, Mary (c. 1690–c. 1762)
Collier, Patience (1910–1987)
Collingwood, Elizabeth (1924—)
Collins, Ann (fl. mid–17th c.)
Collins, Diana (1917–2003)
Collins, Jackie (1937—)
Collins, Joan (1933—)
Collins, José (1887–1958)
Collins, Lottie (c. 1866–1910)
Collins, Pauline (1940—)
Collyer, Mary (d. 1763)
Colquhoun, Ithell (1906–1988)
Colvin, Brenda (1897–1981)
Colyer, Evelyn (1902–1930)
Comberti, Micaela (1952–2003)
Compton, Betty (1907–1944)
Compton, Fay (1894–1978)
Compton, Katherine (1853–1928)
Compton, Madge (c. 1892–1970)
Compton, Viola (1886–1971)
Compton, Virginia (1853–1940)
Compton-Burnett, Ivy (1884–1969)
Comstock, Elizabeth Leslie (1815–1891)
Comyn, Alice (fl. 1318)
Conley, Sandra (1943—)
Conran, Shirley (1932—)
Cons, Emma (1838–1912)
Constance (c. 1374–1416)
Constance (fl. 1100)
Constance Jones, E.E. (1848–1922)
Constance of Castile (1354–1394)
Conti, Italia (1874–1946)
Conway, Verona (1910–1986)
Coockburn, Catharine Trotter (1679–1749)
Cook, Beryl (1926—)
Cook, Edith Maud (d. 1910)
Cook, Eliza (1818–1889)
Cook, Freda Mary (1896–1990)
Cook, Judith (1933–2004)
Cookson, Catherine (1906–1998)
Coomber, Alex (1973—)
Coombs, Claire (1974—)
Cooper, Charlotte (1871–1966)
Cooper, Diana Duff (1892–1986)
Cooper, Edith Emma (1862–1913)
Cooper, Eileen (1953—)
Cooper, Elizabeth (fl. 1737)
Cooper, Gladys (1888–1971)
Cooper, Jilly (1937—)
Cooper, Lillian Kemble (1891–1977)
Cooper, Margaret Joyce (b. 1909)
Cooper, Susie (1902–1995)
Cooper, Violet Kemble (1886–1961)
Cooper, Yvette (1969—)
Corbaux, Fanny (1812–1883)
Corbert, Sybilla (fl. 11th century)
Corbett, Leonora (1908–1960)
Corbett, Marie (1859–1932)
Corbett-Ashby, Margery (1882–1981)
Corelli, Marie (1855–1924)
Cornford, Frances Crofts (1886–1960)
Cornish, Mary (c. 1899–?)
Cornwallis, C.F. (1786–1858)
Corradi, Doris (1922—)
Corston, Jean (1942—)
Cory, Annie Sophie (1868–1952)
Cosway, Maria (1759–1838)
Cotton, Mary Ann (1822–1873)
Cotton, Priscilla (d. 1664)
Court, Hazel (1926—)
Courtauld, Katherine (1856–1935)
Courtauld, Louisa (1729–1807)
Courtenay, Gertrude (c. 1504–1558)
Courtenay, Margaret (fl. 1330)
Courtneidge, Cicely (1893–1980)
Courtneidge, Rosaline (1903–1926)
Courtney, Kathleen (1878–1974)
Couzyn, Jeni (1942—)
Covell, Phyllis (1895–1982)
Coventry, Anne (1673–1763)
Coventry, Pamela (d. 1939)

Cowie, Eliza Jane (1835–1902)
Cowley, Hannah (1743–1809)
Cowper, Mary (1685–1724)
Cradock, Fanny (1909–1994)
Cradock, Mrs. H.C. (1863–1941)
Craig, Edith (1869–1947)
Craig, Sandra (1942—)
Craik, Dinah Maria Mulock (1826–1887)
Crane, Eva (1911—)
Craske, Margaret (1892–1990)
Craven, Elizabeth (1750–1828)
Crawford, Louise Macartney (1790–1858)
Crawford, Mimi (d. 1966)
Cripps, Isobel (1891–1979)
Cripps, Sarah Ann (c. 1821–1892)
Croft, June (1963—)
Croker, Bithia May (c. 1849–1920)
Croly, Jane Cunningham (1829–1901)
Cromwell, Bridget (1624–c. 1660)
Cromwell, Elizabeth (1598–1665)
Cromwell, Mary (1636–1712)
Cropley, Eileen (1932—)
Cropper, Hilary (1941–2004)
Crosby, Caresse (1892–1970)
Cross, Joan (1900–1993)
Crossley, Ada Jemima (1871–1929)
Crouch, Anna Maria (1763–1805)
Crowdy, Rachel (1884–1964)
Crowe, Catherine Anne (c. 1800–1876)
Crowe, Sylvia (1901–1997)
Cruft, Catherine Holway (1927—)
Cruso, Thalassa (1908–1997)
Crutchley, Rosalie (1921–1997)
Cryer, Ann (1939—)
Cryer, Sarah (1848–1929)
Cullis, Winifred Clara (1875–1956)
Cummings, Constance (b. 1910)
Cunard, Maud (1872–1948)
Cunard, Nancy (1896–1965)
Cuneswith (fl. 7th c.)
Cunliffe, Stella (1917—)
Cunningham, Ann (d. 1647)
Currie, Edwina (1946—)
Currie, Mary Montgomerie (1843–1905)
Curtis-Thomas, Claire (1958—)
Curzon, Grace Hinds (1878–1958)
Curzon, Irene (1896–1966)
Curzon, Sarah Anne (1833–1898)
Cust, Aleen (1868–1937)
Custance, Olive (1874–1944)
Cutler, Kate (1870–1955)
Cutts, Patricia (1926–1974)
Cyneburg of Gloucester (c. 660–710)
Cyneburg of Mercia (fl. 655)
Cynethryth (fl. 736–796)
Cynewise (fl. 7th c.)
Cyniburg (fl. 8th c.)
Dacre, Barbarina (1768–1854)
Dacre, Charlotte (c. 1772–1825)
Dacre, Elizabeth (b. before 1566)
Dacre, Marie (1563–1578)
Dagoe, Hannah (d. 1763)
Dainton, Marie (1881–1938)
Daldy, Amey (c. 1829–1920)
Dale, Daphne (1931–1982)
Dale, Kathleen (1895–1984)
Dale, Margaret (1922—)
Dalton, Katharina (1916–2004)
Damer, Anne Seymour (1748–1828)
Dando, Jill (1961–1999)
Dando, Suzanne (1961—)
Dane, Clemence (1888–1965)
Daniels, Maxine (1930–2003)
Daniels, Sarah (1957—)
Danvers, Magdalene (1561–1627)
D'Arcy, Ella (c. 1856–1937)
D'Arcy, Margaretta (1934—)
Dare, Phyllis (1890–1975)
Darling, Grace (1815–1842)
Darragh, Miss (d. 1917)
Darton, Patience (1911–1996)
Daryush, Elizabeth (1887–1977)
Dashwood, Elizabeth Monica (1890–1943)
Da Silva, Ana (1949—)
Datta, Naomi (1922—)
Daunt, Yvonne (b. around 1900)
Davey, Nuna (1902–1977)
Davey, Valerie (1940—)
David, Caroline Edgeworth (1856–1951)
David, Elizabeth (1913–1992)
Davies, Betty (1935—)
Davies, Betty Ann (1910–1955)
Davies, Eleanor (1590–1652)
Davies, Elizabeth Valerie (b. 1912)
Davies, Emily (1830–1921)
Davies, Fanny (1861–1934)
Davies, Laura (1963—)
Davies, Lillian (1895–1932)
Davies, Moll (fl. 1673)
Davies, Sharron (1962—)
Davies, Siobhan (1950—)
Davis, Gladys (b. 1893)
Davison, Emily (1872–1913)
Davy, Sarah (c. 1639–1670)
Davys, Mary (1674–1731)
Dawson, Mary Elizabeth (1833–1924)
Dawson, Nancy (c. 1735–1767)
Day, Edith (1896–1971)
Day, Frances (1907–1984)
Dean, Brenda (1943—)
Dean, Janet (1949—)
de Banzie, Brenda (1915–1981)
Debenham, Cicely (1891–1955)
De Brémont, Anna (1864–1922)
De Casalis, Jeanne (1897–1966)
de Havilland, Olivia (1916—)
De La Haye, Ina (1906–1972)
Delaney, Shelagh (1939—)
Delany, Mary Granville (1700–1788)
de la Pasture, Mrs. Henry (d. 1945)
de Lara, Adelina (1872–1961)
De Mille, Beatrice (1853–1923)
DeMorgan, Evelyn (1850–1919)
Dench, Judy (1934—)
Denham, Isolde (1920—)
Denis, Michaela (1914–2003)
Denman, Gertrude (1884–1954)
Denny, Sandy (1947–1978)
Dent, Edith (1863–1948)
Denton, Jean (1935–2001)
De Reyes, Consuelo (1893–1948)
Derman, Vergie (1942—)
Desforges, Jean Catherine (1929—)
Desmier, Eleanor (1639–1722)
Desmond, Astra (1893–1973)
Desmond, Florence (1905–1993)
Desmond, Lucy (b. 1889)
Despenser, Elizabeth (d. 1408)
Despenser, Isabel (1400–1439)
Devereux, Frances (d. 1674)
Devorgilla (d. 1290)
Devoy, Susan (1964—)
Diana (1961–1997)
Dickens, Monica (1915–1992)
Dickin, Maria (1870–1951)
Dickson, Barbara (1947—)
Dickson, Dorothy (1893–1995)
Digby, Lettice (c. 1588–1658)
Digby el Mesrab, Jane (1807–1881)
Dilke, Emily (1840–1904)
Disraeli, Mary Anne (1792–1872)
Diver, Jenny (1700–1740)
Dix, Dorothy (1892–1970)
Dixie, Florence (1857–1905)
Dixie, Lady Florence (1857–1905)
Dixon, Adele (1908–1992)
Dixon, Victoria (1959—)
Doble, Frances (1902–1969)
Dod, Charlotte (1871–1960)
Dolores (c. 1890–1975)
Donaldson, Mary (1921–2003)
Donisthorpe, G. Sheila (1898–1946)
Dony, Christina Mayne (1910–1995)
D'Orme, Aileen (1877–1939)
Dormer, Daisy (1889–1947)
Doughty, Sue (1948—)
Douglas, Margaret (1515–1578)
Douglas, Marjory (d. 1420)
Douglas, Mary Tew (1921—)
Douglas, Sandra (1967—)
Dowding, Angela (1919—)
Dowling, Joan (1928–1954)
Downing, Lucy Winthrop (c. 1600–1679)
Dowriche, Anne (before 1560–after 1613)
Drabble, Margaret (1939—)
Drake, Elizabeth (fl. 1625–1656)
Drake, Fabia (1904–1990)
Drake, Judith (fl. 1696)
Drane, Augusta Theodosia (1823–1894)
Draper, Margaret (d. around 1800)
Dresdel, Sonia (1909–1976)
Drew, Jane (1911–1996)
Drew, Louisa Lane (1820–1897)
Drew-Baker, Kathleen M. (1901–1957)
Drewery, Corinne (1959—)
Drower, E.S. (1879–1972)
Drower, Margaret S. (c. 1913—)
Drown, Julia (1962—)
Drummond, Dolores (1834–1926)
Dryburgh, Margaret (1890–1945)
Du Boulay, Christine (c. 1923—)
Duclaux, Agnes Mary F. (1856–1944)
Dudley-Ward, Penelope (1914–1982)
Duff, Mary Ann Dyke (1794–1857)
Duff-Gordon, Lucie (1821–1869)
Duff Gordon, Lucy (1862–1935)
Duffy, Maureen (1933—)
du Maurier, Daphne (1907–1989)
Duncombe, Susanna (1725–1812)
Dunkeld, Ada (c. 1195–after 1241)
Dunn, Barbara (c. 1910—)
Dunn, Emma (1875–1966)
Dunn, Nell (1936—)
Dunscombe, Adaliza (1867–1943)
Dunwoody, Gwyneth (1930—)
du Pré, Jacqueline (1945–1987)
Duprez, June (1918–1984)
Durham, Mary Edith (1863–1944)
Du Verger, Susan (before 1625–after 1657)
Duvernay, Pauline (1813–1894)
Duxbury, Elspeth (1909–1967)
Dyer, Amelia Elizabeth (1839–1896)
Eadburgh (c. 773–after 802)
Eadburh (fl. 9th century)
Eadgyth Swanneshals (c. 1012–?)
Eagle, Angela (1961—)
Eagle, Maria (1961—)
Ealdgyth (fl. 1016)
Eales, Nellie B. (1889–1989)
Eanfleda (626–?)
Eardley, Joan (1921–1963)
Eastlake, Elizabeth (1809–1893)
Eastlake-Smith, Gladys (1883–1941)
Easton, Florence (1882–1955)
Eaton, Shirley (1937—)
Eccles, Janet (1895–1966)
Eccles, Mary Hyde (1912–2003)
Ecgwynn (d. around 901)

Edburga (d. 751)
Edburga (d. 960)
Edburga of Bicester (d. 650)
Eden, Clarissa (1920—)
Eden, Emily (1797–1869)
Edflaed (c. 900–?)
Edger, Kate (1857–1935)
Edgifu (d. 968)
Edginton, May (1883–1957)
Edgitha (c. 912–946)
Edhild (d. 946)
Ediss, Connie (1871–1934)
Edith (d. 871)
Edith (d. 937)
Edith (c. 961–984)
Edith (fl. 1009)
Edith (c. 1025–1075)
Edith (fl. 1040)
Edith (fl. 1063)
Edith of Aylesbury (fl. 7th c.)
Edmunds, Christiana (1835–1907)
Edwards, Amelia B. (1831–1892)
Edwards, Margaret (1939—)
Edwards, Tracey (1962—)
Egerton, Sarah Fyge (c. 1670–1723)
Eggar, Samantha (1938—)
Eisinger, Irene (1903–1994)
Eleanor, the Maid of Brittany (1184–1241)
Eleanor de Warrenne (c. 1250–?)
Eleanor of Aquitaine (1122–1204)
Eleanor of Castile (1241–1290)
Eleanor of Montfort (1215–1275)
Eleanor of Montfort (1252–1282)
Eleanor of Provence (c. 1222–1291)
Eleanor of Woodstock (1318–1355)
Eleanor Plantagenet (1264–1297)
Eleanor Plantagenet (c. 1318–1372)
Elfgifu (c. 914–?)
Elfgifu (d. 944)
Elfgifu (c. 945–1002)
Elfgifu (d. 959)
Elfgifu (c. 963–1002)
Elfgifu (c. 997–?)
Elflaed (d. 714)
Elflaed (c. 905–c. 963)
Elflaed (d. 920)
Elfthrith (fl. 7th c.)
Elfthrith (c. 945–1002)
Elfwyn (c. 882–?)
Elgar, Alice (1848–1920)
Elgiva (fl. 1020)
Elgood, Cornelia (1874–1960)
Eliot, Vivienne (1889–1947)
Elizabeth (1770–1840)
Elizabeth Blount (c. 1502–c. 1540)
Elizabeth Bowes-Lyon (1900–2002)
Elizabeth Caroline (1740–1759)
Elizabeth I (1533–1603)
Elizabeth II (1926—)
Elizabeth of Lancaster (1364–1425)
Elizabeth of Nevers (fl. 1460)
Elizabeth of York (1466–1503)
Elizabeth Plantagenet (1282–1316)
Elizabeth Stuart (1635–1650)
Ellen of Wales (d. 1253)
Ellerman, Winifred (1894–1983)
Elliott, Charlotte (1789–1871)
Elliott, Madge (1896–1955)
Ellis, Mary (1897–2003)
Ellis, Sarah Stickney (c. 1799–1872)
Ellis-Fermor, Una Mary (1894–1958)
Elliston, Daisy (b. 1894)
Ellman, Louise (1945—)
Elsie, Lily (1886–1962)
Elsom, Isobel (1893–1981)
Elstob, Elizabeth (1683–1756)
Elswitha (d. 902)
Elthelthrith (630–679)
Emerald, Connie (1891–1959)
Emery, Pollie (1875–1958)
Emery, Winifred (1862–1924)
Emma (fl. 600s)
Emma of Norfolk (d. 1100)
Emmett, Dorothy Mary (b. 1904)
Emms, Gail (1977—)
England, Maud Russell (1863–1956)
Engyth (fl. 7th c.)
Ephelia (fl. 1660s–1680s)
Ermenburga (fl. late 600s)
Ermenilda (d. around 700)
Escott, Cicely Margaret (1908–1977)
Esmond, Annie (1873–1945)
Esmond, Jill (1908–1990)
Espinosa, Judith (1877–1949)
Espinosa, Mimi (1893–1936)
Estaugh, Elizabeth Haddon (1680–1762)
Esteve-Coll, Elizabeth (1938—)
Ethelberga of Northumbria (d. 647)
Ethelburg (fl. 722)
Ethelburga (d. 676?)
Etheldreda (d. around 840)
Ethelflaed (869–918)
Ethelflaed (d. 962)
Ethelflaed (d. after 975)
Ethelflaeda (fl. 900s)
Ethelflaeda (c. 963–c. 1016)
Ethelgeofu (d. around 896)
Ethelswyth (c. 843–889)
Evans, Ann (c. 1836–1916)
Evans, Edith (1888–1976)
Evans, Kathy (1948–2003)
Evans, Mary Anne (1819–1880)
Evans, Nancy (1915–2000)
Evdokimova, Eva (1948—)
Evelyn, Mary (1665–1685)
Everest, Barbara (1890–1968)
Ewing, Annabelle (1960—)
Ewing, Juliana Horatia (1841–1885)
Eyles, Joan M. (1907–1986)
Eyles, Leonora (1889–1960)
Faber, Beryl (d. 1912)
Fachiri, Adila (1886–1962)
Fainlight, Ruth (1931—)
Fairbairns, Zöe (1948—)
Fairbrother, Nicola (1970—)
Fairbrother, Sydney (1872–1941)
Fairfax, Lettice (1876–1948)
Faithfull, Emily (1835–1895)
Faithfull, Marianne (1946—)
Faiz, Alys (1914–2003)
Falconbridge, Anna Maria (fl. 1790–1794)
Falkender, Marcia (1932—)
Fanshawe, Anne (1625–1680)
Fanshawe, Catherine Maria (1765–1834)
Fanthorpe, U.A. (1929—)
Farebrother, Violet (1888–1969)
Farjeon, Annabel (1919—)
Farjeon, Eleanor (1881–1965)
Farmborough, Florence (1887–1978)
Farningham, Marianne (1834–1909)
Farrally, Betty (1915–1989)
Farrar, Gwen (1899–1944)
Farren, Elizabeth (c. 1759–1829)
Farren, Nellie (1848–1904)
Farrer, Margaret (1914–1997)
Farron, Julia (1922—)
Faucit, Helena Saville (1817–1898)
Fawcett, Millicent Garrett (1847–1929)
Fawcett, Philippa (1868–1948)
Fay, Eliza (1756–1816)
Fazan, Eleanor (1930—)
Fedorovitch, Sophie (1893–1953)
Feinstein, Elaine (1930—)
Fell, Honor (1900–1986)
Fell, Margaret (1614–1702)
Fenning, Elizabeth (1792–1815)
Fenton, Lavinia (1708–1760)
Fenwick, Eliza (1766–1840)
Fenwick, Ethel Gordon (1857–1947)
Ferguson, Sarah (1959—)
Ferland, Barbara (1919—)
Fermor, Arabella (d. 1738)
Fermor, Henrietta Louisa (d. 1761)
Ferrers, Anne (d. 1342)
Ferrers, Elizabeth (1392–1434)
Ferrers, Helen (1869–1943
Ferrers, Mary (d. 1457)
Ferrier, Kathleen (1912–1953)
Ferris, Elizabeth (1940—)
Feuchères, Sophie, Baronne de (c. 1795–1841)
Field, Mary (1896–c. 1968)
Field, Shirley Anne (1936—)
Field, Virginia (1917–1992)
Fielding, Sarah (1710–1768)
Fields, Gracie (1898–1979)
Fiennes, Anne (d. 1595)
Fiennes, Celia (1662–1741)
Fiennes, Virginia (1947–2004)
Fifield, Elaine (1930–1999)
Figes, Eva (1932—)
Filippi, Rosina (1866–1930)
Finch, Anne (1631–1679)
Finch, Anne (1661–1720)
Finch, Flora (1867–1940)
Firsova, Elena Olegovna (1950—)
Fisher, Allison (1968—)
Fisher, Cicely Corbett (1885–1959)
Fisher, Clara (1811–1898)
Fisher, Margaret (b. 1689)
Fisher, Mary (c. 1623–1698)
Fitton, Mary (c. 1578–1647)
Fitzalan, Alice (fl. 1285)
Fitzalan, Alice (d. around 1338)
Fitzalan, Alice (1352–1416)
Fitzalan, Amy (fl. 1440)
Fitzalan, Elizabeth (d. 1385)
Fitzalan, Elizabeth (fl. 1408–1417)
Fitzalan, Elizabeth (d. 1425)
Fitzalan, Joan (d. 1419)
Fitzalan, Joan (fl. 1325)
Fitzalan, Katherine (b. around 1520)
Fitzalan, Katherine (fl. 1530s)
Fitzalan, Margaret (b. around 1388)
Fitzalan, Mary (d. 1557)
Fitzalan, Maud (fl. 1200s)
Fitzclarence, Amelia (1807–1858)
Fitzgerald, Elizabeth (c. 1528–1589)
Fitzgerald, Katherine (c. 1500–1604)
Fitzgerald, Penelope (1916–2000)
FitzGilbert, Constance (fl. 12th c.)
Fitzhammon, Amabel (d. 1157)
Fitzherbert, Maria Anne (1756–1837)
Fitzhugh, Anne (fl. 1466)
Fitzrobert, Amicia (d. 1225)
Fitzroy, Charlotte (1664–1717)
Fitzroy, Isabel (1726–1782)
Fitzroy, Mary (c. 1519–1557)
Fitzsimons, Lorna (1967—)
Fitzwilliam, Fanny Elizabeth (1801–1854)
Fleming, Jane (fl. 1550s)
Fleming, Margaret (1803–1811)
Fletcher, Jennie (1890–1968)
Flint, Caroline (1961—)
Flood, Debbie (1980—)
Florence, Mary Sargant (1857–1954)
Florey, Margaret (1904–1994)
Flower, Eliza (1803–1846)

Fogerty, Elsie (1865–1945)
Follett, Barbara (1942—)
Fonaroff, Nina (1914–2003)
Fontaine, Joan (1917—)
Fontaine, Lillian (1886–1975)
Fonteyn, Margot (1919–1991)
Foot, Philippa (1920—)
Foote, Maria (c. 1797–1867)
Forbes, Brenda (1909–1996)
Forbes, Mary (1880–1974)
Forbes, Rosita (1893–1967)
Forbes-Robertson, Beatrice (1883–1967)
Forbes-Robertson, Jean (1905–1962)
Ford, Isabella O. (1855–1924)
Ford, Lita (1958—)
Forde, Florrie (1876–1940)
Fordham, Julia (1962—)
Forgan, Liz (1944—)
Forster, Margaret (1938—)
Fortescue, May (1862–1950)
Fortesque-Brickdale, Eleanor (1872–1945)
Foster, Emily Sophia (1842–1897)
Foster, Jacqueline (1947—)
Fothergill, Jessie (1851–1891)
Fountaine, Margaret (1862–1940)
Fox, Caroline (1819–1871)
Fox, Elizabeth Vassall (1770–1845)
Fox, Mary (b. 1817)
Foyle, Christina (d. 1999)
Franca, Celia (1921—)
Francis, Catherine Augusta (1836–1916)
Francis, Clare (1946—)
Francisca of Portugal (1800–1834)
Frankau, Pamela (1908–1967)
Frankland, Agnes (1726–1783)
Franklin, Eleanor (1795–1825)
Franklin, Jane (1792–1875)
Franklin, Rosalind (1920–1958)
Franks, Rebecca (c. 1760–1823)
Fraser, Antonia (1932—)
Fraser, Mary Crawford (1851–1922)
Fraser, Roslin (1927–1997)
Fraser, Shelagh (1922–2000)
Fraser, Wendy (1963—)
Frederick, Lynne (1954–1994)
Freeman, Caroline (c. 1855–1914)
Freeman, Gillian (1929—)
Freeman, Muriel (1897—)
Fremantle, Anne (1909–2002)
French, Annie (1872–1965)
French, Dawn (1957—)
French, Ruth (b. 1906)
French, Valerie (1932–1990)
Fretter, Vera (1905–1992)
Frideswide (d. 735?)
Frink, Elisabeth (1930–1993)
Frischmann, Justine (1969—)
Frith, Mary (c. 1584–1659)
Frost, Constance Helen (c. 1862–1920)
Fry, Elizabeth (1780–1845)
Fry, Margery (1874–1958)
Fulhame, Elizabeth (fl. 1780)
Fuller, Rosalinde (1901–1982)
Fullerton, Georgiana Charlotte (1812–1885)
Fulton, Catherine (1829–1919)
Fulton, Margaret Barr (1900–1989)
Funnell, Pippa (1968—)
Furley, Matilda (1813–1899)
Furlong, Monica (1930–2003)
Furneaux, Yvonne (1928—)
Furness, Vera (1921–2002)
Furse, Katharine (1875–1952)
Furse, Margaret (1911–1974)
Gabain, Ethel Leontine (1883–1950)
Gardiner, Antoinette (1941—)
Gardiner, Kate (1885–1974)
Gardiner, Margaret (1904–2005)
Gardner, Frances (1913–1989)
Gardner, Helen Louise (1908–1986)
Gardner, Maureen (1928–1974)
Garnett, Constance (1862–1946)
Garrett, Maureen (1922—)
Garrod, Dorothy A. (1892–1969)
Gaskell, Elizabeth (1810–1865)
Gatty, Margaret (1809–1873)
Gaunt, Mary (1861–1942)
Gay, Maisie (1883–1945)
Gems, Pam (1925—)
George, Elizabeth (c. 1814–1902)
George, Muriel (1883–1965)
Gethin, Grace Norton (1676–1697)
Gibbons, E. Joan (1902–1988)
Gibbons, Stella (1902–1989)
Gibbs, Mary Elizabeth (1836–1920)
Gidley, Sandra (1957—)
Gielgud, Maina (1945—)
Gilks, Gillian (1959—)
Gill, Neena (1956—)
Gill, Zillah Smith (1859–1937)
Gillan, Cheryl (1952—)
Gilliatt, Penelope (1932–1993)
Gillmore, Margalo (1897–1986)
Gilmour, Sally (1921–2004)
Gilroy, Beryl (1924–2001)
Gilroy, Linda (1949—)
Ginner, Ruby (c. 1886–1978)
Gipps, Ruth (1921—)
Gitana, Gertie (1887–1957)
Gladstone, Catherine (1812–1900)
Glasse, Hannah (1708–1770)
Gleichen, Feodora (1861–1922)
Glover, Jane Allison (1949—)
Gluck (1895–1978)
Glyn, Elinor (1864–1943)
Goddard, Arabella (1836–1922)
Godgifu (c. 1010–c. 1049)
Godiva (c. 1040–1080)
Godley, Charlotte (1821–1907)
Goffin, Cora (1902–2004)
Goodall, Jane (1934—)
Goodbody, Buzz (1946–1975)
Goodson, Katharine (1872–1958)
Goossens, Marie (1894–1991)
Goossens, Sidonie (1899–2004)
Gordon, Isabella (1901–1988)
Gordon, Kitty (1878–1974)
Gordon, Noele (1923–1985)
Gordon-Watson, Mary (1948—)
Gore, Catherine (1799–1861)
Gosse, Sylvia (1881–1968)
Goudge, Elizabeth (1900–1984)
Gower, Pauline (1910–1947)
Gowing, Margaret (1921–1998)
Graham, Sheila (1904–1988)
Grahame, Margot (1911–1982)
Grahame Johnstone, Anne (1928–1998)
Grahame Johnstone, Janet (1928–1979)
Grandison, Katharine (fl. 1305–1340)
Grann, Phyllis (1937—)
Grant, Pauline (1915—)
Grant Duff, Shiela (1913–2004)
Granville-Barker, Helen (d. 1950)
Graves, Beryl (1915–2003)
Gray, Dulcie (1919—)
Gray, Eve (1900–1983)
Gray, Nicolete (1911–1997)
Gray, Sally (1916—)
Greaves, Mary Ann (1834–1897)
Green, Dorothy (1886–1961)
Green, Janet (1914–1993)
Green, Lucinda (1953—)
Green, Mary Anne Everett (1818–1895)
Greenaway, Kate (1846–1901)
Greenaway, Margaret (fl. 15th c.)
Greene, Angela (1879—)
Greener, Dorothy (1917–1971)
Greenhough, Dorothy (1875–1965)
Greenwell, Dora (1821–1882)
Greenwood, Ellen Sarah (1837–1917)
Greenwood, Joan (1921–1987)
Greenwood, Sarah (c. 1809–1889)
Greer, Germaine (1939—)
Greet, Clare (1871–1939)
Greig, Margaret (1922–1999)
Grenfell, Joyce (1910–1979)
Greville, Frances Evelyn (1861–1938)
Grey, Beryl (1927—)
Grey, Catherine (c. 1540–1568)
Grey, Elizabeth (fl. 1482–1530)
Grey, Elizabeth (1505–1526)
Grey, Elizabeth (1581–1651)
Grey, Elizabeth (d. 1818)
Grey, Elizabeth (d. 1822)
Grey, Lady Jane (1537–1554)
Grey, Maria Georgina (1816–1906)
Grey, Mary (1545–1578)
Grierson, Mary (1912—)
Grieve, Elizabeth Harriet (1735–?)
Griffies, Ethel (1878–1975)
Griffin, Jane (1680–1720)
Griffith, Phyllis (c. 1922—)
Griffiths, Jane (1954—)
Grigson, Jane (1928–1990)
Grinham, Judith (1939—)
Grote, Harriet (1792–1878)
Grubb, Sarah Lynes (1773–1842)
Grubb, Sarah Tuke (1756–1790)
Grymeston, Elizabeth Bernye (d. 1603)
Guinevere (d. 470 or 542)
Guinness, Heather (1910—)
Gundred (d. 1085)
Gunnell, Sally (1966—)
Gunning, Elizabeth (1734–1790)
Gunning, Elizabeth (1769–1823)
Gunning, Maria (1733–1760)
Gunning, Susannah Minifie (c. 1740–1800)
Guppy, Eileen M. (1903–1980)
Gurney, Rachel (1920–2001)
Gwynn, Nell (1650–1687)
Gwynne-Vaughan, Helen (1879–1967)
Gynt, Greta (1916–2000)
Gyseth (fl. 1070)
Hack, Maria (1777–1844)
Hadid, Zaha (1950—)
Haffenden, Elizabeth (1906–1976)
Haldane, Charlotte (1894–1969)
Halkett, Anne (1622–1699)
Hall, Radclyffe (1880–1943)
Halliwell, Geri (1972—)
Halstead, Nellie (1910–1991)
Hames, Mary (1827–1919)
Hamilton, Anne (1636–1716)
Hamilton, Anne (1766–1846)
Hamilton, Catherine (1738–1782)
Hamilton, Cicely (1872–1952)
Hamilton, Elizabeth (c. 1480–?)
Hamilton, Elizabeth (1641–1708)
Hamilton, Elizabeth (1758–1816)
Hamilton, Emma (1765–1815)
Hamilton, Mary (1613–1638)
Hamilton, Mary (1705–?)
Hamilton, Mary (1739–1816)
Hamlett, Dilys (1928–2002)
Hammond, Dorothy (c. 1876–1950)
Hammond, Kay (1909–1980)
Hamnett, Katherine (1952—)
Hampshire, Margaret (1918–2004)
Hampshire, Susan (1938—)

Geographic Index

Hanbury, Elizabeth (1793–1901)
Hancock, Florence (1893–1974)
Handl, Irene (1901–1987)
Hands, Elizabeth (fl. 1789)
Hankford, Anne (1431–1485)
Hannam, Edith (1878–1951)
Hanson, Jean (1919–1973)
Hanway, Mary Ann (c. 1755–c. 1823)
Hardcastle, Sarah (1969—)
Harding, Jan (1925—)
Harding, Phyllis (b. 1907)
Hardy, Barbara (1924—)
Harland, Georgina (1978—)
Harley, Brilliana (c. 1600–1643)
Harlowe, Sarah (1765–1852)
Harman, Harriet (1950—)
Harraden, Beatrice (1864–1936)
Harriman, Pamela (1920–1997)
Harris, Charlotte (1819–?)
Harris, Emily Cumming (c. 1836–1925)
Harris, Jane Elizabeth (c. 1852–1942)
Harris, Joan (1920—)
Harris, Julie (1921—)
Harris, Phoebe (1755–1786)
Harris, Rosemary (1927—)
Harrison, Beatrice (1892–1965)
Harrison, Jane Ellen (1850–1928)
Harrison, Joan (c. 1908–1994)
Harrison, Kathleen (1892–1995)
Harrison, May (1891–1959)
Hart, Alice (fl. late-19th c.)
Hart, Judith (1924—)
Hartigan, Anne Le Marquand (1931—)
Hartley, Donna-Marie (1955—)
Hartley, Margaret
Harvey, Lilian (1906–1968)
Harvey, P.J. (1969—)
Harwood, Elizabeth (1938–1990)
Haselden, Frances Isabella (c. 1841–1936)
Hashman, Judy (1935—)
Haslett, Caroline (1895–1957)
Hassall, Joan (1906–1988)
Hastings, Anne (c. 1487–?)
Hastings, Anne (d. after 1506)
Hastings, Denise (1958—)
Hastings, Elizabeth (1682–1739)
Hastings, Flora (1806–1839)
Hastings, Selina (1707–1791)
Hathaway, Anne (1556–1623)
Hathaway, Sibyl (1884–1974)
Hatton, Marion (1835–1905)
Havergal, Frances Ridley (1836–1879)
Hawarden, Clementina (1822–1865)
Hawker, Lilian E. (1908–1991)
Hawkes, Jacquetta (1910–1996)
Hawkins, Laetitia Matilda (1759–1835)
Hawley, Christine (1949—)
Hawtrey, Marjory (1900–1952)
Hay, Lucy (1599–1660)
Haycraft, Anna Margaret (1932–2005)
Haye, Helen (1874–1957)
Haye, Nicolaa de la (1160–1218)
Hayes, Catherine (1690–1726)
Hayes, Patricia (1909–1998)
Hayles, Alice (d. after 1326)
Haynes, Margery (fl. 15th c.)
Hays, Mary (1760–1843)
Haywood, Eliza (c. 1693–1756)
Heal, Sylvia (1942—)
Heap, Sarah (1870–1960)
Hearnshaw, Susan (1961—)
Heaton, Anne (1930—)
Hector, Annie French (1825–1902)
Heilbron, Rose (1914–2005)
Helena (1846–1923)
Helena Victoria (1870–1948)
Hellaby, Amy Maria (1864–1955)
Helliwell, Ethel (c. 1905—)
Hemans, Felicia D. (1793–1835)
Heming, Violet (1895–1981)
Hemingway, Marie (c. 1893–1939)
Henderson, Mary (1919–2004)
Henrietta Maria (1609–1669)
Henrion, Daphne Hardy (1917–2003)
Hepworth, Barbara (1903–1975)
Herbert, Jocelyn (1917–2003)
Herbert, Katherine (c. 1471–?)
Herbert, Lucy (1669–1744)
Herbert, Mary (1561–1621)
Hereswitha (d. around 690)
Herford, Beatrice (c. 1868–1952)
Hermes, Gertrude (1901–1983)
Hervey, Elizabeth (c. 1748–c. 1820)
Hervey, Mary (1700–1768)
Heslop, Mary Kingdon (1885–1955)
Hess, Myra (1890–1965)
Hetherington, Jessie Isabel (1882–1971)
Hetley, Georgina Burne (1832–1898)
Hewett, Ellen Anne (1843–1926)
Hewett, Mary Elizabeth Grenside (1857–1892)
Hewitt, Patricia (1948—)
Hewlett, Hilda Beatrice (1864–1943)
Heyer, Georgette (1902–1974)
Heyhoe-Flint, Rachael (1939—)
Heywood, Anne (1932—)
Heywood, Joan (1923—)
Hibbert, Eleanor (1906–1993)
Hickling, Grace (1908–1986)
Hicks, Adelaide (1845–1930)
Hicks, Amie (c. 1839–1917)
Hicks, Betty Seymour (1904—)
Hicks, Elizabeth (1705–1716)
Hicks, Mary (d. 1716)
Hickson, Joan (1906–1998)
Higgins, Rosalyn (1937—)
Higgins, Sarah (1830–1923)
Hilda of Hartlepool (fl. 8th c.)
Hilda of Whitby (614–680)
Hill, Emily (1847–1930)
Hill, Joan (fl. 1460)
Hill, Mabel (1872–1956)
Hill, Octavia (1838–1912)
Hill, Susan (1942—)
Hiller, Wendy (1912–2003)
Hilliard, Patricia (1916–2001)
Hill-Lowe, Beatrice
Hillyard, Blanche Bingley (1864–1938)
Hindley, Myra (1942–2002)
Hippisley, E. (fl. 1741–1766)
Hippisley, Jane (d. 1791)
Hirst, Grace (1805–1901)
Hiscock, Eileen (1909—)
Hobhouse, Emily (1860–1926)
Hobson, Valerie (1917–1998)
Hoby, Margaret (1571–1633)
Hodge, Annie Mabel (1862–1938)
Hodge, Margaret (1944—)
Hodges, Faustina Hasse (1822–1895)
Hodgkin, Dorothy (1910–1994)
Hodgson, Elizabeth (1814–1877)
Hodson, Henrietta (1841–1910)
Hoey, Iris (1885–1979)
Hoey, Kate (1946—)
Hogg, Sarah (1946—)
Holden, Edith B. (1871–1920)
Holden, Effie M. (b. 1867)
Holden, Evelyn (1877–c. 1969)
Holden, Fay (1893–1973)
Holden, Gloria (1908–1991)
Holden, Molly (1927–1981)
Holden, Violet (b. 1873)
Holford, Ingrid (1920—)
Holland, Alianor (c. 1373–1405)
Holland, Anne (fl. 1440–1462)
Holland, Anne (d. 1474)
Holland, Annie (1965—)
Holland, Catherine (1637–1720)
Holland, Constance (1387–1437)
Holland, Eleanor (c. 1385–?)
Holland, Elizabeth (c. 1383–?)
Holland, Joan (c. 1380–1434)
Holland, Margaret (1385–1429)
Holland, Mary (1935–2004)
Hollingsworth, Margaret (1940—)
Holman, Dorothy (1883–?)
Holmes, Kelly (1970—)
Holst, Imogen (1907–1984)
Holtby, Winifred (1898–1935)
Honeyball, Mary (1952—)
Honeyman, Susie
Hoo, Anne (c. 1425–1484)
Hood, Mary (c. 1822–1902)
Hopkins, Ellice (1836–1904)
Hopkins, Thelma (1936—)
Hopper, Victoria (1909—)
Hopton, Susanna Harvey (1627–1708)
Horniman, Annie (1860–1937)
Horovitz, Frances (1938–1983)
Horrell, Elizabeth (1826–1913)
Horsbrugh, Florence (1889–1969)
Horton, Ann (1743–1808)
Horton, Christiana (c. 1696–c. 1756)
Hotot, Agnes (fl. 14th c.)
Houghton, Frances (1980—)
Housden, Jane (d. 1714)
Houston, Lucy (1858–1936)
Howard, Anne (1475–1511)
Howard, Anne (d. 1559)
Howard, Caroline Cadette (1821–?)
Howard, Catherine (fl. 1450)
Howard, Catherine (d. 1452)
Howard, Catherine (d. after 1478)
Howard, Catherine (1520/22–1542)
Howard, Catherine (d. 1548)
Howard, Catherine (d. 1596)
Howard, Catherine (d. 1672)
Howard, Catherine (d. 1874)
Howard, Dorothy (fl. 1500)
Howard, Elizabeth (c. 1410–1475)
Howard, Elizabeth (1494–1558)
Howard, Elizabeth (?–1538)
Howard, Elizabeth (d. 1534)
Howard, Elizabeth Ann (1823–1865)
Howard, Elizabeth Jane (1923—)
Howard, Frances (1593–1632)
Howard, Henrietta (1688–1767)
Howard, Isabel (fl. 1500s)
Howard, Jane (d. 1593)
Howard, Joyce (fl. 1500s)
Howard, Margaret (fl. 1450)
Howard, Margaret (fl. 1500s)
Howard, Mary (fl. 1500s)
Howard, Muriel (d. 1512)
Howard, Rosalind Frances (1845–1921)
Howatch, Susan (1940—)
Howes, Sally Ann (1930—)
Howey, Kate Louise (1973—)
Howitt, Mary (1799–1888)
How-Martyn, Edith (1875–1954)
Hoyte-Smith, Joslyn Y. (1954—)
Hughes, Annie (1869–1954)
Hughes, Beverley (1950—)
Hughes, Edna (1916—)
Hull, Eleanor (fl. 15th c.)
Hull, Eleanor Henrietta (1860–1935)
Hulme, Juliet Marion (1938—)
Humble, Joan (1951—)

Hume, Benita (1906–1967)
Hume, Elizabeth (c. 1599–1633)
Humphrey, Edith (1875–1977)
Hungerford, Agnes (d. 1524)
Hunt, Martita (1900–1969)
Hunt, Violet (1866–1942)
Hunte, Heather (1959—)
Hunter, Rita (1933–2001)
Hurst, Margery (1913–1989)
Hutchinson, Amy (1733–1750)
Hutchinson, Amy May (1888–1985)
Hutchinson, Anne (1591–1643)
Hutchinson, Lucy (1620–post 1675)
Huxley, Elspeth (1907–1997)
Huxley, Julia Arnold (1862–1908)
Hyde, Anne (1638–1671)
Hyde, Catherine (1701–1777)
Hyde, Jane (d. 1725)
Hygeburg (fl. 8th c.)
Hylton, Jane (1927–1979)
Hyman, Dorothy (1941—)
Hyman, Prudence (1914–1995)
Hyson, Dorothy (1914–1996)
Ida Plantagenet (fl. 1175)
Imlay, Fanny (1794–1816)
Inchbald, Elizabeth (1753–1821)
Inescort, Elaine (c. 1877–1964)
Ingelow, Jean (1820–1897)
Inglesby, Mona (1918—)
Inglis, Elsie Maud (1864–1917)
Inglis, Esther (1571–1624)
Ingoldsthorp, Isabel (fl. 15th c.)
Ingoldsthorp, Isabel
Innes, Catherine Lucy (1839/40–1900)
Ireland, Jill (1936–1990)
Irving, Ethel (1869–1963)
Isaacs, Stella (1894–1971)
Isaacs, Susan (1885–1948)
Isabel (1386–1402)
Isabel (1409–1484)
Isabel (d. 1457?)
Isabel de Warrenne (c. 1137–1203)
Isabel de Warrenne (d. 1282)
Isabella (1332–1382)
Isabella de Redvers (1237–1293)
Isabella of Angoulême (1186–1246)
Isabella of France (1296–1358)
Isabella of Valois (1389–c. 1410)
Isabel of Beaumont (fl. 1150)
Isabel of Castile (1355–1392)
Isabel of Vermandois (d. before 1147)
Isabel Plantagenet (c. 1317–c. 1347)
Ivan, Rosalind (1880–1959)
Izzard, Molly (1919–2004)
Jabavu, Noni (1919—)
Jackson, Ann Fletcher (1833–1903)
Jackson, Caroline F. (1946—)
Jackson, Freda (1909–1990)
Jackson, Glenda (1936—)
Jackson, Helen (1939—)
Jackson, Mary Percy (1904–2000)
Jackson, Rowena (1926—)
Jackson, Sarah Elizabeth (1858–1946)
Jacob, Naomi Ellington (1889–1964)
Jacobi, Mary Putnam (1842–1906)
Jacobs, Simmone (1966—)
Jacques, Hattie (1922–1980)
Jagger, Amy
Jahoda, Marie (1907–2001)
James, Elinor (c. 1645–1719)
James, Hilda (b. 1904)
James, P.D. (1920—)
Jameson, Helen (1963—)
Jameson, Storm (1891–1986)
Jamieson, Penny (1942—)
Jansen, Elly (1929—)
Jay, Harriett (1863–1932)
Jay, Isabel (1879–1927)
Jeans, Constance (b. 1899)
Jeans, Isabel (1891–1985)
Jeans, Ursula (1906–1973)
Jebb, Eglantyne (1876–1928)
Jeffreys, Ellis (1872–1943)
Jeffries, Elizabeth (d. 1752)
Jeffs, Doreen (d. 1965)
Jekyll, Gertrude (1843–1932)
Jellicoe, Ann (1927—)
Jenkin, Penelope M. (1902–1994)
Jenner, Ann (1944—)
Jenner, Caryl (1917—)
Jennings, Elizabeth Joan (1926–2001)
Jennings, Frances (d. 1730)
Jennings, Gertrude E. (d. 1958)
Jermy, Louie (1864–1934)
Jerome, Helen (b. 1883)
Jerome, Rowena (1889–?)
Jerrold, Mary (1877–1955)
Jesse, Fryniwyd Tennyson (1888–1958)
Jessel, Patricia (1929–1968)
Jewsbury, Geraldine (1812–1880)
Jewsbury, Maria Jane (1800–1833)
Jex-Blake, Sophia (1840–1912)
Joan (1384–1400)
Joan de Clare (c. 1268–after 1322)
Joan de Quinci (d. 1283)
Joan de Vere (fl. 1280s)
Joanna (1333–1348)
Joanna of Navarre (c. 1370–1437)
Joan of Acre (1272–1307)
Joan of Kent (1328–1385)
Joan Plantagenet (c. 1312–c. 1345)
Jocelin, Elizabeth (1596–1622)
Johansen, Aud (1930—)
John, Rosamund (1913–1998)
Johns, Ethel (1879–1968)
Johns, Glynis (1923—)
Johnson, Amy (1903–1941)
Johnson, Celia (1908–1982)
Johnson, Kathryn (1967—)
Johnson, Katie (1878–1957)
Johnson, Melanie (1955—)
Johnson, Pamela Hansford (1912–1981)
Johnson, Phyllis (1886–1967)
Johnstone, Hilda Lorne (b. 1902)
Jolley, Elizabeth (1923—)
Jones, Ann Haydon (1938—)
Jones, Hazel (1896–1974)
Jones, Helen (1954—)
Jones, Lynne (1951—)
Joseph, Helen (1905–1992)
Joseph, Jenefer (1932—)
Joshua, Joan O. (1912–1993)
Jowell, Tessa (1947—)
Judd, Isabel
Julian of Norwich (c. 1342–c. 1416)
June (1901–c. 1984)
Kaberry, Phyllis (1910–1977)
Kane, Sarah (1971–1999)
Kar, Ida (1908–1970)
Katherine (fl. 13th c.)
Katherine of Sutton (d. 1376)
Katherine Plantagenet (1253–1257)
Katherine Plantagenet (1479–1527)
Kaye, M.M. (1908–2004)
Kaye-Smith, Sheila (1887–1956)
Kazantzis, Judith (1940—)
Kean, Ellen (1805–1880)
Keane, Fiorella (1930–1976)
Keeble, Sally (1951—)
Keeler, Christine (1942—)
Keeley, Mary Anne (c. 1806–1899)
Keen, Ann (1948—)
Keene, Laura (c. 1826–1873)
Kelly, Jo Ann (1944–1990)
Kelly, Margaret (1910–2004)
Kelly, Margaret (1956—)
Kelly, Ruth (1968—)
Kelsey, Lavinia Jane (1856–1948)
Kemble, Adelaide (1814–1879)
Kemble, Eliza (1761–1836)
Kemble, Elizabeth (c. 1763–1841)
Kemble, Fanny (1809–1893)
Kemble, Maria Theresa (1774–1838)
Kemble, Priscilla (1756–1845)
Kemp, Charlotte (1790–1860)
Kempe, Margery (c. 1373–after 1438)
Kempson, Rachel (1910–2003)
Kemp-Welch, Joan (1906–1999)
Kendal, Felicity (1946—)
Kendal, Madge (1849–1935)
Kendall, Kay (1926–1959)
Kennard, Olga (1924—)
Kennedy, Jane (1958—)
Kennedy, Margaret (1896–1967)
Kennett, Margaret Brett (fl. 1723–1725)
Kenney, Annie (1879–1953)
Kent, Constance (1844–?)
Kent, Jean (1921—)
Kenyon, Kathleen (1906–1978)
Keppel, Alice (1869–1947)
Kéroüalle, Louise de (1649–1734)
Kerr, Deborah (1921—)
Ker-Seymer, Barbara (b. 1905)
Kielmansegge, Sophia Charlotte von (1673–1725)
Kilbourn, Annelisa (1967–2002)
Killigrew, Anne (1660–1685)
Killigrew, Catherine (c. 1530–1583)
Killigrew, Elizabeth (c. 1622–?)
Kimenye, Barbara (1940—)
King, Anne (1621–after 1684)
King, Ellen (b. 1909)
King, Mary (1961—)
King, Oona (1967—)
Kingsford, Anna (1846–1888)
Kingsley, Mary H. (1862–1900)
Kingsley, Mary St. Leger (1852–1931)
Kingston, Winifred (1894–1967)
Kinnaird, Mary Jane (1816–1888)
Kinsella, Kathleen (d. 1961)
Kipling, Charlotte (1919–1992)
Kirkaldy, Jane Willis (c. 1869–1932)
Kirkbride, Julie (1960—)
Kirkeby, Elizabeth (fl. 1482)
Kirkhoven, Catherine (d. 1667)
Kirkwhite, Iris (c. 1900–1975)
Kirkwood, Pat (1921—)
Kissling, Margaret (1808–1891)
Kite, Jessie
Kitzinger, Sheila (1929—)
Knight, Ellis Cornelia (1758–1837)
Knight, Laura (1877–1970)
Knight, Mary (1749–1788)
Knipp, Mrs. (fl. 1670)
Knollys, Elizabeth (c. 1586–1658)
Knollys, Lettice (c. 1541–1634)
Knorr, Frances (1868–1894)
Knyvett, Catherine (d. 1633)
Kohary, Antoinette (1797–1862)
Konstam, Phyllis (1907–1976)
Lacey, Janet (1903–1988)
Lacey, Maud (fl. 1230–1250)
Lacy, Alice (1281–1348)
Lacy, Harriette Deborah (1807–1874)
Laine, Cleo (1927—)
Laing, Eleanor (1958—)
Lait, Jacqui (1947—)
Lamb, Caroline (1785–1828)

Lamb, Emily (d. 1869)
Lamb, Mary Anne (1764–1847)
Lambert, Jean (1950—)
Lamburn, Richmal Crompton (1890–1969)
Lancaster, Nancy (1897–1994)
Lancaster-Wallis, Ellen (1856–?)
Lanchester, Elsa (1902–1986)
Landon, Letitia Elizabeth (1802–1838)
Landseer, Jessica (1810–1880)
Lane, Elizabeth (1905–1988)
Lane, Grace (1876–1956)
Lane, Jane (d. 1689)
Lane, Maryon (1931—)
Lang, Leonora (1851–1933)
Langford, Bonnie (1964—)
Langton, Jane (fl. 15th c.)
Langtry, Lillie (1853–1929)
Lannaman, Sonia M. (1956—)
Lanner, Katti (1829–1908)
Lansbury, Angela (1925—)
La Plante, Lynda (1946—)
Larpent, Anna Margaretta (fl. 1815–1830)
Lascelles, Ernita (1890–1972)
Laski, Marghanita (1915–1988)
Lathbury, Kathleen Culhane (1900–1993)
Latimer, Elizabeth W. (1822–1904)
Latimer, Sally (1910—)
Laverick, Elise (1975—)
Laverick, Elizabeth (1925—)
Law, Leslie (1965—)
Lawrence, Gertrude (1898–1952)
Lawrence, Susan (1871–1947)
Lawrie, Jean Grant (1914—)
Lawson, Joan (1907–2002)
Lawson, Mary (1910–1941)
Lawson, Winifred (1892–1961)
Laye, Evelyn (1900–1996)
Lead, Jane Ward (1623–1704)
Leakey, Caroline Woolmer (1827–1881)
Leakey, Mary Nicol (1913–1996)
Leapor, Mary (1722–1746)
Leavis, Q.D. (1906–1981)
Le Blond, Elizabeth (1861–1934)
Lebour, Marie (1877–1971)
Leclercq, Carlotta (c. 1840–1893)
Leclercq, Rose (c. 1845–1899)
Lee, Ann (1736–1784)
Lee, Anna (1913–2004)
Lee, Auriol (1880–1941)
Lee, Belinda (1935–1961)
Lee, Gina (1943–2002)
Lee, Harriet (1757–1851)
Lee, Jennie (c. 1846–1930)
Lee, Sarah (1791–1856)
Lee, Sophia (1750–1824)
Lee, Tanith (1947—)
Lees, Sue (1941–2003)
Lee Smith, Jenny (1948—)
Lefanu, Alicia (1753–1817)
Lefanu, Alicia (c. 1795–c. 1826)
Lefanu, Elizabeth (1758–1837)
Lefanu, Nicola (1947—)
Le Gallienne, Eva (1899–1991)
Legat, Nadine (c. 1895–?)
Legh, Alice (1855–1948)
Leginska, Ethel (1886–1970)
Lehmann, Beatrix (1903–1979)
Lehmann, Liza (1862–1918)
Lehmann, Rosamond (1901–1990)
Leigh, Adèle (1928–2004)
Leigh, Augusta (1784–1851)
Leigh, Dorothy Kempe (fl. 1616)
Leigh, Vivien (1913–1967)
Leighton, Clare (1899–1989)
Leighton, Margaret (1922–1976)
Leitch, Cecil (1891–1977)
Lejeune, C.A. (1897–1973)
Lemon, Margaretta Louisa (1860–1953)
Leng, Virginia (1955—)
Lennox, Avril (1956—)
Lennox, Caroline (1723–1774)
Lennox, Charlotte (1720–1804)
Lennox, Emily (1731–1814)
Lennox, Louisa (1743–1821)
Lennox, Sarah (1745–1826)
Lennox Sisters
Le Noir, Elizabeth Anne (c. 1755–1841)
Leonowens, Anna (c. 1831–1914)
Lerwill, Sheila (1928—)
Leslie, May Sybil (1887–1937)
Lessing, Doris (1919—)
Lessore, Thérèse (1884–1945)
Le Sueur, Frances (1919–1995)
Leverson, Ada (1862–1933)
Levertov, Denise (1923–1997)
Leveson-Gower, Harriet (1785–1862)
Leveson-Gower, Harriet Elizabeth Georgiana (1806–1868)
Levison, Mary (1923—)
Levy, Amy (1861–1889)
Lewis, Bertha (1887–1931)
Lewis, Denise (1972—)
Lewis, Ethelreda (1875–1946)
Lewson, Jane (c. 1700–1816)
Leyburne, Elizabeth (d. 1567)
Leyel, Hilda (1880–1957)
Liddell, Alice (1852–1934)
Liddell, Helen (1950—)
Lightfoot, Hannah (fl. 1768)
Lillie, Beatrice (1894–1989)
Lind, Letty (1862–1923)
Lindo, Olga (1899–1968)
Line, Anne (d. 1601)
Linley, Elizabeth (1754–1792)
Linley, Maria (1763–1784)
Linskill, Mary (1840–1891)
Linton, Eliza Lynn (1822–1898)
Lioba (700–779)
Lipkin, Jean (1926—)
Lipman, Maureen (1946—)
Lipson, Edna (1914–1996)
Lisle, Alice (c. 1614–1685)
Lisle, Honora Grenville (c. 1495–1566)
Lister, Anne (1791–1840)
Lister, Sandra (1961—)
Litchfield, Harriett (1777–1854)
Littlewood, Joan (1914–2002)
Litton, Marie (1847–1884)
Litvinov, Ivy (1889–1977)
Lively, Penelope (1933—)
Livingstone, Mary Moffatt (1820–1862)
Lloyd, Alice (1873–1949)
Lloyd, Doris (1896–1968)
Lloyd, Dorothy Jordan (1889–1946)
Lloyd, Gweneth (1901–1993)
Lloyd, Marie (1870–1922)
Lloyd, Maude (1908–2004)
Lloyd, Rosie (b. 1879)
Lloyd-Davies, Vanessa (1960–2005)
Lloyd George, Frances Stevenson (1888–1972)
Lloyd George, Margaret (d. 1941)
Locke, Anne Vaughan (c. 1530–c. 1590)
Lockhart, Kathleen (1894–1978)
Lockwood, Margaret (1916–1990)
Logic, Lora (c. 1961—)
Logue, Jenny (c. 1982—)
Lohman, Ann Trow (1812–1878)
Long, Kathleen (1896–1968)
Longfield, Cynthia (1896–1991)
Longford, Elizabeth (1906–2002)
Longstaff, Mary Jane (c. 1855–1935)
Lonsbrough, Anita (1941—)
Lonsdale, Kathleen (1903–1971)
Loraine, Violet (1886–1956)
Lorraine, Emily (c. 1878–1944)
Lorrayne, Vyvyan (1939—)
Loudon, Jane Webb (1807–1858)
Loughlin, Anne (1894–1979)
Louisa Anne (1749–1768)
Louise (1692–1712)
Louise (1848–1939)
Louise Victoria (1867–1931)
Love, Mabel (1874–1953)
Lovelace, Ada Byron, Countess of (1815–1852)
Lovell, Ann (1803/11–1869)
Lovell, Maria Anne (1803–1877)
Lowe-McConnell, Rosemary (1921—)
Loy, Mina (1882–1966)
Lucas, Caroline (1960—)
Lucas, Margaret Bright (1818–1890)
Luckner, Gertrud (1900–1995)
Lucy, Elizabeth (fl. 1460s)
Ludford, Sarah (1951—)
Luke, Jemima (1813–1906)
Lumley, Joanna (1946—)
Lumley, Joanna (c. 1537–1576)
Lupino, Ida (1914–1995)
Lutyens, Elisabeth (1906–1983)
Lutyens, Mary (1908–1999)
Lwin, Annabella (1965—)
Lyell, Mary Horner (1808–1873)
Lympany, Moura (1916–2005)
Lynn, Vera (1917—)
Lynne, Elizabeth (1948—)
Lynne, Gillian (1926—)
Lyon, Mary Frances (1925—)
Lyttelton, Edith (1865–1948)
Lytton, Constance (1869–1923)
Lytton, Emily (1874–1964)
Mabel of Bury St. Edmunds (fl. 1230)
Macarthur, Elizabeth (1767–1850)
MacArthur, Ellen (1976—)
Macaulay, Catharine (1731–1791)
Macaulay, Rose (1881–1958)
MacColl, Kirsty (1959–2000)
MacDonald, Frances (1874–1921)
Macdonald, Georgiana (1840–1920)
MacDonald, Margaret (c. 1907–1956)
Macfarlane, Edith Mary (1871–1948)
MacGrath, Leueen (1914–1992)
MacGregor, Sue (1941—)
Mackaill, Dorothy (1903–1990)
Mackay, Elizabeth Ann Louisa (1843–1908)
Mackenzie, Midge (1938–2004)
MacKinlay, Jean Sterling (1882–1958)
Mackintosh, Margaret (1865–1933)
Maclean, Ida Smedley (1877–1944)
Macnaghten, Anne (1908–2002)
Macpherson, Margaret Louisa (1895–1974)
Mactaggart, Fiona (1953—)
Mahon, Alice (1937—)
Mairet, Ethel (1872–1952)
Maitland, Agnes Catherine (1850–1906)
Major, Clare Tree (d. 1954)
Major, Ethel Lillie (1890–1934)
Makin, Bathsua (1608–1675)
Malcolm, Emilie Monson (1829/30–1905)
Mallaber, Judy (1951—)
Malleson, Joan (1900–1956)
Malyon, Eily (1879–1961)
Man, Judith (fl. 1640s)
Manley, Dorothy (1927—)
Manley, Mary de la Rivière (1663–1724)
Mann, Ida (1893–1983)
Mannering, Mary (1876–1953)
Manners, Martha (1924–1977)

Mannin, Ethel (1900–1984)
Manning, Anne (1807–1879)
Manning, Leah (1886–1977)
Manning, Maria (c. 1821–1849)
Manning, Olivia (1908–1980)
Manny, Anne (b. 1355)
Mansel, Lucy (c. 1830–1915)
Mansour, Joyce (1928–1987)
Mantle, Winifred Langford (1911–1983)
Manton, Irene (1904–1988)
Manton, Sidnie (1902–1979)
Mar, Frances, Countess of (1690–1761)
Marcet, Jane (1769–1858)
Marchant, Bessie (1862–1941)
Margaret (d. 1228)
Margaret (d. 1275)
Margaret (1275–1318)
Margaret (c. 1320–1400)
Margaret (1346–1361)
Margaret de Burgh (c. 1226–1243)
Margaret of Anjou (1429–1482)
Margaret of France (c. 1282–1318)
Margaret of Kent (1327–before 1352)
Margaret Rose (1930–2002)
Margaret Wake of Liddell (c. 1299–1349)
Marie (fl. 13th c.)
Marie Louise (1879–1948)
Marie of Rumania (1875–1938)
Marina of Greece (1906–1968)
Marjory (fl. 13th c.)
Markham, Beryl (1902–1986)
Markham, Pauline (d. 1919)
Markham, Violet Rosa (1872–1959)
Markova, Alicia (1910–2004)
Marlowe, Julia (1866–1950)
Marrack, Philippa (1945—)
Marryat, Florence (1837–1899)
Marsden, Kate (1859–1931)
Marsh, Jean (1934—)
Marsh, Ngaio (1899–1982)
Marshall, Maud (d. 1248)
Marshall, Sybilla (fl. 1230)
Marsh-Caldwell, Anne (1791–1874)
Marson, Aileen (1912–1939)
Martin, Dorcas Eglestone (fl. 16th c.)
Martin, Emma (1812–1851)
Martin, Hannah (1830–1903)
Martin, Mary (1907–1969)
Martin, Mary Ann (1817–1884)
Martin, Millicent (1934—)
Martindale, Hilda (1875–1952)
Martineau, Harriet (1802–1876)
Martin-Spencer, Lilly (1822–1902)
Marx, Laura (1845–1911)
Marx-Aveling, Eleanor (1855–1898)
Mary (b. 1718)
Mary (1278–1332)
Mary (1344–1362)
Mary (1776–1857)
Mary (1897–1965)
Mary de Bohun (1369–1394)
Mary de Coucy (fl. 1370)
Mary de Monthermer (1298–after 1371)
Mary I (1516–1558)
Mary II (1662–1694)
Mary of Hesse-Cassel (1723–1772)
Mary of Modena (1658–1718)
Mary of Orange (1631–1660)
Mary of Teck (1867–1953)
Mary Plantagenet (1467–1482)
Mary Tudor (1673–1726)
Masham, Abigail (1670–1734)
Masham, Damaris (1658–1708)
Maskell, Virginia (1936–1968)
Mason, Elizabeth (d. 1712)
Mason, Lisa (1982—)
Mason, Monica (1941—)
Mason, Pamela (1918–1996)
Masset, Louise (c. 1863–1900)
Massingham, Dorothy (1889–1933)
Matera, Barbara (1929–2001)
Mathé, Carmen (1938—)
Mathers, Helen (1853–1920)
Mathew, Sarah Louise (c. 1805–1890)
Mathews, Vera Laughton (1888–1959)
Matilda, Empress (1102–1167)
Matilda de Burgh (d. 1315)
Matilda of Boulogne (c. 1103–1152)
Matilda of Flanders (c. 1031–1083)
Matilda of Scotland (1080–1118)
Matthews, Jessie (1907–1981)
Matthison, Edith (1875–1955)
Mattocks, Isabella (1746–1826)
Maude, Margery (1889–1979)
Maud of Lusignan (d. 1241)
Maud of Mandeville (d. 1236)
Maule, Annabel (1922—)
Maxtone Graham, Joyce (1901–1953)
May, Fiona (1969—)
May, Isabella (1850–1926)
May, Pamela (1917–2005)
May, Theresa (1956—)
Maybrick, Florence Elizabeth (c. 1853–1941)
Mayne, Ethel Colburn (1865–1941)
Mayor, Flora M. (1872–1932)
McAvan, Linda (1962—)
McCafferty, Chris (1945—)
McCarthy, Lillah (1875–1960)
McColgan-Lynch, Elizabeth (1964—)
McCormick, Anne O'Hare (1880–1954)
McCracken, Esther Helen (1902–1971)
McDonagh, Siobhain (1960—)
McEwan, Geraldine (1932—)
McGregor, Yvonne (1961—)
McGuire, Anne (1949—)
McIntosh, Anne (1954—)
McIntosh, Madge (1875–1950)
McIsaac, Shona (1960—)
McKain, Douglas Mary (1789–1873)
McKane, Kitty (1896–1992)
McKechin, Ann (1961—)
McKechnie, Sheila (1948–2004)
McKenna, Rosemary (1941—)
McKenna, Virginia (1931—)
McKenzie, Grace (b. 1903)
McKenzie, Julia (1941—)
McKisack, May (1900–1981)
McLachlan, Laurentia (1866–1953)
McLennan, Margo (1938–2004)
McMillan, Margaret (1860–1931)
McMillan, Rachel (1859–1917)
McNair, Winifred (1877–1954)
McPartland, Marian (1920—)
McVie, Christine (1943—)
McWilliams, Jackie (1964—)
Medina, Patricia (1919—)
Mee, Margaret (1909–1988)
Meech, Matilda (c. 1825–1907)
Meeke, Mary (d. 1816)
Melbourne, Elizabeth (d. 1818)
Mellanby, Helen (1911–2001)
Mellanby, May (1882–1978)
Mellish, Edith Mary (1861–1922)
Mellon, Harriot (c. 1777–1837)
Mellon, Sarah Jane (1824–1909)
Melmoth, Charlotte (1749–1823)
Melnotte, Violet (1856–1935)
Melville, June (1915–1970)
Menchik, Vera (1906–1944)
Menuhin, Diana (1912–2003)
Mercer, Beryl (1882–1939)
Mercer, Mabel (1900–1983)
Merchant, Vivien (1929–1983)
Mercier, Margaret (1937—)
Merrall, Mary (1890–1973)
Merrick, Myra King (1825–1899)
Merron, Gillian (1959—)
Merry, Ann Brunton (1769–1808)
Merry, Katharine (1974—)
Messenger, Margaret (1948—)
Metcalfe, Alexandra (1903–1995)
Mew, Charlotte (1869–1928)
Meynell, Alice (1847–1922)
Meynell, Alicia (fl. 1804–1805)
Meynell, Viola (1886–1956)
Milbanke, Anne (1792–1860)
Milburg (d. 722?)
Mildgyth (fl. early 700s)
Mildmay, Audrey (1900–1953)
Mildmay, Grace (1553–1620)
Mildred (d. 700?)
Miles, Sarah (1941—)
Millar, Gertie (1879–1952)
Millard, Ursula (b. 1901)
Miller, Anna Riggs (1741–1781)
Miller, Florence Fenwick (1854–1935)
Miller, Patricia (1927—)
Miller, Tammy (1967—)
Mills, Barbara (1940—)
Mills, Hayley (1946—)
Milner, Brenda Atkinson (1918—)
Milner, Marion (1900–1998)
Mirren, Helen (1945—)
Mitchell, Gladys (1901–1983)
Mitchell, Hannah (1871–1956)
Mitchell, Juliet (1934—)
Mitchell, Yvonne (1925–1979)
Mitchison, Naomi (1897–1999)
Mitchison, Rosalind (1919–2002)
Mitford, Deborah (1920—)
Mitford, Diana (1910–2003)
Mitford, Jessica (1917–1996)
Mitford, Mary Russell (1787–1855)
Mitford, Nancy (1904–1973)
Mitford, Unity (1914–1948)
Moders, Mary (1643–1673)
Moffat, Gwen (1924—)
Moffatt, Laura (1954—)
Moffatt, Mary Smith (1795–1870)
Moggridge, Jackie (1922–2004)
Mohl, Mary (1793–1883)
Mohun, Elizabeth (fl. 14th c.)
Mohun, Joan (fl. 14th c.)
Mohun, Philippa (d. 1431)
Moiseiwitsch, Tanya (1914–2003)
Molesworth, Martha (1577–1646)
Molesworth, Mary Louisa (1839–1921)
Monck, Mary (c. 1678–1715)
Moncrieff, Pérrine (1893–1979)
Monkman, Phyllis (1892–1976)
Montacute, Alice (c. 1406–1463)
Montacute, Anne (d. 1457)
Montacute, Joan (fl. 1300s)
Montacute, Margaret (fl. 1400s)
Montacute, Maud (fl. 1380s)
Montacute, Philippa (fl. 1352)
Montagu, Elizabeth (1720–1800)
Montagu, Elizabeth (1909–2002)
Montagu, Helen (1928–2004)
Montagu, Lady Mary Wortley (1689–1762)
Montagu-Douglas-Scott, Alice (1901–2004)
Montalba, Clara (1842–1929)
Montalba, Henrietta Skerrett (1856–1893)
Montfort, Amicia (fl. 1208)
Montgomery, Margaret (fl. 1438)
Monthermer, Margaret (fl. 1350)
Moodie, Susanna (1803–1885)

Moody, Agnes Claypole (1870–1954)
Moody, Deborah (c. 1583–c. 1659)
Moody, Elizabeth (1737–1814)
Moody, Emma Revell (1842–1903)
Moore, Ann (1950—)
Moore, Decima (1871–1964)
Moore, Eva (1870–1955)
Moore, Jane Elizabeth (1738–?)
Moore, Jessie (1865–1910)
Moran, Margaret (1955—)
More, Agnes (1591–1656)
More, Alice (c. 1472–1545)
More, Gertrude (1606–1633)
More, Hannah (1745–1833)
More, Jane Colt (c. 1488–1511)
More, Mary (d. 1713/15)
Moreman, Marjorie
Moreton, Ursula (1903–1973)
Morgan, Helen (1966—)
Morgan, Joan (1905–2004)
Morgan, Julie (1944—)
Morin, Nea (1906–1986)
Morrell, Ottoline (1873–1938)
Morris, Estelle (1952—)
Morris, Jan (1926—)
Morris, Jane Burden (1839–1914)
Morris, Margaret (1890–1981)
Morris, Mary (1915–1988)
Morris, May (1862–1938)
Morris, Pamela (1906–2002)
Mortimer, Agnes (fl. 1347)
Mortimer, Angela (1932—)
Mortimer, Anne (1390–1411)
Mortimer, Beatrice (d. 1383)
Mortimer, Catherine (c. 1313–1369)
Mortimer, Catherine (d. before 1413)
Mortimer, Eleanor (c. 1395–1418)
Mortimer, Isabel (fl. 1267)
Mortimer, Joan (fl. 1300)
Mortimer, Margaret (d. around 1296)
Mortimer, Maud (c. 1229–1301)
Mortimer, Philippa (1355–1382)
Mortimer, Philippa (1375–1401)
Morton, Lucy (1898–1980)
Moser, Mary (1744–1819)
Mosley, Cynthia (1898–1933)
Moss, Kate (1974—)
Moss, Marjorie (c. 1895–1935)
Mossetti, Carlotta (1890–?)
Mountbatten, Irene (1890–1956)
Mountford, Kali (1954—)
Mowbray, Alison (1971—)
Mowbray, Anne (1472–1481)
Mowbray, Isabel (fl. late 1300s)
Mowbray, Margaret (fl. 1400)
Mowlam, Mo (1949–2005)
Moyet, Alison (1961—)
Muckelt, Ethel (c. 1900—)
Muir, Helen (1920–2005)
Muir, Jean (1928–1995)
Muir-Wood, Helen (1895–1968)
Munda, Constantia (fl. early 17th c.)
Munn, Meg (1959—)
Munro, Janet (1934–1972)
Murdoch, Iris (1919–1999)
Murray, Elizabeth (1626–1698)
Murray, Lilian (1871–1960)
Murray, Margaret (1863–1963)
Murray, Rosemary (1913–2004)
Murrell, Christine (1874–1933)
Murrell, Hilda (c. 1906–1984)
Musgrave, Thea (1928—)
Myddelton, Jane (1645–1692)
Naden, Constance Caroline Woodhill (1858–1889)
Natalie, Mlle (c. 1895–1922)
Neagle, Anna (1904–1986)
Needham, Dorothy (1896–1987)
Needham, Elizabeth (d. 1731)
Neilson, Adelaide (1846–1880)
Neilson, Julia Emilie (1868–1957)
Neilson-Terry, Phyllis (1892–1977)
Nerina, Nadia (1927—)
Nesbit, Edith (1858–1924)
Nesbitt, Cathleen (1888–1982)
Nesta Tewdr (fl. 1090)
Nethersole, Olga (1863–1951)
Nevada, Mignon (1885–1970)
Nevill, Dorothy Fanny (1826–1913)
Nevill, Mary (1961—)
Neville, Alice (fl. 1480s)
Neville, Anne (d. 1480)
Neville, Catherine (c. 1397–1483)
Neville, Catherine (fl. 1460)
Neville, Cecily (1415–1495)
Neville, Cecily (fl. 1480s)
Neville, Eleanor (c. 1413–1472)
Neville, Eleanor (fl. 1480s)
Neville, Isabel (1451–1476)
Neville, Jane (d. 1538)
Neville, Joan (fl. 1468)
Neville, Joan (fl. 1480s)
Neville, Lucy (fl. 15th c.)
Neville, Margaret (d. 1372)
Neville, Margaret (c. 1377–c. 1424)
Neville, Margaret (b. 1466)
Neville, Margaret (d. 1506)
Neville-Jones, Pauline (1939—)
Newall, Sybil (1854–1929)
Newcomb, Mary (1893–1966)
Newman, Mehetabel (c. 1822–1908)
Newman, Nanette (1934—)
Newton, Joy (1913–1996)
Newton, Lily (1893–1981)
Newton-John, Olivia (1948—)
Ney, Marie (1895–1981)
Ngcobo, Lauretta (1932—)
Nicholas, Alison (1962—)
Nicholas, Charlotte (fl. 1915)
Nicholls, Mandy (1968—)
Nicholls, Rhoda Holmes (1854–1930)
Nichols, Dandy (1907–1986)
Nicholson, Emma (1941—)
Nicholson, Margaret (c. 1750–c. 1828)
Nicholson, Nora (1889–1973)
Nicholson, Winifred (1893–1981)
Nicolson, Adela Florence (1865–1904)
Nightingale, Florence (1820–1910)
Nihell, Elizabeth (1723–after 1772)
Ninnoc (fl. 6th c.)
Nisbett, Louisa Cranstoun (1812–1858)
Norden, Christine (1924–1988)
Norgate, Kate (1853–1935)
Normanton, Helena (1883–1957)
North, Marianne (1830–1890)
Norton, Caroline (1808–1877)
Norton, Frances (1640–1731)
Norton, Mary (1903–1992)
Nott, Kathleen (1909–1999)
Novello, Clara (1818–1908)
Nunneley, Kathleen Mary (1872–1956)
Nuthall, Betty (1911—)
Nuthall, Betty (1911–1983)
Oakley, Ann (1944—)
O'Connor, Ellen (1857–1933)
O'Doherty, Mignon (1890–1961)
Ogilvie Farquharson, Marian (1846–1912)
Oldfield, Anne (1683–1730)
Oliphant, Betty (1918–2004)
Oliphant, Margaret (1828–1897)
Olivier, Edith (c. 1879–1948)
Olney, Violet (1911—)
Olrich, April (1931—)
O'Malley, Mary Dolling (1889–1974)
Oman, Julia Trevelyan (1930–2003)
Opie, Amelia (1769–1853)
Opie, Iona (1923—)
Orchard, Sadie (c. 1853–1943)
Orczy, Emma (1865–1947)
Organ, Diana (1952—)
Ormerod, Eleanor A. (1828–1901)
Orthryth of Mercia (fl. 7th c.)
Orton, Beth (1970—)
Osborn, Emily Mary (1834–c. 1885)
Osborne, Dorothy (1627–1695)
Osborne, Sandra (1956—)
Osburga (?–c. 855)
Osburn, Lucy (1835–1891)
Osgerby, Ann (1963—)
O'Shea, Katherine (1845–1921)
Osith (died c. 700)
Ostler, Emma Brignell (c. 1848–1922)
Ostrith (d. 697)
O'Toole, Barbara (1960—)
Owen, Jane (fl. 1617–1634)
Packer, Ann E. (1942—)
Page, Annette (1952—)
Paget, Dorothy (1905–1960)
Paget, Mary (1865–1919)
Paget, Muriel (1876–1938)
Paget, Rosalind (1855–1948)
Paget, Violet (1856–1935)
Paige, Elaine (1948—)
Pakington, Dorothy (d. 1679)
Palladino, Emma (c. 1860–1922)
Palmer, Anne (1661–1722)
Palmer, Barbara (1672–1737)
Palmer, Elizabeth Mary (1832–1897)
Palmer, Frances Flora (1812–1876)
Palmer, Mary (1716–1794)
Palmolive (1955—)
Pankhurst, Adela (1885–1961)
Pankhurst, Christabel (1880–1958)
Pankhurst, Emmeline (1858–1928)
Pankhurst, Sylvia (1882–1960)
Panter-Downes, Mollie (1906–1997)
Pardoe, Julia (1804–1862)
Parepa-Rosa, Euphrosyne (1836–1874)
Pargeter, Edith (c. 1913–1995)
Parke, Mary (1908–1989)
Parker, Bridget (1939—)
Parker, Jane (d. 1542?)
Parker, Mary Ann (fl. 1795)
Parker-Bowles, Camilla (1947—)
Parkes, Bessie Rayner (1829–1925)
Parkinson, Georgina (1938—)
Parr, Anne (d. 1552)
Parr, Catherine (1512–1548)
Parr, Harriet (1828–1900)
Parr, Maud Greene (1495–1529)
Parr, Susanna (fl. 1659)
Parsons, Eliza (c. 1748–1811)
Parsons, Elizabeth (1846–1924)
Parsons, Nancie (1904–1968)
Parton, Mabel (b. 1881)
Partridge, Frances (1900–2004)
Partridge, Margaret (b. 1891)
Pashley, Anne (1935—)
Pasternak, Josephine (1900–1993)
Paston, Agnes (c. 1405–1479)
Paston, Margaret (1423–1484)
Paterson, Emma (1848–1886)
Paterson, Jennifer (1928–1999)
Paterson, Pat (1911–1978)
Patey, Janet Monach (1842–1894)
Paton Walsh, Jill (1937—)
Patten, Marguerite (1915—)
Patterson, Marie (1934—)

Pattison, Dorothy W. (1832–1878)
Paul-Foulds, June (1934—)
Pavlow, Muriel (1921—)
Payne, Sylvia (1880–1974)
Peacock, Lucy (fl. 1785–1816)
Peake, Felicity (1913–2002)
Pearce, Philippa (1920—)
Pearcey, Mary Eleanor (1866–1890)
Pearl, Cora (c. 1837–1886)
Pearsall, Phyllis (1906–1996)
Pearson, Issette (fl. 1893)
Pechey-Phipson, Edith (1845–1908)
Penn, Gulielma Springett (1644–1694)
Penney, Jennifer (1946—)
Pennington, Winifred (1915—)
Penson, Lillian Margery (1896–1963)
Pentreath, Dolly (1685–1777)
Pepys, Elizabeth (1640–1669)
Percy, Agnes (fl. 1120s)
Percy, Anne (fl. 1470s)
Percy, Eleanor (d. 1530)
Percy, Elizabeth (1371–1417)
Percy, Elizabeth (d. 1437)
Percy, Elizabeth (1667–1722)
Percy, Elizabeth (d. 1704)
Percy, Elizabeth (d. 1776)
Percy, Katherine (b. 1423)
Percy, Mary (1320–1362)
Perham, Linda (1947—)
Perham, Margery (1895–1982)
Perrers, Alice (d. 1400)
Perry, Frances (1907–1993)
Pery, Angela Olivia (1897–1981)
Pery, Sylvia (1935—)
Petherick, Mary (fl. 1887)
Pethick-Lawrence, Emmeline (1867–1954)
Petre, Maude (1863–1942)
Petrie, Hilda (1871–1957)
Pfeiffer, Emily Jane (1827–1890)
Philippa de Coucy (fl. 1300s)
Philippa of Hainault (1314–1369)
Philips, Katherine (1631–1664)
Phillipps, Adelaide (1833–1882)
Phillips, Marion (1881–1932)
Phillips, Zara (1981—)
Phillpotts, Bertha Surtees (1877–1932)
Pickford, Mary (1902–2002)
Picking, Anne (1958—)
Pickles, Edith Carrie
Pierce, Judith (1930–2003)
Pike, Mervyn (1918–2004)
Pilcher, Rosamunde (1924—)
Pilkington, Laetitia (c. 1708–1750)
Pilkington, Mary (1766–1839)
Pilley, Dorothy (1893–1986)
Piozzi, Hester Lynch (1741–1821)
Piper, Myfanwy (1911–1997)
Pirie, Antoinette (1905–1991)
Pitman, Jenny (1946—)
Pitter, Ruth (1897–1992)
Pitt-Rivers, Rosalind (1907–1990)
Pix, Mary Griffith (1666–1709)
Pizzey, Erin (1939—)
Platt of Writtle, Baroness (1923—)
Pledge, Sarah (d. 1752)
Plowright, Joan (1929—)
Pole, Elizabeth de la (1444–1503)
Pole, Margaret (1473–1541)
Pole, Ursula (d. 1570)
Pollak, Anna (1912–1996)
Pollard, Marjorie (1899–1982)
Polwhele, Elizabeth (fl. mid-to-late 17th c.)
Poole, Elizabeth (fl. 1648)
Poole, Monica (1921–2003)
Pope, Maria Sophia (1818–1909)
Porter, Anna Maria (1780–1832)
Porter, Annie (1880–1963)
Porter, Gwendoline (c. 1909—)
Porter, Helen Kemp (1899–1987)
Porter, Jane (1776–1850)
Porter, Marguerite (c. 1956—)
Porter, Mary (d. 1765)
Porter, Mary Winearls (1886–1980)
Porter, Sarah (1791–1862)
Poston, Elizabeth (1905–1987)
Potter, Beatrix (1866–1943)
Potter, Sally (1949—)
Pounder, Cheryl
Powell, Dilys (1901–1995)
Powell, Mary Sadler (1854/55?–1946)
Powell, Sandy (1960—)
Power, Eileen (1889–1940)
Poynings, Eleanor (d. 1483)
Pratt, Anne (1806–1893)
Prentice, Bridget (1952—)
Preshaw, Jane (1839–1926)
Price, Hayley
Price, Nancy (1880–1970)
Primarolo, Dawn (1954—)
Prince, Mary (c. 1788–after 1833)
Pringle, Mia Lilly (1920–1983)
Prior, Maddy (1947—)
Pritchard, Hannah (1711–1768)
Probert, Michelle (1960—)
Procter, Adelaide (1825–1864)
Pudney, Elizabeth Jane (1862–1938)
Pulling, Mary Etheldred (1871–1951)
Pulman, Elizabeth (1836–1900)
Pye, Edith (1876–1965)
Pyke, Margaret (1893–1966)
Pym, Barbara (1913–1980)
Quant, Mary (1934—)
Quass, Margaret (1926–2003)
Quatro, Suzi (1950—)
Quin, Ann (1936–1973)
Quin, Joyce (1944—)
Quinton, Carol (1936—)
Radcliffe, Ann (1764–1823)
Radcliffe, Charlotte (b. 1903)
Radcliffe, Charlotte Maria (d. 1755)
Radcliffe, Paula (1973—)
Raine, Kathleen (1908–2003)
Raisin, Catherine (1855–1945)
Ramée, Louise de la (1839–1908)
Rampling, Charlotte (1945—)
Ramsay, Patricia (1886–1974)
Ramsey, Alicia (1864–1933)
Rand, Mary (1940—)
Randolph, Elsie (1904–1982)
Ratcliffe, Jane (1917–1999)
Rathbone, Eleanor (1872–1946)
Rathbone, Hannah Mary (1798–1878)
Rattenbury, Alma (c. 1904–1935)
Ravan, Genya (1942—)
Ravenscroft, Gladys (1888–1960)
Raverat, Gwen (1885–1957)
Ray, Martha (d. 1779)
Ray, René (1911–1993)
Rayner, M.C. (c. 1894–1948)
Read, Imelda Mary (1939—)
Read, Mary (1680–1721)
Rebuck, Gail (1950—)
Redburga (fl. 825)
Redgrave, Lynn (1943—)
Redgrave, Vanessa (1937—)
Reed, Esther De Berdt (1746–1780)
Reeve, Clara (1729–1807)
Reeves, Helen (1980—)
Reeves, Magdalene Stuart (1865–1953)
Reger, Janet (1935–2005)
Rego, Paula (1935—)
Reid, Beryl (1918–1996)
Reid, Kate (1930–1993)
Reignolds, Catherine Mary (1836–1911)
Remington, Barbara (1936—)
Renault, Mary (1905–1983)
Rendell, Ruth (1930—)
Rendle, Sharon (1966—)
Reville, Alma (1899–1982)
Rhodes, Zandra (1940—)
Rhys, Jean (1890–1979)
Rhys-Jones, Sophie (1965—)
Riano, Renie (1899–1971)
Rice, Joan (1930–1997)
Rice-Davies, Mandy (1944—)
Rich, Elizabeth (fl. 1710)
Rich, Penelope (c. 1562–1607)
Richards, Audrey Isabel (1899–1984)
Richardson, Dorothy (1873–1957)
Richardson, Katy (1864–1927)
Richardson, Miranda (1958—)
Richter, Gisela (1882–1972)
Rickett, Mary Ellen (1861–1925)
Riddell, Charlotte (1832–1906)
Ridler, Anne (1912–2001)
Rie, Lucie (1902–1995)
Rigg, Diana (1938—)
Riley, Bridget (1931—)
Rimington, Stella (1935—)
Risdon, Elisabeth (1887–1958)
Ritchie, Anne Isabella (1837–1919)
Ritchie, Harriet Maria (1818–1907)
Roache, Viola (1885–1961)
Robb, Mary Anne (1829–1912)
Roberts, Eirlys (b. 1911)
Roberts, Mary (1788–1864)
Robertson, E. Arnot (1903–1961)
Robertson, Grace (1930—)
Robins, Denise Naomi (1897–1985)
Robins, Elizabeth (1862–1952)
Robinson, Anastasia (c. 1692–1755)
Robinson, Joan Violet (1903–1983)
Robinson, Madeleine (b. 1908)
Robinson, Mary (1758–1800)
Robinson, Mary (d. 1837)
Robsart, Amy (c. 1532–1560)
Robson, Flora (1902–1984)
Roc, Patricia (1915–2003)
Roche, Barbara (1954—)
Roddick, Anita (1942—)
Roe, Marion (1936—)
Rogers, Clara Kathleen (1844–1931)
Rolleston, Elizabeth Mary (1845–1940)
Romero, Rebecca (1980—)
Rooke, Irene (c. 1878–1958)
Roope, Clover (1937—)
Roos, Margaret (fl. 1420)
Roper, Margaret More (1505–1544)
Rorke, Kate (1866–1945)
Rorke, Mary (1858–1938)
Rose, Ernestine (1810–1892)
Rose of Burford (fl. 15th c.)
Ross, Annie (1930—)
Ross, Charlotte Whitehead (1843–1916)
Ross, Forrestina Elizabeth (1860–1936)
Ross, Martin (1862–1915)
Ross-Craig, Stella (1906—)
Rossetti, Christina (1830–1894)
Rossetti, Maria Francesca (1827–1876)
Rothschild, Constance de (1843–1931)
Rothschild, Jeanne de (1908–2003)
Rothschild, Miriam (1908–2005)
Rothwell, Evelyn (b. 1911)
Round, Dorothy (1908–1982)
Routledge, Patricia (1929—)
Rover, Constance (1910–2005)
Rowbotham, Sheila (1943—)
Rowe, Elizabeth Singer (1674–1737)

Geographic Index

Rowling, J.K. (1965—)
Rowson, Susanna (1762–1824)
Royce, Sarah (1819–1891)
Royden, A. Maude (1876–1956)
Royde-Smith, Naomi Gwladys (c. 1880–1964)
Ruck, Berta (1878–1978)
Ruddock, Joan (1943—)
Rudman, Annie (1844–1928)
Rue, Rosemary (1928–2004)
Rule, Margaret (1928—)
Rumbold, Freda (1913—)
Russell, Anna (b. 1911)
Russell, Annie (1864–1936)
Russell, Christine (1945—)
Russell, Dora (1894–1986)
Russell, Dorothy Stuart (1895–1983)
Russell, Elizabeth (1540–1609)
Russell, Lucy (c. 1581–1627)
Russell, Margery (d. around 1380)
Russell, Mary du Caurroy (1865–1937)
Russell, Rachel (1636–1723)
Rutherford, Margaret (1892–1972)
Ryan, Joan (1955—)
Ryder, Sue (1923–2000)
Rye, Daphne (1916—)
Rye, Maria Susan (1829–1903)
Ryman, Brenda (1922–1983)
Rymill, Mary Ann (c. 1817–1897)
Sach, Amelia (1873–1902)
Sackville-West, Vita (1892–1962)
Sade (1959—)
Sadeler, Agnes (fl. 1386)
Saewara (fl. 630)
Saint, Dora Jessie (1913—)
Sale, Florentia (c. 1790–1853)
Salt, Barbara (1904–1975)
Sampson, Kathleen (1892–1980)
Sancha of Provence (c. 1225–1261)
Sandahl, Ingrid (1924—)
Sandars, Nancy K. (1914—)
Sandes, Flora (1876–1956)
Sansom, Odette (1912–1995)
Sansome, Eva (1906–?)
Sargant, Ethel (1863–1918)
Saunders, Cicely (1918–2005)
Saunders, Edith (1865–1945)
Saunders, Jennifer (1958—)
Saunders, Vivien (1946—)
Saunderson, Mary (d. 1712)
Saw, Ruth (1901–1983)
Sawyer, Ivy (1898–1999)
Sayer, Ettie (1875–1923)
Sayers, Dorothy L. (1893–1957)
Scala, Gia (1934–1972)
Scales, Prunella (1932—)
Scharlieb, Mary Ann (1845–1930)
Scharrer, Irene (1888–1971)
Schnackenberg, Annie Jane (1835–1905)
Schooling, Elizabeth (1919—)
Schulenburg, Ehrengard Melusina von der (1667–1743)
Schuster, Norah (1892–1991)
Scott, Anne (1651–1731)
Scott, Charlotte Angas (1858–1931)
Scott, Elizabeth Whitworth (1898–1972)
Scott, Janette (1938—)
Scott, Margaret (1875–1938)
Scott, Margaret (1922—)
Scott, Margaretta (1912–2005)
Scott, Mary (1751–1793)
Scott, Sarah (1723–1795)
Scott, Sheila (1927–1988)
Scott-Maxwell, Florida (1883–1979)
Scovell, E.J. (1907–1999)
Scripps, Ellen Browning (1836–1932)
Scrivens, Jean (1935—)
Scudamore, Margaret (1884–1958)
Seager, Esther (c. 1835–1911)
Sedgwick, Anne Douglas (1873–1935)
Sedley, Catharine (1657–1717)
Segrave, Anne (d. around 1377)
Segrave, Elizabeth (1338–1399)
Segrave, Margaret (c. 1280–?)
Sergeant, Adeline (1851–1904)
Serota, Beatrice (1919–2002)
Serres, Olivia (1772–1834)
Seville, Carolina Ada (1874–1955)
Seward, Anna (1742–1809)
Sewell, Anna (1820–1878)
Sewell, Elizabeth Missing (1815–1906)
Sewell, Mary Wright (1797–1884)
Sexburga (c. 627–673)
Sexburga (d. around 699)
Sexton, Elsie Wilkins (1868–1959)
Seyler, Athene (1889–1990)
Seymour, Anne (c. 1532–1587)
Seymour, Ethel (1881–1963)
Seymour, Frances (d. 1679)
Seymour, Frances Thynne (1699–1754)
Seymour, Jane (c. 1509–1537)
Seymour, Jane (1541–1560)
Seymour, Jane (1951—)
Seymour, Jane (d. 1679)
Seymour, Margaret (c. 1533–?)
Sharman, Helen (1963—)
Sharp, Jane (fl. 1671)
Sharp, Margery (1905–1991)
Shaw, Anna Howard (1847–1919)
Shaw, Flora (1852–1929)
Shaw, Susan (1929–1978)
Shayle George, Frances (c. 1827–1890)
Sheen, Gillian (1928—)
Sheepshanks, Mary (1872–1958)
Shelley, Barbara (1933—)
Shelley, Mary (1797–1851)
Shepard, Mary (1909–2000)
Shephard, Gillian (1940—)
Shepherd, Dolly (d. 1983)
Shepherd-Barron, Dorothy (1897–1953)
Sheppard, Kate (1847–1934)
Sheridan, Caroline Henrietta Callander (1779–1851)
Sheridan, Clare (1885–1970)
Sheridan, Dinah (1920—)
Sherlock, Sheila (1918–2001)
Sherwood, Mary Martha (1775–1851)
Sherwood, Sheila (1945—)
Shields, Ella (1879–1952)
Shilling, Beatrice (1909–1990)
Shipley, Debra (1957—)
Shipton, Mother (1488–1561)
Shirley, Dorothy (1939—)
Shirley, Elizabeth (c. 1568–1641)
Shirreff, Emily (1814–1897)
Shore, Jane (c. 1445–c. 1527)
Short, Clare (1946—)
Shorten, Monica (1923–1993)
Shoshi (fl. 990–1010)
Shrimpton, Jean (1942—)
Sibley, Antoinette (1939—)
Siddal, Elizabeth (1829–1862)
Siddons, Harriet (1783–1844)
Siddons, Sarah (1755–1831)
Sidney, Dorothy (1617–1684)
Sim, Sheila (1922—)
Simcox, Edith (1844–1901)
Simmons, Jean (1929—)
Simpson, Helen (1897–1940)
Simpson, Janet (1944—)
Sims, Joan (1930–2001)
Sinclair, Betty (1907–1983)
Sinclair, Catherine (1817–1891)
Sinclair, May (1863–1946)
Sinden, Topsy (1878–1951)
Singer, Eleanor (1903–1999)
Singer, Winnaretta (1865–1943)
Sitwell, Edith (1887–1964)
Sixsmith, Jane (1967—)
Six Wives of Henry VIII
Skipworth, Alison (1863–1952)
Sly, Wendy (1959—)
Small, Mary Elizabeth (1812/13–1908)
Smallwood-Cook, Kathryn (1960—)
Smart, Elizabeth (1913–1986)
Smedley, Menella Bute (c. 1820–1877)
Smieton, Mary (1902–2005)
Smith, Ada
Smith, Angela (1959—)
Smith, Annie Lorrain (1854–1937)
Smith, Charlotte (1749–1806)
Smith, Delia (1941—)
Smith, Dodie (1896–1990)
Smith, Geraldine (1961—)
Smith, Hilda
Smith, Jacqui (1962—)
Smith, Maggie (1934—)
Smith, Pauline (1882–1959)
Smith, Phylis (1965—)
Smith, Stevie (1902–1971)
Smithson, Alison (1928–1993)
Smyth, Ethel (1858–1944)
Smythe, Emily Anne (c. 1845–1887)
Smythe, Pat (1928–1996)
Snell, Hannah (1723–1792)
Snelling, Lilian (1879–1972)
Sokolova, Lydia (1896–1974)
Somerset, Anne (1631–1662)
Somerset, Elizabeth (fl. 1650)
Somerset, Henrietta (1669–1715)
Somerset, Henrietta (d. 1726)
Somerset, Isabella (1851–1921)
Somerville, E. (1858–1949)
Somerville and Ross
Sophia Dorothea of Brunswick-Celle (1666–1726)
Sophia Matilda (1773–1844)
Sophia Matilda (1777–1848)
Sophia of Greece (b. 1914)
Sotherton, Kelly (1976—)
Southcott, Joanna (1750–1814)
Southey, Caroline Anne (1786–1854)
Southworth, Helen (1956—)
Sowerby, Githa (1876–1970)
Sowerby, Millicent (1878–1967)
Spain, Elsie (1879–1970)
Spark, Muriel (1918–2006)
Speght, Rachel (1597–c. 1630)
Speirs, Annie (1889–1926)
Spelman, Caroline (1958—)
Spencer, Barbara (d. 1721)
Spencer, Lilly Martin (1822–1902)
Spencer Bower, Olivia (1905–1982)
Spencer Smith, Joan (1891–1965)
Spong, Hilda (1875–1955)
Spooner, Molly (1914–1997)
Springfield, Dusty (1939–1999)
Spry, Constance (1886–1960)
Spurgeon, Caroline F.E. (1869–1942)
Squire, Rachel (1954—)
Squires, Catharine (1843–1912)
St. George, Katharine (1894–1983)
St. John, Florence (1854–1912)
Stafford, Anne (c. 1400–1432)
Stafford, Anne (d. 1472)
Stafford, Catherine (d. 1419)
Stafford, Catherine (d. 1476)
Stafford, Catherine (fl. 1530)

Stafford, Constance (d. 1474)
Stafford, Elizabeth (1494–1558)
Stafford, Elizabeth (d. 1532)
Stafford, Margaret (d. 1396)
Stafford, Philippa (d. before 1386)
Stammers, Kay (1914–2005)
Stamp Taylor, Edith (1904–1946)
Stanhope, Hester (1776–1839)
Stanley, Margaret (fl. 16th c.)
Stansfield, Lisa (1966—)
Stark, Freya (1893–1993)
Starkey, Phyllis (1947—)
Starkie, Enid (1897–1970)
Statham, Edith May (1853–1951)
Staveley, Dulcie (1898–1995)
Stebbing, L. Susan (1885–1943)
Steel, Dorothy (1884–1965)
Steel, Flora Annie (1847–1929)
Steele, Anne (1717–1778)
Steele, Barbara (1937—)
Steer, Irene (1889–1947)
Stephen, Julia Prinsep (1846–1895)
Stephens, Catherine (1794–1882)
Stephens, Frances (1924–1978)
Stephenson, Elsie (1916–1967)
Stephenson, Marjory (1885–1948)
Stepney, Catherine (1785–1845)
Stern, G.B. (1890–1973)
Stevenson, Anne (1933—)
Stevenson, Juliet (1956—)
Steward, Natalie (1943—)
Stewart, Adela Blanche (1846–1910)
Stewart, Alice (1906–2002)
Stewart, Beatrice (d. around 1424)
Stewart, Elizabeth (fl. 1300s)
Stewart, Katherine (c. 1861–1949)
Stewart, Mary (1916—)
Stirling, Mary Anne (1815–1895)
Stjernstedt, Rosemary (1912–1998)
Stocks, Mary Danvers (1891–1975)
Stopes, Marie (1880–1958)
Storace, Nancy (1765–1817)
Stothard, Sarah Sophia (1825/26–1901)
Stoute, Jennifer (1965—)
Strachey, Pippa (1872–1968)
Straker, Karen (1964—)
Stratton, Helen (fl. 1891–1925)
Streatfeild, Noel (1895–1986)
Streeter, Alison (1964—)
Stretton, Hesba (1832–1911)
Strickland, Agnes (1796–1874)
Strong, Shirley (1958—)
Stuart, Arabella (1575–1615)
Stuart, Elizabeth (d. 1673)
Stuart, Gisela (1955—)
Stuart, Louisa (1757–1851)
Stuart-Wortley, Emmeline (1806–1855)
Styrene, Poly (c. 1962—)
Suisted, Laura Jane (1840–1903)
Summersby, Kay (1908–1975)
Summerskill, Edith (1901–1980)
Sutcliff, Rosemary (1920–1992)
Sutcliffe, Alice (c. 1600–?)
Sutherland, Lucy Stuart (1903–1980)
Sutherland, Mary (1893–1955)
Suzman, Janet (1939—)
Swainson, Mary Anne (c. 1833–1897)
Swanwick, Anna (1813–1899)
Swanwick, Helena (1864–1939)
Swift, Anne (1829/35–?)
Swinburne, Nora (1902–2000)
Swynford, Catherine (c. 1350–1403)
Syers, Madge Cave (1881–1917)
Syms, Sylvia (1934—)
Szabo, Violette (1921–1945)
Talbot, Anne (d. 1440)
Talbot, Catherine (1721–1770)
Talbot, Elizabeth (d. 1487)
Talbot, Elizabeth (d. around 1506)
Talbot, Elizabeth (1518–1608)
Talbot, Mary (d. 1632)
Talbot, Mary Anne (1778–1808)
Talbot, Nadine (1913–2003)
Talvace, Adela (d. 1174)
Tandy, Jessica (1909–1994)
Tanner, Vera (b. 1906)
Tarrant, Margaret (1888–1959)
Tasker, Marianne Allen (1852–1911)
Tate, Mavis (1893–1947)
Tate, Phyllis (1911–1987)
Tattersall, Philippa (c. 1975—)
Taverner, Sonia (1936—)
Taylor, Alma (1895–1974)
Taylor, Ann (1782–1866)
Taylor, Ann (1947—)
Taylor, Annie Royle (1855–c. 1920)
Taylor, Ann Martin (1757–1830)
Taylor, Brenda (1934—)
Taylor, Dari (1944—)
Taylor, Elizabeth (d. 1708)
Taylor, Elizabeth (1912–1975)
Taylor, Eva (1879–1966)
Taylor, Florence M. (1879–1969)
Taylor, Harriet (1807–1858)
Taylor, Helen (1831–1907)
Taylor, Jane (1783–1824)
Taylor, Janet (1804–1870)
Taylor, Louisa Jane (1846–1883)
Taylor, Mary (1817–1893)
Taylor, Mary (1898–1984)
Taylor, Megan (1920–1993)
Taylor, Stella (1929–2003)
Taylor, Valerie (1902–1988)
Tempest, Marie (1864–1942)
Tennant, Emma (1937—)
Tennant, Margaret Mary (1869–1946)
Tennant, Veronica (1946—)
Tennent, Madge Cook (1889–1972)
Tennyson, Emily (1813–1896)
Ternan, Frances Eleanor (c. 1803–1873)
Terry, Beatrice (b. 1890)
Terry, Ellen (1847–1928)
Terry, Hazel (1918–1974)
Terry, Kate (1844–1924)
Terry, Marion (1852–1930)
Terry, Minnie (b. 1882)
Terry, Olive (1884—)
Terry-Lewis, Mabel (1872–1957)
Texidor, Greville (1902–1964)
Tey, Josephine (1896–1952)
Teyte, Maggie (1888–1976)
Thatcher, Margaret (1925—)
Thimelby, Gertrude Aston (c. 1617–1668)
Thirkell, Angela (1890–1961)
Thomas, Agnes (fl. 1878–1926)
Thomas, Caitlin (1913–1994)
Thomas, Elizabeth (1675–1731)
Thompson, Edith (c. 1894–1923)
Thompson, Emma (1959—)
Thompson, Flora (1876–1947)
Thompson, Joanne (1965—)
Thompson, Lydia (1836–1908)
Thompson, May (d. 1978)
Thompson, Sylvia (1902–1968)
Thorburn, June (1930–1967)
Thorn, Tracey (1962—)
Thorndike, Eileen (1891–1954)
Thorndike, Sybil (1882–1976)
Thornton, Alice (1626–c. 1707)
Thorogood, Alfreda (1942—)
Thurston, Mabel (1869–1960)
Thyra (d. 1018)
Tilberis, Liz (1947–1999)
Tilbury, Zeffie (1863–1950)
Tilley, Vesta (1864–1952)
Timms, Sally (1959—)
Tindall, Gillian (1938—)
Tinsley, Annie Turner (1808–1885)
Tinsley, Pauline (1928—)
Tipper, Constance (1894–1995)
Tipper, Elizabeth (fl. late 17th c.)
Titheradge, Madge (1887–1961)
Todd, Ann (1909–1993)
Tofts, Catherine (c. 1685–1756)
Tonge, Jenny (1941—)
Tonna, Charlotte Elizabeth (1790–1846)
Topham, Mirabel (d. 1980)
Torvill, Jayne (1957—)
Toumine, Nesta (c. 1912–1995)
Tourtel, Mary (1874–1948)
Townsend, Sue (1946—)
Toye, Wendy (1917—)
Tracy, Honor (1913–1989)
Traill, Catherine Parr (1802–1899)
Trapnel, Anna (fl. 1642–1661)
Travers, Linden (1913–2001)
Travers, P.L. (1906–1996)
Tree, Maud Holt (1858–1937)
Tree, Viola (1884–1938)
Trefusis, Violet (1894–1972)
Tremain, Rose (1943—)
Trewavas, Ethelwynn (1900–1992)
Trimmer, Sarah (1741–1810)
Tripp, Grace (1691–1710)
Trollope, Frances Milton (c. 1779–1863)
Trollope, Theodosia (1825–1865)
Trussel, Elizabeth (1496–1527)
Tucker, Charlotte Maria (1821–1893)
Tuckwell, Gertrude (1861–1951)
Tudor-Hart, Edith (1908–1978)
Tufnell, Meriel (1948–2002)
Tullis, Julie (1939–1986)
Turner, Anne (1576–1615)
Turner, Elizabeth (1774–1846)
Turner, Eva (1892–1990)
Turner, Jane (before 1640–after 1660)
Turner-Warwick, Margaret (1924—)
Tussaud, Marie (1761–1850)
Tutin, Dorothy (1930–2001)
Tweedie, Jill (1936–1993)
Twiggy (1946—)
Twining, Louisa (1820–1912)
Tyler, Dorothy J. (1920—)
Tyler, Margaret (d. 1595)
Tylney, Agnes (1476–1545)
Tylney, Elizabeth (d. 1497)
Tynan, Kathleen (1937–1995)
Ufford, Margaret de (fl. 14th c.)
Ullman, Tracey (1959—)
Underhill, Evelyn (1875–1941)
Up, Ari (1962—)
Ure, Mary (1933–1975)
Utley, Freda (1898–1977)
Uttley, Alison (1884–1976)
Uvarov, Olga (1910–2001)
Vanbrugh, Irene (1872–1949)
Vanbrugh, Prudence (1902—)
Vanbrugh, Violet (1867–1942)
Vandamm, Florence (1883–1966)
van Praagh, Peggy (1910–1990)
Vansittart, Henrietta (1840–1883)
Varcoe, Helen (b. 1907)
Varden, Norma (1898–1989)
Vardill, Anna Jane (1781–1852)
Vaughan, Janet (1899–1993)
Vaughan, Kate (c. 1852–1903)
Vaux, Anne (fl. 1605–1635)
Vaz Dias, Selma (1911–1977)

Geographic Index

Veigel, Eva-Maria (1724–1822)
Veley, Margaret (1843–1887)
Verbruggen, Susanna (c. 1667–1703)
Vere, Diana de (d. 1742)
Vere, Frances de (d. 1577)
Vere, Margaret de (fl. 14th c.)
Vere, Maud de (fl. 1360s)
Verey, Rosemary (1918–2001)
Verne, Mathilde (1865–1936)
Verney, Margaret Maria (1844–1930)
Vestris, Lucia (1797–1856)
Vezin, Jane Elizabeth (1827–1902)
Victoria (1819–1901)
Victoria (1868–1935)
Victoria Adelaide (1840–1901)
Victoria of Coburg (1786–1861)
Vidal, Mary Theresa (1815–1869 or 1873)
Villiers, Anne (d. 1688)
Villiers, Barbara (c. 1641–1709)
Villiers, Barbara (d. 1708)
Villiers, Elizabeth (c. 1657–1733)
Villiers, Frances (c. 1633–1677)
Villiers, Margaret Elizabeth Child- (1849–1945)
Villiers, Susan (fl. 17th c.)
Villiers, Theresa (1968—)
Vincent, Madge (b. 1884)
Vincent, Mary Ann (1818–1887)
Vincent, Ruth (1877–1955)
Visconti, Violet (c. 1353–1386)
Vitelli, Annie (c. 1837–?)
Vivian, Ruth (c. 1883–1949)
Vivien, Renée (1877–1909)
Voynich, Ethel (1864–1960)
Waddingham, Dorothea (1899–1936)
Wade, Virginia (1945—)
Wagner, Winifred (1897–1980)
Wakefield, Priscilla (1751–1832)
Waldegrave, Frances (1821–1879)
Walker, Lucy (1836–1916)
Walker, Mary Broadfoot (c. 1888–1974)
Walker, Michelle (1952—)
Waller, Anne (c. 1603–1662)
Waller, Florence (1862–1912)
Walley, Joan (1949—)
Wallis, Diana (1954—)
Wallis, Mary Ann Lake (1821–1910)
Wallis, Shani (1933—)
Wallmoden, Amalie Sophie Marianne (1704–1765)
Wallwork, Elizabeth (1883–1969)
Walpole, Maria (1736–1807)
Walpurgis (c. 710–777)
Walsh, Kay (1914–2005)
Walsingham, Frances (d. 1631)
Walters, Catherine (1839–1920)
Walters, Julie (1950—)
Wandor, Michelene (1940—)
Warburg, Agnes (1872–1953)
Ward, Anne (c. 1825–1896)
Ward, Barbara (1914–1981)
Ward, Claire (1972—)
Ward, Dorothy (1890–1987)
Ward, Harriet (1808–c. 1860)
Ward, Henrietta (1832–1924)
Ward, Ida Caroline (1880–1949)
Ward, Irene (1895–1980)
Ward, Maisie (1889–1975)
Ward, Mary (1586–1645)
Ward, Mrs. Humphry (1851–1920)
Ward, Polly (1908–1987)
Warder, Ann Head (1758–1829)
Waring, Anna Letitia (1823–1910)
Warington, Katherine (1897–1993)
Warner, Deborah (1959—)
Warner, Marina (1946—)
Warner, Sylvia Townsend (1893–1978)
Warnock, Mary (1924—)
Washbourne, Mona (1903–1988)
Watkinson, Angela (1941—)
Watson, Janet Vida (1923–1985)
Watson, Maud (b. 1864)
Watson, Rosamund (1860–1911)
Watts Russell, Elizabeth Rose Rebecca (1833/34–1905)
Weamys, Anna (fl. 1650s)
Weaver, Harriet Shaw (1876–1961)
Webb, Beatrice (1858–1943)
Webb, Catherine (1859–1947)
Webb, Mary (1881–1927)
Webb, Sarah (1977—)
Webb, Violet (1915—)
Webster, Augusta (1837–1894)
Webster, Clara Vestris (1821–1844)
Webster, Mary McCallum (1906–1985)
Wedgwood, C.V. (1910–1997)
Wedgwood, Camilla H. (1901–1955)
Weir, Judith (1954—)
Welch, Ann (1917–2002)
Welch, Barbara (c. 1904–1986)
Welch, Elisabeth (1904–2003)
Welch, Georgiana (1792–1879)
Welch, Priscilla (1944—)
Weldon, Fay (1931—)
Wellesley, Dorothy (1889–1956)
Wells, Ada (1863–1933)
Wells, Catherine (d. 1927)
Wells, Doreen (1937—)
Welsh, Jane (1905–2001)
Wenham, Jane (d. 1730)
Wentworth, Henrietta Maria (c. 1657–1686)
Wentworth, Margaret (d. 1550)
Werburga (d. 700?)
Wesley, Emilia (1692–1771)
Wesley, Martha (1706–1791)
Wesley, Mary (1912–2002)
Wesley, Mehetabel (1697–1750)
Wesley, Susanna (1669–1742)
West, Elizabeth (1927–1962)
West, Jane (1758–1852)
West, Rebecca (1892–1983)
West, Rosemary (1953—)
West, Winifred (1881–1971)
Westbrook, Harriet (1795–1816)
Weston, Agnes (1840–1918)
Weston, Elizabeth Jane (1582–1612)
Weston, Jessie Laidlay (1850–1928)
Westwood, Vivienne (1941—)
Wethered, Joyce (1901–1997)
Wharton, Anne (1659–1685)
Wheeldon, Alice (fl. 1917)
Whiffin, Blanche (1845–1936)
Whitbread, Fatima (1961—)
White, Antonia (1899–1980)
White, Carol (1942–1991)
White, Chrissie (1894–1989)
White, Emily Louisa Merielina (1839–1936)
White, Isabella (1894–1972)
White, Margaret (c. 1888–1977)
White, Maude Valerie (1855–1937)
Whitehouse, Davina (1912–2002)
Whitelaw, Billie (1932—)
Whitney, Isabella (fl. 1567–1575)
Whitty, May (1865–1948)
Wickham, Anna (1883–1947)
Widdecombe, Ann (1947—)
Widdowson, Elsie (1906–2000)
Wieniawska, Irene Regine (1880–1932)
Wilberforce, Octavia (1888–1963)
Wilding, Dorothy (1893–1976)
Wilkinson, Ellen (1891–1947)
Willcox, Sheila (1936—)
Williams, Ann (d. 1753)
Williams, Anna (1706–1783)
Williams, Betty (1944—)
Williams, Cicely (1893–1992)
Williams, Ethel (1863–1948)
Williams, Helen Maria (1762–1827)
Williams, Ivy (1877–1966)
Williams, Jane (c. 1801–1896)
Williams, Marianne (1793–1879)
Williams, Sarah (1841–1868)
Williams, Shirley (1930—)
Williamson, Alison (1971—)
Williamson, Audrey (1926—)
Willmott, Ellen (c. 1859–1934)
Wilmot, Olivia (d. 1774)
Wilson, Catherine (1842–1862)
Wilson, Charlotte (1854–1944)
Wilson, Enid (b. 1910)
Wilson, Fiammetta Worthington (1864–1920)
Wilson, Harriette (1786–1855)
Wilson, Mary (1916—)
Wilson, Romer (1891–1930)
Wilson, Sarah (1750–?)
Wiman, Anna Deere (1924–1963)
Winch, Hope (1895–1944)
Winch, Joan
Winckless, Sarah (1973—)
Windsor, Wallis Warfield, duchess of (1895–1986)
Winkworth, Catherine (1827–1878)
Winkworth, Susanna (1820–1884)
Winter, John Strange (1856–1911)
Winterton, Ann (1941—)
Winterton, Rosie (1958—)
Wintour, Anna (1949—)
Winwood, Estelle (1883–1984)
Wiseman, Jane (fl. 17th c.)
Wiskemann, Elizabeth Meta (1899–1971)
Withburga
Withers, Googie (1917—)
Wohlers, Eliza (c. 1812–1891)
Wollstonecraft, Mary (1759–1797)
Wolstenholme-Elmy, Elizabeth (1834–1913)
Wood, Audrey (1908–1998)
Wood, Daisey (1877–?)
Wood, Ellen Price (1814–1887)
Wood, Florence (c. 1854–1954)
Wood, Marjorie (1882–1955)
Wood, Matilda (1831–1915)
Woodham-Smith, Cecil (1896–1977)
Woods, Doris
Woodville, Anne
Woodville, Elizabeth (1437–1492)
Woodville, Jacquetta
Woodville, Katherine (c. 1442–1512)
Woodville, Margaret (fl. 1450s)
Woodville, Mary (c. 1443–c. 1480)
Woolf, Virginia (1882–1941)
Woolley, Hannah (1623–1677)
Woolliams, Anne (1926–1999)
Wootton, Barbara (1897–1988)
Wordsworth, Dorothy (1771–1855)
Wordsworth, Elizabeth (1840–1932)
Wormeley, Katharine Prescott (1830–1908)
Worsley, Katherine (1933—)
Wotton, Margaret
Wright, Belinda (1927—)
Wright, Haidée (1868–1943)
Wright, Helena (1887–1982)
Wrinch, Dorothy (1894–1976)
Wriothesly, Elizabeth (d. 1690)
Wroth, Mary (c. 1587–c. 1651)
Wulfthryth (fl. 860s)
Wulfthryth (c. 945–1000)

Wyatt, Rachel (1929—)
Wycherly, Margaret (1881–1956)
Wychingham, Elizabeth
Wylie, Ida A.R. (1885–1959)
Wyndham, Mary (1861–1931)
Wynyard, Diana (1906–1964)
Xenia Alexandrovna (1876–1960)
Yarde, Margaret (1878–1944)
Yates, Elizabeth (1799–1860)
Yates, Frances Amelia (1899–1981)
Yates, Mary Ann (1728–1787)
Yearsley, Ann (1752–1806)
Yevonde (1893–1975)
Yonge, Charlotte Mary (1823–1901)
York, Susannah (1941—)
Young, Cecilia (c. 1711–1789)
Young, E.H. (1880–1949)
Young, Elizabeth (fl. 1558)
Young, Esther (1717–1795)
Young, Grace Chisholm (1868–1944)
Young, Isabella (d. 1795)
Young, Janet (1926–2002)
Younghusband, Eileen Louise (1902–1981)
Zabell, Theresa (1965—)
Zanfretta, Francesca (1862–1952)
Ziegler, Anne (1910–2003)
Zimmermann, Agnes (1847–1925)

EPHESUS

Ancient Ionian city in western Asia Minor
See Asia Minor.

EPIRUS

Ancient country in northwestern Greece
Became a republic (c. 200 BCE)
Set up as a Roman province (146 BCE)
Under Byzantine Empire until becoming independent state (1204)
Under Albania (14th c.)
Conquered by Turks (15th c.)
Eastern part to Greece (1881)
Captured Ioannina (1913)
Northern part now in southern Albania
See Albania.
See Greece.

ERFURT

District of East Germany
Founded (6th c.)
Passed to elector of Mainz (17th c.)
Taken by Prussia (1813)
See Germany.
See Prussia.

ESSEX

Former county in southeastern England
See England.

ESTONIA

Settled by Finno-Ugric tribes from the East (c. 3000 BCE)
Conquered by the Germans, Danish, Swedish, and Russians (13th c.)
Small feudal states formed (13th–16th c.)
Invaded by Moscow (16th c.)
Became Swedish territory (17th–18th c.)
Conquered by Russia (18th c.)
Declared the Republic of Estonia (1918)
Invaded and occupied by the Soviet Union (1940)
Occupied by German forces (1941–1944)
Independence achieved (1991)

Koidula, Lydia (1843–1886)
Lauristin, Marju (1940—)
Parek, Lagle (1941—)
Taba, Hilda (1902–1967)
Under, Marie (1883–1980)
Wuolijoki, Hella (1886–1954)

ETHIOPIA

Also called Abyssinia
Ancient country in northeast Africa, now independent state
Dominated by Egypt from 11th dynasty
Became independent of Egypt during 23rd dynasty
Converted to Christianity (4th c.)
Cut off from Christian world by Muslim conquest of Egypt and Nubia (7th c.)
Expelled Muslim sultan of the Somali (16th c.)
Colonized by Italy (1890–1896)
Formally annexed to Italy (1935)
Liberated by British (1941)
Became federated with Eritrea (1952)
Adopted constitution (1955)
Abolished crown (1975)

Defar, Meseret (1983—)
Dibaba, Ejigayehu (1982—)
Dibaba, Tirunesh (1985—)
Judith (fl. 10th c.)
Menen (1899–1962)
Menetewab (c. 1720–1770)
Roba, Fatuma (1973—)
Sheba, Queen of (fl. 10th c. BCE)
Taytu (c. 1850–1918)
Tenagneworq (1913–2003)
Tsahai Haile Selassie (1919–1942)
Tulu, Derartu (1969—)
Wami, Gete (1974—)
Zauditu (1876–1930)

ETRURIA

Ancient country in central Italy
Inhabited by Etruscans probably from Asia Minor (c. 900 BCE)
Established as confederation of 12 cities
Power declined (3rd c. BCE)
Kingdom of Etruria established by Napoleon (1801)
Incorporated into French empire (1808)
Region comprises Tuscany and part of Umbria
See Italy.

EXETER

Borough of Devonshire in southwestern England
See England.

FALKLAND ISLANDS

British colony in South Atlantic Ocean
Discovered 1592
Settled briefly by the French (1764)
English settlement expelled by Spanish (1770)
Claimed by Argentina after its independence but occupied by British (1833)

Terriss, Ellaline (1871–1971)

FERRARA

Province of Emilia-Romagna in northern Italy
Ruled by d'Este family (13th c.)
Became a duchy (15th c.)
Brought under rule of papacy (16th c.)
Ceded to French (18th c.)
Returned to pope (1815)
Joined Sardinia (1859)
See Italy.

FIFE

County in eastern Scotland
See Scotland.

FIGI ISLANDS

Martin, Hannah (1830–1903)

FINLAND

Republic in northern Europe
Conquered by Sweden (12th c.)
Eastern part ceded to Russia (18th c.)
Organized as autonomous grand duchy (1899)
Proclaimed independence (1917)

Ackté, Aino (1876–1944)
Anttila, S. Inkeri (1916—)
Bergroth, Kersti (1886–1975)
Bryk, Rut (1916–1999)
Bulich, Vera Sergeevna (1898–1954)
Canth, Minna (1844–1897)
Elg, Taina (1931—)
Fisk, Sari
Furuhjelm, Annie (1854–1937)
Grotell, Maija (1899–1973)
Hagman, Lucina (1853–1946)
Halonen, Tarja (1943—)
Hautala, Heidi Anneli (1955—)
Heikel, Karin Alice (1901–1944)
Hietamies, Mirja
Huttunen, Eevi (1922—)
Hyytianen, Eija
Iivari, Ulpu (1948—)
Jaatteenmaki, Anneli (1955—)
Jakobsson, Ludowika (1884–1968)
Jansson, Tove (1914–2001)
Jarvela, Satu
Joenpelto, Eeva (1921–2004)
Jotuni, Maria (1880–1943)
Juvonen, Helvi (1919–1959)
Kajosmaa, Marjatta
Kauppi, Piia-Noora (1975—)
Kilpi, Eeva (1928—)
Kirvesniemi, Marja-Liisa (1955—)
Korhola, Eija-Riitta Anneli (1959—)
Laine, Doris (1959—)
Lehtonen, Mirja (1942—)
Leviska, Helvi Lemmiki (1902–1982)
Lillak, Tiina (1961—)
Lukkarinen, Marjut (1966—)
Määttä, Pirkko (1959—)
Manner, Eeva-Liisa (1921–1995)
Matikainen, Marjo (1965—)
Meriluoto, Paivi (1952—)
Mustonen, Kaija (1941—)
Myller, Riita (1956—)
Nordi, Cleo (b. 1899)
Olsson, Hagar (1893–1978)
Parviainen, Katri (1914–2002)
Polkunen, Sirkka (1927—)
Porn, Hanna (1860–1913)
Poysti, Toini K.
Procopé, Ulla (1921–1968)
Pusula, Senja (1941—)
Rantanen, Heli Orvokki (1970—)
Rantanen, Siiri (1924—)
Ratia, Armi (1912–1979)
Rehn, Elisabeth (1935—)
Riihivuori, Hilkka (1952—)
Runeberg, Fredrika (1807–1879)
Ruoppa, Eeva (1932—)
Saariaho, Kaija (1952—)
Saarinen, Loja (1879–1968)
Saimo, Sylvi (1914–2004)
Salminen, Sally (1906–1976)
Savolainen, Jaana (1964—)
Schoultz, Solveig von (1907–1996)
Sillanpää, Miina (1866–1952)
Sipilä, Helvi (1915—)
Södergran, Edith (1892–1923)
Strengell, Marianne (1909–1998)
Suihkonen, Liisa (1943—)
Swanson, Pipsan Saarinen (1905–1979)
Takalo, Helena (1947—)
Talvo, Tyyne (b. 1919)
Thors, Astrid (1957—)
Tikkanen, Märta (1935—)
Van Grippenberg, Alexandra (1859–1913)
Vartio, Marja-Liisa (1924–1966)
Wideman, Lydia (1920—)

Wrede, Mathilda (1864–1928)
Wuolijoki, Hella (1886–1954)

FLANDERS

Medieval country extending along coast of Low Countries
Now consitutes Belgian provinces of East and West Flanders, and part of French Nord

Adelaide of Schaerbeck (d. 1250)
Adelicia of Louvain (c. 1102–1151)
Bentley, Catherine (fl. 1635)
Bijns, Anna (1493/94–1575)
Bourignon, Antoinette (1616–1680)
Cary, Lucy (1619–1650)
Colette (1381–1447)
Eleanor of Normandy (fl. 1000s)
Elfthrith (d. 929)
Eyck, Margaretha van (fl. 1420s–1430s)
Gertrude of Saxony (fl. 1070)
Hadewijch (fl. 13th c.)
Hemessen, Caterina van (c. 1528–c. 1587)
Jacqueline of Hainault (1401–1436)
Jeanne de Montfort (c. 1310–c. 1376)
Joan (fl. 1100)
Joan of Montferrat (d. 1127)
Johanna of Flanders (c. 1200–1244)
Lutgard (1182–1246)
Margaret of Alsace (c. 1135–1194)
Margaret of Brabant (1323–1368)
Margaret of Flanders (d. 1285)
Margaret of Flanders (1350–1405)
Marie of Champagne (c. 1180–1203)
Ogive of Luxemburg (d. 1030)
Patiniere, Agnes (fl. 1286)
Peeters, Clara (1594–after 1657)
Ponten, Clare van der (fl. 14th c.)
Reinhild (fl. 8th c.)
Richilde (1034–1086)
Teerlinc, Levina (c. 1520–1576)

FLORENCE

Commune of Firenze province, Tuscany, in central Italy
Governed by members of wealthy guilds
Ruled by the Medici (15th–16th c.)
Became capital of Italy (19th c.)
See Italy.

FORLÌ

Province of Emilia-Romagna in northern Italy
See Italy.

FORMOSA

See Taiwan.

FRANCE

Republic in western Europe
Conquered by Romans (1st c. BCE)
Southern part became Roman province of Gaul (2nd c. BCE)
Conquered by Julius Caesar (58–51 BCE)
Became Kingdom of Burgundy (5th c. CE)
Became part of the Kingdom of the Franks (8th–9th c.)
Medieval division into domains
Became duchy of Burgundy (10th c.)
Ruled by Capetians (10th–14th c.)
Ruled by House of Valois (14th–16th c.)
Ruled by House of Bourbon (16th–18th c.)
Royal government overthrown by French Revolution (1789)
Became First Republic (1792–1799)
Became consulate (1799–1804)
Became First Empire (1804–1815)
Restoration of Bourbons to throne (1814)
Became Second Republic (1848–1852)
Became Second Empire (1852–1870)
Became Third Republic (1870)
Under Vichy government (1940–1944)
Under provisional government (1944–1946)
Became Fourth Republic (1946–1958)
Became Fifth Republic (1958)

Abbéma, Louise (1858–1927)
Abboud, Simonne (c. 1930—)
Abegg, Elisabeth (1882–1974)
Abrantès, Laure d' (1784–1838)
Acarie, Barbe (1566–1618)
Ackermann, Louise Victorine (1813–1890)
Adam, Juliette la Messine (1836–1936)
Adela Capet (c. 1010–1079)
Adelaide (c. 794–after 852)
Adelaide (fl. 860s)
Adelaide (1777–1847)
Adelaide, Madame (1732–1800)
Adelaide Judith (fl. 879)
Adelaide of Anjou (fl. 10th c.)
Adelaide of Burgundy (931–999)
Adelaide of Burgundy (d. 1273)
Adelaide of Maurienne (1092–1154)
Adelaide of Montserrat (fl. 1100)
Adelaide of Poitou (c. 950–c. 1004)
Adela of Blois (1062–c. 1137)
Adele (r. 1017–1031)
Adele of Champagne (1145–1206)
Adele of Normandy (c. 917–c. 962)
Adelicia (1029–1090)
Adelicia of Louvain (c. 1102–1151)
Adorée, Renée (1898–1933)
Adret, Françoise (1920—)
Aelith de Poitiers (c. 1123–?)
Aemilia Hilaria (fl. 350)
Aénor of Châtellerault (d. 1130)
Agatha of Lorraine (fl. 1100s)
Agnes, Saint (d. possibly c. 304)
Agnes-Anne of France (b. 1171)
Agnes Capet (1260–1327)
Agnes de Dampierre (1237–1288)
Agnes de Nevers (r. 1181–1192)
Agnes of Aquitaine (c. 995–1068)
Agnes of Beaujeu (d. 1231)
Agnes of Bourbon (d. 1287)
Agnes of Burgundy (d. 1476)
Agnes of Jouarre (fl. early 13th c.)
Agnes of Looss (fl. 1150–1175)
Agnes of Meran (d. 1201)
Agnes of Poitou (1024–1077)
Agnes of Poitou (1052–1078)
Agoult, Marie d' (1805–1876)
Ahrweiler, Hélène (1916—)
Aimée, Anouk (1932—)
Ainardi, Sylviane H. (1947—)
Alacoque, Marguerite Marie (1647–1690)
Alain, Marie-Claire (1926—)
Alais (fl. 12th c.)
Alais of France (1160–?)
Alamanda of France (fl. late 12th c.)
Albertina Agnes (d. 1696)
Albertine (1797–1838)
Albertine, Viv (1955—)
Albin-Guillot, Laure (c. 1880–1962)
Albrecht, Bertie (?–1943)
Alençon, Emilienne d' (fl. late 1800s)
Algeranova, Claudie (1924—)
Alice (1150–c. 1197)
Alice (1201–1221)
Alice de Courtenay (d. 1211)
Alice of Normandy (fl. 1017–1037)
Alicia of Parma (1849–1935)
Alix of Vergy (d. after 1218)
Alix of Vergy (r. 1248–c. 1290)
Allard, Marie (1742–1802)
Allart, Hortense (1801–1879)
Almucs de Castelnau (fl. 12th c.)
Amboise, Francise d' (1427–1485)
Amelia of Solms (1602–1675)
Amicie de Courtenay (d. 1275)
Amiel, Josette (1930—)
Anastaise (fl. 1400)
Ancelot, Marguerite (1792–1875)
André, Valerie (1922—)
Anissina, Marina (1975—)
Annabella (1909–1996)
Anna of Savoy (1455–1480)
Anna Victoria of Savoy (fl. 18th c.)
Anne de la Tour (c. 1496–1524)
Anne Henriette Louise (1647–1723)
Anne of Austria (1601–1666)
Anne of Beaujeu (c. 1460–1522)
Anne of Bourbon-Parma (1923—)
Anne of Brittany (c. 1477–1514)
Anne of Chatillon-Antioche (c. 1155–c. 1185)
Anne of Ferrara (1531–1607)
Anne of Kiev (1024–1066)
Anne of Savoy (c. 1320–1353)
Anne Valois (c. 1405–1432)
Ansgard (fl. 863)
Antoinette of Bourbon (1494–1583)
Aouchal, Leila (1937—)
Archambault, Mademoiselle (c. 1724–?)
aret, Jeanne (1740–after 1795)
Arlette (fl. c. 1010)
Arletty (1898–1992)
Armentières, Péronelle d' (fl. 14th c.)
Arnauld, Angélique (1624–1684)
Arnauld, Jacqueline Marie (1591–1661)
Arnauld, Jeanne Catherine (1593–1671)
Arnothy, Christine (1930—)
Arnoul, Françoise (1931—)
Arnould, Sophie (1740–1802)
Arnould-Plessy, Jeanne (1819–1897)
Arron, Christine (1973—)
Arsinde (fl. 934–957)
Arvanitaki, Angélique (1901–1983)
Aubert, Constance (1803–?)
Aubert, Mary Joseph (1835–1926)
Aubespine, Madeleine de l' (1546–1596)
Aubrac, Lucie (1912—)
Aubry, Cécile (1928—)
Auclert, Hubertine (1848–1914)
Audouard, Olympe (1830–1890)
Audoux, Marguerite (1863–1937)
Audovera (d. 580)
Audran, Stéphane (1932—)
Audry, Jacqueline (1908–1977)
Augusta, Mlle (1806–1901)
Augusta Maria of Baden-Baden (1704–1726)
Aulnoy, Marie Catherine, Countess d' (c. 1650–1705)
Auriol, Jacqueline (1917–2000)
Auroi, Danielle (1944—)
Aury, Dominique (1907–1998)
Auzou, Pauline Desmarquets (1775–1835)
Avril, Jane (1868–1943)
Avril, Suzanne (fl. 1920s)
Babois, Marguerite-Victoire (1760–1839)
Balachova, Alexandra (1887–1905)
Balin, Mireille (1911–1968)
Ballanger, Felicia (1971—)
Barat, Madeleine Sophie (1779–1865)
Barbier, Adèle Euphrasie (1829–1893)
Barbier, Marie-Anne (c. 1670–1742)
Bardet, Anne-Lise (1974—)
Bardin, Madeleine (c. 1920—)
Bardotte, Brigitte (1934—)
Barine, Arvède (1840–1908)
Barlois, Valerie (1969—)
Barney, Natalie Clifford (1876–1972)
Baron, Emilie (c. 1834–1852)
Barot, Madeleine (1909–1995)
Barraine, Elsa (1910–1999)

Barrault, Marie-Christine (1944—)
Barre, Margot de la (d. 1390)
Bartet, Jeanne Julia (1854–1941)
Bartolini-Badelli, Giustina
Basine (fl.465)
Basseporte, Magdalene (?–c. 1780)
Baume, Madame de la (fl. 17th c.)
Bavent, Madeleine (fl. 1642)
Baverel, Myriam (1981—)
Bawr, Alexandrine de (1773–1860)
Bayard, Sylviane (1957—)
Bazin, Janine (1923–2003)
Bazincourt, Mlle Thomas de (fl. 18th c.)
Beatrice (1242–1275)
Beatrice of Lorraine (c. 1020–1076)
Beatrice of Savoy (d. 1268)
Beatrice of Vermandois (880–931)
Beatrix de Bourgogne (1257–1310)
Beatrix of Lens (d. around 1216)
Beaugrand, Léontine (1842–1925)
Beauharnais, Fanny de (1737–1813)
Beaumer, Madame de (d. 1766)
Beauvain d'Althenheim, Gabrielle (1814–1886)
Beauvau, Marie Charlotte (1729–1807)
Beauvoir, Simone de (1908–1986)
Beccary, Madame (fl. 18th c.)
Begard, Isabelle (1960—)
Begue, Laetitia (1980—)
Bejart, Armande (c. 1642–1700)
Bejart, Geneviève (c. 1622–1675)
Bejart, Madeleine (1618–1672)
Bell, Marie (1900–1985)
Belleville-Oury, Anna Caroline de (1808–1880)
Bellil, Samira (1972–2004)
Belloc, Louise (1796–1881)
Bellon, Denise (1902–1999)
Belot, Madame (1719–1804)
Benitez-Rexach, Lucienne (1905–1968)
Benoist, Françoise-Albine (1724–1809)
Benoist, Marie (1768–1826)
Benzoni, Juliette (1920—)
Berbie, Jane (1931—)
Berendt, Rachel (d. 1957)
Berès, Pervenche (1957—)
Berger, Nicole (1934–1967)
Bergere, Valerie (1872–1938)
Bernadette of Lourdes (1844–1879)
Bernard, Catherine (1662–1712)
Bernhardt, Sarah (1844–1923)
Bertaud, Marie Rosalie (c. 1700–?)
Bertha of Avenay (c. 830–c. 852)
Bertha of Blangy (d. 725)
Bertha of Brittany (d. 1163)
Bertha of Burgundy (964–1024)
Bertha of Chartres (d. 1084)
Bertha of Holland (1055–1094)
Bertha of Kent (c. 565–c. 616)
Bertha of Marbais (d. 1247)
Bertha of Swabia (fl. 900s)
Bertille (d. 705/713)
Bertin, Louise Angélique (1805–1877)
Bertrada of Montfort (d. after 1117)
Besserer, Eugénie (1868–1934)
Besson, Colette (1946—)
Bias, Fanny (1789–1825)
Bigot de Morogues, Marie (1786–1820)
Biheron, Marie-Catherine (1719–1786)
Binoche, Juliette (1964—)
Bishop, Claire Huchet (1898–1993)
Blanc, Isabelle (1975—)
Blanc, Marie-Thérèse (1840–1907)
Blancard, Jacqueline (1909—)
Blanchard, Madeleine Sophie (1778–1819)
Blanchecotte, Augustine-Malvina (1830–1895)
Blanche of Artois (c. 1247–1302)
Blanche of Boulogne (1326–1360)
Blanche of Bourbon (c. 1338–1361)
Blanche of Burgundy (1288–1348)
Blanche of Burgundy (1296–1326)
Blanche of Castile (1188–1252)
Blanche of Dreux (c. 1396–c. 1418)
Blanche of France (1253–1321)
Blanche of France (c. 1266–1305)
Blanche of France (1328–1392)
Blanche of Navarre (d. 1229)
Blanche of Navarre (fl. 1239)
Blanche of Navarre (1331–1398)
Blangy, Hermine (c. 1820–c. 1865)
Blaze de Bury, Rose (?–1894)
Bocage, Marie-Anne Le Page du (1710–1802)
Bodard, Mag (1916—)
Bodet, Stéphanie (1976—)
Bodin de Boismortier, Suzanne (c. 1722–?)
Boivin, Marie Anne (1773–1847)
Boizot, Marie (1748–?)
Bolland, Adrienne (1895–1975)
Bompard, Gabrielle (1869–?)
Bonaly, Surya (1973—)
Bonaparte, Alexandrine Jouberthon (1778–1855)
Bonaparte, Carolina (1782–1839)
Bonaparte, Christine (1773–1800)
Bonaparte, Letizia (1750–1836)
Bonaparte, Pauline (1780–1825)
Boneta, Prous (d. 1323)
Bonheur, Juliette (1830–1891)
Bonheur, Rosa (1822–1899)
Bonne of Armagnac (d. 1415)
Bonne of Artois (d.1425)
Bordes, Armonia (1945—)
Bordoni, Irene (1895–1953)
Borrel, Andrée (1919–1944)
Boudjenah, Yasmine (1970—)
Boufflers, Madeleine-Angelique, Duchesse de (1707–1787)
Boufflers, Marie (1706–1747)
Boufflers-Rouvrel, Marie Charlotte Hippolyte, Countess de (1724–c. 1800)
Boulanger, Lili (1893–1918)
Boulanger, Nadia (1887–1979)
Bouliar, Marie Geneviève (1762–1825)
Boumediene-Thiery, Alima (1956—)
Bourdic-Viot, Marie-Henriette Payad d'Estang de (1746–1802)
Bourette, Charlotte Rouyer (1714–1784)
Bourgeois, Louise (1563–1636)
Bourgeois, Louise (b. 1911)
Bourgeoys, Marguerite (1620–1700)
Bourin, Jeanne (1922–2004)
Bouvier, Jeanne (1865–1964)
Bouvier, Léone (c. 1929—)
Bovy, Berthe (1887–1977)
Bracquemond, Marie (1840–1916)
Bradley, Jenny
Bradna, Olympe (1920—)
Brandés, Marthe (1862–1930)
Brécourt, Jeanne (b. 1837)
Brennan, Fanny (1921–2001)
Brésil, Marguerite (1880–1923)
Brézé, Charlotte de (c. 1444/49–?)
Brézé, Claire-Clémence de Maillé de (1628–1694)
Briand, Anne (1968—)
Briche, Adelaide de la (1755–1844)
Briet, Marguerite de (c. 1510–c. 1550)
Brigue, Jehenne de (d. 1391)
Brinvilliers, Marie de (1630–1676)
Brion, Hélène (1882–1962)
Brohan, Augustine Suzanne (1807–1887)
Brohan, Émilie Madeleine (1833–1900)
Brohan, Josephine Félicité Augustine (1824–1893)
Brohon, Jacqueline-Aimée (1731–1778)
Brooke-Rose, Christine (1923—)
Broquedis, Marguerite (1893–1983)
Brough, Fanny Whiteside (1854–1914)
Brouquier, Veronique (1957—)
Brûlon, Angélique (1772–1859)
Brun, Marie-Marguerite de Maison-Forte (1713–1794)
Brunschvicg, Cécile (1877–1946)
Buffet, Marguerite (d. 1680)
Bujold, Geneviève (1942—)
Burani, Michelette (1882–1957)
Burlet, Delphyne (1966—)
Cadière, Catherine (b. 1709)
Cahun, Claude (1894–1954)
Caillaux, Henriette (?–1943)
Calvet, Corinne (1921–2001)
Camargo, Marie-Anne Cupis de (1710–1770)
Campan, Jeanne Louise Henriette (1752–1822)
Canal, Marguerite (1890–1978)
Candeille, Julie (1767–1834)
Capet, Gabrielle (1761–1817)
Capucine (1931–1990)
Cardinal, Marie (1929–2001)
Carère, Christine (1930—)
Carles, Emilie (1900–1979)
Carlier, Madeleine (c. 1876–?)
Carlotti, Marie-Arlette (1952—)
Caro, Pauline (1835–1901)
Carol, Martine (1922–1967)
Caroline of Bourbon (1822–1869)
Caron, Christine (1948—)
Caron, Leslie (1931—)
Carré, Mathilde (1908–c. 1970)
Carrel, Dany (1935—)
Carrelet de Marron, Marie-Anne (1725–1778)
Carton, Pauline (1884–1974)
Carven (b. 1909)
Cary, Anne (1615–1671)
Casadesus, Gaby (1901–1999)
Casanova, Danielle (1909–1943)
Casares, Maria (1922–1996)
Castelloza, Na (fl. early 13th c.)
Catherine de Clermont (fl. 16th c.)
Catherine de Courtenay (d. 1307)
Catherine de Foix (c. 1470–1517)
Catherine de France (1428–1446)
Catherine of Bourbon (c. 1555–1604)
Catherine of Cleves (fl. 1550s)
Catherine of Guise (1552–c. 1594)
Catherine of Lorraine (fl. 1600s)
Catherine of Lorraine
Catherine of Spain (1567–1597)
Catherine of Vendôme (r. 1374–1412)
Caulier, Madeleine (d. 1712)
Caullery, Isabelle (1955—)
Cauquil, Chantal (1949—)
Cavagnoud, Regine (1970–2001)
Cayla, Comtesse du (1785–1852)
Caylus, Marthe M. (1673–1729)
Cecilia (c. 1059–1126)
Cecilia of France (fl. 1100s)
Celeste, Madame (1811–1882)
Chabrillan, Céleste de (1824–1909)
Chambefort, Marie (fl. 1850)
Chaminade, Cécile (1857–1944)
Champagneux, Madame (1781–1858)
Champmesle, Marie (c. 1642–1698)

Chanel, Coco (1883–1971)
Chantal, Jeanne de (1572–1641)
Chardonnet, Michele (1956—)
Charlotte (1516–1524)
Charlotte de Montmorency (1594–1650)
Charlotte of Bourbon (d. 1582)
Charlotte of Savoy (c. 1442–1483)
Charlotte of Vendôme (fl. 15th c.)
Charpentier, Constance Marie (1767–1841)
Charrat, Janine (1924—)
Chartroule, Marie-Amélie (1848–1912)
Chastenay, Victorine de (1771–1855)
Châteaubriant, Comtesse de (c. 1490–1537)
Châteauroux, Marie Anne de Mailly-Nesle, Duchesse de (1717–1744)
Châtelet, Émilie du (1706–1749)
Chausson, Anne-Caroline (1977—)
Chauvin, Jeanne (1862–1926)
Chauviré, Yvette (1917—)
Chawaf, Chantal (1943—)
Chazal, Aline-Marie (1825–1869)
Chedid, Andrée (1921—)
Chéri, Rose (1824–1861)
Chéron, Elisabeth-Sophie (1648–1711)
Chevigné, Laure de (1860–1936)
Chirac, Bernadette (1933—)
Choiseul-Meuse, Félicité de (fl. 19th c.)
Choquet-Bruhat, Yvonne (1923—)
Christian (d. 1246)
Christina the Astonishing (c. 1150–c. 1224)
Christine de Pizan (c. 1363–c. 1431)
Christine of France (1606–1663)
Chrodielde (fl. 590)
Cicot, Christine (1964—)
Cigna, Gina (1900–2001)
Cinti-Damoreau, Laure (1801–1863)
Cixous, Hélène (1938—)
Clairon, Mlle (1723–1802)
Claude de France (1499–1524)
Claude de France (1547–1575)
Claude des Armoises (fl. 1400s)
Claudel, Camille (1864–1943)
Claudel, Véronique (1966—)
Clemence of Hungary (1293–1328)
Clément, Catherine (1939—)
Clementia (d. 1133)
Clementine of Orleans (1817–1907)
Clermont, Claude-Catherine de (1545–1603)
Clicquot, Mme (1777–1866)
Clidat, France (1932—)
Clignet, Marion (1964—)
Clotsinda (fl. 6th c.)
Cocéa, Alice (1899–1970)
Coicy, Madame de (fl. 18th c.)
Coignard, Gabrielle de (c. 1550–1586)
Coignet, Clarisse (1823–?)
Colet, Louise (1810–1876)
Colette (1873–1954)
Coligny, Henriette de (1618–1683)
Colleville, Anne-Hyacinthe de Saint-Léger de (1761–1824)
Collot, Marie-Anne (1748–1821)
Condorcet, Sophie Marie Louise, Marquise de (1764–1822)
Constance (c. 1066–1090)
Constance Capet (c. 1128–1176)
Constance de Cezelli (d. 1617)
Constance of Arles (c. 980–1032)
Constance of Brittany (1161–1201)
Constance of Castile (d. 1160)
Constance of France (fl. 1100s)
Contat, Louise (1760–1813)
Contat, Marie (1769–1846)
Coquillard-Albrier, Albertine (c. 1810–1846)
Corbin, Lucidor (fl. 18th c.)
Corday, Charlotte (1768–1793)
Cordelier, Jeanne (1944—)
Cornescou, Irina Soltanovna (1916—)
Cortin, Hélène (1972—)
Cosson de La Cressonière, Charlotte Cathérine (1740–1813)
Cottin, Sophie (1770–1807)
Coudreau, Octavie (c. 1870–c. 1910)
Coulon, Anne-Jacqueline (fl. 18th c.)
Courau, Clotilde (1969—)
Courcel, Nicole (1930—)
Courtauld, Louisa (1729–1807)
Craven, Pauline (1808–1891)
Crequy, Renée Caroline de Froulay, Marquise de (1714–1803)
Crespé, Marie-Madeleine (1760–1796)
Crespin, Régine (1927—)
Cresson, Edith (1934—)
Crochet, Evelyne (1934—)
Croizette, Sophie Alexandrine (1847–1901)
Cunigunde of France (c. 900–?)
Curie, Ève (b. 1904)
Daché, Lilly (1898–1989)
Dacier, Anne (1654–1720)
d'Albert, Marie-Madeleine Bonafous (fl. 18th c.)
D'Alessandri-Valdine, Blanche (c. 1862–1948)
Dalibard, Françoise-Thérèse Aumerle de Saint-Phalier (d. 1757)
Dalida (1933–1987)
Damita, Lili (c. 1901–1994)
d'Angeville, Henriette (1795–1871)
Daninthe, Sarah (1980—)
Danton, Gabrielle (d. 1793)
Danton, Louise (1777–1856)
Darcel, Denise (1925—)
d'Arconville, Geneviève (1720–1805)
Darras, Danielle (1943—)
Darré, Jeanne-Marie (1905–1999)
Darrieux, Danielle (1917—)
Darsonval, Lycette (1912–1996)
Darvi, Bella (1927–1971)
Dassault, Madeleine (1901–1992)
Daubié, Julie-Victoire (1824–1874)
Daudet, Julia (1844–1940)
Daumier, Sophie (1934–2004)
Daunt, Yvonne (b. around 1900)
David, Catherine (fl. 15th c.)
David, Catherine.
David-Neel, Alexandra (1868–1969)
d'Avril, Yola (1907–1984)
Day, Josette (1914–1978)
Daydé, Liane (1932—)
de Almania, Jacqueline Felicia (fl. 1322)
Debernard, Danielle (1954—)
de Bettignies, Louise (d. 1918)
de Bray, Yvonne (1889–1954)
de Brunhoff, Cécile (1903–2003)
De Cespedes, Alba (1911–1997)
de Dia, Beatrice (c. 1160–1212)
Dedieu, Virginie (1979—)
Deffand, Marie Anne de Vichy-Chamrond, marquise du (1697–1780)
de Galard, Geneviève (1925—)
de Gaulle, Geneviève (1921–2002)
de Gaulle, Yvonne (1900–1979)
Déjazet, Pauline-Virginie (1797–1875)
Delanoue, Jeanne (1666–1736)
Delarue-Mardrus, Lucie (1880–1945)
Delaye, Marguerite (fl. 1569)
Delbo, Charlotte (1913–1985)
Delorme, Marion (c. 1613–1650)
Delphy, Christine (1941—)
Delysia, Alice (1889–1979)
Demandols de la Palud, Madeleine (fl. 17th century)
Démar, Claire (1800–1833)
Demessieux, Jeanne (1921–1968)
Demongeot, Mylène (1936—)
Deneuve, Catherine (1943—)
Denis, Louise (c. 1710–1790)
Deraismes, Maria (1828–1894)
de Rivery, Aimee Dubucq (c. 1762–1817)
De Rivoyre, Christine (1921—)
Deroche, Elise-Raymonde (1886–1919)
Deroin, Jeanne-Françoise (1805–1894)
des Anges, Jeanne (fl. 1632)
De Sarnez, Marielle (1951—)
Desbordes-Valmore, Marceline (1785–1859)
Descamps, Marie-Hélène (1938—)
Descard, Maria (1847–1927)
Desclée, Aimée Olympe (1836–1874)
Desgarcins, Magdeleine Marie (1769–1797)
Deshayes, Catherine (d. 1680)
Deshoulières, Antoinette (1638–1694)
Deslys, Gaby (1884–1920)
Desmares, Christine (1682–1753)
Desmoulins, Lucile (1771–1794)
Desprès, Suzanne (1875–1951)
Destivelle, Catherine (1960—)
De Veyrac, Christine (1959—)
de Veyrinas, Françoise (1943—)
Diane de France (1538–1619)
Diane de Poitiers (1499–1566)
Diebold, Laure (1915–1964)
Dieulafoy, Jane (1851–1916)
Dissard, Marie Louise (b. 1880)
Dmitrieff, Elizabeth (1851–1910)
Doda (fl. 1040)
D'Or, Henrietta (1844–1886)
Dorléac, Françoise (1942–1967)
Dorval, Marie (1798–1849)
Dorziat, Gabrielle (1886–1979)
Douce I (d. 1190)
Doudet, Célestine (b. 1817)
Douvillier, Suzanne (1778–1826)
Dreyfuss, Anne (1957—)
Droiturière, Marion la (d. 1390)
Drouet, Juliette (1806–1883)
du Barry, Jeanne Bécu, Comtesse (1743–1793)
du Bief, Jacqueline
Dubois, Marie (1937—)
Dubuisson, Pauline (1926—)
Duchêne, Gabrielle (1870–1954)
Duchesnay, Isabelle (1973—)
Duchesne, Rose Philippine (1769–1852)
Duci, Filippa (fl. 16th c.)
Du Coudray, Angélique (1712–1789)
Dufrénoy, Adelaïde de (1765–1825)
du Guillet, Pernette (c. 1520–1545)
Dulac, Germaine (1882–1942)
Dumée, Jeanne (fl. 1680)
Dumesnil, Marie Françoise (1713–1803)
Dumilâtre, Adèle (1821–1909)
Dumolard, Marie (1816–?)
Dumont, Brigitte (1944—)
du Noyer, Anne-Marguérite Petit (1663–1719)
Duparc, Françoise (1726–1778)
Dupureur, Maryvonne (1937—)
Durand, Catherine (d. 1736)
Durand, Marguerite (1864–1936)
Duras, Claire de (1777–1828)
Duras, Marguerite (1914–1996)
Durocher, Marie (1809–1893)
Durr, Françoise (1942—)
Duvernay, Pauline (1813–1894)
Dux, Emilienne (b. 1874)

Dynalix, Paulette (1917—)
Eaubonne, Françoise d' (1920–2005)
Edgifu (902–951)
Edgifu (c. 917–?)
Ega, Françoise (1920–1976)
Ehrlich, Aline (1928–1991)
Eisner, Lotte (1896–1983)
Eleanor of Aquitaine (1122–1204)
Eleanor of Portugal (1498–1558)
Eleonore of Savoy (d. 1324)
Elie de Beaumont, Anne Louise (1730–1783)
Élisabeth, Madame (1764–1794)
Elisabeth of Habsburg (1554–1592)
Elizabeth-Charlotte (1676–1744)
Elizabeth de Bourbon (1614–1664)
Elizabeth of Courtenay (d. 1205)
Elizabeth of Lorraine (1711–1741)
Elizabeth of the Trinity (1880–1906)
Elvira (fl. 1080s)
Emma of Burgundy (d. 939)
Emma of Italy (948–after 990)
Emma of Paris (d. 968)
Engelberga of Aquitaine (877–917)
Entragues, Henriette d' (1579–1633)
Épinay, Louise-Florence-Pétronille, Madame la Live d' (1726–1783)
Epstein, Marie (c. 1899–1995)
Ermengarde (c. 778–818)
Ermengarde of Anjou (1018–1076)
Ermengarde of Anjou (d. 1147)
Ermengarde of Carcassonne (d. 1070)
Ermengarde of Narbonne (c. 1120–c. 1194)
Ermengarde of Provence (fl. 876)
Ermentrude (d. 869)
Ermentrude de Roucy (d. 1005)
Ernaux, Annie (1940—)
Espaze, Martiale
Estienne, Nicole d' (c. 1544–c. 1596)
Estrées, Angélique, d' (fl. 16th c.)
Estrées, Diane, d' (b. 1572)
Estrées, Françoise Babou de la Bourdaisière, Dame d' (fl. 16th c.)
Estrées, Gabrielle d' (1573–1599)
Étampes, Anne de Pisseleu d'Heilly, Duchesse d' (1508–c. 1580)
Etcherelli, Claire (1934—)
Ethelburga (d. 665)
Eugénie (1826–1920)
Euphrosine (d. 1102)
Fabian, Françoise (1932—)
Fagnan, Marie-Antoinette (d. 1770)
Fahmy, Marguérite Laurent (b. around 1900)
Faileuba (fl. 586–587)
Faith (290–303)
Falcon, Marie Cornélie (1814–1897)
Falconetti, Renée (1892–1946)
Falconnet, Françoise-Cécile de Chaumont (1738–1819)
Famose, Annie (1944—)
Farrenc, Louise (1804–1875)
Fauques, Marianne-Agnès Pillement, Dame de (1721–1773)
Favart, Edmée (1886–1941)
Favart, Marie (1727–1772)
Favart, Marie (b. 1833)
Favre, Julie Velten (1834–1896)
Fel, Marie (1713–1794)
Félix, Lia (b. 1830)
Felix, Sylviane (1977—)
Fenayrou, Gabrielle (b. 1850)
Fénelon, Fania (1918–1983)
Fernig, Félicité de (c. 1776–after 1831)
Fernig, Théophile de (c. 1779–c. 1818)
Ferrais, Amalia (1830–1904)
Ferrari, Gabrielle (1851–1921)
Ferreira, Anne (1961—)
Feuchères, Sophie, Baronne de (c. 1795–1841)
Feuillère, Edwige (1907–1998)
Figues de Saint Marie, Solenne (1979—)
Figueur, Thérèse (1774–1861)
Filleul, Jeanne (1424–1498)
Finas, Lucette (1921—)
Fiocre, Eugénie (1845–1908)
Fitzgerald, Pamela (1773–1831)
Fitzjames, Louise (b. 1809)
Fitzjames, Natalie (b. 1819)
Flautre, Hélène (1958—)
Flessel, Laura (1971—)
Fleury, Catherine (1966—)
Flon, Suzanne (1918–2005)
Flore, Jeanne (fl. early 16th c.)
Flory, Regine (1894–1926)
Foix, Germaine de (1488–1538)
Foix, Janine-Marie de (fl. 1377)
Fontaine, Mlle de la (1655–1738)
Fontaines, Marie-Louise-Charlotte de Pelard de Givry, Comtesse de (1660–1730)
Fontanges, Duchesse de (1661–1681)
Fontette de Sommery, Mademoiselle (fl. 18th c.)
Fourqueux, Madame de (fl. 18th c.)
Fourtou, Janelly (1939—)
Fox-Jerusalmi, Myriam (1961—)
Fragonard, Marie Anne (1745–c. 1823)
Fraisse, Geneviève (1948—)
Francey, Henriette (b. around 1859)
Francis, Eve (1886–1980)
Françoise d'Orleans (1844–1925)
Françoise d'Orleans (fl. 1650)
Françoise-Marie de Bourbon (1677–1749)
Fratellini, Annie (1932–1997)
Frederona (d. 917)
Freist, Greta (1904–1993)
Freund, Gisèle (1912–2000)
Freytag-Loringhoven, Elsa von (1875–1927)
Fuller, Loïe (1862–1928)
Fumelh, Madame de (fl. 18th c.)
Furneaux, Yvonne (1928—)
Furneria of Mirepoix (fl. 13th c.)
Gabain, Ethel Leontine (1883–1950)
Gacon-Dufour, Marie Armande Jeanne (1753–c. 1835)
Gagneur, Louise (1832–1902)
Gagneur, Marguerite (1857–1945)
Galigaï, Leonora (c. 1570–1617)
Galli-Marié, Célestine (1840–1905)
Garaud, Marie-Françoise (1934—)
Garilhe, Renee (1923—)
Garsenda (1170–c. 1257)
Gaudin-Latrille, Brigitte (1958—)
Gauthier, Xavière (1942—)
Gautier, Judith (1845–1917)
Gay, Sophie (1776–1852)
Geneviève (c. 422–512)
Geneviève de Brabant (fl. 8th c.)
Géniat, Marcelle (1879–1959)
Genlis, Stéphanie-Félicité, Comtesse de (1746–1830)
Geoffrin, Marie Thérèse (1699–1777)
Georges, Marguerite J. (c. 1787–1867)
Georgia (d. 6th c.)
Gérard, Marguerite (1761–1837)
Gerberga of Saxony (c. 910–969)
Gerloc (d. 963)
Germain, Sophie (1776–1831)
Gertrude of Flanders (d. 1117)
Gertrude of Metz (d. 1225)
Gibault, Claire (1945—)
Gilette of Narbonne (fl. 1300)
Gillig, Marie-Hélène (1946—)
Gilot, Françoise (1922—)
Gineste, Marie-Rose (1911—)
Girard, Patricia (1968—)
Girardin, Delphine (1804–1855)
Girardot, Annie (1931—)
Giriat, Madame (b. 1866)
Giroud, Françoise (1916–2003)
Gisela of Burgundy (fl. 100s)
Goitschel, Christine (1944—)
Goitschel, Marielle (1945—)
Goll, Claire (1891–1977)
Gomis, Anna (1973—)
Gonzaga, Margherita (1591–1632)
Gonzalès, Eva (1849–1883)
Goold, Maria Vere (1877–1908)
Gordon-Lazareff, Hélène (1909–1988)
Gosse, Christine (1964—)
Gouault-Haston, Laurence
Gouel, Eva (d. 1915)
Gouges, Olympe de (1748–1793)
Goulue, La (1869–1929)
Gournay, Marie le Jars de (1565–1645)
Graffigny, Françoise de (1695–1758)
Gramont, Elizabeth de (fl. 1875–1935)
Grandval, Marie Felicia (1830–1907)
Grantzow, Adele (1845–1877)
Gréco, Juliette (1926—)
Grès, Alix (1910–1993)
Grétry, Lucile (1772–1790)
Gréville, Alice (1842–1903)
Grey, Denise (1896–1996)
Grignan, Françoise-Marguerite de Sévigné, Countess de (1646–1705)
Grillet, Louise Hortense (1865–1952)
Grossetête, Françoise (1946—)
Groult, Benoîte (1921—)
Groult, Flora (1925—)
Guérin, Eugénie de (1805–1848)
Guette, Catherine de la (1613–1676)
Guibal, Brigitte (1971—)
Guibert, Elisabeth (1725–1788)
Guibert, Louise-Alexandrine, Comtesse de (d. 1826)
Guilbert, Yvette (1865–1944)
Guillard, Charlotte (d. 1556)
Guillelma de Rosers (fl. 1240–1260)
Guillemete du Luys (fl. 1479)
Guillemot, Agnès (1931—)
Guimard, Marie Madeleine (1743–1816)
Guirande de Lavaur (d. 1211)
Guizot, Pauline (1773–1827)
Gunnor of Denmark (d. 1031)
Guy-Blaché, Alice (1875–1968)
Guyon, Jeanne Marie Bouviéres de la Mothe (1648–1717)
Guy-Quint, Catherine (1949—)
Guy-Stéphan, Marie (1818–1873)
Haas, Monique (1906–1987)
Hachette, Jeanne (c. 1454–?)
Hachin-Trinquet, Pascale (1958—)
Hading, Jane (1859–1933)
Haigneré, Claudie (1957—)
Halimi, Gisèle (1927—)
Hanau, Marthe (c. 1884–1935)
Harcourt, Johanna (d. 1488)
Harel, Marie (fl. 1790)
Harry, Myriam (1869–1958)
Hausset, Nicole Colleson du (1713–1801)
Hautval, Adelaide (1906–1988)
Hawise (d. after 1135)
Hawise of Brittany (d. 1072)
Hawise of Normandy (d. 1034)
Hawise of Salisbury (fl. 12th c.)
Hazan, Adeline (1956—)
Hébert, Madame (d. 1794)

Hedwig (c. 915–965)
Helaria (fl. 6th c.)
Helene Louise of Mecklenburg-Schwerin (1814–1858)
Heloise (c. 1100–1163)
Helvétius, Madame (1719–1800)
Helvidis (fl. 1136)
Henrietta Anne (1644–1670)
Henrietta Maria (1609–1669)
Henrietta of Cleves (r. 1564–1601)
Henriette (1727–1752)
Henriot-Schweitzer, Nicole (1925–2001)
Herbelin, Jeanne Mathilde (1820–1904)
Héricourt, Jenny Poinsard (1809–1875)
Hermange, Marie-Thérèse (1947—)
Hersende of Champagne (fl. 12th c.)
Hersende of France (fl. 1250)
Hicks, Sheila (1934—)
Hildegard (c. 802–841)
Hildegarde de Beaugency (fl. 1080)
Hildegard of Burgundy (1050–after 1104)
Hildeletha (fl. 700)
Hilsz, Maryse (1903–1946)
Hiltrude of Liessies (d. late 700s)
Holland, Joan (c. 1356–1384)
Holmès, Augusta (1847–1903)
Hombelina (1092–1141)
Hortense de Beauharnais (1783–1837)
Houdetot, Sophie, Comtesse d' (1730–1813)
Huber, Marie (1695–1753)
Hugo, Adèle (1830–1915)
Huppert, Isabelle (1953—)
Hurtis, Muriel (1979—)
Ida de Macon (d. 1224)
Ida of Lorraine (1040–1113)
Ida of Louvain (d. 1260)
Ida of Lower Lorraine (d. 1162)
Ida of Namur (fl. 12th c.)
Ide d'Alsace (c. 1161–1216)
Ily, Nicole (1932—)
Imlay, Fanny (1794–1816)
Ingeborg (c. 1176–1237/38)
Ingoberge (519–589)
Irigaray, Luce (1930—)
Isabeau of Bavaria (1371–1435)
Isabel de Limoges (1283–1328)
Isabella (b. 1180)
Isabella (r. 1398–1412)
Isabella Capet (fl. 1250)
Isabella of Aragon (1243–1271)
Isabella of Guise (1900–1983)
Isabella of Hainault (1170–1190)
Isabella of Orleans (1878–1961)
Isabella of Orleans (1911–2003)
Isabella of Portugal (1397–1471)
Isabelle (1225–1270)
Isabelle of Bourbon (d. 1465)
Isabelle of France (1349–1372)
Isabelle of Savoy (d. 1383)
Iselda, Lady (fl. 12th c.)
Iseut de Capio (1140–?)
Isler Béguin, Marie Anne (1956—)
Jacobson, Louise (1924–1943)
Jacot, Michele (1952—)
Jacquet de la Guerre, Elisabeth-Claude (c. 1666–1729)
Jamet, Marie (1820–1893)
Jane of Bourbon-Vendome (d. 1511)
Jane of France (1343–1373)
Jeanmaire, Zizi (1924—)
Jeanne d'Albret (1528–1572)
Jeanne de Belleville (fl. 1343)
Jeanne de Bourbon (1338–1378)
Jeanne de Castile (r. 1366–1374)
Jeanne de Chatillon (d. 1292)
Jeanne de France (c. 1464–1505)
Jeanne de Laval (d. 1498)
Jeanne de Lestonac (1556–1640)
Jeanne de Penthièvre (c. 1320–1384)
Jeanne de Sarmaize (fl. 1456)
Jeanne des Armoises (fl. 1438)
Jeanne I (d. 1346)
Jeanne II (r. 1346–1355)
Jeanne I of Burgundy (c. 1291–1330)
Jeanne II of Burgundy (1308–1347)
Jeanne of Bourbon (1434–1482)
Jeanne of Bourbon (d. 1493)
Jeanne of Burgundy (1293–1348)
Jeanne of Burgundy (1344–1360)
Jeanne of Chalon (1300–1333)
Jeanne of Lorraine (1458–1480)
Jeanne of Nemours (1644–1724)
Jeanne of Valois (c. 1294–1342)
Jeanne of Valois (c. 1304–?)
Jegado, Hélène (1803–1851)
Joan Holland (c. 1356–1384)
Joan I of Navarre (1273–1305)
Joan II of Navarre (1309–1349)
Joanna of Ponthieu (d. 1251)
Joan of Arc (c. 1412–1431)
Joan of Evreux (d. 1370)
Joan of Toulouse (d. 1271)
Joan Valois (1391–1433)
Jodin, Mademoiselle (fl. 18th c.)
Jolas, Betsy (1926—)
Joliot-Curie, Irène (1897–1956)
Joly, Andrée (1901–1993)
Josephine (1763–1814)
Josland, Claudie (1946—)
Jossinet, Frederique (1975—)
Joy, Génèviève (1919—)
Joyeux, Odette (1914–2000)
Jugan, Jeanne (1792–1879)
Julianna du Guesdin (fl. 1370)
Julie (fl. 1770)
Kaplan, Nelly (1931—)
Kavan, Anna (1901–1968)
Kedrova, Lila (1918—)
Kelly, Margaret (1910–2004)
Kendall, Marie Hartig (1854–1943)
King, Andrea (1919–2003)
Kiraly Picot, Hajnalka (1971—)
Klarsfeld, Beate (1939—)
Kleeberg, Clotilde (1866–1909)
Kogan, Claude (1919–1959)
Kolb, Thérèse (1856–1935)
Kristeva, Julia (1941—)
Kuntz, Florence (1969—)
Kurys, Diane (1948—)
Laage, Barbara (1920–1988)
Labbé, Denise (1926—)
Labé, Louise (c. 1523–1566)
Labille-Guiard, Adelaide (1749–1803)
Labouré, Catherine (1806–1875)
Lachapelle, Marie (1769–1821)
Lachman, Thérèse (1819–1884)
Lacombe, Claire (1765–?)
Lacore, Suzanne (1875–1975)
Lacoste, Catherine (1945—)
Lafarge, Marie (1816–1852)
Lafayette, Marie Adrienne de (1760–1807)
La Fayette, Marie-Madeleine de (1634–1693)
Lafite, Marie-Elisabeth Bouée de (c. 1750–1794)
Lafon, Madeleine (1924–1967)
Lafont, Bernadette (1938—)
La Force, Charlotte-Rose de Caumont de (1650–1724)
La Grange, Anna de (1825–1905)
Lagrave, Comtesse de (1770–1820)
La Guesnerie, Charlotte Charbonnier de (1710–1785)
Laguiller, Arlette (1940—)
La Hye, Louise (1810–1838)
Laisse, Madame de (fl. 18th c.)
Lalande, Amélie Lefrançais de (fl. 1790)
Lalumiere, Catherine (1935—)
Lamballe, Marie Thérèse Louise of Savoy-Carignano, Princesse de (1749–1792)
Lambert, Anne Thérèse de Marguenat de Courcelles, Marquise de (1647–1733)
Lamorlière, Rosalie (fl. 1793–1837)
La Motte, Jeanne de Valois, countess de (1756–1791)
Lancien, Nathalie (1970—)
Lange, Anne Françoise Elizabeth (1772–1816)
Lanvin, Jeanne (1867–1946)
Lany, Louise-Madeleine (1733–1777)
Lapauze, Jeanne (1860–1920)
La Roche, Guilhem (1644–1710)
La Rochefoucauld, Edmée, Duchesse de (1895–1991)
La Rochejacquelein, Marie Louise Victoire, marquise de (1772–1857)
Larrimore, Francine (1898–1975)
La Sablière, Marguerite de (1640–1693)
Laskine, Lily (1893–1988)
La Tour du Pin, Henriette de (1770–1853)
Laurencin, Marie (1883–1956)
Laurette de St. Valery (fl. 1200)
Laval, Josée (c. 1906—1990)
Lavallière, Eve (c. 1866–1929)
La Vallière, Louise de (1644–1710)
Lavoisier, Marie (1758–1836)
Leblanc, Georgette (c. 1875–1941)
Lebrun, Céline (1976—)
Le Camus, Madame (fl. 17th c.)
Leclerc, Annie (1940—)
Leclerc, Ginette (1912–1992)
Le Clercq, Tanaquil (1929–2000)
Lecouvreur, Adrienne (1690–1730)
Ledermann, Alexandra (1969—)
Ledoux, Jeanne Philiberte (1767–1840)
Leduc, Violette (1907–1972)
Lefaucheux, Marie-Helene (1904–1964)
Lefebvre, Catherine (c. 1764–after 1820)
Lefebvre, Janou (1945—)
Le Garrec, Evelyne
Le Givre de Richebourg, Madame (1710–1780)
Legrand, Lise (1976—)
Lehmann, Adelaide (c. 1830–1851)
Leigh, Augusta (1784–1851)
Lemel, Nathalie (1827–1921)
Lemoine, Angélina (1843–?)
Lemoine, Marie Victoire (1754–1820)
Lemoine-Luccioni, Eugénie (1912—)
Lenclos, Ninon de (1623–1705)
Lender, Marcelle (fl. 1890–1914)
Lenglen, Suzanne (1899–1938)
Lenormand, Marie Anne Adélaïde (1772–1843)
Léo, André (1832–1900)
Léon, Léonie (1838–1906)
Léon, Pauline (1758–?)
Lepaute, Hortense (1723–1788)
Lepennec, Emilie (1987—)
Le Prince de Beaumont, Marie (1711–1780)
Leroux, Pauline (1809–1891)
Leskova, Tatiana (1922—)
Lespinasse, Julie de (1732–1776)
Levesque, Louise Cavelier (1703–1743)
Lézardière, Pauline de (1754–1835)
Lezay Marnezia, Charlotte Antoinette de Bressy, Marquise de (c. 1705–1785)

L'Héritier, Marie-Jeanne (1664–1734)
Lignot, Myriam (1975—)
Lissiardi, Sibille (fl. 13th c.)
Livry, Emma (1842–1863)
Lombarda (b. 1190)
Long, Marguerite (1874–1966)
Longo, Jeannie (1958—)
Longueville, Anne Geneviève, Duchesse de (1619–1679)
Lorcia, Suzanne (1902–1999)
Loriod, Yvonne (1924–2001)
Louisa Henrietta de Conti (1726–1759)
Louise-Adelaide (1698–1743)
Louise Adelaide de Bourbon (1757–1824)
Louise de Brézé (fl. 1555)
Louise de Montmorency (fl. 1498–1525)
Louise-Diana (1716–1736)
Louise-Elisabeth de Bourbon Condé (1693–1775)
Louise Elizabeth (1727–1759)
Louise Marie (1737–1787)
Louise Marie of Bourbon (1753–1821)
Louise of Lorraine (1554–1601)
Louise of Orleans (1882–1952)
Louise of Savoy (1476–1531)
Loynes, Antoinette de (fl. 16th c.)
Loynes, Camille de (fl. 16th c.)
Lualdi, Antonella (1931—)
Lubert, Mlle de (c. 1710–c. 1779)
Lubin, Germaine (1890–1979)
Luchaire, Corinne (1921–1950)
Lucy de Blois (d. 1120)
Lupino, Natalina (1963—)
Lussac, Elodie (1979—)
Lussan, Marguerite de (1682–1758)
Maar, Dora (1907–1997)
Madeleine de Saint-Nectaire (fl. 1575)
Madeleine of France (1520–1537)
Mahaut (c. 1270–1329)
Mahaut de Chatillon (d. 1358)
Mahaut de Courtenay (d. 1257)
Mahaut I (r. 1215–1242)
Mahaut II de Dampierre (1234–1266)
Mahaut of Burgundy (d. 1202)
Maillart, Ella (1903–1997)
Maillé, Jeanne-Marie de (1331–1414)
Mailly, Louise Julie de Mailly-Nesle, Comtesse de (1710–1751)
Maintenon, Françoise d'Aubigné, Marquise de (1635–1719)
Malibran, Maria (1808–1836)
Mallet-Joris, Françoise (1930—)
Malraux, Clara (c. 1897–1982)
Manaudou, Laure (1986—)
Mang, Veronique (1984—)
Mangolte, Babette (c. 1945—)
Mannoury d'Ectot, Madame de (fl. 1880)
Mansenée, Desle la (c. 1502–1529)
Mansour, Joyce (1928–1987)
Manès, Gina (1893–1989)
Maracineanu, Roxana (1975—)
Marchal, Arlette (1902–1984)
Marchand, Collette (1925—)
Marchand, Corinne (1937—)
Marchesi, Blanche (1863–1940)
Margaret Capet (d. 1271)
Margaret de Foix (d. 1258)
Margaret de Rohan (1397–1428)
Margaret le Brun (d. 1283)
Margaret of Angoulême (1492–1549)
Margaret of Anjou (c. 1272–1299)
Margaret of Artois (d. 1382)
Margaret of Bavaria (fl. 1390–1410)
Margaret of Bourbon (d. 1483)
Margaret of Burgundy (1290–1315)
Margaret of Limburg (d. 1172)
Margaret of Lorraine (1463–1521)
Margaret of Provence (1221–1295)
Margaret of Savoy (1523–1574)
Margaret of Turenne (fl. 12th c.)
Margaret of Valois (1553–1615)
Margaret of Vendôme (fl. 16th c.)
Margaret of Ypres (fl. 1322)
Marguerite (r. 1218–1230)
Marguerite de Bressieux (d. 1450)
Marguerite de l'Aigle (d. 1141)
Marguerite de Thouars (r. 1365–1377)
Marguerite of Lorraine (c. 1561–?)
Marguerite of Lorraine (fl. 1632)
Marguerite of Orleans (d. 1466)
Maria Amalia (1782–1866)
Maria Anna of Bavaria (1660–1690)
Maria de Ventadour (b. 1165)
Maria Isabella (1834–1901)
Maria Teresa of Savoy (1756–1805)
Maria Teresa of Spain (1638–1683)
Maria Theresa of Spain (1726–1746)
Maria Theresa of Wurttemberg (1934—)
Marie (1393–1438)
Marie Adelaide of Savoy (1685–1712)
Marie-Anne de la Trémouille (c. 1642–1722)
Marie Antoinette (1755–1793)
Marie de Bourbon (fl. 1350s)
Marie de Bourbon (1606–1627)
Marie de Brabant (c. 1530–c. 1600)
Marie de Champagne (1145–1198)
Marie de Chatillon (r. 1230–1241)
Marie de France (c. 1140–1200)
Marie de l'Incarnation (1599–1672)
Marie d'Orleans (1813–1839)
Marie Josephe of Saxony (1731–1767)
Marie Leczinska (1703–1768)
Marie Louise (1695–1719)
Marie Louise d'Orleans (1750–1822)
Marie Louise of Austria (1791–1847)
Marie of Anjou (1404–1463)
Marie of Brabant (c. 1260–1321)
Marie of Cleves (1426–1486)
Marie of Evreux (d. 1335)
Marie of France (1198–c. 1223)
Marie of Guise (d. 1404)
Marie of Orleans (d. 1493)
Marie Thérèse Charlotte (1778–1851)
Marie-Thérèse de Soubiran (1834–1889)
Marillac, Louise de (1591–1660)
Marin, Maguy (1951—)
Maritain, Raïssa (1883–1960)
Marken, Jeanne (1895–1976)
Marnière, Jeanne (1854–1910)
Marquet, Mary (1895–1979)
Marquets, Anne de (1533–1588)
Mars, Ann Françoise (1779–1847)
Martel, Judith (c. 844–?)
Martel de Janville, Comtesse de (1850–1932)
Martinod, Marie (c. 1984—)
Mary of Guise (1515–1560)
Mary of Luxemburg (1305–1323)
Mary Tudor (1496–1533)
Masnada, Florence (1968—)
Masset, Louise (c. 1863–1900)
Mathieu, Simone (1908–1980)
Mathieu, Véronique (1955—)
Matilda of Germany (d. before 1044)
Maud Carinthia (c. 1105–1160)
Mauduit, Louise (1784–1862)
Maupin, d'Aubigny (c. 1670–1707)
Mauresmo, Amelie (1979—)
Maurey, Nicole (1925—)
Mauri, Rosita (1856–1923)
Mayer, Constance (c. 1778–1821)
Medici, Marie de (c. 1573–1642)
Meignan, Laetitia (1960—)
Melikova, Genia (c. 1930–2004)
Melisande (fl. 1100)
Mell, Marisa (1939–1992)
Merard de Saint-Just, Anne-Jeanne-Félicité d'Ormoy (1765–1830)
Mercier, Euphrasie (1823–?)
Mercoeur, Elisa (1809–1835)
Merle, Carole (1964—)
Mermet, Karine (1974—)
Mérode, Cléo de (c. 1875–1966)
Merret, Faustine (1978—)
Mestre, Audrey (1974–2002)
Metella, Malia (1982—)
Metzger, Hélène (1889–1944)
Meurdrac, Marie (fl. 17th c.)
Meygret, Anne (1965—)
Michel, Louise (1830–1905)
Michelle Valois (1394–1422)
Mignot, Claudine Françoise (c. 1617–1711)
Mink, Paule (1839–1901)
Miolan-Carvalho, Marie (1827–1895)
Miou-Miou (1950—)
Mir, Isabelle (1949—)
Mirabeau, Comtesse de (1827–1914)
Miramion, Madame de (1629–1696)
Mireille (1906–1996)
Miremont, Anne d'Aubourg de La Bove, Comtesse de (1735–1811)
Miremont, Jacqueline de (fl. 16th c.)
Misme, Jane (1865–1935)
Mistinguett (1875–1956)
Mitterrand, Danielle (1924—)
Mnouchkine, Ariane (1938—)
Modesta of Trier (d. about 680)
Moillon, Louise (1610–1696)
Monbart, Marie-Joséphine de Lescun (1758–1800)
Monegunde (fl. 6th c.)
Monnet, Marie Moreau (1752–1798)
Monnier, Adrienne (c. 1892–1955)
Monnot, Marguerite (1903–1961)
Monod, Sarah (1836–1912)
Montanclos, Marie-Emilie Maryon de (1736–1812)
Montansier, Marguerite (1730–1820)
Montespan, Françoise, Marquise de (1640–1707)
Montesson, Charlotte Jeanne Béraud de la Haye de Riou, marquise de (1737–1805)
Montfort, Elizabeth (1954—)
Montillet, Carole (1973—)
Montpensier, Anne Marie Louise d'Orléans, Duchesse de (1627–1693)
Montrelay, Michèle
Moreau, Jeanne (1928—)
Moreau, Mady (1928—)
Morency, Barbe-Suzanne-Aimable Giroux de (1770–?)
Moreno, Marguerite (1871–1948)
Moressee-Pichot, Sophie (1962—)
Morgan, Michèle (1920—)
Morin, Micheline (fl. 1930s)
Morisot, Berthe (1841–1895)
Morlay, Gaby (1893–1964)
Moss, Kate (1974—)
Motte, Claire (1937—)
Motteville, Françoise Bertaut de (c. 1621–1689)
Munia Elvira (995–1067)
Murat, Henriette Julie de (1670–1716)
Murat, Princess Eugène (1878–1936)
Musidora (1884–1957)
Muzio, Christine (1951—)
Myrtel, Hera (b. 1868)
Myrtil, Odette (1898–1978)
Nadja (c. 1900–1945)

Napierkowska, Stacia (1886–1945)
Nat, Marie-José (1940—)
Necker, Suzanne (1739–1794)
Nemenoff, Genia (1905–1989)
Nemours, Marie d'Orleans, duchess de (c. 1625–1707)
Neufvic, Madame de (fl. 17th c.)
Neveu, Ginette (1919–1949)
Newman, Julia St. Clair (1818–?)
Niboyet, Eugénie (1797–1883)
Nico (1938–1988)
Nicole of Lorraine (c. 1608–1657)
Niepce, Janine (1921—)
Nin, Anais (1903–1977)
Ninnoc (fl. 6th c.)
Niogret, Corinne (1972—)
Nisima, Maureen (1981—)
Noailles, Anna de (1876–1933)
Noailles, Anne Claude Laurence, duchesse de (d. 1793)
Noailles, Marie-Laure de (1902–1970)
Noblet, Lise (1801–1852)
Noves, Laure de (1308–1348)
Nowak, Cecile (1967—)
Noziere, Violette (1915–1966)
Nuyen, France (1939—)
Oddon, Yvonne (1902–1982)
Odette de Pougy (fl. 1266)
Ogier, Bulle (1939—)
Oignt, Marguerite d' (d. 1310)
Oldenburg, Margaret (b. 1895)
Olivier, Fernande (1884–1966)
O'Meara, Kathleen (1839–1888)
Ostermeyer, Micheline (1922–2001)
Otto-Crepin, Margit (1945—)
Ousset, Cécile (1936—)
Pagava, Ethery (1932—)
Page, Geneviève (1930—)
Palcy, Euzhan (1957—)
Palli, Anne-Marie (1955—)
Palm, Etta Aelders (1743–1799)
Paradis, Marie (fl. 1808)
Parain-Vial, Jeanne (b. 1912)
Parthenay, Anne de (fl. 16th c.)
Parthenay, Catherine de (1554–1631)
Parturier, Françoise (1919—)
Pascal, Christine (1953–1996)
Pascal, Gilberte (1620–1687)
Pascal, Jacqueline (1625–1661)
Patrie, Béatrice (1957—)
Pelen, Perrine (1960—)
Pelletier, Madeleine (1874–1939)
Pequegnot, Laure (1975—)
Perec, Marie-Jose (1968—)
Perey, Marguerite (1909–1975)
Périer, Marguerite (c. 1645–?)
Perriand, Charlotte (1903–1999)
Phalle, Niki de Saint (1930–2002)
Philiberta of Savoy (c. 1498–1524)
Philippa de Rouergue (c. 1074–1118)
Philippa-Elizabeth (1714–1734)
Philippa of Foix (fl. 13th c.)
Philippa of Guelders (d. 1547)
Philippart, Nathalie (c. 1926—)
Piaf, Edith (1915–1963)
Pia of Sicily (1849–1882)
Picasso, Paloma (1949—)
Pierce, Mary (1975—)
Pieronne of Brittany (d. 1430)
Pisier, Marie-France (1944—)
Placencia (fl. 1068)
Plessis, Alphonsine (1824–1847)
Plewinski, Catherine (1968—)
Pleyel, Maria Felicite (1811–1875)
Plisson, Marie-Prudence (1727–1788)
Poinso-Chapuis, Germaine (1901–1981)
Poirot, Catherine (1963—)
Poisson, Madeleine-Angelique (1684–1770)
Polaire (1879–1939)
Pole, Elizabeth de la (1444–1503)
Poliakoff, Olga (c. 1935—)
Polignac, Yolande Martine Gabrielle de (1749–1793)
Pompadour, Jeanne-Antoinette Poisson, Duchesse de (1721–1764)
Pons, Lily (1898–1976)
Ponthiey, Adelaide (fl. 1248)
Pontois, Noëlla (1943—)
Poppa of Normandy (fl. 880)
Porete, Marguerite (d. 1310)
Port Royal des Champs, Abbesses of
Postel-Vinay, Anise (1928—)
Potonié-Pierre, Eugénie (1844–1898)
Pougy, Liane de (1866–c. 1940)
Poulain, Mme (c. 1750–c. 1800)
Presle, Micheline (1922—)
Presti, Ida (1924–1967)
Prévost, Françoise (1680–1741)
Prevost, Hélène
Prie, Jeanne Agnes Berthelot de Pléneuf, Marquise de (1698–1727)
Printemps, Yvonne (1894–1977)
Prou, Suzanne (1920–1995)
Puisieux, Madeleine de (1720–1798)
Questiaux, Nicole (1931—)
Rachel (1821–1858)
Racinet, Delphine (1973—)
Radegonde (d. 1445)
Rahon, Alice (1904–1987)
Rambouillet, Catherine de Vivonne, Marquise de (1588–1665)
Randall, Amelia Mary (1844–1930)
Ranfaing, Élizabeth of (d. 1649)
Raucourt, Mlle (1756–1815)
Rayet, Jacqueline (1932—)
Récamier, Juliette (1777–1849)
Réjane, Gabrielle (1857–1920)
Rémusat, Claire, comtesse de (1780–1821)
Renaud, Madeleine (1903–1994)
Renée de Bourbon (fl. 1477)
Renée of France (1510–1575)
Renée of Montpensier (fl. 1500s)
Renneville, Sophie de (1772–1822)
Restoux, Marie-Claire (1968—)
Reybaud, Fanny (1802–1871)
Reymond, Claire (c. 1868–?)
Reza, Yasmina (1959—)
Ricard, Marthe (1889–1982)
Ricci, Nina (1883–1970)
Riccoboni, Marie-Jeanne (1713–1792)
Richesa of Lorraine (d. 1067)
Richier, Germaine (1904–1959)
Richilde (d. 894)
Richilde of Autun (d. around 910)
Ringart (fl. 822–825)
Riva, Emmanuelle (1927—)
Robert, Marie-Anne de Roumier (1705–1771)
Robert-Kéralio, Louise (1758–1821)
Robespierre, Charlotte (1760–1840)
Robin, Dany (1927–1995)
Robin, Mado (1918–1960)
Robine, Marie (d. 1399)
Robinson, Madeleine (1916–2004)
Roch, Madeleine (1884–1930)
Rochechouart, Gabrielle de (1645–1704)
Rochefort, Christiane (1917–1998)
Roches, Catherine des (1542–1587)
Roches, Madeleine des (1520–1587)
Rohan-Montbazon, Marie de (1600–1679)
Roland, Madame (1754–1793)
Roland, Pauline (1805–1852)
Romance, Viviane (1909–1991)
Romieu, Marie de (c. 1545–c. 1590)
Roque, Jacqueline (d. 1986)
Rosay, Françoise (1891–1974)
Ross, Marie-Henriette LeJeune (1762–1860)
Rothelin, Jacqueline de Rohan, Marquise de (c. 1520–1587)
Rothild (c. 871–c. 928)
Rothschild, Mathilde de (1874–1926)
Rotrud (800–841)
Roudy, Yvette (1929—)
Rouet, Philippa (c. 1348–c. 1387)
Roure, Martine (1948—)
Rousanne, Mme (1894–1958)
Roussel, Nelly (1878–1922)
Roux, Aline (1935—)
Roy de Clotte le Barillier, Berthe (1868–1927)
Royer, Clémence (1830–1902)
Ruby, Karine (1978—)
Ruilly, Macette de (d. 1391)
Rute, Mme de (1831–1902)
Saariaho, Kaija (1952—)
Sablé, Madeleine de Souvré, Marquise de (c. 1599–1678)
Sagan, Françoise (1935–2004)
Saint-Chamond, Claire-Marie Mazarelli, Marquise de La Vieuville de (1731–?)
Saint-Cyr, Renée (1904–2004)
Saint Mars, Gabrielle de (1804–1872)
Salaberga of Laon (d. around 665)
Salete, Mme de (fl. 1600)
Sallé, Marie (1707–1756)
Salm-Dyck, Constance de (1767–1845)
Salonnières (fl. 17th and 18th c.)
Sand, George (1804–1876)
Sand, Monique (1944—)
Sanda, Dominique (1948—)
Sansom, Odette (1912–1995)
Sarah of St. Gilles (fl. 1326)
Sarraute, Nathalie (1900–1999)
Sarrazin, Albertine (1937–1967)
Savignac, Alida de (1790–1847)
Schaffner, Anne-Marie (1945—)
Scherchen, Tona (1938—)
Schiaparelli, Elsa (1890–1973)
Schiffman, Suzanne (1929–2001)
Schmahl, Jeanne (1846–1916)
Schneider, Hortense (1833–1920)
Scholastica of Champagne (d. 1219)
Schwarz, Solange (1910–2000)
Schwarz-Bart, Simone (1938—)
Scieri, Antoinette (fl. 1920s)
Scrivener, Christiane (1925—)
Scudéry, Madeleine de (1607–1701)
Scudéry, Marie-Madeleine du Moncel de Montinvall de (1627–1711)
Sebbar, Leila (1941—)
Sedova, Julia (1880–1969)
Ségalas, Anais (1814–1895)
Ségur, Sophie Rostopchine, Comtesse de (1799–1874)
Seigneuret, Michele (1934—)
Selva, Blanche (1884–1942)
Serreau, Coline (1947—)
Serreau, Geneviève (1915–1981)
Sert, Misia (1872–1950)
Séverine (1855–1929)
Sévigné, Marie de (1626–1696)
Seyrig, Delphine (1932–1990)
Shakhovskaya, Zinaida (1906–2001)
Sibylle of Burgundy (1065–1102)
Sibylle of Burgundy (1126–1150)
Signoret, Simone (1921–1985)
Sigolena of Albi (fl. 7th c.)
Simon, Simone (1910–2005)

Simone, Madame (1877–1985)
Skorik, Irene (1928—)
Soleil, Germaine (1913–1996)
Sologne, Madeleine (1912–1995)
Sophie (1734–1782)
Sophie of Bayern (1847–1897)
Sorel, Agnes (1422–1450)
Sorel, Cécile (1873–1966)
Sorel, Claudette (1930—)
Sourdis, Isabelle de (fl. 16th c.)
Souza-Botelho, Adélaïde Filleul, marquise of (1761–1836)
Staal de Launay, Madame de (1684–1750)
Staël, Germaine de (1766–1817)
Stanley, Charlotte (1599–1664)
Stella, Claudine Bousonnet (1636–1697)
Steurer, Florence (1949—)
Stewart, Alexandra (1939—)
Stewart, Isabel (d. 1494)
Stoecklin, Stephane (1969—)
Suavegotta (fl. 504)
Subligny, Marie-Thérèse Perdou de (1666–1736)
Sudre, Margie (1943—)
Sullerot, Evelyne (1924—)
Surville, Laure (1800–1871)
Svetlova, Marina (1922—)
Sybilla of Anjou (1112–1165)
Sybil of Conversano (d. 1103)
Sylvie (1883–1970)
Szabo, Violette (1921–1945)
Tabouis, Geneviève (1892–1985)
Tagliaferro, Magda (1893–1986)
Taglioni, Louisa (1823–1893)
Tailleferre, Germaine (1892–1983)
Takahashi, Takako (1932—)
Tallien, Thérésa (1773–1835)
Talma, Louise (1906–1996)
Talma, Madame (1771–1860)
Tastu, Amable (1798–1885)
Tavernier, Nicole (fl. 1594)
Tcherina, Ludmilla (1924–2004)
Tencin, Claudine Alexandrine Guérin de (1685–1749)
Theodorade (fl. 9th c.)
Theodrada (b. between 783 and 794)
Théot, Catherine (d. 1794)
Therese of Bourbon (1817–1886)
Thérèse of Lisieux (1873–1897)
Théroigne de Méricourt, Anne-Josèphe (1762–1817)
Thesmar, Ghislaine (1943—)
Thomas-Mauro, Nicole (1951—)
Thomasse (fl. 1292)
Tibors (b. around 1130)
Tillion, Germaine (b. 1907)
Tinayre, Marcelle (c. 1870–1948)
Tinayre, Marguerite (1831–?)
Tissot, Alice (1895–1971)
Traline, Helen (1928—)
Travers, Susan (1909–2003)
Trigère, Pauline (1912—)
Trinquet, Veronique (1956—)
Trintignant, Nadine (1934—)
Triolet, Elsa (1896–1970)
Tristan, Flora (1803–1844)
Trocmé, Magda (1901–1996)
Trouhanova, Natalia (1885–1956)
Urso, Camilla (1842–1902)
Uzès, Anne, Duchesse d' (1847–1933)
Vachetta, Roseline (1951—)
Valadon, Suzanne (1865–1938)
Valette, Aline (1850–1899)
Vallayer-Coster, Anne (1744–1818)
Vallette, Marguerite (1860–1953)
Vallier, Hélène (1932–1988)
Vallin, Ninon (1886–1961)
Vandenhende, Severine (1974—)
Varda, Agnes (1928—)
Vaussard, Christiane (1923—)
Vaux, Clotilde de (1815–1846)
Védrès, Nicole (1911–1965)
Veil, Simone (1927—)
Velichkovskaia, Tamara Antonovna (1908–1990)
Verdy, Violette (1931—)
Vernon, Anne (1924—)
Vérone, Maria (1874–1938)
Versois, Odile (1930–1980)
Vestris, Thérèse (1726–1808)
Viardot, Louise (1841–1918)
Viardot, Pauline (1821–1910)
Victoire, Madame (1733–1799)
Victoria of Saxe-Coburg (1822–1857)
Vidal, Doriane (1976—)
Vidal, Ginette (b. 1931)
Vieira da Silva, Maria Elena (1908–1992)
Vigée-Le Brun, Elisabeth (1755–1842)
Villameur, Lise (1905–2004)
Villedieu, Catherine des Jardins, Mme de (c. 1640–1683)
Villeneuve, Gabrielle-Suzanne de (c. 1695–1755)
Villers, Mme (fl. late 18th c.)
Vilmorin, Louise de (1902–1969)
Vintimille, Pauline Félicité, Marquise de (1712–1741)
Vionnet, Madeleine (1876–1975)
Visconti, Valentina (1366–1408)
Vivien, Renée (1877–1909)
Vlady, Marina (1938—)
Vlasto, Didi (1903–1985)
Vlasto, Dominique (1946—)
Voilquin, Suzanne (1801–1877)
Vreeland, Diana (1903–1989)
Vultrogotha (fl. 558)
Vyroubova, Nina (1921—)
Walkinshaw, Clementina (c. 1726–1802)
Weber, Jeanne (1875–1910)
Weil, Simone (1909–1943)
Weiss, Louise (1893–1983)
Witherington, Pearl (1914—)
Witt, Henriette de (1829–1908)
Wittig, Monique (1935–2003)
Women Prophets and Visionaries in France at the End of the Middle Ages
Yolande de Dreux (1212–1248)
Yolande de Dreux (d. 1238)
Yolande de Dreux (d. 1272)
Yolande of Aragon (1379–1442)
Yolande of Burgundy (1248–1280)
Yolande of France (1434–1478)
Yolande of Vaudemont (1428–1483)
Yourcenar, Marguerite (1903–1987)
Yuasa, Toshiko (1909–1980)
Zei, Alki (1925—)

FRANKS, KINGDOM OF THE

Germanic settlement along lower and middle Rhine (3rd c. CE)
Salian Franks in the north; Ripuarian Franks in the south
Salian and Ripuarian Franks united under Clovis; Frankish empire founded (5th c.)
Included most of France, the Low Countries, Germany west of the Elbe, Austria, Switzerland, and north and central Italy
Under Merovingians, empire divided into several kingdoms
Under Carolingians, empire achieved height of power
Charlemagne's empire partitioned (843 and 870)
West Franks merged with Gallo-Romans of Gaul and became France
East Franks retained Germanic language and became Germany

See also France.
See also Germany.

Adela (d. 735)
Agnes of Courtenay (1136–1186)
Aldegund (c. 630–684)
Anstrude of Laon (fl. 7th c.)
Aregunde (fl. 6th c.)
Balthild (c. 630–c. 680)
Basine (fl. 428)
Basine (fl. 465)
Beretrude (d. 620)
Bertha (719–783)
Bertha (779–after 823)
Bertha of Avenay (fl. 6th c.)
Bilchilde (d. 675)
Chiltrud (fl. 700s)
Chrotrud (d. 724)
Chunsina (fl. 6th c.)
Clotilda (470–545)
Clotilde (d. 691)
Desiderata (d. 773)
Dhuoda of Septimania (fl. 820-843)
Dode (b. 586)
Edonne (fl. 8th c.)
Fara (d. 667)
Fastrada (d. 794)
Fredegund (c. 547–597)
Fredesendis (fl. 1000)
Galswintha (d. around 568)
Gertrude of Nivelles (626–659)
Gisela (c. 753–807)
Gisela (c. 819–c. 874)
Gisela of Chelles (781–814)
Guntheuca (fl. 525)
Helaria (fl. 6th c.)
Hildegarde of Swabia (c. 757–783)
Hiltrude (fl. 800s)
Himiltrude (fl. 700s)
Ida of Nivelles (597–652)
Ingunde (fl. 517)
Irmina (d. 716)
Liutgard (d. 885)
Luitgarde (d. 800)
Martel, Adeloga (fl. 775)
Muriella (fl. 1000)
Nanthilde (610–642)
Odilia (fl. 620)
Radegund of Poitiers (518–587)
Ragnetrude (fl. 630)
Riguntha (fl. 580s)
Rotrude (c. 778–after 839)
Tanaquille (d. 696)
Viborada (d. 925)

FRENCH CANADA

See Quebec.

GALICIA

Former Austrian crownland in east central Europe
Inhabited by Slavs (6th c.)
Medieval principalities of Halicz and Lodomeria emerged (12th c.)
Separated from Russian territory of Kiev by Mongol invasions
Became part of Poland (1386)
Annexed to Austria (1772 and 1795)
Western Galicia included in grand duchy of Warsaw (1809)
Returned to Austria after uprising in Craców (1846)
Ceded to Poland (1919)
Divided between Germany and U.S.S.R. (1939)
Eastern half returned to U.S.S.R. and made part of Ukrainian S.S.R.; half to Poland

See also Austria.
See also Germany.

See also Poland.
See also Russia.

Kalich, Bertha (1874–1939)
Viertel, Salka (1889–1978)

GALILEE

Northern region of Palestine
Included in Assyrian province of Samaria (722 BCE)
Becane a Roman province (1st c.)

Salome II (fl. 1st c.)

GAUL

Ancient European country
Cisalpine Gaul settled by Celts (c. 4th–3rd c. BCE)
Transalpine Gaul conquered by Julius Caesar; divided into regions of Aquitania in the southwest, Gallia in the west and central area, and Belgica in the northeast (58–51 BCE)
Gallia Narbonensis formed as Roman province (c. 121 BCE)
See also France.
See also Germany.

Faith (290–303)

GEORGIA

Ancient region containing kingdoms of Colchis and Iberia
Portions under Turkish and Persian rule (15th–18th c.)
Absorbed into Russian Empire (19th c.)
Achieved independence following Russian revolution (1918–1921)
Incorporated into U.S.S.R. until dissolution of Soviet Union (1991)
See also Russia.

Meskhi, Leila (1968—)

GERMANY

Country in central Europe
Confined by Roman conquests to region east of Rhine and north of Danube (1st c. BCE–1st c. CE)
German tribes inhabited most of Roman Empire; Slavic tribes inhabited Germany east of Elbe (4th–5th c.)
Anglo-Saxons conquered Britain; Franks conquered most of France, west and south Germany, and Thuringia (6th c.)
Dukes of Franconia, Swabia, Bavaria, Saxony, and Lorraine gained power (8th–9th c.)
Included, with Italy, in Holy Roman Empire (10th c.)
Ruled by Habsburgs (13th c.)
Conquered Prussia (13th c.)
After Reformation, Germany split into Catholic and Protestant states (16th c.)
Empire yielded territory to France, Sweden, and Brandenburg (17th c.)
German states became dependents of France (1806)
German Empire dominated by Prussia (1866)
Allied with Austria and Italy in colonial expansion (1879 and 1882)
Lost territory in Treaty of Versailles and adopted Weimar constitution (1919)
Dominated by National Socialist party (1935)
Began World War II with Poland, Great Britain, and France (1939)
Conquered Norway, Netherlands, Belgium, and France (1940)
Defeated by Russians (1943–1944)
Surrendered to Allies and divided into East and West Germany (1945)
East and West Germany reintegrated (1989)
See also Germany, East.

Abarbanell, Lina (1879–1963)
Abrahamowitsch, Ruth (1907–1974)
Adasse (fl. 1348)
Adelaide (1821–1899)
Adelaide of Burgundy (931–999)
Adelaide of Burgundy (d. 1273)
Adelaide of Hohenlohe-Langenburg (1835–1900)
Adelaide of Kiev (c. 1070–1109)
Adelaide of Quedlinburg (977–1045)
Adelaide of Saxe-Meiningen (1792–1849)
Adelaide of Saxe-Meiningen (1891–1971)
Adelaide of Vohburg (fl. 1140s)
Adela of Meissen (fl. 1100s)
Adelgunde of Bavaria (1823–1914)
Afra (fl. c. 304)
Agatha of Hungary (c. 1025–?)
Agnes, Lore (1876–1953)
Agnes Capet (1260–1327)
Agnes of Aquitaine (c. 995–1068)
Agnes of Austria (fl. 1100s)
Agnes of Austria (1281–1364)
Agnes of Barby (1540–1569)
Agnes of Bohemia (1205–1282)
Agnes of Bohemia (1269–1297)
Agnes of Germany (1074–1143)
Agnes of Habsburg (c. 1257–1322)
Agnes of Hesse (1527–1555)
Agnes of Looss (fl. 1150–1175)
Agnes of Poitou (1024–1077)
Agnes of Quedlinburg (1184–1203)
Agnes of Saarbrucken (fl. 1130)
Agnes of Saxony (fl. 1200s)
Ahlefeld, Charlotte von (1781–1849)
Ahlers, Anny (1906–1933)
Ajzenberg-Selove, Fay (1926—)
Albers, Anni (1899–1994)
Alberti, Sophie (1826–1892)
Albertina Agnes (d. 1696)
Albertina of Baden-Durlach (1682–1755)
Albrecht, Angele (1942—)
Albrecht, Sophie (1757–1840)
Alexander, Leni (1924—)
Alexandra Feodorovna (1872–1918)
Alexandra Guelph (1882–1963)
Alexandra Nikolaevna (1825–1844)
Alexandra of Oldenburg (1838–1900)
Alexandra of Saxe-Altenburg (1830–1911)
Alexandra Saxe-Coburg (1878–1942)
Alexandra Victoria of Schleswig-Holstein (1887–1957)
Alexandrina of Mecklenburg-Schwerin (1879–1952)
Alf, Fé (c. 1910—)
Alice Maud Mary (1843–1878)
Alice of Athlone (1883–1981)
Alice of Normandy (fl. 1017–1037)
Alix of Vergy (d. after 1218)
Alix of Vergy (r. 1248–c. 1290)
Amalia of Bavaria (1801–1877)
Amalie Auguste (1788–1851)
Amalie of Greece (1818–1875)
Amalie of Hesse-Darmstadt (1754–1832)
Amalie of Saxe-Coburg-Gotha (1848–1894)
Amalie of Saxony (1794–1870)
Ambrosius, Johanna (b. 1854)
Amelia of Anhalt-Dessau (1666–1726)
Amelia of Cleves (1517–1586)
Amelia of Denmark (1580–1639)
Amelia of Leuchtenburg (1812–1873)
Amelia of Wurttemberg (1799–1848)
Amlingyn, Katherine (fl. late-15th c.)
Anastasia Romanova (1860–1922)
Andersen, Lale (1905–1972)
Anderson, Evelyn N. (1909–1977)
Angerer, Nadine (1978—)
Anna Amalia of Prussia (1723–1787)
Anna Amalia of Saxe-Weimar (1739–1807)
Anna Constancia (1619–1651)
Anna Maria of Saxony (1836–1859)
Anna Maria of the Palatinate (1561–1589)
Anna Maria Theresa (1879–1961)
Anna of Bohemia and Hungary (1503–1547)
Anna of Brandenburg (1507–1567)
Anna of Brunswick (fl. 1400s)
Anna of Brunswick (1528–1590)
Anna of Byzantium (fl. 901)
Anna of Denmark (1532–1585)
Anna of Habsburg (d. 1327)
Anna of Hohenberg (c. 1230–1281)
Anna of Saxony (1420–1462)
Anna of Saxony (1544–1577)
Anna of Schweidnitz (c. 1340–?)
Anna of Silesia
Anna of the Palatinate (fl. 1300s)
Anna Sophia of Denmark (1647–1717)
Anna Sophia of Prussia (1527–1591)
Anna von Munzingen (fl. 1327)
Anne-Eleanor of Hesse-Darmstadt (1601–1659)
Anneke, Mathilde Franziska (1817–1884)
Anne Marie of Brunswick (1532–1568)
Anne of Austria (1601–1666)
Anne of Saxony (1437–1512)
Anne Valois (c. 1405–1432)
Ansgard (fl. 863)
Antoinette of Luxemburg (1899–1954)
Antoinette Saxe-Coburg (1779–1824)
Antonia of Portugal (1845–1913)
Antonini, Theresa (1785–1809)
Apel, Katrin (1973—)
Appel, Gabriele (1958—)
Arendsee, Martha (1885–1953)
Arendt, Gisela (1918–1969)
Arendt, Hannah (1906–1975)
Arndt, Judith (1976—)
Arnim, Bettine von (1785–1859)
Arnold, Emmy (1884–1980)
Assing, Ludmilla (1821–1880)
Assing, Ottilie (1819–1884)
Aston, Luise (1814–1871)
Astor, Sarah Todd (1761–1832)
Auer, Judith (1905–1944)
Auerbach, Charlotte (1899–1994)
Auerbach, Edith (1903—)
Augspurg, Anita (1857–1943)
Augusta Guelph (1737–1813)
Augusta Guelph (1822–1916)
Augusta Maria of Baden-Baden (1704–1726)
Augusta Maria of Holstein-Gottorp (1649–1728)
Augusta of Brunswick-Wolfenbuttel (1764–1788)
Augusta of Hesse-Cassel (1797–1889)
Augusta of Reuss-Ebersdorf (1757–1831)
Augusta of Saxe-Weimar (1811–1890)
Augusta of Schleswig-Holstein (1858–1921)
Augusta of Wurttemberg (1826–1898)
Augustat, Elise (1889–1940)
Augusta Victoria (1890–1966)
Aus der Ohe, Adele (1864–1937)
Ausländer, Rose (1901–1988)
Aussem, Cilly (1909–1963)
Austrebertha (635–704)
Ava of Melk (d. 1127)
Baader, Amalie (b. 1763)
Baarova, Lida (1914–2000)
Bach, Anna Magdalena (1701–1760)
Bach, Maria Barbara (d. 1720)
Bacheracht, Therese von (1804–1852)
Bachmann, Tina (1978—)
Bachor, Isabell (1983—)
Baldus, Brita Pia (1965—)
Ballestrem, Eufemia von (1859–1941)
Barbara of Poland (1478–1534)
Barbara of Saxe-Wittenberg (c. 1405–1465)
Barwirth, Anita (1918—)

Bathildis of Schaumburg-Lippe (1873–1962)
Bau, Sabine (1969—)
Bauer, Karoline (1807–1877)
Bauer, Klara (1836–1876)
Bauer, Viola (1976—)
Baum, Marianne (1912–1942)
Baum, Marie (1874–1964)
Baum, Vicki (1888–1960)
Baumann, Edith (1909–1973)
Bäumer, Gertrud (1873–1954)
Baur, Clara (1835–1912)
Bausch, Pina (1940—)
Baxter, Jane (1909–1996)
Bayard, Sylviane (1957—)
Beatrice of Cenci (1577-1599)
Beatrice of Silesia (fl. 1300s)
Beatrice of Swabia (1198–1235)
Beatrice of Upper Burgundy (1145–1184)
Becher, Hilla (1934—)
Becher, Lilly (1901–1976)
Becker, Britta (1973—)
Becker, Christiane (1778–1797)
Becker, Ellen (1960—)
Becker-Steiner, Marion (1950—)
Beckmann, Gudrun (1955—)
Bedford, Sybille (1911–2006)
Beese, Lotte (1903–1988)
Behle, Petra (1969—)
Behrens, Hildegard (1937—)
Beig, Maria (1920—)
Beimler-Herker, Centa (1909—)
Beinhorn, Elly (1907—)
Bejarano, Esther (1924—)
Benario, Olga (1908–1942)
Benjamin, Hilde (1902–1989)
Berber, Anita (1899–1928)
Berens-Totenohl, Josefa (1891–1969)
Berg, Helene (b. 1906)
Berger, Erna (1900–1990)
Berghaus, Ruth (1927–1996)
Bergmann-Pohl, Sabine (1946—)
Berk, Lotte (1913–2003)
Berlepsch, Emilie von (1755–1830)
Bernauer, Agnes (d. 1435)
Bernays, Marie (1883–1939)
Bernhard, Ruth (1905—)
Bernhardi, Sophie (1775–1833)
Bertha of Biburg (d. 1151)
Bertha of Savoy (1051-1087)
Bertha of Swabia (fl. 900s)
Beutler, Margarete (1876–1949)
Bey, Hannelore (1941—)
Beyer, Helga (1920–1942)
Beyermann, Ina (1967—)
Biebl, Heidi (1941—)
Biechi, Anni (1940—)
Biermann, Aenne (1898–1933)
Bing, Ilse (1899–1998)
Birch-Pfeiffer, Charlotte (1800–1868)
Birell, Tala (1907–1958)
Bischoff, Sabine (1958—)
Bismarck, Johanna von (1824–1894)
Blanche (c. 1392–1409)
Blanche of Valois (c. 1316–?)
Blasberg, Claudia (1975—)
Bleschke, Johanna (1894–1936)
Blind, Mathilde (1841–1896)
Blum, Klara (1904–1971)
Bobath, Berta (1907–1991)
Boedding-Eckhoff, Inge (1947—)
Boehm, Annett (1980—)
Boenisch, Yvonne (1980—)
Böhlau, Helene (1859–1940)
Bohley, Bärbel (1945—)
Bohm-Schuch, Clara (1879–1936)
Bokel, Claudia (1973—)
Boleyn, Anne (c. 1507–1536)
Bollmann, Minna (1876–1935)
Bolte, Amely (1811–1891)
Bonhoeffer, Emmi (1905–1991)
Bonne of Artois (d. 1425)
Bora, Katharina von (1499–1550)
Borchert, Katrin (1969—)
Bormann, Gerda (1909–1946)
Boron, Kathrin (1969—)
Boveri, Margret (1900–1975)
Boy-Ed, Ida (1852–1928)
Brachmann, Louise (1777–1822)
Brachvogel, Carry (1864–1942)
Brandebusemeyer, Nicole (1974—)
Brandt, Marianne (1893–1983)
Braumueller, Ellen (1910—)
Braun, Eva (1912–1945)
Braun, Lily (1865–1916)
Braun, Sabine (1965—)
Braunschweig-Lüneburg, Elisabeth von (1519–1558)
Braunschweig-Lüneburg, Sibylle Ursula von (1629–1671)
Braunschweig-Lüneburg, Sophie Elisabeth von (1613–1676)
Braun-Vogelstein, Julie (1883–1971)
Bré, Ruth (1862–1911)
Breiken, Dagmar (1963—)
Brendel, Daniela (1973—)
Breslauer, Marianne (1909–2001)
Breuer-Dukat, Renate (1939—)
Breyer, Hiltrud (1957—)
Brion, Friederike Elisabeth (1752–1813)
Bronsart, Ingeborg von (1840–1913)
Brück, Christa-Anita (1899–?)
Brückner, Christine (1921–1996)
Brühne, Vera (1910—)
Brun, Friederike (1765–1835)
Brunner, Ursula (1941—)
Buber-Neumann, Margarete (1901–1989)
Buchner, Annemarie
Büchner, Luise (1821–1877)
Buerger, Erna (1909–1958)
Buff, Charlotte (1753–1828)
Bühler, Charlotte (1893–1974)
Bülbring, Edith (1903–1990)
Bülow, Frieda von (1857–1909)
Bülow, Margarete von (1860–1884)
Burgess, Renate (1910–1988)
Buschschulte, Antje (1978—)
Bussman, Gabriele (1959—)
Capellmann, Nadine (1965—)
Cardus, Ana (1943—)
Caroline Augusta of Bavaria (1792–1873)
Caroline Elizabeth (1713–1757)
Caroline Louise of Saxe-Weimar (1786–1816)
Caroline Matilda of Schleswig-Holstein (1860–1932)
Caroline of Baden (1776–1841)
Caroline of Birkenfeld-Zweibrucken (1721–1774)
Caroline of Hesse-Darmstadt (1746–1821)
Caroline of Mecklenburg-Strelitz (1821–1876)
Caroline of Nassau (fl. 1730s)
Caroline of Nassau-Usingen (1762–1823)
Caroline of Orange (1743–1787)
Caroline of Saxony (1833–1907)
Carus, Emma (1879–1927)
Casaretto, Caroline (1978—)
Catherine (1584–1638)
Catherine Charlotte of Hildburghausen (1787–1847)
Catherine Frederica of Wurttemberg (1821–1898)
Catherine of Brunswick-Wolfenbuttel (1488–1563)
Catherine of Custrin (1549–1602)
Catherine of Gorizia (fl. late 1300s)
Catherine of Habsburg (c. 1254–1282)
Catherine of Mecklenburg-Schwerin (1692–1733)
Catherine of Pomerania (d. 1526)
Catherine of Russia (1788–1819)
Catherine of Saxony (1421–1476)
Catherine of Wurttemberg (1783–1835)
Cauer, Minna (1841–1922)
Cecilia of Baden (1839–1891)
Cecilia of Mecklenburg-Schwerin (1886–1954)
Charlotte (1769–1818)
Charlotte Frederica of Mecklenburg-Schwerin (1784–1840)
Charlotte of Bourbon (d. 1582)
Charlotte of Brunswick-Wolfenbüttel (1694–1715)
Charlotte of Hesse (1627–1687)
Charlotte of Hesse-Darmstadt (1755–1785)
Charlotte of Saxe-Meiningen (1860–1919)
Chézy, Helmina von (1783–1856)
Chotek, Sophie (1868–1914)
Christaller, Helene (1872–1953)
Christina Casimir (fl. 1640–1660)
Christine of Baden-Durlach (1645–1705)
Christine of Gandersheim (d. 919)
Christine of Hesse (1543–1604)
Christine of Hesse-Cassel (1933—)
Christine of Saxony (1505–1549)
Claricia of Augsburg (fl. 1220)
Clementia of Habsburg (d. 1293)
Clementina of Zahringen (fl. 1150s)
Conrad-Martius, Hedwig (1888–1966)
Constance of Aragon (d.1222)
Cope, Mother Marianne (1838–1918)
Coppi, Hilde (1909–1943)
Corda, Maria (1898–1975)
Cordua, Beatrice (1943—)
Courths-Mahler, Hedwig (1867–1950)
Cranz, Christl (1914–2004)
Cremer, Erika (1900–1996)
Cruvelli, Sofia (1826–1907)
Cunigunde (d. 1040?)
Cunegunde (d. 1357)
Cunegunde (d. after 1370)
Cunegunde (1465–1520)
Cunigunde of Hungary (d. 1285)
Cunigunde of Swabia (fl. 900s)
Cunigunde Sobieska (fl. 1690s)
Cunitz, Maria (1610–1664)
Czobel, Lisa (1906–1992)
Dagover, Lil (1897–1980)
Daisy, Princess (1873–1943)
Dallmann, Petra (1978—)
Danzi, Maria Margarethe (1768–1800)
Dauthendey, Elisabeth (1854–1943)
Daves, Joan (1919–1997)
Deininger, Beate (1962—)
de Mello, Theresa (1913–1997)
Demleitner, Elisabeth
Deutschkron, Inge (1922—)
Dickenscheid, Tanja (1969—)
Dietrich, Marlene (1901–1992)
Dinescu, Violeta (1953—)
Disl, Ursula (1970—)
Dittmar, Louise (1807–1884)
Dobmeier, Annette (1968—)
Dobson, Deborah (c. 1950—)
Doerdelmann, Sylvia (1970—)
Doerries, Jana (1975—)

Dohm, Hedwig (1831–1919)
Dombeck, Carola (1960—)
Domin, Hilde (1909–2006)
Dönhoff, Marion, Countess (1909–2002)
Dorn, Erna (1912–1953)
Dornemann, Luise (1901–1992)
Dorothea Hedwig of Brunswick-Wolfenbuttel (1587–1609)
Dorothea of Bavaria (1920—)
Dorothea of Brandenburg (1446–1519)
Dorothea of Saxony (1563-1587)
Dörrie, Doris (1955—)
Dransfeld, Hedwig (1871–1925)
Drechsler, Heike (1964—)
Dressel, Vally (1893—)
Drewitz, Ingeborg (1923–1986)
Drexel, Constance (1894–1956)
Dronke, Minnie Maria (1904–1987)
Droste-Hülshoff, Annette von (1797–1848)
Duncan, Elizabeth (c. 1874–1948)
Duncan, Irma (1897–1978)
Duncan, Maria Teresa (1895–1987)
Dünhaupt, Angelika
Duplitzer, Imke (1975—)
Durieux, Tilla (1880–1971)
Düringsfeld, Ida von (1815–1876)
Eberle, Verena (1950—)
Ebner, Christine (1277–1355)
Ebner, Margarethe (1291–1351)
Eckbauer-Baumann, Edith (1949—)
Edinger, Tilly (1897–1967)
Eduardova, Eugenia (1882–1980)
Eggerth, Marta (1912—)
Ehre, Ida (1900–1989)
Ehrlich, Aline (1928–1991)
Eilika of Oldenburg (1928—)
Eilika of Oldenburg (1972—)
Einoder-Straube, Thea (1951—)
Eisenblätter, Charlotte (1903–1944)
Eisenschneider, Elvira (1924–c. 1944)
Eisner, Lotte (1896–1983)
Eleanor of Pfalz-Neuburg (1655–1720)
Eleanor of Saxe-Eisenach (1662–1696)
Eleanor of Solms-Hohensolms-Lich (1871–1937)
Eleonore Hohenzollern (1583–1607)
Elisabeth of Pomerania (1347-1393)
Elisabeth of Saxe-Altenburg (1826–1896)
Elizabeth Amalia of Hesse (1635–1709)
Elizabeth Charlotte of the Palatinate (fl. 1620)
Elizabeth Christina of Brunswick-Wolfenbuttel (1691-1750)
Elizabeth Frederike of Bayreuth (fl. 1750)
Elizabeth Henrietta of Hesse-Cassel (1661–1683)
Elizabeth Hohenzollern (1815–1885)
Elizabeth Maria of Thurn and Taxis (1860–1881)
Elizabeth of Anhalt (1563–1607)
Elizabeth of Anhalt-Dessau (1857–1933)
Elizabeth of Austria (1743–1808)
Elizabeth of Baden (1779–1826)
Elizabeth of Bavaria (fl. 1200s)
Elizabeth of Bavaria (1801–1873)
Elizabeth of Bavaria (1876–1965)
Elizabeth of Bavaria-Landshut (1383–1442)
Elizabeth of Bohemia (1292–1339)
Elizabeth of Bohemia (1596–1662)
Elizabeth of Bohemia (1618–1680)
Elizabeth of Brandenburg (1510–1558)
Elizabeth of Brunswick-Wolfenbuttel (1593–1650)
Elizabeth of Denmark (1485–1555)
Elizabeth of Denmark (1524–1586)
Elizabeth of Denmark (1573–1626)
Elizabeth of Gorlitz (c. 1380–c. 1444)
Elizabeth of Habsburg (1293–1352)
Elizabeth of Hungary (fl. 1250s)
Elizabeth of Poland (fl. 1298–1305)
Elizabeth of Poland (d. 1361)
Elizabeth of Pomerania (1347–1393)
Elizabeth of Saxe-Hildburghausen (1713–1761)
Elizabeth of Schönau (c. 1129–1164)
Elizabeth of Sicily (d. 1349)
Elizabeth of Silesia (fl. 1257)
Elizabeth of Thurn and Taxis (1903–1976)
Elizabeth of Tyrol (c. 1262–1313)
Elizabeth of Wittelsbach (1540–1594)
Elizabeth of Wurttemberg (1767–1790)
Elizabeth of Wurttemberg (1802–1864)
Elizabeth Sophie of Saxe-Altenburg (1619–1680)
Elizabeth the Good (1386–1420)
Ella (1864–1918)
Elsner, Gisela (1937–1992)
Elstob, Elizabeth (1683–1756)
Eluard, Nusch (1906–1946)
Emilia of Orange (1569–1629)
Emma of Bavaria (d. 876)
Emmerich, Anna Katharina (1774–1824)
Ender, Kornelia (1958–)
Engelberga (c. 840-890)
Engelhard, Magdalene Philippine (1756–1831)
Engel-Kramer, Ingrid (1943—)
Epple, Irene (1957—)
Epple, Maria (1959—)
Erdmann, Susi-Lisa (1968—)
Ermengarde (c. 778-818)
Ermentrude de Roucy (d. 1005)
Ernsting-Krienke, Nadine (1974—)
Ertl, Martina (1973—)
Erxleben, Dorothea (1715–1762)
Eschstruth, Nataly von (1860–1939)
Esser, Roswitha (1941—)
Eugénie Hortense (1808–1847)
Evdokimova, Eva (1948—)
Evers, Meike (1977—)
Everts, Sabine (1961—)
Fabian, Dora (1901–1935)
Faileuba (fl. 586–587)
Falck, Hildegard (1949—)
Falk, Ria
Falkenhayn, Benita von (d. 1935)
Falkestein, Beatrice von (c. 1253–1277)
Fassbaender, Brigitte (1939—)
Feodore of Hohenlohe-Langenburg (1866–1932)
Feodore of Leiningen (1807–1872)
Ferneck, Christine (1969—)
Fichtel, Anja (1968—)
Fiebiger, Christel (1946—)
Figes, Eva (1932—)
Fingerin, Agnes (d. 1515)
Fiorenza, Elisabeth Schuessler (1938—)
Fischer, Caroline Auguste (1764–1834)
Fischer, Ruth (1895–1961)
Fitschen, Doris (1968—)
Fleischer, Ottilie (1911—)
Fleischmann, Trude (1895–1990)
Fleisser, Marieluise (1901–1974)
Flügge-Lotz, Irmgard (1903–1974)
Folcheid
Forkel, Karen (1970—)
Förster-Nietzsche, Elisabeth (1846–1935)
Fouqué, Karoline Freifrau de la Motte (1774–1831)
François, Louise von (1817–1893)
Frank, Antje (1968—)
Frederica Louise (1770–1819)
Frederica of Hesse-Darmstadt (1752–1782)
Frederica of Mecklenburg-Strelitz (1778–1841)
Fredericka of Hanover (1848–1926)
Freier, Recha (1892–1984)
Freund, Gisèle (1912–2000)
Fris, Maria (1932–1961)
Froelian, Isolde (1908–1957)
Frohberg, Regina (1783–1850)
Frölich, Henriette (1768–1833)
Frommater, Uta (1948—)
Fromm-Reichmann, Frieda (1889–1957)
Fuchs, Anna Rupertina (1657–1722)
Fuchs, Ruth (1946—)
Fugger, Barbara Baesinger (d. 1497)
Führer, Charlotte (1834–1907)
Funkenhauser, Zita-Eva (1966—)
Furr, Sonja (1978—)
Galdikas, Biruté (1948—)
Galitzin, Amalie von (1748–1806)
Garbrecht-Enfeldt, Monique (1968—)
Garefrekes, Kerstin (1979—)
Gaugel, Heide-Elke (1959—)
Gebhardt, Evelyne (1954—)
Geiringer, Hilda (1893–1973)
Genenger, Martha (1911—)
Georgi, Yvonne (1903–1975)
Gerberga (d. 896)
Gerberga (r. 959–1001)
Gerg, Hilde (1975—)
Gerhardt, Elena (1883–1961)
Gert, Valeska (1900–1978)
Gertrude of Hackeborne (1232–1292)
Gertrude of Meissen (d. 1117)
Gertrude of Saxony (1115–1143)
Gertrude of Sulzbach (d.1146)
Gertrude of Swabia (c. 1104–1191)
Gertrude the Great (1256–1302)
Geyra (fl. 980s)
Gisela (1856–1932)
Gisela of Bavaria (c. 975–1033)
Gisela of Burgundy (d. 1006)
Gisela of Burgundy (fl. 1100s)
Gisela of Swabia (d. 1043)
Glase, Anne-Karin (1954—)
Glockshuber, Margot
Glückel of Hameln (1646–1724)
Glümer, Claire von (1825–1906)
Goebbels, Magda (d. 1945)
Goering, Emmy (1893–1973)
Goethe, Cornelia (c. 1751–c. 1778)
Goethe, Elisabeth (1730–1808)
Goetz, Janina (1981—)
Göhr, Marlies (1958—)
Goldberg, Lea (1911–1970)
Goll, Claire (1891–1977)
Gonzaga, Anna (1585–1618)
Gonzaga, Anne de (1616–1684)
Gonzaga, Barbara (1455–1505)
Gonzaga, Eleonora I (1598–1655)
Gonzaga, Eleonora II (1628–1686)
Goslar, Lotte (1907–1997)
Götte, Jeannette (1979—)
Gottfried, Gesina Margaretha (d. 1828)
Gottsched, Luise Adelgunde (1713–1762)
Gottschlich, Stefanie (1978—)
Gotz, Daniela (1987—)
Gradante, Anna-Maria (1976—)
Graf, Steffi (1969—)
Grantzow, Adele (1845–1877)
Grasegger, Käthe
Gray, Hanna Holborn (1930—)
Greiner-Petter-Memm, Simone (1967—)
Grese, Irma (1923–1945)
Grillo, Gabriela (1952—)
Grings, Inka (1978—)

Groener, Lissy (1954—)
Grothaus, Gisela (1955—)
Gruber, Lilo (1915–1992)
Grumbach, Argula von (1492–after 1563)
Grundig, Lea (1906–1977)
Gsovsky, Tatiana (1901–1993)
Guda (fl. late 12th c.)
Gude, Franziska (1976—)
Guenther, Sarah (1983—)
Günderrode, Karoline von (1780–1806)
Gutheil-Schoder, Marie (1874–1935)
Haas, Dolly (1910–1994)
Haase, Mandy (1982—)
Hadding, Annette (1975—)
Hagen, Birgit (1957—)
Hagen, Uta (1919–2004)
Hagenbaumer, Eva (1967—)
Hagn, Johanna
Hahn, Anna Marie (1906–1938)
Hahn, Birgit (1958—)
Hahn-Hahn, Ida, Countess von (1805–1880)
Halbsguth, Ruth (1916—)
Hanisch, Cornelia (1952—)
Hanke, Henriette (1785–1862)
Hanke, Suzanne (1948—)
Happe-Krey, Ursula (1926—)
Harstick, Sara (1981—)
Hartlaub, Geno (1915—)
Hartmann, Ingrid (1930—)
Harvey, Antje (1967—)
Harvey, Lilian (1906–1968)
Harzendorf, Christiane (1967—)
Hase, Dagmar (1969—)
Hasse, Ute (1963—)
Hatheburg (fl. 906)
Hathumoda (d. 874)
Hatzler, Clara (fl. 1452)
Haug, Jutta D. (1951—)
Hauptmann, Anna (1898–1994)
Heck, Barbara Ruckle (1734–1804)
Hedvig (d. 1436)
Hedwig (d. 903)
Hedwig (c. 915–965)
Hedwig of Denmark (1581–1641)
Hedwig of Eberhard (930–992)
Hedwig of Habsburg (d. 1286)
Hedwig of Poland (1513–1573)
Hedwig of Silesia (1174–1243)
Hedwig Wittelsbach (fl. late 1600s)
Heidemann, Britta (1982—)
Heine, Jutta (1940—)
Heinel, Anna (1753–1808)
Helene (1903–1924)
Helene of Bavaria (1834–1890)
Helene of Brunswick-Luneburg (d. 1273)
Helen of Denmark (d. 1233)
Helen of Nassau (1831–1888)
Helen of Schleswig-Holstein (1888–1962)
Helen of Waldeck and Pyrmont (1861–1922)
Helen of Waldeck and Pyrmont (1899–1948)
Helia de Semur (fl. 1020–1046)
Helm, Brigitte (1908–1996)
Helten, Inge (1950—)
Helwig of Prague (fl. 14th c.)
Hempel, Frieda (1885–1955)
Hendel, Henriette (1772–1849)
Hendrix, Brunhilde (1938—)
Henke, Jana (1973—)
Henkel, Andrea (1977—)
Henkel, Manuela (1974—)
Henkel-Redetzky, Heike (1964—)
Henneberger, Barbi (d. 1964)
Hennings, Emmy (1885–1948)
Henrietta Catherine of Nassau (1637–1708)
Henrietta Maria (1626–1651)
Henrietta of Nassau-Weilburg (1780–1857)
Henrietta of Savoy (c. 1630–?)
Hensel, Luise (1798–1876)
Hentschel, Franziska (1970—)
Herber, Maxi (1920—)
Hermine of Reuss (1887–1947)
Hermine of Waldeck and Pyrmont (1827–1910)
Herrad of Hohenberg (c. 1130–1195)
Herrmann, Liselotte (1909–1938)
Herschel, Caroline (1750–1848)
Herschmann, Nicole (1975—)
Hertha of Ysenburg and Budingen (1883–1972)
Herwegh, Emma (1817–1904)
Herz, Henriette (1764–1847)
Hesse, Eva (1936–1970)
Hesse, Fanny Angelina (1850–1934)
Heyking, Elisabeth von (1861–1925)
Heymair, Magdalena (c. 1545–after 1586)
Heymann, Lida (1867–1943)
Hieronymi, Ruth (1947—)
Hilaria (fl. 304)
Hildegarde of Bavaria (c. 840–?)
Hildegarde of Swabia (fl. 1050)
Hildegard of Bingen (1098–1179)
Hildegund (d. 1188)
Hillern, Wilhelmine von (1836–1916)
Hingst, Ariane (1979—)
Hipp, Jutta (1925–2003)
Hirsch, Rachel (1870–1953)
Höch, Hannah (1889–1978)
Hofer, Evelyn (1922—)
Hoff, Magdalene (1940—)
Hoff, Ursula (1909–2005)
Hoffmann, Gertrude (1871–1966)
Hoffmann, Melanie (1974—)
Hohenhausen, Elizabeth (1789–1857)
Hohn, Annette (1966—)
Holdmann, Anni (1900–1960)
Holm, Hanya (1888–1992)
Holmer, Ulrike (1967—)
Holzner, Ulrike
Honecker, Margot (1927—)
Hoppe, Marianne (1909–2002)
Horn, Camilla (1903–1996)
Horneber, Petra (1965—)
Horney, Brigitte (1911–1988)
Horney, Karen (1885–1952)
Hoy, Bettina (1962—)
Hoya, Katherina von (d. around 1470)
Hoyer, Dore (1911–1967)
Hoyers, Anna Ovena (1584–1655)
Hrotsvitha of Gandersheim (c. 935–1001)
Huber, Therese (1764–1829)
Huch, Ricarda (1864–1947)
Huebler, Anna (1885–1976)
Hummel, Berta (1909–1946)
Hustede, Heike (1946—)
Ida of Saxe-Coburg-Meiningen (1794–1852)
Ida of Schaumburg-Lippe (1852–1891)
Ida of Swabia (d. 986)
Idem, Josefa (1964—)
Ihrer, Emma (1857–1911)
Ildico (fl. 453)
Imagi of Luxemburg (c. 1000–1057)
Immerwahr, Clara (1870–1915)
Impekoven, Niddy (1904–2002)
Irene Angela of Byzantium (d. 1208)
Irene of Hesse-Darmstadt (1866–1953)
Irma of Hohenlohe-Langenburg (1902–1986)
Irmengard (c. 800–851)
Irmengard of Oettingen (fl. 14th c.)
Irmentrude (d. 820)
Irmingard of Zelle (c. 1200–1260)
Isabel (1772–1827)
Isabella of Aragon (c. 1300–1330)
Isabella of England (1214–1241)
Isabella of Portugal (1503–1539)
Jacobi, Lotte (1896–1990)
Jagemann, Karoline (1777–1848)
Janowitz, Gundula (1937—)
Japha, Louise (1826–1889)
Jeggle, Elisabeth (1947—)
Jhabvala, Ruth Prawer (1927—)
Joens, Karin (1953—)
Johanna Elizabeth of Baden-Durlach (1651–1680)
Johanna Elizabeth of Holstein-Gottorp (1712–1760)
Johansen, Hanna (1939—)
Jolanthe of Lorraine (d. 1500)
Jonas, Regina (1902–1944)
Jones, Steffi (1972—)
Juchacz, Marie (1879–1956)
Judith of Bavaria (802-843)
Judith of Bavaria (c. 925–987)
Judith of Bavaria (fl. 1120s)
Judith of Bavaria (fl. 1390s–1400)
Judith of Fiuli (fl. 910–925)
Judith of Flanders (1032–1094)
Junge, Traudel (1920–2002)
Jungjohann, Caren (1970—)
Jungmann, Elisabeth (d. 1959)
Junker, Helen (1905—)
Junker, Karin (1940—)
Jutta of Saxony (d. around 1267)
Jutta of Sponheim (d. 1136)
Kahn, Lilly (c. 1898–1978)
Kania-Enke, Karin (1961—)
Karlstadt, Liesl (1892–1960)
Karsch, Anna Luise (1722–1791)
Kaschnitz, Marie Luise (1901–1974)
Katharina von Gebweiler (fl. c. 1340)
Kaufmann, Sylvia-Yvonne (1955—)
Kaun, Elfriede (1914—)
Kauschke, Katrin (1971—)
Keil, Birgit (1944—)
Keller, Natascha (1977—)
Kellner, Rosa (1910—)
Kelly, Petra (1947–1992)
Kemmer, Heike (1962—)
Keppelhoff-Wiechert, Hedwig (1939—)
Kessler, Margot (1948—)
Keun, Irmgard (1905–1982)
Kiehl, Marina (1965—)
Kieler, Laura (1849–1932)
Kielgass, Kerstin (1969—)
Kiermayer, Susanne (1968—)
Kilius, Marika (1943—)
Kinkel, Johanna (1810–1858)
Kinshofer, Christa (1961—)
Kira of Leiningen (b. 1930)
Kirch, Maria Winkelmann (1670–1720)
Kirchgessner, Marianne (1769–1808)
Kirschner, Lola (1854–1934)
Kisabaka, Linda (1969—)
Klamt, Ewa (1950—)
Klarsfeld, Beate (1939—)
Klass, Christa (1951—)
Klecker, Denise (1972—)
Klein, Helga (1931—)
Kleinert, Nadine (1975—)
Klier-Schaller, Johanna (1952—)
Klug, Annette (1969—)
Knab, Ursula (1929–1989)
Knef, Hildegard (1925—)
Knef, Hildegard (1925–2002)

Knuth, Maria (d. 1954)
Koch, Ilse (1906–1967)
Koch, Marianne (1930—)
Koch, Marita (1957—)
Koch, Martina (1959—)
Koehler, Kathe (1913—)
Koenig, Rita
Koeppen, Kerstin (1967—)
Koering, Dorothea (1880–1945)
Kohde-Kilsch, Claudia (1963—)
Kohl, Hannelore (1933–2001)
Köhler-Richter, Emmy (1918—)
Kolb, Annette (1870–1967)
Kollwitz, Käthe (1867–1945)
Kolmar, Gertrud (1894–1943)
Köth, Erika (1925–1989)
Kowalski, Kerstin (1976—)
Kowalski, Manja (1976—)
Kraus, Angelika (1950—)
Kraus-Boelté, Maria (1836–1918)
Krause, Barbara (1959—)
Krause, Christiane (1950—)
Kraushaar, Silke (1970—)
Krauss, Kathe (1906–1970)
Krebs-Brenning, Marie (1851–1900)
Krehl, Constanze Angela (1956—)
Kremnitz, Marie (1852–1916)
Kronauer, Brigitte (1940—)
Kroniger, Annegret (1952—)
Krueger, Katrin (1959—)
Krueger, Luise (1915—)
Krull, Germaine (1897–1985)
Krupp, Bertha (1886–1957)
Kuckhoff, Greta (1902–1981)
Kuehn, Anke (1981—)
Kuenzel, Claudia (1978—)
Kuhnt, Irina (1968—)
Kukuck, Felicitas (1914–2001)
Kumbernuss, Astrid (1970—)
Kunisch, Kornelia (1959—)
Kuntsch, Margaretha Susanna von (1651–1716)
Kupfernagel, Hanka (1964—)
Küppers, Anneliese (1929—)
Kurz, Isolde (1853–1944)
Kwast, Frieda Hodapp (1880–1949)
Lambert, Margaret Bergmann (1914—)
Landgraf, Sigrid (1959—)
Lang, Josephine (1815–1880)
Langbein, Martha (1941—)
Lange, Aloysia (c. 1761–1839)
Lange, Helene (1848–1930)
Langenhagen, Brigitte (1939—)
Langgässer, Elisabeth (1899–1950)
Langmann, Adelheid (d. 1375)
Langner, Ilse (1899–1987)
La Roche, Sophie von (1730–1807)
La Roe, Else K. (1900–1970)
Lask, Berta (1878–1967)
Lasker-Schüler, Else (1869–1945)
Latif, Badri (1977—)
Latzsch, Heike (1973—)
Laurien, Hanna-Renate (1928—)
Lawrence, Frieda (1879–1956)
Le Beau, Luise Adolpha (1850–1927)
Lebrun, Franziska (1756–1791)
Lecavella, Mabilia (fl. 1206)
Lederer, Gretchen (1891–1955)
Le Fort, Gertrud von (1876–1971)
Lehmann, Christa (1922—)
Lehmann, Lilli (1848–1929)
Lehmann, Lotte (1888–1976)
Lehmann, Sonja (1979—)
Leider, Frida (1888–1975)
Leistenschneider, Nicole (1967—)
Leitzel, Lillian (1892–1931)
Lemnitz, Tiana (1897–1994)
Lemp, Rebecca (d. 1590)
Leonhardt, Carolin (1984—)
Lermontova, Julia (1846–1919)
Lewald, Fanny (1811–1889)
Lichnowsky, Mechthilde (1879–1958)
Lindner, Dorte
Lindner, Herta (1920–1943)
Lingnau, Corinna (1960—)
Lingor, Renate (1975—)
Linsenhoff, Ann-Kathrin (1960—)
Linsenhoff, Liselott (1927—)
Lipsius, Marie (1837–1927)
Lisiewska, Anna (1721–1782)
Lisiewska, Rosina (1716–1783)
Litten, Irmgard (1879–1953)
Litwinde (fl. 850)
Loebinger, Lotte (1905–1999)
Lohmar, Leni (1914—)
Long, Tania (1913–1998)
Losch, Claudia (1960—)
Louisa Henrietta of Orange (1627–1667)
Louisa Juliana (1576–1644)
Louise Augusta (1771–1843)
Louise Charlotte of Mecklenburg-Schwerin (1779–1801)
Louise of Baden (1811–1854)
Louise of Baden (1838–1923)
Louise of Hesse-Cassel (1688–1765)
Louise of Hesse-Darmstadt (d. 1830)
Louise of Saxe-Gotha (1756–1808)
Louise of Saxe-Gotha-Altenburg (1800–1831)
Löwenstein, Helga Maria zu (1910–2004)
Lucic, Mirjana (1982—)
Luckner, Gertrud (1900–1995)
Lüders, Marie-Elizabeth (1888–1966)
Ludmilla of Bohemia (fl. 1100s)
Ludovica (1808–1892)
Ludwig, Christa (1924—)
Ludwig, Paula (1900–1974)
Lurz, Dagmar (1959—)
Lutze, Manuela (1974—)
Lux, Amelie (1977—)
Luxemburg, Rosa (1870–1919)
Magdalena (1532–1590)
Magdalena (fl. late 1500s)
Magdalena Sybilla (1587–1659)
Magdalena Sybilla of Holstein-Gottorp (1631–1719)
Magdalene of Brandenburg (1582–1616)
Magdalene of Oldenburg (1585–1657)
Magdalene of Saxony (1507–1534)
Makaryeva, Nadiezhda (1925—)
Mamlok, Ursula (1928—)
Mann, Elisabeth (1918–2002)
Mann, Erika (1905–1969)
Mann, Erika (1950—)
Mannheim, Lucie (1899–1976)
Mara, Gertrud (1749–1833)
Marchesi, Mathilde (1821–1913)
Margaret Beatrice (1872–1954)
Margaret Clementine (1870–1955)
Margaret-Mary of Hungary (c. 1177–?)
Margaret Maultasch (1318–1369)
Margaret of Austria (fl. 1200s)
Margaret of Baden (1932—)
Margaret of Baden (d. 1457)
Margaret of Bavaria (d. 1424)
Margaret of Bavaria (1445–1479)
Margaret of Brabant (d. 1311)
Margaret of Brandenburg (c. 1450–1489)
Margaret of Burgundy (c. 1376–1441)
Margaret of Burgundy (d. 1441)
Margaret of Cleves (fl. early 1400s)
Margaret Theresa of Spain (1651–1673)
Maria Anna of Spain (1606–1646)
Maria Antonia of Austria (1724–1780)
Maria Leopoldina (1776–1848)
Maria Leopoldine (1632–1649)
Maria Louisa of Spain (1743–1792)
Maria of Bavaria (1805–1877)
Maria Teresa of Naples (1772–1807)
Maria Theresa of Austria (1717–1780)
Marie Alexandra of Baden (1902–1944)
Marie Melita of Hohenlohe-Langenburg (1899–1967)
Marie of Austria (1528–1603)
Marie of Brabant (fl. 1250)
Marie of Brandenburg-Kulmbach (1519–1567)
Marie of Swabia (c. 1201–1235)
Maritza, Sari (1910–1987)
Marlitt, Eugenie (1825–1887)
Marozia Crescentii (885–938)
Märten, Lu (1879–1970)
Marwedel, Emma (1818–1893)
Marx, Laura (1845–1911)
Mary (b. 1718)
Mary Adelaide (1833–1897)
Mary of Brabant (c. 1191–c. 1260)
Mary of Hanover (1849–1904)
Matijass, Julia (1973—)
Matilda of Leiningen (b. 1936)
Matilda of Nassau (fl. 1285–1310)
Matilda of Quedlinburg (c. 953–999)
Matilda of Saxony (978–1025)
Matilda of Saxony (c. 892–968)
Mauermayer, Gisela (b. 1913)
May, Gisela (1924—)
Mayer, Emilie (1821–1883)
Mayer, Helene (1910–1953)
Mayer, Maria Goeppert (1906–1972)
Mechtel, Angelika (1943–2000)
Mechtild of Driessen (d. 1160)
Mechtild of Hackeborne (1241–1298)
Mechtild of Magdeburg (c. 1207–c. 1282)
Medici, Anna Maria Luisa de (1667–1743)
Mees, Helga (1937—)
Mehl, Gabriele (1967—)
Mehlig, Anna (1846–1928)
Meinert, Maren (1973—)
Meinhof, Ulrike (1934–1972)
Mendelssohn, Dorothea (1764–1839)
Mendelssohn, Henriette (1768–1831)
Mendelssohn-Hensel, Fanny (1805–1847)
Mensing, Barbara (1960—)
Menter, Sophie (1846–1918)
Mereau-Brentano, Sophie (1770–1806)
Merian, Maria Sybilla (1647–1717)
Merkel, Angela (1954—)
Meyer, Gertrud (1914—)
Meyfarth, Ulrike (1956—)
Meysel, Inge (1910–2004)
Meysenburg, Malwida von (1816–1903)
Micheler, Elisabeth (1966—)
Mickler, Ingrid (1942—)
Miegel, Agnes (1879–1964)
Miller, Susanne (1915—)
Minnert, Sandra (1973—)
Mittermaier, Rosi (1950—)
Mittermayer, Tatjana (1964—)
Mlakar, Pia (1908–2000)
Modersohn-Becker, Paula (1876–1907)
Modesta of Trier (d. about 680)
Mödl, Martha (1912–2001)
Modthryth (fl. 520)
Moholy-Nagy, Sibyl (1903–1971)
Mollenhauer, Paula (1908–1988)
Moosdorf, Johanna (1911–2000)
Morgenstern, Lina B. (1830–1909)
Moser, Christina (1960—)

Moser, Mary (1744–1819)
Mosheim, Grete (1905–1986)
Mozart, Constanze (1762–1842)
Mucke, Manuela (1975—)
Muehe, Lotte (1910–1981)
Mueller, Claudia (1974—)
Mueller, Kerstin (1969—)
Mueller, Martina (1980—)
Mueller, Silke (1978—)
Mueller, Susanne (1972—)
Müller, Clara (1860–1905)
Müller, Emilia Franziska (1951—)
Müller, Renate (1907–1937)
Müller, Rosemarie (1949—)
Münchow, Kirsten (1977—)
Mundt, Klara Müller (1814–1873)
Munk, Kirsten (1598–1658)
Münter, Gabriele (1877–1962)
Nadejda of Bulgaria (1899–1958)
Natalie of Hesse-Darmstadt (1755–1776)
Naubert, Christiane Benedikte (1756–1819)
Neher, Carola (1900–1942)
Neimke, Kathrin (1966—)
Nerius, Steffi (1972—)
Neuber, Caroline (1697–1760)
Neumann, Annett (1970—)
Neumann, Hanna (1914–1971)
Neumann, Theresa (1898–1962)
Neunast, Daniela (1966—)
Ney, Elisabet (1833–1907)
Ney, Elly (1882–1968)
Nico (1938–1988)
Niebler, Angelika (1963—)
Niederkirchner, Käte (1909–1944)
Niedernhuber, Barbara (1974—)
Niehaus, Jutta (1964—)
Niemann, Gunda (1966—)
Niese, Charlotte (1854–1935)
Noddack, Ida (1896–1978)
Noether, Emmy (1882–1935)
Nollen, Maike (1977—)
Noskowiak, Sonya (1900–1975)
Nüsslein-Volhard, Christiane (1942—)
Oberheuser, Herta (1911–1978)
Oda (806–913)
Oda of Bavaria (fl. 890s)
Oda of Germany and North Marck (fl. 900s)
Oda of Lorraine (fl. mid-1000)
Odebrecht, Viola (1983—)
Oelkers-Caragioff, Olga (1887–1969)
Oelschlagel, Charlotte (c. 1899–after 1948)
Olberg, Oda (1872–1955)
Oldenburg, Margaret (1905–1981)
Olga of Russia (1822–1892)
Omilade, Navina (1981—)
Oppelt, Britta (1978—)
Oppenheim, Méret (1913–1985)
Ortrud of Schleswig-Holstein-Sonderburg-Glucksburg (1925—)
Osten, Maria (1908–1942)
Oswalda, Ossi (1897–1948)
Osygus, Simone (1968—)
Ott, Patricia (1960—)
Ottendorfer, Anna Uhl (1815–1884)
Otto, Kristin (1966—)
Otto, Louise (1896—)
Otto, Sylke (1969—)
Otto-Peters, Luise (1819–1895)
Overlach, Helene (1894–1983)
Paalzow, Henriette (1788–1847)
Paasche, Maria (1909–2000)
Pack, Doris (1942—)
Palfi, Marion (1907–1978)
Palmer, Lilli (1914–1986)
Palucca, Gret (1902–1993)
Parlo, Dita (1906–1971)
Pascalina, Sister (1894–1983)
Pauline of Saxe-Weimar (1852–1904)
Pauline of Wurttemberg (1800–1873)
Pauline of Wurttemberg (1810–1856)
Pechstein, Claudia (1972—)
Peters, Kristina (1968—)
Petersen-Kallensee, Marga (1919—)
Petersmann, Cerstin (1964—)
Pfeiffer, Anna Ursula (1813–1863)
Pflug, Monika (1954—)
Pfohl, Cornelia (1971—)
Philippine Charlotte (1716–1801)
Phillipps, Adelaide (1833–1882)
Pielen, Silke (1955—)
Pielke, Christiane (1963—)
Pippig, Uta (1965—)
Pirckheimer, Caritas (1467–1532)
Ploennies, Luise von (1803–1872)
Poehlsen, Paula (1913—)
Poewe, Sarah (1983—)
Pohlers, Conny (1978—)
Poleska, Anne (1980—)
Poley, Viola (1955—)
Pollack, Andrea (1961—)
Porten, Henny (1888–1960)
Portwich, Ramona (1967—)
Posseckel, Elvira (1953—)
Pötzsch, Anett (1961—)
Prinz, Birgit (1977—)
Prokoff, Sandra (1975—)
Pyritz, Dana (1970—)
Quisthoudt-Rowohl, Godelieve (1947—)
Radke, Lina (1903–1983)
Randzio-Plath, Christa (1940—)
Rasp, Renate (1935—)
Raubal, Geli (c. 1908–1931)
Rebay, Hilla (1890–1967)
Recke, Elisa von der (1754–1833)
Reich, Lilly (1885–1947)
Reichardt, Louise (1779–1826)
Reiche, Maria (1903–1998)
Reichert, Ossi
Reimer, Daniela (1982—)
Reineck, Heidemarie (1952—)
Reinig, Christa (1926—)
Reiniger, Lotte (1899–1981)
Reinshagen, Gerlind (1926—)
Reitsch, Hanna (1912–1979)
Rendschmidt, Elsa (1886–1969)
Renger, Annemarie (1919—)
Renk, Silke (1967—)
Renoth, Heidi Maria (1978—)
Reschke, Karin (1940—)
Rethberg, Elisabeth (1894–1976)
Reuter, Gabriele (1859–1941)
Reventlow, Franziska von (1871–1918)
Rey, Margret (1906–1996)
Richensia of Nordheim (1095–1141)
Richesa of Lorraine (d. 1067)
Richilde (d. 984)
Richter, Annegret (1950—)
Richter, Emma (1888–1956)
Richter, Ulrike (1959—)
Riefenstahl, Leni (1902–2003)
Rinne, Fanny (1980—)
Rinser, Luise (1911–2002)
Robinson, Therese Albertine Louise von Jakob (1797–1870)
Robscheit-Robbins, Frieda (1888–1973)
Rodewald, Marion (1976—)
Rohländer, Uta (1969—)
Rökk, Marika (1913–2004)
Romanov, Catherine (1827–1894)
Rosa (1906–1983)
Rosa Manus (1881–1942)
Rosenberg, Grete (1896–1979)
Rosendahl, Heidemarie (1947—)
Rossner, Petra (1966—)
Roth, Hella (1963—)
Roth-Behrendt, Dagmar (1953—)
Rothe, Mechtild (1947—)
Rothenberger, Anneliese (1924—)
Rothenburger-Luding, Christa (1959—)
Rothilde (fl. 840)
Rottenberg, Silke (1972—)
Rücker, Anja (1972—)
Rueckes, Anette (1951—)
Rühle, Heide (1948—)
Rund, Cathleen (1977—)
Rutschow, Katrin (1975—)
Sabine of Bavaria (1492–1564)
Saburova, Irina (1907–1979)
Sachenbacher, Evi (1980—)
Sachs, Nelly (1891–1970)
Saenger von Mossau, Renata (1680–1749)
Sagan, Leontine (1889–1974)
Sakharoff, Clotilde (1892–1974)
Salomon, Alice (1872–1948)
Salomon, Charlotte (1917–1943)
Salzgeber, Ulla (1958—)
Sancha of Provence (c. 1225–1261)
Sander, Helke (1937—)
Sander, Jil (1943—)
Sander, Maria (1924—)
Sanders-Brahms, Helma (1940—)
Sarah of Görlitz (fl. 1388)
Scharrer, Berta (1906–1995)
Schaumann, Ruth (1899–1975)
Schenk, Franziska (1974—)
Scherberger-Weiss, Rosemarie (1935—)
Schiffer, Claudia (1970—)
Schirmacher, Käthe (1859–1930)
Schlegel-Schelling, Caroline (1763–1809)
Schleicher, Ursula (1933—)
Schley, Gabriela (1964—)
Schlicht, Svenja (1967—)
Schlösinger, Rose (1907–1943)
Schlueter-Schmidt, Karin (1937—)
Schmid, Adelheid (1938—)
Schmid, Susanne (1960—)
Schmidt, Auguste (1833–1902)
Schmidt, Helene (1906–1985)
Schmidt, Sybille (1967—)
Schmitt, Julie (b. 1913)
Schmitt, Sandra (c. 1982–2000)
Schmitz, Ingeborg (1922—)
Schmuck, Christa
Schneider, Magda (1909–1996)
Schoenberg, Bessie (1906–1997)
Scholl, Inge (c. 1917–1998)
Scholl, Sophie (1921–1943)
Scholtz-Klink, Gertrud (1902—)
Scholz, Anke (1978—)
Schöne, Andrea Mitscherlich (1961—)
Schopenhauer, Adele (1797–1849)
Schopenhauer, Johanna (1766–1838)
Schrader, Catharina Geertuida (1656–1745)
Schrader, Hilde (1910–1966)
Schramm, Bernardina Adriana (1900–1987)
Schröder-Devrient, Wilhelmine (1804–1860)
Schroeder, Ilka (1978—)
Schroeder, Louise (1887–1957)
Schroedter, Elisabeth (1959—)
Schuck, Anett (1970—)
Schulter-Mattler, Heike (1958—)
Schulze-Boysen, Libertas (1913–1942)
Schumacher, Elisabeth (1904–1942)
Schumacher, Sandra (1966—)
Schumann, Elisabeth (1885–1952)
Schurz, Margarethe Meyer (1833–1876)
Schuster, Susanne (1963—)

Schuttpelz, Barbara (1956—)
Schwarz, Sybilla (1621–1638)
Schwarzenbach, Annemarie (1908–1942)
Schwarzhaupt, Elisabeth (1901–1986)
Schwarzkopf, Elisabeth (1915—)
Schwerin, Jeanette (1852–1899)
Schwerzmann, Ingeburg (1967—)
Seefried, Irmgard (1919–1988)
Seghers, Anna (1900–1983)
Seick, Karin (1961—)
Seidel, Ina (1885–1974)
Seizinger, Katja (1972—)
Selbert, Elisabeth (1896–1986)
Sender, Toni (1888–1964)
Seyfert, Gabriele (c. 1948—)
Sforza, Bianca Maria (1472–1510)
Sibylle Elizabeth of Wurttemberg (1584–1606)
Sibylle of Anhalt (1564–1614)
Sibylle of Brunswick-Luneburg (1584–1652)
Siebold, Charlotte Heidenreich von (1788–1859)
Siebold, Josepha von (1771–1849)
Siech, Birte (1967—)
Siems, Margarethe (1879–1952)
Sieveking, Amalie (1794–1859)
Simons de Ridder, Alexandra (1963—)
Sintenis, Renée (1888–1965)
Sohnemann, Kate (1913—)
Sommer, Renate (1958—)
Sontag, Henriette (c. 1803–1854)
Sophia (c. 525–after 600)
Sophia (fl. 1211)
Sophia (fl. 1500s)
Sophia (1630–1714)
Sophia Carlotte (1673–1725)
Sophia Dorothea of Brandenburg (1736–1798)
Sophia Dorothea of Brunswick-Celle (1666–1726)
Sophia Dorothea of Brunswick-Lüneburg-Hanover (1687–1757)
Sophia Dorothea of Wurttemberg (1759–1828)
Sophia of Bayreuth (1700–1770)
Sophia of Gandersheim (c. 975–1039)
Sophia of Mecklenburg (1508–1541)
Sophia of Mecklenburg (1758–1794)
Sophia of Nassau (1824–1897)
Sophia of Nassau (1836–1913)
Sophia of Sweden (1801–186 [14] 5)
Sophia of Thuringia (1224–1284)
Sophia of Wurttemberg (1818 1877)
Sophia of Zahringen (fl. 12th c.)
Sophie Amalie of Brunswick-Lüneberg (1628–1685)
Sophie Charlotte of Oldenburg (1879–1964)
Sophie Louise of Mecklenburg (1685–1735)
Sophie of Brandenburg (1568–1622)
Sophie of Holstein-Gottorp (1569–1634)
Sophie of Hungary (d. 1095)
Sophie of Nassau (1902–1941)
Sophie Valdemarsdottir (d. 1241)
Sorma, Agnes (1862–1927)
Sperber, Sylvia (1965—)
Sperling, Hilde (1908–1981)
Spies, Daisy (1905–2000)
Spira, Camilla (1906–1997)
Spira, Steffie (1908–1995)
Spitz, Sabine (1971—)
Sponer, Hertha (1895–1968)
Stade, Richardis von (d. 1152)
Stauffenberg, Litta von (c. 1905–1945)
Stauner, Gabriele (1948—)
Stecher, Renate (1950—)
Stegemann, Kerstin (1977—)
Steiff, Margarete (1847–1909)
Stein, Charlotte von (1742–1827)
Stein, Edith (1891–1942)
Steinbach, Angela (1955—)
Steinwachs, Ginka (1942—)
Stephanie de Beauharnais (1789–1860)
Stern, Catherine Brieger (1894–1973)
Steuer, Anni (b. 1913)
Stiefl, Regina (1966—)
Stindt, Hermine (1888–1974)
Stöbe, Ilse (1911–1942)
Stockbauer, Hannah (1982—)
Stockfleth, Maria Katharina (c. 1633–1692)
Stoecker, Helene (1869–1943)
Strauch, Annegret (1968—)
Strauss und Torney, Lulu von (1873–1956)
Streich, Rita (1920–1987)
Stritt, Marie (1856–1928)
Sucher, Rosa (1847–1927)
Sussiek, Christine (1960—)
Süssmuth, Rita (1937—)
Sybilla of Brandenburg (fl. 1500)
Sybilla of Cleves (1514–1554)
Sybilla of Saxe-Coburg-Gotha (1908–1972)
Taglioni, Marie (1833–1891)
Tarnow, Fanny (1779–1862)
Taro, Gerda (1910–1937)
Taschau, Hannelies (1937—)
Tergit, Gabrielle (1894–1982)
Teske, Charlotte (1949—)
Tetberga (fl. 9th c.)
Theato, Diemut R. (1937—)
Theodelinde (1814–1857)
Theodora of Rome (c. 875–c. 925)
Theodora the Younger (c. 900–c. 950)
Theodorescu, Monica (1963—)
Theophano of Byzantium (c. 955–991)
Theresa (1767–1827)
Theresa of Saxe-Altenburg (1836–1914)
Theresa of Saxony (1792–1854)
Therese of Nassau (1815–1871)
Theuerkauff-Vorbrich, Gudrun (1937—)
Thielemann, Ursula (1958—)
Thieme, Jana (1970—)
Thiess, Ursula (1924—)
Thimm-Finger, Ute (1958—)
Thomaschinski, Simone (1970—)
Thost, Nicola (1977—)
Tietjens, Therese (1831–1877)
Toselli, Louisa (1870–1947)
Traurig, Christine (1957—)
Tschechowa, Olga (1897–1980)
Tussaud, Marie (1761–1850)
Uca, Feleknas (1976—)
Ulfhild of Denmark (d. before 1070)
Unzer, Johanne Charlotte (1725–1782)
Up, Ari (1962—)
Uphoff, Nicole (1967—)
Urselmann, Wiltrud (1942—)
Ursinus, Sophie (1760–1836)
Ursula of Brandenburg (1488–1510)
Ustrowski, Betina (1976—)
Valli, Valli (1882–1927)
Van Almsick, Franziska (1978—)
Vandenhoeck, Anna (1709–1787)
Varnhagen, Rahel (1771–1833)
Vera Constantinovna (1854–1912)
Verne, Kaaren (1918–1967)
Victoria Adelaide (1840–1901)
Victoria Adelaide of Schleswig-Holstein (1885–1970)
Victoria Louise (1892–1980)
Victoria Melita of Saxe-Coburg (1876–1936)
Victoria of Baden (1862–1930)
Victoria of Coburg (1786–1861)
Victoria of Hesse-Darmstadt (1863–1950)
Victoria of Mecklenburg-Strelitz (1878–1948)
Victoria of Saxe-Coburg (1822–1857)
Viebig, Clara (1860–1952)
Viehoff, Valerie (1976—)
Villinger, Hermine (1849–1917)
Voelker, Sabine (1973—)
Voelkner, Iris (1960—)
Voigt, Franka (1963—)
Voigt-Diederichs, Helene (1875–1961)
Völker, Sandra (1974—)
von Aroldingen, Karin (1941—)
Von Ertmann, Dorothea (1781–1849)
von Harbou, Thea (1888–1954)
von Moltke, Freya (b. 1911)
von Nagel, Ida (1917–1971)
Von Nagy, Käthe (1909–1973)
von Richthofen, Else (1874–1973)
Von Seck-Nothnagel, Anke (1966—)
Von Trotta, Margarethe (1942—)
Voznesenskaya, Julia (1940—)
Wagner, Cosima (1837–1930)
Wagner, Friedelind (1918–1991)
Wagner, Johanna (1826–1894)
Wagner, Katrin (1977—)
Wagner, Minna (c. 1800–1866)
Wagner, Sandra (1969—)
Wagner-Stange, Ute (1966—)
Waldrada (fl. 9th c.)
Waleska, Peggy (1980—)
Wallenda, Helen (1910–1996)
Wallmann, Margarethe (1901–1992)
Walter, Annika (1975—)
Walter, Louisa (1978—)
Walter-Martin, Steffi (1962—)
Warnicke, Heike (1966—)
Watteville, Benigna von (1725–1789)
Weber, Christiane (1962—)
Weber, Helene (1881–1962)
Weber, Jutta (1954—)
Weber, Regina (1963—)
Weber-Koszto, Monika (1966—)
Wedemeyer, Maria von (c. 1924–1977)
Wehr-Hásler, Sábine (1967—)
Weiermann-Lietz, Andrea (1958—)
Weigel, Helene (1900–1971)
Weiler, Barbara (1946—)
Weiss, Bianca (1968—)
Wentscher, Dora (1883–1964)
Wenzel, Hanni (1951—)
Wenzel-Perillo, Brigitta (1949—)
Werner, Ilse (1918—)
Werner, Marianne (1924—)
Werremeier, Stefani (1968—)
Werth, Isabell (1969—)
Wessel, Helene (1898–1969)
Wessel-Kirchels, Ute (1953—)
Westermann, Liesel (1944—)
Weygand, Hannelore (1924—)
Wieck, Dorothea (1908–1986)
Wiegmann, Bettina (1971—)
Wigman, Mary (1886–1973)
Wild, Anke (1967—)
Wilden, Rita (1947—)
Wildermuth, Ottilie (1817–1877)
Wilhelm, Anja (1968—)
Wilhelm, Kati (1976—)
Wilhelmina (1709–1758)
Wilhelmina of Prussia (1751–1820)
Wilhelmine (1650–1706)
Wilhelmine (1747–1820)
Wilhelmine (1808–1891)
Wimbersky, Petra (1982—)
Winsloe, Christa (1888–1944)
Winter, Liane (1942—)

Witt, Katarina (1965—)
Wobeser, Caroline von (1769–1807)
Wöckel-Eckert, Bärbel (1955—)
Woetzel, Mandy (1973—)
Wohmann, Gabriele (1932—)
Wolf, Christa (1929—)
Wolff, Helen (1906–1994)
Wolff, Victoria (1903–1992)
Wollerin, Cecilie (d. 1341)
Wollschlaeger, Susanne (1967—)
Wolzogen, Karoline von (1763–1847)
Woolliams, Anne (1926–1999)
Wörishöffer, Sophie (1838–1890)
Wulfhild
Wunderlich, Frieda (1884–1965)
Wunderlich, Magdalena (1952—)
Wunderlich, Pia (1975—)
Wunderlich, Tina (1977—)
Wyludda, Ilke (1969—)
Yolande of Brienne (1212–1228)
Yva (1900–1942)
Zaczkiewicz, Claudia (1962—)
Zakrzewska, Marie (1829–1902)
Zange, Gabi Schönbrunn
Zaunemann, Sidonia Hedwig (1714–1740)
Zeidler, Judith (1968—)
Zeidler, Susanna Elisabeth (1657–1706)
Zell, Katharina Schütz (c. 1497–1562)
Zeller, Eva (1923—)
Zellner, Martina (1974—)
Zenz, Therese (1932—)
Zetkin, Clara (1857–1933)
Ziegler, Christiane Mariane von (1695–1760)
Zillman, Bertha (d. 1893)
Zimmermann, Agnes (1847–1925)
Zimmermann, Gerda (1927—)
Zimmermann-Weber, Annemarie (1940—)
Zindler, Petra (1966—)
Zinner, Hedda (1902–1990)
Zissener, Sabine (1970—)
Zitz, Kathinka (1801–1877)
Zorina, Vera (1917–2003)
Zscherpe, Iris (1967—)
Zürn, Unica (1916–1970)
Zwehl, Julia (1976—)

GERMANY, EAST

German Democratic Republic in northern central Europe
Created after partition of Germany (1945)
Allied with U.S.S.R. and established as Communist state (1949)
Reintegrated with West Germany (1989)

Abel, Irene (1953—)
Ackermann, Rosemarie (1952—)
Ahrenholz, Brigitte (1952—)
Albrecht, Sylvia (1962—)
Anding, Carola (1960—)
Anke, Hannelore (1957—)
Auerswald, Ingrid (1957—)
Badorek, Gabriele (1952—)
Bahmann, Angelika (1952—)
Baier, Anke (1972—)
Balthasar, Ramona (1964—)
Balzer, Karin (1938—)
Bauerschmidt, Maritta (1950—)
Becker, Sabine (1959—)
Behmer-Vater, Anke (1961—)
Behrendt, Kerstin (1967—)
Behrendt-Hampe, Jutta (1960—)
Beier, Roswitha (1956—)
Bischof, Martina (1957—)
Bodendorf, Carla (1953—)
Boesler, Martina (1957—)
Boesler, Petra (1955—)
Boom, Christel (1927–2004)
Borchmann, Anke (1954—)
Börner, Jacqueline (1965—)
Braun, Johanna (1929—)
Breuer, Grit (1972—)
Brüning, Elfriede (1910—)
Buhr-Weigelt, Liane (1956—)
Bullin, Katharina (1959—)
Burosch, Hannelore (1947—)
Busch, Sabine (1962—)
Claus, Hildrun (1939—)
Czekalla, Barbara (1951—)
Dahne, Heike (1961—)
Dahne, Sabine (1950—)
Debertshäuser, Monika
Diers, Ines (1963—)
Doberschuetz-Mey, Gerlinde (1964—)
Dombeck, Carola (1960—)
Donath, Ursula (1931—)
Dörre, Katrin (1961—)
Ebert, Henrietta (1954—)
Ehrhardt, Anneliese (1950—)
Eife, Andrea (1956—)
Emmelmann-Siemon, Kirsten (1961—)
Ender, Kornelia (1958–)
Enderlein, Ortrun (1943–)
Engel-Kramer, Ingrid (1943—)
Errath, Christine (1956—)
Escher, Gitta (1957—)
Fahnrich, Gabriele (1968—)
Felke, Petra (1959—)
Fetzer, Brigitte (1956—)
Fiedler, Ellen (1958—)
Fischer, Birgit (1962—)
Forster-Pieloth, Kerstin (1965—)
Friedrich, Heike (1970—)
Froehlich, Silvia (1959—)
Fuchs, Ruth (1946—)
Fuhrmann, Barbel (1940—)
Gabriel-Koether, Rosemarie (1956—)
Gansky-Sachse, Diana (1963—)
Garisch-Culmberger, Renate (1939—)
Geisler, Ilse
Geissler, Ines (1963—)
Genauss, Carsta (1959—)
Gerschau, Kerstin (1958—)
Gertrude of Sulzbach (d. 1146)
Geweniger, Ute (1964—)
Gnauck, Maxi (1964—)
Goebel, Barbara (1943—)
Göhr, Marlies (1958—)
Goretzki, Viola (1956—)
Grabowski, Petra (1952—)
Grunert, Martina (1949—)
Gummel-Helmboldt, Margitte (1941—)
Guthke, Karin (1956—)
Haacker, Kathrin (1967—)
Haase, Helga (1934–1989)
Hagen, Nina (1955—)
Heim, Andrea (1961—)
Heinecke, Birgit (1957—)
Heinrich, Christina (1949—)
Hellmann, Angelika (1954—)
Hellmann-Opitz, Martina (1960—)
Hempel, Claudia (1958—)
Herbst, Christine (1957—)
Hess, Sabine (1958—)
Hindorff, Silvia (1961—)
Hinzmann, Gabriele (1947—)
Hoffmeister, Gunhild (1944—)
Hommola, Ute (1952—)
Honecker, Margot (1927—)
Hörner, Silke (1965—)
Hornig-Miseler, Carola (1962—)
Huelsenbeck, Sarina (1962—)
Hunger, Daniela (1972—)
Jahl, Evelin (1956—)
Jahn, Sabine (1953—)
Janicke, Marina (1954—)
Janz, Karen (1952—)
Jaschke, Martina (1960—)
Jentsch, Martina (1968—)
John-Paetz-Moebius, Sabine (1957—)
Kaesling, Dagmar (1947—)
Kallies, Monika (1956—)
Kania-Enke, Karin (1961—)
Kapheim, Ramona (1958—)
Kaschube, Ilse (1953—)
Kaufer, Evelyn (1953—)
Kermer, Romy (1956—)
Kersten, Dagmar (1970—)
Kirsch, Sarah (1935—)
Kirst, Jutta (1954—)
Kische, Marion (1958—)
Klapezynski, Ulrike (1953—)
Kleber, Ina (1964—)
Klier, Cornelia (1957—)
Klier-Schaller, Johanna (1952—)
Klotz, Ulrike (1970—)
Kluge, Anja (1964—)
Knacke, Christiane (1962—)
Koch, Beate (1967—)
Koch, Marita (1957—)
Koehler, Christa (1951—)
Koehler, Gisela (1931—)
Koepke-Knetsch, Christiane (1956—)
Königsdorf, Helga (1938—)
Koster, Barbel (1957—)
Kostrzewa, Ute (1961—)
Kraker, Steffi (1960—)
Krause, Roswitha (1949—)
Krause, Sigrun
Kretzschmar, Waltraud (1948—)
Krug, Barbara (1956—)
Kuehne, Rita (1947—)
Kuehn-Lohs, Gabriele (1957—)
Kueper, Ursula (1937—)
Kurth, Andrea (1957—)
Lange, Marita (1943—)
Laser, Christine (1951—)
Lathan-Brehmer, Christina (1958—)
Lau, Jutta (1955—)
Lehmann, Heike (1962—)
Lehmann, Helma (1953—)
Lindner, Helga (1951—)
Linse, Cornelia (1959—)
Loewe, Gabriele (1958—)
Lotz, Ingrid (1934—)
Luettge, Johanna (1936—)
Mager, Manuela (1962—)
Maletzki, Doris (1952—)
Maron, Monika (1941—)
Matz, Evelyn (1955—)
Meissner, Katrin (1973—)
Metschuck, Caren (1963—)
Metz, Karin (1956—)
Michaelis, Liane (1953—)
Moehring, Anke (1969—)
Moeller-Gladisch, Silke (1964—)
Morgner, Irmtraud (1933–1990)
Mueller, Irina (1951—)
Mueller, Petra (1965—)
Mueller, Romy (1958—)
Müller, Anna-Maria (1949—)
Mummhardt, Christine (1951—)
Mundt, Kristina (1966—)
Neisser, Kersten (1956—)
Neubauer-Ruebsam, Dagmar (1962—)
Noack, Angelika (1952—)
Noack, Marianne (1951—)
Nord, Kathleen (1965—)
Nothnagel, Anke (1966—)

Geographic Index

Novak, Helga (1935—)
Oberhoffner, Ute
Otto, Kristin (1966—)
Paskuy, Eva (1948—)
Pechstein, Heidi (1944—)
Peter, Birgit (1964—)
Petzold, Barbara (1955—)
Ploch, Jutta (1960—)
Polit, Cornelia (1963—)
Pollack, Andrea (1961—)
Pollak, Burglinde (1951—)
Pötzsch, Anett (1961—)
Priemer, Petra (1961—)
Proeber, Martina (1963—)
Pueschel, Karin (1958—)
Pufe, Margitta (1952—)
Radochla, Birgit (1945—)
Reimann, Brigitte (1933–1973)
Reinhardt, Sybille (1957—)
Reinisch, Rica (1965—)
Rensch, Katharina (1964—)
Richter, Ilona (1953—)
Richter, Kristina (1946—)
Richter, Ulrike (1959—)
Riedel, Petra (1964—)
Roether, Sabine (1957—)
Roffeis, Karla (1958—)
Rohde, Brigitte (1954—)
Rose, Sylvia (1962—)
Rost, Christina (1952—)
Rostock, Marlies
Rothenburger-Luding, Christa (1959—)
Rudolph, Renate (1949—)
Rühroid, Ute
Runge, Erika (1939—)
Saalfeld, Romy (1960—)
Sandig, Marita (1958—)
Scheiblich, Christine (1954—)
Schieferdecker, Bettina (1968—)
Schmeisser, Richarda (1954—)
Schmidt, Carmela (1962—)
Schmidt, Cerstin
Schmidt, Ingrid (1945—)
Schmidt, Magdalena (1949—)
Schmidt, Martina (1960—)
Schmidt, Veronika
Schmitt, Christine (1953—)
Schmuck, Uta (1949—)
Schneider, Petra (1963—)
Schoenrock, Sybille (1964—)
Schöne, Andrea Mitscherlich (1961—)
Schramm, Beate (1966—)
Schroer-Lehmann, Beatrix (1963—)
Schroeter, Martina (1960—)
Schubert, Helga (1940—)
Schultz, Annette (1957—)
Schulze, Sabina (1972—)
Schumann, Margit (1952—)
Schütz, Birgit (1958—)
Schütz, Helga (1937—)
Schwede, Bianka (1953—)
Sehmisch, Elke (1955—)
Seidler, Helga (1949—)
Seyfert, Gabriele (c. 1948—)
Siebert, Gloria (1964—)
Siefert, Silvia (1953—)
Siegl, Siegrun (1954—)
Singer, Heike (1964—)
Sirch, Cornelia (1966—)
Slupianek, Ilona (1956—)
Sollmann, Melitta
Sorgers, Jana (1967—)
Starke, Ute (1939—)
Stecher, Renate (1950—)
Steffin, Christel (1940—)
Steinbach, Sabine (1952—)
Steindorf, Ute (1957—)
Stellmach, Manuela (1970—)
Strauss, Astrid (1968—)
Streidt, Ellen (1952—)
Struppert, Barbel (1950—)
Stubnick, Christa (1933—)
Sube, Karola (1964—)
Suess, Birgit (1962—)
Tauber, Ulrike (1958—)
ten Elsen, Eva-Maria (1937—)
Tetzner, Gerti (1936—)
Thuemer, Petra (1961—)
Thuemmler-Pawlak, Doerte (1971—)
Tietz, Marion (1952—)
Todten, Jaqueline (1954—)
Treiber, Birgit (1960—)
Uhlig, Petra (1954—)
Vogel, Renate (1955—)
Voigt, Angela (1951—)
Voss, Christina (1952—)
Wachtel, Christine (1965—)
Walter, Martina (1963—)
Walter-Martin, Steffi
Wartenberg, Christiane (1956—)
Wegner, Gudrun (1955—)
Weigang, Birte (1968—)
Weiss, Gisela (1943—)
Wenzel, Kirsten (1961—)
Westendorf, Anke (1954—)
Westphal, Heidi (1959—)
Wetzko, Gabriele (1954—)
Wild, Ute (1965—)
Wilke, Marina (1958—)
Witt, Katarina (1965—)
Wöckel-Eckert, Bärbel (1955—)
Wodars, Sigrun (1965—)
Wujak, Brigitte (1955—)
Wunderlich, Claudia (1956—)
Zange, Gabi Schönbrunn
Zange-Schönbrunn, Gabi (1961—)
Zehrt, Monika (1952—)
Zimmermann, Kathrin (1966—)
Zinn, Elfi (1953—)
Zirzow, Carola (1954—)
Zobelt, Roswietha (1954—)
Zober, Hannelore (1946—)
Zuchold, Erika (1947—)

GHANA

Formerly Ashanti Kingdom
Claimed by Britain (19th c.)
Colonized as British Gold Coast (20th c.)
Became Ghana (1957)

Afua Koba (fl. 1834–1884)
Aidoo, Ama Ata (1942—)
Andam, Aba A. Bentil (c. 1960—)
Jiagge, Annie (1918–1996)
Mugabe, Sally (1932–1992)
Nkrumah, Fathia (c. 1931—)
Ocloo, Esther (1919–2002)
Pokou (c. 1700–c. 1760)
Sutherland, Efua (1924–1996)
Yaa Akyaa (c. 1837–c. 1921)
Yaa Asantewaa (c. 1850–1921)

GIBRALTAR

Reid, Maria (1895–1979)
Wilson, Helen Ann (1793/94–1871)

GLOUCESTER

County borough of Gloucestershire in southwestern central England
See England.

GOTHA

City in Erfurt district of eastern Germany
Received charter (1189)
Residence of dukes of Saxony-Gotha (17th–19th c.)
Residence of dukes of Saxe-Coburg-Gotha (19th–20th c.)
See Germany.

GOTTORP

Castle in Schleswig-Holstein in western Germany
Gave its name to Holstein-Gottorp line of Oldenburg family (16th c.)
Residence of dukes of Schleswig (13th c.)
See Germany.

GRASSE

Commune in Alpes-Maritimes department of southeastern France
See France.

GREAT BRITAIN, UNITED KINGDOM OF

Kingdom in western Europe
See England.
See Ireland, Northern.
See Scotland.
See Wales.

GREECE

Republic in southern Europe
Ancient Hellas divided into independent kingdoms of Thrace, Macedonia, Epirus, Thessaly, and Peloponnesus (c. 1500–1000 BCE)
Southern Greece comprised provinces or states, e.g., Attica, Boeotia, Phocis, Aetolia, Achaea, Corinth, Elis, Arcadia, Laconia, and Messenia (c. 750–550 BCE)
Athenian empire developed (5th c. BCE)
Greek states became dependent upon Macedon (4th c. BCE)
Gradual Roman conquests set up provinces of Epirus, Achaea, and Macedonia (c. 1st c. BCE)
Became part of Byzantine Empire until Constantinople captured (1204)
Returned to Byzantine Empire until its fall (1453)
Became part of Ottoman Empire until conquered by Turks (1456)
Achieved independence from Turkey and established modern Greek kingdom (1821–1829)
Became a republic (1924)
Restored monarchy (1935)
Invaded by Italy (1940)
Conquered by Germany (1941)
Abolished monarchy (1974)

Aesara of Lucania (fl. 400s–300s BCE)
Agariste (fl. 515 BCE–490 BCE)
Agnodice (fl. 4th c. BCE)
Aindili, Eirini (1983—)
Ainianos, Aganice (1838–1892)
Aldredge, Theoni V. (1932—)
Alexandra (1921–1993)
Alexandra Oldenburg (1870–1891)
Alexiou, Elli (1894–1988)
Aliberty, Soteria (1847–1929)
Alice of Battenberg (1885–1969)
Amalie (1818–1875)
Anagnostaki, Loula (1940—)
Anastasia (d. about 860)
Angelopoulos-Daskalaki, Gianna (1955—)
Anghelaki-Rooke, Katerina (1939—)
Anna Comnena (1083–1153/55)
Anna Paleologina (d. 1340)
Anna Paleologina-Cantacuzene (fl. 1270–1313)
Anne-Marie Oldenburg (1946—)
Antonakakis, Suzana (1935—)
Anyte of Tegea (fl. 3rd c. BCE)
Apostoloy, Electra (1911–1944)
Arete of Cyrene (fl. 4th c. BCE)

Argiriadou, Chryssoula (1901–1998)
Aristarete
Asclepignia (c. 375–?)
Asilian, Dimitra (1972—)
Aspasia of Miletus (c. 464 BCE–c. 420 BCE)
Aspasia the Younger (fl. 415–370 BCE)
Axioti, Melpo (1906–1973)
Bachauer, Gina (1913–1976)
Bakogianni, Niki (1968—)
Bekatorou, Sofia (1977—)
Benizelos, Philothey (fl. 1650)
Bonaparte, Marie (1882–1962)
Bouboulina, Laskarina (1771–1825)
Calypso (fl. c. 200 BCE)
Charisse, Calliope (c. 1880–1946)
Chatziioannou, Ioanna (1973—)
Christodoulou, Evangelia
Chryssa (1933—)
Cleobulina of Rhodes (fl. 570 BCE)
Corinna (fl. 5th or 3rd c. BCE)
Cynisca (fl. 396–392 BCE)
Delta, Penelope (1871–1941)
Devetzi, Hrysopiyi (1975—)
Diotima of Mantinea (fl. 400s BCE)
Dracopoulou, Theony (1883–1968)
Elisabeth (1894–1956)
Elizabeth Oldenburg (1904–1955)
Ellinaki, Georgia (1974—)
Erinna (fl. 7th c. BCE)
Eriphanis
Eskenazi, Roza (c. 1900–1980)
Fleming, Amalia (1912–1986)
Françoise of Guise (1902–1953)
Fredericka (1917–1981)
Gatehouse, Eleanor Wright (1886–1973)
Gattilusi, Caterina (fl. 1440)
Gattilusi, Eugenia (fl. late 1390s)
Georgatou, Maria (c. 1983—)
Goulandris, Niki (1925—)
Gritsi-Milliex, Tatiana (1920—)
Halkia, Fani (1979—)
Hatzimichali, Angeliki (1895–1956)
Hedyle (fl. 3rd century BCE)
Helena (fl. after 333 BCE)
Helen of Greece (1896–1982)
Henderson, Mary (1919–2004)
Herophile
Hill, Frances Mulligan (1799–1884)
Hipparchia (fl. 300s BCE)
Iaia (fl. c. 100 BCE)
Iordanidou, Maria (1897–1989)
Irene (fl. 200 BCE?)
Irene (fl. 1310)
Irene (1904–1974)
Irene (1942—)
Issaia, Nana (1934—)
Ivanova, Olimpiada (1970—)
Kairi, Evanthia (1797–1866)
Karagianni, Eftychia (1973—)
Karamanou, Anna (1947—)
Karatza, Rallou (1778–1830)
Karyami, Zacharoula (1983—)
Kazantzaki, Eleni (1903–2004)
Kazantzaki, Galateia (1886–1962)
Kehajia, Kalliopi (1839–1905)
Kelesidou, Anastasia (1972—)
Kotopoúli, Maríka (1887–1954)
Kozompoli, Stavroula (1974—)
Kratsa-Tsagaropoulou, Rodi (1953—)
Lais (fl. 1st c. BCE)
Lais (fl. 385 BCE)
Lais (fl. 425 BCE)
Lara, Georgia (1980—)
Laskaridou, Aikaterini (1842–1916)
Leontias, Sappho (1832–1900)
Leontium (fl. 300–250 BCE)
Liberáki, Margaríta (1919—)
Liosi, Kyriaki (1979—)
Macurdy, Grace Harriet (1866–1946)
Mageras, Georgia Lathouris (1867–1950)
Malliori, Minerva Melpomeni (1952—)
Manjani, Miréla (1976—)
Manos, Aspasia (1896–1972)
Marie (1876–1940)
Marietta (fl. 1430s)
Marina of Greece (1906–1968)
Mavrogenous, Manto (d. 1848)
Mavrokordatou, Alexandra (1605–1684)
Megalostrata (fl. 6 BCE)
Melidoni, Aniopi (1977—)
Melissa (fl. around 3 BCE)
Melissanthi (c. 1907–c. 1991)
Melpomene (fl. 1896)
Mercouri, Melina (1923–1994)
Messene (fl. early 12th c. BCE)
Moschine (fl. 4 BCE)
Mouskouri, Nana (1934—)
Moutza-Martinengou, Elisavet (1801–1832)
Mylonaki, Anthoula (1984—)
Myrtis (fl. early 5th c. BCE)
Mystakidou, Elisavet (1977—)
Nákou, Lilika (1903–1989)
Nelly (1899–1998)
Nicaea (fl. 300 BCE)
Nicarete of Megara (fl. 300 BCE)
Nicesipolis (d. around 345 BCE)
Nossis of Locri (fl. 300 BCE)
Oikonomopoulou, Aikaterini (1978—)
Oldenburg, Cecily (1911–1937)
Oldenburg, Margaret (1905–1981)
Olga Constantinovna (1851–1926)
Olga Oldenburg (1903–1981)
Olympias (c. 371–316 BCE)
Olympias (fl. 1st c.)
Onassis, Christina (1950–1988)
Palli, Angelica (1798–1875)
Pamphila (fl. 1st c.)
Panagiotatou, Angeliki (1878–1954)
Pantazi, Chariklcia (1985—)
Papadopoulou, Alexandra (1867–1906)
Papariga, Alexandra (1945—)
Papas, Irene (1926—)
Parren, Kalliroe (1861–1940)
Parthenis (fl. 2nd c. BCE)
Patoulidou, Paraskevi (1965—)
Paxinou, Katina (1900–1973)
Perictione (fl. 400 BCE)
Philaenis (fl. 2nd c.)
Philinna (c. 380–after c. 356 BCE)
Phintys of Sparta (fl. c. 400 BCE)
Phoebe of Cenchreas (fl. 1st c.)
Phryne (c. 365–c. 295 BCE)
Polidouri, Maria (1902–1930)
Pollatou, Anna (1983—)
Praxilla (fl. 450 BCE)
Rhodopis (fl. 6th c. BCE)
Roumpesi, Antigoni (1983—)
Sanson, Yvonne (1926—)
Sappho (c. 612–c. 557 BCE)
Saranti, Galateia (1920—)
Sophia of Greece (b. 1914)
Sophia of Greece (1938—)
Sophie of Prussia (1870–1932)
Sotiriou, Dido (1909–2004)
Stewart, Anastasia (1883–1923)
Svolou, Maria (d. 1976)
Tarsouli, Athena (1884–1974)
Telesilla (fl. 6th or 5th c. BCE)
Thais (fl. 331 BCE)
Thánou, Ekateríni (1975—)
Theano (fl. 6th c. BCE)
Theano II (fl. 5th c. BCE)
Theodora Oldenburg (1906–1969)
Theodoropoulou, Avra (1880–1963)
Timarete (fl. 3rd c. BCE)
Timoxena (fl. 2nd c.)
Tsoulfa, Emilia (1973—)
Tsoumeleka, Athanasia (1982—)
Tzavella, Moscho (1760–1803)
Vakalo, Eleni (1921—)
Vlachos, Helen (1911–1995)
Xanthippe (c. 435 BCE–?)
Zei, Alki (1925—)
Zographou, Lili
Zorba, Myrsini (1949—)

GREENLAND

Island in northeastern North America
Discovered and colonized by Norsemen (10th c.)
Made Danish crown colony (1924)
Became Danish province (1953)

Rask, Gertrud (fl. 1721)

GUADELOUPE

Bébel-Gisler, Dany (1935–2003)
Condé, Maryse (1937—)
Lacrosil, Michèle (1915—)
Manicom, Jacqueline (1938–1976)
Schwarz-Bart, Simone (1938—)

GUATEMALA

Republic in Central America
Conquered by Alvarado (1524)
Revolted against Spain (1821)
Joined Mexican empire (1822–1823)
Became independent republic (1839)

Hall, Elisa (1900–1982)
Moreno, Luisa (1906–1992)

GUELDERS OR GUELDERLAND

Province in eastern central Netherlands
Duchy of Gelderland conquered Charles the Bold of Burgundy (1473)
Regained independence (1477)
Passed to the House of Habsburg (1543)
Joined Union of Utrecht of the Netherlands against Spain (1579)
Part of Gelderland ceded by the Netherlands to Prussia (1715)
See Netherlands.

GUIENNE

Historic region of southwestern France
Passed to England through the marriage of Eleanor of Aquitaine to Henry II (1152)
Synonymous with Aquitaine until the Hundred Years War (1337–1453)
Reconquered by France (1453)
Formed part of province of Guienne and Gascony under Bordeaux (17th–18th c.)
See England.
See France.

GUINEA

Coastal region of West Africa
Formerly French Guinea
Proclaimed French protectorate (1849)
Boundary agreements with Britain (1882) and Portugal (1886)
Administered with Senegal as Rivières du Sud until established as separate colony (1893)
Became part of West Africa (1895)
Became overseas territory of France (1946)
Achieved independence (1958)

Cisse, Jeanne-Martin (1926—)

GUISE

Commune in Aisne department of northern France
See France.

GUYANA

Republic in northern South American
Formerly British Guiana
Founded by Dutch (c. 1620)
Captured by British (18th c.)
Recaptured by Dutch (19th c.)
Ceded to British (1814)
Essequibo, Berbice, and Demerara united as crown colony of British Buiana (1831)
Achieved independence (1966)
Became a republic (1970)

Burnham, Viola (1930–2003)
Gilroy, Beryl (1924–2001)
Jagan, Janet (1920—)

HABSBURG

Hamlet in Aargau canton in northern central Switzerland
Original seat of the Habsburgs
See Austria.
See Germany.
See Switzerland.

HAINAULT

Medieval country in the Low Countries (now included in Belgium and northern France)
Originated (9th c.)
United with county of Flanders and later with Holland
Held by Wittelsbach house of Bavaria (14th c.)
Taken by Philip of Burgundy (15th c.)
Became part of Spanish and Austrian Netherlands and a province in kingdom of Belgium
See Belgium.
See Flanders.
See France.
See Netherlands.

HAITI

Republic in western part of Hispaniola Island in West Indies
Ruled by the French (17th c.)
Challenged French rule of Hispaniola (18th c.)
Dominated by native rulers (19th c.)
Became a republic (1820)
Became a protectorate of United States (1915)
Adopted constitution (1964)

Anacáona (fl. 1492)
Chauvet, Marie (1916–1973)
Pascal-Trouillot, Ertha (1943—)
Williams, Lavinia (1916–1989)

HAITIAN INDIAN

Indigenous group

Anacáona (fl. 1492)

HANOVER

Former state of northwest Germany
Chartered (1241)
Became residence of dukes Brunswick-Lüneburg (1636)
Became electorate of Holy Roman Empire (1692–1806)
Succeeded to English throne as House of Hanover (1714)
Occupied by French and made part of Westphalia (1807–1813)
Separated from England (1837)
Kingdom incorporated with Prussia (1866)
See England.
See Germany.
See Prussia.

HAUSA EMPIRE

See Nigeria.

HAWAIIAN ISLANDS

Formerly Sandwich Islands in north central Pacific Ocean
Reached by Polynesians (c. 500 CE)
Discovered by Captain Cook (1778)
Under rule of Kamehameha dynasty (1795–1872)
Annexed to United States (1893)
Became a republic (1894)
Admitted as a state (1959)

Aluli, Irmgard (c. 1912–2001)
Baldwin, Charlotte Fowler (1805–1873)
Baldwin, Ethel Frances (1879–1967)
Baraquio, Angela Perez (1976—)
Bishop, Bernice Pauahi (1831–1884)
Cooke, Anna Rice (1853–1934)
Cowie, Bessie Lee (1860–1950)
Emma (1836–1885)
Kaahumanu (1777–1832)
Kaiulani (1875–1899)
Kalama (c. 1820–1870)
Kamamalu (c. 1803–1824)
Kamamalu, Victoria (1838–1866)
Kanahele, Helen Lake (1916–1976)
Kapiolani (c. 1781–1841)
Kapiolani (1834–1899)
Kapule, Deborah (c. 1798–1853)
Kennelly, Keala (1978—)
Keopuolani (c. 1778–1823)
Kinau (c. 1805–1839)
Liliuokalani (1838–1917)
Luahine, Iolani (1915–1978)
Nahienaena (c. 1815–1836)
Namakelua, Alice K. (1892–1987)
Nelson, Clara Meleka (1901–1979)
Pukui, Mary Kawena (1895–1986)
Sinclair, Elizabeth McHutcheson (1800–1892)
Wilcox, Elsie Hart (1879–1954)
Wilson, Kini (1872–1962)

HERTFORD

Borough of Hertfordshire in southeastern England
See England.

HERZEGOVINA

Part of republic of Bosnia and Herzegovina, Yugoslavia
See Bosnia.

HESSE

Region in southwestern Germany
Medieval landgraviate
Residence of houses of Hesse-Darmstadt and Hesse-Cassel (1567)
Extended territory and became grand duchy of Hesse (1806)
Hesse-Cassel became part of kingdom of Westphalia (1807–1813)
Hesse-Cassel united with Prussia (1866)
Hesse-Nassau formed from annexed territories (1866)
Joined North German Confederation (1867)
Electoral Hessse, duchy of Nassau, became part of landgraviate of Hesse-Homburg and republic of Waldeck (after 1929)
Electoral Hesse lost sovereignty (1934)
Partitioned between states of Hesse and Rhineland-Palatinate (1945)
See Germany.

HIDATSA

Native North American Great Plains indigenous group

Sacajawea (c. 1787–c. 1812 or 1884)

HOHENZOLLERN

Historic region and province of Prussia and Germany
Formed from territories of Hohenzollern-Heckhigen and Hohenzollern-Sigmaringen (1849)
Ceded to Prussia (19th–20th c.)
Became part of Baden-Württemberg (1952)
See Germany.
See Prussia.

HOLDERNESS

Peninsula in East Riding, Yorkshire, in northern England
See England.

HOLLAND

See also Netherlands.

De Jong, Bettie (1933—)
De La Bije, Willy (1934—)

HOLSTEIN

Southern part of western German state of Schleswig Holstein
Part of German duchy of Saxony in Carolingian Empire (c. 800 CE)
Became fief of Denmark (1460)
Raised to a duchy (1747)
Became member of German Confederation (1815)
Administered by Austria (1864)
Incorporated by Prussia (1866)
Became a West German state (1946)
See Denmark.
See Germany.

HONDURAS

Alvarado, Elvia (1938—)
Díaz Lozano, Argentina (1912–1999)
Edgell, Zee (1941—)
Eisemann-Schier, Ruth (c. 1942—)

HOPI-TEWA

Native North American Southwest indigenous group

Nampeyo (c. 1860–1942)
Piestewa, Lori Ann (1980–2003)

HUNGARY

Republic in central Europe
Occupied by Magyars (c. 893–901 CE)
Defeated by Germany (955)
Became independent kingdom (c. 1000)
Acquired Dalmatia, Slavonia, and Croatia (11th c.)
Invaded by Mongols (1241)
Died out after Árpád dynasty (997–1301)
Ruled by house of Anjou (1308–1382)
Ruled by Germany (1382–1437)
Lost territory to Turkish invasions (15th–16th c.)
Most of Hungary divided between Turkey and Austria (16th c.)
Came under Habsburgs (1687)
Most of Hungary ceded to Austrian crown (1699)
Part of dual monarchy of Austria-Hungary (1867–1918)
Became independent republic (1918)
Lost additional territories with defeat of Axis (1945)
Established a republic (1945)
Declared a people's republic (1949)
Invaded Czechoslovakia (1968)
See also Austria.
See also Turkey.

Adelaide of Hungary (d. 1062)
Adelaide of Rheinfelden (c. 1065–?)
Adler, Emma (1858–1935)
Agnes of Austria (1281–1364)
Agnes of Austria (fl. 1100s)
Agnes of Bohemia (1205–1282)
Alpar, Gitta (1900–1991)
Anastasia of Russia (c. 1023–after 1074)
Andics, Erzsebet (1902–1986)
Angyal, Eva (1955—)
Anna of Bohemia and Hungary (1503–1547)
Anna of Hungary (fl. 1244)
Anna of Hungary (d. around 1284)

Anne of Chatillon-Antioche (c. 1155–c. 1185)
Apponyi, Geraldine (1915—)
Aranyi, Jelly d' (1895–1966)
Ausländer, Rose (1901–1988)
Baker, Florence von Sass (1841–1916)
Balazs, Erzsebet (1920—)
Balogh, Beatrix (1974—)
Banky, Vilma (1898–1991)
Barbara of Cilli (fl. 1390–1410)
Bartok, Ditta Pasztory (1902–1982)
Bartok, Eva (1926–1998)
Bathory, Elizabeth (1560–1614)
Beatrice of Naples (1457–1508)
Bekesi, Ilona (1953—)
Beniczky-Bajza, Helene (1840–1905)
Besnyö, Eva (1910–2003)
Bobis, Ildiko (1945—)
Bogen, Erna (1906—)
Boros, Ferike (1880–1951)
Bota, Kinga (1977—)
Budapest, Z. (1940—)
Bujdoso, Agota (1943—)
Christina (fl. 1086)
Cicciolina (1951—)
Constance of Hungary (d. 1240)
Corda, Maria (1898–1975)
Csák, Ibolya (b. 1915)
Csaszar, Monika (1954—)
Csikne-Horvath, Klara (1947—)
Csillik, Margit (b. 1914)
Csisztu, Zsuzsa (1970—)
Czigany, Kinga (1952—)
Czobel, Lisa (1906–1992)
Darvas, Julia (c. 1919—)
Darvas, Lili (1902–1974)
Deli, Rita (c. 1972—)
De Putti, Lya (1899–1932)
Deseo, Suzanne (1913–2003)
Dobo, Katica (fl. 1552)
Donusz, Eva (1967—)
Duna, Steffi (1910–1992)
Egerszegi, Krisztina (1974—)
Egervári, Márti (1956—)
Eggerth, Marta (1912—)
Egresi, Vilma (1936–1979)
Egri, Susanna (1926—)
Eibenschütz-Dernbourg, Ilona (1872–1967)
Elizabeth of Bavaria (1837–1898)
Elizabeth of Bosnia (c. 1345–1387)
Elizabeth of Hungary (1207–1231)
Elizabeth of Kumania (c. 1242–?)
Elizabeth of Luxemburg (1409–1442)
Elizabeth of Poland (1305–1380)
Elizabeth of Sicily (fl. 1200s)
Erdos, Eva
Este, Beatrice d' (d. 1245)
Euphemia of Kiev (d. 1139)
Euphrosyne of Kiev (fl. 1130–1180)
Fachiri, Adila (1886–1962)
Farkas, Agnes (1973—)
Farkas, Andrea (c. 1969—)
Farnadi, Edith (1921–1973)
Fazekas, Mrs. Julius (d. 1929)
Feher, Anna (1921—)
Fischer, Annie (1914–1995)
Foix, Anne de (fl. 1480–1500)
Friedne-Banfalvi, Klara (1931—)
Gaal, Franciska (1904–1972)
Gabor, Eva (1919–1995)
Gabor, Jolie (1894–1997)
Gabor, Magda (1914–1997)
Gabor, Zsa Zsa (1917—)
Gabors, The
Galgóczi, Erzsébet (1930–1989)
Geczi, Erika (1959—)
Gerster, Etelka (1855–1920)
Gertrude of Andrechs-Meran (c. 1185–1213)
Gulacsy, Maria (1941—)
Gulyasne-Koeteles, Erzsebet (1924—)
Gyarmati, Andrea (1954—)
Gyarmati, Olga (1924—)
Gyenge, Valeria (1933—)
Haraszty, Eszter (1920–1994)
Hatvany, Lili (1890–1967)
Helena of Serbia (fl. 1100s)
Hoffmann, Beata
Horna, Kati (1912–2000)
Hugonnay, Vilma (1847–1922)
Hunyady, Emese (1966—)
Igaly, Diana (1965—)
Iolande of Hungary (1215–1251)
Isabella of Croy-Dulmen (1856–1931)
Isabella of Poland (1519–1559)
Ivogün, Maria (1891–1987)
Janics, Natasa (1982—)
Janosi, Zsuzsanna (1963—)
Janosine-Ducza, Aniko (1942—)
Johann, Zita (1904–1993)
Jolanta (fl. 1100s)
Judith of Hungary (fl. late 900s)
Juhaszne-Nagy, Katalin (1932—)
Kabos, Ilona (1893–1973)
Kaffka, Margit (1880–1918)
Kalocsai, Margit (b. 1909)
Kanner-Rosenthal, Hedwig (1882–1959)
Kantor, Aniko
Karpati Karcsics, Iren (1927—)
Kékessy, Andrea
Kelemen, Marta (1954—)
Keleti, Ágnes (1921—)
Kelety, Julia (d. 1972)
Kertesz, Aliz (1935—)
Kery, Aniko (1956—)
Kéthly, Anna (1889–1976)
Kezine-Pethoe, Zsuzsanna (1945—)
Kiraly Picot, Hajnalka (1971—)
Klafsky, Katharina (1855–1896)
Kleiberne-Kontsek, Jolan (1939—)
Koban, Rita (1965—)
Kocsis, Erzsebet
Kokeny, Beatrix
Kovach, Nora (1931—)
Kovacs, Agnes (1981—)
Kovacs, Edit (1954—)
Kovacs, Katalin (1976—)
Kovacsne-Nyari, Magdolna (1921—)
Kraus, Lili (1903–1986)
Kronberger, Lily
Krutzler, Eszter (1981—)
Kulcsar, Anita (1976—)
Lakine-Toth Harsanyi, Katalin (1948—)
Lelkesne-Tomann, Rozalia (1950—)
Lemhenyine-Tass, Olga (1929—)
Lipka, Juliane (c. 1860–c. 1929)
Lowy, Dora (1977—)
Madary, Ilona (1916—)
Madeleine of France (1443–1486)
Makray, Katalin (1945—)
Margaret of France (1158–1198)
Maria Anna of Bavaria (1574–1616)
Maria Lascaris (fl. 1234–1242)
Maria of Byzantium (fl. 12th c.)
Maria of Hungary (1371–1395)
Marie of Hungary (d. 1323)
Markus, Erzsebet (1969—)
Maros, Magda (1951—)
Marosi, Paula (1936—)
Mary of Hungary (1505–1558)
Massey, Ilona (1910–1974)
Matefi, Eszter
Matuscsakne-Ronay, Ildiko (1946—)
Matyas, Auguszta
Matzenauer, Margaret (1881–1963)
Medveczky, Krisztina (1958—)
Megyerine-Pacsai, Marta (1952—)
Meksz, Aniko (1965—)
Mendelenyine-Agoston, Judit (1937—)
Mero, Yolanda (1887–1963)
Meszaros, Erika (1966—)
Meszaros, Gabriella (b. 1913)
Mészáros, Márta (1931—)
Molnar, Andrea (1975—)
Molnarne-Bodo, Andrea (1934—)
Nagy, Aniko
Nagy, Annamaria (1982—)
Nagy, Ilona (1951—)
Nagy, Marianna (1957—)
Nagy, Timea (1970—)
Nagy, Zsuzsanna (1951—)
Nemes Nagy, Agnes (1922–1991)
Nemeth, Angela (1946—)
Nemeth, Erzsebet (1953—)
Nemeth, Helga (1973—)
Nijinska, Romola (1891–1978)
Novak, Eva (1930—)
Novak, Ilona (1925—)
Olah, Susanna (d. around 1929)
Onodi, Henrietta (1974—)
Orczy, Emma (1865–1947)
Ovari, Eva (1961—)
Padar, Ildiko (1970—)
Palinger, Katalin (1978—)
Pekli, Maria (1972—)
Petrass, Sari (1890–1930)
Pfeffer, Anna (1945—)
Pigniczki, Krisztina (1975—)
Plachyne-Korondi, Margit (1932—)
Polcz, Alaine (1921—)
Polgar, Judit (1976—)
Predeslava of Hungary (fl. 960)
Preslava of Russia (fl. 1100)
Priska-Irene of Hungary (c. 1085–1133)
Radulovic, Bojana (c. 1973—)
Rajnai, Klara (1953—)
Rakusz, Eva (1961—)
Regoczy, Krisztina
Richesa of Poland (fl. 1030–1040)
Rosenberg, Anna M. (1902–1983)
Rotter, Emilia
Rozsnyoi, Katalin (1942—)
Rudasne-Antal, Marta (1937—)
Ryksa of Poland (1288–1335)
Sagine-Ujlakine-Rejto, Ildiko (1937—)
Sakovitsne-Domolky, Lidia (1936—)
Salome of Hungary (1201–c. 1270)
Sandorne-Nagy, Margit (1921—)
Sarolta (fl. 900s)
Sarolta (fl. 1000s)
Schacherer-Elek, Ilona (1907–1988)
Schwimmer, Rosika (1877–1948)
Senesh, Hannah (1921–1944)
Sinko, Andrea (1967—)
Siti, Beata (c. 1974—)
Sophie of Hungary (d. 1095)
Stefanek, Gertrud (1959—)
Sterbinszky, Amalia (1950—)
Storczer, Beata (1969—)
Sulner, Hanna (1917–1999)
Synadene of Byzantium (c. 1050–?)
Szabó, Magda (1917—)
Szabo, Szilvia (1978—)
Szabo, Tünde (1974—)
Szalay Horvathne, Gyongyi
Szanto, Anna
Szekely, Eva (1927—)
Szekelyne-Marvalics, Gyorgyi (1924—)

Szenes, Katalin (b. 1899)
Szilagyi, Katalin
Szocs, Zsuzsanna (1962—)
Szoke, Katalin (1935—)
Szolnoki, Maria (1947—)
Szönyi, Erzsebet (1924—)
Takács, Eva (1779–1845)
Tanner, Ilona (1895–1955)
Teleki, Blanka (1806–1862)
Telkes, Maria (1900–1995)
Temes, Judit (1930—)
Tordasi Schwarczenberger, Ildiko (1951—)
Toth, Beatrix
Toth, Judit (b. 1906)
Toth, Noemi (1976—)
Toth Harsanyi, Borbala (1946—)
Tothne-Kovacs, Annamaria (1945—)
Troes, Olga (1914—)
Tuschak, Katalin (1959—)
Vadaszne-Vanya, Maria (1950—)
Vasarhelyi Weckinger, Edit (1923—)
Viski, Erzsebet (1980—)
Voit, Eszter (1916—)
Voros, Zsuzsanna (1977—)
Ylla (1911–1955)
Yolanda of Gnesen (d. 1299)
Yolande de Courtenay (d. 1233)
Zakarias, Maria (1952—)
Zalaine-Koevi, Maria (1923—)
Zeisel, Eva (1906—)
Zita of Parma (1892–1989)
Zrinyi, Ilona (1643–1703)
Zsembery, Tamasne (1967—)

HUNTINGDON

Borough in former county of Huntingdonshire in eastern central England

See England.

ICELAND

Island between North Atlantic and Arctic oceans
Settled by Norwegians (9th c.)
United with Norway (1262)
United with Denmark, later became independent kingdom under Denmark (1380)
Became independent republic (1944)

See also Denmark.
See also Norway.

Bjarklind, Unnur Benediktsdóttir (1881–1946)
Bjork (1965—)
Finnbogadóttir, Vigdís (1930—)
Flosadottir, Vala (1978—)
Gísladóttir, Sólrún
Jakobsdóttir, Svava (1930—)
Matthiasdottir, Louisa (1917–2000)
Vidar, Jorunn (1918—)

IGBOLAND

See Nigeria.

ILLYRIA

Ancient country on eastern Adriatic coast
Inhabited by Illyrians who pirated Roman shipping
Conquered by Romans after series of conflicts (3rd–1st c. BCE)
Kingdom of Illyria (Carinthia, Carniola, and Küstenland) became a division of Austria (19th c.)

Teuta (c. 260–after 228 BCE)
Thalestris (fl. 334 BCE)

INCAN EMPIRE

See Peru.

INDIA

Republic in southern Asia
Invaded from Iranian plateau (c. 18th–13th c. BCE)
Invaded by Aryans who developed Vedic religion and social caste system
Developed religious systems of Buddhism and Jainism (6th c. BCE)
Invaded in northwest (Punjab) by Alexander the Great (4th c. BCE)
Northern India consolidated with Afghanistan into empire under Maurya dynasty, adding kingdoms of Bengal and Orissa (4th–2nd c. BCE)
Northern India united by Gupta dynasty (4th–5th c. CE)
Muslim invasions began (10th c.)
Earliest muslim kingdom (Sultanate of Delhi) founded (1206)
Muslim dynasty of Bahmani flourished in the Deccan (14th c.)
Peninsula open to European trade by Vasco da Gama (15th c.)
Gradually conquered by Moguls (16th–18th c.)
Controlled by British (17th–19th c.)
British India divided into 11 provinces (1935)
Military clash with Pakistan over Jammu and Kashmir (1947–1949)
Inaugurated republic (1950)

Adrienne, Jean (b. 1905)
Ali, Aruna Asaf (c. 1909–1996)
Ambapali (fl. c. 540 BCE)
Amritanandamayi, Mata (1953—)
Antarjanam, Lalitambika (1909–1987)
Bannerjee, Karuna (1919–2001)
Bayne, Margaret (1798–1835)
Bhandari, Mannu (1931—)
Bose, Abala (1865–1951)
Brown, Edith Mary (1864–1956)
Brown, Margaret Elizabeth (1918—)
Cama, Bhikaiji (1861–1936)
Carmichael, Amy (1867–1971)
Chand Bibi (1550–1599)
Chattopadhyaya, Kamaladevi (1903–1988)
Chawla, Kalpana (1961–2003)
Chitnis, Leela (1909–2003)
Chowdhury, Eulie (1923—)
Christie, Julie (1941—)
Chugtai, Ismat (1915–1991)
Cooke, Hope (1940—)
Das, Kamala (1934—)
Desai, Anita (1937—)
Deshpande, Shashi (1938—)
Devi, Ashapurna (1909–1995)
Devi, Mahasveta (1926—)
Devi, Maitreyi (1914–1990)
Durgawati (d. 1564)
Farrar, Cynthia (1795–1862)
Fullam, Augusta Fairfield (1876–1914)
Gaidinliu, Rani (1915–1993)
Gandhi, Indira (1917–1984)
Gandhi, Kasturba (1869–1944)
Gandhi, Sonia (1946—)
Garg, Mridula (1938—)
Gayatri Devi (c. 1897–1995)
Gayatri Devi (1919—)
Gulbadan (c. 1522–1603)
Hazrat Mahal (c. 1820–1879)
Heywood, Joan (1923—)
Hosain, Attia (1913–1998)
Hossain, Rokeya Sakhawat (1880–1932)
Hyder, Qurratulain (1927—)
Jahanara (1614–1681)
Jayakar, Pupul (1915–1999)
Jeffreys, Ellen Penelope (1827–1904)
Jodha Bai (d. 1613)
Joshi, Anandibai (1865–1887)
Kamal, Sufia (1911–1999)
Kanwar, Roop (c. 1969–1987)
Kaur, Rajkumari Amrit (1889–1964)
Kaye, M.M. (1908–2004)
Khambatta, Persis (1950–1998)
Khan, Noor Inayat (1914–1944)
Kripalani, Sucheta (1908–1974)
Lakshmibai (c. 1835–1858)
Lal Ded (b. 1355)
Lalla Rookh (fl. 1600s)
Mahapajapati (fl. 570 BCE)
Malinche (c. 1500–1531)
Malleswari, Karnam (1975—)
Maloney, Lucia (c. 1950–1978)
Mangeshkar, Lata (1929—)
Manmati (d. 1619)
Maya (d. around 563 BCE)
Mayawati (1956—)
McLaren, Agnes (1837–1913)
Mehta, Hansa (1897–1995)
Mira Bai (1498–1547)
Mountbatten, Edwina Ashley (1901–1960)
Mountbatten, Pamela (1929—)
Mountbatten, Patricia (1924—)
Mukherjee, Bharati (1938—)
Mumtaz Mahal (c. 1592–1631)
Murray, Margaret (1863–1963)
Naidu, Sarojini (1879–1949)
Nair, Mira (1957—)
Namjoshi, Suniti (1941—)
Nayar, Sushila (1914–2001)
Nikambe, Shevantibai M. (b. 1865)
Nur Jahan (1577–1645)
Oberon, Merle (1911–1979)
Pandit, Vijaya Lakshmi (1900–1990)
Patil, Smita (1955–1986)
Phoolan Devi (c. 1956—)
Phule, Savitribai (1831–1897)
Pritam, Amrita (1919–2005)
Putli Bai (1929–1958)
Rajalakshmi, R. (1926—)
Ramabai, Pandita (1858–1922)
Rama Rau, Dhanvanthi (1893–1987)
Rama Rau, Santha (1923—)
Razia (1211–1240)
Rekha (1954—)
Roshanara (1849–1926)
Roy, Arundhati (1961—)
Sahgal, Nayantara (1927—)
Sarabhai, Anusyabehn (1885–1972)
Satthianadhan, Krupabai (1862–1894)
Sobti, Krishna (1925—)
Sohonie, Kamala (1911—)
Sorabji, Cornelia (1866–1954)
Soundarya (1972–2004)
Subbulakshmi, M.S. (1916–2004)
Suraiya (1929–2004)
Taylor, Kamala (1924–2004)
Tyabji, Kamila (1918–2004)
Udham Bai (fl. 1748–1754)
Yasodhara (fl. 547 BCE)
Zeb-un-Nissa (1639–1702)
Zia, Khaleda (1946—)

INDIGENOUS WOMEN

Akers, Dolly Smith (1902—)
Anacáona (fl. 1492)
Aquash, Anna Mae (1945–1976)
Awashonks (fl. mid-late 17th c.)
Bandler, Faith (1918—)
Bonnin, Gertrude Simmons (1876–1938)
Brant, Molly (c. 1736–1796)
Buffalo-Calf-Road-Woman (fl. 1876)
Cameron, Bessy (c. 1851–1895)
Cooper, Whina (1895–1994)
Dann, Mary (d. 2005)
Dat So La Lee (c. 1835–1925)
Deloria, Ella (1888–1971)
Durgawati (d. 1564)

Gibbs, Pearl (1901–1983)
Goolagong Cawley, Evonne (1951—)
Jemison, Alice Lee (1901–1964)
Johnson, E. Pauline (1861–1913)
La Flesche, Susan (1865–1915)
La Flesche, Susette (1854–1902)
Lefanu, Nicola (1947—)
Mankiller, Wilma (1945—)
Martinez, Maria Montoya (1887–1980)
Medicine, Beatrice A. (1923—)
Minoka-Hill, Rosa (1876–1952)
Mmanthatisi (c. 1780–c. 1836)
Mourning Dove (c. 1888–1936)
Musgrove, Mary (c. 1690–c. 1763)
Nampeyo (c. 1860–1942)
Nanye'hi (1738–1822)
Nongqause (c. 1840–c. 1900)
Odozi Obodo, Madam (1909–1995)
Peña, Tonita (1893–1949)
Peratrovich, Elizabeth Wanamaker (1911–1958)
Pitseolak (c. 1900–1983)
Pocahontas (c. 1596–1617)
Riley, Mary Velasquez (1908–1987)
Sacajawea (c. 1787–c. 1812 or 1884)
Sainte-Marie, Buffy (1941—)
Tekakwitha, Kateri (1656–1680)
Truganini (1812–1876)
Velarde, Pablita (1918—)
Victor, Wilma (1919–1987)
Walker, Kath (1920–1993)
Wauneka, Annie Dodge (1910–1997)
Wetamoo (c. 1650–1676)
Winnemucca, Sarah (1844–1891)
Wright, Muriel Hazel (1889–1975)

INDONESIA

Malay Archipelago in southwestern Asia
First visited by the Dutch (16th–17th c.)
Turned over to the Netherlands (18th c.)
Under Japanese control (1942)
Declared an independent republic (1945)
United States of Indonesia established (1949)
Dissolved union with Netherlands (1954)

Audina, Mia (1979—)
Boylen, Christilot (1947—)
De Jong, Bettie (1933—)
Galdikas, Biruté (1948—)
Handayani, Lilies (1965—)
Hendrawati, Agung (1975—)
Kartini (1879–1904)
MacLeod, Juana-Luisa (1898–1919)
Rumbewas, Raema Lisa (1980—)
Saiman, Nurfitriyana (1962—)
Slamet, Winarni Binti (1975—)
Sri, Indriyani (1978—)
Suharto, Siti (1923–1996)
Sukarnoputri, Megawati (1947—)
Susanti, Susi (1971—)
Vuyk, Beb (1905–1991)
Wardhani, Kusuma (1964—)

INUIT

Native North American Arctic indigenous group
Canadian First Nations indigenous group

Pedersen, Lena (1940—)
Pitseolak (c. 1900–1983)

INUPIAK

Cournoyea, Nellie J. (1940—)

IOWA

Native North American Great Plains indigenous group

Dorion, Marie (c. 1790–1850)
La Flesche, Susette (1854–1902)

IRAN

Islamic republic in southwestern Asia
Formerly Persia
Occupied by Iranian peoples (c. 21st c. BCE)
Under Cyrus the Great, founded Persian Empire (6th c. BCE)
Conquered by Alexander the Great (4th c. BCE)
Neo-Persian Empire of the Sassanidae founded (3rd c. CE)
Territories included Mesopotamia, Armenia, Azerbaijan, Syria, Egypt and parts of Asia Minor (7th c.)
Conquered by Muslim Arabs (633–651)
Founded separate Mongol dynasty of the Il-khans (1260–1353)
Modern Persia founded by Safawid rulers (1502–1736)
Overcome by Afghans and lost territory to Russia (1722)
Invaded India (1736–1757)
Ruled by Kjar dynasty (1794–1925)
Officially renamed Iran (1935)
Empire abolished and Islamic republic established (1979)

Abassa (fl. 8th c.)
Aghdashloo, Shohreh (1952—)
Amanpour, Christiane (1958—)
Atossa (c. 545–c. 470s BCE)
Cassandane (fl. 500s BCE)
Ebadi, Shirin (1947—)
Ebtekar, Massoumeh (1960—)
Esmat (d. 1995)
Farrokhzad, Forugh (1935–1967)
Fiske, Fidelia (1816–1864)
Hashemi, Faezeh (1963—)
Mumtaz Mahal (c. 1592–1631)
Pahlavi, Ashraf (1919—)
Pahlavi, Farah (1938—)
Pahlavi, Soraya (1932–2001)
Parysatis I (fl. 440–385 BCE)
Parysatis II (c. 350–323 BCE)
Rabi'a (c. 714–801)
Sati Beg (c. 1300–after 1342)
Sherkat, Shahla (c. 1956—)
Statira I (c. 425–? BCE)
Statira II (c. 360–331 BCE)
Tajolmolouk (1896–1981)
Vashti (fl. 5th c. BCE)

IRAQ

Republic in southwestern Asia
As ancient Babylonia
Under British mandate (1920)
Kingdom established out of former Turkish territory (1921)
Became limited monarchy (1924)
Became independent under King Faisal I (1932)
Became a republic (1950)

Bederkhan, Leila (b. around 1903)
Hadid, Zaha (1950—)
Hashimi, Aquila al- (1953–2003)
Hassan, Margaret (1944–2004)
Khirniq (fl. late 6th c.)
Malaika, Nazik al- (1923–1992)
Malaika, Salma al- (1908–1953)
Rabi'a (c. 714–801)
Radi, Nuha al- (1941–2004)
Shariyya (b. around 815)

IRELAND

Republic
Celtic invasions (c. 500 BCE)
Organized into clans and governed by kingdoms of Ulster, Leinster, Connaught, Munster, and Meath (5th c. CE)
Converted to Christianity (6th–9th c.)
Raided by Vikings (8th c.)
Clan warfare (12th c.)
Conquered by Normans who established English strip (the Pale) on Dublin coast (12th c.)
Occupied by the English (13th c.)
Catholics driven from land; Irish culture supressed through Penal Laws (16th–17th c.)
Colonized by Scots, Welsh, and English (17th c.)
"Irish Question" of civil rights for Catholics (1829)
Great Potato Famine forces mass emigration (1847–1849)
Renewed efforts to achieve Home Rule (1886)
Unsuccessful attempt to repel English in Easter Rising (1916)
Achieved independence as Irish Free State (1922–1937)
As Republic of Ireland (1938)
Six counties of Ulster remain under British rule as Northern Ireland

See also Ireland, Northern.

Acheson, Anne Crawford (1882–1962)
Acheson, Carrie (1934—)
Ahearn, Theresa (1951–2000)
Ahern, Catherine Ita (1915—)
Ahern, Nuala (1949—)
Aikenhead, Mary (1787–1858)
Alexander, Cecil Frances (1818–1895)
Alexander, Muriel (1898–1975)
Allgood, Sara (1883–1950)
Antrim, Angela (1911–1984)
Aron, Geraldine (1941—)
Bagenal, Mabel (c. 1571–1595)
Ball, Anne Elizabeth (1808–1872)
Ball, Frances (1794–1861)
Banahan, Mary Gertrude (1855/56?–1932)
Banotti, Mary (1939—)
Barber, Fanny (c. 1864–1952)
Barber, Mary (c. 1690–1757)
Bardwell, Leland (1928—)
Barlow, Jane (c. 1857–1917)
Barnes, Monica (1936—)
Barrington, Margaret (1896–1982)
Barron, Hannah Ward (1829–1898)
Barry, Ann Street (1734–1801)
Barry, Myra (1957—)
Bates, Daisy May (1859–1951)
Beckett, Mary (1926—)
Beere, Thekla (1901–1991)
Begga of Egremont (fl. 7th c.)
Bell, Laura (1829–1894)
Bellamy, George Anne (1727–1788)
Bennett, Louie (1870–1956)
Bennett, Olga (1947—)
Bhreathnach, Naimh (1945—)
Binchy, Maeve (1940—)
Blachford, Theodosia (1745–1817)
Blackburn, Helen (1842–1903)
Blackham, Dorothy Isabel (1896–1975)
Blackwood, Hariot (c. 1845–1891)
Blackwood, Helen Selina (1807–1867)
Bland, Lilian (1878–1971)
Blessington, Marguerite, Countess of (1789–1849)
Boland, Eavan (1944—)
Bolger, Deirdre (1938—)
Bonney, Anne (1700–?)
Booth, Evelyn Mary (1897–1988)
Bowen, Elizabeth (1899–1973)
Bowen, Gretta (1880–1981)
Boyle, Helen (1869–1957)
Brady, Mary (1821–1864)
Brady, Veronica (1890–1964)
Brandt, Muriel (1909–1981)
Brennan, Maire (1952—)
Bridget (c. 453–c. 524)
Brooke, Charlotte (1740–1793)
Browne, Augusta (1820–1882)
Browne, Frances (1816–1879)
Browne, Kathleen Anne (b. 1878)
Brugha, Caitlin (1879–1959)

Geographic Index

Bryant, Sophie (1850–1922)
Bulbulia, Katharine (1943—)
Bunbury, Selina (1802–1882)
Burke, Joan T. (1929—)
Burton, Joan (1949—)
Butler, Eleanor (c. 1738–1829)
Butler, Eleanor (c. 1915–1997)
Butters, Mary (fl. 1839)
Cadden, Mamie (c. 1894–1959)
Caffyn, Kathleen (1853–1926)
Campbell, Beatrice (1922–1979)
Campbell, Lady Colin (1857–1911)
Carmichael, Amy (1867–1971)
Carse, Matilda Bradley (1835–1917)
Cashman, Nellie (1844–1925)
Cassidy, Eileen (1932–1995)
Cavanagh, Kit (1667–1739)
Chancellor, Joyce (1906—)
Charleson, Mary (1890–1961)
Chemis, Annie (1862–1939)
Chevenix, Helen (1886–1963)
Christie, Susan (c. 1969—)
Clarke, Kathleen (1878–1972)
Clerke, Agnes Mary (1842–1907)
Clerke, Ellen Mary (1840–1906)
Clive, Kitty (1711–1785)
Clune, Deirdre (1959—)
Cluysenaar, Anne (1936—)
Cobbe, Frances Power (1822–1904)
Cockburn, Patricia (1914–1989)
Cole, Mary (c. 1913—)
Coleman, Kit (1864–1915)
Colley, Anne (1951—)
Collinge, Patricia (1892–1974)
Collins-O'Driscoll, Margaret (1878–1945)
Colum, Mary Gunning (1884–1957)
Concannon, Helena (1878–1952)
Connolly-O'Brien, Nora (1893–1981)
Cooper-Flynn, Beverley (1966—)
Copley, Clara (d. 1949)
Corrigan, Mairead (1944—)
Cosgrave, Niamh (1964—)
Costello, Eileen (1870–1962)
Costello, Louisa Stuart (1799–1870)
Coughlan, Mary (1965—)
Cousins, Margaret (1878–1954)
Cox, Margaret (1963—)
Craig, May (1889–1972)
Crawford, Louise Macartney (1790–1858)
Crowe, Ellen (c. 1845–1930)
Crowley, Honor Mary (1903–1966)
Cusack, Margaret Anne (1832–1899)
Cust, Aleen (1868–1937)
Dagoe, Hannah (d. 1763)
Daly, Mary (c. 1861–1901)
Daly, Mary Agnes
D'Arcy, Margaretta (1934—)
Darragh, Lydia Barrington (1729–1789)
Davidson, Mary Frances (1902–1986)
Davys, Mary (1674–1731)
Deevy, Teresa (1894–1963)
Delany, Maureen (d. 1961)
Denny, Arbella (1707–1792)
Desmond, Eileen (1932—)
de Valera, Sile (1954—)
de Valois, Ninette (1898–2001)
Devorgilla (1109–1193)
Diamond, Ann (c. 1827–1881)
Dougherty, Sarah (c. 1817–1898)
Dowdall, Jane (1899–1974)
Doyle, Avril (1949—)
Dunlop, Eliza Hamilton (1796–1880)
Durgan, Bridget (c. 1845–1867)
Edgeworth, Maria (1768–1849)
English, Ada (c. 1878–1944)
Enya (1961—)
Farrell, Peggy (1920—)
Farren, Elizabeth (c. 1759–1829)
Fennell, Nuala (1935—)
Fergusa (fl. 800s)
FitzGerald, Eithne (1950—)
Fitzgerald, Frances (1950—)
Fitzgerald, Geraldine (1913–2005)
Fitzhenry, Mrs. (d. 1790?)
Flaherty, Mary (1953—)
Flanagan, Sinéad (1878–1975)
Flanagan, Sinéad (b. around 1878)
Fox, Charlotte Milligan (1864–1916)
Fox, Mildred (1971—)
Fricker, Brenda (1945—)
Frost, Winifred (1902–1979)
Fuller, Anne (fl. late 18th c.)
Gallagher, Ann (1967—)
Gallagher, Kitty (fl. mid-19th c.)
Galvin, Sheila (1914–1983)
Garmson, Aileen (c. 1861–1951)
Geddes, Wilhelmina (1887–1955)
Geoghegan-Quinn, Máire (1950—)
Gibson, Emily Patricia (1863/64?–1947)
Gill, Mary Gabriel (1837–1905)
Gilliland, Helen (1897–1942)
Glenn, Alice (1927—)
Glover, Julia (1779–1850)
Gonne, Maud (1866–1953)
Goodwin, Bridget (c. 1802/27–1899)
Gore-Booth, Eva (1870–1926)
Gormflaith (c. 870–925)
Gormflaith of Ireland (fl. 980–1015)
Goulding, Valerie (1918–2003)
Graves, Clotilde Inez Mary (1863–1932)
Gray, Eileen (1878–1976)
Greatorex, Eliza (1820–1897)
Green, Alice Stopford (1847–1929)
Greene, Angela (1921–1978)
Greevy, Bernadette (1939—)
Gregory, Augusta (1852–1932)
Grierson, Constantia (c. 1706–c. 1732)
Griffith, Elizabeth (c. 1720–1793)
Grimshaw, Beatrice (c. 1870–1953)
Guerin, Veronica (1960–1996)
Hall, Anna Maria (1800–1881)
Hanafin, Mary (1959—)
Hannon, Camilla (1936—)
Harney, Mary (1953—)
Hartigan, Anne Le Marquand (1931—)
Haslam, Anna (1829–1922)
Haughery, Margaret Gaffney (1813–1882)
Hawthorne, Margaret Jane Scott (1869–1958)
Hayden, Mary (1862–1942)
Hayden, Mother Mary Bridget (1814–1890)
Hayes, Catherine (1825–1861)
Heath, Sophie (1896–1939)
Hector, Annie French (1825–1902)
Hederman, Carmencita (1939—)
Henry, Mary E.F. (1940—)
Henrys, Catherine (c. 1805–1855)
Heron, Matilda (1830–1877)
Hickey, Emily Henrietta (1845–1924)
Hogan, Brigid (1932—)
Holmès, Augusta (1847–1903)
Honan, Cathy (1951—)
Honan, Tras (1930—)
Hone, Evie (1894–1955)
Honner, Maria (1812–1870)
Hopkins, Thelma (1936—)
Hoult, Norah (1898–1984)
Howard, Caroline Cadette (1821–?)
Howley, Calasanctius (1848–1933)
Huggins, Margaret (1848–1915)
Hull, Eleanor Henrietta (1860–1935)
Humphries, Carmel (1909–1986)
Hungerford, Margaret Wolfe (c. 1855–1897)
Hussey, Gemma (1938—)
Ita of Ireland (d. 570)
Jackman, Mary (1943—)
Jacob, Rosamund (1888–1960)
Jameson, Anna Brownell (1794–1860)
Jellett, Mainie (1897–1944)
Jellicoe, Anne (1823–1880)
Johnson, Esther (1681–1728)
Johnston, Henrietta (c. 1670–1728)
Johnston, Jennifer (1930—)
Jones, Mary Harris (1830–1930)
Jordan, Dora (1761–1816)
Joyce, Lucia (1907–1982)
Joyce, Nora (1884–1951)
Kavanagh, Julia (1824–1877)
Keane, Molly (1904–1996)
Kearney, Miriam (1959—)
Kearns-MacWhinney, Linda (1888–1951)
Keaveney, Cecilia (1968—)
Keeley, Mary Anne (c. 1806–1899)
Kelly, Maeve (1930—)
Kelly, Margaret (1910–2004)
Kelly, Mary (1952—)
Kennedy, Geraldine (1951—)
Kennedy, Margaret L. (b. 1892)
Keogh, Helen (1951—)
King, Martha (1802/03–1897)
Kirby, Mary Kostka (1863–1952)
Kyteler, Alice (fl. 1324)
Ladies of Llangollen, The
Laverty, Maura (1907–1966)
Lavin, Mary (1912–1996)
Lawless, Emily (1845–1913)
Lawlor, Patsy (1933–1998)
Leadbetter, Mary (1758–1826)
Lee, Mary (1821–1909)
Lemass, Eileen (1932—)
Liadan (fl. 7th c.)
Longfield, Cynthia (1896–1991)
Longworth, Maria Theresa (c. 1832–1881)
Lonsdale, Kathleen (1903–1971)
Lowry-Corry, Dorothy (1885–1967)
Lynch, Celia (1908–1989)
Lynch, Eliza (1835–1886)
Lynch, Kathleen (1953—)
Lynn, Kathleen (1874–1955)
Macardle, Dorothy (1889–1958)
MacGill, Moyna (1895–1975)
MacManus, Anna Johnston (1866–1902)
Maconchy, Elizabeth (1907–1994)
MacSwiney, Mary (1872–1942)
Magdalen women (c. 1820s–early 1970s)
Maher, Mary Cecilia (1799–1878)
Malcolm, Sarah (c. 1710–1733)
Mallon, Mary (1867–1938)
Malone, Bernie (1948—)
Manning, Mary (1906–1999)
Mansel, Lucy (c. 1830–1915)
Margaret de Burgh (d. 1303)
Markievicz, Constance (1868–1927)
Martin, Mary Letitia (1815–1850)
Martin, Mother Mary (1892–1975)
Martin, Violet (1862–1915)
Massy, Annie (1867–1931)
Maude, Caitlín (1941–1982)
Maunder, Annie Russell (1868–1947)
Maxwell, Constantia (1886–1962)
McAleese, Mary (1951—)
McAliskey, Bernadette Devlin (1947—)
McAuley, Catherine (1778–1841)
McAuliffe-Ennis, Helena (1951—)
McCracken, Mary Ann (1770–1866)
McGennis, Marian (1953—)
McGroarty, Sister Julia (1827–1901)

McGuinness, Catherine (1934—)
McKenna, Patricia (1957—)
McKiernan, Catherina (1969—)
McManus, Liz (1947—)
McNeill, Janet (1907–1994)
McWilliams, Jackie (1964—)
Mhac An tSaoi, Máire (1922—)
Milne, Mary Jane (1840–1921)
Mitchel, Jenny (1820–1899)
Mitchell, Olivia (1947—)
Modwenna (d. 518)
Molony, Helena (1884–1967)
Monckton, Mary (1746–1840)
Montez, Lola (1818–1861)
Mooney, Mary (1958—)
Mooney, Ria (1904–1973)
Morgan, Sydney (1780–1859)
Morrice, Jane (1954—)
Moyes, Patricia (1923–2000)
Moynihan, Mary (c. 1903–?)
Moynihan-Cronin, Breeda (1953—)
Mulally, Teresa (1728–1803)
Mulkerns, Val (1925—)
Murphy, Dervla (1931—)
Murray, Anna Maria (1808–1899)
Nagle, Nano (1718–1784)
Ni Chuilleanáin, Eiléan (1942—)
Ni Dhomhnaill, Nuala (1952—)
O'Brien, Catherine (1881–1963)
O'Brien, Edna (1930—)
O'Brien, Kate (1897–1974)
O'Callaghan, Kathleen (1888–1961)
O'Carroll, Maureen (1913–1984)
O'Casey, Eileen (1900–1995)
O'Connell, Eileen (c. 1743–c. 1800)
O'Connell, Mary (1814–1897)
O'Connell, Sarah (c. 1822–1870)
O'Connor, Ellen (1857–1933)
O'Connor, Kathleen (1935—)
O'Connor, Sinéad (1966—)
O'Connor, Una (1880–1959)
O'Doherty, Eileen (b. 1891)
O'Doherty, Mary Anne (1826–1910)
O'Donnell, Ann (c. 1857–1934)
O'Donnell, Liz (1956—)
O'Donnell, Mary Stuart (fl. early 1600s)
O'Faolain, Julia (1932—)
O'Faolain, Nuala (1940—)
O'Farrell, Bernadette (1924–1999)
O'Hagan, Mary (1823–1876)
O'Hara, Maureen (1920—)
O'Keeffe, Adelaide (1776–c. 1855)
O'Malley, Grace (c. 1530–1603)
O'Malley, Grania (1885–1973)
O'Meara, Kathleen (1839–1888)
O'Meara, Kathleen (1960—)
O'Murphy, Marie-Louise (1737–1814)
O'Neil, Peggy (1898–1960)
O'Neill, Eliza (1791–1872)
O'Neill, Maire (1885–1952)
O'Rourke, Mary (1937—)
O'Sullivan, Jan (1950—)
O'Sullivan, Mairan D. (1919–1987)
O'Sullivan, Maureen (1911–1998)
O'Sullivan, Sonia (1969—)
Otway-Ruthven, Jocelyn (1909–1989)
Owen, Nora (1945—)
Owens, Evelyn P. (1931—)
Panter-Downes, Mollie (1906–1997)
Parnell, Anna (1852–1911)
Parsons, Mary (1813–1885)
Pearse, Margaret (1857–1932)
Pearse, Margaret Mary (1878–1968)
Pelham, Mary Singleton Copley (c. 1710–1789)
Percy, Eileen (1899–1973)
Philbin, Eva (1914—)
Pirrie, Margaret Montgomery (1857–1935)
Player, Mary Josephine (c. 1857–1924)
Ponsonby, Sarah (1755–1831)
Potter, Maureen (1925–2004)
Potts, Mary Florence (c. 1853–?)
Praeger, Sophia Rosamund (1867–1954)
Price, Kate (1872–1943)
Purser, Sarah (1848–1943)
Quill, Máirin (1940—)
Ralfe, Catherine Hester (c. 1831–1912)
Ralph, Margaret (c. 1822–1913)
Read, Mary (1680–1721)
Redmond, Bridget Mary (1905–1952)
Rehan, Ada (1857–1916)
Reynolds, Jane (c. 1897—)
Reynolds, Mary (c. 1890–1974)
Rhind, Ethel (c. 1879–1952)
Rice, Bridget Mary (1885–1967)
Rich, Mary (1625–1678)
Richards, Shelah (1903–1985)
Riddell, Charlotte (1832–1906)
Ridge, Lola (1873–1941)
Ridge, Therese (1941—)
Robinson, Mary (1944—)
Roche, Regina Maria (c. 1764–1845)
Rodgers, Brid (1935—)
Rodgers, Elizabeth Flynn (1847–1939)
Ros, Amanda (1860–1939)
Ross, Martin (1862–1915)
Runciman, Jane Elizabeth (1873–1950)
Russell, Mother Mary Baptist (1829–1898)
Ryan, Catherine O'Connell (1865–1936)
Ryan, Kathleen (1922–1985)
Ryan, Mary Bridget (1898–1981)
Sadlier, Mary Anne (1820–1903)
Sayers, Peig (1873–1958)
Scallon, Dana Rosemary (1950—)
Shaw, Fiona (1958—)
Sheehy-Skeffington, Hanna (1877–1946)
Sheridan, Frances (1724–1766)
Sheridan, Margaret (1889–1958)
Shiubhlaigh, Maire Nic (1884–1958)
Shortall, Róisín (1954—)
Sigerson, Dora (1866–1918)
Sigerson, Hester (d. 1898)
Skrine, Agnes (c. 1865–1955)
Smith, Michelle (1969—)
Smithson, Harriet Constance (1800–1854)
Somerville, E. (1858–1949)
Somerville and Ross
Starkie, Enid (1897–1970)
Steevens, Grissell (1653–1746)
Stopford Green, Alice (1847–1929)
Strong, Eithne (1923–1999)
Stuart, Miranda (c. 1795–1865)
Tautphoeus, Baroness von (1807–1893)
Taylor-Quinn, Madeleine (1951—)
Teresa, Mother (c. 1766–1846)
Thurston, Katherine (1875–1911)
Tighe, Mary (1772–1810)
Tone, Matilda (c. 1769–1849)
Tonna, Charlotte Elizabeth (1790–1846)
Torlesse, Elizabeth Henrietta (1835/36–1922)
Trench, Melesina (1768–1827)
Tweedy, Hilda (b. 1911)
Tynan, Katharine (1861–1931)
Upton, Mary (1946—)
Vane-Tempest, Frances Anne Emily (d. 1865)
Vane-Tempest-Stewart, Edith (1878–1949)
Vane-Tempest-Stewart, Theresa (1856–1919)
Vesey, Elizabeth (c. 1715–1791)
Vincent, Mother (1819–1892)
Voynich, Ethel (1864–1960)
Waddell, Helen (1889–1965)
Wallace, Mary (1959—)
Walsh, Mary (1929–1976)
Ward, Mary (1827–1869)
Watts Russell, Elizabeth Rose Rebecca (1833/34–1905)
Webster, Kate (1849–1879)
Weldon, Barbara (1829/30–1882)
Wheeler, Anna Doyle (1785–c. 1850)
Whiteside, Jane (1855–1875)
Wilde, Jane (1821–1896)
Williamson, Jessie Marguerite (c. 1855–1937)
Woffington, Peg (c. 1714–1760)
Wyse Power, Jennie (1858–1941)
Yeats, Elizabeth (1868–1940)
Yeats, Lily (1866–1949)
Young, Ella (1867–1951)
Young, Rose Maud (1865–1947)

IRELAND, NORTHERN

Six northern counties of Ireland (Antrim, Armagh, Down, Fermanagh, Londonderry [formerly Derry], and Tyrone) under British rule

Alice Maud Mary, princess of Great Britain and Ireland (1843–1878)
Alice of Athlone (1883–1981)
Anne of Great Britain and Ireland (1665–1714)
Armitage, Pauline
Bell, Eileen (1943—)
Burnell, Jocelyn Bell (1943—)
Byers, Margaret (1832–1912)
Calvert, Lilian (1909–2000)
Carney, Winifred (1887–1943)
Carson, Joan (1935—)
Clare, Isabel de (c. 1174–1220)
Conn, Shena
Corrigan, Mairead (b. 1944)
Coulter, Jean
Courtney, Annie
de Brún, Bairbre (1954—)
Denton, Jean (1935–2001)
Despard, Charlotte (1844–1939)
Dickson, Anne (1928—)
Diver, Jenny (1700–1740)
Elizabeth de Burgh (1332–1363)
Elizabeth II of Great Britain and Northern Ireland (1926—)
Ford, Patricia (1921—)
Gallagher, Rosie (1970–2003)
Garson, Greer (1904–1996)
Gildernew, Michelle (1970—)
Greeves, Marion Janet (1894–1979)
Hanna, Carmel (1946—)
Hermon, Sylvia (1955—)
Hickey, Eileen (1886–1960)
Hobhouse, Violet (1864–1902)
Hoey, Kate (1946—)
Larkin, Delia (1878–1949)
Lewsley, Patricia (1957—)
MacFall, Frances E. (1854–1943)
Maconachie, Bessie
Magee, Martha Maria (d. 1846)
McAliskey, Bernadette Devlin (1947—)
McAliskey, Roisin (1971—)
McCarthy, Arlene (1960—)
McCoubrey, Margaret (1880–1955)
McCracken, Elizabeth (c. 1865–1944)
McGuinness, Norah (1901–1980)
McKenna, Siobhan (1922–1986)
McKenzie, Margaret (c. 1837–1925)
McLaughlin, Florence (1916—)
McMordie, Julia (1860–1942)
McNabb, Dinah

McTier, Martha (c. 1743–1837)
McWilliams, Monica (1954—)
Milligan, Alice (1866–1953)
Montgomery, Mary (fl. 1891–1914)
Mowlam, Mo (1949—)
Mulholland, Clara (d. 1934)
Mulholland, Rosa (1841–1921)
Murnaghan, Sheelagh (1924–1993)
Murray, Ruby (1935–1996)
Nelis, Mary (1935—)
Nivedita, Sister (1867–1911)
O'Hagan, Dara (1964—)
Paisley, Eileen (1934—)
Parker, Dehra (1882–1963)
Peters, Mary (1939—)
Ramsey, Sue (1970—)
Robinson, Iris (1949—)
Rodgers, Brid (1935—)
Shaw, Elizabeth (1920–1992)
Taggart, Edith Ashover (1909–1997)
Tod, Isabella (1836–1896)
Waring, Margaret (1887–1968)
Williams, Betty (1943—)

ISLE OF MAN

Burgin, Annie Mona (1903–1985)

ISLE OF WIGHT

Mansel, Lucy (c. 1830–1915)
Neill, Elizabeth Grace (1846–1926)

ISRAEL, MODERN

Republic in southwestern Asia
Established in partition of Palestine between Jews and Arabs (1948)
Signed armistice with Arab states retaining city of Jerusalem, yielding Gaza coastal region to Egypt (1949)
Warred with Arab countries (1956–1957)
Occupied adjoining parts of Syria, parts of Jordan, and the entire Sinai Peninsula (1967)

Almog, Ruth (1936—)
Arad, Yael (1967—)
Arbatova, Mia (c. 1910—)
Baron, Devorah (1887–1956)
Bat-Miriam, Yocheved (1901–1980)
Ben-Yehuda, Hemda (1873–1951)
Ben Zvi, Rachel Yanait (1886–1979)
Bluwstein, Rachel (1890–1931)
Cohen, Shula (fl. 1960s)
Cohen, Ze'eva (1940—)
Eshkol, Noa (1927—)
Fraenkel, Naomi (1920—)
Freier, Recha (1892–1984)
Gluck, Rena (1933—)
Goldberg, Lea (1911–1970)
Grossman, Haika (1919–1996)
Harareet, Haya (1931—)
Hareven, Shulamit (1930–2003)
Haza, Ofra (1957–2001)
Hendel, Yehudit (1926—)
Kahana-Carmon, Amalia (1930—)
Katznelson, Shulamit (1919–1999)
Katznelson-Shazar, Rachel (1888–1975)
Krauss, Gertrud (1903–1977)
Lapid, Shulamit (1934—)
Liebrecht, Savyon (1948—)
Meir, Golda (1898–1978)
Mishkowsky, Zelda Shneurson (1914–1984)
Raab, Esther (1894–1981)
Rabin, Leah (1928–2000)
Rafael, Sylvia (1938–2005)
Ran, Shulamit (1949—)
Ravikovitch, Dahlia (1936—)
Senesh, Hannah (1921–1944)
Shochat, Manya (1878–1961)
Ticho, Anna (1894–1980)
Vered, Ilana (1939—)
Wallach, Yonah (1944–1985)
Weizmann, Vera (1881–1966)

ISRAEL AND JUDAH

Republic in southwestern Asia
Ancient kingdom in Palestine occupied by Hebrew tribes of Jacob (12th c. BCE)
Formed under Saul, comprising lands in Canaan (c. 1025 BCE)
Consolidated by David (c. 1013 BCE)
Kingdom divided into Northern Kingdom of Israel; Southern Kingdom of Judah (c. 931 BCE)
Overthrown by Assyrians (721 BCE)
Under Maccabees (2nd c. BCE)
Under Tetrarchs (1st c. BCE)
Under Kings of Jerusalem (1099–1244)
Jerusalem under Egypt (1244–1518)
Palestine under Turkish rule (1518–1917)
Palestine under British rule (1917–1918)
Palestine under League of Nations (1923)
Palestine divided into Israel and Jordan (1948)
See also Israel, Modern.
See also Palestine, Modern.

Abigail (fl. 1000 BCE)
Abigail (fl. 1010 BCE)
Adelaide of Savona (d. 1118)
Agnes of Courtenay (1136–1186)
Ahinoam (fl. 1020 BCE)
Ahinoam of Jezreel (fl. 1000 BCE)
Alexandra (r. 76–67 BCE)
Alice of Champagne (fl. 1200s)
Alice of Jerusalem (c. 1106–?)
Aloni, Shulamit (1931—)
Anne (fl. 1st c.)
Athaliah (r. 842–836 BCE)
Azubah (fl. 860 BCE)
Beatrice (fl. c. 1100s)
Berenice (28–after 80)
Berenice (c. 35 BCE–?)
Isabella I of Jerusalem (d. 1205)
Isabella of Cyprus (fl. 1230s)
Isabella of Cyprus (fl. 1250s)
Jehosheba (fl. 9th c.)
Leah (fl. c. 1500 BCE)
Maacah (fl. 1000 BCE)
Malthace (fl. 40 BCE)
Maria Comnena (fl. 1100s)
Marie of Montferrat (d. 1212)
Melisande (1105–1161)
Morphia of Melitene (fl. 1085–1120)
Plaisance of Antioch (d. 1261)
Rachel (fl. c. 1500 BCE)
Sibylla (1160–1190)
Theodora Comnena (1145–after 1183)
Yolande of Brienne (1212–1228)

ITALY

Republic in southern Europe
Greeks colonize in the south and in Sicily (8th c. BCE)
Etruscans arrive in central Italy and the Po Valley (7th c. BCE)
Rome founded (c. 753 BCE)
Foundation of the Roman republic began unification of Italy (509 BCE)
Roman Empire initiated by Emperor Augustus (31 BCE)
Emperor Constantine I transferred capital from Rome to Constantinople (330)
Founding of bishoprics in Rome, Milan, Ravenna, Naples, Benevento, and elsewhere (2nd c. CE)
Under rule of Ostrogoths (r. 493-526)
Byzantine Empire regained control (553)
Lombards arrived in Italy; controlled from north to Tuscany and Umbria (568)
Lombards resisted chiefly by the popes who held land that became Papal States (6th–7th c.)
Frankish invasion of Italy expelled Lombards (8th c.)
Charlemagne crowned emperor in Rome (800)
Feuding between Franks and Byzantines, rise of Saracens from North Africa (900s)
Carolingian Empire collapsed (9th c.)
Under Roman Empire (961–1254)
Individual Italian cities assert autonomy (11th c.)
Kingdom of Sicily established (12th c.)
Norman Sicily and German thrones united (13th c.)
Kingdoms of Naples and Sicily united as Kingdom of the Two Sicilies (15th c.)
Weakening of papacy in Italy gave rise to Renaissance (after 14th c.)
In Milan, the Visconti family rose to power (13th c.)
In Florence, the Sforza family rose to power, surpassed by Medici family (mid–15th c.)
In Ferrara, the Este family ruled (13th–16th c.)
Italian Wars began with invasion of France (15th–19th c.)
Almost all of Italy controlled by the Habsburgs (16th c.)
Passed to Spain upon abdication of Charles V (16th c.)
Austria replaced Spain as dominant power after War of Spanish Succession (1701–1714)
Kingdom of Sardinia and Kingdom of Two Sicilies achieved independence (18th c.)
Italy ruled by France after invasion by Napoleon (1814)
Peace restored in Europe, Italy comprised kingdoms of Sardinia and the Two Sicilies; the Papal States, Tuscany and smaller duchies in north central Italy (1815)
Lombardy and Venetia controlled by Austria (1815)
Italy unified as the Kingdom of Italy (1870)
Joined Germany and Austria in the Triple Alliance (1882)
Declared war on Turkey to obtain Libya (1890s)
Fascism introduced by Benito Mussolini (1920s)
Entered World War II on side of Germany (1943)
Allies pushed German armies out of Italy (1945)
Monarchy abolished and a republic established (1946)

Abba, Marta (1900–1988)
Abrabanel, Benvenida (d. 1560)
Accoramboni, Vittoria (c. 1557–1585)
Adamova, Adela (1927—)
Adelaide of Burgundy (931–999)
Adelaide of Maurienne (1092–1154)
Adelaide of Savona (d. 1118)
Adelgunde of Bavaria (1823–1914)
Aesara of Lucania (fl. 400s–300s BCE)
Agatha (d. 251)
Agatha, Saint (d. 251)
Agnelli, Susanna (1922—)
Agnes, Saint (d. possibly c. 304)
Agnesi, Maria Gaetana (1718–1799)
Agnesi, Maria Teresa (1720–1795)
Agnes of Assisi (1207–1232)
Agnes of Monte Pulciano (1274–1317)
Albanese, Licia (1913—)
Alberghetti, Anna Maria (1936—)
Alboni, Marietta (1823–1894)
Albrizzi, Isabella Teotochi, Contessa d' (1770–1836)
Aldrude (fl. 1172)
Aleotti, Raffaella (c. 1570–c. 1646)
Aleotti, Vittoria (c. 1573–c. 1620)
Alexander, Francesca (1837–1917)
Alicia of Parma (1849–1935)
Alisia of Antioch (fl. 1100s)
Allucci, Carmela (1970—)
Amalasuntha (c. 498–535)
Amalie of Hesse-Darmstadt (1754–1832)
Amati, Olga (1924—)
Ambrosetti, Bianca (1914–1929)
Anagnos, Julia (1844–1886)
Andreini, Isabella (1562–1604)
Angela of Brescia (1474–1540)
Angela of Foligno (1249–1309)
Angeli, Pier (1932–1971)
Angelilli, Roberta (1965—)

Angiolini, Giuseppina (c. 1800–?)
Anguissola, Anna Maria (c. 1545–?)
Anguissola, Elena (c. 1525–after 1584)
Anguissola, Europa (c. 1542–?)
Anguissola, Lucia (c. 1536–1565)
Anguissola, Sofonisba (1532–1625)
Anna Maria of Saxony (1836–1859)
Anna of Savoy (1455–1480)
Anna Victoria of Savoy (fl. 18th c.)
Anne de la Tour (d. 1512)
Anne-Marie d'Bourbon-Orleans (1669–1728)
Anne of Bourbon-Parma (1923—)
Anne of Ferrara (1531–1607)
Anne of Lusignan (b. before 1430)
Anne of Savoy (c. 1320–1353)
Anselmi, Tina (1927—)
Antonelli, Laura (1941—)
Antonia (1456–1491)
Antonia (1858–1883)
Aragona, Tullia d' (1510–1556)
Araujo, Alexandra (1972—)
Arignote (fl. 6th c. BCE)
Ascarelli, Devora (fl. 1601)
Asensio, Manola (1946—)
Assandra, Caterina (fl. 1580–1609)
Aubrey of Buonalbergo (fl. 1000s)
Audofleda (c. 470–?)
Augusta of Tuscany (1825–1864)
Aulenti, Gae (1927—)
Baccelli, Giovanna (c. 1753–1801)
Bacinetti-Florenzi, Marianna (1802–1870)
Bandettini, Teresa (1763–1837)
Banti, Brigitta (c. 1756–1806)
Barbara of Brandenburg (1422–1481)
Barbi, Alice (1862–1948)
Barbieri, Fedora (1919–2003)
Baroni, Leonora (1611–1670)
Barr, Margaret Scolari (1901–1987)
Basile, Adriana (c. 1590–c. 1640)
Bassi, Laura (1711–1778)
Battaglia, Letizia (1935—)
Beatrice of Anjou (d. 1275)
Beatrice of Cenci (1577–1599)
Beatrice of Lorraine (c. 1020–1076)
Beatrice of Provence (d. 1267)
Beatrice of Rethel (fl. 1150s)
Beatrice of Savoy (fl. 1240s)
Beatrice of Upper Burgundy (1145–1184)
Beatrice Portinari (c. 1265–1290)
Belgioso, Cristina (1808–1871)
Bella, Antoinetta (b. 1863)
Bellincioni, Gemma (1864–1950)
Bellonci, Maria (1902–1986)
Bellutti, Antonella (1968—)
Belmondo, Stefania (1969—)
Bembo, Antonia (1643–1715)
Benci, Ginevra de' (b. 1457)
Bene, Adriana Gabrieli del (c. 1755–1799)
Benedicta of Assisi (d. 1260)
Benetton, Guiliana (1935—)
Benincasa, Ursula (1547–1618)
Beretta, Caterina (1839–1911)
Bergalli, Luisa (1703–1779)
Bertha of Toulouse (fl. late 700s)
Bertini, Francesca (1888–1985)
Bertolini, Livia (fl. 1920s–1930s)
Bevilacqua, Alma (1910–1988)
Bianchedi, Diana (1969—)
Bianchini, Angela (1921—)
Bigottini, Emilie (1784–1858)
Blanche of Bourbon (1868–1949)
Blanche of Naples (d. 1310)
Blanche of Navarre (1385–1441)
Blanche of Rossi (d. 1237)
Blanche of Savoy (c. 1337–?)
Blanchi, Elisa (1987—)
Bocchi, Dorotea (fl. 1390–1430)
Bodard, Mag (1916—)
Boiardi, Helen (1905–1995)
Bolkan, Florinda (1941—)
Bonacci Brunamonti, Maria Alinda (1841–1903)
Bonanni, Laudomia (1907–2002)
Bona of Pisa (c. 1156–1207)
Bona of Savoy (c. 1450–c. 1505)
Bonaparte, Carolina (1782–1839)
Bonaparte, Elisa (1777–1820)
Bonaparte, Pauline (1780–1825)
Bonfanti, Marietta (1845–1921)
Bonino, Emma (1948—)
Boninsegna, Celestina (1877–1947)
Bonmartini, Linda (1873–?)
Borboni, Paola (1900–1995)
Bordoni, Faustina (c. 1700–1781)
Borgese Freschi, Maria (1881–1947)
Borgia, Lucrezia (1480–1519)
Boronat, Olimpia (1867–1934)
Bortolozzi, Francesca (1968—)
Boschetti, Amina (1836–1881)
Bosé, Lucia (1931—)
Bosurgi, Silvia (1979—)
Bozzacchi, Giuseppina (1853–1870)
Bozzino, Tina (fl. 1920s–30s)
Braggiotti, Berthe (c. 1900–c. 1925)
Braggiotti, Francesca (1902–1998)
Braggiotti, Gloria (c. 1905—)
Brianza, Carlotta (1862–1930)
Brugnoli, Amalia (c. 1808–?)
Brunet, Roberta (1965—)
Bulnes, Esmée (1900–1986)
Busoni, Anna (1833–1909)
Cabrini, Frances Xavier (1850–1917)
Cacchi, Paola (1945—)
Caccini, Francesca (1587–c. 1626)
Calamai, Clara (1915–1998)
Calligaris, Novella (1954—)
Camber, Irene (1926—)
Campanini, Barbara (1721–1799)
Canale, Gianna Maria (1927—)
Canins, Maria (1949—)
Cantofoli, Ginevra (1618–1672)
Cappello, Bianca (1548–1587)
Cappiello, Rosa (1942—)
Carabella, Flora (1926–1999)
Cardinale, Claudia (1939—)
Caroline (1793–1812)
Caroline of Naples (1798–1870)
Caroline of Parma (1770–1804)
Caroline of Sicily (1820–1861)
Carosio, Margherita (1908–2005)
Carpinteri, Laura (b. 1910)
Carrel, Felicite (fl. 1860s)
Carriera, Rosalba (1675–1757)
Casagrande, Anna (1958—)
Casalina, Lucia (1677–1762)
Castiglione, Virginie, Countess de (1837–1899)
Casulana, Maddalena (c. 1540–1583)
Catalani, Angelica (1780–1849)
Catherine of Bologna (1413–1463)
Catherine of Genoa (1447–1510)
Catherine of Ricci (c. 1522–1589)
Catherine of Siena (1347–1380)
Cattanei, Vannozza (1442–1518)
Cavalieri, Lina (1874–1944)
Cavallazzi, Malvina (c. 1852–1924)
Cavalleri, Silvia (1972—)
Cavani, Liliana (1933—)
Ceccarelli, Daniela (1975—)
Cecchi D'Amico, Suso (1914—)
Cederna, Camilla (1921–1997)
Cereta, Laura, of Brescia (1469–1499)
Cerri, Cecilie (1872–1931)
Cerrito, Fanny (1817–1909)
Cesari, Welleda (1920—)
Charlotte-Aglae (1700–1761)
Chenal-Minuzzo, Giuliana (1931—)
Chiappa, Imelda (1966—)
Chiesa, Laura (1971—)
Christina of Denmark (1521–1590)
Christina of Sardinia (1812–1836)
Christine of Bourbon (1779–1849)
Christine of Lorraine (c. 1571–1637)
Cialente, Fausta (1898–1994)
Ciano, Edda (1910–1995)
Cibò, Caterina (fl. 1533)
Cicciolina (1951—)
Cigna, Gina (1900–2001)
Ciocca, Giovanna (c. 1825–?)
Clara (1697–1744)
Clare of Assisi (c. 1194–1253)
Claudia Felicitas (fl. 17th c.)
Clementine of Austria (1798–1881)
Clotilde of Savoy (1843–1911)
Collino, Maria (1947—)
Colombetti, Bruna (1936—)
Colonna, Catherine (d. around 1440)
Colonna, Vittoria (c. 1490–1547)
Columba of Rieti (1467–1501)
Compagnoni, Deborah (1970—)
Constance of Aragon (d. 1222)
Constance of Sicily (1154–1198)
Conti, Francesca (1972—)
Cornaro, Caterina (1454–1510)
Cornaro Piscopia, Elena Lucretia (1646–1684)
Cornelisen, Ann (1926–2003)
Cornelys, Theresa (1723–1797)
Cortesa, Valentina (1924—)
Corti, Maria (1915–2002)
Cossotto, Fiorenza (1935—)
Cosway, Maria (1759–1838)
Crisi, Maria (1892–1953)
Cristina, Ines (b. 1875)
Cucchi, Claudine (1834–1913)
Cunegunde (fl. 800s)
Cuzzoni, Francesca (c. 1698–1770)
Dal Monte, Toti (1893–1975)
Damo (fl. 6th c. BCE)
Dampierre, Emmanuela del (b. 1913)
Dandolo, Giovanna (fl. 1457)
d'Andrea, Novella (d. 1333)
Danieli, Cecilia (1943—)
De Cespedes, Alba (1911–1997)
Deledda, Grazia (1871–1936)
del Giocondo, Lisa (1474–?)
della Scala, Beatrice (1340–1384)
Dell'Era, Antoinetta (1861–?)
del Maino, Agnes (fl. 1420s)
Denis, María (1916–2004)
De Stefani, Livia (1913—)
De Vito, Gioconda (1907–1994)
Diane de France (1538–1619)
Dianti, Laura (fl. 1527)
Di Centa, Manuela (1963—)
di Lorenzo, Tina (1872–1930)
di Mario, Tania (1979—)
Di Robilant, Daisy, Countess (fl. 1922–1933)
Donatella (fl. 1271)
Dorio, Gabriella (1957—)
D'Ottavio, Frazia (1985—)
Duranti, Francesca (1935—)
Duse, Eleonora (1858–1924)
Dutt, Toru (1856–1877)
Egri, Susanna (1926—)

Geographic Index

Eleanor d'Arborea (c. 1360–c. 1404)
Elena of Montenegro (1873–1952)
Eleonora of Austria (1534–1594)
Elizabeth of Saxony (1830–1912)
Elvira (d. 1135)
Épine, Margherita de l' (c. 1683–1746)
Este, Alda d' (1333–1381)
Este, Alda d' (fl. 1300s)
Este, Beata Beatrice I d' (d. 1226)
Este, Beata Beatrice II d' (d. 1262)
Este, Beatrice d' (fl. 1290s)
Este, Beatrice d' (fl. 1300s)
Este, Beatrice d' (d. 1334)
Este, Beatrice d' (fl. 1350s)
Este, Beatrice d' (1427–1497)
Este, Beatrice d' (1475–1497)
Este, Bianca Maria d' (1440–1506)
Este, Catherine d' (fl. 1700)
Este, Costanza d' (fl. 1200s)
Este, Cunegunda d' (c. 1012–1055)
Este, Eleonora d' (1515–1575)
Este, Eleonora d' (1537–1581)
Este, Elisabetta d' (fl. 1500)
Este, Elisa d' (?–1329)
Este, Giacoma d' (fl. 1300)
Este, Ginevra d' (1414–1440)
Este, Giovanna d' (fl. 1240s)
Este, Giovanna d' (fl. 1280s)
Este, Giovanna d' (fl. 1300s)
Este, Isabella d' (1474–1539)
Este, Isotta d' (1425–1456)
Este, Isotta d' (fl. 1300s)
Este, Lippa d'
Este, Lucia d' (1419–1437)
Este, Lucrezia d' (d. 1516/18)
Este, Lucrezia d' (1535–1598)
Este, Mambilia d' (fl. 1200s)
Este, Margherita d' (d. 1452)
Este, Parisina d' (fl. 1400)
Este, Pizzocara d' (fl. 1400s)
Este, Ricciarda d'
Este, Taddea d' (1365–1404)
Este, Verde d' (fl. 1300s)
Este, Virginia d' (b. 1573?)
Eustochia (1444–1469)
Fabbri, Flora (c. 1807–c. 1857)
Falca, Marinella (1986—)
Falconieri, Juliana (1270–1341)
Fallaci, Oriana (1930—)
Farnese, Giulia (1474–1518?)
Fedele, Cassandra Fidelis (1465–1558)
Ferragamo, Fiamma (1941–1998)
Ferrais, Amalia (1830–1904)
Ferrari, Carlotta (1837–1907)
Ferrero, Anna-Maria (1931—)
Fetti, Lucrina (fl. 1614–1651)
Fiacconi, Franca (1965—)
Filippi, Rosina (1866–1930)
Fini, Leonor (1908–1996)
Firenze, Francesca da (fl. 15th c.)
Foix, Germaine de (1488–1538)
Fontana, Giovanna (1915–2004)
Fontana, Lavinia (1552–1614)
Fornari, Maria Victoria (1562–1617)
Fornaroli, Cia (1888–1954)
Forti, Simone (c. 1935—)
Fracci, Carla (1936—)
Francesca da Rimini (d. 1285?)
Frances of Rome (1384–1440)
Franchi, Anna (1866–1954)
Franco, Veronica (1546–1591)
Françoise d'Orleans (fl. 1650)
Freni, Mirella (1935—)
Fuocco, Sofia (1830–1916)
Fusar-Poli, Barbara (1972—)
Gabrielli, Caterina (1730–1796)
Galilei, Maria Celeste (1600–1634)
Galizia, Fede (1578–1630)
Galli, Caterina (c. 1723–1804)
Galli, Rosina (1896–1940)
Galli-Curci, Amelita (1882–1963)
Gambara, Veronica (1485–1550)
Gambarelli, Maria (1900–1990)
Gandhi, Sonia (1946—)
Gandolfi, Annapia (1964—)
Garibaldi, Anita (c. 1821–1849)
Garufi, Bianca (1920—)
Garzoni, Giovanna (1600–1670)
Gattilusi, Caterina (fl. 1440)
Gattilusi, Eugenia (fl. late 1390s)
Gattinoni, Fernanda (1906–2002)
Gelisio, Deborah (1976—)
Gentile-Cordiale, Edera (1920–1993)
Gentileschi, Artemisia (1593–c. 1653)
Ghilardotti, Fiorella (1946—)
Ghisi, Diana (c. 1530–1590)
Giacobbe, Maria (1928—)
Giaconi, Luisa (1870–1908)
Gianoni, Lavinia (1911—)
Giavotti, Luigina (1916–1976)
Gigli, Elena (1985—)
Giliani, Allessandra (1307–1326)
Ginzburg, Natalia (1916–1991)
Giordani, Claudia (1955—)
Giorgi, Virginia (1914—)
Giovanna of Italy (1907–2000)
Giuranna, Barbara (1902–1998)
Gonzaga, Antonia (d. 1538)
Gonzaga, Cecilia (1426–1451)
Gonzaga, Cecilia (1451–1472)
Gonzaga, Chiara (1465–1505)
Gonzaga, Dorotea (1449–1462)
Gonzaga, Eleonora (1493–1543)
Gonzaga, Ippolita (1503–1570)
Gonzaga, Ippolita (1535–1563)
Gonzaga, Isabella (1537–1579)
Gonzaga, Isabella (d. 1559)
Gonzaga, Isabella (fl. 1600s)
Gonzaga, Margherita (d. 1399)
Gonzaga, Margherita (1418–1439)
Gonzaga, Margherita (1510–1566)
Gonzaga, Margherita (1561–1628)
Gonzaga, Margherita (1564–1618)
Gonzaga, Margherita (1591–1632)
Gonzaga, Maria (1609–1660)
Gonzaga, Paola (1393–1453)
Gonzaga, Paola (1463–1497)
Gonzaga, Paola (1508–1569)
Gramatica, Emma (1875–1965)
Gramatica, Irma (1873–1962)
Gray, Teresa Corinna Ubertis (1877–1964)
Grego, Melania (1973—)
Griselda (fl. 11th c.)
Grisi, Carlotta (1819–1899)
Grisi, Giuditta (1805–1840)
Grisi, Giulia (1811–1869)
Guacci, Giuseppina (1807–1848)
Gufler, Edith (1962—)
Guglielma of Milan (d. 1282)
Guglielminetti, Amalia (1881–1941)
Guicciardini, Isabella (fl. 16th c.)
Guiccioli, Teresa (c. 1801–1873)
Guidacci, Margherita (1921–1992)
Guidi, Rachele (1891–1979)
Guiducci, Armanda (1923–1992)
Guntrud of Bavaria (fl. 715)
Guzman, Eleonore de (d. 1512)
Helena of Epirus (fl. 1250s)
Humilitas of Faenza (1226–1310)
Invernizio, Carolina (1858–1916)
Iotti, Nilde (1920–1999)
Ippolita (1446–1484)
Isabel de Clermont (d. 1465)
Isabella del Balzo (d. 1533)
Isabella of Naples (1470–1524)
Isabelle of Cornwall (fl. 14th c.)
Isabelle of Lorraine (1410–1453)
Jacobini, Maria (1890–1944)
Joan (d. 858)
Joanna II of Naples (1374–1435)
Joanna I of Naples (1326–1382)
Joanna of Aragon (1454–1517)
Joanna of Naples (1478–1518)
Joanna of Sicily (1165–1199)
Josephine of Lorraine (1753–1757)
Justina (d. 64)
Kostner, Isolde (1975—)
Kuliscioff, Anna (c. 1854–1925)
Lagorio, Gina (1930—)
La Gratiosa (d. 1659)
Lama, Giulia (c. 1685–c. 1753)
Lambertini, Imelda (1320–1333)
Landi, Elissa (1904–1948)
Landriani, Lucrezia (fl. 1450s)
Lechner, Erica
Legnani, Pierina (1863–1923)
Lenore of Sicily (1289–1341)
Leonarda, Isabella (1620–1704)
Leone, Giuseppina (1934—)
Leonora of Aragon (1450–1493)
Leonora of Savoy (fl. 1200)
Levi-Montalcini, Rita (b. 1909)
Lipperini, Guendalina (c. 1862–1914)
Lisi, Virna (1936—)
Lollobrigida, Gina (1927—)
Lombardi, Lella (1941–1992)
Longabarba, Bona (fl. 15th c.)
Longhi, Lucia Lopresti (1895–1985)
Lonzi-Ragno, Antonella (1940—)
Loren, Sophia (1934—)
Louisa Amelia (1773–1802)
Louisa Carlotta of Naples (1804–1844)
Loy, Rosetta (1931—)
Lualdi, Antonella (1931—)
Lucia of Narni (1476–1544)
Lussu, Joyce Salvadori (1912–1988)
Maddalena of Canossa (1774–1833)
Madeleine de la Tour d'Auvergne (1501–1519)
Mafalda of Hesse (1902–1944)
Magnani, Anna (1908–1973)
Magoni, Paoletta (1964—)
Malabarba, Germana (1913–2002)
Malaspina, Ricciarda
Malatesta, Anna (fl. 15th c.)
Malatesta, Battista da Montefeltro (1383–1450)
Malato, Giusy (1971—)
Mancini, Evelina (1849–1896)
Mancini, Hortense (1646–1699)
Mancini, Laura (1823–1869)
Mancini, Laure (1635–1657)
Mancini, Marie (1640–1715)
Mancini, Marie-Anne (1649–1714)
Mangano, Silvana (1930–1989)
Manzini, Gianna (1896–1974)
Manzolini, Anna Morandi (1716–1774)
Maraini, Dacia (1936—)
Marangoni, Clara (1915—)
Maratti Zappi, Faustina (c. 1680–1745)
Mareri, Filippa (c. 1190–1236)
Margaret of Attenduli (1375–?)
Margaret of Corigliano
Margaret of Cortona (1247–1297)
Margaret of Naples (fl. late 1300s)
Margaret of Navarre (fl. 1154–1172)
Margaret of Parma (b. 1612)
Margaret of Savoy (d. 1483)

Margaret of Savoy (1523–1574)
Margaret of Savoy (fl. 1609–1612)
Margaret of Savoy (1851–1926)
Marghieri, Clotilde (1897–1981)
Marguerite de Bourgogne (1250–1308)
Marguerite Louise of Orleans (c. 1645–1721)
Maria (fl. 995–1025)
Maria Anna of Saxony (1795–1865)
Maria Anna of Saxony (1799–1832)
Maria Annunziata (1843–1871)
Maria Antonia of Naples (1784–1806)
Maria Antonia of Sicily (1814–1898)
Maria Antonia of Spain (1729–1785)
Maria Carolina (1752–1814)
Maria Clementina of Austria (1777–1801)
Maria de la Esperanza (1914—)
Maria Ludovica (1798–1857)
Maria Ludovica (1845–1917)
Maria Luisa of Etruria (1782–1824)
Maria Magdalena of Austria (1589–1631)
Mariani, Felice (1954—)
Maria of Aragon (fl. 1311)
Maria of Aragon (fl. 1440)
Maria of Castile (1401–1458)
Maria of Savoy (fl. 1400s)
Maria of Savoy (1914—)
Maria of Sicily (d. 1402)
Maria Teresa of Austria (1773–1832)
Maria Theresa of Tuscany (1801–1855)
Marie Adelaide of Austria (1822–1855)
Marie Clotilde (d. 1794)
Marie José of Belgium (1906–2001)
Marie of Valois (fl. 14th c.)
Marinetti, Benedetta Cappa (1897–1977)
Martelli, Camilla (fl. 1570s)
Martinelli, Elsa (1932—)
Marzia (fl. 1357)
Masina, Giulietta (1920–1994)
Massari, Lea (1933—)
Masseroni, Daniela (1985—)
Massimi, Petronilla Paolini (1663–1726)
Mauri, Rosita (1856–1923)
May, Fiona (1969—)
Mayfreda de Pirovano (d. 1300)
Medici, Alfonsina de (d. 1520)
Medici, Anna de (1616–?)
Medici, Anna Maria de (d. 1741)
Medici, Bianca de (fl. late 1400s)
Medici, Caterina de (1593–1629)
Medici, Catherine de (1519–1589)
Medici, Clarice de (c. 1453–1487)
Medici, Clarice de (1493–1528)
Medici, Claudia de (1604–1648)
Medici, Contessina de (fl. 15th c.)
Medici, Eleonora de (1522–1562)
Medici, Eleonora de (1556–1576)
Medici, Eleonora de (1567–1611)
Medici, Eleonora de (1591–1617)
Medici, Eleonora de (fl. 1690)
Medici, Ginevra de (fl. 15th c.)
Medici, Isabella de (1542–1576)
Medici, Laudomia de (fl. 1460s)
Medici, Laudomia de (fl. 1530s)
Medici, Lucrezia de (1425–1482)
Medici, Lucrezia de (b. around 1480)
Medici, Lucrezia de (c. 1544–1561)
Medici, Luisa de (fl. 15th c.)
Medici, Maddalena de (d. 1519)
Medici, Maddalena de (1600–1633)
Medici, Maria Cristina de (1610–1632)
Medici, Maria de (fl. late 1400s)
Medici, Maria Soderini de (fl. 16th c.)
Medici, Marie de (c. 1573–1642)
Medici, Nannina de (fl. 15th c.)
Medici, Piccarda de (fl. 15th c.)
Medici, Semiramide de (fl. 1480s)
Medici, Violante Beatrice de (d. 1731)
Medici, Vittoria de (d. 1694)
Mei-Figner, Medea (1859–1952)
Mendoza, Ana de (1540–1592)
Mercuriade of Salerno (fl. 1200)
Michelina of Pesaro (1300–1356)
Migliaccio, Lucia (1770–1826)
Mila, Adriana (fl. 1469–1502)
Milani, Milena (1922—)
Milo, Sandra (1935—)
Miranda, Isa (1909–1982)
Modotti, Tina (1896–1942)
Molza, Tarquinia (1542–1617)
Montanaria (fl. 1272)
Montefeltro, Elisabetta (fl. 15th c.)
Montefeltro, Giovanna (fl. 15th c.)
Montesi, Wilma (1932–1953)
Montessori, Maria (1870–1952)
Morace, Carolina (1964—)
Morandini, Giuliana (1938—)
Morante, Elsa (1912–1985)
Morata, Fulvia Olympia (1526–1555)
Morgantini, Luisa (1940—)
Morico, Lucia (1975—)
Moroder, Karin (1974—)
Morpurgo, Rachel (1790–1871)
Mozzoni, Anna Maria (1837–1920)
Musa, Gilda (1926–1999)
Muscardini, Cristiana (1948—)
Musi, Maria Maddalena (1669–1751)
Mussolini, Alessandra (1962—)
Musumeci, Maddalena (1976—)
Muzio, Claudia (1889–1936)
Myia (fl. 6th c. BCE)
Naldi, Nita (1897–1961)
Napoletano, Pasqualina (1949—)
Negri, Ada (1870–1945)
Negrone, Carina (1911—)
Noce, Teresa (1900–1980)
Nogarola, Isotta (c. 1416–1466)
Nossis of Locri (fl. 300 BCE)
Notari, Elvira (1875–1946)
Novella (d. 1333)
Odaldi, Annalena (1572–1638)
Oldenburg, Margaret (b. 1895)
Olivero, Magda (b. 1910)
Ombres, Rossana (1931—)
Ormani, Maria (fl. 1453)
Orsini, Belleza (d. 1528)
Ortese, Anna Maria (1914–1998)
Orvieto, Laura (1876–1953)
Paciotti, Elena Ornella (1941—)
Padovani, Lea (1920–1991)
Pagliero, Camilia (1859–1925)
Palladino, Emma (c. 1860–1922)
Palladino, Eusapia (1854–1918)
Pallerini, Antonia (1790–1870)
Palli, Angelica (1798–1875)
Pampanini, Silvana (1925—)
Paruzzi, Gabriella (1969—)
Pasini, Claudia (1939—)
Pasta, Giuditta (1797–1865)
Pavan, Marisa (1932—)
Pellegrini, Federica (1988—)
Percoto, Caterina (1812–1887)
Perrone, Elisabetta (1968—)
Perversi, Luigina (1914–1983)
Petacci, Clara (1912–1945)
Pezzo, Paola (1969—)
Pia of Sicily (1849–1882)
Piccinini, Amelia (1917–1979)
Pico, Caterina (d. 1501)
Pierangeli, Rina Faccio (1876–1960)
Pierantozzi, Emanuela (1968—)
Pimentel, Eleonora (c. 1768–1799)
Pisano, Nicola (fl. 1278)
Pizzavini, Diana (1911–1989)
Podestà, Rossana (1934—)
Poli Bortone, Adriana (1943—)
Pompilj, Vittoria Aganoor (1855–1910)
Pozzi, Antonia (1912–1938)
Pozzo, Modesta (1555–1592)
Pretinha (1975—)
Proba (fl. 4th c.)
Prosperi, Carola (1883–1975)
Putzer, Karen (1978—)
Quaranta, Isabella (1892–1975)
Quaranta, Letizia (1892–1974)
Quaranta, Lidia (1891–1928)
Quaretti, Lea (1912–1981)
Rafanelli, Leda (1880–1971)
Ragusa, Cinzia (1977—)
Rame, Franca (1929—)
Ramondino, Fabrizia (1936—)
Ravera, Camilla (1889–1988)
Renzi, Anna (c. 1620–1660)
Respighi, Elsa (1894–1996)
Ricci, Nina (1883–1970)
Rinaldi, Angela (c. 1916—)
Ristori, Adelaide (1822–1906)
Rita of Cascia (1381–1457)
Robert-Angelini, Enif (1886–1976)
Rodiani, Onorata (d. 1452)
Rogatis, Teresa de (1893–1979)
Romano, Francesca (fl. 1321)
Romano, Lalla (1906–2001)
Rosa, Anella de (1613–1649)
Rosati, Carolina (1826–1905)
Rose of Viterbo (1235–1252)
Rosselli, Amelia (1930–1996)
Rossi, Properzia de (c. 1490–1530)
Rossi Drago, Eleonora (1925—)
Rovere, Giulia della (fl. 16th c.)
Sacchetto, Rita (1879–1959)
Sagan, Ginetta (1923–2000)
Salerno-Sonnenberg, Nadja (1961—)
Salviati, Elena (fl. early 1500s)
Salviati, Maria (1499–1543)
Salvini-Donatelli, Fanny (c. 1815–1891)
Salvioni, Guglierma (1842–?)
Sancha of Aragon (1478–1506)
Sangalli, Rita (1849–1909)
Sanson, Yvonne (1926—)
Santoni, Elisa (1987—)
Sanuti, Nicolosa (fl. 1453)
Sanvitale, Francesca (1928—)
Sarfatti, Margherita (1880–1961)
Sartori, Amalia (1947—)
Savorgnan, Maria (fl. 1500)
Sbarbati, Luciana (1946—)
Scapin, Ylenia (1975—)
Schiaffino, Rosanna (1938—)
Scholastica (c. 480–543)
Scieri, Antoinette (fl. 1920s)
Sciocchetti, Marina (1954—)
Sciolti, Gabriella (1974—)
Sciutti, Graziella (1927–2001)
Scotto, Renata (1933—)
Sensini, Alessandra (1970—)
Serao, Matilde (1856–1927)
Sforza, Angela (fl. 1500s)
Sforza, Anna (1473–1497)
Sforza, Battista (1446–1472)
Sforza, Bianca Simonetta (fl. 15th c.)
Sforza, Bona (1493–1557)
Sforza, Cammilla (fl. 15th c.)
Sforza, Caterina (c. 1462–1509)
Sforza, Chiara (b. around 1464)
Sforza, Costanza (fl. 1445)
Sforza, Ginevra (d. 1507)
Sforza, Ginevra Tiepolo (fl. 16th c.)

Sforza, Ippolita (fl. 15th c.)
Sforza, Maddalena (1472–1490)
Sforza, Polissena (fl. 15th c.)
Sforza, Seraphina (1434–1478)
Sichelgaita of Salerno (1040–1090)
Sigurana, Caterina (fl. 1543)
Simeoni, Sara (1953—)
Simionato, Giulietta (1910—)
Sirani, Elizabetta (1638–1665)
Solinas Donghi, Beatrice (1923—)
Sophie of Montferrat (fl. 15th c.)
Spara, Hieronyma (d. 1659)
Spaziani, Maria Luisa (1924—)
Speraz, Beatrice (1843–1923)
Stampa, Gaspara (1523–1554)
Stignani, Ebe (1903–1975)
Storchio, Rosina (1876–1945)
Strepponi, Giuseppina (1815–1897)
Strozzi, Alessandra (1406–1469)
Strozzi, Barbara (1619–1664)
Strozzi, Marietta Palla (fl. 1468)
Sullam, Sara Coppia (1590–1641)
Tagliabue, Elena (1977—)
Taglioni, Louisa (1823–1893)
Taglioni, Maria (1804–1884)
Tanaquil (fl. late 7th–early 6th BCE)
Tanzini, Luisa (b. 1914)
Tarabotti, Arcangela (1604–1652)
Tebaldi, Renata (1922–2004)
Terabust, Elisabetta (1946—)
Tess, Giulia (1889–1976)
Tetrazzini, Eva
(1862–1938)
Tetrazzini, Luisa (1871–1940)
Theodelinda (568–628)
Theresa of Savoy (1803–1879)
Tipo, Maria (1931—)
Tofana (1653–1723)
Tonelli, Annalena (1943–2003)
Tonolli, Livia (1909–1985)
Torriani, Maria Antonietta (1840–1920)
Tosatti, Barbara Maria (1891–1934)
Toselli, Louisa (1870–1947)
Toth, Noemi (1976—)
Trapani, Antonia von (b. 1851)
Traversa, Lucia (1965—)
Trentini, Emma (1878–1959)
Trettel, Lidia (1973—)
Trillini, Giovanna (1970—)
Trocmé, Magda (1901–1996)
Tronconi, Carolina (b. 1913)
Trotula (c. 1040s–1097)
Tumiati, Lucia (1926—)
Turisini, Valentina (1969—)
Uga, Elisa (1968—)
Vaccaroni, Dorina (1963—)
Valla, Trebisonda (1916—)
Valli, Alida (1921–2006)
Vanzetta, Bice (1961—)
Veigel, Eva-Maria (1724–1822)
Vercesi, Ines (1916–1997)
Vernizzi, Laura (1985—)
Vertua Gentile, Anna (1850–1927)
Vespucci, Simonetta (d. 1476)
Vestris, Thérèse (1726–1808)
Vezzali, Valentina (1974—)
Victoria (d. around 253)
Viganò, Renata (1900–1976)
Viola, Emilia Ferretti (1844–1929)
Visconti, Agnes (c. 1365–1391)
Visconti, Bianca Maria (1423–1470)
Visconti, Catherine (c. 1360–1404)
Vittadini, Rita (1914–2000)
Vitti, Monica (1931—)
Vivanti, Annie (1868–1942)
Volpi, Giulia (1970—)
von Haynau, Edith (1884–1978)
Weissensteiner, Gerda (1969—)
Wertmüller, Lina (1928—)
Wulz, Wanda (1903–1984)
Yolanda Margherita of Italy (b. 1901)
Yolande of Aragon
Yolande of France (1434–1478)
Zalaffi, Margherita (1966—)
Zambelli, Carlotta (1875–1968)
Zanchi, Manuela (1977—)
Zanfretta, Francesca (1862–1952)
Zanfretta, Marietta (c. 1837–1898)
Zita of Lucca (1218–1275)
Zuccari, Anna Radius (1846–1918)
Zucchi, Virginia (1849–1930)

JAMAICA

Independent state, island in West Indies
Discovered by Columbus (1494)
Became Spanish colony (1509–1655)
Under English rule (1655–1958)
Became a territory of West Indies Federation (1958–1962)
Achieved independence (1962)

Bailey, Aleen (1980—)
Barker, Mary Anne (1831–1911)
Bell, Vera (1906—)
Bennett, Louise Simone (1919—)
Brodber, Erna (1936—)
Burgher, Michelle (1977—)
Campbell, Juliet (1970—)
Campbell, Lady Colin (1949—)
Campbell, Veronica (1982—)
Cliff, Michelle (1946—)
Craig, Christine (1943—)
Cuthbert, Juliet (1964—)
Davy, Nadia (1980—)
D'Costa, Jean (1937—)
Denton, Sandy (1969—)
Escoffery, Gloria (1923–2002)
Ferland, Barbara (1919—)
Fox, Elizabeth Vassall (1770–1845)
Freeman, Michele
Garvey, Amy Jacques (1896–1973)
Graham-Fenton, Lorraine (1973—)
Hemmings, Deon (1968—)
Hollar, Constance (1881–1945)
Iremonger, Lucille (c. 1916–1989?)
Jackson, Grace (1961—)
Jones, Grace (1952—)
Killingbeck, Molly (1959—)
Lawrence, Tayna (1975—)
Marley, Cedella (1967—)
Marson, Una (1905–1965)
McDonald, Beverly (1970—)
Mitchell, Nikole
Mordecai, Pamela (1942—)
Mowatt, Judy (1952—)
Nanny (fl. 1730s)
Ottey, Merlene (1960—)
Ottey-Page, Merlene (1960—)
Pollard, Velma (1937—)
Prendergast, Sharon Marley (1964—)
Richards, Sandie (1968—)
Sanderson, Tessa (1956—)
Scott-Pomales, Catherine
Seacole, Mary Jane (c. 1805–1881)
Senior, Olive (1941—)
Simpson, Sherone (1984—)
Sinclair, Madge (1938–1995)
Smith, Ronetta (1980—)
Thomas, Elean (1947–2004)
Williams, Novlene (1982—)
Wynter, Sylvia (1928—)

JAPAN

Independent state comprising island chain in west Pacific Ocean
Early Ainu inhabitants driven north by invaders
Accession of Jimmu Tenno (660 BCE)
Buddhism introduced (552 CE)
Shogunates founded (1192)
Invaded by Mongols (13th c.)
Feudalism broken (15th c.)
Visited by Portuguese (1542–1543)
Christianity introduced (1549–1551)
Japanese Empire united (16th c.)
Adopted constitution (1889)
Warred with China over Korea (1894–1895)
Annexed Korea (1910)
Occupied Manchuria and Shanghai (1930s)
Allied with Gemany and Italy in World War II (1940)
Attacked Pearl Harbor, Hawaii, and occupied Manilla (1941)
Seized Hong Kong and invaded Malay Peninsula (1941)
Siezed coastal Ambon, Borneo, Sumatra, and Java (1942)
Invaded Siam and Burma (1942)
Surrendered after United States dropped atomic bombs on Hiroshima and Nagasaki (1945)
Adopted new constitution (1947)

Aihara, Toshiko (1939—)
Akazome Emon (d. 1027)
Akimoto, Matsuyo (1911—)
Akiyoshi, Toshiko (1929—)
Ando, Misako (1971—)
Anno, Noriko (1976—)
Aoki, Mayumi (1953—)
Aoki, Tsuru (1892–1961)
Aoki, Yayoi (1927—)
Arakida, Yuko (1954—)
Arimori, Yuko (1966—)
Ariyoshi, Sawako (1931–1984)
Asakawa, Hitomi (1948)
Asakawa, Takako (1938—)
Bacon, Alice Mabel (1858–1918)
Chand, Meira (1942—)
Chiba, Ginko (1938—)
Chichibu Setsuko (1909–1995)
Daini no Sanmi (999–after 1078)
Doi, Takako (1928—)
Egami, Ayano
Egami, Yumi (1957—)
Emoto, Yuko (1972—)
Enchi, Fumiko (1905–1986)
Enoki, Miswo (1939—)
Fubuki, Koshiji (1924–1980)
Fujii, Raika (1974—)
Fujii, Yumiko (c. 1972—)
Fujiki, Mayuko (1975—)
Fujimaru, Michiyo (1979—)
Fujimoto, Yuko (1943—)
Fukuda, Hideko (1865–1927)
Fukunaka, Sachiko (1946—)
Furukawa, Makiko (1947—)
Gemmei (c. 661–721)
Genshō (680–748)
Go, Shizuko (1929—)
Go-Sakuramachi (1740–1814)
Hagiwara, Yoko (1920—)
Hama, Keiko (1947—)
Hamaguchi, Kyoko (1978—)
Handa, Yuriko (1940—)
Hani, Motoko (1873–1957)
Hara, Kazuko (1935—)
Hara, Setsuko (1920—)
Harada, Saho (1982—)
Harada, Yasuko (1928—)
Haruko (1850–1914)
Hasegawa, Itsuko (1941—)
Hasegawa, Tomoko (1963—)
Hashiguchi, Miho (1977—)
Hashimoto, Seiko (1964—)

Hattori, Michiko (1968—)
Hayashi, Fumiko (1903–1951)
Hayashi, Kyoko (1930—)
Hidari, Sachiko (1930–2001)
Higuchi, Chako (1945—)
Higuchi, Ichiyo (1872–1896)
Hikage, Atsuko (1954—)
Hiratsuka, Raichō (1886–1971)
Hiro, Norie (1965—)
Hirose, Miyoko (1959—)
Hitomi, Kinue (1908–1931)
Hitomi Kinue (1908–1931)
Hōjo Masako (1157–1225)
Ichikawa, Fusae (1893–1981)
Icho, Chiharu (1981—)
Icho, Kaori (1984—)
Iida, Takako (1946—)
Ikeda, Hiroko
Ikeda, Keiko (1933—)
Inoue, Setsuko (1946—)
Inui, Emi (1983—)
Ise (877–940)
Ishida, Kyoko (1960—)
Ishigaki, Rin (1920—)
Ishikawa, Taeko (c. 1976—)
Isobe, Sata (1944—)
Isoda, Yoko
Ito, Kazue (1977—)
Ito, Midori (1969—)
Iwabuchi, Yumi (1979—)
Iwahara, Toyoko (1945—)
Iwasaki, Kyoko (1978—)
Izumi Shikibu (c. 975–c. 1027)
Jimbo, Rei
Jingū (c. 201–269)
Jitō (645–702)
Kagabu, Yoko (1960—)
Kanesaka, Katsuko (1954—)
Kasai, Masae (1933—)
Kato, Kiyomi (1953—)
Kawabe, Miho (1974—)
Kawaguchi, Yoriko (1941—)
Kawakubo, Rei (1942—)
Kawasaki, Ayumi (1984—)
Kawase, Akiko (1971—)
Kawashima, Naoko (1981—)
Kawashima, Yoshiko (1906–1947)
Kikuko, Princess (d. 2004)
Kimura, Saeko (1963—)
Kinoshita, Alicia (1967—)
Kishida, Toshiko (1863–1901)
Kitao, Kanako (1982—)
Kobayashi, Yoshimi (c. 1968—)
Kōgyoku-Saimei (594–661)
Kojima, Yukiyo (1945—)
Kōken-Shōtoku (718–770)
Kondo, Masako (1941—)
Kono, Taeko (1926—)
Koseki, Shiori (c. 1972—)
Kosuge, Mari (1975—)
Kotani, Mikako (1966—)
Kurahashi, Yumiko (1935—)
Kurishima, Sumiko (1902–1987)
Kuroda, Chika (1884–1968)
Kuroyanagi, Tetsuko (1933—)
Kusakabe, Kie
Kushida Fuki (1899–2001)
Kyo, Machiko (1924—)
Maeda, Echiko (1952—)
Maehata, Hideko (1914–1995)
Maruoka, Hideko (1903–1990)
Masako (1963—)
Masubuchi, Mariko (1980—)
Matsuda, Noriko (1952—)
Matsui, Yayori (1934–2002)
Matsumoto, Naomi (1968—)
Matsumura, Katsumi (1944—)
Matsumura, Yoshiko (1941—)
Matsutani, Miyoko (1926—)
Meisho (1624–1696)
Michiko (1934—)
Michitsuna no haha (c. 936–995)
Midori (1971—)
Minamoto, Sumika (1979—)
Minijima, Kiyo (1833–1919)
Mishina, Masumi (1982—)
Mitsuya, Yuko (1958—)
Miura, Ayako (1922–1999)
Miura, Hanako (1975—)
Miura, Tamaki (1884–1946)
Miyajima, Keiko (1965—)
Miyamoto, Emiko (1937—)
Miyao, Tomiko (1926—)
Mizoguchi, Noriko (1971—)
Mizuta, Tamae (1929—)
Mochizuki, Noriko (1967—)
Mori, Mari (1903–1987)
Morio, Maiko (1967—)
Morisaki, Kazue (1927—)
Morishita, Yoko (1948—)
Morita, Kimie (1958—)
Motoyoshi, Miwako (1960—)
Mukai, Chiaki (1952—)
Mukoda, Kuniko (1929–1981)
Murasaki Shikibu (c. 973–c. 1015)
Nagako (1903–2000)
Naito, Emi (1979—)
Nakada, Kumi (1965—)
Nakajima, Riho (1978—)
Nakamura, Kiharu (1913–2004)
Nakamura, Mai (1979—)
Nakamura, Reiko (1982—)
Nakamura, Taniko (1943—)
Nakanishi, Yuko (1981—)
Nakao, Miki (1978—)
Namba, Yasuko (1949–1996)
Nogami, Yaeko (1885–1985)
Noguchi, Mizuki (1978—)
Oba, Minako (1930—)
Oda, Cheko
Odaka, Emiko (1962—)
Ohara, Tomie (b. 1912)
Ohsako, Tatsuko (1952—)
Oinuma, Sumie (1946—)
Okamoto, Ayako (1951—)
Okamoto, Mariko (1951—)
Okamoto, Yoriko (1971—)
Okazaki, Tomomi (1971—)
Okuno, Fumiko (1972—)
Onishi, Junko (1974—)
Ono, Kiyoko (1936—)
Ono, Yoko (1933—)
Ono no Komachi (c. 830–?)
Onshi (872–907)
Otake, Eiko (1952—)
Otani, Sachiko (1965—)
Reischauer, Haru (c. 1915–1998)
Rinshi (fl. 900s)
Sadako (1885–1951)
Sadako (r. 976–1001)
Saga, Michiko (1934—)
Saito, Haruka (1970—)
Sakai, Hiroko (1978—)
Sakamoto, Naoko (1985—)
Sakaue, Yoko (1968—)
Sarashina (c. 1008–1060)
Saruhashi, Katsuko (1920—)
Sasaki, Setsuko (1944—)
Sata, Ineko (1904–1998)
Sato, Aiko (1923—)
Sato, Rie (1980—)
Sato, Yuka (1973—)
Sato, Yuki (1980—)
Satoya, Tae (c. 1977—)
Sawachi, Hisae (1930—)
Sawako Noma (c. 1944—)
Sei Shonagon (c. 965–?)
Setouchi, Jakucho (1922—)
Shibaki, Yoshiko (b. 1914)
Shibata, Ai (1982—)
Shibuki, Ayano (1941—)
Shige, Yumiko (1965—)
Shigeko (1925–1961)
Shimakage, Seiko (1949—)
Shinoda, Miho (1972—)
Shinozaki, Yoko (1945—)
Shiokawa, Michiko (1951—)
Shiono, Nanami (1937—)
Shirai, Takako (1952—)
Shishikura, Kunie (1946—)
Shizuka Gozen (fl. 12th c.)
Shoshi (fl. 990–1010)
Sono, Ayako (1931—)
Sugawara, Noriko (1972—)
Sugawara, Risa (1977—)
Sugimoto, Sonoko (1925—)
Sugiyama, Kayoko (1961—)
Suiko (554–628)
Sumako, Matsui (1886–1919)
Sumii, Sue (1902–1997)
Suzuki, Emiko (1981—)
Tabei, Junko (1939—)
Tachibana, Miya (1974—)
Tae, Satoya (1976—)
Tajima, Yasuko (1981—)
Takagi, Tokuko Nagai (1891–1919)
Takahashi, Kaori (1974—)
Takahashi, Naoko (1972—)
Takahashi, Takako (1932—)
Takamine Hideko (1924—)
Takayama, Aki (1970—)
Takayama, Juri (1976—)
Takayama, Suzue (1946—)
Takayanagi, Shoko (1954—)
Takeda, Miho (1976—)
Takei, Kei (1946—)
Takenishi, Hiroko (1929—)
Tamoto, Hiroko (c. 1974—)
Tamura, Ryoko (1975—)
Tanabe, Seiko (1928—)
Tanabe, Yoko (1966—)
Tanaka, Junko (1973—)
Tanaka, Kinuyo (1907–1977)
Tanaka, Masami (1979—)
Tanaka, Miyako (1967—)
Tanaka, Satoko (1942—)
Tanida, Kuniko (1939—)
Tanimoto, Ayumi (1981—)
Tateno, Chiyori (1970—)
Tatsumi, Juri (1979—)
Toguri, Iva (1916—)
Tomioka, Taeko (1937—)
Tomoe Gozen (fl. c. 12th c.)
Tsukada, Maki (1982—)
Tsukasa, Yoko (1934—)
Tsumura, Setsuko (1928—)
Tsunoda, Fusako (1914—)
Tsushima, Yuko (1947—)
Uchida, Mitsuko (1948—)
Ueno, Chizuko (1948—)
Ueno, Masae (1979—)
Ueno, Yukiko (1982—)
Uma no Naishi (fl. 10th c.)
Umeki, Miyoshi (1929—)
Uno, Chiyo (1897–1996)
Utsugi, Reika (1963—)
Watanabe, Yoko (1953–2004)
Watkins, Yoko Kawashima (1933—)

Yabe, Sayaka
Yakko, Sada (d. 1946)
Yamada, Eri (1984—)
Yamada, Isuzu (1917—)
Yamada, Mitsuye (1923—)
Yamada, Miyo (c. 1976—)
Yamada Waka (1879–1956)
Yamaji, Noriko (1970—)
Yamamoto, Hiromi (1970—)
Yamamoto, Michiko (1936—)
Yamamoto, Noriko (1945—)
Yamazaki, Tomoko (1931—)
Yamazaki, Toyoko (1924—)
Yamazaki, Yaeko (1950—)
Yano, Hiromi (1955—)
Yasui, Kono (1880–1971)
Yokosawa, Yuki (1980—)
Yokoyama, Juri (1955—)
Yoneda, Yuko (1979—)
Yosano Akiko (1878–1942)
Yoshida, Mariko (1954—)
Yoshida, Saori (1982—)
Yoshida, Setsuko (1942—)
Yoshiko
Yoshioka Yayoi (1871–1959)
Yuasa, Toshiko (1909–1980)
Zetterlund, Yoko (1969—)

JERUSALEM

Fortress of Jubusites captured by David (c. 1000 BCE)
Made capital of Kingdom of Israel and later of Judah
Restored to Jews (538 BCE)
As city of Palestine, ruled by Alexander the Great, Ptolemies, Seleucids, and Romans
Partially destroyed by Titus (70 CE) and Hadrian (135); rebuilt as Aelia Capitolina
Taken by Muslim Arabs (638)
Captured by Seljuks (1077)
Captured by Crusaders and established as Kingdom of Jerusalem (1099–1187)
Held by Muslims (1244–1917)
Occupied by British (1917)
Old city taken over by Transjordan Arabs (1948)
Captured by Israeli forces (1948)
Declared part of new state (1950)
See also Israel, Modern.
See also Israel and Judah.

Egeria (fl. 4th c.)
Isabella I of Jerusalem (d. 1205)
Isabella of Cyprus (fl. 1230s)
Isabella of Cyprus (fl. 1250s)
Joveta of Jerusalem (1120–?)

JORDAN

Kingdom in southwest Asia
Created from former Turkish territory (1921)
Proclaimed independent state (1923)
Became independent kingdom (1946)
Warred with Israel (1948)
Held central part of Palestine, adopted name of Jordan (1949)
Participated in Arab-Israel War, lost territory to Israel (1967)
See also Palestine.

Gardiner, Antoinette (1941—)
Noor al-Hussein (1951—)
Rania (1970—)

JUDAH

See Israel and Judah.

JUDEA

Southern division of Palestine under Persian, Greek, and Roman rule
Succeeded kingdom of Judah
See Israel and Judah.

KANEM-BORNU

Kanem a former protected state of French Equatorial Africa
Founded (9th c.)
Became Muslim (11th c.)
Under Bornu, formed strong empire (13th–19th c.)
Part of Chad (1958)

Aissa Koli (1497–1504)

KAZAKHSTAN

Asian republic
Turkic Kaganate emerged (6th c. CE)
Oghuz Turks controlled western Kazakstan; Kimak and Kipchak peoples, the east (9th–11th c.)
Qarluq state destroyed by Qarakhanid invaders (9th c.)
Qarakhanids conquered by the Karakitai from northern China (1130s)
Mongol invasions (13th c.)
Kazaks divided into: Great Horde controlled Semirech'ye and southern Kazakstan; Middle Horde occupied north-central Kazakstan; Lesser Horde occupied western Kazakstan (16th c.)
Came under Russian control (18th–19th c.)
Established independent national government but surrendered to Bolsheviks (1918–1920)
Established Kyrgyz Autonomous Soviet Socialist Republic (1920)
Renamed Kazak Autonomous Soviet Socialist Republic (1925)
Territory made a full Soviet republic (1936)
Gained independence as Republic of Kazakstan (1991)

Evdokimova, Irina (1978—)
Nurpeissova, Dina (1861–1955)
Prokasheva, Lyudmila (1969—)
Shishigina, Olga (1968—)

KENDAL

Borough of Westmorland in northwestern England
See England.

KENT

County in southeastern England
See England.

KENYA

Republic in East Africa
Formerly East Africa Protectorate
Coastal strip belonged to ruler of Zanaibar and leased to British East Africa (1887)
Boundaries with German East Africa fixed (1886 and 1890)
Region made British colony (1920)
Became independent member of Commonwealth of Nations (1963)
Established as a republic (1964)
Formed with Tanzania and Uganda the East African Community (1967)

Chepchumba, Joyce (1970—)
Creider, Jane Tapsubei (c. 1940s—)
Dale, Daphne (1931–1982)
Kenyatta, Margaret (1928—)
Kiplagat, Lornah (1974—)
Kola, Pamela
Konga, Pauline (c. 1971—)
Likimani, Muthoni (c. 1940—)
Loroupe, Tegla (1973—)
Maathai, Wangari (1940—)
Macgoye, Marjorie Oludhe (1928—)
Mbogo, Jael (1939—)
Mugo, Micere Githae (1942—)
Ndereba, Catherine (1972—)
Njau, Rebeka (1932—)
Ochichi, Isabella (1979—)
Odaga, Asenath (1938—)
Ogot, Grace (1930—)
Okayo, Margaret (1976—)
Onyango, Grace (1934—)
Waciuma, Charity (1936—)
Were, Miriam (1940—)

KIEV

One of oldest cities in Russia
Became capital of a Varangian principality (9th c.)
Became seat of metropolitan Russian Christianity (10th c.)
Power and wealth declined (12th c.)
Overrun and ruined by Mongol invasion (1240)
Became part of Lithuania (14th c.)
Became part of Poland (16th c.)
Incorporated by Russia (17th c.)
See Russia.

KOREA

Republic in eastern Asia
Kingdom of Choson established (c. 12th c. BCE)
Conquered and annexed by China (108 BCE)
Buddhism introduced (4th c.)
Mongol invasion (13th c.)
Invaded by Japan (16th c.)
Achieved independence (19th c.)
Annexed to Japan as province (1910)
Divided into North and South Korea (1945)
North Korea (Democratic People's Republic of Korea)
South Korea (Republic of Korea)
Communist invasion of South precipitated Korean War (1950–1953)

An Sang-Mi
Baik Myung-Sun (1956—)
Bang, Soo-Hyun (1972—)
Byon Kyung-Ja (1956—)
Cha, Theresa Hak Kyung (1951–1982)
Cha Jae-Kyung (1971—)
Chang Eun-Jung (1970—)
Chang Hee-Sook (1955—)
Cho (1809–1890)
Cho Eun-Hee (1972—)
Cho Eun-Jung
Choi, Sook Nyul (1937—)
Choi Aei-Young (1959—)
Choi Choon-Ok (1965—)
Choi Eun-Kyung (1984—)
Choi Im-Jeong (1981—)
Choi Kyung-Hee (1966—)
Choi Min-Kyung
Choi Mi-Soon
Cho Ki-Hyang (1963—)
Cho Min-Sun
Cho Youn-Jeong (1969—)
Chung, Kyung-Wha (1948—)
Chung, Myung-wha (1944—)
Chung Eun-Kyung (1965—)
Chung Sang-Hyun (1963—)
Chung So-Young (1967—)
Chun Lee-Kyung (c. 1976—)
Gil Young-Ah (1970—)
Han Hwa-Soo (1963—)
Han Hyun-Sook (1970—)
Han Keum-Sil (1968—)
Han Ok-Kyung (1965—)
Han Pil-Hwa (1942—)
Han Sun-Hee (1973—)
Hong, Lady (1735–1850)
Hong Ch-Ok (1970—)
Hong Jeong-Ho (1974—)
Huh Soon-Young (1975—)
Huh Young-Sook (1975—)
Hwang Hae-Young (1966—)
Hwang He-Suk (1945—)
Hwang Keum-Sook (1963—)
Hwang Kyung-Sun (1978—)
Hwang Ok-Sil (c. 1972—)
Hyun Jung-Hwa (1969—)
Hyun Sook-Hee
Jang Hye-Ock
Jang Ji-Won (1979—)
Jang Mi-Ran (1983—)
Jang Ok-Rim (1948—)
Jang Ri-Ra (1969—)

Jang So-Hee (1978—)
Jang Yong-Ho
Jeong Hyoi-Soon (1964—)
Jeong Myung-Hee (1964—)
Jeon Young-Sun
Jeung Soon-Bok (1960—)
Jin Deok San
Jin Won-Sim (1965—)
Jo Hea-Jung (1953—)
Joo Min-Jin (1983—)
Jung Jae-Eun (c. 1981—)
Jung Soo-Nok (1955—)
Jung Sung-Sook
Jung Sun Yong
Kang Cho-Hyun (1982—)
Kang Jae-Won (1965—)
Kang Ok-Sun (1946—)
Kim Bo-Ram
Kim Cha-Youn (1981—)
Kim Cheong-Shim (1976—)
Kim Choon-Rye (1966—)
Kim Eun-Mi (1975—)
Kim Eun-Sook (1963—)
Kim Gwang Suk (c. 1976—)
Kim Hwa-Sook (1971—)
Kim Hwa-Soon (1962—)
Kim Hyang-Mi (1979—)
Kim Hyun-Mi (1967—)
Kim Hyun-Ok (1974—)
Ki Mi-Sook (1967—)
Kim Jeong-Mi (1975—)
Kim Jin Ho (1961—)
Kim Jo-Sun
Kim Jum-Sook (c. 1968—)
Kim Kyung-Ah (1977—)
Kim Kyung-Soon (1965—)
Kim Kyung-Wook
Kim Mi-Hyun (1977—)
Kim Mi-Jung (1971—)
Kim Mi-Sim (1970—)
Kim Mi-Sook (1962—)
Kim Mi-Sun (1964—)
Kim Moo-Kyo
Kim Myong-Soon (1964—)
Kim Myong-Suk (1947—)
Kim Myung-Ok
Kim Nam-Soon
Kim Ok-Hwa (1958—)
Kim Rang (1974—)
Kim Ryang-Hee
Kim So-Hee
Kim Soon-Duk (1967—)
Kim Soo-Nyung (1971—)
Kim Su-Dae (1942—)
Kim Yeun-Ja (1943—)
Kim Young-Hee (1963—)
Kim Young-Sook (1965—)
Kim Yun-Mi
Kim Zung-Bok (1945—)
Ko Gi-Hyun (1986—)
Kown Soo-Hyun
Kwag Hye-Jeong (1975—)
Kwon Chang Sook
Kye Sun-Hui (1979—)
Lee Bo-Na (1981—)
Lee Eun-Kyung (1972—)
Lee Eun Kyung
Lee Eun-Sil (1976—)
Lee Eun-Young
Lee Gong-Joo (1980—)
Lee Ho-Youn (1971—)
Lee Hyung-Sook (1964—)
Lee Ji-Young
Lee Ki-Soon (1966—)
Lee Kyung-Won (1980—)
Lee Mi-Ja (1963—)
Lee Mi-Young (1969—)
Lee Sang-Eun (1975—)
Lee Soon-Bok (1950—)
Lee Soon-Ei (1965—)
Lee Soo-Nok (1955—)
Lee Sung-Jin (1985—)
Lee Sun-Hee
Lee Young-Ja (1964—)
Li Bun-Hui (1968—)
Lim Jeong-Sook
Lim Kye-Sook (1964—)
Lim Mi-Kyung (1967—)
Lim O-Kyung (1971—)
Ma Kum-Ja (1955—)
Min (1851–1895)
Min Hye-Sook (1970—)
Moon Hyang-Ja (1972—)
Moon Kyeong-Ha (1980—)
Moon Kyung-Ja (1965—)
Moon Pil-Hee (1982—)
Myoung Bok-Hee (1979—)
Nam Eun-Young (1970—)
Oh Kyo-Moon
Oh Seung-Shin
Oh Sung-Ok (1972—)
Oh Yong-Ran (1972—)
Paek Myong-Suk (1954—)
Pak, Se Ri (1977—)
Park, Grace (1979—)
Park Chan-Sook (1959—)
Park Hae-Jung
Park Hye-Won (1983—)
Park Jeong-Lim (1970—)
Park Kap-Sook (1970—)
Park Mi Kum (1955—)
Park Soon-Ja (1966—)
Park Sung-Hyun (1983—)
Ra Kyung-Min (1976—)
Ri Chun-Ok (1947—)
Ri Song Hui (1978—)
Ryom Chun-Ja (1942—)
Ryu Ji-Hae (1976—)
Shim Eun-Jung (1971—)
Shon Mi-Na (1964—)
Sinn, Pearl (1967—)
Song Ji-Hyun (1969—)
Suh Hyo-Sun (1966—)
Suh Kwang-Mi (1965—)
Suk Eun-Mi (1976—)
Suk Min-Hee (1968—)
Sung Jung-A (1965—)
Sung Kyung-Hwa (1965—)
Wang Hee-Kyung (1970—)
Watkins, Yoko Kawashima (1933—)
Won Hye-Kyung
Woo Hyun-Jung
Woo Sun-Hee (1978—)
Yang Young-Ja (1964—)
Yeo Kab-Soon (1974—)
Yoon Byung-Soon (1963—)
Yoon Hye-Young
Yoon Soo-Kyung (1964—)
Yoon Young-Sook (1971—)
You Jae-Sook
Yu Jung-Hye (1954—)
Yu Kyung-Hwa (1953—)
Yun Mi-Jin (1983—)
Yun Young-Nae (1952—)
Yu Sun-Bok (1970—)

LAKOTA

Native North American Great Plains indigenous group

Crow Dog, Mary (1953—)
Medicine, Beatrice A. (1923—)

LANCASTER

Borough of Lancashire in England
See England.

LAON

Commune of Aisne department in northern France
See France.

LATVIA

Baltic tribes arrived (2000 BCE)
Invaded by Russia and lost territory to Lithuania and Poland (16th c.)
Part of Latvia under Swedish rule (17th c.)
Northern provinces under Russian rule (18th c.)
Latvia Social Democratic Labor Party founded (1904)
National uprising (1906)
Independence declared (1918)
Constitution passed (1922)
Russia declared Latvia a Soviet Republic (1940)
Latvians deported to Siberia (1940s and 1950s)
Independence declared (1991)

Anna Ivanovna (1693–1740)
Apinée, Irena (c. 1930—)
Arbatova, Mia (c. 1910—)
Bellanca, Dorothy (1894–1946)
Chiriaeff, Ludmilla (1924–1996)
Johansson, Ronny (b. 1891)
Lacis, Asja (1891–1979)
Rublevska, Jelena (1976—)
Sazonenkova, Elena (1973—)
Semjonova, Uljana (1952—)
Skobtsova, Maria (1891–1945)
Vike-Freiberga, Vaira (1937—)
Zozula, Vera

LEBANON

Republic in eastern Mediterranean Sea
Inhabited by Maronites, a Syrian Christian sect (7th c.)
Under Roman rule (until 12th c.)
Maronites killed by Druses (19th c.)
Declared autonomous under French mandate (1920)
Reorganized as Lebanese Republic (1926)
Declared independent (1941)
Participated in Arab-Israeli War (1948–1949)

Adnan, Etel (1925—)
Ashrawi, Hanan (1946—)
Coory, Shirefie (c. 1864–1950)
Eschiva of Ibelin (fl. late 1100s)
Eschiva of Ibelin (r. 1282–c. 1284)
Fairuz (1935—)
Lipkowska, Lydia (1882–1958)
Nasralla, Emily (1931—)
Ordonówna, Hanka (1904–1950)
Ostermeyer, Micheline (1922—)
Samman, Ghada al- (1942—)
Seyrig, Delphine (1932–1990)
Shaykh, Hanan al- (1945—)
Stanhope, Hester (1776–1839)
Tueni, Nadia (1935–1983)
Ziyada, Mayy (1886–1941)

LEICESTER

County borough of Leicestershire in central England
See England.

LEÓN

Region and ancient kingdom in northwestern Spain
Ruled by Moors until conquest by Asturias (10th c.)
United with Castile (1037–1157)
Became independent kingdom (1157–1230)
Reunited with Castile (1230)
See Spain.

LIBERIA

West African republic
Project established for settlement of freed American slaves (1817)

Became Free and Independent Republic of Liberia (1847)
Placed under U.S. protection (1911)

Brooks, Angie (1928—)
Newport, Matilda (c. 1795–1837)
Perry, Ruth (1939—)

LIBYA

Ancient Greek name for North Africa
Occupied by Italians (1914)
Provinces of Cyrenaica and Tripolitania united (1934)
Incorporated into Italy (1939)
Achieved independence as Kingdom of Libya (1951)
Monarchy overthrown (1969)
Formed confederation with Egypt and Syria (1971)
See North Africa.

LIECHTENSTEIN

Independent principality on east bank of Rhine
Counties of Schellenberg and Vaduz united to become Liechtenstein (1719)
Became part of Confederation of the Rhine (1806)
Became part of Germanic Confederation (1815–1866)
Belonged to Austrian customs union before collapse of Habsburgs (1918)
Entered Swiss customs union (1924)

Konzett, Ursula (1959—)
Theresa of Liechtenstein (1850–1938)
Wenzel, Hanni (1951—)

LIEGNITZ

City in Wroc[lstrok]aw district of southwestern Poland
See Poland.

LITHUANIA

United as grand duchy to oppose Teutonic Knights (c. 1250)
United with Poland (1386)
Acquired by Russia in partitions of Poland (1772, 1793, 1795)
Joined Polish revolt (1863)
Occupied by Germans during World War I
Proclaimed independent republic (1918)
Annexed as Lithuanian Soviet Socialist Republic (1940)
Incorporated into U.S.S.R. (1944)
Achieved independence (1990)
See also Poland.
See also Russia.

Aldona of Lithuania
Binkiene, Sofija (1902–1984)
Borchers, Cornell (1925—)
Catherine I (1684–1727)
Degutiene, Irena (1949—)
Gaskell, Sonia (1904–1974)
Gimbutas, Marija (1921–1994)
Godowsky, Dagmar (1897–1975)
Gudzineviciute, Daina (1965—)
Halicka, Antonina (1908–1973)
Jagiello, Appolonia (1825–1866)
Julianna of Ruthenia (fl. 1377)
Kalediene, Birute (1934—)
Kutkaite, Dalia (1965—)
Mašiotene, Ona (1883–1949)
Millin, Sarah (1888–1968)
Neris, Salomeja (1904–1945)
Philippa de Dreux (d. 1240)
Plater, Emilja (1806–1831)
Poplavskaja, Kristina (1972—)
Prunskiene, Kazimiera (1943—)
Reisenberg, Nadia (1904–1983)
Rockmore, Clara (1911–1998)
Rutkiewicz, Wanda (1943—)
Sakickiene, Birute (1968—)
Simaite, Ona (1899–1970)
Skujyte, Austra (1979—)
Sophie of Lithuania (1370–1453)
Venciené, Vida
Yolande of Vaudemont (1428–1483)
Ziliute, Diana (1976—)

LOMBARDY

Region in northern Italy
Center of kingdom located in Po valley (6th c.)
Crushed by Charlemagne (8th c.)
Part of Carolingian and Holy Roman Empires
Became seat of duchy of Milan, ruled by Spain (16th c.), and by Austria (18th c.)
Became part of Napoleon's Cisalpine Republic (1797)
Became part of Kingdom of Italy (1805)
Received limited autonomy (1970)
See Italy.

LOOSS

Commune in Nord department of France
See France.

LORRAINE

Medieval kingdom
Originally part of Austrasia
Became German-controlled Lotharingia (9th c.)
Kingdom of Lorraine divided into two duchies (10th c.)
Lower Lorraine claimed by Germany
Upper Lorraine claimed by France
Portions of Upper Lorraine ceded to Germany as Alsace-Lorraine (1871)
See France.
See Germany.

LOTHARINGIA

See Germany.

LOUVAIN

Commune in Brabant province of Belgium
See Belgium.

LÜNEBERG

City in Lower Saxony in western Germany
See Germany.

LUXEMBURG

Medieval county and duchy in western Europe
Part of Holy Roman Empire (10th c.)
Became a duchy (1354)
Passed to Spanish and then to Austrian Habsburgs (15th c.)
Occupied by the French (1794)
Became Grand Duchy of Luxembourg (1815)
Western half acquired by Belgium (1830)
Broke connection with Netherlands (1890)
Occupied by Germany (1940–1944)
Formed customs union with Belgium and Netherlands (1947)
See also Austria.
See also Belgium.
See also Netherlands.

Charlotte (1896–1985)
Flesch, Colette (1937—)
Lulling, Astrid (1929—)

MACEDONIA

Ancient country and kingdom in central Balkan Peninsula
Included Thrace, Chalcidice, Tessaly, and Epirus
Attained domination over Greece (338 BCE)
Macedonian Empire defeated by Rome (197
Part of Byzantine Empire (148 BCE)
Invaded by Slavic peoples (6th c. CE)
Part of Ottoman Empire (15th c.)
Partitioned as result of Balkan Wars (1912–1913)
Part of Yugoslavia and Greece (1920s and 1930s)
See also Greece.
See also Yugoslavia.

Arsinoe (fl. 4th c. BCE)
Arsinoe I (d. 247 BCE)
Arsinoe III (fl. c. 250–210/05 BCE)
Arsinoe II Philadelphus (c. 316–270 BCE)
Arsinoe IV (d. 41 BCE)
Berenice I (c. 345 BCE–c. 275 BCE)
Cleopatra (b. 354 BCE)
Cynnane (c. 357–322 BCE)
Eurydice (fl. 321 BCE)
Eurydice (c. 337–317 BCE)
Eurydice (c. 410–350s BCE)
Lysandra (fl. 300 BCE)
Maria of Macedonia (d. around 864)
Nicaea (fl. 300 BCE)
Phila I (fl. c. 320 BCE)
Phila II (c. 300 BCE–?)
Roxana (fl. 350 BCE)
Statira III (fl. 324 BCE)
Theoxena (fl. 315 BCE)
Thessalonike (c. 345–297 BCE)

MACON

City in Saône-et-Loire department of eastern central France
See France.

MADAGASCAR

Island in western Indian Ocean off southeastern coast of Africa
Discovered by the Portuguese (1500)
French posts held by the British (18101811)
Tribal rule (19th c.)
Made a French colony (1886)
Monarchy abolished by the French (1887)
Occupied by the British (1942)
Became territory within the French union (1946)
Established as Malagasy Republic (1958)

Ranavalona I (1792–1861)
Ranavalona II (1829–1883)
Ranavalona III (1861–1917)

MAINE

Historic region of northwestern France
Became a countship (10th c.)
Ruled by England (1154)
Passed to House of Anjou, reverted to the French crown (1481)
Made a duchy under Louis XIV
See England.
See France.

MALAWI

Republic in southeastern Africa
Became a British protectorate (1891)
Part of Federation of Rhodesia and Nyasaland (1953–1963)
Achieved independence (1964)
Became a republic (1966)

Chirwa, Vera (1933—)

MALAYSIA

Amin, Adibah (1936—)
Rashid, Saleha Abdul (1939—)

MALI

Republic in West Africa
Territories of Senegambia and Niger formed French colony (1904–1920)
Anglo-Egyptian Sudan frontier settled (1924)
Became republic within French Community (1958)
Joined Senegal in Mali Federation (1959–1960)
Became independent republic (1960)

Kassi (1241–?)
Kéita, Aoua (1912–1979)
Pokou (c. 1700–c. 1760)

MALINES

Commune in Antwerp province of northern Belgium
See Belgium.

MALTA

Independent state comprising three islands in Mediterranea Sea
Became a Phoenician and Carthaginian colony
Captured by Romans (218 BCE)
Part of Byzantine holdings when conquered by Saracens (870 CE)
Taken by Norman kingdom of Sicily (1090)
Held by Napoleon (1798–1800)
Captured by British (1800–1814)
Became British crown colony (1933)
Achieved independence (1964)

Agatha, Saint (d. 251)
Barbara, Agatha (1923–2002)
Leng, Virginia (1955—)
Marie of Rumania (1875–1938)
Sharp, Margery (1905–1991)
Strickland, Mabel (1899–1988)
Victoria Melita of Saxe-Coburg (1876–1936)

MANTUA

Commune in Mantova province of Lombardy in northern Italy
See Italy.

MAORI

New Zealand indigenous group

Carroll, Heni Materoa (1852/56?–1930)
Cherrington, Te Paea (c. 1877–1937)
Cooper, Whina (1895–1994)
Faulkner, Ruawahine Irihapeti (?–1855)
Hato, Ana Matawhaura (1907–1953)
Hei, Akenehi (1877/78?–1910)
Herangi, Te Kirihaehae Te Puea (1883–1952)
Hikapuhi (1860/71?–1934)
Hine-i-paketia (fl. 1850–1870)
Hine-i-turama (c. 1818–1864)
Hinematioro (d. 1823)
Hinerangi, Sophia (c. 1830–1911)
Howie, Fanny Rose (1868–1916)
Jury, Te Aitu-o-te-rangi (c. 1820–1854)
Kaaro, Ani (fl. 1885–1901)
Kahutia, Riperata (c. 1838–1887)
Kokoro-Barrett, Hiria (1870–1943)
Lord, Lucy Takiora (c. 1842–1893)
Love, Ripeka Wharawhara (1882–1953)
Mahupuku, Maata (1890–1952)
Maihi, Rehutai (1895–1967)
Mangakahia, Meri Te Tai (1868–1920)
Mataira, Katarina Te Heikoko (1932—)
Matenga, Huria (1840/42–1909)
Menzies, Trixie Te Arama (1936—)
Mihi-ki-te-kapua (?–1872/80)
Morete, Maraea (1844–1907)
Nehua, Katerina (1903–1948)
Newton, Wharetutu Anne (fl. 1827–1870)
Nga-kahu-whero (fl. 1800–1836)
Ngata, Arihia Kane (1879–1929)
Niniwa-i-te-rangi (1854–1929)
Papakura, Makereti (1873–1930)
Parata, Katherine Te Rongokahira (1873–1939)
Pinepine Te Rika (1857/58–1954)
Pitini-Morera, Hariata Whakatau (1871/72?–1938)
Pomare, Hariata (fl. 1863–1864)
Puhiwahine Te Rangi-hirawea, Rihi (d. 1906)
Ratana, Iriaka (1905–1981)
Rere-o-maki (d. 1868)
Rikiriki, Atareta Kawana Ropiha Mere (c. 1855–1926)
Riwai, Kiti Karaka (1870–1927)
Rongonui, Kahupake (1868/69?–1947)
Stirling, Mihi Kotukutuku (1870–1956)
Sturm, J.C. (1927—)
Taiaroa, Tini Kerei (c. 1846–1934)
Tamairangi (fl. 1820–1828)
Tapsell, Ngatai Tohi Te Ururangi (1844–1928)
Te Kahuhiapo, Rahera (1820s?–1910)
Te Kakapi, Ripeka Wharawhara-i-te-rangi (?–1880)
Te Kiri Karamu, Heni (1840–1933)
Tenetahi, Rahui Te Kiri (d. 1913)
Te Paea Tiaho (1820s?–1875)
Te Pikinga (c. 1800–after 1868)
Te Rangi-i-paia II (fl. 1818–1829)
Te Rangimarie, Puna Himene (fl. 1908–1911)
Te Rau-o-te-rangi, Kahe (?–c. 1871)
Te Rohu (fl. 1820–1850)
Te Taiawatea Rangitukehu, Maata (1848/49?–1929)
Te Whaiti, Kaihau Te Rangikakapi Maikara (1863–1937)
Te Wherowhero, Piupiu (1886/87?–1937)
Tirikatene-Sullivan, Whetu (1932—)
Topeora, Rangi Kuini Wikitoria (?–1865/73)
Turikatuku (d. 1827)
Waitaoro (c. 1848–1929)
Waitohi (?–1839)
Wyllie, Kate (d. 1913)
Yates, Ngawini (1852/53?–1910)

MARCH

District in Cambridgeshire in eastern England
See England.

MARCHE

Historic region in central France
Became a countship (10th c.)
Possessed by Lusignan family (13th c.)
Province of France until revolution
See France.

MAROON

See Jamaica.

MARTINIQUE

Capécia, Mayotte (1928–1953)
Ega, Françoise (1920–1976)
Monplaisir, Emma (1918—)
Palcy, Euzhan (1957—)

MASSA

Commune of Massa-Carrara province in Tuscany, Italy
See Italy.

MAURITIUS

Mellish, Edith Mary (1861–1922)

MAYA

Southern Mexican and Central American indigenous group

Menchú, Rigoberta (1959—)
Xoc, Lady (c. 660–c. 720)

MECKLENBURG

Former state in eastern Germany
Ruled briefly by Denmark (13th c.)
Became a duchy (1348)
Became duchies of Mecklenburg-Schwerin and Mechlenburg-Strelitz (1701)
Both became grand duchies (1815)
Joined North Germany Confederation (1867)
Became separate republics (1918)
Reunited (1934); lost soverign rights and divided into districts (1952)
See Germany.

MEININGEN

City in Suhl district of eastern Germany
Capital of the dukes of Saxe-Meiningen
See Germany.

MEISSEN

City in Dresden district of eastern Germany
See Germany.

MELITENE

Ancient province of eastern Turkey
See Turkey.

MERCIA

Ancient Anglian kingdom in central England
One of seven kingdoms of Anglo-Saxon Heptarchy
Northumbrian king overthrown (8th c.)
Conquered by Wessex (829)
English Mercia separated from Danish Mercia in Danelaw (9th c.)
Danelaw reconquered (10th c.)
See England.

MEROE

Ancient city and kingdom on east bank of Nile
Capital of Ethiopian kings (c. 750 BCE)
Capital of Nubia (500–300 BCE)

Amanishakhete (r. c. 41–12 BCE)

MESOPOTAMIA

Region in southwestern Asia
Seat of early civilizations of Babylonia and Assyria (c. 3000–625 BCE)
Upper Mesopotamia was kingdom of the Mitanni (c. 1475–1360 BCE)
Part of Persian Empire (538–331 BCE)
Conquered by Arabs (7th c. CE)
Declined in political power (13th c.)
Part of Ottoman Empire (17th c.)
Became British mandate (1920)
Became kingdom of Iraq (1921)

Rebekah (fl. around 18th c. BCE)

METZ

Pre-Roman foundation
Sacked by Attila (5th c.)
Capital of Austrasia under Franks
See Austrasia.

MEXICAN-AMERICAN

Anzaldúa, Gloria E. (1942–2004)
Bañuelos, Romana Acosta (1925—)
Carr, Vikki (1941—)
Cisneros, Sandra (1954—)
de Hoyos, Angela (1940—)
Hernández, Maria (1896–1986)
Huerta, Dolores (1930—)
Idar, Jovita (1885–1946)
Lopez, Nancy (1957—)
Martinez, Vilma (1943—)
Mendoza, Lydia (1916—)
Montemayor, Alice Dickerson (1902–1989)
Pérez, Eulalia Arrila de (c. 1773–c. 1878)
Portillo, Lourdes
Selena (1971–1995)

MEXICO

Republic in southern North America
Controlled by the Aztec (1430–1519)
Yucatán discovered by Córdoba (1517)
Coast to Veracruz discovered by Grijalva (1518)
Veracruz founded by Cortes (1519)
Spanish authority extended (16th c.)
Revolted against Spain (1821)
Joined by other Central American states (1822–1823)
Established a federal republic (1824)
Defeated by Republic of Texas (1836)

Geographic Index

Warred with United States over annexation of Texas (1846–1848)
Ceded Upper California, New Mexico, and northern Mexico to United States (1848)
Invaded by Spain, Britain, and France (1861)
Overthrew dictatorship of Porfirio Diaz (1911)
Adopted revised constitution (1917)
See also Aztec Empire.

Amor, Guadalupe (1920—)
Barcelo, Gertrudis (c. 1820–1852)
Beltran, Lola (1932–1996)
Bocanegra, Gertrudis (1765–1817)
Calvillo, María del Carmen (1765–1856)
Cárdenas, Nancy (1934–1994)
Cardus, Ana (1943—)
Castellanos, Rosario (1925–1974)
Christian, Linda (1923—)
Contreras, Gloria (1934—)
Cotera, Martha (1938—)
Del Rio, Dolores (1905–1983)
D'Erzell, Catalina (1897–1937)
Duby-Blom, Gertrude (1901–1993)
Esquivel, Laura (1950—)
Felix, Maria (1914–2002)
Fernandez, Adriana (1971—)
Galeana, Benita (1904–1995)
Galindo de Topete, Hermila (1896–1954)
Garro, Elena (1916–1998)
Gaytan, Andrea
Glantz, Margo (1930—)
Greenwood, Marion (1909–1980)
Guerrero Mendez, Belem (1974—)
Guevara, Ana (1977—)
Guraieb Kuri, Rosa (1931—)
Gutiérrez de Mendoza, Juana Belén (1875–1942)
Hayek, Salma (1966—)
Hernandez, Amelia (c. 1930—)
Hernández, Luisa Josefina (1928—)
Hernández, Maria (1896–1986)
Ibarra de Piedra, Rosario (1927—)
Idar, Jovita (1885–1946)
Jimenez Mendivil, Soraya (1977—)
Juana Inés de la Cruz (1651–1695)
Juarez, Margarita (1826–1871)
Jurado, Katy (1924–2002)
Kahlo, Frida (1907–1954)
Landeta, Matilde (1910–1999)
Lupita, Madre (1878–1963)
Margo (1918–1985)
Mendoza, Amalia (1923–2001)
Mexia, Ynes (1870–1938)
Ortíz de Dominguez, Josefa (c. 1768–1829)
Paz Paredes, Margarita (1922–1980)
Pellicer, Pina (1935–1964)
Poniatowska, Elena (1932—)
Portillo, Lourdes
Ramirez, Maria Teresa (1953—)
Ramirez, Sara Estela (1881–1910)
Randall, Marta (1948—)
Roldan Reyna, Pilar (1944—)
Salazar Blanco, Iridia (1982—)
Serrano, Lupe (1930—)
Torres, Raquel (1908–1987)
Vargas, Chavela (1919—)
Velazquez, Consuelo (1916–2005)
Velez, Lupe (1908–1944)
Vicario, Leona (1789–1842)
Yampolsky, Mariana (1925—)

MICMAC

Native North American Eastern indigenous group
Canadian First Nations indigenous group

Aquash, Anna Mae (1945–1976)

MILAN

Ancient Gallic city captured by Romans (222 BCE)
Chief city of Western Roman Empire (4th c.)
Conquered by Huns and Ostragoths (6th c.)
Ruled by the Visconti as dukes of Milan (1349–1447)
Ruled by the Sforza family (1447–1535)
Duchy became Spanish (1535)
Ceded to Austria (1713)
Under Napoleon (1796–1814)
Became part of Italy (1860)
See Italy.

MOAB

Ancient kingdom in Syria
See Syria.

MODENA

Province of Emilia-Romagna in northern Italy
See Italy.

MOESIA

See Bulgaria.

MOHAWK

Native North American Eastern indigenous group
Canadian First Nations indigenous group

Brant, Molly (c. 1736–1796)
Johnson, E. Pauline (1861–1913)
Minoka-Hill, Rosa (1876–1952)
Tekakwitha, Kateri (1656–1680)

MONACO

Independent principality on Mediterranean Sea
Ruled by Grimaldi family (from 10th c.)
Annexed to France (1793–1814)
Under protection of Sardinia (1815–1860)
Sovereignty restored (1861)
Adopted new constitution (1962)

Begue, Laetitia (1980—)
Caroline of Monaco (1957—)
Claudine (1451–1514)
Kelly, Grace (1928–1982)
Stephanie of Monaco (1965—)

MONGOLIA

Region in eastern central Asia
Genghis Khan began Mongol expansion (12th–13th c.)
Became part of China, Russia, and Persia at end of Mongol Empire
Brief empire established by Tamerlane (14th c.)
Became Mongolian People's Republic (1911)

Munkhbayar, Dorzhsuren (1969—)
Tuyaa, Nyam-Osoryn (1958—)
Yanjmaa, Sühbaataryn (1893–1962)

MONTENEGRO

Former kingdom in southeastern Europe
Originated after battle of Kosova (1389)
Ruled by prince-bishops
Allied with Russia against Turkey (18th c.)
Achieved independence (1799)
Became kingdom (1910)
United to form Kingdom of the Serbs, Croats, and Slovenes (1918)

Anastasia Petrovitch-Njegos (1868–1935)
Jutta of Mecklenburg-Strelitz (1880–1946)
Milena (1847–1923)
Militza of Montenegro (1866–1951)
Zorka of Montenegro (1864–1890)

MONTE PULCIANO

Commune in Tuscany in central Italy
See Italy.

MONTFERRAT

Former marquisate and duchy in Italy
See Italy.

MONTSERRAT

Island in West Indies
Discovered by Columbus (1493)
Colonized by the British (1632)
Held by the French (1664–1668 and 1782–1784)
Part of Colony of Leeward Islands (1871–1956)
Part of West Indies Federation (1958–1962)

Adelaide of Montserrat (fl. 1100)

MOORS

Muslim people of mixed Berber and the Saracens who invaded Spain (8th c.)
See also Spain.

Casilda (d. about 1007)
Galiana
Zaida (d. 1107)

MORAVIA

Region in central Czechoslovakia
Settled by a Slavic people (6th c.)
Part of Charlemagne's empire (c. 843)
Revolted against German rule and became independent kingdom (870)
Conquered by Magyars (906)
Part of Bohemian and Polish kingdoms (10th c.)
Became crownland of Austria (1849)
Organized as province of Czechoslovakia (1918)
United with Silesia as Moravia and Silesia (1927)
Restored to Czechoslovakia (1945)
See Czechoslovakia.

MOROCCO

Kingdom in northwestern Africa
Roman province of Mauretainia invaded by Muslims (7th c.)
Founded independent kingdom under Berber dynasty (11th c.)
Taken by Portuguese (1415)
Engaged in piracy as one of Barbary States (until 19th c.)
Warred with France and Spain (19th c.)
Protectorates of French Morocco and Spanish Morocco established (1912)
Achieved independence (1956)
Joined Arab League (1958)

Ben Haddou, Halima (fl. 1980s)
Benhassi, Hasna (1978—)
Bidiouane, Nouzha (1969—)
Binnuna, Khanatta (1940—)
El Moutawakel, Nawal (1962—)
Menebhi, Saïda (1952–1977)
Mernissi, Fatima (1940—)

MOSCOW

Former principality in western central Russia
Incorporated principality of Valdmir (1341)
Defeated Tatars and invaded Lithuania (15th c.)
Occupied by the French under Napoleon (1812)
Became capital of U.S.S.R. (1918)
See Russia.

MOZAMBIQUE

de Sousa, Noémia (1926—)
Diogo, Luisa (1958—)
Machel, Graca (1946—)
Mutola, Maria (1972—)
Tavares, Salette (1922–1994)

NAMIBIA

See South-West Africa.

NAMUR

Province in southern Belgium
See Belgium.

NAPLES

Commune of Napoli province in southern Italy
Founded by refugees from Greek colony of Cumae (c. 600 BCE)
Conquered by Romans (4th c. BCE)
Included in kingdoms of Ostrogoths, Byzantines, and Muslims
Conquered by Norman Sicily, becoming part of Kingdom of the Two Sicilies
Included in Papal States (13th c.)
Remained under Angevin house (1268–1435)
Crown of Naples reunited with Sicily (15th c.)
Claimed by the French (15th c.)
Conquered by the Spanish (1503)
Ceded to Austria (1713)
Ceded to Spain with Sicily as Kingdom of Two Sicilies under house of Bourbon (1735)
Capital of Napoleon's Parthenopean Republic (1799), and Sicilian kingdom (1806)
Joined Italian kingdom (1860)
See Italy.

NARRAGANSETT

Native North American Northeast indigenous group

Magnus (d. 1676)

NASSAU

Former duchy and later Wiesbaden district of Hesse-Nassau province in Prussia
See Germany.
See Prussia.

NATIVE NORTH AMERICAN WOMEN

Akers, Dolly Smith (1901–1986)
Awashonks (fl. mid–late 17th c.)
Awiakta (1936—)
Bonnin, Gertrude Simmons (1876–1938)
Brant, Beth (1941—)
Brant, Molly (c. 1736–1796)
Buffalo-Calf-Road-Woman (fl. 1876)
Callahan, Sophia Alice (1868–1894)
Chona, Maria (1845–1936)
Dann, Mary (d. 2005)
Dat So La Lee (c. 1835–1925)
Deloria, Ella (1888–1971)
La Flesche, Susan (1865–1915)
La Flesche, Susette (1854–1902)
Mourning Dove (c. 1888–1936)
Peña, Tonita (1893–1949)
Pocahontas (c. 1596–1617)
Riley, Mary Velasquez (1908–1987)
Sacajawea (c. 1787–c. 1812 or 1884)
Schoolcraft, Jane Johnston (1800–1841)
Tallchief, Maria (1925—)
Tallchief, Marjorie (1927—)
Tekakwitha, Kateri (1656–1680)
Velarde, Pablita (1918—)
Victor, Wilma (1919–1987)
Wauneka, Annie Dodge (1910–1997)
Wetamoo (c. 1650–1676)
Winnemucca, Sarah (1844–1891)
Wright, Muriel Hazel (1889–1975)

NAVAJO

Native North American Southwest indigenous group

Wauneka, Annie Dodge (1910–1997)

NAVARRE

Ancient kingdom of northern Spain
Conquered by Romans and Visigoths (5th c.)
Conquered by Charlemagne (8th c.)
Became independent kingdom (10th c.)
United with Castile and León (11th c.)
Divided into kingdoms of Navarre, Aragon, and Castile (1035)
Reunited with Aragon (1976–1134)
Annexed by France (1234–1328)
Conquered by Aragon (1512)
Incorporated with Castile (1515)
Passed to France (1589)
See France.
See Spain.

NEMOURS

Town in Seine-et-Marne department of northern France
Countship created (14th c.)
Dukedom held by Armagnac brance of house of Orléans (16th c.)
Dukedom held by a branch of house of Savoy (16th–17th c.)
See France.

NETHERLANDS

Kingdom in northwestern Europe
Included in Charlemagne's empire
Part of medieval kingdom of Lotharingia
Split into several counties and duchies first united under dukes of Burgundy (14th c.)
Eventually passed to Spanish branch of Habsburgs
Union of Utrecht formed (1579)
Independence recognized (1648)
Warred with the English and French (17th–18th c.)
Spanish Netherlands awarded to Austria (1713)
Organized as French-controlled Batavian Republic (1795–1806)
Organized as French-controlled Kingdom of Holland (1805)
Established as United Kingdom of Netherlands (1815)
Broken up by revolt of Belgium (1830)
See also France.
See also Germany.

Adelaide of Burgundy (931–999)
Adelicia of Louvain (c. 1102–1151)
Agsteribbe, Estella (1909–1943)
Albertina Agnes (d. 1696)
Aldegund (c. 630–684)
Ambree, Mary (fl. 1584)
Amelia of Anhalt-Dessau (1666–1726)
Ameling, Elly (1938—)
Ammers-Küller, Johanna van (1884–1966)
Andriesse, Emmy (1914–1953)
Anker-Doedens, Alida van der (1922—)
Anna of Egmont (1533–1558)
Anna Pavlovna (1795–1865)
Appeldoorn, Tessa (1973—)
Audina, Mia (1979—)
Baas-Kaiser, Christina (1938—)
Bari, Tania (1936—)
Baron, Mietje (1908–1948)
Bartels, Tineke (1951—)
Beatrix (b. 1938)
Bekker, Elizabeth (1738–1804)
Benninga, Carina (1962—)
Bentum, Cornelia van (1965—)
Berg, Jacomina van den (1909—)
Bertha of Holland (1055–1094)
Bertken, Sister (c. 1427–1514)
Besnyö, Eva (1910–2003)
Beumer, Catharina (1947—)
Bimolt, Klena (1945—)
Blankers-Koen, Fanny (1918–2004)
Bleeker, Caroline Emilie (1897–1985)
Boekhorst, Josephine (1957—)
Boissevain, Mia (1878–1959)
Bolhuis-Eysvogel, Marjolein (1961—)
Bontje, Ellen (1958—)
Boogerd-Quaak, Johanna L.A. (1944—)
Boogert, Kristie (1973—)
Booij, Minke (1977—)
Boomgaardt, Ageeth (1972—)
Borckink, Annie (1951—)
Borst-Eilers, Els (1932—)
Bos, Alida van den (1902—)
Bosboom-Toussaint, Anna (1812–1886)
Bosch, Edith (1980—)
Bosshardt, Alida M. (1913—)
Bouman, Kea (1903–1998)
Brandes-Brilleslijper, Janny (c. 1918–2003)
Braun, Maria-Johanna (1911–1982)
Brico, Antonia (1902–1989)
Brienese, Karin (1969—)
Brigitha, Enith Salle (1955—)
Brouwenstijn, Gré (1915–1999)
Brouwer, Bertha (1930—)
Bruggen, Carry van (1881–1932)
Buitenweg, Kathalijne Maria (1970—)
Buter, Yvonne (1959—)
Catherine of Bourbon (d. 1469)
Catherine of Cleves (1417–1479)
Charlotte of Bourbon (d. 1582)
Charriere, Isabelle de (1740–1805)
Coligny, Louise de (1555–1620)
Corbey, Dorette (1957—)
Cornet, Lynda (1962—)
Cottenjé, Mireille (1933—)
Cox, Annemarie (1966—)
Davies, Lilian May (1915—)
de Beus, Bernadette de (1958—)
de Bruijn, Chantal (1976—)
de Bruijn, Inge (1973—)
Deelstra, Atje (1938—)
de Haan, Annemiek (1981—)
de Heij, Stella
Deiters, Julie (1975—)
de Jong, Dola (1911–2003)
de Jong, Reggie (1964—)
Deken, Aagje (1741–1804)
Dekker, Inge (1985—)
Dekkers, Hurnet (1974—)
de Kok, Irene (1963—)
de Leeuw, Dianne
de Levie, Elka (1905–1979)
De Mist, Augusta (1783–1832)
Derckx, Annemiek (1954—)
Dermoût, Maria (1888–1962)
de Roever, Lisanne (1979—)
de Rover, Jolanda (1963—)
de Ruiter, Wietske
Dessaur, C.I. (1931–2002)
de Vries, Dorien (1965—)
D'haen, Christine (1923—)
Dijkstra, Sjoukje (1942—)
Donners, Wilhelmina (1974—)
Dullemen, Inez van (1925—)
Dunkeld, Ada (c. 1145–1206)
Duyster, Willemijn
Dyson, Elizabeth Geertruida (1897–1951)
Eijs, Irene (1966—)
Elizabeth of Brabant (1243–1261)
Emma of Waldeck (1858–1934)
Eybers, Elisabeth (1915—)
Eymers, Truus (1903–1988)
Foch, Nina (1924—)
Fokke, Annemieke (1967—)
Fortuyn-Leenmans, Margaretha Droogleever (1909–1998)
Frank, Anne (1929–1945)
Frank, Margot (1926–1945)
Frederica Wilhelmina of Prussia (1774–1837)
Gal, Jenny (1969—)
Gal, Jessica (1971—)
Gaskell, Sonia (1904–1974)
Geijssen, Carolina (1947—)
Georgi, Yvonne (1903–1975)
Gerhardt, Ida (1905–1997)

Gertrude of Ostend (d. 1358)
Gheenst, Johanna van der (fl. 16th c.)
Gies, Miep (1909—)
Gisolf, Carolina (1910—)
Gommers, Maria (1939—)
Gorris, Marleen (1948—)
Goslar, Hannah (1928—)
Goudal, Jetta (1891–1985)
Gravenstijn, Deborah (1974—)
Groenewold, Renate (1976—)
Groot, Chantal (1982—)
Habets, Marie-Louise (1905–1986)
Haesaert, Clara (1924—)
Haringa, Ingrid (1964—)
Heemskerk, Marianne (1944—)
Heijting-Schuhmacher, Irma (1925—)
Hellemans, Greet (1959—)
Hellemans, Nicolette (1961—)
Hendriks, Irene (1958—)
Henneken, Thamar (1979—)
Henrietta Adrienne (1792–1864)
Hepburn, Audrey (1929–1993)
Herzberg, Judith (1934—)
Hillen, Francisca (1959—)
Hillesum, Etty (1914–1943)
Holsboer, Noor (1967—)
Holtrop-van Gelder, Betty (1866–1962)
Hommes, Nienke (1977—)
Houter, Marleen (1961—)
Irene Emma (1939—)
Isabella Clara Eugenia of Austria (1566–1633)
Jaapies, Mieke (1943—)
Jacobs, Aletta (1854–1929)
Jacqueline of Hainault (1401–1436)
Jans, Annetje (c. 1605–1663)
Jansen, Elly (1929—)
Jeanne of Valois (c. 1294–1342)
Joanna of Brabant (1322–1406)
Joan of Hainault (c. 1310–?)
Juliana (1909–2004)
Juliane of Nassau-Dillenburg (1546–1588)
Juliane of Stolberg-Wernigrode (1506–1580)
Jurrilëns, Henny (1949—)
Karres, Sylvia (1976—)
Katherine of Holland (d. 1401)
Kint, Cor (d. 2002)
Kiplagat, Lornah (1974—)
Knol, Monique (1964—)
Kok, Ada (1947—)
Koolen, Nicole (1972—)
Kuipers, Ellen
Ladde, Cornelia (1915—)
Lagerberg, Catherina (1941—)
Laurijsen, Martha (1954—)
Lejeune, Elisabeth (1963—)
Le Mair, H. Willebeek (1889–1966)
LePoole, Alexandra (1959—)
Lewin, Jeannette
Leyster, Judith (1609–1660)
Lidwina of Schiedam (1380–1433)
Linssen-Vaessen, Marie-Louise (1928–1993)
Louisa (1622–1709)
Maas, Annelies (1960—)
MacGillavry, Carolina H. (1904–1993)
Maij-Weggen, Hanja (1943—)
Manus, Rosa (1881–1942)
Margaret of Austria (1480–1530)
Margaret of Burgundy (c. 1376–1441)
Margaret of Holland (d. 1356)
Margaret of Parma (1522–1586)
Margriet Francisca (1943—)
Maria Christina (1742–1798)
Maria Christina (1947—)
Maria Elisabeth (1680–1741)
Marianne of the Netherlands (1810–1883)
Marie of Nassau (1841–1910)
Marsman, Margot (1932—)
Martens, Maria (1955—)
Mary of Hungary (1505–1558)
Mastenbroek, Rie (1919–2003)
Matthijsse, Margriet (1977—)
Meijer, Elien (1970—)
Menco, Sara (1920—)
Mendels, Josepha (1902–1995)
Merian, Maria Sybilla (1647–1717)
Merken, Lucretia Wilhelmina van (1721–1789)
Mia Boissevain (1878–1959)
Michaelis, Hanny (1922—)
Moreira de Melo, Fatima (1978—)
Muis, Marianne (1968—)
Muis, Mildred (1968—)
Mulder, Eefke (1977—)
Neelissen, Catharina (1961—)
Nienhuys, Janna
Nieuwenhuizen, Anneloes (1963—)
Nordheim, Helena (1903–1943)
Oda of Lorraine (fl. mid-1000)
Ogive of Luxemburg (d. 1030)
Ohr, Martine (1964—)
Oomen-Ruijten, Ria G.H.C. (1950—)
Oosterwyck, Maria van (1630–1693)
Oremans, Miriam (1972—)
Ouden, Willemijntje den (1918–1997)
Oversloot, Maria (1914—)
Palm, Etta Aelders (1743–1799)
Peijs, Karla M.H. (1944—)
Pels, Auguste van (1900–1945)
Penninx, Nelleke (1971—)
Philippa of Guelders (d. 1547)
Philippine of Luxemburg (d. 1311)
Plesman, Suzanne
Plooij-Van Gorsel, Elly (1947—)
Polak, Anna (1906–1943)
Portnoy, Ethel (1927–2004)
Pos, Alette (1962—)
Quik, Martijntje (1973—)
Quist, Anne Marie (1957—)
Richilde (1034–1086)
Rijker, Lucia (1967—)
Roland Holst, Henriëtte (1869–1952)
Romein-Verschoor, Annie (1895–1978)
Ronner-Knip, Henriette (1821–1909)
Rothenberger, Gonnelien
Rubinstein, Renate (1929–1990)
Ruysch, Rachel (1664–1750)
Sanders, Annemarie (1958—)
Sanders-Ten Holte, Maria Johanna (1941—)
Sarstadt, Marian (1942—)
Schaft, Hannie (1920–1945)
Scheepstra, Maartje (1980—)
Schopman, Janneke (1977—)
Schrader, Catharina Geertuida (1656–1745)
Schrieck, Louise van der (1813–1886)
Schut, Johanna (1944—)
Selbach, Johanna (1918—)
Senff, Dina (1920—)
Sevens, Elizabeth (1949—)
Siegelaar, Sarah (1981—)
Sinnige, Clarinda (1973—)
Smabers, Hanneke (1973—)
Smabers, Minke (1979—)
Smit, Gretha (1976—)
Smulders, Marlies (1982—)
Snoeks, Jiske (1978—)
Sophia of Malines (d. 1329)
Sophia of Wurttemberg (1818–1877)
Sorgdrager, Winnie (1948—)
Stad-de Jong, Xenia (1922—)
Stalman, Ria (1951—)
Steenberghe, Florentine (1967—)
Stelma, Jacoba (1907—)
Stove, Betty (1945—)
Swiebel, Joke (1941—)
Talma, Madame (1771–1860)
Tammes, Tine (1871–1947)
Tanger, Helen (1978—)
Teeuwen, Josepha (1974—)
ten Boom, Corrie (1892–1983)
ter Beek, Carin (1970—)
Termeulen, Johanna (1929–2001)
Terpstra, Erica (1943—)
Thate, Carole (1971—)
Themans-Simons, Judikje (1904–1943)
Timmer, Marianne (1974—)
Timothy, Elizabeth (d. 1757)
Tinné, Alexandrine (1839–1869)
Touw, Daphne (1970—)
Toxopeus, Jacqueline (1968—)
Vaandrager, Wiljon (1957—)
van Baalen, Coby (1957—)
Van Cortlandt, Annettje Lockermans (c. 1620–after 1665)
van de Kieft, Fleur (1973—)
van den Boogaard, Dillianne (1974—)
van den Burg, Ieke (1952—)
van der Ben, Helena (1964—)
van der Kade-Koudijs, Gerda (1923—)
van Der Kolk, Kirsten (1975—)
van der Plaats, Adriana (1971—)
van der Vaart, Macha (1972—)
van der Vegt, Anna (1903–1983)
van der Wielen, Suzan (1971—)
van der Wildt, Paulina (1944—)
Van Dishoeck, Pieta (1972—)
van Doorn, Marieke (1960—)
van Drogenbroek, Marieke (1964—)
van Ettekoven, Harriet (1961—)
van Eupen, Marit (1969—)
van Geenhuizen, Miek (1981—)
Van Gennip, Yvonne (1964—)
van Grunsven, Anky (1968—)
Van Hamel, Martine (1945—)
van Kessel, Lieve (1977—)
van Langen, Ellen (1966—)
van Manen, Aletta (1958—)
van Moorsel, Leontien (1970—)
Van Nes, Eeke (1969—)
Van Randwijk, Petronella (1905–1978)
van Rijn, Wilma (1971—)
van Rooijen, Manon (1982—)
van Rumpt, Annemarieke (1980—)
van Rumt, Hendrika (b. 1897)
van Schurmann, Anna Maria (1607–1678)
van Staveren, Petra (1966—)
van Stockum, Hilda (b. 1908)
van Velsen, Wilma (1964—)
van Vliet, Petronella (1926—)
van Voorn, Koosje (1935—)
van Weerdenburg, Wilhelmina (1946—)
Vaz Dias, Selma (1911–1977)
Veenstra, Myrna (1975—)
Veldhuis, Marleen (1979—)
Venema, Anneke (1971—)
Verstappen, Annemarie (1965—)
Vierdag, Maria (b. 1905)
Visser, Adriana (1961—)
Vlieghuis, Kirsten (1976—)
von Weiler, Sophie (1958—)
Voorbij, Aartje (1940—)
Voskes, Elles (1964—)
Voskuijl, Bep (d. 1983)
Vrugt, Johanna Petronella (1905–1960)
Vuyk, Beb (1905–1991)
Waard, Elly de (1940—)
Wagner, Catherina (1919—)

Warmond, Ellen (1930—)
Wegman, Froukje (1979—)
Westerhof, Marieke (1974—)
Wielema, Geertje (1934—)
Wijnberg, Rosalie (1887–1973)
Wijsmuller-Meijer, Truus (c. 1896–1978)
Wilhelmina (1880–1962)
Winkel, Kornelia (1944—)
Witziers-Timmer, Jeanette (1923–2005)
Wolff, Ingrid (1964—)
Worhel, Esther (1975—)
Zeghers, Margriet (1954—)
Zelle, Margaretha (1876–1917)
Zwiers, Claudia

NEUSTRIA

Western part of the Kingdom of the Franks

See Austrasia.
See Franks, Kingdom of the.

NEVERS

Commune of Nièvre department in central France

See France.

NEW ZEALAND

Independent state comprising several islands in southwest Pacific Ocean
Discovered by Tasman (1642)
Circumnavigated by Captain Cook (1769)
Colonized by New Zealand Company and claimed by British (1840)
Maori Wars (1843–1852)
Provincial government abolished (1875)
Colonial status terminated (1907)
Adopted unicameral government (1950)

See also Maori.

Abraham, Caroline Harriet (1809–1877)
Abraham, Constance Palgrave (1864–1942)
Adams, Nancy M. (1926—)
Adamson, Catherine (1868–1925)
Adcock, Fleur (1934—)
Addison, Agnes (c. 1841–1903)
Aitken, Jessie (1867–1934)
Alabaster, Ann O'Connor (1842–1915)
Alda, Frances (1879–1952)
Aldous, Lucette (1938—)
Alexander, Jessie (1876–1962)
Allan, Stella (1871–1962)
Allen, Betty Molesworth (1913–2002)
Allen, Pamela Kay (1934—)
Amohau, Merekotia (1898–1978)
Andersen, Catherine Ann (1870–1957)
Anderson, Barbara (1926—)
Anderson, Ellen Alice (1882–1978)
Anderson, Mary Patricia (1887–1966)
Andrews, Elsie Euphemia (1888–1948)
Angus, Rita (1908–1970)
Anstice, Sophia (1849–1926)
Armitage, Rachelina Hepburn (1873–1955)
Armstrong, Jenny (1970—)
Arndt, Hermina (1885–1926)
Arnim, Elizabeth von (1866–1941)
Ashton-Warner, Sylvia (1908–1984)
Atkinson, Jane Maria (1824–1914)
Atkinson, Lily May (1866–1921)
Aubert, Mary Joseph (1835–1926)
Austin, Margaret (1933—)
Aves, Isabel Annie (1887–1938)
Baber, Esther Mary (1871–1956)
Badger, Charlotte (fl. 1806–1808)
Bagley, Amelia (1870–1956)
Bain, Wilhelmina Sherriff (1848–1944)
Baker, Isabel Noeline (1878–1958)
Baker, Louisa Alice (1856–1926)
Baker McLaglan, Eleanor Southey (1879–1969)
Banahan, Mary Gertrude (1855/56?–1932)
Bannerman, Jane (c. 1835–1923)
Barbier, Adèle Euphrasie (1829–1893)
Barnicoat, Constance Alice (1872–1922)
Barraud, Sarah Maria (c. 1823–1895)
Barrer, Nina Agatha Rosamond (1879–1965)
Barron, Hannah Ward (1829–1898)
Barth, Beatrice Mary (1877–1966)
Basham, Maud Ruby (1879–1963)
Basten, Alice (1876–1955)
Batchelor, Mary (1927—)
Bates, Sophia Ann (1817–1899)
Batten, Jean Gardner (1909–1982)
Baughan, Blanche Edith (1870–1958)
Baume, Rosetta Lulah (1871–1934)
Baxter, Millicent Amiel (1888–1984)
Beatty, May (1880–1945)
Beere, Estelle Girda (1875–1959)
Bell, Elizabeth Viola (1897–1990)
Bell, Margaret Brenda (1891–1979)
Bell, Muriel Emma (1898–1974)
Bellamy, Elizabeth (1845–1940)
Benjamin, Ethel Rebecca (1875–1943)
Bennett, Agnes Elizabeth Lloyd (1872–1960)
Bennett, Mary Jane (c. 1816–1885)
Benson, Gertrude (1886–1964)
Bethell, Mary Ursula (1874–1945)
Bethell, Thyra Talvase (1882–1972)
Bettjeman, Agnes Muir (1885–1964)
Bews, Mary Ellen (1856–1945)
Bibby, Mary Ann (c. 1832–1910)
Bicknell, Jessie (1871–1956)
Birchfield, Constance Alice (1898–1994)
Black, Helen McKenzie (1896–1963)
Blackett, Annie Maude (1889–1956)
Blackie, Jeannetta Margaret (1864–1955)
Blackwell, Ellen Wright (1864–1952)
Bloodworth, Rhoda Alice (1889–1980)
Bock, Amy Maud (1859–1943)
Boyce, Ann (c. 1827–1914)
Boys-Smith, Winifred Lily (1865–1939)
Bridger, Bub (1924—)
Briggs, Margaret Jane (1892–1961)
Brooke, Evelyn Gertrude (1879–1962)
Brown, Charlotte (c. 1795–1855)
Browne, Harriet Louisa (1829–1906)
Buckingham, Rosetta (c. 1843–1864)
Buckland, Jessie Lillian (1878–1939)
Buckman, Rosina (1881–1948)
Bullock, Margaret (1845–1903)
Bulstrode, Emily Mary (1867–1959)
Bulstrode, Jane Helena (1862–1946)
Burgess, Georgina Jane (c. 1839–1904)
Burgin, Annie Mona (1903–1985)
Burn, Margaret Gordon (1825–1918)
Burns, Violet Alberta Jessie (1893–1972)
Butler, Grace Ellen (1886–1862)
Butler, Margaret Mary (1883–1947)
Button, Isabel (1863–1921)
Buxton, Mary Ann (c. 1795–1888)
Cabot, Dolce Ann (1862–1943)
Calder, Liz (1938—)
Cameron, Donaldina (1869–1968)
Cameron, Robina Thomson (1892–1971)
Campbell, Laurel (1902–1971)
Campbell, Meg (1937—)
Campion, Jane (1954—)
Candy, Alice (1888–1977)
Canty, Mary Agnes (1879–1950)
Caradus, Elizabeth (1832–1912)
Cardale, Effie (1873–1960)
Carey, Ida Harriet (1891–1982)
Carnachan, Blanche Eleanor (1871–1954)
Caro, Margaret (1848–1938)
Carran, Catherine (1842–1935)
Carroll, Heni Materoa (1852/56?–1930)
Carter, Una Isabel (1890–1954)
Cassie, Alice Mary (1887–1963)
Cassie Cooper, Vivienne (1926—)
Castle, Amy (1880–?)
Chamberlain, Ann Marie (1935—)
Chapman, Anne Maria (1791–1855)
Chapman, Pansy (1892–1973)
Chapman, Sylvia (1896–1995)
Cheeseman, Clara (1852–1943)
Chemis, Annie (1862–1939)
Cherrington, Te Paea (c. 1877–1937)
Cherry, Frances (1937—)
Chevalier, Caroline (c. 1832–1917)
Clark, Cora Maris (1885–1967)
Clark, Helen Elizabeth (1950—)
Clark, Kate Emma (1847–1926)
Clark, Sally (1958–)
Coad, Nellie (1883–1974)
Coberger, Annelise (1971—)
Cohen, Myra (1892–1959)
Colclough, Mary Ann (1836–1885)
Colenso, Elizabeth (1821–1904)
Collier, Edith (1885–1964)
Collier, Jane Annie (1869–1955)
Collier, Jeanie (c. 1791–1861)
Collins, Anne (1951—)
Connon, Helen (c. 1859–1903)
Cook, Freda Mary (1896–1990)
Cooper, Whina (1895–1994)
Coory, Shirefie (c. 1864–1950)
Cossey, Alice Eleanor (1879–1970)
Cossgrove, Selina (1849–1929)
Cottrell, Violet May (1887–1971)
Coulton, Mary Rose (1906–2002)
Cowie, Bessie Lee (1860–1950)
Cowie, Eliza Jane (1835–1902)
Cowie, Helen Stephen (1875–1956)
Cowley, Joy (1936—)
Cripps, Sarah Ann (c. 1821–1892)
Crocombe, Marjorie Tuainekore (fl. 1970s)
Crowe, Ellen (c. 1845–1930)
Cruickshank, Margaret Barnet (1873–1918)
Cryer, Sarah (1848–1929)
Cuddie, Mary (1823–1889)
Cunnington, Eveline Willert (1849–1916)
Curtis, Kathleen Maisey (1892–1994)
Daldy, Amey (c. 1829–1920)
Dallas, Ruth (1919—)
Dalrymple, Learmonth White (1827–1906)
Dalziel, Lianne (1960—)
Davies, Dorothy Ida (1899–1987)
Davies, Sonja (1923–2005)
Davis, Pa Tepaeru Ariki (1923–1990)
Dawson, Mary Elizabeth (1833–1924)
Deamer, Dulcie (1890–1972)
Dean, Williamina (1844–1895)
Deans, Jane (1823–1911)
Devoy, Susan (1964—)
Dewe, Colleen (1930–1993)
Diamond, Ann (c. 1827–1881)
Dickson, Mary Bernard (c. 1810–1895)
Dodd, Lynley Stuart (1941—)
Don, Rachel (1866–1941)
Donald, Janet (c. 1819–1892)
Donaldson, Viva (1893–1970)
Doo, Unui (1873/75?–1940)
Dougherty, Ellen (c. 1843–1919)
Dougherty, Sarah (c. 1817–1898)
Dreaver, Mary (1887–1964)
Dronke, Minnie Maria (1904–1987)
Duckworth, Marilyn (1935—)
Duder, Tessa (1940—)
Du Faur, Emmeline Freda (1882–1935)
du Fresne, Yvonne (1929—)
Duggan, Eileen May (1894–1972)

Dyson, Elizabeth Geertruida (1897–1951)
Edger, Kate (1857–1935)
Edmond, Lauris (1924–2000)
Egnot, Leslie (1963—)
Eise, Ida Gertrude (1891–1978)
Elder, Anne (1918–1976)
Ellen, Mary Ann (1897–1949)
Ellis, Ellen (1829–1895)
Elsom, Sarah Ann (1867–1962)
England, Maud Russell (1863–1956)
Ensing, Riemke (1939—)
Escott, Cicely Margaret (1908–1977)
Evans, Ann (c. 1836–1916)
Evers-Swindell, Caroline (1978—)
Evers-Swindell, Georgina (1978—)
Fabish, Agnes (1873–1947)
Faulkner, Ruawahine Irihapeti (?–1855)
Fergusson, Elizabeth (1867–1930)
Ferner, Ellen Elizabeth (1869–1930)
Field, Ethel Maude (1882–1967)
Finnie, Jessie (c. 1821–?)
FitzGibbon, Hanorah Philomena (1889–1979)
Fletcher, Chris (1955—)
Flint, Elizabeth (b. 1909)
Forbes, Margaret (c. 1807–1877)
Foster, Emily Sophia (1842–1897)
Frame, Janet (1924–2004)
France, Ruth (1913–1968)
Francis, Catherine Augusta (1836–1916)
Frank, Rosaline Margaret (1864–1954)
Fraser, Annie Isabel (1868–1939)
Fraser, Isabella (1857–1932)
Fraser, Janet (1883–1945)
Fraser, Margaret (1866–1951)
Fraser, Mary Isabel (1863–1942)
Freeman, Caroline (c. 1855–1914)
Frost, Constance Helen (c. 1862–1920)
Fulton, Catherine (1829–1919)
Furley, Matilda (1813–1899)
Gant, Phyllis (1922—)
Gardiner, Kate (1885–1974)
Gard'ner, Elizabeth Anne (1858–1926)
Gardner, Margaret (1844–1929)
Gardner, Maria Louisa (1879–1968)
Garlick, Eunice Harriett (1883–1951)
Garmson, Aileen (c. 1861–1951)
Geddes, Annabella Mary (1864–1955)
George, Elizabeth (c. 1814–1902)
Gibb, Helen (1838–1914)
Gibbs, Mary Elizabeth (1836–1920)
Gibson, Emily Patricia (1863/64?–1947)
Gibson, Helena Fannie (1868–1938)
Gibson, Mary Victoria (1864–1929)
Gilbert, Ruth (1917—)
Gill, Mary Gabriel (1837–1905)
Gill, Zillah Smith (1859–1937)
Gillies, Janet (1864–1947)
Gilmer, Elizabeth May (1880–1960)
Gittos, Marianne (1830–1908)
Glen, Esther (1881–1940)
Goddard, Victorine (1844–1935)
Godley, Charlotte (1821–1907)
Goodwin, Bridget (c. 1802/27–1899)
Gordon, Annie Elizabeth (1873–1951)
Gordon, Doris Clifton (1890–1956)
Gordon, Eliza (1877–1938)
Grace, Patricia (1937—)
Graham, Rose (1879–1974)
Greaves, Mary Ann (1834–1897)
Green, Grace Winifred (1907–1976)
Greenwood, Ellen Sarah (1837–1917)
Greenwood, Sarah (c. 1809–1889)
Gregg, Christina (c. 1814–1882)
Griffin, Elsie Mary (1884–1968)
Grigg, Mary (1897–1971)
Grimm, Cherry Barbara (1930–2002)
Grossmann, Edith Searle (1863–1931)
Guard, Elizabeth (1814–1870)
Gunn, Elizabeth Catherine (1879–1963)
Halcombe, Edith Stanway (1844–1903)
Hale, Maria Selina (1864–1951)
Hall, Cara Vincent (1922—)
Hall, Theodora Clemens (1902–1980)
Halliday, Margaret (1956—)
Hames, Mary (1827–1919)
Hammond, Joan (1912–1996)
Hanan, Susanna (1870–1970)
Hannen, Lynley (1964—)
Harris, Emily Cumming (c. 1836–1925)
Harris, Jane Elizabeth (c. 1852–1942)
Harrold, Agnes (c. 1830–1903)
Harsant, Florence Marie (1891–1994)
Haselden, Frances Isabella (c. 1841–1936)
Hasler, Marie (1945—)
Haszard, Rhona (1901–1931)
Hato, Ana Matawhaura (1907–1953)
Hatton, Marion (1835–1905)
Hawthorne, Margaret Jane Scott (1869–1958)
Hay, Jean Emily (1903–1984)
Heap, Sarah (1870–1960)
Hei, Akenehi (1877/78?–1910)
Hellaby, Amy Maria (1864–1955)
Henderson, Christina Kirk (1861–1953)
Henry, Annie (1879–1971)
Herangi, Te Kirihaehae Te Puea (1883–1952)
Hercus, Ann (1942—)
Herrick, Hermione Ruth (1889–1983)
Hetherington, Jessie Isabel (1882–1971)
Hetley, Georgina Burne (1832–1898)
Hewett, Ellen Anne (1843–1926)
Hewett, Mary Elizabeth Grenside (1857–1892)
Hewlett, Hilda Beatrice (1864–1943)
Hickey, Mary St. Domitille (1882–1958)
Hicks, Adelaide (1845–1930)
Higgins, Sarah (1830–1923)
Hikapuhi (1860/71?–1934)
Hill, Emily (1847–1930)
Hill, Mabel (1872–1956)
Hine-i-paketia (fl. 1850–1870)
Hineira, Arapera (1932—)
Hine-i-turama (c. 1818–1864)
Hinematioro (d. 1823)
Hinerangi, Sophia (c. 1830–1911)
Hirst, Grace (1805–1901)
Hodge, Annie Mabel (1862–1938)
Hodgkins, Frances (1869–1947)
Hodgson, Tasha (1974—)
Holford, Alice Hannah (1867–1966)
Hood, Mary (c. 1822–1902)
Hooper, Kate Challis (1894–1982)
Horrell, Elizabeth (1826–1913)
Horsley, Alice Woodward (1871–1957)
Howard, Caroline Cadette (1821–?)
Howard, Mabel (1893–1972)
Howes, Edith Annie (1872–1954)
Howie, Fanny Rose (1868–1916)
Howley, Calasanctius (1848–1933)
Hulme, Keri (1947—)
Hunt, Frances Irwin (1890–1981)
Hurd-Wood, Kathleen Gertrude (1886–1965)
Hutchinson, Amy Hadfield (1874–1971)
Hutchinson, Amy May (1888–1985)
Imison, Rachel (1978—)
Inglis, Helen Clyde (1867–1945)
Innes, Catherine Lucy (1839/40–1900)
Innes, Mary Jane (1852–1941)
Irvine-Smith, Fanny Louise (1878–1948)
Isitt, Kathleen (1876–?)
Jackson, Ann Fletcher (1833–1903)
Jackson, Rowena (1926—)
Jackson, Sarah Elizabeth (1858–1946)
Jacobsen, Inger Kathrine (1867–1939)
Jacobson, Ethel May (1877–1965)
James, Annie Isabella (1884–1965)
James, Esther Marion Pretoria (1900–1990)
James, Florence (1902–1993)
James, Naomi (1949—)
Jamieson, Penny (1942—)
Jeffreys, Ellen Penelope (1827–1904)
Jelicich, Dorothy (1928—)
Joel, Grace Jane (1865–1924)
Johnston, Amy Isabella (1872–1908)
Jury, Te Aitu-o-te-rangi (c. 1820–1854)
Kaaro, Ani (fl. 1885–1901)
Kahutia, Riperata (c. 1838–1887)
Kane, Amy Grace (1879–1979)
Keall, Judy (1942—)
Kefala, Antigone (1935—)
Keller, Nettie Florence (1875–1974)
Kells, Isabella (1861–1938)
Kelly, Annie Elizabeth (1877–1946)
Kelsey, Lavinia Jane (1856–1948)
Kelso, Elizabeth (1889–1967)
Kemp, Charlotte (1790–1860)
Kendall, Barbara Anne (1967—)
Kenny, Alice Annie (1875–1960)
Kent, Thelma Rene (1899–1946)
Kidman, Fiona (1940—)
Kidson, Elsa Beatrice (1905–1979)
King, Annette (1947—)
King, Martha (1802/03–1897)
Kirby, Mary Kostka (1863–1952)
Kirk, Cybele Ethel (1870–1957)
Kirk, Jenny (1945—)
Kissling, Margaret (1808–1891)
Knighton, Margaret (1955—)
Koea, Shonagh (1939—)
Kokoro-Barrett, Hiria (1870–1943)
Latta, Victoria (1951—)
Law, Alice Easton (1870–1942)
Law, Mary Blythe (1873–1955)
Leahy, Mary Gonzaga (1870–1958)
Lee, Mary Isabella (1871–1939)
Lissaman, Elizabeth Hazel (1901–1991)
Locke, Elsie (1912–2001)
Lockwood, Annea F. (1939—)
Lo Keong, Matilda (c. 1854–1915)
Lord, Lucy Takiora (c. 1842–1893)
Lorimer, Margaret (1866–1954)
Love, Ripeka Wharawhara (1882–1953)
Lovell, Ann (1803/11–1869)
Lovell-Smith, Rata Alice (1894–1969)
Low, Caroline Sarah (1876–1934)
Luxford, Nola (1895–1994)
Lynch, Margaret (fl. 1867–1868)
Lyttelton, Edith Joan (1873–1945)
Macandrew, Jennie (1866–1949)
Macfarlane, Edith Mary (1871–1948)
Mackay, Catherine Julia (1864–1944)
Mackay, Elizabeth (c. 1845–1897)
Mackay, Elizabeth Ann Louisa (1843–1908)
Mackay, Jessie (1864–1938)
Mackay, Maria Jane (1844–1933)
MacKinnon, Joanna (1878–1966)
Maclean, Hester (1859–1932)
MacLean, Vida (1881–1970)
Macpherson, Margaret Louisa (1895–1974)
Mactier, Susie (1854–1936)
Maher, Mary Cecilia (1799–1878)
Mahupuku, Maata (1890–1952)
Mahy, Margaret (1936—)
Maihi, Rehutai (1895–1967)
Malcolm, Emilie Monson (1829/30–1905)

Mander, Jane (1877–1949)
Mangakahia, Meri Te Tai (1868–1920)
Mansel, Lucy (c. 1830–1915)
Mansfield, Katherine (1888–1923)
Marchant, Maria Élise Allman (1869–1919)
Marsh, Ngaio (1895–1982)
Martin, Hannah (1830–1903)
Martin, Mary Ann (1817–1884)
Massey, Christina Allan (1863–1932)
Mataira, Katarina Te Heikoko (1932—)
Matenga, Huria (1840/42–1909)
Mathew, Sarah Louise (c. 1805–1890)
Mathieson, Catherine (1818–1883)
Maude, Sibylla Emily (1862–1935)
Maxwell, Alice Heron (1860–1949)
May, Isabella (1850–1926)
McAlpine, Rachel (1940—)
McCarthy, Mary Ann Recknall (1866–1933)
McCombs, Elizabeth Reid (1873–1935)
McDonald, Agnes (1829–1906)
McDonald, Hedwick Wilhelmina (1893–1959)
McHugh, Fanny (1861–1943)
McIntosh, Gail (1955—)
McKain, Douglas Mary (1789–1873)
McKenzie, Jean (1901–1964)
McKenzie, Margaret (c. 1837–1925)
McLauchlan, Joy (1948—)
McLean, Mary Jane (1866–1949)
McMillan, Ethel (1904–1987)
McPherson, Heather (1942—)
McQueen, Mary (1860–1945)
McVicar, Annie (1862–1954)
Meech, Matilda (c. 1825–1907)
Mellish, Edith Mary (1861–1922)
Melville, Eliza Ellen (1882–1946)
Menzies, Trixie Te Arama (1936—)
Mihi-ki-te-kapua (?–1872/80)
Millar, Annie Cleland (1855–1939)
Milne, Mary Jane (1840–1921)
Minchin, Alice Ethel (1889–1966)
Mitchell, Juliet (1934—)
Mitchell, Marion (1876–1955)
Moir, Margaret (1941—)
Moller, Lorraine (1955—)
Moncrieff, Pérrine (1893–1979)
Moore, Mary Emelia (1869–1951)
Morete, Maraea (1844–1907)
Morison, Harriet (1862–1925)
Morrison, Annie Christina (1870–1953)
Morton, Katherine E. (1885–1968)
Müller, Mary Ann (c. 1819–1902)
Mulvany, Josephine (1901–1967)
Mulvany, Sybil Mary (1899–1983)
Myers, Phoebe (1866–1947)
Nehua, Katerina (1903–1948)
Neill, Elizabeth Grace (1846–1926)
Newman, Mehetabel (c. 1822–1908)
Newton, Wharetutu Anne (fl. 1827–1870)
Nga-kahu-whero (fl. 1800–1836)
Ngata, Arihia Kane (1879–1929)
Nicholls, Marjory Lydia (1890–1930)
Nicol, Helen Lyster (1854–1932)
Niniwa-i-te-rangi (1854–1929)
Northcroft, Hilda Margaret (1882–1951)
Nowland, Mary Josepha (1863–1935)
Nunneley, Kathleen Mary (1872–1956)
O'Connell, Sarah (c. 1822–1870)
O'Donnell, Ann (c. 1857–1934)
Okin, Susan Moller (1946–2004)
Orbell, Margaret (1934—)
O'Regan, Katherine (1946—)
Osborn, Daisy (1888–1957)
Osborne, Fanny (1852–1934)
Ostler, Emma Brignell (c. 1848–1922)
Page, Evelyn (1899–1987)
Paget, Nielsine (1858–1932)
Palmer, Alice May (1886–1977)
Palmer, Elizabeth Mary (1832–1897)
Papakura, Makereti (1873–1930)
Parata, Katherine Te Rongokahira (1873–1939)
Park, Ruth (1923—)
Parker, Pauline Yvonne (1938—)
Parkinson, Alice May (1889–1949)
Parsons, Elizabeth (1846–1924)
Paterson, Ada Gertrude (1880–1937)
Paul, Annette (1863–1952)
Paul, Joanna (1945–2003)
Payne, Nicola (1960—)
Peacocke, Isabel Maud (1881–1973)
Penfold, Merimeri (1924—)
Pengelly, Edna (1874–1959)
Pickerill, Cecily Mary Wise (1903–1988)
Pilgrim, Ada (1867–1965)
Pinepine Te Rika (1857/58–1954)
Pitini-Morera, Hariata Whakatau (1871/72?–1938)
Platts-Mills, Daisy Elizabeth (1868–1956)
Player, Mary Josephine (c. 1857–1924)
Polson, Florence Ada Mary Lamb (1877–1941)
Pomare, Hariata (fl. 1863–1864)
Pope, Maria Sophia (1818–1909)
Porter, Nyree Dawn (1936–2001)
Pottinger, Judith (1956—)
Powell, Mary Sadler (1854/55?–1946)
Preshaw, Jane (1839–1926)
Pudney, Elizabeth Allen (1894–1976)
Puhiwahine Te Rangi-hirawea, Rihi (d. 1906)
Pulling, Mary Etheldred (1871–1951)
Pulman, Elizabeth (1836–1900)
Purcell, Samuelene (1898–1982)
Ralfe, Catherine Hester (c. 1831–1912)
Ralph, Margaret (c. 1822–1913)
Randall, Amelia Mary (1844–1930)
Ratana, Iriaka (1905–1981)
Rattray, Lizzie Frost (1855–1931)
Rawlinson, Gloria (1918–1995)
Rees, Annie Lee (1864–1949)
Rees, Rosemary (c. 1876–1963)
Reeve, Elsie (1885–1927)
Reeves, Magdalene Stuart (1865–1953)
Renée (1926—)
Rere-o-maki (d. 1868)
Retter, Hannah (1839–1940)
Reynolds, Rachel Selina (1838–1928)
Richardson, Effie Newbigging (1849/50?–1928)
Richardson, Ruth (1950—)
Richmond, Dorothy Kate (1861–1935)
Richmond, Mary Elizabeth (1853–1949)
Rikiriki, Atareta Kawana Ropiha Mere (c. 1855–1926)
Ritchie, Harriet Maria (1818–1907)
Riwai, Kiti Karaka (1870–1927)
Roberts, Mary Louise (1886–1968)
Robertson, Ann (1825–1922)
Roe, Allison (1957—)
Rolleston, Elizabeth Mary (1845–1940)
Rollett, Hilda (1873–1970)
Rongonui, Kahupake (1868/69?–1947)
Ross, Forrestina Elizabeth (1860–1936)
Ross, Frances Jane (1869–1950)
Ross, Hilda (1883–1959)
Rout, Ettie Annie (1877–1936)
Rudman, Annie (1844–1928)
Runciman, Jane Elizabeth (1873–1950)
Rymill, Mary Ann (c. 1817–1897)
Salmond, Sarah (1864–1956)
Savell, Edith Alma Eileen (1883–1970)
Scales, Helen Flora Victoria (1887–1975)
Scanlan, Nelle (1882–1968)
Schnackenberg, Annie Jane (1835–1905)
Schramm, Bernardina Adriana (1900–1987)
Schroeder, Bertha (1872–1953)
Scott, Jessie Ann (1883–1959)
Scott, Mary Edith (1888–1979)
Scott, Rosie (1948—)
Seager, Esther (c. 1835–1911)
Seville, Carolina Ada (1874–1955)
Shaw, Helen (1913–1985)
Shayle George, Frances (c. 1827–1890)
Shearer, Janet (1958—)
Sheppard, Kate (1847–1934)
Sherwood, Maud Winifred (1880–1956)
Shields, Margaret (1941—)
Shipley, Jenny (1952—)
Siedeberg, Emily Hancock (1873–1968)
Sievwright, Margaret Home (1844–1905)
Simpson, Mary Elizabeth (1865–1948)
Sinclair, Elizabeth McHutcheson (1800–1892)
Siteman, Isabella Flora (c. 1842–1919)
Small, Mary Elizabeth (1812/13–1908)
Smith, Frances Hagell (1877–1948)
Smith, Helen Hay (1873–1918)
Smith, Lucy Masey (1861–1936)
Smither, Elizabeth (1941—)
Snow, Sarah Ellen Oliver (1864–1939)
Soljak, Miriam Bridelia (1879–1971)
Soper, Eileen Louise (1900–1989)
Spencer Bower, Olivia (1905–1982)
Spencer Smith, Joan (1891–1965)
Sperrey, Eleanor Catherine (1862–1893)
Squires, Catharine (1843–1912)
Stace, Helen McRae (1850–1926)
Stanley, Mary (1919–1980)
Statham, Edith May (1853–1951)
Stevenson, Greta Barbara (1911–1990)
Stevenson, Margaret Beveridge (1865–1941)
Stevenson, Rona (1911–1988)
Stewart, Adela Blanche (1846–1910)
Stewart, Catherine Campbell (1881–1957)
Stewart, Frances Ann (1840–1916)
Stewart, Jean (1930—)
Stewart, Mary Downie (1876–1957)
Stirling, Mihi Kotukutuku (1870–1956)
Stoddart, Margaret Olrog (1865–1934)
Stothard, Sarah Sophia (1825/26–1901)
Stout, Anna Paterson (1858–1931)
Strong, Ann Monroe Gilchrist (1875–1957)
Stuart, Bathia Howie (1893–1987)
Stuart, Wilhelmina Magdalene (1895–1985)
Sturm, J.C. (1927—)
Suckling, Sophia Lois (1893–1990)
Suisted, Laura Jane (1840–1903)
Summers, Essie (1912–1998)
Sutherland, Margaret (1941—)
Sutherland, Mary (1893–1955)
Sutherland, Mary Ann (1864–1948)
Sutherland, Selina Murray McDonald (1839–1909)
Sutton, Eve (1906—)
Swainson, Mary Anne (c. 1833–1897)
Swift, Anne (1829/35–?)
Taiaroa, Tini Kerei (c. 1846–1934)
Tamairangi (fl. 1820–1828)
Tapsell, Ngatai Tohi Te Ururangi (1844–1928)
Tasker, Marianne Allen (1852–1911)
Tautari, Mary (d. 1906)
Taylor, Elizabeth Best (1868–1941)
Taylor, Sophia Louisa (1847–1903)
Te Kahuhiapo, Rahera (1820s?–1910)
Te Kakapi, Ripeka Wharawhara-i-te-rangi (?–1880)

Te Kanawa, Kiri (1944—)
Te Kiri Karamu, Heni (1840–1933)
Tenetahi, Rahui Te Kiri (d. 1913)
Tennet, Elizabeth
Te Paea Tiaho (1820s?–1875)
Te Pikinga (c. 1800–after 1868)
Te Rangi-i-paia II (fl. 1818–1829)
Te Rangimarie, Puna Himene (fl. 1908–1911)
Te Rau-o-te-rangi, Kahe (?–c. 1871)
Te Rohu (fl. 1820–1850)
Te Taiawatea Rangitukehu, Maata (1848/49?–1929)
Te Whaiti, Kaihau Te Rangikakapi Maikara (1863–1937)
Te Wherowhero, Piupiu (1886/87?–1937)
Texidor, Greville (1902–1964)
Thompson, Blanche Edith (1874–1963)
Thompson, Marion Beatrice (1877–1964)
Thomson, Jane (1858–1944)
Thurston, Mabel (1869–1960)
Tirikatene-Sullivan, Whetu (1932—)
Tizard, Catherine (1931—)
Tizard, Judith (1956—)
Tombleson, Esmé (1917—)
Topeora, Rangi Kuini Wikitoria (?–1865/73)
Torlesse, Elizabeth Henrietta (1835/36–1922)
Tracy, Mona Innis (1892–1959)
Tripe, Mary Elizabeth (1870–1939)
Turikatuku (d. 1827)
Ulmer, Sarah (1976—)
Valentine, Winifred Annie (1886–1968)
Van Chu-Lin (1893/94?–1946)
Vautier, Catherine (1902–1989)
Vitelli, Annie (c. 1837–?)
Waitaoro (c. 1848–1929)
Waitohi (?–1839)
Wallis, Mary Ann Lake (1821–1910)
Wallwork, Elizabeth (1883–1969)
Ward, Anne (c. 1825–1896)
Waring, Marilyn (1952—)
Watkins, Gladys Elinor (1884–1939)
Watson, Jean (1933—)
Watts Russell, Elizabeth Rose Rebecca (1833/34–1905)
Weldon, Barbara (1829/30–1882)
Wells, Ada (1863–1933)
Weston, Jessie Edith (1867–1944)
Whitaker, Mabel (1884–1976)
White, Anna Lois (1903–1984)
White, Emily Louisa Merielina (1839–1936)
Whitehouse, Davina (1912–2002)
Whiteside, Jane (1855–1875)
Wilde, Fran (1948—)
Wilding, Cora (1888–1982)
Wilkinson, Iris (1906–1939)
Williams, Anna Maria (1839–1929)
Williams, Eileen Hope (1884–1958)
Williams, Jane (c. 1801–1896)
Williams, Marianne (1793–1879)
Williams, Matilda Alice (1875–1973)
Williams, Yvette (1929—)
Williamson, Jessie Marguerite (c. 1855–1937)
Wilson, Fanny (1874–1958)
Wilson, Helen Ann (1793/94–1871)
Wilson, Helen Mary (1869–1957)
Wiseman, Hilda Alexandra (1894–1982)
Wohlers, Eliza (c. 1812–1891)
Wood, Susan (1836–1880)
Wyllie, Kate (d. 1913)
Yates, Elizabeth (c. 1844–1918)
Yates, Ngawini (1852/53?–1910)
Younghusband, Adela Mary (1878–1969)

NICAEA

Empire in Asia Minor (13th c.)
See Asia Minor.

NICARAGUA

Republic in Central America
Part of captain-generalcy of Guatemala
Declared independence from Spain (1821)
Part of United Provinces of Central America (1823–1838)

Alegría, Claribel (1924—)
Araúz, Blanca (d. 1933)
Astorga, Nora (1949–1988)
Chamorro, Violeta (1929—)
Richardson, Michelle (1969—)
Tellez, Dora Maria (1957—)
Zamora, Daisy (1950—)

NIGERIA

Republic in West Africa
Explored by Europeans (18th–19th c.)
Lagos ceded to Britain by native king (1861)
Administered by Sierra Leone (1861–1874)
Administered by Gold Coast Colony (1874)
Reconstituted as Colony and Protectorate of Lagos (1886)
Formed into Protectorates of Northern and Southern Nigeria (1899)
Became Colony and Protectorate of Nigeria (1914)
Achieved independence (1960)

Abayomi, Oyinkansola (1897–1990)
Afolabi, Bisi
Ajakaiye, Deborah Enilo (c. 1940—)
Ajunwa, Chioma (1970—)
Alakija, Aduke (1921—)
Alozie, Glory (1977—)
Amachree, Mactabene (1978—)
Amina (c. 1533–c. 1598)
Awolowo, Hannah (1915—)
Emecheta, Buchi (1944—)
Idehen, Faith (1973—)
Ighodaro, Irene (1916–1995)
Inyama, Rosemary (b. 1903)
Nwapa, Flora (1931–1993)
Nzimiro, Mary (1898–1993)
Odozi Obodo, Madam (1909–1995)
Ogbeifo, Ruth (1967—)
Ogunkoya, Falilat (1969—)
Okoye, Ifeoma
Okwei of Osomari (1872–1943)
Onyali, Mary (1968—)
Opara, Charity (1972—)
Opara-Thompson, Christy (1971—)
Ransome-Kuti, Funmilayo (1900–1978)
Sade (1959—)
Segun, Mabel (1930—)
Sofola, Zulu (1935–1995)
Turunku Bakwa (fl. 1530s)
Ulasi, Adaora Lily (1932—)
Utondu, Beatrice (1969—)
Yusuf, Fatima (1971—)

NIVELLES

Commune in Brabant province of Belgium
See Belgium.

NORFOLK

County in eastern England
See England.

NORMANDY

Historic region in northwestern France
Part of Lugdunensis under Romans
Part of kingdom of Neustria after Frankish invasions
Invaded by Norsemen (9th c.)
Established as a French duchy (10th c.)
United with England (11th c.)
Conquered by the French (1204)
Conquered by the English (1417)
Conquered by the French (1450)
See also England.
See also France.

Adelaide of Montserrat (fl. 1100)
Adela of Blois (1062–c. 1137)
Adele of Normandy (c. 917–c. 962)
Adelicia (1029–1090)
Adeliza (d. 1066?)
Alice of Normandy (fl. 1017–1037)
Corday, Charlotte (1768–1793)
Emma of Normandy (c. 985–1052)
Emma of Paris (d. 968)
Gisela Martel (d. 919)
Gunhild (c. 1020–1038)
Gunnor of Denmark (d. 1031)
Judith of Normandy (c. 1054–after 1086)
Judith of Rennes (c. 982–1018)
Papia of Envermeu (fl. 1020)
Poppa of Normandy (fl. 880)
Sybil of Conversano (d. 1103)

NORTHUMBERLAND

County in northern England
See England.

NORTHUMBRIA

Anglo-Saxon kingdom of Britain
Leading kingdom of the Anglo-Saxon Heptarchy (7th c.)
Subjugated by Mercia
Subjugated by Celtic missionaries
Southern part ruled by Danes (9th c.)
Annexed to Wessex (10th c.)
See also Denmark.
See also England.

Ebba (c. 610–c. 683)

NORWAY

Kingdom in northwestern Europe
Colonized islands off Scotland and Ireland, Iceland, and Greenland (9th c.)
Invaded England (1066)
Ruled by Denmark (14th c.)
Ceded by Denmark to Sweden (1814)
Dissolved union with Sweden (1905)

Aarones, Ann Kristin (1973—)
Ahlander, Thecla (1855–1925)
Andersen, Astrid Hjertenaes (1915–1985)
Andersen, Kjerstin (1958—)
Andersen, Linda (1969—)
Andreassen, Gunn Margit (1973—)
Anker, Nini Roll (1873–1942)
Anna Catherina of Brandenburg (1575–1612)
Anna of Denmark (1532–1585)
Arnesen, Liv (1953—)
Asa (c. 800–c. 850)
Astrid (fl. 1100s)
Aufles, Inger
Aunli, Berit
Backer, Harriet (1845–1932)
Backer-Grondahl, Agathe (1847–1907)
Begga of Egremont (fl. 7th c.)
Bekkevold, Kristin (1977—)
Bjerkrheim, Susann Goksoer (1970—)
Bjoergen, Marit (1980—)
Blanche of Namur (d. 1363)
Boe, Anette
Bonnevie, Kristine (1872–1948)
Bonnevie, Margarete Ottilie (1884–1970)
Bosse, Harriet (1878–1961)
Brantenberg, Gerd (1941—)
Bruce, Isabel (c. 1278–1358)

Bruntland, Gro Harlem (1939—)
Bryn, Alexia (1889–1983)
Carlsen, Agnete (1971—)
Christina of Saxony (1461–1521)
Colban, Marie (1814–1884)
Collett, Camilla (1813–1895)
Dahl, Aslaug
Dahle, Gunn-Rita (1973—)
Dahle, Mona (1970—)
Dahlmo, Marianne
Dal, Ingerid (1895–1985)
d'Aulaire, Ingri (1904–1980)
Devold, Kristin Krohn (1961—)
Digre, Berit (1967—)
Dorothea of Brandenburg (1430–1495)
Dorothea of Saxe-Lauenburg (1511–1571)
Duvholt, Kristine (1974—)
Dybendahl Hartz, Trude (1966—)
Dybwad, Johanne (1867–1950)
Eftedal, Siri (1966—)
Elfgifu of Northampton (c. 1000–1044)
Eliasson, Marthe (1969—)
Elisabeth of Habsburg (1501–1526)
Elizabeth of Kiev (fl. 1045)
Engelbretsdatter, Dorothe (1634–1716)
Enger, Babben
Eriksen, Ann (1971—)
Eriksen, Gunn (1956—)
Espeseth, Gro (1972—)
Euphemia of Rugen (d. 1312)
Fedde, Sister Elizabeth (1850–1921)
Flagstad, Kirsten (1895–1962)
Frederica Amalie (1649–1704)
Frithpoll, Margaret (d. 1130)
Froeseth, Hege (1969—)
Frustol, Tone Gunn (1975—)
Garborg, Hulda (1862–1934)
Gleditsch, Ellen (1879–1968)
Goksoer, Susann (1970—)
Grieg, Nina (1845–1935)
Grini, Kjersti (1971—)
Gulbrandsen, Ragnhild (1977—)
Gulbrandsen, Solveig (1981—)
Gundersen, Trude (1977—)
Gunness, Belle (1860–c. 1908)
Gunnhild (fl. 1150s)
Gurie, Sigrid (1911–1969)
Gynt, Greta (1916–2000)
Hagerup, Inger (1905–1985)
Haltvik, Trine (1965—)
Hansteen, Aasta (1824–1908)
Hansteen, Kirsten (1903–1974)
Hattestad, Stine Lise
Hattestad, Trine (1966—)
Haugen, Tone (1964—)
Haugenes, Margunn (1970—)
Hegh, Hanne (1960—)
Heiberg, Marianne (1945–2004)
Henie, Sonja (1912–1969)
Henriksen, Henriette (1970—)
Hilmo, Elisabeth (1976—)
Hofmo, Gunvor (1921–1995)
Hogness, Hanne (1967—)
Holst, Clara (1868–1935)
Holter, Harriet (1922–1997)
Hovland, Ingeborg (1969—)
Hundvin, Mia (1977—)
Inga (fl. 1204)
Ingeborg (c. 1300–c. 1360)
Ingeborg of Denmark (d. 1287)
Ingigerd Haraldsdottir (fl. 1075)
Ingirid (fl. 1067)
Ingstad, Anne-Stine (c. 1918–1997)
Jahren, Anne
Jensen, Bjorg Eva (1960—)
Jensen, Christine Boe (1975—)
Johansen, Aud (1930—)
Johnsen, Vibeke (1968—)
Jorgensen, Silje (1977—)
Kanga (fl. 1220)
Kielland, Kitty L. (1843–1914)
Kittelsen, Grete Prytz (1917—)
Kjeldaas, Stine Brun (1975—)
Knudsen, Monica (1975—)
Kolstad, Eva (1918–1998)
Korsmo, Lisbeth (1948—)
Kringen, Goril (1972—)
Kristiansen, Ingrid (1956—)
Krog, Gina (1847–1916)
Kvitland, Bente (1974—)
Larsen, Gerd (1920–2001)
Larsen, Tonje (1975—)
Leganger, Cecilie (1975—)
Lehn, Unni (1977—)
Lid, Hilde Synnove
Lorentzen, Ingeborg (1957—)
Lorentzen, Ragnhild (1968—)
Louise of England (1724–1751)
Louise of Mecklenburg-Gustrow (1667–1721)
Løveid, Cecilie (1951—)
Löwenstein, Helga Maria zu (1910–2004)
Lunde, Vibeke (1921–1962)
Mallory, Molla (1884–1959)
Margaret (d. 1209)
Margaret (d. 1270)
Margaret of Norway (1261–1283)
Maria Juliana of Brunswick (1729–1796)
Martha de Freitas (1958—)
Martha of Sweden (1901–1954)
Martinsen, Bente (1972—)
Maud (1869–1938)
Medalen, Linda (1965—)
Mellgren, Dagny (1978—)
Mette-Marit (1973—)
Midthun, Kristin (1961—)
Mikkelsplass, Marit (1965—)
Moen-Guidon, Anita (1967—)
Molin-Kongsgard, Anne (1977—)
Mørdre, Berit
Myklebust, Merete (1973—)
Myrmael, Marit
Nedreaas, Torborg (1906–1987)
Nilsen, Elin (1968—)
Nilsen, Jeanette (1972—)
Nissen, Erika (1845–1903)
Nissen, Greta (1906–1988)
Nordby, Bente (1974—)
Nybraaten, Inger-Helene (1960—)
Nymark Andersen, Nina (1972—)
Oestvold, Line (1978—)
Oldenburg, Astrid (1932—)
Oldenburg, Martha (1971—)
Oldenburg, Ragnhild (1930—)
Ottesen-Jensen, Elise (1886–1973)
Pedersen, Hilde G. (1964—)
Pedersen, Solveig
Pettersen, Brit
Pettersen, Karin (1964—)
Pettersen, Marianne (1975—)
Philippa (1394–1430)
Plaetzer, Kjersti (1972—)
Poiree, Liv Grete (1974—)
Przybyszewska, Dagny Juel (1867–1901)
Rapp, Anita (1977—)
Resvoll, Thekla (1871–1948)
Resvoll-Holmsen, Hanna (1873–1943)
Reventlow, Anne Sophie (1693–1743)
Richiza (fl. 1251)
Riise, Hege (1969—)
Rokne, Marianne (1978—)
Saettem, Birgitte (1978—)
Sagstuen, Tonje (1971—)
Sandaune, Brit (1972—)
Sandel, Cora (1880–1974)
Sandve, Monica (1973—)
Schou Nilsen, Laila (1919–1998)
Seth, Reidun (1966—)
Sikveland, Annette (1972—)
Singstad, Karin (1958—)
Skjelbreid, Ann-Elen (1971—)
Skotvoll, Annette (1968—)
Skram, Amalie (1846–1905)
Sonja (1937—)
Sophia of Bayreuth (1700–1770)
Sophia of Mecklenburg (1557–1631)
Sophia of Pomerania (1498–1568)
Sørlie, Else-Marthe (1978—)
Stephansen, Elizabeth (1872–1961)
Stoere, Heidi (1973—)
Sundal, Heidi (1962—)
Sundby, Siren (1982—)
Svendsen, Cathrine (1967—)
Svensson, Tina (1970—)
Tangeraas, Trine (1971—)
Thora (fl. 1100s)
Thora Johnsdottir (fl. 1000s)
Thoresen, Cecilie (1858–1911)
Thun, Kjersti (1974—)
Thyra of Denmark (d. 1000)
Tjoerhom, Linda (1979—)
Tjugum, Heidi (1973—)
Traa, Kari (1974—)
Ullmann, Liv (1939—)
Undset, Sigrid (1882–1949)
Vaa, Aslaug (1889–1965)
Valle, Inger-Louise (1921—)
Vesaas, Halldis Moren (1907–1995)
Vestly, Anne-Cath (1920—)
Vieregg, Elizabeth Helene (fl. 17th c.)
Vik, Bjørg (1935—)
Waitz, Grete (1953—)
Zorina, Vera (1917–2003)

NUMIDIA

Ancient country in North Africa
Became Roman province (46 BCE)
Later became part of Mauretania
Flourished until invasion by Vandals (428 CE)

Cleopatra V Selene (c. 40 BCE–?)

OJIBWE

LaDuke, Winona (1959—)

OLDENBURG

Former German state
See Germany.

OMAHA

Native North American Great Plains indigenous group

La Flesche, Susan (1865–1915)
La Flesche, Susette (1854–1902)

ORANGE

City in Vaucluse department in southeastern France
Gave name to Dutch princes of Orange
Ruled by house of Nassau
Passed to princes of Orange-Nassau (1530)
Acquired by France
Now the royal line of the Netherlands
See France.
See Germany.
See Netherlands.

ORKNEY

Region in northern Scotland
See Scotland.

Geographic Index

ORLÉANS

Commune of Loiret department in northern central France
Conquered by Caesar (52 BCE)
Major cultural center in early Middle Ages
Center of a royal duchy (1344)
See France.

OSAGE

Native North American Great Plains indigenous group

Tallchief, Maria (1925—)
Tallchief, Marjorie (1927—)

OTTOMAN EMPIRE

Established by Turks from central Asia (13th c.)
Included Balkan region and Egypt (15th c.)
Took western Asian countries and European territory of Holy Roman Empire (16th c.)
Warred with Poland, Austria, and Russia (17th–18th c.)
Expelled from Hungary and northern shores of Black Sea (19th c.)
Completely dissolved (1923)
See Turkey.

OXFORD

Borough in Oxfordshire in central England
See England.

PADUA

Commune of Padova province in northeastern Italy
See Italy.

PAIUTE

Native North American Breat Basin indigenous group

Winnemucca, Sarah (1844–1891)

PAKISTAN

Republic in southern Asia
Established (1947)
Comprises provinces of Baluchistan, North-West Frontier, Punjab, and Sind
Clashed with India over Kashmir (1947–1949)
Became a republic (1956)

Bhutto, Benazir (1953—)
Bhutto, Nusrat (1929—)
Faiz, Alys (1914–2003)
Jehan, Noor (1926–2000)
Jinnah, Fatima (1893–1967)
Khan, Begum Liaquat Ali (1905–1990)
Lodhi, Maleeha (c. 1953—)
Naheed, Kishwar (1940—)
Sidhwa, Bapsi (1938—)
Suraiya (1929–2004)

PALATINATE

Historic region of western Germany
Under jurisdiction of counts palatine who became electors of Holy Roman Empire (14th c.)
See Germany.

PALESTINE, ANCIENT

Conquered by Egypt (1479 BCE)
Occupied by Canaanites prior to Hebrew invasion
Southern coast settled by Philistines
Became part of Assyrian, Chaldean, and Persian Empires (from 8th c. BCE)
Conquered by Pompey (64 BCE)
Became part of Roman province of Syria (c. 4 BCE–29 CE)
Conquered by Arabs
Ruled by various Muslim dynasties
Under Ottoman Empire (1516–1917)
See Israel and Judah.

PALESTINE, MODERN

Conquered by British (1917)
Assigned as British mandate (1920–1948)
Under Israeli administration (1967)

Aaronsohn, Sarah (1890–1917)
Ashrawi, Hanan (1946—)
Harry, Myriam (1869–1958)
Khalifa, Sahar (1941—)
Tuqan, Fadwa (1917—)

PALMYRA

City in Syria
Under Roman rule (1st c. CE)
Kingdom became independent (3rd c. CE)
City destroyed (273 CE)

Zenobia (r. 267–272)

PANAMA

Britton, Rosa María (1936—)
Moscoso, Mireya (1946—)
Sierra, Stella (1917–1997)

PAPUA NEW GUINEA

Southeastern section of New Guinea
Visited by Portuguese, Spanish, French, and English navigators (16th–17th c.)
Region proclaimed by British (1883 and 1884)
Annexed as British New Guinea (1888)
Australian territory proclaimed (1906)
Became independent country (1975)
Member of British Commonwealth

Abaijah, Josephine (1942—)
Burgess, Annie (1969—)
Kouza, Loujaya M.

PARAGUAY

Acuña, Dora (fl. 1940s)
Plá, Josefina (1909–1999)

PARIS

Pre-Roman settlement (52 BCE)
Made bishopric (3rd c.)
Came to Kingdom of the Franks (486)
Established as capital of France (987)
See France.

PARMA

Province of Emilia-Romagna in northern Italy
Founded by Romans (183 BCE)
Made bishopric (4th c. CE)
Passed as duchy of Parma and Piacenza to Farnese, then to Austrians
Held by France (1815)
Became part of kingdom of Italy (1861)
See Italy.

PARTHIA

Ancient country in western Asia
Formed a province of Assyrian and Persian Empires
Became part of empire of Alexander
New Parthian kingdom founded (c. 250 BCE)

Laodice (fl. 129 BCE)
Rhodogune (fl. 2nd c. BCE)

PEMBROKE

Borough of Pembrokeshire in southwestern Wales
See Wales.

PERGAMUM

See Asia Minor.

PERSIA

See Iran.

Gauhar Shad (c. 1378–1459)

PERU

Republic in western South America
Seat of Inca Empire (c. 1230)
Conquered by the Spanish (1542)
Achieved independence from Spain (1824)

Amarilis (fl. 17th c.)
Bastidas, Micaela (1745–1781)
Borja, Ana de (c. 1640–1706)
Cabello de Carbonera, Mercedes (1845–1909)
Cassandane (fl. 500s BCE)
Cervera, Luisa (1964—)
De La Guerra, Alejandra (1968—)
Escot, Pozzi (1933—)
Fajardo, Demisse (1964—)
Gallardo, Miriam (1968—)
Garcia, Rosa (1964—)
Godin des Odonais, Isabel (1728–d. after 1773)
Heredia, Isabel (1963—)
Horny, Katherine (1969—)
Malaga, Natalia (1964—)
Mama-Ocllo (fl. around 12th c.)
Matto de Turner, Clorinda (1854–1909)
Perez del Solar, Gabriela (1968—)
Portal, Magda (1903–1989)
Rose of Lima (1586–1617)
Santolalla, Irene Silva de (1902–1992)
Sumac, Yma (1927—)
Tiit, Cecilia (1962—)
Torrealva, Gina (1961—)
Uribe, Cenaida (1964—)
Vargas, Virginia (1945—)
Villegas, Micaela (1748–1819)

PESARO

Seaport in Pesaro e Urbino province in Marches in central Italy
Ruled by Umbrians, Etruscans, and Senonian Gauls
Became Roman colony (184 BCE)
Destroyed by Ostrogoths (535 CE)
Passed to Malatestas (1285)
Passed to Sforzas (1445)
Passed to Roveres (1512)
Part of Papal Staes (1631)
Became part of kingdom of Italy (1860)
See Italy.

PHILIPPINES

Republic off southeastern coast of Asia
Southern Philippines settled by Muslims (15th c.)
Manila captured and held by British (18th c.)
Spanish control strengthened (18th–19th c.)
Commonwealth of the Philippines established (1935)
Ruled by Japan (1941–1942)
Independent government established (1946)

Abiertas, Josepha (1894–1929)
Alfon, Estrella (1917–1982)
Aquino, Corazon (1933—)
Aquino, Melchora (1812–1919)
Arceo, Liwayway (1924—)
Arroyo, Gloria Macapagal (1947—)
Barros, Lorena (d. 1976)
Blanca, Nida (1936–2001)
Fernando, Gilda Cordero (1930—)
Fitton, Doris (1897–1985)
Florentino, Leona (1849–1884)
Jalandoni, Magdalena (1891–1978)
Jesus, Gregoria de (1875–1943)
Kasilag, Lucrecia R. (1918—)
Lewis, Loida (c. 1943—)
Marcos, Imelda (1929—)
Moreno, Virginia R. (1925—)
Ocampo-Friedmann, Roseli (1937—)
Ochoa, Elisa
Rosca, Ninotchka (1941—)
Silang, Gabriela (1731–1763)

Tescon, Trinidad (1848–1928)
Tiempo, Edith L. (1919—)
Ty-Casper, Linda (1931—)

PHOENICIA

Ancient maritime country in western Syria
Composed of city-states (c. 1600 BCE)
Under rule of Tyre (11th–8th c. BCE)
Conquered by Assyrians, Chaldeans, Persians, and by Alexander the Great (4th c. BCE)
Ruled by Ptolemies of Egypt and Seleucid kingdom of Syria (286–197 BCE)
Included in Roman province of Syria
See Syria.

PIACENZA

Province of Emilia-Romagna in northern Italy
See Italy.

POCASSET

Native North American Northeastern indigenous group

Wetamoo (c. 1650–1676)

POITOU

Historic region in western central France
Conquered by Romans and made part of Aquitania
Conquered by Visigoths (418 CE)
Defeated by the Franks (507 CE)
Made countship by Charlemagne (778)
Part of the duchy of Aquitaine (990)
Passed to France and then to England (12th c.)
Reunited with French crown (15th c.)
Province of France until Revolution, then divided into districts
See France.

POLAND

Republic in central Europe
Slavic duchy under Piast dynasty (10th c.)
Invaded by Mongols (1241)
United with Lithuania (1386)
Obtained West Prussia and East Prussia (1466)
Strong nobility made Polish crown elective (16th c.)
Territory lost to war (17th c.)
Partitioned among Russia, Prussia, and Austria (18th c.)
Partly reestablished by Napoleon as Grand Duchy of Warsaw (1807–1815)
Under Russian crown (19th c.)
Invaded by Germans and Austrians in World War I
Proclaimed independent republic (1918)
Eastern and central parts subjugated by Germany and Russia (1939)
Establishment of Soviet-dominated government (1947)
Achieved independence (1990)

Abakanowicz, Magdalena (1930—)
Agnes of Poland (1137–after 1181)
Aldona of Lithuania (d. 1339)
Anderson, Anna (1902–1984)
Anna Jagello (1523–1596)
Anna of Bohemia (fl. 1230s)
Anna of Schweidnitz (c. 1340–?)
Anna of Styria (1573–1598)
Aszkielowiczowna, Halina (1947—)
Babilenska, Gertruda (1902–1997)
Bacewicz, Grazyna (1909–1969)
Badarzewski-Baranowska, Tekla (1834–1861)
Barbara of Poland (1478–1534)
Barbara Radziwell (1520–1551)
Barbara Zapolya (fl. 1500)
Benislawska, Konstancja (1747–1806)
Beyer, Ursel (b. 1918)
Blumental, Felicja (1908–1991)
Bohuszewiczowna, Maria (1865–1887)
Botwinska, Adela (b. 1904)
Bozyk, Reizl (1914–1993)
Broniewska, Janina (1904–1981)
Brystygierowa, Julia (1902–1980)
Budzynska-Tylicka, Justyna (1876–1936)
Burton, Sala (1925–1987)
Catherine of Habsburg (1533–1572)
Cecilia Renata of Austria (1611–1644)
Chmielnicka, Lidia (1939—)
Chojnowska-Liskiewicz, Krystyna (1937—)
Choms, Wladyslawa Laryssa (1891–1966)
Cieply-Wieczorkowna, Teresa (1937—)
Constance of Styria (1588–1631)
Cunegunde (1234–1292)
Cunegunde (d. after 1370)
Curie, Marie (1867–1934)
Czajkowska, Krystyna (1936—)
Czartoryska, Isabella (1746–1835)
Czerny-Stefanska, Halina (1922—)
Czerny-Stefanska, Halina (1922–2001)
Czopek, Agnieszka (1964—)
Dabrowska, Maria (1889–1965)
Darvi, Bella (1927–1971)
Deutsch, Helene (1884–1982)
Deutscher, Tamara (1913–1990)
Dluzewska, Malgorzata (1958—)
Dobravy of Bohemia (d. 977)
Domanska, Janina (1912–1995)
Donska, Maria (1912–1996)
Dylewska, Izabella (1968—)
Dzerzhinska, Sofia (1882–1968)
Dzieciol, Iwona (1975—)
Eleanor Habsburg (1653–1697)
Elizabeth of Bosnia (d. 1339)
Elizabeth of Habsburg (d. 1545)
Elizabeth of Hungary (c. 1430–1505)
Elizabeth of Silesia (fl. 1257)
Emnilde (fl. 986)
Euphrosyne of Opole (d. 1293)
Fabish, Agnes (1873–1947)
Fornalska, Malgorzata (1902–1944)
Gersten, Berta (c. 1896–1972)
Glinska, Teofila (c. 1765–1799)
Golimowska, Maria (1932—)
Gorecka, Halina (1938—)
Gorka (fl. 920s)
Grabowski, Halina (1928–2003)
Granville, Christine (1915–1952)
Gray, Gilda (1901–1959)
Grossman, Haika (1919–1996)
Gruchala, Sylwia (1981—)
Gunhilda of Poland (d. around 1015)
Halicka, Antonina (1908–1973)
Hanska, Éveline, Countess (1801–1882)
Hartwig, Julia (1921—)
Hauke, Julie von (1825–1895)
Hedwig of Poland (1513–1573)
Held, Anna (c. 1865–1918)
Helene of Moscow (1474–1513)
Hesse-Bukowska, Barbara (1930—)
Holland, Agnieszka (1948—)
Jaczynowska, Katarzyna (1875–1920)
Jadwiga (1374–1399)
Jadwiga of Glogow (fl. late 1300s)
Jagiello, Appolonia (1825–1866)
Jakubowska, Krystyna (1942—)
Jakubowska, Wanda (1907–1998)
Janiszewska, Barbara (1936—)
Janotha, Natalia (1856–1932)
Jedrzejczak, Otylia (1983—)
Jesionowska, Celina (1933—)
Jokielowa, Dorota (1934–1993)
Jonas, Maryla (1911–1959)
Jozwiakowska, Jaroslawa (1937—)
Judith of Hungary (fl. late 900s)
Karpinski, Stephanie (1912–2005)
Kielan, Urszula (1960—)
Klata, Katarzyna (1972—)
Klobukowska, Ewa (1946—)
Konopacka, Halina (1900–1989)
Konopnicka, Maria (1842–1910)
Kordaczukowna, Danuta (1939–1988)
Korjus, Miliza (1900–1980)
Korolewicz-Waydowa, Janina (1875–1955)
Koscianska, Czeslawa (1959—)
Kossak, Zofia (1890–1968)
Koszutska, Maria (1876–1939)
Kotowna-Walowa, Natalia (1938—)
Krall, Hanna (1937—)
Krull, Germaine (1897–1985)
Krupowa, Krystyna (1939—)
Krystyna Rokiczanska (fl. 1300s)
Krzesinska, Elzbieta (1934—)
Ksiazkiewicz, Malgorzata (1967—)
Kulesza, Kasia (1976—)
Kuncewicz, Maria (1899–1989)
Kwadzniewska, Maria (1913—)
Landowska, Wanda (1877–1959)
Langer, Lucyna (1956—)
Ledwigowa, Jozefa (1935—)
Lempicka, Tamara de (1898–1980)
Louise Marie de Gonzague (1611–1667)
Lubetkin, Zivia (1914–1978)
Lucia of Rugia (fl. 1220)
Ludgarda (fl. 1200s)
Luxemburg, Rosa (1870–1919)
Malgorzata (fl. 1290s)
Maria of Kiev (d. 1087)
Marie Casimir (1641–1716)
Marie Josepha (1699–1757)
Marko, Jadwiga (1939—)
Mauer, Renata (1969—)
Maurizio, Anna (1900–1993)
Miller, Alice (1923—)
Mniszek, Marina (c. 1588–1614)
Modjeska, Helena (1840–1909)
Moszumanska-Nazar, Krystyna (1924—)
Mroczkiewicz, Magdalena (1979—)
Nalkowska, Zofia (1884–1954)
Negri, Pola (1894–1987)
Niemczykowa, Barbara (1943—)
Novak, Nina (1927—)
Nowicka, Joanna (1966—)
Oda (fl. 1000)
Oda of Germany and North Marck (fl. 900s)
Ondra, Anny (1902–1987)
Opdyke, Irene (1918–2003)
Ordonówna, Hanka (1904–1950)
Orzeszkowa, Eliza (1841–1910)
Ostromecka, Krystyna (1948—)
Panfil, Wanda (1959—)
Pastuszka, Aneta (1978—)
Pawlikowska, Maria (1891–1945)
Pienkowska, Alina (1952–2002)
Pilejczyk, Helena (1931—)
Piszczek, Renata (1969—)
Polignac, Yolande Martine Gabrielle de (1749–1793)
Porzecowna, Elzbieta (1945—)
Przybyszewska, Stanislawa (1901–1935)
Radziwill, Francisca (1705–1753)
Raisa, Rosa (1893–1963)
Rakoczy, Helena (1921—)
Rambert, Marie (1888–1982)
Ravan, Genya (1942—)
Richesa of Lorraine (d. 1067)
Richizza of Poland (1116–1185)
Roberti, Lyda (1906–1938)
Rogowska, Anna (1981—)
Rose, Ernestine (1810–1892)
Rubinstein, Helena (1870–1965)
Rubinstein, Mala (1905–1999)
Rutkiewicz, Wanda (1943—)

Rutkowska, Jadwiga (1934—)
Rybicka, Anna (1977—)
Ryksa of Poland (d. 1185)
Ryksa of Poland (1288–1335)
Salomea (d. 1144)
Schneiderman, Rose (1882–1972)
Sembrich, Marcella (1858–1935)
Sendler, Irena (b. 1910)
Seroczynska, Elwira (1931—)
Sforza, Bona (1493–1557)
Simon, Kate (1912–1990)
Skolimowska, Kamila (1982—)
Sliwkowa, Maria (1935—)
Slizowska, Barbara (1938—)
Smendzianka, Regina (1924—)
Smosarska, Jadwiga (1898–1971)
Sobieski, Clementina (1702–1735)
Sokolowska, Beata (1974—)
Sophia of Kiev (fl. 1420s)
Sophia of Pomerania (1498–1568)
Sophie of Liegnitz (1525–1546)
Sophie of Poland (1464–1512)
Stachow, Danuta (1934—)
Staw, Sala (d. 1972)
Stokes, Rose Pastor (1879–1933)
Suchocka, Hanna (1946—)
Szczepanska, Aneta (1972—)
Szczerbinska-Krolowa, Lidia (1935—)
Szczesniewska, Zofia (1943–1988)
Szewczyk, Barbara (1970—)
Szewinska, Irena (1946—)
Szumowska, Antoinette (1868–1938)
Szwajger, Adina Blady (1917–1993)
Szydlowska, Irena (1928–1983)
Szymanowska, Maria Agata (1789–1831)
Szymborska, Wislawa (1923—)
Telalkowska, Wanda (1905–1986)
Tomaszewicz-Dobrska, Anna (1854–1918)
Viertel, Salka (1889–1978)
Wajs, Jadwiga (1912–1990)
Walentynowicz, Anna (1929—)
Walewska, Marie (1786–1817)
Walkowiak, Daniela (1935—)
Walsh, Stella (1911–1980)
Wanda of Poland (fl. 730)
Wasilewska, Wanda (1905–1964)
Wiechowna, Wanda (1946—)
Wrobel, Agata (1981—)
Wysoczanska, Barbara (1949—)
Zakrzewska, Marie (1829–1902)
Zaleska, Katherine (1919—)
Zapolska, Gabriela (1857–1921)
Zimetbaum, Mala (1920–1944)
Zlatin, Sabina (1907–1996)
Żmichowska, Narcyza (1819–1876)
Zurek, Natasza (1978—)

POMERANIA

Historic region on Baltic Sea
Invaded by Germans who erected duchy (12th c.)
Eastern part ceded to Poland (1466)
Duchy came under Brandenburg, which divided it with Sweden (1648)
Ceded to Prussia (1720 and 1815)
Occupied by U.S.S.R. (1945)
Assigned to Poland (1945)
See Poland.

PONTHIEU

Ancient region in northern France
Became countship (9th c.)
Passed to Castile (1251)
Held by England (13th–14th c.)
Passed to French crown (1690)
See England.
See France.

PONTUS

See Asia Minor.

PORTLAND

District in Dorsetshire in southern England
See England.

PORTUGAL

Republic in western section of Iberian Peninsula
Conquered by Visigoths (5th c.)
Conquered by Moors
Reconquered by León and Castile (11th c.)
Became independent kingdom (12th c.)
Became Spanish dependency (1580–1640)
Lost much of empire to the Dutch and English (17th–18th c.)
Became dependent ally of England (17th c.)
Occupied by French (1807–1814)
Proclaimed republic (1910)
See also England.
See also Netherlands.
See also Spain.

Acevedo, Angela de (d. 1644)
Adelheid (1831–1909)
Alcoforado, Mariana (1640–1723)
Almada, Filipa de (fl. 15th c.)
Almeida, Brites de (fl. 1385)
Almeida Garrett, Teresa (1953—)
Alorna, Marquesa de (1750–c. 1839)
Andresen, Sophia de Mello Breyner (1919–2004)
Anne of Velasquez (1585–1607)
Antonia of Portugal (1845–1913)
Archer, Maria (1905–1982)
Barreno, Maria Isabel (1939—)
Bastos, Regina (1960—)
Beatrice of Beja (1430–1506)
Beatrice of Castile and Leon (1242–1303)
Beatrice of Castile and Leon (1293–1359)
Beatrice of Portugal (c. 1347–1381)
Beatrice of Portugal (1372–after 1409)
Beatrice of Portugal (d. 1439)
Beatrice of Portugal (1504–1538)
Bessa-Luís, Agustina (1922—)
Botelho, Fernanda (1926—)
Braga, Maria Ondina (1932–2003)
Branca (c. 1192–1240)
Branca (1259–1321)
Brandão, Fiama Hasse País (1938—)
Browne, Maria da Felicidade do Couto (c. 1797–1861)
Cabete, Adelaide (1867–1935)
Carlota Joaquina (1775–1830)
Carrilho, Maria (1943—)
Carvajal, Luisa de (1568–1614)
Carvalho, Maria Judite de (1921–1998)
Castro, Fernanda de (1900–1994)
Castro, Públia Hortênsia de (1548–1595)
Catherine (1507–1578)
Catherine of Braganza (1638–1705)
Catherine of Portugal (1540–1614)
Centeno, Yvette (1940—)
Colaço, Branca de Gonta (1880–1944)
Constance of Castile (1323–1345)
Constance of Portugal (1290–1313)
Correia, Hélia (1939—)
Correia, Natália (1923–1993)
Costa, Emília de Sousa (1877–1957)
Costanza (1182–1202)
Damião, Elisa Maria (1946—)
Da Silva, Ana (1949—)
de Ayala, Josefa (1630–1684)
Douce of Aragon (1160–1198)
Eleanor of Portugal (1434–1467)
Eleanor of Portugal (1458–1525)
Eleanor of Portugal (1498–1558)
Elisa, Henriqueta (1843–1885)
Elizabeth of Portugal (1271–1336)
Espanca, Florbela (1894–1930)
Figueiredo, Ilda (1948—)
Gersão, Teolinda (1940—)
Goncalves, Olga (1937—)
Guimarães, Elina (1904–1991)
Hatherly, Ana Maria (1929—)
Hayes, Nevada (1885–1941)
Horta, Maria Teresa (1937—)
Isabella of Asturias (1471–1498)
Isabella of Braganza (1402–1465)
Isabella of Braganza (1459–1521)
Isabella of Braganza (c. 1512–1576)
Isabel la Paloma (1432–1455)
Isabel Maria (1801–1876)
Isabel of Aragon (1409–1443)
Janny, Amélia (1838–1914)
Joana de Mendoza (d. 1580)
Joanna (1452–1490)
Joanna of Portugal (1636–1653)
Lamas, Maria (1893–1983)
Leonora of Aragon (1405–1445)
Leonora Telles (c. 1350–1386)
Lisboa, Irene (1892–1958)
Lorenzo, Teresa (fl. 1358)
Lucia, Sister (1907–2005)
Luisa de Guzman (1613–1666)
Mafalda (c. 1197–1257)
Maria Ana Victoria (1718–1781)
Maria Anna of Portugal (1843–1884)
Maria Antonia of Austria (1683–1754)
Maria de Fonte (fl. 1846)
Maria de Portugal (1521–1577)
Maria do Céu (1658–1753)
Maria II da Gloria (1819–1853)
Maria I of Braganza (1734–1816)
Maria Isabel of Portugal (1797–1818)
Maria Josepha of Portugal (1857–1943)
Mariana Victoria (1768–1788)
Maria of Castile (1482–1517)
Maria Pia (1847–1911)
Maria Sophia of Neuberg (1666–1699)
Marie-Amelie of Orleans (1865–1951)
Marie-Anne of Braganza (1861–1942)
Marie Elizabeth of Saxony (1610–1684)
Mary of Portugal (1527–1545)
Matilda of Maurienne (c. 1125–1157)
Mencia de Haro (d. 1270)
Mendoza, Ana de (fl. late 1400s)
Meneres, Maria Alberta (1930—)
Meneses, Juana Josefa de (1651–1709)
Mota, Rosa (1958—)
Nasi, Gracia Mendes (1510–1569)
Nóbrega, Isabel da (1925—)
Nunes, Natália (1921—)
Osório, Ana de Castro (1872–1935)
Perestrello-Moniz, Filippa (d. 1483)
Pestana, Alice (1860–1929)
Philippa of Lancaster (c. 1359–1415)
Pintasilgo, Maria de Lurdes (1930–2004)
Pires, Maria-Joao (1944—)
Pusich, Antónia Gertrudes (1805–1883)
Rego, Paula (1935—)
Ribeiro, Fernanda (1969—)
Rodrigues, Amalia (1921–1999)
Sancha (c. 1178–1229)
Silva e Orta, Teresa M. da (c. 1711–1793)
Souza e Mello, Beatriz de (c. 1650–1700)
Stephanie (1837–1859)
Suggia, Guilhermina (1888–1950)
Tavares, Salette (1922–1994)
Teresa of Castile (c. 1080–1130)
Teresa of Portugal (1157–1218)
Teresa of Portugal (1793–1874)
Theresa Henriques (c. 1176–1250)

Three Marias, The
Todi, Luiza Rosa (1753–1833)
Torres Marques, Helena (1941—)
Torrezão, Guiomar (1844–1898)
Urraca of Castile (c. 1186–1220)
Urraca of Portugal (c. 1151–1188)
Vasconcellos, Karoline Michaëlis de (1851–1925)
Vaz de Carvalho, Maria Amália (1847–1921)
Velho da Costa, Maria (1938—)
Vicente, Paula (1519–1576)
Vieira da Silva, Maria Elena (1908–1992)
Violante do Céu (1601–1693)
Vitorino, Virginia (1897–1967)

PORTUGUESE WEST AFRICA

See Angola.

POWHATAN

Native North American Northeast indigenous group

Pocahontas (c. 1596–1617)

PROVENCE

Historic region in southeastern France
Invaded by Visigoths, Burgundians, Ostrogoths, and Franks
Became part of realm of Lothair I (843)
With Transjurane Burgundy, became kingdom of Arles (933)
Made countship (1113)
Under Angevin rule until it passed to France (1481)
Province of France until Revolution

See France.

PRUSSIA

Former German state
East Prussia colonized by Teutonic Knights (13th c.)
West Prussia ceded by Teutonic Knights to Poland (15th c.)
East Prussia became Polish fief and erected into duchy (16th c.)
Duchy of East Prussia achieved independence from Poland (17th c.)
Kingdom of Prussia erected from all holdings of Brandenburg (17th c.)
Prussia expanded territory to include Pomerania, Silesia, and western Poland (18th c.)
East and west Prussia united (1824–1878)
Gained additional territory in war with Austria (1866)
Led North German Confederation (1867–1871)
Became republic (1918)
Lost territory to Poland and Russia (1945)
Formally abolished (1947)

See also Germany.
See also Poland.
See also Russia.

Agnes of Brandenburg (d. 1304)
Albertina Agnes (d. 1696)
Alexandrine of Prussia (1803–1892)
Amelia of Anhalt-Dessau (1666–1726)
Anna Amalia of Prussia (1723–1787)
Anna Catherina of Brandenburg (1575–1612)
Anna of Brandenburg (1487–1514)
Anna of Brandenburg (1507–1567)
Anna of Prussia (1576–1625)
Anna of Saxony (1544–1577)
Anna Sophia of Prussia (1527–1591)
Anne Marie of Brunswick (1532–1568)
Antoinette of Luxemburg (1899–1954)
Augusta of Saxe-Weimar (1811–1890)
Dorothea Oldenburg (1504–1547)
Elizabeth Christina of Brunswick-Wolfenbuttel (1715–1797)
Elizabeth of Brunswick (1746–1840)
Fabish, Agnes (1873–1947)
Frederica Louise (1715–1784)
Frederica of Hesse (1751–1805)
Frederica of Prussia (1767–1820)
Gadski, Johanna (1872–1932)
Herzeleide (1918–1989)
Ina Maria of Bassewitz-Levitzow (1888–1973)
Lichtenau, Countess von (1753–1820)
Louise (1808–1870)
Louise Dorothea of Brandenburg (1680–1705)
Louise of Brunswick-Wolfenbuttel (1722–1780)
Louise of Prussia (1776–1810)
Maria Eleanora (1550–1608)
Marie-Cecile Hohenzollern (1942—)
Marie of Anhalt (1898–1983)
Marie of Saxe-Weimar-Eisenach (1808–1877)
Marx, Jenny von Westphalen (1814–1881)
Mary of Hesse-Homburg (1785–1846)
Menzelli, Elisabetta (c. 1860–c. 1929)
Palm, Etta Aelders (1743–1799)
Pauline of Wurttemberg (1810–1856)
Philipse, Margaret Hardenbrook (d. 1690)
Sabine of Brandenburg-Ansbach (1529–1575)
Sophia Dorothea of Brandenburg (1736–1798)
Sophia Dorothea of Brunswick-Lüneburg-Hanover (1687–1757)
Sophia of Nassau (1824–1897)
Sophia of Nassau (1836–1913)
Sophie Caroline (1737–1817)
Sophie Charlotte of Hanover (1668–1705)
Sophie Louise of Mecklenburg (1685–1735)
Sophie of Brandenburg (1568–1622)
Sophie of Liegnitz (1525–1546)
Sophie of Nassau (1902–1941)
Sophie of Poland (1464–1512)
Sophie of Prussia (1870–1932)
Sophie of Solms-Laubach (1594–1651)
Suzanne of Bavaria (1502–1543)
Sybilla of Brandenburg (fl. 1500)
Therese of Nassau (1815–1871)
Tiedemann, Charlotte (1919–1979)
Ursula of Brandenburg (1488–1510)
Victoria (1866–1929)
Victoria of Mecklenburg-Strelitz (1878–1948)

PUEBLO

Native North American Southwest indigenous group

Peña, Tonita (1893–1949)
Velarde, Pablita (1918—)

PUERTO RICO

Self-governing commonwealth in union with United States
Discovered by Columbus (1493)
Colonized by Spain (16th c.)
Occupied by United States (1898)
Adopted constitution (1952)

Barbosa, Pilar (1898–1997)
Bracetti, Mariana (1840–c. 1904)
Cadilla de Martínez, Maria (1886–1951)
Calderón, Sila M. (1942—)
Calzada, Alba (1945—)
de Burgos, Julia (1914–1953)
Diaz, Eileen (1979—)
Fernandez, Gigi (1964—)
Ferré, Rosario (1938—)
Gautier, Felisa Rincón de (1897–1994)
Hills, Tina S. (1921—)
Lebron, Lolita (1919—)
Moreno, Rita (1931—)
Negron Muñoz, Mercedes (1895–1973)
Pantoja, Antonia (1922–2002)
Rexach, Sylvia (1922–1961)
Rodríguez de Tió, Lola (1843–1924)
Vega, Ana Lydia (1946—)

QUEBEC

Explored by Jacques Cartier (1500s)
Trading post built by Samuel de Champlain (1608)
Declared the colony of New France by Louis XIV (1663)
French protection of fur trade ended with British victory (1759)
Great Britain acquired New France by Treaty of Paris (1763)
Quebec settled by British Loyalists after the American Revolution
British divided area into Upper Canada (now Ontario); Quebec became Lower Canada (1791)
French community revolted against British (1837)
Upper and Lower Canada reunited as Canadian confederation (1841)
Quebec became known as Canada East
French became official language of province of Quebec (1974)
Separatist group gained provincial parliamentary power (1976)
Supreme Court of Canada decided that Quebec could not secede (1998)

Alarie, Pierrette (1921—)
Albani, Emma (c. 1847–1930)
Bolduc, Marie (1894–1941)
Casgrain, Thérèse (1896–1981)
Gérin-Lajoie, Marie (1867–1945)
Hébert, Anne (1916–2000)
La Montagne-Beauregard, Blanche (1899–1960)
Roy, Gabrielle (1909–1983)
Tanguay, Eva (1878–1947)

QUEDLINBURG

City in Halle district of eastern Germany

See Germany.

REIMS

City in Marne department in northeastern France

See France.

REUSS-EBERSDORF

County of Germany
Became part of Thuringia (1918)

See Germany.

RHEINFELDEN

Commune in Aargau canton of northern Switzerland

See Switzerland.

ROMAN EMPIRE

Empire of ancient Rome (27 BCE)
Founded by Octavian, who gained control of Italy and the west and east (1st c. BCE)
Annexed Egypt (30 BCE)
Pressured from Persia and Germany (3rd c.)
Divided for administration from Danube to Adriatic Sea, Byzantine Empire (4th c.)
Invaded by Visigoths, Huns, Vandals, Ostrogoths, and others (5th c.)
End of Western Empire (476)

See also Byzantine Empire.

Acte (fl. 55–69)
Aemilia (fl. 195 BCE)
Aemilia Hilaria (fl. 350)
Agape of Thessalonica (d.304)
Agnes, Saint (d. possibly c. 304)
Agrippina the Elder (c. 14 BCE–33 CE)
Agrippina the Younger (15–59)
Amanishakhete (r. c. 41–12 BCE)
Anastasia (fl. 54–68)

Geographic Index

Anastasia (d. 304)
Anastasia, Saint (d. 304)
Anthusa (c. 324/334–?)
Antistia (fl. 80 BCE)
Antonia Major (39 BCE–?)
Antonia Minor (36 BCE–37 CE)
Arria Major (d. 42)
Atia the Elder (c. 80 BCE–?)
Aurelia (c. 120 BCE–54 BCE)
Aurelia Fadilla (d. before 138)
Basilissa (fl. 54–68)
Bertha of Savoy (1051–1087)
Bibiana (d. 363)
Bruttia Crispina (d. 185)
Calpurnia (c. 70 BCE–?)
Cecilia (c. 154–c. 207)
Charito (fl. 300s)
Chionia (d. 304)
Claudia Antonia (27–66)
Claudia Quinta (fl. 220–206 BCE)
Clodia (c. 60 BCE–?)
Clodia (c. 94–post 45 BCE)
Cloelia (c. 508 BCE)
Constance (d. 305 CE)
Constantia (c. 293–?)
Constantina (c. 321–c. 354)
Cornelia (c. 75–after 48 BCE)
Cornelia (fl. 1st c. BCE)
Cornelia (c. 100–68 BCE)
Cornelia (c. 195–c. 115 BCE)
Cornificia (b. 160)
Cunigunde (d. 1040?)
Cunigunde of Swabia (fl. 900s)
Domitia Faustina (b. 147)
Domitia Lepida (c. 19 BCE–?)
Domitia Longina (fl. 80s)
Domitia Lucilla
Domitia Paulina I (fl. 76)
Domitia Paulina II (fl. 80–100)
Drusilla (15–38)
Drusilla (c. 37–c. 41 CE)
Eponina (40–78)
Eudocia (c. 400–460)
Eugenia (d. around 258)
Eulalia (290–304)
Eustochium (c. 368–c. 419)
Eutropia (fl. 270–300)
Eutropia (fl. 330s)
Fadilla (b. 159)
Fannia (fl. mid–1st c.)
Fausta (d. 324)
Fausta, Cornelia (b. 88 BCE)
Faustina I (c. 90–141)
Faustina II (130–175)
Faustina III (b. 151)
Felicitas of Rome (d. 162?)
Flaccilla (c. 355–386)
Flaccilla (d. 431)
Flavia Domitilla (fl. 39)
Flavia Domitilla (fl. 60)
Flavia Domitilla (c. 60–96)
Fulvia (c. 85/80–40 BCE)
Galla (fl. 320)
Galla (c. 365–394)
Helena (c. 255–329)
Helena (c. 320–?)
Honoria (c. 420–?)
Hortensia (fl. 1st c. BCE)
Irene (d. 304)
Julia (c. 18 BCE–28 CE)
Julia (39 BCE–14 CE)
Julia (d. 54 BCE)
Julia (d. 68 BCE)
Julia Domna (c. 170–217)
Julia Livilla (c. 16–after 38)
Julia Maesa (c. 170–224)
Julia Maior (fl. 1st. c. BCE)
Julia Mamaea (c. 190–235)
Julia Minor (c. 100–51 BCE)
Julia Paula (fl. 220)
Julia Soaemias (d. 222)
Junia Claudilla (fl. 32)
Junia I (fl. 1st c. BCE)
Junia II (fl. 1st c. BCE)
Junia III (fl. 1st c. BCE)
Justina (fl. 350–370)
Laelia (fl. 2nd c. BCE)
Larentia, Acca (fl. 9th, 8th, or 7th c. BCE)
Lea, St. (d. about 383)
Licinia Eudoxia (422–before 490)
Livia (fl. 100 BCE)
Livia Drusilla (58 BCE–29 CE)
Livia Orestilla (fl. 32)
Livilla (c. 14/11 BCE–c. 31 CE)
Locusta (fl. 54)
Lollia Paulina (fl. 38–39)
Lucilla (b. 150)
Lucretia (?–510 BCE)
Marcella of Rome (c. 325–410)
Marcella the Elder (fl. 25 BCE)
Marcella the Younger (fl. 20 BCE)
Marcia (fl. 100 BCE)
Marcia (fl. 177–192)
Margaret-Mary of Hungary (c. 1177–?)
Matidia I (d. 119)
Matidia II (fl. 110)
Melania the Elder (c. 350–c. 410)
Melania the Younger (c. 385–439)
Messalina, Statilia (fl. 66–68)
Messalina, Valeria (c. 23–48)
Milonia Caesonia (d. 41)
Minervina (fl. 290–307)
Mucia (fl. 80 BCE)
Octavia (c. 69–11 BCE)
Octavia (39–62)
Paetina (fl. 30)
Paula (347–404)
Phoebe of Cenchreae (fl. 1st c.)
Placidia (fl. 440s)
Placidia, Galla (c. 390–450)
Plautia Urgulanilla (fl. 25)
Plotina (d. 122)
Pompeia (c. 87 BCE–?)
Pompeia (fl. 60 BCE)
Pomponia (fl. 25 BCE)
Poppaea Sabina (d. 47)
Poppaea Sabina (d. 65)
Portia (fl. 80 BCE)
Priscilla (fl. 1st c.)
Pulcheria (c. 376–385)
Pulcheria (c. 398–453)
Pulcheria (fl. 800s)
Rupilia Faustina (fl. 90)
Sabina (88–136)
Salome (c. 65 BCE–10 CE)
Salonina (r. 254–268)
Scribonia (c. 75 BCE–after 16 CE)
Sempronia (c. 168 BCE–?)
Sempronia (fl. 2nd–1st c. BCE)
Serena (d. 410)
Servilia I (fl. 100 BCE)
Servilia II (c. 100–after 42 BCE)
Sophia (fl. early 2nd c.)
Sulpicia I (fl. 1st c. BCE)
Sulpicia II (fl. 1st c.)
Terentia (fl. 69–45 BCE)
Theodora (fl. 290s)
Tullia (c. 79–45 BCE)
Tullia (fl. 535 BCE)
Ulpia Marciana (fl. 98–117)
Vespasia Polla (fl. 50)
Veturia (late 6th c.–mid-5th c. BCE)
Vibia Aurelia Sabina (b. 166)
Vipsania Agrippina (?–20 CE)
Volumnia (late 6th c.–mid-5th c. BCE)
Zenobia (r. 267–272)

ROMANIA

Republic in southeastern Europe
Danubian Principalities united and took name of Rumania (1861)
Invaded by Russia (1877–1878)
Gained independence from Turkey (1878)
Became kingdom (1881)
Lost territory to Russia, Hungary, and Bulgaria (1940)
Overrun by U.S.S.R. (1944)
Proclaimed people's republic (1947)

Afrasiloaia, Felicia (1954—)
Agache, Lavinia (1966—)
Alupei, Angela (1972—)
Amanar, Simona (1979—)
Anitas, Herta (1967—)
Aposteanu, Angelica (1954—)
Apostol, Chira (1960—)
Appel, Anna (1888–1963)
Arba-Puscatu, Rodica (1962—)
Armasescu, Mihaela (1963—)
Astafei, Galina (1968—)
Badea, Ioana (1964—)
Badea, Laura (1970—)
Balas, Iolanda (1936—)
Ban, Oana (1986—)
Banus, Maria (1914–1999)
Barascu, Aurica (1974—)
Bazon-Chelariu, Adriana (1963—)
Beclea-Szekely, Violeta (1965—)
Bibesco, Marthe Lucie (1887–1973)
Birell, Tala (1907–1958)
Bobeica, Iulia (1967—)
Boboc, Loredana (1984—)
Bondar, Elena (1958—)
Bonner, Antoinette (1892–1920)
Bontas, Cristina (1973—)
Bucur, Florica (1959—)
Bufanu, Valeria (1946—)
Bularda-Homeghi, Olga (1958—)
Burcica, Constanta (1971—)
Caslaru, Beatrice (1975—)
Cassian, Nina (1924—)
Catuna, Anuta (1968—)
Ceausescu, Elena (1916–1989)
Chica, Elena (1828–1888)
Cioncan, Maria (1977—)
Cocéa, Alice (1899–1970)
Cochelea, Veronica (1965—)
Cojocaru, Christiana (1962—)
Coman, Otilia (1942—)
Comaneci, Nadia (1961—)
Constantin, Mariana (1960—)
Constantin-Buhaev, Agafia (1955—)
Constantinescu, Mariana (1956—)
Corban-Banovici, Sofia (1956—)
Cotrubas, Ileana (1939—)
Craciunescu, Florenta (1955—)
Cutina, Laura (1968—)
Damian, Georgeta (1976—)
Dan, Aurora (1955—)
Darclée, Hariclea (1860–1939)
Diaconescu, Camelia (1963—)
Dinescu, Violeta (1953—)
Dobre, Aurelia (1972—)
Dobre-Balan, Anisoara (1966—)
Dobritoiu, Elena (1957—)
Donescu, Anghelache (1945—)
Dumitrache, Maria Magdalena (1977—)
Dumitrescu, Roxana (1967—)
Dumitrescu-Doletti, Joanna (1902–1963)

Dumitru, Viorica (1946—)
Dunca, Rodica (1965—)
Eberle, Emilia (1964—)
Elizabeth of Wied (1843–1916)
Eremia, Alexandra (1987—)
Florea, Rodica (1983—)
Fricioiu, Maria (1960—)
Frintu, Rodica (1960—)
Gabor, Georgeta (1962—)
Gafencu, Liliana (1975—)
Georgescu, Elena (1964—)
Giurca, Elena (1946—)
Gluck, Alma (1884–1938)
Gogean, Gina (1977—)
Golea, Eugenia (1969—)
Grigoras, Anca (1957—)
Grigoras, Cristina (1966—)
Grigorescu, Claudia (1968—)
Groza, Maria (1918—)
Gyulai-Drimba, Ileana (1946—)
Hadarean, Vanda (1976—)
Haskil, Clara (1895–1960)
Helen (b. 1950)
Horvat-Florea, Elena (1958—)
Hurmuzachi, Georgeta (1936—)
Ignat, Doina (1968—)
Iliuta, Ana (1958—)
Ionescu, Atanasia (1935—)
Ionescu, Nastasia (1954—)
Ionescu, Valeria (1960—)
Ionita, Raluca (1976—)
Iovan, Sonia (1935—)
Ipatescu, Ana (1805–1855)
Irene (1953—)
Isarescu, Andreea (1984—)
Ivan, Paula (1963—)
Josephine of Baden (1813–1900)
Karatza, Rallou (1778–1830)
Lambrino, Jeanne (1898–1953)
Lauer, Hilde (1943—)
Lavric, Florica (1962—)
Lazar, Elisabeta (1950—)
Leonida, Florica (1987—)
Lepadatu, Viorica (1971—)
Leusteanu, Elena (1935—)
Limbau, Mariana (1977—)
Lipa, Elisabeta (1964—)
Lita-Vatasoiu, Emilia (1933—)
Loaies, Ionela (1979—)
Loghin, Mihaela (1952—)
Lovin, Fita (1951—)
Lung, Noemi Ildiko (1968—)
Lupescu, Elena (c. 1896–1977)
Macoviciuc, Camelia (1968—)
Manoliu, Lia (1932–1998)
Maracineanu, Roxana (1975—)
Margaret (1949—)
Marie of Rumania (1875–1938)
Marinescu, Alexandra (1981—)
Marinescu-Borcanea, Tecla (1960—)
Mary (b. 1964)
Melinte, Doina (1956—)
Menis, Argentina (1948—)
Micsa, Maria (1953—)
Mihaly, Aneta (1957—)
Milosovici, Lavinia (1976—)
Minea-Sorohan, Anisoara (1963—)
Mocanu, Diana (1984—)
Muratova, Kira (1934—)
Necula, Veronica (1967—)
Neculai, Viorica (1967—)
Neculita, Maria (1974—)
Nichiforov, Maria (1951—)
Niculescu-Margarit, Elena (1936—)
Oancia, Ecaterina (1954—)
Olaru, Maria (1982—)
Olteanu, Ioana (1966—)
Oros, Rozalia (1963—)
Paduraru, Maria (1970—)
Pantelimon, Oana (1972—)
Papadat-Bengescu, Hortensia (1876–1955)
Papuc, Ioana (1984—)
Pasca, Mirela (1975—)
Pascu-Ene-Dersidan, Ana (1944—)
Patrascoiu, Aneta (1957—)
Pauca, Simona (1969—)
Pauker, Ana (c. 1893–1960)
Petrovschi, Oana (1986—)
Pipota, Constanta (1971—)
Plesca, Aurora (1963—)
Ponor, Catalina (1987—)
Popa, Celestina (1970—)
Popa, Eugenia (1973—)
Popescu, Marioara (1962—)
Popovici, Elise (1921—)
Poreceanu, Uta (1936—)
Potec, Camelia Alina (1982—)
Potorac, Gabriela (1973—)
Presacan, Claudia (1979—)
Puica, Maricica (1950—)
Radu, Elena (1975—)
Raducan, Andreea (1983—)
Richter, Simona Marcela (1972—)
Rizea, Elisabeta (1912–2003)
Robu, Doina (1967—)
Rosca-Racila, Valeria (1957—)
Rosu, Monica (1987—)
Rozeanu, Angelica (1921–2006)
Ruehn, Melita (1965—)
Sacalici, Elena (1937—)
Sauca, Lucia (1963—)
Scarlat, Roxana (1975—)
Schileru, Dacia W.
Schnitzer, Henriette (1891–1979)
Sideri, Cornelia (1938—)
Silai, Ileana (1941—)
Silivas, Daniela (1970—)
Simon, Lidia (1973—)
Snep-Balan, Doina Liliana (1963—)
Sofronie, Daniela (1988—)
Sophia (b. 1957)
Spewack, Bella (1899–1990)
Spircu, Doina (1970—)
Stahl-Iencic, Ecaterina (1946—)
Staiculescu, Doina (1967—)
Stanciu, Anisoara (1962—)
Stanulet, Mihaela (1966—)
Stefan, Maria (1954—)
Stroescu, Silvia (1985—)
Susanu, Viorica (1975—)
Szabo, Ecaterina (1966—)
Szabo, Gabriela (1975—)
Szabo, Reka (1967—)
Szabo-Orban, Olga (1938—)
Tanase, Anca (1968—)
Taran-Iordache, Maricica Titie (1962—)
Tirlea-Manolache, Ionela (1976—)
Toma, Sanda (1956—)
Toma, Sanda (1970—)
Trasca, Marioara (1962—)
Trusca, Gabriela (1957—)
Tudoran, Ioana (1948—)
Tufan-Guzganu, Elisabeta (1964—)
Tugurlan, Mirela (1980—)
Turner, Dumitrita (1964—)
Ungureanu, Corina (1980—)
Ungureanu, Teodora (1960—)
Ursuleac, Viorica (1894–1985)
Varady, Julia (1941—)
Veres-Ioja, Viorica (1962—)
Vicol, Maria (1935—)
Viscopoleanu, Viorica (1939—)
Voinea, Camelia (1970—)
Zagoni-Predescu, Marlena (1951—)
Zsak, Marcela (1956—)

RUSSIA

Former empire in eastern Europe and northern and western Asia
Settled by eastern Slavs (3rd–8th c.)
Varagians from Scandinavia entered from north (9th c.)
Invaded and conquered by Mongols (13th c.)
Princes of Russia subjugated rival principalities and pushed into Siberia (16th c.)
Warred with Poland for Ukraine (17th c.)
Annexed Lithuania and Ukraine from partitioned Poland (18th c.)
Acquired Finland and Bessarabia (19th c.)
Invaded by French (1812)
Annexed Georgia and other territories (1813)
Received most of grand duchy of Warsaw (1815)
Advanced against Ottoman Empire
Sold Alaska to United States (1867)
Advanced to Afghanistan borders
Defeated by Japan (1904–1905)
Lost hold in Manchuria
Set up government of soviets (1917)
Territorial independence granted (1990)
See also Russia, Soviet.

Abassova, Tamilla (1982—)
Abramova, Anastasia (1902—)
Abrosimova, Svetlana (1980—)
Achkina, Rita (fl. 1968)
Adelaide of Kiev (c. 1070–1109)
Adler, Sara (1858–1953)
Agnes of Poland (1137–after 1181)
Aisse (c. 1694–1733)
Akhatova, Albina (1976—)
Akhmadulina, Bella (1937—)
Akhmatova, Anna (1889–1966)
Akobia, Marina (1975—)
Akselrod, Liubo (1868–1946)
Aleksandrovna, Vera (1895–1966)
Alekseeva, Lidiya (1909—)
Alexandra Feodorovna (1872–1918)
Alexandra Nikolaevna (1825–1844)
Alexandra of Oldenburg (1838–1900)
Alexandra of Saxe-Altenburg (1830–1911)
Allagulova, Yulia
Almedingen, E.M. (1898–1971)
Amantova, Ingrida
Amosova, Zinaida (fl. 1976)
Anastasia (1901–1918)
Anastasia of Russia (c. 1023–after 1074)
Anastasia Petrovitch-Njegos (1868–1935)
Anastasia Romanova (d. 1560)
Anastasia Romanova (1860–1922)
Anderson, Anna (1902–1984)
Andjaparidze, Veriko (1900–1987)
Andreas-Salomé, Lou (1861–1937)
Andreeva, Maria Fedorovna (1868–1953)
Andreyanova, Yelena Ivanovna (1816–1857)
Aníchkova, Anna (1868–1935)
Anikeeva, Ekaterina (1965—)
Anissina, Marina (1975—)
Anna Ivanovna (1693–1740)
Anna Juliana of Saxe-Coburg-Saalfeld (1781–1860)
Anna Leopoldovna (1718–1746)
Anna of Byzantium (963–1011)
Anna of Cumin (d. 1111)
Anna of Moscow (1393–1417)
Anna Pavlovna (1795–1865)
Anna Petrovna (1757–1758)
Annenkova-Bernár, Nina Pávlovna (1859/64–1933)
Anne of Kiev (1024–1066)
Anne Petrovna (1708–1728)
Anstei, Olga Nikolaevna (1912–1985)

Antin, Mary (1881–1949)
Antonova, Elena (1974–)
Antyukh, Natalia (1981—)
Apréleva, Elena Ivanovna (1846–1923)
Arbenina, Stella (1885–1976)
Arkhipova, Anna (1973—)
Armand, Inessa (1874–1920)
Arteshina, Olga (1982—)
Arzhannikova, Tatiana (1964—)
Astafieva, Serafima (1876–1934)
Averina, Tatiana (1950–2001)
Averkova, Oksana (1970—)
Avilova, Lidya (c. 1864–1943)
Azarova, Elena (1973—)
Aznavourian, Karina (1974—)
Babanova, Maria (b. 1900)
Baclanova, Olga (1899–1974)
Balabanoff, Angelica (1878–1965)
Baldycheva, Nina
Baraksanova, Irina (1969—)
Baranova, Elena (1972—)
Baranova, Lyubov
Baranovskaya, Vera (c. 1870–1935)
Baranskaya, Natalia (b. 1908)
Barbara of Byzantium (d. 1125)
Bari, Nina K. (1901–1961)
Barkova, Anna Aleksandrovna (1901–1976)
Baron, Devorah (1887–1956)
Baronova, Irina (1919—)
Barsukova, Yulia (1978—)
Barykova, Anna Pavlovna (1839–1893)
Bashkirtseff, Marie (1859–1884)
Batyrchina, Jana (1979—)
Bazhanova, Svetlana (1972—)
Bechke, Elena (1966—)
Bechtereva, Natalia (1924—)
Beckman-Shcherbina, Elena (1881–1951)
Belikova, Anastasia (1979—)
Beloglazova, Galina (1967—)
Belova, Elena (1965—)
Belova, Irina (1968—)
Belova, Irina (1980—)
Beluguina, Olesia (1984—)
Benois, Nadia (1896–1975)
Ben Zvi, Rachel Yanait (1886–1979)
Berberova, Nina (1901–1993)
Berezhnaya, Elena (1977—)
Berggolts, Olga (1910–1975)
Bestemianova, Natalia (1960—)
Bichovsky, Elisheva (1888–1949)
Blavatsky, Helena (1831–1891)
Bluffstein, Sophie (1854–1891)
Boginskaya, Svetlana (1973—)
Boronat, Olimpia (1867–1934)
Botchkareva, Evguenia
Botchkareva, Maria (1889–?)
Boyarskikh, Claudia (1939—)
Brandstrom, Elsa (1888–1948)
Branitzka, Nathalie (1905–1977)
Breshkovsky, Catherine (1844–1934)
Bronskaya, Eugenia (1882–1953)
Brouletova, Lioubov
Brovar, Anna Iakovlevna (1887–1917)
Brusnikina, Olga (1978—)
Budberg, Moura (1892–1974)
Bulich, Vera Sergeevna (1898–1954)
Bunina, Anna Petrovna (1774–1829)
Butyrskaya, Maria (1972—)
Catherine II the Great (1729–1796)
Catherine Romanov (1878–1959)
Cebotari, Maria (1910–1949)
Chachkova, Lioubov (1977—)
Charlotte of Prussia (1798–1860)
Chepeleva, Anna (1984—)
Cherkasova, Marina
Chervinskaya, Lidiya Davydovna (1907–1988)
Chiumina, Olga Nikolaevna (1865–1909)
Chizhova, Nadezhda (1945—)
Christina of Sweden (d. 1122)
Chukanova, Olga (1980—)
Chukovskaya, Lidiya (1907–1996)
Churilova, L.A. (1875–1937)
Cohen, Rose (1880–1925)
Dainton, Marie (1881–1938)
Dali, Gala (1894–1982)
Danilova, Maria (1793–1810)
Danilova, Olga (1970—)
Dashkova, Ekaterina (1744–1810)
Davidow, Ruth (1911–1999)
Davydova, Anastasia (1983—)
Daykarhanova, Tamara (1889–1980)
Dean, Vera Micheles (1903–1972)
De La Haye, Ina (1906–1972)
Delaunay, Sonia (1885–1979)
Dell'Era, Antoinetta (1861–?)
Dembo, Tamara (1902–1993)
Dementieva, Elena (1981—)
Demina, Svetlana (c. 1960—)
Deren, Maya (1908–1961)
Derzhinskaya, Zeniya (1889–1951)
De Swirska, Tamara (c. 1890–?)
Diakonova, Elizaveta (1874–1902)
Dizhur, Bella (b. 1906)
Dmitrieff, Elizabeth (1851–1910)
Dmitrieva, Elizaveta Ivanovna (1887–1928)
Dmitrieva, Valentina (1859–1948)
Dogonadze, Anna (1973—)
Dolgopolova, Elena (1980—)
Dolgorukaia, Alexandra (1836–c. 1914)
Dolgorukaia, Natalia Borisovna (1714–1771)
Dolgorukova, Ekaterina (1847–1922)
Dolgorukova, Marie (d. 1625)
Donchenko, Natalya (1932—)
Donguzashvili, Tea (1976—)
Dorfmann, Ania (1899–1984)
Dorodnova, Oksana (1974—)
Dorothea, Princess of Lieven (1785–1857)
Dostoevsky, Anna (1846–1918)
Dudarova, Veronika (1916—)
Dudinskaya, Natalya (1912–2003)
Dudnik, Olesia (1974—)
Durant, Ariel (1898–1981)
Durova, Nadezhda (1783–1866)
Dyachenko, Tatyana (1960—)
Dzerzhinska, Sofia (1882–1968)
Dziouba, Irina
Eckhardt-Gramatté, S.C. (1899–1974)
Eduardova, Eugenia (1882–1980)
Egorova, Lyubov (1880–1972)
Egorova, Lyubov (1966—)
Elizabeth of Baden (1779–1826)
Elizabeth Petrovna (1709–1762)
Ella (1864–1918)
Elvin, Violetta (1925—)
Engelgardt, Sofia Vladimirovna (1828–1894)
Engquist, Ludmila (1964—)
Eristavi-Xostaria, Anastasia (1868–1951)
Ermakova, Anastasia (1983—)
Ermakova, Oxana (1973—)
Ermolaeva, Galina
Ermoleva, Zinaida (1898–1974)
Ermolova, Mariia (1853–1928)
Esau, Katherine (1898–1997)
Essipova, Annette (1851–1914)
Eudoxia Jaroslavovna (1534–1581)
Eudoxia Lopukhina (1669–1731)
Eudoxia of Moscow (1483–1513)
Eudoxia Streshnev (1608–1645)
Exter, Alexandra (1882–1949)
Ezhova, Ljudmilla (1982—)
Federova, Sophia (1879–1963)
Fedicheva, Kaleria (1936—)
Fedorovitch, Sophie (1893–1953)
Fedotova, Irina (1975—)
Feklistova, Maria (1976—)
Feofanova, Svetlana (1980—)
Figner, Vera (1852–1942)
Filosofova, Anna (1837–1912)
Fireva, Tatyana (1982—)
Firsova, Elena Olegovna (1950—)
Fokina, Vera (1886–1958)
Forsh, Olga (1873–1961)
Friedberg, Berta (1864–1944)
Froman, Margareta (1890–1970)
Furtseva, Ekaterina (1910–1974)
Fyodorova, Olga (1983—)
Gaigerova, Varvara Andrianovna (1903–1944)
Galieva, Roza (1977—)
Galkina, Lioubov (1973—)
Gamova, Ekaterina (1980—)
Gan, Elena Andreevna (1814–1842)
Gánina, Maja (1927—)
Garayeva, Yuliya
Gavriljuk, Nina (1965—)
Gelfman, Gesia (d. 1882)
Gelman, Polina (1919—)
Géniat, Marcelle (1879–1959)
Gerasimenok, Irina (1970—)
Gerdt, Elizaveta (1891–1975)
Gertrude of Poland (d. 1107)
Gertsyk, Adelaida (1874–1925)
Geva, Tamara (1906–1997)
Ginzburg, Evgenia (1896–1980)
Ginzburg, Lidiia (1902–1990)
Gippius, Zinaida (1869–1945)
Gladisheva, Svetlana (1971—)
Glatskikh, Olga (1989—)
Glinka, Avdotia Pavlovna (1795–1863)
Glinskaia, Anna (d. 1553)
Glinski, Elena (c. 1506–1538)
Godina, Elena (1977—)
Godunova, Irene (d. 1603)
Godunova, Xenia (1582–1622)
Gogoberidze, Lana (1928—)
Goldman, Emma (1869–1940)
Goldobina, Tatiana (1975—)
Golovkina, Sofia (1915–2004)
Golubkina, Anna (1864–1927)
Goncharenko, Svetlana (1971—)
Goncharova, Natalia (1881–1962)
Gorbacheva, Raisa (1932–1999)
Gorbanevskaya, Natalya Yevgenevna (1936—)
Gordeeva, Ekaterina (1971–)
Gordon, Vera (1886–1948)
Grantzow, Adele (1845–1877)
Gratcheva, Tatiana (1973—)
Gray, Nadia (1923–1994)
Green, Dorothy (1892–1963)
Grigorieva, Tatiana (1975—)
Grinberg, Maria (1908–1979)
Grishina, Oksana (1968—)
Grishuk, Pasha (1972—)
Grizodubova, Valentina (1910–1993)
Gromova, Maria (1984—)
Gromova, Vera (1891–1973)
Grosheva, Yelena (1979—)
Groshkova, Tatiana (1973—)
Grushevski, Agraphia (1662–1681)
Gubaidulina, Sofia (1931—)
Gurevich, Liubov (1866–1940)
Gurina, Elena
Guro, Elena (1877–1913)

Gurova, Elena (1972—)
Gusakova, Maria
Guseva, Klara (1937—)
Gustilina, Diana (1974—)
Gutsu, Tatyana (1976—)
Halicka, Antonina (1908–1973)
Halpert, Edith Gregor (c. 1900–1970)
Harari, Manya (1905–1969)
Helen (b.1950)
Helena of Russia (1882–1957)
Helena Pavlovna (1784–1803)
Helene of Moldavia (d. 1505)
Helene of Wurttemberg (1807–1873)
Hillman, Bessie (1889–1970)
Holmes, Anna-Marie (1943—)
Ichtchenko, Natalia (1986—)
Ilienko, Natalia (1967—)
Ilyina, Vera (1974—)
Inber, Vera (1890–1972)
Iouchkova, Angelina
Irene of Kiev (fl. 1122)
Irina (1895–1970)
Isakova, Maria (1918—)
Ishmouratova, Svetlana (1972—)
Isinbayeva, Yelena (1982—)
Issakova, Natalia
Istomina, Avdotia (1799–1848)
Itkina, Maria (1932—)
Ivanova, Ioulia
Ivanova, Kira (c. 1963–2001)
Ivanova, Natalia (c. 1971—)
Ivanova, Natalya (1981—)
Ivanova, Svetlana (1974—)
Ivanovskaia, Praskovia (1853–1935)
Ivinskaya, Olga (1912–1995)
Jaclard, Anna (1843–1887)
Johansson, Anna (1860–1917)
Kabaeva, Alina (1983—)
K'alandadze, Ana (1924—)
Kalinina, Natalia (1973—)
Kalmykova, Maria (1978—)
Kaminska, Ida (1899–1980)
Kaplan, Fanya (1883–1918)
Kar, Ida (1908–1970)
Karadjordjevic, Helen (1884–1962)
Karavaeva, Irina (1975—)
Karinska, Barbara (1886–1983)
Karpova, Elena (1980—)
Karsavina, Tamara (1885–1978)
Kasaeva, Zarema (1987—)
Katznelson-Shazar, Rachel (1888–1975)
Kazakova, Oksana (1975—)
Kazankina, Tatyana (1951—)
Kedrova, Lila (1918—)
Khabarova, Irina (1966—)
Khasyanova, Elvira (1981—)
Khoklova, Olga (d. 1955)
Kholodnya, Vera (1893–1919)
Khomiakova, Valeriia (d. 1942)
Khorkina, Svetlana (1979—)
Khudorozhkina, Irina (1968—)
Khvoshchinskaia, Nadezhda (1824–1889)
Khvoshchinskaia, Sofia (1828–1865)
Kim, Nelli (1957—)
Kira of Russia (1909–1967)
Kirpishchikova, Anna (1848–1927)
Kisseleva, Maria (1974—)
Kleegman, Sophia (1901–1971)
Klimova, Marina (1966—)
Klochneva, Olga (1968—)
Knipper-Chekova, Olga (1870–1959)
Kobiakova, Aleksandra (1823–1892)
Kochetkova, Dina (1977—)
Kojevnikova, Elizaveta
Kolesnikova, Anastasia (1984—)
Kolesnikova, Vera (1968—)
Kollontai, Alexandra (1872–1952)
Kolokoltseva, Berta (1937—)
Koltunova, Julia (1989—)
Komarova, Stanislava (1986—)
Komarova, Varvara (1862–1942)
Komarovsky, Mirra (1906–1999)
Komissarzhevskaya, Vera (1864–1910)
Kondakova, Yelena (c. 1955—)
Kondratyeva, Lyudmila (1958—)
Königsmark, Aurora von (1662–1728)
Konoukh, Sofia (1980—)
Korbut, Olga (1955—)
Korchinska, Maria (1895–1979)
Koroleva, Maria (1974—)
Korstin, Ilona (1980—)
Korty, Sonia (1892–1955)
Korukovets, Alexandra (1976—)
Kosmodemyanskaya, Zoya (1923–1941)
Kostina, Oksana (1972–1993)
Kotlyarova, Olga (1976—)
Kotova, Tatyana (1976—)
Koujela, Olga (1985—)
Koukleva, Galina (1972—)
Kournikova, Anna (1981—)
Koutouzova, Natalia (1975—)
Kouzina, Svetlana (1975—)
Kovalevskaya, Sophia (1850–1891)
Kovalskaia, Elizaveta (1851–1943)
Kovalyova, Anna (1983—)
Kozlova, Anna (1972—)
Krandievskaya, Anastasiia (1865–1938)
Krandievskaya, Natalia (1888–1963)
Krandievskaya, Natalia (1923—)
Krasnomovets, Olesya (1979—)
Krasnova, Vera (1950—)
Krasovskaya, Vera (d. 1999)
Krestovskaya, Maria V. (1862–1910)
Krieger, Victorina (b. 1896)
Krivochei, Elena
Krüdener, Julie de (1764–1824)
Kruglova, Larisa (1972—)
Krupskaya, Nadezhda (1869–1939)
Krylova, Anjelika (1973—)
Kryuchkova, Maria (1988—)
Kryzhanovskaia, Vera Ivanovna (1861–1924)
Kshesinskaia, Matilda (1872–1971)
Kuchinskaya, Natalia (1949—)
Kuczinski, Ruth (1907–2000)
Kulakova, Galina (1942—)
Kulman, Elisabeth (1808–1825)
Kurbakova, Tatiana (1986—)
Kuzenkova, Olga (1970—)
Kuznetsova, Evgenia (1980—)
Kuznetsova, Maria (1880–1966)
Kuznetsova, Svetlana (1985—)
Kyasht, Lydia (1885–1959)
Ladynina, Marina (1908–2003)
Landau, Klavdia Gustavovna (1922–1990)
Lappo-Danilevskaia, N.A. (c. 1875–1951)
Lasovskaya, Inna (1969—)
Latynina, Larissa (1934—)
Lavrova, Natalia (1984—)
Lazutina, Larissa (1965—)
Lebedeva, Sarra (1892–1967)
Lebedeva, Tatyana (1976—)
Legat, Nadine (c. 1895–?)
Lemlich, Clara (1888–1982)
Leonida (b. 1914)
Leontovich, Eugénie (1894–1993)
Lepeshinskaya, Olga (1916—)
Leporska, Zoya (1918–1996)
Lermontova, Julia (1846–1919)
Lermontova, Nadezhda Vladimirovna (1885–1921)
Levi, Natalia (1901–1972)
Levien, Sonya (1888–1960)
Levina, Ioulia (1973—)
Lhevinne, Rosina (1880–1976)
Lidova, Irene (1907–2002)
Linichuk, Natalia
Lipkovskay, Natalia (1979—)
Lipkowska, Lydia (1882–1958)
Lisnianskaya, Inna (1928—)
Litvyak, Lidiya (1921–1943)
Liubatovich, Olga (1853–1917)
Liubatovich, Vera (1855–1907)
Lobacheva, Irina (1973—)
Lobazniuk, Ekaterina (1983—)
Loeb, Sophie Irene (1876–1929)
Logounova, Tatiana (1980—)
Lokhvitskaia, Mirra (1869–1905)
Lopokova, Lydia (c. 1892–1981)
Lopukhova, Evgenia (1884–1941)
Lukhmanova, N.A. (1840–1907)
Lukom, Elena (1891–1968)
Lyapina, Oksana (1980—)
Makarova, Elena (1951—)
Makarova, Natalia (1940—)
Makarova, Tamara (1907–1997)
Malakhovskaya, Natalia (1947—)
Mamoshina, Glafira Adolfovna (c. 1870–1942)
Mandelstam, Nadezhda (1899–1980)
Maniourova, Gouzel (1978—)
Marchenko, Anastasiia Iakovlevna (1830–1880)
Maretskaya, Vera (1906–1978)
Maria Nagaia (d. 1612)
Maria Nikolaevna (1819–1876)
Maria of Circassia (d. 1569)
Maria of Tver (c. 1440–1467)
Maria Skuratova (d. 1605)
Marie (1899–1918)
Marie Alexandrovna (1853–1920)
Marie Feodorovna (1847–1928)
Marie of Hesse-Darmstadt (1824–1880)
Marie of Russia (1907–1951)
Marie Pavlovna (1786–1859)
Marie Pavlovna (1890–1958)
Marinoff, Fania (1890–1971)
Maritain, Raïssa (1883–1960)
Markova, Olga (c. 1969—)
Marpha (1664–1716)
Marquet, Mary (1895–1979)
Martha the Nun (1560–1631)
Massevitch, Alla G. (1918—)
Masterkova, Svetlana (1968—)
Matveyeva, Novella Niklayevna (1934—)
Mazina, Maria (1964—)
Mekshilo, Eudokia
Melnik, Olga (1974—)
Melnikova, Elena
Menuhin, Marutha (1896–1996)
Merk, Larisa (1971—)
Messerer, Sulamith (1908–2004)
Mikhaylova, Maria (1866–1943)
Milashkina, Tamara Andreyevna (1934—)
Militsyna, Elizaveta Mitrofanovna (1869–1930)
Miloslavskaia, Maria (1626–1669)
Miramova, Elena (c. 1905—)
Mishkutenok, Natalia (1970—)
Misnik, Alla (1967—)
Mniszek, Marina (c. 1588–1614)
Moiseeva, Irina (1955—)
Mons, Anna (d. 1714)
Montvid, A.S. (b. 1845)
Morits, Yunna (1937—)
Morozova, Theodosia (d. 1675)
Mosolova, Vera (1875–1949)
Mukhacheva, Lubov

Mukhina, Vera (1889–1953)
Murzina, Elena (1984—)
Myskina, Anastasia (1981—)
Nadejda Michaelovna (1896–1963)
Nagejkina, Svetlana (1965—)
Nagródskaia, Evdokiia (1866–1930)
Narishkina, Natalya (1651–1694)
Natalie, Mlle (c. 1895–1922)
Natalie of Hesse-Darmstadt (1755–1776)
Nazáreva, Kapitolina Valerianovna (1847–1900)
Nazarova, Natalya (1979—)
Nazimova, Alla (1879–1945)
Nelidova, Lydia (1863–1929)
Nemchinova, Vera (1899–1984)
Netessova, Maria (1983—)
Nezhdanova, Antonia (1873–1950)
Nezhdanova, Antonina (1873–1950)
Nijinska, Bronislava (1891–1972)
Nikitina, Alice (1909–1978)
Nikolaeva, Klavdiia (1893–1944)
Nikolaeva, Olga (1972—)
Nikolayeva, Tatiana (1924–1993)
Noris, Assia (1912–1998)
Noskova, Luiza (1968—)
Novokshchenova, Olga (1974—)
Odoevtseva, Irina (c. 1895–1990)
Olenewa, Maria (1893–1965)
Olga (c. 890–969)
Olga (1895–1918)
Olga, Princess Paley (1865–1929)
Olga Alexandrovna (1882–1960)
Olga Iurevskaya (1873–1925)
Olga of Russia (1822–1892)
Olunina, Alevtina (1930—)
Orlova, Liubov (1902–1975)
Osipenko, Polina (1907–1939)
Osipova, Irina (1981—)
Oswald, Marina (1941—)
Ouspenskaya, Maria (1876–1949)
Ovchinnikova, Elena (1982—)
Pakhalina, Yulia (1977—)
Pakhmutova, Alexandra (1929—)
Pakhomova, Ludmila (d. 1986)
Panaeva, Avdotia (c. 1819–1893)
Panova, Vera (1905–1973)
Parnok, Sophia (1885–1933)
Pasternak, Josephine (1900–1993)
Pavlova, Anna (1881–1931)
Pavlova, Anna (1987—)
Pavlova, Karolina (1807–1893)
Pecherskaya, Svetlana (1968—)
Peleshenko, Larisa (1964—)
Penkinson, Sophie (fl. late 1890s)
Perchina, Irina (1978—)
Perovskaya, Sonia (1853–1881)
Pesotta, Rose (1896–1965)
Petipa, Marie (1836–1882)
Petipa, Marie (1857–1930)
Petrova, Ioulia (1979—)
Petrova, Ludmila (1968—)
Petrova, Tatiana (1973—)
Petrovýkh, Mariia (1908–1979)
Petruseva, Natalia (1955—)
Petrushevskaya, Ludmilla (1938—)
Pious, Minerva (1903–1979)
Pitoëff, Ludmilla (1896–1951)
Plisetskaya, Maya (1925—)
Plotnikova, Elena (1978—)
Poliakova, Elena (1884–1972)
Ponomareva-Romashkova, Nina (1929—)
Popova, Liubov (1889–1924)
Popova, Valentina (1972—)
Portapovitch, Anna Knapton (1890–1974)
Posevina, Elena (1986—)
Potachova, Olga (1976—)
Predeslava of Hungary (fl. 960)
Preobrazhenska, Olga (1871–1962)
Privalova, Irina (1968—)
Produnova, Elena (1980—)
Prokhorova, Yelena (1978—)
Protopopov, Ludmila (1935—)
Ptaschkina, Nelly (1903–1920)
Pugacheva, Alla (1949—)
Pyleva, Olga (1975—)
Raikh, Zinaida (1894–1939)
Rakhmatulina, Oxana (1976—)
Raskova, Marina (1912–1943)
Ratushinskaya, Irina (1954—)
Reisner, Larissa (1895–1926)
Reztsova, Anfisa (1964—)
Riabouchinska, Tatiana (1917–2000)
Rocheva, Nina
Rodnina, Irina (1949—)
Romanov, Anna (fl. 1550)
Romanov, Anna (1632–1692)
Romanov, Euphamia (fl. 1550)
Romanov, Irina (fl. 1601)
Romanov, Irina (1627–1679)
Romanov, Martha (fl. 1550)
Romanov, Natalya (1674–1716)
Romanov, Sophie (1634–1676)
Romanova, Maria (1886–1954)
Romasko, Olga (1968—)
Rosenfeld, Fanny "Bobbie" (1903–1969)
Rosenthal, Ida Cohen (1886–1973)
Rostopchina, Evdokiya (1811–1858)
Rousanne, Mme (1894–1958)
Rozanova, Olga (1886–1918)
Rozengolts-Levina, Eva (1898–1975)
Rozhanskaya, Mariam (1928—)
Rubinstein, Ida (1880–1960)
Rusudani (b. 1195)
Rylova, Tamara (1931—)
Rytova, Galina (1975—)
Saburova, Irina (1907–1979)
Sadova, Natalya (1972—)
Safronova, Natalia (1979—)
Salhias de Tournemire, Elizaveta (1815–1892)
Saltykova, Praskovya (1664–1723)
Samoilova, Konkordiya (1876–1921)
Sankova, Galina (b. 1904)
Sankovskaya, Yekaterina (c. 1816–1878)
Sargsian, Inessa (1972—)
Sazonenkova, Elena (1973—)
Schennikova, Angelika (1969—)
Scriabin, Vera (1875–1920)
Sedakova, Olga (c. 1972—)
Sedova, Julia (1880–1969)
Ségur, Sophie Rostopchine, Comtesse de (1799–1874)
Seifullina, Lydia (1889–1954)
Selezneva, Larisa (1963—)
Semenova, Ekaterina (1786–1849)
Serebryakova, Zinaida (1884–1967)
Sergava, Katharine (1910–2005)
Sert, Misia (1872–1950)
Shabanova, Anna (1848–1932)
Shabelska, Maria (1898–1980)
Shaginian, Marietta (1888–1982)
Shakhovskaya, Eugenie M. (1889–?)
Shakhovskaya, Zinaida (1906–2001)
Shalamova, Elena (1982—)
Shapir, Olga (1850–1916)
Shaposhnikova, Natalia (1961—)
Sharapova, Maria (1987—)
Shayne, Tamara (1902–1983)
Shchegoleva, Tatiana (1982—)
Shchepkina-Kupernik, Tatiana (1874–1952)
Shelest, Alla (1919–1998)
Shepitko, Larissa (1938–1979)
Sheremetskaia, Natalia (1880–1952)
Sheshenina, Marina (1985—)
Shimanskaya, Vera (1981—)
Shishova, Albina (1966—)
Shive, Natalya (1963—)
Shkapskaia, Mariia (1891–1952)
Shorina, Anna (1982—)
Shtern, Lina (1878–1968)
Shub, Esther (1894–1959)
Sidorova, Evgenyia (c. 1935—)
Sidorova, Tatyana (1936—)
Simagina, Irina (1982—)
Simonovich-Efimova, Nina (1877–1948)
Sivkova, Anna (1982—)
Skoblikova, Lydia (1939—)
Skobtsova, Maria (1891–1945)
Slesarenko, Yelena (1982—)
Slutskaya, Irina (1979—)
Slutskaya, Vera (1874–1917)
Slyusareva, Olga (1969—)
Smetanina, Raisa (1929—)
Smirnova, Ludmila (1949—)
Smirnova, Sofia (1852–1921)
Smirnow, Zoya (fl. 1914)
Smurova, Elena (1973—)
Snytina, Natalia (1971—)
Sobakin, Marta (d. 1571)
Sofronova, Antonina (1892–1966)
Soia, Elena (1981—)
Sokhanskaia, Nadezhda (1823–1884)
Sokolova, Elena (1980—)
Sokolova, Eugenia (1850–1925)
Solntseva, Yulia (1901–1989)
Sophia (1868–1927)
Sophia Alekseyevna (1657–1704)
Sophia Dorothea of Wurttemberg (1759–1828)
Sophia of Byzantium (1448–1503)
Sophia of Kiev (fl. 1420s)
Sophie of Lithuania (1370–1453)
Sophie of Russia (c. 1140–1198)
Sotnikova, Yuliya (1970—)
Spessivtzeva, Olga (1895–1980)
Spiridonova, Maria (1884–1941)
Stanislavski, Maria Lilina (b. around 1870)
Starovoitova, Galina (1946–1998)
Stasova, Elena (1873–1966)
Stasova, Nadezhda (1822–1895)
Sten, Anna (1908–1993)
Stenina, Valentina (1936—)
Stepanova, Maria (1979—)
Stepanova, Varvara (1894–1958)
Stepanskaya, Galina (1949—)
Stolitsa, Liubov (1884–1934)
Stovbchataya, Ludmila (1974—)
Struchkova, Raissa (1925–2005)
Suslova, Nadezhda (1845–1916)
Svilova, Elizaveta (1900–1975)
Swetchine, Anne Sophie (1782–1857)
Tabakova, Yuliya (1980—)
Talanova, Nadejda (1967—)
Tamara (1160–1212)
Tamara (1907–1943)
Tamiris (fl. 550–530 BCE)
Taranina, Viktoria
Tarasova, Alla (1898–1973)
Tarnowska, Maria (1878–1923)
Tatiana (1897–1918)
Tchachina, Irina (1982—)
Tchepalova, Julija (1976—)
Tchernicheva, Lubov (1890–1976)
Tebenikhina, Irina (1978—)
Teffi, N.A. (1872–1952)
Teplova, Nadezhda Sergeevna (1814–1848)
Tereshchuk-Antipova, Tetiana (1969—)
Tereshkova, Valentina (1937—)

Theodosia (fl. 1220)
Theodosia of Moscow (1475–1501)
Tichtchenko, Elizaveta (1975—)
Tikhonova, Tamara (1964—)
Timanoff, Vera (1855–1942)
Tiourina, Elena (1971—)
Titova, Ludmila (1962—)
Tokareva, Viktoria (1937—)
Tokoun, Elena (1974—)
Tolkacheva, Irina (1982—)
Tolkounova, Irina (1971—)
Tolstaya, Tatyana (1951—)
Tolstoy, Alexandra (1884–1979)
Tolstoy, Sonya (1844–1919)
Tomashova, Tatyana (1975—)
Toumanova, Tamara (1919–1996)
Tourischeva, Ludmila (1952—)
Trefilova, Vera (1875–1943)
Trotsky, Natalia Ivanovna (1882–1962)
Trouhanova, Natalia (1885–1956)
Trubnikova, Mariia (1835–1897)
Tschechowa, Olga (1897–1980)
Tsebrikova, M.K. (1835–1917)
Tsvetaeva, Marina (1892–1941)
Udaltsova, Nadezhda (1885–1961)
Ulanova, Galina (1910–1998)
Ulyanova, Marie (1878–1937)
Usova, Maia (1964—)
Ustvolskaya, Galina (1919—)
Uvarov, Olga (1910–2001)
Vaganova, Agrippina (1879–1951)
Välbe, Elena (1968—)
Valentina (1899–1989)
Valova, Elena (1963—)
Vasilevskaia, Elena (1978—)
Vasilieva, Yulia (1978—)
Vassilieva, Ekaterina (1976—)
Vassiltschikov, Anna (16th c.)
Vassioukova, Olga (1980—)
Vazem, Ekaterina (1848–1937)
Velichkovskaia, Tamara Antonovna (1908–1990)
Venciené, Vida
Vengerova, Isabelle (1877–1956)
Vengerova, Zinaida (1867–1941)
Venttsel, Elena Sergeevna (1907–2002)
Verbitskaia, Anastasiia (1861–1928)
Verchinina, Nina (1910–1995)
Veselitskaia, Lidiia Ivanovna (1857–1936)
Veselkova-Kil'shtet, M.G. (1861–1931)
Veysberg, Yuliya (1878–1942)
Vishnevskaya, Galina (1926—)
Vlasova, Yulia
Vodopyanova, Natalia (1981—)
Volchetskaya, Yelena (1943—)
Volkonskaya, Maria (1805–1863)
Volkova, Vera (1904–1975)
von Meck, Nadezhda (1831–1894)
Voznesenskaya, Julia (1940—)
Vronsky, Vitya (1909–1992)
Vyroubova, Nina (1921—)
Wasilewska, Wanda (1905–1964)
Willson, Rini Zarova (d. 1966)
Xenia Alexandrovna (1876–1960)
Yakunchikova, Maria (1870–1901)
Yavorska, Lydia (1869–1921)
Yegorova, Irina (1940—)
Yelesina, Yelena (1970—)
Yeroshina, Radya
Youshkevitch, Nina (c. 1921–1998)
Yudina, Maria (1899–1970)
Zabirova, Zulfia (1973—)
Zabolotnaia, Natalia (1985—)
Zakharova, Svetlana (1970—)
Zamolodchikova, Elena (1982—)
Zasipkina, Maria (1985—)
Zasulich, Vera (1849–1919)
Zaturenska, Marya Alexandrovna (1902–1982)
Zbyslawa (fl. 1100)
Zhadovskaia, Iuliia Valerianovna (1824–1883)
Zhuk, Tatiana
Zhukova, Maria (1804–1855)
Zhurova, Svetlana (1972—)
Ziganshina, Natalia (1985—)
Zilber, Irina (c. 1980—)
Zinóveva-Annibal, Lidiia Dmitrievna (1866–1907)
Zozula, Vera
Zykina, Olesya (1980—)

RUSSIA, SOVIET

Former republic in eastern Europe and northern and central Asia
Organized from soviet republics of Russian S.F.S.R., Ukrainian S.S.R., Belorussian S.S.R., and Transcaucasian Federation (1922)
Struggle for power after death of Lenin resulted in victor for Stalin (1926)
Trotsky expelled from country (1929)
Adopted new constitution (1936)
Occupied eastern Poland (1939)
Took other territories from Finland and Baltic countries (1939–1940)
Invaded by Germany (1942–1945)
One of four powers occupying Germany after end of World War II (1945)
Invaded Manchuria (1945)
Established Communist regimes throughout eastern Europe (1945–1948)
Withdrew from Austria (1955)
Suppressed anti-Communist revolt in Hungary (1956)
Invaded Czechoslovakia (1968)
Dissolved and independence granted to territories (1990s)

Abramova, Nelli (1940—)
Akhaminova, Yelena (1961—)
Akhmerova, Leylya (1957—)
Aksyonova-Shapovalova, Lyudmila (1947—)
Alekseyeva, Galina (1946—)
Alekseyeva-Kreft, Galina (1950—)
Alfeyeva, Lidiya (1946—)
Aliger, Margarita Iosifovna (1915–1992)
Alliluyeva, Svetlana (1926—)
Alliluyeva-Stalin, Nadezhda (1901–1932)
Anchutina, Leda (1915–1989)
Anderson-Ivantzova, Elizabeth (c. 1893–1973)
Andreeva-Babakhan, Anna Misaakovna (1923—)
Andreyuk, Yelena (1958—)
Anisimova, Natalya (1960—)
Anisimova, Nina (1909—)
Anisimova, Tatyana (1949—)
Anisimova, Vera (1952—)
Annenkova, Julia (c. 1898–c. 1938)
Antonova, Yelena (1952—)
Ardzhannikova, Lyudmila (1958—)
Artamonova, Evguenia (1975—)
Artyukhina, Aleksandra (1889–1969)
Asanova, Dinara (1942–1985)
Babanina, Svetlana (1943—)
Badulina, Svetlana (1960—)
Bagryantseva, Yelizaveta (1920—)
Baikauskaite, Laimute (1956—)
Balachova, Alexandra (1887–1905)
Baldina, Alexandra Maria (1885–1977)
Barel, Olesya (1960—)
Barskaya, Margarita A. (1903–1938)
Barysheva, Olga (1954—)
Bazanova, Marina (1962—)
Beglyakova, Irina (1933—)
Belova-Novikova, Yelena (1947—)
Bergen, Larisa (1949—)
Beseliene, Vida (1956—)
Besfamilnaya, Nadezhda (1950—)
Bessmertnova, Natalia (1941—)
Bicherova, Olga (1966—)
Biltauere, Astra (1944—)
Biryukova, Alexandra (1929—)
Bobrova, Natalia (1978—)
Bocharova, Nina (1924—)
Bochina, Natalya (1962—)
Bogdanova, Svetlana (1964—)
Bogdanova, Yuliya (1964—)
Bogomolova, Ludmilla (1932—)
Bogoraz, Larisa (c. 1930–2004)
Bogoslovskaya, Olga (1964—)
Bondarenko, Olga (1960—)
Bonner, Elena (1923—)
Borozna, Lyudmila (1954—)
Borzenkova, Galina (1964—)
Bovt, Violette (1927—)
Bragina, Lyudmila (1943—)
Brezhneva, Galina (1929—)
Brezhneva, Viktoriya (1908–1995)
Bryunina, Mira (1951—)
Bryzgina, Olga (1963—)
Bugrimova, Irina (1910–2001)
Bukharina, Galina (1945—)
Buldakova, Lyudmila (1938—)
Bunatyants, Elen (1970—)
Burda, Lyubov (1953—)
Buryakina, Olga (1958—)
Buruzova, Natalya (1954—)
Bykova, Natalya (1958—)
Bykova, Tamara (1958—)
Bystrova, Galina (1934—)
Chaikina, Liza (d. 1941)
Chamie, Tatiana (d. 1953)
Chebukina, Yelena (1965—)
Chen, Si-Lan (1909—)
Chenchik, Taisiya (1936—)
Cheremisina, Nina (1946—)
Cherkasova, Valentina (1958—)
Chernyshova, Lyudmila (1952—)
Chernyshova, Nadezhda (1951—)
Chiaureli, Sofiko (1937—)
Chudina, Alexandra (1923–1990)
Chunikhovskaya, Irina (1968—)
Chusovitina, Oksana (1975—)
Cistjakova, Galina (1962—)
Cohen, Lona (1913–1993)
Cornescou, Irina Soltanovna (1916—)
Danilova, Alexandra (1903–1997)
Danilova, Pelageya (1918—)
Dauniene, Tamara (1951—)
Davidovich, Bella (1928—)
Davydova, Yelena (1961—)
Dementyeva, Yelizaveta (1928—)
Dendeberova, Yelena (1969—)
Deryugina, Natalya (1971—)
Devyatova, Tatyana (1949—)
Doubrovska, Felia (1896–1981)
Dronova, Nina
Dumbadze, Nina (1919–1983)
Dumcheva, Antonina (1958—)
Dzhandzhgava, Tatyana (1964—)
Dzhigalova, Lyudmila (1962—)
Dzhugeli, Medeya (1925—)
Emirzyan, Sirvard (1966—)
Fadeyeva, Mariya (1958—)
Fedotkina, Svetlana (1967—)
Feryabnikova, Nelli (1949—)
Filatova, Maria (1961—)
Filipova, Nadya (1959—)
Franklyn, Lidije (1922—)

Frolova, Inna (1965—)
Frolova, Lyudmila (1953—)
Frolova, Nina (1948—)
Frolova, Tatiana (1967—)
Furtseva, Ekaterina (1910–1974)
Galushka, Vera (1945—)
Gapchenko, Emma (1938—)
Gelman, Polina (1919—)
Geltzer, Ykaterina (1876–1962)
Gerlits, Irina (1966—)
Gilyazova, Nailiya (1953—)
Glubokova, Lidiya (1953—)
Glushchenko, Tatyana (1956—)
Gogoberidze, Lana (1928—)
Golubnichaya, Mariya (1924—)
Gonobobleva, Tatyana Pavlovna (1948—)
Gorb, Tatyana (1965—)
Gorbacheva, Raisa (1932–1999)
Gorbyatkova, Nelli (1958–1981)
Gorchakova, Yelena (1933—)
Gordeeva, Ekaterina (1971–)
Gorokhova, Galina (1938—)
Gorokhovskaya, Mariya (1921—)
Goyshchik-Nasanova, Tatyana (1952—)
Grinberg, Maria (1908–1979)
Grishchenkova, Alla (1961—)
Grizodubova, Valentina (1910–1993)
Gromova, Lyudmila (1942—)
Grozdeva, Svetlana (1959—)
Grudneva, Yelena (1974—)
Gsovsky, Tatiana (1901–1993)
Gubaidulina, Sofia (1931—)
Gudz, Lyudmila (1969—)
Gunda, Saida (1959—)
Gureyeva, Lyudmila (1943—)
Guryeva, Yelena (1958—)
Guseva, Elina (1964—)
Gutsu, Tatyana (1976—)
Guzenko, Olga (1956—)
Ilyina-Kolesnikova, Nadezhda (1949—)
Inzhuvatova, Galina (1952—)
Isakova, Maria (1920—)
Ivanova-Kalinina, Lidiya (1937—)
Ivinskaya, Tatyana (1958—)
Jaunzeme, Ineze (1932—)
Kaciusyte, Lina (1963—)
K'alandadze, Ana (1924—)
Kalediene, Birute (1934—)
Kalimbet, Irina (1968—)
Kalinchuk, Yekaterina (1922—)
Kalinina, Irina (1959—)
Kaminskaite, Leonora (1951–1986)
Karalli, Vera (1889–1972)
Karasyova, Olga (1949—)
Karlova, Larisa (1958—)
Kasatkina, Natalia (1934—)
Katusheva, Marita (1938—)
Kazankina, Tatyana (1951—)
Kham, Alina (1959—)
Khloptseva, Yelena (1960—)
Khnykina, Nadezhda (1933–1994)
Khodotovich, Ekaterina (1972—)
Khomiakova, Valeriia (d. 1942)
Khudashova, Yelena (1965—)
Kirichenko, Olga (1976—)
Kiselyova, Larisa (1970—)
Klimova, Natalya (1951—)
Klimovica-Drevina, Inta (1951—)
Knuth, Maria (d. 1954)
Knyazeva, Olga (1954—)
Kochergina-Makarets, Tatyana (1956—)
Kolkova, Olga (1955—)
Kolpakova, Irina (1933—)
Kolpakova, Tatyana (1959—)
Komisova, Vera (1953—)
Kondakova, Yelena (c. 1955—)
Kondrashina, Anna (1955—)
Kondratieva, Marina (1934—)
Kondratyeva, Lyudmila (1958—)
Konyayeva, Nadezhda (1931—)
Korbut, Olga (1955—)
Korshunova, Tatyana (1956—)
Korytova, Svetlana (1968—)
Kosenkova, Klavdiya (1949—)
Koshel, Antonina (1954—)
Koshevaya, Marina (1960—)
Kosmodemyanskaya, Zoya (1923–1941)
Kovpan, Valentina (1950—)
Kozakova, Olga (1951—)
Kozyr, Valentina (1950—)
Kozyreva, Lyubov (1956—)
Krachevskaya-Dolzhenko, Svetlana (1944—)
Krasnikova, Natella (1953—)
Krassovska, Nathalie (1918–2005)
Kravets, Inessa (1966—)
Kraynova, Tatyana (1967—)
Krepkina, Vera (1933—)
Krivelyova, Svetlana (1969—)
Krivosheyeva, Olga (1961—)
Krokhina, Lyudmila (1954—)
Kruglova, Yelena (1962—)
Krutova, Ninel (1926—)
Krylova, Lidiya (1951—)
Kuchinskaya, Natalia (1949—)
Kuczinski, Ruth (1907–2000)
Kudreva, Natalya (1942—)
Kumysh, Marina (1964—)
Kurgapkina, Ninel (1929—)
Kurvyakova, Raisa (1945—)
Kuryshko-Nagirnaya, Yekatarina (1949—)
Kushner, Natalya (1954—)
Kvrivichvili, Khatuna (1974—)
Lantratov, Vera (1947—)
Lapitskaya, Natalya (1962—)
Laschenova, Natalia (1973—)
Lashko, Irina (1973—)
Lazakovich, Tamara (1954—)
Lebedeva, Natalya (1949—)
Lebedeva, Sarra (1892–1967)
Ledovskaya, Tatyana (1966—)
Leonova, Aleksandra (1964—)
Leontyeva, Galina (1941—)
Lepeshinskaya, Olga (1916—)
Lesovaya, Tatyana (1956—)
Levi, Natalia (1901–1972)
Lisovskaya, Natalya (1962—)
Litoshenko, Mariya (1949—)
Litvyak, Lidiya (1921–1943)
Lobanova, Natalya (1947—)
Lobatch, Marina (1970—)
Lobova, Nina (1957—)
Loginova, Lidiya (1951—)
Logvinenko, Marina (1961—)
Losaberidze, Ketevan (1949—)
Lukanina, Ninel (1937—)
Lutayeva-Berzina, Valentina (1956—)
Lysenko, Tatiana (1975—)
Lyubimova, Nadezhda (1959—)
Lyukhina, Tamara (1939—)
Makarova, Inna (1928—)
Makaryeva, Nadiezhda (1925—)
Makhina, Antonina (1958—)
Makogonova, Irina (1959—)
Malchugina-Mikheyeva, Galina (1962—)
Malinovska, Valentina
Malukhina, Anna (1958—)
Manina, Tamara (1934—)
Mankova, Svetlana (1962—)
Maretskaya, Vera (1906–1978)
Maslakova-Zharkova, Lyudmila (1952—)
Massevitch, Alla G. (1918—)
Matiyevskaya, Yelena (1961—)
Maximova, Ekaterina (1939—)
Melnikova, Antonina (1958—)
Meshcheryakova, Natalya (1972—)
Meskhi, Leila (1968—)
Mikhaylovskaya, Lyudmila (1937—)
Milashkina, Tamara Andreyevna (1934—)
Minaicheva, Galina (1929—)
Mineyeva, Olga (1952—)
Minkh, Irina (1964—)
Miroshina, Yelena (1974—)
Misevich, Vera (1945—)
Mishak, Valentina (1942—)
Mishenina, Galina (1950—)
Mitryuk, Natalya (1959—)
Morozova, Natalia (1973—)
Morskova, Natalya (1966—)
Moskalenko, Larisa (1963—)
Mostepanova, Olga (1968—)
Mukhina, Elena (1960—)
Mukhina, Vera (1889–1953)
Muradyan, Nina (1954—)
Muratova, Kira (1934—)
Muratova, Sofiya (1929—)
Nadezhdina, Nadezhda (1908–1979)
Naimushina, Elena (1964—)
Nazarova, Olga (1955—)
Nazarova-Bagryantseva, Irina (1957—)
Nemashkalo, Yelena (1963—)
Neneniene-Casaitite, Aldona (1949—)
Nikishina, Svetlana (1958—)
Nikolayeva, Margarita (1935—)
Nikolayeva, Yelena (1966—)
Nikonova, Valentina (1952—)
Nikulina, Marina (1963—)
Nurutdinova, Liliya (1963—)
Odinokova-Berezhnaya, Lyubov (1955—)
Ogiyenko, Valentina (1965—)
Olizarenko, Nadezhda (1953—)
Omelianchik, Oksana (1970—)
Onoprienko, Galina (1963—)
Orlova, Liubov (1902–1975)
Osadchaya, Liliya (1953—)
Osipenko, Alla (1932—)
Osipenko, Polina (1907–1939)
Ovechkina, Nadezhda (1958—)
Ovechkina, Tatyana (1950—)
Ozolina, Elvira (1939—)
Pakhmutova, Alexandra (1929—)
Palchikova, Irina (1959—)
Panchuk, Lyudmila (1956—)
Panov, Galina (1949—)
Panova, Vera (1905–1973)
Parkhomchuk, Irina (1965—)
Parnok, Sophia (1885–1933)
Pasokha, Anna (1949—)
Pavlova, Nadezhda (1956—)
Pazyun, Mariya (1953—)
Pechenkina, Natalya (1946—)
Pereyaslavec, Valentina (1907–1998)
Petrik, Larissa (1949—)
Petrova, Yelena (1966—)
Petruseva, Natalia
Petushkova, Yelena (1940—)
Pinayeva-Khvedosyuk, Lyudmila (1936—)
Pinigina-Kulchunova, Mariya (1958—)
Pisareva, Mariya (1934—)
Pivovarova, Olga (1956—)
Plisetskaya, Maya (1925—)
Pogosheva-Safonova, Tamara (1946—)
Pomoshchnikova, Natalya (1965—)
Ponomareva-Romashkova, Nina (1929—)
Ponyaeva, Tatyana (1946—)
Popkova, Vera (1943—)
Popova, Nina (1922—)
Popova-Aleksandrova, Larisa (1957—)
Poradnik-Bobrus, Lyudmila (1946—)

Preobrazhenskaya, Nina (1956—)
Press, Irina (1939—)
Press, Tamara (1939—)
Prishchepa, Nadezhda (1956—)
Prorochenko-Burakova, Tatyana (1952—)
Providokhina-Fyodorenko, Tatyana (1953—)
Prozumenshchykova, Galina (1948—)
Prudskova, Valentina (1938—)
Pryakhina, Svetlana (1970—)
Pugacheva, Alla (1949—)
Pugovskaya, Olga (1942—)
Pustovit, Antonina (1955—)
Radyonska, Tanya (1924—)
Radzevich, Nadezhda (1953—)
Raikh, Zinaida (1894–1939)
Ramoskiene, Genovaite (1945—)
Raskova, Marina (1912–1943)
Rastvorova, Valentina (1933—)
Razumova, Natalya (1961—)
Reisner, Larissa (1895–1926)
Rinaldi, Angela (c. 1916—)
Rodnina, Irina (1949—)
Rogachyova, Lyudmila (1966—)
Rogozhina, Lyudmila (1959—)
Romanova, Maria (1886–1954)
Romanova, Yelena (1963—)
Rosenfeld, Fanny (1905–1969)
Roshchina, Nadezhda (1954—)
Roshchina, Tatyana (1941—)
Roslavleva, Natalia (1907–1977)
Rostova, Anna (1950—)
Rozengolts-Levina, Eva (1898–1975)
Rozgon, Nadezhda (1952—)
Rudkovskaya, Yelena (1973—)
Rudovskaya, Lyubov (1950—)
Rukavishnikova, Olga (1955—)
Rupshiene, Angele (1952—)
Rusanova, Lyubov (1954—)
Rusnachenko, Natalya (1969—)
Rustamova, Zebinisso (1955—)
Ruzina, Yelena (1964—)
Ryabchinskaya, Yuliya (1947–1973)
Ryskal, Inna (1944—)
Ryzhova, Antonina (1934—)
Saadi, Elvira (1952—)
Sabaite, Nijole (1950—)
Sadovskaya, Tatyana (1966—)
Safina, Yuliya (1950—)
Salikhova, Roza (1944—)
Salukvadze, Nino (1969—)
Salumae, Erika (1962—)
Samolenko, Tatyana (1961—)
Samotesova, Lyudmila (1939—)
Samusenko-Petrenko, Tatyana (1938—)
Sankova, Galina (b. 1904)
Sarycheva, Tatyana (1949—)
Savelyeva, Tatyana (1947—)
Savina, Nina (1915–1965)
Savitskaya, Galina (1961—)
Savitskaya, Svetlana (1948—)
Savkina, Larisa (1955—)
Schollar, Ludmilla (c. 1888–1978)
Semjonova, Uljana (1952—)
Semyonova, Marina (b. 1908)
Semyonova, Olga (1964—)
Semyonova, Svetlana (1958—)
Seredina, Antonina (1930—)
Sevostyanova, Nadezhda (1953—)
Shabanova, Rafiga (1943—)
Shamray-Rudko, Galina (1931—)
Shaposhnikova, Natalia (1961—)
Sharmay, Lyubov (1956—)
Shchelkanova, Tatyana (1937—)
Shchetinina, Lyudmila (1951—)
Sheina, Svetlana (1918–2005)
Shelest, Alla (1919–1998)
Shepitko, Larissa (1938–1979)
Shevchenko, Elena (1971—)
Shevtsova, Lyudmila (1934—)
Shikolenko, Natalya (1964—)
Shilova, Irina (1960—)
Shishova, Lyudmila (1940—)
Shkurnova, Olga (1962—)
Shmonina, Marina (1965—)
Shtern, Lina (1878–1968)
Shub, Esther (1894–1959)
Shubina, Lyudmila (1948—)
Shubina, Mariya (1930—)
Shubina, Yelena (1974—)
Shushunova, Elena (1969—)
Shuvayeva, Nadezhda (1952—)
Shvaybovich, Yelena (1966—)
Shvyganova, Tatyana (1960—)
Sidorenko, Tatyana (1966—)
Sidorova-Burochkina, Valentina (1954—)
Simonovich-Efimova, Nina (1877–1948)
Sizova, Alla (1939—)
Skachko-Pakhovskaya, Tatyana (1954—)
Skaldina, Oksana (1972—)
Skoblikova, Lydia (1939—)
Slutskaya, Vera (1874–1917)
Smirnova, Irina (1968—)
Smoleyeva, Nina (1948—)
Sofronova, Antonina (1892–1966)
Sokolova, Lyubov (1921–2001)
Sokolova-Kulichkova, Natalya (1949—)
Solntseva, Yulia (1901–1989)
Solovova, Olga (1953—)
Sorokina, Nina (1942—)
Sovetnikova, Galina (1955—)
Spessivtzeva, Olga (1895–1980)
Starovoitova, Galina (1946–1998)
Stasova, Elena (1873–1966)
Stepanova, Varvara (1894–1958)
Stetsenko, Tatyana (1957—)
Strazheva, Olga (1972—)
Strecen-Maseikaite, Sigita (1958—)
Stroyeva, Vera (b. 1903)
Strunnikova, Natalya (1964—)
Studneva, Marina (1959—)
Sukharnova, Olga (1955—)
Sumnikova, Irina (1964—)
Svilova, Elizaveta (1900–1975)
Talalayeva, Lyubov (1953—)
Talysheva-Tregub, Tatyana (1937—)
Tarakanova, Nelli (1954—)
Tereshkova, Valentina (1937—)
Teryoshina, Yelena (1959—)
Tikhonina, Tamara (1934—)
Timochenko, Alexandra (1972—)
Timoshkina-Sherstyuk, Natalya (1952—)
Tkachenko, Marina (1965—)
Tkachenko, Nadezhda (1948—)
Tochenova, Klavdiya (1921—)
Tornikidu, Yelena (1965—)
Tovstogan, Yevgeniya (1965—)
Trandenkova-Krivosheva, Marina (1967—)
Trofimova-Gopova, Nina (1953—)
Tsagarayeva, Larisa (1958—)
Tsirkova, Svetlana (1945—)
Tsotadze, Liana (1961—)
Tuomaite, Vitalija (1964—)
Turchina, Zinaida (1946—)
Tyshkevich, Tamara (1931—)
Tyurina, Lyubov (1943—)
Ulanova, Galina (1910–1998)
Umanets, Nina (1956—)
Urbanovich, Galina (1917—)
Ushakova, Irina (1954—)
Ustinova, Natalya (1944—)
Ustyuzhanina, Tatyana (1965—)
Vaganova, Agrippina (1879–1951)
Valeyeva, Natalya (1969—)
Varganova, Svetlana (1964—)
Vasilchenko, Olga (1956—)
Vasilkova, Elvira (1962—)
Vaytsekhovskaya, Yelena (1958—)
Vecheslova, Tatiana (1910–1991)
Volchetskaya, Yelena (1943—)
Volkova, Yelena (1960—)
Vyroubova, Nina (1921—)
Vyuzhanina, Galina (1952—)
Yakovleva, Olga (1963—)
Yegorova, Lyudmila (1931—)
Yegorova, Valentina (1964—)
Yembakhtova, Tatyana (1956—)
Yermolayeva, Galina (1948—)
Yevkova, Olga (1965—)
Yudina, Maria (1899–1970)
Yurchenko, Natalia (1965—)
Yurchenya, Marina (1959—)
Yurina, Esfir (1923—)
Yusova, Zoya (1948—)
Zabelina, Aleksandra (1937—)
Zaboluyeva, Svetlana (1966—)
Zakharova, Galina (1947—)
Zakharova, Nadezhda (1945—)
Zakharova, Stella (1963—)
Zakharova, Tatyana (1951—)
Zaslavskaya, Tatyana (1924—)
Zasulskaya, Natalya (1969—)
Zazdravnykh, Valentina (1954—)
Zelikovich-Dumcheva, Antonina (1958—)
Zhirko, Yelena (1968—)
Zhirova, Marina (1963—)
Zhivanevskaya, Nina (1977—)
Zhulina, Valentina (1953—)
Zhupiyeva, Yelena (1960—)
Zilporite, Laima (1967—)
Zubareva, Olga (1958—)
Zubko, Yelena (1953—)
Zvereva, Natasha (1971—)
Zybina, Galina (1931—)
Zyuskova, Nina (1952—)

RWANDA

Republic in eastern central Africa
Formerly part of Belgian trust territory of Ruanda-Urundi
Achieved independence (1962)

Uwilingiyimana, Agathe (1953–1994)

SAINT VINCENT

Self-governing state of Windward Islands, West Indies
Became independent as Saint Vincent and the Grenadines (1979)

Francois, Elma (1897–1944)

SAKONNET

Native North American Northeastern indigenous group of Wampanoag Confederacy

Awashonks (fl. mid–late 17th c.)

SALERNO

Province of Campania in southern Italy
See Italy.

SALISBURY

Borough of Wiltshire in southern England
See England.

SANTA CLARA PUEBLO

Native North American Southwest indigenous group

Velarde, Pablita (1918—)

SARDINIA

Island in Mediterranean Sea, autonomous region of Italy
Settled by Phoenicians and Greeks
Ruled by Carthage (6th c. BCE)
Taken by Romans (3rd c. BCE)
Part of Vandal kingdom (5th c. CE)
Reconquered by Byzantine Empire (6th c.)
Raided by Muslims (8th–11th c.)
Held by Austria (1713–1720)
Ceded to Savoy for Sicily (1720)
See Italy.

SAUDI ARABIA

Kingdom on Arabian Peninsula in southwestern Asia
Dual kingdom formed by king of Nejd and Hejaz (1926)
Single kingdom renamed Saudi Arabia (1932)
Entered treaty with Iraq (1936)
Formed agreement with Egypt (1937)

Iffat (1916–2000)
Karioka, Tahiya (c. 1921–1999)

SAVONA

Province of Liguria in northwestern Italy
Destroyed by Lombards (7th c.)
Under Genoese rule (16th c.)
Under French rule (1805–1815)
Passed to Savoy (1815)
See Italy.

SAVOY

Historic region of southeastern France and northwestern Italy
Counts of Savoy ruled as part of kingdom of Arles (from 11th c.)
Became independent and expanded territory to include Piedmont
Elevated to duchy (1416)
Allied alternately with France and Italy
Involved in wars between France and Spain
Joined Grand Alliance (1704)
Kingdom of Sardinia (Piedmont, Savoy, and Sardinia) formed (1720)
Genoa added (1815)
Joined other states to form kingdom of Italy, ruled by house of Savoy (1860)
Territory of Savoy and Nice ceded to France
See France.
See Italy.

SAXE

French name for Saxony
Used chiefly in names of former duchies in Thuringia (15th–16th c.)
Duchy of Saxe-Altenburg
Duchy of Saxe-Weimar-Eisenach
Duchy of Saxe-Meiningen
Duchy of Saxe-Gotha
Duchy of Saxe-Coburg
See Germany.

SAXONY

Former German state
Occupied by the Saxons until subdued by Charlemagne (7th–8th c.)
As duchy of East Frankish kingdom, repelled Wends and incorporated Thuringia
Became an electorate (15th c.)
Became kingdom (1806)
Received rule of grand duchy of Warsaw (1807)
Lost territory to Prussia (1815)
Rest of kingdom a free state in German Empire (1871–1918)
Became a republic (1918)
Part of Soviet-occupied sector of Germany (1945)
See Germany.

SCANDINAVIA

Ancient name of the country of the Norsemen

Richeza Eriksdottir (fl. 1200s)
Sophie (fl. 1200s)

SCHAERBECK

Commune in Brabant province of central Belgium
See Belgium.

SCHLESWIG

Historic region of northwestern Germany
Former duchy of Danish crown
Attached to Holy Roman Empire (934–1027)
Ceded to Denmark and ruled by Holstein (14th c.)
Part of German Empire
Ruled by Danish royal house of Oldenburg
Administered by Prussia (1865–1866)
Awarded to Denmark (1920)
See Denmark.
See Germany.

SCHWEIDNITZ

Town in Lublin province of eastern Poland
See Poland.

SCHWERIN

District in eastern Germany
See Germany.

SCOTLAND

Northern part of island of Great Britain
Occupied by Picts when invaded by Romans (80 CE)
Kingdom of the Picts in highlands north of River Forth
Kingdom of Scots (of Irish extraction) in western highlands
Kingdom of Strathclyde in the south
Kingdom in southeast belonging to Anglo-Saxon kingdom of Northumbria
Picts broke Anglo-Saxon power on border
Invaded by Norse (8th c.)
Picts conquered Scots (9th c.)
Lothian and Strathclyde added to united Scottish kingdom
Forced rule by English crown (11th c.)
Won independence of England (1314)
Ruled by house of Stuart (1371–1688)
Acquired Orkneys and Shetlands (1472)
Accession of James VI of Scotland as James I of England united kingdoms (1603)

Aberdeen, Ishbel Maria Gordon, Lady (1857–1939)
Adam, Jean (1710–1765)
Adams, Irene (1947—)
Adam Smith, Janet (1905–1999)
Addison, Agnes (c. 1841–1903)
Aitken, Jessie (1867–1934)
Alcock, Nora (1874–1972)
Alexander, Wendy
Alexandra Victoria (1891–1959)
Allen, Betty (1936—)
Angelus, Muriel (1909–2004)
Angus, Dorothy (1891–1979)
Anne de la Tour (c. 1496–1524)
Anne de la Tour (d. 1512)
Anne of Denmark (1574–1619)
Armour, Mary Nicol Neill (1902–2000)
Attwooll, Elspeth (1943—)
Auerbach, Charlotte (1899–1994)
Baillie, Grisell (1822–1921)
Baillie, Grizel (1665–1746)
Baillie, Isobel (1895–1983)
Baillie, Jackie (1964—)
Bain, Wilhelmina Sherriff (1848–1944)
Baldwin, Sally (1940–2003)
Balfour, Alison (d. 1596)
Balfour, Jean (1927—)
Ballinger, Margaret (1894–1980)
Balliol, Ada (fl. 1256)
Balliol, Cecily (d. before 1273)
Balliol, Eleanor (fl. 1230)
Balliol, Margaret (c. 1255–?)
Balliol, Margaret (fl. 1300s)
Bannerman, Helen (1862–1946)
Bannerman, Jane (c. 1835–1923)
Barns-Graham, Wilhelmina (1912–2004)
Bayne, Margaret (1798–1835)
Beat, Janet Eveline (1937—)
Beaufort, Joan (c. 1410–1445)
Begg, Anne (1955—)
Bell, Maggie (1945—)
Bethoc (fl. 1000)
Bethoc (fl. 11th c.)
Bethune, Elizabeth (fl. 16th c.)
Betjeman, Agnes Muir (1885–1964)
Bews, Mary Ellen (1856–1945)
Black, Helen McKenzie (1896–1963)
Blackadder, Elizabeth (1931—)
Blackburn, Jemima (1823–1909)
Blair, Catherine (1872–1946)
Bond, Mary (1939—)
Borrowman, Agnes (1881–1955)
Bottomley, Virginia (1948—)
Boyack, Sarah (1961—)
Boyd, Mary (fl. 1487)
Boyd, Megan (1915–2001)
Boyd, Susan (1949–2004)
Brankin, Rhona
Bright, Mary (1954–2002)
Brown, Anna (1747–1810)
Brown, Hilary (1952—)
Browne, Harriet Louisa (1829–1906)
Bruce, Christian (d. 1356)
Bruce, Margaret (c. 1286–?)
Bruce, Margaret (1296–1316)
Bruce, Margaret (d. 1346)
Bruce, Mary (fl. 1290–1316)
Bruce, Matilda (c. 1285–c. 1326)
Bruce, Matilda (d. 1353)
Brunton, Mary (1778–1818)
Buchan, Anna (1878–1948)
Buchan, Elspeth (1738–1791)
Buchanan, Dorothy (1899–1985)
Buchanan, Isobel Wilson (1954—)
Burgess, Georgina Jane (c. 1839–1904)
Burn, Margaret Gordon (1825–1918)
Burnford, Sheila (1918–1984)
Cadell, Jean (1884–1967)
Cairns, Elizabeth (1685–1714)
Calderón de la Barca, Frances (1804–1882)
Calderwood, Margaret (1715–1774)
Cameron, Kate (1874–1965)
Cameron, Robina Thomson (1892–1971)
Caradus, Elizabeth (1832–1912)
Cardny, Marion (fl. 1300s)
Carlyle, Jane Welsh (1801–1866)
Carmichael, Elizabeth (fl. 1530s)
Carnegie, Caroline (1934—)
Carswell, Catherine (1879–1946)
Cassie, Alice Mary (1887–1963)
Casson, Margaret MacDonald (1913–1999)
Chambers, Norah (1905–1989)
Charteris, Catherine Morice (1835–1918)
Clare, Isabel de (1226–1254)
Clark, Lynda (1949—)
Cockburn, Alicia (1713–1794)
Coleridge, Georgina (1916–2003)
Collier, Jeanie (c. 1791–1861)
Colville, Elizabeth (c. 1571–1600s)
Colville, Meg (1918–2004)
Cook, Stephanie (1972—)
Corri, Adrienne (1930—)
Cossgrove, Selina (1849–1929)
Cowie, Laura (1892–1969)
Craigie, Cathie (1954—)
Cranston, Kate (1850–1934)
Cruft, Catherine Holway (1927—)

Cuddie, Mary (1823–1889)
Cunningham, Roseanna (1951—)
Curran, Margaret (c. 1962—)
Currie, Ethel Dobbie (1898–1963)
Dalrymple, Grace (1758–1823)
Davies, Betty (1935—)
Deacon, Susan
Dean, Williamina (1844–1895)
Deans, Jane (1823–1911)
De Burgh, Aimée (d. 1946)
Dickson, Barbara (1947—)
Dickson, Joan (1921–1994)
Dixon, Margaret (1670–1753)
Doada (fl. 990–1005)
Donald, Janet (c. 1819–1892)
Donaldson, Margaret Caldwell (1926—)
Donata (fl. 11th century)
Douglas, Elizabeth (d. before 1451)
Douglas, Margaret (b. around 1427)
Downie, Dorothy G. (1894–1960)
Drummond, Annabella (1350–1401)
Drummond, Flora (1869–1949)
Drummond, Margaret (d. 1375)
Drummond, Margaret (c. 1472–1502)
Dunbar, Agnes (1312–1369)
Dunbar, Christine (c. 1350–?)
Dunedin, Maudie (c. 1888–1937)
Dunnett, Dorothy (1923–2001)
Eadie, Helen
Eardley, Joan (1921–1963)
Easton, Sheena (1959—)
Elder, Dorothy-Grace
Elflaed (fl. 1030)
Elizabeth de Burgh (d. 1327)
Ellen, Mary Ann (1897–1949)
Elphinstone, Eupheme (fl. 1500s)
Elphinstone, Eupheme
Eriksen, Gunn (1956—)
Ermengarde of Beaumont (d. 1234)
Erskine, Margaret (fl. 1530s)
Erskine, Mary (1629–1707)
Ethelreda (fl. 1090)
Euphemia (fl. 1100s)
Ewing, Annabelle (1960—)
Ewing, Margaret (1945–2006)
Ewing, Winnie (1929—)
Fabiani, Linda (1956—)
Fawcett, Marion (1886–1957)
Ferguson, Patricia (1958—)
Fergusson, Elizabeth (1867–1930)
Fergusson, Mary (1914–1997)
Ferrier, Susan Edmonstone (1782–1854)
Finnie, Jessie (c. 1821–?)
Finnie, Linda (1952—)
Fleming, Williamina Paton (1857–1911)
Flemming, Mary (fl. 1540s)
Forbes, Margaret (c. 1807–1877)
Forbes-Sempill, Elizabeth (1912–1965)
Forgan, Liz (1944—)
Fraser, Agnes (1877–1968)
Fraser, Elizabeth (1963—)
Fraser, Isabella (1857–1932)
Fraser, Janet (1883–1945)
Fraser, Margaret (1866–1951)
Fraser, Susan (1966—)
French, Annie (1872–1965)
Garden, Mary (1874–1967)
Gardner, Margaret (1844–1929)
Garvie, Sheila (fl. 1960s)
Geddes, Janet (fl. 1637)
Gibb, Helen (1838–1914)
Gibson, Catherine (1931—)
Gillon, Karen (1967—)
Gilmour, Christina (c. 1824–c. 1911)
Glennie, Evelyn (1965—)
Godman, Trish (1939—)
Goldie, Annabel (1950—)
Gordon, Eliza (1877–1938)
Gordon, Hannah (1941—)
Gordon, Helen (1934—)
Gordon, Mary (1882–1963)
Gordon Baille, Mary Ann (1857–?)
Gordon-Cumming, Eka (1837–1924)
Graham, Euphemia (d. 1469)
Graham, Isabella (1742–1814)
Graham, Margaret (d. 1380)
Grahame, Christine (1944—)
Grainger, Katherine (1975—)
Grange, Rachel (1682–1745)
Grant, Anne (1755–1838)
Grant, Rhoda (1963—)
Gregg, Christina (c. 1814–1882)
Gruaidh (fl. 11 c.)
Gruoch (fl. 1020–1054)
Haldane, Elizabeth S. (1862–1937)
Hale, Maria Selina (1864–1951)
Hamilton, Mary (1882–1966)
Hargreaves, Alison (1962–1995)
Harvie Anderson, Betty (1913–1979)
Helen (fl. 1275)
Herlie, Eileen (1919—)
Heywood, Joan (1923—)
Hodierna (fl. 1100s)
Hopekirk, Helen (1856–1945)
Horne, Janet (d. 1727)
Hughes, Janis (1958—)
Hume, Anna (fl. 1644)
Hunter, Mollie (1922—)
Hutchison, Isobel Wylie (1899–1982)
Hyslop, Fiona (1964—)
Illington, Marie (d. 1927)
Inescort, Frieda (1900–1976)
Ingebiorge (fl. 1045–1068)
Inman, Elizabeth Murray (c. 1724–1785)
Irvine, Jean Kennedy (c. 1877–1962)
Isaac, Joan (fl. 1300s)
Isabel (fl. 1183)
Isabel (fl. 1225)
Isabel (d. 1457?)
Isabel de Warrenne (b. 1253)
Isabella (1206–1251)
Isabella of Buchan (fl. 1290–1310)
Isabella of Mar (d. 1296)
Isabel of Fife (c. 1332–1389)
Jackson, Sylvia (c. 1951—)
Jamieson, Cathy (1956—)
Jamieson, Margaret (1953—)
Jenkin, Penelope M. (1902–1994)
Joan (1210–1238)
Joan of the Tower (1321–1362)
Johnstone, Isobel (1781–1857)
Jull, Roberta (1872–1961)
Keith, Margaret (fl. 1395)
Keith, Muriel (d. 1449)
Kelso, Elizabeth (1889–1967)
Kennedy, Helena (1950—)
Kennedy-Fraser, Marjorie (1857–1930)
Kidd, Margaret Henderson (1900–1989)
Kincaid, Jean (1579–1600)
King, Jessie Marion (1875–1949)
Knox, Debbie (1968—)
Knox, Elizabeth (1899–1963)
Knox, Isa (1831–1903)
Lait, Jacqui (1947—)
Lamont, Johann (1957—)
Law, Alice Easton (1870–1942)
Law, Mary Blythe (1873–1955)
Lee, Jane (c. 1912–1957)
Lee, Jennie (1904–1988)
Lee, Mary Isabella (1871–1939)
Leitch, Moira (fl. late 1300s)
Lennox, Annie (1954—)
Lennox, Avril (1956—)
Leveson-Gower, Elizabeth (1765–1839)
Lewis, Agnes Smith (1843–1926)
Liddell, Helen (1950—)
Lindsay, Anne (1750–1825)
Lindsay, Gillian Anne (1973—)
Little, Janet (1759–1813)
Livingstone, Marilyn (1952—)
Lochhead, Liz (1947—)
Loftus, Cissie (1876–1943)
Loftus, Kitty (1867–1927)
Loftus, Marie (1857–1940)
Logan, Ella (1913–1969)
Lorimer, Margaret (1866–1954)
Low, Bet (1924—)
Lucy of Scotland (d. 1090)
Lulu (1948—)
Macarthur, Mary Reid (1880–1921)
MacDonald, Elaine (1943—)
MacDonald, Finula (fl. 1569–1592)
MacDonald, Fiona (1974—)
Macdonald, Flora (1722–1790)
MacDonald, Frances (1874–1921)
Macdonald, Linsey (1964—)
MacDonald, Margo (c. 1948—)
MacInnes, Helen (1907–1985)
Mackay, Elizabeth (c. 1845–1897)
MacKenzie, Jane (1825–1893)
MacKinnon, Joanna (1878–1966)
Mackintosh, Margaret (1865–1933)
Maclean, Kate (1958—)
Maclehose, Agnes (1759–1841)
MacLeod, Mary (c. 1615–c. 1706)
MacLeod, Sheila (1939—)
Macmillan, Chrystal (1871–1937)
Macmillan, Maureen (1943—)
Macphail, Katherine Stewart (1888–1974)
Macquarie, Elizabeth (1778–1835)
MacRobert, Rachel (1884–1954)
Macruari, Amy (fl. 1300s)
Margaret (fl. 1000s)
Margaret (1240–1275)
Margaret (d. 1993)
Margaret, Maid of Norway (c. 1283–1290)
Margaret, St. (c. 1046–1093)
Margaret de Burgh (c. 1193–1259)
Margaret of Denmark (1456–1486)
Margaret of Scotland (1424–1445)
Margaret Tudor (1489–1541)
Marjorie of Carrick (c. 1254–1292)
Marjory (fl. 13th c.)
Marshall, Margaret (1949—)
Marshall, Sheina (1896–1977)
Martin, Rhona (1966—)
Marwick, Tricia (1953—)
Mary (b. 1718)
Mary de Coucy (c. 1220–c. 1260)
Mary of Burgundy (c. 1400–1463)
Mary of Guise (1515–1560)
Mary Stuart (1542–1587)
Mathieson, Catherine (1818–1883)
Matilda of Northumberland (c. 1074–1131)
McAllister, Anne Hunter (1892–1983)
McCoubrey, Margaret (1880–1955)
McDermid, Val (1955—)
McDonald, Agnes (1829–1906)
McGugan, Irene (1952—)
McGuire, Anne (1949—)
McIntosh, Lyndsay (1955—)
McIntyre, Molly (c. 1886–1952)
McKain, Douglas Mary (1789–1873)
McKechin, Ann (1961—)
McKechnie, Sheila (1948–2004)
McKenna, Lesley (1974—)
McKenna, Rosemary (1941—)
McLaren, Agnes (1837–1913)

McLeod, Fiona (1957—)
McLeod, Mrs. (d. 1727)
McMillan, Rachel (1859–1917)
McNeill, Florence Marian (1885–1973)
McNeill, Pauline (c. 1967—)
McVicar, Annie (1862–1954)
Mellanby, Helen (1911–2001)
Millar, Annie Cleland (1855–1939)
Mitchison, Naomi (1897–1999)
M'Lachlan, Jessie (c. 1834–1899)
Moon, Lorna (1886–1930)
Moore, Isabella (1894–1975)
Morris, Margaret (1890–1981)
Morton, Margaret (1968—)
Muir, Elizabeth (d. before 1355)
Muir, Willa (1890–1970)
Mulligan, Mary (1960—)
Murray, Elaine (1954—)
Murray, Elizabeth (1626–1698)
Murray, Yvonne (1964—)
Myles, Lynda (1947—)
Nairne, Carolina (1766–1845)
Neill, Elizabeth Grace (1846–1926)
Newbigin, Marion I. (1869–1934)
Newell, Susan (1893–1923)
Nicol, Helen Lyster (1854–1932)
Nisbet, Mary (1778–1855)
Noble, Mary (1911–2002)
Ogilvie, Catherine (1746–?)
Ogilvie Gordon, Maria M. (1864–1939)
Oldfather, Irene (1954—)
Osborne, Sandra (1956—)
Pagan, Isobel (c. 1742–1821)
Panton, Catherine (1955—)
Parker, Agnes Miller (1895–1980)
Pearson, Molly (d. 1959)
Peattie, Cathy (c. 1956—)
Picking, Anne (1958—)
Pierce, Judith (1930–2003)
Pilcher, Rosamunde (1924—)
Prentice, Bridget (1952—)
Radcliffe, Mary Ann (c. 1746–after 1810)
Radcliffe, Nora (1946—)
Raeburn, Agnes Middleton (1872–1955)
Ramsay, Alison (1959—)
Rankin, Janice (1972—)
Redpath, Anne (1895–1965)
Redpath, Jean (1937—)
Richardson, Effie Newbigging (1849/50?–1928)
Robertson, Agnes (1833–1916)
Robertson, Ann (1825–1922)
Robertson, Jeannie (1908–1975)
Robertson, Margaret Murray (1823–1897)
Robertson, Muriel (1883–1973)
Robertson, Shirley (1968—)
Robison, Shona (1966—)
Ross, Euphemia (d. 1387)
Ross, Euphemia (d. after 1394)
Ross, Ishbel (1895–1975)
Ross, Ishobel (1890–1965)
Salmond, Sarah (1864–1956)
Sampson, Agnes (d. 1591)
Scanlon, Mary (1947—)
Schaw, Janet (d. around 1801)
Scott-Maxwell, Florida (1883–1979)
Sellars, Elizabeth (1923—)
Shaw, Elizabeth (fl. 1500s)
Shearer, Moira
Shepherd, Mary (c. 1780–1847)
Sidgwick, Eleonora Mildred (1845–1936)
Sievwright, Margaret Home (1844–1905)
Sinclair, Catherine (fl. 1475)
Sinclair, Catherine (1780–1864)
Sinclair, Eleanor (d. 1518)
Sinclair, Elizabeth McHutcheson (1800–1892)
Siteman, Isabella Flora (c. 1842–1919)
Slessor, Mary (1848–1915)
Smith, Annie Lorrain (1854–1937)
Smith, Elaine (1963—)
Smith, Madeleine Hamilton (1835–1928)
Smith, Margaret (1961—)
Somerville, Mary Fairfax (1780–1872)
Spence, Catherine (1825–1910)
Spottiswoode, Alicia Ann (1810–1900)
Squire, Rachel (1954—)
St. Denis, Teddie (b. 1909)
Stewart, Annabella (d. after 1471)
Stewart, Anne (fl. 1515)
Stewart, Beatrice (d. around 1424)
Stewart, Catherine Campbell (1881–1957)
Stewart, Egidia (d. after 1388)
Stewart, Egidia
Stewart, Elizabeth (c. 1390–?)
Stewart, Elizabeth (d. before 1411)
Stewart, Elizabeth (fl. 1578)
Stewart, Euphemia (c. 1375–1415)
Stewart, Isabel (d. around 1410)
Stewart, Isabel (fl. 1390–1410)
Stewart, Jean (d. after 1404)
Stewart, Jean (d. 1486)
Stewart, Joan (fl. 15th c.)
Stewart, Katherine (d. after 1394)
Stewart, Margaret (fl. 1350)
Stewart, Margaret (d. before 1456)
Stewart, Margaret (fl. 1460–1520)
Stewart, Marjorie (d. after 1417)
Stewart, Marjory (d. before 1432)
Stewart, Mary (1916—)
Stewart, Mary (c. 1451–1488)
Stewart, Mary (d. 1458)
Stewart, Mary (d. 1465)
Stewart, Olga Margaret (1920–1998)
Stewart, Sarah (1911—)
Stewart, Sophie (1908–1977)
Stewart-Mackenzie, Maria (1783–1862)
Stewart-Murray, Katharine (1874–1960)
Stewart-Richardson, Lady Constance (1883–1932)
Stihler, Catherine (1973—)
Storm, Lesley (1898–1975)
Stuart, Aimée (c. 1885–1981)
Stuart, Frances (1647–1702)
Sturgeon, Nicola (1970—)
Sutherland, Selina Murray McDonald (1839–1909)
Sybilla (d. 1122)
Tattersall, Philippa (c. 1975—)
Taylor, Ann (1947—)
Thompson, Linda (1948—)
Thomson, Elaine (1957—)
Thomson, Muriel (1954—)
Todd, Margaret G. (1859–1918)
Trout, Jenny Kidd (1841–1921)
Ullrich, Kay (1943—)
Ure, Mary (1933–1975)
Vassar, Queenie (1870–1960)
Victoria Adelaide of Schleswig-Holstein (1885–1970)
Villiers, Elizabeth (c. 1657–1733)
Walford, Lucy (1845–1915)
Walker, Ethel (1861–1951)
Walker, Helen (1710–1791)
Walker, Mary Broadfoot (c. 1888–1974)
Walkinshaw, Clementina (c. 1726–1802)
Wallace, Nellie (1870–1948)
Wardlaw, Elizabeth (1677–1727)
Watkins, Margaret (1884–1969)
Webster, Mary McCallum (1906–1985)
Webster, Mary Morison (1894–1980)
Weir, Molly (1910–2004)
West, Elizabeth (fl. early 18th c.)
White, Sandra (1951—)
Whitefield, Karen (1970—)
Whyte, Kathleen (1909–1996)
Wilson, Bertha (1923—)
Wright, Frances (1795–1852)
Yates, Elizabeth (c. 1844–1918)
Yolande de Dreux (d. 1323)
Zinkeisen, Doris (1898–1991)

SCYTHIA

Ancient name of sections of Europe and Asia
See Russia.

SEGOVIA

Commune of Segovia Province in central Spain
Founded (c. 700 BCE)
Taken by Moors (8th c.)
Medieval residence of kings of Castile and León
Sacked by the French (1808)
See Spain.

SELEUCIA

See Asia Minor.
See Syria.

SENECA

Native North American Northeast indigenous group

Jemison, Alice Lee (1901–1964)

SENEGAL

West African republic
Settled by Portuguese (15th c.)
Settled by French (17th c.)
Conflicts between French and Portuguese (18th–19th c.)
Became a republic within French Community (1958)
Member of Mali Federation (1959–1960)
Achieved independence (1960)

Aline Sitoe (c. 1920–1944)
Bâ, Mariama (1929–1981)
Diallo, Nafissatou (1941–1982)
Maiga-Ka, Aminata (1940—)
Sow Fall, Aminata (1941—)
Thiam, Awa (1936—)

SENEGHUN

See Sierra Leone.

SERBIA

A constituent republic of Yugoslavia
Settled by Serbs who were pushed into Moesia by Avars (7th c.)
Part of Byzantine Empire
Became independent (12th c.)
Lost territory to Hungary and Bulgaria
Defeated by Turks (1389)
Part of Ottoman Empire (1459)
Northern Serbia held by Austria (1718–1739)
Independent of Turkey but lost Bosnia and Herzegovina (1878)
Defeated by Bulgaria (1885)
Proclaimed Kingdom of Serbs, Croats, and Slovenes (1918)
Made constituent republic of Yugoslavia (1946)
Achieved independence (1991–1992)

Bugarinovic, Melanija (1905–1986)
Catargi, Marie (fl. 1850s)
Dejanović, Draga (1843–1870)
Dokic, Jelena (1983—)
Draga (1867–1903)
Einstein-Maríc, Mileva (1875–1948)
Maksimovic, Desanka (1898–1993)
Maric, Ljubica (1909–2003)
Markovic, Mirjana (1942—)

Nathalia Keshko (1859–1941)
Nenadovich, Persida (1813–1873)
Nikola, Helene Knez (1765–1842)
Plavsic, Biljana (1930—)
Savić-Rebac, Anica (1892–1935)
Sekulić, Isadora (1877–1958)
Stojadinović-Srpkinja, Milica (1830–1878)

SHEPPEY, ISLE OF

See England.

SHOSHONI

Native North American Great Basin indigenous group

Dann, Mary (d. 2005)
Sacajawea (c. 1787–c. 1812 or 1884)

SHREWSBURY

Borough of Shropshire in western England
See England.

SICILY

Largest island in Mediterranean Sea
Inhabited by Sicani
Settled by Greeks (8th c. BCE)
Conquered by Rome (3rd c. BCE)
Part of Vandal and Ostrogothic kingdoms and of Byzantine Empire
Overrun by Muslims (9th c. CE)
Conquered by Normans who founded Kingdom of Two Sicilies (1072–1091)
Conquered by Charles of Anjou, who was expelled from Sicily (13th c.)
Ruled by house of Aragon (until 1302)
Reunited with Naples (15th c.)
Held by Spain, Savoy, and Austria (18th c.)
Received autonomy (1948)

Adelaide of Savona (d. 1118)
Agatha, Saint (d. 251)
Maria of Aragon (fl. 1311)
Maria of Sicily (d. 1402)
Maria Sophia Amalia (1841–1925)
Marie Isabella of Spain (1789–1848)
Migliaccio, Lucia (1770–1826)
Pia of Sicily (1849–1882)
Theresa of Austria (1816–1867)
Virdimura of Sicily (fl. 1376)
Yolande of Aragon (1379–1442)

SIERRA LEONE

West African republic
Visited by Portuguese (15th c.)
Settlements for runaway and freed slaves established by English (18th c.)
Proclaimed a French protectorate (1896)
Achieved independence (1961)
Became a republic (1971)

Casely-Hayford, Adelaide (1868–1960)
Casely-Hayford, Gladys (1904–1950)
Yoko (c. 1849–1906)

SIGMARINGEN

City in Baden-Württemberg in western Germany
See Germany.

SIKKIM

Cooke, Hope (1940—)

SILESIA

Region in eastern central Europe
See Czechoslovakia.
See Germany.
See Poland.

SINGAPORE

Baker, Carlee (1978—)
Chand, Meira (1942—)
Choy, Elizabeth (b. 1910)

SLOVAKIA

Republic in eastern Europe
Settled by Slovaks (6th–7th c.)
Part of Great Moravia (9th c.)
Conquered by Magyars (10th c.)
Part of Kingdom of Hungary (until 1918)
Joined Czechs in forming Czechoslovakia (1918)
Achieved atonomy (1938)
Established as constituent republic of Czechoslovakia (1945)
Achieved independence (1993)
See also Czechoslovakia.
See also Hungary.

Bukovec, Brigita (1970—)
Figuli, Margita (1909–1995)
Jurca, Branca (1914—)
Kaliska, Elena (1972—)
Moravcova, Martina (1976—)
Reik, Haviva (1914–1944)
Slancikova, Bozena (1867–1951)
Svobodova, Martina (1983—)
Vadkerti-Gavorníková, Lydia (1932–1999)
Vansova, Terezia (1857–1942)
Zelinová, Hana (1914—)

SLOVENIA

Ceplak, Jolanda (1976—)
Dovzan, Alenka (1976—)
Koren, Katja (1975—)
Svet, Mateja (1968—)
Zolner, Urska (1982—)

SOMALIA

Dirie, Waris (1967—)
Tonelli, Annalena (1943–2003)

SOMERSET

County in southwestern England
See England.

SONDERBURG

Former county in Denmark
See Denmark.

SOUTH AFRICA

Republic in southern Africa
Dutch East India Company arrived at Cape of Good Hope (1652)
British forces occupied Cape (1795 and 1806)
Cape region ceded by Dutch to British (1814)
Dutch settlers (Boers or Afrikaaners) left Cape, founded Orange Free State and Transvall (1836)
British declared coastal region of Natal a crown colony (1843)
Natal annexed to Cape Colony (1844)
Natal split from Cape Colony (1856)
British annexed Bechuanaland (1885)
British annexed South African Republic (1877)
Boers defeated in South African War (1899–1902)
Orange Free State and Transvall annexed by British (1902)
Apartheid instituted (1948–1993)
Rejoined Commonwealth of Nations (1994)

Abernethy, Moira (1939—)
Ames, Frances (1920–2002)
Aron, Geraldine (1941—)
Baard, Francina (1901–1997)
Ballinger, Margaret (1894–1980)
Barbieri, Margaret (1947—)
Becker, Jillian (1932—)
Bedford, Marie (1907—)
Benson, Mary (1919–2000)
Bergsma, Deanne (1941—)
Bernard, Dorothy (1890–1955)
Bernstein, Hilda (1915—)
Blackburn, Molly (c. 1931–1985)
Bliss, Anna (1843–1925)
Botha, Wendy (1965—)
Brand, Esther (1924—)
Bryceland, Yvonne (1926–1992)
Budd, Zola (1966—)
Burgess, Yvonne (1936—)
Clark, Marjorie (b. 1909)
Cloete, Hestrie (1978—)
Coetzer, Amanda (1971—)
Coles, Joyce (b, around 1904)
Courtenay-Latimer, Marjorie (1907–2004)
Couzyn, Jeni (1942—)
Cussons, Sheila (1922–2004)
De Brémont, Anna (1864–1922)
De Casalis, Jeanne (1897–1966)
de Keyser, Ethel (1926–2004)
de Klerk, Marike (1937–2001)
De Melker, Daisy Louisa (1886–1932)
De Mist, Augusta (1783–1832)
De Reuck, Colleen (1964—)
Derman, Vergie (1942—)
Duncan, Sheena (1932—)
Eybers, Elisabeth (1915—)
Fassie, Brenda (1964–2004)
Fawcett, Philippa (1868–1948)
Ferguson, Abbie Park (1837–1919)
First, Ruth (1925–1982)
Fugard, Sheila (1932—)
Gibson, Perla Siedle (d. 1971)
Gordimer, Nadine (1923—)
Goudvis, Bertha (1876–1966)
Grahame, Margot (1911–1982)
Groesbeek, Maria (1937–1970)
Grové, Henriette (1922—)
Haddon, Eileen (1921–2003)
Harrison, Joan (1935—)
Hasenjager-Robb, Daphne (1929—)
Head, Bessie (1937–1986)
Heyns, Penny (1974—)
Howes, Dulcie (1908–1993)
Jabavu, Noni (1919—)
Jonker, Ingrid (1933–1965)
Joseph, Helen (1905–1992)
Joubert, Elsa (1922—)
Karodia, Farida (1942—)
Kriel, Marianne
Kuper, Hilda B. (1911–1992)
Kuzwayo, Ellen (1914–2006)
Lane, Maryon (1931—)
Lipkin, Jean (1926—)
Lister, Moira (1923—)
Little, Sally (1951—)
Livingstone, Mary Moffatt (1820–1862)
Lloyd, Maude (1908–2004)
Lorrayne, Vyvyan (1939—)
Louw, Anna M. (1913–2003)
Maakal, Jenny (1913—)
Machel, Graca (1946—)
Madikizela-Mandela, Winnie (1934—)
Magogo ka Dinizulu, Constance (1900–1984)
Makeba, Miriam (1932—)
Mason, Monica (1941—)
Meer, Fatima (1928—)
Meyer, Elana (1966—)
Miller, Patricia (1927—)
Miller, Ruth (1919–1969)
Millin, Sarah (1888–1968)
Mitford, Unity (1914–1948)
Mmanthatisi (c. 1780–c. 1836)
Mntwana, Ida (1903–1960)
Moggridge, Jackie (1922–2004)
Mounsey, Yvonne (c. 1921—)
Myburgh, Jeanette (1940—)

Geographic Index

Myburgh, Natalie (1940—)
Nandi (c. 1760s–1827)
Naudé, Adèle (1910–1981)
Nerina, Nadia (1927—)
Ngcobo, Lauretta (1932—)
Ngoyi, Lilian (1911–1980)
Nonteta Bungu (c. 1875–1935)
Nyembe, Dorothy (1930–1998)
Packer, Joy (1905–1977)
Prowse, Juliet (1936–1996)
Rainier, Priaulx (1903–1986)
Ramphele, Mamphela (1947—)
Rathebe, Dolly (1928–2004)
Rennie, Rhoda
Roberts, Sheila (1937—)
Roberts, Susan (1939—)
Rooke, Daphne (1914—)
Rothmann, Maria Elisabeth (1875–1975)
Russell, Kathleen
Sagan, Leontine (1889–1974)
Salmons, Josephine (b. 1904)
Schreiner, Olive (1855–1920)
Scott, Margaret (1922—)
September, Dulcie (1935–1988)
Sikakane, Joyce Nomafa (1943—)
Silinga, Annie (1910–1983)
Sisulu, Albertina (1918—)
Slater, Frances Charlotte (1892–1947)
Smith, Pauline (1882–1959)
Stern, Irma (1894–1966)
Stockenström, Wilma (1933—)
Stoneman, Bertha (1866–1943)
Suzman, Helen (1917—)
Suzman, Janet (1939—)
Tlali, Miriam (1933—)
van der Goes, Frederica
Vrba, Elisabeth (1942—)
Ward, Harriet (1808–c. 1860)
Webster, Mary Morison (1894–1980)
Weston, Cecil (1889–1976)
Wilman, Maria (1867–1957)
Wilson, Ethel (1888–1980)
Wilson, Monica Hunter (1908–1982)
Winterbach, Ingrid (1948—)
Zwi, Rose (1928—)

SOUTH-WEST AFRICA

Territory in southwest Africa
Annexed by Germany (1885)
Captured from South Africa in World War I
To South Africa as a mandate from League of Nations (1919)
Mandate terminated (1966)
Called Namibia by United Nations

Abrahams, Ottilie Grete (1937—)
Amathila, Libertine Appolus (1940—)

SOVIET UNION

See Russia, Soviet

SPAIN

Kingdom in southwestern Europe
Southern and eastern coasts colonized by Phoenicians and Greeks
Mediterranean coastal region ruled by Carthage and ceded to Rome (201 BCE)
Tarraconensis, Boetica, and Lusitania provinces of Roman Empire
Invaded by Vandals (409)
Toledo seat of Visigothic kingdom (534–712)
Conquered by Muslims from North Africa (711–719)
Most of Spain ruled by Ommiad dynasty of Córdoba (756–1031)
Northern states Christian (Asturias, León, Galicia, Navarre, Barcelona)
Moorish Spain ruled by Almoravides (after 1090)
Moorish Spain ruled by Almohades (after 1147)
Moorish Spain gradually reconquered by Christian states of Castile and Aragon
Spain united (1479)
Conquered Granada, last kingdom of Moors (1492)
Annexed southern Navarre (1515)
Part of Holy Roman Empire (1519)
Acquired large colonial empire in New World, Philippines, and Northern Africa (16th c.)
Lost territory to France (17th c.)
Relinquished central Italian holdings for Kingdom of the Two Sicilies (1735–1738)
Established first republic (1873–1874)
Lost Cuba, Puerto Rico, Philippines, and Guam to United States (1898)
Established second republic (1931)
Joined United Nations (1955)
Adopted new constitution (1966)
Monarchy returned (1975)

Abarca, Maria Francisca de (fl. 1640–1656)
Acedo, Carmen (1975—)
Acevedo, Angela de (d. 1644)
Agnes de Poitiers (fl. 1135)
Agnes of Poitou (1052–1078)
Agostina (1788–1857)
Agreda, Sor María de (1602–1665)
Albert, Caterina (1869–1966)
Alcantara, Dolores Jimenez (1909–1999)
Aldecoa, Josefina R. (1926—)
Alós, Concha (1922—)
Alozie, Glory (1977—)
Alvarez, Lili de (1905—)
Alvarez de Toledo, Luisa Isabel (1936—)
Amaya, Carmen (1913–1963)
Andreu, Blanca (1959—)
Anglada, Maria Angels (1930–1999)
Anne of Austria (c. 1550–1580)
Anne of Austria (1601–1666)
Arderiu, Clementina (1899–1976)
Arenal, Concepción (1820–1893)
Arquimbau, Rosa Maria (1910—)
Atencia, Maria Victoria (1931—)
Avilés Perea, María Antonia
Ayuso González, María del Pilar (1942—)
Azon, Sandra (1973—)
Baldo, Marta
Ballesteros, Mercedes (1913–1995)
Barea Cobos, Maria (1966—)
Barrientos, Maria (1884–1946)
Barrio Gutierrez, Sonia (1969—)
Beatrice of Swabia (1198–1235)
Beatrix da Silva (1424–1490)
Beatriz of Spain (1909–2002)
Berengaria of Castile (1180–1246)
Berengaria of Navarre (c. 1163–c. 1230)
Berengaria of Provence (1108–1149)
Berganza, Teresa (1934—)
Bertha of Burgundy (d. 1097)
Bertrana, Aurora (1899–1974)
Blanche of Bourbon (c. 1338–1361)
Blanche of Naples (d. 1310)
Blanche of Navarre (d. 1158)
Blanche of Navarre (1424–1464)
Blasco Soto, Miriam (1963—)
Böhl von Faber, Cecilia (1796–1877)
Bonaparte, Julie Clary (1771–1845)
Bori, Lucrezia (1887–1960)
Burgos Seguí, Carmen de (1867–1932)
Caballé, Montserrat (1933—)
Cabanillas, Nuria (1980—)
Cajal, Rosa María (1920—)
Calvé, Emma (1858–1942)
Calvo de Aguilar, Isabel (1916—)
Camargo, Marie-Anne Cupis de (1710–1770)
Campoamor, Clara (1888–1972)
Cansino, Elisa (b. 1895)
Capmany Farnes, Maria Aurèlia (1918—)
Caro Mallén de Soto, Ana (c. 1590–1650)
Cartagena, Teresa de (c. 1420–1470)
Carvajal, Mariana de (c. 1620–1680)
Casares, Maria (1922–1996)
Castro, Inez de (c. 1320–1355)
Castroviejo, Concha (1915–1995)
Catalina (1403–1439)
Catherine of Lancaster (1372–1418)
Cayetana, Maria del Pilar Teresa (1762–1802)
Cayetana Fitz-James Stuart y Silva, Maria del Rosario (1926—)
Cerdeira Morterero, Carmen (1958—)
Chacel, Rosa (1898–1994)
Chacón, Dulce (1954–2003)
Chinchon, Ana, countess of (1576–1639)
Coghen Alberdingk, Mercedes (1962—)
Colbran, Isabella (1785–1845)
Columba of Cordova (d. 853)
Columba of Sens (d. 274?)
Conde, Carmen (1907–1996)
Constance of Aragon (d. 1283)
Constance of Aragon (d. 1327)
Constance of Aragon (c. 1350–?)
Constance of Burgundy (1046–c. 1093)
Constance of Castile (1354–1394)
Constance of Sicily (d. 1302)
Constance of Toulouse (fl. 12th century)
Coronado, Carolina (1820–1911)
Cristina (1965—)
Crusat, Paulina (1900–1981)
Dali, Gala (1894–1982)
de la Cerda, Blanche (c. 1311–1347)
Del Vando, Amapola (1910–1988)
Diaz, Jimena (fl. 1074–1100)
Díez González, Rosa M. (1952—)
Diosdado, Ana (1938—)
Domenech i Escate de Canellas, Maria (1877–1952)
Dorado Gomez, Natalia (1967—)
Dührkop Dührkop, Bárbara (1945—)
Egeria (fl. 4th c.)
Egual, Maria (1698–1735)
Eleanor of Albuquerque (1374–1435)
Eleanor of Aragon (1358–1382)
Eleanor of Castile (1162–1214)
Eleanor of Castile (1202–1244)
Eleanor of Castile (1241–1290)
Eleanor of Castile (1307–1359)
Eleanor of Navarre (1425–1479)
Eleanor of Portugal (1328–1348)
Eleanor of Sicily (d. 1375)
Eleanor Trastamara (d. 1415)
Elena (1963—)
Elizabeth of Valois (1545–1568)
Elizabeth Valois (1602–1644)
Elvira (1038–1101)
Elvira Gonzalez of Galicia (d. 1022)
Ena (1887–1969)
Enríquez de Guzmán, Feliciana (c. 1580–1640)
Erauso, Catalina de (1592–1635)
Espert, Nuria (1935—)
Espina, Concha (1869–1955)
Estefania of Barcelona (fl. 1038)
Eulalia (1864–1958)
Falcón, Lidia (1935—)
Falkenburg, Jinx (1919–2003)
Farnese, Elizabeth (1692–1766)
Farrés, Carmen (1931–1976)
Fernandez, Isabel (1972—)
Fernández Ochoa, Blanca (1963—)
Ferrer, Concepció (1938—)
Ferrer Salat, Beatriz (1966—)
Figueras-Dotti, Marta (1957—)
Flora of Cordova (d. 851)
Florentina (d. 7th c.)

Flores, Lola (1924–1995)
Foix, Germaine de (1488–1538)
Fórmica, Mercedes (1916—)
Fornaroli, Cia (1888–1954)
Franco, Carmen Polo de (1902–1988)
Fuertes, Gloria (1917–1998)
Fullana, Margarita (1972—)
Gabellanes Marieta, Nagore (1973—)
Galiana
Galindo, Beatriz (1475–1534)
Galvarriato, Eulalia (1905–1997)
Garcia, Sancha (fl. 1230)
García-Orcoyen Tormo, Cristina (1948—)
Garro, Elena (1916–1998)
Gersenda (fl. 1000)
Gilberga (d. 1054)
Gimenez, Estela
Godden, Rumer (1907–1998)
Gomez, Elena (1985—)
Gómez de Avellaneda, Gertrudis (1814–1873)
González Álvarez, Laura (1941—)
Gonzalez Laguillo, Maria (1961—)
Guerra Cabrera, Patricia (1965—)
Guerrero, Maria (1867–1928)
Guidosalvi, Sancia (fl. early 12th c.)
Guilló, Magdalena (1940—)
Gurendez, Lorena (1981—)
Gutiérrez-Cortines, Cristina (1939—)
Guy-Stéphan, Marie (1818–1873)
Guzman, Eleonore de (d. 1512)
Guzman, Leonora de (1310–1351)
Guzman, Mayor de (d. 1262)
Hernandez, Angela (c. 1949—)
Herranz García, Maria Esther (1969—)
Herrera Garrido, Francisca (1869–1950)
Hidalgo, Elvira de (1892–1980)
Horna, Kati (1912–2000)
Ibárruri, Dolores (1895–1989)
Icaza, Carmen de (1899–1979)
Iolande of Hungary (1215–1251)
Irene of Santarem (fl. 7th c.)
Irene of Spain (fl. 300s)
Isabella Clara Eugenia of Austria (1566–1633)
Isabella I (1451–1504)
Isabella II (1830–1904)
Isabella of Parma (1741–1763)
Isabella of Portugal (1503–1539)
Isabel of Castile (1355–1392)
Isabel of Portugal (1428–1496)
Isabel of Urgel (fl. 1065)
Iturbi, Amparo (1898–1969)
Izquierdo Rojo, Maria (1946—)
Janés, Clara (1940—)
Jiménez, Soledad (1874–1966)
Joanna Enriquez (1425–1468)
Joanna of Castile (1339–1381)
Joanna of Ponthieu (d. 1279)
Joanna of Portugal (1439–1475)
Juana la Beltraneja (1462–1530)
Juana la Loca (1479–1555)
Karr, Carme (1865–1943)
Kent, Victoria (1898–1987)
Kurtz, Carmen (1911—)
Kurtz, Carmen (1911–1999)
Laffitte, María (1902–1986)
Laforet, Carmen (1921–2004)
Lamarca, Tania (1980—)
Larrocha, Alicia de (1923—)
Leocadia (d. about 303)
Leodegundia (fl. 10th c.)
León, Maria Teresa (1903–1988)
Lloret, Maria Isabel (1971—)
López de Córdoba, Leonor (1362–1412)
Lorengar, Pilar (1928—)
Los Angeles, Victoria de (1923–2005)
Louise Elizabeth (1709–1750)
Luisa Fernanda (1832–1897)
Maiques Dern, Ana (1967—)
Malibran, Maria (1808–1836)
Manrique Perez, Silvia (1973—)
Maragall Verge, Elisabeth (1970—)
March, Susana (1918–1991)
Margaret of Austria (c. 1577–1611)
Margarita Maria (1939—)
Maria Amalia of Saxony (1724–1760)
Maria Anna of Austria (c. 1634–1696)
Maria Anna of Neuberg (1667–1740)
Maria Barbara of Braganza (1711–1758)
Maria Beatrice of Modena (1750–1829)
Maria Christina of Austria (1858–1929)
Maria Cristina (1911–1996)
Maria Cristina I of Naples (1806–1878)
Maria de la Paz (1862–1946)
Maria de las Mercedes (1860–1878)
Maria de las Mercedes (1880–1904)
Maria de las Mercedes (1910–2000)
Maria de Molina (d. 1321)
Maria do Céu (1658–1753)
Maria Isabel Francisca (1851–1931)
Maria Josepha of Saxony (1803–1829)
Maria Luisa Teresa of Parma (1751–1819)
Mariana of Jesus (1565–1624)
Maria of Aragon (1403–1445)
Maria of Castile (1401–1458)
Maria of Cordova (d. 851)
Maria of Montpellier (1181–1213)
Maria of Navarre (fl. 1340)
Maria Teresa (1882–1912)
Marie de Padilla (1335–1361)
Marie Louise d'Orleans (1662–1689)
Marie Louise of Savoy (1688–1714)
Martinez, Conchita (1972—)
Martinez, Estibaliz
Martínez Sierra, Maria de la O (1874–1974)
Martín Gaite, Carmen (1925—)
Matilda of Narbonne (d. after 1348)
Matute, Ana Maria (1926—)
Maura, Carmen (1945—)
Mauri, Rosita (1856–1923)
Medio, Dolores (1914–1996)
Meller, Raquel (1888–1962)
Mendoza, Ana de (1540–1592)
Miguélez Ramos, Rosa (1953—)
Miró, Pilar (1940–1997)
Monserdà de Macía, Dolors (1845–1919)
Montez, Maria (1918–1951)
Montiel, Sarita (1928—)
Montoriol i Puig, Carme (1893–1966)
Montseny, Federica (1905–1994)
Mora, Constancia de la (1906–1950)
Moreno, Patricia (1988—)
Motos Iceta, Teresa (1963—)
Mulder, Elisabeth (1904–1987)
Munia Elvira (995–1067)
Muñoz, Jimena (c. 1065–1128)
Munoz Martinez, Almudena (1968—)
Muria, Anna (1904–2002)
Nelken, Margarita (1896–1968)
Neumann, Liselotte (1966—)
Nillson, Carlotta (c. 1878–1951)
Nilsmark, Catrin (1967—)
Nilsson, Karin (b. 1904)
Nordin, Hjoerdis (1932—)
Noren, Svea (1895–1985)
Nyberg, Katarina (1965—)
Ochoa, Blanca Fernández (c. 1964—)
Odena, Lina (1911–1936)
Olive Vancells, Nuria (1968—)
Orantes, Ana (c. 1937–1997)
Ortiz, Letizia (1972—)
Otero, Caroline (1868–1965)
Paca (1825–1860)
Padilla, Maria Pacheco (c. 1496–1531)
Palencia, Isabel de (1878–c. 1950)
Palmolive (1955—)
Pàmies, Teresa (1919—)
Pardo Bazán, Emilia (1852–1921)
Pascual, Carolina (1976—)
Patti, Adelina (1843–1919)
Pepa, Mari (1913–2004)
Perez, Maria (fl. 13th c.)
Peri Rossi, Cristina (1941—)
Pino, Rosario (d. 1933)
Plá, Josefina (1909–1999)
Placencia (fl. 1068)
Pompeia, Núria (1938—)
Portal, Marta (1930—)
Primo de Rivera, Pilar (1913–1991)
Queizán, María Xosé (1938—)
Quintanal, Maria (1969—)
Quiroga, Elena (1919–1995)
Ramirez Merino, Virginia (1964—)
Redondo Jiménez, Encarnación (1944—)
Resino, Carmen (1941—)
Ridruejo, Mónica (1963—)
Rodoreda, Mercè (1909–1983)
Rodríguez Ramos, María (1963—)
Rodriguez Suarez, Maria (1957—)
Roldán, Luisa (1656–1704)
Ruano Pascual, Virginia (1973—)
Rueda, Eva (1971—)
Ryksa of Poland (d. 1185)
Sabuco, Oliva de Nantes Barrera (1562–1625)
Saenz-Alonso, Mercedes (1916–2000)
Salisachs, Mercedes (1916—)
Sancha de Aybar (fl. 11th c.)
Sancha of Castile and Leon (1164–1208)
Sancha of Leon (1013–1067)
Sánchez, Cristina (1972—)
San Félix, Sor Marcela de (1605–1688)
Sauquillo Pérez Del Arco, Francisca (1943—)
Serrahima, Nuria (1937—)
Serrano, Eugenia (1918—)
Sevilla, Carmen (1930—)
Sigea, Luisa (c. 1531–1560)
Silang, Gabriela (1731–1763)
Sinués, Maria del Pilar (1835–1893)
Six Wives of Henry VIII
Soler, Yolanda
Sophia of Greece (1938—)
Soriano, Elena (1917–1996)
Sornosa Martínez, María (1949—)
Supervia, Conchita (1895–1936)
Telleria Goni, Maider (1973—)
Teresa de Cartagena (fl. 1400)
Teresa of Avila (1515–1582)
Terrón i Cusí, Anna (1962—)
Theresa Henriques (c. 1176–1250)
Tiedemann, Charlotte (1919–1979)
Torres, Xohana (1931—)
Trava, Teresa Fernandez de (fl. 1170)
Tusquets, Esther (1936—)
Urraca (1033–1101)
Urraca (c. 1079–1126)
Urraca of Castile (d. 1179)
Urraca of Castile (c. 1186–1220)
Urraca of Portugal (c. 1151–1188)
Valenciano Martínez-Orozco, María Elena (1960—)
Valentí, Helena (1940—)
Varo, Remedios (1906–1963)
Vasco, María (1975—)
Vega, Elvira de la (fl. late 1300s)
Ventós i Cullell, Palmira (1862–1917)

Via Dufresne, Begona (1971—)
Via Dufresne, Natalia (1973—)
Viardot, Pauline (1821–1910)
Villena, Isabel de (1430–1490)
Wallada (fl. 11th c.)
Xirinacs, Olga (1936—)
Yolande of Aragon (d. 1300)
Zabell, Theresa (1965—)
Zambrano, María (1904–1991)
Zardoya, Concha (1914—)
Zayas y Sotomayor, María de (1590–c. 1650)
Zhivanevskaya, Nina (1977—)

SRI LANKA

See also Ceylon.

Jayasinghe, Susanthika (1975—)
Wijenaike, Punyakanthi (1935—)

STAFFORD

Borough of Staffordshire in western central England
See England.

STRASSBURG

City of Bas-Rhin department in northeastern France
Celtic settlement passed to Romans
Destroyed by Attila
Restored by Franks (5th c.)
Linked to Germany (10th c.)
Occupied by French (1681)
Ceded to French (1697)
Under German rule (1871–1918)
See France.
See Germany.

STYRIA

Austrian state
Part of Carinthia under Charlemagne (9th c.)
Became separate as a mark (1085)
Became a duchy (1180)
Came under Habsburgs (1246)
See Austria.

SUDAN

Republic in northeastern Africa
Conquered by Egypt under Hussein (1820–1822)
Ravaged by slave trade
Jointly administered by Egypt and Britain (after 1899)
Achieved independence (1956)
Purged Communists (1971)

Arol, Victoria Yar (1948—)
Kéita, Aoua (1912–1979)

SUFFOLK

County in eastern England
See England.

SUMER

Southern division of ancient Babylonia
Kingdom of non-Semitic people (c. 4000 BCE)
United gradually with Akkadians (c. 2600–2400 BCE)
Combined empire overcome by Semitic Babylonian kingdom (c. 1950 BCE)
See Babylonia.

SUNDERLAND

County borough of Durham in northern England
See England.

SURREY

Former county in southeastern England
See England.

SUSA

Ancient city of Elam in Babylonia
Winter residence of Achaemenian kings (7th–4th c. BCE)
Made Persian capital
See Babylonia.

SWABIA

Duchy in medieval Germany
Conquered by the Franks (5th c.)
Became a duchy (10th c.)
Ruled by Hohenstaufen kings and emperors (1105–1254)
Divided (1268)
Leagues of Swabian cities formed (1331 and 1488–1534)
See Germany.

SWAZILAND

South African kingdom
Settled by Swazi branch of Zulu nation (1880s)
Following Boer War, administered by British governor of Transvaal (1899–1902)
Achieved independence (1968)

Kuper, Hilda B. (1911–1992)
Labotsibeni Gwamile laMdluli (c. 1858–1925)
Makhubu, Lydia (1937—)

SWEDEN

Kingdom in northwestern Europe
Inhabitants among Scandinavian raiders (9th c.)
United and converted to Christianity (11th c.)
Conquered Finns (12th c.)
United with Denmark and Norway (1397)
Broke away under house of Vasa (1523–1654)
Sweden began expansion
Defeated in Great Northern War and lost most German territories (1700–1721)
Exchanged Pomerania for Norway (1814)
Acknowledged independence of Norway (1905)

Aakesson, Birgit (1908–2001)
ABBA (1974–1982)
Adlerstrahle, Maertha (1868–1956)
Ahlander, Thecla (1855–1925)
Akesson, Sonja (1926–1977)
Albertina of Baden-Durlach (1682–1755)
Albertine (1753–1829)
Alshammar, Therese (1977—)
Anckarsvard, Karin (1915–1969)
Anderson, Mary (1872–1964)
Andersson, Agneta (1961—)
Andersson, Bibi (1935—)
Andersson, Gerd (1932—)
Andersson, Harriet (1932—)
Andree, Elfrida (1841–1929)
Anna of Styria (1573–1598)
Ann-Margret (1941—)
Ari, Carina (1897–1970)
Asp, Anna (1946—)
Astrid of Sweden (1905–1935)
Astrid of the Obotrites (c. 979–?)
Av-Paul, Annette (1944—)
Backander, Helge (1891–1958)
Baryard, Malin (1975—)
Beatrice of Wittelsbach (1344–1359)
Benedictsson, Victoria (1850–1888)
Bengtsson, Birgitta (1965—)
Berg, Aina (b. 1902)
Berggren, Evy (1934—)
Bergman, Ingrid (1915–1982)
Bergqvist, Kajsa (1976—)
Beskow, Elsa (1874–1953)
Birgitta of Sweden (1937—)
Björk, Anita (1923—)
Blanche of Namur (d. 1363)
Blomberg, Vanja (1929—)
Borgström, Hilda (1871–1953)
Bosse, Harriet (1878–1961)
Boye, Karin (1900–1941)
Brandstrom, Elsa (1888–1948)
Branzell, Karin (1891–1974)
Bremer, Fredrika (1801–1865)
Bridget of Sweden (1303–1373)
Britt, May (1933—)
Bullinger, Anna (c. 1504–1564)
Bylund, Ingamay (1949—)
Carlén, Emilia (1807–1892)
Carlén, Rosa (1836–1883)
Catherine Jagello (1525–1583)
Catherine of Sweden (c. 1330–1381)
Cederqvist, Jane (1945—)
Cederschiöld, Charlotte (1944—)
Charlotte of Oldenburg (1759–1818)
Cherry, Neneh (1963—)
Christina Bernadotte (b. 1943)
Christina of Holstein-Gottorp (1573–1625)
Christina of Sweden (1626–1689)
Christina Stigsdottir (fl. 1160s)
Cullberg, Birgit (1908–1999)
Dahlbeck, Eva (1920—)
Désirée (1777–1860)
Desiree Bernadotte (1938—)
Dorothea of Brandenburg (1430–1495)
Edgren, Anne Charlotte (1849–1892)
Edla (fl. 900s)
Edstrom, Sonja
Ekberg, Anita (1931—)
Ekman, Kirsten (1933—)
Engquist, Ludmila (1964—)
Ericsson, Ingela (1968—)
Eriksson, Agneta (1965—)
Eriksson, Anna-Lisa
Eriksson, Marianne (1952—)
Eugenie (1830–1889)
Euphemia (1317–after 1336)
Everlund, Gurli (1902–1985)
Fältskog, Agnetha (1950—)
Fick, Sigrid (1887–1979)
Forsberg, Magdalena (1967—)
Frederica Dorothea of Baden (1781–1826)
Fredriksson, Marie (1958—)
Fremstad, Olive (1871–1951)
Friederike of Hesse-Cassel (1722–1787)
Garbo, Greta (1905–1990)
Gard'ner, Elizabeth Anne (1858–1926)
Gentzel, Inga (1908–1991)
Gripe, Maria (1923—)
Grönfeldt Bergman, Lisbeth (1948—)
Gulbranson, Ellen (1863–1947)
Gunnarsson, Susanne (1963—)
Gustafson, Elisabet (1964—)
Gustafsson, Tina (1962—)
Gustafsson, Toini (1938—)
Gylling, Jane (1902–1961)
Hagan, Ellen (1873–1958)
Haglund, Maria (1972—)
Hakanson, Ulla (1937—)
Hansen, Pia (1965—)
Hasselqvist, Jenny (1894–1978)
Hasso, Signe (1910—)
Hatz, Elizabeth (1952—)
Hedberg, Doris (1936—)
Hedkvist Petersen, Ewa (1952—)
Hedman, Martha (1883–1974)
Hedwig of Holstein (d. 1325)
Hedwig of Holstein-Gottorp (1636–1715)
Hedwig Sophia (1681–1708)
Helen (fl. 1100s)
Henning, Eva (1920—)
Hermodsson, Elisabet Hermine (1927—)
Hesselgren, Kerstin (1872–1962)
Hulten, Vivi-Anne (1911–2003)
Ingeborg (d. 1254)
Ingeborg of Denmark (1878–1958)
Ingeborg of Sweden (fl. 1070)
Ingigerd Olafsdottir (c. 1001–1050)

Jacobsson, Ulla (1929–1982)
Johanson, Margareta (1895–1978)
Johansson, Irma
Johansson, Ronny (b. 1891)
Jöhncke, Louise (1976—)
Jonsson, Magdalena (1969—)
Josephine Beauharnais (1807–1876)
Julin-Mauroy, Magda (1894–1990)
Kammerling, Anna-Karin (1980—)
Karlen, Maud (1932—)
Karlsson, Eva (1961—)
Katarina of Saxe-Lüneburg (1513–1535)
Katarina Stenbock (1536–1621)
Key, Ellen (1849–1926)
Kluft, Carolina (1983—)
Knape, Ulrika (1955—)
Kock, Karin (1891–1976)
Kristina (fl. 1150)
Krusenstjerna, Agnes von (1894–1940)
Lagerlöf, Selma (1858–1940)
Lang, Maria (1948—)
Lathgertha (b. around 665)
Leander, Zarah (1907–1981)
Lenngren, Anna Maria (1754–1817)
Leyman, Ann-Britt (1922—)
Lidman, Sara (1923–2004)
Lind, Jenny (1820–1887)
Lindahl, Margaretha (c. 1971—)
Lindberg, Karin (1929—)
Lindblom, Gunnel (1931—)
Lindfors, Viveca (1920–1995)
Lindgren, Astrid (1907–2002)
Lindgren, Marie
Lindh, Anna (1957–2003)
Ljungdahl, Carina (1960—)
Louisa Ulrica of Prussia (1720–1782)
Louise Mountbatten (1889–1965)
Louise of the Netherlands (1828–1871)
Lundberg, Emma (1881–1954)
Lundequist, Gerda (1871–1959)
Lyngstad, Frida (1945—)
Maansdatter, Katherine (1550–1612)
Maas-Fjetterstrom, Marta (1873–1941)
Machnow, Emy (1897–1974)
Madeleine (b. 1982)
Malmström, Cecilia (1968—)
Margareta Leijonhufvud (1514–1551)
Margaret Bernadotte (1934—)
Margaretha of Sweden (1899–1977)
Margaret of Connaught (1882–1920)
Maria Eleonora of Brandenburg (1599–1655)
Marmont, Louise (1967—)
Martensson, Agneta (1961—)
Martha of Denmark (c. 1272–1341)
Martinson, Moa (1890–1964)
Martinsson, Barbro
Merete Ulfsdatter (fl. 1320–1370)
Molander, Karin (1889–1978)
Montgomery, Charlotte (1958—)
Myrdal, Alva (1902–1986)
Nathhorst, Louise (1955—)
Nilsson, Anna Q. (1889–1974)
Nilsson, Birgit (1918–2005)
Nilsson, Christine (1843–1921)
Norelius, Martha (1908–1955)
Odhnoff, Camilla (1923—)
Olin, Lena (1955—)
Olliwier, Eva (1904–1955)
Olsson, Anna (1964—)
Orlando, Mariane (1934—)
Ottesen-Jensen, Elise (1886–1973)
Paerson, Anja (1981—)
Paulsen, Marit (1939—)
Persson, Elisabeth (1964—)
Pettersson, Ann-Sofi (1932—)
Pettersson, Goeta (1926—)
Pettersson, Wivan (1904–1976)
Philippa (1394–1430)
Pleijel, Agneta (1940—)
Regnell, Lisa (1887–1979)
Richizza of Denmark (d. 1220)
Roenstroem, Eva (1932—)
Roering, Gun (1930—)
Rosenqvist, Susanne (1967—)
Sandberg-Fries, Yvonne (1950—)
Schörling, Inger (1946—)
Sigurdsen, Gertrud (1923—)
Silvia Sommerlath (1943—)
Sjöberg, Johanna (1978—)
Sjoeqvist, Laura (1903–1964)
Sköld, Berit (1939—)
Söderbaum, Kristina (1912—)
Söderström, Elisabeth (1927—)
Söderström, Marit (1962—)
Sophia of Denmark (1746–1813)
Sophia of Nassau (1836–1913)
Sophia of Sweden (1801–1865)
Sophie of Denmark (d. 1286)
Sorenstam, Annika (1970—)
Sorenstam, Charlotta (1973—)
Stevens, Inger (1934–1970)
Stjernstedt, Rosemary (1912–1998)
Strandberg, Britt
Sundhage, Pia (1960—)
Svedberg, Ruth (1903–2004)
Swaab, Ninna (1940—)
Sylwan, Kari (1959—)
Theorin, Maj Britt (1932—)
Thorborg, Kerstin (1896–1970)
Thulin, Ingrid (1926–2004)
Toren, Marta (1926–1957)
Torgersson, Therese (1976—)
Trotzig, Birgitta (1929—)
Ulfhild (fl. 1112)
Ulrica Eleanora (1688–1741)
Ulrica Eleanora of Denmark (1656–1693)
Várnay, Astrid (1918—)
Victoria (1977—)
Victoria of Baden (1862–1930)
von Essen, Siri (1850–1912)
Von Rosen, Elsa Marianne (1924—)
von Rosen, Maud (1925—)
Waara, Jennie (1975—)
Wägner, Elin (1882–1949)
Warington, Katherine (1897–1993)
Wiberg, Pernilla (1970—)
Wifstrand, Naima (1890–1968)
Zachrisson, Vendela (1978—)
Zetterling, Mai (1925–1994)
Zetterlund, Monica (1937–2005)

SWITZERLAND

Federal republic in central Europe
Occupied by Helvetians; conquered by Romans
Invaded by Burgundians and Alamanni
Part of Frankish Empire
Part of kingdom of Arles
Formed anti-Habsburg league, nucleus of Swiss Confederation
Added territories (14th–15th c.)
Organized by French as Helvetic Republic (1798–1803)
Perpetual neutrality guaranteed by international agreement (1815)
Adopted new constitutions (1848 and 1874)

Adelaide of Rheinfelden (c. 1065–?)
Albrecht-Loretan, Brigitte (1970—)
Andersen-Scheiss, Gabriela (1945—)
Andress, Ursula (1936—)
Andujar, Claudia (1931—)
Asensio, Manola (1946—)
Auer, Judith (1905–1944)
Barnicoat, Constance Alice (1872–1922)
Baumer, Daniela
Baur, Margrit (1937—)
Berthod, Madeleine (1931—)
Berthod, Sylviane (1977—)
Beutler, Maja (1936—)
Bidaud, Laurence (1968—)
Blatter, Barbara (1970—)
Bloch, Suzanne (1907–2002)
Bochatay, Fernande (1946—)
Borkh, Inge (1917—)
Boulaz, Loulou (1912—)
Brand, Colette
Breslau, Louise (1857–1927)
Burkart, Erika (1922—)
Bögli, Lina (1858–1941)
Caduff, Sylvia (1937—)
Carton, Pauline (1884–1974)
Colliard, Renée (fl. 1950s)
Corday, Rita (1920–1992)
Dänzer, Frieda
de Bary, Amy-Catherine (1944—)
Della Casa, Lisa (1919—)
Dreifuss, Ruth (1940—)
Duby-Blom, Gertrude (1901–1993)
Eberhardt, Isabelle (1877–1904)
Ebnoether, Luzia (1971—)
Ehrmann, Marianne (1755–1795)
Eichenberger, Sabine
Engel, Regula (1761–1853)
Figini, Michela (1966—)
Frei, Tanya (1972—)
Goegg, Marie (1826–1899)
Gossweiler, Marianne (1943—)
Gourd, Emilie (1879–1946)
Hablützel-Bürki, Gianna (1969—)
Haralamow, Ingrid
Heer, Anna (1863–1918)
Hersch, Jeanne (1910–2000)
Hess, Erika (1962—)
Hingis, Martina (1980—)
Huber, Andrea (1975—)
Huber, Marie (1695–1753)
Huxley, Juliette (1896–1994)
Jeanneret, Marie (d. 1884)
Kaiser, Isabella (1866–1925)
Kauffmann, Angelica (1741–1807)
Kessler, Romi (1963—)
Kübler-Ross, Elisabeth (1926–2004)
Lamon, Sophie (1985—)
Lauber, Cécile (1887–1981)
Lavater-Sloman, Mary (1891–1980)
Lendorff, Gertrud (1900–1986)
Leonardi Cortesi, Natascia (1971—)
Leu, Evelyne (1976—)
Loos, Cécile Ines (1883–1959)
Maillart, Ella (1903–1997)
Maurizio, Anna (1900–1993)
McMahon, Brigitte (1967—)
McNaught, Lesley (1966—)
Messmer, Magali (1971—)
Meyer, Antoinette
Meyer, Olga (1889–1972)
Miller, Alice (1923—)
Montolieu, Pauline (1751–1832)
Morerod, Lise-Marie (1956—)
Mueller, Gabi
Nadig, Marie-Thérése (1954—)
Necker, Suzanne (1739–1794)
Necker de Saussure, Albertine (1766–1841)
Nef, Sonja (1972—)
Oertli, Brigitte (1962—)
Oppenheim, Méret (1913–1985)
Orelli, Susanna (1845–1939)
Ott, Mirjam (1972—)
Pedretti, Erica (1930—)

Geographic Index

Polier, Marie-Elizabeth (1742–1817)
Pulver, Lilo (1929—)
Ramseier, Doris (1939—)
Reuteler, Fabienne (1979—)
Robbiani, Heidi (1950—)
Rochat, Laurence (1979—)
Rochat-Moser, Franziska (1966–2002)
Roethlisberger, Nadia (1972—)
Romagnoli, Diana (1977—)
Rüegg, Annelise (1879–1934)
Ruegg, Yvonne
Salis-Marschlins, Meta (1855–1929)
Scherchen, Tona (1938—)
Schlunegger, Hedy (1923–2003)
Schneider, Vreni (1964—)
Schriber, Margrit (1939—)
Schwarzenbach, Annemarie (1908–1942)
Shaw, Pauline Agassiz (1841–1917)
Skoronel, Vera (1909–1932)
Spyri, Emily Kempin (1853–1901)
Spyri, Johanna (1827–1901)
Stagel, Elsbeth (c. 1300–c. 1366)
Stefan, Verena (1947—)
Stöcklin, Franziska (1894–1931)
Stückelberger, Christine (1947—)
Tauber-Arp, Sophie (1889–1943)
Thuerig, Karin (1972—)
Tone, Lel (c. 1971—)
Ullmann, Regina (1884–1961)
Vaucher, Yvette (1929—)
Vögtlin, Marie (1845–1916)
Walliser, Maria (1963—)
Walter, Silja (1919—)
Waser, Anna (1678–1714)
Waser, Maria (1878–1939)
Wenger, Lisa (1858–1941)
Wieck, Dorothea (1908–1986)
Wilker, Gertrud (1924–1984)
Zwingli, Anna Reinhard (1487–c. 1538)

SYRIA

Ancient country in Asia
Conquered by Egypt (c. 1471 BCE)
Part of Babylonian, Assyrian, and Persian Empires
Conquered by Alexander the Great (4th c. BCE)
Made a Roman province by Pompey (64 BCE)
Invaded and conquered by Persians (611 CE)
Overrun by Muslim Arabs (635 CE)
Seat of Ommiad dynasty (661–750)
Ruled by Seljuks and Fatimids during early Crusades
Ruled by Ottoman Turks (1516)
Invaded by French (1798–1799)
Achieved independence from Turkey (1917)

Agnes of Courtenay (1136–1186)
Akhat-milki (fl. 1265 BCE)
Alexandra (d. 27 BCE)
Anastasia (fl. 500s)
Attar, Samar (1940—)
Badi'a Masabnik
Beatrice (fl. c. 1100s)
Berenice Syra (c. 280–246 BCE)
Cleopatra Selene (c. 130–69 BCE)
Cleopatra Thea (c. 165–121 BCE)
Cleopatra Tryphaena (d. after 112 BCE)
Comitona (fl. 500s)
Dido (fl. 800 BCE)
Fatima, Djemille (c. 1890–1921)
Idlibi, 'Ulfah al- (1912—)
Khuri, Colette (1937—)
Laodice I (c. 285–c. 236 BCE)
Laodice III (fl. 200 BCE)
Mavia (c. 350–c. 430)
Nawfal, Hind (fl. 1890s)
Phila II (c. 300 BCE–?)
Ruth (fl. 1100 BCE)
Shouaa, Ghada (1972—)
Stratonice I (c. 319–254 BCE)
Stratonice II (c. 285–228 BCE)
Stratonice III (fl. 250 BCE)

TAIWAN

Island off Fukien province in southeastern China
Visited by Portuguese (1590)
Settled by Chinese (17th c.)
Dutch driven out (17th c.)
Ceded to Japan (1895)
Returned to China (1945)

Chen Jing (1968—)
Chen Li Ju (1981—)
Chen Ruoxi (1938—)
Chiang, Faina (1916–2004)
Chi Shu-Ju (c. 1983—)
Kuo Yi-Hang (1975—)
Li Feng-Ying (1975—)
Nieh Hualing (1925—)
Qiong Yao (1938—)
Reel, Chi Cheng (1944—)
Su Hsueh-lin (1897–1999)
Teng, Teresa (1953–1995)
Wu Hui Ju (1982—)
Yuan Shu Chi (1984—)

TANGANYIKA

See Tanzania.

TANZANIA

Republic in eastern Africa
Coast dominated by Arabs, Portuguese and rulers of Oman and Zanzibar
German East Africa Company received charter (1887)
Declared German East Africa (1891)
Declared a British protectorate (1890)
Native risings suppressed (1888, 18911893, 1905)
Captured by British (1914–1916)
Renamed Tanganyika when it became a British mandate (1920)
Achieved independence (1961)
Became a republic (1962)
United with Zanzibar as Tanzania (1964)

Mongella, Gertrude (1945—)
Mvungi, Martha
Olrich, April (1931—)
Saad, Siti binti (c. 1880–1950)

TASMANIA

Island and state of Australia
Discovered and named Van Dieman's Land (1642)
Renamed Tasmania (1853)
Taken over by Great Britain as a penal colony (1803)
Federated as state of Australian Commonwealth (1901)
Aboriginal Tasmanians became extinct (1876)
See also Australia.

Lyttelton, Edith Joan (1873–1945)

TASMANIAN ABORIGINE

Truganini (1812–1876)

TEWA PUEBLO

Native North American Southwest indigenous group

Martinez, Maria Montoya (1887–1980)
Tafoya, Margaret (1904–2001)

THAILAND

Kingdom in southeastern Asia
Formerly Siam
Part of the Mon-Khmer kingdom
Separate state formed by Thai people (1350)
Frequently overrun by Burmese (15th–16th c.)
Visited by Portuguese and Dutch (16th–17th c.)
Visited by British and French who seized territory (18th c.)
Renounced claim to Cambodia (1863)
Ceded territory to French (1893)
Yielded Britain its rights to four Unfederated Malay States (1909)
Became constitutional monarchy (1932)
Attacked Indochina (1940)
Seized by Japan (1941)
Participated in Korean War (1950–1953)
Abolished constitution (1971)

Boorapolchai, Yaowapa (1984—)
Chulabhorn, Princess (1957—)
Debyasuvan, Boonlua Kunjara (1911–1982)
Kameaim, Wandee (1978—)
Kiengsiri, Kanha (1911—)
Nimmanhemin, M.L. Bupha Kunjara (1905–1963)
Polsak, Udomporn (1981—)
Sirikit (1932—)
Suta, Khassaraporn (1971—)
Thongsuk, Pawina (1979—)
Vejjabul, Pierra (b. 1909)
Wiratthaworn, Aree (1980—)
Yanaranop, Sukanya (1931—)

THEBES

Roman province of Upper Egypt
Settled by Boeotians (before 1500 BCE)
Headed Boeotian League (c. 600–550 BCE)
Under Athenian rule (456–447 BCE)
Under Spartan rule (382–379 BCE)
Destroyed Spartan supremacy (371 BCE)
Destroyed by Alexander (336 BCE)

Nitocris (c. 660–584 BCE)
Timoclea (c. 370–? BCE)

THESSALY

Administrative region of Greece
Subject to Macedonia (4th–2nd c. BCE)
Ceded to modern Greece (1881)
See Greece.

THRACE

Region in eastern Balkan Peninsula in southeastern Europe
Became a Roman province (69–79 CE)
Overrun by Goths, Huns, and other barbarian invaders
Part of Byzantine Empire, part fell to Turks (1361)
Ruled by Turkey (after 1453)
Northern part separated as Eastern Rumelia (1878)
Western Thrace an administrative region of Greece
Eastern Thrace became Turkey
All Thrace became Greece (1920–1923)
See Bulgaria.
See Greece.
See Turkey.

THUBURBO

Ancient city in North Africa

Felicitas (d. 203)
Perpetua (181–203)

THURINGIA

Former German state
Conquered by Franks (6th c.)
Under Frankish rule (634–804)
Identified with duchy and kingdom of Saxony (1485–1918)
States combined under Weimar republic (1919–1933)
Became part of East Germany (1945)
See Germany.

TIBET

Autonomous region of China
Buddhism introduced (7th c.)
Under Chinese control 1720)
Anglo-Tibetan Convention signed (1904)
Invaded by Communist Chinese (1950)

Dolma, Pachen (c. 1933–2002)
Ma-gcig Lab-sgron (c. 1055–c. 1149)

TLINGIT

Native North American Pacific Northwest indigenous group

Peratrovich, Elizabeth Wanamaker (1911–1958)

TOBAGO

Island in West Indies
Discovered by Columbus (1498)
First settled by English (1616)
Held also by Dutch and French, remained English (after 1814)
Made part of colony of Trinidad and Tobago (1898)
Became part of independent state of Trinidad and Tobago (1962)

Atwell, Winifred (1914–1983)
Calypso Rose (1940—)
Francois, Elma (1897–1944)

TONGA ISLANDS

Kingdom in southwestern Pacific Ocean
Discovered by Dutch (1616)
Became British protectorate (1900)
Achieved independence (1970)

Rawlinson, Gloria (1918–1995)
Salote Topou III (1900–1965)

TREBIZOND

Greek empire (1204–1461)
See Byzantine Empire.

TRIER

City in Rhineland-Palatinate in western Germany
Seat of independent archbishops (5th–19th c.)
Capital of French department of the Sarre under Napoleon
Under Prussia (1815)
See Germany.
See Prussia.

TRIESTE

Province of Friuli-Venezia Giulia in Italy
Came under Rome (c. 177 BCE)
Under episcopal rule (948–1202)
Under Austrian rule (1382)
Held by French (1809–1814)
Returned to Italy (1954)
See Italy.

TRINIDAD

Island of the West Indies
Discovered by Columbus (1498)
Spanish settlement (1577)
Occupied by British (1797)
Ceced to Great Britain (1802)
Made part of colony of Trinidad and Tobago (1898)
Became part of independent state of Trinidad and Tobago (1962)
See also Tobago.

Calypso Rose (1940—)
Dai, Ailian (1916–2006)
De Lima, Clara Rosa (1923—)
Francois, Elma (1897–1944)
Guy, Rosa (1925—)
Harris, Claire (1937—)
Jones, Marion Patrick (1934—)
Marsh, Marian (1913—)
May, Pamela (1917–2005)
Richardson, Jillian (1965—)

TRIPOLI

Region in northern Africa
Founded (7th c.)
Capital of Tripolis
Held by Seleucids and Romans and taken by Muslims (638 CE)
Conquered by Crusaders
Retaken by Mamelukes and destroyed (1289)

Hodierna of Jerusalem (c. 1115–after 1162)
Sibylla of Armenia (fl. 1200s)

TROY

Ancient city in Troas in northwestern Asia Minor
See Asia Minor.

TUNISIA

Chaibi, Aïcha
Guellouz, Souad (1937—)

TURKEY

Republic in southeastern Europe
Established Ottoman Empire (13th c.)
Included Balkan region and Egypt (15th c.)
Took western Asian countries and European territory of Holy Roman Empire (16th c.)
Warred with Poland, Austria, and Russia (17th–18th c.)
Expelled from Hungary and northern shores of Black Sea (19th c.)
Defeated Greece (1920–1922)
Adopted constitution (1922)
Ottoman Empire dissolved (1923)
Proclaimed Turkish republic (1923)
Abolished caliphate (1924)
Abolished Islam as state religion (1928)
Joined Balkan Pact (1934)
Joined nonagression pact with Iraq, Iran, and Afghanistan (1937)
Adopted new constitution (1961)

Ada (c. 380–c. 323 BCE)
Adivar, Halide Edib (c. 1884–1964)
Agaoglu, Adalet (1929—)
Akin, Gülten (1933—)
Aliye, Fatima (1862–1936)
Anna Anachoutlou (r. 1341–1342)
Araz, Nezihe (1922—)
Artemisia I (c. 520–? BCE)
Artemisia II (c. 395–351 BCE)
Aspasia of Miletus (c. 464 BCE–c. 420 BCE)
Ayverdi, Samiha (1906–1993)
Ba_ar, Sukufe Nihal (1896–1973)
Berksoy, Semiha (1910–2004)
Bikcin, Hamide (1978—)
Biret, Idil (1941—)
Çiller, Tansu (1946—)
Darvas, Julia (c. 1919—)
Dervis, Suat (1905–1972)
Ener, Güner (1935—)
Erbil, Leyla (1931—)
Fitnat-Khanim (c. 1725–1780)
Frame, Alice (1878–1941)
Fürüzan (1935—)
Gencer, Leyla (1924—)
Gülabahar (fl. 1521)
Hadice Turhan (1627–1683)
Hafsa (d. 1534)
Halim, Tahiya (1919–2003)
Hanim, Latife (1898–1975)
Hanim, Leyla (1850–1936)
Hanim, Nigar (1862–1918)
Khanim, Leyla (d. 1847/48)
Koptagel, Yuksel (1931—)
Kösem (1589–1651)
Mihri Khatun (fl. 15/16th c.)
Mihrimah (1522–1575)
Morphia of Melitene (fl. 1085–1120)
Nöel, Magali (1932—)
Nurbanu (1525–1583)
Osmanoglu, Gevheri (1904–1980)
Paletzi, Juliane (d. 1569)
Reign of Women (1520–1683)
Roxelana (c. 1504–1558)
Safiye (d. 1603)
Sah (fl. 1500s)
Senyurt, Hulya (1973—)
Soray, Turkan (1945—)
Soysal, Sevgi (1936–1976)
Taylan, Nurcan (1983—)
Ucok, Bahriye (d. 1990)
Yener, Aslihan (1946—)
Zabel (b. around 1210)
Zabelle, Flora (1880–1968)
Zorlutuna, Halidé Nusret (1901–1984)

TUSCANY

Autonomous region in western Italy
A margravate (9th c.)
Became a duchy (10th c.)
Divided into independent city-states (12th–13th c.)
Reunited under Medici dukes of Florence
Passed to house of Lorraine, to Sardinia, and kingdom of Italy
See Italy.

UGANDA

Kimenye, Barbara (1940—)
Lakwena, Alice (1960—)
Zirimu, Elvania Namukwaya (1938–1979)

UKRAINE

Republic in eastern Europe
Settled by Ukrainians and Ruthenians (6th–7th c.)
Principality of Russia until Tatar conquest (13th c.)
Taken by Lithuania (1667)
Region of Cossaks and that east of Dnieper acquired by Russia (1680)
Rest of Ukraine acquired by Russia through partitions (1793)
Ukrainian People's Republic established (1917)
Declared its independence from Russia (1918)
Part taken by Poland (1919–1938)
Remainder conquered by Russia (1923)
Achieved independence (1992)

Abrashitova, Elena (1974—)
Astakhova, Polina (1936—)
Babakova, Inga (1967—)
Baiul, Oksana (1977—)
Balabanova, Hanna (1969—)
Bessonova, Anna (1984—)
Borysenko, Nataliya (1975—)
Burdeyna, Nataliya (1974—)
Burmystrova, Ganna (1977—)
Cherevatova, Olena (1970—)
Dudnik, Olesia (1974—)
Frolova, Inna (1965—)
Govorova, Olena (1973—)
Grishuk, Pasha (1972—)
Honcharova, Iryna (1974—)
Hupalo, Katherine (1890–1974)
Kalinina, Ganna (1979—)
Kalinina, Natalia (1973—)
Karinska, Barbara (1886–1983)
Karpenko, Viktoria (1984—)
Klochkova, Yana (1982—)
Kobrynska, Natalia Ivanovna (1855–1920)
Kobylianska, Olha (1863–1942)
Kostevych, Olena (1985—)
Kravets, Inessa (1966—)
Krusceniski, Salomea (1873–1952)
Kuliscioff, Anna (c. 1854–1925)
Lyapina, Nataliya (1976—)
Lysenko, Tatiana (1975—)
Markova, Olga
Markushevska, Galyna (1976—)
Matevusheva, Svitlana (1981—)
Maziy, Svetlana (1968—)
Melnik, Faina (1945—)
Merleni, Irini (1982—)

Geographic Index

Miftakhutdinova, Diana (1973—)
Misnik, Alla (1967—)
Morits, Yunna (1937—)
Osypenko, Inna (1982—)
Pakholchik, Olena (1964—)
Petrova, Olena (1972—)
Podkopayeva, Lilia (1978—)
Press, Irina (1939—)
Press, Tamara (1939—)
Prozumenshchykova, Galina (1948—)
Radchenko, Olena (1973—)
Rayhel, Oxana (1977—)
Repko, Elena (1975—)
Ronzhina, Olena (1970—)
Roslavleva, Natalia (1907–1977)
Sadovnycha, Olena (1967—)
Semykina, Tetyana (1973—)
Serdyuk, Kateryna
Serebrianskaya, Yekaterina (1977—)
Sheremeta, Liubov (1980—)
Shevchenko, Lyudmyla (1975—)
Shynkarenko, Tetyana (1978—)
Siukalo, Ganna (1976—)
Skakun, Nataliya (1981—)
Skaldina, Oksana (1972—)
Slyusareva, Olga (1969—)
Sokhanskaia, Nadezhda (1823–1884)
Sorokina, Anna (1976—)
Stovbchataya, Ludmila (1974—)
Stroyeva, Vera (b. 1903)
Styopina, Viktoriya (1976—)
Tamara (1907–1943)
Taran, Ruslana (1970—)
Tarasova, Alla (1898–1973)
Teslenko, Olga (1981—)
Tichtchenko, Elizaveta (1975—)
Timochenko, Alexandra (1972—)
Tserbe-Nessina, Valentyna (1969—)
Tsygitsa, Olena (1975—)
Tsyhuleva, Oksana
Tymoshenko, Yulia (1960—)
Ukrainka, Lesya (1871–1913)
Vergelyuk, Maryna (1978—)
Vilinska, Mariya (1834–1907)
Vitrichenko, Elena (1976—)
Yanovych, Iryna (1976—)
Yatsenko, Olena (1977—)
Youshkevitch, Nina (c. 1921–1998)
Zabar, Lillian (c. 1905–1995)
Zakharova, Olga (1973—)
Zaslavskaya, Tatyana (1924—)
Zaspa, Larysa (1971—)
Zelepukina, Svetlana (1980—)
Zhupina, Olena (1973—)

UMBRIA

Autonomous region in central Italy
Conquered by Etruscans
Came under Rome (c. 300 BCE)
See Italy.

UNITED STATES OF AMERICA

Federal republic in North America
First permanent settlement by the Spanish in St. Augustine, Florida (1565)
English settlement in Virginia (1607), Massachusetts (1620), Maryland (1634), Pennsylvania (1681)
English victory in French and Indian War (1754–1763)
Atlantic seaboard colonies under British control until American Revolution (1775–1783)
Adopted constitution (1787)
Purchased Louisiana Territory from France (1803)
Warred with Britain (1812)
Purchased Florida from Spain (1819)
Expanded westward into Middle West and to Far West after discovery of gold in California (1848)
Annexed Texas (1845)
Northwest boundary established with Britain (1846)
New Mexico and California ceded by Mexico (1848)
Acquired Arizona from Mexico (1853)
War between the States (1861–1865)
Purchased Alaska from Russia (1867)
Annexed Hawaiian Islands (1898)
Spanish American War ended with acquisition of Philippine Islands, Puerto Rico, and Guam (1898–1899)
Occupied Wake Island (1898–1899)
Acquired American Samoa from Germany (1899)
Purchased Panama Canal Zone from Panama (1903)
Purchased Virgin Islands from Denmark (1917)
Granted independence to Philippine Islands (1946)
Established autonomous commonwealth of Puerto Rico (1952)

Aadland, Beverly (1943—)
Aaliyah (1979–2001)
Aarons, Ruth Hughes (1918–1980)
Abady, Josephine (c. 1950–2002)
Abarca, Lydia (1951—)
Abbe, Kathryn (1919—)
Abbott, Berenice (1898–1991)
Abbott, Bessie (d. 1937)
Abbott, Diahnne (1945—)
Abbott, Edith (1876–1957)
Abbott, Elenore Plaisted (1873–1935)
Abbott, Emma (1850–1891)
Abbott, Grace (1878–1939)
Abbott, Lorraine (1937—)
Abbott, Margaret (1878–1955)
Abbott, Merriel (c. 1893–1977)
Abdallah, Nia (1984—)
Abdellah, Faye Glenn (1919—)
Abel, Annie Heloise (1873–1947)
Abel, Hazel (1888–1966)
Abel, Theodora (1899–1998)
Abrahams, Doris Cole (1925—)
Abzug, Bella (1920–1998)
Ace, Jane (1905–1974)
Acker, Jean (1893–1978)
Acker, Kathy (1943–1997)
Ackerman, Paula (1893–1989)
Ackerman, Val (1959—)
Acquanetta (1921–2004)
Adair, Jean (1872–1953)
Adair, Virginia Hamilton (1913–2004)
Adamek, Donna (1957—)
Adams, Abigail (1744–1818)
Adams, Abigail (1765–1813)
Adams, Abigail Brooks (1808–1889)
Adams, Adrienne (1906–2002)
Adams, Alice (1926–1999)
Adams, Annette (1877–1956)
Adams, Carolyn (1943—)
Adams, Charity (1917–2002)
Adams, Clara (born c. 1899)
Adams, Clover (1843–1885)
Adams, Constance (1874–1960)
Adams, Diana (1927–1993)
Adams, Dorothy (1900–1988)
Adams, Edie (1927—)
Adams, Evangeline Smith (1873–1932)
Adams, Fae Margaret (1918—)
Adams, Hannah (1755–1831)
Adams, Harriet Chalmers (1875–1937)
Adams, Harriet Stratemeyer (c. 1893–1982)
Adams, Ida (c. 1888–1960)
Adams, Jane (1921—)
Adams, Julie (1926—)
Adams, Kathryn (1893–1959)
Adams, Léonie Fuller (1899–1988)
Adams, Louisa Catherine (1775–1852)
Adams, Lynn (c. 1958—)
Adams, Maude (1872–1953)
Adams, Millicent (1942—)
Adams, Sharon Sites (c. 1930—)
Adams, Susan Boylston (d. 1797)
Adams, Susanna Boylston (1769–1828)
Adato, Perry Miller
Addams, Jane (1860–1935)
Addor, Ady (c. 1935—)
Adelaide (c. 1884–1959)
Adler, Alexandra (1901–2001)
Adler, C.S. (1932—)
Adler, Celia (1890–1979)
Adler, Frances (d. 1964)
Adler, Julia (1897–1995)
Adler, Polly (1899–1962)
Adler, Renata (1938—)
Adler, Sara (1858–1953)
Adler, Stella (1902–1993)
Adolf, Helen (1895–1998)
Adrian, Iris (1912–1994)
Aebi, Tania (1966—)
Agassiz, Elizabeth Cary (1822–1907)
Ahern, Kathy (1949–1996)
Ahern, Mary Eileen (1860–1938
Ahmann-Leighton, Crissy (1970—)
Ahmanson, Caroline (1918–2005)
Aiken, Kimberly (c. 1975—)
Aikens, Charlotte (c. 1868–1949)
Aitken, Jane (1764–1832)
Ajzenberg-Selove, Fay (1926—)
Akeley, Delia J. (1875–1970)
Akeley, Mary Jobe (1878–1966)
Akers, Dolly Smith (1902—)
Akers, Michelle (1966—)
Akin, Susan (c. 1964—)
Akins, Zoe (1886–1958)
Akiyoshi, Toshiko (1929—)
Alba, Nanina (1915–1968)
Albers, Anni (1899–1994)
Albert, Octavia V.R. (1853–c. 1899)
Albertson, Lillian (1881–1962)
Albertson, Mabel (1901–1982)
Albright, Lola (1925—)
Albright, Madeleine (1937—)
Albright, Tenley (1935—)
Alcott, Amy (1956—)
Alcott, Anna Bronson (1831–1893)
Alcott, Louisa May (1832–1888)
Alcott, May (1840–1879)
Alden, Cynthia Westover (1862–1931)
Alden, Hortense (1903–1999)
Alden, Isabella (1841–1930)
Alden, Mary (1883–1946)
Alden, Priscilla (c. 1602–c. 1685)
Aldis, Dorothy (1896–1966)
Aldis, Mary (1872–1949)
Aldredge, Theoni V. (1932—)
Aldrich, Anne Reeve (1866–1892)
Aldrich, Bess Streeter (1881–1954)
Aleandro, Norma (1936—)
Alenikoff, Frances (1920—)
Alexander, Annie Montague (1867–1949)
Alexander, Claire (1898–1927)
Alexander, Dorothy (1904–1986)
Alexander, Florence (1904–1993)
Alexander, Francesca (1837–1917)
Alexander, Hattie (1901–1968)
Alexander, Jane (1939—)
Alexander, Katherine (1898–1981)
Alexander, Lucy Maclay (fl. 1950s)
Alexander, Mary (1693–1760)
Alexander, Sadie (1898–1989)
Alf, Fé (c. 1910—)
Alkhateeb, Sharifa (1946–2004)
Allan, Maude (1883–1956)
Allan-Shetter, Liz (1947—)
Allbritton, Louise (1920–1979)
Allbut, Barbara (1940—)

Allbut, Phyllis (1942—)
Allen, Charlotte Vale (1941—)
Allen, Debbie (1950—)
Allen, Dede (1923—)
Allen, Elizabeth Chase (1832–1911)
Allen, Florence Ellinwood (1884–1966)
Allen, Frances S. (1854–1941)
Allen, Gracie (1902–1964)
Allen, Jay Presson (1922–2006)
Allen, Mary E. (1858–1941)
Allen, Maryon (1925—)
Allen, Paula Gunn (1939—)
Allen, Rita (d. 1968)
Allen, Rosalie (1924–2003)
Allen, Sadie (c. 1868–?)
Allen, Sarita (1954—)
Allen, Susan Westford (c. 1865–1944)
Allen, Tori (1988—)
Allen, Vera (1897–1987)
Allen, Viola (1867–1948)
Allenby, Peggy (1905–1967)
Allende, Isabel (1942—)
Allison, Fran (1907–1989)
Allison, May (1890–1989)
Allred, Gloria (1941—)
Allwyn, Astrid (1905–1978)
Allyson, June (1917—)
Almon, Baylee (1994–1995)
Almond, Linda (1881–1987)
Almy, Mary Gould (1735–1808)
Almy, Millie (1915–2001)
Alonso, Dora (1910–2001)
Alsop, Susan Mary (d. 2004)
Alston, Barbara (1945—)
Aluli, Irmgard (c. 1912–2001)
Alvarez, Anita (1920—)
Alvarez, Carmen (c. 1936—)
Amanpour, Christiane (1958—)
Ambler, Mary Cary (fl. 1700s)
Ambrosie, Christie (1976—)
America³ Team (1995—)
Ames, Adrienne (1907–1947)
Ames, Blanche (1878–1969)
Ames, Eleanor Maria (1830–1908)
Ames, Fanny Baker (1840–1931)
Ames, Jessie Daniel (1883–1972)
Ames, Mary Clemmer (1831–1884)
Ames, Rosemary (1906–1988)
Amico, Leah (1974—)
Amini-Hudson, Johari (1935—)
Amory, Katherine (1731–1777)
Amos, Tori (1963—)
Amparo Ruiz de Burton, Maria (1832–1895)
Anable, Gloria Hollister (1903–1988)
Anastasi, Anne (1908–2001)
Anchutina, Leda (1915–1989)
Ancker-Johnson, Betsy (1927—)
Anders, Beth (1951—)
Anders, Luana (1938–1996)
Anders, Merry (1932—)
Andersen, Dorothy Hansine (1901–1963)
Andersen, Lisa (1969—)
Anderson, Bella (1864–?)
Anderson, Beth (1950—)
Anderson, Bette B. (c. 1929—)
Anderson, Caroline Still (1848–1919)
Anderson, Chantelle (1981—)
Anderson, Claire (1895–1964)
Anderson, Claire (fl. 1940s)
Anderson, Elda E. (1899–1961)
Anderson, Elizabeth Milbank (1850–1921)
Anderson, Erica (1914–1976)
Anderson, Ernestine (1928—)
Anderson, Eugenie Moore (1909–1997)
Anderson, Evelyn (1907–1994)
Anderson, Isabel Perkins (1876–1948)
Anderson, Ivie (1904–1949)
Anderson, Janet (1956—)
Anderson, Jodi (1957—)
Anderson, Katherine (1944—)
Anderson, Laurie (1947—)
Anderson, Margaret Carolyn (1886–1973)
Anderson, Marian (1897–1993)
Anderson, Mary (1859–1940)
Anderson, Mary (1872–1964)
Anderson, Mignon (1892–1983)
Anderson, Regina M. (1901–1993)
Anderson-Ivantzova, Elizabeth (c. 1893–1973)
Anderson-Scott, Carol (1935–2003)
Andra, Fern (1893–1974)
Andrews, Ann (1890–1986)
Andrews, Barbara (c. 1934–1978)
Andrews, Doris (1920–2003)
Andrews, Elizabeth Bullock (1911–2002)
Andrews, Eliza Frances (1840–1931)
Andrews, Fannie Fern (1867–1950)
Andrews, Jane (1833–1887)
Andrews, LaVerne (1911–1967)
Andrews, Lois (1924–1968)
Andrews, Mary Raymond (1860–1936)
Andrews, Maxene (1916–1995)
Andrews, Nancy (1924–1989)
Andrews, Patti (1918—)
Andrews, Theresa (1962—)
Andrews Sisters (1932–1953)
Andrus, Ethel Percy (1884–1967)
Angelica, Mother (1923—)
Angelou, Maya (1928—)
Anglin, Margaret (1876–1958)
Annabelle (1878–1961)
Anneke, Mathilde Franziska (1817–1884)
Ann-Margret (1941—)
Anson, Laura (1892–1968)
Anthony, Bessie (1880–1912)
Anthony, Katharine Susan (1877–1965)
Anthony, Mary (c. 1920—)
Anthony, Susan B. (1820–1906)
Anthony, Susan B., II (1916–1991)
Antin, Mary (1881–1949)
Antolin, Jeanette (1981—)
Anzaldúa, Gloria E. (1942–2004)
Apgar, Virginia (1909–1974)
Appel, Anna (1888–1963)
Applebee, Constance (1873–1981)
Appleby, Dorothy (1906–1990)
Aptheker, Bettina (1944—)
Aragon, Jesusita (1908—)
Arbus, Diane (1923–1971)
Arbuthnot, May Hill (1884–1969)
Archer-Gilligan, Amy (1869–1928)
Arden, Elizabeth (1878–1966)
Arden, Eve (1907–1990)
Arden, Toni (fl. 1950s)
Arenal, Julie (1942—)
Arendt, Hannah (1906–1975)
Aresty, Esther B. (1908–2000)
Arlington, Lizzie (1876–1917)
Armbrust, Roma (1927–2003)
Armen, Kay (1920—)
Armen, Margaret (1921–2003)
Armer, Laura Adams (1874–1963)
Armitage, Goody (fl. 1643)
Armitage, Karole (1954—)
Armour, Toby (1936—)
Armstead, Izora (1942–2004)
Armstrong, Anne L. (1927—)
Armstrong, Debbie (1963—)
Armstrong, Lil Hardin (1898–1971)
Armstrong, Margaret Neilson (1867–1944)
Armstrong, Penny (1946—)
Arne, Sigrid (1894–1973)
Arnell, Amy (1919—)
Arnold, Becky (1936—)
Arnold, Bené (1953—)
Arnold, Dorothy (1917–1984)
Arnold, Eve (1913—)
Arnold, June (1926–1982)
Arnold, Mary Beth (1981—)
Arnow, Harriette Simpson (1908–1986)
Arnst, Bobbe (1903–1980)
Arnstein, Margaret (1904–1972)
Arova, Sonia (1927–2001)
Arroyo, Martina (1935—)
Arsenault, Samantha (1981—)
Arthur, Bea (1923—)
Arthur, Charthel (1946—)
Arthur, Ellen Herndon (1837–1880)
Arthur, Jean (1900–1991)
Arthur, Julia (1869–1950)
Arvidson, Linda (1884–1949)
Arzner, Dorothy (1897–1979)
Asakawa, Takako (1938—)
Ash, Mary Kay (1918–2001)
Ashbrook, Jean (1934—)
Ashcraft, Juanita (1921—2000)
Asher, Elise (c. 1912–2004)
Ashford, Evelyn (1957—)
Ashley, Elizabeth (1939—)
Ashley, Merrill (1950—)
Ashworth, Jeanne (1938—)
Askew, Sarah B. (c. 1863–1942)
Aspinall, Nan Jane (fl. 1911)
Asquith, Ruby (c. 1910—)
Assing, Ottilie (1819–1884)
Ast, Pat (1941–2001)
Astaire, Adele (1898–1981)
Astor, Augusta (fl. 1820s–1890s)
Astor, Brooke (b. 1902)
Astor, Caroline Schermerhorn (1830–1908)
Astor, Gertrude (1887–1977)
Astor, Madeleine Talmadge (c. 1893–1940)
Astor, Mary (1906–1987)
Astor, Sarah Todd (1761–1832)
Astrologes, Maria (1951—)
Atherton, Gertrude (1857–1948)
Atkins, Mary (1819–1882)
Atkins, Susan (1948—)
Atkinson, Eleanor (1863–1942)
Atkinson, Eudora Clark (1831–?)
Atkinson, Juliette P. (1873–1944)
Atkinson, Ti-Grace (1939—)
Atlas, Consuelo (1944–1979)
Atler, Vanessa (1982—)
Atwater, Edith (1911–1986)
Atwater, Helen (1876–1947)
Atwood, Donna (c. 1923—)
Atwood, Susan (1953—)
Auel, Jean (1936—)
Auerbach, Beatrice Fox (1887–1968)
Auerbach, Ellen (1906–2004)
August, Bonnie (1947–2003)
Augustine, Rose (1910–2003)
Austen, Alice (1866–1952)
Austin, Debbie (1948—)
Austin, Debra (1955—)
Austin, Jane Goodwin (1831–1894)
Austin, Lovie (1887–1972)
Austin, Mary Hunter (1868–1934)
Austin, Tracy (1962—)
Avedon, Barbara Hammer (1930–1994)
Avery, Martha (1851–1929)
Avery, Mary Ellen (1927—)
Avery, Rachel G. (1858–1919)
Av-Paul, Annette (1944—)
Awiakta (1936—)
Axton, Estelle (1918–2004)
Axton, Mae Boren (1914–1997)

Axum, Donna (c. 1924—)
Ay, Evelyn (c. 1934—)
Ayer, Harriet Hubbard (1849–1903)
Ayres, Agnes (1896–1940)
Ayres, Mary Andrews (fl. 1970s)
Ayscough, Florence (1875/78–1942)
Azzi, Jennifer (1968—)
Babashoff, Shirley (1957—)
Babbin, Jacqueline (1921–2001)
Babb-Sprague, Kristen (1968—)
Babcock, Maud May (1867–1954)
Babilonia, Tai (1959—)
Bacall, Lauren (1924—)
Bache, Sarah (1743–1808)
Bachrach, Elise Wald (1899–1940)
Bacon, Albion Fellows (1865–1933)
Bacon, Alice Mabel (1858–1918)
Bacon, Delia Salter (1811–1859)
Bacon, Faith (1909–1956)
Bacon, Josephine Dodge (1876–1961)
Bacon, Mabel (fl. 1910)
Bacon, Mary (1948–1991)
Bacon, Peggy (1895–1987)
Badgley, Helen (1908–1977)
Badham, Mary (1952—)
Baez, Joan (1941—)
Bagley, Sarah (b. 1806)
Bagnold, Lisbeth (1947—)
Bahrke, Shannon (1980—)
Bailes, Margaret Johnson (1951—)
Bailey, Abigail Abbott (1746–1815)
Bailey, Anna Warner (1758–1851)
Bailey, Carolyn Sherwin (1875–1961)
Bailey, Chris (1972—)
Bailey, Elizabeth (1938—)
Bailey, Florence (1863–1948)
Bailey, Frankie (1859–1953)
Bailey, Hannah Johnston (1839–1923)
Bailey, Mildred (1903–1951)
Bailey, Pearl (1918–1990)
Bailey, Temple (c. 1869–1953)
Bailin, Gladys (1930—)
Bainter, Fay (1891–1968)
Baird, Cora (c. 1912–1967)
Baird, Leah (1883–1971)
Bakanic, Ladislava (1924—)
Baker, Anita (1958—)
Baker, Augusta (1911–1998)
Baker, Belle (1893–1957)
Baker, Bonnie (b. 1917)
Baker, Carroll (1931—)
Baker, Diane (1938—)
Baker, Dorothy (1907–1968)
Baker, Ella (1903–1986)
Baker, Harriette Newell (1815–1893)
Baker, Irene Bailey (1901–1994)
Baker, Josephine (1906–1975)
Baker, Kate (1861–1953)
Baker, Kathy (1961—)
Baker, Laurie (1976—)
Baker, LaVern (1929–1997)
Baker, Nina Brown (1888–1957)
Baker, S. Josephine (1873–1945)
Bakken, Jill (1977—)
Balch, Emily Greene (1867–1961)
Baldina, Alexandra Maria (1885–1977)
Baldwin, Charlotte Fowler (1805–1873)
Baldwin, Faith (1893–1978)
Baldwin, Maria Louise (1856–1922)
Baldwin, Ruth Ann (fl. 1915–1921)
Balfour, Katharine (c. 1921–1990)
Balin, Ina (1937–1990)
Ball, Catherine (1951—)
Ball, Lucille (1911–1989)
Ball, Suzan (1933–1950)
Ballantyne, Sara (c. 1964—)
Ballard, Florence (1943–1976)
Ballard, Kaye (1926—)
Ballard, Lucinda (1906–1993)
Ballard, Martha Moore (1735–1812)
Ballin, Mabel (1887–1958)
Balliser, Helen (fl. 1914)
Ballou, Esther Williamson (1915–1973)
Ballou, Germaine (b. 1899)
Bambace, Angela (1898–1975)
Bambara, Toni Cade (1939–1995)
Bampton, Rose (1907—)
Bancroft, Ann (1955—)
Bancroft, Anne (1931–2005)
Bancroft, Jessie (1867–1952)
Baniszewski, Gertrude Wright (1929–1990)
Bankhead, Tallulah (1902–1968)
Bannerman, Margaret (1896–1976)
Banning, Margaret Culkin (1891–1982)
Bannon, Ann (1932—)
Bañuelos, Romana Acosta (1925—)
Bara, Theda (1885–1955)
Baraquio, Angela Perez (1976—)
Barberi, Maria (1880–?)
Barcelo, Gertrudis (c. 1820–1852)
Bard, Mary (1904–1970)
Bardin, Madeleine (c. 1920—)
Bari, Judi (1949–1997)
Bari, Lynn (1913–1989)
Barkentin, Marjorie (c. 1891–1974)
Barker, Francine (1947—)
Barker, Kylene (c. 1956—)
Barker, M.C. (1879–1963)
Barker, Ma (1872–1935)
Barkley, Jane Hadley (1911–1964)
Barkman, Jane (1951—)
Barnard, Hannah Jenkins (d. 1825)
Barnard, Kate (1875–1930)
Barnes, Binnie (1903–1998)
Barnes, Charlotte Mary Sanford (1818–1863)
Barnes, Debra Dene (c. 1947—)
Barnes, Djuna (1892–1982)
Barnes, Jhane (1954—)
Barnes, Margaret Ayer (1886–1967)
Barnes, Mary Downing (1850–1898)
Barnes, Pancho (1901–1975)
Barnett, Pamela (1944—)
Barney, Alice Pike (1857–1931)
Barney, Natalie Clifford (1876–1972)
Barney, Nora (1883–1971)
Barns, Cornelia Baxter (1888–1941)
Barnum, Gertrude (1866–1948)
Barnwell, Barbara Olive (c. 1919–c. 1977)
Barone, Marian E. (1924–1996)
Barr, Amelia Huddleston (1831–1919)
Barr, Beth (1971—)
Barr, Margaret Scolari (1901–1987)
Barret, Dorothy (1917–1987)
Barrett, Edith (1906–1977)
Barrett, Janie Porter (1865–1948)
Barrett, Kate Waller (1857–1925)
Barrett, Minnette (1880–1964)
Barrett, Rona (1934—)
Barrett, Rose Tyler (b. 1889)
Barrie, Elaine (1915–2003)
Barrie, Mona (1909–1964)
Barrie, Wendy (1912–1978)
Barringer, Emily Dunning (1876–1961)
Barriscale, Bessie (1884–1965)
Barron, Gayle (c. 1947—)
Barron, Jennie Loitman (1891–1969)
Barrow, Frances Elizabeth (1822–1894)
Barrows, Isabel Hayes (1845–1913)
Barry, Deidre (1972—)
Barry, Elaine (d. 1948)
Barry, Iris (1895–1969)
Barry, Leonora M. (1849–1930)
Barrymore, Diana (1921–1960)
Barrymore, Ethel (1879–1959)
Barstow, Edith (1907–1960)
Bartel, Jean (c. 1924—)
Bartelme, Mary (1866–1954)
Bartholomew, Susan (1969—)
Bartkowicz, Peaches (1949—)
Bartlett, Mary (d. 1789)
Barton, Clara (1821–1912)
Barton, Donna (c. 1967—)
Bartosik, Alison (1983—)
Bascom, Florence (1862–1945)
Basich, Tina (1969—)
Basquette, Lina (1907–1995)
Bass, Charlotta Spears (1880–1969)
Bass, Mary Elizabeth (1876–1956)
Bassett, Angela (1958—)
Bassett, Ann (1878–1956)
Bateham, Josephine (1829–1901)
Bateman, Kate (1842–1917)
Bates, Barbara (1925–1969)
Bates, Blanche (1873–1941)
Bates, Charlotte Fiske (1838–1916)
Bates, Clara Doty (1838–1895)
Bates, Daisy Lee (1914—)
Bates, Elizabeth (1947–2003)
Bates, Florence (1888–1954)
Bates, Harriet Leonora (1856–1886)
Bates, Katherine Lee (1859–1929)
Bates, Kathy (1948—)
Bates, Mary (1861–1954)
Bates, Ruby (1913–1976)
Bates, Vietta M. (1922–1972)
Batson, Flora (1864–1906)
Battelle, Ann (1968—)
Batten, Kim (1969—)
Batterham, Mary Rose (c. 1870–1927)
Battle, Kathleen (1948—)
Bauchens, Anne (1881–1967)
Bauer, Alice (1927–2002)
Bauer, Catherine Krouse (1905–1964)
Bauer, Charita (1922–1985)
Bauer, Marion (1887–1955)
Bauer, Sybil (1903–1927)
Bauersmith, Paula (1909–1987)
Baugh, Laura (1955—)
Baume, Rosetta Lulah (1871–1934)
Baumgartner, Ann (c. 1923—)
Baur, Clara (1835–1912)
Bavier, Frances (1902–1989)
Baxley, Barbara (1923–1990)
Baxter, Anne (1923–1985)
Bay, Josephine Perfect (1900–1962)
Bayer, Adèle (1814–1892)
Bayes, Nora (1880–1928)
Baylis, Meredith (1929–2002)
Bayliss, Blanche (fl. 1894)
Bayne, Beverly (1894–1982)
Beach, Amy Cheney (1867–1944)
Beach, Cyprian (1893–1951)
Beach, Holly (b. 1884)
Beach, Sylvia (1887–1962)
Beals, Jessie Tarbox (1870–1942)
Beaman, Hana (1982—)
Bean, Janet Beveridge (1964—)
Beard, Amanda (1981—)
Beard, Betsy (1961—)
Beard, Mary (1876–1946)
Beard, Mary Ritter (1876–1958)
Bearden, Bessye (1888–1943)
Beattie, Ann (1947—)
Beattie, Mollie (1947–1996)
Beatty, Bessie (1886–1947)
Beatty, May (1880–1945)
Beaudet, Louise (1861–1947)

Beaumont, Florence (c. 1912–1967)
Beauprey, Jeanne (1961—)
Beauregard, Robin (1979—)
Beaux, Cecilia (1855–1942)
Beavers, Louise (1902–1962)
Bechtel, Louise Seaman (1894–1985)
Beck, Audrey P. (1931–1983)
Beck, Emily Morison (1915–2004)
Beck, Martha (c. 1921–1951)
Beck, Sophie (1858–?)
Becker, Carolyn (1958—)
Becker, May Lamberton (1873–1958)
Becker-Dey, Courtenay (1965—)
Becker-Pinkston, Elizabeth (1903–1989)
Beckwith, Martha Warren (1871–1959)
Bedell, Harriet M. (1875–1969)
Bedford, B.J. (1972—)
Bedford, Barbara (1903–1981)
Beech, Olive Ann (1903–1993)
Beecher, Catharine (1800–1878)
Beecher, Janet (1884–1955)
Beechman, Laurie (c. 1955–1998)
Beeman, Ruth Coates (1925—)
Beers, Ethel Lynn (1827–1879)
Beglin, Elizabeth (1957—)
Beland, Lucy (1871–1941)
Belfrage, Sally (1936–1994)
Bel Geddes, Barbara (1922–2005)
Bell, Elizabeth Viola (1897–1990)
Bell, Lilian (1867–1929)
Bell, Mabel Hubbard (1857–1923)
Bell, Marion (1919–1997)
Bell, Nora Kizer (1941–2004)
Bell, Peggy Kirk (1921—)
Bell, Teresa Z. (1966—)
Bellamy, Elizabeth Whitfield (1839–1900)
Bellamy, Madge (1899–1990)
Bellanca, Dorothy (1894–1946)
Belle, Anne (1935–2003)
Belle, Regina (1963—)
Belmont, Alva Smith (1853–1933)
Belmont, Eleanor Robson (1879–1979)
Belote, Melissa (1956—)
Beltran, Lola (c. 1931–1996)
Benaderet, Bea (1906–1968)
Benatar, Pat (1953—)
Benchley, Belle (1882–1973)
Bender, Kate (1849–?)
Benedict, Ruth (1887–1948)
Benerito, Ruth (1916—)
Benet, Laura (1884–1979)
Benham, Dorothy (c. 1956—)
Benko, Lindsay (1976—)
Bennett, Alice (1851–1925)
Bennett, Alma (1889–1958)
Bennett, Barbara (1906–1958)
Bennett, Belle (1891–1932)
Bennett, Belle Harris (1852–1922)
Bennett, Brooke (1980—)
Bennett, Constance (1904–1965)
Bennett, Estelle (1944—)
Bennett, Evelyn (b. 1905)
Bennett, Isadora (d. 1980)
Bennett, Joan (1910–1990)
Bennett, Marjorie (1896–1982)
Bennett, Mary Katharine (1864–1950)
Bennett, Patricia (1947—)
Bennett, Wilda (1894–1967)
Bennion, Lianne (1972—)
Benson, Linda (c. 1944—)
Benson, Mildred (1905–2002)
Benson, Rita Romilly (1900–1980)
Benson, Sally (1900–1972)
Bentley, Elizabeth Turrill (1908–1963)
Bentley, Gladys (1907–1960)
Bentley, Helen Delich (1923—)
Bentley, Irene (1904–1965)
Bentley, Irene (d. 1940)
Bentley, Muriel (1917–1999)
Benzell, Mimi (1922–1970)
Beranger, Clara (1886–1956)
Berberian, Cathy (1925–1983)
Berberova, Nina (1901–1993)
Berenson, Berry (1948–2001)
Berenson, Marisa (1946—)
Berenson, Mary (1864–1944)
Berenson, Senda (1868–1954)
Berg, Edith (d. 1931)
Berg, Gertrude (1899–1966)
Berg, Laura (1975—)
Berg, Patty (1918—)
Bergen, Candice (1946—)
Bergen, Nella (1873–1919)
Bergen, Polly (1929—)
Bergere, Ouida (1885–1974)
Bergere, Valerie (1872–1938)
Bergeron, Marian (1918–2002)
Bergman, Marilyn (1929—)
Beri, Beth (c. 1904—)
Beringer, Aimée Daniell (1856–1936)
Berke, Dorothea (c. 1900—)
Berkeley, Frances (1634–after 1695)
Berman, Sara Mae (1936—)
Bernard, Dorothy (1890–1955)
Bernard, Jessie (1903–1996)
Bernard, Karen (1948—)
Bernhard, Ruth (1905—)
Berning, Susie Maxwell (1941—)
Bernson, Kathryn (1950—)
Bernstein, Aline (1882–1955)
Bernstein, Sylvia (1915–2003)
Bernstein, Theresa Ferber (1890–2002)
Berry, Halle (1966—)
Berry, Harriet Morehead (1877–1940)
Berry, Martha McChesney (1866–1942)
Bertsch, Marguerite (1889–1967)
Besserer, Eugénie (1868–1934)
Betbeze, Yolande (1930—)
Betham-Edwards, Matilda (1836–1919)
Bethune, Joanne (1770–1860)
Bethune, Louise Blanchard (1856–1913)
Bettis, Valerie (1919–1982)
Betts, Anna Whelan (1873–1959)
Betts, Doris (1932—)
Betts, Ethel Franklin (1878–?)
Betz, Pauline (1919—)
Bevier, Isabel (1860–1942)
Bewley, Lois (c. 1936—)
Bhardwaj, Mohini (1978—)
Bianco, Suzannah (1973—)
Bible, Frances L. (1919–2001)
Bickerdyke, Mary Ann (1817–1901)
Biehl, Amy (1967–1993)
Bigelow, Kathryn (1951—)
Bilansky, Ann (1820–1860)
Bileck, Pamela (1968—)
Billington, Francelia (1895–1934)
Bingham, Amelia (1869–1927)
Bingham, Anne Willing (1764–1801)
Bingham, Henrietta (1901–1968)
Bingham, Millicent Todd (1880–1968)
Bingham, Sybil Moseley (1792–1848)
Binney, Constance (1896–1989)
Biracree, Thelma (1904–1997)
Birch, Patricia (c. 1930—)
Bird, Billie (1908–2002)
Bird, Bonnie (1914–1995)
Bird, Dorothy (c. 1913—)
Bird, Sue (1980—)
Birdsong, Cindy (1939—)
Birmingham Four
Birney, Alice McLellan (1858–1907)
Bischoff, Ilse (1903–1976)
Bishop, Claire Huchet (1898–1993)
Bishop, Elizabeth (1911–1979)
Bishop, Georgianna M. (1878–1971)
Bishop, Harriet E. (1817–1883)
Bishop, Hazel (1906–1998)
Bishop, Isabel (1902–1988)
Bishop, Julie (1914–2001)
Bishop, Kelly (1944—)
Bisland, Elizabeth (1863–1929)
Bissell, Emily (1861–1948)
Bittenbender, Ada Matilda (1848–1925)
Bjorkland, Penny (1941—)
Black, Shirley Temple (1928—)
Black, Winifred Sweet (1863–1936)
Blackwell, Alice Stone (1857–1950)
Blackwell, Emily (1826–1910)
Blahoski, Alana (1974—)
Blaine, Anita McCormick (1866–1954)
Blaine, Vivian (1921–1995)
Blair, Betsy (1923—)
Blair, Bonnie (1964—)
Blair, Emily Newell (1877–1951)
Blair, Janet (1921—)
Blair, Mary (c. 1895–1947)
Blair, Pamela (1949—)
Blais, Marie-Claire (1939—)
Blake, Amanda (1929–1989)
Blake, Lillie Devereux (1833–1913)
Blaker, Eliza Ann (1854–1926)
Blalock, Jane (1945—)
Blanchard, Mari (1927–1970)
Blanchard, Theresa Weld (1893–1978)
Blanchfield, Florence (1884–1971)
Blanco, Kathleen (1942—)
Bland, Harriet (1915–1991)
Blandick, Clara (1880–1962)
Blane, Sally (1910–1997)
Blangy, Hermine (c. 1820–c. 1865)
Blank, Carla (c. 1940—)
Blankenburg, Lucretia L. (1845–1937)
Blazejowski, Carol (1957—)
Blecher, Miriam (1912–1979)
Bleecker, Ann Eliza (1752–1783)
Bleibtrey, Ethelda M. (1902–1978)
Bleiler, Gretchen (1981—)
Bley, Carla (1938—)
Blige, Mary J. (1971—)
Blinks, Susan (1957—)
Bliss, Anna (1843–1925)
Bliss, Lillie (1864–1931)
Bliss, Mary Elizabeth (1824–1909)
Bliss, Mildred Barnes (1879–1969)
Blitch, Iris Faircloth (1912–1993)
Bloch, Suzanne (1907–2002)
Blodgett, Katharine Burr (1898–1979)
Bloede, Gertrude (1845–1905)
Blondeau, Barbara (1938–1974)
Blondell, Joan (1906–1979)
Bloom, Verna (1939—)
Bloomer, Amelia Jenks (1818–1894)
Bloor, Ella Reeve (1862–1951)
Blow, Susan Elizabeth (1843–1916)
Blue, Rita Hassan (c. 1905–1973)
Blum, Arlene (1945—)
Blume, Judy (1938—)
Blunt, Katharine (1876–1954)
Blyth, Ann (1928—)
Blythe, Betty (1893–1972)
Boardman, Diane (c. 1950—)
Boardman, Eleanor (1898–1991)
Boardman, Mabel (1860–1946)
Bober, Phyllis (1920–2002)
Boddie, Barbara White (1940—)
Bodley, Rachel (1831–1888)
Boehm, Helen F. (b. early 1920s)

Boehm, Mary Louise (1924–2002)
Bofill, Angela (1954—)
Bogan, Louise (1897–1970)
Bogan, Lucille (1897–1948)
Boggs, Lindy (1916—)
Bogle, Helen McDermott (1871–?)
Bogle, Sarah C.N. (1870–1932)
Boglioli, Wendy (1955—)
Boiardi, Helen (1905–1995)
Boissevain, Inez M. (1886–1916)
Boit, Elizabeth Eaton (1849–1932)
Boland, Mary (1880–1965)
Boland, Veronica Grace (1899–1982)
Bolden, Jeanette (1960—)
Bolen, Lin (1941—)
Boley, May (1881–1963)
Bollinger, Anne (c. 1923–1962)
Bolton, Frances Payne (1885–1977)
Bolton, Mildred Mary (1886–1943)
Bolton, Ruthie (1967—)
Bolton, Sarah Knowles (1841–1916)
Bolton, Sarah T. (1814–1893)
Bolton-Holifield, Ruthie (1967—)
Bombeck, Erma (1927–1996)
Bonaparte, Elizabeth Patterson (1785–1879)
Bond, Carrie Jacobs (1862–1946)
Bond, Elizabeth Powell (1841–1926)
Bond, Sheila (1928—)
Bond, Sudie (1928–1984)
Bond, Victoria (1950—)
Bondi, Beulah (1892–1981)
Bonds, Margaret (1913–1972)
Bonds, Rosie (c. 1944—)
Bonfanti, Marietta (1845–1921)
Bonfils, Helen (c. 1890–1972)
Bonner, Antoinette (1892–1920)
Bonner, Beth (1952–1998)
Bonner, Isabel (1907–1955)
Bonner, Margerie (1905–1988)
Bonner, Marita (1899–1971)
Bonner, Mary (1885–1935)
Bonner, Priscilla (1899–1996)
Bonner, Sherwood (1849–1883)
Bonney, Mary Lucinda (1816–1900)
Bonney, Thérèse (1894–1978)
Bonnin, Gertrude Simmons (1876–1938)
Bono, Mary (1961—)
Bonoff, Karla (1952—)
Bonstelle, Jessie (1871–1932)
Bontecou, Lee (1931—)
Boole, Ella (1858–1952)
Boone, Debby (1956—)
Booth, Adrian (1918—)
Booth, Agnes (1843–1910)
Booth, Edwina (1904–1991)
Booth, Ellen Scripps (1863–1948)
Booth, Jane Bastanchury (1948—)
Booth, Karin (1919–1992)
Booth, Margaret (1898–2002)
Booth, Mary Louise (1831–1889)
Booth, Maud Ballington (1865–1948)
Booth, Shirley (1907–1992)
Booth-Tucker, Emma Moss (1860–1903)
Borchardt, Selma Munter (1895–1968)
Borda, Deborah (1949—)
Borden, Amanda (1977—)
Borden, Lizzie (1860–1927)
Borden, Olive (1906–1947)
Borders, Ila (1975—)
Bordoni, Irene (1895–1953)
Borelli, LaVerne (1909—)
Borg, Anita (1949–2003)
Borg, Dorothy (1901–1993)
Borg, Veda Ann (1915–1973)
Boring, Alice Middleton (1883–1955)
Boris, Ruthanna (1918—)
Borne, Bonita (1952—)
Boros, Ferike (1880–1951)
Bosone, Reva Beck (1895–1983)
Boswell, Cathy (1962—)
Boswell, Connee (1907–1976)
Botkin, Cordelia (c. 1854–1910)
Botsford, Beth (1981—)
Botta, Anne C.L. (1815–1891)
Bottome, Margaret McDonald (1827–1906)
Boudin, Kathy (1943—)
Boughton, Alice (1866–1943)
Bourgeois, Louise (b. 1911)
Bourke-White, Margaret (1904–1971)
Boutilier, Joy (1939—)
Bouvet, Marguerite (1865–1915)
Bovasso, Julie (1930–1991)
Bove, Joan (1901–2001)
Bovt, Violette (1927—)
Bow, Clara (1904–1965)
Bowden, Sally (c. 1948—)
Bowen, Catherine Drinker (1897–1973)
Bowen, Louise (1859–1953)
Bower, Alberta (1922—)
Bower, Beverly (d. 2002)
Bower, Carol (1956—)
Bowers, Bathsheba (c. 1672–1718)
Bowers, Elizabeth Crocker (1830–1895)
Bowles, Eva del Vakia (1875–1943)
Bowles, Jane (1917–1973)
Bowman, Patricia (1904–1999)
Bowne, Eliza Southgate (1783–1809)
Bowring, Eva Kelly (1892–1985)
Box, Betty E. (1915–1999)
Boxer, Barbara (1940—)
Boxx, Gillian (1973—)
Boxx, Shannon (1977—)
Boyce, Johanna (1954—)
Boyce, Neith (1872–1951)
Boyd, Belle (1844–1900)
Boyd, Eva (1945–2003)
Boyd, Louise Arner (1887–1972)
Boylan, Mary (1913–1984)
Boyle, Darian (c. 1968—)
Boyle, Kay (1902–1992)
Brace, Julia (1806–1884)
Brackeen, JoAnne (1938—)
Brackett, Anna Callender (1836–1911)
Brackett, Leigh (1915–1978)
Braden, Anne (1924–2006)
Bradford, Barbara Taylor (1933—)
Bradford, Cornelia Foster (1847–1935)
Bradford, Cornelia Smith (d. 1755)
Bradley, Amy Morris (1823–1904)
Bradley, Grace (1913—)
Bradley, Lillian Trimble (1875–?)
Bradley, Lisa (1941—)
Bradley, Lydia Moss (1816–1908)
Bradley, Marion Zimmer (1930–1999)
Bradley, Pat (1951—)
Bradstreet, Anne (1612–1672)
Bradwell, Myra (1831–1894)
Brady, Alice (1892–1939)
Brady, Mary (1821–1864)
Brady, Mildred Edie (1906–1965)
Braggiotti, Berthe (c. 1900–c. 1925)
Braggiotti, Francesca (1902–1998)
Braggiotti, Gloria (c. 1905—)
Bramlett, Bonnie (1944—)
Bramley, Jenny Rosenthal (1910–1997)
Branch, Anna Hempstead (1875–1937)
Branch, Mary Lydia Bolles (1840–1922)
Brand, Phoebe (1907–2004)
Brand, Sybil (c. 1899–2004)
Brandegee, Mary Katharine (1844–1920)
Brandstrom, Elsa (1888–1948)
Brandy (1979—)
Branham, Sara Elizabeth (1888–1962)
Branigan, Laura (1957–2004)
Branitzka, Nathalie (1905–1977)
Branscombe, Gena (1881–1977)
Brant, Beth (1941—)
Brant, Molly (c. 1736–1796)
Braslau, Sophie (1888–1935)
Braun, Carol Mosely (1947—)
Braun, E. Lucy (1889–1971)
Braxton, Toni (1967—)
Brayley, Sally (1937—)
Breamer, Sylvia (1897–1943)
Breckinridge, Madeline McDowell (1872–1920)
Breckinridge, Margaret E. (d. 1864)
Breckinridge, Mary (1881–1965)
Breckinridge, Mary Martin (b. 1905)
Breckinridge, Sophonisba Preston (1866–1948)
Bredahl, Charlotte (1957—)
Breen, Nellie (c. 1898–1986)
Breer, Murle MacKenzie (1939—)
Brehm, Marie Caroline (1859–1926)
Bremer, Edith (1885–1964)
Bremer, Lucille (1923–1996)
Brennan, Eileen (1935—)
Brennan, Fanny (1921–2001)
Brenner, Dori (1946–2000)
Brent, Evelyn (1899–1975)
Brent, Margaret (c. 1601–1671)
Brewer, Lucy (fl. 1812)
Brewer, Margaret A. (1930—)
Brewer, Teresa (1931—)
Brewster, Anne Hampton (1818–1892)
Brewster, Barbara (1918–2005)
Brewster, Gloria (1918–1996)
Brewster, Martha Wadsworth (fl. 1725–1757)
Brian, Mary (1906–2002)
Brice, Carol (1918–1985)
Brice, Elizabeth (c. 1885–1965)
Brice, Fanny (1891–1951)
Brickell, Edie (1966—)
Brico, Antonia (1902–1989)
Bridges, Alice (1916—)
Bridges, Fidelia (1834–1923)
Bridges, Ruby (c. 1954—)
Bridgman, Eliza Jane (1805–1871)
Bridgman, Laura (1829–1889)
Briggs, Emily Edson (1830–1910)
Briggs, Margaret Jane (1892–1961)
Brigham, Emma Frances (1855–1881)
Brigham, Mary Ann (1829–1889)
Brigman, Anne W. (1869–1950)
Brill, Patti (1923–1963)
Brink, Carol Ryrie (1895–1981)
Brinker, Nancy G. (1946—)
Brinkley, Christie (1953—)
Briscoe, Lottie (1870–1950)
Brisco-Hooks, Valerie (1960—)
Brissac, Virginia (1883–1979)
Britain, Radie (1897–1994)
Britton, Barbara (1919–1980)
Britton, Elizabeth Knight (1858–1934)
Britton, Nan (1896–1991)
Britton, Pamela (1923–1974)
Britz, Jerilyn (1943—)
Broad, Molly Corbett (c. 1941—)
Broadwick, Tiny (1893–1978)
Broccoli, Dana (1922–2004)
Brock, Karena (1942—)
Brockovich, Erin (1960—)
Brockwell, Gladys (1894–1929)
Brodbeck, May (1917–1983)
Broder, Jane (d. 1977)
Broderick, Helen (1890–1959)

Brogden, Cindy (1957—)
Bromley, Dorothy Dunbar (1896–1986)
Broner, E.M. (1930—)
Bronner, Augusta Fox (1881–1966)
Bronson, Betty (1906–1971)
Bronson, Lillian (1902–1995)
Brooke, Hillary (1914–1999)
Brooks, Charlotte (1918—)
Brooks, Dolores (1946—)
Brooks, Geraldine (1925–1977)
Brooks, Gwendolyn (1917–2000)
Brooks, Hadda (1916–2002)
Brooks, Louise (1906–1985)
Brooks, Maria Gowen (c. 1794–1845)
Brooks, Matilda M. (1888–1981)
Brooks, Pauline (1912–1967)
Brooks, Phyllis (1914–1995)
Brooks, Romaine (1874–1970)
Broomall, Anna (1847–1931)
Brothers, Joyce (1928—)
Brotherton, Alice Williams (1848–1930)
Brough, Louise (1923—)
Brousse, Amy (1910–1963)
Brown, Abbie Farwell (1871–1927)
Brown, Ada (1889–1950)
Brown, Alice (1856–1948)
Brown, Alice Regina (1960—)
Brown, Alice Van Vechten (1862–1949)
Brown, Beverly (1941–2002)
Brown, Carol Page (1953—)
Brown, Carolyn (1927—)
Brown, Charlotte (1846–1904)
Brown, Charlotte Emerson (1838–1895)
Brown, Charlotte Hawkins (c. 1883–1961)
Brown, Cindy (1965—)
Brown, Cleo (1905–1995)
Brown, Dorothy L. (1919–2004)
Brown, Earlene Dennis (1935—)
Brown, Elaine (1943—)
Brown, Elizabeth (1753–1812)
Brown, Foxy (1979—)
Brown, Hallie Quinn (c. 1845–1949)
Brown, Helen Gurley (1922—)
Brown, Jessica (c. 1900–?)
Brown, Jessie (1892–1985)
Brown, Josephine (1892–1976)
Brown, Judi (1961—)
Brown, Karen (1955—)
Brown, Katie (1982—)
Brown, Kay (1903–1995)
Brown, Leah (1975—)
Brown, Linda (1943—)
Brown, Lucy (fl. 1895)
Brown, Marcia (1918—)
Brown, Margaret Wise (1910–1952)
Brown, Martha McClellan (1838–1916)
Brown, Mary Jane (1917–1997)
Brown, Minnijean (1942—)
Brown, Molly (1867–1932)
Brown, Olympia (1835–1926)
Brown, Rachel Fuller (1898–1980)
Brown, Rita Mae (1944—)
Brown, Rosel George (1926–1967)
Brown, Rosellen (1939—)
Brown, Ruth (1928—)
Brown, Tina (1953—)
Brown, Trisha (1936—)
Brown, Vanessa (1928–1999)
Brown, Vida (1922—)
Brown, Virginia Mae (1923–1991)
Brown Blackwell, Antoinette (1825–1921)
Browne, Augusta (1820–1882)
Browne, Helen Edith (1911–1987)
Browne, Leslie (1958—)
Browne, Mary K. (1891–1971)
Browne, Rosalind Bengelsdorf (1916–1979)
Brownell, Kady (b. 1842)
Browner, Carol M. (1956—)
Brown-Miller, Lisa (1966—)
Brownscombe, Jennie Augusta (1850–1936)
Brownson, Josephine (1880–1942)
Brownstein, Carrie (1974—)
Broxon, Mildred Downey (1944—)
Bruce, Betty (1920–1974)
Bruce, Catherine Wolfe (1816–1900)
Bruce, Kate (1858–1946)
Bruce, Tonie Edgar (1892–1966)
Bruce, Virginia (1910–1982)
Bruce, Wendy (1973—)
Brues, Alice (1913—)
Brunauer, Esther C. (1901–1959)
Brundage, Jennifer (1973—)
Bruno, Gioia Carmen (1965—)
Brunswick, Ruth Mack (1897–1946)
Brustein, Norma (c. 1929–1979)
Brutsaert, Elke (1968—)
Bryan, Anna E. (1858–1901)
Bryan, Jane (1918—)
Bryan, Mary Edwards (1838–1913)
Bryant, Alice Gertrude (c. 1862–1942)
Bryant, Bonnie (1943—)
Bryant, Deborah (c. 1946—)
Bryant, Dorothy (1930—)
Bryant, Felice (1925–2003)
Bryant, Hazel (1939–1983)
Bryant, Lane (1879–1951)
Bryant, Louise (1885–1936)
Bryant, Rosalyn (1956—)
Bryner, Vera (d. 1967)
Bryson, Bernarda (1903–2004)
Bubley, Esther (1921–1998)
Buchanan, Vera Daerr (1902–1955)
Buck, Carrie (d. 1983)
Buck, Kitty (1907–2001)
Buck, Linda B. (1947—)
Buck, Pearl S. (1892–1973)
Buckel, C. Annette (1833–1912)
Budapest, Z. (1940—)
Budke, Mary Anne (1953—)
Buehrmann, Elizabeth (1886–1954)
Buell, Marjorie Henderson (1905–1993)
Bufalino, Brenda (1937—)
Buferd, Marilyn (1925–1990)
Buffington, Adele (1900–1973)
Buford-Bailey, Tonja (1970—)
Bugbee, Emma (1888–1981)
Buggy, Regina (1959—)
Buglisi, Jacqulyn (1951—)
Bühler, Charlotte (1893–1974)
Bulfinch, Hannah Apthorp (1768–1841)
Bullett, Vicky (1967—)
Bullette, Julia (d. 1867)
Bullowa, Emilie (1869–1942)
Bumbry, Grace (1937—)
Bunker, Carol Laise (1918–1991)
Bunting, Mary Ingraham (1910–1998)
Bunzel, Ruth (1898–1990)
Burani, Michelette (1882–1957)
Burchenal, Elizabeth (1876–1959)
Burfeindt, Betty (1945—)
Burford, Anne Gorsuch (1942–2004)
Burgess, Dorothy (1907–1961)
Burke, Billie (1885–1970)
Burke, Frances (c. 1921—)
Burke, Georgia (1880–1986)
Burke, Kathleen (1913–1980)
Burke, Lynn (1943—)
Burke, Selma Hortense (1900–1995)
Burke, Yvonne Brathwaite (1932—)
Burleigh, Celia C. (1826–1875)
Burlin, Natalie Curtis (1875–1921)
Burnett, Carol (1933—)
Burnett, Frances Hodgson (1849–1924)
Burnett, Hallie Southgate (1908–1991)
Burns, Lindsay
Burns, Louise (1949—)
Burns, Lucy (1879–1966)
Burnside, Cara-Beth (1968—)
Burr, Esther Edwards (1732–1758)
Burr, Leslie (1956—)
Burr, Theodosia (1783–1813)
Burras, Anne (fl. 1609)
Burroughs, Margaret Taylor (1917—)
Burroughs, Nannie Helen (c. 1878–1961)
Burrows-Fontaine, Evan (1898–1984)
Burstyn, Ellen (1932—)
Burton, Annie L. (fl. 19th c.)
Burton, Pearlie (1904–1993)
Burton, Sala (1925–1987)
Burton, Virginia Lee (1909–1968)
Busby, Amy (c. 1872–1957)
Busch, Mae (1891–1946)
Bush, Barbara (1924—)
Bush, Dorothy V. (1916–1991)
Bush, Frances Cleveland (d. 1967)
Bush, Kate (1958—)
Bush, Laura (1946—)
Bush, Lesley (1947—)
Bush, Pauline (1886–1969)
Bushfield, Vera Cahalan (1889–1976)
Busley, Jessie (1869–1950)
Bustos, Crystl (1977—)
Butcher, Susan (1954—)
Bute, Mary Ellen (1906–1983)
Butler, Elizabeth Beardsley (c. 1885–1911)
Butler, Helen May (1867–1957)
Butler, Ida (1868–1949)
Butler, Mother Marie Joseph (1860–1940)
Butler, Octavia E. (1947—)
Butler, Selena Sloan (1872–1964)
Butterworth, Mary Peck (1686–1775)
Buzonas, Gail Johnson (1954—)
Byars, Betsy (1928—)
Bye, Karyn (1971—)
Byington, Spring (1886–1971)
Byrd, Mary Willing (1740–1814)
Byrne, Jane (1934—)
Byron, Beverly Butcher (1932—)
Byron, Katharine Edgar (1903–1976)
Byron, Marion (1911–1985)
Cabot, Susan (1927–1986)
Caccialanza, Gisella (1914–1998)
Cachat, Beth (1951—)
Cady, H. Emilie (1848–1941)
Caesar, Doris Porter (1892–1971)
Cagney, Frances (1901–1994)
Cagney, Jeanne (1919–1984)
Cahan, Cora (1940—)
Cahill, Lily (1885–1955)
Cahill, Mabel E. (1863–?)
Cahill, Marie (1870–1933)
Calderón de la Barca, Frances (1804–1882)
Calderone, Mary Steichen (1904–1998)
Caldicott, Helen (1938—)
Caldwell, Anne (1876–1936)
Caldwell, Mary Gwendolin (1863–1909)
Caldwell, Sarah (1924–2006)
Caldwell, Taylor (1900–1985)
Calhoun, Alice (1900–1966)
Calhoun, Marge (fl. 1950s)
Calisher, Hortense (b. 1911)
Calkins, Mary Whiton (1863–1930)
Callahan, Sophia Alice (1868–1894)
Callas, Maria (1923–1977)
Callen, Maude (1899–1990)
Callender, Hannah (1737–1801)
Callender, Marie (1907–1995)
Callison, Carole Jo (1938—)

Calloway, Blanche (1902–1973)
Calvert, Catherine (1890–1971)
Calvert, Patricia (1906–1978)
Calvet, Corinne (1921–2001)
Calvillo, María del Carmen (1765–1856)
Calzada, Alba (1945—)
Cameron, Donaldina (1869–1968)
Cameron, Dorothy (d. 1958)
Cameron, Julia (c. 1947—)
Cammermeyer, Margarethe (1942—)
Campanelli, Pauline (1943–2001)
Campbell, Beatrice (1922–1979)
Campbell, Charlotte C. (1914–1993)
Campbell, Edith (d. 1945)
Campbell, Helen Stuart (1839–1918)
Campbell, Louise (1911–1997)
Campbell, Mary Katherine (1905–1990)
Campbell, Maude B. (c. 1908–?)
Campbell, Persia (1898–1974)
Camps, Miriam (1916–1994)
Canary, Christa (1962—)
Cannary, Martha Jane (1852–1903)
Cannon, Annie Jump (1863–1941)
Cannon, Dyan (1937—)
Cannon, Harriet Starr (1823–1896)
Cannon, Ida (1877–1960)
Canova, Judy (1916–1983)
Cansino, Elisa (b. 1895)
Capers, Virginia (1925–2004)
Caperton, Harriette (c. 1913—)
Caponi, Donna (1945—)
Capps, Lois (1938—)
Capriati, Jennifer (1976—)
Caprice, June (1899–1936)
Carabillo, Toni (1926–1997)
Caramagno, Denise (1961—)
Caraway, Hattie Wyatt (1878–1950)
Carew, Mary (1913–2002)
Carew, Ora (1893–1955)
Carey, Eva (fl. 1921)
Carey, Mariah (1970—)
Carey, Miriam E. (1858–1937)
Carey, Olive (1896–1988)
Carhart, Georgiana (d. 1959)
Carleton, Claire (1913–1979)
Carlin, Cynthia (d. 1973)
Carlisle, Alexandra (1886–1936)
Carlisle, Belinda (1958—)
Carlisle, Kitty (b. 1910)
Carlisle, Mary (b. 1912)
Carlson, Carolyn (1943—)
Carlson, Gretchen (c. 1966—)
Carlson, Violet (d. 1997)
Carmen, Jewel (1897–1984)
Carnegie, Hattie (1886–1956)
Carnegie, Louise Whitfield (1857–1946)
Carner, JoAnne (1939—)
Carnes, Kim (1945—)
Carol, Sue (1906–1982)
Caron, Margaret Pettibone (b. around 1904)
Carothers, E. Eleanor (1882–1957)
Carpenter, Karen (1950–1983)
Carpenter, Marion (1920–2002)
Carpenter, Mary Chapin (1958—)
Carpenter, Thelma (1922–1997)
Carpenter-Phinney, Connie (1957—)
Carr, Ann (1958—)
Carr, Catherine (1954—)
Carr, Emma Perry (1880–1972)
Carr, Mary (1874–1973)
Carr, Vikki (1941—)
Carrighar, Sally (1898–1985)
Carroll, Anna Ella (1815–1894)
Carroll, Dee (1925–1980)
Carroll, Diahann (1935—)
Carroll, Gladys Hasty (1904–1999)
Carroll, Nancy (1903–1965)
Carroll, Vinnette (1922–2002)
Carruthers, Kitty (1962—)
Carse, Matilda Bradley (1835–1917)
Carson, Ann (d. 1824)
Carson, Julia (1938—)
Carson, Rachel (1907–1964)
Carter, Amy (1967—)
Carter, Anita (1933–1999)
Carter, Ann Shaw (1922—)
Carter, Betty (1929–1998)
Carter, Carlene (1955—)
Carter, Eunice Hunton (1899–1970)
Carter, Helen (1927–1998)
Carter, Helena (1923–2000)
Carter, Janis (1913–1994)
Carter, Jeanette (1923–2006)
Carter, Maybelle (1909–1978)
Carter, Mrs. Leslie (1862–1937)
Carter, Nell (1948–2003)
Carter, Rosalynn (1927—)
Carter, Sarah (1898–1979)
Cartier, Diana (1939—)
Carus, Emma (1879–1927)
Carver, Kathryn (1899–1947)
Carver, Louise (1869–1956)
Carver, Lynne (1909–1955)
Carver, Tina (c. 1923–1982)
Cary, Alice (1820–1871)
Cary, Annie Louise (1841–1921)
Cary, Elisabeth Luther (1867–1936)
Cary, Mary Ann Shadd (1823–1893)
Cary, Phoebe (1824–1871)
Casals, Rosemary (1948—)
Case, Adelaide (1887–1948)
Caselotti, Adriana (1916–1997)
Cash, June Carter (1929–2003)
Cash, Kellye (c. 1965—)
Cash, Rosalind (1938–1995)
Cash, Rosanne (1955—)
Cash, Swin (1979—)
Cashin, Bonnie (1915–2000)
Cashman, Karen
Cashman, Nellie (1844–1925)
Cason, Barbara (1928–1990)
Caspary, Vera (1899–1987)
Cass, Peggy (1924–1999)
Cassatt, Mary (1844–1926)
Castle, Irene (c. 1893–1969)
Castle, Peggie (1926–1973)
Caswell, Maude (c. 1880–?)
Catchings, Tamika (1979—)
Cather, Willa (1873–1947)
Catherwood, Mary Hartwell (1847–1902)
Catlett, Elizabeth (b. 1915)
Catt, Carrie Chapman (1859–1947)
Catterson, Pat (1946—)
Caulfield, Joan (1922–1921)
Caulkins, Frances Manwaring (1795–1869)
Caulkins, Tracy (1963—)
Cavallazzi, Malvina (c. 1852–1924)
Cayvan, Georgia (1857–1906)
Cazneau, Jane McManus (1807–1878)
Cha, Theresa Hak Kyung (1951–1982)
Chabot, Maria (1913–2001)
Chace, Elizabeth Buffum (1806–1899)
Chace, Marian (1896–1970)
Chadwick, Florence (1918–1995)
Chadwick, Helene (1897–1940)
Chaffee, Suzy (1946—)
Chai, Ling (1966—)
Chambers, Anne Cox (1919—)
Chambers, Charlotte (d. 1821)
Chamblit, Rebekah (d. 1733)
Chamie, Tatiana (d. 1953)
Champion, Marge (1919—)
Champlin, Jane (1917–1943)
Chandler, Dorothy Buffum (1901–1997)
Chandler, Elizabeth Margaret (1807–1834)
Chandler, Helen (1906–1965)
Chandler, Janet (1915–1994)
Chandler, Jennifer (1959—)
Chaney, Frances (1915–2004)
Chang, Diana (1934—)
Chang, Iris (1968–2004)
Chanler, Margaret (b. 1862)
Channing, Carol (1921—)
Channing, Stockard (1944—)
Chapelle, Dickey (1919–1972)
Chapin, Anne Morrison (1892–1967)
Chapin, Augusta (1836–1905)
Chapin, Sallie F. (c. 1830–1896)
Chaplin, Geraldine (1944—)
Chaplin, Lita Grey (1908–1995)
Chaplin, Oona O'Neill (1925–1991)
Chapman, Caroline (c. 1818–1876)
Chapman, Edythe (1863–1948)
Chapman, Marguerite (1918–1999)
Chapman, Maria (1806–1885)
Chapman, Merilyn (1962—)
Chapman, Tracy (1964—)
Charisse, Cyd (1921—)
Charles, Daedra (1969—)
Charles, Suzette (1963—)
Charleson, Mary (1890–1961)
Charnas, Suzy McKee (1939—)
Chase, Agnes Meara (1869–1963)
Chase, Alison Becker (c. 1948—)
Chase, Arline (1900–1926)
Chase, Barrie (1933—)
Chase, Edna Woolman (1877–1957)
Chase, Ilka (1905–1978)
Chase, Lucia (1897–1986)
Chase, Martha (1927–2003)
Chase, Mary Coyle (1907–1981)
Chase, Mary Ellen (1887–1973)
Chase, Pauline (1885–1962)
Chasen, Maude (1904–2001)
Chase-Riboud, Barbara (1936—)
Chast, Roz (1954—)
Chastain, Brandi (1968—)
Chatterton, Ruth (1893–1961)
Chavez-Thompson, Linda (1944—)
Chawla, Kalpana (1961–2003)
Cheeseborough, Chandra (1959—)
Cheeseman, Gwen (1951—)
Chelgren, Pamela (c. 1949—)
Chen, Joyce (1918–1994)
Cheney, Dorothy Bundy (1916—)
Cheney, Ednah Dow (1824–1904)
Cheney, Leona Pressler (1904–1982)
Cheney, Lynne (1941—)
Chennault, Anna (1923—)
Chenoweth, Helen (1938—)
Cher (1946—)
Cherrill, Virginia (1908–1996)
Cherry, Addie (c. 1859–1942)
Cherry, Effie (d. 1944)
Cherry, Neneh (1963—)
Cherryh, C.J. (1942—)
Chesebrough, Caroline (1825–1873)
Chesimard, Joanne (1948—)
Chesler, Phyllis (1940—)
Chesnut, Mary Boykin (1823–1886)
Cheung, Katherine (1904–2003)
Chicago, Judy (1939—)
Child, Julia (1912–2004)
Child, Lydia Maria (1802–1880)
Childers, Naomi (1892–1964)
Childress, Alice (1916–1994)
Childs, Lucinda (1940—)
Ching, Laura Blears (c. 1951—)

Chinn, May Edward (1896–1980)
Chisholm, Linda (1957—)
Chisholm, Shirley (1924–2005)
Chladek, Dana (1963—)
Choate, Mrs. Allison (b. 1910)
Choate, Pearl (1907–1983)
Choi, Sook Nyul (1937—)
Chona, Maria (1845–1936)
Chopin, Kate (1850–1904)
Chopra, Joyce (1938—)
Chouteau, Yvonne (1929—)
Chow, Amy (1978—)
Chow, Tina (1950–1992)
Christian, Meg (1946—)
Christine, Virginia (1920–1996)
Christman, Elisabeth (1881–1975)
Christopher, Patricia (c. 1934—)
Christy, Barrett (1971—)
Christy, June (1925–1990)
Chryssa (1933—)
Chu, Julie (1982—)
Chung, Connie (1946—)
Chung, Kyung-Wha (1948—)
Church, Ellen (c. 1905–1965)
Church, Marguerite Stitt (1892–1990)
Churchill, Jennie Jerome (1854–1921)
Churchill, Marguerite (1909–2000)
Churchill, May (1876–1929)
Chute, B.J. (1913–1987)
Chute, Carolyn (1947—)
Chute, Marchette (1909–1994)
Cicierska, Margaret
Ciocca, Giovanna (c. 1825–?)
Cisneros, Eleonora de (1878–1934)
Cisneros, Evelyn (1958—)
Cisneros, Sandra (1954—)
Claflin, Tennessee (1846–1923)
Claiborne, Liz (1929—)
Claire, Helen (1911–1974)
Claire, Ina (1892–1985)
Clampitt, Amy (1920–1994)
Clapp, Cornelia Maria (1849–1934)
Clapp, Louise (1819–1906)
Clapp, Margaret (1910–1974)
Clare, Ada (1836–1874)
Clark, Cheryl (1950—)
Clark, Eleanor (1913–1996)
Clark, Eugenie (1922—)
Clark, Georgia Neese (1900–1995)
Clark, Kelly (1983—)
Clark, Laurel (1961–2003)
Clark, Mamo (1914–1986)
Clark, Marguerite (1883–1940)
Clark, Mary Ellen (1962—)
Clark, Mary Higgins (1929—)
Clark, Mattie Moss (1925–1994)
Clark, Nancy Talbot (1825–1901)
Clark, Peggy (c. 1916–1996)
Clark, Septima Poinsette (1898–1987)
Clarke, Betty Ross (1896–1947)
Clarke, Edith (1883–1959)
Clarke, Grace Julian (1865–1938)
Clarke, Helen (c. 1897–?)
Clarke, Helen Archibald (1860–1926)
Clarke, Julia (d. 1912)
Clarke, Mae (1907–1992)
Clarke, Martha (1944—)
Clarke, Mary (1924—)
Clarke, Mary Bayard (1827–1886)
Clarke, Mary Frances (1803–1887)
Clarke, Maura (1931—)
Clarke, Rebecca Sophia (1833–1906)
Clarke, Sarah Jones (1840–1929)
Clarke, Shirley (1925–1997)
Clark Sisters (fl. 1940s)
Claster, Nancy (1915–1997)
Claxton, Kate (1848–1924)
Clay, Laura (1849–1941)
Clay, Virginia Tunstall (1825–1915)
Clayburgh, Alma (d. 1958)
Claypole, Edith Jane (1870–1915)
Clayton, Bessie (c. 1878–1948)
Clayton, Ethel (1882–1966)
Clayton, Eva M. (1934—)
Clayton, Jan (1917–1983)
Clayton, Marguerite (1891–1968)
Clayton, S. Lillian (1876–1930)
Cleare, Ivy (1948—)
Cleary, Beverly (1916—)
Cleaves, Jessica (1948—)
Cleaves, Margaret (1848–1917)
Cleland, Tammy (1975—)
Cleveland, Emeline Horton (1829–1878)
Cleveland, Frances Folsom (1864–1947)
Cleveland, Rose Elizabeth (b. 1846)
Cleveland, Ruth (1891–1904)
Cliff, Michelle (1946—)
Cliff, Theresa (1978—)
Clifford, Kathleen (1887–1962)
Clifford, Ruth (1900–1998)
Clift, Martha (fl. 1930s)
Clifton, Lucille (1936—)
Cline, Genevieve (1879–1959)
Cline, Maggie (1857–1934)
Cline, Patsy (1932–1963)
Clinton, Chelsea (1980—)
Clinton, Hillary Rodham (1947—)
Clooney, Rosemary (1928–2002)
Close, Glenn (1947—)
Clyde, June (1909–1987)
Clymer, Eleanor (1906–2001)
Coachman, Alice (1923—)
Coates, Dorothy Love (1928–2002)
Coates, Florence Nicholson (1850–1927)
Coates, Gloria (1938—)
Coatsworth, Elizabeth (1893–1986)
Cobb, Jerrie (1931—)
Cobb, Jewell Plummer (1924—)
Cobbs, Janet (1967—)
Cobos, Antonia (c. 1920—)
Coburn, Doris (fl. 1970s)
Coburn-Carroll, Cindy (fl. 1980s)
Coca, Imogene (1909–2001)
Cochran, Angela (1965—)
Cochran, Barbara (1951—)
Cochran, Jacqueline (1906–1980)
Cochran, Linda (1953—)
Cochran, Marilyn (1950—)
Cockerill, Kay (1964—)
Coffee, Lenore (1896–1984)
Coghlan, Gertrude (1876–1952)
Coghlan, Rose (1852–1932)
Cohan, Georgette (b. 1900)
Cohan, Helen F. (1910–1996)
Cohan, Josephine (1876–1916)
Cohen, Lona (1913–1993)
Cohen, Rose (1880–1925)
Cohen, Tiffany (1966—)
Cohen, Ze'eva (1940—)
Cohn, Fannia (c. 1885–1962)
Coit, Margaret L. (1919–2003)
Coit, Mehetabel Chandler (1673–1758)
Colander-Richardson, LaTasha (1976—)
Colbert, Claudette (1903–1996)
Colborn, Theodora (1927—)
Colby, Christine (c. 1950—)
Colby, Clara Bewick (1846–1916)
Colcord, Joanna Carver (1882–1960)
Colden, Jane (1724–1766)
Cole, Anna Russell (1846–1926)
Cole, Johnnetta B. (1936—)
Cole, Kay (1948—)
Cole, Natalie (1950—)
Cole, Paula (1968—)
Cole, Rebecca J. (1846–1922)
Colella, Lynn (1950—)
Coleman, Alice Merriam (1858–1936)
Coleman, Ann Rancy Thomas (1810–1897)
Coleman, Bessie (1892–1926)
Coleman, Corrine Grad (1927–2004)
Coleman, Georgia (1912–1940)
Coleman, Mary (1914–2001)
Coleman, Mary Sue (1943—)
Coleman, Nancy (1912–2000)
Coley, Doris (1941–2000)
Collier, Jeanne (1946—)
Collier, Lois (1919–1999)
Collinge, Patricia (1892–1974)
Collins, Addie Mae (d. 1963)
Collins, Barbara-Rose (1939—)
Collins, Cardiss (1931—)
Collins, Christine (1969—)
Collins, Cora Sue (1927—)
Collins, Eileen (1956—)
Collins, Ellen (1828–1912)
Collins, Gail (1945—)
Collins, Janet (1917–2003)
Collins, Jennie (1828–1887)
Collins, Kathleen (1942—1988)
Collins, Martha Layne (1936—)
Collins, Marva (1936—)
Collyer, June (1907–1968)
Colman, Julia (1828–1909)
Colt, Ethel Barrymore (1912–1977)
Colter, Mary Elizabeth (1869–1949)
Colton, Elizabeth Avery (1872–1924)
Coltrane, Alice (1937—)
Colum, Mary Gunning (1884–1957)
Columbo, Patricia (1957—)
Colvin, Shawn (1956—)
Colwell, Rita R. (1934—)
Colwin, Laurie (1944–1992)
Coman, Katharine (1857–1915)
Comden, Betty (1915—)
Comfort, Anna Manning (1845–1931)
Comingore, Dorothy (1913–1971)
Compson, Betty (1897–1974)
Compton, Betty (1907–1944)
Compton, Virginia (1853–1940)
Comstock, Ada Louise (1876–1973)
Comstock, Anna Botsford (1854–1930)
Comstock, Elizabeth Leslie (1815–1891)
Comstock, Nanette (1873–1942)
Conant, Hannah Chaplin (1809–1865)
Conboy, Sara McLaughlin (1870–1928)
Conde, Felisa (c. 1920—)
Condé, Maryse (1937—)
Cone, Carin (1940—)
Cone, Claribel (1864–1929)
Cone, Etta (1870–1949)
Cones, Nancy Ford (1869–1962)
Conklin, Peggy (1902–2003)
Conley, Peggy (1947—)
Conn, Elenor (fl. 1980s)
Connally, Nellie (1919—)
Connelly, Cornelia (1809–1879)
Conner, Nadine (1907–2003)
Connolly, Maureen (1934–1969)
Connor, Chris (1927—)
Conrad, Karen (1919–1976)
Conradt, Jody (1941—)
Content, Marjorie (1895–1984)
Converse, Harriet Maxwell (1836–1903)
Conway, Jill Ker (1934—)
Coo, Eva (d. 1935)
Cook, Barbara (1927—)
Cook, Cordelia E. (1919–1996)
Cook, Sheri (1953—)

Cooke, Emma
Cooke, Flora (1864–1953)
Cooke, Rose Terry (1827–1892)
Coolbrith, Ina Donna (1841–1928)
Coolidge, Elizabeth Sprague (1863–1953)
Coolidge, Grace Goodhue (1879–1957)
Coolidge, Martha (1946—)
Coolidge, Priscilla
Coolidge, Rita (1944—)
Coombs, Patricia (1926—)
Cooney, Barbara (1917–2000)
Cooney, Cecelia (1904–1969)
Cooney, Joan Ganz (1929—)
Cooper, Anna J. (c. 1858–1964)
Cooper, Bette (c. 1920—)
Cooper, Christin (1961—)
Cooper, Cynthia (1963—)
Cooper, Cynthia (1964—)
Cooper, Dulcie (1903–1981)
Cooper, Edna Mae (1900–1986)
Cooper, J. California (1940s—)
Cooper, Lillian Kemble (1891–1977)
Cooper, Mary Wright (1714–1778)
Cooper, Miriam (1891–1976)
Cooper, Sarah Ingersoll (1835–1896)
Cooper, Susan Fenimore (1813–1894)
Cooper, Violet Kemble (1886–1961)
Cope, Mother Marianne (1838–1918)
Copeland, Lillian (1904–1964)
Copeland-Durham, Emily (1984—)
Copley, Helen (1922–2004)
Coppin, Fanny Jackson (1837–1913)
Corbin, Hazel (1894–1988)
Corbin, Margaret Cochran (1751–c. 1800)
Corbin, Virginia Lee (1910–1942)
Corby, Ellen (1911–1998)
Corday, Mara (1930—)
Cordell, Cathleen (1915–1997)
Cori, Gerty T. (1896–1957)
Corio, Ann (1914–1999)
Corkle, Francesca (1952—)
Cormier, Lucia M. (1909–1993)
Cornelisen, Ann (1926–2003)
Cornelius, Kathy (1932—)
Cornell, Katharine (1893–1974)
Cornell, Sheila (1962—)
Cornett, Leanza (1971—)
Cornfield, Ellen (1948—)
Cornwall, Anne (1897–1980)
Corridon, Marie (1930—)
Corrock, Susan (1951—)
Corson, Juliet (1841–1897)
Cortesa, Valentina (1924—)
Cortez, Jayne (1936—)
Cosby, Camille (1945—)
Costello, Dolores (1905–1979)
Costello, Helene (1903–1957)
Costie, Candace (1963—)
Cotera, Martha (1938—)
Cothran, Shirley (c. 1953—)
Cotten, Elizabeth (c. 1893–1987)
Cotten, Sallie Southall (1846–1929)
Cotton, Lucy (c. 1891–1948)
Coughlin, Natalie (1982—)
Coughlin, Paula A. (c. 1961—)
Coulson, Juanita (1933—)
Couric, Katie (1957—)
Courtney, Inez (1908–1975)
Courtney, Patricia (c. 1932–2003)
Couzins, Phoebe Wilson (1842–1913)
Cowan, Ruth (1901–1993)
Cowart, Juanita (1944—)
Cowen, Donna (c. 1950—)
Cowie, Bessie Lee (1860–1950)
Cowl, Jane (1883–1950)
Cowles, Anna Roosevelt (1855–1931)
Cowles, Betsey Mix (1810–1876)
Cowles, Fleur (1910—)
Cowles, Julia (1785–1803)
Cowles, Virginia (1912–1983)
Cowsill, Barbara (1929–1985)
Cowsill, Susan (1960—)
Cox, Alison (1979—)
Cox, Crystal (1979—)
Cox, Gertrude Mary (1900–1978)
Cox, Hazel (b. 1887)
Cox, Ida (1896–1967)
Cox, Louise H.K. (1865–1945)
Cox, Lynne (1957—)
Cox, Ray (b. 1880)
Coyle, Grace Longwell (1892–1962)
Coyle, Rose (1914–1988)
Coyne, Colleen (1971—)
Crabtree, Lotta (1847–1924)
Craft, Ellen (1826–c. 1891)
Craig, Edith (1907–1979)
Craig, Helen (1912–1986)
Craig, Jenny (1932—)
Craig, Judy (1946—)
Craig, May (1888–1975)
Craig, Minnie D. (1883–1965)
Craig, Nell (1891–1965)
Craighill, Margaret (1898–1977)
Craigie, Pearl Mary Teresa (1867–1906)
Crain, Jeanne (1925–2003)
Cranch, Elizabeth (1743–1811)
Cranch, Mary Smith (1741–1811)
Crandall, Ella Phillips (1871–1938)
Crandall, Prudence (1803–1890)
Crane, Caroline Bartlett (1858–1935)
Crane, Norma (1928–1973)
Crapsey, Adelaide (1878–1914)
Craske, Margaret (1892–1990)
Cratty, Mabel (1868–1928)
Craven, Margaret (1901–1980)
Crawford, Cheryl (1902–1986)
Crawford, Cindy (1966—)
Crawford, Jane Todd (1763–1842)
Crawford, Jean Ashley (1939—)
Crawford, Joan (1906–1977)
Crawford, Ruth (1901–1953)
Creed, Clifford Anne (1938—)
Creighton, Mary Frances (1899–1936)
Crews, Laura Hope (1879–1942)
Crimmins, Alice (1941—)
Crisler, Lois (1897–1971)
Crispell, Marilyn (1947—)
Crist, Judith (1922—)
Critchfield, Lee (c. 1909—)
Crocker, Hannah Mather (1752–1829)
Crocker, Lucretia (1829–1886)
Crocker, Mary Lou (1944—)
Crockett, Jean A. (1919–1998)
Crockett, Rita Louise (1957—)
Croll, Tina (1943—)
Croly, Jane Cunningham (1829–1901)
Cropley, Eileen (1932—)
Crosby, Caresse (1892–1970)
Crosby, Elizabeth (1888–1983)
Crosby, Fanny (1820–1915)
Crosman, Henrietta (1861–1944)
Cross, Jessica (b. 1909)
Cross-Battle, Tara (1968—)
Crosson, Marvel (1904–1929)
Croteau, Julie (1970—)
Crothers, Rachel (1878–1958)
Crow, Sheryl (1962—)
Crow, Tamara (1977—)
Crow Dog, Mary (1953—)
Crowley, Pat (1929—)
Crozier, Catharine (1914–2003)
Crump, Diane (1949—)
Crumpler, Rebecca Lee (1831–1895)
Cruso, Thalassa (1908–1997)
Cryer, Gretchen (1935—)
Csizmazia, Kim (c. 1968—)
Cudone, Carolyn (1918—)
Cullen, Betsy (1938—)
Cumming, Adelaide Hawley (1905–1998)
Cumming, Dorothy (1899–1983)
Cumming, Kate (c. 1828–1909)
Cumming, Ruth (c. 1904–1967)
Cummings, Alma (b. 1890)
Cummings, Blondell (c. 1948—)
Cummings, Constance (1910–2005)
Cummings, Edith (1899–1984)
Cummings, Marian (c. 1892–1984)
Cummings, Ruth (1894–1984)
Cummings, Vicki (1913–1969)
Cummins, Maria Susanna (1827–1866)
Cunard, Grace (c. 1891–1967)
Cunard, Maud (1872–1948)
Cunningham, Agnes (1909–2004)
Cunningham, Ann Pamela (1816–1875)
Cunningham, Imogen (1883–1976)
Cunningham, Letitia (fl. 1783)
Cunningham, Minnie Fisher (1882–1964)
Cunningham, Sarah (1918–1986)
Cuoco, Joyce (1953—)
Curless, Ann (1965—)
Curley, Wilma (1937—)
Currie, Cherie (1959—)
Currier, Ruth (1926—)
Curry, Denise (1959—)
Curry, Jenny (1984—)
Curtis, Ann (1926—)
Curtis, Charlotte (1928–1987)
Curtis, Doris Malkin (1914–1991)
Curtis, Harriot (1881–1974)
Curtis, Jamie Lee (1958—)
Curtis, Peggy (1883–1965)
Curtright, Jorja (1923–1985)
Curzon, Mary Leiter (1870–1906)
Cushier, Elizabeth (1837–1932)
Cushing, Catherine Chisholm (1874–1952)
Cushing, Justine B. (b. 1918)
Cushing Sisters
Cushman, Charlotte Saunders (1816–1876)
Cushman, Pauline (1833–1893)
Cushman, Vera (1876–1946)
Custer, Elizabeth Bacon (1842–1933)
Custis, Eleanor "Nellie" Calvert (fl. 1775)
Custis, Eleanor "Nelly" Parke (1779–1852)
Cutler, Hannah Conant (1815–1896)
Cutler, Robyn (1948—)
Cutter, Kiki (1951—)
Daché, Lilly (1898–1989)
Dagmar (1921–2001)
Dahl, Arlene (1924—)
Dahl-Wolfe, Louise (1895–1989)
Dakides, Tara (1975—)
Dale, Esther (1885–1961)
Dale, Margaret (1876–1972)
Dale, Virginia (1917–1994)
Daley, Cass (1915–1975)
Dall, Caroline Wells (1822–1912)
Dalrymple, Jean (1910–1998)
Dalton, Doris (1910–1984)
Dalton, Dorothy (1893–1972)
Dalton, Dorothy (1922–1973)
Daly, Mary (1928—)
Daly, Tyne (1946—)
Damita, Lili (1901–1994)
Damon, Cathryn (1930–1987)
Dana, Leora (1923–1983)
Dana, Marie Louise (c. 1876–1946)
Dana, Viola (1897–1987)
Dandridge, Dorothy (1923–1965)

Danias, Starr (1949—)
Daniel, Annie Sturges (1858–1944)
Daniel, Beth (1956—)
Daniel, Ellie (1950—)
Daniele, Graciela (1939—)
Daniels, Bebe (1901–1971)
Daniels, Isabelle Frances (1937—)
Daniels, Mabel Wheeler (1878–1971)
Dann, Mary (d. 2005)
Danner, Blythe (1943—)
Danner, Margaret (1910–1984)
D'Antuono, Eleanor (1939—)
Dantzscher, Jamie (1982—)
Danziger, Paula (1944–2004)
Darby, Eileen (1916–2004)
Darc, Mireille (1938—)
Dare, Zena (1887–1975)
Dargan, Olive Tilford (1869–1968)
Darling, Flora (1840–1910)
Darling, May (1887–1971)
Darlington, Jennie (c. 1925—)
Darmond, Grace (1898–1963)
Darnell, Linda (1921–1965)
d'Arnell, Nydia (d. 1970)
Darragh, Lydia Barrington (1729–1789)
Darrow, Anna (1876–1959)
Darvas, Julia (c. 1919—)
Darvas, Lili (1902–1974)
Darwell, Jane (1879–1967)
Darwitz, Natalie (1982—)
Dash, Julie (1952—)
Dash, Sarah (1945—)
Daubechies, Ingrid (1954—)
d'Aulaire, Ingri (1904–1980)
Dauser, Sue (1888–1972)
Davenport, Fanny (1850–1898)
Davenport, Gwen (1909–2002)
Davenport, Lindsay (1976—)
Davenport, Marcia (1903–1996)
Daves, Joan (1919–1997)
Davidow, Ruth (1911–1999)
Davidson, Lucretia Maria (1808–1825)
Davidson, Margaret Miller (1823–1838)
Davies, Caryn (1982—)
Davies, Marion (1897–1961)
Davis, Adelle (1904–1974)
Davis, Alice Brown (1852–1935)
Davis, Angela (1944—)
Davis, Bette (1908–1989)
Davis, Clarissa (1967—)
Davis, Dorothy Hilliard (1917–1994)
Davis, Fay (1872–1945)
Davis, Frances Elliott (1882–1965)
Davis, Gail (1925–1997)
Davis, Hilda (1905–2001)
Davis, Jessica (1978—)
Davis, Joan (1907–1961)
Davis, Katharine Bement (1860–1935)
Davis, Marguerite (1889–1980)
Davis, Mary
Davis, Mary E.P. (c. 1840–1924)
Davis, Mary Fenn (1824–1886)
Davis, Mollie Moore (1844–1909)
Davis, Paulina Wright (1813–1876)
Davis, Rebecca Harding (1831–1910)
Davis, Skeeter (1931–2004)
Davis, Theresa (1950—)
Davis, Varina Howell (1826–1906)
d'Avril, Yola (1907–1984)
Daw, Evelyn (1912–1970)
Daw, Marjorie (1902–1979)
Dawes, Dominique (1976—)
Dawidowicz, Lucy (1915–1990)
Dawn, Dolly (1916–2002)
Dawn, Hazel (1891–1988)
Dawn, Isabel (1905–1966)
Day, Alice (1905–1995)
Day, Doris (1924—)
Day, Dorothy (1897–1980)
Day, Edith (1896–1971)
Day, Frances (1907–1984)
Day, Laraine (1917—)
Day, Marceline (1907–2000)
Daykarhanova, Tamara (1889–1980)
Dazie, Mademoiselle (1882–1952)
de Acosta, Mercedes (1893–1968)
Dean, Dora (c. 1872–1950)
Dean, Jennie (1852–1913)
Dean, Julia (1830–1868)
Dean, Julia (1878–1952)
Dean, Laura (1945—)
Dean, Margie (1896–1918)
Dean, Priscilla (1896–1987)
Dean, Vera Micheles (1903–1972)
Deane, Doris (1900–1974)
Deane, Helen Wendler (1917–1966)
De Angeli, Marguerite (1889–1987)
De Angelo, Ana Marie (1955—)
Deardurff, Deena (1957—)
Dearie, Blossom (1926—)
de Blois, Natalie (1921—)
Debo, Angie (1890–1988)
DeCamp, Rosemary (1910–2001)
De Carlo, Yvonne (1922—)
DeCastro, Peggy (1921–2004)
Decker, Sarah Platt (1852–1912)
de Cleyre, Voltairine (1866–1912)
DeCosta, Sara (1977—)
Dee, Frances (1907–2004)
Dee, Ruby (1923—)
Dee, Sandra (1942–2005)
Deer, Ada (1935—)
Deering, Olive (1918–1986)
DeFrantz, Anita (1952—)
DeGaetani, Jan (1933–1989)
DeGeneres, Ellen (1958—)
De Graffenried, Clare (1849–1921)
DeHaven, Flora (1883–1950)
DeHaven, Gloria (1924—)
Dehner, Dorothy (1901–1994)
de Hoyos, Angela (1940—)
De Jong, Bettie (1933—)
de Jong, Dola (1911–2003)
de Kooning, Elaine Fried (1918–1989)
de Laguna, Frederica (b. around 1874)
de Laguna, Frederica (1906–2004)
de Laguna, Grace Mead (1878–1978)
De La Motte, Marguerite (1902–1950)
Deland, Margaret (1857–1945)
Delander, Lois (1911–1985)
Delano, Jane Arminda (1862–1919)
Delany, Annie Elizabeth (1891–1995)
Delany, Sarah Louise (1889–1999)
De Lappe, Gemze (1922—)
Delarverié, Stormé (1922—)
De Lauretis, Teresa (1938—)
DeLauro, Rosa L. (1943—)
De Lavallade, Carmen (1931—)
DeLay, Dorothy (1917–2002)
De Leath, Vaughan (1900–1943)
de Leeuw, Dianne
De Leporte, Rita (c. 1910—)
Delf, Juliet (d. 1962)
Delille, Henriette (1813–1862)
Delmar, Viña (1903–1990)
Deloria, Ella (1888–1971)
Delroy, Irene (1898–?)
De Luce, Virginia (1921–1997)
de Lussan, Zélie (1861–1949)
Del Vando, Amapola (1910–1988)
Delza, Elizabeth (c. 1903—)
De Marco, Renée (c. 1913—)
De Marco, Sally (1921—)
DeMarinis, Anne
De Mattei, Susan (1962—)
Dembo, Tamara (1902–1993)
DeMent, Iris (1961—)
de Mille, Agnes (1905–1993)
De Mille, Beatrice (1853–1923)
DeMille, Katherine (1911–1995)
Deming, Dorothy (1893–1972)
Demorest, Ellen Curtis (1824–1898)
Dempsey, Sister Mary Joseph (1856–1939)
Dempster, Carol (1901–1991)
Denenberg, Gail (1947—)
Denison, Mary Andrews (1826–1911)
Deniz, Leslie (1962—)
Dennett, Mary Ware (1872–1947)
Dennie, Abigail (1715–1745)
Dennis, Sandy (1937–1992)
Dennison, Jo-Carroll (c. 1924—)
Densen-Gerber, Judianne (1934–2003)
Densmore, Frances (1867–1957)
Denton, Mary Florence (1857–1947)
Denton, Sandy (1969—)
de Passe, Suzanne (1946—)
Deren, Maya (1908–1961)
Derickson, Uli (1944–2005)
deRiel, Emily (1974—)
Derricotte, Juliette (1897–1931)
De Rue, Carmen (1908–1986)
Desha (1892–1965)
DeShannon, Jackie (1944—)
De Sousa, May (1887–1948)
Dessoff, Margarethe (1874–1944)
De Swirska, Tamara (c. 1890–?)
Dettweiler, Helen (1914–1990)
Deutsch, Babette (1895–1982)
Deutsch, Helen (1906–1992)
Deutsch, Helene (1884–1982)
de Varona, Donna (1947—)
Devers, Gail (1966—)
DeVoe, Emma Smith (1848–1927)
de Voie, Bessie (b. around 1888)
Devore, Dorothy (1899–1976)
Dewees, Mary Coburn (fl. 1787–1788)
Dewey, Alice Chipman (1858–1927)
De Witt, Lydia (1859–1928)
de Wolfe, Elsie (1865–1950)
Dewson, Molly (1874–1962)
Diachenko, Nada (1946—)
Diamant, Anita (1917–1996)
Diaz, Abby (1821–1904)
Diaz, Mary F. (c. 1962–2004)
Di Bona, Linda (1946—)
Dick, Gladys (1881–1963)
Dickason, Gladys (1903–1971)
Dickens, Helen Octavia (1909–2001)
Dickerson, Nancy (1927–1997)
Dickey, Nancy Wilson (1950—)
Dickey, Sarah (1838–1904)
Dickinson, Angie (1931—)
Dickinson, Anna E. (1842–1932)
Dickinson, Emily (1830–1886)
Dickinson, Frances (1755–1830)
Dickinson, Judy (1950—)
Dickson, Amanda America (1849–1893)
Dickson, Dorothy (1893–1995)
Dickson, Gloria (1916–1945)
Didion, Joan (1934—)
Diemer, Emma Lou (1927—)
DiFranco, Ani (1970—)
Diggs, Annie LePorte (1848–1916)
Diggs, Irene (1906—)
Dill, Mary Lou (1948—)
Dillard, Annie (1945—)
Diller, Angela (1877–1968)
Diller, Phyllis (1917—)

Dilley, Dorothy (b. around 1907)
Dillon, Diane (1933—)
Dillon, Melinda (1939—)
Dimock, Susan (1847–1875)
Dingeldein, Margaret (1980—)
Dinnerstein, Dorothy (1923–1992)
Dinsdale, Shirley (c. 1928–1999)
Dinwiddie, Emily (1879–1949)
Di Prima, Diane (1934—)
Dirkmaat, Megan (1976—)
Disney, Lillian (1899–1997)
Dix, Beulah Marie (1876–1970)
Dix, Dorothea Lynde (1802–1887)
Dixon, Diane (1964—)
Dixon, Jean (1896–1981)
Dixon, Jeane (1918–1997)
Dixon, Medina (1962—)
Dixon, Heather (1945—)
Dixon, Tina (1976—)
Dixon Jones, Mary Amanda (1828–1908)
Dlugoszewski, Lucia (1925–2000)
Dobbins, Georgia (1944–1980)
Dobratz, Erin (1982—)
Dobson, Deborah (c. 1950—)
Dock, Lavinia L. (1858–1956)
Doda, Carol
Dodd, Claire (1908–1973)
Dodge, Eva F. (1896–1990)
Dodge, Grace Hoadley (1856–1914)
Dodge, Josephine (1855–1928)
Dodge, Mary Abigail (1833–1896)
Dodge, Mary Mapes (1831–1905)
Doering, Jane (c. 1922—)
Doerr, Harriet (1910–2002)
Dohan, Edith Hall (1877–1943)
Dohnal, Darcie
Dohrn, Bernardine (1942—)
Dole, Elizabeth Hanford (1936—)
Dolley, Sarah Adamson (1829–1909)
Dolly, Jenny (1892–1941)
Dolly, Rosie (1892–1970)
Domanska, Janina (1912–1995)
Domergue, Faith (1924–1999)
Donadio, Candida (1929–2001)
Donahue, Hessie (fl. 1892)
Donahue, Margaret (c. 1893–1978)
Donaldson, Norma (1928–1994)
Donegan, Dorothy (1922–1998)
Doner, Kitty (1895–1988)
DonHowe, Gwyda (1933–1988)
Donlon, Mary H. (1894–1977)
Donnell, Jeff (1921–1988)
Donnelly, Dorothy (1880–1928)
Donnelly, Euphrasia (b. 1906)
Donnelly, Lucy (1870–1948)
Donnelly, Patricia (c. 1920—)
Donnelly, Ruth (1896–1982)
Donner, Vyvyan (1895–1965)
Donohoe, Shelagh (1965—)
Donovan, Anne (1961—)
Donovan, Carrie (1928–2001)
Donovan, Jean (1953—)
Doolittle, Hilda (1886–1961)
Doraldina (c. 1893–c. 1925)
Doran, Ann (1911–2000)
Doremus, Sarah Platt (1802–1877)
Dorfmann, Ania (1899–1984)
Dorion, Marie (c. 1790–1850)
Dorman, Sonya (1924—)
Dormon, Carrie (1888–1971)
Doro, Marie (1882–1956)
Dorr, Julia Caroline (1825–1913)
Dorr, Rheta Childe (1866–1948)
Dorsey, Sarah Anne (1829–1879)
Dorsey, Susan Miller (1857–1946)
Doscher, Doris (1882–1970)
Doss, Nannie (1905–1965)
Doucet, Catherine (1875–1958)
Douglas, Adèle Cutts (1835–1899)
Douglas, Amanda Minnie (1831–1916)
Douglas, Ann (b. 1901)
Douglas, Emily Taft (1899–1994)
Douglas, Helen Gahagan (1900–1980)
Douglas, Helyn (c. 1945—)
Douglas, Lizzie (1897–1973)
Douglas, Marjory Stoneman (1890–1998)
Douglass, Anna Murray (1813–1882)
Douglass, Helen Pitts (1838–1903)
Douglass, Margaret (d. 1949)
Douglass, Sarah Mapps (1806–1882)
Douvillier, Suzanne (1778–1826)
Dove, Billie (1900–1997)
Dove, Rita (1952—)
Dovey, Alice (1884–1969)
Dow, Peggy (1928—)
Dowd, Nancy (1944—)
Dowling, Constance (1920–1969)
Dowling, Doris (1921–2004)
Downey, June Etta (1875–1932)
Downing, Lucy Winthrop (c. 1600–1679)
Downing, Virginia (1904–1996)
Downs, Cathy (1924–1976)
Downs, Deirdre (c. 1980—)
Doyle, Patricia (d. 1975)
Dragila, Stacy (1971—)
Dragonette, Jessica (1900–1980)
Drake, Betsy (1923—)
Drake, Dona (1914–1989)
Drake, Frances (1908–2000)
Drake, Frances Denny (1797–1875)
Draper, Dorothy (1888–1969)
Draper, Elisabeth (1900–1993)
Draper, Helen (1871–1951)
Draper, Margaret (d. around 1800)
Draper, Mary Anna Palmer (1839–1914)
Draper, Ruth (1884–1956)
Draves, Victoria (1924—)
Drayton, Grace Gebbie (1877–1936)
Dreier, Katherine Sophie (1877–1952)
Dreier, Mary Elisabeth (1875–1963)
Dresser, Louise (1878–1965)
Dressler, Marie (1869–1934)
Drew, Ellen (1914–2003)
Drew, Georgiana Emma (1854–1893)
Drew, Lucille (1890–1925)
Drexel, Constance (1894–1956)
Drexel, Mary Katharine (1858–1955)
Dreyfuss, Anne (1957—)
Drinker, Catherine Ann (1841–1922)
Drinker, Elizabeth Sandwith (1734–1807)
Drinker, Ernesta (1852–1939)
Drinkwater, Jennie M. (1841–1900)
Driscoll, Clara (1881–1945)
Driscoll, Jean (1966—)
Driver, Senta (1942—)
Dru, Joanne (1923–1996)
Druse, Roxana (1846–1889)
Drylie, Patricia (c. 1928–1993)
Duane, Diane (1952—)
Du Bois, Cora (1903–1991)
Du Boulay, Christine (c. 1923—)
Duckering, Florence West (1869–1951)
Dudleston, Penny (1952—)
Dudley, Doris (1917–1985)
Dudley, Dorothy (fl. 1775)
Dudley, Jane (1912–2001)
Duenkel, Ginny (1947—)
Duerk, Alene B. (1920—)
Duff, Mary Ann Dyke (1794–1857)
Duffy, Martha (c. 1936–1997)
Dukakis, Olympia (1931—)
Duke, Doris (1912–1993)
Duke, Patty (1946—)
Dulles, Eleanor Lansing (1895–1996)
Dumm, Edwina (1893–1990)
Dummer, Ethel Sturges (1866–1954)
Dumont, Margaret (1889–1965)
Dunaway, Faye (1941—)
Dunbar, Diane
Dunbar, Dixie (1915–1991)
Dunbar, Flanders (1902–1959)
Dunbar-Nelson, Alice (1875–1935)
Duncan, Elizabeth (c. 1874–1948)
Duncan, Irma (1897–1978)
Duncan, Isadora (1878–1927)
Duncan, Lois (1934—)
Duncan, Maria Teresa (1895–1987)
Duncan, Mary (1895–1993)
Duncan, Rosetta (1890–1959)
Duncan, Sandy (1946—)
Duncan, Vivian (1902–1986)
Dunedin, Maudie (c. 1888–1937)
Dunfield, Sonya Klopfer (c. 1936—)
Dunham, Ethel Collins (1883–1969)
Dunham, Katherine (1909–2006)
Duniway, Abigail Scott (1834–1915)
Dunkle, Nancy (1955—)
Dunlap, Ericka (1982—)
Dunlap, Jane (fl. 1771)
Dunn, Gertrude (c. 1932–2004)
Dunn, Josephine (1906–1983)
Dunn, Loula Friend (1896–1977)
Dunn, Natalie (1956—)
Dunn, Shannon (1972—)
Dunn, Tricia (1974—)
Dunn, Velma (1918—)
Dunne, Irene (1898–1990)
Dunne, Jean Gilligan (1951—)
Dunnock, Mildred (1900–1991)
Du Pont, Patricia (1894–1973)
Dupree, Minnie (1873–1947)
Dupuy, Eliza Ann (1814–1881)
Durant, Ariel (1898–1981)
Durfee, Minta (1897–1975)
Durgan, Bridget (c. 1845–1867)
Durham, Dianne (1968—)
Dusserre, Michelle (1968—)
Dutton, Anne (fl. 1743)
Duval, Helen (1916—)
Dvorak, Ann (1912–1979)
Dwan, Dorothy (1907–1981)
Dworkin, Andrea (1946–2005)
Dwyer, Ada (1863–1952)
Dwyer, Doriot Anthony (1922—)
Dwyer, Florence Price (1902–1976)
Dyer, Mary Barrett (c. 1591–1660)
Dyk, Ruth (1901–2000)
Dyroen-Lancer, Becky (1971—)
Eagels, Jeanne (1894–1929)
Eakins, Susan Hannah (1851–1938)
Eames, Clare (1896–1930)
Eames, Emma (1865–1952)
Eames, Ray (1912–1988)
Eames, Virginia (1889–1971)
Earhart, Amelia (1897–1937)
Earle, Alice Morse (1851–1911)
Earle, Virginia (1875–1937)
Early, Penny Ann (c. 1946—)
Eastman, Annis Ford (1852–1910)
Eastman, Carole (1934–2004)
Eastman, Crystal (1881–1928)
Eastman, Elaine Goodale (1863–1953)
Eastman, Linda A. (1867–1963)
Easton, Sheena (1959—)
Eastwood, Alice (1859–1953)
Eaton, Edith (1865–1914)
Eaton, Mary (1901–1948)
Eaton, Pearl (1898–1958)

Eaton, Peggy (c. 1799–1879)
Eaves, Elsie (1898–1983)
Eberhart, Mignon G. (1899–1996)
Eberle, Abastenia St. Leger (1878–1942)
Ebert, Joyce (1933–1997)
Ebsen, Vilma (1911—)
Echols, Sheila Ann (1964—)
Eckart, Jean (1921–1993)
Eckerson, Sophia H. (d. 1954)
Eckert, Cynthia (1965—)
Eckford, Elizabeth (1942—)
Eckstorm, Fannie Pearson Hardy (1865–1946)
Eddy, Bernice (b. 1903)
Eddy, Helen Jerome (1897–1990)
Eddy, Mary Baker (1821–1910)
Edelman, Marian Wright (1939—)
Eden, Barbara (1934—)
Ederle, Gertrude (1905–2003)
Edinger, Tilly (1897–1967)
Edmonds, Emma (1841–1898)
Edmunds, Elizabeth M. (c. 1941—)
Edson, Katherine Philips (1870–1933)
Eduardova, Eugenia (1882–1980)
Edwards, Edna Park (c. 1895–1967)
Edwards, Gloria (1944–1988)
Edwards, India (1895–1990)
Edwards, Penny (1928–1998)
Edwards, Sarah Pierpont (1710–1758)
Edwards, Teresa (1964—)
Edwards, Torri (1977—)
Ehrenreich, Barbara (1941—)
Ehret, Gloria (1941—)
Ehrlich, Ida Lublenski (d. 1986)
Eigenmann, Rosa Smith (1858–1947)
Eilber, Janet (1951—)
Eilberg, Amy (1954—)
Eilers, Sally (1908–1978)
Einstein, Hannah Bachman (1862–1929)
Eisemann-Schier, Ruth (c. 1942—)
Eisenberg, Mary Jane (1951—)
Eisenhower, Mamie (1896–1979)
Eisenstein, Judith (1909–1996)
Eisenstein, Phyllis (1946—)
Elder, Kate (fl. 1881)
Elder, Ruth (1902–1977)
Elders, Joycelyn (1933—)
Eldred, Pam (c. 1948—)
Eldridge, Florence (1901–1988)
Elg, Taina (1931—)
Elgin, Suzette Haden (1936—)
Elias, Rosalind (1930—)
Eline, Grace (1898—)
Eline, Marie (1902–1981)
Elion, Gertrude B. (1918–1999)
Eliot, Martha May (1891–1978)
Elizabeth of Yugoslavia (1936—)
Ellerbee, Linda (1944—)
Ellet, Elizabeth (c. 1812–1877)
Elliot, Cass (1941–1974)
Elliott, Cheri (1970—)
Elliott, Gertrude (1874–1950)
Elliott, Harriet Wiseman (1884–1947)
Elliott, Maud Howe (1854–1948)
Elliott, Maxine (1868–1940)
Elliott, Missy (1971—)
Elliott, Sarah Barnwell (1848–1928)
Ellis, Betty (c. 1941—)
Ellis, Edith (c. 1874–1960)
Ellis, Evelyn (1894–1958)
Ellis, Florence Hawley (1906–1991)
Ellis, Kathleen (1946—)
Ellis, Lucille (c. 1915—)
Ellis, Mary (1897–2003)
Ellis, Patricia (1916–1970)
Ellis, Terry (1966—)
Ellmann, Barbara (1950—)
Elmendorf, Theresa West (1855–1932)
Elseeta (1883–1903)
Elsener, Patricia (1929—)
Elsom, Isobel (1893–1981)
Elste, Meta (1921—)
Emerson, Ellen Russell (1837–1907)
Emerson, Ellen Tucker (1811–1831)
Emerson, Ellen Tucker (1839–1909)
Emerson, Faye (1917–1983)
Emerson, Gladys Anderson (1903–1984)
Emerson, Gloria (1929–2004)
Emerson, Hope (1897–1960)
Emerson, Mary Moody (1774–1863)
Emery, Katherine (1906–1980)
Emmet, Katherine (c. 1882–1960)
Emmons, Chansonetta Stanley (1858–1937)
Emshwiller, Carol (1921—)
Endicott, Lori (1967—)
Engdahl, Sylvia (1933—)
Engelhard, Jane (1917–2004)
England, Lynndie (1982—)
Englehorn, Shirley (1940—)
Enright, Elizabeth (1909–1968)
Ensler, Eve (1953—)
Entenmann, Martha (1906–1996)
Enters, Angna (1907–1989)
Enthoven, Gabrielle (1868–1950)
Ephron, Nora (1941—)
Ephron, Phoebe (1914–1971)
Eppes, Maria Jefferson (1778–1804)
Epstein, Charlotte (1884–1938)
Epstein, Selma (1927—)
Erbesfield, Robyn (1963—)
Erdman, Jean (1917—)
Erickson, Hilda (1859–1968)
Erikson, Joan (c. 1902–1997)
Ernst, Kitty (1926—)
Esau, Katherine (1898–1997)
Escovedo, Sheila (1957—)
Essen, Viola (1926–1969)
Esserman, Carol (c. 1945—)
Estaugh, Elizabeth Haddon (1680–1762)
Estefan, Gloria (1957—)
Estes, Ellen (1978—)
Estópinal, Renee (1949—)
Estrich, Susan R. (1952—)
Etheridge, Melissa (1961—)
Ethridge, Mary Camille (1964—)
Etting, Ruth (1896–1978)
Eustis, Dorothy (1886–1946)
Evan, Blanche (1909–1982)
Evans, Alice Catherine (1881–1975)
Evans, Elizabeth Glendower (1856–1937)
Evans, Janet (1971—)
Evans, Joan (1934—)
Evans, Madge (1909–1981)
Evans, Mari (1923—)
Evans, Matilda Arabella (1872–1935)
Evans, Minnie (1892–1987)
Evans, Renee (1908–1971)
Evdokimova, Eva (1948—)
Evelyn, Judith (1913–1967)
Everett, Betty (1939–2001)
Everett, Eva (1942—)
Everleigh, Aida (1864–1960)
Everleigh, Minna (1866–1948)
Evers-Williams, Myrlie (1933—)
Evert, Chris (1954—)
Exene (1956—)
Exner, Judith Campbell (d. 1999)
Eyton, Bessie (1890–1965)
Ezekiel, Denise Tourover (1903–1980)
Ezzell, Cheryl (c. 1979—)
Fabray, Nanette (1920—)
Fadiman, Annalee (1916–2002)
Faggs, Mae (1932—)
Fagin, Claire (1926—)
Fainlight, Ruth (1931—)
Fair, Elinor (1902–1957)
Fair, Lorrie (1978—)
Fairbanks, Madeline (1900–1989)
Fairbanks, Marion (1900–1973)
Faire, Virginia Brown (1904–1980)
Fairfax, Marion (1875–1979)
Falconer, Martha Platt (1862–1941)
Falkenburg, Jinx (1919–2003)
Fallis, Barbara (1924–1980)
Farber, Viola (1931–1998)
Farenthold, Frances "Sissy" (1926—)
Farina, Mimi (1945–2001)
Farkas, Ruth L. (1906–1996)
Farley, Harriet (1813–1907)
Farmer, Fannie Merritt (1857–1915)
Farmer, Frances (1913–1970)
Farmer, Virginia (1898–1988)
Farmer-Patrick, Sandra (1962—)
Farnham, Eliza W. (1815–1864)
Farnsworth, Emma J. (1860–1952)
Farquhar, Marilyn (1928—)
Farr, Wanda K. (1895–1983)
Farrand, Beatrix Jones (1872–1959)
Farrar, Cynthia (1795–1862)
Farrar, Eliza Rotch (1791–1870)
Farrar, Geraldine (1882–1967)
Farrar, Margaret (1897–1984)
Farrell, Eileen (1920–2002)
Farrell, Glenda (1904–1971)
Farrell, Suzanne (1945—)
Farrow, Mia (1945—)
Fassett, Cornelia (1831–1898)
Fatima, Djemille (c. 1890–1921)
Faugeres, Margaretta V. (1771–1801)
Faulk, Mary Lena (1926–1995)
Fauntz, Jane (1910–1989)
Fauset, Crystal Bird (1893–1965)
Fauset, Jessie Redmon (1882–1961)
Faust, Lotta (1880–1910)
Faut, Jean (1925—)
Favor, Suzy (1968—)
Fawcett, Joy (1968—)
Fay, Amy (1844–1928)
Fay, Vivien (b. around 1908)
Faye, Alice (1912–1998)
Faye, Julia (1893–1966)
Fazenda, Louise (1895–1962)
Fealy, Maude (1883–1971)
Fearn, Anne Walter (1865–1939)
Fedde, Sister Elizabeth (1850–1921)
Federova, Nina (1958—)
Fedicheva, Kaleria (1936—)
Feeney, Carol (1964—)
Feigenheimer, Irene (1946—)
Feinstein, Dianne (1933—)
Feldman, Andrea (1948–1972)
Feldman, Gladys (1891–1974)
Felice, Cynthia (1942—)
Felix, Allyson (1985—)
Fellows, Edith (1923—)
Felton, Rebecca Latimer (1835–1930)
Felton, Verna (1890–1966)
Feng, Amy (1969—)
Fenley, Molissa (1954—)
Fenno, Jenny (c. 1765–?)
Fenwick, Irene (1887–1936)
Fenwick, Millicent (1910–1992)
Ferber, Edna (1885–1968)
Ferdinand, Marie (1978—)
Fergerson, Mable (1955—)
Ferguson, Abbie Park (1837–1919)
Ferguson, Cathy Jean (1948—)
Ferguson, Dottie (1923–2003)

Ferguson, Elizabeth Graeme (1737–1801)
Ferguson, Elsie (1883–1961)
Ferguson, Helen (1901–1977)
Ferguson, Margaret Clay (1863–1951)
Ferguson, Miriam A. (1875–1961)
Fern, Fanny (1811–1872)
Fernandez, Bijou (1877–1961)
Fernandez, Lisa (1971—)
Fernandez, Mary Joe (1971—)
Fernandez, Mrs. E.L. (1852–1909)
Ferraris, Jan (1947—)
Ferraro, Geraldine (1935—)
Ferrell, Barbara (1947—)
Ferrin, Mary Upton (1810–1881)
Feury, Peggy (1924–1985)
Fichandler, Zelda (1924—)
Fiebig, Cora (c. 1934—)
Fiedler, Bobbi (1937—)
Field, Betty (1918–1973)
Field, Jessie (1881–1971)
Field, Kate (1838–1896)
Field, Pattie H. (b. around 1902)
Field, Rachel Lyman (1894–1942)
Field, Sally (1946—)
Field, Sara Bard (1882–1974)
Field, Sylvia (1901–1998)
Fields, Annie Adams (1834–1915)
Fields, Crystal (1969—)
Fields, Debbi (1956—)
Fields, Dorothy (1904–1974)
Fields, Evelyn J.
Fields, Julia (1938—)
Fields, Mary (c. 1832–1914)
Fields, Verna (1918–1982)
Fikotová, Olga (1932—)
Filkins, Grace (c. 1865–1962)
Fillmore, Abigail Powers (1798–1853)
Fillmore, Myrtle Page (1845–1931)
Finch, Flora (1867–1940)
Finch, Jennie (1980—)
Finch, Jennifer (1966—)
Findlay, Ruth (1904–1949)
Fine, Perle (1908–1988)
Fine, Sylvia (1913–1991)
Fine, Vivian (1913–2000)
Fingerhut, Arden (1945–1994)
Finley, Martha (1828–1909)
Finn-Burrell, Michelle (1965—)
Finneran, Sharon (1946—)
Finney, Joan (1925–2001)
Fiorenza, Elisabeth Schuessler (1938—)
Fischer, Alice (1869–1947)
Fischer, Ann (1919–1971)
Fischer, Margarita (1886–1975)
Fischer, Mary Ann (1933—)
Fischer, Ruth (1895–1961)
Fish, Jennifer (1949—)
Fish, Marian (1853–1915)
Fisher, Aileen (19096–2002)
Fisher, Anna L. (1949—)
Fisher, Clara (1811–1898)
Fisher, Doris (1915–2003)
Fisher, Dorothy Canfield (1879–1958)
Fisher, M.F.K. (1908–1992)
Fisher, Mary (c. 1623–1698)
Fisher, Mary (c. 1946—)
Fisher, Nellie (1920–1994)
Fisher, Sarah (1980—)
Fisher, Sarah Logan (1751–1796)
Fiske, Fidelia (1816–1864)
Fiske, Minnie Maddern (1865–1932)
Fiske, Sarah Symmes (1652–1692)
Fitzgerald, Benita (1961—)
Fitzgerald, Ella (1917–1996)
Fitzgerald, Eugenia Tucker (c. 1834–1928)
Fitzgerald, Frances Scott (1921–1986)
Fitzgerald, Geraldine (1913–2005)
Fitzgerald, Lillian (d. 1947)
Fitzgerald, Zelda (1900–1948)
Fitz-Gibbon, Bernice (c. 1895–1982)
Fitzhugh, Louise (1928–1974)
Flachmeier, Laurie (1959—)
Flack, Roberta (1937—)
Flagg, Elise (1951—)
Flagg, Fannie (1941—)
Flaherty, Frances Hubbard (c. 1886–1972)
Flanagan, Hallie (1889–1969)
Flanagan, Jeanne (1957—)
Flanner, Janet (1892–1978)
Flannery, Judy (1939–1997)
Fleeson, Doris (1901–1970)
Fleischmann, Torrance (1949—)
Fleischmann, Trude (1895–1990)
Fleming, Alice (1882–1952)
Fleming, Nancy (c. 1941—)
Fleming, Peggy (1948—)
Fleming, Renée (1959—)
Fleming, Rhonda (1922—)
Fleming, Williamina Paton (1857–1911)
Fletcher, Alice Cunningham (1838–1923)
Fletcher, Caroline (1906—)
Fletcher, Louise (1934—)
Fletcher, Maria (c. 1942—)
Flexner, Anne Crawford (1874–1955)
Flexner, Jennie M. (1882–1944)
Flikke, Julia Otteson (1879–1965)
Flint, Helen (1898–1967)
Florence, Malvina Pray (1830–1906)
Flower, Lucy (1837–1921)
Flowers, Bess (1898–1984)
Flowers, Tairia (1981—)
Flowers, Vonetta (1973—)
Flowerton, Consuelo (1900–1965)
Flynn, Elizabeth Gurley (1890–1964)
Flynn, Jeannie
Foch, Nina (1924—)
Foley, Edna (1878–1943)
Foley, Margaret (c. 1827–1877)
Foley, Martha (c. 1897–1977)
Folger, Emily (1858–1936)
Follansbee, Elizabeth A. (1839–1917)
Follen, Eliza (1787–1860)
Follett, Mary Parker (1868–1933)
Foltz, Clara (1849–1934)
Fonaroff, Nina (1914–2003)
Fonda, Jane (1937—)
Fontanne, Lynn (1887–1983)
Foot, Katherine (c. 1852–?)
Foote, Mary Hallock (1847–1938)
Forbes, Brenda (1909–1996)
Forbes, Esther (1891–1967)
Forbes, Mary Elizabeth (1879–1964)
Force, Julia (1860–?)
Force, Juliana (1876–1948)
Ford, Betty (1918—)
Ford, Eileen (1922—)
Ford, Harriet (c. 1863–1949)
Ford, Ita (1940—)
Ford, Judith (c. 1950—)
Ford, Mary (1924–1977)
Ford, Penny (1964—)
Ford, Susan (1957—)
Forde, Eugenie (1879–1940)
Forde, Victoria (1896–1964)
Forman, Ada (b. around 1895)
Formby, Margaret (1929–2003)
Fornaroli, Cia (1888–1954)
Fornia, Rita (1878–1922)
Forrest, Ann (1895–1985)
Forrest, Helen (1918–1999)
Forrest, Sally (1928—)
Fort, Cornelia (1919–1943)
Fort, Syvilla (c. 1917–1975)
Forten, Margaretta (1808–1875)
Forti, Simone (c. 1935—)
Fosburgh, Minnie Astor (1906–1978)
Fossey, Dian (1932–1985)
Foster, Frances (1924–1997)
Foster, Gae (b. 1903)
Foster, Gloria (1933–2001)
Foster, Hannah Webster (1758–1840)
Foster, J. Ellen (1840–1910)
Foster, Jodie (1962—)
Foster, Lillian (d. 1949)
Foster, Marie (1917–2003)
Foster, Susanna (1924—)
Fothergill, Dorothy (1945—)
Foudy, Julie (1971—)
Fout, Nina (1959—)
Fowle, Elida Rumsey (1842–1919)
Fowler, Lydia Folger (1822–1879)
Fowler, Marjorie (1920–2003)
Fowler, Tillie (1942–2005)
Fox, Carol (1926–1981)
Fox, Catherine (1977—)
Fox, Della (1870–1913)
Fox, Dorothy (b. around 1914)
Fox, Francine (1949—)
Fox, Jackie (1959—)
Fox, Kate (c. 1839–1892)
Fox, Leah (c. 1818–1890)
Fox, Margaret (c. 1833–1893)
Fox, Paula (1923—)
Fox, Ruby (1945—)
Fox, Sidney (1910–1942)
Foy, Madeline (1903–1988)
Foy, Mary (1901–1987)
Fradon, Ramona (1926—)
Fraley, Ingrid (1949—)
Frame, Alice (1878–1941)
Frampton, Eleanor (1896–1973)
Francine, Anne (1917–1999)
Francis, Anne (1930—)
Francis, Arlene (1908–2001)
Francis, Connie (1938—)
Francis, Kay (1899–1968)
Francis, Milly (c. 1802–1848)
Francisco, Betty (1900–1950)
Frank, Dottie (1941—)
Frank, Jacqueline (1980—)
Frank, Mary K. (1911–1988)
Frank, Nance (1949—)
Franken, Rose (c. 1895–1988)
Frankenthaler, Helen (1928—)
Frankland, Agnes (1726–1783)
Franklin, Alberta (1896–1976)
Franklin, Ann (1696–1763)
Franklin, Aretha (1942—)
Franklin, Erma (1938–2002)
Franklin, Irene (1876–1941)
Franklin, Martha Minerva (1870–1968)
Franklin, Shirley (1945—)
Franklyn, Beth (c. 1873–1956)
Franklyn, Lidije (1922—)
Franks, Lucinda (1946—)
Franks, Rebecca (c. 1760–1823)
Frantz, Virginia Kneeland (1896–1967)
Frasca, Mary (d. 1973)
Fraser, Alexa Stirling (1897–1977)
Fraser, Gretchen (1919–1994)
Fratianne, Linda (1960—)
Frazee, Jane (1918–1985)
Frazier, Maude (1881–1963)
Frederick, Christine (1883–1970)
Frederick, Marcia (1963—)
Frederick, Pauline (1881–1938)
Frederick, Pauline (1908–1990)
Freed, Amanda (1979—)

Freedman, Nancy (1920—)
Freeman, Emma B. (1880–1927)
Freeman, Kathleen (1919–2001)
Freeman, Lucy (1916–2004)
Freeman, Mary E. Wilkins (1852–1930)
Freeman, Mavis (1918—)
Freeman, Mona (1926—)
Freeman, Ruth B. (1906–1982)
Freer, Agnes Rand (1878–1972)
Fremantle, Anne (1909–2002)
Frémont, Jessie Benton (1824–1902)
Fremstad, Olive (1871–1951)
French, Alice (1850–1934)
French, Heather (1974—)
French, Marilyn (1929—)
French, Mary (fl. 1703)
French, Michelle (1977—)
Friday, Dallas J. (1986—)
Friday, Nancy (1937—)
Friebus, Florida (1909–1988)
Friedan, Betty (1921–2006)
Friedl, Ernestine (1920—)
Friedman, Elizebeth (d. 1980)
Friedman, Esther Pauline (1918–2002)
Friend, Charlotte (1921–1987)
Friesinger, Anni (1977—)
Frietschie, Barbara (1766–1862)
Friganza, Trixie (1870–1955)
Frings, Ketti (1909–1981)
Frissell, Toni (1907–1988)
Froman, Jane (1907–1980)
Fromm, Erika (1909–2003)
Fromme, Lynette (1948—)
Fromm-Reichmann, Frieda (1889–1957)
Frostic, Gwen (1906–2001)
Fry, Laura Ann (1857–1943)
Fry, Shirley (1927—)
Frye, Mary E. (1905–2004)
Fuerstner, Fiona (1936—)
Fuld, Carrie (1864–1944)
Fuller, Amy (1968—)
Fuller, Elizabeth (1775–1856)
Fuller, Frances (1907–1980)
Fuller, Ida (1874–1975)
Fuller, Loïe (1862–1928)
Fuller, Lucia Fairchild (1870–1924)
Fuller, Margaret (1810–1850)
Fuller, Mary (1888–1973)
Fuller, Meta Warrick (1877–1968)
Fuller, Minnie Rutherford (1868–1946)
Fuller, Rosalinde (1901–1982)
Fuller, Sarah (1836–1927)
Fulton, Mary Hannah (1854–1927)
Fulton, Maude (1881–1950)
Funicello, Annette (1942—)
Funk, Wally (1939—)
Furbish, Kate (1834–1931)
Furman, Bess (1894–1969)
Furness, Betty (1916–1994)
Furse, Judith (1912–1974)
Furtado, Juliana (1967—)
Furtsch, Evelyn (1911—)
Gabarra, Carin (1965—)
Gabor, Eva (1919–1995)
Gabor, Magda (1914–1997)
Gabor, Zsa Zsa (1917—)
Gabors, The
Gacioch, Rose (1915—)
Gacioch, Rose (1915–2004)
Gág, Wanda (1893–1946)
Gage, Frances D. (1808–1884)
Gage, Matilda Joslyn (1826–1898)
Gage, Susanna Phelps (1857–1915)
Gaines, Chryste (1970—)
Gaines, Irene McCoy (1892–1964)
Gaines, Myra Clark (1805–1885)
Gale, Tristan (1980—)
Gale, Zona (1874–1938)
Gallagher, Helen (1926—)
Gallagher, Kim (1964–2002)
Galland, Bertha (1876–1932)
Gallatin, Alberta (c. 1861–1948)
Gallina, Juliane (1970—)
Galloway, Grace Growden (d. 1782)
Galloway, Louise (d. 1949)
Gam, Rita (1928—)
Gambarelli, Maria (1900–1990)
Gamson, Annabelle (1928—)
Gandy, Kim A. (c. 1954—)
Ganser, Marge (c. 1948–1996)
Ganser, Mary Ann (c. 1948–1971)
Gantt, Rosa (1875–1935)
Garatti-Saville, Eleanor (1909—)
Garbousova, Raya (1909–1997)
Garcia-O'Brien, Tanya (c. 1973—)
Garde, Betty (1905–1989)
Gardella, Tess (1897–1950)
Garden, Mary (1874–1967)
Gardener, Helen Hamilton (1853–1925)
Gardiner, Lisa (c. 1896–1958)
Gardiner, Muriel (1901–1985)
Gardner, Ava (1922–1990)
Gardner, Helen (1878–1946)
Gardner, Helen (1884–1968)
Gardner, Isabella (1915–1981)
Gardner, Isabella Stewart (1840–1924)
Gardner, Janet (1962—)
Gardner, Julia Anna (1882–1960)
Gardner, Kay (1941–2002)
Gardner, Mary Sewall (1871–1961)
Gardner, Suzi (1960—)
Garfield, Lucretia (1832–1918)
Garfield, Viola (1899–1983)
Garland, Judy (1922–1969)
Garner, Peggy Ann (1931–1984)
Garner, Sarah (1971—)
Garnet, Sarah (1831–1911)
Garon, Pauline (1900–1965)
Garrett, Betty (1919—)
Garrett, Emma (c. 1846–1893)
Garrett, Mary Elizabeth (1854–1915)
Garrett, Mary Smith (1839–1925)
Garrison, Lucy McKim (1842–1877)
Garrison, Mabel (1886–1963)
Garrison, Zina (1963—)
Garth, Midi (1920—)
Gaskin, Ina May (1940—)
Gates, Eleanor (1871–1951)
Gates, Nancy (1926—)
Gates, Ruth (1886–1966)
Gateson, Marjorie (1891–1977)
Gathers, Helen (1943—)
Gaughin, Lorraine (1924–1974)
Gault, Alma Elizabeth (1891–1981)
Gauntier, Gene (1885–1966)
Gaxton, Madeline (1897–1990)
Gayle, Crystal (1951—)
Gaynor, Gloria (1949—)
Gaynor, Janet (1906–1984)
Gaynor, Mitzi (1930—)
Gaytan, Andrea
Gear, Luella (1897–1980)
Geddes, Jane (1960—)
Gee, Dolly (1897–1978)
Gee, Helen (1919–2004)
Geer, Charlotte (1957—)
Geise, Sugar (1909–1988)
Geister, Janet M. (1885–1964)
Geller, Margaret Joan (1947—)
Gellhorn, Edna (1878–1970)
Gellhorn, Martha (1908–1998)
Geneviève (1920–2004)
Genhart, Cecile Staub (1898–1983)
Genovese, Kitty (1935–1964)
Genth, Lillian (1876–1953)
Gentle, Alice (1889–1958)
Gentry, Bobbie (1944—)
Gentry, Eva (c. 1920—)
George, Carolyn (1927—)
George, Gladys (1900–1954)
George, Grace (1879–1961)
George, Maude (1888–1963)
George, Phyllis (1949—)
George, Zelma Watson (1904–1994)
Geppi-Aikens, Diane (c. 1963–2003)
Geraghty, Agnes (1906–1974)
Geraghty, Carmelita (1901–1966)
Geraldine (1916—)
Germaine, Diane (1944—)
Gerould, Katharine (1879–1944)
Gersten, Berta (c. 1896–1972)
Gestefeld, Ursula Newell (1845–1921)
Gestring, Marjorie (1922–1992)
Geva, Tamara (1906–1997)
Giannini, Dusolina (1900–1986)
Gianulias, Nikki (1959—)
Gibb, Roberta (1942—)
Gibbons, Abby Hopper (1801–1893)
Gibbs, Georgia (1920—)
Gibbs, Lois (1946—)
Gibson, Althea (1927–2003)
Gibson, Deborah (1970—)
Gibson, Dorothy (1889–1946)
Gibson, Helen (1892–1977)
Gibson, Irene Langhorne (1873–1956)
Gibson, Michelle (1969—)
Gibson, Wynne (1903–1987)
Giddens, Rebecca (1977—)
Gideon, Miriam (1906–1996)
Gifford, Frances (1920–1994)
Gilbert, Anne (1821–1904)
Gilbert, Jody (1916–1979)
Gilbert, Katherine Everett (1886–1952)
Gilbert, Linda (1847–1895)
Gilbert, Mercedes (1894–1952)
Gilbert, Ronnie (1926—)
Gilbert, Ruth (d. 1993)
Gilbert, Sandra M. (1936—)
Gilberto, Astrud (1940—)
Gilbreth, Lillian Moller (1878–1972)
Gilchrist, Connie (1901–1985)
Gilchrist, Ellen (1935—)
Gilder, Jeannette Leonard (1849–1916)
Gilder, Virginia (1958—)
Gildersleeve, Virginia Crocheron (1877–1965)
Gillars, Mildred E. (1900–1988)
Gillespie, Mabel (1877–1923)
Gillespie, Mother Angela (1824–1887)
Gillett, Emma (1852–1927)
Gillette, Genevieve (1898–1986)
Gilligan, Carol (1936—)
Gillmor, Frances (1903–1993)
Gillmore, Margalo (1897–1986)
Gillmore, Ruth (d. 1976)
Gillom, Jennifer (1964—)
Gilman, Caroline Howard (1794–1888)
Gilman, Charlotte Perkins (1860–1935)
Gilman, Elisabeth (1867–1950)
Gilmer, Elizabeth Meriwether (1861–1951)
Gilmore, Virginia (1919–1986)
Gilpin, Laura (1891–1979)
Gimbutas, Marija (1921–1994)
Gingold, Hermione (1897–1987)
Ginsburg, Mirra (1909–2000)
Ginsburg, Ruth Bader (1933—)
Giovanni, Nikki (1943—)
Giove, Missy (1972—)

Gish, Dorothy (1898–1968)
Gish, Lillian (1893–1993)
Gisolo, Margaret (1914–2003)
Gitelman, Claudia (1938—)
Givney, Kathryn (1896–1978)
Glabe, Karen (1942—)
Gladney, Edna (1886–1961)
Glanville-Hicks, Peggy (1912–1990)
Glaser, Elizabeth (1947–1994)
Glaser, Lulu (1874–1958)
Glaser, Pease (1961—)
Glasgow, Ellen (1873–1945)
Glaspell, Susan (1876–1948)
Glass, Bonnie (b. around 1895)
Glass, Julie (1979—)
Glaum, Louise (1894–1970)
Gleason, Kate (1865–1933)
Gleason, Lucile (1886–1947)
Gleason, Rachel Brooks (1820–1905)
Glenn, Laura (1945—)
Glenn, Mary Willcox (1869–1940)
Gless, Sharon (1943—)
Glover, Amelia (c. 1873–?)
Glover, Elizabeth Harris (d. 1643)
Glück, Louise (1943—)
Gluck, Rena (1933—)
Glueck, Eleanor Touroff (1898–1972)
Glutting, Charlotte E. (1910–1996)
Goddard, Mary Katherine (1738–1816)
Goddard, Paulette (1905–1990)
Goddard, Sarah Updike (c. 1700–1770)
Godowsky, Dagmar (1897–1975)
Godwin, Gail (1937—)
Goetze, Vicki (1972—)
Goggans, Lalla (1906–1987)
Golda, Natalie (1981—)
Goldberg, Rose (d. 1966)
Goldberg, Whoopi (1949—)
Golden, Diana (1963–2001)
Goldfrank, Esther S. (1896–1997)
Goldman, Emma (1869–1940)
Goldman, Hetty (1881–1972)
Goldman-Rakic, Patricia S. (1937–2003)
Goldmark, Josephine (1877–1950)
Goldring, Winifred (1888–1971)
Goldsmith, Grace Arabell (1904–1975)
Goldstein, Jennie (1896–1960)
Goldthwaite, Anne Wilson (1869–1944)
Gollner, Nana (1919–1980)
Gombell, Minna (1892–1973)
Goodenough, Florence Laura (1886–1959)
Goodhue, Sarah Whipple (1641–1681)
Goodman, Ellen (1941—)
Goodman, Shirley (1936–2005)
Goodrich, Annie Warburton (1866–1954)
Goodrich, Edna (1883–1971)
Goodrich, Frances (1891–1984)
Goodridge, Sarah (1788–1853)
Goodson, Sadie (c. 1900—)
Goodwin, Doris Kearns (1943—)
Goodwin, Michelle (1966—)
Goose, Elizabeth (1665–1757)
Gordon, Anna Adams (1853–1931)
Gordon, Bridgette (1967—)
Gordon, Caroline (1895–1981)
Gordon, Dorothy (1889–1970)
Gordon, Gale Ann (1943—)
Gordon, Jean Margaret (1865–1931)
Gordon, Julia Swayne (1878–1933)
Gordon, Kate M. (1861–1932)
Gordon, Kim (1953—)
Gordon, Laura de Force (1838–1907)
Gordon, Mary (1882–1963)
Gordon, Ruth (1896–1985)
Gordon, Vera (1886–1948)
Gore, Altovise (1935—)
Gore, Leslie (1946—)
Goring, Sonia (1940—)
Gorman, Margaret (1905–1995)
Gorman, Miki (1935—)
Gormé, Eydie (1931—)
Gorton, Bettina (c. 1916–1983)
Gossick, Sue (1947—)
Goudal, Jetta (1891–1985)
Gougar, Helen (1843–1907)
Gould, Beatrice Blackmar (c. 1899–1989)
Gould, Lois (1932?–2002?)
Gould, Sandra (1916–1999)
Govrin, Gloria (1942—)
Goyette, Cynthia (1946—)
Grable, Betty (1916–1973)
Grabowski, Halina (1928–2003)
Gracen, Elizabeth (1960—)
Grafton, Sue (1940)
Graham, Barbara Wood (1923–1955)
Graham, Bette Nesmith (1924–1980)
Graham, Georgia (1900–1988)
Graham, Isabella (1742–1814)
Graham, Katharine (1917–2001)
Graham, Kim (1971—)
Graham, Martha (1894–1991)
Graham, Sheila (1904–1988)
Graham, Shirley (1896–1977)
Grahame, Gloria (1924–1981)
Grahn, Judy (1940—)
Granahan, Kathryn E. (1894–1979)
Granato, Cammi (1971—)
Grandin, Ethel (1894–1988)
Grandy, Maria (1937–1998)
Granger, Josie (1853–1934)
Granger, Michele (1970—)
Granholm, Jennifer M. (1959—)
Grann, Phyllis (1937—)
Grant, Amy (1960—)
Grant, Jane (1895–1972)
Grant, Julia (1826–1902)
Grant, Kathryn (1933—)
Grant, Lee (1927—)
Grant, Valentine (1881–1949)
Grant, Zilpah (1794–1874)
Granville, Bonita (1923–1988)
Granville, Louise (1895–1968)
Grasso, Ella (1919–1981)
Gratz, Rebecca (1781–1869)
Grau, Shirley Ann (1929—)
Graves, Carie (1953—)
Graves, Nancy (1940–1995)
Gray, Coleen (1922—)
Gray, Dolores (1924–2002)
Gray, Hanna Holborn (1930—)
Gray, Macy (1970—)
Grayson, Betty Evans (1925–1979)
Grayson, Kathryn (1922—)
Greatorex, Eliza (1820–1897)
Greeley-Smith, Nixola (1880–1919)
Green, Anna Katharine (1846–1935)
Green, Anne Catherine (c. 1720–1775)
Green, Constance McLaughlin (1897–1975)
Green, Debbie (1958—)
Green, Debora (c. 1951—)
Green, Dorothy (1892–1963)
Green, Edith Starrett (1910–1987)
Green, Elizabeth Shippen (1871–1954)
Green, Hetty (1834–1916)
Green, Mitzi (1920–1969)
Green, Tammie (1959—)
Green, Vera Mae (1928–1982)
Greenbaum, Dorothea Schwarcz (1893–1986)
Greene, Belle da Costa (1883–1950)
Greene, Catharine Littlefield (1755–1814)
Greene, Catharine Ray (d. 1794)
Greene, Cordelia A. (1831–1905)
Greene, Gertrude Glass (1904–1956)
Greene, Sarah Pratt (1856–1935)
Greener, Dorothy (1917–1971)
Greenfield, Elizabeth Taylor (c. 1819–1876)
Greenfield, Meg (1930–1999)
Greenhow, Rose O'Neal (c. 1817–1864)
Greenway, Isabella Selmes (1886–1953)
Greenwood, Charlotte (1890–1978)
Greenwood, Edith
Greenwood, Marion (1909–1980)
Greer, Jane (1924–2001)
Gregg, Virginia (1916–1986)
Gregory, Cynthia (1946—)
Greig, Marion (1954—)
Grenard, Lizz (1965—)
Grenfell, Helen L. (b. 1868)
Gresser, Gisela (1906–2000)
Grew, Mary (1902–1971)
Grew, Mary A. (1813–1896)
Grey, Jane (1883–1944)
Grey, Katherine (1873–1950)
Grey, Nan (1918–1993)
Grey, Virginia (1917–2004)
Grier, Pam (1949—)
Griffin, Eleanore (1904–1995)
Griffin, Ellen (1918–1986)
Griffing, Josephine White (1814–1872)
Griffith, Corinne (1894–1979)
Griffith, Emily (c. 1880–1947)
Griffith, Nanci (1953—)
Griffith, Yolanda (1970—)
Griffiths, Martha Wright (1912–2003)
Griffitts, Hannah (1727–1817)
Grillo, Joann (1939–1999)
Grimes, Tammy (1934—)
Grimké, Angelina E. (1805–1879)
Grimké, Angelina Weld (1880–1958)
Grimké, Charlotte L. Forten (1837–1914)
Grimké, Sarah Moore (1792–1873)
Grinder, Martha (1815–1866)
Griscom, Frances C. (1880–1973)
Griswold, Denny (1908–2001)
Groody, Louise (1897–1961)
Grossfeld, Muriel Davis (1941—)
Grossinger, Jennie (1892–1972)
Grossman, Edith (1936—)
Grotell, Maija (1899–1973)
Gruber, Ruth (1911—)
Gruenberg, Sidonie (1881–1974)
Grumbach, Doris (1918—)
Guérin, Mother Theodore (1798–1856)
Guest, C.Z. (1920–2003)
Guest, Irene (1900–1979)
Guggenheim, Florence Shloss (1863–1944)
Guggenheim, Irene (1868–1954)
Guggenheim, Olga H. (1877–1970)
Guggenheim, Peggy (1898–1979)
Guggenheimer, Minnie (1882–1966)
Guidry, Carlette (1969—)
Guild, Nancy (1925–1999)
Guinan, Texas (1884–1933)
Guiney, Louise Imogen (1861–1920)
Guion, Connie M. (1882–1971)
Guisewite, Cathy (1950—)
Gulick, Alice Gordon (1847–1903)
Gulick, Charlotte Vetter (1865–1928)
Gulliver, Julia Henrietta (1856–1940)
Gund, Agnes (1938—)
Gunnarsson, Martine (1927—)
Gunness, Belle (1860–c. 1908)
Gunning, Louise (1879–1960)
Gunther, Erna (1896–1982)
Gurie, Sigrid (1911–1969)
Gurney, Eliza (1801–1881)
Gurney, Hilda (1943—)

Gurney, Nella Hooper (1838–1887)
Gustavson, Linda (1949—)
Guthrie, Janet (1938—)
Guthrie, Mary Jane (1895–1975)
Gutridge, Molly (fl. 1778)
Guy, Rosa (1925—)
Gwynne, Anne (1918–2003)
Hacker, Marilyn (1942—)
Hackett, Jeanette (c. 1898–1979)
Hackett, Joan (1942–1983)
Hackley, E. Azalia Smith (1867–1922)
Haden, Sara (1897–1981)
Hagen, Jean (1923–1977)
Hagen, Uta (1919–2004)
Hagge, Marlene Bauer (1934—)
Hagood, Margaret (1907–1963)
Hahn, Anna Marie (1906–1938)
Hahn, Dorothy (1876–1950)
Hahn, Emily (1905–1997)
Hahn, Helene B. (c. 1940—)
Haig, Emma (1898–1939)
Haines, Helen (1872–1961)
Haislett, Nicole (1972—)
Hale, Barbara (1921—)
Hale, Binnie (1899–1984)
Hale, Clara (1905–1992)
Hale, Ellen Day (1855–1940)
Hale, Georgia (1905–1985)
Hale, Lilian Westcott (1881–1963)
Hale, Louise Closser (1872–1933)
Hale, Lucretia Peabody (1820–1900)
Hale, Mamie O. (1911–c. 1968)
Hale, Nancy (1908–1988)
Hale, Ruth (1886–1934)
Hale, Sarah Josepha (1788–1879)
Hale, Sarah Preston (1796–1866)
Hale, Sue Sally (1937–2003)
Hale, Susan (1833–1910)
Haley, Margaret A. (1861–1939)
Hall, Adelaide (1904–1993)
Hall, Anne (1792–1863)
Hall, Ella (1896–1982)
Hall, Emma Amelia (1837–1884)
Hall, Evelyne (1909–1993)
Hall, Geraldine (1905–1970)
Hall, Grayson (1923–1985)
Hall, Juanita (1901–1968)
Hall, Katie Beatrice (1938—)
Hall, Kaye (1951—)
Hall, Lydia E. (1906–1969)
Hall, Natalie (1904–1994)
Hall, Rosetta Sherwood (1865–1951)
Hallam, Mrs. Lewis (?–1774)
Hallaren, Mary A. (1907–2005)
Hallowell, Anna (1831–1905)
Halls, Ethel May (1882–1967)
Halpert, Edith Gregor (c. 1900–1970)
Halprin, Ann (1920—)
Hamer, Fannie Lou (1917–1977)
Hamill, Dorothy (1956—)
Hamilton, Alice (1869–1970)
Hamilton, Carrie (1963–2002)
Hamilton, Edith (1867–1963)
Hamilton, Elizabeth Schuyler (1757–c. 1854)
Hamilton, Gordon (1892–1967)
Hamilton, Margaret (1902–1985)
Hamilton, Nancy (1908–1985)
Hamilton, Tara (1982—)
Hamilton, Virginia (1936–2002)
Hamlin, Shelley (1949—)
Hamm, Mia (1972—)
Hammarberg, Gretchen
Hammerstein, Dorothy (1899–1987)
Hammerstein, Elaine (1897–1948)
Hammon, Mary (c. 1633–?)
Hammond, Blodwen (1908–1973)
Hammond, Kathleen (1951—)
Hammond, Virginia (1893–1972)
Hamper, Geneviève (c. 1889–1971)
Hampton, Hope (1897–1982)
Hampton, Mabel (1902–1989)
Hanaford, Phebe Ann (1829–1921)
Hancock, Cornelia (1840–1927)
Hancock, Joy (1898–1986)
Handler, Ruth (1916–2002)
Handzlic, Jean (d. 1963)
Haney, Carol (1924–1964)
Hanks, Jane Richardson (b. 1908)
Hanks, Nancy (1783–1818)
Hanks, Nancy (1927–1983)
Hansberry, Lorraine (1930–1965)
Hanscom, Adelaide (1876–1932)
Hansen, Jacqueline A. (c. 1949—)
Hansen, Juanita (1895–1961)
Hansen, Julia Butler (1907–1988)
Hanshaw, Annette (1910–1985)
Hanson, Beverly (1924—)
Hanson, Elizabeth Meader (1684–1737)
Hanson, Gladys (1883–1973)
Hanson, Luise V. (1913–2003)
Hanson, Marla (c. 1962—)
Hapgood, Isabel (1850–1928)
Haraszty, Eszter (c. 1910–1994)
Hard, Darlene (1936—)
Harden, Cecil Murray (1894–1984)
Hardey, Mary Aloysia (1809–1886)
Harding, Ann (1902–1981)
Harding, Florence K. (1860–1924)
Harding, Tonya (1970—)
Hardwick, Elizabeth (1916—)
Hardy, Anna Eliza (1839–1934)
Hardy, Catherine (1930—)
Harjo, Joy (1951—)
Harkness, Anna M. Richardson (1837–1926)
Harkness, Georgia (1891–1974)
Harkness, Mary Stillman (1874–1950)
Harkness, Rebekah (1915–1982)
Harley, Katherine (1881–1961)
Harlow, Jean (1911–1937)
Harman, Katie Marie (c. 1980—)
Harnack, Mildred (1902–1943)
Harned, Virginia (1872–1946)
Harold, Erika (c. 1980—)
Harper, Frances E.W. (1825–1911)
Harper, Ida Husted (1851–1931)
Harper, Valerie (1940—)
Harrigan, Lori (1970—)
Harrigan, Nedda (1899–1989)
Harriman, Florence Jaffray (1870–1967)
Harriman, Mary (1851–1932)
Harriman, Pamela (1920–1997)
Harrington, Penny (c. 1943—)
Harris, Addie (1940–1982)
Harris, Barbara (1930—)
Harris, Barbara (1935—)
Harris, Barbara (1945—)
Harris, Corra May (1869–1935)
Harris, Dionna (1968—)
Harris, Edna Mae (1910–1997)
Harris, Emmylou (1947—)
Harris, Jackie
Harris, Julie (1925—)
Harris, Lois (1940—)
Harris, Lusia Mae (1955—)
Harris, Marjorie Silliman (1890–1976)
Harris, Mary Belle (1874–1957)
Harris, Mildred (1901–1944)
Harris, Patricia Roberts (1924–1985)
Harris, Renee (1885–1969)
Harris, Rosemary (1927—)
Harris, Sylvia (d. 1966)
Harrison, Anna Symmes (1775–1864)
Harrison, Barbara Grizzuti (1934–2002)
Harrison, Caroline Scott (1832–1892)
Harrison, Constance Cary (1843–1920)
Harrison, Elizabeth (1849–1927)
Harrison, Hazel (1883–1969)
Harrison, Jane Irwin (1804–1846)
Harrison, June (1925–1974)
Harrison, Marguerite (1879–1967)
Harrison, Mary Scott Dimmick (1858–1948)
Harrison, Ruth (1911–1974)
Harry, Deborah (1945—)
Harshaw, Margaret (1909–1997)
Hart, Annie (d. 1947)
Hart, Dolores (1938—)
Hart, Doris (1925—)
Hart, Flo (c. 1896–1960)
Hart, Jane (1920—)
Hart, Margie (1916—)
Hart, Nancy (c. 1735–1830)
Hart, Nancy (c. 1846–1902)
Hart, Pearl (c. 1875–c. 1924)
Harte, Betty (c. 1882–1965)
Hartigan, Grace (1922—)
Hartley, Mariette (1940—)
Hartman, Elizabeth (1941–1987)
Hartman, Grace (1907–1955)
Harvey, Ethel Browne (1885–1965)
Harvey, Georgette (c. 1882–1952)
Harvey, Mary (1965—)
Hasbrouck, Lydia Sayer (1827–1910)
Hashman, Judy (1935—)
Hasoutra (1906–1978)
Hasso, Signe (1910–2002)
Hastings, Caroline (1841–1922)
Hatch, Annia (1978—)
Hatcher, Orie Latham (1868–1946)
Hatfield, Juliana (1967—)
Hatton, Fanny (c. 1870–1939)
Hatvany, Lili (1890–1967)
Haughery, Margaret Gaffney (1813–1882)
Hauk, Minnie (1851–1929)
Hauptmann, Anna (1898–1994)
Havemeyer, Louisine (1855–1929)
Haven, Emily Bradley Neal (1827–1863)
Haver, June (1926–2005)
Haver, Phyllis (1899–1960)
Haviland, Laura S. (1808–1898)
Havoc, June (1916—)
Hawes, Elizabeth (1903–1971)
Hawes, Harriet Boyd (1871–1945)
Hawkes, Sharlene (c. 1964—)
Hawkins, Mary Ann (1919–1993)
Hawkins, Paula Fickes (1927—)
Hawley, Wanda (1895–1963)
Hawn, Goldie (1945—)
Haworth, Cheryl (1983—)
Hawthorne, Sophia Peabody (1809–1871)
Hay, Elizabeth Dexter (1927—)
Hay, Mary (1901–1957)
Hay, Mary Garrett (1857–1928)
Hay, Vanessa Briscoe (1955—)
Hayden, Anna Tompson (1648–after 1720)
Hayden, Esther Allen (c. 1713–1758)
Hayden, Mother Mary Bridget (1814–1890)
Hayden, Sophia (1868–1953)
Haydon, Julie (1910–1994)
Hayes, Allison (1930–1977)
Hayes, Helen (1900–1993)
Hayes, Joanna (1976—)
Hayes, Lucy Webb (1831–1889)
Hayes, Maggie (1916–1977)
Hayes, Nevada (1885–1941)
Hayes, Patty (1955—)
Haygood, Laura Askew (1845–1900)

Hayman, Lillian (1922–1994)
Haynes, Elizabeth Ross (1883–1953)
Haynie, Sandra B. (1943—)
Hayward, Lillie (1891–1978)
Hayward, Susan (1917–1975)
Haywood, Claire (c. 1916–1978)
Hayworth, Rita (1918–1987)
Hazard, Caroline (1856–1945)
Hazeltine, Mary (1868–1949)
Hazen, Elizabeth Lee (1883–1975)
Hazlett, Olive C. (1890–1974)
Hazzard, Shirley (1931—)
Head, Edith (1897–1981)
Heady, Bonnie (1912–1953)
Healey, Eunice (c. 1920—)
Healy, Pamela (1963—)
Heap, Jane (1887–1964)
Hearst, Catherine Campbell (1917–1998)
Hearst, Millicent (1882–1974)
Hearst, Patricia Campbell (1954—)
Hearst, Phoebe A. (1842–1919)
Heath, Clarita (c. 1916–2003)
Heath, Sophia (1896–1936)
Heaton, Hannah Cook (1721–1794)
Hebard, Grace Raymond (1861–1936)
Heckart, Eileen (1919–2001)
Hecker, Genevieve (1884–1960)
Heckler, Margaret M. (1931—)
Hedgepeth, Whitney L. (1971—)
Hedren, Tippi (1931—)
Hedrick, Heather (c. 1972—)
Heenan, Frances (1910–1956)
Heenan, Katie (1985—)
Heffernan, Fallon (1986—)
Heflin, Alma (fl. 1930s)
Hegamin, Lucille (1894–1970)
Heiden, Beth (1959—)
Height, Dorothy (1912—)
Heilbrun, Carolyn Gold (1926–2003)
Heinemann, Barbara (1795–1883)
Heinrichs, April (1964—)
Heiss-Jenkins, Carol (1940—)
Helburn, Theresa (1887–1959)
Held, Anna (c. 1865–1918)
Heldman, Gladys (1922–2003)
Heldman, Julie (1945—)
Hellman, Lillian (1905–1984)
Helm, June (1924—)
Helmer, Bessie Bradwell (1858–1927)
Helmond, Katherine (1934—)
Helser, Brenda (1926—)
Hemenway, Abby (1828–1890)
Hemenway, Mary Porter Tileston (1820–1894)
Heming, Violet (1895–1981)
Hemings, Sally (1773–1835)
Hemingway, Margaux (1955–1996)
Hemingway, Mariel (1961—)
Hempel, Frieda (1885–1955)
Hemsley, Estelle (1887–1968)
Henderlite, Rachel (1905–1991)
Henderson, Alice Corbin (1881–1949)
Henderson, Danielle (1977—)
Henderson, Jo (1934–1988)
Henderson, Monique (1983—)
Henderson, Virginia (1897–1996)
Henderson, Zenna (1917–1983)
Hendl, Susan (1949—)
Hendrix, Wanda (1928–1981)
Hendryx, Nona (1945—)
Hengler, Flora (c. 1887–1965)
Hengler, May (c. 1884–1952)
Henley, Beth (1952—)
Henmyer, Annie W. (1827–1900)
Hennagan, Monique (1976—)
Henne, Jan (1947—)
Henneberg, Jill
Henning, Anne (1955—)
Henning, Eva (1920—)
Hennock, Frieda B. (1904–1960)
Henri, Florence (1895–1982)
Henrich, Christy (1973–1994)
Henrotin, Ellen Martin (1847–1922)
Henry, Alice (1857–1943)
Henry, Charlotte (1913–1980)
Henry, Gale (1893–1972)
Henry, Lea (1961—)
Henry, Marguerite (1902–1997)
Henson, Lisa (1960—)
Hentz, Caroline Lee (1800–1856)
Hepburn, Katharine (1907–2003)
Herbst, Josephine (1892–1969)
Heritage, Doris Brown (1942—)
Herman, Barbara (c. 1952—)
Herman, Robin (c. 1952—)
Hernández, Maria (1896–1986)
Herne, Chrystal (1882–1950)
Herne, Katharine Corcoran (1857–1943)
Heron, Matilda (1830–1877)
Herrick, Christine Terhune (1859–1944)
Herrick, Elinore Morehouse (1895–1964)
Herrick, Genevieve Forbes (1894–1962)
Herron, Carrie Rand (1867–1914)
Herron, Cindy (1965—)
Herscher, Sylvia (1913–2004)
Hervey, Irene (1910–1998)
Hesse, Eva (1936–1970)
Hesse, Fanny Angelina (1850–1934)
Hewins, Caroline Maria (1846–1926)
Heyman, Katherine Ruth (1877–1944)
Heyward, Dorothy (1890–1961)
Hibbard, Edna (c. 1895–1942)
Hibbard, Hope (1893–1988)
Hickman, Libbie (1965—)
Hickok, Lorena A. (1893–1968)
Hicks, Betty (1920—)
Hicks, Helen (1911–1974)
Hicks, Louise Day (1916–2003)
Hicks, Sheila (1934—)
Hier, Ethel Glenn (1889–1971)
Higgins, Marguerite (1920–1966)
Higgins, Pam (1945—)
Highsmith, Patricia (1921–1995)
Hightower, Rosella (1920—)
Hildebrand, Sara (1979—)
Hill, Anita (1956—)
Hill, Betty (1919–2004)
Hill, Cindy (1948—)
Hill, Debra (1950–2005)
Hill, Frances Mulligan (1799–1884)
Hill, Grace Livingston (1865–1947)
Hill, Hannah, Jr (1703–1714)
Hill, Lauryn (1975—)
Hill, Lynn (1961—)
Hill, Martha (1900–1995)
Hill, Opal S. (1892–1981)
Hill, Patty Smith (1868–1946)
Hill, Thelma (1925–1977)
Hill, Virginia (1907–1967)
Hill, Virginia (1916–1966)
Hilliard, Harriet (1909–1994)
Hillis, Margaret (1921—)
Hillman, Bessie (1889–1970)
Hills, Carla (1934—)
Hills, Tina S. (1921—)
Hinderas, Natalie (1927–1987)
Hines, Elizabeth (1899–1971)
Hinkle, Beatrice M. (1874–1953)
Hinkson, Mary (1930—)
Hinson, Lois E. (1926—)
Hipp, Jutta (1925–2003)
Hird, Judith (c. 1946—)
Hird, Thora (1911–2003)
Hirsch, Mary (c. 1913—)
Hite, Shere (1943—)
Hoban, Lillian (1925–1998)
Hobart, Rose (1906–2000)
Hobby, Gladys Lounsbury (1910–1993)
Hobby, Oveta Culp (1905–1995)
Hobson, Elizabeth Christophers (1831–1912)
Hobson, Laura Z. (1900–1986)
Hockaday, Margaret (1907–1992)
Hockfield, Susan (1951—)
Hoctor, Harriet (1905–1977)
Hodder, Jessie Donaldson (1867–1931)
Hodges, Faustina Hasse (1822–1895)
Hodges, Joy (1914–2003)
Hodgkins, Sarah Perkins (c. 1750–1803)
Hoefly, Ethel Ann (1919–2003)
Hoey, Jane M. (1892–1968)
Hoff, Vanda (b. around 1900)
Hoffleit, E. Dorrit (1907—)
Hoffman, Alice (1952—)
Hoffman, Claire Giannini (1904–1997)
Hoffman, Joyce (c. 1948—)
Hoffman, Malvina (1885–1966)
Hoffmann, Gertrude (1871–1966)
Hofmann, Adele (d. 2001)
Hogan, Linda (1947—)
Hoge, Jane (1811–1890)
Hogg, Ima (1882–1975)
Hogshead, Nancy (1962—)
Hokinson, Helen E. (1893–1949)
Holden, Joan (1939—)
Holden, Mari (1971—)
Holdsclaw, Chamique (1977—)
Holiday, Billie (c. 1915–1959)
Holladay, Wilhelmina Cole (1922—)
Holland, Cecelia (1943—)
Holland, Tara Dawn (c. 1972—)
Holley, Marietta (1836–1926)
Holley, Mary Austin (1784–1846)
Holley, Sallie (1818–1893)
Holliday, Jennifer (1960—)
Holliday, Judy (1921–1965)
Hollingworth, Leta Stetter (1886–1939)
Hollins, Marion B. (1892–1944)
Hollinshead, Ariel (1929—)
Holly, J. Hunter (1932–1982)
Holm, Celeste (1919—)
Holm, Eleanor (1913–2004)
Holm, Hanya (1888–1992)
Holm, Jeanne (1921—)
Holman, Libby (1904–1971)
Holmes, Helen (1892–1950)
Holmes, Julia Archibald (1838–1887)
Holmes, Mary Jane (1825–1907)
Holst, Clara (1868–1935)
Holt, Jennifer (1920–1997)
Holt, Marjorie Sewell (1920—)
Holt, Stella (d. 1967)
Holt, Winifred (1870–1945)
Holtzman, Elizabeth (1941—)
Holtzmann, Fanny (c. 1900–1980)
Holum, Dianne (1951—)
Holum, Kirsten (c. 1981—)
Holyoke, Mary Vial (1737–1802)
Homan, Gertrude (1880–1951)
Homer, Louise (1871–1947)
Honeyman, Nan Wood (1881–1970)
Honeyman, Susie
Hoobler, Icie Macy (1892–1984)
Hood, Darla (1931–1979)
Hooker, Evelyn (1907–1996)
Hooker, Isabella Beecher (1822–1907)
Hooper, Ellen Sturgis (1812–1848)
Hooper, Jessie Jack (1865–1935)

Hoover, H.M. (1935—)
Hoover, Katherine (1937—)
Hoover, Lou Henry (1874–1944)
Hopkins, Emma Curtis (1853–1925)
Hopkins, Juliet (1818–1890)
Hopkins, Miriam (1902–1972)
Hopkins, Pauline E. (1859–1930)
Hopper, Edna Wallace (1864–1959)
Hopper, Grace Murray (1906–1992)
Hopper, Hedda (1885–1966)
Horn, Miriam Burns (1904–1951)
Horne, Alice Merrill (1868–1948)
Horne, Katharyn (1932—)
Horne, Lena (1917—)
Horne, Marilyn (1929—)
Horne, Myrtle (1892–1969)
Horney, Karen (1885–1952)
Horstmann, Dorothy M. (1911–2001)
Horton, Gladys (1944—)
Horton, Mildred McAfee (1900–1994)
Horvath, Julia (1924–1947)
Horwich, Frances (1908–2001)
Hoskens, Jane Fenn (1694–c. 1750)
Hoskins, Olive (1882–1975)
Hosmer, Harriet (1830–1908)
Hotchkiss, Avis (fl. 1915)
Hotchkiss, Effie (fl. 1915)
Houghton, Edith (1912—)
Housden, Nina (1916—)
Houston, Cissy (1933—)
Houston, Margaret Lea (1819–1867)
Houston, Thelma (1946—)
Houston, Whitney (1963—)
Howard, Ada Lydia (1829–1907)
Howard, Blanche Willis (1847–1898)
Howard, Cordelia (1848–1941)
Howard, Denean (1964—)
Howard, Esther (1892–1965)
Howard, Frances (1903–1976)
Howard, Jane (1934–1996)
Howard, Jean (1910–2000)
Howard, Jessica (1984—)
Howard, Kathleen (1879–1956)
Howard, Kathy (c. 1961—)
Howard, Sherri (1962—)
Howe, Fanny (1942—)
Howe, Julia Ward (1819–1910)
Howe, Lois (c. 1864–1964)
Howe, Susan (1937—)
Howe, Tina (1937—)
Howell, Alice (1888–1961)
Howell, Lida (1859–1939)
Howell, Mary (1932–1998)
Howes, Barbara (1914–1996)
Howland, Emily (1827–1929)
Howland, Jobyna (1880–1936)
Hoyt, Beatrix (1880–1963)
Hoyt, Julia (c. 1897–1955)
Hoyt, Mary F. (1858–1958)
Hubbard, Ruth (1924—)
Huck, Winnifred Sprague Mason (1882–1936)
Hucles, Angela (1978—)
Hudson, Martha (1939—)
Hudson, Rochelle (1916–1972)
Hudson, Winson (1916–2004)
Huebner, Robin (1961—)
Huerta, Dolores (1930—)
Huff, Louise (1895–1973)
Hufstedler, Shirley Mount (1925—)
Hughan, Jessie (1875–1955)
Hughes, Adelaide (1884–1960)
Hughes, Adella (1869–1950)
Hughes, Karen (1956—)
Hughes, Kathleen (1928—)
Hughes, Mary Beth (1919–1995)
Hughes, Sarah (1985—)
Hughes, Sarah T. (1896–1985)
Hulette, Gladys (1896–1991)
Hull, Hannah (1872–1958)
Hull, Helen Rose (1888–1971)
Hull, Josephine (1886–1957)
Hull, Peggy (1889–1967)
Hulme, Kathryn (1900–1981)
Hume, Sophia Wigington (1702–1774)
Hummert, Anne (1905–1996)
Humphrey, Doris (1895–1958)
Humphrey, Muriel (1912–1998)
Humphrey, Terin (1986—)
Hunt, Eva (1934–1980)
Hunt, Harriot Kezia (1805–1875)
Hunt, Helen (1963—)
Hunt, Marsha (1917—)
Hunt, Mary Hanchett (1830–1906)
Hunter, Alberta (1895–1984)
Hunter, Clementine (1886–1988)
Hunter, Holly (1958—)
Hunter, Kim (1922–2002)
Hunter, Kristin (1931—)
Hunter-Gault, Charlayne (1942—)
Huntington, Anna Hyatt (1876–1973)
Huntington, Anne Huntington (d. 1790)
Huntington, Emily (1841–1909)
Huntley, Joni (1956—)
Hunton, Addie D. Waites (1875–1943)
Hupalo, Katherine (1890–1974)
Hurd, Dorothy Campbell (1883–1945)
Hurd, Edith Thacher (1910–1997)
Hurd, Gale Anne (1955—)
Hurd-Mead, Kate Campbell (1867–1941)
Hurdon, Elizabeth (1868–1941)
Hurlock, Madeline (1899–1989)
Hurst, Fannie (1889–1968)
Hurston, Zora Neale (c. 1891–1960)
Huson, Florence (1857–1915)
Hussey, Ruth (1911–2005)
Husted, Marjorie Child (c. 1892–1986)
Huston, Anjelica (1951—)
Hutchins, Colleen Kay (c. 1927—)
Hutchins, Grace (1885–1969)
Hutchinson, Abigail (1829–1892)
Hutchinson, Jeanette (1951—)
Hutchinson, Josephine (1903–1998)
Hutchinson, Pamela (1958—)
Hutchinson, Sheila (1953—)
Hutchinson, Wanda (1951—)
Hutchison, Kay Bailey (1943—)
Hutchison, Muriel (1915–1975)
Hutson, Jean (1914–1998)
Hutton, Barbara (1912–1979)
Hutton, Betty (1921—)
Hutton, Ina Ray (1916–1984)
Hutton, Lauren (1943—)
Huxtable, Ada Louise (1921—)
Hyams, Leila (1905–1977)
Hyde, Ida (1857–1945)
Hyer, Martha (1924—)
Hyland, Diana (1936–1977)
Hyman, Flo (1954–1986)
Hyman, Libbie Henrietta (1888–1969)
Hyman, Misty (1979—)
Hyman, Phyllis (1949–1995)
Hyman, Trina Schart (1939–2004)
Hynde, Chrissie (1951—)
Hyslop, Beatrice Fry (1899–1973)
Hyson, Dorothy (1914–1996)
Iams, Lucy (1855–1924)
Ian, Janis (1951—)
Ichino, Yoko (c. 1954—)
Ickes, Anna Thompson (1873–1935)
Idar, Jovita (1885–1946)
Ide, Letitia (1909–1993)
Ifill, Gwen (1955—)
Iko, Momoko (1940—)
Illington, Margaret (1881–1934)
Ingalls, Laura H. (c. 1900–c. 1988)
Ingham, Mary Hall (1866–1937)
Ingraham, Mary Shotwell (1887–1981)
Ingram, Sheila Rena (1957—)
Inkster, Juli (1960—)
Inman, Elizabeth Murray (c. 1724–1785)
Inness, Jean (1900–1978)
Intropodi, Ethel (d. 1946)
Ireland, Patricia (1945—)
Irene (1901–1962)
Irene, Sister (1823–1896)
Ireys, Alice (1911–2000)
Irving, Isabel (1871–1944)
Irving, Margaret (1898–1988)
Irwin, Agnes (1841–1914)
Irwin, Elisabeth (1880–1942)
Irwin, Estelle Mae (1923—)
Irwin, Flo (born c. 1860)
Irwin, Inez Haynes (1873–1970)
Irwin, May (1862–1938)
Isaacs, Edith (1878–1956)
Isaksen, Lone (1941—)
Isler, Jennifer (1963—)
Isom, Mary Frances (1865–1920)
Ivey, Jean Eichelberger (1923—)
Ivins, Molly (c. 1944—)
Iyall, Debora (1954—)
Jackson, Anne (1926—)
Jackson, Cordell (1923–2004)
Jackson, Ethel (1877–1957)
Jackson, Helen Hunt (1830–1885)
Jackson, Janet (1966—)
Jackson, Julia (fl. 19th c.)
Jackson, Mahalia (1911–1972)
Jackson, Mary Jane (b. 1836)
Jackson, Mercy B. (1802–1877)
Jackson, Nell (1929–1988)
Jackson, Rachel Donelson (1767–1828)
Jackson, Rebecca Cox (1795–1871)
Jackson, Shirley (1916–1965)
Jackson, Shirley Ann (1946—)
Jackson, Tammy (1962—)
Jackson, Trina (1977—)
Jackson, Wanda (1937—)
Jacobellis, Lindsey (1985—)
Jacobi, Lotte (1896–1990)
Jacobs, Frances Wisebart (1843–1892)
Jacobs, Harriet A. (1813–1897)
Jacobs, Helen Hull (1908–1997)
Jacobs, Pattie Ruffner (1875–1935)
Jacobsen, Josephine (1908–2003)
Jacobson, Helen (d. 1974)
Jacobson, Henrietta (1906–1988)
Jacobson, Sada (1983—)
Jacquin, Lisa (1962—)
Jagan, Janet (1920—)
James, Alice (1848–1892)
James, Alice Gibbens (1849–1922)
James, Cheryl (1964—)
James, Claire (1920–1986)
James, Etta (1938—)
James, Mary Walsh (1810–1882)
James, Zerelda (c. 1824–1911)
Jameson, Betty (1919—)
Jameson, Joyce (1932–1987)
Jamison, Cecilia V. (1837–1909)
Jamison, Judith (1943—)
Janeway, Elizabeth (1913–2005)
Janis, Elsie (1889–1956)
Jans, Annetje (c. 1605–1663)
Jansen, Linda
Jarboro, Caterina (1908–1986)
Jarrell, Ira (1896–1973)

Jarrett, Mary Cromwell (1877–1961)
Jarvis, Anna M. (1864–1948)
Jarvis, Lucy (1919—)
Jasontek, Rebecca (1975—)
Jeakins, Dorothy (1914–1995)
Jean, Gloria (1926—)
Jean, Sally Lucas (1878–1971)
Jeanes, Anna Thomas (1822–1907)
Jefferson, Martha (1748–1782)
Jeffrey, Mildred (1910–2004)
Jeffrey, Rhi (1986—)
Jeffreys, Anne (1923—)
Jelsma, Clara Mitsuko (1931—)
Jemison, Mae (1956—)
Jemison, Mary (1742–1833)
Jenckes, Virginia Ellis (1877–1975)
Jenkins, Helen Hartley (1860–1934)
Jennings, Lynn (1960—)
Jens, Salome (1935—)
Jenssen, Elois (1922–2004)
Jentzer, Emma R.H. (c. 1883–1972)
Jepson, Helen (1904–1997)
Jergens, Adele (1917–2002)
Jervey, Caroline Howard (1823–1877)
Jessen, Ruth (1936—)
Jessup, Marion (b. 1897)
Jessye, Eva (1895–1992)
Jett, Joan (1958—)
Jewell, Isabel (1907–1972)
Jewell, Lynne (1959—)
Jewell, Wanda (1954—)
Jewett, Sarah Orne (1849–1909)
Jezek, Linda (1960—)
Jiles, Pamela (1955—)
Jillana (1934—)
Jiménez, Soledad (1874–1966)
Johann, Zita (1904–1993)
Johansson, Ronny (b. 1891)
Johns, Helen (1914—)
Johnson, Adelaide (1859–1955)
Johnson, Brandy (1973—)
Johnson, Chris (1958—)
Johnson, Courtney (1974—)
Johnson, Eleanor Murdoch (1892–1987)
Johnson, Eliza McCardle (1810–1876)
Johnson, Ella (1923–2004)
Johnson, Ellen Cheney (1829–1899)
Johnson, Georgia Douglas (1877–1966)
Johnson, Halle (1864–1901)
Johnson, Helene (1906–1995)
Johnson, Helen Kendrick (1844–1917)
Johnson, Jenna (1967—)
Johnson, Josephine Winslow (1910–1990)
Johnson, Julie (1903–1973)
Johnson, Kate (1978—)
Johnson, Kathy (1959—)
Johnson, Kay (1904–1975)
Johnson, Lady Bird (1912—)
Johnson, Luci Baines (1947—)
Johnson, Lynda Bird (1944—)
Johnson, Nancy (1935—)
Johnson, Nicole (c. 1974—)
Johnson, Opha Mae (c. 1899—)
Johnson, Osa (1894–1953)
Johnson, Rita (1912–1965)
Johnson, Shannon (1974—)
Johnson, Sheryl (1957—)
Johnson, Sunny (1953–1984)
Johnson, Susannah Willard (1729–1810)
Johnson, Tish (1962—)
Johnson, Virginia E. (1925—)
Johnston, Annie Fellows (1863–1931)
Johnston, Frances Benjamin (1864–1952)
Johnston, Henrietta (c. 1670–1728)
Johnston, Jill (1929—)
Johnston, Julanne (1900–1988)
Johnston, Mary (1870–1936)
Johnstone, Anna Hill (1913–1992)
Johnstone, Ann Casey (1921—)
Johnstone, Justine (1895–1982)
Johnston-Forbes, Cathy (1963—)
Jolas, Betsy (1926—)
Jolas, Maria (1893–1987)
Jolly, Allison (1956—)
Jones, Amanda Theodosia (1835–1914)
Jones, Anissa (1958–1976)
Jones, Barbara (1937—)
Jones, Caroline R. (1942–2001)
Jones, Carolyn (1929–1983)
Jones, Carolyn (1969—)
Jones, Elizabeth (c. 1935—)
Jones, Esther (1969—)
Jones, Etta (1928—)
Jones, Etta (1928–2001)
Jones, Jane Elizabeth (1813–1896)
Jones, Jennifer (1919—)
Jones, Linda (1944–1972)
Jones, Lois M. (1934–2000)
Jones, Loïs Mailou (1905–1998)
Jones, Marcia (1941—)
Jones, Margo (1911–1955)
Jones, Marion (1879–1965)
Jones, Marion (1975—)
Jones, Mary Harris (1830–1930)
Jones, Maxine (1966—)
Jones, Rebecca (1739–1818)
Jones, Shirley (1934—)
Jones, Sissieretta (1869–1933)
Jones, Susan (1952—)
Jones, Sybil (1808–1873)
Jong, Erica (1942—)
Jonrowe, DeeDee (1953—)
Joplin, Janis (1943–1970)
Jordan, Barbara (1936–1996)
Jordan, Dorothy (1906–1988)
Jordan, Elizabeth Garver (1865–1947)
Jordan, June (1936–2002)
Jordan, Marian (1896–1961)
Jordan, Sara Murray (1884–1959)
Jordan, Sheila (1928—)
Jorgensen, Janel (1971—)
Joseph, Mother (1823–1902)
Josephson, Karen (1964—)
Josephson, Sarah (1964—)
Joshi, Anandibai (1865–1887)
Joy, Leatrice (1893–1985)
Joyce, Alice (1889–1955)
Joyce, Brenda (1915—)
Joyce, Joan (1940—)
Joyce, Kara Lynn (1985—)
Joyce, Peggy Hopkins (1893–1957)
Joyner, Florence Griffith (1959–1998)
Joyner, Marjorie Stewart (1896–1994)
Joyner-Kersee, Jackie (1962—)
Juch, Emma (1860–1939)
Judd, Ashley (1968—)
Judd, Naomi (1946—)
Judd, Winnie Ruth (1905–1998)
Judd, Wynonna (1964—)
Judge, Arline (1912–1974)
Judson, Ann Hasseltine (1789–1826)
Judson, Emily Chubbuck (1817–1854)
Judson, Sarah Boardman (1803–1845)
Jumel, Eliza Bowen (1775–1865)
Jumper, Betty Mae (1923—)
Jung, Lovieanne (1980—)
Junger, Esther (c. 1915—)
Jurado, Jeanette (1966—)
Jurado, Katy (1927—)
Jurney, Dorothy Misener (1909–2002)
Justin, Enid (1894–1990)
Kael, Pauline (1919–2001)
Kagan, Elena (1960—)
Kahn, Florence (1878–1951)
Kahn, Florence Prag (1866–1948)
Kahn, Madeline (1942–1999)
Kai, Una (1928—)
Kaiser, Natasha (1967—)
Kajiwara, Mari (1952—)
Kalama, Thelma (1931–1999)
Kallen, Kitty (1922—)
Kallen, Lucille (1922–1999)
Kalmus, Natalie (1878–1965)
Kamali, Norma (1945—)
Kamenshek, Dorothy (1925—)
Kanaga, Consuelo (1894–1978)
Kanahele, Helen Lake (1916–1976)
Kanakaole, Edith K. (1913–1979)
Kander, Lizzie Black (1858–1940)
Kane, Gail (1887–1966)
Kane, Helen (1903–1966)
Kane, Marjorie (1909–1992)
Kanin, Fay (1917—)
Kankus, Roberta A. (1953—)
Kaptur, Marcy (1946—)
Karan, Donna (1948—)
Karle, Isabella (1921—)
Karnilova, Maria (1920–2001)
Karpatkin, Rhoda Hendrick (1930—)
Kasabian, Linda (1949—)
Käsebier, Gertrude (1852–1934)
Kashfi, Anna (1934—)
Kassebaum, Nancy Landon (1932—)
Kasten, Barbara (1936—)
Kastor, Deena (1973—)
Katz, Lillian (1927—)
Kaufman, Beatrice (1894–1945)
Kawamoto, Evelyn (1933—)
Kay, Beatrice (1907–1986)
Kaye, Nora (1920–1987)
Kazel, Dorothy (1931—)
Kean, Betty (1915–1986)
Kean, Jane (1924—)
Keane, Doris (1881–1945)
Keane, Fiorella (1930–1976)
Kearney, Belle (1863–1939)
Keaton, Diane (1946—)
Keckley, Elizabeth (c. 1824–1907)
Kee, Elizabeth (1895–1975)
Keefe, Zena (1896–1977)
Keeler, Kathryn (1956—)
Keeler, Ruby (1909–1993)
Keen, Dora (1871–1963)
Keene, Constance (1921–2005)
Keene, Laura (c. 1826–1873)
Kehew, Mary Morton (1859–1918)
Keith, Agnes Newton (1901–1982)
Keith, Marcia (1859–1950)
Kelety, Julia (d. 1972)
Kellas, Eliza (1864–1943)
Keller, Evelyn Fox (1936—)
Keller, Helen (1880–1968)
Keller, Nettie Florence (1875–1974)
Kellerman, Sally (1936—)
Kelley, Abby (1810–1887)
Kelley, Beverly Gwinn (c. 1952—)
Kelley, Edith Summers (1884–1956)
Kelley, Florence (1859–1932)
Kellogg, Clara Louise (1842–1916)
Kellogg, Louise Phelps (1862–1942)
Kellor, Frances Alice (1873–1952)
Kelly, Dorothy (1894–1966)
Kelly, Edna Flannery (1906–1997)
Kelly, Fanny Wiggins (1845–1904)
Kelly, Florence Finch (1858–1939)
Kelly, Grace (1928–1982)
Kelly, Isabel (1906–1983)
Kelly, Kathryn Thorne (1904–1998?)

Kelly, Kitty (1902–1968)
Kelly, Leontine (1920—)
Kelly, Nancy (1921–1995)
Kelly, Patsy (1910–1981)
Kelly, Paula (1939—)
Kelsey, Frances O. (1914—)
Kelton, Pert (1907–1968)
Kemner, Caren (1965—)
Kemp, Jennifer (1955—)
Kempfer, Hannah Jensen (1880–1943)
Kempner, Patty (1942—)
Kendall, Marie Hartig (1854–1943)
Kendrick, Pearl L. (1890–1980)
Kennedy, Adrienne (1931—)
Kennedy, Courtney (1979—)
Kennedy, Ethel (1928—)
Kennedy, Florynce (1916–2000)
Kennedy, Jacqueline (1929–1994)
Kennedy, Joan (1936—)
Kennedy, Karol (1932–2004)
Kennedy, Kate (1827–1890)
Kennedy, Kathleen (1920–1948)
Kennedy, Kathleen (1954—)
Kennedy, Madge (1890–1987)
Kennedy, Merna (1908–1944)
Kennedy, Rose Fitzgerald (1890–1995)
Kennedy, Rosemary (1918–2005)
Kennedy, Suzanne (c. 1955—)
Kennelly, Barbara (1936—)
Kennelly, Keala (1978—)
Kennibrew, Dee Dee (1945—)
Kent, Allegra (1937—)
Kent, Leslie (1981—)
Kent, Linda (1946—)
Kenworthy, Marion E. (c. 1891–1980)
Kenyon, Doris (1897–1979)
Kenyon, Dorothy (1888–1972)
Keohane, Nannerl (1940—)
Kerr, Anita (1927—)
Kerr, Jean (1923–2003)
Kerr, Sophie (1880–1965)
Kerrigan, Nancy (1969—)
Kershaw, Willette (1890–1960)
Keur, Dorothy (1904–1989)
Keyes, Evelyn (1919—)
Keys, Martha Elizabeth (1930—)
Khan, Chaka (1953—)
Khote, Durga (c. 1905–1991)
Khouri, Callie (1957—)
Kibbee, Lois (1922–1993)
Kidder, Kathryn (1867–1939)
Kies, Mary Dixon (fl. 19th c.)
Kight-Wingard, Lenore (1911–2000)
Kilbourn, Annelisa (1967–2002)
Kilbourne, Andrea (1980—)
Kilgallen, Dorothy (1913–1965)
Kilgore, Carrie B. (1838–1908)
Killough, Lee (1942—)
Kim, Ronyoung (1926–1987)
Kimball, Judy (1938—)
Kimball, Martha G. (1840–1894)
Kincaid, Jamaica (1949—)
Kinch, Myra (1904–1981)
King, Alberta Williams (1903–1974)
King, Andrea (1919–2003)
King, Anita (1891–1963)
King, Betsy (1955—)
King, Billie Jean (1943—)
King, Carole (1942—)
King, Carol Weiss (1895–1952)
King, Coretta Scott (1927–2006)
King, Dottie (c. 1896–1923)
King, Eleanor (1906–1991)
King, Grace Elizabeth (c. 1852–1932)
King, Helen Dean (1869–1955)
King, Henrietta Chamberlain (1832–1925)
King, Jane (d. 1971)
King, Katie (1975—)
King, Lida Shaw (1868–1932)
King, Louisa Yeomans (1863–1948)
King, Mabel (1932–1999)
King, Mazie (b. around 1880)
King, Micki (1944—)
King, Mollie (1885–1981)
King, Nellie (1895–1935)
King, Rebecca (c. 1950—)
Kingsbury, Susan (1870–1949)
Kingsley, Dorothy (1909–1997)
Kingsley, Elizabeth (1871–1957)
Kingsley, Susan (1946–1984)
Kingsolver, Barbara (1955—)
Kingston, Maxine Hong (1940—)
Kingston, Winifred (1894–1967)
Kinnan, Mary (1763–1848)
Kinney, Dita Hopkins (1854–1921)
Kinsella, Kathleen (d. 1961)
Kinzie, Juliette Magill (1806–1870)
Kirby, Dorothy (1920—)
Kirchwey, Freda (1893–1976)
Kirk, Phyllis (1926—)
Kirkland, Caroline Matilda (1801–1864)
Kirkland, Gelsey (1952—)
Kirkland, Johnna (1950—)
Kirkland, Muriel (1903–1971)
Kirkpatrick, Helen (1909–1997)
Kirkpatrick, Jeane (1926—)
Kirkus, Virginia (1893–1980)
Kirouac, Martha Wilkinson (1948—)
Kirsten, Dorothy (1910–1992)
Kitchell, Iva (1908–1983)
Kitson, Theo A.R. (1871–1932)
Kitt, Eartha (1928—)
Kittrell, Flemmie (1904–1980)
Kizer, Carolyn (1925—)
Kleegman, Sophia (1901–1971)
Klein, Anne (1923–1974)
Klein, Kit (1910–1985)
Kleine, Megan (1974—)
Klepfisz, Irena (1941—)
Klimek, Tillie (1865–1936)
Klumpke, Anna Elizabeth (1856–1942)
Klumpke, Augusta (1859–1927)
Klumpke, Dorothea (1861–1942)
Knapp, Evalyn (1908–1981)
Knight, Gladys (1944—)
Knight, June (1913–1987)
Knight, Margaret (1838–1914)
Knight, Sarah Kemble (1666–1727)
Knight, Shirley (1936—)
Knoll, Florence Schust (1917—)
Knopf, Blanche (1894–1966)
Knopf, Eleanora Bliss (1883–1974)
Knowles, Beyoncé (1981—)
Knowlton, Helen Mary (1832–1918)
Knox, Elyse (1917—)
Knox, Rose Markward (1857–1950)
Knudsen, Peggy (1923–1980)
Knutson, Coya Gjesdal (1912–1996)
Kobart, Ruth (1924–2002)
Kober, Alice Elizabeth (1906–1950)
Koesun, Ruth Ann (1928—)
Kohner, Kathy (1941—)
Kohner, Susan (1936—)
Kohut, Rebekah (1864–1951)
Kolb, Barbara (1939—)
Kolb, Claudia (1949—)
Koleva, Elizabeth (1972—)
Komarovsky, Mirra (1906–1999)
Komen, Susan G. (1944–1980)
Komisarz, Rachel (1976—)
Koner, Pauline (1912–2001)
Koontz, Elizabeth (1919–1989)
Kopsky, Doris
Korholz, Laurel (1970—)
Kornman, Mary (1915–1973)
Kosta, Tessa (1893–1981)
Kowal, Kristy (1978—)
Kozlova, Anna (1972—)
Koznick, Kristina (1975—)
Kraft, Karen (1969—)
Krainik, Ardis (1929–1997)
Krantz, Judith (1928—)
Krasner, Lee (1908–1984)
Kraus-Boelté, Maria (1836–1918)
Krauss, Alison (1971—)
Kremer, Mitzi (1968—)
Krenwinkel, Patricia (1947—)
Kreps, Juanita (1921—)
Kretschman, Kelly (1979—)
Krim, Mathilde (1926—)
Kroc, Joan (1928–2003)
Kroeber, Theodora (1897–1979)
Kroeger, Alice (1864–1909)
Krone, Julie (1963—)
Kronold, Selma (1861–1920)
Kruger, Alma (1868–1960)
Kruger, Barbara (1945—)
Kruse, Pamela (1950—)
Kryszak, Mary Olszewski (1875–1945)
Kuehne, Kelli (1977—)
Kuehnemund, Jan (1961—)
Kugler, Anna Sarah (1856–1930)
Kuhlman, Kathryn (1907–1976)
Kuhn, Irene Corbally (1898–1995)
Kuhn, Maggie (1905–1995)
Kulikowski, Theresa (1980—)
Kulp, Nancy (1921–1991)
Kumin, Maxine (1925—)
Kummer, Clare (1873–1958)
Kunin, Madeleine (1933—)
Kuper, Hilda B. (1911–1992)
Kupets, Courtney (1986—)
Kuragina, Olga (1959—)
Kursinski, Anne (1959—)
Kurys, Sophie (1925—)
Kuscsik, Nina (c. 1940—)
Kusner, Kathy (1940—)
Kwan, Michelle (1980—)
Kyrk, Hazel (1886–1957)
La Badie, Florence (1888–1917)
La Barbara, Joan (1947—)
LaBelle, Patti (1944—)
La Belle Marie (c. 1882–1935)
LaBelle Oceana (c. 1835–?)
Lacey, Venus (1967—)
Lackie, Ethel (1907—)
Lackie, Ethel (1907–1979)
Lacuesta, Natalie (1981—)
Ladd, Anna Coleman (1878–1939)
Ladd, Diane (1932—)
Ladd, Kate Macy (1863–1945)
Ladd-Franklin, Christine (1847–1930)
Ladewig, Marion (1914—)
LaDuke, Winona (1959—)
Laemmle, Carla (b. 1909)
La Flesche, Susan (1865–1915)
La Flesche, Susette (1854–1902)
La Follette, Belle Case (1859–1931)
La Follette, Fola (1882–1970)
LaForge, Margaret Getchell (1841–1880)
Laidlaw, Harriet Burton (1873–1949)
Laing, Elizabeth (1959—)
Laird, Carobeth (1895–1983)
Lake, Alice (1895–1967)
Lake, Florence (1904–1980)
Lake, Veronica (1919–1973)
Lakey, Alice (1857–1935)
Lalaurie, Delphine (c. 1790–?)

Lalive, Caroline (1979—)
La Marr, Barbara (c. 1896–1926)
Lamarr, Hedy (1913–2000)
Lamb, Martha J.R. (1826–1893)
Lambert, Adelaide (1907–1996)
Lambine, Janna (c. 1951—)
La Meri (1899–1988)
Lamour, Dorothy (1914–1996)
Lampert, Rachel (1948—)
Lampert, Zohra (1937—)
Lampkin, Daisy (1883–1965)
Lancaster, Nancy (1897–1994)
Lancefield, Rebecca Craighill (1895–1981)
Lander, Louisa (1826–1923)
Landes, Bertha Knight (1868–1943)
Landes, Ruth (1908–1991)
Landin, Hope (1893–1973)
Landis, Carole (1919–1948)
Landis, Jessie Royce (1904–1972)
Landon, Margaret (1903–1993)
Landry, Jackie (1940–1997)
Lane, Gertrude B. (1874–1941)
Lane, Harriet (1830–1903)
Lane, Lola (1909–1981)
Lane, Pinkie Gordon (1925—)
Lane, Priscilla (1917–1995)
Lane, Rosemary (1914–1974)
Lane, Rose Wilder (1886–1968)
Laney, Lucy Craft (1854–1933)
Lang, June (1915—)
Lang, K.D. (1961—)
Lang, Margaret Ruthven (1867–1972)
Lang, Raven (1942—)
Lange, Dorothea (1895–1965)
Lange, Elizabeth Clovis (1784–1882)
Lange, Hope (1931–2003)
Lange, Jessica (1949—)
Langer, Susanne Knauth (1895–1985)
Langford, Frances (1914—)
Langford, Frances (1914–2005)
Langley, Katherine (1888–1948)
Langley, Neva (c. 1934—)
Lanphier, Fay (1906–1959)
Lansbury, Angela (1925—)
Lansing, Joi (1928–1972)
Lansing, Sherry (1944—)
LaPlanche, Rosemary (1923–1979)
La Plante, Laura (1904–1996)
Lapp, Bernice (1917—)
Larcom, Lucy (1824–1893)
Laredo, Ruth (1937–2005)
La Roe, Else K. (1900–1970)
La Roy, Rita (1907–1993)
Larrieu, Francie (1952—)
Larrimore, Francine (1898–1975)
Larsen, Nella (1891–1964)
Larson, Nicolette (1952–1997)
Larson-Mason, Christine (1956—)
LaRue, Florence (1944—)
La Rue, Grace (1880–1956)
Lascelles, Ernita (1890–1972)
Lasker, Mary (1900–1994)
Lasser, Louise (1939—)
La Sylphe (c. 1900—)
Lathrop, Julia Clifford (1858–1932)
Lathrop, Rose Hawthorne (1851–1926)
Latimer, Elizabeth W. (1822–1904)
Lauder, Estée (1908–2004)
Lauer, Bonnie (1951—)
Laughlin, Clara E. (1873–1941)
Laughlin, Gail (1868–1952)
Lauper, Cyndi (1953—)
Laurel, Kay (1890–1927)
Laurie, Piper (1932—)
Laveau, Marie (1801–1881)
Laveau, Marie (1827–1897)
Lavell, Carol (1943—)
Lavenson, Alma (1897–1989)
La Verne, Lucille (1869–1945)
Lavi, Daliah (1940—)
Lavin, Mary (1912–1996)
LaVine, Jacqueline (1929—)
LaVoe, Spivy (1906–1971)
Law, Ruth (1887–1970)
Law, Sallie Chapman (1805–1894)
Lawanson, Ruth (1963—)
Lawford, Patricia Kennedy (1924—)
Lawrance, Jody (1930–1986)
Lawrence, Andrea Mead (1932—)
Lawrence, Carol (1932—)
Lawrence, Chiara (1975—)
Lawrence, Daisy Gordon (c. 1900—)
Lawrence, Eleanor (1936–2001)
Lawrence, Elizabeth (1904–1985)
Lawrence, Florence (1886–1938)
Lawrence, Janice (1962—)
Lawrence, Margaret (1889–1929)
Lawrence, Mary Wells (1928—)
Lawrence, Pauline (1900–1971)
Lawrence, Viola (1894–1973)
Lawrenson, Helen (1907–1982)
Laws, Annie (1855–1927)
Lawson, Priscilla (1914–1958)
Lawson, Roberta Campbell (1878–1940)
Lawyer, April (1975—)
Laybourne, Geraldine (1947—)
Laybourne, Roxie (1910–2003)
Lazarus, Emma (1849–1887)
Lazzari, Carolina (c. 1889–1946)
Leach, Abby (1855–1918)
Leach, Christiana (fl. 1765–1796)
Leachman, Cloris (1926—)
Leacock, Eleanor Burke (1922–1987)
Leadbetter, Mary (1758–1826)
Lear, Evelyn (1926—)
Lear, Frances (1923–1996)
Lease, Mary Elizabeth (1853–1933)
Leatherwood, Lillie (1964—)
Leaver, Henrietta (c. 1916–1993)
Leavitt, Henrietta Swan (1868–1921)
Leavitt, Mary (1830–1912)
Le Clercq, Tanaquil (1929–2001)
Lecompte, Eugenie Anna (c. 1798–c. 1850)
Lederer, Gretchen (1891–1955)
Lee, Agnes (1841–1873)
Lee, Anna (1913–2004)
Lee, Anne Carter (1839–1862)
Lee, Barbara (1946—)
Lee, Barbara (1947–1992)
Lee, Beverly (1941—)
Lee, Brenda (1944—)
Lee, Dixie (1911–1952)
Lee, Gwen (1904–1961)
Lee, Gypsy Rose (1914–1970)
Lee, Hannah Farnham (1780–1865)
Lee, Harper (1926—)
Lee, Jane (c. 1912–1957)
Lee, Jarena (1783–c. 1849)
Lee, Jennie (1848–1925)
Lee, Lila (1901–1973)
Lee, Lucinda (fl. 1787)
Lee, Mary Ann (1823–1899)
Lee, Mary Custis (1835–1918)
Lee, Mary Custis (c. 1808–1873)
Lee, Mildred Childe (1846–1905)
Lee, Muna (1895–1965)
Lee, Peggy (1920–2002)
Lee, Rose Hum (1904–1964)
Lee, Ruth (1895–1975)
Leech, Margaret (1893–1974)
Leeds, Andrea (1913–1984)
Leete, Harriet L. (c. 1875–1927)
Le Gallienne, Eva (1899–1991)
LeGon, Jeni (1916—)
Le Guin, Ursula K. (1929—)
Lehmann, Adelaide (c. 1830–1851)
Lehr, Anna (1890–1974)
Leibovitz, Annie (1949—)
Leigh, Carolyn (1926–1983)
Leigh, Frances Butler (1838–1910)
Leigh, Janet (1927–2004)
Leighton, Clare (1899–1989)
Leighton, Dorothea (1908–1989)
Leland, Sara (1941—)
Lemlich, Clara (1888–1982)
Lemmon, Sarah Plummer (1836–1923)
Lenczyk, Grace (1927—)
L'Engle, Madeleine (1918—)
Lenihan, Winifred (1898–1964)
Lennart, Isobel (1915–1971)
Lennox, Charlotte (1720–1804)
LeNoire, Rosetta (1911–2002)
Lenski, Lois (1893–1974)
Lenya, Lotte (1898–1981)
Lenz, Consetta (1918–1980)
Leonard, Carol L. (1950—)
Leonard, Marion (1881–1956)
Leporska, Zoya (1918–1996)
Lerner, Gerda (1920—)
LeShan, Eda J. (1922–2002)
Leslie, Amy (1855–1939)
Leslie, Annie (1869–1948)
Leslie, Bethel (1929–1999)
Leslie, Eliza (1787–1858)
Leslie, Gladys (1899–1976)
Leslie, Joan (1925—)
Leslie, Lisa (1972—)
Leslie, Miriam Folline Squier (1836–1914)
L'Esperance, Elise Strang (c. 1879–1959)
Lesser, Patricia (1933—)
LeSueur, Emily Porter (1972—)
Le Sueur, Meridel (1900–1996)
Le Vert, Octavia Walton (1811–1877)
Leverton, Irene (1924—)
Levey, Ethel (1880–1955)
Levien, Sonya (1888–1960)
Levi-Montalcini, Rita (b. 1909)
Levine, Lena (1903–1965)
Levinson, Tamara (1976—)
Levitt, Helen (1913—)
Levy, Chandra (1977–2001)
Levy, Florence Nightingale (1870–1947)
Levy, Jerre (1938—)
Lew, Bird (c. 1966—)
Lewis, Abby (1910–1997)
Lewis, Bobo (1926–1998)
Lewis, Cathy (1916–1968)
Lewis, Charlotte (1955—)
Lewis, Edmonia (c. 1845–c. 1909)
Lewis, Edna (1916–2006)
Lewis, Elma (1921–2004)
Lewis, Estelle Anna (1824–1880)
Lewis, Flora (1922–2002)
Lewis, Graceanna (1821–1912)
Lewis, Ida (1842–1911)
Lewis, Loida (c. 1943—)
Lewis, Margaret Reed (1881–1970)
Lewis, Shari (1933–1998)
Lewis, Vera (1873–1956)
Lewisohn, Alice (1883–1972)
Lewisohn, Irene (1892–1944)
Lewitzky, Bella (1915–2004)
Lhevinne, Rosina (1880–1976)
Libbey, Laura Jean (1862–1925)
Lichtenberg, Jacqueline (1942—)
Lieberman-Cline, Nancy (1958—)
Liebes, Dorothy (1897–1972)

Liebling, Estelle (1880–1970)
Lightner, A.M. (1904–1988)
Lightner, Candy (1946—)
Lightner, Winnie (1899–1971)
Lignell, Kristen (c. 1965—)
Liley, Tammy (1965—)
Lil' Kim (1975—)
Lilly, Kristine (1971—)
Lin, Hazel (1913–1986)
Lin, Maya (1959—)
Lin, Tai-yi (1926—)
Lincoln, Abbey (1930—)
Lincoln, Mary Johnson (1844–1921)
Lincoln, Mary Todd (1818–1882)
Lind, Joan (1952—)
Lindbergh, Anne Morrow (1906–2001)
Lindh, Hilary (1969—)
Lindley, Audra (1918–1997)
Lindsay, Margaret (1910–1981)
Lindsey, Estelle Lawton (1868–1955)
Lindstrom, Pia (1938—)
Lingle, Linda (1953—)
Linley, Mary (1758–1787)
Linn, Bambi (1926—)
Lipinski, Tara (1982—)
Lipman, Clara (1869–1952)
Lippincott, Sara Clarke (1823–1904)
Lipson-Gruzen, Berenice (1925–1998)
Lisa, Mary Manuel (1782–1869)
Liston, Melba (1926—)
Little, Ann (1891–1984)
Little, Tawny (c. 1957—)
Littledale, Clara (1891–1956)
Littlefield, Caroline (c. 1882–1957)
Littlefield, Catherine (1904–1951)
Littlefield, Dorothie (c. 1908–1953)
Littlefield, Nancy (c. 1929—)
Litz, Katharine (c. 1918–1978)
Liu, Nienling (1934—)
Liuzzo, Viola (1925–1965)
Livermore, Harriet (1788–1868)
Livermore, Mary A. (1820–1905)
Livingston, Alida Schuyler (1656–1727)
Livingston, Anne Shippen (1763–1841)
Livingston, Margaret (1896–1984)
Llanes, Tara (1976—)
Lloyd, Alice (1876–1962)
Lloyd, Andrea (1965—)
Lloyd, Marilyn Laird (1929—)
Lobo, Rebecca (1973—)
Locke, Bessie (1865–1952)
Locke, Katherine (1910–1995)
Lockhart, June (1925—)
Lockhart, Kathleen (1894–1978)
Lockrey, Sarah Hunt (1863–1929)
Lockwood, Belva Ann (1830–1917)
Loden, Barbara (1932–1980)
Loeb, Sophie Irene (1876–1929)
Logan, Deborah Norris (1761–1839)
Logan, Jacqueline (1901–1983)
Logan, Laura R. (1879–1974)
Logan, Martha (1704–1779)
Logan, Mary Cunningham (1838–1923)
Logan, Olive (1839–1909)
Logan, Onnie Lee (c. 1910–1995)
Lohman, Ann Trow (1812–1878)
Lokelani, Princess Lei (c. 1898–1921)
Lombard, Carole (1908–1942)
London, Julie (1926–2000)
Long, Catherine Small (1924—)
Long, Jill Lynette (1952—)
Longfellow, Frances Appleton (1819–1861)
Longman, Evelyn Beatrice (1874–1954)
Longshore, Hannah E. (1819–1901)
Longworth, Alice Roosevelt (1884–1980)
Looney, Shelley (1972—)
Loos, Anita (1893–1981)
Lopes, Lisa (1971–2002)
Lopez, Nancy (1957—)
Lord, Bette Bao (1938—)
Lord, Marjorie (1918—)
Lord, Pauline (1890–1950)
Lorde, Athena (1915–1973)
Lorde, Audre (1934–1992)
Lorenz, Ericka (1981—)
Lorne, Marion (1888–1968)
Lorraine, Emily (c. 1878–1944)
Lorraine, Louise (1901–1981)
Lortel, Lucille (1902–1999)
Lothrop, Alice (1870–1920)
Lothrop, Harriet (1844–1924)
Lotsey, Nancy (c. 1955—)
Lott, Elsie S. (fl. 1940s)
Loudon, Dorothy (1933–2003)
Loughran, Beatrix (1896–1975)
Louise, Anita (1915–1970)
Louise, Ruth Harriet (1906–1944)
Louise, Tina (1934—)
Love, Barbara (1941—)
Love, Bessie (1898–1986)
Love, Darlene (1938—)
Love, Nancy (1914–1976)
Love, Susan (1948—)
Lovejoy, Esther Pohl (1869–1967)
Lovelace, Linda (1952–2002)
Lovelace, Maud Hart (1892–1980)
Loveless, Lea (1971—)
Loveman, Amy (1881–1955)
Loveridge, Emily Lemoine (1860–1941)
Low, Juliette Gordon (1860–1927)
Low, Mary Fairchild (1858–1946)
Lowe, Sara (1984—)
Lowell, Amy (1874–1925)
Lowell, Josephine Shaw (1843–1905)
Lowell, Maria White (1821–1853)
Lowe-Porter, Helen (1876–1963)
Lowey, Nita M. (1937—)
Lowney, Shannon (1969–1994)
Lowry, Edith (1897–1970)
Lowry, Judith (1890–1976)
Lowry, Lois (1937—)
Loy, Mina (1882–1966)
Loy, Myrna (1905–1993)
Lozier, Clemence S. (1813–1888)
Luahine, Iolani (1915–1978)
Lubic, Ruth Watson (1927—)
Lucas, Joy (1917—)
Luce, Claire (1903–1989)
Luce, Lila (1899–1999)
Lucid, Shannon (1943—)
Luckett, LeToya (1981—)
Lucy, Autherine Juanita (1929—)
Ludington, Nancy
Ludington, Sybil (1761–1839)
Luhan, Mabel Dodge (1879–1962)
Lukens, Rebecca (1794–1854)
Lundberg, Emma (1881–1954)
Lundeberg, Helen (1908–1999)
Lupino, Ida (1914–1995)
Lurie, Alison (1926—)
Lurie, Nancy O. (1924—)
Lusk, Georgia Lee (1893–1971)
Lusk, Grace (1878–1938)
Lyall, Katharine C. (1941—)
Lyles, Anjette (1917–1977)
Lyman, Mary Ely (1887–1975)
Lynch, Laura (1958—)
Lynn, Barbara (1942—)
Lynn, Diana (1926–1971)
Lynn, Elizabeth A. (1946—)
Lynn, Janet (1953—)
Lynn, Loretta (1935—)
Lynn, Sharon (1901–1963)
Lyon, Annabelle (c. 1915—)
Lyon, Genevieve (c. 1893–1916)
Lyon, Mary (1797–1849)
Lyons, Sophie (1848–1924)
Lytle, Nancy A. (1924–1987)
Maass, Clara (1876–1901)
Mabley, Jackie (1894–1975)
MacArthur, Mary (1930–1949)
MacDonald, Barbara K. (1957—)
MacDonald, Betty (1908–1958)
MacDonald, Blossom (1895–1978)
MacDonald, Christie (1875–1962)
MacDonald, Jeanette (1903–1965)
MacDonald, Katherine (1881–1956)
MacDowell, Marian (1857–1956)
MacFadden, Gertrude (c. 1900–1967)
MacGibbon, Harriet (1905–1987)
MacGrath, Leueen (1914–1992)
MacGraw, Ali (1938—)
MacIver, Loren (1909–1998)
Mack, Helen (1913–1986)
Mack, Marion (1902–1989)
Mack, Nila (1891–1953)
Mackenzie, Jean Kenyon (1874–1936)
Mackin, Catherine (1939–1982)
Mackinnon, Catherine A. (1946—)
Macklin, Madge (1893–1962)
MacLaine, Shirley (1934—)
MacLaren, Mary (1896–1985)
MacLean, Katherine (1925—)
MacLeish, Martha Hillard (1856–1947)
Macleod, Charlotte (1852–1950)
Macleod, Jaime (1976—)
MacMahon, Aline (1899–1991)
MacMillan, Shannon (1974—)
Macomber, Mary Lizzie (1861–1916)
Macpherson, Jeanie (1887–1946)
Macpherson, Wendy (1968—)
MacRobert, Rachel (1884–1954)
Macurdy, Grace Harriet (1866–1946)
Macy, Anne Sullivan (1866–1936)
Macy, Gertrude (1904–1983)
Macy, Robin Lynn (1958—)
Madar, Olga (1915–1996)
Madden, Beezie (1963—)
Maddern, Merle (1887–1984)
Maddox, Rose (1925–1998)
Madeleva, Sister Mary (1887–1964)
Madgett, Naomi Long (1923—)
Madison, Cleo (1883–1964)
Madison, Dolley Payne (1768–1849)
Madison, Helene (1913–1970)
Madonna (1958—)
Maffett, Debra Sue (c. 1957—)
Magafan, Ethel (1916–1993)
Magafan, Jenne (1916–1952)
Magee, Joni (1941—)
Magee, Samantha (1983—)
Mageras, Georgia Lathouris (1867–1950)
Magers, Rose (1960—)
Magnes, Frances (1919—)
Magoffin, Susan Shelby (1827–c. 1855)
Magruder, Julia (1854–1907)
Maher, Kim (1971—)
Mahoney, Mary Eliza (1845–1926)
Mahony, Marion (1871–1961)
Main, Marjorie (1890–1975)
Maines, Natalie (1974—)
Major, Clare Tree (d. 1954)
Major, Maeghan (1984—)
Makemson, Maud Worcester (1891–1977)
Malcomson, Ruth (1906–1988)
Malina, Judith (1926—)
Malison, Joyce (c. 1935—)
Mallon, Mary (1867–1938)

Mallon, Meg (1963—)
Mallory, Boots (1913–1958)
Malo, Gina (1909–1963)
Malone, Annie Turnbo (1869–1957)
Malone, Dorothy (1925—)
Malone, Maicel (1969—)
Maloney, Kristen (1981—)
Maloney, Lucia (c. 1950–1978)
Malpede, Karen (1945—)
Maltby, Margaret E. (1860–1944)
Malyon, Eily (1879–1961)
Mamlok, Ursula (1928—)
Mana-Zucca (1887–1981)
Manchester, Melissa (1951—)
Mandame, Mary (fl. 1639)
Mandrell, Barbara (1948—)
Mangolte, Babette (c. 1945—)
Manigault, Ann Ashby (1703–1782)
Mankin, Helen Douglas (1894–1956)
Manley, Effa (1900–1981)
Mann, Aimee (1960—)
Mann, Carol (1941—)
Mann, Elisabeth (1918–2002)
Mann, Mary Peabody (1806–1887)
Mann, Shelley (1937—)
Manners, Martha (1924–1977)
Mannes, Clara Damrosch (1869–1948)
Mannes, Marya (1904–1990)
Manning, Irene (1912–2004)
Manning, Katharine (1904–1974)
Manning, Madeline (1948—)
Manning, Marie (c. 1873–1945)
Manning, Mary (1906–1999)
Mansfield, Arabella (1846–1911)
Mansfield, Jayne (1933–1967)
Mansfield, Martha (1899–1923)
Mansfield, Portia (1887–1979)
Mansour, Agnes Mary (c. 1931–2004)
Mar, Sabrina (1970—)
Mara, Adele (1923—)
Maracci, Carmelita (1911–1988)
Marble, Alice (1913–1990)
Marble, Mary (d. 1965)
Marbury, Elisabeth (1856–1933)
March, Eve (1910–1974)
Marchand, Nancy (1928–2000)
Marcus, Adele (1905–1995)
Marcus, Marie (1914–2003)
Marcus, Ruth Barcan (1921—)
Marden, Adrienne (1909–1978)
Marden, Anne (1958—)
Margo (1918–1985)
Margolin, Janet (1943–1993)
Margulis, Lynn (1938—)
Marie, Teena (1956—)
Marinoff, Fania (1890–1971)
Marinova, Mila (1974—)
Mario, Queena (1896–1951)
Marion, Frances (1888–1973)
Marisol (1930—)
Maritza, Sari (1910–1987)
Mark, Mary Ellen (1940—)
Markey, Enid (1891–1981)
Markham, Pauline (d. 1919)
Marks, Rita (c. 1908–1976)
Marlatt, Abby (1916—)
Marlatt, Abby L. (1869–1943)
Marley, Cedella (1967—)
Marlowe, June (1903–1984)
Marlowe, Missy (1971—)
Marlowe, Nora (1915–1977)
Marmein, Irene (1894–1972)
Marmein, Miriam (1897–1970)
Marmein, Phyllis (1908–1994)
Marot, Helen (1865–1940)
Marquardt, Melissa (1983—)
Marquis, Gail (1956—)
Marr, Sally (1906–1997)
Marrack, Philippa (1945—)
Marriott, Alice Sheets (1907–2000)
Marron, Eugenie (1899–1999)
Marsh, Joan (1913–2000)
Marsh, Mae (1895–1968)
Marsh, Marian (1913—)
Marshall, Brenda (1915–1992)
Marshall, Catherine (1914–1983)
Marshall, Clara (1847–1931)
Marshall, Paule Burke (1929—)
Marshall, Penny (1942—)
Marshall, Susan (1958—)
Marshall, Trudy (1922–2004)
Martin, Agnes (1912—)
Martin, Anne Henrietta (1875–1951)
Martin, Georgia (1866–1946)
Martin, Helen (1909–2000)
Martin, LaVonna (1966—)
Martin, Lillien Jane (1851–1943)
Martin, Lynn (1939—)
Martin, Maria (1796–1863)
Martin, Marianne (1961—)
Martin, Marion (1908–1985)
Martin, Mary (1913–1990)
Martin, Patricia J. (1928—)
Martin, Sara (1884–1955)
Martin, Vivian (1893–1987)
Martinez, Vilma (1943—)
Martino, Angel (1967—)
Martin-Spencer, Lilly (1822–1902)
Marvelettes (fl. 1960s)
Marwedel, Emma (1818–1893)
Marx, Susan Fleming (1908–2002)
Masakayan, Liz (1964—)
Masaryk, Charlotte Garrigue (1850–1923)
Maslow, Sophie (1911—)
Mason, Alice Trumbull (1904–1971)
Mason, Ann (c. 1898–1948)
Mason, Biddy (1818–1891)
Mason, Bobbie Ann (1940—)
Mason, Lucy Randolph (1882–1959)
Mason, Marge (1918–1974)
Mason, Marsha (1942—)
Mason, Shirley (1900–1979)
Massary, Fritzi (1882–1969)
Massee, May (1881–1966)
Massey, Debbie (1950—)
Massey, Edith (1918–1984)
Massey, Ilona (1910–1974)
Master, Edith (1932—)
Masters, Sybilla (d. 1720)
Matalin, Mary (1953—)
Matera, Barbara (1929–2001)
Mathé, Carmen (1938—)
Mather, Margrethe (c. 1885–1952)
Mathews, Ann Teresa (1732–1800)
Mathews, Carmen (1914–1995)
Mathieu, Susie
Mathis, June (1892–1927)
Mathison, Melissa (1950—)
Matteson, Ruth (1909–1975)
Matthews, Burnita S. (1894–1988)
Matthews, Janet (1965—)
Matthews, Kelly (1982—)
Matthews, Margaret (1935—)
Matthews, Victoria Earle (1861–1907)
Matthiasdottir, Louisa (1917–2000)
Mattox, Martha (1879–1933)
Matzinger, Polly (1947—)
Maude, Margery (1889–1979)
Mauermayer, Gisela (1913–1995)
Maurice, Mary (1844–1918)
Maury, Antonia (1866–1952)
Maury, Carlotta (1874–1938)
Maxwell, Anna Caroline (1851–1929)
Maxwell, Elsa (1883–1963)
Maxwell, Kate (fl. 1886)
Maxwell, Marilyn (1921–1972)
Maxwell, Vera (1901–1995)
Maxwell, Vera (c. 1892–1950)
Maxwell-Pierson, Stephanie (1964—)
May, Abby W. (1829–1888)
May, Catherine Dean (1914–2004)
May, Doris (1902–1984)
May, Edna (1875–1948)
May, Elaine (1932—)
May, Geraldine (1895–1997)
May, Misty (1977—)
Maybrick, Florence Elizabeth (c. 1853–1941)
Mayer, Diana K. (c. 1947—)
Mayer, Jacquelyn (c. 1942—)
Mayer, Maria Goeppert (1906–1972)
Mayfair, Mitzi (1914–1976)
Mayhar, Ardath (1930—)
Mayhew, Kate (1853–1944)
Maynard, Mary (c. 1938—)
Maynor, Dorothy (1910–1996)
Mayo, Katherine (1867–1940)
Mayo, Margaret (1882–1951)
Mayo, Mary Anne (1845–1903)
Mayo, Sara Tew (1869–1930)
Mayo, Virginia (1920–2005)
Maywood, Augusta (1825–1876)
Mazeas, Jacqueline (1920—)
McAllister, Susie (1947—)
McAuliffe, Christa (1948–1986)
McAvoy, May (1901–1984)
McBeth, Susan Law (1830–1893)
McBride, Mary Margaret (1899–1976)
McBride, Patricia (1942—)
McCaffrey, Anne (1926—)
McCambridge, Mercedes (1916–2004)
McCardell, Claire (1905–1958)
McCarthy, Carolyn (1944—)
McCarthy, Kathryn O'Loughlin (1894–1952)
McCarthy, Mary (1912–1989)
McCarthy, Patricia (1911–1943)
McCarthy, Peggy (1956—)
McCartney, Linda (1941–1998)
McCarty, Mary (1923–1980)
McCarty, Patti (1921–1985)
McCauley, Mary Ludwig Hays (1754–1832)
McClain, Katrina (1965—)
McClellan, Catharine (1921—)
McClendon, Rosalie (1884–1936)
McClendon, Sarah (1910–2003)
McClintock, Barbara (1902–1992)
McCollum, Ruby (1915—)
McComas, Carroll (1886–1962)
McConnell, Lulu (1882–1962)
McConnell, Suzanne (1966—)
McCoo, Marilyn (1943—)
McCool, Courtney (1988—)
McCord, Joan (1930–2004)
McCord, Louisa S. (1810–1879)
McCorkle, Susannah (1946–2001)
McCormack, Patty (1945—)
McCormick, Edith Rockefeller (1872–1932)
McCormick, Katharine Dexter (1875–1967)
McCormick, Katherine Medill (d. 1932)
McCormick, Kelly (1960—)
McCormick, Nettie Fowler (1835–1923)
McCormick, Patricia (1930—)
McCormick, Ruth Hanna (1880–1944)
McCoy, Bessie (1888–1931)
McCoy, Elizabeth (1903–1978)
McCoy, Gertrude (1890–1967)
McCoy, Iola Fuller (1906–1993)

McCracken, Joan (1922–1961)
McCrackin, Josephine Clifford (1838–1920)
McCray, Nikki (1971—)
McCrea, Jane (c. 1752–1777)
McCreery, Maria (1883–1938)
McCue, Lillian de la Torre Bueno (1902–1993)
McCullers, Carson (1917–1967)
McCulloch, Catharine (1862–1945)
McCully, Emily Arnold (1939—)
McCusker, Marilyn Wehrle (1944–1979)
McCutcheon, Floretta (1888–1967)
McDaniel, Hattie (1895–1952)
McDaniel, Mildred (1933–2004)
McDevitt, Ruth (1895–1976)
McDonald, Audra (1970—)
McDonald, Deborah (1954—)
McDonald, Gabrielle Kirk (1942—)
McDonald, Grace (1918–1999)
McDonald, Marie (1923–1965)
McDormand, Frances (1957—)
McDowell, Anne E. (1826–1901)
McDowell, Claire (1877–1966)
McDowell, Mary Eliza (1854–1936)
McElderry, Margaret K. (1912—)
McElmury, Audrey (1943—)
McElroy, Mary Arthur (d. 1916)
McEntire, Reba (1955—)
McFall, Lauren (1980—)
McFalls, Jennifer (1971—)
McFarland, Beulah (c. 1898–1964)
McFarland, Irene (fl. 1925)
McFarlane, Elaine (1942—)
McFarlane, Tracey (1966—)
McGahey, Kathleen (1960—)
McGee, Anita Newcomb (1864–1940)
McGee, Pamela (1962—)
McGehee, Helen (1921—)
McGhee, Carla (1968—)
McGinley, Phyllis (1905–1978)
McGrath, Kathleen (1952–2002)
McGraw, Eloise Jarvis (1915–2000)
McGroarty, Sister Julia (1827–1901)
McGrory, Mary (1918–2004)
McGuire, Dorothy (1916–2001)
McGuire, Edith (1944—)
McGuire, Kathryn (1903–1978)
McGuire, Phyllis (1931—)
McIntire, Barbara (1935—)
McIntosh, Caroline C. (1813–1881)
McIntosh, Maria (1803–1878)
McIntosh, Millicent Carey (1898–2001)
McIntyre, Elizabeth (1965—)
McIntyre, Leila (1882–1953)
McIntyre, Molly (c. 1886–1952)
McIntyre, Vonda N. (1948—)
McKane, Alice Woodby (1865–1948)
McKean, Olive (1915—)
McKechnie, Donna (1940—)
McKee, Maria (1964—)
McKenna, Rollie (1918–2003)
McKenney, Ruth (1911–1972)
McKenzie, Ella (1911–1987)
McKenzie, Eva B. (1889–1967)
McKenzie, Ida Mae (1911–1986)
McKim, Ann (d. 1875)
McKim, Josephine (1910—)
McKinley, Ida Saxton (1847–1907)
McKinney, Cynthia (1955—)
McKinney, Nina Mae (c. 1912–1967)
McKinney, Tamara (1962—)
McKnight, Kim
McKnight, Marian (c. 1937—)
McLaren, Louise Leonard (1885–1968)
McLaughlin, M. Louise (1847–1939)
McLaughlin-Gill, Frances (1919—)
McLean, Alice (1886–1968)
McLean, Barbara (1903–1996)
McLean, Evalyn Walsh (1886–1947)
McLean, Kathryn (1909–1966)
McLean, Mary Hancock (1861–1930)
McLeod, Catherine (1921–1997)
McLeod, Mary Adelia (1938—)
McLerie, Allyn Ann (1926—)
McLish, Rachel (1958—)
MC Lyte (1971—)
McMain, Eleanor Laura (1866–1934)
McMann, Sara (1980—)
McMein, Neysa (1888–1949)
McMillan, Clara Gooding (1894–1976)
McMillan, Kathy (1957—)
McMillan, Margaret (1860–1931)
McMillan, Rachel (1859–1917)
McMillan, Terry (1951—)
McMurry, Lillian Shedd (1921–1999)
McNair, Denise (d. 1963)
McNally, Karen Cook (1940—)
McNamara, Julianne (1966—)
McNamara, Maggie (1928–1978)
McNaught, Rose (1893–1978)
McNeil, Claudia (1917–1993)
McNeil, Loretta T. (1907–1988)
McNulty, Faith (1918–2005)
McPeak, Holly (1969—)
McQueen, Thelma (1911–1995)
McRae, Carmen (1920–1994)
McWhinney, Madeline H. (1922—)
McWhinnie, Mary Alice (1922–1980)
Mead, Elizabeth Storrs (1832–1917)
Mead, Lucia Ames (1856–1936)
Mead, Lynda Lee (c. 1939—)
Mead, Margaret (1901–1978)
Mead, Sylvia Earle (1935—)
Meadows, Audrey (1922–1996)
Meadows, Jayne (1920—)
Meagher, Mary T. (1964—)
Meaker, Marijane (1927—)
Means, Jacqueline (1936—)
Means, Marianne (1934—)
Meany, Helen (1904–1991)
Mearig, Kim (1963—)
Mears, Elizabeth (1900–1988)
Mears, Helen Farnsworth (1872–1916)
Mechlin, Leila (1874–1949)
Mecom, Jane Franklin (1712–1794)
Medford, Kay (1914–1980)
Medina, Patricia (1919—)
Meeuwsen, Terry (1949—)
Meigs, Cornelia Lynde (1884–1973)
Meili, Launi (1963—)
Meiselas, Susan (1948—)
Meiser, Edith (1898–1993)
Mekeel, Joyce (1931—)
Melendez, Jolinda (1954—)
Melikova, Genia (c. 1930–2004)
Mellon, Gwen Grant (1911–2000)
Melmoth, Charlotte (1749–1823)
Meloney, Marie (1878–1943)
Melville, Rose (1873–1946)
Memmel, Chellsie (1988—)
Mendenhall, Dorothy Reed (1874–1964)
Mendes, Jonna (1979—)
Mendoza, Jessica (1980—)
Mendoza, Lydia (1916—)
Menken, Adah Isaacs (1835–1868)
Menken, Helen (1901–1966)
Menken, Marie (1909–1970)
Menken-Schaudt, Carol (1957—)
Menten, Maude (1879–1960)
Menuhin, Hephzibah (1920–1981)
Menuhin, Yaltah (1921–2001)
Menzelli, Elisabetta (c. 1860–c. 1929)
Menzelli, Lola (c. 1898–1951)
Merande, Doro (1892–1975)
Mercer, Frances (1915–2000)
Mercer, Jacque (1931–1982)
Mercer, Mabel (1900–1983)
Merchant, Natalie (1963—)
Mercier, Margaret (1937—)
Meredith, Iris (1915–1980)
Meredyth, Bess (1890–1969)
Mergler, Marie Josepha (1851–1901)
Meriwether, Lee Ann (1935—)
Meriwether, Louise (1923—)
Merkel, Una (1903–1986)
Merman, Ethel (1912–1984)
Mermey, Fayvelle (1916–1977)
Merrell, Mary (1938—)
Merriam, Charlotte (1906–1972)
Merrick, Caroline (1825–1908)
Merrick, Myra King (1825–1899)
Merril, Judith (1923–1997)
Merrill, Beth (1892–1986)
Merrill, Dina (1925—)
Merrill, Gretchen (1925–1965)
Merrill, Jan (1956—)
Merrill, Mary (1853–1924)
Merriman, Nan (1920—)
Merritt, Anna Lea (1844–1930)
Merritt, Kim (c. 1955—)
Merritt, Theresa (1924–1998)
Merry, Ann Brunton (1769–1808)
Mersereau, Violet (1892–1975)
Merten, Lauri (1960—)
Merz, Sue (1972—)
Meseke, Marilyn (1916–2001)
Messenger-Harris, Beverly (1947—)
Messick, Dale (1906–2005)
Mesta, Perle (1889–1975)
Metalious, Grace (1924–1964)
Metcalf, Augusta Isabella Corson (1881–1971)
Metcalf, Harriet (1958—)
Metheny, Linda (1948—)
Methot, Mayo (1904–1951)
Metraux, Rhoda (1914–2003)
Mexia, Ynes (1870–1938)
Meyen, Janna (1977—)
Meyer, Agnes (1887–1970)
Meyer, Annie Nathan (1867–1951)
Meyer, Debbie (1952—)
Meyer, Helen (1907–2003)
Meyer, Joyce (1943—)
Meyer, Lucy (1849–1922)
Meyerhoff, Jane (1924–2004)
Meyers, Ann (1955—)
Meyers, Jan (1928—)
Meyers, Mary (1946—)
Meyner, Helen Stevenson (1929–1997)
Michael, Gertrude (1910–1965)
Michelena, Beatriz (1890–1942)
Michelman, Kate (1942—)
Mickelson, Anna (1980—)
Midler, Bette (1945—)
Midori (1971—)
Mieth, Hansel (1909–1998)
Mikulski, Barbara (1936—)
Milbrett, Tiffeny (1972—)
Miles, Jearl (1966—)
Miles, Lizzie (1895–1963)
Miles, Sylvia (1932—)
Miles, Vera (1929—)
Miley, Marion (c. 1914–1941)
Millar, Margaret (1915–1994)
Millard, Evelyn (1869–1941)
Millay, Edna St. Vincent (1892–1950)
Millay, Norma (d. 1986)
Miller, Alice (1956—)

Geographic Index

Miller, Alice Duer (1874–1942)
Miller, Anita (1951—)
Miller, Ann (1919–2004)
Miller, Annie Jenness (b. 1859)
Miller, Bebe (1950—)
Miller, Bertha Mahony (1882–1969)
Miller, Caroline (1903–1992)
Miller, Cheryl (1964—)
Miller, Colleen (1932—)
Miller, Dorothy Canning (1904–2003)
Miller, Elizabeth Smith (1822–1911)
Miller, Emily Huntington (1833–1913)
Miller, Emma Guffey (1874–1970)
Miller, Freda (c. 1910–1960)
Miller, Frieda S. (1889–1973)
Miller, Inger (1972—)
Miller, Jane (1945—)
Miller, Joyce D. (1928—)
Miller, Lee (1907–1977)
Miller, Lucille (1930—)
Miller, Marilyn (1898–1936)
Miller, Olive Thorne (1831–1918)
Miller, Patsy Ruth (1904–1995)
Miller, Shannon (1977—)
Miller, Sharon Kay (1941—)
Millett, Kate (1934—)
Millican, Arthenia J. Bates (1920—)
Millikin, Kerry
Millington, Jean (1949—)
Millington, June (1950—)
Millman, Bird (1895–1940)
Mills, Amy (c. 1949—)
Mills, Eleanor (1888–1922)
Mills, Florence (1895–1927)
Mills, Lorna H. (1916–1998)
Mills, Mary (1940—)
Mills, Phoebe (1972—)
Mills, Stephanie (1957—)
Mills, Susan Tolman (1825–1912)
Milne, Leslie (1956—)
Milton, DeLisha (1974—)
Milton, Gladys (1924–1999)
Miner, Dorothy (1904–1973)
Miner, Jan (1917–2004)
Miner, Myrtilla (1815–1864)
Miner, Sarah Luella (1861–1935)
Mink, Patsy (1927–2002)
Minnelli, Liza (1946—)
Minner, Ruth Ann (1935—)
Minnigerode, Lucy (1871–1935)
Minor, Virginia L. (1824–1894)
Minter, Mary Miles (1902–1984)
Minus, Rene (1943—)
Mirabella, Erin (1978—)
Miramova, Elena (c. 1905—)
Miranda, Patricia (1979—)
Mitchell, Abbie (1884–1960)
Mitchell, Elizabeth (1966—)
Mitchell, Jackie (1912–1987)
Mitchell, Joan (1926–1992)
Mitchell, Lucy (1845–1888)
Mitchell, Lucy Sprague (1878–1967)
Mitchell, Margaret (1900–1949)
Mitchell, Margaret J. (1832–1918)
Mitchell, Maria (1818–1889)
Mitchell, Martha (1918–1976)
Mitchell, Michelle (1962—)
Mitchell, Rhea (1890–1957)
Mitchell, Ruth (c. 1888–1969)
Mitford, Jessica (1917–1996)
Mitts, Heather (1978—)
Mixer, Elizabeth (fl. 1707–1720)
Mladova, Milada (c. 1918—)
Mlakar, Veronika (1935—)
Mleczko, A.J. (1975—)
Mobley, Mamie Till (1921–2003)
Mobley, Mary Ann (1939—)
Moceanu, Dominique (1981—)
Mock, Jerrie (1925—)
Model, Lisette (1901–1983)
Moe, Karen (1952—)
Moffo, Anna (1932–2006)
Mofford, Rose (1922—)
Moholy-Nagy, Sibyl (1903–1971)
Mohr, Nicholasa (1935—)
Moisant, Matilde (c. 1877–1964)
Moïse, Penina (1797–1880)
Molinari, Susan (1958—)
Molton, Flora (1908–1990)
Moneymaker, Kelly (1965—)
Monica (1980—)
Monk, Meredith (1942—)
Monroe, Elizabeth (1768–1830)
Monroe, Eliza Kortright (1786–1840)
Monroe, Harriet (1860–1936)
Monroe, Maria Hester (1803–1850)
Monroe, Marilyn (1926–1962)
Montana, Patsy (1909–1996)
Montealegre, Felicia (d. 1978)
Montemayor, Alice Dickerson (1902–1989)
Montez, Lola (1818–1861)
Montgomery, Elizabeth (1933–1995)
Montgomery, Goodee (1906–1978)
Montgomery, Helen Barrett (1861–1934)
Montgomery, Peggy (1917—)
Montiero, June (1946—)
Montour, Isabelle (1667–c. 1750)
Moody, Agnes Claypole (1870–1954)
Moody, Anne (1940—)
Moody, Deborah (c. 1583–c. 1659)
Moody, Emma Revell (1842–1903)
Moody, Heather (1973—)
Moon, Lorna (1886–1930)
Moon, Lottie (1840–1912)
Mooney, Julie (1888–1915)
Moore, Anne Carroll (1871–1961)
Moore, Aubertine Woodward (1841–1929)
Moore, Audley (1898–1997)
Moore, C.L. (1911–1987)
Moore, Clara (1824–1899)
Moore, Cleo (1928–1973)
Moore, Colleen (1900–1988)
Moore, Constance (1919–2005)
Moore, Elisabeth H. (1876–1959)
Moore, Ellie Durall (1940—)
Moore, Grace (1898–1947)
Moore, Ida (1882–1964)
Moore, Juanita (1922—)
Moore, Julia A. (1847–1920)
Moore, Lilian (1909–2004)
Moore, Lillian (1911–1967)
Moore, Maggie (1847–1929)
Moore, Marianne (1887–1972)
Moore, Mary Tyler (1936—)
Moore, Sara Jane (1930—)
Moore, Terry (1929—)
Moorehead, Agnes (1900–1974)
Moorhead, Sarah Parsons (fl. 1741–1742)
Morales, Hilda (1946—)
Moran, Dolores (1924–1982)
Moran, Gussie (1923—)
Moran, Lois (1907–1990)
Moran, Mary Nimmo (1842–1899)
Moran, Patsy (1903–1968)
Moran, Peggy (1918–2002)
Moran, Polly (1884–1952)
Morani, Alma Dea (1907–2001)
Morawetz, Cathleen Synge (1923—)
Moreau, Janet (1927—)
Morella, Constance A. (1931—)
Moreno, Rita (1931—)
Morett, Charlene (1957—)
Morgan, Agnes Fay (1884–1968)
Morgan, Anna (1851–1936)
Morgan, Anne (1873–1952)
Morgan, Ann Haven (1882–1966)
Morgan, Barbara (1900–1992)
Morgan, Claudia (1912–1974)
Morgan, Frances Louisa (1845–1924)
Morgan, Helen (1900–1941)
Morgan, Jane (1924—)
Morgan, Jane Norton Grew (1868–1925)
Morgan, Jaye P. (1931—)
Morgan, Julia (1872–1957)
Morgan, Marion (c. 1887–1971)
Morgan, Mary Kimball (1861–1948)
Morgan, Maud (1903–1999)
Morgan, Robin (1941—)
Morini, Erica (1904–1995)
Morison, Patricia (1914—)
Morissette, Alanis (1974—)
Morkis, Dorothy (1942—)
Morlacchi, Guiseppina (1836–1886)
Morley, Karen (1905–2003)
Morley, Ruth (1925–1991)
Morris, Anita (1943–1994)
Morris, Betty (1948—)
Morris, Clara (1847–1925)
Morris, Esther Hobart (1814–1902)
Morris, Janet E. (1946—)
Morris, Margaret Hill (1737–1816)
Morris, Mary (1895–1970)
Morrison, Adrienne (1889–1940)
Morrison, Ann (1916–1978)
Morrison, Melissa (1971—)
Morrison, Toni (1931—)
Morrow, Doretta (1927–1968)
Morrow, Elizabeth Cutter (1873–1955)
Morse, Ella Mae (1925–1999)
Mortimer, Dorothy (1898–1950)
Mortimer, Mary (1816–1877)
Morton, Azie Taylor (c. 1936–2003)
Morton, Clara (c. 1882–1948)
Morton, Martha (1865–1925)
Morton, Rosalie Slaughter (1876–1968)
Moses, Anna "Grandma" (1860–1961)
Mosher, Clelia Duel (1863–1940)
Mosher, Eliza Maria (1846–1928)
Moskowitz, Belle (1877–1933)
Mosquini, Marie (1899–1983)
Moss, Cynthia (1940—)
Moss, Emma Sadler (1898–1970)
Moss, Kate (1974—)
Mostel, Kate (1918–1986)
Moten, Etta (1901–2004)
Moten, Lucy Ellen (1851–1933)
Motley, Constance Baker (1921–2005)
Mott, Lucretia (1793–1880)
Moulton, Barbara (1915–1997)
Moulton, Louise Chandler (1835–1908)
Mounsey, Tara (1978—)
Mounsey, Yvonne (c. 1921—)
Movsessian, Vicki (1972—)
Mowatt, Anna Cora (1819–1870)
Moyd, Pauline
Moyer, Diane (1958—)
Moylan, Mary-Ellen (1926—)
Mudge, Isadore (1875–1957)
Mueller, Leah Poulos (1951—)
Muir, Esther (1903–1995)
Muir, Florabel (1889–1970)
Muir, Jean (1928–1995)
Mukherjee, Bharati (1938—)
Muldowney, Shirley (1940—)
Mulkey, Kim (1962—)
Mullany, Kate (1845–1906)
Mullen, Barbara (1914–1979)
Muller, Gertrude (1887–1954)

Muller, Jennifer (1949—)
Muller-Schwarze, Christine
Mullinix, Siri (1978—)
Mullins, Aimee (c. 1973—)
Mumford, Mary Bassett (1842–1935)
Mundinger, Mary O. (1937—)
Munro, Mimi (1952—)
Munro, Thalia (1982—)
Munsel, Patrice (1925—)
Munson, Audrey (1891–1996)
Munson, Ona (1894–1955)
Munz, Diana (1982—)
Murdaugh, Angela (1940—)
Murden, Tori (1963—)
Murdock, Margaret (1942—)
Murfin, Jane (1893–1955)
Murfree, Mary N. (1850–1922)
Murie, Margaret (1902–2003)
Murphy, Brianne (1933–2003)
Murphy, Edna (1899–1974)
Murphy, Lizzie (1894–1964)
Murphy, Mary (1931—)
Murphy, Sara (1883–1975)
Murray, Elizabeth (1871–1946)
Murray, Elizabeth (1940—)
Murray, Judith Sargent (1751–1820)
Murray, Katherine (1894–1974)
Murray, Kathleen (d. 1969)
Murray, Kathryn (1906–1999)
Murray, Mae (1885–1965)
Murray, Patty (1950—)
Murray, Pauli (1910–1985)
Murtfeldt, Mary (1848–1913)
Musser, Tharon (1925—)
Mussey, Ellen Spencer (1850–1936)
Mydans, Shelley (1915–2002)
Myers, Carmel (1899–1980)
Myers, Caroline Clark (c. 1888–1980)
Myers, Dee Dee (1961—)
Myers, Paula Jean (1934—)
Myerson, Bess (1924—)
Myrtil, Odette (1898–1978)
Nadja (c. 1900–1945)
Nagel, Anne (1915–1966)
Naldi, Nita (1897–1961)
Nall, Anita (1976—)
Namakelua, Alice K. (1892–1987)
Napolitano, Johnette (1957—)
Napolski, Nancy (1974—)
Nash, Diane (1938—)
Nash, Florence (1888–1950)
Nash, June (1911–1979)
Nash, Mary (1885–1976)
Nassif, Anna (1933—)
Natalie, Mlle (c. 1895–1922)
Nathan, Maud (1862–1946)
Nathaniel, Cathy (1949—)
Nation, Carry (1846–1911)
Natwick, Mildred (1908–1994)
Navratilova, Martina (1956—)
Naylor, Genevieve (1915–1989)
Naylor, Gloria (1950—)
Naylor, Phyllis Reynolds (1933—)
Neal, Patricia (1926—)
Nealy, Frances (1918–1997)
Near, Holly (1949—)
Nearing, Helen (1904–1995)
Neary, Colleen (1952—)
Neary, Patricia (1942—)
Neel, Alice (1900–1984)
Negri, Pola (1894–1987)
Neilson, Nellie (1873–1947)
Neilson, Sandy (1956—)
Nelson, Cindy (1955—)
Nelson, Clara Meleka (1901–1979)
Nelson, Jodie (1976—)
Nelson, Maud (1881–1944)
Nelson, Ruth (1905–1992)
Nelson, Tracy (1944—)
Nelsova, Zara (1917–2002)
Nesbit, Evelyn (1884–1967)
Nesbitt, Miriam (1873–1954)
Nesbitt, Stephanie (1985—)
Nessim, Barbara (1939—)
Nestle, Joan (1940—)
Nestor, Agnes (1880–1948)
Netter, Mildrette (1948—)
Nettleton, Lois (1929—)
Neuberger, Maurine B. (1906–2000)
Neufeld, Elizabeth F. (1928—)
Neuffer, Elizabeth (1956–2003)
Neuffer, Judy (1949—)
Neumann, Vera (1907–1993)
Nevada, Emma (1859–1940)
Nevelson, Louise (1899–1988)
Neville, Phoebe (1941—)
Newberry, Barbara (1910—)
Newby-Fraser, Paula (1962—)
Newcomb, Ethel (1875–1959)
Newcomb, Josephine L. (1816–1901)
Newcomb, Mary (1893–1966)
Newell, Harriet Atwood (1793–1812)
Newhouse, Alice (1924–2004)
Newhouse, Caroline H. (1910–2003)
Newlin, Dika (1923—)
Newman, Angelia L. (1837–1910)
Newman, Frances (1883–1928)
Newman, Pauline (1887–1986)
Newmar, Julie (1935—)
Newport, Matilda (c. 1795–1837)
Newsom, Carol (1946–2003)
Newsom, Ella King (1838–1919)
Newton, Juice (1952—)
Newton-John, Olivia (1948—)
Nice, Margaret Morse (1883–1974)
Nichols, Anne (1891–1966)
Nichols, Barbara (1929–1976)
Nichols, Clarina (1810–1885)
Nichols, Etta Grigsby (1897–1994)
Nichols, Mary Gove (1810–1884)
Nichols, Minerva Parker (1861–1949)
Nichols, Ruth (1901–1960)
Nicholson, Eliza Jane (1849–1896)
Nichtern, Claire (c. 1921–1994)
Nickerson, Camille (1884–1982)
Nicks, Stevie (1948—)
Nico (1938–1988)
Nidetch, Jean (1923—)
Niedecker, Lorine (1903–1970)
Nieh Hualing (1925—)
Nielsen, Alice (c. 1870–1943)
Nielsen, Jerri (1953—)
Nieman, Nancy (1933—)
Niesen, Gertrude (1910–1975)
Niggli, Josefina (1910–1983)
Nigh, Jane (1925–1993)
Niles, Blair (1880–1959)
Niles, Mary Ann (1938–1987)
Nillson, Carlotta (c. 1878–1951)
Nixon, Agnes (1927—)
Nixon, Joan Lowery (1927–2003)
Nixon, Julie (1948—)
Nixon, Marion (1904–1983)
Nixon, Marni (1929—)
Nixon, Pat (1912–1993)
Nixon, Tricia (1946—)
Noble, Cindy (1958—)
Noemi, Lea (1883–1973)
Noguchi, Constance Tom (1948—)
Nolan, Jeanette (1911–1998)
Nolan, Kathleen (1933—)
Noonan, Peggy (1950—)
Nordica, Lillian (1857–1914)
Nordstrom, Ursula (1910–1988)
Norelius, Kristine (1956—)
Norman, Dorothy (1905–1997)
Norman, Goodwife (fl. mid-17th c.)
Norman, Jessye (1945—)
Norman, Maidie (1912–1998)
Norman, Marsha (1947—)
Normand, Mabel (1892–1930)
Norrell, Catherine Dorris (1901–1981)
Norris, Kathleen (1880–1966)
North, Sheree (1933–2005)
Norton, Alice Peloubet (1860–1928)
Norton, Andre (1912–2005)
Norton, Eleanor Holmes (1937—)
Norton, Mary T. (1875–1959)
Noskowiak, Sonya (1900–1975)
Nott, Andrea (1982—)
Nott, Tara (1972—)
Nourse, Elizabeth (1859–1938)
Novak, Eva (1898–1988)
Novak, Jane (1896–1990)
Novak, Kim (1933—)
Novarra-Reber, Sue (1955—)
Novello, Antonia (1944—)
Noyes, Blanche (1900–1981)
Noyes, Clara Dutton (1869–1936)
Nurse, Rebecca (1621–1692)
Nussbaum, Karen (1950—)
Nuthead, Dinah (fl. 1696)
Nutt, Emma M. (c. 1849–1926)
Nuttall, Zelia (1857–1933)
Nutting, Mary Adelaide (1858–1948)
Nuveman, Stacey (1978—)
Nyad, Diana (1949—)
Nyro, Laura (1947–1997)
Oakar, Mary Rose (1940—)
Oakley, Annie (1860–1926)
Oakley, Laura (1880–1957)
Oakley, Violet (1874–1961)
Oates, Joyce Carol (1938—)
Oatman, Olive Ann (c. 1838–1903)
Oberon, Merle (1911–1979)
O'Brien, Margaret (1937—)
O'Brien, Miriam (1898–1976)
O'Brien, Virginia (1896–1987)
O'Brien, Virginia (1919–2001)
O'Brien-Moore, Erin (1902–1979)
Ocampo-Friedmann, Roseli (1937—)
Ochoa, Ellen (1958—)
Ochs, Debra (1966—)
O'Connell, Helen (1920–1993)
O'Connell, Mary (1814–1897)
O'Connell, Patricia (d. 1975)
O'Connor, Colleen
O'Connor, Flannery (1925–1964)
O'Connor, Karen (1958—)
O'Connor, Mary Anne (1953—)
O'Connor, Sandra Day (1930—)
O'Connor, Una (1880–1959)
O'Day, Anita (1919—)
O'Day, Caroline (1869–1943)
O'Day, Molly (1911–1998)
Oden, Elaina (1967—)
Oden, Kimberley (1964—)
Odetta (1930—)
O'Donnell, Cathy (1923–1970)
O'Donnell, May (1906–2004)
O'Donnell, Rosie (1962—)
O'Driscoll, Martha (1922–1998)
Oelschlagel, Charlotte (c. 1899–after 1948)
O'Hair, Madalyn Murray (1919–1995)
O'Hanlon, Virginia (c. 1899–1971)
O'Hara, Mary (1885–1980)
O'Hara, Maureen (1920—)
O'Hara, Shirley (1910–1979)

O'Hara, Shirley (1924–2002)
O'Hare, Kate Richards (1876–1948)
Ohlson, Agnes K. (1902–1991)
Ohta, Tomoko (1933—)
O'Keeffe, Georgia (1887–1986)
O'Kelley, Mattie Lou (c. 1908–1997)
Okin, Susan Moller (1946–2004)
Okino, Betty (1975—)
Okorokova, Antonina (1941—)
Oldfield, Pearl Peden (1876–1962)
Olds, Elizabeth (1896–1991)
Oliver, Edith (1913–1998)
Oliver, Edna May (1883–1942)
Oliver, Mary (1935—)
Oliver, Susan (1937–1990)
Oliver, Thelma (1941—)
Oliveros, Pauline (1932—)
Olivette, Nina (c. 1908–1971)
Olmsted, Gertrude (1897–1975)
Olmsted, Mildred Scott (1890–1990)
Olsen, Tillie (c. 1912—)
Olsen, Zoe Ann (1931—)
Olson, Leslee (1978—)
Olson, Nancy (1928—)
O'Malley, Grania (1885–1973)
Omelenchuk, Jeanne (1931—)
Omens, Estelle (1928–1983)
Omlie, Phoebe Fairgrave (1902–1975)
O'Neal, Christine (1949—)
O'Neal, Tatum (1963—)
O'Neal, Zelma (1903–1989)
O'Neale, Lila M. (1886–1948)
O'Neil, Barbara (1909–1980)
O'Neil, Kitty (1947—)
O'Neil, Nance (1874–1965)
O'Neil, Sally (1908–1968)
O'Neill, Carlotta (1888–1970)
O'Neill, Rose Cecil (1874–1944)
Ono, Yoko (1933—)
Oppenheimer, Jane Marion (1911–1996)
Oppens, Ursula (1944—)
Orchard, Sadie (c. 1853–1943)
Orcutt, Edith (c. 1918–1973)
Orcutt, Maureen (b. 1907)
Ordway, Katharine (1899–1979)
O'Reilly, Heather (1985—)
O'Reilly, Leonora (1870–1927)
Orkin, Ruth (1921–1985)
O'Rourke, Heather (1975–1988)
Orr, Alice Greenough (1902–1995)
Orr, Kay (1939—)
Orr, Vickie (1967—)
Orwig, Bernice (1976—)
Osato, Sono (1919–1953)
Osborn, Sarah (1714–1796)
Osborne, Estelle Massey (1901–1981)
Osborne, Joan (1962—)
Osborne, Margaret (1918—)
Osborne, Marie (1911—)
Osborne, Mary (1921–1992)
Osborne, Mary D. (1875–1946)
Osborne, Susan M. (1858–1918)
Osborne, Vivienne (1896–1961)
Osburn, Ruth (1912–1994)
Osgood, Frances (1811–1850)
Osipowich, Albina (1911–1964)
Oslin, K.T. (1941—)
Osmond, Marie (1959—)
Osserman, Wendy (1942—)
O'Steen, Shyril (1960—)
Ostenso, Martha (1900–1963)
Osterman, Catherine (1983—)
Ostriche, Muriel (1896–1989)
O'Sullivan, Keala (1950—)
O'Sullivan, Mary Kenney (1864–1943)
O'Sullivan, Maureen (1911–1998)
Oswald, Marina (1941—)
Otake, Eiko (1952—)
O'Toole, Maureen (1961—)
Ottenberg, Nettie Podell (1887–1982)
Ottendorfer, Anna Uhl (1815–1884)
Oughton, Diana (1942–1970)
Oughton, Winifred (1890–1964)
Overbeck, Carla (1969—)
Ovington, Mary White (1865–1951)
Ovtchinnikova, Elena (1965—)
Owen, Catherine Dale (1900–1965)
Owen, Laurence (1945–1961)
Owen, Maribel (1941–1961)
Owen, Maribel Vinson (1911–1961)
Owen, Seena (1894–1966)
Owens, Claire Myers (1896–1983)
Owens, Shirley (1941—)
Owens-Adair, Bethenia (1840–1926)
Owings, Margaret Wentworth (1913–1999)
Ozick, Cynthia (1928—)
Packard, Elizabeth (1816–1897)
Packard, Sophia B. (1824–1891)
Paddleford, Clementine (1900–1967)
Page, Dorothy G. (1921–1989)
Page, Estelle Lawson (1907–1983)
Page, Gale (1913–1983)
Page, Geraldine (1924–1987)
Page, LaWanda (1920–2002)
Page, Patti (1927—)
Page, Ruth (1899–1991)
Paget, Debra (1933—)
Paget, Mary (1865–1919)
Paglia, Camille (1947—)
Pagliughi, Lina (1907–1980)
Paige, Janis (1922—)
Paige, Jean (1895–1990)
Paige, Mabel (1879–1954)
Painter, Eleanor (1890–1947)
Paley, Babe (1915–1978)
Paley, Grace (1922—)
Palfi, Marion (1907–1978)
Palfrey, Sarah (1912–1996)
Palmer, Alice Freeman (1855–1902)
Palmer, Bertha Honoré (1849–1918)
Palmer, Frances Flora (1812–1876)
Palmer, Leland (1940—)
Palmer, Lilli (1914–1986)
Palmer, Lizzie Merrill (1838–1916)
Palmer, Phoebe Worrall (1807–1874)
Palmer, Sandra (1941—)
Palmer, Sophia French (1853–1920)
Paltrow, Gwyneth (1972—)
Panov, Galina (1949—)
Pantoja, Antonia (1922–2002)
Paraskevin-Young, Connie (1961—)
Paretsky, Sara (1947—)
Parish, Sister (1910–1994)
Parisien, Julie (1971—)
Park, Ida May (1879–1954)
Park, Maud Wood (1871–1955)
Park, Rosemary (1907–2004)
Parker, Bonnie (1910–1934)
Parker, Claire (1906–1981)
Parker, Cynthia Ann (c. 1827–c. 1864)
Parker, Denise (1973—)
Parker, Dorothy (1893–1967)
Parker, Eleanor (1922—)
Parker, Jean (1915–2005)
Parker, Julia O'Connor (1890–1972)
Parker, Lottie Blair (c. 1858–1937)
Parker, Madeleine (c. 1909–1936)
Parker, Pat (1944–1989)
Parker, Suzy (1932–1932)
Parker, Valeria Hopkins (1879–1959)
Parkhurst, Charlotte (d. 1879)
Parkhurst, Helen (1887–1973)
Parks, Hildy (1926–2004)
Parks, Rosa (1913—)
Parks, Suzan-Lori (1963—)
Parloa, Maria (1843–1909)
Parlow, Cindy (1978—)
Parnis, Mollie (1905–1992)
Parrish, Anne (1760–1800)
Parrish, Anne (1888–1957)
Parrish, Celestia (1853–1918)
Parrish, Helen (1922–1959)
Parritt, Barbara (1944—)
Parsley, Lea Ann (1968—)
Parsons, Betty Pierson (1900–1982)
Parsons, Elsie Clews (1875–1941)
Parsons, Emily Elizabeth (1824–1880)
Parsons, Estelle (1927—)
Parsons, Harriet (1906–1983)
Parsons, Louella (1881–1972)
Parton, Dolly (1946—)
Pascal, Amy (1959—)
Patch, Edith (1876–1954)
Patrick, Gail (1911–1980)
Patrick, Mary Mills (1850–1940)
Patrick, Ruth (1907—)
Patten, Dorothy (1905–1975)
Patten, Luana (1938–1996)
Patten, Mary Ann (1837–1861)
Patterson, Alicia (1906–1963)
Patterson, Audrey (1926–1996)
Patterson, Carly (1988—)
Patterson, Eleanor Medill (1881–1948)
Patterson, Elizabeth (1874–1966)
Patterson, Elizabeth J. (1939—)
Patterson, Francine (1947—)
Patterson, Hannah (1879–1937)
Patterson, Martha Johnson (1828–1901)
Patterson, Mary Jane (1840–1894)
Patterson, Nan (c. 1882–?)
Patterson-Tyler, Audrey (1926–1996)
Patton, Frances Gray (1906–2000)
Paul, Alice (1885–1977)
Pauley, Jane (1950—)
Pauli, Hertha (1909–1973)
Payne, Ethel (1911–1991)
Payne, Freda (1945—)
Payne, Katy (1937—)
Payne, Nicolle (1976—)
Payne, Thelma (1896–1988)
Payne, Virginia (1908–1977)
Payne-Gaposchkin, Cecilia (1900–1979)
Payson, Joan Whitney (1903–1975)
Payson, Sandra (c. 1926–2004)
Payton, Barbara (1927–1967)
Payton, Carolyn Robertson (1925–2001)
Peabody, Elizabeth Palmer (1778–1853)
Peabody, Elizabeth Palmer (1804–1894)
Peabody, Josephine Preston (1874–1922)
Peabody, Lucy (1861–1949)
Peake, Mary S. (1823–1862)
Peale, Anna Claypoole (1791–1878)
Peale, Margaretta Angelica (1795–1882)
Peale, Ruth Stafford (b. 1906)
Peale, Sarah Miriam (1800–1885)
Peale Sisters
Pearce, Alice (1913–1966)
Pearce, Christie (1975—)
Pearce, Louise (1885–1959)
Pearl, Minnie (1912–1996)
Pearson, Molly (d. 1959)
Pearson, Virginia (1886–1958)
Peary, Josephine (1863–1955)
Pease, Heather (1975—)
Peck, Annie Smith (1850–1935)
Peck, Ellen (1829–1915)
Peden, Irene (1925—)
Pedersen, Elaine (1936–2000)

Pedersen, Share (1963—)
Pedersen, Susan (1953—)
Peebles, Ann (1947—)
Peebles, Florence (1874–1956)
Peete, Louise (1883–1947)
Peixotto, Jessica (1864–1941)
Pelish, Thelma (1926–1983)
Pelosi, Nancy (1940—)
Pember, Phoebe Yates (1823–1913)
Pendleton, Ellen Fitz (1864–1936)
Penes, Mihaela (1947—)
Penicheiro, Ticha (1974—)
Penkinson, Sophie (fl. late 1890s)
Penn, Hannah (1671–1726)
Pennell, Elizabeth Robins (1855–1936)
Pennington, Ann (1892–1971)
Pennington, Mary Engle (1872–1952)
Pennison, Marleen (1951—)
Peplau, Hildegard E. (1909–1999)
Pepper, Beverly (1924—)
Pepper, Dottie D. (1965—)
Peppler, Mary Jo (1944—)
Percy, Eileen (1899–1973)
Pereira, Irene Rice (1902–1971)
Pereyaslavec, Valentina (1907–1998)
Pérez, Eulalia Arrila de (c. 1773–c. 1878)
Perkins, Elizabeth Peck (c. 1735–1807)
Perkins, Frances (1880–1965)
Perkins, Lucy Fitch (1865–1937)
Perkins, Millie (1938—)
Perkins, Susan (c. 1954—)
Perreau, Gigi (1941—)
Perrier, Glorianne (1929—)
Perrin, Ethel (1871–1962)
Perrot, Kim (c. 1967–1999)
Perry, Antoinette (1888–1946)
Perry, Elaine (1921–1986)
Perry, Eleanor (1915–1981)
Perry, Julia (1924–1979)
Perry, Katherine (1897–1983)
Perry, Lilla Cabot (c. 1848–1933)
Perry, Margaret (1913—)
Perry, Nanceen (1977—)
Perry, Wanda (1917–1985)
Pert, Candace B. (1946—)
Pesotta, Rose (1896–1965)
Peter, Sarah Worthington (1800–1877)
Peterkin, Julia (1880–1961)
Peters, Bernadette (1948—)
Peters, Jean (1926–2000)
Peters, Roberta (1930—)
Peters, Roumania (1917–2003)
Peters, Susan (1921–1952)
Peterson, Amy (1971—)
Peterson, Ann (1947—)
Peterson, Esther (1906–1997)
Peterson, Marjorie (1906–1974)
Peterson, Mary (1927—)
Peterson, Sylvia (1946—)
Petri, Heather (1978—)
Petrucci, Roxy (1962—)
Petry, Ann (1908–1997)
Petry, Lucile (1902–1999)
Pettis, Bridget (1971—)
Pettis, Shirley Neil (1924—)
Pettit, Katherine (1868–1936)
Petty, Mary (1899–1976)
Peyton, Kim (1957–1986)
Pfeiffer, Jane Cahill (1932—)
Pfeiffer, Michelle (1957—)
Pflueger, Joan (1931—)
Pfost, Gracie (1906–1965)
Phagan, Mary (c. 1899–1913)
Phair, Liz (1967—)
Phelps, Almira Lincoln (1793–1884)
Phelps, Elizabeth Porter (1747–1817)
Phelps, Elizabeth Wooster Stuart (1815–1852)
Phelps, Jaycie (1979—)
Philbin, Mary (1903–1993)
Philips, Mary (1901–1975)
Philipse, Margaret Hardenbrook (d. 1690)
Phillips, Chynna (1968—)
Phillips, Clara (1899Phillips, Dorothy (1889–1980)
Phillips, Esther (1935–1984)
Phillips, Frances L. (1896–1986)
Phillips, Harriet Newton (1819–1901)
Phillips, Irna (1901–1973)
Phillips, Julia (1944–2002)
Phillips, Kristie (1972—)
Phillips, Lena Madesin (1881–1955)
Phillips, Margaret (1923–1984)
Phillips, Michelle (1944—)
Phillpotts, Adelaide (1896–c. 1995)
Phipps, Sally (1909–1978)
Phranc (1957—)
Pickens, Helen (1910—)
Pickens, Jane (1908–1992)
Pickens, Lucy (1832–1899)
Pickens, Patti (1914–1995)
Pickersgill, Mary (1776–1857)
Pickett, Fuchsia T. (1918–2004)
Pickford, Lottie (1895–1936)
Pickford, Mary (1893–1979)
Picon, Molly (1898–1992)
Pierce, Jane Means (1806–1863)
Pierce, Joanne E. (c. 1941—)
Pierce, Sarah (1767–1852)
Piercy, Marge (1936—)
Piestewa, Lori Ann (1980–2003)
Pigeon, Anna (fl. 1860s)
Pigeon, Ellen (fl. 1860s)
Pike, Mary (1824–1908)
Pinchot, Cornelia (1881–1960)
Pinckney, Eliza Lucas (1722–1793)
Pinkham, Lydia E. (1819–1883)
Pinney, Eunice Griswold (1770–1849)
Pious, Minerva (1903–1979)
Piper, Carly (1983—)
Piper, Leonora E. (1859–1950)
Piserchia, Doris (1928—)
Pitot, Genevieve (c. 1920—)
Pitou, Penny (1938—)
Pitts, ZaSu (1898–1963)
Place, Etta (fl. 1896–1905)
Place, Marcella (1959—)
Place, Martha (1848–1899)
Plath, Sylvia (1932–1963)
Plato, Ann (c. 1820–?)
Platt, Louise (1915–2003)
Platz, Elizabeth
Player, Willa B. (1909–2003)
Pleasant, Mary Ellen (c. 1814–1904)
Pleshette, Suzanne (1937—)
Plummer, Mary Wright (1856–1916)
Poe, Elizabeth (c. 1787–1811)
Poe, Virginia Clemm (1822–1847)
Pointer, Anita (1948—)
Pointer, Bonnie (1950—)
Pointer, June (1954–2006)
Pointer, Ruth (1946—)
Pointer Sisters (1973—)
Polis, Carol
Polite, Carlene Hatcher (1932—)
Polk, Sarah Childress (1803–1891)
Pollitzer, Anita (1894–1975)
Pollock, Jessie
Pollock, Nancy (1905–1979)
Polyblank, Ellen Albertina (1840–1930)
Ponselle, Carmela (1892–1977)
Ponselle, Rosa (1897–1981)
Pool, Judith Graham (1919–1975)
Pool, Maria Louise (1841–1898)
Poor, Anne (1918–2002)
Popova, Diana (1976—)
Popova, Nina (1922)
Poppler, Jericho (1951—)
Porn, Hanna (1860–1913)
Portapovitch, Anna Knapton (1890–1974)
Porter, Charlotte Endymion (1857–1942)
Porter, Dorothy Germain (1924—)
Porter, Eleanor H. (1868–1920)
Porter, Elizabeth Kerr (1894–1989)
Porter, Eliza Chappell (1807–1888)
Porter, Jean (1924—)
Porter, Katherine Anne (1890–1980)
Porter, Mary Bea (1949—)
Porter, Sarah (fl. 1791)
Porter, Sarah (1813–1900)
Porter, Sylvia (1913–1991)
Portillo, Lourdes
Portillo-Trambley, Estela (1936–1999)
Portnoy, Ethel (1927–2004)
Post, Emily (1872–1960)
Post, Lydia Minturn (fl. 1776–1783)
Post, Marjorie Merriweather (1887–1973)
Postell, Ashley (1986—)
Postlewait, Kathy (1949—)
Potter, Cora (1857–1936)
Potter, Cynthia (1950—)
Potts, Mary Florence (c. 1853–?)
Pought, Emma (1942—)
Pought, Jannie (1944–1980)
Pound, Louise (1872–1958)
Powdermaker, Hortense (1896–1970)
Powell, Dawn (1897–1965)
Powell, Eleanor (1910–1982)
Powell, Jane (1929—)
Powell, Kristy (1980—)
Powell, Louise Mathilde (1871–1943)
Powell, Maud (1867–1920)
Powell, Susan (c. 1959—)
Powers, Georgia Davis (1923—)
Powers, Harriet (1837–1911)
Powers, Leona (1896–1970)
Powers, Mala (1931—)
Powers, Marie (1902–1973)
Poynton, Dorothy (1915—)
Poyntz, Juliet Stuart (1886–c. 1937)
Prang, Mary D. Hicks (1836–1927)
Pratt, Anna Beach (1867–1932)
Pratt, Daria (1861–1938)
Pratt, Eliza Jane (1902–1981)
Pratt, Ruth (1877–1965)
Preisser, Cherry (1918–1964)
Preisser, June (1920–1984)
Prejean, Helen (1939—)
Premice, Josephine (1926–2001)
Prendergast, Sharon Marley (1964—)
Prentice, Jo Ann (1933—)
Prentiss, Elizabeth Payson (1818–1878)
Prentiss, Paula (1939—)
Preston, Ann (1813–1872)
Preston, Margaret Junkin (1820–1897)
Preston, May Wilson (1873–1949)
Pretty, Arline (1885–1978)
Preuss, Phyllis (1939—)
Prewitt, Cheryl (c. 1957—)
Price, Eugenia (1916–1996)
Price, Florence B. (1888–1953)
Price, Kate (1872–1943)
Price, Leontyne (1927—)
Prickett, Maudie (1914–1976)
Priesand, Sally Jane (1946—)
Priest, Ivy Baker (1905–1975)
Primrose-Smith, Elizabeth (c. 1948—)
Primus, Pearl (1919–1994)

Prince, Lucy Terry (c. 1730–1821)
Pringle, Aileen (1895–1989)
Pringle, Elizabeth Allston (1845–1921)
Prior, Margaret (1773–1842)
Prophet, Elizabeth (1890–1960)
Prophet, Elizabeth Clare (1940—)
Proskouriakoff, Tatiana (1909–1985)
Proulx, E. Annie (1935—)
Prout, Mary Ann (1801–1884)
Prouty, Olive Higgins (1882–1974)
Provine, Dorothy (1937—)
Pryor, Sara Agnes (b. 1830)
Puck, Eva (1892–1979)
Pugh, Madelyn (c. 1921—)
Pugh, Sarah (1800–1884)
Pung, Jackie (1921—)
Purcell, Irene (1902–1972)
Purviance, Edna (1894–1958)
Purvis, Harriet Forten (1810–1875)
Purvis, Sarah Forten (c. 1811–c. 1898)
Putnam, Alice Whiting (1841–1919)
Putnam, Bertha Haven (1872–1960)
Putnam, Emily James (1865–1944)
Putnam, Helen (1857–1951)
Putnam, Mary T.S. (1810–1898)
Qualter, Tot (1894–1974)
Quance, Kristine (1975—)
Quann, Megan (1984—)
Quatro, Suzi (1950—)
Queen Latifah (1970—)
Queler, Eve (1936—)
Questel, Mae (1908–1998)
Quimby, Edith (1891–1982)
Quimby, Harriet (1875–1912)
Quindlen, Anna (1953—)
Quinlan, Karen Ann (1954–1985)
Quinn, Helen (1943—)
Quinn, Jane Bryant (1939—)
Quinn, Mary Ann (c. 1928—)
Quinton, Amelia S. (1833–1926)
Quinton, Cornelia B. Sage (1876–1936)
Rabbani, Ruhiyyih (1910–2000)
Rablen, Eva (1905—)
Racine, Jean (1978—)
Radner, Gilda (1946–1989)
Rafferty, Frances (1922–2004)
Rafko, Kaye Lani (c. 1963—)
Ragghianti, Marie (1942—)
Rahn, Muriel (1911–1961)
Raiche, Bessica (c. 1874–1932)
Rainer, Yvonne (1934—)
Raines, Ella (1920–1988)
Rainey, Barbara Allen (1948–1982)
Rainey, Ma (1886–1939)
Raisa, Rosa (1893–1963)
Raitt, Bonnie (1949—)
Ralph, Jessie (1864–1944)
Ralston, Esther (1902–1994)
Ralston, Jobyna (1900–1967)
Ralston, Vera Hruba (1921–2003)
Rambeau, Marjorie (1889–1970)
Rambova, Natacha (1897–1966)
Ramenofsky, Marilyn (1946—)
Ramey, Nancy (1940—)
Ramey, Venus (c. 1925—)
Ramo, Roberta Cooper (1942—)
Ramsay, Martha Laurens (1759–1811)
Ramsey, Alice Huyler (1886–1983)
Ramsey, Anne (1929–1988)
Ramsey, Elizabeth M. (1906–1993)
Ran, Shulamit (1949—)
Rand, Ayn (1905–1982)
Rand, Caroline Amanda (1828–1905)
Rand, Ellen (1875–1941)
Rand, Gertrude (1886–1970)
Rand, Sally (1904–1979)
Randall, Claire (1919—)
Randall, Marta (1948—)
Randall, Martha (1948—)
Randolph, Amanda (1896–1967)
Randolph, Barbara (d. 2002)
Randolph, Isabel (1889–1973)
Randolph, Lillian (1898–1980)
Randolph, Martha Jefferson (1775–1836)
Randolph, Virginia (1874–1958)
Rankin, Jeannette (1880–1973)
Rankin, Judy (1945—)
Rankin, Nell (1924–2005)
Rapoport, Lydia (1923–1971)
Rapp, Susan (1965—)
Rasch, Albertina (1896–1967)
Rashad, Phylicia (1948—)
Raskin, Judith (1928–1984)
Rathbone, Josephine Adams (1864–1941)
Rathbun, Mary Jane (1860–1943)
Rathgeber, Lisa (1961—)
Ratner, Anna (c. 1892–1967)
Ravan, Genya (1942—)
Rawle, Anna (c. 1757–1828)
Rawlings, Marjorie Kinnan (1896–1953)
Rawls, Betsy (1928—)
Rawls, Katherine (1918–1982)
Ray, Charlotte E. (1850–1911)
Ray, Dixy Lee (1914–1994)
Ray, Elise (1982—)
Ray, H. Cordelia (c. 1849–1916)
Raye, Martha (1916–1994)
Raymond, Eleanor (1887–1989)
Raymond, Helen (c. 1885–1965)
Raymond, Lisa (1973—)
Raymond, Paula (1923–2003)
Read, Deborah (1707–1774)
Reagan, Maureen (1941–2001)
Reagan, Nancy (1921—)
Reals, Gail (c. 1937—)
Ream, Vinnie (1847–1914)
Rebay, Hilla (1890–1967)
Reddick, Cat (1982—)
Redgrave, Lynn (1943—)
Redpath, Christine (1951—)
Redpath, Jean (1937—)
Reece, Gabrielle (1970—)
Reece, Louise Goff (1898–1970)
Reed, Alma (1889–1966)
Reed, Donna (1921–1986)
Reed, Florence (1883–1967)
Reed, Janet (1916–2000)
Reed, Kit (1932—)
Reed, Mary (1854–1943)
Reed, Myrtle (1874–1911)
Reed, Rowena (1900–1988)
Reel, Chi Cheng (1944—)
Reese, Della (1931—)
Reese, Gail (1946—)
Reese, Lizette Woodworth (1856–1935)
Reeves, Connie (1901–2003)
Reeves, Martha (1941—)
Regan, Agnes (1869–1943)
Regan, Sylvia (1908–2003)
Rehan, Ada (1857–1916)
Reichard, Gladys (1893–1955)
Reid, Charlotte Thompson (b. 1913)
Reid, Clarice D. (1931—)
Reid, Dorothy Davenport (1895–1977)
Reid, Elisabeth Mills (1858–1931)
Reid, Frances (b. 1913)
Reid, Helen Rogers (1882–1970)
Reid, Maria (1895–1979)
Reignolds, Catherine Mary (1836–1911)
Reiman, Elise (c. 1910—)
Reinders, Agnes (1913–1993)
Reiner, Ethel Linder (d. 1971)
Reinhardt, Aurelia Henry (1877–1948)
Reinking, Ann (1949—)
Reischauer, Haru (c. 1915–1998)
Reisenberg, Nadia (1904–1983)
Reiter, Frances (1904–1977)
Reitz, Dana (1948—)
Remey, Ethel (1895–1979)
Remick, Lee (1935–1991)
Remington, Barbara (1936—)
Remler, Emily (1957–1990)
Remond, Sarah Parker (1826–1894)
Reno, Janet (1938—)
Repplier, Agnes (1855–1950)
Resnik, Judith (1949–1986)
Resnik, Muriel (c. 1917–1995)
Resnik, Regina (1922—)
Retton, Mary Lou (1968—)
Revere, Anne (1903–1990)
Revier, Dorothy (1904–1993)
Revsin, Leslie (1944–2004)
Rey, Margret (1906–1996)
Reynolds, Adeline DeWalt (1862–1961)
Reynolds, Belle (fl. 1860s)
Reynolds, Debbie (1932—)
Reynolds, Malvina (1900–1978)
Reynolds, Marjorie (1917–1997)
Reynolds, Myra (1853–1936)
Reynolds, Vera (1899–1962)
Rhode, Kim (1979—)
Rhodes, Betty (c. 1935–1987)
Rhodes, Billie (1894–1988)
Rhodes, Mary (c. 1782–1853)
Riale, Karen (c. 1949—)
Riano, Renie (1899–1971)
Ricarda, Ana (c. 1925—)
Rice, Alice Hegan (1870–1942)
Rice, Anne (1941—)
Rice, Condoleezza (1954—)
Rice, Florence (1907–1974)
Rich, Adrienne (1929—)
Rich, Irene (1891–1988)
Rich, Louise Dickinson (1903–1991)
Richards, Ann Willis (1933—)
Richards, Beah (1920–2000)
Richards, Ellen Swallow (1842–1911)
Richards, Julie Burns (1970—)
Richards, Laura E. (1850–1943)
Richards, Linda (1841–1930)
Richards, Renée (1934—)
Richards, Sanya (1985—)
Richardson, Dot (1961—)
Richardson, Gloria (1922—)
Richardson, Luba Lyons (1949—)
Richardson, Michelle (1969—)
Richey, Helen (1910–1947)
Richman, Julia (1855–1912)
Richmond, Mary E. (1861–1928)
Richter, Gisela (1882–1972)
Richter, Marga (1926—)
Ricker, Marilla (1840–1920)
Rickert, Edith (1871–1938)
Ricketson, Gail (1953—)
Rickon, Kelly (1959—)
Riddles, Libby (1956—)
Ride, Sally (1951—)
Rider-Kelsey, Corinne (1877–1947)
Ridge, Lola (1873–1941)
Ridgley, Cleo (1893–1962)
Ridgway, Rozanne Lejeanne (1935—)
Riding, Laura (1901–1991)
Riepp, Mother Benedicta (1825–1862)
Rigby, Cathy (1952—)
Riggin, Aileen (1906–2002)
Riggs, Katherine Witchie (d. 1967)
Riley, Corinne Boyd (1893–1979)
Riley, Dawn (1964—)

Riley, Jeannie C. (1945—)
Riley, Mary Velasquez (1908–1987)
Riley, Polly Ann (1926–2002)
Riley, Ruth (1979—)
Rind, Clementina (c. 1740–1774)
Rinehart, Mary Roberts (1876–1958)
Ring, Blanche (1877–1961)
Ring, Frances (1882–1951)
Ringgold, Faith (1934—)
Rinker, Laurie (1962—)
Riperton, Minnie (1947–1979)
Ripley, Martha Rogers (1843–1912)
Ripley, Sarah Alden (1793–1867)
Ripley, Sophia (1803–1861)
Rippin, Jane Deeter (1882–1953)
Risdon, Elisabeth (1887–1958)
Ritchie, Jean (1922—)
Ritchie, Sharon Kay (c. 1937—)
Rittenhouse, Jessie Belle (1869–1948)
Ritter, Louise (1958—)
Ritter, Thelma (1905–1969)
Riva, Maria (1924—)
Rivé-King, Julie (1854–1937)
Rivera, Chita (1933—)
Rives, Amélie (1863–1945)
Rizzo, Patti (1960—)
Rizzotti, Jennifer (1974—)
Robb, Isabel Hampton (1860–1910)
Robbins, Gale (1921–1980)
Robbins, Jane Elizabeth (1860–1946)
Robbins, Kelly (1969—)
Roberson, LaTavia (1981—)
Roberti, Lyda (1906–1938)
Roberts, Cokie (1943—)
Roberts, Doris (1929—)
Roberts, Edith (1899–1935)
Roberts, Elizabeth Madox (1881–1941)
Roberts, Flora (c. 1921–1998)
Roberts, Florence (1861–1940)
Roberts, Florence (1871–1927)
Roberts, Julia (1967—)
Roberts, Lydia (1879–1965)
Roberts, Lynne (1919–1978)
Roberts, Marguerite (1905–1989)
Roberts, Mary May (1877–1959)
Roberts, Patricia (1955—)
Roberts, Robin (1960—)
Roberts, Sheila (1937—)
Roberts, Sue (1948—)
Roberts, Tiffany (1977—)
Robertson, Alice Mary (1854–1931)
Robertson, Ann Worcester (1826–1905)
Robertson, Carol (d. 1963)
Robeson, Eslanda Goode (1896–1965)
Robins, Elizabeth (1862–1952)
Robins, Margaret Dreier (1868–1945)
Robinson, Betty (1911–1997)
Robinson, Cynthia (1946—)
Robinson, Dawn (1968—)
Robinson, Dot (1912–1999)
Robinson, Gertrude (1890–1962)
Robinson, Harriet Hanson (1825–1911)
Robinson, Henrietta (1816–1905)
Robinson, Jane Bancroft (1847–1932)
Robinson, Jo Ann (1911–1992)
Robinson, Julia B. (1919–1985)
Robinson, Moushaumi (1981—)
Robinson, Ruby Doris Smith (1942–1967)
Robinson, Sarah Jane (d. 1905)
Robinson, Shawna (1964—)
Robinson, Vicki Sue (1954–2000)
Robison, Emily (1972—)
Robison, Paula (1941—)
Robscheit-Robbins, Frieda (1888–1973)
Robson, May (1858–1942)
Roche, Josephine (1886–1976)
Roche, Maggie (1951—)
Roche, Suzzy (1956—)
Roche, Terre (1953—)
Rochester, Anna (1880–1966)
Rockefeller, Abby Aldrich (1874–1948)
Rockefeller, Blanchette Hooker (1909–1992)
Rockefeller, Laura Spelman (1839–1915)
Rockefeller, Margaret (1915–1996)
Rockefeller, Margaretta (1926—)
Rockefeller, Martha Baird (1895–1971)
Rockefeller, Mary Todhunter (1907–1999)
Rockford Peaches (1940–1954)
Rodgers, Elizabeth Flynn (1847–1939)
Rodin, Judith (1944—)
Rodríguez, Ana (1938—)
Rodriguez, Jennifer (1976—)
Roebling, Emily (1844–1903)
Roebling, Mary G. (1906–1994)
Roffe, Diann (1967—)
Rogers, Annette (b. 1913)
Rogers, Dale Evans (1912–2001)
Rogers, Edith Nourse (1881–1960)
Rogers, Elizabeth Ann (1829–1921)
Rogers, Ginger (1911–1995)
Rogers, Grace Rainey (1867–1943)
Rogers, Harriet B. (1834–1919)
Rogers, Jean (1916–1991)
Rogers, Martha E. (1914–1994)
Rogers, Mother Mary Joseph (1882–1955)
Rogge, Florence (b. 1904)
Rohde, Lisa (1955—)
Rohde, Ruth Bryan Owen (1885–1954)
Rojcewicz, Susan (1953—)
Roland, Ruth (1892–1937)
Roles, Barbara
Roley, Susan Lynn (c. 1947—)
Rolle, Esther (1920–1998)
Rollins, Charlemae Hill (1897–1979)
Romack, Barbara (1932—)
Roman, Ruth (1922–1999)
Romary, Janice-Lee (1927—)
Rombauer, Irma S. (1877–1962)
Rome, Esther (1945–1995)
Ronne, Edith (1919—)
Ronstadt, Linda (1946—)
Rood, Florence (1873–1944)
Rooney, Josie (b. 1892)
Rooney, Julia (b. 1893)
Roosevelt, Alice Lee (1861–1884)
Roosevelt, Anna Hall (1863–1892)
Roosevelt, Edith Kermit Carow (1861–1948)
Roosevelt, Eleanor (1884–1962)
Roosevelt, Ethel Carow (1891–1977)
Roosevelt, Sara Delano (1854–1941)
Roper, Marion
Rorer, Sarah Tyson (1849–1937)
Rork, Ann (1908–1988)
Rosazza, Joan (1935—)
Rosca, Ninotchka (1941—)
Rose, Helen (1904–1985)
Rose, Kay (1922–2002)
Rose, Margo (1903–1997)
Roseanne (1952—)
Rosenberg, Anna M. (1902–1983)
Rosenberg, Ethel (1915–1953)
Rosenthal, Ida Cohen (1886–1973)
Rosenthal, Jean (1912–1969)
Rosenthal, Jody (1962—)
Ros-Lehtinen, Ileana (1952—)
Ross, Betsy (1752–1836)
Ross, Diana (1944—)
Ross, Ishbel (1895–1975)
Ross, Lillian (1926—)
Ross, Nellie Tayloe (1876–1977)
Ross, Shirley (1909–1975)
Roth, Ann (1931—)
Roth, Lillian (1910–1980)
Rothhammer, Keena (1957—)
Rothlein, Arlene (1939–1976)
Rothman, Stephanie (1936—)
Rothschild, Judith (1921–1993)
Roudenko, Lubov (1915—)
Roukema, Margaret (1929—)
Roulstone, Elizabeth (fl. 1804)
Rountree, Martha (1911–1999)
Rourke, Constance (1885–1941)
Rowell, Mary (1958—)
Rowland, Kelly (1981—)
Rowlands, Gena (1934—)
Rowson, Susanna (1762–1824)
Roy, Julie (c. 1938—)
Royce, Sarah (1819–1891)
Royle, Selena (1904–1983)
Roys-Gavitt, Elmina M. (1828–1898)
Rubens, Alma (1897–1931)
Rubenstein, Blanche (c. 1897–1969)
Rubin, Barbara Jo (1949—)
Rubin, Chandra (1976—)
Rubin, Vera (1911–1985)
Rubin, Vera Cooper (1928—)
Rubinstein, Helena (1870–1965)
Ruddins, Kimberly (1963—)
Rudishauser, Corrie (1973—)
Rudkin, Margaret (1897–1967)
Rudner, Sara (1944—)
Rudolph, Wilma (1940–1994)
Ruether, Rosemary (1936—)
Ruffin, Josephine St. Pierre (1842–1924)
Ruggiero, Angela (1980—)
Ruick, Barbara (1930–1974)
Ruiz, Brunhilda (1936—)
Ruiz, Rosie (c. 1954—)
Ruiz, Tracie (1963—)
Rukeyser, Muriel (1913–1980)
Rule, Jane (1931—)
Rule, Janice (1931–2003)
Rulon, Kelly (1984—)
Rumsey, Mary Harriman (1881–1934)
Runcie, Constance Faunt Le Roy (1836–1911)
Rush, Barbara (1927—)
Rush, Cathy
Rush, Rebecca (1779–1850)
Russ, Joanna (1937—)
Russell, Alys Smith (1866–1951)
Russell, Anna (b. 1911)
Russell, Annie (1864–1936)
Russell, Elizabeth S. (1913—)
Russell, Francia (1938—)
Russell, Gail (1924–1961)
Russell, Jane (1921—)
Russell, Jane Anne (1911–1967)
Russell, Lillian (1861–1922)
Russell, Mother Mary Baptist (1829–1898)
Russell, Rosalind (1908–1976)
Rutherford, Ann (1917—)
Rutherford, Frances Armstrong (1842–1922)
Rutherford, Mildred (1851–1928)
Rutledge, Ann (1813–1835)
Ruuska, Sylvia (1942—)
Ruzicka, Marla (1976–2005)
Ryan, Anne (1889–1954)
Ryan, Catherine O'Connell (1865–1936)
Ryan, Elizabeth (1891–1979)
Ryan, Fran (1916–2000)
Ryan, Irene (1902–1973)
Ryan, Mary (1885–1948)
Ryan, Meg (1961—)
Ryan, Peggy (1924–2004)

Ryan, Sheila (1921–1975)
Ryon, Luann (1953—)
Saarinen, Aline (1914–1972)
Sabin, Ellen (1850–1949)
Sabin, Florence (1871–1953)
Sabin, Pauline Morton (1887–1955)
Safford, Mary Jane (1834–1891)
Safier, Gloria (d. 1985)
Sagan, Ginetta (1923–2000)
Sage, Kay (1898–1963)
Sage, Margaret Olivia (1828–1918)
Sager, Ruth (1918–1997)
Saiki, Patricia Fukuda (1930—)
Saint, Eva Marie (1924—)
Sais, Marin (1890–1971)
Sale, Virginia (1899–1992)
Salerno-Sonnenberg, Nadja (1961—)
Salmon, Lucy Maynard (1853–1927)
Salm-Salm, Agnes, Princess (1840–1912)
Salsberg, Germain Merle (1950—)
Salt, Barbara (1904–1975)
Salter, Susanna Medora (1860–1961)
Samaroff, Olga (1882–1948)
Samoilova, Tatania (1934—)
Sampson, Deborah (1760–1827)
Sampson, Edith S. (1901–1979)
Sampson, Teddy (1898–1970)
Sampter, Jessie (1883–1938)
Sams, Doris (1927—)
Samuelson, Joan Benoit (1957—)
Sanchez, Carol Lee (1934—)
Sanchez, Linda T. (1969—)
Sanchez, Loretta (1960—)
Sanchez, Sonia (1934—)
Sanchez Vicario, Arantxa (1971—)
Sandelin, Lucy Giovinco (c. 1958—)
Sandeno, Kaitlin (1983—)
Sander, Anne Quast (1937—)
Sanders, Elizabeth Elkins (1762–1851)
Sanders, Marlene (1931—)
Sanders, Summer (1972—)
Sanders, Tonya (1968—)
Sanderson, Julia (1887–1975)
Sanderson, Sybil (1865–1903)
Sandoz, Mari (1896–1966)
Sands, Diana (1934–1973)
Sands, Dorothy (1893–1980)
Sanford, Isabel (1917–2004)
Sanford, Katherine (1915—)
Sanford, Maria Louise (1836–1920)
Sangalli, Rita (1849–1909)
Sanger, Alice B.
Sanger, Margaret (1879–1966)
Sangster, Margaret (1838–1912)
San Juan, Olga (1927—)
Sansay, Leonora (fl. 1807–1823)
Santiglia, Peggy (1944—)
Sapenter, Debra (1952—)
Sapp, Carolyn (1967—)
Sappington, Margo (1947—)
Saralegui, Cristina (1948—)
Sarandon, Susan (1946—)
Sargeant, N.C. (fl. 1895)
Sargent, Pamela (1948—)
Sarry, Christine (1946—)
Sartain, Emily (1841–1927)
Sarton, May (1912–1995)
Sato, Liane (1964—)
Saubert, Jean
Saunders, Doris (1921—)
Saunders, Jackie (1892–1954)
Savage, Augusta (1892–1962)
Savery, Jill (1972—)
Saville, Kathleen (1956—)
Savitch, Jessica (1947–1983)
Sawyer, Caroline M. Fisher (1812–1894)
Sawyer, Ivy (1898–1999)
Sawyer, Laura (1885–1970)
Sawyer, Ruth (1880–1970)
Saxe, Susan (1947—)
Saxon, Marie (1904–1941)
Say, Lucy Sistare (1801–1885)
Sayre, Nora (1932–2001)
Sayres, Aurelie (1977—)
Scales, Jessie Sleet (fl. 1900)
Scarborough, Dorothy (1878–1935)
Schaefer, Laurel Lea (c. 1949—)
Schaeffer, Rebecca (1967–1989)
Schafer, Natalie (1900–1991)
Scharff-Goldhaber, Gertrude (1911–1998)
Scharrer, Berta (1906–1995)
Schary, Hope Skillman (1908–1981)
Schau, Virginia M. (1915–1989)
Scheff, Fritzi (1879–1954)
Schekeryk, Melanie (1947—)
Schenk, Lynn (1945—)
Schifano, Helen (1922—)
Schiff, Dorothy (1903–1989)
Schileru, Dacia W.
Schlamme, Martha (1922–1985)
Schlein, Miriam (1926–2004)
Schleper, Sarah (1979—)
Schlossberg, Caroline Kennedy (1957—)
Schlotfeldt, Rozella M. (b. 1914—)
Schmich, Mary Teresa (1954—)
Schmidgall, Jenny (1979—)
Schmidt, Kathryn (1953—)
Schneider, Claudine (1947—)
Schneiderman, Rose (1882–1972)
Schneyder, Nathalie (1968—)
Schnitzer, Henriette (1891–1979)
Schoenberg, Bessie (1906–1997)
Schoenfield, Dana (1953—)
Schoff, Hannah Kent (1853–1940)
Schofield, Martha (1839–1916)
Schollar, Ludmilla (c. 1888–1978)
Schonthal, Ruth (1924—)
Schoolcraft, Jane Johnston (1800–1841)
Schoonmaker, Thelma (1940—)
Schrieck, Louise van der (1813–1886)
Schroeder, Patricia (1940—)
Schroth, Clara (1920—)
Schroth, Frances (b. 1893)
Schuler, Carolyn (1943—)
Schultz, Sigrid (1893–1980)
Schumann-Heink, Ernestine (1861–1936)
Schurz, Margarethe Meyer (1833–1876)
Schuyler, Catherine Van Rensselaer (1734–1803)
Schuyler, Louisa Lee (1837–1926)
Schuyler, Philippa Duke (1931–1967)
Schwandt, Rhonda (1963—)
Schwartz, Anna Jacobson (1915—)
Schwen, Missy (1972—)
Schwikert, Tasha (1984—)
Scidmore, Eliza Ruhamah (1856–1928)
Scott, Ann London (1929–1975)
Scott, Blanche (1885–1970)
Scott, Esther Mae (1893–1979)
Scott, Evelyn (1893–1963)
Scott, Hazel (1920–1981)
Scott, Ivy (1886–1947)
Scott, Lizabeth (1922—)
Scott, Martha (1914–2003)
Scott, Sherry (c. 1948—)
Scott, Shirley (1934–2002)
Scott-Brown, Denise (1931—)
Scott-Maxwell, Florida (1883–1979)
Scripps, Ellen Browning (1836–1932)
Scudder, Ida (1870–1960)
Scudder, Janet (1869–1940)
Scudder, Laura Clough (1881–1959)
Scudder, Vida (1861–1954)
Scurry, Briana (1971—)
Seaman, Elizabeth Cochrane (1864–1922)
Sears, Eleanora (1881–1968)
Sears, Mary (1905–1997)
Sears, Mary (1939—)
Sears, Zelda (1873–1935)
Seastrand, Andrea (1941—)
Seaton, Anna (1964—)
Sebastian, Dorothy (1903–1957)
Sebastiani, Sylvia (1916–2003)
Seberg, Jean (1938–1979)
Seda, Dori (1951–1988)
Seddon, Margaret (1872–1968)
Seddon, Rhea (1947—)
Sedgwick, Anne Douglas (1873–1935)
Sedgwick, Catharine (1789–1867)
Sedgwick, Edie (1943–1971)
Sedgwick, Josie (1898–1973)
Seeger, Peggy (1935—)
Seeley, Blossom (1891–1974)
Segal, Vivienne (1897–1992)
Seibert, Florence B. (1897–1991)
Seid, Ruth (1913–1995)
Seidel, Martie (1969—)
Seidelman, Susan (1952—)
Selby, Sarah (1905–1980)
Selena (1971–1995)
Seles, Monica (1973—)
Sell, Janie (1941—)
Sellers, Kathryn (1870–1939)
Selznick, Irene Mayer (1910–1990)
Sembrich, Marcella (1858–1935)
Semple, Ellen Churchill (1863–1932)
Semple, Letitia Tyler (1821–1907)
Sender, Toni (1888–1964)
Sergava, Katharine (1910–2005)
Serlenga, Nikki (1978—)
Serrano, Lupe (1930—)
Servoss, Mary (1881–1968)
Sessions, Almira (1888–1974)
Sessions, Kate O. (1857–1940)
Sessions, Patty Bartlett (1795–1892)
Seton, Elizabeth Ann (1774–1821)
Seton, Grace Gallatin (1872–1959)
Seufert, Christina (1957—)
Severance, Caroline M. (1820–1914)
Severn, Margaret (1901–1997)
Severson, Kim (1973—)
Sewall, Lucy Ellen (1837–1890)
Sewall, May Wright (1844–1920)
Sewell, Edna (1881–1967)
Sexton, Anne (1928–1974)
Sey, Jennifer (1969—)
Seyfert, Gabriele (1948—)
Seymour, Anne (1909–1988)
Seymour, Clarine (1898–1920)
Seymour, Jane (1951—)
Seymour, Jane (c. 1898–1956)
Seymour, Mary F. (1846–1893)
Seymour, May Davenport (d. 1967)
Shabazz, Betty (1936–1997)
Shabelska, Maria (1898–1980)
Shafer, Helen Almira (1839–1894)
Shaffer, Alexandra (1976—)
Shaheen, Jeanne (1947—)
Shain, Eva (1917–1999)
Shalala, Donna (1941—)
Shaler, Eleanor (1900–1989)
Shane, Mary Driscoll (c. 1949—)
Shange, Ntozake (1948—)
Shannon, Effie (1867–1954)
Shannon, Peggy (1907–1941)
Shanté, Roxanne (1970—)
Shapiro, Betty Kronman (1907–1989)
Sharaff, Irene (1910–1993)

Sharp, Katharine Lucinda (1865–1914)
Sharp, Susie M. (1907–1996)
Shattuck, Lydia (1822–1889)
Shaver, Dorothy (1897–1959)
Shaw, Anna Howard (1847–1919)
Shaw, Mary G. (1854–1929)
Shaw, Pauline Agassiz (1841–1917)
Shaw, Reta (1912–1982)
Shaw, Wini (1910–1982)
Shawlee, Joan (1926–1987)
Sheahan, Marion (1892–1994)
Shealey, Courtney (c. 1978—)
Shearer, Norma (1900–1983)
Sheehan, Margaret Flavin (d. 1969)
Sheehan, Patty (1956—)
Sheehy, Kathy (1970—)
Sheldon, May French (1847–1936)
Shelton, Karen (1957—)
Shepard, Helen Miller (1868–1938)
Shepardson, Mary Thygeson (1906–1997)
Shepherd, Cybill (1949—)
Shepherd, Karen (1940—)
Shepley, Ruth (1892–1951)
Sher, Lisa (1969—)
Sheridan, Ann (1915–1967)
Sherif, Carolyn Wood (1922–1982)
Sherman, Lydia (d. 1878)
Sherman, Yvonne (1930–2005)
Sherman-Kauf, Patti (1963—)
Sherwin, Belle (1868–1955)
Sherwood, Katharine Margaret (1841–1914)
Sherwood, Mary (1856–1935)
Sherwood, Mary Elizabeth (1826–1903)
Shields, Carol (1935–2003)
Shields, Ella (1879–1952)
Shields, Susan (1952—)
Shiley, Jean (1911–1998)
Shindle, Kate (1979—)
Shinn, Millicent Washburn (1858–1940)
Shipley, Ruth B. (1885–1966)
Shipman, Nell (1892–1970)
Shipp, Ellis Reynolds (1847–1939)
Shippen, Peggy (1760–1804)
Shirley, Anne (1917–1993)
Shockley, Ann Allen (1925—)
Shockley, Marian (1911–1981)
Shoemaker, Ann (1891–1978)
Shoemaker, Carolyn (1929—)
Shopp, BeBe (1930—)
Shore, Dinah (1917–1994)
Shore, Henrietta (1880–1963)
Short, Elizabeth (1925–1947)
Short, Florence (1889–1946)
Short, Gertrude (1902–1968)
Shoshi (fl. 990–1010)
Shouse, Kay (1896–1994)
Showalter, Elaine (1941—)
Shriver, Eunice Kennedy (1921—)
Shriver, Maria (1955—)
Shriver, Pam (1962—)
Shuler, Nettie Rogers (1862–1939)
Shulman, Alix Kates (1932—)
Shurr, Gertrude (c. 1920—)
Shutta, Ethel (1896–1976)
Sidhwa, Bapsi (1938—)
Sidney, Sylvia (1910–1999)
Siebert, Muriel (1932—)
Sierens, Gayle (1954—)
Siering, Lauri (1957—)
Sigourney, Lydia H. (1791–1865)
Silko, Leslie Marmon (1948—)
Silkwood, Karen (1946–1974)
Sill, Anna Peck (1816–1889)
Silliman, Lynn (1959—)
Sills, Beverly (1929—)
Silver, Joan Micklin (1935—)
Simkhovitch, Mary (1867–1951)
Simkins, Modjeska M. (1899–1992)
Simmons, Coralie (1977—)
Simmons, Ruth J. (1945—)
Simmons-Carrasco, Heather (1970—)
Simms, Florence (1873–1923)
Simms, Ginny (1915–1994)
Simms, Hilda (1920–1994)
Simon, Carly (1945—)
Simon, Kate (1912–1990)
Simone, Nina (1933–2003)
Simonis, Anita (1926—)
Simons, Nancy (1938—)
Simpson, Adele (1903–1995)
Simpson, Carole (1940—)
Simpson, Edna Oakes (1891–1984)
Simpson, Juliene (1953—)
Simpson, Mary Michael (1925—)
Simpson, Nicole Brown (1959–1994)
Simpson, Valerie (1946—)
Simpson-Serven, Ida (c. 1850s–c. 1896)
Sims, Naomi (1948—)
Sinatra, Nancy (1940—)
Sinclair, Betty (1907–1983)
Sinclair, Catherine (1817–1891)
Sinclair, Madge (1938–1995)
Singer, Margaret (1921–2003)
Singer, Winnaretta (1865–1943)
Sipprell, Clara (1885–1975)
Sirota, Beate (1923—)
Sirridge, Marjorie S. (1921—)
Sitterly, Charlotte Moore (1898–1990)
Skillman, Melanie (1954—)
Skinner, Constance Lindsay (1877–1939)
Skinner, Cornelia Otis (1901–1979)
Slagle, Eleanor Clarke (1871–1942)
Slancy, Mary Decker (1958—)
Slaton, Danielle (1980—)
Slaughter, Lenora S. (1906–2000)
Slaughter, Louise M. (1929—)
Sledge, Debra (1955—)
Sledge, Joni (1957—)
Sledge, Kathy (1959—)
Sledge, Kim (1958—)
Sleeper, Martha (1907–1983)
Slenczynska, Ruth (1925—)
Slesinger, Tess (1905–1945)
Slick, Grace (1939—)
Slocum, Frances (1773–1847)
Slosson, Annie Trumbull (1838–1926)
Slowe, Lucy Diggs (1885–1937)
Slye, Maud (1869–1954)
Smallwood, Norma (c. 1908–1966)
Smart, Pamela Wojas (1967—)
Smeal, Eleanor (1939—)
Smedley, Agnes (1892–1950)
Smiley, Jane (1949—)
Smith, Abby (1797–1878)
Smith, Ada (1894–1984)
Smith, Alexis (1921–1993)
Smith, Amanda Berry (1837–1915)
Smith, Anna Deavere (1950—)
Smith, Anna Young (1756–1780)
Smith, Annette
Smith, Arlene (1941—)
Smith, Bathsheba (1822–1910)
Smith, Bessie (1894–1937)
Smith, Betty (1896–1972)
Smith, Caroline (1906—)
Smith, Chloethiel Woodard (1910–1992)
Smith, Clara (1894–1935)
Smith, Elizabeth "Betsy" (1750–1815)
Smith, Elizabeth Oakes (1806–1893)
Smith, Elizabeth Quincy (1721–1775)
Smith, Eliza Roxey Snow (1804–1887)
Smith, Emma Hale (1804–1879)
Smith, Erminnie A. Platt (1836–1886)
Smith, Evelyn E. (1922–2000)
Smith, Hannah Whitall (1832–1911)
Smith, Hazel Brannon (1914–1994)
Smith, Jean Kennedy (1928—)
Smith, Jessie Willcox (1863–1935)
Smith, Julia Frances (1911–1989)
Smith, Julie (1968—)
Smith, Kate (1907–1986)
Smith, Katie (1974—)
Smith, Keely (1932—)
Smith, Kendra (1960—)
Smith, Lillian (1897–1966)
Smith, Liz (1923—)
Smith, Mabel (1924–1972)
Smith, Mamie (1883–1946)
Smith, Margaret (fl. 1660)
Smith, Margaret Bayard (1778–1844)
Smith, Margaret Charles (b. 1906)
Smith, Margaret Chase (1897–1995)
Smith, Marilynn (1929—)
Smith, Mary Louise (1914–1997)
Smith, Michele (1967—)
Smith, Muriel Burrell (1923–1985)
Smith, Nora Archibald (1859?–1934)
Smith, Patti (1946—)
Smith, Queenie (1898–1978)
Smith, Robyn (1942—)
Smith, Samantha (1972–1985)
Smith, Sammi (1943–2005)
Smith, Shawntel (1971—)
Smith, Sophia (1796–1870)
Smith, Trixie (1895–1943)
Smith, Virginia Dodd (1911–2006)
Smith, Virginia Thrall (1836–1903)
Smith, Wiffi (1936—)
Smith, Willie Mae Ford (1904–1994)
Smith, Zilpha Drew (1851–1926)
Smith-Rosenberg, Carroll
Smoller, Dorothy (c. 1901–1926)
Smucker, Barbara (1915–2003)
Smyth, Patty (1957—)
Snite, Betsy (1938–1984)
Snow, Helen Foster (1907–1997)
Snow, Marguerite (1889–1958)
Snow, Phoebe (1952—)
Snow, Valaida (c. 1903–1956)
Snowden, Leigh (1929–1982)
Snowe, Olympia J. (1947—)
Snyder, Alice D. (1887–1943)
Snyder, Ruth (1893–1928)
Sobotka, Ruth (1925–1967)
Sobrero, Kate (1976—)
Soccer: Women's World Cup, 1999
Sohier, Elizabeth Putnam (1847–1926)
Sokolow, Anna (1910–2000)
Solano, Solita (1888–1975)
Solomon, Hannah Greenebaum (1858–1942)
Somerville, Nellie Nugent (1863–1952)
Somogi, Judith (1937–1988)
Sondergaard, Gale (1899–1985)
Sontag, Susan (1933–2004)
Sorel, Felicia (1904–1972)
Sorenson, Carol (1942—)
Sorkin, Naomi (1948—)
Sothern, Ann (1909–2001)
Sothern, Georgia (1912–1981)
Souez, Ina (1903–1992)
Soule, Caroline White (1824–1903)
Southern, Eileen Jackson (1920–2002)
Southern, Jeri (1926–1991)
Southworth, E.D.E.N. (1819–1899)
Soyer, Ida (1909–1970)
Spacek, Sissy (1949—)
Spafford, Belle Smith (1895–1982)

Spagnuolo, Filomena (1903–1987)
Spain, Fay (1932–1983)
Spain, Jayne (1927—)
Spalding, Catherine (1793–1858)
Spalding, Eliza (1807–1851)
Sparks, Donita (1963—)
Speare, Elizabeth George (1908–1994)
Spears, Britney (1981—)
Spector, Ronnie (1943—)
Spellman, Gladys Noon (1918–1988)
Spencer, Anna (1851–1931)
Spencer, Anne (1882–1975)
Spencer, Cornelia Phillips (1825–1908)
Spencer, Dorothy (b. 1909)
Spencer, Elizabeth (1921—)
Spencer, Lilly Martin (1822–1902)
Spewack, Bella (1899–1990)
Speyer, Ellin Prince (1849–1921)
Speyer, Leonora (1872–1956)
Spheeris, Penelope (1945—)
Spillane, Joan (1943—)
Spinelli, Evelita Juanita (1889–1941)
Spivak, Gayatri Chakravorty (1942—)
Spivey, Victoria (1906–1976)
Spofford, Grace Harriet (1887–1974)
Spofford, Harriet Prescott (1835–1921)
Spolin, Viola (1906–1994)
Sponer, Hertha (1895–1968)
Spong, Hilda (1875–1955)
Spooner, Cecil (1875–1953)
Spooner, Edna May (1873–1953)
Sprague, Kate Chase (1840–1899)
Spurgin, Patricia (1965—)
Spuzich, Sandra (1937—)
St. Clair, Lydia (1898–1970)
St. Clair, Sallie (1842–1867)
St. Clair, Stephanie (fl. 1920s–30s)
St. Clair, Yvonne (1914–1971)
St. Denis, Ruth (1877–1968)
St. George, Katharine (1894–1983)
St. James, Lyn (1947—)
St. Johns, Adela Rogers (1894–1988)
Stabenow, Debbie (1950—)
Stacey, Kim (1980—)
Stachowski, Amber (1983—)
Stack, Chelle (1973—)
Stacker, Brenann (1987—)
Stacy, Hollis (1954—)
Stafford, Jean (1915–1979)
Stafford, Jo (1920—)
Stahl, Lesley (1941—)
Stahl, Rose (1870–1955)
Staley, Dawn (1970—)
Stanford, Jane (1828–1905)
Stang, Dorothy (1931–2005)
Stanley, Kim (1925–2001)
Stanley, Louise (1883–1954)
Stanley, Martha M. (1867–1950)
Stanley, Winifred Claire (1909–1996)
Stanton, Elizabeth Cady (1815–1902)
Stanwood, Cordelia (1865–1958)
Stanwyck, Barbara (1907–1990)
Staples, Cleo (1934—)
Staples, Mavis (1940—)
Staples, Yvonne (1939—)
Stapleton, Maureen (1925–2006)
Stapleton, Ruth Carter (1929–1983)
Starbird, Kate (1975—)
Starbuck, Mary Coffyn (1644/45–1717)
Starke, Pauline (1900–1977)
Starr, Belle (1848–1889)
Starr, Eliza Allen (1824–1901)
Starr, Ellen Gates (1859–1940)
Starr, Frances Grant (1886–1973)
Starr, Kay (1922—)
Stauffer, Brenda (1961—)
Staupers, Mabel (1890–1989)
Staver, Julie (1952—)
Staw, Sala (d. 1972)
Stearns, Lutie (1866–1943)
Stearns, Sally (c. 1915—)
Stebbins, Emma (1815–1882)
Steber, Eleanor (1914–1990)
Steding, Katy (1967—)
Stedman, Myrtle (1885–1938)
Steed, Gitel P. (1914–1977)
Steel, Dawn (1946–1997)
Steele, Alison (c. 1937–1995)
Steele, Danielle (1947—)
Steele, Micki (1954—)
Stein, Gertrude (1874–1946)
Steinem, Gloria (1934—)
Steinseifer, Carrie (1968—)
Steloff, Frances (1887–1989)
Sten, Anna (1908–1993)
Stepan, Mary Louise (1935—)
Stephens, Alice Barber (1858–1932)
Stephens, Ann S. (1810–1886)
Stephens, Helen (1918–1994)
Stephens, Kate (1853–1938)
Sterkel, Jill (1961—)
Sterling, Jan (1921–2004)
Stern, Catherine Brieger (1894–1973)
Stern, Edith Rosenwald (1895–1980)
Stern, Elizabeth (1915–1980)
Stern, Frances (1873–1947)
Sternhagen, Frances (1930—)
Stetson, Augusta (1842–1928)
Stetson, Helen (1887–1982)
Stettheimer, Florine (1871–1944)
Stevens, Alzina (1849–1900)
Stevens, Connie (1938—)
Stevens, Emily (1882–1928)
Stevens, Georgia Lydia (1870–1946)
Stevens, Inger (1934–1970)
Stevens, Julie (1916–1984)
Stevens, K.T. (1919–1994)
Stevens, Lillian (1844–1914)
Stevens, May (1924—)
Stevens, Nettie Maria (1861–1912)
Stevens, Risë (1913—)
Stevens, Rochelle (1966—)
Stevens, Stella (1936—)
Stevenson, Anne (1933—)
Stevenson, Fanny (1840–1914)
Stevenson, Matilda (1849–1915)
Stevenson, Sarah Hackett (1841–1909)
Stevenson, Sara Yorke (1847–1921)
Steward, Susan McKinney (1847–1918)
Stewart, Anita (1895–1961)
Stewart, Cora Wilson (1875–1958)
Stewart, Elaine (1929—)
Stewart, Eliza Daniel (1816–1908)
Stewart, Ellen (c. 1920—)
Stewart, Katherine (c. 1861–1949)
Stewart, Maria W. (1803–1879)
Stewart, Martha (1941—)
Stewart, Sarah (1906–1976)
Stich-Randall, Teresa (1927—)
Stickles, Terri Lee (1946—)
Stickney, Dorothy (1896–1998)
Stimson, Julia (1881–1948)
Stinson, Katherine (1891–1977)
Stinson, Marjorie (1894–1975)
Stives, Karen (1950—)
Stobs, Shirley (1942—)
Stockton, Annis Boudinot (1736–1801)
Stockton, Betsey (c. 1798–1865)
Stoddard, Cora Frances (1872–1936)
Stoddard, Elizabeth Drew (1823–1902)
Stoeckel, Ellen Battell (1851–1939)
Stokes, Olivia Phelps (1847–1927)
Stokes, Rose Pastor (1879–1933)
Stokes, Shelly (1967—)
Stoler, Shirley (1929–1999)
Stone, Beth (1940—)
Stone, Carol (1915—)
Stone, Dorothy (1905–1974)
Stone, Grace Zaring (1896–1991)
Stone, Hannah (1893–1941)
Stone, Lucinda Hinsdale (1814–1900)
Stone, Lucy (1818–1893)
Stone, Nikki (1971—)
Stone, Paula (1912–1997)
Stone, Rosie (1945—)
Stone, Ruth (1915—)
Stone, Sharon (1958—)
Stone, Toni (1921–1996)
Stonehouse, Ruth (1892–1941)
Stoneman, Abigail (c. 1740–?)
Stoneman, Bertha (1866–1943)
Stopa, Wanda (1899–1925)
Storer, Maria (1849–1932)
Storey, Edith (1892–1955)
Storm, Gale (1922—)
Stouder, Sharon (1948—)
Stout, Juanita Kidd (1919–1998)
Stover, Mary Johnson (1832–1883)
Stover-Irwin, Juno (1928—)
Stowe, Harriet Beecher (1811–1896)
Stradner, Rose (1913–1958)
Straight, Beatrice (1914–2001)
Strang, Ruth (1895–1971)
Strange, Michael (1890–1950)
Strasberg, Paula (1911–1966)
Strasberg, Susan (1938–1999)
Stratton, Dorothy (b. 1899)
Stratton-Porter, Gene (1863–1924)
Straus, Ida (1849–1912)
Strauss, Sara Milford (1896–1979)
Streb, Elizabeth (1950—)
Streb, Marla (1965—)
Streep, Meryl (1949—)
Street, Picabo (1971—)
Streeter, Ruth Cheney (1895–1990)
Streisand, Barbra (1942—)
Strengell, Marianne (1909–1998)
Stringer, C. Vivian (1948—)
Stringfield, Bessie B. (1912–1993)
Stritch, Elaine (1925—)
Stroganova, Nina (1919—)
Strong, Anna Louise (1885–1970)
Strong, Ann Monroe Gilchrist (1875–1957)
Strong, Harriet (1844–1929)
Strong, Judy (1960—)
Strossen, Nadine (1950—)
Strozzi, Kay (1899–1996)
Strug, Kerri (1977—)
Stuart, Gloria (1909—)
Stuart, Jane (1812–1888)
Stuart, Mary (1926–2002)
Stuart, Ruth McEnery (c. 1849–1917)
Stunyo, Jeanne (1936—)
Sturgis, Katharine Boucot (1903–1987)
Suckow, Ruth (1892–1960)
Sudduth, Jill (1971—)
Sudlow, Joan (1892–1970)
Suesse, Dana (1909–1987)
Suggs, Louise (1923—)
Sulka, Elaine (1933–1994)
Sullavan, Margaret (1911–1960)
Sullivan, Cynthia Jan (1937—)
Sullivan, Jean (1923–2003)
Sullivan, Kathryn (1951—)
Sullivan, Leonor Kretzer (1902–1988)
Sullivan, Mary Quinn (1877–1939)
Sullivan, Maxine (1911–1987)
Sulzberger, I.O. (1892–1990)

Summer, Donna (1948—)
Summers, Leonora (1897–1976)
Summitt, Pat (1952—)
Sumner, Jessie (1898–1994)
Sumners, Rosalynn (1964—)
Sunderland, Nan (1898–1973)
Sundstrom, Becky (1976—)
Sundstrom, Shana (1973—)
Sunn, Rell (1951–1998)
Sunshine, Marion (1894–1963)
Supremes, The (1964–1977)
Surratt, Mary E. (c. 1820–1865)
Susann, Jacqueline (1921–1974)
Sutliffe, Irene H. (1850–1936)
Sutter, Linda (1941–1995)
Sutton, Carol (1933–1985)
Sutton, May (1887–1975)
Svetlova, Marina (1922—)
Swagerty, Jane (1951—)
Swail, Julie (1972—)
Swain, Clara A. (1834–1910)
Swank, Hilary (1974—)
Swann, Caroline Burke (d. 1964)
Swanson, Gloria (1897–1983)
Swanson, Pipsan Saarinen (1905–1979)
Swarthout, Gladys (1904–1969)
Swartz, Maud O'Farrell (1879–1937)
Sweet, Blanche (1895–1986)
Sweet, Rachel (1963—)
Swenson, May (1913–1989)
Swett, Jane (b. 1805)
Swift, Delia (fl. 1850s)
Swift, Jane M. (1965—)
Swindler, Mary Hamilton (1884–1967)
Swisshelm, Jane Grey (1815–1884)
Switzer, Kathy (1947—)
Switzer, Mary E. (1900–1971)
Swoopes, Sheryl (1971—)
Syms, Nancy Roth (1939—)
Syms, Sylvia (1916–1992)
Taba, Hilda (1902–1967)
Tabankin, Margery Ann (c. 1948—)
Taber, Gladys (1899–1980)
Taeuber, Irene Barnes (1906–1974)
Tafoya, Margaret (1904–2001)
Taft, Helen Herron (1861–1943)
Taft, Jessie (1882–1960)
Taft, Lydia (c. 1711–1778)
Taggard, Genevieve (1894–1948)
Taggart, Michele (1970—)
Tait, Agnes (c. 1897–1981)
Tait, Dorothy (1905–1972)
Takei, Kei (1946—)
Talavera, Tracee (1966—)
Talbert, Mary Morris (1866–1923)
Talbot, Marion (1858–1948)
Talbott, Gloria (1931–2000)
Talcott, Eliza (1836–1911)
Taliaferro, Edith (1893–1958)
Taliaferro, Mabel (1887–1979)
Tallchief, Maria (1925—)
Tallchief, Marjorie (1927—)
Talley, Marion (1906–1983)
Talley, Nedra (1946—)
Talma, Louise (1906–1996)
Talmadge, Constance (1897–1973)
Talmadge, Natalie (1897–1969)
Talmadge, Norma (1893–1957)
Tamiris, Helen (1902–1966)
Tan, Amy (1952—)
Tandy, Jessica (1909–1994)
Tanguay, Eva (1878–1947)
Tannenbaum, Jane Belo (1904–1968)
Tanner, Clara Lee (1905–1997)
Tanner, Marion (1891–1985)
Tanning, Dorothea (b. 1910)
Taormina, Sheila (1969—)
Tapley, Rose (1881–1956)
Tappan, Caroline Sturgis (1819–1888)
Tappan, Eva March (1854–1930)
Tappin, Ashley T. (1974—)
Tarbell, Ida (1857–1944)
Tarpley, Lindsay (1983—)
Tarry, Ellen (b. 1906)
Tashman, Lilyan (1899–1934)
Tate, Sharon (1943–1969)
Taurasi, Diana (1982—)
Tauskey, Mary Anne (1955—)
Taussig, Helen Brooke (1898–1986)
Taylor, Anna Edson (c. 1858–c. 1921)
Taylor, Elizabeth (1932—)
Taylor, Estelle (1894–1958)
Taylor, Eva (1895–1977)
Taylor, June (1917–2004)
Taylor, Kamala (1924–2004)
Taylor, Koko (1935—)
Taylor, Laurette (1884–1946)
Taylor, Lily Ross (1886–1969)
Taylor, Lucy Hobbs (1833–1910)
Taylor, Margaret Smith (1788–1852)
Taylor, Melanie Smith (1949—)
Taylor, Renée (1933—)
Taylor, Ruth (1908–1984)
Taylor, Stella (1929–2003)
Taylor, Susie King (1848–1912)
Taymor, Julie (1952—)
Tcherkassky, Marianna (1955—)
Teale, Nellie (1900–1993)
Team USA: Women's Ice Hockey at Nagano
Teasdale, Sara (1884–1933)
Teasdale, Verree (1904–1987)
Teer, Barbara Ann (1937—)
Teeters, Nancy Hays (1930—)
Teitel, Carol (1923–1986)
Telkes, Maria (1900–1995)
Tell, Alma (1892–1937)
Tell, Olive (1894–1951)
Telva, Marion (1897–1962)
Tempest, Florence (c. 1891–?)
Templeton, Fay (1865–1939)
Templeton, Olive (1883–1979)
Templeton, Rini (1935–1986)
Tennant, Eleanor (1895–1974)
Tenney, Tabitha Gilman (1762–1837)
Tennille, Toni (1943—)
Teresa, Mother (c. 1766–1846)
Terhune, Mary Virginia (1830–1922)
Terrell, Mary Church (1863–1954)
Terrell, Tammi (1946–1970)
Terris, Norma (1904–1989)
Terry, Alice (1899–1987)
Terry, Megan (1932—)
Terwillegar, Erica (1963—)
Teter, Hannah (1987—)
Tetzel, Joan (1921–1977)
Teuscher, Cristina (1978—)
Tewkesbury, Joan (1936—)
Thaden, Louise (1905–1979)
Thane, Elswyth (1900–1984)
Tharp, Twyla (1941—)
Tharpe, Rosetta (1915–1973)
Thatcher, Molly Day (d. 1963)
Thaxter, Celia Laighton (1835–1894)
Thaxter, Phyllis (1921—)
Thebom, Blanche (1918—)
Thebom, Blanche (b. 1918)
Thien, Margot (1971—)
Thigpen, Lynne (1948–2003)
Thoburn, Isabella (1840–1901)
Thomas, Alice (fl. 1670s)
Thomas, Alma (1891–1978)
Thomas, Carla (1942—)
Thomas, Debi (1967—)
Thomas, Edith Matilda (1854–1925)
Thomas, Edna (1885–1974)
Thomas, Helen (1920—)
Thomas, Joyce Carol (1938—)
Thomas, Lera Millard (1900–1993)
Thomas, M. Carey (1857–1935)
Thomas, Marlo (1937—)
Thomas, Mary (1946—)
Thomas, Mary Myers (1816–1888)
Thomas, Olive (1884–1920)
Thomas, Rozonda (1971—)
Thompson, Carol Semple (1948—)
Thompson, Clara (1893–1958)
Thompson, Donielle (1981—)
Thompson, Dorothy (1893–1961)
Thompson, Eliza (1816–1905)
Thompson, Elizabeth Rowell (1821–1899)
Thompson, Eloise Bibb (1878–1928)
Thompson, Era Bell (1906–1986)
Thompson, Gertrude Hickman (1877–1950)
Thompson, Helen (1908–1974)
Thompson, Jennie (1981—)
Thompson, Jenny (1973—)
Thompson, Kay (1908–1998)
Thompson, Louise (1901–1999)
Thompson, Mary Harris (1829–1895)
Thompson, May (d. 1978)
Thompson, Ruth (1887–1970)
Thompson, Sada (1929—)
Thompson, Sarah (1774–1852)
Thompson, Tina (1975—)
Thoms, Adah B. (c. 1863–1943)
Thorne, Florence (1877–1973)
Thorne, Harriet V.S. (1843–1926)
Thornton, Kathryn (1952—)
Thornton, Willie Mae (1926–1984)
Thorpe, Rose Hartwick (1850–1939)
Thorsness, Kristen (1960—)
Thurber, Jeannette (1850–1946)
Thurman, Karen L. (1951—)
Thurman, Sue (1903–1996)
Thurman, Tracey
Thurman, Uma (1970—)
Thursby, Emma (1845–1931)
Thurston, Lucy (1795–1876)
Thurston, Matilda (1875–1958)
Thygeson, Sylvie Thompson (1868–1975)
Tibbetts, Margaret Joy (1919—)
Tiburzi, Bonnie (1948—)
Tickey, Bertha (1925—)
Ticknor, Anna Eliot (1823–1896)
Tidd, Rachel (1984—)
Tidwell-Lucas, Gypsy (c. 1975—)
Tiernan, Frances Fisher (1846–1920)
Tierney, Gene (1920–1991)
Tietjens, Eunice (1884–1944)
Tiffany (1971—)
Tighe, Virginia (1923–1995)
Tilghman, Shirley M. (1946—)
Tilly, Dorothy (1883–1970)
Tilton, Elizabeth (1834–c. 1896)
Tilton, Martha (1915—)
Timms, Sally (1959—)
Timothy, Ann (c. 1727–1792)
Timothy, Elizabeth (d. 1757)
Tingley, Katherine (1847–1929)
Tipton, Billy (1914–1989)
Titus, Shirley Carew (1892–1967)
Tobey, Beatrice (d. 1993)
Tobin, Genevieve (1899–1995)
Tobin, Vivian (1902–2002)
Todd, Ann (1931—)
Todd, E.L. (fl. early 1900s)
Todd, Mabel Loomis (1858–1932)

Todd, Marion Marsh (1841–post 1913)
Todd, Olga Taussky (1906–1995)
Todd, Thelma (1905–1935)
Toguri, Iva (1916—)
Toklas, Alice B. (1877–1967)
Tomlin, Lily (1939—)
Tompkins, Sally Louisa (1833–1916)
Tone, Lel (c. 1971—)
Toor, Frances (1890–1956)
Toppan, Jane (1854–1938)
Topperwein, Elizabeth "Plinky" (c. 1886–1945)
Topping, Jenny (1980—)
Torrence, Gwen (1965—)
Torres, Dara (1967—)
Torres, Raquel (1908–1987)
Torres, Vanessa (1986—)
Toumanova, Tamara (1919–1996)
Tourel, Jennie (1899–1973)
Toussaint, Cheryl (1952—)
Tower, Joan (1938—)
Towle, Charlotte (1896–1966)
Towle, Katherine (1898–1986)
Towne, Laura Matilda (1825–1901)
Tracy, Martha (1876–1942)
Tracy, Paula (1939—)
Trask, Kate Nichols (1853–1922)
Traske, Mary (fl. 1660)
Traubel, Helen (1899–1972)
Traurig, Christine (1957—)
Travell, Janet G. (1901–1997)
Travers, Mary (1936—)
Traverse, Madlaine (1875–1964)
Tree, Dolly (1899–1962)
Tree, Dorothy (1906–1992)
Tree, Marietta (1917–1991)
Treen, Mary (1907–1989)
Trevor, Claire (1909–2000)
Trigère, Pauline (1912–2002)
Trilling, Diana (1905–1996)
Trisler, Joyce (1934–1979)
Trotman, Julia (1968—)
Trotter, Deedee (1982—)
Trotter, Mildred (1899–1991)
Trotter, Virginia Yapp (1921–1998)
Troup, Augusta Lewis (c. 1848–1920)
Trout, Jenny Kidd (1841–1921)
Troy, Doris (1937–2004)
Troy, Louise (1933–1994)
Troyanos, Tatiana (1938–1993)
Truax, Sarah (1877–1958)
Trueman, Paula (1900–1994)
Truitt, Anne (1921–2004)
Truman, Bess (1885–1982)
Truman, Margaret (1924—)
Trunnelle, Mabel (1879–1981)
Truth, Sojourner (c. 1797–1883)
Tryon, Amy (1970—)
Tubbs, Alice (1851–1930)
Tubman, Harriet (1821–1913)
Tuchman, Barbara (1912–1989)
Tucker, C. DeLores (1927–2005)
Tucker, Corin (1972—)
Tucker, Sophie (1884–1966)
Tucker, Tanya (1958—)
Tueting, Sarah (1976—)
Tufty, Esther Van Wagoner (1896–1986)
Tully, Alice (1902–1993)
Tully, Mary Jean Crenshaw (1925–2003)
Tureck, Rosalyn (1914–2003)
Turell, Jane (1708–1735)
Turlington, Christy (1969—)
Turnbull, Julia Anne (1822–1887)
Turner, Cathy (1962—)
Turner, Debbye (1966—)
Turner, Eliza Sproat (1826–1903)
Turner, Florence E. (c. 1888–1946)
Turner, Kathleen (1954—)
Turner, Kim (1961—)
Turner, Lana (1921–1995)
Turner, Mary (d. 1918)
Turner, Sherri (1956—)
Turner, Tina (1938—)
Turpie, Marion (d. 1967)
Tuthill, Louisa Huggins (1799–1879)
Tuttle, Lurene (1906–1986)
Tutwiler, Julia Strudwick (1841–1916)
Tuve, Rosemond (1903–1964)
Twain, Shania (1965—)
Twelvetrees, Helen (1908–1958)
Twigg, Rebecca (1963—)
Two "Mollies"
Ty-Casper, Linda (1931—)
Tyler, Adeline Blanchard (1805–1875)
Tyler, Alice S. (1859–1944)
Tyler, Anne (1941—)
Tyler, Danielle (1974—)
Tyler, Judy (1933–1957)
Tyler, Julia Gardiner (1820–1889)
Tyler, Letitia (1790–1842)
Tyler, Odette (1869–1936)
Tyler, Priscilla Cooper (1816–1889)
Tyler-Sharman, Lucy (1965—)
Tyson, Cicely (1933—)
Tyus, Wyomia (1945—)
Uchida, Christine (1952—)
Uchida, Yoshiko (1921–1992)
Ueland, Clara Hampson (1860–1927)
Uggams, Leslie (1943—)
Ulion, Gretchen (1972—)
Ulmann, Doris (1882–1934)
Ulric, Lenore (1892–1970)
Umeki, Miyoshi (1929—)
Underhill, Ruth Murray (1883–1984)
Underwood, Agness Wilson (1902–1984)
Underwood, Lillias (1851–1921)
Unger, Gladys B. (c. 1885–1940)
Unger, Mary Ann (1945–1998)
Unsoeld, Jolene (1931—)
Upton, Harriet Taylor (1853–1945)
Urecal, Minerva (1894–1966)
Utley, Freda (1898–1977)
Vaccaro, Brenda (1939—)
Vague, Vera (1906–1974)
Vail, Myrtle (1888–1978)
Valentina (1899–1989)
Valentine, Grace (1884–1964)
Valentine, Lila (1865–1921)
Valenzuela, Luisa (1938—)
Valerie, Joan (1911–1983)
Valli, Virginia (1895–1968)
Van Blarcom, Carolyn (1879–1960)
Van Buren, Adeline (1894–1949)
Van Buren, Angelica (1816–1878)
Van Buren, Augusta
Van Buren, Hannah Hoes (1783–1819)
Van Buren, Mabel (1878–1947)
VanCaspel, Venita (1922—)
Vance, Danitra (1954–1994)
Vance, Norma (1927–1956)
Vance, Vivian (1909–1979)
Van Cleve, Edith (1894–1985)
Van Cott, Margaret (1830–1914)
Van Deman, Esther (1862–1937)
Van Deman, Irene (1889–1961)
Vanderbeck, Florence (1884–1935)
Vanderbilt, Alice Gwynne (1845–1934)
Vanderbilt, Amy (1908–1974)
Vanderbilt, Consuelo (1877–1964)
Vanderbilt, Gertrude (1880–1960)
Vanderbilt, Gladys Moore (1886–1965)
Vanderbilt, Gloria (1924—)
Vanderbilt, Maria (1821–1896)
Vanderbilt, Sophia Johnson (1797–1868)
Van Derbur, Marilyn (c. 1937—)
Vanderpool, Sylvia (1936—)
Van de Vate, Nancy (1930—)
Van Doren, Irita (1891–1966)
Van Doren, Mamie (1931—)
Van Dover, Cindy (1954—)
Van Duyn, Mona (1921–2004)
Van Dyke, Vonda Kay (c. 1944—)
Van Dyken, Amy (1973—)
Vane, Daphne (1918–1966)
Van Gordon, Cyrena (1896–1964)
Van Hamel, Martine (1945—)
Van Hoosen, Bertha (1863–1952)
Van Houten, Leslie (1949—)
Van Kleeck, Mary Abby (1883–1972)
Van Lew, Elizabeth (1818–1900)
Vann, Jesse Matthews (c. 1890–1967)
Vano, Donna (c. 1955—)
Van Rensselaer, Mariana (1851–1934)
Van Rensselaer, Martha (1864–1932)
Van Runkle, Theadora (1940—)
van Stockum, Hilda (b. 1908)
Van Studdiford, Grace (1873–1927)
Van Upp, Virginia (1902–1970)
Van Valkenburgh, Elizabeth (1799–1846)
Van Vorst, Marie Louise (1867–1936)
Van Waters, Miriam (1887–1974)
Van Wie, Virginia (1909–1997)
Van Zandt, Marie (1858–1919)
Varden, Evelyn (1893–1958)
Vare, Glenna Collett (1903–1989)
Várnay, Astrid (1918—)
Varsi, Diane (1937–1992)
Vassar, Queenie (1870–1960)
Vaughan, Gladys (d. 1987)
Vaughan, Sarah (1924–1990)
Vaughn, Hilda (1898–1957)
Vaught, Wilma L. (1930—)
Vautrin, Minnie (1886–1941)
Veazie, Carol (1895–1984)
Vega, Suzanne (1959—)
Velarde, Pablita (1918—)
Velásquez, Loreta (1842–1897)
Velez, Lisa (1967—)
Velez, Lupe (1908–1944)
Venable, Evelyn (1913–1993)
Ventre, Fran (1941—)
Venturella, Michelle (1973—)
Venturini, Tisha (1973—)
Venuta, Benay (1911–1995)
Vera-Ellen (1920–1981)
Verdon, Gwen (1925–2000)
Verdugo, Elena (1926—)
Verdy, Violette (1931—)
Vernon, Mabel (1883–1975)
Verrett, Shirley (1931—)
Vestoff, Floria (1920–1963)
Vickers, Janeene (1968—)
Vickers, Martha (1925–1971)
Victor, Frances (1826–1902)
Victor, Lucia (1912–1986)
Victor, Metta (1831–1885)
Victor, Wilma (1919–1987)
Vidali, Lynn (1952—)
Vidor, Florence (1895–1977)
Villa, Brenda (1980—)
Villard, Fanny Garrison (1844–1928)
Vince, Marion Lloyd (1906–1969)
Vincent, Marjorie (c. 1965—)
Vincent, Mary Ann (1818–1887)
Vinge, Joan D. (1948—)
Vining, Elizabeth Gray (1902–1999)
Vinson, Helen (1907–1999)
Vise, Hollie (1987—)

Vogel, Dorothy (1935—)
Vokes, May (d. 1957)
Vollertsen, Julie (1959—)
Vollmar, Jocelyn (1925—)
Vollmer, Dana (1987—)
Vollmer, Lula (d. 1955)
von Aroldingen, Karin (1941—)
Von Bremen, Wilhelmina (1909–1976)
von Busing, Fritzi (c. 1884–1948)
von Furstenberg, Diane (1946—)
Vonnoh, Bessie Potter (1872–1955)
von Saltza, Chris (1944—)
Von Stade, Frederica (1945—)
von Wiegand, Charmion (1896–1993)
Voronina, Zinaida (1947—)
Vorse, Mary Heaton (1874–1966)
Voutilainen, Katrina (1975—)
Vrba, Elisabeth (1942—)
Vucanovich, Barbara F. (1921—)
Waddles, Charleszetta (1912–2001)
Waddy, Harriet (1904–1999)
Wade, Margaret (1912–1995)
Wagner, Allison (1977—)
Wagner, Aly (1980—)
Wagstaff, Elizabeth (1974—)
Wainwright, Helen (1906—)
Waite, Catherine (1829–1913)
Wakeling, Gwen (1901–1982)
Wakoski, Diane (1937—)
Walcamp, Marie (1894–1936)
Walcott, Mary Morris (1860–1940)
Wald, Florence (1917—)
Wald, Lillian D. (1867–1940)
Wald, Patricia McGowan (1928—)
Waldo, Ruth Fanshaw (1885–1975)
Waldorf, Wilella (c. 1900–1946)
Wales, Ethel (1878–1952)
Walker, Ada Overton (1870–1914)
Walker, Alice (1944—)
Walker, Barbara Jo (1926–2000)
Walker, Betty (1928–1982)
Walker, Charlotte (1876–1958)
Walker, Colleen (1956—)
Walker, Edyth (1867–1950)
Walker, Helen (1920–1968)
Walker, June (1900–1966)
Walker, Laura (1970—)
Walker, Lillian (1887–1975)
Walker, Madame C.J. (1867–1919)
Walker, Maggie Lena (1867–1934)
Walker, Margaret (1915–1998)
Walker, Mary Edwards (1832–1919)
Walker, Nancy (1922–1992)
Walker, Nella (1880–1971)
Walker, Olene S. (1930—)
Walker, Polly (b. 1908)
Wall, Geraldine (1912–1970)
Wall, Lyndsay (1985—)
Wallace, Jean (1923–1990)
Wallace, Lila Acheson (1889–1984)
Wallace, Lucille (1898–1977)
Wallace, Regina (1886–1978)
Wallace, Sippie (1898–1986)
Wallace, Zerelda G. (1817–1901)
Wallenda, Helen (1910–1996)
Waller, Judith Cary (1889–1973)
Wallis, Ruth Sawtell (1895–1978)
Waln, Nora (1895–1964)
Walsh, Kerri (1978—)
Walsh, Loretta (1898–c. 1988)
Walsh, Stella (1911–1980)
Walter, Cornelia Wells (1813–1898)
Walters, Barbara (1929—)
Walters, Bernice R. (1912–1975)
Walton, Angie (1966—)
Walton, Florence (1891–1981)
Walworth, Ellen Hardin (1832–1915)
Wambach, Abby (1980—)
Wambaugh, Sarah (1882–1955)
Wang, Vera (1949—)
Ward, Catharine Barnes (1851–1913)
Ward, Clara Mae (1924–1973)
Ward, Elizabeth Stuart Phelps (1844–1911)
Ward, Fannie (1865–1952)
Ward, Geneviève (1838–1922)
Ward, Hortense (1872–1944)
Ward, Winifred Louise (1884–1975)
Warder, Ann Head (1758–1829)
Warfield, Irene (c. 1896–1961)
Waring, Laura Wheeler (1887–1948)
Warmus, Carolyn (1964—)
Warner, Anna Bartlett (1827–1915)
Warner, Anne (1954—)
Warner, Bonny (1962—)
Warner, Estella Ford (1891–1974)
Warner, Gloria (c. 1914–1934)
Warner, Susan Bogert (1819–1885)
Warnes, Jennifer (1947—)
Warren, Althea (1886–1958)
Warren, Caroline Matilda (1785–1844)
Warren, Elinor Remick (1900–1991)
Warren, Lavinia (1841–1919)
Warrick, Ruth (1915–2005)
Warwick, Dionne (1940—)
Wash, Martha
Washam, Jo Ann (1950—)
Washburn, Margaret Floy (1871–1939)
Washburn, Mary (1907–1994)
Washington, Bennetta (1918–1991)
Washington, Dinah (1924–1963)
Washington, Fredi (1903–1994)
Washington, Josephine (1861–1949)
Washington, Margaret Murray (c. 1861–1925)
Washington, Martha (1731–1802)
Washington, Olivia Davidson (1854–1889)
Washington, Ora (1899–1971)
Washington, Sarah Spencer (1889–?)
Wasserstein, Wendy (1950–2006)
Waters, Alice (1944—)
Waters, Ethel (1896–1977)
Waters, Maxine (1938—)
Watkins, Linda (1908–1976)
Watkins, Tionne (1970—)
Watkins, Yoko Kawashima (1933—)
Watley, Jody (1959—)
Watley, Natasha (1981—)
Watson, Edith (1861–1943)
Watson, Ellen (1861–1889)
Watson, Jill (1963—)
Watson, Lucile (1879–1962)
Watson, Pokey (1950—)
Watteville, Benigna von (1725–1789)
Wattleton, Faye (1943—)
Watts, Heather (1953—)
Wauneka, Annie Dodge (1910–1997)
Way, Amanda M. (1828–1914)
Wayburn, Peggy (1917–2002)
Wayne, Carol (1942–1985)
Wayte, Mary (1965—)
Weatherspoon, Teresa (1965—)
Weaver, Marjorie (1913–1994)
Weaver, Sigourney (1949—)
Webb, Electra Havemeyer (1888–1960)
Webb, Elida (1895–1975)
Webb, Laura (1941–2001)
Webb, Sharon (1936—)
Weber, Lois (1881–1939)
Webster, Jean (1876–1916)
Webster, Margaret (1905–1972)
Weddington, Sarah R. (1945—)
Wedemeyer, Maria von (c. 1924–1977)
Weed, Ella (1853–1894)
Weed, Ethel (1906–1975)
Weeks, Ada May (1898–1978)
Weeks, Dorothy (1893–1990)
Weeks, Marion (1886–1968)
Weeks-Shaw, Clara S. (1857–1940)
Wehselau, Mariechen (1906–1992)
Weidenbach, Lisa Larsen (c. 1962—)
Weidler, Virginia (1926–1968)
Weigl, Vally (1889–1982)
Weinberg, Wendy (1958—)
Weinbrecht, Donna (1965—)
Weingarten, Violet (1915–1976)
Weinstein, Hannah (1911–1984)
Weir, Amanda (1986—)
Weir, Irene (1862–1944)
Weis, Jessica McCullough (1901–1963)
Weisberger, Barbara (c. 1926—)
Weishoff, Paula (1962—)
Weiss, Alta (1889–1964)
Weiss, Janet (1965—)
Weiss, Liz
Weiss, Mary
Weissman, Dora (1881–1974)
Welch, Elisabeth (1904–2003)
Welch, Raquel (1940—)
Weld, Tuesday (1943—)
Welles, Gwen (1951–1993)
Wellman, Emily Ann (d. 1946)
Wells, Alice (1927–1987)
Wells, Alice Stebbins (1873–1957)
Wells, Carolyn (1862–1942)
Wells, Charlotte Fowler (1814–1901)
Wells, Emmeline B. (1828–1921)
Wells, Fay Gillis (1908–2002)
Wells, Kate Gannett (1838–1911)
Wells, Kitty (b. 1919)
Wells, Marguerite Milton (1872–1959)
Wells, Mary (1943–1992)
Wells, Mary Ann (c. 1895–1971)
Wells, Melissa Foelsch (1932—)
Wells-Barnett, Ida (1862–1931)
Welsh, Lilian (1858–1938)
Welter, Ariadna (1930–1998)
Weltfish, Gene (1902–1980)
Welty, Eudora (1909–2001)
Wendell, Krissy (1981—)
Wendt, Julia Bracken (1871–1942)
Wentworth, Cecile de (c. 1853–1933)
Werlein, Elizebeth Thomas (1883–1946)
Wesley, Cynthia
West, Claire (1893–1980)
West, Dorothy (1907–1998)
West, Dottie (1932–1991)
West, Jessamyn (1902–1984)
West, Mae (1893–1980)
West, Sandy (1960—)
West, Vera (1900–1947)
Westcott, Helen (1928–1998)
Westley, Helen (1875–1942)
Westman, Nydia (1902–1970)
Weston, Cecil (1889–1976)
Weston, Ruth (1906–1955)
Westover, Winifred (1899–1978)
Wetherill, Louisa Wade (1877–1945)
Wetmore, Joan (1911–1989)
Wexler, Nancy (1945—)
Weymouth, Tina (1950—)
Whalen, Sara (1976—)
Wharton, Anne Hollingsworth (1845–1928)
Wharton, Edith (1862–1937)
Wheatley, Phillis (c. 1752–1784)
Wheaton, Anne (1892–1977)
Wheeler, Anna Pell (1883–1966)
Wheeler, Candace (1827–1923)
Wheeler, Ruth (1877–1948)

Wheelock, Lucy (1857–1946)
Whelan, Arleen (1916–1993)
Whelan, Cyprienne Gabel (d. 1985)
Whipple, Mary (1980—)
Whitcher, Frances Miriam Berry (1811–1852)
White, Alice (1904–1983)
White, Alma Bridwell (1862–1946)
White, Amy (1968—)
White, Anna (1831–1910)
White, Donna (1954—)
White, Eartha M. (1876–1974)
White, Edna Noble (1879–1954)
White, Eliza Orne (1856–1947)
White, Ellen Gould (1827–1915)
White, Frances (1896–1969)
White, Helen C. (1896–1967)
White, Helen Magill (1853–1944)
White, Karyn (1965—)
White, Katharine S. (1892–1977)
White, Marilyn Elaine (1944—)
White, Morgan (1983—)
White, Pearl (1889–1938)
White, Ruth (1914–1969)
White, Sue Shelton (1887–1943)
White, Willye B. (1939—)
Whitestone, Heather (c. 1973—)
Whiting, Lilian (1847–1942)
Whiting, Margaret (1924—)
Whiting, Sarah F. (1847–1927)
Whitman, Christine Todd (1946—)
Whitman, Narcissa (1808–1847)
Whitman, Sarah Helen (1803–1878)
Whitmire, Kathy (1946—)
Whitney, Adeline Dutton (1824–1906)
Whitney, Anne (1821–1915)
Whitney, Betsey Cushing Roosevelt (1908–1998)
Whitney, Charlotte Anita (1867–1955)
Whitney, Dorothy Payne (1887–1968)
Whitney, Eleanore (1917—)
Whitney, Flora Payne (1897–1986)
Whitney, Gertrude Vanderbilt (1875–1942)
Whitney, Helen Hay (1876–1944)
Whitney, Mary Watson (1847–1921)
Whitney, Phyllis A. (1903—)
Whitney, Ruth (1928–1999)
Whittelsey, Abigail Goodrich (1788–1858)
Whittier, Polly (1877–1946)
Whitworth, Kathy (1939—)
Whyte, Edna Gardner (1902–1992)
Whyte, Sandra (1970—)
Wichman, Sharon (1952—)
Wickes, Mary (1916–1995)
Wickwire, Nancy (1925–1974)
Widdemer, Margaret (1884–1978)
Widnall, Sheila (1938—)
Wiesman, Linden (1975—)
Wiggin, Kate Douglas (1856–1923)
Wiggins, Myra Albert (1869–1956)
Wightman, Hazel Hotchkiss (1886–1974)
Wilber, Doreen (1930—)
Wilcox, Ella Wheeler (1850–1919)
Wilcox, Lisa (1966—)
Wilder, Laura Ingalls (1867–1957)
Wiley, Lee (1915–1975)
Wiley, Mildred (1901–2000)
Wilhelm, Kate (1928—)
Wilkinson, Jemima (1752–1819)
Wilkinson, Laura (1977—)
Wilkinson, Marguerite Ogden (1883–1928)
Willard, Emma Hart (1787–1870)
Willard, Frances E. (1839–1898)
Willard, Mary (1941—)
Willebrandt, Mabel Walker (1889–1963)
Willeford, Mary B. (1900–1941)
Williams, Anna Wessels (1863–1954)
Williams, Camilla (1922—)
Williams, Cara (1925—)
Williams, Christa (1978—)
Williams, Clara (1888–1928)
Williams, Deniece (1951—)
Williams, Elizabeth Sprague (1869–1922)
Williams, Esther (1923—)
Williams, Fannie Barrier (1855–1944)
Williams, Frances (1903–1959)
Williams, Hattie (1872–1942)
Williams, Hope (1897–1990)
Williams, Jody (1950—)
Williams, Kathlyn (1888–1960)
Williams, Lauryn (1983—)
Williams, Lavinia (1916–1989)
Williams, Lucinda (1937—)
Williams, Lucinda (1953—)
Williams, Marion (1927–1994)
Williams, Mary Lou (1910–1981)
Williams, Mary Wilhelmine (1878–1944)
Williams, Michelle (1980—)
Williams, Natalie (1970—)
Williams, Serena (1981—)
Williams, Sherley Anne (1944–1999)
Williams, Vanessa (1963—)
Williams, Venus (1980—)
Williams, Victoria (1958—)
Williams, Wendy Lian (1967—)
Williams, Wendy O. (1951–1998)
Williamson, Sarah Eileen (1974—)
Willing, Jennie Fowler (1834–1916)
Willis, Connie (1945—)
Willis, Frances (1899–1983)
Willits, Mary (1855–1902)
Willoughby, Frances L. (c. 1906–1984)
Wills, Helen Newington (1905–1998)
Willson, Rini Zarova (d. 1966)
Wilson, Augusta Evans (1835–1909)
Wilson, Carnie (1968—)
Wilson, Deborah (1955—)
Wilson, Edith (1896–1981)
Wilson, Edith Bolling (1872–1961)
Wilson, Elizabeth (d. 1786)
Wilson, Ellen Axson (1860–1914)
Wilson, Ethel (d. 1980)
Wilson, Harriet E. Adams (c. 1827–c. 1870)
Wilson, Heather (1960—)
Wilson, Lois (1894–1988)
Wilson, Margaret Bush (1919—)
Wilson, Margaret W. (1882–1973)
Wilson, Margery (1896–1986)
Wilson, Marie (1916–1972)
Wilson, Mary (1944—)
Wilson, Nancy (1937—)
Wilson, Peggy (1934—)
Wilson, Sallie (1932—)
Wilson, Staci (1976—)
Wilson, Wendy (1969—)
Wiman, Anna Deere (1924–1963)
Winant, Ethel (1922–2003)
Windsor, Claire (1897–1972)
Windsor, Marie (1919–2000)
Windsor, Wallis Warfield, duchess of (1895–1986)
Wine-Banks, Jill (1943—)
Winfrey, Oprah (1954—)
Wing, Toby (1915–2001)
Winger, Debra (1955—)
Wingo, Effiegene Locke (1883–1962)
Winlock, Anna (1857–1904)
Winser, Beatrice (1869–1947)
Winslow, Anna Green (1759–1779)
Winslow, Ola Elizabeth (c. 1885–1977)
Winsor, Kathleen (1919—)
Winter, Alice Ames (1865–1944)
Winter, Ethel (1924—)
Winter, Joanne (1924—)
Winters, Marian (1924–1978)
Winters, Shelley (1920–2006)
Winton, Jane (1905–1959)
Wintour, Anna (1949—)
Winwood, Estelle (1883–1984)
Wise, Brownie (1913–1992)
Wise, Louise Waterman (1874–1947)
Wister, Sarah (1761–1804)
Wister, Sarah Butler (1835–1908)
Witchcraft Trials in Salem Village (1692–1693)
Withee, Mabel (d. 1952)
Withers, Jane (1926—)
Witherspoon, Cora (1890–1957)
Withington, Alfreda (1860–1951)
Withington, Eliza (1825–1877)
Wittenmyer, Annie Turner (1827–1900)
Wittpenn, Caroline Stevens Alexander (1859–1932)
Witty, Chris (1975—)
Woerishoffer, Carola (1885–1911)
Woizikowska, Sonia (1919—)
Wolcott, Marion Post (1910–1990)
Wolf, Hazel (1898–2000)
Wolf, Kate (1942–1986)
Wolfe, Catherine L. (1828–1887)
Wolfenstein, Martha (1869–1905)
Wolff, Helen (1906–1994)
Wolff, Victoria (1903–1992)
Wolfson, Theresa (1897–1972)
Wollstein, Martha (1868–1939)
Wolters, Kara (1975—)
Wong, Anna May (1907–1961)
Wong, Betty Ann (1938—)
Wong, Jade Snow (1919–2006)
Wong-Staal, Flossie (1946—)
Wood, Audrey (1905–1985)
Wood, Beatrice (1893–1998)
Wood, Carolyn (1945—)
Wood, Edith Elmer (1871–1945)
Wood, Evelyn (1909–1995)
Wood, Mary Elizabeth (1861–1931)
Wood, Natalie (1938–1981)
Wood, Peggy (1892–1978)
Wood, Sally Sayward Barrell Keating (1759–1855)
Wood, Thelma (b. 1901)
Wood, Yvonne (1914—)
Woodard, Lynette (1959—)
Woodbridge, Louise Deshong (1848–1925)
Woodbridge, Margaret (1902—)
Woodbury, Clare (c. 1880–1949)
Woodbury, Helen Sumner (1876–1933)
Woodbury, Joan (1915–1989)
Woodhead, Cynthia (1964—)
Woodhouse, Margaret Chase Going (1890–1984)
Woodhull, Victoria (1838–1927)
Woodrow, Nancy Mann Waddel (c. 1866–1935)
Woods, Katharine Pearson (1853–1923)
Woodsmall, Ruth F. (1883–1963)
Woodstra, Susan (1957—)
Woodward, Ellen Sullivan (1887–1971)
Woodward, Joanne (1930—)
Woolley, Helen (1874–1947)
Woolley, Mary E. (1863–1947)
Woolman, Mary Schenck (1860–1940)
Woolsey, Abby Howland (1828–1893)
Woolsey, Georgeanna Muirson (1833–1906)
Woolsey, Jane Stuart (1830–1891)
Woolsey, Lynn C. (1937—)
Woolsey, Sarah Chauncey (1835–1905)

Woolson, Abba Goold (1838–1921)
Woolson, Constance Fenimore (1840–1894)
Wootten, Bayard (1875–1959)
Workman, Fanny (1859–1925)
Wormeley, Katharine Prescott (1830–1908)
Wormington, H. Marie (1914–1994)
Worms, Pamela Lee (d. 1852)
Worth, Irene (1916—)
Wray, Fay (1907—)
Wright, Betty (1953—)
Wright, Camille (1955—)
Wright, Cobina (1887–1970)
Wright, Cobina Jr. (1921—)
Wright, Frances (1795–1852)
Wright, Helen (1914–1997)
Wright, Jane Cooke (1919—)
Wright, Laura Maria (1809–1886)
Wright, Lucy (1760–1821)
Wright, Mabel Osgood (1859–1934)
Wright, Maginel (1881–1966)
Wright, Martha Coffin (1806–1875)
Wright, Mary Clabaugh (1917–1970)
Wright, Mickey (1935—)
Wright, Muriel Hazel (1889–1975)
Wright, Patience Lovell (1725–1786)
Wright, Patricia (1945—)
Wright, Rebecca (1942—)
Wright, Sarah Elizabeth (1928—)
Wright, Sophie Bell (1866–1912)
Wright, Syreeta (1946–2004)
Wright, Teresa (1918—)
Wu, Chien-Shiung (1912–1997)
Wunderlich, Frieda (1884–1965)
Wuornos, Aileen (1956–2002)
Wurdemann, Audrey Mary (1911–1960)
Wyatt, Jane (1912—)
Wyeth, Henriette (1907–1997)
Wyland, Wendy (1964–2003)
Wylie, Elinor (1885–1928)
Wyman, Jane (1914—)
Wymore, Patrice (1926—)
Wynekoop, Alice (1870–1952)
Wynette, Tammy (1942–1998)
Wynter, Dana (1927—)
Yakko, Sada (d. 1946)
Yale, Caroline A. (1848–1933)
Yalow, Rosalyn (1921—)
Yamada, Mitsuye (1923—)
Yamaguchi, Kristi (1971—)
Yamauchi, Wakako (1924—)
Yampolsky, Mariana (1925—)
Yarborough, Sara (1950—)
Yarbro, Chelsea Quinn (1942—)
Yard, Molly (1912–2005)
Yarros, Rachelle (1869–1946)
Yasui, Kono (1880–1971)
Yaw, Ellen Beach (1868–1947)
Yeager, Jeana (1952—)
Yearwood, Trisha (1964—)
Yener, Aslihan (1946—)
Yezierska, Anzia (c. 1881–1970)
Ylla (1911–1955)
Yohé, May (1869–1938)
Yorkin, Nicole (1958—)
Yorkin, Peg (b. 1927)
Young, Ann Eliza (b. 1844)
Young, Anne Sewell (1871–1961)
Young, Clara Kimball (1890–1960)
Young, Dannette (1964—)
Young, Ella Flagg (1845–1918)
Young, Loretta (1913–2000)
Young, Marguerite (1908–1995)
Young, Mary Marsden (1880–1971)
Young, Mary Sophie (1872–1919)
Young, Rida Johnson (1875–1926)
Young, Sheila (1950—)
Young, Wanda (1944—)
Younger, Maud (1870–1936)
Youngs, Elaine (1970—)
Youskevitch, Maria (c. 1946—)
Yow, Kay (1942—)
Yuan, Tina (c. 1950—)
Yu Lihua (1932—)
Yuriko (b. 1920)
Yurka, Blanche (1887–1974)
Zabar, Lillian (c. 1905–1995)
Zabelle, Flora (1880–1968)
Zabriskie, Louise (1887–1957)
Zachry, Caroline B. (1894–1945)
Zagunis, Mariel (1985—)
Zaharias, Babe Didrikson (1911–1956)
Zakrzewska, Marie (1829–1902)
Zamba, Frieda (1965—)
Zane, Betty (c. 1766–c. 1831)
Zanotto, Kendra (1981—)
Zaturenska, Marya Alexandrovna (1902–1982)
Zayak, Elaine (1965—)
Zeisel, Eva (1906—)
Zeisler, Fanny Bloomfield (1863–1927)
Zemina, Kathryn (1968—)
Zenger, Anna Catharina (c. 1704–1751)
Zetterlund, Yoko (1969—)
Zide, Rochelle (1938—)
Ziegelmeyer, Nikki (c. 1975—)
Zimbalist, Mary Louise Curtis (1876–1970)
Zimmerman, Mary Beth (1960—)
Zimmerman, Suzanne (1925—)
Zimmermann, Gerda (1927—)
Zintkala Nuni (c. 1890–c. 1919)
Zipprodt, Patricia (1925–1999)
Zmeskal, Kim (1976—)
Zoch, Jacqueline (1949—)
Zolotow, Charlotte (b. 1915)
Zorach, Marguerite Thompson (1887–1968)
Zorina, Vera (1917–2003)
Zwilich, Ellen Taaffe (1939—)
Zwink, Tara (1973—)

URBINO

Commune in Pesaro e Urbino Province of central Italy
Under Rome (3rd c. BCE)
Ruled by church (9th–13th c.)
Capital of Duchy of Urbino (15th c.)
Came under Papacy (17th c.)
Part of kingdom of Italy (1860)
See Italy.

URUGUAY

Republic in southeastern central South America
Rio de la Plata discovered by Solís (1516)
Colonia founded by Portuguese (1680)
Montevideo founded by Portugal (1726)
Spanish viceroyalty of La Plata established (1776)
La Plata, with Buenos Aires, obtained independence from Spain (1811–1814)
Incorporated in Brazil as Cisplatine Province (1821)
Revolted against Brazil (1825)
Recognized as independent state (1828)
Adopted new constitution (1966)

Agustini, Delmira (1886–1914)
Berenguer, Amanda (1924—)
Cáceres, Esther de (1903–1971)
Crocker, Fay (1914—)
de Ibáñez, Sara (1909–1971)
Ibarbourou, Juana de (1895–1979)
Luna, Rosa (1937–1993)
Maracci, Carmelita (1911–1988)
Peri Rossi, Cristina (1941—)
Russell, Dora Isella (1925—)
Sabalsajaray, Nibuya (1951–1974)
Santos Arrascaeta, Beatriz (1947—)
Silva, Clara (1905–1976)
Silva Vila, María Inés (1926—)
Somers, Armonía (1914–1994)
Vaz Ferreira, María Eugenia (1875–1924)
Vilariño, Idea (1920—)
Zani, Giselda (1909–1975)

UZBEKISTAN

Baraksanova, Irina (1969—)
Batyrchina, Jana (1979—)
Cheryazova, Lina (1968—)
Chusovitina, Oksana (1975—)
Galieva, Roza (1977—)
Saadi, Elvira (1952—)
Zabirova, Zulfia (1973—)
Zaripova, Amina (1976—)

VENDÔME

Town in Loir-et-Cher department in northern central France
Ancient countship
Made a duchy (1515)
See France.

VENEZUELA

Republic in northern South America
Settled by Spanish (1520)
Independence from Spain proclaimed (1811)
Part of Greater Colombia (1819–1829)
Separated from Colombia (1830)
Lost territory to British Guiana (1895–1896)
Adopted new constitution (1961)

Allende, Isabel (1942—)
Aretz, Isabel (1909—)
Arvelo Larriva, Enriqueta (1886–1963)
Carreño, Teresa (1853–1917)
Esperanza, Maria (1928–2004)
Gramcko, Ida (1924–1994)
Machado, Luz (1916–1999)
Marisol (1930—)
Palacios, Lucila (1902–1994)
Parra, Teresa de la (1889–1936)
Rodriguez, Zhandra (1947—)
Sáez, Irene (1961—)
Schön, Elizabeth (1921–2001)
Stolk, Gloria (1918–1979)
Terán, Ana Enriqueta (1919—)
Toro, Maria Teresa (d. 1803)
Valle Silva, Luisa del (1896–1962)
Velásquez, Lucila (1928—)

VENICE

City in Venezia province of northeastern Italy
Elected first doge (697)
Vassal of Byzantine Empire (until 10th c.)
Ruler of colonial empire (13th c.)
Gradually lost territory to Ottoman Turks (15th–18th c.)
Ceded territory to Austria (1797)
Incorporated in Napoleon's kingdom of Italy (1805)
Restored to Austria (1815)
Ceded to Italy (1866)
See Italy.

VERONA

Province of Veneto in northeastern Italy
Under Roman rule (89 BCE)
Captured by Goths
Captured by Charlemagne (774)
Became independent republic (1107)
Ruled by della Scala family (1260–1387)
Ruled by Visconti family of Milan (1387–1405)
Ruled by Venice (1405–1797)
Passed to Austria (19th c.)
Became part of kingdom of Italy (1866)
See Italy.

VIETNAM

Republic in southeastern Asia
Came under Chinese influence (221 BCE)
Made province of Chinese Empire (111 BCE)
Under Chinese control (until 939 CE)
Cambodia conquered by Vietnamese (1698–1757)
Wall built by South Vietnamese dividing region into two parts (1613)
Visted by Spanish and Portuguese traders (16th c.)
Visited by English and Dutch traders (17th c.)
North and South unified under single dynasty (1802)
Saigon captured by Franco-Spanish naval force (1859)
Provinces ceded to France (1862)
French protectorate established (1884)
Occupied by Japanese (1940–1945)
Vietnam partitioned (1954)
North and South Vietnam unified under Communist regime (1976)

A Nong (c. 1005–1055)
Ba Trieu (225–248)
Bui Thi Xuan (d. 1771)
Ho Xuan Huong (fl. late 18th c.)
Nguyen Thi Dinh (1920–1992)
Nhu, Madame (1924—)
Nuyen, France (1939—)
Phuc, Kim (c. 1963—)
Tran Hieu Ngan (1974—)
Trung Sisters (d. 43)

WALES

Principality of Great Britain
Inhabited by the Cymric Celts
Conquered by Romans
Norman occupation (12th c.)
Made an English principality (1284)

Angharad (d. 1162)
Angharad (fl. 13th c.)
Ashley, Laura (1925–1985)
Augusta of Saxe-Gotha (1719–1772)
Bassey, Shirley (1937—)
Bate, Dorothea (1879–1951)
Braose, Isabel de (d. 1248?)
Broughton, Rhoda (1840–1920)
Butler, Eleanor (c. 1738–1829)
Cave, Jane (c. 1754–1813)
Charlotte Augusta (1796–1817)
Clarke, Gillian (1937—)
Clarke, Patricia Hannah (1919—)
Clwyd, Ann (1937—)
Cummins, Peggy (1925—)
Cunnington, Eveline Willert (1849–1916)
Curtis-Thomas, Claire (1958—)
Daisy, Princess (1873–1943)
Davies, Gwendoline (1882–1951)
Davies, Margaret (1884–1963)
Davies, Margaret (1914–1982)
Dillwyn, Amy (1845–1935)
Eleanor of Montfort (1252–1282)
Emma de Gatinais (fl. 1150–1170)
Entwhistle, Peg (1908–1932)
Evans, Jillian (1959—)
French, Dawn (1957—)
Gladstone, Catherine (1812–1900)
Gladys (fl. 1075)
Gladys (fl. 1100s)
Gladys the Black (d. 1251)
Glendower, Margaret (fl. late 1300s)
Glynne, Mary (1895–1954)
Griffiths, Ann (1776–1805)
Guest, Lady Charlotte (1812–1895)
Gwenllian of Wales (fl. 1137)
Hall, Augusta (1802–1896)
Hamnett, Nina (1890–1956)
Hardy, Barbara (1924—)
Haycraft, Anna Margaret (1932–2005)
Heal, Sylvia (1942—)
Innes, Mary Jane (1852–1941)
Joan of England (d. 1237)
John, Gwen (1876–1939)
Jones, Elizabeth Marina (1926—)
Jones, Gwyneth (1936—)
Keen, Ann (1948—)
Kinnock, Glenys (1944—)
Ladies of Llangollen, The
Lawrence, Jackie (1948—)
Lilly, Gweneth (1920–2004)
Lloyd George, Margaret (1866–1941)
Lloyd George, Megan (1902–1966)
Marared (fl. 1173)
Marshall, Isabel (1200–1240)
Matthews, Donna (1971—)
McLaren, Anne Laura (1927—)
McNally, Eryl Margaret (1942—)
Morgan, Eluned (1967—)
Morgan, Julie (1944—)
Morris, Jan (1926—)
Mortimer, Agnes (fl. 1347)
Mortimer, Penelope (1918–1999)
Mulford, Wendy (1941—)
Novello-Davies, Clara (1861–1943)
O'Shea, Tessie (1913–1995)
Parr, Anne (d. 1552)
Phillips, Margaret (1923–1984)
Phillips, Siân (1934—)
Piozzi, Hester Lynch (1741–1821)
Ponsonby, Sarah (1755–1831)
Price, Margaret (1941—)
Rees, Gwendolen (1906–1994)
Rhondda, Margaret (1883–1958)
Roberts, Kate (1891–1985)
Roberts, Rachel (1927–1980)
Rubens, Bernice (1928–2004)
Ruddock, Joan (1943—)
Sampson, Kathleen (1892–1980)
Senena (fl. 1200s)
Sheehan, Margaret Flavin (d. 1969)
Stjernstedt, Rosemary (1912–1998)
Susan of Powys (fl. 1100s)
Tangwystl (fl. 1180–1210)
Thomas, Mary (1932–1997)
Vachell, Eleanor (1879–1948)
van Heyningen, Ruth (1917—)
Vaughan, Hilda (1892–1985)
Walter, Lucy (c. 1630–1658)
Watts, Helen (1927—)
Williams, Betty (1944—)
Williams, Grace (1906–1977)

WARWICK

Borough in Warwickshire in central England
See England.

WASHO

Native North American Great Basin indigenous group

Dat So La Lee (c. 1835–1925)

WEIMAR

City in Erfurt district of eastern Germany
Seat of the duchy of Saxe-Weimar (1547–1918)
See Germany.

WESSEX

Ancient Anglo-Saxon kingdom
Founded by Saxon invaders of Britain
Leader of Anglo-Saxon Heptarchy (9th c.)
Reconquered the Danelaw and ruled all England (10th c.)
See England.

WEST INDIES

See Antigua.
See Bahama Islands.
See Barbados.
See Cuba.
See Dominica.
See Grenada.
See Guyana.
See Hispaniola (Haiti and Dominican Republic).
See Jamaica.
See Montserrat.
See Puerto Rico.
See Saint Vincent.
See Trinidad and Tobago.
See Virgin Islands.

WESTMORELAND

Former county in northwestern England
See England.

WILTSHIRE

Former county in southern England
See England.

WURTTEMBERG

Former German state
Became duchy of Swabia
Ruled by counts (11th–15th c.)
Became a duchy (1495)
Became an electorate (1803)
Became a kingdom (1806)
Became a constitutional monarchy (1819–1918)
Became a republic (1918–1934)
Lost sovereignty to Reich (1934)
Made part of Baden-Wurttemberg (1952)
See Germany.

XHOSA

Bantu indigenous group of Cape of Good Hope Province, South Africa

Nongqause (c. 1840–c. 1900)

YANKTON

Native North American Great Plains indigenous group

Bonnin, Gertrude Simmons (1876–1938)
Deloria, Ella (1888–1971)

YEMEN

Republic in southern Arabian Peninsula
Seat of ancient Minaean kingdom
Conquered by Egypt (c. 1600 BCE)
Invaded by Ethiopians and Romans
Converted to Islam (628 CE)
Ruled under caliphate
Under Turkish control (16th c.)
Under Egyptian control (1819)
Overthrew monarchy (1962)

Arwa (1052–1137)
Asmā (c. 1028–1084)

YORK

County in northern England
See England.

YUGOSLAVIA

Republic in southeastern Europe
Proclaimed Kingdom of Serbs, Croats, and Slovenes (1918)
Ruled by absolute monarchy (1929–1931)
Invaded by German forces (1941)
Established a Communist republic (1945)
Adopted new constitution (1963)
Became federation of Slovenia, Croatia, Serbia, Bosnia, Montenegro, and Macedonia (1990)

Alexandra (1921–1993)
Anastasovski, Svetlana (1961—)
Arbutina, Andjelija (1967—)

Aurora of San Donato (1873–1904)
Bajkusa, Vesna (1970—)
Basch, Anamarija (1893–after 1945)
Becirspahic, Mirsada (1957—)
Binder, Aranka (1966—)
Bjedov, Djurdica (1947—)
Bjedov, Mira (1955—)
Bonney, Linda (1949—)
Bursac, Marija (1921–1943)
Cuderman, Alenka (1961—)
Dasic-Kitic, Svetlana (1960—)
Desha (1892–1965)
Despotovic, Vesna (1961—)
Djukica, Slavic (1960—)
Djuraskovic, Vera (1949—)
Djurica, Mirjana (1961—)
Djurkovic, Zorica (1957—)
Dornik, Polona (1962—)
Drljaca, Radmila (1959—)
Elizabeth of Yugoslavia (1936—)
Ercic, Emilija (1962—)
Fazlic, Jasna (1970—)
Froman, Margareta (1890–1970)
Golic, Sladjana (1960—)
Iles, Katica (1946—)
Ivosev, Aleksandra (1974—)
Jankovic, Ljubinka (1958—)
Jeremic, Slavica (1957—)
Jurca, Branca (1914–1999)
Jurinac, Sena (1921—)
Kastl, Sonja (1929—)
Kira of Leiningen (b. 1930)
Kolar-Merdan, Jasna (1956—)
Komnenovic, Jelica (1960—)
Koscina, Sylva (1933–1994)
Kvesic, Kornelija (1964—)
Lakic, Mara (1963—)
Lang-Beck, Ivana (1912–1983)
Lelas, Zana (1970—)
Majstorovic, Biljana (1959—)
Marie (1900–1961)
Markovic, Vera (1931—)
Milolevic, Vesna (1955—)
Milosavljeric, Ljubinka (1917—)
Milosevic, Bojana (1965—)
Mitic, Vukica (1953—)
Mlakar, Pia (1908–2000)
Mlakar, Veronika (1935—)
Mugosa, Ljiljana (1962—)
Mugosa, Svetlana (1964—)
Mujanovic, Razija (1967—)
Mulroney, Mila (1953—)
Nakic, Danira (1969—)
Ognjenovic, Mirjana (1953—)
Ozegovic, Sanja (1959—)
Pavicevic, Zorica (1956—)
Pekic, Sofija (1953—)
Perazic, Jasmina (1960—)
Perkucin, Gordana (1962—)
Planinc, Milka (1924—)
Poliakova, Elena
(1884–1972)
Ptujec, Jasna (1959—)
Radovic, Vesna (1950—)
Reljin, Milena (1967—)
Roje, Ana (1909—)
Savic, Rada (1961—)
Sekaric, Jasna (1965—)
Seles, Monica (1973—)
Slavenska, Mia (1914–2000)
Svet, Mateja (1968—)
Titlic, Ana (1952—)
Tito, Jovanka Broz (1924—)
Tonkovic, Marija (1959—)
Vangelovska, Stojna (1965—)
Visnjic, Biserka (1953—)
Vojinovic, Zorica (1958—)
Wild, Eleonora (1969—)
Yuric, Dragica (1963—)

ZAMBIA

Republic in southern central Africa
Under jurisdiction of British South Africa Company (1889–1924)
Became British protectorate (1924)
Part of Federation of Rhodesia and Nyasaland (1953–1963)
Became independent republic (1964)

Chibesakunda, Lombe Phyllis (1944—)
Konie, Gwendoline (1938—)
Mulenga, Alice (1924–1978)
Nakatindi, Princess (c. 1943—)

ZANZIBAR

Former sultanate in eastern Africa
Dominated by Portuguese (c. 1505)
Conquered by ruler of Oman (18th c.)
Became independent sultanate (1963)
United with Tanganyika to form Tanzania (1964)
See Tanzania.

ZIMBABWE

Republic in southern central Africa

Chase, Elizabeth (1950—)
Chick, Sandra (1947—)
Coventry, Kirsty (1983—)
Cowley, Gillian (1955—)
Davies, Patricia (1956—)
English, Sarah (1955—)
George, Maureen (1955—)
Grant, Ann (1955—)
Huggett, Susan (1954—)
Kuper, Hilda B.
(1911–1992)
McKillop, Patricia (1956—)
Mugabe, Sally (1932–1992)
Mujuru, Joyce (1955—)
Newby-Fraser, Paula (1962—)
Nhiwatiwa, Naomi (1940—)
Page, Gertrude (1873–1922)
Park, Merle (1937—)
Phillips, Brenda (1958—)
Prinsloo, Christine (1952—)
Robertson, Sonia (1947—)
Sithole-Niang, Idah (1957—)
Stockley, Cynthia (1872–1936)
Stowell, Belinda (1971—)
Volk, Helen (1954—)
Watson, Linda (1955—)

ZULU

Bantu indigenous group of southeastern Africa

Nandi (c. 1760s–1827)

OCCUPATIONAL INDEX

ABBESS
See Nun/Abbess.

ABOLITIONIST
Alcott, Louisa May (1832–1888)
Anthony, Susan B. (1820–1906)
Augspurg, Anita (1857–1943)
Bradwell, Myra (1831–1894)
Brown Blackwell, Antoinette (1825–1921)
Cary, Mary Ann Shadd (1823–1893)
Cary, Phoebe (1824–1871)
Chace, Elizabeth Buffum (1806–1899)
Chandler, Elizabeth Margaret (1807–1834)
Chapman, Maria (1806–1885)
Cheney, Ednah Dow (1824–1904)
Child, Lydia Maria (1802–1880)
Cowles, Betsey Mix (1810–1876)
Craft, Ellen (1826–c. 1891)
Davis, Paulina Wright (1813–1876)
de Cleyre, Voltairine (1866–1912)
Dickinson, Anna E. (1842–1932)
Douglass, Anna Murray (1813–1882)
Douglass, Sarah Mapps (1806–1882)
Falconbridge, Anna Maria (fl. 1790–1794)
Field, Kate (1838–1896)
Follen, Eliza (1787–1860)
Forten, Margaretta (1808–1875)
Gage, Frances D. (1808–1884)
Gibbons, Abby Hopper (1801–1893)
Gonzaga, Chiquinha (1847–1935)
Grajales, Mariana (1808–1893)
Grew, Mary A. (1813–1896)
Griffing, Josephine White (1814–1872)
Grimké, Angelina E. (1805–1879)
Grimké, Charlotte L. Forten (1837–1914)
Grimké, Sarah Moore (1792–1873)
Hale, Sarah Josepha (1788–1879)
Hallowell, Anna (1831–1905)
Hanbury, Elizabeth (1793–1901)
Harper, Frances E.W. (1825–1911)
Haviland, Laura S. (1808–1898)
Hayes, Lucy Webb (1831–1889)
Heymann, Lida (1867–1943)
Holley, Sallie (1818–1893)
Howe, Julia Ward (1819–1910)
Isabel of Brazil (1846–1921)
Jackson, Helen Hunt (1830–1885)
Jacobs, Harriet A. (1813–1897)
Jones, Jane Elizabeth (1813–1896)
Kelley, Abby (1810–1887)
Kelley, Florence (1859–1932)
Kemble, Fanny (1809–1893)
Lewis, Graceanna (1821–1912)
Livermore, Mary A. (1820–1905)
Lockwood, Belva Ann (1830–1917)
Lowell, Maria White (1821–1853)
Martineau, Harriet (1802–1876)
McCracken, Mary Ann (1770–1866)
McDowell, Mary Eliza (1854–1936)
Miner, Myrtilla (1815–1864)
Mott, Lucretia (1793–1880)
Ovington, Mary White (1865–1951)
Peabody, Elizabeth Palmer (1778–1853)
Plato, Ann (c. 1820–?)
Pleasant, Mary Ellen (c. 1814–1904)
Preston, Ann (1813–1872)
Pugh, Sarah (1800–1884)
Purvis, Harriet Forten (1810–1875)
Purvis, Sarah Forten (c. 1811–c. 1898)
Putnam, Mary T.S. (1810–1898)
Ray, Charlotte E. (1850–1911)
Ray, H. Cordelia (c. 1849–1916)
Remond, Sarah Parker (1826–1894)
Robinson, Harriet Hanson (1825–1911)
Rose, Ernestine (1810–1892)
Schofield, Martha (1839–1916)
Severance, Caroline M. (1820–1914)
Sewall, Lucy Ellen (1837–1890)
Smith, Abby (1797–1878)
Smith, Julia (1792–1886)
Stanton, Elizabeth Cady (1815–1902)
Stewart, Maria W. (1803–1879)
Stoecker, Helene (1869–1943)
Stone, Lucy (1818–1893)
Swisshelm, Jane Grey (1815–1884)
Taylor, Susie King (1848–1912)
Thomas, Mary Myers (1816–1888)
Towne, Laura Matilda (1825–1901)
Trollope, Frances Milton (1779–1863)
Truth, Sojourner (c. 1797–1883)
Tubman, Harriet (1821–1913)
Van Lew, Elizabeth (1818–1900)
Walker, Mary Edwards (1832–1919)
Whitney, Anne (1821–1915)
Wright, Frances (1795–1852)

ABORIGINAL-RIGHTS ACTIVIST
Bandler, Faith (1918—)
Bennett, Mary Montgomerie (1881–1961)
Gibbs, Pearl (1901–1983)
Gilmore, Mary (1865–1962)
Parker, Catherine Langloh (c. 1856–1940)
Street, Jessie (1889–1970)
Sykes, Bobbi (1943—)
Walker, Kath (1920–1993)
Wright, Judith (1915–2000)

ABORTION-RIGHTS ACTIVIST
See Reproductive-rights activist.

ACCOUNTANT
Basten, Alice (1876–1955)
Erauso, Catalina de (1592–1635)
Fairclough, Ellen (1905–2004)
Kolstad, Eva (1918–1998)
Papariga, Alexandra (1945—)

ACTING TEACHER
Adams, Maude (1872–1953)
Adler, Stella (1902–1993)
Benson, Rita Romilly (1900–1980)
Conti, Italia (1874–1946)
Daykarhanova, Tamara (1889–1980)
Escott, Cicely Margaret (1908–1977)
Feury, Peggy (1924–1985)
Fitton, Doris (1897–1985)
Flanagan, Hallie (1889–1969)
Foch, Nina (1924—)
Fogerty, Elsie (1865–1945)
Fontanne, Lynn (1887–1983)
Fuller, Frances (1907–1980)
Hagen, Uta (1919–2004)
Hurston, Zora Neale (c. 1891–1960)
Leontovich, Eugénie (1894–1993)
Lewisohn, Alice (1883–1972)
Lewisohn, Irene (1892–1944)
Makarova, Tamara (1907–1997)
Margo (1918–1985)
Mooney, Ria (1904–1973)
Nicholls, Marjory Lydia (1890–1930)
Oughton, Winifred (1890–1964)
Piscator, Maria Ley (1899–1999)
Reignolds, Catherine Mary (1836–1911)
Sands, Dorothy (1893–1980)
Spolin, Viola (1906–1994)
Strasberg, Paula (1911–1966)
Suzman, Janet (1939—)
Thimig, Helene (1889–1974)
von Essen, Siri (1850–1912)
Whelan, Cyprienne Gabel (d. 1985)

ACTIVIST/ADVOCATE/REFORMER
See Aboriginal-rights activist.
See AIDS activist.
See Animal-rights activist.
See Anti-apartheid activist.
See Child-welfare advocate.
See Civil-rights activist.
See Consumers' advocate.
See Dress reformer.
See Education reformer.
See Gay-rights activist.
See Humanitarian/Human-rights activist.
See Labor activist.
See Literacy activist.
See Mental-health reformer.
See Native-rights activist.
See Political reformer/activist.
See Prison reformer.
See Public-health reformer.
See Religious reformer.
See Reproductive-rights activist.
See Social activist/reformer.
See Temperance reformer.
See Women's-rights activist.

ACTRESS
Aadland, Beverly (1943—)
Aaliyah (1979–2001)
Abarbanell, Lina (1879–1963)
Abba, Marta (1900–1988)
Abbott, Diahnne (1945—)
Abington, Frances (1737–1815)
Achurch, Janet (1864–1916)
Acker, Jean (1893–1978)
Acquanetta (1921–2004)
Adair, Jean (1872–1953)
Adamova, Adela (1927—)
Adams, Constance (1874–1960)
Adams, Dorothy (1900–1988)
Adams, Ida (c. 1888–1960)
Adams, Jane (1921—)
Adams, Julie (1926—)

Adams, Maude (1872–1953)
Adams, Miriam (1907—)
Addams, Dawn (1930–1985)
Addison, Carlotta (1849–1914)
Addison, Laura (d. 1852)
Adler, Celia (1890–1979)
Adler, Frances (d. 1964)
Adler, Julia (1897–1995)
Adler, Sara (1858–1953)
Adler, Stella (1902–1993)
Adorée, Renée (1898–1933)
Adrian, Iris (1912–1994)
Adrienne, Jean (b. 1905)
Agate, May (1892–1960)
Aghdashloo, Shohreh (1952—)
Ahlander, Thecla (1855–1925)
Ahlers, Anny (1906–1933)
Aimée, Anouk (1932—)
Aked, Muriel (1887–1955)
Akerman, Chantal (1950—)
Albanesi, Meggie (1899–1923)
Alberghetti, Anna Maria (1936—)
Albertson, Lillian (1881–1962)
Albertson, Mabel (1901–1982)
Albrecht, Sophie (1757–1840)
Albright, Lola (1925—)
Alden, Hortense (1903–1999)
Aldredge, Theoni V. (1932—)
Aleandro, Norma (1936—)
Alexander, Claire (1898–1927)
Alexander, Jane (1939—)
Alexander, Janet (d. 1961)
Alexander, Julie (1938–2003)
Alexander, Katherine (1898–1981)
Alexander, Muriel (1898–1975)
Allan, Elizabeth (1908–1990)
Allbritton, Louise (1920–1979)
Allen, Adrianne (1907–1993)
Allen, Debbie (1950—)
Allen, Gracie (1902–1964)
Allen, Vera (1897–1987)
Allen, Viola (1867–1948)
Allenby, Peggy (1905–1967)
Allgood, Sara (1883–1950)
Allison, May (1890–1989)
Allwyn, Astrid (1905–1978)
Allyson, June (1917—)
Alvarez, Anita (1920—)
Alvarez, Carmen (c. 1936—)
Ames, Adrienne (1907–1947)
Ames, Rosemary (1906–1988)
Amin, Adibah (1936—)
Anders, Luana (1938–1996)
Anders, Merry (1932—)
Anderson, Claire (fl. 1940s)
Anderson, Judith (1898–1992)
Anderson, Mary (1859–1940)
Andersson, Bibi (1935—)
Andersson, Harriet (1932—)
Andjaparidze, Veriko (1900–1987)
Andre, Gwili (1908–1959)
Andreeva, Maria Fedorovna (1868–1953)
Andreeva-Babakhan, Anna Misaakovna (1923—)
Andreini, Isabella (1562–1604)
Andress, Ursula (1936—)
Andrews, Ann (1890–1986)
Andrews, Julie (1935—)
Andrews, Lois (1924–1968)
Andrews, Nancy (1924–1989)
Angel, Heather (1909–1986)
Angeli, Pier (1932–1971)
Angelou, Maya (1928—)
Angelus, Muriel (1909–2004)
Anglin, Margaret (1876–1958)
Ankers, Evelyn (1918–1985)
Annabella (1909–1996)
Annabelle (1878–1961)
Annenkova-Bernár, Nina Pávlovna (1859/64–1933)
Annis, Francesca (1944—)
Ann-Margret (1941—)
Antonelli, Laura (1941—)
Antony, Hilda (1896–?)
Aoki, Tsuru (1892–1961)
Appleby, Dorothy (1906–1990)
Arbenina, Stella (1885–1976)
Archer, Robyn (1948—)
Arden, Eve (1907–1990)
Argyle, Pearl (1910–1947)
Arletty (1898–1992)
Arliss, Florence (1871–1950)
Armand, Inessa (1874–1920)
Arnaud, Yvonne (1892–1958)
Arnold, Dorothy (1917–1984)
Arnoul, Françoise (1931—)
Arnould-Plessy, Jeanne (1819–1897)
Arnst, Bobbe (1903–1980)
Arthur, Bea (1923—)
Arthur, Daphne (1925—)
Arthur, Jean (1900–1991)
Arthur, Julia (1869–1950)
Arundale, Sybil (1882–1965)
Arvidson, Linda (1884–1949)
Ash, Maie (b. 1888)
Ashcroft, Peggy (1907–1991)
Asherson, Renée (1915—)
Ashley, Elizabeth (1939—)
Ashwell, Lena (1872–1957)
Ast, Pat (1941–2001)
Astaire, Adele (1898–1981)
Astor, Gertrude (1887–1977)
Astor, Mary (1906–1987)
Atkins, Eileen (1934—)
Atwater, Edith (1911–1986)
Aubrey, Madge (1902–1970)
Aubry, Cécile (1928—)
Audley, Maxine (1923–1992)
Audran, Stéphane (1932—)
Augarde, Adrienne (d. 1913)
Augarde, Amy (1868–1959)
Augarde, Louise (1863–1909)
Ault, Marie (1870–1951)
Avril, Suzanne (fl. 1920s)
Ayres, Agnes (1896–1940)
Baarova, Lida (1914–2000)
Babanova, Maria (b. 1900)
Bacall, Lauren (1924—)
Baclanova, Olga (1899–1974)
Baddeley, Angela (1904–1976)
Baddeley, Hermione (1906–1986)
Baddeley, Sophia (1745–1786)
Badham, Mary (1952—)
Bai Fengxi (1934—)
Bailey, Pearl (1918–1990)
Bainter, Fay (1891–1968)
Baird, Cora (c. 1912–1967)
Baird, Dorothea (1875–1933)
Baird, Leah (1883–1971)
Baker, Belle (1893–1957)
Baker, Carroll (1931—)
Baker, Diane (1938—)
Baker, Iris (b. 1901)
Baldwin, Ruth Ann (fl. 1915–1921)
Balfour, Betty (1903–1979)
Balfour, Katharine (c. 1921–1990)
Balin, Ina (1937–1990)
Balin, Mireille (1911–1968)
Ball, Lucille (1911–1989)
Ball, Suzan (1933–1950)
Bancroft, Anne (1931–2005)
Bancroft, Lady (1839–1921)
Bankhead, Tallulah (1902–1968)
Banky, Vilma (1898–1991)
Bannerjee, Karuna (1919–2001)
Bannerman, Kay (1919–1991)
Bannerman, Margaret (1896–1976)
Bara, Theda (1885–1955)
Baranovskaya, Vera (c. 1870–1935)
Barbour, Joyce (1901–1977)
Bardotte, Brigitte (1934—)
Bari, Lynn (1913–1989)
Barlow, Billie (1862–1937)
Barnes, Binnie (1903–1998)
Barnes, Charlotte Mary Sanford (1818–1863)
Barnes, Winifred (1894–1935)
Barrault, Marie-Christine (1944—)
Barrett, Edith (1906–1977)
Barrett, Minnette (1880–1964)
Barrie, Elaine (1915–2003)
Barrie, Mona (1909–1964)
Barrie, Wendy (1912–1978)
Barriscale, Bessie (1884–1965)
Barry, Ann Street (1734–1801)
Barry, Elizabeth (1658–1713)
Barrymore, Diana (1921–1960)
Barrymore, Ethel (1879–1959)
Barskaya, Margarita A. (1903–1938)
Bartel, Jean (c. 1924—)
Bartet, Jeanne Julia (1854–1941)
Bartok, Eva (1926–1998)
Barton, Dora (1884–1966)
Barton, Mary (d. 1970)
Basquette, Lina (1907–1995)
Bassett, Angela (1958—)
Bateman, Jessie (1877–1940)
Bateman, Kate (1842–1917)
Bates, Barbara (1925–1969)
Bates, Blanche (1873–1941)
Bates, Florence (1888–1954)
Bates, Kathy (1948—)
Bauer, Charita (1922–1985)
Bauer, Karoline (1807–1877)
Bauersmith, Paula (1909–1987)
Bauld, Alison (1944—)
Bavier, Frances (1902–1989)
Baxley, Barbara (1923–1990)
Baxter, Anne (1923–1985)
Baxter, Jane (1909–1996)
Bayes, Nora (1880–1928)
Bayliss, Blanche (fl. 1894)
Bayne, Beverly (1894–1982)
Beach, Cyprian (1893–1951)
Beatty, May (1880–1945)
Beaudet, Louise (1861–1947)
Beaumont, Diana (1909–1964)
Beaumont, Muriel (1881–1957)
Beavers, Louise (1902–1962)
Becker, Christiane (1778–1797)
Beckham, Victoria (1974—)
Beecher, Janet (1884–1955)
Beechman, Laurie (c. 1955–1998)
Behrens, Hildegard (1937—)
Bejart, Armande (c. 1642–1700)
Bejart, Geneviève (c. 1622–1675)
Bejart, Madeleine (1618–1672)
Bel Geddes, Barbara (1922–2005)
Bell, Maggie (1945—)
Bell, Marie (1900–1985)
Bell, Marion (1919–1997)
Bell, Mary Hayley (1911–2005)
Bellamy, George Anne (1727–1788)
Bellamy, Madge (1899–1990)
Bellew, Kyrle (1887–1948)
Belmont, Eleanor Robson (1879–1979)
Belmore, Bertha (1882–1953)
Bennett, Barbara (1906–1958)
Bennett, Belle (1891–1932)
Bennett, Constance (1904–1965)

Bennett, Eileen (1920—)
Bennett, Enid (1893–1969)
Bennett, Jill (1931–1990)
Bennett, Joan (1910–1990)
Bennett, Louise Simone (1919—)
Bennett, Marjorie (1896–1982)
Bennett, Wilda (1894–1967)
Benson, Rita Romilly (1900–1980)
Bent, Buena (c. 1890–1957)
Bentley, Irene (1904–1965)
Bentley, Irene (d. 1940)
Benzell, Mimi (1922–1970)
Berendt, Rachel (d. 1957)
Berenson, Berry (1948–2001)
Berenson, Marisa (1946—)
Berg, Gertrude (1899–1966)
Berganza, Teresa (1934—)
Bergen, Candice (1946—)
Bergen, Nella (1873–1919)
Bergen, Polly (1929—)
Berger, Nicole (1934–1967)
Berger, Senta (1941—)
Bergere, Ouida (1885–1974)
Bergere, Valerie (1872–1938)
Bergman, Ingrid (1915–1982)
Bergner, Elisabeth (1897–1986)
Beringer, Esmé (1875–1972)
Beringer, Vera (1879–1964)
Bernard, Dorothy (1890–1955)
Bernhardt, Sarah (1844–1923)
Berry, Halle (1966—)
Bertini, Francesca (1888–1985)
Besserer, Eugénie (1868–1934)
Best, Edna (1900–1974)
Bevans, Philippa (1913–1968)
Billington, Adeline (1825–1917)
Bingham, Amelia (1869–1927)
Binoche, Juliette (1964—)
Birch-Pfeiffer, Charlotte (1800–1868)
Birell, Tala (1907–1958)
Birkett, Viva (1887–1934)
Bishop, Julie (1914–2001)
Bishop, Kate (b. 1847)
Bishop, Kelly (1944—)
Björk, Anita (1923—)
Black, Shirley Temple (1928—)
Blackler, Betty (1929—)
Blackman, Honor (1926—)
Blaine, Vivian (1921–1995)
Blair, Betsy (1923—)
Blair, Janet (1921—)
Blair, Mary (c. 1895–1947)
Blake, Amanda (1929–1989)
Blanca, Nida (1936–2001)
Blanchard, Mari (1927–1970)
Blanche, Ada (1862–1953)
Blanche, Marie (1893—)
Blandick, Clara (1880–1962)
Blane, Sally (1910–1997)
Blayney, May (1875–1953)
Bleibtreu, Hedwig (1868–1958)
Bleschke, Johanna (1894–1936)
Blondell, Joan (1906–1979)
Bloom, Claire (1931—)
Bloom, Verna (1939—)
Blower, Elizabeth (1763–after 1816)
Blue, Rita Hassan (c. 1905–1973)
Blyth, Ann (1928—)
Blythe, Betty (1893–1972)
Blythe, Coralie (1880–1928)
Boardman, Eleanor (1898–1991)
Boland, Mary (1880–1965)
Boley, May (1881–1963)
Bolkan, Florinda (1941—)
Bond, Jessie (1853–1942)
Bond, Lilian (1908–1991)
Bond, Sheila (1928—)
Bond, Sudie (1928–1984)
Bondi, Beulah (1892–1981)
Bonfils, Helen (c. 1890–1972)
Bonner, Isabel (1907–1955)
Bonner, Priscilla (1899–1996)
Bonstelle, Jessie (1871–1932)
Boone, Debby (1956—)
Booth, Adrian (1918—)
Booth, Agnes (1843–1910)
Booth, Edwina (1904–1991)
Booth, Karin (1919–1992)
Booth, Sarah (1793–1867)
Booth, Shirley (1907–1992)
Borboni, Paola (1900–1995)
Borchers, Cornell (1925—)
Borg, Veda Ann (1915–1973)
Borgström, Hilda (1871–1953)
Boros, Ferike (1880–1951)
Bosé, Lucia (1931—)
Bosse, Harriet (1878–1961)
Boucicault, Nina (1867–1950)
Boulter, Rosalyn (1916–1997)
Bovasso, Julie (1930–1991)
Bovy, Berthe (1887–1977)
Bow, Clara (1904–1965)
Bowers, Elizabeth Crocker (1830–1895)
Bowers, Lally (1917–1984)
Bowes, Alice (c. 1890–1969)
Bowman, Nellie (b. 1878)
Boylan, Mary (1913–1984)
Boyne, Eva Leonard (1886–1960)
Bozyk, Reizl (1914–1993)
Bracegirdle, Anne (1671–1748)
Bradley, Grace (1913—)
Bradna, Olympe (1920—)
Bradshaw, Maria (1801–1862)
Brady, Alice (1892–1939)
Brady, Veronica (1890–1964)
Braga, Sonia (1950—)
Braggiotti, Francesca (1902–1998)
Braham, Leonora (1853–1931)
Braithwaite, Lilian (1873–1948)
Brand, Phoebe (1907–2004)
Brandés, Marthe (1862–1930)
Brandy (1979—)
Brayton, Lily (1876–1953)
Brejchová, Hana (c. 1943—)
Brejchová, Jana (1940—)
Bremer, Lucille (1923–1996)
Brennan, Eileen (1935—)
Brenner, Dori (1946–2000)
Brent, Evelyn (1899–1975)
Brésil, Marguerite (1880–1923)
Brian, Mary (1906–2002)
Brice, Elizabeth (c. 1885–1965)
Brice, Fanny (1891–1951)
Briercliffe, Nellie (1889–1966)
Brightman, Sarah (1960—)
Brill, Patti (1923–1963)
Briscoe, Lottie (1870–1950)
Brissac, Virginia (1883–1979)
Britt, May (1933—)
Britton, Barbara (1919–1980)
Britton, Hutin (1876–1965)
Britton, Pamela (1923–1974)
Broccoli, Dana (1922–2004)
Brockwell, Gladys (1894–1929)
Brogden, Gwendoline (1891–?)
Brohan, Augustine Suzanne (1807–1887)
Brohan, Émilie Madeleine (1833–1900)
Brohan, Josephine Félicité Augustine (1824–1893)
Bron, Eleanor (1934—)
Bronson, Betty (1906–1971)
Bronson, Lillian (1902–1995)
Brooke, Cynthia (1875–1949)
Brooke, Hillary (1914–1999)
Brooks, Geraldine (1925–1977)
Brooks, Louise (1906–1985)
Brooks, Pauline (1912–1967)
Brooks, Phyllis (1914–1995)
Brough, Fanny Whiteside (1854–1914)
Brough, Mary (1863–1934)
Broughton, Phyllis (1862–1926)
Brouwenstijn, Gré (1915—)
Brown, Georgia (1933–1992)
Brown, Jessica (c. 1900–?)
Brown, Jessie (1892–1985)
Brown, Josephine (1892–1976)
Brown, Melanie (1975—)
Brown, Pamela (1917–1975)
Brown, Vanessa (1928–1999)
Browne, Coral (1913–1991)
Browne, Irene (1896–1965)
Browne, Marjorie (1910–1990)
Bruce, Tonie Edgar (1892–1966)
Bruce, Virginia (1910–1982)
Brune, Adrienne (b. 1892)
Brune, Gabrielle (b. 1912)
Brunton, Dorothy (1893–1977)
Brunton, Louisa (c. 1785–1860)
Brustein, Norma (c. 1929–1979)
Bryan, Jane (1918—)
Bryceland, Yvonne (1926–1992)
Buckingham, Rosetta (c. 1843–1864)
Buferd, Marilyn (1925–1990)
Bujold, Geneviève (1942—)
Bunton, Emma (1976—)
Burani, Michelette (1882–1957)
Burgess, Dorothy (1907–1961)
Burke, Billie (1885–1970)
Burke, Georgia (1880–1986)
Burke, Kathleen (1913–1980)
Burke, Patricia (1917–2003)
Burnand, Lily (1865–?)
Burne, Nancy (1912–1954)
Burrell, Daisy (b. 1893)
Burstyn, Ellen (1932—)
Burt, Laura (1872–1952)
Busby, Amy (c. 1872–1957)
Busch, Mae (1891–1946)
Bush, Frances Cleveland (d. 1967)
Bush, Pauline (1886–1969)
Busley, Jessie (1869–1950)
Byington, Spring (1886–1971)
Byron, Kathleen (1922—)
Cabot, Susan (1927–1986)
Cadell, Jean (1884–1967)
Cagney, Jeanne (1919–1984)
Cahill, Lily (1885–1955)
Cahill, Marie (1870–1933)
Calamai, Clara (1915–1998)
Caldwell, Marianne (1866–1933)
Caldwell, Zoë (1933—)
Callas, Maria (1923–1977)
Calvé, Emma (1858–1942)
Calvert, Mrs. Charles (1837–1921)
Calvert, Patricia (1906–1978)
Calvert, Phyllis (1915–2002)
Calvet, Corinne (1921–2001)
Cameron, Violet (1862–1919)
Campbell, Beatrice (1922–1979)
Campbell, Edith (d. 1945)
Campbell, Judy (1916–2004)
Campbell, Louise (1911–1997)
Campbell, Mrs. Patrick (1865–1940)
Campbell, Naomi (1970—)
Campbell, Stella Tanner (b. 1886)
Campbell, Violet (1892–1970)
Canale, Gianna Maria (1927—)
Candeille, Julie (1767–1834)

Cannon, Dyan (1937—)
Capers, Virginia (1925–2004)
Capucine (1931–1990)
Carabella, Flora (1926–1999)
Cardinale, Claudia (1939—)
Carère, Christine (1930—)
Carew, Ora (1893–1955)
Carey, Olive (1896–1988)
Carleton, Claire (1913–1979)
Carlier, Madeleine (c. 1876–?)
Carlin, Cynthia (d. 1973)
Carlisle, Alexandra (1886–1936)
Carlisle, Kitty (b. 1910)
Carlisle, Mary (b. 1912)
Carlson, Violet (d. 1997)
Carmen, Jewel (1897–1984)
Carne, Judy (1939—)
Carol, Martine (1922–1967)
Carol, Sue (1906–1982)
Caron, Leslie (1931—)
Carpenter, Constance (1904–1992)
Carpenter, Thelma (1922–1997)
Carr, Mary (1874–1973)
Carr, Vikki (1941—)
Carr-Cook, Madge (1856–1933)
Carrel, Dany (1935—)
Carrington, Ethel (1889–1962)
Carroll, Dee (1925–1980)
Carroll, Diahann (1935—)
Carroll, Madeleine (1906–1987)
Carroll, Nancy (1903–1965)
Carson, Violet (1898–1983)
Carten, Audrey (b. 1900)
Carter, Helena (1923–2000)
Carter, Janis (1913–1994)
Carter, Mrs. Leslie (1862–1937)
Carter, Nell (1894–1965)
Carter, Nell (1948–2003)
Cartlidge, Katrin (1961–2002)
Carton, Pauline (1884–1974)
Cartwright, Peggy (1912–2001)
Carver, Kathryn (1899–1947)
Carver, Louise (1869–1956)
Carver, Lynne (1909–1955)
Carver, Tina (c. 1923–1982)
Casares, Maria (1922–1996)
Caselotti, Adriana (1916–1997)
Cash, June Carter (1929–2003)
Cash, Rosalind (1938–1995)
Cason, Barbara (1928–1990)
Casson, Ann (1915–1990)
Casson, Mary (b. 1914)
Castle, Peggie (1926–1973)
Catley, Ann (1745–1789)
Caulfield, Joan (1922–1921)
Cavendish, Ada (1839–1895)
Cayvan, Georgia (1857–1906)
Cecil, Sylvia (1906–1983)
Celeste, Madame (1815–1882)
Celli, Faith (1888–1942)
Centlivre, Susanna (c. 1669–1723)
Chabrillan, Céleste de (1824–1909)
Champion, Marge (1919—)
Champmesle, Marie (c. 1642–1698)
Chancellor, Joyce (1906—)
Chandler, Helen (1906–1965)
Chandler, Janet (1915–1994)
Chaney, Frances (1915–2004)
Channing, Carol (1921—)
Channing, Stockard (1944—)
Chapin, Anne Morrison (1892–1967)
Chaplin, Geraldine (1944—)
Chaplin, Lita Grey (1908–1995)
Chapman, Caroline (c. 1818–1876)
Chapman, Edythe (1863–1948)
Chapman, Marguerite (1918–1999)
Charisse, Cyd (1921—)
Charke, Charlotte Cibber (1713–1760)
Charleson, Mary (1890–1961)
Chase, Arline (1900–1926)
Chase, Barrie (1933—)
Chase, Ilka (1905–1978)
Chase, Lucia (1897–1986)
Chase, Pauline (1885–1962)
Chatterton, Ruth (1893–1961)
Chatwin, Margaret (c. 1881–1937)
Chen, Joan (1961—)
Chen Hong (1968—)
Cher (1946—)
Cherrill, Virginia (1908–1996)
Cherry, Helen (1915–2001)
Chester, Betty (1895–1943)
Chiaureli, Sofiko (1937—)
Childress, Alice (1916–1994)
Chin, Tsai (1937—)
Chisholm, Melanie (1974—)
Chitnis, Leela (1909–2003)
Christian, Linda (1923—)
Christians, Mady (1900–1951)
Christie, Julie (1941—)
Christine, Virginia (1920–1996)
Church, Esmé (1893–1972)
Churchill, Diana (1913–1994)
Churchill, Marguerite (1909–2000)
Churchill, Sarah (1914–1982)
Churilova, L.A. (1875–1937)
Cibber, Susannah (1714–1766)
Cicciolina (1951—)
Cigna, Gina (b. 1900)
Cilento, Diane (1933—)
Claire, Helen (1911–1974)
Claire, Ina (1892–1985)
Clairon, Mlle (1723–1802)
Clare, Ada (1836–1874)
Clare, Mary (1894–1970)
Clark, Cheryl (1950—)
Clark, Mamo (1914–1986)
Clark, Marguerite (1883–1940)
Clark, Petula (1932—)
Clarke, Mae (1907–1992)
Claxton, Kate (1848–1924)
Clayton, Ethel (1882–1966)
Clayton, Jan (1917–1983)
Clement-Scott, Margaret (fl. 19th c.)
Clifford, Camille (1885–1970)
Clifford, Kathleen (1887–1962)
Clifford, Ruth (1900–1998)
Cline, Maggie (1857–1934)
Clive, Kitty (1711–1785)
Clooney, Rosemary (1928–2002)
Close, Glenn (1947—)
Cloutier, Suzanne (1927–2003)
Clouzot, Vera (1921–1960)
Clyde, June (1909–1987)
Coates, Gloria (1938—)
Coca, Imogene (1909–2001)
Cocéa, Alice (1899–1970)
Coghlan, Gertrude (1876–1952)
Coghlan, Rose (1852–1932)
Cohan, Georgette (b. 1900)
Cohan, Helen F. (1910–1996)
Cohan, Josephine (1876–1916)
Colbert, Claudette (1903–1996)
Colby, Christine (c. 1950—)
Cole, Edith (1870–1927)
Cole, Kay (1948—)
Coleman, Fanny (1840–1919)
Coleman, Nancy (1912–2000)
Coleridge, Ethel (1883–1976)
Colette (1873–1954)
Colin, Jean (1905–1989)
Collier, Constance (1878–1955)
Collier, Lois (1919–1999)
Collier, Patience (1910–1987)
Collinge, Patricia (1892–1974)
Collins, Cora Sue (1927—)
Collins, Dorothy (1926–1994)
Collins, Jackie (1937—)
Collins, Joan (1933—)
Collins, José (1887–1958)
Collins, Pauline (1940—)
Collyer, June (1907–1968)
Colt, Ethel Barrymore (1912–1977)
Comingore, Dorothy (1913–1971)
Compson, Betty (1897–1974)
Compton, Betty (1907–1944)
Compton, Fay (1894–1978)
Compton, Katherine (1853–1928)
Compton, Madge (c. 1892–1970)
Compton, Viola (1886–1971)
Compton, Virginia (1853–1940)
Comstock, Nanette (1873–1942)
Conklin, Peggy (1902–2003)
Conner, Nadine (1907–2003)
Contat, Louise (1760–1813)
Contat, Marie (1769–1846)
Conti, Italia (1874–1946)
Cook, Barbara (1927—)
Cooper, Diana Duff (1892–1986)
Cooper, Dulcie (1903–1981)
Cooper, Elizabeth (fl. 1737)
Cooper, Gladys (1888–1971)
Cooper, Lillian Kemble (1891–1977)
Cooper, Violet Kemble (1886–1961)
Corbin, Virginia Lee (1910–1942)
Corby, Ellen (1911–1998)
Corday, Mara (1930—)
Corday, Rita (1920–1992)
Cordell, Cathleen (1915–1997)
Corio, Ann (1914–1999)
Cornell, Katharine (1893–1974)
Corri, Adrienne (1930—)
Cortesa, Valentina (1924—)
Costello, Dolores (1905–1979)
Costello, Helene (1903–1957)
Cotton, Lucy (c. 1891–1948)
Courau, Clotilde (1969—)
Courcel, Nicole (1930—)
Court, Hazel (1926—)
Courtneidge, Cicely (1893–1980)
Courtneidge, Rosaline (1903–1926)
Courtney, Inez (1908–1975)
Cowie, Laura (1892–1969)
Cowl, Jane (1883–1950)
Cox, Hazel (b. 1887)
Crabtree, Lotta (1847–1924)
Craig, Edith (1869–1947)
Craig, Edith (1907–1979)
Craig, Helen (1912–1986)
Craig, May (1889–1972)
Crain, Jeanne (1925–2003)
Crane, Norma (1928–1973)
Crawford, Cindy (1966—)
Crawford, Joan (1906–1977)
Crawford, Mimi (d. 1966)
Crews, Laura Hope (1879–1942)
Cristina, Ines (b. 1875)
Croizette, Sophie Alexandrine (1847–1901)
Crosman, Henrietta (1861–1944)
Crow, Sheryl (1962—)
Crowley, Pat (1929—)
Crutchley, Rosalie (1921–1997)
Cryer, Gretchen (1935—)
Cumming, Dorothy (1899–1983)
Cumming, Ruth (c. 1904–1967)
Cummings, Constance (1910–2005)
Cummings, Ruth (1894–1984)
Cummings, Vicki (1913–1969)

Cummins, Peggy (1925—)
Cunard, Grace (c. 1891–1967)
Cunningham, Sarah (1918–1986)
Currie, Cherie (1959—)
Curtis, Jamie Lee (1958—)
Curtright, Jorja (1923–1985)
Cushman, Charlotte Saunders (1816–1876)
Cushman, Pauline (1833–1893)
Cutler, Kate (1870–1955)
Cutts, Patricia (1926–1974)
Dagmar (1921–2001)
Dagover, Lil (1897–1980)
Dahl, Arlene (1924—)
Dahlbeck, Eva (1920—)
Dainton, Marie (1881–1938)
Dale, Esther (1885–1961)
Dale, Margaret (1876–1972)
Dale, Virginia (1917–1994)
Dal Monte, Toti (1893–1975)
Dalton, Doris (1910–1984)
Dalton, Dorothy (1893–1972)
Daly, Tyne (1946—)
Damita, Lili (1901–1994)
Damon, Cathryn (1930–1987)
Dana, Leora (1923–1983)
Dana, Marie Louise (c. 1876–1946)
Dandridge, Dorothy (1923–1965)
Daniele, Graciela (1939—)
Daniels, Bebe (1901–1971)
Danner, Blythe (1943—)
Darc, Mireille (1938—)
Darcel, Denise (1925—)
D'Arcy, Margaretta (1934—)
Dare, Phyllis (1890–1975)
Dare, Zena (1887–1975)
Darling, May (1887–1971)
Darnell, Linda (1921–1965)
d'Arnell, Nydia (d. 1970)
Darragh, Miss (d. 1917)
Darrieux, Danielle (1917—)
Darvas, Lili (1902–1974)
Darvi, Bella (1927–1971)
Darwell, Jane (1879–1967)
Daumier, Sophie (1934–2004)
Davenport, Fanny (1850–1898)
Davey, Nuna (1902–1977)
Davies, Betty Ann (1910–1955)
Davies, Lillian (1895–1932)
Davies, Marion (1897–1961)
Davies, Moll (fl. 1673)
Davis, Bette (1908–1989)
Davis, Fay (1872–1945)
Davis, Gail (1925–1997)
Davis, Joan (1907–1961)
Davis, Judy (1955—)
Daw, Evelyn (1912–1970)
Dawn, Dolly (1916–2002)
Dawn, Isabel (1905–1966)
Day, Doris (1924—)
Day, Edith (1896–1971)
Day, Frances (1907–1984)
Day, Josette (1914–1978)
Day, Laraine (1917—)
Daykarhanova, Tamara (1889–1980)
Deamer, Dulcie (1890–1972)
Dean, Julia (1830–1868)
Dean, Julia (1878–1952)
Deane, Doris (1900–1974)
de Banzie, Brenda (1915–1981)
Debenham, Cicely (1891–1955)
de Bray, Yvonne (1889–1954)
De Burgh, Aimée (d. 1946)
DeCamp, Rosemary (1910–2001)
De Carlo, Yvonne (1922—)
Dee, Frances (1907–2004)
Dee, Ruby (1923—)
Dee, Sandra (1942–2005)
Deering, Olive (1918–1986)
DeHaven, Gloria (1924—)
de Havilland, Olivia (1916—)
Déjazet, Pauline-Virginie (1797–1875)
De La Haye, Ina (1906–1972)
Delany, Maureen (d. 1961)
De Lappe, Gemze (1922—)
Del Rio, Dolores (1905–1983)
Del Vando, Amapola (1910–1988)
Delysia, Alice (1889–1979)
DeMille, Katherine (1911–1995)
Demongeot, Mylène (1936—)
Dench, Judy (1934—)
Deneuve, Catherine (1943—)
Denham, Isolde (1920—)
Denis, María (1916–2004)
Dennis, Sandy (1937–1992)
Dennison, Jo-Carroll (c. 1924—)
Denton, Sandy (1969—)
De Putti, Lya (1899–1932)
Deren, Maya (1908–1961)
Desclée, Aimée Olympe (1836–1874)
Desgarcins, Magdeleine Marie (1769–1797)
Deslys, Gaby (1884–1920)
Desmares, Christine (1682–1753)
Desmond, Florence (1905–1993)
De Sousa, May (1887–1948)
Desprès, Suzanne (1875–1951)
de Voie, Bessie (b. around 1888)
Dewhurst, Colleen (1924–1991)
de Wolfe, Elsie (1865–1950)
Diamond, Selma (1920–1985)
Dickinson, Angie (1931—)
Dickinson, Anna E. (1842–1932)
Dickson, Barbara (1947—)
Dickson, Dorothy (1893–1995)
Dickson, Gloria (1916–1945)
Dietrich, Marlene (1901–1992)
Dilley, Dorothy (b. around 1907)
Dillon, Melinda (1939—)
di Lorenzo, Tina (1872–1930)
Di Murska, Ilma (1836–1889)
Ditchburn, Ann (c. 1950—)
Dix, Beulah Marie (1876–1970)
Dix, Dorothy (1892–1970)
Dixon, Adele (1908–1992)
Dixon, Jean (1896–1981)
Doble, Frances (1902–1969)
Dodd, Claire (1908–1973)
Dolores (c. 1890–1975)
Domergue, Faith (1924–1999)
Donaldson, Norma (1928–1994)
DonHowe, Gwyda (1933–1988)
Donnell, Jeff (1921–1988)
Donnelly, Dorothy (1880–1928)
Doran, Ann (1911–2000)
Dorléac, Françoise (1942–1967)
D'Orme, Aileen (1877–1939)
Doro, Marie (1882–1956)
Dors, Diana (1931–1984)
D'Orsay, Fifi (1904–1983)
Dorval, Marie (1798–1849)
Dorziat, Gabrielle (1886–1979)
Dostalova, Leopolda (1879–1972)
Doucet, Catherine (1875–1958)
Douglas, Helen Gahagan (1900–1980)
Douglass, Margaret (d. 1949)
Dove, Billie (1900–1997)
Dovey, Alice (1884–1969)
Dow, Peggy (1928—)
Dowling, Constance (1920–1969)
Dowling, Doris (1921–2004)
Dowling, Joan (1928–1954)
Downing, Virginia (1904–1996)
Downs, Cathy (1924–1976)
Doyle, Patricia (d. 1975)
Dragonette, Jessica (1900–1980)
Drake, Betsy (1923—)
Drake, Dona (1914–1989)
Drake, Fabia (1904–1990)
Drake, Frances (1908–2000)
Drake, Frances Denny (1797–1875)
Draper, Ruth (1884–1956)
Dresdel, Sonia (1909–1976)
Dresser, Louise (1878–1965)
Dressler, Marie (1869–1934)
Drew, Ellen (1914–2003)
Drew, Georgiana Emma (1854–1893)
Drew, Louisa Lane (1820–1897)
Drew, Lucille (1890–1925)
Dronke, Minnie Maria (1904–1987)
Drouet, Juliette (1806–1883)
Dru, Joanne (1923–1996)
Drummond, Dolores (1834–1926)
Dubois, Marie (1937—)
Dudley, Doris (1917–1985)
Dudley-Ward, Penelope (1914–1982)
Duff, Mary Ann Dyke (1794–1857)
Dukakis, Olympia (1931—)
Duke, Patty (1946—)
Dumesnil, Marie Françoise (1713–1803)
Dumont, Margaret (1889–1965)
Duna, Steffi (1910–1992)
Dunaway, Faye (1941—)
Dunbar, Dixie (1915–1991)
Duncan, Mary (1895–1993)
Duncan, Sandy (1946—)
Duncan, Vivian (1902–1986)
Dunn, Emma (1875–1966)
Dunn, Josephine (1906–1983)
Dunne, Irene (1898–1990)
Dunnock, Mildred (1900–1991)
Dupree, Minnie (1873–1947)
Duprez, June (1918–1984)
Durand, Marguerite (1864–1936)
Durbin, Deanna (1921—)
Durieux, Tilla (1880–1971)
Duse, Eleonora (1858–1924)
Dux, Emilienne (b. 1874)
Duxbury, Elspeth (1909–1967)
Dvorak, Ann (1912–1979)
Dwan, Dorothy (1907–1981)
Dwyer, Ada (1863–1952)
Dybwad, Johanne (1867–1950)
Eagels, Jeanne (1894–1929)
Eames, Clare (1896–1930)
Eames, Virginia (1889–1971)
Earle, Virginia (1875–1937)
Eaton, Mary (1901–1948)
Eaton, Shirley (1937—)
Ebert, Joyce (1933–1997)
Eburne, Maude (1875–1960)
Eccles, Janet (1895–1966)
Eden, Barbara (1934—)
Ediss, Connie (1871–1934)
Edwards, Edna Park (c. 1895–1967)
Edwards, Gloria (1944–1988)
Edwards, Penny (1928–1998)
Eggar, Samantha (1938—)
Eggerth, Marta (1912—)
Ehre, Ida (1900–1989)
Eilers, Sally (1908–1978)
Eisinger, Irene (1903–1994)
Ekberg, Anita (1931—)
Eldridge, Florence (1901–1988)
Elg, Taina (1931—)
Eline, Grace (1898—)
Elliott, Gertrude (1874–1950)
Elliott, Madge (1896–1955)
Elliott, Maxine (1868–1940)
Ellis, Edith (c. 1874–1960)

Ellis, Evelyn (1894–1958)
Ellis, Lucille (c. 1915—)
Ellis, Mary (1897–2003)
Ellis, Patricia (1916–1970)
Elliston, Daisy (b. 1894)
Elsie, Lily (1886–1962)
Elsom, Isobel (1893–1981)
Elssler, Fanny (1810–1884)
Emerald, Connie (1891–1959)
Emerson, Faye (1917–1983)
Emerson, Hope (1897–1960)
Emery, Katherine (1906–1980)
Emery, Pollie (1875–1958)
Emery, Winifred (1862–1924)
Emmet, Katherine (c. 1882–1960)
Entwhistle, Peg (1908–1932)
Epstein, Marie (c. 1899–1995)
Ermolova, Mariia (1853–1928)
Esmond, Annie (1873–1945)
Esmond, Jill (1908–1990)
Espert, Nuria (1935—)
Essen, Viola (1926–1969)
Evans, Edith (1888–1976)
Evans, Joan (1934—)
Evans, Madge (1909–1981)
Evans, Renee (1908–1971)
Evelyn, Judith (1913–1967)
Everest, Barbara (1890–1968)
Exene (1956—)
Faber, Beryl (d. 1912)
Fabian, Françoise (1932—)
Fabray, Nanette (1920—)
Fair, Elinor (1902–1957)
Fairbrother, Sydney (1872–1941)
Fairfax, Lettice (1876–1948)
Faithfull, Marianne (1946—)
Falconetti, Renée (1892–1946)
Falkenburg, Jinx (1919–2003)
Farebrother, Violet (1888–1969)
Farmer, Frances (1913–1970)
Farmer, Virginia (1898–1988)
Farrar, Geraldine (1882–1967)
Farrar, Gwen (1899–1944)
Farrell, Glenda (1904–1971)
Farren, Elizabeth (c. 1759–1829)
Farren, Nellie (1848–1904)
Farrokhzad, Forugh (1935–1967)
Farrow, Mia (1945—)
Faucit, Helena Saville (1817–1898)
Favart, Edmée (1886–1941)
Favart, Marie (1727–1772)
Favart, Marie (b. 1833)
Fawcett, Marion (1886–1957)
Faye, Alice (1912–1998)
Faye, Julia (1893–1966)
Fazenda, Louise (1895–1962)
Fealy, Maude (1883–1971)
Feldman, Andrea (1948–1972)
Feldman, Gladys (1891–1974)
Félix, Lia (b. 1830)
Felix, Maria (1914–2002)
Fellows, Edith (1923—)
Felton, Verna (1890–1966)
Fenton, Lavinia (1708–1760)
Fenwick, Irene (1887–1936)
Ferguson, Elsie (1883–1961)
Fernandez, Bijou (1877–1961)
Ferrero, Anna-Maria (1931—)
Ferrers, Helen (1869–1943
Ferrier, Kathleen (1912–1953)
Feuillère, Edwige (1907–1998)
Feury, Peggy (1924–1985)
Field, Betty (1918–1973)
Field, Kate (1838–1896)
Field, Sally (1946—)
Field, Shirley Anne (1936—)
Field, Sylvia (1901–1998)
Field, Virginia (1917–1992)
Fields, Gracie (1898–1979)
Filippi, Rosina (1866–1930)
Filkins, Grace (c. 1865–1962)
Findlay, Ruth (1904–1949)
Fischer, Alice (1869–1947)
Fisher, Clara (1811–1898)
Fiske, Minnie Maddern (1865–1932)
Fitton, Doris (1897–1985)
Fitzgerald, Geraldine (1913–2005)
Fitzhenry, Mrs. (d. 1790?)
Fitzwilliam, Fanny Elizabeth (1801–1854)
Flagg, Fannie (1941—)
Flanagan, Sinéad (1878–1975)
Fleming, Alice (1882–1952)
Fleming, Rhonda (1922—)
Fletcher, Louise (1934—)
Flint, Helen (1898–1967)
Flon, Suzanne (1918–2005)
Flores, Lola (1924–1995)
Flory, Regine (1894–1926)
Flowers, Bess (1898–1984)
Flowerton, Consuelo (1900–1965)
Foch, Nina (1924—)
Fonda, Jane (1937—)
Fontaine, Joan (1917—)
Fontaine, Lillian (1886–1975)
Fontanne, Lynn (1887–1983)
Foote, Maria (c. 1797–1867)
Forbes, Brenda (1909–1996)
Forbes, Mary (1880–1974)
Forbes, Mary Elizabeth (1879–1964)
Forbes-Robertson, Beatrice (1883–1967)
Forbes-Robertson, Jean (1905–1962)
Forde, Victoria (1896–1964)
Forrest, Sally (1928—)
Fortescue, May (1862–1950)
Foster, Dianne (1928—)
Foster, Frances (1924–1997)
Foster, Gloria (1933–2001)
Foster, Jodie (1962—)
Foster, Lillian (d. 1949)
Foster, Susanna (1924—)
Fox, Della (1870–1913)
Fox, Sidney (1910–1942)
Foy, Madeline (1903–1988)
Foy, Mary (1901–1987)
Francine, Anne (1917–1999)
Francis, Anne (1930—)
Francis, Arlene (1908–2001)
Francis, Eve (1886–1980)
Francis, Kay (1899–1968)
Franklin, Irene (1876–1941)
Franklyn, Beth (c. 1873–1956)
Frasca, Mary (d. 1973)
Fraser, Agnes (1877–1968)
Fraser, Shelagh (1922–2000)
Frazee, Jane (1918–1985)
Frederick, Lynne (1954–1994)
Frederick, Pauline (1881–1938)
Freeman, Mona (1926—)
French, Dawn (1957—)
French, Valerie (1932–1990)
Fricker, Brenda (1945—)
Friebus, Florida (1909–1988)
Frith, Mary (c. 1584–1659)
Fubuki, Koshiji (1924–1980)
Fuller, Frances (1907–1980)
Fuller, Mary (1888–1973)
Fuller, Rosalinde (1901–1982)
Fulton, Maude (1881–1950)
Funicello, Annette (1942—)
Furneaux, Yvonne (1928—)
Furness, Betty (1916–1994)
Furse, Judith (1912–1974)
Gaal, Franciska (1904–1972)
Gabor, Eva (1919–1995)
Gabor, Magda (1914–1997)
Gabor, Zsa Zsa (1917—)
Gabors, The
Gallagher, Helen (1926—)
Galland, Bertha (1876–1932)
Gallatin, Alberta (c. 1861–1948)
Galloway, Louise (d. 1949)
Gam, Rita (1928—)
Gambarelli, Maria (1900–1990)
Garbo, Greta (1905–1990)
Garde, Betty (1905–1989)
Garden, Mary (1874–1967)
Gardner, Ava (1922–1990)
Gardner, Isabella (1915–1981)
Garland, Judy (1922–1969)
Garner, Peggy Ann (1931–1984)
Garon, Pauline (1900–1965)
Garrett, Betty (1919—)
Garson, Greer (1904–1996)
Gates, Nancy (1926—)
Gates, Ruth (1886–1966)
Gateson, Marjorie (1891–1977)
Gaughin, Lorraine (1924–1974)
Gauntier, Gene (1885–1966)
Gaynor, Janet (1906–1984)
Gaynor, Mitzi (1930—)
Geise, Sugar (1909–1988)
Geistinger, Marie (1833–1903)
Gencer, Leyla (1924—)
Géniat, Marcelle (1879–1959)
George, Gladys (1900–1954)
George, Grace (1879–1961)
George, Maude (1888–1963)
George, Muriel (1883–1965)
Georges, Marguerite J. (c. 1787–1867)
Geraghty, Carmelita (1901–1966)
Gersten, Berta (c. 1896–1972)
Gert, Valeska (1900–1978)
Gessner, Adrienne (1896–1987)
Geva, Tamara (1906–1997)
Gibson, Althea (1927—)
Gibson, Deborah (1970—)
Gibson, Dorothy (1889–1946)
Gibson, Helen (1892–1977)
Gibson, Wynne (1903–1987)
Gifford, Frances (1920–1994)
Gilbert, Anne (1821–1904)
Gilbert, Jody (1916–1979)
Gilbert, Mercedes (1894–1952)
Gilbert, Ronnie (1926—)
Gilbert, Ruth (d. 1993)
Gilchrist, Connie (1901–1985)
Gilliland, Helen (1897–1942)
Gillmore, Margalo (1897–1986)
Gillmore, Ruth (d. 1976)
Gilmore, Virginia (1919–1986)
Gingold, Hermione (1897–1987)
Girardot, Annie (1931—)
Gish, Dorothy (1898–1968)
Gish, Lillian (1893–1993)
Gitana, Gertie (1887–1957)
Givney, Kathryn (1896–1978)
Gladney, Edna (1886–1961)
Glaspell, Susan (1876–1948)
Gleason, Lucile (1886–1947)
Gless, Sharon (1943—)
Glover, Julia (1779–1850)
Glynne, Mary (1895–1954)
Goddard, Paulette (1905–1990)
Goering, Emmy (1893–1973)
Goffin, Cora (1902–2004)
Goldberg, Whoopi (1949—)
Gombell, Minna (1892–1973)
Gonne, Maud (1866–1953)

Goodrich, Edna (1883–1971)
Gordon, Hannah (1941—)
Gordon, Kitty (1878–1974)
Gordon, Mary (1882–1963)
Gordon, Noele (1923–1985)
Gordon, Ruth (1896–1985)
Gordon, Vera (1886–1948)
Goslar, Lotte (1907–1997)
Gould, Sandra (1916–1999)
Grable, Betty (1916–1973)
Gracen, Elizabeth (1960—)
Grahame, Gloria (1924–1981)
Grahame, Margot (1911–1982)
Gramatica, Emma (1875–1965)
Gramatica, Irma (1873–1962)
Grant, Kathryn (1933—)
Grant, Lee (1927—)
Grant, Valentine (1881–1949)
Granville, Bonita (1923–1988)
Gray, Coleen (1922—)
Gray, Dolores (1924–2002)
Gray, Dulcie (1919—)
Gray, Eve (1900–1983)
Gray, Gilda (1901–1959)
Gray, Sally (1916—)
Grayson, Kathryn (1922—)
Gréco, Juliette (1926—)
Green, Dorothy (1886–1961)
Green, Janet (1914–1993)
Green, Mitzi (1920–1969)
Greene, Angela (1921–1978)
Greenwood, Joan (1921–1987)
Greer, Jane (1924–2001)
Greet, Clare (1871–1939)
Gregg, Virginia (1916–1986)
Gregor, Nora (1901–1949)
Grenfell, Joyce (1910–1979)
Grew, Mary (1902–1971)
Grey, Denise (1896–1996)
Grey, Jane (1883–1944)
Grey, Katherine (1873–1950)
Grey, Nan (1918–1993)
Grey, Virginia (1917–2004)
Grier, Pam (1949—)
Griffies, Ethel (1878–1975)
Griffith, Corinne (1894–1979)
Grimes, Tammy (1934—)
Grisi, Giulia (1811–1869)
Groody, Louise (1897–1961)
Gueden, Hilde (1915–1988)
Guerrero, Maria (1867–1928)
Guilbert, Yvette (1865–1944)
Guild, Nancy (1925–1999)
Guimard, Marie Madeleine (1743–1816)
Guinan, Texas (1884–1933)
Gunning, Louise (1879–1960)
Gurie, Sigrid (1911–1969)
Gurney, Rachel (1920–2001)
Gwynn, Nell (1650–1687)
Gwynne, Anne (1918–2003)
Gynt, Greta (1916–2000)
Haas, Dolly (1910–1994)
Hackett, Joan (1942–1983)
Haden, Sara (1897–1981)
Hading, Jane (1859–1933)
Hagen, Jean (1923–1977)
Hagen, Nina (1955—)
Hagen, Uta (1919–2004)
Hale, Barbara (1921—)
Hale, Louise Closser (1872–1933)
Hall, Adelaide (1904–1993)
Hall, Geraldine (1905–1970)
Hall, Grayson (1923–1985)
Hall, Juanita (1901–1968)
Hall, Natalie (1904–1994)
Hallam, Mrs. Lewis (?–1774)
Halliwell, Geri (1972—)
Halls, Ethel May (1882–1967)
Hamilton, Carrie (1963–2002)
Hamilton, Cicely (1872–1952)
Hamilton, Emma (1765–1815)
Hamilton, Margaret (1902–1985)
Hamlett, Dilys (1928–2002)
Hammerstein, Dorothy (1899–1987)
Hammerstein, Elaine (1897–1948)
Hammond, Dorothy (c. 1876–1950)
Hammond, Kay (1909–1980)
Hammond, Virginia (1893–1972)
Hamper, Geneviève (c. 1889–1971)
Hampshire, Susan (1938—)
Hampton, Hope (1897–1982)
Hanson, Gladys (1883–1973)
Hara, Setsuko (1920—)
Harareet, Haya (1931—)
Harding, Ann (1902–1981)
Harlow, Jean (1911–1937)
Harlowe, Sarah (1765–1852)
Harned, Virginia (1872–1946)
Harper, Valerie (1940—)
Harrigan, Nedda (1899–1989)
Harris, Barbara (1935—)
Harris, Edna Mae (1910–1997)
Harris, Julie (1925—)
Harris, Mildred (1901–1944)
Harris, Rosemary (1927—)
Harrison, June (1925–1974)
Harrison, Kathleen (1892–1995)
Harry, Deborah (1945—)
Hart, Dolores (1938—)
Hartley, Mariette (1940—)
Hartman, Elizabeth (1941–1987)
Hartman, Grace (1907–1955)
Harvey, Georgette (c. 1882–1952)
Harvey, Lilian (1906–1968)
Hasselqvist, Jenny (1894–1978)
Hasso, Signe (1910—)
Haver, June (1926—)
Havoc, June (1916—)
Hawn, Goldie (1945—)
Hawtrey, Marjory (1900–1952)
Hay, Mary (1901–1957)
Haydon, Ethel (1878–1954)
Haydon, Julie (1910–1994)
Haye, Helen (1874–1957)
Hayek, Salma (1966—)
Hayes, Allison (1930–1977)
Hayes, Helen (1900–1993)
Hayes, Maggie (1916–1977)
Hayes, Patricia (1909–1998)
Hayman, Lillian (1922–1994)
Hayward, Susan (c. 1917–1975)
Haywood, Eliza (c. 1693–1756)
Hayworth, Rita (1918–1987)
Heckart, Eileen (1919–2001)
Hedman, Martha (1883–1974)
Hedren, Tippi (1931—)
Heiberg, Johanne Luise (1812–1890)
Held, Anna (c. 1865–1918)
Helm, Brigitte (1908–1996)
Helmond, Katherine (1934—)
Heming, Violet (1895–1981)
Hemingway, Margaux (1955–1996)
Hemingway, Marie (c. 1893–1939)
Hemingway, Mariel (1961—)
Hemsley, Estelle (1887–1968)
Hendel, Henriette (1772–1849)
Henderson, Jo (1934–1988)
Hendrix, Wanda (1928–1981)
Henie, Sonja (1912–1969)
Henley, Beth (1952—)
Henning, Eva (1920—)
Hennings, Betty (1850–1939)
Hennings, Emmy (1885–1948)
Henry, Charlotte (1913–1980)
Hepburn, Audrey (1929–1993)
Hepburn, Katharine (1907—)
Herford, Beatrice (c. 1868–1952)
Herlie, Eileen (1919—)
Herne, Chrystal (1882–1950)
Herne, Katharine Corcoran (1857–1943)
Heron, Matilda (1830–1877)
Hervey, Irene (1910–1998)
Hessling, Catherine (1899–1979)
Heywood, Anne (1932—)
Hicks, Betty Seymour (1904—)
Hickson, Joan (1906–1998)
Hidari, Sachiko (1930–2001)
Hidari Sachiko (1930—)
Hiller, Wendy (1912—)
Hilliard, Harriet (1909–1994)
Hilliard, Patricia (1916–2001)
Hines, Elizabeth (1899–1971)
Hippisley, E. (fl. 1741–1766)
Hippisley, Jane (d. 1791)
Hird, Thora (1911–2003)
Hobart, Rose (1906–2000)
Hobson, Valerie (1917–1998)
Hodges, Joy (1914–2003)
Hodson, Henrietta (1841–1910)
Hoey, Iris (1885–1979)
Holden, Fay (1893–1973)
Holden, Gloria (1908–1991)
Holliday, Jennifer (1960—)
Holliday, Judy (1921–1965)
Holm, Celeste (1919—)
Holman, Libby (1904–1971)
Holmes, Helen (1892–1950)
Holt, Jennifer (1920–1997)
Holtrop-van Gelder, Betty (1866–1962)
Homan, Gertrude (1880–1951)
Honner, Maria (1812–1870)
Hood, Darla (1931–1979)
Hopkins, Miriam (1902–1972)
Hopkins, Pauline E. (1859–1930)
Hoppe, Marianne (1909–2002)
Hopper, Victoria (1909—)
Horn, Camilla (1903–1996)
Horne, Lena (1917—)
Horney, Brigitte (1911–1988)
Horton, Christiana (c. 1696–c. 1756)
Hosain, Attia (1913–1998)
Howard, Cordelia (1848–1941)
Howard, Esther (1892–1965)
Howard, Frances (1903–1976)
Howard, Jean (1910–2000)
Howard, Kathleen (1879–1956)
Howes, Sally Ann (1930—)
Howland, Jobyna (1880–1936)
Hoyt, Julia (c. 1897–1955)
Huang Zongying (1925—)
Huber, Gusti (1914–1993)
Hu Die (1908–1989)
Hudson, Rochelle (1916–1972)
Huff, Louise (1895–1973)
Hughes, Annie (1869–1954)
Hughes, Kathleen (1928—)
Hughes, Mary Beth (1919–1995)
Hughes, Wendy (1950—)
Hull, Josephine (1886–1957)
Hume, Benita (1906–1967)
Hunt, Helen (1963—)
Hunt, Marsha (1917—)
Hunt, Martita (1900–1969)
Hunter, Holly (1958—)
Hunter, Kim (1922–2002)
Hupalo, Katherine (1890–1974)
Huppert, Isabelle (1953—)
Hurst, Fannie (1889–1968)

Hussey, Ruth (1911–2005)
Huston, Anjelica (1951—)
Hutchinson, Josephine (1903–1998)
Hutchison, Muriel (1915–1975)
Hutton, Betty (1921—)
Hutton, Lauren (1943—)
Hyams, Leila (1905–1977)
Hyer, Martha (1924—)
Hyland, Diana (1936–1977)
Hyland, Frances (1927–2004)
Hylton, Jane (1927–1979)
Hyman, Phyllis (1949–1995)
Hyson, Dorothy (1914–1996)
Illington, Margaret (1881–1934)
Illington, Marie (d. 1927)
Inchbald, Elizabeth (1753–1821)
Inescort, Elaine (c. 1877–1964)
Inescort, Frieda (1900–1976)
Inness, Jean (1900–1978)
Intropodi, Ethel (d. 1946)
Ireland, Jill (1936–1990)
Irving, Ethel (1869–1963)
Irving, Isabel (1871–1944)
Irving, Margaret (1898–1988)
Irwin, May (1862–1938)
Ivan, Rosalind (1880–1959)
Jackson, Anne (1926—)
Jackson, Ethel (1877–1957)
Jackson, Freda (1909–1990)
Jackson, Glenda (1936—)
Jackson, Janet (1966—)
Jacob, Naomi Ellington (1889–1964)
Jacobini, Maria (1890–1944)
Jacobson, Henrietta (1906–1988)
Jacobsson, Ulla (1929–1982)
Jagemann, Karoline (1777–1848)
James, Cheryl (1964—)
James, Claire (1920–1986)
Jameson, Joyce (1932–1987)
Janauschek, Fanny (1829–1904)
Janis, Elsie (1889–1956)
Jay, Harriett (1863–1932)
Jay, Isabel (1879–1927)
Jean, Gloria (1926—)
Jeanmaire, Zizi (1924—)
Jeans, Isabel (1891–1985)
Jeans, Ursula (1906–1973)
Jeffreys, Anne (1923—)
Jeffreys, Ellis (1872–1943)
Jehan, Noor (1926–2000)
Jenner, Andrea (1891–1985)
Jens, Salome (1935—)
Jergens, Adele (1917–2002)
Jeritza, Maria (1887–1982)
Jerome, Helen (b. 1883)
Jerome, Rowena (1889–?)
Jerrold, Mary (1877–1955)
Jessel, Patricia (1929–1968)
Jett, Joan (1958—)
Jewell, Isabel (1907–1972)
Jiang Qing (1914–1991)
Jiménez, Soledad (1874–1966)
Johann, Zita (1904–1993)
Johansen, Aud (1930—)
John, Rosamund (1913–1998)
Johns, Glynis (1923—)
Johnson, Celia (1908–1982)
Johnson, Katie (1878–1957)
Johnson, Kay (1904–1975)
Johnson, Rita (1912–1965)
Johnson, Sunny (1953–1984)
Johnston, Julanne (1900–1988)
Johnston, Margaret (1917–2002)
Johnstone, Justine (1895–1982)
Jones, Anissa (1958–1976)
Jones, Carolyn (1929–1983)
Jones, Gwyneth (1936—)
Jones, Hazel (1896–1974)
Jones, Jennifer (1919—)
Jones, Shirley (1934—)
Jordan, Dora (1761–1816)
Jordan, Dorothy (1906–1988)
Joy, Leatrice (1893–1985)
Joyce, Alice (1889–1955)
Joyce, Brenda (1915—)
Joyce, Peggy Hopkins (1893–1957)
Joyeux, Odette (1914–2000)
Judd, Ashley (1968—)
Judge, Arline (1912–1974)
Jurado, Katy (1924–2002)
Jurinac, Sena (1921—)
Kahn, Florence (1878–1951)
Kahn, Lilly (c. 1898–1978)
Kahn, Madeline (1942–1999)
Kalich, Bertha (1874–1939)
Kaminska, Ida (1899–1980)
Kane, Gail (1887–1966)
Kane, Helen (1903–1966)
Kane, Marjorie (1909–1992)
Kanin, Fay (1917—)
Kaplan, Nelly (1931—)
Karalli, Vera (1889–1972)
Karina, Anna (1940—)
Karioka, Tahiya (c. 1921–1999)
Karnilova, Maria (1920–2001)
Kashfi, Anna (1934—)
Kautsky, Minna (1837–1912)
Kean, Ellen (1805–1880)
Kean, Jane (1924—)
Keane, Doris (1881–1945)
Keaton, Diane (1946—)
Kedrova, Lila (1918–2000)
Keeler, Ruby (1909–1993)
Keeley, Mary Anne (c. 1806–1899)
Keene, Laura (c. 1826–1873)
Kelety, Julia (d. 1972)
Kellerman, Annette (1886–1975)
Kellerman, Sally (1936—)
Kelly, Dorothy (1894–1966)
Kelly, Ethel (1875–1949)
Kelly, Grace (1928–1982)
Kelly, Judy (1913–1991)
Kelly, Kitty (1902–1968)
Kelly, Nancy (1921–1995)
Kelly, Patsy (1910–1981)
Kelly, Paula (1939—)
Kelton, Pert (1907–1968)
Kemble, Eliza (1761–1836)
Kemble, Elizabeth (c. 1763–1841)
Kemble, Fanny (1809–1893)
Kemble, Maria Theresa (1774–1838)
Kemble, Priscilla (1756–1845)
Kempson, Rachel (1910–2003)
Kemp-Welch, Joan (1906–1999)
Kendal, Felicity (1946—)
Kendal, Madge (1849–1935)
Kendall, Kay (1926–1959)
Kennedy, Madge (1890–1987)
Kennedy, Merna (1908–1944)
Kent, Allegra (1937—)
Kent, Barbara (b. 1906)
Kent, Jean (1921—)
Kenyon, Doris (1897–1979)
Kerima (1925—)
Kerr, Deborah (1921—)
Kershaw, Willette (1890–1960)
Keyes, Evelyn (1919—)
Khambatta, Persis (1950–1998)
Kholodnya, Vera (1893–1919)
Khote, Durga (c. 1905–1991)
Kibbee, Lois (1922–1993)
Kidder, Kathryn (1867–1939)
Kidder, Margot (1948—)
Kidman, Nicole (1967—)
King, Andrea (1919–2003)
King, Jane (d. 1971)
King, Mabel (1932–1999)
King, Mollie (1885–1981)
King, Nellie (1895–1935)
Kingsley, Susan (1946–1984)
Kinsella, Kathleen (d. 1961)
Kirk, Phyllis (1926—)
Kirkland, Muriel (1903–1971)
Kirkwood, Pat (1921—)
Kitt, Eartha (1928—)
Knapp, Evalyn (1908–1981)
Knef, Hildegard (1925—)
Knef, Hildegard (1925–2002)
Knight, June (1913–1987)
Knight, Shirley (1936—)
Knipp, Mrs. (fl. 1670)
Knipper-Chekova, Olga (1870–1959)
Knowles, Beyoncé (1981—)
Knox, Elyse (1917—)
Knudsen, Peggy (1923–1980)
Kobart, Ruth (1924–2002)
Koch, Marianne (1930—)
Kohner, Susan (1936—)
Kolb, Thérèse (1856–1935)
Komissarzhevskaya, Vera (1864–1910)
Konstam, Phyllis (1907–1976)
Korjus, Miliza (1900–1980)
Kornman, Mary (1915–1973)
Koscina, Sylva (1933–1994)
Kosta, Tessa (1893–1981)
Kotopoúli, Maríka (1887–1954)
Krestovskaya, Maria V. (1862–1910)
Kruger, Alma (1868–1960)
Kulp, Nancy (1921–1991)
Kurishima, Sumiko (1902–1987)
Kuznetsova, Maria (1880–1966)
Kvapilova, Hana (1860–1907)
Kwan, Nancy (1939—)
Kyo, Machiko (1924—)
Laage, Barbara (1920–1988)
La Badie, Florence (1888–1917)
Lacis, Asja (1891–1979)
Lacombe, Claire (1765–?)
Lacy, Harriette Deborah (1807–1874)
Ladd, Diane (1932—)
La Follette, Fola (1882–1970)
Lafont, Bernadette (1938—)
Lake, Alice (1895–1967)
Lake, Florence (1904–1980)
Lake, Veronica (1919–1973)
Lamarque, Libertad (1908–2000)
La Marr, Barbara (c. 1896–1926)
Lamarr, Hedy (1913–2000)
Lamour, Dorothy (1914–1996)
Lampert, Zohra (1937—)
Lancaster-Wallis, Ellen (1856–?)
Lanchester, Elsa (1902–1986)
Landi, Elissa (1904–1948)
Landin, Hope (1893–1973)
Landis, Carole (1919–1948)
Landis, Jessie Royce (1904–1972)
Lane, Grace (1876–1956)
Lane, Lola (1909–1981)
Lane, Priscilla (1917–1995)
Lane, Rosemary (1914–1974)
Lang, June (1915—)
Lang, K.D. (1961—)
Lange, Anne Françoise Elizabeth (1772–1816)
Lange, Hope (1931–2003)
Lange, Jessica (1949—)
Langford, Frances (1914–2005)
Langtry, Lillie (1853–1929)
Lanphier, Fay (1906–1959)

Lansbury, Angela (1925—)
Lansing, Joi (1928–1972)
LaPlanche, Rosemary (1923–1979)
La Plante, Laura (1904–1996)
La Plante, Lynda (1946—)
La Roy, Rita (1907–1993)
Larrimore, Francine (1898–1975)
Larsen, Gerd (1920–2001)
La Rue, Grace (1880–1956)
Lascelles, Ernita (1890–1972)
Latimer, Sally (1910—)
Laurie, Piper (1932—)
Lavallière, Eve (c. 1866–1929)
La Verne, Lucille (1869–1945)
Lavi, Daliah (1940—)
LaVoe, Spivy (1906–1971)
Lawrance, Jody (1930–1986)
Lawrence, Carol (1932—)
Lawrence, Florence (1886–1938)
Lawrence, Gertrude (1898–1952)
Lawrence, Margaret (1889–1929)
Lawrence, Marjorie (1908–1979)
Lawson, Mary (1910–1941)
Lawson, Priscilla (1914–1958)
Lawson, Winifred (1892–1961)
Laye, Evelyn (1900–1996)
Lazzari, Carolina (c. 1889–1946)
Leachman, Cloris (1926—)
Leander, Zarah (1907–1981)
Leblanc, Georgette (c. 1875–1941)
Leclerc, Ginette (1912–1992)
Leclercq, Carlotta (c. 1840–1893)
Leclercq, Rose (c. 1845–1899)
Lecouvreur, Adrienne (1690–1730)
Lederer, Gretchen (1891–1955)
Lee, Anna (1913–2004)
Lee, Auriol (1880–1941)
Lee, Belinda (1935–1961)
Lee, Dixie (1911–1952)
Lee, Gwen (1904–1961)
Lee, Gypsy Rose (1914–1970)
Lee, Jennie (c. 1846–1930)
Lee, Lila (1901–1973)
Lee, Peggy (1920–2002)
Lee, Ruth (1895–1975)
Leeds, Andrea (1913–1984)
Le Gallienne, Eva (1899–1991)
LeGon, Jeni (1916—)
Lehmann, Beatrix (1903–1979)
Leigh, Janet (1927–2004)
Leigh, Vivien (1913–1967)
Leighton, Margaret (1922–1976)
Lender, Marcelle (fl. 1890–1914)
Lenihan, Winifred (1898–1964)
LeNoire, Rosetta (1911–2002)
Lenya, Lotte (1898–1981)
Leontovich, Eugénie (1894–1993)
Leslie, Bethel (1929–1999)
Leslie, Gladys (1899–1976)
Leslie, Joan (1925—)
Leslie, Miriam Folline Squier (1836–1914)
Levey, Ethel (1880–1955)
Levi, Natalia (1901–1972)
Lewis, Abby (1910–1997)
Lewis, Bertha (1887–1931)
Lewis, Bobo (1926–1998)
Lewis, Cathy (1916–1968)
Lewis, Elma (1921—)
Lewis, Vera (1873–1956)
Lillie, Beatrice (1894–1989)
Lincoln, Abbey (1930—)
Lind, Jenny (1820–1887)
Lind, Letty (1862–1923)
Lindblom, Gunnel (1931—)
Lindfors, Viveca (1920–1995)
Lindley, Audra (1918–1997)
Lindo, Olga (1899–1968)
Lindsay, Margaret (1910–1981)
Linn, Bambi (1926—)
Lipkowska, Lydia (1882–1958)
Lipman, Clara (1869–1952)
Lipman, Maureen (1946—)
Lisi, Virna (1936—)
Lister, Moira (1923—)
Litchfield, Harriett (1777–1854)
Littlewood, Joan (1914–2002)
Litton, Marie (1847–1884)
Livingston, Margaret (1896–1984)
Lloyd, Doris (1896–1968)
Lloyd, Marie (1870–1922)
Locke, Katherine (1910–1995)
Lockhart, June (1925—)
Lockhart, Kathleen (1894–1978)
Lockwood, Margaret (1916–1990)
Loden, Barbara (1932–1980)
Loebinger, Lotte (1905–1999)
Loftus, Cissie (1876–1943)
Loftus, Kitty (1867–1927)
Logan, Ella (1913–1969)
Logan, Olive (1839–1909)
Löhr, Marie (1890–1975)
Lollobrigida, Gina (1927—)
Lombard, Carole (1908–1942)
London, Julie (1926–2000)
Loos, Anita (1893–1981)
Lopez, Encarnación (1898–1945)
Loraine, Violet (1886–1956)
Lord, Marjorie (1918—)
Lord, Pauline (1890–1950)
Lorde, Athena (1915–1973)
Loren, Sophia (1934—)
Lorraine, Emily (c. 1878–1944)
Losch, Tilly (1903–1975)
Loudon, Dorothy (1933–2003)
Louise, Anita (1915–1970)
Louise, Tina (1934—)
Love, Bessie (1898–1986)
Love, Darlene (1938—)
Love, Mabel (1874–1953)
Lovelace, Linda (1952–2002)
Lovell, Maria Anne (1803–1877)
Lovely, Louise (1895–1980)
Lowry, Judith (1890–1976)
Loy, Myrna (1905–1993)
Lualdi, Antonella (1931—)
Luce, Claire (1903–1989)
Luchaire, Corinne (1921–1950)
Lulu (1948—)
Lumley, Joanna (1946—)
Lundequist, Gerda (1871–1959)
Lupino, Ida (1914–1995)
Luxford, Nola (1895–1994)
Lyell, Lottie (1890–1925)
Lynn, Diana (1926–1971)
Lynn, Sharon (1901–1963)
Lynn, Vera (1917—)
Lynne, Elizabeth (1948—)
Lynne, Gillian (1926—)
MacArthur, Mary (1930–1949)
MacDonald, Blossom (1895–1978)
MacDonald, Christie (1875–1962)
MacDonald, Jeanette (1903–1965)
MacFadden, Gertrude (c. 1900–1967)
MacGibbon, Harriet (1905–1987)
MacGill, Moyna (1895–1975)
MacGrath, Leueen (1914–1992)
MacGraw, Ali (1938—)
Mack, Helen (1913–1986)
Mack, Nila (1891–1953)
Mackaill, Dorothy (1903–1990)
MacKinlay, Jean Sterling (1882–1958)
MacLaine, Shirley (1934—)
MacMahon, Aline (1899–1991)
Macpherson, Jeanie (1887–1946)
Maddern, Merle (1887–1984)
Madison, Cleo (1883–1964)
Madison, Helene (1913–1970)
Madonna (1958—)
Magnani, Anna (1908–1973)
Main, Marjorie (1890–1975)
Major, Clare Tree (d. 1954)
Makarova, Inna (1928—)
Makarova, Natalia (1940—)
Makarova, Tamara (1907–1997)
Malibran, Maria (1808–1836)
Malina, Judith (1926—)
Mallory, Boots (1913–1958)
Malo, Gina (1909–1963)
Malone, Dorothy (1925—)
Malyon, Eily (1879–1961)
Manchester, Melissa (1951—)
Mangano, Silvana (1930–1989)
Mann, Erika (1905–1969)
Mannering, Mary (1876–1953)
Mannheim, Lucie (1899–1976)
Manning, Irene (1912–2004)
Mansfield, Jayne (1933–1967)
Mansfield, Martha (1899–1923)
Manès, Gina (1893–1989)
Mara, Adele (1923—)
Marble, Mary (d. 1965)
March, Eve (1910–1974)
Marchal, Arlette (1902–1984)
Marchand, Corinne (1937—)
Marchand, Nancy (1928–2000)
Marden, Adrienne (1909–1978)
Maretskaya, Vera (1906–1978)
Margo (1918–1985)
Margolin, Janet (1943–1993)
Marinoff, Fania (1890–1971)
Maris, Mona (1903–1991)
Maritza, Sari (1910–1987)
Marken, Jeanne (1895–1976)
Markey, Enid (1891–1981)
Marley, Cedella (1967—)
Marlowe, Julia (1866–1950)
Marlowe, June (1903–1984)
Marlowe, Nora (1915–1977)
Marly, Florence (1918–1978)
Marquet, Mary (1895–1979)
Mars, Ann Françoise (1779–1847)
Marsh, Jean (1934—)
Marsh, Joan (1913–2000)
Marsh, Mae (1895–1968)
Marsh, Marian (1913—)
Marshall, Brenda (1915–1992)
Marshall, Penny (1942—)
Marshall, Trudy (1922–2004)
Marson, Aileen (1912–1939)
Martin, Helen (1909–2000)
Martin, Marion (1908–1985)
Martin, Mary (1913–1990)
Martin, Millicent (1934—)
Martin, Vivian (1893–1987)
Martinelli, Elsa (1932—)
Marx, Susan Fleming (1908–2002)
Masina, Giulietta (1920–1994)
Maskell, Virginia (1936–1968)
Mason, Ann (c. 1898–1948)
Mason, Marsha (1942—)
Mason, Pamela (1918–1996)
Mason, Shirley (1900–1979)
Massari, Lea (1933—)
Massary, Fritzi (1882–1969)
Massen, Osa (1916–2006)
Massey, Edith (1918–1984)
Massey, Ilona (1910–1974)
Massingham, Dorothy (1889–1933)

Mathews, Carmen (1914–1995)
Mathis, June (1892–1927)
Matteson, Ruth (1909–1975)
Matthews, Jessie (1907–1981)
Matthison, Edith (1875–1955)
Mattocks, Isabella (1746–1826)
Mattox, Martha (1879–1933)
Maude, Margery (1889–1979)
Maule, Annabel (1922—)
Maura, Carmen (1945—)
Maurey, Nicole (1925—)
Maurice, Mary (1844–1918)
Maxwell, Lois (1927—)
Maxwell, Marilyn (1921–1972)
Maxwell, Vera (c. 1892–1950)
May, Edna (1875–1948)
May, Elaine (1932—)
May, Gisela (1924—)
Mayhew, Kate (1853–1944)
Mayo, Margaret (1882–1951)
Mayo, Virginia (1920–2005)
McAliskey, Roisin (1971—)
McAvoy, May (1901–1984)
McCambridge, Mercedes (1916–2004)
McCarthy, Lillah (1875–1960)
McCarthy, Patricia (1911–1943)
McCarty, Mary (1923–1980)
McCarty, Patti (1921–1985)
McComas, Carroll (1886–1962)
McCormack, Patty (1945—)
McCracken, Esther Helen (1902–1971)
McCracken, Joan (1922–1961)
McDaniel, Hattie (1895–1952)
McDevitt, Ruth (1895–1976)
McDonagh, Isobel (1899–1982)
McDonald, Audra (1970—)
McDonald, Grace (1918–1999)
McDonald, Marie (1923–1965)
McDormand, Frances (1957—)
McDowell, Claire (1877–1966)
McEntire, Reba (1955—)
McEwan, Geraldine (1932—)
McGuire, Dorothy (1916–2001)
McGuire, Kathryn (1903–1978)
McIntosh, Madge (1875–1950)
McIntyre, Molly (c. 1886–1952)
McKenna, Siobhan (1922–1986)
McKenna, Virginia (1931—)
McKenzie, Ella (1911–1987)
McKenzie, Eva B. (1889–1967)
McKenzie, Ida Mae (1911–1986)
McKenzie, Julia (1941—)
McKinney, Nina Mae (c. 1912–1967)
McKnight, Marian (c. 1937—)
McLennan, Margo (1938–2004)
McLeod, Catherine (1921–1997)
McLerie, Allyn Ann (1926—)
McNamara, Maggie (1928–1978)
McNeil, Claudia (1917–1993)
McQueen, Thelma (1911–1995)
Meadows, Audrey (1922–1996)
Meadows, Jayne (1920—)
Medford, Kay (1914–1980)
Medina, Patricia (1919—)
Meiser, Edith (1898–1993)
Mell, Marisa (1939–1992)
Meller, Raquel (1888–1962)
Mellon, Sarah Jane (1824–1909)
Melmoth, Charlotte (1749–1823)
Melnotte, Violet (1856–1935)
Melville, June (1915–1970)
Melville, Rose (1873–1946)
Menken, Adah Isaacs (1835–1868)
Menken, Helen (1901–1966)
Menken, Marie (1909–1970)
Merande, Doro (1892–1975)
Mercer, Beryl (1882–1939)
Mercer, Frances (1915–2000)
Merchant, Vivien (1929–1983)
Mercouri, Melina (1923–1994)
Meredith, Iris (1915–1980)
Meriwether, Lee Ann (1935—)
Merkel, Una (1903–1986)
Merman, Ethel (1912–1984)
Merrall, Mary (1890–1973)
Merriam, Charlotte (1906–1972)
Merrill, Beth (1892–1986)
Merrill, Dina (1925—)
Merritt, Theresa (1924–1998)
Merry, Ann Brunton (1769–1808)
Methot, Mayo (1904–1951)
Meysel, Inge (1910–2004)
Michael, Gertrude (1910–1965)
Michelena, Beatriz (1890–1942)
Midler, Bette (1945—)
Mikey, Fanny (1931—)
Miles, Sarah (1941—)
Miles, Sylvia (1932—)
Miles, Vera (1929—)
Millar, Gertie (1879–1952)
Millard, Evelyn (1869–1941)
Millard, Ursula (b. 1901)
Millay, Norma (d. 1986)
Miller, Ann (1919–2004)
Miller, Colleen (1932—)
Miller, Marilyn (1898–1936)
Miller, Patsy Ruth (1904–1995)
Mills, Hayley (1946—)
Mills, Stephanie (1957—)
Milo, Sandra (1935—)
Miner, Jan (1917–2004)
Minnelli, Liza (1946—)
Minter, Mary Miles (1902–1984)
Miou-Miou (1950—)
Miramova, Elena (c. 1905—)
Miranda, Carmen (1909–1955)
Miranda, Isa (1909–1982)
Mireille (1906–1996)
Mirren, Helen (1945—)
Mistinguett (1875–1956)
Mitchell, Abbie (1884–1960)
Mitchell, Margaret J. (1832–1918)
Mitchell, Yvonne (1925–1979)
Mobley, Mary Ann (1939—)
Modjeska, Helena (1840–1909)
Moholy-Nagy, Sibyl (1903–1971)
Molander, Karin (1889–1978)
Moncrieff, Gladys (1892–1976)
Monica (1980—)
Monroe, Marilyn (1926–1962)
Montagu, Elizabeth (1909–2002)
Montansier, Marguerite (1730–1820)
Montealegre, Felicia (d. 1978)
Montez, Lola (1818–1861)
Montez, Maria (1918–1951)
Montgomery, Elizabeth (1933–1995)
Montgomery, Goodee (1906–1978)
Montgomery, Peggy (1917—)
Montiel, Sarita (1928—)
Mooney, Ria (1904–1973)
Moore, Cleo (1928–1973)
Moore, Colleen (1900–1988)
Moore, Constance (1919–2005)
Moore, Decima (1871–1964)
Moore, Eva (1870–1955)
Moore, Ida (1882–1964)
Moore, Jessie (1865–1910)
Moore, Juanita (1922—)
Moore, Maggie (1847–1929)
Moore, Mary Tyler (1936—)
Moore, Terry (1929—)
Moorehead, Agnes (1900–1974)
Moran, Dolores (1924–1982)
Moran, Lois (1907–1990)
Moran, Peggy (1918–2002)
Moran, Polly (1884–1952)
More, Jane Colt (c. 1488–1511)
Moreau, Jeanne (1928—)
Moreno, Marguerite (1871–1948)
Moreno, Rita (1931—)
Morgan, Claudia (1912–1974)
Morgan, Helen (1900–1941)
Morgan, Joan (1905–2004)
Morgan, Michèle (1920—)
Morgan, Robin (1941—)
Morison, Patricia (1914—)
Morissette, Alanis (1974—)
Morlay, Gaby (1893–1964)
Morley, Karen (1905–2003)
Morris, Anita (1943–1994)
Morris, Clara (1847–1925)
Morris, Mary (1895–1970)
Morris, Mary (1915–1988)
Morrison, Adrienne (1889–1940)
Morrison, Ann (1916–1978)
Morrow, Doretta (1927–1968)
Mortimer, Dorothy (1898–1950)
Morton, Clara (c. 1882–1948)
Mosheim, Grete (1905–1986)
Mosquini, Marie (1899–1983)
Mostel, Kate (1918–1986)
Moten, Etta (1901–2004)
Mowatt, Anna Cora (1819–1870)
Muir, Esther (1903–1995)
Muir, Jean (1928–1995)
Mullen, Barbara (1914–1979)
Müller, Renate (1907–1937)
Munro, Janet (1934–1972)
Munson, Ona (1894–1955)
Murphy, Edna (1899–1974)
Murphy, Mary (1931—)
Murray, Katherine (1894–1974)
Murray, Kathleen (d. 1969)
Murray, Mae (1885–1965)
Musidora (1884–1957)
Mussolini, Alessandra (1962—)
Myrtil, Odette (1898–1978)
Nagel, Anne (1915–1966)
Naldi, Nita (1897–1961)
Nansen, Betty (1873–1943)
Napierkowska, Stacia (1886–1945)
Nash, Florence (1888–1950)
Nash, June (1911–1979)
Nash, Mary (1885–1976)
Nat, Marie-José (1940—)
Natwick, Mildred (1908–1994)
Nazimova, Alla (1879–1945)
Neagle, Anna (1904–1986)
Neal, Patricia (1926—)
Negri, Pola (1894–1987)
Neher, Carola (1900–1942)
Neilson, Adelaide (1846–1880)
Neilson, Julia Emilie (1868–1957)
Neilson-Terry, Phyllis (1892–1977)
Nelson, Ruth (1905–1992)
Nesbit, Evelyn (1884–1967)
Nesbitt, Cathleen (1888–1982)
Nesbitt, Miriam (1873–1954)
Nethersole, Olga (1863–1951)
Nettleton, Lois (1929—)
Neuber, Caroline (1697–1760)
Newcomb, Mary (1893–1966)
Newman, Nanette (1934—)
Newmar, Julie (1935—)
Newton-John, Olivia (1948—)
Ney, Marie (1895–1981)
Nichols, Barbara (1929–1976)
Nichols, Dandy (1907–1986)

Nicholson, Nora (1889–1973)
Nico (1938–1988)
Nielsen, Asta (1881–1972)
Niese, Hansi (1875–1934)
Nigh, Jane (1925–1993)
Niles, Mary Ann (1938–1987)
Nillson, Carlotta (c. 1878–1951)
Nilsson, Anna Q. (1889–1974)
Nisbett, Louisa Cranstoun (1812–1858)
Nissen, Greta (1906–1988)
Nixon, Marion (1904–1983)
Nixon, Marni (1929—)
Nöel, Magali (1932—)
Nolan, Jeanette (1911–1998)
Nolan, Kathleen (1933—)
Norden, Christine (1924–1988)
Noris, Assia (1912–1998)
Norman, Maidie (1912–1998)
Normand, Mabel (1892–1930)
North, Sheree (1933–2005)
Norton, Mary (1903–1992)
Novak, Eva (1898–1988)
Novak, Jane (1896–1990)
Novak, Kim (1933—)
Novotna, Jarmila (1907–1994)
Nuyen, France (1939—)
Oberon, Merle (1911–1979)
O'Brien, Margaret (1937—)
O'Brien, Virginia (1896–1987)
O'Brien-Moore, Erin (1902–1979)
O'Casey, Eileen (1900–1995)
O'Connell, Patricia (d. 1975)
O'Connor, Sinéad (1966—)
O'Connor, Una (1880–1959)
O'Day, Molly (1911–1998)
O'Doherty, Eileen (b. 1891)
O'Doherty, Mignon (1890–1961)
O'Donnell, Cathy (1923–1970)
O'Donnell, Rosie (1962—)
O'Driscoll, Martha (1922–1998)
O'Farrell, Bernadette (1924–1999)
Ogier, Bulle (1939—)
O'Hara, Maureen (1920—)
O'Hara, Shirley (1910–1979)
O'Hara, Shirley (1924–2002)
Oldfield, Anne (1683–1730)
Olin, Lena (1955—)
Oliver, Edna May (1883–1942)
Oliver, Susan (1937–1990)
Oliver, Thelma (1941—)
Olivette, Nina (c. 1908–1971)
Olrich, April (1931—)
Olson, Nancy (1928—)
O'Malley, Grania (1885–1973)
Omens, Estelle (1928–1983)
Ondra, Anny (1902–1987)
O'Neal, Tatum (1963—)
O'Neil, Barbara (1909–1980)
O'Neil, Nance (1874–1965)
O'Neil, Nancy (1911–1995)
O'Neil, Peggy (1898–1960)
O'Neil, Sally (1908–1968)
O'Neill, Carlotta (1888–1970)
O'Neill, Eliza (1791–1872)
O'Neill, Maire (1885–1952)
Ordonówna, Hanka (1904–1950)
Orlova, Liubov (1902–1975)
O'Rourke, Heather (1975–1988)
Osborne, Marie (1911—)
Osborne, Vivienne (1896–1961)
O'Shea, Tessie (1913–1995)
Oslin, K.T. (1941—)
O'Sullivan, Mairan D. (1919–1987)
O'Sullivan, Maureen (1911–1998)
Oswalda, Ossi (1897–1948)
Oughton, Winifred (1890–1964)
Ouspenskaya, Maria (1876–1949)
Owen, Catherine Dale (1900–1965)
Owens, Patricia (1925–2000)
Padovani, Lea (1920–1991)
Page, Gale (1913–1983)
Page, Geneviève (1930—)
Page, Geraldine (1924–1987)
Paget, Debra (1933—)
Paige, Elaine (1948—)
Paige, Janis (1922—)
Paige, Jean (1895–1990)
Paige, Mabel (1879–1954)
Painter, Eleanor (1890–1947)
Palencia, Isabel de (1878–c. 1950)
Palmer, Lilli (1914–1986)
Palmer, Maria (1917–1981)
Paltrow, Gwyneth (1972—)
Pampanini, Silvana (1925—)
Papas, Irene (1926—)
Parepa-Rosa, Euphrosyne (1836–1874)
Park, Ida May (1879–1954)
Parker, Cecilia (1905–1993)
Parker, Eleanor (1922—)
Parker, Jean (1915–2005)
Parker, Lottie Blair (c. 1858–1937)
Parker, Suzy (1932–1932)
Parks, Hildy (1926–2004)
Parlo, Dita (1906–1971)
Parrish, Helen (1922–1959)
Parsons, Estelle (1927—)
Parsons, Nancie (1904–1968)
Parton, Dolly (1946—)
Pascal, Christine (1953–1996)
Pasta, Giuditta (1797–1865)
Paterson, Pat (1911–1978)
Patil, Smita (1955–1986)
Patrick, Dorothy (1921–1987)
Patrick, Gail (1911–1980)
Patten, Dorothy (1905–1975)
Patten, Luana (1938–1996)
Patterson, Elizabeth (1874–1966)
Pauli, Hertha (1909–1973)
Pavan, Marisa (1932—)
Pavlova, Anna (1881–1931)
Pavlow, Muriel (1921—)
Paxinou, Katina (1900–1973)
Payne, Freda (1945—)
Payne, Virginia (1908–1977)
Payton, Barbara (1927–1967)
Pearce, Vera (1896–1966)
Pearson, Molly (d. 1959)
Pelish, Thelma (1926–1983)
Pellicer, Pina (1935–1964)
Pennington, Ann (1892–1971)
Perkins, Millie (1938—)
Perón, Eva (1919–1952)
Perreau, Gigi (1941—)
Perry, Antoinette (1888–1946)
Perry, Elaine (1921–1986)
Perry, Katherine (1897–1983)
Perry, Margaret (1913—)
Perry, Wanda (1917–1985)
Peters, Bernadette (1948—)
Peters, Jean (1926–2000)
Peters, Susan (1921–1952)
Peterson, Marjorie (1906–1974)
Petrass, Sari (1890–1930)
Petrova, Olga (1886–1977)
Pfeiffer, Michelle (1957—)
Phair, Liz (1967—)
Philips, Mary (1901–1975)
Phillipps, Adelaide (1833–1882)
Phillips, Chynna (1968—)
Phillips, Margaret (1923–1984)
Phillips, Michelle (1944—)
Phillips, Siân (1934—)
Phillpotts, Adelaide (1896–c. 1995)
Pickens, Jane (1908–1992)
Pickford, Lottie (1895–1936)
Pickford, Mary (1893–1979)
Picon, Molly (1898–1992)
Pino, Rosario (d. 1933)
Pious, Minerva (1903–1979)
Piscator, Maria Ley (1899–1999)
Piseth Pilika (1965–1999)
Pisier, Marie-France (1944—)
Pitoëff, Ludmilla (1896–1951)
Pitts, ZaSu (1898–1963)
Platt, Louise (1915–2003)
Pleshette, Suzanne (1937—)
Plowright, Joan (1929—)
Podestà, Rossana (1934—)
Poe, Elizabeth (c. 1787–1811)
Polaire (1879–1939)
Poliakoff, Olga (c. 1935—)
Pollak, Anna (1912–1996)
Pollock, Nancy (1905–1979)
Pollock, Sharon (1936—)
Ponselle, Rosa (1897–1981)
Pontoppidan, Clara (1883–1975)
Popp, Lucia (1939–1993)
Porten, Henny (1888–1960)
Porter, Jean (1924—)
Porter, Katherine Anne (1890–1980)
Porter, Mary (d. 1765)
Porter, Nyree Dawn (1936–2001)
Potter, Cora (1857–1936)
Potter, Maureen (1925–2004)
Pounder, Cheryl
Powell, Eleanor (1910–1982)
Powell, Jane (1929—)
Powers, Leona (1896–1970)
Powers, Mala (1931—)
Preisser, June (1920–1984)
Premice, Josephine (1926–2001)
Prendergast, Sharon Marley (1964—)
Prentiss, Paula (1939—)
Presle, Micheline (1922—)
Prevost, Marie (1895–1937)
Price, Nancy (1880–1970)
Prickett, Maudie (1914–1976)
Pringle, Aileen (1895–1989)
Printemps, Yvonne (1894–1977)
Pritchard, Hannah (1711–1768)
Provine, Dorothy (1937—)
Prowse, Juliet (1936–1996)
Puck, Eva (1892–1979)
Pulver, Lilo (1929—)
Purcell, Irene (1902–1972)
Purviance, Edna (1894–1958)
Queen Latifah (1970—)
Queeny, Mary (1913–2003)
Questel, Mae (1908–1998)
Rachel (1821–1858)
Radner, Gilda (1946–1989)
Rafferty, Frances (1922–2004)
Rahn, Muriel (1911–1961)
Raikh, Zinaida (1894–1939)
Rainer, Luise (1910—)
Raines, Ella (1920–1988)
Ralph, Jessie (1864–1944)
Ralston, Esther (1902–1994)
Ralston, Jobyna (1900–1967)
Ralston, Vera Hruba (1921–2003)
Rambeau, Marjorie (1889–1970)
Rambova, Natacha (1897–1966)
Rame, Franca (1929—)
Rampling, Charlotte (1945—)
Ramsey, Anne (1929–1988)
Rand, Sally (1904–1979)
Randolph, Amanda (1896–1967)
Randolph, Barbara (d. 2002)

Occupational Index

Randolph, Isabel (1889–1973)
Randolph, Lillian (1898–1980)
Rashad, Phylicia (1948—)
Rathebe, Dolly (1928–2004)
Raucourt, Mlle (1756–1815)
Ray, René (1911–1993)
Raye, Martha (1916–1994)
Raymond, Helen (c. 1885–1965)
Raymond, Paula (1923–2003)
Reagan, Nancy (1921—)
Reddy, Helen (1941—)
Redgrave, Lynn (1943—)
Redgrave, Vanessa (1937—)
Reed, Donna (1921–1986)
Reed, Florence (1883–1967)
Rees, Rosemary (c. 1876–1963)
Reese, Della (1931—)
Regan, Sylvia (1908–2003)
Rehan, Ada (1857–1916)
Reid, Beryl (1918–1996)
Reid, Dorothy Davenport (1895–1977)
Reid, Frances (b. 1913)
Reid, Kate (1930–1993)
Reid, Maria (1895–1979)
Reignolds, Catherine Mary (1836–1911)
Réjane, Gabrielle (1857–1920)
Rekha (1954—)
Remey, Ethel (1895–1979)
Remick, Lee (1935–1991)
Renaud, Madeleine (1903–1994)
Retton, Mary Lou (1968—)
Revere, Anne (1903–1990)
Revier, Dorothy (1904–1993)
Reynolds, Adeline DeWalt (1862–1961)
Reynolds, Debbie (1932—)
Reynolds, Marjorie (1917–1997)
Rhodes, Betty (c. 1935–1987)
Riano, Renie (1899–1971)
Rice, Florence (1907–1974)
Rice, Joan (1930–1997)
Richards, Ann (1917—)
Richards, Beah (1920–2000)
Richards, Shelah (1903–1985)
Richardson, Miranda (1958—)
Riefenstahl, Leni (1902–2003)
Rigg, Diana (1938—)
Ring, Blanche (1877–1961)
Ring, Frances (1882–1951)
Risdon, Elisabeth (1887–1958)
Ristori, Adelaide (1822–1906)
Ritchie, Sharon Kay (c. 1937—)
Ritter, Thelma (1905–1969)
Riva, Emmanuelle (1927—)
Riva, Maria (1924—)
Rivera, Chita (1933—)
Rizk, Amina (1910–2003)
Roache, Viola (1885–1961)
Robbins, Gale (1921–1980)
Robert-Angelini, Enif (1886–1976)
Roberti, Lyda (1906–1938)
Roberts, Doris (1929—)
Roberts, Edith (1899–1935)
Roberts, Florence (1861–1940)
Roberts, Florence (1871–1927)
Roberts, Julia (1967—)
Roberts, Lynne (1919–1978)
Roberts, Rachel (1927–1980)
Robertson, Agnes (1833–1916)
Robin, Dany (1927–1995)
Robins, Elizabeth (1862–1952)
Robinson, Gertrude (1890–1962)
Robinson, Madeleine (1916–2004)
Robinson, Madeleine (b. 1908)
Robinson, Mary (1758–1800)
Robson, Flora (1902–1984)
Robson, May (1858–1942)
Roc, Patricia (1915–2003)
Roch, Madeleine (1884–1930)
Roche, Suzzy (1956—)
Rodriguez, Estelita (1928–1966)
Rogers, Dale Evans (1912–2001)
Rogers, Ginger (1911–1995)
Rogers, Jean (1916–1991)
Rökk, Marika (1913–2004)
Roland, Ruth (1892–1937)
Rolle, Esther (1920–1998)
Roman, Ruth (1922–1999)
Romance, Viviane (1909–1991)
Rooke, Irene (c. 1878–1958)
Rork, Ann (1908–1988)
Rorke, Kate (1866–1945)
Rorke, Mary (1858–1938)
Rosay, Françoise (1891–1974)
Roseanne (1952—)
Ross, Annie (1930—)
Ross, Shirley (1909–1975)
Rossi Drago, Eleonora (1925—)
Roth, Lillian (1910–1980)
Rothenberger, Anneliese (1924—)
Rothlein, Arlene (1939–1976)
Rothschild, Jeanne de (1908–2003)
Routledge, Patricia (1929—)
Rowlands, Gena (1934—)
Rowson, Susanna (1762–1824)
Royle, Selena (1904–1983)
Rubens, Alma (1897–1931)
Rubenstein, Blanche (c. 1897–1969)
Ruick, Barbara (1930–1974)
Rule, Janice (1931–2003)
Rush, Barbara (1927—)
Russell, Annie (1864–1936)
Russell, Gail (1924–1961)
Russell, Jane (1921—)
Russell, Lillian (1861–1922)
Russell, Rosalind (1908–1976)
Rutherford, Ann (1917—)
Rutherford, Margaret (1892–1972)
Ryan, Fran (1916–2000)
Ryan, Irene (1902–1973)
Ryan, Kathleen (1922–1985)
Ryan, Mary (1885–1948)
Ryan, Meg (1961—)
Ryan, Peggy (1924–2004)
Ryan, Sheila (1921–1975)
Saga, Michiko (1934—)
Sagan, Leontine (1889–1974)
Saint, Eva Marie (1924—)
Saint-Cyr, Renée (1904–2004)
Sais, Marin (1890–1971)
Sale, Virginia (1899–1992)
Salmonova, Lyda (1889–1968)
Samoilova, Tatania (1934—)
Sampson, Teddy (1898–1970)
Sanda, Dominique (1948—)
Sanders, Summer (1972—)
Sanderson, Julia (1887–1975)
Sands, Diana (1934–1973)
Sands, Dorothy (1893–1980)
Sanford, Isabel (1917–2004)
San Juan, Olga (1927—)
Sanson, Yvonne (1926—)
Santos Arrascaeta, Beatriz (1947—)
Sapp, Carolyn (1967—)
Sarandon, Susan (1946—)
Saunders, Jackie (1892–1954)
Saunderson, Mary (d. 1712)
Scala, Gia (1934–1972)
Scales, Prunella (1932—)
Schaefer, Laurel Lea (c. 1949—)
Schaeffer, Rebecca (1967–1989)
Schafer, Natalie (1900–1991)
Schell, Maria (1926–2005)
Schiaffino, Rosanna (1938—)
Schlamme, Martha (1922–1985)
Schneider, Magda (1909–1996)
Schneider, Romy (1938–1982)
Schnitzer, Henriette (1891–1979)
Schratt, Katharina (1853–1940)
Schulze-Boysen, Libertas (1913–1942)
Scott, Hazel (1920–1981)
Scott, Janette (1938—)
Scott, Lizabeth (1922—)
Scott, Margaretta (1912–2005)
Scott, Martha (1914–2003)
Scudamore, Margaret (1884–1958)
Sears, Zelda (1873–1935)
Sebastian, Dorothy (1903–1957)
Seberg, Jean (1938–1979)
Seddon, Margaret (1872–1968)
Sedgwick, Edie (1943–1971)
Seeley, Blossom (1891–1974)
Segal, Vivienne (1897–1992)
Seidl, Lea (1895–1987)
Selby, Sarah (1905–1980)
Sell, Janie (1941—)
Sellars, Elizabeth (1923—)
Semenova, Ekaterina (1786–1849)
Sergava, Katharine (1910–2005)
Serreau, Coline (1947—)
Servoss, Mary (1881–1968)
Sessions, Almira (1888–1974)
Sevilla, Carmen (1930—)
Seyler, Athene (1889–1990)
Seymour, Anne (1909–1988)
Seymour, Clarine (1898–1920)
Seymour, Jane (c. 1898–1956)
Seymour, Jane (1951—)
Seymour, May Davenport (d. 1967)
Seyrig, Delphine (1932–1990)
Shaler, Eleanor (1900–1989)
Shannon, Effie (1867–1954)
Shannon, Peggy (1907–1941)
Shaw, Fiona (1958—)
Shaw, Mary G. (1854–1929)
Shaw, Reta (1912–1982)
Shaw, Susan (1929–1978)
Shaw, Victoria (1935–1988)
Shawlee, Joan (1926–1987)
Shayne, Tamara (1902–1983)
Shearer, Moira (1926–2006)
Shearer, Norma (1900–1983)
Sheehan, Margaret Flavin (d. 1969)
Shelley, Barbara (1933—)
Shepherd, Cybill (1949—)
Shepley, Ruth (1892–1951)
Sheridan, Ann (1915–1967)
Sheridan, Dinah (1920—)
Sheridan, Margaret (1889–1958)
Shindle, Kate (1979—)
Shipman, Nell (1892–1970)
Shirley, Anne (1917–1993)
Shiubhlaigh, Maire Nic (1884–1958)
Shockley, Marian (1911–1981)
Shoemaker, Ann (1891–1978)
Shore, Dinah (1917–1994)
Short, Florence (1889–1946)
Shutta, Ethel (1896–1976)
Siddons, Harriet (1783–1844)
Siddons, Sarah (1755–1831)
Sidney, Sylvia (1910–1999)
Signoret, Simone (1921–1985)
Sim, Sheila (1922—)
Simmons, Jean (1929—)
Simms, Ginny (1915–1994)
Simms, Hilda (1920–1994)
Simon, Simone (1910–2005)
Simone, Madame (1877–1985)
Sinatra, Nancy (1940—)

Sinclair, Betty (1907–1983)
Sinclair, Catherine (1817–1891)
Sinclair, Madge (1938–1995)
Sinden, Topsy (1878–1951)
Singleton, Penny (1908–2003)
Skala, Lilia (1896–1994)
Skinner, Cornelia Otis (1901–1979)
Skipworth, Alison (1863–1952)
Sleeper, Martha (1907–1983)
Smith, Alexis (1921–1993)
Smith, Anna Deavere (1950—)
Smith, Maggie (1934—)
Smith, Mamie (1883–1946)
Smith, Muriel Burrell (1923–1985)
Smith, Queenie (1898–1978)
Smithson, Harriet Constance (1800–1854)
Smosarska, Jadwiga (1898–1971)
Snowden, Leigh (1929–1982)
Söderbaum, Kristina (1912—)
Söderström, Elisabeth (1927—)
Sokolova, Lyubov (1921–2001)
Solntseva, Yulia (1901–1989)
Sologne, Madeleine (1912–1995)
Sondergaard, Gale (1899–1985)
Sontag, Henriette (c. 1803–1854)
Soray, Turkan (1945—)
Sorel, Cécile (1873–1966)
Sorma, Agnes (1862–1927)
Sothern, Ann (1909–2001)
Soundarya (1972–2004)
Spacek, Sissy (1949—)
Spagnuolo, Filomena (1903–1987)
Spain, Elsie (1879–1970)
Spain, Fay (1932–1983)
Spears, Britney (1981—)
Spira, Camilla (1906–1997)
Spira, Steffie (1908–1995)
Spolin, Viola (1906–1994)
Spong, Hilda (1875–1955)
Spooner, Cecil (1875–1953)
Spooner, Edna May (1873–1953)
St. Clair, Lydia (1898–1970)
St. Clair, Yvonne (1914–1971)
St. Denis, Teddie (b. 1909)
St. John, Florence (1854–1912)
Stahl, Rose (1870–1955)
Stamp Taylor, Edith (1904–1946)
Stanislavski, Maria Lilina (b. around 1870)
Stanley, Kim (1925–2001)
Stansfield, Lisa (1966—)
Stanwyck, Barbara (1907–1990)
Stapleton, Maureen (1925–2006)
Starr, Frances Grant (1886–1973)
Starr, Muriel (1888–1950)
Staw, Sala (d. 1972)
Stedman, Myrtle (1885–1938)
Steele, Barbara (1937—)
Sten, Anna (1908–1993)
Stephens, Catherine (1794–1882)
Sterling, Jan (1921–2004)
Sternhagen, Frances (1930—)
Stevens, Connie (1938—)
Stevens, Emily (1882–1928)
Stevens, Inger (1934–1970)
Stevens, Julie (1916–1984)
Stevens, K.T. (1919–1994)
Stevens, Stella (1936—)
Stevenson, Juliet (1956—)
Stewart, Alexandra (1939—)
Stewart, Anita (1895–1961)
Stewart, Elaine (1929—)
Stewart, Katherine (c. 1861–1949)
Stewart, Nellie (1858–1931)
Stewart, Sophie (1908–1977)
Stickney, Dorothy (1896–1998)
Stirling, Mary Anne (1815–1895)
Stockenström, Wilma (1933—)
Stoler, Shirley (1929–1999)
Stone, Carol (1915—)
Stone, Dorothy (1905–1974)
Stone, Paula (1912–1997)
Stone, Sharon (1958—)
Stonehouse, Ruth (1892–1941)
Storey, Edith (1892–1955)
Storm, Gale (1922—)
Stradner, Rose (1913–1958)
Straight, Beatrice (1914–2001)
Strange, Michael (1890–1950)
Strasberg, Paula (1911–1966)
Strasberg, Susan (1938–1999)
Stratas, Teresa (1938—)
Streatfeild, Noel (1895–1986)
Streep, Meryl (1949—)
Streisand, Barbra (1942—)
Stritch, Elaine (1925—)
Stroyeva, Vera (b. 1903)
Strozzi, Kay (1899–1996)
Stuart, Bathia Howie (1893–1987)
Stuart, Gloria (1909—)
Stuart, Mary (1926–2002)
Sucher, Rosa (1847–1927)
Sudlow, Joan (1892–1970)
Sulka, Elaine (1933–1994)
Sullavan, Margaret (1911–1960)
Sullivan, Jean (1923–2003)
Sumako, Matsui (1886–1919)
Sunderland, Nan (1898–1973)
Sunshine, Marion (1894–1963)
Suraiya (1929–2004)
Susann, Jacqueline (1921–1974)
Sutherland, Joan (1926—)
Suzman, Janet (1939—)
Swank, Hilary (1974—)
Swann, Caroline Burke (d. 1964)
Swanson, Gloria (1897–1983)
Sweet, Blanche (1895–1986)
Sweet, Rachel (1963—)
Swinburne, Nora (1902–2000)
Sylvie (1883–1970)
Sylwan, Kari (1959—)
Syms, Sylvia (1916–1992)
Syms, Sylvia (1934—)
Takagi, Tokuko Nagai (1891–1919)
Takamine, Hideko (1924—)
Talbott, Gloria (1931–2000)
Taliaferro, Edith (1893–1958)
Talma, Madame (1771–1860)
Talmadge, Constance (1897–1973)
Talmadge, Natalie (1897–1969)
Talmadge, Norma (1893–1957)
Tamara (1907–1943)
Tanaka, Kinuyo (1907–1977)
Tandy, Jessica (1909–1994)
Tanguay, Eva (1878–1947)
Tanner, Marion (1891–1985)
Tapley, Rose (1881–1956)
Tarasova, Alla (1898–1973)
Tashman, Lilyan (1899–1934)
Tate, Sharon (1943–1969)
Taylor, Alma (1895–1974)
Taylor, Elizabeth (1932—)
Taylor, Laurette (1884–1946)
Taylor, Ruth (1908–1984)
Taylor, Valerie (1902–1988)
Tcherina, Ludmilla (1924–2004)
Teasdale, Verree (1904–1987)
Teer, Barbara Ann (1937—)
Teitel, Carol (1923–1986)
Tell, Alma (1892–1937)
Tell, Olive (1894–1951)
Tempest, Marie (1864–1942)
Templeton, Fay (1865–1939)
Templeton, Olive (1883–1979)
Tennant, Veronica (1946—)
Ternan, Frances Eleanor (c. 1803–1873)
Terris, Norma (1904–1989)
Terriss, Ellaline (1871–1971)
Terry, Alice (1899–1987)
Terry, Beatrice (b. 1890)
Terry, Ellen (1847–1928)
Terry, Hazel (1918–1974)
Terry, Kate (1844–1924)
Terry, Marion (1852–1930)
Terry, Minnie (b. 1882)
Terry, Olive (1884—)
Terry-Lewis, Mabel (1872–1957)
Tetzel, Joan (1921–1977)
Thaxter, Phyllis (1921—)
Thiess, Ursula (1924—)
Thigpen, Lynne (1948–2003)
Thimig, Helene (1889–1974)
Thomas, Agnes (fl. 1878–1926)
Thomas, Edna (1885–1974)
Thomas, Marlo (1937—)
Thomas, Olive (1884–1920)
Thompson, Emma (1959—)
Thompson, Kay (1908–1998)
Thompson, Lydia (1836–1908)
Thompson, May (d. 1978)
Thompson, Sada (1929—)
Thorburn, June (1930–1967)
Thoresen, Cecilie (1858–1911)
Thorndike, Eileen (1891–1954)
Thorndike, Sybil (1882–1976)
Thulin, Ingrid (1926–2004)
Thurman, Uma (1970—)
Tierney, Gene (1920–1991)
Tilbury, Zeffie (1863–1950)
Tiller, Nadja (1929—)
Tilton, Martha (1915—)
Tissot, Alice (1895–1971)
Titheradge, Madge (1887–1961)
Tobin, Genevieve (1899–1995)
Tobin, Vivian (1902–2002)
Todd, Ann (1909–1993)
Todd, Ann (1931—)
Todd, Thelma (1905–1935)
Todi, Luiza Rosa (1753–1833)
Tomlin, Lily (1939—)
Toren, Marta (1926–1957)
Torres, Lolita (1930–2002)
Torres, Raquel (1908–1987)
Toumanova, Tamara (1919–1996)
Travers, Linden (1913–2001)
Travers, P.L. (1906–1996)
Tree, Dorothy (1906–1992)
Tree, Maud Holt (1858–1937)
Tree, Viola (1884–1938)
Treen, Mary (1907–1989)
Trefilova, Vera (1875–1943)
Trevor, Claire (1909–2000)
Troy, Louise (1933–1994)
Truax, Sarah (1877–1958)
Trueman, Paula (1900–1994)
Trunnelle, Mabel (1879–1981)
Tschechowa, Olga (1897–1980)
Tsukasa, Yoko (1934—)
Tucker, Tanya (1958—)
Turnbull, Julia Anne (1822–1887)
Turner, Florence E. (c. 1888–1946)
Turner, Kathleen (1954—)
Turner, Lana (1921–1995)
Tutin, Dorothy (1930–2001)
Tuttle, Lurene (1906–1986)
Twelvetrees, Helen (1908–1958)
Twiggy (1946—)
Tyler, Judy (1933–1957)
Tyler, Odette (1869–1936)

Tyler, Priscilla Cooper (1816–1889)
Tyson, Cicely (1933—)
Uggams, Leslie (1943—)
Ulanova, Galina (1910–1998)
Ullmann, Liv (1939—)
Ullrich, Luise (1911–1985)
Ulric, Lenore (1892–1970)
Umeki, Miyoshi (1929—)
Ure, Mary (1933–1975)
Urecal, Minerva (1894–1966)
Vaccaro, Brenda (1939—)
Vail, Myrtle (1888–1978)
Valentine, Grace (1884–1964)
Valerie, Joan (1911–1983)
Valli, Alida (1921–2006)
Valli, Valli (1882–1927)
Vallier, Hélène (1932–1988)
Vanbrugh, Irene (1872–1949)
Vanbrugh, Prudence (1902—)
Vanbrugh, Violet (1867–1942)
Van Buren, Mabel (1878–1947)
Vance, Vivian (1909–1979)
Van Cleve, Edith (1894–1985)
Vanderbilt, Gloria (1924—)
Van Doren, Mamie (1931—)
Van Fleet, Jo (1919–1996)
Van Studdiford, Grace (1873–1927)
Varden, Evelyn (1893–1958)
Varden, Norma (1898–1989)
Varsi, Diane (1937–1992)
Vassar, Queenie (1870–1960)
Vaughan, Kate (c. 1852–1903)
Vaughn, Hilda (1898–1957)
Vaz Dias, Selma (1911–1977)
Veazie, Carol (1895–1984)
Veigel, Eva-Maria (1724–1822)
Velez, Lisa (1967—)
Velez, Lupe (1908–1944)
Venable, Evelyn (1913–1993)
Venuta, Benay (1911–1995)
Vera-Ellen (1920–1981)
Verbruggen, Susanna (c. 1667–1703)
Verdon, Gwen (1925–2000)
Verdugo, Elena (1926—)
Verne, Kaaren (1918–1967)
Vernon, Anne (1924—)
Versois, Odile (1930–1980)
Vestoff, Floria (1920–1963)
Vestris, Lucia (1797–1856)
Vezin, Jane Elizabeth (1827–1902)
Viardot, Pauline (1821–1910)
Vicente, Paula (1519–1576)
Vickers, Martha (1925–1971)
Viertel, Salka (1889–1978)
Villegas, Micaela (1748–1819)
Vincent, Madge (b. 1884)
Vincent, Mary Ann (1818–1887)
Vincent, Ruth (1877–1955)
Vinson, Helen (1907–1999)
Vitti, Monica (1931—)
Vivian, Ruth (c. 1883–1949)
Vlady, Marina (1938—)
von Busing, Fritzi (c. 1884–1948)
von Essen, Siri (1850–1912)
von Harbou, Thea (1888–1954)
Von Nagy, Käthe (1909–1973)
Von Trotta, Margarethe (1942—)
Wagner, Minna (c. 1800–1866)
Walcamp, Marie (1894–1936)
Wales, Ethel (1878–1952)
Walker, Ada Overton (1870–1914)
Walker, Charlotte (1876–1958)
Walker, Helen (1920–1968)
Walker, June (1900–1966)
Walker, Nancy (1922–1992)
Walker, Nella (1880–1971)
Walker, Polly (b. 1908)
Wall, Geraldine (1912–1970)
Wallace, Jean (1923–1990)
Wallace, Regina (1886–1978)
Waller, Florence (1862–1912)
Wallis, Shani (1933—)
Walsh, Kay (1914–2005)
Walters, Julie (1950—)
Ward, Dorothy (1890–1987)
Ward, Geneviève (1838–1922)
Ward, Polly (1908–1987)
Warner, Gloria (c. 1914–1934)
Warrick, Ruth (1915–2005)
Washbourne, Mona (1903–1988)
Washington, Fredi (1903–1994)
Waters, Ethel (1896–1977)
Watkins, Linda (1908–1976)
Watson, Lucile (1879–1962)
Wayne, Carol (1942–1985)
Weaver, Marjorie (1913–1994)
Weaver, Sigourney (1949—)
Weber, Lois (1881–1939)
Webster, Margaret (1905–1972)
Weeks, Ada May (1898–1978)
Weeks, Marion (1886–1968)
Weidler, Virginia (1926–1968)
Weigel, Helene (1900–1971)
Weir, Molly (1910–2004)
Weissman, Dora (1881–1974)
Welch, Elisabeth (1904–2003)
Welch, Raquel (1940—)
Weld, Tuesday (1943—)
Welles, Gwen (1951–1993)
Wellman, Emily Ann (d. 1946)
Welsh, Jane (1905–2001)
Welter, Ariadna (1930–1998)
Werbezirk, Gisela (1875–1956)
Werner, Ilse (1918—)
Wessely, Paula (1907–2000)
West, Mae (1893–1980)
Westcott, Helen (1928–1998)
Westley, Helen (1875–1942)
Westman, Nydia (1902–1970)
Weston, Cecil (1889–1976)
Weston, Ruth (1906–1955)
Wetmore, Joan (1911–1989)
Whelan, Arleen (1916–1993)
Whelan, Cyprienne Gabel (d. 1985)
Whiffin, Blanche (1845–1936)
White, Alice (1904–1983)
White, Antonia (1899–1980)
White, Carol (1942–1991)
White, Pearl (1889–1938)
White, Ruth (1914–1969)
Whitehouse, Davina (1912–2002)
Whitelaw, Billie (1932—)
Whitty, May (1865–1948)
Wickwire, Nancy (1925–1974)
Wieck, Dorothea (1908–1986)
Wifstrand, Naima (1890–1968)
Wiley, Lee (1915–1975)
Williams, Cara (1925—)
Williams, Clara (1888–1928)
Williams, Esther (1923—)
Williams, Frances (1903–1959)
Williams, Hope (1897–1990)
Williams, Kathlyn (1888–1960)
Williams, Victoria (1958—)
Williams, Wendy O. (1951–1998)
Willson, Rini Zarova (d. 1966)
Wilson, Ethel (d. 1980)
Wilson, Lois (1894–1988)
Wilson, Margery (1896–1986)
Wilson, Nancy (1937—)
Windsor, Claire (1897–1972)
Windsor, Marie (1919–2000)
Winfrey, Oprah (1954—)
Wing, Toby (1915–2001)
Winger, Debra (1955—)
Winn, Anona (1907–1994)
Winters, Marian (1924–1978)
Winters, Shelley (1920–2005)
Winton, Jane (1905–1959)
Winwood, Estelle (1883–1984)
Withers, Googie (1917—)
Withers, Jane (1926—)
Witherspoon, Cora (1890–1957)
Woffington, Peg (c. 1714–1760)
Wolter, Charlotte (1834–1897)
Women of the Harlem Renaissance
Wong, Anna May (1907–1961)
Wood, Florence (c. 1854–1954)
Wood, Marjorie (1882–1955)
Wood, Matilda (1831–1915)
Wood, Natalie (1938–1981)
Wood, Peggy (1892–1978)
Woodbury, Clare (c. 1880–1949)
Woodbury, Joan (1915–1989)
Woodhull, Victoria (1838–1927)
Woodward, Joanne (1930—)
Worth, Irene (1916–2002)
Wray, Fay (1907–2004)
Wright, Cobina Jr. (1921—)
Wright, Haidée (1868–1943)
Wright, Teresa (1918–2005)
Wyatt, Jane (1911—)
Wycherly, Margaret (1881–1956)
Wyman, Jane (1914—)
Wymore, Patrice (1926—)
Wyndham, Mary (1861–1931)
Wynter, Dana (1927—)
Wynyard, Diana (1906–1964)
Yakko, Sada (d. 1946)
Yamada, Isuzu (1917—)
Yarde, Margaret (1878–1944)
Yates, Elizabeth (1799–1860)
Yates, Mary Ann (1728–1787)
Yavorska, Lydia (1869–1921)
Yohé, May (1869–1938)
York, Susannah (1941—)
Young, Clara Kimball (1890–1960)
Young, Loretta (1913–2000)
Young, Mary Marsden (1880–1971)
Young, Rida Johnson (1869–1926)
Yurka, Blanche (1887–1974)
Zabelle, Flora (1880–1968)
Zapolska, Gabriela (1857–1921)
Zetterling, Mai (1925–1994)
Zetterlund, Monica (1937–2005)
Zhang Ruifang (1918—)
Ziegler, Anne (1910–2003)
Zoff, Marianne (1893–1984)
Zorina, Vera (1917–2003)

ADVENTURER

Adams, Harriet Chalmers (1875–1937)
Akeley, Delia J. (1875–1970)
Akeley, Mary Jobe (1878–1966)
Allen, Sadie (c. 1868–?)
Anable, Gloria Hollister (1903–1988)
Baret, Jeanne (1740–after 1795)
Benham, Gertrude (fl. 1909)
Bishop, Isabella (1831–1904)
Blum, Arlene (1945—)
Blunt, Anne (1837–1917)
Boyd, Louise Arner (1887–1972)
Cannary, Martha Jane (1852–1903)
Carrel, Felicite (fl. 1860s)
Chudleigh, Elizabeth (1720–1788)
David-Neel, Alexandra (1868–1969)
Digby el Mesrab, Jane (1807–1881)
Dixie, Lady Florence (1857–1905)

Eberhardt, Isabelle (1877–1904)
Ellis, Mina A. (1870–1956)
Franklin, Jane (1792–1875)
Fraser, Eliza (c. 1798–1858)
Harrison, Marguerite (1879–1967)
Holmes, Julia Archibald (1838–1887)
Johnson, Osa (1894–1953)
Keen, Dora (1871–1963)
Kelly, Emily (d. 1922)
Kingsley, Mary H. (1862–1900)
Kogan, Claude (1919–1959)
La Motte, Jeanne de Valois, countess de (1756–1791)
Le Blond, Elizabeth (1861–1934)
Markham, Beryl (1902–1986)
Mexia, Ynes (1870–1938)
Mignot, Claudine Françoise (c. 1617–1711)
Moffat, Gwen (1924—)
Montez, Lola (1818–1861)
Morin, Nea (1906–1986)
Murden, Tori (1963—)
O'Brien, Miriam (1898–1976)
O'Donnell, Mary Stuart (fl. early 1600s)
Paradis, Marie (fl. 1808)
Peary, Josephine (1863–1955)
Peck, Annie Smith (1850–1935)
Petherick, Mary (fl. 1887)
Pfeiffer, Ida (1797–1858)
Pigeon, Anna and Ellen (fl. 1860s)
Pilley, Dorothy (1893–1986)
Ramsey, Alice Huyler (1886–1983)
Richardson, Katy (1864–1927)
Royce, Sarah (1819–1891)
Rutkiewicz, Wanda (1943—)
Seacole, Mary Jane (c. 1805–1881)
Seton, Grace Gallatin (1872–1959)
Shepherd, Dolly (d. 1983)
Stanhope, Hester (1776–1839)
Stark, Freya (1893–1993)
Tabei, Junko (1939—)
Taylor, Anna Edson (c. 1858–c. 1921)
Tinné, Alexandrine (1839–1869)
Vaucher, Yvette (1929—)
Walker, Lucy (1836–1916)
Wilson, Sarah (1750–?)
Workman, Fanny (1859–1925)

ADVERTISING EXECUTIVE
Ayres, Mary Andrews (fl. 1970s)
Cowles, Fleur (1910—)
Fitz-Gibbon, Bernice (c. 1895–1982)
Hockaday, Margaret (1907–1992)
Husted, Marjorie Child (c. 1892–1986)
Jones, Caroline R. (1942–2001)
Lawrence, Mary Wells (1928—)
Martin, Patricia J. (1928—)
Waldo, Ruth Fanshaw (1885–1975)

AERONAUTICAL ENGINEER
Chapelle, Dickey (1919–1972)
Flügge-Lotz, Irmgard (1903–1974)
Guthrie, Janet (1938—)
MacGill, Elsie (d. 1980)
Mock, Jerrie (1925—)
Platt of Writtle, Baroness (1923—)
Savitskaya, Svetlana (b. 1948)
Shilling, Beatrice (1909–1990)
Widnall, Sheila (1938—)

AGRICULTURIST
Aitkin, Yvonne (1911—)
Ayuso González, María del Pilar (1942—)
Balfour, Eve (1898–1990)
Courtauld, Katherine (1856–1935)
Cruso, Thalassa (1908–1997)
Fiebiger, Christel (1946—)
Redondo Jiménez, Encarnación (1944—)
Schierhuber, Agnes (1946—)
Sessions, Kate O. (1857–1940)
Sommer, Renate (1958—)
Strong, Harriet (1844–1929)

AIDS ACTIVIST
Chytilova, Vera (1929—)
Cornett, Leanza (1971—)
Dewhurst, Colleen (1924–1991)
Diana (1961–1997)
Elion, Gertrude B. (1918–1999)
Fisher, Mary (c. 1946—)
Gao Yaojie (c. 1927—)
Glaser, Elizabeth (1947–1994)
Havel, Olga (1933–1996)
Kübler-Ross, Elisabeth (1926–2004)
Lasker, Mary (1900–1994)
Makeba, Miriam (1932—)
Montgomery, Elizabeth (1933–1995)
Novello, Antonia (1944—)
O'Brien, Margaret (1937—)
Shindle, Kate (1979—)
Stone, Sharon (1958—)
Taylor, Elizabeth (1932—)
Varda, Agnes (1928—)
Veil, Simone (1927—)
Verrett, Shirley (1931—)
Warwick, Dionne (1940—)
Yorkin, Peg (1927—)

AIRPLANE DESIGNER
Moisant, Matilde (c. 1877–1964)

AIRPLANE MANUFACTURER
Beech, Olive Ann (1903–1993)

ALCHEMIST
Mary the Jewess (fl. 1st, 2nd or 3rd c.)

AMBASSADOR
See Diplomat.

ANAESTHETIST
Horsley, Alice Woodward (1871–1957)
Siedeberg, Emily Hancock (1873–1968)
Sudre, Margie (1943—)

ANATOMIST
Biheron, Marie-Catherine (1719–1786)

ANIMAL-RIGHTS ACTIVIST
Dickin, Maria (1870–1951)
Hedren, Tippi (1931—)

ANIMAL TAMER
Bugrimova, Irina (1910–2001)

ANTHROPOLOGIST
Bates, Daisy May (1859–1951)
Benedict, Ruth (1887–1948)
Berndt, Catherine Webb (1918–1994)
Blackwood, Beatrice (1889–1975)
Brues, Alice (1913—)
Bunzel, Ruth (1898–1990)
Chilver, Sally (1914—)
Cole, Johnnetta B. (1936—)
de Laguna, Frederica (1906–2004)
Deloria, Ella (1888–1971)
Densmore, Frances (1867–1957)
Diggs, Irene (1906—)
Douglas, Mary Tew (1921—)
Du Bois, Cora (1903–1991)
Dunham, Katherine (1909–2006)
Durham, Mary Edith (1863–1944)
Ellis, Florence Hawley (1906–1991)
Fischer, Ann (1919–1971)
Fletcher, Alice Cunningham (1838–1923)
Friedl, Ernestine (1920—)
Garfield, Viola (1899–1983)
Gillmor, Frances (1903–1993)
Goldfrank, Esther S. (1896–1997)
Green, Vera Mae (1928–1982)
Gunther, Erna (1896–1982)
Hammond, Blodwen (1908–1973)
Hanks, Jane Richardson (b. 1908)
Helm, June (1924—)
Hunt, Eva (1934–1980)
Hurston, Zora Neale (c. 1891–1960)
Kaberry, Phyllis (1910–1977)
Kelly, Isabel (1906–1983)
Keur, Dorothy (1904–1989)
Kingsley, Mary H. (1862–1900)
Kitzinger, Sheila (1929—)
Kroeber, Theodora (1897–1979)
Kuper, Hilda B. (1911–1992)
Landes, Ruth (1908–1991)
Leacock, Eleanor Burke (1922–1987)
Leighton, Dorothea (1908–1989)
Lurie, Nancy O. (1924—)
McClellan, Catharine (1921—)
Mead, Margaret (1901–1978)
Medicine, Beatrice A. (1923—)
Mekeel, Joyce (1931—)
Merril, Judith (1923–1997)
Metraux, Rhoda (1914–2003)
O'Neale, Lila M. (1886–1948)
Parsons, Elsie Clews (1875–1941)
Powdermaker, Hortense (1896–1970)
Primus, Pearl (1919–1994)
Ramphele, Mamphela (1947—)
Reichard, Gladys (1893–1955)
Richards, Audrey Isabel (1899–1984)
Rubin, Vera (1911–1985)
Salmons, Josephine (b. 1904)
Shepardson, Mary Thygeson (1906–1997)
Steed, Gitel P. (1914–1977)
Stevenson, Matilda (1849–1915)
Tanner, Clara Lee (1905–1997)
Tillion, Germaine (b. 1907)
Toor, Frances (1890–1956)
Trotter, Mildred (1899–1991)
Wallis, Ruth Sawtell (1895–1978)
Wedgwood, Camilla H. (1901–1955)
Weltfish, Gene (1902–1980)
Wilson, Monica Hunter (1908–1982)
Zapata Olivella, Delia (1926–2001)

ANTI-APARTHEID ACTIVIST
Ames, Frances (1920–2002)
Baard, Francina (1901–1997)
Ballinger, Margaret (1894–1980)
Barrow, Nita (1916–1995)
Benson, Mary (1919–2000)
Biehl, Amy (1967–1993)
Blackburn, Molly (c. 1931–1985)
Brown, Rosemary (1930—)
Castle, Barbara (1910–2002)
Collins, Diana (1917–2003)
de Keyser, Ethel (1926–2004)
Duncan, Sheena (1932—)
First, Ruth (1925–1982)
Gordimer, Nadine (1923—)
Haddon, Eileen (1921–2003)
Jiagge, Annie (1918–1996)
Jonker, Ingrid (1933–1965)
Joseph, Helen (1905–1992)
Kuzwayo, Ellen (1914–2006)
Madikizela-Mandela, Winnie (1934—)
Makeba, Miriam (1932—)
Meer, Fatima (1928—)
Mitchison, Naomi (1897–1999)
Mntwana, Ida (1903–1960)

Ngoyi, Lilian (1911–1980)
Nyembe, Dorothy (1930–1998)
Ramphele, Mamphela (1947—)
September, Dulcie (1935–1988)
Sikakane, Joyce Nomafa (1943—)
Silinga, Annie (1910–1983)
Sisulu, Albertina (1918—)
Suzman, Helen (1917—)

ANTI-NUCLEAR ACTIVIST
Brown, Rosemary (1930—)
Caldicott, Helen (1938—)
Casgrain, Thérèse (1896–1981)
Chevenix, Helen (1886–1963)
Collins, Diana (1917–2003)
Cook, Judith (1933–2004)
Douglas, Helen Gahagan (1900–1980)
Dreier, Mary Elisabeth (1875–1963)
Elizabeth of Bavaria (1876–1965)
Fittko, Lisa (1909–2005)
Kelly, Petra (1947–1992)
Kushida Fuki (1899–2001)
Levertov, Denise (1923–1997)
Mitchison, Naomi (1897–1999)
Murrell, Hilda (c. 1906–1984)
Myrdal, Alva (1902–1986)
Paley, Grace (1922—)
Roosevelt, Eleanor (1884–1962)
Ruddock, Joan (1943—)
Russell, Dora (1894–1986)
Stewart, Alice (1906–2002)
Ward, Barbara (1914–1981)

ANTI-SLAVERY ACTIVIST
See Abolitionist.

ANTI-WAR ACTIVIST
See Pacifist.

APIARIST
Maurizio, Anna (1900–1993)

ARABIAN SINGER
Azza al-Maila (?–c. 707)
Bid'a (856–915)
Dananir al Barmakiyya (fl. late 8th c.)
Fadl (d. around 870)
Habbaba (d. 724)
Hind bint 'Utba (d. 610)
Inan (fl. c. 800)
Irfan (fl. mid–800s)
Mahbuba (fl. 9th c.)
Milh al-Attara (fl. 840s)
Mutayyam al-Hashimiyya (fl. 8th c.)
Oraib (797–890)
Shariyya (b. around 815)
Ubaida (fl. c. 830)
Ulayya (fl. 800s)

ARCHAEOLOGIST
Armitage, Ella (1841–1931)
Bell, Gertrude (1868–1926)
Caton-Thompson, Gertrude (1888–1985)
Davies, Margaret (1914–1982)
de Laguna, Frederica (1906–2004)
Dohan, Edith Hall (1877–1943)
Duby-Blom, Gertrude (1901–1993)
Eady, Dorothy (1904–1981)
Ellis, Florence Hawley (1906–1991)
Garrod, Dorothy A. (1892–1969)
Gimbutas, Marija (1921–1994)
Goldman, Hetty (1881–1972)
Hawes, Harriet Boyd (1871–1945)
Hawkes, Jacquetta (1910–1996)
Ingstad, Anne-Stine (c. 1918–1997)
Kelly, Isabel (1906–1983)
Kenyon, Kathleen (1906–1978)
Leakey, Mary Nicol (1913–1996)
Lowry-Corry, Dorothy (1885–1967)
Mitchell, Lucy (1845–1888)
Murray, Margaret (1863–1963)
Nuttall, Zelia (1857–1933)
Papariga, Alexandra (1945—)
Peck, Annie Smith (1850–1935)
Petrie, Hilda (1871–1957)
Proskouriakoff, Tatiana (1909–1985)
Richter, Gisela (1882–1972)
Rule, Margaret (1928—)
Sandars, Nancy K. (1914—)
Stevenson, Sara Yorke (1847–1921)
Swindler, Mary Hamilton (1884–1967)
Van Deman, Esther (1862–1937)
Wormington, H. Marie (1914–1994)
Yener, Aslihan (1946—)

ARCHDUCHESS
Alexandra Pavlovna (1783–1801)
Augusta of Tuscany (1825–1864)
Carlota (1840–1927)
Chotek, Sophie (1868–1914)
Clotilde of Saxe-Coburg-Gotha (1846–1927)
Elisabeth of Habsburg (1554–1592)
Elizabeth (1831–1903)
Elizabeth (fl. 1850s)
Elizabeth of Savoy-Carignan (1800–1856)
Elizabeth von Habsburg (1883–1963)
Gonzaga, Anna Caterina (1566–1621)
Hildegarde of Bavaria (1825–1864)
Ileana (1909–1991)
Isabella Clara Eugenia of Austria (1566–1633)
Isabella of Croy-Dulmen (1856–1931)
Joanna of Austria (1546–1578)
Margaret of Austria (c. 1577–1611)
Maria Annunziata (1843–1871)
Maria Antonia of Austria (1683–1754)
Maria Beatrice of Modena (1750–1829)
Maria Christina (1742–1798)
Maria Cristina of Sicily (1877–1947)
Maria Immaculata of Sicily (1844–1899)
Maria Josepha of Saxony (1867–1944)
Maria of Wurttemberg (1797–1855)
Maria Theresa of Austria (1717–1780)
Maria Theresa of Portugal (1855–1944)
Maria Theresa of Tuscany (1801–1855)
Marie Louise of Austria (1791–1847)
Marie Valerie (1868–1924)
Mary of Burgundy (1457–1482)
Medici, Claudia de (1604–1648)
Sophie of Bavaria (1805–1872)
Stewart, Eleanor (1427–1496)
Visconti, Virida (c. 1354–1414)

ARCHER
Ardzhannikova, Lyudmila (1958—)
Burdeyna, Nataliya (1974—)
Butuzova, Natalya (1954—)
Chen Li Ju (1981—)
Cho Youn-Jeong (1969—)
Cooke, Emma
Dzieciol, Iwona (1975—)
Gapchenko, Emma (1938—)
Griffith, Phyllis (c. 1922—)
Handayani, Lilies (1965—)
He Ying (1977—)
Hill-Lowe, Beatrice
Howell, Lida (1859–1939)
Jang Yong-Ho
Kim Bo-Ram
Kim Jin-Ho (1961—)
Kim Jo-Sun
Kim Kyung-Wook
Kim Nam-Soon
Kim Soo-Nyung (1971—)
Klata, Katarzyna (1972—)
Kovpan, Valentina (1950—)
Kvrivichvili, Khatuna (1974—)
Lee Eun-Kyung (1972—)
Lee Sung-Jin (1985—)
Legh, Alice (1855–1948)
Lidstone, Dorothy (1938—)
Li Lingjuan (1966—)
Lin Sang (1977—)
Losaberidze, Ketevan (1949—)
Ma Xiangjun (1964—)
Mensing, Barbara (1960—)
Meriluoto, Paivi (1952—)
Newall, Sybil (1854–1929)
Nowicka, Joanna (1966—)
Ochs, Debra (1966—)
Oh Kyo-Moon
Parker, Denise (1973—)
Park Sung-Hyun (1983—)
Pfohl, Cornelia (1971—)
Pollock, Jessie
Rustamova, Zebinisso (1955—)
Ryon, Luann (1953—)
Sadovnycha, Olena (1967—)
Saiman, Nurfitriyana (1962—)
Serdyuk, Kateryna
Skillman, Melanie (1954—)
Szydlowska, Irena (1928–1983)
Valeyeva, Natalya (1969—)
Wagner, Sandra (1969—)
Wang Hee-Kyung (1970—)
Wang Hong (1965—)
Wang Xiaozhu (1973—)
Wardhani, Kusuma (1964—)
Wilber, Doreen (1930—)
Williamson, Alison (1971—)
Wu Hui Ju (1982—)
Yoon Hye-Young
Yoon Young-Sook (1971—)
Yuan Shu Chi (1984—)
Yun Mi-Jin (1983—)
Zhang Juanjuan (1981—)

ARCHITECT/ARCHITECTURAL DESIGNER
Antonakakis, Suzana (1935—)
Aulenti, Gae (1927—)
Barney, Nora (1883–1971)
Beese, Lotte (1903–1988)
Belmont, Alva Smith (1853–1933)
Bethune, Louise Blanchard (1856–1913)
Butler, Eleanor (c. 1915–1997)
Casson, Margaret MacDonald (1913–1999)
Chowdhury, Eulie (1923—)
Colter, Mary Elizabeth (1869–1949)
Crowe, Sylvia (1901–1997)
de Blois, Natalie (1921—)
Drew, Jane (1911–1996)
Eames, Ray (1912–1988)
Farrand, Beatrix Jones (1872–1959)
Gisbert Carbonell de Mesa, Teresa (1926—)
Gray, Eileen (1878–1976)
Hadid, Zaha (1950—)
Hasegawa, Itsuko (1941—)
Hatz, Elizabeth (1952—)
Hawley, Christine (1949—)
Hayden, Sophia (1868–1953)
Howe, Lois (c. 1864–1964)
Jiricna, Eva (1939—)
Joseph, Mother (1823–1902)
Kennedy, Louise St. John (1950—)
Lawrence, Elizabeth (1904–1985)
Lin, Maya (1959—)
Mackintosh, Margaret (1865–1933)
Mahony, Marion (1871–1961)
Morgan, Julia (1872–1957)

Nichols, Minerva Parker (1861–1949)
Nur Jahan (1577–1645)
Parek, Lagle (1941—)
Raymond, Eleanor (1887–1989)
Reich, Lilly (1885–1947)
Schütte-Lihotzky, Margarete (1897–2000)
Scott, Elizabeth Whitworth (1898–1972)
Scott-Brown, Denise (1931—)
Smith, Chloethiel Woodard (1910–1992)
Smithson, Alison (1928–1993)
Stjernstedt, Rosemary (1912–1998)
Taylor, Florence M. (1879–1969)
Vecsei, Eva (1930—)

ARCHITECTURAL CRITIC
Bauer, Catherine Krouse (1905–1964)
Moholy-Nagy, Sibyl (1903–1971)

ART COLLECTOR
Bliss, Lillie (1864–1931)
Bliss, Mildred Barnes (1879–1969)
Cone, Claribel (1864–1929)
Cone, Etta (1870–1949)
Davies, Gwendoline (1882–1951)
Davies, Margaret (1884–1963)
Engelhard, Jane (1917–2004)
Folger, Emily (1858–1936)
Frank, Nance (1949—)
Gardner, Isabella Stewart (1840–1924)
Guggenheim, Irene (1868–1954)
Guggenheim, Peggy (1898–1979)
Gund, Agnes (1938—)
Halpert, Edith Gregor (c. 1900–1970)
Havemeyer, Louisine (1855–1929)
Howard, Henrietta (1688–1767)
Mary of Teck (1867–1953)
Medici, Anna Maria Luisa de (1667–1743)
Meyerhoff, Jane (1924–2004)
Noailles, Marie-Laure de (1902–1970)
Ordway, Katharine (1899–1979)
Rogers, Grace Rainey (1867–1943)
Stein, Gertrude (1874–1946)
Sullivan, Mary Quinn (1877–1939)
Vogel, Dorothy (1935—)
Webb, Electra Havemeyer (1888–1960)

ART CRITIC
Brookner, Anita (1928—)
Cary, Elisabeth Luther (1867–1936)
Cato, Nancy (1917–2000)
de Kooning, Elaine Fried (1918–1989)
Dilke, Emily (1840–1904)
Escoffery, Gloria (1923–2002)
Hoff, Ursula (1909–2005)
Mayreder, Rosa (1858–1938)
Mechlin, Leila (1874–1949)
Monroe, Harriet (1860–1936)
Mulally, Teresa (1728–1803)
Nelken, Margarita (1896–1968)
Paoli, Betty (1814–1894)
Pennell, Elizabeth Robins (1855–1936)
Piper, Myfanwy (1911–1997)
Plá, Josefina (1909–1999)
Raverat, Gwen (1885–1957)
Rollett, Hilda (1873–1970)
Saarinen, Aline (1914–1972)
Sarfatti, Margherita (1880–1961)
Trotzig, Birgitta (1929—)
Vakalo, Eleni (1921—)
Van Rensselaer, Mariana (1851–1934)

ART DEALER
England, Maud Russell (1863–1956)

ARTISAN
Barlow, Hannah (1851–1916)
Dat So La Lee (c. 1835–1925)
Kirkeby, Elizabeth (fl. 1482)
Kokoro-Barrett, Hiria (1870–1943)
Mabel of Bury St. Edmunds (fl. 1230)
Martinez, Maria Montoya (1887–1980)
Nampeyo (c. 1860–1942)
Patiniere, Agnes (fl. 1286)
Pitter, Ruth (1897–1992)
Powers, Harriet (1837–1911)
Raverat, Gwen (1885–1957)
Rie, Lucie (1902–1995)
Simonovich-Efimova, Nina (1877–1948)
Storer, Maria (1849–1932)
Whyte, Kathleen (1909–1996)
Wood, Beatrice (1893–1998)
Yeats, Elizabeth (1868–1940)
Yeats, Lily (1866–1949)
Zeisel, Eva (b. 1906)

ARTIST
See also Artisan.
See also Cartoonist.
See also Collage artist.
See also Engraver.
See also Etcher.
See also Film animation artist.
See also Folk artist.
See also Goldsmith.
See also Graphic artist/illustrator.
See also Illustrator.
See also Manuscript illuminator.
See also Mosaic artist.
See also Native artist.
See also Painter.
See also Photographer.
See also Sculptor.
See also Silk-screen artist.
See also Silversmith.
See also Textile artist/designer.
Alexander, Francesca (1837–1917)
Blackham, Dorothy Isabel (1896–1975)
Borrero, Dulce María (1883–1945)
Borrero, Juana (1877–1896)
Clark, Kate Emma (1847–1926)
Cockburn, Patricia (1914–1989)
Gardner, Maria Louisa (1879–1968)
Greenwood, Sarah (c. 1809–1889)
Hipp, Jutta (1925–2003)
Jeffreys, Ellen Penelope (1827–1904)
Kruger, Barbara (1945—)
Wilson, Helen Ann (1793/94–1871)

ARTS ADMINISTRATOR
Archer, Robyn (1948—)
Brown, Alice Van Vechten (1862–1949)
Carlisle, Kitty (b. 1910)
de Valois, Ninette (1898–2001)
Gee, Helen (1919–2004)
Gund, Agnes (1938—)
Jameson, Storm (1891–1986)
Le Gallienne, Eva (1899–1991)
Levy, Florence Nightingale (1870–1947)
Lewis, Elma (1921—)
McDonagh, Phyllis (1900–1978)
Santamaría, Haydée (1922–1980)
van Praagh, Peggy (1910–1990)

ARTS PATRON/PHILANTHROPIST/ BENEFACTOR
Adelaide de Condet (fl. 12th c.)
Adelicia of Louvain (c. 1102–1151)
Agnes of Poitou (1024–1077)
Ahmanson, Caroline (1918–2005)
Albrizzi, Isabella Teotochi, Contessa d' (1770–1836)
Alexander, Francesca (1837–1917)
Anderson, Regina M. (1900–1993)
Anguissola, Sofonisba (1532–1625)
Anna Amalia of Prussia (1723–1787)
Anna Amalia of Saxe-Weimar (1739–1807)
Anne of Bohemia (1366–1394)
Anne of Brittany (c. 1477–1514)
Anne of Denmark (1574–1619)
Arnstein, Fanny von (1758–1818)
Augustine, Rose (1910–2003)
Beaufort, Margaret (1443–1509)
Beech, Olive Ann (1903–1993)
Bliss, Lillie (1864–1931)
Bliss, Mildred Barnes (1879–1969)
Bonaparte, Elisa (1777–1820)
Borgia, Lucrezia (1480–1519)
Braunschweig-Lüneburg, Sophie Elisabeth von (1613–1676)
Braun-Vogelstein, Julie (1883–1971)
Casey, Maie (1892–1983)
Cavendish, Georgiana, duchess of Devonshire (1757–1806)
Chabot, Maria (1913–2001)
Chanel, Coco (1883–1971)
Christina of Sweden (d. 1122)
Clark, Kate Emma (1847–1926)
Clodia (c. 94–post 45 BCE)
Cooke, Anna Rice (1853–1934)
Coolidge, Elizabeth Sprague (1863–1953)
Cornaro, Caterina (1454–1510)
Cranston, Kate (1850–1934)
Cunard, Maud (1872–1948)
Dandolo, Giovanna (fl. 1457)
Danvers, Lady Magdalene (1561–1627)
Danvers, Magdalene (1561–1627)
Davies, Gwendoline (1882–1951)
Davies, Margaret (1884–1963)
Deffand, Marie Anne de Vichy-Chamrond, Marquise du (1697–1780)
Deffand, Marie du (1697–1780)
Dexter, Caroline (1819–1884)
Diane de Poitiers (1499–1566)
Duke, Doris (1912–1993)
Eccles, Mary Hyde (1912–2003)
Eleanor of Aquitaine (1122–1204)
Eleanor of Portugal (1458–1525)
Elizabeth of Bavaria (1876–1965)
Engelhard, Jane (1917–2004)
Ermengarde of Narbonne (c. 1120–c. 1194)
Este, Beatrice d' (1475–1497)
Este, Isabella d' (1474–1539)
FitzGilbert, Constance (fl. 12th c.)
Folger, Emily (1858–1936)
Fosburgh, Minnie Astor
Freier, Recha (1892–1984)
Fuld, Carrie (1864–1944)
Gambara, Veronica (1485–1550)
Gardiner, Margaret (1904–2005)
Geoffrin, Marie Thérèse (1699–1777)
Gonzaga, Eleonora (1493–1543)
Gregory, Augusta (1852–1932)
Guggenheim, Peggy (1898–1979)
Guggenheimer, Minnie (1882–1966)
Hall, Augusta (1802–1896)
Hanska, Eveline, Countess (1801–1882)
Hanson-Dyer, Louise (1884–1962)
Harkness, Anna M. Richardson (1837–1926)
Harkness, Mary Stillman (1874–1950)
Harkness, Rebekah (1915–1982)
Henrietta Anne of England, and duchess of Orléans (1644–1670)
Hird, Thora (1911–2003)
Horniman, Annie (1860–1937)
Howard, Henrietta (1688–1767)
Isabeau of Bavaria (1371–1435)
Isabel de Warrenne (d. 1282)
Isabelle of Lorraine (1410–1453)
Jeanne de Bourbon (1338–1378)

Jitō (645–702)
Joyner, Marjorie Stewart (1896–1994)
Judith of Flanders (1032–1094)
Kennedy, Jacqueline (1929–1994)
La Sablière, Marguerite de (1640–1693)
Louisa Ulrica of Prussia (1720–1782)
Luhan, Mabel Dodge (1879–1962)
Mahaut (c. 1270–1329)
Mancini, Marie-Anne (1649–1714)
Margaret of Angoulême (1492–1549)
Margaret of Austria (1480–1530)
Margaret of Savoy (1523–1574)
Maria Antonia of Austria (1724–1780)
Maria Barbara of Braganza (1711–1758)
Maria de Ventadour (b. 1165)
Maria of Castile (1401–1458)
Marie de Champagne (1145–1198)
Martinez, Marianne (1744–1812)
Mary of Burgundy (1457–1482)
Matilda (d. 1252)
McCormick, Edith Rockefeller (1872–1932)
Medici, Maria de (fl. late 1400s)
Medici, Violante Beatrice de (d. 1731)
Melisande (fl. 1100)
Montagu, Elizabeth (1720–1800)
Montefeltro, Elisabetta (fl. 15th c.)
Montespan, Françoise, Marquise de (1640–1707)
Morgan, Julia (1872–1957)
Morrell, Ottoline (1873–1938)
Nasi, Gracia Mendes (1510–1569)
Noailles, Marie-Laure de (1902–1970)
Nur Jahan (1577–1645)
Ocampo, Victoria (1890–1979)
Parsons, Betty Pierson (1900–1982)
Payson, Sandra (c. 1926–2004)
Perry, Antoinette (1888–1946)
Philippa of Hainault (1314–1369)
Phoebe of Cenchreae (fl. 1st c.)
Pompadour, Jeanne-Antoinette Poisson, Duchesse de (1721–1764)
Purser, Sarah (1848–1943)
Razia (1211–1240)
Richilde of Autun (d. around 910)
Rockefeller, Abby Aldrich (1874–1948)
Rogers, Grace Rainey (1867–1943)
Russell, Lucy (c. 1581–1627)
Sagan, Leontine (1889–1974)
Sert, Misia (1872–1950)
Seymour, Frances Thynne (1699–1754)
Sforza, Bona (1493–1557)
Shepard, Helen Miller (1868–1938)
Shouse, Kay (1896–1994)
Singer, Winnaretta (1865–1943)
Sophia of Greece (1938—)
Sophie Charlotte of Hanover (1668–1705)
Stanford, Jane (1828–1905)
Steloff, Frances (1887–1989)
Stoeckel, Ellen Battell (1851–1939)
Storer, Maria (1849–1932)
Sullivan, Mary Quinn (1877–1939)
Thompson, Elizabeth Rowell (1821–1899)
Thurber, Jeannette (1850–1946)
Tully, Alice (1902–1993)
Ulrica Eleanora (1688–1741)
Vanderbilt, Gloria (1924—)
Visconti, Bianca Maria (1423–1470)
Visconti, Catherine (c. 1360–1404)
von Meck, Nadezhda (1831–1894)
Walker, A'Lelia (1885–1931)
Wallada (fl. 11th c.)
Wheeler, Candace (1827–1923)
Whitney, Flora Payne (1897–1986)
Whitney, Gertrude Vanderbilt (1875–1942)
Wroth, Mary (c. 1587–c. 1651)
Zeb-un-Nissa (1639–1702)
Zimbalist, Mary Louise Curtis (1876–1970)

ART TEACHER
Bridgman, Laura (1829–1889)
Brown, Alice Van Vechten (1862–1949)
Brown Blackwell, Antoinette (1825–1921)
Carey, Ida Harriet (1891–1982)
Deland, Margaret (1857–1945)
Eise, Ida Gertrude (1891–1978)
Emmons, Chansonetta Stanley (1858–1937)
Gardner, Helen (1878–1946)
Hill, Mabel (1872–1956)
Knowlton, Helen Mary (1832–1918)
Lovell-Smith, Rata Alice (1894–1969)
Osborn, Daisy (1888–1957)
Prang, Mary D. Hicks (1836–1927)
Richmond, Dorothy Kate (1861–1935)
Sartain, Emily (1841–1927)
Savage, Augusta (1892–1962)
Tripe, Mary Elizabeth (1870–1939)
Wallwork, Elizabeth (1883–1969)
Ward, Henrietta (1832–1924)
Weir, Irene (1862–1944)
White, Anna Lois (1903–1984)
Younghusband, Adela Mary (1878–1969)

ASSASSIN (ACCUSED)
Anna Comnena (1083–1153/55)
Astorga, Nora (1949–1988)
Corday, Charlotte (1768–1793)
Domitia Longina (fl. 80s)
Figner, Vera (1852–1942)
Fromme, Lynette (1948—)
Ivanovskaia, Praskovia (1853–1935)
Kaplan, Fanya (1883–1918)
Moore, Sara Jane (1930—)
Perovskaya, Sonia (1853–1881)
Schaft, Hannie (1920–1945)
Spiridonova, Maria (1884–1941)
Theophano (c. 940–?)
Wheeldon, Alice (fl. 1917)
Zasulich, Vera (1849–1919)
Zetkin, Clara (1857–1933)

ASTROLOGER
See Prophet/sibyl/visionary.

ASTRONAUT
Bondar, Roberta (1945—)
Chawla, Kalpana (1961–2003)
Clark, Laurel (1961–2003)
Cobb, Jerrie (1931—)
Collins, Eileen (1956—)
Fisher, Anna L. (1949—)
Haigneré, Claudie (1957—)
Jemison, Mae (1956—)
Kondakova, Yelena (c. 1955—)
Lucid, Shannon (1943—)
McAuliffe, Christa (1948–1986)
Mukai, Chiaki (1952—)
Ochoa, Ellen (1958—)
Resnik, Judith (1949–1986)
Ride, Sally (1951—)
Savitskaya, Svetlana (1948—)
Seddon, Rhea (1947—)
Sharman, Helen (1963—)
Sullivan, Kathryn (1951—)
Tereshkova, Valentina (1937—)
Thornton, Kathryn (1952—)

ASTRONOMER
Adam, Madge (1912–2001)
Blagg, Mary Adela (1858–1944)
Brahe, Sophia (1556–1643)
Burbidge, Margaret (1919—)
Burnell, Jocelyn Bell (1943—)
Cannon, Annie Jump (1863–1941)
Clerke, Agnes Mary (1842–1907)
Cunitz, Maria (1610–1664)
Dumée, Jeanne (fl. 1680)
Fleming, Williamina Paton (1857–1911)
Geller, Margaret Joan (1947—)
Herschel, Caroline (1750–1848)
Hoffleit, E. Dorrit (1907—)
Huggins, Margaret (1848–1915)
Hypatia (c. 375–415)
Kirch, Maria Winkelmann (1670–1720)
Klumpke, Dorothea (1861–1942)
Lalande, Amélie Lefrançais de (fl. 1790)
Leavitt, Henrietta Swan (1868–1921)
Lepaute, Hortense (1723–1788)
Makemson, Maud Worcester (1891–1977)
Maunder, Annie Russell (1868–1947)
Maury, Antonia (1866–1952)
Mitchell, Maria (1818–1889)
Payne-Gaposchkin, Cecilia (1900–1979)
Rubin, Vera Cooper (1928—)
Salmond, Sarah (1864–1956)
Shoemaker, Carolyn (1929—)
Sitterly, Charlotte Moore (1898–1990)
Ward, Mary (1827–1869)
Whiting, Sarah F. (1847–1927)
Whitney, Mary Watson (1847–1921)
Wilson, Fiammetta Worthington (1864–1920)
Winlock, Anna (1857–1904)
Wright, Helen (1914–1997)
Young, Anne Sewell (1871–1961)

ASTROPHYSICIST
Burbidge, Margaret (1919—)
Burnell, Jocelyn Bell (1943—)
Cannon, Annie Jump (1863–1941)
Huggins, Margaret (1848–1915)
Massevitch, Alla G. (1918—)
Payne-Gaposchkin, Cecilia (1900–1979)
Whiting, Sarah F. (1847–1927)

ASYLUM MATRON
Seager, Esther (c. 1835–1911)

ATHLETE
See Baseball player.
See Basketball player.
See Biathlon athlete.
See Bowler.
See Bullfighter.
See Curler.
See Cyclist.
See Decathlon athlete.
See Disabled athlete.
See Diver.
See Equestrian.
See Fencer.
See Field-hockey player.
See Golfer.
See Gymnast.
See Harness racer.
See Heptathlete.
See Horse racer.
See Ice skater.
See Ice-Hockey player.
See Luge athlete.
See Olympic chariot racer.
See Pentathlete.
See Pugilist.
See Race-car driver.
See Runner.
See Sculler.
See Skier.
See Sleddog racer.
See Soccer player.
See Softball player.

See Squash player.
See Swimmer.
See Table-tennis player.
See Tennis player.
See Track-and-field athlete.
See Triathlon athlete.
See Volleyball player.

ATHLETIC COACH/INSTRUCTOR
See Basketball coach.
See Field-hockey coach.
See Ice-hockey coach.
See Ice-skating coach.
See Skiing instructor.
See Softball coach.
See Swimming coach/instructor.
See Tennis coach/instructor.
See Track-and-field coach.

ATTORNEY
See Lawyer.

AUTOMOBILE RACER
See Race-car driver.

AVIATION EXECUTIVE
Beech, Olive Ann (1903–1993)
Greenway, Isabella Selmes (1886–1953)
Moisant, Matilde (c. 1877–1964)
Nichols, Ruth (1901–1960)
Stinson, Katherine (1891–1977)

AVIATION INSTRUCTOR
Fort, Cornelia (1919–1943)
Hillis, Margaret (1921—)
Omlie, Phoebe Fairgrave (1902–1975)
Rainey, Barbara Allen (1948–1982)
Richey, Helen (1910–1947)
Stinson, Katherine (1891–1977)
Whyte, Edna Gardner (1902–1992)

AVIATOR
Auriol, Jacqueline (1917–2000)
Bailey, Mary (1890–1960)
Barnes, Pancho (1901–1975)
Batten, Jean Gardner (1909–1982)
Baumgartner, Ann (c. 1923—)
Beinhorn, Elly (1907—)
Benson, Mildred (1905–2002)
Bird, Nancy (1915—)
Blackburn, Jessy (1894–1995)
Blanchard, Madeleine Sophie (1778–1819)
Bland, Lilian (1878–1971)
Bolland, Adrienne (1895–1975)
Bonney, Lores (1897–1994)
Bryant, Millicent (1878–1927)
Carter, Ann Shaw (1922—)
Casey, Maie (1892–1983)
Champlin, Jane (1917–1943)
Cheung, Katherine (1904–2003)
Clarke, Julia (d. 1912)
Cobb, Jerrie (1931—)
Cochran, Jacqueline (1906–1980)
Coleman, Bessie (1892–1926)
Cook, Edith Maud (d. 1910)
Cooper, Edna Mae (1900–1986)
Coughlin, Paula A. (c. 1961—)
Crosson, Marvel (1904–1929)
Cummings, Marian (c. 1892–1984)
Davis, Dorothy Hilliard (1917–1994)
Deroche, Elise-Raymonde (1886–1919)
Deroche, Elise-Raymonde (b. 1886)
Duigan, Suzanne Lawless (1924–1993)
Dutrieu, Hélène (1877–1961)
Earhart, Amelia (1897–1937)
Elder, Ruth (1904–1977)
Flynn, Jeannie
Fort, Cornelia (1919–1943)
Funk, Wally (1939—)
Gelman, Polina (1919—)
Gordon, Gale Ann (1943—)
Gower, Pauline (1910–1947)
Grizodubova, Valentina (1910–1993)
Hart, Jane (1920—)
Heath, Sophie (1896–1939)
Heflin, Alma (fl. 1930s)
Hewlett, Hilda Beatrice (1864–1943)
Hilsz, Maryse (1903–1946)
Ingalls, Laura H. (c. 1900–c. 1988)
Johnson, Amy (1903–1941)
Karpinski, Stephanie (1912–2005)
Kennard, Gaby (1944—)
Khomiakova, Valeriia (d. 1942)
Lambine, Janna (c. 1951—)
Law, Ruth (1887–1970)
Leverton, Irene (1924—)
Lindbergh, Anne Morrow (1906–2001)
Litvyak, Lidiya (1921–1943)
Love, Nancy (1914–1976)
Macpherson, Jeanie (1887–1946)
Markham, Beryl (1902–1986)
McFarland, Irene (fl. 1925)
McKillop, Peggy (1909–1998)
Miller, Jessie Maude (1910–1972)
Mock, Jerrie (1925—)
Moggridge, Jackie (1922–2004)
Moisant, Matilde (c. 1877–1964)
Negrone, Carina (1911—)
Neuffer, Judy (1949—)
Nichols, Ruth (1901–1960)
Noyes, Blanche (1900–1981)
Oliver, Susan (1937–1990)
Omlie, Phoebe Fairgrave (1902–1975)
Osipenko, Polina (1907–1939)
Peake, Felicity (1913–2002)
Pepa, Mari (1913–2004)
Quimby, Harriet (1875–1912)
Raiche, Bessica (c. 1874–1932)
Rainey, Barbara Allen (1948–1982)
Raskova, Marina (1912–1943)
Rawls, Katherine (1918–1982)
Reitsch, Hanna (1912–1979)
Richey, Helen (1910–1947)
Russell, Mary du Caurroy (1865–1937)
Rutledge, Margaret Fane (1914–2004)
Scott, Blanche (1885–1970)
Scott, Sheila (1927–1988)
Shakhovskaya, Eugenie M. (1889–?)
Stauffenberg, Litta von (c. 1905–1945)
Stinson, Katherine (1891–1977)
Stinson, Marjorie (1894–1975)
Streeter, Ruth Cheney (1895–1990)
Thaden, Louise (1905–1979)
Thompson, Freda (1906–1980)
Tiburzi, Bonnie (1948—)
Tourtel, Mary (1874–1948)
Welch, Ann (1917–2002)
Wells, Fay Gillis (1908–2002)
Whyte, Edna Gardner (1902–1992)
Yeager, Jeana (1952—)

BACTERIOLOGIST
Branham, Sara Elizabeth (1888–1962)
Datta, Naomi (1922—)
Evans, Alice Catherine (1881–1975)
Fleming, Amalia (1912–1986)
Freeman, Mavis (1907—)
Frost, Constance Helen (c. 1862–1920)
Hamilton, Alice (1869–1970)
Hazen, Elizabeth Lee (1883–1975)
Hobby, Gladys Lounsbury (1910–1993)
Horsley, Alice Woodward (1871–1957)
Lancefield, Rebecca Craighill (1895–1981)
McCoy, Elizabeth (1903–1978)
Moulton, Barbara (1915–1997)
Williams, Anna Wessels (1863–1954)

BADMINTON PLAYER
Audina, Mia (1979—)
Bang, Soo-Hyun (1972—)
Chung So-Young (1967—)
Emms, Gail (1977—)
Gao Ling (1979—)
Ge Fei (1975—)
Gilks, Gillian (1959—)
Gil Young-Ah (1970—)
Gong Zhichao (1977—)
Guan Weizhen (1964—)
Gu Jun (1975—)
Hashman, Judy (1935—)
Hill, Virginia (1907–1967)
Huang Hua (1969—)
Huang Nanyan (1977—)
Huang Sui (1982—)
Hwang Hae-Young (1966—)
Jang Hye-Ock
Lee Kyung-Won (1980—)
Lin Yanfen (1971—)
Martin, Camilla (1974—)
Nong Qunhua (1966—)
Pi Hongyan (1979—)
Qin Yiyuan
Ra Kyung-Min (1976—)
Schjoldager, Mette (1977—)
Shim Eun-Jung (1971—)
Susanti, Susi (1971—)
Tang Jiuhong (1969—)
Tang Yongshu
Walton, Dorothy (1908—)
Yang Wei (1979—)
Yao Fen (1967—)
Ye Zhaoying (1974—)
Zhang Jiewen (1981—)
Zhang Ning (1975—)
Zhou Mi (1979—)

BAKER
Furley, Matilda (1813–1899)

BALLET DANCER
Aakesson, Birgit (c. 1908–2001)
Abarca, Lydia (1951—)
Abramova, Anastasia (b. 1902)
Adamova, Adela (1927—)
Adams, Diana (1927–1993)
Addor, Ady (c. 1935—)
Adelaide (c. 1884–1959)
Adret, Françoise (1920—)
Agoglia, Esmeralda (1926—)
Albrecht, Angele (1942—)
Aldous, Lucette (1938—)
Alexander, Dorothy (1904–1986)
Algeranova, Claudie (1924—)
Allard, Marie (1742–1802)
Alonso, Alicia (1921—)
Amati, Olga (1924—)
Amiel, Josette (1930—)
Anchutina, Leda (1915–1989)
Anderson-Ivantzova, Elizabeth (c. 1893–1973)
Andersson, Gerd (1932—)
Anderton, Elizabeth (1938—)
Andreae, Felicity (1914—)
Andreyanova, Yelena Ivanovna (1816–1857)
Angiolini, Giuseppina (c. 1800–?)
Anisimova, Nina (1909—)
Apinée, Irena (c. 1930—)
Arbatova, Mia (c. 1910—)
Argyle, Pearl (1910–1947)
Ari, Carina (1897–1970)

Occupational Index

Arnold, Bené (1953—)
Arova, Sonia (1927–2001)
Arthur, Charthel (1946—)
Asakawa, Hitomi (1948)
Asensio, Manola (1946—)
Ashley, Merrill (1950—)
Asquith, Ruby (c. 1910—)
Astafieva, Serafima (1876–1934)
Augusta, Mlle (1806–1901)
Austin, Debra (1955—)
Av-Paul, Annette (1944—)
Baccelli, Giovanna (c. 1753–1801)
Balachova, Alexandra (1887–1905)
Baldina, Alexandra Maria (1885–1977)
Ballou, Germaine (b. 1899)
Banks, Margaret (1924—)
Barbieri, Margaret (1947—)
Bardin, Madeleine (c. 1920—)
Bari, Tania (1936—)
Baron, Emilie (c. 1834–1852)
Baronova, Irina (1919—)
Bauer, Margaret (1927—)
Bayard, Sylviane (1957—)
Beaugrand, Léontine (1842–1925)
Belfiore, Liliana (1952—)
Bella, Antoinetta (b. 1863)
Bentley, Muriel (1917–1999)
Beretta, Caterina (1839–1911)
Bergsma, Deanne (1941—)
Beriosova, Svetlana (1932–1998)
Bessmertnova, Natalia (1941—)
Bewley, Lois (c. 1936—)
Bey, Hannelore (1941—)
Bias, Fanny (1789–1825)
Bigottini, Emilie (1784–1858)
Biracree, Thelma (1904–1997)
Bjørn, Dinna (1947—)
Blangy, Hermine (c. 1820–c. 1865)
Bogomolova, Ludmilla (1932—)
Bonfanti, Marietta (1845–1921)
Boris, Ruthanna (1918—)
Borne, Bonita (1952—)
Bosch, Aurora (c. 1940—)
Boschetti, Amina (1836–1881)
Bovt, Violette (1927—)
Bowman, Patricia (1904–1999)
Bozzacchi, Giuseppina (1853–1870)
Brabants, Jeanne (1920—)
Bradley, Lisa (1941—)
Brae, June (1917–2000)
Branitzka, Nathalie (1905–1977)
Brayley, Sally (1937—)
Brexner, Edeltraud (1927—)
Brianza, Carlotta (1862–1930)
Brock, Karena (1942—)
Brown, Jessie (1892–1985)
Brown, Karen (1955—)
Brown, Vida (1922—)
Browne, Leslie (1958—)
Bruce, Betty (1920–1974)
Brugnoli, Amalia (c. 1808–?)
Bulnes, Esmée (1900–1986)
Burr, Marilyn (1933—)
Bush, Noreen (1905–1977)
Butsova, Hilda (1896–1976)
Caccialanza, Gisella (1914–1998)
Calzada, Alba (1945—)
Camargo, Marie-Anne Cupis de (1710–1770)
Campanini, Barbara (1721–1799)
Cardus, Ana (1943—)
Cartier, Diana (1939—)
Cavallazzi, Malvina (c. 1852–1924)
Celeste, Madame (1815–1882)
Cerri, Cecilie (1872–1931)
Cerrito, Fanny (1817–1909)
Chamie, Tatiana (d. 1953)
Charrat, Janine (1924—)
Chase, Lucia (1897–1986)
Chauviré, Yvette (1917—)
Chiriaeff, Ludmilla (1924–1996)
Chouteau, Yvonne (1929—)
Ciocca, Giovanna (c. 1825–?)
Cisneros, Evelyn (1958—)
Clayden, Pauline (1922—)
Cleare, Ivy (1948—)
Colby, Christine (c. 1950—)
Coles, Joyce (b. around 1904)
Collier, Lesley (1947—)
Collins, Janet (1917—)
Conley, Sandra (1943—)
Conrad, Karen (1919–1976)
Consuelo, Beatriz (c. 1930—)
Contreras, Gloria (1934—)
Cook, Sheri (1955—)
Coquillard-Albrier, Albertine (c. 1810–1846)
Cordua, Beatrice (1943—)
Corkle, Francesca (1952—)
Coulon, Anne-Jacqueline (fl. 18th c.)
Cowen, Donna (c. 1950—)
Craig, Sandra (1942—)
Craske, Margaret (1892–1990)
Crespé, Marie-Madeleine (1760–1796)
Cucchi, Claudine (1834–1913)
Cullberg, Birgit (1908–1999)
Cuoco, Joyce (1953—)
Curley, Wilma (1937—)
Dale, Daphne (1931–1982)
Dale, Margaret (1922—)
D'Alessandri-Valdine, Blanche (c. 1862–1948)
Danias, Starr (1949—)
Daniele, Graciela (1939—)
Danilova, Alexandra (1903–1997)
Danilova, Maria (1793–1810)
D'Antuono, Eleanor (1939—)
Darsonval, Lycette (1912–1996)
Daunt, Yvonne (b. around 1900)
Daydé, Liane (1932—)
De Angelo, Ana Marie (1955—)
De La Bije, Willy (1934—)
De Lappe, Gemze (1922—)
De Lavallade, Carmen (1931—)
De Leporte, Rita (c. 1910—)
Dell'Era, Antoinetta (1861–?)
Derman, Vergie (1942—)
Di Bona, Linda (1946—)
Ditchburn, Ann (c. 1950—)
Dobson, Deborah (c. 1950—)
Doering, Jane (c. 1922—)
D'Or, Henrietta (1844–1886)
Doubrovska, Felia (1896–1981)
Douglas, Helyn (c. 1945—)
Douvillier, Suzanne (1778–1826)
Drylie, Patricia (c. 1928–1993)
Du Boulay, Christine (c. 1923—)
Dudinskaya, Natalya (1912–2003)
Dudleston, Penny (1952—)
Dumilâtre, Adèle (1821–1909)
Duna, Steffi (1910–1992)
Duvernay, Pauline (1813–1894)
Dynalix, Paulette (1917—)
Eduardova, Eugenia (1882–1980)
Egorova, Lyubov (1880–1972)
Egri, Susanna (1926—)
Elder, Anne (1918–1976)
Eldred, Pam (c. 1948—)
Elliston, Daisy (b. 1894)
Elseeta (1883–1903)
Elssler, Fanny (1810–1884)
Elssler, Thérèse (1808–1878)
Elvin, Violetta (1925—)
Espinosa, Judith (1877–1949)
Essen, Viola (1926–1969)
Estópinal, Renee (1949—)
Evdokimova, Eva (1948—)
Everett, Eva (1942—)
Fabbri, Flora (c. 1807–c. 1857)
Fallis, Barbara (1924–1980)
Farjeon, Annabel (1919—)
Farrally, Betty (1915–1989)
Farrell, Suzanne (1945—)
Farron, Julia (1922—)
Fay, Vivien (b. around 1908)
Federova, Nina (1958—)
Federova, Sophia (1879–1963)
Fedicheva, Kaleria (1936—)
Ferrais, Amalia (1830–1904)
Ferri, Olga (1928—)
Fifield, Elaine (1930–1999)
Fiocre, Eugénie (1845–1908)
Fitzjames, Natalie (b. 1819)
Flagg, Elise (1951—)
Flindt, Vivi (1943—)
Fokina, Vera (1886–1958)
Fonaroff, Nina (1914–2003)
Fontaine, Mlle de la (1655–1738)
Fonteyn, Margot (1919–1991)
Fornaroli, Cia (1888–1954)
Fracci, Carla (1936—)
Fraley, Ingrid (1949—)
Franca, Celia (1921—)
French, Ruth (b. 1906)
Fris, Maria (1932–1961)
Froman, Margareta (1890–1970)
Fuerstner, Fiona (1936—)
Fuocco, Sofia (1830–1916)
Galli, Rosina (1896–1940)
Gambarelli, Maria (1900–1990)
García, Marta (c. 1945—)
Gardie, Anna (c. 1760–1798)
Gardiner, Lisa (c. 1896–1958)
Geltzer, Ykaterina (1876–1962)
Genée, Adeline (1878–1970)
George, Carolyn (1927—)
Gerdt, Elizaveta (1891–1975)
Geva, Tamara (1906–1997)
Gielgud, Maina (1945—)
Gilmour, Sally (1921–2004)
Glover, Amelia (c. 1873–?)
Gollner, Nana (1919–1980)
Golovkina, Sofia (1915–2004)
Gorham, Kathleen (1932–1983)
Govrin, Gloria (1942—)
Grahn, Lucile (1819–1907)
Grandy, Maria (1937–1998)
Granger, Josie (1853–1934)
Grant, Pauline (1915—)
Grantzow, Adele (1845–1877)
Gregory, Cynthia (1946—)
Grey, Beryl (1927—)
Grisi, Carlotta (1819–1899)
Gruber, Lilo (1915–1992)
Gsovsky, Tatiana (1901–1993)
Guimard, Marie Madeleine (1743–1816)
Guy-Stéphan, Marie (1818–1873)
Haig, Emma (1898–1939)
Hanka, Erika (1905–1958)
Hanke, Suzanne (1948—)
Harris, Joan (1920—)
Hasselqvist, Jenny (1894–1978)
Haydée, Marcia (1939—)
Hayden, Melissa (1923—)
Heaton, Anne (1930—)
Heberle, Thérèse (1806–1840)
Heinel, Anna (1753–1808)
Hendl, Susan (1949—)
Hennings, Betty (1850–1939)
Hightower, Rosella (1920—)
Holmes, Anna-Marie (1943—)

Honningen, Mette (1944—)
Horne, Katharyn (1932—)
Horvath, Julia (1924–1947)
Howes, Dulcie (1908–1993)
Hyman, Prudence (1914–1995)
Ichino, Yoko (c. 1954—)
Inglesby, Mona (1918—)
Isaksen, Lone (1941—)
Istomina, Anna (1925—)
Istomina, Avdotia (1799–1848)
Jackson, Rowena (1926—)
Jarvis, Lilian (1931—)
Jeanmaire, Zizi (1924—)
Jenner, Ann (1944—)
Jillana (1934—)
Johansson, Anna (1860–1917)
Jones, Marilyn (1940—)
Jones, Susan (1952—)
June (1901–c. 1984)
Jurrilëns, Henny (1949—)
Kai, Una (1928—)
Kain, Karen (1951—)
Karalli, Vera (1889–1972)
Karnilova, Maria (1920–2001)
Karsavina, Tamara (1885–1978)
Karstens, Gerda (1903–1988)
Kasatkina, Natalia (1934—)
Kastl, Sonja (1929—)
Kaye, Nora (1920–1987)
Keane, Fiorella (1930–1976)
Keil, Birgit (1944—)
Kent, Allegra (1937—)
Khoklova, Olga (d. 1955)
Kirkland, Gelsey (1952—)
Kirkland, Johnna (1950—)
Kirkwhite, Iris (c. 1900–1975)
Kirsova, Helene (1910–1962)
Kocsun, Ruth Ann (1928—)
Köhler-Richter, Emmy (1918—)
Kolpakova, Irina (1933—)
Kondratieva, Marina (1934—)
Korty, Sonia (1892–1955)
Kovach, Nora (1931—)
Krassovska, Nathalie (1918–2005)
Krieger, Victorina (b. 1896)
Kshesinskaia, Matilda (1872–1971)
Kurgapkina, Ninel (1929—)
Kyasht, Lydia (1885–1959)
LaBelle Oceana (c. 1835–?)
Laemmle, Carla (b. 1909)
Laerkesen, Anna (1942—)
Lafon, Madeleine (1924–1967)
Laine, Doris (1959—)
Laing, Elizabeth (1959—)
Lander, Margot (1910–1961)
Lander, Toni (1931–1985)
Lane, Maryon (1931—)
Lang, Maria (1948—)
Lanner, Katti (1829–1908)
Lany, Louise-Madeleine (1733–1777)
Larsen, Gerd (1920–2001)
Lawson, Joan (1907–2002)
Le Clercq, Tanaquil (1929–2000)
Lecompte, Eugenie Anna (c. 1798–c. 1850)
Lee, Mary Ann (1823–1899)
Lee, Sondra (1930—)
Legat, Nadine (c. 1895–?)
Legnani, Pierina (1863–1923)
Leland, Sara (1941—)
Lepeshinskaya, Olga (1916—)
Leporska, Zoya (1918–1996)
Leroux, Pauline (1809–1891)
Leskova, Tatiana (1922—)
Littlefield, Caroline (c. 1882–1957)
Littlefield, Catherine (1904–1951)
Littlefield, Dorothie (c. 1908–1953)
Livry, Emma (1842–1863)
Lloyd, Maude (1908–2004)
Lopokova, Lydia (c. 1892–1981)
Lopukhova, Evgenia (1884–1941)
Lorcia, Suzanne (1902–1999)
Lorrayne, Vyvyan (1939—)
Lukom, Elena (1891–1968)
Lynne, Gillian (1926—)
Lyon, Annabelle (c. 1915—)
MacDonald, Elaine (1943—)
Makarova, Natalia (1940—)
Marchand, Collette (1925—)
Markova, Alicia (1910–2004)
Markovic, Vera (1931—)
Mason, Monica (1941—)
Mathé, Carmen (1938—)
Mauri, Rosita (1856–1923)
Maximova, Ekaterina (1939—)
May, Pamela (1917–2005)
Maywood, Augusta (1825–1876)
McBride, Patricia (1942—)
Mears, Elizabeth (1900–1988)
Melendez, Jolinda (1954—)
Melikova, Genia (c. 1930–2004)
Méndez, Josefina (c. 1940—)
Menuhin, Diana (1912–2003)
Menzelli, Elisabetta (c. 1860–c. 1929)
Menzelli, Lola (c. 1898–1951)
Mercier, Margaret (1937—)
Mérode, Cléo de (c. 1875–1966)
Messerer, Sulamith (1908–2004)
Miller, Jane (1945—)
Miller, Patricia (1927—)
Miramova, Elena (c. 1905—)
Mladova, Milada (c. 1918—)
Mlakar, Pia (1908–2000)
Mlakar, Veronika (1935—)
Monkman, Phyllis (1892–1976)
Morales, Hilda (1946—)
Moreton, Ursula (1903–1973)
Morishita, Yoko (1948—)
Morlacchi, Guiseppina (1836–1886)
Mosolova, Vera (1875–1949)
Moss, Marjorie (c. 1895–1935)
Mossetti, Carlotta (1890–?)
Motte, Claire (1937—)
Mounsey, Yvonne (c. 1921—)
Moylan, Mary-Ellen (1926—)
Nadezhdina, Nadezhda (1908–1979)
Neary, Colleen (1952—)
Neary, Patricia (1942—)
Nelidova, Lydia (1863–1929)
Nemchinova, Vera (1899–1984)
Nerina, Nadia (1927—)
Newton, Joy (1913–1996)
Nielsen, Augusta (1822–1902)
Nijinska, Bronislava (1891–1972)
Nikitina, Alice (1909–1978)
Noblet, Lise (1801–1852)
Nordi, Cleo (b. 1899)
Novak, Nina (1927—)
Olenewa, Maria (1893–1965)
Oliphant, Betty (1918–2004)
Olrich, April (1931—)
O'Neal, Christine (1949—)
Orlando, Mariane (1934—)
Osato, Sono (1919–1953)
Ostergaard, Solveig (1939—)
Pagava, Ethery (1932—)
Page, Annette (1952—)
Page, Ruth (1899–1991)
Palladino, Emma (c. 1860–1922)
Pallerini, Antonia (1790–1870)
Panov, Galina (1949—)
Park, Merle (1937—)
Parker, Madeleine (c. 1909–1936)
Parkinson, Georgina (1938—)
Pavlova, Anna (1881–1931)
Pavlova, Nadezhda (1956—)
Penney, Jennifer (1946—)
Pereyaslavec, Valentina (1907–1998)
Petipa, Marie (1836–1882)
Petipa, Marie (1857–1930)
Philippart, Nathalie (c. 1926—)
Plá, Mirta (1940–2003)
Plisetskaya, Maya (1925—)
Poelvoorde, Rita (1951—)
Poliakova, Elena (1884–1972)
Pontois, Noëlla (1943—)
Popova, Nina (1922—)
Portapovitch, Anna Knapton (1890–1974)
Porter, Marguerite (c. 1956—)
Preobrazhenska, Olga (1871–1962)
Prévost, Françoise (1680–1741)
Price, Ellen (1878–1968)
Price, Juliette (1831–1906)
Ralov, Kirsten (1922–1999)
Rambert, Marie (1888–1982)
Rambova, Natacha (1897–1966)
Rasch, Albertina (1896–1967)
Rayet, Jacqueline (1932—)
Redpath, Christine (1951—)
Reed, Janet (1916–2000)
Reiman, Elise (c. 1910—)
Remington, Barbara (1936—)
Riabouchinska, Tatiana (1917–2000)
Rode, Lizzie (1933—)
Rodriguez, Zhandra (1947—)
Roje, Ana (1909—)
Romanova, Maria (1886–1954)
Rosati, Carolina (1826–1905)
Roudenko, Lubov (1915—)
Roux, Aline (1935—)
Rowe, Marilyn (1946—)
Rubenstein, Ida (1875–1961)
Rubinstein, Ida (1880–1960)
Ruiz, Brunhilda (1936—)
Russell, Francia (1938—)
Sallé, Marie (1707–1756)
Salvioni, Guglierma (1842–?)
Sand, Inge (1928–1974)
Sand, Monique (1944—)
Sangalli, Rita (1849–1909)
Sankovskaya, Yekaterina (c. 1816–1878)
Sappington, Margo (1947—)
Sarry, Christine (1946—)
Sarstadt, Marian (1942—)
Schanne, Margrethe (1921—)
Schollar, Ludmilla (c. 1888–1978)
Schooling, Elizabeth (1919—)
Schwarz, Solange (1910–2000)
Scott, Margaret (1922—)
Sedova, Julia (1880–1969)
Seigneuret, Michele (1934—)
Semyonova, Marina (b. 1908)
Sergava, Katharine (1910–2005)
Serrano, Lupe (1930—)
Severn, Margaret (1901–1997)
Seymour, Lynn (1939—)
Shabelska, Maria (1898–1980)
Shearer, Moira (1911–2006)
Sheina, Svetlana (1918–2005)
Shelest, Alla (1919–1998)
Sibley, Antoinette (b. 1939)
Simone, Kirsten (1934—)
Sizova, Alla (1939—)
Sköld, Berit (1939—)
Skorik, Irene (1928—)
Slavenska, Mia (1914–2000)
Smith, Queenie (1898–1978)
Smoller, Dorothy (c. 1901–1926)
Sobotka, Ruth (1925–1967)

Sokolova, Eugenia (1850–1925)
Sokolova, Lydia (1896–1974)
Sorkin, Naomi (1948—)
Sorokina, Nina (1942—)
Spessivtzeva, Olga (1895–1980)
Spies, Daisy (1905–2000)
St. Clair, Sallie (1842–1867)
Stroganova, Nina (1919—)
Struchkova, Raissa (1925–2005)
Subligny, Marie-Thérèse Perdou de (1666–1736)
Sullivan, Jean (1923–2003)
Svetlova, Marina (1922—)
Sylwan, Kari (1959—)
Taglioni, Louisa (1823–1893)
Taglioni, Maria (1804–1884)
Taglioni, Marie (1833–1891)
Tallchief, Maria (1925—)
Tallchief, Marjorie (1927—)
Talvo, Tyyne (b. 1919)
Taverner, Sonia (1936—)
Taylor, Brenda (1934—)
Tcherina, Ludmilla (1924–2004)
Tcherkassky, Marianna (1955—)
Tchernicheva, Lubov (1890–1976)
Tennant, Veronica (1946—)
Terabust, Elisabetta (1946—)
Theilade, Nini (b. 1915)
Thesmar, Ghislaine (1943—)
Thorogood, Alfreda (1942—)
Toumanova, Tamara (1919–1996)
Toumine, Nesta (c. 1912–1995)
Tracy, Paula (1939—)
Trailine, Helen (1928—)
Trefilova, Vera (1875–1943)
Turnbull, Julia Anne (1822–1887)
Uchida, Christine (1952—)
Ulanova, Galina (1910–1998)
Vaganova, Agrippina (1879–1951)
Vance, Norma (1927–1956)
Vane, Daphne (1918–1966)
Vangsaae, Mona (1920–1983)
Van Hamel, Martine (1945—)
van Praagh, Peggy (1910–1990)
Vaussard, Christiane (1923—)
Vazem, Ekaterina (1848–1937)
Vecheslova, Tatiana (1910–1991)
Verchinina, Nina (1910–1995)
Verdy, Violette (1931—)
Vessel, Anne Marie (1949—)
Vestris, Thérèse (1726–1808)
Volkova, Vera (1904–1975)
Vollmar, Jocelyn (1925—)
von Aroldingen, Karin (1941—)
Von Rosen, Elsa Marianne (1924—)
Vyroubova, Nina (1921—)
Watts, Heather (1953—)
Webster, Clara Vestris (1821–1844)
Weisberger, Barbara (c. 1926—)
Weiss, Josephine (1805–1852)
Wells, Doreen (1937—)
West, Elizabeth (1927–1962)
Wilson, Sallie (1932—)
Woizikowska, Sonia (1919—)
Woolliams, Anne (1926–1999)
Wright, Belinda (1927—)
Wright, Rebecca (1942—)
Yarborough, Sara (1950—)
Youshkevitch, Nina (c. 1921–1998)
Youskevitch, Maria (c. 1946—)
Yuan, Tina (c. 1950—)
Zambelli, Carlotta (1875–1968)
Zanfretta, Francesca (1862–1952)
Zide, Rochelle (1938—)
Zimmermann, Gerda (1927—)
Zorina, Vera (1917–2003)
Zucchi, Virginia (1849–1930)

BALLET DIRECTOR
Alonso, Alicia (1921—)
Chase, Lucia (1897–1986)
Cullberg, Birgit (1908–1999)
Danilova, Alexandra (1903–1997)
de Valois, Ninette (1898–2001)
Dunham, Katherine (1909–2006)
Franca, Celia (1921—)
Haydée, Marcia (1939—)
Hightower, Rosella (1920—)
MacDonald, Elaine (1943—)
Markova, Alicia (1910–2004)
Page, Ruth (1899–1991)
Park, Merle (1937—)
Pavlova, Anna (1881–1931)
Plisetskaya, Maya (1925—)
Rambert, Marie (1888–1982)
Tallchief, Maria (1925—)
Tallchief, Marjorie (1927—)
van Praagh, Peggy (1910–1990)

BALLET TEACHER
Adams, Diana (1927–1993)
Anderson-Ivantzova, Elizabeth (c. 1893–1973)
Astafieva, Serafima (1876–1934)
Bonfanti, Marietta (1845–1921)
Bulnes, Esmée (1900–1986)
Bush, Noreen (1905–1977)
Cavallazzi, Malvina (c. 1852–1924)
Collins, Janet (1917–2003)
Craske, Margaret (1892–1990)
Danilova, Alexandra (1903–1997)
de Valois, Ninette (1898–2001)
Du Boulay, Christine (c. 1923—)
Dudinskaya, Natalya (1912–2003)
Eduardova, Eugenia (1882–1980)
Egorova, Lyubov (1880–1972)
Espinosa, Judith (1877–1949)
Farrell, Suzanne (1945—)
French, Ruth (b. 1906)
Gardiner, Lisa (c. 1896–1958)
Gerdt, Elizaveta (1891–1975)
Golovkina, Sofia (1915–2004)
Gorham, Kathleen (1932–1983)
Grandy, Maria (1937–1998)
Harris, Joan (1920—)
Haywood, Claire (c. 1916–1978)
Hightower, Rosella (1920—)
Howes, Dulcie (1908–1993)
Karsavina, Tamara (1885–1978)
Keane, Fiorella (1930–1976)
Kent, Allegra (1937—)
Korty, Sonia (1892–1955)
Kovach, Nora (1931—)
Kshesinskaia, Matilda (1872–1971)
LaBelle Oceana (c. 1835–?)
Le Clercq, Tanaquil (1929–2000)
Legat, Nadine (c. 1895–?)
Littlefield, Caroline (c. 1882–1957)
Lloyd, Gweneth (1901–1993)
Markova, Alicia (1910–2004)
Melikova, Genia (c. 1930–2004)
Menzelli, Elisabetta (c. 1860–c. 1929)
Nelidova, Lydia (1863–1929)
Newton, Joy (1913–1996)
Nijinska, Bronislava (1891–1972)
Nordi, Cleo (b. 1899)
Olenewa, Maria (1893–1965)
Oliphant, Betty (1918–2004)
Page, Ruth (1899–1991)
Park, Merle (1937—)
Pereyaslavec, Valentina (1907–1998)
Poliakova, Elena (1884–1972)
Popova, Nina (1922—)
Portapovitch, Anna Knapton (1890–1974)
Preobrazhenska, Olga (1871–1962)
Prévost, Françoise (1680–1741)
Rambert, Marie (1888–1982)
Reiman, Elise (c. 1910—)
Romanova, Maria (1886–1954)
Rousanne, Mme (1894–1958)
Sedova, Julia (1880–1969)
Shabelska, Maria (1898–1980)
Slavenska, Mia (1914–2000)
Sokolova, Lydia (1896–1974)
Taglioni, Maria (1804–1884)
Tallchief, Marjorie (1927—)
Tchernicheva, Lubov (1890–1976)
Toumine, Nesta (c. 1912–1995)
Ulanova, Galina (1910–1998)
Vaganova, Agrippina (1879–1951)
van Praagh, Peggy (1910–1990)
Volkova, Vera (1904–1975)
Vyroubova, Nina (1921—)
Wells, Mary Ann (c. 1895–1971)
Woolliams, Anne (1926–1999)
Youshkevitch, Nina (c. 1921–1998)
Zanfretta, Francesca (1862–1952)

BALLOONIST
Blanchard, Madeleine Sophie (1778–1819)
Conn, Elenor (fl. 1980s)
Shepherd, Dolly (d. 1983)

BANDIT
Bonita, Maria (c. 1908–1938)
Cooney, Cecelia (1904–1969)
Dean, Margie (1896–1918)
Phoolan Devi (1963–2001)
Place, Etta (fl. 1896–1905)
Putli Bai (1929–1958)
Starr, Belle (1848–1889)

BANDLEADER
Akiyoshi, Toshiko (1929—)
Armstrong, Lil Hardin (1898–1971)
Austin, Lovie (1887–1972)
Calloway, Blanche (1902–1973)
Hutton, Ina Ray (1916–1984)

BAND SINGER
Bergeron, Marian (1918–2002)
Blair, Janet (1921—)
Boswell, Connee (1907–1976)
Connor, Chris (1927—)
Daniels, Maxine (1930–2003)
Dawn, Dolly (1916–2002)
Johnson, Ella (1923–2004)
Maxwell, Marilyn (1921–1972)
Moore, Constance (1919–2005)
Morse, Ella Mae (1925–1999)
O'Connell, Helen (1920–1993)
O'Day, Anita (1919—)
Ross, Shirley (1909–1975)
Simms, Ginny (1915–1994)
Tilton, Martha (1915—)

BANKER/FINANCIER
Adasse (fl. 1348)
Bay, Josephine Perfect (1900–1962)
Burdett-Coutts, Angela (1814–1906)
Clark, Georgia Neese (1900–1995)
Crockett, Jean A. (1919–1998)
Driscoll, Clara (1881–1945)
Dunne, Jean Gilligan (1951—)
Erskine, Mary (1629–1707)
Gee, Dolly (1897–1978)
Gleason, Kate (1865–1933)
Green, Hetty (1834–1916)
Ishigaki, Rin (1920—)
McWhinney, Madeline H. (1922—)
Mills, Lorna H. (1916–1998)
Minijima, Kiyo (1833–1919)

Ramphele, Mamphela (1947—)
Roebling, Mary G. (1906–1994)
Song Ailing (1890–1973)
Streeter, Alison (1964—)
Walker, Maggie Lena (1867–1934)

BANKING COMMISSIONER
Siebert, Muriel (1932—)

BANKROBBER (ACCUSED)
Barker, Ma (1872–1935)
Churchill, May (1876–1929)
Hearst, Patricia Campbell (1954—)
Irwin, Estelle Mae (1923—)
Parker, Bonnie (1910–1934)

BARBER
Cohen, Myra (1892–1959)

BARONESS
Arnstein, Fanny von (1758–1818)
Arundel, Blanche (1583–1649)
Audley, Alice (d. 1374)
Bawr, Alexandrine de (1773–1860)
Beauchamp, Elizabeth (fl. 1400s)
Blackstone, Tessa (1942—)
Blaze de Bury, Rose (?–1894)
Blunt, Anne (1837–1917)
Bol Poel, Martha (1877–1956)
Bonham-Carter, Violet (1887–1969)
Bonville, Cecily (1460–1530)
Bourchier, Anne (1512–1571)
Brandon, Anne (d. 1557)
Braose, Maud de (d. 1211)
Brassey, Anna (1839–1887)
Budberg, Moura (1892–1974)
Bülow, Frieda von (1857–1909)
Burdett-Coutts, Angela (1814–1906)
Castle, Barbara (1910–2002)
Chantal, Jeanne Françoise de (1572–1641)
Christian de Plessetis (c. 1250–?)
Churchill, Clementine (1885–1977)
Clive, Margaret (1735–1817)
Comyn, Alice (fl. 1318)
Craven, Elizabeth (1750–1828)
Currie, Mary Montgomerie (1843–1905)
Curzon, Grace Hinds (1878–1958)
Curzon, Irene (1896–1966)
Curzon, Mary Leiter (1870–1906)
Dacre, Barbarina (1768–1854)
Dean, Brenda (1943—)
Desiree Bernadotte (1938—)
Desiree Bernadotte (b. 1938)
Despenser, Isabel (1400–1439)
Digby, Lettice (c. 1588–1658)
Digby el Mesrab, Jane (1807–1881)
Droste-Hülshoff, Annette von (1797–1848)
Ebner-Eschenbach, Marie (1830–1916)
Elphinstone, Margaret Mercer (1788–1867)
Falkenhayn, Benita von (d. 1935)
Feuchères, Sophie, Baronne de (c. 1795–1841)
Fitzalan, Margaret (b. around 1388)
Freytag-Loringhoven, Baroness Elsa von (1875–1927)
Goodall, Jane (1934—)
Greiffenberg, Catharina Regina von (1633–1694)
Grey, Elizabeth (fl. 1482–1530)
Grey, Elizabeth (1505–1526)
Gyllembourg-Ehrensvärd, Thomasine (1773–1856)
Handel-Mazzetti, Enrica von (1871–1955)
Heemstra, Ella van (1900–1984)
Hervey, Mary (1700–1768)
Hogg, Sarah (1946—)
Hohenhausen, Elizabeth (1789–1857)
Horsbrugh, Florence (1889–1969)
Howard, Catherine (fl. 1450)
Howard, Catherine (d. after 1478)
Isaacs, Stella (1894–1971)
James, P.D. (1920—)
Jeanne de Lestonac (1556–1640)
Joan Plantagenet (c. 1312–c. 1345)
Kielmansegge, Sophia Charlotte von (1673–1725)
Kinnaird, Mary Jane (1816–1888)
Krüdener, Julie de (1764–1824)
Latimer, Elizabeth (d. 1395)
Lawrence, Frieda (1879–1956)
Lee, Jennie (1904–1988)
Lempicka, Tamara de (1898–1980)
Lennox, Caroline (1723–1774)
Lennox, Sarah (1745–1826)
Ludford, Sarah (1951—)
MacRobert, Rachel (1884–1954)
Mahaut II de Dampierre (1234–1266)
Marchesi, Blanche (1863–1940)
Margaret Wake of Liddell (c. 1299–1349)
Mohun, Joan (fl. 14th c.)
Montacute, Margaret (fl. 1400s)
Monthermer, Margaret (fl. 1350)
Mortimer, Joan (fl. 1300)
Mortimer, Maud (c. 1229–1301)
Mountbatten, Patricia (1924—)
Mowbray, Isabel (fl. late 1300s)
Nairne, Carolina (1766–1845)
Neville, Jane (d. 1538)
Nicholson, Emma (1941—)
Orczy, Emma (1865–1947)
Paemel, Monika van (1945—)
Patti, Adelina (1843–1919)
Percy, Elizabeth (1716–1776)
Percy, Mary (1320–1362)
Pike, Mervyn (1918–2004)
Pole, Ursula (d. 1570)
Rebay, Hilla (1890–1967)
Rich, Elizabeth (fl. 1710)
Rothschild, Constance de (1843–1931)
Rothschild, Jeanne de (1908–2003)
Rothschild, Mathilde de (1874–1926)
Ryder, Sue (1923–2000)
Schulenburg, Ehrengard Melusina von der (1667–1743)
Sedley, Catharine (1657–1717)
Segrave, Margaret (c. 1280–?)
Serota, Beatrice (1919–2002)
Somerset, Elizabeth (fl. 1650)
Staël, Germaine de (1766–1817)
Stein, Charlotte von (1742–1827)
Stocks, Mary Danvers (1891–1975)
Summerskill, Edith (1901–1980)
Suttner, Bertha von (1843–1914)
Talbot, Elizabeth (d. 1487)
Tautphoeus, Baroness von (1807–1893)
Tennyson, Emily (1813–1896)
Ufford, Margaret de (fl. 14th c.)
Van Grippenberg, Alexandra (1859–1913)
Vere, Margaret de (fl. 14th c.)
Vetsera, Marie (1871–1889)
Villiers, Barbara (d. 1708)
Von Trapp, Maria (1905–1987)
Ward, Barbara (1914–1981)
Ward, Irene (1895–1980)
Warnock, Mary (1924—)
Wentworth, Henrietta Maria (c. 1657–1686)
Williams, Shirley (1930—)
Wootton, Barbara (1897–1988)
Young, Janet (1926–2002)

BARRISTER
See Lawyer.

BASEBALL PLAYER
Arlington, Lizzie (1876–1917)
Arlington, Lizzie (b. 1876)
Borders, Ila (1975—)
Courtney, Patricia (c. 1932–2003)
Croteau, Julie (1970—)
Dunn, Gertrude (c. 1932–2004)
Faut, Jean (1925—)
Ferguson, Dottie (1923–2003)
Fields, Crystal (1969—)
Gacioch, Rose (1915–2004)
Gisolo, Margaret (1914–2003)
Houghton, Edith (1912—)
Kamenshek, Dorothy (1925—)
Kurys, Sophie (1925—)
Lotsey, Nancy (c. 1955—)
Mitchell, Jackie (1912–1987)
Murphy, Lizzie (1894–1964)
Nelson, Maud (1881–1944)
Rockford Peaches (1940–1954)
Sams, Doris (1927—)
Stone, Toni (1921–1996)
Weiss, Alta (1889–1964)
Winter, Joanne (1924—)
Zaharias, Babe Didrikson (1911–1956)

BASKETBALL COACH
Applebee, Constance (1873–1981)
Berenson, Senda (1868–1954)
Conradt, Jody (1941—)
Lieberman-Cline, Nancy (1958—)
Miller, Cheryl (1964—)
Mulkey, Kim (1962—)
Rush, Cathy
Staley, Dawn (1970—)
Vautier, Catherine (1902–1989)
Wade, Margaret (1912–1995)
Yow, Kay (1942—)

BASKETBALL PLAYER
Abrosimova, Svetlana (1980—)
Ackerman, Val (1959—)
Amachree, Mactabene (1978—)
Anderson, Chantelle (1981—)
Arbutina, Andjelija (1967—)
Arcain, Janeth (1969—)
Arkhipova, Anna (1973—)
Arteshina, Olga (1982—)
Azzi, Jennifer (1968—)
Bajkusa, Vesna (1970—)
Baranova, Elena (1972—)
Barel, Olesya (1960—)
Barysheva, Olga (1954—)
Batkovic, Suzy (1980—)
Ba Yan (1962—)
Becirspahic, Mirsada (1957—)
Beseliene, Vida (1956—)
Bird, Sue (1980—)
Bjedov, Mira (1955—)
Blazejowski, Carol (1957—)
Bogdanova, Krasimira (1949—)
Bolton, Ruthie (1967—)
Bolton-Holifield, Ruthie (1967—)
Boswell, Cathy (1962—)
Boyd, Carla (1975—)
Brogan, Michelle (1973—)
Brogden, Cindy (1957—)
Brondello, Sandy (1968—)
Brown, Cindy (1965—)
Bullett, Vicky (1967—)
Bunatyants, Elen (1970—)
Burgess, Annie (1969—)
Buryakina, Olga (1958—)
Cash, Swin (1979—)
Catchings, Tamika (1979—)
Chandler, Michelle

Occupational Index

Charles, Daedra (1969—)
Chen Yuefang (1963—)
Choi Aei-Young (1959—)
Choi Kyung-Hee (1966—)
Cong Xued (1963—)
Cook, Allison (1972—)
Cooper, Cynthia (1963—)
Cooper, Cynthia (1964—)
Curry, Denise (1959—)
Dauniene, Tamara (1951—)
David, Ilisaine Karen (1977—)
Davis, Clarissa (1967—)
Dermendzhieva, Vanya (1952—)
Despotovic, Vesna (1961—)
Dilova, Diana (1952—)
Dixon, Medina (1962—)
Djuraskovic, Vera (1949—)
Djurkovic, Zorica (1957—)
Donovan, Anne (1961—)
Dornik, Polona (1962—)
dos Santos, Cintia (1975—)
Dunkle, Nancy (1955—)
Edmonton Grads (1915–1940)
Edwards, Teresa (1964—)
Ethridge, Mary Camille (1964—)
Fallon, Trisha (1972—)
Ferdinand, Marie (1978—)
Feryabnikova, Nelli (1949—)
Gerlits, Irina (1966—)
Germanova, Silviya (1961—)
Gillom, Jennifer (1964—)
Golcheva, Nadka (1952—)
Golic, Sladjana (1960—)
Goncalves, Lilian Cristina (1979—)
Gordon, Bridgette (1967—)
Griffith, Yolanda (1970—)
Gustavo, Roseli (1971—)
Gustilina, Diana (1974—)
Gyurova, Krasimira (1953—)
Harris, Lusia Mae (1955—)
Harrower, Kristi (1975—)
He Jun (1969—)
Henry, Lea (1961—)
Hill, Jo (1963—)
Holdsclaw, Chamique (1977—)
Ivinskaya, Tatyana (1958—)
Jackson, Lauren (1981—)
Jackson, Tammy (1962—)
Jeong Myung-Hee (1964—)
Johnson, Shannon (1974—)
Jones, Carolyn (1969—)
Joyce, Joan (1940—)
Kalmykova, Maria (1978—)
Kamenshek, Dorothy (1925—)
Karpova, Elena (1980—)
Khudashova, Yelena (1965—)
Kim Eun-Sook (1963—)
Kim Hwa-Soon (1962—)
Kim Young-Hee (1963—)
Klimova, Natalya (1951—)
Komnenovic, Jelica (1960—)
Korstin, Ilona (1980—)
Kurvyakova, Raisa (1945—)
Kurys, Sophie (1925—)
Kvesic, Kornelija (1964—)
Lacey, Venus (1967—)
Lakic, Mara (1963—)
Lawrence, Janice (1962—)
Lee Hyung-Sook (1964—)
Lee Mi-Ja (1963—)
Lelas, Zana (1970—)
Leonova, Aleksandra (1964—)
Leslie, Lisa (1972—)
Lewis, Charlotte (1955—)
Li Dongmei (1969—)
Lieberman-Cline, Nancy (1958—)
Li Lan (1961—)
Liu Jun (1969—)
Liu Qing (1964—)
Li Xiaoqin (1961—)
Li Xin (1969—)
Lloyd, Andrea (1965—)
Lobo, Rebecca (1973—)
Luz, Helen (1972—)
Luz, Silvia (1975—)
MacDonald, Noel (1915—)
Maher, Robyn (1959—)
Majstorovic, Biljana (1959—)
Makaveeva, Petkana (1952—)
Marcari Oliva, Hortencia (1959—)
Marquis, Gail (1956—)
McClain, Katrina (1965—)
McConnell, Suzanne (1966—)
McCray, Nikki (1971—)
McGee, Pamela (1962—)
McGhee, Carla (1968—)
Menken-Schaudt, Carol (1957—)
Metodieva, Penka (1950—)
Meyers, Ann (1955—)
Mikhaylova, Angelina (1960—)
Mikhaylova, Snezhana (1954—)
Miller, Cheryl (1964—)
Milosevic, Bojana (1965—)
Milton, DeLisha (1974—)
Minkh, Irina (1964—)
Mitic, Vukica (1953—)
Moon Kyung-Ja (1965—)
Mujanovic, Razija (1967—)
Mulkey, Kim (1962—)
Nakic, Danira (1969—)
Neves, Claudia (1975—)
Noble, Cindy (1958—)
O'Connor, Mary Anne (1953—)
Oliveira, Alessandra (1973—)
Orr, Vickie (1967—)
Osipova, Irina (1981—)
Ovechkina, Tatyana (1950—)
Ozegovic, Sanja (1959—)
Park Chan-Sook (1959—)
Pastor, Claudia (1971—)
Pekic, Sofija (1953—)
Peng Ping (1967—)
Penicheiro, Ticha (1974—)
Perazic, Jasmina (1960—)
Perrot, Kim (c. 1967–1999)
Pettis, Bridget (1971—)
Pinto, Adriana (1978—)
Porter, Natalia (1980—)
Poto, Alicia (1978—)
Qiu Chen (1963—)
Radkova, Kostadinka (1962—)
Rakhmatulina, Oxana (1976—)
Riley, Ruth (1979—)
Rizzotti, Jennifer (1974—)
Roberts, Patricia (1955—)
Robinson, Fiona (1969—)
Rogozhina, Lyudmila (1959—)
Rojcewicz, Susan (1953—)
Rupshiene, Angele (1952—)
Sandie, Shelley (1969—)
Santos, Adriana (1971—)
Santos, Kelly (1979—)
Savitskaya, Galina (1961—)
Semjonova, Uljana (1952—)
Sharmay, Lyubov (1956—)
Shchegoleva, Tatiana (1982—)
Shtarkelova, Margarita (1951—)
Shuvayeva, Nadezhda (1952—)
Shvaybovich, Yelena (1966—)
Silva, Maria Angelica (1966—)
Silva, Paula (1962—)
Simpson, Juliene (1953—)
Skerlatova, Girgina (1954—)
Slavcheva, Evladiya (1962—)
Smith, Bev (1960—)
Smith, Katie (1974—)
Snell, Belinda (1981—)
Sobral, Leila (1974—)
Sobral, Marta (1964—)
Song Xiaobo (1958—)
Sporn, Rachael (1968—)
Staley, Dawn (1970—)
Starbird, Kate (1975—)
Steding, Katy (1967—)
Stepanova, Maria (1979—)
Stephens, Helen (1918–1994)
Stoyanova, Mariya (1947—)
Stoyanova, Penka (1950—)
Sukharnova, Olga (1955—)
Summerton, Laura (1983—)
Summitt, Pat (1952—)
Sumnikova, Irina (1964—)
Sung Jung-A (1965—)
Swoopes, Sheryl (1971—)
Taurasi, Diana (1982—)
Taylor, Penny (1981—)
Thompson, Tina (1975—)
Timms, Michelle (1965—)
Tkachenko, Marina (1965—)
Tonkovic, Marija (1959—)
Tornikidu, Yelena (1965—)
Tuomaite, Vitalija (1964—)
Vangelovska, Stojna (1965—)
Vautier, Catherine (1902–1989)
Vodopyanova, Natalia (1981—)
Wade, Margaret (1912–1995)
Wang Fang (1967—)
Wang Jun (1963—)
Washington, Ora (1899–1971)
Weatherspoon, Teresa (1965—)
Whittle, Jenny (1973—)
Wild, Eleonora (1969—)
Williams, Natalie (1970—)
Wilson, Ruth (1919–2001)
Wolters, Kara (1975—)
Woodard, Lynette (1959—)
Xiu Lijuan (1957—)
Yakovleva, Olga (1963—)
Yevkova, Olga (1965—)
Yordanova, Todorka (1956—)
Zaboluyeva, Svetlana (1966—)
Zaharias, Babe Didrikson (1911–1956)
Zakharova, Nadezhda (1945—)
Zakharova, Tatyana (1951—)
Zasulskaya, Natalya (1969—)
Zhang Hui (1959—)
Zhang Yueqin (1960—)
Zhan Shuping (1964—)
Zheng Dongmei (1967—)
Zheng Haixia (1967—)
Zhirko, Yelena (1968—)

BASKETMAKER
Chona, Maria (1845–1936)
Dat So La Lee (c. 1835–1925)

BEAUTY PAGEANT DIRECTOR
Slaughter, Lenora S. (1906–2000)

BELLY DANCER
See Exotic dancer.

BENEFACTOR
See Patron/philanthropist/benefactor.

BIATHLETE
Akhatova, Albina (1976—)
Andreassen, Gunn Margit (1973—)
Apel, Katrin (1973—)

Bedard, Myriam (1969—)
Behle, Petra (1969—)
Belova, Elena (1965—)
Briand, Anne (1968—)
Burlet, Delphyne (1966—)
Claudel, Véronique (1966—)
Dafovska, Ekaterina (1976—)
Disl, Ursula (1970—)
Forsberg, Magdalena (1967—)
Greiner-Petter-Memm, Simone (1967—)
Harvey, Antje (1967—)
Henkel, Andrea (1977—)
Ishmouratova, Svetlana (1972—)
Koukleva, Galina (1972—)
Melnik, Olga (1974—)
Melnikova, Elena
Nikoultchina, Irina (1974—)
Niogret, Corinne (1972—)
Noskova, Luiza (1968—)
Paramygina, Svetlana (1965—)
Pecherskaya, Svetlana (1968—)
Petrova, Olena (1972—)
Poiree, Liv Grete (1974—)
Pyleva, Olga (1975—)
Reztsova, Anfisa (1964—)
Romasko, Olga (1968—)
Sikveland, Annette (1972—)
Skjelbreid, Ann-Elen (1971—)
Snytina, Natalia (1971—)
Talanova, Nadejda (1967—)
Tjoerhom, Linda (1979—)
Tserbe-Nessina, Valentyna (1969—)
Wilhelm, Kati (1976—)
Zellner, Martina (1974—)

BIBLICAL WOMEN
Abigail (fl. 1000 BCE)
Abigail (fl. 1010 BCE)
Abihail (fl. 970 BCE)
Abishag of Shunem (fl. 1000 BCE)
Abital (fl. 1000 BCE)
Achsah
Adah
Ahinoam (fl. 1020 BCE)
Ahinoam of Jezreel (fl. 1000 BCE)
Anna
Apphia
Asenath
Athaliah (r. 842–836 BCE)
Azubah (fl. 860 BCE)
Azubah
Bashemath (fl. 900 BCE)
Bashemath
Bathsheba (fl. 1010–975 BCE)
Bilhah
Claudia (fl. 26–36)
Cypros (fl. 28 CE)
Cyprus (c. 90 BCE–?)
Deborah (fl. 12th c. BCE)
Delilah (1200–1000 BCE?)
Dinah (fl. 1730 BCE)
Dorcas (fl. 37)
Eglah (fl. 1000 BCE)
Elisheba
Elizabeth (fl. 1st c.)
Esther (fl. 475 BCE)
Eunice
Eve
Hagar (fl. 3rd, 2nd, or 1st c. BCE)
Haggith (fl. 1000 BCE)
Hannah (fl. 11th c. BCE)
Herodias (c. 14 BCE–after 40 CE)
Iscah
Jael (fl. c. 1125 BCE)
Jecholiah
Jedidah
Jehosheba (fl. 9th c.)
Jehudijah
Jemima
Jerusha
Jezebel (d. 884 BCE)
Joanna
Jochebed
Judith (fl. early 6th c. BCE)
Judith
Kerenhappuch (fl. 2000 BCE)
Keturah (fl. 3rd, 2nd, or 1st c. BCE)
Keziah (fl. 2000 BCE)
Leah (fl. c. 1500 BCE)
Lois
Lo-Ruhamah
Lydia (fl. 53)
Maacah (fl. 931 BCE)
Maachah (fl. 1575 BCE)
Mahlah
Malthace (fl. 40 BCE)
Mariamne (fl. 1st c.)
Martha of Bethany (fl. early 1st c.)
Mary Magdalene (fl. early 1st c.)
Mary of Bethany (fl. early 1st c.)
Mary of Cleophas
Mary of Jerusalem
Mary the Virgin (20 BCE–40 CE)
Mehetabel
Merab (fl. 1000 BCE)
Meshullemeth
Michal (fl. 1000 BCE)
Milcah
Miriam
Miriam the Prophet (fl. c. 13th or 14th c. BCE)
Naamah (fl. 900 BCE)
Naamah
Naarah
Naomi (fl. 1100 BCE)
Nehushta (fl. 610 BCE)
Noadiah
Noah
Orpah (fl. 1100 BCE)
Peninnah
Persis
Phoebe of Cenchreae (fl. 1st c.)
Rachel (fl. c. 1500 BCE)
Rahab (fl. 1100 BCE)
Rebekah (fl. around 18th c. BCE)
Rhoda
Rizpah
Ruth (fl. 1100 BCE)
Salome (c. 65 BCE–10 CE)
Salome II (fl. 1st c.)
Salome III (c. 15–?)
Sapphira (fl. 1st c.)
Sarah (fl. 3rd, 2nd, or 1st c. BCE)
Sheba, Queen of (fl. 10th c. BCE)
Susanna (fl. 6th c. BCE)
Syntyche
Syro-Phoenician
Tamar (fl. 1000 BCE)
Tamar (fl. 1100 BCE)
Tirzah
Vashti (fl. 5th c. BCE)
Zilpah
Zipporah

BIGAMIST (ACCUSED)
Chudleigh, Elizabeth (1720–1788)
Hamilton, Mary (1705–?)
Menken, Adah Isaacs (1835–1868)
Moders, Mary (1643–1673)

BIG-GAME HUNTER
Akeley, Delia J. (1875–1970)
Johnson, Osa (1894–1953)
Uzès, Anne, Duchesse d' (1847–1933)

BIOCHEMIST
See Organic chemist.

BIOGRAPHER
Adam, Juliette la Messine (1836–1936)
Aikin, Lucy (1781–1864)
Aliye, Fatima (1862–1936)
Allen, Hannah Archer (fl. 1680s)
Almedingen, E.M. (1898–1971)
Andreas-Salomé, Lou (1861–1937)
Anna von Munzingen (fl. 1327)
Anthony, Katharine Susan (1877–1965)
Armstrong, Margaret Neilson (1867–1944)
Ashbridge, Elizabeth (1713–1755)
Asquith, Cynthia (1887–1960)
Baker, Nina Brown (1888–1957)
Barine, Arvède (1840–1908)
Benger, Elizabeth (1778–1827)
Benson, Mary (1919–2000)
Berberova, Nina (1901–1993)
Blackwell, Alice Stone (1857–1950)
Blind, Mathilde (1841–1896)
Bowen, Catherine Drinker (1897–1973)
Boy-Ed, Ida (1852–1928)
Bramwell-Booth, Catherine (1883–1987)
Brittain, Vera (1893–1970)
Brown, Alice (1856–1948)
Brown, Hallie Quinn (c. 1845–1949)
Burton, Annie L. (fl. 19th c.)
Campbell, Maria (1940—)
Carles, Emilie (1900–1979)
Carswell, Catherine (1879–1946)
Cary, Lucy (1619–1650)
Cederna, Camilla (1921–1997)
Chabrillan, Céleste de (1824–1909)
Chapman, Maria (1806–1885)
Churchill, Mary (1922—)
Chute, Marchette (1909–1994)
Clapp, Margaret (1910–1974)
Clifford, Anne (1590–1676)
Cohen, Rose (1880–1925)
Coignet, Clarisse (1823–?)
Coit, Margaret L. (1919–2003)
Cook, Judith (1933–2004)
Cooper, Susan Fenimore (1813–1894)
Costa, Emília de Sousa (1877–1957)
Curie, Ève (b. 1904)
Dall, Caroline Wells (1822–1912)
d'Alpuget, Blanche (1944—)
d'Arconville, Geneviève (1720–1805)
Davenport, Marcia (1903–1996)
Dornemann, Luise (1901–1992)
Dorr, Rheta Childe (1866–1948)
Douglas, Emily Taft (1899–1994)
Durack, Mary (1913–1994)
Eckstorm, Fannie Pearson Hardy (1865–1946)
Elliott, Maud Howe (1854–1948)
Elliott, Sarah Barnwell (1848–1928)
Farjeon, Annabel (1919—)
Farrar, Eliza Rotch (1791–1870)
Fields, Annie Adams (1834–1915)
First, Ruth (1925–1982)
Follen, Eliza (1787–1860)
Forbes, Esther (1891–1967)
Förster-Nietzsche, Elisabeth (1846–1935)
Frame, Janet (1924–2004)
Fraser, Antonia (1932—)
Fukuda Hideko (1865–1927)
Furlong, Monica (1930–2003)
Gaskell, Elizabeth (1810–1865)
Goodwin, Doris Kearns (1943—)
Gourd, Emilie (1879–1946)
Grote, Harriet (1792–1878)
Grumbach, Doris (1918—)

Hahn, Emily (1905–1997)
Haldane, Charlotte (1894–1969)
Hale, Nancy (1908–1988)
Hamilton, Virginia (1936–2002)
Hanaford, Phebe Ann (1829–1921)
Haynes, Elizabeth Ross (1883–1953)
Hays, Mary (1760–1843)
Hickok, Lorena A. (1893–1968)
Howard, Jane (1934–1996)
Hunt, Violet (1866–1942)
Hutchinson, Lucy (1620–post 1675)
Huxley, Elspeth (1907–1997)
Jayakar, Pupul (1915–1999)
Jurca, Branca (1914–1999)
Kaus, Gina (1894–1985)
Kavanagh, Julia (1824–1877)
Kazantzaki, Eleni (1903–2004)
Keller, Helen (1880–1968)
Kempe, Margery (c. 1373–after 1438)
Komarova, Varvara (1862–1942)
La Rochefoucauld, Edmée, Duchesse de (1895–1991)
Laski, Marghanita (1915–1988)
Lavater-Sloman, Mary (1891–1980)
Leduc, Violette (1907–1972)
Leech, Margaret (1893–1974)
Lerner, Gerda (1920—)
Lindbergh, Anne Morrow (1906–2001)
Lipsius, Marie (1837–1927)
Longhi, Lucia Lopresti (1895–1985)
Lowell, Amy (1874–1925)
Lutyens, Mary (1908–1999)
Machar, Agnes Maule (1837–1927)
Mannin, Ethel (1900–1984)
Marshall, Catherine (1914–1983)
Meigs, Cornelia Lynde (1884–1973)
Meriwether, Louise (1923—)
Meynell, Viola (1886–1956)
Millin, Sarah (1888–1968)
Mitchison, Naomi (1897–1999)
Mitford, Nancy (1904–1973)
Mortimer, Penelope (1918–1999)
Norman, Dorothy (1905–1997)
Nováková, Teréza (1853–1912)
Ocampo, Victoria (1890–1979)
Oliphant, Margaret (1828–1897)
Olivier, Edith (c. 1879–1948)
O'Meara, Kathleen (1839–1888)
Paget, Violet (1856–1935)
Palencia, Isabel de (1878–c. 1950)
Pankhurst, Sylvia (1882–1960)
Parr, Harriet (1828–1900)
Pascal, Gilberte (1620–1687)
Pauli, Hertha (1909–1973)
Pennell, Elizabeth Robins (1855–1936)
Périer, Marguerite (c. 1645–?)
Repplier, Agnes (1855–1950)
Respighi, Elsa (1894–1996)
Reuter, Gabriele (1859–1941)
Richards, Laura E. (1850–1943)
Ritchie, Anne Isabella (1837–1919)
Ross, Ishbel (1895–1975)
Rourke, Constance (1885–1941)
Royde-Smith, Naomi Gwladys (c. 1880–1964)
Rukeyser, Muriel (1913–1980)
Sackville-West, Vita (1892–1962)
Sandoz, Mari (1896–1966)
Sarfatti, Margherita (1880–1961)
Shaginian, Marietta (1888–1982)
Shields, Carol (1935–2003)
Shirley, Elizabeth (c. 1568–1641)
Simpson, Helen (1897–1940)
Smedley, Agnes (1892–1950)
Spark, Muriel (1918—)
Spiel, Hilde (1911–1990)
Stockert-Meynert, Dora von (1870–1947)
Stocks, Mary Danvers (1891–1975)
Strachey, Ray (1887–1940)
Strauss und Torney, Lulu von (1873–1956)
Strickland, Agnes (1796–1874)
Surville, Laure (1800–1871)
Taggard, Genevieve (1894–1948)
Tait, Dorothy (1905–1972)
Tarbell, Ida (1857–1944)
Tarry, Ellen (b. 1906)
Tindall, Gillian (1938—)
Truman, Margaret (1924—)
Tynan, Kathleen (1937–1995)
Vining, Elizabeth Gray (1902–1999)
Wägner, Elin (1882–1949)
Ward, Maisie (1889–1975)
Warner, Sylvia Townsend (1893–1978)
Wedgwood, C.V. (1910–1997)
Winslow, Ola Elizabeth (c. 1885–1977)
Witt, Henriette de (1829–1908)
Wolzogen, Karoline von (1763–1847)
Woodham-Smith, Cecil (1896–1977)
Wright, Helen (1914–1997)
Yonge, Charlotte Mary (1823–1901)
Young, Marguerite (1908–1995)
Zaturenska, Marya Alexandrovna (1902–1982)
Ziyada, Mayy (1886–1941)

BIOLOGIST
Alexander, Annie Montague (1867–1949)
Alexander, Hattie (1901–1968)
Anable, Gloria Hollister (1903–1988)
Andrews, Eliza Frances (1840–1931)
Arber, Agnes (1879–1960)
Armstrong, Margaret Neilson (1867–1944)
Atkins, Anna (1797–1871)
Auerbach, Charlotte (1899–1994)
Bage, Freda (1883–1970)
Bailey, Florence (1863–1948)
Becker, Lydia (1827–1890)
Beddington, Rosa (1956–2001)
Beloff-Chain, Anne (1921–1991)
Bennett, Isobel (b. 1909)
Bodley, Rachel (1831–1888)
Bonnevie, Kristine (1872–1948)
Boring, Alice Middleton (1883–1955)
Brandegee, Mary Katharine (1844–1920)
Branham, Sara Elizabeth (1888–1962)
Braun, E. Lucy (1889–1971)
Britton, Elizabeth Knight (1858–1934)
Brooks, Matilda M. (1888–1981)
Brown, Margaret Elizabeth (1918—)
Brown, Rachel Fuller (1898–1980)
Campbell, Charlotte C. (1914–1993)
Carson, Rachel (1907–1964)
Chase, Agnes Meara (1869–1963)
Cobb, Jewell Plummer (1924—)
Colden, Jane (1724–1766)
Dick, Gladys (1881–1963)
Dormon, Carrie (1888–1971)
Eastwood, Alice (1859–1953)
Ehrlich, Aline (1928–1991)
Ermoleva, Zinaida (1898–1974)
Esau, Katherine (1898–1997)
Farquhar, Marilyn (1928—)
Farr, Wanda K. (1895–1983)
Fell, Honor (1900–1986)
Ferguson, Margaret Clay (1863–1951)
Fleming, Amalia (1912–1986)
Fossey, Dian (1932–1985)
Franklin, Rosalind (1920–1958)
Frost, Winifred (1902–1979)
Furbish, Kate (1834–1931)
Harvey, Ethel Browne (1885–1965)
Hay, Elizabeth Dexter (1927—)
Hazen, Elizabeth Lee (1883–1975)
Hobby, Gladys Lounsbury (1910–1993)
Hodgkin, Dorothy (1910–1994)
Hubbard, Ruth (1924—)
Humphries, Carmel (1909–1986)
Hyde, Ida (1857–1945)
Hyman, Libbie Henrietta (1888–1969)
Kann, Edith (1907–1987)
Keller, Evelyn Fox (1936—)
King, Helen Dean (1869–1955)
Kipling, Charlotte (1919–1992)
Krim, Mathilde (1926—)
Lancefield, Rebecca Craighill (1895–1981)
Lemmon, Sarah Plummer (1836–1923)
Levy, Jerre (1938—)
Lewis, Graceanna (1821–1912)
Lloyd, Dorothy Jordan (1889–1946)
Lowe-McConnell, Rosemary (1921—)
Lucid, Shannon (1943—)
Macklin, Madge (1893–1962)
Manton, Sidnie (1902–1979)
Maurizio, Anna (1900–1993)
McClintock, Barbara (1902–1992)
McCoy, Elizabeth (1903–1978)
McLaren, Anne Laura (1927—)
Mead, Sylvia Earle (1935—)
Meredith, Louisa Anne (1812–1895)
Morgan, Agnes Fay (1884–1968)
Neufeld, Elizabeth F. (1928—)
Newbigin, Marion I. (1869–1934)
Nüsslein-Volhard, Christiane (1942—)
Ohta, Tomoko (1933—)
Oppenheimer, Jane Marion (1911–1996)
Ordway, Katharine (1899–1979)
Panagiotatou, Angeliki (1878–1954)
Peebles, Florence (1874–1956)
Pennington, Winifred (1915—)
Pool, Judith Graham (1919–1975)
Pratt, Anne (1806–1893)
Rathbun, Mary Jane (1860–1943)
Ray, Dixy Lee (1914–1994)
Russell, Jane Anne (1911–1967)
Ruttner-Kolisko, Agnes (1911–1991)
Sager, Ruth (1918–1997)
Sargant, Ethel (1863–1918)
Scharrer, Berta (1906–1995)
Seibert, Florence B. (1897–1991)
Shattuck, Lydia (1822–1889)
Shtern, Lina (1878–1968)
Stephenson, Marjory (1885–1948)
Stevens, Nettie Maria (1861–1912)
Tizard, Catherine (1931—)
Tonolli, Livia (1909–1985)
Traill, Catherine Parr (1802–1899)
Trewavas, Ethelwynn (1900–1992)
Welch, Barbara (c. 1904–1986)
Williams, Anna Wessels (1863–1954)
Wrinch, Dorothy (1894–1976)
Yasui, Kono (1880–1971)
Young, Mary Sophie (1872–1919)

BIOPHYSICIST
Hanson, Jean (1919–1973)
Telkes, Maria (1900–1995)

BIRTH-CONTROL ACTIVIST
See Reproductive-rights activist.

BISHOP
Harris, Barbara (1930—)
Jamieson, Penny (1942—)
Kelly, Leontine (1920—)
Matthews, Victoria (1954—)
McLeod, Mary Adelia (1938—)
White, Alma Bridwell (1862–1946)

BLACKLISTED
Baker, S. Josephine (1873–1945)
Boyle, Kay (1902–1992)

Braden, Anne (1924—)
Christians, Mady (1900–1951)
Comingore, Dorothy (1913–1971)
El Saadawi, Nawal (1931—)
Gellhorn, Martha (1908–1998)
Gilbert, Ronnie (1926—)
Hagen, Uta (1919–2004)
Han, Suyin (1917—)
Head, Bessie (1937–1986)
Hellman, Lillian (1905–1984)
Hillman, Bessie (1889–1970)
Holliday, Judy (1921–1965)
Horne, Lena (1917—)
Hunt, Marsha (1917—)
Hunter, Kim (1922–2002)
Lee, Jennie (1904–1988)
Lemlich, Clara (1888–1982)
Le Sueur, Meridel (1900–1996)
Muir, Jean (1928–1995)
Parker, Dorothy (1893–1967)
Perry, Eleanor (1915–1981)
Preston, Ann (1813–1872)
Revere, Anne (1903–1990)
Reynolds, Malvina (1900–1978)
Riefenstahl, Leni (1902–2003)
Roberts, Marguerite (1905–1989)
Schütte-Lihotzky, Margarete (1897–2000)
Schwimmer, Rosika (1877–1948)
Sheehy-Skeffington, Hanna (1877–1946)
Sondergaard, Gale (1899–1985)
Taylor, Elizabeth (1912–1975)
Tizard, Catherine (1931—)
Webster, Margaret (1905–1972)
Weinstein, Hannah (1911–1984)
Whitton, Charlotte (1896–1975)
Wrinch, Dorothy (1894–1976)

BLACKMAILER (ACCUSED)
Brécourt, Jeanne (b. 1837)
Churchill, Deborah (1677–1708)
Lyons, Sophie (1848–1924)
Mercier, Euphrasie (1823–?)
Messalina, Valeria (c. 23–48)
Moders, Mary (1643–1673)

BLUES SINGER
Bell, Maggie (1945—)
Bentley, Gladys (1907–1960)
Bogan, Lucille (1897–1948)
Brown, Ada (1889–1950)
Cox, Ida (1896–1967)
Douglas, Lizzie (1897–1973)
Holiday, Billie (c. 1915–1959)
Hunter, Alberta (1895–1984)
Joplin, Janis (1943–1970)
Kelly, Jo Ann (1944–1990)
Martin, Sara (1884–1955)
Miles, Lizzie (1895–1963)
Molton, Flora (1908–1990)
Rainey, Ma (1886–1939)
Scott, Esther Mae (1893–1979)
Smith, Bessie (1894–1937)
Smith, Clara (1894–1935)
Smith, Mabel (1924–1972)
Smith, Mamie (1883–1946)
Smith, Trixie (1895–1943)
Spivey, Victoria (1906–1976)
Taylor, Koko (1935—)
Tharpe, Rosetta (1915–1973)
Thornton, Willie Mae (1926–1984)
Wallace, Sippie (1898–1986)
Washington, Dinah (1924–1963)
Waters, Ethel (1896–1977)
Wilson, Edith (1896–1981)

BOBSLEDDER
Bakken, Jill (1977—)
Engquist, Ludmila (1964—)
Erdmann, Susi-Lisa (1968—)
Flowers, Vonetta (1973—)
Herschmann, Nicole (1975—)
Holzner, Ulrike
Prokoff, Sandra (1975—)
Racine, Jean (1978—)
Warner, Bonny (1962—)

BODYBUILDER
McLish, Rachel (1958—)

BOOK COLLECTOR
Eccles, Mary Hyde (1912–2003)

BOOK EDITOR
Abdel-Aziz, Malak (1923—)
Adam Smith, Janet (1905–1999)
Arbuthnot, May Hill (1884–1969)
Bechtel, Louise Seaman (1894–1985)
Beck, Emily Morison (1915–2004)
Berg, Leila (1917—)
Brant, Beth (1941—)
Clarke, Mary Bayard (1827–1886)
Gacon-Dufour, Marie Armande Jeanne (1753–c. 1835)
Graves, Beryl (1915–2003)
Kaufman, Beatrice (1894–1945)
Krasnohorska, Eliska (1847–1926)
Lang, Leonora (1851–1933)
Lin, Tai-yi (1926—)
McNeil, Florence (1937—)
Miner, Dorothy (1904–1973)
Moore, Lilian (1909–2004)
Mordecai, Pamela (1942—)
Phillips, Frances L. (1896–1986)
Sargent, Pamela (1948—)
Tonna, Charlotte Elizabeth (1790–1846)
Wen Jieruo (1927—)

BOOK ILLUSTRATOR/DESIGNER
Abbott, Berenice (1898–1991)
Adams, Adrienne (1906–2002)
Adamson, Joy (1910–1980)
Ahlberg, Janet (1944–1994)
Albin-Guillot, Laure (c. 1880–1962)
Allen, Pamela Kay (1934—)
Allingham, Helen Patterson (1848–1926)
Anderson, Anne (1874–1930)
Appleton, Honor C. (1879–1951)
Armer, Laura Adams (1874–1963)
Ashton-Warner, Sylvia (1908–1984)
Atkins, Anna (1797–1871)
Attwell, Mabel Lucie (1879–1964)
Bacon, Peggy (1895–1987)
Barker, Cicely Mary (1895–1973)
Barnes, Djuna (1892–1982)
Baynes, Pauline (1922—)
Bell, Vanessa (1879–1961)
Benson, Stella (1892–1933)
Beskow, Elsa (1874–1953)
Betts, Anna Whelan (1873–1959)
Betts, Ethel Franklin (1878–?)
Bianco, Pamela (1906–1994)
Bischoff, Ilse (1903–1976)
Bishop, Isabel (1902–1988)
Bonney, Thérèse (1894–1978)
Boyle, Eleanor Vere (1825–1916)
Brown, Marcia (1918—)
Bryson, Bernarda (1903–2004)
Burton, Virginia Lee (1909–1968)
Buss, Frances Mary (1827–1894)
Butler, Elizabeth Thompson (1846–1933)
Cahun, Claude (1894–1954)
Cameron, Julia Margaret (1815–1879)
Carter, Amy (1967—)
Casey, Maie (1892–1983)
Cavell, Edith (1865–1915)
Chase, Agnes Meara (1869–1963)
Chute, Marchette (1909–1994)
Comstock, Anna Botsford (1854–1930)
Coombs, Patricia (1926—)
Cooney, Barbara (1917–2000)
d'Aulaire, Ingri (1904–1980)
Davis, Marguerite (1889–1980)
Davis, Marguerite (b. 1889)
De Angeli, Marguerite (1889–1987)
Delaunay, Sonia (1885–1979)
Dillon, Diane (1933—)
Dodd, Lynley Stuart (1941—)
Domanska, Janina (1912–1995)
Drayton, Grace Gebbie (1877–1936)
Earle, Alice Morse (1851–1911)
Edwards, Amelia B. (1831–1892)
Ener, Güner (1935—)
Enright, Elizabeth (1909–1968)
Enters, Angna (1907–1989)
Exter, Alexandra (1882–1949)
Fini, Leonor (1908–1996)
Fitzhugh, Louise (1928–1974)
Fletcher, Alice Cunningham (1838–1923)
Foote, Mary Hallock (1847–1938)
Frink, Elisabeth (1930–1993)
Frissell, Toni (1907–1988)
Furbish, Kate (1834–1931)
Gág, Wanda (1893–1946)
Gatty, Margaret (1809–1873)
Gibbs, May (1877–1969)
Gilot, Françoise (1922—)
Gilpin, Laura (1891–1979)
Goncharova, Natalia (1881–1962)
Green, Elizabeth Shippen (1871–1954)
Greenaway, Kate (1846–1901)
Grimshaw, Beatrice (c. 1870–1953)
Guest, Lady Charlotte (1812–1895)
Hall, Augusta (1802–1896)
Hamnett, Nina (1890–1956)
Hassall, Joan (1906–1988)
Hentz, Caroline Lee (1800–1856)
Hoban, Lillian (1925–1998)
Hofer, Evelyn
Holden, Edith B. (1871–1920)
Holden, Evelyn (1877–c. 1969)
Holden, Violet (b. 1873)
Hyman, Trina Schart (1939–2004)
Jansson, Tove (1914–2001)
Jekyll, Gertrude (1843–1932)
Johnston, Frances Benjamin (1864–1952)
Khan, Noor Inayat (1914–1944)
King, Jessie Marion (1875–1949)
La Flesche, Susette (1854–1902)
Lange, Dorothea (1895–1965)
Lathrop, Rose Hawthorne (1851–1926)
Laurencin, Marie (1883–1956)
Leakey, Mary Nicol (1913–1996)
Leighton, Clare (1899–1989)
Le Mair, H. Willebeek (1889–1966)
Lenski, Lois (1893–1974)
MacDonald, Frances (1874–1921)
Mackintosh, Margaret (1865–1933)
Margrethe II of Denmark (1940—)
McGuinness, Norah (1901–1980)
Meredith, Louisa Anne (1812–1895)
Merian, Maria Sybilla (1647–1717)
Montanaria (fl. 1272)
Nicholls, Rhoda Holmes (1854–1930)
Oakley, Violet (1874–1961)
Olds, Elizabeth (1896–1991)
O'Neill, Rose Cecil (1874–1944)
Orczy, Emma (1865–1947)
Orkin, Ruth (1921–1985)

Outhwaite, Ida Rentoul (1888–1960)
Parrish, Anne (1888–1957)
Peck, Annie Smith (1850–1935)
Perkins, Lucy Fitch (1865–1937)
Potter, Beatrix (1866–1943)
Praeger, Sophia Rosamund (1867–1954)
Rathbone, Hannah Mary (1798–1878)
Raverat, Gwen (1885–1957)
Ringgold, Faith (1934—)
Rozanova, Olga (1886–1918)
Ruck, Berta (1878–1978)
Say, Lucy Sistare (1801–1885)
Scepens, Elizabeth (fl. 1476)
Scholl, Sophie (1921–1943)
Shaw, Elizabeth (1920–1992)
Shepard, Mary (1909–2000)
Smith, Jessie Willcox (1863–1935)
Smith, Stevie (1902–1971)
Sowerby, Millicent (1878–1967)
Spencer, Lilly Martin (1822–1902)
Stephens, Alice Barber (1858–1932)
Stratton, Helen (fl. 1891–1925)
Tait, Agnes (c. 1897–1981)
Tarrant, Margaret (1888–1959)
Taylor, Ann (1782–1866)
Taylor, Jane (1783–1824)
Thomasse (fl. 1292)
Toyen (1902–1980)
Trimmer, Sarah (1741–1810)
Uchida, Yoshiko (1921–1992)
van Stockum, Hilda (b. 1908)
Velarde, Pablita (1918—)
Walcott, Mary Morris (1860–1940)
Ward, Mary (1827–1869)
Weil, Simone (1909–1943)
Wootten, Bayard (1875–1959)
Wright, Maginel (1881–1966)
Yampolsky, Mariana (1925–2002)

BOOK PUBLISHER
Adams, Harriet Stratemeyer (c. 1893–1982)
Arnold, June (1926–1982)
Beach, Amy Cheney (1867–1944)
Buttrose, Ita (1942—)
Calder, Liz (1938—)
Callil, Carmen (1938—)
Chen, Joyce (1918–1994)
Child, Lydia Maria (1802–1880)
Crosby, Fanny (1820–1915)
Cunard, Nancy (1896–1965)
Goddard, Mary Katherine (1738–1816)
Grann, Phyllis (1937—)
Guiney, Louise Imogen (1861–1920)
Gurevich, Liubov (1866–1940)
Knopf, Blanche (1894–1966)
McElderry, Margaret K. (1912—)
Meyer, Helen (1907–2003)
Monnier, Adrienne (c. 1892–1955)
Morris, Pamela (1906–2002)
Ocampo, Victoria (1890–1979)
Phillips, Frances L. (1896–1986)
Rebuck, Gail (1950—)
Saunders, Doris (1921—)
Sawako Noma (c. 1944—)
Scepens, Elizabeth (fl. 1476)
Vandenhoeck, Anna (1709–1787)
Ward, Maisie (1889–1975)
Weaver, Harriet Shaw (1876–1961)
Wolff, Helen (1906–1994)
Yeats, Elizabeth (1868–1940)
Yeats, Lily (1866–1949)
Zolotow, Charlotte (b. 1915)
Zorba, Myrsini (1949—)

BOOK REVIEWER
Berberova, Nina (1901–1993)
Bowen, Elizabeth (1899–1973)
Figes, Eva (1932—)
Haines, Helen (1872–1961)
Hapgood, Isabel (1850–1928)
Jewsbury, Geraldine (1812–1880)
Johnson, Pamela Hansford (1912–1981)
Kael, Pauline (1919–2001)
Lowell, Amy (1874–1925)
Manning, Olivia (1908–1980)
McGrory, Mary (1918–2004)
Merril, Judith (1923–1997)
Moore, Marianne (1887–1972)
Porter, Katherine Anne (1890–1980)
Schlegel-Schelling, Caroline (1763–1809)
Sheehy-Skeffington, Hanna (1877–1946)
Skrine, Agnes (c. 1865–1955)
Smith, Stevie (1902–1971)
Snow, Helen Foster (1907–1997)
Travers, P.L. (1906–1996)
Trilling, Diana (1905–1996)
White, Katharine S. (1892–1977)
Wilkinson, Marguerite Ogden (1883–1928)
Wollstonecraft, Mary (1759–1797)
Zapolska, Gabriela (1857–1921)

BOOKSELLER
Beach, Sylvia (1887–1962)
Bertram, Elsie (1912–2003)
Birchfield, Constance Alice (1898–1994)
Foyle, Christina (d. 1999)
Goddard, Mary Katherine (1738–1816)
Miller, Bertha Mahony (1882–1969)
Monnier, Adrienne (c. 1892–1955)
Peabody, Elizabeth Palmer (1804–1894)
Peacock, Lucy (fl. 1785–1816)
Steloff, Frances (1887–1989)
Vandenhoeck, Anna (1709–1787)
Zenger, Anna Catharina (c. 1704–1751)

BOOT MANUFACTURER
Justin, Enid (1894–1990)

BORDELLO OPERATOR
Adler, Polly (1899–1962)
Cornelys, Theresa (1723–1797)
Everleigh, Aida (1864–1960)
Everleigh, Minna (1866–1948)
Needham, Elizabeth (d. 1731)
Pleasant, Mary Ellen (c. 1814–1904)
Watson, Ellen (1861–1889)

BOSSA-NOVA SINGER
Gilberto, Astrud (1940—)

BOTANICAL ARTIST
King, Martha (1802/03–1897)

BOTANIST
Alexander, Annie Montague (1867–1949)
Allen, Betty Molesworth (1913–2002)
Andrews, Eliza Frances (1840–1931)
Arber, Agnes (1879–1960)
Armstrong, Margaret Neilson (1867–1944)
Atkins, Anna (1797–1871)
Atkinson, Louisa (1834–1872)
Basford, Kathleen (1916–1998)
Becker, Lydia (1827–1890)
Blackburn, Kathleen (1892–1968)
Blackwell, Ellen Wright (1864–1952)
Blackwood, Margaret (1909–1986)
Bodley, Rachel (1831–1888)
Booth, Evelyn Mary (1897–1988)
Borrowman, Agnes (1881–1955)
Brandegee, Mary Katharine (1844–1920)
Braun, E. Lucy (1889–1971)
Brenchley, Winifred (1883–1953)
Britton, Elizabeth Knight (1858–1934)
Cadbury, Dorothy Adlington (1892–1987)
Campbell, Charlotte C. (1914–1993)
Cassie Cooper, Vivienne (1926—)
Chase, Agnes Meara (1869–1963)
Colden, Jane (1724–1766)
Conway, Verona (1910–1986)
Dent, Edith (1863–1948)
Dony, Christina Mayne (1910–1995)
Dormon, Carrie (1888–1971)
Downie, Dorothy G. (1894–1960)
Drew-Baker, Kathleen M. (1901–1957)
Duigan, Suzanne Lawless (1924–1993)
Eastwood, Alice (1859–1953)
Eckerson, Sophia H. (d. 1954)
Esau, Katherine (1898–1997)
Farr, Wanda K. (1895–1983)
Fawcett, Maisie (1902–1988)
Ferguson, Margaret Clay (1863–1951)
Flint, Elizabeth (b. 1909)
Furbish, Kate (1834–1931)
Gatty, Margaret (1809–1873)
Gibbons, E. Joan (1902–1988)
Goss, Olga May (1916–1994)
Gwynne-Vaughan, Helen (1879–1967)
Hindmarsh, Mary (1921–2000)
Hodgson, Elizabeth (1814–1877)
Hofmann, Elise (1889–1955)
Hutchison, Isobel Wylie (1899–1982)
Knox, Elizabeth (1899–1963)
Lee, Alma (1912–1990)
Lemmon, Sarah Plummer (1836–1923)
Le Sueur, Frances (1919–1995)
Loudon, Jane Webb (1807–1858)
Manton, Irene (1904–1988)
May, Valerie (c. 1915/16—)
Meredith, Louisa Anne (1812–1895)
Mexia, Ynes (1870–1938)
Molloy, Georgiana (1805–1842)
Newton, Lily (1893–1981)
Noble, Mary (1911–2002)
Ocampo-Friedmann, Roseli (1937—)
Ogilvie Farquharson, Marian (1846–1912)
Patrick, Ruth (1907—)
Pinckney, Eliza Lucas (1722–1793)
Porter, Helen Kemp (1899–1987)
Pratt, Anne (1806–1893)
Rayner, M.C. (c. 1894–1948)
Resvoll, Thekla (1871–1948)
Resvoll-Holmsen, Hanna (1873–1943)
Robb, Mary Anne (1829–1912)
Sampson, Kathleen (1892–1980)
Sargant, Ethel (1863–1918)
Saunders, Edith (1865–1945)
Shattuck, Lydia (1822–1889)
Smith, Annie Lorrain (1854–1937)
Stevenson, Greta Barbara (1911–1990)
Stewart, Olga Margaret (1920–1998)
Stoneman, Bertha (1866–1943)
Stopes, Marie (1880–1958)
Sutherland, Mary (1893–1955)
Traill, Catherine Parr (1802–1899)
Vachell, Eleanor (1879–1948)
Vickery, Joyce (1908–1979)
Warington, Katherine (1897–1993)
Webster, Mary McCallum (1906–1985)
Wilman, Maria (1867–1957)
Young, Mary Sophie (1872–1919)

BOWLER
Adamek, Donna (1957—)
Coburn, Doris (fl. 1970s)
Coburn-Carroll, Cindy (fl. 1980s)
Duval, Helen (1916—)
Faut, Jean (1925—)
Fiebig, Cora (c. 1934—)
Fothergill, Dorothy (1945—)

Gacioch, Rose (1915—)
Gianulias, Nikki (1959—)
Johnson, Tish (1962—)
Ladewig, Marion (1914—)
Macpherson, Wendy (1968—)
McCutcheon, Floretta (1888–1967)
Morris, Betty (1948—)
Rathgeber, Lisa (1961—)
Sandelin, Lucy Giovinco (c. 1958—)
Townsend, Cathy (1937—)

BOXER
See Pugilist.

BROADCASTING
See Television/radio.

BULLFIGHTER
Cintrón, Conchita (1922—)
Hernandez, Angela (c. 1949—)
Sánchez, Cristina (1972—)

BURLESQUE PERFORMER
See Vaudeville/Burlesque/Variety performer.

BUSINESS EXECUTIVE
Ackerman, Val (1959—)
Ahmanson, Caroline (1918–2005)
Alexander, Mary (1693–1760)
Alice of Battenberg (1885–1969)
Angelopoulos-Daskalaki, Gianna (1955—)
Archer, Violet Balestreri (1913–2000)
Arden, Elizabeth (1878–1966)
Auerbach, Beatrice Fox (1887–1968)
Augustine, Rose (1910–2003)
Awolowo, Hannah (1915—)
Bañuelos, Romana Acosta (1925—)
Barrett, Rose Tyler (b. 1889)
Bartel, Jean (c. 1924—)
Bay, Josephine Perfect (1900–1962)
Beech, Olive Ann (1903–1993)
Benetton, Guiliana (1935—)
Bishop, Hazel (1906–1998)
Boehm, Helen F. (b. early 1920s)
Boiardi, Helen (1905–1995)
Bradwell, Myra (1831–1894)
Callender, Marie (1907–1995)
Ching Shih (fl. 1807–1810)
Claiborne, Liz (1929—)
Cochran, Jacqueline (1906–1980)
Cooney, Joan Ganz (1929—)
Cooper, Whina (1895–1994)
Cowles, Fleur (1910—)
Cropper, Hilary (1941–2004)
Denny, Arbella (1707–1792)
Donahue, Margaret (c. 1893–1978)
Duniway, Abigail Scott (1834–1915)
Entenmann, Martha (1906–1996)
Fairclough, Ellen (1905–2004)
Faithfull, Emily (1835–1895)
Ferragamo, Fiamma (1941–1998)
Fingerin, Agnes (d. 1515)
Fitz-Gibbon, Bernice (c. 1895–1982)
Flöge, Emilie (1874–1952)
Foyle, Christina (d. 1999)
Fugger, Barbara Baesinger (d. 1497)
Fuller, Loïe (1862–1928)
Gabor, Magda (1914–1997)
Gautier, Felisa Rincón de (1897–1994)
Glasse, Hannah (1708–1770)
Gleason, Kate (1865–1933)
Glückel of Hameln (1646–1724)
Granville, Bonita (1923–1988)
Greenaway, Kate (1846–1901)
Greenaway, Margaret (fl. 15th c.)
Halpert, Edith Gregor (c. 1900–1970)
Hampshire, Margaret (1918–2004)
Handler, Ruth (1916–2002)
Haughery, Margaret Gaffney (1813–1882)
Haynes, Margery (fl. 15th c.)
Helmer, Bessie Bradwell (1858–1927)
Henie, Sonja (1912–1969)
Henson, Lisa (1960—)
Hills, Tina S. (1921—)
Hoffman, Claire Giannini (1914—)
Hurst, Margery (1913–1989)
Husted, Marjorie Child (c. 1892–1986)
Inyama, Rosemary (b. 1903)
Joyner, Marjorie Stewart (1896–1994)
Justin, Enid (1894–1990)
Keckley, Elizabeth (c. 1824–1907)
Khadijah (c. 555–619)
Kirkeby, Elizabeth (fl. 1482)
Knopf, Blanche (1894–1966)
Knox, Rose Markward (1857–1950)
LaForge, Margaret Getchell (1841–1880)
Lawrence, Mary Wells (1928—)
Lear, Frances (1923–1996)
Lecavella, Mabilia (fl. 1206)
Leslie, Miriam Folline Squier (1836–1914)
Lewis, Loida (c. 1943—)
Liebes, Dorothy (1897–1972)
Loy, Mina (1882–1966)
Lydia (fl. 53)
Macarthur, Elizabeth (1767–1850)
Macarthur-Onslow, Elizabeth (1840–1911)
Malone, Annie Turnbo (1869–1957)
Manley, Effa (1900–1981)
Mason, Biddy (1818–1891)
Mayer, Diana K. (c. 1947—)
McCartney, Linda (1941–1998)
McCormick, Nettie Fowler (1835–1923)
McEntire, Reba (1955—)
McWhinney, Madeline H. (1922—)
Medici, Lucrezia de (1425–1482)
Meyer, Helen (1907–2003)
Millar, Annie Cleland (1855–1939)
Minijima, Kiyo (1833–1919)
Mitford, Deborah (1920—)
Moore, Ellie Durall (1940—)
Muller, Gertrude (1887–1954)
Murray, Kathryn (1906–1999)
Nasi, Gracia Mendes (1510–1569)
Newton-John, Olivia (1948—)
Norman, Decima (1909–1983)
O'Hara, Maureen (1920—)
Okwei of Osomari (1872–1943)
Osmond, Marie (1959—)
Parton, Dolly (1946—)
Pfeiffer, Jane Cahill (1932—)
Phoebe of Cenchreae (fl. 1st c.)
Pirrie, Margaret Montgomery (1857–1935)
Post, Marjorie Merriweather (1887–1973)
Primrose-Smith, Elizabeth (c. 1948—)
Queen Latifah (1970—)
Ratia, Armi (1912–1979)
Reid, Rose Marie (1906–1978)
Rhondda, Margaret (1883–1958)
Roche, Josephine (1886–1976)
Rosenberg, Anna M. (1902–1983)
Rosenthal, Ida Cohen (1886–1973)
Ross, Betsy (1752–1836)
Rubinstein, Helena (1870–1965)
Rubinstein, Mala (1905–1999)
Rudkin, Margaret (1897–1967)
Schary, Hope Skillman (1908–1981)
Seacole, Mary Jane (c. 1805–1881)
Sebastiani, Sylvia (1916–2003)
Shaver, Dorothy (1897–1959)
Siebert, Muriel (1932—)
Sims, Naomi (1948—)
Spain, Jayne (1927—)
Stanwyck, Barbara (1907–1990)
Surratt, Mary E. (c. 1820–1865)
Talbot, Elizabeth (1518–1608)
Thaden, Louise (1905–1979)
Thompson, Gertrude Hickman (1877–1950)
Towne, Laura Matilda (1825–1901)
Tucker, Tanya (1958—)
Turner, Lana (1921–1995)
VanCaspel, Venita (1922—)
Vanderbilt, Amy (1908–1974)
Vanderbilt, Gloria (1924—)
Vucanovich, Barbara F. (1921—)
Waldo, Ruth Fanshaw (1885–1975)
Walker, Madame C.J. (1867–1919)
Walker, Maggie Lena (1867–1934)
Waller, Judith Cary (1889–1973)
Washington, Sarah Spencer (b. 1889)
Wells, Charlotte Fowler (1814–1901)
Wilding, Dorothy (1893–1976)
Wise, Brownie (1913–1992)
Wolff, Helen (1906–1994)

BUTCHER
Furley, Matilda (1813–1899)

CABARET PERFORMER
Andersen, Lale (1910–1972)
Baker, Josephine (1906–1975)
Benitez-Rexach, Lucienne (1905–1968)
Berber, Anita (1899–1928)
Brooks, Romaine (1874–1970)
Brown, Georgia (1933–1992)
Cook, Barbara (1927—)
DeCastro, Peggy (1921–2004)
Dietrich, Marlene (1901–1992)
Dors, Diana (1931–1984)
Etting, Ruth (1896–1978)
Fénelon, Fania (1918–1983)
Fields, Gracie (1898–1979)
Francis, Connie (1938—)
Guilbert, Yvette (1865–1944)
Holiday, Billie (c. 1915–1959)
Horne, Lena (1917—)
Karlstadt, Liesl (1892–1960)
Keeler, Christine (1942—)
Keeler, Ruby (1909–1993)
Kitt, Eartha (1928—)
Lavallière, Eve (c. 1866–1929)
LaVoe, Spivy (1906–1971)
Lawrence, Gertrude (1898–1952)
Lenya, Lotte (1898–1981)
Lynn, Vera (1917—)
Mann, Erika (1905–1969)
Martin, Sara (1884–1955)
May, Gisela (1924—)
McCorkle, Susannah (1946–2001)
McKinney, Nina Mae (c. 1912–1967)
McNeil, Claudia (1917–1993)
Merman, Ethel (1912–1984)
Miles, Lizzie (1895–1963)
Mireille (1906–1996)
Molton, Flora (1908–1990)
Morgan, Helen (1900–1941)
Nesbit, Evelyn (1884–1967)
Ordonówna, Hanka (1904–1950)
Otero, Caroline (1868–1965)
Palmer, Lilli (1914–1986)
Potter, Maureen (1925–2004)
Rosé, Alma (1906–1944)
Roussel, Nelly (1878–1922)
Smith, Bessie (1894–1937)
Smith, Trixie (1895–1943)
Snow, Valaida (c. 1903–1956)
Spira, Steffie (1908–1995)
Tilley, Vesta (1864–1952)
Turner, Tina (1938—)
Welch, Elisabeth (1904–2003)

Werbezirk, Gisela (1875–1956)
West, Mae (1893–1980)
Whiting, Margaret (1924—)
Wiesenthal, Grete (1885–1970)
Wilson, Edith (1896–1981)

CABINET OFFICIAL (GOVERNMENT)

Albright, Madeleine (1937—)
Aloni, Shulamit (1931—)
Amathila, Libertine Appolus (1940—)
Anderson, Elizabeth Garrett (1836–1917)
Anselmi, Tina (1927—)
Anttila, S. Inkeri (1916—)
Armstrong, Anne L. (1927—)
Ashrawi, Hanan (1946—)
Bang, Nina (1866–1928)
Bergmann-Pohl, Sabine (1946—)
Bondfield, Margaret (1873–1953)
Brunschvicg, Cécile (1877–1946)
Castle, Barbara (1910–2002)
Çiller, Tansu (1946—)
Clark, Georgia Neese (1900–1995)
Devold, Kristin Krohn (1961—)
Dragoicheva, Tsola (1893–1993)
Fairclough, Ellen (1905–2004)
Furtseva, Ekaterina (1910–1974)
Giroud, Françoise (1916–2003)
Granahan, Kathryn E. (1894–1979)
Haigneré, Claudie (1957—)
Hansteen, Kirsten (1903–1974)
Harris, Patricia Roberts (1924–1985)
Hills, Carla (1934—)
Hobby, Oveta Culp (1905–1995)
Honecker, Margot (1927—)
Horsbrugh, Florence (1889–1969)
Howard, Mabel (1893–1972)
Joliot-Curie, Irène (1897–1956)
Kaur, Rajkumari Amrit (1889–1964)
Kéthly, Anna (1889–1976)
Kock, Karin (1891–1976)
Kreps, Juanita (1921—)
Lacore, Suzanne (1875–1975)
Lee, Jennie (1904–1988)
Markievicz, Constance (1868–1927)
Martin, Lynn (1939—)
Meir, Golda (1898–1978)
Mercouri, Melina (1923–1994)
Montseny, Federica (1905–1994)
Myrdal, Alva (1902–1986)
Pandit, Vijaya Lakshmi (1900–1990)
Parlby, Irene (1868–1965)
Pauker, Ana (c. 1893–1960)
Perkins, Frances (1880–1965)
Peterson, Esther (1906–1997)
Poinso-Chapuis, Germaine (1901–1981)
Priest, Ivy Baker (1905–1975)
Rehor, Grete (1910–1987)
Reno, Janet (1938—)
Rice, Condoleezza (1954—)
Ruth-Rolland, J.M. (1937–1995)
Sauvé, Jeanne (1922–1993)
Schwarzhaupt, Elisabeth (1901–1986)
Shalala, Donna (1941—)
Shephard, Gillian (1940—)
Summerskill, Edith (1901–1980)
Veil, Simone (1927—)
Wilkinson, Ellen (1891–1947)
Williams, Shirley (1930—)
Wu Yi (1938—)
Zhivkova, Lyudmila (1942–1981)

CALLIGRAPHER

Catherine of Bologna (1413–1463)
Guan Daosheng (1262–1319)
Hatzler, Clara (fl. 1452)
Inglis, Esther (1571–1624)
Montanaria (fl. 1272)
Wei Shuo (272–349)
Wiseman, Hilda Alexandra (1894–1982)

CAN-CAN DANCER

Goulue, La (1869–1929)
Grey, Denise (1897–1996)

CANOEIST/KAYAKER

Alekseyeva-Kreft, Galina (1930—)
Andersson, Agneta (1961—)
Anker-Doedens, Alida van der (1922—)
Bahmann, Angelika (1952—)
Balabanova, Hanna (1969—)
Bardet, Anne-Lise (1974—)
Barre, Alexandra (1958—)
Baumer, Daniela
Bischof, Martina (1957—)
Borchert, Katrin (1969—)
Bota, Kinga (1977—)
Breuer-Dukat, Renate (1939—)
Brunet, Caroline (1969—)
Cherevatova, Olena (1970—)
Chladek, Dana (1963—)
Constantin-Buhaev, Agafia (1955—)
Cox, Annemarie (1966—)
Czigany, Kinga (1952—)
Dementyeva, Yelizaveta (1928—)
Derckx, Annemiek (1954—)
Donusz, Eva (1967—)
Dumitru, Viorica (1946—)
Dylewska, Izabella (1968—)
Egresi, Vilma (1936–1979)
Eichenberger, Sabine
Ericsson, Ingela (1968—)
Esser, Roswitha (1941—)
Fischer, Birgit (1962—)
Fox, Francine (1949—)
Fox-Jerusalmi, Myriam (1961—)
Friedne-Banfalvi, Klara (1931—)
Geczi, Erika (1959—)
Genauss, Carsta (1959—)
Gesheva-Tsvetkova, Vanya (1960—)
Giddens, Rebecca (1977—)
Grabowski, Petra (1952—)
Grothaus, Gisela (1955—)
Guay, Lucie (1958—)
Guibal, Brigitte (1971—)
Gunnarsson, Susanne (1963—)
Haglund, Maria (1972—)
Haralamow, Ingrid
Hartmann, Ingrid (1930—)
Hilgertova, Stepanka (1968—)
Hoff, Karen (1921—)
Holloway, Sue (1955—)
Idem, Josefa (1964—)
Ionescu, Nastasia (1954—)
Ionita, Raluca (1976—)
Ivanova, Borislava (1966—)
Jaapies, Mieke (1943—)
Janics, Natasa (1982—)
Jones, Marcia (1941—)
Kaliska, Elena (1972—)
Karlsson, Eva (1961—)
Kaschube, Ilse (1953—)
Koban, Rita (1965—)
Korshunova, Tatyana (1956—)
Koster, Barbel (1957—)
Kovacs, Katalin (1976—)
Kuryshko-Nagirnaya, Yekatarina (1949—)
Lauer, Hilde (1943—)
Leonhardt, Carolin (1984—)
Liebhart, Gertrude (1928—)
Limbau, Mariana (1977—)
Marinescu-Borcanea, Tecla (1960—)
Melnikova, Antonina (1958—)
Meszaros, Erika (1966—)
Micheler, Elisabeth (1966—)
Mucke, Manuela (1975—)
Mueller, Gabi
Nichiforov, Maria (1951—)
Nollen, Maike (1977—)
Nothnagel, Anke (1966—)
Olmsted, Barbara (1959—)
Olsson, Anna (1964—)
Osypenko, Inna (1982—)
Paliyska, Diana (1966—)
Pastuszka, Aneta (1978—)
Perrier, Glorianne (1929—)
Petkova, Ognyana (1964—)
Pfeffer, Anna (1945—)
Pinayeva-Khvedosyuk, Lyudmila (1936—)
Portwich, Ramona (1967—)
Radu, Elena (1975—)
Rajnai, Klara (1953—)
Rakusz, Eva (1961—)
Reeves, Helen (1980—)
Rosenqvist, Susanne (1967—)
Rozsnyoi, Katalin (1942—)
Ryabchinskaya, Yuliya (1947–1973)
Saimo, Sylvi (1914–2004)
Savina, Nina (1915–1965)
Schuck, Anett (1970—)
Schuttpelz, Barbara (1956—)
Semykina, Tetyana (1973—)
Seredina, Antonina (1930—)
Shubina, Mariya (1930—)
Sideri, Cornelia (1938—)
Singer, Heike (1964—)
Sokolowska, Beata (1974—)
Stefan, Maria (1954—)
Szabo, Szilvia (1978—)
Toma, Sanda (1970—)
Trofimova-Gopova, Nina (1953—)
Viski, Erzsebet (1980—)
Von Seck-Nothnagel, Anke (1966—)
Wagner, Katrin (1977—)
Walkowiak, Daniela (1935—)
Wood, Anna (1966—)
Woodward, Danielle (1965—)
Wunderlich, Magdalena (1952—)
Zakarias, Maria (1952—)
Zenz, Therese (1932—)
Zimmermann-Weber, Annemarie (1940—)
Zirzow, Carola (1954—)

CARDIOLOGIST

Abbott, Maude (1869–1940)
Gardner, Frances (1913–1989)
Taussig, Helen Brooke (1898–1986)

CARILLONIST

Watkins, Gladys Elinor (1884–1939)

CARTOGRAPHER

Pearsall, Phyllis (1906–1996)
Williams, Mary Wilhelmine (1878–1944)
Workman, Fanny (1859–1925)

CARTOONIST

Barns, Cornelia Baxter (1888–1941)
Blankers-Koen, Fanny (1918—)
Buell, Marjorie Henderson (1905–1993)
Chast, Roz (1954—)
Drayton, Grace Gebbie (1877–1936)
Dumm, Edwina (1893–1990)
Fradon, Ramona (1926—)
Gibbs, May (1877–1969)
Guisewite, Cathy (1950—)
Hokinson, Helen E. (1893–1949)
Marucha (1944–1991)
Messick, Dale (1906–2005)
O'Neill, Rose Cecil (1874–1944)

Outhwaite, Ida Rentoul (1888–1960)
Pompeia, Núria (1938—)
Schmich, Mary Teresa (1954—)
Seda, Dori (1951–1988)
Shaw, Elizabeth (1920–1992)
Sutter, Linda (1941–1995)
Tourtel, Mary (1874–1948)
Whitcher, Frances Miriam Berry (1811–1852)

CATTLE RUSTLER (ACCUSED)
Baker, Mary Ann (1834–1905)
Bassett, Ann (1878–1956)
Watson, Ellen (1861–1889)

CELLIST
Chung, Myung-wha (1944—)
Dickson, Joan (1921–1994)
du Pré, Jacqueline (1945–1987)
Garbousova, Raya (1909–1997)
Harrison, Beatrice (1892–1965)
Holland, Dulcie Sybil (1913—)
Nelsova, Zara (1917–2002)
Suggia, Guilhermina (1888–1950)

CERAMIST/POTTER
Adams, Truda (1890–1958)
Baudisch-Wittke, Gudrun (1907–1982)
Britton, Alison (1948—)
Carr, Emily (1871–1945)
Cliff, Clarice (1899–1972)
Cooper, Susie (1902–1995)
Eriksen, Gunn (1956—)
Fry, Laura Ann (1857–1943)
Gardner, Maria Louisa (1879–1968)
Gibbs, May (1877–1969)
Grotell, Maija (1899–1973)
Krebs, Nathalie (1895–1978)
Lissaman, Elizabeth Hazel (1901–1991)
Martinez, Maria Montoya (1887–1980)
McLaughlin, M. Louise (1847–1939)
Nampeyo (c. 1860–1942)
Pitter, Ruth (1897–1992)
Plá, Josefina (1909–1999)
Procopé, Ulla (1921–1968)
Rie, Lucie (1902–1995)
Saad, Siti binti (c. 1880–1950)
Storer, Maria (1849–1932)
Tafoya, Margaret (1904–2001)
Telalkowska, Wanda (1905–1986)
Templeton, Rini (1935–1986)
Velarde, Pablita (1918—)
Wong, Jade Snow (1919–2006)
Wood, Beatrice (1893–1998)
Zeisel, Eva (b. 1906)

CHEF
Alexander, Lucy Maclay (fl. 1950s)
Allen, Betty (1936—)
Brown, Hilary (1952—)
Chen, Joyce (1918–1994)
Child, Julia (1912–2004)
Eriksen, Gunn (1956—)
Lewis, Edna (1916–2006)
Mackay, Catherine Julia (1864–1944)
Mallon, Mary (1867–1938)
Paterson, Jennifer (1928–1999)
Revsin, Leslie (1944–2004)
Waters, Alice (1944—)

CHEMICAL ENGINEER
Espín de Castro, Vilma (1934—)
Pintasilgo, Maria de Lurdes (1930–2004)

CHEMIST
Beloff-Chain, Anne (1921–1991)
Benerito, Ruth (1916—)
Bishop, Hazel (1906–1998)
Blodgett, Katharine Burr (1898–1979)
Blum, Arlene (1945—)
Blunt, Katharine (1876–1954)
Bodley, Rachel (1831–1888)
Brahe, Sophia (1556–1643)
Brown, Rachel Fuller (1898–1980)
Buchanan, Margaret (1864–1940)
Carr, Emma Perry (1880–1972)
Chulabhorn, Princess (1957—)
Clark, Eugenie (1922—)
Cori, Gerty T. (1896–1957)
Cremer, Erika (1900–1996)
Cunningham, Imogen (1883–1976)
Curie, Marie (1867–1934)
Deane, Helen Wendler (1917–1966)
Eckerson, Sophia H. (d. 1954)
Elion, Gertrude B. (1918–1999)
Emerson, Gladys Anderson (1903–1984)
Franklin, Rosalind (1920–1958)
Fulhame, Elizabeth (fl. 1780)
Furness, Vera (1921–2002)
Gleditsch, Ellen (1879–1968)
Hazen, Elizabeth Lee (1883–1975)
Hodgkin, Dorothy (1910–1994)
Humphrey, Edith (1875–1977)
Immerwahr, Clara (1870–1915)
Joliot-Curie, Irène (1897–1956)
Jones, Lois M. (1934–2000)
Karle, Isabella (1921—)
Kuroda, Chika (1884–1968)
Lavoisier, Marie (1758–1836)
Lermontova, Julia (1846–1919)
Leslie, May Sybil (1887–1937)
Lloyd, Dorothy Jordan (1889–1946)
Lonsdale, Kathleen (1903–1971)
Lucid, Shannon (1943—)
Makhubu, Lydia (1937—)
Menten, Maude (1879–1960)
Metzger, Hélène (1889–1944)
Meurdrac, Marie (fl. 17th c.)
Morgan, Agnes Fay (1884–1968)
Murray, Rosemary (1913–2004)
Noddack, Ida (1896–1978)
Pennington, Mary Engle (1872–1952)
Perey, Marguerite (1909–1975)
Pockels, Agnes (1862–1935)
Richards, Ellen Swallow (1842–1911)
Russell, Jane Anne (1911–1967)
Saruhashi, Katsuko (1920—)
Seibert, Florence B. (1897–1991)
Sharman, Helen (1963—)
Stephenson, Marjory (1885–1948)
Telkes, Maria (1900–1995)
Wrinch, Dorothy (1894–1976)

CHESS PLAYER
Gresser, Gisela (1906–2000)
Menchik, Vera (1906–1944)
Polgar, Judit (1976—)

CHIEFESS
Bishop, Bernice Pauahi (1831–1884)
Davis, Alice Brown (1852–1935)
Keopuolani (c. 1778–1823)
Nanny (fl. 1730s)

CHILDREN'S WRITER
Adams, Adrienne (1906–2002)
Adams, Harriet Stratemeyer (c. 1893–1982)
Adler, C.S. (1932—)
Ahlberg, Janet (1944–1994)
Aiken, Joan (1924–2004)
Ainsworth, Ruth (1908–1984)
Alcock, Vivien (1924–2003)
Aldis, Dorothy (1896–1966)
Alexander, Cecil Frances (1818–1895)
Allen, Pamela Kay (1934—)
Almond, Linda (1881–1987)
Anckarsvard, Karin (1915–1969)
Andresen, Sophia de Mello Breyner (1919–2004)
Andrews, Jane (1833–1887)
Apréleva, Elena Ivanovna (1846–1923)
Araz, Nezihe (1922—)
Ashford, Daisy (1881–1972)
Atkinson, Eleanor (1863–1942)
Attwell, Mabel Lucie (1879–1964)
Bailey, Carolyn Sherwin (1875–1961)
Baker, Harriette Newell (1815–1893)
Baker, Nina Brown (1888–1957)
Banks, Lynne Reid (1929—)
Bannerman, Helen (1862–1946)
Barbauld, Anna Letitia (1743–1825)
Bates, Clara Doty (1838–1895)
Bates, Katherine Lee (1859–1929)
Bawden, Nina (1925—)
Bechtel, Louise Seaman (1894–1985)
Belloc, Louise (1796–1881)
Berg, Leila (1917—)
Beskow, Elsa (1874–1953)
Bianco, Margery Williams (1881–1944)
Bishop, Claire Huchet (1898–1993)
Blume, Judy (1938—)
Blyton, Enid (1897–1968)
Booth, Maud Ballington (1865–1948)
Boston, Lucy Maria (1892–1990)
Bouvet, Marguerite (1865–1915)
Branch, Mary Lydia Bolles (1840–1922)
Brent-Dyer, Elinor M. (1894–1969)
Brink, Carol Ryrie (1895–1981)
Brlić-Mažuranić, Ivana (1874–1938)
Brown, Abbie Farwell (1871–1927)
Brown, Marcia (1918—)
Brown, Margaret Wise (1910–1952)
Bruce, Mary Grant (1878–1958)
Burnett, Frances Hodgson (1849–1924)
Burnford, Sheila (1918–1984)
Burton, Virginia Lee (1909–1968)
Byars, Betsy (1928—)
Cameron, Eleanor (1912–1996)
Carey, Rosa Nouchette (1840–1909)
Carpenter, Mary Chapin (1958—)
Catherwood, Mary Hartwell (1847–1902)
Chauncy, Nan (1900–1970)
Choi, Sook Nyul (1937—)
Clark, Catherine Anthony (1892–1977)
Clark, Joan (1934—)
Clarke, Rebecca Sophia (1833–1906)
Clarke, Sarah Jones (1840–1929)
Cleary, Beverly (1916—)
Clifford, Mrs. W.K. (1846–1929)
Clifton, Lucille (1936—)
Clymer, Eleanor (1906–2001)
Coatsworth, Elizabeth (1893–1986)
Comstock, Anna Botsford (1854–1930)
Coombs, Patricia (1926—)
Cooney, Barbara (1917–2000)
Costa, Emília de Sousa (1877–1957)
Couzyn, Jeni (1942—)
Cowley, Joy (1936—)
Cradock, Mrs. H.C. (1863–1941)
Danziger, Paula (1944–2004)
Davis, Mollie Moore (1844–1909)
D'Costa, Jean (1937—)
De Angeli, Marguerite (1889–1987)
de Brunhoff, Cécile (1903–2003)
de Jong, Dola (1911–2003)
Delta, Penelope (1871–1941)
Deming, Dorothy (1893–1972)
Desai, Anita (1937—)
Diaz, Abby (1821–1904)
Dodd, Lynley Stuart (1941—)

Occupational Index

Dodge, Mary Mapes (1831–1905)
Domanska, Janina (1912–1995)
Douglas, Amanda Minnie (1831–1916)
Downie, Mary Alice (1934—)
Drinkwater, Jennie M. (1841–1900)
Duder, Tessa (1940—)
Duncan, Lois (1934—)
Duncan, Sandy Frances (1942—)
Durand, Lucile (1930—)
Enright, Elizabeth (1909–1968)
Ewing, Juliana Horatia (1841–1885)
Farjeon, Eleanor (1881–1965)
Fenwick, Eliza (1766–1840)
Field, Rachel Lyman (1894–1942)
Finley, Martha (1828–1909)
Fisher, Aileen (19096–2002)
Fisher, Dorothy Canfield (1879–1958)
Fitzhugh, Louise (1928–1974)
Follen, Eliza (1787–1860)
Fox, Paula (1923—)
Freeman, Mary E. Wilkins (1852–1930)
Gág, Wanda (1893–1946)
Ge Cuilin (1930—)
Gilroy, Beryl (1924–2001)
Ginsburg, Mirra (1909–2000)
Glen, Esther (1881–1940)
Godden, Rumer (1907–1998)
Goldberg, Lea (1911–1970)
Goose, Elizabeth (1665–1757)
Goudge, Elizabeth (1900–1984)
Guy, Rosa (1925—)
Hack, Maria (1777–1844)
Hagerup, Inger (1905–1985)
Hamilton, Virginia (1936–2002)
Harris, Christie (1907–2002)
Haven, Emily Bradley Neal (1827–1863)
Henry, Marguerite (1902–1997)
Hoban, Lillian (1925–1998)
Hoffman, Alice (1952—)
Howes, Edith Annie (1872–1954)
Huang Qingyun (1920—)
Hughes, Monica (1925–2003)
Hunter, Mollie (1922—)
Hurd, Edith Thacher (1910–1997)
Hyman, Trina Schart (1939–2004)
Jaburkova, Jozka (d. 1944)
James, Florence (1902–1993)
Jamison, Cecilia V. (1837–1909)
Johnson, Helen Kendrick (1844–1917)
Johnston, Annie Fellows (1863–1931)
Ke Yan (1929—)
Kimenye, Barbara (1940—)
Klein, Robin (1936—)
Kogawa, Joy (1935—)
Kumin, Maxine (1925—)
Kurtz, Carmen (1911–1999)
Lamburn, Richmal Crompton (1890–1969)
Laurence, Margaret (1926–1987)
L'Engle, Madeleine (1918—)
Lenski, Lois (1893–1974)
Le Prince de Beaumont, Marie (1711–1780)
Lightner, A.M. (1904–1988)
Lilly, Gweneth (1920–2004)
Lindgren, Astrid (1907–2002)
Little, Jean (1932—)
Lively, Penelope (1933—)
Locke, Elsie (1912–2001)
Lothrop, Harriet (1844–1924)
Lovelace, Maud Hart (1892–1980)
Lowry, Lois (1937—)
Lunn, Janet (1928—)
MacDonald, Betty (1908–1958)
MacEwen, Gwendolyn (1941–1987)
Mack, Louise (1874–1935)
Madonna (1958—)
Mahy, Margaret (1936—)
Mamoshina, Glafira Adolfovna (c. 1870–1942)
Marchant, Bessie (1862–1941)
Mataira, Katarina Te Heikoko (1932—)
Matsutani, Miyoko (1926—)
Mayröcker, Friederike (1924—)
McCully, Emily Arnold (1939—)
McGinley, Phyllis (1905–1978)
McGraw, Eloise Jarvis (1915–2000)
McNeil, Florence (1937—)
McNeill, Janet (1907–1994)
Meaker, Marijane (1927—)
Meneres, Maria Alberta (1930—)
Miller, Olive Thorne (1831–1918)
Mitchell, Elyne (1913–2002)
Mitchell, Lucy Sprague (1878–1967)
Molesworth, Mary Louisa (1839–1921)
Montgomery, Lucy Maud (1874–1942)
Moore, Lilian (1909–2004)
Mordecai, Pamela (1942—)
Morgan, Sally (1951—)
Naylor, Phyllis Reynolds (1933—)
Nesbit, Edith (1858–1924)
Newman, Nanette (1934—)
Nixon, Joan Lowery (1927–2003)
Norton, Mary (1903–1992)
Nöstlinger, Christine (1936—)
Ocampo, Silvina (1903–1993)
Odaga, Asenath (1938—)
O'Hara, Mary (1885–1980)
Okoye, Ifeoma
Opie, Iona (1923—)
Orvieto, Laura (1876–1953)
Ośorio, Ana de Castro (1872–1935)
Park, Ruth (1923—)
Parrish, Anne (1888–1957)
Paton Walsh, Jill (1937—)
Pauli, Hertha (1909–1973)
Peacock, Lucy (fl. 1785–1816)
Peacocke, Isabel Maud (1881–1973)
Pearce, Philippa (1920—)
Perkins, Lucy Fitch (1865–1937)
Phipson, Joan (1912–2003)
Poletti, Syria (1919–1991)
Porter, Eleanor H. (1868–1920)
Potter, Beatrix (1866–1943)
Praeger, Sophia Rosamund (1867–1954)
Prentiss, Elizabeth Payson (1818–1878)
Ravikovitch, Dahlia (1936—)
Rawlings, Marjorie Kinnan (1896–1953)
Rey, Margret (1906–1996)
Rice, Alice Hegan (1870–1942)
Rich, Louise Dickinson (1903–1991)
Ringgold, Faith (1934—)
Roberts, Kate (1891–1985)
Robertson, Margaret Murray (1823–1897)
Roland, Betty (1903–1996)
Rollins, Charlemae Hill (1897–1979)
Rooke, Daphne (1914—)
Rowling, J.K. (1965—)
Saranti, Galateia (1920—)
Sawyer, Ruth (1880–1970)
Schlein, Miriam (1926–2004)
Segun, Mabel (1930—)
Ségur, Sophie Rostopchine, Comtesse de (1799–1874)
Sewell, Anna (1820–1878)
Sewell, Elizabeth Missing (1815–1906)
Shange, Ntozake (1948—)
Sharp, Margery (1905–1991)
Sherwood, Mary Martha (1775–1851)
Shkapskaia, Mariia (1891–1952)
Simon, Carly (1945—)
Sinclair, Catherine (1780–1864)
Smith, Dodie (1896–1990)
Smith, Pauline (1882–1959)
Smucker, Barbara (1915–2003)
Speare, Elizabeth George (1908–1994)
Spyri, Johanna (1827–1901)
Stephen, Julia Prinsep (1846–1895)
Streatfeild, Noel (1895–1986)
Stretton, Hesba (1832–1911)
Sutcliff, Rosemary (1920–1992)
Sutton, Eve (1906—)
Tan, Amy (1952—)
Tappan, Eva March (1854–1930)
Thompson, Kay (1908–1998)
Townsend, Sue (1946—)
Tracy, Mona Innis (1892–1959)
Travers, P.L. (1906–1996)
Trimmer, Sarah (1741–1810)
Tucker, Charlotte Maria (1821–1893)
Tumiati, Lucia (1926—)
Turner, Elizabeth (1774–1846)
Turner, Ethel (1872–1958)
Uchida, Yoshiko (1921–1992)
Uttley, Alison (1884–1976)
Van Dyke, Vonda Kay (c. 1944—)
van Stockum, Hilda (b. 1908)
Vestly, Anne-Cath (1920—)
Vining, Elizabeth Gray (1902–1999)
Waciuma, Charity (1936—)
Wakefield, Priscilla (1751–1832)
Walsh, María Elena (1930—)
Warner, Marina (1946—)
Warren, Caroline Matilda (1785–1844)
Wasserstein, Wendy (1950–2006)
Watkins, Yoko Kawashima (1933—)
Webster, Jean (1876–1916)
Wells, Carolyn (1862–1942)
White, Eliza Orne (1856–1947)
Whitney, Adeline Dutton (1824–1906)
Widdemer, Margaret (1884–1978)
Wiggin, Kate Douglas (1856–1923)
Wilder, Laura Ingalls (1867–1957)
Wildermuth, Ottilie (1817–1877)
Williams, Deniece (1951—)
Wiseman, Hilda Alexandra (1894–1982)
Wrightson, Patricia (1921—)
Xie Wanying (1900–1999)
York, Susannah (1941—)
Young, Ella (1867–1951)
Zei, Alki (1925—)
Zolotow, Charlotte (b. 1915)

CHILD-WELFARE ADVOCATE

Abbott, Grace (1878–1939)
Addams, Jane (1860–1935)
Baker, S. Josephine (1873–1945)
Bäumer, Gertrud (1873–1954)
Birney, Alice McLellan (1858–1907)
Bondfield, Margaret (1873–1953)
Brown, Vera Scantlebury (1889–1946)
Burjan, Hildegard (1883–1933)
Butler, Selena Sloan (1872–1964)
Campbell, Kate (1899–1986)
Chisholm, Shirley (1924–2005)
Cowan, Edith (1861–1932)
Di Robilant, Daisy, Countess (fl. 1922–1933)
Ebadi, Shirin (1947—)
Edelman, Marian Wright (1939—)
Eliot, Martha May (1891–1978)
Elizabeth of Bavaria (1876–1965)
Evans, Matilda Arabella (1872–1935)
Ezekiel, Denise Tourover (1903–1980)
Fischer, Greta (1909–1988)
Garrett, Emma (c. 1846–1893)
Garrett, Mary Smith (1839–1925)
Gladney, Edna (1886–1961)
Hallowell, Anna (1831–1905)
Hepburn, Audrey (1929–1993)
Jebb, Eglantyne (1876–1928)
Kelley, Florence (1859–1932)

Kuzwayo, Ellen (1914–2006)
Lacore, Suzanne (1875–1975)
Lathrop, Julia Clifford (1858–1932)
Loeb, Sophie Irene (1876–1929)
Lowney, Shannon (1969–1994)
Lundberg, Emma (1881–1954)
Lynn, Kathleen (1874–1955)
Marot, Helen (1865–1940)
Mendenhall, Dorothy Reed (1874–1964)
Metcalfe, Alexandra (1903–1995)
Nevejean, Yvonne (1900–1987)
Richman, Julia (1855–1912)
Shriver, Eunice Kennedy (1921—)
Smith, Virginia Thrall (1836–1903)
Stevens, Alzina (1849–1900)
Taft, Jessie (1882–1960)
Van Derbur, Marilyn (c. 1937—)
Wilding, Cora (1888–1982)
Windeyer, Mary (1836–1912)
Wise, Louise Waterman (1874–1947)

CHOREOGRAPHER

Aakesson, Birgit (1908–2001)
Adret, Françoise (1920—)
Alexander, Dorothy (1904–1986)
Allan, Maude (1883–1956)
Anderson, Lea (1959—)
Anisimova, Nina (1909—)
Anthony, Mary (c. 1920—)
Arenal, Julie (1942—)
Armitage, Karole (1954—)
Armour, Toby (1936—)
Arnold, Becky (1936—)
Asakawa, Takako (1938—)
Bailin, Gladys (1930—)
Banks, Margaret (1924—)
Barret, Dorothy (1917–1987)
Barstow, Edith (1907–1960)
Bausch, Pina (1940—)
Beatty, Patricia (1936—)
Berke, Dorothea (c. 1900—)
Bernard, Karen (1948—)
Bernson, Kathryn (1950—)
Bettis, Valerie (1919–1982)
Birch, Patricia (c. 1930—)
Bird, Bonnie (1914–1995)
Bjørn, Dinna (1947—)
Blank, Carla (c. 1940—)
Blecher, Miriam (1912–1979)
Boardman, Diane (c. 1950—)
Bodenwieser, Gertrud (1886–1959)
Boris, Ruthanna (1918—)
Boschetti, Amina (1836–1881)
Boutilier, Joy (1939—)
Bowden, Sally (c. 1948—)
Boyce, Johanna (1954—)
Brabants, Jeanne (1920—)
Brown, Beverly (1941–2002)
Brown, Carolyn (1927—)
Brown, Trisha (1936—)
Butcher, Rosemary (1947—)
Cachat, Beth (1951—)
Carlson, Carolyn (1943—)
Caron, Margaret Pettibone (b. around 1904)
Catterson, Pat (1946—)
Cerrito, Fanny (1817–1909)
Charrat, Janine (1924—)
Chase, Alison Becker (c. 1948—)
Childs, Lucinda (1940—)
Chiriaeff, Ludmilla (1924–1996)
Cicierska, Margaret
Clarke, Martha (1944—)
Cobos, Antonia (c. 1920—)
Cohen, Ze'eva (1940—)
Collins, Janet (1917–2003)
Contreras, Gloria (1934—)
Cullberg, Birgit (1908–1999)
Currier, Ruth (1926—)
Dai, Ailian (1916–2006)
Dale, Margaret (1922—)
Danilova, Alexandra (1903–1997)
Davies, Siobhan (1950—)
Dean, Laura (1945—)
De Keersmaeker, Anne Teresa (1960—)
Delza, Elizabeth (c. 1903—)
De Marco, Renée (c. 1913—)
de Mille, Agnes (1905–1993)
de Valois, Ninette (1898–2001)
Diachenko, Nada (1946—)
Dudinskaya, Natalya (1912–2003)
Dudley, Jane (1912–2001)
Duncan, Irma (1897–1978)
Duncan, Isadora (1878–1927)
Duncan, Maria Teresa (1895–1987)
Dunham, Katherine (1909–2006)
Eaton, Pearl (1898–1958)
Egri, Susanna (1926—)
Eisenberg, Mary Jane (1951—)
Elssler, Thérèse (1808–1878)
Erdman, Jean (1917—)
Evan, Blanche (1909–1982)
Farber, Viola (1931–1998)
Feigenheimer, Irene (1946—)
Fenley, Molissa (1954—)
Fisher, Nellie (1920–1994)
Fonaroff, Nina (1914–2003)
Fornaroli, Cia (1888–1954)
Forti, Simone (c. 1935—)
Foster, Gae (b. 1903)
Franca, Celia (1921—)
Garth, Midi (1920—)
Gentry, Eva (c. 1920—)
Germaine, Diane (1944—)
Gitelman, Claudia (1938—)
Gluck, Rena (1933—)
Gore, Altovise (1935—)
Goslar, Lotte (1907–1997)
Graham, Martha (1894–1991)
Grant, Pauline (1915—)
Gruber, Lilo (1915–1992)
Gsovsky, Tatiana (1901–1993)
Hackett, Jeanette (c. 1898–1979)
Haney, Carol (1924–1964)
Hanka, Erika (1905–1958)
Hernandez, Amelia (c. 1930—)
Hinkson, Mary (1930—)
Hoctor, Harriet (1905–1977)
Hoffmann, Gertrude (1871–1966)
Holm, Hanya (1888–1992)
Hoyer, Dore (1911–1967)
Humphrey, Doris (1895–1958)
Inglesby, Mona (1918—)
Jamison, Judith (1943—)
Junger, Esther (c. 1915—)
Kasatkina, Natalia (1934—)
Kastl, Sonja (1929—)
Kelly, Margaret (1910–2004)
Kinch, Myra (1904–1981)
King, Eleanor (1906–1991)
Köhler-Richter, Emmy (1918—)
Koner, Pauline (1912–2001)
Krassovska, Nathalie (1918–2005)
Krauss, Gertrud (1903–1977)
Lampert, Rachel (1948—)
Leporska, Zoya (1918–1996)
Lewis, Elma (1921—)
Lewis, Elma (1921–2004)
Lewitzky, Bella (1915–2004)
Littlefield, Catherine (1904–1951)
Lloyd, Gweneth (1901–1993)
Losch, Tilly (1903–1975)
Lynne, Gillian (1926—)
Mansfield, Portia (1887–1979)
Maracci, Carmelita (1911–1988)
Maracci, Carmelita (b. 1911)
Marin, Maguy (1951—)
Marshall, Susan (1958—)
Maslow, Sophie (1911—)
McGehee, Helen (1921—)
Messerer, Sulamith (1908–2004)
Miller, Bebe (1950—)
Mlakar, Pia (1908–2000)
Monk, Meredith (1942—)
Moore, Lillian (1911–1967)
Morgan, Marion (c. 1887–1971)
Morris, Margaret (1890–1981)
Muller, Jennifer (1949—)
Neville, Phoebe (1941—)
Newberry, Barbara (1910—)
Nijinska, Bronislava (1891–1972)
O'Donnell, May (1906–2004)
Osserman, Wendy (1942—)
Otake, Eiko (1952—)
Page, Ruth (1899–1991)
Palmer, Leland (1940—)
Palucca, Gret (1902–1993)
Pennison, Marleen (1951—)
Plisetskaya, Maya (1925—)
Primus, Pearl (1919–1994)
Rainer, Yvonne (1934—)
Ralov, Kirsten (1922–1999)
Rasch, Albertina (1896–1967)
Reinking, Ann (1949—)
Reitz, Dana (1948—)
Ricarda, Ana (c. 1925—)
Rogge, Florence (b. 1904)
Roope, Clover (1937—)
Rothlein, Arlene (1939–1976)
Sacchetto, Rita (1879–1959)
Sallé, Marie (1707–1756)
Salsberg, Germain Merle (1950—)
Sappington, Margo (1947—)
Severn, Margaret (1901–1997)
Skoronel, Vera (1909–1932)
Slavenska, Mia (1914–2000)
Sokolow, Anna (1910–2000)
Sorel, Felicia (1904–1972)
Spies, Daisy (1905–2000)
St. Denis, Ruth (1877–1968)
Stewart-Richardson, Lady Constance (1883–1932)
Strauss, Sara Milford (1896–1979)
Streb, Elizabeth (1950—)
Takei, Kei (1946—)
Tamiris, Helen (1902–1966)
Taylor, June (1917–2004)
Tharp, Twyla (1941—)
Theilade, Nini (b. 1915)
Toumanova, Tamara (1919–1996)
Toye, Wendy (1917—)
Von Rosen, Elsa Marianne (1924—)
Wallmann, Margarethe (1901–19922)
Webb, Elida (1895–1975)
Weiss, Josephine (1805–1852)
White, Oona (1922–2005)
Wiesenthal, Grete (1885–1970)
Wigman, Mary (1886–1973)
Winter, Ethel (1924—)
Yuriko (b. 1920)
Zapata Olivella, Delia (1926–2001)

CHORUS/CHORALE CONDUCTOR

Branscombe, Gena (1881–1977)
Chambers, Norah (1905–1989)
Dessoff, Margarethe (1874–1944)
Glover, Jane Allison (1949—)
Hillis, Margaret (1921—)
Jessye, Eva (1895–1992)
Kinkel, Johanna (1810–1858)

Kukuck, Felicitas (1914–2001)
Novello-Davies, Clara (1861–1943)
Reichardt, Louise (1779–1826)
Somogi, Judith (1937–1988)
Szönyi, Erzsebet (1924—)

CHORUS/CHORALE FOUNDER
Branscombe, Gena (1881–1977)
Chambers, Norah (1905–1989)
Dessoff, Margarethe (1874–1944)
Diller, Angela (1877–1968)
Hillis, Margaret (1921—)
Novello-Davies, Clara (1861–1943)

CHURCH ADMINISTRATOR
Blackie, Jeannetta Margaret (1864–1955)

CINEMATOGRAPHER
Mangolte, Babette (c. 1945—)
Murphy, Brianne (1933–2003)
Tokareva, Viktoria (1937—)

CIRCUS/FLYING-CIRCUS PERFORMER
Adorée, Renée (1898–1933)
Fratellini, Annie (1932–1997)
Greenwood, Joan (1921–1987)
Law, Ruth (d. 1970)
Leitzel, Lillian (1892–1931)
Lenya, Lotte (1898–1981)
Miles, Lizzie (1895–1963)
Millman, Bird (1895–1940)
Moisant, Matilde (c. 1877–1964)
Nichols, Ruth (1901–1960)
Scott, Blanche (1885–1970)
Stinson, Katherine (1891–1977)
Valadon, Suzanne (1865–1938)
Wallenda, Helen (1910–1996)
White, Pearl (1889–1938)

CIVIL ENGINEER
Barney, Nora (1883–1971)
Buchanan, Dorothy (1899–1985)
Chitty, Letitia (1897–1982)
Eaves, Elsie (1898–1983)
Fergusson, Mary (1914–1997)
Hebard, Grace Raymond (1861–1936)
Qian Zhengying (1923—)
Roebling, Emily (1844–1903)
Stauffenberg, Litta von (c. 1905–1945)

CIVIL-RIGHTS ACTIVIST
Abbott, Diane (1953—)
Abzug, Bella (1920–1998)
Alexander, Sadie (1898–1989)
Ames, Jessie Daniel (1883–1972)
Baez, Joan (1941—)
Baker, Ella (1903–1986)
Baker, Josephine (1906–1975)
Bandler, Faith (1918—)
Bass, Charlotta Spears (1880–1969)
Bates, Daisy Lee (1914—)
Bennett, Gwendolyn B. (1902–1981)
Bernstein, Sylvia (1915–2003)
Bethune, Mary McCleod (1875–1955)
Blackburn, Doris Amelia (1889–1970)
Blackburn, Molly (c. 1931–1985)
Bonner, Elena (1923—)
Braden, Anne (1924–2006)
Bridges, Ruby (c. 1954—)
Brown, Hallie Quinn (c. 1845–1949)
Brown, Linda (1943—)
Brown, Minnijean (1942—)
Cary, Mary Ann Shadd (1823–1893)
Catlett, Elizabeth (b. 1915)
Chandler, Elizabeth Margaret (1807–1834)
Cheney, Ednah Dow (1824–1904)
Child, Lydia Maria (1802–1880)
Chisholm, Shirley (1924–2005)
Clark, Septima Poinsette (1898–1987)
Cooper, Whina (1895–1994)
Cotera, Martha (1938—)
Craft, Ellen (1826–c. 1891)
Crandall, Prudence (1803–1890)
Cunard, Nancy (1896–1965)
Curtis, Harriot (1881–1974)
Curtis, Peggy (1883–1965)
Dee, Ruby (1923—)
Derricotte, Juliette (1897–1931)
Dickinson, Anna E. (1842–1932)
Douglas, Emily Taft (1899–1994)
Duncan, Sheena (1932—)
Dunham, Katherine (1909–2006)
Eckford, Elizabeth (1942—)
Evers-Williams, Myrlie (1933—)
Fauset, Jessie Redmon (1882–1961)
Forten, Margaretta (1808–1875)
Foster, Marie (1917–2003)
Fuller, Meta Warrick (1877–1968)
Gaines, Irene McCoy (1892–1964)
Garnet, Sarah (1831–1911)
Hamer, Fannie Lou (1917–1977)
Harris, Barbara (1930—)
Harris, Patricia Roberts (1924–1985)
Haviland, Laura S. (1808–1898)
Height, Dorothy (1912—)
Hernández, Maria (1896–1986)
Hudson, Winson (1916–2004)
Hunton, Addie D. Waites (1875–1943)
Idar, Jovita (1885–1946)
Jackson, Mahalia (1911–1972)
Jacobs, Harriet A. (1813–1897)
Jeffrey, Mildred (1910–2004)
Johnson, Georgia Douglas (1877–1966)
Johnson, Helene (1906–1995)
Jones, Marion Patrick (1934—)
Joseph, Helen (1905–1992)
Kelley, Abby (1810–1887)
Kenyon, Dorothy (1888–1972)
King, Coretta Scott (1927–2006)
Lampkin, Daisy (1883–1965)
Liuzzo, Viola (1925–1965)
Lorde, Audre (1934–1992)
Lucy, Autherine Juanita (1929—)
Manley, Effa (1900–1981)
Mann, Erika (1905–1969)
Marlatt, Abby (1916—)
Martinez, Vilma (1943—)
McAliskey, Bernadette Devlin (1947—)
McClendon, Rosalie (1884–1936)
Millett, Kate (1934—)
Mills, Florence (1895–1927)
Mobley, Mamie Till (1921–2003)
Moore, Audley (1898–1997)
Moreno, Luisa (1906–1992)
Motley, Constance Baker (1921–2005)
Mott, Lucretia (1793–1880)
Murray, Pauli (1910–1985)
Nash, Diane (1938—)
Norman, Dorothy (1905–1997)
Nyembe, Dorothy (1930–1998)
Ovington, Mary White (1865–1951)
Parks, Rosa (1913—)
Pleasant, Mary Ellen (c. 1814–1904)
Powers, Georgia Davis (1923—)
Pugh, Sarah (1800–1884)
Purvis, Harriet Forten (1810–1875)
Purvis, Sarah Forten (c. 1811–c. 1898)
Richardson, Gloria (1922—)
Robeson, Eslanda Goode (1896–1965)
Robinson, Jo Ann (1911–1992)
Robinson, Ruby Doris Smith (1942–1967)
Santos Arrascaeta, Beatriz (1947—)
Severance, Caroline M. (1820–1914)
Shabazz, Betty (1936–1997)
Sikakane, Joyce Nomafa (1943—)
Simkins, Modjeska M. (1899–1992)
Simone, Nina (1933—)
Sisulu, Albertina (1918—)
Smith, Hazel Brannon (1914–1994)
Smith, Lillian (1897–1966)
Spencer, Anne (1882–1975)
Staupers, Mabel (1890–1989)
Stone, Lucy (1818–1893)
Talbert, Mary Morris (1866–1923)
Tarry, Ellen (b. 1906)
Terrell, Mary Church (1863–1954)
Thompson, Louise (1901–1999)
Thoms, Adah B. (c. 1863–1943)
Tilly, Dorothy (1883–1970)
Towne, Laura Matilda (1825–1901)
Tree, Marietta (1917–1991)
Tucker, C. DeLores (1927–2005)
Walker, A'Lelia (1885–1931)
Washington, Fredi (1903–1994)
Williams, Fannie Barrier (1855–1944)
Wilson, Margaret Bush (1919—)
Winters, Shelley (1920–2005)
Yard, Molly (1912–2005)
Yourcenar, Marguerite (1903–1987)

CLASSICAL-MUSIC SINGER
See Opera/Classical-music singer.

CLASSICAL SCHOLAR
Abbott, Evelyn (1843–1901)
Barbauld, Anna Letitia (1743–1825)
Carter, Elizabeth (1717–1806)
Hamilton, Edith (1867–1963)
Harrison, Jane Ellen (1850–1928)
King, Lida Shaw (1868–1932)
Kober, Alice Elizabeth (1906–1950)
Leach, Abby (1855–1918)
Macurdy, Grace Harriet (1866–1946)
Peck, Annie Smith (1850–1935)
Ripley, Sarah Alden (1793–1867)

CLERGY
See also Lay minister.
Andreas-Salomé, Lou (1861–1937)
Andrews, Barbara (c. 1934–1978)
Barnard, Hannah Jenkins (d. 1825)
Beaufort, Margaret (1443–1509)
Bell, Laura (1829–1894)
Booth, Catherine (1829–1890)
Booth, Evangeline (1865–1950)
Brown, Charlotte (c. 1795–1855)
Brown, Olympia (1835–1926)
Brown Blackwell, Antoinette (1825–1921)
Brunauer, Esther C. (1901–1959)
Chapin, Augusta (1836–1905)
Comstock, Elizabeth Leslie (1815–1891)
Conway, Verona (1910–1986)
Crane, Caroline Bartlett (1858–1935)
Eastman, Annis Ford (1852–1910)
Eddy, Mary Baker (1821–1910)
Eilberg, Amy (1954—)
Grubb, Sarah Lynes (1773–1842)
Grubb, Sarah Tuke (1756–1790)
Gurney, Eliza (1801–1881)
Harris, Barbara (1930—)
Henderlite, Rachel (1905–1991)
Hird, Judith (c. 1946—)
Hume, Sophia Wigington (1702–1774)
Jamieson, Penny
Joan (d. 858)
Jonas, Regina (1902–1944)
Jones, Rebecca (1739–1818)
Jones, Sybil (1808–1873)
Lee, Ann (1736–1784)

Levison, Mary (1923—)
Li, Florence Tim Oi (1907–1992)
Matthews, Victoria (1954—)
Means, Jacqueline (1936—)
Meyer, Joyce (1943—)
Murray, Pauli (1910–1985)
Odozi Obodo, Madam (1909–1995)
Pickett, Fuchsia T. (1918–2004)
Platz, Elizabeth
Priesand, Sally Jane (1946—)
Rose of Viterbo (1235–1252)
Royden, A. Maude (1876–1956)
Shaw, Anna Howard (1847–1919)
Simpson, Mary Michael (1925—)
Smith, Amanda Berry (1837–1915)
Soule, Caroline White (1824–1903)
Southcott, Joanna (1750–1814)
Spencer, Anna (1851–1931)
Starbuck, Mary Coffyn (1644/45–1717)
Stetson, Augusta (1842–1928)
Truth, Sojourner (c. 1797–1883)
Way, Amanda M. (1828–1914)
White, Alma Bridwell (1862–1946)
Wilkinson, Jemima (1752–1819)
Willing, Jennie Fowler (1834–1916)

CLIMBER
Brown, Katie (1982—)
Csizmazia, Kim (c. 1968—)
Destivelle, Catherine (1960—)
Erbesfield, Robyn (1963—)
Gouault-Haston, Laurence
Grenard, Lizz (1965—)
Hendrawati, Agung (1975—)
Kim Jum-Sook (c. 1968—)
Lew, Bird (c. 1966—)
Ovtchinnikova, Elena (1965—)
Piszczek, Renata (1969—)
Repko, Elena (1975—)
Zakharova, Olga (1973—)

CLOTHING DESIGNER
See Costume designer.
See Couturiere.
See Fashion designer.
See Milliner.
See Seamstress/dressmaker.
See Shoe designer.
See Sportswear designer.

COACH (ATHLETICS)
See Athletic coach/instructor.

COAL MINER
Lee, Mary Isabella (1871–1939)

COINER
Harris, Phoebe (1755–1786)
Housden, Jane (d. 1714)
Spencer, Barbara (d. 1721)

COLLAGE ARTIST
Chicago, Judy (1939—)
Delaunay, Sonia (1885–1979)
Fine, Perle (1908–1988)
Hartigan, Grace (1922—)
Henri, Florence (1895–1982)
Hesse, Eva (1936–1970)
Höch, Hannah (1889–1978)
Krasner, Lee (1908–1984)
Loy, Mina (1882–1966)
Morgan, Maud (1903–1999)
Popova, Liubov (1889–1924)
Rego, Paula (1935—)
Rozanova, Olga (1886–1918)
Ryan, Anne (1889–1954)
Sage, Kay (1898–1963)
Stepanova, Varvara (1894–1958)
Tauber-Arp, Sophie (1889–1943)
Vanderbilt, Gloria (1924—)
von Wiegand, Charmion (1896–1993)

COLLEGE/UNIVERSITY ADMINISTRATOR
Abbott, Edith (1876–1957)
Agassiz, Elizabeth Cary (1822–1907)
Aldrich-Blake, Louisa (1865–1925)
Anderson, Elizabeth Garrett (1836–1917)
Apgar, Virginia (1909–1974)
Ashrawi, Hanan (1946—)
Attwell, Mabel Lucie (1879–1964)
Batten, Mollie (1905–1985)
Bell, Nora Kizer (1941–2004)
Blackstone, Tessa (1942—)
Blackwell, Emily (1826–1910)
Bliss, Anna (1843–1925)
Blunt, Katharine (1876–1954)
Bodley, Rachel (1831–1888)
Breckinridge, Sophonisba Preston (1866–1948)
Broad, Molly Corbett (c. 1941—)
Brodbeck, May (1917–1983)
Brown, Hallie Quinn (c. 1845–1949)
Browne, Sidney Jane (1850–1941)
Bullwinkel, Vivian (1915–2000)
Bunting, Mary Ingraham (1910–1998)
Chowdhury, Eulie (1923—)
Clapp, Margaret (1910–1974)
Cleveland, Emeline Horton (1829–1878)
Cobb, Jewell Plummer (1924—)
Cole, Johnnetta B. (1936—)
Coleman, Mary Sue (1943—)
Colwell, Rita R. (1934—)
Comstock, Ada Louise (1876–1973)
Conway, Jill Ker (1934—)
Curtis, Harriot (1881–1974)
Curtis, Peggy (1883–1965)
Davis, Hilda (1905–2001)
Derricotte, Juliette (1897–1931)
Engelbretsdatter, Dorothe (1634–1716)
Esteve-Coll, Elizabeth (1938—)
Evatt, Elizabeth (1933—)
Farenthold, Frances "Sissy" (1926—)
Ferguson, Abbie Park (1837–1919)
Flanagan, Hallie (1889–1969)
Flower, Lucy (1837–1921)
Frame, Alice (1878–1941)
Gault, Alma Elizabeth (1891–1981)
George, Zelma Watson (1904–1994)
Gildersleeve, Virginia Crocheron (1877–1965)
Goldsmith, Grace Arabell (1904–1975)
Gray, Hanna Holborn (1930—)
Gulliver, Julia Henrietta (1856–1940)
Harris, Patricia Roberts (1924–1985)
Harrison, Elizabeth (1849–1927)
Hay, Elizabeth Dexter (1927—)
Hazard, Caroline (1856–1945)
Hetherington, Jessie Isabel (1882–1971)
Hockfield, Susan (1951—)
Horney, Karen (1885–1952)
Horton, Mildred McAfee (1900–1994)
Howard, Ada Lydia (1829–1907)
Howell, Mary (1932–1998)
Irwin, Agnes (1841–1914)
Jackson, Shirley Ann (1946—)
James, Susan Gail (1953—)
Jex-Blake, Sophia (1840–1912)
Johns, Ethel (1879–1968)
Kagan, Elena (1960—)
Kasilag, Lucrecia R. (1918—)
Kellas, Eliza (1864–1943)
Kennedy, Helena (1950—)
Kenyon, Kathleen (1906–1978)
Keohane, Nannerl (1940—)
King, Lida Shaw (1868–1932)
Kittrell, Flemmie (1904–1980)
Kollontai, Alexandra (1872–1952)
Kreps, Juanita (1921—)
Lin Qiaozhi (1901–1983)
Livingston, Nora G.E. (1848–1927)
Logan, Laura R. (1879–1974)
Lozier, Clemence S. (1813–1888)
Lyall, Katharine C. (1941—)
MacLeish, Martha Hillard (1856–1947)
Madeleva, Sister Mary (1887–1964)
Maitland, Agnes Catherine (1850–1906)
Mansfield, Arabella (1846–1911)
Matthews, Victoria (1954—)
McIntosh, Millicent Carey (1898–2001)
Mead, Elizabeth Storrs (1832–1917)
Merrick, Myra King (1825–1899)
Miner, Sarah Luella (1861–1935)
Mitchell, Lucy Sprague (1878–1967)
Mortimer, Mary (1816–1877)
Mosher, Eliza Maria (1846–1928)
Mundinger, Mary O. (1937—)
Murdaugh, Angela (1940—)
Murray, Pauli (1910–1985)
Murray, Rosemary (1913–2004)
Mussey, Ellen Spencer (1850–1936)
Otway-Ruthven, Jocelyn (1909–1989)
Palmer, Alice Freeman (1855–1902)
Park, Rosemary (1907–2004)
Patrick, Mary Mills (1850–1940)
Pearce, Louise (1885–1959)
Pendleton, Ellen Fitz (1864–1936)
Penson, Lillian Margery (1896–1963)
Petry, Lucile (1902–1999)
Preston, Ann (1813–1872)
Putnam, Emily James (1865–1944)
Raisin, Catherine (1855–1945)
Ramphele, Mamphela (1947—)
Reinhardt, Aurelia Henry (1877–1948)
Rice, Condoleezza (1954—)
Robinson, Jane Bancroft (1847–1932)
Rodin, Judith (1944—)
Rogers, Martha E. (1914–1994)
Sabin, Ellen (1850–1949)
Shafer, Helen Almira (1839–1894)
Shalala, Donna (1941—)
Sidgwick, Eleonora Mildred (1845–1936)
Simmons, Ruth J. (1945—)
Slowe, Lucy Diggs (1885–1937)
Stevens, Risë (1913—)
Stimson, Julia (1881–1948)
Stocks, Mary Danvers (1891–1975)
Stoneman, Bertha (1866–1943)
Stratton, Dorothy (b. 1899)
Sutherland, Lucy Stuart (1903–1980)
Sutliffe, Irene H. (1850–1936)
Talbot, Marion (1858–1948)
Taylor, Lily Ross (1886–1969)
Thomas, M. Carey (1857–1935)
Thurston, Matilda (1875–1958)
Tilghman, Shirley M. (1946—)
Towle, Katherine (1898–1986)
Trotter, Virginia Yapp (1921–1998)
Tutwiler, Julia Strudwick (1841–1916)
Tyler, Alice S. (1859–1944)
Ucok, Bahriye (d. 1990)
Wald, Florence (1917—)
Washington, Margaret Murray (c. 1861–1925)
Weed, Ella (1853–1894)
White, Helen Magill (1853–1944)
Winslow, Ola Elizabeth (c. 1885–1977)
Woolley, Mary E. (1863–1947)
Wordsworth, Elizabeth (1840–1932)
Wunderlich, Frieda (1884–1965)
Yoshioka Yayoi (1871–1959)
Zimbalist, Mary Louise Curtis (1876–1970)

COLLEGE/UNIVERSITY FOUNDER
See Educational institution/program founder.

COLLEGE/UNIVERSITY PROFESSOR/ INSTRUCTOR/LECTURER

Abakanowicz, Magdalena (1930—)
Abbott, Grace (1878–1939)
Abbott, Maude (1869–1940)
Abdel Rahman, Aisha (1913–1998)
Abel, Annie Heloise (1873–1947)
Adams, Maude (1872–1953)
Adivar, Halide Edib (c. 1884–1964)
Adler, Stella (1902–1993)
Adnan, Etel (1925—)
Adolf, Helen (1895–1998)
Agnesi, Maria Gaetana (1718–1799)
Ahrweiler, Hélène (1916—)
Ajzenberg-Selove, Fay (1926—)
Akselrod, Liubo (1868–1946)
Alba, Nanina (1915–1968)
Albers, Anni (1899–1994)
Alexander, Hattie (1901–1968)
Allen, Paula Gunn (1939—)
Almedingen, E.M. (1898–1971)
Ambrose, Alice (1906–2001)
Andersen, Dorothy Hansine (1901–1963)
Anderson, Elizabeth Garrett (1836–1917)
Anscombe, G.E.M. (1919–2001)
Anttila, S. Inkeri (1916—)
Apgar, Virginia (1909–1974)
Arber, Agnes (1879–1960)
Arbuthnot, May Hill (1884–1969)
Archer, Violet Balestreri (1913–2000)
Aretz, Isabel (1909—)
Ashrawi, Hanan (1946—)
Ashton-Warner, Sylvia (1908–1984)
Ashur, Radwa (1946—)
Atkinson, Ti-Grace (1939—)
Auerbach, Charlotte (1899–1994)
Babcock, Maud May (1867–1954)
Baker, Augusta (1911–1998)
Baker, S. Josephine (1873–1945)
Balch, Emily Greene (1867–1961)
Baldwin, Sally (1940–2003)
Ballinger, Margaret (1894–1980)
Barraine, Elsa (1910—)
Bascom, Florence (1862–1945)
Bass, Mary Elizabeth (1876–1956)
Bassi, Laura (1711–1778)
Bates, Katherine Lee (1859–1929)
Bateson, Mary (1865–1906)
Bauer, Catherine Krouse (1905–1964)
Bauer, Marion (1887–1955)
Beach, Amy Cheney (1867–1944)
Bell, Muriel Emma (1898–1974)
Bell, Nora Kizer (1941–2004)
Benario, Olga (1908–1942)
Benedict, Ruth (1887–1948)
Benson, Gertrude (1886–1964)
Berg, Helene (b. 1906)
Bernard, Jessie (1903–1996)
Bevier, Isabel (1860–1942)
Blackwell, Elizabeth (1821–1910)
Blackwell, Emily (1826–1910)
Bliss, Catherine (1908–1989)
Blow, Susan Elizabeth (1843–1916)
Bocchi, Dorotea (fl. 1390–1430)
Bodkin, Maud (1875–1967)
Bonnevie, Kristine (1872–1948)
Boring, Alice Middleton (1883–1955)
Boyle, Kay (1902–1992)
Boys-Smith, Winifred Lily (1865–1939)
Braun, E. Lucy (1889–1971)
Breckinridge, Sophonisba Preston (1866–1948)
Brodbeck, May (1917–1983)
Brooks, Gwendolyn (1917–2000)
Brown, Dorothy (1919—)
Brown, Hallie Quinn (c. 1845–1949)
Brown, Olympia (1835–1926)
Bunting, Mary Ingraham (1910–1998)
Burbidge, Margaret (1919—)
Burnell, Jocelyn Bell (1943—)
Cadilla de Martínez, Maria (1886–1951)
Calkins, Mary Whiton (1863–1930)
Cam, Helen M. (1885–1968)
Campbell, Charlotte C. (1914–1993)
Campbell, Kate (1899–1986)
Campbell, Persia (1898–1974)
Candy, Alice (1888–1977)
Cannon, Annie Jump (1863–1941)
Carr, Emma Perry (1880–1972)
Carus-Wilson, Eleanora Mary (1897–1977)
Carvalho, Dinora de (1905—)
Case, Adelaide (1887–1948)
Cassian, Nina (1924—)
Catlett, Elizabeth (b. 1915)
Chase, Mary Ellen (1887–1973)
Chesler, Phyllis (1940—)
Chisholm, Shirley (1924–2005)
Çiller, Tansu (1946—)
Cinti-Damoreau, Laure (1801–1863)
Clapp, Cornelia Maria (1849–1934)
Clarke, Edith (1883–1959)
Clément, Catherine (1939—)
Clerke, Agnes Mary (1842–1907)
Cleveland, Emeline Horton (1829–1878)
Clinton, Hillary Rodham (1947—)
Cluysenaar, Anne (1936—)
Cobb, Jewell Plummer (1924—)
Cole, Johnnetta B. (1936—)
Coleman, Mary Sue (1943—)
Colton, Elizabeth Avery (1872–1924)
Colwell, Rita R. (1934—)
Comstock, Ada Louise (1876–1973)
Comstock, Anna Botsford (1854–1930)
Conrad-Martius, Hedwig (1888–1966)
Constance Jones, E.E. (1848–1922)
Cori, Gerty T. (1896–1957)
Coyle, Grace Longwell (1892–1962)
Crozier, Catharine (1914–2003)
Cullis, Winifred Clara (1875–1956)
Curie, Marie (1867–1934)
Dai Houying (1938–1996)
David, Caroline Edgeworth (1856–1951)
Davis, Angela (1944—)
Dawidowicz, Lucy (1915–1990)
Deane, Helen Wendler (1917–1966)
de Ibáñez, Sara (1909–1971)
de Laguna, Grace Mead (1878–1978)
De Lauretis, Teresa (1938—)
Demessieux, Jeanne (1921–1968)
De Vito, Gioconda (1907–1994)
Dianda, Hilda (1925—)
Dickason, Gladys (1903–1971)
Donaldson, Margaret Caldwell (1926—)
Donnelly, Lucy (1870–1948)
Dove, Rita (1952—)
Downey, June Etta (1875–1932)
Drew, Jane (1911–1996)
Dulles, Eleanor Lansing (1895–1996)
Dunlop, Florence (c. 1896–1963)
Dworkin, Andrea (1946–2005)
Eames, Ray (1912–1988)
Ebadi, Shirin (1947—)
Ehre, Ida (1900–1989)
Elders, Joycelyn (1933—)
Elion, Gertrude B. (1918–1999)
Eliot, Martha May (1891–1978)
Elliott, Harriet Wiseman (1884–1947)
Ellis-Fermor, Una Mary (1894–1958)
El Saadawi, Nawal (1931—)
Emerson, Gladys Anderson (1903–1984)
Emmett, Dorothy Mary (b. 1904)
Enright, Elizabeth (1909–1968)
Estrich, Susan R. (1952—)
Farr, Wanda K. (1895–1983)
Farrell, Eileen (1920–2002)
Feng Yuanjun (1900–1974)
Fern, Fanny (1811–1872)
Fine, Perle (1908–1988)
Fiorenza, Elisabeth Schuessler (1938—)
First, Ruth (1925–1982)
Florey, Margaret (1904–1994)
Flügge-Lotz, Irmgard (1903–1974)
Foot, Philippa (1920—)
Fossey, Dian (1932–1985)
Fowler, Lydia Folger (1822–1879)
Frantz, Virginia Kneeland (1896–1967)
Frenkel-Brunswik, Else (1908–1958)
Friedan, Betty (1921–2006)
Fry, Laura Ann (1857–1943)
Galdikas, Biruté (1948—)
Gardner, Frances (1913–1989)
Gardner, Helen (1878–1946)
Garrod, Dorothy A. (1892–1969)
Gauthier, Xavière (1942—)
Gebara, Ivone (1944—)
Geiringer, Hilda (1893–1973)
Gelman, Polina (1919—)
Gersão, Teolinda (1940—)
Gilbert, Katherine Everett (1886–1952)
Gilbert, Sandra M. (1936—)
Gilbreth, Lillian Moller (1878–1972)
Gildersleeve, Virginia Crocheron (1877–1965)
Gilligan, Carol (1936—)
Gimbutas, Marija (1921–1994)
Ginsburg, Ruth Bader (1933—)
Gipps, Ruth (1921—)
Gisbert Carbonell de Mesa, Teresa (1926—)
Glantz, Margo (1930—)
Glanville-Hicks, Peggy (1912–1990)
Gleditsch, Ellen (1879–1968)
Glover, Jane Allison (1949—)
Gogoberidze, Lana (1928—)
Goldberg, Lea (1911–1970)
Goldman, Hetty (1881–1972)
Goodenough, Florence Laura (1886–1959)
Gorbacheva, Raisa (1932–1999)
Gordon, Doris Clifton (1890–1956)
Gray, Hanna Holborn (1930—)
Green, Constance McLaughlin (1897–1975)
Greenwood, Marion (1909–1980)
Grotell, Maija (1899–1973)
Gruenberg, Sidonie (1881–1974)
Grundig, Lea (1906–1977)
Guion, Connie M. (1882–1971)
Gwynne-Vaughan, Helen (1879–1967)
Hadid, Zaha (1950—)
Hagood, Margaret (1907–1963)
Haines, Helen (1872–1961)
Hale, Susan (1833–1910)
Hamilton, Alice (1869–1970)
Hamilton, Edith (1867–1963)
Hamilton, Gordon (1892–1967)
Hanson, Jean (1919–1973)
Hara, Kazuko (1935—)
Hardwick, Elizabeth (1916—)
Hardy, Barbara (1924—)
Harjo, Joy (1951—)
Harkness, Georgia (1891–1974)
Harnack, Mildred (1902–1943)
Harper, Frances E.W. (1825–1911)
Harris, Jane Elizabeth (c. 1852–1942)
Harris, Marjorie Silliman (1890–1976)
Harris, Patricia Roberts (1924–1985)
Harrison, Jane Ellen (1850–1928)

Hasegawa, Itsuko (1941—)
Hastings, Caroline (1841–1922)
Hatcher, Orie Latham (1868–1946)
Hatz, Elizabeth (1952—)
Hawker, Lilian E. (1908–1991)
Hawley, Christine (1949—)
Hay, Elizabeth Dexter (1927—)
Hayden, Mary (1862–1942)
Hazlett, Olive C. (1890–1974)
Hebard, Grace Raymond (1861–1936)
Henderson, Virginia (1897–1996)
Henley, Beth (1952—)
Hersch, Jeanne (1910—)
Heslop, Mary Kingdon (1885–1955)
Hetherington, Jessie Isabel (1882–1971)
Hibbard, Hope (1893–1988)
Higgins, Rosalyn (1937—)
Hill, Anita (1956—)
Hill, Dorothy (1907–1997)
Hill, Patty Smith (1868–1946)
Hills, Carla (1934—)
Hinderas, Natalie (1927–1987)
Hirsch, Rachel (1870–1953)
Hobby, Gladys Lounsbury (1910–1993)
Hodgkin, Dorothy (1910–1994)
Hoffleit, E. Dorrit (1907—)
Hofmann, Elise (1889–1955)
Hogan, Linda (1947—)
Hollingworth, Leta Stetter (1886–1939)
Holst, Clara (1868–1935)
Holter, Harriet (1922–1997)
Hopper, Grace Murray (1906–1992)
Horton, Mildred McAfee (1900–1994)
How-Martyn, Edith (1875–1954)
Hubbard, Ruth (1924—)
Humphries, Carmel (1909–1986)
Hyde, Ida (1857–1945)
Hypatia (c. 375–415)
Hyslop, Beatrice Fry (1899–1973)
Irvine-Smith, Fanny Louise (1878–1948)
Isaacs, Susan (1885–1948)
Jackson, Nell (1929–1988)
Jacobi, Mary Putnam (1842–1906)
Jahoda, Marie (1907–2001)
James, Susan Gail (1953—)
Jenkin, Penelope M. (1902–1994)
Jolas, Betsy (1926—)
Jolley, Elizabeth (1923—)
Kasilag, Lucrecia R. (1918—)
Katznelson, Shulamit (1919–1999)
Keller, Evelyn Fox (1936—)
Keller, Nettie Florence (1875–1974)
Kennard, Olga (1924—)
Kenworthy, Marion E. (c. 1891–1980)
Kenyon, Kathleen (1906–1978)
Key, Ellen (1849–1926)
Khan, Begum Liaquat Ali (1905–1990)
King, Helen Dean (1869–1955)
Kirkpatrick, Jeane (1926—)
Kirkwood, Julieta (1936–1985)
Kock, Karin (1891–1976)
Kolb, Barbara (1939—)
Kollwitz, Käthe (1867–1945)
Komarovsky, Mirra (1906–1999)
Korchinska, Maria (1895–1979)
Köth, Erika (1925–1989)
Kovalevskaya, Sophia (1850–1891)
Kovalskaia, Elizaveta (1851–1943)
Kramer, Leonie (1924—)
Kreps, Juanita (1921—)
Kripalani, Sucheta (1908–1974)
Kübler-Ross, Elisabeth (1926–2004)
Kuroda, Chika (1884–1968)
Kyrk, Hazel (1886–1957)
La Barbara, Joan (1947—)
Laby, Jean (1915—)
Ladd-Franklin, Christine (1847–1930)
La Meri (b. 1898)
Lang-Beck, Ivana (1912–1983)
Laskine, Lily (1893–1988)
Lawrence, Marjorie (1908–1979)
Leach, Abby (1855–1918)
Lee, Rose Hum (1904–1964)
Lefanu, Nicola (1947—)
Leider, Frida (1888–1975)
Lerner, Gerda (1920—)
Leslie, Miriam Folline Squier (1836–1914)
Levi-Montalcini, Rita (b. 1909)
Li, Florence Tim Oi (1907–1992)
Lind, Jenny (1820–1887)
Ling Shuhua (1904–1990)
Littlefield, Nancy (c. 1929—)
Long, Jill Lynette (1952—)
Long, Marguerite (1874–1966)
Lonsdale, Kathleen (1903–1971)
Lorde, Audre (1934–1992)
Loudov, Ivana (1941—)
Lozier, Clemence S. (1813–1888)
Lyman, Mary Ely (1887–1975)
Maathai, Wangari (1940—)
MacDonald, Margaret (c. 1907–1956)
MacGillavry, Carolina H. (1904–1993)
Mackinnon, Catherine A. (1946—)
Macklin, Madge (1893–1962)
Macurdy, Grace Harriet (1866–1946)
Madgett, Naomi Long (1923—)
Makarova, Tamara (1907–1997)
Makemson, Maud Worcester (1891–1977)
Maksimovic, Desanka (1898–1993)
Malpede, Karen (1945—)
Maltby, Margaret E. (1860–1944)
Mann, Ida (1893–1983)
Manton, Irene (1904–1988)
Manzolini, Anna Morandi (1716–1774)
Marchesi, Mathilde (1821–1913)
Marcus, Ruth Barcan (1921—)
Markovic, Mirjana (1942—)
Marlatt, Abby (1916—)
Martin, Lillien Jane (1851–1943)
Martin, Lynn (1939—)
Massevitch, Alla G. (1918—)
Maury, Antonia (1866–1952)
Maury, Carlotta (1874–1938)
Maxwell, Constantia (1886–1962)
Mayer, Maria Goeppert (1906–1972)
McAllister, Anne Hunter (1892–1983)
McClintock, Barbara (1902–1992)
McCoy, Iola Fuller (1906–1993)
McKisack, May (1900–1981)
McLaren, Anne Laura (1927—)
McMillan, Terry (1951—)
Mead, Margaret (1901–1978)
Meer, Fatima (1928—)
Meinhof, Ulrike (1934–1972)
Meireles, Cecélia (1901–1964)
Meitner, Lise (1878–1968)
Mekeel, Joyce (1931—)
Mendenhall, Dorothy Reed (1874–1964)
Mercuriade of Salerno (fl. 1200)
Mernissi, Fatima (1940—)
Merrick, Myra King (1825–1899)
Meyer, Lucy (1849–1922)
Millis, Nancy (1922—)
Milner, Brenda Atkinson (1918—)
Mistral, Gabriela (1889–1957)
Mitchell, Juliet (1934—)
Mitchell, Maria (1818–1889)
Mitchison, Naomi (1897–1999)
Moholy-Nagy, Sibyl (1903–1971)
Moody, Agnes Claypole (1870–1954)
Morani, Alma Dea (1907–2001)
Morgan, Agnes Fay (1884–1968)
Morgan, Ann Haven (1882–1966)
Morrison, Toni (1931—)
Mosher, Clelia Duel (1863–1940)
Mosher, Eliza Maria (1846–1928)
Moszumanska-Nazar, Krystyna (1924—)
Moulton, Barbara (1915–1997)
Mugo, Micere Githae (1942—)
Murdoch, Iris (1919–1999)
Murray, Margaret (1863–1963)
Murray, Pauli (1910–1985)
Musgrave, Thea (1928—)
Mutafchieva, Vera P. (1929—)
Nashar, Beryl (1923—)
Naylor, Gloria (1950—)
Neilson, Nellie (1873–1947)
Neruda, Wilma (c. 1838–1911)
Neumann, Hanna (1914–1971)
Newlin, Dika (1923—)
Newton, Lily (1893–1981)
Nickerson, Camille (1884–1982)
Nikolayeva, Tatiana (1924–1993)
Noach, Ilse (1908–1998)
Noether, Emmy (1882–1935)
Norman, Marsha (1947—)
Novella (d. 1333)
Novello, Antonia (1944—)
Nutting, Mary Adelaide (1858–1948)
Nwapa, Flora (1931–1993)
Oakley, Ann (1944—)
Oates, Joyce Carol (1938—)
O'Callaghan, Kathleen (1888–1961)
Odio Benito, Elizabeth (1939—)
O'Hare, Kate Richards (1876–1948)
Okin, Susan Moller (1946–2004)
Okoye, Ifeoma
Oliver, Mary (1935—)
Oliveros, Pauline (1932—)
Olsen, Tillie (c. 1912—)
Opie, Iona (1923—)
Oppenheimer, Jane Marion (1911–1996)
Ormerod, Eleanor A. (1828–1901)
Osborne, Estelle Massey (1901–1981)
Ostermeyer, Micheline (1922—)
Otway-Ruthven, Jocelyn (1909–1989)
Overlach, Helene (1894–1983)
Paglia, Camille (1947—)
Paley, Grace (1922—)
Panagiotatou, Angeliki (1878–1954)
Pardo Bazán, Emilia (1852–1921)
Parkhurst, Helen (1887–1973)
Parrish, Celestia (1853–1918)
Parsons, Elsie Clews (1875–1941)
Payne-Gaposchkin, Cecilia (1900–1979)
Pearce, Louise (1885–1959)
Peck, Annie Smith (1850–1935)
Peebles, Florence (1874–1956)
Peixotto, Jessica (1864–1941)
Pendleton, Ellen Fitz (1864–1936)
Pennington, Mary Engle (1872–1952)
Pennington, Winifred (1915—)
Penson, Lillian Margery (1896–1963)
Peplau, Hildegard E. (1909–1999)
Perey, Marguerite (1909–1975)
Perham, Margery (1895–1982)
Phillpotts, Bertha Surtees (1877–1932)
Pickford, Mary (1902–2002)
Pool, Judith Graham (1919–1975)
Portal, Marta (1930—)
Porter, Annie (1880–1963)
Porter, Helen Kemp (1899–1987)
Pound, Louise (1872–1958)
Powdermaker, Hortense (1896–1970)
Power, Eileen (1889–1940)
Preston, Ann (1813–1872)
Primus, Pearl (1919–1994)
Putnam, Bertha Haven (1872–1960)

Putnam, Emily James (1865–1944)
Quimby, Edith (1891–1982)
Raine, Kathleen (1908–2003)
Raisin, Catherine (1855–1945)
Rajalakshmi, R. (1926—)
Rand, Gertrude (1886–1970)
Rapoport, Lydia (1923–1971)
Ray, Dixy Lee (1914–1994)
Redpath, Jean (1937—)
Rees, Gwendolen (1906–1994)
Rego, Paula (1935—)
Reichard, Gladys (1893–1955)
Reinders, Agnes (1913–1993)
Reynolds, Myra (1853–1936)
Richardson, Henry Handel (1870–1946)
Richter, Elise (1865–1943)
Rickert, Edith (1871–1938)
Rickett, Mary Ellen (1861–1925)
Ripley, Martha Rogers (1843–1912)
Ritter, Erika (1948—)
Roberts, Lydia (1879–1965)
Roberts, Rachel (1927–1980)
Robinson, Jane Bancroft (1847–1932)
Robinson, Jo Ann (1911–1992)
Robinson, Joan Violet (1903–1983)
Robinson, Julia B. (1919–1985)
Robinson, Mary (1944—)
Rogers, Clara Kathleen (1844–1931)
Rothwell, Evelyn (b. 1911)
Rubin, Vera Cooper (1928—)
Ruether, Rosemary (1936—)
Rukeyser, Muriel (1913–1980)
Russell, Annie (1864–1936)
Russell, Dorothy Stuart (1895–1983)
Russell, Jane Anne (1911–1967)
Saariaho, Kaija (1952—)
Sabin, Ellen (1850–1949)
Sadat, Jehan (1933—)
Safford, Mary Jane (1834–1891)
Sager, Ruth (1918–1997)
Salmon, Lucy Maynard (1853–1927)
Sampson, Kathleen (1892–1980)
Sandars, Nancy K. (1914—)
Sandel, Cora (1880–1974)
Sanford, Maria Louise (1836–1920)
Sansome, Eva (1906–?)
Santolalla, Irene Silva de (1902–1992)
Savić-Rebac, Anica (1892–1935)
Savitch, Jessica (1947–1983)
Saw, Ruth (1901–1983)
Scharff-Goldhaber, Gertrude (1911–1998)
Scharrer, Berta (1906–1995)
Scott-Brown, Denise (1931—)
Scudder, Vida (1861–1954)
Seibert, Florence B. (1897–1991)
Semple, Ellen Churchill (1863–1932)
Sexton, Anne (1928–1974)
Shabazz, Betty (1936–1997)
Shange, Ntozake (1948—)
Shattuck, Lydia (1822–1889)
Sherif, Carolyn Wood (1922–1982)
Sherlock, Sheila (1918–2001)
Shoemaker, Carolyn (1929—)
Showalter, Elaine (1941—)
Shtern, Lina (1878–1968)
Silko, Leslie Marmon (1948—)
Sintenis, Renée (1888–1965)
Slowe, Lucy Diggs (1885–1937)
Slye, Maud (1869–1954)
Smiley, Jane (1949—)
Smith-Rosenberg, Carroll
Sofola, Zulu (1935–1995)
Spafford, Belle Smith (1895–1982)
Spain, Jayne (1927—)
Spencer, Anna (1851–1931)
Spencer, Elizabeth (1921—)
Spender, Dale (1943—)
Spivak, Gayatri Chakravorty (1942—)
Sponer, Hertha (1895–1968)
Spurgeon, Caroline F.E. (1869–1942)
Starovoitova, Galina (1946–1998)
Stein, Edith (1891–1942)
Stephens, Kate (1853–1938)
Stephenson, Elsie (1916–1967)
Stevenson, Sarah Hackett (1841–1909)
Stoneman, Bertha (1866–1943)
Stopes, Marie (1880–1958)
Storni, Alfonsina (1892–1938)
Strang, Ruth (1895–1971)
Stratton, Dorothy (b. 1899)
Strauss, Jennifer (1933—)
Strickland, Shirley (1925—)
Strong, Ann Monroe Gilchrist (1875–1957)
Strossen, Nadine (1950—)
Sturgis, Katharine Boucot (1903–1987)
Sullerot, Evelyne (1924—)
Suzman, Helen (1917—)
Swenson, May (1913–1989)
Swindler, Mary Hamilton (1884–1967)
Taba, Hilda (1902–1967)
Taeuber, Irene Barnes (1906–1974)
Taft, Jessie (1882–1960)
Talbot, Marion (1858–1948)
Tammes, Tine (1871–1947)
Taussig, Helen Brooke (1898–1986)
Taylor, Eva (1879–1966)
Taylor, Janet (1804–1870)
Taylor, Lily Ross (1886–1969)
Terrell, Mary Church (1863–1954)
Thomas, Clara (1919—)
Thomas, M. Carey (1857–1935)
Thompson, Mary Harris (1829–1895)
Thursby, Emma (1845–1931)
Tibbetts, Margaret Joy (1919—)
Tizard, Catherine (1931—)
Towle, Charlotte (1896–1966)
Travell, Janet G. (1901–1997)
Trotula (c. 1040s–1097)
Tuve, Rosemond (1903–1964)
Tyler, Alice S. (1859–1944)
Udaltsova, Nadezhda (1885–1961)
Underhill, Evelyn (1875–1941)
Ustvolskaya, Galina (1919—)
Vaganova, Agrippina (1879–1951)
Valette, Aline (1850–1899)
Van Deman, Esther (1862–1937)
Van de Vate, Nancy (1930—)
Van Dover, Cindy (1954—)
Van Hoosen, Bertha (1863–1952)
Van Rensselaer, Martha (1864–1932)
Vargas, Virginia (1945—)
Vasconcellos, Karoline Michaëlis de (1851–1925)
Vega, Ana Lydia (1946—)
Vérone, Maria (1874–1938)
Vike-Freiberga, Vaira (1937—)
Vilariño, Idea (1920—)
Wagner, Friedelind (1918–1991)
Walker, Margaret (1915–1998)
Wambaugh, Sarah (1882–1955)
Ward, Barbara (1914–1981)
Warner, Marina (1946—)
Washburn, Margaret Floy (1871–1939)
Webster, Margaret (1905–1972)
Weddington, Sarah R. (1945—)
Weizmann, Vera (1881–1966)
Welsh, Lilian (1858–1938)
Welty, Eudora (1909–2001)
West, Jessamyn (1902–1984)
Wexler, Nancy (1945—)
Wheeler, Anna Pell (1883–1966)
White, Edna Noble (1879–1954)
White, Helen C. (1896–1967)
White, Margaret (c. 1888–1977)
Whitelaw, Billie (1932—)
Whitney, Mary Watson (1847–1921)
Whyte, Kathleen (1909–1996)
Wiesenthal, Grete (1885–1970)
Williams, Cicely (1893–1992)
Williams, Ivy (1877–1966)
Williams, Mary Wilhelmine (1878–1944)
Williams, Sherley Anne (1944–1999)
Willing, Jennie Fowler (1834–1916)
Winslow, Ola Elizabeth (c. 1885–1977)
Wiskemann, Elizabeth Meta (1899–1971)
Wolf, Christa (1929—)
Wolfson, Theresa (1897–1972)
Wood, Evelyn (1909–1995)
Woodhouse, Margaret Chase Going (1890–1984)
Woolley, Helen (1874–1947)
Woolley, Mary E. (1863–1947)
Wootton, Barbara (1897–1988)
Wright, Jane Cooke (1919—)
Wright, Mary Clabaugh (1917–1970)
Wrinch, Dorothy (1894–1976)
Wu, Chien-Shiung (1912–1997)
Xie Xide (1921–2000)
Yalow, Rosalyn (1921—)
Yamada, Mitsuye (1923—)
Yang Jiang (b. 1911)
Yasui, Kono (1880–1971)
Ye Jiayin (1924—)
Yener, Aslihan (1946—)
Yessayan, Zabel (1878–1943)
Young, Anne Sewell (1871–1961)
Young, Ella Flagg (1845–1918)
Younghusband, Eileen Louise (1902–1981)
Yuasa, Toshiko (1909–1980)
Yudina, Maria (1899–1970)
Zabriskie, Louise (1887–1957)
Zapata Olivella, Delia (1926–2001)
Zhao Luorui (b. 1912)
Zhao Yufen (1948—)
Zheng Min (1920—)

COLUMNIST

Adams, Evangeline Smith (1873–1932)
Allen, Rosalie (1924–2003)
Aubert, Constance (1803–?)
Auclert, Hubertine (1848–1914)
Bass, Mary Elizabeth (1876–1956)
Becker, May Lamberton (1873–1958)
Blyton, Enid (1897–1968)
Boardman, Eleanor (1898–1991)
Bombeck, Erma (1927–1996)
Bottome, Margaret McDonald (1827–1906)
Bromley, Dorothy Dunbar (1896–1986)
Bronson, Betty (1906–1971)
Cartland, Barbara (1901–2000)
Cashman, Mel (1891–1979)
Cather, Willa (1873–1947)
Clare, Ada (1836–1874)
Collins, Gail (1945—)
Colwin, Laurie (1944–1992)
Connolly, Maureen (1934–1969)
Craig, May (1888–1975)
Croly, Jane Cunningham (1829–1901)
Cross, Zora (1890–1964)
Cruso, Thalassa (1908–1997)
Diggs, Annie LePorte (1848–1916)
Dorr, Rheta Childe (1866–1948)
Douglas, Marjory Stoneman (1890–1998)
Dunbar-Nelson, Alice (1875–1935)
Durand, Marguerite (1864–1936)
Felton, Rebecca Latimer (1835–1930)
Fern, Fanny (1811–1872)
Field, Kate (1838–1896)

Fleeson, Doris (1901–1970)
Freeman, Alice (1857–1936)
Friday, Nancy (1937—)
Friedman, Esther Pauline (1918–2002)
Friedman, Pauline Esther (1918—)
Gilmer, Elizabeth Meriwether (1861–1951)
Glaspell, Susan (1876–1948)
Goodman, Ellen (1941—)
Graham, Sheila (1904–1988)
Greenfield, Meg (1930–1999)
Guest, C.Z. (1920–2003)
Hale, Sarah Preston (1796–1866)
Harper, Ida Husted (1851–1931)
Head, Bessie (1937–1986)
Higgins, Marguerite (1920–1966)
Hobby, Oveta Culp (1905–1995)
Hopper, Hedda (1885–1966)
Ivins, Molly (c. 1944—)
Jemison, Alice Lee (1901–1964)
Kelly, Florence Finch (1858–1939)
Kilgallen, Dorothy (1913–1965)
Kirchwey, Freda (1893–1976)
Kuhn, Irene Corbally (1898–1995)
La Follette, Belle Case (1859–1931)
Leslie, Annie (1869–1948)
Lewis, Flora (1922–2002)
Lieberman-Cline, Nancy (1958—)
Loveman, Amy (1881–1955)
Luce, Clare Boothe (1903–1987)
Lyons, Enid (1897–1981)
Lyons, Sophie (1848–1924)
Macaulay, Rose (1881–1958)
Macphail, Agnes (1890–1954)
Manning, Marie (c. 1873–1945)
McCormick, Anne O'Hare (1880–1954)
McGrory, Mary (1918–2004)
McKenney, Ruth (1911–1972)
Mead, Margaret (1901–1978)
Meinhof, Ulrike (1934–1972)
Misme, Jane (1865–1935)
Muir, Florabel (1889–1970)
Norman, Dorothy (1905–1997)
O'Faolain, Nuala (1940—)
O'Hare, Kate Richards (1876–1948)
Paddleford, Clementine (1900–1967)
Parker, Dorothy (1893–1967)
Parsons, Harriet (1906–1983)
Parsons, Louella (1881–1972)
Patterson, Alicia (1906–1963)
Paulsen, Marit (1939—)
Pennell, Elizabeth Robins (1855–1936)
Pettis, Shirley Neil (1924—)
Porter, Katherine Anne (1890–1980)
Porter, Sylvia (1913–1991)
Potonié-Pierre, Eugénie (1844–1898)
Rand, Ayn (1905–1982)
Retton, Mary Lou (1968—)
Rubinstein, Renate (1929–1990)
Russell, Lillian (1861–1922)
Scott, Mary Edith (1888–1979)
Scott-Maxwell, Florida (1883–1979)
Seaman, Elizabeth Cochrane (1864–1922)
Séverine (1855–1929)
Smith, Lillian (1897–1966)
Smith, Liz (1923—)
Soper, Eileen Louise (1900–1989)
Stratton-Porter, Gene (1863–1924)
Taber, Gladys (1899–1980)
Tabouis, Geneviève (1892–1985)
Tarry, Ellen (b. 1906)
Thompson, Dorothy (1893–1961)
Tierney, Gene (1920–1991)
Trilling, Diana (1905–1996)
Tweedie, Jill (1936–1993)
Valette, Aline (1850–1899)
Vanderbilt, Amy (1908–1974)
Vengerova, Zinaida (1867–1941)
Vérone, Maria (1874–1938)
Washington, Fredi (1903–1994)
Wells-Barnett, Ida (1862–1931)
West, Dorothy (1907–1998)
Whitton, Charlotte (1896–1975)
Wilder, Laura Ingalls (1867–1957)
Wright, Cobina (1887–1970)

COMBAT AVIATOR

André, Valerie (1922—)
Bailey, Mary (1890–1960)
Cochran, Jacqueline (1906–1980)
Davis, Dorothy Hilliard (1917–1994)
Fort, Cornelia (1919–1943)
Gelman, Polina (1919—)
Gower, Pauline (1910–1947)
Grizodubova, Valentina (1910–1993)
Johnson, Amy (1903–1941)
Karpinski, Stephanie (1912–2005)
Khomiakova, Valeriia (d. 1942)
Litvyak, Lidiya (1921–1943)
Moggridge, Jackie (1922–2004)
Osipenko, Polina (1907–1939)
Quimby, Harriet (1875–1912)
Rainey, Barbara Allen (1948–1982)
Raskova, Marina (1912–1943)

COMBAT CORRESPONDENT

Adams, Harriet Chalmers (1875–1937)
Bonney, Thérèse (1894–1978)
Broniewska, Janina (1904–1981)
Bryant, Louise (1885–1936)
Carpenter, Iris (b. 1906)
Chapelle, Dickey (1919–1972)
Colette (1873–1954)
Cowan, Ruth (1901–1993)
Cowles, Virginia (1912–1983)
Craig, May (1888–1975)
Davis, Rebecca Harding (1831–1910)
Deutscher, Tamara (1913–1990)
Dixie, Lady Florence (1857–1905)
Emerson, Gloria (1929–2004)
Fadiman, Annalee (1916–2002)
Flanner, Janet (1892–1978)
Fleeson, Doris (1901–1970)
Frederick, Pauline (1908–1990)
Gauntier, Gene (1885–1966)
Gellhorn, Martha (1908–1998)
Glyn, Elinor (1864–1943)
Haldane, Charlotte (1894–1969)
Higgins, Marguerite (1920–1966)
Hull, Peggy (1889–1967)
Jesse, Fryniwyd Tennyson (1888–1958)
Kirkpatrick, Helen (1909–1997)
Krull, Germaine (1897–1985)
Kuhn, Irene Corbally (1898–1995)
Littledale, Clara (1891–1956)
Long, Tania (1913–1998)
Luce, Clare Boothe (1903–1987)
Miller, Lee (1907–1977)
Neuffer, Elizabeth (1956–2003)
Osten, Maria (1908–1942)
Reid, Helen Rogers (1882–1970)
Rinehart, Mary Roberts (1876–1958)
Schultz, Sigrid (1893–1980)
Smedley, Agnes (1892–1950)
Strickland, Mabel (1899–1988)
Tietjens, Eunice (1884–1944)
Tufty, Esther Van Wagoner (1896–1986)
Ward, Mrs. Humphry (1851–1920)

COMBAT NURSE

Abdellah, Faye Glenn (1919—)
Agnelli, Susanna (1922—)
Alexandra Feodorovna (1872–1918)
Ashton, Helen (1891–1958)
Aston, Luise (1814–1871)
Bagnold, Enid (1889–1981)
Barton, Clara (1821–1912)
Basch, Anamarija (1893–after 1945)
Bernhardt, Sarah (1844–1923)
Bickerdyke, Mary Ann (1817–1901)
Blanchfield, Florence (1884–1971)
Bonner, Elena (1923—)
Boston, Lucy Maria (1892–1990)
Bradley, Amy Morris (1823–1904)
Brady, Mary (1821–1864)
Breckinridge, Mary (1881–1965)
Brown, Molly (1867–1932)
Brownell, Kady (b. 1842)
Bruha, Antonia (1915—)
Bullwinkel, Vivian (1915–2000)
Cammermeyer, Margarethe (1942—)
Carré, Mathilde (1908–c. 1970)
Cavell, Edith (1865–1915)
Churchill, Diana Spencer (1909–1963)
Churchill, Jennie Jerome (1854–1921)
Colette (1873–1954)
Cook, Cordelia E. (1919–1996)
Darragh, Lydia Barrington (1729–1789)
Darton, Patience (1911–1996)
Dauser, Sue (1888–1972)
Davidow, Ruth (1911–1999)
de Galard, Geneviève (1925—)
Delano, Jane Arminda (1862–1919)
de Wolfe, Elsie (1865–1950)
Dix, Dorothea Lynde (1802–1887)
Drexel, Constance (1894–1956)
Edmonds, Emma (1841–1898)
Elliott, Maxine (1868–1940)
Farmborough, Florence (1887–1978)
Fenwick, Ethel Gordon (1857–1947)
Flikke, Julia Otteson (1879–1965)
Fu Hao (fl. 1040 BCE)
Gardner, Julia Anna (1882–1960)
Gellhorn, Martha (1908–1998)
Gibbons, Abby Hopper (1801–1893)
Goldman, Hetty (1881–1972)
Gonne, Maud (1866–1953)
Hamm, Margherita (1867–1907)
Holtby, Winifred (1898–1935)
Kenny, Elizabeth (1880–1952)
Keppel, Alice (1869–1947)
Kimball, Martha G. (1840–1894)
Kingsley, Mary H. (1862–1900)
Larkin, Delia (1878–1949)
Larsen, Nella (1891–1964)
Lemmon, Sarah Plummer (1836–1923)
Levertov, Denise (1923–1997)
Lott, Elsie S. (fl. 1940s)
Loy, Mina (1882–1966)
Maass, Clara (1876–1901)
Mance, Jeanne (1606–1673)
Marie Feodorovna (1847–1928)
Martin, Mother Mary (1892–1975)
McCarthy, Maud (1858–1949)
McGee, Anita Newcomb (1864–1940)
McKenna, Marthe (1893–1969)
Michel, Louise (1830–1905)
Nienhuys, Janna
Nightingale, Florence (1820–1910)
O'Connell, Mary (1814–1897)
Overlach, Helene (1894–1983)
Paget, Mary (1865–1919)
Parsons, Emily Elizabeth (1824–1880)
Petre, Maude (1863–1942)
Petry, Lucile (1902–1999)
Putnam, Bertha Haven (1872–1960)
Reynolds, Belle (fl. 1860s)
Rohde, Ruth Bryan Owen (1885–1954)
Safford, Mary Jane (1834–1891)

Sampson, Deborah (1760–1827)
Sandes, Flora (1876–1956)
Sankova, Galina (b. 1904)
Stimson, Julia (1881–1948)
Svolou, Maria (d. 1976)
Swisshelm, Jane Grey (1815–1884)
Taylor, Susie King (1848–1912)
Thomas, Mary Myers (1816–1888)
Tompkins, Sally Louisa (1833–1916)
Uzès, Anne, Duchesse d' (1847–1933)
Wilkinson, Iris (1906–1939)
Wittenmyer, Annie Turner (1827–1900)
Woolson, Constance Fenimore (1840–1894)
Zlatin, Sabina (1907–1996)

COMBAT PHOTOGRAPHER
Bourke-White, Margaret (1904–1971)
Bubley, Esther (1921–1998)
Frissell, Toni (1907–1988)
Horna, Kati (1912—)
Sankova, Galina (b. 1904)
Taro, Gerda (1910–1937)

COMEDIAN/COMEDIC ACTRESS
Adams, Edie (1927—)
Allen, Gracie (1902–1964)
Allen, Susan Westford (c. 1865–1944)
Ball, Lucille (1911–1989)
Ballard, Kaye (1926—)
Bayes, Nora (1880–1928)
Bird, Billie (1908–2002)
Bozyk, Reizl (1914–1993)
Breen, Nellie (c. 1898–1986)
Brice, Fanny (1891–1951)
Broderick, Helen (1890–1959)
Bruce, Betty (1920–1974)
Burnett, Carol (1933—)
Byron, Marion (1911–1985)
Canova, Judy (1916–1983)
Carney, Kate (1870–1950)
Carter, Maybelle (1909–1978)
Carus, Emma (1879–1927)
Cass, Peggy (1924–1999)
Chéri, Rose (1824–1861)
Claire, Ina (1892–1985)
Clive, Kitty (1711–1785)
Coca, Imogene (1909–2001)
Compton, Fay (1894–1978)
Corbett, Leonora (1908–1960)
Courtneidge, Cicely (1893–1980)
Cox, Ray (b. 1880)
Crabtree, Lotta (1847–1924)
Daley, Cass (1915–1975)
Davies, Marion (1897–1961)
Davis, Joan (1907–1961)
De Casalis, Jeanne (1897–1966)
DeGeneres, Ellen (1958—)
Diller, Phyllis (1917—)
Donnelly, Ruth (1896–1982)
Dormer, Daisy (1889–1947)
Dressler, Marie (1869–1934)
Durfee, Minta (1897–1975)
Fields, Gracie (1898–1979)
Finch, Flora (1867–1940)
Fitzgerald, Lillian (d. 1947)
Flagg, Fannie (1941—)
Florence, Malvina Pray (1830–1906)
Forde, Florrie (1876–1940)
Fox, Della (1870–1913)
Freeman, Kathleen (1919–2001)
French, Dawn (1957—)
Friganza, Trixie (1870–1955)
Gardella, Tess (1897–1950)
Garland, Judy (1922–1969)
Gay, Maisie (1883–1945)
Gear, Luella (1897–1980)
Geistinger, Marie (1833–1903)
Gingold, Hermione (1897–1987)
Glaser, Lulu (1874–1958)
Glover, Julia (1779–1850)
Goldberg, Whoopi (1949—)
Greener, Dorothy (1917–1971)
Greenwood, Charlotte (1890–1978)
Hale, Binnie (1899–1984)
Handl, Irene (1901–1987)
Harlow, Jean (1911–1937)
Hart, Annie (d. 1947)
Heiberg, Johanne Luise (1812–1890)
Held, Anna (c. 1865–1918)
Henry, Gale (1893–1972)
Hibbard, Edna (c. 1895–1942)
Hilliard, Harriet (1909–1994)
Hopper, Edna Wallace (1864–1959)
Howell, Alice (1888–1961)
Jacques, Hattie (1922–1980)
Jordan, Marian (1896–1961)
Kahn, Madeline (1942–1999)
Kay, Beatrice (1907–1986)
Kean, Betty (1915–1986)
Kelly, Patsy (1910–1981)
Kendal, Madge (1849–1935)
Kendall, Kay (1926–1959)
Ladynina, Marina (1908–2003)
Lasser, Louise (1939—)
Lavallière, Eve (c. 1866–1929)
Lightner, Winnie (1899–1971)
Lillie, Beatrice (1894–1989)
Lloyd, Alice (1873–1949)
Lloyd, Marie (1870–1922)
Lloyd, Rosie (b. 1879)
Loftus, Marie (1857–1940)
Lombard, Carole (1908–1942)
Lorne, Marion (1888–1968)
Mabley, Jackie (1894–1975)
Marr, Sally (1906–1997)
Mars, Ann Françoise (1779–1847)
Mattocks, Isabella (1746–1826)
McConnell, Lulu (1882–1962)
McIntyre, Leila (1882–1953)
Monkman, Phyllis (1892–1976)
Moran, Patsy (1903–1968)
Moran, Polly (1884–1952)
Murray, Elizabeth (1871–1946)
Neuber, Caroline (1697–1760)
Niesen, Gertrude (1910–1975)
Normand, Mabel (1892–1930)
O'Brien, Virginia (1919–2001)
O'Neal, Zelma (1903–1989)
Page, LaWanda (1920–2002)
Pearce, Alice (1913–1966)
Pearl, Minnie (1912–1996)
Picon, Molly (1898–1992)
Price, Kate (1872–1943)
Radner, Gilda (1946–1989)
Randolph, Elsie (1904–1982)
Raye, Martha (1916–1994)
Rhodes, Billie (1894–1988)
Ritter, Erika (1948—)
Roseanne (1952—)
Routledge, Patricia (1929—)
Russell, Anna (b. 1911)
Russell, Lillian (1861–1922)
Russell, Rosalind (1908–1976)
Saunders, Jennifer (1958—)
Scott, Ivy (1886–1947)
Sheridan, Dinah (1920—)
Short, Gertrude (1902–1968)
Sims, Joan (1930–2001)
Summers, Leonora (1897–1976)
Taylor, Renée (1933—)
Tempest, Marie (1864–1942)
Thompson, Emma (1959—)
Tomlin, Lily (1939—)
Ullman, Tracey (1959—)
Vague, Vera (1906–1974)
Vance, Danitra (1954–1994)
Vanderbilt, Gertrude (1880–1960)
Vestris, Lucia (1797–1856)
Villegas, Micaela (1748–1819)
Vincent, Mary Ann (1818–1887)
Vokes, May (d. 1957)
Von Nagy, Käthe (1909–1973)
Walker, Betty (1928–1982)
Walker, Nancy (1922–1992)
Wallace, Nellie (1870–1948)
Waters, Ethel (1896–1977)
West, Mae (1893–1980)
Wickes, Mary (1916–1995)
Williams, Hattie (1872–1942)
Wilson, Marie (1916–1972)
Withee, Mabel (d. 1952)
Wood, Daisey (1877–?)

COMEDY WRITER
Pugh, Madelyn (c. 1921—)

COMMUNITY LEADER
Halcombe, Edith Stanway (1844–1903)

COMPOSER
See Hymn writer.
See Librettist.
See Lyricist.
See Music composer.
See Songwriter.

COMPUTER ENGINEER
Borg, Anita (1949–2003)
Bramley, Jenny Rosenthal (1910–1997)
Hopper, Grace Murray (1906–1992)
Wedemeyer, Maria von (c. 1924–1977)

COMTESS
See Countess.

CONCHOLOGIST
Cockburn, Patricia (1914–1989)
Lyell, Mary Horner (1808–1873)

CONCUBINE
Arsinoe (fl. 4th c. BCE)
Aspasia of Miletus (c. 464 BCE–c. 420 BCE)
Aspasia the Younger (fl. 415–370 BCE)
Cixi (1835–1908)
Eadgyth Swanneshals (c. 1012–?)
Fredegund (c. 547–597)
Hazrat Mahal (c. 1820–1879)
Hemings, Sally (1773–1835)
Ise (877–940)
Keturah (fl. 3rd, 2nd, or 1st c. BCE)
Maachah (fl. 1575 BCE)
Marcia (fl. 177–192)
Rizpah
Thora Johnsdottir (fl. 1000s)
Tomoe Gozen (fl. c. 12th c.)
Wang Zhaojun (52 BCE–18 CE)
Wu Zetian (624–705)
Zilpah

CONDUCTOR
See Bandleader.
See Chorus/chorale conductor.
See Orchestra conductor.

CONFIDENCE ARTIST (ACCUSED)
Beck, Sophie (1858–?)
Bluffstein, Sophie (1854–1891)
Bock, Amy Maud (1859–1943)
Chadwick, Cassie L. (1859–1907)

Churchill, May (1876–1929)
Gordon-Baille, Mary Ann (1857–?)
Grieve, Elizabeth Harriet (1735–?)
Hanau, Marthe (c. 1884–1935)
Lyons, Sophie (1848–1924)
Moders, Mary (1643–1673)
Newman, Julia St. Clair (1818–?)
Peck, Ellen (1829–1915)
Serres, Olivia (1772–1834)

CONGRESSIONAL REPRESENTATIVE
See Politician.

CONSERVATIONIST
Armbrust, Roma (1927–2003)
Atkins, Babs (1917–2004)
Balfour, Jean (1927—)
Barclay-Smith, Phyllis (1903–1980)
Bingham, Millicent Todd (1880–1968)
Braun, E. Lucy (1889–1971)
Caldicott, Helen (1938—)
Carles, Emilie (1900–1979)
Carson, Rachel (1907–1964)
Davies, Margaret (1914–1982)
Denman, Gertrude (1884–1954)
Dormon, Carrie (1888–1971)
Duby-Blom, Gertrude (1901–1993)
Fossey, Dian (1932–1985)
Galdikas, Biruté (1948—)
Gibbs, May (1877–1969)
Gillette, Genevieve (1898–1986)
Gilmer, Elizabeth May (1880–1960)
Goodall, Jane (1934—)
Huxley, Elspeth (1907–1997)
Kilbourn, Annelisa (1967–2002)
Lemon, Margaretta Louisa (1860–1953)
McCrackin, Josephine Clifford (1838–1920)
Moncrieff, Pérrine (1893–1979)
Morgan, Ann Haven (1882–1966)
Murie, Margaret (1902–2003)
Ordway, Katharine (1899–1979)
Owings, Margaret Wentworth (1913–1999)
Rawlings, Marjorie Kinnan (1896–1953)
Reiche, Maria (1903–1998)
Rockefeller, Margaret (1915–1996)
Stratton-Porter, Gene (1863–1924)
Wayburn, Peggy (1917–2002)
Wolf, Hazel (1898–2000)
Wright, Judith (1915–2000)
Wright, Mabel Osgood (1859–1934)

CONSORT
Adelaide of Maurienne (1092–1154)
Adelaide of Savona (d. 1118)
Alexandra of Denmark (1844–1925)
Anne of Denmark (1574–1619)
Balthild (c. 630–c. 680)
Bonita, Maria (c. 1908–1938)
Brant, Molly (c. 1736–1796)
Catherine I (1684–1727)
Charlotte of Mecklenburg-Strelitz (1744–1818)
Cleopatra Berenice III (c. 115–80 BCE)
Draga (1867–1903)
Eleanor of Castile (1307–1359)
Eleanor of Provence (c. 1222–1291)
Elizabeth Bowes-Lyon (1900–2002)
Emma (1836–1885)
Engelberga (c. 840–890)
Fredegund (c. 547–597)
Fredericka (1917–1981)
Fu Hao (fl. 1040 BCE)
Geraldine (1916—)
Gülabahar (fl. 1521)
Gunhilda of Poland (d. around 1015)
Gunnhild (fl. 1150s)
Hafsa (d. 1534)
Helena (c. 255–329)
Isabella of France (1296–1358)
Isabel of Portugal (1428–1496)
Josephine (1763–1814)
Kelly, Grace (1928–1982)
Livia Drusilla (58 BCE–29 CE)
Margaret of France (c. 1282–1318)
Margaret of Navarre (fl. 1154–1172)
Maria Carolina (1752–1814)
Marie Louise d'Orleans (1662–1689)
Martel, Judith (c. 844–?)
Matilda, Empress (1102–1167)
Min (1851–1895)
Minervina (fl. 290–307)
Nagako (1903–2000)
Onshi (872–907)
Philippa of Hainault (1314–1369)
Pulcheria (c. 398–453)
Rachel (1821–1858)
Roxelana (c. 1504–1558)
Sophia Dorothea of Brunswick-Celle (1666–1726)
Sosipatra (fl. 4th c.)
Suiko (554–628)
Ulrica Eleanora (1688–1741)
Zoë Porphyrogenita (980–1050)

CONSUMERS' ADVOCATE
Baker, Ella (1903–1986)
Brady, Mildred Edie (1906–1965)
Butler, Elizabeth Beardsley (c. 1885–1911)
Campbell, Persia (1898–1974)
Dewson, Molly (1874–1962)
Furness, Betty (1916–1994)
Hamilton, Alice (1869–1970)
Hiratsuka Raichō (1886–1971)
Kelley, Florence (1859–1932)
Mason, Lucy Randolph (1882–1959)
McKechnie, Sheila (1948–2004)
Myerson, Bess (1924—)
Nathan, Maud (1862–1946)
Richards, Ellen Swallow (1842–1911)
Roberts, Eirlys (b. 1911)
Rumsey, Mary Harriman (1881–1934)
Sherwin, Belle (1868–1955)
Simkhovitch, Mary (1867–1951)
Tweedy, Hilda (b. 1911)
White, Sue Shelton (1887–1943)
Woerishoffer, Carola (1885–1911)

COSMETICS/HAIR-CARE ENTREPRENEUR
Arden, Elizabeth (1878–1966)
Ash, Mary Kay (1918–2001)
Ayer, Harriet Hubbard (1849–1903)
Bishop, Hazel (1906–1998)
Bove, Joan (1901–2001)
Calloway, Blanche (1902–1973)
Carnegie, Hattie (1886–1956)
Cochran, Jacqueline (1906–1980)
Joyner, Marjorie Stewart (1896–1994)
Lauder, Estée (1908–2004)
Malone, Annie Turnbo (1869–1957)
Quant, Mary (1934—)
Rubinstein, Helena (1870–1965)
Rubinstein, Mala (1905–1999)
Tschechowa, Olga (1897–1980)
Vanderbilt, Gloria (1924—)
Walker, A'Lelia (1885–1931)
Walker, Madame C.J. (1867–1919)
Washington, Sarah Spencer (1889–?)

COSMETIC SURGEON
See Plastic/reconstructive surgeon.

COSMONAUT
See Astronaut.

COSTUME DESIGNER
Ballard, Lucinda (1906–1993)
Bernstein, Aline (1882–1955)
Bewley, Lois (c. 1936—)
Bjornson, Maria (1949–2002)
Cashin, Bonnie (1915–2000)
Craig, Edith (1869–1947)
Delaunay, Sonia (1885–1979)
Duff Gordon, Lucy (1862–1935)
Dunham, Katherine (1909–2006)
Eckart, Jean (1921–1993)
Ellmann, Barbara (1950—)
Exter, Alexandra (1882–1949)
Fuller, Loïe (1862–1928)
Furse, Margaret (1911–1974)
Graham, Martha (1894–1991)
Haffenden, Elizabeth (1906–1976)
Haraszty, Eszter (c. 1910–1994)
Harris, Julie (1921—)
Head, Edith (1897–1981)
Irene (1901–1962)
Jeakins, Dorothy (1914–1995)
Jenssen, Elois (1922–2004)
Johnstone, Anna Hill (1913–1992)
Karinska, Barbara (1886–1983)
Lawrence, Pauline (1900–1971)
Lewisohn, Alice (1883–1972)
Lewisohn, Irene (1892–1944)
Margrethe II of Denmark (1940—)
Matera, Barbara (1929–2001)
Moiseiwitsch, Tanya (1914–2003)
Morley, Ruth (1925–1991)
Mukhina, Vera (1889–1953)
Powell, Sandy (1960—)
Rambova, Natacha (1897–1966)
Rose, Helen (1904–1985)
Roth, Ann (1931—)
Sharaff, Irene (1910–1993)
Sobotka, Ruth (1925–1967)
Stepanova, Varvara (1894–1958)
Tanning, Dorothea (b. 1910)
Taylor, Laurette (1884–1946)
Taymor, Julie (1952—)
Tree, Dolly (1899–1962)
Van Runkle, Theadora (1940—)
Wakeling, Gwen (1901–1982)
West, Claire (1893–1980)
West, Vera (1900–1947)
Wood, Yvonne (b. 1914)
Zinkeisen, Doris (1898–1991)
Zipprodt, Patricia (1925–1999)

COUNTERFEITER (ACCUSED)
Butterworth, Mary Peck (1686–1775)
Carson, Ann (d. 1824)

COUNTESS
Aberdeen, Ishbel Maria Gordon, Lady (1857–1939)
Adela Capet (c. 1010–1079)
Adelaide (fl. 860s)
Adelaide of Savona (d. 1118)
Adelaide of Saxe-Meiningen (1891–1971)
Adela of Blois (1062–c. 1137)
Adele of Normandy (c. 917–c. 962)
Adelicia (1029–1090)
Adelicia de Warrenne (d. 1178)
Agatha of Lorraine (fl. 1100s)
Agatha of Lorraine
Agnelli, Susanna (1922—)
Agnes de Nevers (r. 1181–1192)
Agnes of Aquitaine (c. 995–1068)
Agnes of Bourbon (d. 1287)

Agnes of Saxony (fl. 1200s)
Aldrude (fl. 1172)
Alexandra Victoria of Schleswig-Holstein (1887–1957)
Alice (1150–c. 1197)
Alice de Courtenay (d. 1211)
Alice de Joinville (fl. 14th c.)
Alice le Brun (d. 1255)
Alice of Athlone (1883–1981)
Alice of Normandy (fl. 1017–1037)
Alix of Vergy (r. 1248–c. 1290)
Amicie de Courtenay (d. 1275)
Anna of Egmont (1533–1558)
Anna of Saxony (1544–1577)
Anne de la Tour (c. 1496–1524)
Anne Plantagenet (1383–1438)
Anning, Mary (1799–1847)
Antrim, Angela (1911–1984)
Apponyi, Geraldine (1915—)
Arnim, Elizabeth von (1866–1941)
Arsinde (fl. 934–957)
Arundel, Ann (1557–1630)
Arundel, Anne (d. 1642)
Audley, Margaret (fl. 1340s)
Augusta, Mlle (1806–1901)
Augusta Victoria (1890–1966)
Avelina de Forz (1259–1274)
Badlesmere, Elizabeth (fl. 1315–1342)
Badlesmere, Maud (d. 1366)
Barry, Elizabeth (1658–1713)
Barry, Leonora M. (1849–1930)
Bathory, Elizabeth (1560–1614)
Bauer, Karoline (1807–1877)
Bawr, Alexandrine de (1773–1860)
Beatrice (fl. c. 1100s)
Beatrice of Portugal (c. 1347–1381)
Beatrice of Portugal (d. 1439)
Beatrice of Savoy (d. 1268)
Beauchamp, Anne (1426–1492)
Beauchamp, Elizabeth (fl. 1420)
Beauchamp, Isabel (fl. 1285)
Beauchamp, Margaret (d. 1482)
Beaufort, Eleanor (d. 1501)
Beaufort, Joan (c. 1379–1440)
Beaufort, Margaret (c. 1407–?)
Beaufort, Margaret (1443–1509)
Beaufort, Margaret (d. 1474)
Beauharnais, Fanny de (1737–1813)
Beaumont, Hawise (d. 1197)
Beaumont, Isabel (c. 1104–d. after 1172)
Beaumont, Mary (d. 1632)
Belgioso, Cristina (1808–1871)
Benoist, Marie (1768–1826)
Bertha of Chartres (d. 1084)
Bertrada of Evreux (fl. 1170s)
Bertrada of Montfort (d. after 1117)
Blanche of Artois (c. 1247–1302)
Blanche of Boulogne (1326–1360)
Blanche of Burgundy (1288–1348)
Blanche of Dreux (c. 1396–c. 1418)
Blanche of France (1328–1392)
Blanche of Navarre (d. 1229)
Blessington, Marguerite, Countess of (1789–1849)
Bohun, Alianore (d. 1313)
Bohun, Eleanor (fl. 1327–1340)
Bohun, Maud (fl. 1240s)
Bohun, Maud (fl. 1275)
Bonaparte, Carolina (1782–1839)
Bonmartini, Linda (1873–?)
Boufflers-Rouvrel, Marie Charlotte Hippolyte, Countess de (1724–c. 1800)
Bourchier, Anne (1512–1571)
Bruce, Christian (d. 1356)
Bruce, Margaret (c. 1286–?)
Bruce, Matilda (c. 1285–c. 1326)
Brunton, Louisa (c. 1785–1860)
Butler, Eleanor (c. 1915–1997)
Campanini, Barbara (1721–1799)
Carnegie, Maud (1893–1945)
Caroline of Nassau (fl. 1730s)
Castiglione, Virginie, Countess de (1837–1899)
Catherine (1584–1638)
Catherine de Clermont (fl. 16th c.)
Catherine de Courtenay (d. 1307)
Catherine of Pomerania (d. 1426)
Catherine of Vendôme (r. 1374–1412)
Cavendish, Christiana (1595–1675)
Cavendish, Elizabeth (d. 1582)
Cavendish, Georgiana (1783–1858)
Cavendish, Henrietta (d. 1755)
Cavendish-Bentinck, Nina (c. 1860–?)
Caylus, Marthe M. (1673–1729)
Cecil, Georgiana (1827–1899)
Chabrillan, Céleste de (1824–1909)
Charlotte (1896–1985)
Charlotte of Bourbon (d. 1582)
Châteaubriant, Comtesse de (c. 1490–1537)
Châteauroux, Marie Anne de Mailly-Nesle, Duchesse de (1717–1744)
Chaworth, Maud (1282–c. 1322)
Chinchon, Ana, countess of (1576–1639)
Chotek, Sophie (1868–1914)
Christian (d. 1246)
Chudleigh, Elizabeth (1720–1788)
Churchill, Anne (1684–1716)
Clare, Elizabeth de (1295–1360)
Clare, Isabel de (c. 1174–1220)
Clare, Margaret de (1249–1313)
Clare, Margaret de (c. 1293–1342)
Clementina of Zahringen (fl. 1150s)
Clifford, Anne (1590–1676)
Clifford, Margaret (c. 1560–1616)
Clifford, Margaret (d. 1596)
Clifford, Maud (d. 1446)
Coke, Alexandra (1891–1984)
Coligny, Henriette de (1618–1683)
Coligny, Louise de (1555–1620)
Colonna, Catherine (d. around 1440)
Constance (c. 1066–1090)
Constance Capet (c. 1128–1176)
Constance of Brittany (1161–1201)
Constance of France (fl. 1100s)
Courtenay, Margaret (fl. 1330)
Coventry, Anne (1673–1763)
Cowper, Mary (1685–1724)
Cromwell, Mary (1636–1712)
Cunigunde of France (c. 900–?)
Czartoryska, Isabella (1746–1835)
Dat So La Lee (c. 1835–1925)
De Brémont, Anna (1864–1922)
de Gaulle, Yvonne (1900–1979)
Desmier, Eleanor (1639–1722)
Despenser, Isabel (1400–1439)
Digby el Mesrab, Jane (1807–1881)
Di Robilant, Daisy, Countess (fl. 1922–1933)
Dönhoff, Marion, Countess (1909–2002)
Douce I (d. 1190)
Douglas, Elizabeth (d. before 1451)
Douglas, Margaret (b. around 1427)
du Barry, Jeanne Bécu, Comtesse (1743–1793)
Dunbar, Agnes (1312–1369)
Dunbar, Christine (c. 1350–?)
Dunkeld, Ada (c. 1145–1206)
Dunkeld, Ada (c. 1195–after 1241)
Ebner-Eschenbach, Marie (1830–1916)
Edgifu (902–951)
Eleanor of Montfort (1215–1275)
Eleanor of Normandy (fl. 1000s)
Eleanor Plantagenet (c. 1318–1372)
Eleonore of Savoy (d. 1324)
Elfgifu (c. 997–?)
Elfthrith (d. 929)
Elizabeth de Burgh (1332–1363)
Elizabeth of Bohemia (1292–1339)
Ellen of Wales (d. 1253)
Elphinstone, Margaret Mercer (1788–1867)
Elvira (fl. 1080s)
Emma of Norfolk (d. 1100)
Ermengarde of Carcassonne (d. 1070)
Ermentrude (d. 1126)
Ermentrude de Roucy (d. 1005)
Ermesind of Luxemburg (fl. 1200)
Ermesind of Luxemburg (d. 1247)
Eugénie (1826–1920)
Euphrosine (d. 1102)
Farren, Elizabeth (c. 1759–1829)
Fermor, Henrietta Louisa (d. 1761)
Finch, Anne (1661–1720)
Fitzalan, Alice (fl. 1285)
Fitzalan, Alice (d. around 1338)
Fitzalan, Alice (1352–1416)
Fitzalan, Amy (fl. 1440)
Fitzalan, Elizabeth (d. 1385)
Fitzalan, Joan (fl. 1325)
Fitzalan, Joan (d. 1419)
Fitzalan, Katherine (b. around 1520)
Fitzalan, Mary (d. 1557)
Fitzgerald, Katherine (c. 1500–1604)
Fitzhammon, Amabel (d. 1157)
Fitzrobert, Amicia (d. 1225)
Fitzroy, Charlotte (1664–1717)
Foote, Maria (c. 1797–1867)
Françoise-Marie de Bourbon (1677–1749)
Friederike of Hesse-Cassel (1722–1787)
Garsenda (1170–c. 1257)
Genlis, Stéphanie-Félicité, Comtesse de (1746–1830)
Gersenda (fl. 1000)
Gertrude of Saxony (fl. 1070)
Gertrude of Swabia (c. 1104–1191)
Gisela (c. 819–c. 874)
Gisela of Burgundy (fl. 1100s)
Gleichen, Feodora (1861–1922)
Gonzaga, Anne de (1616–1684)
Gonzaga, Maria (1609–1660)
Gonzaga, Paola (1463–1497)
Graham, Euphemia (d. 1469)
Graham, Margaret (d. 1380)
Grandison, Katharine (fl. 1305–1340)
Granville, Christine (1915–1952)
Greville, Frances Evelyn (1861–1938)
Grey, Catherine (c. 1540–1568)
Grey, Elizabeth (1581–1651)
Grey, Elizabeth (d. 1818)
Grey, Elizabeth (d. 1822)
Gruaidh (fl. 11 c.)
Guiccioli, Teresa (c. 1801–1873)
Gundred (d. 1085)
Gunning, Maria (1733–1760)
Guzman, Leonora de (1310–1351)
Gytha (fl. 1022–1042)
Hahn-Hahn, Ida, Countess von (1805–1880)
Hamilton, Elizabeth (c. 1480–?)
Hamilton, Elizabeth (1641–1708)
Hankford, Anne (1431–1485)
Hanska, Éveline, Countess (1801–1882)
Hastings, Anne (c. 1487–?)
Hastings, Anne (d. after 1506)
Hastings, Selina (1707–1791)
Hauke, Julie von (1825–1895)
Hawise (d. after 1135)
Hawise of Salisbury (fl. 12th c.)
Hay, Lucy (1599–1660)
Hayles, Alice (d. after 1326)
Hedvig (d. 1436)
Hedwig (c. 915–965)
Hedwig of Eberhard (930–992)

Helen (fl. 1275)
Herbert, Katherine (c. 1471–?)
Herbert, Mary (1561–1621)
Hildegard (c. 802–841)
Hildegarde de Beaugency (fl. 1080)
Hodierna of Jerusalem (c. 1115–after 1162)
Holland, Alianor (c. 1373–1405)
Holland, Anne (fl. 1440–1462)
Holland, Constance (1387–1437)
Holland, Eleanor (c. 1385–?)
Holland, Margaret (1385–1429)
Howard, Anne (d. 1559)
Howard, Blanche Willis (1847–1898)
Howard, Catherine (d. 1672)
Howard, Dorothy (fl. 1500)
Howard, Elizabeth (?–1538)
Howard, Elizabeth (c. 1410–1475)
Howard, Elizabeth (d. 1534)
Howard, Elizabeth Ann (1823–1865)
Howard, Frances (1593–1632)
Howard, Henrietta (1688–1767)
Howard, Jane (d. 1593)
Howard, Rosalind Frances (1845–1921)
Hume, Elizabeth (c. 1599–1633)
Hyde, Jane (d. 1725)
Ida of Lorraine (1040–1113)
Ida Plantagenet (fl. 1175)
Ide d'Alsace (c. 1161–1216)
Imagi of Luxemburg (c. 1000–1057)
Ina Maria of Bassewitz-Levitzow (1888–1973)
Ingoldsthorp, Isabel (fl. 15th c.)
Irmengard of Oettingen (fl. 14th c.)
Irmentrude (d. 820)
Isabel (fl. 1225)
Isabel (1409–1484)
Isabel (d. 1457?)
Isabel (1772–1827)
Isabel de Warrenne (c. 1137–1203)
Isabel de Warrenne (d. 1282)
Isabella (1332–1382)
Isabella (r. 1398–1412)
Isabella de Redvers (1237–1293)
Isabella of Buchan (fl. 1290–1310)
Isabella of Guise (1900–1983)
Isabella of Orleans (1911–2003)
Isabelle of Bourbon (d. 1465)
Isabel of Brazil (1846–1921)
Isabel of Fife (c. 1332–1389)
Isabel of Vermandois (d. before 1147)
Jacqueline of Hainault (1401–1436)
Jane of Bourbon-Vendome (d. 1511)
Januaria (1822–1901)
Jeanne de Chatillon (d. 1292)
Jeanne de Montfort (c. 1310–c. 1376)
Jeanne de Penthièvre (c. 1320–1384)
Jeanne I (d. 1346)
Jeanne II (r. 1346–1355)
Jeanne I of Burgundy (c. 1291–1330)
Jeanne II of Burgundy (1308–1347)
Jeanne of Burgundy (1293–1348)
Jeanne of Chalon (1300–1333)
Jeanne of Lorraine (1458–1480)
Jeanne of Valois (c. 1294–1342)
Jeanne of Valois (c. 1304–?)
Joan (fl. 1100)
Joan de Quinci (d. 1283)
Joan de Vere (fl. 1280s)
Joan I of Navarre (1273–1305)
Joanna of Brabant (1322–1406)
Joanna of Ponthieu (d. 1251)
Joan of Kent (1328–1385)
Joan of Montferrat (d. 1127)
Joan of Toulouse (d. 1271)
Johanna of Flanders (c. 1200–1244)
Josephine (1763–1814)
Judith of Normandy (c. 1054–after 1086)
Juliane of Nassau-Dillenburg (1546–1588)
Juliane of Stolberg-Wernigrode (1506–1580)
Katherine of Holland (d. 1401)
Kielmansegge, Sophia Charlotte von (1673–1725)
Knollys, Lettice (c. 1541–1634)
Knyvett, Catherine (d. 1633)
Königsmark, Aurora von (1662–1728)
Lacey, Maud (fl. 1230–1250)
Lacy, Alice (1281–1348)
La Fayette, Marie-Madeleine de (1634–1693)
La Grange, Anna de (1825–1905)
Lamb, Emily (d. 1869)
La Motte, Jeanne de Valois, countess de (1756–1791)
Lascelles, Patricia (1926—)
Laval, Josée (c. 1906—1990)
Lavoisier, Marie (1758–1836)
Leslie, Euphemia (d. after 1424)
Leslie, Mary (d. 1429)
Leveson-Gower, Elizabeth (1765–1839)
Leveson-Gower, Harriet (1785–1862)
Lloyd George, Frances Stevenson (1888–1972)
Longford, Elizabeth (1906–2002)
Louise of Stolberg-Gedern (1752–1824)
Lovelace, Ada Byron, Countess of (1815–1852)
Lucia (r. 1288–1289)
Madeleine de Saint-Nectaire (fl. 1575)
Magdalena (fl. late 1500s)
Mahaut (c. 1270–1329)
Mahaut de Chatillon (d. 1358)
Mahaut de Courtenay (d. 1257)
Mahaut II de Dampierre (1234–1266)
Mahaut of Burgundy (d. 1202)
Mancini, Olympia (c. 1639–1708)
Manny, Anne (b. 1355)
Mar, Frances, Countess of (1690–1761)
Margaret (d. 1228)
Margaret (d. 1275)
Margaret (c. 1320–1400)
Margaret de Burgh (d. 1303)
Margaret del Balzo (fl. 15th c.)
Margaret de Rohan (fl. 1449)
Margaret Maultasch (1318–1369)
Margaret of Alsace (c. 1135–1194)
Margaret of Anjou (c. 1272–1299)
Margaret of Artois (d. 1382)
Margaret of Brabant (1323–1368)
Margaret of Burgundy (c. 1376–1441)
Margaret of Flanders (1202–1280)
Margaret of Flanders (1350–1405)
Margaret of Geneva (fl. late 1100s–early 1200s)
Margaret of Hainault (d. 1342)
Margaret of Holland (d. 1356)
Margaret of Huntingdon (c. 1140–1201)
Margaret of Savoy (d. 1483)
Margaret of Turenne (fl. 12th c.)
Margaret Rose (1930–2002)
Marguerite (r. 1218–1230)
Marguerite de Bourgogne (1250–1308)
Marguerite de Brabant (c. 1192–?)
Marguerite of Orleans (d. 1466)
Maria de las Mercedes (1910–2000)
Maria Isabella (1834–1901)
Maria Isabella (1848–1919)
Maria Teresa of Spain (1638–1683)
Maria Theresa of Wurttemberg
Marie de Champagne (1145–1198)
Marie de Chatillon (r. 1230–1241)
Marie de St. Pol (1304–1377)
Marie José of Belgium (1906–2001)
Marie Josephine of Savoy (d. 1810)
Marie of Boulogne (d. 1182)
Marie of Brabant (fl. 1250)
Marie of Champagne (c. 1180–1203)
Marie of France (1344–1404)
Marie of Guelders (1325–1399)
Marie of Guise (d. 1404)
Marie of Hainault (fl. 1300)
Marie of Hohenzollern-Sigmaringen (1845–1912)
Marie of Lusignan (d. 1260)
Marie of Luxemburg (fl. 16th c.)
Marie of Orleans (d. 1493)
Marie of Salerno (fl. 1000s)
Marie Thérèse Charlotte (1778–1851)
Marjorie of Carrick (c. 1254–1292)
Marjory (fl. 13th c.)
Markievicz, Constance (1868–1927)
Marr, Margaret (d. after 1384)
Marshall, Isabel (1200–1240)
Marshall, Maud (d. 1248)
Marshall, Sybilla (fl. 1230)
Martel, Judith (c. 844–?)
Martel de Janville, Comtesse de (1850–1932)
Mary (b. 1718)
Mary (1897–1965)
Mary of Atholl (d. 1116)
Mary of Brabant (c. 1191–c. 1260)
Mary of Burgundy (1457–1482)
Mary Tudor (1673–1726)
Mathilde of Bavaria (1843–1925)
Matilda (d. 1252)
Matilda (1813–1862)
Matilda de Blois (d. 1120)
Matilda de Burgh (d. 1315)
Matilda de Dammartin (d. 1258)
Matilda of Boulogne (c. 1103–1152)
Matilda of Chëteau-du-Loir
Matilda of Habsburg (1251–1304)
Matilda of Nassau (fl. 1285–1310)
Matilda of Saxony (978–1025)
Matilda of Tuscany (1046–1115)
Matilde of Vienne (d. after 1145)
Maud Carinthia (c. 1105–1160)
Maude of Brabant (1224–1288)
Maude of Chester (1171–1233)
Maud of Lusignan (d. 1241)
Maud of Mandeville (d. 1236)
Maud of Normandy (d. 1017)
Maud Plantagenet (1335–1362)
Maud Plantagenet (c. 1310–c. 1377)
Maxwell, Mary (fl. 1715)
Maxwell, Winifred (1672–1749)
Modjeska, Helena (1840–1909)
Mohun, Elizabeth (fl. 14th c.)
Monckton, Mary (1746–1840)
Montacute, Joan (fl. 1300s)
Montacute, Maud (fl. 1380s)
Montacute, Philippa (fl. 1352)
Montez, Lola (1818–1861)
Montfort, Amicia (fl. 1208)
Montgomery, Margaret (fl. 1438)
Mortimer, Agnes (fl. 1347)
Mortimer, Anne (1390–1411)
Mortimer, Catherine (c. 1313–1369)
Mortimer, Catherine (d. before 1413)
Mortimer, Isabel (fl. 1267)
Mortimer, Margaret (d. around 1296)
Mortimer, Philippa (1355–1382)
Mortimer, Philippa (1375–1401)
Mountbatten, Edwina Ashley (1901–1960)
Munck, Ebba (1858–1946)
Munk, Kirsten (1598–1658)
Murray, Elizabeth (1626–1698)
Nadejda Michaelovna (1896–1963)
Neville, Cecily (fl. 1480s)
Neville, Eleanor (c. 1413–1472)
Neville, Eleanor (fl. 1480s)
Neville, Joan (fl. 1468)
Neville, Margaret (d. 1372)
Nisbet, Mary (1778–1855)

Noailles, Anna de (1876–1933)
Novello, Clara (1818–1908)
Oda (806–913)
Oda of Lorraine (fl. mid-1000)
Ogive of Luxemburg (d. 1030)
Olga Iurevskaya (1873–1925)
Palmer, Anne (1661–1722)
Parr, Anne (d. 1552)
Parsons, Mary (1813–1885)
Pejacevic, Dora (1885–1923)
Percy, Anne (fl. 1470s)
Percy, Elizabeth (d. 1437)
Percy, Elizabeth (1667–1722)
Percy, Elizabeth (d. 1704)
Percy, Katherine (b. 1423)
Pery, Angela Olivia (1897–1981)
Pery, Sylvia (1935—)
Philippa de Coucy (fl. 1300s)
Philippa de Dreux (d. 1240)
Philippine of Luxemburg (d. 1311)
Pole, Margaret (1473–1541)
Polignac, Yolande Martine Gabrielle de (1749–1793)
Ponthon, Louise de (d. 1821)
Poynings, Eleanor (d. 1483)
Radcliffe, Charlotte Maria (d. 1755)
Rasmussen, Louise Christine (1815–1874)
Rémusat, Claire, comtesse de (1780–1821)
Rhys-Jones, Sophie (1965—)
Rich, Mary (1625–1678)
Richesa of Lorraine (d. 1067)
Richilde (1034–1086)
Robinson, Anastasia (c. 1692–1755)
Ross, Euphemia (d. after 1394)
Rostopchina, Evdokiya (1811–1858)
Rothild (c. 871–c. 928)
Russell, Dora (1894–1986)
Russell, Lucy (c. 1581–1627)
Rute, Mme de (1831–1902)
Salhias de Tournemire, Elizaveta (1815–1892)
Sancha of Aragon (d. 1073)
Schiaparelli, Elsa (1890–1973)
Scholastica of Champagne (d. 1219)
Scott, Anne (1651–1731)
Sedley, Catharine (1657–1717)
Seymour, Frances (d. 1679)
Seymour, Frances Thynne (1699–1754)
Seymour, Mary (d. 1673)
Sforza, Caterina (c. 1462–1509)
Sheremetskaia, Natalia (1880–1952)
Sibylla of Armenia (fl. 1200s)
Sidney, Dorothy (1617–1684)
Sinclair, Eleanor (d. 1518)
Somerset, Henrietta (1669–1715)
Sontag, Henriette (c. 1803–1854)
Sophia (1868–1927)
Sophia Carlotte (1673–1725)
Spencer, Henrietta Frances (1761–1821)
Stafford, Anne (d. 1472)
Stafford, Catherine (d. 1419)
Stafford, Catherine (d. 1476)
Stafford, Catherine (fl. 1530)
Stafford, Constance (d. 1474)
Stafford, Elizabeth (d. 1532)
Stafford, Margaret (d. 1396)
Stafford, Philippa (d. before 1386)
Stanley, Margaret (fl. 16th c.)
Stauffenberg, Litta von (c. 1905–1945)
Stein, Marion (1926—)
Stephanie de Beauharnais (1789–1860)
Stephens, Catherine (1794–1882)
Stewart, Annabella (d. after 1471)
Stewart, Beatrice (d. around 1424)
Stewart, Elizabeth (fl. 1578)
Stewart, Euphemia (c. 1375–1415)
Stewart, Marjorie (d. after 1417)
Stuart, Elizabeth (d. 1673)
Suttner, Bertha von (1843–1914)
Sybilla of Anjou (1112–1165)
Taglioni, Maria (1804–1884)
Talbot, Nadine (1913–2003)
Tallien, Thérésa (1773–1835)
Tarnowska, Maria (1878–1923)
Teleki, Blanka (1806–1862)
Thompson, Sarah (1774–1852)
Tolstoy, Sonya (1844–1919)
Vanderbilt, Gladys Moore (1886–1965)
Vane-Tempest, Frances Anne Emily (d. 1865)
Villiers, Margaret Elizabeth Child- (1849–1945)
Wallmoden, Amalie Sophie Marianne (1704–1765)
Watteville, Benigna von (1725–1789)
Zrinyi, Ilona (1643–1703)

COUNTRY-AND-WESTERN SINGER

Allen, Rosalie (1924–2003)
Carpenter, Mary Chapin (1958—)
Carter, Anita (1933–1999)
Carter, Carlene (1955—)
Carter, Helen (1927–1998)
Carter, Jeanette (1923–2006)
Carter, Maybelle (1909–1978)
Carter, Sarah (1898–1979)
Cash, June Carter (1929–2003)
Cash, Rosanne (1955—)
Cline, Genevieve (1879–1959)
Cline, Patsy (1932–1963)
Coolidge, Rita (1944—)
Davis, Skeeter (1931–2004)
DeMent, Iris (1961—)
Ford, Mary (1924–1977)
Gayle, Crystal (1951—)
Gentry, Bobbie (1944—)
Grant, Amy (1960—)
Harris, Emmylou (1947—)
Jackson, Wanda (1937—)
Judd, Naomi (1946—)
Judd, Wynonna (1964—)
Larson, Nicolette (1952–1997)
Lee, Brenda (1944—)
Lynch, Laura (1958—)
Lynn, Loretta (1935—)
Macy, Robin Lynn (1958—)
Maddox, Rose (1925–1998)
Maines, Natalie (1974—)
Mandrell, Barbara (1948—)
McEntire, Reba (1955—)
Montana, Patsy (1909–1996)
Nelson, Tracy (1944—)
Newton, Juice (1952—)
Newton-John, Olivia (1948—)
Oslin, K.T. (1941—)
Osmond, Marie (1959—)
Page, Patti (1927—)
Parton, Dolly (1946—)
Pearl, Minnie (1912–1996)
Riley, Jeannie C. (1945—)
Robison, Emily (1972—)
Ronstadt, Linda (1946—)
Seidel, Martie (1969—)
Smith, Sammi (1943–2005)
Sweet, Rachel (1963—)
Tucker, Tanya (1958—)
Twain, Shania (1965—)
Wells, Kitty (b. 1919)
West, Dottie (1932–1991)
Williams, Lucinda (1953—)
Williams, Victoria (1958—)
Wynette, Tammy (1942–1998)
Yearwood, Trisha (1964—)

COURIER

Lovell, Ann (1803/11–1869)

COURTESAN

Acte (fl. 55–69)
Alençon, Emilienne d' (fl. late 1800s)
Ambapali (fl. c. 540 BCE)
Anastasia (fl. 500s)
Aragona, Tullia d' (1510–1556)
Aspasia of Miletus (c. 464 BCE–c. 420 BCE)
Aspasia the Younger (fl. 415–370 BCE)
Ban Jieyu (c. 48–c. 6 BCE)
Bell, Laura (1829–1894)
Bilistiche (fl. 268–264 BCE)
Boufflers, Marie (1706–1747)
Braun, Eva (1912–1945)
Brécourt, Jeanne (b. 1837)
Bullette, Julia (d. 1867)
Cardny, Marion (fl. 1300s)
Carmichael, Elizabeth (fl. 1530s)
Castro, Inez de (c. 1320–1355)
Chabrillan, Céleste de (1824–1909)
Châteaubriant, Comtesse de (c. 1490–1537)
Churchill, Arabella (1648–1714)
Clarke, Mary Anne (c. 1776–1852)
Clifford, Rosamund (c. 1145–1176)
Comitona (fl. 500s)
Corbert, Sybilla
Dalrymple, Grace (1758–1823)
Delorme, Marion (c. 1613–1650)
Diane de Poitiers (1499–1566)
Dolgorukaia, Alexandra (1836–c. 1914)
Drummond, Margaret (fl. 1490s)
Duci, Filippa
Franco, Veronica (1546–1591)
Gouges, Olympe de (1748–1793)
Goulue, La (1869–1929)
Gwynn, Nell (1650–1687)
Labé, Louise (c. 1523–1566)
Lachman, Thérèse (1819–1884)
Lais (fl. 385 BCE)
Lais (fl. 425 BCE)
Langtry, Lillie (1853–1929)
Larentia, Acca (fl. 9th, 8th, or 7th c. BCE)
Lempicka, Tamara de (1898–1980)
Lenclos, Ninon de (1623–1705)
Lynch, Eliza (1835–1886)
Malatesta (fl. 1504–1505)
Montez, Lola (1818–1861)
Nicarete of Megara (fl. 300 BCE)
Otero, Caroline (1868–1965)
Palm, Etta Aelders (1743–1799)
Pearl, Cora (c. 1837–1886)
Pelagia, Saint
Phoebe of Cenchreae (fl. 1st c.)
Phryne (c. 365–c. 295 BCE)
Plessis, Alphonsine (1824–1847)
Pougy, Liane de (1866–c. 1940)
Rhodopis (fl. 6th c. BCE)
Sammuramat (fl. 8th c. BCE)
Stampa, Gaspara (1523–1554)
Thais (fl. 331 BCE)
Théroigne de Méricourt, Anne-Josèphe (1762–1817)
Vestris, Thérèse (1726–1808)
Walters, Catherine (1839–1920)
Wilson, Harriette (1786–1855)
Zelle, Margaretha (1876–1917)

COURTIER

Astell, Mary (1666–1731)
Balbilla (fl. 130)
Ban Zhao (c. 45–c. 120)
Feuchères, Sophie, Baronne de (c. 1795–1841)
Kottanner, Helene (fl. 1440)

COUTURIÈRE
Carnegie, Hattie (1886–1956)
Chanel, Coco (1883–1971)
Demorest, Ellen Curtis (1824–1898)
Flöge, Emilie (1874–1952)
Grès, Alix (1910–1993)
Head, Edith (1897–1981)
Lanvin, Jeanne (1867–1946)
Quant, Mary (1934—)
Rambova, Natacha (1897–1966)
Schiaparelli, Elsa (1890–1973)
Trigère, Pauline (1912–2002)

CRICKETER
Heyhoe-Flint, Rachael (1939—)

CRIME/DECTECTIVE-FICTION WRITER
Christie, Agatha (1890–1976)
Fortune, Mary (fl. 1866–1910)
Grafton, Sue (1940)
Gray, Dulcie (1919—)
Green, Anna Katharine (1846–1935)
Highsmith, Patricia (1921–1995)
James, P.D. (1920—)
Jesse, Fryniwyd Tennyson (1888–1958)
Lee, Muna (1895–1965)
Marsh, Ngaio (1895–1982)
McDermid, Val (1955—)
Millar, Margaret (1915–1994)
Mitchell, Gladys (1901–1983)
Moffat, Gwen (1924—)
Moyes, Patricia (1923–2000)
Paretsky, Sara (1947—)
Rinehart, Mary Roberts (1876–1958)
Sayers, Dorothy L. (1893–1957)
Simpson, Helen (1897–1940)
Tey, Josephine (1896–1952)
Wells, Carolyn (1862–1942)

CRIMINAL
Fenning, Elizabeth (1792–1815)

CRIMINOLOGIST
Anttila, S. Inkeri (1916—)
Glueck, Eleanor Touroff (1898–1972)
McCord, Joan (1930–2004)
Sulner, Hanna (1917–1999)

CRITIC
See Architectural critic.
See Art critic.
See Dance critic.
See Literary critic.
See Music critic.
See Theater critic.

CROQUET PLAYER
Steel, Dorothy (1884–1965)

CROSS-COUNTRY SKIER
See Skier.

CROSS-DRESSER
Baret, Jeanne (1740–after 1795)
Eberhardt, Isabelle (1877–1904)
Edmonds, Emma (1841–1898)
Erauso, Catalina de (1592–1635)
Hamilton, Mary (1705–?)
Maupin, d'Aubigny (c. 1670–1707)
Parkhurst, Charlotte (d. 1879)
Sampson, Deborah (1760–1827)
Sand, George (1804–1876)
Stuart, Miranda (c. 1795–1865)
Tilley, Vesta (1864–1952)
Tipton, Billy (1914–1989)

CROSSWORD-PUZZLE EDITOR
Farrar, Margaret (1897–1984)
Kingsley, Elizabeth (1871–1957)

CROWN PRINCESS
Carlota Joaquina (1775–1830)
Donaldson, Mary (1972—)
Juana la Loca (1479–1555)
Margaret of Connaught (1882–1920)
Margarita Maria (b. 1939)
Martha of Sweden (1901–1954)
Masako (1963—)
Mathilde of Belgium (1973—)
Mette-Marit (1973—)
Ortiz, Letizia (1972—)
Salote Topou III (1900–1965)
Sonja (1937—)
Victoria (1977—)
Victoria Adelaide (1840–1901)

CRYPTOGRAPHER
Friedman, Elizebeth (d. 1980)

CRYSTALLOGRAPHER
Karle, Isabella (1921—)
Kennard, Olga (1924—)
Lonsdale, Kathleen (1903–1971)
MacGillavry, Carolina H. (1904–1993)
Porter, Mary Winearls (1886–1980)

CULINARY-ARTS EXPERT
Cumming, Adelaide Hawley (1905–1998)

CULINARY-ARTS TEACHER
Barker, Mary Anne (1831–1911)
Carter, Una Isabel (1890–1954)
Chen, Joyce (1918–1994)
Child, Julia (1912–2004)
Corson, Juliet (1841–1897)
Cradock, Fanny (1909–1994)
Farmer, Fannie Merritt (1857–1915)
Hemenway, Mary Porter Tileston (1820–1894)
Lincoln, Mary Johnson (1844–1921)
Parloa, Maria (1843–1909)
Price, Roberta MacAdams (1881–1959)
Smith, Virginia Thrall (1836–1903)
Spry, Constance (1886–1960)

CULINARY-ARTS WRITER
Acton, Eliza (1799–1859)
Aresty, Esther B. (1908–2000)
Barker, Mary Anne (1831–1911)
Beeton, Isabella Mary (1836–1865)
Brown, Hilary (1952—)
Carter, Una Isabel (1890–1954)
Chen, Joyce (1918–1994)
Child, Julia (1912–2004)
Colwin, Laurie (1944–1992)
Corson, Juliet (1841–1897)
Croly, Jane Cunningham (1829–1901)
David, Elizabeth (1913–1992)
Farmer, Fannie Merritt (1857–1915)
Fisher, M.F.K. (1908–1992)
Gard'ner, Elizabeth Anne (1858–1926)
Glasse, Hannah (1708–1770)
Grigson, Jane (1928–1990)
Hahn, Emily (1905–1997)
Hale, Sarah Josepha (1788–1879)
Hemenway, Mary Porter Tileston (1820–1894)
Herrick, Christine Terhune (1859–1944)
Hunter, Kim (1922–2002)
Johnstone, Isobel (1781–1857)
Jordan, Sara Murray (1884–1959)
Kander, Lizzie Black (1858–1940)
Kaye-Smith, Sheila (1887–1956)
Laverty, Maura (1907–1966)
Leslie, Eliza (1787–1858)
Lincoln, Mary Johnson (1844–1921)
Maitland, Agnes Catherine (1850–1906)
McCartney, Linda (1941–1998)
McNeill, Florence Marian (1885–1973)
Miller, Elizabeth Smith (1822–1911)
Newman, Nanette (1934)
Nidetch, Jean (1923—)
Parloa, Maria (1843–1909)
Patten, Marguerite (1915—)
Rawlings, Marjorie Kinnan (1896–1953)
Reed, Myrtle (1874–1911)
Rombauer, Irma S. (1877–1962)
Rorer, Sarah Tyson (1849–1937)
Rudkin, Margaret (1897–1967)
Shore, Dinah (1917–1994)
Smith, Delia (1941—)
Steel, Flora Annie (1847–1929)
Taber, Gladys (1899–1980)
Waddles, Charleszetta (1912–2001)
Waters, Alice (1944—)
Woolley, Hannah (1623–1677)

CURATOR
Abbott, Maude (1869–1940)
Barry, Iris (1895–1969)
Boissevain, Mia (1878–1959)
Brandegee, Mary Katharine (1844–1920)
Britton, Alison (1948—)
Britton, Elizabeth Knight (1858–1934)
Burgess, Renate (1910–1988)
Cannon, Annie Jump (1863–1941)
Courtenay-Latimer, Marjorie (1907–2004)
Cruft, Catherine Holway (1927—)
Debo, Angie (1890–1988)
Eastwood, Alice (1859–1953)
Edinger, Tilly (1897–1967)
Eisner, Lotte (1896–1983)
Fleming, Williamina Paton (1857–1911)
Gray, Nicolete (1911–1997)
Halpert, Edith Gregor (c. 1900–1970)
Han, Suyin (1917—)
Hutson, Jean (1914–1998)
Huxtable, Ada Louise (1921—)
John, Gwen (1876–1939)
Manus, Rosa (1881–1942)
Mead, Margaret (1901–1978)
Miller, Dorothy Canning (1904–2003)
Moholy, Lucia (1894–1989)
Ottenberg, Nettie Podell (1887–1982)
Plummer, Mary Wright (1856–1916)
Rathbun, Mary Jane (1860–1943)
Reinig, Christa (1926—)
Richter, Gisela (1882–1972)
Seymour, May Davenport (d. 1967)
Tolstoy, Alexandra (1884–1979)
Unger, Mary Ann (1945–1998)
Wright, Mary Clabaugh (1917–1970)
Yakunchikova, Maria (1870–1901)
Young, Mary Sophie (1872–1919)

CURLER
Betker, Jan (c. 1960—)
Bidaud, Laurence (1968—)
Bidstrup, Jane (c. 1956—)
Bidstrup, Lene (1966—)
Ebnoether, Luzia (1971—)
Ford, Atina (c. 1972—)
Frei, Tanya (1972—)
Gudereit, Marcia (c. 1966—)
Gustafson, Elisabet (1964—)
Holm, Dörthe (c. 1973—)
Knox, Debbie (1968—)
Lavrsen, Helena (c. 1963—)
Law, Kelley (1966—)
Lindahl, Margaretha (c. 1971—)
MacDonald, Fiona (1974—)

Marmont, Louise (1967—)
Martin, Rhona (1966—)
McCusker, Joan (c. 1966—)
Morton, Margaret (1968—)
Nelson, Diane (1958—)
Noble, Cheryl (1956—)
Nyberg, Katarina (1965—)
Ott, Mirjam (1972—)
Persson, Elisabeth (1964—)
Pörtner, Margit (c. 1973—)
Qvist, Trine (c. 1967—)
Rankin, Janice (1972—)
Roethlisberger, Nadia (1972—)
Schmirler, Sandra (1963–2000)
Skinner, Julie (1968—)
Wheatcroft, Georgina (1965—)

CYCLIST
Abassova, Tamilla (1982—)
Arndt, Judith (1976—)
Augspurg, Anita (1857–1943)
Ballanger, Felicia (1971—)
Ballantyne, Sara (c. 1964—)
Barry, Deidre (1972—)
Bellutti, Antonella (1968—)
Blair, Bonnie (1964—)
Blatter, Barbara (1970—)
Burka, Sylvia (1954—)
Burton, Beryl (1937–1996)
Burton, Denise (1956—)
Canins, Maria (1949—)
Carpenter-Phinney, Connie (1957—)
Carrigan, Sara (1980—)
Chiappa, Imelda (1966—)
Clignet, Marion (1964—)
Dahle, Gunn-Rita (1973—)
De Mattei, Susan (1962—)
Ermolaeva, Galina
Ferris, Michelle (1976—)
Fullana, Margarita (1972—)
Furtado, Juliana (1967—)
Giove, Missy (1972—)
Grimshaw, Beatrice (c. 1870–1953)
Grishina, Oksana (1968—)
Guerrero Mendez, Belem (1974—)
Haringa, Ingrid (1964—)
Heiden, Beth (1959—)
Heymann, Lida (1867–1943)
Holden, Mari (1971—)
Hughes, Clara (1972—)
Jensen, Bjorg Eva (1960—)
Jiang Cuihua
Jiang Yonghua (1973—)
Knol, Monique (1964—)
Kopsky, Doris
Kupfernagel, Hanka (1964—)
Lancien, Nathalie (1970—)
Lawyer, April (1975—)
Longo, Jeannie (1958—)
Mactier, Kate (1975—)
Martin, Marianne (1961—)
McElmury, Audrey (1943—)
McGregor, Yvonne (1961—)
Meares, Anna (1983—)
Mirabella, Erin (1978—)
Muenzer, Lori-Ann (1966—)
Neumann, Annett (1970—)
Neumannova, Katerina (1973—)
Niehaus, Jutta (1964—)
Nieman, Nancy (1933—)
Novarra-Reber, Sue (1955—)
Oakley, Annie (1860–1926)
Omelenchuk, Jeanne (1931—)
O'Neil, Kitty (1947—)
Paraskevin-Young, Connie (1961—)
Pezzo, Paola (1969—)
Pound, Louise (1872–1958)
Premont, Marie-Hélene (1977—)
Rossner, Petra (1966—)
Rothenburger-Luding, Christa (1959—)
Salumae, Erika (1962—)
Schumacher, Sandra (1966—)
Slyusareva, Olga (1969—)
Spitz, Sabine (1971—)
Stiefl, Regina (1966—)
Sydor, Alison (1966—)
Szabo, Violette (1921–1945)
Thompson, Blanche Edith (1874–1963)
Thuerig, Karin (1972—)
Tsylinskaya, Natallia (1975—)
Twigg, Rebecca (1963—)
Tyler-Sharman, Lucy (1965—)
Ulmer, Sarah (1976—)
van Moorsel, Leontien (1970—)
Watt, Kathryn (1964—)
Yanovych, Iryna (1976—)
Young, Sheila (1950—)
Zabirova, Zulfia (1973—)
Ziliute, Diana (1976—)
Zilporite, Laima (1967—)

CYTOLOGIST
Boring, Alice Middleton (1883–1955)
Farr, Wanda K. (1895–1983)
Foot, Katherine (c. 1852–?)
Harvey, Ethel Browne (1885–1965)
Yasui, Kono (1880–1971)

DAIRY PRODUCER
Mathieson, Catherine (1818–1883)

DAIRY WORKER
Chemis, Annie (1862–1939)

DANCE-COMPANY/TROUPE FOUNDER
Brown, Trisha (1936—)
Chase, Lucia (1897–1986)
Danilova, Alexandra (1903–1997)
de Valois, Ninette (1898–2001)
Dunham, Katherine (1909–2006)
Franca, Celia (1921—)
Graham, Martha (1894–1991)
Gregory, Cynthia (1946—)
Harkness, Rebekah (1915–1982)
Inglesby, Mona (1918—)
Jamison, Judith (1943—)
Jones, Sissieretta (1869–1933)
Lidova, Irene (1907–2002)
Lloyd, Gweneth (1901–1993)
Markova, Alicia (1910–2004)
Morgan, Marion (c. 1887–1971)
Page, Ruth (1899–1991)
Rainer, Yvonne (1934—)
Tallchief, Maria (1925—)
Tallchief, Marjorie (1927—)
Wallmann, Margarethe (1901–19922)

DANCE CRITIC
Farjeon, Annabel (1919—)
Krasovskaya, Vera (d. 1999)
Lidova, Irene (1907–2002)
Lloyd, Maude (1908–2004)
Roslavleva, Natalia (1907–1977)

DANCE DIRECTOR
Abbott, Merriel (c. 1893–1977)
Alonso, Alicia (1921—)
Bausch, Pina (1940—)
Chace, Marian (1896–1970)
Chase, Lucia (1897–1986)
Cullberg, Birgit (1908–1999)
de Mille, Agnes (1905–1993)
de Valois, Ninette (1898–2001)
Dunham, Katherine (b. 1909)
Fazan, Eleanor (1930—)
Franca, Celia (1921—)
Haydée, Marcia (1939—)
Helliwell, Ethel (c. 1905—)
Holm, Hanya (1888–1992)
Humphrey, Doris (1895–1958)
Jamison, Judith (1943—)
Kaye, Nora (1920–1987)
Kent, Allegra (1937—)
Lewis, Elma (1921—)
Markova, Alicia (1910–2004)
Nijinska, Bronislava (1891–1972)
Page, Ruth (1899–1991)
Plisetskaya, Maya (1925—)
van Praagh, Peggy (1910–1990)

DANCER
Aakesson, Birgit (c. 1908–2001)
Abarca, Lydia (1951—)
Abramova, Anastasia (1902—)
Adams, Carolyn (1943—)
Adams, Diana (1927–1993)
Addor, Ady (c. 1935—)
Adorée, Renée (1898–1933)
Adrienne, Jean (b. 1905)
Alenikoff, Frances (1920—)
Alexander, Claire (1898–1927)
Alf, Fé (c. 1910—)
Allard, Marie (1742–1802)
Allen, Debbie (1950—)
Allen, Gracie (1902–1964)
Allen, Sarita (1954—)
Alonso, Alicia (1921—)
Alvarez, Anita (1920—)
Alvarez, Carmen (c. 1936—)
Amaya, Carmen (1913–1963)
Anderson, Claire (1895–1964)
Anderson, Claire (fl. 1940s)
Anderson, Evelyn (1907–1994)
Anderson, Ivie (1904–1949)
Anderson, Lea (1959—)
Angelou, Maya (1928—)
Anisimova, Nina (1909—)
Annabelle (1878–1961)
Ann-Margret (1941—)
Anthony, Mary (c. 1920—)
Arenal, Julie (1942—)
Argyle, Pearl (1910–1947)
Arletty (1898–1992)
Armitage, Karole (1954—)
Armour, Toby (1936—)
Arnold, Becky (1936—)
Arnst, Bobbe (1903–1980)
Asakawa, Takako (1938—)
Astafieva, Serafima (1876–1934)
Astaire, Adele (1898–1981)
Atlas, Consuelo (1944–1979)
Augusta, Mlle (1806–1901)
Avril, Jane (1868–1943)
Baccelli, Giovanna (c. 1753–1801)
Bacon, Faith (1909–1956)
Bagnold, Lisbeth (1947—)
Bailey, Frankie (1859–1953)
Bailey, Pearl (1918–1990)
Bailin, Gladys (1930—)
Baker, Janet (1933—)
Baker, Josephine (1906–1975)
Bampton, Rose (1909—)
Bari, Lynn (1913–1989)
Bari, Tania (1936—)
Baronova, Irina (1919—)
Barret, Dorothy (1917–1987)
Barry, Elaine (d. 1948)
Barstow, Edith (1907–1960)
Baylis, Meredith (1929–2002)

Beatty, Patricia (1936—)
Bedells, Phyllis (1893–1985)
Bederkhan, Leila (b. around 1903)
Belita (1923–2005)
Bell, Marilyn (1937—)
Benesh, Joan (1920—)
Bennett, Barbara (1906–1958)
Bennett, Evelyn (b. 1905)
Bentley, Muriel (1917–1999)
Berber, Anita (1899–1928)
Berghaus, Ruth (1927–1996)
Beri, Beth (c. 1904—)
Berk, Lotte (1913–2003)
Berke, Dorothea (c. 1900—)
Bernard, Karen (1948—)
Bernson, Kathryn (1950—)
Bettis, Valerie (1919–1982)
Bigottini, Emilie (1784–1858)
Birch, Patricia (c. 1930—)
Bird, Bonnie (1914–1995)
Bird, Dorothy (c. 1913—)
Bishop, Kelly (1944—)
Black, Shirley Temple (1928—)
Blair, Pamela (1949—)
Blank, Carla (c. 1940—)
Blecher, Miriam (1912–1979)
Boardman, Diane (c. 1950—)
Bodenwieser, Gertrud (1886–1959)
Bond, Sheila (1928—)
Bond, Sudie (1928–1984)
Bonfanti, Marietta (1845–1921)
Boutilier, Joy (1939—)
Bowden, Sally (c. 1948—)
Bowman, Patricia (1904–1999)
Boyce, Johanna (1954—)
Bradley, Grace (1913—)
Braggiotti, Berthe (c. 1900–c. 1925)
Braggiotti, Francesca (1902–1998)
Braggiotti, Gloria (c. 1905—)
Breen, Nellie (c. 1898–1986)
Bremer, Lucille (1923–1996)
Brewster, Barbara (1918–2005)
Brewster, Gloria (1918–1996)
Brianza, Carlotta (1862–1930)
Brice, Elizabeth (c. 1885–1965)
Brill, Patti (1923–1963)
Brooks, Louise (1906–1985)
Broughton, Phyllis (1862–1926)
Brown, Beverly (1941–2002)
Brown, Carolyn (1927—)
Brown, Jessica (c. 1900–?)
Browne, Marjorie (1910–1990)
Buglisi, Jacqulyn (1951—)
Burke, Patricia (1917–2003)
Burne, Nancy (1912–1954)
Burns, Louise (1949—)
Burrows-Fontaine, Evan (1898–1984)
Busby, Amy (c. 1872–1957)
Butcher, Rosemary (1947—)
Cachat, Beth (1951—)
Cagney, Frances (1901–1994)
Cahan, Cora (1940—)
Camargo, Marie-Anne Cupis de (1710–1770)
Cameron, Dorothy (d. 1958)
Campanini, Barbara (1721–1799)
Cansino, Elisa (b. 1895)
Caperton, Harriette (c. 1913—)
Carlson, Carolyn (1943—)
Caron, Leslie (1931—)
Caron, Margaret Pettibone (b. around 1904)
Carroll, Nancy (1903–1965)
Cartwright, Peggy (1912–2001)
Castle, Irene (c. 1893–1969)
Caswell, Maude (c. 1880–?)
Catterson, Pat (1946—)
Celeste, Madame (1815–1882)
Cerrito, Fanny (1817–1909)
Chabrillan, Céleste de (1824–1909)
Chace, Marian (1896–1970)
Champion, Marge (1919—)
Charisse, Calliope (c. 1880–1946)
Charisse, Cyd (1921—)
Chase, Alison Becker (c. 1948—)
Chase, Arline (1900–1926)
Chase, Barrie (1933—)
Chase, Lucia (1897–1986)
Chen, Si-Lan (1909—)
Childs, Lucinda (1940—)
Christopher, Patricia (c. 1934—)
Cicierska, Margaret
Clark, Cheryl (1950—)
Clarke, Helen (c. 1897–?)
Clarke, Mae (1907–1992)
Clarke, Martha (1944—)
Clarke, Shirley (1925–1997)
Clayton, Bessie (c. 1878–1948)
Coca, Imogene (1909–2001)
Cohan, Josephine (1876–1916)
Cohen, Ze'eva (1940—)
Cole, Kay (1948—)
Collins, Cora Sue (1927—)
Collins, Janet (1917–2003)
Collins, Lottie (c. 1866–1910)
Conde, Felisa (c. 1920—)
Cornfield, Ellen (1948—)
Cox, Hazel (b. 1887)
Cox, Ray (b. 1880)
Crespé, Marie-Madeleine (1760–1796)
Critchfield, Lee (c. 1909—)
Croll, Tina (1943—)
Cropley, Eileen (1932—)
Cullberg, Birgit (1908–1999)
Cummings, Alma (b. 1890)
Cummings, Blondell (c. 1948—)
Curley, Wilma (1937—)
Currier, Ruth (1926—)
Cutler, Robyn (1948—)
Czobel, Lisa (1906–1992)
Dai, Ailian (1916–2006)
Dale, Virginia (1917–1994)
Dalida (1933–1987)
Dana, Viola (1897–1987)
Dandridge, Dorothy (1923–1965)
Daniels, Mabel Wheeler (1878–1971)
Danilova, Alexandra (1903–1997)
Darling, May (1887–1971)
Darvas, Julia (c. 1919—)
Daunt, Yvonne (b. around 1900)
Davies, Moll (fl. 1673)
Davies, Siobhan (1950—)
Dawson, Nancy (c. 1735–1767)
Day, Edith (1896–1971)
Dazie, Mademoiselle (1882–1952)
Dean, Dora (c. 1872–1950)
Dean, Laura (1945—)
DeHaven, Flora (1883–1950)
De Jong, Bettie (1933—)
De Keersmaeker, Anne Teresa (1960—)
De Lavallade, Carmen (1931—)
Delroy, Irene (1898–?)
De Luce, Virginia (1921–1997)
Delza, Elizabeth (c. 1903—)
De Marco, Renée (c. 1913—)
De Marco, Sally (1921—)
de Mille, Agnes (1905–1993)
Dempster, Carol (1901–1991)
De Putti, Lya (1899–1932)
Desha (1892–1965)
Deslys, Gaby (1884–1920)
Desmond, Florence (1905–1993)
De Swirska, Tamara (c. 1890–?)
de Valois, Ninette (1898–2001)
de Voie, Bessie (b. around 1888)
Diachenko, Nada (1946—)
Dickson, Dorothy (1893–1995)
Dilley, Dorothy (b. around 1907)
Dolly, Jenny (1892–1941)
Dolly, Rosie (1892–1970)
Doner, Kitty (1895–1988)
Doraldina (c. 1893–c. 1925)
Douglas, Ann (b. 1901)
Doyle, Patricia (d. 1975)
Dreyfuss, Anne (1957—)
Driver, Senta (1942—)
Drylie, Patricia (c. 1928–1993)
Dudinskaya, Natalya (1912–2003)
Dudley, Jane (1912–2001)
Dunbar, Dixie (1915–1991)
Duncan, Irma (1897–1978)
Duncan, Isadora (1878–1927)
Duncan, Maria Teresa (1895–1987)
Duncan, Sandy (1946—)
Dunedin, Maudie (c. 1888–1937)
Dunham, Katherine (1909–2006)
Eaton, Mary (1901–1948)
Eaton, Pearl (1898–1958)
Eilber, Janet (1951—)
Eisenberg, Mary Jane (1951—)
Elg, Taina (1931—)
Eline, Grace (1898—)
Elliott, Madge (1896–1955)
Ellis, Lucille (c. 1915—)
Ellmann, Barbara (1950—)
Elsie, Lily (1886–1962)
Elssler, Fanny (1810–1884)
Enters, Angna (1907–1989)
Erdman, Jean (1917—)
Eshkol, Noa (1927—)
Espinosa, Mimi (1893–1936)
Evan, Blanche (1909–1982)
Evans, Renee (1908–1971)
Fabray, Nanette (1920—)
Fairbanks, Madeline (1900–1989)
Fairbanks, Marion (1900–1973)
Farber, Viola (1931–1998)
Farrell, Suzanne (1945—)
Faust, Lotta (1880–1910)
Fazan, Eleanor (1930—)
Feigenheimer, Irene (1946—)
Fenley, Molissa (1954—)
Fisher, Nellie (1920–1994)
Fitzgerald, Zelda (1900–1948)
Fletcher, Maria (c. 1942—)
Florence, Malvina Pray (1830–1906)
Flores, Lola (1924–1995)
Flory, Regine (1894–1926)
Fokina, Vera (1886–1958)
Fontaine, Mlle de la (1655–1738)
Fonteyn, Margot (1919–1991)
Forman, Ada (b. around 1895)
Forrest, Sally (1928—)
Fort, Syvilla (c. 1917–1975)
Fox, Dorothy (b. around 1914)
Frampton, Eleanor (1896–1973)
Franca, Celia (1921—)
Frank, Dottie (1941—)
Franklyn, Lidije (1922—)
Friganza, Trixie (1870–1955)
Fuller, Loïe (1862–1928)
Furtseva, Ekaterina (1910–1974)
Gallagher, Helen (1926—)
Gamson, Annabelle (1928—)
Garborg, Hulda (1862–1934)
Gardner, Maureen (1928–1974)
Garland, Judy (1922–1969)
Garrett, Betty (1919—)
Garth, Midi (1920—)
Gaskell, Sonia (1904–1974)

Gaxton, Madeline (1897–1990)
Gaynor, Mitzi (1930—)
Geise, Sugar (1909–1988)
Geistinger, Marie (1833–1903)
Genée, Adeline (1878–1970)
Gentry, Eva (c. 1920—)
Georgi, Yvonne (1903–1975)
Germaine, Diane (1944—)
Gert, Valeska (1900–1978)
Geva, Tamara (1906–1997)
Gilbert, Anne (1821–1904)
Ginner, Ruby (c. 1886–1978)
Gitelman, Claudia (1938—)
Glass, Bonnie (b. around 1895)
Glenn, Laura (1945—)
Gluck, Rena (1933—)
Goldsmith, Grace Arabell (1904–1975)
Gore, Altovise (1935—)
Gorham, Kathleen (1932–1983)
Goulue, La (1869–1929)
Grable, Betty (1916–1973)
Graham, Georgia (1900–1988)
Graham, Martha (1894–1991)
Grahn, Lucile (1819–1907)
Granger, Josie (1853–1934)
Gray, Gilda (1901–1959)
Greenwood, Charlotte (1890–1978)
Gregory, Cynthia (1946—)
Grey, Beryl (1927—)
Grey, Denise (1897–1996)
Grisi, Carlotta (1819–1899)
Groody, Louise (1897–1961)
Guimard, Marie Madeleine (1743–1816)
Gynt, Greta (1916–2000)
Halprin, Ann (1920—)
Haney, Carol (1924–1964)
Harkness, Rebekah (1915–1982)
Harrison, Ruth (1911–1974)
Hart, Flo (c. 1896–1960)
Hartman, Grace (1907–1955)
Hasoutra (1906–1978)
Hay, Mary (1901–1957)
Haydée, Marcia (1939—)
Hayden, Melissa (1923—)
Hayworth, Rita (1918–1987)
Healey, Eunice (c. 1920—)
Heinel, Anna (1753–1808)
Hemsley, Estelle (1887–1968)
Hengler, Flora (c. 1887–1965)
Hengler, May (c. 1884–1952)
Hepburn, Audrey (1929–1993)
Hernandez, Amelia (c. 1930—)
Hill, Martha (1900–1995)
Hill, Thelma (1925–1977)
Hines, Elizabeth (1899–1971)
Hinkson, Mary (1930—)
Hoctor, Harriet (1905–1977)
Hoey, Iris (1885–1979)
Hoff, Vanda (b. around 1900)
Hoffmann, Gertrude (1871–1966)
Holm, Hanya (1888–1992)
Howland, Jobyna (1880–1936)
Hoyer, Dore (1911–1967)
Hudson, Rochelle (1916–1972)
Hughes, Adelaide (1884–1960)
Humphrey, Doris (1895–1958)
Ide, Letitia (1909–1993)
Impekoven, Niddy (1904—)
Impekoven, Niddy (1904–2002)
Ireland, Jill (1936–1990)
Irving, Margaret (1898–1988)
Jamison, Judith (1943—)
Jeanmaire, Zizi (1924—)
Johansen, Aud (1930—)
Johansson, Ronny (b. 1891)
Johnson, Julie (1903–1973)
Johnston, Julanne (1900–1988)
Johnstone, Justine (1895–1982)
Joyce, Lucia (1907–1982)
Judge, Arline (1912–1974)
Junger, Esther (c. 1915—)
Kajiwara, Mari (1952—)
Kanahele, Helen Lake (1916–1976)
Kanakaole, Edith K. (1913–1979)
Kane, Helen (1903–1966)
Kane, Marjorie (1909–1992)
Karioka, Tahiya (c. 1921–1999)
Karsavina, Tamara (1885–1978)
Kaye, Nora (1920–1987)
Keeler, Ruby (1909–1993)
Kelly, Margaret (1910–2004)
Kelly, Patsy (1910–1981)
Kelly, Paula (1939—)
Kennedy, Merna (1908–1944)
Kent, Allegra (1937—)
Kent, Linda (1946—)
Khoklova, Olga (d. 1955)
Kinch, Myra (1904–1981)
King, Dottie (c. 1896–1923)
King, Eleanor (1906–1991)
King, Mazie (b. around 1880)
King, Mollie (1885–1981)
King, Nellie (1895–1935)
Kirkland, Gelsey (1952—)
Kitchell, Iva (1908–1983)
Kitt, Eartha (1928—)
Knight, June (1913–1987)
Koner, Pauline (1912–2001)
Korbut, Olga (1955—)
Krauss, Gertrud (1903–1977)
Kshesinskaia, Matilda (1872–1971)
Kurishima, Sumiko (1902–1987)
Kyo, Machiko (1924—)
Lafont, Bernadette (1938—)
La Marr, Barbara (c. 1896–1926)
La Meri (1899–1988)
Lampert, Rachel (1948—)
Landi, Elissa (1904–1948)
Lang, June (1915—)
La Rue, Grace (1880–1956)
La Sylphe (c. 1900—)
Laurel, Kay (1890–1927)
Lawrence, Carol (1932—)
Lawrence, Gertrude (1898–1952)
Lawrence, Pauline (1900–1971)
Le Clercq, Tanaquil (1929–2000)
Lee, Dixie (1911–1952)
Lee, Gypsy Rose (1914–1970)
Lee, Mary Ann (1823–1899)
Lee, Sondra (1930—)
Legnani, Pierina (1863–1923)
Lehmann, Adelaide (c. 1830–1851)
Lepeshinskaya, Olga (1916—)
Lewis, Elma (1921—)
Lewitzky, Bella (1915–2004)
Lind, Letty (1862–1923)
Linn, Bambi (1926—)
Litz, Katharine (c. 1918–1978)
Livry, Emma (1842–1863)
Loftus, Kitty (1867–1927)
Lopez, Encarnación (1898–1945)
Lopokova, Lydia (c. 1892–1981)
Lopukhova, Evgenia (1884–1941)
Losch, Tilly (1903–1975)
Luahine, Iolani (1915–1978)
Luce, Claire (1903–1989)
Luna, Rosa (1937–1993)
MacLaine, Shirley (1934—)
Macpherson, Jeanie (1887–1946)
Makarova, Natalia (1940—)
Malo, Gina (1909–1963)
Maloney, Lucia (c. 1950–1978)
Mangano, Silvana (1930–1989)
Manners, Martha (1924–1977)
Manning, Katharine (1904–1974)
Mansfield, Portia (1887–1979)
Mara, Adele (1923—)
Maracci, Carmelita (b. 1911)
Marchand, Collette (1925—)
Margo (1918–1985)
Marin, Maguy (1951—)
Markham, Pauline (d. 1919)
Markova, Alicia (1910–2004)
Marks, Rita (c. 1908–1976)
Marmein, Irene (1894–1972)
Marmein, Miriam (1897–1970)
Marmein, Phyllis (1908–1994)
Marshall, Susan (1958—)
Martin, Mary (1913–1990)
Marx, Susan Fleming (1908–2002)
Maslow, Sophie (1911—)
Matthews, Jessie (1907–1981)
Maxwell, Vera (c. 1892–1950)
Mayfair, Mitzi (1914–1976)
Maywood, Augusta (1825–1876)
McCarthy, Patricia (1911–1943)
McCoy, Bessie (1888–1931)
McCracken, Joan (1922–1961)
McDonald, Grace (1918–1999)
McFarland, Beulah (c. 1898–1964)
McGehee, Helen (1921—)
McKechnie, Donna (1940—)
McKinney, Nina Mae (c. 1912–1967)
McLerie, Allyn Ann (1926—)
McQueen, Thelma (1911–1995)
Mears, Elizabeth (1900–1988)
Mercé, Antonia (c. 1886–1936)
Mérode, Cléo de (c. 1875–1966)
Miller, Ann (1919–2004)
Miller, Bebe (1950—)
Millman, Bird (1895–1940)
Mills, Florence (1895–1927)
Miramova, Elena (c. 1905—)
Mistinguett (1875–1956)
Monk, Meredith (1942—)
Montez, Lola (1818–1861)
Mooney, Julie (1888–1915)
Moore, Lillian (1911–1967)
Moreno, Rita (1931—)
Morgan, Marion (c. 1887–1971)
Moss, Marjorie (c. 1895–1935)
Muller, Jennifer (1949—)
Murray, Kathryn (1906–1999)
Nassif, Anna (1933—)
Natalie, Mlle (c. 1895–1922)
Nelson, Clara Meleka (1901–1979)
Nemchinova, Vera (1899–1984)
Neville, Phoebe (1941—)
Newberry, Barbara (1910—)
Nijinska, Bronislava (1891–1972)
Niles, Mary Ann (1938–1987)
Norden, Christine (1924–1988)
North, Sheree (1933–2005)
Novak, Nina (1927—)
O'Donnell, May (1906–2004)
Oelschlagel, Charlotte (c. 1899–after 1948)
Oliver, Thelma (1941—)
Olivette, Nina (c. 1908–1971)
O'Neal, Zelma (1903–1989)
Orcutt, Edith (c. 1918–1973)
Ordonówna, Hanka (1904–1950)
Osato, Sono (1919–1953)
Osipenko, Alla (1932—)
Osserman, Wendy (1942—)
Otake, Eiko (1952—)
Otero, Caroline (1868–1965)
Page, Ruth (1899–1991)
Palmer, Leland (1940—)

Palucca, Gret (1902–1993)
Parker, Madeleine (c. 1909–1936)
Patterson, Nan (c. 1882–?)
Pavlova, Anna (1881–1931)
Pennington, Ann (1892–1971)
Pennison, Marleen (1951—)
Peterson, Marjorie (1906–1974)
Piseth Pilika (1965–1999)
Plisetskaya, Maya (1925—)
Porter, Jean (1924—)
Potter, Maureen (1925–2004)
Powell, Eleanor (1910–1982)
Preisser, Cherry (1918–1964)
Preisser, June (1920–1984)
Preobrazhenska, Olga (1871–1962)
Prévost, Françoise (1680–1741)
Primus, Pearl (1919–1994)
Printemps, Yvonne (1894–1977)
Provine, Dorothy (1937—)
Prowse, Juliet (1936–1996)
Putli Bai (1929–1958)
Qualter, Tot (1894–1974)
Rainer, Yvonne (1934—)
Rambert, Marie (1888–1982)
Rambova, Natacha (1897–1966)
Rand, Sally (1904–1979)
Randolph, Elsie (1904–1982)
Ratner, Anna (c. 1892–1967)
Reese, Gail (1946—)
Reinking, Ann (1949—)
Reitz, Dana (1948—)
Reynolds, Marjorie (1917–1997)
Riabouchinska, Tatiana (1917–2000)
Riggs, Katherine Witchie (d. 1967)
Rivera, Chita (1933—)
Rogers, Ginger (1911–1995)
Rogge, Florence (b. 1904)
Rökk, Marika (1913–2004)
Romanova, Maria (1886–1954)
Rooney, Josie (b. 1892)
Rooney, Julia (b. 1893)
Roope, Clover (1937—)
Roshanara (1849–1926)
Ross, Shirley (1909–1975)
Rothlein, Arlene (1939–1976)
Rubenstein, Ida (1875–1961)
Rudner, Sara (1944—)
Rule, Janice (1931–2003)
Ryan, Peggy (1924–2004)
Sacchetto, Rita (1879–1959)
Sakharoff, Clotilde (1892–1974)
Sallé, Marie (1707–1756)
Salsberg, Germain Merle (1950—)
Sawyer, Ivy (1898–1999)
Saxon, Marie (1904–1941)
Schoenberg, Bessie (1906–1997)
Severn, Margaret (1901–1997)
Sevilla, Carmen (1930—)
Shaler, Eleanor (1900–1989)
Shaw, Wini (1910–1982)
Shearer, Moira (1926—)
Shelest, Alla (1919–1998)
Shizuka Gozen (fl. 12th c.)
Shurr, Gertrude (c. 1920—)
Sibley, Antoinette (1939—)
Sinden, Topsy (1878–1951)
Singleton, Penny (1908–2003)
Skoronel, Vera (1909–1932)
Slavenska, Mia (1914–2000)
Smith, Bessie (1894–1937)
Smith, Mamie (1883–1946)
Smoller, Dorothy (c. 1901–1926)
Snow, Valaida (c. 1903–1956)
Sokolova, Lydia (1896–1974)
Sokolow, Anna (1910–2000)
Sorel, Felicia (1904–1972)
Soyer, Ida (1909–1970)
Spessivtzeva, Olga (1895–1980)
St. Clair, Yvonne (1914–1971)
St. Denis, Ruth (1877–1968)
Stewart-Richardson, Lady Constance (1883–1932)
Stone, Dorothy (1905–1974)
Stonehouse, Ruth (1892–1941)
Strauss, Sara Milford (1896–1979)
Streatfeild, Noel (1895–1986)
Streb, Elizabeth (1950—)
Subligny, Marie-Thérèse Perdou de (1666–1736)
Summers, Leonora (1897–1976)
Taglioni, Maria (1804–1884)
Takagi, Tokuko Nagai (1891–1919)
Takei, Kei (1946—)
Tallchief, Maria (1925—)
Tallchief, Marjorie (1927—)
Tamiris, Helen (1902–1966)
Tauber-Arp, Sophie (1889–1943)
Tauhida (?–1932)
Taylor, Eva (1895–1977)
Taylor, June (1917–2004)
Tchernicheva, Lubov (1890–1976)
Teer, Barbara Ann (1937—)
Tempest, Florence (c. 1891–?)
Theano (fl. 6th c. BCE)
Thomas, Caitlin (1913–1994)
Thomas, Olive (1884–1920)
Tofts, Catherine (c. 1685–1756)
Toumanova, Tamara (1919–1996)
Toye, Wendy (1917—)
Travers, P.L. (1906–1996)
Trefilova, Vera (1875–1943)
Trisler, Joyce (1934–1979)
Trouhanova, Natalia (1885–1956)
Trueman, Paula (1900–1994)
Turnbull, Julia Anne (1822–1887)
Ukrainka, Lesya (1871–1913)
Ulanova, Galina (1910–1998)
Vaganova, Agrippina (1879–1951)
Vanbrugh, Violet (1867–1942)
van Praagh, Peggy (1910–1990)
Vaughan, Kate (c. 1852–1903)
Veigel, Eva-Maria (1724–1822)
Velez, Lupe (1908–1944)
Venuta, Benay (1911–1995)
Vera-Ellen (1920–1981)
Verdon, Gwen (1925–2000)
Vestoff, Floria (1920–1963)
Vestris, Lucia (1797–1856)
Vestris, Thérèse (1726–1808)
Vezin, Jane Elizabeth (1827–1902)
Villegas, Micaela (1748–1819)
Volkova, Vera (1904–1975)
Vyroubova, Nina (1921—)
Walker, Ada Overton (1870–1914)
Wallmann, Margarethe (1901–19922)
Walsh, Kay (1914–2005)
Walton, Florence (1891–1981)
Ward, Polly (1908–1987)
Warner, Gloria (c. 1914–1934)
Washington, Fredi (1903–1994)
Watley, Jody (1959—)
Weaver, Marjorie (1913–1994)
Webb, Elida (1895–1975)
Weeks, Ada May (1898–1978)
Whelan, Cyprienne Gabel (d. 1985)
White, Alice (1904–1983)
White, Frances (1896–1969)
White, Oona (1922–2005)
Wiesenthal, Grete (1885–1970)
Wigman, Mary (1886–1973)
Williams, Hattie (1872–1942)
Williams, Lavinia (1916–1989)
Wilson, Kini (1872–1962)
Wing, Toby (1915–2001)
Winter, Ethel (1924—)
Wright, Rebecca (1942—)
Yarborough, Sara (1950—)
Yuan, Tina (c. 1950—)
Yuriko (b. 1920)
Zanfretta, Marietta (c. 1837–1898)
Zapata Olivella, Delia (1926–2001)
Zelle, Margaretha (1876–1917)
Zorina, Vera (1917—)

DANCE SATIRIST
Cullberg, Birgit (1908–1999)
de Mille, Agnes (1905–1993)
Geistinger, Marie (1833–1903)
Holm, Hanya (1888–1992)
Kitchell, Iva (1908–1983)
Maracci, Carmelita (b. 1911)
Nelson, Clara Meleka (1901–1979)

DANCE TEACHER
Abbott, Merriel (c. 1893–1977)
Adams, Diana (1927–1993)
Astafieva, Serafima (1876–1934)
Baldina, Alexandra Maria (1885–1977)
Ballou, Germaine (b. 1899)
Baylis, Meredith (1929–2002)
Beatty, Patricia (1936—)
Beere, Estelle Girda (1875–1959)
Beretta, Caterina (1839–1911)
Berk, Lotte (1913–2003)
Bird, Bonnie (1914–1995)
Bonfanti, Marietta (1845–1921)
Brianza, Carlotta (1862–1930)
Brown, Mary Jane (1917–1997)
Collins, Janet (1917–2003)
Dai, Ailian (1916–2006)
Danilova, Alexandra (1903–1997)
de Valois, Ninette (1898–2001)
Dudinskaya, Natalya (1912–2003)
Duncan, Elizabeth (c. 1874–1948)
Farrell, Suzanne (1945—)
Fonaroff, Nina (1914–2003)
Fort, Syvilla (c. 1917–1975)
Gisolo, Margaret (1914—)
Gorham, Kathleen (1932–1983)
Graham, Martha (1894–1991)
Hill, Martha (1900–1995)
Hill, Thelma (1925–1977)
Holm, Hanya (1888–1992)
Humphrey, Doris (1895–1958)
Karsavina, Tamara (1885–1978)
Kent, Allegra (1937—)
Kshesinskaia, Matilda (1872–1971)
Le Clercq, Tanaquil (1929–2000)
Manning, Katharine (1904–1974)
Markova, Alicia (1910–2004)
Maywood, Augusta (1825–1876)
Nijinska, Bronislava (1891–1972)
O'Donnell, May (1906–2004)
Page, Ruth (1899–1991)
Palucca, Gret (1902–1993)
Preobrazhenska, Olga (1871–1962)
Prévost, Françoise (1680–1741)
Rambert, Marie (1888–1982)
Romanova, Maria (1886–1954)
Schoenberg, Bessie (1906–1997)
Schollar, Ludmilla (c. 1888–1978)
Shurr, Gertrude (c. 1920—)
Simpson-Serven, Ida (c. 1850s–c. 1896)
Slavenska, Mia (1914–2000)
Sokolova, Lydia (1896–1974)
Sokolow, Anna (1910–2000)
Taglioni, Maria (1804–1884)
Tallchief, Marjorie (1927—)

Tchernicheva, Lubov (1890–1976)
Ulanova, Galina (1910–1998)
Vaganova, Agrippina (1879–1951)
van Praagh, Peggy (1910–1990)
Volkova, Vera (1904–1975)
Vyroubova, Nina (1921—)
Wallmann, Margarethe (1901–19922)

DAUPHINE
Maria Anna of Bavaria (1660–1690)
Maria Theresa of Spain (1726–1746)
Mary Stuart (1542–1587)
Montpensier, Anne Marie Louise d'Orléans, Duchesse de (1627–1693)

DEACONESS
Alexander, Jessie (1876–1962)
Boole, Ella (1858–1952)
Fedde, Sister Elizabeth (1850–1921)
Helaria (fl. 6th c.)
Macrina (327–379)
McQueen, Mary (1860–1945)
Mellish, Edith Mary (1861–1922)
Olympias (c. 365–408)
Radegund of Poitiers (518–587)
Sigolena of Albi (fl. 7th c.)
Spencer Smith, Joan (1891–1965)
Williams, Matilda Alice (1875–1973)

DECATHLON ATHLETE
Belova, Irina (1968—)

DECORATIVE-ARTS DESIGNER
Barlow, Hannah (1851–1916)
Baynes, Pauline (1922—)
Carrington, Dora (1893–1932)
Claudel, Camille (1864–1943)
Cliff, Clarice (1899–1972)
Cooper, Susie (1902–1995)
Fry, Laura Ann (1857–1943)
Gray, Eileen (1878–1976)
King, Jessie Marion (1875–1949)
Morris, May (1862–1938)
Pompadour, Jeanne-Antoinette Poisson, Duchesse de (1721–1764)
Sarfatti, Margherita (1880–1961)
Tauber-Arp, Sophie (1889–1943)
Wheeler, Candace (1827–1923)
Whyte, Kathleen (1909–1996)
Woodsmall, Ruth F. (1883–1963)

DEMOGRAPHER
Hagood, Margaret (1907–1963)
Taeuber, Irene Barnes (1906–1974)

DENTAL ASSISTANT
Cohen, Myra (1892–1959)

DENTAL SURGEON
Murray, Lilian (1871–1960)

DENTIST
Apgar, Virginia (1909–1974)
Caro, Margaret (1848–1938)
Delany, Annie Elizabeth (1891–1995)
Johnston, Amy Isabella (1872–1908)
Murray, Lilian (1871–1960)
Price, Eugenia (1916–1996)
Slutskaya, Vera (1874–1917)
Taylor, Lucy Hobbs (1833–1910)

DESIGNER
See Airplane designer.
See Book illustrator/designer.
See Clothing designer.
See Decorative-arts designer.
See Floral designer.
See Furnishings designer.
See Furniture designer.
See Garden designer.
See Glassware designer.
See Graphic artist/designer.
See Interior designer.
See Jewelry designer.
See Landscape architect/designer.
See Lighting designer.
See Sportswear designer.
See Stained-glass artist/designer.
See Tapestry designer.
See Textile artist/designer.
See Theatrical designer.

DETECTIVE-FICTION WRITER
See Crime/Detective-fiction writer.

DEVELOPER
See Innovator.

DIARIST
Adamson, Catherine (1868–1925)
Alcott, Louisa May (1832–1888)
Allen, Florence Ellinwood (1884–1966)
Almy, Mary Gould (1735–1808)
Ambler, Mary Cary (fl. 1700s)
Amory, Katherine (1731–1777)
Arnstein, Fanny von (1758–1818)
Asquith, Cynthia (1887–1960)
Asquith, Margot Tennant (1864–1945)
Astor, Nancy Witcher (1879–1964)
Atkinson, Jane Maria (1824–1914)
Bacheracht, Therese von (1804–1852)
Ballard, Martha Moore (1735–1812)
Bashkirtseff, Marie (1859–1884)
Bates, Katherine Lee (1859–1929)
Beach, Amy Cheney (1867–1944)
Belloc-Lowndes, Marie (1868–1947)
Berenson, Mary (1864–1944)
Betham-Edwards, Matilda (1836–1919)
Bibesco, Marthe Lucie (1887–1973)
Blackburn, Jemima (1823–1909)
Boscawen, Fanny (1719–1805)
Boye, Karin (1900–1941)
Brassey, Anna (1839–1887)
Bulfinch, Hannah Apthorp (1768–1841)
Burney, Fanny (1752–1840)
Burr, Esther Edwards (1732–1758)
Butler, Eleanor (c. 1738–1829)
Caesar, Mary (1677–1741)
Calderwood, Margaret (1715–1774)
Callender, Hannah (1737–1801)
Carrington, Dora (1893–1932)
Castle, Barbara (1910–2002)
Chambers, Charlotte (d. 1821)
Chaminade, Cécile (1857–1944)
Chesnut, Mary Boykin (1823–1886)
Chopin, Kate (1850–1904)
Clifford, Anne (1590–1676)
Coit, Mehetabel Chandler (1673–1758)
Cooper, Mary Wright (1714–1778)
Cowles, Julia (1785–1803)
Cowper, Mary (1685–1724)
Cranch, Elizabeth (1743–1811)
Crawford, Ruth (1901–1953)
Cumming, Kate (c. 1828–1909)
Cunard, Nancy (1896–1965)
Dabrowska, Maria (1889–1965)
Dark, Eleanor (1901–1985)
Dawbin, Annie Maria (1816–1905)
De Mist, Augusta (1783–1832)
Deutsch, Helene (1884–1982)
Dewees, Mary Coburn (fl. 1787–1788)
Diakonova, Elizaveta (1874–1902)
Dostoevsky, Anna (1846–1918)
Drinker, Elizabeth Sandwith (1734–1807)
Dudley, Dorothy (fl. 1775)
Durova, Nadezhda (1783–1866)
Edwards, Sarah Pierpont (1710–1758)
Emerson, Mary Moody (1774–1863)
Farmborough, Florence (1887–1978)
Ferguson, Elizabeth Graeme (1737–1801)
Filipović, Zlata (1981—)
Fisher, Sarah Logan (1751–1796)
Fitzgerald, Zelda (1900–1948)
Fleming, Margaret (1803–1811)
Fort, Cornelia (1919–1943)
Fox, Caroline (1819–1871)
Frank, Anne (1929–1945)
Franklin, Jane (1792–1875)
Fuller, Elizabeth (1775–1856)
Fulton, Catherine (1829–1919)
Gág, Wanda (1893–1946)
Galloway, Grace Growden (d. 1782)
Gilman, Charlotte Perkins (1860–1935)
Gippius, Zinaida (1869–1945)
Gluck (1895–1978)
Glyn, Elinor (1864–1943)
Gregory, Augusta (1852–1932)
Guérin, Eugénie de (1805–1848)
Guest, Lady Charlotte (1812–1895)
Harris, Emily Cumming (c. 1836–1925)
Hillesum, Etty (1914–1943)
Hoby, Margaret (1571–1633)
Holyoke, Mary Vial (1737–1802)
Horney, Karen (1885–1952)
Huch, Ricarda (1864–1947)
Hugo, Adèle (1830–1915)
Huntington, Anna Hyatt (1876–1973)
Inman, Elizabeth Murray (c. 1724–1785)
James, Alice (1848–1892)
Jarnević, Dragojla (1812–1875)
Jex-Blake, Sophia (1840–1912)
Jolley, Elizabeth (1923—)
Katznelson-Shazar, Rachel (1888–1975)
Knight, Sarah Kemble (1666–1727)
Ladies of Llangollen, The
Lamburn, Richmal Crompton (1890–1969)
Lane, Rose Wilder (1886–1968)
Larpent, Anna Margaretta (fl. 1815–1830)
Leach, Christiana (fl. 1765–1796)
Lee, Lucinda (fl. 1787)
Lindbergh, Anne Morrow (1906–2001)
Lindsay, Anne (1750–1825)
Lister, Anne (1791–1840)
Livingston, Anne Shippen (1763–1841)
Longfellow, Frances Appleton (1819–1861)
Macarthur, Elizabeth (1767–1850)
Mackellar, Dorothea (1885–1968)
Macquarie, Elizabeth (1778–1835)
Magoffin, Susan Shelby (1827–c. 1855)
Mahler, Alma (1879–1964)
Manigault, Ann Ashby (1703–1782)
Mansfield, Katherine (1888–1923)
Mathew, Sarah Louise (c. 1805–1890)
Maupin, d'Aubigny (c. 1670–1707)
McCrae, Georgiana Huntly (1804–1890)
Michitsuna no haha (c. 936–995)
Mildmay, Grace (1553–1620)
Mitchell, Maria (1818–1889)
Montgomery, Lucy Maud (1874–1942)
Morgan, Sydney (1780–1859)
Morris, Margaret Hill (1737–1816)
Mott, Lucretia (1793–1880)
Nalkowska, Zofia (1884–1954)
Nin, Anais (1903–1977)
Osborn, Sarah (1714–1796)
Pakington, Dorothy (d. 1679)
Pardo Bazán, Emilia (1852–1921)
Pengelly, Edna (1874–1959)

Pfeiffer, Ida (1797–1858)
Phelps, Elizabeth Porter (1747–1817)
Piozzi, Hester Lynch (1741–1821)
Post, Lydia Minturn (fl. 1776–1783)
Powell, Dawn (1897–1965)
Prentiss, Elizabeth Payson (1818–1878)
Ptaschkina, Nelly (1903–1920)
Purser, Sarah (1848–1943)
Pym, Barbara (1913–1980)
Radi, Nuha al- (1941–2004)
Ralfe, Catherine Hester (c. 1831–1912)
Ramsay, Martha Laurens (1759–1811)
Rawle, Anna (c. 1757–1828)
Ream, Vinnie (1847–1914)
Recke, Elisa von der (1754–1833)
Reventlow, Franziska von (1871–1918)
Reynolds, Belle (fl. 1860s)
Rhys, Jean (1890–1979)
Rich, Mary (1625–1678)
Rinser, Luise (1911–2002)
Robins, Elizabeth (1862–1952)
Rockefeller, Abby Aldrich (1874–1948)
Sackville-West, Vita (1892–1962)
Sale, Florentia (c. 1790–1853)
Sarashina (c. 1008–1060)
Sarrazin, Albertine (1937–1967)
Sarton, May (1912–1995)
Scholl, Sophie (1921–1943)
Schopenhauer, Johanna (1766–1838)
Schumann, Clara (1819–1896)
Senesh, Hannah (1921–1944)
Seton, Elizabeth Ann (1774–1821)
Stewart, Adela Blanche (1846–1910)
Thompson, Flora (1876–1947)
Turner, Ethel (1872–1958)
Victoria (1819–1901)
Wagner, Cosima (1837–1930)
Waller, Anne (c. 1603–1662)
Wander, Maxie (1933–1977)
Warder, Ann Head (1758–1829)
Warner, Sylvia Townsend (1893–1978)
West, Elizabeth (fl. early 18th c.)
White, Antonia (1899–1980)
Whitney, Gertrude Vanderbilt (1875–1942)
Winslow, Anna Green (1759–1779)
Wister, Sarah (1761–1804)
Wolf, Christa (1929—)
Wordsworth, Dorothy (1771–1855)

DIETITIAN

See Nutritionist.

DIPLOMAT

Albright, Madeleine (1937—)
Anderson, Eugenie Moore (1909–1997)
Anttila, S. Inkeri (1916—)
Armstrong, Anne L. (1927—)
Astorga, Nora (1949–1988)
Bailey, Pearl (1918–1990)
Balch, Emily Greene (1867–1961)
Barrow, Nita (1916–1995)
Begtrup, Bodil (1903–1987)
Bernardino, Minerva (1907–1998)
Black, Shirley Temple (1928—)
Blagoeva, Stella Dimitrova (1887–1954)
Boggs, Lindy (1916—)
Bolton, Frances Payne (1885–1977)
Bouboulina, Laskarina (1771–1825)
Brinker, Nancy G. (1946—)
Brooks, Angie (1928—)
Brunschvicg, Cécile (1877–1946)
Bruntland, Gro Harlem (1939—)
Bunker, Carol Laise (1918–1991)
Castellanos, Rosario (1925–1974)
Castle, Barbara (1910–2002)
Chambers, Anne Cox (1919—)
Chibesakunda, Lombe Phyllis (1944—)
Chiepe, Gaositwe (c. 1924—)
Cisse, Jeanne-Martin (1926—)
Clouzot, Vera (1921–1960)
Darton, Patience (1911–1996)
Dobson, Ruth (1918–1989)
Dorothea, Princess of Lieven (1785–1857)
Douglas, Helen Gahagan (1900–1980)
Dulles, Eleanor Lansing (1895–1996)
Dunne, Irene (1898–1990)
El Saadawi, Nawal (1931—)
Farkas, Ruth L. (1906–1996)
Fenwick, Millicent (1910–1992)
Figueroa, Ana (1907–1970)
Freundlich, Emmy (1878–1948)
George, Zelma Watson (1904–1994)
Gildersleeve, Virginia Crocheron (1877–1965)
Glinski, Elena (c. 1506–1538)
Greenhow, Rose O'Neal (c. 1817–1864)
Gueiler Tejada, Lydia (1921—)
Harriman, Florence Jaffray (1870–1967)
Harriman, Pamela (1920–1997)
Harris, Patricia Roberts (1924–1985)
Hashimi, Aquila al- (1953–2003)
Hawkes, Jacquetta (1910–1996)
Heckler, Margaret M. (1931—)
Horsbrugh, Florence (1889–1969)
Hulme, Kathryn (1900–1981)
Jagan, Janet (1920—)
Kasilag, Lucrecia R. (1918—)
Khan, Begum Liaquat Ali (1905–1990)
Kirkpatrick, Jeane (1926—)
Klimova, Rita (1931–1993)
Kollontai, Alexandra (1872–1952)
Konie, Gwendoline (1938—)
Lefaucheux, Marie-Helene (1904–1964)
Lodhi, Maleeha (c. 1953—)
Luce, Clare Boothe (1903–1987)
Makeba, Miriam (1932—)
Malinche (c. 1500–1531)
Margaret of Austria (1480–1530)
Mary of Guise (1515–1560)
McCormick, Anne O'Hare (1880–1954)
McKenzie, Jean (1901–1964)
Meir, Golda (1898–1978)
Menchú, Rigoberta (1959—)
Mesta, Perle (1889–1975)
Miller, Frieda S. (1889–1973)
Min of Korea (1851–1895)
Mistral, Gabriela (1889–1957)
Mongella, Gertrude (1945—)
Musgrove, Mary (c. 1690–c. 1763)
Myrdal, Alva (1902–1986)
Neville-Jones, Pauline (1939—)
Nur Jahan (1577–1645)
Ogot, Grace (1930—)
Palacios, Lucila (1902–1994)
Palencia, Isabel de (1878–c. 1950)
Palm, Etta Aelders (1743–1799)
Pandit, Vijaya Lakshmi (1900–1990)
Pintasilgo, Maria de Lurdes (1930–2004)
Rankin, Annabelle (1908–1986)
Rapoport, Lydia (1923–1971)
Rāteb, Aisha (1928—)
Reisner, Larissa (1895–1926)
Ridgway, Rozanne Lejeanne (1935—)
Rohde, Ruth Bryan Owen (1885–1954)
Roosevelt, Eleanor (1884–1962)
Roxelana (c. 1504–1558)
Salt, Barbara (1904–1975)
Sampson, Edith S. (1901–1979)
Schwimmer, Rosika (1877–1948)
Sipilä, Helvi (1915—)
Smith, Jean Kennedy (1928—)
Street, Jessie (1889–1970)
Tamara (1160–1212)
Tibbetts, Margaret Joy (1919—)
Tree, Marietta (1917–1991)
Wells, Melissa Foelsch (1932—)
Willis, Frances (1899–1983)
Wilson, Cairine (1885–1962)
Wuolijoki, Hella (1886–1954)

DIRECTOR

See also Ballet director.
See also Dance director.
See also Film director.
See also Music director.
See also Opera director.
See also Television/radio director.
See also Theatre director.

Aleandro, Norma (1936—)
Bovasso, Julie (1930–1991)
Dybwad, Johanne (1867–1950)
Furse, Judith (1912–1974)
Grant, Lee (1927—)
Helmond, Katherine (1934—)
Jenner, Caryl (1917—)
Kaplan, Nelly (1931—)
Lindblom, Gunnel (1931—)
May, Elaine (1932—)
Pascal, Christine (1953–1996)
Stevens, Stella (1936—)
Tewkesbury, Joan (1936—)
Toye, Wendy (1917—)
Védrès, Nicole (1911–1965)

DISABLED ATHLETE

Binns, Hilda May (1945—)
Driscoll, Jean (1967—)
Golden, Diana (1963—)

DISC JOCKEY

Steele, Alison (c. 1937–1995)

DISCOVERER

See Innovator.

DISCUS THROWER

See Track-and-field athlete.

DIVER

Alekseyeva, Galina (1946—)
Armstrong, Eileen (1894–1981)
Baldus, Brita Pia (1965—)
Becker-Pinkston, Elizabeth (1903–1989)
Bernier, Sylvie (1964—)
Boys, Beverly (1951—)
Bush, Lesley (1947—)
Chandler, Jennifer (1959—)
Christoffersen, Birte (1924—)
Clark, Mary Ellen (1962—)
Clausen, Stefanie (1900–1981)
Coleman, Georgia (1912–1940)
Collier, Jeanne (1946—)
Draves, Victoria (1924—)
Duchkova, Milena (1952—)
Dunn, Velma (1918—)
Elsener, Patricia (1929—)
Emirzyan, Sirvard (1966—)
Engel-Kramer, Ingrid (1943—)
Fauntz, Jane (1910–1989)
Ferris, Elizabeth (1940—)
Fletcher, Caroline (1906—)
Fu Mingxia (1978—)
Gao Min (1970—)
Gestring, Marjorie (1922–1992)
Gilmore, Rebecca
Goncharova, Natalia (1988—)
Gossick, Sue (1947—)
Guo Jingjing (1981—)
Guthke, Karin (1956—)
Hartley, Blythe (1982—)

Occupational Index

Heymans, Emilie (1981—)
Hildebrand, Sara (1979—)
Ilyina, Vera (1974—)
Janicke, Marina (1954—)
Jaschke, Martina (1960—)
Johanson, Margareta (1895–1978)
Kalinina, Irina (1959—)
Kellerman, Annette (1886–1975)
King, Micki (1944—)
Knape, Ulrika (1955—)
Koehler, Christa (1951—)
Koehler, Kathe (1913—)
Koltunova, Julia (1989—)
Krutova, Ninel (1926—)
Lao Lishi (1987—)
Lashko, Irina (1973—)
Li Na (1984—)
Lindner, Dorte
Li Qing (1972—)
Li Ting (1987—)
Lobanova, Natalya (1947—)
MacDonald, Irene (1933–2002)
McCormick, Kelly (1960—)
McCormick, Patricia (1930—)
Meany, Helen (1904–1991)
Mestre, Audrey (1974–2002)
Miroshina, Yelena (1974—)
Mitchell, Michelle (1962—)
Montminy, Anne (1975—)
Moreau, Mady (1928—)
Myers, Paula Jean (1934—)
Newbery, Chantelle (1977—)
Olliwier, Eva (1904–1955)
Olsen, Zoe Ann (1931—)
O'Sullivan, Keala (1950—)
Pakhalina, Yulia (1977—)
Payne, Thelma (1896–1988)
Pelletier, Annie (1973—)
Peterson, Ann (1947—)
Pogosheva-Safonova, Tamara (1946—)
Potter, Cynthia (1950—)
Poynton, Dorothy (1915—)
Proeber, Martina (1963—)
Rawls, Katherine (1918–1982)
Regnell, Lisa (1887–1979)
Riggin, Aileen (1906–2002)
Roper, Marion
Sang Xue (1984—)
Seufert, Christina (1957—)
Sjoeqvist, Laura (1903–1964)
Smith, Caroline (1906—)
Sorokina, Anna (1976—)
Stover-Irwin, Juno (1928—)
Stunyo, Jeanne (1936—)
Taylor, Valerie (1935—)
Tourky, Loudy (1979—)
Tsotadze, Liana (1961—)
Vare, Glenna Collett (1903–1989)
Vaytsekhovskaya, Yelena (1958—)
Wainwright, Helen (1906—)
Walter, Annika (1975—)
White, Isabella (1894–1972)
Wilkinson, Laura (1977—)
Willard, Mary (1941—)
Williams, Wendy Lian (1967—)
Wilson, Deborah (1955—)
Wu Minxia (1985—)
Wyland, Wendy (1964–2003)
Xu Yanmei (1971—)
Zhou Jihong (1965—)
Zhupina, Olena (1973—)

DOCUMENT ANALYST
Sulner, Hanna (1917–1999)

DOCUMENTARY PHOTOGRAPHER
Abbott, Berenice (1898–1991)
Andriesse, Emmy (1914–1953)
Arbus, Diane (1923–1971)
Besnyö, Eva (1910–2003)
Bourke-White, Margaret (1904–1971)
Brooks, Charlotte (1918—)
Broom, Christina (1863–1939)
Bubley, Esther (1921–1998)
Dahl-Wolfe, Louise (1895–1989)
Flaherty, Frances Hubbard (c. 1886–1972)
Frissell, Toni (1907–1988)
Gilpin, Laura (1891–1979)
Hofer, Evelyn
Johnston, Frances Benjamin (1864–1952)
Kanaga, Consuelo (1894–1978)
Kar, Ida (1908–1970)
Kasten, Barbara (1936—)
Kendall, Marie Hartig (1854–1943)
Krull, Germaine (1897–1985)
Lange, Dorothea (1895–1965)
Levitt, Helen (1913—)
Modotti, Tina (1896–1942)
Naylor, Genevieve (1915–1989)
Palfi, Marion (1907–1978)
Watson, Edith (1861–1943)
Wolcott, Marion Post (1910–1990)

DOGARESSA
Maria (fl. 995–1025)

DOMBRA PLAYER
Nurpeissova, Dina (1861–1955)

DOMESTIC SERVANT
Fraser, Margaret (1866–1951)
Tasker, Marianne Allen (1852–1911)

DOWNHILL SKIER
See Skier.

DRAMA TEACHER
See Acting teacher.

DRAMATIST
Condé, Maryse (1937—)

DRAPER
Addison, Agnes (c. 1841–1903)
Anstice, Sophia (1849–1926)

DRESSMAKER
See Seamstress/dressmaker.

DRESS REFORMER
Bloomer, Amelia Jenks (1818–1894)
Croly, Jane Cunningham (1829–1901)
Dexter, Caroline (1819–1884)
Hasbrouck, Lydia Sayer (1827–1910)
May, Isabella (1850–1926)
Miller, Annie Jenness (b. 1859)
Nesbit, Edith (1858–1924)
Pelletier, Madeleine (1874–1939)
Pfeiffer, Emily Jane (1827–1890)
Potonié-Pierre, Eugénie (1844–1898)
Safford, Mary Jane (1834–1891)
Seacole, Mary Jane (c. 1805–1881)
Sewall, May Wright (1844–1920)
Stanton, Elizabeth Cady (1815–1902)
Walker, Mary Edwards (1832–1919)
Ward, Elizabeth Stuart Phelps (1844–1911)
Willard, Frances E. (1839–1898)
Woolson, Abba Goold (1838–1921)

DRUMMER
Escovedo, Sheila (1957—)

DUCHESS
Abrantès, Laure d' (1784–1838)
Accoramboni, Vittoria (c. 1557–1585)
Adelaide (1821–1899)
Adelaide of Burgundy (d. 1273)
Adelaide of Hohenlohe-Langenburg (1835–1900)
Adelaide of Saxe-Meiningen (1891–1971)
Adelaide of Vohburg (fl. 1140s)
Adelgunde of Bavaria (1823–1914)
Aénor of Châtellerault (d. 1130)
Agnes Capet (1260–1327)
Agnes of Aquitaine (c. 995–1068)
Agnes of Bohemia (1269–1297)
Agnes of Burgundy (d. 1476)
Agnes of Looss (fl. 1150–1175)
Agnes of Saarbrucken (fl. 1130)
Agnes of Saxony (fl. 1200s)
Albertina of Baden-Durlach (1682–1755)
Albertine (1797–1838)
Alexandra Feodorovna (1872–1918)
Alexandra Guelph (1882–1963)
Alexandra Pavlovna (1783–1801)
Alexandra Victoria (1891–1959)
Alexandra Victoria of Schleswig-Holstein (1887–1957)
Alexandrina of Baden (1820–1904)
Alexandrine of Prussia (1803–1892)
Alice (1201–1221)
Alice Maud Mary (1843–1878)
Alicia of Parma (1849–1935)
Alix of Vergy (d. after 1218)
Alvarez de Toledo, Luisa Isabel (1936—)
Amalie Auguste (1788–1851)
Amalie of Saxe-Coburg-Gotha (1848–1894)
Amalie of Saxony (1794–1870)
Amboise, Francise d' (1427–1485)
Amelia of Denmark (1580–1639)
Amelia of Wurttemberg (1799–1848)
Anastasia (1901–1918)
Anastasia Romanova (1860–1922)
Anna Amalia of Saxe-Weimar (1739–1807)
Anna Ivanovna (1693–1740)
Anna Maria of Saxony (1836–1859)
Anna of Bohemia (fl. 1230s)
Anna of Brandenburg (1507–1567)
Anna of Brunswick (fl. 1400s)
Anna of Brunswick (1528–1590)
Anna of Byzantium (963–1011)
Anna of Silesia (fl. 1200s)
Anna Pavlovna (1795–1865)
Anna Sophia of Prussia (1527–1591)
Anne de la Tour (c. 1496–1524)
Anne de la Tour (d. 1512)
Anne-Eleanor of Hesse-Darmstadt (1601–1659)
Anne Marie of Brunswick (1532–1568)
Anne of Austria (1432–1462)
Anne of Brittany (c. 1477–1514)
Anne of Ferrara (1531–1607)
Anne of Lusignan (b. before 1430)
Anne of Velasquez (1585–1607)
Anne Plantagenet (1439–1476)
Anne Valois (c. 1405–1432)
Antoinette of Bourbon (1494–1583)
Antoinette Saxe-Coburg (1779–1824)
Aptheker, Bettina (1944—)
Aubrey of Buonalbergo (fl. 1000s)
Audley, Margaret (d. 1564)
Augusta Guelph (1737–1813)
Augusta Guelph (1822–1916)
Augusta Maria of Baden-Baden (1704–1726)
Augusta of Hesse-Cassel (1797–1889)
Augusta of Reuss-Ebersdorf (1757–1831)
Augusta of Tuscany (1825–1864)
Baird, Frances (d. 1708)
Barbara of Poland (1478–1534)

Beatrice (1242–1275)
Beatrice of Beja (1430–1506)
Beatrice of Brandenburg (1360–1414)
Beatrice of Portugal (1504–1538)
Beatrice of Saxe-Coburg (1884–1966)
Beatrix de Bourgogne (1257–1310)
Beauchamp, Eleanor (1408–1468)
Beaufort, Eleanor (d. 1501)
Beaumont, Isabel (d. 1368)
Bentinck, Margaret (1714–1785)
Bertha of Brittany (d. 1163)
Bertie, Catharine (1519–1580)
Blanche (c. 1392–1409)
Blanche of Artois (c. 1247–1302)
Blanche of Bourbon (1868–1949)
Blanche of France (1328–1392)
Blanche of Lancaster (1341–1369)
Blanche of Navarre (fl. 1239)
Bohun, Eleanor (1366–1399)
Bona of Savoy (c. 1450–c. 1505)
Bonaparte, Elisa (1777–1820)
Bonaparte, Pauline (1780–1825)
Bonne of Armagnac (d. 1415)
Bonne of Artois (d. 1425)
Borgia, Lucrezia (1480–1519)
Boufflers, Madeleine-Angelique, Duchesse de (1707–1787)
Bourchier, Anne (c. 1417–1474)
Brandon, Eleanor (c. 1520–1547)
Brandon, Frances (1517–1559)
Braunschweig-Lüneburg, Sophie Elisabeth von (1613–1676)
Browne, Anne (d. 1511)
Cadogan, Sarah (1706–1751)
Cappello, Bianca (1548–1587)
Carlota (1840–1927)
Carnegie, Caroline (1934—)
Caroline Louise of Saxe-Weimar (1786–1816)
Caroline Matilda of Schleswig-Holstein (1860–1932)
Caroline of Bourbon (1822–1869)
Caroline of Naples (1798–1870)
Catalina (1403–1439)
Catherine Charlotte of Hildburghausen (1787–1847)
Catherine II the Great of Russia (1729–1796)
Catherine of Bourbon (d. 1469)
Catherine of Bourbon (c. 1555–1604)
Catherine of Brunswick-Wolfenbuttel (1488–1563)
Catherine of Burgundy (1378–1425)
Catherine of Cleves (1417–1479)
Catherine of Cleves (fl. 1550s)
Catherine of Gorizia (fl. late 1300s)
Catherine of Guise (1552–c. 1594)
Catherine of Habsburg (1533–1572)
Catherine of Lorraine (fl. 1600s)
Catherine of Mecklenburg-Schwerin (1692–1733)
Catherine of Pomerania (d. 1526)
Catherine of Portugal (1540–1614)
Catherine of Russia (1788–1819)
Catherine of Spain (1567–1597)
Cavendish, Christiana (1595–1675)
Cavendish, Elizabeth (1759–1824)
Cavendish, Georgiana (1757–1806)
Cavendish, Margaret (1623–1673)
Cayetana, Maria del Pilar Teresa (1762–1802)
Cayetana Fitz-James Stuart y Silva, Maria del Rosario (1926—)
Cecilia of Mecklenburg-Schwerin (1886–1954)
Charlotte (1769–1818)
Charlotte (1896–1985)
Charlotte-Aglae (1700–1761)
Charlotte Elizabeth of Bavaria (1652–1722)
Charlotte of Vendôme (fl. 15th c.)
Châteauroux, Marie Anne de Mailly-Nesle, Duchesse de (1717–1744)
Chaucer, Alice (fl. 1400s)
Chotek, Sophie (1868–1914)
Christina of Denmark (1521–1590)
Christine of Baden-Durlach (1645–1705)
Christine of Bourbon (1779–1849)
Christine of France (1606–1663)
Christine of Hesse (1543–1604)
Christine of Lorraine (c. 1571–1637)
Chudleigh, Elizabeth (1720–1788)
Churchill, Fanny (1822–1899)
Churchill, Henrietta (1681–1733)
Churchill, Mary (1689–1751)
Churchill, Sarah Jennings (1660–1744)
Cibò, Caterina (fl. 1533)
Cimburca of Masovia (c. 1396–1429)
Claude de France (1499–1524)
Clementia (d. 1133)
Clementia
Clermont, Claude-Catherine de (1545–1603)
Clotilde of Saxe-Coburg-Gotha (1846–1927)
Cobham, Eleanor (d. 1452)
Constance (c. 1374–1416)
Constance of Aragon (d. 1327)
Constance of Brittany (1161–1201)
Constance of Castile (d. 1160)
Constance of Castile (1354–1394)
Cristina (1965—)
Cunegunde (d. after 1370)
Cunegunde (1465–1520)
Dampierre, Emmanuela del (b. 1913)
Davies, Lilian May (1915—)
de la Cerda, Blanche (c. 1311–1347)
Devereux, Frances (d. 1674)
Diane de France (1538–1619)
Diane de Poitiers (1499–1566)
Dobravy of Bohemia (d. 977)
Doda (fl. 1040)
Dorothea of Brandenburg (1446–1519)
Dorothea Oldenburg (1504–1547)
Dorothy of Denmark (1546–1617)
Douglas, Margaret (b. around 1427)
Douglas, Margaret (1515–1578)
Douglas, Marjory (d. 1420)
Drahomira of Bohemia (d. after 932)
Duras, Claire de (1777–1828)
Edgifu (902–951)
Edgren, Anne Charlotte (1849–1892)
Eilika of Oldenburg (1928—)
Eilika of Oldenburg (1972—)
Eleanor of Solms-Hohensolms-Lich (1871–1937)
Eleanor of Woodstock (1318–1355)
Elena (b. 1963)
Eleonora of Austria (1534–1594)
Elisabeth of Habsburg (1554–1592)
Elisabeth of Saxe-Altenburg (1826–1896)
Elizabeth (1831–1903)
Elizabeth (fl. 1850s)
Elizabeth Bowes-Lyon (1900–2002)
Elizabeth-Charlotte (1676–1744)
Elizabeth Charlotte of the Palatinate (fl. 1620)
Elizabeth de Bourbon (1614–1664)
Elizabeth Frederike of Bayreuth (fl. 1750)
Elizabeth Hohenzollern (1815–1885)
Elizabeth Maria of Thurn and Taxis (1860–1881)
Elizabeth of Anhalt-Dessau (1857–1933)
Elizabeth of Bavaria (1876–1965)
Elizabeth of Bohemia (1358–1373)
Elizabeth of Brandenburg (1510–1558)
Elizabeth of Brunswick-Wolfenbuttel (1593–1650)
Elizabeth of Denmark (1524–1586)
Elizabeth of Denmark (1573–1626)
Elizabeth of Gorlitz (c. 1380–c. 1444)
Elizabeth of Habsburg (1293–1352)
Elizabeth of Hungary (fl. 1250s)
Elizabeth of Lancaster (1364–1425)
Elizabeth of Luxemburg (1409–1442)
Elizabeth of Nevers (fl. 1460)
Elizabeth of Poland (d. 1361)
Elizabeth of Savoy-Carignan (1800–1856)
Elizabeth of Saxe-Hildburghausen (1713–1761)
Elizabeth of Saxony (1830–1912)
Elizabeth of Sicily (d. 1349)
Elizabeth of Wurttemberg (1767–1790)
Elizabeth Plantagenet (1282–1316)
Elizabeth Sophie of Saxe-Altenburg (1619–1680)
Elizabeth von Habsburg (1883–1963)
Elvira (d. 1135)
Emma of Paris (d. 968)
Engelberga of Aquitaine (877–917)
Ermengarde of Anjou (1018–1076)
Ermengarde of Anjou (d. 1147)
Este, Beatrice d' (1475–1497)
Este, Catherine d' (fl. 1700)
Este, Lucrezia d' (1535–1598)
Este, Virginia d' (b. 1573?)
Estrées, Gabrielle d' (1573–1599)
Étampes, Anne de Pisseleu d'Heilly, Duchesse d' (1508–c. 1580)
Euphemia (1317–after 1336)
Fenton, Lavinia (1708–1760)
Ferguson, Sarah (1959—)
Fitzalan, Elizabeth (d. 1425)
Fitzroy, Mary (c. 1519–1557)
Folcheid (fl. 7th c.)
Francisca of Portugal (1800–1834)
Françoise d'Orleans (fl. 1650)
Françoise d'Orleans (1844–1925)
Frederica Amalie (1649–1704)
Frederica of Hesse-Darmstadt (1752–1782)
Frederica of Mecklenburg-Strelitz (1778–1841)
Frederica of Prussia (1767–1820)
Friederike of Hesse-Cassel (1722–1787)
Gerloc (d. 963)
Gertrude of Flanders (d. 1117)
Gertrude of Meissen (d. 1117)
Gertrude of Saxony (1115–1143)
Gisela Martel (d. 919)
Gisela of Burgundy (d. 1006)
Gonzaga, Anna Caterina (1566–1621)
Gonzaga, Barbara (1455–1505)
Gonzaga, Eleonora (1493–1543)
Gonzaga, Isabella (fl. 1600s)
Gonzaga, Margherita (1510–1566)
Gonzaga, Margherita (1561–1628)
Gonzaga, Margherita (1564–1618)
Gonzaga, Margherita (1591–1632)
Gunning, Elizabeth (1734–1790)
Gunnor of Denmark (d. 1031)
Guzman, Eleonore de (d. 1512)
Hamilton, Anne (1636–1716)
Hamilton, Mary (1613–1638)
Harcourt, Johanna (d. 1488)
Hawise of Brittany (d. 1072)
Hawise of Normandy (d. 1034)
Hayes, Nevada (1885–1941)
Hedwig (d. 903)
Hedwig (c. 915–965)
Hedwig of Silesia (1174–1243)
Hedwig Sophia (1681–1708)
Helena (1846–1923)
Helena of Russia (1882–1957)
Helene (1903–1924)
Helene Louise of Mecklenburg-Schwerin (1814–1858)
Helene of Brunswick-Luneburg (d. 1273)
Helene of Wurttemberg (1807–1873)

Helen of Denmark (d. 1233)
Helen of Nassau (1831–1888)
Helen of Waldeck and Pyrmont (1861–1922)
Helia de Semur (fl. 1020–1046)
Hemma of Bohemia (c. 930–c. 1005)
Henrietta Anne (1644–1670)
Henrietta of Belgium (1870–1948)
Henrietta of Cleves (r. 1564–1601)
Henrietta of Nassau-Weilburg (1780–1857)
Hildegarde of Bavaria (1825–1864)
Hildegarde of Swabia (fl. 1050)
Hildegard of Burgundy (1050–after 1104)
Holland, Joan (c. 1356–1384)
Holland, Joan (c. 1380–1434)
Horton, Ann (1743–1808)
Howard, Anne (1475–1511)
Howard, Elizabeth (1494–1558)
Howard, Margaret (fl. 1450)
Hyde, Anne (1638–1671)
Hyde, Catherine (1701–1777)
Hyde, Jane (d. 1725)
Ida de Macon (d. 1224)
Ida of Namur (fl. 12th c.)
Ida of Swabia (d. 986)
Ileana (1909–1991)
Ingeborg (c. 1300–c. 1360)
Ingeborg of Russia (fl. 1118–1131)
Irene (1904–1974)
Isabel (d. 1457?)
Isabel de Limoges (1283–1328)
Isabella of Braganza (1459–1521)
Isabella of Braganza (c. 1512–1576)
Isabella of Croy-Dulmen (1856–1931)
Isabella of Naples (1470–1524)
Isabella of Orleans (1878–1961)
Isabella of Portugal (1397–1471)
Isabelle of Lorraine (1410–1453)
Isabelle of Savoy (d. 1383)
Isabel of Aragon (1409–1443)
Isabel of Castile (1355–1392)
Jeanne de Laval (d. 1498)
Jeanne de Montfort (c. 1310–c. 1376)
Jeanne of Bourbon (1434–1482)
Jeanne of Nemours (1644–1724)
Joana de Mendoza (d. 1580)
Joan de Clare (c. 1268–after 1322)
Joan Holland (c. 1356–1384)
Joanna of Austria (1546–1578)
Joanna of Brabant (1322–1406)
Joan of Acre (1272–1307)
Joan of Hainault (c. 1310–?)
Joan Valois (1391–1433)
Johanna of Bavaria (c. 1373–1410)
Johanna of Pfirt (1300–1351)
Josephine-Charlotte of Belgium (1927—)
Judith of Bavaria (c. 925–987)
Judith of Bavaria (fl. 1120s)
Judith of Fiuli (fl. 910–925)
Judith of Flanders (1032–1094)
Judith of Rennes (c. 982–1018)
Karadjordjevic, Helen (1884–1962)
Katherine Plantagenet (1479–1527)
Keith, Muriel (d. 1449)
Kéroüalle, Louise de (1649–1734)
La Rochefoucauld, Edmée, Duchesse de (1895–1991)
La Vallière, Louise de (1644–1710)
Lefebvre, Catherine (c. 1764–after 1820)
Lennox, Emily (1731–1814)
Leonora of Aragon (1450–1493)
Leveson-Gower, Harriet Elizabeth Georgiana (1806–1868)
Leyburne, Elizabeth (d. 1567)
Liutgard of Saxony (d. 953)
Longueville, Anne Geneviève, Duchesse de (1619–1679)
Louisa Amelia (1773–1802)
Louisa Christina of Bavaria (fl. 1726)
Louisa Henrietta de Conti (1726–1759)
Louise (1848–1939)
Louise Augusta (1771–1843)
Louise Charlotte of Mecklenburg-Schwerin (1779–1801)
Louise de Brézé (fl. 1555)
Louise Elizabeth (1727–1759)
Louise Margaret of Prussia (1860–1917)
Louise Marie of Bourbon (1753–1821)
Louise of Baden (1838–1923)
Louise of Bourbon-Berry (1819–1864)
Louise of Denmark (1750–1831)
Louise of Hesse-Cassel (1688–1765)
Louise of Hesse-Darmstadt (d. 1830)
Louise of Hohenlohe-Langenburg (1763–1837)
Louise of Parma (1802–1857)
Louise of Savoy (1476–1531)
Louise of Saxe-Gotha (1756–1808)
Louise of Saxe-Gotha-Altenburg (1800–1831)
Louise Victoria (1867–1931)
Lucia (1908–2001)
Ludmila (859–920)
Ludmilla of Bohemia (fl. 1100s)
Luisa de Guzman (1613–1666)
Luisa Fernanda (1832–1897)
Lutgardis (fl. 1139)
Madeleine (b. 1982)
Madeleine de la Tour d'Auvergne (1501–1519)
Madeleine of Anhalt-Zerbst (1679–1740)
Magdalena Sybilla of Holstein-Gottorp (1631–1719)
Mancini, Hortense (1646–1699)
Mancini, Laure (1635–1657)
Mancini, Marie-Anne (1649–1714)
Margaret (1275–1318)
Margaret (c. 1320–1400)
Margaret (1395–1447)
Margaret (d. 1993)
Margaret de Burgh (c. 1193–1259)
Margaret Maultasch (1318–1369)
Margaret of Angoulême (1492–1549)
Margaret of Austria (1480–1530)
Margaret of Babenberg (fl. 1252)
Margaret of Baden (1932—)
Margaret of Bavaria (fl. 1390–1410)
Margaret of Bavaria (d. 1424)
Margaret of Bavaria (1445–1479)
Margaret of Bourbon (d. 1483)
Margaret of Brandenburg (c. 1450–1489)
Margaret of Burgundy (d. 1441)
Margaret of Cleves (fl. early 1400s)
Margaret of Flanders (d. 1285)
Margaret of Flanders (1350–1405)
Margaret of Huntingdon (c. 1140–1201)
Margaret of Limburg (d. 1172)
Margaret of Lorraine (1463–1521)
Margaret of Parma (1522–1586)
Margaret of Parma (b. 1612)
Margaret of Parma (1847–1893)
Margaret of Savoy (1523–1574)
Margaret of Savoy (fl. 1609–1612)
Margaret of Saxony (c. 1416–1486)
Margaret of Saxony (1469–1528)
Margaret of Valois (1553–1615)
Margaret of Vendôme (fl. 16th c.)
Margaret of York (1446–1503)
Margaret Sophie (1870–1902)
Margaret Wake of Liddell (c. 1299–1349)
Marguerite de Foix (fl. 1456–1477)
Marguerite Louise of Orleans (c. 1645–1721)
Marguerite of Lorraine (c. 1561–?)
Marguerite of Lorraine (fl. 1632)
Maria Amalia (1746–1804)
Maria Anna of Saxony (1795–1865)
Maria Anna of Saxony (1799–1832)
Maria Annunziata (1843–1871)
Maria Antonia of Austria (1683–1754)
Maria Antonia of Portugal (1862–1959)
Maria Antonia of Sicily (1814–1898)
Maria Antonia of Spain (1729–1785)
Maria Augusta of Thurn and Taxis (1706–1756)
Maria Beatrice of Modena (1750–1829)
Maria Beatrice of Sardinia (1792–1840)
Maria Carolina (1752–1814)
Maria Christina (1742–1798)
Maria Christina of Saxony (1779–1851)
Maria Cristina of Sicily (1877–1947)
Maria dal Pozzo (fl. 19th c.)
Maria del Pilar (1936—)
Maria Dorothea of Austria (1867–1932)
Maria Eleanora (1550–1608)
Maria Immaculata (1878–1968)
Maria Immaculata of Sicily (1844–1899)
Maria Josepha of Saxony (1867–1944)
Maria Louisa of Spain (1745–1792)
Maria Luisa of Etruria (1782–1824)
Maria Magdalena of Austria (1589–1631)
Maria Nikolaevna (1819–1876)
Maria of Bavaria (1872–1954)
Maria of Julich-Berg (fl. 1515)
Maria of Mecklenburg-Schwerin (1854–1920)
Maria of Portugal (1538–1577)
Maria of Savoy (fl. 1400s)
Maria of Wurttemberg (1797–1855)
Maria Sophia Amalia (1841–1925)
Maria Theresa of Portugal (1855–1944)
Maria Theresa of Tuscany (1801–1855)
Marie (1899–1918)
Marie Adelaide of Luxemburg (1894–1924)
Marie Adelaide of Savoy (1685–1712)
Marie Alexandrovna (1853–1920)
Marie-Anne de la Trémouille (c. 1642–1722)
Marie de Bourbon (fl. 1440s)
Marie de Bourbon (1606–1627)
Marie d'Orleans (1813–1839)
Marie Elizabeth of Saxony (1610–1684)
Marie Laetitia (1866–1890)
Marie Louise (1695–1719)
Marie Louise d'Orleans (1750–1822)
Marie Louise of Austria (1791–1847)
Marie Melita of Hohenlohe-Langenburg (1899–1967)
Marie of Baden (1817–1888)
Marie of Brandenburg-Kulmbach (1519–1567)
Marie of Cleves (1426–1486)
Marie of Dreux (1391–1446)
Marie of Evreux (d. 1335)
Marie of France (1198–c. 1223)
Marie of Guelders (1325–1399)
Marie of Luxemburg (fl. 16th c.)
Marie of Mecklenburg-Gustrow (1659–1701)
Marie Pavlovna (1786–1859)
Marie Pavlovna (1890–1958)
Marie Thérèse Charlotte (1778–1851)
Marie Valerie (1868–1924)
Marina of Greece (1906–1968)
Martelli, Camilla (fl. 1570s)
Martinozzi, Laura (fl. 1658)
Mary (1531–1581)
Mary (1776–1857)
Mary Adelaide (1833–1897)
Mary de Monthermer (1298–after 1371)
Mary-Elizabeth of Padua (1782–1808)
Mary of Bavaria (1551–1608)
Mary of Burgundy (c. 1400–1463)
Mary of Burgundy (d. 1428)
Mary of Burgundy (1457–1482)
Mary of Guelders (d. 1405)
Mary of Guise (1515–1560)
Mary of Hesse-Cassel (1796–1880)

Mary of Teck (1867–1953)
Mary of Wurttemberg (1799–1860)
Mary Tudor (1496–1533)
Mathilda (1925–1997)
Mathilde de Mayenne (fl. 12th c.)
Mathilde of Belgium (1973—)
Matilda (fl. 1100s)
Matilda (1813–1862)
Matilda of Anjou (1107–1154)
Matilda of Brandenburg (d. 1261)
Matilda of England (1156–1189)
Matilda of Habsburg (1251–1304)
Maude of Alsace (1163–c. 1210)
Medici, Anna Maria de (d. 1741)
Medici, Caterina de (1593–1629)
Medici, Claudia de (1604–1648)
Medici, Eleonora de (1522–1562)
Medici, Eleonora de (1567–1611)
Medici, Vittoria de (d. 1694)
Mellon, Harriot (c. 1777–1837)
Michelle Valois (1394–1422)
Mitford, Deborah (1920—)
Mohun, Philippa (d. 1431)
Montacute, Alice (c. 1406–1463)
Montacute, Anne (d. 1457)
Montagu-Douglas-Scott, Alice (1901–2004)
Montefeltro, Elisabetta (fl. 15th c.)
Montesson, Charlotte Jeanne Béraud de la Haye de Riou, marquise de (1737–1805)
Montpensier, Anne Marie Louise d'Orléans, Duchesse de (1627–1693)
Mowbray, Anne (1472–1481)
Muir, Elizabeth (d. before 1355)
Murray, Elizabeth (1626–1698)
Nadejda of Bulgaria (1899–1958)
Nemours, Marie d'Orleans, duchess de (c. 1625–1707)
Neville, Anne (d. 1480)
Neville, Catherine (fl. 1460)
Neville, Cecily (1415–1495)
Neville, Isabel (1451–1476)
Neville, Margaret (c. 1377–c. 1424)
Neville, Margaret (b. 1466)
Nicole of Lorraine (c. 1608–1657)
Noailles, Anne Claude Laurence, duchesse de (d. 1793)
Noailles, Marie-Laure de (1902–1970)
Oda of Germany and North Marck (fl. 900s)
Olga (1895–1918)
Olga Alexandrovna (1882–1960)
Olga of Russia (1822–1892)
Paca (1825–1860)
Papia of Envermeu (fl. 1020)
Pauline of Saxe-Weimar (1852–1904)
Pauline of Wurttemberg (1810–1856)
Percy, Eleanor (d. 1530)
Percy, Elizabeth (1667–1722)
Percy, Elizabeth (1716–1776)
Philiberta of Savoy (c. 1498–1524)
Philippa de Rouergue (c. 1074–1118)
Philippa of Guelders (d. 1547)
Philippine Charlotte (1716–1801)
Pia of Sicily (1849–1882)
Pole, Elizabeth de la (1444–1503)
Polignac, Yolande Martine Gabrielle de (1749–1793)
Pompadour, Jeanne-Antoinette Poisson, Duchesse de (1721–1764)
Poppa of Normandy (fl. 880)
Regintrud (fl. 8th c.)
Renée of France (1510–1575)
Renée of Montpensier (fl. 1500s)
Rohan-Montbazon, Marie de (1600–1679)
Romanov, Catherine (1827–1894)
Romanov, Elizabeth (1826–1845)
Romanov, Natalya (1674–1716)
Rosa (1906–1983)
Rovere, Giulia della (fl. 16th c.)
Russell, Mary du Caurroy (1865–1937)
Sabine of Bavaria (1492–1564)
Sancha of Provence (c. 1225–1261)
Sarolta (fl. 900s)
Schulenburg, Ehrengard Melusina von der (1667–1743)
Scott, Anne (1651–1731)
Seymour, Frances Thynne (1699–1754)
Seymour, Georgiana (d. 1884)
Sforza, Anna (1473–1497)
Sforza, Battista (1446–1472)
Sforza, Bona (1493–1557)
Sibylle of Anhalt (1564–1614)
Sibylle of Brunswick-Luneburg (1584–1652)
Sibylle of Burgundy (1065–1102)
Sichelgaita of Salerno (1040–1090)
Sinclair, Catherine (fl. 1475)
Somerset, Henrietta (d. 1726)
Sophia (fl. 1500s)
Sophia (1630–1714)
Sophia Dorothea of Brandenburg (1736–1798)
Sophia Dorothea of Brunswick-Celle (1666–1726)
Sophia Dorothea of Wurttemberg (1759–1828)
Sophia of Malines (d. 1329)
Sophia of Mecklenburg (1508–1541)
Sophia of Nassau (1824–1897)
Sophia of Sweden (1801–1865)
Sophia of Thuringia (1224–1284)
Sophie Charlotte of Oldenburg (1879–1964)
Sophie of Bavaria (1805–1872)
Sophie of Bayern (1847–1897)
Sophie of Holstein-Gottorp (1569–1634)
Sophie of Hungary (d. 1095)
Stafford, Anne (d. 1472)
Stafford, Elizabeth (1494–1558)
Stanhope, Anne (1497–1587)
Stephanie de Beauharnais (1789–1860)
Stewart, Eleanor (1427–1496)
Stewart, Isabel (d. 1494)
Stewart, Mary (d. 1465)
Stewart-Murray, Katharine (1874–1960)
Stuart, Frances (1647–1702)
Suzanne of Bourbon (1491–1521)
Swynford, Catherine (c. 1350–1403)
Sybilla of Brandenburg (fl. 1500)
Sybilla of Saxe-Coburg-Gotha (1908–1972)
Sybil of Conversano (d. 1103)
Talbot, Anne (d. 1440)
Talbot, Elizabeth (d. around 1506)
Talvace, Adela (d. 1174)
Tatiana (1897–1918)
Telles, Maria (d. 1379)
Teresa of Portugal (1793–1874)
Theresa of Savoy (1803–1879)
Therese of Nassau (1815–1871)
Thyra Oldenburg (1853–1933)
Tiedemann, Charlotte (1919–1979)
Tylney, Agnes (1476–1545)
Ulfhild of Denmark (d. before 1070)
Ursula of Brandenburg (1488–1510)
Uta of Passau (fl. 11th c.)
Vanderbilt, Consuelo (1877–1964)
van Deurs, Brigitte (1946—)
Vera Constantinovna (1854–1912)
Victoria (1977—)
Victoria Adelaide of Schleswig-Holstein (1885–1970)
Victoria Louise (1892–1980)
Victoria Melita of Saxe-Coburg (1876–1936)
Victoria of Coburg (1786–1861)
Victoria of Saxe-Coburg (1822–1857)
Villiers, Barbara (c. 1641–1709)
Villiers, Frances (c. 1633–1677)
Visconti, Bianca Maria (1423–1470)
Visconti, Catherine (c. 1360–1404)
Visconti, Elizabeth (d. 1432)
Visconti, Thaddaea (d. 1381)
Visconti, Valentina (1366–1408)
Visconti, Violet (c. 1353–1386)
Visconti, Virida (c. 1354–1414)
Walpole, Maria (1736–1807)
Wellesley, Dorothy (1889–1956)
Wilhelmine of Baden (1788–1836)
Wilmot, Olivia (d. 1774)
Windsor, Wallis Warfield, duchess of (1895–1986)
Wolfida of Saxony (c. 1075–1126)
Woodville, Katherine (c. 1442–1512)
Worsley, Katherine (1933—)
Wuldetrada of the Lombards (fl. 6th c.)
Xenia Alexandrovna (1876–1960)
Yolanda of Gnesen (d. 1299)
Yolande de Dreux (d. 1238)
Yolande of Aragon (1379–1442)
Yolande of France (1434–1478)
Yolande of Vaudemont (1428–1483)

DUELIST

Maupin, d'Aubigny (c. 1670–1707)

EARTH SCIENTIST

Alexander, Annie Montague (1867–1949)
Anning, Mary (1799–1847)
Bascom, Florence (1862–1945)
Benett, Etheldred (1776–1845)
Bingham, Millicent Todd (1880–1968)
Boyd, Louise Arner (1887–1972)
Curtis, Doris Malkin (1914–1991)
Edinger, Tilly (1897–1967)
Lehmann, Inge (1888–1993)
Lyell, Mary Horner (1808–1873)
Sears, Mary (1905–1997)
Semple, Ellen Churchill (1863–1932)
Watson, Janet Vida (1923–1985)

ECOLOGIST

Braun, E. Lucy (1889–1971)
Colborn, Theodora (1927—)
Dormon, Carrie (1888–1971)
Jorge Pádua, Maria Tereza (1943—)
Maathai, Wangari (1940—)
Patrick, Ruth (1907—)

ECONOMIST

Bailey, Elizabeth (1938—)
Beck, Audrey P. (1931–1983)
Boserup, Esther (1910–1999)
Campbell, Persia (1898–1974)
Çiller, Tansu (1946—)
Collet, Clara (1860–1948)
Coman, Katharine (1857–1915)
Cooper, Yvette (1969—)
Cresson, Edith (1934—)
Dewson, Molly (1874–1962)
Dickason, Gladys (1903–1971)
Dreifuss, Ruth (1940—)
Dulles, Eleanor Lansing (1895–1996)
Groza, Maria (1918—)
Hogg, Sarah (1946—)
Jensen, Anne Elisabet (1951—)
Kelly, Ruth (1968—)
Kock, Karin (1891–1976)
Kreps, Juanita (1921—)
Kyrk, Hazel (1886–1957)
Luxemburg, Rosa (1870–1919)
Lyall, Katharine C. (1941—)
McCoubrey, Margaret (1880–1955)
Peixotto, Jessica (1864–1941)
Quinn, Jane Bryant (1939—)
Robinson, Joan Violet (1903–1983)

Occupational Index

Rochester, Anna (1880–1966)
Schwartz, Anna Jacobson (1915—)
Scrivener, Christiane (1925—)
Sender, Toni (1888–1964)
Switzer, Mary E. (1900–1971)
Teeters, Nancy Hays (1930—)
Ward, Barbara (1914–1981)
Wolfson, Theresa (1897–1972)
Woodhouse, Margaret Chase Going (1890–1984)
Wootton, Barbara (1897–1988)
Zaslavskaya, Tatyana (1924—)

EDITOR
See Book editor.
See Crossword-puzzle editor.
See Film editor.
See Information-services editor.
See Newspaper editor.
See Periodical editor.
See Publishing-house editor.
See Television/radio editor.

EDUCATION ADMINISTRATOR
See College/university administrator.
See School administrator.

EDUCATIONAL INSTITUTION/ PROGRAM FOUNDER
Agassiz, Elizabeth Cary (1822–1907)
Alabaster, Ann O'Connor (1842–1915)
Aldecoa, Josefina R. (1926—)
Anderson, Elizabeth Garrett (1836–1917)
Anneke, Mathilde Franziska (1817–1884)
Arbuthnot, May Hill (1884–1969)
Augspurg, Anita (1857–1943)
Bacon, Alice Mabel (1858–1918)
Barbauld, Anna Letitia (1743–1825)
Barnes, Mary Downing (1850–1898)
Barton, Clara (1821–1912)
Baur, Clara (1835–1912)
Bayne, Margaret (1798–1835)
Beecher, Catharine (1800–1878)
Beere, Thekla (1901–1991)
Benizelos, Philothey (fl. 1650)
Bernays, Marie (1883–1939)
Besant, Annie (1847–1933)
Bethune, Joanne (1770–1860)
Bethune, Mary McCleod (1875–1955)
Bettis, Valerie (1919–1982)
Bews, Mary Ellen (1856–1945)
Bijns, Anna (1493/94–1575)
Bishop, Hazel (1906–1998)
Blackwell, Elizabeth (1821–1910)
Blaine, Anita McCormick (1866–1954)
Blaker, Eliza Ann (1854–1926)
Bliss, Anna (1843–1925)
Bocanegra, Gertrudis (1765–1817)
Booth, Ellen Scripps (1863–1948)
Brackett, Anna Callender (1836–1911)
Brown, Charlotte Hawkins (c. 1883–1961)
Brunschvicg, Cécile (1877–1946)
Bühler, Charlotte (1893–1974)
Butler, Mother Marie Joseph (1860–1940)
Buxton, Mary Ann (c. 1795–1888)
Byers, Margaret (1832–1912)
Cabrini, Frances Xavier (1850–1917)
Calkins, Mary Whiton (1863–1930)
Carter, Betty (1929–1998)
Cary, Mary Ann Shadd (1823–1893)
Chisholm, Caroline (1808–1877)
Clare, Elizabeth de (1295–1360)
Cohn, Fannia (c. 1885–1962)
Collett, Camilla (1813–1895)
Cooke, Flora (1864–1953)
Cosway, Maria (1759–1838)
Crandall, Prudence (1803–1890)
Crosby, Fanny (1820–1915)
Cross, Joan (1900–1993)
Davies, Gwendoline (1882–1951)
Davies, Margaret (1884–1963)
Day, Dorothy (1897–1980)
Deroin, Jeanne-Françoise (1805–1894)
de Valois, Ninette (1898–2001)
Dewey, Alice Chipman (1858–1927)
Dexter, Caroline (1819–1884)
Diller, Angela (1877–1968)
Duniway, Abigail Scott (1834–1915)
Einstein-Marić, Mileva (1875–1948)
Elizabeth of Portugal (1271–1336)
Elizabeth Petrovna (1709–1762)
Erskine, Mary (1629–1707)
Falconer, Martha Platt (1862–1941)
Farrar, Cynthia (1795–1862)
Fearn, Anne Walter (1865–1939)
Ferguson, Abbie Park (1837–1919)
Fogerty, Elsie (1865–1945)
Franca, Celia (1921—)
Fuld, Carrie (1864–1944)
Gayatri Devi (1919—)
Gilligan, Carol (1936—)
Goldsmith, Grace Arabell (1904–1975)
Goldthwaite, Anne Wilson (1869–1944)
Goodall, Jane (1934—)
Grey, Maria Georgina (1816–1906)
Griffith, Emily (c. 1880–1947)
Guilbert, Yvette (1865–1944)
Gulick, Alice Gordon (1847–1903)
Gulick, Charlotte Vetter (1865–1928)
Gund, Agnes (1938—)
Hagman, Lucina (1853–1946)
Hani, Motoko (1873–1957)
Hastings, Selina (1707–1791)
Heymann, Lida (1867–1943)
Hill, Frances Mulligan (1799–1884)
Hobson, Elizabeth Christophers (1831–1912)
Holley, Sallie (1818–1893)
Horney, Karen (1885–1952)
Huxley, Julia Arnold (1862–1908)
Hyslop, Beatrice Fry (1899–1973)
Irwin, Elisabeth (1880–1942)
Jadwiga (1374–1399)
Jameson, Storm (1891–1986)
Jellicoe, Anne (1823–1880)
Jex-Blake, Sophia (1840–1912)
Joan I of Navarre (1273–1305)
Joyner, Marjorie Stewart (1896–1994)
Kanakaole, Edith K. (1913–1979)
Kartini (1879–1904)
Katznelson, Shulamit (1919–1999)
Kaur, Rajkumari Amrit (1889–1964)
Kelley, Florence (1859–1932)
Kelsey, Lavinia Jane (1856–1948)
Kennard, Olga (1924—)
Kennedy, Florynce (1916–2000)
Kenyon, Kathleen (1906–1978)
King, Coretta Scott (1927—)
Kohut, Rebekah (1864–1951)
Kraus-Boelté, Maria (1836–1918)
Kroeger, Alice (1864–1909)
Lacore, Suzanne (1875–1975)
Landowska, Wanda (1877–1959)
Lane, Rose Wilder (1886–1968)
Laney, Lucy Craft (1854–1933)
Lange, Elizabeth Clovis (1784–1882)
Lange, Helene (1848–1930)
Lenglen, Suzanne (1899–1938)
Leontovich, Eugénie (1894–1993)
Lewis, Elma (1921—)
Lloyd, Alice (1876–1962)
Lockwood, Belva Ann (1830–1917)
Long, Marguerite (1874–1966)
Love, Susan (1948—)
Loveridge, Emily Lemoine (1860–1941)
Löwenstein, Helga Maria zu (1910–2004)
Lozier, Clemence S. (1813–1888)
Lubic, Ruth Watson (1927—)
Lyon, Mary (1797–1849)
Lytle, Nancy A. (1924–1987)
Macleod, Charlotte (1852–1950)
Mannes, Clara Damrosch (1869–1948)
Margaret of Anjou (1429–1482)
Marie de St. Pol (1304–1377)
Martin, Anne Henrietta (1875–1951)
Marwedel, Emma (1818–1893)
Maynor, Dorothy (1910–1996)
Maywood, Augusta (1825–1876)
McAllister, Anne Hunter (1892–1983)
McCormick, Edith Rockefeller (1872–1932)
McCormick, Katharine Dexter (1875–1967)
McCormick, Ruth Hanna (1880–1944)
McGroarty, Sister Julia (1827–1901)
McKane, Alice Woodby (1865–1948)
McLaren, Louise Leonard (1885–1968)
McMillan, Rachel (1859–1917)
Meyer, Lucy (1849–1922)
Michel, Louise (1830–1905)
Milbanke, Anne (1792–1860)
Mills, Susan Tolman (1825–1912)
Miner, Myrtilla (1815–1864)
Mireille (1906–1996)
Montespan, Françoise, Marquise de (1640–1707)
Montessori, Maria (1870–1952)
Moody, Emma Revell (1842–1903)
Morgan, Mary Kimball (1861–1948)
Morgenstern, Lina B. (1830–1909)
Mosher, Eliza Maria (1846–1928)
Mulally, Teresa (1728–1803)
Myrdal, Alva (1902–1986)
Noyes, Clara Dutton (1869–1936)
Nzimiro, Mary (1898–1993)
Page, Ruth (1899–1991)
Palmer, Lizzie Merrill (1838–1916)
Palmer, Sophia French (1853–1920)
Palucca, Gret (1902–1993)
Paradis, Maria Theresia von (1759–1824)
Parkhurst, Helen (1887–1973)
Peabody, Elizabeth Palmer (1804–1894)
Peebles, Florence (1874–1956)
Pennington, Mary Engle (1872–1952)
Peter, Sarah Worthington (1800–1877)
Phule, Savitribai (1831–1897)
Porter, Sarah (1813–1900)
Post, Emily (1872–1960)
Powdermaker, Hortense (1896–1970)
Prout, Mary Ann (1801–1884)
Purser, Sarah (1848–1943)
Quimby, Edith (1891–1982)
Ramabai, Pandita (1858–1922)
Ransome-Kuti, Funmilayo (1900–1978)
Russell, Dora (1894–1986)
Salomon, Alice (1872–1948)
Sappho (c. 612–c. 557 BCE)
Sartain, Emily (1841–1927)
Scharrer, Berta (1906–1995)
Schurz, Margarethe Meyer (1833–1876)
Scudder, Ida (1870–1960)
Sears, Mary (1905–1997)
Semple, Ellen Churchill (1863–1932)
Sewall, May Wright (1844–1920)
Shaw, Pauline Agassiz (1841–1917)
Sill, Anna Peck (1816–1889)
Smith, Sophia (1796–1870)
Sosipatra (fl. 4th c.)
Spry, Constance (1886–1960)
St. Denis, Ruth (1877–1968)
Stasova, Nadezhda (1822–1895)

Stetson, Augusta (1842–1928)
Stevens, Georgia Lydia (1870–1946)
Stevenson, Sarah Hackett (1841–1909)
Stockton, Betsey (c. 1798–1865)
Stopes, Marie (1880–1958)
Sutliffe, Irene H. (1850–1936)
Szold, Henrietta (1860–1945)
Taylor, Janet (1804–1870)
Thebom, Blanche (1918—)
Theodoropoulou, Avra (1880–1963)
Thomas, M. Carey (1857–1935)
Thompson, Clara (1893–1958)
Thompson, Mary Harris (1829–1895)
Thurston, Matilda (1875–1958)
Tolstoy, Alexandra (1884–1979)
Towne, Laura Matilda (1825–1901)
Trocmé, Magda (1901–1996)
Tureck, Rosalyn (1914—)
Vakalo, Eleni (1921—)
Victoria Adelaide (1840–1901)
Volkova, Vera (1904–1975)
Wallmann, Margarethe (1901–19922)
Washington, Olivia Davidson (1854–1889)
Watteville, Benigna von (1725–1789)
Weir, Irene (1862–1944)
Weiss, Louise (1893–1983)
West, Winifred (1881–1971)
Wheelock, Lucy (1857–1946)
White, Edna Noble (1879–1954)
White, Ellen Gould (1827–1915)
Whittelsey, Abigail Goodrich (1788–1858)
Willard, Emma Hart (1787–1870)
Williams, Fannie Barrier (1855–1944)
Willing, Jennie Fowler (1834–1916)
Wormeley, Katharine Prescott (1830–1908)
Wright, Helen (1914–1997)
Wright, Mary Clabaugh (1917–1970)
Wright, Sophie Bell (1866–1912)
Yale, Caroline A. (1848–1933)
Zakrzewska, Marie (1829–1902)

EDUCATIONAL PSYCHOLOGIST
Height, Dorothy (1912—)
Hollingworth, Leta Stetter (1886–1939)
Jones, Margo (1911–1955)
Pringle, Mia Lilly (1920–1983)
Zachry, Caroline B. (1894–1945)

EDUCATION REFORMER
Abbott, Maude (1869–1940)
Beale, Dorothea (1831–1906)
Bevier, Isabel (1860–1942)
Bose, Abala (1865–1951)
Calderone, Mary Steichen (1904–1998)
Cavendish, Lucy Caroline (1841–1925)
Colton, Elizabeth Avery (1872–1924)
Crocker, Lucretia (1829–1886)
Dalrymple, Learmonth White (1827–1906)
Dunlop, Florence (c. 1896–1963)
Edger, Kate (1857–1935)
England, Maud Russell (1863–1956)
Erskine, Mary (1629–1707)
Fewings, Eliza Anne (1857–1940)
Fraser, Mary Isabel (1863–1942)
Grey, Maria Georgina (1816–1906)
Gruenberg, Sidonie (1881–1974)
Harrison, Elizabeth (1849–1927)
Hatcher, Orie Latham (1868–1946)
Hill, Patty Smith (1868–1946)
Hossain, Rokeya Sakhawat (1880–1932)
Jellicoe, Anne (1823–1880)
Jex-Blake, Sophia (1840–1912)
Ladd-Franklin, Christine (1847–1930)
Lange, Helene (1848–1930)
Macaulay, Catharine (1731–1791)
McMillan, Rachel (1859–1917)
Miner, Myrtilla (1815–1864)
Montessori, Maria (1870–1952)
Mumford, Mary Bassett (1842–1935)
Mussey, Ellen Spencer (1850–1936)
Myers, Phoebe (1866–1947)
Pantoja, Antonia (1922–2002)
Peabody, Elizabeth Palmer (1804–1894)
Putnam, Alice Whiting (1841–1919)
Schurz, Margarethe Meyer (1833–1876)
Schwarzwald, Eugenie (1872–1940)
Shabazz, Betty (1936–1997)
Shaw, Pauline Agassiz (1841–1917)
Spencer, Cornelia Phillips (1825–1908)
Stern, Catherine Brieger (1894–1973)
Takács, Eva (1779–1845)
Teleki, Blanka (1806–1862)
Thomas, M. Carey (1857–1935)
Ticknor, Anna Eliot (1823–1896)
Valentine, Lila (1865–1921)
Valentine, Winifred Annie (1886–1968)
Wiggin, Kate Douglas (1856–1923)
Wolstenholme-Elmy, Elizabeth (1834–1913)
Woolley, Mary E. (1863–1947)
Wootton, Barbara (1897–1988)
Wordsworth, Elizabeth (1840–1932)

EDUCATOR
See Acting teacher.
See Art teacher.
See Athletic coach/instructor.
See Aviation instructor.
See Ballet teacher.
See College/university professor/instructor/lecturer.
See Culinary arts teacher.
See Decorative arts teacher.
See Fine arts teacher.
See Medical/Health educator.

EGYPTOLOGIST
Caton-Thompson, Gertrude (1888–1985)
Drower, Margaret S. (c. 1913—)
Eady, Dorothy (1904–1981)
Edwards, Amelia B. (1831–1892)
Murray, Margaret (1863–1963)
Rambova, Natacha (1897–1966)

ELECTRESS
Agnes of Habsburg (c. 1257–1322)
Agnes of Hesse (1527–1555)
Anna Constancia (1619–1651)
Anna of Denmark (1532–1585)
Anna of Prussia (1576–1625)
Anna of Prussia
Anna Sophia of Denmark (1647–1717)
Anne of Saxony (1437–1512)
Caroline of Baden (1776–1841)
Catherine of Custrin (1549–1602)
Catherine of Saxony (1421–1476)
Cunegunde (d. 1357)
Cunigunde Sobieska (fl. 1690s)
Dorothea of Denmark (1520–1580)
Eleonore Hohenzollern (1583–1607)
Elizabeth Amalia of Hesse (1635–1709)
Elizabeth Charlotte of the Palatinate (fl. 1620)
Elizabeth of Anhalt (1563–1607)
Elizabeth of Bavaria-Landshut (1383–1442)
Elizabeth of Bohemia (1596–1662)
Elizabeth of Denmark (1485–1555)
Elizabeth of Wittelsbach (1540–1594)
Hedwig of Denmark (1581–1641)
Hedwig of Poland (1513–1573)
Henrietta of Savoy (c. 1630–?)
Louisa Henrietta of Orange (1627–1667)
Louisa Juliana (1576–1644)
Ludovica (1808–1892)
Magdalena Sybilla (1587–1659)
Margaret of Saxony (c. 1416–1486)
Margaret of Saxony (1449–1501)
Maria Anna of Bavaria (1610–1665)
Maria Antonia (1669–1692)
Maria Antonia of Austria (1724–1780)
Maria Leopoldina (1776–1848)
Mariana Victoria (1768–1788)
Marie of Brandenburg-Kulmbach (1519–1567)
Medici, Anna Maria Luisa de (1667–1743)
Sabine of Brandenburg-Ansbach (1529–1575)
Sibylle Elizabeth of Wurttemberg (1584–1606)
Sophia (1630–1714)
Sophia Dorothea of Brunswick-Celle (1666–1726)
Sophie of Brandenburg (1568–1622)
Wilhelmine (1650–1706)
Wilhelmine (1747–1820)

ELECTRICAL ENGINEER
Ayrton, Hertha Marks (1854–1923)
Clarke, Edith (1883–1959)
Haslett, Caroline (1895–1957)
Laverick, Elizabeth (1925—)
MacGill, Elsie (d. 1980)
Manoliu, Lia (1932–1998)
Ochoa, Ellen (1958—)
Partridge, Margaret (b. 1891)
Peden, Irene (1925—)
Resnik, Judith (1949–1986)

EMBROIDERER
Angus, Dorothy (1891–1979)
Mabel of Bury St. Edmunds (fl. 1230)
MacDonald, Frances (1874–1921)
Mackintosh, Margaret (1865–1933)
Morris, May (1862–1938)
Tauber-Arp, Sophie (1889–1943)
Whyte, Kathleen (1909–1996)
Yeats, Lily (1866–1949)
Zorach, Marguerite Thompson (1887–1968)

EMBRYOLOGIST
Beddington, Rosa (1956–2001)
Gage, Susanna Phelps (1857–1915)
Harvey, Ethel Browne (1885–1965)
Hay, Elizabeth Dexter (1927—)

EMPLOYMENT AGENT
Howard, Caroline Cadette (1821–?)

EMPRESS
Adelaide of Burgundy (931–999)
Adelaide of Kiev (c. 1070–1109)
Agnes-Anne of France (b. 1171)
Agnes of Poitou (1024–1077)
Albia Domnica (fl. 4th c.)
Alexandra Feodorovna (1872–1918)
Amelia of Leuchtenburg (1812–1873)
Anastasia (fl. 600s)
Anastasia Romanova (d. 1560)
Anna Angelina (d. 1210?)
Anna Dalassena (c. 1025–1105)
Anna Ivanovna (1693–1740)
Anna Maria of the Palatinate (1561–1589)
Anna of Bohemia and Hungary (1503–1547)
Anna of Byzantium (fl. 901)
Anna of Hohenberg (c. 1230–1281)
Anna of Hungary (d. around 1284)
Anna of Schweidnitz (c. 1340–?)
Anna of the Palatinate (fl. 1300s)
Anne of Savoy (c. 1320–1353)
Ariadne (fl. 457–515)
Augusta of Saxe-Weimar (1811–1890)
Augusta of Schleswig-Holstein (1858–1921)
Barca-Theodosia (fl. 800s)
Beatrice of Anjou (d. 1275)
Beatrice of Silesia (fl. 1300s)

Beatrice of Upper Burgundy (1145–1184)
Berengaria of Castile (b. around 1199)
Bertha-Eudocia the Frank (fl. 900s)
Bertha-Irene of Sulzbach (d. 1161)
Bertha of Savoy (1051–1087)
Blanche of Valois (c. 1316–?)
Bruttia Crispina (d. 185)
Carlota (1840–1927)
Catherine I (1684–1727)
Catherine II the Great (1729–1796)
Catherine of Bulgaria (fl. 1050)
Catherine of Tarento (fl. early 1300s)
Chabi (fl. 13th c.)
Charito (fl. 300s)
Charlotte of Prussia (1798–1860)
Cixi (1835–1908)
Constance (d. 305 CE)
Constance-Anna of Hohenstaufen (fl. 13th century)
Constance of Aragon (d. 1222)
Constance of Sicily (1154–1198)
Constantia (c. 293–?)
Constantina (c. 321–c. 354)
Constantina (fl. 582–602)
Cunigunde (d. 1040?)
Cunigunde of Swabia (fl. 900s)
Deng (r. 105–121)
Dolgorukova, Marie (d. 1625)
Edgitha (c. 912–946)
Eleanor of Pfalz-Neuburg (1655–1720)
Eleanor of Portugal (1434–1467)
Elizabeth Christina of Brunswick-Wolfenbuttel (1691–1750)
Elizabeth of Baden (1779–1826)
Elizabeth of Bavaria (1837–1898)
Elizabeth of Pomerania (1347–1393)
Elizabeth Petrovna (1709–1762)
Engelberga (c. 840–890)
Ermengarde (c. 778–818)
Eudocia (c. 400–460)
Eudocia (fl. 700s)
Eudocia Angelina (fl. 1204)
Eudocia Baiane (d. 902)
Eudocia Decapolita (fl. 800s)
Eudocia Ingerina (fl. 800s)
Eudocia Macrembolitissa (1021–1096)
Eudocia of Byzantium (d. 404)
Eudoxia Lopukhina (1669–1731)
Eudoxia Streshnev (1608–1645)
Eugénie (1826–1920)
Euphrosyne (c. 790–840)
Euphrosyne (d. 1203)
Eusebia of Macedonia (fl. 300)
Eutropia (fl. 270–300)
Fabia-Eudocia (fl. 600s)
Fausta (d. 324)
Fausta (fl. 600s)
Faustina I (c. 90–141)
Faustina II (130–175)
Faustina of Antioch (fl. 300s)
Flaccilla (c. 355–386)
Fulvia (c. 85/80–40 BCE)
Galla (fl. 320)
Galla (c. 365–394)
Gemmei (c. 661–721)
Gertrude of Sulzbach (d. 1146)
Gisela of Swabia (d. 1043)
Godunova, Irene (d. 1603)
Gonzaga, Anna (1585–1618)
Gonzaga, Eleonora I (1598–1655)
Gonzaga, Eleonora II (1628–1686)
Go-Sakuramachi (1740–1814)
Gregoria-Anastasia (fl. 640s)
Grushevski, Agraphia (1662–1681)
Haruko (1850–1914)
Helena (c. 255–329)
Helena (c. 320–?)
Helena Cantacuzene (fl. 1340s)
Helena Dragas (fl. 1400)
Helena Lekapena (c. 920–961)
Helena of Alypia (fl. 980s)
Helen Asen of Bulgaria (d. 1255?)
Ino-Anastasia (fl. 575–582)
Irene (fl. 700s)
Irene Angela of Byzantium (d. 1208)
Irene Asen (fl. 1300s)
Irene Ducas (c. 1066–1133)
Irene Lascaris (fl. 1222–1235)
Irene of Athens (c. 752–803)
Irene of Brunswick (fl. 1300s)
Irene of Montferrat (fl. 1300)
Irene of the Khazars (d. 750?)
Irmengard (c. 800–851)
Isabella of Aragon (c. 1300–1330)
Isabella of England (1214–1241)
Isabella of Portugal (1503–1539)
Jingū (c. 201–269)
Jitō (645–702)
Josephine (1763–1814)
Judith of Bavaria (802–843)
Julia Domna (c. 170–217)
Julia Maesa (c. 170–224)
Julia Mamaea (c. 190–235)
Julia Paula (fl. 220)
Julia Soaemias (d. 222)
Justina (fl. 350–370)
Kassi (1241–?)
Kōgyoku-Saimei (594–661)
Kōken-Shōtoku (718–770)
Leontia (fl. 602–610)
Leopoldina of Austria (1797–1826)
Licinia Eudoxia (422–before 490)
Livia Drusilla (58 BCE–29 CE)
Lollia Paulina (fl. 38–39)
Lü Hou (r. 195–180 BCE)
Lupicinia-Euphemia (d. 523)
Margaret-Mary of Hungary (c. 1177–?)
Margaret of Brabant (d. 1311)
Margaret Theresa of Spain (1651–1673)
Maria (fl. 700s)
Maria Anna of Savoy (1803–1884)
Maria Anna of Spain (1606–1646)
Maria Josepha of Bavaria (1739–1767)
Maria-Kyratza Asen (fl. late 1300s)
Maria Leopoldine (1632–1649)
Maria Louisa of Spain (1745–1792)
Maria Ludovica of Modena (1787–1816)
Maria Nagaia (d. 1612)
Maria of Alania (fl. 1070–1081)
Maria of Amnia (fl. 782)
Maria of Armenia (fl. 1300)
Maria of Circassia (d. 1569)
Maria of Trebizond (d. 1439)
Maria Teresa of Naples (1772–1807)
Marie de Courtenay (fl. 1215)
Marie Feodorovna (1847–1928)
Marie Louise of Austria (1791–1847)
Marie of Antioch (d. 1183)
Marie of Austria (1528–1603)
Marie of Hesse-Darmstadt (1824–1880)
Marpha (1664–1716)
Martina (fl. 600s)
Mary of Brabant (c. 1191–c. 1260)
Matilda of Boulogne (c. 1103–1152)
Matilda of Saxony (c. 892–968)
Meisho (1624–1696)
Menen (1899–1962)
Menetewab (c. 1720–1770)
Messalina, Statilia (fl. 66–68)
Messalina, Valeria (c. 23–48)
Michiko (1934—)
Miloslavskaia, Maria (1626–1669)
Min (1851–1895)
Mniszek, Marina (c. 1588–1614)
Mumtaz Mahal (c. 1592–1631)
Nagako (1903–2000)
Narishkina, Natalya (1651–1694)
Nur Jahan (1577–1645)
Octavia (39–62)
Oda of Bavaria (fl. 890s)
Onshi (872–907)
Pahlavi, Farah (1938—)
Pahlavi, Soraya (1932—)
Philippa of Lesser Armenia (fl. 1200s)
Placidia, Galla (c. 390–450)
Plotina (d. 122)
Poppaea Sabina (d. 65)
Priska-Irene of Hungary (c. 1085–1133)
Prokopia (fl. 800s)
Pulcheria (c. 398–453)
Richensia of Nordheim (1095–1141)
Richilde (d. 894)
Roxelana (c. 1504–1558)
Sabina (88–136)
Sadako (r. 976–1001)
Sadako (1885–1951)
Salonina (r. 254–268)
Saltykova, Praskovya (1664–1723)
Sforza, Bianca Maria (1472–1510)
Sheremetskaia, Natalia (1880–1952)
Shoshi (fl. 990–1010)
Sobakin, Marta (d. 1571)
Sophia (c. 525–after 600)
Sophia Dorothea of Wurttemberg (1759–1828)
Sophia of Byzantium (1448–1503)
Sophie of Montferrat (fl. 15th c.)
Suiko (554–628)
Taytu (c. 1850–1918)
Teresa Cristina of Bourbon (1822–1889)
Thecla (c. 775–c. 823)
Theodora (c. 500–548)
Theodora (fl. early 900s)
Theodora (fl. late 900s)
Theodora Ducas (fl. 11th c.)
Theodora of the Khazars (fl. 700s)
Theodora Porphyrogenita (c. 989–1056)
Theodora the Blessed (c. 810–c. 860)
Theodota (c. 775–early 800s)
Theophano (c. 866–c. 897)
Theophano (c. 940–?)
Theophano of Athens (fl. 800s)
Theophano of Byzantium (c. 955–991)
Vassiltschikov, Anna (16th c.)
Verina (fl. 437–483)
Victoria Adelaide (1840–1901)
Wang Zhaojun (52 BCE–18 CE)
Wilhelmina of Brunswick (1673–1742)
Wu Zetian (624–705)
Yolande of Brienne (1212–1228)
Yolande of Courtenay (d. 1219)
Yoshiko (1834–1907)
Zita of Parma (1892–1989)
Zoë Carbopsina (c. 890–920)
Zoe Ducas (fl. 11th c.)
Zoë Porphyrogenita (980–1050)
Zoë Zautzina (c. 870–c. 899)

ENDOCRINOLOGIST

Elders, Joycelyn (1933—)
Russell, Jane Anne (1911–1967)

ENGINEER

See Aeronautical engineer.
See Chemical engineer.
See Civil engineer.
See Computer engineer.
See Electrical engineer.
See Industrial engineer.

See Mechanical engineer.
See Military engineer.
See Mining engineer.

ENGRAVER

Baader, Amalie (b. 1763)
Barlow, Hannah (1851–1916)
Bertaud, Marie Rosalie (c. 1700–?)
Comstock, Anna Botsford (1854–1930)
Gág, Wanda (1893–1946)
Ghisi, Diana (c. 1530–1590)
Hassall, Joan (1906–1988)
Hermes, Gertrude (1901–1983)
Jones, Elizabeth (c. 1935—)
Leighton, Clare (1899–1989)
Merian, Maria Sybilla (1647–1717)
Parker, Agnes Miller (1895–1980)
Poole, Monica (1921–2003)
Raverat, Gwen (1885–1957)
Sartain, Emily (1841–1927)
Sintenis, Renée (1888–1965)
Stella, Claudine Bousonnet (1636–1697)
Taylor, Ann (1782–1866)
Taylor, Jane (1783–1824)
Yeats, Lily (1866–1949)

ENTERTAINER

Vitelli, Annie (c. 1837–?)

ENTOMOLOGIST

Castle, Amy (1880–?)
Cheesman, Lucy Evelyn (1881–1969)
Clay, Theresa (1911–1995)
Fountaine, Margaret (1862–1940)
Longfield, Cynthia (1896–1991)
Merian, Maria Sybilla (1647–1717)
Murtfeldt, Mary (1848–1913)
Ormerod, Eleanor A. (1828–1901)
Patch, Edith (1876–1954)
Rothschild, Miriam (1908–2005)
Slosson, Annie Trumbull (1838–1926)

ENTREPRENEUR

Abaijah, Josephine (1942—)
Abrabanel, Benvenida (d. 1560)
Adler, Polly (1899–1962)
Arden, Elizabeth (1878–1966)
Ashley, Laura (1925–1985)
Astor, Sarah Todd (1761–1832)
Awolowo, Hannah (1915—)
Axton, Estelle (1918–2004)
Ayer, Harriet Hubbard (1849–1903)
Barcelo, Gertrudis (c. 1820–1852)
Barker, Kylene (c. 1956—)
Beech, Olive Ann (1903–1993)
Berk, Lotte (1913–2003)
Bertram, Elsie (1912–2003)
Bishop, Hazel (1906–1998)
Boiardi, Helen (1905–1995)
Bryant, Lane (1879–1951)
Buck, Kitty (1907–2001)
Cabrini, Frances Xavier (1850–1917)
Callender, Marie (1907–1995)
Calloway, Blanche (1902–1973)
Carabillo, Toni (1926–1997)
Carpenter, Karen (1950–1983)
Cashin, Bonnie (1915–2000)
Chai, Ling (1966—)
Chanel, Coco (1883–1971)
Chennault, Anna (1923—)
Claiborne, Liz (1929—)
Clicquot, Mme (1777–1866)
Cochran, Jacqueline (1906–1980)
Connolly, Maureen (1934–1969)
Cooper, Susie (1902–1995)
Copley, Clara (d. 1949)
Cornelys, Theresa (1723–1797)
Cosby, Camille (1945—)
Craig, Jenny (1932—)
Cranston, Kate (1850–1934)
Davies, Betty (1935—)
Demel, Anna (1872–1956)
de Passe, Suzanne (1946—)
Deseo, Suzanne (1913–2003)
Dickson, Amanda America (1849–1893)
Dulac, Germaine (1882–1942)
Edwards, Tracey (1962—)
Entenmann, Martha (1906–1996)
Erskine, Mary (1629–1707)
Fields, Debbi (1956—)
Fisher, Doris
Fontana, Giovanna (1915–2004)
Ford, Eileen (1922—)
Gilbreth, Lillian Moller (1878–1972)
Gleason, Kate (1865–1933)
Glückel of Hameln (1646–1724)
Goddard, Mary Katherine (1738–1816)
Graham, Bette Nesmith (1924–1980)
Greenaway, Margaret (fl. 15th c.)
Greenway, Isabella Selmes (1886–1953)
Handler, Ruth (1916–2002)
Hanson, Luise V. (1913–2003)
Harding, Jan (1925—)
Haughery, Margaret Gaffney (1813–1882)
Haynes, Margery (fl. 15th c.)
Hellaby, Amy Maria (1864–1955)
Innes, Mary Jane (1852–1941)
Irene (1901–1962)
Joyner, Marjorie Stewart (1896–1994)
Justin, Enid (1894–1990)
Kalmus, Natalie (1878–1965)
Kamali, Norma (1945—)
Karan, Donna (1948—)
Katz, Lillian (1927—)
Kingsley, Dorothy (1909–1997)
Langton, Jane (fl. 15th c.)
Lauder, Estée (1908–2004)
Lawrence, Mary Wells (1928—)
Leigh, Frances Butler (1838–1910)
Lil' Kim (1975—)
Lockwood, Belva Ann (1830–1917)
Macarthur, Elizabeth (1767–1850)
MacGill, Helen Gregory (1871–1947)
Malone, Annie Turnbo (1869–1957)
Manley, Effa (1900–1981)
Marriott, Alice Sheets (1907–2000)
Matthews, Burnita S. (1894–1988)
McCartney, Linda (1941–1998)
McKnight, Marian (c. 1937—)
McMurry, Lillian Shedd (1921–1999)
McPartland, Marian (1920—)
Mead, Lynda Lee (c. 1939—)
Minijima, Kiyo (1833–1919)
Mitford, Deborah (1920—)
Muller, Gertrude (1887–1954)
Murray, Kathryn (1906–1999)
Nathoy, Lalu (1853–1933)
Nidetch, Jean (1923—)
Ocloo, Esther (1919–2002)
Okwei of Osomari (1872–1943)
Parish, Sister (1910–1994)
Payson, Joan Whitney (1903–1975)
Perkins, Elizabeth Peck (c. 1735–1807)
Perry, Ruth (1939—)
Pettis, Shirley Neil (1924—)
Pinkham, Lydia E. (1819–1883)
Pleasant, Mary Ellen (c. 1814–1904)
Quant, Mary (1934—)
Ratia, Armi (1912–1979)
Reibey, Mary (1777–1855)
Rhodes, Zandra (1940—)
Rhodopis (fl. 6th c. BCE)
Riefenstahl, Leni (1902–2003)
Roddick, Anita (1942—)
Rosenthal, Ida Cohen (1886–1973)
Rubinstein, Helena (1870–1965)
Rubinstein, Mala (1905–1999)
Rudkin, Margaret (1897–1967)
Saunders, Doris (1921—)
Schary, Hope Skillman (1908–1981)
Scudder, Laura Clough (1881–1959)
Seacole, Mary Jane (c. 1805–1881)
Seymour, Mary F. (1846–1893)
Sims, Naomi (1948—)
Smith, Chloethiel Woodard (1910–1992)
Song Ailing (1890–1973)
Steiff, Margarete (1847–1909)
Steloff, Frances (1887–1989)
Stewart, Martha (1941—)
Stratton-Porter, Gene (1863–1924)
Strozzi, Alessandra (1406–1469)
Toor, Frances (1890–1956)
Topham, Mirabel (d. 1980)
Trigère, Pauline (1912–2002)
Tschechowa, Olga (1897–1980)
Tussaud, Marie (1761–1850)
Vandenhoeck, Anna (1709–1787)
Walker, Madame C.J. (1867–1919)
Walker, Maggie Lena (1867–1934)
Washington, Sarah Spencer (1889–?)
Weinstein, Hannah (1911–1984)
Westwood, Vivienne (1941—)
Wheeler, Candace (1827–1923)
White, Eartha M. (1876–1974)
Whitney, Helen Hay (1876–1944)
Whyte, Edna Gardner (1902–1992)
Williams, Mary Lou (1910–1981)
Wise, Brownie (1913–1992)
Youville, Marie Marguerite d' (1701–1771)
Zabar, Lillian (1905–1995)
Zinner, Hedda (1902–1990)

ENVIRONMENTALIST

Bari, Judi (1949–1997)
Beattie, Mollie (1947–1996)
Bingham, Millicent Todd (1880–1968)
Brockovich, Erin (1960—)
Browner, Carol M. (1956—)
Carson, Rachel (1907–1964)
Douglas, Marjory Stoneman (1890–1998)
Duby-Blom, Gertrude (1901–1993)
Eastwood, Alice (1859–1953)
Ebtekar, Massoumeh (1960—)
Gibbs, Lois (1946—)
Kelly, Petra (1947–1992)
King, Carole (1942—)
LaDuke, Winona (1959—)
Maathai, Wangari (1940—)
Mann, Elisabeth (1918–2002)
Nearing, Helen (1904–1995)
Paley, Grace (1922—)
Ray, Dixy Lee (1914–1994)
Richards, Ellen Swallow (1842–1911)
Roddick, Anita (1942—)
Ward, Barbara (1914–1981)
Wayburn, Peggy (1917–2002)
Wolf, Hazel (1898–2000)

EPIDEMIOLOGIST

Horstmann, Dorothy M. (1911–2001)
Stewart, Alice (1906–2002)

EQUESTRIAN

Abraham, Constance Palgrave (1864–1942)
Adivar, Halide Edib (c. 1884–1964)
Alexandra of Denmark (1844–1925)
Anne, Princess (1950—)
Aspinall, Nan Jane (fl. 1911)
Bartels, Tineke (1951—)

Baryard, Malin (1975—)
Benario, Olga (1908–1942)
Blinks, Susan (1957—)
Bontje, Ellen (1958—)
Boylen, Christilot (1947—)
Brakewell, Jeanette (1974—)
Bredahl, Charlotte (1957—)
Briggs, Margaret Jane (1892–1961)
Burr, Leslie (1956—)
Button, Isabel (1863–1921)
Bylund, Ingamay (1949—)
Capellmann, Nadine (1965—)
Carlota Joaquina (1775–1830)
Casagrande, Anna (1958—)
Catchpole, Margaret (1762–1819)
Chabrillan, Céleste de (1824–1909)
Clapham, Diana (1957—)
Clark, Sally (1958–)
Coakes, Marion (1947—)
Connolly, Maureen (1934–1969)
de Bary, Amy-Catherine (1944—)
Donescu, Anghelache (1945—)
Edmonds, Emma (1841–1898)
Ferrer Salat, Beatriz (1966—)
Fleischmann, Torrance (1949—)
Fout, Nina (1959—)
Funnell, Pippa (1968—)
Gibson, Michelle (1969—)
Gordon-Watson, Mary (1948—)
Gossweiler, Marianne (1943—)
Green, Lucinda (1953—)
Grillo, Gabriela (1952—)
Gurney, Hilda (1943—)
Hakanson, Ulla (1937—)
Hart, Nancy (c. 1846–1902)
Hartel, Lis (1921—)
Henneberg, Jill
Howard, Elizabeth Ann (1823–1865)
Hoy, Bettina (1962—)
Huntington, Anna Hyatt (1876–1973)
Ishoy, Cynthia (1952—)
Jacquin, Lisa (1962—)
Jensen, Anne Grethe (1951—)
Johnstone, Hilda Lorne (b. 1902)
Kelly, Kate (1862–1898)
Kemmer, Heike (1962—)
Kennedy, Ethel (1928—)
Kennedy, Jacqueline (1929–1994)
King, Mary (1961—)
Knighton, Margaret (1955—)
Krone, Julie (1963—)
Küppers, Anneliese (1929—)
Kursinski, Anne (1959—)
Kusner, Kathy (1940—)
Lakshmibai (c. 1835–1858)
Latta, Victoria (1951—)
Lavell, Carol (1943—)
Law, Leslie (1965—)
Ledermann, Alexandra (1969—)
Lefebvre, Janou (1945—)
Leng, Virginia (1955—)
Linsenhoff, Ann-Kathrin (1960—)
Linsenhoff, Liselott (1927—)
Lloyd-Davies, Vanessa (1960–2005)
Lyell, Lottie (1890–1925)
Madden, Beezie (1963—)
Margaret of Parma (1522–1586)
Marie of Rumania (1875–1938)
Master, Edith (1932—)
McDonald, Deborah (1954—)
McKinney, Tamara (1962—)
McLean, Alice (1886–1968)
McNaught, Lesley (1966—)
Melba, Nellie (1861–1931)
Meynell, Alicia (fl. 1804–1805)
Millikin, Kerry
Misevich, Vera (1945—)
Mitchell, Ruth (c. 1888–1969)
Moore, Ann (1950—)
Morkis, Dorothy (1942—)
Nathhorst, Louise (1955—)
Nicoll, Ashley (1963—)
Niederkirchner, Käte (1909–1944)
Oakley, Annie (1860–1926)
O'Connor, Karen (1958—)
Otto-Crepin, Margit (1945—)
Parker, Bridget (1939—)
Parlby, Irene (1868–1965)
Petushkova, Yelena (1940—)
Place, Etta (fl. 1896–1905)
Pottinger, Judith (1956—)
Pracht, Eva-Maria (1937—)
Ramseier, Doris (1939—)
Reeves, Connie (1901–2003)
Richards, Julie Burns (1970—)
Robbiani, Heidi (1950—)
Rolton, Gillian (1956—)
Rothenberger, Gonnelien
Sáenz, Manuela (1797–1856)
Salzgeber, Ulla (1958—)
Sanders, Annemarie (1958—)
Schaeffer, Wendy (c. 1975—)
Schlueter-Schmidt, Karin (1937—)
Sciocchetti, Marina (1954—)
Scott, Barbara Ann (1929—)
Sears, Eleanora (1881–1968)
Seizinger, Katja (1972—)
Severson, Kim (1973—)
Simons de Ridder, Alexandra (1963—)
Smith, Bathsheba (1822–1910)
Smith, Gina (1957—)
Smythe, Pat (1928–1996)
Stives, Karen (1950—)
Straker, Karen (1964—)
Stückelberger, Christine (1947—)
Swaab, Ninna (1940—)
Syers, Madge Cave (1881–1917)
Tauskey, Mary Anne (1955—)
Taylor, Melanie Smith (1949—)
Theodorescu, Monica (1963—)
Theurer, Elisabeth (1956—)
Traurig, Christine (1957—)
Tryon, Amy (1970—)
Uphoff, Nicole (1967—)
van Baalen, Coby (1957—)
van Grunsven, Anky (1968—)
von Nagel, Ida (1917–1971)
von Rosen, Maud (1925—)
Werth, Isabell (1969—)
Weygand, Hannelore (1924—)
Wiesman, Linden (1975—)
Wilcox, Lisa (1966—)
Willcox, Sheila (1936—)
Wu Zetian (624–705)

ESPIONAGE AGENT
See Spy.

ESSAYIST
Adam, Juliette la Messine (1836–1936)
Adams, Sarah Flower (1805–1848)
Adnan, Etel (1925—)
Aguilar, Grace (1816–1847)
Aguirre, Mirta (1912—)
Akhmadulina, Bella (1937—)
Albrizzi, Isabella Teotochi, Contessa d' (1770–1836)
Alice Meynell (1847–1922)
Allart, Hortense (1801–1879)
Ambrose, Alice (1906–2001)
Andreas-Salomé, Lou (1861–1937)
Angelou, Maya (1928—)
Anger, Jane (fl. c. 1580)
Anichkova, Anna (1868–1935)
Anker, Nini Roll (1873–1942)
Anscombe, G.E.M. (1919–2001)
Anzaldúa, Gloria E. (1942–2004)
Aptheker, Bettina (1944—)
Archambault, Mademoiselle (c. 1724–?)
Archer, Maria (1905–1982)
Archer, Robyn (1948—)
Arenal, Concepción (1820–1893)
Argiriadou, Chryssoula (1901–1998)
Arnim, Bettine von (1785–1859)
Arnstein, Fanny von (1758–1818)
Asquith, Margot Tennant (1864–1945)
Assing, Ottilie (1819–1884)
Awiakta (1936—)
Ayverdi, Samiha (1906–1993)
Bâ, Mariama (1929–1981)
Beauvoir, Simone de (1908–1986)
Bedregal, Yolanda (1916–1999)
Belot, Madame (1719–1804)
Benson, Stella (1892–1933)
Berberova, Nina (1901–1993)
Berlepsch, Emilie von (1755–1830)
Bevington, L.S. (1845–1895)
Bianchini, Angela (1921—)
Bibesco, Marthe Lucie (1887–1973)
Blackwell, Elizabeth (1821–1910)
Boland, Eavan (1944—)
Bonhote, Elizabeth (1744–1818)
Bosco, María Angélica (1917—)
Botta, Anne C.L. (1815–1891)
Bourdic-Viot, Marie-Henriette Payad d'Estang de (1746–1802)
Boveri, Margret (1900–1975)
Bowen, Catherine Drinker (1897–1973)
Bowen, Elizabeth (1899–1973)
Boyle, Kay (1902–1992)
Brachvogel, Carry (1864–1942)
Brant, Beth (1941—)
Bremer, Fredrika (1801–1865)
Brewster, Anne Hampton (1818–1892)
Brittain, Vera (1893–1970)
Brøgger, Suzanne (1944—)
Brohon, Jacqueline-Aimée (1731–1778)
Broner, E.M. (1930—)
Brophy, Brigid (1929–1995)
Brossard, Nicole (1943—)
Brown, Olympia (1835–1926)
Brown, Rita Mae (1944—)
Brown, Tina (1953—)
Brüll, Ilse (1925–1942)
Cabete, Adelaide (1867–1935)
Cáceres, Esther de (1903–1971)
Cadilla de Martínez, Maria (1886–1951)
Caird, Mona Alison (1858–1932)
Canth, Minna (1844–1897)
Carson, Rachel (1907–1964)
Castellanos, Rosario (1925–1974)
Cather, Willa (1873–1947)
Cereta, Laura, of Brescia (1469–1499)
Cha, Theresa Hak Kyung (1951–1982)
Chang, Eileen (1920–1995)
Charriere, Isabelle de (1740–1805)
Chase, Mary Ellen (1887–1973)
Chastenay, Victorine de (1771–1855)
Châtelet, Émilie du (1706–1749)
Chervinskaya, Lidiya Davydovna (1907–1988)
Child, Lydia Maria (1802–1880)
Chopin, Kate (1850–1904)
Christensen, Inger (1935—)
Christine de Pizan (c. 1363–c. 1431)
Chudleigh, Mary Lee (1656–1710)
Clark, Eleanor (1913–1996)
Clarke, Gillian (1937—)
Clarke, Mary Cowden (1809–1898)

Cobbe, Frances Power (1822–1904)
Cockburn, Catharine Trotter (1679–1749)
Coicy, Madame de (fl. 18th c.)
Coleridge, Mary Elizabeth (1861–1907)
Coleridge, Sara (1802–1852)
Colette (1873–1954)
Collett, Camilla (1813–1895)
Costello, Louisa Stuart (1799–1870)
Cotten, Elizabeth (c. 1893–1987)
Craigie, Pearl Mary Teresa (1867–1906)
Craik, Dinah Maria Mulock (1826–1887)
Croly, Jane Cunningham (1829–1901)
Cunningham, Letitia (fl. 1783)
Currie, Mary Montgomerie (1843–1905)
Curzon, Sarah Anne (1833–1898)
Dai Qing (1941—)
Dall, Caroline Wells (1822–1912)
d'Arconville, Geneviève (1720–1805)
Daubié, Julie-Victoire (1824–1874)
Daudet, Julia (1844–1940)
Davies, Emily (1830–1921)
Davis, Angela (1944—)
Dawidowicz, Lucy (1915–1990)
Debyasuvan, Boonlua Kunjara (1911–1982)
Dejanović, Draga (1843–1870)
de Kooning, Elaine Fried (1918–1989)
de Laguna, Grace Mead (1878–1978)
Démar, Claire (1800–1833)
Deren, Maya (1908–1961)
Dessaur, C.I. (1931–2002)
Deutscher, Tamara (1913–1990)
D'haen, Christine (1923—)
Diakonova, Elizaveta (1874–1902)
Dillard, Annie (1945—)
Dinesen, Isak (1885–1962)
Ding Ling (1904–1985)
Dittmar, Louise (1807–1884)
Dodge, Mary Abigail (1833–1896)
Dominguez, María Alicia (1908—)
Doolittle, Hilda (1886–1961)
Dougall, Lily (1858–1923)
Douglas, Marjory Stoneman (1890–1998)
Duclaux, Agnes Mary F. (1856–1944)
Dunbar-Nelson, Alice (1875–1935)
Duras, Marguerite (1914–1996)
Dutt, Toru (1856–1877)
Eaubonne, Françoise d' (1920–2005)
Eberhardt, Isabelle (1877–1904)
Eckstorm, Fannie Pearson Hardy (1865–1946)
Ehrenreich, Barbara (1941—)
Eisner, Lotte (1896–1983)
Elizabeth of Wied (1843–1916)
Emerson, Mary Moody (1774–1863)
Ephron, Nora (1941—)
Épinay, Louise-Florence-Pétronille, Madame la Live d' (1726–1783)
Evans, Mary Anne (1819–1880)
Exter, Alexandra (1882–1949)
Farley, Harriet (1813–1907)
Fawcett, Millicent Garrett (1847–1929)
Fern, Fanny (1811–1872)
Fisher, Dorothy Canfield (1879–1958)
Fisher, M.F.K. (1908–1992)
Fleisser, Marieluise (1901–1974)
Fontette de Sommery, Mademoiselle (fl. 18th c.)
Foot, Philippa (1920—)
Fouqué, Karoline Freifrau de la Motte (1774–1831)
Franchi, Anna (1866–1954)
Fremantle, Anne (1909–2002)
French, Alice (1850–1934)
Freud, Anna (1895–1982)
Freund, Gisèle (1912–2000)
Fuller, Margaret (1810–1850)
Gacon-Dufour, Marie Armande Jeanne (1753–c. 1835)
Gale, Zona (1874–1938)
Galindo, Beatriz (1475–1534)
Gándara, Carmen (1900–1977)
García Marruz, Fina (1923—)
Gardner, Kay (1941–2002)
Gauthier, Xavière (1942—)
Gilmer, Elizabeth Meriwether (1861–1951)
Gilmore, Mary (1865–1962)
Ginzburg, Evgenia (1896–1980)
Ginzburg, Natalia (1916–1991)
Giovanni, Nikki (1943—)
Glasgow, Ellen (1873–1945)
Glaspell, Susan (1876–1948)
Goldberg, Lea (1911–1970)
Goldman, Emma (1869–1940)
Gordimer, Nadine (1923—)
Gordon, Caroline (1895–1981)
Gould, Lois (1932–2002)
Gournay, Marie le Jars de (1565–1645)
Grant, Anne (1755–1838)
Gray, Nicolete (1911–1997)
Grenfell, Joyce (1910–1979)
Grimké, Charlotte L. Forten (1837–1914)
Grimké, Sarah Moore (1792–1873)
Groult, Benoîte (1921—)
Guiney, Louise Imogen (1861–1920)
Gutiérrez de Mendoza, Juana Belén (1875–1942)
Gutteridge, Helena Rose (1879–1960)
Hagiwara, Yoko (1920—)
Hale, Susan (1833–1910)
Hamilton, Edith (1867–1963)
Hansberry, Lorraine (1930–1965)
Hardwick, Elizabeth (1916—)
Harris, Claire (1937—)
Harrison, Barbara Grizzuti (1934–2002)
Hartwig, Julia (1921—)
Hays, Mary (1760–1843)
Hazard, Caroline (1856–1945)
Head, Bessie (1937–1986)
Herbst, Josephine (1892–1969)
Hickey, Emily Henrietta (1845–1924)
Hill, Octavia (1838–1912)
Hofer, Evelyn
Hogan, Linda (1947—)
Horney, Karen (1885–1952)
Howitt, Mary (1799–1888)
Huber, Marie (1695–1753)
Hunter, Mollie (1922—)
Hurst, Fannie (1889–1968)
Hurston, Zora Neale (c. 1891–1960)
Jackson, Helen Hunt (1830–1885)
Jacobi, Mary Putnam (1842–1906)
Jacobs, Aletta (1854–1929)
Jameson, Anna Brownell (1794–1860)
Jameson, Storm (1891–1986)
Jayakar, Pupul (1915–1999)
Jelsma, Clara Mitsuko (1931—)
Jhabvala, Ruth Prawer (1927—)
Jordan, June (1936–2002)
Juana Inés de la Cruz (1651–1695)
Jurado, Alicia (1915—)
Kael, Pauline (1919–2001)
Kaschnitz, Marie Luise (1901–1974)
Katznelson-Shazar, Rachel (1888–1975)
Keller, Helen (1880–1968)
Kelly, Petra (1947–1992)
Kerr, Jean (1923–2003)
Key, Ellen (1849–1926)
Killigrew, Anne (1660–1685)
Kingsolver, Barbara (1955—)
Kinkel, Johanna (1810–1858)
Kirchwey, Freda (1893–1976)
Kolb, Annette (1870–1967)
Kronauer, Brigitte (1940—)
Lamas, Maria (1893–1983)
Lamb, Martha J.R. (1826–1893)
Lange, Dorothea (1895–1965)
Lange, Norah (1906–1972)
La Rochefoucauld, Edmée, Duchesse de (1895–1991)
Lars, Claudia (1899–1974)
Lawrence, Frieda (1879–1956)
Lazarus, Emma (1849–1887)
Lee, Harper (1926—)
León, Maria Teresa (1903–1988)
Leslie, Miriam Folline Squier (1836–1914)
Levertov, Denise (1923–1997)
Lewald, Fanny (1811–1889)
Lichnowsky, Mechthilde (1879–1958)
Lidman, Sara (1923–2004)
Lindbergh, Anne Morrow (1906–2001)
Lin Haiyin (1918–2001)
Linton, Eliza Lynn (1822–1898)
Li Qingzhao (1083–c. 1151)
Lisboa, Henriquetta (1904–1985)
Livermore, Mary A. (1820–1905)
Loos, Anita (1893–1981)
Lorde, Audre (1934–1992)
Lowell, Amy (1874–1925)
Lowe-Porter, Helen (1876–1963)
Lukhmanova, N.A. (1840–1907)
Lussu, Joyce Salvadori (1912–1988)
Lyons, Enid (1897–1981)
Macaulay, Rose (1881–1958)
Machado, Luz (1916–1999)
Madeleva, Sister Mary (1887–1964)
Mannes, Marya (1904–1990)
Marghieri, Clotilde (1897–1981)
Marinetti, Benedetta Cappa (1897–1977)
Maritain, Raïssa (1883–1960)
Marlowe, Julia (1866–1950)
Martineau, Harriet (1802–1876)
Martinson, Moa (1890–1964)
Matto de Turner, Clorinda (1854–1909)
Mayreder, Rosa (1858–1938)
McClung, Nellie L. (1873–1951)
McCullers, Carson (1917–1967)
McDowell, Mary Eliza (1854–1936)
McGinley, Phyllis (1905–1978)
McTeer, Maureen (1952—)
Mercoeur, Elisa (1809–1835)
Mew, Charlotte (1869–1928)
Meyer, Annie Nathan (1867–1951)
Michaelis, Hanny (1922—)
Miller, Olive Thorne (1831–1918)
Millin, Sarah (1888–1968)
Mitchell, Juliet (1934—)
Mitchison, Naomi (1897–1999)
Monbart, Marie-Joséphine de Lescun (1758–1800)
Monroe, Harriet (1860–1936)
Montagu, Lady Mary Wortley (1689–1762)
Moore, Anne Carroll (1871–1961)
Moore, Marianne (1887–1972)
Morante, Elsa (1912–1985)
Morata, Fulvia Olympia (1526–1555)
Morath, Inge (1923–2002)
Morgan, Robin (1941—)
Mori, Mari (1903–1987)
Morrison, Toni (1931—)
Mourning Dove (c. 1888–1936)
Mowatt, Anna Cora (1819–1870)
Mukhina, Vera (1889–1953)
Mukoda, Kuniko (1929–1981)
Mundt, Klara Müller (1814–1873)
Murray, Judith Sargent (1751–1820)
Musa, Gilda (1926–1999)
Mutafchieva, Vera P. (1929—)
Naden, Constance Caroline Woodhill (1858–1889)
Nákou, Lilika (1903–1989)

Nalkowska, Zofia (1884–1954)
Naranjo, Carmen (1928—)
Naylor, Gloria (1950—)
Necker, Suzanne (1739–1794)
Nestle, Joan (1940—)
Noailles, Anna de (1876–1933)
Nogami, Yaeko (1885–1985)
Norman, Dorothy (1905–1997)
Norton, Mary (1903–1992)
Nováková, Teréza (1853–1912)
Oba, Minako (1930—)
Ocampo, Victoria (1890–1979)
Oliphant, Margaret (1828–1897)
Oliver, Mary (1935—)
Olsen, Tillie (c. 1912—)
Olsson, Hagar (1893–1978)
Opie, Amelia (1769–1853)
Oppenheimer, Jane Marion (1911–1996)
Osório, Ana de Castro (1872–1935)
Ozick, Cynthia (1928—)
Paget, Violet (1856–1935)
Paglia, Camille (1947—)
Palmer, Alice Freeman (1855–1902)
Palmer, Nettie (1885–1964)
Paoli, Betty (1814–1894)
Pardo Bazán, Emilia (1852–1921)
Parker, Pat (1944–1989)
Parkes, Bessie Rayner (1829–1925)
Parturier, Françoise (1919—)
Pauli, Hertha (1909–1973)
Pereira, Irene Rice (1902–1971)
Peterkin, Julia (1880–1961)
Petit, Magdalena (1900–1968)
Pfeiffer, Emily Jane (1827–1890)
Pichler, Karoline (1769–1843)
Pierangeli, Rina Faccio (1876–1960)
Plath, Sylvia (1932–1963)
Plato, Ann (c. 1820–?)
Plisson, Marie-Prudence (1727–1788)
Pool, Maria Louise (1841–1898)
Porter, Katherine Anne (1890–1980)
Portnoy, Ethel (1927–2004)
Post, Emily (1872–1960)
Poulain, Mme (c. 1750–c. 1800)
Prichard, Katharine Susannah (1883–1969)
Putnam, Emily James (1865–1944)
Rambova, Natacha (1897–1966)
Ramée, Louise de la (1839–1908)
Ramirez, Sara Estela (1881–1910)
Ransome-Kuti, Funmilayo (1900–1978)
Rawlings, Marjorie Kinnan (1896–1953)
Reed, Myrtle (1874–1911)
Repplier, Agnes (1855–1950)
Reuter, Gabriele (1859–1941)
Rich, Adrienne (1929—)
Richardson, Dorothy (1873–1957)
Ricker, Marilla (1840–1920)
Rind, Clementina (c. 1740–1774)
Rinser, Luise (1911–2002)
Ritchie, Anne Isabella (1837–1919)
Ritter, Erika (1948—)
Robins, Elizabeth (1862–1952)
Robinson, Joan Violet (1903–1983)
Robinson, Therese Albertine Louise von Jakob (1797–1870)
Rochefort, Christiane (1917–1998)
Roland, Pauline (1805–1852)
Roland Holst, Henriëtte (1869–1952)
Roosevelt, Eleanor (1884–1962)
Rothmann, Maria Elisabeth (1875–1975)
Rourke, Constance (1885–1941)
Rowson, Susanna (1762–1824)
Rubinstein, Renate (1929–1990)
Rukeyser, Muriel (1913–1980)
Russell, Dora Isella (1925—)
Saenz-Alonso, Mercedes (1916–2000)
Saint-Chamond, Claire-Marie Mazarelli, Marquise de La Vieuville de (1731–?)
Salis-Marschlins, Meta (1855–1929)
Samaroff, Olga (1882–1948)
Sampter, Jessie (1883–1938)
Sanchez, Carol Lee (1934—)
Sand, George (1804–1876)
Sanders, Elizabeth Elkins (1762–1851)
Sangster, Margaret (1838–1912)
Santos Arrascaeta, Beatriz (1947—)
Sanuti, Nicolosa (fl. 1453)
Sarraute, Nathalie (1900–1999)
Sarton, May (1912–1995)
Sato, Aiko (1923—)
Saw, Ruth (1901–1983)
Sawachi, Hisae (1930—)
Sayers, Dorothy L. (1893–1957)
Sayre, Nora (1932–2001)
Schlesinger, Therese (1863–1940)
Schmahl, Jeanne (1846–1916)
Scholl, Sophie (1921–1943)
Scholtz-Klink, Gertrud (1902–1999)
Schreiner, Olive (1855–1920)
Schütte-Lihotzky, Margarete (1897–2000)
Seidel, Ina (1885–1974)
Sei Shōnagon (c. 965–?)
Sewell, Anna (1820–1878)
Sexton, Anne (1928–1974)
Shaginian, Marietta (1888–1982)
Shelley, Mary (1797–1851)
Shepherd, Mary (c. 1780–1847)
Shoshi (fl. 990–1010)
Sigourney, Lydia H. (1791–1865)
Silko, Leslie Marmon (1948—)
Sinclair, May (1863–1946)
Skinner, Constance Lindsay (1877–1939)
Skinner, Cornelia Otis (1901–1979)
Skobtsova, Maria (1891–1945)
Smiley, Jane (1949—)
Smith, Charlotte (1749–1806)
Smith, Lillian (1897–1966)
Song Meiling (b. 1897)
Sontag, Susan (1933–2004)
Spiel, Hilde (1911–1990)
Spofford, Harriet Prescott (1835–1921)
Stafford, Jean (1915–1979)
Starr, Eliza Allen (1824–1901)
Stein, Edith (1891–1942)
Steinem, Gloria (1934—)
Stephen, Julia Prinsep (1846–1895)
Stephens, Kate (1853–1938)
Stewart, Maria W. (1803–1879)
Stratton-Porter, Gene (1863–1924)
Strickland, Mabel (1899–1988)
Su Hsueh-lin (1897–1999)
Szymborska, Wislawa (1923—)
Taber, Gladys (1899–1980)
Taggard, Genevieve (1894–1948)
Talbot, Catherine (1721–1770)
Tarabotti, Arcangela (1604–1652)
Taylor, Ann (1782–1866)
Taylor, Ann Martin (1757–1830)
Taylor, Harriet (1807–1858)
Taylor, Jane (1783–1824)
Taymuriyya, 'A'isha 'Ismat al- (1840–1902)
Teffi, N.A. (1872–1952)
Terhune, Mary Virginia (1830–1922)
Thompson, Flora (1876–1947)
Traba, Marta (1930–1983)
Trench, Melesina (1768–1827)
Trier Mørch, Dea (1941—)
Trilling, Diana (1905–1996)
Troll-Borostyani, Irma von (1847–1912)
Trotzig, Birgitta (1929—)
Tsvetaeva, Marina (1892–1941)
Tuchman, Barbara (1912–1989)
Turell, Jane (1708–1735)
Underhill, Evelyn (1875–1941)
Undset, Sigrid (1882–1949)
Uttley, Alison (1884–1976)
Vaa, Aslaug (1889–1965)
Védrès, Nicole (1911–1965)
Velāsquez, Lucila (1928—)
Vengerova, Zinaida (1867–1941)
Vesaas, Halldis Moren (1907–1995)
Vilariño, Idea (1920—)
Villedieu, Catherine des Jardins, Mme de (c. 1640–1683)
Viola, Emilia Ferretti (1844–1929)
von Haynau, Edith (1884–1978)
Walker, Margaret (1915–1998)
Ward, Elizabeth Stuart Phelps (1844–1911)
Waser, Maria (1878–1939)
Watson, Rosamund (1860–1911)
Webb, Mary (1881–1927)
Webster, Augusta (1837–1894)
Wedgwood, C.V. (1910–1997)
Weil, Simone (1909–1943)
Welty, Eudora (1909–2001)
West, Rebecca (1892–1983)
Wharton, Edith (1862–1937)
Wheeler, Candace (1827–1923)
White, Katharine S. (1892–1977)
Whitman, Sarah Helen (1803–1878)
Whitney, Adeline Dutton (1824–1906)
Wilcox, Ella Wheeler (1850–1919)
Williams, Fannie Barrier (1855–1944)
Wolf, Christa (1929—)
Wolff, Victoria (1903–1992)
Woolf, Virginia (1882–1941)
Woolson, Abba Goold (1838–1921)
Wordsworth, Elizabeth (1840–1932)
Wright, Judith (1915–2000)
Wynter, Sylvia (1928—)
Xiang Jingyu (1895–1928)
Xie Wanying (1900–1999)
Yamada Waka (1879–1956)
Yates, Frances Amelia (1899–1981)
Young, Marguerite (1908–1995)
Yourcenar, Marguerite (1903–1987)
Zambrano, María (1904–1991)
Ziyada, Mayy (1886–1941)
Zographou, Lili
Zuzoric, Cvijeta (c. 1555–1600)

ETCHER

Airy, Anna (1882–1964)
Arndt, Hermina (1885–1926)
Bacon, Peggy (1895–1987)
Bishop, Isabel (1902–1988)
Bonner, Mary (1885–1935)
Cameron, Kate (1874–1965)
Cassatt, Mary (1844–1926)
Delaunay, Sonia (1885–1979)
Frink, Elisabeth (1930–1993)
Goldthwaite, Anne Wilson (1869–1944)
Gosse, Sylvia (1881–1968)
Graves, Nancy (1940–1995)
Greatorex, Eliza (1820–1897)
Grundig, Lea (1906–1977)
Hermes, Gertrude (1901–1983)
Jacobi, Lotte (1896–1990)
Knight, Laura (1877–1970)
Kollwitz, Käthe (1867–1945)
Landseer, Jessica (1810–1880)
Laurencin, Marie (1883–1956)
Mason, Alice Trumbull (1904–1971)
Merritt, Anna Lea (1844–1930)
Moran, Mary Nimmo (1842–1899)
Nessim, Barbara (1939—)
Nevelson, Louise (1899–1988)
Rego, Paula (1935—)

Sirani, Elizabetta (1638–1665)
Templeton, Rini (1935–1986)
Yakunchikova, Maria (1870–1901)

ETHNOLOGIST/ETHNOGRAPHER
Bébel-Gisler, Dany (1935–2003)
Beckwith, Martha Warren (1871–1959)
Cabrera, Lydia (1899–1991)
de Laguna, Frederica (1906–2004)
Deloria, Ella (1888–1971)
Dunlop, Eliza Hamilton (1796–1880)
Ellis, Florence Hawley (1906–1991)
Emerson, Ellen Russell (1837–1907)
Fletcher, Alice Cunningham (1838–1923)
Gomez, Sara (1943–1974)
Hanks, Jane Richardson (b. 1908)
Laird, Carobeth (1895–1983)
Mead, Margaret (1901–1978)
Michel, Louise (1830–1905)
Nováková, Teréza (1853–1912)
Papakura, Makereti (1873–1930)
Powdermaker, Hortense (1896–1970)
Primus, Pearl (1919–1994)
Smith, Erminnie A. Platt (1836–1886)
Starovoitova, Galina (1946–1998)
Tillion, Germaine (b. 1907)
Toor, Frances (1890–1956)
Underhill, Ruth Murray (1883–1984)

ETIQUETTE WRITER
Brown, Charlotte Hawkins (c. 1883–1961)
Farrar, Eliza Rotch (1791–1870)
Leslie, Eliza (1787–1858)
Moore, Clara (1824–1899)
Post, Emily (1872–1960)
Sherwood, Mary Elizabeth (1826–1903)
Vanderbilt, Amy (1908–1974)

EUGENICIST
Apgar, Virginia (1909–1974)
Barrer, Nina Agatha Rosamond (1879–1965)
Braun, Lily (1865–1916)
Macklin, Madge (1893–1962)
Owens-Adair, Bethenia (1840–1926)
Rumsey, Mary Harriman (1881–1934)
Stoecker, Helene (1869–1943)
Stopes, Marie (1880–1958)
Vejjabul, Pierra (b. 1909)
Vérone, Maria (1874–1938)

EVANGELICAL
Aylward, Gladys (1902–1970)
Bäumer, Gertrud (1873–1954)
Bell, Laura (1829–1894)
Booth, Evangeline (1865–1950)
Bridgman, Laura (1829–1889)
Buchan, Elspeth (1738–1791)
Burrows, Eva (1929—)
Cairns, Elizabeth (1685–1714)
Crosby, Fanny (1820–1915)
Finley, Martha (1828–1909)
Fisher, Mary (c. 1623–1698)
Harkness, Georgia (1891–1974)
Hastings, Selina (1707–1791)
Hopkins, Ellice (1836–1904)
Howe, Julia Ward (1819–1910)
Jackson, Ann Fletcher (1833–1903)
Jiagge, Annie (1918–1996)
Judson, Sarah Boardman (1803–1845)
Kapiolani (c. 1781–1841)
Kemble, Fanny (1809–1893)
Krüdener, Julie de (1764–1824)
Kuhlman, Kathryn (1907–1976)
Livermore, Harriet (1788–1868)
Margaret of Angoulême (1492–1549)
McPherson, Aimee Semple (1890–1944)
Meyer, Joyce (1943—)
More, Hannah (1745–1833)
Nation, Carry (1846–1911)
Palmer, Phoebe Worrall (1807–1874)
Pankhurst, Christabel (1880–1958)
Peabody, Lucy (1861–1949)
Pickett, Fuchsia T. (1918–2004)
Porter, Anna Maria (1780–1832)
Priscilla (fl. 1st c.)
Richards, Linda (1841–1930)
Schreiner, Olive (1855–1920)
Smith, Amanda Berry (1837–1915)
Smith, Willie Mae Ford (1904–1994)
Stapleton, Ruth Carter (1929–1983)
Stretton, Hesba (1832–1911)
ten Boom, Corrie (1892–1983)
Thoburn, Isabella (1840–1901)
Van Cott, Margaret (1830–1914)
Walker, Mary Edwards (1832–1919)
Ward, Mrs. Humphry (1851–1920)
Warner, Anna Bartlett (1827–1915)
Warner, Susan Bogert (1819–1885)
White, Ellen Gould (1827–1915)
Whitman, Narcissa (1808–1847)
Wilcox, Elsie Hart (1879–1954)

EVENT FOUNDER
Height, Dorothy (1912—)
Hess, Myra (1890–1965)
Lutyens, Elisabeth (1906–1983)
Maconchy, Elizabeth (1907–1994)
Markova, Alicia (1910–2004)
McCormick, Ruth Hanna (1880–1944)
Storer, Maria (1849–1932)
Winter, Joanne (1924—)

EXOTIC DANCER
Corio, Ann (1914–1999)
Doda, Carol
Hart, Margie (1916—)
Karioka, Tahiya (c. 1921–1999)
Lee, Gypsy Rose (1914–1970)
Rand, Sally (1904–1979)
Sothern, Georgia (1912–1981)
Williams, Wendy O. (1951–1998)
Zelle, Margaretha (1876–1917)

EXPATRIATE/EXILE
Barney, Natalie Clifford (1876–1972)
Boyle, Kay (1902–1992)
Breshkovsky, Catherine (1844–1934)
Bryant, Louise (1885–1936)
Cassatt, Mary (1844–1926)
Dmitrieff, Elizabeth (1851–1910)
Doolittle, Hilda (1886–1961)
Dzerzhinska, Sofia (1882–1968)
Flanner, Janet (1892–1978)
Gardiner, Muriel (1901–1985)
Hahn, Emily (1905–1997)
Highsmith, Patricia (1921–1995)
Hosmer, Harriet (1830–1908)
Hulme, Kathryn (1900–1981)
Jolas, Maria (1893–1987)
Joyce, Nora (1884–1951)
Laurencin, Marie (1883–1956)
Lewis, Edmonia (c. 1845–c. 1909)
Liubatovich, Olga (1853–1917)
Loy, Mina (1882–1966)
Massey, Ilona (1910–1974)
Merritt, Anna Lea (1844–1930)
Nourse, Elizabeth (1859–1938)
O'Neill, Rose Cecil (1874–1944)
Richardson, Henry Handel (1870–1946)
Schiaparelli, Elsa (1890–1973)
Solano, Solita (1888–1975)
Stein, Gertrude (1874–1946)
Taylor, Elizabeth (1932—)
Volkonskaya, Maria (1805–1863)
Yourcenar, Marguerite (1903–1987)

EXPERIMENTAL AVIATOR
Auriol, Jacqueline (1917–2000)
Cobb, Jerrie (b. 1931)
Collins, Eileen (1956—)
Love, Nancy (1914–1976)
Reitsch, Hanna (1912–1979)
Savitskaya, Svetlana (b. 1948)
Stauffenberg, Litta von (c. 1905–1945)
Todd, E.L. (fl. early 1900s)

EXPLORER/TRAVELER
Adams, Harriet Chalmers (1875–1937)
Agassiz, Elizabeth Cary (1822–1907)
Akeley, Delia J. (1875–1970)
Akeley, Mary Jobe (1878–1966)
Anable, Gloria Hollister (1903–1988)
Arnesen, Liv (1953—)
Audouard, Olympe (1830–1890)
Baker, Florence von Sass (1841–1916)
Bancroft, Ann (1955—)
Baret, Jeanne (1740–after 1795)
Bell, Gertrude (1868–1926)
Bishop, Isabella (1831–1904)
Blanc, Marie-Thérèse (1840–1907)
Blunt, Anne (1837–1917)
Boyd, Louise Arner (1887–1972)
Bunbury, Selina (1802–1882)
Burton, Isabel (1831–1896)
Calderón de la Barca, Frances (1804–1882)
Cameron, Agnes Deans (1863–1912)
Campbell, Maude B. (c. 1908–?)
Cheesman, Lucy Evelyn (1881–1969)
Coudreau, Octavie (c. 1870–c. 1910)
Darlington, Jennie (c. 1925—)
David-Neel, Alexandra (1868–1969)
Digby el Mesrab, Jane (1807–1881)
Dixie, Lady Florence (1857–1905)
Dorion, Marie (c. 1790–1850)
Eberhardt, Isabelle (1877–1904)
Ellis, Mina A. (1870–1956)
Fiennes, Celia (1662–1741)
Fiennes, Virginia (1947–2004)
Forbes, Rosita (1893–1967)
Franklin, Jane (1792–1875)
Godin des Odonais, Isabel (1728–d. after 1773)
Hahn, Emily (1905–1997)
Johnson, Osa (1894–1953)
Keen, Dora (1871–1963)
Kingsley, Mary H. (1862–1900)
Krüdener, Julie de (1764–1824)
Maillart, Ella (1903–1997)
Manley, Effa (1900–1981)
Marsden, Kate (1859–1931)
Mead, Margaret (1901–1978)
Mee, Margaret (1909–1988)
Merian, Maria Sybilla (1647–1717)
Mexia, Ynes (1870–1938)
Montez, Lola (1818–1861)
Niles, Blair (1880–1959)
Peary, Josephine (1863–1955)
Peck, Annie Smith (1850–1935)
Pfeiffer, Ida (1797–1858)
Ronne, Edith (1919—)
Saville, Kathleen (1956—)
Scidmore, Eliza Ruhamah (1856–1928)
Seton, Grace Gallatin (1872–1959)
Sheldon, May French (1847–1936)
Stanhope, Hester (1776–1839)
Stark, Freya (1893–1993)
Taylor, Annie Royle (1855–c. 1920)
Taylor, Mary (1817–1893)
Tinné, Alexandrine (1839–1869)

Wetherill, Louisa Wade (1877–1945)
Workman, Fanny (1859–1925)

EXTREME ATHLETE
Allen, Tori (1988—)
Baker, Carlee (1978—)
Basich, Tina (1969—)
Beaman, Hana (1982—)
Bleiler, Gretchen (1981—)
Bodet, Stéphanie (1976—)
Boyle, Darian (c. 1968—)
Brown, Katie (1982—)
Brutsaert, Elke (1968—)
Burke, Sarah (1982—)
Burnside, Cara-Beth (1968—)
Chausson, Anne-Caroline (1977—)
Christy, Barrett (1971—)
Clark, Kelly (1983—)
Cliff, Theresa (1978—)
Cline, Aleisha (1970—)
Copeland-Durham, Emily (1984—)
Csizmazia, Kim (c. 1968—)
Curry, Jenny (1984—)
Dakides, Tara (1975—)
da Silva, Fabiola (1979—)
Demers, Anik (1972—)
Dixon, Tina (1976—)
Drouin, Candice (1976—)
Dunn, Shannon (1972—)
Elliott, Cheri (1970—)
Erbesfield, Robyn (1963—)
Ezzell, Cheryl (c. 1979—)
Fisher, Sarah (1980—)
Friday, Dallas J. (1986—)
Garcia-O'Brien, Tanya (c. 1973—)
Gaytan, Andrea
Giove, Missy (1972—)
Glass, Julie (1979—)
Gouault-Haston, Laurence
Grenard, Lizz (1965—)
Hamilton, Tara (1982—)
Hammarberg, Gretchen
Heffernan, Fallon (1986—)
Hendrawati, Agung (1975—)
Hill, Lynn (1961—)
Hodgson, Tasha (1974—)
Jacobellis, Lindsey (1985—)
Jarvela, Satu
Jonsson, Magdalena (1969—)
Kawasaki, Ayumi (1984—)
Kent, Leslie (1981—)
Kim Jum-Sook (c. 1968—)
Kjeldaas, Stine Brun (1975—)
Lawrence, Chiara (1975—)
Lawyer, April (1975—)
Lew, Bird (c. 1966—)
Llanes, Tara (1976—)
Logue, Jenny (c. 1982—)
Macleod, Jaime (1976—)
Major, Maeghan (1984—)
Marquardt, Melissa (1983—)
Martinod, Marie (c. 1984—)
Matthews, Janet (1965—)
Matthews, Kelly (1982—)
McKenna, Lesley (1974—)
McKnight, Kim
Meyen, Janna (1977—)
Miller, Katrina (1975—)
Molin-Kongsgard, Anne (1977—)
Oestvold, Line (1978—)
Olson, Leslee (1978—)
Ovtchinnikova, Elena (1965—)
Piszczek, Renata (1969—)
Poetzl, Ine (1976—)
Repko, Elena (1975—)
Ricker, Maelle (1978—)
Rodriguez, Jennifer (1976—)
Rudishauser, Corrie (1973—)
Sayres, Aurelie (1977—)
Sher, Lisa (1969—)
Sherman-Kauf, Patti (1963—)
Simmons, Erin (1976—)
Stacey, Kim (1980—)
Streb, Marla (1965—)
Svobodova, Martina (1983—)
Taggart, Michele (1970—)
Teter, Hannah (1987—)
Tidwell-Lucas, Gypsy (c. 1975—)
Tone, Lel (c. 1971—)
Torres, Vanessa (1986—)
Vano, Donna (c. 1955—)
Voutilainen, Katrina (1975—)
Waara, Jennie (1975—)
Walton, Angie (1966—)
Wehr-Hásler, Sábine (1967—)
Yabe, Sayaka
Zakharova, Olga (1973—)
Zwink, Tara (1973—)

FACTORY WORKER
Anderson, Mary (1872–1964)
Apostoloy, Electra (1911–1944)
Aquash, Anna Mae (1945–1976)
Aylward, Gladys (1902–1970)
Boschek, Anna (1874–1957)
Burgess, Renate (1910–1988)
Hayashi Fumiko (1903–1951)
Huck, Winnifred Sprague Mason (1882–1936)
Jemison, Alice Lee (1901–1964)
Jochmann, Rosa (1901–1994)
Kosmodemyanskaya, Zoya (1923–1941)
Kuderikova, Marie (1921–1943)
Larcom, Lucy (1824–1893)
Le Sueur, Meridel (1900–1996)
Nielsen, Asta (1881–1972)
Reinig, Christa (1926—)
Renault, Mary (1905–1983)
Ridge, Lola (1873–1941)
Sanders-Brahms, Helma (1940—)

FADO SINGER
Rodrigues, Amalia (1921–1999)

FAITH HEALER
McPherson, Aimee Semple (1890–1944)
Stapleton, Ruth Carter (1929–1983)
Te Rangimarie, Puna Himene (fl. 1908–1911)

FANTASY/SCIENCE-FICTION WRITER
Brackett, Leigh (1915–1978)
Bradley, Marion Zimmer (1930–1999)
Braun, Johanna (1929—)
Brown, Rosel George (1926–1967)
Broxon, Mildred Downey (1944—)
Burdekin, Katharine (1896–1963)
Butler, Octavia E. (1947—)
Cavendish, Margaret (1623–1673)
Chapman, Vera (1898–1996)
Charnas, Suzy McKee (1939—)
Cherryh, C.J. (1942—)
Coulson, Juanita (1933—)
Dorman, Sonya (1924—)
Duane, Diane (1952—)
Eisenstein, Phyllis (1946—)
Elgin, Suzette Haden (1936—)
Emshwiller, Carol (1921—)
Engdahl, Sylvia (1933—)
Fairbairns, Zöe (1948—)
Felice, Cynthia (1942—)
Freedman, Nancy (1920—)
Gotlieb, Phyllis (1926—)
Grimm, Cherry Barbara (1930–2002)
Haldane, Charlotte (1894–1969)
Henderson, Zenna (1917–1983)
Holland, Cecelia (1943—)
Holly, J. Hunter (1932–1982)
Hoover, H.M. (1935—)
Hughes, Monica (1925–2003)
Kavan, Anna (1901–1968)
Killough, Lee (1942—)
Lee, Tanith (1947—)
Le Guin, Ursula K. (1929—)
L'Engle, Madeleine (1918—)
Lessing, Doris (1919—)
Lichtenberg, Jacqueline (1942—)
Lightner, A.M. (1904–1988)
Lynn, Elizabeth A. (1946—)
MacLean, Katherine (1925—)
MacLeod, Sheila (1939—)
Mayhar, Ardath (1930—)
McCaffrey, Anne (1926—)
McIntyre, Vonda N. (1948—)
Merril, Judith (1923–1997)
Mitchison, Naomi (1897–1999)
Moore, C.L. (1911–1987)
Morris, Janet E. (1946—)
Norton, Andre (1912–2005)
Piserchia, Doris (1928—)
Randall, Marta (1948—)
Reed, Kit (1932—)
Russ, Joanna (1937—)
Sanders-Brahms, Helma (1940—)
Sargent, Pamela (1948—)
Seghers, Anna (1900–1983)
Shelley, Mary (1797–1851)
Smith, Evelyn E. (1922–2000)
Tennant, Emma (1937—)
Vinge, Joan D. (1948—)
Webb, Sharon (1936—)
Wilhelm, Kate (1928—)
Willis, Connie (1945—)
Wrightson, Patricia (1921—)
Yarbro, Chelsea Quinn (1942—)

FARMER
Cryer, Sarah (1848–1929)
Fabish, Agnes (1873–1947)
Gibb, Helen (1838–1914)
Gregg, Christina (c. 1814–1882)
Halcombe, Edith Stanway (1844–1903)
Hames, Mary (1827–1919)
Hirst, Grace (1805–1901)
Jury, Te Aitu-o-te-rangi (c. 1820–1854)
Mackay, Elizabeth Ann Louisa (1843–1908)
O'Donnell, Ann (c. 1857–1934)
Savell, Edith Alma Eileen (1883–1970)
Sinclair, Elizabeth McHutcheson (1800–1892)
Siteman, Isabella Flora (c. 1842–1919)
Small, Mary Elizabeth (1812/13–1908)
Sutherland, Mary Ann (1864–1948)
Wilson, Helen Mary (1869–1957)

FASHION COMMENTATOR
Donner, Vyvyan (1895–1965)

FASHION DESIGNER
Ashley, Laura (1925–1985)
August, Bonnie (1947–2003)
Barnes, Jhane (1954—)
Benetton, Guiliana (1935—)
Bryant, Lane (1879–1951)
Carnegie, Hattie (1886–1956)
Carven (b. 1909)
Cashin, Bonnie (1915–2000)
Chanel, Coco (1883–1971)
Claiborne, Liz (1929—)
Davies, Betty (1935—)
Demorest, Ellen Curtis (1824–1898)
Duff Gordon, Lucy (1862–1935)

Etting, Ruth (1896–1978)
Flöge, Emilie (1874–1952)
Fontana, Giovanna (1915–2004)
Gattinoni, Fernanda (1906–2002)
Grès, Alix (1910–1993)
Hamnett, Katherine (1952—)
Hawes, Elizabeth (1903–1971)
Irene (1901–1962)
Kamali, Norma (1945—)
Karan, Donna (1948—)
Kawakubo, Rei (1942—)
Klein, Anne (1923–1974)
Lanvin, Jeanne (1867–1946)
Maxwell, Vera (1901–1995)
McCardell, Claire (1905–1958)
McMein, Neysa (1888–1949)
Muir, Jean (1928–1995)
Myrtil, Odette (1898–1978)
Parnis, Mollie (1905–1992)
Rambova, Natacha (1897–1966)
Ratia, Armi (1912–1979)
Reger, Janet (1935–2005)
Reich, Lilly (1885–1947)
Reid, Rose Marie (1906–1978)
Rhodes, Zandra (1940—)
Ricci, Nina (1883–1970)
Sander, Jil (1943—)
Schiaparelli, Elsa (1890–1973)
Simon, Simone (1910–2005)
Simpson, Adele (1903–1995)
Stepanova, Varvara (1894–1958)
Tilberis, Liz (1947–1999)
Trigère, Pauline (1912—)
Valentina (1899–1989)
Vionnet, Madeleine (1876–1975)
von Furstenberg, Diane (1946—)
Vreeland, Diana (1903–1989)
Wang, Vera (1949—)
West, Claire (1893–1980)
Westwood, Vivienne (1941—)

FASHION MODEL
Alexander, Julie (1938–2003)
Ast, Pat (1941–2001)
Berenson, Marisa (1946—)
Berry, Halle (1966—)
Brinkley, Christie (1953—)
Burke, Frances (c. 1921—)
Capucine (1931–1990)
Falkenburg, Jinx (1919–2003)
Hanson, Marla (c. 1962—)
Hedren, Tippi (1931—)
Hemingway, Margaux (1955–1996)
Holden, Gloria (1908–1991)
Hutton, Lauren (1943—)
James, Esther Marion Pretoria (1900–1990)
La Badie, Florence (1888–1917)
Lange, Jessica (1949—)
Leaver, Henrietta (c. 1916–1993)
MacGraw, Ali (1938—)
McNamara, Maggie (1928–1978)
Meseke, Marilyn (1916–2001)
Miller, Lee (1907–1977)
Moss, Kate (1974—)
Novak, Kim (1933—)
Parker, Suzy (1932–1932)
Shepherd, Cybill (1949—)
Shrimpton, Jean (1942—)
Simon, Simone (1910–2005)
Sims, Naomi (1948—)
Stone, Sharon (1958—)
Thomas, Olive (1884–1920)
Turlington, Christy (1969—)
Twiggy (1946—)

FASHION PHOTOGRAPHER
Abbe, Kathryn (1919—)
Andriesse, Emmy (1914–1953)
Berenson, Berry (1948–2001)
Besnyö, Eva (1910–2003)
Dahl-Wolfe, Louise (1895–1989)
Fleischmann, Trude (1895–1990)
Frissell, Toni (1907–1988)
Hofer, Evelyn
Naylor, Genevieve (1915–1989)

FEDERAL COMMUNICATIONS COMMISSIONER (U.S.)
Hennock, Frieda B. (1904–1960)
Reid, Charlotte Thompson (b. 1913)

FEMINIST
Abaijah, Josephine (1942—)
Abayomi, Oyinkansola (1897–1990)
Abiertas, Josepha (1894–1929)
Abzug, Bella (1920–1998)
Achurch, Janet (1864–1916)
Adam, Juliette la Messine (1836–1936)
Aesara of Lucania (fl. 400s–300s BCE)
Aikin, Lucy (1781–1864)
Akerman, Chantal (1950—)
Akhmatova, Anna (1889–1966)
Aliberty, Soteria (1847–1929)
Alkhateeb, Sharifa (1946–2004)
Allart, Hortense (1801–1879)
Allred, Gloria (1941—)
Ames, Jessie Daniel (1883–1972)
Anderson, Maybanke (1845–1927)
Angelou, Maya (1928—)
Anneke, Mathilde Franziska (1817–1884)
Anselmi, Tina (1927—)
Anthony, Katharine Susan (1877–1965)
Anthony, Susan B. (1820–1906)
Anthony, Susan B., II (1916–1991)
Aoki, Yayoi (1927—)
Aptheker, Bettina (1944—)
Arceo, Liwayway (1924—)
Archambault, Mademoiselle (c. 1724–?)
Armand, Inessa (1874–1920)
Astell, Mary (1666–1731)
Aston, Luise (1814–1871)
Astorga, Nora (1949–1988)
Atkinson, Lily May (1866–1921)
Atkinson, Ti-Grace (1939—)
Auclert, Hubertine (1848–1914)
Bain, Wilhelmina Sherriff (1848–1944)
Bajer, Matilde (1840–1934)
Barakat, Hidiya Afifi (1898–1969)
Baranskaya, Natalia (b. 1908)
Barker, Jane (1652–1732)
Barnes, Djuna (1892–1982)
Barney, Natalie Clifford (1876–1972)
Baume, Rosetta Lulah (1871–1934)
Bear-Crawford, Annette (1853–1899)
Beard, Mary Ritter (1876–1958)
Beauvoir, Simone de (1908–1986)
Bellamy, Madge (1899–1990)
Bemberg, Maria Luisa (1922–1995)
Benedict, Ruth (1887–1948)
Benson, Mildred (1905–2002)
Benson, Stella (1892–1933)
Bernardino, Minerva (1907–1998)
Besnyö, Eva (1910–2003)
Betbeze, Yolande (1930—)
Bethune, Louise Blanchard (1856–1913)
Blackwell, Alice Stone (1857–1950)
Blair, Emily Newell (1877–1951)
Bloodworth, Rhoda Alice (1889–1980)
Bloomer, Amelia Jenks (1818–1894)
Bodichon, Barbara (1827–1891)
Boissevain, Mia (1878–1959)
Bol Poel, Martha (1877–1956)
Bonnevie, Margarete Ottilie (1884–1970)
Booth, Angela Elizabeth (1869–1954)
Boucherett, Jessie (1825–1905)
Bouvier, Jeanne (1865–1964)
Brantenberg, Gerd (1941—)
Bré, Ruth (1862–1911)
Brinvilliers, Marie de (1630–1676)
Brion, Hélène (1882–1962)
Brittain, Vera (1893–1970)
Brooks, Romaine (1874–1970)
Brown, Rosemary (1930—)
Brunschvicg, Cécile (1877–1946)
Bryant, Dorothy (1930—)
Budzynska-Tylicka, Justyna (1876–1936)
Bullock, Margaret (1845–1903)
Butler, Josephine (1828–1906)
Cabete, Adelaide (1867–1935)
Cabot, Dolce Ann (1862–1943)
Calkins, Mary Whiton (1863–1930)
Callwood, June (1924—)
Calypso Rose (1940—)
Cambridge, Ada (1844–1926)
Cameron, Agnes Deans (1863–1912)
Campoamor, Clara (1888–1972)
Canth, Minna (1844–1897)
Capmany Farnes, Maria Aurèlia (1918—)
Carabillo, Toni (1926–1997)
Carlén, Emilia (1807–1892)
Carney, Winifred (1887–1943)
Carter, Angela (1940–1992)
Casgrain, Thérèse (1896–1981)
Cassie, Alice Mary (1887–1963)
Castellanos, Rosario (1925–1974)
Catt, Carrie Chapman (1859–1947)
Cauer, Minna (1841–1922)
Chapin, Augusta (1836–1905)
Châtelet, Émilie du (1706–1749)
Chattopadhyaya, Kamaladevi (1903–1988)
Chawaf, Chantal (1943—)
Chen Tiejun (1904–1928)
Chesler, Phyllis (1940—)
Chicago, Judy (1939—)
Chitnis, Leela (1909–2003)
Christine de Pizan (c. 1363–c. 1431)
Clément, Catherine (1939—)
Clisby, Harriet (1830–1931)
Cobbe, Frances Power (1822–1904)
Colclough, Mary Ann (1836–1885)
Coleman, Corrine Grad (1927–2004)
Collet, Clara (1860–1948)
Collett, Camilla (1813–1895)
Cook, Freda Mary (1896–1990)
Cooper, Anna J. (c. 1858–1964)
Corbett-Ashby, Margery (1882–1981)
Costa, Maria Velho de (b. 1938)
Cotera, Martha (1938—)
Cousins, Margaret (1878–1954)
Crocker, Hannah Mather (1752–1829)
Cullis, Winifred Clara (1875–1956)
Cunnington, Eveline Willert (1849–1916)
Daldy, Amey (c. 1829–1920)
Dalrymple, Learmonth White (1827–1906)
Daly, Mary (1928—)
D'Arcy, Margaretta (1934—)
Davey, Constance (1882–1963)
David, Caroline Edgeworth (1856–1951)
Davies, Sonja (1923–2005)
Davis, Paulina Wright (1813–1876)
Dawson, Alice Madge (c. 1980–2003)
Debo, Angie (1890–1988)
de Cleyre, Voltairine (1866–1912)
De Costa, Maria Velho (b. 1938)
Dejanović, Draga (1843–1870)
Delarue-Mardrus, Lucie (1880–1945)
De Lauretis, Teresa (1938—)

Delphy, Christine (1941—)
Démar, Claire (1800–1833)
Deng Yuzhi (1900–1996)
Denison, Flora MacDonald (1867–1921)
Deraismes, Maria (1828–1894)
Deroin, Jeanne-Françoise (1805–1894)
Despard, Charlotte (1844–1939)
Deutsch, Helene (1884–1982)
Devanny, Jean (1894–1962)
Dexter, Caroline (1819–1884)
Di Robilant, Daisy, Countess (fl. 1922–1933)
Dittmar, Louise (1807–1884)
Dohm, Hedwig (1831–1919)
Doolittle, Hilda (1886–1961)
Dorr, Rheta Childe (1866–1948)
Douglass, Helen Pitts (1838–1903)
Drake, Judith (fl. 1696)
Drew, Jane (1911–1996)
Duchêne, Gabrielle (1870–1954)
Duff Gordon, Lucy (1862–1935)
Dugdale, Henrietta (1826–1918)
Dulac, Germaine (1882–1942)
Durack, Fanny (1889–1956)
Durand, Lucile (1930—)
Durand, Marguerite (1864–1936)
Dworkin, Andrea (1946–2005)
Earhart, Amelia (1897–1937)
Eastman, Annis Ford (1852–1910)
Eaubonne, Françoise d' (1920–2005)
Efflatoun, Inji (1923–1989)
Egyptian Feminism (1800–1980)
Ellen, Mary Ann (1897–1949)
El Saadawi, Nawal (1931—)
England, Maud Russell (1863–1956)
Enoki, Miswo (1939—)
Estrich, Susan R. (1952—)
Faithfull, Emily (1835–1895)
Falcón, Lidia (1935—)
Farrokhzad, Forugh (1935–1967)
Fawcett, Millicent Garrett (1847–1929)
Fennell, Nuala (1935—)
Fiedler, Bobbi (1937—)
Figes, Eva (1932—)
Filosofova, Anna (1837–1912)
Firestone, Shulamith (1945—)
First, Ruth (1925–1982)
Fisher, Dorothy Canfield (1879–1958)
Flanagan, Hallie (1889–1969)
Fleeson, Doris (1901–1970)
Flynn, Elizabeth Gurley (1890–1964)
Foltz, Clara (1849–1934)
Ford, Isabella O. (1855–1924)
Freeman, Alice (1857–1936)
Friday, Nancy (1937—)
Friedan, Betty (1921–2006)
Fukuda Hideko (1865–1927)
Fuller, Margaret (1810–1850)
Furlong, Monica (1930–2003)
Gage, Frances D. (1808–1884)
Gagneur, Louise (1832–1902)
Gale, Zona (1874–1938)
Galindo de Topete, Hermila (1896–1954)
Galvão, Patricia (1910–1962)
Gandy, Kim A. (c. 1954—)
Gardener, Helen Hamilton (1853–1925)
Garvey, Amy Jacques (1896–1973)
Geddes, Annabella Mary (1864–1955)
Gérin-Lajoie, Marie (1867–1945)
Gibson, Emily Patricia (1863/64?–1947)
Gillett, Emma (1852–1927)
Gilligan, Carol (1936—)
Gilman, Charlotte Perkins (1860–1935)
Gilmore, Mary (1865–1962)
Gísladóttir, Sólrún
Goegg, Marie (1826–1899)
Goldstein, Vida (1869–1949)
Gomez, Sara (1943–1974)
Gonne, Maud (1866–1953)
Goodbody, Buzz (1946–1975)
Gore-Booth, Eva (1870–1926)
Gourd, Emilie (1879–1946)
Grant, Jane (1895–1972)
Gray, Hanna Holborn (1930—)
Greer, Germaine (1939—)
Gress, Elsa (1919–1989)
Grimké, Angelina E. (1805–1879)
Grimké, Charlotte L. Forten (1837–1914)
Grimké, Sarah Moore (1792–1873)
Grossmann, Edith Searle (1863–1931)
Groza, Maria (1918—)
Guiducci, Armanda (1923–1992)
Gutiérrez de Mendoza, Juana Belén (1875–1942)
Gutteridge, Helena Rose (1879–1960)
Hagan, Ellen (1873–1958)
Hagman, Lucina (1853–1946)
Hainisch, Marianne (1839–1936)
Haldane, Charlotte (1894–1969)
Halimi, Gisèle (1927—)
Hall, Radclyffe (1880–1943)
Hamilton, Cicely (1872–1952)
Hamilton, Mary (1882–1966)
Hanaford, Phebe Ann (1829–1921)
Hanim, Latife (1898–1975)
Harjo, Joy (1951—)
Harman, Harriet (1950—)
Hart, Jane (1920—)
Haslam, Anna (1829–1922)
Haushofer, Marlen (1920–1970)
Havemeyer, Louisine (1855–1929)
Hawes, Elizabeth (1903–1971)
Hays, Mary (1760–1843)
Heilbrun, Carolyn Gold (1926–2003)
Henderson, Stella (1871–1962)
He Xiangning (1879–1972)
Heymann, Lida (1867–1943)
Higuchi, Ichiyo (1872–1896)
Hiratsuka, Raichō (1886–1971)
Hirsch, Rachel (1870–1953)
Hite, Shere (1943—)
Hogan, Linda (1947—)
Holley, Marietta (1836–1926)
Hollins, Marion B. (1892–1944)
Holmes, Julia Archibald (1838–1887)
Holt, Winifred (1870–1945)
Holtby, Winifred (1898–1935)
Hooper, Kate Challis (1894–1982)
Hopkins, Ellice (1836–1904)
Horney, Karen (1885–1952)
Horta, Maria Teresa (b. 1937)
How-Martyn, Edith (1875–1954)
Hrotsvitha of Gandersheim (c. 935–1001)
Hughes, Sarah T. (1896–1985)
Hull, Helen Rose (1888–1971)
Hurst, Fannie (1889–1968)
Hutchinson, Abigail (1829–1892)
Hutton, Lauren (1943—)
Ibarbourou, Juana de (1895–1979)
Ichikawa Fusae (1893–1981)
Idar, Jovita (1885–1946)
Ihrer, Emma (1857–1911)
Ireland, Patricia (1945—)
Irigaray, Luce (1930—)
Irwin, Inez Haynes (1873–1970)
Jaburkova, Jozka (d. 1944)
Jacob, Rosamund (1888–1960)
Jacobs, Aletta (1854–1929)
Jacobs, Harriet A. (1813–1897)
Jakobsdóttir, Svava (1930—)
Jalandoni, Magdalena (1891–1978)
Jameson, Storm (1891–1986)
Janeway, Elizabeth (1913–2005)
Jesenská, Milena (1896–1945)
Jesse, Fryniwyd Tennyson (1888–1958)
Jewett, Sarah Orne (1849–1909)
Jewsbury, Geraldine (1812–1880)
Johnson, Adelaide (1859–1955)
Johnston, Mary (1870–1936)
Juana Inés de la Cruz (1651–1695)
Judd, Ashley (1968—)
Kairi, Evanthia (1797–1866)
Kamal, Sufia (1911–1999)
Karr, Carme (1865–1943)
Kartini (1879–1904)
Kazantzis, Judith (1940—)
Kehajia, Kalliopi (1839–1905)
Kéita, Aoua (1912–1979)
Kelley, Abby (1810–1887)
Kelly, Petra (1947–1992)
Kennedy, Florynce (1916–2000)
Kennedy, Helena (1950—)
Kenyon, Dorothy (1888–1972)
Késhly, Anna (1889–1976)
Key, Ellen (1849–1926)
Khan, Begum Liaquat Ali (1905–1990)
King, Billie Jean (1943—)
Kirchwey, Freda (1893–1976)
Kirkwood, Julieta (1936–1985)
Kitzinger, Sheila (1929—)
Klepfisz, Irena (1941—)
Kobrynska, Natalia Ivanovna (1855–1920)
Kollontai, Alexandra (1872–1952)
Kollwitz, Käthe (1867–1945)
Konopnicka, Maria (1842–1910)
Kovalskaia, Elizaveta (1851–1943)
Kreps, Juanita (1921—)
Kruger, Barbara (1945—)
Kuhn, Maggie (1905–1995)
Kushida Fuki (1899–2001)
Labé, Louise (c. 1523–1566)
Landeta, Matilde (1913—)
Lang, Marie (1858–1934)
Lange, Helene (1848–1930)
La Rochefoucauld, Edmée, Duchesse de (1895–1991)
Laskaridou, Aikaterini (1842–1916)
Laughlin, Gail (1868–1952)
Lawrence, Susan (1871–1947)
Lawson, Louisa (1848–1920)
Lear, Frances (1923–1996)
Leclerc, Annie (1940—)
Lee, Muna (1895–1965)
Lees, Sue (1941–2003)
Lefaucheux, Marie-Helene (1904–1964)
Le Garrec, Evelyne
Leginska, Ethel (1886–1970)
Lehmann, Rosamond (1901–1990)
Lemel, Nathalie (1827–1921)
Léo, André (1832–1900)
Léon, Pauline (1758–?)
Lerner, Gerda (1920—)
Le Sueur, Meridel (1900–1996)
Lorde, Audre (1934–1992)
Lovejoy, Esther Pohl (1869–1967)
Lowney, Shannon (1969–1994)
Lüders, Marie-Elizabeth (1888–1966)
Lutz, Berta (1894–1976)
MacFall, Frances E. (1854–1943)
MacGill, Elsie (d. 1980)
MacGill, Helen Gregory (1871–1947)
Mackay, Elizabeth Ann Louisa (1843–1908)
Mackenzie, Midge (1938–2004)
Mackinnon, Catherine A. (1946—)
Macmillan, Chrystal (1871–1937)
Macphail, Agnes (1890–1954)
Majerová, Marie (1882–1967)
Malaika, Nazik al- (1923–1992)
Malaika, Salma al- (1908–1953)

Malakhovskaya, Natalia (1947—)
Malpede, Karen (1945—)
Manus, Rosa (1881–1942)
Maraini, Dacia (1936—)
Martin, Emma (1812–1851)
Martin, Lillien Jane (1851–1943)
Martinson, Moa (1890–1964)
Marzouk, Zahia (1906–1988)
Mason, Lucy Randolph (1882–1959)
Mayreder, Rosa (1858–1938)
McCracken, Mary Ann (1770–1866)
McIntosh, Millicent Carey (1898–2001)
McLaren, Agnes (1837–1913)
McPherson, Heather (1942—)
Meena (1956–1987)
Melville, Eliza Ellen (1882–1946)
Mészáros, Márta (1931—)
Meyer, Annie Nathan (1867–1951)
Michaëlis, Karin (1872–1950)
Michel, Louise (1830–1905)
Millay, Edna St. Vincent (1892–1950)
Miller, Alice Duer (1874–1942)
Miller, Emma Guffey (1874–1970)
Millett, Kate (1934—)
Mink, Paule (1839–1901)
Mirabal de González, Patria (1924–1960)
Mirabal de Guzmán, María Teresa (1936–1960)
Mirabal de Tavárez, Minerva (1927–1960)
Miró, Pilar (1940–1997)
Misme, Jane (1865–1935)
Mitchell, Juliet (1934—)
Mitchell, Roma (1913–2000)
Mitchison, Rosalind (1919–2002)
Mizuta, Tamae (1929—)
Monod, Sarah (1836–1912)
Montanclos, Marie-Emilie Maryon de (1736–1812)
Montoriol i Puig, Carme (1893–1966)
Montreal Massacre (1989)
Montseny, Federica (1905–1994)
Moreau de Justo, Alicia (1885–1986)
Morgan, Robin (1941—)
Morgner, Irmtraud (1933–1990)
Morison, Harriet (1862–1925)
Mott, Lucretia (1793–1880)
Mozzoni, Anna Maria (1837–1920)
M'rabet, Fadéla (1935—)
Mulford, Wendy (1941—)
Müller, Mary Ann (c. 1819–1902)
Murphy, Emily (1868–1933)
Murray, Judith Sargent (1751–1820)
Murray, Margaret (1863–1963)
Murray, Pauli (1910–1985)
Namjoshi, Suniti (1941—)
Nasrin, Taslima (1962—)
Nasser, Tahia (1923—)
Nassif, Malak Hifni (1886–1918)
Near, Holly (1949—)
Nedreaas, Torborg (1906–1987)
Negri, Ada (1870–1945)
Nelken, Margarita (1896–1968)
Nin, Anais (1903–1977)
Noce, Teresa (1900–1980)
Noronha, Joana de (fl. c. 1850)
Norton, Eleanor Holmes (1937—)
Nováková, Teréza (1853–1912)
Oakley, Ann (1944—)
O'Brien, Kate (1897–1974)
Ocampo, Victoria (1890–1979)
Okin, Susan Moller (1946–2004)
Olberg, Oda (1872–1955)
Orzeszkowa, Eliza (1841–1910)
Ośorio, Ana de Castro (1872–1935)
Ottesen-Jensen, Elise (1886–1973)
Otto-Peters, Luise (1819–1895)
Ovington, Mary White (1865–1951)
Paglia, Camille (1947—)
Palm, Etta Aelders (1743–1799)
Palmer, Alice May (1886–1977)
Pankhurst, Adela (1885–1961)
Pankhurst, Christabel (1880–1958)
Pankhurst, Emmeline (1858–1928)
Pankhurst, Sylvia (1882–1960)
Pappenheim, Bertha (1859–1936)
Pardo Bazán, Emilia (1852–1921)
Parker, Pat (1944–1989)
Parkes, Bessie Rayner (1829–1925)
Parlby, Irene (1868–1965)
Parren, Kalliroe (1861–1940)
Parturier, Françoise (1919—)
Pelham, Mary Singleton Copley (c. 1710–1789)
Pelletier, Madeleine (1874–1939)
Peri Rossi, Cristina (1941—)
Perovskaya, Sonia (1853–1881)
Perry, Eleanor (1915–1981)
Pestana, Alice (1860–1929)
Phillips, Lena Madesin (1881–1955)
Phillips, Marion (1881–1932)
Pierangeli, Rina Faccio (1876–1960)
Pinkham, Lydia E. (1819–1883)
Pitt, Marie E.J. (1869–1948)
Plaminkova, Frantiska (1875–1942)
Player, Mary Josephine (c. 1857–1924)
Pollitzer, Anita (1894–1975)
Pompeia, Núria (1938—)
Poniatowska, Elena (1932—)
Portal, Magda (1903–1989)
Potonié-Pierre, Eugénie (1844–1898)
Pritam, Amrita (1919–2005)
Procter, Adelaide (1825–1864)
Prosperi, Carola (1883–1975)
Prou, Suzanne (1920–1995)
Ptaschkina, Nelly (1903–1920)
Puisieux, Madeleine de (1720–1798)
Qiu Jin (c. 1875–1907)
Queizán, María Xosé (1938—)
Rafanelli, Leda (1880–1971)
Ramirez, Sara Estela (1881–1910)
Ransome-Kuti, Funmilayo (1900–1978)
Rathbone, Eleanor (1872–1946)
Ravera, Camilla (1889–1988)
Reagan, Maureen (1941–2001)
Reddy, Helen (1942—)
Reinig, Christa (1926—)
Remond, Sarah Parker (1826–1894)
Reuter, Gabriele (1859–1941)
Rhondda, Margaret (1883–1958)
Ricard, Marthe (1889–1982)
Rich, Adrienne (1929—)
Rifaat, Alifa (1930–1996)
Robins, Elizabeth (1862–1952)
Robinson, Mary (1944—)
Rochefort, Christiane (1917–1998)
Rodríguez, Evangelina (1879–1947)
Rodríguez de Tió, Lola (1843–1924)
Rohde, Ruth Bryan Owen (1885–1954)
Roland, Pauline (1805–1852)
Rome, Esther (1945–1995)
Roudy, Yvette (1929—)
Roussel, Nelly (1878–1922)
Rover, Constance (1910–2005)
Rowbotham, Sheila (1943—)
Rowson, Susanna (1762–1824)
Roxon, Lillian (1932–1973)
Royer, Clémence (1830–1902)
Ruddock, Joan (1943—)
Ruether, Rosemary (1936—)
Runeberg, Fredrika (1807–1879)
Russ, Joanna (1937—)
Russell, Dora (1894–1986)
Rye, Maria Susan (1829–1903)
Sabin, Florence (1871–1953)
Sackville-West, Vita (1892–1962)
Salis-Marschlins, Meta (1855–1929)
Samoilova, Konkordiya (1876–1921)
Sanford, Maria Louise (1836–1920)
Sanger, Margaret (1879–1966)
Sangster, Margaret (1838–1912)
Sarfatti, Margherita (1880–1961)
Sauvé, Jeanne (1922–1993)
Savary, Olga (1933—)
Schirmacher, Käthe (1859–1930)
Schlesinger, Therese (1863–1940)
Schmahl, Jeanne (1846–1916)
Schmidt, Auguste (1833–1902)
Schreiber, Adele (1872–1957)
Schreiner, Olive (1855–1920)
Schwimmer, Rosika (1877–1948)
Scott, Ann London (1929–1975)
Scott, Mary (1751–1793)
Scott, Rose (1847–1925)
Seton, Grace Gallatin (1872–1959)
Séverine (1855–1929)
Sewall, Lucy Ellen (1837–1890)
Seyrig, Delphine (1932–1990)
Shaarawi, Huda (1879–1947)
Shabanova, Anna (1848–1932)
Shafik, Doria (1908–1975)
Shange, Ntozake (1948—)
Shapir, Olga (1850–1916)
Shapiro, Betty Kronman (1907–1989)
Shaver, Dorothy (1897–1959)
Sheehy-Skeffington, Hanna (1877–1946)
Sheepshanks, Mary (1872–1958)
Sheppard, Kate (1847–1934)
Sherkat, Shahla (c. 1956—)
Shulman, Alix Kates (1932—)
Sievwright, Margaret Home (1844–1905)
Simcox, Edith (1844–1901)
Sinclair, May (1863–1946)
Smeal, Eleanor (1939—)
Smedley, Agnes (1892–1950)
Smith, Lucy Masey (1861–1936)
Snow, Sarah Ellen Oliver (1864–1939)
Soljak, Miriam Bridelia (1879–1971)
Sotiriou, Dido (1909–2004)
Spence, Catherine (1825–1910)
Spencer, Anne (1882–1975)
Spender, Dale (1943—)
Staël, Germaine de (1766–1817)
Stasova, Nadezhda (1822–1895)
Stead, Christina (1902–1983)
Steel, Dawn (1946–1997)
Stefan, Verena (1947—)
Steinem, Gloria (1934—)
Stephens, Kate (1853–1938)
Stevens, May (1924—)
Stewart, Alice (1906–2002)
Stocks, Mary Danvers (1891–1975)
Stoecker, Helene (1869–1943)
Stone, Constance (1856–1902)
Storni, Alfonsina (1892–1938)
Stout, Anna Paterson (1858–1931)
Stowe, Emily Howard (1831–1903)
Strachey, Pippa (1872–1968)
Strachey, Ray (1887–1940)
Street, Jessie (1889–1970)
Stritt, Marie (1856–1928)
Strong, Harriet (1844–1929)
Strossen, Nadine (1950—)
Sullerot, Evelyne (1924—)
Suplicy, Marta (c. 1946—)
Svetla, Caroline (1830–1899)
Svolou, Maria (d. 1976)
Swanwick, Anna (1813–1899)
Tabouis, Geneviève (1892–1985)
Taggard, Genevieve (1894–1948)
Tasker, Marianne Allen (1852–1911)

Taylor, Harriet (1807–1858)
Taymuriyya, 'A'isha 'Ismat al- (1840–1902)
Théoret, France (1942—)
Théroigne de Méricourt, Anne-Josèphe (1762–1817)
Thiam, Awa (1936—)
Thomas, M. Carey (1857–1935)
Thomas, Marlo (1937—)
Thompson, Clara (1893–1958)
Tinayre, Marcelle (c. 1870–1948)
Tod, Isabella (1836–1896)
Torrezão, Guiomar (1844–1898)
Toyen (1902–1980)
Traba, Marta (1930–1983)
Trubnikova, Mariia (1835–1897)
Truth, Sojourner (c. 1797–1883)
Tucker, C. DeLores (1927—)
Tully, Mary Jean Crenshaw (1925–2003)
Tuqan, Fadwa (1917–2003)
Tusap, Srbuhi (1841–1901)
Tweedie, Jill (1936–1993)
Tweedy, Hilda (b. 1911)
Ueno, Chizuko (1948—)
Uzès, Anne, Duchesse d' (1847–1933)
Vaa, Aslaug (1889–1965)
Valette, Aline (1850–1899)
Van Grippenberg, Alexandra (1859–1913)
van Schurmann, Anna Maria (1607–1678)
Varda, Agnes (1928—)
Vargas, Virginia (1945—)
Vasconcellos, Karoline Michaëlis de (1851–1925)
Veil, Simone (1927—)
Vengerova, Zinaida (1867–1941)
Vernon, Mabel (1883–1975)
Vérone, Maria (1874–1938)
Vik, Bjørg (1935—)
Voilquin, Suzanne (1801–1877)
Wägner, Elin (1882–1949)
Wald, Lillian D. (1867–1940)
Wandor, Michelene (1940—)
Waring, Marilyn (1952—)
Warner, Marina (1946—)
Weber, Helene Marie (b. 1824)
Webster, Augusta (1837–1894)
Weiss, Louise (1893–1983)
Wells, Ada (1863–1933)
West, Rebecca (1892–1983)
Wheeler, Anna Doyle (1785–c. 1850)
Whitney, Anne (1821–1915)
Whitton, Charlotte (1896–1975)
Wickham, Anna (1883–1947)
Wieland, Joyce (1931–1998)
Wilhelmine of Darmstadt (1765–1796)
Wilkinson, Ellen (1891–1947)
Willard, Emma Hart (1787–1870)
Williams, Mary Wilhelmine (1878–1944)
Williamson, Jessie Marguerite (c. 1855–1937)
Wilson, Charlotte (1854–1944)
Wilson, Margaret W. (1882–1973)
Wittig, Monique (1935–2003)
Wolf, Christa (1929—)
Wollstonecraft, Mary (1759–1797)
Wolstenholme-Elmy, Elizabeth (1834–1913)
Woodward, Joanne (1930—)
Woolf, Virginia (1882–1941)
Woolley, Mary E. (1863–1947)
Wootton, Barbara (1897–1988)
Workman, Fanny (1859–1925)
Wu, Chien-Shiung (1912–1997)
Wunderlich, Frieda (1884–1965)
Wu Zetian (624–705)
Xiao Hong (1911–1942)
Yamada, Mitsuye (1923—)
Yard, Molly (1912–2005)
Yorkin, Peg (1927—)
Yosano, Akiko (1878–1942)
Yosano Akiko (1878–1942)
Zagorka (1873–1957)
Zayas y Sotomayor, María de (1590–c. 1650)
Zayyat, Latifa al- (1923—)
Zetkin, Clara (1857–1933)
Ziyada, Mayy (1886–1941)

FENCER
Aznavourian, Karina (1974—)
Badea, Laura (1970—)
Barlois, Valerie (1969—)
Bau, Sabine (1969—)
Begard, Isabelle (1960—)
Belova-Novikova, Yelena (1947—)
Bianchedi, Diana (1969—)
Bischoff, Sabine (1958—)
Bobis, Ildiko (1945—)
Bogen, Erna (1906—)
Bokel, Claudia (1973—)
Bortolozzi, Francesca (1968—)
Brouquier, Veronique (1957—)
Camber, Irene (1926—)
Cesari, Welleda (1920—)
Chiesa, Laura (1971—)
Collino, Maria (1947—)
Colombetti, Bruna (1936—)
Dan, Aurora (1955—)
Daninthe, Sarah (1980—)
Davis, Gladys (b. 1893)
Dobmeier, Annette (1968—)
Dumitrescu, Roxana (1967—)
Dumont, Brigitte (1944—)
Duplitzer, Imke (1975—)
Ermakova, Oxana (1973—)
Fichtel, Anja (1968—)
Flessel, Laura (1971—)
Freeman, Muriel (1897—)
Funkenhauser, Zita-Eva (1966—)
Gandolfi, Annapia (1964—)
Garayeva, Yuliya
Garilhe, Renee (1923—)
Gaudin-Latrille, Brigitte (1958—)
Gilyazova, Nailiya (1953—)
Gorokhova, Galina (1938—)
Grigorescu, Claudia (1968—)
Gruchala, Sylwia (1981—)
Guinness, Heather (1910—)
Gulacsy, Maria (1941—)
Gyulai-Drimba, Ileana (1946—)
Hablützel-Bürki, Gianna (1969—)
Hachin-Trinquet, Pascale (1958—)
Hanisch, Cornelia (1952—)
Heckscher, Grete (1901–1987)
Heidemann, Britta (1982—)
Jacobson, Sada (1983—)
Janosi, Zsuzsanna (1963—)
Josland, Claudie (1946—)
Juhaszne-Nagy, Katalin (1932—)
Kiraly Picot, Hajnalka (1971—)
Klug, Annette (1969—)
Knyazeva, Olga (1954—)
Koenig, Rita
Kovacs, Edit (1954—)
Kovacsne-Nyari, Magdolna (1921—)
Lachmann, Karen (1916–1962)
Lambert, Margaret Bergmann (1914—)
Lamon, Sophie (1985—)
Liang Qin
Li Na
Logounova, Tatiana (1980—)
Lonzi-Ragno, Antonella (1940—)
Luan Jujie (1958—)
Maros, Magda (1951—)
Marosi, Paula (1936—)
Matuscsakne-Ronay, Ildiko (1946—)
Mayer, Helene (1910–1953)
Mazina, Maria (1964—)
Mees, Helga (1937—)
Mendelenyine-Agoston, Judit (1937—)
Meygret, Anne (1965—)
Moressee-Pichot, Sophie (1962—)
Mroczkiewicz, Magdalena (1979—)
Muzio, Christine (1951—)
Nagy, Annamaria (1982—)
Nagy, Timea (1970—)
Nikonova, Valentina (1952—)
Nisima, Maureen (1981—)
Oelkers-Caragioff, Olga (1887–1969)
Oros, Rozalia (1963—)
Osiier, Ellen (1890–1962)
Pascu-Ene-Dersidan, Ana (1944—)
Pasini, Claudia (1939—)
Preis, Ellen (1912—)
Prudskova, Valentina (1938—)
Rastvorova, Valentina (1933—)
Roldan Reyna, Pilar (1944—)
Romagnoli, Diana (1977—)
Romary, Janice-Lee (1927—)
Rybicka, Anna (1977—)
Sadovskaya, Tatyana (1966—)
Sagine-Ujlakine-Rejto, Ildiko (1937—)
Sakovitsne-Domolky, Lidia (1936—)
Samusenko-Petrenko, Tatyana (1938—)
Scarlat, Roxana (1975—)
Schacherer-Elek, Ilona (1907–1988)
Scherberger-Weiss, Rosemarie (1935—)
Schmid, Adelheid (1938—)
Sheen, Gillian (1928—)
Shishova, Lyudmila (1940—)
Sidorova-Burochkina, Valentina (1954—)
Sivkova, Anna (1982—)
Stahl-Iencic, Ecaterina (1946—)
Stefanek, Gertrud (1959—)
Szabo, Reka (1967—)
Szabo-Orban, Olga (1938—)
Szalay Horvathne, Gyongyi
Szekelyne-Marvalics, Gyorgyi (1924—)
Szewczyk, Barbara (1970—)
Szocs, Zsuzsanna (1962—)
Szolnoki, Maria (1947—)
Tan Xue (1984—)
Theuerkauff-Vorbrich, Gudrun (1937—)
Traversa, Lucia (1965—)
Trillini, Giovanna (1970—)
Trinquet, Veronique (1956—)
Tsagarayeva, Larisa (1958—)
Tsirkova, Svetlana (1945—)
Tufan-Guzganu, Elisabeta (1964—)
Tuschak, Katalin (1959—)
Uga, Elisa (1968—)
Ushakova, Irina (1954—)
Vaccaroni, Dorina (1963—)
Vezzali, Valentina (1974—)
Vicol, Maria (1935—)
Vince, Marion Lloyd (1906–1969)
Wang Huifeng (1968—)
Weber, Christiane (1962—)
Weber-Koszto, Monika (1966—)
Wessel-Kirchels, Ute (1953—)
Wysoczanska, Barbara (1949—)
Yang Shaoqi
Zabelina, Aleksandra (1937—)
Zagunis, Mariel (1985—)
Zalaffi, Margherita (1966—)
Zsak, Marcela (1956—)

FICTION WRITER
See Crime/Detective-fiction writer.
See Fantasy/Science-fiction writer.
See Gothic-fiction writer.
See Historical-fiction writer.

See Mystery/Suspense-fiction writer.
See Novelist.
See Romance-fiction writer.
See Short-fiction writer.

FIELD-AND-TRACK
See Track-and-field.

FIELD-HOCKEY COACH
Applebee, Constance (1873–1981)
Clark, Cora Maris (1885–1967)

FIELD-HOCKEY PLAYER
Aicega, Magdalena (1973—)
Akhmerova, Leylya (1957—)
Allen, Kate (1974—)
Anders, Beth (1951—)
Andrews, Michelle (1971—)
Annan, Alyson (1973—)
Antoniska, Mariela (1975—)
Appel, Gabriele (1958—)
Applebee, Constance (1873–1981)
Arrondo, Ines (1977—)
Atkins, Gillian (1963—)
Aymar, Luciana (1977—)
Bachmann, Tina (1978—)
Barea Cobos, Maria (1966—)
Barrio Gutierrez, Sonia (1969—)
Bayliss, Lisa (1966—)
Becker, Britta (1973—)
Beglin, Elizabeth (1957—)
Belbin, Tracey (1967—)
Benninga, Carina (1962—)
Blazkova, Milada (1958—)
Boekhorst, Josephine (1957—)
Bolhuis-Eysvogel, Marjolein (1961—)
Booij, Minke (1977—)
Boomgaardt, Ageeth (1972—)
Bowman, Deborah (1963—)
Breiken, Dagmar (1963—)
Brown, Karen (1963—)
Buggy, Regina (1959—)
Burkart, Claudia (1980—)
Buter, Yvonne (1959—)
Buzunova, Natalya (1958—)
Bykova, Natalya (1958—)
Capes, Lee (1961—)
Capes, Michelle (1966—)
Carbon, Sally (1967—)
Casaretto, Caroline (1978—)
Cermakova, Jirina (1944—)
Chang Eun-Jung (1970—)
Chase, Elizabeth (1950—)
Cheeseman, Gwen (1951—)
Chick, Sandra (1947—)
Cho Eun-Jung
Choi Choon-Ok (1965—)
Choi Eun-Kyung
Choi Mi-Soon
Cho Ki-Hyang (1963—)
Chung Eun-Kyung (1965—)
Chung Sang-Hyun (1963—)
Clark, Cora Maris (1885–1967)
Clement, Elspeth (1956—)
Coghen Alberdingk, Mercedes (1962—)
Cowley, Gillian (1955—)
Davies, Patricia (1956—)
de Beus, Bernadette de (1958—)
de Bruijn, Chantal (1976—)
de Heij, Stella
Deininger, Beate (1962—)
Deiters, Julie (1975—)
de Roever, Lisanne (1979—)
de Ruiter, Wietske
Dickenscheid, Tanja (1969—)
di Giacomo, Marina (1976—)
Dixon, Victoria (1959—)
Dobson, Louise (1972—)
Dod, Charlotte (1871–1960)
Donners, Wilhelmina (1974—)
Dorado Gomez, Natalia (1967—)
Dorman, Loretta (1963—)
Dunn, Gertrude (c. 1932–2004)
Duyster, Willemijn
English, Sarah (1955—)
Ernsting-Krienke, Nadine (1974—)
Farrell, Renita (1972—)
Ferneck, Christine (1969—)
Ferrari, Maria Paz (1973—)
Filipova, Nadya (1959—)
Fish, Maree (1963—)
Fokke, Annemieke (1967—)
Fraser, Susan (1966—)
Fraser, Wendy (1963—)
Frolova, Lyudmila (1953—)
Gabellanes Marieta, Nagore (1973—)
Gambero, Anabel (1972—)
Garcia, Agustina Soledad (1981—)
George, Maureen (1955—)
Glubokova, Lidiya (1953—)
Gonzalez Laguillo, Maria (1961—)
Gonzalez Oliva, Mariana (1976—)
Gorbyatkova, Nelli (1958–1981)
Grant, Ann (1955—)
Gude, Franziska (1976—)
Gulla, Alejandra (1977—)
Guryeva, Yelena (1958—)
Haase, Mandy (1982—)
Hagen, Birgit (1957—)
Hagenbaumer, Eva (1967—)
Hahn, Birgit (1958—)
Hajkova, Jirina (1954—)
Han Keum-Sil (1968—)
Han Ok-Kyung (1965—)
Haslam, Juliet (1969—)
Hawkes, Rechelle (1967—)
Hendriks, Irene (1958—)
Hentschel, Franziska (1970—)
Hernandez, Maria de la Paz (1977—)
Hillas, Lorraine (1961—)
Hillen, Francisca (1959—)
Holsboer, Noor (1967—)
Hopper, Grace Murray (1906–1992)
Hruba, Berta (1946—)
Hubackova, Ida (1954—)
Hudson, Nikki (1976—)
Huggett, Susan (1954—)
Hwang Keum-Sook (1963—)
Imison, Rachel (1978—)
Inzhuvatova, Galina (1952—)
Jeon Young-Sun
Jin Deok San
Jin Won-Sim (1965—)
Johnson, Kathryn (1967—)
Johnson, Sheryl (1957—)
Jungjohann, Caren (1970—)
Kadlecova, Jirina (1948—)
Karres, Sylvia (1976—)
Kauschke, Katrin (1971—)
Keller, Natascha (1977—)
Kham, Alina (1959—)
Kim Mi-Sun (1964—)
Kim Myung-Ok
Kim Soon-Duk (1967—)
Kim Young-Sook (1965—)
Klecker, Denise (1972—)
Koch, Martina (1959—)
Koolen, Nicole (1972—)
Kown Soo-Hyun
Kralickova, Jarmila (1944—)
Krasnikova, Natella (1953—)
Krizova, Jirina (1948—)
Kuehn, Anke (1981—)
Kuhnt, Irina (1968—)
Kuipers, Ellen
Kwon Chang Sook
Kyselicova, Alena (1957—)
Lahodova, Jana (1957—)
Landgraf, Sigrid (1959—)
Larson-Mason, Christine (1956—)
Latif, Badri (1977—)
Latzsch, Heike (1973—)
Lee Eun Kyung
Lee Eun-Young
Lee Ji-Young
Lehmann, Sonja (1979—)
Lejeune, Elisabeth (1963—)
LePoole, Alexandra (1959—)
Lewin, Jeannette
Lim Jeong-Sook
Lim Kye-Sook (1964—)
Lingnau, Corinna (1960—)
Lister, Sandra (1961—)
Maillart, Ella (1903–1997)
Maiques Dern, Ana (1967—)
Maitland, Clover (1972—)
Maiztegui, Laura
Manrique Perez, Silvia (1973—)
Maragall Verge, Elisabeth (1970—)
Margalot, Mercedes (1975—)
Marsden, Karen (1962—)
Masotta, Paula Karina (1972—)
McGahey, Kathleen (1960—)
McKay, Heather (1941—)
McKillop, Patricia (1956—)
McWilliams, Jackie (1964—)
Meyers, Ann (1955—)
Miller, Anita (1951—)
Miller, Tammy (1967—)
Milne, Leslie (1956—)
Mitchell-Taverner, Claire (1970—)
Moreira de Melo, Fatima (1978—)
Morett, Charlene (1957—)
Morgan, Helen (1966—)
Morris, Jenny (1972—)
Moser, Christina (1960—)
Motos Iceta, Teresa (1963—)
Moyer, Diane (1958—)
Mueller, Silke (1978—)
Mueller, Susanne (1972—)
Mulder, Eefke (1977—)
Nevill, Mary (1961—)
Nicholls, Mandy (1968—)
Nieuwenhuizen, Anneloes (1963—)
Ohr, Martine (1964—)
Oh Seung-Shin
Olive Vancells, Nuria (1968—)
Oneto, Vanina (1973—)
Ott, Patricia (1960—)
Ovechkina, Nadezhda (1958—)
Park Soon-Ja (1966—)
Parlby, Irene (1868–1965)
Partridge, Kathleen (1963—)
Patmore, Sharon (1963—)
Pearce, Caroline (1925—)
Pearce, Jean (1921—)
Pearce, May (1915–1981)
Pearce, Morna (1932—)
Peek, Alison (1969—)
Pereira, Jacqueline (1964—)
Peris-Kneebone, Nova (1971—)
Peters, Kristina (1968—)
Petrickova, Kvetoslava (1952—)
Phillips, Brenda (1958—)
Pisani, Sandra (1959—)
Place, Marcella (1959—)
Plesman, Suzanne
Podhanyiova, Viera (1960—)

Occupational Index

Pollard, Marjorie (1899–1982)
Pos, Alette (1962—)
Powell, Katrina (1972—)
Powell, Lisa (1970—)
Prinsloo, Christine (1952—)
Ramirez Merino, Virginia (1964—)
Ramsay, Alison (1959—)
Rimoldi, Jorgelina (1972—)
Rinne, Fanny (1980—)
Robertson, Sonia (1947—)
Roche, Danni (1970—)
Rodewald, Marion (1976—)
Rodriguez Suarez, Maria (1957—)
Rognoni, Cecilia (1976—)
Roth, Hella (1963—)
Russo, Marine (1980—)
Scheepstra, Maartje (1980—)
Schley, Gabriela (1964—)
Schmid, Susanne (1960—)
Schopman, Janneke (1977—)
Sears, Eleanora (1881–1968)
Sevens, Elizabeth (1949—)
Shelton, Karen (1957—)
Shvyganova, Tatyana (1960—)
Sinnige, Clarinda (1973—)
Sixsmith, Jane (1967—)
Skirving, Angie (1981—)
Smabers, Hanneke (1973—)
Smabers, Minke (1979—)
Small, Kim (1965—)
Snoeks, Jiske (1978—)
Sramkova, Iveta (1963—)
Starre, Katie (1971—)
Stauffer, Brenda (1961—)
Staver, Julie (1952—)
Steenberghe, Florentine (1967—)
Stepnik, Ayelen (1975—)
Strickland, Shirley (1925—)
Stringer, C. Vivian (1948—)
Strong, Judy (1960—)
Suh Hyo-Sun (1966—)
Suh Kwang-Mi (1965—)
Sykorova, Marie (1952—)
Teeuwen, Josepha (1974—)
Telleria Goni, Maider (1973—)
Thate, Carole (1971—)
Thielemann, Ursula (1958—)
Thomaschinski, Simone (1970—)
Thompson, Joanne (1965—)
Tooth, Liane (1962—)
Touw, Daphne (1970—)
Towers, Julie (1976—)
Toxopeus, Jacqueline (1968—)
Urbanova, Marta (1960—)
van de Kieft, Fleur (1973—)
van den Boogaard, Dillianne (1974—)
van der Ben, Helena (1964—)
van der Vaart, Macha (1972—)
van der Wielen, Suzan (1971—)
van Doorn, Marieke (1960—)
van Geenhuizen, Miek (1981—)
van Kessel, Lieve (1977—)
van Manen, Aletta (1958—)
Veenstra, Myrna (1975—)
Volk, Helen (1954—)
von Weiler, Sophie (1958—)
Vukojicic, Paola (1974—)
Vymazalova, Lenka (1959—)
Vyuzhanina, Galina (1952—)
Walter, Louisa (1978—)
Watson, Linda (1955—)
Weiermann-Lietz, Andrea (1958—)
Weiss, Bianca (1968—)
Wild, Anke (1967—)
Wolff, Ingrid (1964—)
Wollschlaeger, Susanne (1967—)
Woo Hyun-Jung
Yembakhtova, Tatyana (1956—)
You Jae-Sook
Zazdravnykh, Valentina (1954—)
Zeghers, Margriet (1954—)
Zwehl, Julia (1976—)

FIGHTER PILOT
See Combat aviator.

FIGURATIVE PAINTER
Backer, Harriet (1845–1932)
Bacon, Peggy (1895–1987)
Beale, Mary (1632–1699)
Bishop, Isabel (1902–1988)
Boughton, Alice (1866–1943)
Brooks, Romaine (1874–1970)
Butler, Elizabeth Thompson (1846–1933)
Genth, Lillian (1876–1953)
Hall, Anne (1792–1863)
Knight, Laura (1877–1970)
Lama, Giulia (c. 1685–c. 1753)
Lempicka, Tamara de (1898–1980)
Low, Mary Fairchild (1858–1946)
Martin, Agnes (1912–2004)
Modersohn-Becker, Paula (1876–1907)
Pinney, Eunice Griswold (1770–1849)
Popova, Liubov (1889–1924)
Rothschild, Judith (1921–1993)
Serebryakova, Zinaida (1884–1967)
Valadon, Suzanne (1865–1938)

FIGURE SKATER
See Ice skater.

FILM ANIMATION ARTIST
Batchelor, Joy (1914–1991)
Parker, Claire (1906–1981)
Reiniger, Lotte (1899–1981)
Wieland, Joyce (1931–1998)

FILM CRITIC
Adler, Renata (1938—)
Barry, Iris (1895–1969)
Benson, Sally (1900–1972)
Berberova, Nina (1901–1993)
Carpenter, Iris (b. 1906)
Crist, Judith (1922—)
Curie, Ève (b. 1904)
Eisner, Lotte (1896–1983)
Gilliatt, Penelope (1932–1993)
Kael, Pauline (1919—)
Kirchwey, Freda (1893–1976)
Lawrenson, Helen (b. 1907)
Lejeune, C.A. (1897–1973)
McDonagh, Paulette (1901–1978)
Powell, Dilys (1901–1995)
Robertson, E. Arnot (1903–1961)
Rochefort, Christiane (1917–1998)
Sayre, Nora (1932–2001)
Sheehy-Skeffington, Hanna (1877–1946)

FILM DESIGNER
Oman, Julia Trevelyan (1930–2003)

FILM DIRECTOR
Adato, Perry Miller
Akerman, Chantal (1950—)
Armstrong, Gillian (1950—)
Arzner, Dorothy (1897–1979)
Asanova, Dinara (1942–1985)
Audry, Jacqueline (1908–1977)
Baldwin, Ruth Ann (fl. 1915–1921)
Barskaya, Margarita A. (1903–1938)
Bemberg, Maria Luisa (1922–1995)
Beranger, Clara (1886–1956)
Bertsch, Marguerite (1889–1967)
Bigelow, Kathryn (1951—)
Box, Muriel (1905–1991)
Campion, Jane (1954—)
Cannon, Dyan (1937—)
Cavani, Liliana (1933—)
Chopra, Joyce (1938—)
Chytilova, Vera (1929—)
Coolidge, Martha (1946—)
Crawford, Cheryl (1902–1986)
Dash, Julie (1952—)
Deren, Maya (1908–1961)
Donner, Vyvyan (1895–1965)
Dörrie, Doris (1955—)
Drew, Lucille (1890–1925)
Dulac, Germaine (1882–1942)
Ephron, Nora (1941—)
Epstein, Marie (c. 1899–1995)
Field, Mary (1896–c. 1968)
Field, Sally (1946—)
Foster, Jodie (1962—)
Franken, Rose (c. 1895–1988)
Gardner, Helen (1884–1968)
Giroud, Françoise (1916–2003)
Gomez, Sara (1943–1974)
Gorris, Marleen (1948—)
Guy-Blaché, Alice (1875–1968)
Henning-Jensen, Astrid (1914—)
Hidari Sachiko (1930—)
Holland, Agnieszka (1948—)
Huston, Anjelica (1951—)
Imaleyene, Fatime-Zohra (1936—)
Jakubowska, Wanda (1907–1998)
Kurys, Diane (1948—)
Landeta, Matilde (1913—)
Littlefield, Nancy (c. 1929—)
Loden, Barbara (1932–1980)
Lupino, Ida (1914–1995)
Lyell, Lottie (1890–1925)
Macpherson, Jeanie (1887–1946)
Madison, Cleo (1883–1964)
Marion, Frances (1888–1973)
Marshall, Penny (1942—)
Matthews, Jessie (1907–1981)
McDonagh, Paulette (1901–1978)
McLaughlin-Gill, Frances (1919—)
Mészáros, Márta (1931—)
Miró, Pilar (1940–1997)
Moreau, Jeanne (1928—)
Muratova, Kira (1934—)
Murfin, Jane (1893–1955)
Musidora (1884–1957)
Nair, Mira (1957—)
Nazimova, Alla (1879–1945)
Normand, Mabel (1892–1930)
Notari, Elvira (1875–1946)
Palcy, Euzhan (1957—)
Park, Ida May (1879–1954)
Perry, Antoinette (1888–1946)
Pisier, Marie-France (1944—)
Potter, Sally (1949—)
Reid, Dorothy Davenport (1895–1977)
Riefenstahl, Leni (1902–2003)
Rothman, Stephanie (1936—)
Sagan, Leontine (1889–1974)
Sander, Helke (1937—)
Sanders-Brahms, Helma (1940—)
Schiffman, Suzanne (1929–2001)
Seidelman, Susan (1952—)
Serreau, Coline (1947—)
Shepitko, Larissa (1938–1979)
Shub, Esther (1894–1959)
Silver, Joan Micklin (1935—)
Solntseva, Yulia (1901–1989)
Sontag, Susan (1933–2004)
Spheeris, Penelope (1945—)
Stonehouse, Ruth (1892–1941)

Streisand, Barbra (1942—)
Svilova, Elizaveta (1900–1975)
Takamine Hideko (1924—)
Tanaka, Kinuyo (1907–1977)
Taymor, Julie (1952—)
Trintignant, Nadine (1934—)
Turner, Florence E. (c. 1888–1946)
Ullmann, Liv (1939—)
Varda, Agnes (1928—)
Viertel, Salka (1889–1978)
Vitti, Monica (1931—)
von Harbou, Thea (1888–1954)
Von Trotta, Margarethe (1942—)
Warner, Deborah (1959—)
Weber, Lois (1881–1939)
Wertmüller, Lina (1928—)
Wieland, Joyce (1931–1998)
Wilson, Margery (1896–1986)
Zetterling, Mai (1925–1994)

FILM EDITOR
Allen, Dede (1923—)
Arzner, Dorothy (1897–1979)
Bauchens, Anne (1881–1967)
Booth, Margaret (1898–2002)
Coates, Anne V. (1925—)
Collins, Kathleen (1942–1988)
Farrokhzad, Forugh (1935–1967)
Fields, Verna (1918–1982)
Flaherty, Frances Hubbard (c. 1886–1972)
Fowler, Marjorie (1920–2003)
Guillemot, Agnès (1931—)
Lawrence, Viola (1894–1973)
McLean, Barbara (1903–1996)
Nazimova, Alla (1879–1945)
Reville, Alma (1899–1982)
Rey, Margret (1906–1996)
Schoonmaker, Thelma (1940—)
Shub, Esther (1894–1959)
Spencer, Dorothy (b. 1909)
Spheeris, Penelope (1945—)
Svilova, Elizaveta (1900–1975)
Trintignant, Nadine (1934—)
Varda, Agnes (1928—)

FILM PRODUCER
Anderson, Erica (1914–1976)
Anderson, Robin (1948–2002)
Andra, Fern (1893–1974)
Arzner, Dorothy (1897–1979)
Asanova, Dinara (1942–1985)
Atkins, Eileen (1934—)
Audry, Jacqueline (1908–1977)
Babbin, Jacqueline (1921–2001)
Bambara, Toni Cade (1939–1995)
Barskaya, Margarita A. (1903–1938)
Bazin, Janine (1923–2003)
Beavers, Louise (1902–1962)
Belle, Anne (1935–2003)
Bemberg, Maria Luisa (1922–1995)
Bodard, Mag (1916—)
Box, Betty E. (1915–1999)
Box, Muriel (1905–1991)
Broccoli, Dana (1922–2004)
Brown, Kay (1903–1995)
Bute, Mary Ellen (1906–1983)
Chopra, Joyce (1938—)
Chytilova, Vera (1929—)
Clarke, Shirley (1925–1997)
Collins, Jackie (1937—)
Collins, Kathleen (1942–1988)
Crawford, Cheryl (1902–1986)
Cunard, Grace (c. 1891–1967)
Denis, Michaela (1914–2003)
Deren, Maya (1908–1961)
Donner, Vyvyan (1895–1965)
Dulac, Germaine (1882–1942)
Duras, Marguerite (1914–1996)
Eames, Ray (1912–1988)
Falconetti, Renée (1892–1946)
Farrokhzad, Forugh (1935–1967)
Field, Mary (1896–c. 1968)
Field, Sally (1946—)
Fox, Beryl (1931—)
Franken, Rose (c. 1895–1988)
Gam, Rita (1928—)
Gardner, Helen (1884–1968)
Gogoberidze, Lana (1928—)
Goldberg, Whoopi (1949—)
Gomez, Sara (1943–1974)
Graves, Nancy (1940–1995)
Guy-Blaché, Alice (1875–1968)
Harrison, Joan (c. 1908–1994)
Hawn, Goldie (1945—)
Henson, Lisa (1960—)
Hidari, Sachiko (1930–2001)
Hidari Sachiko (1930—)
Hill, Debra (1950–2005)
Hurd, Gale Anne (1955—)
Jakubowska, Wanda (1907—)
Johnson, Osa (1894–1953)
Kennedy, Helena (1950—)
Kennedy, Kathleen (1954—)
Landeta, Matilde (1913—)
Littlefield, Nancy (c. 1929—)
Loden, Barbara (1932–1980)
Lupino, Ida (1914–1995)
Mack, Marion (1902–1989)
Mangeshkar, Lata (1929—)
Marshall, Penny (1942—)
McDonagh, Paulette (1901–1978)
McKinney, Nina Mae (c. 1912–1967)
McLaughlin-Gill, Frances (1919—)
Menken, Marie (1909–1970)
Moholy, Lucia (1894–1989)
Musidora (1884–1957)
Myles, Lynda (1947—)
Nazimova, Alla (1879–1945)
Notari, Elvira (1875–1946)
Orkin, Ruth (1921–1985)
Parsons, Harriet (1906–1983)
Perry, Antoinette (1888–1946)
Phillips, Julia (1944–2002)
Portillo, Lourdes
Queeny, Mary (1913–2003)
Rainer, Yvonne (1934—)
Reid, Dorothy Davenport (1895–1977)
Richards, Beah (1920–2000)
Riefenstahl, Leni (1902—)
Saint-Cyr, Renée (1904–2004)
Sander, Helke (1937—)
Scott, Hazel (1920–1981)
Shepitko, Larissa (1938–1979)
Shipman, Nell (1892–1970)
Silver, Joan Micklin (1935—)
Spheeris, Penelope (1945—)
Streisand, Barbra (1942—)
Stuart, Bathia Howie (1893–1987)
Sutherland, Efua (1924–1996)
Svilova, Elizaveta (1900–1975)
Tanaka, Kinuyo (1907–1977)
Taylor, Valerie (1935—)
Turner, Florence E. (c. 1888–1946)
Van Upp, Virginia (1902–1970)
Varda, Agnes (1928—)
von Harbou, Thea (1888–1954)
Weinstein, Hannah (1911–1984)
Weiss, Louise (1893–1983)
Wertmüller, Lina (1928—)
Wieland, Joyce (1931–1998)
Winfrey, Oprah (1954—)
Zetterling, Mai (1925–1994)

FILM SOUND EDITOR
Rose, Kay (1922–2002)

FILM-STUDIO EXECUTIVE
Dulac, Germaine (1882–1942)
Lansing, Sherry (1944—)
Pascal, Amy (1959—)
Pickford, Mary (1893–1979)
Riefenstahl, Leni (1902–2003)
Steel, Dawn (1946–1997)
Stratton-Porter, Gene (1863–1924)
Weinstein, Hannah (1911–1984)

FINANCIAL WRITER
Driscoll, Clara (1881–1945)
Porter, Sylvia (1913–1991)

FINANCIER
See Banker/financier.

FIRST DAUGHTER
Adams, Abigail (1765–1813)
Bliss, Mary Elizabeth (1824–1909)
Carter, Amy (1967—)
Churchill, Diana Spencer (1909–1963)
Churchill, Mary (1922—)
Cleveland, Ruth (1891–1904)
Clinton, Chelsea (1980—)
Fernandez, Alina (1956—)
Ford, Susan (1957—)
Johnson, Luci Baines (1947—)
Johnson, Lynda Bird (1944—)
Longworth, Alice Roosevelt (1884–1980)
Monroe, Eliza Kortright (1786–1840)
Monroe, Maria Hester (1803–1850)
Nixon, Julie (1948—)
Nixon, Tricia (1946—)
Randolph, Martha Jefferson (1775–1836)
Reagan, Maureen (1941–2001)
Roosevelt, Ethel Carow (1891–1977)
Schlossberg, Caroline Kennedy (1957—)
Taylor, Knox (1814–1835)
Truman, Margaret (1924—)

FIRST LADY
Abbott, Mary Martha (1823–1898)
Adams, Abigail (1744–1818)
Adams, Louisa Catherine (1775–1852)
Arthur, Ellen Herndon (1837–1880)
Ben Zvi, Rachel Yanait (1886–1979)
Bhutto, Nusrat (1929—)
Borden, Laura (1862–1940)
Brezhneva, Viktoriya (1908–1995)
Bush, Barbara (1924—)
Bush, Laura (1946—)
Carter, Rosalynn (1927—)
Ceausescu, Elena (1916–1989)
Chiang, Faina (1916–2004)
Chirac, Bernadette (1933—)
Chrétien, Aline (1936—)
Churchill, Clementine (1885–1977)
Cleveland, Frances Folsom (1864–1947)
Clinton, Hillary Rodham (1947—)
Coolidge, Grace Goodhue (1879–1957)
Davis, Varina Howell (1826–1906)
de Gaulle, Yvonne (1900–1979)
de Klerk, Marike (1937–2001)
Diefenbaker, Olive (1902–1976)
Eisenhower, Mamie (1896–1979)
Fillmore, Abigail Powers (1798–1853)
Flanagan, Sinéad (1878–1975)
Ford, Betty (1918—)
Franco, Carmen Polo de (1902–1988)
Gandhi, Indira (1917–1984)
Garfield, Lucretia (1832–1918)
Gorbacheva, Raisa (1932–1999)
Grant, Julia (1826–1902)

Harding, Florence K. (1860–1924)
Harrison, Anna Symmes (1775–1864)
Harrison, Caroline Scott (1832–1892)
Havel, Olga (1933–1996)
Hayes, Lucy Webb (1831–1889)
Hoover, Lou Henry (1874–1944)
Jefferson, Martha (1748–1782)
Johnson, Eliza McCardle (1810–1876)
Juarez, Margarita (1826–1871)
Katznelson-Shazar, Rachel (1888–1975)
Kennedy, Jacqueline (1929–1994)
Khieu Ponnary (1920–2003)
Kohl, Hannelore (1933–2001)
Laurier, Zoé (1841–1921)
Lincoln, Mary Todd (1818–1882)
Lloyd George, Margaret (d. 1941)
Lynch, Eliza (1835–1886)
Macdonald, Susan Agnes (1836–1920)
Machel, Graca (1946—)
MacKenzie, Jane (1825–1893)
Madison, Dolley Payne (1768–1849)
Marcos, Imelda (1929—)
Markovic, Mirjana (1942—)
McKinley, Ida Saxton (1847–1907)
McTeer, Maureen (1952—)
Meighen, Isabel J. (1883–1985)
Mitterrand, Danielle (1924—)
Monroe, Elizabeth (1768–1830)
Mugabe, Sally (1932–1992)
Mulroney, Mila (1953—)
Napier, Geills (1937—)
Nasser, Tahia (1923—)
Nhu, Madame (1924—)
Nixon, Pat (1912–1993)
Nkrumah, Fathia (c. 1931—)
Pearson, Maryon (1901–1989)
Perón, Eva (1919–1952)
Pierce, Jane Means (1806–1863)
Polk, Sarah Childress (1803–1891)
Rabin, Leah (1928–2000)
Reagan, Nancy (1921—)
Roosevelt, Edith Kermit Carow (1861–1948)
Roosevelt, Eleanor (1884–1962)
Rosas, Encarnación de (1795–1838)
Sadat, Jehan (1933—)
Saint-Laurent, Jeanne (1887–1966)
Song Meiling (1897–2003)
Suharto, Siti (1923–1996)
Taft, Helen Herron (1861–1943)
Taylor, Margaret Smith (1788–1852)
Thompson, Annie E. (1845–1913)
Tito, Jovanka Broz (1924—)
Trudeau, Margaret (1948—)
Truman, Bess (1885–1982)
Tupper, Frances (1826–1912)
Tyler, Julia Gardiner (1820–1889)
Tyler, Letitia (1790–1842)
Van Buren, Hannah Hoes (1783–1819)
Washington, Martha (1731–1802)
Weizmann, Vera (1881–1966)
Wilson, Edith Bolling (1872–1961)
Wilson, Ellen Axson (1860–1914)
Winthrop, Margaret (c. 1591–1647)
Zhivkova, Lyudmila (1942–1981)

FISHMONGER
Pentreath, Dolly (1685–1777)

FLAMENCO DANCER
Amaya, Carmen (1913–1963)
Flores, Lola (1924–1995)
Lopez, Encarnación (1898–1945)
Mercé, Antonia (c. 1886–1936)
Sullivan, Jean (1923–2003)

FLAMENCO SINGER
Alcantara, Dolores Jimenez (1909–1999)
Flores, Lola (1924–1995)

FLORAL DESIGNER
Spry, Constance (1886–1960)

FLORAL PAINTER
Adamson, Joy (1910–1980)
Airy, Anna (1882–1964)
Anastaise (fl. 1400)
Barker, Cicely Mary (1895–1973)
Basseporte, Magdalene (?–c. 1780)
Bridges, Fidelia (1834–1923)
Carrington, Dora (1893–1932)
Content, Marjorie (1895–1984)
Edwards, Henrietta Muir (1849–1933)
Garzoni, Giovanna (1600–1670)
Gluck (1895–1978)
Guan Daosheng (1262–1319)
Hall, Anne (1792–1863)
Hunter, Clementine (1886–1988)
Laurencin, Marie (1883–1956)
Lemmon, Sarah Plummer (1836–1923)
Leyster, Judith (1609–1660)
Macomber, Mary Lizzie (1861–1916)
Martin, Maria (1796–1863)
Mayreder, Rosa (1858–1938)
Moser, Mary (1744–1819)
Neel, Alice (1900–1984)
Nicholson, Winifred (1893–1981)
North, Marianne (1830–1890)
O'Keeffe, Georgia (1887–1986)
Oosterwyck, Maria van (1630–1693)
Peale, Anna Claypoole (1791–1878)
Peale, Margaretta Angelica (1795–1882)
Peale, Sarah Miriam (1800–1885)
Peeters, Clara (1594–after 1657)
Redpath, Anne (1895–1965)
Ruysch, Rachel (1664–1750)
Sowerby, Millicent (1878–1967)
Stettheimer, Florine (1871–1944)
Valadon, Suzanne (1865–1938)
Walcott, Mary Morris (1860–1940)
Weir, Irene (1862–1944)

FLORIST
Elsom, Sarah Ann (1867–1962)

FLUTIST
Boyd, Anne (1946—)
Dwyer, Doriot Anthony (1922—)
Gardner, Kay (1941–2002)
Hoover, Katherine (1937—)
Lawrence, Eleanor (1936–2001)
Ochoa, Ellen (1958—)
Robison, Paula (1941—)

FOLK ARTIST
Hunter, Clementine (1886–1988)
Kalvak, Helen (1901–1984)
Moses, Anna "Grandma" (1860–1961)
O'Kelley, Mattie Lou (c. 1908–1997)
Pinney, Eunice Griswold (1770–1849)
Powers, Harriet (1837–1911)

FOLKLORIST
Alexander, Francesca (1837–1917)
Amrouche, Marie-Louise (1913–1976)
Aretz, Isabel (1909—)
Beckwith, Martha Warren (1871–1959)
Bennett, Louise Simone (1919—)
Cadilla de Martínez, Maria (1886–1951)
Campbell, Maria (1940—)
Costello, Eileen (1870–1962)
Eckstorm, Fannie Pearson Hardy (1865–1946)
Fowke, Edith (1913–1996)
Gillmor, Frances (1903–1993)
Gregory, Augusta (1852–1932)
Hatzimichali, Angeliki (1895–1956)
Hurston, Zora Neale (c. 1891–1960)
McNeill, Florence Marian (1885–1973)
Millican, Arthenia J. Bates (1920—)
Mourning Dove (c. 1888–1936)
Ritchie, Jean (1922—)
Rourke, Constance (1885–1941)
Schoolcraft, Jane Johnston (1800–1841)
Weston, Jessie Laidlay (1850–1928)

FOLKSINGER
Amrouche, Fadhma Mansour (1882–1967)
Baez, Joan (1941—)
Christian, Meg (1946—)
Carter, Jeanette (1923–2006)
Colvin, Shawn (1956—)
Cotten, Elizabeth (c. 1893–1987)
DeMent, Iris (1961—)
Denny, Sandy (1947–1978)
Farina, Mimi (1945–2001)
Fox, Charlotte Milligan (1864–1916)
Gilbert, Ronnie (1926—)
Griffith, Nanci (1953—)
Harris, Emmylou (1947—)
Hatfield, Juliana (1967—)
Ian, Janis (1951—)
Kennedy-Fraser, Marjorie (1857–1930)
Mitchell, Joni (1943—)
Odetta (1930—)
Phranc (1957—)
Prior, Maddy (1947—)
Raitt, Bonnie (1949—)
Redpath, Jean (1937—)
Reynolds, Malvina (1900–1978)
Ritchie, Jean (1922—)
Robertson, Jeannie (1908–1975)
Sainte-Marie, Buffy (1941—)
Schekeryk, Melanie (1947—)
Seeger, Peggy (b. 1935)
Sosa, Mercedes (1935—)
Thompson, Linda (1948—)
Travers, Mary (1936—)
Vega, Suzanne (1959—)
Williams, Lucinda (1953—)
Williams, Victoria (1958—)
Wolf, Kate (1942–1986)

FOOTBALL PLAYER
See Soccer player.

FOREIGN CORRESPONDENT
Brewster, Anne Hampton (1818–1892)
Carpenter, Iris (b. 1906)
Emerson, Gloria (1929–2004)
Flanner, Janet (1892–1978)
Foley, Martha (c. 1897–1977)
Fuller, Margaret (1810–1850)
Gellhorn, Martha (1908–1998)
Higgins, Marguerite (1920–1966)
Kirkpatrick, Helen (1909–1997)
Kuhn, Irene Corbally (1898–1995)
Lewis, Flora (1922–2002)
McCormick, Anne O'Hare (1880–1954)
Neuffer, Elizabeth (1956–2003)
Olberg, Oda (1872–1955)
Palencia, Isabel de (1878–c. 1950)
Rinehart, Mary Roberts (1876–1958)
Schultz, Sigrid (1893–1980)
Smedley, Agnes (1892–1950)
Snow, Helen Foster (1907–1997)
Spewack, Bella (1899–1990)
Thompson, Dorothy (1893–1961)
Tufty, Esther Van Wagoner (1896–1986)
Ward, Mrs. Humphry (1851–1920)

FORESTER
Sutherland, Mary (1893–1955)

FORTUNE TELLER
See Prophet/sibyl/visionary.

FOUNDER
See Chorale founder.
See Dance-company/troupe founder.
See Educational-institution/program founder.
See Entrepreneur.
See Event founder.
See Hospital/Health-center founder.
See Library/museum founder.
See Movement founder.
See Newspaper founder.
See Opera-company founder.
See Orchestra founder.
See Periodical founder.
See Professional-organization founder.
See Reform-organization founder.
See Religious-community/institution founder.
See Social-welfare organization founder.
See Theater or Theatrical company/troupe founder.

FREESTYLE SKIER
See Skier.

FRONTIER SCOUT
See Scout/guide.

FRONTIERSWOMAN/HOMESTEADER
Bailey, Ann (1742–1825)
Bassett, Ann (1878–1956)
Cannary, Martha Jane (1852–1903)
Edwards, Sarah Pierpont (1710–1758)
Elder, Kate (fl. 1881)
Estaugh, Elizabeth Haddon (1680–1762)
Greenway, Isabella Selmes (1886–1953)
Jackson, Rachel Donelson (1767–1828)
Kanahele, Helen Lake (1916–1976)
Maxwell, Kate (fl. 1886)
Nearing, Helen (1904–1995)
Orchard, Sadie (c. 1853–1943)
Royce, Sarah (1819–1891)
Tubbs, Alice (1851–1930)
Watson, Ellen (1861–1889)
Wilder, Laura Ingalls (1867–1957)
Zane, Betty (c. 1766–c. 1831)

FURNISHINGS DESIGNER
Loy, Mina (1882–1966)
Neumann, Vera (1907–1993)
Strengell, Marianne (1909–1998)

FURNITURE DESIGNER
Ditzel, Nana (1923—)
Eames, Ray (1912–1988)
Knoll, Florence Schust (1917—)
Perriand, Charlotte (1903–1999)
Strengell, Marianne (1909–1998)
Tauber-Arp, Sophie (1889–1943)

FUR TRADER
Astor, Sarah Todd (1761–1832)

GAMBLER
McTier, Martha (c. 1743–1837)
Tubbs, Alice (1851–1930)

GARDEN DESIGNER
Cruso, Thalassa (1908–1997)
Farrand, Beatrix Jones (1872–1959)
Jekyll, Gertrude (1843–1932)
Nur Jahan (1577–1645)
Sackville-West, Vita (1892–1962)
Verey, Rosemary (1918–2001)
White, Emily Louisa Merielina (1839–1936)

GARDENER
Baker, Isabel Noeline (1878–1958)
King, Martha (1802/03–1897)

GAY-RIGHTS ACTIVIST
Atkinson, Ti-Grace (1939—)
Calderone, Mary Steichen (1904–1998)
Cammermeyer, Margarethe (1942—)
Delarverié, Stormé (1922—)
Hall, Radclyffe (1880–1943)
Hampton, Mabel (1902–1989)
Lorde, Audre (1934–1992)
Navratilova, Martina (1956—)
Rich, Adrienne (1929—)
Sarton, May (1912–1995)
Stone, Sharon (1958—)

GEISHA
Nakamura, Kiharu (1913–2004)

GENEALOGIST
Lowry Corry, Dorothy (1885–1967)
Pitini-Morera, Hariata Whakatau (1871/72?–1938)
Snow, Helen Foster (1907–1997)

GENETICIST
Andersen, Dorothy Hansine (1901–1963)
Apgar, Virginia (1909–1974)
Auerbach, Charlotte (1899–1994)
Blackwood, Margaret (1909–1986)
Bonnevie, Kristine (1872–1948)
Boring, Alice Middleton (1883–1955)
Esau, Katherine (1898–1997)
Friedman, Elizebeth (d. 1980)
Lyon, Mary Frances (1925—)
Macklin, Madge (1893–1962)
Margulis, Lynn (1938—)
McClintock, Barbara (1902–1992)
McLaren, Anne Laura (1927—)
Newton Turner, Helen (1908–1995)
Nüsslein-Volhard, Christiane (1942—)
Ohta, Tomoko (1933—)
Russell, Elizabeth S. (1913—)
Sager, Ruth (1918–1997)
Sithole-Niang, Idah (1957—)
Stevens, Nettie Maria (1861–1912)
Tammes, Tine (1871–1947)
Wong-Staal, Flossie (1946—)

GEOGRAPHER
Adams, Harriet Chalmers (1875–1937)
Bingham, Millicent Todd (1880–1968)
Bishop, Isabella (1831–1904)
Blum, Arlene (1945—)
Boyd, Louise Arner (1887–1972)
Harrison, Marguerite (1879–1967)
Heslop, Mary Kingdon (1885–1955)
Leakey, Mary Nicol (1913–1996)
Newbigin, Marion I. (1869–1934)
Pearsall, Phyllis (1906–1996)
Pfeiffer, Ida (1797–1858)
Semple, Ellen Churchill (1863–1932)
Taylor, Eva (1879–1966)
Walcott, Mary Morris (1860–1940)

GEOLOGIST
Ajakaiye, Deborah Enilo (c. 1940—)
Anning, Mary (1799–1847)
Bascom, Florence (1862–1945)
Bate, Dorothea (1879–1951)
Benett, Etheldred (1776–1845)
Currie, Ethel Dobbie (1898–1963)
Curtis, Doris Malkin (1914–1991)
Edinger, Tilly (1897–1967)
Ehrlich, Aline (1928–1991)
Eyles, Joan M. (1907–1986)
Gardner, Julia Anna (1882–1960)
Guppy, Eileen M. (1903–1980)
Halicka, Antonina (1908–1973)
Heslop, Mary Kingdon (1885–1955)
Hill, Dorothy (1907–1997)
Hodgson, Elizabeth (1814–1877)
Hofmann, Elise (1889–1955)
Knopf, Eleanora Bliss (1883–1974)
Lyell, Mary Horner (1808–1873)
MacRobert, Rachel (1884–1954)
Maury, Carlotta (1874–1938)
McNally, Karen Cook (1940—)
Moyd, Pauline
Nashar, Beryl (1923—)
Ogilvie Gordon, Maria M. (1864–1939)
Raisin, Catherine (1855–1945)
Saruhashi, Katsuko (1920—)
Slavikova, Ludmila (1890–1943)
Watson, Janet Vida (1923–1985)
Welch, Barbara (c. 1904–1986)
Wilman, Maria (1867–1957)

GEOPHYSICIST
Ajakaiye, Deborah Enilo (c. 1940—)
Gallagher, Rosie (1970–2003)
Lehmann, Inge (1888–1993)

GIRL SCOUT/GUIDES MEMBER/LEADER
See Scouting movement member/leader.

GOLD MINER
Cashman, Nellie (1844–1925)
Goodwin, Bridget (c. 1802/27–1899)
Royce, Sarah (1819–1891)

GOLDSMITH
Kirkeby, Elizabeth (fl. 1482)
Kittelsen, Grete Prytz (1917—)

GOLFER
Abbott, Lorraine (1937—)
Abbott, Margaret (1878–1955)
Abraham, Constance Palgrave (1864–1942)
Ahern, Kathy (1949–1996)
Alcott, Amy (1956—)
Anthony, Bessie (1880–1912)
Astrologes, Maria (1951—)
Austin, Debbie (1948—)
Baker, Kathy (1961—)
Barnett, Pamela (1944—)
Barton, Pam (1917–1943)
Bauer, Alice (1927–2002)
Baugh, Laura (1955—)
Bell, Peggy Kirk (1921—)
Berg, Patty (1918—)
Berning, Susie Maxwell (1941—)
Bertolaccini, Silvia (1959—)
Bishop, Georgianna M. (1878–1971)
Blalock, Jane (1945—)
Boddie, Barbara White (1940—)
Booth, Jane Bastanchury (1948—)
Bourassa, Jocelyn (1947—)
Bower, Alberta (1922—)
Bradley, Pat (1951—)
Breer, Murle MacKenzie (1939—)
Britz, Jerilyn (1943—)
Brown, Lucy (fl. 1895)
Browne, Mary K. (1891–1971)
Bryant, Bonnie (1943—)
Budke, Mary Anne (1953—)
Burfeindt, Betty (1945—)
Callison, Carole Jo (1938—)
Caponi, Donna (1945—)
Carner, JoAnne (1939—)
Cavalleri, Silvia (1972—)
Cheney, Leona Pressler (1904–1982)

Occupational Index

Choate, Mrs. Allison (b. 1910)
Cockerill, Kay (1964—)
Coe, Dawn (1960—)
Conley, Peggy (1947—)
Cornelius, Kathy (1932—)
Crafter, Jane (1955—)
Crawford, Jean Ashley (1939—)
Creed, Clifford Anne (1938—)
Crocker, Fay (1914—)
Crocker, Mary Lou (1944—)
Cudone, Carolyn (1918—)
Cullen, Betsy (1938—)
Cummings, Edith (1899–1984)
Curtis, Harriot (1881–1974)
Curtis, Peggy (1883–1965)
Cushing, Justine B. (b. 1918)
Daniel, Beth (1956—)
Davies, Laura (1963—)
Denenberg, Gail (1947—)
Dettweiler, Helen (1914–1990)
Dickinson, Judy (1950—)
Dill, Mary Lou (1948—)
Ehret, Gloria (1941—)
Englehorn, Shirley (1940—)
Faulk, Mary Lena (1926–1995)
Ferraris, Jan (1947—)
Figueras-Dotti, Marta (1957—)
Fontaine, Joan (b. 1917)
Fraser, Alexa Stirling (1897–1977)
Garrett, Maureen (1922—)
Gatehouse, Eleanor Wright (1886–1973)
Geddes, Jane (1960—)
Gibson, Althea (1927–2003)
Glutting, Charlotte E. (1910–1996)
Goetze, Vicki (1972—)
Green, Tammie (1959—)
Griffin, Ellen (1918–1986)
Griscom, Frances C. (1880–1973)
Hagge, Marlene Bauer (1934—)
Hamlin, Shelley (1949—)
Hammond, Joan (1912–1996)
Hanson, Beverly (1924—)
Harley, Katherine (1881–1961)
Hastings, Denise (1958—)
Hattori, Michiko (1968—)
Hayes, Patty (1955—)
Haynie, Sandra B. (1943—)
Hecker, Genevieve (1884–1960)
Hicks, Betty (1920—)
Hicks, Helen (1911–1974)
Higgins, Pam (1945—)
Higuchi, Chako (1945—)
Hikage, Atsuko (1954—)
Hill, Cindy (1948—)
Hill, Opal S. (1892–1981)
Hollins, Marion B. (1892–1944)
Horn, Miriam Burns (1904–1951)
Hoyt, Beatrix (1880–1963)
Hurd, Dorothy Campbell (1883–1945)
Inkster, Juli (1960—)
Jameson, Betty (1919—)
Jessen, Ruth (1936—)
Johnson, Chris (1958—)
Johnstone, Ann Casey (1921—)
Johnston-Forbes, Cathy (1963—)
Kimball, Judy (1938—)
Kim Mi-Hyun (1977—)
King, Betsy (1955—)
Kirby, Dorothy (1920—)
Kirouac, Martha Wilkinson (1948—)
Kuehne, Kelli (1977—)
Lacoste, Catherine (1945—)
Lauer, Bonnie (1951—)
Lee Smith, Jenny (1948—)
Leitch, Cecil (1891–1977)
Lenczyk, Grace (1927—)
Lesser, Patricia (1933—)
Little, Sally (1951—)
Lock, Jane (1954—)
Lopez, Nancy (1957—)
Mackenzie, Ada (1891–1973)
Malison, Joyce (c. 1935—)
Mallon, Meg (1963—)
Mann, Carol (1941—)
Mason, Marge (1918–1974)
Massey, Debbie (1950—)
Masters, Margaret (1934—)
McAllister, Susie (1947—)
McIntire, Barbara (1935—)
Merten, Lauri (1960—)
Miley, Marion (c. 1914–1941)
Miller, Alice (1956—)
Miller, Sharon Kay (1941—)
Mills, Mary (1940—)
Montgomery, Charlotte (1958—)
Neumann, Liselotte (1966—)
Nicholas, Alison (1962—)
Nilsmark, Catrin (1967—)
Ohsako, Tatsuko (1952—)
Okamoto, Ayako (1951—)
Orcutt, Maureen (b. 1907)
Page, Estelle Lawson (1907–1983)
Pak, Se Ri (1977—)
Palli, Anne-Marie (1955—)
Palmer, Sandra (1941—)
Panton, Catherine (1955—)
Park, Grace (1979—)
Pearson, Issette (fl. 1893)
Pepper, Dottie D. (1965—)
Pooley, Violet (1886–1965)
Porter, Dorothy Germain (1924—)
Porter, Mary Bea (1949—)
Post, Sandra (1948—)
Postlewait, Kathy (1949—)
Pound, Louise (1872–1958)
Pratt, Daria (1861–1938)
Prentice, Jo Ann (1933—)
Preuss, Phyllis (1939—)
Pulz, Penny (1953—)
Pung, Jackie (1921—)
Rankin, Judy (1945—)
Ravenscroft, Gladys (1888–1960)
Rawls, Betsy (1928—)
Riley, Polly Ann (1926–2002)
Rinker, Laurie (1962—)
Rizzo, Patti (1960—)
Robbins, Kelly (1969—)
Roberts, Sue (1948—)
Romack, Barbara (1932—)
Rosenthal, Jody (1962—)
Sander, Anne Quast (1937—)
Sargeant, N.C. (fl. 1895)
Saunders, Vivien (1946—)
Scherbak, Barb (1958—)
Scott, Margaret (1875–1938)
Sears, Eleanora (1881–1968)
Sheehan, Patty (1956—)
Sherk, Cathy (1950—)
Shore, Dinah (1917–1994)
Sinn, Pearl (1967—)
Smith, Marilynn (1929—)
Smith, Wiffi (1936—)
Sorenson, Carol (1942—)
Sorenstam, Annika (1970—)
Sorenstam, Charlotta (1973—)
Spuzich, Sandra (1937—)
Stacy, Hollis (1954—)
Stephens, Frances (1924–1978)
Stephenson, Jan (1951—)
Stetson, Helen (1887–1982)
Stone, Beth (1940—)
Streit, Marlene Stewart (1934—)
Suggs, Louise (1923—)
Sullivan, Cynthia Jan (1937—)
Syms, Nancy Roth (1939—)
Teske, Rachel (1972—)
Thompson, Carol Semple (1948—)
Thomson, Muriel (1954—)
Trevor-Jones, Mabel (fl. 1904–1921)
Turner, Sherri (1956—)
Turpie, Marion (d. 1967)
Vanderbeck, Florence (1884–1935)
Van Wie, Virginia (1909–1997)
Vare, Glenna Collett (1903–1989)
Walker, Colleen (1956—)
Walker, Michelle (1952—)
Walters, Lisa (1960—)
Washam, Jo Ann (1950—)
Webb, Karrie (1974—)
Wethered, Joyce (1901–1997)
White, Donna (1954—)
Whittier, Polly (1877–1946)
Whitworth, Kathy (1939—)
Williams, Eileen Hope (1884–1958)
Wilson, Enid (b. 1910)
Wilson, Peggy (1934—)
Wilson, Ruth (1919–2001)
Wright, Mickey (1935—)
Zaharias, Babe Didrikson (1911–1956)
Zimmerman, Mary Beth (1960—)

GOSPEL SINGER

Clark, Mattie Moss (1925–1994)
Coates, Dorothy Love (1928–2002)
Grant, Amy (1960—)
Houston, Cissy (1933—)
Jackson, Mahalia (1911–1972)
Jones, Linda (1944–1972)
Martin, Sara (1884–1955)
Robinson, Vicki Sue (1954–2000)
Simone, Nina (1933–2003)
Smith, Willie Mae Ford (1904–1994)
Staples, Cleo (1934—)
Staples, Mavis (1940—)
Staples, Yvonne (1939—)
Tharpe, Rosetta (1915–1973)
Ward, Clara Mae (1924–1973)
Washington, Dinah (1924–1963)
Williams, Deniece (1951—)
Williams, Marion (1927–1994)

GOTHIC-FICTION WRITER

Barney, Natalie Clifford (1876–1972)
Benedictsson, Victoria (1850–1888)
Dacre, Charlotte (c. 1772–1825)
Dinesen, Isak (1885–1962)
Durova, Nadezhda (1783–1866)
Eberhart, Mignon G. (1899–1996)
Jackson, Shirley (1916–1965)
James, P.D. (1920—)
Jolley, Elizabeth (1923—)
Lee, Sophia (1750–1824)
McCullers, Carson (1917–1967)
O'Neill, Rose Cecil (1874–1944)
Parsons, Eliza (c. 1748–1811)
Radcliffe, Ann (1764–1823)
Reeve, Clara (1729–1807)
Roche, Regina Maria (c. 1764–1845)
Shelley, Mary (1797–1851)
Southworth, E.D.E.N. (1819–1899)
Spofford, Harriet Prescott (1835–1921)
Tennant, Emma (1937—)
Wood, Ellen Price (1814–1887)
Wylie, Elinor (1885–1928)

GOVERNESS

Anguissola, Sofonisba (1532–1625)
Bates, Daisy May (1859–1951)

Besant, Annie (1847–1933)
Betham-Edwards, Matilda (1836–1919)
Bloomer, Amelia Jenks (1818–1894)
Blyton, Enid (1897–1968)
Brazil, Angela (1868–1947)
Breshkovsky, Catherine (1844–1934)
Bridget of Sweden (1303–1373)
Brontë, Anne (1820–1849)
Brontë, Charlotte (1816–1855)
Brontë, Emily (1818–1848)
Carpenter, Mary (1807–1877)
Cavell, Edith (1865–1915)
Cooper, Sarah Ingersoll (1835–1896)
Curie, Marie (1867–1934)
Deken, Aagje (1741–1804)
Doudet, Célestine (b. 1817)
Elstob, Elizabeth (1683–1756)
Evans, Mary Anne (1819–1880)
Fletcher, Alice Cunningham (1838–1923)
Fuller, Margaret (1810–1850)
Genlis, Stéphanie-Félicité, Comtesse de (1746–1830)
Hanan, Susanna (1870–1970)
Holley, Mary Austin (1784–1846)
Huxley, Juliette (1896–1994)
Jameson, Anna Brownell (1794–1860)
Kellas, Eliza (1864–1943)
Leonowens, Anna (c. 1831–1914)
Le Sueur, Meridel (1900–1996)
Livermore, Mary A. (1820–1905)
Luxemburg, Rosa (1870–1919)
MacKillop, Mary Helen (1842–1909)
Maintenon, Françoise d'Aubigné, Marquise de (1635–1719)
Margaret of Austria (1480–1530)
Maxwell, Winifred (1672–1749)
Mayer, Helene (1910–1953)
Morgan, Sydney (1780–1859)
Paoli, Betty (1814–1894)
Peabody, Elizabeth Palmer (1804–1894)
Pilkington, Mary (1766–1839)
Prichard, Katharine Susannah (1883–1969)
Przybyszewska, Dagny Juel (1867–1901)
Radcliffe, Mary Ann (c. 1746–after 1810)
Richardson, Dorothy (1873–1957)
Rowson, Susanna (1762–1824)
Salmond, Sarah (1864–1956)
Schreiner, Olive (1855–1920)
Sergeant, Adeline (1851–1904)
Smith, Eliza Roxey Snow (1804–1887)
Spence, Catherine (1825–1910)
Staal de Launay, Madame de (1684–1750)
Suttner, Bertha von (1843–1914)
Taylor, Elizabeth (1912–1975)
Théroigne de Méricourt, Anne-Josèphe (1762–1817)
Tinayre, Marguerite (1831–?)
Under, Marie (1883–1980)
Utley, Freda (1898–1977)
Vejjabul, Pierra (b. 1909)
Von Trapp, Maria (1905–1987)
Wesley, Mehetabel (1697–1750)
Wollstonecraft, Mary (1759–1797)

GOVERNMENT OFFICIAL
Abakanowicz, Magdalena (1930—)
Abzug, Bella (1920–1998)
Agnelli, Susanna (1922—)
Akers, Dolly Smith (1901–1986)
Alegría, Claribel (1924—)
Aloni, Shulamit (1931—)
Amathila, Libertine Appolus (1940—)
Ancker-Johnson, Betsy (1927—)
Andersen, Lale (1910–1972)
Anderson, Mary (1872–1964)
Anselmi, Tina (1927—)
Anttila, S. Inkeri (1916—)
Armand, Inessa (1874–1920)
Armstrong, Anne L. (1927—)
Ashrawi, Hanan (1946—)
Astorga, Nora (1949–1988)
Baker, S. Josephine (1873–1945)
Balabanoff, Angelica (1878–1965)
Balch, Emily Greene (1867–1961)
Bandaranaike, Sirimavo (1916–2000)
Bang, Nina (1866–1928)
Batten, Mollie (1905–1985)
Becher, Lilly (1901–1976)
Beere, Thekla (1901–1991)
Benjamin, Hilde (1902–1989)
Bergmann-Pohl, Sabine (1946—)
Bhutto, Benazir (1953—)
Bhutto, Nusrat (1929—)
Biryukova, Alexandra (1929—)
Bondfield, Margaret (1873–1953)
Boserup, Esther (1910–1999)
Brown, Virginia Mae (1923–1991)
Browner, Carol M. (1956—)
Brunauer, Esther C. (1901–1959)
Bruntland, Gro Harlem (1939—)
Brystygierowa, Julia (1902–1980)
Bunke, Tamara (1937–1967)
Caillaux, Henriette (?–1943)
Campbell, Persia (1898–1974)
Camps, Miriam (1916–1994)
Carter, Eunice Hunton (1899–1970)
Castle, Barbara (1910–2002)
Catherine II the Great of Russia (1729–1796)
Ceausescu, Elena (1916–1989)
Charles, Eugenia (1919—)
Cheney, Lynne (1941—)
Çiller, Tansu (1946—)
Cisse, Jeanne-Martin (1926—)
Clapp, Margaret (1910–1974)
Clark, Georgia Neese (1900–1995)
Deer, Ada (1935—)
Dole, Elizabeth Hanford (1936—)
Dragoicheva, Tsola (1893–1993)
Elders, Joycelyn (1933—)
Elliott, Harriet Wiseman (1884–1947)
Fairclough, Ellen (1905–2004)
Field, Pattie H. (b. around 1902)
Furtseva, Ekaterina (1910–1974)
Gandhi, Indira (1917–1984)
Hale, Maria Selina (1864–1951)
Hanks, Nancy (1927–1983)
Harris, Patricia Roberts (1924–1985)
Hart, Judith (1924—)
Hashimi, Aquila al- (1953–2003)
Hawthorne, Margaret Jane Scott (1869–1958)
Hetherington, Jessie Isabel (1882–1971)
Hills, Carla (1934—)
Hobby, Oveta Culp (1905–1995)
Hoey, Jane M. (1892–1968)
Honecker, Margot (1927—)
Horsbrugh, Florence (1889–1969)
Horton, Mildred McAfee (1900–1994)
Howard, Caroline Cadette (1821–?)
Howard, Mabel (1893–1972)
Hoxha, Nexhmije (1920—)
Isaacs, Stella (1894–1971)
Jagan, Janet (1920—)
Jarrell, Ira (1896–1973)
Jentzer, Emma R.H. (c. 1883–1972)
Jiang Qing (1914–1991)
Joliot-Curie, Irène (1897–1956)
Kéthly, Anna (1889–1976)
Khan, Begum Liaquat Ali (1905–1990)
Kock, Karin (1891–1976)
Kreps, Juanita (1921—)
Kripalani, Sucheta (1908–1974)
Lathrop, Julia Clifford (1858–1932)
Leakey, Mary Nicol (1913–1996)
Lee, Jennie (1904–1988)
Lee, Muna (1895–1965)
Li Qingzhao (1083–c. 1151)
Martin, Lynn (1939—)
Martindale, Hilda (1875–1952)
Matalin, Mary (1953—)
Meir, Golda (1898–1978)
Mercouri, Melina (1923–1994)
Miller, Frieda S. (1889–1973)
Mongella, Gertrude (1945—)
Montseny, Federica (1905–1994)
Morris, Esther Hobart (1814–1902)
Mugabe, Sally (1932–1992)
Myers, Dee Dee (1961—)
Naranjo, Carmen (1928—)
Neill, Elizabeth Grace (1846–1926)
Neville-Jones, Pauline (1939—)
Nikolaeva, Klavdiia (1893–1944)
Novello, Antonia (1944—)
Odio Benito, Elizabeth (1939—)
Pandit, Vijaya Lakshmi (1900–1990)
Parlby, Irene (1868–1965)
Patterson, Hannah (1879–1937)
Pauker, Ana (c. 1893–1960)
Perkins, Frances (1880–1965)
Peterson, Esther (1906–1997)
Pintasilgo, Maria de Lurdes (1930–2004)
Planinc, Milka (1924—)
Priest, Ivy Baker (1905–1975)
Prokop, Liese (1941—)
Prunskiene, Kazimiera (1943—)
Qian Zhengying (1923—)
Questiaux, Nicole (1931—)
Rankin, Annabelle (1908–1986)
Ratebzad, Anahita (1931—)
Ray, Dixy Lee (1914–1994)
Reeves, Magdalene Stuart (1865–1953)
Rehn, Elisabeth (1935—)
Rehor, Grete (1910–1987)
Reno, Janet (1938—)
Rimington, Stella (1935—)
Roche, Josephine (1886–1976)
Ross, Nellie Tayloe (1876–1977)
Ruth-Rolland, J.M. (1937–1995)
Sanger, Alice B.
Sauvé, Jeanne (1922–1993)
Schroeder, Bertha (1872–1953)
Schwarzhaupt, Elisabeth (1901–1986)
Shephard, Gillian (1940—)
Shipley, Ruth B. (1885–1966)
Sillanpää, Miina (1866–1952)
Smieton, Mary (1902–2005)
Smith, Mary Ellen (1861–1933)
Sorgdrager, Winnie (1948—)
Strickland, Mabel (1899–1988)
Suchocka, Hanna (1946—)
Summerskill, Edith (1901–1980)
Süssmuth, Rita (1937—)
Switzer, Mary E. (1900–1971)
Thatcher, Margaret (1925—)
Uwilingiyimana, Agathe (1953–1994)
Veil, Simone (1927—)
Wasilewska, Wanda (1905–1964)
White, Sue Shelton (1887–1943)
Whitman, Christine Todd (1946—)
Wilkinson, Ellen (1891–1947)
Willebrandt, Mabel Walker (1889–1963)
Williams, Shirley (1930—)
Woodward, Ellen Sullivan (1887–1971)
Yanjmaa, Sühbaataryn (1893–1962)
Zamora, Daisy (1950—)
Zia, Khaleda (1946—)

GOVERNMENT PETITIONER
Chemis, Annie (1862–1939)

GOVERNOR
Anne of Austria (1601–1666)
Barrow, Nita (1916–1995)
Bashir, Marie (1930—)
Beere, Thekla (1901–1991)
Borgia, Lucrezia (1480–1519)
Constance de Cezelli (d. 1617)
Ferguson, Miriam A. (1875–1961)
Finney, Joan (1925–2001)
Forde, Leneen (1935—)
Granholm, Jennifer M. (1959—)
Grasso, Ella (1919–1981)
Hamilton, Mary (1882–1966)
Lingle, Linda (1953—)
Medici, Violante Beatrice de (d. 1731)
Minner, Ruth Ann (1935—)
Mitchell, Roma (1913–2000)
Mofford, Rose (1922—)
Nestor, Agnes (1880–1948)
Odhnoff, Camilla (1923—)
Pandit, Vijaya Lakshmi (1900–1990)
Ray, Dixy Lee (1914–1994)
Richards, Ann Willis (1933—)
Roebling, Mary G. (1906–1994)
Rosas, Encarnación de (1795–1838)
Ross, Nellie Tayloe (1876–1977)
Sáez, Irene (1961—)
Sauvé, Jeanne (1922–1993)
Swift, Jane M. (1965—)
Tizard, Catherine (1931—)
Walker, Olene S. (1930—)
Whitman, Christine Todd (1946—)

GRAND DUCHESS
Alexandra Feodorovna (1872–1918)
Alexandra Guelph (1882–1963)
Alexandrine of Prussia (1803–1892)
Alice Maud Mary (1843–1878)
Alicia of Parma (1849–1935)
Anastasia (1901–1918)
Anastasia Romanova (1860–1922)
Anna Maria of Saxony (1836–1859)
Anna of Byzantium (963–1011)
Anna Pavlovna (1795–1865)
Blanche of Bourbon (1868–1949)
Bonaparte, Elisa (1777–1820)
Cappello, Bianca (1548–1587)
Catherine II the Great (1729–1796)
Catherine of Russia (1788–1819)
Charlotte (1896–1985)
Charlotte of Hesse-Darmstadt (1755–1785)
Christine of Lorraine (c. 1571–1637)
Eleanor of Solms-Hohensolms-Lich (1871–1937)
Elizabeth (fl. 1850s)
Elizabeth Hohenzollern (1815–1885)
Elizabeth of Anhalt-Dessau (1857–1933)
Ella (1864–1918)
Helena of Russia (1882–1957)
Helene of Wurttemberg (1807–1873)
Helen of Waldeck and Pyrmont (1899–1948)
Joanna of Austria (1546–1578)
Josephine-Charlotte of Belgium (1927—)
Karadjordjevic, Helen (1884–1962)
Loughlin, Anne (1894–1979)
Louisa Amelia (1773–1802)
Louise of Baden (1838–1923)
Lutz, Berta (1894–1976)
Margaret of Baden (1932—)
Marguerite Louise of Orleans (c. 1645–1721)
Maria Anna of Saxony (1795–1865)
Maria Anna of Saxony (1799–1832)
Maria Antonia of Sicily (1814–1898)
Maria Magdalena of Austria (1589–1631)
Maria of Mecklenburg-Schwerin (1854–1920)
Marie (1899–1918)
Marie (1900–1961)
Marie Adelaide of Luxemburg (1894–1924)
Marie Alexandrovna (1853–1920)
Marie Feodorovna (1847–1928)
Martelli, Camilla (fl. 1570s)
Mary of Hesse-Cassel (1796–1880)
Matilda (1813–1862)
Medici, Anna Maria de (d. 1741)
Medici, Vittoria de (d. 1694)
Olga (1895–1918)
Olga Alexandrovna (1882–1960)
Olga of Russia (1822–1892)
Pauline of Saxe-Weimar (1852–1904)
Romanov, Elizabeth (1826–1845)
Romanov, Natalya (1674–1716)
Sophia Dorothea of Wurttemberg (1759–1828)
Sophia of Nassau (1824–1897)
Sophia of Sweden (1801–1865)
Stephanie de Beauharnais (1789–1860)
Tatiana (1897–1918)
Victoria Melita of Saxe-Coburg (1876–1936)
Wilhelmine of Baden (1788–1836)
Xenia Alexandrovna (1876–1960)

GRAND PRINCESS
Barbara of Byzantium (d. 1125)
Christina of Sweden (d. 1122)
Gertrude of Poland (d. 1107)
Glinski, Elena (c. 1506–1538)
Julianna of Ruthenia (fl. 1377)
Maria of Tver (c. 1440–1467)
Marie of Kiev (d. 1179)
Solomonia (fl. 16th c.)

GRAPHIC ARTIST/DESIGNER
Albers, Anni (1899–1994)
Bacon, Peggy (1895–1987)
Bishop, Isabel (1902–1988)
Burton, Virginia Lee (1909–1968)
Carabillo, Toni (1926–1997)
Cassatt, Mary (1844–1926)
Coe, Sue (1951—)
Eames, Ray (1912–1988)
Frostic, Gwen (1906–2001)
Gág, Wanda (1893–1946)
Grahame Johnstone, Anne (1928–1998)
Grahame Johnstone, Janet (1928–1979)
Graves, Nancy (1940–1995)
Grundig, Lea (1906–1977)
Hadid, Zaha (1950—)
Haydon, Julie (1910–1994)
Höch, Hannah (1889–1978)
Hoffman, Malvina (1885–1966)
Huntington, Anna Hyatt (1876–1973)
Jacobi, Lotte (1896–1990)
King, Jessie Marion (1875–1949)
Marucha (1944–1991)
Massee, May (1881–1966)
McCully, Emily Arnold (1939—)
McMein, Neysa (1888–1949)
Moran, Mary Nimmo (1842–1899)
Morgan, Barbara (1900–1992)
Mukhina, Vera (1889–1953)
O'Neill, Rose Cecil (1874–1944)
Parker, Agnes Miller (1895–1980)
Pitseolak (c. 1900–1983)
Preston, Margaret Rose (c. 1875–1963)
Roland Holst, Henriëtte (1869–1952)
Ross-Craig, Stella (1906—)
Rosser, Celia E. (1930—)
Sintenis, Renée (1888–1965)
Stepanova, Varvara (1894–1958)
Tanning, Dorothea (b. 1910)
Varo, Remedios (1906–1963)
von Haynau, Edith (1884–1978)
Wiseman, Hilda Alexandra (1894–1982)
Yampolsky, Mariana (1925–2002)

GROCER
Wallis, Mary Ann Lake (1821–1910)

GUIDE
See Scout/guide.

GUITARIST
Albertine, Viv (1955—)
Aluli, Irmgard (c. 1912–2001)
Armatrading, Joan (1947—)
Boyd, Liona (1950—)
Brownstein, Carrie (1974—)
Carter, Maybelle (1909–1978)
Cotten, Elizabeth (c. 1893–1987)
Da Silva, Ana (1949—)
DeMent, Iris (1961—)
Douglas, Lizzie (1897–1973)
Exene (1956—)
Finch, Jennifer (1966—)
Gardner, Janet (1962—)
Gardner, Suzi (1960—)
Gilbert, Ronnie (1926—)
Gordon, Kim (1953—)
Harvey, P.J. (1969—)
Hynde, Chrissie (1951—)
Jackson, Cordell (1923–2004)
Kelly, Jo Ann (1944–1990)
Kuehnemund, Jan (1961—)
Lynn, Barbara (1942—)
McKee, Maria (1964—)
Mendoza, Lydia (1916—)
Millington, Jean (1949—)
Millington, June (1950—)
Namakelua, Alice K. (1892–1987)
Newton, Juice (1952—)
Osborne, Mary (1921–1992)
Presti, Ida (1924–1967)
Raitt, Bonnie (1949—)
Remler, Emily (1957–1990)
Roche, Maggie (1951—)
Roche, Suzzy (1956—)
Roche, Terre (1953—)
Rogatis, Teresa de (1893–1979)
Sparks, Donita (1963—)
Tharpe, Rosetta (1915–1973)
Tucker, Corin (1972—)
Vanderpool, Sylvia (1936—)
West, Sandy (1960—)
Williams, Lucinda (1953—)
Wolf, Kate (1942–1986)

GYMNAST
Abel, Irene (1953—)
Abrashitova, Elena (1974—)
Acedo, Carmen (1975—)
Agache, Lavinia (1966—)
Agsteribbe, Estella (1909–1943)
Aihara, Toshiko (1939—)
Aindili, Eirini (1983—)
Allen, Monique (1971—)
Amanar, Simona (1979—)
Ambrosetti, Bianca (1914–1929)
Ananko, Tatyana (1984—)
Annenkova-Bernár, Nina Pávlovna (1859/64–1933)
Antolin, Jeanette (1981—)
Arnold, Mary Beth (1981—)
Arzhannikova, Tatiana (1964—)
Astakhova, Polina (1936—)
Atler, Vanessa (1982—)
Averkova, Oksana (1970—)
Backander, Helge (1891–1958)
Baitova, Svetlana (1972—)
Bakanic, Ladislava (1924—)
Balazs, Erzsebet (1920—)
Baldo, Marta

Ban, Oana (1986—)
Baraksanova, Irina (1969—)
Barone, Marian E. (1924–1996)
Barsukova, Yulia (1978—)
Barwirth, Anita (1918—)
Batyrchina, Jana (1979—)
Begue, Laetitia (1980—)
Bekesi, Ilona (1953—)
Belan, Tatyana (1982—)
Beloglazova, Galina (1967—)
Belova, Irina (1980—)
Beluguina, Olesia (1984—)
Berenson, Senda (1868–1954)
Berg, Jacomina van den (1909—)
Berggren, Evy (1934—)
Bessonova, Anna (1984—)
Bhardwaj, Mohini (1978—)
Bicherova, Olga (1966—)
Bileck, Pamela (1968—)
Bi Wenjing (1981—)
Blair, Bonnie (1964—)
Blanchi, Elisa (1987—)
Blomberg, Vanja (1929—)
Bobkova, Hana (1929—)
Boboc, Loredana (1984—)
Bobrova, Natalia (1978—)
Bocharova, Nina (1924—)
Boginskaya, Svetlana (1973—)
Bontas, Cristina (1973—)
Borden, Amanda (1977—)
Bos, Alida van den (1902—)
Bosakova-Vechtova, Eva (1931–1991)
Botchkareva, Evguenia
Brown, Leah (1975—)
Bruce, Wendy (1973—)
Buerger, Erna (1909–1958)
Bunke, Tamara (1937–1967)
Burda, Lyubov (1953—)
Cabanillas, Nuria (1980—)
Canary, Christa (1962—)
Carr, Ann (1958—)
Caslavska, Vera (1942—)
Chadimova, Alena (1931—)
Chapman, Merilyn (1962—)
Chen Cuiting (1971—)
Chen Yongyan (1962—)
Chepeleva, Anna (1984—)
Chiba, Ginko (1938—)
Chow, Amy (1978—)
Christodoulou, Evangelia
Chtyrenko, Olga
Chusovitina, Oksana (1975—)
Clisby, Harriet (1830–1931)
Cochran, Linda (1953—)
Comaneci, Nadia (1961—)
Constantin, Mariana (1960—)
Csaszar, Monika (1954—)
Csillik, Margit (b. 1914)
Csisztu, Zsuzsa (1970—)
Cutina, Laura (1968—)
Dalton, Dorothy (1922–1973)
Dando, Suzanne (1961—)
Danilova, Pelageya (1918—)
Dantzscher, Jamie (1982—)
Davis, Jessica (1978—)
Davydova, Yelena (1961—)
Dawes, Dominique (1976—)
Dekanova, Vlasta (1909–1974)
de Levie, Elka (1905–1979)
Deltcheva, Ina (1977–)
Demireva, Bojanka (1969—)
Desmond, Lucy (b. 1889)
Diaz, Eileen (1979—)
Dobesova, Bozena (1914—)
Dobre, Aurelia (1972—)
Dolgopolova, Elena (1980—)
Dombeck, Carola (1960—)
Dong Fangxiao (1983—)
D'Ottavio, Frazia (1985—)
Drevjana, Alena (1969—)
Dronova, Nina
Dudeva, Diana (1968—)
Dudnik, Olesia (1974—)
Dunavska, Adriana (1970—)
Dunbar, Diane
Dunca, Rodica (1965—)
Durham, Dianne (1968—)
Dusserre, Michelle (1968—)
Dzhugeli, Medeya (1925—)
Dziouba, Irina
Eberle, Emilia (1964—)
Egervári, Márti (1956—)
Elste, Meta (1921—)
Eremia, Alexandra (1987—)
Escher, Gitta (1957—)
Evdokimova, Irina (1978—)
Ezhova, Ljudmilla (1982—)
Fahnrich, Gabriele (1968—)
Falca, Marinella (1986—)
Feher, Anna (1921—)
Filatova, Maria (1961—)
Foltova, Vlasta (1913—)
Frederick, Marcia (1963—)
Friesinger, Anni (1977—)
Froelian, Isolde (1908–1957)
Frolova, Tatiana (1967—)
Fung, Lori (1963—)
Gabor, Georgeta (1962—)
Galieva, Roza (1977—)
Georgatou, Maria (c. 1983—)
Gerschau, Kerstin (1958—)
Gianoni, Lavinia (1911—)
Giavotti, Luigina (1916–1976)
Gimenez, Estela
Giorgi, Virginia (1914—)
Glatskikh, Olga (1989—)
Glazkova, Anna (1981—)
Gnauck, Maxi (1964—)
Goermann, Monica (1964—)
Gogean, Gina (1977—)
Golea, Eugenia (1969—)
Gomez, Elena (1985—)
Goodwin, Michelle (1966—)
Gorokhovskaya, Mariya (1921—)
Grancharova, Zoya (1966—)
Grigoras, Anca (1957—)
Grigoras, Cristina (1966—)
Grimké, Angelina Weld (1880–1958)
Gromova, Lyudmila (1942—)
Grosheva, Yelena (1979—)
Groshkova, Tatiana (1973—)
Grossfeld, Muriel Davis (1941—)
Grozdeva, Svetlana (1959—)
Grudneva, Yelena (1974—)
Gueorguieva, Diliana (1965—)
Guigova, Maria (1947—)
Gulyasne-Koeteles, Erzsebet (1924—)
Gurendez, Lorena (1981—)
Gurina, Elena
Gurova, Elena (1972—)
Gutsu, Tatyana (1976—)
Hadarean, Vanda (1976—)
Hartley, Margaret
Hashiguchi, Miho (1977—)
Hatch, Annia (1978—)
Hawco, Sherry (d. 1991)
Hedberg, Doris (1936—)
Heenan, Katie (1985—)
Hellmann, Angelika (1954—)
Hemenway, Mary Porter Tileston (1820–1894)
Henrich, Christy (1973–1994)
Hindorff, Silvia (1961—)
Honsova, Zdeka (1927–1994)
Houter, Marleen (1961—)
Howard, Jessica (1984—)
Howard, Kathy (c. 1961—)
Hrebrinova, Anna (1908—)
Huang Mandan (1983—)
Huang Qun (1969—)
Huebner, Robin (1961—)
Hughes, Joanna (1977—)
Humphrey, Terin (1986—)
Hurmuzachi, Georgeta (1936—)
Ignatova, Lilia (1965—)
Ikeda, Hiroko
Ikeda, Keiko (1933—)
Ilienko, Natalia (1967—)
Ilieva, Zhaneta (1984—)
Ilyenkova, Irina (1980—)
Impekoven, Niddy (1904—)
Ionescu, Atanasia (1935—)
Iouchkova, Angelina
Iovan, Sonia (1935—)
Isarescu, Andreea (1984—)
Ivanova, Ioulia
Ivanova, Svetlana (1974—)
Ivanova-Kalinina, Lidiya (1937—)
Jagger, Amy
Janosinc-Ducza, Aniko (1942—)
Janz, Karen (1952—)
Jentsch, Martina (1968—)
Ji Liya (1981—)
Johnson, Brandy (1973—)
Johnson, Kathy (1959—)
Johnston, Carol (1958—)
Jokielowa, Dorota (1934–1993)
Judd, Isabel
Kabaeva, Alina (1983—)
Kalinchuk, Yekaterina (1922—)
Kalinina, Natalia (1973—)
Kalocsai, Margit (b. 1909)
Karasyova, Olga (1949—)
Karlen, Maud (1932—)
Karpati-Karcsics, Iren (1927—)
Karpenko, Viktoria (1984—)
Karyami, Zacharoula (1983—)
Kelemen, Marta (1954—)
Keleti, Ágnes (1921—)
Kelsall, Karen (1962—)
Kersten, Dagmar (1970—)
Kertesz, Aliz (1935—)
Kery, Aniko (1956—)
Kessler, Romi (1963—)
Kevlian, Valentina (1980—)
Kezhova, Eleonora (1985—)
Khorkina, Svetlana (1979—)
Kim, Nelli (1957—)
Kim Gwang Suk (c. 1976—)
Kische, Marion (1958—)
Kite, Jessie
Klotz, Ulrike (1970—)
Kochetkova, Dina (1977—)
Kolesnikova, Anastasia (1984—)
Kolesnikova, Vera (1968—)
Koleva, Elizabeth (1972—)
Koleva, Maria
Korbut, Olga (1955—)
Koshel, Antonina (1954—)
Kostina, Oksana (1972–1993)
Kosuge, Mari (1975—)
Kotowna-Walowa, Natalia (1938—)
Kovalova, Marie (1927—)
Kovalyova, Anna (1983—)
Krajcirova, Maria (1948—)
Kraker, Steffi (1960—)
Krivochei, Elena
Kryuchkova, Maria (1988—)
Kubickova-Posnerova, Jana (1945—)

Kuchinskaya, Natalia (1949—)
Kui Yuanyuan (1981—)
Kulikowski, Theresa (1980—)
Kupets, Courtney (1986—)
Kurbakova, Tatiana (1986—)
Kutkaite, Dalia (1965—)
Kuznetsova, Evgenia (1980—)
Labakova, Jana (1966—)
Lacuesta, Natalie (1981—)
Lamarca, Tania (1980—)
Laschenova, Natalia (1973—)
Latynina, Larissa (1934—)
Lavrova, Natalia (1984—)
Lazakovich, Tamara (1954—)
Lazuk, Maria (1983—)
Leitzel, Lillian (1892–1931)
Lemhenyine-Tass, Olga (1929—)
Lennox, Avril (1956—)
Lenz, Consetta (1918–1980)
Leonida, Florica (1987—)
Lepennec, Emilie (1987—)
Leusteanu, Elena (1935—)
Levinson, Tamara (1976—)
Lindberg, Karin (1929—)
Ling Jie (1982—)
Lipkovskay, Natalia (1979—)
Liskova, Hana (1952—)
Lita-Vatasoiu, Emilia (1933—)
Liu Xuan (1979—)
Lloret, Maria Isabel (1971—)
Loaies, Ionela (1979—)
Lobatch, Marina (1970—)
Lobazniuk, Ekaterina (1983—)
Lockwood, Belva Ann (1830–1917)
Lu Li (1976—)
Lussac, Elodie (1979—)
Lyapina, Oksana (1980—)
Lysenko, Tatiana (1975—)
Lyukhina, Tamara (1939—)
Madary, Ilona (1916—)
Makray, Katalin (1945—)
Malabarba, Germana (1913–2002)
Maloney, Kristen (1981—)
Manina, Tamara (1934—)
Mar, Sabrina (1970—)
Marangoni, Clara (1915—)
Mareckova, Eva (1964—)
Marinescu, Alexandra (1981—)
Marinova, Mila (1974—)
Marinova, Zornitsa (1987—)
Marlowe, Missy (1971—)
Martens, Camille (1976—)
Martinez, Estibaliz
Mason, Lisa (1982—)
Masseroni, Daniela (1985—)
Matouskova-Sinova, Matylda (1933—)
Ma Yanhong (1963—)
McCool, Courtney (1988—)
McNamara, Julianne (1966—)
Medveczky, Krisztina (1958—)
Memmel, Chellsie (1988—)
Mermet, Karine (1974—)
Meszaros, Gabriella (b. 1913)
Metheny, Linda (1948—)
Meyer, Gertrud (1914—)
Miller, Shannon (1977—)
Mills, Phoebe (1972—)
Milosovici, Lavinia (1976—)
Minaicheva, Galina (1929—)
Misakova, Miloslava (1922—)
Misnik, Alla (1967—)
Mitova, Silvia (1976—)
Miura, Hanako (1975—)
Moceanu, Dominique (1981—)
Mochizuki, Noriko (1967—)
Mo Huilan (1979—)
Molnar, Andrea (1975—)
Molnarne-Bodo, Andrea (1934—)
Moreman, Marjorie
Moreno, Patricia (1988—)
Morio, Maiko (1967—)
Mostepanova, Olga (1968—)
Muellerova, Milena (1923—)
Mukhina, Elena (1960—)
Muratova, Sofiya (1929—)
Murzina, Elena (1984—)
Nagy, Zsuzsanna (1951—)
Naimushina, Elena (1964—)
Nakamura, Taniko (1943—)
Neculita, Maria (1974—)
Netessova, Maria (1983—)
Niculescu-Margarit, Elena (1936—)
Nikolayeva, Margarita (1935—)
Noack, Marianne (1931—)
Nordheim, Helena (1903–1943)
Nordin, Hjoerdis (1932—)
Oda, Cheko
Okino, Betty (1975—)
Olaru, Maria (1982—)
Omelianchik, Oksana (1970—)
Ono, Kiyoko (1936—)
Onodi, Henrietta (1974—)
Oulehlova, Lenka (1973—)
Ovari, Eva (1961—)
Palfyova, Matylda (1912–1944)
Panova, Bianca (1970—)
Pantazi, Charikleia (1985—)
Pasca, Mirela (1975—)
Pascual, Carolina (1976—)
Patterson, Carly (1988—)
Pauca, Simona (1969—)
Pavlina, Yevgenia (1979—)
Pavlova, Anna (1987—)
Perversi, Luigina (1914–1983)
Petrik, Larissa (1949—)
Petrova, Maria (1975—)
Petrovschi, Oana (1986—)
Pettersson, Ann-Sofi (1932—)
Pettersson, Goeta (1926—)
Phelps, Jaycie (1979—)
Phillips, Kristie (1972—)
Pickles, Edith Carrie
Pimnacova, Bohumila (1947—)
Piskun, Elena (1978—)
Pizzavini, Diana (1911–1989)
Plachyne-Korondi, Margit (1932—)
Podkopayeva, Lilia (1978—)
Poehlsen, Paula (1913—)
Polak, Anna (1906–1943)
Pollatou, Anna (1983—)
Polokova, Iveta (1970—)
Polozkova, Alëna (1979—)
Ponor, Catalina (1987—)
Popa, Celestina (1970—)
Popa, Eugenia (1973—)
Popova, Diana (1976—)
Poreceanu, Uta (1936—)
Posevina, Elena (1986—)
Postell, Ashley (1986—)
Potorac, Gabriela (1973—)
Powell, Kristy (1980—)
Presacan, Claudia (1979—)
Price, Hayley
Produnova, Elena (1980—)
Puzhevich, Olga (1983—)
Rabasova, Jana (1933—)
Radochla, Birgit (1945—)
Raducan, Andreea (1983—)
Raeva, Iliana (1963—)
Rakoczy, Helena (1921—)
Ralenkova, Anelia (1963—)
Ranguelova, Kristina (1985—)
Raskina, Yulia (1982—)
Ray, Elise (1982—)
Reichova, Alena (1933—)
Reljin, Milena (1967—)
Rensch, Katharina (1964—)
Retton, Mary Lou (1968—)
Ricna, Hana (1968—)
Rigby, Cathy (1952—)
Roenstroem, Eva (1932—)
Roering, Gun (1930—)
Rosu, Monica (1987—)
Rueda, Eva (1971—)
Ruehn, Melita (1965—)
Russell, Ernestine (1938—)
Ruzickova, Hana (1941–1981)
Ruzickova, Vera (1928—)
Saadi, Elvira (1952—)
Sacalici, Elena (1937—)
Salapatyska, Stella (1979—)
Sandahl, Ingrid (1924—)
Sandorne-Nagy, Margit (1921—)
Sang Lan (1981—)
Santoni, Elisa (1987—)
Sazonenkova, Elena (1973—)
Schennikova, Angelika (1969—)
Schieferdecker, Bettina (1968—)
Schifano, Helen (1922—)
Schlegel, Elfi (1964—)
Schmeisser, Richarda (1954—)
Schmidt, Magdalena (1949—)
Schmitt, Christine (1953—)
Schmitt, Julie (b. 1913)
Schroth, Clara (1920—)
Schwandt, Rhonda (1963—)
Schwikert, Tasha (1984—)
Sedlackova, Jaroslava (1946—)
Serebrianskaya, Yekaterina (1977—)
Sey, Jennifer (1969—)
Seymour, Ethel (1881–1963)
Shalamova, Elena (1982—)
Shamray-Rudko, Galina (1931—)
Shaposhnikova, Natalia (1961—)
Sheremeta, Liubov (1980—)
Shevchenko, Elena (1971—)
Shimanskaya, Vera (1981—)
Shinoda, Miho (1972—)
Shishova, Albina (1966—)
Shushunova, Elena (1969—)
Silhanova, Olga (1920–1986)
Silivas, Daniela (1970—)
Simonis, Anita (1926—)
Sinko, Andrea (1967—)
Skaldina, Oksana (1972—)
Sklenickova, Miroslava (1951—)
Slizowska, Barbara (1938—)
Smith, Ada
Smith, Hilda
Sofronie, Daniela (1988—)
Sohnemann, Kate (1913—)
Sokolova, Elena
Srncova, Bozena (1925—)
Stachow, Danuta (1934—)
Stack, Chelle (1973—)
Stacker, Brenann (1987—)
Staiculescu, Doina (1967—)
Stanulet, Mihaela (1966—)
Starke, Ute (1939—)
Stelma, Jacoba (1907—)
Storczer, Beata (1969—)
Stovbchataya, Ludmila (1974—)
Stoyanova, Boriana (1968—)
Strazheva, Olga (1972—)
Stroescu, Silvia (1985—)
Strong, Lori (1972—)
Strug, Kerri (1977—)
Sube, Karola (1964—)

Suess, Birgit (1962—)
Sugawara, Risa (1977—)
Svedova-Schoenova, Lydmila (1936—)
Szabo, Ecaterina (1966—)
Szabo, Violette (1921–1945)
Szczerbinska-Krolowa, Lidia (1935—)
Tabakova, Maja (1978—)
Talavera, Tracee (1966—)
Taleva, Ivelina (1979—)
Tancheva, Galina (1987—)
Tancheva, Vladislava (1987—)
Tanzini, Luisa (b. 1914)
Tchachina, Irina (1982—)
Teslenko, Olga (1981—)
Themans-Simons, Judikje (1904–1943)
Thompson, Donielle (1981—)
Thompson, Jennie (1981—)
Thuemmler-Pawlak, Doerte (1971—)
Tidd, Rachel (1984—)
Timochenko, Alexandra (1972—)
Tkacikova-Tacova, Adolfina (1939—)
Toth, Judit (b. 1906)
Tourischeva, Ludmila (1952—)
Tousek, Yvonne (1980—)
Troes, Olga (1914—)
Tronconi, Carolina (b. 1913)
Trusca, Gabriela (1957—)
Tugurlan, Mirela (1980—)
Turner, Dumitrita (1964—)
Umeh, Stella (1975—)
Ungureanu, Corina (1980—)
Ungureanu, Teodora (1960—)
Urbanovich, Galina (1917—)
Vancurova, Vera (1932—)
van der Vegt, Anna (1903–1983)
Van Randwijk, Petronella (1905–1978)
van Rumt, Hendrika (b. 1897)
Vasarhelyi Weckinger, Edit (1923—)
Vatachka, Vjara (1980—)
Vercesi, Ines (1916–1997)
Vermirovska, Zdena (1913—)
Vernizzi, Laura (1985—)
Vetrovska, Marie (1912–1987)
Vise, Hollie (1987—)
Vitrichenko, Elena (1976—)
Vittadini, Rita (1914–2000)
Voigt, Franka (1963—)
Voinea, Camelia (1970—)
Voit, Eszter (1916—)
Volchetskaya, Yelena (1943—)
Volpi, Giulia (1970—)
Weber, Regina (1963—)
White, Morgan (1983—)
Whiteside, Jane (1855–1875)
Wilhelm, Anja (1968—)
Woods, Doris
Wu Jiani (1966—)
Xiaojiao Sun (1984—)
Yang Bo (1973—)
Yang Yun (c. 1984—)
Yegorova, Lyudmila (1931—)
Yurchenko, Natalia (1965—)
Yurkina, Olga (1976—)
Zakharova, Stella (1963—)
Zalaine-Koevi, Maria (1923—)
Zamolodchikova, Elena (1982—)
Zaripova, Amina (1976—)
Zasipkina, Maria (1985—)
Zelepukina, Svetlana (1980—)
Zhang Nan (1986—)
Zhou Ping (1968—)
Zhou Qiurui (1967—)
Ziganshina, Natalia (1985—)
Zilber, Irina (c. 1980—)
Zmeskal, Kim (1976—)
Zuchold, Erika (1947—)

GYNECOLOGICAL SURGEON
Scharlieb, Mary Ann (1845–1930)

GYNECOLOGIST
Adams, Fae Margaret (1918—)
Barnes, Josephine (1912–1999)
Barringer, Emily Dunning (1876–1961)
Cilento, Phyllis (1894–1987)
Cleveland, Emeline Horton (1829–1878)
Gao Yaojie (c. 1927—)
Hurd-Mead, Kate Campbell (1867–1941)
Hurdon, Elizabeth (1868–1941)
Kleegman, Sophia (1901–1971)
Levine, Lena (1903–1965)
Lin Qiaozhi (1901–1983)
MacMurchy, Helen (1862–1953)
Putnam, Helen (1857–1951)
Ramsey, Elizabeth M. (1906–1993)
Stone, Hannah (1893–1941)
Sulner, Hanna (1917–1999)
Vögtlin, Marie (1845–1916)
Wijnberg, Rosalie (1887–1973)
Wright, Helena (1887–1982)

HANDBALL PLAYER
Anastasovski, Svetlana (1961—)
Andersen, Anja Jul (1969—)
Andersen, Camilla (1973—)
Andersen, Kjerstin (1958—)
Andersen, Kristine (1976—)
Angyal, Eva (1955—)
Anisimova, Natalya (1960—)
Astrup, Heidi (1972—)
Badorek, Gabriele (1952—)
Balogh, Beatrix (1974—)
Bazanova, Marina (1962—)
Bjerkrheim, Susann Goksoer (1970—)
Bogdanova, Svetlana (1964—)
Borysenko, Nataliya (1975—)
Borzenkova, Galina (1964—)
Bottzau, Tina (1971—)
Brodsgaard, Karen (1978—)
Bujdoso, Agota (1943—)
Burmystrova, Ganna (1977—)
Burosch, Hannelore (1947—)
Cha Jae-Kyung (1971—)
Chen Zhen (1963—)
Cho Eun-Hee (1972—)
Choi Im-Jeong (1981—)
Csikne-Horvath, Klara (1947—)
Cuderman, Alenka (1961—)
Dahle, Mona (1970—)
Dasic-Kitic, Svetlana (1960—)
Daugaard, Line (1978—)
Deli, Rita (c. 1972—)
Deryugina, Natalya (1971—)
Digre, Berit (1967—)
Djukica, Slavic (1960—)
Djurica, Mirjana (1961—)
Drljaca, Radmila (1959—)
Duvholt, Kristine (1974—)
Dzhandzhgava, Tatyana (1964—)
Eftedal, Siri (1966—)
Eliasson, Marthe (1969—)
Ercic, Emilija (1962—)
Erdos, Eva
Eriksen, Ann (1971—)
Farkas, Agnes (1973—)
Farkas, Andrea (c. 1969—)
Florman, Marianne (1964—)
Froeseth, Hege (1969—)
Fruelund, Katrine (1978—)
Gao Xiumin (1963—)
Glushchenko, Tatyana (1956—)
Goksoer, Susann (1970—)
Gorb, Tatyana (1965—)
Grini, Kjersti (1971—)
Gronbek, Maja (1971—)
Gudz, Lyudmila (1969—)
Guseva, Elina (1964—)
Haltvik, Trine (1965—)
Hamann, Conny (1969—)
Han Hwa-Soo (1963—)
Han Hyun-Sook (1970—)
Hansen, Anja (1973—)
Hansen, Christina Roslyng (1978—)
Han Sun-Hee (1973—)
Hegh, Hanne (1960—)
Heinecke, Birgit (1957—)
He Jianping (1963—)
Henriksen, Henriette (1970—)
Hilmo, Elisabeth (1976—)
Hoffman, Anette (1971—)
Hoffmann, Beata
Hogness, Hanne (1967—)
Honcharova, Iryna (1974—)
Hong Jeong-Ho (1974—)
Huh Soon-Young (1975—)
Huh Young-Sook (1975—)
Hundvin, Mia (1977—)
Iles, Katica (1946—)
Jang Ri-Ra (1969—)
Jang So-Hee (1978—)
Jankovic, Ljubinka (1958—)
Jensen, Trine (1980—)
Jeong Hyoi-Soon (1964—)
Jeremic, Slavica (1957—)
Jeung Soon-Bok (1960—)
Johnsen, Vibeke (1968—)
Jorgensen, Rikke Horlykke (1976—)
Kang Jae-Won (1965—)
Kantor, Aniko
Karlova, Larisa (1958—)
Kezine-Pethoe, Zsuzsanna (1945—)
Kiaerskou, Lotte (1975—)
Kim Cha-Youn (1981—)
Kim Cheong-Shim (1976—)
Kim Choon-Rye (1966—)
Kim Eun-Mi (1975—)
Kim Hwa-Sook (1971—)
Kim Hyun-Mi (1967—)
Kim Hyun-Ok (1974—)
Ki Mi-Sook (1967—)
Kim Jeong-Mi (1975—)
Kim Kyung-Soon (1965—)
Kim Mi-Sim (1970—)
Kim Mi-Sook (1962—)
Kim Myong-Soon (1964—)
Kim Ok-Hwa (1958—)
Kim Rang (1974—)
Kiselyova, Larisa (1970—)
Kjaergaard, Tonje (1975—)
Kochergina-Makarets, Tatyana (1956—)
Kocsis, Erzsebet
Kokeny, Beatrix
Kolar-Merdan, Jasna (1956—)
Kolling, Janne (1968—)
Krause, Roswitha (1949—)
Kretzschmar, Waltraud (1948—)
Krueger, Katrin (1959—)
Kulcsar, Anita (1976—)
Kunisch, Kornelia (1959—)
Kwag Hye-Jeong (1975—)
Lakine-Toth Harsanyi, Katalin (1948—)
Lapitskaya, Natalya (1962—)
Larsen, Tonje (1975—)
Lauritsen, Susanne (1967—)
Lee Gong-Joo (1980—)
Lee Ho-Youn (1971—)
Lee Ki-Soon (1966—)
Lee Mi-Young (1969—)
Lee Sang-Eun (1975—)

Lee Soon-Ei (1965—)
Lee Young-Ja (1964—)
Leganger, Cecilie (1975—)
Lelkesne-Tomann, Rozalia (1950—)
Lim Mi-Kyung (1967—)
Lim O-Kyung (1971—)
Litoshenko, Mariya (1949—)
Liu Liping (1958—)
Liu Yumei (1961—)
Lobova, Nina (1957—)
Lowy, Dora (1977—)
Lutayeva-Berzina, Valentina (1956—)
Lyapina, Nataliya (1976—)
Madsen, Gitte (1969—)
Mankova, Svetlana (1962—)
Markushevska, Galyna (1976—)
Matefi, Eszter
Matyas, Auguszta
Matz, Evelyn (1955—)
Megyerine-Pacsai, Marta (1952—)
Meksz, Aniko (1965—)
Michaelis, Liane (1953—)
Midthun, Kristin (1961—)
Mikkelsen, Henriette Roende (1980—)
Milolevic, Vesna (1955—)
Min Hye-Sook (1970—)
Mitryuk, Natalya (1959—)
Moon Hyang-Ja (1972—)
Moon Kyeong-Ha (1980—)
Moon Pil-Hee (1982—)
Morskova, Natalya (1966—)
Mortensen, Karin (1977—)
Mugosa, Ljiljana (1962—)
Mugosa, Svetlana (1964—)
Myoung Bok-Hee (1979—)
Nagy, Aniko
Nagy, Ilona (1951—)
Nagy, Marianna (1957—)
Nam Eun-Young (1970—)
Nemashkalo, Yelena (1963—)
Nemeth, Erzsebet (1953—)
Nemeth, Helga (1973—)
Neneniene-Casaitite, Aldona (1949—)
Nielsen, Anja (1975—)
Nilsen, Jeanette (1972—)
Noergaard, Louise Bager (1982—)
Odinokova-Berezhnaya, Lyubov (1955—)
Ognjenovic, Mirjana (1953—)
Oh Sung-Ok (1972—)
Oh Yong-Ran (1972—)
Onoprienko, Galina (1963—)
Padar, Ildiko (1970—)
Palchikova, Irina (1959—)
Palinger, Katalin (1978—)
Panchuk, Lyudmila (1956—)
Park Jeong-Lim (1970—)
Park Kap-Sook (1970—)
Paskuy, Eva (1948—)
Pavicevic, Zorica (1956—)
Pettersen, Karin (1964—)
Pigniczki, Krisztina (1975—)
Poradnik-Bobrus, Lyudmila (1946—)
Pryakhina, Svetlana (1970—)
Ptujec, Jasna (1959—)
Radchenko, Olena (1973—)
Radovic, Vesna (1950—)
Radulovic, Bojana (c. 1973—)
Rantala, Lene (1968—)
Rayhel, Oxana (1977—)
Richter, Kristina (1946—)
Roether, Sabine (1957—)
Rokne, Marianne (1978—)
Rost, Christina (1952—)
Rudolph, Renate (1949—)
Rusnachenko, Natalya (1969—)
Saettem, Birgitte (1978—)
Safina, Yuliya (1950—)
Sagstuen, Tonje (1971—)
Sandve, Monica (1973—)
Savic, Rada (1961—)
Savkina, Larisa (1955—)
Schmidt, Rikke (1975—)
Semyonova, Olga (1964—)
Shabanova, Rafiga (1943—)
Shevchenko, Lyudmyla (1975—)
Shon Mi-Na (1964—)
Shubina, Lyudmila (1948—)
Shynkarenko, Tetyana (1978—)
Siefert, Silvia (1953—)
Singstad, Karin (1958—)
Siti, Beata (c. 1974—)
Siukalo, Ganna (1976—)
Skotvoll, Annette (1968—)
Skov, Rikke (1980—)
Song Ji-Hyun (1969—)
Sørlie, Else-Marthe (1978—)
Sterbinszky, Amalia (1950—)
Stoecklin, Stephane (1969—)
Strecen-Maseikaite, Sigita (1958—)
Suk Min-Hee (1968—)
Sundal, Heidi (1962—)
Sunesen, Gitte (1971—)
Sung Kyung-Hwa (1965—)
Sun Xiulan (1961—)
Svendsen, Cathrine (1967—)
Szanto, Anna
Szilagyi, Katalin
Tanderup, Anne Dorthe (1972—)
Thomsen, Camilla Ingemann (1974—)
Tietz, Marion (1952—)
Timoshkina-Sherstyuk, Natalya (1952—)
Titlic, Ana (1952—)
Tjugum, Heidi (1973—)
Toth, Beatrix
Toth Harsanyi, Borbala (1946—)
Touray, Josephine (1979—)
Tovstogan, Yevgeniya (1965—)
Tsygitsa, Olena (1975—)
Turchina, Zinaida (1946—)
Uhlig, Petra (1954—)
Vadaszne-Vanya, Maria (1950—)
Vergelyuk, Maryna (1978—)
Vestergaard, Mette (1975—)
Visnjic, Biserka (1953—)
Vojinovic, Zorica (1958—)
Voss, Christina (1952—)
Wang Linwei (1956—)
Wang Mingxing (1961—)
Woo Sun-Hee (1978—)
Wunderlich, Claudia (1956—)
Wu Xingjiang (1957—)
Yatsenko, Olena (1977—)
Yoon Byung-Soon (1963—)
Yoon Soo-Kyung (1964—)
Yuric, Dragica (1963—)
Zakharova, Galina (1947—)
Zaspa, Larysa (1971—)
Zhang Meihong (1963—)
Zhang Peijun (1958—)
Zhu Juefeng (1964—)
Zober, Hannelore (1946—)
Zsembery, Tamasne (1967—)
Zubareva, Olga (1958—)

HARNESS RACER
Kelly, Pearl (1894–1983)
Uzès, Anne, Duchesse d' (1847–1933)

HARPIST
Coltrane, Alice (1937—)
Goossens, Marie (1894–1991)
Goossens, Sidonie (1899–2004)
Korchinska, Maria (1895–1979)
Laskine, Lily (1893–1988)
Palmer, Bertha Honoré (1849–1918)
Visconti, Valentina (1366–1408)

HARPSICHORDIST
Agnesi, Maria Teresa (1720–1795)
Aleotti, Raffaella (c. 1570–c. 1646)
Aleotti, Vittoria (c. 1573–c. 1620)
Amalie of Saxony (1794–1870)
Anna Amalia of Prussia (1723–1787)
Bach, Anna Magdalena (1701–1760)
Caccini, Francesca (1587–c. 1626)
Carr-Boyd, Ann (1938—)
Jacquet de la Guerre, Elisabeth-Claude (c. 1666–1729)
Jefferson, Martha (1748–1782)
Joyce, Eileen (1912—)
Kleeberg, Clotilde (1866–1909)
Kraus, Greta (1907–1998)
Landowska, Wanda (1877–1959)
Lavoisier, Marie (1758–1836)
Maria Antonia of Austria (1724–1780)
Mariana Victoria (1768–1788)
Martinez, Marianne (1744–1812)
Mekeel, Joyce (1931—)
Pinckney, Eliza Lucas (1722–1793)
Pompadour, Jeanne-Antoinette Poisson, Duchesse de (1721–1764)
Sullam, Sara Coppia (1590–1641)
Wallace, Lucille (1898–1977)

HAWAIIAN DANCER
Landis, Carole (1919–1948)
Lokelani, Princess Lei (c. 1898–1921)
Wilson, Kini (1872–1962)

HEADMISTRESS
See School administrator.

HEALTH-CENTER FOUNDER
See Hospital/health-center founder.

HEALTH EDUCATOR
See Medical/Health educator.

HEIRESS
Alexandra of Denmark (1844–1925)
Anne of Brittany (c. 1477–1514)
Anne of Warwick (1456–1485)
Beaufort, Margaret (1443–1509)
Bethoc (fl. 1000)
Brooks, Romaine (1874–1970)
Burdett-Coutts, Angela (1814–1906)
Carlyle, Jane Welsh (1801–1866)
Charlotte of Lusignan (1442–1487)
Chase, Lucia (1897–1986)
Clare, Elizabeth de (1295–1360)
Drexel, Constance (1894–1956)
Duke, Doris (1912–1993)
Eleanor of Aquitaine (1122–1204)
Elizabeth of Luxemburg (1409–1442)
Ermengarde of Narbonne (c. 1120–c. 1194)
Gomez-Acebo, Margaret (fl. 20th c.)
Harkness, Rebekah (1915–1982)
Hutton, Barbara (1912–1979)
Isabel de Warrenne (c. 1137–1203)
Isabella de Redvers (1237–1293)
Isabel of Brazil (1846–1921)
Jacqueline of Hainault (1401–1436)
Krupp, Bertha (1886–1957)
Mansfield, Katherine (1888–1923)
Marie Feodorovna (1847–1928)
Mary of Burgundy (1457–1482)
Matilda de Dammartin (d. 1258)
McCormick, Edith Rockefeller (1872–1932)
McLean, Evalyn Walsh (1886–1947)

Melisande (fl. 1100)
Mitford, Mary Russell (1787–1855)
Montpensier, Anne Marie Louise d'Orléans, Duchesse de (1627–1693)
Nightingale, Florence (1820–1910)
Onassis, Christina (1950–1988)
Sage, Kay (1898–1963)
Sand, George (1804–1876)
Staël, Germaine de (1766–1817)
Strozzi, Marietta Palla (fl. 1468)
Tinné, Alexandrine (1839–1869)
Uzès, Anne, Duchesse d' (1847–1933)
Vanderbilt, Consuelo (1877–1964)
Vanderbilt, Gloria (1924—)
Vicario, Leona (1789–1842)
Whitney, Dorothy Payne (1887–1968)
Whitney, Gertrude Vanderbilt (1875–1942)

HEPTATHLETE
Behmer-Vater, Anke (1961—)
Belova, Irina (1968—)
Braun, Sabine (1965—)
Everts, Sabine (1961—)
John-Paetz-Moebius, Sabine (1957—)
Joyner, Florence Griffith (1959–1998)
Joyner-Kersee, Jackie (1962—)
Kluft, Carolina (1983—)
Lewis, Denise (1972—)
Nunn, Glynis (1960—)
Prokhorova, Yelena (1978—)
Sanderson, Tessa (1956—)
Sazanovich, Natalya (1973—)
Shouaa, Ghada (1972—)
Skujyte, Austra (1979—)
Sotherton, Kelly (1976—)

HERBALIST
Aubert, Mary Joseph (1835–1926)
Boyce, Ann (c. 1827–1914)

HERETIC (ACCUSED)
Askew, Anne (c. 1521–1546)
Elizabeth I of England (1533–1603)
Furneria of Mirepoix (fl. 13th c.)
Gippius, Zinaida (1869–1945)
Guglielma of Milan (d. 1282)
Guyon, Jeanne Marie Bouviéres de la Mothe (1648–1717)
Hutchinson, Anne (1591–1643)
Jeanne d'Albret (1528–1572)
Joan of Arc (c. 1412–1431)
Julian of Norwich (c. 1342–c. 1416)
Line, Anne (d. 1601)
Lombarda (b. 1190)
Margaret of Angoulême (1492–1549)
Mayfreda de Pirovano (d. 1300)
Mniszek, Marina (c. 1588–1614)
Philippa of Foix (fl. 13th c.)
Pompadour, Jeanne-Antoinette Poisson, Duchesse de (1721–1764)
Zell, Katharina Schütz (c. 1497–1562)

HEROINE
Aaronsohn, Sarah (1890–1917)
Adela of Blois (1062–c. 1137)
Agostina (1788–1857)
Alice of Battenberg (1885–1969)
Almeida, Brites de (fl. 1385)
Aquino, Melchora (1812–1919)
Arnstein, Fanny von (1758–1818)
Askew, Anne (c. 1521–1546)
Astorga, Nora (1949–1988)
Azurduy de Padilla, Juana (1781–1862)
Bailey, Anna Warner (1758–1851)
Barton, Clara (1821–1912)
Ba Trieu (225–248)
Béltran, Manuela (fl. 18th c.)
Besant, Annie (1847–1933)
Botchkareva, Maria (1889–?)
Bouboulina, Laskarina (1771–1825)
Bouhired, Djamila (1937—)
Boyd, Belle (1844–1900)
Brandstrom, Elsa (1888–1948)
Brousse, Amy (1910–1963)
Brownell, Kady (b. 1842)
Brûlon, Angélique (1772–1859)
Brusselsmans, Anne
Bryant, Mary (1765–?)
Bueno, Maria (1939—)
Bursac, Marija (1921–1943)
Cannary, Martha Jane (1852–1903)
Carré, Mathilde (1908–c. 1970)
Casanova, Danielle (1909–1943)
Catherine de Clermont (fl. 16th c.)
Cavell, Edith (1865–1915)
Choy, Elizabeth (b. 1910)
Cloelia (c. 508 BCE)
Cohn, Marianne (1921–1944)
Corbin, Margaret Cochran (1751–c. 1800)
Cornish, Mary (c. 1899–?)
Darling, Grace (1815–1842)
Darragh, Lydia Barrington (1729–1789)
David-Neel, Alexandra (1868–1969)
de Galard, Geneviève (1925—)
Delaye, Marguerite (fl. 1569)
Demorest, Ellen Curtis (1824–1898)
Derickson, Uli (1944–2005)
Diaz, Jimena (fl. 1074–1100)
Dimitrova, Blaga (1922—)
Dobo, Katica (fl. 1552)
Dorion, Marie (c. 1790–1850)
Dunbar, Agnes (1312–1369)
Dustin, Hannah (1657–c. 1736)
Earhart, Amelia (1897–1937)
Elizabeth of Bavaria (1876–1965)
Fischer, Greta (1909–1988)
Francis, Milly (c. 1802–1848)
Francois, Elma (1897–1944)
Fraser, Eliza (c. 1798–1858)
Frietschie, Barbara (1766–1862)
Garibaldi, Anita (c. 1821–1849)
Gelman, Polina (1919—)
Gies, Miep (b. 1909)
Godiva (c. 1040–1080)
Grossman, Haika (1919–1996)
Gwenllian of Wales (fl. 1137)
Hachette, Jeanne (c. 1454–?)
Hale, Clara (1905–1992)
Hart, Nancy (c. 1735–1830)
Hart, Nancy (c. 1846–1902)
Herrmann, Liselotte (1909–1938)
Hess, Myra (1890–1965)
Hilsz, Maryse (1903–1946)
Jaburkova, Jozka (d. 1944)
Jacobs, Aletta (1854–1929)
Jadwiga (1374–1399)
Jagiello, Appolonia (1825–1866)
Jesus, Gregoria de (1875–1943)
Joan of Arc (c. 1412–1431)
Judith (fl. early 6th c. BCE)
Khan, Noor Inayat (1914–1944)
Kosmodemyanskaya, Zoya (1923–1941)
Lacombe, Claire (1765–?)
Lakshmibai (c. 1835–1858)
Lane, Jane (d. 1689)
Lewis, Ida (1842–1911)
Litvyak, Lidiya (1921–1943)
Ludington, Sybil (1761–1839)
Macdonald, Flora (1722–1790)
Marie of Rumania (1875–1938)
McCauley, Mary Ludwig Hays (1754–1832)
Messene (fl. early 12th c. BCE)
Michel, Louise (1830–1905)
Mink, Paule (1839–1901)
Mirabal de González, Patria (1924–1960)
Mirabal de Guzmán, María Teresa (1936–1960)
Mirabal Sisters
Mugabe, Sally (1932–1992)
Nevejean, Yvonne (1900–1987)
Newport, Matilda (c. 1795–1837)
Niederkirchner, Käte (1909–1944)
Nightingale, Florence (1820–1910)
Nijinska, Romola (1891–1978)
Odena, Lina (1911–1936)
Opdyke, Irene (1918–2003)
Paasche, Maria (1909–2000)
Pimentel, Eleonora (c. 1768–1799)
Qiu Jin (c. 1875–1907)
Reed, Alma (1889–1966)
Rodríguez de Tió, Lola (1843–1924)
Salavarrieta, Pola (1795–1817)
Sandes, Flora (1876–1956)
Sansom, Odette (1912–1995)
Secord, Laura (1775–1868)
Sendler, Irena (b. 1910)
Senesh, Hannah (1921–1944)
Shizuka Gozen (fl. 12th c.)
Sigurana, Caterina (fl. 1543)
Simaite, Ona (1899–1970)
Spiridonova, Maria (1884–1941)
Stanley, Charlotte (1599–1664)
Tescon, Trinidad (1848–1928)
Truganini (1812–1876)
Tzavella, Moscho (1760–1803)
Vercheres, Madeleine de (1678–1747)
Villameur, Lise (1905–2004)
Walker, Helen (1710–1791)
Wrede, Mathilda (1864–1928)
Yaa Asantewaa (c. 1850–1921)
Zane, Betty (c. 1766–c. 1831)
Zrinyi, Ilona (1643–1703)

HIGH JUMPER
See Track-and-field athlete.

HISTORIAN
Abbott, Evelyn (1843–1901)
Abel, Annie Heloise (1873–1947)
Adam-Smith, Patsy (1924–2001)
Ahrweiler, Hélène (1916—)
Aikin, Lucy (1781–1864)
Albert, Octavia V.R. (1853–c. 1899)
Aleksandrovna, Vera (1895–1966)
Alvarez de Toledo, Luisa Isabel (1936—)
Angers, Félicité (1845–1924)
Anna Comnena (1083–1153/55)
Baly, Monica E. (1914–1998)
Bang, Nina (1866–1928)
Ban Zhao (c. 45–c. 120)
Barbauld, Anna Letitia (1743–1825)
Barbosa, Pilar (1898–1997)
Barine, Arvède (1840–1908)
Barr, Margaret Scolari (1901–1987)
Barry, Iris (1895–1969)
Beard, Mary Ritter (1876–1958)
Becker, Jillian (1932—)
Bell, Gertrude (1868–1926)
Benson, Mary (1919–2000)
Berenson, Mary (1864–1944)
Bessa-Luís, Agustina (1922—)
Bonds, Margaret (1913–1972)
Borg, Dorothy (1901–1993)
Bourin, Jeanne (1922–2004)
Braun-Vogelstein, Julie (1883–1971)
Burgess, Renate (1910–1988)
Burkholder, Mabel (1881–1973)
Butler, Helen May (1867–1957)
Cam, Helen M. (1885–1968)

Occupational Index

Carabillo, Toni (1926–1997)
Carter, Elizabeth (1717–1806)
Cartwright, Julia (1851–1924)
Carus-Wilson, Eleanora Mary (1897–1977)
Caton-Thompson, Gertrude (1888–1985)
Caulkins, Frances Manwaring (1795–1869)
Chacón Nardi, Rafaela (1926–2001)
Chang, Iris (1968–2004)
Christine de Pizan (c. 1363–c. 1431)
Clapp, Margaret (1910–1974)
Coignet, Clarisse (1823–?)
Colcord, Joanna Carver (1882–1960)
Concannon, Helena (1878–1952)
Cruft, Catherine Holway (1927—)
Dawidowicz, Lucy (1915–1990)
Debo, Angie (1890–1988)
Dilke, Emily (1840–1904)
Drake-Brockman, Henrietta (1901–1968)
Durant, Ariel (1898–1981)
Eady, Dorothy (1904–1981)
Eaubonne, Françoise d' (1920–2005)
Eckstorm, Fannie Pearson Hardy (1865–1946)
Edwards, Amelia B. (1831–1892)
Eisner, Lotte (1896–1983)
Ellet, Elizabeth (c. 1812–1877)
Elliott, Maud Howe (1854–1948)
Ellis, Florence Hawley (1906–1991)
Enthoven, Gabrielle (1868–1950)
Eyles, Joan M. (1907–1986)
Fisher, Dorothy Canfield (1879–1958)
Forbes, Esther (1891–1967)
Fuller, Margaret (1810–1850)
Gage, Frances D. (1808–1884)
Gisbert Carbonell de Mesa, Teresa (1926—)
Goodwin, Doris Kearns (1943—)
Gowing, Margaret (1921–1998)
Gray, Nicolete (1911–1997)
Green, Alice Stopford (1847–1929)
Green, Constance McLaughlin (1897–1975)
Green, Mary Anne Everett (1818–1895)
Gulbadan (c. 1522–1603)
Gund, Agnes (1938—)
Gurevich, Liubov (1866–1940)
Hamilton, Edith (1867–1963)
Harrison, Jane Ellen (1850–1928)
Hawes, Harriet Boyd (1871–1945)
Hawkes, Jacquetta (1910–1996)
Hayden, Mary (1862–1942)
Hemenway, Abby (1828–1890)
Hickey, Mary St. Domitille (1882–1958)
Howitt, Mary (1799–1888)
Hrotsvitha of Gandersheim (c. 935–1001)
Hyslop, Beatrice Fry (1899–1973)
Ingstad, Anne-Stine (c. 1918–1997)
Kavanagh, Julia (1824–1877)
Kellogg, Louise Phelps (1862–1942)
Kiddle, Margaret (1914–1958)
King, Grace Elizabeth (c. 1852–1932)
Krasovskaya, Vera (d. 1999)
Kuncewicz, Maria (1899–1989)
Lamb, Martha J.R. (1826–1893)
Leach, Abby (1855–1918)
Lee, Ida (1865–1943)
Leech, Margaret (1893–1974)
Lehmann, Rosamond (1901–1990)
Lerner, Gerda (1920—)
Lesik, Vera (1910–1975)
Le Sueur, Meridel (1900–1996)
Lézardière, Pauline de (1754–1835)
Litchfield, Jessie (1883–1956)
Logan, Deborah Norris (1761–1839)
Longford, Elizabeth (1906—)
Lowry-Corry, Dorothy (1885–1967)
Macardle, Dorothy (1889–1958)
Macaulay, Catharine (1731–1791)
Macaulay, Rose (1881–1958)
Macurdy, Grace Harriet (1866–1946)
Martín Gaite, Carmen (1925—)
Maxwell, Constantia (1886–1962)
McKisack, May (1900–1981)
Metzger, Hélène (1889–1944)
Miller, Susanne (1915—)
Miner, Dorothy (1904–1973)
Mitchell, Lucy (1845–1888)
Mitchison, Rosalind (1919–2002)
Mizuta, Tamae (1929—)
Moholy-Nagy, Sibyl (1903–1971)
Morris, Jan (1926—)
Mutafchieva, Vera P. (1929—)
Neilson, Nellie (1873–1947)
Nestle, Joan (1940—)
Norgate, Kate (1853–1935)
Nuttall, Zelia (1857–1933)
Otway-Ruthven, Jocelyn (1909–1989)
Pamphila (fl. 1st c.)
Papariga, Alexandra (1945—)
Peck, Annie Smith (1850–1935)
Penson, Lillian Margery (1896–1963)
Pérez, Eulalia Arrila de (c. 1773–c. 1878)
Petre, Maude (1863–1942)
Pitini-Morera, Hariata Whakatau (1871/72?–1938)
Power, Eileen (1889–1940)
Putnam, Bertha Haven (1872–1960)
Robert-Kéralio, Louise (1758–1821)
Rochester, Anna (1880–1966)
Romein-Verschoor, Annie (1895–1978)
Roslavleva, Natalia (1907–1977)
Rover, Constance (1910–2005)
Rowbotham, Sheila (1943—)
Rozhanskaya, Mariam (1928—)
Rutherford, Mildred (1851–1928)
Salmon, Lucy Maynard (1853–1927)
Sandoz, Mari (1896–1966)
Shakhovskaya, Zinaida (1906–2001)
Skinner, Constance Lindsay (1877–1939)
Smith-Rosenberg, Carroll
Spender, Dale (1943—)
Spiel, Hilde (1911–1990)
Stanton, Elizabeth Cady (1815–1902)
Stevenson, Sara Yorke (1847–1921)
Stopford Green, Alice (1847–1929)
Strickland, Agnes (1796–1874)
Sutherland, Lucy Stuart (1903–1980)
Taylor, Eva (1879–1966)
Tremain, Rose (1943—)
Tuchman, Barbara (1912–1989)
Vaz de Carvalho, Maria Amália (1847–1921)
Victor, Frances (1826–1902)
Warner, Marina (1946—)
Warren, Mercy Otis (1728–1814)
Wedgwood, C.V. (1910–1997)
Welch, Ann (1917–2002)
Wharton, Anne Hollingsworth (1845–1928)
Whitaker, Mabel (1884–1976)
Williams, Mary Wilhelmine (1878–1944)
Winslow, Ola Elizabeth (c. 1885–1977)
Wiskemann, Elizabeth Meta (1899–1971)
Woodbury, Helen Sumner (1876–1933)
Woodham-Smith, Cecil (1896–1977)
Wordsworth, Dorothy (1771–1855)
Wright, Mary Clabaugh (1917–1970)
Wright, Muriel Hazel (1889–1975)
Yamazaki, Tomoko (1931—)
Yates, Frances Amelia (1899–1981)

HISTORICAL-FICTION WRITER

Andrews, Mary Raymond (1860–1936)
Atherton, Gertrude (1857–1948)
Aulnoy, Marie Catherine, Countess d' (c. 1650–1705)
Barr, Amelia Huddleston (1831–1919)
Bibesco, Marthe Lucie (1887–1973)
Bombal, María Luisa (1910–1980)
Bourin, Jeanne (1922–2004)
Colegate, Isabel (1931—)
Dark, Eleanor (1901–1985)
Dunnett, Dorothy (1923–2001)
Eberhart, Mignon G. (1899–1996)
Evans, Mary Anne (1819–1880)
Figuli, Margita (1909–1995)
Forbes, Esther (1891–1967)
Gaskell, Elizabeth (1810–1865)
Goudge, Elizabeth (1900–1984)
Hébert, Anne (1916—)
Huch, Ricarda (1864–1947)
Jesse, Fryniwyd Tennyson (1888–1958)
Johnston, Mary (1870–1936)
Kaffka, Margit (1880–1918)
Kossak, Zofia (1890–1968)
Lovelace, Maud Hart (1892–1980)
Macaulay, Rose (1881–1958)
Martinson, Moa (1890–1964)
McCoy, Iola Fuller (1906–1993)
McCue, Lillian de la Torre Bueno (1902–1993)
Mitchison, Naomi (1897–1999)
Mundt, Klara Müller (1814–1873)
Murfree, Mary N. (1850–1922)
Mutafchieva, Vera P. (1929—)
Mydans, Shelley (1915–2002)
Niese, Charlotte (1854–1935)
Paget, Violet (1856–1935)
Pardoe, Julia (1804–1862)
Pargeter, Edith (c. 1913–1995)
Porter, Jane (1776–1850)
Rathbone, Hannah Mary (1798–1878)
Renault, Mary (1905–1983)
Riding, Laura (1901–1991)
Roberts, Elizabeth Madox (1881–1941)
Sackville-West, Vita (1892–1962)
Shelley, Mary (1797–1851)
Stead, Christina (1902–1983)
Strauss und Torney, Lulu von (1873–1956)
Sutcliff, Rosemary (1920–1992)
Taber, Gladys (1899–1980)
Tey, Josephine (1896–1952)
Verney, Margaret Maria (1844–1930)
Vining, Elizabeth Gray (1902–1999)
Walker, Margaret (1915–1998)
West, Jane (1758–1852)
Wilkinson, Iris (1906–1939)
Yearsley, Ann (1752–1806)
Yonge, Charlotte Mary (1823–1901)

HOLOCAUST RESCUER

Babilenska, Gertruda (1902–1997)
Binkiene, Sofija (1902–1984)
Nevejean, Yvonne (1900–1987)
Schindler, Emilie (1909–2001)
ten Boom, Corrie (1892–1983)
Trocmé, Magda (1901–1996)
Voskuijl, Bep (d. 1983)

HOLOCAUST VICTIM

Brüll, Ilse (1925–1942)
Hautval, Adelaide (1906–1988)
Schindler, Emilie (1909–2001)
Zimetbaum, Mala (1920–1944)

HOME ECONOMIST

Atwater, Helen (1876–1947)
Beeton, Isabella Mary (1836–1865)
Bevier, Isabel (1860–1942)
Blunt, Katharine (1876–1954)
Campbell, Helen Stuart (1839–1918)
Coachman, Alice (1923—)
Delany, Sarah Louise (1889–1999)
Duncan, Sheena (1932—)

Emerson, Gladys Anderson (1903–1984)
Frederick, Christine (1883–1970)
Hesselgren, Kerstin (1872–1962)
Husted, Marjorie Child (c. 1892–1986)
Jarvis, Lucy (1919—)
Kittrell, Flemmie (1904–1980)
Kyrk, Hazel (1886–1957)
Marlatt, Abby L. (1869–1943)
Maynor, Dorothy (1910–1996)
Mendenhall, Dorothy Reed (1874–1964)
Morgan, Agnes Fay (1884–1968)
Nutting, Mary Adelaide (1858–1948)
Parloa, Maria (1843–1909)
Patten, Marguerite (1915—)
Pennington, Mary Engle (1872–1952)
Richards, Ellen Swallow (1842–1911)
Roberts, Lydia (1879–1965)
Robertson, Brenda May (1929—)
Stanley, Louise (1883–1954)
Stern, Frances (1873–1947)
Strang, Ruth (1895–1971)
Strong, Ann Monroe Gilchrist (1875–1957)
Talbot, Marion (1858–1948)
Terhune, Mary Virginia (1830–1922)
Valette, Aline (1850–1899)
Van Rensselaer, Martha (1864–1932)
Wheeler, Ruth (1877–1948)
White, Edna Noble (1879–1954)
Woodhouse, Margaret Chase Going (1890–1984)
Woolman, Mary Schenck (1860–1940)

HOMEMAKER
Mackay, Elizabeth (c. 1845–1897)
McKenzie, Margaret (c. 1837–1925)
Paget, Nielsine (1858–1932)

HOMESTEADER
See Frontierswoman/Homesteader.

HORROR-FICTION WRITER
Jackson, Shirley (1916–1965)
Rice, Anne (1941—)

HORSE BREEDER
Cynisca (fl. 396–392 BCE)
Euryleonis (fl. 368 BCE)
Hirsch, Mary (c. 1913—)
Paget, Dorothy (1905–1960)
Pitman, Jenny (1946—)
Sears, Eleanora (1881–1968)

HORSE DRIVER
Button, Isabel (1863–1921)

HORSE RACER
Campbell, Laurel (1902–1971)
McDonald, Hedwick Wilhelmina (1893–1959)
Paget, Dorothy (1905–1960)
Sears, Eleanora (1881–1968)
Smith, Bill (1886–1975)
Smith, Robyn (1942—)

HORSE THIEF (ACCUSED)
Starr, Belle (1848–1889)

HORSE TRAINER
Button, Isabel (1863–1921)
Campbell, Laurel (1902–1971)
Pitman, Jenny (1946—)

HORTICULTURIST
Blodgett, Katharine Burr (1898–1979)
Brahe, Sophia (1556–1643)
Comstock, Anna Botsford (1854–1930)
Cruso, Thalassa (1908–1997)
Dormon, Carrie (1888–1971)
Eastwood, Alice (1859–1953)
Farrand, Beatrix Jones (1872–1959)
Fleming, Nancy (c. 1941—)
Guest, C.Z. (1920–2003)
Jekyll, Gertrude (1843–1932)
King, Louisa Yeomans (1863–1948)
Lawrence, Elizabeth (1904–1985)
Logan, Martha (1704–1779)
Loudon, Jane Webb (1807–1858)
Mahony, Marion (1871–1961)
Molloy, Georgiana (1805–1842)
Nevill, Dorothy Fanny (1826–1913)
Ormerod, Eleanor A. (1828–1901)
Perry, Frances (1907–1993)
Sackville-West, Vita (1892–1962)
Sessions, Kate O. (1857–1940)
Verey, Rosemary (1918–2001)
Willmott, Ellen (c. 1859–1934)

HOSPITAL/HEALTH-CENTER FOUNDER
Bacon, Alice Mabel (1858–1918)
Bishop, Isabella (1831–1904)
Blackwell, Elizabeth (1821–1910)
Elizabeth of Hungary (1207–1231)
Fedde, Sister Elizabeth (1850–1921)
Gunn, Elizabeth Catherine (1879–1963)
Hall, Rosetta Sherwood (1865–1951)
Hegan, Eliza Parks (1861–1917)
Kaur, Rajkumari Amrit (1889–1964)
Kugler, Anna Sarah (1856–1930)
L'Esperance, Elise Strang (c. 1879–1959)
Mahaut (c. 1270–1329)
Mance, Jeanne (1606–1673)
Martin, Mother Mary (1892–1975)
McMaster, Elizabeth Jennet (1847–1903)
Montespan, Françoise, Marquise de (1640–1707)
Newman, Pauline (1887–1986)
Osburn, Lucy (1835–1891)
Palmer, Lizzie Merrill (1838–1916)
Parren, Kalliroe (1861–1940)
Parton, Dolly (1946—)
Payson, Joan Whitney (1903–1975)
Preston, Ann (1813–1872)
Ramphele, Mamphela (1947—)
Richards, Linda (1841–1930)
Ripley, Martha Rogers (1843–1912)
Russell, Mother Mary Baptist (1829–1898)
Scudder, Ida (1870–1960)
Seville, Carolina Ada (1874–1955)
Speyer, Ellin Prince (1849–1921)
Stone, Constance (1856–1902)
Tallien, Thérésa (1773–1835)
Thompson, Gertrude Hickman (1877–1950)
Thompson, Mary Harris (1829–1895)
Tolstoy, Alexandra (1884–1979)
Weiss, Louise (1893–1983)
White, Ellen Gould (1827–1915)
Wilding, Cora (1888–1982)
Zakrzewska, Marie (1829–1902)

HOSPITAL ADMINISTRATOR
Abbott, Mother (1846–1934)
Bagley, Amelia (1870–1956)
Bicknell, Jessie (1871–1956)
Brooke, Evelyn Gertrude (1879–1962)
Chapman, Pansy (1892–1973)
Chapman, Sylvia (1896–1995)
Cheney, Ednah Dow (1824–1904)
Cope, Mother Marianne (1838–1918)
Cumming, Kate (c. 1828–1909)
Darton, Patience (1911–1996)
Dempsey, Sister Mary Joseph (1856–1939)
Dimock, Susan (1847–1875)
Dougherty, Ellen (c. 1843–1919)
Evans, Matilda Arabella (1872–1935)
Fearn, Anne Walter (1865–1939)
Fergusson, Elizabeth (1867–1930)
FitzGibbon, Hanorah Philomena (1889–1979)
Fraser, Isabella (1857–1932)
Hegan, Eliza Parks (1861–1917)
Holford, Alice Hannah (1867–1966)
Hopkins, Juliet (1818–1890)
Inglis, Helen Clyde (1867–1945)
Jordan, Sara Murray (1884–1959)
Leahy, Mary Gonzaga (1870–1958)
Maclean, Hester (1859–1932)
MacLean, Vida (1881–1970)
Mance, Jeanne (1606–1673)
Maude, Sibylla Emily (1862–1935)
Neill, Elizabeth Grace (1846–1926)
Newsom, Ella King (1838–1919)
Nightingale, Florence (1820–1910)
O'Connell, Mary (1814–1897)
Osburn, Lucy (1835–1891)
Palmer, Sophia French (1853–1920)
Parsons, Emily Elizabeth (1824–1880)
Pattison, Dorothy W. (1832–1878)
Pechey-Phipson, Edith (1845–1908)
Pember, Phoebe Yates (1823–1913)
Pengelly, Edna (1874–1959)
Preshaw, Jane (1839–1926)
Scott, Jessie Ann (1883–1959)
Siedeberg, Emily Hancock (1873–1968)
Smythe, Emily Anne (c. 1845–1887)
Thurston, Mabel (1869–1960)
Tomaszewicz-Dobrska, Anna (1854–1918)
Tompkins, Sally Louisa (1833–1916)
Tyler, Adeline Blanchard (1805–1875)
Wilson, Fanny (1874–1958)
Yoshioka Yayoi (1871–1959)

HOSPITAL MATRON
Ritchie, Harriet Maria (1818–1907)
Seville, Carolina Ada (1874–1955)

HOSTESS
See Political hostess.
See Salonnière.

HOTEL ADMINISTRATOR
Grossinger, Jennie (1892–1972)
Marriott, Alice Sheets (1907–2000)
Rubenstein, Blanche (c. 1897–1969)
Sacher, Anna (1859–1930)

HOUSING REFORMER
Bacon, Albion Fellows (1865–1933)
Bauer, Catherine Krouse (1905–1964)
Cons, Emma (1838–1912)
Dinwiddie, Emily (1879–1949)
Hancock, Cornelia (1840–1927)
Hill, Octavia (1838–1912)
Simkhovitch, Mary (1867–1951)
Wood, Edith Elmer (1871–1945)

HUMANITARIAN/HUMAN-RIGHTS ACTIVIST
Agnelli, Susanna (1922—)
Allen, Florence Ellinwood (1884–1966)
Anderson, Marian (1897–1993)
Anderson, Regina M. (1900–1993)
Ashcroft, Peggy (1907–1991)
Aung San Suu Kyi (1945—)
Babilenska, Gertruda (1902–1997)
Barot, Madeleine (1909–1995)
Barton, Clara (1821–1912)
Bay, Josephine Perfect (1900–1962)
Begtrup, Bodil (1903–1987)
Berg, Patty (1918—)
Bohm-Schuch, Clara (1879–1936)
Bonhoeffer, Emmi (1905–1991)
Brown, Rosemary (1930—)
Buck, Pearl S. (1892–1973)

Occupational Index

Bühler, Charlotte (1893–1974)
Cammermeyer, Margarethe (1942—)
Carles, Emilie (1900–1979)
Cassidy, Sheila (1937—)
Chai, Ling (1966—)
Chase, Mary Coyle (1907–1981)
Clark, Septima Poinsette (1898–1987)
Denny, Arbella (1707–1792)
Deutscher, Tamara (1913–1990)
Diaz, Mary F. (c. 1962–2004)
Dohm, Hedwig (1831–1919)
Duncan, Sheena (1932—)
Duniway, Abigail Scott (1834–1915)
Durieux, Tilla (1880–1971)
Ebadi, Shirin (1947—)
Elders, Joycelyn (1933—)
Elizabeth of Bavaria (1876–1965)
Enthoven, Gabrielle (1868–1950)
Evans, Matilda Arabella (1872–1935)
Evatt, Elizabeth (1933—)
Ezekiel, Denise Tourover (1903–1980)
Faiz, Alys (1914–2003)
Fenwick, Millicent (1910–1992)
Ferraro, Geraldine (1935—)
Figueroa, Ana (1907–1970)
Fisher, Dorothy Canfield (1879–1958)
Fleming, Amalia (1912–1986)
Forten, Margaretta (1808–1875)
Franklin, Jane (1792–1875)
French, Heather (1974—)
Frost, Phyllis (1917–2004)
Fu Yuehua (c. 1947—)
Gandhi, Indira (1917–1984)
Gibbs, Pearl (1901–1983)
Goldberg, Whoopi (1949—)
Goldman, Hetty (1881–1972)
Grimké, Angelina E. (1805–1879)
Hainisch, Marianne (1839–1936)
Hamer, Fannie Lou (1917–1977)
Harris, Patricia Roberts (1924–1985)
Hautval, Adelaide (1906–1988)
Haviland, Laura S. (1808–1898)
Height, Dorothy (1912—)
Hellman, Lillian (1905–1984)
Hepburn, Audrey (1929–1993)
Hobhouse, Emily (1860–1926)
Holden, Edith B. (1871–1920)
Ibárruri, Dolores (1895–1989)
Irene Lascaris (fl. 1222–1235)
Jacob, Rosamund (1888–1960)
Jiagge, Annie (1918–1996)
Kanahele, Helen Lake (1916–1976)
Kelly, Petra (1947–1992)
Kennedy, Ethel (1928—)
Kéthly, Anna (1889–1976)
Khan, Begum Liaquat Ali (1905–1990)
Kilmury, Diana (1948—)
King, Carol Weiss (1895–1952)
Kübler-Ross, Elisabeth (1926–2004)
Kuhn, Maggie (1905–1995)
Kuzwayo, Ellen (1914–2006)
Léo, André (1832–1900)
Lewis, Graceanna (1821–1912)
Lindgren, Astrid (1907–2002)
Liuzzo, Viola (1925–1965)
Lonsdale, Kathleen (1903–1971)
Löwenstein, Helga Maria zu (1910–2004)
Lowney, Shannon (1969–1994)
Lyons, Enid (1897–1981)
Macaulay, Catharine (1731–1791)
Macphail, Agnes (1890–1954)
Malpede, Karen (1945—)
Masaryk, Alice Garrigue (1879–1966)
Mason, Lucy Randolph (1882–1959)
Mayer, Helene (1910–1953)
McClung, Nellie L. (1873–1951)
McDowell, Mary Eliza (1854–1936)
Menchú, Rigoberta (1959—)
Mitchell, Roma (1913–2000)
Mitterrand, Danielle (1924—)
Moodie, Susanna (1803–1885)
Mountbatten, Edwina Ashley (1901–1960)
Mugabe, Sally (1932–1992)
Murnaghan, Sheelagh (1924–1993)
Murray, Judith Sargent (1751–1820)
Murray, Pauli (1910–1985)
Myddelton, Jane (1645–1692)
Ngoyi, Lilian (1911–1980)
O'Day, Caroline (1869–1943)
Odio Benito, Elizabeth (1939—)
Pahlavi, Ashraf (1919—)
Palencia, Isabel de (1878–c. 1950)
Peabody, Josephine Preston (1874–1922)
Pedersen, Helga (1911–1980)
Pelletier, Madeleine (1874–1939)
Peratrovich, Elizabeth Wanamaker (1911–1958)
Potonié-Pierre, Eugénie (1844–1898)
Powers, Georgia Davis (1923—)
Prince, Nancy Gardner (1799–?)
Questiaux, Nicole (1931—)
Ratebzad, Anahita (1931—)
Raye, Martha (1916–1994)
Rehn, Elisabeth (1935—)
Remond, Sarah Parker (1826–1894)
Renger, Annemarie (1919—)
Ripley, Martha Rogers (1843–1912)
Robinson, Mary (1944—)
Robinson, Ruby Doris Smith (1942–1967)
Roddick, Anita (1942—)
Roland Holst, Henriëtte (1869–1952)
Roosevelt, Eleanor (1884–1962)
Rose, Ernestine (1810–1892)
Royden, A. Maude (1876–1956)
Russell, Rosalind (1908–1976)
Sagan, Ginetta (1923–2000)
Sampson, Edith S. (1901–1979)
Schroeder, Louise (1887–1957)
Séverine (1855–1929)
Sieveking, Amalie (1794–1859)
Sipilä, Helvi (1915—)
Sirikit (1932—)
Sophia of Greece (1938—)
Stanhope, Hester (1776–1839)
Stevenson, Sarah Hackett (1841–1909)
Stoecker, Helene (1869–1943)
Stone, Sharon (1958—)
Suzman, Helen (1917—)
Taussig, Helen Brooke (1898–1986)
Teresa, Mother (1910–1997)
Tillion, Germaine (b. 1907)
Tolstoy, Alexandra (1884–1979)
Tonelli, Annalena (1943–2003)
Towne, Laura Matilda (1825–1901)
Traba, Marta (1930–1983)
Tree, Marietta (1917–1991)
Valette, Aline (1850–1899)
Veil, Simone (1927—)
Vejjabul, Pierra (b. 1909)
Waddles, Charleszetta (1912–2001)
Warwick, Dionne (1940—)
Wheatley, Phillis (c. 1752–1784)
Williams, Jody (1950—)
Wilson, Cairine (1885–1962)
Wilson, Nancy (1937—)
Wolf, Christa (1929—)
Woodhull, Victoria (1838–1927)
Yamada, Mitsuye (1923—)
Yorkin, Peg (1927—)
Zaharias, Babe Didrikson (1911–1956)

HUMORIST
Ivins, Molly (c. 1944—)

HURDLER
See Track-and-field athlete.

HYMN WRITER
Adams, Sarah Flower (1805–1848)
Alexander, Cecil Frances (1818–1895)
Blomfield, Dorothy (1858–1932)
Crosby, Fanny (1820–1915)
Elliott, Charlotte (1789–1871)
Engelbretsdatter, Dorothe (1634–1716)
Farningham, Marianne (1834–1909)
Ferguson, Elizabeth Graeme (1737–1801)
Havergal, Frances Ridley (1836–1879)
Howe, Julia Ward (1819–1910)
Kassia (c. 800/810–before 867)
Luke, Jemima (1813–1906)
Moïse, Penina (1797–1880)
Steele, Anne (1717–1778)
Waring, Anna Letitia (1823–1910)
Warner, Anna Bartlett (1827–1915)
Wittenmyer, Annie Turner (1827–1900)

ICE DANCER
Xue Shen (1978—)

ICE-HOCKEY COACH
Brown-Miller, Lisa (b. 1966)

ICE-HOCKEY PLAYER
Antal, Dana (1977—)
Bailey, Chris (1972—)
Baker, Laurie (1976—)
Bechard, Kelly (1978—)
Blahoski, Alana (1974—)
Botterill, Jennifer (1979—)
Brisson, Therese (1966—)
Brown-Miller, Lisa (1966—)
Campbell, Cassie (1973—)
Canadian Women's National Ice Hockey Team (1998)
Chartrand, Isabelle (1978—)
Chu, Julie (1982—)
Coyne, Colleen (1971—)
Darwitz, Natalie (1982—)
DeCosta, Sara (1977—)
Diduck, Judy (1966—)
Drolet, Nancy (1973—)
Dunn, Tricia (1974—)
Dupuis, Lori (1972—)
Fisk, Sari
Goyette, Danielle (1966—)
Granato, Cammi (1971—)
Heaney, Geraldine (1967—)
Hefford, Jayna (1977—)
Kellar, Becky (1975—)
Kennedy, Courtney (1979—)
Kilbourne, Andrea (1980—)
King, Katie (1975—)
Looney, Shelley (1972—)
McCormack, Katheryn (1974—)
Merz, Sue (1972—)
Mleczko, A.J. (1975—)
Mounsey, Tara (1978—)
Movsessian, Vicki (1972—)
Nystrom, Karen (1969—)
Ouellette, Caroline (1979—)
Piper, Cherie (1981—)
Pounder, Cheryl (1976—)
Reddon, Lesley (1970—)
Rheaume, Manon (1972—)
Ruggiero, Angela (1980—)
Schuler, Laura (1970—)
Shewchuk, Tammy Lee (1977—)
Small, Sami Jo (1976—)
Smith, Fiona (1973—)
Sostorics, Colleen (1979—)
St. Louis, France (1959—)

St. Pierre, Kim (1978—)
Sunohara, Vicky (1970—)
Team USA: Women's Ice Hockey at Nagano
Tueting, Sarah (1976—)
Ulion, Gretchen (1972—)
Wall, Lyndsay (1985—)
Wendell, Krissy (1981—)
Whyte, Sandra (1970—)
Wickenheiser, Hayley (1978—)
Wilson, Stacy (1965—)

ICE SKATER
Albrecht, Sylvia (1962—)
Albright, Tenley (1935—)
Allagulova, Yulia
Altwegg, Jeanette (1930—)
Anissina, Marina (1975—)
Ashworth, Jeanne (1938—)
Atwood, Donna (c. 1923—)
Averina, Tatiana (1951—)
Baas-Kaiser, Christina (1938—)
Babilonia, Tai (1959—)
Baiul, Oksana (1977—)
Bechke, Elena (1966—)
Becker, Sabine (1959—)
Belita (1923–2005)
Berezhnaya, Elena (1977—)
Berg, Patty (1918—)
Bestemianova, Natalia (1960—)
Blair, Bonnie (1964—)
Blanchard, Theresa Weld (1893–1978)
Bonaly, Surya (1973—)
Borckink, Annie (1951—)
Brasseur, Isabelle (1970—)
Brooks, Lela (b. 1908)
Brunner, Melitta (1907—)
Bryn, Alexia (1889–1983)
Burger, Fritzi
Burka, Ellen Petra (1921—)
Burka, Petra (1946—)
Burka, Sylvia (1954—)
Butyrskaya, Maria (1972—)
Carpenter-Phinney, Connie (1957—)
Carruthers, Kitty (1962—)
Cashman, Karen
Caslavska, Vera (1942—)
Charest, Isabelle (1971—)
Chen, Lu (1976—)
Cherkasova, Marina
Choi Eun-Kyung (1984—)
Choi Min-Kyung
Chun Lee-Kyung (c. 1976—)
Colledge, Cecilia (1920—)
Cutrone, Angela
Dafoe, Frances (1929—)
Daigle, Sylvie (1962—)
Deelstra, Atje (1938—)
de Leeuw, Dianne
Dijkstra, Sjoukje (1942—)
Dod, Charlotte (1871–1960)
Dohnal, Darcie
Donchenko, Natalya (1932—)
Drolet, Marie-Eve (1982—)
du Bief, Jacqueline
Duchesnay, Isabelle (1973—)
Dunfield, Sonya Klopfer (c. 1936—)
Engelmann, Helene
Errath, Christine (1956—)
Falk, Ria
Fedotkina, Svetlana (1967—)
Fish, Jennifer (1949—)
Fleming, Peggy (1948—)
Fratianne, Linda (1960—)
Fusar-Poli, Barbara (1972—)
Garbrecht-Enfeldt, Monique (1968—)
Geijssen, Carolina (1947—)
Glockshuber, Margot
Gordeeva, Ekaterina (1971—)
Goulet-Nadon, Amelie (1983—)
Greenhough, Dorothy (1875–1965)
Grishuk, Pasha (1972—)
Groenewold, Renate (1976—)
Guseva, Klara (1937—)
Haase, Helga (1934–1989)
Hamill, Dorothy (1956—)
Han Pil-Hwa (1942—)
Harding, Tonya (1970—)
Haringa, Ingrid (1964—)
Hashimoto, Seiko (1964—)
Heiden, Beth (1959—)
Heiss-Jenkins, Carol (1940—)
Heitzer, Regine (fl. 1960s)
Henie, Sonja (1912–1969)
Henning, Anne (1955—)
Herber, Maxi (1920—)
Holum, Dianne (1951—)
Holum, Kirsten (c. 1981—)
Huebler, Anna (1885–1976)
Hughes, Clara (1972—)
Hughes, Sarah (1985—)
Hulten, Vivi-Anne (1911–2003)
Hunyady, Emese (1966—)
Hunyady, Emese (1967—)
Huttunen, Eevi (1922—)
Hwang Ok-Sil (c. 1972—)
Isakova, Maria (1918—)
Issakova, Natalia
Ito, Midori (1969—)
Ivanova, Kira (c. 1963–2001)
Jakobsson, Ludowika (1884–1968)
Jensen, Bjorg Eva (1960—)
Johnson, Phyllis (1886–1967)
Joly, Andrée (1901–1993)
Joo Min-Jin (1983—)
Julin-Mauroy, Magda (1894–1990)
Kania-Enke, Karin (1961—)
Kazakova, Oksana (1975—)
Kékessy, Andrea
Kennedy, Karol (1932–2004)
Kermer, Romy (1956—)
Kerrigan, Nancy (1969—)
Kilius, Marika (1943—)
Kim Ryang-Hee
Kim So-Hee
Kim Yun-Mi
Klassen, Cindy (1979—)
Klimova, Marina (1966—)
Ko Gi-Hyun (1986—)
Kolokoltseva, Berta (1937—)
Korsmo, Lisbeth (1948—)
Krasnova, Vera (1950—)
Kraus, Alanna (1977—)
Kronberger, Lily
Krylova, Anjelika (1973—)
Kwan, Michelle (1980—)
Lambert, Nathalie (1963—)
Lannoy, Micheline
Le May Doan, Catriona (1970—)
Linichuk, Natalia
Lipinski, Tara (1982—)
Li Yan
Lobacheva, Irina (1973—)
Loughran, Beatrix (1896–1975)
Ludington, Nancy
Lurz, Dagmar (1959—)
Lynn, Janet (1953—)
Mager, Manuela (1962—)
Magnussen, Karen (1952—)
Manley, Elizabeth (1965—)
Markova, Olga (1974—)
Maskova, Hana (1949–1972)
McLennan, Margo (1938–2004)
Merrell, Mary (1938—)
Merrill, Gretchen (1925–1965)
Meyers, Mary (1946—)
Mishkutenok, Natalia (1970—)
Moiseeva, Irina (1955—)
Morrow, Suzanne
Muckelt, Ethel (c. 1900—)
Mueller, Leah Poulos (1951—)
Mustonen, Kaija (1941—)
Nagy, Marianna
Niemann, Gunda (1966—)
Noren, Svea (1895–1985)
O'Connor, Colleen
Oelschlagel, Charlotte (c. 1899–after 1948)
Okazaki, Tomomi (1971—)
Omelenchuk, Jeanne (1931—)
Owen, Laurence (1945–1961)
Owen, Maribel (1941–1961)
Owen, Maribel Vinson (1911–1961)
Pakhomova, Ludmila (d. 1986)
Paraskevin-Young, Connie (1961—)
Park Hye-Won (1983—)
Pausin, Ilse (1919—)
Pawlik, Eva (1927–1983)
Pechstein, Claudia (1972—)
Perreault, Annie (1971—)
Peterson, Amy (1971—)
Petruseva, Natalia (1955—)
Pflug, Monika (1954—)
Pilejczyk, Helena (1931—)
Planck-Szabó, Herma (1902–1986)
Pötzsch, Anett (1961—)
Pound, Louise (1872–1958)
Priestner, Cathy (1958—)
Protopopov, Ludmila (1935—)
Radanova, Evgenia (1977—)
Ralston, Vera Hruba (1921–2003)
Regoczy, Krisztina
Rendschmidt, Elsa (1886–1969)
Rodnina, Irina (1949—)
Rodriguez, Jennifer (1976—)
Roles, Barbara
Rothenburger-Luding, Christa (1959—)
Rotter, Emilia
Rylova, Tamara (1931—)
Sale, Jamie (1977—)
Sato, Yuka (1973—)
Schenk, Franziska (1974—)
Scholz, Lilly
Schöne, Andrea Mitscherlich (1961—)
Schou Nilsen, Laila (1919–1998)
Schuba, Beatrix (1951—)
Schut, Johanna (1944—)
Schwarz, Elisabeth (1936—)
Scott, Barbara Ann (1929—)
Selezneva, Larisa (1963—)
Seroczynska, Elwira (1931—)
Seyfert, Gabriele (1948—)
Sherman, Yvonne (1930–2005)
Shive, Natalya (1963—)
Sidorova, Tatyana (1936—)
Skoblikova, Lydia (1939—)
Slutskaya, Irina (1979—)
Smirnova, Ludmila (1949—)
Smit, Gretha (1976—)
Sokolova, Elena (1980—)
Stenina, Valentina (1936—)
Stepanskaya, Galina (1949—)
Sumners, Rosalynn (1964—)
Sun Dandan
Sundstrom, Becky (1976—)
Sundstrom, Shana (1973—)
Syers, Madge Cave (1881–1917)
Taranina, Viktoria
Taylor, Megan (1920–1993)
Thomas, Debi (1967—)

Timmer, Marianne (1974—)
Titova, Ludmila (1962—)
Torvill, Jayne (1957—)
Turner, Cathy (1962—)
Usova, Maia (1964—)
Valova, Elena (1963—)
Van Gennip, Yvonne (1964—)
Vicent, Tania (1976—)
Visser, Adriana (1961—)
Vlasova, Yulia
Voelker, Sabine (1973—)
Wagner, Barbara (1938—)
Wang Chunlu (1978—)
Warnicke, Heike (1966—)
Watson, Jill (1963—)
Wendl, Ingrid (1940—)
Wilkes, Debbi (c. 1947—)
Wilson, Jean (1910–1933)
Wilson, Tracy
Witt, Katarina (1965—)
Witty, Chris (1975—)
Woetzel, Mandy (1973—)
Won Hye-Kyung
Yamaguchi, Kristi (1971—)
Yamamoto, Hiromi (1970—)
Yang Yang (1976—)
Yang Yang (1977—)
Yegorova, Irina (1940—)
Ye Qiaobo (1964—)
Young, Sheila (1950—)
Zange, Gabi Schönbrunn
Zange-Schönbrunn, Gabi (1961—)
Zayak, Elaine (1965—)
Zhang Yanmei
Zhuk, Tatiana
Zhurova, Svetlana (1972—)
Ziegelmeyer, Nikki (c. 1975—)

ICE-SKATING COACH

Burka, Ellen Petra (1921—)
Fratianne, Linda (1960—)
Owen, Maribel Vinson (1911–1961)
Rodnina, Irina (1949—)

ILLUMINATOR

See Manuscript illuminator.

ILLUSTRATOR

Abbe, Kathryn (1919—)
Abbott, Berenice (1898–1991)
Abbott, Elenore Plaisted (1873–1935)
Adams, Nancy M. (1926—)
Adamson, Joy (1910–1980)
Albin-Guillot, Laure (c. 1880–1962)
Allingham, Helen Patterson (1848–1926)
Ames, Blanche (1878–1969)
Anderson, Anne (1874–1930)
Armer, Laura Adams (1874–1963)
Ashton-Warner, Sylvia (1908–1984)
Atkins, Anna (1797–1871)
Attwell, Mabel Lucie (1879–1964)
Austen, Winifred (1876–1964)
Bacon, Peggy (1895–1987)
Bailey, Barbara Vernon (1910–2003)
Barker, Cicely Mary (1895–1973)
Barnes, Djuna (1892–1982)
Barns, Cornelia Baxter (1888–1941)
Baynes, Pauline (1922—)
Bell, Vanessa (1879–1961)
Benson, Stella (1892–1933)
Beskow, Elsa (1874–1953)
Bianco, Pamela (1906–1994)
Bishop, Isabel (1902–1988)
Bonney, Thérèse (1894–1978)
Boys-Smith, Winifred Lily (1865–1939)
Brown, Marcia (1918—)
Burton, Virginia Lee (1909–1968)
Buss, Frances Mary (1827–1894)
Butler, Elizabeth Thompson (1846–1933)
Cahun, Claude (1894–1954)
Cameron, Julia Margaret (1815–1879)
Cameron, Kate (1874–1965)
Cavell, Edith (1865–1915)
Chase, Agnes Meara (1869–1963)
Chute, Marchette (1909–1994)
Comstock, Anna Botsford (1854–1930)
Davis, Marguerite (b. 1889)
Delaunay, Sonia (1885–1979)
Demorest, Ellen Curtis (1824–1898)
Donatella (fl. 1271)
Drayton, Grace Gebbie (1877–1936)
Dumm, Edwina (1893–1990)
Durham, Mary Edith (1863–1944)
Earle, Alice Morse (1851–1911)
Edwards, Amelia B. (1831–1892)
Enright, Elizabeth (1909–1968)
Enters, Angna (1907–1989)
Exter, Alexandra (1882–1949)
Fini, Leonor (1908–1996)
Fitzhugh, Louise (1928–1974)
Fletcher, Alice Cunningham (1838–1923)
Foote, Mary Hallock (1847–1938)
Fortesque-Brickdale, Eleanor (1872–1945)
French, Annie (1872–1965)
Frink, Elisabeth (1930–1993)
Frissell, Toni (1907–1988)
Fuller, Meta Warrick (1877–1968)
Furbish, Kate (1834–1931)
Gág, Wanda (1893–1946)
Gatty, Margaret (1809–1873)
Geddes, Wilhelmina (1887–1955)
Gibbs, May (1877–1969)
Gilot, Françoise (1922—)
Gilpin, Laura (1891–1979)
Goncharova, Natalia (1881–1962)
Goulandris, Niki (1925—)
Green, Elizabeth Shippen (1871–1954)
Greenaway, Kate (1846–1901)
Grierson, Mary (1912—)
Grimshaw, Beatrice (c. 1870–1953)
Guest, Lady Charlotte (1812–1895)
Hale, Sarah Josepha (1788–1879)
Hall, Augusta (1802–1896)
Hamnett, Nina (1890–1956)
Hanscom, Adelaide (1876–1932)
Hartigan, Grace (1922—)
Hassall, Joan (1906–1988)
Hentz, Caroline Lee (1800–1856)
Hermodsson, Elisabet Hermine (1927—)
Hesse, Fanny Angelina (1850–1934)
Hofer, Evelyn
Hoffman, Malvina (1885–1966)
Holden, Edith B. (1871–1920)
Holden, Evelyn (1877–c. 1969)
Holden, Violet (b. 1873)
Hummel, Berta (1909–1946)
Huntington, Anna Hyatt (1876–1973)
Ida of Nivelles (d. 1232)
Jansson, Tove (1914–2001)
Jekyll, Gertrude (1843–1932)
Johnston, Frances Benjamin (1864–1952)
Khan, Noor Inayat (1914–1944)
King, Jessie Marion (1875–1949)
La Flesche, Susette (1854–1902)
Lange, Dorothea (1895–1965)
Lathrop, Rose Hawthorne (1851–1926)
Laurencin, Marie (1883–1956)
Leakey, Mary Nicol (1913–1996)
Lee, Sarah (1791–1856)
Leighton, Clare (1899–1989)
Le Mair, H. Willebeek (1889–1966)
Lenski, Lois (1893–1974)
Lewis, Graceanna (1821–1912)
Leyster, Judith (1609–1660)
Liddell, Alice (1852–1934)
Lovelace, Ada Byron, Countess of (1815–1852)
MacDonald, Frances (1874–1921)
Mackintosh, Margaret (1865–1933)
Margrethe II of Denmark (1940—)
McGuinness, Norah (1901–1980)
McMein, Neysa (1888–1949)
Meredith, Louisa Anne (1812–1895)
Merian, Maria Sybilla (1647–1717)
Model, Lisette (1901–1983)
Montanaria (fl. 1272)
Nessim, Barbara (1939—)
Neuberger, Maurine B. (1906–2000)
Nicholls, Rhoda Holmes (1854–1930)
Oakley, Violet (1874–1961)
O'Day, Caroline (1869–1943)
Olds, Elizabeth (1896–1991)
O'Neill, Rose Cecil (1874–1944)
Orczy, Emma (1865–1947)
Orkin, Ruth (1921–1985)
Ormani, Maria (fl. 1453)
Outhwaite, Ida Rentoul (1888–1960)
Parke, Mary (1908–1989)
Parrish, Anne (1888–1957)
Peck, Annie Smith (1850–1935)
Perkins, Lucy Fitch (1865–1937)
Petty, Mary (1899–1976)
Potter, Beatrix (1866–1943)
Praeger, Sophia Rosamund (1867–1954)
Pratt, Anne (1806–1893)
Preston, May Wilson (1873–1949)
Raeburn, Agnes Middleton (1872–1955)
Rambova, Natacha (1897–1966)
Rathbone, Hannah Mary (1798–1878)
Raverat, Gwen (1885–1957)
Rego, Paula (1935—)
Ridge, Lola (1873–1941)
Rowan, Ellis (1848–1922)
Rozanova, Olga (1886–1918)
Ruck, Berta (1878–1978)
Sangster, Margaret (1838–1912)
Say, Lucy Sistare (1801–1885)
Scepens, Elizabeth (fl. 1476)
Scholl, Sophie (1921–1943)
Sexton, Elsie Wilkins (1868–1959)
Sharaff, Irene (1910–1993)
Shaw, Elizabeth (1920–1992)
Shepard, Mary (1909–2000)
Smith, Jessie Willcox (1863–1935)
Smith, Stevie (1902–1971)
Snelling, Lilian (1879–1972)
Somerville, E. (1858–1949)
Sowerby, Millicent (1878–1967)
Spencer, Lilly Martin (1822–1902)
Stepanova, Varvara (1894–1958)
Stephens, Alice Barber (1858–1932)
Stewart, Olga Margaret (1920–1998)
Stones, Margaret (1920—)
Stratton, Helen (fl. 1891–1925)
Tait, Agnes (c. 1897–1981)
Tarrant, Margaret (1888–1959)
Taylor, Ann (1782–1866)
Taylor, Jane (1783–1824)
Thomasse (fl. 1292)
Tourtel, Mary (1874–1948)
Toyen (1902–1980)
Trier Mørch, Dea (1941—)
Trimmer, Sarah (1741–1810)
Uchida, Yoshiko (1921–1992)
van Stockum, Hilda (b. 1908)
Velarde, Pablita (1918—)
von Haynau, Edith (1884–1978)
Walcott, Mary Morris (1860–1940)

Walker, A'Lelia (1885–1931)
Ward, Mary (1827–1869)
Weil, Simone (1909–1943)
West, Winifred (1881–1971)
Whitcher, Frances Miriam Berry (1811–1852)
Whitney, Anne (1821–1915)
Wootten, Bayard (1875–1959)
Wright, Maginel (1881–1966)
Yampolsky, Mariana (1925–2002)

IMMUNOLOGIST
Buck, Linda B. (1947—)
Lancefield, Rebecca Craighill (1895–1981)
Levy, Julia (1934—)
Marrack, Philippa (1945—)
Matzinger, Polly (1947—)
Turner-Warwick, Margaret (1924—)

IMPERSONATOR
Anderson, Anna (1902–1984)
Delarverié, Stormé (1922—)
Desmond, Florence (1905–1993)
Fields, Gracie (1898–1979)
Jeanne de Sarmaize (fl. 1456)
Loftus, Cissie (1876–1943)
Stuart, Miranda (c. 1795–1865)
Wilson, Sarah (1750–?)

INDIAN CAPTIVE
Dustin, Hannah (1657–c. 1736)
Jemison, Mary (1742–1833)
Kelly, Fanny Wiggins (1845–1904)
Oatman, Olive Ann (c. 1838–1903)
Parker, Cynthia Ann (c. 1827–c. 1864)
Rowlandson, Mary (c. 1635–after 1682)
Slocum, Frances (1773–1847)
Tekakwitha, Kateri (1656–1680)

INDUSTRIAL DESIGNER
Eames, Ray (1912–1988)

INDUSTRIAL ENGINEER
Chojnowska-Liskiewicz, Krystyna (1937—)
Gilbreth, Lillian Moller (1878–1972)
Pintasilgo, Maria de Lurdes (1930–2004)

INDUSTRIALIST
Beech, Olive Ann (1903–1993)
Danieli, Cecilia (1943—)
Dassault, Madeleine (1901–1992)
Dillwyn, Amy (1845–1935)
Guest, Lady Charlotte (1812–1895)
Lukens, Rebecca (1794–1854)

INDUSTRIAL TOXICOLOGIST
Hamilton, Alice (1869–1970)

INFORMATION-SERVICES EDITOR
Anderson, Evelyn N. (1909–1977)
Bachmann, Ingeborg (1926–1973)
Carson, Rachel (1907–1964)
Hopper, Hedda (1885–1966)
Levitt, Helen (1913—)
May, Catherine Dean (1914–2004)
Morath, Inge (1923–2002)
Ogot, Grace (1930—)
Parsons, Louella (1881–1972)
Roche, Josephine (1886–1976)
Saarinen, Aline (1914–1972)

INLINE SKATER
Cliff, Theresa (1978—)
Curry, Jenny (1984—)
da Silva, Fabiola (1979—)
Ezzell, Cheryl (c. 1979—)
Glass, Julie (1979—)
Heffernan, Fallon (1986—)
Hodgson, Tasha (1974—)
Kawasaki, Ayumi (1984—)
Logue, Jenny (c. 1982—)
Matthews, Kelly (1982—)
Rodriguez, Jennifer (1976—)
Svobodova, Martina (1983—)
Taggart, Michele (1970—)
Tidwell-Lucas, Gypsy (c. 1975—)
Vano, Donna (c. 1955—)
Walton, Angie (1966—)
Yabe, Sayaka

INNKEEPER
Armitage, Goody (fl. 1643)
Barron, Hannah Ward (1829–1898)
Burgess, Georgina Jane (c. 1839–1904)
Diamond, Ann (c. 1827–1881)
Forbes, Margaret (c. 1807–1877)
Furley, Matilda (1813–1899)
George, Elizabeth (c. 1814–1902)
Gibb, Helen (1838–1914)
Goddard, Victorine (1844–1935)
Graham, Rose (1879–1974)
Harrold, Agnes (c. 1830–1903)
McDonald, Agnes (1829–1906)
Millar, Annie Cleland (1855–1939)
O'Donnell, Ann (c. 1857–1934)
Ralph, Margaret (c. 1822–1913)
Robertson, Ann (1825–1922)
Stoneman, Abigail (c. 1740–?)
Surratt, Mary E. (c. 1820–1865)
Te Rau-o-te-rangi, Kahe (?–c. 1871)
Thomasse (fl. 1292)

INNOVATOR
Ames, Blanche (1878–1969)
Ashcroft, Peggy (1907–1991)
Benerito, Ruth (1916—)
Blodgett, Katharine Burr (1898–1979)
Bramley, Jenny Rosenthal (1910–1997)
Brown, Rachel Fuller (1898–1980)
Bryant, Alice Gertrude (c. 1862–1942)
Cecilia (c. 154–c. 207)
Colledge, Cecilia (1920—)
Crosby, Caresse (1892–1970)
Demorest, Ellen Curtis (1824–1898)
Dlugoszewski, Lucia (1925–2000)
Dodge, Mary Mapes (1831–1905)
Du Coudray, Angélique (1712–1789)
Elion, Gertrude B. (1918–1999)
Field, Mary (1896–c. 1968)
Fleming, Williamina Paton (1857–1911)
Flügge-Lotz, Irmgard (1903–1974)
Gilbert, Linda (1847–1895)
Gluck (1895–1978)
Graham, Bette Nesmith (1924–1980)
Greene, Catharine Littlefield (1755–1814)
Harel, Marie (fl. 1790)
Hazen, Elizabeth Lee (1883–1975)
Herrick, Elinore Morehouse (1895–1964)
Hopper, Grace Murray (1906–1992)
Humphrey, Doris (1895–1958)
Hyde, Ida (1857–1945)
James, Esther Marion Pretoria (1900–1990)
Jones, Amanda Theodosia (1835–1914)
Joyner, Marjorie Stewart (1896–1994)
Kies, Mary Dixon (fl. 19th c.)
Kirch, Maria Winkelmann (1670–1720)
Knight, Margaret (1838–1914)
Lamarr, Hedy (1913–2000)
Lillie, Beatrice (1894–1989)
Lovelace, Ada Byron, Countess of (1815–1852)
Mackay, Elizabeth Ann Louisa (1843–1908)
Mary the Jewess (fl. 1st, 2nd or 3rd c.)
Masters, Sybilla (d. 1720)
McClintock, Barbara (1902–1992)
McCormick, Nettie Fowler (1835–1923)
McCoy, Elizabeth (1903–1978)
Meitner, Lise (1878–1968)
Merian, Maria Sybilla (1647–1717)
Mitchell, Maria (1818–1889)
Morton, Rosalie Slaughter (1876–1968)
Mosher, Clelia Duel (1863–1940)
Mosher, Eliza Maria (1846–1928)
Muller, Gertrude (1887–1954)
Nicholas, Charlotte (fl. 1915)
Noddack, Ida (1896–1978)
O'Neill, Rose Cecil (1874–1944)
Parker, Claire (1906–1981)
Pennington, Mary Engle (1872–1952)
Perey, Marguerite (1909–1975)
Potts, Mary Florence (c. 1853–?)
Quimby, Edith (1891–1982)
Rand, Gertrude (1886–1970)
Reid, Rose Marie (1906–1978)
Rosenthal, Jean (1912–1969)
Ryan, Catherine O'Connell (1865–1936)
Shtern, Lina (1878–1968)
Sims, Naomi (1948—)
Spewack, Bella (1899–1990)
Steiff, Margarete (1847–1909)
Todd, E.L. (fl. early 1900s)
Ulfeldt, Leonora Christina (1621–1698)
Van Cortlandt, Annettje Lockermans (c. 1620–after 1665)
Vansittart, Henrietta (1840–1883)
Walker, Madame C.J. (1867–1919)
Weizmann, Vera (1881–1966)
Wheeler, Candace (1827–1923)
Williams, Cicely (1893–1992)
Wilson, Fiammetta Worthington (1864–1920)

INSTRUMENTALIST
See also Cellist.
See also Dombra player.
See also Flutist.
See also Guitarist.
See also Harpist.
See also Harpsichordist.
See also Latva player.
See also Oboist.
See also Ondes Martenot player.
See also Organist.
See also Oud player.
See also Pianist.
See also Saxaphonist.
See also Tanbur player.
See also Theremin player.
See also Trombonist.
See also Trumpeter.
See also Tunbur player.
See also Ugubhu player.
See also Violinist.
Bloch, Suzanne (1907–2002)
Cunningham, Agnes (1909–2004)
Davis, Mary
DeMarinis, Anne
Farrar, Gwen (1899–1944)
Fox, Jackie (1959—)
Glennie, Evelyn (1965—)
Harjo, Joy (1951—)
Henriot-Schweitzer, Nicole (1925–2001)
Kirchgessner, Marianne (1769–1808)
Lee, Gina (1943–2002)
MacDonald, Barbara K. (1957—)
Palmolive (1955—)
Pedersen, Share (1963—)
Petrucci, Roxy (1962—)
Riale, Karen (c. 1949—)
Smith, Kendra (1960—)

Steele, Micki (1954—)
Sullivan, Jean (1923–2003)
Weiss, Janet (1965—)
West, Sandy (1960—)
Weymouth, Tina (1950—)

INTELLIGENCE AGENT
See Spy.

INTERIOR DESIGNER
Brice, Fanny (1891–1951)
de Wolfe, Elsie (1865–1950)
Draper, Dorothy (1888–1969)
Draper, Elisabeth (1900–1993)
Frederick, Christine (1883–1970)
Hammerstein, Dorothy (1899–1987)
Haraszty, Eszter (c. 1910–1994)
Howard, Henrietta (1688–1767)
Knoll, Florence Schust (1917—)
Lancaster, Nancy (1897–1994)
Parish, Sister (1910–1994)
Perriand, Charlotte (1903–1999)
Rambova, Natacha (1897–1966)
Swanson, Pipsan Saarinen (1905–1979)
Wheeler, Candace (1827–1923)

INTERLOCUTOR
See Translator/Interpreter.

INTERPRETATIVE DANCER
Allan, Maude (1883–1956)
Alonso, Alicia (1921—)
Collins, Janet (1917–2003)
de Mille, Agnes (1905–1993)
Deren, Maya (1908–1961)
Duncan, Isadora (1878–1927)
Graham, Martha (1894–1991)
Holm, Hanya (1888–1992)
Humphrey, Doris (1895–1958)
Impekoven, Niddy (1904—)
La Meri (b. 1898)
Lyon, Genevieve (c. 1893–1916)
Morris, Margaret (1890–1981)
Nadja (c. 1900–1945)
Nevelson, Louise (1899–1988)
Palucca, Gret (1902–1993)
Primus, Pearl (1919–1994)
Rainer, Yvonne (1934—)
Riefenstahl, Leni (1902–2003)
Slavenska, Mia (1914–2000)
Sokolow, Anna (1910–2000)
St. Denis, Ruth (1877–1968)
Tamiris, Helen (1902–1966)
Wallmann, Margarethe (1901–1922)
Wigman, Mary (1886–1973)

INTERPRETER
See Translator/Interpreter.

INVENTOR
See Innovator.

IRON MANUFACTURER
Lukens, Rebecca (1794–1854)

JAVELIN THROWER
See Track-and-field athlete.

JAZZ MUSICIAN
Akiyoshi, Toshiko (1929—)
Armstrong, Lil Hardin (1898–1971)
Brown, Ada (1889–1950)
Brown, Cleo (1905–1995)
Hipp, Jutta (1925–2003)
Lee, Gina (1943–2002)
Liston, Melba (1926—)
Martin, Sara (1884–1955)
McPartland, Marian (1920—)
Osborne, Mary (1921–1992)
Tipton, Billy (1914–1989)
Williams, Mary Lou (1910–1981)

JAZZ PIANIST
Donegan, Dorothy (1922–1998)

JAZZ SINGER
Anderson, Ernestine (1928—)
Anderson, Ivie (1904–1949)
Andrade, Leny (1943—)
Bailey, Mildred (1903–1951)
Bailey, Pearl (1918–1990)
Bofill, Angela (1954—)
Boswell, Connee (1907–1976)
Brown, Ada (1889–1950)
Brown, Ruth (1928—)
Carpenter, Thelma (1922–1997)
Carter, Betty (1929–1998)
Christy, June (1925–1990)
Connor, Chris (1927—)
Daniels, Maxine (1930–2003)
Dearie, Blossom (1926—)
Fitzgerald, Ella (1917–1996)
Flack, Roberta (1937—)
Goodson, Sadie (c. 1900—)
Hanshaw, Annette (1910–1985)
Hegamin, Lucille (1894–1970)
Holiday, Billie (c. 1915–1959)
Johnson, Ella (1923–2004)
Jones, Etta (1928–2001)
Jordan, Sheila (1928—)
Kelly, Jo Ann (1944–1990)
Krall, Diana (1964—)
Laine, Cleo (1927—)
Lee, Peggy (1920—)
Lee, Peggy (1920–2002)
Lincoln, Abbey (1930—)
London, Julie (1926–2000)
McRae, Carmen (1920–1994)
Molton, Flora (1908–1990)
Morse, Ella Mae (1925–1999)
Mouskouri, Nana (1934—)
O'Day, Anita (1919—)
Payne, Freda (1945—)
Rathebe, Dolly (1928–2004)
Ross, Annie (1930—)
Scott, Hazel (1920–1981)
Scott, Sherry (c. 1948—)
Simone, Nina (1933–2003)
Smith, Ada (1894–1984)
Smith, Bessie (1894–1937)
Smith, Keely (1932—)
Snow, Valaida (c. 1903–1956)
Southern, Jeri (1926–1991)
Vaughan, Sarah (1924–1990)
Waters, Ethel (1896–1977)
Wiley, Lee (1915–1975)
Wilson, Nancy (1937—)
Zetterlund, Monica (1937–2005)

JEWELER
Reeve, Elsie (1885–1927)

JEWELRY DESIGNER
Chow, Tina (1950–1992)
Ditzel, Nana (1923—)
Morris, May (1862–1938)
Picasso, Paloma (1949—)

JOCKEY
Bacon, Mary (1948–1991)
Barton, Donna (c. 1967—)
Crump, Diane (1949—)
Early, Penny Ann (c. 1946—)
Krone, Julie (1963—)
Kusner, Kathy (1940—)
Rubin, Barbara Jo (1949—)
Smith, Bill (1886–1975)
Smith, Robyn (1942—)
Tufnell, Meriel (1948–2002)

JOURNALIST
Acosta de Samper, Soledad (1833–1913)
Adam, Juliette la Messine (1836–1936)
Adams, Harriet Chalmers (1875–1937)
Adams, Mary Grace (1898–1984)
Adam Smith, Janet (1905–1999)
Adler, Renata (1938—)
Alden, Cynthia Westover (1862–1931)
Aleksandrovna, Vera (1895–1966)
Aliger, Margarita Iosifovna (1915–1992)
Alkhateeb, Sharifa (1946–2004)
Allan, Stella (1871–1962)
Allen, Maryon (1925—)
Allende, Isabel (1942—)
Almog, Ruth (1936—)
Amanpour, Christiane (1958—)
Ames, Mary Clemmer (1831–1884)
Amin, Adibah (1936—)
Anckarsvard, Karin (1915–1969)
Anderson, Doris (1921—)
Anderson, Evelyn N. (1909–1977)
Annenkova, Julia (c. 1898–c. 1938)
Anthony, Susan B., II (1916–1991)
Araz, Nezihe (1922—)
Arne, Sigrid (1894–1973)
Arnold, Eve (1913—)
Arnothy, Christine (1930—)
Arquimbau, Rosa Maria (1910—)
Assing, Ludmilla (1821–1880)
Assing, Ottilie (1819–1884)
Aubert, Constance (1803–?)
Auclert, Hubertine (1848–1914)
Audouard, Olympe (1830–1890)
Awolowo, Hannah (1915—)
Ayer, Harriet Hubbard (1849–1903)
Bacon, Gertrude (1874–1949)
Bain, Wilhelmina Sherriff (1848–1944)
Baker, Louisa Alice (1856–1926)
Baldwin, Ruth Ann (fl. 1915–1921)
Ballesteros, Mercedes (1913–1995)
Barkova, Anna Aleksandrovna (1901–1976)
Barnes, Djuna (1892–1982)
Barnicoat, Constance Alice (1872–1922)
Barns, Cornelia Baxter (1888–1941)
Barrett, Rona (1934—)
Bates, Daisy Lee (1914–1999)
Bates, Daisy May (1859–1951)
Bauer, Helene (1871–1942)
Beals, Jessie Tarbox (1870–1942)
Beatty, Bessie (1886–1947)
Beaumer, Madame de (d. 1766)
Becker, May Lamberton (1873–1958)
Beinhorn, Elly (1907—)
Belfrage, Sally (1936–1994)
Belloc-Lowndes, Marie (1868–1947)
Bellonci, Maria (1902–1986)
Beloff, Nora (1919–1997)
Benson, Mildred (1905–2002)
Bentley, Helen Delich (1923—)
Beranger, Clara (1886–1956)
Berberova, Nina (1901–1993)
Besant, Annie (1847–1933)
Betham-Edwards, Matilda (1836–1919)
Beynon, Francis Marion (1884–1951)
Binchy, Maeve (1940—)
Bing, Ilse (1899–1998)
Bins, Patrícia (1930—)
Black, Winifred Sweet (1863–1936)
Blanc, Marie-Thérèse (1840–1907)

Blaze de Bury, Rose (?–1894)
Bloom, Ursula (1893–1984)
Bloor, Ella Reeve (1862–1951)
Bonanni, Laudomia (1907–2002)
Bonney, Thérèse (1894–1978)
Booth, Mary Louise (1831–1889)
Bourke-White, Margaret (1904–1971)
Boveri, Margret (1900–1975)
Braden, Anne (1924–2006)
Brady, Mildred Edie (1906–1965)
Breckinridge, Mary Martin (b. 1905)
Brewster, Anne Hampton (1818–1892)
Briggs, Emily Edson (1830–1910)
Broniewska, Janina (1904–1981)
Broom, Christina (1863–1939)
Brown, Margaret A. (1867–?)
Brown, Tina (1953—)
Browne, Augusta (1820–1882)
Bruce, Mary Grant (1878–1958)
Bryan, Mary Edwards (1838–1913)
Bryant, Louise (1885–1936)
Bugbee, Emma (1888–1981)
Bullock, Margaret (1845–1903)
Bullrich, Silvina (1915–1990)
Burkholder, Mabel (1881–1973)
Burns, Violet Alberta Jessie (1893–1972)
Buttrose, Ita (1942—)
Cabot, Dolce Ann (1862–1943)
Caldwell, Taylor (1900–1985)
Callwood, June (1924—)
Campbell, Lady Colin (1857–1911)
Campbell, Lady Jeanne (1928—)
Canto, Estela (1919–1994)
Carpenter, Iris (b. 1906)
Carranza, María Mercedes (1945–2003)
Carter, Angela (1940–1992)
Carvajal, María Isabel (1888–1949)
Cary, Mary Ann Shadd (1823–1893)
Castle, Barbara (1910–2002)
Castro Alves, Diná Silveira de (1911–1983)
Cather, Willa (1873–1947)
Cato, Nancy (1917–2000)
Cazneau, Jane McManus (1807–1878)
Cederna, Camilla (1921–1997)
Chapelle, Dickey (1919–1972)
Chattopadhyaya, Kamaladevi (1903–1988)
Chennault, Anna (1923—)
Cilento, Phyllis (1894–1987)
Clément, Catherine (1939—)
Clift, Charmian (1923–1969)
Clisby, Harriet (1830–1931)
Cobbe, Frances Power (1822–1904)
Coit, Margaret L. (1919–2003)
Coleman, Kit (1864–1915)
Coleridge, Georgina (1916–2003)
Colet, Louise (1810–1876)
Colette (1873–1954)
Collins, Gail (1945—)
Commins, Kathleen (1909–2003)
Conran, Shirley (1932—)
Cook, Freda Mary (1896–1990)
Cooney, Joan Ganz (1929—)
Cooper, Yvette (1969—)
Copps, Sheila (1952—)
Cottrell, Dorothy (1902–1957)
Cowan, Ruth (1901–1993)
Cowles, Fleur (1910—)
Cowles, Virginia (1912–1983)
Craig, May (1888–1975)
Craigie, Pearl Mary Teresa (1867–1906)
Craik, Dinah Maria Mulock (1826–1887)
Crane, Caroline Bartlett (1858–1935)
Craven, Margaret (1901–1980)
Crist, Judith (1922—)
Croly, Jane Cunningham (1829–1901)
Cross, Zora (1890–1964)
Cunard, Nancy (1896–1965)
Curie, Ève (b. 1904)
Curtis, Charlotte (1928–1987)
Dabrowska, Maria (1889–1965)
Dai Qing (1941—)
Dando, Jill (1961–1999)
Das, Kamala (1934—)
Davis, Rebecca Harding (1831–1910)
Daw Khin Myo Chit (1915–2003)
Day, Dorothy (1897–1980)
Deamer, Dulcie (1890–1972)
Dean, Vera Micheles (1903–1972)
de Burgos, Julia (1914–1953)
De Cespedes, Alba (1911–1997)
de Jong, Dola (1911–2003)
Dervis, Suat (1905–1972)
de Sousa, Noémia (1926—)
Deutscher, Tamara (1913–1990)
Deutschkron, Inge (1922—)
Devanny, Jean (1894–1962)
Dickerson, Nancy (1927–1997)
Didion, Joan (1934—)
Dixie, Lady Florence (1857–1905)
Dönhoff, Marion, Countess (1909–2002)
Donovan, Carrie (1928–2001)
Dorr, Rheta Childe (1866–1948)
Douglas, Marjory Stoneman (1890–1998)
Drexel, Constance (1894–1956)
Duby-Blom, Gertrude (1901–1993)
Duder, Tessa (1940—)
Duff Gordon, Lucy (1862–1935)
Dulac, Germaine (1882–1942)
Duncan, Sara Jeanette (1861–1922)
du Noyer, Anne-Marguérite Petit (1663–1719)
Durand, Marguerite (1864–1936)
Dyson, Elizabeth Geertruida (1897–1951)
Eaton, Edith (1865–1914)
Eberhardt, Isabelle (1877–1904)
Eden, Clarissa (1920—)
Edwards, Henrietta Muir (1849–1933)
Ehrmann, Marianne (1755–1795)
Elder, Dorothy-Grace
Ellerbee, Linda (1944—)
El Saadawi, Nawal (1931—)
Emerson, Gloria (1929–2004)
Evangelista, Linda (1965—)
Evans, Kathy (1948–2003)
Fabian, Dora (1901–1935)
Fairbairn, Joyce (1939—)
Faiz, Alys (1914–2003)
Fallaci, Oriana (1930—)
Farjeon, Annabel (1919—)
Farningham, Marianne (1834–1909)
Felton, Rebecca Latimer (1835–1930)
Fennell, Nuala (1935—)
Ferber, Edna (1885–1968)
Fern, Fanny (1811–1872)
Field, Kate (1838–1896)
Figes, Eva (1932—)
First, Ruth (1925–1982)
Fischer, Ruth (1895–1961)
Flanner, Janet (1892–1978)
Fleeson, Doris (1901–1970)
Forgan, Liz (1944—)
Franchi, Anna (1866–1954)
Frankau, Pamela (1908–1967)
Franks, Lucinda (1946—)
Frederick, Pauline (1908–1990)
Freeman, Alice (1857–1936)
Freeman, Lucy (1916–2004)
Fremantle, Anne (1909–2002)
Freund, Gisèle (1912–2000)
Friedan, Betty (1921–2006)
Friedman, Esther Pauline (1918–2002)
Friedman, Pauline Esther (1918—)
Fuller, Margaret (1810–1850)
Furlong, Monica (1930–2003)
Furman, Bess (1894–1969)
Furness, Betty (1916–1994)
Gale, Zona (1874–1938)
Galindo de Topete, Hermila (1896–1954)
Galvão, Patricia (1910–1962)
Garro, Elena (1916–1998)
Gaunt, Mary (1861–1942)
Gellhorn, Martha (1908–1998)
Ge Yang (1916—)
Gibbons, Stella (1902–1989)
Gilder, Jeannette Leonard (1849–1916)
Gilmore, Mary (1865–1962)
Giroud, Françoise (1916–2003)
Gísladóttir, Sólrún
Glanville-Hicks, Peggy (1912–1990)
Glaspell, Susan (1876–1948)
Glen, Esther (1881–1940)
Glyn, Elinor (1864–1943)
Goldberg, Lea (1911–1970)
Gomez, Sara (1943–1974)
Gonne, Maud (1866–1953)
Goodman, Ellen (1941—)
Gordon, Caroline (1895–1981)
Gordon-Lazareff, Hélène (1909–1988)
Gould, Beatrice Blackmar (c. 1899–1989)
Graham, Katharine (1917–2001)
Granata, Maria (1921—)
Grant Duff, Shiela (1913–2004)
Greeley-Smith, Nixola (1880–1919)
Green, Grace Winifred (1907–1976)
Greenfield, Meg (1930–1999)
Gréville, Alice (1842–1903)
Grimshaw, Beatrice (c. 1870–1953)
Grossmann, Edith Searle (1863–1931)
Gruber, Ruth (1911—)
Guerin, Veronica (1960–1996)
Guglielminetti, Amalia (1881–1941)
Gutiérrez de Mendoza, Juana Belén (1875–1942)
Haddon, Eileen (1921–2003)
Hagan, Ellen (1873–1958)
Haldane, Charlotte (1894–1969)
Hale, Ruth (1886–1934)
Hale, Sarah Josepha (1788–1879)
Hall, Cara Vincent (1922—)
Hamilton, Cicely (1872–1952)
Hamilton, Mary (1882–1966)
Hamm, Margherita (1867–1907)
Hani, Motoko (1873–1957)
Hansberry, Lorraine (1930–1965)
Harper, Ida Husted (1851–1931)
Harrison, Marguerite (1879–1967)
Hawes, Elizabeth (1903–1971)
Haycraft, Anna Margaret (1932–2005)
Head, Bessie (1937–1986)
Henderson, Mary (1919–2004)
Henry, Alice (1857–1943)
Herbst, Josephine (1892–1969)
Herman, Robin (c. 1952—)
Herrick, Elinore Morehouse (1895–1964)
Herrick, Genevieve Forbes (1894–1962)
Hickok, Lorena A. (1893–1968)
Higgins, Marguerite (1920–1966)
Hind, Cora (1861–1942)
Hobson, Laura Z. (1900–1986)
Hogg, Sarah (1946—)
Holland, Mary (1935–2004)
Holm, Eleanor (1913—)
Holtby, Winifred (1898–1935)
Hopper, Hedda (1885–1966)
Hosain, Attia (1913–1998)
Hoult, Norah (1898–1984)
Howard, Caroline Cadette (1821–?)
Huang Zongying (1925—)

Hughes, Karen (1956—)
Hull, Eleanor Henrietta (1860–1935)
Hull, Peggy (1889–1967)
Hulme, Kathryn (1900–1981)
Hummert, Anne (1905–1996)
Hunter-Gault, Charlayne (1942—)
Hyder, Qurratulain (1927—)
Ichikawa Fusae (1893–1981)
Idar, Jovita (1885–1946)
Ifill, Gwen (1955—)
Inber, Vera (1890–1972)
Jaburkova, Jozka (d. 1944)
Jackson, Alice (1887–1974)
Jacob, Rosamund (1888–1960)
Jacobson, Ethel May (1877–1965)
Jagan, Janet (1920—)
Jemison, Alice Lee (1901–1964)
Jenner, Andrea (1891–1985)
Jensen, Anne Elisabet (1951—)
Jesenská, Milena (1896–1945)
Jesse, Fryniwyd Tennyson (1888–1958)
Jessye, Eva (1895–1992)
Johnston, Jill (1929—)
Johnstone, Isobel (1781–1857)
Jolas, Maria (1893–1987)
Jordan, Elizabeth Garver (1865–1947)
Jurney, Dorothy Misener (1909–2002)
Kanaga, Consuelo (1894–1978)
Kane, Amy Grace (1879–1979)
Kantůrkova, Eva (1930—)
Kar, Ida (1908–1970)
Katznelson-Shazar, Rachel (1888–1975)
Kautsky, Luise (1864–1944)
Kazantzaki, Eleni (1903–2004)
Kee, Elizabeth (1895–1975)
Keeble, Sally (1951—)
Kelly, Florence Finch (1858–1939)
Kelso, Elizabeth (1889–1967)
Kennedy, Geraldine (1951—)
Kennedy, Jacqueline (1929–1994)
Kéthly, Anna (1889–1976)
Khan, Begum Liaquat Ali (1905–1990)
Kilgallen, Dorothy (1913–1965)
Kincaid, Jamaica (1949—)
Kingsolver, Barbara (1955—)
Kirchwey, Freda (1893–1976)
Kirkbride, Julie (1960—)
Kirkpatrick, Helen (1909–1997)
Koea, Shonagh (1939—)
Krall, Hanna (1937—)
Krull, Germaine (1897–1985)
Kuhn, Irene Corbally (1898–1995)
La Flesche, Susette (1854–1902)
Lane, Rose Wilder (1886–1968)
Laski, Marghanita (1915–1988)
Laurence, Margaret (1926–1987)
Lauristin, Marju (1940—)
Lawson, Louisa (1848–1920)
Lee, Jennie (1904–1988)
Le Garrec, Evelyne
Léo, André (1832–1900)
Lesik, Vera (1910–1975)
Levien, Sonya (1888–1960)
Lewald, Fanny (1811–1889)
Lewis, Flora (1922–2002)
Liddell, Helen (1950—)
Lidman, Sara (1923–2004)
Likimani, Muthoni (c. 1940—)
Lindsey, Estelle Lawton (1868–1955)
Lindstrom, Pia (1938—)
Linton, Eliza Lynn (1822–1898)
Lippincott, Sara Clarke (1823–1904)
Lispector, Clarice (1920–1977)
Littledale, Clara (1891–1956)
Livermore, Mary A. (1820–1905)
Lodhi, Maleeha (c. 1953—)
Loeb, Sophie Irene (1876–1929)
Long, Tania (1913–1998)
Luce, Clare Boothe (1903–1987)
Luxemburg, Rosa (1870–1919)
Luxford, Nola (1895–1994)
Macaulay, Rose (1881–1958)
MacGill, Helen Gregory (1871–1947)
Machado, Luz (1916–1999)
Mack, Louise (1874–1935)
Mackay, Catherine Julia (1864–1944)
Mackin, Catherine (1939–1982)
MacMurchy, Marjory (1869–1938)
Macpherson, Margaret Louisa (1895–1974)
Madgett, Naomi Long (1923—)
Maihi, Rehutai (1895–1967)
Maillart, Ella (1903–1997)
Makemson, Maud Worcester (1891–1977)
Mander, Jane (1877–1949)
Manley, Mary de la Rivière (1663–1724)
Mann, Erika (1905–1969)
Mannes, Marya (1904–1990)
Mannin, Ethel (1900–1984)
Manning, Marie (c. 1873–1945)
Manzini, Gianna (1896–1974)
Mario, Queena (1896–1951)
Marion, Frances (1888–1973)
Martin, C.E.M. (1847–1937)
Masters, Olga (1919–1986)
Mathews, Vera Laughton (1888–1959)
Matsui, Yayori (1934–2002)
Matthews, Victoria Earle (1861–1907)
McBride, Mary Margaret (1899–1976)
McCarthy, Mary (1912–1989)
McClendon, Sarah (1910–2003)
McCormick, Anne O'Hare (1880–1954)
McDermid, Val (1955—)
McGrory, Mary (1918–2004)
McKenney, Ruth (1911–1972)
McNeill, Florence Marian (1885–1973)
Means, Marianne (1934—)
Meinhof, Ulrike (1934–1972)
Melissanthi (c. 1907–c. 1991)
Meloney, Marie (1878–1943)
Mermey, Fayvelle (1916–1977)
Meyer, Agnes (1887–1970)
Miller, Cheryl (1964—)
Miller, Florence Fenwick (1854–1935)
Miller, Lee (1907–1977)
Mink, Paule (1839–1901)
Mirabeau, Comtesse de (1827–1914)
Misme, Jane (1865–1935)
Model, Lisette (1901–1983)
Modotti, Tina (1896–1942)
Molinari, Susan (1958—)
Montanclos, Marie-Emilie Maryon de (1736–1812)
Monte, Hilda (1914–1945)
Montgomery, Peggy (1917—)
Moon, Lorna (1886–1930)
Morath, Inge (1923–2002)
Moreno, Luisa (1906–1992)
Morrice, Jane (1954—)
Morton, Katherine E. (1885–1968)
Muir, Florabel (1889–1970)
Murdoch, Nina (1890–1976)
Muria, Anna (1904–2002)
Mutafchieva, Vera P. (1929—)
Mydans, Shelley (1915–2002)
Naheed, Kishwar (1940—)
Nawfal, Hind (fl. 1890s)
Naylor, Genevieve (1915–1989)
Neill, Elizabeth Grace (1846–1926)
Neuffer, Elizabeth (1956–2003)
Niboyet, Eugénie (1797–1883)
Nichols, Clarina (1810–1885)
Nicholson, Eliza Jane (1849–1896)
Niepce, Janine (1921—)
Nivedita, Sister (1867–1911)
Noce, Teresa (1900–1980)
Noonan, Peggy (1950—)
Norman, Marsha (1947—)
Noronha, Joana de (fl. c. 1850)
Norris, Kathleen (1880–1966)
Odena, Lina (1911–1936)
Olberg, Oda (1872–1955)
Orkin, Ruth (1921–1985)
Ortese, Anna Maria (1914–1998)
Osten, Maria (1908–1942)
Ostenso, Martha (1900–1963)
Ottesen-Jensen, Elise (1886–1973)
Otto-Peters, Luise (1819–1895)
Overlach, Helene (1894–1983)
Palmer, Nettie (1885–1964)
Panova, Vera (1905–1973)
Panter-Downes, Mollie (1906–1997)
Paoli, Betty (1814–1894)
Parren, Kalliroe (1861–1940)
Parsons, Louella (1881–1972)
Parturier, Françoise (1919—)
Patterson, Alicia (1906–1963)
Payne, Ethel (1911–1991)
Peacocke, Isabel Maud (1881–1973)
Pelletier, Madeleine (1874–1939)
Peri Rossi, Cristina (1941—)
Petre, Maude (1863–1942)
Petry, Ann (1908–1997)
Plá, Josefina (1909–1999)
Polier, Marie-Elizabeth (1742–1817)
Pollard, Marjorie (1899–1982)
Poniatowska, Elena (1932—)
Popp, Adelheid (1869–1939)
Portal, Marta (1930—)
Porter, Katherine Anne (1890–1980)
Prichard, Katharine Susannah (1883–1969)
Quimby, Harriet (1875–1912)
Quindlen, Anna (1953—)
Quinn, Jane Bryant (1939—)
Ramirez, Sara Estela (1881–1910)
Rattray, Lizzie Frost (1855–1931)
Rawlings, Marjorie Kinnan (1896–1953)
Reed, Alma (1889–1966)
Reid, Helen Rogers (1882–1970)
Reischauer, Haru (c. 1915–1998)
Reisner, Larissa (1895–1926)
Rey, Margret (1906–1996)
Rinehart, Mary Roberts (1876–1958)
Rippin, Jane Deeter (1882–1953)
Roberts, Kate (1891–1985)
Robertson, Heather (1942—)
Roland, Betty (1903–1996)
Roland, Madame (1754–1793)
Roland, Pauline (1805–1852)
Rollett, Hilda (1873–1970)
Ronne, Edith (1919—)
Rooke, Daphne (1914—)
Roosevelt, Eleanor (1884–1962)
Ross, Forrestina Elizabeth (1860–1936)
Ross, Ishbel (1895–1975)
Ross, Lillian (1926—)
Rountree, Martha (1911–1999)
Rout, Ettie Annie (1877–1936)
Roxon, Lillian (1932–1973)
Roy, Gabrielle (1909–1983)
Royall, Anne (1769–1854)
Royde-Smith, Naomi Gwladys (c. 1880–1964)
Rudel-Zeynek, Olga (1871–1948)
Ruffin, Josephine St. Pierre (1842–1924)
Rukeyser, Muriel (1913–1980)
Saenz-Alonso, Mercedes (1916–2000)
Sahgal, Nayantara (1927—)
Saint Mars, Gabrielle de (1804–1872)
Sanders, Marlene (1931—)

Sankova, Galina (b. 1904)
Sanvitale, Francesca (1928—)
Saralegui, Cristina (1948—)
Sarfatti, Margherita (1880–1961)
Sarrazin, Albertine (1937–1967)
Saunders, Doris (1921—)
Sauvé, Jeanne (1922–1993)
Savary, Olga (1933—)
Savitch, Jessica (1947–1983)
Scanlan, Nelle (1882–1968)
Schirmacher, Käthe (1859–1930)
Schlesinger, Therese (1863–1940)
Schmich, Mary Teresa (1954—)
Schreiber, Adele (1872–1957)
Schultz, Sigrid (1893–1980)
Schulze-Boysen, Libertas (1913–1942)
Seaman, Elizabeth Cochrane (1864–1922)
Selbert, Elisabeth (1896–1986)
Sender, Toni (1888–1964)
Serao, Matilde (1856–1927)
Serrano, Eugenia (1918—)
Séverine (1855–1929)
Sexton, Anne (1928–1974)
Seymour, Mary F. (1846–1893)
Shaginian, Marietta (1888–1982)
Shaw, Flora (1852–1929)
Sheehy-Skeffington, Hanna (1877–1946)
Sheridan, Clare (1885–1970)
Sherkat, Shahla (c. 1956—)
Sherwood, Katharine Margaret (1841–1914)
Shkapskaia, Mariia (1891–1952)
Sikakane, Joyce Nomafa (1943—)
Sillanpää, Miina (1866–1952)
Simcox, Edith (1844–1901)
Simpson, Carole (1940—)
Skinner, Constance Lindsay (1877–1939)
Smedley, Agnes (1892–1950)
Smith, Hazel Brannon (1914–1994)
Smith, Margaret Bayard (1778–1844)
Solano, Solita (1888–1975)
Soljak, Miriam Bridelia (1879–1971)
Soper, Eileen Louise (1900–1989)
Sotiriou, Dido (1909–2004)
Spaziani, Maria Luisa (1924—)
Spence, Catherine (1825–1910)
Spencer, Elizabeth (1921—)
Spewack, Bella (1899–1990)
Spiel, Hilde (1911–1990)
St. Johns, Adela Rogers (1894–1988)
Stafford, Jean (1915–1979)
Stanton, Elizabeth Cady (1815–1902)
Stead, Christina (1902–1983)
Steinem, Gloria (1934—)
Stenzel, Ursula (1945—)
Stevens, Alzina (1849–1900)
Stoddard, Elizabeth Drew (1823–1902)
Storni, Alfonsina (1892–1938)
Strickland, Mabel (1899–1988)
Strong, Anna Louise (1885–1970)
Stuart, Bathia Howie (1893–1987)
Suisted, Laura Jane (1840–1903)
Sullerot, Evelyne (1924—)
Sutton, Carol (1933–1985)
Swisshelm, Jane Grey (1815–1884)
Taber, Gladys (1899–1980)
Tabouis, Geneviève (1892–1985)
Tarbell, Ida (1857–1944)
Taro, Gerda (1910–1937)
Tarry, Ellen (b. 1906)
Taylor, Kamala (1924–2004)
Tennant, Kylie (1912–1988)
Tergit, Gabrielle (1894–1982)
Thant, Mme (1900–1989)
Thomas, Helen (1920—)
Thompson, Dorothy (1893–1961)
Thompson, Eloise Bibb (1878–1928)
Thompson, Era Bell (1906–1986)
Tietjens, Eunice (1884–1944)
Tinayre, Marcelle (c. 1870–1948)
Tod, Isabella (1836–1896)
Tracy, Mona Innis (1892–1959)
Trilling, Diana (1905–1996)
Troup, Augusta Lewis (c. 1848–1920)
Tuchman, Barbara (1912–1989)
Tufty, Esther Van Wagoner (1896–1986)
Tweedie, Jill (1936–1993)
Tynan, Katharine (1861–1931)
Tynan, Kathleen (1937–1995)
Uhl, Frida (1872–1943)
Ulasi, Adaora Lily (1932—)
Ulyanova, Marie (1878–1937)
Underwood, Agness Wilson (1902–1984)
Utley, Freda (1898–1977)
Vallette, Marguerite (1860–1953)
Vérone, Maria (1874–1938)
Vicario, Leona (1789–1842)
Viganò, Renata (1900–1976)
Vlachos, Helen (1911–1995)
von Wiegand, Charmion (1899–1993)
Vorse, Mary Heaton (1874–1966)
Vuyk, Beb (1905–1991)
Wägner, Elin (1882–1949)
Waln, Nora (1895–1964)
Walter, Cornelia Wells (1813–1898)
Walters, Barbara (1929—)
Ward, Barbara (1914–1981)
Ward, Hortense (1872–1944)
Ward, Mrs. Humphry (1851–1920)
Weed, Ethel (1906–1975)
Weiss, Louise (1893–1983)
Wells, Fay Gillis (1908–2002)
West, Rebecca (1892–1983)
Wetherald, Ethelwyn (1857–1940)
Wheaton, Anne (1892–1977)
White, Sue Shelton (1887–1943)
Whiting, Lilian (1847–1942)
Whitman, Sarah Helen (1803–1878)
Whitney, Ruth (1928–1999)
Whittelsey, Abigail Goodrich (1788–1858)
Wilcox, Ella Wheeler (1850–1919)
Wilkinson, Iris (1906–1939)
Williams, Shirley (1930—)
Winfrey, Oprah (1954—)
Winsor, Kathleen (1919–2003)
Winter, John Strange (1856–1911)
Wiskemann, Elizabeth Meta (1899–1971)
Wright, L.R. (1939–2001)
Zagorka (1873–1957)
Zani, Giselda (1909–1975)
Zapolska, Gabriela (1857–1921)
Zetkin, Clara (1857–1933)
Zinner, Hedda (1902–1990)

JUDGE

Adams, Annette (1877–1956)
Allen, Florence Ellinwood (1884–1966)
Ashton, Helen (1891–1958)
Barron, Jennie Loitman (1891–1969)
Bartelme, Mary (1866–1954)
Benjamin, Hilde (1902–1989)
Blair, Cherie (1954—)
Bosone, Reva Beck (1895–1983)
Butler-Sloss, Elizabeth (1933—)
Chibesakunda, Lombe Phyllis (1944—)
Cline, Genevieve (1879–1959)
Coleman, Mary (1914–2001)
Deborah (fl. 12th c. BCE)
Donlon, Mary H. (1894–1977)
Ebadi, Shirin (1947—)
Ermengarde of Narbonne (c. 1120–c. 1194)
Evatt, Elizabeth (1933—)
Gaudron, Mary Genevieve (1943—)
Ginsburg, Ruth Bader (1933—)
Gonne, Maud (1866–1953)
Griffiths, Martha Wright (1912–2003)
Hazan, Adeline (1956—)
Heilbron, Rose (1914—)
Higgins, Rosalyn (1937—)
Hufstedler, Shirley Mount (1925—)
Hughes, Sarah T. (1896–1985)
Jiagge, Annie (1918–1996)
Kenyon, Dorothy (1888–1972)
Lane, Elizabeth (1905—)
MacGill, Helen Gregory (1871–1947)
Matthews, Burnita S. (1894–1988)
McDonald, Gabrielle Kirk (1942—)
McGuinness, Catherine (1934—)
Mitchell, Roma (1913–2000)
Motley, Constance Baker (1921–2005)
Murphy, Emily (1868–1933)
O'Connor, Sandra Day (1930—)
Odio Benito, Elizabeth (1939—)
Paciotti, Elena Ornella (1941—)
Patrie, Béatrice (1957—)
Pedersen, Helga (1911–1980)
Perry, Ruth (1939—)
Sampson, Edith S. (1901–1979)
Scharlieb, Mary Ann (1845–1930)
Schwarzhaupt, Elisabeth (1901–1986)
Sellers, Kathryn (1870–1939)
Sharp, Susie M. (1907–1996)
Sheehy-Skeffington, Hanna (1877–1946)
Sipilä, Helvi (1915—)
Stout, Juanita Kidd (1919–1998)
Sumner, Jessie (1898–1994)
Thompson, Ruth (1887–1970)
Veil, Simone (1927—)
Wald, Patricia McGowan (1928—)
Ward, Hortense (1872–1944)
Wilson, Bertha (1923—)
Wunderlich, Frieda (1884–1965)

JUDOIST

Anno, Noriko (1976—)
Arad, Yael (1967—)
Beltran, Daima (1972—)
Berghmans, Ingrid (1961—)
Blasco Soto, Miriam (1963—)
Boehm, Annett (1980—)
Boenisch, Yvonne (1980—)
Bosch, Edith (1980—)
Briggs, Karen (1963—)
Brouletova, Lioubov
Cho Min-Sun
Cicot, Christine (1964—)
de Kok, Irene (1963—)
Donguzashvili, Tea (1976—)
Emoto, Yuko (1972—)
Fairbrother, Nicola (1970—)
Fernandez, Isabel (1972—)
Fleury, Catherine (1966—)
Gal, Jenny (1969—)
Gal, Jessica (1971—)
Gao Feng (1982—)
Gonzalez Morales, Driulys (1973—)
Gradante, Anna-Maria (1976—)
Gravenstijn, Deborah (1974—)
Hagn, Johanna
Heill, Claudia (1982—)
Heylen, Ilse (1977—)
Howey, Kate Louise (1973—)
Hyun Sook-Hee
Jossinet, Frederique (1975—)
Jung Sung-Sook
Jung Sun Yong
Kim Mi-Jung (1971—)
Kusakabe, Kie
Kye Sun-Hui (1979—)

Laborde Duanes, Yurisel (1979—)
Lebrun, Céline (1976—)
Li Shufang (1979—)
Liu Xia (1979—)
Liu Yuxiang (1975—)
Li Zhongyun (1967—)
Lomba, Marisabel
Luna Castellano, Diadenis
Lupetey Cobas, Yurieleidys (1981—)
Lupino, Natalina (1963—)
Mariani, Felice (1954—)
Matijass, Julia (1973—)
Meignan, Laetitia (1960—)
Mizoguchi, Noriko (1971—)
Morico, Lucia (1975—)
Munoz Martinez, Almudena (1968—)
Nowak, Cecile (1967—)
Pekli, Maria (1972—)
Petrova, Yelena (1966—)
Pierantozzi, Emanuela (1968—)
Qin Dongya (1978—)
Rakels, Heidi (1968—)
Rendle, Sharon (1966—)
Restoux, Marie-Claire (1968—)
Reve Jimenez, Odalis (1970—)
Richter, Simona Marcela (1972—)
Rodriguez Villanueva, Estela (1967—)
Sakaue, Yoko (1968—)
Savon Carmenate, Amarilys (1974—)
Scapin, Ylenia (1975—)
Senyurt, Hulya (1973—)
Simons, Ann (1980—)
Soler, Yolanda
Sugawara, Noriko (1972—)
Sun Fuming (1974—)
Szczepanska, Aneta (1972—)
Tamura, Ryoko (1975—)
Tanabe, Yoko (1966—)
Tang Lin (1975—)
Tanimoto, Ayumi (1981—)
Tateno, Chiyori (1970—)
Tsukada, Maki (1982—)
Ueno, Masae (1979—)
Vandecaveye, Gella (1973—)
Vandenhende, Severine (1974—)
Veranes, Sibelis (1974—)
Verdecia, Legna (1972—)
Wang Xianbo
Werbrouck, Ulla (1972—)
Xian Dongmei (1975—)
Yokosawa, Yuki (1980—)
Yuan Hua (1974—)
Zhang Di (1968—)
Zhuang Xiaoyan (1969—)
Zolner, Urska (1982—)
Zwiers, Claudia

JUSTICE, CANADIAN SUPREME COURT
McLachlin, Beverley (1943—)
Wilson, Bertha (1923—)

JUSTICE, U.S. SUPREME COURT
Ginsburg, Ruth Bader (1933—)
O'Connor, Sandra Day (1930—)

JUSTICE OF THE PEACE
Ahern, Lizzie (1877–1969)
Bates, Daisy May (1859–1951)
Beaufort, Margaret (1443–1509)
Couchman, Elizabeth (1876–1982)
Cowan, Edith (1861–1932)
Haldane, Elizabeth S. (1862–1937)
Huxley, Elspeth (1907–1997)
Litchfield, Jessie (1883–1956)
McCulloch, Catharine (1862–1945)
Morris, Esther Hobart (1814–1902)
Onians, Edith (1866–1955)
Pirrie, Margaret Montgomery (1857–1935)
Tuckwell, Gertrude (1861–1951)

KIDNAPPER (ACCUSED)
Anderson, Bella (1864–?)
Barker, Ma (1872–1935)
Bogle, Helen McDermott (1871–?)
Carson, Ann (d. 1824)
Eisemann-Schier, Ruth (c. 1942—)
Heady, Bonnie (1912–1953)
Kelly, Kathryn Thorne (1904–1998?)
Parker, Bonnie (1910–1934)

LABOR ACTIVIST
Aitken, Jessie (1867–1934)
Anderson, Mary (1872–1964)
Anderson, Mary Patricia (1887–1966)
Anselmi, Tina (1927—)
Baard, Francina (1901–1997)
Bagley, Sarah (b. 1806)
Balabanoff, Angelica (1878–1965)
Balch, Emily Greene (1867–1961)
Bambace, Angela (1898–1975)
Barker, M.C. (1879–1963)
Barnard, Kate (1875–1930)
Barnum, Gertrude (1866–1948)
Barrios de Chúngara, Domitila (1937—)
Barry, Leonora M. (1849–1930)
Beeby, Doris (1894–1948)
Bellanca, Dorothy (1894–1946)
Bennett, Louie (1870–1956)
Besant, Annie (1847–1933)
Birchfield, Constance Alice (1898–1994)
Black, Clementina (1854–1922)
Blatch, Harriot Stanton (1856–1940)
Bloodworth, Rhoda Alice (1889–1980)
Bloor, Ella Reeve (1862–1951)
Bondfield, Margaret (1873–1953)
Borchardt, Selma Munter (1895–1968)
Boschek, Anna (1874–1957)
Bouvier, Jeanne (1865–1964)
Brion, Hélène (1882–1962)
Buller, Annie (1896–1973)
Butler, Elizabeth Beardsley (c. 1885–1911)
Carney, Winifred (1887–1943)
Cashman, Mel (1891–1979)
Catt, Carrie Chapman (1859–1947)
Chavez-Thompson, Linda (1944—)
Chevenix, Helen (1886–1963)
Christman, Elisabeth (1881–1975)
Cohn, Fannia (c. 1885–1962)
Collins, Jennie (1828–1887)
Conboy, Sara McLaughlin (1870–1928)
Cossey, Alice Eleanor (1879–1970)
Dean, Brenda (1943—)
De Graffenried, Clare (1849–1921)
Deng Yuzhi (1900–1996)
Dickason, Gladys (1903–1971)
Dilke, Emily (1840–1904)
Dreier, Katherine Sophie (1877–1952)
Dreier, Mary Elisabeth (1875–1963)
Duchêne, Gabrielle (1870–1954)
Durand, Marguerite (1864–1936)
Edson, Katherine Philips (1870–1933)
Emhart, Maria (1901–1981)
Evans, Elizabeth Glendower (1856–1937)
Fabian, Dora (1901–1935)
First, Ruth (1925–1982)
Flynn, Elizabeth Gurley (1890–1964)
Francois, Elma (1897–1944)
Freundlich, Emmy (1878–1948)
Garmson, Aileen (c. 1861–1951)
Gillespie, Mabel (1877–1923)
Gilmore, Mary (1865–1962)
Goldman, Emma (1869–1940)
Goldmark, Josephine (1877–1950)
Gore-Booth, Eva (1870–1926)
Gutteridge, Helena Rose (1879–1960)
Hale, Maria Selina (1864–1951)
Hamilton, Alice (1869–1970)
Hancock, Florence (1893–1974)
Hawes, Elizabeth (1903–1971)
Hawthorne, Margaret Jane Scott (1869–1958)
Haynes, Elizabeth Ross (1883–1953)
Henrotin, Ellen Martin (1847–1922)
Henry, Alice (1857–1943)
Hicks, Amie (c. 1839–1917)
Hillman, Bessie (1889–1970)
Huerta, Dolores (1930—)
Hutchins, Grace (1885–1969)
Ichikawa Fusae (1893–1981)
Ickes, Anna Thompson (1873–1935)
Ihrer, Emma (1857–1911)
Jacobs, Aletta (1854–1929)
Jarrell, Ira (1896–1973)
Jeffrey, Mildred (1910–2004)
Jochmann, Rosa (1901–1994)
Jones, Mary Harris (1830–1930)
Kanahele, Helen Lake (1916–1976)
Katznelson-Shazar, Rachel (1888–1975)
Kehew, Mary Morton (1859–1918)
Kéita, Aoua (1912–1979)
Keller, Helen (1880–1968)
Kelley, Florence (1859–1932)
Kenney, Annie (1879–1953)
Kéthly, Anna (1889–1976)
Kilmury, Diana (1948—)
King, Carol Weiss (1895–1952)
Kollontai, Alexandra (1872–1952)
Kovalskaia, Elizaveta (1851–1943)
Larkin, Delia (1878–1949)
Lease, Mary Elizabeth (1853–1933)
Lee, Jennie (1904–1988)
Lee, Mary (1821–1909)
Lemlich, Clara (1888–1982)
Loughlin, Anne (1894–1979)
Luxemburg, Rosa (1870–1919)
Macarthur, Mary Reid (1880–1921)
Macphail, Agnes (1890–1954)
Madar, Olga (1915–1996)
Manning, Leah (1886–1977)
Markievicz, Constance (1868–1927)
Marot, Helen (1865–1940)
Martinson, Moa (1890–1964)
Marx-Aveling, Eleanor (1855–1898)
Mason, Lucy Randolph (1882–1959)
Maynard, Mary (c. 1938—)
McCoubrey, Margaret (1880–1955)
McCreery, Maria (1883–1938)
McDowell, Mary Eliza (1854–1936)
McLaren, Louise Leonard (1885–1968)
Michel, Louise (1830–1905)
Miller, Frieda S. (1889–1973)
Miller, Joyce D. (1928—)
Molony, Helena (1884–1967)
Moreno, Luisa (1906–1992)
Morison, Harriet (1862–1925)
Mullany, Kate (1845–1906)
Murray, Pauli (1910–1985)
Nalkowska, Zofia (1884–1954)
Nestor, Agnes (1880–1948)
Newman, Pauline (1887–1986)
Noce, Teresa (1900–1980)
Nussbaum, Karen (1950—)
O'Hare, Kate Richards (1876–1948)
Olsen, Tillie (c. 1912—)
O'Reilly, Leonora (1870–1927)
O'Sullivan, Mary Kenney (1864–1943)
Palmer, Alice May (1886–1977)
Parker, Julia O'Connor (1890–1972)
Paterson, Emma (1848–1886)

Patterson, Marie (1934—)
Pesotta, Rose (1896–1965)
Peterson, Esther (1906–1997)
Phillips, Marion (1881–1932)
Pienkowska, Alina (1952–2002)
Popp, Adelheid (1869–1939)
Powdermaker, Hortense (1896–1970)
Purcell, Samuelene (1898–1982)
Rehor, Grete (1910–1987)
Robins, Margaret Dreier (1868–1945)
Robinson, Harriet Hanson (1825–1911)
Roche, Josephine (1886–1976)
Rodgers, Elizabeth Flynn (1847–1939)
Rood, Florence (1873–1944)
Runciman, Jane Elizabeth (1873–1950)
Sabalsajaray, Nibuya (1951–1974)
Sanger, Margaret (1879–1966)
Sarabhai, Anusyabehn (1885–1972)
Sauvé, Jeanne (1922–1993)
Schlesinger, Therese (1863–1940)
Schneiderman, Rose (1882–1972)
Schreiner, Olive (1855–1920)
Scudder, Vida (1861–1954)
Seidel, Amalie (1876–1952)
Shochat, Manya (1878–1961)
Simcox, Edith (1844–1901)
Simms, Florence (1873–1923)
Snow, Helen Foster (1907–1997)
Spencer, Anna (1851–1931)
Spira, Steffie (1908–1995)
Starr, Ellen Gates (1859–1940)
Stevens, Alzina (1849–1900)
Strachey, Pippa (1872–1968)
Strachey, Ray (1887–1940)
Suchocka, Hanna (1946—)
Swartz, Maud O'Farrell (1879–1937)
Tasker, Marianne Allen (1852–1911)
Templeton, Rini (1935–1986)
Thompson, Louise (1901–1999)
Thorndike, Sybil (1882–1976)
Thorne, Florence (1877–1973)
Tristan, Flora (1803–1844)
Troup, Augusta Lewis (c. 1848–1920)
Tuckwell, Gertrude (1861–1951)
Van Kleeck, Mary Abby (1883–1972)
Van Vorst, Marie Louise (1867–1936)
Vorse, Mary Heaton (1874–1966)
Wald, Lillian D. (1867–1940)
Walentynowicz, Anna (1929—)
Ward, Irene (1895–1980)
Webb, Beatrice (1858–1943)
Weil, Simone (1909–1943)
Whitney, Charlotte Anita (1867–1955)
Whitty, May (1865–1948)
Wilkinson, Ellen (1891–1947)
Willard, Frances E. (1839–1898)
Wilson, Helen Mary (1869–1957)
Woerishoffer, Carola (1885–1911)
Wolfson, Theresa (1897–1972)
Woodbury, Helen Sumner (1876–1933)
Woodhouse, Margaret Chase Going (1890–1984)
Woodhull, Victoria (1838–1927)
Wootton, Barbara (1897–1988)
Xiang Jingyu (1895–1928)
Yard, Molly (1912–2005)
Younger, Maud (1870–1936)
Zetkin, Clara (1857–1933)

LABOR-RELATIONS EXPERT
Herrick, Elinore Morehouse (1895–1964)
Kreps, Juanita (1921—)
Rosenberg, Anna M. (1902–1983)

LACROSSE COACH
Geppi-Aikens, Diane (c. 1963–2003)

LACROSSE PLAYER
Hashman, Judy (1935—)

LADY-IN-WAITING
Abrantès, Laure d' (1784–1838)
Anastasia the Patrician (d. 567)
Aubespine, Madeleine de l' (1546–1596)
Boleyn, Anne (c. 1507–1536)
Bridget of Sweden (1303–1373)
Castro, Inez de (c. 1320–1355)
Colville, Meg (1918–2004)
Courtenay, Gertrude (c. 1504–1558)
Diane de Poitiers (1499–1566)
Dolgorukaia, Alexandra (1836–c. 1914)
Genlis, Stéphanie-Félicité, Comtesse de (1746–1830)
Hamilton, Anne (1766–1846)
Juana Inés de la Cruz (1651–1695)
Kishida Toshiko (1863–1901)
Kottanner, Helene (fl. 1440)
La Fayette, Marie-Madeleine de (1634–1693)
La Tour du Pin, Henriette de (1770–1853)
López de Córdoba, Leonor (1362–1412)
Maintenon, Françoise d'Aubigné, Marquise de (1635–1719)
Motteville, Françoise Bertaut de (c. 1621–1689)
Murasaki Shikibu (c. 973–c. 1015)
Parr, Anne (d. 1552)
Rémusat, Claire, comtesse de (1780–1821)
Sei Shōnagon (c. 965–?)
Sorel, Agnes (1422–1450)
Stein, Charlotte von (1742–1827)
Stuart, Frances (1647–1702)
Talbot, Elizabeth (1518–1608)
Villiers, Barbara (c. 1641–1709)

LAKOTA
Zintkala Nuni (c. 1890–c. 1919)

LANDGRAVINE
Alexandra Nikolaevna (1825–1844)
Anna of Saxony (1420–1462)
Caroline of Birkenfeld-Zweibrucken (1721–1774)
Caroline of Hesse-Darmstadt (1746–1821)
Caroline of Nassau-Usingen (1762–1823)
Charlotte of Hesse (1627–1687)
Charlotte Oldenburg (1789–1864)
Christine of Saxony (1505–1549)
Elizabeth (1770–1840)
Elizabeth of Hungary (1207–1231)
Hesse, Eva (1936–1970)
Jolanthe of Lorraine (d. 1500)
Louise Dorothea of Brandenburg (1680–1705)
Mafalda of Hesse (1902–1944)
Magdalene of Brandenburg (1582–1616)
Margaret Beatrice (1872–1954)
Margaret of Germany (1237–1270)
Marie Louise Albertine of Leiningen-Heidesheim (1729–1818)
Mary of Hesse-Cassel (1723–1772)
Sophia (fl. 1211)
Sophia (1957—)
Sophia of Sweden (1801–1875)
Sophia of Thuringia (1224–1284)

LANDOWNER
Collier, Jeanie (c. 1791–1861)
Dawson, Mary Elizabeth (1833–1924)
Faulkner, Ruawahine Irihapeti (?–1855)
Gardner, Margaret (1844–1929)
Jury, Te Aitu-o-te-rangi (c. 1820–1854)
Matenga, Huria (1840/42–1909)
McKain, Douglas Mary (1789–1873)
O'Connell, Sarah (c. 1822–1870)
Ostler, Emma Brignell (c. 1848–1922)
Ralph, Margaret (c. 1822–1913)
Randall, Amelia Mary (1844–1930)
Richardson, Effie Newbigging (1849/50?–1928)
Sutherland, Mary Ann (1864–1948)
Taylor, Sophia Louisa (1847–1903)
Yates, Ngawini (1852/53?–1910)

LANDSCAPE ARCHITECT/DESIGNER
Bliss, Mildred Barnes (1879–1969)
Chowdhury, Eulie (1923—)
Colvin, Brenda (1897–1981)
Crowe, Sylvia (1901–1997)
Farrand, Beatrix Jones (1872–1959)
Gillette, Genevieve (1898–1986)
Huntington, Anna Hyatt (1876–1973)
Ireys, Alice (1911–2000)
Jekyll, Gertrude (1843–1932)
Lawrence, Elizabeth (1904–1985)
Raymond, Eleanor (1887–1989)

LANDSCAPE PAINTER
Bacon, Peggy (1895–1987)
Brice, Fanny (1891–1951)
Bugbee, Emma (1888–1981)
Cassatt, Mary (1844–1926)
Content, Marjorie (1895–1984)
Dashkova, Ekaterina (1744–1810)
Galizia, Fede (1578–1630)
Gentileschi, Artemisia (1593–c. 1653)
Gluck (1895–1978)
Graves, Nancy (1940–1995)
Greatorex, Eliza (1820–1897)
Guan Daosheng (1262–1319)
Hamnett, Nina (1890–1956)
Hodgkins, Frances (1869–1947)
Jones, Loïs Mailou (1905–1998)
Klumpke, Anna Elizabeth (1856–1942)
Knight, Laura (1877–1970)
Landseer, Jessica (1810–1880)
Laurencin, Marie (1883–1956)
Low, Mary Fairchild (1858–1946)
Lundeberg, Helen (1908–1999)
MacIver, Loren (1909–1998)
Martin, Agnes (1912–2004)
Mayreder, Rosa (1858–1938)
McGuinness, Norah (1901–1980)
Mitchell, Joan (1926–1992)
Modersohn-Becker, Paula (1876–1907)
Montalba, Clara (1842–1929)
Morgan, Barbara (1900–1992)
Münter, Gabriele (1877–1962)
Neel, Alice (1900–1984)
Nourse, Elizabeth (1859–1938)
O'Keeffe, Georgia (1887–1986)
Osborn, Emily Mary (1834–c. 1885)
Outhwaite, Ida Rentoul (1888–1960)
Perry, Lilla Cabot (c. 1848–1933)
Pike, Mary (1824–1908)
Pinney, Eunice Griswold (1770–1849)
Rahon, Alice (1904–1987)
Redpath, Anne (1895–1965)
Rothschild, Judith (1921–1993)
Rozanova, Olga (1886–1918)
Sandel, Cora (1880–1974)
Sewell, Anna (1820–1878)
Shore, Henrietta (1880–1963)
Sofronova, Antonina (1892–1966)
Stephens, Alice Barber (1858–1932)
Tarrant, Margaret (1888–1959)
Udaltsova, Nadezhda (1885–1961)
Valadon, Suzanne (1865–1938)
Vigée-Le Brun, Elisabeth (1755–1842)
Walcott, Mary Morris (1860–1940)
Waring, Laura Wheeler (1887–1948)
Weir, Irene (1862–1944)
Yakunchikova, Maria (1870–1901)

LAVTA PLAYER
Osmanoglu, Gevheri (1904–1980)

LAWYER
Abiertas, Josepha (1894–1929)
Abzug, Bella (1920–1998)
Adams, Annette (1877–1956)
Alakija, Aduke (1921—)
Alexander, Sadie (1898–1989)
Allen, Florence Ellinwood (1884–1966)
Allred, Gloria (1941—)
Almeida Garrett, Teresa (1953—)
Astorga, Nora (1949–1988)
Barron, Jennie Loitman (1891–1969)
Bartelme, Mary (1866–1954)
Bastos, Regina (1960—)
Bates, Florence (1888–1954)
Benjamin, Ethel Rebecca (1875–1943)
Benjamin, Hilde (1902–1989)
Bickerdyke, Mary Ann (1817–1901)
Bittenbender, Ada Matilda (1848–1925)
Blair, Cherie (1954—)
Boissevain, Inez M. (1886–1916)
Borchardt, Selma Munter (1895–1968)
Bradwell, Myra (1831–1894)
Brennan, Anna Teresa (1879–1962)
Brooks, Angie (1928—)
Brooks, Louise (1906–1985)
Brown, Virginia Mae (1923–1991)
Browner, Carol M. (1956—)
Bullowa, Emilie (1869–1942)
Burke, Yvonne Brathwaite (1932—)
Campoamor, Clara (1888–1972)
Carter, Eunice Hunton (1899–1970)
Cary, Mary Ann Shadd (1823–1893)
Cerdeira Morterero, Carmen (1958—)
Charles, Eugenia (1919—)
Chauvin, Jeanne (1862–1926)
Chibesakunda, Lombe Phyllis (1944—)
Chirwa, Vera (1933—)
Clerke, Agnes Mary (1842–1907)
Clinton, Hillary Rodham (1947—)
d'Andrea, Novella (d. 1333)
DeFrantz, Anita (1952—)
Densen-Gerber, Judianne (1934–2003)
Dohrn, Bernardine (1942—)
Dole, Elizabeth Hanford (1936—)
Donlon, Mary H. (1894–1977)
Ebadi, Shirin (1947—)
Estrich, Susan R. (1952—)
Evatt, Elizabeth (1933—)
Farenthold, Frances "Sissy" (1926—)
Ferraro, Geraldine (1935—)
Foltz, Clara (1849–1934)
Foster, J. Ellen (1840–1910)
Fuller, Margaret (1810–1850)
Garaud, Marie-Françoise (1934—)
Gaudron, Mary Genevieve (1943—)
Gibb, Roberta (1943—)
Gillett, Emma (1852–1927)
Ginsburg, Ruth Bader (1933—)
Gordon, Laura de Force (1838–1907)
Guimarães, Elina (1904–1991)
Hahn, Helene B. (c. 1940—)
Halimi, Gisèle (1927—)
Harris, Patricia Roberts (1924–1985)
Heilbron, Rose (1914–2005)
Heldman, Julie (1945—)
Helmer, Bessie Bradwell (1858–1927)
Hennock, Frieda B. (1904–1960)
Hicks, Louise Day (1923—)
Higgins, Rosalyn (1937—)
Hill, Anita (1956—)
Hills, Carla (1934—)
Holtzman, Elizabeth (1941—)
Holtzmann, Fanny (1895–1980)
Hughes, Sarah T. (1896–1985)
Ireland, Patricia (1945—)
Jiagge, Annie (1918–1996)
Jordan, Barbara (1936–1996)
Kagan, Elena (1960—)
Karpatkin, Rhoda Hendrick (1930—)
Kennedy, Florynce (1916–2000)
Kennedy, Helena (1950—)
Kent, Victoria (1898–1987)
Kenyon, Dorothy (1888–1972)
Kidd, Margaret Henderson (1900–1989)
Kilgore, Carrie B. (1838–1908)
King, Carol Weiss (1895–1952)
King, Rebecca (c. 1950—)
Kuntz, Florence (1969—)
Lalumiere, Catherine (1935—)
Lane, Elizabeth (1905–1988)
Laughlin, Gail (1868–1952)
Lease, Mary Elizabeth (1853–1933)
Lewis, Loida (c. 1943—)
Lockwood, Belva Ann (1830–1917)
Loynaz, Dulce María (1902–1997)
MacGill, Helen Gregory (1871–1947)
Machel, Graca (1946—)
Mackinnon, Catherine A. (1946—)
Malone, Bernie (1948—)
Mankin, Helen Douglas (1894–1956)
Mansfield, Arabella (1846–1911)
Martinez, Vilma (1943—)
McAleese, Mary (1951—)
McCulloch, Catharine (1862–1945)
McDonald, Gabrielle Kirk (1942—)
McGuinness, Catherine (1934—)
McLachlin, Beverley (1943—)
McTeer, Maureen (1952—)
Melville, Eliza Ellen (1882–1946)
Mills, Barbara (1940—)
Mink, Patsy (1927–2002)
Mitchell, Roma (1913–2000)
Motley, Constance Baker (1921–2005)
Murnaghan, Sheelagh (1924–1993)
Murray, Pauli (1910–1985)
Mussey, Ellen Spencer (1850–1936)
Niebler, Angelika (1963—)
Normanton, Helena (1883–1957)
O'Connor, Sandra Day (1930—)
Odio Benito, Elizabeth (1939—)
O'Hair, Madalyn Murray (1919–1995?)
Pascal-Trouillot, Ertha (1943—)
Pedersen, Helga (1911–1980)
Phillips, Lena Madesin (1881–1955)
Pintasilgo, Maria de Lurdes (1930–2004)
Ramo, Roberta Cooper (1942—)
Randzio-Plath, Christa (1940—)
Ray, Charlotte E. (1850–1911)
Rees, Annie Lee (1864–1949)
Reno, Janet (1938—)
Richards, Ann Willis (1933—)
Ricker, Marilla (1840–1920)
Riis-Jorgensen, Karin (1952—)
Robinson, Mary (1944—)
Rodríguez Ramos, María (1963—)
Roth-Behrendt, Dagmar (1953—)
Sampson, Edith S. (1901–1979)
Sauquillo Pérez Del Arco, Francisca (1943—)
Schlossberg, Caroline Kennedy (1957—)
Schreiner, Olive (1855–1920)
Schroeder, Patricia (1940—)
Selbert, Elisabeth (1896–1986)
Sellers, Kathryn (1870–1939)
Sipilä, Helvi (1915—)
Sorabji, Cornelia (1866–1954)
Spyri, Emily Kempin (1853–1901)
Stanley, Winifred Claire (1909–1996)
Stauner, Gabriele (1948—)
Strossen, Nadine (1950—)
Sumner, Jessie (1898–1994)
Telles, Lygia Fagundes (1923—)
Thatcher, Margaret (1925—)
Thompson, Ruth (1887–1970)
Thors, Astrid (1957—)
Thyssen, Marianne L.P. (1956—)
Todd, Marion Marsh (1841–post 1913)
Tully, Mary Jean Crenshaw (1925–2003)
Tyabji, Kamila (1918–2004)
Ty-Casper, Linda (1931—)
Vérone, Maria (1874–1938)
Villiers, Theresa (1968—)
Waite, Catherine (1829–1913)
Wald, Patricia McGowan (1928—)
Ward, Hortense (1872–1944)
Weddington, Sarah R. (1945—)
White, Sue Shelton (1887–1943)
Willebrandt, Mabel Walker (1889–1963)
Williams, Ivy (1877–1966)
Wilson, Bertha (1923—)
Wilson, Margaret Bush (1919—)
Wine-Banks, Jill (1943—)

LAY MINISTER
Holland, Tara Dawn (c. 1972—)
Prewitt, Cheryl (c. 1957—)
Shopp, BeBe (1930—)

LECTURER (COLLEGE/UNIVERSITY)
See College/university professor/instructor/lecturer.

LECTURER/ORATOR
Abzug, Bella (1920–1998)
Adams, Harriet Chalmers (1875–1937)
Adivar, Halide Edib (c. 1884–1964)
Ahern, Lizzie (1877–1969)
Aiken, Kimberly (c. 1975—)
Akeley, Delia J. (1875–1970)
Akeley, Mary Jobe (1878–1966)
Andrews, Eliza Frances (1840–1931)
Armand, Inessa (1874–1920)
Aubin, Penelope (c. 1685–1731)
Auclert, Hubertine (1848–1914)
Augspurg, Anita (1857–1943)
Austin, Mary Hunter (1868–1934)
Ay, Evelyn (c. 1934—)
Ayscough, Florence (1875/78–1942)
Bacon, Gertrude (1874–1949)
Baker, Ella (1903–1986)
Balabanoff, Angelica (1878–1965)
Baldwin, Maria Louise (1856–1922)
Barnard, Marjorie (1897–1987)
Barry, Leonora M. (1849–1930)
Barton, Clara (1821–1912)
Bear-Crawford, Annette (1853–1899)
Berg, Patty (1918—)
Besant, Annie (1847–1933)
Bethune, Mary McLeod (1875–1955)
Bloomer, Amelia Jenks (1818–1894)
Bloor, Ella Reeve (1862–1951)
Bondfield, Margaret (1873–1953)
Bonds, Margaret (1913–1972)
Bonnevie, Kristine (1872–1948)
Booth, Evangeline (1865–1950)
Bottome, Phyllis (1884–1963)
Bowen, Elizabeth (1899–1973)
Boys-Smith, Winifred Lily (1865–1939)
Braddock, Bessie (1899–1970)
Brown, Hallie Quinn (c. 1845–1949)
Brown, Martha McClellan (1838–1916)
Brown, Olympia (1835–1926)
Brown Blackwell, Antoinette (1825–1921)
Buller, Annie (1896–1973)
Caldicott, Helen (1938—)
Campbell, Mrs. Patrick (1865–1940)
Cannon, Annie Jump (1863–1941)

Castle, Barbara (1910–2002)
Castro, Públia Hortênsia de (1548–1595)
Catt, Carrie Chapman (1859–1947)
Channing, Carol (1921—)
Chattopadhyaya, Kamaladevi (1903–1988)
Churchill, Clementine (1885–1977)
Colclough, Mary Ann (1836–1885)
Colette (1873–1954)
Cooper, Sarah Ingersoll (1835–1896)
Cousins, Margaret (1878–1954)
Cowan, Edith (1861–1932)
Cowie, Bessie Lee (1860–1950)
Crowdy, Rachel Eleanor (1884–1964)
Cunnington, Eveline Willert (1849–1916)
de Cleyre, Voltairine (1866–1912)
de Mille, Agnes (1905–1993)
Demorest, Ellen Curtis (1824–1898)
Deraismes, Maria (1828–1894)
Deren, Maya (1908–1961)
Derricotte, Juliette (1897–1931)
de Valois, Ninette (1898–2001)
Devanny, Jean (1894–1962)
Dickerson, Nancy (1927–1997)
Dickinson, Anna E. (1842–1932)
Douglas, Helen Gahagan (1900–1980)
Dransfeld, Hedwig (1871–1925)
Duby-Blom, Gertrude (1901–1993)
Earhart, Amelia (1897–1937)
Ebtekar, Massoumeh (1960—)
Edwards, Tracey (1962—)
Emhart, Maria (1901–1981)
Fabian, Dora (1901–1935)
Farningham, Marianne (1834–1909)
Fawcett, Millicent Garrett (1847–1929)
Ferraro, Geraldine (1935—)
Field, Kate (1838–1896)
Fischer, Ruth (1895–1961)
Fisher, Dorothy Canfield (1879–1958)
Fletcher, Alice Cunningham (1838–1923)
Flynn, Elizabeth Gurley (1890–1964)
Fowler, Lydia Folger (1822–1879)
Freundlich, Emmy (1878–1948)
Fuller, Loïe (1862–1928)
Gage, Matilda Joslyn (1826–1898)
Gardner, Kay (1941–2002)
Gilbreth, Lillian Moller (1878–1972)
Gilman, Charlotte Perkins (1860–1935)
Goldman, Emma (1869–1940)
Green, Constance McLaughlin (1897–1975)
Grimké, Angelina E. (1805–1879)
Grossman, Haika (1919–1996)
Gutteridge, Helena Rose (1879–1960)
Hansteen, Aasta (1824–1908)
Harper, Frances E.W. (1825–1911)
Harrison, Elizabeth (1849–1927)
Harrison, Marguerite (1879–1967)
Hewins, Caroline Maria (1846–1926)
Heymann, Lida (1867–1943)
Holtby, Winifred (1898–1935)
Hoover, Katherine (1937—)
Hoover, Lou Henry (1874–1944)
Horne, Myrtle (1892–1969)
Howard, Caroline Cadette (1821–?)
Howe, Julia Ward (1819–1910)
Huck, Winnifred Sprague Mason (1882–1936)
Jackson, Helen Hunt (1830–1885)
Jagan, Janet (1920—)
Janeway, Elizabeth (1913–2005)
Jensen, Thit (1876–1957)
Jinnah, Fatima (1893–1967)
Jodin, Mademoiselle (fl. 18th c.)
Johnson, Osa (1894–1953)
Johnston, Frances Benjamin (1864–1952)
Jordan, Barbara (1936–1996)
Joseph, Helen (1905–1992)
Keller, Helen (1880–1968)
Kelley, Abby (1810–1887)
Kellogg, Louise Phelps (1862–1942)
Key, Ellen (1849–1926)
King, Coretta Scott (1927—)
Kirkpatrick, Helen (1909–1997)
Kishida Toshiko (1863–1901)
Kollontai, Alexandra (1872–1952)
Krupskaya, Nadezhda (1869–1939)
Lacis, Asja (1891–1979)
La Flesche, Susette (1854–1902)
La Hye, Louise (1810–1838)
Laughlin, Clara E. (1873–1941)
Laumann, Silken (1964—)
Lazarus, Emma (1849–1887)
Lease, Mary Elizabeth (1853–1933)
Lee, Jennie (1904–1988)
L'Engle, Madeleine (1918—)
Leslie, Miriam Folline Squier (1836–1914)
Lippincott, Sara Clarke (1823–1904)
Livermore, Mary A. (1820–1905)
Lloyd George, Megan (1902–1966)
Lockwood, Belva Ann (1830–1917)
Long, Marguerite (1874–1966)
Loughlin, Anne (1894–1979)
Lowell, Amy (1874–1925)
Löwenstein, Helga Maria zu (1910–2004)
Luxemburg, Rosa (1870–1919)
Macphail, Agnes (1890–1954)
Main, Marjorie (1890–1975)
Mann, Erika (1905–1969)
Marx-Aveling, Eleanor (1855–1898)
Mayer, Jacquelyn (c. 1942—)
McAliskey, Roisin (1971—)
McClung, Nellie L. (1873–1951)
McCoubrey, Margaret (1880–1955)
McCulloch, Catharine (1862–1945)
McHugh, Fanny (1861–1943)
McKinney, Louise (1868–1931)
McMein, Neysa (1888–1949)
McPherson, Aimee Semple (1890–1944)
McTeer, Maureen (1952—)
Mead, Lucia Ames (1856–1936)
Melba, Nellie (1861–1931)
Miller, Annie Jenness (b. 1859)
Miller, Florence Fenwick (1854–1935)
Mink, Paule (1839–1901)
Montez, Lola (1818–1861)
Montseny, Federica (1905–1994)
Moore, Anne Carroll (1871–1961)
Moorehead, Agnes (1900–1974)
Mumtaz Mahal (c. 1592–1631)
Myrdal, Alva (1902–1986)
Naidu, Sarojini (1879–1949)
Nation, Carry (1846–1911)
Newman, Angelia L. (1837–1910)
Ngoyi, Lilian (1911–1980)
Nicholls, Marjory Lydia (1890–1930)
Nichols, Clarina (1810–1885)
Nichols, Mary Gove (1810–1884)
Nichols, Ruth (1901–1960)
Noyes, Clara Dutton (1869–1936)
O'Hare, Kate Richards (1876–1948)
O'Reilly, Leonora (1870–1927)
Ottesen-Jensen, Elise (1886–1973)
Palmer, Alice Freeman (1855–1902)
Pankhurst, Adela (1885–1961)
Pankhurst, Christabel (1880–1958)
Pankhurst, Emmeline (1858–1928)
Pankhurst, Sylvia (1882–1960)
Peabody, Elizabeth Palmer (1804–1894)
Popovici, Elise (1921—)
Popp, Adelheid (1869–1939)
Prichard, Katharine Susannah (1883–1969)
Prince, Lucy Terry (c. 1730–1821)
Qiu Jin (c. 1875–1907)
Rafko, Kaye Lani (c. 1963—)
Remond, Sarah Parker (1826–1894)
Rich, Adrienne (1929—)
Richman, Julia (1855–1912)
Robins, Elizabeth (1862–1952)
Robinson, Betty (1911–1997)
Rogatis, Teresa de (1893–1979)
Rohde, Ruth Bryan Owen (1885–1954)
Roosevelt, Eleanor (1884–1962)
Rose, Ernestine (1810–1892)
Ross, Nellie Tayloe (1876–1977)
Roussel, Nelly (1878–1922)
Rutherford, Mildred (1851–1928)
Sampson, Deborah (1760–1827)
Sauvé, Jeanne (1922–1993)
Savitch, Jessica (1947–1983)
Sayers, Dorothy L. (1893–1957)
Scarborough, Dorothy (1878–1935)
Schaefer, Laurel Lea (c. 1949—)
Schlafly, Phyllis (1924—)
Schlesinger, Therese (1863–1940)
Schneiderman, Rose (1882–1972)
Scholtz-Klink, Gertrud (1902–1999)
Schütte-Lihotzky, Margarete (1897–2000)
Schuyler, Philippa Duke (1931–1967)
Schwimmer, Rosika (1877–1948)
Seidel, Amalie (1876–1952)
Seton, Grace Gallatin (1872–1959)
Séverine (1855–1929)
Sewall, May Wright (1844–1920)
Shaw, Anna Howard (1847–1919)
Shaw, Mary G. (1854–1929)
Shearer, Moira (1926—)
Sheppard, Kate (1847–1934)
Sherif, Carolyn Wood (1922–1982)
Slutskaya, Vera (1874–1917)
Smedley, Agnes (1892–1950)
Smith, Abby (1797–1878)
Smith, Hazel Brannon (1914–1994)
Smith, Julia (1792–1886)
Smith, Shawntel (1971—)
Somerville, Nellie Nugent (1863–1952)
Soule, Caroline White (1824–1903)
Spence, Catherine (1825–1910)
Spencer, Anna (1851–1931)
Spry, Constance (1886–1960)
Stanton, Elizabeth Cady (1815–1902)
Starbuck, Mary Coffyn (1644/45–1717)
Starr, Eliza Allen (1824–1901)
Stein, Edith (1891–1942)
Steinem, Gloria (1934—)
Stewart, Maria W. (1803–1879)
Stokes, Rose Pastor (1879–1933)
Stone, Lucy (1818–1893)
Strange, Michael (1890–1950)
Stuart, Ruth McEnery (c. 1849–1917)
Swisshelm, Jane Grey (1815–1884)
Szönyi, Erzsebet (1924—)
Tabouis, Geneviève (1892–1985)
Taylor, Helen (1831–1907)
Tennant, Kylie (1912–1988)
Terrell, Mary Church (1863–1954)
Terzian, Alicia (1938—)
Thompson, Dorothy (1893–1961)
Todd, Mabel Loomis (1858–1932)
Tolstoy, Alexandra (1884–1979)
Truth, Sojourner (c. 1797–1883)
Tusap, Srbuhi (1841–1901)
Uzès, Anne, Duchesse d' (1847–1933)
Valette, Aline (1850–1899)
Van Derbur, Marilyn (c. 1937—)
Velásquez, Loreta (1842–1897)
Vérone, Maria (1874–1938)
Von Trapp, Maria (1905–1987)
Wagner, Friedelind (1918–1991)
Walker, Kath (1920–1993)
Walker, Maggie Lena (1867–1934)

Walker, Mary Edwards (1832–1919)
Wambaugh, Sarah (1882–1955)
Ward, Catharine Barnes (1851–1913)
Washington, Margaret Murray (c. 1861–1925)
Weigl, Vally (1889–1982)
Wells-Barnett, Ida (1862–1931)
Whitestone, Heather (c. 1973—)
Whitton, Charlotte (1896–1975)
Willard, Frances E. (1839–1898)
Williams, Fannie Barrier (1855–1944)
Wilson, Charlotte (1854–1944)
Winfrey, Oprah (1954—)
Winnemucca, Sarah (1844–1891)
Wise, Louise Waterman (1874–1947)
Wong, Betty Ann (1938—)
Woolley, Helen (1874–1947)
Wright, Frances (1795–1852)
Wynyard, Diana (1906–1964)
Yates, Frances Amelia (1899–1981)
Young, Ann Eliza (b. 1844)
Zell, Katharina Schütz (c. 1497–1562)
Ziyada, Mayy (1886–1941)

LEGAL-PRECEDENT SETTER
Gaines, Myra Clark (1805–1885)
Quinlan, Karen Ann (1954–1985)
Remond, Sarah Parker (1826–1894)
Robertson, Ann (1825–1922)

LEGISLATOR
See Politician.

LETTER WRITER
Adams, Abigail (1744–1818)
Alcoforado, Mariana (1640–1723)
Arnim, Bettine von (1785–1859)
Ascham, Margaret Howe (c. 1535–1590)
Atkinson, Jane Maria (1824–1914)
Bacon, Alice Mabel (1858–1918)
Barraud, Sarah Maria (c. 1823–1895)
Bartlett, Mary (d. 1789)
Berthgyth (fl. 8th c.)
Boscawen, Fanny (1719–1805)
Bowne, Eliza Southgate (1783–1809)
Brown, Eliza (d. 1896)
Brown, Elizabeth (1753–1812)
Browne, Harriet Louisa (1829–1906)
Bulfinch, Hannah Apthorp (1768–1841)
Burdett-Coutts, Angela (1814–1906)
Butler, Eleanor (c. 1738–1829)
Byrd, Mary Willing (1740–1814)
Caesar, Mary (1677–1741)
Carlyle, Jane Welsh (1801–1866)
Cely, Margery (fl. late 15th c.)
Çentlivre, Susanna (c. 1669–1723)
Černínová z Harasova, Zuzana (1601–1654)
Charlotte Elizabeth of Bavaria (1652–1722)
Clapp, Louise (1819–1906)
Cockburn, Alicia (1713–1794)
Crequy, Renée Caroline de Froulay, Marquise de (1714–1803)
Darling, Flora (1840–1910)
Delany, Mary Granville (1700–1788)
Downing, Lucy Winthrop (c. 1600–1679)
Duff-Gordon, Lucie (1821–1869)
Dunbar, Christine (c. 1350–?)
Dutton, Anne (fl. 1743)
Emerson, Mary Moody (1774–1863)
Fay, Eliza (1756–1816)
Fell, Margaret (1614–1702)
Fermor, Henrietta Louisa (d. 1761)
Fraser, Margaret (1866–1951)
Godley, Charlotte (1821–1907)
Gottsched, Luise Adelgunde (1713–1762)
Gratz, Rebecca (1781–1869)
Greene, Catharine Ray (d. 1794)
Greenwood, Sarah (c. 1809–1889)
Griffitts, Hannah (1727–1817)
Grubb, Sarah Lynes (1773–1842)
Head, Bessie (1937–1986)
Henning, Rachel (1826–1914)
Hodgkins, Sarah Perkins (c. 1750–1803)
Huntington, Anne Huntington (d. 1790)
Imlay, Fanny (1794–1816)
Inman, Elizabeth Murray (c. 1724–1785)
Jacobson, Louise (1924–1943)
Kartini (1879–1904)
Ladies of Llangollen, The
Lisle, Honora Grenville (c. 1495–1566)
Livingston, Alida Schuyler (1656–1727)
Locke, Anne Vaughan (c. 1530–c. 1590)
Macarthur, Elizabeth (1767–1850)
Maclehose, Agnes (1759–1841)
Margaret of Angouleme (1492–1549)
McTier, Martha (c. 1743–1837)
Mead, Lucia Ames (1856–1936)
Mitford, Mary Russell (1787–1855)
Montagu, Lady Mary Wortley (1689–1762)
Newman, Mehetabel (c. 1822–1908)
Osborne, Dorothy (1627–1695)
Ponsonby, Sarah (1755–1831)
Porter, Katherine Anne (1890–1980)
Ramirez, Sara Estela (1881–1910)
Riding, Laura (1901–1991)
Sablé, Madeleine de Souvré, Marquise de (c. 1599–1678)
Sévigné, Marie de (1626–1696)
Shaginian, Marietta (1888–1982)
Smith, Margaret (fl. 1660)
Staal de Launay, Madame de (1684–1750)
Strozzi, Alessandra (1406–1469)
Stuart, Louisa (1757–1851)
Talbot, Catherine (1721–1770)
Thimelby, Gertrude Aston (c. 1617–1668)
Ticknor, Anna Eliot (1823–1896)
Traske, Mary (fl. 1660)
Trench, Melesina (1768–1827)
Varnhagen, Rahel (1771–1833)
Wander, Maxie (1933–1977)
Wheatley, Phillis (c. 1752–1784)
Williams, Helen Maria (1762–1827)
Williams, Marianne (1793–1879)
Winthrop, Margaret (c. 1591–1647)

LIBRARIAN
Ahern, Mary Eileen (1860–1938
Aliger, Margarita Iosifovna (1915–1992)
Anderson, Regina M. (1900–1993)
Apgar, Virginia (1909–1974)
Askew, Sarah B. (c. 1863–1942)
Bain, Wilhelmina Sherriff (1848–1944)
Baker, Augusta (1911–1998)
Barnard, Marjorie (1897–1987)
Barry, Iris (1895–1969)
Benedict, Ruth (1887–1948)
Blackett, Annie Maude (1889–1956)
Bogle, Sarah C.N. (1870–1932)
Bush, Laura (1946—)
Carey, Miriam E. (1858–1937)
Clampitt, Amy (1920–1994)
Constance Jones, E.E. (1848–1922)
Coolbrith, Ina Donna (1841–1928)
Corson, Juliet (1841–1897)
Diggs, Annie LePorte (1848–1916)
Eastman, Linda A. (1867–1963)
Elmendorf, Theresa West (1855–1932)
Esteve-Coll, Elizabeth (1938—)
Flexner, Jennie M. (1882–1944)
Garnett, Constance (1862–1946)
Greene, Belle da Costa (1883–1950)
Haines, Helen (1872–1961)
Hawes, Harriet Boyd (1871–1945)
Hazeltine, Mary (1868–1949)
Hebard, Grace Raymond (1861–1936)
Hewins, Caroline Maria (1846–1926)
Huch, Ricarda (1864–1947)
Hutson, Jean (1914–1998)
Isom, Mary Frances (1865–1920)
Kenny, Alice Annie (1875–1960)
Kroeger, Alice (1864–1909)
Larsen, Nella (1891–1964)
L'Engle, Madeleine (1918—)
Leviska, Helvi Lemmiki (1902–1982)
Litchfield, Jessie (1883–1956)
Lorde, Audre (1934–1992)
MacInnes, Helen (1907–1985)
Marie de Bourbon (1606–1627)
Marot, Helen (1865–1940)
Massee, May (1881–1966)
Mauermayer, Gisela (b. 1913)
Minchin, Alice Ethel (1889–1966)
Miner, Dorothy (1904–1973)
Mitchell, Maria (1818–1889)
Moore, Anne Carroll (1871–1961)
Mudge, Isadore (1875–1957)
Newman, Frances (1883–1928)
Niedecker, Lorine (1903–1970)
Norris, Kathleen (1880–1966)
Nunneley, Kathleen Mary (1872–1956)
Oddon, Yvonne (1902–1982)
Pickthall, Marjorie (1883–1922)
Plummer, Mary Wright (1856–1916)
Rathbone, Josephine Adams (1864–1941)
Rimington, Stella (1935—)
Robins, Elizabeth (1862–1952)
Rollins, Charlemae Hill (1897–1979)
Saunders, Doris (1921—)
Sharp, Katharine Lucinda (1865–1914)
Shearer, Moira (1926—)
Spencer, Anne (1882–1975)
Stearns, Lutie (1866–1943)
Stevens, Nettie Maria (1861–1912)
Taylor, Elizabeth (1912–1975)
Tyler, Alice S. (1859–1944)
Vogel, Dorothy (1935—)
Warren, Althea (1886–1958)
Winser, Beatrice (1869–1947)
Wood, Mary Elizabeth (1861–1931)

LIBRARY/MUSEUM FOUNDER
Alexander, Annie Montague (1867–1949)
Folger, Emily (1858–1936)
Formby, Margaret (1929–2003)
Fowle, Elida Rumsey (1842–1919)
Haldane, Elizabeth S. (1862–1937)
Holladay, Wilhelmina Cole (1922—)
Jadwiga (1374–1399)
Lewisohn, Alice (1883–1972)
Lewisohn, Irene (1892–1944)
Marie-Amelie of Orleans (1865–1951)
Marot, Helen (1865–1940)
McDowell, Anne E. (1826–1901)
Vanderbilt, Gloria (1924—)
Victoria Adelaide (1840–1901)
Whitney, Gertrude Vanderbilt (1875–1942)
Winser, Beatrice (1869–1947)

LIBRETTIST
Agnesi, Maria Teresa (1720–1795)
Chézy, Helmina von (1783–1856)
Fitzgerald, Geraldine (1913–2005)
Hara, Kazuko (1935—)
Krasnohorska, Eliska (1847–1926)
Mayreder, Rosa (1858–1938)
Piper, Myfanwy (1911–1997)
Stein, Gertrude (1874–1946)
Young, Rida Johnson (1869–1926)

LIGHTHOUSE KEEPER
Bennett, Mary Jane (c. 1816–1885)
Lewis, Ida (1842–1911)

LIGHTING DESIGNER
Adams, Maude (1872–1953)
Clark, Peggy (c. 1916–1996)
Eckart, Jean (1921–1993)
Fingerhut, Arden (1945–1994)
Kalmus, Natalie (1878–1965)
Musser, Tharon (1925—)
Rosenthal, Jean (1912–1969)

LINGUIST
Adolf, Helen (b. 1895)
Aliye, Fatima (1862–1936)
Aníchkova, Anna (1868–1935)
Anscombe, G.E.M. (1919–2001)
Anstei, Olga Nikolaevna (1912–1985)
Aubin, Penelope (c. 1685–1731)
Ayscough, Florence (1875/78–1942)
Bacinetti-Florenzi, Marianna (1802–1870)
Barney, Natalie Clifford (1876–1972)
Basset, Mary Roper (fl. 1544–1572)
Bayne, Margaret (1798–1835)
Bianco, Margery Williams (1881–1944)
Booth, Mary Louise (1831–1889)
Braunschweig-Lüneburg, Sibylle Ursula von (1629–1671)
Budberg, Moura (1892–1974)
Buffet, Marguerite (d. 1680)
Carter, Elizabeth (1717–1806)
Cassian, Nina (1924—)
Clerke, Ellen Mary (1840–1906)
Dacier, Anne (1654–1720)
Dal, Ingerid (1895–1985)
d'Arconville, Geneviève (1720–1805)
Deloria, Ella (1888–1971)
Duff-Gordon, Lucie (1821–1869)
Dutt, Toru (1856–1877)
Elizabeth of Wied (1843–1916)
Fisher, Dorothy Canfield (1879–1958)
Goldberg, Lea (1911–1970)
Gournay, Marie le Jars de (1565–1645)
Hartwig, Julia (1921—)
Holst, Clara (1868–1935)
Howitt, Mary (1799–1888)
Jolas, Maria (1893–1987)
Kolmar, Gertrud (1894–1943)
Kristeva, Julia (1941—)
Laird, Carobeth (1895–1983)
Latimer, Elizabeth W. (1822–1904)
Lehmann, Rosamond (1901–1990)
Levertov, Denise (1923–1997)
Lewis, Agnes Smith (1843–1926)
Longhi, Lucia Lopresti (1895–1985)
Malinche (c. 1500–1531)
Malraux, Clara (c. 1897–1982)
Manner, Eeva-Liisa (1921–1995)
Mansfield, Katherine (1888–1923)
McKenna, Siobhan (1922–1986)
Montgomery, Helen Barrett (1861–1934)
Morris, Pamela (1906–2002)
Murray, Margaret (1863–1963)
Pavlova, Karolina (1807–1893)
Pound, Louise (1872–1958)
Pukui, Mary Kawena (1895–1986)
Royde-Smith, Naomi Gwladys (c. 1880–1964)
Royer, Clémence (1830–1902)
Russell, Elizabeth (1540–1609)
Sayers, Dorothy L. (1893–1957)
Sirota, Beate (1923—)
Solano, Solita (1888–1975)
Sullam, Sara Coppia (1590–1641)
Swanwick, Anna (1813–1899)
Szymborska, Wislawa (1923—)
Thomas, Edith Matilda (1854–1925)
Vesaas, Halldis Moren (1907–1995)
Voynich, Ethel (1864–1960)
Ward, Ida Caroline (1880–1949)
White, Antonia (1899–1980)
Winkworth, Catherine (1827–1878)
Winkworth, Susanna (1820–1884)
Wormeley, Katharine Prescott (1830–1908)
Wright, Laura Maria (1809–1886)
Yamada Waka (1879–1956)
Yourcenar, Marguerite (1903–1987)
Zrinska, Ana Katarina (1625–1673)

LITERACY ACTIVIST
Bush, Barbara (1924—)
Clark, Septima Poinsette (1898–1987)
Gandhi, Indira (1917–1984)
Gasteazoro, Ana (1950–1993)
Hamer, Fannie Lou (1917–1977)
Hunton, Addie D. Waites (1875–1943)
Ransome-Kuti, Funmilayo (1900–1978)
Reisner, Larissa (1895–1926)
Rose, Margo (1903–1997)
Sohier, Elizabeth Putnam (1847–1926)
Stewart, Cora Wilson (1875–1958)
Zia, Khaleda (1946—)

LITERARY AGENT
Bradley, Jenny
Budberg, Moura (1892–1974)
Daves, Joan (1919–1997)
Diamant, Anita (1917–1996)
Donadio, Candida (1929–2001)
Herscher, Sylvia (1913–2004)
Morrison, Adrienne (1889–1940)
Pauli, Hertha (1909–1973)
Safier, Gloria (d. 1985)
Wood, Audrey (1905–1985)

LITERARY/ARTISTIC INSPIRATION
Beatrice Portinari (c. 1265–1290)
Bosse, Harriet (1878–1961)
Chevigné, Laure de (1860–1936)
Claudel, Camille (1864–1943)
Eliot, Vivienne (1889–1947)
Fermor, Arabella (d. 1738)
Gonne, Maud (1866–1953)
Graves, Beryl (1915–2003)
Habets, Marie-Louise (1905–1986)
Heiberg, Johanne Luise (1812–1890)
Houdetot, Sophie, Comtesse d' (1730–1813)
Jermy, Louie (1864–1934)
Johnson, Esther (1681–1728)
Joyce, Lucia (1907–1982)
Joyce, Nora (1884–1951)
Kieler, Laura (1849–1932)
Laurencin, Marie (1883–1956)
Lefebvre, Catherine (c. 1764–after 1820)
Lenya, Lotte (1898–1981)
Lewson, Jane (c. 1700–1816)
Liddell, Alice (1852–1934)
Mahupuku, Maata (1890–1952)
Manning, Maria (c. 1821–1849)
Murphy, Sara (1883–1975)
Noves, Laure de (1308–1348)
O'Hanlon, Virginia (c. 1899–1971)
Plessis, Alphonsine (1824–1847)
Poe, Virginia Clemm (1822–1847)
Rich, Penelope (c. 1562–1607)
Robinson, Mary (d. 1837)
Vaux, Clotilde de (1815–1846)
Von Trapp, Maria (1905–1987)
Zuzoric, Cvijeta (c. 1555–1600)

LITERARY CRITIC
Abdel Rahman, Aisha (1913–1998)
Akselrod, Liubo (1868–1946)
Aleksandrovna, Vera (1895–1966)
Allen, Paula Gunn (1939—)
Anderson, Margaret Carolyn (1886–1973)
Aoki, Yayoi (1927—)
Arbuthnot, May Hill (1884–1969)
Atwood, Margaret (1939—)
Beer, Patricia (1919–1999)
Bergroth, Kersti (1886–1975)
Bianchini, Angela (1921—)
Bianco, Margery Williams (1881–1944)
Blanc, Marie-Thérèse (1840–1907)
Bodkin, Maud (1875–1967)
Bogan, Louise (1897–1970)
Brooke-Rose, Christine (1923—)
Brophy, Brigid (1929–1995)
Byatt, A.S. (1936—)
Centeno, Yvette (1940—)
César, Ana Cristina (1952–1983)
Chervinskaya, Lidiya Davydovna (1907–1988)
Chukovskaya, Lidiya (1907–1996)
Cixous, Hélène (1938—)
Colaço, Branca de Gonta (1880–1944)
Coleridge, Mary Elizabeth (1861–1907)
Colum, Mary Gunning (1884–1957)
Condé, Maryse (1937—)
Cooper, Elizabeth (fl. 1737)
Corti, Maria (1915–2002)
Croly, Jane Cunningham (1829–1901)
D'Arcy, Margaretta (1934—)
D'Costa, Jean (1937—)
Deutsch, Babette (1895–1982)
Deutscher, Tamara (1913–1990)
Drabble, Margaret (1939—)
Duclaux, Agnes Mary F. (1856–1944)
Eldershaw, Flora (1897–1956)
Ellis-Fermor, Una Mary (1894–1958)
Feng Yuanjun (1900–1974)
Finas, Lucette (1921—)
Fuller, Margaret (1810–1850)
Gardner, Helen Louise (1908–1986)
Gertsyk, Adelaida (1874–1925)
Gilbert, Sandra M. (1936—)
Ginzburg, Lidiia (1902–1990)
Gippius, Zinaida (1869–1945)
Glantz, Margo (1930—)
Goldberg, Lea (1911–1970)
Gordon, Caroline (1895–1981)
Gournay, Marie le Jars de (1565–1645)
Green, Dorothy (1915–1991)
Greer, Germaine (1939—)
Guiducci, Armanda (1923–1992)
Gurevich, Liubov (1866–1940)
Hansberry, Lorraine (1930–1965)
Hardwick, Elizabeth (1916—)
Hardy, Barbara (1924—)
Hatherly, Ana Maria (1929—)
Hébert, Anne (1916—)
Heilbrun, Carolyn Gold (1926–2003)
Hodrova, Daniela (1946—)
Howe, Susan (1937—)
Jacobsen, Josephine (1908–2003)
Jameson, Storm (1891–1986)
Janeway, Elizabeth (1913–2005)
Johnson, Pamela Hansford (1912–1981)
Jolas, Maria (1893–1987)
Keesing, Nancy (1923–1993)
Kennedy, Margaret (1896–1967)
Key, Ellen (1849–1926)
Khvoshchinskaia, Nadezhda (1824–1889)
Kirkus, Virginia (1893–1980)
Kristeva, Julia (1941—)
Lacis, Asja (1891–1979)
Laski, Marghanita (1915–1988)
Leavis, Q.D. (1906–1981)
Lemoine-Luccioni, Eugénie (1912—)
Liu, Nienling (1934—)

Occupational Index

Loveman, Amy (1881–1955)
Lowell, Amy (1874–1925)
Luft, Lia (1938—)
Lurie, Alison (1926—)
Macaulay, Rose (1881–1958)
Malaika, Nazik al- (1923–1992)
Malraux, Clara (c. 1897–1982)
Manning, Olivia (1908–1980)
Mansfield, Katherine (1888–1923)
Marothy-Soltesova, Elena (1855–1939)
McCarthy, Mary (1912–1989)
McIlwraith, Jean Newton (1859–1938)
Medio, Dolores (1914–1996)
Morandini, Giuliana (1938—)
Mulford, Wendy (1941—)
Nedreaas, Torborg (1906–1987)
Noronha, Joana de (fl. c. 1850)
Palmer, Nettie (1885–1964)
Parker, Dorothy (1893–1967)
Paterson, Isabel (c. 1886–1961)
Patterson, Alicia (1906–1963)
Plá, Josefina (1909–1999)
Pollard, Velma (1937—)
Queizán, María Xosé (1938—)
Raine, Kathleen (1908–2003)
Riding, Laura (1901–1991)
Rittenhouse, Jessie Belle (1869–1948)
Rochefort, Christiane (1917–1998)
Romein-Verschoor, Annie (1895–1978)
Saenz-Alonso, Mercedes (1916–2000)
Salhias de Tournemire, Elizaveta (1815–1892)
Sekulić, Isadora (1877–1958)
Shaginian, Marietta (1888–1982)
Shields, Carol (1935–2003)
Shockley, Ann Allen (1925—)
Showalter, Elaine (1941—)
Sinclair, May (1863–1946)
Spark, Muriel (1918—)
Spence, Catherine (1825–1910)
Spender, Dale (1943—)
Spiel, Hilde (1911–1990)
Spivak, Gayatri Chakravorty (1942—)
Starkie, Enid (1897–1970)
Steinwachs, Ginka (1942—)
Strauss, Jennifer (1933—)
Su Hsueh-lin (1897–1999)
Tastu, Amable (1798–1885)
Théoret, France (1942—)
Thomas, Clara (1919—)
Traba, Marta (1930–1983)
Travers, P.L. (1906–1996)
Trilling, Diana (1905–1996)
Trotzig, Birgitta (1929—)
Tsebrikova, M.K. (1835–1917)
Vallette, Marguerite (1860–1953)
Velichkovskaia, Tamara Antonovna (1908–1990)
Vengerova, Zinaida (1867–1941)
Ward, Mrs. Humphry (1851–1920)
Warner, Marina (1946—)
West, Rebecca (1892–1983)
Williams, Sherley Anne (1944–1999)
Wright, Judith (1915–2000)
Ye Jiayin (1924—)
Zardoya, Concha (1914–2004)
Zwicky, Fay (1933—)

LITERARY FIGURE

Jungmann, Elisabeth (d. 1959)

LITERARY HOSTESS

See Salonnière.

LITERARY INSPIRATION

Luxford, Nola (1895–1994)
Reeves, Magdalene Stuart (1865–1953)

LITHOGRAPHER

Albers, Anni (1899–1994)
Bacon, Peggy (1895–1987)
Blackburn, Jemima (1823–1909)
Bonner, Mary (1885–1935)
Bourgeois, Louise (b. 1911)
Catlett, Elizabeth (b. 1915)
Gabain, Ethel Leontine (1883–1950)
Goldthwaite, Anne Wilson (1869–1944)
Gosse, Sylvia (1881–1968)
Greenwood, Marion (1909–1980)
Grundig, Lea (1906–1977)
Hale, Ellen Day (1855–1940)
Olds, Elizabeth (1896–1991)
Palmer, Frances Flora (1812–1876)
Pitseolak (c. 1900–1983)
Preston, Margaret Rose (c. 1875–1963)
Ryan, Anne (1889–1954)
Tait, Agnes (c. 1897–1981)
Telalkowska, Wanda (1905–1986)
Templeton, Rini (1935–1986)
Ticho, Anna (1894–1980)
Toyen (1902–1980)

LOGICIAN

Ladd-Franklin, Christine (1847–1930)
Robinson, Julia B. (1919–1985)

LONG JUMPER

See Track-and-field athlete.

LUGE ATHLETE

Amantova, Ingrida
Demleitner, Elisabeth
Dünhaupt, Angelika
Enderlein, Ortrun (1943–)
Erdmann, Susi-Lisa (1968—)
Geisler, Ilse
Kraushaar, Silke (1970—)
Lechner, Erica
Müller, Anna-Maria (1949—)
Neuner, Angelika (1969—)
Neuner, Doris (1970—)
Niedernhuber, Barbara (1974—)
Oberhoffner, Ute
Otto, Sylke (1969—)
Rührold, Ute
Schmidt, Cerstin
Schmuck, Christa
Schumann, Margit (1952—)
Sollmann, Melitta
Tagwerker, Andrea
Terwillegar, Erica (1963—)
Thurner, Helene
Walter-Martin, Steffi (1962—)
Warner, Bonny (1962—)
Weissensteiner, Gerda (1969—)
Zozula, Vera

LYRICIST

Bergman, Marilyn (1929—)
Caldwell, Anne (1876–1936)
Comden, Betty (1915—)
Cryer, Gretchen (1935—)
Donnelly, Dorothy (1880–1928)
Dove, Rita (1952—)
Fields, Dorothy (1904–1974)
Fine, Sylvia (1913–1991)
Fitzgerald, Geraldine (1913–2005)
Hale, Sarah Josepha (1788–1879)
Hamilton, Nancy (1908–1985)
Johnson, Georgia Douglas (1877–1966)
Lee, Peggy (1920—)
Leigh, Carolyn (1926–1983)
Nairne, Carolina (1766–1845)
Pagan, Isobel (c. 1742–1821)
Reynolds, Malvina (1900–1978)
Rowson, Susanna (1762–1824)
Young, Rida Johnson (1869–1926)

MAGICIAN

Whiteside, Jane (1855–1875)

MAMMOLOGIST

Alexander, Annie Montague (1867–1949)

MANAGEMENT THEORIST

Follett, Mary Parker (1868–1933)
Gilbreth, Lillian Moller (1878–1972)

MANUFACTURER

Beale, Mary (1632–1699)
Beech, Olive Ann (1903–1993)
Bishop, Hazel (1906–1998)
Boit, Elizabeth Eaton (1849–1932)
Gleason, Kate (1865–1933)
Hewlett, Hilda Beatrice (1864–1943)
Justin, Enid (1894–1990)
Knox, Rose Markward (1857–1950)
Lukens, Rebecca (1794–1854)
Merian, Maria Sybilla (1647–1717)
Reid, Rose Marie (1906–1978)
Schary, Hope Skillman (1908–1981)
Smith, Helen Hay (1873–1918)
Spain, Jayne (1927—)

MANUSCRIPT ILLUMINATOR

Anastaise (fl. 1400)
Claricia of Augsburg (fl. 1220)
Donatella (fl. 1271)
Leodegundia (fl. 10th c.)
Montanaria (fl. 1272)
Ormani, Maria (fl. 1453)
Thomasse (fl. 1292)

MAPMAKER

See Cartographer.

MARCHIONESS

Alorna, Marquesa de (1750–c. 1839)
Barbara of Brandenburg (1422–1481)
Beatrice of Lorraine (c. 1020–1076)
Blackwood, Hariot (c. 1845–1891)
Boufflers, Marie (1706–1747)
Brinvilliers, Marie de (1630–1676)
Calderón de la Barca, Frances (1804–1882)
Caldwell, Mary Gwendolin (1863–1909)
Cavendish-Bentinck, Elizabeth (1735–1825)
Caylus, Marthe M. (1673–1729)
Châtelet, Émilie du (1706–1749)
Colonna, Vittoria (c. 1490–1547)
Condorcet, Sophie Marie Louise, Marquise de (1764–1822)
Courtenay, Gertrude (c. 1504–1558)
Crequy, Renée Caroline de Froulay, Marquise de (1714–1803)
Deffand, Marie Anne de Vichy-Chamrond, Marquise du (1697–1780)
Deffand, Marie du (1697–1780)
Emma (fl. 1080s)
Entragues, Henriette d' (1579–1633)
Este, Cunegunda d' (c. 1012–1055)
Este, Gigliola d'
Este, Isabella d' (1474–1539)
Este, Parisina d' (fl. 1400)
Este, Ricciarda d'
Estrées, Gabrielle d' (1573–1599)
Fitzroy, Isabel (1726–1782)
Fuller, Margaret (1810–1850)
Gonzaga, Margherita (1418–1439)
Gonzaga, Paola (1393–1453)
Griselda (fl. 11th c.)
Holland, Anne (d. 1474)
Isaacs, Stella (1894–1971)

Isabelle of Cornwall (fl. 14th c.)
Julie (fl. 1770)
Kennedy, Kathleen (1920–1948)
Lafayette, Marie Adrienne de (1760–1807)
Lambert, Anne Thérèse de Marguenat de Courcelles (1647–1733)
La Rochejacquelein, Marie Louise Victoire, marquise de (1772–1857)
La Tour du Pin, Henriette de (1770–1853)
Maintenon, Françoise d'Aubigné, Marquise de (1635–1719)
Margaret of Bavaria (1445–1479)
Maria of Aragon (fl. 1440)
Massimi, Petronilla Paolini (1663–1726)
Masters, Sybilla (1720–?)
Montespan, Françoise, Marquise de (1640–1707)
Montesson, Charlotte Jeanne Béraud de la Haye de Riou, marquise de (1737–1805)
Mountbatten, Irene (1890–1956)
Patti, Adelina (1843–1919)
Pimentel, Eleonora (c. 1768–1799)
Pompadour, Jeanne-Antoinette Poisson, Duchesse de (1721–1764)
Prie, Jeanne Agnes Berthelot de Pléneuf, Marquise de (1698–1727)
Rambouillet, Catherine de Vivonne, Marquise de (1588–1665)
Rothelin, Jacqueline de Rohan, Marquise de (c. 1520–1587)
Sablé, Madeleine de Souvré, Marquise de (c. 1599–1678)
Saint Mars, Gabrielle de (1804–1872)
Sévigné, Marie de (1626–1696)
Souza-Botelho, Adélaïde Filleul, marquise of (1761–1836)
Tallien, Thérésa (1773–1835)
Tencin, Claudine Alexandrine Guérin de (1685–1749)
Vane-Tempest, Frances Anne Emily (d. 1865)
Vane-Tempest-Stewart, Edith (1878–1949)
Victoria of Hesse-Darmstadt (1863–1950)
Vintimille, Pauline Félicité, Marquise de (1712–1741)
Wotton, Margaret (fl. 16th c.)

MARGRAVINE
Augusta Maria of Holstein-Gottorp (1649–1728)
Barbara of Saxe-Wittenberg (c. 1405–1465)
Christina Casimir (fl. 1640–1660)
Craven, Elizabeth (1750–1828)
Eleanor of Saxe-Eisenach (1662–1696)
Frederica Louise (1715–1784)
Hedwig of Habsburg (d. 1286)
Ida of Austria (d. 1101?)
Irmingard of Zelle (c. 1200–1260)
Johanna Elizabeth of Baden-Durlach (1651–1680)
Jutta of Saxony (d. around 1267)
Margarethe (1370–c. 1400)
Marie Louise (1879–1948)
Sophia of Denmark (1217–1248)
Sophie Caroline (1737–1817)
Sophie of Poland (1464–1512)
Sophie of Solms-Laubach (1594–1651)
Suzanne of Bavaria (1502–1543)
Theodora Oldenburg (1906–1969)
Wilhelmina (1709–1758)

MARINE BIOLOGIST
Bennett, Isobel (b. 1909)
Bidder, Anna McClean (1903–2001)
Carson, Rachel (1907–1964)
Clark, Eugenie (1922—)
Lebour, Marie (1877–1971)
Marshall, Sheina (1896–1977)
Massy, Annie (1867–1931)
Mead, Sylvia Earle (1935—)
Mestre, Audrey (1974–2002)
Parke, Mary (1908–1989)
Rathbun, Mary Jane (1860–1943)
Spooner, Molly (1914–1997)
Van Dover, Cindy (1954—)

MARKET PRODUCE GARDENER
Small, Mary Elizabeth (1812/13–1908)

MARQUISE/MARQUESA
See Marchioness.

MARTYR
See also Political martyr.
See also Religious martyr.
Barbara (fl. 3rd c.)
Bibiana (d. 363)
Bocher, Joan (d. 1550)
Constance (d. 305)
Eusebia of Bergamo (fl. 3rd c.)
Flora of Cordova (d. 851)
Maria of Cordova (d. 851)

MASSEUSE
Roberts, Mary Louise (1886–1968)

MATHEMATICAL PHYSICIST
Somerville, Mary Fairfax (1780–1872)

MATHEMATICIAN
Agnesi, Maria Gaetana (1718–1799)
Bari, Nina K. (1901–1961)
Cartwright, Mary L. (1900–1998)
Choquet-Bruhat, Yvonne (1923—)
Daubechies, Ingrid (1954—)
Einstein-Maríc, Mileva (1875–1948)
Fawcett, Philippa (1868–1948)
Geiringer, Hilda (1893–1973)
Germain, Sophie (1776–1831)
Greig, Margaret (1922–1999)
Hazlett, Olive C. (1890–1974)
Hoffleit, E. Dorrit (1907—)
Hopper, Grace Murray (1906–1992)
Hypatia (c. 375–415)
Königsdorf, Helga (1938—)
Kovalevskaya, Sophia (1850–1891)
Ladd-Franklin, Christine (1847–1930)
Lama, Giulia (c. 1685–c. 1753)
Lehmann, Inge (1888–1993)
Lepaute, Hortense (1723–1788)
Lovelace, Ada Byron, Countess of (1815–1852)
Morawetz, Cathleen Synge (1923—)
Neumann, Hanna (1914–1971)
Newton Turner, Helen (1908–1995)
Noether, Emmy (1882–1935)
Reiche, Maria (1903–1998)
Rickett, Mary Ellen (1861–1925)
Robinson, Julia B. (1919–1985)
Scott, Charlotte Angas (1858–1931)
Somerville, Mary Fairfax (1780–1872)
Stephansen, Elizabeth (1872–1961)
Taylor, Mary (1898–1984)
Todd, Olga Taussky (1906–1995)
Venttsel, Elena Sergeevna (1907–2002)
Wedemeyer, Maria von (c. 1924–1977)
Weeks, Dorothy (1893–1990)
Wheeler, Anna Pell (1883–1966)
Winlock, Anna (1857–1904)
Wrinch, Dorothy (1894–1976)
Young, Grace Chisholm (1868–1944)

MAYOR
Agnelli, Susanna (1922—)
Ali, Aruna Asaf (c. 1909–1996)
Anderson, Elizabeth Garrett (1836–1917)
Arendsee, Martha (1885–1953)
Byrne, Jane (1934—)
Clarke, Kathleen (1878–1972)
Cresson, Edith (1934—)
Emhart, Maria (1901–1981)
Fairclough, Ellen (1905–2004)
Fergusson, Muriel McQueen (1899–1997)
Franklin, Shirley (1945—)
Gautier, Felisa Rincón de (1897–1994)
Kenyatta, Margaret (1928—)
Kernohan, Liz (1939–2004)
Landes, Bertha Knight (1868–1943)
Lindsey, Estelle Lawton (1868–1955)
MacFall, Frances E. (1854–1943)
Markham, Violet Rosa (1872–1959)
Page, Dorothy G. (d. 1989)
Porter, Gladys M. (1894–1967)
Salter, Susanna Medora (1860–1961)
Schroeder, Louise (1887–1957)
Spiridonova, Maria (1884–1941)
Suplicy, Marta (c. 1946—)
Tizard, Catherine (1931—)
Weber, Lois (1881–1939)
Whitmire, Kathy (1946—)
Whitton, Charlotte (1896–1975)
Wilde, Fran (1948—)

MECHANICAL ENGINEER
Gleason, Kate (1865–1933)
Hartigan, Grace (1922—)
Kankus, Roberta A. (1953—)

MEDICAL-CLINIC FOUNDER
See Hospital/Health-center founder.

MEDICAL/HEALTH EDUCATOR
Abaijah, Josephine (1942—)
Abbott, Maude (1869–1940)
Amathila, Libertine Appolus (1940—)
Broomall, Anna (1847–1931)
Brown, Edith Mary (1864–1956)
Cannon, Ida (1877–1960)
Dunbar, Flanders (1902–1959)
Dunham, Ethel Collins (1883–1969)
Fenwick, Ethel Gordon (1857–1947)
Goldsmith, Grace Arabell (1904–1975)
Guion, Connie M. (1882–1971)
Hurd-Wood, Kathleen Gertrude (1886–1965)
Jarrett, Mary Cromwell (1877–1961)
Johnson, Nicole (c. 1974—)
Leyel, Hilda (1880–1957)
Marshall, Clara (1847–1931)
Maxwell, Anna Caroline (1851–1929)
Mayer, Jacquelyn (c. 1942—)
Perrin, Ethel (1871–1962)
Pery, Sylvia (1935—)
Powell, Louise Mathilde (1871–1943)
Roberts, Lydia (1879–1965)
Rout, Ettie Annie (1877–1936)
Stephenson, Elsie (1916–1967)
Tracy, Martha (1876–1942)
Yarros, Rachelle (1869–1946)

MEDICAL PRACTITIONER
See Anaesthetist.
See Dentist.
See Gynecologist.
See Midwife.
See Nurse.
See Nutritionist.
See Obstetrician.
See Physician.
See Psychiatrist.
See Surgeon.

MEDICAL WRITER

Bourgeois, Louise (1563–1636)
Cannon, Ida (1877–1960)
Dunham, Ethel Collins (1883–1969)
Fromm-Reichmann, Frieda (1889–1957)
Jarrett, Mary Cromwell (1877–1961)
Sabuco, Oliva de Nantes Barrera (1562–1625)
Sharp, Jane (fl. 1671)

MEDIUM (PSYCHIC)

See Spiritualist.

MEMOIRIST

Abrantès, Laure d' (1784–1838)
Acland, Lady Harriet (1750–1815)
Adam, Juliette la Messine (1836–1936)
Adams, Louisa Catherine (1775–1852)
Adıvar, Halide Edib (c. 1884–1964)
Aikin, Lucy (1781–1864)
Ajzenberg-Selove, Fay (1926—)
Aldecoa, Josefina R. (1926—)
Alice of Athlone (1883–1981)
Alliluyeva, Svetlana (1926—)
Andreas-Salomé, Lou (1861–1937)
Arletty (1898–1992)
Aubrac, Lucie (1912—)
Augspurg, Anita (1857–1943)
Aulnoy, Marie Catherine, Countess d' (c. 1650–1705)
Avilova, Lidya (c. 1864–1943)
Bailey, Abigail Abbott (1746–1815)
Balabanoff, Angelica (1878–1965)
Balfour, Frances (1858–1931)
Barbauld, Anna Letitia (1743–1825)
Barkley, Jane Hadley (1911–1964)
Barney, Natalie Clifford (1876–1972)
Bates, Daisy Lee (1914–1999)
Bauer, Karoline (1807–1877)
Baum, Vicki (1888–1960)
Bäumer, Gertrud (1873–1954)
Beach, Sylvia (1887–1962)
Beaumont, Agnes (1652–1720)
Beauvau, Marie Charlotte (1729–1807)
Beauvoir, Simone de (1908–1986)
Behn, Aphra (1640?–1689)
Beinhorn, Elly (1907—)
Belfrage, Sally (1936–1994)
Bellil, Samira (1972–2004)
Belloc-Lowndes, Marie (1868–1947)
Berg, Gertrude (1899–1966)
Bergmann-Pohl, Sabine (1946—)
Bergner, Elisabeth (1897–1986)
Bernhardt, Sarah (1844–1923)
Bernstein, Hilda (1915—)
Bishop, Elizabeth (1911–1979)
Blessington, Marguerite, Countess of (1789–1849)
Boggs, Lindy (1916—)
Boissevain, Mia (1878–1959)
Bonaparte, Letizia (1750–1836)
Bondfield, Margaret (1873–1953)
Boswell, Annabella (1826–1916)
Botta, Anne C.L. (1815–1891)
Bowen, Elizabeth (1899–1973)
Boyd, Belle (1844–1900)
Brewer, Lucy (fl. 1812)
Brice, Fanny (1891–1951)
Briche, Adelaide de la (1755–1844)
Brittain, Vera (1893–1970)
Brooks, Romaine (1874–1970)
Bruha, Antonia (1915—)
Buber-Neumann, Margarete (1901–1989)
Burke, Billie (1885–1970)
Cairns, Elizabeth (1685–1714)
Carpenter, Iris (b. 1906)
Carr, Emily (1871–1945)
Carré, Mathilde (1908–c. 1970)
Carter, Elizabeth (1717–1806)
Casgrain, Thérèse (1896–1981)
Catherine II the Great of Russia (1729–1796)
Catley, Ann (1745–1789)
Cavendish, Margaret (1623–1673)
Caylus, Marthe M. (1673–1729)
Chabrillan, Céleste de (1824–1909)
Chastenay, Victorine de (1771–1855)
Chichibu Setsuko (1909–1995)
Choi, Sook Nyul (1937—)
Chowdhury, Eulie (1923—)
Christie, Agatha (1890–1976)
Chukovskaya, Lidiya (1907–1996)
Churchill, Jennie Jerome (1854–1921)
Clairon, Mlle (1723–1802)
Clark, Eleanor (1913–1996)
Coffee, Lenore (1896–1984)
Cohen, Harriet (1895–1967)
Coleman, Ann Raney Thomas (1810–1897)
Coleman, Bessie (1892–1926)
Coleridge, Sara (1802–1852)
Colette (1873–1954)
Comden, Betty (1915—)
Connally, Nellie (1919—)
Conway, Jill Ker (1934—)
Coolidge, Grace Goodhue (1879–1957)
Cooper, Gladys (1888–1971)
Corbett-Ashby, Margery (1882–1981)
Corelli, Marie (1855–1924)
Courtneidge, Cicely (1893–1980)
Cousins, Margaret (1878–1954)
Cowles, Fleur (1910—)
Crawford, Cheryl (1902–1986)
Crow Dog, Mary (1953—)
Custer, Elizabeth Bacon (1842–1933)
Dabrowska, Maria (1889–1965)
Daisy, Princess (1873–1943)
Danilova, Alexandra (1903–1997)
Dashkova, Ekaterina (1744–1810)
Davidson, Robyn (1950—)
Deans, Jane (1823–1911)
de Galard, Geneviève (1925—)
Delany, Annie Elizabeth (1891–1995)
Deutschkron, Inge (1922—)
de Valois, Ninette (1898–2001)
Diallo, Nafissatou (1941–1982)
Dinesen, Isak (1885–1962)
Ditlevsen, Tove (1917–1976)
Dolgorukaia, Natalia Borisovna (1714–1771)
Dors, Diana (1931–1984)
Dostalova, Leopolda (1879–1972)
Dostoevsky, Anna (1846–1918)
Dulles, Eleanor Lansing (1895–1996)
Durieux, Tilla (1880–1971)
Durova, Nadezhda (1783–1866)
Dzerzhinska, Sofia (1882–1968)
Eaton, Peggy (c. 1799–1879)
Edmonds, Emma (1841–1898)
Eisner, Lotte (1896–1983)
El Saadawi, Nawal (1931—)
Emhart, Maria (1901–1981)
Engel, Regula (1761–1853)
Épinay, Louise-Florence-Pétronille, Madame la Live d' (1726–1783)
Erauso, Catalina de (1592–1635)
Eugénie (1826–1920)
Falconbridge, Anna Maria (fl. 1790–1794)
Fanshawe, Anne (1625–1680)
Farjeon, Eleanor (1881–1965)
Farmborough, Florence (1887–1978)
Farnese, Elizabeth (1692–1766)
Farrar, Eliza Rotch (1791–1870)
Fawcett, Millicent Garrett (1847–1929)
Felton, Rebecca Latimer (1835–1930)
Fernandez, Alina (1956—)
Figner, Vera (1852–1942)
Fittko, Lisa (1909–2005)
Flagstad, Kirsten (1895–1962)
Fox, Paula (1923—)
Freeman, Lucy (1916–2004)
Fuller, Margaret (1810–1850)
Fulton, Mary Hannah (1854–1927)
Gardiner, Muriel (1901–1985)
Gay, Sophie (1776–1852)
Genlis, Stéphanie-Félicité, Comtesse de (1746–1830)
Gildersleeve, Virginia Crocheron (1877–1965)
Ginzburg, Evgenia (1896–1980)
Gippius, Zinaida (1869–1945)
Glückel of Hameln (1646–1724)
Gonne, Maud (1866–1953)
Gorbanevskaya, Natalya Yevgenevna (1936—)
Gordon, Caroline (1895–1981)
Gordon, Ruth (1896–1985)
Graham, Katharine (1917–2001)
Graham, Martha (1894–1991)
Gramont, Elizabeth de (fl. 1875–1935)
Grant, Anne (1755–1838)
Grant, Julia (1826–1902)
Greenhow, Rose O'Neal (c. 1817–1864)
Gress, Elsa (1919–1989)
Grundig, Lea (1906–1977)
Guette, Catherine de la (1613–1676)
Guilbert, Yvette (1865–1944)
Guy-Blaché, Alice (1875–1968)
Hamilton, Elizabeth Schuyler (1757–c. 1854)
Hani, Motoko (1873–1957)
Hanim, Nigar (1862–1918)
Harrison, Constance Cary (1843–1920)
Harrison, Marguerite (1879–1967)
Hauk, Minnie (1851–1929)
Hausset, Nicole Colleson du (1713–1801)
Hautval, Adelaide (1906–1988)
Hawkins, Laetitia Matilda (1759–1835)
Hayes, Helen (1900–1993)
Heiberg, Johanne Luise (1812–1890)
Held, Anna (c. 1865–1918)
Hellman, Lillian (1905–1984)
Henie, Sonja (1912–1969)
Henningsen, Agnes (1868–1962)
Henry, Alice (1857–1943)
Herbst, Josephine (1892–1969)
Herwegh, Emma (1817–1904)
Herz, Henriette (1764–1847)
Heymann, Lida (1867–1943)
Hong, Lady (1735–1850)
Hoskens, Jane Fenn (1694–c. 1750)
Hu Die (1908–1989)
Inchbald, Elizabeth (1753–1821)
Izzard, Molly (1919–2004)
Jabavu, Noni (1919—)
Jeanne d'Albret (1528–1572)
Jenner, Andrea (1891–1985)
Johnson, Pamela Hansford (1912–1981)
Judson, Emily Chubbuck (1817–1854)
Kalama (c. 1820–1870)
Kellogg, Clara Louise (1842–1916)
Kelly, Ethel (1875–1949)
Kemble, Fanny (1809–1893)
Kempe, Margery (c. 1373–after 1438)
Kenney, Annie (1879–1953)
King, Coretta Scott (1927—)
Kingston, Maxine Hong (1940—)
Kinnan, Mary (1763–1848)
Kirkland, Caroline Matilda (1801–1864)
Knef, Hildegard (1925—)
Kohut, Rebekah (1864–1951)
Kovalskaia, Elizaveta (1851–1943)
Krandievskaya, Natalia (1888–1963)
Kshesinskaia, Matilda (1872–1971)
Kuckhoff, Greta (1902–1981)

Lacis, Asja (1891–1979)
Lafarge, Marie (1816–1852)
La Fayette, Marie-Madeleine de (1634–1693)
Lake, Veronica (1919–1973)
La Rochefoucauld, Edmée, Duchesse de (1895–1991)
Lars, Claudia (1899–1974)
La Tour du Pin, Henriette de (1770–1853)
Laurencin, Marie (1883–1956)
Lawrence, Frieda (1879–1956)
Lawrenson, Helen (b. 1907)
Leander, Zarah (1907–1981)
Leduc, Violette (1907–1972)
Lee, Gypsy Rose (1914–1970)
Lee, Jarena (1783–c. 1849)
Lehmann, Lotte (1888–1976)
Lenclos, Ninon de (1623–1705)
Levertov, Denise (1923–1997)
Lewald, Fanny (1811–1889)
Litten, Irmgard (1879–1953)
Liubatovich, Olga (1853–1917)
Logan, Mary Cunningham (1838–1923)
Longford, Elizabeth (1906—)
Longworth, Alice Roosevelt (1884–1980)
Loos, Anita (1893–1981)
Lubetkin, Zivia (1914–1978)
Luhan, Mabel Dodge (1879–1962)
Lynn, Vera (1917—)
MacDowell, Marian (1857–1956)
Mackenzie, Jean Kenyon (1874–1936)
Madison, Dolley Payne (1768–1849)
Mahony, Marion (1871–1961)
Malraux, Clara (c. 1897–1982)
Mana-Zucca (1887–1981)
Mancini, Hortense (1646–1699)
Mandelstam, Nadezhda (1899–1980)
Manning, Olivia (1908–1980)
Manus, Rosa (1881–1942)
Marble, Alice (1913–1990)
Margaret of Valois (1553–1615)
Marie of Rumania (1875–1938)
Maritain, Raïssa (1883–1960)
Markham, Beryl (1902–1986)
Markova, Alicia (1910–2004)
Marlowe, Julia (1866–1950)
Mary II (1662–1694)
Masaryk, Alice Garrigue (1879–1966)
McBride, Mary Margaret (1899–1976)
McCarthy, Mary (1912–1989)
McGinley, Phyllis (1905–1978)
McKenna, Siobhan (1922–1986)
Mead, Margaret (1901–1978)
Meir, Golda (1898–1978)
Menken, Adah Isaacs (1835–1868)
Merman, Ethel (1912–1984)
Merritt, Anna Lea (1844–1930)
Meysenburg, Malwida von (1816–1903)
Michaëlis, Karin (1872–1950)
Michel, Louise (1830–1905)
Milligan, Alice (1866–1953)
Min, Anchee (1957—)
Mistinguett (1875–1956)
Mitchison, Naomi (1897–1999)
Modjeska, Helena (1840–1909)
Monroe, Harriet (1860–1936)
Montagu-Douglas-Scott, Alice (1901–2004)
Montez, Lola (1818–1861)
Montiel, Sarita (1928—)
Montpensier, Anne Marie Louise d'Orléans, Duchesse de (1627–1693)
Moody, Anne (1940—)
Moore, Jane Elizabeth (1738–?)
Morgan, Sydney (1780–1859)
Morrell, Ottoline (1873–1938)
Mortimer, Penelope (1918–1999)
Motteville, Françoise Bertaut de (c. 1621–1689)
Murasaki Shikibu (c. 973–c. 1015)
Murat, Henriette Julie de (1670–1716)
Murphy, Emily (1868–1933)
Negri, Pola (1894–1987)
Nemours, Marie d'Orleans, duchess de (c. 1625–1707)
Nguyen Thi Dinh (1920–1992)
Niboyet, Eugénie (1797–1883)
Nielsen, Asta (1881–1972)
Nielsen, Jerri (1953—)
Nilsson, Birgit (1918—)
O'Casey, Eileen (1900–1995)
Odoevtseva, Irina (c. 1895–1990)
O'Faolain, Nuala (1940—)
Oldfield, Anne (1683–1730)
Olivier, Fernande (1884–1966)
O'Neill, Eliza (1791–1872)
önhoff, Marion, Countess (1909–2002)
Opie, Amelia (1769–1853)
Otero, Caroline (1868–1965)
Pàmies, Teresa (1919—)
Panaeva, Avdotia (c. 1819–1893)
Pankhurst, Sylvia (1882–1960)
Partridge, Frances (1900–2004)
Pelletier, Madeleine (1874–1939)
Perkins, Frances (1880–1965)
Peter, Sarah Worthington (1800–1877)
Pichler, Karoline (1769–1843)
Pilkington, Laetitia (c. 1708–1750)
Rachel (1821–1858)
Radcliffe, Mary Ann (c. 1746–after 1810)
Rainer, Luise (1910—)
Rama Rau, Santha (1923—)
Ramsay, Martha Laurens (1759–1811)
Ratushinskaya, Irina (1954—)
Reagan, Nancy (1921—)
Récamier, Juliette (1777–1849)
Reynolds, Rachel Selina (1838–1928)
Rich, Mary (1625–1678)
Richardson, Henry Handel (1870–1946)
Richter, Gisela (1882–1972)
Riding, Laura (1901–1991)
Ristori, Adelaide (1822–1906)
Robespierre, Charlotte (1760–1840)
Robins, Elizabeth (1862–1952)
Robinson, Mary (1758–1800)
Roland, Betty (1903–1996)
Roland, Madame (1754–1793)
Rowlandson, Mary (c. 1635–after 1682)
Saint Mars, Gabrielle de (1804–1872)
Salomon, Alice (1872–1948)
Samaroff, Olga (1882–1948)
Sarton, May (1912–1995)
Schopenhauer, Johanna (1766–1838)
Seeley, Blossom (1891–1974)
Sert, Misia (1872–1950)
Shaarawi, Huda (1879–1947)
Shafik, Doria (1908–1975)
Shaginian, Marietta (1888–1982)
Sheridan, Frances (1724–1766)
Sherwood, Mary Elizabeth (1826–1903)
Shiubhlaigh, Maire Nic (1884–1958)
Signoret, Simone (1921–1985)
Singer, Winnaretta (1865–1943)
Sitwell, Edith (1887–1964)
Smyth, Ethel (1858–1944)
Söderbaum, Kristina (1912—)
Somerville, Mary Fairfax (1780–1872)
Sorabji, Cornelia (1866–1954)
Soysal, Sevgi (1936–1976)
Spiel, Hilde (1911–1990)
Staal de Launay, Madame de (1684–1750)
Stanhope, Hester (1776–1839)
Stein, Gertrude (1874–1946)
Stern, G.B. (1890–1973)
Strauss und Torney, Lulu von (1873–1956)
Street, Jessie (1889–1970)
Stuart, Louisa (1757–1851)
Suttner, Bertha von (1843–1914)
Suzman, Helen (1917—)
Swarthout, Gladys (1904–1969)
Tarbell, Ida (1857–1944)
Taylor, Ann (1782–1866)
Taylor, Jane (1783–1824)
Taylor, Susie King (1848–1912)
Teffi, N.A. (1872–1952)
Tennant, Emma (1937—)
Tergit, Gabrielle (1894–1982)
Terry, Ellen (1847–1928)
Thaden, Louise (1905–1979)
Thatcher, Margaret (1925—)
Thirkell, Angela (1890–1961)
Thomas, Caitlin (1913–1994)
Thompson, Marion Beatrice (1877–1964)
Thornton, Alice (1626–c. 1707)
Trefusis, Violet (1894–1972)
Trench, Melesina (1768–1827)
Truth, Sojourner (c. 1797–1883)
Tsebrikova, M.K. (1835–1917)
Tsunoda, Fusako (1914—)
Tussaud, Marie (1761–1850)
Tynan, Katharine (1861–1931)
Ullrich, Luise (1911–1985)
Utley, Freda (1898–1977)
Vallette, Marguerite (1860–1953)
Vanderbilt, Gloria (1924—)
Verne, Mathilde (1865–1936)
Verney, Margaret Maria (1844–1930)
Vestris, Lucia (1797–1856)
Vigée-Le Brun, Elisabeth (1755–1842)
von Moltke, Freya (b. 1911)
Vreeland, Diana (1903–1989)
Waciuma, Charity (1936—)
Wald, Lillian D. (1867–1940)
Wallmann, Margarethe (1901–19922)
Ward, Mrs. Humphry (1851–1920)
Washburn, Margaret Floy (1871–1939)
Weiss, Louise (1893–1983)
Werner, Ilse (1918—)
West, Jessamyn (1902–1984)
West, Mae (1893–1980)
Wilhelmina (1880–1962)
Windsor, Wallis Warfield, duchess of (1895–1986)
Wiskemann, Elizabeth Meta (1899–1971)
Wong, Jade Snow (1919—)
Wood, Peggy (1892–1978)
Yang Jiang (b. 1911)
Young, Ella (1867–1951)
Zapolska, Gabriela (1857–1921)
Zlatin, Sabina (1907–1996)

MENOMINEE
Deer, Ada (1935—)

MENTAL-HEALTH REFORMER
Anderson, Elizabeth Milbank (1850–1921)
Barnard, Kate (1875–1930)
Bear-Crawford, Annette (1853–1899)
Bradwell, Myra (1831–1894)
Bridgman, Laura (1829–1889)
Calderone, Mary Steichen (1904–1998)
Carey, Miriam E. (1858–1937)
Carter, Rosalynn (1927—)
Dix, Dorothea Lynde (1802–1887)
Grossinger, Jennie (1892–1972)
Hobson, Valerie (1917–1998)
Hogg, Ima (1882–1975)
Holm, Celeste (1919—)
Horney, Karen (1885–1952)
Jacobi, Mary Putnam (1842–1906)
Jansen, Elly (1929—)

Jarvis, Lucy (1919—)
Jones, Jennifer (1919—)
Kübler-Ross, Elisabeth (1926–2004)
Kuhn, Maggie (1905–1995)
Lasker, Mary (1900–1994)
Marina of Greece (1906–1968)
Martin, Lillien Jane (1851–1943)
Mead, Margaret (1901–1978)
Packard, Elizabeth (1816–1897)
Perry, Eleanor (1915–1981)
Rapoport, Lydia (1923–1971)
Roosevelt, Eleanor (1884–1962)
Rye, Maria Susan (1829–1903)
Seaman, Elizabeth Cochrane (1864–1922)
Shriver, Eunice Kennedy (1921—)
Silvia Sommerlath (1943—)
Slagle, Eleanor Clarke (1871–1942)
Stafford, Jo (1920—)
Taft, Jessie (1882–1960)
Tierney, Gene (1920–1991)
Towle, Charlotte (1896–1966)
Vance, Vivian (1909–1979)
Wald, Florence (1917—)
Wald, Patricia McGowan (1928—)

MERCHANT/TRADER
See also Merchant/Trader.
Amlingyn, Katherine (fl. late-15th c.)
Astor, Sarah Todd (1761–1832)
Barron, Hannah Ward (1829–1898)
Bibby, Mary Ann (c. 1832–1910)
Coory, Shirefie (c. 1864–1950)
Cripps, Sarah Ann (c. 1821–1892)
Cuddie, Mary (1823–1889)
Diamond, Ann (c. 1827–1881)
Doo, Unui (1873/75?–1940)
Durgawati (d. 1564)
Fingerin, Agnes (d. 1515)
Fugger, Barbara Baesinger (d. 1497)
Furley, Matilda (1813–1899)
Glückel of Hameln (1646–1724)
Goddard, Mary Katherine (1738–1816)
Greenaway, Margaret (fl. 15th c.)
Hirst, Grace (1805–1901)
Hood, Mary (c. 1822–1902)
Inyama, Rosemary (b. 1903)
Khadijah (c. 555–619)
Kirkeby, Elizabeth (fl. 1482)
LaForge, Margaret Getchell (1841–1880)
Langton, Jane (fl. 15th c.)
Lecavella, Mabilia (fl. 1206)
Lo Keong, Matilda (c. 1854–1915)
Lovell, Ann (1803/11–1869)
McHugh, Fanny (1861–1943)
Meech, Matilda (c. 1825–1907)
Milne, Mary Jane (1840–1921)
Monnier, Adrienne (c. 1892–1955)
Musgrove, Mary (c. 1690–c. 1763)
Nasi, Gracia Mendes (1510–1569)
Nzimiro, Mary (1898–1993)
O'Donnell, Ann (c. 1857–1934)
Okwei of Osomari (1872–1943)
Pelham, Mary Singleton Copley (c. 1710–1789)
Philipse, Margaret Hardenbrook (d. 1690)
Ponten, Clare van der (fl. 14th c.)
Pope, Maria Sophia (1818–1909)
Ralfe, Catherine Hester (c. 1831–1912)
Richards, Ellen Swallow (1842–1911)
Rose of Burford (fl. 15th c.)
Russell, Margery (d. around 1380)
Smith, Helen Hay (1873–1918)
Taylor, Mary (1817–1893)
Te Rau-o-te-rangi, Kahe (?–c. 1871)
Toguri, Iva (1916—)
Van Chu-Lin (1893/94?–1946)
Wetherill, Louisa Wade (1877–1945)
Wollerin, Cecilie (d. 1341)
Yates, Ngawini (1852/53?–1910)

METALLURGIST
Tipper, Constance (1894–1995)

METEOROLOGIST
White, Margaret (c. 1888–1977)

MICROBIOLOGIST
Alexander, Hattie (1901–1968)
Branham, Sara Elizabeth (1888–1962)
Colwell, Rita R. (1934—)
Dick, Gladys (1881–1963)
Eddy, Bernice (b. 1903)
Ermoleva, Zinaida (1898–1974)
Evans, Alice Catherine (1881–1975)
Fleming, Amalia (1912–1986)
Franklin, Rosalind (1920–1958)
Friend, Charlotte (1921–1987)
Hobby, Gladys Lounsbury (1910–1993)
Kendrick, Pearl L. (1890–1980)
Lancefield, Rebecca Craighill (1895–1981)
Levy, Julia (1934—)
Margulis, Lynn (1938—)
McCoy, Elizabeth (1903–1978)
Millis, Nancy (1922—)
Panagiotatou, Angeliki (1878–1954)
Stewart, Sarah (1906–1976)
Williams, Anna Wessels (1863–1954)

MICROSCOPIST
Ward, Mary (1827–1869)

MIDWIFE
Agnodice (fl. 4th c. BCE)
Aragon, Jesusita (1908—)
Armstrong, Penny (1946—)
Bagley, Amelia (1870–1956)
Ballard, Martha Moore (1735–1812)
Beeman, Ruth Coates (1925—)
Bettjeman, Agnes Muir (1885–1964)
Boivin, Marie Anne (1773–1847)
Bourgeois, Louise (1563–1636)
Breckinridge, Mary (1881–1965)
Brownrigg, Elizabeth (1720–1767)
Burgess, Georgina Jane (c. 1839–1904)
Burgess, Renate (1910–1988)
Burton, Pearlie (1904–1993)
Callen, Maude (1899–1990)
Carran, Catherine (1842–1935)
Catchpole, Margaret (1762–1819)
Cellier, Elizabeth (fl. 1679)
Cripps, Sarah Ann (c. 1821–1892)
Cuddie, Mary (1823–1889)
Darragh, Lydia Barrington (1729–1789)
Darton, Patience (1911–1996)
Diamond, Ann (c. 1827–1881)
Du Coudray, Angélique (1712–1789)
Erickson, Hilda (1859–1968)
Ernst, Kitty (1926—)
Evans, Ann (c. 1836–1916)
Farrer, Margaret (1914–1997)
Fergusson, Elizabeth (1867–1930)
Figner, Vera (1852–1942)
Fowler, Lydia Folger (1822–1879)
Führer, Charlotte (1834–1907)
Gaskin, Ina May (1940—)
Goggans, Lalla (1906–1987)
Gordon, Eliza (1877–1938)
Hale, Mamie O. (1911–c. 1968)
Hamilton, Elizabeth Jane (1805–1897)
Harrold, Agnes (c. 1830–1903)
Hei, Akenehi (1877/78?–1910)
Héricourt, Jenny Poinsard d' (1809–1875)
Hersende of France (fl. 1250)
Hicks, Adelaide (1845–1930)
Higgins, Sarah (1830–1923)
Hirst, Grace (1805–1901)
Hogan, Aileen I. (1899–1981)
Holford, Alice Hannah (1867–1966)
Hutchinson, Anne (1591–1643)
Inglis, Helen Clyde (1867–1945)
Jacobsen, Inger Kathrine (1867–1939)
James, Susan Gail (1953—)
Kéita, Aoua (1912–1979)
Lais (fl. 1st c. BCE)
Lang, Raven (1942—)
Leonard, Carol L. (1950—)
Logan, Onnie Lee (c. 1910–1995)
Lubic, Ruth Watson (1927—)
Mackay, Maria Jane (1844–1933)
Mageras, Georgia Lathouris (1867–1950)
Manicom, Jacqueline (1938–1976)
Martin, Mother Mary (1892–1975)
Mason, Biddy (1818–1891)
McDougall, Adelaide (1909–2000)
McHugh, Fanny (1861–1943)
McKain, Douglas Mary (1789–1873)
McNaught, Rose (1893–1978)
Milton, Gladys (1924–1999)
Murdaugh, Angela (1940—)
Nichols, Etta Grigsby (1897–1994)
Nihell, Elizabeth (1723–after 1772)
Osburn, Lucy (1835–1891)
Paget, Nielsine (1858–1932)
Paget, Rosalind (1855–1948)
Pelletier, Henriette (c. 1864–1961)
Pérez, Eulalia Arrila de (c. 1773–c. 1878)
Peterson, Mary (1927—)
Player, Mary Josephine (c. 1857–1924)
Porn, Hanna (1860–1913)
Preshaw, Jane (1839–1926)
Reinders, Agnes (1913–1993)
Retter, Hannah (1839–1940)
Richardson, Luba Lyons (1949—)
Ross, Marie-Henriette LeJeune (1762–1860)
Schmahl, Jeanne (1846–1916)
Schrader, Catharina Geertuida (1656–1745)
Sessions, Patty Bartlett (1795–1892)
Smith, Margaret Charles (b. 1906)
Stephenson, Elsie (1916–1967)
Trotula (c. 1040s–1097)
Van Blarcom, Carolyn (1879–1960)
Ventre, Fran (1941—)
Voilquin, Suzanne (1801–1877)
Wattleton, Faye (1943—)
Willeford, Mary B. (1900–1941)
Willums, Sigbrit (fl. 1507–1523)
Wood, Audrey (1908–1998)
Zakrzewska, Marie (1829–1902)

MILITARY ENGINEER
Tereshkova, Valentina (1937—)

MILITARY LEADER
Abdellah, Faye Glenn (1919—)
Adams, Charity (1917–2002)
Aldrude (fl. 1172)
Almeida, Brites de (fl. 1385)
Ambree, Mary (fl. 1584)
André, Valerie (1922—)
Ashcraft, Juanita (1921—2000)
Azurduy de Padilla, Juana (1781–1862)
Botchkareva, Maria (1889–?)
Bouboulina, Laskarina (1771–1825)
Brewer, Margaret A. (1930—)
Brownell, Kady (b. 1842)
Brûlon, Angélique (1772–1859)
Bui Thi Xuan (d. 1771)
Catherine de Clermont (fl. 16th c.)
Cloelia (c. 508 BCE)
Constance de Cezelli (d. 1617)

Davis, Dorothy Hilliard (1917–1994)
Duerk, Alene B. (1920—)
Durova, Nadezhda (1783–1866)
Erauso, Catalina de (1592–1635)
Fields, Evelyn J.
Flikke, Julia Otteson (1879–1965)
Fu Hao (fl. 1040 BCE)
Furse, Katharine (1875–1952)
Gallina, Juliane (1970—)
Gambara, Veronica (1485–1550)
Hallaren, Mary A. (1907–2005)
Herrick, Hermione Ruth (1889–1983)
Hetha (fl. 10th c.)
Hobby, Oveta Culp (1905–1995)
Hōjo Masako (1157–1225)
Holm, Jeanne (1921—)
Hopper, Grace Murray (1906–1992)
Horton, Mildred McAfee (1900–1994)
Isabelle of Lorraine (1410–1453)
Jacqueline of Hainault (1401–1436)
Jeanne des Armoises (fl. 1438)
Jingū (c. 201–269)
Joan of Arc (c. 1412–1431)
Kelley, Beverly Gwinn (c. 1952—)
Kuczinski, Ruth (1907–2000)
Longabarba, Bona (fl. 15th c.)
Margaret of Attenduli (1375–?)
Marzia (fl. 1357)
Mathews, Vera Laughton (1888–1959)
May, Geraldine (1895–1997)
Nur Jahan (1577–1645)
Peake, Felicity (1913–2002)
Read, Deborah (1707–1774)
Reals, Gail (c. 1937—)
Rodiani, Onorata (d. 1452)
Stimson, Julia (1881–1948)
Stratton, Dorothy (b. 1899)
Streeter, Ruth Cheney (1895–1990)
Tamara (1160–1212)
Towle, Katherine (1898–1986)
Valasca (fl. 738)
Waddy, Harriet (1904–1999)
Wa Shi (1498–1560)
Weed, Ethel (1906–1975)
Widnall, Sheila (1938—)

MILITARY NURSE
See Combat nurse.

MILITARY STRATEGIST
Nur Jahan (1577–1645)
Thusnelda (fl. 1st c.)

MILLINER
Bagley, Sarah (b. 1806)
Carnegie, Hattie (1886–1956)
Chandler, Mary (1687–1745)
Chanel, Coco (1883–1971)
Cohen, Myra (1892–1959)
Daché, Lilly (1898–1989)
Demorest, Ellen Curtis (1824–1898)
Duniway, Abigail Scott (1834–1915)
Edmonds, Emma (1841–1898)
Evans, Edith (1888–1976)
Hyde, Ida (1857–1945)
Ihrer, Emma (1857–1911)
Manley, Effa (1900–1981)
Mansfield, Arabella (1846–1911)
McCracken, Mary Ann (1770–1866)
McMein, Neysa (1888–1949)
Milne, Mary Jane (1840–1921)
Miranda, Carmen (1909–1955)
Tailleferre, Germaine (1892–1983)
Way, Amanda M. (1828–1914)

MILLOWNER
Gardner, Margaret (1844–1929)

MILLWORKER
Cochran, Jacqueline (1906–1980)
Conboy, Sara McLaughlin (1870–1928)
Cope, Mother Marianne (1838–1918)
Corrigan, Mairead (b. 1944)
Emhart, Maria (1901–1981)
Farley, Harriet (1813–1907)
Fields, Gracie (1898–1979)
Knight, Margaret E. (1838–1914)
Larcom, Lucy (1824–1893)
Lee, Ann (1736–1784)
Murphy, Lizzie (1894–1964)
Robinson, Harriet Hanson (1825–1911)
Van Vorst, Marie Louise (1867–1936)

MIME
Colette (1873–1954)
Enters, Angna (1907–1989)
Genée, Adeline (1878–1970)
Goslar, Lotte (1907–1997)
Hendel, Henriette (1772–1849)
Kshesinskaia, Matilda (1872–1971)
Lopez, Encarnación (1898–1945)
Markham, Pauline (d. 1919)
Masina, Giulietta (1920–1994)
Nielsen, Asta (1881–1972)
Pagliero, Camilia (1859–1925)
Picon, Molly (1898–1992)
Regina, Elis (1945–1982)
Turner, Florence E. (c. 1888–1946)
Ulanova, Galina (1910–1998)

MINIATURIST
Beale, Mary (1632–1699)
Capet, Gabrielle (1761–1817)
Carriera, Rosalba (1675–1757)
Cosway, Maria (1759–1838)
Donatella (fl. 1271)
Edwards, Henrietta Muir (1849–1933)
Firenze, Francesca da (fl. 15th c.)
Fragonard, Marie Anne (1745–c. 1823)
Fuller, Lucia Fairchild (1870–1224)
Goodridge, Sarah (1788–1853)
Hall, Anne (1792–1863)
Herbelin, Jeanne Mathilde (1820–1904)
Landseer, Jessica (1810–1880)
Peale, Anna Claypoole (1791–1878)
Peale, Margaretta Angelica (1795–1882)
Peale, Sarah Miriam (1800–1885)
Teerlinc, Levina (c. 1520–1576)
Vandamm, Florence (1883–1966)

MINING ENGINEER
Hahn, Emily (1905–1997)
Richards, Ellen Swallow (1842–1911)

MINING ENTREPRENEUR
Ralph, Margaret (c. 1822–1913)

MINISTER
See Clergy.
See Government official.

MISS AMERICA
Aiken, Kimberly (c. 1975—)
Akin, Susan (c. 1964—)
Axum, Donna (c. 1924—)
Ay, Evelyn (c. 1934—)
Baraquio, Angela Perez (1976—)
Barker, Kylene (c. 1956—)
Barnes, Debra Dene (c. 1947—)
Bartel, Jean (c. 1924—)
Benham, Dorothy (c. 1956—)
Bergeron, Marian (1918–2002)
Betbeze, Yolande (1930—)
Bryant, Deborah (c. 1946—)
Buferd, Marilyn (1925–1990)
Burke, Frances (c. 1921—)
Campbell, Mary Katherine (1905–1990)
Carlson, Gretchen (c. 1966—)
Cash, Kellye (c. 1965—)
Charles, Suzette (1963—)
Cooper, Bette (c. 1920—)
Cornett, Leanza (1971—)
Cothran, Shirley (c. 1953—)
Coyle, Rose (1914–1988)
Delander, Lois (1911–1985)
Dennison, Jo-Carroll (c. 1924—)
Donnelly, Patricia (c. 1920—)
Downs, Deirdre (c. 1980—)
Dunlap, Ericka (1982—)
Eldred, Pam (c. 1948—)
Fleming, Nancy (c. 1941—)
Fletcher, Maria (c. 1942—)
Ford, Judith (c. 1950—)
French, Heather (1974—)
George, Phyllis (1949—)
Gorman, Margaret (1905–1995)
Gracen, Elizabeth (1960—)
Harman, Katie Marie (c. 1980—)
Harold, Erika (c. 1980—)
Hawkes, Sharlene (c. 1964—)
Holland, Tara Dawn (c. 1972—)
Hutchins, Colleen Kay (c. 1927—)
Johnson, Nicole (c. 1974—)
King, Rebecca (c. 1950—)
Langley, Neva (c. 1934—)
Lanphier, Fay (1906–1959)
LaPlanche, Rosemary (1923–1979)
Leaver, Henrietta (c. 1916–1993)
Little, Tawny (c. 1957—)
Maffett, Debra Sue (c. 1957—)
Malcomson, Ruth (1906–1988)
Mayer, Jacquelyn (c. 1942—)
McKnight, Marian (c. 1937—)
Mead, Lynda Lee (c. 1939—)
Meeuwsen, Terry (1949—)
Mercer, Jacque (1931–1982)
Meriwether, Lee Ann (1935—)
Meseke, Marilyn (1916–2001)
Mobley, Mary Ann (1939—)
Perkins, Susan (c. 1954—)
Powell, Susan (c. 1959—)
Prewitt, Cheryl (c. 1957—)
Rafko, Kaye Lani (c. 1963—)
Ramey, Venus (c. 1925—)
Ritchie, Sharon Kay (c. 1937—)
Sapp, Carolyn (1967—)
Schaefer, Laurel Lea (c. 1949—)
Shindle, Kate (1979—)
Shopp, BeBe (1930—)
Smallwood, Norma (c. 1908–1966)
Smith, Shawntel (1971—)
Turner, Debbye (1966—)
Van Derbur, Marilyn (c. 1937—)
Van Dyke, Vonda Kay (c. 1944—)
Vincent, Marjorie (c. 1965—)
Walker, Barbara Jo (1926–2000)
Whitestone, Heather (c. 1973—)
Williams, Vanessa (1963—)

MISSIONARY
Alexander, Jessie (1876–1962)
Avery, Martha (1851–1929)
Aylward, Gladys (1902–1970)
Bailey, Hannah Johnston (1839–1923)
Baldwin, Charlotte Fowler (1805–1873)
Bayne, Margaret (1798–1835)
Bedell, Harriet M. (1875–1969)
Bell, Laura (1829–1894)
Bellamy, Elizabeth (1845–1940)
Berthgyth (fl. 8th c.)
Bethune, Mary McLeod (1875–1955)

Bickerdyke, Mary Ann (1817–1901)
Bingham, Sybil Moseley (1792–1848)
Bishop, Harriet E. (1817–1883)
Bonney, Mary Lucinda (1816–1900)
Booth-Tucker, Emma Moss (1860–1903)
Bridgman, Eliza Jane (1805–1871)
Bulstrode, Emily Mary (1867–1959)
Bulstrode, Jane Helena (1862–1946)
Cable, Mildred (1878–1952)
Cameron, Donaldina (1869–1968)
Carmichael, Amy (1867–1971)
Carvajal, Luisa de (1568–1614)
Chapman, Anne Maria (1791–1855)
Colenso, Elizabeth (1821–1904)
Cope, Mother Marianne (1838–1918)
Coppin, Fanny Jackson (1837–1913)
Dean, Jennie (1852–1913)
Denton, Mary Florence (1837–1947)
Doremus, Sarah Platt (1802–1877)
Dryburgh, Margaret (1890–1945)
Duchesne, Rose Philippine (1769–1852)
Farrar, Cynthia (1795–1862)
Fisher, Mary (c. 1623–1698)
Fiske, Fidelia (1816–1864)
Frame, Alice (1878–1941)
French, Evangeline (1869–1960)
French, Francesca (1871–1960)
Fulton, Mary Hannah (1854–1927)
Gittos, Marianne (1830–1908)
Gulick, Alice Gordon (1847–1903)
Hall, Rosetta Sherwood (1865–1951)
Hayden, Mother Mary Bridget (1814–1890)
Haygood, Laura Askew (1845–1900)
Henry, Annie (1879–1971)
Hill, Frances Mulligan (1799–1884)
Hobhouse, Emily (1860–1926)
James, Annie Isabella (1884–1965)
Jones, Sybil (1808–1873)
Judson, Ann Hasseltine (1789–1826)
Judson, Emily Chubbuck (1817–1854)
Judson, Sarah Boardman (1803–1845)
Kemp, Charlotte (1790–1860)
Kissling, Margaret (1808–1891)
Krüdener, Julie de (1764–1824)
Kugler, Anna Sarah (1856–1930)
Leavitt, Mary (1830–1912)
Lee, Ann (1736–1784)
Lioba (700–779)
Livingstone, Mary Moffatt (1820–1862)
Mackenzie, Jean Kenyon (1874–1936)
Mance, Jeanne (1606–1673)
Martin, Mother Mary (1892–1975)
McBeth, Susan Law (1830–1893)
Mills, Susan Tolman (1825–1912)
Miner, Sarah Luella (1861–1935)
Moffatt, Mary Smith (1795–1870)
Montgomery, Helen Barrett (1861–1934)
Moon, Lottie (1840–1912)
Moore, Mary Emelia (1869–1951)
Nagle, Nano (1718–1784)
Newell, Harriet Atwood (1793–1812)
Newman, Angelia L. (1837–1910)
Newman, Mehetabel (c. 1822–1908)
Patrick, Mary Mills (1850–1940)
Peabody, Lucy (1861–1949)
Polyblank, Ellen Albertina (1840–1930)
Priscilla (fl. 1st c.)
Rask, Gertrud (fl. 1721)
Reed, Mary (1854–1943)
Robertson, Ann Worcester (1826–1905)
Rogers, Elizabeth Ann (1829–1921)
Rymill, Mary Ann (c. 1817–1897)
Schnackenberg, Annie Jane (1835–1905)
Schuyler, Philippa Duke (1931–1967)
Scudder, Ida (1870–1960)
Slessor, Mary (1848–1915)
Smith, Amanda Berry (1837–1915)
Smith, Frances Hagell (1877–1948)
Soule, Caroline White (1824–1903)
Spalding, Eliza (1807–1851)
Stockton, Betsey (c. 1798–1865)
Swain, Clara A. (1834–1910)
Talcott, Eliza (1836–1911)
Taylor, Annie Royle (1855–c. 1920)
Teresa, Mother (1910–1997)
Thoburn, Isabella (1840–1901)
Thurston, Lucy (1795–1876)
Thurston, Matilda (1875–1958)
Tucker, Charlotte Maria (1821–1893)
Underwood, Lillias (1851–1921)
Vautrin, Minnie (1886–1941)
Vincent, Mother (1819–1892)
Von Trapp, Maria (1905–1987)
Walpurgis (c. 710–777)
Whitman, Narcissa (1808–1847)
Williams, Jane (c. 1801–1896)
Williams, Marianne (1793–1879)
Wilson, Margaret Bush (1919—)
Wohlers, Eliza (c. 1812–1891)
Wood, Mary Elizabeth (1861–1931)
Wright, Helena (1887–1982)
Wright, Laura Maria (1809–1886)

MISTRESS
See Paramour.

MODEL
Adams, Jane (1921—)
Arletty (1898–1992)
Brooks, Romaine (1874–1970)
Calder, Liz (1938—)
Campbell, Naomi (1970—)
Collier, Constance (1878–1955)
Crawford, Cindy (1966—)
Dali, Gala (1894–1982)
del Giocondo, Lisa (1474–?)
Dirie, Waris (1967—)
Dolores (c. 1890–1975)
Doscher, Doris (1882–1970)
Dove, Billie (1900–1997)
Drinker, Ernesta (1852–1939)
Eluard, Nusch (1906–1946)
Emmons, Chansonetta Stanley (1858–1937)
Evangelista, Linda (1965—)
Fenwick, Millicent (1910–1992)
Fernandez, Alina (1956—)
Flöge, Emilie (1874–1952)
Forbes, Mary Elizabeth (1879–1964)
Ford, Betty (1918—)
Gibson, Irene Langhorne (1873–1956)
Gonzalès, Eva (1849–1883)
Goulue, La (1869–1929)
Greene, Angela (1921–1978)
Hessling, Catherine (1899–1979)
Hite, Shere (1943—)
Jones, Grace (1952—)
King, Dottie (c. 1896–1923)
Leslie, Lisa (1972—)
Maar, Dora (1907–1997)
MacDonald, Jeanette (1903–1965)
McNamara, Maggie (1928–1978)
Merkel, Una (1903–1986)
Miller, Lee (1907–1977)
Monica (1980—)
Montesi, Wilma (1932–1953)
Morris, Jane Burden (1839–1914)
Munson, Audrey (1891–1996)
Nesbit, Evelyn (1884–1967)
Nico (1938–1988)
Nin, Anais (1903–1977)
Novak, Kim (1933—)
Olivier, Fernande (1884–1966)
Parker, Suzy (1932–1932)
Phryne (c. 365–c. 295 BCE)
Quirot, Ana (1963—)
Rhys, Jean (1890–1979)
Schiffer, Claudia (1970—)
Sert, Misia (1872–1950)
Shrimpton, Jean (1942—)
Siddal, Elizabeth (1829–1862)
Simon, Simone (1910–2005)
Sims, Naomi (1948—)
Twiggy (1946—)
Valadon, Suzanne (1865–1938)
Vespucci, Simonetta (d. 1476)
Wright, Patience Lovell (1725–1786)

MONEYLENDER
See Banker/financier.

MOSAIC ARTIST
Hermes, Gertrude (1901–1983)
Hone, Evie (1894–1955)
Lundeberg, Helen (1908–1999)
Oakley, Violet (1874–1961)
Rhind, Ethel (c. 1879–1952)

MOTORCYCLIST
Halliday, Margaret (1956—)
Hotchkiss, Avis (fl. 1915)
Hotchkiss, Effie (fl. 1915)
O'Neil, Kitty (1947—)
Robinson, Dot (1912–1999)
Stringfield, Bessie B. (1912–1993)
Van Buren, Adeline (1894–1949)
Van Buren, Augusta

MOUNTAIN BIKER
Brutsaert, Elke (1968—)
Chausson, Anne-Caroline (1977—)
Cline, Aleisha (1970—)
Csizmazia, Kim (c. 1968—)
Elliott, Cheri (1970—)
Giove, Missy (1972—)
Llanes, Tara (1976—)
Miller, Katrina (1975—)
Sher, Lisa (1969—)
Streb, Marla (1965—)

MOUNTAINEER
Allen, Tori (1988—)
Barnicoat, Constance Alice (1872–1922)
Bell, Gertrude (1868–1926)
Benham, Gertrude (1867–1938)
Bertolini, Livia (fl. 1920s–1930s)
Blum, Arlene (1945—)
Bodet, Stéphanie (1976—)
Boulaz, Loulou (1912—)
Bozzino, Tina (fl. 1920s–30s)
Bristow, Lily (fl. 1890s)
Brooks, Matilda M. (1888–1981)
Carrel, Felicite (fl. 1860s)
d'Angeville, Henriette (1795–1871)
de Gaulle, Yvonne (1900–1979)
Destivelle, Catherine (1960—)
Du Faur, Emmeline Freda (1882–1935)
Gardiner, Kate (1885–1974)
Geiringer, Hilda (1893–1973)
Hargreaves, Alison (1962–1995)
Holmes, Julia Archibald (1838–1887)
Keen, Dora (1871–1963)
Kelly, Emily (d. 1922)
Kogan, Claude (1919–1959)
Le Blond, Elizabeth (1861–1934)
Lehmann, Inge (1888–1993)
Lignell, Kristen (c. 1965—)
Lindner, Herta (1920–1943)
Lorimer, Margaret (1866–1954)
MacInnes, Helen (1907–1985)

Moffat, Gwen (1924—)
Morin, Micheline (fl. 1930s)
Morin, Nea (1906–1986)
Namba, Yasuko (1949–1996)
O'Brien, Miriam (1898–1976)
Paradis, Marie (fl. 1808)
Peck, Annie Smith (1850–1935)
Petherick, Mary (fl. 1887)
Pigeon, Anna (fl. 1860s)
Pigeon, Ellen (fl. 1860s)
Pilley, Dorothy (1893–1986)
Richardson, Katy (1864–1927)
Roberts, Mary Louise (1886–1968)
Ross, Forrestina Elizabeth (1860–1936)
Rutkiewicz, Wanda (1943—)
Stevenson, Greta Barbara (1911–1990)
Tabei, Junko (1939—)
Thomson, Jane (1858–1944)
Tullis, Julie (1939–1986)
Vaucher, Yvette (1929—)
Walker, Lucy (1836–1916)
Workman, Fanny (1859–1925)

MOVEMENT FOUNDER
Abaijah, Josephine (1942—)
Angela of Brescia (1474–1540)
Balabanoff, Angelica (1878–1965)
Ben Zvi, Rachel Yanait (1886–1979)
Dalrymple, Learmonth White (1827–1906)
Darling, Flora (1840–1910)
David, Caroline Edgeworth (1856–1951)
Dennett, Mary Ware (1872–1947)
Dransfeld, Hedwig (1871–1925)
Hopkins, Emma Curtis (1853–1925)
Li Qingzhao (1083–c. 1151)
Low, Juliette Gordon (1860–1927)
Saunders, Cicely (1918–2005)

MURALIST
Barker, Cicely Mary (1895–1973)
Cassatt, Mary (1844–1926)
Delaunay, Sonia (1885–1979)
Florence, Mary Sargant (1857–1954)
Goldthwaite, Anne Wilson (1869–1944)
Greenwood, Marion (1909–1980)
Krasner, Lee (1908–1984)
Low, Mary Fairchild (1858–1946)
Magafan, Ethel (1916–1993)
Magafan, Jenne (1916–1952)
Oakley, Violet (1874–1961)
Pankhurst, Sylvia (1882–1960)
Perkins, Lucy Fitch (1865–1937)
Shore, Henrietta (1880–1963)
Smith, Jessie Willcox (1863–1935)
Spencer, Lilly Martin (1822–1902)
Tait, Agnes (c. 1897–1981)
Velarde, Pablita (1918—)
Vieira da Silva, Maria Elena (1908–1992)
Weir, Irene (1862–1944)
Zorach, Marguerite Thompson (1887–1968)

MURDERER (ACCUSED)
Adams, Millicent (1942—)
Adler, Lydia (1704–?)
Allen, Margaret (1906–1949)
Allitt, Beverley Gail (1969—)
Ansell, Mary (1877–1899)
Antonini, Theresa (1785–1809)
Archer-Gilligan, Amy (1869–1928)
Arden, Alice (1516–1551)
Atkins, Susan (1948—)
Baniszewski, Gertrude Wright (1929–1990)
Barber, Fanny (c. 1864–1952)
Barberi, Maria (1880–?)
Barney, Elvira Dolores (c. 1905–c. 1936)
Barry, Mary Ann (1855–1874)
Bartlett, Adelaide (c. 1856–?)
Bateman, Mary (1768–1809)
Bathory, Elizabeth (1560–1614)
Beck, Martha (c. 1921–1951)
Becker, Marie Alexander (1877–194?)
Beddingfield, Ann (1742–1763)
Bell, Mary (c. 1957—)
Bender, Kate (1849–?)
Bilansky, Ann (1820–1860)
Bjorkland, Penny (1941—)
Blandy, Mary (1719–1752)
Bolton, Mildred Mary (1886–1943)
Bompard, Gabrielle (1869–?)
Bonmartini, Linda (1873–?)
Borden, Lizzie (1860–1927)
Borelli, LaVerne (1909—)
Botkin, Cordelia (c. 1854–1910)
Bouvier, Léone (c. 1929—)
Branch, Elizabeth (1673–1740)
Bravo, Florence (1845–1878)
Brinvilliers, Marie de (1630–1676)
Broadingham, Elizabeth (d. 1776)
Brownrigg, Elizabeth (1720–1767)
Brühne, Vera (1910—)
Bryant, Charlotte (c. 1902–1936)
Burdock, Mary Ann (1805–1835)
Butchill, Elizabeth (1758–1780)
Byron, Kitty (c. 1879–?)
Cadden, Mamie (c. 1894–1959)
Caillaux, Henriette (?–1943)
Calvert, Louie (c. 1893–1926)
Carew, Edith Mary (1868–?)
Chamberlain, Lindy (1948—)
Chamblit, Rebekah (d. 1733)
Chard-Williams, Ada (c. 1876–1900)
Chesimard, Joanne (1948—)
Chivers, Elizabeth (1682–1712)
Choate, Pearl (1907–1983)
Christie, Susan (c. 1969—)
Christofi, Styllou (c. 1900–1954)
Clift, Martha (fl. 1930s)
Cole, Mary (c. 1913—)
Columbo, Patricia (1957—)
Coo, Eva (d. 1935)
Corday, Charlotte (1768–1793)
Cotton, Mary Ann (1822–1873)
Creighton, Mary Frances (1899–1936)
Crimmins, Alice (1941—)
Daly, Mary (c. 1861–1901)
Daly, Mary Agnes
Dean, Williamina (1844–1895)
De Melker, Daisy Louisa (1886–1932)
Dick, Evelyn (1922—)
Dixon, Margaret (1670–1753)
Doss, Nannie (1905–1965)
Doudet, Célestine (b. 1817)
Druse, Roxana (1846–1889)
Dubuisson, Pauline (1926—)
Dumolard, Marie (1816–?)
Durgan, Bridget (c. 1845–1867)
Dyer, Amelia Elizabeth (1839–1896)
Edmunds, Christiana (1835–1907)
Ellis, Ruth (1927–1955)
Fahmy, Marguérite Laurent (b. around 1900)
Fazekas, Mrs. Julius (d. 1929)
Fenayrou, Gabrielle (b. 1850)
Force, Julia (1860–?)
Francey, Henriette (b. around 1859)
Fromme, Lynette (1948—)
Fullam, Augusta Fairfield (1876–1914)
Garvie, Sheila (fl. 1960s)
Gilmour, Christina (c. 1824–c. 1911)
Giriat, Madame (b. 1866)
Glabe, Karen (1942—)
Goold, Maria Vere (1877–1908)
Gottfried, Gesina Margaretha (d. 1828)
Graham, Barbara Wood (1923–1955)
Green, Debora (c. 1951—)
Gregg, Christina (c. 1814–1882)
Griffin, Jane (1680–1720)
Grinder, Martha (1815–1866)
Groesbeek, Maria (1937–1970)
Gunness, Belle (1860–c. 1908)
Hahn, Anna Marie (1906–1938)
Harris, Charlotte (1819–?)
Hayes, Catherine (1690–1726)
Hindley, Myra (1942–2002)
Housden, Jane (d. 1714)
Housden, Nina (1916—)
Howard, Frances (1593–1632)
Hulme, Juliet Marion (1938—)
Hungerford, Agnes (d. 1524)
Hutchinson, Amy (1733–1750)
Ily, Nicole (1932—)
Jackson, Mary Jane (b. 1836)
Jeanneret, Marie (d. 1884)
Jeffries, Elizabeth (d. 1752)
Jeffs, Doreen (d. 1965)
Jegado, Hélène (1803–1851)
Jones, Elizabeth Marina (1926—)
Judd, Winnie Ruth (1905–1998)
Kasabian, Linda (1949—)
Kent, Constance (1844–?)
Kincaid, Jean (1579–1600)
Klimek, Tillie (1865–1936)
Knight, Mary (1749–1788)
Knorr, Frances (1868–1894)
Krenwinkel, Patricia (1947—)
Labbé, Denise (1926—)
Lacoste, Catherine
Lafarge, Marie (1816–1852)
Lalaurie, Delphine (c. 1790–?)
Lehmann, Christa (1922—)
Lemoine, Angélina (1843–?)
Lipka, Juliane (c. 1860–c. 1929)
Lusk, Grace (1878–1938)
Lyles, Anjette (1917–1977)
Major, Ethel Lillie (1890–1934)
Malcolm, Sarah (c. 1710–1733)
Manning, Maria (c. 1821–1849)
Marek, Martha Lowenstein (1904–1938)
Mason, Elizabeth (d. 1712)
Masset, Louise (c. 1863–1900)
Maybrick, Florence Elizabeth (c. 1853–1941)
McCollum, Ruby (1915—)
Mercier, Euphrasie (1823–?)
Miller, Lucille (1930—)
Milosavljeric, Ljubinka (1917—)
M'Lachlan, Jessie (c. 1834–1899)
Moynihan, Mary (c. 1903–?)
Myrtel, Hera (b. 1868)
Nathaniel, Cathy (1949—)
Newell, Susan (1893–1923)
Noziere, Violette (1915–1966)
Ogilvie, Catherine (1746–?)
Olah, Susanna (d. around 1929)
Parker, Pauline Yvonne (1938—)
Parkinson, Alice May (1889–1949)
Patterson, Nan (c. 1882–?)
Pearcey, Mary Eleanor (1866–1890)
Peete, Louise (1883–1947)
Phillips, Clara (1899Place, Martha (1848–1899)
Pledge, Sarah (d. 1752)
Rablen, Eva (1905—)
Rattenbury, Alma (c. 1904–1935)
Rendall, Martha (d. 1909)
Reymond, Claire (c. 1868–?)
Reynolds, Jane (c. 1897—)
Robinson, Henrietta (1816–1905)
Robinson, Sarah Jane (d. 1905)
Rumbold, Freda (1913—)
Sach, Amelia (1873–1902)

Saxe, Susan (1947—)
Scieri, Antoinette (fl. 1920s)
Sherman, Lydia (d. 1878)
Smart, Pamela Wojas (1967—)
Smith, Madeleine Hamilton (1835–1928)
Snyder, Ruth (1893–1928)
Spinelli, Evelita Juanita (1889–1941)
Stopa, Wanda (1899–1925)
Swett, Jane (b. 1805)
Swift, Delia (fl. 1850s)
Tarnowska, Maria (1878–1923)
Taylor, Louisa Jane (1846–1883)
Thompson, Edith (c. 1894–1923)
Tofana (1653–1723)
Toppan, Jane (1854–1938)
Tripp, Grace (1691–1710)
Turner, Anne (1576–1615)
Ursinus, Sophie (1760–1836)
Van Houten, Leslie (1949—)
Van Valkenburgh, Elizabeth (1799–1846)
Vidal, Ginette (b. 1931)
Waddingham, Dorothea (1899–1936)
Warmus, Carolyn (1964—)
Weber, Jeanne (1875–1910)
Webster, Kate (1849–1879)
Weiss, Jeanne Daniloff (1868–1891)
West, Rosemary (1953—)
Williams, Ann (d. 1753)
Wilson, Catherine (1842–1862)
Wilson, Elizabeth (d. 1786)
Worms, Pamela Lee (d. 1852)
Wuornos, Aileen (1956–2002)
Wynekoop, Alice (1870–1952)
Zillman, Bertha (d. 1893)

MURDER VICTIM (KNOWN AS)
Chotek, Sophie (1868–1914)
Collins, Addie Mae (d. 1963)
Coventry, Pamela (d. 1939)
Genovese, Kitty (1935–1964)
King, Dottie (c. 1896–1923)
Liuzzo, Viola (1925–1965)
Mills, Eleanor (1888–1922)
Montesi, Wilma (1932–1953)
Montreal Massacre (1989)
Phagan, Mary (c. 1899–1913)
Rafael, Sylvia (1938–2005)
Short, Elizabeth (1925–1947)
Simpson, Nicole Brown (1959–1994)
Tate, Sharon (1943–1969)

MUSEUM ADMINISTRATOR
Alexander, Annie Montague (1867–1949)
Barry, Iris (1895–1969)
Esteve-Coll, Elizabeth (1938—)
Force, Juliana (1876–1948)
Miller, Dorothy Canning (1904–2003)
Miner, Dorothy (1904–1973)
Quinton, Cornelia B. Sage (1876–1936)
Rebay, Hilla (1890–1967)
Winser, Beatrice (1869–1947)

MUSEUM FOUNDER
See Library/museum founder.

MUSIC ARRANGER
Austin, Lovie (1887–1972)
Crawford, Ruth (1901–1953)
Kennedy-Fraser, Marjorie (1857–1930)
Kerr, Anita (1927—)
Liston, Melba (1926—)
Suesse, Dana (1909–1987)
Thompson, Kay (1908–1998)
Vaughan, Sarah (1924–1990)
Williams, Mary Lou (1910–1981)

MUSIC COMPOSER
See also Hymn writer.
See also Librettist.
See also Lyricist.
See also Music composer.
See also Songwriter.
Abrams, Harriett (c. 1758–c. 1822)
Akiyoshi, Toshiko (1929—)
Alain, Marie-Claire (1926—)
Aleotti, Raffaella (c. 1570–c. 1646)
Aleotti, Vittoria (c. 1573–c. 1620)
Alexander, Leni (1924—)
Ali-Zadeh, Franghiz (1947—)
Amalie of Saxony (1794–1870)
Amohau, Merekotia (1898–1978)
Anderson, Beth (1950—)
Anderson, Laurie (1947—)
Andree, Elfrida (1841–1929)
Anna Amalia of Prussia (1723–1787)
Anna Amalia of Saxe-Weimar (1739–1807)
Archer, Violet Balestreri (1913–2000)
Aretz, Isabel (1909—)
Armstrong, Lil Hardin (1898–1971)
Assandra, Caterina (fl. 1580–1609)
Azza al-Maila (fl. c. 707)
Bacewicz, Grazyna (1909–1969)
Bach, Maria (1896–1978)
Backer-Grondahl, Agathe (1847–1907)
Badarzewski-Baranowska, Tekla (1834–1861)
Ballou, Esther Williamson (1915–1973)
Barraine, Elsa (1910—)
Barraine, Elsa (1910–1999)
Bartholomew, Ann Sheppard (1811–1891)
Bauer, Marion (1887–1955)
Bauld, Alison (1944—)
Beach, Amy Cheney (1867–1944)
Beat, Janet Eveline (1937—)
Beath, Betty (1932—)
Belleville-Oury, Anna Caroline de (1808–1880)
Bembo, Antonia (1643–1715)
Berberian, Cathy (1925–1983)
Bergman, Marilyn (1929—)
Bernstein, Theresa Ferber (1890–2002)
Bertin, Louise Angélique (1805–1877)
Bid'a (856–915)
Blahetka, Marie Leopoldine (1811–1887)
Bley, Carla (1938—)
Bond, Carrie Jacobs (1862–1946)
Bond, Victoria (1950—)
Bonds, Margaret (1913–1972)
Bonoff, Karla (1952—)
Boulanger, Lili (1893–1918)
Boulanger, Nadia (1887–1979)
Boyd, Anne (1946—)
Boyd, Liona (1950—)
Brackeen, JoAnne (1938—)
Branscombe, Gena (1881–1977)
Braunschweig-Lüneburg, Sophie Elisabeth von (1613–1676)
Bright, Dora Estella (1863–1951)
Britain, Radie (1897–1994)
Bronsart, Ingeborg von (1840–1913)
Browne, Augusta (1820–1882)
Butler, Helen May (1867–1957)
Caccini, Francesca (1587–c. 1626)
Cai Yan (c. 162–239)
Caldwell, Anne (1876–1936)
Canal, Marguerite (1890–1978)
Candeille, Julie (1767–1834)
Carr-Boyd, Ann (1938—)
Carvalho, Dinora de (1905—)
Cassian, Nina (1924—)
Casulana, Maddalena (c. 1540–1583)
Chaminade, Cécile (1857–1944)
Clarke, Rebecca (1886–1979)
Coates, Gloria (1938—)
Cockburn, Alicia (1713–1794)
Coleridge-Taylor, Avril (1903–1998)
Cotten, Elizabeth (c. 1893–1987)
Crawford, Ruth (1901–1953)
Crispell, Marilyn (1947—)
Daniels, Mabel Wheeler (1878–1971)
Danzi, Maria Margarethe (1768–1800)
De Leath, Vaughan (1900–1943)
Demessieux, Jeanne (1921–1968)
Destinn, Emmy (1878–1930)
Dianda, Hilda (1925—)
Diemer, Emma Lou (1927—)
Dinescu, Violeta (1953—)
Dlugoszewski, Lucia (1925—)
Dlugoszewski, Lucia (1925–2000)
Droste-Hülshoff, Annette von (1797–1848)
Eckhardt-Gramatté, S.C. (1899–1974)
Eisenstein, Judith (1909–1996)
Erinna (fl. 7th c. BCE)
Escot, Pozzi (1933—)
Eugenie (1830–1889)
Fadl (d. ca. 870)
Farrenc, Louise (1804–1875)
Ferrari, Carlotta (1837–1907)
Ferrari, Gabrielle (1851–1921)
Fine, Sylvia (1913–1991)
Fine, Vivian (1913–2000)
Firsova, Elena Olegovna (1950—)
Flower, Eliza (1803–1846)
Fontyn, Jacqueline (1930—)
Gaigerova, Varvara Andrianovna (1903–1944)
Gardner, Kay (1941–2002)
Gideon, Miriam (1906–1996)
Gipps, Ruth (1921—)
Giuranna, Barbara (1902–1998)
Glanville-Hicks, Peggy (1912–1990)
Gonzaga, Chiquinha (1847–1935)
Graham, Shirley (1896–1977)
Grandval, Marie Felicia (1830–1907)
Grétry, Lucile (1772–1790)
Gubaidulina, Sofia (1931—)
Guraieb Kuri, Rosa (1931—)
Gyring, Elizabeth (1906–1970)
Haas, Monique (1906–1987)
Hall, Elsie (1877–1976)
Hamilton, Catherine (1738–1782)
Hanim, Leyla (1850–1936)
Hara, Kazuko (1935—)
Harkness, Rebekah (1915–1982)
Hermodsson, Elisabet Hermine (1927—)
Hier, Ethel Glenn (1889–1971)
Hildegard of Bingen (1098–1179)
Hodges, Faustina Hasse (1822–1895)
Holland, Dulcie Sybil (1913—)
Holmès, Augusta (1847–1903)
Holst, Imogen (1907–1984)
Hoover, Katherine (1937—)
Hopekirk, Helen (1856–1945)
Hortense de Beauharnais (1783–1837)
Hoya, Katherina von (d. around 1470)
Hyde, Miriam Beatrice (1913—)
Hyde, Miriam Beatrice (1913–2005)
Inan (fl. c. 800)
Inanna (fl. c. 3000 BCE)
Irfan (fl. mid-800s)
Ivey, Jean Eichelberger (1923—)
Jacquet de la Guerre, Elisabeth-Claude (c. 1666–1729)
Janis, Elsie (1889–1956)
Jessye, Eva (1895–1992)
Jolas, Betsy (1926—)
Kanakaole, Edith K. (1913–1979)
Kapralova, Vitezslava (1915–1940)
Kasilag, Lucrecia R. (1918—)
King, Carole (1942—)
Kinkel, Johanna (1810–1858)

Kolb, Barbara (1939—)
Koptagel, Yuksel (1931—)
Kukuck, Felicitas (1914–2001)
La Barbara, Joan (1947—)
La Hye, Louise (1810–1838)
Landowska, Wanda (1877–1959)
Lang, Josephine (1815–1880)
Lang, Margaret Ruthven (1867–1972)
Larrocha, Alicia de (1923—)
Le Beau, Luise Adolpha (1850–1927)
Lebrun, Franziska (1756–1791)
Lefanu, Nicola (1947—)
Leginska, Ethel (1886–1970)
Lehmann, Liza (1862–1918)
Leigh, Carolyn (1926–1983)
Leonarda, Isabella (1620–1704)
Levi, Natalia (1901–1972)
Leviska, Helvi Lemmiki (1902–1982)
Lockwood, Annea F. (1939—)
Loudov, Ivana (1941—)
Lutyens, Elisabeth (1906–1983)
Maconchy, Elizabeth (1907–1994)
Macrina (327–379)
Mahler, Alma (1879–1964)
Mamlok, Ursula (1928—)
Mana-Zucca (1887–1981)
Maria Antonia of Austria (1724–1780)
Maric, Ljubica (1909–2003)
Martinez, Marianne (1744–1812)
Mayer, Emilie (1821–1883)
Mekeel, Joyce (1931—)
Mendelssohn-Hensel, Fanny (1805–1847)
Menter, Sophie (1846–1918)
Mihi-ki-te-kapua (?–1872/80)
Miller, Freda (c. 1910–1960)
Mireille (1906–1996)
Molza, Tarquinia (1542–1617)
Monk, Meredith (1942—)
Moszumanska-Nazar, Krystyna (1924—)
Musgrave, Thea (1928—)
Namakelua, Alice K. (1892–1987)
Newlin, Dika (1923—)
Nickerson, Camille (1884–1982)
Nicks, Stevie (1948—)
Nikolayeva, Tatiana (1924–1993)
Nurpeissova, Dina (1861–1955)
Oliveros, Pauline (1932—)
Osmanoglu, Gevheri (1904–1980)
Pakhmutova, Alexandra (1929—)
Palmer, Elizabeth Mary (1832–1897)
Paradis, Maria Theresia von (1759–1824)
Pejacevic, Dora (1885–1923)
Pentland, Barbara (1912–2000)
Perez, Maria (fl. 13th c.)
Perry, Julia (1924–1979)
Pitot, Genevieve (c. 1920—)
Popovici, Elise (1921—)
Poston, Elizabeth (1905–1987)
Price, Florence B. (1888–1953)
Puhiwahine Te Rangi-hirawea, Rihi (d. 1906)
Pukui, Mary Kawena (1895–1986)
Rainier, Priaulx (1903–1986)
Ran, Shulamit (1949—)
Reichardt, Louise (1779–1826)
Respighi, Elsa (1894–1996)
Rexach, Sylvia (1922–1961)
Richter, Marga (1926—)
Rivé-King, Julie (1854–1937)
Rogatis, Teresa de (1893–1979)
Rogers, Clara Kathleen (1844–1931)
Runcie, Constance Faunt Le Roy (1836–1911)
Saariaho, Kaija (1952—)
Scherchen, Tona (1938—)
Schonthal, Ruth (1924—)
Schumann, Clara (1819–1896)
Schuyler, Philippa Duke (1931–1967)
Simon, Carly (1945—)
Smith, Julia Frances (1911–1989)
Smyth, Ethel (1858–1944)
Spottiswoode, Alicia Ann (1810–1900)
Strozzi, Barbara (1619–1664)
Suesse, Dana (1909–1987)
Sutherland, Margaret (1897–1984)
Szönyi, Erzsebet (1924—)
Szymanowska, Maria Agata (1789–1831)
Tailleferre, Germaine (1892–1983)
Talma, Louise (1906–1996)
Tate, Phyllis (1911–1987)
Terzian, Alicia (1938—)
Theano (fl. 6th c. BCE)
Thompson, Kay (1908–1998)
Topeora, Rangi Kuini Wikitoria (?–1865/73)
Tower, Joan (1938—)
Ustvolskaya, Galina (1919—)
Van de Vate, Nancy (1930—)
Velazquez, Consuelo (1916–2005)
Veysberg, Yuliya (1878–1942)
Viardot, Pauline (1821–1910)
Vidar, Jorunn (1918—)
Vorlova, Slavka (1894–1973)
Warren, Elinor Remick (1900–1991)
Watkins, Gladys Elinor (1884–1939)
Weigl, Vally (1889–1982)
Weir, Judith (1954—)
White, Maude Valerie (1855–1937)
Wieniawska, Irene Regine (1880–1932)
Williams, Grace (1906–1977)
Williams, Mary Lou (1910–1981)
Wong, Betty Ann (1938—)
Zwilich, Ellen Taaffe (1939—)

MUSIC CRITIC

Davenport, Marcia (1903–1996)
Glanville-Hicks, Peggy (1912–1990)
Leviska, Helvi Lemmiki (1902–1982)
Newlin, Dika (1923—)
Roxon, Lillian (1932–1973)
Samaroff, Olga (1882–1948)
Skinner, Constance Lindsay (1877–1939)
Spofford, Grace Harriet (1887–1974)

MUSIC DIRECTOR

Armstrong, Margaret Neilson (1867–1944)
Barnes, Debra Dene (c. 1947—)
Bonds, Margaret (1913–1972)
Butler, Helen May (1867–1957)
Daniels, Mabel Wheeler (1878–1971)
Fine, Vivian (1913–2000)
Hackley, E. Azalia Smith (1867–1922)
Jessye, Eva (1895–1992)
Poston, Elizabeth (1905–1987)
Schwarzkopf, Elisabeth (1915—)
Ward, Clara Mae (1924–1973)

MUSICIAN

See Composer.
See Conductor.
See Instrumentalist.
See Singer.

MUSICOLOGIST

Aretz, Isabel (1909—)
Burlin, Natalie Curtis (1875–1921)
Coates, Gloria (1938—)
Densmore, Frances (1867–1957)
Dianda, Hilda (1925—)
Eisenstein, Judith (1909–1996)
Fletcher, Alice Cunningham (1838–1923)
Garrison, Lucy McKim (1842–1877)
George, Zelma Watson (1904–1994)
Kennedy-Fraser, Marjorie (1857–1930)
Landowska, Wanda (1877–1959)
Moore, Aubertine Woodward (1841–1929)
Newlin, Dika (1923—)
Scarborough, Dorothy (1878–1935)
Southern, Eileen Jackson (1920–2002)
Terzian, Alicia (1938—)
Tureck, Rosalyn (1914–2003)

MUSIC PRODUCER

McMurry, Lillian Shedd (1921–1999)
Ravan, Genya (1942—)
Vanderpool, Sylvia (1936—)

MUSIC SATIRIST

Russell, Anna (b. 1911)

MUSIC TEACHER

Abayomi, Oyinkansola (1897–1990)
Armstrong, Lil Hardin (1898–1971)
Barr, Amelia Huddleston (1831–1919)
Barth, Beatrice Mary (1877–1966)
Baur, Clara (1835–1912)
Bloch, Suzanne (1907–2002)
Boulanger, Nadia (1887–1979)
Bowen, Catherine Drinker (1897–1973)
Canal, Marguerite (1890–1978)
Crozier, Catharine (1914–2003)
Davies, Dorothy Ida (1899–1987)
de Brunhoff, Cécile (1903–2003)
de Cleyre, Voltairine (1866–1912)
DeLay, Dorothy (1917–2002)
Dickson, Joan (1921–1994)
Diller, Angela (1877–1968)
Dlugoszewski, Lucia (1925–2000)
Donalda, Pauline (1882–1970)
Donska, Maria (1912–1996)
Essipova, Annette (1851–1914)
Farrenc, Louise (1804–1875)
Gillars, Mildred E. (1900–1988)
Gittos, Marianne (1830–1908)
Greenfield, Elizabeth Taylor (c. 1819–1876)
Guraieb Kuri, Rosa (1931—)
Hidari Sachiko (1930—)
Hier, Ethel Glenn (1889–1971)
Hoffman, Malvina (1885–1966)
Holst, Imogen (1907–1984)
Hyde, Miriam Beatrice (1913—)
Iturbi, Amparo (1898–1969)
Janotha, Natalia (1856–1932)
Kanner-Rosenthal, Hedwig (1882–1959)
Kasilag, Lucrecia R. (1918—)
Keene, Constance (1921–2005)
Korchinska, Maria (1895–1979)
Kukuck, Felicitas (1914–2001)
Landowska, Wanda (1877–1959)
Lawrence, Eleanor (1936–2001)
Lenya, Lotte (1898–1981)
Lhevinne, Rosina (1880–1976)
Macandrew, Jennie (1866–1949)
Macrina (327–379)
Marcus, Adele (1905–1995)
Martinez, Marianne (1744–1812)
Millin, Sarah (1888–1968)
Nelson, Clara Meleka (1901–1979)
Nickerson, Camille (1884–1982)
Nissen, Erika (1845–1903)
Palmer, Elizabeth Mary (1832–1897)
Reisenberg, Nadia (1904–1983)
Roche, Terre (1953—)
Rogers, Clara Kathleen (1844–1931)
Samaroff, Olga (1882–1948)
Schramm, Bernardina Adriana (1900–1987)
Schumann, Clara (1819–1896)
Sirota, Beate (1923—)
Sorel, Claudette (1930—)
Spofford, Grace Harriet (1887–1974)
Szönyi, Erzsebet (1924—)
Szymanowska, Maria Agata (1789–1831)

Thompson, Blanche Edith (1874–1963)
Ustvolskaya, Galina (1919—)
Vengerova, Isabelle (1877–1956)
Vidar, Jorunn (1918—)
Vorlova, Slavka (1894–1973)
Walker, Edyth (1867–1950)
Waring, Laura Wheeler (1887–1948)
Wilson, Fiammetta Worthington (1864–1920)
Wong, Betty Ann (1938—)

MYCOLOGIST
Allingham, Margery (1904–1966)
Bacon, Peggy (1895–1987)
Brackett, Leigh (1915–1978)
Campbell, Charlotte C. (1914–1993)
Canter-Lund, Hilda M. (1922—)
Christie, Agatha (1890–1976)
Curtis, Kathleen Maisey (1892–1994)
du Maurier, Daphne (1907–1989)
Eberhart, Mignon G. (1899–1996)
Hawker, Lilian E. (1908–1991)
Hazen, Elizabeth Lee (1883–1975)
Highsmith, Patricia (1921–1995)
James, P.D. (1920—)
Marsh, Ngaio (1895–1982)
McCue, Lillian de la Torre Bueno (1902–1993)
Pargeter, Edith (c. 1913–1995)
Rinehart, Mary Roberts (1876–1958)
Sampson, Kathleen (1892–1980)
Sansome, Eva (1906–?)
Sayers, Dorothy L. (1893–1957)
Simpson, Helen (1897–1940)
Stevenson, Greta Barbara (1911–1990)
Tey, Josephine (1896–1952)
Wells, Carolyn (1862–1942)
Whitney, Phyllis A. (b. 1903)

MYSTERY/SUSPENSE-FICTION WRITER
Caspary, Vera (1899–1987)
Clark, Mary Higgins (1929—)
Cook, Judith (1933–2004)
de Jong, Dola (1911–2003)
Duncan, Lois (1934—)
Fraser, Antonia (1932—)
Hulme, Juliet Marion (1938—)
Nixon, Joan Lowery (1927–2003)
Rendell, Ruth (1930—)
Wilhelm, Kate (1928—)
Wright, L.R. (1939–2001)

MYSTIC (RELIGIOUS)
Acarie, Barbe (1566–1618)
Angela of Brescia (1474–1540)
Barber, Margaret Fairless (1869–1901)
Beatrice of Nazareth (c. 1200–1268)
Blavatsky, Helena (1831–1891)
Boneta, Prous
Bourignon, Antoinette (1616–1680)
Castillo y Guevara, Francisca Josefa del (1671–1742)
Catherine of Genoa (1447–1510)
Catherine of La Rochelle (fl. 1429)
Catherine of Siena (1347–1380)
Catherine of Sweden (c. 1330–1381)
Claude des Armoises
Columba of Rieti (1467–1501)
Constance of Rabastens (fl. 1384)
Daubenton, Jeanne or Peronne (d. 1372)
Delphine of Puimichel (1284–1360)
Ebner, Christine (1277–1355)
Edwards, Sarah Pierpont (1710–1758)
Elizabeth of Schönau (c. 1129–1164)
Emmerich, Anna Katharina (1774–1824)
Esperanza, Maria (1928–2004)
Gertrude of Hackeborne (1232–1292)
Gertrude of Ostend (d. 1358)
Gertrude the Great (1256–1302)
Griffiths, Ann (1776–1805)
Guglielma of Milan (d. 1282)
Guyon, Jeanne Marie Bouviéres de la Mothe (1648–1717)
Hadewijch (fl. 13th c.)
Hildegard of Bingen (1098–1179)
Inanna (fl. c. 3000 BCE)
Jackson, Rebecca Cox (1795–1871)
Jeanne-Marie de Maillé
Jingū (c. 201–269)
Julian of Norwich (c. 1342–c. 1416)
Jutta of Sponheim (d. 1136)
Kempe, Margery (c. 1373–after 1438)
Krüdener, Julie de (1764–1824)
Lal Ded (b. 1355)
La Rochelle, Catherine
Lead, Jane Ward (1623–1704)
Lidwina of Schiedam (1380–1433)
Lutgard (1182–1246)
Maillé, Jeanne-Marie de (1331–1414)
Margaret of Hungary (1242–1270)
Marie de l'Incarnation (1599–1672)
Mary of Oignies (1177–1213)
Mechtild of Hackeborne (1241–1298)
Mechtild of Magdeburg (c. 1207–c. 1282)
Oignt, Marguerite d' (d. 1310)
Porete, Marguerite (d. 1310)
Rabi'a (c. 714–801)
Robine, Marie (d. 1399)
Rose of Lima (1586–1617)
Swetchine, Anne Sophie (1782–1857)
Teresa de Cartagena (fl. 1400)
Teresa of Avila (1515–1582)
Viborada (d. 925)
Weil, Simone (1909–1943)

MYTHOLOGIST
Young, Ella (1867–1951)

NATIVE ARTIST
Dat So La Lee (c. 1835–1925)
Harjo, Joy (1951—)
Peña, Tonita (1893–1949)
Velarde, Pablita (1918—)

NATIVE-RIGHTS ACTIVIST
Akers, Dolly Smith (1901–1986)
Aquash, Anna Mae (1945–1976)
Bonney, Mary Lucinda (1816–1900)
Bonnin, Gertrude Simmons (1876–1938)
Converse, Harriet Maxwell (1836–1903)
Cooper, Whina (1895–1994)
Cournoyea, Nellie J. (1940—)
Dann, Mary (d. 2005)
Debo, Angie (1890–1988)
Deloria, Ella (1888–1971)
Duby-Blom, Gertrude (1901–1993)
Ellis, Florence Hawley (1906–1991)
Fletcher, Alice Cunningham (1838–1923)
Jackson, Helen Hunt (1830–1885)
Jemison, Alice Lee (1901–1964)
Johnson, E. Pauline (1861–1913)
La Flesche, Susan (1865–1915)
La Flesche, Susette (1854–1902)
Mankiller, Wilma (1945—)
Medicine, Beatrice A. (1923—)
Menchú, Rigoberta (1959—)
Mourning Dove (c. 1888–1936)
Peabody, Elizabeth Palmer (1804–1894)
Peratrovich, Elizabeth Wanamaker (1911–1958)
Quinton, Amelia S. (1833–1926)
Sainte-Marie, Buffy (1941—)
Victor, Wilma (1919–1987)
Wauneka, Annie Dodge (1910–1997)
Winnemucca, Sarah (1844–1891)
Wright, Muriel Hazel (1889–1975)

NATURALIST
Adamson, Joy (1910–1980)
Agassiz, Elizabeth Cary (1822–1907)
Akeley, Delia J. (1875–1970)
Alexander, Annie Montague (1867–1949)
Ball, Anne Elizabeth (1808–1872)
Banks, Sarah Sophia (1744–1818)
Bennett, Isobel (b. 1909)
Blackburne, Anna (1726–1793)
Brightwen, Eliza (1830–1906)
Buckland, Mary Morland (d. 1857)
Carrighar, Sally (1898–1985)
Carson, Rachel (1907–1964)
Comstock, Anna Botsford (1854–1930)
Cooper, Susan Fenimore (1813–1894)
Crisler, Lois (1897–1971)
Dormon, Carrie (1888–1971)
Eastwood, Alice (1859–1953)
Kingsley, Mary H. (1862–1900)
Lewis, Graceanna (1821–1912)
Morgan, Ann Haven (1882–1966)
North, Marianne (1830–1890)
Ratcliffe, Jane (1917–1999)
Rothschild, Miriam (1908–2005)
Shattuck, Lydia (1822–1889)
Stratton-Porter, Gene (1863–1924)
Teale, Nellie (1900–1993)
Traill, Catherine Parr (1802–1899)
Walcott, Mary Morris (1860–1940)
Ward, Mary (1827–1869)

NATURE WRITER
Bailey, Florence (1863–1948)
Barber, Margaret Fairless (1869–1901)
Miller, Olive Thorne (1831–1918)
Roberts, Mary (1788–1864)
Stratton-Porter, Gene (1863–1924)
Wright, Mabel Osgood (1859–1934)

NEEDLEWORK ARTIST
Alford, Marianne Margaret (1817–1888)
Mabel of Bury St. Edmunds (fl. 1230)
MacDonald, Frances (1874–1921)
Ross, Betsy (1752–1836)
Whyte, Kathleen (1909–1996)
Yeats, Elizabeth (1868–1940)
Yeats, Lily (1866–1949)

NEUROSCIENTIST
Arvanitaki, Angélique (1901–1983)
Bechtereva, Natalia (1924—)
Goldman-Rakic, Patricia S. (1937–2003)
Hockfield, Susan (1951—)
Levi-Montalcini, Rita (b. 1909)
Scharrer, Berta (1906–1995)
Yalow, Rosalyn (1921—)

NEUROSURGEON
André, Valerie (1922—)

NEWSPAPER EDITOR
Adnan, Etel (1925—)
Alegría, Claribel (1924—)
Allfrey, Phyllis Shand (1915–1986)
Angelou, Maya (1928—)
Annenkova, Julia (c. 1898–c. 1938)
Araz, Nezihe (1922—)
Baker, Ella (1903–1986)
Balabanoff, Angelica (1878–1965)
Barry, Iris (1895–1969)
Bass, Charlotta Spears (1880–1969)
Beatty, Bessie (1886–1947)
Becher, Lilly (1901–1976)
Beloff, Nora (1919–1997)
Bentley, Helen Delich (1923—)

Bloomer, Amelia Jenks (1818–1894)
Bradford, Cornelia Smith (d. 1755)
Bradwell, Myra (1831–1894)
Brown, Martha McClellan (1838–1916)
Bryant, Louise (1885–1936)
Cary, Mary Ann Shadd (1823–1893)
Cather, Willa (1873–1947)
Chase, Mary Coyle (1907–1981)
Coignet, Clarisse (1823–?)
Coleman, Kit (1864–1915)
Crane, Caroline Bartlett (1858–1935)
Croly, Jane Cunningham (1829–1901)
Curtis, Charlotte (1928–1987)
de Kooning, Elaine Fried (1918–1989)
Diggs, Annie LePorte (1848–1916)
Dimock, Susan (1847–1875)
Dönhoff, Marion, Countess (1909–2002)
Donnelly, Patricia (c. 1920—)
Dorr, Rheta Childe (1866–1948)
Douglas, Marjory Stoneman (1890–1998)
Driscoll, Clara (1881–1945)
Edwards, India (1895–1990)
Farley, Harriet (1813–1907)
First, Ruth (1925–1982)
Flanner, Janet (1892–1978)
Fleeson, Doris (1901–1970)
Fort, Cornelia (1919–1943)
Freundlich, Emmy (1878–1948)
Garvey, Amy Jacques (1896–1973)
Gilder, Jeannette Leonard (1849–1916)
Gilmore, Mary (1865–1962)
Goldman, Emma (1869–1940)
Graham, Katharine (1917–2001)
Greenfield, Meg (1930–1999)
Haldane, Charlotte (1894–1969)
Hani, Motoko (1873–1957)
Hapgood, Isabel (1850–1928)
Helmer, Bessie Bradwell (1858–1927)
Herrick, Elinore Morehouse (1895–1964)
Hickok, Lorena A. (1893–1968)
Hobby, Oveta Culp (1905–1995)
Hollingworth, Leta Stetter (1886–1939)
Hoult, Norah (1898–1984)
Huber, Therese (1764–1829)
Hull, Peggy (1889–1967)
Ibárruri, Dolores (1895–1989)
Jackson, Alice (1887–1974)
Jacobson, Ethel May (1877–1965)
Jagan, Janet (1920—)
Jolas, Betsy (1926—)
Jordan, Elizabeth Garver (1865–1947)
Jurney, Dorothy Misener (1909–2002)
Katznelson-Shazar, Rachel (1888–1975)
Kelly, Kathryn Thorne (1904–1998?)
Kerr, Sophie (1880–1965)
Kirchwey, Freda (1893–1976)
Koszutska, Maria (1876–1939)
La Flesche, Susette (1854–1902)
Loos, Anita (1893–1981)
MacGill, Helen Gregory (1871–1947)
Macpherson, Margaret Louisa (1895–1974)
Maihi, Rehutai (1895–1967)
McCormick, Anne O'Hare (1880–1954)
McDowell, Anne E. (1826–1901)
Meyer, Agnes (1887–1970)
Meynell, Alice (1847–1922)
Mitchel, Jenny (1820–1899)
Moreau de Justo, Alicia (1885–1986)
Nichols, Clarina (1810–1885)
Nicholson, Eliza Jane (1849–1896)
Niniwa-i-te-rangi (1854–1929)
Norris, Kathleen (1880–1966)
Olberg, Oda (1872–1955)
Osten, Maria (1908–1942)
Ottendorfer, Anna Uhl (1815–1884)
Otto-Peters, Luise (1819–1895)
Overlach, Helene (1894–1983)
Paddleford, Clementine (1900–1967)
Park, Ruth (1923—)
Parnell, Anna (1852–1911)
Parren, Kalliroe (1861–1940)
Patterson, Alicia (1906–1963)
Patterson, Eleanor Medill (1881–1948)
Petry, Ann (1908–1997)
Popp, Adelheid (1869–1939)
Porter, Sylvia (1913–1991)
Reed, Alma (1889–1966)
Rind, Clementina (c. 1740–1774)
Ross, Ishbel (1895–1975)
Ruffin, Josephine St. Pierre (1842–1924)
Samoilova, Konkordiya (1876–1921)
Sarfatti, Margherita (1880–1961)
Schiff, Dorothy (1903–1989)
Schurz, Margarethe Meyer (1833–1876)
Serao, Matilde (1856–1927)
Shaw, Flora (1852–1929)
Sherwood, Katharine Margaret (1841–1914)
Slesinger, Tess (1905–1945)
Smart, Elizabeth (1913–1986)
Smith, Hazel Brannon (1914–1994)
Smith, Margaret Chase (1897–1995)
Solano, Solita (1888–1975)
Strong, Anna Louise (1885–1970)
Sutton, Carol (1933–1985)
Swisshelm, Jane Grey (1815–1884)
Szymborska, Wislawa (1923—)
Tabouis, Geneviève (1892–1985)
Tarbell, Ida (1857–1944)
Templeton, Rini (1935–1986)
Thorne, Florence (1877–1973)
Tinayre, Marcelle (c. 1870–1948)
Tufty, Esther Van Wagoner (1896–1986)
Turner, Ethel (1872–1958)
Underwood, Agness Wilson (1902–1984)
Van Doren, Irita (1891–1966)
Washington, Fredi (1903–1994)
Wasilewska, Wanda (1905–1964)
Whiting, Lilian (1847–1942)
Wilkinson, Iris (1906–1939)
Willard, Frances E. (1839–1898)
Woodhull, Victoria (1838–1927)
Wright, Frances (1795–1852)
Zasulich, Vera (1849–1919)
Zenger, Anna Catharina (c. 1704–1751)

NEWSPAPER FOUNDER

Anneke, Mathilde Franziska (1817–1884)
Brown, Olympia (1835–1926)
Field, Kate (1838–1896)
Patterson, Alicia (1906–1963)
Timothy, Elizabeth (d. 1757)
Wilson, Charlotte (1854–1944)

NEWSPAPER PUBLISHER

Abayomi, Oyinkansola (1897–1990)
Anneke, Mathilde Franziska (1817–1884)
Bates, Daisy Lee (1914–1999)
Bradwell, Myra (1831–1894)
Brown, Olympia (1835–1926)
Chamorro, Violeta (1929—)
Chandler, Dorothy Buffum (1901–1997)
Copley, Helen (1922–2004)
Curie, Ève (b. 1904)
Dönhoff, Marion, Countess (1909–2002)
Field, Kate (1838–1896)
Goddard, Mary Katherine (1738–1816)
Graham, Katharine (1917–2001)
Hills, Tina S. (1921—)
Hobby, Oveta Culp (1905–1995)
Maihi, Rehutai (1895–1967)
Meyer, Agnes (1887–1970)
Nicholson, Eliza Jane (1849–1896)
Ottendorfer, Anna Uhl (1815–1884)
Patterson, Alicia (1906–1963)
Patterson, Eleanor Medill (1881–1948)
Reid, Helen Rogers (1882–1970)
Rind, Clementina (c. 1740–1774)
Roberts, Kate (1891–1985)
Schiff, Dorothy (1903–1989)
Scripps, Ellen Browning (1836–1932)
Smith, Hazel Brannon (1914–1994)
Strickland, Mabel (1899–1988)
Sulzberger, I.O. (1892–1990)
Swisshelm, Jane Grey (1815–1884)
Timothy, Ann (c. 1727–1792)
Timothy, Elizabeth (d. 1757)
Vann, Jesse Matthews (c. 1890–1967)
Villard, Fanny Garrison (1844–1928)
Vlachos, Helen (1911–1995)
Wilson, Charlotte (1854–1944)
Zenger, Anna Catharina (c. 1704–1751)

NOBEL LAUREATE

Addams, Jane (1860–1935)
Aung San Suu Kyi (1945—)
Balch, Emily Greene (1867–1961)
Buck, Linda B. (1947—)
Buck, Pearl S. (1892–1973)
Cori, Gerty T. (1896–1957)
Corrigan, Mairead (1944—)
Curie, Marie (1867–1934)
Deledda, Grazia (1871–1936)
Ebadi, Shirin (1947—)
Elion, Gertrude B. (1918–1999)
Gordimer, Nadine (1923—)
Hodgkin, Dorothy (1910–1994)
Joliot-Curie, Irène (1897–1956)
Lagerlöf, Selma (1858–1940)
Levi-Montalcini, Rita (b. 1909)
Mayer, Maria Goeppert (1906–1972)
McClintock, Barbara (1902–1992)
Menchú, Rigoberta (1959—)
Mistral, Gabriela (1889–1957)
Morrison, Toni (1931—)
Myrdal, Alva (1902–1986)
Nüsslein-Volhard, Christiane (1942—)
Sachs, Nelly (1891–1970)
Suttner, Bertha von (1843–1914)
Szymborska, Wislawa (1923—)
Teresa, Mother (1910–1997)
Undset, Sigrid (1882–1949)
Williams, Betty (1943—)
Williams, Jody (1950—)
Yalow, Rosalyn (1921—)

NONFICTION WRITER

Cornelisen, Ann (1926–2003)
Dworkin, Andrea (1946–2005)
Friday, Nancy (1937—)
Gardner, Kay (1941–2002)
Gilligan, Carol (1936—)
Grey, Maria Georgina (1816–1906)
Hite, Shere (1943—)
Kennedy, Helena (1950—)
Kincaid, Jamaica (1949—)
Lees, Sue (1941–2003)
Mackinnon, Catherine A. (1946—)
McNulty, Faith (1918–2005)
Oakley, Ann (1944—)
Okin, Susan Moller (1946–2004)
Paglia, Camille (1947—)
Runge, Erika (1939—)
Sawachi, Hisae (1930—)
Shirreff, Emily (1814–1897)
Warner, Marina (1946—)

NORDIC SKIER

See Skier.

NOVELIST

Abaijah, Josephine (1942—)
Abdel Rahman, Aisha (1913–1998)
Abrantès, Laure d' (1784–1838)
Acker, Kathy (1943–1997)
Acosta de Samper, Soledad (1833–1913)
Adam, Juliette la Messine (1836–1936)
Adams, Alice (1926–1999)
Adams, Glenda (1939—)
Adivar, Halide Edib (c. 1884–1964)
Adler, Renata (1938—)
Agaoglu, Adalet (1929—)
Aguilar, Grace (1816–1847)
Ahlefeld, Charlotte von (1781–1849)
Aichinger, Ilse (1921—)
Aiken, Joan (1924–2004)
Alcott, Louisa May (1832–1888)
Alden, Isabella (1841–1930)
Aldrich, Anne Reeve (1866–1892)
Aldrich, Bess Streeter (1881–1954)
Alexiou, Elli (1894–1988)
Aliye, Fatima (1862–1936)
Allart, Hortense (1801–1879)
Allen, Charlotte Vale (1941—)
Allen, Paula Gunn (1939—)
Allende, Isabel (1942—)
Allfrey, Phyllis Shand (1915–1986)
Allingham, Margery (1904–1966)
Almeida, Julia Lopes de (1862–1934)
Almog, Ruth (1936—)
Alonso, Dora (1910–2001)
Alós, Concha (1922—)
Alvarez de Toledo, Luisa Isabel (1936—)
Ames, Mary Clemmer (1831–1884)
Amin, Adibah (1936—)
Ammers-Küller, Johanna van (1884–1966)
Amparo Ruiz de Burton, Maria (1832–1895)
Amrane, Djamila (1939—)
Amrouche, Marie-Louise (1913–1976)
Anderson, Barbara (1926—)
Anderson, Doris (1921—)
Anderson, Jessica (1916—)
Andreas-Salomé, Lou (1861–1937)
Angel, Albalucía (1939—)
Angers, Félicité (1845–1924)
Anglada, Maria Angels (1930–1999)
Anker, Nini Roll (1873–1942)
Aouchal, Leila (1937—)
Apréleva, Elena Ivanovna (1846–1923)
Arceo, Liwayway (1924—)
Ariyoshi, Sawako (1931–1984)
Armour, Rebecca (1846–1891)
Arnim, Elizabeth von (1866–1941)
Arnold, June (1926–1982)
Arnothy, Christine (1930—)
Arnow, Harriette Simpson (1908–1986)
Arquimbau, Rosa Maria (1910—)
Ashford, Daisy (1881–1972)
Ashton, Helen (1891–1958)
Ashton-Warner, Sylvia (1908–1984)
Ashur, Radwa (1946—)
Astley, Thea (1925–2004)
Atherton, Gertrude (1857–1948)
Atkinson, Louisa (1834–1872)
Attar, Samar (1940—)
Atwood, Margaret (1939—)
Aubert, Constance (1803–?)
Aubin, Penelope (c. 1685–1731)
Audouard, Olympe (1830–1890)
Audoux, Marguerite (1863–1937)
Auel, Jean (1936—)
Austen, Jane (1775–1817)
Austin, Jane Goodwin (1831–1894)
Austin, Mary Hunter (1868–1934)
Axioti, Melpo (1906–1973)
Ayres, Ruby Mildred (1883–1955)
Ayverdi, Samiha (1906–1993)
Bâ, Mariama (1929–1981)
Babcock, Winnifred (1875–1954)
Bacheracht, Therese von (1804–1852)
Bachmann, Ingeborg (1926–1973)
Bagnold, Enid (1889–1981)
Bailey, Temple (c. 1869–1953)
Bainbridge, Beryl (1933—)
Baird, Irene (1901–1981)
Baker, Dorothy (1907–1968)
Baker, Louisa Alice (1856–1926)
Baldwin, Faith (1893–1978)
Ballesteros, Mercedes (1913–1995)
Ballestrem, Eufemia von (1859–1941)
Bambara, Toni Cade (1939–1995)
Banks, Isabella (1821–1897)
Banks, Lynne Reid (1929—)
Banning, Margaret Culkin (1891–1982)
Bannon, Ann (1932—)
Barandas, Ana Eurídice Eufrosina de (1806–1856)
Bardwell, Leland (1928—)
Barfoot, Joan (1946—)
Barker, A.L. (1918–2002)
Barker, Jane (1652–1732)
Barnes, Charlotte Mary Sanford (1818–1863)
Barnes, Djuna (1892–1982)
Barnes, Margaret Ayer (1886–1967)
Barnes, Zadel (1841–1917)
Baron, Devorah (1887–1956)
Barr, Amelia Huddleston (1831–1919)
Barra, Emma de la (1861–1947)
Barreno, Maria Isabel (1939—)
Barroso, Maria Alice (1926—)
Bates, Harriet Leonora (1856–1886)
Batson, Henrietta M. (1859–1943)
Bauer, Klara (1836–1876)
Baum, Vicki (1888–1960)
Baur, Margrit (1937—)
Bawden, Nina (1925—)
Bawr, Alexandrine de (1773–1860)
Bayly, Ada Ellen (1857–1903)
Baynton, Barbara (1857–1929)
Ba_ar, Sukufe Nihal (1896–1973)
Beattie, Ann (1947—)
Beauharnais, Fanny de (1737–1813)
Beaumer, Madame de (d. 1766)
Beauvain d'Althenheim, Gabrielle (1814–1886)
Beauvoir, Simone de (1908–1986)
Beccary, Madame (fl. 18th c.)
Beck, Beatrix (1914—)
Becker, Jillian (1932—)
Beckett, Mary (1926—)
Behn, Aphra (1640?–1689)
Beig, Maria (1920—)
Bekker, Elizabeth (1738–1804)
Bell, Lilian (1867–1929)
Bell, Mary Hayley (1911–2005)
Bellamy, Elizabeth Whitfield (1839–1900)
Belloc-Lowndes, Marie (1868–1947)
Bellonci, Maria (1902–1986)
Benedictsson, Victoria (1850–1888)
Ben Haddou, Halima (fl. 1980s)
Ben-Haim, Marylise (1928–2001)
Beniczky-Bajza, Helene (1840–1905)
Bennett, Anna Maria (c. 1750–1808)
Benoist, Françoise-Albine (1724–1809)
Benson, Mary (1919–2000)
Benson, Stella (1892–1933)
Bentley, Phyllis (1894–1977)
Bentley, Ursula (1945–2004)
Berberova, Nina (1901–1993)
Berens-Totenohl, Josefa (1891–1969)
Beresford-Howe, Constance (1922—)
Bergroth, Kersti (1886–1975)
Beringer, Aimée Daniell (1856–1936)
Bernard, Catherine (1662–1712)
Bernhardi, Sophie (1775–1833)
Bernstein, Hilda (1915—)
Bertrana, Aurora (1899–1974)
Bessa-Luís, Agustina (1922—)
Betham-Edwards, Matilda (1836–1919)
Betts, Doris (1932—)
Beutler, Maja (1936—)
Bevilacqua, Alma (1910–1988)
Beynon, Francis Marion (1884–1951)
Bhandari, Mannu (1931—)
Bhatia, June (1919—)
Bianchini, Angela (1921—)
Bianco, Margery Williams (1881–1944)
Bibesco, Marthe Lucie (1887–1973)
Biehl, Charlotta Dorothea (1731–1788)
Binchy, Maeve (1940—)
Binnuna, Khanatta (1940—)
Bins, Patrícia (1930—)
Bjelke-Petersen, Marie (1874–1969)
Blais, Marie-Claire (1939—)
Blanc, Marie-Thérèse (1840–1907)
Blaze de Bury, Rose (?–1894)
Bleschke, Johanna (1894–1936)
Blessington, Marguerite, Countess of (1789–1849)
Bloede, Gertrude (1845–1905)
Blondal, Patricia (1926–1959)
Bloom, Ursula (1893–1984)
Blower, Elizabeth (1763–after 1816)
Blume, Judy (1938—)
Bodin de Boismortier, Suzanne (c. 1722–?)
Böhl von Faber, Cecilia (1796–1877)
Bolte, Amely (1811–1891)
Bonanni, Laudomia (1907–2002)
Bonhote, Elizabeth (1744–1818)
Bonner, Margerie (1905–1988)
Bonner, Sherwood (1849–1883)
Borgese Freschi, Maria (1881–1947)
Bormann, Maria Benedita Câmara de (1853–1895)
Bosboom-Toussaint, Anna (1812–1886)
Bosco, María Angélica (1917—)
Bosco, Monique (1927—)
Botelho, Fernanda (1926—)
Bottome, Phyllis (1884–1963)
Bowen, Elizabeth (1899–1973)
Bowles, Jane (1917–1973)
Boye, Karin (1900–1941)
Boy-Ed, Ida (1852–1928)
Boyle, Kay (1902–1992)
Brachvogel, Carry (1864–1942)
Brackett, Leigh (1915–1978)
Braddon, Mary Elizabeth (1835–1915)
Bradford, Barbara Taylor (1933—)
Braga, Maria Ondina (1932–2003)
Brantenberg, Gerd (1941—)
Bray, Anna Eliza (1790–1883)
Bregendahl, Marie (1867–1940)
Bremer, Fredrika (1801–1865)
Brewster, Elizabeth (1922—)
Briet, Marguerite de (c. 1510–c. 1550)
Brink, Carol Ryrie (1895–1981)
Brinsmead, Hesba Fay (1922–2003)
Brittain, Vera (1893–1970)
Britton, Rosa María (1936—)
Broccoli, Dana (1922–2004)
Brodber, Erna (1936—)
Brøgger, Suzanne (1944—)
Brohon, Jacqueline-Aimée (1731–1778)
Broner, E.M. (1930—)
Brontë, Anne (1820–1849)
Brontë, Charlotte (1816–1855)
Brontë, Emily (1818–1848)
Brooke, Frances (1724–1789)
Brooke-Rose, Christine (1923—)

Brookner, Anita (1928—)
Brooks, Gwendolyn (1917–2000)
Brophy, Brigid (1929–1995)
Brossard, Nicole (1943—)
Broughton, Rhoda (1840–1920)
Brown, Alice (1856–1948)
Brown, Margaret A. (1867–?)
Brown, Rita Mae (1944—)
Brown, Rosellen (1939—)
Brown, Tina (1953—)
Brück, Christa-Anita (1899–?)
Brückner, Christine (1921–1996)
Bruggen, Carry van (1881–1932)
Brunet, Marta (1897–1967)
Brüning, Elfriede (1910—)
Brunton, Mary (1778–1818)
Bryan, Mary Edwards (1838–1913)
Buchan, Anna (1878–1948)
Büchner, Luise (1821–1877)
Buck, Pearl S. (1892–1973)
Bullrich, Silvina (1915–1990)
Bülow, Frieda von (1857–1909)
Bülow, Margarete von (1860–1884)
Bulwer-Lytton, Rosina, Lady (1802–1882)
Bunbury, Selina (1802–1882)
Bunge de Gálvez, Delfina (1881–1952)
Burford, Barbara (1944—)
Burgess, Yvonne (1936—)
Burgos Seguí, Carmen de (1867–1932)
Burkart, Erika (1922—)
Burnett, Frances Hodgson (1849–1924)
Burnett, Hallie Southgate (1908–1991)
Burney, Fanny (1752–1840)
Burney, Sarah Harriet (1772–1844)
Bury, Charlotte (1775–1861)
Butala, Sharon (1940—)
Byatt, A.S. (1936—)
Cabello de Carbonera, Mercedes (1845–1909)
Caffyn, Kathleen (1853–1926)
Caird, Mona Alison (1858–1932)
Cajal, Rosa María (1920—)
Caldwell, Taylor (1900–1985)
Calisher, Hortense (b. 1911)
Callahan, Sophia Alice (1868–1894)
Calvo de Aguilar, Isabel (1916—)
Campbell, Grace MacLennan (1895–1963)
Canth, Minna (1844–1897)
Canto, Estela (1919–1994)
Capécia, Mayotte (1928–1953)
Capmany Farnes, Maria Aurèlia (1918—)
Cappiello, Rosa (1942—)
Cardinal, Marie (1929–2001)
Carlén, Emilia (1807–1892)
Carlén, Rosa (1836–1883)
Caro, Pauline (1835–1901)
Carpinteri, Laura (b. 1910)
Carrington, Leonora (1917—)
Carswell, Catherine (1879–1946)
Carter, Angela (1940–1992)
Cartland, Barbara (1901–2000)
Cartwright, Julia (1851–1924)
Carvajal, María Isabel (1888–1949)
Carvajal, Mariana de (c. 1620–1680)
Carvalho, Maria Judite de (1921–1998)
Castellanos, Rosario (1925–1974)
Castro, Fernanda de (1900–1994)
Castro Alves, Diná Silveira de (1911–1983)
Castroviejo, Concha (1915–1995)
Cather, Willa (1873–1947)
Catherwood, Mary Hartwell (1847–1902)
Cato, Nancy (1917–2000)
Centeno, Yvette (1940—)
Chabrillan, Céleste de (1824–1909)
Chacón, Dulce (1954–2003)
Chaibi, Aïcha
Chand, Meira (1942—)
Chang, Diana (1934—)
Chang, Eileen (1920–1995)
Charke, Charlotte Cibber (1713–1760)
Charriere, Isabelle de (1740–1805)
Chartroule, Marie-Amélie (1848–1912)
Chase, Mary Coyle (1907–1981)
Chase, Mary Ellen (1887–1973)
Chase-Riboud, Barbara (1936—)
Chauvet, Marie (1916–1973)
Chawaf, Chantal (1943—)
Chedid, Andrée (1921—)
Cheeseman, Clara (1852–1943)
Chen Duansheng (1751–1796)
Cheney, Lynne (1941—)
Chen Ruoxi (1938—)
Cherry, Frances (1937—)
Chesebrough, Caroline (1825–1873)
Child, Lydia Maria (1802–1880)
Choiseul-Meuse, Félicité de (fl. 19th c.)
Cholmondeley, Mary (1859–1925)
Chopin, Kate (1850–1904)
Christaller, Helene (1872–1953)
Christensen, Inger (1935—)
Christie, Agatha (1890–1976)
Chugtai, Ismat (1915–1991)
Chukovskaya, Lidiya (1907–1996)
Churilova, L.A. (1875–1937)
Chute, Carolyn (1947—)
Cialente, Fausta (1898–1994)
Cilento, Diane (1933—)
Cisneros, Sandra (1954—)
Cixous, Hélène (1938—)
Clare, Ada (1836–1874)
Clark, Joan (1934—)
Clément, Catherine (1939—)
Cliff, Michelle (1946—)
Clifford, Mrs. W.K. (1846–1929)
Clift, Charmian (1923–1969)
Codina, Iverna (1918—)
Coffee, Lenore (1896–1984)
Colban, Marie (1814–1884)
Coleridge, Mary Elizabeth (1861–1907)
Colette (1873–1954)
Collett, Camilla (1813–1895)
Colleville, Anne-Hyacinthe de Saint-Léger de (1761–1824)
Collins, Jackie (1937—)
Collins, Joan (1933—)
Collyer, Mary (d. 1763)
Colwin, Laurie (1944–1992)
Compton-Burnett, Ivy (1884–1969)
Conde, Carmen (1907–1996)
Condé, Maryse (1937—)
Conran, Shirley (1932—)
Cookson, Catherine (1906–1998)
Cordelier, Jeanne (1944—)
Corelli, Marie (1855–1924)
Correia, Hélia (1939—)
Correia, Natália (1923–1993)
Corti, Maria (1915–2002)
Cory, Annie Sophie (1868–1952)
Costello, Louisa Stuart (1799–1870)
Cottenjé, Mireille (1933—)
Cottin, Sophie (1770–1807)
Coulton, Mary Rose (1906–2002)
Courths-Mahler, Hedwig (1867–1950)
Coutinho, Sônia (1939—)
Couvreur, Jessie (1848–1897)
Cowley, Joy (1936—)
Craigie, Pearl Mary Teresa (1867–1906)
Craik, Dinah Maria Mulock (1826–1887)
Craven, Elizabeth (1750–1828)
Craven, Margaret (1901–1980)
Craven, Pauline (1808–1891)
Creider, Jane Tapsubei (c. 1940s—)
Crisi, Maria (1892–1953)
Croker, Bithia May (c. 1849–1920)
Crowe, Catherine Anne (c. 1800–1876)
Crusat, Paulina (1900–1981)
Cummins, Maria Susanna (1827–1866)
Currie, Mary Montgomerie (1843–1905)
Cusack, Dymphna (1902–1981)
Dai Houying (1938–1996)
d'Albert, Marie-Madeleine Bonafous (fl. 18th c.)
Dalibard, Françoise-Thérèse Aumerle de Saint-Phalier (d. 1757)
Dallas, Ruth (1919—)
d'Alpuget, Blanche (1944—)
Dane, Clemence (1888–1965)
Daong Khin Khin Lay (1913—)
d'Arconville, Geneviève (1720–1805)
Dargan, Olive Tilford (1869–1968)
Dark, Eleanor (1901–1985)
Darling, Flora (1840–1910)
Dauthendey, Elisabeth (1854–1943)
Davenport, Gwen (1909–2002)
Davis, Rebecca Harding (1831–1910)
Davys, Mary (1674–1731)
Daw San San (1944–1990)
Day, Dorothy (1897–1980)
de Alonso, Carmen (1909—)
Debeche, Jamila (1925—)
De Brémont, Anna (1864–1922)
Debyasuvan, Boonlua Kunjara (1911–1982)
De Cespedes, Alba (1911–1997)
De Costa, Maria Velho (b. 1938)
de Jong, Dola (1911–2003)
Deken, Aagje (1741–1804)
Deland, Margaret (1857–1945)
de la Pasture, Mrs. Henry (d. 1945)
de la Roche, Mazo (1879–1961)
Delarue-Mardrus, Lucie (1880–1945)
Deledda, Grazia (1871–1936)
De Lima, Clara Rosa (1923—)
Delmar, Viña (1903–1990)
Delta, Penelope (1871–1941)
Denison, Mary Andrews (1826–1911)
De Rivoyre, Christine (1921—)
Dermoût, Maria (1888–1962)
Dervis, Suat (1905–1972)
Desai, Anita (1937—)
Descard, Maria (1847–1927)
Deshpande, Shashi (1938—)
Dessaur, C.I. (1931–2002)
De Stefani, Livia (1913—)
Destinn, Emmy (1878–1930)
Deutsch, Babette (1895–1982)
Devanny, Jean (1894–1962)
Devi, Ashapurna (1909–1995)
Devi, Mahasveta (1926—)
Diallo, Nafissatou (1941–1982)
Díaz Lozano, Argentina (1912–1999)
Dickens, Monica (1915–1992)
Dickinson, Anna E. (1842–1932)
Didion, Joan (1934—)
Dieulafoy, Jane (1851–1916)
Dillard, Annie (1945—)
Dimitrova, Blaga (1922—)
Ditlevsen, Tove (1917–1976)
Dmitrieva, Valentina (1859–1948)
Dodge, Mary Mapes (1831–1905)
Doerr, Harriet (1910–2002)
Dohm, Hedwig (1831–1919)
Domin, Hilde (1909–2006)
Dominguez, María Alicia (1908—)
Doolittle, Hilda (1886–1961)
Dorr, Julia Caroline (1825–1913)
Dougall, Lily (1858–1923)
Douglas, Amanda Minnie (1831–1916)
Dove, Rita (1952—)
Drabble, Margaret (1939—)

Drake-Brockman, Henrietta (1901–1968)
Drewitz, Ingeborg (1923–1986)
Drif, Zohra (1941—)
Drinkwater, Jennie M. (1841–1900)
Driscoll, Clara (1881–1945)
Duckworth, Marilyn (1935—)
Duff, Mary Ann Dyke (1794–1857)
Duffy, Maureen (1933—)
Dufrénoy, Adelaïde de (1765–1825)
du Fresne, Yvonne (1929—)
Duley, Margaret (1894–1968)
Dullemen, Inez van (1925—)
du Maurier, Daphne (1907–1989)
Duncan, Lois (1934—)
Duncan, Sara Jeanette (1861–1922)
Duniway, Abigail Scott (1834–1915)
Dunn, Nell (1936—)
Dunnett, Dorothy (1923–2001)
Dupuy, Eliza Ann (1814–1881)
Durack, Mary (1913–1994)
Durand, Catherine (d. 1736)
Durand, Lucile (1930—)
Duranti, Francesca (1935—)
Duras, Claire de (1777–1828)
Duras, Marguerite (1914–1996)
Düringsfeld, Ida von (1815–1876)
Dutt, Toru (1856–1877)
Dworkin, Andrea (1946–2005)
Eastman, Elaine Goodale (1863–1953)
Eberhardt, Isabelle (1877–1904)
Eberhart, Mignon G. (1899–1996)
Ebner-Eschenbach, Marie (1830–1916)
Edgell, Zee (1941—)
Edginton, May (1883–1957)
Edgren, Anne Charlotte (1849–1892)
Ega, Françoise (1920–1976)
Ehrmann, Marianne (1755–1795)
Ekman, Kirsten (1933—)
Elie de Beaumont, Anne Louise (1730–1783)
Elizabeth of Wied (1843–1916)
Ellerman, Winifred (1894–1983)
Elliott, Maud Howe (1854–1948)
Elliott, Sarah Barnwell (1848–1928)
Ellis, Ellen (1829–1895)
Ellis, Sarah Stickney (c. 1799–1872)
El Saadawi, Nawal (1931—)
Elsner, Gisela (1937–1992)
Emecheta, Buchi (1944—)
Enchi, Fumiko (1905–1986)
Ener, Güner (1935—)
Engel, Marian (1933–1985)
Èngelgardt, Sofia Vladimirovna (1828–1894)
Ephron, Nora (1941—)
Épinay, Louise-Florence-Pétronille, Madame la Live d' (1726–1783)
Erbil, Leyla (1931—)
Eristavi-Xostaria, Anastasia (1868–1951)
Ernaux, Annie (1940—)
Eschstruth, Nataly von (1860–1939)
Escott, Cicely Margaret (1908–1977)
Esquivel, Laura (1950—)
Etcherelli, Claire (1934—)
Evans, Mary Anne (1819–1880)
Fairbairns, Zöe (1948—)
Falcón, Lidia (1935—)
Fallaci, Oriana (1930—)
Farmer, Beverley (1941—)
Farnham, Eliza W. (1815–1864)
Farrar, Eliza Rotch (1791–1870)
Farrés, Carmen (1931–1976)
Fauques, Marianne-Agnès Pillement, Dame de (1721–1773)
Fauset, Jessie Redmon (1882–1961)
Feinstein, Elaine (1930—)
Ferber, Edna (1885–1968)
Fern, Fanny (1811–1872)
Ferrier, Susan Edmonstone (1782–1854)
Field, Rachel Lyman (1894–1942)
Fielding, Sarah (1710–1768)
Figuli, Margita (1909–1995)
Filippi, Rosina (1866–1930)
Finas, Lucette (1921—)
Fischer, Caroline Auguste (1764–1834)
Fisher, Dorothy Canfield (1879–1958)
Fitzgerald, Penelope (1916–2000)
Fitzgerald, Zelda (1900–1948)
Flagg, Fannie (1941—)
Flanner, Janet (1892–1978)
Fleming, May Agnes (1840–1880)
Flexner, Anne Crawford (1874–1955)
Fontaines, Marie-Louise-Charlotte de Pelard de Givry, Comtesse de (1660–1730)
Fontette de Sommery, Mademoiselle (fl. 18th c.)
Forbes, Esther (1891–1967)
Forbes, Rosita (1893–1967)
Fórmica, Mercedes (1916—)
Forsh, Olga (1873–1961)
Forster, Margaret (1938—)
Fothergill, Jessie (1851–1891)
Fouqué, Karoline Freifrau de la Motte (1774–1831)
Fourqueux, Madame de (fl. 18th c.)
Fox, Paula (1923—)
Fraenkel, Naomi (1920—)
Frame, Janet (1924–2004)
France, Ruth (1913–1968)
Franchi, Anna (1866–1954)
Francis, Clare (1946—)
François, Louise von (1817–1893)
Frankau, Pamela (1908–1967)
Franklin, Miles (1879–1954)
Franks, Lucinda (1946—)
Fraser, Antonia (1932—)
Fraser, Mary Crawford (1851–1922)
Fraser, Sylvia (1935—)
Freedman, Nancy (1920—)
Freeman, Gillian (1929—)
Freeman, Lucy (1916–2004)
Freeman, Mary E. Wilkins (1852–1930)
Fremantle, Anne (1909–2002)
French, Alice (1850–1934)
French, Marilyn (1929—)
Frigerio, Marta Lía (1925–1985)
Frings, Ketti (1909–1981)
Frischmuth, Barbara (1941—)
Frohberg, Regina (1783–1850)
Frölich, Henriette (1768–1833)
Fugard, Sheila (1932—)
Fuller, Anne (fl. late 18th c.)
Fullerton, Georgiana Charlotte (1812–1885)
Fumelh, Madame de (fl. 18th c.)
Furlong, Monica (1930–2003)
Fürüzan (1935—)
Fussenegger, Gertrud (1912—)
Gacon-Dufour, Marie Armande Jeanne (1753–c. 1835)
Gagneur, Louise (1832–1902)
Galgóczi, Erzsébet (1930–1989)
Gallant, Mavis (1922—)
Gallardo, Sara (1931–1988)
Galvão, Patricia (1910–1962)
Galvarriato, Eulalia (1905–1997)
Gambaro, Griselda (1928—)
Gan, Elena Andreevna (1814–1842)
Gándara, Carmen (1900–1977)
Gant, Phyllis (1922—)
Gardener, Helen Hamilton (1853–1925)
Gare, Nene (1919–1994)
Garg, Mridula (1938—)
Garner, Helen (1942—)
Garro, Elena (1916–1998)
Garufi, Bianca (1920—)
Gaskell, Elizabeth (1810–1865)
Gates, Eleanor (1871–1951)
Gaunt, Mary (1861–1942)
Gauthier, Xavière (1942—)
Gautier, Judith (1845–1917)
Gay, Sophie (1776–1852)
Gellhorn, Martha (1908–1998)
Gerould, Katharine (1879–1944)
Gersão, Teolinda (1940—)
Ghalem, Nadia (1941—)
Giacobbe, Maria (1928—)
Gibbons, Stella (1902–1989)
Gilchrist, Ellen (1935—)
Gilliatt, Penelope (1932–1993)
Gillmor, Frances (1903–1993)
Gilman, Charlotte Perkins (1860–1935)
Gilroy, Beryl (1924–2001)
Ginzburg, Natalia (1916–1991)
Gippius, Zinaida (1869–1945)
Glantz, Margo (1930—)
Glasgow, Ellen (1873–1945)
Glaspell, Susan (1876–1948)
Glyn, Elinor (1864–1943)
Go, Shizuko (1929—)
Godden, Rumer (1907–1998)
Godwin, Gail (1937—)
Goncalves, Olga (1937—)
Gordimer, Nadine (1923—)
Gordon, Caroline (1895–1981)
Gore, Catherine (1799–1861)
Gorriti, Juana Manuela (1816–1892)
Goudge, Elizabeth (1900–1984)
Goudvis, Bertha (1876–1966)
Gould, Lois (1932–2002)
Gournay, Marie le Jars de (1565–1645)
Grace, Patricia (1937—)
Graffigny, Françoise de (1695–1758)
Grafton, Sue (1940)
Grahn, Judy (1940—)
Granata, Maria (1921—)
Granville-Barker, Helen (d. 1950)
Grau, Shirley Ann (1929—)
Graves, Clotilde Inez Mary (1863–1932)
Gray, Teresa Corinna Ubertis (1877–1964)
Greene, Sarah Pratt (1856–1935)
Gréville, Alice (1842–1903)
Grey, Maria Georgina (1816–1906)
Griffith, Elizabeth (c. 1720–1793)
Grillet, Louise Hortense (1865–1952)
Gripe, Maria (1923—)
Gritsi-Milliex, Tatiana (1920—)
Grogger, Paula (1892–1984)
Grossmann, Edith Searle (1863–1931)
Grossmann, Judith (1931—)
Groult, Benoîte (1921—)
Groult, Flora (1925—)
Grové, Henriette (1922—)
Grumbach, Doris (1918—)
Guellouz, Souad (1937—)
Guibert, Louise-Alexandrine, Comtesse de (d. 1826)
Guido, Beatriz (1924—)
Guilló, Magdalena (1940—)
Guizot, Pauline (1773–1827)
Gunn, Jeannie (1870–1961)
Gunning, Susannah Minifie (c. 1740–1800)
Guy, Rosa (1925—)
Gyllembourg-Ehrensvärd, Thomasine (1773–1856)
Hagiwara, Yoko (1920—)
Hahn, Emily (1905–1997)
Hahn-Hahn, Ida, Countess von (1805–1880)
Haldane, Charlotte (1894–1969)
Hale, Louise Closser (1872–1933)
Hale, Nancy (1908–1988)
Hale, Sarah Josepha (1788–1879)

Hall, Elisa (1900–1982)
Hall, Radclyffe (1880–1943)
Hamilton, Mary (1739–1816)
Handel-Mazzetti, Enrica von (1871–1955)
Handzová, Viera (1931–1997)
Hanke, Henriette (1785–1862)
Hanrahan, Barbara (1939–1991)
Hanway, Mary Ann (c. 1755–c. 1823)
Harada, Yasuko (1928—)
Hardwick, Elizabeth (1916—)
Hareven, Shulamit (1930–2003)
Harford, Lesbia (1891–1927)
Harraden, Beatrice (1864–1936)
Harris, Corra May (1869–1935)
Harrison, Constance Cary (1843–1920)
Harrower, Elizabeth (1928—)
Harry, Myriam (1869–1958)
Hart, Julia Catherine (1796–1867)
Hartlaub, Geno (1915—)
Haushofer, Marlen (1920–1970)
Haven, Emily Bradley Neal (1827–1863)
Hawkins, Laetitia Matilda (1759–1835)
Hayashi, Kyoko (1930—)
Haycraft, Anna Margaret (1932–2005)
Hays, Mary (1760–1843)
Haywood, Eliza (c. 1693–1756)
Hazzard, Shirley (1931—)
Head, Bessie (1937–1986)
Hébert, Anne (1916—)
Hector, Annie French (1825–1902)
Heilbrun, Carolyn Gold (1926–2003)
Hendel, Yehudit (1926—)
Hentz, Caroline Lee (1800–1856)
Hernández, Luisa Josefina (1928—)
Herrera Garrido, Francisca (1869–1950)
Hervey, Elizabeth (c. 1748–c. 1820)
Hewett, Dorothy (1923–2002)
Heyer, Georgette (1902–1974)
Heyking, Elisabeth von (1861–1925)
Hibbert, Eleanor (1906–1993)
Highsmith, Patricia (1921–1995)
Higuchi, Ichiyo (1872–1896)
Hill, Ernestine (1899–1972)
Hill, Susan (1942—)
Hillern, Wilhelmine von (1836–1916)
Hilst, Hilda (1930—)
Hobson, Laura Z. (1900–1986)
Hodrova, Daniela (1946—)
Hoffman, Alice (1952—)
Hogan, Linda (1947—)
Hohenhausen, Elizabeth (1789–1857)
Holden, Helene (1935—)
Holden, Molly (1927–1981)
Holmes, Mary Jane (1825–1907)
Holtby, Winifred (1898–1935)
Hopkins, Pauline E. (1859–1930)
Horta, Maria Teresa (1937—)
Hosain, Attia (1913–1998)
Hospital, Janette Turner (1942—)
Hoult, Norah (1898–1984)
Howard, Blanche Willis (1847–1898)
Howard, Elizabeth Jane (1923—)
Howatch, Susan (1940—)
Howe, Fanny (1942—)
Huber, Therese (1764–1829)
Huch, Ricarda (1864–1947)
Hull, Helen Rose (1888–1971)
Hulme, Keri (1947—)
Hungerford, Margaret Wolfe (c. 1855–1897)
Hunt, Violet (1866–1942)
Hunter, Kristin (1931—)
Hunter, Mollie (1922—)
Hurst, Fannie (1889–1968)
Hurston, Zora Neale (c. 1891–1960)
Hyder, Qurratulain (1927—)
Icaza, Carmen de (1899–1979)
Imaleyene, Fatime-Zohra (1936—)
Inchbald, Elizabeth (1753–1821)
Ingelow, Jean (1820–1897)
Invernizio, Carolina (1858–1916)
Iordanidou, Maria (1897–1989)
Iremonger, Lucille (c. 1916–1989?)
Irwin, Inez Haynes (1873–1970)
Isitt, Kathleen (1876–?)
Jaburkova, Jozka (d. 1944)
Jackson, Helen Hunt (1830–1885)
Jackson, Shirley (1916–1965)
Jacob, Naomi Ellington (1889–1964)
Jakobsdóttir, Svava (1930—)
Jalandoni, Magdalena (1891–1978)
Jameson, Storm (1891–1986)
Jamison, Cecilia V. (1837–1909)
Janés, Clara (1940—)
Janeway, Elizabeth (1913–2005)
Janitschek, Maria (1859–1927)
Jelinek, Elfriede (1946—)
Jensen, Thit (1876–1957)
Jervey, Caroline Howard (1823–1877)
Jesse, Fryniwyd Tennyson (1888–1958)
Jewett, Sarah Orne (1849–1909)
Jewsbury, Geraldine (1812–1880)
Jhabvala, Ruth Prawer (1927—)
Joenpelto, Eeva (1921–2004)
Johansen, Hanna (1939—)
Johnson, Josephine Winslow (1910–1990)
Johnson, Pamela Hansford (1912–1981)
Johnston, Jennifer (1930—)
Johnston, Mary (1870–1936)
Johnstone, Isobel (1781–1857)
Jolley, Elizabeth (1923—)
Jones, Marion Patrick (1934—)
Jong, Erica (1942—)
Joubert, Elsa (1922—)
Joudry, Patricia (1921–2000)
Jurado, Alicia (1915—)
Kaffka, Margit (1880–1918)
Kahana-Carmon, Amalia (1930—)
Kaiser, Isabella (1866–1925)
Kantůrkova, Eva (1930—)
Karodia, Farida (1942—)
Kaus, Gina (1894–1985)
Kautsky, Minna (1837–1912)
Kavan, Anna (1901–1968)
Kavanagh, Julia (1824–1877)
Kaye, M.M. (1908–2004)
Kaye-Smith, Sheila (1887–1956)
Kazantzaki, Galateia (1886–1962)
Keane, Molly (1904–1996)
Kefala, Antigone (1935—)
Kelley, Edith Summers (1884–1956)
Kelly, Ethel (1875–1949)
Kelly, Gwen (1922—)
Kelly, Maeve (1930—)
Kennedy, Adrienne (1931—)
Kennedy, Margaret (1896–1967)
Kenny, Alice Annie (1875–1960)
Kerr, Sophie (1880–1965)
Keun, Irmgard (1905–1982)
Keyes, Evelyn (1919—)
Khalifa, Sahar (1941—)
Khuri, Colette (1937—)
Khvoshchinskaia, Nadezhda (1824–1889)
Kidman, Fiona (1940—)
Kiengsiri, Kanha (1911—)
Kilpi, Eeva (1928—)
Kim, Ronyoung (1926–1987)
Kimenye, Barbara (1940—)
Kincaid, Jamaica (1949—)
King, Grace Elizabeth (c. 1852–1932)
Kingsolver, Barbara (1955—)
Kingston, Maxine Hong (1940—)
Kinzie, Juliette Magill (1806–1870)
Kirschner, Lola (1854–1934)
Knight, Ellis Cornelia (1758–1837)
Knox, Isa (1831–1903)
Kobiakova, Aleksandra (1823–1892)
Kobylianska, Olha (1863–1942)
Koea, Shonagh (1939—)
Kogawa, Joy (1935—)
Kolb, Annette (1870–1967)
Komarova, Varvara (1862–1942)
König, Alma Johanna (1887–c. 1942)
Königsdorf, Helga (1938—)
Kono, Taeko (1926—)
Kossak, Zofia (1890–1968)
Krall, Hanna (1937—)
Krandievskaya, Anastasiia (1865–1938)
Krantz, Judith (1928—)
Kremnitz, Marie (1852–1916)
Krestovskaya, Maria V. (1862–1910)
Kronauer, Brigitte (1940—)
Krusenstjerna, Agnes von (1894–1940)
Kryzhanovskaia, Vera Ivanovna (1861–1924)
Kumin, Maxine (1925—)
Kuncewicz, Maria (1899–1989)
Kurahashi, Yumiko (1935—)
Kurz, Isolde (1853–1944)
Lacrosil, Michèle (1915—)
La Fayette, Marie-Madeleine de (1634–1693)
Laffitte, María (1902–1986)
La Force, Charlotte-Rose de Caumont de (1650–1724)
Laforet, Carmen (1921–2004)
Lagerlöf, Selma (1858–1940)
Lagorio, Gina (1930—)
Lagrave, Comtesse de (1770–1820)
La Guesnerie, Charlotte Charbonnier de (1710–1785)
Lamb, Caroline (1785–1828)
Lambert, Betty (1933–1983)
Lamburn, Richmal Crompton (1890–1969)
Landau, Klavdia Gustavovna (1922–1990)
Landon, Letitia Elizabeth (1802–1838)
Landon, Margaret (1903–1993)
Lane, Rose Wilder (1886–1968)
Lange, Norah (1906–1972)
Langgässer, Elisabeth (1899–1950)
Langley, Eve (1908–1974)
Langner, Ilse (1899–1987)
Lapauze, Jeanne (1860–1920)
Lapid, Shulamit (1934—)
La Plante, Lynda (1946—)
Lappo-Danilevskaia, N.A. (c. 1875–1951)
La Roche, Guilhem (1644–1710)
La Roche, Sophie von (1730–1807)
Larsen, Nella (1891–1964)
Laski, Marghanita (1915–1988)
Lauber, Cécile (1887–1981)
Lavater-Sloman, Mary (1891–1980)
Laverty, Maura (1907–1966)
Lawless, Emily (1845–1913)
Lazarová, Katarina (1914—)
Leakey, Caroline Woolmer (1827–1881)
Leclerc, Annie (1940—)
Lee, Hannah Farnham (1780–1865)
Lee, Harper (1926—)
Lee, Harriet (1757–1851)
Lee, Sophia (1750–1824)
Le Fort, Gertrud von (1876–1971)
Le Givre de Richebourg, Madame (1710–1780)
Lehmann, Rosamond (1901–1990)
Lemsine, Aicha (1942—)
Lendorff, Gertrud (1900–1986)
Lennox, Charlotte (1720–1804)
Le Noir, Elizabeth Anne (c. 1755–1841)
Léo, André (1832–1900)
León, Maria Teresa (1903–1988)
Leonardos, Stela (1923—)

Leprohon, Rosanna (1832–1879)
Lesik, Vera (1910–1975)
Lessing, Doris (1919—)
Leverson, Ada (1862–1933)
Levesque, Louise Cavelier (1703–1743)
Levinson, Luisa Mercedes (1909–1988)
Levy, Amy (1861–1889)
Lewald, Fanny (1811–1889)
Lewis, Agnes Smith (1843–1926)
Lewis, Ethelreda (1875–1946)
L'Héritier, Marie-Jeanne (1664–1734)
Libbey, Laura Jean (1862–1925)
Liberáki, Margaríta (1919—)
Lidman, Sara (1923–2004)
Likimani, Muthoni (c. 1940—)
Lin, Hazel (1913–1986)
Lin, Tai-yi (1926—)
Lindbergh, Anne Morrow (1906–2001)
Lindgren, Astrid (1907–2002)
Linskill, Mary (1840–1891)
Linton, Eliza Lynn (1822–1898)
Lipperini, Guendalina (c. 1862–1914)
Lipson, Edna (1914–1996)
Lispector, Clarice (1920–1977)
Litvinov, Ivy (1889–1977)
Liu, Nienling (1934—)
Lively, Penelope (1933—)
Lizars, Kathleen MacFarlane (d. 1931)
Locke, Sumner (1881–1917)
Logan, Olive (1839–1909)
Longhi, Lucia Lopresti (1895–1985)
Loos, Anita (1893–1981)
Loos, Cécile Ines (1883–1959)
Lord, Bette Bao (1938—)
Louw, Anna M. (1913–2003)
Løveid, Cecilie (1951—)
Lovelace, Maud Hart (1892–1980)
Loveling, Virginie (1836–1923)
Loy, Rosetta (1931—)
Lubert, Mlle de (c. 1710–c. 1779)
Luft, Lia (1938—)
Lurie, Alison (1926—)
Lusarreta, Pilar de (1914–1967)
Lussan, Marguerite de (1682–1758)
Lussu, Joyce Salvadori (1912–1988)
Lütken, Hulda (1896–1947)
Lutyens, Mary (1908–1999)
Lyttelton, Edith Joan (1873–1945)
Macardle, Dorothy (1889–1958)
Macaulay, Rose (1881–1958)
MacDonald, Betty (1908–1958)
MacEwen, Gwendolyn (1941–1987)
MacFall, Frances E. (1854–1943)
Macgoye, Marjorie Oludhe (1928—)
MacGregor, Esther Miller (1874–1961)
MacInnes, Helen (1907–1985)
Mack, Louise (1874–1935)
Mactier, Susie (1854–1936)
Magruder, Julia (1854–1907)
Maiga-Ka, Aminata (1940—)
Maillet, Antonine (1929—)
Maitland, Agnes Catherine (1850–1906)
Majerovç, Marie (1882–1967)
Mallet-Joris, Françoise (1930—)
Malpede, Karen (1945—)
Malraux, Clara (c. 1897–1982)
Mancini, Evelina (1849–1896)
Mander, Jane (1877–1949)
Manicom, Jacqueline (1938–1976)
Manley, Mary de la Rivière (1663–1724)
Manner, Eeva-Liisa (1921–1995)
Manning, Anne (1807–1879)
Manning, Olivia (1908–1980)
Mannoury d'Ectot, Madame de (fl. 1880)
Mansilla de García, Eduarda (1838–1892)
Mansour, Joyce (1928–1987)
Manzini, Gianna (1896–1974)
Maraini, Dacia (1936—)
Maranhão, Heloísa (1925—)
March, Susana (1918–1991)
Marchenko, Anastasiia Iakovlevna (1830–1880)
Marghieri, Clotilde (1897–1981)
Marion, Frances (1888–1973)
Marlitt, Eugenie (1825–1887)
Marnière, Jeanne (1854–1910)
Maron, Monika (1941—)
Marothy-Soltesova, Elena (1855–1939)
Marryat, Florence (1837–1899)
Marsh, Ngaio (1895–1982)
Marshall, Joyce (1913—)
Marshall, Paule Burke (1929—)
Marsh-Caldwell, Anne (1791–1874)
Martel de Janville, Comtesse de (1850–1932)
Martin, C.E.M. (1847–1937)
Martin, Claire (1914—)
Martin, Georgia (1866–1946)
Martin, Mary Letitia (1815–1850)
Martínez Sierra, Maria de la O (1874–1974)
Martín Gaite, Carmen (1925—)
Martinson, Moa (1890–1964)
Mason, Bobbie Ann (1940—)
Masters, Olga (1919–1986)
Mathers, Helen (1853–1920)
Matto de Turner, Clorinda (1854–1909)
Matute, Ana Maria (1926—)
Mayne, Ethel Colburn (1865–1941)
Mayo, Katherine (1867–1940)
Mayor, Flora M. (1872–1932)
Mayröcker, Friederike (1924—)
McAlpine, Rachel (1940—)
McCarthy, Mary (1912–1989)
McClung, Nellie L. (1873–1951)
McCoy, Iola Fuller (1906–1993)
McCullers, Carson (1917–1967)
McCullough, Colleen (1937—)
McCully, Emily Arnold (1939—)
McIlwraith, Jean Newton (1859–1938)
McIntosh, Maria (1803–1878)
McKenna, Marthe (1893–1969)
McKenney, Ruth (1911–1972)
McManus, Liz (1947—)
McMillan, Terry (1951—)
McNeill, Florence Marian (1885–1973)
McNeill, Janet (1907–1994)
McNulty, Faith (1918–2005)
Meaker, Marijane (1927—)
Mechtel, Angelika (1943–2000)
Meeke, Mary (d. 1816)
Menco, Sara (1920—)
Mendels, Josepha (1902–1995)
Merard de Saint-Just, Anne-Jeanne-Félicité d'Ormoy (1765–1830)
Mereau-Brentano, Sophie (1770–1806)
Meredith, Gwen (b. 1907)
Meriwether, Louise (1923—)
Merril, Judith (1923–1997)
Metalious, Grace (1924–1964)
Meyer, Olga (1889–1972)
Michaëlis, Karin (1872–1950)
Milani, Milena (1922—)
Millar, Margaret (1915–1994)
Miller, Alice Duer (1874–1942)
Miller, Caroline (1903–1992)
Miller, Emily Huntington (1833–1913)
Millican, Arthenia J. Bates (1920—)
Milligan, Alice (1866–1953)
Millin, Sarah (1888–1968)
Mirabeau, Comtesse de (1827–1914)
Miranda, Isa (1909–1982)
Miremont, Anne d'Aubourg de La Bove, Comtesse de (1735–1811)
Mitchell, Margaret (1900–1949)
Mitchison, Naomi (1897–1999)
Miura, Ayako (1922–1999)
Miyao, Tomiko (1926—)
Mohr, Nicholasa (1935—)
Molesworth, Mary Louisa (1839–1921)
Monbart, Marie-Joséphine de Lescun (1758–1800)
Monplaisir, Emma (1918—)
Monserdà de Macía, Dolors (1845–1919)
Montgomery, Lucy Maud (1874–1942)
Montolieu, Pauline (1751–1832)
Montoriol i Puig, Carme (1893–1966)
Montseny, Federica (1905–1994)
Moon, Lorna (1886–1930)
Moore, Clara (1824–1899)
Moosdorf, Johanna (1911–2000)
Morandini, Giuliana (1938—)
Morante, Elsa (1912–1985)
More, Hannah (1745–1833)
Morency, Barbe-Suzanne-Aimable Giroux de (1770–?)
Morgan, Joan (1905–2004)
Morgan, Sally (1951—)
Morgan, Sydney (1780–1859)
Morgner, Irmtraud (1933–1990)
Mori, Mari (1903–1987)
Morisaki, Kazue (1927—)
Morris, Jan (1926—)
Morrison, Toni (1931—)
Mortimer, Penelope (1918–1999)
Mourning Dove (c. 1888–1936)
Muir, Willa (1890–1970)
Mukherjee, Bharati (1938—)
Mulder, Elisabeth (1904–1987)
Mulholland, Clara (d. 1934)
Mulholland, Rosa (1841–1921)
Mulkerns, Val (1925—)
Müller, Clara (1860–1905)
Mundt, Klara Müller (1814–1873)
Murasaki Shikibu (c. 973–c. 1015)
Murat, Henriette Julie de (1670–1716)
Murdoch, Iris (1919–1999)
Murfree, Mary N. (1850–1922)
Muria, Anna (1904–2002)
Murray, Anna Maria (1808–1899)
Musa, Gilda (1926–1999)
Mutafchieva, Vera P. (1929—)
Mvungi, Martha
Myles, Lynda (1947—)
Myrtel, Hera (b. 1868)
Nagródskaia, Evdokiia (1866–1930)
Nákou, Lilika (1903–1989)
Nalkowska, Zofia (1884–1954)
Namjoshi, Suniti (1941—)
Naranjo, Carmen (1928—)
Nasralla, Emily (1931—)
Nasrin, Taslima (1962—)
Naubert, Christiane Benedikte (1756–1819)
Naylor, Gloria (1950—)
Nazáreva, Kapitolina Valerianovna (1847–1900)
Nesbit, Edith (1858–1924)
Ngcobo, Lauretta (1932—)
Niboyet, Eugénie (1797–1883)
Nieh Hualing (1925—)
Niese, Charlotte (1854–1935)
Nikambe, Shevantibai M. (b. 1865)
Niles, Blair (1880–1959)
Nimmanhemin, M.L. Bupha Kunjara (1905–1963)
Njau, Rebeka (1932—)
Noailles, Marie-Laure de (1902–1970)
Nóbrega, Isabel da (1925—)
Nogami, Yaeko (1885–1985)
Norman, Marsha (1947—)
Norris, Kathleen (1880–1966)
Norton, Caroline (1808–1877)

Norton, Mary (1903–1992)
Nöstlinger, Christine (1936—)
Nott, Kathleen (1909–1999)
Novak, Helga (1935—)
Nováková, Teréza (1853–1912)
Nunes, Natália (1921—)
Nwapa, Flora (1931–1993)
Oakley, Ann (1944—)
Oates, Joyce Carol (1938—)
Oba, Minako (1930—)
O'Brien, Edna (1930—)
O'Brien, Kate (1897–1974)
O'Connor, Flannery (1925–1964)
Odaga, Asenath (1938—)
Odoevtseva, Irina (c. 1895–1990)
O'Faolain, Julia (1932—)
O'Faolain, Nuala (1940—)
Ogot, Grace (1930—)
O'Hara, Mary (1885–1980)
Ohara, Tomie (b. 1912)
O'Keeffe, Adelaide (1776–c. 1855)
Okoye, Ifeoma
Oliphant, Margaret (1828–1897)
Olivier, Edith (c. 1879–1948)
Olsen, Tillie (c. 1912—)
Olsson, Hagar (1893–1978)
O'Malley, Mary Dolling (1889–1974)
Ombres, Rossana (1931—)
O'Meara, Kathleen (1839–1888)
O'Neill, Rose Cecil (1874–1944)
Orphee, Elvira (1930—)
Ortese, Anna Maria (1914–1998)
Orzeszkowa, Eliza (1841–1910)
Ostenso, Martha (1900–1963)
Otto-Peters, Luise (1819–1895)
Owens, Claire Myers (1896–1983)
Ozick, Cynthia (1928—)
Paalzow, Henriette (1788–1847)
Packer, Joy (1905–1977)
Paemel, Monika van (1945—)
Page, Gertrude (1873–1922)
Paget, Violet (1856–1935)
Palacios, Lucila (1902–1994)
Palli, Angelica (1798–1875)
Palmer, Lilli (1914–1986)
Panova, Vera (1905–1973)
Panter-Downes, Mollie (1906–1997)
Papadat-Bengescu, Hortensia (1876–1955)
Papadopoulou, Alexandra (1867–1906)
Pardo Bazán, Emilia (1852–1921)
Pardoe, Julia (1804–1862)
Paretsky, Sara (1947—)
Pargeter, Edith (c. 1913–1995)
Park, Ruth (1923—)
Parr, Harriet (1828–1900)
Parra, Teresa de la (1889–1936)
Parren, Kalliroe (1861–1940)
Parrish, Anne (1888–1957)
Parsons, Eliza (c. 1748–1811)
Parturier, Françoise (1919—)
Paterson, Isabel (c. 1886–1961)
Paton Walsh, Jill (1937—)
Patton, Frances Gray (1906–2000)
Peacocke, Isabel Maud (1881–1973)
Pedretti, Erica (1930—)
Peri Rossi, Cristina (1941—)
Pestana, Alice (1860–1929)
Peterkin, Julia (1880–1961)
Petit, Magdalena (1900–1968)
Petrushevskaya, Ludmilla (1938—)
Petry, Ann (1908–1997)
Phelps, Elizabeth Wooster Stuart (1815–1852)
Pichler, Karoline (1769–1843)
Pichler, Magdalena (1881–1920)
Pickthall, Marjorie (1883–1922)
Pierangeli, Rina Faccio (1876–1960)
Piercy, Marge (1936—)
Pike, Mary (1824–1908)
Pilcher, Rosamunde (1924—)
Piñon, Nélida (1937—)
Pizzey, Erin (1939—)
Plath, Sylvia (1932–1963)
Pleijel, Agneta (1940—)
Polcz, Alaine (1921—)
Poletti, Syria (1919–1991)
Polite, Carlene Hatcher (1932—)
Pompeia, Núria (1938—)
Poniatowska, Elena (1932—)
Portal, Marta (1930—)
Porter, Anna Maria (1780–1832)
Porter, Jane (1776–1850)
Porter, Katherine Anne (1890–1980)
Post, Emily (1872–1960)
Poulain, Mme (c. 1750–c. 1800)
Powell, Dawn (1897–1965)
Powell, Dilys (1901–1995)
Praed, Rosa (1851–1935)
Preradovic, Paula von (1887–1951)
Price, Eugenia (1916–1996)
Prichard, Katharine Susannah (1883–1969)
Pritam, Amrita (1919–2005)
Prosperi, Carola (1883–1975)
Prou, Suzanne (1920–1995)
Proulx, E. Annie (1935—)
Prouty, Olive Higgins (1882–1974)
Przybyszewska, Dagny Juel (1867–1901)
Puisieux, Madeleine de (1720–1798)
Pym, Barbara (1913–1980)
Qiong Yao (1938—)
Quaretti, Lea (1912–1981)
Queirós, Raquel de (1910–2003)
Queizán, María Xosé (1938—)
Quin, Ann (1936–1973)
Quindlen, Anna (1953—)
Quiroga, Elena (1919–1995)
Radcliffe, Ann (1764–1823)
Radcliffe, Mary Ann (c. 1746–after 1810)
Rafanelli, Leda (1880–1971)
Rama Rau, Santha (1923—)
Ramée, Louise de la (1839–1908)
Ramondino, Fabrizia (1936—)
Rand, Ayn (1905–1982)
Rashid, Saleha Abdul (1939—)
Rasp, Renate (1935—)
Rathbone, Hannah Mary (1798–1878)
Rawlings, Marjorie Kinnan (1896–1953)
Rawlinson, Gloria (1918–1995)
Ray, René (1911–1993)
Reed, Myrtle (1874–1911)
Reeve, Clara (1729–1807)
Reimann, Brigitte (1933–1973)
Reinig, Christa (1926—)
Reinshagen, Gerlind (1926—)
Reis, Maria Firmina dos (1825–1917)
Renault, Mary (1905–1983)
Rendell, Ruth (1930—)
Renée (1926—)
Renneville, Sophie de (1772–1822)
Reschke, Karin (1940—)
Resnik, Muriel (c. 1917–1995)
Reuter, Gabriele (1859–1941)
Reventlow, Franziska von (1871–1918)
Reybaud, Fanny (1802–1871)
Reza, Yasmina (1959—)
Rhys, Jean (1890–1979)
Riccoboni, Marie-Jeanne (1713–1792)
Rice, Alice Hegan (1870–1942)
Rice, Anne (1941—)
Rich, Louise Dickinson (1903–1991)
Richards, Laura E. (1850–1943)
Richardson, Dorothy (1873–1957)
Richardson, Henry Handel (1870–1946)
Rickert, Edith (1871–1938)
Riddell, Charlotte (1832–1906)
Rimington, Stella (1935—)
Rinehart, Mary Roberts (1876–1958)
Rinser, Luise (1911–2002)
Ritchie, Anne Isabella (1837–1919)
Ritter, Erika (1948—)
Rives, Amélie (1863–1945)
Robert, Marie-Anne de Roumier (1705–1771)
Robert-Angelini, Enif (1886–1976)
Robert-Kéralio, Louise (1758–1821)
Roberts, Elizabeth Madox (1881–1941)
Roberts, Sheila (1937—)
Robertson, E. Arnot (1903–1961)
Robertson, Heather (1942—)
Robins, Denise Naomi (1897–1985)
Robins, Elizabeth (1862–1952)
Robinson, Therese Albertine Louise von Jakob (1797–1870)
Roche, Regina Maria (c. 1764–1845)
Rochefort, Christiane (1917–1998)
Rodoreda, Mercè (1909–1983)
Romano, Lalla (1906–2001)
Romein-Verschoor, Annie (1895–1978)
Rooke, Daphne (1914—)
Ros, Amanda (1860–1939)
Rosca, Ninotchka (1941—)
Rosman, Alice Grant (1887–1961)
Rothmann, Maria Elisabeth (1875–1975)
Rowson, Susanna (1762–1824)
Roy, Arundhati (1961—)
Roy, Gabrielle (1909–1983)
Roy de Clotte le Barillier, Berthe (1868–1927)
Royde-Smith, Naomi Gwladys (c. 1880–1964)
Rubens, Bernice (1928–2004)
Ruck, Berta (1878–1978)
Rukeyser, Muriel (1913–1980)
Rule, Jane (1931—)
Runeberg, Fredrika (1807–1879)
Rush, Rebecca (1779–1850)
Rute, Mme de (1831–1902)
Ryum, Ulla (1937—)
Saburova, Irina (1907–1979)
Sackville-West, Vita (1892–1962)
Sadlier, Mary Anne (1820–1903)
Saenz-Alonso, Mercedes (1916–2000)
Sagan, Françoise (1935–2004)
Sahgal, Nayantara (1927—)
Saint, Dora Jessie (1913—)
Saint Mars, Gabrielle de (1804–1872)
Salhias de Tournemire, Elizaveta (1815–1892)
Salisachs, Mercedes (1916—)
Salm-Dyck, Constance de (1767–1845)
Salminen, Sally (1906–1976)
Salverson, Laura Goodman (1890–1970)
Samman, Ghada al- (1942—)
Sand, George (1804–1876)
Sandel, Cora (1880–1974)
Sanders, Dorothy Lucie (1903–1987)
Sangster, Margaret (1838–1912)
Sansay, Leonora (fl. 1807–1823)
Sanvitale, Francesca (1928—)
Saranti, Galateia (1920—)
Sarraute, Nathalie (1900–1999)
Sarrazin, Albertine (1937–1967)
Sarton, May (1912–1995)
Sata, Ineko (1904–1998)
Sato, Aiko (1923—)
Saunders, Marshall (1861–1947)
Savignac, Alida de (1790–1847)
Sayers, Dorothy L. (1893–1957)
Scanlan, Nelle (1882–1968)
Scarborough, Dorothy (1878–1935)
Schopenhauer, Adele (1797–1849)
Schopenhauer, Johanna (1766–1838)
Schreiner, Olive (1855–1920)

Schriber, Margrit (1939—)
Schütz, Helga (1937—)
Schwarz-Bart, Simone (1938—)
Scott, Evelyn (1893–1963)
Scott, Mary Edith (1888–1979)
Scott, Rosie (1948—)
Scott, Sarah (1723–1795)
Scudder, Vida (1861–1954)
Scudéry, Madeleine de (1607–1701)
Sebbar, Leila (1941—)
Sedgwick, Anne Douglas (1873–1935)
Sedgwick, Catharine (1789–1867)
Seghers, Anna (1900–1983)
Seid, Ruth (1913–1995)
Seidel, Ina (1885–1974)
Sekulić, Isadora (1877–1958)
Senior, Olive (1941—)
Serao, Matilde (1856–1927)
Sergeant, Adeline (1851–1904)
Serrahima, Nuria (1937—)
Serrano, Eugenia (1918—)
Serreau, Geneviève (1915–1981)
Setouchi, Jakucho (1922—)
Séverine (1855–1929)
Sewell, Anna (1820–1878)
Sewell, Elizabeth Missing (1815–1906)
Shaginian, Marietta (1888–1982)
Shakhovskaya, Zinaida (1906–2001)
Shaler, Eleanor (1900–1989)
Shange, Ntozake (1948—)
Shapir, Olga (1850–1916)
Shaykh, Hanan al- (1945—)
Shelley, Mary (1797–1851)
Shen Rong (1935—)
Sheridan, Caroline Henrietta Callander (1779–1851)
Sheridan, Frances (1724–1766)
Sherwood, Mary Elizabeth (1826–1903)
Shibaki, Yoshiko (b. 1914)
Shields, Carol (1935–2003)
Shiono, Nanami (1937—)
Shirreff, Emily (1814–1897)
Shockley, Ann Allen (1925—)
Shulman, Alix Kates (1932—)
Sidhwa, Bapsi (1938—)
Sigerson, Dora (1866–1918)
Sigerson, Hester (d. 1898)
Silko, Leslie Marmon (1948—)
Silva, Clara (1905–1976)
Silva e Orta, Teresa M. da (c. 1711–1793)
Silva Vila, María Inés (1926—)
Simpson, Helen (1897–1940)
Sinclair, Catherine (1780–1864)
Sinclair, May (1863–1946)
Sinués, Maria del Pilar (1835–1893)
Skinner, Mollie (1876–1955)
Skrine, Agnes (c. 1865–1955)
Slater, Frances Charlotte (1892–1947)
Slesinger, Tess (1905–1945)
Smart, Elizabeth (1913–1986)
Smedley, Agnes (1892–1950)
Smedley, Menella Bute (c. 1820–1877)
Smiley, Jane (1949—)
Smirnova, Sofia (1852–1921)
Smith, Betty (1896–1972)
Smith, Charlotte (1749–1806)
Smith, Dodie (1896–1990)
Smith, Lillian (1897–1966)
Smith, Pauline (1882–1959)
Smith, Stevie (1902–1971)
Smither, Elizabeth (1941—)
Smyth, Donna (1943—)
Sobti, Krishna (1925—)
Solano, Solita (1888–1975)
Solinas Donghi, Beatrice (1923—)
Somers, Armonía (1914–1994)
Sono, Ayako (1931—)
Sontag, Susan (1933–2004)
Soriano, Elena (1917–1996)
Sotiriou, Dido (1909–2004)
Southworth, E.D.E.N. (1819–1899)
Souza-Botelho, Adélaïde Filleul, marquise of (1761–1836)
Sow Fall, Aminata (1941—)
Soysal, Sevgi (1936–1976)
Spark, Muriel (1918–2006)
Spence, Catherine (1825–1910)
Spencer, Elizabeth (1921—)
Speraz, Beatrice (1843–1923)
Spiel, Hilde (1911–1990)
St. Johns, Adela Rogers (1894–1988)
Staël, Germaine de (1766–1817)
Stafford, Jean (1915–1979)
Stead, Christina (1902–1983)
Steel, Flora Annie (1847–1929)
Steele, Danielle (1947—)
Stefan, Verena (1947—)
Stein, Gertrude (1874–1946)
Steinwachs, Ginka (1942—)
Stepney, Catherine (1785–1845)
Stern, G.B. (1890–1973)
Stettheimer, Florine (1871–1944)
Stewart, Mary (1916—)
Stockenström, Wilma (1933—)
Stockfleth, Maria Katharina (c. 1633–1692)
Stockley, Cynthia (1872–1936)
Stoddard, Elizabeth Drew (1823–1902)
Stolk, Gloria (1918–1979)
Stone, Grace Zaring (1896–1991)
Storm, Lesley (1898–1975)
Stowe, Harriet Beecher (1811–1896)
Stratton-Porter, Gene (1863–1924)
Streatfeild, Noel (1895–1986)
Stretton, Hesba (1832–1911)
Strong, Eithne (1923–1999)
Stuart, Ruth McEnery (c. 1849–1917)
Suckow, Ruth (1892–1960)
Sugimoto, Sonoko (1925—)
Sumii, Sue (1902–1997)
Summers, Essie (1912–1998)
Susann, Jacqueline (1921–1974)
Sutcliff, Rosemary (1920–1992)
Sutherland, Margaret (1941—)
Suttner, Bertha von (1843–1914)
Szabó, Magda (1917—)
Taber, Gladys (1899–1980)
Tait, Dorothy (1905–1972)
Takahashi, Takako (1932—)
Takenishi, Hiroko (1929—)
Tan, Amy (1952—)
Tanabe, Seiko (1928—)
Tanner, Ilona (1895–1955)
Taschau, Hannelies (1937—)
Tautphoeus, Baroness von (1807–1893)
Taylor, Elizabeth (1912–1975)
Taylor, Kamala (1924–2004)
Taylor, Mary (1817–1893)
Telles, Lygia Fagundes (1923—)
Tennant, Kylie (1912–1988)
Tergit, Gabrielle (1894–1982)
Terhune, Mary Virginia (1830–1922)
Tesky, Adeline Margaret (c. 1850–1924)
Tetzner, Gerti (1936—)
Tey, Josephine (1896–1952)
Thane, Elswyth (1900–1984)
Thirkell, Angela (1890–1961)
Thomas, Audrey (1935—)
Thomas, Joyce Carol (1938—)
Thompson, Sylvia (1902–1968)
Thorpe, Rose Hartwick (1850–1939)
Thorup, Kirsten (1942—)
Three Marias, The
Thurston, Katherine (1875–1911)
Tiempo, Edith L. (1919—)
Tiernan, Frances Fisher (1846–1920)
Tikkanen, Märta (1935—)
Tinayre, Marcelle (c. 1870–1948)
Tindall, Gillian (1938—)
Tinsley, Annie Turner (1808–1885)
Tlali, Miriam (1933—)
Todd, Margaret G. (1859–1918)
Tomioka, Taeko (1937—)
Tonna, Charlotte Elizabeth (1790–1846)
Torres, Xohana (1931—)
Torrezão, Guiomar (1844–1898)
Torriani, Maria Antonietta (1840–1920)
Townsend, Sue (1946—)
Traba, Marta (1930–1983)
Tracy, Honor (1913–1989)
Tracy, Mona Innis (1892–1959)
Travers, P.L. (1906–1996)
Trefusis, Violet (1894–1972)
Tremain, Rose (1943—)
Trier Mørch, Dea (1941—)
Triolet, Elsa (1896–1970)
Tristan, Flora (1803–1844)
Trollope, Frances Milton (c. 1779–1863)
Trotzig, Birgitta (1929—)
Tsumura, Setsuko (1928—)
Tsushima, Yuko (1947—)
Tumiati, Lucia (1926—)
Turner, Ethel (1872–1958)
Tusap, Srbuhi (1841–1901)
Tusquets, Esther (1936—)
Ty-Casper, Linda (1931—)
Tyler, Anne (1941—)
Tynan, Katharine (1861–1931)
Tynan, Kathleen (1937–1995)
Ulasi, Adaora Lily (1932—)
Ullmann, Regina (1884–1961)
Underhill, Evelyn (1875–1941)
Undset, Sigrid (1882–1949)
Uno, Chiyo (1897–1996)
Uttley, Alison (1884–1976)
Valentí, Helena (1940—)
Valenzuela, Luisa (1938—)
Vallette, Marguerite (1860–1953)
Van der Mark, Christine (1917–1969)
Vansova, Terezia (1857–1942)
Vartio, Marja-Liisa (1924–1966)
Vaughan, Hilda (1892–1985)
Vaz de Carvalho, Maria Amália (1847–1921)
Védrès, Nicole (1911–1965)
Vega, Ana Lydia (1946—)
Veley, Margaret (1843–1887)
Ventós i Cullell, Palmira (1862–1917)
Verbitskaia, Anastasiia (1861–1928)
Vernon, Barbara (1916–1978)
Vertua Gentile, Anna (1850–1927)
Veselkova-Kil'shtet, M.G. (1861–1931)
Victor, Frances (1826–1902)
Victor, Metta (1831–1885)
Vidal, Mary Theresa (1815–1869 or 1873)
Viebig, Clara (1860–1952)
Viganò, Renata (1900–1976)
Villedieu, Catherine des Jardins, Mme de (c. 1640–1683)
Villeneuve, Gabrielle-Suzanne de (c. 1695–1755)
Villinger, Hermine (1849–1917)
Vilmorin, Louise de (1902–1969)
Viola, Emilia Ferretti (1844–1929)
Vivanti, Annie (1868–1942)
Voigt-Diederichs, Helene (1875–1961)
von Harbou, Thea (1888–1954)
von Haynau, Edith (1884–1978)
Vorse, Mary Heaton (1874–1966)
Voynich, Ethel (1864–1960)

Voznesenskaya, Julia (1940—)
Vrugt, Johanna Petronella (1905–1960)
Vuyk, Beb (1905–1991)
Wägner, Elin (1882–1949)
Walford, Lucy (1845–1915)
Walker, Alice (1944—)
Walker, Margaret (1915–1998)
Ward, Elizabeth Stuart Phelps (1844–1911)
Ward, Harriet (1808–c. 1860)
Ward, Mrs. Humphry (1851–1920)
Warner, Marina (1946—)
Warner, Sylvia Townsend (1893–1978)
Warren, Caroline Matilda (1785–1844)
Waser, Maria (1878–1939)
Watson, Jean (1933—)
Watson, Sheila (1909–1998)
Webb, Mary (1881–1927)
Webster, Mary Morison (1894–1980)
Weingarten, Violet (1915–1976)
Weinzweig, Helen (1915—)
Weiss, Louise (1893–1983)
Weldon, Fay (1931—)
Wells, Carolyn (1862–1942)
Welty, Eudora (1909–2001)
Wenger, Lisa (1858–1941)
Wentscher, Dora (1883–1964)
Were, Miriam (1940—)
Wesley, Mary (1912–2002)
West, Jane (1758–1852)
West, Jessamyn (1902–1984)
West, Rebecca (1892–1983)
Weston, Jessie Edith (1867–1944)
Wharton, Edith (1862–1937)
White, Antonia (1899–1980)
White, Eliza Orne (1856–1947)
Whitney, Phyllis A. (b. 1903)
Widdecombe, Ann (1947—)
Widdemer, Margaret (1884–1978)
Wied, Martina (1882–1957)
Wijenaike, Punyakanthi (1935—)
Wilker, Gertrud (1924–1984)
Wilkinson, Ellen (1891–1947)
Wilkinson, Iris (1906–1939)
Williams, Sherley Anne (1944–1999)
Willumsen, Dorrit (1940—)
Wilson, Anne Glenny (1848–1930)
Wilson, Augusta Evans (1835–1909)
Wilson, Ethel (1888–1980)
Wilson, Harriet E. Adams (c. 1827–c. 1870)
Wilson, Margaret W. (1882–1973)
Wilson, Romer (1891–1930)
Winsloe, Christa (1888–1944)
Winsor, Kathleen (1919–2003)
Winter, Alice Ames (1865–1944)
Winter, John Strange (1856–1911)
Winterbach, Ingrid (1948—)
Wittig, Monique (1935–2003)
Wobeser, Caroline von (1769–1807)
Wohmann, Gabriele (1932—)
Wolf, Christa (1929—)
Wolff, Victoria (1903–1992)
Wollstonecraft, Mary (1759–1797)
Wolzogen, Karoline von (1763–1847)
Wood, Edith Elmer (1871–1945)
Wood, Ellen Price (1814–1887)
Wood, Peggy (1892–1978)
Wood, Sally Sayward Barrell Keating (1759–1855)
Woodrow, Nancy Mann Waddel (c. 1866–1935)
Woods, Katharine Pearson (1853–1923)
Woolf, Virginia (1882–1941)
Woolson, Abba Goold (1838–1921)
Wörishöffer, Sophie (1838–1890)
Wright, Mabel Osgood (1859–1934)
Wright, Sarah Elizabeth (1928—)
Wrightson, Patricia (1921—)
Wyatt, Rachel (1929—)
Wylie, Elinor (1885–1928)
Wylie, Ida A.R. (1885–1959)
Wynter, Sylvia (1928—)
Xiao Hong (1911–1942)
Xirinacs, Olga (1936—)
Yamamoto, Michiko (1936—)
Yamazaki, Toyoko (1924—)
Yanaranop, Sukanya (1931—)
Yáñez, María Flora (1898–1982)
Yazova, Yana (1912–1974)
Yessayan, Zabel (1878–1943)
Yezierska, Anzia (c. 1881–1970)
Yonge, Charlotte Mary (1823–1901)
Young, E.H. (1880–1949)
Young, Marguerite (1908–1995)
Yourcenar, Marguerite (1903–1987)
Yuan Jing (b. 1914)
Yu Lihua (1932—)
Zamudio, Adela (1854–1928)
Zapolska, Gabriela (1857–1921)
Zayas y Sotomayor, María de (1590–c. 1650)
Zayyat, Latifa al- (1923—)
Zei, Alki (1925—)
Zelinová, Hana (b. 1914)
Zeller, Eva (1923—)
Zetterling, Mai (1925–1994)
Zguriška, Zuska (1900–1984)
Zhang Jie (1937—)
Zhukova, Maria (1804–1855)
Zinner, Hedda (1902–1990)
Żmichowska, Narcyza (1819–1876)
Zographou, Lili
Zorlutuna, Halidé Nusret (1901–1984)
Zuccari, Anna Radius (1846–1918)
Zur Mühlen, Hermynia (1883–1951)
Zwi, Rose (1928—)

NUCLEAR SCIENTIST

Ajzenberg-Selove, Fay (1926—)
Brooks, Harriet (1876–1933)
Curie, Marie (1867–1934)
Freeman, Joan (1918–1998)
Joliot-Curie, Irène (1897–1956)
Mayer, Maria Goeppert (1906–1972)
Meitner, Lise (1878–1968)
Perey, Marguerite (1909–1975)
Quimby, Edith (1891–1982)
Scharff-Goldhaber, Gertrude (1911–1998)
Wu, Chien-Shiung (1912–1997)
Yalow, Rosalyn (1921—)

NUN/ABBESS

Abbott, Mother (1846–1934)
Acarie, Barbe (1566–1618)
Adela, Saint (d. 735)
Adelaide of Quedlinburg (977–1045)
Adelaide of Schaerbeck (d. 1250)
Adeliza (d. 1066?)
Agnesi, Maria Gaetana (1718–1799)
Agnes of Assisi (1207–1232)
Agnes of Bohemia (1205–1282)
Agnes of Jouarre (fl. early 13th c.)
Agnes of Monte Pulciano (1274–1317)
Agnes of Quedlinburg (1184–1203)
Agreda, Sor María de (1602–1665)
Aikenhead, Mary (1787–1858)
Alacoque, Marguerite Marie (1647–1690)
Alcoforado, Mariana (1640–1723)
Aldegund (c. 630–684)
Aldetrude (fl. 7th c)
Angela of Brescia (1474–1540)
Angelica, Mother (1923—)
Anguissola, Elena
Anna Dalassena (c. 1025–1105)
Anna von Munzingen (fl. 1327)
Anstrude of Laon (fl. 7th c.)
Antonia (1456–1491)
Arnauld, Angélique (1624–1684)
Arnauld, Jacqueline Marie (1591–1661)
Arnauld, Jeanne Catherine (1593–1671)
Assandra, Caterina (fl. 1580–1609)
Aubert, Mary Joseph (1835–1926)
Austrebertha (635–704)
Ball, Frances (1794–1861)
Balthild (c. 630–c. 680)
Banahan, Mary Gertrude (1855/56?–1932)
Barat, Madeleine Sophie (1779–1865)
Barbier, Adèle Euphrasie (1829–1893)
Barton, Elizabeth (c. 1506–1534)
Basilissa (d. 780)
Beatrice of Kent (d. after 1280)
Beatrice of Nazareth (c. 1200–1268)
Benedicta of Assisi (d. 1260)
Benincasa, Ursula (1547–1618)
Benizelos, Philothey (fl. 1650)
Bentley, Catherine (fl. 1635)
Bernadette of Lourdes (1844–1879)
Bertha of Biburg (d. 1151)
Bertha of Marbais (d. 1247)
Berthgyth (fl. 8th c.)
Bertille (d. 705/713)
Bertken, Sister (c. 1427–1514)
Bertrada of Montfort (d. after 1117)
Bourgeoys, Marguerite (1620–1700)
Branca (1259–1321)
Bridget (c. 453–c. 524)
Bridget of Sweden (1303–1373)
Butler, Mother Marie Joseph (1860–1940)
Cabrini, Frances Xavier (1850–1917)
Canty, Mary Agnes (1879–1950)
Cartagena, Teresa de (c. 1420–1470)
Castillo y Guevara, Francisca Josefa del (1671–1742)
Catherine of Bologna (1413–1463)
Catherine of Ricci (c. 1522–1589)
Catherine of Sweden (c. 1330–1381)
Cecilia (c. 1059–1126)
Christina (fl. 1086)
Christine of Gandersheim (d. 919)
Chrodielde (fl. 590)
Clara (1697–1744)
Clare of Assisi (c. 1194–1253)
Clarke, Maura (1931—)
Clemence of Barking (fl. 12th c.)
Clotilda (470–545)
Columba of Cordova (d. 853)
Columba of Rieti (1467–1501)
Connelly, Cornelia (1809–1879)
Cope, Mother Marianne (1838–1918)
Cunigunde (d. 1040?)
Cusack, Margaret Anne (1832–1899)
Cyneburg of Gloucester (c. 660–710)
Cyneburg of Mercia (fl. 655)
Cyniburg (fl. 8th c.)
Dashwood, Elizabeth Monica (1890–1943)
Demandols de La Palud, Madeleine
des Anges, Jeanne (fl. 1632)
Dickson, Mary Bernard (c. 1810–1895)
Dolma, Pachen (c. 1933–2002)
Donovan, Jean (1953—)
Drexel, Mary Katharine (1858–1955)
Duchesne, Rose Philippine (1769–1852)
Ebba (c. 610–c. 683)
Ebner, Christine (1277–1355)
Ebner, Margarethe (1291–1351)
Edburga (d. 751)
Edburga (d. 960)
Edburga of Bicester (d. 650)
Edflaed (c. 900–?)
Edith (d. 871)

Edith (d. 937)
Edith (c. 961–984)
Edmunds, Elizabeth M. (c. 1941—)
Eleanor of Provence (c. 1222–1291)
Elflaed (d. 714)
Elflaed (c. 905–c. 963)
Elfthrith (fl. 7th c.)
Elfthrith (c. 945–1002)
Elizabeth of Austria (1743–1808)
Elizabeth of Bohemia (1618–1680)
Elizabeth of Schönau (c. 1129–1164)
Elizabeth of the Trinity (1880–1906)
Elizabeth the Good (1386–1420)
Elswitha (d. 902)
Elthelthrith (630–679)
Emmerich, Anna Katharina (1774–1824)
Erauso, Catalina de (1592–1635)
Ermengarde of Anjou (d. 1147)
Este, Eleonora d' (1515–1575)
Estrées, Angélique, d' (fl. 16th c.)
Ethelburga (d. 665)
Ethelburga (d. 676?)
Ethelflaeda (fl. 900s)
Ethelflaeda (c. 963–c. 1016)
Ethelswyth (c. 843–889)
Euphrasia of Constantinople (d. around 412)
Euphrosyne (c. 790–840)
Eustochium (c. 368–c. 419)
Fara (d. 667)
Fetti, Lucrina (fl. 1614–1651)
Firenze, Francesca da (fl. 15th c.)
Florentina (d. 7th c.)
Ford, Ita (1940—)
Fornari, Maria Victoria (1562–1617)
Galilei, Maria Celeste (1600–1634)
Garcia, Sancha (fl. 1230)
Gerberga (d. 896)
Gerberga (r. 959–1001)
Gertrude of Hackeborne (1232–1292)
Gertrude of Nivelles (626–659)
Gertrude the Great (1256–1302)
Gillespie, Mother Angela (1824–1887)
Gisela (c. 753–807)
Godunova, Irene (d. 1603)
Godunova, Xenia (1582–1622)
Gonzaga, Ippolita (1503–1570)
Gonzaga, Paola (1508–1569)
Guda (fl. late 12th c.)
Habets, Marie Louise (1905–1986)
Hart, Dolores (1938—)
Hathumoda (d. 874)
Hayden, Mother Mary Bridget (1814–1890)
Heloise (c. 1100–1163)
Herlind of Maasryck (fl. 8th c.)
Herrad of Hohenberg (c. 1130–1195)
Hersende of Champagne (fl. 12th c.)
Hickey, Mary St. Domitille (1882–1958)
Hilda of Hartlepool (fl. 8th c.)
Hilda of Whitby (614–680)
Hildegard of Bingen (1098–1179)
Hildegund (d. 1188)
Hōjo Masako (1157–1225)
Hombelina (1092–1141)
Howley, Calasanctius (1848–1933)
Hoya, Katherina von (d. around 1470)
Hrotsvitha of Gandersheim (c. 935–1001)
Hummel, Berta (1909–1946)
Hygeburg (fl. 8th c.)
Ida of Louvain (d. 1260)
Ida of Nivelles (597–652)
Ida of Nivelles (d. 1232)
Ileana (1909–1991)
Irene, Sister (1823–1896)
Irene of Constantinople (d. around 921)
Irmina, Saint (d. 716?)
Isabel (1386–1402)
Isabella of France (1296–1358)
Isabel Plantagenet (c. 1317–c. 1347)
Jamet, Marie (1820–1893)
Joseph, Mother (1823–1902)
Joveta of Jerusalem (1120–?)
Juana Inés de la Cruz (1651–1695)
Juana la Beltraneja (1462–1530)
Jugan, Jeanne (1792–1879)
Juliana of Cornillon (1192–1258)
Julianna du Guesdin (fl. 1370)
Kassia (c. 800/810–before 867)
Katharina von Gebweiler (fl. c. 1340)
Katherine of Sutton (d. 1376)
Kazel, Dorothy (1931—)
Kirby, Mary Kostka (1863–1952)
Langmann, Adelheid (d. 1375)
Lathrop, Rose Hawthorne (1851–1926)
Laura
Lavallière, Eve (c. 1866–1929)
Lea, St. (d. about 383)
Leahy, Mary Gonzaga (1870–1958)
Leonarda, Isabella (1620–1704)
Leslie, Euphemia (d. after 1424)
Lioba (700–779)
Louise-Adelaide (1698–1743)
Louise Marie (1737–1787)
Lucia, Sister (1907–2005)
Lucia of Narni (1476–1544)
Lupita, Madre (1878–1963)
MacKillop, Mary Helen (1842–1909)
Macrina (327–379)
Madelberte (fl. 7th c.)
Madeleva, Sister Mary (1887–1964)
Mahapajapati (fl. 570 BCE)
Maher, Mary Cecilia (1799–1878)
Mansour, Agnes Mary (c. 1931–2004)
Mareri, Filippa (c. 1190–1236)
Margaret of Cortona (1247–1297)
Margaret of Hungary (1242–1270)
Maria do Céu (1658–1753)
Mariana of Jesus (1565–1624)
Marie (fl. 13th c.)
Marie Clotilde (d. 1794)
Marie de Bourbon (fl. 1350s)
Marie de France (c. 1140–1200)
Marie de l'Incarnation (1599–1672)
Marie of Boulogne (d. 1182)
Marie-Thérèse de Soubiran (1834–1889)
Marillac, Louise de (1591–1660)
Mariscotti, Hyacintha (d. 1640)
Marquets, Anne de (1533–1588)
Martel, Adeloga (fl. 775)
Martha the Nun (1560–1631)
Martin, Mother Mary (1892–1975)
Mary (1278–1332)
Massimi, Petronilla Paolini (1663–1726)
Mathews, Ann Teresa (1732–1800)
Mathilde de Mayenne (fl. 12th c.)
Matilda of Quedlinburg (c. 953–999)
Matilda of Saxony (c. 892–968)
Maud Plantagenet (c. 1310–c. 1377)
McAuley, Catherine (1778–1841)
McGroarty, Sister Julia (1827–1901)
McLachlan, Laurentia (1866–1953)
Mechtild of Hackeborne (1241–1298)
Mechtild of Magdeburg (c. 1207–c. 1282)
Medici, Maddalena de (1600–1633)
Melania the Elder (c. 350–c. 410)
Mexia, Ynes (1870–1938)
Milburg (d. 722?)
Mildgyth (fl. early 700s)
Mildred (d. 700?)
Monk, Maria (1816–1849)
Montespan, Françoise, Marquise de (1640–1707)
Murasaki Shikibu (c. 973–c. 1015)
Nagle, Nano (1718–1784)
Ninnoc (fl. 6th c.)
Nowland, Mary Josepha (1863–1935)
O'Connell, Mary (1814–1897)
Odette de Pougy (fl. 1266)
Odilia (fl. 620)
O'Hagan, Mary (1823–1876)
Oignt, Marguerite d' (d. 1310)
Olympias (c. 365–408)
Ormani, Maria (fl. 1453)
Osith (died c. 700)
Pascal, Jacqueline (1625–1661)
Pascalina, Sister (1894–1983)
Petre, Maude (1863–1942)
Pirckheimer, Caritas (1467–1532)
Pontes, Sister Dulce Lopes (1914–1992)
Port Royal des Champs, Abbesses of
Prejean, Helen (1939—)
Radegund of Poitiers (518–587)
Reinders, Agnes (1913–1993)
Reinhild (fl. 8th c.)
Renée de Bourbon (fl. 1477)
Restituta, Sister (1894–1943)
Rhodes, Mary (c. 1782–1853)
Riepp, Mother Benedicta (1825–1862)
Rochechouart, Gabrielle de (1645–1704)
Rogers, Mother Mary Joseph (1882–1955)
Romanov, Martha (fl. 1550)
Rossetti, Maria Francesca (1827–1876)
Russell, Mother Mary Baptist (1829–1898)
Salaberga of Laon (d. around 665)
Sancha (c. 1178–1229)
Schrieck, Louise van der (1813–1886)
Segrave, Anne (d. around 1377)
Sei Shōnagon (c. 965–?)
Seton, Elizabeth Ann (1774–1821)
Sexburga (d. around 699)
Shizuka Gozen (fl. 12th c.)
Sigolena of Albi (fl. 7th c.)
Simpson, Mary Michael (1925—)
Skobtsova, Maria (1891–1945)
Sophia of Gandersheim (c. 975–1039)
Spalding, Catherine (1793–1858)
Stade, Richardis von (d. 1152)
Stagel, Elsbeth (c. 1300–c. 1366)
Stang, Dorothy (1931–2005)
Stein, Edith (1891–1942)
Stevens, Georgia Lydia (1870–1946)
Tarabotti, Arcangela (1604–1652)
Taylor, Stella (1929—)
Tekakwitha, Kateri (1656–1680)
Teresa, Mother (1910–1997)
Teresa de Cartagena (fl. 1400)
Teresa of Avila (1515–1582)
Theoctista (c. 740–c. 802)
Theodora Porphyrogenita (c. 989–1056)
Theodrada (b. between 783 and 794)
Theophano of Athens (fl. 800s)
Thérèse of Lisieux (1873–1897)
Tomoe Gozen (fl. c. 12th c.)
Urraca of Aragon (fl. 11th c.)
Ursula (fl. 3rd or 5th c.)
Villena, Isabel de (1430–1490)
Vincent, Mother (1819–1892)
Von Trapp, Maria (1905–1987)
Walpurgis (c. 710–777)
Walter, Silja (1919—)
Ward, Mary (1586–1645)
Werburga (d. 700?)
Withburga (fl. 7th c.)
Wulfetrud of Nivelles (fl. 7th c.)
Wu Zetian (624–705)
Xenia Alexandrovna (1876–1960)
Yonge, Charlotte Mary (1823–1901)
Youville, Marie Marguerite d' (1701–1771)
Zoë Porphyrogenita (980–1050)

NURSE

Abdellah, Faye Glenn (1919—)
Agnelli, Susanna (1922—)
Aikens, Charlotte (c. 1868–1949)
Alexandra Feodorovna (1872–1918)
Allitt, Beverley Gail (1969—)
Anderson, Ellen Alice (1882–1978)
Armstrong, Penny (1946—)
Arnstein, Margaret (1904–1972)
Ashton, Helen (1891–1958)
Aston, Luise (1814–1871)
Aubert, Mary Joseph (1835–1926)
Baly, Monica E. (1914–1998)
Banotti, Mary (1939—)
Barrow, Nita (1916–1995)
Barton, Clara (1821–1912)
Basch, Anamarija (1893–after 1945)
Batterham, Mary Rose (c. 1870–1927)
Beard, Mary (1876–1946)
Beeman, Ruth Coates (1925—)
Bell, Jane (1873–1959)
Bernadette of Lourdes (1844–1879)
Betjeman, Agnes Muir (1885–1964)
Bickerdyke, Mary Ann (1817–1901)
Bicknell, Jessie (1871–1956)
Birtles, Mary (1859–1943)
Blanchfield, Florence (1884–1971)
Bonner, Elena (1923—)
Boston, Lucy Maria (1892–1990)
Botwinska, Adela (b. 1904)
Bradley, Amy Morris (1823–1904)
Brady, Mary (1821–1864)
Brandstrom, Elsa (1888–1948)
Breckinridge, Margaret E. (d. 1864)
Breckinridge, Mary (1881–1965)
Brooke, Evelyn Gertrude (1879–1962)
Brown, Molly (1867–1932)
Browne, Helen Edith (1911–1987)
Browne, Sidney Jane (1850–1941)
Buckel, C. Annette (1833–1912)
Bullwinkel, Vivian (1915–2000)
Bulstrode, Emily Mary (1867–1959)
Burgess, Renate (1910–1988)
Burke, Selma Hortense (1900–1995)
Butler, Ida (1868–1949)
Caffyn, Kathleen (1853–1926)
Callen, Maude (1899–1990)
Cameron, Robina Thomson (1892–1971)
Cammermeyer, Margarethe (1942—)
Carré, Mathilde (1908–c. 1970)
Carvajal, Luisa de (1568–1614)
Catchpole, Margaret (1762–1819)
Cavell, Edith (1865–1915)
Christie, Agatha (1890–1976)
Churchill, Jennie Jerome (1854–1921)
Clark, Cora Maris (1885–1967)
Clayton, S. Lillian (1876–1930)
Clisby, Harriet (1830–1931)
Colette (1873–1954)
Corbey, Dorette (1957—)
Corbin, Hazel (1894–1988)
Crandall, Ella Phillips (1871–1938)
Darragh, Lydia Barrington (1729–1789)
Darton, Patience (1911–1996)
Dauser, Sue (1888–1972)
Davidow, Ruth (1911–1999)
Davis, Frances Elliott (1882–1965)
Davis, Mary E.P. (c. 1840–1924)
de Galard, Geneviève (1925—)
Delano, Jane Arminda (1862–1919)
Deming, Dorothy (1893–1972)
de Wolfe, Elsie (1865–1950)
Dickson, Mary Bernard (c. 1810–1895)
Dix, Dorothea Lynde (1802–1887)
Dock, Lavinia L. (1858–1956)
Donaldson, Viva (1893–1970)
Dougherty, Ellen (c. 1843–1919)
Dougherty, Sarah (c. 1817–1898)
Dowdall, Jane (1899–1974)
Drexel, Constance (1894–1956)
Durieux, Tilla (1880–1971)
Dyke, Eunice (1883–1969)
Earhart, Amelia (1897–1937)
Edmonds, Emma (1841–1898)
Elizabeth of Hungary (1207–1231)
Elliott, Maxine (1868–1940)
Ernst, Kitty (1926—)
Evans, Ann (c. 1836–1916)
Fabiola (1928—)
Fagin, Claire (1926—)
Farmborough, Florence (1887–1978)
Fedde, Sister Elizabeth (1850–1921)
Fenwick, Ethel Gordon (1857–1947)
Fergusson, Elizabeth (1867–1930)
FitzGibbon, Hanorah Philomena (1889–1979)
Flikke, Julia Otteson (1879–1965)
Foley, Edna (1878–1943)
Franklin, Martha Minerva (1870–1968)
Fraser, Isabella (1857–1932)
Fraser, Roslin (1927–1997)
Freeman, Ruth B. (1906–1982)
Fu Hao (fl. 1040 BCE)
Gallagher, Kitty (fl. mid–19th c.)
Gardner, Julia Anna (1882–1960)
Gardner, Mary Sewall (1871–1961)
Gault, Alma Elizabeth (1891–1981)
Geister, Janet M. (1885–1964)
Gellhorn, Martha (1908–1998)
Gibbons, Abby Hopper (1801–1893)
Gillies, Janet (1864–1947)
Gilpin, Laura (1891–1979)
Goggans, Lalla (1906–1987)
Goldman, Emma (1869–1940)
Goldman, Hetty (1881–1972)
Gonne, Maud (1866–1953)
Goodrich, Annie Warburton (1866–1954)
Gordon, Eliza (1877–1938)
Greene, Catharine Littlefield (1755–1814)
Greenwood, Edith
Hale, Mamie O. (1911–c. 1968)
Hall, Lydia E. (1906–1969)
Hallowell, Anna (1831–1905)
Hamm, Margherita (1867–1907)
Hancock, Cornelia (1840–1927)
Harrold, Agnes (c. 1830–1903)
Harsant, Florence Marie (1891–1994)
Harvey, Lilian (1906–1968)
Haughery, Margaret Gaffney (1813–1882)
Hegamin, Lucille (1894–1970)
Hegan, Eliza Parks (1861–1917)
Hei, Akenehi (1877/78?–1910)
Henderson, Virginia (1897–1996)
Hicks, Adelaide (1845–1930)
Hikapuhi (1860/71?–1934)
Hirst, Grace (1805–1901)
Hoefly, Ethel Ann (1919–2003)
Hogan, Aileen I. (1899–1981)
Hoge, Jane (1811–1890)
Holford, Alice Hannah (1867–1966)
Holtby, Winifred (1898–1935)
Hooper, Kate Challis (1894–1982)
Horne, Myrtle (1892–1969)
Howes, Mary (1941—)
Hunter, Alberta (1895–1984)
Hutchinson, Anne (1591–1643)
Inglis, Helen Clyde (1867–1945)
James, Susan Gail (1953—)
Jean, Sally Lucas (1878–1971)
Jemison, Alice Lee (1901–1964)
Johns, Ethel (1879–1968)
Jumper, Betty Mae (1923—)
Kearns-MacWhinney, Linda (1888–1951)
Kenny, Elizabeth (1880–1952)
Kent, Constance (1844–?)
Keppel, Alice (1869–1947)
Khan, Noor Inayat (1914–1944)
Kimball, Martha G. (1840–1894)
Kingsley, Mary H. (1862–1900)
Kinney, Dita Hopkins (1854–1921)
Köstler, Marie (1879–1965)
Larkin, Delia (1878–1949)
Larsen, Nella (1891–1964)
Lathrop, Rose Hawthorne (1851–1926)
Lavallière, Eve (c. 1866–1929)
Law, Sallie Chapman (1805–1894)
Leete, Harriet L. (c. 1875–1927)
Lemmon, Sarah Plummer (1836–1923)
Levertov, Denise (1923–1997)
Li Shuxian (1924–1997)
Livingston, Nora G.E. (1848–1927)
Logan, Laura R. (1879–1974)
Loveridge, Emily Lemoine (1860–1941)
Loy, Mina (1882–1966)
Lubic, Ruth Watson (1927—)
Lytle, Nancy A. (1924–1987)
Maass, Clara (1876–1901)
Mackay, Maria Jane (1844–1933)
MacKinnon, Joanna (1878–1966)
Maclean, Hester (1859–1932)
MacLean, Vida (1881–1970)
Macleod, Charlotte (1852–1950)
Mahoney, Mary Eliza (1845–1926)
Mance, Jeanne (1606–1673)
Marsden, Kate (1859–1931)
Martin, Mother Mary (1892–1975)
Maude, Sibylla Emily (1862–1935)
McCarthy, Carolyn (1944—)
McCarthy, Maud (1858–1949)
McDonald, Agnes (1829–1906)
McGee, Anita Newcomb (1864–1940)
McHugh, Fanny (1861–1943)
McKain, Douglas Mary (1789–1873)
McKenna, Marthe (1893–1969)
McMaster, Elizabeth Jennet (1847–1903)
McNaught, Rose (1893–1978)
Means, Jacqueline (1936—)
Michel, Louise (1830–1905)
Miegel, Agnes (1879–1964)
Millet, Cleusa (c. 1931–1998)
Minnigerode, Lucy (1871–1935)
Mitchison, Naomi (1897–1999)
Monod, Sarah (1836–1912)
Mundinger, Mary O. (1937—)
Murdaugh, Angela (1940—)
Neill, Elizabeth Grace (1846–1926)
Nienhuys, Janna
Nightingale, Florence (1820–1910)
Noyes, Clara Dutton (1869–1936)
Nutting, Mary Adelaide (1858–1948)
O'Connell, Mary (1814–1897)
Ohlson, Agnes K. (1902–1991)
Olberg, Oda (1872–1955)
Osborne, Estelle Massey (1901–1981)
Osborne, Mary D. (1875–1946)
Osburn, Lucy (1835–1891)
Osipenko, Polina (1907–1939)
Overlach, Helene (1894–1983)
Paget, Mary (1865–1919)
Paget, Nielsine (1858–1932)
Paget, Rosalind (1855–1948)
Palmer, Sophia French (1853–1920)
Parsons, Emily Elizabeth (1824–1880)
Pattison, Dorothy W. (1832–1878)
Pengelly, Edna (1874–1959)
Peplau, Hildegard E. (1909–1999)
Peterson, Mary (1927—)
Petre, Maude (1863–1942)
Petry, Lucile (1902–1999)

Phillips, Harriet Newton (1819–1901)
Porter, Elizabeth Kerr (1894–1989)
Preradovic, Paula von (1887–1951)
Preshaw, Jane (1839–1926)
Pudney, Elizabeth Allen (1894–1976)
Putnam, Bertha Haven (1872–1960)
Pye, Edith (1876–1965)
Rafko, Kaye Lani (c. 1963—)
Reinders, Agnes (1913–1993)
Reiter, Frances (1904–1977)
Renault, Mary (1905–1983)
Restituta, Sister (1894–1943)
Reynolds, Belle (fl. 1860s)
Richards, Linda (1841–1930)
Richardson, Luba Lyons (1949—)
Rinehart, Mary Roberts (1876–1958)
Robb, Isabel Hampton (1860–1910)
Roberts, Mary May (1877–1959)
Rogers, Martha E. (1914–1994)
Rohde, Ruth Bryan Owen (1885–1954)
Ross, Ishobel (1890–1965)
Rozengolts-Levina, Eva (1898–1975)
Rymill, Mary Ann (c. 1817–1897)
Safford, Mary Jane (1834–1891)
Sandes, Flora (1876–1956)
Sanger, Margaret (1879–1966)
Sankova, Galina (b. 1904)
Saunders, Cicely (1918–2005)
Savell, Edith Alma Eileen (1883–1970)
Scales, Jessie Sleet (fl. 1900)
Schlotfeldt, Rozella M. (b. 1914—)
Schöne, Andrea Mitscherlich (1961—)
Seacole, Mary Jane (c. 1805–1881)
Seville, Carolina Ada (1874–1955)
Shaw, Flora Madeline (1864–1927)
Sheahan, Marion (1892–1994)
Sieveking, Amalie (1794–1859)
Sisulu, Albertina (1918—)
Slessor, Mary (1848–1915)
Smellie, Elizabeth Lawrie (1884–1968)
Snively, Mary Agnes (1847–1933)
Staupers, Mabel (1890–1989)
Stephenson, Elsie (1916–1967)
Stewart, Isabel Maitland (1878–1963)
Stimson, Julia (1881–1948)
Stone, Toni (1921–1996)
Sutherland, Selina Murray McDonald (1839–1909)
Sutliffe, Irene H. (1850–1936)
Svolou, Maria (d. 1976)
Swisshelm, Jane Grey (1815–1884)
Talcott, Eliza (1836–1911)
Taylor, Susie King (1848–1912)
Te Rangimarie, Puna Himene (fl. 1908–1911)
Thomas, Mary Myers (1816–1888)
Thoms, Adah B. (c. 1863–1943)
Thurston, Mabel (1869–1960)
Tillion, Germaine (b. 1907)
Titus, Shirley Carew (1892–1967)
Tolstoy, Alexandra (1884–1979)
Tompkins, Sally Louisa (1833–1916)
Toppan, Jane (1854–1938)
Tsahai Haile Selassie (1919–1942)
Tubman, Harriet (1821–1913)
Tyler, Adeline Blanchard (1805–1875)
Uzès, Anne, Duchesse d' (1847–1933)
Van Blarcom, Carolyn (1879–1960)
Ventre, Fran (1941—)
Vögtlin, Marie (1845–1916)
Wald, Florence (1917—)
Wald, Lillian D. (1867–1940)
Wallace, Sippie (1898–1986)
Wattleton, Faye (1943—)
Way, Amanda M. (1828–1914)
Weeks-Shaw, Clara S. (1857–1940)
Whyte, Edna Gardner (1902–1992)
Wilkinson, Iris (1906–1939)
Willeford, Mary B. (1900–1941)
Wilson, Cairine (1885–1962)
Wilson, Catherine (1842–1862)
Wilson, Fanny (1874–1958)
Wilson, Helen Ann (1793/94–1871)
Wittenmyer, Annie Turner (1827–1900)
Wohlers, Eliza (c. 1812–1891)
Woolson, Constance Fenimore (1840–1894)
Wormeley, Katharine Prescott (1830–1908)
Zabriskie, Louise (1887–1957)
Zaleska, Katherine (1919—)
Zlatin, Sabina (1907–1996)

NURSING ADMINISTRATOR
Bagley, Amelia (1870–1956)
Barrow, Nita (1916–1995)
Bradley, Amy Morris (1823–1904)
Cammermeyer, Margarethe (1942—)
Cavell, Edith (1865–1915)
Chapman, Pansy (1892–1973)
Delano, Jane Arminda (1862–1919)
Dix, Dorothea Lynde (1802–1887)
Fenwick, Ethel Gordon (1857–1947)
FitzGibbon, Hanorah Philomena (1889–1979)
Gardner, Mary Sewall (1871–1961)
Gillies, Janet (1864–1947)
Hooper, Kate Challis (1894–1982)
McGee, Anita Newcomb (1864–1940)
Noyes, Clara Dutton (1869–1936)
Nutting, Mary Adelaide (1858–1948)
Parsons, Emily Elizabeth (1824–1880)
Petry, Lucile (1902–1999)
Richards, Linda (1841–1930)
Robb, Isabel Hampton (1860–1910)
Stephenson, Elsie (1916–1967)
Stewart, Isabel Maitland (1878–1963)
Stimson, Julia (1881–1948)
Thoms, Adah B. (c. 1863–1943)
Thurston, Mabel (1869–1960)
Van Blarcom, Carolyn (1879–1960)
Vögtlin, Marie (1845–1916)
Wittenmyer, Annie Turner (1827–1900)
Wormeley, Katharine Prescott (1830–1908)

NUTRITIONIST
Amathila, Libertine Appolus (1940—)
Andersen, Dorothy Hansine (1901–1963)
Beeton, Isabella Mary (1836–1865)
Bell, Muriel Emma (1898–1974)
Bevier, Isabel (1860–1942)
Blunt, Katharine (1876–1954)
Chick, Harriette (1875–1977)
Davis, Adelle (1904–1974)
Davis, Katharine Bement (1860–1935)
Emerson, Gladys Anderson (1903–1984)
Farmer, Fannie Merritt (1857–1915)
Freundlich, Emmy (1878–1948)
Goldsmith, Grace Arabell (1904–1975)
Kendall, Marie Hartig (1854–1943)
Kittrell, Flemmie (1904–1980)
Minoka-Hill, Rosa (1876–1952)
Morgan, Agnes Fay (1884–1968)
Muller, Gertrude (1887–1954)
Nightingale, Florence (1820–1910)
Richards, Ellen Swallow (1842–1911)
Roberts, Lydia (1879–1965)
Rorer, Sarah Tyson (1849–1937)
Santolalla, Irene Silva de (1902–1992)
Seddon, Margaret Rhea (b. 1947)
Stanley, Louise (1883–1954)
Stern, Frances (1873–1947)
Villard, Fanny Garrison (1844–1928)
Wheeler, Ruth (1877–1948)
Widdowson, Elsie (1906–2000)
Williams, Cicely (1893–1992)

OBOIST
Gipps, Ruth (1921—)
Johnson, Celia (1908–1982)
Rothwell, Evelyn (b. 1911)

OBSTETRICIAN
Adams, Fae Margaret (1918—)
Barnes, Josephine (1912–1999)
Broomall, Anna (1847–1931)
Du Coudray, Angélique (1712–1789)
Durocher, Marie (1809–1893)
Gordon, Doris Clifton (1890–1956)
Huson, Florence (1857–1915)
Kleegman, Sophia (1901–1971)
Lachapelle, Marie (1769–1821)
Levine, Lena (1903–1965)
Lin Qiaozhi (1901–1983)
MacMurchy, Helen (1862–1953)
Ramsey, Elizabeth M. (1906–1993)
Siebold, Josepha von (1771–1849)

OCCUPATIONAL THERAPIST
Fulton, Margaret Barr (1900–1989)
Slagle, Eleanor Clarke (1871–1942)

OCEANOGRAPHER
Sears, Mary (1905–1997)

OLYMPIC-CHARIOT RACER
Bilistiche (fl. 268–264 BCE)
Cynisca (fl. 396–392 BCE)

OLYMPIC-GOLD MEDALIST
Abbott, Margaret (1878–1955)
Ackermann, Rosemarie (1952—)
Agache, Lavinia (1966—)
Agsteribbe, Estella (1909–1943)
Aguero, Taimaris (1977—)
Ahmann-Leighton, Crissy (1970—)
Ahrenholz, Brigitte (1952—)
Ajunwa, Chioma (1970—)
Akers, Michelle (1966—)
Akhaminova, Yelena (1961—)
Albright, Tenley (1935—)
Alekseyeva-Kreft, Galina (1950—)
Allen, Kate (1974—)
Allen, Katherine (1970—)
Allucci, Carmela (1970—)
Altwegg, Jeanette (1930—)
Alupei, Angela (1972—)
Amanar, Simona (1979—)
Ambrosie, Christie (1976—)
Amico, Leah (1974—)
Amosova, Zinaida (fl. 1976)
Anastasovski, Svetlana (1961—)
Andersen, Anja Jul (1969—)
Andersen, Camilla (1973—)
Andersen, Greta (1927—)
Andersen, Kristine (1976—)
Andersen, Linda (1969—)
Anderson, Chantelle (1981—)
Andersson, Agneta (1961—)
Anding, Carola (1960—)
Andrews, Michelle (1971—)
Andrews, Theresa (1962—)
Andreyuk, Yelena (1958—)
Anissina, Marina (1975—)
Anke, Hannelore (1957—)
Annan, Alyson (1973—)
Anno, Noriko (1976—)
An Sang-Mi
Antal, Dana (1977—)
Antonova, Elena (1974–)
Aoki, Mayumi (1953—)
Apel, Katrin (1973—)
Apostol, Chira (1960—)
Arakida, Yuko (1954—)

Araujo, Alexandra (1972—)
Arba-Puscatu, Rodica (1962—)
Armbrust, Barbara (1963—)
Armstrong, Debbie (1963—)
Armstrong, Jenny (1970—)
Arsenault, Samantha (1981—)
Ashford, Evelyn (1957—)
Astakhova, Polina (1936—)
Astrup, Heidi (1972—)
Auerswald, Ingrid (1957—)
Aufles, Inger
Averina, Tatiana (1950–2001)
Ayton, Sarah (1980—)
Azarova, Elena (1973—)
Aznavourian, Karina (1974—)
Azzi, Jennifer (1968—)
Baas-Kaiser, Christina (1938—)
Babb-Sprague, Kristen (1968—)
Bachmann, Tina (1978—)
Backander, Helge (1891–1958)
Badea, Ioana (1964—)
Badea, Laura (1970—)
Badulina, Svetlana (1960—)
Bahmann, Angelika (1952—)
Bailes, Margaret Johnson (1951—)
Bailey, Aleen (1980—)
Bailey, Chris (1972—)
Baitova, Svetlana (1972—)
Baiul, Oksana (1977—)
Baker, Laurie (1976—)
Bakken, Jill (1977—)
Balas, Iolanda (1936—)
Baldo, Marta
Baldycheva, Nina
Ball, Catherine (1951—)
Ballanger, Felicia (1971—)
Balogh, Suzanne (1973—)
Balthasar, Ramona (1964—)
Balzer, Karin (1938—)
Ban, Oana (1986—)
Bang, Soo-Hyun (1972—)
Baranova, Elena (1972—)
Baranova, Lyubov
Barascu, Aurica (1974—)
Barbulova-Kelbecheva, Siyka (1951—)
Barea Cobos, Maria (1966—)
Barkman, Jane (1951—)
Barlois, Valerie (1969—)
Barnes, Kirsten (1968—)
Barrio Gutierrez, Sonia (1969—)
Barros, Zoila (1976—)
Barsukova, Yulia (1978—)
Barwirth, Anita (1918—)
Barysheva, Olga (1954—)
Bau, Sabine (1969—)
Bauer, Sybil (1903–1927)
Bauer, Viola (1976—)
Bauma, Herma (1915–2003)
Bazhanova, Svetlana (1972—)
Beard, Amanda (1981—)
Beard, Betsy (1961—)
Bechard, Kelly (1978—)
Becker-Pinkston, Elizabeth (1903–1989)
Bedard, Myriam (1969—)
Bedford, B.J. (1972—)
Behle, Petra (1969—)
Behrendt-Hampe, Jutta (1960—)
Beiser, Trude (1927—)
Bekatorou, Sofia (1977—)
Bekkevold, Kristin (1977—)
Belbin, Tracey (1967—)
Bell, Florence (1909—)
Bell, Regla (1971—)
Bellutti, Antonella (1968—)
Belmondo, Stefania (1969—)
Belote, Melissa (1956—)
Belova, Irina (1980—)
Belova-Novikova, Yelena (1947—)
Beluguina, Olesia (1984—)
Benida, Nouria (1970—)
Benko, Lindsay (1976—)
Bennett, Brooke (1980—)
Benninga, Carina (1962—)
Berg, Jacomina van den (1909—)
Berg, Laura (1975—)
Berggren, Evy (1934—)
Berghmans, Ingrid (1961—)
Bernier, Sylvie (1964—)
Berthod, Madeleine (1931—)
Beseliene, Vida (1956—)
Besson, Colette (1946—)
Bestemianova, Natalia (1960—)
Betker, Jan (c. 1960—)
Bianchedi, Diana (1969—)
Bianco, Suzannah (1973—)
Biebl, Heidi (1941—)
Bird, Sue (1980—)
Bischof, Martina (1957—)
Bischoff, Sabine (1958—)
Bjedov, Djurdica (1947—)
Blahoski, Alana (1974—)
Blair, Bonnie (1964—)
Blanc, Isabelle (1975—)
Bland, Harriet (1915–1991)
Blankers-Koen, Fanny (1918—)
Blankers-Koen, Fanny (1918–2004)
Blasco Soto, Miriam (1963—)
Bleibtrey, Ethelda M. (1902–1978)
Blomberg, Vanja (1929—)
Boboc, Loredana (1984—)
Bocharova, Nina (1924—)
Bodendorf, Carla (1953—)
Boekhorst, Josephine (1957—)
Boenisch, Yvonne (1980—)
Boesler, Martina (1957—)
Boginskaya, Svetlana (1973—)
Boglioli, Wendy (1955—)
Bolden, Jeanette (1960—)
Bolhuis-Eysvogel, Marjolein (1961—)
Bolton, Ruthie (1967—)
Bondarenko, Olga (1960—)
Borchmann, Anke (1954—)
Borckink, Annie (1951—)
Borden, Amanda (1977—)
Börner, Jacqueline (1965—)
Boron, Kathrin (1969—)
Borozna, Lyudmila (1954—)
Bortolozzi, Francesca (1968—)
Bos, Alida van den (1902—)
Bosakova-Vechtova, Eva (1931–1991)
Bosurgi, Silvia (1979—)
Boswell, Cathy (1962—)
Botsford, Beth (1981—)
Botterill, Jennifer (1979—)
Bottzau, Tina (1971—)
Boulmerka, Hassiba (1968—)
Bower, Carol (1956—)
Bowman, Deborah (1963—)
Boxx, Gillian (1973—)
Boxx, Shannon (1977—)
Boyarskikh, Claudia (1939—)
Bragina, Lyudmila (1943—)
Brain, Marilyn (1959—)
Brand, Esther (1924—)
Braun, Maria-Johanna (1911–1982)
Briand, Anne (1968—)
Brisco-Hooks, Valerie (1960—)
Brisson, Therese (1966—)
Brodsgaard, Karen (1978—)
Broquedis, Marguerite (1893–1983)
Brouquier, Veronique (1957—)
Brown, Alice Regina (1960—)
Brown, Cindy (1965—)
Brown-Miller, Lisa (1966—)
Brundage, Jennifer (1973—)
Brusnikina, Olga (1978—)
Bryzgina, Olga (1963—)
Buerger, Erna (1909–1958)
Buhr-Weigelt, Liane (1956—)
Bularda-Homeghi, Olga (1958—)
Buldakova, Lyudmila (1938—)
Bullett, Vicky (1967—)
Bunatyants, Elen (1970—)
Burcica, Constanta (1971—)
Burda, Lyubov (1953—)
Burke, Lynn (1943—)
Burns, Lauren (1974—)
Burr, Leslie (1956—)
Bush, Lesley (1947—)
Bustos, Crystl (1977—)
Bye, Karyn (1971—)
Cabanillas, Nuria (1980—)
Caird, Maureen (1951—)
Calderon Martinez, Mercedes (1965—)
Camber, Irene (1926—)
Cameron, Michelle (1962—)
Campbell, Cassie (1973—)
Campbell, Veronica (1982—)
Capellmann, Nadine (1965—)
Capes, Lee (1961—)
Capes, Michelle (1966—)
Capriati, Jennifer (1976—)
Carbon, Sally (1967—)
Carew, Mary (1913–2002)
Carpenter-Phinney, Connie (1957—)
Carr, Catherine (1954—)
Carrigan, Sara (1980—)
Carvajal Rivera, Magaly Esther (1968—)
Casaretto, Caroline (1978—)
Cash, Swin (1979—)
Caslavska, Vera (1942—)
Castle, Naomi (1974—)
Catchings, Tamika (1979—)
Catherwood, Ethel (1910–1987)
Caulkins, Tracy (1963—)
Ceccarelli, Daniela (1975—)
Cha Jae-Kyung (1971—)
Chambers, Dorothea Lambert (1878–1960)
Chandler, Jennifer (1959—)
Chartrand, Isabelle (1978—)
Chase, Elizabeth (1950—)
Chastain, Brandi (1968—)
Chebukina, Yelena (1965—)
Cheeseborough, Chandra (1959—)
Chen Jing (1968—)
Chen Jing (1975—)
Chen Shih Hsin (1978—)
Chen Xiaomin (1977—)
Chen Yanqing (1979—)
Chen Yueling (1968—)
Chen Zhong (1982—)
Chernyshova, Lyudmila (1952—)
Cheryazova, Lina (1968—)
Chick, Sandra (1947—)
Choi Eun-Kyung (1984—)
Choi Min-Kyung
Cho Min-Sun
Chow, Amy (1978—)
Cho Youn-Jeong (1969—)
Chung So-Young (1967—)
Chun Lee-Kyung (c. 1976—)
Chusovitina, Oksana (1975—)
Cieply-Wieczorkowna, Teresa (1937—)
Clark, Kelly (1983—)
Claudel, Véronique (1966—)
Clausen, Stefanie (1900–1981)
Cleland, Tammy (1975—)

Clement, Elspeth (1956—)
Coachman, Alice (1923—)
Coghen Alberdingk, Mercedes (1962—)
Cohen, Tiffany (1966—)
Colander-Richardson, LaTasha (1976—)
Coleman, Georgia (1912–1940)
Colliard, Renée (fl. 1950s)
Colon, Maria (1958—)
Comaneci, Nadia (1961—)
Constantin-Buhaev, Agafia (1955—)
Conti, Francesca (1972—)
Cook, Myrtle (1902–1985)
Cook, Natalie (1975—)
Cook, Stephanie (1972—)
Cooper, Charlotte (1871–1966)
Cooper, Cynthia (1964—)
Copeland, Lillian (1904–1964)
Corban-Banovici, Sofia (1956—)
Cornell, Sheila (1962—)
Corridon, Marie (1930—)
Costa, Marlenis (1973—)
Costie, Candace (1963—)
Coughlin, Natalie (1982—)
Coventry, Kirsty (1983—)
Cowley, Gillian (1955—)
Cox, Crystal (1979—)
Coyne, Colleen (1971—)
Cranz, Christl (1914—)
Cranz, Christl (1914–2004)
Crapp, Lorraine J. (1938—)
Crawford, Shannon (1963—)
Croker, Norma (1934—)
Cuderman, Alenka (1961—)
Cumba Jay, Yumileidi (1975—)
Cuthbert, Betty (1938—)
Cutina, Laura (1968—)
Cutrone, Angela
Czigany, Kinga (1952—)
Dafovska, Ekaterina (1976—)
Dahle, Gunn-Rita (1973—)
Damian, Georgeta (1976—)
Dangalakova-Bogomilova, Tanya (1964—)
Daniel, Ellie (1950—)
Danilova, Olga (1970—)
Danilova, Pelageya (1918—)
Dasic-Kitic, Svetlana (1960—)
Daugaard, Line (1978—)
Dauniene, Tamara (1951—)
Davenport, Lindsay (1976—)
Davies, Patricia (1956—)
Davis-Thompson, Pauline (1966—)
Davydova, Anastasia (1983—)
Dawes, Dominique (1976—)
Deardurff, Deena (1957—)
de Beus, Bernadette de (1958—)
de Bruijn, Inge (1973—)
DeCosta, Sara (1977—)
Defar, Meseret (1983—)
Delehanty, Megan (1968—)
de Levie, Elka (1905–1979)
Dementyeva, Yelizaveta (1928—)
Deng Yaping (1973—)
Dennis, Clare (1916–1971)
de Rover, Jolanda (1963—)
de Varona, Donna (1947—)
Devers, Gail (1966—)
Di Centa, Manuela (1963—)
Diers, Ines (1963—)
Dijkstra, Sjoukje (1942—)
di Mario, Tania (1979—)
Ding Meiyuan (1979—)
Disl, Ursula (1970—)
Dixon, Diane (1964—)
Djukica, Slavic (1960—)
Djurica, Mirjana (1961—)
Doberschuetz-Mey, Gerlinde (1964—)
Dobson, Louise (1972—)
Dogonadze, Anna (1973—)
Donkova, Yordanka (1961—)
Donnelly, Euphrasia (b. 1906)
Donusz, Eva (1967—)
Dorado Gomez, Natalia (1967—)
Dorio, Gabriella (1957—)
Dorman, Loretta (1963—)
Dragila, Stacy (1971—)
Draves, Victoria (1924—)
Drechsler, Heike (1964—)
Duchkova, Milena (1952—)
Duenkel, Ginny (1947—)
Dumitrache, Maria Magdalena (1977—)
Dunn, Tricia (1974—)
Dupuis, Lori (1972—)
Durack, Fanny (1889–1956)
Dyroen Lancer, Becky (1971—)
Dzhigalova, Lyudmila (1962—)
Dzhugeli, Medeya (1925—)
Eastlake-Smith, Gladys (1883–1941)
Ebert, Henrietta (1954—)
Echols, Sheila Ann (1964—)
Ederle, Gertrude (1905–2003)
Edstrom, Sonja
Egerszegi, Krisztina (1974—)
Egorova, Lyubov (1966—)
Ehrhardt, Anneliese (1950—)
Ellis, Kathleen (1946—)
El Moutawakel, Nawal (1962—)
Emoto, Yuko (1972—)
Ender, Kornelia (1958–)
Enderlein, Ortrun (1943–)
Engel-Kramer, Ingrid (1943—)
Engelmann, Helene
Enger, Babben
English, Sarah (1955—)
Engquist, Ludmila (1964—)
Ercic, Emilija (1962—)
Eremia, Alexandra (1987—)
Ermakova, Anastasia (1983—)
Ermakova, Oxana (1973—)
Ernsting-Krienke, Nadine (1974—)
Espeseth, Gro (1972—)
Esser, Roswitha (1941—)
Ethridge, Mary Camille (1964—)
Evans, Janet (1971—)
Evers, Meike (1977—)
Evers-Swindell, Caroline (1978—)
Evers-Swindell, Georgina (1978—)
Faggs, Mae (1932—)
Falck, Hildegard (1949—)
Falk, Ria
Farrell, Renita (1972—)
Fawcett, Joy (1968—)
Felke, Petra (1959—)
Feng Kun (1978—)
Ferdinand, Marie (1978—)
Ferguson, Debbie (1976—)
Fernandez, Ana Ivis (1973—)
Fernandez, Gigi (1964—)
Fernandez, Isabel (1972—)
Ferrell, Barbara (1947—)
Feryabnikova, Nelli (1949—)
Fichtel, Anja (1968—)
Figini, Michela (1966—)
Fikotová, Olga (1932—)
Finch, Jennie (1980—)
Finn-Burrell, Michelle (1965—)
Fischer, Birgit (1962—)
Fish, Maree (1963—)
Fitzgerald, Benita (1961—)
Flanagan, Jeanne (1957—)
Fleischer, Ottilie (1911—)
Fleischmann, Torrance (1949—)
Fleming, Peggy (1948—)
Flessel, Laura (1971—)
Fletcher, Jennie (1890–1968)
Fleury, Catherine (1966—)
Flintoff, Debra (1960—)
Florea, Rodica (1983—)
Florman, Marianne (1964—)
Flowers, Tairia (1981—)
Flowers, Vonetta (1973—)
Ford, Atina (c. 1972—)
Ford, Michelle Jan (1962—)
Forster-Pieloth, Kerstin (1965—)
Foudy, Julie (1971—)
Fox, Catherine (1977—)
Fox, Joanne (1979—)
Francia, Mirka (1975—)
Fraser, Dawn (1937—)
Fraser, Gretchen (1919–1994)
Frechette, Sylvie (1967—)
Freed, Amanda (1979—)
Fricioiu, Maria (1960—)
Friedrich, Heike (1970—)
Friesinger, Anni (1977—)
Froehlich, Silvia (1959—)
Froelian, Isolde (1908–1957)
Fruelund, Katrine (1978—)
Fuchs, Ruth (1946—)
Fujimoto, Yuko (1943—)
Fu Mingxia (1978—)
Fung, Lori (1963—)
Funkenhauser, Zita-Eva (1966—)
Furtsch, Evelyn (1911—)
Fynes, Sevatheda (1974—)
Gabarra, Carin (1965—)
Gabellanes Marieta, Nagore (1973—)
Gafencu, Liliana (1975—)
Gaines, Chryste (1970—)
Gale, Tristan (1980—)
Galieva, Roza (1977—)
Galkina, Lioubov (1973—)
Galushka, Vera (1945—)
Gao Ling (1979—)
Gao Min (1970—)
Garatti-Saville, Eleanor (1909—)
Gato, Idalmis (1971—)
Gaudin-Latrille, Brigitte (1958—)
Gavriljuk, Nina (1965—)
Ge Fei (1975—)
Geijssen, Carolina (1947—)
Geissler, Ines (1963—)
Genauss, Carsta (1959—)
George, Maureen (1955—)
Georgescu, Elena (1964—)
Gerg, Hilde (1975—)
Gerlits, Irina (1966—)
Gesheva-Tsvetkova, Vanya (1960—)
Geweniger, Ute (1964—)
Gigli, Elena (1985—)
Gillom, Jennifer (1964—)
Gilyazova, Nailiya (1953—)
Gimenez, Estela
Glatskikh, Olga (1989—)
Glushchenko, Tatyana (1956—)
Gnauck, Maxi (1964—)
Golden, Diana (1963–2001)
Gomis, Anna (1973—)
Gong Zhichao (1977—)
Gonobobleva, Tatyana Pavlovna (1948—)
Gonzalez Laguillo, Maria (1961—)
Gonzalez Morales, Driulys (1973—)
Gordeeva, Ekaterina (1971—)
Gordon, Bridgette (1967—)
Gordon-Watson, Mary (1948—)
Gorecka, Halina (1938—)
Goretzki, Viola (1956—)
Gorokhova, Galina (1938—)
Gorokhovskaya, Mariya (1921—)

Gossick, Sue (1947—)
Gould, Shane (1956—)
Goyette, Cynthia (1946—)
Goyette, Danielle (1966—)
Goyshchik-Nasanova, Tatyana (1952—)
Graf, Steffi (1969—)
Graham, Kim (1971—)
Granato, Cammi (1971—)
Granger, Michele (1970—)
Grant, Ann (1955—)
Graves, Carie (1953—)
Greene, Nancy (1943—)
Grego, Melania (1973—)
Griffith, Yolanda (1970—)
Grigoras, Cristina (1966—)
Grillo, Gabriela (1952—)
Grinham, Judith (1939—)
Grishuk, Pasha (1972—)
Gromova, Lyudmila (1942—)
Gromova, Maria (1984—)
Gronbek, Maja (1971—)
Grozdeva, Maria (1972—)
Grozdeva, Svetlana (1959—)
Grudneva, Yelena (1974—)
Gude, Franziska (1976—)
Gudereit, Marcia (c. 1966—)
Gudzineviciute, Daina (1965—)
Guerra Cabrera, Patricia (1965—)
Guest, Irene (1900–1979)
Guidry, Carlette (1969—)
Gu Jun (1975—)
Gulbrandsen, Ragnhild (1977—)
Gulbrandsen, Solveig (1981—)
Gulyasne-Koeteles, Erzsebet (1924—)
Gummel-Helmboldt, Margitte (1941—)
Gunnarsson, Susanne (1963—)
Guo Jingjing (1981—)
Gurendez, Lorena (1981—)
Gusakova, Maria
Guseva, Klara (1937—)
Gustafsson, Toini (1938—)
Gustavson, Linda (1949—)
Gutsu, Tatyana (1976—)
Gyarmati, Olga (1924—)
Gyenge, Valeria (1933—)
Haacker, Kathrin (1967—)
Haas, Christl (1943–2001)
Haase, Helga (1934–1989)
Haase, Mandy (1982—)
Hachin-Trinquet, Pascale (1958—)
Haislett, Nicole (1972—)
Halkia, Fani (1979—)
Hall, Kaye (1951—)
Hamann, Conny (1969—)
Hamill, Dorothy (1956—)
Hamm, Mia (1972—)
Handa, Yuriko (1940—)
Han Hyun-Sook (1970—)
Hannam, Edith (1878–1951)
Hansen, Anja (1973—)
Hansen, Christina Roslyng (1978—)
Hansen, Pia (1965—)
Hanson, Brooke (1978—)
Happe-Krey, Ursula (1926—)
Hardy, Catherine (1930—)
Harrigan, Lori (1970—)
Harris, Dionna (1968—)
Harrison, Joan (1935—)
Harup, Karen-Margrete (1924—)
Harvey, Antje (1967—)
Harvey, Mary (1965—)
Hase, Dagmar (1969—)
Haslam, Juliet (1969—)
Hattestad, Stine Lise
Hattestad, Trine (1966—)
Haugenes, Margunn (1970—)
Hawkes, Rechelle (1967—)
Hayes, Joanna (1976—)
Heaney, Geraldine (1967—)
Heddle, Kathleen (1965—)
Hefford, Jayna (1977—)
Heggtveit, Anne (1939—)
Heiss-Jenkins, Carol (1940—)
Hellmann-Opitz, Martina (1960—)
Helser, Brenda (1926—)
Hemmings, Deon (1968—)
Henderson, Danielle (1977—)
Henderson, Monique (1983—)
Hendriks, Irene (1958—)
Henie, Sonja (1912–1969)
Henin-Hardenne, Justine (1982—)
Henkel, Andrea (1977—)
Henkel, Manuela (1974—)
Henkel-Redetzky, Heike (1964—)
Hennagan, Monique (1976—)
Henne, Jan (1947—)
Henning, Anne (1955—)
Henry, Jodie (1983—)
Henry, Lea (1961—)
Herber, Maxi (1920—)
Hess, Sabine (1958—)
Heyns, Penny (1974—)
Hietamies, Mirja
Higgins, Yvette (1978—)
Hilgertova, Stepanka (1968—)
Hillas, Lorraine (1961—)
Hillen, Francisca (1959—)
Hoff, Karen (1921—)
Hoffman, Anette (1971—)
Hogshead, Nancy (1962—)
Holm, Eleanor (1913–2004)
Holmes, Kelly (1970—)
Holum, Dianne (1951—)
Hong Jeong-Ho (1974—)
Honsova, Zdeka (1927–1994)
Hooper, Kate
Hörner, Silke (1965—)
Hornig-Miseler, Carola (1962—)
Horvat-Florea, Elena (1958—)
Hou Yuzhu (1963—)
Hovland, Ingeborg (1969—)
Howard, Denean (1964—)
Howard, Sherri (1962—)
Howell, Lida (1859–1939)
Hoy, Bettina (1962—)
Hucles, Angela (1978—)
Hudson, Martha (1939—)
Hudson, Nikki (1976—)
Huebler, Anna (1885–1976)
Huelsenbeck, Sarina (1962—)
Huggett, Susan (1954—)
Hughes, Sarah (1985—)
Hunger, Daniela (1972—)
Hunyady, Emese (1966—)
Hunyady, Emese (1967—)
Hwang Hae-Young (1966—)
Hyman, Misty (1979—)
Hyun Jung-Hwa (1969—)
Icho, Kaori (1984—)
Ichtchenko, Natalia (1986—)
Idem, Josefa (1964—)
Igaly, Diana (1965—)
Ignat, Doina (1968—)
Iida, Takako (1946—)
Ilyina, Vera (1974—)
Imison, Rachel (1978—)
Ionescu, Nastasia (1954—)
Isarescu, Andreea (1984—)
Isinbayeva, Yelena (1982—)
Isobe, Sata (1944—)
Ivan, Paula (1963—)
Ivanova-Kalinina, Lidiya (1937—)
Ivinskaya, Tatyana (1958—)
Ivosev, Aleksandra (1974—)
Iwasaki, Kyoko (1978—)
Izquierdo, Lilia (1967—)
Jackson, Marjorie (1931—)
Jackson, Trina (1977—)
Jahl, Evelin (1956—)
Jahren, Anne
Jakobsson, Ludowika (1884–1968)
Jang Ji-Won (1979—)
Jang Ri-Ra (1969—)
Jang Yong-Ho
Janics, Natasa (1982—)
Jankovic, Ljubinka (1958—)
Janz, Karen (1952—)
Jaschke, Martina (1960—)
Jaunzeme, Ineze (1932—)
Jedrzejczak, Otylia (1983—)
Jeffrey, Rhi (1986—)
Jensen, Bjorg Eva (1960—)
Jensen, Christine Boe (1975—)
Jensen, Trine (1980—)
Jewell, Lynne (1959—)
Jiang Ying (1963—)
Jimenez Mendivil, Soraya (1977—)
Johanson, Margareta (1895–1978)
Johansson, Irma
Johns, Helen (1914—)
Johnson, Jenna (1967—)
Johnson, Shannon (1974—)
Jolly, Allison (1956—)
Jones, Barbara (1937—)
Jones, Esther (1969—)
Jones, Leisel (1985—)
Joo Min-Jin (1983—)
Jorgensen, Rikke Horlykke (1976—)
Jorgensen, Silje (1977—)
Josephson, Karen (1964—)
Josephson, Sarah (1964—)
Joyner, Florence Griffith (1959–1998)
Joyner-Kersee, Jackie (1962—)
Juhaszne-Nagy, Katalin (1932—)
Julin-Mauroy, Magda (1894–1990)
Jung, Lovieanne (1980—)
Jung Jae-Eun (c. 1981—)
Kabaeva, Alina (1983—)
Kaciusyte, Lina (1963—)
Kaesling, Dagmar (1947—)
Kalama, Thelma (1931–1999)
Kalinchuk, Yekaterina (1922—)
Kalinina, Irina (1959—)
Kaliska, Elena (1972—)
Kallies, Monika (1956—)
Kanesaka, Katsuko (1954—)
Kania-Enke, Karin (1961—)
Kapheim, Ramona (1958—)
Karasyova, Olga (1949—)
Karavaeva, Irina (1975—)
Karlova, Larisa (1958—)
Kasai, Masae (1933—)
Kato, Kiyomi (1953—)
Kazakova, Oksana (1975—)
Kazankina, Tatyana (1951—)
Keeler, Kathryn (1956—)
Keleti, Ágnes (1921—)
Kellar, Becky (1975—)
Keller, Natascha (1977—)
Kemmer, Heike (1962—)
Kemp, Jennifer (1955—)
Kempner, Patty (1942—)
Kendall, Barbara Anne (1967—)
Kertesz, Aliz (1935—)
Khasyanova, Elvira (1981—)
Khloptseva, Yelena (1960—)
Khorkina, Svetlana (1979—)
Khristova, Ivanka (1941—)

Occupational Index

Khudashova, Yelena (1965—)
Kiaerskou, Lotte (1975—)
Kim Bo-Ram
Kim Choon-Rye (1966—)
Kim Hwa-Sook (1971—)
Kim Hyun-Mi (1967—)
Ki Mi-Sook (1967—)
Kim Jo-Sun
Kim Kyung-Soon (1965—)
Kim Kyung-Wook
Kim Mi Jung (1971—)
Kim Myong-Soon (1964—)
Kim Nam-Soon
Kim Ryang-Hee
Kim So-Hee
Kim Soo-Nyung (1971—)
Kim Yun-Mi
King, Katie (1975—)
King, Micki (1944—)
Kirvesniemi, Marja-Liisa (1955—)
Kisseleva, Maria (1974—)
Kjaergaard, Tonje (1975—)
Klecker, Denise (1972—)
Kleine, Megan (1974—)
Klier, Cornelia (1957—)
Klier-Schaller, Johanna (1952—)
Klimova, Marina (1966—)
Klimova, Natalya (1951—)
Klobukowska, Ewa (1946—)
Klochkova, Yana (1982—)
Klochneva, Olga (1968—)
Kluft, Carolina (1983—)
Klug, Annette (1969—)
Kluge, Anja (1964—)
Knape, Ulrika (1955—)
Knol, Monique (1964—)
Knudsen, Monica (1975—)
Knyazeva, Olga (1954—)
Koban, Rita (1965—)
Koch, Marita (1957—)
Kochergina-Makarets, Tatyana (1956—)
Koepke-Knetsch, Christiane (1956—)
Koeppen, Kerstin (1967—)
Koering, Dorothea (1880–1945)
Ko Gi-Hyun (1986—)
Kok, Ada (1947—)
Kolar-Merdan, Jasna (1956—)
Kolb, Claudia (1949—)
Kolling, Janne (1968—)
Kolpakova, Tatyana (1959—)
Komisarz, Rachel (1976—)
Komisova, Vera (1953—)
Kondo, Masako (1941—)
Kondratyeva, Lyudmila (1958—)
Konopacka, Halina (1900–1989)
Korbut, Olga (1955—)
Korolchik, Yanina (1976—)
Korytova, Svetlana (1968—)
Koshel, Antonina (1954—)
Koshevaya, Marina (1960—)
Kostelic, Janica (1982—)
Kostevych, Olena (1985—)
Koujela, Olga (1985—)
Koukleva, Galina (1972—)
Kovacs, Agnes (1981—)
Kovacs, Katalin (1976—)
Kovalova, Marie (1927—)
Kowalski, Kerstin (1976—)
Kowalski, Manja (1976—)
Kozyreva, Lyubov (1956—)
Krause, Barbara (1959—)
Krause, Christiane (1950—)
Kraushaar, Silke (1970—)
Kravets, Inessa (1966—)
Kraynova, Tatyana (1967—)
Kreiner, Kathy (1954—)
Krepkina, Vera (1933—)
Kretschman, Kelly (1979—)
Kringen, Goril (1972—)
Krivelyova, Svetlana (1969—)
Krivosheyeva, Olga (1961—)
Kronberger, Petra (1969—)
Krzesinska, Elzbieta (1934—)
Kuchinskaya, Natalia (1949—)
Kudreva, Natalya (1942—)
Kuehn, Anke (1981—)
Kuehne, Rita (1967—)
Kuehn-Lohs, Gabriele (1957—)
Kuenzel, Claudia (1978—)
Kulakova, Galina (1942—)
Kumbernuss, Astrid (1970—)
Kumysh, Marina (1964—)
Kurbakova, Tatiana (1986—)
Kurbatova-Gruycheva, Stoyanka (1955—)
Kurth, Andrea (1957—)
Kurvyakova, Raisa (1945—)
Kuryshko-Nagirnaya, Yekatarina (1949—)
Kuzenkova, Olga (1970—)
Kvitland, Bente (1974—)
Kye Sun-Hui (1979—)
Lacey, Venus (1967—)
Lackie, Ethel (1907–1979)
Lambert, Adelaide (1907–1996)
Lambert, Nathalie (1963—)
Lancien, Nathalie (1970—)
Lang Ping (1960—)
Lantratov, Vera (1947—)
Lao Lishi (1987—)
Laschenova, Natalia (1973—)
Latamblet Daudinot, Norka (1962—)
Lathan-Brehmer, Christina (1958—)
Latif, Badri (1977—)
Latynina, Larissa (1934—)
Latzsch, Heike (1973—)
Lau, Jutta (1955—)
Lauritsen, Susanne (1967—)
Lavric, Florica (1962—)
Lavrova, Natalia (1984—)
Lawrence, Andrea Mead (1932—)
Lawrence, Janice (1962—)
Lawrence, Tayna (1975—)
Lazakovich, Tamara (1954—)
Lazutina, Larissa (c. 1966—)
Leatherwood, Lillie (1964—)
Lebedeva, Tatyana (1976—)
Ledovskaya, Tatyana (1966—)
Leech, Faith (1941—)
Lee Eun-Kyung (1972—)
Lee-Gartner, Kerrin (1966—)
Lee Ho-Youn (1971—)
Lee Ki-Soon (1966—)
Lee Lai-shan (1970—)
Lee Mi-Young (1969—)
Lee Sung-Jin (1985—)
Lee Sun-Hee
Lehmann, Helma (1953—)
Lehmann, Sonja (1979—)
Lehn, Unni (1977—)
Le May Doan, Catriona (1970—)
Lemhenyine-Tass, Olga (1929—)
Leng, Virginia (1955—)
Lenton, Lisbeth (1985—)
Leonhardt, Carolin (1984—)
Leontyeva, Galina (1941—)
Lepennec, Emilie (1987—)
LePoole, Alexandra (1959—)
Leslie, Lisa (1972—)
LeSueur, Emily Porter (1972—)
Liang Yan (1961—)
Li Du (1982—)
Li Duihong (1970—)
Li Ju (1976—)
Lim Mi-Kyung (1967—)
Lim O-Kyung (1971—)
Li Na (1984—)
Lindberg, Karin (1929—)
Linichuk, Natalia
Lin Li (1970—)
Linsenhoff, Ann-Kathrin (1960—)
Linsenhoff, Liselott (1927—)
Lin Weining (1979—)
Lipa, Elisabeta (1964—)
Lipinski, Tara (1982—)
Li Shan (1980—)
Lisovskaya, Natalya (1962—)
Li Ting (1980—)
Li Ting (1987—)
Litoshenko, Mariya (1949—)
Liu Chunhong (1985—)
Liu Xuan (1979—)
Liu Yanan (1980—)
Li Yanjun (1963—)
Lloyd, Andrea (1965—)
Lobatch, Marina (1970—)
Lobo, Rebecca (1973—)
Lobova, Nina (1957—)
Loginova, Lidiya (1951—)
Logounova, Tatiana (1980—)
Logvinenko, Marina (1961—)
Longo, Jeannie (1958—)
Lonsbrough, Anita (1941—)
Lonzi-Ragno, Antonella (1940—)
Looney, Shelley (1972—)
Losaberidze, Ketevan (1949—)
Losch, Claudia (1960—)
Loveless, Lea (1971—)
Luan Jujie (1958—)
Luis, Alejandrina (1967—)
Lukkarinen, Marjut (1966—)
Lukkarinen, Marjut
Lu Li (1976—)
Luo Wei (1983—)
Luo Xuejuan (1984—)
Lutayeva-Berzina, Valentina (1956—)
Lutze, Manuela (1974—)
Lysenko, Tatiana (1975—)
Lyukhina, Tamara (1939—)
MacMillan, Shannon (1974—)
Macoviciuc, Camelia (1968—)
Madison, Helene (1913–1970)
Madsen, Gitte (1969—)
Maeda, Echiko (1952—)
Maehata, Hideko (1914–1995)
Maher, Kim (1971—)
Maiques Dern, Ana (1967—)
Maitland, Clover (1972—)
Makogonova, Irina (1959—)
Malato, Giusy (1971—)
Maletzki, Doris (1952—)
Malone, Maicel (1969—)
Manaudou, Laure (1986—)
Manina, Tamara (1934—)
Mann, Shelley (1937—)
Manning, Madeline (1948—)
Manoliu, Lia (1932–1998)
Manrique Perez, Silvia (1973—)
Maragall Verge, Elisabeth (1970—)
Marinescu-Borcanea, Tecla (1960—)
Marinova, Tereza (1977—)
Marosi, Paula (1936—)
Marsden, Karen (1962—)
Marten Garcia, Maritza (1963—)
Martino, Angel (1967—)
Martinsen, Bente (1972—)
Mastenbroek, Rie (1919—)
Mastenbroek, Rie (1919–2003)
Masterkova, Svetlana (1968—)
Mathews, Marlene (1934—)

Matikainen, Marjo (c. 1966—)
Matsuda, Noriko (1952—)
Matsumura, Katsumi (1944—)
Matsumura, Yoshiko (1941—)
Mauer, Renata (1969—)
Mauermayer, Gisela (1913–1995)
Mauresmo, Amelie (1979—)
May, Misty (1977—)
Ma Yanhong (1963—)
Mayer, Helene (1910–1953)
Mazina, Maria (1964—)
Mbango Etone, Françoise (1976—)
McBean, Marnie (1968—)
McConnell, Suzanne (1966—)
McCormick, Patricia (1930—)
McCray, Nikki (1971—)
McCusker, Joan (c. 1966—)
McDaniel, Mildred (1933–2004)
McDonald, Beverly (1970—)
McFalls, Jennifer (1971—)
McGee, Pamela (1962—)
McGhee, Carla (1968—)
McGuire, Edith (1944—)
McKane, Kitty (1896–1992)
McKillop, Patricia (1956—)
McKim, Josephine (1910—)
McMahon, Brigitte (1967—)
McMann, Sara (1980—)
McNair, Winifred (1877–1954)
McNamara, Julianne (1966—)
Meagher, Mary T. (1964—)
Meany, Helen (1904–1991)
Meares, Anna (1983—)
Meftakhetdinova, Zemfira (1963—)
Meili, Launi (1963—)
Meissner, Katrin (1973—)
Mekshilo, Eudokia
Melinte, Doina (1956—)
Mellgren, Dagny (1978—)
Mellor, Fleur (1936—)
Melnik, Faina (1945—)
Mendelenyine Agoston, Judit (1937—)
Mendoza, Jessica (1980—)
Menendez, Osleidys (1979—)
Menken-Schaudt, Carol (1957—)
Merleni, Irini (1982—)
Merret, Faustine (1978—)
Merz, Sue (1972—)
Meszaros, Erika (1966—)
Metcalf, Harriet (1958—)
Metschuck, Caren (1963—)
Metz, Karin (1956—)
Meyer, Debbie (1952—)
Meyer, Gertrud (1914—)
Meyfarth, Ulrike (1956—)
Micheler, Elisabeth (1966—)
Mickler, Ingrid (1942—)
Mikhaylovskaya, Lyudmila (1937—)
Mikkelsen, Henriette Roende (1980—)
Milbrett, Tiffeny (1972—)
Miles, Jearl (1966—)
Miller, Cheryl (1964—)
Miller, Inger (1972—)
Mills, Alice (1986—)
Milosovici, Lavinia (1976—)
Milton, DeLisha (1974—)
Minaicheva, Galina (1929—)
Minea-Sorohan, Anisoara (1963—)
Min Hye-Sook (1970—)
Minkh, Irina (1964—)
Misakova, Miloslava (1922—)
Misevich, Vera (1945—)
Mishkutenok, Natalia (1970—)
Mitchell, Elizabeth (1966—)
Mitchell-Taverner, Claire (1970—)
Mittermaier, Rosi (1950—)
Mitts, Heather (1978—)
Miyamoto, Emiko (1937—)
Mleczko, A.J. (1975—)
Mocanu, Diana (1984—)
Moceanu, Dominique (1981—)
Moe, Karen (1952—)
Molik, Alicia (1981—)
Molnarne-Bodo, Andrea (1934—)
Monroe, Jessica (1966—)
Montillet, Carole (1973—)
Moon Hyang-Ja (1972—)
Moore, Isabella (1894–1975)
Mørdre, Berit
Moreau, Janet (1927—)
Moressee-Pichot, Sophie (1962—)
Morgan, Sandra (1942—)
Morris, Jenny (1972—)
Mortensen, Karin (1977—)
Morton, Lucy (1898–1980)
Mota, Rosa (1958—)
Motos Iceta, Teresa (1963—)
Mounsey, Tara (1978—)
Movsessian, Vicki (1972—)
Mucke, Manuela (1975—)
Mueller, Irina (1951—)
Mueller, Kerstin (1969—)
Mueller, Romy (1958—)
Mueller, Silke (1978—)
Muellerova, Milena (1923—)
Muenzer, Lori-Ann (1966—)
Mugosa, Ljiljana (1962—)
Mugosa, Svetlana (1964—)
Mukhacheva, Lubov
Mulkey, Kim (1962—)
Müller, Anna-Maria (1949—)
Mundt, Kristina (1966—)
Munoz Martinez, Almudena (1968—)
Munz, Diana (1982—)
Muratova, Sofiya (1929—)
Murzina, Elena (1984—)
Mustonen, Kaija (1941—)
Musumeci, Maddalena (1976—)
Muzio, Christine (1951—)
Nadig, Marie-Thérése (1954—)
Nagejkina, Svetlana (1965—)
Nagy, Annamaria (1982—)
Nagy, Timea (1970—)
Naimushina, Elena (1964—)
Nall, Anita (1976—)
Nam Eun-Young (1970—)
Napolski, Nancy (1974—)
Nazarova, Olga (1955—)
Nazarova-Bagryantseva, Irina (1957—)
Neall, Gail (1955—)
Neilson, Sandy (1956—)
Neisser, Kersten (1956—)
Nemeth, Angela (1946—)
Neneniene-Casaitite, Aldona (1949—)
Nesterenko, Yuliya (1979—)
Netessova, Maria (1983—)
Netter, Mildrette (1948—)
Neunast, Daniela (1966—)
Newall, Sybil (1854–1929)
Newbery, Chantelle (1977—)
Nielsen, Anja (1975—)
Niemann, Gunda (1966—)
Nieuwenhuizen, Anneloes (1963—)
Nikishina, Svetlana (1958—)
Nikolayeva, Margarita (1935—)
Nikolayeva, Yelena (1966—)
Nikonova, Valentina (1952—)
Nikulina, Marina (1963—)
Niogret, Corinne (1972—)
Noack, Angelika (1952—)
Noble, Cindy (1958—)
Noergaard, Louise Bager (1982—)
Noguchi, Mizuki (1978—)
Nollen, Maike (1977—)
Nord, Kathleen (1965—)
Nordby, Bente (1974—)
Nordheim, Helena (1903–1943)
Nordin, Hjoerdis (1932—)
Norelius, Kristine (1956—)
Norelius, Martha (1908–1955)
Nothnagel, Anke (1966—)
Novak, Eva (1930—)
Novak, Ilona (1925—)
Novokshchenova, Olga (1974—)
Nowak, Cecile (1967—)
Nunn, Glynis (1960—)
Nuveman, Stacey (1978—)
Nybraaten, Inger-Helene (1960—)
Oancia, Ecaterina (1954—)
Ochoa, Blanca Fernández (c. 1964—)
Odinokova-Berezhnaya, Lyubov (1955—)
O'Farrill, Raisa (1972—)
Ogiyenko, Valentina (1965—)
Ognjenovic, Mirjana (1953—)
Oh Kyo-Moon
Ohr, Martine (1964—)
Oh Sung-Ok (1972—)
Okamoto, Mariko (1951—)
Olaru, Maria (1982—)
Olive Vancells, Nuria (1968—)
Olizarenko, Nadezhda (1953—)
Olsson, Anna (1964—)
Olteanu, Ioana (1966—)
Olunina, Alevtina (1930—)
O'Neill, Susie (1973—)
Onodi, Henrietta (1974—)
O'Reilly, Heather (1985—)
Ortiz Calvo, Tania (1965—)
Osiier, Ellen (1890–1962)
Osipowich, Albina (1911–1964)
O'Steen, Shyril (1960—)
Osterman, Catherine (1983—)
Ostermeyer, Micheline (1922–2001)
Otsetova, Svetlana (1950—)
Ottenbrite, Anne (1966—)
Otto, Kristin (1966—)
Otto, Sylke (1969—)
Ouden, Willemijntje den (1918–1997)
Ouellette, Caroline (1979—)
Ovchinnikova, Elena (1982—)
Ovechkina, Tatyana (1950—)
Ozolina, Elvira (1939—)
Packer, Ann E. (1942—)
Pakhalina, Yulia (1977—)
Pakhomova, Ludmila (d. 1986)
Palchikova, Irina (1959—)
Pall, Olga (1947—)
Panchuk, Lyudmila (1956—)
Papuc, Ioana (1984—)
Parker, Bridget (1939—)
Parkhomchuk, Irina (1965—)
Park Hye-Won (1983—)
Park Jeong-Lim (1970—)
Park Sung-Hyun (1983—)
Parlow, Cindy (1978—)
Partridge, Kathleen (1963—)
Paruzzi, Gabriella (1969—)
Patmore, Sharon (1963—)
Patoulidou, Paraskevi (1965—)
Patterson, Carly (1988—)
Pauca, Simona (1969—)
Pavicevic, Zorica (1956—)
Pease, Heather (1975—)
Pedersen, Susan (1953—)
Peek, Alison (1969—)
Penes, Mihaela (1947—)
Perchina, Irina (1978—)
Perec, Marie-Jose (1968—)

Pereira, Jacqueline (1964—)
Peris-Kneebone, Nova (1971—)
Perreault, Annie (1971—)
Peter, Birgit (1964—)
Peters, Mary (1939—)
Petrik, Larissa (1949—)
Petruseva, Natalia (1955—)
Pettersen, Marianne (1975—)
Pettersson, Ann-Sofi (1932—)
Pettersson, Goeta (1926—)
Petushkova, Yelena (1940—)
Petzold, Barbara (1955—)
Peyton, Kim (1957–1986)
Pezzo, Paola (1969—)
Phelps, Jaycie (1979—)
Phillips, Brenda (1958—)
Pinayeva-Khvedosyuk, Lyudmila (1936—)
Pinigina-Kulchunova, Mariya (1958—)
Piper, Carly (1983—)
Piper, Cherie (1981—)
Pires Tavares, Sandra (1973—)
Pisani, Sandra (1959—)
Plachyne-Korondi, Margit (1932—)
Planck-Szabó, Herma (1902–1986)
Ploch, Jutta (1960—)
Podkopayeva, Lilia (1978—)
Poehlsen, Paula (1913—)
Polak, Anna (1906–1943)
Poley, Viola (1955—)
Polkunen, Sirkka (1927—)
Poll, Claudia (1972—)
Pollack, Andrea (1961—)
Polsak, Udomporn (1981—)
Ponomareva-Romashkova, Nina (1929—)
Ponor, Catalina (1987—)
Ponyaeva, Tatyana (1946—)
Popescu, Marioara (1962—)
Popova-Aleksandrova, Larisa (1957—)
Poradnik-Bobrus, Lyudmila (1946—)
Portwich, Ramona (1967—)
Pos, Alette (1962—)
Posevina, Elena (1986—)
Potec, Camelia Alina (1982—)
Pottharst, Kerri-Ann (1965—)
Pötzsch, Anett (1961—)
Pounder, Cheryl (1976—)
Powell, Katrina (1972—)
Powell, Lisa (1970—)
Poynton, Dorothy (1915—)
Preis, Ellen (1912—)
Presacan, Claudia (1979—)
Press, Irina (1939—)
Press, Tamara (1939—)
Prinsloo, Christine (1952—)
Proell-Moser, Annemarie (1953—)
Prorochenko-Burakova, Tatyana (1952—)
Protopopov, Ludmila (1935—)
Prozumenshchykova, Galina (1948—)
Prudskova, Valentina (1938—)
Ptujec, Jasna (1959—)
Puica, Maricica (1950—)
Qian Hong (1971—)
Quann, Megan (1984—)
Radke, Lina (1903–1983)
Raducan, Andreea (1983—)
Radzevich, Nadezhda (1953—)
Ragusa, Cinzia (1977—)
Ramirez Merino, Virginia (1964—)
Rand, Mary (1940—)
Rantala, Lene (1968—)
Rantanen, Heli Orvokki (1970—)
Rantanen, Siiri (1924—)
Rapp, Anita (1977—)
Rapp, Susan (1965—)
Rastvorova, Valentina (1933—)
Razumova, Natalya (1961—)

Reddick, Cat (1982—)
Reichert, Ossi
Reinhardt, Sybille (1957—)
Reinisch, Rica (1965—)
Renk, Silke (1967—)
Restoux, Marie-Claire (1968—)
Retton, Mary Lou (1968—)
Reve Jimenez, Odalis (1970—)
Rezkova, Miloslava (1950—)
Reztsova, Anfisa (1964—)
Rhode, Kim (1979—)
Richards, Sanya (1985—)
Richardson, Dot (1961—)
Richter, Annegret (1950—)
Richter, Ilona (1953—)
Richter, Ulrike (1959—)
Riggin, Aileen (1906–2002)
Riise, Hege (1969—)
Riley, Ruth (1979—)
Rinne, Fanny (1980—)
Ritter, Louise (1958—)
Roberts, Tiffany (1977—)
Robertson, Shirley (1968—)
Robertson, Sonia (1947—)
Robinson, Betty (1911–1997)
Robinson, Moushaumi (1981—)
Roche, Danni (1970—)
Rodewald, Marion (1976—)
Rodnina, Irina (1949—)
Rodriguez Suarez, Maria (1957—)
Roering, Gun (1930—)
Roffe, Diann (1967—)
Rogers, Annette (b. 1913)
Rogozhina, Lyudmila (1959—)
Rohde, Brigitte (1954—)
Rolton, Gillian (1956—)
Romanova, Yelena (1963—)
Rooney, Giaan (1982—)
Rosca-Racila, Valeria (1957—)
Rose, Sylvia (1962—)
Rosendahl, Heidemarie (1947—)
Rosenfeld, Fanny (1905–1969)
Rossner, Petra (1966—)
Rostock, Marlies
Rosu, Monica (1987—)
Rothenburger-Luding, Christa (1959—)
Rothhammer, Keena (1957—)
Ruby, Karine (1978—)
Rudkovskaya, Yelena (1973—)
Rudolph, Wilma (1940–1994)
Ruegg, Yvonne
Ruggiero, Angela (1980—)
Ruiz, Tracie (1963—)
Ruiz, Yumilka (1978—)
Rupshiene, Angele (1952—)
Rutschow, Katrin (1975—)
Ruzickova, Vera (1928—)
Ruzina, Yelena (1964—)
Ryabchinskaya, Yuliya (1947–1973)
Ryon, Luann (1953—)
Ryskal, Inna (1944—)
Saadi, Elvira (1952—)
Saalfeld, Romy (1960—)
Sachenbacher, Evi (1980—)
Sadova, Natalya (1972—)
Safina, Yuliya (1950—)
Sagine-Ujlakine-Rejto, Ildiko (1937—)
Saimo, Sylvi (1914–2004)
Sakovitsne-Domolky, Lidia (1936—)
Salikhova, Roza (1944—)
Salukvadze, Nino (1969—)
Salumae, Erika (1962—)
Salzgeber, Ulla (1958—)
Samolenko, Tatyana (1961—)
Samuelson, Joan Benoit (1957—)
Samusenko-Petrenko, Tatyana (1938—)

Sanchez Salfran, Marta (1973—)
Sandahl, Ingrid (1924—)
Sandaune, Brit (1972—)
Sandeno, Kaitlin (1983—)
Sanders, Summer (1972—)
Sanderson, Tessa (1956—)
Sandig, Marita (1958—)
Sang Xue (1984—)
Sarycheva, Tatyana (1949—)
Sasaki, Setsuko (1944—)
Savery, Jill (1972—)
Savkina, Larisa (1955—)
Schacherer-Elek, Ilona (1907–1988)
Schaeffer, Wendy (c. 1975—)
Scheiblich, Christine (1954—)
Schlunegger, Hedy (1923–2003)
Schmid, Adelheid (1938—)
Schmidgall, Jenny (1979—)
Schmidt, Rikke (1975—)
Schmidt, Sybille (1967—)
Schmidt, Veronika
Schmirler, Sandra (1963–2000)
Schmitt, Julie (b. 1913)
Schneider, Petra (1963—)
Schneider, Vreni (1964—)
Schneyder, Nathalie (1968—)
Schöne, Andrea Mitscherlich (1961—)
Schrader, Hilde (1910–1966)
Schramm, Beate (1966—)
Schröer-Lehmann, Beatrix (1963—)
Schroeter, Martina (1960—)
Schroth, Frances (b. 1893)
Schuba, Beatrix (1951—)
Schuck, Anett (1970—)
Schuler, Carolyn (1943—)
Schulze, Sabina (1972—)
Schumann, Margit (1952—)
Schut, Johanna (1944—)
Schütz, Birgit (1958—)
Schwarz, Elisabeth (1936—)
Schwede, Bianka (1953—)
Sciolti, Gabriella (1974—)
Scott, Barbara Ann (1928—)
Scott, Barbara Ann (1929—)
Seidler, Helga (1949—)
Seizinger, Katja (1972—)
Sekaric, Jasna (1965—)
Selbach, Johanna (1918—)
Semjonova, Uljana (1952—)
Senff, Dina (1920—)
Sensini, Alessandra (1970—)
Serebrianskaya, Yekaterina (1977—)
Seredina, Antonina (1930—)
Sevens, Elizabeth (1949—)
Shabanova, Rafiga (1943—)
Shalamova, Elena (1982—)
Shamray-Rudko, Galina (1931—)
Shaposhnikova, Natalia (1961—)
Sharmay, Lyubov (1956—)
Shealey, Courtney (c. 1978—)
Sheen, Gillian (1928—)
Shevchenko, Elena (1971—)
Shevtsova, Lyudmila (1934—)
Shewchuk, Tammy Lee (1977—)
Shibata, Ai (1982—)
Shibuki, Ayano (1941—)
Shiley, Jean (1911–1998)
Shilova, Irina (1960—)
Shimanskaya, Vera (1981—)
Shinozaki, Yoko (1945—)
Shirai, Takako (1952—)
Shishigina, Olga (1968—)
Shishova, Lyudmila (1940—)
Shkurnova, Olga (1962—)
Shmonina, Marina (1965—)
Shon Mi-Na (1964—)

Shorina, Anna (1982—)
Shouaa, Ghada (1972—)
Shriver, Pam (1962—)
Shubina, Lyudmila (1948—)
Shubina, Mariya (1930—)
Shushunova, Elena (1969—)
Shuvayeva, Nadezhda (1952—)
Shvaybovich, Yelena (1966—)
Sidorenko, Tatyana (1966—)
Sidorova-Burochkina, Valentina (1954—)
Siech, Birte (1967—)
Siegl, Siegrun (1954—)
Silhanova, Olga (1920–1986)
Silivas, Daniela (1970—)
Silva, Jackie (1962—)
Simeoni, Sara (1953—)
Simmons-Carrasco, Heather (1970—)
Simons de Ridder, Alexandra (1963—)
Simpson, Sherone (1984—)
Singer, Heike (1964—)
Sirch, Cornelia (1966—)
Sivkova, Anna (1982—)
Skakun, Nataliya (1981—)
Skirving, Angie (1981—)
Skoblikova, Lydia (1939—)
Skolimowska, Kamila (1982—)
Skov, Rikke (1980—)
Slatter, Kate (1971—)
Slesarenko, Yelena (1982—)
Slupianek, Ilona (1956—)
Slyusareva, Olga (1969—)
Small, Kim (1965—)
Small, Sami Jo (1976—)
Smirnova, Irina (1968—)
Smith, Caroline (1906—)
Smith, Ethel (1907–1979)
Smith, Julie (1968—)
Smith, Katie (1974—)
Smith, Michele (1967—)
Smith, Michelle (1969—)
Smoleyeva, Nina (1948—)
Sobrero, Kate (1976—)
Soccer: Women's World Cup, 1999
Sofronie, Daniela (1988—)
Sohnemann, Kate (1913—)
Soia, Elena (1981—)
Solovova, Olga (1953—)
Song Ji-Hyun (1969—)
Song Nina (1980—)
Sorgers, Jana (1967—)
Sostorics, Colleen (1979—)
Speirs, Annie (1889–1926)
Sperber, Sylvia (1965—)
Spillane, Joan (1943—)
Spircu, Doina (1970—)
Spurgin, Patricia (1965—)
Srncova, Bozena (1925—)
St. Pierre, Kim (1978—)
Stad-de Jong, Xenia (1922—)
Staley, Dawn (1970—)
Stalman, Ria (1951—)
Stanciu, Anisoara (1962—)
Stanulet, Mihaela (1966—)
Starre, Katie (1971—)
Stecher, Renate (1950—)
Steding, Katy (1967—)
Steer, Irene (1889–1947)
Stefan, Maria (1954—)
Steindorf, Ute (1957—)
Steinseifer, Carrie (1968—)
Stellmach, Manuela (1970—)
Stelma, Jacoba (1907—)
Sterkel, Jill (1961—)
Stevens, Rochelle (1966—)
Still, Megan (1972—)
Stives, Karen (1950—)
Stobs, Shirley (1942—)
Stokes, Shelly (1967—)
Stone, Nikki (c. 1971—)
Stouder, Sharon (1948—)
Stowell, Belinda (1971—)
Strandberg, Britt
Strauch, Annegret (1968—)
Strazheva, Olga (1972—)
Strecen-Maseikaite, Sigita (1958—)
Street, Picabo (1971—)
Streidt, Ellen (1952—)
Strickland, Shirley (1925–2004)
Stroescu, Silvia (1985—)
Strug, Kerri (1977—)
Stückelberger, Christine (1947—)
Sturrup, Chandra (1971—)
Sudduth, Jill (1971—)
Su Huijuan (1964—)
Sukharnova, Olga (1955—)
Suk Min-Hee (1968—)
Sumnikova, Irina (1964—)
Sundby, Siren (1982—)
Sunesen, Gitte (1971—)
Sun Fuming (1974—)
Sung Kyung-Hwa (1965—)
Sunohara, Vicky (1970—)
Sun Tian Tian (1981—)
Susanti, Susi (1971—)
Susanu, Viorica (1975—)
Swoopes, Sheryl (1971—)
Syers, Madge Cave (1881–1917)
Szabo, Ecaterina (1966—)
Szabo, Gabriela (1975—)
Szekely, Eva (1927—)
Szewinska, Irena (1946—)
Szoke, Katalin (1935—)
Takahashi, Naoko (1972—)
Takalo, Helena (1947—)
Takayanagi, Shoko (1954—)
Tamura, Ryoko (1975—)
Tanase, Anca (1968—)
Tanderup, Anne Dorthe (1972—)
Tang Gonghong (1979—)
Tang Lin (1975—)
Tanida, Kuniko (1939—)
Tanimoto, Ayumi (1981—)
Tao Luna (1974—)
Taormina, Sheila (1969—)
Tappin, Ashley T. (1974—)
Taran-Iordache, Maricica Titie (1962—)
Tarpley, Lindsay (1983—)
Tauber, Ulrike (1958—)
Tauskey, Mary Anne (1955—)
Taylan, Nurcan (1983—)
Taylor, Brenda (1962—)
Taylor, Melanie Smith (1949—)
Tchachina, Irina (1982—)
Team USA: Women's Ice Hockey at Nagano
Telleria Goni, Maider (1973—)
Temes, Judit (1930—)
Teuscher, Cristina (1978—)
Themans-Simons, Judikje (1904–1943)
Theodorescu, Monica (1963—)
Theurer, Elisabeth (1956—)
Thieme, Jana (1970—)
Thien, Margot (1971—)
Thom, Linda (1943—)
Thomas, Petria (1975—)
Thompson, Jenny (1973—)
Thompson, Lesley (1959—)
Thompson, Tina (1975—)
Thomsen, Camilla Ingemann (1974—)
Thongsuk, Pawina (1979—)
Thorsness, Kristen (1960—)
Thost, Nicola (1977—)
Thuemer, Petra (1961—)
Tikhonova, Tamara (1964—)
Timmer, Marianne (1974—)
Timochenko, Alexandra (1972—)
Timoshkina-Sherstyuk, Natalya (1952—)
Titova, Ludmila (1962—)
Tkachenko, Marina (1965—)
Tkachenko, Nadezhda (1948—)
Tolkacheva, Irina (1982—)
Toma, Sanda (1956—)
Tooth, Liane (1962—)
Topping, Jenny (1980—)
Tordasi Schwarczenberger, Ildiko (1951—)
Tornikidu, Yelena (1965—)
Torrence, Gwen (1965—)
Torres, Dara (1967—)
Torres, Regla (1975—)
Torvill, Jayne (1957—)
Toth, Noemi (1976—)
Touray, Josephine (1979—)
Tourischeva, Ludmila (1952—)
Towers, Julie (1976—)
Traa, Kari (1974—)
Trillini, Giovanna (1970—)
Trofimova-Gopova, Nina (1953—)
Trotter, Deedee (1982—)
Tsirkova, Svetlana (1945—)
Tsoulfa, Emilia (1973—)
Tsoumeleka, Athanasia (1982—)
Tsukada, Maki (1982—)
Tueting, Sarah (1976—)
Tulu, Derartu (1969—)
Turchina, Zinaida (1946—)
Turner, Cathy (1962—)
Tyler, Danielle (1974—)
Tyshkevich, Tamara (1931—)
Tyurina, Lyubov (1943—)
Tyus, Wyomia (1945—)
Ueno, Masae (1979—)
Ulion, Gretchen (1972—)
Ulmer, Sarah (1976—)
Uphoff, Nicole (1967—)
Urbanovich, Galina (1917—)
Urrutia, Maria Isabel (1965—)
Vaccaroni, Dorina (1963—)
Välbe, Elena (1968—)
Valla, Trebisonda (1916—)
Valova, Elena (1963—)
Vandenhende, Severine (1974—)
van der Kade-Koudijs, Gerda (1923—)
van der Vegt, Anna (1903–1983)
van Doorn, Marieke (1960—)
Van Dyken, Amy (1973—)
Van Gennip, Yvonne (1964—)
van Grunsven, Anky (1968—)
van Langen, Ellen (1966—)
van Manen, Aletta (1958—)
van Moorsel, Leontien (1970—)
Van Randwijk, Petronella (1905–1978)
van Rumt, Hendrika (b. 1897)
van Staveren, Petra (1966—)
van Vliet, Petronella (1926—)
Vasilieva, Yulia (1978—)
Vassioukova, Olga (1980—)
Vaytsekhovskaya, Yelena (1958—)
Venciené, Vida
Venturella, Michelle (1973—)
Venturini, Tisha (1973—)
Veranes, Sibelis (1974—)
Verdecia, Legna (1972—)
Veres-Ioja, Viorica (1962—)
Vermirovska, Zdena (1913—)
Vestergaard, Mette (1975—)
Vezzali, Valentina (1974—)
Via Dufresne, Begona (1971—)
Viscopoleanu, Viorica (1939—)
Visnjic, Biserka (1953—)

Occupational Index

Voigt, Angela (1951—)
Volchetskaya, Yelena (1943—)
Volk, Helen (1954—)
Volkova, Yelena (1960—)
Vollmer, Dana (1987—)
Von Bremen, Wilhelmina (1909–1976)
von Saltza, Chris (1944—)
Von Seck-Nothnagel, Anke (1966—)
von Weiler, Sophie (1958—)
Voronina, Zinaida (1947—)
Voros, Zsuzsanna (1977—)
Wachter, Anita (1967—)
Wagner, Aly (1980—)
Wagner, Catherina (1919—)
Wagner, Katrin (1977—)
Wagstaff, Elizabeth (1974—)
Waldo, Carolyn (1964—)
Walsh, Kerri (1978—)
Walsh, Stella (1911–1980)
Walter, Louisa (1978—)
Walter, Martina (1963—)
Wambach, Abby (1980—)
Wang Hee-Kyung (1970—)
Wang Junxia (1973—)
Wang Lina (1978—)
Wang Liping (1976—)
Wang Nan (1978—)
Wang Xu (1985—)
Watley, Natasha (1981—)
Watson, Debbie (1965—)
Watson, Linda (1955—)
Watson, Pokey (1950—)
Watt, Kathryn (1964—)
Wayte, Mary (1965—)
Webb, Sarah (1977—)
Weber, Christiane (1962—)
Wehselau, Mariechen (1906—)
Wehselau, Mariechen (1906–1992)
Weigang, Birte (1968—)
Weinbrecht, Donna (1965—)
Weissensteiner, Gerda (1969—)
Wenzel, Hanni (1951—)
Wenzel, Kirsten (1961—)
Werbrouck, Ulla (1972—)
Werth, Isabell (1969—)
Wessel-Kirchels, Ute (1953—)
Wheeler, Lucille (1935—)
Whitfield, Beverly (1954–1996)
Whyte, Sandra (1970—)
Wiberg, Pernilla (1970—)
Wichman, Sharon (1952—)
Wickenheiser, Hayley (1978—)
Wideman, Lydia (1920—)
Wightman, Hazel Hotchkiss (1886–1974)
Wilber, Doreen (1930—)
Wild, Ute (1965—)
Wilhelm, Kati (1976—)
Wilke, Marina (1958—)
Wilkinson, Laura (1977—)
Williams, Christa (1978—)
Williams, Lucinda (1937—)
Williams, Natalie (1970—)
Williams, Serena (1981—)
Williams, Tonique (1976—)
Williams, Venus (1980—)
Williams, Yvette (1929—)
Wills, Helen Newington (1905–1998)
Wilson, Staci (1976—)
Witt, Katarina (1965—)
Witziers-Timmer, Jeanette (1923–2005)
Wöckel-Eckert, Bärbel (1955—)
Wodars, Sigrun (1965—)
Wolf, Sigrid (1964—)
Wolters, Kara (1975—)
Won Hye-Kyung
Wood, Carolyn (1945—)
Woodard, Lynette (1959—)
Woodbridge, Margaret (b. 1902)
Worthington, Kay (1959—)
Wu Minxia (1985—)
Wu Xiaoxuan (1958—)
Wyludda, Ilke (1969—)
Xian Dongmei (1975—)
Xing Huina (1984—)
Xu Yanmei (1971—)
Yamaguchi, Kristi (1971—)
Yang Hao (1980—)
Yang Wei (1979—)
Yang Wenyi (1972—)
Yang Xia (1977—)
Yang Xiaojun (1963—)
Yang Xilan (1961—)
Yang Yang (1976—)
Yang Young-Ja (1964—)
Yano, Hiromi (1955—)
Yegorova, Lyudmila (1931—)
Yegorova, Valentina (1964—)
Yelesina, Yelena (1970—)
Yeo Kab-Soon (1974—)
Yokoyama, Juri (1955—)
Yoon Hye-Young
Yoon Young-Sook (1971—)
Yordanova, Zdravka (1950—)
Yoshida, Mariko (1954—)
Yoshida, Saori (1982—)
Young, Dannette (1964—)
Young, Sheila (1950—)
Yuan Hua (1974—)
Yun Mi-Jin (1983—)
Yuric, Dragica (1963—)
Zabelina, Aleksandra (1937—)
Zabell, Theresa (1965—)
Zabirova, Zulfia (1973—)
Zaboluyeva, Svetlana (1966—)
Zagunis, Mariel (1985—)
Zaharias, Babe Didrikson (1911–1956)
Zakharova, Galina (1947—)
Zakharova, Nadezhda (1945—)
Zakharova, Stella (1963—)
Zakharova, Tatyana (1951—)
Zalaffi, Margherita (1966—)
Zanchi, Manuela (1977—)
Zasulskaya, Natalya (1969—)
Zatopek, Dana (1922—)
Zeghers, Margriet (1954—)
Zehrt, Monika (1952—)
Zeidler, Judith (1968—)
Zellner, Martina (1974—)
Zhang Jiewen (1981—)
Zhang Na (1980—)
Zhang Ning (1975—)
Zhang Ping (1982—)
Zhang Rongfang (1957—)
Zhang Shan (1968—)
Zhang Yining (1981—)
Zhang Yuehong (1975—)
Zhao Ruirui (1981—)
Zheng Meizhu (1962—)
Zhirko, Yelena (1968—)
Zhou Jihong (1965—)
Zhou Suhong (1979—)
Zhou Xiaolan (1957—)
Zhuang Xiaoyan (1969—)
Zhuang Yong (1972—)
Zhu Ling (1957—)
Zilber, Irina (c. 1980—)
Zimmermann-Weber, Annemarie (1940—)
Zirzow, Carola (1954—)
Zmeskal, Kim (1976—)
Zobelt, Roswietha (1954—)
Zozula, Vera
Zubareva, Olga (1958—)
Zvereva, Ellina (1960—)
Zwehl, Julia (1976—)
Zybina, Galina (1931—)
Zyuskova, Nina (1952—)

ONDES MARTENOT PLAYER

Loriod, Yvonne (1924–2001)

OPERA ADMINISTRATOR

Carte, Bridget D'Oyly (1908–1985)
Cross, Joan (1900–1993)
Krainik, Ardis (1929–1997)
Ponselle, Rosa (1897–1981)
Resnik, Regina (1922—)
Sills, Beverly (1929—)
Wagner, Winifred (1897–1980)
Yates, Mary Ann (1728–1787)

OPERA/CLASSICAL-MUSIC SINGER

Abbott, Bessie (d. 1937)
Abbott, Emma (1850–1891)
Abrams, Harriett (c. 1758–c. 1822)
Ackté, Aino (1876–1944)
Ahlers, Anny (1906–1933)
Ajzenberg-Selove, Fay (1926—)
Alarie, Pierrette (1921—)
Albanese, Licia (1913—)
Albani, Emma (c. 1847–1930)
Alboni, Marietta (1823–1894)
Alda, Frances (1879–1952)
Alpar, Gitta (1900–1991)
Ameling, Elly (1938—)
Anderson, Marian (1897–1993)
Arnould, Sophie (1740–1802)
Arroyo, Martina (1935—)
Artôt, Désirée (1835–1907)
Austral, Florence (1894–1968)
Bahr-Mildenburg, Anna (1872–1947)
Baillie, Isobel (1895–1983)
Baker, Janet (1933—)
Balkanska, Mimi (b. 1902)
Bampton, Rose (1907—)
Banti, Brigitta (c. 1756–1806)
Barbi, Alice (1862–1948)
Barbieri, Fedora (1919–2003)
Baroni, Leonora (1611–1670)
Barrientos, Maria (1884–1946)
Basile, Adriana (c. 1590–c. 1640)
Battle, Kathleen (1948—)
Behrens, Hildegard (1937—)
Bellincioni, Gemma (1864–1950)
Bene, Adriana Gabrieli del (c. 1755–1799)
Benham, Dorothy (c. 1956—)
Bennett, Mavis (1900–1990)
Benzell, Mimi (1922–1970)
Berbie, Jane (1931—)
Berganza, Teresa (1934—)
Berger, Erna (1900–1990)
Berksoy, Semiha (1910–2004)
Bible, Frances L. (1919–2001)
Billington, Elizabeth (c. 1765/68–1818)
Bishop, Ann Rivière (1810–1884)
Bland, Maria Theresa (1769–1838)
Bollinger, Anne (c. 1923–1962)
Boninsegna, Celestina (1877–1947)
Bordoni, Faustina (c. 1700–1781)
Bori, Lucrezia (1887–1960)
Borkh, Inge (1917—)
Boronat, Olimpia (1867–1934)
Bowden, Pamela (1925–2003)
Bower, Beverly (d. 2002)
Brandt, Marianne (1842–1921)
Branzell, Karin (1891–1974)
Braslau, Sophie (1888–1935)
Brema, Marie (1856–1925)
Brice, Carol (1918–1985)

Brightman, Sarah (1960—)
Bronhill, June (1929–2005)
Bronskaya, Eugenia (1882–1953)
Brouwenstijn, Gré (1915—)
Brouwenstijn, Gré (1915–1999)
Bryner, Vera (d. 1967)
Buckman, Rosina (1881–1948)
Bugarinovic, Melanija (1905–1986)
Bumbry, Grace (1937—)
Butt, Clara (1872–1936)
Caballé, Montserrat (1933—)
Callas, Maria (1923–1977)
Calvé, Emma (1858–1942)
Carden, Joan (1937—)
Carhart, Georgiana (d. 1959)
Carlisle, Kitty (b. 1910)
Carosio, Margherita (1908–2005)
Carreño, Teresa (1853–1917)
Cary, Annie Louise (1841–1921)
Castles, Amy (1880–1951)
Catalani, Angelica (1780–1849)
Cavalieri, Caterina (1760–1801)
Cavalieri, Lina (1874–1944)
Cebotari, Maria (1910–1949)
Chilcott, Susan (1963–2003)
Cibber, Susannah (1714–1766)
Cigna, Gina (1900–2001)
Cinti-Damoreau, Laure (1801–1863)
Cisneros, Eleonora de (1878–1934)
Clayburgh, Alma (d. 1958)
Colbran, Isabella (1785–1845)
Conner, Nadine (1907–2003)
Cossotto, Fiorenza (1935—)
Cotrubas, Ileana (1939—)
Crespin, Régine (1927—)
Cross, Joan (1900–1993)
Crouch, Anna Maria (1763–1805)
Cruvelli, Sofia (1826–1907)
Cuzzoni, Francesca (c. 1698–1770)
Dal Monte, Toti (1893–1975)
Danco, Suzanne (1911—)
Danco, Suzanne (1911–2000)
Darclée, Hariclea (1860–1939)
David-Neel, Alexandra (1868–1969)
DeGaetani, Jan (1933–1989)
Della Casa, Lisa (1919—)
de Lussan, Zélie (1861–1949)
Dernesch, Helga (1939—)
Derzhinskaya, Zeniya (1889–1951)
Desmond, Astra (1893–1973)
Dimitrova, Ghena (1941–2005)
Di Murska, Ilma (1836–1889)
Donalda, Pauline (1882–1970)
Douglas, Helen Gahagan (1900–1980)
Eames, Emma (1865–1952)
Easton, Florence (1882–1955)
Edvina, Louise (1878–1948)
Elias, Rosalind (1930—)
Elms, Lauris (1931—)
Épine, Margherita de l' (c. 1683–1746)
Evans, Nancy (1915–2000)
Falcon, Marie Cornélie (1814–1897)
Farrar, Geraldine (1882–1967)
Farrell, Eileen (1920–2002)
Fassbaender, Brigitte (1939—)
Favart, Marie (1727–1772)
Fel, Marie (1713–1794)
Ferrier, Kathleen (1912–1953)
Finnie, Linda (1952—)
Flagstad, Kirsten (1895–1962)
Fleming, Renée (1959—)
Fornia, Rita (1878–1922)
Fremstad, Olive (1871–1951)
Freni, Mirella (1935—)
Gadski, Johanna (1872–1932)
Galli, Caterina (c. 1723–1804)
Galli-Curci, Amelita (1882–1963)
Galli-Marié, Célestine (1840–1905)
Garden, Mary (1874–1967)
Garrison, Mabel (1886–1963)
Gauthier, Eva (1885–1958)
Gentle, Alice (1889–1958)
Gerhardt, Elena (1883–1961)
Giannini, Dusolina (1900–1986)
Gorr, Rita (1926—)
Greevy, Bernadette (1939—)
Grillo, Joann (1939–1999)
Grisi, Giuditta (1805–1840)
Gruberová, Edita (1946—)
Hale, Una (1922–2005)
Hammond, Joan (1912–1996)
Hampton, Hope (1897–1982)
Handzlic, Jean (d. 1963)
Harshaw, Margaret (1909–1997)
Hauk, Minnie (1851–1929)
Hayes, Catherine (1825–1861)
Heldy, Fanny (1888–1973)
Helmrich, Dorothy (1889–1984)
Hempel, Frieda (1885–1955)
Hidalgo, Elvira de (1892–1980)
Homer, Louise (1871–1947)
Horne, Marilyn (1929—)
Howard, Kathleen (1879–1956)
Howie, Fanny Rose (1868–1916)
Hunter, Rita (1933–2001)
Ivogün, Maria (1891–1987)
Janowitz, Gundula (1937—)
Jarboro, Caterina (1908–1986)
Jepson, Helen (1904–1997)
Jeritza, Maria (1887–1982)
Jones, Gwyneth (1936—)
Jones, Sissieretta (1869–1933)
Juch, Emma (1860–1939)
Jurinac, Sena (1921—)
Kellogg, Clara Louise (1842–1916)
Kemble, Adelaide (1814–1879)
Kirsten, Dorothy (1910–1992)
Klafsky, Katharina (1855–1896)
Konetzni, Anny (1902–1968)
Konetzni, Hilde (1905–1980)
Korjus, Miliza (1900–1980)
Korolewicz-Waydowa, Janina (1875–1955)
Köth, Erika (1925–1989)
Kronold, Selma (1861–1920)
Krusceniski, Salomea (1873–1952)
Kurz, Selma (1874–1933)
Kuznetsova, Maria (1880–1966)
La Grange, Anna de (1825–1905)
Lange, Aloysia (c. 1761–1839)
La Palme, Béatrice (1878–1921)
Lawrence, Marjorie (1908–1979)
Lazzari, Carolina (c. 1889–1946)
Lear, Evelyn (1926—)
Leblanc, Georgette (c. 1875–1941)
Lehmann, Lilli (1848–1929)
Lehmann, Lotte (1888–1976)
Leider, Frida (1888–1975)
Leigh, Adèle (1928–2004)
Lemnitz, Tiana (1897–1994)
Liebling, Estelle (1880–1970)
Lind, Jenny (1820–1887)
Linley, Elizabeth (1754–1792)
Linley, Maria (1763–1784)
Linley, Mary (1758–1787)
Lipkowska, Lydia (1882–1958)
Löhr, Marie (1890–1975)
Lorengar, Pilar (1928—)
Los Angeles, Victoria de (1923–2005)
Lubin, Germaine (1890–1979)
Lucca, Pauline (1841–1908)
Ludwig, Christa (1924—)
Malibran, Maria (1808–1836)
Mallinger, Mathilde (1847–1920)
Mana-Zucca (1887–1981)
Manning, Irene (1912–2004)
Mara, Gertrud (1749–1833)
Marchesi, Blanche (1863–1940)
Marchesi, Mathilde (1821–1913)
Mario, Queena (1896–1951)
Markova, Olga
Marshall, Lois (1924–1997)
Marshall, Margaret (1949—)
Massary, Fritzi (1882–1969)
Materna, Amalie (1844–1918)
Matzenauer, Margaret (1881–1963)
Maupin, d'Aubigny (c. 1670–1707)
Maynor, Dorothy (1910–1996)
Mei-Figner, Medea (1859–1952)
Melba, Nellie (1861–1931)
Merriman, Nan (1920—)
Mikhaylova, Maria (1866–1943)
Milanov, Zinka (1906–1989)
Milashkina, Tamara Andreyevna (1934—)
Milder-Hauptmann, Anna (1785–1838)
Mildmay, Audrey (1900–1953)
Minton, Yvonne (1938—)
Miolan-Carvalho, Marie (1827–1895)
Miura, Tamaki (1884–1946)
Mödl, Martha (1912–2001)
Moffo, Anna (1932–2006)
Moncrieff, Gladys (1892–1976)
Moore, Grace (1898–1947)
Munsel, Patrice (1925—)
Musi, Maria Maddalena (1669–1751)
Muzio, Claudia (1889–1936)
Nevada, Emma (1859–1940)
Nevada, Mignon (1885–1970)
Nezhdanova, Antonia (1873–1950)
Nezhdanova, Antonina (1873–1950)
Nielsen, Alice (c. 1870–1943)
Nilsson, Birgit (1918–2005)
Nilsson, Christine (1843–1921)
Nordica, Lillian (1857–1914)
Norman, Jessye (1945—)
Novello, Clara (1818–1908)
Novotna, Jarmila (1907–1994)
O'Connell, Patricia (d. 1975)
Olivero, Magda (b. 1910)
Oraib (797–890)
Pagliughi, Lina (1907–1980)
Painter, Eleanor (1890–1947)
Parepa-Rosa, Euphrosyne (1836–1874)
Pashley, Anne (1935—)
Pasta, Giuditta (1797–1865)
Patey, Janet Monach (1842–1894)
Patti, Adelina (1843–1919)
Peters, Roberta (1930—)
Phillipps, Adelaide (1833–1882)
Pierce, Judith (1930–2003)
Pollak, Anna (1912–1996)
Pons, Lily (1898–1976)
Ponselle, Carmela (1892–1977)
Popp, Lucia (1939–1993)
Powers, Marie (1902–1973)
Price, Leontyne (1927—)
Price, Margaret (1941—)
Raisa, Rosa (1893–1963)
Rankin, Nell (1924–2005)
Raskin, Judith (1928–1984)
Renzi, Anna (c. 1620–1660)
Resnik, Regina (1922—)
Respighi, Elsa (1894–1996)
Rethberg, Elisabeth (1894–1976)
Robin, Mado (1918–1960)
Robinson, Anastasia (c. 1692–1755)
Rothenberger, Anneliese (1924—)
Russell, Anna (b. 1911)
Rysanek, Leonie (1926–1998)

Salvini-Donatelli, Fanny (c. 1815–1891)
Sanderson, Sybil (1865–1903)
Sass, Marie Constance (1834–1907)
Sayao, Bidu (1902–1999)
Scheff, Fritzi (1879–1954)
Schneider, Hortense (1833–1920)
Schröder-Devrient, Wilhelmine (1804–1860)
Schumann, Elisabeth (1885–1952)
Schumann-Heink, Ernestine (1861–1936)
Schwarz, Vera (1888–1964)
Schwarzkopf, Elisabeth (1915—)
Sciutti, Graziella (1927–2001)
Scott, Ivy (1886–1947)
Scotto, Renata (1933—)
Seefried, Irmgard (1919–1988)
Sembrich, Marcella (1858–1935)
Sheridan, Margaret (1889–1958)
Siems, Margarethe (1879–1952)
Sills, Beverly (1929—)
Simionato, Giulietta (1910—)
Söderström, Elisabeth (1927—)
Sontag, Henriette (c. 1803–1854)
Souez, Ina (1903–1992)
Steber, Eleanor (1914–1990)
Stephens, Catherine (1794–1882)
Stevens, Risë (1913—)
Stewart, Nellie (1858–1931)
Stich-Randall, Teresa (1927—)
Stignani, Ebe (1903–1975)
Stolz, Teresa (1834–1902)
Storace, Nancy (1765–1817)
Storchio, Rosina (1876–1945)
Stratas, Teresa (1938—)
Streich, Rita (1920–1987)
Strepponi, Giuseppina (1815–1897)
Sucher, Rosa (1847–1927)
Supervia, Conchita (1895–1936)
Sutherland, Joan (1926—)
Swarthout, Gladys (1904–1969)
Talbot, Nadine (1913–2003)
Talley, Marion (1906–1983)
Tebaldi, Renata (1922–2004)
Te Kanawa, Kiri (1944—)
Telva, Marion (1897–1962)
Ternina, Milka (1863–1941)
Tess, Giulia (1889–1976)
Tetrazzini, Eva
(1862–1938)
Tetrazzini, Luisa (1871–1940)
Teyte, Maggie (1888–1976)
Thebom, Blanche (b. 1918)
Thomas, Mary (1932–1997)
Thorborg, Kerstin (1896–1970)
Thursby, Emma (1845–1931)
Tietjens, Therese (1831–1877)
Tinsley, Pauline (1928—)
Todi, Luiza Rosa (1753–1833)
Tofts, Catherine (c. 1685–1756)
Tourel, Jennie (1899–1973)
Traubel, Helen (1899–1972)
Trentini, Emma (1878–1959)
Troyanos, Tatiana (1938–1993)
Tully, Alice (1902–1993)
Turner, Eva (1892–1990)
Unger, Caroline (1803–1877)
Ursuleac, Viorica (1894–1985)
Vallin, Ninon (1886–1961)
Van Gordon, Cyrena (1896–1964)
Van Studdiford, Grace (1873–1927)
Van Zandt, Marie (1858–1919)
Varady, Julia (1941—)
Várnay, Astrid (1918—)
Verrett, Shirley (1931—)
Vestris, Lucia (1797–1856)
Viardot, Louise (1841–1918)
Viardot, Pauline (1821–1910)
Vincent, Ruth (1877–1955)
Vishnevskaya, Galina (1926—)
Von Stade, Frederica (1945—)
Wagner, Johanna (1826–1894)
Waldmann, Maria (1842–1920)
Walker, Edyth (1867–1950)
Ward, Geneviève (1838–1922)
Watanabe, Yoko (1953–2004)
Watts, Helen (1927—)
Welitsch, Ljuba (1913–1996)
Williams, Camilla (1922—)
Yaw, Ellen Beach (1868–1947)
Young, Cecilia (c. 1711–1789)
Young, Esther (1717–1795)
Young, Isabella (d. 1795)
Zoff, Marianne (1893–1984)

OPERA-COMPANY FOUNDER
Abbott, Emma (1850–1891)
Ackté, Aino (1876–1944)
Brice, Carol (1918–1985)
Caldwell, Sarah (1924–2006)
Carreño, Teresa (1853–1917)
Fox, Carol (1926–1981)
Hauk, Minnie (1851–1929)
Kellogg, Clara Louise (1842–1916)
Kuznetsova, Maria (1880–1966)
McCormick, Edith Rockefeller (1872–1932)
Melba, Nellie (1861–1931)
Nielsen, Alice (c. 1870–1943)
Parepa-Rosa, Euphrosyne (1836–1874)
Thurber, Jeannette (1850–1946)

OPERA DIRECTOR
Ackté, Aino (1876–1944)
Balkanska, Mimi (b. 1902)
Berghaus, Ruth (1927–1996)
Bori, Lucrezia (1887–1960)
Caldwell, Sarah (1924–2006)
Cross, Joan (1900–1993)
Flagstad, Kirsten (1895–1962)
Frank, Dottie (1941—)
Garden, Mary (1874–1967)
Geistinger, Marie (1833–1903)
Glover, Jane Allison (1949—)
Gutheil-Schoder, Marie (1874–1935)
Hammond, Joan (1912—)
Janowitz, Gundula (1937—)
Kellogg, Clara Louise (1842–1916)
Korolewicz-Waydowa, Janina (1875–1955)
Krainik, Ardis (1929–1997)
Kuznetsova, Maria (1880–1966)
Lemnitz, Tiana (1897–1994)
Mayer, Emilie (1821–1883)
Ponselle, Rosa (1897–1981)
Resnik, Regina (1922—)
Sciutti, Graziella (1927–2001)
Sills, Beverly (1929—)
Stevens, Risë (1913—)
Wallmann, Margarethe (1901–19922)
Warner, Deborah (1959—)
Zorina, Vera (1917—)

OPERA PRODUCER
Berghaus, Ruth (1927–1996)
Fox, Carol (1926–1981)

OPERETTA/LIGHT-OPERA SINGER
Alpar, Gitta (1903—)
Amohau, Merekotia (1898–1978)
Baker, Josephine (1906–1975)
Balkanska, Mimi (b. 1902)
Blyth, Ann (1928—)
Carter, Mrs. Leslie (1862–1937)
Christians, Mady (1900–1951)
Cooper, Gladys (1888–1971)
Flagstad, Kirsten (1895–1962)
Fox, Della (1870–1913)
Gaynor, Mitzi (1930—)
Geistinger, Marie (1833–1903)
Grayson, Kathryn (1922—)
Hading, Jane (1859–1941)
Harvey, Lilian (1906–1968)
Holman, Libby (1904–1971)
Jones, Shirley (1934—)
Kahn, Madeline (1942–1999)
Kuznetsova, Maria (1880–1966)
Laye, Evelyn (1900–1996)
Leander, Zarah (1907–1981)
Leslie, Amy (1855–1939)
Loebinger, Lotte (1905–1999)
Lopokova, Lydia (c. 1892–1981)
Lorengar, Pilar (1928—)
MacDonald, Jeanette (1903–1965)
Mana-Zucca (1887–1981)
Marlowe, Julia (1866–1950)
Martin, Mary (1913–1990)
Meadows, Audrey (1922–1996)
Moore, Grace (1898–1947)
Nielsen, Alice (c. 1870–1943)
Niese, Hansi (1875–1934)
Orlova, Liubov (1902–1975)
Palmer, Lilli (1914–1986)
Rothenberger, Anneliese (1924—)
Russell, Lillian (1861–1922)
Scheff, Fritzi (1879–1954)
Schneider, Hortense (1833–1920)
Schneider, Magda (1909–1996)
Schwarz, Vera (1888–1964)
Schwarzkopf, Elisabeth (1915—)
Sills, Beverly (1929—)
Teyte, Maggie (1888–1976)
Vestris, Lucia (1797–1856)

OPHTHALMOLOGIST
Barrows, Isabel Hayes (1845–1913)
Mann, Ida (1893–1983)
Pirie, Antoinette (1905–1991)
Richards, Renée (1934—)
van Heyningen, Ruth (1917—)

OPTHALMIC SURGEON
Barrows, Isabel Hayes (1845–1913)
Maxwell, Constantia (1886–1962)

OPTICIAN
Dunscombe, Adaliza (1867–1943)

OPTOMETRIST
Suckling, Sophia Lois (1893–1990)

ORAL SURGEON
See Dental surgeon.

ORATOR
See Lecturer/Orator.

ORCHESTRA ADMINISTRATOR
Borda, Deborah (1949—)
Caduff, Sylvia (1937—)
Caldwell, Sarah (1924—)
Hughes, Adella (1869–1950)
Leginska, Ethel (1886–1970)
Thompson, Helen (1908–1974)

ORCHESTRA CONDUCTOR
Bond, Victoria (1950—)
Boulanger, Nadia (1887–1979)
Branscombe, Gena (1881–1977)
Brico, Antonia (1902–1989)
Brown, Iona (1941–2004)
Butler, Helen May (1867–1957)
Caduff, Sylvia (1937—)
Caldwell, Sarah (1924–2006)

Canal, Marguerite (1890–1978)
Carreño, Teresa (1853–1917)
Carvalho, Dinora de (1905—)
Coleridge-Taylor, Avril (1903–1998)
Dianda, Hilda (1925—)
Dudarova, Veronika (1916—)
Dudarova, Veronika Borisovna (1916—)
Gardner, Kay (1941–2002)
Gibault, Claire (1945—)
Gipps, Ruth (1921—)
Glover, Jane Allison (1949—)
Hillis, Margaret (1921—)
Holst, Imogen (1907–1984)
Kapralova, Vitezslava (1915–1940)
Kinkel, Johanna (1810–1858)
Leginska, Ethel (1886–1970)
Macandrew, Jennie (1866–1949)
Maric, Ljubica (1909–2003)
Mills, Amy (c. 1949—)
Musgrave, Thea (1928—)
Popovici, Elise (1921—)
Queler, Eve (1936—)
Rosé, Alma (1906–1944)
Somogi, Judith (1937–1988)
Terzian, Alicia (1938—)
Tureck, Rosalyn (1914—)
Vorlova, Slavka (1894–1973)
Zeng Xiaoying (1929—)

ORCHESTRA FOUNDER
Brico, Antonia (1902–1989)
Carvalho, Dinora de (1905—)
Coleridge-Taylor, Avril (1903–1998)
Gipps, Ruth (1921—)
Hillis, Margaret (1921—)
Leginska, Ethel (1886–1970)

ORGANIC CHEMIST
Anderson, Margaret (1900–1997)
Beloff-Chain, Anne (1921–1991)
Clarke, Patricia Hannah (1919—)
Cori, Gerty T. (1896–1957)
Elion, Gertrude B. (1918–1999)
Emerson, Gladys Anderson (1903–1984)
Freeman, Mavis (1907—)
Hahn, Dorothy (1876–1950)
Hodgkin, Dorothy (1910–1994)
Hoobler, Icie Macy (1892–1984)
Lathbury, Kathleen Culhane (1900–1993)
Lloyd, Dorothy Jordan (1889–1946)
Lucid, Shannon (1943—)
Maclean, Ida Smedley (1877–1944)
Morgan, Agnes Fay (1884–1968)
Muir, Helen (1920–2005)
Needham, Dorothy (1896–1987)
Philbin, Eva (1914—)
Rajalakshmi, R. (1926—)
Russell, Jane Anne (1911–1967)
Ryman, Brenda (1922–1983)
Seibert, Florence B. (1897–1991)
Sithole-Niang, Idah (1957—)
Sohonie, Kamala (1911—)
Stephenson, Marjory (1885–1948)
Tilghman, Shirley M. (1946—)
Wrinch, Dorothy (1894–1976)
Zhao Yufen (1948—)

ORGANIST
Alain, Marie-Claire (1926—)
Andree, Elfrida (1841–1929)
Bartholomew, Ann Sheppard (1811–1891)
Bright, Dora Estella (1863–1951)
Browne, Augusta (1820–1882)
Cameron, Bessy (c. 1851–1895)
Coltrane, Alice (1937—)
Connolly, Maureen (1934–1969)
Crozier, Catharine (1914–2003)
Demessieux, Jeanne (1921–1968)
Densmore, Frances (1867–1957)
Fremstad, Olive (1871–1951)
George, Zelma Watson (1904–1994)
Harris, Barbara (1930—)
Hassall, Joan (1906–1988)
Hodges, Faustina Hasse (1822–1895)
Jolas, Betsy (1926—)
King, Alberta Williams (1903–1974)
La Hye, Louise (1810–1838)
Macandrew, Jennie (1866–1949)
Melba, Nellie (1861–1931)
Norrell, Catherine Dorris (1901–1981)
Respighi, Elsa (1894–1996)
Scott, Shirley (1934–2002)
Somogi, Judith (1937–1988)
Spivey, Victoria (1906–1976)
Uzès, Anne, Duchesse d' (1847–1933)

ORGANIZED-CRIME ASSOCIATE (ACCUSED)
Hill, Virginia (1916–1966)

ORIGINATOR
See Innovator.

ORNITHOLOGIST
Alexander, Annie Montague (1867–1949)
Bailey, Florence (1863–1948)
Barclay-Smith, Phyllis (1903–1980)
Dormon, Carrie (1888–1971)
Eckstorm, Fannie Pearson Hardy (1865–1946)
Hickling, Grace (1908–1986)
Laybourne, Roxie (1910–2003)
Lemon, Margaretta Louisa (1860–1953)
Le Sueur, Frances (1919–1995)
Lewis, Graceanna (1821–1912)
Moncrieff, Pérrine (1893–1979)
Nice, Margaret Morse (1883–1974)
Stanwood, Cordelia (1865–1958)
Wright, Mabel Osgood (1859–1934)

ORPHANAGE ADMINISTRATOR
Wallis, Mary Ann Lake (1821–1910)

ORTHOPEDIC SURGEON
Richardson, Dot (1961—)
Thomas, Debi (1967—)

OUD PLAYER
Osmanoglu, Gevheri (1904–1980)

PACIFIST
Abegg, Elisabeth (1882–1974)
Abzug, Bella (1920–1998)
Addams, Jane (1860–1935)
Agnes, Lore (1876–1953)
Allen, Florence Ellinwood (1884–1966)
Andrews, Elsie Euphemia (1888–1948)
Andrews, Fannie Fern (1867–1950)
Arletty (1898–1992)
Arnold, Emmy (1884–1980)
Aubrac, Lucie (1912—)
Augspurg, Anita (1857–1943)
Avedon, Barbara Hammer (1930–1994)
Bailey, Pearl (1918–1990)
Bain, Wilhelmina Sherriff (1848–1944)
Balabanoff, Angelica (1878–1965)
Balch, Emily Greene (1867–1961)
Barney, Natalie Clifford (1876–1972)
Baum, Marianne (1912–1942)
Baxter, Millicent Amiel (1888–1984)
Beaumont, Florence (c. 1912–1967)
Boissevain, Mia (1878–1959)
Boyle, Kay (1902–1992)
Braddock, Bessie (1899–1970)
Brion, Hélène (1882–1962)
Brittain, Vera (1893–1970)
Brown, Rosemary (1930—)
Buller, Annie (1896–1973)
Butts, Mary (1890–1937)
Cadbury, Rachel (b. 1894)
Caldicott, Helen (1938—)
Calkins, Mary Whiton (1863–1930)
Casgrain, Thérèse (1896–1981)
Catt, Carrie Chapman (1859–1947)
Chevenix, Helen (1886–1963)
Clark, Hilda (1881–1955)
Coppi, Hilde (1909–1943)
Corrigan, Mairead (1944—)
Courtney, Kathleen (1878–1974)
Day, Dorothy (1897–1980)
Dennett, Mary Ware (1872–1947)
Despard, Charlotte (1844–1939)
Duchêne, Gabrielle (1870–1954)
Duncan, Sheena (1932—)
Earhart, Amelia (1897–1937)
Eastman, Crystal (1881–1928)
Ehre, Ida (1900–1989)
Esau, Katherine (1898–1997)
Evans, Elizabeth Glendower (1856–1937)
Fittko, Lisa (1909–2005)
Ford, Isabella O. (1855–1924)
Franklin, Miles (1879–1954)
Gale, Zona (1874–1938)
Gilmore, Mary (1865–1962)
Gore-Booth, Eva (1870–1926)
Hainisch, Marianne (1839–1936)
Harkness, Georgia (1891–1974)
Hatshepsut (c. 1515–1468 BCE)
Herrmann, Liselotte (1909–1938)
Heymann, Lida (1867–1943)
Hiratsuka Raichō (1886–1971)
Hobhouse, Emily (1860–1926)
Hodgkin, Dorothy (1910–1994)
Holtby, Winifred (1898–1935)
Hooper, Jessie Jack (1865–1935)
Howe, Julia Ward (1819–1910)
Howland, Emily (1827–1929)
Hughan, Jessie (1875–1955)
Hull, Hannah (1872–1958)
Jacob, Rosamund (1888–1960)
Jacobs, Aletta (1854–1929)
Jameson, Storm (1891–1986)
Kaffka, Margit (1880–1918)
Kelley, Florence (1859–1932)
Kelly, Petra (1947–1992)
Key, Ellen (1849–1926)
Kuhn, Maggie (1905–1995)
Kulcsar, Ilse (1902–1973)
Levertov, Denise (1923–1997)
Lindbergh, Anne Morrow (1906–2001)
Lonsdale, Kathleen (1903–1971)
Low, Caroline Sarah (1876–1934)
Luckner, Gertrud (1900–1995)
Luxemburg, Rosa (1870–1919)
Macarthur, Mary Reid (1880–1921)
Macmillan, Chrystal (1871–1937)
Mannin, Ethel (1900–1984)
Manus, Rosa (1881–1942)
Martin, Anne Henrietta (1875–1951)
Mayreder, Rosa (1858–1938)
McAliskey, Bernadette Devlin (1947—)
McCoubrey, Margaret (1880–1955)
Mead, Lucia Ames (1856–1936)
Mitchell, Hannah (1871–1956)
Morrell, Ottoline (1873–1938)
Near, Holly (1949—)
Niboyet, Eugénie (1797–1883)
Noether, Emmy (1882–1935)
Norris, Kathleen (1880–1966)
O'Day, Caroline (1869–1943)

Occupational Index

O'Hare, Kate Richards (1876–1948)
Olmsted, Mildred Scott (1890–1990)
O'Reilly, Leonora (1870–1927)
O'Sullivan, Mary Kenney (1864–1943)
Paley, Grace (1922—)
Pankhurst, Sylvia (1882–1960)
Parsons, Elsie Clews (1875–1941)
Pelletier, Madeleine (1874–1939)
Phillips, Lena Madesin (1881–1955)
Prichard, Katharine Susannah (1883–1969)
Pye, Edith (1876–1965)
Rankin, Jeannette (1880–1973)
Roussel, Nelly (1878–1922)
Rüegg, Annelise (1879–1934)
Russell, Dora (1894–1986)
Sainte-Marie, Buffy (1941—)
Salmon, Lucy Maynard (1853–1927)
Salomon, Alice (1872–1948)
Schlesinger, Therese (1863–1940)
Scholl, Inge (c. 1917–1998)
Schwimmer, Rosika (1877–1948)
Scudder, Vida (1861–1954)
Séverine (1855–1929)
Sewall, May Wright (1844–1920)
Shaw, Anna Howard (1847–1919)
Sheehy-Skeffington, Hanna (1877–1946)
Sheepshanks, Mary (1872–1958)
Smedley, Agnes (1892–1950)
Smith, Samantha (1972–1985)
Song Ailing (1890–1973)
Song Meiling (b. 1897)
Song Qingling (1893–1981)
Spencer, Anna (1851–1931)
Stoecker, Helene (1869–1943)
Stokes, Rose Pastor (1879–1933)
Suttner, Bertha von (1843–1914)
Svolou, Maria (d. 1976)
Swanwick, Helena (1864–1939)
Szold, Henrietta (1860–1945)
Tarbell, Ida (1857–1944)
Thorndike, Sybil (1882–1976)
Trask, Kate Nichols (1853–1922)
Vernon, Mabel (1883–1975)
Villard, Fanny Garrison (1844–1928)
Wägner, Elin (1882–1949)
Walentynowicz, Anna (1929—)
Weiss, Louise (1893–1983)
Wheeldon, Alice (fl. 1917)
Williams, Betty (1943—)
Williams, Mary Wilhelmine (1878–1944)
Woolley, Mary E. (1863–1947)
Zetkin, Clara (1857–1933)

PAINTER

Abarca, Maria Francisca de (fl. 1640–1656)
Abbéma, Louise (1858–1927)
Abraham, Caroline Harriet (1809–1877)
Adamson, Joy (1910–1980)
Adnan, Etel (1925—)
Agnes of Quedlinburg (1184–1203)
Airy, Anna (1882–1964)
Aldis, Mary (1872–1949)
Allingham, Helen Patterson (1848–1926)
Anastaise (fl. 1400)
Ancher, Anna (1859–1935)
Anderson, Anne (1874–1930)
Anderson, Sophie (1823–1903)
Angell, Helen Cordelia (1847–1884)
Anguissola, Anna Maria (c. 1545–?)
Anguissola, Elena (c. 1525–after 1584)
Anguissola, Europa (c. 1542–?)
Anguissola, Lucia (c. 1536–1565)
Anguissola, Sofonisba (1532–1625)
Angus, Rita (1908–1970)
Antonia (1456–1491)
Appleton, Jean (1911–2003)
Aristarete
Armour, Mary Nicol Neill (1902–2000)
Arndt, Hermina (1885–1926)
Asher, Elise (c. 1912–2004)
Austen, Winifred (1876–1964)
Auzou, Pauline Desmarquets (1775–1835)
Bachrach, Elise Wald (1899–1940)
Backer, Harriet (1845–1932)
Bacon, Peggy (1895–1987)
Bailey, Barbara Vernon (1910–2003)
Barker, Cicely Mary (1895–1973)
Barney, Alice Pike (1857–1931)
Barney, Natalie Clifford (1876–1972)
Barns-Graham, Wilhelmina (1912–2004)
Barra, Emma de la (1861–1947)
Bashkirtseff, Marie (1859–1884)
Basseporte, Magdalene (?–c. 1780)
Beale, Mary (1632–1699)
Beaux, Cecilia (1855–1942)
Bell, Vanessa (1879–1961)
Ben-Haim, Marylise (1928–2001)
Bennett, Gwendolyn B. (1902–1981)
Benois, Nadia (1896–1975)
Benoist, Marie (1768–1826)
Bernstein, Aline (1882–1955)
Bernstein, Hilda (1915—)
Bertin, Louise Angélique (1805–1877)
Best, Mary Ellen (1809–1891)
Bianco, Pamela (1906–1994)
Bishop, Isabel (1902–1988)
Blackadder, Elizabeth (1931—)
Blackburn, Jemima (1823–1909)
Blair, Catherine (1872–1946)
Bodichon, Barbara (1827–1891)
Boehm, Mary Louise (1924–2002)
Boizot, Marie (1748–?)
Bond, Mary (1939—)
Bonheur, Juliette (1830–1891)
Bonheur, Rosa (1822–1899)
Boughton, Alice (1866–1943)
Bouliar, Marie Geneviève (1762–1825)
Bourgeois, Louise (b. 1911)
Bowen, Gretta (1880–1981)
Boyle, Eleanor Vere (1825–1916)
Bracquemond, Marie (1840–1916)
Brandt, Muriel (1909–1981)
Bremer, Fredrika (1801–1865)
Brennan, Fanny (1921–2001)
Breslau, Louise (1857–1927)
Brice, Fanny (1891–1951)
Bridges, Fidelia (1834–1923)
Brooks, Romaine (1874–1970)
Browne, Rosalind Bengelsdorf (1916–1979)
Brownscombe, Jennie Augusta (1850–1936)
Bugbee, Emma (1888–1981)
Buresova, Charlotte (1904–1984)
Burroughs, Margaret Taylor (1917—)
Butler, Elizabeth Thompson (1846–1933)
Butler, Grace Ellen (1886–1862)
Calypso (fl. c. 200 BCE)
Cam, Helen M. (1885–1968)
Campanelli, Pauline (1943–2001)
Cantofoli, Ginevra (1618–1672)
Capet, Gabrielle (1761–1817)
Carey, Ida Harriet (1891–1982)
Carline, Nancy (1909–2004)
Carpinteri, Laura (b. 1910)
Carr, Emily (1871–1945)
Carrelet de Marron, Marie-Anne (1725–1778)
Carriera, Rosalba (1675–1757)
Carrington, Dora (1893–1932)
Carrington, Joanna (1931–2003)
Carrington, Leonora (1917—)
Casey, Maie (1892–1983)
Cassab, Judy (1920—)
Cassatt, Mary (1844–1926)
Catherine of Bologna (1413–1463)
Cavell, Edith (1865–1915)
Charpentier, Constance Marie (1767–1841)
Chéron, Elisabeth-Sophie (1648–1711)
Chryssa (1933—)
Churchill, Sarah (1914–1982)
Collier, Edith (1885–1964)
Colquhoun, Ithell (1906–1988)
Content, Marjorie (1895–1984)
Cook, Beryl (1926—)
Cooper, Eileen (1953—)
Corbaux, Fanny (1812–1883)
Costello, Louisa Stuart (1799–1870)
Cowles, Fleur (1910—)
Cox, Louise H.K. (1865–1945)
Dashkova, Ekaterina (1744–1810)
de Ayala, Josefa (1630–1684)
de Kooning, Elaine Fried (1918–1989)
Delaunay, Sonia (1885–1979)
DeMorgan, Evelyn (1850–1919)
Dicker-Brandeis, Friedl (1898–1944)
Dillon, Diane (1933—)
Donatella (fl. 1271)
Drayton, Grace Gebbie (1877–1936)
Drinker, Catherine Ann (1841–1922)
Dunnett, Dorothy (1923–2001)
Duparc, Françoise (1726–1778)
Eakins, Susan Hannah (1851–1938)
Eames, Ray (1912–1988)
Eardley, Joan (1921–1963)
Edwards, Henrietta Muir (1849–1933)
Efflatoun, Inji (1923–1989)
Eise, Ida Gertrude (1891–1978)
Elizabeth of Wied (1843–1916)
Emmons, Chansonetta Stanley (1858–1937)
Enters, Angna (1907–1989)
Escoffery, Gloria (1923–2002)
Evans, Minnie (1892–1987)
Exter, Alexandra (1882–1949)
Eyck, Margaretha van (fl. 1420s–1430s)
Fanshawe, Catherine Maria (1765–1834)
Fassett, Cornelia (1831–1898)
Ferner, Ellen Elizabeth (1869–1930)
Fetti, Lucrina (fl. 1614–1651)
Fine, Perle (1908–1988)
Fini, Leonor (1908–1996)
Firenze, Francesca da (fl. 15th c.)
Fitzhugh, Louise (1928–1974)
Fletcher, Alice Cunningham (1838–1923)
Florence, Mary Sargant (1857–1954)
Fontana, Lavinia (1552–1614)
Fortesque-Brickdale, Eleanor (1872–1945)
Fragonard, Marie Anne (1745–c. 1823)
Frankenthaler, Helen (1928—)
Freist, Greta (1904–1993)
French, Annie (1872–1965)
Frink, Elisabeth (1930–1993)
Fuller, Lucia Fairchild (1870–1924)
Gabain, Ethel Leontine (1883–1950)
Gág, Wanda (1893–1946)
Galizia, Fede (1578–1630)
Garzoni, Giovanna (1600–1670)
Genth, Lillian (1876–1953)
Gentileschi, Artemisia (1593–c. 1653)
Gérard, Marguerite (1761–1837)
Gibbs, May (1877–1969)
Gilot, Françoise (1922—)
Gluck (1895–1978)
Goldthwaite, Anne Wilson (1869–1944)
Goncharova, Natalia (1881–1962)
Gonzalès, Eva (1849–1883)
González, Beatriz (1938—)
Goodridge, Sarah (1788–1853)
Gosse, Sylvia (1881–1968)
Graves, Nancy (1940–1995)
Greatorex, Eliza (1820–1897)

Green, Elizabeth Shippen (1871–1954)
Greenaway, Kate (1846–1901)
Greenbaum, Dorothea Schwarcz (1893–1986)
Greene, Gertrude Glass (1904–1956)
Greenwood, Marion (1909–1980)
Guan Daosheng (1262–1319)
Hadid, Zaha (1950—)
Halcombe, Edith Stanway (1844–1903)
Hale, Ellen Day (1855–1940)
Hale, Lilian Westcott (1881–1963)
Halim, Tahiya (1919–2003)
Hall, Anne (1792–1863)
Hamnett, Nina (1890–1956)
Hanrahan, Barbara (1939–1991)
Hansteen, Aasta (1824–1908)
Hardy, Anna Eliza (1839–1934)
Harris, Emily Cumming (c. 1836–1925)
Harrison, Caroline Scott (1832–1892)
Hartigan, Anne Le Marquand (1931—)
Hartigan, Grace (1922—)
Haszard, Rhona (1901–1931)
Helena (fl. after 333 BCE)
Hemessen, Caterina van (c. 1528–c. 1587)
Hepworth, Barbara (1903–1975)
Herbelin, Jeanne Mathilde (1820–1904)
Hetley, Georgina Burne (1832–1898)
Heyking, Elisabeth von (1861–1925)
Hill, Mabel (1872–1956)
Hodgkins, Frances (1869–1947)
Hoffman, Malvina (1885–1966)
Hokinson, Helen E. (1893–1949)
Holden, Evelyn (1877–c. 1969)
Hunt, Frances Irwin (1890–1981)
Hunter, Clementine (1886–1988)
Iaia (fl. c. 100 BCE)
Irene (fl. 200 BCE?)
Isabel of Brazil (1846–1921)
Jamison, Cecilia V. (1837–1909)
Jekyll, Gertrude (1843–1932)
Jellett, Mainie (1897–1944)
Joel, Grace Jane (1865–1924)
John, Gwen (1876–1939)
Johnston, Henrietta (c. 1670–1728)
Jones, Loïs Mailou (1905–1998)
Kahlo, Frida (1907–1954)
Kauffmann, Angelica (1741–1807)
Kaye, M.M. (1908–2004)
Kelly, Annie Elizabeth (1877–1946)
Khvoshchinskaia, Sofia (1828–1865)
Kielland, Kitty L. (1843–1914)
Killigrew, Anne (1660–1685)
Kim, Ronyoung (1926–1987)
King, Jessie Marion (1875–1949)
Klumpke, Anna Elizabeth (1856–1942)
Knight, Laura (1877–1970)
Knowlton, Helen Mary (1832–1918)
Krandievskaya, Natalia (1923—)
Krasner, Lee (1908–1984)
Labille-Guiard, Adelaide (1749–1803)
Lama, Giulia (c. 1685–c. 1753)
Landseer, Jessica (1810–1880)
La Rochefoucauld, Edmée, Duchesse de (1895–1991)
Laurencin, Marie (1883–1956)
Ledoux, Jeanne Philiberte (1767–1840)
Lehmann, Lotte (1888–1976)
Lemmon, Sarah Plummer (1836–1923)
Lemoine, Marie Victoire (1754–1820)
Lempicka, Tamara de (1898–1980)
Leopoldina of Austria (1797–1826)
Lermontova, Nadezhda Vladimirovna (1885–1921)
Lessore, Thérèse (1884–1945)
Leveson-Gower, Elizabeth (1765–1839)
Lewis, Graceanna (1821–1912)
Leyster, Judith (1609–1660)
Lisiewska, Anna (1721–1782)
Lisiewska, Rosina (1716–1783)
Lollobrigida, Gina (1927—)
Losch, Tilly (1903–1975)
Lovell Smith, Rata Alice (1894–1969)
Low, Bet (1924—)
Low, Mary Fairchild (1858–1946)
Loy, Mina (1882–1966)
Lundeberg, Helen (1908–1999)
Maar, Dora (1907–1997)
MacDonald, Frances (1874–1921)
Macdonald, Georgiana (1840–1920)
MacIver, Loren (1909–1998)
Mackintosh, Margaret (1865–1933)
Macomber, Mary Lizzie (1861–1916)
Magafan, Ethel (1916–1993)
Magafan, Jenne (1916–1952)
Maria Antonia of Austria (1683–1754)
Marie d'Orleans (1813–1839)
Marinetti, Benedetta Cappa (1897–1977)
Marisol (1930—)
Martin, Agnes (1912–2004)
Martin, Maria (1796–1863)
Martin, Mary (1907–1969)
Martin-Spencer, Lilly (1822–1902)
Marzouk, Zahia (1906–1988)
Mason, Alice Trumbull (1904–1971)
Matthiasdottir, Louisa (1917–2000)
Mauduit, Louise (1784–1862)
Mayer, Constance (c. 1778–1821)
Mayreder, Rosa (1858–1938)
McGuinness, Norah (1901–1980)
McKenna, Rollie (1918–2003)
McMein, Neysa (1888–1949)
Mee, Margaret (1909–1988)
Menken, Marie (1909–1970)
Merritt, Anna Lea (1844–1930)
Metcalf, Augusta Isabella Corson (1881–1971)
Milani, Milena (1922—)
Mirabal de González, Patria (1924–1960)
Mirabal de Guzmán, María Teresa (1936–1960)
Mirabal de Tavárez, Minerva (1927–1960)
Miranda, Isa (1909–1982)
Mitchell, Joan (1926–1992)
Modersohn-Becker, Paula (1876–1907)
Moillon, Louise (1610–1696)
Monroe, Elizabeth (1768–1830)
Montalba, Clara (1842–1929)
Montemayor, Alice Dickerson (1902–1989)
Moran, Mary Nimmo (1842–1899)
Morgan, Barbara (1900–1992)
Morgan, Maud (1903–1999)
Morgan, Sally (1951—)
Morisot, Berthe (1841–1895)
Moser, Mary (1744–1819)
Moses, Anna "Grandma" (1860–1961)
Münter, Gabriele (1877–1962)
Murray, Elizabeth (1940—)
Neel, Alice (1900–1984)
Nelken, Margarita (1896–1968)
Nessim, Barbara (1939—)
Neumann, Vera (1907–1993)
Nicholls, Rhoda Holmes (1854–1930)
Nicholson, Winifred (1893–1981)
North, Marianne (1830–1890)
Nourse, Elizabeth (1859–1938)
Oakley, Violet (1874–1961)
O'Keeffe, Georgia (1887–1986)
O'Kelley, Mattie Lou (c. 1908–1997)
Olympias
Oosterwyck, Maria van (1630–1693)
Oppenheim, Méret (1913–1985)
Osborn, Daisy (1888–1957)
Osborn, Emily Mary (1834–c. 1885)
Osborne, Fanny (1852–1934)
Ostenso, Martha (1900–1963)
Outhwaite, Ida Rentoul (1888–1960)
Page, Evelyn (1899–1987)
Page, P.K. (1916—)
Palmer, Frances Flora (1812–1876)
Palmer, Lilli (1914–1986)
Pankhurst, Sylvia (1882–1960)
Parra, Violeta (1917–1967)
Parsons, Betty Pierson (1900–1982)
Paul, Joanna (1945–2003)
Peale, Anna Claypoole (1791–1878)
Peale, Margaretta Angelica (1795–1882)
Peale, Sarah Miriam (1800–1885)
Peeters, Clara (1594–after 1657)
Peña, Tonita (1893–1949)
Pepper, Beverly (1924—)
Pereira, Irene Rice (1902–1971)
Perkins, Lucy Fitch (1865–1937)
Perry, Lilla Cabot (c. 1848–1933)
Phalle, Niki de Saint (1930–2002)
Pike, Mary (1824–1908)
Pinney, Eunice Griswold (1770–1849)
Poor, Anne (1918–2002)
Popova, Liubov (1889–1924)
Potter, Beatrix (1866–1943)
Preston, Margaret Rose (c. 1875–1963)
Purser, Sarah (1848–1943)
Radi, Nuha al- (1941–2004)
Raeburn, Agnes Middleton (1872–1955)
Rahon, Alice (1904–1987)
Rand, Ellen (1875–1941)
Rebay, Hilla (1890–1967)
Redpath, Anne (1895–1965)
Rego, Paula (1935—)
Reinhild (fl. 8th c.)
Rentoul, Annie Isobel (c. 1855–1928)
Rey, Margret (1906–1996)
Richmond, Dorothy Kate (1861–1935)
Riley, Bridget (1931—)
Rodiani, Onorata (d. 1452)
Ronner-Knip, Henriette (1821–1909)
Rosa, Anella de (1613–1649)
Rothschild, Judith (1921–1993)
Rozanova, Olga (1886–1918)
Rozengolts-Levina, Eva (1898–1975)
Ruysch, Rachel (1664–1750)
Ryan, Anne (1889–1954)
Sachs, Nelly (1891–1970)
Sage, Kay (1898–1963)
Salomon, Charlotte (1917–1943)
Sanchez, Carol Lee (1934—)
Sandel, Cora (1880–1974)
Sartain, Emily (1841–1927)
Scales, Helen Flora Victoria (1887–1975)
Schacherer-Elek, Ilona (1907–1988)
Schaumann, Ruth (1899–1975)
Serebryakova, Zinaida (1884–1967)
Serres, Olivia (1772–1834)
Sewell, Anna (1820–1878)
Sherwood, Maud Winifred (1880–1956)
Shore, Henrietta (1880–1963)
Siddal, Elizabeth (1829–1862)
Simonovich-Efimova, Nina (1877–1948)
Singer, Winnaretta (1865–1943)
Sirani, Elizabetta (1638–1665)
Smith, Bathsheba (1822–1910)
Smith, Grace Cossington (1892–1984)
Smith, Jessie Willcox (1863–1935)
Sofronova, Antonina (1892–1966)
Sowerby, Millicent (1878–1967)
Spencer, Lilly Martin (1822–1902)
Spencer Bower, Olivia (1905–1982)
Stebbins, Emma (1815–1882)
Sten, Anna (1908–1993)
Stephens, Alice Barber (1858–1932)
Stern, Irma (1894–1966)
Stettheimer, Florine (1871–1944)

Stevens, May (1924—)
Stöcklin, Franziska (1894–1931)
Stoddart, Margaret Olrog (1865–1934)
Stuart, Jane (1812–1888)
Summer, Donna (1948—)
Tait, Agnes (c. 1897–1981)
Tallien, Thérésa (1773–1835)
Tanning, Dorothea (b. 1910)
Tarrant, Margaret (1888–1959)
Tauber-Arp, Sophie (1889–1943)
Teerlinc, Levina (c. 1520–1576)
Templeton, Rini (1935–1986)
Tennent, Madge Cook (1889–1972)
Thomas, Alma (1891–1978)
Ticho, Anna (1894–1980)
Timarete (fl. 3rd c. BCE)
Tobey, Beatrice (d. 1993)
Toyen (1902–1980)
Tripe, Mary Elizabeth (1870–1939)
Truitt, Anne (1921–2004)
Udaltsova, Nadezhda (1885–1961)
Valadon, Suzanne (1865–1938)
Vallayer-Coster, Anne (1744–1818)
Vandamm, Florence (1883–1966)
van Stockum, Hilda (b. 1908)
Varo, Remedios (1906–1963)
Velarde, Pablita (1918—)
Vieira da Silva, Maria Elena (1908–1992)
Vigée-Le Brun, Elisabeth (1755–1842)
Villers, Mme (fl. late 18th c.)
von Wiegand, Charmion (1896–1993)
Walcott, Mary Morris (1860–1940)
Walker, Ethel (1861–1951)
Wallwork, Elizabeth (1883–1969)
Ward, Henrietta (1832–1924)
Waring, Laura Wheeler (1887–1948)
Waser, Anna (1678–1714)
Weir, Irene (1862–1944)
Welty, Eudora (1909–2001)
Wenger, Lisa (1858–1941)
Wentscher, Dora (1883–1964)
Wentworth, Cecile de (c. 1853–1933)
White, Anna Lois (1903–1984)
Wieland, Joyce (1931–1998)
Wilding, Cora (1888–1982)
Wood, Beatrice (1893–1998)
Wood, Thelma (1901–1970)
Wright, Patience Lovell (1725–1786)
Wyeth, Henriette (1907–1997)
Yakunchikova, Maria (1870–1901)
Younghusband, Adela Mary (1878–1969)
Zhukova, Maria (1804–1855)
Zinkeisen, Doris (1898–1991)
Zorach, Marguerite Thompson (1887–1968)

PAINT MANUFACTURER
Merian, Maria Sybilla (1647–1717)

PAIRS SKATER
See Ice skater.

PALEONTOLOGIST
Alexander, Annie Montague (1867–1949)
Anning, Mary (1799–1847)
Bascom, Florence (1862–1945)
Curtis, Doris Malkin (1914–1991)
Edinger, Tilly (1897–1967)
Gardner, Julia Anna (1882–1960)
Goldring, Winifred (1888–1971)
Gromova, Vera (1891–1973)
Hill, Dorothy (1907–1997)
King, Helen Dean (1869–1955)
Longstaff, Mary Jane (c. 1855–1935)
Maury, Carlotta (1874–1938)
Muir-Wood, Helen (1895–1968)
Richter, Emma (1888–1956)
Vrba, Elisabeth (1942—)

PARACHUTIST
Broadwick, Tiny (1893–1978)
Chapelle, Dickey (1919–1972)
Cook, Edith Maud (d. 1910)
Niederkirchner, Käte (1909–1944)
Rinaldi, Angela (c. 1916—)
Shepherd, Dolly (d. 1983)

PARAMOUR
Acte (fl. 55–69)
Agnes of Meran (d. 1201)
Armand, Inessa (1874–1920)
Aspasia of Miletus (c. 464 BCE–c. 420 BCE)
Baccelli, Giovanna (c. 1753–1801)
Berenice (c. 35 BCE–?)
Bethune, Elizabeth (fl. 16th c.)
Bilistiche (fl. 268–264 BCE)
Blount, Elizabeth (c. 1502–c. 1540)
Boleyn, Anne (c. 1507–1536)
Boufflers, Marie (1706–1747)
Boufflers, Stanislas-Jean
Boufflers-Rouvrel, Marie Charlotte Hippolyte, Countess de (1724–c. 1800)
Boyd, Mary (fl. 1487)
Bracegirdle, Anne (1671–1748)
Braun, Eva (1912–1945)
Britton, Nan (1896–1991)
Camargo, Marie-Anne Cupis de (1710–1770)
Campanini, Barbara (1721–1799)
Cappello, Bianca (1548–1587)
Cardny, Marion (fl. 1300s)
Carmichael, Elizabeth (fl. 1530s)
Castiglione, Virginie, Countess de (1837–1899)
Castro, Inez de (c. 1320–1355)
Catherine I of Russia (1684–1727)
Cattanei, Vannozza (1442–1518)
Cayla, Comtesse du (1785–1852)
Châteaubriant, Comtesse de (c. 1490–1537)
Châteauroux, Marie Anne de Mailly-Nesle, Duchesse de (1717–1744)
Churchill, Arabella (1648–1714)
Clairmont, Claire (1798–1879)
Clarke, Mary Anne (c. 1776–1852)
Cleopatra VII (69–30 BCE)
Clifford, Rosamund (c. 1145–1176)
Corbert, Sybilla (fl. 11th century)
Currie, Edwina (1946—)
Davies, Moll (fl. 1673)
del Maino, Agnes (fl. 1420s)
Diane de Poitiers (1499–1566)
Dianti, Laura (fl. 1527)
Dolgorukaia, Alexandra (1836–c. 1914)
Dolgorukova, Ekaterina (1847–1922)
Dostoevsky, Anna (1846–1918)
Draga (1867–1903)
Drouet, Juliette (1806–1883)
Drummond, Margaret (c. 1472–1502)
Drusilla (15–38)
du Barry, Jeanne Bécu, Comtesse (1743–1793)
Duci, Filippa (fl. 16th c.)
Dyveke (c. 1491–1517)
Eadgyth Swanneshals (c. 1012–?)
Ecgwynn (d. around 901)
Edla (fl. 900s)
Elfgifu of Northampton (c. 1000–1044)
Elizabeth Blount (c. 1502–c. 1540)
Elizabeth of Kiev (fl. 1045)
Elphinstone, Eupheme (fl. 1500s)
Elssler, Fanny (1810–1884)
Entragues, Henriette d' (1579–1633)
Erskine, Margaret (fl. 1530s)
Estrées, Gabrielle d' (1573–1599)
Étampes, Anne de Pisseleu d' Heilly, Duchesse d' (1508–c. 1580)
Eudocia Ingerina (fl. 800s)
Exner, Judith Campbell (d. 1999)
Farnese, Giulia (1474–1518?)
Feuchères, Sophie, Baronne de (c. 1795–1841)
Fitzherbert, Maria Anne (1756–1837)
Fleming, Jane (fl. 1550s)
Flemming, Mary (fl. 1540s)
Fontanges, Duchesse de (1661–1681)
Frankland, Agnes (1726–1783)
Fredegund (c. 547–597)
Gheenst, Johanna van der (fl. 16th c.)
Gilot, Françoise (1922—)
Gouel, Eva (d. 1915)
Gunhilda of Poland (d. around 1015)
Gunhild of Norway (d. 1054)
Guzman, Leonora de (1310–1351)
Guzman, Mayor de (d. 1262)
Gwynn, Nell (1650–1687)
Hamilton, Emma (1765–1815)
Heloise (c. 1100–1163)
Hemings, Sally (1773–1835)
Hill, Joan (fl. 1460)
Howard, Elizabeth Ann (1823–1865)
Howard, Henrietta (1688–1767)
Jagemann, Karoline (1777–1848)
Jordan, Dora (1761–1816)
Kawashima, Yoshiko (1906–1947)
Keeler, Christine (1942—)
Keppel, Alice (1869–1947)
Kéroüalle, Louise de (1649–1734)
Killigrew, Elizabeth (c. 1622–?)
Königsmark, Aurora von (1662–1728)
Kshesinskaia, Matilda (1872–1971)
Landriani, Lucrezia (fl. 1450s)
Langtry, Lillie (1853–1929)
La Vallière, Louise de (1644–1710)
Lecouvreur, Adrienne (1690–1730)
Leitch, Moira (fl. late 1300s)
Lenclos, Ninon de (1623–1705)
Léon, Léonie (1838–1906)
Leonora Telles (c. 1350–1386)
Lichtenau, Countess von (1753–1820)
Lorenzo, Teresa (fl. 1358)
Lucy, Elizabeth (fl. 1460s)
Lupescu, Elena (c. 1896–1977)
Lynch, Eliza (1835–1886)
Maansdatter, Katherine (1550–1612)
Maar, Dora (1907–1997)
Mailly, Louise Julie de Mailly-Nesle, Comtesse de (1710–1751)
Maintenon, Françoise d'Aubigné, Marquise de (1635–1719)
Malinche (c. 1500–1531)
Mancini, Hortense (1646–1699)
Mancini, Olympia (c. 1639–1708)
Marcia (fl. 177–192)
Margaret of Cortona (1247–1297)
Marie de Padilla (1335–1361)
Marie of Anjou (1404–1463)
Marietta (fl. 1430s)
Melbourne, Elizabeth (d. 1818)
Mendoza, Ana de (fl. late 1400s)
Mérode, Cléo de (c. 1875–1966)
Migliaccio, Lucia (1770–1826)
Mons, Anna (d. 1714)
Montespan, Françoise, Marquise de (1640–1707)
Montez, Lola (1818–1861)
Moth, Sophie Amalie (fl. 1670s)
Muñoz, Jimena (c. 1065–1128)
Nesta Tewdr (fl. 1090)
Olivier, Fernande (1884–1966)
O'Murphy, Marie-Louise (1737–1814)

Parker-Bowles, Camilla (1947—)
Pegge, Catherine (fl. 1657)
Perez, Gontrada (fl. 1100s)
Perez, Inez (fl. 1400)
Perrers, Alice (d. 1400)
Petacci, Clara (1912–1945)
Pickford, Mary (1893–1979)
Plessis, Alphonsine (1824–1847)
Pompadour, Jeanne-Antoinette Poisson, Duchesse de (1721–1764)
Poppaea Sabina (d. 65)
Rasmussen, Louise Christine (1815–1874)
Ray, Martha (d. 1779)
Regina (d. around 251)
Richilde of Autun (d. around 910)
Robinson, Mary (1758–1800)
Sancha de Aybar (fl. 11th c.)
Sarfatti, Margherita (1880–1961)
Schratt, Katharina (1853–1940)
Schulenburg, Ehrengard Melusina von der (1667–1743)
Sedley, Catharine (1657–1717)
Servilia II (c. 100–after 42 BCE)
Shaw, Elizabeth (fl. 1500s)
Shizuka Gozen (fl. 12th c.)
Shore, Jane (c. 1445–c. 1527)
Sophia Carlotte (1673–1725)
Sorel, Agnes (1422–1450)
Sourdis, Isabelle de (fl. 16th c.)
Souza-Botelho, Adélaïde Filleul, marquise of (1761–1836)
Stafford, Elizabeth (d. 1532)
Stein, Charlotte von (1742–1827)
Stewart, Elizabeth
Summersby, Kay (1908–1975)
Swynford, Catherine (c. 1350–1403)
Tallien, Thérésa (1773–1835)
Tangwystl (fl. 1180–1210)
Tewdwr, Nesta (fl. 1090)
Thecla (c. 823–c. 870)
Thora (fl. 1100s)
Thora Johnsdottir (fl. 1000s)
Tilton, Elizabeth (1834–c. 1896)
Vega, Elvira de la (fl. late 1300s)
Vetsera, Marie (1871–1889)
Villegas, Micaela (1748–1819)
Villiers, Barbara (c. 1641–1709)
Villiers, Elizabeth (c. 1657–1733)
Vintimille, Pauline Félicité, Marquise de (1712–1741)
Walewska, Marie (1786–1817)
Walkinshaw, Clementina (c. 1726–1802)
Wallmoden, Amalie Sophie Marianne (1704–1765)
Walter, Lucy (c. 1630–1658)
Wentworth, Henrietta Maria (c. 1657–1686)
Wilson, Harriette (1786–1855)
Windsor, Wallis Warfield, duchess of (1895–1986)
Wulfthryth (c. 945–1000)
Zaida (d. 1107)
Zoë Carbopsina (c. 890–920)
Zoë Zautzina (c. 870–c. 899)

PARLIAMENTARY REPRESENTATIVE

See Politician.

PATHOLOGIST

Andersen, Dorothy Hansine (1901–1963)
Barber, Mary (1911–1965)
Claypole, Edith Jane (1870–1915)
Clayton, Barbara (1922—)
Cori, Gerty T. (1896–1957)
Dalyell, Elsie (1881–1948)
De Witt, Lydia (1859–1928)
Florey, Margaret (1904–1994)
Frost, Constance Helen (c. 1862–1920)
Hamilton, Alice (1869–1970)
Heseltine, Mary J. (1910–2002)
Horsley, Alice Woodward (1871–1957)
Hurdon, Elizabeth (1868–1941)
Johnstone, Justine (1895–1982)
Menten, Maude (1879–1960)
Moss, Emma Sadler (1898–1970)
Pearce, Louise (1885–1959)
Ramsey, Elizabeth M. (1906–1993)
Robscheit-Robbins, Frieda (1888–1973)
Russell, Dorothy Stuart (1895–1983)
Schuster, Norah (1892–1991)
Slye, Maud (1869–1954)
Stern, Elizabeth (1915–1980)
Vaughan, Janet (1899–1993)
Williams, Anna Wessels (1863–1954)
Wollstein, Martha (1868–1939)

PATRON/PHILANTHROPIST/ BENEFACTOR

See also Arts patron/philanthropist/benefactor.
See also Religious patron/philanthropist/benefactor.
See also Sciences patron/philanthropist/benefactor.
Aberdeen, Ishbel Maria Gordon, Lady (1857–1939)
Ahmanson, Caroline (1918–2005)
Alexander, Francesca (1837–1917)
Baillie, Grisell (1822–1921)
Baldwin, Ethel Frances (1879–1967)
Bannerman, Jane (c. 1835–1923)
Barnett, Henrietta (1851–1936)
Bell, Mabel Hubbard (1857–1923)
Blaine, Anita McCormick (1866–1954)
Bowen, Louise (1859–1953)
Brand, Sybil (c. 1899–2004)
Carnegie, Louise Whitfield (1857–1946)
Cole, Anna Russell (1846–1926)
Colton, Mary (1822–1898)
Copley, Helen (1922–2004)
Cosby, Camille (1945—)
Cryer, Sarah (1848–1929)
Daldy, Amey (c. 1829–1920)
Disney, Lillian (1899–1997)
Dummer, Ethel Sturges (1866–1954)
Elizabeth of Yugoslavia (1936—)
Fulton, Catherine (1829–1919)
Guggenheim, Florence Shloss (1863–1944)
Guggenheim, Olga H. (1877–1970)
Hanson, Luise V. (1913–2003)
Harriman, Mary (1851–1932)
Hastings, Elizabeth (1682–1739)
Hearst, Phoebe A. (1842–1919)
Jeanes, Anna Thomas (1822–1907)
Kroc, Joan (1928–2003)
Lacey, Janet (1903–1988)
Luce, Lila (1899–1999)
Mellon, Gwen Grant (1911–2000)
Newhouse, Alice (1924–2004)
Newhouse, Caroline H. (1910–2003)
Perkins, Elizabeth Peck (c. 1735–1807)
Pickersgill, Mary (1776–1857)
Randall, Amelia Mary (1844–1930)
Rockefeller, Blanchette Hooker (1909–1992)
Siteman, Isabella Flora (c. 1842–1919)
Weston, Agnes (1840–1918)

PATRON SAINT

Agatha, Saint (d. 251)
Barbara (fl. 3rd c.)
Bona of Pisa (c. 1156–1207)
Bridget of Ireland (c. 453–c. 524)
Bridget of Sweden (1303–1373)
Catherine of Alexandria (?–305)
Cecilia (c. 154–c. 207)
Dympna (fl. 650)
Geneviève (c. 422–512)
Gertrude the Great (1256–1302)
Gudula of Brussels (d. 712?)
Hedwig of Silesia (1174–1243)
Inanna (fl. c. 3000 BCE)
Joan of Arc (c. 1412–1431)
Justina (d. 64)
Lucy (d. 303)
Mary Magdalene (fl. early 1st c.)
Rita of Cascia (1381–1457)
Ursula (fl. 3rd or 5th c.)
Wandru (c. 628–688)

PEDIATRICIAN

Alexander, Hattie (1901–1968)
Andersen, Dorothy Hansine (1901–1963)
Avery, Mary Ellen (1927—)
Bonner, Elena (1923—)
Caldicott, Helen (1938—)
Campbell, Kate (1899–1986)
Diallo, Nafissatou (1941–1982)
Dunham, Ethel Collins (1883–1969)
Hofmann, Adele (d. 2001)
Howell, Mary (1932–1998)
MacMurchy, Helen (1862–1953)
Szwajger, Adina Blady (1917–1993)
Taussig, Helen Brooke (1898–1986)
Vögtlin, Marie (1845–1916)
Williams, Cicely (1893–1992)

PENOLOGIST

Barrows, Isabel Hayes (1845–1913)
Davis, Katharine Bement (1860–1935)
Grenfell, Helen L. (b. 1868)
O'Hare, Kate Richards (1876–1948)

PENTATHLETE

Allenby, Kate (1974—)
Blankers-Koen, Fanny (1918—)
Bystrova, Galina (1934—)
Cook, Stephanie (1972—)
deRiel, Emily (1974—)
Harland, Georgina (1978—)
Joyner-Kersee, Jackie (1962—)
Konihowski, Diane Jones (1951—)
Kuragina, Olga (1959—)
Laser, Christine (1951—)
Metheny, Linda (1948—)
Peters, Mary (1939—)
Pollak, Burglinde (1951—)
Press, Irina (1939—)
Prokop, Liese (1941—)
Rand, Mary (1940—)
Rosendahl, Heidemarie (1947—)
Rublevska, Jelena (1976—)
Rukavishnikova, Olga (1955—)
Siegl, Siegrun (1954—)
Tkachenko, Nadezhda (1948—)
Tothne-Kovacs, Annamaria (1945—)
Voros, Zsuzsanna (1977—)
Walsh, Stella (1911–1980)

PERFORMANCE ARTIST

Acker, Kathy (1943–1997)
Anderson, Laurie (1947—)
Cha, Theresa Hak Kyung (1951–1982)
Chadwick, Helen (1953–1996)
Ono, Yoko (1933—)

PERFORMANCE-ARTS TEACHER

Henriot-Schweitzer, Nicole (1925–2001)

PERFUMIERE

Arden, Elizabeth (1878–1966)
Carnegie, Hattie (1886–1956)
Chanel, Coco (1883–1971)
Lanvin, Jeanne (1867–1946)

Occupational Index

Lauder, Estée (1908–2004)
Picasso, Paloma (1949—)
Pugacheva, Alla (1949—)
Taylor, Elizabeth (1932—)

PERIODICAL EDITOR

See also Newspaper editor.
Abbott, Berenice (1898–1991)
Abbott, Grace (1878–1939)
Abzug, Bella (1920–1998)
Adnan, Etel (1925—)
Ahern, Mary Eileen (1860–1938
Aikens, Charlotte (c. 1868–1949)
Alegría, Claribel (1924—)
Allen, Florence Ellinwood (1884–1966)
Allen, Mary Sophia (1878–1964)
Allfrey, Phyllis Shand (1915–1986)
Anderson, Doris (1921—)
Anderson, Margaret Carolyn (1886–1973)
Andrus, Ethel Percy (1884–1967)
Angelou, Maya (1928—)
Annenkova, Julia (c. 1898–c. 1938)
Apostoloy, Electra (1911–1944)
Applebee, Constance (1873–1981)
Araz, Nezihe (1922—)
Arendsee, Martha (1885–1953)
Aston, Luise (1814–1871)
Astor, Brooke (b. 1902)
Atwater, Helen (1876–1947)
Aubert, Constance (1803–?)
Augspurg, Anita (1857–1943)
Bacon, Josephine Dodge (1876–1961)
Bagley, Sarah (b. 1806)
Bailey, Hannah Johnston (1839–1923)
Baker, Ella (1903–1986)
Balabanoff, Angelica (1878–1965)
Balch, Emily Greene (1867–1961)
Barns, Cornelia Baxter (1888–1941)
Barrows, Isabel Hayes (1845–1913)
Barry, Iris (1895–1969)
Bascom, Florence (1862–1945)
Bauer, Helene (1871–1942)
Bäumer, Gertrud (1873–1954)
Beard, Mary Ritter (1876–1958)
Beatty, Bessie (1886–1947)
Becher, Lilly (1901–1976)
Beloff, Nora (1919–1997)
Benedict, Ruth (1887–1948)
Bentley, Helen Delich (1923—)
Bergroth, Kersti (1886–1975)
Besant, Annie (1847–1933)
Beyer, Helga (1920–1942)
Bisland, Elizabeth (1863–1929)
Black, Clementina (1854–1922)
Blackburn, Helen (1842–1903)
Blackwell, Alice Stone (1857–1950)
Blair, Emily Newell (1877–1951)
Blanchard, Theresa Weld (1893–1978)
Blavatsky, Helena (1831–1891)
Bloomer, Amelia Jenks (1818–1894)
Bogan, Louise (1897–1970)
Booth, Mary Louise (1831–1889)
Boucherett, Jessie (1825–1905)
Boye, Karin (1900–1941)
Bradwell, Myra (1831–1894)
Brady, Mildred Edie (1906–1965)
Braun, Lily (1865–1916)
Breckinridge, Mary (1881–1965)
Brewster, Anne Hampton (1818–1892)
Broniewska, Janina (1904–1981)
Brown, Helen Gurley (1922—)
Brown, Martha McClellan (1838–1916)
Brown, Tina (1953—)
Bryant, Louise (1885–1936)
Buber-Neumann, Margarete (1901–1989)
Burnett, Hallie Southgate (1908–1991)
Buttrose, Ita (1942—)
Campbell, Helen Stuart (1839–1918)
Cary, Mary Ann Shadd (1823–1893)
Castle, Barbara (1910–2002)
Cather, Willa (1873–1947)
Cauer, Minna (1841–1922)
Chapelle, Dickey (1919–1972)
Chase, Edna Woolman (1877–1957)
Chase, Mary Coyle (1907–1981)
Child, Lydia Maria (1802–1880)
Christman, Elisabeth (1881–1975)
Clarke, Mary Cowden (1809–1898)
Clisby, Harriet (1830–1931)
Coignet, Clarisse (1823–?)
Coleman, Kit (1864–1915)
Coleridge, Georgina (1916–2003)
Colette (1873–1954)
Colum, Mary Gunning (1884–1957)
Comstock, Anna Botsford (1854–1930)
Corbett-Ashby, Margery (1882–1981)
Corson, Juliet (1841–1897)
Coulson, Juanita (1933—)
Cousins, Margaret (1878–1954)
Cowles, Fleur (1910—)
Crane, Caroline Bartlett (1858–1935)
Croly, Jane Cunningham (1829–1901)
Dall, Caroline Wells (1822–1912)
Dashwood, Elizabeth Monica (1890–1943)
Davenport, Marcia (1903–1996)
Davies, Emily (1830–1921)
de Kooning, Elaine Fried (1918–1989)
Deledda, Grazia (1871–1936)
Demorest, Ellen Curtis (1824–1898)
Dennett, Mary Ware (1872–1947)
Deutschkron, Inge (1922—)
Diggs, Annie LePorte (1848–1916)
Dimock, Susan (1847–1875)
Dodge, Mary Abigail (1833–1896)
Dönhoff, Marion, Countess (1909–2002)
Donlon, Mary H. (1894–1977)
Doolittle, Hilda (1886–1961)
Dorr, Rheta Childe (1866–1948)
Douglas, Marjory Stoneman (1890–1998)
Dransfeld, Hedwig (1871–1925)
Driscoll, Clara (1881–1945)
Duczynska, Ilona (1897–1978)
Duffy, Martha (c. 1936–1997)
Duncan, Sheena (1932—)
Dyson, Elizabeth Geertruida (1897–1951)
Dzerzhinska, Sofia (1882–1968)
Earhart, Amelia (1897–1937)
Edwards, India (1895–1990)
Ehrmann, Marianne (1755–1795)
El Saadawi, Nawal (1931—)
Ermoleva, Zinaida (1898–1974)
Evans, Mary Anne (1819–1880)
Farley, Harriet (1813–1907)
Farningham, Marianne (1834–1909)
Fauset, Jessie Redmon (1882–1961)
Fenwick, Millicent (1910–1992)
Ferré, Rosario (1938—)
Firestone, Shulamith (1945—)
First, Ruth (1925–1982)
Flanner, Janet (1892–1978)
Fleeson, Doris (1901–1970)
Foley, Martha (c. 1897–1977)
Fort, Cornelia (1919–1943)
Frederick, Christine (1883–1970)
Fremantle, Anne (1909–2002)
Freundlich, Emmy (1878–1948)
Fukuda Hideko (1865–1927)
Fuller, Margaret (1810–1850)
Gage, Frances D. (1808–1884)
Galindo de Topete, Hermila (1896–1954)
Gardener, Helen Hamilton (1853–1925)
Gardner, Isabella (1915–1981)
Garvey, Amy Jacques (1896–1973)
Gatty, Margaret (1809–1873)
Geiringer, Hilda (1893–1973)
Gilbert, Katherine Everett (1886–1952)
Gilder, Jeannette Leonard (1849–1916)
Gilman, Charlotte Perkins (1860–1935)
Gilmore, Mary (1865–1962)
Ginsburg, Ruth Bader (1933—)
Giroud, Françoise (1916–2003)
Goldman, Emma (1869–1940)
Gordon, Laura de Force (1838–1907)
Gould, Beatrice Blackmar (c. 1899–1989)
Graham, Katharine (1917–2001)
Greenfield, Meg (1930–1999)
Greville, Frances Evelyn (1861–1938)
Griswold, Denny (1908–2001)
Guglielminetti, Amalia (1881–1941)
Gutiérrez de Mendoza, Juana Belén (1875–1942)
Gutteridge, Helena Rose (1879–1960)
Hagan, Ellen (1873–1958)
Haldane, Charlotte (1894–1969)
Hale, Sarah Josepha (1788–1879)
Hamilton, Gordon (1892–1967)
Hamm, Margherita (1867–1907)
Hani, Motoko (1873–1957)
Hapgood, Isabel (1850–1928)
Harari, Manya (1905–1969)
Harris, Patricia Roberts (1924–1985)
Harrison, Constance Cary (1843–1920)
Hasbrouck, Lydia Sayer (1827–1910)
Haslett, Caroline (1895–1957)
Haywood, Eliza (c. 1693–1756)
Hazlett, Olive C. (1890–1974)
Head, Edith (1897–1981)
Heap, Jane (1887–1964)
Heldman, Gladys (1922—)
Heldman, Gladys (1922–2003)
Helmer, Bessie Bradwell (1858–1927)
Henderson, Alice Corbin (1881–1949)
Henry, Alice (1857–1943)
Herrick, Elinore Morehouse (1895–1964)
Heymann, Lida (1867–1943)
Hickok, Lorena A. (1893–1968)
Hiratsuka Raichō (1886–1971)
Hobby, Gladys Lounsbury (1910–1993)
Hobby, Oveta Culp (1905–1995)
Hockaday, Margaret (1907–1992)
Hollingworth, Leta Stetter (1886–1939)
Hopkins, Pauline E. (1859–1930)
Horna, Kati (1912—)
Horney, Karen (1885–1952)
Hoult, Norah (1898–1984)
Howes, Barbara (1914–1996)
Huber, Therese (1764–1829)
Hull, Peggy (1889–1967)
Huxtable, Ada Louise (1921—)
Ibárruri, Dolores (1895–1989)
Ichikawa Fusae (1893–1981)
Ihrer, Emma (1857–1911)
Irwin, Inez Haynes (1873–1970)
Isaacs, Edith (1878–1956)
Ivinskaya, Olga (1912–1995)
Jaburkova, Jozka (d. 1944)
Jackson, Alice (1887–1974)
Jackson, Shirley (1916–1965)
Jacobi, Lotte (1896–1990)
Jagan, Janet (1920—)
Jameson, Storm (1891–1986)
Janeway, Elizabeth (1913–2005)
Jarvis, Lucy (1919—)
Jekyll, Gertrude (1843–1932)
Jemison, Mary (1742–1833)
Jesenská, Milena (1896–1945)
Johnson, Celia (1908–1982)
Johnson, Eleanor Murdoch (1892–1987)

Johnson, Helen Kendrick (1844–1917)
Jolas, Betsy (1926—)
Jolas, Maria (1893–1987)
Jordan, Elizabeth Garver (1865–1947)
Juchacz, Marie (1879–1956)
Katznelson-Shazar, Rachel (1888–1975)
Kavan, Anna (1901–1968)
Kelly, Ethel (1875–1949)
Kelly, Kathryn Thorne (1904–1998?)
Kelso, Elizabeth (1889–1967)
Kennedy, Jacqueline (1929–1994)
Kerr, Sophie (1880–1965)
Kéthly, Anna (1889–1976)
Kirchwey, Freda (1893–1976)
Kirkland, Caroline Matilda (1801–1864)
Kirkus, Virginia (1893–1980)
Konopnicka, Maria (1842–1910)
Koszutska, Maria (1876–1939)
Kovalevskaya, Sophia (1850–1891)
Kuhn, Irene Corbally (1898–1995)
La Flesche, Susette (1854–1902)
La Follette, Belle Case (1859–1931)
Lamas, Maria (1893–1983)
Landon, Letitia Elizabeth (1802–1838)
Lane, Gertrude B. (1874–1941)
Langgässer, Elisabeth (1899–1950)
Larcom, Lucy (1824–1893)
Lawrenson, Helen (1907–1982)
Lawrenson, Helen (b. 1907)
Lear, Frances (1923–1996)
Lehmann, Rosamond (1901–1990)
Leslie, Miriam Folline Squier (1836–1914)
Litchfield, Jessie (1883–1956)
Littledale, Clara (1891–1956)
Livermore, Mary A. (1820–1905)
Lloyd, Alice (1876–1962)
Longhi, Lucia Lopresti (1895–1985)
Lonsdale, Kathleen (1903–1971)
Loos, Anita (1893–1981)
Loveman, Amy (1881–1955)
Luce, Clare Boothe (1903–1987)
Luxemburg, Rosa (1870–1919)
Macarthur, Mary Reid (1880–1921)
MacDonald, Margaret (c. 1907–1956)
MacGill, Helen Gregory (1871–1947)
Maclean, Hester (1859–1932)
Manley, Mary de la Rivière (1663–1724)
Mannes, Marya (1904–1990)
Mansfield, Katherine (1888–1923)
Manzini, Gianna (1896–1974)
Marot, Helen (1865–1940)
Marshall, Catherine (1914–1983)
Massee, May (1881–1966)
Mathews, Vera Laughton (1888–1959)
Maunder, Annie Russell (1868–1947)
McCormick, Anne O'Hare (1880–1954)
McDowell, Anne E. (1826–1901)
McGinley, Phyllis (1905–1978)
McIsaac, Shona (1960—)
Meinhof, Ulrike (1934–1972)
Meloney, Marie (1878–1943)
Merril, Judith (1923–1997)
Meyer, Agnes (1887–1970)
Meynell, Alice (1847–1922)
Miller, Annie Jenness (b. 1859)
Miller, Bertha Mahony (1882–1969)
Miner, Dorothy (1904–1973)
Mitchel, Jenny (1820–1899)
Molony, Helena (1884–1967)
Monod, Sarah (1836–1912)
Monroe, Harriet (1860–1936)
Moodie, Susanna (1803–1885)
Moore, Marianne (1887–1972)
Moreau de Justo, Alicia (1885–1986)
Mosher, Eliza Maria (1846–1928)
Moskowitz, Belle (1877–1933)
Murphy, Emily (1868–1933)
Myers, Caroline Clark (c. 1888–1980)
Nice, Margaret Morse (1883–1974)
Nichols, Clarina (1810–1885)
Nicholson, Eliza Jane (1849–1896)
Noce, Teresa (1900–1980)
Norris, Kathleen (1880–1966)
Norton, Caroline (1808–1877)
Ocampo, Victoria (1890–1979)
O'Connor, Sandra Day (1930—)
O'Hair, Madalyn Murray (1919–1995)
O'Hare, Kate Richards (1876–1948)
Olberg, Oda (1872–1955)
Osten, Maria (1908–1942)
Ottendorfer, Anna Uhl (1815–1884)
Otto-Peters, Luise (1819–1895)
Overlach, Helene (1894–1983)
Paddleford, Clementine (1900–1967)
Paley, Babe (1915–1978)
Palmer, Alice May (1886–1977)
Palmer, Helen (1917–1979)
Palmer, Phoebe Worrall (1807–1874)
Palmer, Sophia French (1853–1920)
Pankhurst, Christabel (1880–1958)
Park, Ruth (1923—)
Parkes, Bessie Rayner (1829–1925)
Parnell, Anna (1852–1911)
Parren, Kalliroe (1861–1940)
Parsons, Elsie Clews (1875–1941)
Patterson, Alicia (1906–1963)
Patterson, Eleanor Medill (1881–1948)
Pennington, Mary Engle (1872–1952)
Petry, Ann (1908–1997)
Pollard, Marjorie (1899–1982)
Popp, Adelheid (1869–1939)
Porter, Sylvia (1913–1991)
Pound, Louise (1872–1958)
Pusich, Antónia Gertrudes (1805–1883)
Pym, Barbara (1913–1980)
Raine, Kathleen (1908–2003)
Rama Rau, Santha (1923—)
Rand, Ayn (1905–1982)
Reed, Alma (1889–1966)
Reisner, Larissa (1895–1926)
Rhondda, Margaret (1883–1958)
Richmond, Mary E. (1861–1928)
Rickert, Edith (1871–1938)
Ridge, Lola (1873–1941)
Rind, Clementina (c. 1740–1774)
Robinson, Mary (1944—)
Roland Holst, Henriëtte (1869–1952)
Roosevelt, Eleanor (1884–1962)
Rosman, Alice Grant (1887–1961)
Ross, Ishbel (1895–1975)
Rountree, Martha (1911–1999)
Rourke, Constance (1885–1941)
Royden, A. Maude (1876–1956)
Royde-Smith, Naomi Gwladys (1875–1964)
Ruffin, Josephine St. Pierre (1842–1924)
Russell, Jane Anne (1911–1967)
Salhias de Tournemire, Elizaveta (1815–1892)
Samoilova, Konkordiya (1876–1921)
Sangster, Margaret (1838–1912)
Sarfatti, Margherita (1880–1961)
Sartain, Emily (1841–1927)
Schary, Hope Skillman (1908–1981)
Schiff, Dorothy (1903–1989)
Schroeder, Louise (1887–1957)
Schurz, Margarethe Meyer (1833–1876)
Sears, Mary (1905–1997)
Serao, Matilde (1856–1927)
Shaw, Flora (1852–1929)
Sheehy-Skeffington, Hanna (1877–1946)
Sherif, Carolyn Wood (1922–1982)
Sherkat, Shahla (c. 1956—)
Sherwood, Katharine Margaret (1841–1914)
Shinn, Millicent Washburn (1858–1940)
Shirreff, Emily (1814–1897)
Shtern, Lina (1878–1968)
Simon, Kate (1912–1990)
Sitwell, Edith (1887–1964)
Slesinger, Tess (1905–1945)
Smart, Elizabeth (1913–1986)
Smith, Hazel Brannon (1914–1994)
Smith, Lucy Masey (1861–1936)
Smith, Margaret Chase (1897–1995)
Solano, Solita (1888–1975)
Soule, Caroline White (1824–1903)
Spafford, Belle Smith (1895–1982)
Spark, Muriel (1918—)
Spiridonova, Maria (1884–1941)
St. Denis, Ruth (1877–1968)
Stasova, Elena (1873–1966)
Steinem, Gloria (1934—)
Stevens, Alzina (1849–1900)
Stoecker, Helene (1869–1943)
Stone, Lucy (1818–1893)
Strong, Anna Louise (1885–1970)
Strossen, Nadine (1950—)
Stuart, Ruth McEnery (c. 1849–1917)
Sutton, Carol (1933–1985)
Svolou, Maria (d. 1976)
Swenson, May (1913–1989)
Swindler, Mary Hamilton (1884–1967)
Swisshelm, Jane Grey (1815–1884)
Szymborska, Wislawa (1923—)
Taber, Gladys (1899–1980)
Tabouis, Geneviève (1892–1985)
Taeuber, Irene Barnes (1906–1974)
Taggard, Genevieve (1894–1948)
Tarbell, Ida (1857–1944)
Teffi, N.A. (1872–1952)
Templeton, Rini (1935–1986)
Terhune, Mary Virginia (1830–1922)
Thompson, Era Bell (1906–1986)
Thompson, Helen (1908–1974)
Thorne, Florence (1877–1973)
Thorpe, Rose Hartwick (1850–1939)
Tietjens, Eunice (1884–1944)
Tilberis, Liz (1947–1999)
Tinayre, Marcelle (c. 1870–1948)
Todd, Marion Marsh (1841–post 1913)
Toor, Frances (1890–1956)
Torrezão, Guiomar (1844–1898)
Travers, P.L. (1906–1996)
Tree, Marietta (1917–1991)
Trilling, Diana (1905–1996)
Tuchman, Barbara (1912–1989)
Tufty, Esther Van Wagoner (1896–1986)
Turner, Ethel (1872–1958)
Tyler, Alice S. (1859–1944)
Underwood, Agness Wilson (1902–1984)
Van Blarcom, Carolyn (1879–1960)
Van Doren, Irita (1891–1966)
Van Rensselaer, Martha (1864–1932)
Vérone, Maria (1874–1938)
Victor, Metta (1831–1885)
Voilquin, Suzanne (1801–1877)
Vorse, Mary Heaton (1874–1966)
Vreeland, Diana (1903–1989)
Walter, Cornelia Wells (1813–1898)
Walworth, Ellen Hardin (1832–1915)
Ward, Barbara (1914–1981)
Ward, Catharine Barnes (1851–1913)
Washburn, Margaret Floy (1871–1939)
Washington, Fredi (1903–1994)
Wasilewska, Wanda (1905–1964)
Weaver, Harriet Shaw (1876–1961)
Weber, Helene (1881–1962)
Wedgwood, C.V. (1910–1997)
Weiss, Louise (1893–1983)
Wells, Emmeline B. (1828–1921)

Wells-Barnett, Ida (1862–1931)
West, Jessamyn (1902–1984)
Wheeler, Anna Pell (1883–1966)
White, Antonia (1899–1980)
White, Katharine S. (1892–1977)
Whiting, Lilian (1847–1942)
Whitney, Ruth (1928–1999)
Whittelsey, Abigail Goodrich (1788–1858)
Whitton, Charlotte (1896–1975)
Wilkinson, Iris (1906–1939)
Willard, Frances E. (1839–1898)
Williams, Mary Wilhelmine (1878–1944)
Willing, Jennie Fowler (1834–1916)
Wilson, Charlotte (1854–1944)
Winter, John Strange (1856–1911)
Wintour, Anna (1949—)
Wolf, Christa (1929—)
Woodhull, Victoria (1838–1927)
Wright, Frances (1795–1852)
Wright, Mabel Osgood (1859–1934)
Wright, Muriel Hazel (1889–1975)
Wrightson, Patricia (1921—)
Yonge, Charlotte Mary (1823–1901)
Zasulich, Vera (1849–1919)
Zenger, Anna Catharina (c. 1704–1751)
Zetkin, Clara (1857–1933)

PERIODICAL FOUNDER
See also Newspaper founder.
Adam, Juliette la Messine (1836–1936)
Alden, Isabella (1841–1930)
Ali, Aruna Asaf (c. 1909–1996)
Allen, Mary Sophia (1878–1964)
Allfrey, Phyllis Shand (1915–1986)
Anderson, Margaret Carolyn (1886–1973)
Anneke, Mathilde Franziska (1817–1884)
Anthony, Susan B. (1820–1906)
Auclert, Hubertine (1848–1914)
Audouard, Olympe (1830–1890)
Augustine, Rose (1910–2003)
Awolowo, Hannah (1915—)
Bailey, Hannah Johnston (1839–1923)
Baker, Ella (1903–1986)
Belgioso, Cristina (1808–1871)
Besant, Annie (1847–1933)
Brandegee, Mary Katharine (1844–1920)
Brown, Olympia (1835–1926)
Child, Lydia Maria (1802–1880)
Churchill, Jennie Jerome (1854–1921)
Clarke, Helen Archibald (1860–1926)
Cobbe, Frances Power (1822–1904)
Cooper, Gladys (1888–1971)
Dashkova, Ekaterina (1744–1810)
Deroin, Jeanne-Françoise (1805–1894)
Dittmar, Louise (1807–1884)
Dodge, Mary Mapes (1831–1905)
Eddy, Mary Baker (1821–1910)
Field, Kate (1838–1896)
Fillmore, Myrtle Page (1845–1931)
Firestone, Shulamith (1945—)
Foltz, Clara (1849–1934)
Fuertes, Gloria (1917–1998)
Fukuda Hideko (1865–1927)
Galindo de Topete, Hermila (1896–1954)
Gatty, Margaret (1809–1873)
Gilder, Jeannette Leonard (1849–1916)
Gilman, Charlotte Perkins (1860–1935)
Gippius, Zinaida (1869–1945)
Giroud, Françoise (1916–2003)
Goldman, Emma (1869–1940)
Gonne, Maud (1866–1953)
Gourd, Emilie (1879–1946)
Gutiérrez de Mendoza, Juana Belén (1875–1942)
Harand, Irene (1900–1975)
Haslett, Caroline (1895–1957)
Heap, Jane (1887–1964)
Holt, Winifred (1870–1945)
Ihrer, Emma (1857–1911)
Jesenská, Milena (1896–1945)
Johnson, Eleanor Murdoch (1892–1987)
Jolas, Betsy (1926—)
Jolas, Maria (1893–1987)
Katznelson-Shazar, Rachel (1888–1975)
Kent, Victoria (1898–1987)
King, Billie Jean (1943—)
King, Carol Weiss (1895–1952)
Kirchwey, Freda (1893–1976)
Kirkus, Virginia (1893–1980)
Kuliscioff, Anna (c. 1854–1925)
Lange, Helene (1848–1930)
Larcom, Lucy (1824–1893)
Lawson, Louisa (1848–1920)
Lear, Frances (1923–1996)
Léo, André (1832–1900)
Lisboa, Irene (1892–1958)
Loeb, Sophie Irene (1876–1929)
Longhi, Lucia Lopresti (1895–1985)
Loveman, Amy (1881–1955)
MacManus, Anna Johnston (1866–1902)
McDowell, Anne E. (1826–1901)
McPherson, Aimee Semple (1890–1944)
Meynell, Alice (1847–1922)
Miller, Bertha Mahony (1882–1969)
Milligan, Alice (1866–1953)
Monroe, Harriet (1860–1936)
Musidora (1884–1957)
Niboyet, Eugénie (1797–1883)
Ocampo, Victoria (1890–1979)
O'Hair, Madalyn Murray (1919–1995)
Palmer, Helen (1917–1979)
Pankhurst, Sylvia (1882–1960)
Parker, Dorothy (1893–1967)
Parren, Kalliroe (1861–1940)
Paterson, Emma (1848–1886)
Patterson, Alicia (1906–1963)
Peabody, Lucy (1861–1949)
Pelletier, Madeleine (1874–1939)
Phillips, Lena Madesin (1881–1955)
Pimentel, Eleonora (c. 1768–1799)
Popp, Adelheid (1869–1939)
Porter, Charlotte Endymion (1857–1942)
Pound, Louise (1872–1958)
Qiu Jin (c. 1875–1907)
Raine, Kathleen (1908–2003)
Ramirez, Sara Estela (1881–1910)
Respighi, Elsa (1894–1996)
Rhondda, Margaret (1883–1958)
Roys-Gavitt, Elmina M. (1828–1898)
Sand, George (1804–1876)
Sarfatti, Margherita (1880–1961)
Sayers, Dorothy L. (1893–1957)
Serao, Matilde (1856–1927)
Sherkat, Shahla (c. 1956—)
Slesinger, Tess (1905–1945)
Smith, Lillian (1897–1966)
Spark, Muriel (1918—)
Stanton, Elizabeth Cady (1815–1902)
Steinem, Gloria (1934—)
Stephens, Ann S. (1810–1886)
Stoecker, Helene (1869–1943)
Strong, Anna Louise (1885–1970)
Suttner, Bertha von (1843–1914)
Tabouis, Geneviève (1892–1985)
Tallien, Thérésa (1773–1835)
Tauber-Arp, Sophie (1889–1943)
Taylor, Florence M. (1879–1969)
Thurman, Sue (1903–1996)
Timothy, Elizabeth (d. 1757)
Traba, Marta (1930–1983)
Uno, Chiyo (1897–1996)
Vallette, Marguerite (1860–1953)
Van Duyn, Mona (1921–2004)
Walker, Maggie Lena (1867–1934)
Wallace, Lila Acheson (1889–1984)
Weaver, Harriet Shaw (1876–1961)
Webb, Beatrice (1858–1943)
Weiss, Louise (1893–1983)
West, Dorothy (1907–1998)
Whitty, May (1865–1948)
Wilson, Charlotte (1854–1944)
Winter, John Strange (1856–1911)
Woodhull, Victoria (1838–1927)
Wright, Helen (1914–1997)
Wright, Mary Clabaugh (1917–1970)
Zamora, Daisy (1950—)

PERIODICAL PUBLISHER
See also Newspaper publisher.
Abayomi, Oyinkansola (1897–1990)
Abbott, Berenice (1898–1991)
Anderson, Margaret Carolyn (1886–1973)
Anneke, Mathilde Franziska (1817–1884)
Arnold, Eve (1913—)
Bates, Daisy Lee (1914–1999)
Bradwell, Myra (1831–1894)
Brown, Olympia (1835–1926)
Buttrose, Ita (1942—)
Chamorro, Violeta (1929—)
Chandler, Dorothy Buffum (1901–1997)
Coleridge, Georgina (1916–2003)
Cunningham, Agnes (1909–2004)
Curie, Ève (b. 1904)
Dönhoff, Marion, Countess (1909–2002)
Faithfull, Emily (1835–1895)
Field, Kate (1838–1896)
Goddard, Mary Katherine (1738–1816)
Graham, Katharine (1917–2001)
Hani, Motoko (1873–1957)
Henmyer, Annie W. (1827–1900)
Hobby, Oveta Culp (1905–1995)
Jolas, Maria (1893–1987)
Kirchwey, Freda (1893–1976)
La Roche, Sophie von (1730–1807)
Leslie, Miriam Folline Squier (1836–1914)
Meyer, Agnes (1887–1970)
Nicholson, Eliza Jane (1849–1896)
Ottendorfer, Anna Uhl (1815–1884)
Patterson, Alicia (1906–1963)
Patterson, Eleanor Medill (1881–1948)
Reid, Helen Rogers (1882–1970)
Rind, Clementina (c. 1740–1774)
Roberts, Kate (1891–1985)
Saunders, Doris (1921—)
Schiff, Dorothy (1903–1989)
Scripps, Ellen Browning (1836–1932)
Sherkat, Shahla (c. 1956—)
Smith, Hazel Brannon (1914–1994)
Strickland, Mabel (1899–1988)
Swisshelm, Jane Grey (1815–1884)
Timothy, Ann (c. 1727–1792)
Timothy, Elizabeth (d. 1757)
Toor, Frances (1890–1956)
Vann, Jesse Matthews (c. 1890–1967)
Villard, Fanny Garrison (1844–1928)
Vlachos, Helen (1911–1995)
Wallace, Lila Acheson (1889–1984)
Whittelsey, Abigail Goodrich (1788–1858)
Wilson, Charlotte (1854–1944)
Zenger, Anna Catharina (c. 1704–1751)

PHARAOH
Hatshepsut (c. 1515–1468 BCE)
Sobek-neferu (fl. 1680–1674 BCE)

PHARMACIST/PHARMACOLOGIST
Bülbring, Edith (1903–1990)
Dougherty, Ellen (c. 1843–1919)

Elion, Gertrude B. (1918–1999)
Enoki, Miswo (1939—)
Hollinshead, Ariel (1929—)
Irvine, Jean Kennedy (c. 1877–1962)
Jex-Blake, Sophia (1840–1912)
Kelsey, Frances O. (1914—)
Long, Catherine Small (1924—)
Petry, Ann (1908–1997)
Walker, Mary Broadfoot (c. 1888–1974)
Winch, Hope (1895–1944)
Wright, Mickey (1935—)

PHILOLOGIST
Corti, Maria (1915–2002)
Dashkova, Ekaterina (1744–1810)
Stafford, Jean (1915–1979)

PHILOSOPHER
Aesara of Lucania (fl. 400s–300s BCE)
Akselrod, Liubo (1868–1946)
Ambrose, Alice (1906–2001)
Anscombe, G.E.M. (1919–2001)
Arendt, Hannah (1906–1975)
Arete of Cyrene (fl. 4th c. BCE)
Arignote (fl. 6th c. BCE)
Asclepignia (c. 375–?)
Bacinetti-Florenzi, Marianna (1802–1870)
Bassi, Laura (1711–1778)
Beatrice of Nazareth (c. 1200–1268)
Brodbeck, May (1917–1983)
Calkins, Mary Whiton (1863–1930)
Cavendish, Margaret (1623–1673)
Châtelet, Emilie du (1706–1749)
Cleobulina of Rhodes (fl. 570 BCE)
Cockburn, Catharine Trotter (1679–1749)
Coignet, Clarisse (1823–?)
Colonna, Vittoria (c. 1490–1547)
Conrad-Martius, Hedwig (1888–1966)
Constance Jones, E.E. (1848–1922)
Cornaro Piscopia, Elena Lucretia (1646–1684)
Daly, Mary (1928—)
Damo (fl. 6th c. BCE)
de Laguna, Grace Mead (1878–1978)
Diotima of Mantinea (fl. 400s BCE)
Dittmar, Louise (1807–1884)
Elizabeth of Bohemia (1618–1680)
Emmett, Dorothy Mary (b. 1904)
Favre, Julie Velten (1834–1896)
Finch, Anne (1631–1679)
Fisher, Dorothy Canfield (1879–1958)
Foot, Philippa (1920—)
Gilbert, Katherine Everett (1886–1952)
Gournay, Marie le Jars de (1565–1645)
Haldane, Elizabeth S. (1862–1937)
Harris, Marjorie Silliman (1890–1976)
Héricourt, Jenny Poinsard d' (1809–1875)
Herrad of Hohenberg (c. 1130–1195)
Hersch, Jeanne (1910—)
Hipparchia (fl. 300s BCE)
Hypatia (c. 375–415)
Irigaray, Luce (1930—)
Ladd-Franklin, Christine (1847–1930)
Langer, Susanne Knauth (1895–1985)
Leclerc, Annie (1940—)
Leontium (fl. 300–250 BCE)
MacDonald, Margaret (c. 1907–1956)
Marcus, Ruth Barcan (1921—)
Maritain, Raïssa (1883–1960)
Melissa (fl. around 3 BCE)
Molza, Tarquinia (1542–1617)
Murdoch, Iris (1919–1999)
Myia (fl. 6th c. BCE)
Naden, Constance Caroline Woodhill (1858–1889)
Nicarete of Megara (fl. 300 BCE)
Nott, Kathleen (1909–1999)
O'Hair, Madalyn Murray (1919–1995)
Okin, Susan Moller (1946–2004)
Parain-Vial, Jeanne (b. 1912)
Pasternak, Josephine (1900–1993)
Phintys of Sparta (fl. c. 400 BCE)
Rand, Ayn (1905–1982)
Royer, Clémence (1830–1902)
Sabuco, Oliva de Nantes Barrera (1562–1625)
Saw, Ruth (1901–1983)
Shepherd, Mary (c. 1780–1847)
Sinclair, May (1863–1946)
Sosipatra (fl. 4th c.)
Stebbing, L. Susan (1885–1943)
Stein, Edith (1891–1942)
Taylor, Harriet (1807–1858)
Theano (fl. 6th c. BCE)
Timoxena (fl. 2nd c.)
van Schurmann, Anna Maria (1607–1678)
Warnock, Mary (1924—)
Wrinch, Dorothy (1894–1976)
Zambrano, María (1904–1991)

PHONETICIAN
Ward, Ida Caroline (1880–1949)

PHOTOGRAPHER
Abbe, Kathryn (1919—)
Abbott, Berenice (1898–1991)
Akeley, Mary Jobe (1878–1966)
Albin-Guillot, Laure (c. 1880–1962)
Allen, Frances S. (1854–1941)
Allen, Mary E. (1858–1941)
Andriesse, Emmy (1914–1953)
Andujar, Claudia (1931—)
Arbus, Diane (1923–1971)
Arnold, Eve (1913—)
Atkins, Anna (1797–1871)
Austen, Alice (1866–1952)
Barton, Emma (1872–1938)
Beals, Jessie Tarbox (1870–1942)
Becher, Hilla (1934—)
Beese, Lotte (1903–1988)
Bellon, Denise (1902–1999)
Ben-Yusuf, Zaida (fl. 1897–1907)
Bernhard, Ruth (1905—)
Besnyö, Eva (1910–2003)
Biermann, Aenne (1898–1933)
Bing, Ilse (1899–1998)
Bishop, Isabel (1902–1988)
Bland, Lilian (1878–1971)
Blondeau, Barbara (1938–1974)
Bonney, Thérèse (1894–1978)
Boughton, Alice (1866–1943)
Bourke-White, Margaret (1904–1971)
Braggiotti, Gloria (c. 1905—)
Breckinridge, Mary Martin (b. 1905)
Breslauer, Marianne (1909–2001)
Brigman, Anne W. (1869–1950)
Brooks, Charlotte (1918—)
Brooks, Geraldine (1925–1977)
Broom, Christina (1863–1939)
Bubley, Esther (1921–1998)
Buckland, Jessie Lillian (1878–1939)
Buehrmann, Elizabeth (1886–1954)
Cahun, Claude (1894–1954)
Cameron, Julia Margaret (1815–1879)
Canter-Lund, Hilda M. (1922—)
Carpenter, Marion (1920–2002)
Chabot, Maria (1913–2001)
Chadwick, Helen (1953–1996)
Chambefort, Marie (fl. 1850)
Chapelle, Dickey (1919–1972)
Charles, Lallie (1869–1919)
Cones, Nancy Ford (1869–1962)
Content, Marjorie (1895–1984)
Cunningham, Imogen (1883–1976)
Dahl-Wolfe, Louise (1895–1989)
Darby, Eileen (1916–2004)
Duby-Blom, Gertrude (1901–1993)
Eakins, Susan Hannah (1851–1938)
Eames, Ray (1912–1988)
Earhart, Amelia (1897–1937)
Emerson, Gladys Anderson (1903–1984)
Emmons, Chansonetta Stanley (1858–1937)
Farnsworth, Emma J. (1860–1952)
Ferner, Ellen Elizabeth (1869–1930)
Flaherty, Frances Hubbard (c. 1886–1972)
Fleischmann, Trude (1895–1990)
Frank, Rosaline Margaret (1864–1954)
Freeman, Emma B. (1880–1927)
Freund, Gisèle (1912–2000)
Frissell, Toni (1907–1988)
Garlick, Eunice Harriett (1883–1951)
George, Carolyn (1927—)
Gilpin, Laura (1891–1979)
Grimshaw, Beatrice (c. 1870–1953)
Gruber, Ruth (1911—)
Hanscom, Adelaide (1876–1932)
Hawarden, Clementina (1822–1865)
Henri, Florence (1895–1982)
Hofer, Evelyn (1922—)
Horna, Kati (1912–2000)
Howard, Jean (1910–2000)
Jacobi, Lotte (1896–1990)
Jekyll, Gertrude (1843–1932)
Johnston, Frances Benjamin (1864–1952)
Kanaga, Consuelo (1894–1978)
Kar, Ida (1908–1970)
Käsebier, Gertrude (1852–1934)
Kasten, Barbara (1936—)
Keaton, Diane (1946—)
Kendall, Marie Hartig (1854–1943)
Kent, Thelma Rene (1899–1946)
Ker-Seymer, Barbara (b. 1905)
Kruger, Barbara (1945—)
Krull, Germaine (1897–1985)
Lange, Dorothea (1895–1965)
Lavenson, Alma (1897–1989)
Leibovitz, Annie (1949—)
Levitt, Helen (1913—)
Lollobrigida, Gina (1927—)
Louise, Ruth Harriet (1906–1944)
Maillart, Ella (1903–1997)
Mark, Mary Ellen (1940—)
Marucha (1944–1991)
Mather, Margrethe (c. 1885–1952)
McAliskey, Roisin (1971—)
McCartney, Linda (1941–1998)
McKenna, Rollie (1918–2003)
McLaughlin-Gill, Frances (1919—)
Meiselas, Susan (1948—)
Mieth, Hansel (1909–1998)
Miller, Lee (1907–1977)
Model, Lisette (1901–1983)
Modotti, Tina (1896–1942)
Moholy, Lucia (1894–1989)
Moodie, Geraldine (1853–1945)
Morath, Inge (1923–2002)
Morgan, Barbara (1900–1992)
Naylor, Genevieve (1915–1989)
Nelly (1899–1998)
Neuberger, Maurine B. (1906–2000)
Newsom, Carol (1946–2003)
Niepce, Janine (1921—)
Norman, Dorothy (1905–1997)
Noskowiak, Sonya (1900–1975)
Orkin, Ruth (1921–1985)
Palfi, Marion (1907–1978)
Parsons, Mary (1813–1885)
Peck, Annie Smith (1850–1935)
Pulman, Elizabeth (1836–1900)
Resvoll-Holmsen, Hanna (1873–1943)

Rey, Margret (1906–1996)
Robertson, Grace (1930—)
Sankova, Galina (b. 1904)
Schau, Virginia M. (1915–1989)
Sipprell, Clara (1885–1975)
Tannenbaum, Jane Belo (1904–1968)
Taro, Gerda (1910–1937)
Thorne, Harriet V.S. (1843–1926)
Tudor-Hart, Edith (1908–1978)
Ulmann, Doris (1882–1934)
Vandamm, Florence (1883–1966)
Varda, Agnes (1928—)
Warburg, Agnes (1872–1953)
Ward, Catharine Barnes (1851–1913)
Watkins, Margaret (1884–1969)
Watson, Edith (1861–1943)
Wells, Alice (1927–1987)
Wiggins, Myra Albert (1869–1956)
Wilding, Dorothy (1893–1976)
Withington, Eliza (1825–1877)
Wolcott, Marion Post (1910–1990)
Woodbridge, Louise Deshong (1848–1925)
Wootten, Bayard (1875–1959)
Wulz, Wanda (1903–1984)
Yampolsky, Mariana (1925–2002)
Yevonde (1893–1975)
Ylla (1911–1955)
Younghusband, Adela Mary (1878–1969)
Yva (1900–1942)

PHOTOJOURNALIST
Arnold, Eve (1913—)
Battaglia, Letizia (1935—)
Beals, Jessie Tarbox (1870–1942)
Bing, Ilse (1899–1998)
Bland, Lilian (1878–1971)
Bourke-White, Margaret (1904–1971)
Breckinridge, Mary Marvin (1905–2002)
Brooks, Charlotte (1918—)
Broom, Christina (1863–1939)
Chapelle, Dickey (1919–1972)
Freund, Gisèle (1912–2000)
Horna, Kati (1912—)
Kanaga, Consuelo (1894–1978)
Kar, Ida (1908–1970)
Mark, Mary Ellen (1940—)
Meiselas, Susan (1948—)
Model, Lisette (1901–1983)
Morath, Inge (1923–2002)
Naylor, Genevieve (1915–1989)
Niepce, Janine (1921—)
Orkin, Ruth (1921–1985)
Robertson, Grace (1930—)
Sankova, Galina (b. 1904)
Taro, Gerda (1910–1937)

PHRENOLOGIST
Wells, Charlotte Fowler (1814–1901)

PHYSICAL CHEMIST
Carr, Emma Perry (1880–1972)
Franklin, Rosalind (1920–1958)
Immerwahr, Clara (1870–1915)
Noddack, Ida (1896–1978)
Telkes, Maria (1900–1995)

PHYSICAL-EDUCATION INSTRUCTOR
Applebee, Constance (1873–1981)
Babcock, Maud May (1867–1954)
Bancroft, Jessie (1867–1952)
Baraquio, Angela Perez (1976—)
Berenson, Senda (1868–1954)
Cai Chang (1900–1990)
Coachman, Alice (1923—)
Cobb, Jewell Plummer (1924—)
Colon, Maria (1958—)
Gibson, Althea (1927—)
Gisolo, Margaret (1914—)
Goldsmith, Grace Arabell (1904–1975)
Jackson, Nell (1929–1988)
Jones, Barbara (1937—)
Kuzwayo, Ellen (1914—)
Mosher, Eliza Maria (1846–1928)
Neuberger, Maurine B. (1906–2000)
Perrin, Ethel (1871–1962)
Peterson, Esther (1906–1997)
Potonié-Pierre, Eugénie (1844–1898)
Prets, Christa (1947—)
Sabin, Florence (1871–1953)
Summitt, Pat (1952—)
Tyus, Wyomia (1945—)
West, Winifred (1881–1971)
Williams, Lucinda (1937—)

PHYSICIAN
Abbott, Maude (1869–1940)
Abrahams, Ottilie Grete (1937—)
Aemilia Hilaria (fl. 350)
Agnes of Huntingdonshire (fl. 13th c.)
Albright, Tenley (1935—)
Aldrich-Blake, Louisa (1865–1925)
Alexander, Hattie (1901–1968)
Ames, Frances (1920–2002)
Andersen, Dorothy Hansine (1901–1963)
Anderson, Caroline Still (1848–1919)
Anderson, Elizabeth Garrett (1836–1917)
André, Valerie (1922—)
Angwin, Maria L. (1849–1898)
Anne of York (fl. 13th c.)
Apgar, Virginia (1909–1974)
Ashton, Helen (1891–1958)
Auerbach, Edith (1903—)
Bagshaw, Elizabeth (1881–1982)
Baker, S. Josephine (1873–1945)
Baker McLaglan, Eleanor Southey (1879–1969)
Balliser, Helen (fl. 1914)
Barrett, Kate Waller (1857–1925)
Barringer, Emily Dunning (1876–1961)
Barrows, Isabel Hayes (1845–1913)
Bass, Mary Elizabeth (1876–1956)
Bates, Mary (1861–1954)
Bechtereva, Natalia (1924—)
Bell, Muriel Emma (1898–1974)
Benchley, Belle (1882–1973)
Bennett, Agnes Elizabeth Lloyd (1872–1960)
Bennett, Alice (1851–1925)
Bentham, Ethel (1861–1931)
Bergmann-Pohl, Sabine (1946—)
Biggs, Rosemary (1912–2001)
Black, Elinor F.E. (1905–1982)
Blackwell, Elizabeth (1821–1910)
Blackwell, Emily (1826–1910)
Blanc, Marie-Thérèse (1840–1907)
Bodley, Rachel (1831–1888)
Boivin, Marie Anne (1773–1847)
Bondar, Roberta (b. 1945)
Bonner, Elena (1923—)
Borst-Eilers, Els (1932—)
Brandegee, Mary Katharine (1844–1920)
Branham, Sara Elizabeth (1888–1962)
Britton, Rosa María (1936—)
Broomall, Anna (1847–1931)
Brown, Charlotte (1846–1904)
Brown, Dorothy (1919—)
Brown, Vera Scantlebury (1889–1946)
Buckel, C. Annette (1833–1912)
Budzynska-Tylicka, Justyna (1876–1936)
Cabete, Adelaide (1867–1935)
Calderone, Mary Steichen (1904–1998)
Caldicott, Helen (1938—)
Callender, Sheila (1914–2004)
Campbell, Kate (1899–1986)
Cassidy, Sheila (1937—)
Chapman, Sylvia (1896–1995)
Chinn, May Edward (1896–1980)
Cilento, Phyllis (1894–1987)
Clark, Hilda (1881–1955)
Clark, Nancy Talbot (1825–1901)
Cleaves, Margaret (1848–1917)
Cleopatra (fl. 1st c. BCE)
Cleveland, Emeline Horton (1829–1878)
Clisby, Harriet (1830–1931)
Clubb, Elizabeth (1922—)
Cole, Rebecca J. (1846–1922)
Comfort, Anna Manning (1845–1931)
Cori, Gerty T. (1896–1957)
Cowie, Helen Stephen (1875–1956)
Craighill, Margaret (1898–1977)
Cruickshank, Margaret Barnet (1873–1918)
Crumpler, Rebecca Lee (1831–1895)
Cushier, Elizabeth (1837–1932)
Dalton, Katharina (1916–2004)
Dalyell, Elsie (1881–1948)
Daniel, Annie Sturges (1858–1944)
Darrow, Anna (1876–1959)
de Almania, Jacqueline Felicia (fl. 1322)
Deutsch, Helene (1884–1982)
Dick, Gladys (1881–1963)
Dickey, Nancy Wilson (1950—)
Dimock, Susan (1847–1875)
Dixon Jones, Mary Amanda (1828–1908)
Dodge, Eva F. (1896–1990)
Dolley, Sarah Adamson (1829–1909)
Duckering, Florence West (1869–1951)
Du Coudray, Angélique (1712–1789)
Edmunds, Elizabeth M. (c. 1941—)
Elders, Joycelyn (1933—)
Elgood, Cornelia (1874–1960)
Elion, Gertrude B. (1918–1999)
Eliot, Martha May (1891–1978)
El Saadawi, Nawal (1931—)
English, Ada (c. 1878–1944)
Erxleben, Dorothea (1715–1762)
Evans, Matilda Arabella (1872–1935)
Fearn, Anne Walter (1865–1939)
Florey, Margaret (1904–1994)
Follansbee, Elizabeth A. (1839–1917)
Forbes-Sempill, Elizabeth (1912–1965)
Fowler, Lydia Folger (1822–1879)
Frantz, Virginia Kneeland (1896–1967)
Frost, Constance Helen (c. 1862–1920)
Fulton, Mary Hannah (1854–1927)
Gantt, Rosa (1875–1935)
Gao Yaojie (c. 1927—)
Gardiner, Muriel (1901–1985)
Gardner, Frances (1913–1989)
Gilette of Narbonne (fl. 1300)
Gleason, Rachel Brooks (1820–1905)
Goldsmith, Grace Arabell (1904–1975)
Gordon, Doris Clifton (1890–1956)
Greene, Cordelia A. (1831–1905)
Guillemete du Luys (fl. 1479)
Guion, Connie M. (1882–1971)
Gullen, Augusta Stowe (1857–1943)
Gunn, Elizabeth Catherine (1879–1963)
Hall, Rosetta Sherwood (1865–1951)
Hall, Theodora Clemens (1902–1980)
Han, Suyin (1917—)
Hastings, Caroline (1841–1922)
Hautval, Adelaide (1906–1988)
Heer, Anna (1863–1918)
Helvidis (fl. 1136)
Hersende of France (fl. 1250)
Hickey, Eileen (1886–1960)
Hinkle, Beatrice M. (1874–1953)
Hirsch, Rachel (1870–1953)
Horsley, Alice Woodward (1871–1957)
Howell, Mary (1932–1998)
Hugonnay, Vilma (1847–1922)

Hunt, Harriot Kezia (1805–1875)
Hurd-Mead, Kate Campbell (1867–1941)
Hurdon, Elizabeth (1868–1941)
Huson, Florence (1857–1915)
Ighodaro, Irene (1916–1995)
Inglis, Elsie Maud (1864–1917)
Jackson, Mary Percy (1904–2000)
Jackson, Mercy B. (1802–1877)
Jacobi, Mary Putnam (1842–1906)
Jacobs, Aletta (1854–1929)
Jemison, Mae C. (b. 1956)
Jex-Blake, Sophia (1840–1912)
Johnson, Halle (1864–1901)
Jordan, Sara Murray (1884–1959)
Joshi, Anandibai (1865–1887)
Jull, Roberta (1872–1961)
Katherine (fl. 13th c.)
Keller, Nettie Florence (1875–1974)
Kelsey, Frances O. (1914—)
Kingsford, Anna (1846–1888)
Kleegman, Sophia (1901–1971)
Klumpke, Augusta (1859–1927)
Kübler-Ross, Elisabeth (1926–2004)
Lachapelle, Marie (1769–1821)
La Flesche, Susan (1865–1915)
Lais (fl. 1st c. BCE)
La Roe, Else K. (1900–1970)
Laurette de St. Valery (fl. 1200)
Lawrie, Jean Grant (1914—)
L'Esperance, Elise Strang (c. 1879–1959)
Levi-Montalcini, Rita (b. 1909)
Levine, Lena (1903–1965)
Li Huixin (1937—)
Lingens-Reiner, Ella (1908–2002)
Lin Qiaozhi (1901–1983)
Lissiardi, Sibille (fl. 13th c.)
Lloyd Davies, Vanessa (1960–2005)
Lockrey, Sarah Hunt (1863–1929)
Longshore, Hannah E. (1819–1901)
Love, Susan (1948—)
Lovejoy, Esther Pohl (1869–1967)
Lozier, Clemence S. (1813–1888)
Lynn, Kathleen (1874–1955)
Macklin, Madge (1893–1962)
MacMurchy, Helen (1862–1953)
Macnamara, Jean (1899–1968)
Macphail, Katherine Stewart (1888–1974)
Magee, Joni (1941—)
Malleson, Joan (1900–1956)
Margaret of Ypres (fl. 1322)
Marshall, Clara (1847–1931)
Matheson, Elizabeth (1866–1958)
Mayo, Sara Tew (1869–1930)
McGee, Anita Newcomb (1864–1940)
McKane, Alice Woodby (1865–1948)
McLaren, Agnes (1837–1913)
McLean, Mary Hancock (1861–1930)
Mellanby, Helen (1911–2001)
Mendenhall, Dorothy Reed (1874–1964)
Menten, Maude (1879–1960)
Mercuriade of Salerno (fl. 1200)
Mergler, Marie Josepha (1851–1901)
Merrick, Myra King (1825–1899)
Meyer, Lucy (1849–1922)
Minoka-Hill, Rosa (1876–1952)
Montessori, Maria (1870–1952)
Morani, Alma Dea (1907–2001)
Moreau de Justo, Alicia (1885–1986)
Morton, Rosalie Slaughter (1876–1968)
Mosher, Clelia Duel (1863–1940)
Mosher, Eliza Maria (1846–1928)
Murrell, Christine (1874–1933)
Nasrin, Taslima (1962—)
Nayar, Sushila (1914–2001)
Nichols, Mary Gove (1810–1884)
Nielsen, Jerri (1953—)
Northcroft, Hilda Margaret (1882–1951)
Novello, Antonia (1944—)
Oberheuser, Herta (1911–1978)
Owens-Adair, Bethenia (1840–1926)
Panagiotatou, Angeliki (1878–1954)
Parker, Valeria Hopkins (1879–1959)
Paterson, Ada Gertrude (1880–1937)
Pearce, Louise (1885–1959)
Pechey-Phipson, Edith (1845–1908)
Pelletier, Madeleine (1874–1939)
Pickerill, Cecily Mary Wise (1903–1988)
Platts-Mills, Daisy Elizabeth (1868–1956)
Preston, Ann (1813–1872)
Putnam, Helen (1857–1951)
Raiche, Bessica (c. 1874–1932)
Ramphele, Mamphela (1947—)
Ramsey, Elizabeth M. (1906–1993)
Ratebzad, Anahita (1931—)
Reid, Clarice D. (1931—)
Remond, Sarah Parker (1826–1894)
Richardson, Dot (1961—)
Ripley, Martha Rogers (1843–1912)
Robbins, Jane Elizabeth (1860–1946)
Rodríguez, Evangelina (1879–1947)
Romano, Francesca (fl. 1321)
Ross, Charlotte Whitehead (1843–1916)
Roys-Gavitt, Elmina M. (1828–1898)
Rue, Rosemary (1928–2004)
Russell, Dorothy Stuart (1895–1983)
Rutherford, Frances Armstrong (1842–1922)
Sabin, Florence (1871–1953)
Safford, Mary Jane (1834–1891)
Sarah of St. Gilles (fl. 1326)
Saunders, Cicely (1918–2005)
Sayer, Ettie (1875–1923)
Scharlieb, Mary Ann (1845–1930)
Scott, Jessie Ann (1883–1959)
Scudder, Ida (1870–1960)
Seacole, Mary Jane (c. 1805–1881)
Seddon, Rhea (1947—)
Sewall, Lucy Ellen (1837–1890)
Shabanova, Anna (1848–1932)
Shaw, Anna Howard (1847–1919)
Sherlock, Sheila (1918–2001)
Sherwood, Mary (1856–1935)
Shipp, Ellis Reynolds (1847–1939)
Shortt, Elizabeth Smith (1859–1949)
Siebold, Charlotte Heidenreich von (1788–1859)
Siedeberg, Emily Hancock (1873–1968)
Singer, Eleanor (1903–1999)
Sirridge, Marjorie S. (1921—)
Slye, Maud (1869–1954)
Staveley, Dulcie (1898–1995)
Stevenson, Sarah Hackett (1841–1909)
Steward, Susan McKinney (1847–1918)
Stone, Constance (1856–1902)
Stone, Hannah (1893–1941)
Stowe, Emily Howard (1831–1903)
Stuart, Miranda (c. 1795–1865)
Sturgis, Katharine Boucot (1903–1987)
Summerskill, Edith (1901–1980)
Suslova, Nadezhda (1845–1916)
Swain, Clara A. (1834–1910)
Taussig, Helen Brooke (1898–1986)
Thomas, Mary Myers (1816–1888)
Thompson, Clara (1893–1958)
Thompson, Mary Harris (1829–1895)
Todd, Margaret G. (1859–1918)
Tomaszewicz-Dobrska, Anna (1854–1918)
Tracy, Martha (1876–1942)
Travell, Janet G. (1901–1997)
Trotula (c. 1040s–1097)
Trout, Jenny Kidd (1841–1921)
Turner-Warwick, Margaret (1924—)
Underwood, Lillias (1851–1921)
Uvarov, Olga (1910–2001)
Van Hoosen, Bertha (1863–1952)
Vejjabul, Pierra (b. 1909)
Virdimura of Sicily (fl. 1376)
Vögtlin, Marie (1845–1916)
Wald, Florence (1917—)
Walker, Mary Broadfoot (c. 1888–1974)
Walker, Mary Edwards (1832–1919)
Walters, Bernice R. (1912–1975)
Warner, Estella Ford (1891–1974)
Weiss, Alta (1889–1964)
Welsh, Lilian (1858–1938)
Wilberforce, Octavia (1888–1963)
Williams, Anna Wessels (1863–1954)
Williams, Cicely (1893–1992)
Williams, Ethel (1863–1948)
Willits, Mary (1855–1902)
Willoughby, Frances L. (c. 1906–1984)
Willums, Sigbrit (fl. 1507–1523)
Withington, Alfreda (1860–1951)
Wollstein, Martha (1868–1939)
Yarros, Rachelle (1869–1946)
Yeomans, Amelia (1842–1913)
Yoshioka, Yayoi (1871–1959)
Zakrzewska, Marie (1829–1902)

PHYSICIST

Ajzenberg-Selove, Fay (1926—)
Ancker-Johnson, Betsy (1927—)
Andam, Aba A. Bentil (c. 1960—)
Anderson, Elda E. (1899–1961)
Anderson, Elizabeth Garrett (1836–1917)
Ayrton, Hertha Marks (1854–1923)
Bleeker, Caroline Emilie (1897–1985)
Blodgett, Katharine Burr (1898–1979)
Brooks, Harriet (1876–1933)
Burbidge, Margaret (1919—)
Choquet-Bruhat, Yvonne (1923—)
Cremer, Erika (1900–1996)
Daubechies, Ingrid (1954—)
Entragues, Henriette d' (1579–1633)
Eymers, Truus (1903–1988)
Franklin, Rosalind (1920–1958)
Freeman, Joan (1918–1998)
Guthrie, Janet (1938—)
Hanson, Jean (1919–1973)
Héricourt, Jenny Poinsard d' (1809–1875)
Horney, Karen (1885–1952)
Hunt, Harriot Kezia (1805–1875)
Jackson, Shirley Ann (1946—)
Jex-Blake, Sophia (1840–1912)
Joliot-Curie, Irène (1897–1956)
Keith, Marcia (1859–1950)
Laby, Jean (1915—)
Lehmann, Inge (1888–1993)
Macnamara, Jean (1899–1968)
Maltby, Margaret E. (1860–1944)
Massevitch, Alla G. (1918—)
Mayer, Maria Goeppert (1906–1972)
Meitner, Lise (1878–1968)
Merkel, Angela (1954—)
Nichols, Mary Gove (1810–1884)
Payne-Gaposchkin, Cecilia (1900–1979)
Perey, Marguerite (1909–1975)
Quimby, Edith (1891–1982)
Quinn, Helen (1943—)
Scharff-Goldhaber, Gertrude (1911–1998)
Scott, Ruby Payne (1912–1981)
Somerville, Mary Fairfax (1780–1872)
Sponer, Hertha (1895–1968)
Telkes, Maria (1900–1995)
Weeks, Dorothy (1893–1990)
Whiting, Sarah F. (1847–1927)
Wright, Helena (1887–1982)
Wrinch, Dorothy (1894–1976)
Wu, Chien-Shiung (1912–1997)

Xie Xide (1921–2000)
Yalow, Rosalyn (1921—)
Yuasa, Toshiko (1909–1980)

PHYSIOLOGIST

Bidder, Marion Greenwood (1862–1932)
Bobath, Berta (1907–1991)
Bülbring, Edith (1903–1990)
Chick, Harriette (1875–1977)
Claypole, Edith Jane (1870–1915)
Cullis, Winifred Clara (1875–1956)
Esau, Katherine (1898–1997)
Hyde, Ida (1857–1945)
Lewis, Margaret Reed (1881–1970)
Pickford, Mary (1902–2002)
Pitt-Rivers, Rosalind (1907–1990)
Pool, Judith Graham (1919–1975)
Rand, Gertrude (1886–1970)
Shtern, Lina (1878–1968)

PHYSIOTHERAPIST

Pilgrim, Ada (1867–1965)
Roberts, Mary Louise (1886–1968)
Wilding, Cora (1888–1982)

PIANIST

Akiyoshi, Toshiko (1929—)
Albanesi, Meggie (1899–1923)
Albani, Emma (c. 1847–1930)
Alda, Frances (1879–1952)
Alexander, Leni (1924—)
Allen, Florence Ellinwood (1884–1966)
Amos, Tori (1963—)
Anderson, Beth (1950—)
Anderson, Eugenie Moore (1909–1997)
Anderson, Lucy (1797–1878)
Anna Amalia of Prussia (1723–1787)
Archer, Violet Balestreri (1913–2000)
Aretz, Isabel (1909—)
Argerich, Martha (1941—)
Armand, Inessa (1874–1920)
Armstrong, Lil Hardin (1898–1971)
Arnaud, Yvonne (1892–1958)
Atwell, Winifred (1914–1983)
Aus der Ohe, Adele (1864–1937)
Austin, Lovie (1887–1972)
Bach, Maria (1896–1978)
Bachauer, Gina (1913–1976)
Backer-Grondahl, Agathe (1847–1907)
Ballon, Ellen (1898–1969)
Ballou, Esther Williamson (1915–1973)
Bartholomew, Ann Sheppard (1811–1891)
Bartlett, Ethel (1896–1978)
Bartok, Ditta Pasztory (1902–1982)
Batten, Jean Gardner (1909–1982)
Beach, Amy Cheney (1867–1944)
Beckman-Shcherbina, Elena (1881–1951)
Beeton, Isabella Mary (1836–1865)
Belleville-Oury, Anna Caroline de (1808–1880)
Bentley, Gladys (1907–1960)
Bergman, Marilyn (1929—)
Bigot de Morogues, Marie (1786–1820)
Biret, Idil (1941—)
Bishop, Bernice Pauahi (1831–1884)
Blahetka, Marie Leopoldine (1811–1887)
Blancard, Jacqueline (1909—)
Bloom, Ursula (1893–1984)
Blumental, Felicja (1908–1991)
Blumental, Felicja (1918—)
Boehm, Mary Louise (1924–2002)
Bonds, Margaret (1913–1972)
Bonnin, Gertrude Simmons (1876–1938)
Boulanger, Nadia (1887–1979)
Brackeen, JoAnne (1938—)
Branscombe, Gena (1881–1977)
Bremer, Fredrika (1801–1865)
Brico, Antonia (1902–1989)
Bright, Dora Estella (1863–1951)
Bronsart, Ingeborg von (1840–1913)
Brooks, Hadda (1916–2002)
Brooks, Louise (1906–1985)
Brown, Ada (1889–1950)
Busoni, Anna (1833–1909)
Cameron, Bessy (c. 1851–1895)
Campbell, Mrs. Patrick (1865–1940)
Canal, Marguerite (1890–1978)
Candeille, Julie (1767–1834)
Cannon, Annie Jump (1863–1941)
Carrel, Felicite (fl. 1860s)
Carreño, Teresa (1853–1917)
Carter, Betty (1929–1998)
Carvalho, Dinora de (1905—)
Casadesus, Gaby (1901–1999)
Casadesus, Gaby (b. 1901)
Chambers, Norah (1905–1989)
Chaminade, Cécile (1857–1944)
Clarke, Rebecca (1886–1979)
Clauss-Szárvady, Wilhelmina (1834–1907)
Clidat, France (1932—)
Cohen, Harriet (1895–1967)
Coleridge-Taylor, Avril (1903–1998)
Collett, Camilla (1813–1895)
Coltrane, Alice (1937—)
Connolly, Maureen (1934–1969)
Coolidge, Elizabeth Sprague (1863–1953)
Crawford, Ruth (1901–1953)
Crispell, Marilyn (1947—)
Crochet, Evelyne (1934—)
Curie, Ève (b. 1904)
Czerny-Stefanska, Halina (1922-2001)
Dale, Kathleen (1895–1984)
Darré, Jeanne-Marie (1905–1999)
Davidovich, Bella (1928—)
Davies, Dorothy Ida (1899–1987)
Davies, Fanny (1861–1934)
Dearie, Blossom (1926—)
de Brunhoff, Cécile (1903–2003)
de Lara, Adelina (1872–1961)
Demessieux, Jeanne (1921–1968)
Densmore, Frances (1867–1957)
De Swirska, Tamara (c. 1890–?)
Dlugoszewski, Lucia (1925–2000)
Donska, Maria (1912–1996)
Dorfmann, Ania (1899–1984)
Droste-Hülshoff, Annette von (1797–1848)
Eakins, Susan Hannah (1851–1938)
Eckhardt-Gramatté, S.C. (1899–1974)
Eibenschütz-Dernbourg, Ilona (1872–1967)
Eisler, Charlotte (1894–1970)
Elgar, Alice (1848–1920)
Epstein, Selma (1927—)
Essipova, Annette (1851–1914)
Farnadi, Edith (1921–1973)
Farrenc, Louise (1804–1875)
Fay, Amy (1844–1928)
Fénelon, Fania (1918–1983)
Ferrari, Carlotta (1837–1907)
Ferrari, Gabrielle (1851–1921)
Ferrier, Kathleen (1912–1953)
Fine, Vivian (1913–2000)
Fischer, Annie (1914–1995)
Flack, Roberta (1937—)
Fremstad, Olive (1871–1951)
Gaigerova, Varvara Andrianovna (1903–1944)
Garbousova, Raya (1909–1997)
Gardner, Kay (1941–2002)
Genhart, Cecile Staub (1898–1983)
Gibson, Perla Siedle (d. 1971)
Gipps, Ruth (1921—)
Giuranna, Barbara (1902–1998)
Glanville-Hicks, Peggy (1912–1990)
Goddard, Arabella (1836–1922)
Gonzaga, Chiquinha (1847–1935)
Goodson, Katharine (1872–1958)
Goodson, Sadie (c. 1900—)
Grinberg, Maria (1908–1979)
Gubaidulina, Sofia (1931—)
Guggenheimer, Minnie (1882–1966)
Guraieb Kuri, Rosa (1931—)
Haas, Monique (1906–1987)
Hackley, E. Azalia Smith (1867–1922)
Haebler, Ingrid (1926—)
Hall, Cara Vincent (1922—)
Hanim, Leyla (1850–1936)
Harding, Florence K. (1860–1924)
Harrison, Hazel (1883–1969)
Harrison, Susie Frances (1859–1935)
Haskil, Clara (1895–1960)
Haver, June (1926—)
Henriot-Schweitzer, Nicole (1925—)
Hess, Myra (1890–1965)
Hesse-Bukowska, Barbara (1930—)
Heyman, Katherine Ruth (1877–1944)
Hier, Ethel Glenn (1889–1971)
Hillesum, Etty (1914–1943)
Hinderas, Natalie (1927–1987)
Hipp, Jutta (1925–2003)
Hodges, Faustina Hasse (1822–1895)
Hodgkins, Frances (1869–1947)
Hofer, Evelyn
Hogg, Ima (1882–1975)
Holland, Dulcie Sybil (1913—)
Holley, Marietta (1836–1926)
Holmès, Augusta (1847–1903)
Holst, Imogen (1907–1984)
Hopekirk, Helen (1856–1945)
Hyde, Miriam Beatrice (1913–2005)
Iturbi, Amparo (1898–1969)
Ivey, Jean Eichelberger (1923—)
Jaczynowska, Katarzyna (1875–1920)
Janotha, Natalia (1856–1932)
Japha, Louise (1826–1889)
Jefferson, Martha (1748–1782)
Jolas, Betsy (1926—)
Jonas, Maryla (1911–1959)
Jordan, Marian (1896–1961)
Joy, Génèviève (1919—)
Joyce, Eileen (1908–1991)
Kabos, Ilona (1893–1973)
Kallir, Lilian (1931–2004)
Kanner-Rosenthal, Hedwig (1882–1959)
Kasilag, Lucrecia R. (1918—)
Keene, Constance (1921–2005)
Kennedy, Joan (1936—)
Kerr, Anita (1927—)
Khan, Noor Inayat (1914–1944)
Kinkel, Johanna (1810–1858)
Kleeberg, Clotilde (1866–1909)
Koptagel, Yuksel (1931—)
Krall, Diana (1964—)
Kraus, Greta (1907–1998)
Kraus, Lili (1903–1986)
Krebs-Brenning, Marie (1851–1900)
Kwast, Frieda Hodapp (1880–1949)
Lafarge, Marie (1816–1852)
La Hye, Louise (1810–1838)
Landowska, Wanda (1877–1959)
Lane, Lola (1909–1981)
Lang, Josephine (1815–1880)
Lang-Beck, Ivana (1912–1983)
Langley, Neva (c. 1934—)
Laredo, Ruth (1937–2005)
Larrocha, Alicia de (1923—)
Lear, Evelyn (1926—)
Le Beau, Luise Adolpha (1850–1927)
Lebrun, Franziska (1756–1791)
Lee, Gypsy Rose (1914–1970)
Lefaucheux, Marie-Helene (1904–1964)

Leginska, Ethel (1886–1970)
Lehmann, Liza (1862–1918)
Lenya, Lotte (1898–1981)
Leviska, Helvi Lemmiki (1902–1982)
Lhevinne, Rosina (1880–1976)
Lipson-Gruzen, Berenice (1925–1998)
Long, Kathleen (1896–1968)
Long, Marguerite (1874–1966)
Loriod, Yvonne (1924–2001)
Lowney, Shannon (1969–1994)
Lympany, Moura (1916–2005)
Lynn, Diana (1926–1971)
Macandrew, Jennie (1866–1949)
MacDowell, Marian (1857–1956)
Maconchy, Elizabeth (1907–1994)
Malibran, Maria (1808–1836)
Mana-Zucca (1887–1981)
Mannes, Clara Damrosch (1869–1948)
Marcus, Adele (1905–1995)
Marcus, Marie (1914–2003)
Maria Antonia of Austria (1724–1780)
Mariana Victoria (1768–1788)
Marlowe, Julia (1866–1950)
Martin, Sara (1884–1955)
Martinez, Marianne (1744–1812)
Matzenauer, Margaret (1881–1963)
Maxwell, Elsa (1883–1963)
Mayer, Emilie (1821–1883)
McCullers, Carson (1917–1967)
McMein, Neysa (1888–1949)
McPartland, Marian (1920—)
McRae, Carmen (1920–1994)
Mead, Lucia Ames (1856–1936)
Mehlig, Anna (1846–1928)
Mekeel, Joyce (1931—)
Melba, Nellie (1861–1931)
Mendelssohn-Hensel, Fanny (1805–1847)
Menter, Sophie (1846–1918)
Menuhin, Hephzibah (1920–1981)
Menuhin, Yaltah (1921–2001)
Merman, Ethel (1912–1984)
Mero, Yolanda (1887–1963)
Miller, Freda (c. 1910–1960)
Mireille (1906–1996)
Mitchell, Joni (1943—)
Model, Lisette (1901–1983)
Monnot, Marguerite (1903–1961)
Moszumanska-Nazar, Krystyna (1924—)
Mozart, Constanze (1762–1842)
Mozart, Maria Anna (1751–1829)
Nemenoff, Genia (1905–1989)
Newcomb, Ethel (1875–1959)
Newlin, Dika (1923—)
Ney, Elly (1882–1968)
Nickerson, Camille (1884–1982)
Nikolayeva, Tatiana (1924–1993)
Nissen, Erika (1845–1903)
Norrell, Catherine Dorris (1901–1981)
Novaës, Guiomar (1895–1979)
Oppens, Ursula (1944—)
Ortiz, Cristina (1950—)
Ostermeyer, Micheline (1922–2001)
Ousset, Cécile (1936—)
Pachler-Koschak, Marie (1792–1855)
Paradis, Maria Theresia von (1759–1824)
Parker, Dorothy (1893–1967)
Pearl, Minnie (1912–1996)
Pentland, Barbara (1912–2000)
Pires, Maria-Joao (1944—)
Pitot, Genevieve (c. 1920—)
Pleyel, Maria Felicite (1811–1875)
Popovici, Elise (1921—)
Poston, Elizabeth (1905–1987)
Powell, Maud (1867–1920)
Price, Florence B. (1888–1953)
Price, Leontyne (1927—)
Przybyszewska, Dagny Juel (1867–1901)
Rainier, Priaulx (1903–1986)
Reisenberg, Nadia (1904–1983)
Renard, Rosita (1894–1949)
Respighi, Elsa (1894–1996)
Richardson, Henry Handel (1870–1946)
Richter, Marga (1926—)
Rivé-King, Julie (1854–1937)
Rockefeller, Martha Baird (1895–1971)
Rogatis, Teresa de (1893–1979)
Royer, Clémence (1830–1902)
Runcie, Constance Faunt Le Roy (1836–1911)
Rutherford, Margaret (1892–1972)
Samaroff, Olga (1882–1948)
Scharrer, Irene (1888–1971)
Schonthal, Ruth (1924—)
Schramm, Bernardina Adriana (1900–1987)
Schumann, Clara (1819–1896)
Schuyler, Philippa Duke (1931–1967)
Scott, Hazel (1920–1981)
Scriabin, Vera (1875–1920)
Sellick, Phyllis (b. 1911)
Selva, Blanche (1884–1942)
Sembrich, Marcella (1858–1935)
Sert, Misia (1872–1950)
Séverine (1855–1929)
Simon, Kate (1912–1990)
Simone, Nina (1933–2003)
Slenczynska, Ruth (1925—)
Smendzianka, Regina (1924—)
Smith, Mabel (1924–1972)
Somer, Hilde (1922–1979)
Somogi, Judith (1937–1988)
Sorel, Claudette (1930—)
Southern, Eileen Jackson (1920–2002)
Southern, Jeri (1926–1991)
Spivey, Victoria (1906–1976)
St. James, Lyn (1947—)
Starr, Belle (1848–1889)
Steber, Eleanor (1914–1990)
Stone, Rosie (1945—)
Suesse, Dana (1909–1987)
Sutherland, Margaret (1897–1984)
Suttner, Bertha von (1843–1914)
Szönyi, Erzsebet (1924—)
Szumowska, Antoinette (1868–1938)
Szymanowska, Maria Agata (1789–1831)
Tagliaferro, Magda (1893–1986)
Tailleferre, Germaine (1892–1983)
Tallchief, Maria (1925—)
Talma, Louise (1906–1996)
Tennent, Madge Cook (1889–1972)
Tennyson, Emily (1813–1896)
Terzian, Alicia (1938—)
Theodoropoulou, Avra (1880–1963)
Thompson, Kay (1908–1998)
Thorndike, Sybil (1882–1976)
Timanoff, Vera (1855–1942)
Tipo, Maria (1931—)
Tipton, Billy (1914–1989)
Tureck, Rosalyn (1914–2003)
Uchida, Mitsuko (1948—)
Ukrainka, Lesya (1871–1913)
Várnay, Astrid (1918—)
Velazquez, Consuelo (1916–2005)
Vengerova, Isabelle (1877–1956)
Vered, Ilana (1939—)
Verne, Mathilde (1865–1936)
Viardot, Pauline (1821–1910)
Vidar, Jorunn (1918—)
Villard, Fanny Garrison (1844–1928)
Von Ertmann, Dorothea (1781–1849)
von Meck, Nadezhda (1831–1894)
Vorlova, Slavka (1894–1973)
Vronsky, Vitya (1909–1992)
Wallace, Lucille (1898–1977)
Wallace, Sippie (1898–1986)
Warren, Elinor Remick (1900–1991)
Warwick, Dionne (1940—)
Washington, Dinah (1924–1963)
Watkins, Gladys Elinor (1884–1939)
Weber, Lois (1881–1939)
Wieniawska, Irene Regine (1880–1932)
Williams, Mary Lou (1910–1981)
Wong, Betty Ann (1938—)
Yudina, Maria (1899–1970)
Zeisler, Fannie Bloomfield (1863–1927)
Zimmermann, Agnes (1847–1925)
Zwilich, Ellen Taaffe (1939—)

PILOT
See Aviator.

PIONEER
George, Phyllis (1949—)

PIRATE
Bonney, Anne
Ching Shih (fl. 1807–1810)
Jeanne de Belleville (fl. 1343)
O'Malley, Grace (c. 1530–1603)
Read, Mary

PLACENTOLOGIST
Ramsey, Elizabeth M. (1906–1993)

PLANTATION OWNER
Estaugh, Elizabeth Haddon (1680–1762)
McCord, Louisa S. (1810–1879)
Pinckney, Eliza Lucas (1722–1793)
Pringle, Elizabeth Allston (1845–1921)
Sinclair, Elizabeth McHutcheson (1800–1892)

PLANT PHYSIOLOGIST
Esau, Katherine (1898–1997)
Farr, Wanda K. (1895–1983)
Pennington, Mary Engle (1872–1952)
Sager, Ruth (1918–1997)

PLASTIC/RECONSTRUCTIVE SURGEON
Morani, Alma Dea (1907–2001)
Pickerill, Cecily Mary Wise (1903–1988)

PLAYWRIGHT
Acevedo, Angela de (d. 1644)
Agaoglu, Adalet (1929—)
Aidoo, Ama Ata (1942—)
Akimoto, Matsuyo (1911—)
Akins, Zoe (1886–1958)
Alexiou, Elli (1894–1988)
Allen, Jay Presson (1922–2006)
Alonso, Dora (1910–2001)
Alvarez Rios, Maria (1919—)
Amin, Adibah (1936—)
Ammers-Küller, Johanna van (1884–1966)
Anagnostaki, Loula (1940—)
Anderson, Isabel Perkins (1876–1948)
Anderson, Regina M. (1900–1993)
Angel, Albalucía (1939—)
Annenkova-Bernár, Nina Pávlovna (1859/64–1933)
Archer, Robyn (1948—)
Argiriadou, Chryssoula (1901–1998)
Ariadne (fl. 1696)
Aron, Geraldine (1941—)
Atkins, Eileen (1934—)
Bagnold, Enid (1889–1981)
Bai Fengxi (1934—)
Baillie, Joanna (1762–1851)
Bai Wei (1894–1987)
Baker, Elizabeth (d. 1962)
Barbier, Marie-Anne (c. 1670–1742)
Bardwell, Leland (1928—)

Barkentin, Marjorie (c. 1891–1974)
Barnes, Charlotte Mary Sanford (1818–1863)
Barnes, Djuna (1892–1982)
Barnes, Margaret Ayer (1886–1967)
Bawr, Alexandrine de (1773–1860)
Beauvain d'Althenheim, Gabrielle (1814–1886)
Behn, Aphra (1640?–1689)
Bell, Mary Hayley (1911–2005)
Belloc-Lowndes, Marie (1868–1947)
Benoist, Françoise-Albine (1724–1809)
Bergalli, Luisa (1703–1779)
Bergere, Ouida (1885–1974)
Berggolts, Olga (1910–1975)
Bergroth, Kersti (1886–1975)
Beringer, Aimée Daniell (1856–1936)
Beringer, Vera (1879–1964)
Bessa-Luís, Agustina (1922—)
Beutler, Margarete (1876–1949)
Biehl, Charlotta Dorothea (1731–1788)
Birch-Pfeiffer, Charlotte (1800–1868)
Blais, Marie-Claire (1939—)
Bocage, Marie-Anne Le Page du (1710–1802)
Boland, Bridget (1904–1988)
Bolt, Carol (1941–2000)
Bonner, Marita (1899–1971)
Boothby, Frances (fl. 1669)
Boucher, Denise (1935—)
Bovasso, Julie (1930–1991)
Boylan, Mary (1913–1984)
Bradley, Katharine Harris (1846–1914)
Bradley, Lillian Trimble (1875–?)
Brand, Mona (1915—)
Brandão, Fiama Hasse País (1938—)
Braunschweig-Lüneburg, Sophie Elisabeth von (1613–1676)
Britton, Rosa María (1936—)
Brooke, Frances (1724–1789)
Brophy, Brigid (1929–1995)
Brown, Alice (1856–1948)
Brown, Tina (1953—)
Burford, Barbara (1944—)
Burney, Fanny (1752–1840)
Canth, Minna (1844–1897)
Cárdenas, Nancy (1934–1994)
Caro Mallén de Soto, Ana (c. 1590–1650)
Carrelet de Marron, Marie-Anne (1725–1778)
Carroll, Vinnette (1922–2002)
Carten, Audrey (b. 1900)
Carvajal, Mariana de (c. 1620–1680)
Cary, Elizabeth (1586–1639)
Caspary, Vera (1899–1987)
Castro Alves, Diná Silveira de (1911–1983)
Cavendish, Elizabeth (1626–1663)
Cavendish, Jane (1621–1669)
Centlivre, Susanna (c. 1669–1723)
Chapin, Anne Morrison (1892–1967)
Charriere, Isabelle de (1740–1805)
Chase, Mary Coyle (1907–1981)
Chauvet, Marie (1916–1973)
Chedid, Andrée (1921—)
Childress, Alice (1916–1994)
Chiumina, Olga Nikolaevna (1865–1909)
Christensen, Inger (1935—)
Christie, Agatha (1890–1976)
Christie, Dorothy (b. 1896)
Chugtai, Ismat (1915–1991)
Churchill, Caryl (1938—)
Cixous, Hélène (1938—)
Clifford, Mrs. W.K. (1846–1929)
Cockburn, Catharine Trotter (1679–1749)
Colleville, Anne-Hyacinthe de Saint-Léger de (1761–1824)
Collins, Kathleen (1942–1988)
Comden, Betty (1915—)
Cooper, Edith Emma (1862–1913)
Cooper, Elizabeth (fl. 1737)
Cooper, J. California (1940s—)
Correia, Natália (1923–1993)
Cottenjé, Mireille (1933—)
Cowl, Jane (1883–1950)
Cowley, Hannah (1743–1809)
Craig, Christine (1943—)
Craigie, Pearl Mary Teresa (1867–1906)
Craven, Elizabeth (1750–1828)
Crisi, Maria (1892–1953)
Crothers, Rachel (1878–1958)
Cusack, Dymphna (1902–1981)
Cushing, Catherine Chisholm (1874–1952)
Dacre, Barbarina (1768–1854)
Dalibard, Françoise-Thérèse Aumerle de Saint-Phalier (d. 1757)
Dane, Clemence (1888–1965)
Daniels, Sarah (1957—)
D'Arcy, Margaretta (1934—)
Davenport, Gwen (1909–2002)
Davys, Mary (1674–1731)
Deamer, Dulcie (1890–1972)
De Casalis, Jeanne (1897–1966)
Deevy, Teresa (1894–1963)
De Groen, Alma (1941—)
Delaney, Shelagh (1939—)
de la Pasture, Mrs. Henry (d. 1945)
Delmar, Viña (1903–1990)
De Reyes, Consuelo (1893–1948)
D'Erzell, Catalina (1897–1937)
Deutsch, Helen (1906–1992)
Devi, Mahasveta (1926—)
Dimitrova, Blaga (1922—)
Diosdado, Ana (1938—)
Di Prima, Diane (1934—)
Donisthorpe, G. Sheila (1898–1946)
Donnelly, Dorothy (1880–1928)
Drake-Brockman, Henrietta (1901–1968)
Drewitz, Ingeborg (1923–1986)
Duffy, Maureen (1933—)
du Maurier, Daphne (1907–1989)
Dunbar-Nelson, Alice (1875–1935)
Dunn, Nell (1936—)
Durand, Lucile (1930—)
Ebner-Eschenbach, Marie (1830–1916)
Edginton, May (1883–1957)
Edgren, Anne Charlotte (1849–1892)
Edmond, Lauris (1924–2000)
Egual, Maria (1698–1735)
Ehrlich, Ida Lublenski (d. 1986)
Elliott, Sarah Barnwell (1848–1928)
Ellis, Edith (c. 1874–1960)
Ensler, Eve (1953—)
Enthoven, Gabrielle (1868–1950)
Ephelia (fl. 1660s–1680s)
Ephron, Phoebe (1914–1971)
Eschstruth, Nataly von (1860–1939)
Evans, Mari (1923—)
Fairfax, Marion (1875–1979)
Falcón, Lidia (1935—)
Falconnet, Françoise-Cécile de Chaumont (1738–1819)
Favart, Marie (1727–1772)
Fleisser, Marieluise (1901–1974)
Flexner, Anne Crawford (1874–1955)
Florentino, Leona (1849–1884)
Ford, Harriet (c. 1863–1949)
Forsh, Olga (1873–1961)
Franken, Rose (c. 1895–1988)
Friedberg, Berta (1864–1944)
Frings, Ketti (1909–1981)
Fulton, Maude (1881–1950)
Gambaro, Griselda (1928—)
Garro, Elena (1916–1998)
Gates, Eleanor (1871–1951)
Gems, Pam (1925—)
Gippius, Zinaida (1869–1945)
Glaspell, Susan (1876–1948)
Glass, Joanna (1936—)
Gómez de Avellaneda, Gertrudis (1814–1873)
Goodrich, Frances (1891–1984)
Gore, Catherine (1799–1861)
Goudvis, Bertha (1876–1966)
Gouges, Olympe de (1748–1793)
Graffigny, Françoise de (1695–1758)
Graham, Shirley (1896–1977)
Gramcko, Ida (1924–1994)
Granville-Barker, Helen (d. 1950)
Graves, Clotilde Inez Mary (1863–1932)
Gray, Oriel (1920–2003)
Green, Janet (1914–1993)
Gregory, Augusta (1852–1932)
Gress, Elsa (1919–1989)
Griffith, Elizabeth (c. 1720–1793)
Grové, Henriette (1922—)
Guibert, Elisabeth (1725–1788)
Guido, Beatriz (1924—)
Guro, Elena (1877–1913)
Hagerup, Inger (1905–1985)
Hamilton, Cicely (1872–1952)
Hansberry, Lorraine (1930–1965)
Hartigan, Anne Le Marquand (1931—)
Hatton, Fanny (c. 1870–1939)
Hatvany, Lili (1890–1967)
Haywood, Eliza (c. 1693–1756)
Helburn, Theresa (1887–1959)
Hellman, Lillian (1905–1984)
Hemans, Felicia D. (1793–1835)
Henley, Beth (1952—)
Hernández, Luisa Josefina (1928—)
Herzberg, Judith (1934—)
Hewett, Dorothy (1923–2002)
Heyward, Dorothy (1890–1961)
Hogan, Linda (1947—)
Hohenhausen, Elizabeth (1789–1857)
Holden, Joan (1939—)
Hollingsworth, Margaret (1940—)
Holtby, Winifred (1898–1935)
Hopkins, Pauline E. (1859–1930)
Howe, Tina (1937—)
Hrotsvitha of Gandersheim (c. 935–1001)
Hunter, Mollie (1922—)
Iko, Momoko (1940—)
Inchbald, Elizabeth (1753–1821)
Jakobsdóttir, Svava (1930—)
Jameson, Storm (1891–1986)
Jay, Harriett (1863–1932)
Jelinek, Elfriede (1946—)
Jellicoe, Ann (1927—)
Jennings, Gertrude E. (d. 1958)
Jesse, Fryniwyd Tennyson (1888–1958)
Johnson, Georgia Douglas (1877–1966)
Johnson, Pamela Hansford (1912–1981)
Jordan, June (1936–2002)
Joudry, Patricia (1921–2000)
Juana Inés de la Cruz (1651–1695)
Kane, Sarah (1971–1999)
Kanin, Fay (1917—)
Katherine of Sutton (d. 1376)
Kaufman, Beatrice (1894–1945)
Kaus, Gina (1894–1985)
Keane, Molly (1904–1996)
Kennedy, Adrienne (1931—)
Kennedy, Margaret (1896–1967)
Kerr, Jean (1923–2003)
Kidman, Fiona (1940—)
Koidula, Lydia (1843–1886)
Kummer, Clare (1873–1958)
Lambert, Betty (1933–1983)
Lancaster-Wallis, Ellen (1856–?)
Langner, Ilse (1899–1987)
Lapauze, Jeanne (1860–1920)
Lapid, Shulamit (1934—)

Lappo-Danilevskaia, N.A. (c. 1875–1951)
Lascelles, Ernita (1890–1972)
Lask, Berta (1878–1967)
Lauber, Cécile (1887–1981)
Laverty, Maura (1907–1966)
Lee, Rose Hum (1904–1964)
Lee, Sophia (1750–1824)
Lefanu, Alicia (1753–1817)
Leontovich, Eugénie (1894–1993)
Levinson, Luisa Mercedes (1909–1988)
Lewis, Estelle Anna (1824–1880)
Liberáki, Margaríta (1919—)
Lichnowsky, Mechthilde (1879–1958)
Lidman, Sara (1923–2004)
Lipman, Clara (1869–1952)
Lochhead, Liz (1947—)
Locke, Sumner (1881–1917)
Lokhvitskaia, Mirra (1869–1905)
Loos, Anita (1893–1981)
Louw, Anna M. (1913–2003)
Løveid, Cecilie (1951—)
Lovell, Maria Anne (1803–1877)
Lowe-Porter, Helen (1876–1963)
Luce, Clare Boothe (1903–1987)
Lukhmanova, N.A. (1840–1907)
Lusarreta, Pilar de (1914–1967)
Lyttelton, Edith (1865–1948)
MacEwen, Gwendolyn (1941–1987)
MacGrath, Leueen (1914–1992)
Malpede, Karen (1945—)
Manley, Mary de la Rivière (1663–1724)
Manner, Eeva-Liisa (1921–1995)
Manning, Mary (1906–1999)
Mansilla de García, Eduarda (1838–1892)
Maranhão, Heloísa (1925—)
Marion, Frances (1888–1973)
Marnière, Jeanne (1854–1910)
Marson, Una (1905–1965)
Märten, Lu (1879–1970)
Massingham, Dorothy (1889–1933)
Matto de Turner, Clorinda (1854–1909)
May, Elaine (1932—)
Mayo, Margaret (1882–1951)
McAlpine, Rachel (1940—)
McCracken, Esther Helen (1902–1971)
McDermid, Val (1955—)
McNeill, Janet (1907–1994)
Meredith, Gwen (b. 1907)
Merken, Lucretia Wilhelmina van (1721–1789)
Milligan, Alice (1866–1953)
Mitchison, Naomi (1897–1999)
Montanclos, Marie-Emilie Maryon de (1736–1812)
Montoriol i Puig, Carme (1893–1966)
More, Hannah (1745–1833)
Moreno, Virginia R. (1925—)
Morgan, Sally (1951—)
Morton, Martha (1865–1925)
Moutza-Martinengou, Elisavet (1801–1832)
Mowatt, Anna Cora (1819–1870)
Mugo, Micere Githae (1942—)
Murfin, Jane (1893–1955)
Murray, Judith Sargent (1751–1820)
Naylor, Gloria (1950—)
Nazáreva, Kapitolina Valerianovna (1847–1900)
Nichols, Anne (1891–1966)
Niggli, Josefina (1910–1983)
Njau, Rebeka (1932—)
Nóbrega, Isabel da (1925—)
Nogami, Yaeko (1885–1985)
Norman, Marsha (1947—)
Oba, Minako (1930—)
Odaga, Asenath (1938—)
Odaldi, Annalena (1572–1638)
Ozick, Cynthia (1928—)
Palacios, Lucila (1902–1994)
Panova, Vera (1905–1973)
Parker, Lottie Blair (c. 1858–1937)
Parks, Suzan-Lori (1963—)
Parsons, Eliza (c. 1748–1811)
Parthenay, Catherine de (1554–1631)
Parturier, Françoise (1919—)
Paul, Joanna (1945–2003)
Pawlikowska, Maria (1891–1945)
Peabody, Josephine Preston (1874–1922)
Pestana, Alice (1860–1929)
Petrushevskaya, Ludmilla (1938—)
Pilcher, Rosamunde (1924—)
Pix, Mary Griffith (1666–1709)
Pleijel, Agneta (1940—)
Poisson, Madeleine-Angelique (1684–1770)
Pollock, Sharon (1936—)
Polwhele, Elizabeth (fl. mid-to-late 17th c.)
Portillo-Trambley, Estela (1936–1999)
Portnoy, Ethel (1927–2004)
Pozzo, Modesta (1555–1592)
Praed, Rosa (1851–1935)
Preissova, Gabriela (1862–1946)
Przybyszewska, Stanislawa (1901–1935)
Pusich, Antónia Gertrudes (1805–1883)
Queirós, Raquel de (1910–2003)
Rachel (1821–1858)
Radziwill, Francisca (1705–1753)
Rambova, Natacha (1897–1966)
Rame, Franca (1929—)
Ramsey, Alicia (1864–1933)
Rand, Ayn (1905–1982)
Regan, Sylvia (1908–2003)
Reinig, Christa (1926—)
Reinshagen, Gerlind (1926—)
Renée (1926—)
Resino, Carmen (1941—)
Resnik, Muriel (c. 1917–1995)
Reza, Yasmina (1959—)
Richards, Beah (1920–2000)
Ridler, Anne (1912–2001)
Ringwood, Gwen Pharis (1910–1984)
Ritter, Erika (1948—)
Robins, Elizabeth (1862–1952)
Roches, Catherine des (1542–1587)
Roches, Madeleine des (1520–1587)
Roland, Betty (1903–1996)
Rowson, Susanna (1762–1824)
Royde-Smith, Naomi Gwladys (c. 1880–1964)
Ryum, Ulla (1937—)
Sachs, Nelly (1891–1970)
Sagan, Françoise (1935–2004)
Saint-Chamond, Claire-Marie Mazarelli, Marquise de La Vieuville de (1731–?)
Salm-Dyck, Constance de (1767–1845)
Sanchez, Sonia (1934—)
Sand, George (1804–1876)
Schön, Elizabeth (1921–2001)
Schwarz-Bart, Simone (1938—)
Ségalas, Anais (1814–1895)
Serreau, Geneviève (1915–1981)
Shaginian, Marietta (1888–1982)
Shange, Ntozake (1948—)
Sharp, Margery (1905–1991)
Shaykh, Hanan al- (1945—)
Shchepkina-Kupernik, Tatiana (1874–1952)
Shearer, Jill (1936—)
Sheridan, Frances (1724–1766)
Shields, Carol (1935–2003)
Shoshi (fl. 990–1010)
Simons, Beverly (1938—)
Slancikova, Bozena (1867–1951)
Smith, Anna Deavere (1950—)
Smith, Betty (1896–1972)
Smith, Dodie (1896–1990)
Smyth, Donna (1943—)
Sofola, Zulu (1935–1995)
Souza e Mello, Beatriz de (c. 1650–1700)
Sowerby, Githa (1876–1970)
Spewack, Bella (1899–1990)
Stanley, Martha M. (1867–1950)
Stein, Charlotte von (1742–1827)
Stern, G.B. (1890–1973)
Stockert-Meynert, Dora von (1870–1947)
Stolitsa, Liubov (1884–1934)
Storm, Lesley (1898–1975)
Strange, Michael (1890–1950)
Stuart, Aimée (c. 1885–1981)
Sutherland, Efua (1924–1996)
Taylor, Laurette (1884–1946)
Terry, Megan (1932—)
Tey, Josephine (1896–1952)
Thane, Elswyth (1900–1984)
Thatcher, Molly Day (d. 1963)
Thompson, Sylvia (1902–1968)
Torrezão, Guiomar (1844–1898)
Townsend, Sue (1946—)
Travers, P.L. (1906–1996)
Tree, Viola (1884–1938)
Tremain, Rose (1943—)
Tyler, Odette (1869–1936)
Ukrainka, Lesya (1871–1913)
Unger, Gladys B. (c. 1885–1940)
Vaa, Aslaug (1889–1965)
Vansova, Terezia (1857–1942)
Vaughan, Hilda (1892–1985)
Vaz Ferreira, María Eugenia (1875–1924)
Verbitskaia, Anastasiia (1861–1928)
Vernon, Barbara (1916–1978)
Veselkova-Kil'shtet, M.G. (1861–1931)
Vicente, Paula (1519–1576)
Victor, Lucia (1912–1986)
Vik, Bjørg (1935—)
Villedieu, Catherine des Jardins, Mme de (c. 1640–1683)
Vitorino, Virginia (1897–1967)
Vollmer, Lula (d. 1955)
Vorse, Mary Heaton (1874–1966)
Walter, Silja (1919—)
Wandor, Michelene (1940—)
Warren, Mercy Otis (1728–1814)
Wasserstein, Wendy (1950–2006)
Webster, Augusta (1837–1894)
West, Mae (1893–1980)
Williams, Sherley Anne (1944–1999)
Winsloe, Christa (1888–1944)
Winters, Marian (1924–1978)
Wiseman, Jane (fl. 17th c.)
Wray, Fay (1907–2004)
Wyatt, Rachel (1929—)
Wynter, Sylvia (1928—)
Yamauchi, Wakako (1924—)
Yearsley, Ann (1752–1806)
Young, Rida Johnson (1869–1926)
Yourcenar, Marguerite (1903–1987)
Zapolska, Gabriela (1857–1921)
Zelinová, Hana (b. 1914)
Zinner, Hedda (1902–1990)
Zinóveva-Annibal, Lidiia Dmitrievna (1866–1907)
Zirimu, Elvania Namukwaya (1938–1979)
Zur Mühlen, Hermynia (1883–1951)
Zürn, Unica (1916–1970)

POET

Abdel-Aziz, Malak (1923—)
Ackermann, Louise Victorine (1813–1890)
Acton, Eliza (1799–1859)
Acuña, Dora (fl. 1940s)
Adair, Virginia Hamilton (1913–2004)
Adam, Jean (1710–1765)
Adams, Léonie Fuller (1899–1988)
Adams, Sarah Flower (1805–1848)

Adcock, Fleur (1934—)
Adnan, Etel (1925—)
Adolf, Helen (b. 1895)
Aguirre, Mirta (1912—)
Agustini, Delmira (1886–1914)
Aichinger, Ilse (1921—)
Aidoo, Ama Ata (1942—)
Aikin, Lucy (1781–1864)
Ainianos, Aganice (1838–1892)
Akazome Emon (d. 1027)
Akesson, Sonja (1926–1977)
Akhmadulina, Bella (1937—)
Akhmatova, Anna (1889–1966)
Akin, Gülten (1933—)
Alba, Nanina (1915–1968)
Albert, Caterina (1869–1966)
Alcock, Mary (1742–1798)
Alcorta, Gloria (1915—)
Aldrich, Anne Reeve (1866–1892)
Alegría, Claribel (1924—)
Alekseeva, Lidiya (1909—)
Alexander, Cecil Frances (1818–1895)
Alice Meynell (1847–1922)
Aliger, Margarita Iosifovna (1915–1992)
Allen, Elizabeth Chase (1832–1911)
Allen, Paula Gunn (1939—)
Almada, Filipa de (fl. 15th c.)
Almedingen, E.M. (1898–1971)
Almucs de Castelnau (fl. 12th c.)
Alorna, Marquesa de (1750–c. 1839)
Alvarez Rios, Maria (1919—)
Amália, Narcisa (1852–1924)
Amarilis (fl. 17th c.)
Ambrosius, Johanna (b. 1854)
Amini-Hudson, Johari (1935—)
Amor, Guadalupe (1920—)
Amrouche, Fadhma Mansour (1882–1967)
Anagnos, Julia (1844–1886)
Anan (fl. 9th c.)
Andersen, Astrid Hjertenaes (1915–1985)
Anderson, Isabel Perkins (1876–1948)
Andreini, Isabella (1562–1604)
Andresen, Sophia de Mello Breyner (1919–2004)
Andreu, Blanca (1959—)
Angelou, Maya (1928—)
Anghelaki-Rooke, Katerina (1939—)
Anneke, Mathilde Franziska (1817–1884)
Anstei, Olga Nikolaevna (1912–1985)
Antarjanam, Lalitambika (1909–1987)
Anyte of Tegea (fl. 3rd c. BCE)
Anzaldúa, Gloria E. (1942–2004)
Aragona, Tullia d' (1510–1556)
Araz, Nezihe (1922—)
Arderiu, Clementina (1899–1976)
Arenal, Concepción (1820–1893)
Argiriadou, Chryssoula (1901–1998)
Armentières, Péronelle d' (fl. 14th c.)
Arsiennieva, Natalia (1903—)
Arvelo Larriva, Enriqueta (1886–1963)
Ascarelli, Devora (fl. 1601)
Asher, Elise (c. 1912–2004)
Astell, Mary (1666–1731)
Atencia, Maria Victoria (1931—)
Attar, Samar (1940—)
Atwood, Margaret (1939—)
Aubespine, Madeleine de l' (1546–1596)
Aubin, Penelope (c. 1685–1731)
Ausländer, Rose (1901–1988)
Avison, Margaret (1918—)
Awiakta (1936—)
Axioti, Melpo (1906–1973)
Axioti, Melpo (c. 1906–c. 1973)
Ayscough, Florence (1875/78–1942)
Babois, Marguerite-Victoire (1760–1839)
Bachmann, Ingeborg (1926–1973)
Bacon, Peggy (1895–1987)
Bagryana, Elisaveta (1893–1991)
Bailey, Pearl (1918–1990)
Baillie, Joanna (1762–1851)
Balabanoff, Angelica (1878–1965)
Balbilla (fl. 130)
Baldwin, Faith (1893–1978)
Ballestrem, Eufemia von (1859–1941)
Bandettini, Teresa (1763–1837)
Ban Jieyu (c. 48–c. 6 BCE)
Banks, Isabella (1821–1897)
Banus, Maria (1914–1999)
Ban Zhao (c. 45–c. 120)
Barandas, Ana Eurídice Eufrosina de (1806–1856)
Barber, Mary (c. 1690–1757)
Barbi, Alice (1862–1948)
Bardwell, Leland (1928—)
Barker, Jane (1652–1732)
Barkova, Anna Aleksandrovna (1901–1976)
Barlow, Jane (c. 1857–1917)
Barnes, Charlotte Mary Sanford (1818–1863)
Barnes, Djuna (1892–1982)
Barney, Natalie Clifford (1876–1972)
Barreno, Maria Isabel (b. 1939)
Barykova, Anna Pavlovna (1839–1893)
Bates, Charlotte Fiske (1838–1916)
Bates, Harriet Leonora (1856–1886)
Bates, Katherine Lee (1859–1929)
Bat-Miriam, Yocheved (1901–1980)
Baughan, Blanche Edith (1870–1958)
Bazincourt, Mlle Thomas de (fl. 18th c.)
Ba_ar, Sukufe Nihal (1896–1973)
Beals, Jessie Tarbox (1870–1942)
Beatrice of Kent (d. after 1280)
Beauharnais, Fanny de (1737–1813)
Beauvain d'Althenheim, Gabrielle (1814–1886)
Bedregal, Yolanda (1916–1999)
Beer, Patricia (1919–1999)
Beers, Ethel Lynn (1827–1879)
Beig, Maria (1920—)
Bell, Gertrude (1868–1926)
Bell, Vera (1906—)
Benedict, Ruth (1887–1948)
Benet, Laura (1884–1979)
Benger, Elizabeth (1778–1827)
Benislawska, Konstancja (1747–1806)
Bennett, Gwendolyn B. (1902–1981)
Bennett, Louise Simone (1919—)
Benson, Stella (1892–1933)
Berberova, Nina (1901–1993)
Berenguer, Amanda (1924—)
Berens-Totenohl, Josefa (1891–1969)
Beresford, Anne (1919—)
Bergalli, Luisa (1703–1779)
Berggolts, Olga (1910–1975)
Bergman, Marilyn (1929—)
Bernal, Emilia (1884–1964)
Bertin, Louise Angélique (1805–1877)
Bervoets, Marguerite (1914–1944)
Bethell, Mary Ursula (1874–1945)
Beutler, Margarete (1876–1949)
Bevington, L.S. (1845–1895)
Bichovsky, Elisheva (1888–1949)
Bijns, Anna (1493/94–1575)
Bishop, Elizabeth (1911–1979)
Bjarklind, Unnur Benediktsdóttir (1881–1946)
Blackwood, Helen Selina (1807–1867)
Blamire, Susanna (1747–1794)
Blanchecotte, Augustine-Malvina (1830–1895)
Bleecker, Ann Eliza (1752–1783)
Blind, Mathilde (1841–1896)
Bloede, Gertrude (1845–1905)
Blomfield, Dorothy (1858–1932)
Blum, Klara (1904–1971)
Bluwstein, Rachel (1890–1931)
Bocage, Marie-Anne Le Page du (1710–1802)
Bogan, Louise (1897–1970)
Boland, Eavan (1944—)
Bolduc, Marie (1894–1941)
Bolton, Sarah T. (1814–1893)
Bonacci Brunamonti, Maria Alinda (1841–1903)
Bonnin, Gertrude Simmons (1876–1938)
Borgese Freschi, Maria (1881–1947)
Borrero, Dulce María (1883–1945)
Borrero, Juana (1877–1896)
Botelho, Fernanda (1926—)
Botta, Anne C.L. (1815–1891)
Bourdic-Viot, Marie-Henriette Payad d'Estang de (1746–1802)
Bourette, Charlotte Rouyer (1714–1784)
Boyd, Elizabeth (fl. 1727–1745)
Boye, Karin (1900–1941)
Boyle, Kay (1902–1992)
Bošković, Anica (1714–1804)
Brachmann, Louise (1777–1822)
Brackett, Leigh (1915–1978)
Bradley, Katharine Harris (1846–1914)
Bradstreet, Anne (1612–1672)
Branch, Anna Hempstead (1875–1937)
Brand, Mona (1915—)
Brandão, Fiama Hasse Pais (1938—)
Bré, Ruth (1862–1911)
Breden, Christiane von (1839–1901)
Bregendahl, Marie (1867–1940)
Brewster, Anne Hampton (1818–1892)
Brewster, Elizabeth (1922—)
Brewster, Martha Wadsworth (fl. 1725–1757)
Bridger, Bub (1924—)
Brittain, Vera (1893–1970)
Brodber, Erna (1936—)
Brontë, Charlotte (1816–1855)
Brooks, Gwendolyn (1917–2000)
Brooks, Maria Gowen (c. 1794–1845)
Brossard, Nicole (1943—)
Brotherton, Alice Williams (1848–1930)
Brown, Abbie Farwell (1871–1927)
Brown, Anna (1747–1810)
Brown, Audrey Alexandra (1904–1998)
Brown, Margaret Wise (1910–1952)
Brown, Rita Mae (1944—)
Brown, Rosellen (1939—)
Browne, Maria da Felicidade do Couto (c. 1797–1861)
Browning, Elizabeth Barrett (1806–1861)
Brun, Friederike (1765–1835)
Brun, Marie-Marguerite de Maison-Forte (1713–1794)
Büchner, Luise (1821–1877)
Buck, Heather (1926—)
Bulich, Vera Sergeevna (1898–1954)
Bullrich, Silvina (1915–1990)
Bunge de Gálvez, Delfina (1881–1952)
Bunina, Anna Petrovna (1774–1829)
Burford, Barbara (1944—)
Burkart, Erika (1922—)
Burroughs, Margaret Taylor (1917—)
Busta, Christine (1914–1987)
Cáceres, Esther de (1903–1971)
Cai Yan (c. 162–239)
Cambridge, Ada (1844–1926)
Campbell, Meg (1937—)
Candler, Ann (1740–1814)
Cárdenas, Nancy (1934–1994)
Carranza, María Mercedes (1945–2003)
Carter, Elizabeth (1717–1806)
Cary, Alice (1820–1871)
Cary, Anne (1615–1671)
Cary, Elizabeth (1586–1639)
Cary, Phoebe (1824–1871)
Casely-Hayford, Gladys (1904–1950)

Cassian, Nina (1924—)
Castellanos, Rosario (1925–1974)
Castelloza, Na (fl. early 13th c.)
Castro, Fernanda de (1900–1994)
Castro, Rosalía de (1837–1885)
Cato, Nancy (1917–2000)
Cave, Jane (c. 1754–1813)
Cavendish, Elizabeth (1626–1663)
Cavendish, Jane (1621–1669)
Cecil, Anne (1556–1589)
Centeno, Yvette (1940—)
César, Ana Cristina (1952–1983)
Chacón, Dulce (1954–2003)
Chacón Nardi, Rafaela (1926–2001)
Chandler, Elizabeth Margaret (1807–1834)
Chandler, Mary (1687–1745)
Chang, Diana (1934—)
Chedid, Andrée (1921—)
Chen Duansheng (1751–1796)
Chen Jingrong (1917–1989)
Chéron, Elisabeth-Sophie (1648–1711)
Chervinskaya, Lidiya Davydovna (1907–1988)
Chézy, Helmina von (1783–1856)
Chiumina, Olga Nikolaevna (1865–1909)
Christensen, Inger (1935—)
Christie, Agatha (1890–1976)
Christine de Pizan (c. 1363–c. 1431)
Chudleigh, Mary Lee (1656–1710)
Chukovskaya, Lidiya (1907–1996)
Churchill, Sarah (1914–1982)
Churilova, L.A. (1875–1937)
Chute, Marchette (1909–1994)
Cisneros, Sandra (1954—)
Clampitt, Amy (1920–1994)
Clarke, Gillian (1937—)
Clarke, Mary Bayard (1827–1886)
Cleobulina of Rhodes (fl. 570 BCE)
Clermont, Claude-Catherine de (1545–1603)
Clifton, Lucille (1936—)
Clive, Caroline (1801–1873)
Cluysenaar, Anne (1936—)
Coates, Florence Nicholson (1850–1927)
Cobbold, Elizabeth (c. 1764–1824)
Cockburn, Alicia (1713–1794)
Cockburn, Catharine Trotter (1679–1749)
Codina, Iverna (1918—)
Coignard, Gabrielle de (c. 1550–1586)
Colaço, Branca de Gonta (1880–1944)
Coleridge, Mary Elizabeth (1861–1907)
Colet, Louise (1810–1876)
Coligny, Henriette de (1618–1683)
Collier, Mary (c. 1690–c. 1762)
Collins, Ann (fl. mid–17th c.)
Colonia, Regina Célia (1940—)
Colonna, Vittoria (c. 1490–1547)
Colquhoun, Ithell (1906–1988)
Colville, Elizabeth (c. 1571–1600s)
Coman, Otilia (1942—)
Conde, Carmen (1907–1996)
Cook, Eliza (1818–1889)
Coolbrith, Ina Donna (1841–1928)
Cooper, Edith Emma (1862–1913)
Corinna (fl. 5th or 3rd c. BCE)
Cornford, Frances Crofts (1886–1960)
Coronado, Carolina (1820–1911)
Correia, Natália (1923–1993)
Cortez, Jayne (1936—)
Cortines, Júlia (1868–1948)
Cosson de La Cressonière, Charlotte Cathérine (1740–1813)
Costello, Louisa Stuart (1799–1870)
Cottrell, Violet May (1887–1971)
Couzyn, Jeni (1942—)
Craig, Christine (1943—)
Crapsey, Adelaide (1878–1914)
Crawford, Louise Macartney (1790–1858)
Crisi, Maria (1892–1953)
Crosby, Fanny (1820–1915)
Cross, Zora (1890–1964)
Cunard, Nancy (1896–1965)
Currie, Mary Montgomerie (1843–1905)
Cussons, Sheila (1922–2004)
Custance, Olive (1874–1944)
Czartoryska, Isabella (1746–1835)
Dacre, Barbarina (1768–1854)
Daini no Sanmi (999–after 1078)
Dalibard, Françoise-Thérèse Aumerle de Saint-Phalier (d. 1757)
Dallas, Ruth (1919—)
Danner, Margaret (1910–1984)
d'Arconville, Geneviève (1720–1805)
Dargan, Olive Tilford (1869–1968)
Daryush, Elizabeth (1887–1977)
Das, Kamala (1934—)
da Silva, Benedita (1942—)
Daudet, Julia (1844–1940)
Davidson, Lucretia Maria (1808–1825)
Davidson, Margaret Miller (1823–1838)
Davis, Mollie Moore (1844–1909)
D'Costa, Jean (1937—)
De Brémont, Anna (1864–1922)
de Burgos, Julia (1914–1953)
De Cespedes, Alba (1911–1997)
De Costa, Maria Velho (b. 1938)
de Dia, Beatrice (c. 1160–1212)
Dee, Ruby (1923—)
de Hoyos, Angela (1940—)
de Ibáñez, Sara (1909–1971)
Dejanović, Draga (1843–1870)
Deken, Aagje (1741–1804)
Delarue-Mardrus, Lucie (1880–1945)
Delle Grazie, Marie Eugenie (1864–1931)
Dennie, Abigail (1715–1745)
Deren, Maya (1908–1961)
Desbordes-Valmore, Marceline (1785–1859)
Deshoulières, Antoinette (1638–1694)
de Sousa, Noémia (1926—)
Dessaur, C.I. (1931–2002)
De Stefani, Livia (1913—)
Deutsch, Babette (1895–1982)
Devi, Maitreyi (1914–1990)
D'haen, Christine (1923—)
Diakonova, Elizaveta (1874–1902)
Dickinson, Emily (1830–1886)
Dillard, Annie (1945—)
Dinesen, Isak (1885–1962)
Ding Ning (1924—)
Di Prima, Diane (1934—)
Ditlevsen, Tove (1917–1976)
Dizhur, Bella (b. 1906)
Dlugoszewski, Lucia (1925–2000)
Dmitrieva, Elizaveta Ivanovna (1887–1928)
Dobson, Rosemary (1920—)
Dodge, Mary Abigail (1833–1896)
Domin, Hilde (1909–2006)
Doolittle, Hilda (1886–1961)
Dorman, Sonya (1924—)
Dorr, Julia Caroline (1825–1913)
Dove, Rita (1952—)
Dowriche, Anne (before 1560–after 1613)
Dracopoulou, Theony (1883–1968)
Dransfeld, Hedwig (1871–1925)
Droste-Hülshoff, Annette von (1797–1848)
Duclaux, Agnes Mary F. (1856–1944)
Duff, Mary Ann Dyke (1794–1857)
Dufrénoy, Adelaïde de (1765–1825)
Duggan, Eileen May (1894–1972)
du Guillet, Pernette (c. 1520–1545)
Dunbar-Nelson, Alice (1875–1935)
Duncombe, Susanna (1725–1812)
Dunlap, Jane (fl. 1771)
Dunlop, Eliza Hamilton (1796–1880)
Düringsfeld, Ida von (1815–1876)
Dutt, Toru (1856–1877)
Dworkin, Andrea (1946–2005)
Eastman, Elaine Goodale (1863–1953)
Eaubonne, Françoise d' (1920–2005)
Ebner-Eschenbach, Marie (1830–1916)
Eddy, Mary Baker (1821–1910)
Egerton, Sarah Fyge (c. 1670–1723)
Elder, Anne (1918–1976)
Elisa, Henriqueta (1843–1885)
Elizabeth of Wied (1843–1916)
Ellet, Elizabeth (c. 1812–1877)
Engelbretsdatter, Dorothe (1634–1716)
Engelhard, Magdalene Philippine (1756–1831)
Enheduanna (fl. 2300 BCE)
Enríquez de Guzmán, Feliciana (c. 1580–1640)
Ensing, Riemke (1939—)
Ephelia (fl. 1660s–1680s)
Erinna (fl. 7th c. BCE)
Eriphanis
Escoffery, Gloria (1923–2002)
Escott, Cicely Margaret (1908–1977)
Espanca, Florbela (1894–1930)
Espina, Concha (1869–1955)
Estienne, Nicole d' (c. 1544–c. 1596)
Eudocia (c. 400–460)
Evans, Mari (1923—)
Evans, Mary Anne (1819–1880)
Evelyn, Mary (1665–1685)
Exene (1956—)
Eybers, Elisabeth (1915—)
Fadl (d. ca. 870)
Fainlight, Ruth (1931—)
Fanshawe, Catherine Maria (1765–1834)
Fanthorpe, U.A. (1929—)
Farjeon, Eleanor (1881–1965)
Farningham, Marianne (1834–1909)
Farrokhzad, Forugh (1935–1967)
Fauset, Jessie Redmon (1882–1961)
Fedele, Cassandra Fidelis (1465–1558)
Feinstein, Elaine (1930—)
Feng Keng (1907–1931)
Fenno, Jenny (c. 1765–?)
Ferguson, Elizabeth Graeme (1737–1801)
Ferland, Barbara (1919—)
Ferrari, Carlotta (1837–1907)
Fiamengo, Marya (1926—)
Field, Rachel Lyman (1894–1942)
Field, Sara Bard (1882–1974)
Fields, Julia (1938—)
Filleul, Jeanne (1424–1498)
Finch, Anne (1661–1720)
Finnigan, Joan (1925—)
Fischer, Caroline Auguste (1764–1834)
Fitnat-Khanim (c. 1725–1780)
Florentino, Leona (1849–1884)
Fortuyn-Leenmans, Margaretha Droogleever (1909–1998)
Frame, Janet (1924–2004)
France, Ruth (1913–1968)
Franco, Veronica (1546–1591)
Franklin, Eleanor (1795–1825)
Freer, Agnes Rand (1878–1972)
Freier, Recha (1892–1984)
French, Mary (fl. 1703)
Freytag-Loringhoven, Elsa von (1875–1927)
Friedberg, Berta (1864–1944)
Frye, Mary E. (1905–2004)
Fuchs, Anna Rupertina (1657–1722)
Fuertes, Gloria (1917–1998)
Fugard, Sheila (1932—)
Fullerton, Mary Eliza (1868–1946)
Furlong, Monica (1930–2003)
Galindo, Beatriz (1475–1534)
Galloway, Grace Growden (d. 1782)
Galvão, Patricia (1910–1962)

Gambara, Veronica (1485–1550)
García Marruz, Fina (1923—)
Gardner, Isabella (1915–1981)
Garsenda (1170–c. 1257)
Gautier, Judith (1845–1917)
Gemmei (c. 661–721)
Gerhardt, Ida (1905–1997)
Gertsyk, Adelaida (1874–1925)
Ghalem, Nadia (1941—)
Giaconi, Luisa (1870–1908)
Gibbons, Stella (1902–1989)
Gilbert, Ruth (1917—)
Gilbert, Sandra M. (1936—)
Gilman, Caroline Howard (1794–1888)
Gilmore, Mary (1865–1962)
Gilot, Françoise (1922—)
Giovanni, Nikki (1943—)
Gippius, Zinaida (1869–1945)
Girardin, Delphine (1804–1855)
Glinska, Teofila (c. 1765–1799)
Glück, Louise (1943—)
Goldberg, Lea (1911–1970)
Goll, Claire (1891–1977)
Gómez de Avellaneda, Gertrudis (1814–1873)
Goncalves, Olga (1937—)
Gorbanevskaya, Natalya Yevgenevna (1936—)
Gore-Booth, Eva (1870–1926)
Gormflaith (c. 870–925)
Gotlieb, Phyllis (1926—)
Gottsched, Luise Adelgunde (1713–1762)
Grahn, Judy (1940—)
Gramcko, Ida (1924–1994)
Granata, Maria (1921—)
Grant, Anne (1755–1838)
Granville-Barker, Helen (d. 1950)
Gray, Teresa Corinna Ubertis (1877–1964)
Green, Dorothy (1915–1991)
Greenaway, Kate (1846–1901)
Grégoire, Colette Anna (1931–1966)
Greiffenberg, Catharina Regina von (1633–1694)
Grierson, Constantia (c. 1706–c. 1732)
Griffitts, Hannah (1727–1817)
Grimké, Angelina Weld (1880–1958)
Grimké, Charlotte L. Forten (1837–1914)
Gritsi-Milliex, Tatiana (1920—)
Grossmann, Judith (1931—)
Grymeston, Elizabeth Bernye (d. 1603)
Guacci, Giuseppina (1807–1848)
Guan Daosheng (1262–1319)
Guérin, Eugénie de (1805–1848)
Guglielminetti, Amalia (1881–1941)
Guibert, Elisabeth (1725–1788)
Guidacci, Margherita (1921–1992)
Guiducci, Armanda (1923–1992)
Guimarães Peixoto Bretas, Ana Lins do (1889–1985)
Guiney, Louise Imogen (1861–1920)
Günderrode, Karoline von (1780–1806)
Guro, Elena (1877–1913)
Gutridge, Molly (fl. 1778)
Hacker, Marilyn (1942—)
Hadewijch (fl. 13th c.)
Haesaert, Clara (1924—)
Hagerup, Inger (1905–1985)
Halamová, Masa (1908–1995)
Hale, Sarah Josepha (1788–1879)
Hall, Radclyffe (1880–1943)
Hands, Elizabeth (fl. 1789)
Hanim, Leyla (1850–1936)
Hanim, Nigar (1862–1918)
Hansberry, Lorraine (1930–1965)
Hareven, Shulamit (1930–2003)
Harford, Lesbia (1891–1927)
Harjo, Joy (1951—)
Harkness, Georgia (1891–1974)
Harper, Frances E.W. (1825–1911)
Harris, Claire (1937—)
Harrison, Susie Frances (1859–1935)
Hartigan, Anne Le Marquand (1931—)
Hartwig, Julia (1921—)
Haruko (1850–1914)
Harwood, Gwen (1920–1995)
Hastings, Flora (1806–1839)
Hatherly, Ana Maria (1929—)
Hauková, Jiřina (1919—)
Havergal, Frances Ridley (1836–1879)
Hawkes, Jacquetta (1910–1996)
Hayashi Fumiko (1903–1951)
Hayden, Anna Tompson (1648–after 1720)
Hayden, Esther Allen (c. 1713–1758)
Hazard, Caroline (1856–1945)
Head, Bessie (1937–1986)
Hébert, Anne (1916—)
Hedyle (fl. 3rd century BCE)
Heikel, Karin Alice (1901–1944)
Helburn, Theresa (1887–1959)
Hemans, Felicia D. (1793–1835)
Hemenway, Abby (1828–1890)
Henderson, Alice Corbin (1881–1949)
Hennings, Emmy (1885–1948)
Hensel, Luise (1798–1876)
Hermodsson, Elisabet Hermine (1927—)
Herophile
Herrera Garrido, Francisca (1869–1950)
Herzberg, Judith (1934—)
Hewett, Dorothy (1923–2002)
Hickey, Emily Henrietta (1845–1924)
Higuchi, Ichiyo (1872–1896)
Hildegard of Bingen (1098–1179)
Hilst, Hilda (1930—)
Hind bint 'Utba (d. 610)
Hineira, Arapera (1932—)
Hofmo, Gunvor (1921–1995)
Hogan, Linda (1947—)
Hohenhausen, Elizabeth (1789–1857)
Holden, Effie M. (b. 1867)
Holden, Molly (1927–1981)
Hollar, Constance (1881–1945)
Hooper, Ellen Sturgis (1812–1848)
Horovitz, Frances (1938–1983)
Horta, Maria Teresa (b. 1937)
Houdetot, Sophie, Comtesse d' (1730–1813)
Howe, Fanny (1942—)
Howe, Julia Ward (1819–1910)
Howe, Susan (1937—)
Howes, Barbara (1914–1996)
Howes, Mary (1941—)
Howitt, Mary (1799–1888)
Ho Xuan Huong (fl. late 18th c.)
Hoyers, Anna Ovena (1584–1655)
Hrotsvitha of Gandersheim (c. 935–1001)
Huch, Ricarda (1864–1947)
Hulme, Keri (1947—)
Hume, Anna (fl. 1644)
Hutton, Barbara (1912–1979)
Ibarbourou, Juana de (1895–1979)
Inber, Vera (1890–1972)
Ingelow, Jean (1820–1897)
Isabella (b. 1180)
Ise (877–940)
Iseut de Capio (1140–?)
Ishigaki, Rin (1920—)
Issaia, Nana (1934—)
Iyall, Debora (1954—)
Izumi Shikibu (c. 975–c. 1027)
Jackson, Helen Hunt (1830–1885)
Jacobsen, Josephine (1908–2003)
Janés, Clara (1940—)
Janitschek, Maria (1859–1927)
Janny, Amélia (1838–1914)
Jelinek, Elfriede (1946—)
Jennings, Elizabeth Joan (1926–2001)
Jesse, Fryniwyd Tennyson (1888–1958)
Jewsbury, Maria Jane (1800–1833)
Johnson, E. Pauline (1861–1913)
Johnson, Helene (1906–1995)
Johnson, Josephine Winslow (1910–1990)
Johnson, Pamela Hansford (1912–1981)
Johnston, Mary (1870–1936)
Jones, Amanda Theodosia (1835–1914)
Jong, Erica (1942—)
Jonker, Ingrid (1933–1965)
Jordan, June (1936–2002)
Joseph, Jenefer (1932—)
Juana Inés de la Cruz (1651–1695)
Júlia, Francisca (1871–1920)
Juvonen, Helvi (1919–1959)
Kaffka, Margit (1880–1918)
K'alandadze, Ana (1924—)
Kamal, Sufia (1911–1999)
Karsch, Anna Luise (1722–1791)
Kaschnitz, Marie Luise (1901–1974)
Kaye-Smith, Sheila (1887–1956)
Kazantzaki, Galateia (1886–1962)
Kazantzis, Judith (1940—)
Keesing, Nancy (1923–1993)
Kefala, Antigone (1935—)
Kelly, Gwen (1922—)
Kelly, Maeve (1930—)
Kemble, Fanny (1809–1893)
Kenny, Alice Annie (1875–1960)
Ke Yan (1929—)
Khanim, Leyla (d. 1847/48)
Khansa (c. 575–c. 645)
Khirniq (fl. late 6th c.)
Khuri, Colette (1937—)
Khvoshchinskaia, Nadezhda (1824–1889)
Kidman, Fiona (1940—)
Killigrew, Anne (1660–1685)
Kilpi, Eeva (1928—)
King, Anne (1621–after 1684)
Kinkel, Johanna (1810–1858)
Kirsch, Sarah (1935—)
Kizer, Carolyn (1925—)
Klepfisz, Irena (1941—)
Knox, Isa (1831–1903)
Kogawa, Joy (1935—)
Koidula, Lydia (1843–1886)
Kolmar, Gertrud (1894–1943)
Konopnicka, Maria (1842–1910)
Kouza, Loujaya M.
Krandievskaya, Natalia (1888–1963)
Krasnohorska, Eliska (1847–1926)
Kulman, Elisabeth (1808–1825)
Kumin, Maxine (1925—)
Kuntsch, Margaretha Susanna von (1651–1716)
Kurz, Isolde (1853–1944)
Labé, Louise (c. 1523–1566)
Lafarge, Marie (1816–1852)
Lal Ded (b. 1355)
Lamb, Caroline (1785–1828)
Lamb, Mary Anne (1764–1847)
La Montagne-Beauregard, Blanche (1899–1960)
Landon, Letitia Elizabeth (1802–1838)
Lane, Pinkie Gordon (1925—)
Lange, Norah (1906–1972)
Langner, Ilse (1899–1987)
Lapauze, Jeanne (1860–1920)
Larcom, Lucy (1824–1893)
La Rochefoucauld, Edmée, Duchesse de (1895–1991)
Lars, Claudia (1899–1974)
Lask, Berta (1878–1967)
Lasker-Schüler, Else (1869–1945)
Lathrop, Rose Hawthorne (1851–1926)
Lauber, Cécile (1887–1981)
Laurence, Margaret (1926–1987)

Laurencin, Marie (1883–1956)
Lavant, Christine (1915–1973)
Lawless, Emily (1845–1913)
Lawson, Louisa (1848–1920)
Layla al-Akhyaliyya (fl. 650–660)
Lazarus, Emma (1849–1887)
Leadbetter, Mary (1758–1826)
Leakey, Caroline Woolmer (1827–1881)
Leapor, Mary (1722–1746)
Le Camus, Madame (fl. 17th c.)
Lee, Muna (1895–1965)
Lenngren, Anna Maria (1754–1817)
Lennox, Charlotte (1720–1804)
Le Noir, Elizabeth Anne (c. 1755–1841)
Leodegundia (fl. 10th c.)
Leonardos, Stela (1923—)
Le Sueur, Meridel (1900–1996)
Levertov, Denise (1923–1997)
Levesque, Louise Cavelier (1703–1743)
Levy, Amy (1861–1889)
Lewis, Estelle Anna (1824–1880)
Liadan (fl. 7th c.)
Liang Desheng (1771–1847)
Likimani, Muthoni (c. 1940—)
Lindbergh, Anne Morrow (1906–2001)
Lindsay, Anne (1750–1825)
Lipkin, Jean (1926—)
Lippincott, Sara Clarke (1823–1904)
Li Qingzhao (1083–c. 1151)
Lisboa, Henriquetta (1904–1985)
Lisboa, Irene (1892–1958)
Lisnianskaya, Inna (1928—)
Little, Janet (1759–1813)
Livesay, Dorothy (1909–1996)
Lochhead, Liz (1947—)
Locke, Anne Vaughan (c. 1530–c. 1590)
Lokhvitskaia, Mirra (1869–1905)
Lombarda (b. 1190)
Lorde, Audre (1934–1992)
Løveid, Cecilie (1951—)
Loveling, Virginie (1836–1923)
Lowell, Amy (1874–1925)
Lowell, Maria White (1821–1853)
Lowe-Porter, Helen (1876–1963)
Lowther, Patricia Louise (1935–1975)
Loy, Mina (1882–1966)
Loynaz, Dulce María (1902–1997)
Loynes, Antoinette de (fl. 16th c.)
Loynes, Camille de (fl. 16th c.)
Ludwig, Paula (1900–1974)
Luft, Lia (1938—)
Luke, Jemima (1813–1906)
Lussu, Joyce Salvadori (1912–1988)
Lürken, Hulda (1896–1947)
Macaulay, Rose (1881–1958)
MacDonald, Elizabeth Roberts (1864–1922)
MacEwen, Gwendolyn (1941–1987)
Macgoye, Marjorie Oludhe (1928—)
Machado, Gilka (1893–1980)
Machado, Luz (1916–1999)
Machar, Agnes Maule (1837–1927)
Mackay, Jessie (1864–1938)
Mackellar, Dorothea (1885–1968)
MacLeod, Mary (c. 1615–c. 1706)
MacManus, Anna Johnston (1866–1902)
Macpherson, Jay (1931—)
Mactier, Susie (1854–1936)
Madeleva, Sister Mary (1887–1964)
Madgett, Naomi Long (1923—)
Mahbuba (fl. 9th c.)
Maksimovic, Desanka (1898–1993)
Malaika, Nazik al- (1923–1992)
Malaika, Salma al- (1908–1953)
Mamoshina, Glafira Adolfovna (c. 1870–1942)
Mancini, Evelina (1849–1896)
Mancini, Laura (1823–1869)
Mandel, Miriam (1930–1982)
Manner, Eeva-Liisa (1921–1995)
Mannes, Marya (1904–1990)
Mansour, Joyce (1928–1987)
Maratti Zappi, Faustina (c. 1680–1745)
March, Susana (1918–1991)
Marchenko, Anastasiia Iakovlevna (1830–1880)
Margaret of Angoulême (1492–1549)
Margaret of Austria (1480–1530)
Margaret of Geneva (fl. late 1100s–early 1200s)
Margaret of Scotland (1424–1445)
Maria de Ventadour (b. 1165)
Maria do Céu (1658–1753)
Mariana Victoria (1768–1788)
Marie de Brabant (c. 1530–c. 1600)
Marín del Solar, Mercedes (1804–1866)
Maritain, Raïssa (1883–1960)
Marquets, Anne de (1533–1588)
Marriott, Anne (1913–1997)
Marson, Una (1905–1965)
Märten, Lu (1879–1970)
Martin, Agnes (1912–2004)
Martinson, Moa (1890–1964)
Mason, Alice Trumbull (1904–1971)
Massimi, Petronilla Paolini (1663–1726)
Matamoros, Mercedes (1851–1906)
Matveyeva, Novella Niklayevna (1934—)
Maude, Caitlín (1941–1982)
Mayröcker, Friederike (1924—)
McAlpine, Rachel (1940—)
McCormick, Anne O'Hare (1880–1954)
McGinley, Phyllis (1905–1978)
McNeil, Florence (1937—)
McPherson, Heather (1942—)
Medici, Isabella de (1542–1576)
Medio, Dolores (1914–1996)
Megalostrata (fl. 6 BCE)
Meireles, Cecília (1901–1964)
Melissanthi (c. 1907–c. 1991)
Menebhi, Saïda (1952–1977)
Meneres, Maria Alberta (1930—)
Meneses, Juana Josefa de (1651–1709)
Menken, Adah Isaacs (1835–1868)
Menzies, Trixie Te Arama (1936—)
Mercoeur, Elisa (1809–1835)
Mereau-Brentano, Sophie (1770–1806)
Meredith, Louisa Anne (1812–1895)
Merken, Lucretia Wilhelmina van (1721–1789)
Mew, Charlotte (1869–1928)
Meynell, Viola (1886–1956)
Mhac An tSaoi, Máire (1922—)
Michael, Julia Warner (b. 1879)
Michaelis, Hanny (1922—)
Michel, Louise (1830–1905)
Michitsuna no haha (c. 936–995)
Miegel, Agnes (1879–1964)
Mihi-ki-te-kapua (?–1872/80)
Mihri Khatun (fl. 15/16th c.)
Milani, Milena (1922—)
Millay, Edna St. Vincent (1892–1950)
Miller, Alice Duer (1874–1942)
Miller, Ruth (1919–1969)
Milligan, Alice (1866–1953)
Mira Bai (1498–1547)
Miremont, Jacqueline de (fl. 16th c.)
Mishkowsky, Zelda Shneurson (1914–1984)
Mistral, Gabriela (1889–1957)
Mitchison, Naomi (1897–1999)
Mitford, Mary Russell (1787–1855)
Moero (fl. 4th–3rd BCE)
Moïse, Penina (1797–1880)
Monck, Mary (c. 1678–1715)
Monroe, Harriet (1860–1936)
Montagu, Lady Mary Wortley (1689–1762)
Montoriol i Puig, Carme (1893–1966)
Moodie, Susanna (1803–1885)
Moody, Elizabeth (1737–1814)
Moore, Jane Elizabeth (1738–?)
Moore, Julia A. (1847–1920)
Moore, Lilian (1909–2004)
Moore, Marianne (1887–1972)
Moorhead, Sarah Parsons (fl. 1741–1742)
Moosdorf, Johanna (1911–2000)
Morante, Elsa (1912–1985)
Morata, Fulvia Olympia (1526–1555)
Mordecai, Pamela (1942—)
More, Gertrude (1606–1633)
More, Hannah (1745–1833)
Moreno, Virginia R. (1925—)
Morgan, Robin (1941—)
Morisaki, Kazue (1927—)
Morits, Yunna (1937—)
Morpurgo, Rachel (1790–1871)
Moschine (fl. 4 BCE)
Moulton, Louise Chandler (1835–1908)
Moutza-Martinengou, Elisavet (1801–1832)
Mugo, Micere Githae (1942—)
Mulder, Elisabeth (1904–1987)
Mulford, Wendy (1941—)
Müller, Clara (1860–1905)
Murasaki Shikibu (c. 973–c. 1015)
Murdoch, Nina (1890–1976)
Murray, Judith Sargent (1751–1820)
Murray, Pauli (1910–1985)
Musa, Gilda (1926–1999)
Mutayyam al-Hashimiyya (fl. 8th c.)
Myrtis (fl. early 5th c. BCE)
Naden, Constance Caroline Woodhill (1858–1889)
Nagródskaia, Evdokiia (1866–1930)
Naheed, Kishwar (1940—)
Naidu, Sarojini (1879–1949)
Nairne, Carolina (1766–1845)
Namjoshi, Suniti (1941—)
Nasrin, Taslima (1962—)
Naudé, Adèle (1910–1981)
Negri, Ada (1870–1945)
Negron Muñoz, Mercedes (1895–1973)
Nemes Nagy, Agnes (1922–1991)
Neris, Salomeja (1904–1945)
Nesbit, Edith (1858–1924)
Nevelson, Louise (1899–1988)
Nicholls, Marjory Lydia (1890–1930)
Nicholson, Eliza Jane (1849–1896)
Ni Chuilleanáin, Eiléan (1942—)
Nicolson, Adela Florence (1865–1904)
Ni Dhomhnaill, Nuala (1952—)
Niedecker, Lorine (1903–1970)
Niggli, Josefina (1910–1983)
Nin, Anais (1903–1977)
Noailles, Anna de (1876–1933)
Nogarola, Isotta (c. 1416–1466)
Norman, Dorothy (1905–1997)
Norton, Caroline (1808–1877)
Norton, Frances (1640–1731)
Nossis of Locri (fl. 300 BCE)
Nott, Kathleen (1909–1999)
Novak, Helga (1935—)
Nur Jahan (1577–1645)
Oba, Minako (1930—)
Ocampo, Silvina (1903–1993)
O'Connell, Eileen (c. 1743–c. 1800)
Odoevtseva, Irina (c. 1895–1990)
O'Doherty, Mary Anne (1826–1910)
O'Keeffe, Adelaide (1776–c. 1855)
Oliveira, Marli de (1935—)
Oliver, Mary (1935—)
Olsen, Tillie (c. 1912—)
Olsson, Hagar (1893–1978)
Ombres, Rossana (1931—)
O'Neill, Rose Cecil (1874–1944)
Ono no Komachi (c. 830–?)

Opie, Amelia (1769–1853)
Osgood, Frances (1811–1850)
Ostenso, Martha (1900–1963)
Otto-Peters, Luise (1819–1895)
Ozick, Cynthia (1928—)
Page, P.K. (1916—)
Paley, Grace (1922—)
Palli, Angelica (1798–1875)
Palmer, Nettie (1885–1964)
Paoli, Betty (1814–1894)
Papadopoulou, Alexandra (1867–1906)
Pardoe, Julia (1804–1862)
Parker, Dorothy (1893–1967)
Parker, Pat (1944–1989)
Parkes, Bessie Rayner (1829–1925)
Parnok, Sophia (1885–1933)
Parra, Violeta (1917–1967)
Parthenay, Anne de (fl. 16th c.)
Parthenay, Catherine de (1554–1631)
Parthenis (fl. 2nd c. BCE)
Parun, Vesna (1922—)
Pasternak, Josephine (1900–1993)
Paul, Joanna (1945–2003)
Pauli, Hertha (1909–1973)
Pavlova, Karolina (1807–1893)
Pawlikowska, Maria (1891–1945)
Paz Paredes, Margarita (1922–1980)
Peabody, Josephine Preston (1874–1922)
Peale, Sarah Miriam (1800–1885)
Penfold, Merimeri (1924—)
Pereira, Irene Rice (1902–1971)
Peri Rossi, Cristina (1941—)
Perry, Lilla Cabot (c. 1848–1933)
Petrovýkh, Mariia (1908–1979)
Pfeiffer, Emily Jane (1827–1890)
Phantasia
Philips, Katherine (1631–1664)
Pickthall, Marjorie (1883–1922)
Pierangeli, Rina Faccio (1876–1960)
Piercy, Marge (1936—)
Pimentel, Eleonora (c. 1768–1799)
Pitt, Marie E.J. (1869–1948)
Pitter, Ruth (1897–1992)
Pizarnik, Alejandra (1936–1972)
Plá, Josefina (1909–1999)
Plath, Sylvia (1932–1963)
Plato, Ann (c. 1820–?)
Pleijel, Agneta (1940—)
Plisson, Marie-Prudence (1727–1788)
Ploennies, Luise von (1803–1872)
Plummer, Mary Wright (1856–1916)
Polidouri, Maria (1902–1930)
Pollard, Velma (1937—)
Pompilj, Vittoria Aganoor (1855–1910)
Portal, Magda (1903–1989)
Porter, Sarah (fl. 1791)
Poulain, Mme (c. 1750–c. 1800)
Pozzi, Antonia (1912–1938)
Pozzo, Modesta (1555–1592)
Prado, Adélia (1936—)
Praxilla (fl. 450 BCE)
Preradovic, Paula von (1887–1951)
Preston, Margaret Junkin (1820–1897)
Prince, Lucy Terry (c. 1730–1821)
Pritam, Amrita (1919—)
Proba (fl. 4th c.)
Procter, Adelaide (1825–1864)
Przybyszewska, Dagny Juel (1867–1901)
Purvis, Sarah Forten (c. 1811–c. 1898)
Pusich, Antónia Gertrudes (1805–1883)
Qiu Jin (c. 1875–1907)
Raab, Esther (1894–1981)
Rabbani, Ruhiyyih (1910–2000)
Radcliffe, Ann (1764–1823)
Radegund of Poitiers (518–587)
Rahon, Alice (1904–1987)
Raine, Kathleen (1908–2003)
Ramirez, Sara Estela (1881–1910)
Rashid, Saleha Abdul (1939—)
Rasp, Renate (1935—)
Rathbone, Hannah Mary (1798–1878)
Ratushinskaya, Irina (1954—)
Ravikovitch, Dahlia (1936—)
Rawlings, Marjorie Kinnan (1896–1953)
Rawlinson, Gloria (1918–1995)
Ray, H. Cordelia (c. 1849–1916)
Recke, Elisa von der (1754–1833)
Reed, Myrtle (1874–1911)
Reese, Lizette Woodworth (1856–1935)
Reeve, Clara (1729–1807)
Reinig, Christa (1926—)
Reis, Maria Firmina dos (1825–1917)
Reisner, Larissa (1895–1926)
Reynolds, Malvina (1900–1978)
Rich, Adrienne (1929—)
Richards, Ann (1917—)
Richards, Beah (1920–2000)
Richards, Laura E. (1850–1943)
Ridge, Lola (1873–1941)
Riding, Laura (1901–1991)
Ridler, Anne (1912–2001)
Rittenhouse, Jessie Belle (1869–1948)
Roberts, Elizabeth Madox (1881–1941)
Roberts, Sheila (1937—)
Robinson, Mary (1758–1800)
Roches, Catherine des (1542–1587)
Roches, Madeleine des (1520–1587)
Rodríguez, Evangelina (1879–1947)
Rodriguez, Judith (1936—)
Rodríguez de Tió, Lola (1843–1924)
Roland Holst, Henriëtte (1869–1952)
Romieu, Marie de (c. 1545–c. 1590)
Ros, Amanda (1860–1939)
Rosselli, Amelia (1930–1996)
Rossetti, Christina (1830–1894)
Rostopchina, Evdokiya (1811–1858)
Rowe, Elizabeth Singer (1674–1737)
Rowson, Susanna (1762–1824)
Roy de Clotte le Barillier, Berthe (1868–1927)
Royer, Clémence (1830–1902)
Rozanova, Olga (1886–1918)
Rukeyser, Muriel (1913–1980)
Russell, Dora Isella (1925—)
Russell, Elizabeth (1540–1609)
Ryan, Anne (1889–1954)
Saburova, Irina (1907–1979)
Sachs, Nelly (1891–1970)
Sackville-West, Vita (1892–1962)
Sadlier, Mary Anne (1820–1903)
Sage, Kay (1898–1963)
Salete, Mme de (fl. 1600)
Salm-Dyck, Constance de (1767–1845)
Samman, Ghada al- (1942—)
Sampter, Jessie (1883–1938)
Sanchez, Carol Lee (1934—)
Sanchez, Sonia (1934—)
San Félix, Sor Marcela de (1605–1688)
Sangster, Margaret (1838–1912)
Santos Arrascaeta, Beatriz (1947—)
Sappho (c. 612–c. 557 BCE)
Sarfatti, Margherita (1880–1961)
Sarrazin, Albertine (1937–1967)
Sarton, May (1912–1995)
Savary, Olga (1933—)
Savić-Rebac, Anica (1892–1935)
Savorgnan, Maria (fl. 1500)
Sawyer, Caroline M. Fisher (1812–1894)
Schaumann, Ruth (1899–1975)
Schiaparelli, Elsa (1890–1973)
Schön, Elizabeth (1921–2001)
Schoolcraft, Jane Johnston (1800–1841)
Schopenhauer, Adele (1797–1849)
Schoultz, Solveig von (1907–1996)
Schutting, Julian (1937—)
Schwarz, Sybilla (1621–1638)
Scott, Ann London (1929–1975)
Scott, Evelyn (1893–1963)
Scott, Mary (1751–1793)
Scovell, E.J. (1907–1999)
Scudéry, Madeleine de (1607–1701)
Ségalas, Anais (1814–1895)
Seidel, Ina (1885–1974)
Senior, Olive (1941—)
Seward, Anna (1742–1809)
Sewell, Mary Wright (1797–1884)
Sexton, Anne (1928–1974)
Seymour, Anne (c. 1532–1587)
Seymour, Frances Thynne (1699–1754)
Seymour, Jane (1541–1560)
Seymour, Margaret (c. 1533–?)
Shaginian, Marietta (1888–1982)
Shakhovskaya, Zinaida (1906–2001)
Shange, Ntozake (1948—)
Sharp, Margery (1905–1991)
Shaw, Helen (1913–1985)
Shchepkina-Kupernik, Tatiana (1874–1952)
Sherwood, Katharine Margaret (1841–1914)
Sherwood, Mary Elizabeth (1826–1903)
Shields, Carol (1935–2003)
Shkapskaia, Mariia (1891–1952)
Siddal, Elizabeth (1829–1862)
Sierra, Stella (1917–1997)
Sigea, Luisa (c. 1531–1560)
Sigerson, Dora (1866–1918)
Sigerson, Hester (d. 1898)
Sigourney, Lydia H. (1791–1865)
Silko, Leslie Marmon (1948—)
Silva, Clara (1905–1976)
Simpson, Helen (1897–1940)
Sinclair, May (1863–1946)
Sitwell, Edith (1887–1964)
Skinner, Constance Lindsay (1877–1939)
Skobtsova, Maria (1891–1945)
Skrine, Agnes (c. 1865–1955)
Slye, Maud (1869–1954)
Smart, Elizabeth (1913–1986)
Smedley, Menella Bute (c. 1820–1877)
Smith, Abby (1797–1878)
Smith, Anna Young (1756–1780)
Smith, Charlotte (1749–1806)
Smith, Eliza Roxey Snow (1804–1887)
Smith, Julia (1792–1886)
Smith, Patti (1946—)
Smith, Stevie (1902–1971)
Smither, Elizabeth (1941—)
Södergran, Edith (1892–1923)
Solov'eva, Poliksena (1867–1924)
Southey, Caroline Anne (1786–1854)
Souza, Auta de (1876–1901)
Spark, Muriel (1918—)
Spaziani, Maria Luisa (1924—)
Speght, Rachel (1597–c. 1630)
Spencer, Anne (1882–1975)
Speyer, Leonora (1872–1956)
Spofford, Harriet Prescott (1835–1921)
Spottiswoode, Alicia Ann (1810–1900)
St. Denis, Ruth (1877–1968)
Stampa, Gaspara (1523–1554)
Stanley, Mary (1919–1980)
Starr, Eliza Allen (1824–1901)
Stefan, Verena (1947—)
Stein, Gertrude (1874–1946)
Stepanova, Varvara (1894–1958)
Stern, Catherine Brieger (1894–1973)
Stettheimer, Florine (1871–1944)
Stevenson, Anne (1933—)
Stockenström, Wilma (1933—)
Stockfleth, Maria Katharina (c. 1633–1692)

Stöcklin, Franziska (1894–1931)
Stockton, Annis Boudinot (1736–1801)
Stoddard, Elizabeth Drew (1823–1902)
Stojadinović-Srpkinja, Milica (1830–1878)
Stolitsa, Liubov (1884–1934)
Stolk, Gloria (1918–1979)
Stone, Ruth (1915—)
Stopes, Marie (1880–1958)
Storni, Alfonsina (1892–1938)
Strange, Michael (1890–1950)
Strauss, Jennifer (1933—)
Strauss und Torney, Lulu von (1873–1956)
Strong, Eithne (1923–1999)
Stuart-Wortley, Emmeline (1806–1855)
Sturm, J.C. (1927—)
Su Hui (fl. 4th c.)
Sullam, Sara Coppia (1590–1641)
Sulpicia I (fl. 1st c. BCE)
Sulpicia II (fl. 1st c.)
Sutherland, Efua (1924–1996)
Swenson, May (1913–1989)
Sykes, Bobbi (1943—)
Szabó, Magda (1917—)
Szumigalski, Anne (1922–1999)
Szymborska, Wislawa (1923—)
Taber, Gladys (1899–1980)
Taggard, Genevieve (1894–1948)
Tamairangi (fl. 1820–1828)
Tappan, Caroline Sturgis (1819–1888)
Taschau, Hannelies (1937—)
Tastu, Amable (1798–1885)
Tavares, Salette (1922–1994)
Taylor, Ann (1782–1866)
Taylor, Elizabeth (d. 1708)
Taylor, Harriet (1807–1858)
Taylor, Jane (1783–1824)
Taymuriyya, 'A'isha 'Ismat al- (1840–1902)
Teasdale, Sara (1884–1933)
Teffi, N.A. (1872–1952)
Telesilla (fl. 6th or 5th c. BCE)
Teplova, Nadezhda Sergeevna (1814–1848)
Terán, Ana Enriqueta (1919—)
Thaxter, Celia Laighton (1835–1894)
Theano (fl. 6th c. BCE)
Theano II (fl. 5th c. BCE)
Thimelby, Gertrude Aston (c. 1617–1668)
Thomas, Caitlin (1913–1994)
Thomas, Edith Matilda (1854–1925)
Thomas, Elean (1947–2004)
Thomas, Elizabeth (1675–1731)
Thomas, Joyce Carol (1938—)
Thompson, Eloise Bibb (1878–1928)
Thompson, Flora (1876–1947)
Thorpe, Rose Hartwick (1850–1939)
Thorup, Kirsten (1942—)
Tiempo, Edith L. (1919—)
Tietjens, Eunice (1884–1944)
Tighe, Mary (1772–1810)
Tikkanen, Märta (1935—)
Tinsley, Annie Turner (1808–1885)
Tipper, Elizabeth (fl. late 17th c.)
Todd, Mabel Loomis (1858–1932)
Tomioka, Taeko (1937—)
Topeora, Rangi Kuini Wikitoria (?–1865/73)
Tosatti, Barbara Maria (1891–1934)
Tostevin, Lola Lemire (1937—)
Traba, Marta (1930–1983)
Tracy, Mona Innis (1892–1959)
Travers, P.L. (1906–1996)
Tsvetaeva, Marina (1892–1941)
Tueni, Nadia (1935–1983)
Tuqan, Fadwa (1917–2003)
Turell, Jane (1708–1735)
Tusap, Srbuhi (1841–1901)
Tynan, Katharine (1861–1931)
Ukrainka, Lesya (1871–1913)
Uma no Naishi (fl. 10th c.)
Under, Marie (1883–1980)
Underhill, Evelyn (1875–1941)
Unzer, Johanne Charlotte (1725–1782)
Vaa, Aslaug (1889–1965)
Vadkerti-Gavorníková, Lydia (1932–1999)
Vakalo, Eleni (1921—)
Valle Silva, Luisa del (1896–1962)
Vanderbilt, Gloria (1924—)
Van Duyn, Mona (1921–2004)
Van Rensselaer, Mariana (1851–1934)
van Schurmann, Anna Maria (1607–1678)
Van Vorst, Marie Louise (1867–1936)
Vardill, Anna Jane (1781–1852)
Vartio, Marja-Liisa (1924–1966)
Vaz de Carvalho, Maria Amália (1847–1921)
Vaz Ferreira, María Eugenia (1875–1924)
Velâsquez, Lucila (1928—)
Veley, Margaret (1843–1887)
Velichkovskaia, Tamara Antonovna (1908–1990)
Vesaas, Halldis Moren (1907–1995)
Veselkova Kil'shtet, M.G. (1861–1931)
Victor, Frances (1826–1902)
Vieira, Maruja (1922—)
Viganò, Renata (1900–1976)
Vilariño, Idea (1920—)
Villarino, María de (1905–1994)
Villedieu, Catherine des Jardins, Mme de (c. 1640–1683)
Vilmorin, Louise de (1902–1969)
Violante do Céu (1601–1693)
Vitorino, Virginia (1897–1967)
Vivanti, Annie (1868–1942)
Vivien, Renée (1877–1909)
Voigt-Diederichs, Helene (1875–1961)
Voznesenskaya, Julia (1940—)
Waard, Elly de (1940—)
Waddell, Helen (1889–1965)
Waddington, Miriam (1917–2004)
Wakoski, Diane (1937—)
Walker, Alice (1944—)
Walker, Kath (1920–1993)
Walker, Margaret (1915–1998)
Wallace, Bronwen (1945–1989)
Wallach, Yonah (1944–1985)
Wallada (fl. 11th c.)
Walsh, María Elena (1930—)
Walter, Silja (1919—)
Wandor, Michelene (1940—)
Wang Zhaojun (52 BCE–18 CE)
Ward, Elizabeth Stuart Phelps (1844–1911)
Wardlaw, Elizabeth (1677–1727)
Warmond, Ellen (1930—)
Warner, Sylvia Townsend (1893–1978)
Warren, Mercy Otis (1728–1814)
Washington, Josephine (1861–1949)
Watson, Rosamund (1860–1911)
Weamys, Anna (fl. 1650s)
Webb, Mary (1881–1927)
Webb, Phyllis (1927—)
Webster, Augusta (1837–1894)
Webster, Jean (1876–1916)
Webster, Mary Morison (1894–1980)
Wellesley, Dorothy (1889–1956)
Wells, Emmeline B. (1828–1921)
West, Jane (1758–1852)
West, Jessamyn (1902–1984)
Weston, Elizabeth Jane (1582–1612)
Wetherald, Ethelwyn (1857–1940)
Wharton, Anne (1659–1685)
Wheatley, Phillis (c. 1752–1784)
Whiting, Lilian (1847–1942)
Whitman, Sarah Helen (1803–1878)
Whitney, Adeline Dutton (1824–1906)
Whitney, Isabella (fl. 1567–1575)
Wickham, Anna (1883–1947)
Widdemer, Margaret (1884–1978)
Wied, Martina (1882–1957)
Wiggins, Myra Albert (1869–1956)
Wilcox, Ella Wheeler (1850–1919)
Wilde, Jane (1821–1896)
Wilker, Gertrud (1924–1984)
Wilkinson, Anne (1910–1961)
Wilkinson, Iris (1906–1939)
Wilkinson, Marguerite Ogden (1883–1928)
Williams, Anna (1706–1783)
Williams, Helen Maria (1762–1827)
Williams, Sarah (1841–1868)
Williams, Sherley Anne (1944–1999)
Wilson, Anne Glenny (1848–1930)
Wilson, Mary (1916—)
Winkworth, Catherine (1827–1878)
Wister, Sarah (1761–1804)
Wohmann, Gabriele (1932—)
Woolsey, Sarah Chauncey (1835–1905)
Wordsworth, Dorothy (1771–1855)
Wright, Judith (1915–2000)
Wright, Martha Coffin (1806–1875)
Wright, Sarah Elizabeth (1928—)
Wright, Susanna (1697–1784)
Wroth, Mary (c. 1587–c. 1651)
Wurdemann, Audrey Mary (1911–1960)
Wu Zetian (624–705)
Wylie, Elinor (1885–1928)
Xiao Hong (1911–1942)
Xie Wanying (1900–1999)
Xirinacs, Olga (1936—)
Xue Tao (c. 760–c. 832)
Yamada, Mitsuye (1923—)
Yamamoto, Michiko (1936—)
Yazova, Yana (1912–1974)
Yearsley, Ann (1752–1806)
Yosano Akiko (1878–1942)
Young, Ella (1867–1951)
Young, Marguerite (1908–1995)
Yourcenar, Marguerite (1903–1987)
Zamora, Daisy (1950—)
Zamudio, Adela (1854–1928)
Zani, Giselda (1909–1975)
Zardoya, Concha (1914–2004)
Zaturenska, Marya Alexandrovna (1902–1982)
Zaunemann, Sidonia Hedwig (1714–1740)
Zayas y Sotomayor, María de (1590–c. 1650)
Zeb-un-Nissa (1639–1702)
Zeidler, Susanna Elisabeth (1657–1706)
Zeller, Eva (1923—)
Zetterling, Mai (1925–1994)
Zhadovskaia, Iuliia Valerianovna (1824–1883)
Zhao Luorui (b. 1912)
Zheng Min (1920—)
Ziegler, Christiane Mariane von (1695–1760)
Zirimu, Elvania Namukwaya (1938–1979)
Ziyada, Mayy (1886–1941)
Żmichowska, Narcyza (1819–1876)
Zorlutuna, Halidé Nusret (1901–1984)
Zuccari, Anna Radius (1846–1918)
Zürn, Unica (1916–1970)
Zuzoric, Cvijeta (c. 1555–1600)
Zwicky, Fay (1933—)

POET LAUREATE

Brooks, Gwendolyn (1917–2000)
Coates, Florence Nicholson (1850–1927)
Coolbrith, Ina Donna (1841–1928)
Lorde, Audre (1934–1992)
Van Duyn, Mona (1921–2004)

POISONER (ACCUSED)

Becker, Marie Alexander (1877–194?)
Blandy, Mary (1719–1752)
Brinvilliers, Marie de (1630–1676)

Occupational Index

Deshayes, Catherine (d. 1680)
Eadburgh (c. 773–after 802)
Howard, Frances (1593–1632)
Lafarge, Marie (1816–1852)
La Gratiosa (d. 1659)
Locusta (fl. 54)
Parysatis I (fl. 440–385 BCE)
Spara, Hieronyma (d. 1659)
Tofana (1653–1723)
Toppan, Jane (1854–1938)
Turner, Anne (1576–1615)
Ursinus, Sophie (1760–1836)
Wilson, Catherine (1842–1862)

POLICE ADMINISTRATOR
Allen, Mary Sophia (1878–1964)
Harrington, Penny (c. 1943—)
Kidd, Margaret Henderson (1900–1989)

POLICE OFFICER
Allen, Mary Sophia (1878–1964)
Esserman, Carol (c. 1945—)
Harrington, Penny (c. 1943—)
Hughes, Sarah T. (1896–1985)
Roche, Josephine (1886–1976)
Wells, Alice Stebbins (1873–1957)

POLITICAL-CAMPAIGN MANAGER
Carroll, Anna Ella (1815–1894)
Dunbar-Nelson, Alice (1875–1935)
Dyachenko, Tatyana (1960—)
Estrich, Susan R. (1952—)
Felton, Rebecca Latimer (1835–1930)
Hughes, Karen (1956—)
McCormick, Ruth Hanna (1880–1944)
Moore, Audley (1898–1997)
Richards, Ann Willis (1933—)
Sullivan, Leonor Kretzer (1902–1988)
Upton, Harriet Taylor (1853–1945)
Weis, Jessica McCullough (1901–1963)

POLITICAL HOSTESS
Adams, Abigail (1744–1818)
Adams, Louisa Catherine (1775–1852)
Alice de Bryene (d. 1435)
Alice of Athlone (1883–1981)
Alsop, Susan Mary (d. 2004)
Arthur, Ellen Herndon (1837–1880)
Asquith, Margot Tennant (1864–1945)
Bache, Sarah (1743–1808)
Bishop, Bernice Pauahi (1831–1884)
Black, Helen McKenzie (1896–1963)
Blair, Cherie (1954—)
Blessington, Marguerite, Countess of (1789–1849)
Bliss, Mary Elizabeth (1824–1909)
Briggs, Emily Edson (1830–1910)
Browne, Harriet Louisa (1829–1906)
Burr, Theodosia (1783–1813)
Bush, Barbara (1924—)
Carter, Rosalynn (1927—)
Churchill, Clementine (1885–1977)
Cleveland, Frances Folsom (1864–1947)
Cleveland, Rose Elizabeth (b. 1846)
Coolidge, Grace Goodhue (1879–1957)
Davis, Varina Howell (1826–1906)
de Gaulle, Yvonne (1900–1979)
Disraeli, Mary Anne (1792–1872)
Douglas, Adèle Cutts (1835–1899)
Eden, Emily (1797–1869)
Eisenhower, Mamie (1896–1979)
Eppes, Maria Jefferson (1778–1804)
Fillmore, Abigail Powers (1798–1853)
Ford, Betty (1918—)
Forten, Margaretta (1808–1875)
Garfield, Lucretia (1832–1918)
Grant, Julia (1826–1902)
Harding, Florence K. (1860–1924)
Harriman, Pamela (1920–1997)
Harrison, Anna Symmes (1775–1864)
Harrison, Caroline Scott (1832–1892)
Harrison, Jane Irwin (1804–1846)
Hayes, Lucy Webb (1831–1889)
Henderson, Mary (1919–2004)
Herron, Carrie Rand (1867–1914)
Hoover, Lou Henry (1874–1944)
Johnson, Eliza McCardle (1810–1876)
Johnson, Lady Bird (1912—)
Kennedy, Jacqueline (1929–1994)
Lamb, Emily (d. 1869)
Lane, Harriet (1830–1903)
Lincoln, Mary Todd (1818–1882)
Logan, Mary Cunningham (1838–1923)
Madison, Dolley Payne (1768–1849)
Massey, Christina Allan (1863–1932)
Maxwell, Elsa (1883–1963)
McCormick, Ruth Hanna (1880–1944)
McElroy, Mary Arthur (d. 1916)
McKinley, Ida Saxton (1847–1907)
McLean, Evalyn Walsh (1886–1947)
Mesta, Perle (1889–1975)
Mitchell, Marion (1876–1955)
Monroe, Elizabeth (1768–1830)
Moulton, Louise Chandler (1835–1908)
Nhu, Madame (1924—)
Nixon, Pat (1912–1993)
Osborne, Margaret (1918—)
Palmer, Lizzie Merrill (1838–1916)
Patterson, Martha Johnson (1828–1901)
Pierce, Jane Means (1806–1863)
Polk, Sarah Childress (1803–1891)
Rama Rau, Santha (1923—)
Ramsay, Patricia (1886–1974)
Randolph, Martha Jefferson (1775–1836)
Reagan, Nancy (1921—)
Ream, Vinnie (1847–1914)
Reed, Esther De Berdt (1746–1780)
Rockefeller, Abby Aldrich (1874–1948)
Rolleston, Elizabeth Mary (1845–1940)
Roosevelt, Eleanor (1884–1962)
Semple, Letitia Tyler (1821–1907)
Sherwood, Mary Elizabeth (1826–1903)
Stewart, Mary Downie (1876–1957)
Stover, Mary Johnson (1832–1883)
Taft, Helen Herron (1861–1943)
Taylor, Margaret Smith (1788–1852)
Truman, Bess (1885–1982)
Tyler, Julia Gardiner (1820–1889)
Tyler, Priscilla Cooper (1816–1889)
Van Buren, Angelica (1816–1878)
Van Buren, Hannah Hoes (1783–1819)
Vane-Tempest-Stewart, Theresa (1856–1919)
Washington, Martha (1731–1802)
Whitney, Betsey Cushing Roosevelt (1908–1998)
Wilson, Edith Bolling (1872–1961)
Wilson, Ellen Axson (1860–1914)

POLITICAL MARTYR
Aaronsohn, Sarah (1890–1917)
Astorga, Nora (1949–1988)
Bocanegra, Gertrudis (1765–1817)
Bohuszewiczowna, Maria (1865–1887)
Bouhired, Djamila (1937—)
Cavell, Edith (1865–1915)
Christians, Mady (1900–1951)
Constance (d. 305)
Corday, Charlotte (1768–1793)
Cushman, Pauline (1833–1893)
Deng Yingchao (1903–1992)
Eisenblätter, Charlotte (1903–1944)
Eisenschneider, Elvira (1924–c. 1944)
Fornalska, Malgorzata (1902–1944)
Goldman, Emma (1869–1940)
Kosmodemyanskaya, Zoya (1923–1941)
Lindner, Herta (1920–1943)
Liuzzo, Viola (1925–1965)
Marie Clotilde (d. 1794)
Mirabal de González, Patria (1924–1960)
Mirabal de Guzmán, María Teresa (1936–1960)
Niederkirchner, Käte (1909–1944)
Odena, Lina (1911–1936)
Perovskaya, Sonia (1853–1881)
Pimentel, Eleonora (c. 1768–1799)
Qiu Jin (c. 1875–1907)
Schaft, Hannie (1920–1945)
September, Dulcie (1935–1988)
Silang, Gabriela (1731–1763)
Spiridonova, Maria (1884–1941)
Stanley, Charlotte (1599–1664)
Tillion, Germaine (b. 1907)
Turner, Mary (d. 1918)
Ulanova, Galina (1910–1998)
Vashti (fl. 5th c. BCE)
Walentynowicz, Anna (1929—)
Whitman, Narcissa (1808–1847)
Xiang Jingyu (1895–1928)

POLITICAL REFORMER/ACTIVIST
Abaijah, Josephine (1942—)
Adam, Juliette la Messine (1836–1936)
Adivar, Halide Edib (c. 1884–1964)
Agnes, Lore (1876–1953)
Aitken, Jessie (1867–1934)
Ali, Aruna Asaf (c. 1909–1996)
Alvarado, Elvia (1938—)
Alvarez de Toledo, Luisa Isabel (1936—)
Ashley, Pauline (1932–2003)
Aston, Luise (1814–1871)
Auer, Judith (1905–1944)
Aung San Suu Kyi (1945—)
Avedon, Barbara Hammer (1930–1994)
Bailey, Hannah Johnston (1839–1923)
Bang, Nina (1866–1928)
Barnard, Kate (1875–1930)
Barns, Cornelia Baxter (1888–1941)
Barrington, Margaret (1896–1982)
Baumann, Edith (1909–1973)
Bellanca, Dorothy (1894–1946)
Besant, Annie (1847–1933)
Binkiene, Sofija (1902–1984)
Birchfield, Constance Alice (1898–1994)
Blackburn, Molly (c. 1931–1985)
Blair, Emily Newell (1877–1951)
Bogoraz, Larisa (c. 1930–2004)
Bohley, Bärbel (1945—)
Bonafini, Hebe de (1928—)
Bondfield, Margaret (1873–1953)
Bonner, Elena (1923—)
Boupacha, Djamila (1942—)
Brown, Elaine (1943—)
Brusselmans, Anne (c. 1905—)
Bryant, Sophie (1850–1922)
Burns, Violet Alberta Jessie (1893–1972)
Cano, María (1887–1967)
Carranza, María Mercedes (1945–2003)
Casanova, Danielle (1909–1943)
Cassie, Alice Mary (1887–1963)
Coignet, Clarisse (1823–?)
Cole, Margaret (1893–1980)
Cook, Freda Mary (1896–1990)
Corbin, Lucidor (fl. 18th c.)
Darton, Patience (1911–1996)
Davey, Constance (1882–1963)
Davidow, Ruth (1911–1999)
de Burgos, Julia (1914–1953)
Devanny, Jean (1894–1962)
Dimitrova, Blaga (1922—)
Dohrn, Bernardine (1942—)

Duby-Blom, Gertrude (1901–1993)
Duczynska, Ilona (1897–1978)
First, Ruth (1925–1982)
Fleming, Amalia (1912–1986)
Foster, J. Ellen (1840–1910)
Francois, Elma (1897–1944)
Gale, Zona (1874–1938)
Galeana, Benita (1904–1995)
Garmson, Aileen (c. 1861–1951)
Gasteazoro, Ana (1950–1993)
Gibbs, Pearl (1901–1983)
Gibson, Emily Patricia (1863/64?–1947)
Hamer, Fannie Lou (1917–1977)
Hobhouse, Violet (1864–1902)
Horne, Alice Merrill (1868–1948)
Hughan, Jessie (1875–1955)
Ibarra de Piedra, Rosario (1927—)
Inglis, Helen Clyde (1867–1945)
Jakubowska, Wanda (1907—)
Johnson, Georgia Douglas (1877–1966)
Johnson, Helene (1906–1995)
Joyner, Marjorie Stewart (1896–1994)
Kamal, Sufia (1911–1999)
Kaur, Rajkumari Amrit (1889–1964)
Kelly, Petra (1947–1992)
Kirchwey, Freda (1893–1976)
Kirkwood, Julieta (1936–1985)
Kishida Toshiko (1863–1901)
Kuhn, Maggie (1905–1995)
Kuliscioff, Anna (c. 1854–1925)
La Flesche, Susette (1854–1902)
Lampkin, Daisy (1883–1965)
Léo, André (1832–1900)
Lynn, Kathleen (1874–1955)
Manley, Effa (1900–1981)
Mannin, Ethel (1900–1984)
Martinson, Moa (1890–1964)
McCarthy, Mary Ann Recknall (1866–1933)
McCombs, Elizabeth Reid (1873–1935)
McMillan, Rachel (1859–1917)
Miller, Emma Guffey (1874–1970)
Miller, Olive Thorne (1831–1918)
Millett, Kate (1934—)
Modotti, Tina (1896–1942)
Moreau de Justo, Alicia (1885–1986)
Mugabe, Sally (1932–1992)
Olberg, Oda (1872–1955)
Olsen, Tillie (c. 1912—)
Pankhurst, Sylvia (1882–1960)
Paul, Alice (1885–1977)
Peri Rossi, Cristina (1941—)
Portal, Magda (1903–1989)
Prichard, Katharine Susannah (1883–1969)
Ramirez, Sara Estela (1881–1910)
Ramphele, Mamphela (1947—)
Rich, Adrienne (1929—)
Rodríguez, Ana (1938—)
Rodríguez de Tió, Lola (1843–1924)
Rukeyser, Muriel (1913–1980)
Russell, Lillian (1861–1922)
Sabin, Pauline Morton (1887–1955)
Santamaría, Haydée (1922–1980)
Shaarawi, Huda (1879–1947)
Sievwright, Margaret Home (1844–1905)
Smith, Abby (1797–1878)
Smith, Julia (1792–1886)
Smith, Mary Louise (1914–1997)
Snow, Sarah Ellen Oliver (1864–1939)
Soljak, Miriam Bridelia (1879–1971)
Starovoitova, Galina (1946–1998)
Stewart, Catherine Campbell (1881–1957)
Stopford Green, Alice (1847–1929)
Szwajger, Adina Blady (1917–1993)
Tabankin, Margery Ann (c. 1948—)
Todd, Marion Marsh (1841–post 1913)
Tula, María Teresa (1951—)
Vargas, Virginia (1945—)
Warner, Sylvia Townsend (1893–1978)
Weil, Simone (1909–1943)
Weinstein, Hannah (1911–1984)
Wilkinson, Ellen (1891–1947)
Winters, Shelley (1920–2005)
Wunderlich, Frieda (1884–1965)
Yard, Molly (1912–2005)

POLITICAL SCIENTIST/STRATEGIST/ THEORIST

Abbott, Grace (1878–1939)
Akselrod, Liubo (1868–1946)
Allen, Florence Ellinwood (1884–1966)
Anderson, Evelyn N. (1909–1977)
Arendt, Hannah (1906–1975)
Bauer, Helene (1871–1942)
Beard, Mary Ritter (1876–1958)
Beere, Thekla (1901–1991)
Breckinridge, Sophonisba Preston (1866–1948)
Church, Marguerite Stitt (1892–1990)
Clodia (c. 94–post 45 BCE)
de Cleyre, Voltairine (1866–1912)
Dulles, Eleanor Lansing (1895–1996)
Dyachenko, Tatyana (1960—)
Fabian, Dora (1901–1935)
Keohane, Nannerl (1940—)
Kirkpatrick, Jeane (1926—)
Luxemburg, Rosa (1870–1919)
Mann, Elisabeth (1918–2002)
Marx, Jenny von Westphalen (1814–1881)
Miller, Frieda S. (1889–1973)
Nur Jahan (1577–1645)
Pankhurst, Emmeline (1858–1928)
Ranavalona I of Madagascar (1792–1861)
Richards, Audrey Isabel (1899–1984)
Smeal, Eleanor (1939—)
Thorne, Florence (1877–1973)
Wambaugh, Sarah (1882–1955)

POLITICAL TERRORIST

Amrane, Djamila (1939—)
Boudin, Kathy (1943—)
Bouhired, Djamila (1937—)
Chesimard, Joanne (1948—)
Corday, Charlotte (1768–1793)
Figner, Vera (1852–1942)
Ivanovskaia, Praskovia (1853–1935)
Lebron, Lolita (1919—)
Meinhof, Ulrike (1934–1972)
Oughton, Diana (1942–1970)
Pankhurst, Emmeline (1858–1928)
Perovskaya, Sonia (1853–1881)
Saxe, Susan (1947—)
Schaft, Hannie (1920–1945)
Sikakane, Joyce Nomafa (1943—)
Spiridonova, Maria (1884–1941)
Zasulich, Vera (1849–1919)

POLITICIAN

Abbott, Diane (1953—)
Abel, Hazel (1888–1966)
Abzug, Bella (1920–1998)
Acheson, Carrie (1934—)
Adams, Irene (1947—)
Agnelli, Susanna (1922—)
Agnes of Courtenay (1136–1186)
Ahearn, Theresa (1951–2000)
Ahern, Catherine Ita (1915—)
Ahern, Nuala (1949—)
Ainardi, Sylviane H. (1947—)
Akers, Dolly Smith (1901–1986)
Alexander, Wendy
Allen, Florence Ellinwood (1884–1966)
Allen, Maryon (1925—)
Allfrey, Phyllis Shand (1915–1986)
Almeida Garrett, Teresa (1953—)
Aloni, Shulamit (1931—)
Amathila, Libertine Appolus (1940—)
Anderson, Janet (1949—)
Andrews, Elizabeth Bullock (1911–2002)
Angelilli, Roberta (1965—)
Angelopoulos-Daskalaki, Gianna (1955—)
Anselmi, Tina (1927—)
Aquino, Corazon (1933—)
Armitage, Pauline
Armstrong, Anne L. (1927—)
Armstrong, Hilary (1945—)
Arol, Victoria Yar (1948—)
Artyukhina, Aleksandra (1889–1969)
Ashbrook, Jean (1934—)
Astor, Nancy Witcher (1879–1964)
Atherton, Candy (1955—)
Atkins, Charlotte (1950—)
Attwood, Julie Maree (1957—)
Attwooll, Elspeth (1943—)
Auer, Johanna (1950—)
Augustat, Elise (1889–1940)
Auroi, Danielle (1944—)
Austin, Margaret (1933—)
Avilés Perea, María Antonia
Ayuso González, María del Pilar (1942—)
Baard, Francina (1901–1997)
Baillie, Jackie (1964—)
Baird, Vera (1951—)
Baker, Irene Bailey (1901–1994)
Ballinger, Margaret (1894–1980)
Bandaranaike, Sirimavo (1916–2000)
Bang, Nina (1866–1928)
Banotti, Mary (1939—)
Bañuelos, Romana Acosta (1925—)
Barbara, Agatha (1923–2002)
Barnes, Monica (1936—)
Barry, Bonny (1960—)
Barry, Myra (1957—)
Bashir, Marie (1930—)
Basten, Alice (1876–1955)
Bastos, Regina (1960—)
Batchelor, Mary (1927—)
Bäumer, Gertrud (1873–1954)
Bayer, Johanna (1915–2000)
Beck, Audrey P. (1931–1983)
Beckett, Margaret (1943—)
Begg, Anne (1955—)
Belishova, Liri (1923—)
Bell, Eileen (1943—)
Bennedsen, Dorte (1938—)
Bennett, Olga (1947—)
Bentley, Helen Delich (1923—)
Berès, Pervenche (1957—)
Berger, Maria (1956—)
Besant, Annie (1847–1933)
Betancourt, Ingrid (1961—)
Bhreathnach, Naimh (1945—)
Bhutto, Benazir (1953—)
Bird, Lorraine
Biryukova, Alexandra (1929—)
Bjerregaard, Ritt (1941—)
Black, Helen McKenzie (1896–1963)
Black, Martha Louise (1866–1957)
Blackburn, Doris Amelia (1889–1970)
Blackman, Liz (1949—)
Blackstone, Tessa (1942—)
Blanco, Kathleen (1942—)
Blears, Hazel Anne (1956—)
Bligh, Anna Maria
Blitch, Iris Faircloth (1912–1993)
Boggs, Lindy (1916—)
Boland, Veronica Grace (1899–1982)
Bolger, Deirdre (1938—)
Bollmann, Minna (1876–1935)
Bolton, Frances Payne (1885–1977)

Bondfield, Margaret (1873–1953)
Bonino, Emma (1948—)
Bono, Mary (1961—)
Boogerd-Quaak, Johanna L.A. (1944—)
Boothroyd, Betty (1929—)
Bordes, Armonia (1945—)
Borst-Eilers, Els (1932—)
Bosone, Reva Beck (1895–1983)
Bottomley, Virginia (1948—)
Boudjenah, Yasmine (1970—)
Boumediene-Thiery, Alima (1956—)
Bowring, Eva Kelly (1892–1985)
Boxer, Barbara (1940—)
Boyack, Sarah (1961—)
Boyle, Desley (1948—)
Braddock, Bessie (1899–1970)
Brankin, Rhona
Braun, Carol Mosely (1947—)
Breyer, Hiltrud (1957—)
Brooke, Annette (1947—)
Brown, Dorothy L. (1919–2004)
Brown, Rosemary (1930—)
Brownbill, Kay
Browne, Kathleen Anne (b. 1878)
Browner, Carol M. (1956—)
Browning, Angela (1946—)
Brugha, Caitlin (1879–1959)
Bruntland, Gro Harlem (1939—)
Buchanan, Vera Daerr (1902–1955)
Buck, Karen (1958—)
Buitenweg, Kathalijne Maria (1970—)
Bulbulia, Katharine (1943—)
Burford, Anne Gorsuch (1942–2004)
Burke, Joan T. (1929—)
Burke, Yvonne Brathwaite (1932—)
Burnham, Viola (1930–2003)
Burton, Joan (1949—)
Burton, Sala (1925–1987)
Bush, Dorothy V. (1916–1991)
Bushfield, Vera Cahalan (1889–1976)
Butler, Eleanor (c. 1915–1997)
Butler, Helen May (1867–1957)
Buttfield, Nancy (1912—)
Byrne, Jane (1934—)
Byron, Beverly Butcher (1932—)
Byron, Katharine Edgar (1903–1976)
Calderón, Sila M. (1942—)
Calton, Patsy (1948–2005)
Calvert, Lilian (1909–2000)
Campbell, Anne (1940—)
Campoamor, Clara (1888–1972)
Canfield, Ella Jean (1918—)
Capps, Lois (1938—)
Caraway, Hattie Wyatt (1878–1950)
Cardell-Oliver, Florence (1876–1965)
Carlotti, Marie-Arlette (1952—)
Carrilho, Maria (1943—)
Carson, Joan (1935—)
Carson, Julia (1938—)
Casgrain, Thérèse (1896–1981)
Cassidy, Eileen (1932–1995)
Castle, Barbara (1910–2002)
Caullery, Isabelle (1955—)
Cauquil, Chantal (1949—)
Ceausescu, Elena (1916–1989)
Cederschiöld, Charlotte (1944—)
Cerdeira Morterero, Carmen (1958—)
Chalker, Lynda (1942—)
Chamorro, Violeta (1929—)
Champagne, Andrée (1939—)
Chapman, Yvonne (1940—)
Charles, Eugenia (1919—)
Chattopadhyaya, Kamaladevi (1903–1988)
Chen Muhua (c. 1940—)
Chenoweth, Helen (1938—)
Chiepe, Gaositwe (c. 1924—)
Child, Joan (1921—)
Chirwa, Vera (1933—)
Chisholm, Shirley (1924–2005)
Choy, Elizabeth (b. 1910)
Church, Marguerite Stitt (1892–1990)
Cicciolina (1951—)
Çiller, Tansu (1946—)
Clark, Helen (1954—)
Clark, Helen Elizabeth (1950—)
Clark, Lesley Ann (1948—)
Clark, Liddy (1953—)
Clark, Lynda (1949—)
Clayton, Eva M. (1934—)
Clinton, Hillary Rodham (1947—)
Clune, Deirdre (1959—)
Clwyd, Ann (1937—)
Coffey, Ann (1946—)
Colley, Anne (1951—)
Collins, Anne (1951—)
Collins, Barbara-Rose (1939—)
Collins, Cardiss (1931—)
Collins, Martha Layne (1936—)
Collins-O'Driscoll, Margaret (1878–1945)
Conn, Shena
Connolly-O'Brien, Nora (1893–1981)
Cooper, Jessie (1914–1993)
Cooper, Yvette (1969—)
Cooper-Flynn, Beverley (1966—)
Copps, Sheila (1952—)
Corbett-Ashby, Margery (1882–1981)
Corbey, Dorette (1957—)
Cormier, Lucia M. (1909–1993)
Corston, Jean (1942—)
Cosgrave, Niamh (1964—)
Costello, Eileen (1870–1962)
Couchman, Elizabeth (1876–1982)
Coughlan, Mary (1965—)
Coulter, Jean
Cournoyea, Nellie J. (1940—)
Courtney, Annie
Cowan, Edith (1861–1932)
Cox, Margaret (1963—)
Craig, Minnie D. (1883–1965)
Craigie, Cathie (1954—)
Cresson, Edith (1934—)
Croft, Peta-Kaye (1972—)
Crowley, Honor Mary (1903–1966)
Crowley, Rosemary (1938—)
Cryer, Ann (1939—)
Cunningham, Elizabeth Anne
Cunningham, Minnie Fisher (1882–1964)
Cunningham, Roseanna (1951—)
Curran, Margaret (c. 1962—)
Currie, Edwina (1946—)
Curtis-Thomas, Claire (1958—)
Dalziel, Lianne (1960—)
Damião, Elisa Maria (1946—)
Daniels, Martha Catalina (d. 2002)
Darras, Danielle (1943—)
da Silva, Benedita (1942—)
Davey, Valerie (1940—)
Davidson, Mary Frances (1902–1986)
Davies, Sonja (1923–2005)
Deacon, Susan
Dean, Janet (1949—)
de Brún, Bairbre (1954—)
Degutiene, Irena (1949—)
De Keyser, Véronique (1945—)
DeLauro, Rosa L. (1943—)
Denton, Jean (1935–2001)
De Sarnez, Marielle (1951—)
Descamps, Marie-Hélène (1938—)
Desmond, Eileen (1932—)
de Valera, Sile (1954—)
De Veyrac, Christine (1959—)
de Veyrinas, Françoise (1943—)
Dewe, Colleen (1930–1993)
Dewson, Molly (1874–1962)
Dickson, Anne (1928—)
Díez González, Rosa M. (1952—)
Diggs, Annie LePorte (1848–1916)
Dimitrova, Blaga (1922—)
Diogo, Luisa (1958—)
Doi, Takako (1928—)
Dole, Elizabeth Hanford (1936—)
Domitien, Elisabeth (1926—)
Donaldson, Mary (1921–2003)
Donaldson, Viva (1893–1970)
Doughty, Sue (1948—)
Douglas, Emily Taft (1899–1994)
Douglas, Helen Gahagan (1900–1980)
Dowdall, Jane (1899–1974)
Doyle, Avril (1949—)
Dreaver, Mary (1887–1964)
Dreifuss, Ruth (1940—)
Driscoll, Clara (1881–1945)
Drown, Julia (1962—)
Dührkop Dührkop, Bárbara (1945—)
Dunwoody, Gwyneth (1930—)
Dwyer, Florence Price (1902–1976)
Dybkjaer, Lone (1940—)
Eadie, Helen
Eagle, Angela (1961—)
Eagle, Maria (1961—)
Ebtekar, Massoumeh (1960—)
Echerer, Raina A. Mercedes (1963—)
Edmond, Wendy (1946—)
Elder, Dorothy-Grace
Ellman, Louise (1945—)
English, Ada (c. 1878–1944)
Eriksson, Marianne (1952—)
Este, Beatrice d' (1475–1497)
Este, Isabella d' (1474–1539)
Evans, Jillian (1959—)
Ewing, Annabelle (1960—)
Ewing, Margaret (1945–2006)
Ewing, Winnie (1929—)
Fabiani, Linda (1956—)
Fairbairn, Joyce (1939—)
Falkender, Marcia (1932—)
Farrell, Peggy (1920—)
Fauset, Crystal Bird (1893–1965)
Feinstein, Dianne (1933—)
Felton, Rebecca Latimer (1835–1930)
Fennell, Nuala (1935—)
Fenwick, Millicent (1910–1992)
Ferguson, Miriam A. (1875–1961)
Ferguson, Patricia (1958—)
Fergusson, Muriel McQueen (1899–1997)
Ferraro, Geraldine (1935—)
Ferreira, Anne (1961—)
Ferrer, Concepció (1938—)
Fiebiger, Christel (1946—)
Fiedler, Bobbi (1937—)
Figueiredo, Ilda (1948—)
Finnbogadóttir, Vigdís (1930—)
Finney, Joan (1925–2001)
First, Ruth (1925–1982)
FitzGerald, Eithne (1950—)
Fitzgerald, Frances (1950—)
Fitzsimons, Lorna (1967—)
Flaherty, Mary (1953—)
Flautre, Hélène (1958—)
Flemming, Marialiese (1933—)
Flesch, Colette (1937—)
Fletcher, Chris (1955—)
Flint, Caroline (1961—)
Follett, Barbara (1942—)
Follett, Rosemary (1948—)
Ford, Patricia (1921—)
Foster, Jacqueline (1947—)
Fourtou, Janelly (1939—)

Fowler, Tillie (1942–2005)
Fox, Mildred (1971—)
Frahm, Pernille (1954—)
Fraisse, Geneviève (1948—)
Franklin, Shirley (1945—)
Frassoni, Monica (1963—)
Frazier, Maude (1881–1963)
Furtseva, Ekaterina (1910–1974)
Galgóczi, Erzsébet (1930–1989)
Gallagher, Ann (1967—)
Galvin, Sheila (1914–1983)
Gamin, Judith (1930—)
Gandhi, Indira (1917–1984)
Gandhi, Sonia (1946—)
Garaud, Marie-Françoise (1934—)
García-Orcoyen Tormo, Cristina (1948—)
Gebhardt, Evelyne (1954—)
Geoghegan-Quinn, Máire (1950—)
Ghilardotti, Fiorella (1946—)
Gidley, Sandra (1957—)
Gildernew, Michelle (1970—)
Gill, Neena (1956—)
Gill, Zillah Smith (1859–1937)
Gillan, Cheryl (1952—)
Gillig, Marie-Hélène (1946—)
Gillon, Karen (1967—)
Gilmer, Elizabeth May (1880–1960)
Gilroy, Linda (1949—)
Glase, Anne-Karin (1954—)
Glenn, Alice (1927—)
Godman, Trish (1939—)
Goldie, Annabel (1950—)
González Álvarez, Laura (1941—)
Gordimer, Nadine (1923—)
Gordon, Jean (1918—)
Goulding, Valerie (1918–2003)
Grahame, Christine (1944—)
Grant, Rhoda (1963—)
Grasso, Ella (1919–1981)
Gredal, Eva (1927–1995)
Green, Edith Starrett (1910–1987)
Greenway, Isabella Selmes (1886–1953)
Greeves, Marion Janet (1894–1979)
Griffiths, Jane (1954—)
Griffiths, Martha Wright (1912–2003)
Grigg, Mary (1897–1971)
Groener, Lissy (1954—)
Groes, Lis (1910–1074)
Grönfeldt Bergman, Lisbeth (1948—)
Grossetête, Françoise (1946—)
Groza, Maria (1918—)
Gueiler Tejada, Lydia (1921—)
Gutiérrez-Cortines, Cristina (1939—)
Gutteridge, Helena Rose (1879–1960)
Guy-Quint, Catherine (1949—)
Haines, Janine (1945–2004)
Hall, Katie Beatrice (1938—)
Halonen, Tarja (1943—)
Hamilton, Mary (1882–1966)
Hanafin, Mary (1959—)
Hanna, Carmel (1946—)
Hannon, Camilla (1936—)
Hansen, Julia Butler (1907–1988)
Hansteen, Kirsten (1903–1974)
Harden, Cecil Murray (1894–1984)
Harman, Harriet (1950—)
Harney, Mary (1953—)
Harriman, Pamela (1920–1997)
Hart, Judith (1924—)
Harvey, Leisha (1947—)
Harvie Anderson, Betty (1913–1979)
Haselbach, Anna Elisabeth (1942—)
Hashemi, Faezeh (1963—)
Hashimi, Aquila al- (1953–2003)
Hasler, Marie (1945—)
Haug, Jutta D. (1951—)
Hautala, Heidi Anneli (1955—)
Hawkins, Paula Fickes (1927—)
Hayden, Mary (1862–1942)
Hazan, Adeline (1956—)
Head, Bessie (1937–1986)
Heal, Sylvia (1942—)
Heckler, Margaret M. (1931—)
Hederman, Carmencita (1939—)
Hedkvist Petersen, Ewa (1952—)
Henry, Mary E.F. (1940—)
Hercus, Ann (1942—)
Hermange, Marie-Thérèse (1947—)
Hermon, Sylvia (1955—)
Herranz García, Maria Esther (1969—)
Hewitt, Patricia (1948—)
Hickey, Eileen (1886–1960)
Hicks, Louise Day (1916–2003)
Hicks, Louise Day (1923—)
Hieden-Sommer, Helga (1934—)
Hieronymi, Ruth (1947—)
Hodge, Margaret (1944—)
Hoey, Kate (1946—)
Hoff, Magdalene (1940—)
Hogan, Brigid (1932—)
Hogg, Sarah (1946—)
Holt, Marjorie Sewell (1920—)
Holtzman, Elizabeth (1941—)
Honan, Cathy (1951—)
Honan, Tras (1930—)
Honeyball, Mary (1952—)
Honeyman, Nan Wood (1881–1970)
Horne, Alice Merrill (1868–1948)
Horsbrugh, Florence (1889–1969)
Howard, Mabel (1893–1972)
Hoxha, Nexhmije (1920—)
Huck, Winnifred Sprague Mason (1882–1936)
Hughes, Beverley (1950—)
Hughes, Janis (1958—)
Hughes, Sarah T. (1896–1985)
Humble, Joan (1951—)
Humphrey, Muriel (1912–1998)
Hussey, Gemma (1938—)
Hutchison, Kay Bailey (1943—)
Hyslop, Fiona (1964—)
Ichikawa, Fusae (1893–1981)
Ickes, Anna Thompson (1873–1935)
Iivari, Ulpu (1948—)
Inman, Florence (1890–1986)
Inyama, Rosemary (b. 1903)
Iotti, Nilde (1920–1999)
Isler Béguin, Marie Anne (1956—)
Izquierdo Rojo, Maria (1946—)
Jaatteenmaki, Anneli (1955—)
Jackman, Mary (1943—)
Jackson, Caroline F. (1946—)
Jackson, Glenda (1936—)
Jackson, Helen (1939—)
Jackson, Sylvia (c. 1951—)
Jagan, Janet (1920—)
Jakobsdóttir, Svava (1930—)
Jamieson, Cathy (1956—)
Jamieson, Margaret (1953—)
Jarratt, Jan (1958—)
Jeggle, Elisabeth (1947—)
Jelicich, Dorothy (1928—)
Jenckes, Virginia Ellis (1877–1975)
Jensen, Anne Elisabet (1951—)
Jiang Qing (1914–1991)
Jingū (c. 201–269)
Jinnah, Fatima (1893–1967)
Joens, Karin (1953—)
Johnson, Melanie (1955—)
Johnson, Nancy (1935—)
Johnston, Rita Margaret (1935—)
Jones, Helen (1954—)
Jones, Lynne (1951—)
Jordan, Barbara (1936–1996)
Jordan, Vi (d. 1982)
Jowell, Tessa (1947—)
Junker, Karin (1940—)
Kahn, Florence Prag (1866–1948)
Kaptur, Marcy (1946—)
Karamanou, Anna (1947—)
Kassebaum, Nancy Landon (1932—)
Katznelson-Shazar, Rachel (1888–1975)
Kaufmann, Sylvia-Yvonne (1955—)
Kauppi, Piia-Noora (1975—)
Kawaguchi, Yoriko (1941—)
Keall, Judy (1942—)
Kearney, Miriam (1959—)
Kearns-MacWhinney, Linda (1888–1951)
Keaveney, Cecilia (1968—)
Kee, Elizabeth (1895–1975)
Keeble, Sally (1951—)
Keech, Margaret Majella
Keen, Ann (1948—)
Kéita, Aoua (1912–1979)
Kelley, Florence (1859–1932)
Kelly, Edna Flannery (1906–1997)
Kelly, Mary (1952—)
Kelly, Petra (1947–1992)
Kelly, Ruth (1968—)
Kempe, Margery (c. 1373–after 1438)
Kempfer, Hannah Jensen (1880–1943)
Kennedy, Geraldine (1951—)
Kennedy, Jane (1958—)
Kennedy, Margaret L. (b. 1892)
Kennelly, Barbara (1936—)
Kent, Victoria (1898–1987)
Kenyatta, Margaret (1928—)
Keogh, Helen (1951—)
Keppelhoff-Wiechert, Hedwig (1939—)
Kernohan, Liz (1939–2004)
Kessler, Margot (1948—)
Keys, Martha Elizabeth (1930—)
King, Annette (1947—)
King, Oona (1967—)
Kinigi, Sylvie (1953—)
Kinnock, Glenys (1944—)
Kippin, Vicky (1942—)
Kirk, Jenny (1945—)
Kirkbride, Julie (1960—)
Kirkland-Casgrain, Marie-Claire (1924—)
Kirner, Joan (1938—)
Klamt, Ewa (1950—)
Klass, Christa (1951—)
Knutson, Coya Gjesdal (1912–1996)
Kolstad, Eva (1918–1998)
Korhola, Eija-Riitta Anneli (1959—)
Kratsa-Tsagaropoulou, Rodi (1953—)
Krehl, Constanze Angela (1956—)
Kripalani, Sucheta (1908–1974)
Kryszak, Mary Olszewski (1875–1945)
Kumaratunga, Chandrika Bandaranaike (1945—)
Kunin, Madeleine (1933—)
Kuntz, Florence (1969—)
Kyburz, Rosemary (1944—)
Lagorio, Gina (1930—)
Laguiller, Arlette (1940—)
Laing, Eleanor (1958—)
Lait, Jacqui (1947—)
Lalumiere, Catherine (1935—)
Lambert, Jean (1950—)
Lamont, Johann (1957—)
Landes, Bertha Knight (1868–1943)
Langenhagen, Brigitte (1939—)
Langley, Katherine (1888–1948)
Laughlin, Gail (1868–1952)
Laurien, Hanna-Renate (1928—)

Occupational Index

Lauristin, Marju (1940—)
Lavarch, Linda (1958—)
Lawlor, Patsy (1933–1998)
Lawrence, Carmen Mary (1948—)
Lawrence, Jackie (1948—)
Lawrence, Susan (1871–1947)
Lease, Mary Elizabeth (1853–1933)
Lee, Barbara (1946—)
Lee, Jennie (1904–1988)
Lee Long, Rosa
Lehmann, Rosamond (1901–1990)
Lemass, Eileen (1932—)
Lewsley, Patricia (1957—)
Liddell, Helen (1950—)
Lind, Nathalie (1918–1999)
Lindh, Anna (1957–2003)
Lingle, Linda (1953—)
Livingstone, Marilyn (1952—)
Lloyd, Marilyn Laird (1929—)
Lloyd George, Megan (1902–1966)
Long, Catherine Small (1924—)
Long, Jill Lynette (1952—)
Longman, Irene Maud (1877–1964)
Lowey, Nita M. (1937—)
Lucas, Caroline (1960—)
Luce, Clare Boothe (1903–1987)
Lüders, Marie-Elizabeth (1888–1966)
Ludford, Sarah (1951—)
Lulling, Astrid (1929—)
Lusk, Georgia Lee (1893–1971)
Lynch, Celia (1908–1989)
Lynch, Kathleen (1953—)
Lynne, Elizabeth (1948—)
Lyons, Enid (1897–1981)
Maathai, Wangari (1940—)
MacDonald, Margo (c. 1948—)
Maclean, Kate (1958—)
Macmillan, Maureen (1943—)
Maconachie, Bessie
Macphail, Agnes (1890–1954)
MacSwiney, Mary (1872–1942)
Mactaggart, Fiona (1953—)
Maes, Nelly (1941—)
Mahon, Alice (1937—)
Maihi, Rehutai (1895–1967)
Maij-Weggen, Hanja (1943—)
Male, Carolyn Therese (1966—)
Mallaber, Judy (1951—)
Malliori, Minerva Melpomeni (1952—)
Malmström, Cecilia (1968—)
Malone, Bernie (1948—)
Mankin, Helen Douglas (1894–1956)
Mann, Erika (1950—)
Manning, Leah (1886–1977)
Marcos, Imelda (1929—)
Margaret of Attenduli (1375–?)
Marin, Gladys (1941–2005)
Martens, Maria (1955—)
Martin, Lynn (1939—)
Marwick, Tricia (1953—)
Marx, Susan Fleming (1908–2002)
Mathieu, Véronique (1955—)
May, Catherine Dean (1914–2004)
May, Theresa (1956—)
Mayawati (1956—)
Mbogo, Jael (1939—)
McAleese, Mary (1951—)
McAliskey, Bernadette Devlin (1947—)
McAliskey, Roisin (1971—)
McAuliffe-Ennis, Helena (1951—)
McAvan, Linda (1962—)
McCafferty, Chris (1945—)
McCarthy, Arlene (1960—)
McCarthy, Carolyn (1944—)
McCarthy, Kathryn O'Loughlin (1894–1952)
McCauley, Diane (1946—)
McClung, Nellie L. (1873–1951)
McCombs, Elizabeth Reid (1873–1935)
McCormick, Ruth Hanna (1880–1944)
McDonagh, Siobhain (1960—)
McGennis, Marian (1953—)
McGugan, Irene (1952—)
McGuinness, Catherine (1934—)
McGuire, Anne (1949—)
McIntosh, Anne (1954—)
McIntosh, Gail (1955—)
McIntosh, Lyndsay (1955—)
McIsaac, Shona (1960—)
McKechin, Ann (1961—)
McKenna, Patricia (1957—)
McKenna, Rosemary (1941—)
McKinney, Cynthia (1955—)
McKinney, Louise (1868–1931)
McLauchlan, Joy (1948—)
McLaughlin, Audrey (1936—)
McLaughlin, Florence (1916—)
McLeod, Fiona (1957—)
McManus, Liz (1947—)
McMillan, Clara Gooding (1894–1976)
McMillan, Ethel (1904–1987)
McMordie, Julia (1860–1942)
McNabb, Dinah
McNally, Eryl Margaret (1942—)
McNeill, Pauline (c. 1967—)
McVicar, Annie (1862–1954)
McWilliams, Monica (1954—)
Mehta, Hansa (1897–1995)
Meir, Golda (1898–1978)
Melville, Eliza Ellen (1882–1946)
Mercouri, Melina (1923–1994)
Merkel, Angela (1954—)
Merron, Gillian (1959—)
Meyers, Jan (1928—)
Meyner, Helen Stevenson (1929–1997)
Miegel, Agnes (1879–1964)
Miguélez Ramos, Rosa (1953—)
Mikulski, Barbara (1936—)
Miller, Jo-Ann (1958—)
Mink, Patsy (1927—)
Minner, Ruth Ann (1935—)
Mitchell, Hannah (1871–1956)
Mitchell, Olivia (1947—)
Mntwana, Ida (1903–1960)
Moffatt, Laura (1954—)
Mofford, Rose (1922—)
Moir, Margaret (1941—)
Molinari, Susan (1958—)
Molloy, Cate (1955—)
Mongella, Gertrude (1945—)
Montfort, Elizabeth (1954—)
Mooney, Mary (1958—)
Mora, Constancia de la (1906–1950)
Moran, Margaret (1955—)
Morella, Constance A. (1931—)
Morgan, Eluned (1967—)
Morgan, Julie (1944—)
Morgantini, Luisa (1940—)
Morrice, Jane (1954—)
Morris, Estelle (1952—)
Moscoso, Mireya (1946—)
Motley, Constance Baker (1921–2005)
Mountbatten, Edwina Ashley (1901–1960)
Mountford, Kali (1954—)
Mowlam, Mo (1949–2005)
Moynihan-Cronin, Breeda (1953—)
Müller, Emilia Franziska (1951—)
Müller, Rosemarie (1949—)
Mulligan, Mary (1960—)
Munn, Meg (1959—)
Murnaghan, Sheelagh (1924–1993)
Murray, Elaine (1954—)
Murray, Patty (1950—)
Muscardini, Cristiana (1948—)
Mussolini, Alessandra (1962—)
Myller, Riita (1956—)
Naidu, Sarojini (1879–1949)
Nakatindi, Princess (c. 1943—)
Napoletano, Pasqualina (1949—)
Nelis, Mary (1935—)
Nelken, Margarita (1896–1968)
Nelson, Beryce Ann (1947—)
Nelson-Carr, Lindy (1952—)
Neuberger, Maurine B. (1906–2000)
Neville-Jones, Pauline (1939—)
Ngoyi, Lilian (1911–1980)
Nhiwatiwa, Naomi (1940—)
Nicholson, Emma (1941—)
Niebler, Angelika (1963—)
Nolan, Mae Ella (1886–1973)
Nolan, Rachel (1974—)
Norrell, Catherine Dorris (1901–1981)
Norton, Eleanor Holmes (1937—)
Norton, Mary T. (1875–1959)
Nyembe, Dorothy (1930–1998)
Oakar, Mary Rose (1940—)
O'Callaghan, Kathleen (1888–1961)
O'Carroll, Maureen (1913–1984)
Ochoa, Elisa
O'Connor, Ellen (1857–1933)
O'Connor, Kathleen (1935—)
O'Connor, Sandra Day (1930—)
O'Day, Caroline (1869–1943)
Odhnoff, Camilla (1923—)
O'Donnell, Liz (1956—)
Ogot, Grace (1930—)
O'Hagan, Dara (1964—)
Oldfather, Irene (1954—)
Oldfield, Pearl Peden (1876–1962)
O'Meara, Kathleen (1960—)
Onyango, Grace (1934—)
Oomen-Ruijten, Ria G.H.C. (1950—)
O'Regan, Katherine (1946—)
Organ, Diana (1952—)
O'Rourke, Mary (1937—)
Orr, Kay (1939—)
Osborne, Sandra (1956—)
O'Sullivan, Jan (1950—)
O'Toole, Barbara (1960—)
Owen, Nora (1945—)
Owens, Evelyn P. (1931—)
Pacari, Nina (1961—)
Paciotti, Elena Ornella (1941—)
Pack, Doris (1942—)
Page, Dorothy G. (d. 1989)
Paisley, Eileen (1934—)
Pandit, Vijaya Lakshmi (1900–1990)
Papariga, Alexandra (1945—)
Parek, Lagle (1941—)
Parker, Dehra (1882–1963)
Parlby, Irene (1868–1965)
Pascal-Trouillot, Ertha (1943—)
Patrie, Béatrice (1957—)
Patterson, Elizabeth J. (1939—)
Paulsen, Marit (1939—)
Pearse, Margaret (1857–1932)
Pearse, Margaret Mary (1878–1968)
Pearson, Landon Carter (1930—)
Peattie, Cathy (c. 1956—)
Pedersen, Helga (1911–1980)
Pedersen, Lena (1940—)
Peijs, Karla M.H. (1944—)
Pelosi, Nancy (1940—)
Perham, Linda (1947—)
Perkins, Frances (1880–1965)
Perón, Isabel (1931—)
Perry, Ruth (1939—)
Petersen, Alicia O'Shea (1862–1923)
Pettis, Shirley Neil (1924—)

Pfost, Gracie (1906–1965)
Phillips, Anita Frances
Picking, Anne (1958—)
Pienkowska, Alina (1952–2002)
Pike, Mervyn (1918–2004)
Pinchot, Cornelia (1881–1960)
Pintasilgo, Maria de Lurdes (1930–2004)
Plaminkova, Frantiska (1875–1942)
Planinc, Milka (1924—)
Plavsic, Biljana (1930—)
Plooij-Van Gorsel, Elly (1947—)
Poinso-Chapuis, Germaine (1901–1981)
Poli Bortone, Adriana (1943—)
Porter, Gladys M. (1894–1967)
Power, Laurel Jean (1953—)
Powers, Georgia Davis (1923—)
Pratt, Dolly (1955—)
Pratt, Eliza Jane (1902–1981)
Pratt, Ruth (1877–1965)
Prentice, Bridget (1952—)
Prets, Christa (1947—)
Price, Roberta MacAdams (1881–1959)
Primarolo, Dawn (1954—)
Prokop, Liese (1941—)
Prunskiene, Kazimiera (1943—)
Pühringer, Uta Barbara (1943—)
Qian Zhengying (1923—)
Questiaux, Nicole (1931—)
Quill, Máirin (1940—)
Quin, Joyce (1944—)
Quisthoudt-Rowohl, Godelieve (1947—)
Radcliffe, Nora (1946—)
Ramey, Venus (c. 1925—)
Ramsey, Sue (1970—)
Ramsland, Sarah Katherine (1882–1964)
Randzio-Plath, Christa (1940—)
Rankin, Annabelle (1908–1986)
Rankin, Jeannette (1880–1973)
Raschhofer, Daniela (1960—)
Ratana, Iriaka (1905–1981)
Rāteb, Aisha (1928—)
Rathbone, Eleanor (1872–1946)
Read, Imelda Mary (1939—)
Redmond, Bridget Mary (1905–1952)
Redondo Jiménez, Encarnación (1944—)
Reece, Louise Goff (1898–1970)
Rehn, Elisabeth (1935—)
Rehor, Grete (1910–1987)
Reid, Charlotte Thompson (b. 1913)
Reid, Margaret (1935—)
Reilly, Dianne (1969—)
Renger, Annemarie (1919—)
Reynolds, Mary (c. 1890–1974)
Rice, Bridget Mary (1885–1967)
Rice, Condoleezza (1954—)
Richards, Ann Willis (1933—)
Richardson, Ruth (1950—)
Ridge, Therese (1941—)
Ridruejo, Mónica (1963—)
Ries, Frédérique (1959—)
Riis-Jorgensen, Karin (1952—)
Riley, Corinne Boyd (1893–1979)
Roberts, Elisa Mary (1970—)
Robertson, Alice Mary (1854–1931)
Robertson, Brenda May (1929—)
Robinson, Iris (1949—)
Robinson, Mary (1944—)
Robison, Shona (1966—)
Roche, Barbara (1954—)
Rodgers, Brid (1935—)
Rodríguez Ramos, María (1963—)
Roe, Marion (1936—)
Rogers, Edith MacTavish (1876–1947)
Rogers, Edith Nourse (1881–1960)
Rohde, Ruth Bryan Owen (1885–1954)
Rose, Merri (1955—)
Ros-Lehtinen, Ileana (1952—)
Ross, Hilda (1883–1959)
Ross, Nellie Tayloe (1876–1977)
Roth-Behrendt, Dagmar (1953—)
Rothe, Mechtild (1947—)
Roudy, Yvette (1929—)
Roukema, Margaret (1929—)
Roure, Martine (1948—)
Ruddock, Joan (1943—)
Rudel-Zeynek, Olga (1871–1948)
Rühle, Heide (1948—)
Russell, Christine (1945—)
Ryan, Joan (1955—)
Ryan, Mary Bridget (1898–1981)
Sáez, Irene (1961—)
Saiki, Patricia Fukuda (1930—)
Sanchez, Linda T. (1969—)
Sanchez, Loretta (1960—)
Sandbaek, Ulla Margrethe (1943—)
Sandberg-Fries, Yvonne (1950—)
Sanders-Ten Holte, Maria Johanna (1941—)
Santamaría, Haydée (1922–1980)
Santolalla, Irene Silva de (1902–1992)
Sartori, Amalia (1947—)
Sauquillo Pérez Del Arco, Francisca (1943—)
Sauvé, Jeanne (1922–1993)
Sbarbati, Luciana (1946—)
Scallon, Dana Rosemary (1950—)
Scanlon, Mary (1947—)
Schaffner, Anne-Marie (1945—)
Scheele, Karin (1968—)
Schenk, Lynn (1945—)
Schierhuber, Agnes (1946—)
Schleicher, Ursula (1933—)
Schneider, Claudine (1947—)
Schörling, Inger (1946—)
Schreiber, Adele (1872–1957)
Schroeder, Ilka (1978—)
Schroeder, Louise (1887–1957)
Schroeder, Patricia (1940—)
Schroedter, Elisabeth (1959—)
Schwarzhaupt, Elisabeth (1901–1986)
Scott, Christine Margaret (1946—)
Scott, Desley Carleton (1943—)
Scrivener, Christiane (1925—)
Seastrand, Andrea (1941—)
Sender, Toni (1888–1964)
September, Dulcie (1935–1988)
Serota, Beatrice (1919–2002)
Shaheen, Jeanne (1947—)
Sheldon, Joan Mary (1943—)
Shephard, Gillian (1940—)
Shepherd, Karen (1940—)
Sherwood, Katharine Margaret (1841–1914)
Shields, Margaret (1941—)
Shipley, Debra (1957—)
Shipley, Jenny (1952—)
Short, Clare (1946—)
Shortall, Róisín (1954—)
Sigurdsen, Gertrud (1923—)
Silinga, Annie (1910–1983)
Sillanpää, Miina (1866–1952)
Simpson, Edna Oakes (1891–1984)
Simpson, Fiona (1965—)
Sisulu, Albertina (1918—)
Slaughter, Louise M. (1929—)
Smet, Miet (1943—)
Smith, Angela (1959—)
Smith, Christine Anne (1946—)
Smith, Elaine (1963—)
Smith, Geraldine (1961—)
Smith, Jacqui (1962—)
Smith, Margaret (1961—)
Smith, Margaret Chase (1897–1995)
Smith, Mary Ellen (1861–1933)
Smith, Virginia Dodd (1911–2006)
Snowe, Olympia J. (1947—)
Sohier, Elizabeth Putnam (1847–1926)
Somerville, Nellie Nugent (1863–1952)
Sommer, Renate (1958—)
Sorensen, Patsy (1952—)
Sorgdrager, Winnie (1948—)
Sornosa Martínez, María (1949—)
Southworth, Helen (1956—)
Spellman, Gladys Noon (1918–1988)
Spelman, Caroline (1958—)
Spence, Judith (1957—)
Squire, Rachel (1954–2006)
Squires, Helena E. (1879–1959)
St. George, Katharine (1894–1983)
Stabenow, Debbie (1950—)
Stanley, Winifred Claire (1909–1996)
Starkey, Phyllis (1947—)
Starovoitova, Galina (1946–1998)
Stauner, Gabriele (1948—)
Steele, Joyce
Stenzel, Ursula (1945—)
Stevenson, Rona (1911–1988)
Stewart, Catherine Campbell (1881–1957)
Stihler, Catherine (1973—)
Stone, Barbara Gwendoline (1962—)
Struthers, Karen Lee (1963—)
Stuart, Gisela (1955—)
Sturgeon, Nicola (1970—)
Suchocka, Hanna (1946—)
Sudre, Margie (1943—)
Sullivan, Carryn (1955—)
Sullivan, Leonor Kretzer (1902–1988)
Summerskill, Edith (1901–1980)
Sumner, Jessie (1898–1994)
Suplicy, Marta (c. 1946—)
Süssmuth, Rita (1937—)
Suzman, Helen (1917—)
Svolou, Maria (d. 1976)
Swiebel, Joke (1941—)
Swift, Jane M. (1965—)
Taggart, Edith Ashover (1909–1997)
Tangney, Dorothy (1911–1985)
Tate, Mavis (1893–1947)
Taylor, Ann (1947—)
Taylor, Dari (1944—)
Taylor-Quinn, Madeleine (1951—)
Tennet, Elizabeth
Terpstra, Erica (1943—)
Terrón i Cusí, Anna (1962—)
Thatcher, Margaret (1925—)
Theato, Diemut R. (1937—)
Theorin, Maj Britt (1932—)
Thomas, Lera Millard (1900–1993)
Thomas-Mauro, Nicole (1951—)
Thompson, Ruth (1887–1970)
Thomson, Elaine (1957—)
Thorning-Schmidt, Helle (1966—)
Thors, Astrid (1957—)
Thurman, Karen L. (1951—)
Thyssen, Marianne L.P. (1956—)
Tirikatene-Sullivan, Whetu (1932—)
Tizard, Judith (1956—)
Tombleson, Esmé (1917—)
Tonge, Jenny (1941—)
Torres Marques, Helena (1941—)
Tschitschko, Helene (1908–1992)
Tucker, C. DeLores (1927–2005)
Tuyaa, Nyam-Osoryn (1958—)
Tweedy, Hilda (b. 1911)
Tymoshenko, Yulia (1960—)
Uca, Feleknas (1976—)
Ucok, Bahriye (d. 1990)
Ullrich, Kay (1943—)
Unsoeld, Jolene (1931—)
Upton, Harriet Taylor (1853–1945)
Upton, Mary (1946—)

Uwilingiyimana, Agathe (1953–1994)
Vachetta, Roseline (1951—)
Valenciano Martínez-Orozco, María Elena (1960—)
Valle, Inger-Louise (1921—)
Van Brempt, Kathleen (1969—)
van den Burg, Ieke (1952—)
Van Grippenberg, Alexandra (1859–1913)
Van Lancker, Anne E.M. (1954—)
Veil, Simone (1927—)
Vicario, Leona (1789–1842)
Vike-Freiberga, Vaira (1937—)
Villiers, Theresa (1968—)
Vlachos, Helen (1911–1995)
Vlasto, Dominique (1946—)
Vucanovich, Barbara F. (1921—)
Walker, Olene S. (1930—)
Wallace, Mary (1959—)
Walley, Joan (1949—)
Wallis, Diana (1954—)
Walsh, Mary (1929–1976)
Wang Guangmei (1922—)
Ward, Claire (1972—)
Ward, Irene (1895–1980)
Ward, Mrs. Humphry (1851–1920)
Waring, Margaret (1887–1968)
Waring, Marilyn (1952—)
Warner, Anne Marie (1945—)
Warwick, Lyn (1946—)
Wa Shi (1498–1560)
Wasilewska, Wanda (1905–1964)
Waters, Maxine (1938—)
Watkinson, Angela (1941—)
Weddington, Sarah R. (1945—)
Weiler, Barbara (1946—)
Weis, Jessica McCullough (1901–1963)
Wells, Ada (1863–1933)
Wenzel-Perillo, Brigitta (1949—)
Wessel, Helene (1898–1969)
White, Sandra (1951—)
Whitefield, Karen (1970—)
Whitman, Christine Todd (1946—)
Whitton, Charlotte (1896–1975)
Widdecombe, Ann (1947—)
Wilcox, Elsie Hart (1879–1954)
Wilde, Fran (1948—)
Wilkinson, Ellen (1891–1947)
Williams, Betty (1944—)
Williams, Shirley (1930—)
Wilson, Cairine (1885–1962)
Wilson, Heather (1960—)
Wilson, Naomi (1940—)
Wingo, Effiegene Locke (1883–1962)
Winterton, Ann (1941—)
Winterton, Rosie (1958—)
Woodgate, Margaret (1935—)
Woodhouse, Margaret Chase Going (1890–1984)
Woodward, Ellen Sullivan (1887–1971)
Woolley, Mary E. (1863–1947)
Woolsey, Lynn C. (1937—)
Wu Wenying (1932—)
Wu Yi (1938—)
Wu Zetian (624–705)
Wyse Power, Jennie (1858–1941)
Yates, Elizabeth (c. 1844–1918)
Young, Janet (1926–2002)
Zabell, Theresa (1965—)
Zia, Khaleda (1946—)
Zissener, Sabine (1970—)
Zorba, Myrsini (1949—)
Zrihen, Olga (1953—)

POLO PLAYER
Hale, Sue Sally (1937–2003)

POPE (PRESUMED)
Joan (d. 858)

POP SINGER
Allbut, Barbara (1940—)
Allbut, Phyllis (1942—)
Amos, Tori (1963—)
Amphlett, Christina (c. 1960—)
Anderson, Katherine (1944—)
Andrews, Laverne (1911–1967)
Andrews, Maxene (1916-1995)
Andrews, Patti (b.1918)
Armen, Kay (1920—)
Armstead, Izora (1942–2004)
Baker, Anita (1958—)
Ballard, Florence (1943–1976)
Bassey, Shirley (1937—)
Beckham, Victoria (1974—)
Belle, Regina (1963—)
Bennett, Patricia (1947—)
Bethânia, Maria (1946—)
Birdsong, Cindy (1939—)
Bjork (1965—)
Blige, Mary J. (1971—)
Bofill, Angela (1954—)
Bonoff, Karla (1952—)
Boone, Debby (1956—)
Brandy (1979—)
Branigan, Laura (1957–2004)
Braxton, Toni (1967—)
Brewer, Teresa (1931—)
Brickell, Edie (1966—)
Brown, Melanie (1975—)
Bruno, Gioia Carmen (1965—)
Bunton, Emma (1976—)
Bush, Kate (1958—)
Carey, Mariah (1970—)
Carlisle, Belinda (1958—)
Carpenter, Karen (1950–1983)
Carpenter, Mary Chapin (1958—)
Carr, Vikki (1941—)
Cher (1946—)
Chisholm, Melanie (1974—)
Cleaves, Jessica (1948—)
Cline, Patsy (1932–1963)
Clooney, Rosemary (1928–2002)
Cole, Natalie (1950—)
Cole, Paula (1968—)
Colvin, Shawn (1956—)
Cowart, Juanita (1944—)
Cowsill, Barbara (1929–1985)
Cowsill, Susan (1960—)
Craig, Judy (1946—)
Crow, Sheryl (1962—)
Curless, Ann (1965—)
Davis, Theresa (1950—)
Day, Doris (1924—)
Dearie, Blossom (1926—)
DeCastro, Peggy (1921–2004)
DeFranco, Marisa (1955—)
DeFranco, Merlina (1957—)
DeShannon, Jackie (1944—)
Dion, Céline (1968—)
Dixon, Reather (1945—)
Dobbins, Georgia (1944–1980)
Drewery, Corinne (1959—)
Easton, Sheena (1959—)
Elliot, Cass (1941–1974)
Ellis, Terry (1966—)
Escovedo, Sheila (1957—)
Eskenazi, Roza (c. 1900–1980)
Estefan, Gloria (1957—)
Etting, Ruth (1896–1978)
Fältskog, Agnetha (1950—)
Fassie, Brenda (1964–2004)
Fitzgerald, Ella (1917–1996)
Ford, Mary (1924–1977)
Fordham, Julia (1962—)
Forrest, Helen (1918–1999)
Francis, Connie (1938—)
Franklin, Aretha (1942—)
Franklin, Erma (1938–2002)
Fraser, Elizabeth (1963—)
Fredriksson, Marie (1958—)
Frischmann, Justine (1969—)
Froman, Jane (1907–1980)
Gardner, Janet (1962—)
Gathers, Helen (1943—)
Gaynor, Gloria (1949—)
Gibson, Deborah (1970—)
Gilberto, Astrud (1940—)
Gore, Leslie (1946—)
Gormé, Eydie (1931—)
Grant, Amy (1960—)
Gray, Macy (1970—)
Hagen, Nina (1955—)
Halliwell, Geri (1972—)
Harvey, P.J. (1969—)
Haza, Ofra (1957–2001)
Hendryx, Nona (1945—)
Herron, Cindy (1965—)
Hill, Lauryn (1975—)
Holland, Annie (1965—)
Holliday, Jennifer (1960—)
Horne, Lena (1917—)
Horton, Gladys (1944—)
Houston, Thelma (1946—)
Houston, Whitney (1963—)
Hutchinson, Jeanette (1951—)
Hutchinson, Pamela (1958—)
Hutchinson, Sheila (1953—)
Hutchinson, Wanda (1951—)
Jackson, Janet (1966—)
Jansen, Linda
Jones, Etta (1928—)
Jones, Grace (1952—)
Jones, Maxine (1966—)
Joplin, Janis (1943–1970)
Jurado, Jeanette (1966—)
Kallen, Kitty (1922—)
Kerr, Anita (1927—)
Khan, Chaka (1953—)
King, Carole (1942—)
Knight, Gladys (1944—)
Knowles, Beyoncé (1981—)
Kuehnemund, Jan (1961—)
LaRue, Florence (1944—)
Lee, Barbara (1947–1992)
Lee, Brenda (1944—)
Lennox, Annie (1954—)
London, Julie (1926–2000)
Love, Barbara (1941—)
Luckett, LeToya (1981—)
Lynch, Laura (1958—)
Lynn, Vera (1917—)
MacDonald, Barbara K. (1957—)
MacKenzie, Gisele (1927–2003)
Macy, Robin Lynn (1958—)
Madonna (1958—)
Maines, Natalie (1974—)
Manchester, Melissa (1951—)
Mann, Aimee (1960—)
Matthews, Donna (1971—)
Matzenauer, Margaret (1881–1963)
McCoo, Marilyn (1943—)
McFarlane, Elaine (1942—)
McGuire, Phyllis (1931—)
McLachlan, Sarah (1968—)
Mendoza, Lydia (1916—)
Merchant, Natalie (1963—)
Midler, Bette (1945—)
Mireille (1906–1996)

Moneymaker, Kelly (1965—)
Morgan, Jane (1924—)
Morgan, Jaye P. (1931—)
Morissette, Alanis (1974—)
Morse, Ella Mae (1925–1999)
Mouskouri, Nana (1934—)
Murray, Ruby (1935–1996)
Newton-John, Olivia (1948—)
O'Connell, Helen (1920–1993)
O'Connor, Sinéad (1966—)
Page, Patti (1927—)
Parton, Dolly (1946—)
Pedersen, Share (1963—)
Peterson, Sylvia (1946—)
Petrucci, Roxy (1962—)
Phillips, Chynna (1968—)
Piaf, Edith (1915–1963)
Pointer, Anita (1948—)
Pointer, Bonnie (1950—)
Pointer, June (1954–2006)
Pointer, Ruth (1946—)
Pought, Emma (1942—)
Pought, Jannie (1944–1980)
Pugacheva, Alla (1949—)
Raitt, Bonnie (1949—)
Reddy, Helen (1942—)
Reese, Della (1931—)
Regina, Elis (1945–1982)
Riperton, Minnie (1947–1979)
Roberson, LaTavia (1981—)
Robinson, Dawn (1968—)
Robinson, Vicki Sue (1954–2000)
Robison, Emily (1972—)
Ronstadt, Linda (1946—)
Ross, Diana (1944—)
Rowland, Kelly (1981—)
Santiglia, Peggy (1944—)
Schekeryk, Melanie (1947—)
Scott, Sherry (c. 1948—)
Seeley, Blossom (1891–1974)
Seidel, Martie (1969—)
Selena (1971–1995)
Shakira (1977—)
Shariyya (b. around 815)
Shinoda, Miho (1972—)
Shore, Dinah (1917–1994)
Simone, Nina (1933–2003)
Sledge, Debra (1955—)
Sledge, Joni (1957—)
Sledge, Kathy (1959—)
Sledge, Kim (1958—)
Slick, Grace (1939—)
Smith, Kate (1907–1986)
Smith, Keely (1932—)
Smyth, Patty (1957—)
Spears, Britney (1981—)
Spector, Ronnie (1943—)
Springfield, Dusty (1939–1999)
Stafford, Jo (1920—)
Stansfield, Lisa (1966—)
Staples, Cleo (1934—)
Staples, Mavis (1940—)
Staples, Yvonne (1939—)
Starr, Kay (1922—)
Steele, Micki (1954—)
Sullivan, Maxine (1911–1987)
Summer, Donna (1948—)
Sweet, Rachel (1963—)
Talley, Nedra (1946—)
Teng, Teresa (1953–1995)
Tennille, Toni (1943—)
Terriss, Ellaline (1871–1971)
Thorn, Tracey (1962—)
Tiffany (1971—)
Twain, Shania (1965—)
Umeki, Miyoshi (1929—)
Vaughan, Sarah (1924–1990)
Vega, Suzanne (1959—)
Warnes, Jennifer (1947—)
Warwick, Dionne (1940—)
Wash, Martha
Washington, Dinah (1924–1963)
Waters, Ethel (1896–1977)
Watley, Jody (1959—)
Webb, Laura (1941–2001)
White, Karyn (1965—)
Whiting, Margaret (1924—)
Wiley, Lee (1915–1975)
Williams, Deniece (1951—)
Williams, Michelle (1980—)
Wilson, Carnie (1968—)
Wilson, Mary (1944—)
Wilson, Nancy (1937—)
Wilson, Wendy (1969—)
Young, Wanda (1944—)

PORTRAIT PAINTER
Ancher, Anna (1859–1935)
Anguissola, Sofonisba (1532–1625)
Barker, Cicely Mary (1895–1973)
Barney, Natalie Clifford (1876–1972)
Beale, Mary (1632–1699)
Beaux, Cecilia (1855–1942)
Bouliar, Marie Geneviève (1762–1825)
Bremer, Fredrika (1801–1865)
Capet, Gabrielle (1761–1817)
Carriera, Rosalba (1675–1757)
Content, Marjorie (1895–1984)
de Kooning, Elaine Fried (1918–1989)
Duparc, Françoise (1726–1778)
Eakins, Susan Hannah (1851–1938)
Fassett, Cornelia (1831–1898)
Fontana, Lavinia (1552–1614)
Gabain, Ethel Leontine (1883–1950)
Galizia, Fede (1578–1630)
Gentileschi, Artemisia (1593–c. 1653)
Gluck (1895–1978)
Goodridge, Sarah (1788–1853)
Greenwood, Marion (1909–1980)
Hall, Anne (1792–1863)
Hansteen, Aasta (1824–1908)
Hawthorne, Sophia Peabody (1809–1871)
Hepworth, Barbara (1903–1975)
Hodgkins, Frances (1869–1947)
Iaia (fl. c. 100 BCE)
Irene (fl. 200 BCE?)
John, Gwen (1876–1939)
Jones, Loïs Mailou (1905–1998)
Kauffmann, Angelica (1741–1807)
Klumpke, Anna Elizabeth (1856–1942)
Labille-Guiard, Adelaide (1749–1803)
La Rochefoucauld, Edmée, Duchesse de (1895–1991)
Ledoux, Jeanne Philiberte (1767–1840)
Lemoine, Marie Victoire (1754–1820)
Lempicka, Tamara de (1898–1980)
Low, Mary Fairchild (1858–1946)
MacDonald, Frances (1874–1921)
Maria Antonia of Austria (1724–1780)
McKenna, Rollie (1918–2003)
McMein, Neysa (1888–1949)
Merritt, Anna Lea (1844–1930)
Neel, Alice (1900–1984)
Nourse, Elizabeth (1859–1938)
Oakley, Violet (1874–1961)
Osborn, Emily Mary (1834–c. 1885)
Peale, Anna Claypoole (1791–1878)
Peale, Margaretta Angelica (1795–1882)
Peale, Sarah Miriam (1800–1885)
Rand, Ellen (1875–1941)
Sandel, Cora (1880–1974)
Smith, Bathsheba (1822–1910)
Sofronova, Antonina (1892–1966)
Spencer, Lilly Martin (1822–1902)
Sperrey, Eleanor Catherine (1862–1893)
Stebbins, Emma (1815–1882)
Stephens, Alice Barber (1858–1932)
Stern, Irma (1894–1966)
Teerlinc, Levina (c. 1520–1576)
Timarete (fl. 3rd c. BCE)
Vandamm, Florence (1883–1966)
van Stockum, Hilda (b. 1908)
Vigée-Le Brun, Elisabeth (1755–1842)
Waring, Laura Wheeler (1887–1948)
Weir, Irene (1862–1944)
Wentworth, Cecile de (c. 1853–1933)

PORTRAIT PHOTOGRAPHER
Abbe, Kathryn (1919—)
Abbott, Berenice (1898–1991)
Albin-Guillot, Laure (c. 1880–1962)
Allen, Frances S. (1854–1941)
Allen, Mary E. (1858–1941)
Andriesse, Emmy (1914–1953)
Arbus, Diane (1923–1971)
Bernhard, Ruth (1905—)
Biermann, Aenne (1898–1933)
Boughton, Alice (1866–1943)
Cameron, Julia Margaret (1815–1879)
Cunningham, Imogen (1883–1976)
Dahl-Wolfe, Louise (1895–1989)
Fleischmann, Trude (1895–1990)
Hanscom, Adelaide (1876–1932)
Hofer, Evelyn
Jacobi, Lotte (1896–1990)
Johnston, Frances Benjamin (1864–1952)
Kanaga, Consuelo (1894–1978)
Kar, Ida (1908–1970)
Käsebier, Gertrude (1852–1934)
Kendall, Marie Hartig (1854–1943)
Krull, Germaine (1897–1985)
Lange, Dorothea (1895–1965)
McKenna, Rollie (1918–2003)
Modotti, Tina (1896–1942)
Noskowiak, Sonya (1900–1975)
Palfi, Marion (1907–1978)
Sipprell, Clara (1885–1975)
Ulmann, Doris (1882–1934)
Vandamm, Florence (1883–1966)
Warburg, Agnes (1872–1953)
Watson, Edith (1861–1943)
Withington, Eliza (1825–1877)
Wulz, Wanda (1903–1984)

POSTMASTER
Bates, Sophia Ann (1817–1899)
Bloomer, Amelia Jenks (1818–1894)
Burgess, Georgina Jane (c. 1839–1904)
Cripps, Sarah Ann (c. 1821–1892)
Edmonds, Emma (1841–1898)
Fairclough, Ellen (1905–2004)
Gibb, Helen (1838–1914)
Goddard, Mary Katherine (1738–1816)
Kells, Isabella (1861–1938)
McDonald, Agnes (1829–1906)
Thompson, Flora (1876–1947)

POSTMISTRESS
Tautari, Mary (d. 1906)

POTTER
See Ceramist/potter.

PREACHER
See Clergy.
See Evangelical.

PRESERVATIONIST
Alcott, Anna Bronson (1831–1893)

Andrews, Doris (1920–2003)
Cunningham, Ann Pamela (1816–1875)
Epstein, Marie (c. 1899–1995)
Maxwell, Alice Heron (1860–1949)
Ordway, Katharine (1899–1979)
Pitini-Morera, Hariata Whakatau (1871/72?–1938)
Statham, Edith May (1853–1951)
Werlein, Elizebeth Thomas (1883–1946)
Young, Rose Maud (1865–1947)

PRESIDENT (GOVERNMENT)
Aquino, Corazon (1933—)
Arroyo, Gloria Macapagal (1947—)
Barbara, Agatha (1923–2002)
Bergmann-Pohl, Sabine (1946—)
Chamorro, Violeta (1929—)
Finnbogadóttir, Vigdís (1930—)
Gueiler Tejada, Lydia (1921—)
Halonen, Tarja (1943—)
Jagan, Janet (1920—)
Kumaratunga, Chandrika Bandaranaike (1945—)
McAleese, Mary (1951—)
Moscoso, Mireya (1946—)
Perón, Isabel (1931—)
Perry, Ruth (1939—)
Plavsic, Biljana (1930—)
Robinson, Mary (1944—)
Sukarnoputri, Megawati (1947—)
Vike-Freiberga, Vaira (1937—)

PRESS AGENT/SECRETARY
See Publicist.

PRIEST
Baker, Elsie (1909–2003)
Means, Jacqueline (1936—)
Messenger-Harris, Beverly (1947—)
Simpson, Mary Michael (1925—)

PRIESTESS
Agrippina the Younger (15–59)
Ahmose-Nefertari (c. 1570–1535 BCE)
Diotima of Mantinea (fl. 400s BCE)
Enheduanna (fl. 2300 BCE)
Kahina (r. 695–703)
Kapiolani (c. 1781–1841)
Laveau, Marie (1801–1881)
Laveau, Marie (1827–1897)
Livia Drusilla (58 BCE–29 CE)
Millet, Cleusa (c. 1931–1998)
Nitocris (c. 660–584 BCE)

PRIMATOLOGIST
Fossey, Dian (1932–1985)
Galdikas, Biruté (1948—)
Kilbourn, Annelisa (1967–2002)

PRIME MINISTER
Bandaranaike, Sirimavo (1916–2000)
Bhutto, Benazir (1953—)
Bruntland, Gro Harlem (1939—)
Campbell, Kim (1947—)
Charles, Eugenia (1919–2005)
Çiller, Tansu (1946—)
Clark, Helen Elizabeth (1950—)
Cresson, Edith (1934—)
Diogo, Luisa (1958—)
Domitien, Elisabeth (1926—)
Gandhi, Indira (1917–1984)
Jaatteenmaki, Anneli (1955—)
Kumaratunga, Chandrika Bandaranaike (1945—)
Meir, Golda (1898–1978)
Pintasilgo, Maria de Lurdes (1930–2004)
Planinc, Milka (1924—)
Prunskiene, Kazimiera (1943—)
Shipley, Jenny (1952—)
Suchocka, Hanna (1946—)
Thatcher, Margaret (1925—)
Tymoshenko, Yulia (1960—)
Uwilingiyimana, Agathe (1953–1994)
Zia, Khaleda (1946—)

PRIME-MINISTERIAL WIFE
Barton, Jane (1851–1938)
Blair, Cherie (1954—)
Bowell, Harriet (1829–1884)
Bruce, Ethel (1879–1967)
Callaghan, Audrey (1915–2005)
Chifley, Elizabeth (1886–1962)
Cook, Mary (1863–1950)
Curtin, Elsie (1890–1975)
Deakin, Pattie (1863–1934)
Diefenbaker, Olive (1902–1976)
Eden, Clarissa (1920—)
Fadden, Ilma (d. 1987)
Fisher, Margaret (c. 1874–1958)
Forde, Vera (1894–1967)
Fraser, Tamie (1936—)
Gladstone, Catherine (1812–1900)
Gorton, Bettina (c. 1916–1983)
Hawke, Hazel (1929—)
Holt, Zara (1909–1989)
Howard, Janette (1944—)
Hughes, Mary (1874–1958)
Keating, Annita (1949—)
Lloyd George, Margaret (1866–1941)
Massey, Christina Allan (1863–1932)
McEwen, Anne (c. 1903–1967)
McMahon, Sonia (1932—)
Menzies, Pattie (1899–1995)
Page, Ethel (c. 1875–1958)
Reid, Florence (c. 1870–1950)
Scullin, Sarah (1880–1962)
Watson, Ada (1859–1921)
Whitlam, Margaret (1919—)

PRINCESS
Adelaide (c. 794–after 852)
Adelaide (1777–1847)
Adelaide, Madame (1732–1800)
Adeliza (d. 1066?)
Agatha (fl. 1060)
Agnes of Austria (1281–1364)
Agnes of Austria (fl. 1100s)
Agnes of Bohemia (1205–1282)
Agnes of Bohemia (1269–1297)
Agnes of Courtenay (1136–1186)
Agnes of Germany (1074–1143)
Agnes of Poland (1137–after 1181)
Alais of France (1160–?)
Albertina Agnes (d. 1696)
Albertine (1753–1829)
Alexandra (1921–1993)
Alexandra Feodorovna (1872–1918)
Alexandra of Denmark (1844–1925)
Alexandra of Kent (1936—)
Alexandra of Oldenburg (1838–1900)
Alexandra Oldenburg (1870–1891)
Alexandra Saxe-Coburg (1878–1942)
Alexandra Victoria (1891–1959)
Alexandra Victoria of Schleswig-Holstein (1887–1957)
Alice (1280–1291)
Alice Maud Mary (1843–1878)
Alice of Athlone (1883–1981)
Alice of Battenberg (1885–1969)
Alice of Jerusalem (c. 1106–?)
Amalie (1818–1875)
Amalie Auguste (1788–1851)
Amalie of Hesse-Darmstadt (1754–1832)
Amalie of Saxony (1794–1870)
Amelia (1783–1810)
Amelia of Anhalt-Dessau (1666–1726)
Amelia of Solms (1602–1675)
Amelia Sophia (1711–1786)
Anacáona (fl. 1492)
Anastasia (fl. 800s)
Angharad (fl. 13th c.)
Anna Amalia of Prussia (1723–1787)
Anna Comnena (1083–1153/55)
Anna Maria Theresa (1879–1961)
Anna of Bohemia (fl. 1318)
Anna of Cumin (d. 1111)
Anna of Denmark (1532–1585)
Anna of Habsburg (d. 1327)
Anna of Hungary (fl. 1244)
Anna of Saxony (1544–1577)
Anna Palaeologina (d. 1340)
Anna Petrovna (1757–1758)
Anna Victoria of Savoy (fl. 18th c.)
Anne (1709–1759)
Anne, Princess (1950—)
Anne of Austria (1601–1666)
Anne of Beaujeu (c. 1460–1522)
Anne of Bourbon-Parma (1923—)
Anne of Denmark (1574–1619)
Anne Petrovna (1708–1728)
Antoinette of Luxemburg (1899–1954)
Antonia of Portugal (1845–1913)
Apama (c. 290 BCE–?)
Arsinoe (fl. 4th c. BCE)
Arsinoe I (d. 247 BCE)
Arsinoe III (fl. c. 250–210/05 BCE)
Astrid of Sweden (1905–1935)
Augusta Guelph (1737–1813)
Augusta Guelph (1768–1840)
Augusta of Saxe-Gotha (1719–1772)
Augusta of Saxe-Weimar (1811–1890)
Augusta of Wurttemberg (1826–1898)
Aurora of San Donato (1873–1904)
Barbara of Byzantium (d. 1125)
Bathildis of Schaumburg-Lippe (1873–1962)
Beatrice (1242–1275)
Beatrice (1857–1944)
Beatriz of Spain (1909–2002)
Beaufort, Joan (c. 1410–1445)
Benedikte (1944—)
Berengaria of Navarre (c. 1163–c. 1230)
Berenice (28–after 80)
Berenice (c. 35 BCE–?)
Bertha (779–after 823)
Bethoc (fl. 11th c.)
Bibesco, Marthe Lucie (1887–1973)
Birgitta of Sweden (1937—)
Blanche of Burgundy (1296–1326)
Blanche of France (1253–1321)
Blanche of France (c. 1266–1305)
Bona of Bohemia (1315–1349)
Bonaparte, Elisa (1777–1820)
Bonaparte, Marie (1882–1962)
Bonaparte, Pauline (1780–1825)
Bonney, Linda (1949—)
Branca (c. 1192–1240)
Braose, Isabel de (d. 1248?)
Braunschweig-Lüneburg, Elisabeth von (1519–1558)
Brézé, Charlotte de (c. 1444/49–?)
Bruce, Margaret (1296–1316)
Bruce, Margaret (d. 1346)
Bruce, Matilda (d. 1353)
Carlota (1840–1927)
Carlota Joaquina (1775–1830)
Caroline (1793–1881)
Caroline Augusta of Bavaria (1792–1873)
Caroline Elizabeth (1713–1757)
Caroline Matilda of Denmark (1912–1995)

Caroline of Ansbach (1683–1737)
Caroline of Austria (1801–1832)
Caroline of Brunswick (1768–1821)
Caroline of Mecklenburg-Strelitz (1821–1876)
Caroline of Monaco (1957—)
Caroline of Naples (1798–1870)
Caroline of Orange (1743–1787)
Caroline of Parma (1770–1804)
Caroline of Sicily (1820–1861)
Catherine Charlotte of Hildburghausen (1787–1847)
Catherine de France (1428–1446)
Catherine Frederica of Wurttemberg (1821–1898)
Catherine II the Great of Russia (1729–1796)
Catherine of Aragon (1485–1536)
Catherine of Bourbon (c. 1555–1604)
Catherine of Braganza (1638–1705)
Catherine of Brittany (1428–c. 1476)
Catherine of Habsburg (c. 1254–1282)
Catherine of Valois (1401–1437)
Catherine Romanov (1878–1959)
Cecilia (1469–1507)
Cecilia of Baden (1839–1891)
Cecilia of France (fl. 1100s)
Charlotte (1516–1524)
Charlotte (1896–1985)
Charlotte Amalie (1706–1782)
Charlotte Augusta (1796–1817)
Charlotte Augusta Matilda (1766–1828)
Charlotte de Montmorency (1594–1650)
Charlotte de Montmorency (fl. 1600–1621)
Charlotte Frederica of Mecklenburg-Schwerin (1784–1840)
Charlotte of Bourbon (d. 1582)
Charlotte of Brunswick-Wolfenbüttel (1694–1715)
Charlotte of Mecklenburg-Strelitz (1744–1818)
Charlotte of Saxe-Meiningen (1860–1919)
Chewikar, Princess (1876–1947)
Chichibu Setsuko (1909–1995)
Chiltrud (fl. 700s)
Chotek, Sophie (1868–1914)
Christina of Sweden (d. 1122)
Christina of Sweden (1626–1689)
Christine of France (1606–1663)
Christine of Hesse-Cassel (1933—)
Claude de France (1547–1575)
Clementine of Austria (1798–1881)
Clementine of Belgium (1872–1955)
Clementine of Orleans (1817–1907)
Cleopatra (b. 354 BCE)
Clotilde of Savoy (1843–1911)
Coligny, Louise de (1555–1620)
Constance of Aragon (d. 1283)
Constance of France (fl. 1100s)
Constance of Sicily (1154–1198)
Coombs, Claire (1974—)
Costanza (1182–1202)
Courau, Clotilde (1969—)
Cristina (1965—)
Cunigunde of Bohemia (d. 1321)
Czartoryska, Isabella (1746–1835)
Daisy, Princess (1873–1943)
Dashkova, Ekaterina (1744–1810)
Davies, Lilian May (1915—)
de Mello, Theresa (1913–1997)
Dessilava (fl. 1197–1207)
Devorgilla (1109–1193)
Devorgilla (d. 1290)
Diana (1961–1997)
Dido (fl. 800 BCE)
Doada (fl. 990–1005)
Dolgorukova, Ekaterina (1847–1922)
Donata (fl. 11th century)
Dorothea, Princess of Lieven (1785–1857)
Dorothea Hedwig of Brunswick-Wolfenbuttel (1587–1609)
Dorothea of Denmark (1528–1575)
Dorothea of Saxony (1563–1587)
Dumitrescu-Doletti, Joanna (1902–1963)
Durgawati (d. 1564)
Ebba (c. 610–c. 683)
Edgitha (c. 912–946)
Edhild (d. 946)
Edith (fl. 1009)
Eleanor of Castile (1241–1290)
Eleanor of Montfort (1215–1275)
Eleanor of Montfort (1252–1282)
Eleanor of Navarre (1425–1479)
Eleanor of Portugal (1434–1467)
Eleanor of Woodstock (1318–1355)
Elena (1963—)
Elfgifu (c. 914–?)
Elfgifu (c. 997–?)
Elflaed (c. 905–c. 963)
Elizabeth (1770–1840)
Élisabeth, Madame (1764–1794)
Elizabeth Caroline (1740–1759)
Elizabeth Hohenzollern (1815–1885)
Elizabeth of Austria (1743–1808)
Elizabeth of Baden (1779–1826)
Elizabeth of Bavaria (fl. 1200s)
Elizabeth of Bavaria (1801–1873)
Elizabeth of Bavaria (1876–1965)
Elizabeth of Bohemia (1618–1680)
Elizabeth of Brabant (1243–1261)
Elizabeth of Hungary (1207–1231)
Elizabeth of Poland (1305–1380)
Elizabeth of Portugal (1271–1336)
Elizabeth of Saxe-Hildburghausen (1713–1761)
Elizabeth of Silesia (fl. 1257)
Elizabeth of Valois (1545–1568)
Elizabeth of Wurttemberg (1767–1790)
Elizabeth of Wurttemberg (1802–1864)
Elizabeth of Yugoslavia (1936—)
Elizabeth Oldenburg (1904–1955)
Elizabeth Stuart (1635–1650)
Ella (1864–1918)
Elvira (1038–1101)
Emilia of Orange (1569–1629)
Emma de Gatinais (fl. 1150–1170)
Ena (1887–1969)
Este, Beatrice d' (1475–1497)
Este, Eleonora d' (1537–1581)
Este, Isabella d' (1474–1539)
Este, Lucrezia d' (d. 1516/18)
Estrith (fl. 1017–1032)
Ethelgeofu (d. around 896)
Eudocia (c. 1260–?)
Eudocia Comnena (fl. 1100)
Eudoxia of Moscow (1483–1513)
Eugenie (1830–1889)
Eugénie Hortense (1808–1847)
Eulalia (1864–1958)
Euphrosyne (fl. 1200s)
Fadia (1943–2002)
Farial (1938—)
Fausta (fl. 600s)
Fawzia (1921—)
Fawzia (1940–2005)
Feodore of Hohenlohe-Langenburg (1866–1932)
Feodore of Leiningen (1807–1872)
Feuchères, Sophie, Baronne de (c. 1795–1841)
Francisca of Portugal (1824–1898)
Françoise of Guise (1902–1953)
Frederica Louise (1770–1819)
Frederica of Prussia (1767–1820)
Fredericka (1917–1981)
Fredericka of Hanover (1848–1926)
Fredesendis (fl. 1000)
Fredesendis (fl. 1050)
Frideswide (d. 735?)
Galiana
Galitzin, Amalie von (1748–1806)
Galswintha (d. around 568)
Gemmei (c. 661–721)
Genshō (680–748)
Gerberga of Saxony (c. 910–969)
Gertrude of Nivelles (626–659)
Gertrude of Poland (d. 1107)
Geyra (fl. 980s)
Gisela (1856–1932)
Gisela of Bavaria (c. 975–1033)
Gisela of Chelles (781–814)
Gladys (fl. 1100s)
Gladys the Black (d. 1251)
Glinskaia, Anna (d. 1553)
Glinski, Elena (c. 1506–1538)
Godgifu (c. 1010–c. 1049)
Gonzaga, Anne de (1616–1684)
Gonzaga, Isabella (d. 1559)
Gormflaith of Ireland (fl. 980–1015)
Go-Sakuramachi (1740–1814)
Gunhild (c. 1020–1038)
Gunhilda of Denmark (d. 1002)
Gunhilda of Poland (d. around 1015)
Gwenllian of Wales (fl. 1137)
Gyseth (fl. 1070)
Haruko (1850–1914)
Hatheburg (fl. 906)
Hedwig Sophia (1681–1708)
Helen (b. 1950)
Helena (1846–1923)
Helena Pavlovna (1784–1803)
Helen Asen of Bulgaria (d. 1255?)
Helena Victoria (1870–1948)
Helene of Bavaria (1834–1890)
Helene of Brunswick-Luneburg (d. 1273)
Helene of Moldavia (d. 1505)
Helen of Greece (1896–1982)
Helen of Schleswig-Holstein (1888–1962)
Helen of Waldeck and Pyrmont (1861–1922)
Henrietta Anne of England (1644–1670)
Henrietta Catherine of Nassau (1637–1708)
Henrietta Maria (1626–1651)
Henriette (1727–1752)
Hermine of Reuss (1887–1947)
Hermine of Waldeck and Pyrmont (1827–1910)
Herodias (c. 14 BCE–after 40 CE)
Hertha of Ysenburg and Budingen (1883–1972)
Herzeleide (1918–1989)
Hildegarde of Bavaria (c. 840–?)
Hiltrude (fl. 800s)
Hodierna (fl. 1100s)
Honoria (c. 420–?)
Howard, Anne (1475–1511)
Ida of Saxe-Coburg-Meiningen (1794–1852)
Ida of Schaumburg-Lippe (1852–1891)
Ildico (fl. 453)
Ingeborg (d. 1254)
Ingeborg (1347–1370)
Ingeborg of Denmark (1878–1958)
Ingigerd Olafsdottir (c. 1001–1050)
Ingrid of Sweden (1910–2000)
Irene (fl. late 1100s)
Irene (1904–1974)
Irene (1942—)
Irene (1953—)
Irene Emma (1939—)
Irene of Byzantium (d. 1067)
Irene of Hesse-Darmstadt (1866–1953)
Irene of Kiev (fl. 1122)
Irina (1895–1970)
Isabeau of Bavaria (1371–1435)

Isabel (fl. 1225)
Isabella I (1451–1504)
Isabella of Asturias (1471–1498)
Isabella of Braganza (1402–1465)
Isabella of Cyprus (fl. 1230s)
Isabella of France (1296–1358)
Isabella of Parma (1741–1763)
Isabella of Portugal (1503–1539)
Isabelle (1225–1270)
Isabelle of France (1349–1372)
Isabel of Brazil (1846–1921)
Ita of Ireland (d. 570)
Jacquetta of Luxemburg (c. 1416–1472)
Jahanara (1614–1681)
Januaria (1822–1901)
Jeanne of Bourbon (d. 1493)
Jeanne of Burgundy (1344–1360)
Jezebel (d. 884 BCE)
Jitō (645–702)
Joanna (1333–1348)
Joanna of Portugal (1636–1653)
Joan of England (d. 1237)
Joan of Kent (1328–1385)
Jodha Bai (d. 1613)
Johanna Elizabeth of Holstein-Gottorp (1712–1760)
Jolanta (fl. 1100s)
Josephine of Belgium (1872–1958)
Josephine of Lorraine (1753–1757)
Joveta of Jerusalem (1120–?)
Juana la Beltraneja (1462–1530)
Juana la Loca (1479–1555)
Judith of Bavaria (fl. 1390s–1400)
Julianna of Ruthenia (fl. 1377)
Kaiulani (1875–1899)
Kamamalu, Victoria (1838–1866)
Katherine Plantagenet (1253–1257)
Katherine Plantagenet (1479–1527)
Kaur, Rajkumari Amrit (1889–1964)
Kelly, Grace (1928–1982)
Kikuko, Princess (d. 2004)
Kira of Leiningen (b. 1930)
Kira of Russia (1909–1967)
Kshesinskaia, Matilda (1872–1971)
Lalla Rookh (fl. 1600s)
Lamballe, Marie Thérèse Louise of Savoy-Carignano, Princesse de (1749–1792)
Leonida (1914—)
Leopoldine (1837–1903)
Libussa (c. 680–738)
Liliuokalani (1838–1917)
Litwinde (fl. 850)
Longueville, Anne Geneviève, Duchesse de (1619–1679)
Louisa (1622–1709)
Louisa Carlotta of Naples (1804–1844)
Louise (1692–1712)
Louise (1808–1870)
Louise (1848–1939)
Louise Adelaide de Bourbon (1757–1824)
Louise Caroline (1875–1906)
Louise-Diana (1716–1736)
Louise Dorothea of Brandenburg (1680–1705)
Louise-Elisabeth de Bourbon Condé (1693–1775)
Louise Marie (1737–1787)
Louise Marie de Gonzague (1611–1667)
Louise of Baden (1811–1854)
Louise of Belgium (1858–1924)
Louise of Hesse-Cassel (1688–1765)
Louise of Orleans (1882–1952)
Louise of Prussia (1776–1810)
Louise of Saxe-Hilburghausen (1726–1756)
Louise of Stolberg-Gedern (1752–1824)
Louise Victoria (1867–1931)
Löwenstein, Helga Maria zu (1910–2004)
Lucia (r. 1288–1289)
Lucienne of Segni (r. around 1252–1258)
Lucy de Blois (d. 1120)
Lucy of Scotland (d. 1090)
Luisa Fernanda (1832–1897)
Lysandra (fl. 300 BCE)
Maacah (fl. 1000 BCE)
Madeleine of France (1520–1537)
Mafalda (c. 1197–1257)
Mafalda of Hesse (1902–1944)
Magdalena (1532–1590)
Magdalene of Oldenburg (1585–1657)
Magdalene of Saxony (1507–1534)
Magogo ka Dinizulu, Constance (1900–1984)
Malaspina, Ricciarda
Mancini, Marie (1640–1715)
Mancini, Olympia (c. 1639–1708)
Mammati (d. 1619)
Marared (fl. 1173)
Margaret (1346–1361)
Margaret (b. 1949)
Margaret, Saint (c. 1046–1093)
Margaret Capet (d. 1271)
Margaret Christofsdottir (c. 1305–1340)
Margaret Clementine (1870–1955)
Margaret de Burgh (c. 1193–1259)
Margaret I of Denmark (1353–1412)
Margaret of Connaught (1882–1920)
Margaret of Saxony (1840–1858)
Margaret of Valois (1553–1615)
Margaret Rose (1930–2002)
Margaret Tudor (1489–1541)
Margarita Maria (b. 1939)
Margrethe II of Denmark (1940—)
Margriet Francisca (1943—)
Maria (fl. 1200s)
Maria Amalia (1724–1730)
Maria Anna (1718–1744)
Maria Anna of Portugal (1843–1884)
Maria Annunziata (1843–1871)
Maria Antonia of Austria (1724–1780)
Maria Antonia of Naples (1784–1806)
Maria Cantacuzene (fl. 1300s)
Maria Charlotte of Sardinia (c. 1761–c. 1786)
Maria Christina (1947—)
Maria Clementina of Austria (1777–1801)
Maria Comnena (fl. 1090s)
Maria Cristina (1911–1996)
Maria da Gloria (1946—)
Maria dei Conti d'Aquino (fl. 1300s)
Maria de la Esperanza (1914—)
Maria de la Paz (1862–1946)
Maria Gabriele of Bavaria (1878–1912)
Maria I of Braganza (1734–1816)
Maria Isabel Francisca (1851–1931)
Maria Isabel of Portugal (1797–1818)
Maria Josepha of Portugal (1857–1943)
Maria Magdalena (1689–1743)
Maria Magdalena of Austria (1589–1631)
Mariana Victoria (1768–1788)
Marianne of the Netherlands (1810–1883)
Maria of Aragon (fl. 1311)
Maria of Kiev (d. 1146)
Maria of Savoy (1914—)
Maria of Tver (c. 1440–1467)
Maria of Waldeck (1857–1882)
Maria Teresa (1882–1912)
Maria Theresa of Austria (1717–1780)
Marie (1876–1940)
Marie-Anne de la Trémouille (c. 1642–1722)
Marie-Anne of Braganza (1861–1942)
Marie Antoinette (1755–1793)
Marie de Bourbon (fl. 18th c.)
Marie d'Orleans (1813–1839)
Marie Feodorovna (1847–1928)
Marie José of Belgium (1906–2001)
Marie Leczinska (1703–1768)
Marie Louise (1872–1956)
Marie Louise Albertine of Leiningen-Heidesheim (1729–1818)
Marie Louise d'Orleans (1662–1689)
Marie Louise of Bulgaria (1933—)
Marie of Anhalt (1898–1983)
Marie of Baden (1817–1888)
Marie of Bulgaria (c. 1046–?)
Marie of Hesse-Darmstadt (1824–1880)
Marie of Kiev (d. 1179)
Marie of Nassau (1841–1910)
Marie of Rumania (1875–1938)
Marie of Russia (1907–1951)
Marie of Saxe-Weimar-Eisenach (1808–1877)
Marie of Swabia (c. 1201–1235)
Marie Pavlovna (1786–1859)
Marie Thérèse Charlotte (1778–1851)
Marie Therese of Bourbon (1817–1886)
Marjory (fl. 13th c.)
Martel, Adeloga (fl. 775)
Martel, Judith (c. 844–?)
Martha of Sweden (1901–1954)
Martin, Mary Letitia (1815–1850)
Mary (1278–1332)
Mary (1344–1362)
Mary (1776–1857)
Mary (1897–1965)
Mary (b. 1964)
Mary I of England (1516–1558)
Mary II (1662–1694)
Mary of Antioch (d. 1277)
Mary of Baden (1834–1899)
Mary of Hanover (1849–1904)
Mary of Hesse-Cassel (1723–1772)
Mary of Hesse-Homburg (1785–1846)
Mary of Orange (1631–1660)
Mary of Portugal (1527–1545)
Mary of Teck (1867–1953)
Mary Plantagenet (1467–1482)
Mary Stuart (1542–1587)
Mathilde (1820–1904)
Matilda (fl. 680s)
Matilda, Empress (1102–1167)
Matilda of Bavaria (fl. 1300s)
Matilda of Boulogne (c. 1103–1152)
Matilda of Guelders (d. 1380)
Matilda of Saxony (c. 892–968)
Maya (d. around 563 BCE)
Medici, Anna de (1616–?)
Medici, Anna Maria de (d. 1741)
Medici, Catherine de (1519–1589)
Medici, Claudia de (1604–1648)
Medici, Isabella de (1542–1576)
Medici, Maria de (fl. late 1400s)
Melisande (fl. 1100)
Mendoza, Ana de (1540–1592)
Michael of Kent (b. 1945)
Mihrimah (1522–1575)
Mildgyth (fl. early 700s)
Militza of Montenegro (1866–1951)
Modthryth (fl. 520)
Modwenna (d. 518)
Montagu-Douglas-Scott, Alice (1901–2004)
Montpensier, Anne Marie Louise d'Orléans, Duchesse de (1627–1693)
Mutnedjmet (c. 1360–1326 BCE)
Nagako (1903–2000)
Nahienaena (c. 1815–1836)
Nathalia Keshko (1859–1941)
Nenadovich, Persida (1813–1873)
Ninnoc (fl. 6th c.)
Noailles, Anna de (1876–1933)
Oldenburg, Astrid (1932—)
Oldenburg, Cecily (1911–1937)
Oldenburg, Margaret (1895–1992)

Oldenburg, Margaret (1905–1981)
Oldenburg, Martha (1971—)
Oldenburg, Mary (1865–1909)
Oldenburg, Ragnhild (1930—)
Olga (1884–1958)
Olga, Princess Paley (1865–1929)
Olga Alexandrovna (1882–1960)
Olga Oldenburg (1903–1981)
Orthryth of Mercia (fl. 7th c.)
Ortrud of Schleswig-Holstein-Sonderburg-Glucksburg (1925—)
Pahlavi, Ashraf (1919—)
Pahlavi, Soraya (1932–2001)
Paletzi, Juliane (d. 1569)
Parysatis II (c. 350–323 BCE)
Pauline of Wurttemberg (1877–1965)
Phila II (c. 300 BCE–?)
Philippa-Elizabeth (1714–1734)
Philippa of Antioch (fl. 1100s)
Phillips, Zara (1981—)
Placidia, Galla (c. 390–450)
Pocahontas (c. 1596–1617)
Predeslava of Hungary (fl. 960)
Pribyslava (fl. 10th c.)
Ptolemais (c. 315 BCE–?)
Radegonde (d. 1445)
Radegund of Poitiers (518–587)
Radziwill, Francisca (1705–1753)
Ramsay, Patricia (1886–1974)
Ranavalona II of Madagascar (1829–1883)
Ranavalona III of Madagascar (1861–1917)
Reign of Women (1520–1683)
Richeza Eriksdottir (fl. 1200s)
Richilde (d. 894)
Richizza of Poland (1116–1185)
Rigunthа (fl. 580s)
Romanov, Anna (1632–1692)
Romanov, Irina (1627–1679)
Romanov, Sophie (1634–1676)
Rothilde (fl. 840)
Rotrud (800–841)
Rotrude (c. 778–after 839)
Roxane (c. 345–310 BCE)
Sadako (1885–1951)
Sah (fl. 1500s)
Salm-Salm, Agnes, Princess (1840–1912)
Salote Topou III (1900–1965)
Sarolta (fl. 1000s)
Shigeko (1925–1961)
Sibylla (1160–1190)
Sichelgaita of Salerno (1040–1090)
Singer, Winnaretta (1865–1943)
Sirikit (1932—)
Sobieski, Clementina (1702–1735)
Solomonia (fl. 16th c.)
Sonja (1937—)
Sophia (1630–1714)
Sophia (1957—)
Sophia Alekseyevna (1657–1704)
Sophia Dorothea of Brandenburg (1736–1798)
Sophia Dorothea of Brunswick-Celle (1666–1726)
Sophia Matilda (1773–1844)
Sophia of Gandersheim (c. 975–1039)
Sophia of Greece (b. 1914)
Sophia of Mecklenburg (1758–1794)
Sophie (1734–1782)
Sophie Hedwig (1677–1735)
Sophie of Lithuania (1370–1453)
Sophie of Nassau (1902–1941)
Sophie Valdemarsdottir (d. 1241)
Stephanie of Belgium (1864–1945)
Stephanie of Monaco (1965—)
Stewart, Anastasia (1883–1923)
Stewart, Egidia (fl. 14th c.)
Stewart, Isabel (fl. 1390–1410)
Stewart, Jean (d. after 1404)
Stewart, Katherine (d. after 1394)
Stewart, Katherine (fl. 14th c.)
Stewart, Margaret (fl. 1350)
Stewart, Margaret (d. before 1456)
Stewart, Margaret (fl. 1460–1520)
Stewart, Margaret (fl. 14th c.)
Stewart, Mary (c. 1451–1488)
Stewart, Mary (d. 1458)
Stratonice II (c. 285–228 BCE)
Stratonice III (fl. 250 BCE)
Stuart, Arabella (1575–1615)
Sunnichild (d. 741)
Sybilla of Saxe-Coburg-Gotha (1908–1972)
Tallien, Thérésa (1773–1835)
Tecuichpo (d. 1551)
Tenagneworq (1913–2003)
Teresa of Aragon (1037–?)
Teresa of Portugal (1157–1218)
Teresa of Portugal (1793–1874)
Theodora Cantacuzene (fl. 14th c.)
Theodora Comnena (fl. 1080s)
Theodora Ducas (fl. 11th c.)
Theodora Oldenburg (1906–1969)
Theodora Paleologina
Theodora the Blessed (c. 810–c. 860)
Theodosia (fl. 1220)
Theodosia of Moscow (1475–1501)
Theresa of Liechtenstein (1850–1938)
Theresa of Saxe-Altenburg (1836–1914)
Theresa of Saxony (1792–1854)
Thermuthis (fl. 1500 BCE)
Thyra of Denmark (1880–1945)
Thyra Oldenburg (1853–1933)
Toselli, Louisa (1870–1947)
Tsahai Haile Selassie (1919–1942)
Urraca (1033–1101)
Urraca of Aragon (fl. 11th c.)
Ursula (fl. 3rd or 5th c.)
Victoire, Madame (1733–1799)
Victoria (1819–1901)
Victoria (1866–1929)
Victoria (1868–1935)
Victoria (1977—)
Victoria Adelaide (1840–1901)
Victoria Adelaide of Schleswig-Holstein (1885–1970)
Victoria of Hesse-Darmstadt (1863–1950)
Volkonskaya, Maria (1805–1863)
Wencheng (c. 620–680)
Wilhelmina (1880–1962)
Wilhelmina of Prussia (1751–1820)
Wilhelmine (1808–1891)
Withburga (fl. 7th c.)
Wulfhild (fl. 11th c.)
Yasodhara (fl. 547 BCE)
Yolanda Margherita of Italy (1901–1986)
Yolande of Aragon (1379–1442)
Zabel (b. around 1210)
Zauditu (1876–1930)
Zbyslawa (fl. 1100)
Zoe Ducas (fl. 11th c.)
Zorka of Montenegro (1864–1890)

PRINCESS IMPERIAL

Januaria (1822–1901)

PRINCESS ROYAL

Anne, Princess (1950—)
Augusta Guelph (1737–1813)
Charlotte Augusta Matilda (1766–1828)
Charlotte of Saxe-Meiningen (1860–1919)
Frederica of Prussia (1767–1820)
Isabel of Brazil (1846–1921)
Mary (1897–1965)
Mary of Hesse-Cassel (1723–1772)
Mary of Orange (1631–1660)
Sophia Matilda (1773–1844)
Victoria Adelaide (1840–1901)

PRINTER

Aitken, Jane (1764–1832)
Bradford, Cornelia Smith (d. 1755)
Draper, Margaret (d. around 1800)
Durand, Marguerite (1864–1936)
Faithfull, Emily (1835–1895)
Franklin, Ann (1696–1763)
Glover, Elizabeth Harris (d. 1643)
Goddard, Mary Katherine (1738–1816)
Goddard, Sarah Updike (c. 1700–1770)
Green, Anne Catherine (c. 1720–1775)
Guillard, Charlotte (d. 1556)
Gutiérrez de Mendoza, Juana Belén (1875–1942)
James, Elinor (c. 1645–1719)
McKenney, Ruth (1911–1972)
Nuthead, Dinah (fl. 1696)
Phipson, Joan (1912–2003)
Rind, Clementina (c. 1740–1774)
Roulstone, Elizabeth (fl. 1804)
Templeton, Rini (1935–1986)
Timothy, Ann (c. 1727–1792)
Timothy, Elizabeth (d. 1757)
Yeats, Elizabeth (1868–1940)
Yeats, Lily (1866–1949)
Zenger, Anna Catharina (c. 1704–1751)

PRINTMAKER

See Lithographer.

PRIORESS

Beatrice of Nazareth (c. 1200–1268)
Campanini, Barbara (1721–1799)
Catherine of Ricci (c. 1522–1589)
Christina of Markyate (1096–1160)
Drane, Augusta Theodosia (1823–1894)
Fedele, Cassandra Fidelis (1465–1558)
Gill, Mary Gabriel (1837–1905)
Heloise (c. 1100–1163)
Herbert, Lucy (1669–1744)
Jutta (d. 1284)
Lutgard (1182–1246)
Marie (1393–1438)
Marie de Bourbon (fl. 1350s)
Mathews, Ann Teresa (1732–1800)
McLachlan, Laurentia (1866–1953)
Oignt, Marguerite d' (d. 1310)

PRISON ADMINISTRATOR

Arenal, Concepción (1820–1893)
Atkinson, Eudora Clark (1831–?)
Hall, Emma Amelia (1837–1884)
Harris, Mary Belle (1874–1957)
Van Waters, Miriam (1887–1974)

PRISONER

Adelaide of Burgundy (931–999)
Adler, Polly (1899–1962)
Adler, Valentine (1898–1942)
Agnes, Lore (1876–1953)
Ahern, Lizzie (1877–1969)
Alais of France (1160–?)
Albrecht, Bertie (d. 1943)
Allen, Mary Sophia (1878–1964)
Anderson, Evelyn (1907–1994)
Andics, Erzsebet (1902–1986)
Annenkova, Julia (c. 1898–c. 1938)
Apostoloy, Electra (1911–1944)
Aquino, Melchora (1812–1919)
Arendsee, Martha (1885–1953)
Arletty (1898–1992)
Armand, Inessa (1874–1920)
Arnauld, Angélique (1624–1684)

Occupational Index

Arnim, Bettine von (1785–1859)
Askew, Anne (c. 1521–1546)
Assing, Ludmilla (1821–1880)
Auer, Judith (1905–1944)
Augustat, Elise (1889–1940)
Aung San Suu Kyi (1945—)
Awolowo, Hannah (1915—)
Baard, Francina (1901–1997)
Baarova, Lida (1914–2000)
Badger, Charlotte (fl. 1806–1808)
Barkova, Anna Aleksandrovna (1901–1976)
Barykova, Anna Pavlovna (1839–1893)
Bastidas, Micaela (1745–1781)
Bateman, Mary (1768–1809)
Bates, Daisy Lee (1914–1999)
Bathory, Elizabeth (1560–1614)
Baum, Marianne (1912–1942)
Baumann, Edith (1909–1973)
Bavent, Madeleine (fl. 1642)
Beaufort, Joan (c. 1410–1445)
Becker, Marie Alexander (1877–194?)
Behn, Aphra (1640?–1689)
Bejarano, Esther (1924—)
Bell, Gertrude (1868–1926)
Benario, Olga (1908–1942)
Benizelos, Philothey (fl. 1650)
Berengaria of Navarre (c. 1163–c. 1230)
Berenice Syra (c. 280–246 BCE)
Bervoets, Marguerite (1914–1944)
Besant, Annie (1847–1933)
Beyer, Helga (1920–1942)
Bhutto, Benazir (1953—)
Bhutto, Nusrat (1929—)
Billington-Greig, Teresa (1877–1964)
Blanche of Bourbon (c. 1338–1361)
Blanche of Navarre (1424–1464)
Bloor, Ella Reeve (1862–1951)
Bocanegra, Gertrudis (1765–1817)
Bocher, Joan (d. 1550)
Bohley, Bärbel (1945—)
Bohm-Schuch, Clara (1879–1936)
Bohuszewiczowna, Maria (1865–1887)
Boissevain, Mia (1878–1959)
Boleyn, Anne (c. 1507–1536)
Bol Poel, Martha (1877–1956)
Bona of Pisa (c. 1156–1207)
Botchkareva, Maria (1889–?)
Boudin, Kathy (1943—)
Bouhired, Djamila (1937—)
Boyd, Belle (1844–1900)
Bracetti, Mariana (1840–c. 1904)
Braden, Anne (1924—)
Braose, Annora de (d. 1241)
Braose, Maud de (d. 1211)
Brécourt, Jeanne (b. 1837)
Breshkovsky, Catherine (1844–1934)
Brion, Hélène (1882–1962)
Broniewska, Janina (1904–1981)
Bruce, Margaret (1296–1316)
Bruha, Antonia (1915—)
Brüll, Ilse (1925–1942)
Brunner, Josefine (1909–1943)
Buber-Neumann, Margarete (1901–1989)
Budberg, Moura (1892–1974)
Buller, Annie (1896–1973)
Bullwinkel, Vivian (1915–2000)
Buresova, Charlotte (1904–1984)
Cahun, Claude (1894–1954)
Carney, Winifred (1887–1943)
Caroline Matilda (1751–1775)
Carré, Mathilde (1908–c. 1970)
Casanova, Danielle (1909–1943)
Catherine, Queen of Portugal (1507–1578)
Catherine I of Russia (1684–1727)
Cavell, Edith (1865–1915)
Chadwick, Cassie L. (1859–1907)
Chambers, Norah (1905–1989)
Chapelle, Dickey (1919–1972)
Chase, Agnes Meara (1869–1963)
Chattopadhyaya, Kamaladevi (1903–1988)
Chirwa, Vera (1933—)
Christina of Saxony (1461–1521)
Churchill, Deborah (1677–1708)
Clarke, Kathleen (1878–1972)
Clarke, Mary Anne (c. 1776–1852)
Cobham, Eleanor (d. 1452)
Cohn, Marianne (1921–1944)
Corday, Charlotte (1768–1793)
Cornelys, Theresa (1723–1797)
Cousins, Margaret (1878–1954)
Crespé, Marie-Madeleine (1760–1796)
Cuzzoni, Francesca (c. 1698–1770)
Davis, Angela (1944—)
Davison, Emily (1872–1913)
de Bettignies, Louise (d. 1918)
Delbo, Charlotte (1913–1985)
Demandols de La Palud, Madeleine
Deng Yingchao (1903–1992)
Deroin, Jeanne-Françoise (1805–1894)
Deshoulières, Antoinette (1638–1694)
Despard, Charlotte (1844–1939)
Devanny, Jean (1894–1962)
Diebold, Laure (1915–1964)
Ding Ling (1904–1985)
Dorn, Erna (1912–1953)
Dragoicheva, Tsola (1893–1993)
Drexel, Constance (1894–1956)
Drummond, Flora (1869–1949)
Dryburgh, Margaret (1890–1945)
du Barry, Jeanne Bécu, Comtesse (1743–1793)
Duczynska, Ilona (1897–1978)
Dunham, Katherine (1909–2006)
Dustin, Hannah (1657–c. 1736)
Dyer, Mary Barrett (c. 1591–1660)
Dzerzhinska, Sofia (1882–1968)
Ehre, Ida (1900–1989)
Eisenblätter, Charlotte (1903–1944)
Eleanor, the Maid of Brittany (1184–1241)
Eleanor of Aquitaine (1122–1204)
Eleanor of Montfort (1252–1282)
Elizabeth I of England (1533–1603)
Ellis, Ruth (1927–1955)
El Saadawi, Nawal (1931—)
Emhart, Maria (1901–1981)
Erauso, Catalina de (1592–1635)
Fabian, Dora (1901–1935)
Felicitas or Felicitas of Carthage (d. 203)
Fell, Margaret (1614–1702)
Fénelon, Fania (1918–1983)
Figner, Vera (1852–1942)
First, Ruth (1925–1982)
Fischer, Ruth (1895–1961)
Fittko, Lisa (1909–2005)
Fleming, Amalia (1912–1986)
Flora of Cordova (d. 851)
Flynn, Elizabeth Gurley (1890–1964)
Fornalska, Malgorzata (1902–1944)
Frank, Anne (1929–1945)
Fredegund (c. 547–597)
Freundlich, Emmy (1878–1948)
Fukuda Hideko (1865–1927)
Gabrielli, Caterina (1730–1796)
Gaidinliu, Rani (1915–1993)
Gandhi, Indira (1917–1984)
Gasteazoro, Ana (1950–1993)
Gelfman, Gesia (d. 1882)
Gillars, Mildred E. (1900–1988)
Giroud, Françoise (1916–2003)
Goldman, Emma (1869–1940)
Golubkina, Anna (1864–1927)
Gonne, Maud (1866–1953)
Goode, Dorcas
Goode, Sarah
Gore-Booth, Eva (1870–1926)
Goslar, Hannah (1928—)
Gouges, Olympe de (1748–1793)
Grange, Rachel (1682–1745)
Greenhow, Rose O'Neal (c. 1817–1864)
Grey, Catherine (c. 1540–1568)
Grey, Lady Jane (1537–1554)
Grundig, Lea (1906–1977)
Guard, Elizabeth (1814–1870)
Guiney, Louise Imogen (1861–1920)
Gutiérrez de Mendoza, Juana Belén (1875–1942)
Gutteridge, Helena Rose (1879–1960)
Guyon, Jeanne Marie Bouviéres de la Mothe (1648–1717)
Guzman, Leonora de (1310–1351)
Hamer, Fannie Lou (1917–1977)
Hamilton, Emma (1765–1815)
Hanau, Marthe (c. 1884–1935)
Harnack, Mildred (1902–1943)
Harrison, Marguerite (1879–1967)
Hart, Nancy (c. 1846–1902)
Hautval, Adelaide (1906–1988)
Hay, Lucy (1599–1660)
Hayes, Catherine (1690–1726)
Hearst, Patricia Campbell (1954—)
Hébert, Madame (d. 1794)
Henrys, Catherine (c. 1805–1855)
Herrmann, Liselotte (1909–1938)
Hillesum, Etty (1914–1943)
Hindley, Myra (1942—)
Holiday, Billie (c. 1915–1959)
How-Martyn, Edith (1875–1954)
Hoxha, Nexhmije (1920—)
Huck, Winnifred Sprague Mason (1882–1936)
Ibárruri, Dolores (1895–1989)
Ingeborg (c. 1176–1237/38)
Inglis, Elsie Maud (1864–1917)
Irene of Athens (c. 752–803)
Isabella del Balzo (d. 1533)
Isabella of Buchan (fl. 1290–1310)
Ivanovskaia, Praskovia (1853–1935)
Ivinskaya, Olga (1912–1995)
Jacob, Rosamund (1888–1960)
Jacobs, Harriet A. (1813–1897)
Jacobson, Louise (1924–1943)
Jacqueline of Hainault (1401–1436)
Jemison, Mary (1742–1833)
Jenner, Andrea (1891–1985)
Jesenská, Milena (1896–1945)
Jingū (c. 201–269)
Joanna I of Naples (1326–1382)
Joanna of Navarre (c. 1370–1437)
Joan of Arc (c. 1412–1431)
Jochmann, Rosa (1901–1994)
Jones, Mary Harris (1830–1930)
Josephine (1763–1814)
Juana la Loca (1479–1555)
Julia (39 BCE–14 CE)
Kartini (1879–1904)
Keeler, Christine (1942—)
Kelly, Kathryn Thorne (1904–1998?)
Kenney, Annie (1879–1953)
Kent, Constance (1844–?)
Kéthly, Anna (1889–1976)
Khan, Noor Inayat (1914–1944)
Klarsfeld, Beate (1939—)
Koch, Ilse (1906–1967)
Kollontai, Alexandra (1872–1952)
Kosmodemyanskaya, Zoya (1923–1941)
Kossak, Zofia (1890–1968)
Koszutska, Maria (1876–1939)
Kovalskaia, Elizaveta (1851–1943)
Kuderikova, Marie (1921–1943)
Kuliscioff, Anna (c. 1854–1925)

Kunke, Steffi (1908–1942)
Kuzwayo, Ellen (1914–2006)
Lacombe, Claire (1765–?)
Lafarge, Marie (1816–1852)
Lafayette, Marie Adrienne de (1760–1807)
Lamballe, Marie Thérèse Louise of Savoy-Carignano, Princesse de (1749–1792)
Lange, Anne Françoise Elizabeth (1772–1816)
Lavoisier, Marie (1758–1836)
Lebron, Lolita (1919—)
Lee, Ann (1736–1784)
Leichter, Käthe (1895–1942)
Leocadia (d. about 303)
Liliuokalani (1838–1917)
Lindner, Herta (1920–1943)
Lingens-Reiner, Ella (1908–2002)
Liubatovich, Olga (1853–1917)
Liubatovich, Vera (1855–1907)
Lohman, Ann Trow (1812–1878)
Longueville, Anne Geneviève, Duchesse de (1619–1679)
Lonsdale, Kathleen (1903–1971)
López de Córdoba, Leonor (1362–1412)
Lucid, Shannon (1943—)
Luckner, Gertrud (1900–1995)
Ludmila (859–920)
Lupicinia-Euphemia (d. 523)
Luxemburg, Rosa (1870–1919)
Lynch, Eliza (1835–1886)
Lyons, Sophie (1848–1924)
Lytton, Constance (1869–1923)
Macardle, Dorothy (1889–1958)
Macdonald, Flora (1722–1790)
Mafalda of Hesse (1902–1944)
Magnus (d. 1676)
Mahbuba (fl. 9th c.)
Maintenon, Françoise d'Aubigné, Marquise de (1635–1719)
Mansenée, Desle la (c. 1502–1529)
Manus, Rosa (1881–1942)
Marek, Martha Lowenstein (1904–1938)
Margaret (1240–1275)
Margaret of Angoulême (1492–1549)
Margaret of Anjou (c. 1272–1299)
Margaret of Antioch (c. 255–c. 275)
Margaret of Burgundy (1290–1315)
Margaret of Valois (1553–1615)
Marguerite Louise of Orleans (c. 1645–1721)
Maria-Kyratza Asen (fl. late 1300s)
Maria Luisa of Etruria (1782–1824)
Maria of Cordova (d. 851)
Maria of Hungary (1371–1395)
Marie Antoinette (1755–1793)
Marie Feodorovna (1847–1928)
Marie Thérèse Charlotte (1778–1851)
Markievicz, Constance (1868–1927)
Markovic, Mirjana (1942—)
Marx, Jenny von Westphalen (1814–1881)
Mary I of England (1516–1558)
Mary Stuart (1542–1587)
Marzia (fl. 1357)
Masaryk, Alice Garrigue (1879–1966)
Mavrokordatou, Alexandra (1605–1684)
McAliskey, Bernadette Devlin (1947—)
Medici, Catherine de (1519–1589)
Meinhof, Ulrike (1934–1972)
Mendoza, Ana de (1540–1592)
Mercier, Euphrasie (1823–?)
Michel, Louise (1830–1905)
Michelina of Pesaro (1300–1356)
Mink, Paule (1839–1901)
Mirabal de González, Patria (1924–1960)
Mirabal de Guzmán, María Teresa (1936–1960)
Mirabal de Tavárez, Minerva (1927–1960)
Mitchell, Ruth (c. 1888–1969)
Mitford, Diana (1910–2003)
Mniszek, Marina (c. 1588–1614)
Moders, Mary (1643–1673)
Molony, Helena (1884–1967)
Montesson, Charlotte Jeanne Béraud de la Haye de Riou, marquise de (1737–1805)
Mulenga, Alice (1924–1978)
Mydans, Shelley (1915–2002)
Nanye'hi (1738–1822)
Nasi, Gracia Mendes (1510–1569)
Nation, Carry (1846–1911)
Neher, Carola (1900–1942)
Neuber, Caroline (1697–1760)
Newman, Julia St. Clair (1818–?)
Ngoyi, Lilian (1911–1980)
Nguyen Thi Dinh (1920–1992)
Niederkirchner, Käte (1909–1944)
Nienhuys, Janna
Nonteta Bungu (c. 1875–1935)
Nurse, Rebecca (1621–1692)
Nyembe, Dorothy (1930–1998)
Oberheuser, Herta (1911–1978)
Ocampo, Victoria (1890–1979)
O'Hare, Kate Richards (1876–1948)
O'Malley, Grace (c. 1530–1603)
Ordonówna, Hanka (1904–1950)
Ortíz de Dominguez, Josefa (c. 1768–1829)
Osburn, Sarah
Overlach, Helene (1894–1983)
Paasche, Maria (1909–2000)
Palm, Etta Aelders (1743–1799)
Pandit, Vijaya Lakshmi (1900–1990)
Pankhurst, Adela (1885–1961)
Pankhurst, Christabel (1880–1958)
Pankhurst, Emmeline (1858–1928)
Pankhurst, Sylvia (1882–1960)
Parek, Lagle (1941—)
Parker, Dorothy (1893–1967)
Pauker, Ana (c. 1893–1960)
Paul, Alice (1885–1977)
Peck, Ellen (1829–1915)
Pels, Auguste van (1900–1945)
Perpetua (181–203)
Pfeiffer, Ida (1797–1858)
Phoolan Devi (1963–2001)
Pilkington, Laetitia (c. 1708–1750)
Pimentel, Eleonora (c. 1768–1799)
Place, Martha (1848–1899)
Preradovic, Paula von (1887–1951)
Przybyszewska, Stanislawa (1901–1935)
Pulcheria (c. 398–453)
Radegund of Poitiers (518–587)
Rafael, Sylvia (1938–2005)
Raucourt, Mlle (1756–1815)
Razia (1211–1240)
Reibey, Mary (1777–1855)
Reitsch, Hanna (1912–1979)
Renée of France (1510–1575)
Restituta, Sister (1894–1943)
Rhondda, Margaret (1883–1958)
Richilde (1034–1086)
Riefenstahl, Leni (1902–2003)
Rinser, Luise (1911–2002)
Robespierre, Charlotte (1760–1840)
Robinson, Mary (1758–1800)
Rodríguez, Ana (1938—)
Roland, Madame (1754–1793)
Roland, Pauline (1805–1852)
Rosé, Alma (1906–1944)
Rosenberg, Ethel (1915–1953)
Rothelin, Jacqueline de Rohan, Marquise de (c. 1520–1587)
Rubenstein, Blanche (c. 1897–1969)
Ruth-Rolland, J.M. (1937–1995)
Salavarrieta, Pola (1795–1817)
Samoilova, Konkordiya (1876–1921)
Sanger, Margaret (1879–1966)
Sansom, Odette (1912–1995)
Sarrazin, Albertine (1937–1967)
Schaft, Hannie (1920–1945)
Schlösinger, Rose (1907–1943)
Scholl, Sophie (1921–1943)
Schulze-Boysen, Libertas (1913–1942)
Schumacher, Elisabeth (1904–1942)
Scott, Jessie Ann (1883–1959)
Seidel, Amalie (1876–1952)
Senesh, Hannah (1921–1944)
September, Dulcie (1935–1988)
Sforza, Caterina (c. 1462–1509)
Sheehy-Skeffington, Hanna (1877–1946)
Shochat, Manya (1878–1961)
Shtern, Lina (1878–1968)
Sikakane, Joyce Nomafa (1943—)
Sisulu, Albertina (1918—)
Smedley, Agnes (1892–1950)
Smith, Charlotte (1749–1806)
Smyth, Ethel (1858–1944)
Snow, Valaida (c. 1903–1956)
Snyder, Ruth (1893–1928)
Sobieski, Clementina (1702–1735)
Sophia Dorothea of Brunswick-Celle (1666–1726)
Spira, Steffie (1908–1995)
Spiridonova, Maria (1884–1941)
Staal de Launay, Madame de (1684–1750)
Starr, Belle (1848–1889)
Stasova, Elena (1873–1966)
Strong, Anna Louise (1885–1970)
Stuart, Arabella (1575–1615)
Surratt, Mary E. (c. 1820–1865)
Szabo, Violette (1921–1945)
Talbot, Mary Anne (1778–1808)
Tallien, Thérésa (1773–1835)
Taro, Gerda (1910–1937)
ten Boom, Corrie (1892–1983)
Tetberga (fl. 9th c.)
Theoctista (c. 740–c. 802)
Théot, Catherine (d. 1794)
Théroigne de Méricourt, Anne-Josèphe (1762–1817)
Thomas, Elizabeth (1675–1731)
Tillion, Germaine (b. 1907)
Tinayre, Marguerite (1831–?)
Tituba
Toguri, Iva (1916—)
Tolstoy, Alexandra (1884–1979)
Trapnel, Anna (fl. 1642–1661)
Triolet, Elsa (1896–1970)
Trotsky, Natalia Ivanovna (1882–1962)
Tsvetaeva, Marina (1892–1941)
Tussaud, Marie (1761–1850)
Ulfeldt, Leonora Christina (1621–1698)
Ursinus, Sophie (1760–1836)
Varo, Remedios (1906–1963)
Vaux, Anne (fl. 1605–1635)
Veil, Simone (1927—)
Vestris, Lucia (1797–1856)
Vicario, Leona (1789–1842)
Vlachos, Helen (1911–1995)
Volkonskaya, Maria (1805–1863)
Walentynowicz, Anna (1929—)
Walker, Mary Edwards (1832–1919)
Ward, Mary (1586–1645)
Weber, Jeanne (1875–1910)
Webster, Kate (1849–1879)
Wheeldon, Alice (fl. 1917)
Wheeler, Anna Doyle (1785–c. 1850)
White, Sue Shelton (1887–1943)
Williams, Cicely (1893–1992)
Williams, Helen Maria (1762–1827)
Witchcraft Trials in Salem Village (1692–1693)
Wolstenholme-Elmy, Elizabeth (1834–1913)
Women POWs of Sumatra (1942–1945)
Women Prophets and Visionaries in France at the End of the Middle Ages

Yaa Akyaa (c. 1837–c. 1921)
Young, Ella (1867–1951)
Zasulich, Vera (1849–1919)
Zelle, Margaretha (1876–1917)
Zetkin, Clara (1857–1933)
Zimetbaum, Mala (1920–1944)
Zita of Parma (1892–1989)
Zlatin, Sabina (1907–1996)
Zrinyi, Ilona (1643–1703)

PRISON MATRON
Seager, Esther (c. 1835–1911)

PRISON REFORMER
Arenal, Concepción (1820–1893)
Astor, Nancy Witcher (1879–1964)
Barnard, Kate (1875–1930)
Bartelme, Mary (1866–1954)
Braddock, Bessie (1899–1970)
Bradwell, Myra (1831–1894)
Burke, Yvonne Brathwaite (1932—)
Carpenter, Mary (1807–1877)
Carter, Rosalynn (1927—)
Child, Lydia Maria (1802–1880)
Crane, Caroline Bartlett (1858–1935)
Croly, Jane Cunningham (1829–1901)
Davis, Katharine Bement (1860–1935)
Evans, Elizabeth Glendower (1856–1937)
Felton, Rebecca Latimer (1835–1930)
Fenwick, Millicent (1910–1992)
Foltz, Clara (1849–1934)
Ford, Isabella O. (1855–1924)
Franklin, Miles (1879–1954)
Fry, Elizabeth (1780–1845)
Fry, Margery (1874–1958)
Fuller, Margaret (1810–1850)
Gilbert, Linda (1847–1895)
Goldstein, Vida (1869–1949)
Hall, Emma Amelia (1837–1884)
Hallowell, Anna (1831–1905)
Hanbury, Elizabeth (1793–1901)
Hodder, Jessie Donaldson (1867–1931)
Hughes, Sarah T. (1896–1985)
Johnson, Ellen Cheney (1829–1899)
Kenyatta, Margaret (1928—)
Lonsdale, Kathleen (1903–1971)
Lowell, Josephine Shaw (1843–1905)
Lozier, Clemence S. (1813–1888)
MacGill, Helen Gregory (1871–1947)
Macphail, Agnes (1890–1954)
Marion, Frances (1888–1973)
McCracken, Mary Ann (1770–1866)
Mitford, Jessica (1917–1996)
Nalkowska, Zofia (1884–1954)
O'Hare, Kate Richards (1876–1948)
Ottenberg, Nettie Podell (1887–1982)
Parren, Kalliroe (1861–1940)
Pedersen, Helga (1911–1980)
Ragghianti, Marie (1942—)
Ricker, Marilla (1840–1920)
Rodríguez, Ana (1938—)
Sarrazin, Albertine (1937–1967)
Scott, Rose (1847–1925)
Stuart, Miranda (c. 1795–1865)
Suzman, Helen (1917—)
Tutwiler, Julia Strudwick (1841–1916)
Van Waters, Miriam (1887–1974)
Veil, Simone (1927—)
Walentynowicz, Anna (1929—)
Wells, Alice Stebbins (1873–1957)
Willebrandt, Mabel Walker (1889–1963)
Wilson, Charlotte (1854–1944)
Wilson, Margaret W. (1882–1973)
Wrede, Mathilda (1864–1928)

PRISON-RELIEF WORKER
Annabella (1909–1996)
Booth, Evangeline (1865–1950)
Booth, Maud Ballington (1865–1948)
Bremer, Fredrika (1801–1865)
Brooks, Gwendolyn (1917–2000)
Brophy, Brigid (1929–1995)
Byers, Margaret (1832–1912)
Cabrini, Frances Xavier (1850–1917)
Carey, Miriam E. (1858–1937)
Casilda (d. about 1007)
Cousins, Margaret (1878–1954)
Despard, Charlotte (1844–1939)
Doremus, Sarah Platt (1802–1877)
Duncan, Sheena (1932—)
Farnham, Eliza W. (1815–1864)
Figner, Vera (1852–1942)
Foltz, Clara (1849–1934)
Franklin, Jane (1792–1875)
Fukuda Hideko (1865–1927)
Gabrielli, Caterina (1730–1796)
Gaskell, Elizabeth (1810–1865)
Gasteazoro, Ana (1950–1993)
Gilbert, Linda (1847–1895)
Graham, Isabella (1742–1814)
Harris, Barbara (1930—)
Hayes, Lucy Webb (1831–1889)
Jameson, Anna Brownell (1794–1860)
Kingsley, Mary H. (1862–1900)
Koszutska, Maria (1876–1939)
Krupskaya, Nadezhda (1869–1939)
Lagerlöf, Selma (1858–1940)
Lefaucheux, Marie-Helene (1904–1964)
Loebinger, Lotte (1905–1999)
Longueville, Anne Geneviève, Duchesse de (1619–1679)
Lyons, Sophie (1848–1924)
Macphail, Agnes (1890–1954)
Michel, Louise (1830–1905)
Mosher, Eliza Maria (1846–1928)
Newman, Angelia L. (1837–1910)
Nienhuys, Janna
Oddon, Yvonne (1902–1982)
Palmer, Phoebe Worrall (1807–1874)
Ricker, Marilla (1840–1920)
Robinson, Mary (1944—)
Sampson, Edith S. (1901–1979)
Schoff, Hannah Kent (1853–1940)
Scudéry, Madeleine de (1607–1701)
Sheehy-Skeffington, Hanna (1877–1946)
Sikakane, Joyce Nomafa (1943—)
Stuart, Miranda (c. 1795–1865)
ten Boom, Corrie (1892–1983)
Tillion, Germaine (b. 1907)
Tingley, Katherine (1847–1929)
Tod, Isabella (1836–1896)
Tolstoy, Alexandra (1884–1979)
Van Lew, Elizabeth (1818–1900)
Volkonskaya, Maria (1805–1863)
Wald, Florence (1917—)
White, Eartha M. (1876–1974)
Whitney, Dorothy Payne (1887–1968)
Wilson, Charlotte (1854–1944)
Winnemucca, Sarah (1844–1891)
Wright, Helena (1887–1982)
Zell, Katharina Schütz (c. 1497–1562)

PRODUCER
Allen, Jay Presson (1922–2006)
Baker, Diane (1938—)
Bergen, Polly (1929—)
Bovasso, Julie (1930–1991)
Fawcett, Marion (1886–1957)
Gauntier, Gene (1885–1966)
Marly, Florence (1918–1978)
Moore, Terry (1929—)
Nair, Mira (1957—)
Oliver, Susan (1937–1990)

PROFESSIONAL-ORGANIZATION FOUNDER
Albright, Tenley (1935—)
Alice Maud Mary (1843–1878)
Andrus, Ethel Percy (1884–1967)
Applebee, Constance (1873–1981)
Ashcroft, Peggy (1907–1991)
Barker, M.C. (1879–1963)
Bauer, Marion (1887–1955)
Beecher, Catharine (1800–1878)
Breckinridge, Mary (1881–1965)
Burchenal, Elizabeth (1876–1959)
Clarke, Helen Archibald (1860–1926)
Dall, Caroline Wells (1822–1912)
Deutsch, Helen (1906–1992)
Donalda, Pauline (1882–1970)
Douglas, Marjory Stoneman (1890–1998)
El Saadawi, Nawal (1931—)
Epstein, Charlotte (1884–1938)
Evans, Matilda Arabella (1872–1935)
Flaherty, Frances Hubbard (c. 1886–1972)
Fontana, Lavinia (1552–1614)
Franklin, Martha Minerva (1870–1968)
Fromm-Reichmann, Frieda (1889–1957)
Fuller, Lucia Fairchild (1870–1224)
Furbish, Kate (1834–1931)
Gardner, Mary Sewall (1871–1961)
Gibson, Althea (1927—)
Hanson-Dyer, Louise (1884–1962)
Harrison, Elizabeth (1849–1927)
Heath, Sophia (1896–1936)
Hill, Patty Smith (1868–1946)
Jarrett, Mary Cromwell (1877–1961)
Kaur, Rajkumari Amrit (1889–1964)
King, Billie Jean (1943—)
Korchinska, Maria (1895–1979)
Lasker, Mary (1900–1994)
Milligan, Alice (1866–1953)
Morgan, Agnes Fay (1884–1968)
Orr, Alice Greenough (1902–1995)
Pankhurst, Adela (1885–1961)
Parrish, Celestia (1853–1918)
Perry, Lilla Cabot (c. 1848–1933)
Petersen, Alicia O'Shea (1862–1923)
Petry, Lucile (1902–1999)
Phillips, Lena Madesin (1881–1955)
Porter, Charlotte Endymion (1857–1942)
Powell, Maud (1867–1920)
Preston, May Wilson (1873–1949)
Richter, Elise (1865–1943)
Robinson, Jane Bancroft (1847–1932)
Roebling, Mary G. (1906–1994)
Roland, Pauline (1805–1852)
Sarabhai, Anusyabehn (1885–1972)
Stanwyck, Barbara (1907–1990)
Talbot, Marion (1858–1948)
Thaden, Louise (1905–1979)
Ticknor, Anna Eliot (1823–1896)
Triolet, Elsa (1896–1970)
Van Hoosen, Bertha (1863–1952)
Washington, Fredi (1903–1994)
Wells, Emmeline B. (1828–1921)
Wells-Barnett, Ida (1862–1931)
Wheeler, Candace (1827–1923)
Yamada, Mitsuye (1923—)
Zaharias, Babe Didrikson (1911–1956)
Zorach, Marguerite Thompson (1887–1968)

PROOF-READER
Gibson, Emily Patricia (1863/64?–1947)

PROPAGANDIST
Anderson, Evelyn N. (1909–1977)

Arendsee, Martha (1885–1953)
Armand, Inessa (1874–1920)
Baker, Josephine (1906–1975)
Balabanoff, Angelica (1878–1965)
Becher, Lilly (1901–1976)
Belgioso, Cristina (1808–1871)
Benario, Olga (1908–1942)
Berg, Helene (b. 1906)
Billington-Greig, Teresa (1877–1964)
Boissevain, Mia (1878–1959)
Box, Betty E. (1915–1999)
Breshkovsky, Catherine (1844–1934)
Brion, Hélène (1882–1962)
Brunschvicg, Cécile (1877–1946)
Bülow, Frieda von (1857–1909)
Cai Chang (1900–1990)
Deutsch, Helene (1884–1982)
Drexel, Constance (1894–1956)
Dzerzhinska, Sofia (1882–1968)
Exter, Alexandra (1882–1949)
Flanagan, Hallie (1889–1969)
Galindo de Topete, Hermila (1896–1954)
Gasteazoro, Ana (1950–1993)
Gillars, Mildred E. (1900–1988)
Greenhow, Rose O'Neal (c. 1817–1864)
Hamilton, Emma (1765–1815)
Horna, Kati (1912—)
Ibárruri, Dolores (1895–1989)
Kaminska, Ida (1899–1980)
Kang Keqing (1911–1992)
Karatza, Rallou (1778–1830)
Kollontai, Alexandra (1872–1952)
Kovalskaia, Elizaveta (1851–1943)
Krupskaya, Nadezhda (1869–1939)
Lee, Jennie (1904–1988)
Liubatovich, Olga (1853–1917)
Loebinger, Lotte (1905–1999)
Lowell, Amy (1874–1925)
Löwenstein, Helga Maria zu (1910–2004)
Luxemburg, Rosa (1870–1919)
Macaulay, Rose (1881–1958)
Manus, Rosa (1881–1942)
Matthews, Jessie (1907–1981)
Millay, Edna St. Vincent (1892–1950)
Milligan, Alice (1866–1953)
Mukhina, Vera (1889–1953)
Neris, Salomeja (1904–1945)
Noce, Teresa (1900–1980)
Pankhurst, Christabel (1880–1958)
Pauker, Ana (c. 1893–1960)
Porter, Katherine Anne (1890–1980)
Rabin, Leah (1928–2000)
Rambert, Marie (1888–1982)
Riefenstahl, Leni (1902–2003)
Roberts, Marguerite (1905–1989)
Rodríguez, Ana (1938—)
Roland, Pauline (1805–1852)
Roland Holst, Henriëtte (1869–1952)
Salt, Barbara (1904–1975)
Samoilova, Konkordiya (1876–1921)
Sand, George (1804–1876)
Sayers, Dorothy L. (1893–1957)
Sirota, Beate (1923—)
Söderbaum, Kristina (1912—)
Spiridonova, Maria (1884–1941)
Stasova, Elena (1873–1966)
Strong, Anna Louise (1885–1970)
Toguri, Iva (1916—)
Valette, Aline (1850–1899)
von Harbou, Thea (1888–1954)
Warren, Mercy Otis (1728–1814)
Wasilewska, Wanda (1905–1964)
Wessely, Paula (1907–2000)
Wu Zetian (624–705)
Yessayan, Zabel (1878–1943)

PROPHET/SIBYL/VISIONARY
Adams, Evangeline Smith (1873–1932)
Boneta, Prous (d. 1323)
Brigue, Jehenne de (d. 1391)
Butters, Mary (fl. 1839)
Cassandra (possibly fl. around 1200 BCE)
Davies, Eleanor (1590–1652)
Deborah (fl. 12th c. BCE)
Dixon, Jeane (1918–1997)
Frith, Mary (c. 1584–1659)
Guglielma of Milan (d. 1282)
Gushterova, Vangelia (1911–1996)
Hadewijch (fl. 13th c.)
Hannah (fl. 11th c. BCE)
Hikapuhi (1860/71?–1934)
Hildegard of Bingen (1098–1179)
Huldah
Jackson, Rebecca Cox (1795–1871)
Kaaro, Ani (fl. 1885–1901)
Kahina (r. 695–703)
Lenormand, Marie Anne Adélaïde (1772–1843)
Mary the Jewess (fl. 1st, 2nd or 3rd c.)
Miriam the Prophet (fl. c. 13th or 14th c. BCE)
Mulenga, Alice (1924–1978)
Nonteta Bungu (c. 1875–1935)
Odozi Obodo, Madam (1909–1995)
Orsini, Belleza (d. 1528)
Pentreath, Dolly (1685–1777)
Rikiriki, Atareta Kawana Ropiha Mere (c. 1855–1926)
Robine, Marie (d. 1399)
Sambethe
Shipton, Mother (1488–1561)
Soleil, Germaine (1913–1996)
Southcott, Joanna (1750–1814)
Teresa, Mother (1910–1997)
Théot, Catherine (d. 1794)
Trapnel, Anna (fl. 1642–1661)
White, Ellen Gould (1827–1915)

PROSTITUTE
Finnie, Jessie (c. 1821–?)
Greaves, Mary Ann (1834–1897)
Swift, Anne (1829/35–?)
Weldon, Barbara (1829/30–1882)

PSYCHIATRIST
Adler, Alexandra (1901–2001)
Bashir, Marie (1930—)
Boyle, Helen (1869–1957)
Densen-Gerber, Judianne (1934–2003)
Deutsch, Helene (1884–1982)
Dunbar, Flanders (1902–1959)
Fortuyn-Leenmans, Margaretha Droogleever (1909–1998)
Fromm-Reichmann, Frieda (1889–1957)
Hinkle, Beatrice M. (1874–1953)
Horney, Karen (1885–1952)
Kenworthy, Marion E. (c. 1891–1980)
Kübler-Ross, Elisabeth (1926–2004)
Levine, Lena (1903–1965)
Payne, Sylvia (1880–1974)
Pelletier, Madeleine (1874–1939)
Thompson, Clara (1893–1958)
Willoughby, Frances L. (c. 1906–1984)

PSYCHIC
See Spiritualist.

PSYCHOLOGIST/PSYCHOANALYST
Abel, Theodora (1899–1998)
Almy, Millie (1915–2001)
Ames, Frances (1920–2002)
Anastasi, Anne (1908–2001)
Bates, Elizabeth (1947–2003)
Boden, Margaret (1936—)
Bronner, Augusta Fox (1881–1966)
Brothers, Joyce (1928—)
Bühler, Charlotte (1893–1974)
Calkins, Mary Whiton (1863–1930)
Chesler, Phyllis (1940—)
Cullis, Winifred Clara (1875–1956)
Davey, Constance (1882–1963)
De Keyser, Véronique (1945—)
Dembo, Tamara (1902–1993)
Deutsch, Helene (1884–1982)
Dinnerstein, Dorothy (1923–1992)
Donaldson, Margaret Caldwell (1926—)
Downey, June Etta (1875–1932)
Dunbar, Flanders (1902–1959)
Dunlop, Florence (c. 1896–1963)
Dyk, Ruth (1901–2000)
Frenkel-Brunswik, Else (1908–1958)
Freud, Anna (1895–1982)
Fromm, Erika (1909–2003)
Fromm-Reichmann, Frieda (1889–1957)
Gardiner, Muriel (1901–1985)
Garufi, Bianca (1920—)
Gilbreth, Lillian Moller (1878–1972)
Gilligan, Carol (1936—)
Goodenough, Florence Laura (1886–1959)
Hollingworth, Leta Stetter (1886–1939)
Hooker, Evelyn (1907–1996)
Horney, Karen (1885–1952)
Hug-Hellmuth, Hermine (1871–1924)
Irigaray, Luce (1930—)
Isaacs, Susan (1885–1948)
Jahoda, Marie (1907–2001)
Johnson, Virginia E. (1925—)
Klein, Melanie (1882–1960)
Kristeva, Julia (1941—)
Ladd-Franklin, Christine (1847–1930)
Lawrence, Carmen Mary (1948—)
LeShan, Eda J. (1922–2002)
Levy, Jerre (1938—)
Martin, Lillien Jane (1851–1943)
McCormick, Edith Rockefeller (1872–1932)
Miller, Alice (1923—)
Milner, Brenda Atkinson (1918—)
Milner, Marion (1900–1998)
Montrelay, Michèle
Muller-Schwarze, Christine
Myrdal, Alva (1902–1986)
Noach, Ilse (1908–1998)
Patterson, Francine (1947—)
Payne, Sylvia (1880–1974)
Payton, Carolyn Robertson (1925–2001)
Polcz, Alaine (1921—)
Pringle, Mia Lilly (1920–1983)
Rand, Gertrude (1886–1970)
Rodin, Judith (1944—)
Scott-Maxwell, Florida (1883–1979)
Sherif, Carolyn Wood (1922–1982)
Shinn, Millicent Washburn (1858–1940)
Simpson, Mary Michael (1925—)
Singer, Margaret (1921–2003)
Starovoitova, Galina (1946–1998)
Suplicy, Marta (c. 1946—)
Taft, Jessie (1882–1960)
Vike-Freiberga, Vaira (1937—)
Washburn, Margaret Floy (1871–1939)
Wexler, Nancy (1945—)
Woolley, Helen (1874–1947)
Zachry, Caroline B. (1894–1945)

PUBLIC-HEALTH OFFICIAL
Apgar, Virginia (1909–1974)
Barrow, Nita (1916–1995)
Bruntland, Gro Harlem (1939—)
Burgess, Renate (1910–1988)
Calderone, Mary Steichen (1904–1998)
Crandall, Ella Phillips (1871–1938)
Elders, Joycelyn (1933—)

Ermoleva, Zinaida (1898–1974)
Gantt, Rosa (1875–1935)
Gunn, Elizabeth Catherine (1879–1963)
McNeill, Florence Marian (1885–1973)
Novello, Antonia (1944—)
Pandit, Vijaya Lakshmi (1900–1990)
Paterson, Ada Gertrude (1880–1937)
Pery, Sylvia (1935—)
Ratebzad, Anahita (1931—)
Roche, Josephine (1886–1976)
Schwarzhaupt, Elisabeth (1901–1986)
Sigurdsen, Gertrud (1923—)
Strang, Ruth (1895–1971)
Switzer, Mary E. (1900–1971)
Thomas, Mary Myers (1816–1888)
Thoms, Adah B. (c. 1863–1943)
Towle, Charlotte (1896–1966)
Towne, Laura Matilda (1825–1901)
Vejjabul, Pierra (b. 1909)
Williams, Anna Wessels (1863–1954)

PUBLIC-HEALTH REFORMER
Cannon, Ida (1877–1960)
Lakey, Alice (1857–1935)

PUBLICIST
Austin, Mary Hunter (1868–1934)
Bailey, Hannah Johnston (1839–1923)
Baldwin, Ruth Ann (fl. 1915–1921)
Barkentin, Marjorie (c. 1891–1974)
Becher, Lilly (1901–1976)
Bennett, Isadora (d. 1980)
Cooney, Joan Ganz (1929—)
Dalrymple, Jean (1910–1998)
Dawidowicz, Lucy (1915–1990)
Dennett, Mary Ware (1872–1947)
Deutsch, Helen (1906–1992)
Dohm, Hedwig (1831–1919)
Ferguson, Helen (1901–1977)
Fittko, Lisa (1909–2005)
Hickok, Lorena A. (1893–1968)
Jebb, Eglantyne (1876–1928)
Konopnicka, Maria (1842–1910)
Koszutska, Maria (1876–1939)
Macardle, Dorothy (1889–1958)
Myers, Dee Dee (1961—)
Otto-Peters, Luise (1819–1895)
Pennington, Mary Engle (1872–1952)
Ross, Ishbel (1895–1975)
Schwimmer, Rosika (1877–1948)
Smedley, Agnes (1892–1950)
Spewack, Bella (1899–1990)
Strong, Anna Louise (1885–1970)
Terrell, Mary Church (1863–1954)
Upton, Harriet Taylor (1853–1945)
Wertmüller, Lina (1928—)
Whitton, Charlotte (1896–1975)

PUBLIC OFFICIAL
Palmer, Alice May (1886–1977)

PUBLIC-RELATIONS CONSULTANT/ WORKER
Bates, Daisy Lee (1914–1999)
Bethune, Mary McLeod (1875–1955)
Dormon, Carrie (1888–1971)
Griswold, Denny (1908–2001)
Guerin, Veronica (1960–1996)
Guthrie, Janet (1938—)
Husted, Marjorie Child (c. 1892–1986)
Jackson, Alice (1887–1974)
Jacobs, Helen Hull (1908–1997)
Jiagge, Annie (1918–1996)
Knutson, Coya Gjesdal (1912–1996)
Lasker, Mary (1900–1994)
Manley, Effa (1900–1981)
Mathieu, Susie
Meyers, Jan (1928—)
Moskowitz, Belle (1877–1933)
Nidetch, Jean (1923—)
Oakar, Mary Rose (1940—)
Ogot, Grace (1930—)
Parsons, Louella (1881–1972)
Robson, Flora (1902–1984)
Saarinen, Aline (1914–1972)
Sarfatti, Margherita (1880–1961)
Saunders, Doris (1921—)
Shabazz, Betty (1936–1997)
Szold, Henrietta (1860–1945)
Tyler, Alice S. (1859–1944)
Tyus, Wyomia (1945—)
Walters, Barbara (1929—)
Warren, Althea (1886–1958)
Weed, Ella (1853–1894)
Werlein, Elizebeth Thomas (1883–1946)
Wheaton, Anne (1892–1977)

PUBLISHER
See Book publisher.
See Newspaper publisher.
See Periodical founder.

PUBLISHING-HOUSE EDITOR
Arendt, Hannah (1906–1975)
Brittain, Vera (1893–1970)
Bromley, Dorothy Dunbar (1896–1986)
Brown, Margaret Wise (1910–1952)
Clampitt, Amy (1920–1994)
Dimitrova, Blaga (1922—)
Field, Rachel Lyman (1894–1942)
Forbes, Esther (1891–1967)
Ginzburg, Natalia (1916–1991)
Guthrie, Janet (1938—)
Jacobs, Helen Hull (1908–1997)
Kennedy, Jacqueline (1929–1994)
Moholy, Lucia (1894–1989)
Morrison, Toni (1931—)
Nordstrom, Ursula (1910–1988)
Stephens, Kate (1853–1938)
Swenson, May (1913–1989)
Szold, Henrietta (1860–1945)
Tennant, Kylie (1912–1988)
Towle, Katherine (1898–1986)
Wei Junyi (1917–2002)
West, Dorothy (1907–1998)
Wolf, Christa (1929—)
Zolotow, Charlotte (b. 1915)

PUBLISHING-HOUSE FOUNDER
Bates, Daisy Lee (1914–1999)
Box, Muriel (1905–1991)
Callil, Carmen (1938—)
Crosby, Caresse (1892–1970)
Davies, Gwendoline (1882–1951)
Davies, Margaret (1884–1963)
Faithfull, Emily (1835–1895)
Farrar, Margaret (1897–1984)
Hanson-Dyer, Louise (1884–1962)
Harari, Manya (1905–1969)
Martin, Sara (1884–1955)
Massee, May (1881–1966)
Nwapa, Flora (1931–1993)
Otto-Peters, Luise (1819–1895)
Riding, Laura (1901–1991)
Wolff, Helen (1906–1994)

PUGILIST
Donahue, Hessie (fl. 1892)
Rijker, Lucia (1967—)

PUPPETEER
Baird, Cora (c. 1912–1967)
Dinsdale, Shirley (c. 1928–1999)
Exter, Alexandra (1882–1949)
Lewis, Shari (1933–1998)
Rose, Margo (1903–1997)
Simonovich-Efimova, Nina (1877–1948)
Tauber-Arp, Sophie (1889–1943)
Taymor, Julie (1952—)
Van Dyke, Vonda Kay (c. 1944—)

QUEEN
Adelaide Judith (fl. 879)
Adelaide of Anjou (fl. 10th c.)
Adelaide of Burgundy (931–999)
Adelaide of Burgundy (d. 1273)
Adelaide of Hungary (d. 1062)
Adelaide of Maurienne (1092–1154)
Adelaide of Poitou (c. 950–c. 1004)
Adelaide of Rheinfelden (c. 1065–?)
Adelaide of Savona (d. 1118)
Adelaide of Saxe-Meiningen (1792–1849)
Adele of Champagne (1145–1206)
Adelheid (1831–1909)
Adelicia of Louvain (c. 1102–1151)
Agnes de Poitiers (fl. 1135)
Agnes of Austria (fl. 1100s)
Agnes of Austria (1281–1364)
Agnes of Brandenburg (d. 1304)
Agnes of Meran (d. 1201)
Agnes of Poitou (1052–1078)
Ahhotep (r. 1570–1546 BCE)
Ahmose-Nefertari (c. 1570–1535 BCE)
Aissa Koli (1497–1504)
Akhat-milki (fl. 1265 BCE)
Alexandra (r. 76–67 BCE)
Alexandra (1921–1993)
Alexandra of Denmark (1844–1925)
Alexandrina of Mecklenburg-Schwerin (1879–1952)
Alice of Champagne (fl. 1200s)
Aline Sitoe (c. 1920–1944)
Amalia of Bavaria (1801–1877)
Amalie (1818–1875)
Amanishakhete (r. c. 41–12 BCE)
Amelia of Leuchtenburg (1812–1873)
Amina (c. 1533–c. 1598)
Anastasia of Russia (c. 1023–after 1074)
Angharad (d. 1162)
Anna Anachoutlou (r. 1341–1342)
Anna Catherina of Brandenburg (1575–1612)
Anna Jagello (1523–1596)
Anna of Styria (1573–1598)
Anna Pavlovna (1795–1865)
Anne (1665–1714)
Anne-Marie d'Bourbon-Orleans (1669–1728)
Anne-Marie Oldenburg (1946—)
Anne of Austria (c. 1550–1580)
Anne of Austria (1601–1666)
Anne of Bohemia (1366–1394)
Anne of Brittany (c. 1477–1514)
Anne of Chatillon-Antioche (c. 1155–c. 1185)
Anne of Cleves (1515–1557)
Anne of Denmark (1574–1619)
Anne of Kiev (1024–1066)
Anne of Warwick (1456–1485)
Ansgard (fl. 863)
Anula (r. 47–42 BCE)
Apama (fl. 245 BCE)
Apponyi, Geraldine (1915–2002)
Aregunde (fl. 6th c.)
Arsinoe II Philadelphus (c. 316–270 BCE)
Arsinoe IV (d. 41 BCE)
Artemisia I (c. 520–? BCE)
Arwa (1052–1137)
Asa (c. 800–c. 850)
Asmā (c. 1028–1084)
Astrid of Sweden (1905–1935)
Astrid of the Obotrites (c. 979–?)

Atossa (c. 545–c. 470s BCE)
Audofleda (c. 470–?)
Audovera (d. 580)
Augusta of Brunswick-Wolfenbuttel (1764–1788)
Augusta of Saxe-Weimar (1811–1890)
Avisa of Gloucester (c. 1167–1217)
Baels, Liliane (1916–2002)
Balthild (c. 630–c. 680)
Barbara of Cilli (fl. 1390–1410)
Barbara Radziwell (1520–1551)
Barbara Zapolya (fl. 1500)
Basine (fl. 428)
Basine (fl. 465)
Beatrice, Dona (c. 1684–1706)
Beatrice of Castile and Leon (1242–1303)
Beatrice of Castile and Leon (1293–1359)
Beatrice of Naples (1457–1508)
Beatrice of Portugal (1372–after 1409)
Beatrice of Provence (d. 1267)
Beatrice of Rethel (fl. 1150s)
Beatrice of Savoy (fl. 1240s)
Beatrice of Swabia (1198–1235)
Beatrice of Upper Burgundy (1145–1184)
Beatrice of Vermandois (880–931)
Beatrix (b. 1938)
Beaufort, Joan (c. 1410–1445)
Berengaria (1194–1221)
Berengaria of Castile (1180–1246)
Berengaria of Navarre (c. 1163–c. 1230)
Berengaria of Provence (1108–1149)
Berenice I (c. 345 BCE–c. 275 BCE)
Berenice II of Cyrene (c. 273–221 BCE)
Berenice IV (fl. 79–55 BCE)
Berenice Syra (c. 280–246 BCE)
Beretrude (d. 620)
Bertha (719–783)
Bertha-Irene of Sulzbach (d. 1161)
Bertha of Burgundy (964–1024)
Bertha of Burgundy (d. 1097)
Bertha of Holland (1055–1094)
Bertha of Kent (c. 565–c. 616)
Bertha of Swabia (fl. 900s)
Bertha of Toulouse (fl. late 700s)
Bertrada of Montfort (d. after 1117)
Bilchilde (d. 675)
Blanche of Artois (c. 1247–1302)
Blanche of Bourbon (c. 1338–1361)
Blanche of Castile (1188–1252)
Blanche of Namur (d. 1363)
Blanche of Naples (d. 1310)
Blanche of Navarre (d. 1158)
Blanche of Navarre (1331–1398)
Blanche of Navarre (1385–1441)
Blanche of Navarre (1424–1464)
Bodil of Norway (fl. 1000s)
Bodil of Norway (fl. 1090s)
Boleyn, Anne (c. 1507–1536)
Bonaparte, Carolina (1782–1839)
Bonaparte, Julie Clary (1771–1845)
Borja, Ana de (c. 1640–1706)
Boudica (26/30–60)
Braose, Isabel de (d. 1248?)
Bruce, Isabel (c. 1278–1358)
Brunhilda (c. 533–613)
Carlota Joaquina (1775–1830)
Caroline Amelia of Augustenburg (1796–1881)
Caroline Matilda (1751–1775)
Caroline of Ansbach (1683–1737)
Caroline of Baden (1776–1841)
Caroline of Brunswick (1768–1821)
Caroline of Saxony (1833–1907)
Cartimandua (fl. 43–69)
Cassandane (fl. 500s BCE)
Catherine (1507–1578)
Catherine de Foix (c. 1470–1517)
Catherine Jagello (1525–1583)
Catherine of Aragon (1485–1536)
Catherine of Braganza (1638–1705)
Catherine of Habsburg (1533–1572)
Catherine of Lancaster (1372–1418)
Catherine of Russia (1788–1819)
Catherine of Valois (1401–1437)
Catherine of Wurttemberg (1783–1835)
Cecilia Renata of Austria (1611–1644)
Cendrith (fl. 680s)
Chand Bibi (1550–1599)
Charlotte Amalia of Hesse (1650–1714)
Charlotte of Lusignan (1442–1487)
Charlotte of Mecklenburg-Strelitz (1744–1818)
Charlotte of Oldenburg (1759–1818)
Charlotte of Savoy (c. 1442–1483)
Christina of Holstein-Gottorp (1573–1625)
Christina of Sardinia (1812–1836)
Christina of Saxony (1461–1521)
Christina of Sweden (1626–1689)
Christina Stigsdottir (fl. 1160s)
Chunsina (fl. 6th c.)
Ci'an (1837–1881)
Claude de France (1499–1524)
Clemence of Hungary (1293–1328)
Cleopatra Berenice III (c. 115–80 BCE)
Cleopatra I (c. 210–176 BCE)
Cleopatra II (c. 183–116 BCE)
Cleopatra III (c. 155–101 BCE)
Cleopatra IV (c. 135–112 BCE)
Cleopatra VII (69–30 BCE)
Cleopatra V Selene (c. 40 BCE–?)
Cleopatra V Tryphaena (c. 95–c. 57 BCE)
Cleopatra Selene (c. 130–69 BCE)
Cleopatra Thea (c. 165–121 BCE)
Cleopatra Tryphaena (d. after 112 BCE)
Clotilda (470–545)
Clotilde (d. 691)
Clotsinda (fl. 6th c.)
Clotsinda
Constance of Aragon (d. 1222)
Constance of Aragon (c. 1350–?)
Constance of Arles (c. 980–1032)
Constance of Burgundy (1046–c. 1093)
Constance of Castile (d. 1160)
Constance of Castile (1323–1345)
Constance of Hungary (d. 1240)
Constance of Portugal (1290–1313)
Constance of Sicily (1154–1198)
Constance of Sicily (d. 1302)
Constance of Styria (1588–1631)
Constance of Toulouse (fl. 12th century)
Cooke, Hope (1940—)
Cornaro, Caterina (1454–1510)
Cunegunde (fl. 800s)
Cunegunde (1234–1292)
Cuneswith (fl. 7th c.)
Cunigunde of Hohenstaufen (fl. 1215–1230)
Cunigunde of Hungary (d. 1285)
Cyneburg of Mercia (fl. 655)
Cynethryth (fl. 736–796)
Cynewise (fl. 7th c.)
Dagmar of Bohemia (d. 1212)
Deoteria (fl. 535)
Desiderata (d. 773)
Désirée (1777–1860)
Dorothea of Brandenburg (1430–1495)
Dorothea of Saxe-Lauenburg (1511–1571)
Douce of Aragon (1160–1198)
Draga (1867–1903)
Drummond, Annabella (1350–1401)
Drummond, Margaret (d. 1375)
Durgawati (d. 1564)
Eadburgh (c. 773–after 802)
Ealdgyth (fl. 1016)
Eanfleda (626–?)
Edgifu (902–951)
Edgifu (c. 917–?)
Edgifu (d. 968)
Edith (d. 937)
Edith (c. 1025–1075)
Edith (fl. 1063)
Edonne (fl. 8th c.)
Eleanora of Reuss (1860–1917)
Eleanor Habsburg (1653–1697)
Eleanor of Albuquerque (1374–1435)
Eleanor of Aquitaine (1122–1204)
Eleanor of Aragon (1358–1382)
Eleanor of Castile (1162–1214)
Eleanor of Castile (1202–1244)
Eleanor of Castile (1241–1290)
Eleanor of Castile (1307–1359)
Eleanor of Navarre (1425–1479)
Eleanor of Portugal (1328–1348)
Eleanor of Portugal (1434–1467)
Eleanor of Portugal (1458–1525)
Eleanor of Portugal (1498–1558)
Eleanor of Provence (c. 1222–1291)
Eleanor of Sicily (d. 1375)
Eleanor Plantagenet (1264–1297)
Eleanor Trastamara (d. 1415)
Elena of Montenegro (1873–1952)
Elflaed (d. 920)
Elfgifu (d. 944)
Elfgifu (d. 959)
Elfgifu (c. 963–1002)
Elflaed (fl. 1030)
Elfthrith (c. 945–1002)
Elfwyn (c. 882–?)
Elgiva (fl. 1020)
Elisabeth (1894–1956)
Elisabeth of Habsburg (1501–1526)
Elisabeth of Habsburg (1554–1592)
Elizabeth Bowes-Lyon (1900–2002)
Elizabeth Christina of Brunswick-Wolfenbuttel (1715–1797)
Elizabeth de Burgh (d. 1327)
Elizabeth I (1533–1603)
Elizabeth II (1926—)
Elizabeth of Bavaria (1876–1965)
Elizabeth of Bohemia (1596–1662)
Elizabeth of Bosnia (d. 1339)
Elizabeth of Bosnia (c. 1345–1387)
Elizabeth of Habsburg (d. 1545)
Elizabeth of Holstein (fl. 1329)
Elizabeth of Hungary (c. 1430–1505)
Elizabeth of Kiev (fl. 1045)
Elizabeth of Kumania (c. 1242–?)
Elizabeth of Luxemburg (1409–1442)
Elizabeth of Poland (fl. 1298–1305)
Elizabeth of Poland (1305–1380)
Elizabeth of Portugal (1271–1336)
Elizabeth of Sicily (fl. 1200s)
Elizabeth of Tyrol (c. 1262–1313)
Elizabeth of Valois (1545–1568)
Elizabeth of Wied (1843–1916)
Elizabeth of York (1466–1503)
Elizabeth Valois (1602–1644)
Elswitha (d. 902)
Elthelthrith (630–679)
Elvira (d. 1135)
Elvira Gonzalez of Galicia (d. 1022)
Emma (fl. 600s)
Emma (1836–1885)
Emma of Bavaria (d. 876)
Emma of Burgundy (d. 939)
Emma of Italy (948–after 990)
Emma of Normandy (c. 985–1052)
Emma of Waldeck (1858–1934)
Ena (1887–1969)
Ermenburga (fl. late 600s)
Ermengarde (c. 778–818)

Ermengarde of Beaumont (d. 1234)
Ermengarde of Provence (fl. 876)
Ermenilda (d. about 700)
Ermentrude (d. 869)
Eschiva of Ibelin (r. 1282–c. 1284)
Esmat (d. 1995)
Este, Beatrice d' (d. 1245)
Estefania of Barcelona (fl. 1038)
Esther (fl. 475 BCE)
Ethelberga of Northumbria (d. 647)
Ethelburg (fl. 722)
Ethelflaed (d. 962)
Ethelflaed (d. after 975)
Ethelreda (fl. 1090)
Ethelswyth (c. 843–889)
Euphemia of Kiev (d. 1139)
Euphemia of Pomerania (d. 1330)
Euphemia of Rugen (d. 1312)
Euphrosyne of Kiev (fl. 1130–1180)
Fabiola (1928—)
Faileuba (fl. 586–587)
Falkestein, Beatrice von (c. 1253–1277)
Farida (1921–1988)
Farnese, Elizabeth (1692–1766)
Fastrada (d. 794)
Fergusa (fl. 800s)
Foix, Anne de (fl. 1480–1500)
Foix, Germaine de (1488–1538)
Fredegund (c. 547–597)
Frederica Dorothea of Baden (1781–1826)
Frederica of Hesse (1751–1805)
Frederica Wilhelmina of Prussia (1774–1837)
Fredericka (1917–1981)
Frederona (d. 917)
Frithpoll, Margaret (d. 1130)
Gaboimilla
Galswintha (d. around 568)
Gardiner, Antoinette (1941—)
Gauhar Shad (c. 1378–1459)
Gayatri Devi (1919—)
Gerberga of Saxony (c. 910–969)
Gerberge of the Lombards (fl. mid–700s)
Germaine de Foix (1488–1538)
Gertrude of Andrechs-Meran (c. 1185–1213)
Gertrude of Saxony (fl. 1070)
Gertrude of Saxony (c. 1155–1196)
Gilberga (d. 1054)
Giovanna of Italy (1907–2000)
Gisela of Bavaria (c. 975–1033)
Gladys (fl. 1075)
Gonzaga, Eleonora I (1598–1655)
Gonzaga, Eleonora II (1628–1686)
Gorka (fl. 920s)
Gormflaith of Ireland (fl. 980–1015)
Gruoch (fl. 1020–1054)
Guinevere (d. 470 or 542)
Gunhild of Norway (d. 1054)
Guntheuca (fl. 525)
Guntrud of Bavaria (fl. 715)
Gyde (fl. 1054)
Gyrid (fl. 950s)
Hedwig of Holstein (d. 1325)
Hedwig of Holstein-Gottorp (1636–1715)
Helen (fl. 1100s)
Helena of Epirus (fl. 1250s)
Helena of Serbia (fl. 1100s)
Helene of Moscow (1474–1513)
Helen of Hungary (fl. mid–1000s)
Helen Paleologina (c. 1415–1458)
Helvig of Denmark (fl. 1350s)
Henrietta Maria (1609–1669)
Hereswitha (d. around 690)
Hetepheres I (fl. c. 2630 BCE)
Hetha (fl. 10th c.)
Hildegarde of Swabia (c. 757–783)
Himiltrude (fl. 700s)
Himnechildis (r. 662–675)
Hodierna of Jerusalem (c. 1115–after 1162)
Homaira (1916–2002)
Hong, Lady (1735–1850)
Hortense de Beauharnais (1783–1837)
Howard, Catherine (1520/22–1542)
Ida of Nivelles (597–652)
Iffat (1916–2000)
Inga (fl. 1204)
Ingebiorge (fl. 1045–1068)
Ingeborg (c. 1176–1237/38)
Ingeborg (d. 1319)
Ingeborg of Denmark (d. 1287)
Ingirid (fl. 1067)
Ingoberge (519–589)
Ingrid of Sweden (1910–2000)
Ingunde (fl. 517)
Iolande of Hungary (1215–1251)
Ippolita (1446–1484)
Irene (fl. 1310)
Isabeau of Bavaria (1371–1435)
Isabel de Clermont (d. 1465)
Isabel de Warrenne (b. 1253)
Isabella (d. 1282)
Isabella Capet (fl. 1250)
Isabella del Balzo (d. 1533)
Isabella I (1451–1504)
Isabella I of Jerusalem (d. 1205)
Isabella II (1830–1904)
Isabella of Angoulême (1186–1246)
Isabella of Aragon (1243–1271)
Isabella of Asturias (1471–1498)
Isabella of Cyprus (fl. 1250s)
Isabella of France (1296–1358)
Isabella of Hainault (1170–1190)
Isabella of Mar (d. 1296)
Isabella of Poland (1519–1559)
Isabella of Valois (1389–c. 1410)
Isabel la Paloma (1432–1455)
Isabelle of Lorraine (1410–1453)
Isabel of Portugal (1428–1496)
Isabel of Urgel (fl. 1065)
Jadwiga (1374–1399)
Jadwiga of Glogow (fl. late 1300s)
Jane of France (1343–1373)
Jeanne I of Burgundy (c. 1291–1330)
Jeanne de Bourbon (1338–1378)
Jeanne de France (c. 1464–1505)
Jeanne of Burgundy (1293–1348)
Jezebel (d. 884 BCE)
Joan (1210–1238)
Joan I of Navarre (1273–1305)
Joan II of Navarre (1309–1349)
Joanna Enriquez (1425–1468)
Joanna I of Naples (1326–1382)
Joanna II of Naples (1374–1435)
Joanna of Aragon (1454–1517)
Joanna of Castile (1339–1381)
Joanna of Naples (1478–1518)
Joanna of Navarre (c. 1370–1437)
Joanna of Ponthieu (d. 1279)
Joanna of Portugal (1439–1475)
Joanna of Sicily (1165–1199)
Joan of Evreux (d. 1370)
Joan of the Tower (1321–1362)
Jodha Bai (d. 1613)
Josephine Beauharnais (1807–1876)
Josephine of Baden (1813–1900)
Juana la Loca (1479–1555)
Judith (fl. 10th c.)
Judith (1271–1297)
Judith of Hungary (fl. late 900s)
Juliana (1909–2004)
Jutta of Mecklenburg-Strelitz (1880–1946)
Kaahumanu (1777–1832)
Kahina (r. 695–703)
Kalama (c. 1820–1870)
Kamamalu (c. 1803–1824)
Kanga (fl. 1220)
Kapiolani (1834–1899)
Kapule, Deborah (c. 1798–1853)
Katarina of Saxe-Lüneburg (1513–1535)
Katarina Stenbock (1536–1621)
Khaizaran (d. 790)
Khamerernebty I (fl. c. 2600 BCE)
Khamerernebty II (fl. c. 2600 BCE)
Khentkawes (fl. c. 2510 BCE)
Kossamak (1904–1975)
Krystyna Rokiczanska (fl. 1300s)
Lakshmibai (c. 1835–1858)
Laodice I (c. 285–c. 236 BCE)
Laodice II (fl. 250 BCE)
Laodice III (fl. 200 BCE)
Lathgertha (b. around 665)
Lenore of Sicily (1289–1341)
Leonora of Aragon (1405–1445)
Leonora Telles (c. 1350–1386)
Leonor of Portugal (1211–1231)
Libussa (c. 680–738)
Liliuokalani (1838–1917)
Liutgard (d. 885)
Louisa Ulrica of Prussia (1720–1782)
Louise d'Orléans (1812–1850)
Louise Elizabeth (1709–1750)
Louise Marie de Gonzague (1611–1667)
Louise Mountbatten (1889–1965)
Louise of England (1724–1751)
Louise of Hesse-Cassel (1688–1765)
Louise of Lorraine (1554–1601)
Louise of Mecklenburg-Gustrow (1667–1721)
Louise of Prussia (1776–1810)
Louise of Sweden (1851–1926)
Louise of the Netherlands (1828–1871)
Lucia of Rugia (fl. 1220)
Ludovica (1808–1892)
Luisa de Guzman (1613–1666)
Luitgarde (d. 800)
MacDonald, Finula (fl. 1569–1592)
Madeleine of France (1443–1486)
Malgorzata (fl. 1290s)
Malmfrid of Russia (fl. 1100s)
Malthace (fl. 40 BCE)
Mama-Ocllo (fl. around 12th c.)
Manos, Aspasia (1896–1972)
Margaret (fl. 1000s)
Margaret (d. 1209)
Margaret (1240–1275)
Margaret (d. 1270)
Margaret, Maid of Norway (c. 1283–1290)
Margareta Leijonhufvud (1514–1551)
Margaret de Foix (d. 1258)
Margaret I of Denmark (1353–1412)
Margaret of Angoulême (1492–1549)
Margaret of Anjou (1429–1482)
Margaret of Austria (fl. 1200s)
Margaret of Austria (c. 1577–1611)
Margaret of Babenberg (fl. 1252)
Margaret of Burgundy (1290–1315)
Margaret of Denmark (1456–1486)
Margaret of France (1158–1198)
Margaret of France (c. 1282–1318)
Margaret of Naples (fl. late 1300s)
Margaret of Navarre (fl. 1154–1172)
Margaret of Norway (1261–1283)
Margaret of Pomerania (d. 1282)
Margaret of Provence (1221–1295)
Margaret of Savoy (1851–1926)
Margaret of Valois (1553–1615)
Margaret Tudor (1489–1541)
Margrethe II (1940—)
Marguerite de Bourgogne (1250–1308)
Marguerite de l'Aigle (d. 1141)

Maria Amalia (1782–1866)
Maria Amalia of Saxony (1724–1760)
Maria Ana Victoria (1718–1781)
Maria Anna of Austria (c. 1634–1696)
Maria Anna of Bavaria (1574–1616)
Maria Anna of Neuberg (1667–1740)
Maria Anna of Spain (1606–1646)
Maria Antonia of Austria (1683–1754)
Maria Barbara of Braganza (1711–1758)
Maria Carolina (1752–1814)
Maria Christina of Austria (1858–1929)
Maria Comnena (fl. 1100s)
Maria Cristina I of Naples (1806–1878)
Maria de las Mercedes (1860–1878)
Maria de las Mercedes (1880–1904)
Maria de Molina (d. 1321)
Maria de Portugal (1521–1577)
Maria Eleonora of Brandenburg (1599–1655)
Maria Henrietta of Austria (1836–1902)
Maria II da Gloria (1819–1853)
Maria I of Braganza (1734–1816)
Maria Josepha of Saxony (1803–1829)
Maria Juliana of Brunswick (1729–1796)
Maria Lascaris (fl. 1234–1242)
Maria Leopoldine (1632–1649)
Maria Luisa of Etruria (1782–1824)
Maria Luisa Teresa of Parma (1751–1819)
Maria of Aragon (1403–1445)
Maria of Bavaria (1805–1877)
Maria of Byzantium (fl. 12th c.)
Maria of Castile (1401–1458)
Maria of Castile (1482–1517)
Maria of Hungary (1371–1395)
Maria of Kiev (d. 1087)
Maria of Montpellier (1181–1213)
Maria of Navarre (fl. 1340)
Maria of Prussia (1825–1889)
Maria of Sicily (d. 1402)
Maria Pia (1847–1911)
Maria Sophia Amalia (1841–1925)
Maria Sophia of Neuberg (1666–1699)
Maria Teresa of Austria (1773–1832)
Maria Teresa of Este (1849–1919)
Maria Teresa of Savoy (1756–1805)
Maria Teresa of Spain (1638–1683)
Maria Theresa of Spain (1726–1746)
Maria Theresa of Tuscany (1801–1855)
Marie (1900–1961)
Marie Adelaide of Austria (1822–1855)
Marie-Amelie of Orleans (1865–1951)
Marie-Anne of Braganza (1861–1942)
Marie Antoinette (1755–1793)
Marie Casimir (1641–1716)
Marie Clotilde (1759–1802)
Marie Françoise of Savoy (1646–1683)
Marie Isabella of Spain (1789–1848)
Marie José of Belgium (1906–2001)
Marie Josepha (1699–1757)
Marie Leczinska (1703–1768)
Marie Louise d'Orleans (1662–1689)
Marie Louise of Parma (1870–1899)
Marie Louise of Savoy (1688–1714)
Marie of Anjou (1404–1463)
Marie of Brabant (c. 1260–1321)
Marie of Hungary (d. 1323)
Marie of Montferrat (d. 1212)
Marie of Rumania (1875–1938)
Marie Sophie of Hesse-Cassel (1767–1852)
Martha of Denmark (c. 1272–1341)
Mary de Coucy (c. 1220–c. 1260)
Mary I (1516–1558)
Mary of Guelders (1433–1463)
Mary of Guise (1515–1560)
Mary of Hungary (1505–1558)
Mary of Luxemburg (1305–1323)
Mary of Modena (1658–1718)
Mary of Saxe-Altenburg (1818–1907)
Mary of Teck (1867–1953)
Mary Stuart (1542–1587)
Mary Tudor (1496–1533)
Matilda (fl. 680s)
Matilda (1102–1167)
Matilda Martel (943–c. 982)
Matilda of Boulogne (c. 1103–1152)
Matilda of Flanders (c. 1031–1083)
Matilda of Germany (d. before 1044)
Matilda of Maurienne (c. 1125–1157)
Matilda of Northumberland (c. 1074–1131)
Matilda of Portugal (c. 1149–1173)
Matilda of Saxony (c. 892–968)
Matilda of Scotland (1080–1118)
Maud (1869–1938)
Mavia (c. 350–c. 430)
Mechtild of Holstein (d. 1288)
Medea (d. 1440)
Medici, Catherine de (1519–1589)
Medici, Maria de (fl. late 1400s)
Mei (d. 1875)
Melisande (fl. 1100)
Mencia de Haro (d. 1270)
Mer-neith (fl. c. 3100 BCE)
Migliaccio, Lucia (1770–1826)
Milena (1847–1923)
Min (1851–1895)
Mira Bai (1498–1547)
Morphia of Melitene (fl. 1085–1120)
Munia Elvira (995–1067)
Mutnedjmet (c. 1360–1326 BCE)
Nandi (c. 1760s–1827)
Nanthilde (610–642)
Nariman (1934–2005)
Nathalia Keshko (1859–1941)
Nazli (1894–1978)
Nefertari (c. 1295–1256 BCE)
Nefertiti (c. 1375–1336 BCE)
Neithotep (fl. c. 3100 BCE)
Nicaea (fl. 300 BCE)
Nitocris (fl. 6th c. BCE)
Njinga (c. 1580s–1663)
Noor al-Hussein (1951—)
Norodom Monineath Sihanouk (1936—)
Nur Jahan (1577–1645)
Oda (fl. 1000)
Olga Constantinovna (1851–1926)
Olga of Russia (1822–1892)
Orthryth of Mercia (fl. 7th c.)
Osburga (?–c. 855)
Ostrith (d. 697)
Paola (1937—)
Parr, Catherine (1512–1548)
Parysatis I (fl. 440–385 BCE)
Pauline of Wurttemberg (1800–1873)
Petronilla (1135–1174)
Pharandzem (c. 320–c. 364)
Pheretima (fl. 6th c. BCE)
Phila II (c. 300 BCE–?)
Philippa (1394–1430)
Philippa de Rouergue (c. 1074–1118)
Philippa of Hainault (1314–1369)
Philippa of Lancaster (c. 1359–1415)
Phoolan Devi (1963–2001)
Placencia (fl. 1068)
Plaisance of Antioch (d. 1261)
Plectrudis (fl. 665–717)
Preslava of Russia (fl. 1100)
Radegund of Poitiers (518–587)
Ragnetrude (fl. 630)
Ragnhild (fl. 1100s)
Ranavalona I (1792–1861)
Ranavalona II (1829–1883)
Ranavalona III (1861–1917)
Rania (1970—)
Razia (1211–1240)
Redburga (fl. 825)
Reventlow, Anne Sophie (1693–1743)
Rhodogune (fl. 2nd c. BCE)
Richesa of Lorraine (d. 1067)
Richesa of Poland (fl. 1030–1040)
Richilde (d. 894)
Richilde of Autun (d. around 910)
Richiza (fl. 1251)
Richizza of Denmark (d. 1220)
Richizza of Poland (1116–1185)
Ringart (fl. 822–825)
Ross, Euphemia (d. 1387)
Rusudani (b. 1195)
Ryksa (fl. 1288)
Ryksa of Poland (d. 1185)
Ryksa of Poland (1288–1335)
Saewara (fl. 630)
Salomea (d. 1144)
Salome of Hungary (1201–c. 1270)
Salote Topou III (1900–1965)
Sammuramat (fl. 8th c. BCE)
Sancha of Castile and Leon (1164–1208)
Sancha of Castile and Leon (d. 1179)
Sancha of Leon (1013–1067)
Sati Beg (c. 1300–after 1342)
Sexburga (c. 627–673)
Sexburga (d. around 699)
Seymour, Jane (c. 1509–1537)
Sforza, Bona (1493–1557)
Sheba, Queen of (fl. 10th c. BCE)
Sibylla (1160–1190)
Sibylle of Burgundy (1126–1150)
Sigrid the Haughty (d. before 1013)
Silvia Sommerlath (1943—)
Sirikit (1932—)
Sivali (d. 93)
Six Wives of Henry VIII
Sonja (1937—)
Sophia Dorothea of Brunswick-Lüneburg-Hanover (1687–1757)
Sophia of Bavaria (fl. 1390s–1400s)
Sophia of Bayreuth (1700–1770)
Sophia of Denmark (1746–1813)
Sophia of Greece (1938—)
Sophia of Kiev (fl. 1420s)
Sophia of Mecklenburg (1557–1631)
Sophia of Nassau (1836–1913)
Sophia of Pomerania (1498–1568)
Sophia of Wurttemberg (1818–1877)
Sophie Amalie of Brunswick-Lüneberg (1628–1685)
Sophie Charlotte of Hanover (1668–1705)
Sophie Louise of Mecklenburg (1685–1735)
Sophie of Denmark (d. 1286)
Sophie of Prussia (1870–1932)
Sophie of Russia (c. 1140–1198)
Statira I (c. 425–? BCE)
Statira II (c. 360–331 BCE)
Statira III (fl. 324 BCE)
Stephanie (1837–1859)
Stratonice I (c. 319–254 BCE)
Suavegotta (fl. 504)
Susan of Powys (fl. 1100s)
Sybilla (d. 1122)
Synadene of Byzantium (c. 1050–?)
Tajolmolouk (1896–1981)
Tamara (1160–1212)
Tamiris (fl. 550–530 BCE)
Tanaquille (d. 696)
Teresa of Castile (c. 1080–1130)
Tetberga (fl. 9th c.)
Teuta (c. 260–after 228 BCE)
Thalestris (fl. 334 BCE)
Theodelinda (568–628)
Theodora Comnena (1145–after 1183)

Theoxena (fl. 315 BCE)
Theresa (1767–1827)
Theresa Henriques (c. 1176–1250)
Theresa of Austria (1816–1867)
Theresa of Savoy (1803–1879)
Theresa of Saxony (1792–1854)
Thessalonike (c. 345–297 BCE)
Thora (fl. 1100s)
Thyra (d. 940)
Thyra of Denmark (d. 1000)
Tiy (c. 1400–1340 BCE)
Trava, Teresa Fernandez de (fl. 1170)
Tullia (fl. 535 BCE)
Turunku Bakwa (fl. 1530s)
Udham Bai (fl. 1748–1754)
Ulfhild (fl. 1112)
Ulrica Eleanora (1688–1741)
Ulrica Eleanora of Denmark (1656–1693)
Urraca (c. 1079–1126)
Urraca of Castile (c. 1186–1220)
Urraca of Castile (d. 1179)
Urraca of Portugal (c. 1151–1188)
Vashti (fl. 5th c. BCE)
Victoria (1819–1901)
Victoria of Baden (1862–1930)
Vieregg, Elizabeth Helene (fl. 17th c.)
Vuldetrade (fl. 550)
Vultrogotha (fl. 558)
Waldrada (fl. 9th c.)
Wanda of Poland (fl. 730)
Wilhelmina (1880–1962)
Woodville, Elizabeth (1437–1492)
Wulfthryth (fl. 860s)
Yaa Akyaa (c. 1837–c. 1921)
Yaa Asantewaa (c. 1850–1921)
Yoko (c. 1849–1906)
Yolande de Bar (fl. 14th c.)
Yolande de Coucy (d. 1222)
Yolande de Dreux (d. 1323)
Yolande of Aragon (d. 1300)
Yolande of Aragon (1379–1442)
Yolande of Aragon
Yolande of Brienne (1212–1228)
Zabel (b. around 1210)
Zenobia (r. 267–272)
Zita of Parma (1892–1989)
Zubeida (d. 831)

QUEEN CONSORT
Alexandra of Denmark (1844–1925)
Anne of Denmark (1574–1619)
Charlotte of Mecklenburg-Strelitz (1744–1818)
Elizabeth Bowes-Lyon (1900–2002)
Fu Hao (fl. 1040 BCE)
Isabella of France (1296–1358)
Isabel of Portugal (1428–1496)
Margaret of France (c. 1282–1318)
Maria Carolina (1752–1814)
Marie Louise d'Orleans (1662–1689)
Matilda (1102–1167)
Munk, Kirsten (1598–1658)

QUEEN MOTHER
Afua Koba (fl. 1834–1884)
Anne of Austria (1601–1666)
de Rivery, Aimee Dubucq (c. 1762–1817)
Eleanor of Provence (c. 1222–1291)
Elizabeth Bowes-Lyon (1900–2002)
Emma of Normandy (c. 985–1052)
Fredegund (c. 547–597)
Josephine of Baden (1813–1900)
Mary of Teck (1867–1953)
Matilda (1102–1167)
Medici, Catherine de (1519–1589)
Nur Jahan (1577–1645)
Yaa Akyaa (c. 1837–c. 1921)
Yaa Asantewaa (c. 1850–1921)

QUEEN REGENT
Eleanor of Navarre (1425–1479)
Kaahumanu (1777–1832)
Maria de Molina (d. 1321)
Melisande (fl. 1100)
Teresa of Castile (c. 1080–1130)

QUILTER
Powers, Harriet (1837–1911)

RABBI
Ackerman, Paula (1893–1989)
Eilberg, Amy (1954—)
Jonas, Regina (1902–1944)
Priesand, Sally Jane (1946—)

RACE-CAR DRIVER
Denton, Jean (1935–2001)
Fisher, Sarah (1980—)
Guthrie, Janet (1938—)
Lombardi, Lella (1941–1992)
Muldowney, Shirley (1940—)
Robinson, Shawna (1964—)
St. James, Lyn (1947—)

RACKETEER
St. Clair, Stephanie (fl. 1920s–30s)

RACQUETBALL PLAYER
Adams, Lynn (c. 1958—)

RADIO
See Television/radio.

RANCHER
Calvillo, María del Carmen (1765–1856)
Greenway, Isabella Selmes (1886–1953)
King, Henrietta Chamberlain (1832–1925)
Starr, Belle (1848–1889)

RANI
See Queen.

REFEREE
Shain, Eva (1917–1999)

REFORMER
Chichester, Sophia (1795–1847)
Welch, Georgiana (1792–1879)

REFORM-ORGANIZATION FOUNDER
Abayomi, Oyinkansola (1897–1990)
Abrahams, Ottilie Grete (1937—)
Abzug, Bella (1920–1998)
Ahern, Lizzie (1877–1969)
Allfrey, Phyllis Shand (1915–1986)
Aloni, Shulamit (1931—)
Anderson, Mary (1872–1964)
Anthony, Susan B. (1820–1906)
Apostoloy, Electra (1911–1944)
Arendsee, Martha (1885–1953)
Arendt, Hannah (1906–1975)
Auclert, Hubertine (1848–1914)
Aung San Suu Kyi (1945—)
Bagley, Sarah (b. 1806)
Bailey, Hannah Johnston (1839–1923)
Bajer, Matilde (1840–1934)
Bandaranaike, Sirimavo (1916–2000)
Barrett, Janie Porter (1865–1948)
Barry, Leonora M. (1849–1930)
Becker, Lydia (1827–1890)
Bellanca, Dorothy (1894–1946)
Bennett, Louie (1870–1956)
Bethune, Mary McCleod (1875–1955)
Blackburn, Helen (1842–1903)
Blackwell, Alice Stone (1857–1950)
Blackwell, Elizabeth (1821–1910)
Blackwood, Hariot (c. 1845–1891)
Blagoeva, Stella Dimitrova (1887–1954)
Bohley, Bärbel (1945—)
Boissevain, Mia (1878–1959)
Breshkovsky, Catherine (1844–1934)
Brion, Hélène (1882–1962)
Buck, Pearl S. (1892–1973)
Bülow, Frieda von (1857–1909)
Burroughs, Nannie Helen (c. 1878–1961)
Butler, Josephine (1828–1906)
Cai Chang (1900–1990)
Caldicott, Helen (1938—)
Campoamor, Clara (1888–1972)
Casgrain, Thérèse (1896–1981)
Catt, Carrie Chapman (1859–1947)
Charles, Eugenia (1919—)
Chattopadhyaya, Kamaladevi (1903–1988)
Christman, Elisabeth (1881–1975)
Clisby, Harriet (1830–1931)
Cobbe, Frances Power (1822–1904)
Deraismes, Maria (1828–1894)
Deroin, Jeanne-Françoise (1805–1894)
Douglas, Marjory Stoneman (1890–1998)
Duchêne, Gabrielle (1870–1954)
Durand, Marguerite (1864–1936)
Edwards, Henrietta Muir (1849–1933)
Eilberg, Amy (1954—)
Faithfull, Emily (1835–1895)
First, Ruth (1925–1982)
Flower, Lucy (1837–1921)
Flynn, Elizabeth Gurley (1890–1964)
Fossey, Dian (1932–1985)
Francois, Elma (1897–1944)
Friedan, Betty (1921–2006)
Gonne, Maud (1866–1953)
Gratz, Rebecca (1781–1869)
Gutteridge, Helena Rose (1879–1960)
Gwynne-Vaughan, Helen (1879–1967)
Hackley, E. Azalia Smith (1867–1922)
Hagan, Ellen (1873–1958)
Halimi, Gisèle (1927—)
Hamilton, Cicely (1872–1952)
Harand, Irene (1900–1975)
Harriman, Florence Jaffray (1870–1967)
Haslam, Anna (1829–1922)
Hillman, Bessie (1889–1970)
How-Martyn, Edith (1875–1954)
Huerta, Dolores (1930—)
Hughan, Jessie (1875–1955)
Ichikawa Fusae (1893–1981)
Ihrer, Emma (1857–1911)
Inglis, Elsie Maud (1864–1917)
Irwin, Inez Haynes (1873–1970)
Isaacs, Stella (1894–1971)
Jagan, Janet (1920—)
Jiagge, Annie (1918–1996)
Johnston, Mary (1870–1936)
Kehew, Mary Morton (1859–1918)
Kéita, Aoua (1912–1979)
Kellor, Frances Alice (1873–1952)
Kéthly, Anna (1889–1976)
Kobrynska, Natalia Ivanovna (1855–1920)
Kuhn, Maggie (1905–1995)
Kumaratunga, Chandrika Bandaranaike (1945—)
Lampkin, Daisy (1883–1965)
Lathrop, Rose Hawthorne (1851–1926)
Lemlich, Clara (1888–1982)
Léo, André (1832–1900)
Levertov, Denise (1923–1997)
Lightner, Candy (1946—)
Lutz, Berta (1894–1976)
Luxemburg, Rosa (1870–1919)
Macmillan, Chrystal (1871–1937)
Manus, Rosa (1881–1942)

Markievicz, Constance (1868–1927)
Marx-Aveling, Eleanor (1855–1898)
Masiotene, Ona (1883–1949)
McCormick, Ruth Hanna (1880–1944)
McCulloch, Catharine (1862–1945)
McDowell, Mary Eliza (1854–1936)
Mink, Paule (1839–1901)
Misme, Jane (1865–1935)
Mitterrand, Danielle (1924—)
Moore, Audley (1898–1997)
Moreau de Justo, Alicia (1885–1986)
Morgenstern, Lina B. (1830–1909)
Mourning Dove (c. 1888–1936)
Mozzoni, Anna Maria (1837–1920)
Myrdal, Alva (1902–1986)
O'Sullivan, Mary Kenney (1864–1943)
Palm, Etta Aelders (1743–1799)
Pankhurst, Adela (1885–1961)
Pankhurst, Christabel (1880–1958)
Pankhurst, Emmeline (1858–1928)
Pankhurst, Sylvia (1882–1960)
Pantoja, Antonia (1922–2002)
Parks, Rosa (1913—)
Parren, Kalliroe (1861–1940)
Paterson, Emma (1848–1886)
Paul, Alice (1885–1977)
Pintasilgo, Maria de Lurdes (1930–2004)
Potonié-Pierre, Eugénie (1844–1898)
Ramabai, Pandita (1858–1922)
Ramirez, Sara Estela (1881–1910)
Rankin, Jeannette (1880–1973)
Ratebzad, Anahita (1931—)
Rohde, Ruth Bryan Owen (1885–1954)
Roland Holst, Henriëtte (1869–1952)
Rumsey, Mary Harriman (1881–1934)
Sainte-Marie, Buffy (1941—)
Sanger, Margaret (1879–1966)
Santolalla, Irene Silva de (1902–1992)
Schmahl, Jeanne (1846–1916)
Schneider, Claudine (1947—)
Schneiderman, Rose (1882–1972)
Schroeder, Louise (1887–1957)
Schwimmer, Rosika (1877–1948)
Scott, Rose (1847–1925)
Severance, Caroline M. (1820–1914)
Sewall, May Wright (1844–1920)
Shaarawi, Huda (1879–1947)
Shafik, Doria (1908–1975)
Shapiro, Betty Kronman (1907–1989)
Shaw, Pauline Agassiz (1841–1917)
Sheehy-Skeffington, Hanna (1877–1946)
Sheppard, Kate (1847–1934)
Sherwin, Belle (1868–1955)
Shochat, Manya (1878–1961)
Sieveking, Amalie (1794–1859)
Simcox, Edith (1844–1901)
Simkhovitch, Mary (1867–1951)
Smeal, Eleanor (1939—)
Somerville, Nellie Nugent (1863–1952)
Staël, Germaine de (1766–1817)
Stanton, Elizabeth Cady (1815–1902)
Stewart, Eliza Daniel (1816–1908)
Stoddard, Cora Frances (1872–1936)
Stoecker, Helene (1869–1943)
Stone, Lucy (1818–1893)
Stopes, Marie (1880–1958)
Sullerot, Evelyne (1924—)
Suttner, Bertha von (1843–1914)
Svetla, Caroline (1830–1899)
Swain, Clara A. (1834–1910)
Szold, Henrietta (1860–1945)
Theodoropoulou, Avra (1880–1963)
Tod, Isabella (1836–1896)
Trotsky, Natalia Ivanovna (1882–1962)
Troup, Augusta Lewis (c. 1848–1920)
Tuckwell, Gertrude (1861–1951)
Valette, Aline (1850–1899)
Van Grippenberg, Alexandra (1859–1913)
Villard, Fanny Garrison (1844–1928)
Walker, Maggie Lena (1867–1934)
Way, Amanda M. (1828–1914)
Weizmann, Vera (1881–1966)
Werlein, Elizebeth Thomas (1883–1946)
Willard, Frances E. (1839–1898)
Williams, Fannie Barrier (1855–1944)
Williams, Mary Wilhelmine (1878–1944)
Williams, Shirley (1930—)
Wilson, Charlotte (1854–1944)
Wingo, Effiegene Locke (1883–1962)
Woolley, Mary E. (1863–1947)
Wright, Judith (1915–2000)
Wright, Laura Maria (1809–1886)
Yorkin, Peg (1927—)
Zasulich, Vera (1849–1919)

REFUGE FOUNDER

Torlesse, Elizabeth Henrietta (1835/36–1922)

REGENT

Adelaide of Burgundy (931–999)
Adelaide of Montserrat (fl. 1100)
Adelaide of Savona (d. 1118)
Adela of Blois (1062–c. 1137)
Adele of Champagne (1145–1206)
Agnes of Poitou (1024–1077)
Ahhotep (r. 1570–1546 BCE)
Alice of Jerusalem (c. 1106–?)
Alix of Vergy (d. after 1218)
Amalasuntha (c. 498–535)
Anna Amalia of Saxe-Weimar (1739–1807)
Anna Dalassena (c. 1025–1105)
Anna Leopoldovna (1718–1746)
Anna Paleologina (d. 1340)
Anna Paleologina-Cantacuzene (fl. 1270–1313)
Anne of Austria (1601–1666)
Anne of Beaujeu (c. 1460–1522)
Anne of Savoy (c. 1320–1353)
Asa (c. 800–c. 850)
Augusta of Tuscany (1825–1864)
Balthild (c. 630–c. 680)
Beatrice of Lorraine (c. 1020–1076)
Berengaria of Castile (1180–1246)
Blanche of Castile (1188–1252)
Bona of Savoy (c. 1450–c. 1505)
Borgia, Lucrezia (1480–1519)
Boudica (26/30–60)
Caroline of Ansbach (1683–1737)
Catherine of Bourbon (c. 1555–1604)
Catherine of Braganza (1638–1705)
Chand Bibi (1550–1599)
Cho (1809–1890)
Christine of France (1606–1663)
Christine of Lorraine (c. 1571–1637)
Cixi (1835–1908)
Cleopatra I (c. 210–176 BCE)
Cleopatra II (c. 183–116 BCE)
Cleopatra VII (69–30 BCE)
Cleopatra V Tryphaena (c. 95–c. 57 BCE)
Clifford, Rosamund (c. 1145–1176)
della Scala, Beatrice (1340–1384)
Deng (r. 105–121)
Drahomira of Bohemia (d. after 932)
Durgawati (d. 1564)
Eleanor of Aquitaine (1122–1204)
Eleanor of Provence (c. 1222–1291)
Elfgifu of Northampton (c. 1000–1044)
Elizabeth of Bosnia (c. 1345–1387)
Elizabeth of Poland (1305–1380)
Emma of Italy (948–after 990)
Emma of Waldeck (1858–1934)
Engelberga (c. 840–890)
Ermengarde of Anjou (d. 1147)
Ethelflaed (869–918)
Eudocia (c. 400–460)
Eudoxia Lopukhina (1669–1731)
Eugénie (1826–1920)
Farnese, Elizabeth (1692–1766)
Fredegund (c. 547–597)
Garsenda (1170–c. 1257)
Gerberga of Saxony (c. 910–969)
Glinski, Elena (c. 1506–1538)
Gonzaga, Maria (1609–1660)
Hatshepsut (c. 1515–1468 BCE)
Himnechildis (r. 662–675)
Hodierna of Jerusalem (c. 1115–after 1162)
Hōjo Masako (1157–1225)
Hortense de Beauharnais (1783–1837)
Irene of Athens (c. 752–803)
Isabeau of Bavaria (1371–1435)
Isabella Clara Eugenia of Austria (1566–1633)
Isabella of Portugal (1503–1539)
Isabelle of Lorraine (1410–1453)
Isabel Maria (1801–1876)
Isabel of Brazil (1846–1921)
Jeanne de Castile (r. 1366–1374)
Jeanne of Nemours (1644–1724)
Joanna (1452–1490)
Joanna of Austria (1535–1573)
Joanna of Navarre (c. 1370–1437)
Kaahumanu (1777–1832)
Khentkawes (fl. c. 2510 BCE)
Kinau (c. 1805–1839)
Labotsibeni Gwamile laMdluli (c. 1858–1925)
Leonora of Savoy (fl. 1200)
Leonora Telles (c. 1350–1386)
Liliuokalani (1838–1917)
Louise of Bourbon-Berry (1819–1864)
Louise of Savoy (1476–1531)
Lucienne of Segni (r. around 1252–1258)
Luisa de Guzman (1613–1666)
Mahaut (c. 1270–1329)
Margaret I of Denmark (1353–1412)
Margaret of Antioch-Lusignan (fl. 1283–1291)
Margaret of Austria (1480–1530)
Margaret of Navarre (fl. 1154–1172)
Margaret of Parma (1522–1586)
Margaret of Pomerania (d. 1282)
Margaret Tudor (1489–1541)
Maria Ana Victoria (1718–1781)
Maria Anna of Austria (c. 1634–1696)
Maria Antonia of Austria (1683–1754)
Maria Christina of Austria (1858–1929)
Maria Cristina I of Naples (1806–1878)
Maria de Molina (d. 1321)
Maria Luisa of Etruria (1782–1824)
Maria Magdalena of Austria (1589–1631)
Marie Casimir (1641–1716)
Marie Louise of Austria (1791–1847)
Marie Louise of Savoy (1688–1714)
Marie of Antioch (d. 1183)
Marie of Montferrat (d. 1212)
Martinozzi, Laura (fl. 1658)
Mary II (1662–1694)
Mary of Guelders (1433–1463)
Mary of Guise (1515–1560)
Mary of Hungary (1505–1558)
Mary Stuart (1542–1587)
Matilda (1102–1167)
Matilda of Flanders (c. 1031–1083)
Matilda of Quedlinburg (c. 953–999)
Matilda of Saxony (c. 892–968)
Medici, Catherine de (1519–1589)
Medici, Claudia de (1604–1648)
Medici, Maria de (fl. late 1400s)
Melisande (fl. 1100)
Menetewab (c. 1720–1770)
Mer-neith (fl. c. 3100 BCE)
Mmanthatisi (c. 1780–c. 1836)

Narishkina, Natalya (1651–1694)
Nefertiti (c. 1375–1336 BCE)
Neithotep (fl. c. 3100 BCE)
Olga (c. 890–969)
Olga Constantinovna (1851–1926)
Pahlavi, Farah (1938—)
Philippa of Hainault (1314–1369)
Plaisance of Antioch (d. 1261)
Plectrudis (fl. 665–717)
Pulcheria (c. 398–453)
Richilde (1034–1086)
Sancha of Leon (1013–1067)
Seymour, Jane (c. 1509–1537)
Sforza, Caterina (c. 1462–1509)
Shajar al-Durr (d. 1259)
Sirikit (1932—)
Sophia Alekseyevna (1657–1704)
Tamara (1160–1212)
Tauseret (c. 1220–1188 BCE)
Taytu (c. 1850–1918)
Teresa of Castile (c. 1080–1130)
Thecla (c. 823–c. 870)
Theodelinda (568–628)
Theodora (c. 500–548)
Theodora the Blessed (c. 810–c. 860)
Theophano (c. 940–?)
Theophano of Byzantium (c. 955–991)
Tiy (c. 1400–1340 BCE)
Urraca of Castile (c. 1186–1220)
Visconti, Catherine (c. 1360–1404)
Wu Zetian (624–705)
Yolande of Aragon (1379–1442)
Yolande of France (1434–1478)
Zenobia (r. 267–272)
Zoë Carbopsina (c. 890–920)

REGGAE SINGER
Marley, Cedella (1967—)
Marley, Rita (1946—)
Mowatt, Judy (1952—)

REGIONAL WRITER
Arnow, Harriette Simpson (1908–1986)
Bentley, Phyllis (1894–1977)
Blamire, Susanna (1747–1794)
Böhl von Faber, Cecilia (1796–1877)
Bonner, Sherwood (1849–1883)
Carlén, Emilia (1807–1892)
Castro, Rosalía de (1837–1885)
Davis, Mollie Moore (1844–1909)
Davis, Rebecca Harding (1831–1910)
Edgeworth, Maria (1768–1849)
Gale, Zona (1874–1938)
Jewett, Sarah Orne (1849–1909)
Kaye-Smith, Sheila (1887–1956)
Kinzie, Juliette Magill (1806–1870)
Kroeber, Theodora (1897–1979)
Lenski, Lois (1893–1974)
Murfree, Mary N. (1850–1922)
Niese, Charlotte (1854–1935)
Nováková, Teréza (1853–1912)
Sand, George (1804–1876)
Scarborough, Dorothy (1878–1935)
Spencer, Cornelia Phillips (1825–1908)
Suckow, Ruth (1892–1960)
Taggard, Genevieve (1894–1948)

RELIEF-ORGANIZATION FOUNDER
See Social-welfare organization founder.

RELIEF WORKER
See Social-welfare worker.

RELIGIOUS-COMMUNITY/ INSTITUTION FOUNDER
Abbott, Mother (1846–1934)
Adela, Saint (d. 735)
Adelaide of Burgundy (931–999)
Adelaide of Maurienne (1092–1154)
Agnes of Assisi (1207–1232)
Agnes of Bohemia (1205–1282)
Alice of Battenberg (1885–1969)
Amboise, Francise d' (1427–1485)
Anna Comnena (1083–1153/55)
Anna Dalassena (c. 1025–1105)
Arnold, Emmy (1884–1980)
Aubert, Mary Joseph (1835–1926)
Ayres, Anne (1816–1896)
Balthild (c. 630–c. 680)
Barbier, Adèle Euphrasie (1829–1893)
Beale, Dorothea (1831–1906)
Beatrix da Silva (1424–1490)
Beaufort, Joan (c. 1379–1440)
Begga (613–698)
Begga of Egremont (fl. 7th c.)
Benincasa, Ursula (1547–1618)
Bertha of Avenay (fl. 6th c.)
Bertha of Blangy (d. 725)
Bertha of Kent (c. 565–c. 616)
Blanche of Castile (1188–1252)
Booth, Catherine (1829–1890)
Borgia, Lucrezia (1480–1519)
Bridget (c. 453–c. 524)
Brown Blackwell, Antoinette (1825–1921)
Cabrini, Frances Xavier (1850–1917)
Cannon, Harriet Starr (1823–1896)
Clare of Assisi (c. 1194–1253)
Clarke, Mary Frances (1803–1887)
Clotilda (470–545)
Columba of Rieti (1467–1501)
Connelly, Cornelia (1809–1879)
Constantina (c. 321–c. 354)
Delanoue, Jeanne (1666–1736)
Delille, Henriette (1813–1862)
Dickinson, Frances (1755–1830)
Duchesne, Rose Philippine (1769–1852)
Dunbar-Nelson, Alice (1875–1935)
Eddy, Mary Baker (1821–1910)
Edith (c. 1025–1075)
Elisabeth of Habsburg (1554–1592)
Elthelthrith (630–679)
Engelberga (c. 840–890)
Ethelflaed (869–918)
Eugenia (d. around 258)
Falconieri, Juliana (1270–1341)
Fara (d. 667)
Fedde, Sister Elizabeth (1850–1921)
Fillmore, Myrtle Page (1845–1931)
Frances of Rome (1384–1440)
Frideswide (d. 735?)
Fullerton, Georgiana Charlotte (1812–1885)
Galindo, Beatriz (1475–1534)
Gisela (c. 753–807)
Guérin, Mother Theodore (1798–1856)
Hahn-Hahn, Ida, Countess von (1805–1880)
Hardey, Mary Aloysia (1809–1886)
Hedwig of Silesia (1174–1243)
Hersende of Champagne (fl. 12th c.)
Hilda of Whitby (614–680)
Humilitas of Faenza (1226–1310)
Irene Ducas (c. 1066–1133)
Isabelle (1225–1270)
Ita of Ireland (d. 570)
Jadwiga (1374–1399)
Jamet, Marie (1820–1893)
Jeanne de Bourbon (1338–1378)
Joanna of Austria (1535–1573)
Jonas, Regina (1902–1944)
Jugan, Jeanne (1792–1879)
Kingsford, Anna (1846–1888)
Lange, Elizabeth Clovis (1784–1882)
Lathrop, Rose Hawthorne (1851–1926)
Lioba (700–779)
Louise Adelaide de Bourbon (1757–1824)
Lupita, Madre (1878–1963)
Macrina (327–379)
Maddalena of Canossa (1774–1833)
Margaret of Flanders (1202–1280)
Maria Antonia of Austria (1683–1754)
Maria Barbara of Braganza (1711–1758)
Marie de St. Pol (1304–1377)
Marillac, Louise de (1591–1660)
Mary of Guelders (1433–1463)
Mathews, Ann Teresa (1732–1800)
Matilda of Flanders (c. 1031–1083)
McAuley, Catherine (1778–1841)
Melania the Elder (c. 350–c. 410)
Melania the Younger (c. 385–439)
Mellish, Edith Mary (1861–1922)
Mendoza, Ana de (1540–1592)
Modesta of Trier (d. about 680)
Modwenna (d. 518)
Montespan, Françoise, Marquise de (1640–1707)
Mulenga, Alice (1924–1978)
Nagle, Nano (1718–1784)
Ninnoc (fl. 6th c.)
Nonteta Bungu (c. 1875–1935)
Odilia (fl. 620)
Odozi Obodo, Madam (1909–1995)
O'Hagan, Mary (1823–1876)
Olympias (c. 365–408)
Osburga (?–c. 855)
Paula (347–404)
Prophet, Elizabeth Clare (1940—)
Radegund of Poitiers (518–587)
Ranfaing, Élizabeth of (d. 1649)
Rhodes, Mary (c. 1782–1853)
Riepp, Mother Benedicta (1825–1862)
Rogers, Mother Mary Joseph (1882–1955)
Scholastica (c. 480–543)
Sexburga (c. 627–673)
Sigolena of Albi (fl. 7th c.)
Teresa, Mother (c. 1766–1846)
Teresa of Avila (1515–1582)
Tilly, Dorothy (1883–1970)
Wandru (c. 628–688)
White, Alma Bridwell (1862–1946)
White, Ellen Gould (1827–1915)

RELIGIOUS HEALER
Simpson, Mary Elizabeth (1865–1948)

RELIGIOUS MARTYR
Afra (fl. c. 304)
Agatha, Saint (d. 251)
Agnes (d. possibly c. 304)
Agnes, Saint (d. possibly c. 304)
Anastasia, Saint (fl. 54–68)
Anastasia, Saint (d. 304)
Askew, Anne (c. 1521–1546)
Barbara (fl. 3rd c.)
Bibiana (d. 363)
Blandina (d. 177)
Bocher, Joan (d. 1550)
Catherine of Alexandria (?–305)
Cecilia (c. 154–c. 207)
Clarke, Maura (1931—)
Clitherow, Margaret (1556–1586)
Constance (d. 305 CE)
Donovan, Jean (1953—)
Dyer, Mary Barrett (c. 1591–1660)
Elizabeth of Bohemia (1596–1662)
Eulalia (290–304)
Eustochium (c. 368–c. 419)
Faith (290–303)
Felicitas (d. 203)
Felicitas of Rome (d. 162?)
Flora of Cordova (d. 851)

Ford, Ita (1940—)
Gertrude the Great (1256–1302)
Grey, Lady Jane (1537–1554)
Hilaria (fl. 304)
Hildegard of Bingen (1098–1179)
Joan of Arc (c. 1412 1431)
Justina (d. 64)
Justina (d. 304)
Kazel, Dorothy (1931—)
Kempe, Margery (c. 1373–after 1438)
Lucy (d. 303)
Ludmila (859–920)
Maria of Cordova (d. 851)
Marie Clotilde (d. 1794)
Mary Magdalene (fl. early 1st c.)
Michel, Louise (1830–1905)
Odena, Lina (1911–1936)
Perovskaya, Sonia (1853–1881)
Perpetua (181–203)
Perpetua and Felicitas
Regina (d. around 251)
Sophia (fl. early 2nd c.)
Stein, Edith (1891–1942)
Ursula (fl. 3rd or 5th c.)
Victoria (d. around 253)

RELIGIOUS-ORDER FOUNDER
See Religious community/institution founder.

RELIGIOUS PATRON/ PHILANTHROPIST/BENEFACTOR
Adelaide of Burgundy (931–999)
Bannerman, Jane (c. 1835–1923)
Bradley, Lydia Moss (1816–1908)
Catherine of Aragon (1485–1536)
Devorgilla (1109–1193)
Devorgilla (d. 1290)
Eudocia (c. 400–460)
Godiva (c. 1040–1080)
Helvidis (fl. 1136)
Jeanne de Bourbon (1338–1378)
Jitō (645–702)
Judith of Flanders (1032–1094)
Margaret, Saint (c. 1046–1093)
Margaret of York (1446–1503)
Marie de St. Pol (1304–1377)
Matilda (1102–1167)
Matilda, Empress (d. 1252)
Matilda of Flanders (c. 1031–1083)
McCormick, Nettie Fowler (1835–1923)
Melania the Younger (c. 385–439)
Melisande (fl. 1100)
Nagle, Nano (1718 1784)
Parr, Catherine (1512–1548)
Paula (347–404)
Peabody, Lucy (1861–1949)
Phoebe of Cenchreae (fl. 1st c.)
Reibey, Mary (1777–1855)
Sage, Margaret Olivia (1828–1918)
Sforza, Bona (1493–1557)
Visconti, Bianca Maria (1423–1470)

RELIGIOUS REFORMER
Agnes of Jouarre (fl. early 13th c.)
Arnold, Emmy (1884–1980)
Bliss, Catherine (1908–1989)
Braose, Loretta de (d. 1266)
Caro, Margaret (1848–1938)
Catherine of Bourbon (c. 1555–1604)
Colette (1381–1447)
Colonna, Vittoria (c. 1490–1547)
Cunningham, Ann (d. 1647)
Davis, Mary Fenn (1824–1886)
Heck, Barbara Ruckle (1734–1804)
Petre, Maude (1863–1942)
Philippa of Foix (fl. 13th c.)
Randall, Claire (1919—)
Stevenson, Margaret Beveridge (1865–1941)
Teresa of Avila (1515–1582)
Truth, Sojourner (c. 1797–1883)
White, Anna (1831–1910)
Young, Ann Eliza (b. 1844)
Young, Elizabeth (fl. 1558)
Zell, Katharina Schütz (c. 1497–1562)

RELIGIOUS/SPIRITUAL LEADER
Amritanandamayi, Mata (1953—)
Baillie, Grisell (1822–1921)
Bannerman, Jane (c. 1835–1923)
Barot, Madeleine (1909–1995)
Barton, Elizabeth (c. 1506–1534)
Beatrice, Dona (c. 1684–1706)
Bedell, Harriet M. (1875–1969)
Bennett, Mary Katharine (1864–1950)
Blaugdone, Barbara (c. 1609–1705)
Blavatsky, Helena (1831–1891)
Booth, Evangeline (1865–1950)
Bosshardt, Alida M. (1913—)
Bottome, Margaret McDonald (1827 1906)
Bramwell-Booth, Catherine (1883–1987)
Budapest, Z. (1940—)
Burleigh, Celia C. (1826–1875)
Burrows, Eva (1929—)
Cannon, Harriet Starr (1823–1896)
Carey, Eva (fl. 1921)
Case, Adelaide (1887–1948)
Christina of Markyate (1096–1160)
Chrodielde (fl. 590)
Delille, Henriette (1813–1862)
Donald, Janet (c. 1819–1892)
Dryburgh, Margaret (1890–1945)
Eddy, Mary Baker (1821–1910)
Eilberg, Amy (1954—)
Eustochium (c. 368–c. 419)
Fell, Margaret (1614–1702)
Fillmore, Myrtle Page (1845–1931)
Gardner, Kay (1941–2002)
Gayatri Devi (c. 1897–1995)
Gordon, Annie Elizabeth (1873–1951)
Hastings, Selina (1707–1791)
Heinemann, Barbara (1795–1883)
Helaria (fl. 6th c.)
Helwig of Prague (fl. 14th c.)
Hildegard of Bingen (1098–1179)
Hopkins, Emma Curtis (1853–1925)
Hutchinson, Anne (1591 1643)
Lee, Ann (1736–1784)
Lowry, Edith (1897–1970)
MacKillop, Mary Helen (1842–1909)
Marie de Bourbon (fl. 1350s)
Millet, Cleusa (c. 1931–1998)
Mulenga, Alice (1924–1978)
Nanny (fl. 1730s)
Nazaré, Maria Escolástica Da Conceição (1894–1986)
Neumann, Theresa (1898–1962)
Nivedita, Sister (1867–1911)
Nonna (c. 305–c. 374)
Nonteta Bungu (c. 1875–1935)
Odozi Obodo, Madam (1909–1995)
O'Hagan, Mary (1823–1876)
Palmer, Phoebe Worrall (1807–1874)
Paul, Annette (1863–1952)
Peale, Ruth Stafford (b. 1906)
Penn, Gulielma Springett (1644–1694)
Penn, Hannah (1671–1726)
Phoebe of Cenchreae (fl. 1st c.)
Priesand, Sally Jane (1946—)
Pudney, Elizabeth Allen (1894–1976)
Pudney, Elizabeth Jane (1862–1938)
Rabbani, Ruhiyyih (1910–2000)
Ray, Charlotte E. (1850–1911)
Robinson, Jane Bancroft (1847–1932)
Rudman, Annie (1844–1928)
Schroeder, Bertha (1872–1953)
Simpson, Mary Elizabeth (1865–1948)
Smith, Bathsheba (1822–1910)
Smith, Eliza Roxey Snow (1804–1887)
Smith, Hannah Whitall (1832–1911)
Squires, Catharine (1843–1912)
Stetson, Augusta (1842–1928)
Te Rangimarie, Puna Himene (fl. 1908–1911)
Teresa, Mother (c. 1766–1846)
Waddles, Charleszetta (1912–2001)
Wells, Emmeline B. (1828–1921)
White, Alma Bridwell (1862–1946)
White, Anna (1831–1910)
White, Ellen Gould (1827–1915)
Wilkinson, Jemima (1752–1819)
Wittenmyer, Annie Turner (1827–1900)
Wright, Lucy (1760–1821)
Zell, Katharina Schütz (c. 1497–1562)
Zwingli, Anna Reinhard (1487–c. 1538)

RELIGIOUS/SPIRITUAL WRITER
Adams, Sarah Flower (1805–1848)
Agreda, Sor María de (1602–1665)
Alden, Isabella (1841–1930)
Araz, Nezihe (1922—)
Ava of Melk (d. 1127)
Bayly, Ada Ellen (1857–1903)
Beaumont, Agnes (1652–1720)
Biddle, Hester (1629–1696)
Bijns, Anna (1493/94–1575)
Bowers, Bathsheba (c. 1672–1718)
Burnet, Elizabeth (1661–1709)
Carey, Mary (c. 1610–c. 1680)
Carmichael, Amy (1867–1971)
Cary, Mary (c. 1621–after 1653)
Cassidy, Sheila (1937—)
Castillo y Guevara, Francisca Josefa del (1671–1742)
Charles, Elizabeth (1828–1896)
Charlesworth, Maria (1819–1880)
Chidley, Katherine (fl. 1641)
Conant, Hannah Chaplin (1809–1865)
Cotton, Priscilla (d. 1664)
Coventry, Anne (1673–1763)
Davies, Eleanor (1590–1652)
Davy, Sarah (c. 1639–1670)
Deken, Aagje (1741–1804)
Ebner, Christine (1277–1355)
Ebner, Margarethe (1291–1351)
Elizabeth of the Trinity (1880–1906)
Fenno, Jenny (c. 1765–?)
Fiske, Sarah Symmes (1652–1692)
Gebara, Ivone (1944—)
Gestefeld, Ursula Newell (1845–1921)
Gippius, Zinaida (1869–1945)
Goodhue, Sarah Whipple (1641–1681)
Greenwell, Dora (1821–1882)
Grubb, Sarah Tuke (1756–1790)
Grumbach, Argula von (1492–after 1563)
Hadewijch (fl. 13th c.)
Havergal, Frances Ridley (1836–1879)
Heaton, Hannah Cook (1721–1794)
Hensel, Luise (1798–1876)
Herbert, Lucy (1669–1744)
Hill, Hannah, Jr (1703–1714)
Holland, Catherine (1637–1720)
Hopton, Susanna Harvey (1627–1708)
Hume, Sophia Wigington (1702–1774)
Hygeburg (fl. 8th c.)
Jackson, Rebecca Cox (1795–1871)
Katharina von Gebweiler (fl. c. 1340)
Katherine of Sutton (d. 1376)
Kingsford, Anna (1846–1888)
Langmann, Adelheid (d. 1375)

Occupational Index

Lead, Jane Ward (1623–1704)
Lyman, Mary Ely (1887–1975)
MacLaine, Shirley (1934—)
Margaret of Angoulême (1492–1549)
Marie (fl. 13th c.)
Martin, Dorcas Eglestone (fl. 16th c.)
Meeuwsen, Terry (1949—)
Meneses, Juana Josefa de (1651–1709)
Meyer, Lucy (1849–1922)
Mixer, Elizabeth (fl. 1707–1720)
More, Gertrude (1606–1633)
More, Hannah (1745–1833)
Norton, Frances (1640–1731)
Osborn, Sarah (1714–1796)
Owen, Jane (fl. 1617–1634)
Parr, Susanna (fl. 1659)
Petre, Maude (1863–1942)
Pickett, Fuchsia T. (1918–2004)
Poole, Elizabeth (fl. 1648)
Pozzo, Modesta (1555–1592)
Prewitt, Cheryl (c. 1957—)
Price, Eugenia (1916–1996)
Pulling, Mary Etheldred (1871–1951)
Rogers, Dale Evans (1912–2001)
Rossetti, Christina (1830–1894)
Shirley, Elizabeth (c. 1568–1641)
Simpson, Mary Elizabeth (1865–1948)
Smith, Eunice (1757–1823)
Smith, Hannah Whitall (1832–1911)
Stagel, Elsbeth (c. 1300–c. 1366)
Stowe, Harriet Beecher (1811–1896)
Sutcliffe, Alice (c. 1600–?)
Turner, Jane (before 1640–after 1660)
Underhill, Evelyn (1875–1941)
Ward, Maisie (1889–1975)
Waring, Anna Letitia (1823–1910)
West, Elizabeth (fl. early 18th c.)
Williams, Sarah (1841–1868)
Witt, Henriette de (1829–1908)

REPORTER
See Journalist.

REPRODUCTIVE-RIGHTS ACTIVIST
Abzug, Bella (1920–1998)
Anttila, S. Inkeri (1916—)
Beauvoir, Simone de (1908–1986)
Benjamin, Hilde (1902–1989)
Besant, Annie (1847–1933)
Black, Shirley Temple (1928—)
Booth, Angela Elizabeth (1869–1954)
Bromley, Dorothy Dunbar (1896–1986)
Brown, Dorothy (1919—)
Budzynska-Tylicka, Justyna (1876–1936)
Calderone, Mary Steichen (1904–1998)
Chisholm, Shirley (1924–2005)
Davidow, Ruth (1911–1999)
Denison, Flora MacDonald (1867–1921)
Denman, Gertrude (1884–1954)
Dennett, Mary Ware (1872–1947)
Dornemann, Luise (1901–1992)
Elders, Joycelyn (1933—)
Fernando, Sylvia (1904–1983)
Goldman, Emma (1869–1940)
Hawkins, Mary (1875–1950)
Ireland, Patricia (1945—)
Jacobs, Aletta (1854–1929)
Jagan, Janet (1920—)
Jesse, Fryniwyd Tennyson (1888–1958)
Kenyon, Dorothy (1888–1972)
Levine, Lena (1903–1965)
Lohman, Ann Trow (1812–1878)
Lowney, Shannon (1969–1994)
Mansour, Agnes Mary (c. 1931–2004)
Martin, Lynn (1939—)
Martinson, Moa (1890–1964)
Marzouk, Zahia (1906–1988)
McCormick, Katharine Dexter (1875–1967)
Michelman, Kate (1942—)
Millett, Kate (1934—)
Olmsted, Mildred Scott (1890–1990)
Ottesen-Jensen, Elise (1886–1973)
Pelletier, Madeleine (1874–1939)
Pyke, Margaret (1893–1966)
Reagan, Maureen (1941–2001)
Rich, Adrienne (1929—)
Rodríguez, Evangelina (1879–1947)
Roussel, Nelly (1878–1922)
Russell, Dora (1894–1986)
Sanger, Margaret (1879–1966)
Shapiro, Betty Kronman (1907–1989)
Smeal, Eleanor (1939—)
Steinem, Gloria (1934—)
Stoecker, Helene (1869–1943)
Stopes, Marie (1880–1958)
Suckling, Sophia Lois (1893–1990)
Wattleton, Faye (1943—)
Whitman, Christine Todd (1946—)
Wright, Helena (1887–1982)
Yard, Molly (1912–2005)
Yorkin, Peg (1927—)

RESEARCH-INSTITUTE FOUNDER
See Educational institution/program founder.

RESISTANCE LEADER
Abegg, Elisabeth (1882–1974)
Adler, Valentine (1898–1942)
Agnes, Lore (1876–1953)
Agostina (1788–1857)
Albrecht, Bertie (?–1943)
Ali, Aruna Asaf (c. 1909–1996)
Andersen, Lale (1910–1972)
Anderson, Evelyn N. (1909–1977)
Apostoloy, Electra (1911–1944)
Aubrac, Lucie (1912—)
Auer, Judith (1905–1944)
Barot, Madeleine (1909–1995)
Basch, Anamarija (1893–after 1945)
Ba Trieu (225–248)
Baum, Marianne (1912–1942)
Becher, Lilly (1901–1976)
Beimler-Herker, Centa (1909—)
Belishova, Liri (1923—)
Benjamin, Hilde (1902–1989)
Bergner, Elisabeth (1897–1986)
Bervoets, Marguerite (1914–1944)
Beyer, Helga (1920–1942)
Bohm-Schuch, Clara (1879–1936)
Bonhoeffer, Emmi (1905–1991)
Bottome, Phyllis (1884–1963)
Boveri, Margret (1900–1975)
Brandes-Brilleslijper, Janny (c. 1918–2003)
Braun-Vogelstein, Julie (1883–1971)
Bruha, Antonia (1915—)
Brunner, Josefine (1909–1943)
Brusselsmans, Anne
Burger, Hildegard (1905–1943)
Casanova, Danielle (1909–1943)
Christians, Mady (1900–1951)
Coppi, Hilde (1909–1943)
Dassault, Madeleine (1901–1992)
de Gaulle, Geneviève (1921–2002)
de Jongh, Andree (1916—)
Delbo, Charlotte (1913–1985)
Deutsch, Helen (1906–1992)
Diebold, Laure (1915–1964)
Dietrich, Marlene (1901–1992)
Dissard, Marie Louise (b. 1880)
Dönhoff, Marion, Countess (1909–2002)
Douglas, Helen Gahagan (1900–1980)
Duby-Blom, Gertrude (1901–1993)
Durieux, Tilla (1880–1971)
Eisenblätter, Charlotte (1903–1944)
Eisenschneider, Elvira (1924–c. 1944)
Eisner, Lotte (1896–1983)
Emhart, Maria (1901–1981)
Fabian, Dora (1901–1935)
Fénelon, Fania (1918–1983)
Fischer, Ruth (1895–1961)
Fittko, Lisa (1909–2005)
Fleming, Amalia (1912–1986)
Gardiner, Muriel (1901–1985)
Gineste, Marie-Rose (1911—)
Grundig, Lea (1906–1977)
Harand, Irene (1900–1975)
Harnack, Mildred (1902–1943)
Hazrat Mahal (c. 1820–1879)
Heemstra, Ella van (1900–1984)
Herrmann, Liselotte (1909–1938)
Honecker, Margot (1927—)
Jacobi, Lotte (1896–1990)
Juchacz, Marie (1879–1956)
Jurca, Branca (1914–1999)
Kaur, Rajkumari Amrit (1889–1964)
Kripalani, Sucheta (1908–1974)
Kuckhoff, Greta (1902–1981)
Kuderikova, Marie (1921–1943)
Kulcsar, Ilse (1902–1973)
Kunke, Steffi (1908–1942)
Lindner, Herta (1920–1943)
Lingens-Reiner, Ella (1908–2002)
Litten, Irmgard (1879–1953)
Löwenstein, Helga Maria zu (1910–2004)
Lubetkin, Zivia (1914–1978)
Luce, Clare Boothe (1903–1987)
Luckner, Gertrud (1900–1995)
Mann, Erika (1905–1969)
Maric, Ljubica (1909–2003)
Massy-Beresford, Monica (1894–1945)
Meena (1956–1987)
Michaëlis, Karin (1872–1950)
Moholy-Nagy, Sibyl (1903–1971)
Monte, Hilda (1914–1945)
Neher, Carola (1900–1942)
Neumann, Hanna (1914–1971)
Niederkirchner, Käte (1909–1944)
Noce, Teresa (1900–1980)
Oddon, Yvonne (1902–1982)
Olberg, Oda (1872–1955)
Osten, Maria (1908–1942)
Paasche, Maria (1909–2000)
Pauli, Hertha (1909–1973)
Postel-Vinay, Anise (1928—)
Preradovic, Paula von (1887–1951)
Rehor, Grete (1910–1987)
Reik, Haviva (1914–1944)
Rizea, Elisabeta (1912–2003)
Roland Holst, Henriëtte (1869–1952)
Rubenstein, Blanche (c. 1897–1969)
Sagan, Ginetta (1923–2000)
Salomon, Alice (1872–1948)
Sansom, Odette (1912–1995)
Schaft, Hannie (1920–1945)
Schlösinger, Rose (1907–1943)
Scholl, Sophie (1921–1943)
Schroeder, Louise (1887–1957)
Schulze-Boysen, Libertas (1913–1942)
Schumacher, Elisabeth (1904–1942)
Seidel, Amalie (1876–1952)
Sintenis, Renée (1888–1965)
Spira, Steffie (1908–1995)
Stöbe, Ilse (1911–1942)
Stone, Grace Zaring (1896–1991)
Svolou, Maria (d. 1976)
Taro, Gerda (1910–1937)
Tillion, Germaine (b. 1907)
Triolet, Elsa (1896–1970)

Trung Sisters (d. 43)
Undset, Sigrid (1882–1949)
von Moltke, Freya (b. 1911)
Wagner, Friedelind (1918–1991)
Weigel, Helene (1900–1971)
Wichfeld-Muus, Varinka (1922–2002)
Wiesenthal, Grete (1885–1970)
Witherington, Pearl (1914—)
Zaleska, Katherine (1919—)
Zita of Parma (1892–1989)

RESTAURATEUR
Allen, Betty (1936—)
Benjamin, Ethel Rebecca (1875–1943)
Brown, Hilary (1952—)
Burton, Annie L. (fl. 19th c.)
Callender, Marie (1907–1995)
Chasen, Maude (1904–2001)
Chen, Joyce (1918–1994)
Cranston, Kate (1850–1934)
Eriksen, Gunn (1956—)
Zabar, Lillian (1905–1995)

RETAILER
See Merchant/Trader.

REVOLUTIONARY
Adler, Valentine (1898–1942)
Ali, Aruna Asaf (c. 1909–1996)
Anderson, Evelyn N. (1909–1977)
Anneke, Mathilde Franziska (1817–1884)
Apostoloy, Electra (1911–1944)
Aquino, Melchora (1812–1919)
Araúz, Blanca (d. 1933)
Armand, Inessa (1874–1920)
Aston, Luise (1814–1871)
Astorga, Nora (1949–1988)
Auer, Judith (1905–1944)
Balabanoff, Angelica (1878–1965)
Barros, Lorena (d. 1976)
Basch, Anamarija (1893–after 1945)
Bastidas, Micaela (1745–1781)
Baum, Marianne (1912–1942)
Belgioso, Cristina (1808–1871)
Benario, Olga (1908–1942)
Berg, Helene (b. 1906)
Beyer, Helga (1920–1942)
Blagoeva, Stella Dimitrova (1887–1954)
Bohuszewiczowna, Maria (1865–1887)
Bonita, Maria (c. 1908–1938)
Bracetti, Mariana (1840–c. 1904)
Breshkovsky, Catherine (1844–1934)
Brown, Elaine (1943—)
Brunner, Josefine (1909–1943)
Bunke, Tamara (1937–1967)
Cai Chang (1900–1990)
Cama, Bhikaiji (1861–1936)
Carney, Winifred (1887–1943)
Casanova, Danielle (1909–1943)
Chai, Ling (1966—)
Chen Tiejun (1904–1928)
Chen Zongying (1902–2003)
Clarke, Kathleen (1878–1972)
Clodia (c. 94–post 45 BCE)
Cohn, Fannia (c. 1885–1962)
Corbin, Margaret Cochran (1751–c. 1800)
Dai Houying (1938–1996)
Davidow, Ruth (1911–1999)
Davis, Angela (1944—)
Deng Yingchao (1903–1992)
Deutsch, Helene (1884–1982)
de Valois, Ninette (1898–2001)
Dolma, Pachen (c. 1933–2002)
Dragoicheva, Tsola (1893–1993)
Drif, Zohra (1941—)
Duczynska, Ilona (1897–1978)
Dzerzhinska, Sofia (1882–1968)
Eisenblätter, Charlotte (1903–1944)
Eisenschneider, Elvira (1924–c. 1944)
Emhart, Maria (1901–1981)
Espín de Castro, Vilma (1934—)
Figner, Vera (1852–1942)
First, Ruth (1925–1982)
Fischer, Ruth (1895–1961)
Flynn, Elizabeth Gurley (1890–1964)
Fornalska, Malgorzata (1902–1944)
Fukuda Hideko (1865–1927)
Galindo de Topete, Hermila (1896–1954)
Gandhi, Kasturba (1869–1944)
Gasteazoro, Ana (1950–1993)
Gelfman, Gesia (d. 1882)
Goldman, Emma (1869–1940)
Golubkina, Anna (1864–1927)
Gomez, Sara (1943–1974)
Gonne, Maud (1866–1953)
Gouges, Olympe de (1748–1793)
Grajales, Mariana (1808–1893)
Gutiérrez de Mendoza, Juana Belén (1875–1942)
Hébert, Madame (d. 1794)
Héricourt, Jenny Poinsard d' (1809–1875)
He Xiangning (1879–1972)
Ibárruri, Dolores (1895–1989)
Ipatescu, Ana (1805–1855)
Ivanovskaia, Praskovia (1853–1935)
Jesus, Gregoria de (1875–1943)
Jochmann, Rosa (1901–1994)
Kang Keqing (1911–1992)
Kaplan, Fanya (1883–1918)
Kéthly, Anna (1889–1976)
Kollontai, Alexandra (1872–1952)
Koszutska, Maria (1876–1939)
Kovalevskaya, Sophia (1850–1891)
Kovalskaia, Elizaveta (1851–1943)
Krupskaya, Nadezhda (1869–1939)
Kuliscioff, Anna (c. 1854–1925)
Kunke, Steffi (1908–1942)
Lacore, Suzanne (1875–1975)
Lakwena, Alice (1960—)
Leichter, Käthe (1895–1942)
Lemel, Nathalie (1827–1921)
Léo, André (1832–1900)
Léon, Pauline (1758–?)
Liubatovich, Olga (1853–1917)
Liubatovich, Vera (1855–1907)
Luxemburg, Rosa (1870–1919)
Machel, Graca (1946—)
Marin, Gladys (1941–2005)
Markievicz, Constance (1868–1927)
Marot, Helen (1865–1940)
Martinson, Moa (1890–1964)
Marx, Jenny von Westphalen (1814–1881)
McCauley, Mary Ludwig Hays
McCracken, Mary Ann (1770–1866)
Meena (1956–1987)
Michel, Louise (1830–1905)
Mink, Paule (1839–1901)
Mirabal de González, Patria (1924–1960)
Mirabal de Guzmán, María Teresa (1936–1960)
Mirabal de Tavárez, Minerva (1927–1960)
Modotti, Tina (1896–1942)
Mongella, Gertrude (1945—)
Montpensier, Anne Marie Louise d'Orléans, Duchesse de (1627–1693)
Mujuru, Joyce (1955—)
Nguyen Thi Dinh (1920–1992)
Nikolaeva, Klavdiia (1893–1944)
Nivedita, Sister (1867–1911)
Noce, Teresa (1900–1980)
Olsen, Tillie (c. 1912—)
Ortíz de Dominguez, Josefa (c. 1768–1829)
Overlach, Helene (1894–1983)
Padilla, Maria Pacheco (c. 1496–1531)
Pankhurst, Christabel (1880–1958)
Pankhurst, Emmeline (1858–1928)
Pankhurst, Sylvia (1882–1960)
Pelletier, Madeleine (1874–1939)
Perovskaya, Sonia (1853–1881)
Qian Zhengying (1923—)
Qiu Jin (c. 1875–1907)
Rambert, Marie (1888–1982)
Ramirez, Sara Estela (1881–1910)
Reisner, Larissa (1895–1926)
Roland Holst, Henriëtte (1869–1952)
Sáenz, Manuela (1797–1856)
Salavarrieta, Pola (1795–1817)
Samoilova, Konkordiya (1876–1921)
Sanchez, Celia (1920–1980)
Santamaría, Haydée (1922–1980)
Shochat, Manya (1878–1961)
Silang, Gabriela (1731–1763)
Slutskaya, Vera (1874–1917)
Spiridonova, Maria (1884–1941)
Stasova, Elena (1873–1966)
Stoecker, Helene (1869–1943)
Tallien, Thérésa (1773–1835)
Tecson, Trinidad (1848–1928)
Tellez, Dora Maria (1957—)
Templeton, Rini (1935–1986)
Tescon, Trinidad (1848–1928)
Théroigne de Méricourt, Anne-Josèphe (1762–1817)
Tinayre, Marguerite (1831–?)
Tito, Jovanka Broz (1924—)
Trotsky, Natalia Ivanovna (1882–1962)
Ulyanova, Marie (fl. 1880–1930s)
Vicario, Leona (1789–1842)
Wasilewska, Wanda (1905–1964)
Webb, Beatrice (1858–1943)
Wilson, Charlotte (1854–1944)
Wu Lanying (d. 1929)
Xiang Jingyu (1895–1928)
Zamora, Daisy (1950—)
Zasulich, Vera (1849–1919)

RHYTHM-AND-BLUES SINGER
Aaliyah (1979–2001)
Armstead, Izora (1942–2004)
Baker, Anita (1958—)
Belle, Regina (1963—)
Bennett, Patricia (1947—)
Bentley, Gladys (1907–1960)
Blige, Mary J. (1971—)
Bofill, Angela (1954—)
Bogan, Lucille (1897–1948)
Brandy (1979—)
Braxton, Toni (1967—)
Brown, Foxy (1979—)
Brown, Ruth (1928—)
Bruno, Gioia Carmen (1965—)
Cole, Natalie (1950—)
Cox, Ida (1896–1967)
Craig, Judy (1946—)
Curless, Ann (1965—)
Dash, Sarah (1945—)
Davis, Theresa (1950—)
Dixon, Reather (1945—)
Douglas, Lizzie (1897–1973)
Elliott, Missy (1971—)
Ellis, Terry (1966—)
Everett, Betty (1939–2001)
Ford, Penny (1964—)
Franklin, Aretha (1942—)
Franklin, Erma (1938–2002)
Gathers, Helen (1943—)
Goodman, Shirley (1936–2005)
Goring, Sonia (1940—)
Harris, Barbara (1945—)
Harris, Lois (1940—)

Hendryx, Nona (1945—)
Herron, Cindy (1965—)
Houston, Whitney (1963—)
Hutchinson, Jeanette (1951—)
Hutchinson, Pamela (1958—)
Hutchinson, Sheila (1953—)
Hutchinson, Wanda (1951—)
Hyman, Phyllis (1949–1995)
James, Etta (1938—)
Jones, Maxine (1966—)
Jurado, Jeanette (1966—)
Khan, Chaka (1953—)
Knight, Gladys (1944—)
Knowles, Beyoncé (1981—)
LaBelle, Patti (1944—)
Landry, Jackie (1940–1997)
Lee, Barbara (1947–1992)
Lopes, Lisa (1971–2002)
Luckett, LeToya (1981—)
Marie, Teena (1956—)
MC Lyte (1971—)
Mills, Stephanie (1957—)
Minus, Rene (1943—)
Moneymaker, Kelly (1965—)
Monica (1980—)
Montiero, June (1946—)
Nelson, Tracy (1944—)
Parritt, Barbara (1944—)
Peebles, Ann (1947—)
Peterson, Sylvia (1946—)
Phillips, Esther (1935–1984)
Pought, Emma (1942—)
Pought, Jannie (1944–1980)
Queen Latifah (1970—)
Raitt, Bonnie (1949—)
Roberson, LaTavia (1981—)
Robinson, Dawn (1968—)
Rowland, Kelly (1981—)
Sledge, Debra (1955—)
Sledge, Joni (1957—)
Sledge, Kathy (1959—)
Sledge, Kim (1958—)
Smith, Annette
Smith, Arlene (1941—)
Smith, Mabel (1924–1972)
Snow, Phoebe (1952—)
Springfield, Dusty (1939–1998)
Stansfield, Lisa (1966—)
Staples, Cleo (1934—)
Staples, Mavis (1940—)
Staples, Yvonne (1939—)
Terrell, Tammi (1946–1970)
Thomas, Carla (1942—)
Thomas, Rozonda (1971—)
Thornton, Willie Mae (1926–1984)
Troy, Doris (1937–2004)
Turner, Tina (1938—)
Vanderpool, Sylvia (1936—)
Warwick, Dionne (1940—)
Wash, Martha
Washington, Dinah (1924–1963)
Watkins, Tionne (1970—)
Webb, Laura (1941–2001)
Wells, Mary (1943–1992)
White, Karyn (1965—)
Williams, Deniece (1951—)
Williams, Michelle (1980—)
Wilson, Nancy (1937—)
Wright, Betty (1953—)
Wright, Syreeta (1946–2004)

RITUAL PARTNER

Xoc, Lady (c. 660–c. 720)

ROCK-AND-ROLL MUSICIAN/SINGER

Allbut, Barbara (1940—)
Allbut, Phyllis (1942—)
Alston, Barbara (1945—)
Amphlett, Christina (c. 1960—)
Baker, LaVern (1929–1997)
Bean, Janet Beveridge (1964—)
Benatar, Pat (1953—)
Birdsong, Cindy (1939—)
Bley, Carla (1938—)
Bramlett, Bonnie (1944—)
Branigan, Laura (1957–2004)
Brooks, Dolores (1946—)
Brown, Ruth (1928—)
Brownstein, Carrie (1974—)
Bush, Kate (1958—)
Carnes, Kim (1945—)
Carter, Carlene (1955—)
Cherry, Neneh (1963—)
Cole, Paula (1960—)
Colvin, Shawn (1956—)
Coolidge, Rita (1944—)
Cowsill, Barbara (1929–1985)
Cowsill, Susan (1960—)
Currie, Cherie (1959—)
Dash, Sarah (1945—)
DeFranco, Marisa (1955—)
DeFranco, Merlina (1957—)
Denny, Sandy (1947–1978)
DiFranco, Ani (1970—)
Easton, Sheena (1959—)
Elliot, Cass (1941–1974)
Elliott, Missy (1971—)
Etheridge, Melissa (1961—)
Exene (1956—)
Faithfull, Marianne (1946—)
Flack, Roberta (1937—)
Ford, Lita (1958—)
Frischmann, Justine (1969—)
Gordon, Kim (1953—)
Goring, Sonia (1940—)
Harris, Addie (1940–1982)
Harris, Lois (1940—)
Harry, Deborah (1945—)
Holland, Annie (1965—)
Hynde, Chrissie (1951—)
Jackson, Cordell (1923–2004)
Jackson, Wanda (1937—)
Jansen, Linda
Jett, Joan (1958—)
Joplin, Janis (1943–1970)
Kennibrew, Dee Dee (1945—)
King, Carole (1942—)
LaBelle, Patti (1944—)
Landry, Jackie (1940–1997)
Logic, Lora (c. 1961—)
Lwin, Annabella (1965—)
Lynch, Laura (1958—)
MacColl, Kirsty (1959–2000)
Macy, Robin Lynn (1958—)
Maines, Natalie (1974—)
Matthews, Donna (1971—)
Millington, Jean
Minus, Rene (1943—)
Mitchell, Joni (1943—)
Morissette, Alanis (1974—)
Napolitano, Johnette (1957—)
Nicks, Stevie (1948—)
Phillips, Michelle (1944—)
Quatro, Suzi (1950—)
Ravan, Genya (1942—)
Robison, Emily (1972—)
Santiglia, Peggy (1944—)
Seidel, Martie (1969—)
Shakira (1977—)
Slick, Grace (1939—)
Smith, Annette
Smith, Arlene (1941—)
Springfield, Dusty (1939–1998)
Styrene, Poly (c. 1962—)
Supremes, The (1964–1977)
Thomas, Mary (1946—)
Tucker, Corin (1972—)
Tucker, Tanya (1958—)
Turner, Tina (1938—)
Up, Ari (1962—)
Wright, Patricia (1945—)

ROCK CLIMBER

Hill, Lynn (1961—)

RODEO CHAMPION

Orr, Alice Greenough (1902–1995)

ROLLER SKATER

Dunn, Natalie (1956—)

ROMANCE-FICTION WRITER

Acosta de Samper, Soledad (1833–1913)
Bailey, Temple (c. 1869–1953)
Barclay, Florence Louisa (1862–1921)
Beck, Elizabeth Louisa (c. 1862–1931)
Benzoni, Juliette (1920—)
Bloom, Ursula (1893–1984)
Broughton, Rhoda (1840–1920)
Bury, Charlotte (1775–1861)
Caldwell, Taylor (1900–1985)
Cartland, Barbara (1901–2000)
Cooper, Jilly (1937—)
Du Verger, Susan (before 1625–after 1657)
Eberhart, Mignon G. (1899–1996)
Glyn, Elinor (1864–1943)
Mantle, Winifred Langford (1911–1983)
Molesworth, Mary Louisa (1839–1921)
Porter, Jane (1776–1850)
Price, Eugenia (1916–1996)
Rees, Rosemary (c. 1876–1963)
Rinehart, Mary Roberts (1876–1958)
Saint Mars, Gabrielle de (1804–1872)
Taber, Gladys (1899–1980)
Whitney, Phyllis A. (b. 1903)
Wilson, Anne Glenny (1848–1930)
Wright, Mabel Osgood (1859–1934)

ROWER

See Sculler.

RUGBY PLAYER

Gallagher, Rosie (1970–2003)

RULER

Ada (c. 380–c. 323 BCE)
Adele (r. 1017–1031)
Agnes de Dampierre (1237–1288)
Agnes de Nevers (r. 1181–1192)
Alix of Vergy (r. 1248–c. 1290)
Arsinde (fl. 934–957)
Braunschweig-Lüneburg, Elisabeth von (1519–1558)
Claudine (1451–1514)
Cleopatra II (c. 183–116 BCE)
Constance of Antioch (1128–1164)
Eleanor d'Arborea (c. 1360–c. 1404)
Ermesind of Luxemburg (d. 1247)
Ethelflaed (869–918)
Euphrosine (d. 1102)
Henrietta of Cleves (r. 1564–1601)
Herodias (c. 14 BCE–after 40 CE)
Isabella Clara Eugenia of Austria (1566–1633)
Jeanne de Castile (r. 1366–1374)
Labotsibeni Gwamile laMdluli (c. 1858–1925)
Mahaut de Courtenay (d. 1257)
Mahaut I (r. 1215–1242)
Margaret Maultasch (1318–1369)
Margaret of Alsace (c. 1135–1194)

Marguerite de Thouars (r. 1365–1377)
Marozia Crescentii (885–938)
Matilda of Tuscany (1046–1115)
Pokou (c. 1700–c. 1760)
Udham Bai (fl. 1748–1754)

RUNNER

Ashford, Evelyn (1957—)
Bailey, Angela (1962—)
Blankers-Koen, Fanny (1918—)
Boulmerka, Hassiba (1968—)
Brisco-Hooks, Valerie (1960—)
Budd, Zola (1966—)
Cuthbert, Betty (1938—)
Devers, Gail (1966—)
El Moutawakel, Nawal (1962—)
Faggs, Mae (1932—)
Ferrell, Barbara (1947—)
Flintoff, Debra (1960—)
Gardner, Maureen (1928–1974)
Gibb, Roberta (1943—)
Göhr, Marlies (1958—)
Gunnell, Sally (1966—)
Hardy, Catherine (1932—)
Hitomi Kinue (1908–1931)
Hudson, Martha (1939—)
Itkina, Maria (1932—)
Jackson, Grace (1961—)
Jackson, Marjorie (1931—)
Jackson, Nell (1929–1988)
Jones, Barbara (1937—)
Joyner, Florence Griffith (1959–1998)
Joyner-Kersee, Jackie (1962—)
Kazankina, Tatyana (1951—)
King, Joyce (1921—)
Klier-Schaller, Johanna (1952—)
Koch, Marita (1957—)
Kondratyeva, Lyudmila (1958—)
Kristiansen, Ingrid (1956—)
Larrieu, Francie (1952—)
Manley, Dorothy (1927—)
Matthews, Margaret (1935—)
McGuire, Edith (1944—)
Melpomene (fl. 1896)
Moreau, Janet (1927—)
Mota, Rosa (1958—)
Ottey-Page, Merlene (1960—)
Packer, Ann E. (1942—)
Patterson-Tyler, Audrey (1926–1996)
Pedersen, Elaine (1936–2000)
Perec, Marie-Jose (1968—)
Pippig, Uta (1965—)
Quirot, Ana (1963—)
Reel, Chi Cheng (1944—)
Robinson, Betty (1911–1997)
Rosenfeld, Fanny "Bobbie" (1903–1969)
Rudolph, Wilma (1940–1994)
Samuelson, Joan Benoit (1957—)
Slaney, Mary Decker (1958—)
Stecher, Renate (1950—)
Stephens, Helen (1918–1994)
Switzer, Kathy (1947—)
Torrence, Gwen (1965—)
Toussaint, Cheryl (1952—)
Tulu, Derartu (1972—)
Tyus, Wyomia (1945—)
Waitz, Grete (1953—)
Walsh, Stella (1911–1980)
White, Marilyn Elaine (1944—)
Williams, Lucinda (1937—)
Wöckel-Eckert, Bärbel (1955—)
Zatopek, Dana (1922—)

SAILOR

Abboud, Simonne (c. 1930—)
Adams, Sharon Sites (c. 1930—)
Aebi, Tania (1966—)
Amato, Serena (1974—)
America³ Team (1995—)
Andersen, Linda (1969—)
Armstrong, Jenny (1970—)
Ayton, Sarah (1980—)
Azon, Sandra (1973—)
Bacon, Mabel (fl. 1910)
Becker-Dey, Courtenay (1965—)
Bekatorou, Sofia (1977—)
Bengtsson, Birgitta (1965—)
Bonney, Anne (1700–?)
Borregaard Otzen, Christina (1975—)
Bouboulina, Laskarina (1771–1825)
Chelgren, Pamela (c. 1949—)
Chojnowska-Liskiewicz, Krystyna (1937—)
Chunikhovskaya, Irina (1968—)
Cottee, Kay (1954—)
de Vries, Dorien (1965—)
Edwards, Tracey (1962—)
Egnot, Leslie (1963—)
Fields, Evelyn J.
Francis, Clare (1946—)
Frank, Nance (1949—)
Glaser, Pease (1961—)
Guerra Cabrera, Patricia (1965—)
Healy, Pamela (1963—)
Isler, Jennifer (1963—)
James, Naomi (1949—)
Jensen, Dorte (1972—)
Jespersen, Helle (1968—)
Jewell, Lynne (1959—)
Jolly, Allison (1956—)
Kalinina, Ganna (1979—)
Kendall, Barbara Anne (1967—)
Kinoshita, Alicia (1967—)
Lee Lai-shan (1970—)
Livbjerg, Signe (1980—)
Lunde, Vibeke (1921–1962)
Lux, Amelie (1977—)
MacArthur, Ellen (1976—)
Maillart, Ella (1903–1997)
Matevusheva, Svitlana (1981—)
Matthijsse, Margriet (1977—)
Merret, Faustine (1978—)
Moskalenko, Larisa (1963—)
Pakholchik, Olena (1964—)
Patten, Mary Ann (1837–1861)
Read, Mary (1680–1721)
Riley, Dawn (1964—)
Robertson, Shirley (1968—)
Roug, Kristine (1975—)
Sensini, Alessandra (1970—)
Shearer, Janet (1958—)
Shige, Yumiko (1965—)
Smidova, Lenka (1975—)
Söderström, Marit (1962—)
Stowell, Belinda (1971—)
Sundby, Siren (1982—)
Talbot, Mary Anne (1778–1808)
Taran, Ruslana (1970—)
Torgersson, Therese (1976—)
Trotman, Julia (1968—)
Tsoulfa, Emilia (1973—)
Via Dufresne, Begona (1971—)
Via Dufresne, Natalia (1973—)
Webb, Sarah (1977—)
Yin Jian (1978—)
Zabell, Theresa (1965—)
Zachrisson, Vendela (1978—)
Zhang Xiaodong (1964—)

SAINT

Acarie, Barbe (1566–1618)
Adela (d. 735)
Adelaide, Madame (1732–1800)
Adelaide of Burgundy (931–999)
Adelaide of Schaerbeck (d. 1250)
Afra (fl. c. 304)
Agape of Thessalonica (d. 304)
Agatha (d. 251)
Agnes (d. possibly c. 304)
Agnes of Aquitaine (c. 995–1068)
Agnes of Meran (d. 1201)
Agnes of Monte Pulciano (1274–1317)
Aldetrude (fl. 7th c)
Amalia (d. 690)
Anastasia (fl. 54–68)
Anastasia (d. 304)
Anastasia (d. about 860)
Anastasia of Russia (c. 1023–after 1074)
Anastasia the Patrician (d. 567)
Angela of Brescia (1474–1540)
Angela of Foligno (1249–1309)
Anne (fl. 1st c.)
Barat, Madeleine Sophie (1779–1865)
Barbara (fl. 3rd c.)
Basilissa (fl. 54–68)
Beatrix da Silva (1424–1490)
Beatrix of Lens (d. around 1216)
Begga (613–698)
Begga of Egremont (fl. 7th c.)
Benedicta of Assisi (d. 1260)
Bernadette of Lourdes (1844–1879)
Bertha of Avenay (c. 830–c. 852)
Bertha of Avenay (fl. 6th c.)
Bertha of Biburg (d. 1151)
Bertha of Blangy (d. 725)
Bertha of Marbais (d. 1247)
Bertille (d. 705/713)
Blandina (d. 177)
Bona of Pisa (c. 1156–1207)
Bridget (c. 453–c. 524)
Bridget of Sweden (1303–1373)
Cabrini, Frances Xavier (1850–1917)
Casilda (d. about 1007)
Catherine of Alexandria (?–305)
Catherine of Bologna (1413–1463)
Catherine of Genoa (1447–1510)
Catherine of Ricci (c. 1522–1589)
Catherine of Siena (1347–1380)
Catherine of Sweden (c. 1330–1381)
Cecilia (c. 154–c. 207)
Chantal, Jeanne de (1572–1641)
Chionia (d. 304)
Christina the Astonishing (c. 1150–c. 1224)
Clara (1697–1744)
Clare of Assisi (c. 1194–1253)
Clitherow, Margaret (1556–1586)
Clotilda (470–545)
Colette (1381–1447)
Columba of Cordova (d. 853)
Columba of Sens (d. 274?)
Constantina (c. 321–c. 354)
Correa, Deolinda (fl. 1830)
Cunegunde (1234–1292)
Cunigunde (d. 1040?)
Delanoue, Jeanne (1666–1736)
Duchesne, Rose Philippine (1769–1852)
Dympna (fl. 650)
Ebba (c. 610–c. 683)
Edburga (d. 751)
Edburga of Bicester (d. 650)
Edith (d. 937)
Edith (c. 961–984)
Edith of Aylesbury (fl. 7th c.)
Elizabeth (fl. 1st c.)
Elizabeth of Hungary (1207–1231)
Elizabeth of Portugal (1271–1336)
Elizabeth the Good (1386–1420)
Elswitha (d. 902)
Elthelthrith (630–679)

Emma of Werden (d. around 1050)
Ethelburga (d. 665)
Ethelburga (d. 676?)
Etheldreda (d. around 840)
Eugenia (d. around 258)
Eulalia (290–304)
Euphrasia of Constantinople (d. around 412)
Eusebia of Bergamo (fl. 3rd c.)
Eustochia (1444–1469)
Eustochium (c. 368–c. 419)
Fabiola (d. 399)
Falconieri, Juliana (1270–1341)
Fara (d. 667)
Felicitas (d. 203)
Felicitas of Rome (d. 162?)
Flora of Cordova (d. 851)
Florentina (d. 7th c.)
Frances of Rome (1384–1440)
Frideswide (d. 735?)
Galswintha (d. around 568)
Geneviève (c. 422–512)
Geneviève de Brabant (fl. 8th c.)
Georgia (d. 6th c.)
Gertrude of Nivelles (626–659)
Gertrude of Ostend (d. 1358)
Gertrude the Great (1256–1302)
Gisela (c. 753–807)
Gudula of Brussels (d. 712?)
Hedwig of Silesia (1174–1243)
Helena (c. 255–329)
Hereswitha (d. c. 690)
Hilaria (fl. 304)
Hilda of Whitby (614–680)
Hildegarde of Swabia (c. 757–783)
Hildegard of Bingen (1098–1179)
Hildegund (d. 1188)
Hildeletha (fl. 700)
Hiltrude of Liessies (d. late 700s)
Hombelina (1092–1141)
Humilitas of Faenza (1226–1310)
Ida of Lorraine (1040–1113)
Ida of Louvain (d. 1260)
Irene (d. 304)
Irene of Constantinople (d. around 921)
Irene of Santarem (fl. 7th c.)
Irene of Spain (fl. 300s)
Irene of Thessalonica (d. 304)
Irmina (d. 716)
Isabelle (1225–1270)
Ita of Ireland (d. 570)
Ivetta of Huy (1158–1228)
Jacoba di Settesoli (d. about 1273)
Jadwiga (1374–1399)
Jeanne de France (c. 1464–1505)
Jeanne de Lestonac (1556–1640)
Joan of Arc (c. 1412–1431)
Juliana of Cornillon (1192–1258)
Juliana of Nicomedia (d. about 305)
Julitta of Caesarea (d. about 305)
Justina (d. 64)
Justina (d. 304)
Labouré, Catherine (1806–1875)
Laura
Lea, St. (d. about 383)
Leocadia (d. about 303)
Lidwina of Schiedam (1380–1433)
Lioba (700–779)
Lucy (d. 303)
Lucy of Scotland (d. 1090)
Ludmila (859–920)
Lutgard (1182–1246)
Macrina (327–379)
Maddalena of Canossa (1774–1833)
Madelberte (fl. 7th c.)
Marcellina (fl. 4th c.)
Mareri, Filippa (c. 1190–1236)
Margaret, St. (c. 1046–1093)
Margaret of Antioch (c. 255–c. 275)
Margaret of Cortona (1247–1297)
Margaret of Hungary (1242–1270)
Mariamne (fl. 1st c.)
Mariana de Paredes (1618–1645)
Mariana of Jesus (1565–1624)
Marie Clotilde (d. 1794)
Marie-Thérèse de Soubiran (1834–1889)
Marillac, Louise de (1591–1660)
Mariscotti, Hyacintha (d. 1640)
Mary Magdalene (fl. early 1st c.)
Mary Magdalen of Pazzi (1566–1607)
Mary of Cleophas
Mary of Egypt (d. 430)
Mary of Oignies (1177–1213)
Mary the Virgin (20 BCE–40 CE)
Matilda of Saxony (c. 892–968)
Mechtild of Driessen (d. 1160)
Michelina of Pesaro (1300–1356)
Milburg (d. 722?)
Mildred (d. 700?)
Modesta of Trier (d. about 680)
Modwenna (d. 518)
Monegunde (fl. 6th c.)
Monica (331–387)
Ninnoc (fl. 6th c.)
Olga (c. 890–969)
Olympias (c. 365–408)
Pelagia, Saint
Perpetua (181–203)
Philomena
Priscilla (fl. 1st c.)
Rabi'a (c. 714–801)
Radegund of Poitiers (518–587)
Regina (d. around 251)
Regina of Ostrevant
Richilde (d. 894)
Richilde (d. 1100)
Rita of Cascia (1381–1457)
Rose of Lima (1586–1617)
Rose of Viterbo (1235–1252)
Salaberga of Laon (d. around 665)
Salome II (fl. 1st c.)
Salome of Hungary (1201–c. 1270)
Scholastica (c. 480–543)
Seton, Elizabeth Ann (1774–1821)
Sexburga (d. around 699)
Sforza, Seraphina (1434–1478)
Sheba, Queen of (fl. 10th c. BCE)
Sigolena of Albi (fl. 7th c.)
Sophia (fl. early 2nd c.)
Stein, Edith (1891–1942)
Tavernier, Nicole (fl. 1594)
Tekakwitha, Kateri (1656–1680)
Teresa of Avila (1515–1582)
Thecla (fl. 1st c.)
Theodora (d. 304)
Theodora the Blessed (c. 810–c. 860)
Theophano (c. 866–c. 897)
Theophano of Athens (fl. 800s)
Thérèse of Lisieux (1873–1897)
Ursula (fl. 3rd or 5th c.)
Veronica (fl. 1st c.?)
Viborada (d. 925)
Victoria (d. around 253)
Walpurgis (c. 710–777)
Wandru (c. 628–688)
Werburga (d. 700?)
Wulfthryth (c. 945–1000)
Yolanda of Gnesen (d. 1299)
Youville, Marie Marguerite d' (1701–1771)
Zita of Lucca (1218–1275)

SALONNIÈRE

Abrabanel, Benvenida (d. 1560)
Adam, Juliette la Messine (1836–1936)
Adams, Clover (1843–1885)
Agoult, Marie d' (1805–1876)
Alorna, Marquesa de (1750–c. 1839)
Ancelot, Marguerite (1792–1875)
Aníchkova, Anna (1868–1935)
Anna Comnena (1083–1153/55)
Arnim, Bettine von (1785–1859)
Arnould, Sophie (1740–1802)
Arnstein, Fanny von (1758–1818)
Aubespine, Madeleine de l' (1546–1596)
Barney, Natalie Clifford (1876–1972)
Beauharnais, Fanny de (1737–1813)
Belgioso, Cristina (1808–1871)
Bell, Vanessa (1879–1961)
Bingham, Anne Willing (1764–1801)
Blessington, Marguerite, Countess of (1789–1849)
Bocage, Marie-Anne Le Page du (1710–1802)
Botta, Anne C.L. (1815–1891)
Boufflers, Madeleine-Angelique, Duchesse de (1707–1787)
Boufflers-Rouvrel, Marie Charlotte Hippolyte, Countess de (1724–c. 1800)
Bowen, Elizabeth (1899–1973)
Brewster, Anne Hampton (1818–1892)
Briche, Adelaide de la (1755–1844)
Browne, Maria da Felicidade do Couto (c. 1797–1861)
Brun, Marie-Marguerite de Maison-Forte (1713–1794)
Budberg, Moura (1892–1974)
Cary, Alice (1820–1871)
Chézy, Helmina von (1783–1856)
Coligny, Henriette de (1618–1683)
Condorcet, Sophie Marie Louise, Marquise de (1764–1822)
Cornelia (c. 195–c. 115 BCE)
Cushing, Mary Benedict (1906–1978)
Deffand, Marie Anne de Vichy-Chamrond, Marquise du (1697–1780)
Delorme, Marion (c. 1613–1650)
Duff-Gordon, Lucie (1821–1869)
Duras, Claire de (1777–1828)
Fields, Annie Adams (1834–1915)
Frölich, Henriette (1768–1833)
Gautier, Judith (1845–1917)
Gay, Sophie (1776–1852)
Genlis, Stéphanie-Félicité, Comtesse de (1746–1830)
Geoffrin, Marie Thérèse (1699–1777)
Gippius, Zinaida (1869–1945)
Girardin, Delphine (1804–1855)
Gournay, Marie le Jars de (1565–1645)
Hamilton, Elizabeth Schuyler (1757–c. 1854)
Helvétius, Madame (1719–1800)
Herz, Henriette (1764–1847)
Johnson, Georgia Douglas (1877–1966)
La Fayette, Marie-Madeleine de (1634–1693)
Lambert, Anne Thérèse de Marguenat de Courcelles, Marquise de (1647–1733)
Lecouvreur, Adrienne (1690–1730)
Léo, André (1832–1900)
Lespinasse, Julie de (1732–1776)
Lezay Marnezia, Charlotte Antoinette de Bressy, Marquise de (c. 1705–1785)
Loynes, Antoinette de (fl. 16th c.)
Lynch, Eliza (1835–1886)
Mancini, Marie-Anne (1649–1714)
Mandelstam, Nadezhda (1899–1980)
Mathilde (1820–1904)
Mavrokordatou, Alexandra (1605–1684)
Mendelssohn, Dorothea (1764–1839)
Mendelssohn, Henriette (1768–1831)
Menken, Adah Isaacs (1835–1868)
Meysenburg, Malwida von (1816–1903)

Mohl, Mary (1793–1883)
Montansier, Marguerite (1730–1820)
Morgan, Anna (1851–1936)
Morrell, Ottoline (1873–1938)
Moulton, Louise Chandler (1835–1908)
Mundt, Klara Müller (1814–1873)
Nalkowska, Zofia (1884–1954)
Necker, Suzanne (1739–1794)
Noailles, Marie-Laure de (1902–1970)
Norton, Caroline (1808–1877)
Paalzow, Henriette (1788–1847)
Perry, Lilla Cabot (c. 1848–1933)
Philips, Katherine (1631–1664)
Pichler, Karoline (1769–1843)
Preradovic, Paula von (1887–1951)
Rambouillet, Catherine de Vivonne, marquise de (1588–1665)
Récamier, Juliette (1777–1849)
Recke, Elisa von der (1754–1833)
Roches, Catherine des (1542–1587)
Roches, Madeleine des (1520–1587)
Rolleston, Elizabeth Mary (1845–1940)
Rostopchina, Evdokiya (1811–1858)
Royde-Smith, Naomi Gwladys (1875–1964)
Sablé, Madeleine de Souvré, Marquise de (c. 1599–1678)
Salonnières (fl. 17th and 18th c.)
Sarfatti, Margherita (1880–1961)
Schopenhauer, Johanna (1766–1838)
Schwarzwald, Eugenie (1872–1940)
Scudéry, Madeleine de (1607–1701)
Singer, Winnaretta (1865–1943)
Sophie Charlotte of Hanover (1668–1705)
Spencer, Anne (1882–1975)
Stein, Gertrude (1874–1946)
Stone, Grace Zaring (1896–1991)
Sullam, Sara Coppia (1590–1641)
Teffi, N.A. (1872–1952)
Tencin, Claudine Alexandrine Guérin de (1685–1749)
Thaxter, Celia Laighton (1835–1894)
Trefusis, Violet (1894–1972)
Trollope, Theodosia (1825–1865)
Tusap, Srbuhi (1841–1901)
Vanderbilt, Consuelo (1877–1964)
Varnhagen, Rahel (1771–1833)
Vesey, Elizabeth (c. 1715–1791)
Viertel, Salka (1889–1978)
Walker, A'Lelia (1885–1931)
Wheeler, Anna Doyle (1785–c. 1850)
Wilde, Jane (1821–1896)
Williams, Helen Maria (1762–1827)
Wolzogen, Karoline von (1763–1847)
Ziyada, Mayy (1886–1941)
Zuzoric, Cvijeta (c. 1555–1600)

SALSA SINGER
Cruz, Celia (1924—)

SATIRIST
Astley, Thea (1925–2004)
Austen, Jane (1775–1817)
Bacon, Josephine Dodge (1876–1961)
Bacon, Peggy (1895–1987)
Barykova, Anna Pavlovna (1839–1893)
Bekker, Elizabeth (1738–1804)
Benson, Stella (1892–1933)
Burney, Fanny (1752–1840)
Carrington, Leonora (1917—)
Castro, Rosalía de (1837–1885)
Cecchi D'Amico, Suso (1914—)
Centlivre, Susanna (c. 1669–1723)
Collier, Jane (1710–c. 1754)
Crothers, Rachel (1878–1958)
Cullberg, Birgit (1908–1999)
de Mille, Agnes (1905–1993)
Dittmar, Louise (1807–1884)
Eden, Emily (1797–1869)
Engelbretsdatter, Dorothe (1634–1716)
Ferber, Edna (1885–1968)
Fitzhugh, Louise (1928–1974)
Franklin, Miles (1879–1954)
Gaskell, Elizabeth (1810–1865)
Geistinger, Marie (1833–1903)
Gibbons, Stella (1902–1989)
Gibbs, May (1877–1969)
Gilman, Charlotte Perkins (1860–1935)
Glasgow, Ellen (1873–1945)
Gore, Catherine (1799–1861)
Hamilton, Elizabeth Schuyler (1757–c. 1854)
Harrison, Constance Cary (1843–1920)
Höch, Hannah (1889–1978)
Hokinson, Helen E. (1893–1949)
Holm, Hanya (1888–1992)
Holtby, Winifred (1898–1935)
Jameson, Storm (1891–1986)
Laski, Marghanita (1915–1988)
Lawrenson, Helen (b. 1907)
Lessing, Doris (1919—)
Lewald, Fanny (1811–1889)
Lindgren, Astrid (1907–2002)
Li Qingzhao (1083–c. 1151)
Loos, Anita (1893–1981)
Loy, Mina (1882–1966)
Luce, Clare Boothe (1903–1987)
Macaulay, Rose (1881–1958)
Manley, Mary de la Rivière (1663–1724)
Mann, Erika (1905–1969)
Manner, Eeva-Liisa (1921–1995)
Mannes, Marya (1904–1990)
Mannin, Ethel (1900–1984)
Mansfield, Katherine (1888–1923)
Maracci, Carmelita (b. 1911)
Marisol (1930—)
Mitford, Nancy (1904–1973)
Model, Lisette (1901–1983)
Montagu, Lady Mary Wortley (1689–1762)
Moore, Marianne (1887–1972)
Nelson, Clara Meleka (1901–1979)
Norton, Mary (1903–1992)
O'Connor, Flannery (1925–1964)
Paget, Violet (1856–1935)
Parker, Dorothy (1893–1967)
Patterson, Eleanor Medill (1881–1948)
Pavlova, Karolina (1807–1893)
Petty, Mary (1899–1976)
Pix, Mary Griffith (1666–1709)
Powell, Dawn (1897–1965)
Rambova, Natacha (1897–1966)
Rawlings, Marjorie Kinnan (1896–1953)
Reinig, Christa (1926—)
Roberts, Elizabeth Madox (1881–1941)
Robins, Elizabeth (1862–1952)
Rochefort, Christiane (1917–1998)
Ros, Amanda (1860–1939)
Rostopchina, Evdokiya (1811–1858)
Russell, Anna (1911—)
Schreiner, Olive (1855–1920)
Sei Shōnagon (c. 965–?)
Sherwood, Katharine Margaret (1841–1914)
Skinner, Cornelia Otis (1901–1979)
Spark, Muriel (1918—)
Stafford, Jean (1915–1979)
Stead, Christina (1902–1983)
Stettheimer, Florine (1871–1944)
Teffi, N.A. (1872–1952)
Tenney, Tabitha Gilman (1762–1837)
Tweedie, Jill (1936–1993)
Victor, Metta (1831–1885)
Walker, Kath (1920–1993)
Warren, Mercy Otis (1728–1814)
Weed, Ella (1853–1894)
West, Jessamyn (1902–1984)
Wharton, Edith (1862–1937)
Whitcher, Frances Miriam Berry (1811–1852)
Wickham, Anna (1883–1947)
Wroth, Mary (c. 1587–c. 1651)
Yessayan, Zabel (1878–1943)
Zinner, Hedda (1902–1990)

SAXOPHONIST
Gibson, Althea (1927—)
Harjo, Joy (1951—)
Lobo, Rebecca (1973—)
Logic, Lora (c. 1961—)
Snow, Valaida (c. 1903–1956)
Tipton, Billy (1914–1989)

SCENARIST
Adams, Maude (1872–1953)
Barskaya, Margarita A. (1903–1938)
Beranger, Clara (1886–1956)
Box, Muriel (1905–1991)
Buffington, Adele (1900–1973)
Comden, Betty (1915—)
De Acosta, Mercedes (1893–1968)
Devanny, Jean (1894–1962)
Duras, Marguerite (1914–1996)
Harrison, Joan (c. 1908–1994)
Kuhn, Irene Corbally (1898–1995)
Loos, Anita (1893–1981)
Marion, Frances (1888–1973)
Mathis, June (1892–1927)
Park, Ida May (1879–1954)
Parsons, Louella (1881–1972)
Pickford, Mary (1893–1979)
Rand, Ayn (1905–1982)
Shaginian, Marietta (1888–1982)
Shipman, Nell (1892–1970)
Varda, Agnes (1928—)

SCHOLAR
Abbott, Evelyn (1843–1901)
Adolf, Helen (b. 1895)
Aesara of Lucania (fl. 400s–300s BCE)
Agnesi, Maria Gaetana (1718–1799)
Aikin, Lucy (1781–1864)
Akhmatova, Anna (1889–1966)
Akselrod, Liubo (1868–1946)
Albert, Octavia V.R. (1853–c. 1899)
Aleksandrovna, Vera (1895–1966)
Alkhateeb, Sharifa (1946–2004)
Allen, Paula Gunn (1939—)
Ambrose, Alice (1906–2001)
Anna Comnena (1083–1153/55)
Anscombe, G.E.M. (1919–2001)
Aoki, Yayoi (1927—)
Arendt, Hannah (1906–1975)
Arete of Cyrene (fl. 4th c. BCE)
Aretz, Isabel (1909—)
Arignote (fl. 6th c. BCE)
Asclepignia (c. 375–?)
Aspasia of Miletus (c. 464 BCE–c. 420 BCE)
Augusta of Saxe-Weimar (1811–1890)
Aung San Suu Kyi (1945—)
Bang, Nina (1866–1928)
Ban Zhao (c. 45–c. 120)
Barbauld, Anna Letitia (1743–1825)
Barbosa, Pilar (1898–1997)
Bassi, Laura (1711–1778)
Bates, Katherine Lee (1859–1929)
Beard, Mary Ritter (1876–1958)
Bell, Gertrude (1868–1926)
Bernard, Jessie (1903–1996)
Blodgett, Katharine Burr (1898–1979)
Blunt, Anne (1837–1917)
Bober, Phyllis (1920–2002)
Bonds, Margaret (1913–1972)

Occupational Index

Borg, Dorothy (1901–1993)
Braun, E. Lucy (1889–1971)
Brewster, Anne Hampton (1818–1892)
Brodbeck, May (1917–1983)
Bryant, Sophie (1850–1922)
Burgess, Renate (1910–1988)
Calkins, Mary Whiton (1863–1930)
Cam, Helen M. (1885–1968)
Carabillo, Toni (1926–1997)
Carson, Rachel (1907–1964)
Carter, Elizabeth (1717–1806)
Carus-Wilson, Eleanora Mary (1897–1977)
Castro, Públia Hortênsia de (1548–1595)
Caton-Thompson, Gertrude (1888–1985)
Cavendish, Margaret (1623–1673)
Cereta, Laura, of Brescia (1469–1499)
Châtelet, Émilie du (1706–1749)
Chesler, Phyllis (1940—)
Chinn, May Edward (1896–1980)
Christine de Pizan (c. 1363–c. 1431)
Chukovskaya, Lidiya (1907–1996)
Clarke, Mary Cowden (1809–1898)
Cleobulina of Rhodes (fl. 570 BCE)
Cockburn, Catharine Trotter (1679–1749)
Concannon, Helena (1878–1952)
Conrad-Martius, Hedwig (1888–1966)
Constance Jones, E.E. (1848–1922)
Cooper, Anna J. (c. 1858–1964)
Corbaux, Fanny (1812–1883)
Cornaro Piscopia, Elena Lucretia (1646–1684)
Cullis, Winifred Clara (1875–1956)
Dacier, Anne (1654–1720)
Dale, Kathleen (1895–1984)
Damo (fl. 6th c. BCE)
Dashkova, Ekaterina (1744–1810)
David, Caroline Edgeworth (1856–1951)
Dawidowicz, Lucy (1915–1990)
Debo, Angie (1890–1988)
de Cleyre, Voltairine (1866–1912)
de Laguna, Grace Mead (1878–1978)
Dembo, Tamara (1902–1993)
Diggs, Irene (1906—)
Dilke, Emily (1840–1904)
Diotima of Mantinea (fl. 400s BCE)
Dittmar, Louise (1807–1884)
Downey, June Etta (1875–1932)
Drower, E.S. (1879–1972)
Dunbar, Flanders (1902–1959)
Durant, Ariel (1898–1981)
Dzerzhinska, Sofia (1882–1968)
Eady, Dorothy (1904–1981)
Eastwood, Alice (1859–1953)
Edwards, Amelia B. (1831–1892)
Elfthrith (fl. 7th c.)
Elizabeth of Bohemia (1618–1680)
Ellet, Elizabeth (c. 1812–1877)
Elliott, Maud Howe (1854–1948)
Ellis, Florence Hawley (1906–1991)
Elstob, Elizabeth (1683–1756)
Emerson, Mary Moody (1774–1863)
Emmett, Dorothy Mary (b. 1904)
Farrenc, Louise (1804–1875)
Favre, Julie Velten (1834–1896)
Fedele, Cassandra Fidelis (1465–1558)
Finch, Anne (1631–1679)
Fischer, Ruth (1895–1961)
Fisher, Dorothy Canfield (1879–1958)
Folger, Emily (1858–1936)
Foot, Philippa (1920—)
Galindo, Beatriz (1475–1534)
Gardner, Helen Louise (1908–1986)
Gildersleeve, Virginia Crocheron (1877–1965)
Goldberg, Lea (1911–1970)
Goldring, Winifred (1888–1971)
Gournay, Marie le Jars de (1565–1645)
Gray, Hanna Holborn (1930—)
Gray, Nicolete (1911–1997)
Greenfield, Meg (1930–1999)
Griffiths, Martha Wright (1912–2003)
Grignan, Françoise-Marguerite de Sévigné, Countess de (1646–1705)
Guest, Lady Charlotte (1812–1895)
Guilbert, Yvette (1865–1944)
Guiney, Louise Imogen (1861–1920)
Gulliver, Julia Henrietta (1856–1940)
Hamilton, Edith (1867–1963)
Harkness, Georgia (1891–1974)
Harris, Marjorie Silliman (1890–1976)
Harris, Mary Belle (1874–1957)
Harrison, Jane Ellen (1850–1928)
Hatcher, Orie Latham (1868–1946)
Heloise (c. 1100–1163)
Herbert, Mary (1561–1621)
Héricourt, Jenny Poinsard d' (1809–1875)
Hersch, Jeanne (1910—)
Holter, Harriet (1922–1997)
Hug-Hellmuth, Hermine (1871–1924)
Hull, Eleanor Henrietta (1860–1935)
Hypatia (c. 375–415)
Jordan, Barbara (1936–1996)
Jotuni, Maria (1880–1943)
Juana Inés de la Cruz (1651–1695)
K'alandadze, Ana (1924—)
Kavanagh, Julia (1824–1877)
Kellogg, Louise Phelps (1862–1942)
Kiddle, Margaret (1914–1958)
King, Grace Elizabeth (c. 1852–1932)
Kirkpatrick, Jeane (1926—)
Knight, Ellis Cornelia (1758–1837)
Lamb, Martha J.R. (1826–1893)
Langer, Susanne Knauth (1895–1985)
Lazarus, Emma (1849–1887)
Leach, Abby (1855–1918)
Leakey, Mary Nicol (1913–1996)
Lee, Ida (1865–1943)
Leech, Margaret (1893–1974)
Lerner, Gerda (1920—)
Lewis, Agnes Smith (1843–1926)
Li Qingzhao (1083–c. 1151)
Lister, Anne (1791–1840)
Longford, Elizabeth (1906—)
Lowry-Corry, Dorothy (1885–1967)
MacDonald, Margaret (c. 1907–1956)
Mackinnon, Catherine A. (1946—)
Macurdy, Grace Harriet (1866–1946)
Malatesta, Battista da Montefeltro (1383–1450)
Marcet, Jane (1769–1858)
Marcus, Ruth Barcan (1921—)
Margaret Tudor (1489–1541)
Maritain, Raïssa (1883–1960)
Masham, Damaris (1658–1708)
Mayer, Maria Goeppert (1906–1972)
McCoy, Iola Fuller (1906–1993)
McLachlan, Laurentia (1866–1953)
Mead, Sylvia Earle (1935—)
Meyer, Agnes (1887–1970)
Meyer, Lucy (1849–1922)
Miller, Susanne (1915—)
Mitchell, Lucy (1845–1888)
Moholy-Nagy, Sibyl (1903–1971)
Moore, Marianne (1887–1972)
Morata, Fulvia Olympia (1526–1555)
Morpurgo, Rachel (1790–1871)
Murdoch, Iris (1919–1999)
Naden, Constance Caroline Woodhill (1858–1889)
Neilson, Nellie (1873–1947)
Neumann, Hanna (1914–1971)
Nicarete of Megara (fl. 300 BCE)
Nogarola, Isotta (c. 1416–1466)
Oakley, Ann (1944—)
Otway-Ruthven, Jocelyn (1909–1989)
Paglia, Camille (1947—)
Peck, Annie Smith (1850–1935)
Penson, Lillian Margery (1896–1963)
Perham, Margery (1895–1982)
Phillpotts, Bertha Surtees (1877–1932)
Plummer, Mary Wright (1856–1916)
Portal, Marta (1930—)
Pound, Louise (1872–1958)
Pulcheria (c. 398–453)
Putnam, Bertha Haven (1872–1960)
Ramabai, Pandita (1858–1922)
Rambert, Marie (1888–1982)
Rambova, Natacha (1897–1966)
Ray, H. Cordelia (c. 1849–1916)
Reynolds, Myra (1853–1936)
Richter, Elise (1865–1943)
Rickert, Edith (1871–1938)
Ripley, Sarah Alden (1793–1867)
Robinson, Joan Violet (1903–1983)
Roper, Margaret More (1505–1544)
Rourke, Constance (1885–1941)
Royden, A. Maude (1876–1956)
Salmon, Lucy Maynard (1853–1927)
Sayers, Dorothy L. (1893–1957)
Scudder, Vida (1861–1954)
Seghers, Anna (1900–1983)
Selva, Blanche (1884–1942)
Semple, Ellen Churchill (1863–1932)
Sharp, Katharine Lucinda (1865–1914)
Shaw, Anna Howard (1847–1919)
Snyder, Alice D. (1887–1943)
Somers, Armonía (1914–1994)
Stein, Edith (1891–1942)
Stevenson, Sara Yorke (1847–1921)
Stewart-Murray, Katharine (1874–1960)
Sutherland, Lucy Stuart (1903–1980)
Swindler, Mary Hamilton (1884–1967)
Taggard, Genevieve (1894–1948)
Talbot, Catherine (1721–1770)
Taylor, Eva (1879–1966)
Taylor, Lily Ross (1886–1969)
Thomas, M. Carey (1857–1935)
Tibbetts, Margaret Joy (1919—)
Toor, Frances (1890–1956)
Tuve, Rosemond (1903–1964)
van Schurmann, Anna Maria (1607–1678)
Vasconcellos, Karoline Michaëlis de (1851–1925)
Waddell, Helen (1889–1965)
Waddy, Charis (1909–2004)
Ward, Ida Caroline (1880–1949)
Washburn, Margaret Floy (1871–1939)
Wedgwood, C.V. (1910–1997)
Weston, Elizabeth Jane (1582–1612)
Wheeler, Anna Pell (1883–1966)
White, Helen C. (1896–1967)
Wiskemann, Elizabeth Meta (1899–1971)
Woodhouse, Margaret Chase Going (1890–1984)
Wootton, Barbara (1897–1988)
Wormeley, Katharine Prescott (1830–1908)
Wright, Mary Clabaugh (1917–1970)
Wright, Muriel Hazel (1889–1975)
Wyse Power, Jennie (1858–1941)
Yates, Frances Amelia (1899–1981)
Yazova, Yana (1912–1974)
Young, Rose Maud (1865–1947)
Zimmermann, Agnes (1847–1925)

SCHOOL ADMINISTRATOR

Anthony, Susan B. (1820–1906)
Astell, Mary (1666–1731)
Atkins, Mary (1819–1882)
Baber, Esther Mary (1871–1956)
Bancroft, Jessie (1867–1952)
Barker, M.C. (1879–1963)

Beale, Dorothea (1831–1906)
Bews, Mary Ellen (1856–1945)
Bliss, Anna (1843–1925)
Boys-Smith, Winifred Lily (1865–1939)
Brackett, Anna Callender (1836–1911)
Breshkovsky, Catherine (1844–1934)
Brigham, Mary Ann (1829–1889)
Bryan, Anna E. (1858–1901)
Bryant, Sophie (1850–1922)
Bulstrode, Emily Mary (1867–1959)
Bulstrode, Jane Helena (1862–1946)
Burgin, Annie Mona (1903–1985)
Burn, Margaret Gordon (1825–1918)
Byers, Margaret (1832–1912)
Casely-Hayford, Adelaide (1868–1960)
Connon, Helen (c. 1859–1903)
Cooke, Flora (1864–1953)
Cousins, Margaret (1878–1954)
Crocker, Lucretia (1829–1886)
Davies, Emily (1830–1921)
Dewey, Alice Chipman (1858–1927)
Dorsey, Susan Miller (1857–1946)
Farningham, Marianne (1834–1909)
Ferguson, Abbie Park (1837–1919)
Fewings, Eliza Anne (1857–1940)
Foster, Emily Sophia (1842–1897)
Francis, Catherine Augusta (1836–1916)
Fraser, Mary Isabel (1863–1942)
Frazier, Maude (1881–1963)
Freeman, Caroline (c. 1855–1914)
Gard'ner, Elizabeth Anne (1858–1926)
Gibson, Helena Fannie (1868–1938)
Gibson, Mary Victoria (1864–1929)
Hamilton, Edith (1867–1963)
Hampshire, Margaret (1918–2004)
Hewett, Mary Elizabeth Grenside (1857–1892)
Hickey, Mary St. Domitille (1882–1958)
Horwich, Frances (1908–2001)
Huxley, Julia Arnold (1862–1908)
Jackson, Sarah Elizabeth (1858–1946)
Kehajia, Kalliopi (1839–1905)
Kellas, Eliza (1864–1943)
Lacore, Suzanne (1875–1975)
Leontias, Sappho (1832–1900)
Lorimer, Margaret (1866–1954)
Marchant, Maria Élise Allman (1869–1919)
McCoubrey, Margaret (1880–1955)
McLean, Mary Jane (1866–1949)
McMillan, Rachel (1859–1917)
Morrison, Annie Christina (1870–1953)
Morrow, Elizabeth Cutter (1873–1955)
Moten, Lucy Ellen (1851–1933)
Nivedita, Sister (1867–1911)
Parkhurst, Helen (1887–1973)
Parren, Kalliroe (1861–1940)
Peck, Annie Smith (1850–1935)
Pengelly, Edna (1874–1959)
Pierce, Sarah (1767–1852)
Porter, Sarah (1813–1900)
Pulling, Mary Etheldred (1871–1951)
Reed, Mary (1854–1943)
Ross, Frances Jane (1869–1950)
Rowson, Susanna (1762–1824)
Sabin, Ellen (1850–1949)
Shirreff, Emily (1814–1897)
Smith, Nora Archibald (1859?–1934)
Spofford, Grace Harriet (1887–1974)
Stace, Helen McRae (1850–1926)
Swainson, Mary Anne (c. 1833–1897)
Thompson, Marion Beatrice (1877–1964)
Towle, Katherine (1898–1986)
Wallis, Mary Ann Lake (1821–1910)
Washington, Bennetta (1918–1991)
Weber, Helene (1881–1962)
West, Winifred (1881–1971)
Williams, Anna Maria (1839–1929)
Young, Ella Flagg (1845–1918)

SCHOOL FOUNDER

See Educational-institution/program founder.

SCHOOL TEACHER

Alabaster, Ann O'Connor (1842–1915)
Aliberty, Soteria (1847–1929)
Andersen, Catherine Ann (1870–1957)
Andrews, Elsie Euphemia (1888–1948)
Andrews, Jane (1833–1887)
Angwin, Maria L. (1849–1898)
Anthony, Susan B. (1820–1906)
Attar, Samar (1940—)
Aubert, Mary Joseph (1835–1926)
Auerbach, Charlotte (1899–1994)
Augustine, Rose (1910–2003)
Bâ, Mariama (1929–1981)
Baber, Esther Mary (1871–1956)
Bacon, Alice Mabel (1858–1918)
Bailey, Carolyn Sherwin (1875–1961)
Bailey, Hannah Johnston (1839–1923)
Bain, Wilhelmina Sherriff (1848–1944)
Baldwin, Charlotte Fowler (1805–1873)
Banahan, Mary Gertrude (1855/56?–1932)
Barbier, Adèle Euphrasie (1829–1893)
Barrer, Nina Agatha Rosamond (1879–1965)
Bates, Daisy Lee (1914–1999)
Bates, Sophia Ann (1817–1899)
Baume, Rosetta Lulah (1871–1934)
Bäumer, Gertrud (1873–1954)
Beecher, Catharine (1800–1878)
Belishova, Liri (1923—)
Bell, Elizabeth Viola (1897–1990)
Bellamy, Elizabeth (1845–1940)
Bennett, Belle Harris (1852–1922)
Bethune, Joanne (1770–1860)
Bijns, Anna (1493/94–1575)
Blackie, Jeannetta Margaret (1864–1955)
Blagoeva, Stella Dimitrova (1887–1954)
Blaker, Eliza Ann (1854–1926)
Borchardt, Selma Munter (1895–1968)
Bowles, Eva del Vakia (1875–1943)
Bré, Ruth (1862–1911)
Bridgman, Eliza Jane (1805–1871)
Brion, Hélène (1882–1962)
Brown, Charlotte (c. 1795–1855)
Brown, Charlotte Hawkins (c. 1883–1961)
Bryan, Anna E. (1858–1901)
Bryant, Sophie (1850–1922)
Burgin, Annie Mona (1903–1985)
Burn, Margaret Gordon (1825–1918)
Bush, Laura (1946—)
Buxton, Mary Ann (c. 1795–1888)
Cabot, Dolce Ann (1862–1943)
Cabrini, Frances Xavier (1850–1917)
Candy, Alice (1888–1977)
Canty, Mary Agnes (1879–1950)
Carles, Emilie (1900–1979)
Carnachan, Blanche Eleanor (1871–1954)
Cauer, Minna (1841–1922)
Chase, Mary Ellen (1887–1973)
Chilver, Sally (1914—)
Clapp, Louise (1819–1906)
Coad, Nellie (1883–1974)
Colclough, Mary Ann (1836–1885)
Colenso, Elizabeth (1821–1904)
Collier, Jane Annie (1869–1955)
Connon, Helen (c. 1859–1903)
Cook, Freda Mary (1896–1990)
Cooke, Flora (1864–1953)
Cooper, Sarah Ingersoll (1835–1896)
Costa, Maria Velho de (b. 1938)
Cowles, Betsey Mix (1810–1876)
Crocker, Lucretia (1829–1886)
Davison, Emily (1872–1913)
Daw Mi Mi Khaing (1916–1990)
Debo, Angie (1890–1988)
de Burgos, Julia (1914–1953)
de Laguna, Frederica (b. around 1874)
Denison, Flora MacDonald (1867–1921)
Denton, Mary Florence (1857–1947)
Dickey, Sarah (1838–1904)
Dickson, Mary Bernard (c. 1810–1895)
Dimock, Susan (1847–1875)
Donaldson, Viva (1893–1970)
Dorsey, Susan Miller (1857–1946)
Eastman, Annis Ford (1852–1910)
England, Maud Russell (1863–1956)
Eristavi-Xostaria, Anastasia (1868–1951)
Faggs, Mae (1932—)
Farningham, Marianne (1834–1909)
Ferraro, Geraldine (1935—)
Fiske, Fidelia (1816–1864)
Foster, Emily Sophia (1842–1897)
Frame, Alice (1878–1941)
Francis, Catherine Augusta (1836–1916)
Fraser, Mary Isabel (1863–1942)
Frazier, Maude (1881–1963)
Freeman, Alice (1857–1936)
Freeman, Caroline (c. 1855–1914)
Freud, Anna (1895–1982)
Fukuda Hideko (1865–1927)
Fuller, Sarah (1836–1927)
Furman, Bess (1894–1969)
Gág, Wanda (1893–1946)
Gardener, Helen Hamilton (1853–1925)
Gard'ner, Elizabeth Anne (1858–1926)
Garnet, Sarah (1831–1911)
Gibson, Helena Fannie (1868–1938)
Gibson, Mary Victoria (1864–1929)
Gilroy, Beryl (1924–2001)
Grant, Zilpah (1794–1874)
Greenwood, Ellen Sarah (1837–1917)
Greenwood, Sarah (c. 1809–1889)
Griffin, Elsie Mary (1884–1968)
Griffith, Emily (c. 1880–1947)
Grimké, Sarah Moore (1792–1873)
Grossmann, Edith Searle (1863–1931)
Guellouz, Souad (1937—)
Gutiérrez de Mendoza, Juana Belén (1875–1942)
Haley, Margaret A. (1861–1939)
Harding, Jan (1925—)
Harris, Emily Cumming (c. 1836–1925)
Haselden, Frances Isabella (c. 1841–1936)
Hay, Jean Emily (1903–1984)
Haygood, Laura Askew (1845–1900)
Heap, Sarah (1870–1960)
Henderson, Christina Kirk (1861–1953)
Herrick, Genevieve Forbes (1894–1962)
Heslop, Mary Kingdon (1885–1955)
Hetherington, Jessie Isabel (1882–1971)
Heymair, Magdalena (c. 1545–after 1586)
Hickling, Grace (1908–1986)
Hill, Emily (1847–1930)
Hodge, Annie Mabel (1862–1938)
Hopkins, Emma Curtis (1853–1925)
Horrell, Elizabeth (1826–1913)
Howley, Calasanctius (1848–1933)
Hudson, Martha (1939—)
Hughan, Jessie (1875–1955)
Hurston, Zora Neale (c. 1891–1960)
Inglis, Helen Clyde (1867–1945)
Irvine-Smith, Fanny Louise (1878–1948)
Isaacs, Susan (1885–1948)
Jackson, Alice (1887–1974)
Jackson, Sarah Elizabeth (1858–1946)
Jacobson, Ethel May (1877–1965)
Jambrišak, Marija (1847–1937)
Jebb, Eglantyne (1876–1928)
Jiagge, Annie (1918–1996)

Kaffka, Margit (1880–1918)
Kahn, Florence Prag (1866–1948)
Kann, Edith (1907–1987)
Kells, Isabella (1861–1938)
Kelsey, Lavinia Jane (1856–1948)
Kennedy, Kate (1827–1890)
King, Martha (1802/03–1897)
Kirk, Cybele Ethel (1870–1957)
Kissling, Margaret (1808–1891)
Kovalevskaya, Sophia (1850–1891)
Krog, Gina (1847–1916)
Kuzwayo, Ellen (1914–2006)
Lacore, Suzanne (1875–1975)
Lamburn, Richmal Crompton (1890–1969)
Laney, Lucy Craft (1854–1933)
Langgässer, Elisabeth (1899–1950)
Law, Alice Easton (1870–1942)
Law, Mary Blythe (1873–1955)
Lee, Jennie (1904–1988)
Le Sueur, Frances (1919–1995)
Livesay, Dorothy (1909–1996)
Locke, Bessie (1865–1952)
Loeb, Sophie Irene (1876–1929)
Loveridge, Emily Lemoine (1860–1941)
Low, Caroline Sarah (1876–1934)
MacKillop, Mary Helen (1842–1909)
Macleod, Charlotte (1852–1950)
MacMurchy, Helen (1862–1953)
Maher, Mary Cecilia (1799–1878)
Mander, Jane (1877–1949)
Manning, Leah (1886–1977)
Martin, Lynn (1939—)
Martin, Mary Ann (1817–1884)
Mašiotene, Ona (1883–1949)
McAllister, Anne Hunter (1892–1983)
McAuliffe, Christa (1948–1986)
McCarthy, Mary Ann Recknall (1866–1933)
McGinley, Phyllis (1905–1978)
McGuire, Edith (1944—)
Mead, Lucia Ames (1856–1936)
Melissanthi (c. 1907–c. 1991)
Minchin, Alice Ethel (1889–1966)
Miner, Myrtilla (1815–1864)
Montgomery, Lucy Maud (1874–1942)
Mortimer, Mary (1816–1877)
Moten, Lucy Ellen (1851–1933)
Mugabe, Sally (1932–1992)
Myers, Caroline Clark (c. 1888–1980)
Myers, Phoebe (1866–1947)
Negri, Ada (1870–1945)
Nelson, Clara Meleka (1901–1979)
Newman, Mehetabel (c. 1822–1908)
Nivedita, Sister (1867–1911)
Nixon, Pat (1912–1993)
Norton, Alice Peloubet (1860–1928)
Nowland, Mary Josepha (1863–1935)
Ostler, Emma Brignell (c. 1848–1922)
Oughton, Diana (1942–1970)
Pankhurst, Adela (1885–1961)
Pengelly, Edna (1874–1959)
Phipson, Joan (1912–2003)
Pierce, Sarah (1767–1852)
Place, Etta (fl. 1896–1905)
Plaminkova, Frantiska (1875–1942)
Polyblank, Ellen Albertina (1840–1930)
Pool, Maria Louise (1841–1898)
Portillo-Trambley, Estela (1936–1999)
Raeburn, Agnes Middleton (1872–1955)
Ralfe, Catherine Hester (c. 1831–1912)
Ratcliffe, Jane (1917–1999)
Rees, Annie Lee (1864–1949)
Richards, Ellen Swallow (1842–1911)
Richmond, Mary Elizabeth (1853–1949)
Ripley, Sophia (1803–1861)
Robertson, Ann Worcester (1826–1905)
Robertson, Grace (1930—)
Robinson, Jo Ann (1911–1992)
Roddick, Anita (1942—)
Rogers, Elizabeth Ann (1829–1921)
Rogers, Harriet B. (1834–1919)
Rollett, Hilda (1873–1970)
Rood, Florence (1873–1944)
Ross, Forrestina Elizabeth (1860–1936)
Ross, Frances Jane (1869–1950)
Roure, Martine (1948—)
Rymill, Mary Ann (c. 1817–1897)
Sampson, Deborah (1760–1827)
Saunders, Marshall (1861–1947)
Schmidt, Auguste (1833–1902)
Scott, Mary Edith (1888–1979)
Scott, Ruby Payne (1912–1981)
Seymour, Mary F. (1846–1893)
Shayle George, Frances (c. 1827–1890)
Shirreff, Emily (1814–1897)
Shortt, Elizabeth Smith (1859–1949)
Skoblikova, Lydia (1939—)
Smedley, Agnes (1892–1950)
Soljak, Miriam Bridelia (1879–1971)
Somers, Armonía (1914–1994)
Southworth, E.D.E.N. (1819–1899)
Spooner, Molly (1914–1997)
Stasova, Elena (1873–1966)
Stephansen, Elizabeth (1872–1961)
Stevenson, Greta Barbara (1911–1990)
Stothard, Sarah Sophia (1825/26–1901)
Swainson, Mary Anne (c. 1833–1897)
Swisshelm, Jane Grey (1815–1884)
Tautari, Mary (d. 1906)
Taylor, Anna Edson (c. 1858–c. 1921)
Te Kiri Karamu, Heni (1840–1933)
Thompson, Marion Beatrice (1877–1964)
Thorne, Florence (1877–1973)
Todd, Thelma (1905–1935)
Trout, Jenny Kidd (1841–1921)
Uchida, Yoshiko (1921–1992)
Valentine, Winifred Annie (1886–1968)
Vautier, Catherine (1902–1989)
von Richthofen, Else (1874–1973)
Waitz, Grete (1953—)
Walker, Maggie Lena (1867–1934)
Wasilewska, Wanda (1905–1964)
Weber, Helene (1881–1962)
Wells, Ada (1863–1933)
Westwood, Vivienne (1941—)
Whitaker, Mabel (1884–1976)
Williams, Anna Maria (1839–1929)
Wilson, Helen Mary (1869–1957)
Wohlers, Eliza (c. 1812–1891)
Woolley, Hannah (1623–1677)
Woolman, Mary Schenck (1860–1940)
Worth, Irene (1916–2002)
Young, Ella Flagg (1845–1918)

SCIENCES PATRON/PHILANTHROPIST/BENEFACTOR

Aberdeen, Ishbel Maria Gordon, Lady (1857–1939)
Baldwin, Ethel Frances (1879–1967)
Barnett, Henrietta (1851–1936)
Bell, Mabel Hubbard (1857–1923)
Brand, Sybil (c. 1899–2004)
Bruce, Catherine Wolfe (1816–1900)
Christina of Sweden (1626–1689)
Draper, Mary Anna Palmer (1839–1914)
Duke, Doris (1912–1993)
Herron, Carrie Rand (1867–1914)
Jenkins, Helen Hartley (1860–1934)
Ladd, Kate Macy (1863–1945)
La Sablière, Marguerite de (1640–1693)
Lasker, Mary (1900–1994)
Louisa Ulrica of Prussia (1720–1782)
Margaret of Angoulême (1492–1549)
Rand, Caroline Amanda (1828–1905)
Reid, Elisabeth Mills (1858–1931)
Thompson, Elizabeth Rowell (1821–1899)
Treble, Lillian M. (1854–1909)
Ulrica Eleanora (1688–1741)

SCIENTIST

Abbott, Maude (1869–1940)
Abercrombie, M.L.J. (1909–1984)
Abrahams, Ottilie Grete (1937—)
Adam, Madge (1912–2001)
Adams, Nancy M. (1926—)
Aemilia Hilaria (fl. 350)
Agnesi, Maria Gaetana (1718–1799)
Agnes of Huntingdonshire (fl. 13th c.)
Aitkin, Yvonne (1911—)
Ajzenberg-Selove, Fay (1926—)
Albright, Tenley (1935—)
Alcock, Nora (1874–1972)
Aldrich-Blake, Louisa (1865–1925)
Alexander, Annie Montague (1867–1949)
Alexander, Hattie (1901–1968)
Anable, Gloria Hollister (1903–1988)
Andersen, Dorothy Hansine (1901–1963)
Anderson, Caroline Still (1848–1919)
Anderson, Elizabeth Garrett (1836–1917)
Anderson, Margaret (1900–1997)
André, Valerie (1922—)
Andrews, Eliza Frances (1840–1931)
Anne of York (fl. 13th c.)
Anning, Mary (1799–1847)
Apgar, Virginia (1909–1974)
Arber, Agnes (1879–1960)
Armitage, Ella (1841–1931)
Armstrong, Margaret Neilson (1867–1944)
Ashton, Helen (1891–1958)
Atkins, Anna (1797–1871)
Auerbach, Charlotte (1899–1994)
Ayrton, Hertha Marks (1854–1923)
Bailey, Florence (1863–1948)
Baker, S. Josephine (1873–1945)
Balfour, Eve (1898–1990)
Balfour, Jean (1927—)
Ball, Anne Elizabeth (1808–1872)
Baly, Monica E. (1914–1998)
Barber, Mary (1911–1965)
Barclay-Smith, Phyllis (1903–1980)
Barrett, Kate Waller (1857–1925)
Barringer, Emily Dunning (1876–1961)
Barrows, Isabel Hayes (1845–1913)
Bascom, Florence (1862–1945)
Bass, Mary Elizabeth (1876–1956)
Bassi, Laura (1711–1778)
Bate, Dorothea (1879–1951)
Becker, Lydia (1827–1890)
Beloff-Chain, Anne (1921–1991)
Benchley, Belle (1882–1973)
Benett, Etheldred (1776–1845)
Bergmann-Pohl, Sabine (1946—)
Bidder, Anna McClean (1903–2001)
Biggs, Rosemary (1912–2001)
Bingham, Millicent Todd (1880–1968)
Bishop, Ann (1899–1990)
Bishop, Hazel (1906–1998)
Blackwell, Elizabeth (1821–1910)
Blackwell, Emily (1826–1910)
Blackwood, Margaret (1909–1986)
Blagg, Mary Adela (1858–1944)
Blanc, Marie-Thérèse (1840–1907)
Bleeker, Caroline Emilie (1897–1985)
Blodgett, Katharine Burr (1898–1979)
Blum, Arlene (1945—)
Blunt, Katharine (1876–1954)
Bodley, Rachel (1831–1888)
Boivin, Marie Anne (1773–1847)
Bondar, Roberta (1945—)

Bonner, Elena (1923—)
Bonnevie, Kristine (1872–1948)
Boring, Alice Middleton (1883–1955)
Borrowman, Agnes (1881–1955)
Boyd, Louise Arner (1887–1972)
Brahe, Sophia (1556–1643)
Brandegee, Mary Katharine (1844–1920)
Branham, Sara Elizabeth (1888–1962)
Braun, E. Lucy (1889–1971)
Brenchley, Winifred (1883–1953)
Britton, Elizabeth Knight (1858–1934)
Bromhall, Margaret Ann (1890–1967)
Brooks, Harriet (1876–1933)
Brooks, Matilda M. (1888–1981)
Brown, Margaret Elizabeth (1918—)
Brown, Rachel Fuller (1898–1980)
Brown, Vera Scantlebury (1889–1946)
Budzynska-Tylicka, Justyna (1876–1936)
Bühler, Charlotte (1893–1974)
Burbidge, Margaret (1919—)
Burnell, Jocelyn Bell (1943—)
Calderone, Mary Steichen (1904–1998)
Caldicott, Helen (1938—)
Calkins, Mary Whiton (1863–1930)
Campbell, Charlotte C. (1914–1993)
Campbell, Kate (1899–1986)
Cannon, Annie Jump (1863–1941)
Carr, Emma Perry (1880–1972)
Carson, Rachel (1907–1964)
Chase, Agnes Meara (1869–1963)
Chase, Martha (1927–2003)
Chick, Harriette (1875–1977)
Clark, Eugenie (1922—)
Cleopatra (fl. 1st c. BCE)
Clerke, Agnes Mary (1842–1907)
Cleveland, Emeline Horton (1829–1878)
Clisby, Harriet (1830–1931)
Cobb, Jerrie (1931—)
Cobb, Jewell Plummer (1924—)
Colborn, Theodora (1927—)
Colden, Jane (1724–1766)
Cole, Rebecca J. (1846–1922)
Collins, Eileen (1956—)
Cori, Gerty T. (1896–1957)
Crane, Eva (1911—)
Cremer, Erika (1900–1996)
Crosby, Elizabeth (1888–1983)
Cruso, Thalassa (1908–1997)
Cunitz, Maria (1610–1664)
Cunningham, Imogen (1883–1976)
Curie, Marie (1867–1934)
Curtis, Doris Malkin (1914–1991)
Dalton, Katharina (1916–2004)
Dalyell, Elsie (1881–1948)
d'Arconville, Geneviève (1720–1805)
Darlington, Jennie (c. 1925—)
Davey, Constance (1882–1963)
de Almania, Jacqueline Felicia (fl. 1322)
Dembo, Tamara (1902–1993)
Deutsch, Helene (1884–1982)
De Witt, Lydia (1859–1928)
Dick, Gladys (1881–1963)
Dimock, Susan (1847–1875)
Dormon, Carrie (1888–1971)
Downey, June Etta (1875–1932)
Du Coudray, Angélique (1712–1789)
Eastwood, Alice (1859–1953)
Eddy, Bernice (b. 1903)
Edinger, Tilly (1897–1967)
Eigenmann, Rosa Smith (1858–1947)
Einstein-Marić, Mileva (1875–1948)
Elders, Joycelyn (1933—)
Elion, Gertrude B. (1918–1999)
Eliot, Martha May (1891–1978)
El Saadawi, Nawal (1931—)
Emerson, Gladys Anderson (1903–1984)
Entragues, Henriette d' (1579–1633)
Ermoleva, Zinaida (1898–1974)
Erxleben, Dorothea (1715–1762)
Esau, Katherine (1898–1997)
Evans, Matilda Arabella (1872–1935)
Farr, Wanda K. (1895–1983)
Fawcett, Maisie (1902–1988)
Ferguson, Margaret Clay (1863–1951)
Fleming, Amalia (1912–1986)
Fleming, Williamina Paton (1857–1911)
Fletcher, Alice Cunningham (1838–1923)
Fossey, Dian (1932–1985)
Fowler, Lydia Folger (1822–1879)
Franklin, Rosalind (1920–1958)
Frantz, Virginia Kneeland (1896–1967)
Furbish, Kate (1834–1931)
Gage, Susanna Phelps (1857–1915)
Galdikas, Biruté (1948—)
Gardiner, Muriel (1901–1985)
Geiringer, Hilda (1893–1973)
Geller, Margaret Joan (1947—)
Germain, Sophie (1776–1831)
Gilette of Narbonne (fl. 1300)
Giliani, Allessandra (1307–1326)
Gleditsch, Ellen (1879–1968)
Goldsmith, Grace Arabell (1904–1975)
Goodall, Jane (1934—)
Gowing, Margaret (1921–1998)
Guillemete du Luys (fl. 1479)
Guion, Connie M. (1882–1971)
Guthrie, Janet (1938—)
Guthrie, Mary Jane (1895–1975)
Hamilton, Alice (1869–1970)
Han, Suyin (1917—)
Hanson, Jean (1919–1973)
Harvey, Ethel Browne (1885–1965)
Hautval, Adelaide (1906–1988)
Hay, Elizabeth Dexter (1927—)
Hazen, Elizabeth Lee (1883–1975)
Hazlett, Olive C. (1890–1974)
Heer, Anna (1863–1918)
Helvidis (fl. 1136)
Héricourt, Jenny Poinsard d' (1809–1875)
Herschel, Caroline (1750–1848)
Hersende of France (fl. 1250)
Hesse, Fanny Angelina (1850–1934)
Hinkle, Beatrice M. (1874–1953)
Hirsch, Rachel (1870–1953)
Hobby, Gladys Lounsbury (1910–1993)
Hodgkin, Dorothy (1910–1994)
Hoffleit, E. Dorrit (1907—)
Holford, Ingrid (1920—)
Hollinshead, Ariel (1929—)
Hopper, Grace Murray (1906–1992)
Horney, Karen (1885–1952)
Hunt, Harriot Kezia (1805–1875)
Hurd-Mead, Kate Campbell (1867–1941)
Hyde, Ida (1857–1945)
Hyman, Libbie Henrietta (1888–1969)
Hypatia (c. 375–415)
Ighodaro, Irene (1916–1995)
Immerwahr, Clara (1870–1915)
Inglis, Elsie Maud (1864–1917)
Jacobi, Mary Putnam (1842–1906)
Jacobs, Aletta (1854–1929)
Jemison, Mae C. (b. 1956)
Jex-Blake, Sophia (1840–1912)
Joliot-Curie, Irène (1897–1956)
Jordan, Sara Murray (1884–1959)
Jorge Pádua, Maria Tereza (1943—)
Katherine (fl. 13th c.)
Keith, Marcia (1859–1950)
Kelsey, Frances O. (1914—)
Kidson, Elsa Beatrice (1905–1979)
King, Helen Dean (1869–1955)
Kingsford, Anna (1846–1888)
Kirch, Maria Winkelmann (1670–1720)
Kittrell, Flemmie (1904–1980)
Kleegman, Sophia (1901–1971)
Klumpke, Dorothea (1861–1942)
Knox, Elizabeth (1899–1963)
Kondakova, Yelena (c. 1955—)
Kovalevskaya, Sophia (1850–1891)
Kübler-Ross, Elisabeth (1926–2004)
Lachapelle, Marie (1769–1821)
Ladd-Franklin, Christine (1847–1930)
La Flesche, Susan (1865–1915)
Lais (fl. 1st c. BCE)
Lalande, Amélie Lefrançais de (fl. 1790)
Lama, Giulia (c. 1685–c. 1753)
Lancefield, Rebecca Craighill (1895–1981)
Laurette de St. Valery (fl. 1200)
Lavoisier, Marie (1758–1836)
Leavitt, Henrietta Swan (1868–1921)
Lehmann, Inge (1888–1993)
Lemmon, Sarah Plummer (1836–1923)
Lepaute, Hortense (1723–1788)
Lermontova, Julia (1846–1919)
Levi-Montalcini, Rita (b. 1909)
Levine, Lena (1903–1965)
Levy, Jerre (1938—)
Levy, Julia (1934—)
Lewis, Graceanna (1821–1912)
Lewis, Margaret Reed (1881–1970)
Lingens-Reiner, Ella (1908–2002)
Lissiardi, Sibille (fl. 13th c.)
Lloyd, Dorothy Jordan (1889–1946)
Longshore, Hannah E. (1819–1901)
Lonsdale, Kathleen (1903–1971)
Lovejoy, Esther Pohl (1869–1967)
Lovelace, Ada Byron, Countess of (1815–1852)
Lowe-McConnell, Rosemary (1921—)
Lozier, Clemence S. (1813–1888)
Lucid, Shannon (1943—)
Lyell, Mary Horner (1808–1873)
Lynn, Kathleen (1874–1955)
Lyon, Mary Frances (1925—)
Maathai, Wangari (1940—)
Macklin, Madge (1893–1962)
Macnamara, Jean (1899–1968)
Makemson, Maud Worcester (1891–1977)
Maltby, Margaret E. (1860–1944)
Manton, Sidnie (1902–1979)
Manzolini, Anna Morandi (1716–1774)
Margaret of Ypres (fl. 1322)
Massevitch, Alla G. (1918—)
Maunder, Annie Russell (1868–1947)
Maurizio, Anna (1900–1993)
Maury, Carlotta (1874–1938)
May, Valerie (c. 1915/16—)
Mayer, Maria Goeppert (1906–1972)
McAliskey, Roisin (1971—)
McAuliffe, Christa (1948–1986)
McClintock, Barbara (1902–1992)
McCoy, Elizabeth (1903–1978)
McGee, Anita Newcomb (1864–1940)
McKane, Alice Woodby (1865–1948)
McLaren, Anne Laura (1927—)
McWhinnie, Mary Alice (1922–1980)
Mead, Sylvia Earle (1935—)
Meitner, Lise (1878–1968)
Mellanby, May (1882–1978)
Mendenhall, Dorothy Reed (1874–1964)
Mercuriade of Salerno (fl. 1200)
Meredith, Louisa Anne (1812–1895)
Merian, Maria Sybilla (1647–1717)
Mexia, Ynes (1870–1938)
Meyer, Lucy (1849–1922)
Milner, Marion (1900–1998)
Minoka-Hill, Rosa (1876–1952)
Mitchell, Maria (1818–1889)
Montessori, Maria (1870–1952)

Morani, Alma Dea (1907–2001)
Morawetz, Cathleen Synge (1923—)
Moreau de Justo, Alicia (1885–1986)
Morgan, Agnes Fay (1884–1968)
Morgan, Ann Haven (1882–1966)
Mosher, Eliza Maria (1846–1928)
Muller-Schwarze, Christine
Murtfeldt, Mary (1848–1913)
Neumann, Hanna (1914–1971)
Nice, Margaret Morse (1883–1974)
Nichols, Mary Gove (1810–1884)
Noddack, Ida (1896–1978)
Noether, Emmy (1882–1935)
Noguchi, Constance Tom (1948—)
Novello, Antonia (1944—)
Nüsslein-Volhard, Christiane (1942—)
Oberheuser, Herta (1911–1978)
Ochoa, Ellen (1958—)
Ohta, Tomoko (1933—)
Oppenheimer, Jane Marion (1911–1996)
Ormerod, Eleanor A. (1828–1901)
Owens-Adair, Bethenia (1840–1926)
Panagiotatou, Angeliki (1878–1954)
Patch, Edith (1876–1954)
Payne-Gaposchkin, Cecilia (1900–1979)
Pearce, Louise (1885–1959)
Pechey-Phipson, Edith (1845–1908)
Peden, Irene (1925—)
Peebles, Florence (1874–1956)
Pelletier, Madeleine (1874–1939)
Pennington, Mary Engle (1872–1952)
Perey, Marguerite (1909–1975)
Pert, Candace B. (1946—)
Pool, Judith Graham (1919–1975)
Porter, Annie (1880–1963)
Porter, Helen Kemp (1899–1987)
Porter, Mary Winearls (1886–1980)
Pratt, Anne (1806–1893)
Preston, Ann (1813–1872)
Quimby, Edith (1891–1982)
Raiche, Bessica (c. 1874–1932)
Ramphele, Mamphela (1947—)
Ramsey, Elizabeth M. (1906–1993)
Rand, Gertrude (1886–1970)
Ratebzad, Anahita (1931—)
Rathbun, Mary Jane (1860–1943)
Ray, Dixy Lee (1914–1994)
Reiche, Maria (1903–1998)
Reid, Clarice D. (1931—)
Remond, Sarah Parker (1826–1894)
Resnik, Judith (1949–1986)
Richards, Ellen Swallow (1842–1911)
Richardson, Dot (1961—)
Ride, Sally (1951—)
Ripley, Martha Rogers (1843–1912)
Robinson, Julia B. (1919–1985)
Rodríguez, Evangelina (1879–1947)
Romano, Francesca (fl. 1321)
Rothschild, Miriam (1908–2005)
Royer, Clémence (1830–1902)
Russell, Dorothy Stuart (1895–1983)
Russell, Jane Anne (1911–1967)
Sabin, Florence (1871–1953)
Safford, Mary Jane (1834–1891)
Sager, Ruth (1918–1997)
Sanford, Katherine (1915—)
Sanger, Ruth Ann (1918–2001)
Sarah of St. Gilles (fl. 1326)
Sargant, Ethel (1863–1918)
Saunders, Cicely (1918–2005)
Savitskaya, Svetlana (1948—)
Scharff-Goldhaber, Gertrude (1911–1998)
Scharlieb, Mary Ann (1845–1930)
Scharrer, Berta (1906–1995)
Scott, Charlotte Angas (1858–1931)
Scudder, Ida (1870–1960)
Seacole, Mary Jane (c. 1805–1881)
Sears, Mary (1905–1997)
Seddon, Rhea (1947—)
Seibert, Florence B. (1897–1991)
Semple, Ellen Churchill (1863–1932)
Sessions, Kate O. (1857–1940)
Shattuck, Lydia (1822–1889)
Shaw, Anna Howard (1847–1919)
Shoemaker, Carolyn (1929—)
Shtern, Lina (1878–1968)
Slosson, Annie Trumbull (1838–1926)
Slye, Maud (1869–1954)
Somerville, Mary Fairfax (1780–1872)
Stanwood, Cordelia (1865–1958)
Stephenson, Marjory (1885–1948)
Stern, Elizabeth (1915–1980)
Stevens, Nettie Maria (1861–1912)
Stevenson, Sarah Hackett (1841–1909)
Stewart, Alice (1906–2002)
Stewart, Sarah (1906–1976)
Stone, Constance (1856–1902)
Stowe, Emily Howard (1831–1903)
Strong, Harriet (1844–1929)
Stuart, Miranda (c. 1795–1865)
Sullivan, Kathryn (1951—)
Summerskill, Edith (1901–1980)
Suslova, Nadezhda (1845–1916)
Swain, Clara A. (1834–1910)
Taussig, Helen Brooke (1898–1986)
Taylor, Mary (1898–1984)
Telkes, Maria (1900–1995)
Tereshkova, Valentina (1937—)
Thomas, Mary Myers (1816–1888)
Thompson, Clara (1893–1958)
Thompson, Mary Harris (1829–1895)
Thornton, Kathryn (1952—)
Tipper, Constance (1894–1995)
Tizard, Catherine (1931—)
Todd, Olga Taussky (1906–1995)
Tomaszewicz-Dobrska, Anna (1854–1918)
Traill, Catherine Parr (1802–1899)
Trotula (c. 1040s–1097)
Uvarov, Olga (1910–2001)
Van Hoosen, Bertha (1863–1952)
Vansittart, Henrietta (1840–1883)
Vejjabul, Pierra (b. 1909)
Virdimura of Sicily (fl. 1376)
Vögtlin, Marie (1845–1916)
Wald, Florence (1917—)
Walker, Mary Edwards (1832–1919)
Ward, Mary (1827–1869)
Watson, Janet Vida (1923–1985)
Wedemeyer, Maria von (c. 1924–1977)
Weiss, Alta (1889–1964)
Welsh, Lilian (1858–1938)
Wexler, Nancy (1945—)
Wheeler, Anna Pell (1883–1966)
Whiting, Sarah F. (1847–1927)
Whitney, Mary Watson (1847–1921)
Wilberforce, Octavia (1888–1963)
Williams, Anna Wessels (1863–1954)
Williams, Cicely (1893–1992)
Willums, Sigbrit (fl. 1507–1523)
Wilson, Fiammetta Worthington (1864–1920)
Winlock, Anna (1857–1904)
Wollstein, Martha (1868–1939)
Wong-Staal, Flossie (1946—)
Wright, Helen (1914–1997)
Wright, Helena (1887–1982)
Wright, Jane Cooke (1919—)
Wrinch, Dorothy (1894–1976)
Wu, Chien-Shiung (1912–1997)
Yalow, Rosalyn (1921—)
Yoshioka Yayoi (1871–1959)
Young, Anne Sewell (1871–1961)
Young, Grace Chisholm (1868–1944)
Young, Mary Sophie (1872–1919)
Zakrzewska, Marie (1829–1902)

SCOUT/GUIDE

Bailey, Ann (1742–1825)
Cannary, Martha Jane (1852–1903)
Fittko, Lisa (1909–2005)
Hinerangi, Sophia (c. 1830–1911)
Kosmodemyanskaya, Zoya (1923–1941)
Lawrence, Daisy Gordon (c. 1900—)
Lord, Lucy Takiora (c. 1842–1893)
Malinche (c. 1500–1531)
Papakura, Makereti (1873–1930)
Sacajawea (c. 1787–c. 1812 or 1884)
Starr, Belle (1848–1889)
Truganini (1812–1876)
Tubman, Harriet (1821–1913)
Winnemucca, Sarah (1844–1891)

SCOUTING-MOVEMENT MEMBER/ WORKER

Abayomi, Oyinkansola (1897–1990)
Bacon, Josephine Dodge (1876–1961)
Baden-Powell, Agnes (1858–1945)
Brystygierowa, Julia (1902–1980)
Burgin, Annie Mona (1903–1985)
Church, Marguerite Stitt (1892–1990)
Cohn, Marianne (1921–1944)
Cossgrove, Selina (1849–1929)
Follett, Mary Parker (1868–1933)
Gulick, Charlotte Vetter (1865–1928)
Herrick, Hermione Ruth (1889–1983)
Hoover, Lou Henry (1874–1944)
Joplin, Janis (1943–1970)
Klimova, Rita (1931–1993)
Lane, Priscilla (1917–1995)
Low, Juliette Gordon (1860–1927)
Rippin, Jane Deeter (1882–1953)
Ritter, Thelma (1905–1969)
Santolalla, Irene Silva de (1902–1992)
Scholl, Sophie (1921–1943)
Sipilä, Helvi (1915—)
Smith, Kate (1907–1986)
Smith, Samantha (1972–1985)
Soper, Eileen Louise (1900–1989)
Spewack, Bella (1899–1990)
Stratton, Dorothy (b. 1899)
Veil, Simone (1927—)
Wauneka, Annie Dodge (1910–1997)
Yorkin, Peg (1927—)

SCREENWRITER

Akerman, Chantal (1950—)
Akins, Zoe (1886–1958)
Aleandro, Norma (1936—)
Allen, Jay Presson (1922–2006)
Aron, Geraldine (1941—)
Audry, Jacqueline (1908–1977)
Baird, Leah (1883–1971)
Baldwin, Ruth Ann (fl. 1915–1921)
Bannerman, Kay (1919–1991)
Bemberg, Maria Luisa (1922–1995)
Beranger, Clara (1886–1956)
Bergere, Ouida (1885–1974)
Bertsch, Marguerite (1889–1967)
Bigelow, Kathryn (1951—)
Boland, Bridget (1904–1988)
Bombal, María Luisa (1910–1980)
Box, Muriel (1905–1991)
Brackett, Leigh (1915–1978)
Buffington, Adele (1900–1973)
Bullrich, Silvina (1915–1990)
Campion, Jane (1954—)
Caspary, Vera (1899–1987)
Cavani, Liliana (1933—)
Cecchi D'Amico, Suso (1914—)

Chapin, Anne Morrison (1892–1967)
Christie, Dorothy (b. 1896)
Coffee, Lenore (1896–1984)
Collins, Kathleen (1942–1988)
Comden, Betty (1915—)
Cunard, Grace (c. 1891–1967)
Dawn, Isabel (1905–1966)
De Acosta, Mercedes (1893–1968)
Delmar, Viña (1903–1990)
De Mille, Beatrice (1853–1923)
Deutsch, Helen (1906–1992)
Dörrie, Doris (1955—)
Dowd, Nancy (1944—)
Duane, Diane (1952—)
Eastman, Carole (1934–2004)
Edginton, May (1883–1957)
Ephron, Nora (1941—)
Ephron, Phoebe (1914–1971)
Epstein, Marie (c. 1899–1995)
Esquivel, Laura (1950—)
Fadiman, Annalee (1916–2002)
Fairfax, Marion (1875–1979)
Fields, Dorothy (1904–1974)
Flexner, Anne Crawford (1874–1955)
Ford, Harriet (c. 1863–1949)
Franken, Rose (c. 1895–1988)
Freeman, Gillian (1929—)
Frings, Ketti (1909–1981)
Fulton, Maude (1881–1950)
Garro, Elena (1916–1998)
Gauntier, Gene (1885–1966)
Gilliatt, Penelope (1932–1993)
Glyn, Elinor (1864–1943)
Goodrich, Frances (1891–1984)
Gordon, Ruth (1896–1985)
Gorris, Marleen (1948—)
Green, Janet (1914–1993)
Griffin, Eleanore (1904–1995)
Guido, Beatriz (1924—)
Harjo, Joy (1951—)
Harrison, Joan (c. 1908–1994)
Hatton, Fanny (c. 1870–1939)
Hatvany, Lili (1890–1967)
Hayward, Lillie (1891–1978)
Hellman, Lillian (1905–1984)
Henley, Beth (1952—)
Henning-Jensen, Astrid (1914—)
Hoffman, Alice (1952—)
Jhabvala, Ruth Prawer (1927—)
Joyeux, Odette (1914–2000)
Kanin, Fay (1917—)
Kaplan, Nelly (1931—)
Kaus, Gina (1894–1985)
Khouri, Callie (1957—)
Kingsley, Dorothy (1909–1997)
Kurys, Diane (1948—)
La Marr, Barbara (c. 1896–1926)
Landeta, Matilde (1910–1999)
Lennart, Isobel (1915–1971)
Levien, Sonya (1888–1960)
Lindblom, Gunnel (1931—)
Littlefield, Nancy (c. 1929—)
Loos, Anita (1893–1981)
Lupino, Ida (1914–1995)
Lyell, Lottie (1890–1925)
Macpherson, Jeanie (1887–1946)
Malpede, Karen (1945—)
Marion, Frances (1888–1973)
Mathis, June (1892–1927)
Mathison, Melissa (1950—)
May, Elaine (1932—)
Meredyth, Bess (1890–1969)
Mészáros, Márta (1931—)
Millar, Margaret (1915–1994)
Moon, Lorna (1886–1930)
Moreau, Jeanne (1928—)
Morgan, Joan (1905–2004)
Murfin, Jane (1893–1955)
Nair, Mira (1957—)
Naylor, Gloria (1950—)
Nazimova, Alla (1879–1945)
Owen, Seena (1894–1966)
Pauli, Hertha (1909–1973)
Perry, Eleanor (1915–1981)
Pisier, Marie-France (1944—)
Potter, Sally (1949—)
Rand, Ayn (1905–1982)
Reid, Dorothy Davenport (1895–1977)
Reville, Alma (1899–1982)
Reza, Yasmina (1959—)
Roberts, Marguerite (1905–1989)
Rothman, Stephanie (1936—)
Roy, Arundhati (1961—)
Sanders-Brahms, Helma (1940—)
Schiffman, Suzanne (1929–2001)
Scott, Blanche (1885–1970)
Sears, Zelda (1873–1935)
Serreau, Coline (1947—)
Shub, Esther (1894–1959)
Silko, Leslie Marmon (1948—)
Silver, Joan Micklin (1935—)
Slesinger, Tess (1905–1945)
Spewack, Bella (1899–1990)
Spheeris, Penelope (1945—)
Stroyeva, Vera (b. 1903)
Stuart, Aimée (c. 1885–1981)
Tan, Amy (1952—)
Taylor, Renée (1933—)
Tewkesbury, Joan (1936—)
Thompson, Emma (1959—)
Trintignant, Nadine (1934—)
Tynan, Kathleen (1937–1995)
Unger, Gladys B. (c. 1885–1940)
Van Upp, Virginia (1902–1970)
Vernon, Barbara (1916–1978)
Viertel, Salka (1889–1978)
von Harbou, Thea (1888–1954)
Wademant, Annette (1928—)
Wasserstein, Wendy (1950–2006)
West, Jessamyn (1902–1984)
Winsloe, Christa (1888–1944)
Yezierska, Anzia (c. 1881–1970)
York, Susannah (1941—)
Zetterling, Mai (1925–1994)

SCRIBE/TRANSCRIBER
Agassiz, Elizabeth Cary (1822–1907)
Baume, Madame de la (fl. 17th c.)
Elgar, Alice (1848–1920)
Fern, Fanny (1811–1872)
Hatzler, Clara (fl. 1452)
MacDowell, Marian (1857–1956)
Marx, Jenny von Westphalen (1814–1881)
Scepens, Elizabeth (fl. 1476)
Wright, Susanna (1697–1784)
Young, Grace Chisholm (1868–1944)

SCRIPTWRITER
Arzner, Dorothy (1897–1979)
Bachmann, Ingeborg (1926–1973)
Brovar, Anna Iakovlevna (1887–1917)
Carroll, Gladys Hasty (1904–1999)
Chen Ruiqing (1932—)
Day, Dorothy (1897–1980)
Harrison, Joan (c. 1908–1994)
Jenner, Andrea (1891–1985)
Kuhn, Irene Corbally (1898–1995)
Mathis, June (1892–1927)
Ogot, Grace (1930—)
Parks, Hildy (1926–2004)
Pearce, Philippa (1920—)
Phipson, Joan (1912–2003)
Porter, Katherine Anne (1890–1980)
Tokareva, Viktoria (1937—)
Vernon, Barbara (1916–1978)
Wertmüller, Lina (1928—)
Wolff, Victoria (1903–1992)
Yezierska, Anzia (c. 1881–1970)
Yuan Jing (b. 1914)

SCULLER
Afrasiloaia, Felicia (1954—)
Ahrenholz, Brigitte (1952—)
Alexander, Buffy (c. 1977—)
Alupei, Angela (1972—)
America^3 Team
Anitas, Herta (1967—)
Antonova, Yelena (1952—)
Aposteanu, Angelica (1954—)
Apostol, Chira (1960—)
Appeldoorn, Tessa (1973—)
Arba-Puscatu, Rodica (1962—)
Armasescu, Mihaela (1963—)
Armbrust, Barbara (1963—)
Badea, Ioana (1964—)
Bakova, Ani (1957—)
Balthasar, Ramona (1964—)
Barascu, Aurica (1974—)
Barbulova-Kelbecheva, Siyka (1951—)
Barnes, Kirsten (1968—)
Batten, Guin (1967—)
Batten, Miriam (1964—)
Bazon-Chelariu, Adriana (1963—)
Beard, Betsy (1961—)
Becker, Ellen (1960—)
Behrendt-Hampe, Jutta (1960—)
Bell, Teresa Z. (1966—)
Bennion, Lianne (1972—)
Berberova, Lalka (1965—)
Bichyk, Yuliya (1983—)
Biesenthal, Laryssa (1971—)
Bishop, Cath (1971—)
Blasberg, Claudia (1975—)
Bobeica, Iulia (1967—)
Boesler, Martina (1957—)
Boesler, Petra (1955—)
Boncheva, Rumeliana (1957—)
Bondar, Elena (1958—)
Borchmann, Anke (1954—)
Boron, Kathrin (1969—)
Bower, Carol (1956—)
Bradley, Amber (1980—)
Brain, Marilyn (1959—)
Brancourt, Karen (1962—)
Bredael, Annelies (1965—)
Brown, Carol Page (1953—)
Bryunina, Mira (1951—)
Bucur, Florica (1959—)
Buhr-Weigelt, Liane (1956—)
Bularda-Homeghi, Olga (1958—)
Burcica, Constanta (1971—)
Burns, Lindsay
Cao Mianying
Chapman, Susan (1962—)
Cheremisina, Nina (1946—)
Chernyshova, Nadezhda (1951—)
Cochelea, Veronica (1965—)
Collins, Christine (1969—)
Constantinescu, Mariana (1956—)
Corban-Banovici, Sofia (1956—)
Cornet, Lynda (1962—)
Cortin, Hélène (1972—)
Cox, Alison (1979—)
Craig, Betty (1957—)
Crawford, Shannon (1963—)
Dahne, Sabine (1950—)
Damian, Georgeta (1976—)
Davies, Caryn (1982—)

Davis, Heather (1974—)
Davydenko, Tamara
DeFrantz, Anita (1952—)
de Haan, Annemiek (1981—)
Dekkers, Hurnet (1974—)
Delehanty, Megan (1968—)
Diaconescu, Camelia (1963—)
Dirkmaat, Megan (1976—)
Dluzewska, Malgorzata (1958—)
Doberschuetz-Mey, Gerlinde (1964—)
Dobre-Balan, Anisoara (1966—)
Dobritoiu, Elena (1957—)
Doerdelmann, Sylvia (1970—)
Donohoe, Shelagh (1965—)
Dorodnova, Oksana (1974—)
Dumcheva, Antonina (1958—)
Dumitrache, Maria Magdalena (1977—)
Ebert, Henrietta (1954—)
Eckbauer-Baumann, Edith (1949—)
Eckert, Cynthia (1965—)
Eijs, Irene (1966—)
Einoder-Straube, Thea (1951—)
Eriksen, Hanne (1960—)
Evers, Meike (1977—)
Evers-Swindell, Caroline (1978—)
Evers-Swindell, Georgina (1978—)
Fadeyeva, Mariya (1958—)
Faletic, Dana (1977—)
Fedotova, Irina (1975—)
Feeney, Carol (1964—)
Filipova, Nadya (1959—)
Flanagan, Jeanne (1957—)
Flood, Debbie (1980—)
Florea, Rodica (1983—)
Forster-Pieloth, Kerstin (1965—)
Foster, Margot (1958—)
Frank, Antje (1968—)
Fricioiu, Maria (1960—)
Frintu, Rodica (1960—)
Froehlich, Silvia (1959—)
Frolova, Inna (1965—)
Frolova, Nina (1948—)
Fuller, Amy (1968—)
Gafencu, Liliana (1975—)
Garner, Sarah (1971—)
Geer, Charlotte (1957—)
Georgescu, Elena (1964—)
Georgieva, Anka (1959—)
Georgieva, Magdalena (1962—)
Georgieva-Panayotovna, Kapka (1951—)
Gilder, Virginia (1958—)
Giurca, Elena (1946—)
Goretzki, Viola (1956—)
Gosse, Christine (1964—)
Grainger, Katherine (1975—)
Graves, Carie (1953—)
Greig, Marion (1954—)
Grey-Gardner, Robyn (1964—)
Gu Xiaoli (1971—)
Guzenko, Olga (1956—)
Gyurova, Ginka (1954—)
Haacker, Kathrin (1967—)
Haesebrouck, Ann (1963—)
Hanel, Birgitte (1954—)
Hannen, Lynley (1964—)
Hansen, Trine
Han Yaqin (1963—)
Harzendorf, Christiane (1967—)
Heddle, Kathleen (1965—)
Helakh, Natallia (1978—)
Hellemans, Greet (1959—)
Hellemans, Nicolette (1961—)
Hess, Sabine (1958—)
He Yanwen (1966—)
Hohn, Annette (1966—)
Hommes, Nienke (1977—)
Hore, Kerry (1981—)
Hornig-Miseler, Carola (1962—)
Horvat-Florea, Elena (1958—)
Houghton, Frances (1980—)
Hu Yadong (1968—)
Ignat, Doina (1968—)
Iliuta, Ana (1958—)
Jahn, Sabine (1953—)
Jewett, Sarah Orne (1849–1909)
Johnson, Kate (1978—)
Joyce, Rebecca
Kalimbet, Irina (1968—)
Kallies, Monika (1956—)
Kaminskaite, Leonora (1951–1986)
Kapheim, Ramona (1958—)
Keeler, Kathryn (1956—)
Khloptseva, Yelena (1960—)
Khodotovich, Ekaterina (1972—)
Klier, Cornelia (1957—)
Kluge, Anja (1964—)
Koefoed, Charlotte (1957—)
Koepke-Knetsch, Christiane (1956—)
Koeppen, Kerstin (1967—)
Kolkova, Olga (1955—)
Kondrashina, Anna (1955—)
Korholz, Laurel (1970—)
Korn, Alison (1970—)
Koscianska, Czeslawa (1959—)
Kosenkova, Klavdiya (1949—)
Kowalski, Kerstin (1976—)
Kowalski, Manja (1976—)
Kraft, Karen (1969—)
Krokhina, Lyudmila (1954—)
Krylova, Lidiya (1951—)
Kuehn-Lohs, Gabriele (1957—)
Kurbatova-Gruycheva, Stoyanka (1955—)
Kurth, Andrea (1957—)
Lau, Jutta (1955—)
Laumann, Daniele (1961—)
Laumann, Silken (1964—)
Laurijsen, Martha (1954—)
Laverick, Elise (1975—)
Lavric, Florica (1962—)
Lavrinenko, Natalya
Lazar, Elisabeta (1950—)
Lee, Susan (1966—)
Lee, Virginia (1965—)
Lehmann, Helma (1953—)
Lepadatu, Viorica (1971—)
Levina, Ioulia (1973—)
Lind, Joan (1952—)
Lindsay, Gillian Anne (1973—)
Linse, Cornelia (1959—)
Lipa, Elisabeta (1964—)
Li Ronghua (1956—)
Lu Huali (1972—)
Luke, Theresa (1967—)
Lutze, Manuela (1974—)
Lyubimova, Nadezhda (1959—)
Macoviciuc, Camelia (1968—)
Madina, Stefka (1963—)
Magee, Samantha (1983—)
Makhina, Antonina (1958—)
Marden, Anne (1958—)
Matiyevskaya, Yelena (1961—)
Maunder, Maria (1972—)
Maxwell-Pierson, Stephanie (1964—)
Maziy, Svetlana (1968—)
McBean, Marnie (1968—)
McCarthy, Peggy (1956—)
McDermid, Heather (1968—)
Mehl, Gabriele (1967—)
Meijer, Elien (1970—)
Merk, Larisa (1971—)
Metcalf, Harriet (1958—)
Metz, Karin (1956—)
Mickelson, Anna (1980—)
Micsa, Maria (1953—)
Miftakhutdinova, Diana (1973—)
Mihaly, Aneta (1957—)
Mikulich, Alena (1977—)
Minea-Sorohan, Anisoara (1963—)
Mishenina, Galina (1950—)
Modeva, Mariyka (1954—)
Monroe, Jessica (1966—)
Mowbray, Alison (1971—)
Mueller, Irina (1951—)
Mueller, Kerstin (1969—)
Mundt, Kristina (1966—)
Murden, Tori (1963—)
Nakova, Dolores (1957—)
Necula, Veronica (1967—)
Neculai, Viorica (1967—)
Neelissen, Catharina (1961—)
Neisser, Kersten (1956—)
Neunast, Daniela (1966—)
Neykova, Rumyana (1973—)
Ninova, Violeta (1963—)
Noack, Angelika (1952—)
Norelius, Kristine (1956—)
Oancia, Ecaterina (1954—)
O'Grady, Diane (1967—)
Olteanu, Ioana (1966—)
Oppelt, Britta (1978—)
O'Steen, Shyril (1960—)
Otsetova, Svetlana (1950—)
Paduraru, Maria (1970—)
Pankina, Aleksandra
Papuc, Ioana (1984—)
Pasokha, Anna (1949—)
Pavlovich, Yaroslava
Payne, Nicola (1960—)
Pazyun, Mariya (1953—)
Penninx, Nelleke (1971—)
Peter, Birgit (1964—)
Petersmann, Cerstin (1964—)
Pipota, Constanta (1971—)
Pivovarova, Olga (1956—)
Plesca, Aurora (1963—)
Ploch, Jutta (1960—)
Poley, Viola (1955—)
Popescu, Marioara (1962—)
Poplavskaja, Kristina (1972—)
Popova-Aleksandrova, Larisa (1957—)
Preobrazhenskaya, Nina (1956—)
Prishchepa, Nadezhda (1956—)
Pugovskaya, Olga (1942—)
Pustovit, Antonina (1955—)
Pyritz, Dana (1970—)
Quik, Martijntje (1973—)
Quist, Anne Marie (1957—)
Ramoskiene, Genovaite (1945—)
Rasmussen, Bodil Steen (1957—)
Reimer, Daniela (1982—)
Reinhardt, Sybille (1957—)
Richter, Ilona (1953—)
Ricketson, Gail (1953—)
Rickon, Kelly (1959—)
Robinson, Emma (1971—)
Robu, Doina (1967—)
Rohde, Lisa (1955—)
Romero, Rebecca (1980—)
Ronzhina, Olena (1970—)
Rosca-Racila, Valeria (1957—)
Rose, Sylvia (1962—)
Roshchina, Nadezhda (1954—)
Rozgon, Nadezhda (1952—)
Rutschow, Katrin (1975—)
Saalfeld, Romy (1960—)
Sakickiene, Birute (1968—)
Sandig, Marita (1958—)
Sattin, Rebecca (1980—)

Sauca, Lucia (1963—)
Saville, Kathleen (1956—)
Scheiblich, Christine (1954—)
Schmidt, Sybille (1967—)
Schneider, Angela (1959—)
Schramm, Beate (1966—)
Schröer-Lehmann, Beatrix (1963—)
Schroeter, Martina (1960—)
Schütz, Birgit (1958—)
Schwede, Bianka (1953—)
Schwen, Missy (1972—)
Schwerzmann, Ingeburg (1967—)
Seaton, Anna (1964—)
Semyonova, Svetlana (1958—)
Serbezova, Mariana (1959—)
Sevostyanova, Nadezhda (1953—)
Siech, Birte (1967—)
Siegelaar, Sarah (1981—)
Silliman, Lynn (1959—)
Skrabatun, Valentina (1958—)
Slatter, Kate (1971—)
Smith, Tricia (1957—)
Smulders, Marlies (1982—)
Snep-Balan, Doina Liliana (1963—)
Sorensen, Jette Hejli (1961—)
Sorgers, Jana (1967—)
Sovetnikova, Galina (1955—)
Spircu, Doina (1970—)
Stasyuk, Natalia (1969—)
Stearns, Sally (c. 1915—)
Steindorf, Ute (1957—)
Stetsenko, Tatyana (1957—)
Still, Megan (1972—)
Stoyanova, Radka (1964—)
Strauch, Annegret (1968—)
Studneva, Marina (1959—)
Susanu, Viorica (1975—)
Talalayeva, Lyubov (1953—)
Tanase, Anca (1968—)
Tanger, Helen (1978—)
Tarakanova, Nelli (1954—)
Taran-Iordache, Maricica Titie (1962—)
Taylor, Brenda (1962—)
Taylor, Rachael (1976—)
ter Beek, Carin (1970—)
Teryoshina, Yelena (1959—)
Thieme, Jana (1970—)
Thompson, Lesley (1959—)
Thorsness, Kristen (1960—)
Todorova, Rita (1958—)
Toma, Sanda (1956—)
Trasca, Marioara (1962—)
Tregunno, Jane (1962—)
Tsang, Tasha (1970—)
Tudoran, Ioana (1948—)
Umanets, Nina (1956—)
Urbaniak, Dorota (1972—)
Ustyuzhanina, Tatyana (1965—)
Vaandrager, Wiljon (1957—)
Van der Kamp, Anna (1972—)
van Der Kolk, Kirsten (1975—)
Van Dishoeck, Pieta (1972—)
van Drogenbroek, Marieke (1964—)
van Ettekoven, Harriet (1961—)
van Eupen, Marit (1969—)
Van Nes, Eeke (1969—)
van Rumpt, Annemarieke (1980—)
Vaseva, Lilyana (1955—)
Vasilchenko, Olga (1956—)
Velinova, Iskra (1953—)
Venema, Anneke (1971—)
Veres-Ioja, Viorica (1962—)
Viehoff, Valerie (1976—)
Voelkner, Iris (1960—)
Volchek, Natalya
Wagner-Stange, Ute (1966—)
Waleska, Peggy (1980—)
Walter, Martina (1963—)
Warner, Anne (1954—)
Wegman, Froukje (1979—)
Wenzel, Kirsten (1961—)
Werremeier, Stefani (1968—)
Westerhof, Marieke (1974—)
Westphal, Heidi (1959—)
Whipple, Mary (1980—)
Wild, Ute (1965—)
Wilke, Marina (1958—)
Winckless, Sarah (1973—)
Worhel, Esther (1975—)
Worthington, Kay (1959—)
Yang Xiao (1964—)
Yermolayeva, Galina (1948—)
Yordanova, Reni (1953—)
Yordanova, Zdravka (1950—)
Zagoni-Predescu, Marlena (1951—)
Zeidler, Judith (1968—)
Zelikovich-Dumcheva, Antonina (1958—)
Zhang Xianghua (1968—)
Zhang Xiuyun (1976—)
Zhang Yali (1964—)
Zhou Shouying (1969—)
Zhou Xiuhua (1966—)
Zhulina, Valentina (1953—)
Znak, Marina (1961—)
Zobelt, Roswietha (1954—)
Zoch, Jacqueline (1949—)
Zubko, Yelena (1953—)

SCULPTOR

Abakanowicz, Magdalena (1930—)
Abbott, Berenice (1898–1991)
Acheson, Anne Crawford (1882–1962)
Agar, Eileen (1899–1991)
Alcorta, Gloria (1915—)
Antrim, Angela (1911–1984)
Barlow, Hannah (1851–1916)
Barton, Glenys (1944—)
Baudisch-Wittke, Gudrun (1907–1982)
Bontecou, Lee (1931—)
Botta, Anne C.L. (1815–1891)
Bourgeois, Louise (b. 1911)
Brigham, Emma Frances (1855–1881)
Burke, Selma Hortense (1900–1995)
Burroughs, Margaret Taylor (1917—)
Butler, Margaret Mary (1883–1947)
Caesar, Doris Porter (1892–1971)
Catlett, Elizabeth (b. 1915)
Chase-Riboud, Barbara (1936—)
Chryssa (1933—)
Claudel, Camille (1864–1943)
Collot, Marie-Anne (1748–1821)
Damer, Anne Seymour (1748–1828)
Dane, Clemence (1888–1965)
Dehner, Dorothy (1901–1994)
Dunnett, Dorothy (1923–2001)
Eberle, Abastenia St. Leger (1878–1942)
Foley, Margaret (c. 1827–1877)
Frink, Elisabeth (1930–1993)
Fry, Laura Ann (1857–1943)
Fuller, Meta Warrick (1877–1968)
Gagneur, Marguerite (1857–1945)
Ghisi, Diana (c. 1530–1590)
Gibb, Roberta (1943—)
Gleichen, Feodora (1861–1922)
Golubkina, Anna (1864–1927)
Goncharova, Natalia (1881–1962)
Graves, Nancy (1940–1995)
Greenbaum, Dorothea Schwarcz (1893–1986)
Greene, Gertrude Glass (1904–1956)
Guidosalvi, Sancia (fl. early 12th c.)
Harkness, Rebekah (1915–1982)
Henrion, Daphne Hardy (1917–2003)
Hepworth, Barbara (1903–1975)
Hermes, Gertrude (1901–1983)
Hesse, Eva (1936–1970)
Hoffman, Malvina (1885–1966)
Holt, Winifred (1870–1945)
Hosmer, Harriet (1830–1908)
Huntington, Anna Hyatt (1876–1973)
Huxley, Juliette (1896–1994)
Johnson, Adelaide (1859–1955)
Jones, Elizabeth (c. 1935—)
Kidson, Elsa Beatrice (1905–1979)
Kim, Ronyoung (1926–1987)
Kitson, Theo A.R. (1871–1932)
Kollwitz, Käthe (1867–1945)
Ladd, Anna Coleman (1878–1939)
Lander, Louisa (1826–1923)
Lebedeva, Sarra (1892–1967)
Lewis, Edmonia (c. 1845–c. 1909)
Lin, Maya (1959—)
Lollobrigida, Gina (1927—)
Longman, Evelyn Beatrice (1874–1954)
Louise (1848–1939)
Marie d'Orleans (1813–1839)
Marisol (1930—)
Martin, Mary (1907–1969)
Marzouk, Zahia (1906–1988)
Mayer, Emilie (1821–1883)
Mears, Helen Farnsworth (1872–1916)
Millett, Kate (1934—)
Montalba, Henrietta Skerrett (1856–1893)
Montgomery, Mary (fl. 1891–1914)
Mukhina, Vera (1889–1953)
Münter, Gabriele (1877–1962)
Nevelson, Louise (1899–1988)
Newhouse, Caroline H. (1910–2003)
Ney, Elisabet (1833–1907)
Nourse, Elizabeth (1859–1938)
Oppenheim, Méret (1913–1985)
Parsons, Betty Pierson (1900–1982)
Pedretti, Erica (1930—)
Pepper, Beverly (1924—)
Phalle, Niki de Saint (1930–2002)
Pisano, Nicola (fl. 1278)
Praeger, Sophia Rosamund (1867–1954)
Prophet, Elizabeth (1890–1960)
Radi, Nuha al- (1941–2004)
Ream, Vinnie (1847–1914)
Reed, Rowena (1900–1988)
Richier, Germaine (1904–1959)
Ringgold, Faith (1934—)
Roldán, Luisa (1656–1704)
Rossi, Properzia de (c. 1490–1530)
Savage, Augusta (1892–1962)
Schaumann, Ruth (1899–1975)
Scudder, Janet (1869–1940)
Sheridan, Clare (1885–1970)
Sintenis, Renée (1888–1965)
Stebbins, Emma (1815–1882)
Steinbach, Sabina von (fl. 13th c.)
Tanning, Dorothea (b. 1910)
Truitt, Anne (1921–2004)
Unger, Mary Ann (1945–1998)
Uzès, Anne, Duchesse d' (1847–1933)
Vonnoh, Bessie Potter (1872–1955)
Walker, Ethel (1861–1951)
Wendt, Julia Bracken (1871–1942)
Whitney, Anne (1821–1915)
Whitney, Flora Payne (1897–1986)
Whitney, Gertrude Vanderbilt (1875–1942)
Winsloe, Christa (1888–1944)
Wong, Jade Snow (1919–2006)
Wood, Beatrice (1893–1998)
Wood, Thelma (1901–1970)
Wright, Patience Lovell (1725–1786)

SEA CAPTAIN
Ching Shih (fl. 1807–1810)
Hetha (fl. 10th c.)
McGrath, Kathleen (1952–2002)
O'Malley, Grace (c. 1530–1603)

SEAMSTRESS/DRESSMAKER
Anstice, Sophia (1849–1926)
Audoux, Marguerite (1863–1937)
Awolowo, Hannah (1915—)
Bennett, Louise Simone (1919—)
Berg, Helene (b. 1906)
Bonheur, Rosa (1822–1899)
Bonita, Maria (c. 1908–1938)
Brice, Fanny (1891–1951)
Bridgman, Laura (1829–1889)
Bryant, Lane (1879–1951)
Campoamor, Clara (1888–1972)
Carnegie, Hattie (1886–1956)
Chanel, Coco (1883–1971)
Chazal, Aline-Marie (1825–1869)
Cossey, Alice Eleanor (1879–1970)
Craft, Ellen (1826–c. 1891)
de Burgos, Julia (1914–1953)
Denison, Flora MacDonald (1867–1921)
Deroin, Jeanne-Françoise (1805–1894)
Durieux, Tilla (1880–1971)
Fitzhenry, Mrs. (d. 1790?)
Gautier, Felisa Rincón de (1897–1994)
Hale, Maria Selina (1864–1951)
Hames, Mary (1827–1919)
Harris, Julie (1921—)
Hawthorne, Margaret Jane Scott (1869–1958)
Held, Anna (c. 1865–1918)
Herrick, Elinore Morehouse (1895–1964)
Hipp, Jutta (1925–2003)
Ibárruri, Dolores (1895–1989)
Irene (1901–1962)
Jackson, Rebecca Cox (1795–1871)
Jacobs, Harriet A. (1813–1897)
Jemison, Alice Lee (1901–1964)
Johnstone, Anna Hill (1913–1992)
Jones, Mary Harris (1830–1930)
Joyner, Florence Griffith (1959–1998)
Juchacz, Marie (1879–1956)
Kael, Pauline (1919–2001)
Keckley, Elizabeth (c. 1824–1907)
Lanvin, Jeanne (1867–1946)
Lawrence, Marjorie (1908–1979)
Lebron, Lolita (1919—)
Lee, Mary Isabella (1871–1939)
Lohman, Ann Trow (1812–1878)
Mink, Paule (1839–1901)
Mitchell, Hannah (1871–1956)
Niederkirchner, Käte (1909–1944)
O'Neill, Maire (1885–1952)
O'Sullivan, Mary Kenney (1864–1943)
Parks, Rosa (1913—)
Peake, Mary S. (1823–1862)
Pitseolak (c. 1900–1983)
Poole, Elizabeth (fl. 1648)
Popp, Adelheid (1869–1939)
Powers, Harriet (1837–1911)
Ralfe, Catherine Hester (c. 1831–1912)
Rankin, Jeannette (1880–1973)
Reich, Lilly (1885–1947)
Reid, Rose Marie (1906–1978)
Ricci, Nina (1883–1970)
Ritchie, Harriet Maria (1818–1907)
Rosenthal, Ida Cohen (1886–1973)
Rowlandson, Mary (c. 1635–after 1682)
Runciman, Jane Elizabeth (1873–1950)
Salavarrieta, Pola (1795–1817)
Sampson, Deborah (1760–1827)
Schiaparelli, Elsa (1890–1973)
Siddal, Elizabeth (1829–1862)
Stevenson, Fanny (1840–1914)
Storni, Alfonsina (1892–1938)
Vionnet, Madeleine (1876–1975)
Volkonskaya, Maria (1805–1863)
Washington, Sarah Spencer (b. 1889)
Westwood, Vivienne (1941—)
Wohlers, Eliza (c. 1812–1891)
Zardoya, Concha (1914–2004)

SECRET AGENT
See Spy.

SECRETARY
Barnicoat, Constance Alice (1872–1922)

SECRETARY OF LABOR (U.S.)
Martin, Lynn (1939—)
Perkins, Frances (1880–1965)
Peterson, Esther (1906–1997)

SECRETARY OF STATE
Agnelli, Susanna (1922—)
Brooks, Angie (1928—)
Bunker, Carol Laise (1918–1991)
Castle, Barbara (1910–2002)
Fairclough, Ellen (1905–2004)
Grasso, Ella (1919–1981)
Hart, Judith (1924—)
Joliot-Curie, Irène (1897–1956)
Kennelly, Barbara (1936—)
Lacore, Suzanne (1875–1975)
Lee, Jennie (1904–1988)
Mink, Patsy (1927—)
Norrell, Catherine Dorris (1901–1981)
Pascalina, Sister (1894–1983)
Pintasilgo, Maria de Lurdes (1930–2004)
Shephard, Gillian (1940—)
Thatcher, Margaret (1925—)
Tucker, C. DeLores (1927—)
Woodhouse, Margaret Chase Going (1890–1984)

SECURITIES BROKER
Bay, Josephine Perfect (1900–1962)
Bishop, Hazel (1906–1998)
Chadwick, Florence (1918–1995)
Claflin, Tennessee (1846–1923)
Dalrymple, Jean (1910–1998)
Hanau, Marthe (c. 1884–1935)
Post, Marjorie Merriweather (1887–1973)
Rudkin, Margaret (1897–1967)
Siebert, Muriel (1932—)
Woodard, Lynette (1959—)
Woodhull, Victoria (1838–1927)

SENATOR
See Politician.

SERF/SLAVE/SLAVE LABORER
Acte (fl. 55–69)
Aisse (c. 1694–1733)
Albert, Octavia V.R. (1853–c. 1899)
Baum, Marianne (1912–1942)
Blandina (d. 177)
Burton, Annie L. (fl. 19th c.)
Cassandra (possibly fl. around 1200 BCE)
Craft, Ellen (1826–c. 1891)
Dananir al Barmakiyya (fl. late 8th c.)
Dean, Jennie (1852–1913)
de Rivery, Aimee Dubucq (c. 1762–1817)
Farida (c. 830–?)
Felicitas or Felicitas of Carthage (d. 203)
Fields, Mary (c. 1832–1914)
Fraser, Eliza (c. 1798–1858)
Habbaba (d. 724)
Hagar (fl. 3rd, 2nd, or 1st c. BCE)
Hemings, Sally (1773–1835)
Inan (fl. c. 800)
Irfan (fl. mid–800s)
Jacobs, Harriet A. (1813–1897)
Jonas, Regina (1902–1944)
Kovalskaia, Elizaveta (1851–1943)
Lupicinia-Euphemia (d. 523)
Malinche (c. 1500–1531)
Maryam the Egyptian (fl. 7th c.)
Mason, Biddy (1818–1891)
Milh al-Attara (fl. 840s)
Nathoy, Lalu (1853–1933)
Nurbanu (1525–1583)
Oraib (797–890)
Phryne (c. 365–c. 295 BCE)
Pleasant, Mary Ellen (c. 1814–1904)
Powers, Harriet (1837–1911)
Prince, Lucy Terry (c. 1730–1821)
Prince, Mary (c. 1788–after 1833)
Prout, Mary Ann (1801–1884)
Rabi'a (c. 714–801)
Rowlandson, Mary (c. 1635–after 1682)
Roxelana (c. 1504–1558)
Sacajawea (c. 1787–c. 1812 or 1884)
Sadeler, Agnes (fl. 1386)
Shariyya (b. around 815)
Smith, Amanda Berry (1837–1915)
Stockton, Betsey (c. 1798–1865)
Taylor, Susie King (1848–1912)
Truth, Sojourner (c. 1797–1883)
Tubman, Harriet (1821–1913)
Wheatley, Phillis (c. 1752–1784)
Zilpah

SERVANT
Lynch, Margaret (fl. 1867–1868)

SERVANTS' HOME MATRON
Ritchie, Harriet Maria (1818–1907)

SETTLEMENT-HOUSE FOUNDER
Addams, Jane (1860–1935)
Bernstein, Aline (1882–1955)
Dreier, Margaret (1868–1945)
Kander, Lizzie Black (1858–1940)
Ottenberg, Nettie Podell (1887–1982)
Robbins, Jane Elizabeth (1860–1946)
Simkhovitch, Mary (1867–1951)
Szold, Henrietta (1860–1945)
Ward, Mrs. Humphry (1851–1920)
Wells-Barnett, Ida (1862–1931)

SETTLEMENT-HOUSE WORKER
Addams, Jane (1860–1935)
Balch, Emily Greene (1867–1961)
Bernstein, Aline (1882–1955)
Crandall, Ella Phillips (1871–1938)
Dreier, Margaret (1868–1945)
Dreier, Mary Elisabeth (1875–1963)
Earhart, Amelia (1897–1937)
Kander, Lizzie Black (1858–1940)
Lathrop, Rose Hawthorne (1851–1926)
McDowell, Mary Eliza (1854–1936)
McMain, Eleanor Laura (1866–1934)
Moskowitz, Belle (1877–1933)
O'Reilly, Leonora (1870–1927)
Ottenberg, Nettie Podell (1887–1982)
Petre, Maude (1863–1942)
Pettit, Katherine (1868–1936)
Simkhovitch, Mary (1867–1951)
Starr, Ellen Gates (1859–1940)
Stevens, Alzina (1849–1900)
Szold, Henrietta (1860–1945)
Thomas, Alma (1891–1978)
Wald, Lillian D. (1867–1940)
Ward, Mrs. Humphry (1851–1920)
Wells-Barnett, Ida (1862–1931)
Werlein, Elizebeth Thomas (1883–1946)

Wise, Louise Waterman (1874–1947)
Wolfson, Theresa (1897–1972)
Younger, Maud (1870–1936)

SEXOLOGIST
Hite, Shere (1943—)
Johnson, Virginia E. (1925—)

SHAMANESS
A Nong (c. 1005–1055)
Himiko (fl. 3rd c.)
Jingū (c. 201–269)

SHARPSHOOTER
Ashumova, Irada (1958—)
Balogh, Suzanne (1973—)
Baynes, Deserie (1960—)
Binder, Aranka (1966—)
Cherkasova, Valentina (1958—)
Demina, Svetlana (c. 1960—)
Dench, Patricia (1932—)
Feklistova, Maria (1976—)
Forder, Annemarie (1978—)
Fox, Ruby (1945—)
Galkina, Lioubov (1973—)
Gao E (1962—)
Gao Jing (1975—)
Gelisio, Deborah (1976—)
Gerasimenok, Irina (1970—)
Goldobina, Tatiana (1975—)
Grozdeva, Maria (1972—)
Gudzineviciute, Daina (1965—)
Gufler, Edith (1962—)
Gunnarsson, Martine (1927—)
Hansen, Pia (1965—)
Hart, Nancy (c. 1846–1902)
Hasegawa, Tomoko (1963—)
Holmer, Ulrike (1967—)
Horneber, Petra (1965—)
Hykova, Lenka (1985—)
Igaly, Diana (1965—)
Ivosev, Aleksandra (1974—)
Jewell, Wanda (1954—)
Kang Cho-Hyun (1982—)
Kang Keqing (1911–1992)
Kiermayer, Susanne (1968—)
Klochneva, Olga (1968—)
Kostevych, Olena (1985—)
Ksiazkiewicz, Malgorzata (1967—)
Kurkova, Katerina (1983—)
Lecheva, Vesela (1964—)
Lee Bo-Na (1981—)
Li Du (1982—)
Li Duihong (1970—)
Logvinenko, Marina (1961—)
Malukhina, Anna (1958—)
Matova, Nonka (1954—)
Mauer, Renata (1969—)
Meftakhetdinova, Zemfira (1963—)
Meili, Launi (1963—)
Milchina, Lolita
Munkhbayar, Dorzhsuren (1969—)
Murdock, Margaret (1942—)
Napolski, Nancy (1974—)
Nattrass, Susan (1950—)
Oakley, Annie (1860–1926)
Pflueger, Joan (1931—)
Quintanal, Maria (1969—)
Racinet, Delphine (1973—)
Rhode, Kim (1979—)
Salukvadze, Nino (1969—)
Sekaric, Jasna (1965—)
Shilova, Irina (1960—)
Sperber, Sylvia (1965—)
Spurgin, Patricia (1965—)
Tao Luna (1974—)
Thom, Linda (1943—)
Topperwein, Elizabeth "Plinky" (c. 1886–1945)
Turisini, Valentina (1969—)
Wang Chengyi (1983—)
Wei Ning (1982—)
Wu Xiaoxuan (1958—)
Yeo Kab-Soon (1974—)
Yorgova, Diana Vassilleva (1971—)
Zhang Shan (1968—)

SHIPOWNER
O'Malley, Grace (c. 1530–1603)
Philipse, Margaret Hardenbrook (d. 1690)

SHIPYARD WORKER
Hermes, Gertrude (1901–1983)
Hulme, Kathryn (1900–1981)
Walentynowicz, Anna (1929—)

SHOE DESIGNER
Ferragamo, Fiamma (1941–1998)
Wright, Maginel (1881–1966)

SHOP KEEPER
See Merchant/Trader.

SHORT-FICTION WRITER
Adams, Alice (1926–1999)
Agaoglu, Adalet (1929—)
Aichinger, Ilse (1921—)
Aidoo, Ama Ata (1942—)
Alba, Nanina (1915–1968)
Alcott, Louisa May (1832–1888)
Aldecoa, Josefina R. (1926—)
Aldrich, Bess Streeter (1881–1954)
Allingham, Margery (1904–1966)
Anderson, Barbara (1926—)
Andresen, Sophia de Mello Breyner (1919–2004)
Angel, Albalucía (1939—)
Anneke, Mathilde Franziska (1817–1884)
Annenkova-Bernár, Nina Pávlovna (1859/64–1933)
Apréleva, Elena Ivanovna (1846–1923)
Arceo, Liwayway (1924—)
Ariyoshi, Sawako (1931–1984)
Arnow, Harriette Simpson (1908–1986)
Ashton-Warner, Sylvia (1908–1984)
Astley, Thea (1925–2004)
Atherton, Gertrude (1857–1948)
Austen, Jane (1775–1817)
Austin, Mary Hunter (1868–1934)
Avilova, Lidya (c. 1864–1943)
Bacewicz, Grazyna (1909–1969)
Bailey, Carolyn Sherwin (1875–1961)
Bailey, Hannah Johnston (1839–1923)
Bailey, Temple (c. 1869–1953)
Baldwin, Faith (1893–1978)
Bambara, Toni Cade (1939–1995)
Banning, Margaret Culkin (1891–1982)
Baranskaya, Natalia (b. 1908)
Barker, A.L. (1918–2002)
Barnes, Djuna (1892–1982)
Barnes, Zadel (1841–1917)
Barrington, Margaret (1896–1982)
Barroso, Maria Alice (1926—)
Baum, Vicki (1888–1960)
Baynton, Barbara (1857–1929)
Beattie, Ann (1947—)
Beatty, Bessie (1886–1947)
Beauvoir, Simone de (1908–1986)
Becher, Lilly (1901–1976)
Bellamy, Madge (1899–1990)
Belloc-Lowndes, Marie (1868–1947)
Benson, Sally (1900–1972)
Benson, Stella (1892–1933)
Bentley, Phyllis (1894–1977)
Ben-Yehuda, Hemda (1873–1951)
Berggolts, Olga (1910–1975)
Bernard, Catherine (1662–1712)
Bernhardi, Sophie (1775–1833)
Bernstein, Aline (1882–1955)
Besant, Annie (1847–1933)
Betham-Edwards, Matilda (1836–1919)
Betts, Doris (1932—)
Bhandari, Mannu (1931—)
Binnuna, Khanatta (1940—)
Bjarklind, Unnur Benediktsdóttir (1881–1946)
Blanc, Marie-Thérèse (1840–1907)
Blum, Klara (1904–1971)
Böhl von Faber, Cecilia (1796–1877)
Bonanni, Laudomia (1907–2002)
Bonner, Marita (1899–1971)
Bonner, Sherwood (1849–1883)
Bottome, Phyllis (1884–1963)
Bowen, Elizabeth (1899–1973)
Bowles, Jane (1917–1973)
Boyle, Kay (1902–1992)
Brackett, Leigh (1915–1978)
Braga, Maria Ondina (1932–2003)
Brant, Beth (1941—)
Brewster, Anne Hampton (1818–1892)
Brewster, Elizabeth (1922—)
Bridger, Bub (1924—)
Bright, Mary Golding (1857–1945)
Brovar, Anna Iakovlevna (1887–1917)
Brown, Alice (1856–1948)
Brunet, Marta (1897–1967)
Buck, Pearl S. (1892–1973)
Butala, Sharon (1940—)
Cadilla de Martínez, Maria (1886–1951)
Cambridge, Ada (1844–1926)
Campbell, Grace MacLennan (1895–1963)
Campbell, Maria (1940—)
Canth, Minna (1844–1897)
Carey, Miriam E. (1858–1937)
Carrington, Leonora (1917—)
Carter, Angela (1940–1992)
Carvalho, Maria Judite de (1921–1998)
Cary, Alice (1820–1871)
Casely-Hayford, Adelaide (1868–1960)
Cash, Rosanne (1955—)
Castellanos, Rosario (1925–1974)
Cather, Willa (1873–1947)
Chand, Meira (1942—)
Chang, Eileen (1920–1995)
Charriere, Isabelle de (1740–1805)
Cheeseman, Clara (1852–1943)
Chen Ruiqing (1932—)
Chen Ruoxi (1938—)
Cherry, Frances (1937—)
Chesebrough, Caroline (1825–1873)
Chopin, Kate (1850–1904)
Christaller, Helene (1872–1953)
Christie, Agatha (1890–1976)
Christine de Pizan (c. 1363–c. 1431)
Chugtai, Ismat (1915–1991)
Clift, Charmian (1923–1969)
Codina, Iverna (1918—)
Cohen, Rose (1880–1925)
Colette (1873–1954)
Collins, Kathleen (1942–1988)
Colonia, Regina Célia (1940—)
Cooper, J. California (1940s—)
Cooper, Susan Fenimore (1813–1894)
Costa, Maria Velho de (b. 1938)
Cottrell, Dorothy (1902–1957)
Coutinho, Sônia (1939—)
Cowley, Joy (1936—)
Craig, Christine (1943—)
Croker, Bithia May (c. 1849–1920)
Dabrowska, Maria (1889–1965)
Daong Khin Khin Lay (1913—)

D'Arcy, Ella (c. 1856–1937)
Dargan, Olive Tilford (1869–1968)
Dark, Eleanor (1901–1985)
Davis, Rebecca Harding (1831–1910)
Daw Khin Myo Chit (1915–2003)
Daw San San (1944–1990)
de Alonso, Carmen (1909—)
de la Roche, Mazo (1879–1961)
Deledda, Grazia (1871–1936)
De Lima, Clara Rosa (1923—)
Desai, Anita (1937—)
Deshpande, Shashi (1938—)
Deutsch, Helen (1906–1992)
Devanny, Jean (1894–1962)
Díaz Lozano, Argentina (1912–1999)
Dilke, Emily (1840–1904)
Dinesen, Isak (1885–1962)
Ding Ling (1904–1985)
Ditlevsen, Tove (1917–1976)
Dmitrieva, Valentina (1859–1948)
Domenech i Escate de Canellas, Maria (1877–1952)
Dominguez, María Alicia (1908—)
Dörrie, Doris (1955—)
Dove, Rita (1952—)
Downey, June Etta (1875–1932)
Driscoll, Clara (1881–1945)
du Fresne, Yvonne (1929—)
Dullemen, Inez van (1925—)
du Maurier, Daphne (1907–1989)
Dunbar-Nelson, Alice (1875–1935)
Dupuy, Eliza Ann (1814–1881)
Dworkin, Andrea (1946–2005)
Eberhart, Mignon G. (1899–1996)
Edgeworth, Maria (1768–1849)
Elizabeth of Wied (1843–1916)
Elliott, Sarah Barnwell (1848–1928)
Ener, Güner (1935—)
Engel, Marian (1933–1985)
Èngelgardt, Sofia Vladimirovna (1828–1894)
Enright, Elizabeth (1909–1968)
Erbil, Leyla (1931—)
Eristavi-Xostaria, Anastasia (1868–1951)
Espanca, Florbela (1894–1930)
Ewing, Juliana Horatia (1841–1885)
Fagnan, Marie-Antoinette (d. 1770)
Fainlight, Ruth (1931—)
Farjeon, Eleanor (1881–1965)
Farmer, Beverley (1941—)
Fauset, Jessie Redmon (1882–1961)
Feng Keng (1907–1931)
Ferber, Edna (1885–1968)
Fernando, Gilda Cordero (1930—)
Figuli, Margita (1909–1995)
Firestone, Shulamith (1945—)
Fischer, Caroline Auguste (1764–1834)
Fisher, Dorothy Canfield (1879–1958)
Fisher, M.F.K. (1908–1992)
Flanner, Janet (1892–1978)
Fleisser, Marieluise (1901–1974)
Fleming, May Agnes (1840–1880)
Flore, Jeanne (fl. early 16th c.)
Foley, Martha (c. 1897–1977)
Foote, Mary Hallock (1847–1938)
Forbes, Esther (1891–1967)
Forsh, Olga (1873–1961)
Fouqué, Karoline Freifrau de la Motte (1774–1831)
Frame, Janet (1924–2004)
François, Louise von (1817–1893)
Franklin, Miles (1879–1954)
Freeman, Mary E. Wilkins (1852–1930)
French, Alice (1850–1934)
Friedberg, Berta (1864–1944)
Frigerio, Marta Lía (1925–1985)
Frischmuth, Barbara (1941—)
Frohberg, Regina (1783–1850)
Fuertes, Gloria (1917–1998)
Fürüzan (1935—)
Gale, Zona (1874–1938)
Gallant, Mavis (1922—)
Gambaro, Griselda (1928—)
Gándara, Carmen (1900–1977)
Gánina, Maja (1927—)
Gardener, Helen Hamilton (1853–1925)
Garg, Mridula (1938—)
Garner, Helen (1942—)
Garro, Elena (1916–1998)
Gaskell, Elizabeth (1810–1865)
Gaunt, Mary (1861–1942)
Gautier, Judith (1845–1917)
Gellhorn, Martha (1908–1998)
Gerould, Katharine (1879–1944)
Gertsyk, Adelaida (1874–1925)
Gibbons, Stella (1902–1989)
Gilchrist, Ellen (1935—)
Gilliatt, Penelope (1932–1993)
Gilman, Caroline Howard (1794–1888)
Gippius, Zinaida (1869–1945)
Girardin, Delphine (1804–1855)
Giroud, Françoise (1916–2003)
Glaspell, Susan (1876–1948)
Glümer, Claire von (1825–1906)
Glyn, Elinor (1864–1943)
Goldberg, Lea (1911–1970)
Gordimer, Nadine (1923—)
Gordon, Caroline (1895–1981)
Goudge, Elizabeth (1900–1984)
Goudvis, Bertha (1876–1966)
Grace, Patricia (1937—)
Gramcko, Ida (1924–1994)
Grau, Shirley Ann (1929—)
Griffith, Nanci (1953—)
Grimké, Angelina Weld (1880–1958)
Grimshaw, Beatrice (c. 1870–1953)
Gritsi-Milliex, Tatiana (1920—)
Grogger, Paula (1892–1984)
Grossmann, Judith (1931—)
Grové, Henriette (1922—)
Guglielminetti, Amalia (1881–1941)
Guido, Beatriz (1924—)
Guimarães Peixoto Bretas, Ana Lins do (1889–1985)
Guy, Rosa (1925—)
Guy-Blaché, Alice (1875–1968)
Hale, Nancy (1908–1988)
Hall, Radclyffe (1880–1943)
Han Aili (1937—)
Handel-Mazzetti, Enrica von (1871–1955)
Handzová, Viera (1931–1997)
Hanrahan, Barbara (1939–1991)
Hansberry, Lorraine (1930–1965)
Harraden, Beatrice (1864–1936)
Harrison, Susie Frances (1859–1935)
Harry, Myriam (1869–1958)
Haven, Emily Bradley Neal (1827–1863)
Hayashi Fumiko (1903–1951)
Hazzard, Shirley (1931—)
Head, Bessie (1937–1986)
Hébert, Anne (1916—)
Helburn, Theresa (1887–1959)
Hendel, Yehudit (1926—)
Hentz, Caroline Lee (1800–1856)
Herbst, Josephine (1892–1969)
Highsmith, Patricia (1921–1995)
Higuchi, Ichiyo (1872–1896)
Hill, Susan (1942—)
Hilst, Hilda (1930—)
Hindmarch, Gladys (1940—)
Hineira, Arapera (1932—)
Hobson, Laura Z. (1900–1986)
Hoffman, Alice (1952—)
Hogan, Linda (1947—)
Hollingworth, Leta Stetter (1886–1939)
Holtby, Winifred (1898–1935)
Hopkins, Pauline E. (1859–1930)
Hosain, Attia (1913–1998)
Hospital, Janette Turner (1942—)
Hossain, Rokeya Sakhawat (1880–1932)
Hoult, Norah (1898–1984)
Howes, Barbara (1914–1996)
Huang Zongying (1925—)
Huber, Therese (1764–1829)
Huch, Ricarda (1864–1947)
Hull, Helen Rose (1888–1971)
Hunt, Violet (1866–1942)
Hunter, Kristin (1931—)
Hunter, Mollie (1922—)
Hurst, Fannie (1889–1968)
Hurston, Zora Neale (c. 1891–1960)
Idlibi, 'Ulfah al- (1912—)
Inber, Vera (1890–1972)
Ingelow, Jean (1820–1897)
Irwin, Inez Haynes (1873–1970)
Iyall, Debora (1954—)
Jackson, Alice (1887–1974)
Jackson, Shirley (1916–1965)
Jacobsen, Josephine (1908–2003)
Jakobsdóttir, Svava (1930—)
Jalandoni, Magdalena (1891–1978)
Jameson, Storm (1891–1986)
Janitschek, Maria (1859–1927)
Jansson, Tove (1914–2001)
Jelsma, Clara Mitsuko (1931—)
Jesenská, Ružena (1863–1940)
Jesse, Fryniwyd Tennyson (1888–1958)
Jewett, Sarah Orne (1849–1909)
Jewsbury, Maria Jane (1800–1833)
Jhabvala, Ruth Prawer (1927—)
Johnson, E. Pauline (1861–1913)
Johnson, Helene (1906–1995)
Johnson, Josephine Winslow (1910–1990)
Jolley, Elizabeth (1923—)
Jonker, Ingrid (1933–1965)
Jordan, Elizabeth Garver (1865–1947)
Jotuni, Maria (1880–1943)
Jurado, Alicia (1915—)
Kadaré, Elena (1943—)
Kaffka, Margit (1880–1918)
Karodia, Farida (1942—)
Karr, Carme (1865–1943)
Kaschnitz, Marie Luise (1901–1974)
Kautsky, Minna (1837–1912)
Kavan, Anna (1901–1968)
Kavanagh, Julia (1824–1877)
Kazantzis, Judith (1940—)
Kelly, Gwen (1922—)
Kelly, Maeve (1930—)
Kenny, Alice Annie (1875–1960)
Kerr, Sophie (1880–1965)
Khuri, Colette (1937—)
Khvoshchinskaia, Sofia (1828–1865)
Kiengsiri, Kanha (1911—)
Kilpi, Eeva (1928—)
Kimenye, Barbara (1940—)
Kincaid, Jamaica (1949—)
King, Grace Elizabeth (c. 1852–1932)
Kirpishchikova, Anna (1848–1927)
Kirsch, Sarah (1935—)
Kobiakova, Aleksandra (1823–1892)
Kobrynska, Natalia Ivanovna (1855–1920)
Kobylianska, Olha (1863–1942)
Koea, Shonagh (1939—)
Kola, Pamela
Königsdorf, Helga (1938—)
Konopnicka, Maria (1842–1910)
Kossak, Zofia (1890–1968)
Krandievskaya, Anastasiia (1865–1938)

Kryzhanovskaia, Vera Ivanovna (1861–1924)
Kurahashi, Yumiko (1935—)
Kurz, Isolde (1853–1944)
Lafite, Marie-Elisabeth Bouée de (c. 1750–1794)
La Flesche, Susette (1854–1902)
Laforet, Carmen (1921–2004)
Lagerlöf, Selma (1858–1940)
Lagorio, Gina (1930—)
Laisse, Madame de (fl. 18th c.)
Landau, Klavdia Gustavovna (1922–1990)
Langgässer, Elisabeth (1899–1950)
Lapid, Shulamit (1934—)
Lappo-Danilevskaia, N.A. (c. 1875–1951)
Larsen, Nella (1891–1964)
Laskaridou, Aikaterini (1842–1916)
Laurence, Margaret (1926–1987)
Lavin, Mary (1912–1996)
Lawson, Louisa (1848–1920)
Leadbetter, Mary (1758–1826)
Lee, Harper (1926—)
Le Givre de Richebourg, Madame (1710–1780)
Lehmann, Beatrix (1903–1979)
Lehmann, Rosamond (1901–1990)
Leonardos, Stela (1923—)
Lessing, Doris (1919—)
Le Sueur, Meridel (1900–1996)
Levesque, Louise Cavelier (1703–1743)
Levinson, Luisa Mercedes (1909–1988)
Lewald, Fanny (1811–1889)
L'Héritier, Marie-Jeanne (1664–1734)
Liebrecht, Savyon (1948—)
Li Huixin (1937—)
Ling Shuhua (1904–1990)
Lin Haiyin (1918–2001)
Linskill, Mary (1840–1891)
Lipson, Edna (1914–1996)
Lispector, Clarice (1920–1977)
Litchfield, Jessie (1883–1956)
Litvinov, Ivy (1889–1977)
Liu, Nienling (1934—)
Liu Zhen (1930—)
Longhi, Lucia Lopresti (1895–1985)
Loos, Anita (1893–1981)
Louw, Anna M. (1913–2003)
Loy, Rosetta (1931—)
Lubert, Mlle de (c. 1710–c. 1779)
Luce, Clare Boothe (1903–1987)
Lukhmanova, N.A. (1840–1907)
Luo Shu (1903–1938)
Lussan, Marguerite de (1682–1758)
Lu Yin (1899–1934)
Lyttelton, Edith Joan (1873–1945)
Macardle, Dorothy (1889–1958)
MacDonald, Betty (1908–1958)
MacDonald, Elizabeth Roberts (1864–1922)
MacEwen, Gwendolyn (1941–1987)
MacFall, Frances E. (1854–1943)
Machar, Agnes Maule (1837–1927)
MacManus, Anna Johnston (1866–1902)
Majerovç, Marie (1882–1967)
Makarova, Elena (1951—)
Maksimovic, Desanka (1898–1993)
Malpede, Karen (1945—)
Manley, Mary de la Rivière (1663–1724)
Manner, Eeva-Liisa (1921–1995)
Manning, Marie (c. 1873–1945)
Manning, Olivia (1908–1980)
Mansfield, Katherine (1888–1923)
Mansilla de García, Eduarda (1838–1892)
Manzini, Gianna (1896–1974)
Maraini, Dacia (1936—)
Maranhão, Heloísa (1925—)
Marchenko, Anastasiia Iakovlevna (1830–1880)
Marie de France (c. 1140–1200)
Marion, Frances (1888–1973)
Markham, Beryl (1902–1986)
Marriott, Anne (1913–1997)
Marshall, Joyce (1913—)
Marshall, Paule Burke (1929—)
Martineau, Harriet (1802–1876)
Martín Gaite, Carmen (1925—)
Martinson, Moa (1890–1964)
Mason, Bobbie Ann (1940—)
Masters, Olga (1919–1986)
Mathis, June (1892–1927)
Matute, Ana Maria (1926—)
Mayhar, Ardath (1930—)
Mayne, Ethel Colburn (1865–1941)
Mayor, Flora M. (1872–1932)
Mayreder, Rosa (1858–1938)
McCaffrey, Anne (1926—)
McClung, Nellie L. (1873–1951)
McCue, Lillian de la Torre Bueno (1902–1993)
McCullers, Carson (1917–1967)
McIntyre, Vonda N. (1948—)
McLean, Kathryn (1909–1966)
McMein, Neysa (1888–1949)
Mechtel, Angelika (1943–2000)
Medio, Dolores (1914–1996)
Meigs, Cornelia Lynde (1884–1973)
Merril, Judith (1923–1997)
Mew, Charlotte (1869–1928)
Meyer, Annie Nathan (1867–1951)
Meynell, Viola (1886–1956)
Michaëlis, Karin (1872–1950)
Miegel, Agnes (1879–1964)
Militsyna, Elizaveta Mitrofanovna (1869–1930)
Millar, Margaret (1915–1994)
Millican, Arthenia J. Bates (1920—)
Millin, Sarah (1888–1968)
Mitchell, Margaret (1900–1949)
Mitchison, Naomi (1897–1999)
Mohr, Nicholasa (1935—)
Molesworth, Mary Louisa (1839–1921)
Monnet, Marie Moreau (1752–1798)
Montgomery, Lucy Maud (1874–1942)
Montvid, A.S. (b. 1845)
Moon, Lorna (1886–1930)
Morante, Elsa (1912–1985)
Morris, Janet E. (1946—)
Mukherjee, Bharati (1938—)
Mukoda, Kuniko (1929–1981)
Mulkerns, Val (1925—)
Munro, Alice (1931—)
Murat, Henriette Julie de (1670–1716)
Murfree, Mary N. (1850–1922)
Mvungi, Martha
Nagródskaia, Evdokiia (1866–1930)
Naranjo, Carmen (1928—)
Nasralla, Emily (1931—)
Naylor, Gloria (1950—)
Nedreaas, Torborg (1906–1987)
Negri, Ada (1870–1945)
Nesbit, Edith (1858–1924)
Nieh Hualing (1925—)
Niese, Charlotte (1854–1935)
Niles, Blair (1880–1959)
Nin, Anais (1903–1977)
Njau, Rebeka (1932—)
Norris, Kathleen (1880–1966)
Nováková, Teréza (1853–1912)
Oates, Joyce Carol (1938—)
O'Brien, Edna (1930—)
Ocampo, Silvina (1903–1993)
O'Connor, Flannery (1925–1964)
O'Faolain, Julia (1932—)
Ogot, Grace (1930—)
Oliphant, Margaret (1828–1897)
Olivier, Edith (c. 1879–1948)
Olsen, Tillie (c. 1912—)
O'Neill, Rose Cecil (1874–1944)
Opie, Amelia (1769–1853)
Orphee, Elvira (1930—)
Ortese, Anna Maria (1914–1998)
Orzeszkowa, Eliza (1841–1910)
Osten, Maria (1908–1942)
Otto-Peters, Luise (1819–1895)
Owens, Claire Myers (1896–1983)
Ozick, Cynthia (1928—)
Paget, Violet (1856–1935)
Palacios, Lucila (1902–1994)
Paley, Grace (1922—)
Palli, Angelica (1798–1875)
Palmer, Nettie (1885–1964)
Panaeva, Avdotia (c. 1819–1893)
Panova, Vera (1905–1973)
Papadopoulou, Alexandra (1867–1906)
Pardo Bazán, Emilia (1852–1921)
Pardoe, Julia (1804–1862)
Paretsky, Sara (1947—)
Park, Ruth (c. 1923—)
Parker, Dorothy (1893–1967)
Parra, Teresa de la (1889–1936)
Patton, Frances Gray (1906–2000)
Pauli, Hertha (1909–1973)
Peabody, Josephine Preston (1874–1922)
Pearce, Philippa (1920—)
Pelletier, Madeleine (1874–1939)
Percoto, Caterina (1812–1887)
Peri Rossi, Cristina (1941—)
Petit, Magdalena (1900–1968)
Petrushevskaya, Ludmilla (1938—)
Phillips, Lena Madesin (1881–1955)
Pickthall, Marjorie (1883–1922)
Pilcher, Rosamunde (1924—)
Piñon, Nélida (1937—)
Plá, Josefina (1909–1999)
Plath, Sylvia (1932–1963)
Plisson, Marie-Prudence (1727–1788)
Poisson, Madeleine-Angelique (1684–1770)
Poletti, Syria (1919–1991)
Polier, Marie-Elizabeth (1742–1817)
Pollard, Velma (1937—)
Pompeia, Núria (1938—)
Poniatowska, Elena (1932—)
Portal, Marta (1930—)
Porter, Anna Maria (1780–1832)
Porter, Eleanor H. (1868–1920)
Porter, Jane (1776–1850)
Porter, Katherine Anne (1890–1980)
Portillo-Trambley, Estela (1936–1999)
Post, Emily (1872–1960)
Powell, Dawn (1897–1965)
Prado, Adélia (1936—)
Preissova, Gabriela (1862–1946)
Pritam, Amrita (1919–2005)
Prosperi, Carola (1883–1975)
Przybyszewska, Dagny Juel (1867–1901)
Queirós, Raquel de (1910–2003)
Rafanelli, Leda (1880–1971)
Ramondino, Fabrizia (1936—)
Randall, Marta (1948—)
Rashid, Saleha Abdul (1939—)
Ravikovitch, Dahlia (1936—)
Rawlings, Marjorie Kinnan (1896–1953)
Rawlinson, Gloria (1918–1995)
Reed, Kit (1932—)
Reed, Myrtle (1874–1911)
Rendell, Ruth (1930—)
Repplier, Agnes (1855–1950)
Rhys, Jean (1890–1979)
Richards, Laura E. (1850–1943)
Richardson, Henry Handel (1870–1946)
Rickert, Edith (1871–1938)
Riddell, Charlotte (1832–1906)
Rifaat, Alifa (1930–1996)
Rinehart, Mary Roberts (1876–1958)
Rinser, Luise (1911–2002)

Ritter, Erika (1948—)
Roberts, Elizabeth Madox (1881–1941)
Roberts, Kate (1891–1985)
Roberts, Sheila (1937—)
Robins, Elizabeth (1862–1952)
Rodoreda, Mercè (1909–1983)
Rodriguez, Judith (1936—)
Romano, Lalla (1906–2001)
Rosca, Ninotchka (1941—)
Ross, Violet Florence (1862–1915)
Royde-Smith, Naomi Gwladys (1875–1964)
Rubens, Bernice (1928–2004)
Rule, Jane (1931—)
Runeberg, Fredrika (1807–1879)
Ru Zhijuan (1925—)
Ryum, Ulla (1937—)
Saburova, Irina (1907–1979)
Sackville-West, Vita (1892–1962)
Sadlier, Mary Anne (1820–1903)
Sagan, Françoise (1935–2004)
Saint-Chamond, Claire-Marie Mazarelli, Marquise de La Vieuville de (1731–?)
Sandel, Cora (1880–1974)
Sanders, Dorothy Lucie (1903–1987)
Santos Arrascaeta, Beatriz (1947—)
Sanvitale, Francesca (1928—)
Saranti, Galateia (1920—)
Sarton, May (1912–1995)
Satthianadhan, Krupabai (1862–1894)
Savary, Olga (1933—)
Sawyer, Caroline M. Fisher (1812–1894)
Sayers, Dorothy L. (1893–1957)
Schoultz, Solveig von (1907–1996)
Schreiner, Olive (1855–1920)
Schubert, Helga (1940—)
Schutting, Julian (1937—)
Scott, Rosie (1948—)
Scudéry, Madeleine de (1607–1701)
Segun, Mabel (1930—)
Seid, Ruth (1913–1995)
Seifullina, Lydia (1889–1954)
Sekulić, Isadora (1877–1958)
Senior, Olive (1941—)
Serao, Matilde (1856–1927)
Serrano, Eugenia (1918—)
Serreau, Geneviève (1915–1981)
Sewell, Anna (1820–1878)
Shange, Ntozake (1948—)
Shapir, Olga (1850–1916)
Shaw, Flora (1852–1929)
Shaw, Helen (1913–1985)
Sherwood, Mary Elizabeth (1826–1903)
Shields, Carol (1935–2003)
Silko, Leslie Marmon (1948—)
Silva Vila, María Inés (1926—)
Simpson, Helen (1897–1940)
Sinclair, May (1863–1946)
Skinner, Constance Lindsay (1877–1939)
Skram, Amalie (1846–1905)
Slancikova, Bozena (1867–1951)
Slesinger, Tess (1905–1945)
Smiley, Jane (1949—)
Smirnova, Sofia (1852–1921)
Smith, Pauline (1882–1959)
Smith, Stevie (1902–1971)
Sobti, Krishna (1925—)
Sokhanskaia, Nadezhda (1823–1884)
Solano, Solita (1888–1975)
Solinas Donghi, Beatrice (1923—)
Somers, Armonía (1914–1994)
Somerville, E. (1858–1949)
Somerville and Ross
Sontag, Susan (1933–2004)
Soysal, Sevgi (1936–1976)
Spark, Muriel (1918—)
Spencer, Elizabeth (1921—)
Spofford, Harriet Prescott (1835–1921)
St. Johns, Adela Rogers (1894–1988)
Stafford, Jean (1915–1979)
Stead, Christina (1902–1983)
Steel, Flora Annie (1847–1929)
Stein, Gertrude (1874–1946)
Stephens, Ann S. (1810–1886)
Stern, G.B. (1890–1973)
Stockley, Cynthia (1872–1936)
Stolk, Gloria (1918–1979)
Story, Gertrude (1929—)
Stowe, Harriet Beecher (1811–1896)
Strauss und Torney, Lulu von (1873–1956)
Strong, Eithne (1923–1999)
Stuart, Ruth McEnery (c. 1849–1917)
Sturm, J.C. (1927—)
Suckow, Ruth (1892–1960)
Summers, Merna (1933—)
Sutherland, Efua (1924–1996)
Sutherland, Margaret (1941—)
Swenson, May (1913–1989)
Taber, Gladys (1899–1980)
Taggard, Genevieve (1894–1948)
Tan, Amy (1952—)
Tarnow, Fanny (1779–1862)
Taylor, Ann (1782–1866)
Taylor, Elizabeth (1912–1975)
Taylor, Jane (1783–1824)
Teffi, N.A. (1872–1952)
Telles, Lygia Fagundes (1923—)
Tennant, Kylie (1912–1988)
Terán, Ana Enriqueta (1919—)
Terhune, Mary Virginia (1830–1922)
Tesky, Adeline Margaret (c. 1850–1924)
Texidor, Greville (1902–1964)
Thirkell, Angela (1890–1961)
Thomas, Caitlin (1913–1994)
Thompson, Eloise Bibb (1878–1928)
Thorup, Kirsten (1942—)
Tiempo, Edith L. (1919—)
Tinayre, Marcelle (c. 1870–1948)
Tlali, Miriam (1933—)
Tokareva, Viktoria (1937—)
Tolstaya, Tatyana (1951—)
Tracy, Mona Innis (1892–1959)
Travers, P.L. (1906–1996)
Trefusis, Violet (1894–1972)
Triolet, Elsa (1896–1970)
Tsushima, Yuko (1947—)
Turner, Eliza Sproat (1826–1903)
Ty-Casper, Linda (1931—)
Tyler, Anne (1941—)
Tynan, Katharine (1861–1931)
Uchida, Yoshiko (1921–1992)
Ullrich, Luise (1911–1985)
Undset, Sigrid (1882–1949)
Valenzuela, Luisa (1938—)
Vanderbilt, Gloria (1924—)
Vaz Ferreira, María Eugenia (1875–1924)
Vega, Ana Lydia (1946—)
Venttsel, Elena Sergeevna (1907–2002)
Verbitskaia, Anastasiia (1861–1928)
Vertua Gentile, Anna (1850–1927)
Veselitskaia, Lidiia Ivanovna (1857–1936)
Vidal, Mary Theresa (1815–1869 or 1873)
Viebig, Clara (1860–1952)
Vik, Bjørg (1935—)
Vilinska, Mariya (1834–1907)
Villarino, María de (1905–1994)
Villinger, Hermine (1849–1917)
Vinge, Joan D. (1948—)
Vivanti, Annie (1868–1942)
Voigt-Diederichs, Helene (1875–1961)
Von Nagy, Käthe (1909–1973)
Vorse, Mary Heaton (1874–1966)
Voznesenskaya, Julia (1940—)
Vrugt, Johanna Petronella (1905–1960)
Vuyk, Beb (1905–1991)
Walker, Alice (1944—)
Wallace, Bronwen (1945–1989)
Wandor, Michelene (1940—)
Ward, Elizabeth Stuart Phelps (1844–1911)
Warner, Marina (1946—)
Warner, Sylvia Townsend (1893–1978)
Watson, Jean (1933—)
Watson, Sheila (1909–1998)
Webb, Mary (1881–1927)
Webster, Jean (1876–1916)
Wei Junyi (1917–2002)
Weingarten, Violet (1915–1976)
Weinzweig, Helen (1915—)
Wells, Carolyn (1862–1942)
Welty, Eudora (1909–2001)
Wentscher, Dora (1883–1964)
Wen Xiaoyu (1938—)
West, Dorothy (1907–1998)
West, Jessamyn (1902–1984)
Wharton, Edith (1862–1937)
White, Eliza Orne (1856–1947)
Whitney, Gertrude Vanderbilt (1875–1942)
Wiggin, Kate Douglas (1856–1923)
Wijenaike, Punyakanthi (1935—)
Wildermuth, Ottilie (1817–1877)
Wilhelm, Kate (1928—)
Willis, Connie (1945—)
Wilson, Ethel (1888–1980)
Wilson, Margaret W. (1882–1973)
Winter, John Strange (1856–1911)
Wohmann, Gabriele (1932—)
Wolf, Christa (1929—)
Wolfenstein, Martha (1869–1905)
Wolff, Victoria (1903–1992)
Wood, Ellen Price (1814–1887)
Woodrow, Nancy Mann Waddel (c. 1866–1935)
Woolf, Virginia (1882–1941)
Woolson, Constance Fenimore (1840–1894)
Wootton, Barbara (1897–1988)
Wordsworth, Dorothy (1771–1855)
Wright, Judith (1915–2000)
Wright, Martha Coffin (1806–1875)
Wylie, Elinor (1885–1928)
Wylie, Ida A.R. (1885–1959)
Xiao Hong (1911–1942)
Xie Wanying (1900–1999)
Yanaranop, Sukanya (1931—)
Yáñez, María Flora (1898–1982)
Yessayan, Zabel (1878–1943)
Ye Wenling (1942—)
Yezierska, Anzia (c. 1881–1970)
Yonge, Charlotte Mary (1823–1901)
Yu Lihua (1932—)
Zani, Giselda (1909–1975)
Zayas y Sotomayor, María de (1590–c. 1650)
Zelinová, Hana (b. 1914)
Zetterling, Mai (1925–1994)
Zhadovskaia, Iuliia Valerianovna (1824–1883)
Zhang Jie (1937—)
Zhukova, Maria (1804–1855)
Zinner, Hedda (1902–1990)
Zinóveva-Annibal, Lidiia Dmitrievna (1866–1907)
Zitz, Kathinka (1801–1877)
Zong Pu (1928—)
Zürn, Unica (1916–1970)
Zwicky, Fay (1933—)

SHOTPUTTER
See Track-and-field athlete.

SIBYL
See Prophet/sibyl/visionary.

SILENT-FILM ACTRESS

Adams, Claire (1898–1978)
Adams, Kathryn (1893–1959)
Alden, Mary (1883–1946)
Allison, May (1890–1989)
Anderson, Claire (1895–1964)
Anderson, Mignon (1892–1983)
Andra, Fern (1893–1974)
Anson, Laura (1892–1968)
Arthur, Jean (1900–1991)
Arvidson, Linda (1884–1949)
Astor, Gertrude (1887–1977)
Astor, Mary (1906–1987)
Ayres, Agnes (1896–1940)
Badgley, Helen (1908–1977)
Balfour, Betty (1903–1979)
Ball, Lucille (1911–1989)
Ballin, Mabel (1887–1958)
Bankhead, Tallulah (1902–1968)
Banky, Vilma (1898–1991)
Bara, Theda (1885–1955)
Basquette, Lina (1907–1995)
Bayne, Beverly (1894–1982)
Beavers, Louise (1902–1962)
Bedford, Barbara (1903–1981)
Bell, Marie (1900–1985)
Bellamy, Madge (1899–1990)
Bennett, Alma (1889–1958)
Bennett, Constance (1904–1965)
Bergner, Elisabeth (1897–1986)
Bernhardt, Sarah (1844–1923)
Billington, Francelia (1895–1934)
Binney, Constance (1896–1989)
Blane, Sally (1910–1997)
Blythe, Betty (1893–1972)
Boardman, Eleanor (1898–1991)
Bonner, Margerie (1905–1988)
Borden, Olive (1906–1947)
Borgström, Hilda (1871–1953)
Bow, Clara (1904–1965)
Brady, Alice (1892–1939)
Breamer, Sylvia (1897–1943)
Brent, Evelyn (1899–1975)
Brian, Mary (1906–2002)
Brooks, Louise (1906–1985)
Bruce, Kate (1858–1946)
Burke, Billie (1885–1970)
Calhoun, Alice (1900–1966)
Calvert, Catherine (1890–1971)
Caprice, June (1899–1936)
Carter, Mrs. Leslie (1862–1937)
Chadwick, Helene (1897–1940)
Childers, Naomi (1892–1964)
Claire, Ina (1892–1985)
Clark, Marguerite (1883–1940)
Clarke, Betty Ross (1896–1947)
Clayton, Marguerite (1891–1968)
Colbert, Claudette (1903–1996)
Compton, Fay (1894–1978)
Cooper, Edna Mae (1900–1986)
Cooper, Miriam (1891–1976)
Corda, Maria (1898–1975)
Cornwall, Anne (1897–1980)
Costello, Helene (1903–1957)
Craig, Nell (1891–1965)
Crawford, Joan (1906–1977)
Cunard, Grace (c. 1891–1967)
Dagover, Lil (1897–1980)
Damita, Lili (1901–1994)
Dana, Viola (1897–1987)
Daniels, Bebe (1901–1971)
Darmond, Grace (1898–1963)
Darwell, Jane (1879–1967)
Davies, Marion (1897–1961)
d'Avril, Yola (1907–1984)
Daw, Marjorie (1902–1979)
Dawn, Hazel (1891–1988)
Day, Alice (1905–1995)
Day, Marceline (1907–2000)
Dean, Priscilla (1896–1987)
DeHaven, Flora (1883–1950)
De La Motte, Marguerite (1902–1950)
Dempster, Carol (1901–1991)
De Rue, Carmen (1908–1986)
Devore, Dorothy (1899–1976)
Doscher, Doris (1882–1970)
Dove, Billie (1900–1997)
Dressler, Marie (1869–1934)
Du Pont, Patricia (1894–1973)
Duse, Eleonora (1858–1924)
Eddy, Helen Jerome (1897–1990)
Eline, Marie (1902–1981)
Elliott, Maxine (1868–1940)
Eyton, Bessie (1890–1965)
Faire, Virginia Brown (1904–1980)
Falconetti, Renée (1892–1946)
Fischer, Margarita (1886–1975)
Forde, Eugenie (1879–1940)
Forrest, Ann (1895–1985)
Francisco, Betty (1900–1950)
Franklin, Alberta (1896–1976)
Garbo, Greta (1905–1990)
Gardner, Helen (1884–1968)
Gaynor, Janet (1906–1984)
George, Gladys (1900–1954)
Gish, Dorothy (1898–1968)
Gish, Lillian (1893–1993)
Glaum, Louise (1894–1970)
Godowsky, Dagmar (1897–1975)
Gordon, Julia Swayne (1878–1933)
Gordon, Ruth (1896–1985)
Goudal, Jetta (1891–1985)
Grandin, Ethel (1894–1988)
Granville, Louise (1895–1968)
Gray, Gilda (1901–1959)
Green, Dorothy (1892–1963)
Griffith, Corinne (1896–1979)
Guinan, Texas (1884–1933)
Hale, Georgia (1905–1985)
Hall, Ella (1896–1982)
Hansen, Juanita (1895–1961)
Harlow, Jean (1911–1937)
Harris, Mildred (1901–1944)
Harte, Betty (c. 1882–1965)
Haver, Phyllis (1899–1960)
Hawley, Wanda (1895–1963)
Holmes, Helen (1892–1950)
Hu Die (1908–1989)
Hulette, Gladys (1896–1991)
Hurlock, Madeline (1899–1989)
Jacobini, Maria (1890–1944)
Janis, Elsie (1889–1956)
Joy, Leatrice (1893–1985)
Keefe, Zena (1896–1977)
Kennedy, Madge (1890–1987)
Kenyon, Doris (1897–1979)
King, Anita (1891–1963)
Kingston, Winifred (1894–1967)
La Marr, Barbara (c. 1896–1926)
La Plante, Laura (1904–1996)
Lee, Jane (c. 1912–1957)
Lee, Jennie (1848–1925)
Lehr, Anna (1890–1974)
Leonard, Marion (1881–1956)
Little, Ann (1891–1984)
Logan, Jacqueline (1901–1983)
Lombard, Carole (1908–1942)
Lorraine, Louise (1901–1981)
Love, Bessie (1898–1986)
Loy, Myrna (1905–1993)
Lyell, Lottie (1890–1925)
MacDonald, Jeanette (1903–1965)
MacDonald, Katherine (1881–1956)
Mack, Marion (1902–1989)
MacLaren, Mary (1896–1985)
Macpherson, Jeanie (1887–1946)
Madison, Cleo (1883–1964)
Maretskaya, Vera (1906–1978)
Marsh, Mae (1895–1968)
May, Doris (1902–1984)
McAvoy, May (1901–1984)
McCoy, Gertrude (1890–1967)
Mersereau, Violet (1892–1975)
Minter, Mary Miles (1902–1984)
Mistinguett (1875–1956)
Mitchell, Rhea (1890–1957)
Moore, Colleen (1902–1988)
Moran, Lois (1907–1990)
Moran, Polly (1884–1952)
Morgan, Helen (1900–1941)
Murray, Mae (1885–1965)
Myers, Carmel (1899–1980)
Naldi, Nita (1897–1961)
Nansen, Betty (1873–1943)
Nazimova, Alla (1879–1945)
Negri, Pola (1894–1987)
Nielsen, Asta (1881–1972)
Niese, Hansi (1875–1934)
Nilsson, Anna Q. (1889–1974)
Nissen, Greta (1906–1988)
Normand, Mabel (1892–1930)
Novak, Eva (1898–1988)
Novak, Jane (1896–1990)
Oakley, Laura (1880–1957)
Oliver, Edna May (1883–1942)
Olmsted, Gertrude (1897–1975)
Ostriche, Muriel (1896–1989)
Oswalda, Ossi (1897–1948)
Owen, Seena (1894–1966)
Pavlova, Anna (1881–1931)
Pearson, Virginia (1886–1958)
Percy, Eileen (1899–1973)
Petrova, Olga (1886–1977)
Philbin, Mary (1903–1993)
Phillips, Dorothy (1889–1980)
Phipps, Sally (1909–1978)
Pickford, Mary (1893–1979)
Pitts, ZaSu (1898–1963)
Porter, Katherine Anne (1890–1980)
Pretty, Arline (1885–1978)
Purviance, Edna (1894–1958)
Quaranta, Isabella (1892–1975)
Quaranta, Letizia (1892–1974)
Quaranta, Lidia (1891–1928)
Ralston, Esther (1902–1994)
Rand, Sally (1904–1979)
Reid, Dorothy Davenport (1895–1977)
Reynolds, Vera (1899–1962)
Rhodes, Billie (1894–1988)
Rich, Irene (1891–1988)
Ridgley, Cleo (1893–1962)
Robson, May (1858–1942)
Rubens, Alma (1897–1931)
Rubenstein, Blanche (c. 1897–1969)
Sawyer, Laura (1885–1970)
Sedgwick, Josie (1898–1973)
Shearer, Norma (1900–1983)
Shipman, Nell (1892–1970)
Snow, Marguerite (1889–1958)
Stanwyck, Barbara (1907–1990)
Starke, Pauline (1900–1977)
Stewart, Anita (1895–1961)
Stonehouse, Ruth (1892–1941)
Swanson, Gloria (1897–1983)
Sweet, Blanche (1895–1986)
Taliaferro, Mabel (1887–1979)
Talmadge, Constance (1897–1973)
Talmadge, Natalie (1897–1969)

Talmadge, Norma (1893–1957)
Tanaka, Kinuyo (1907–1977)
Tanguay, Eva (1878–1947)
Taylor, Estelle (1894–1958)
Thorndike, Sybil (1882–1976)
Traverse, Madlaine (1875–1964)
Valli, Virginia (1895–1968)
Vidor, Florence (1895–1977)
Von Nagy, Käthe (1909–1973)
Walker, Lillian (1887–1975)
Ward, Fannie (1865–1952)
Warfield, Irene (c. 1896–1961)
Westover, Winifred (1899–1978)
White, Chrissie (1894–1989)
White, Pearl (1889–1938)
Whitty, May (1865–1948)
Windsor, Claire (1897–1972)
Wong, Anna May (1907–1961)
Wray, Fay (1907–2004)
Young, Clara Kimball (1890–1960)

SILK-SCREEN ARTIST
Albers, Anni (1899–1994)
Olds, Elizabeth (1896–1991)
Templeton, Rini (1935–1986)

SILVERSMITH
Bateman, Hester (1709–1794)
Courtauld, Louisa (1729–1807)

SINGER
Abbott, Emma (1850–1891)
Abington, Frances (1737–1815)
Abrams, Harriett (c. 1758–c. 1822)
Ackté, Aino (1876–1944)
Adamova, Adela (1927—)
Adams, Edie (1927—)
Adrienne, Jean (b. 1905)
Agnesi, Maria Teresa (1720–1795)
Agnetha Fältskog (1950—)
Ahmad, Fathiyya (c. 1898–1975)
Alais (fl. 12th c.)
Alarie, Pierrette (1921—)
Albanese, Licia (1913—)
Albani, Emma (c. 1847–1930)
Alberghetti, Anna Maria (1936—)
Albertazzi, Emma (1813–1847)
Alboni, Marietta (1823–1894)
Alcantara, Dolores Jimenez (1909–1999)
Alda, Frances (1879–1952)
Allen, Gracie (1902–1964)
Allen, Rosalie (1924–2003)
Allwyn, Astrid (1905–1978)
Alpar, Gitta (1903—)
Aluli, Irmgard (c. 1912–2001)
Amalie of Saxony (1794–1870)
Ameling, Elly (1938—)
Amohau, Merekotia (1898–1978)
Amrouche, Fadhma Mansour (1882–1967)
Andersen, Lale (1905–1972)
Anderson, Ernestine (1928—)
Anderson, Ivie (1904–1949)
Anderson, Judith (1898–1992)
Anderson, Marian (1897–1993)
Andrews, Julie (1935—)
Andrews, LaVerne (1911–1967)
Andrews, Maxene (1916–1995)
Andrews, Nancy (1924–1989)
Andrews, Patti (1918—)
Angelou, Maya (1928—)
Angelus, Muriel (1909–2004)
Archer, Robyn (1948—)
Arden, Toni (fl. 1950s)
Arletty (1898–1992)
Armatrading, Joan (1947—)
Armstrong, Lil Hardin (1898–1971)
Arnell, Amy (1919—)
Arnold, Dorothy (1917–1984)
Arnould, Sophie (1740–1802)
Arroyo, Martina (1935—)
Arthur, Ellen Herndon (1837–1880)
Artôt, Désirée (1835–1907)
Augarde, Amy (1868–1959)
Augarde, Louise (1863–1909)
Azza al-Maila (fl. c. 707)
Bach, Anna Magdalena (1701–1760)
Bacon, Mary (1948–1991)
Baddeley, Sophia (1745–1786)
Badi'a Masabnik
Bahr-Mildenburg, Anna (1872–1947)
Bailey, Mildred (1903–1951)
Bailey, Pearl (1918–1990)
Baillie, Isobel (1895–1983)
Baker, Belle (1893–1957)
Baker, Bonnie (b. 1917)
Baker, Janet (1933—)
Baker, Josephine (1906–1975)
Baker, LaVern (1929–1997)
Balkanska, Mimi (b. 1902)
Ball, Suzan (1933–1950)
Ballard, Florence (1943–1976)
Bampton, Rose (1909—)
Barbi, Alice (1862–1948)
Barbieri, Fedora (1919—)
Barker, Francine (1947—)
Barlow, Billie (1862–1937)
Barnes, Winifred (1894–1935)
Baroni, Leonora (1611–1670)
Barra, Emma de la (1861–1947)
Barrientos, Maria (1884–1946)
Basham, Maud Ruby (1879–1963)
Basile, Adriana (c. 1590–c. 1640)
Batson, Flora (1864–1906)
Bayes, Nora (1880–1928)
Beatty, May (1880–1945)
Beaudet, Louise (1861–1947)
Beechman, Laurie (c. 1955–1998)
Behrens, Hildegard (1937—)
Bejarano, Esther (1924—)
Bell, Marion (1919–1997)
Bellincioni, Gemma (1864–1950)
Beltran, Lola (1932–1996)
Bene, Adriana Gabrieli del (c. 1755–1799)
Bennett, Estelle (1944—)
Bennett, Louise Simone (1919—)
Bentley, Gladys (1907–1960)
Bentley, Irene (d. 1940)
Berberian, Cathy (1925–1983)
Berganza, Teresa (1934—)
Bergen, Nella (1873–1919)
Bergen, Polly (1929—)
Berger, Erna (1900–1990)
Bid'a (856–915)
Bielenberg, Christabel (1909–2003)
Billington, Elizabeth (c. 1765/68–1818)
Birch, Gina (1956—)
Bishop, Ann Rivière (1810–1884)
Black, Cilla (1943—)
Blair, Janet (1921—)
Blanche, Marie (1893—)
Bland, Maria Theresa (1769–1838)
Blyth, Ann (1928—)
Bogan, Lucille (1897–1948)
Bolduc, Marie (1894–1941)
Bond, Jessie (1853–1942)
Bond, Sheila (1928—)
Bond, Sudie (1928–1984)
Bonds, Margaret (1913–1972)
Boninsegna, Celestina (1877–1947)
Booth, Adrian (1918—)
Bordoni, Faustina (c. 1700–1781)
Bori, Lucrezia (1887–1960)
Borkh, Inge (1917—)
Boswell, Connee (1907–1976)
Boyd, Eva (1945–2003)
Bradshaw, Maria (1801–1862)
Braham, Leonora (1853–1931)
Brandt, Marianne (1842–1921)
Branzell, Karin (1891–1974)
Brennan, Maire (1952—)
Brewer, Teresa (1931—)
Brice, Carol (1918–1985)
Brice, Elizabeth (c. 1885–1965)
Brice, Fanny (1891–1951)
Briercliffe, Nellie (1889–1966)
Brightman, Sarah (1960—)
Broderick, Helen (1890–1959)
Brogden, Gwendoline (1891–?)
Bronhill, June (1929–2005)
Bronskaya, Eugenia (1882–1953)
Brooks, Hadda (1916–2002)
Broughton, Phyllis (1862–1926)
Brouwenstijn, Gré (1915—)
Brown, Ada (1889–1950)
Brown, Anna (1747–1810)
Brown, Cleo (1905–1995)
Brown, Georgia (1933–1992)
Brown, Ruth (1928—)
Browne, Marjorie (1910–1990)
Brune, Adrienne (b. 1892)
Brune, Gabrielle (b. 1912)
Brunton, Dorothy (1893–1977)
Bryant, Hazel (1939–1983)
Buchanan, Isobel Wilson (1954—)
Buckingham, Rosetta (c. 1843–1864)
Buckman, Rosina (1881–1948)
Bugarinovic, Melanija (1905–1986)
Burke, Patricia (1917–2003)
Burnand, Lily (1865–?)
Burne, Nancy (1912–1954)
Burnett, Carol (1933—)
Burrell, Daisy (b. 1893)
Bush, Frances Cleveland (d. 1967)
Butt, Clara (1872–1936)
Caballé, Montserrat (1933—)
Caccini, Francesca (1587–c. 1626)
Callas, Maria (1923–1977)
Calloway, Blanche (1902–1973)
Calvé, Emma (1858–1942)
Calypso Rose (1940—)
Camargo, Marie-Anne Cupis de (1710–1770)
Campbell, Judy (1916–2004)
Campbell, Naomi (1970—)
Candeille, Julie (1767–1834)
Canova, Judy (1916–1983)
Cantrell, Lana (1943—)
Capers, Virginia (1925–2004)
Cappiani, Luisa (1835—?)
Cappiani, Luisa (b. 1835)
Carney, Kate (1870–1950)
Carpenter, Constance (1904–1992)
Carpenter, Karen (1950–1983)
Carreño, Teresa (1853–1917)
Carroll, Diahann (1935—)
Carroll, Nancy (1903–1965)
Carter, Anita (1933—)
Carter, Betty (1929–1998)
Carter, Carlene (1955—)
Carter, Helen (1927–1998)
Carter, Jeanette (1923—)
Carter, Maybelle (1909–1978)
Carter, Nell (1948–2003)
Carter, Sarah (1898–1979)
Carus, Emma (1879–1927)
Cary, Annie Louise (1841–1921)
Cash, June Carter (1929—)
Cash, Kellye (c. 1965—)
Castles, Amy (1880–1951)

Casulana, Maddalena (c. 1540–1583)
Catalani, Angelica (1780–1849)
Catley, Ann (1745–1789)
Cavalieri, Caterina (1760–1801)
Cavalieri, Lina (1874–1944)
Cebotari, Maria (1910–1949)
Cecil, Sylvia (1906–1983)
Chapman, Tracy (1964—)
Charles, Suzette (1963—)
Chatwin, Margaret (c. 1881–1937)
Chester, Betty (1895–1943)
Chilcott, Susan (1963–2003)
Cibber, Susannah (1714–1766)
Cicciolina (1951—)
Cigna, Gina (b. 1900)
Cinti-Damoreau, Laure (1801–1863)
Cisneros, Eleonora de (1878–1934)
Clark, Mattie Moss (1929–1998)
Clark Sisters (fl. 1940s)
Clayton, Jan (1917–1983)
Clifford, Kathleen (1887–1962)
Cline, Patsy (1932–1963)
Clive, Kitty (1711–1785)
Clooney, Rosemary (1928–2002)
Coates, Gloria (1938—)
Coca, Imogene (1909–2001)
Cocéa, Alice (1899–1970)
Colbran, Isabella (1785–1845)
Coley, Doris (1941–2000)
Colin, Jean (1905–1989)
Collins, Dorothy (1926–1994)
Collins, José (1887–1958)
Colt, Ethel Barrymore (1912–1977)
Cook, Barbara (1927—)
Coolidge, Priscilla
Cooper, Lillian Kemble (1891–1977)
Cornelys, Theresa (1723–1797)
Cotrubas, Ileana (1939—)
Cotten, Elizabeth (c. 1893–1987)
Cox, Ida (1896–1967)
Cross, Joan (1900–1993)
Crossley, Ada Jemima (1871–1929)
Crouch, Anna Maria (1763–1805)
Cruvelli, Sofia (1826–1907)
Cruz, Celia (1924—)
Cruz, Celia (1924–2003)
Cumming, Ruth (c. 1904–1967)
Cummings, Vicki (1913–1969)
Cunningham, Agnes (1909–2004)
Cushman, Charlotte Saunders (1816–1876)
Cuzzoni, Francesca (c. 1698–1770)
Daley, Cass (1915–1975)
Dalida (1933–1987)
Dal Monte, Toti (1893–1975)
Dananir al Barmakiyya (fl. late 8th c.)
Danco, Suzanne (1911—)
Dandridge, Dorothy (1923–1965)
Daniels, Maxine (1930–2003)
Danzi, Maria Margarethe (1768–1800)
Darrieux, Danielle (1917—)
Darvas, Julia (c. 1919—)
Da Silva, Ana (1949—)
David-Neel, Alexandra (1868–1969)
Davies, Betty Ann (1910–1955)
Davies, Lillian (1895–1932)
Davis, Mary
Dawn, Hazel (1891–1988)
Day, Doris (1924—)
Day, Edith (1896–1971)
Day, Frances (1907–1984)
Debenham, Cicely (1891–1955)
DeHaven, Gloria (1924—)
De La Haye, Ina (1906–1972)
De Leath, Vaughan (1900–1943)
Della Casa, Lisa (1919—)
De Luce, Virginia (1921–1997)
Delysia, Alice (1889–1979)
Denton, Sandy (1969—)
Dernesch, Helga (1939—)
Derzhinskaya, Zeniya (1889–1951)
Desbordes-Valmore, Marceline (1785–1859)
Desmond, Astra (1893–1973)
Destinn, Emmy (1878–1930)
Dickson, Barbara (1947—)
Di Murska, Ilma (1836–1889)
Dixon, Adele (1908–1992)
Donalda, Pauline (1882–1970)
Donaldson, Norma (1928–1994)
D'Orme, Aileen (1877–1939)
Douglas, Helen Gahagan (1900–1980)
Douglas, Lizzie (1897–1973)
Dovey, Alice (1884–1969)
Dragonette, Jessica (1900–1980)
Dumont, Margaret (1889–1965)
Durbin, Deanna (1921—)
Eames, Emma (1865–1952)
Earle, Virginia (1875–1937)
Eaton, Mary (1901–1948)
Edvina, Louise (1878–1948)
Eggerth, Marta (1912—)
Egyptian Singers and Entrepreneurs (fl. 1920s)
Eisinger, Irene (1903–1994)
Eisler, Charlotte (1894–1970)
Elias, Rosalind (1930—)
Elliot, Cass (1941–1974)
Ellis, Mary (1897–2003)
Elsom, Isobel (1893–1981)
Enya (1961—)
Eskenazi, Roza (c. 1900–1980)
Etting, Ruth (1896–1978)
Evans, Nancy (1915–2000)
Everett, Betty (1939–2001)
Fabray, Nanette (1920—)
Fadl (d. ca. 870)
Fairuz (1935—)
Farida (c. 830–?)
Farrar, Geraldine (1882–1967)
Farrar, Gwen (1899–1944)
Farrell, Eileen (1920–2002)
Fassbaender, Brigitte (1939—)
Fathiyya Ahmad (c. 1898–1975)
Favart, Edmée (1886–1941)
Favart, Marie (1727–1772)
Faye, Alice (1912–1998)
Fel, Marie (1713–1794)
Fénelon, Fania (1918–1983)
Ferrari, Carlotta (1837–1907)
Ferrier, Kathleen (1912–1953)
Fields, Gracie (1898–1979)
Finch, Jennifer (1966—)
Fitzgerald, Ella (1917–1996)
Fitzgerald, Lillian (d. 1947)
Flagstad, Kirsten (1895–1962)
Flores, Lola (1924–1995)
Ford, Mary (1924–1977)
Forde, Florrie (1876–1940)
Fornia, Rita (1878–1922)
Forrest, Helen (1918–1999)
Foster, Susanna (1924—)
Fox, Charlotte Milligan (1864–1916)
Fox, Della (1870–1913)
Francine, Anne (1917–1999)
Francis, Connie (1938—)
Frasca, Mary (d. 1973)
Fraser, Agnes (1877–1968)
Frazee, Jane (1918–1985)
Fremstad, Olive (1871–1951)
Freni, Mirella (1935—)
Friganza, Trixie (1870–1955)
Froman, Jane (1907–1980)
Fubuki, Koshiji (1924–1980)
Gaal, Franciska (1904–1972)
Galli-Curci, Amelita (1882–1963)
Ganser, Marge (c. 1948–1996)
Ganser, Mary Ann (c. 1948–1971)
Gardella, Tess (1897–1950)
Garden, Mary (1874–1967)
Gardner, Suzi (1960—)
Garland, Judy (1922–1969)
Garrett, Betty (1919—)
Garsenda (1170–c. 1257)
Gauthier, Eva (1885–1958)
Gay, Maisie (1883–1945)
Gaynor, Mitzi (1930—)
Geistinger, Marie (1833–1903)
Gencer, Leyla (1924—)
Geneviève (1920–2004)
Gerhardt, Elena (1883–1961)
Gerster, Etelka (1855–1920)
Gibbs, Georgia (1920—)
Gibson, Althea (1927—)
Gibson, Perla Siedle (d. 1971)
Gibson, Wynne (1903–1987)
Gilbert, Jody (1916–1979)
Gilbert, Ronnie (1926—)
Gluck, Alma (1884–1938)
Gordon, Dorothy (1889–1970)
Gordon, Kitty (1878–1974)
Gorr, Rita (1926—)
Gray, Dolores (1924–2002)
Gray, Eve (1900–1983)
Grayson, Kathryn (1922—)
Gréco, Juliette (1926—)
Greener, Dorothy (1917–1971)
Greenfield, Elizabeth Taylor (c. 1819–1876)
Greer, Jane (1924–2001)
Grieg, Nina (1845–1935)
Grimes, Tammy (1934—)
Grisi, Giuditta (1805–1840)
Grisi, Giulia (1811–1869)
Gruberová, Edita (1946–)
Gueden, Hilde (1915–1988)
Guilbert, Yvette (1865–1944)
Guinan, Texas (1884–1933)
Gunning, Louise (1879–1960)
Gutheil-Schoder, Marie (1874–1935)
Habbaba (d. 724)
Hackley, E. Azalia Smith (1867–1922)
Hall, Adelaide (1904–1993)
Hall, Juanita (1901–1968)
Hall, Natalie (1904–1994)
Hamer, Fannie Lou (1917–1977)
Hamilton, Carrie (1963–2002)
Hammond, Joan (1912—)
Hanan, Susanna (1870–1970)
Hara, Kazuko (1935—)
Harris, Jackie
Hart, Annie (d. 1947)
Harwood, Elizabeth (1938–1990)
Hato, Ana Matawhaura (1907–1953)
Hauk, Minnie (1851–1929)
Hay, Vanessa Briscoe (1955—)
Haydon, Ethel (1878–1954)
Hayes, Catherine (1825–1861)
Hayman, Lillian (1922–1994)
Hegamin, Lucille (1894–1970)
Heldy, Fanny (1888–1973)
Helmrich, Dorothy (1889–1984)
Hempel, Frieda (1885–1955)
Herlind of Maasryck (fl. 8th c.)
Hidalgo, Elvira de (1892–1980)
Hilliard, Harriet (1909–1994)
Hind bint 'Utba (d. 610)
Holiday, Billie (c. 1915–1959)
Holland, Tara Dawn (c. 1972—)
Holm, Celeste (1919—)
Holman, Libby (1904–1971)
Homer, Louise (1871–1947)

Hopkins, Pauline E. (1859–1930)
Hopper, Edna Wallace (1864–1959)
Hopper, Victoria (1909—)
Horne, Lena (1917—)
Horne, Marilyn (1929—)
Howes, Sally Ann (1930—)
Hunter, Alberta (1895–1984)
Hutchinson, Abigail (1829–1892)
Hutton, Betty (1921—)
Inan (fl. c. 800)
Irfan (fl. mid–800s)
Irwin, Flo (born c. 1860)
Irwin, May (1862–1938)
Iti (c. 2563–2424 BCE)
Ivogün, Maria (1891–1987)
Iyall, Debora (1954—)
Jackson, Ethel (1877–1957)
Jackson, Mahalia (1911–1972)
Jackson, Wanda (1937—)
Jacquet de la Guerre, Elisabeth-Claude (c. 1666–1729)
Jagemann, Karoline (1777–1848)
James, Cheryl (1964—)
Janowitz, Gundula (1937—)
Jarboro, Caterina (1908–1986)
Jay, Isabel (1879–1927)
Jean, Gloria (1926—)
Jeffreys, Anne (1923—)
Jehan, Noor (1926–2000)
Jepson, Helen (1904–1997)
Jeritza, Maria (1887–1982)
Jessye, Eva (1895–1992)
Jesus, Clementina de (1902–1987)
Johansen, Aud (1930—)
Johnson, Osa (1894–1953)
Jones, Etta (1928—)
Jones, Gwyneth (1936—)
Jones, Linda (1944–1972)
Jones, Shirley (1934—)
Jones, Sissieretta (1869–1933)
Joplin, Janis (1943–1970)
Jurinac, Sena (1921—)
Kahn, Madeline (1942–1999)
Kalich, Bertha (1874–1939)
Kallen, Kitty (1922—)
Kanahele, Helen Lake (1916–1976)
Kane, Helen (1903–1966)
Kay, Beatrice (1907–1986)
Keeler, Ruby (1909–1993)
Kelety, Julia (d. 1972)
Kellogg, Clara Louise (1842–1916)
Kelly, Jo Ann (1944–1990)
Kemble, Adelaide (1814–1879)
Kennedy-Fraser, Marjorie (1857–1930)
Kerr, Anita (1927—)
Kilius, Marika (1943—)
King, Carole (1942—)
King, Coretta Scott (1927—)
King, Jane (d. 1971)
King, Mabel (1932–1999)
Kirkwood, Pat (1921—)
Kirsten, Dorothy (1910–1992)
Kitt, Eartha (1928—)
Klafsky, Katharina (1855–1896)
Knef, Hildegard (1925–2002)
Konetzni, Anny (1902–1968)
Konetzni, Hilde (1905–1980)
Kosta, Tessa (1893–1981)
Köth, Erika (1925–1989)
Krainik, Ardis (1929–1997)
Krauss, Alison (1971—)
Krusceniski, Salomea (1873–1952)
Kurz, Selma (1874–1933)
Kuznetsova, Maria (1880–1966)
La Barbara, Joan (1947—)
La Grange, Anna de (1825–1905)
La Hye, Louise (1810–1838)
La Lupe (1939–1992)
Lamarque, Libertad (1908–2000)
Landis, Carole (1919–1948)
Lang, Josephine (1815–1880)
Lang, K.D. (1961—)
Lange, Aloysia (c. 1761–1839)
Langford, Frances (1914–2005)
La Palme, Béatrice (1878–1921)
Larson, Nicolette (1952–1997)
La Rue, Grace (1880–1956)
Lauper, Cyndi (1953—)
Lavallière, Eve (c. 1866–1929)
Lawrence, Gertrude (1898–1952)
Lawrence, Marjorie (1908–1979)
Lawson, Winifred (1892–1961)
Leander, Zarah (1907–1981)
Lear, Evelyn (1926—)
Leblanc, Georgette (c. 1875–1941)
Lebrun, Franziska (1756–1791)
Lee, Beverly (1941—)
Lee, Brenda (1944—)
Lee, Dixie (1911–1952)
Lee, Peggy (1920—)
Lehmann, Lilli (1848–1929)
Lehmann, Liza (1862–1918)
Lehmann, Lotte (1888–1976)
Leider, Frida (1888–1975)
Lemnitz, Tiana (1897–1994)
Lenya, Lotte (1898–1981)
Levey, Ethel (1880–1955)
Lewis, Bertha (1887–1931)
Lewis, Cathy (1916–1968)
Liebling, Estelle (1880–1970)
Lightner, Winnie (1899–1971)
Lil' Kim (1975—)
Lind, Jenny (1820–1887)
Linley, Elizabeth (1754–1792)
Linley, Maria (1763–1784)
Linley, Mary (1758–1787)
Lipkowska, Lydia (1882–1958)
Lloyd, Alice (1873–1949)
Lloyd, Marie (1870–1922)
Loftus, Kitty (1867–1927)
Logan, Ella (1913–1969)
Löhr, Marie (1890–1975)
London, Julie (1926–2000)
Lopez, Encarnación (1898–1945)
Lorengar, Pilar (1928—)
Los Angeles, Victoria de (1923—)
Love, Darlene (1938—)
Lubin, Germaine (1890–1979)
Lucca, Pauline (1841–1908)
Ludwig, Christa (1924—)
Lulu (1948—)
Lyngstad, Frida (1945—)
Lynn, Barbara (1942—)
Lynn, Loretta (1935—)
Lynn, Vera (1917—)
Lynne, Gillian (1926—)
MacDonald, Christie (1875–1962)
Macdonald, Flora (1722–1790)
MacDonald, Jeanette (1903–1965)
Macrina (327–379)
Madison, Helene (1913–1970)
Magnani, Anna (1908–1973)
Magogo ka Dinizulu, Constance (1900–1984)
Mahbuba (fl. 9th c.)
Mahdiyya, Munira al- (c. 1895–1965)
Makeba, Miriam (1932—)
Malibran, Maria (1808–1836)
Mallinger, Mathilde (1847–1920)
Mana-Zucca (1887–1981)
Mangeshkar, Lata (1929—)
Manning, Irene (1912–2004)
Mara, Adele (1923—)
Mara, Gertrud (1749–1833)
Marchesi, Blanche (1863–1940)
Marchesi, Mathilde (1821–1913)
Marcos, Imelda (1929—)
Maria Antonia of Austria (1724–1780)
Mario, Queena (1896–1951)
Marshall, Lois (1924–1997)
Martin, Mary (1913–1990)
Martin, Millicent (1934—)
Martin, Sara (1884–1955)
Martinez, Marianne (1744–1812)
Materna, Amalie (1844–1918)
Matthews, Jessie (1907–1981)
Mattocks, Isabella (1746–1826)
Matzenauer, Margaret (1881–1963)
Maupin, d'Aubigny (c. 1670–1707)
Maxwell, Kate (fl. 1886)
May, Edna (1875–1948)
May, Gisela (1924—)
Maynor, Dorothy (1910–1996)
McCarty, Mary (1923–1980)
McCorkle, Susannah (1946–2001)
McCoy, Bessie (1888–1931)
McDaniel, Hattie (1895–1952)
McDonald, Audra (1970—)
McDonald, Marie (1923–1965)
McGuire, Phyllis (1931—)
McKee, Maria (1964—)
McKenzie, Julia (1941—)
McKinney, Nina Mae (c. 1912–1967)
McNeil, Claudia (1917–1993)
McRae, Carmen (1920–1994)
McVie, Christine (1943—)
Meeuwsen, Terry (1949—)
Mei-Figner, Medea (1859–1952)
Melba, Nellie (1861–1931)
Meller, Raquel (1888–1962)
Mendoza, Amalia (1923–2001)
Mercer, Mabel (1900–1983)
Merman, Ethel (1912–1984)
Merriman, Nan (1920—)
Merritt, Theresa (1924–1998)
Mesta, Perle (1889–1975)
Milanov, Zinka (1906–1989)
Milashkina, Tamara Andreyevna (1934—)
Milder-Hauptmann, Anna (1785–1838)
Mildmay, Audrey (1900–1953)
Miles, Lizzie (1895–1963)
Milh al-Attara (fl. 840s)
Mills, Eleanor (1888–1922)
Mills, Florence (1895–1927)
Minnelli, Liza (1946—)
Minton, Yvonne (1938—)
Miolan-Carvalho, Marie (1827–1895)
Miranda, Carmen (1909–1955)
Mireille (1906–1996)
Mistinguett (1875–1956)
Mitchell, Abbie (1884–1960)
Mitchell, Joni (1943—)
Mitchell, Marion (1876–1955)
Miura, Tamaki (1884–1946)
Mödl, Martha (1912—)
Moffo, Anna (1932—)
Molton, Flora (1908–1990)
Molza, Tarquinia (1542–1617)
Montana, Patsy (1909–1996)
Montiel, Sarita (1928—)
Moore, Decima (1871–1964)
Moore, Grace (1898–1947)
Moore, Jessie (1865–1910)
Moore, Maggie (1847–1929)
Moreno, Rita (1931—)
Morgan, Helen (1900–1941)
Morison, Patricia (1914—)
Morrow, Doretta (1927–1968)
Morse, Ella Mae (1925–1999)

Moten, Etta (1901–2004)
Moyet, Alison (1961—)
Mozart, Constanze (1762–1842)
Munsel, Patrice (1925—)
Munson, Ona (1894–1955)
Murray, Anne (1945—)
Murray, Katherine (1894–1974)
Murray, Ruby (1935–1996)
Musi, Maria Maddalena (1669–1751)
Mutayyam al-Hashimiyya (fl. 8th c.)
Muzio, Claudia (1889–1936)
Myrtil, Odette (1898–1978)
Nagako (1903–2000)
Na'ima al-Masriyya
Namakelua, Alice K. (1892–1987)
Near, Holly (1949—)
Nelson, Clara Meleka (1901–1979)
Nevada, Emma (1859–1940)
Nevada, Mignon (1885–1970)
Newman, Julia St. Clair (1818–?)
Nezhdanova, Antonia (1873–1950)
Nicks, Stevie (1948—)
Nico (1938–1988)
Nielsen, Alice (c. 1870–1943)
Niese, Hansi (1875–1934)
Niesen, Gertrude (1910–1975)
Nilsson, Birgit (1918—)
Nilsson, Christine (1843–1921)
Nixon, Marni (1929—)
Norden, Christine (1924–1988)
Nordica, Lillian (1857–1914)
Novello, Clara (1818–1908)
Novello-Davies, Clara (1861–1943)
Novotna, Jarmila (1907–1994)
Nyro, Laura (1947–1997)
O'Brien, Virginia (1896–1987)
O'Connell, Helen (1920–1993)
O'Day, Anita (1919—)
Odetta (1930—)
Olivero, Magda (1914—)
Olivette, Nina (c. 1908–1971)
O'Neal, Zelma (1903–1989)
Ono, Yoko (1933—)
Oraib (797–890)
Ordonówna, Hanka (1904–1950)
Orlova, Liubov (1902–1975)
Orton, Beth (1970—)
Osborne, Joan (1962—)
Osborne, Mary (1921–1992)
O'Shea, Tessie (1913–1995)
Oslin, K.T. (1941—)
Owens, Shirley (1941—)
Page, Patti (1927—)
Pagliughi, Lina (1907–1980)
Paige, Elaine (1948—)
Paige, Janis (1922—)
Painter, Eleanor (1890–1947)
Parepa-Rosa, Euphrosyne (1836–1874)
Parra, Violeta (1917–1967)
Parsons, Elizabeth (1846–1924)
Pasta, Giuditta (1797–1865)
Patey, Janet Monach (1842–1894)
Patti, Adelina (1843–1919)
Pearce, Vera (1896–1966)
Perez, Maria (fl. 13th c.)
Perkins, Susan (c. 1954—)
Peters, Bernadette (1948—)
Peters, Roberta (1930—)
Phair, Liz (1967—)
Phillipps, Adelaide (1833–1882)
Phillips, Esther (1935–1984)
Phillips, Michelle (1944—)
Piaf, Edith (1915–1963)
Pickens, Helen (1910—)
Pickens, Jane (1908–1992)
Pickens, Patti (1914–1995)
Picon, Molly (1898–1992)
Piseth Pilika (1965–1999)
Pointer, Anita (1948—)
Pointer, Bonnie (1950—)
Pointer, June (1954—)
Pointer, Ruth (1946—)
Pollak, Anna (1912–1996)
Pons, Lily (1898–1976)
Ponselle, Carmela (1892–1977)
Ponselle, Rosa (1897–1981)
Popp, Lucia (1939–1993)
Pounder, Cheryl
Powell, Jane (1929—)
Prendergast, Sharon Marley (1964—)
Price, Leontyne (1927—)
Provine, Dorothy (1937—)
Pugacheva, Alla (1949—)
Pukui, Mary Kawena (1895–1986)
Rahn, Muriel (1911–1961)
Rainey, Ma (1886–1939)
Raisa, Rosa (1893–1963)
Randolph, Amanda (1896–1967)
Randolph, Barbara (d. 2002)
Raskin, Judith (1928–1984)
Rathebe, Dolly (1928–2004)
Ray, Martha (d. 1779)
Raye, Martha (1916–1994)
Reagan, Maureen (1941–2001)
Reddy, Helen (1941—)
Redpath, Jean (1937—)
Reeves, Martha (1941—)
Regina, Elis (1945–1982)
Resnik, Regina (1922—)
Respighi, Elsa (1894–1996)
Rethberg, Elisabeth (1894–1976)
Reynolds, Debbie (1932—)
Reynolds, Malvina (1900–1978)
Rhodes, Betty (c. 1935–1987)
Rider-Kelsey, Corinne (1877–1947)
Ring, Blanche (1877–1961)
Riperton, Minnie (1947–1979)
Ritchie, Jean (1922—)
Rivera, Chita (1933—)
Robbins, Gale (1921–1980)
Roberti, Lyda (1906–1938)
Robin, Mado (1918–1960)
Robinson, Anastasia (c. 1692–1755)
Roche, Maggie (1951—)
Roche, Suzzy (1956—)
Roche, Terre (1953—)
Rodrigues, Amalia (1921–1999)
Rogers, Clara Kathleen (1844–1931)
Rogers, Dale Evans (1912–2001)
Rökk, Marika (1913–2004)
Ross, Annie (1930—)
Ross, Diana (1944—)
Roth, Lillian (1910–1980)
Rothenberger, Anneliese (1924—)
Ruick, Barbara (1930–1974)
Russell, Anna (1911—)
Ryan, Peggy (1924–2004)
Rysanek, Leonie (1926–1998)
Saad, Siti binti (c. 1880–1950)
Sade (1959—)
Sainte-Marie, Buffy (1941—)
Salvini-Donatelli, Fanny (c. 1815–1891)
Sanderson, Julia (1887–1975)
Sanderson, Sybil (1865–1903)
Santos Arrascaeta, Beatriz (1947—)
Sass, Marie Constance (1834–1907)
Sayao, Bidu (1902–1999)
Scallon, Dana Rosemary (1950—)
Schaefer, Laurel Lea (c. 1949—)
Scheff, Fritzi (1879–1954)
Schlamme, Martha (1922–1985)
Schneider, Hortense (1833–1920)
Schröder-Devrient, Wilhelmine (1804–1860)
Schumann, Elisabeth (1885–1952)
Schumann-Heink, Ernestine (1861–1936)
Schwarz, Vera (1888–1964)
Schwarzkopf, Elisabeth (1915—)
Scott, Esther Mae (1893–1979)
Scott, Hazel (1920–1981)
Seefried, Irmgard (1919–1988)
Seeger, Peggy (b. 1935)
Seeley, Blossom (1891–1974)
Segal, Vivienne (1897–1992)
Seidl, Lea (1895–1987)
Selena (1971–1995)
Sembrich, Marcella (1858–1935)
Sevilla, Carmen (1930—)
Shaler, Eleanor (1900–1989)
Shanté, Roxanne (1970—)
Shariyya (b. around 815)
Shaw, Wini (1910–1982)
Sheridan, Margaret (1889–1958)
Shore, Dinah (1917–1994)
Shutta, Ethel (1896–1976)
Siems, Margarethe (1879–1952)
Sills, Beverly (1929—)
Simionato, Giulietta (1916—)
Simon, Carly (1945—)
Simone, Nina (1933—)
Sinatra, Nancy (1940—)
Sinden, Topsy (1878–1951)
Singleton, Penny (1908–2003)
Smith, Ada (1894–1984)
Smith, Bessie (1894–1937)
Smith, Clara (1894–1935)
Smith, Kate (1907–1986)
Smith, Kendra (1960—)
Smith, Mabel (1924–1972)
Smith, Mamie (1883–1946)
Smith, Muriel Burrell (1923–1985)
Smith, Patti (1946—)
Smith, Queenie (1898–1978)
Smith, Trixie (1895–1943)
Smith, Willie Mae Ford (1904–1994)
Snow, Valaida (c. 1903–1956)
Söderström, Elisabeth (1927—)
Sontag, Henriette (c. 1803–1854)
Sosa, Mercedes (1935—)
Sothern, Ann (1909–2001)
Souez, Ina (1903–1992)
Spain, Elsie (1879–1970)
Sparks, Donita (1963—)
Spivey, Victoria (1906–1976)
Springfield, Dusty (1939–1998)
St. Denis, Ruth (1877–1968)
Stafford, Jo (1920—)
Stamp Taylor, Edith (1904–1946)
Starr, Kay (1922—)
Steber, Eleanor (1914–1990)
Stephens, Catherine (1794–1882)
Stevens, Connie (1938—)
Stevens, Risë (1913—)
Stewart, Nellie (1858–1931)
Stich-Randall, Teresa (1927—)
Stignani, Ebe (1903–1975)
Stolz, Teresa (1834–1902)
Stone, Dorothy (1905–1974)
Stone, Rosie (1945—)
Storace, Nancy (1765–1817)
Storchio, Rosina (1876–1945)
Stratas, Teresa (1938—)
Streich, Rita (1920–1987)
Streisand, Barbra (1942—)
Strepponi, Giuseppina (1815–1897)
Stuart, Bathia Howie (1893–1987)
Subbulakshmi, M.S. (1916–2004)
Sucher, Rosa (1847–1927)
Sullivan, Maxine (1911–1987)

Sumac, Yma (1927—)
Supervia, Conchita (1895–1936)
Suraiya (1929–2004)
Sutherland, Joan (1926—)
Swanson, Gloria (1897–1983)
Swarthout, Gladys (1904–1969)
Syms, Sylvia (1916–1992)
Talley, Marion (1906–1983)
Tanguay, Eva (1878–1947)
Taylor, Eva (1895–1977)
Tebaldi, Renata (1922—)
Tempest, Marie (1864–1942)
Teng, Teresa (1953–1995)
Ternina, Milka (1863–1941)
Terriss, Ellaline (1871–1971)
Tess, Giulia (1889–1976)
Tetrazzini, Eva (1862–1938)
Tetrazzini, Luisa (1871–1940)
Teyte, Maggie (1888–1976)
Tharpe, Rosetta (1915–1973)
Thebom, Blanche (1918—)
Thompson, Kay (1908–1998)
Thorborg, Kerstin (1896–1970)
Thornton, Willie Mae (1926–1984)
Thursby, Emma (1845–1931)
Tibors (b. around 1130)
Tietjens, Therese (1831–1877)
Tilley, Vesta (1864–1952)
Tilton, Martha (1915—)
Timms, Sally (1959—)
Tinsley, Pauline (1928—)
Todd, Mabel Loomis (1858–1932)
Todi, Luiza Rosa (1753–1833)
Tofts, Catherine (c. 1685–1756)
Torres, Lolita (1930–2002)
Tourel, Jennie (1899–1973)
Traubel, Helen (1899–1972)
Tree, Viola (1884–1938)
Troy, Louise (1933–1994)
Troyanos, Tatiana (1938–1993)
Tucker, Sophie (1884–1966)
Tully, Alice (1902–1993)
Turner, Eva (1892–1990)
Turner, Tina (1938—)
Ubaida (fl. c. 830)
Uggams, Leslie (1943—)
Ulayya (fl. 800s)
Ullman, Tracey (1959—)
Umeki, Miyoshi (1929—)
Um Kalthum (c. 1898–1975)
Unger, Caroline (1803–1877)
Ursuleac, Viorica (1894–1985)
Vallin, Ninon (1886–1961)
Van Doren, Mamie (1931—)
Van Dyke, Vonda Kay (c. 1944—)
Van Zandt, Marie (1858–1919)
Vargas, Chavela (1919—)
Várnay, Astrid (1918—)
Vaughan, Sarah (1924–1990)
Velez, Lisa (1967—)
Venuta, Benay (1911–1995)
Verdon, Gwen (1925–2000)
Verrett, Shirley (1931—)
Vestris, Lucia (1797–1856)
Vezin, Jane Elizabeth (1827–1902)
Viardot, Louise (1841–1918)
Viardot, Pauline (1821–1910)
Villegas, Micaela (1748–1819)
Vincent, Madge (b. 1884)
Vishnevskaya, Galina (1926—)
Vitelli, Annie (c. 1837–?)
von Busing, Fritzi (c. 1884–1948)
Von Trapp, Maria (1905–1987)
Vorlova, Slavka (1894–1973)
Wagner, Johanna (1826–1894)
Waldmann, Maria (1842–1920)
Walker, Ada Overton (1870–1914)
Walker, Edyth (1867–1950)
Wallace, Sippie (1898–1986)
Wallis, Shani (1933—)
Ward, Clara Mae (1924–1973)
Ward, Dorothy (1890–1987)
Ward, Geneviève (1838–1922)
Ward, Polly (1908–1987)
Warren, Elinor Remick (1900–1991)
Warwick, Dionne (1940—)
Washington, Dinah (1924–1963)
Waters, Ethel (1896–1977)
Watts, Helen (1927—)
Weaver, Marjorie (1913–1994)
Weeks, Marion (1886–1968)
Weiss, Janet (1965—)
Weiss, Liz
Weiss, Mary
Welch, Elisabeth (1904–2003)
Welitsch, Ljuba (1913–1996)
Wells, Kitty (1919—)
Wells, Mary (1943–1992)
West, Dottie (1932–1991)
West, Mae (1893–1980)
West, Sandy (1960—)
White, Frances (1896–1969)
Whiting, Margaret (1924—)
Wieniawska, Irene Regine (1880–1932)
Wiley, Lee (1915–1975)
Williams, Camilla (1922—)
Williams, Frances (1903–1959)
Williams, Hattie (1872–1942)
Williams, Marion (1927–1994)
Williams, Vanessa (1963—)
Williams, Wendy O. (1951–1998)
Willson, Rini Zarova (d. 1966)
Wilson, Edith (1896–1981)
Wilson, Kini (1872–1962)
Wilson, Mary (1944—)
Wilson, Nancy (1937—)
Winn, Anona (1907–1994)
Wolf, Kate (1942–1986)
Wood, Peggy (1892–1978)
Wright, Cobina (1887–1970)
Wynette, Tammy (1942–1998)
Yaw, Ellen Beach (1868–1947)
Young, Cecilia (c. 1711–1789)
Zabelle, Flora (1880–1968)
Ziegler, Anne (1910–2003)

SIOUX
Zintkala Nuni (c. 1890–c. 1919)

SKATEBOARDER
Torres, Vanessa (1986—)

SKELETON ATHLETE
Gale, Tristan (1980—)

SKIER
Achkina, Rita (fl. 1968)
Albrecht-Loretan, Brigitte (1970—)
Allan-Shetter, Liz (1947—)
Amosova, Zinaida (fl. 1976)
Anding, Carola (1960—)
Armstrong, Debbie (1963—)
Arnesen, Liv (1953—)
Asselin, Marie-Claude
Aufles, Inger
Aunli, Berit
Bahrke, Shannon (1980—)
Baldycheva, Nina
Bancroft, Ann (1955—)
Baranova, Lyubov
Battelle, Ann (1968—)
Bauer, Veronika (1979—)
Bauer, Viola (1976—)
Beiser, Trude (1927—)
Belmondo, Stefania (1969—)
Berthod, Madeleine (1931—)
Berthod, Sylviane (1977—)
Biebl, Heidi (1941—)
Bjoergen, Marit (1980—)
Bochatay, Fernande (1946—)
Boe, Anette
Boyarskikh, Claudia (1939—)
Boyle, Darian (c. 1968—)
Brand, Colette
Brenner, Veronica (1974—)
Buchner, Annemarie
Burke, Sarah (1982—)
Camplin, Alisa (1974—)
Canins, Maria (1949—)
Cavagnoud, Regine (1970–2001)
Ceccarelli, Daniela (1975—)
Chaffee, Suzy (1946—)
Charvatova, Olga (1962—)
Chenal-Minuzzo, Giuliana (1931—)
Cheryazova, Lina (1968—)
Clifford, Betsy (1953—)
Cline, Aleisha (1970—)
Coberger, Annelise (1971—)
Cochran, Barbara (1951—)
Cochran, Marilyn (1950—)
Colliard, Renée (fl. 1950s)
Compagnoni, Deborah (1970—)
Cooper, Christin (1961—)
Cooper, Jacqui (1973—)
Corrock, Susan (1951—)
Cranz, Christl (1914—)
Cranz, Christl (1914–2004)
Csizmazia, Kim (c. 1968—)
Cutter, Kiki (1951—)
Dahl, Aslaug
Dahlmo, Marianne
Danilova, Olga (1970—)
Dänzer, Frieda
Debernard, Danielle (1954—)
Debertshäuser, Monika
Demers, Anik (1972—)
Deseo, Suzanne (1913–2003)
Di Centa, Manuela (1963—)
Dionne, Deidra (1982—)
Dorfmeister, Michaela (1973—)
Dovzan, Alenka (1976—)
Drexel, Wiltrud (1950—)
Drouin, Candice (1976—)
Dybendahl Hartz, Trude (1966—)
Eder, Elfriede (1970—)
Edstrom, Sonja
Egger, Sabine (1977—)
Egorova, Lyubov (1966—)
Enger, Babben
Epple, Irene (1957—)
Epple, Maria (1959—)
Eriksson, Anna-Lisa
Ertl, Martina (1973—)
Famose, Annie (1944—)
Fernández Ochoa, Blanca (1963—)
Figini, Michela (1966—)
Frandl, Josefine
Fraser, Gretchen (1919–1994)
Gabl, Gertrud (1948–1976)
Gavriljuk, Nina (1965—)
Gerg, Hilde (1975—)
Giordani, Claudia (1955—)
Gladisheva, Svetlana (1971—)
Goetschl, Renate (1975—)
Goitschel, Christine (1944—)
Goitschel, Marielle (1945—)
Golden, Diana (1963—)
Golden, Diana (1963–2001)
Grasegger, Käthe

Greene, Nancy (1943—)
Guo Dandan (1977—)
Gusakova, Maria
Gustafsson, Toini (1938—)
Haas, Christl (1943–2001)
Hammerer, Resi (1925—)
Hattestad, Stine Lise
Heath, Clarita (c. 1916–2003)
Hecher, Traudl (1943—)
Heggtveit, Anne (1939—)
Henkel, Manuela (1974—)
Henneberger, Barbi (d. 1964)
Hess, Erika (1962—)
Hietamies, Mirja
Hochleitner, Dorothea
Holloway, Sue (1955—)
Huber, Andrea (1975—)
Hyytianen, Eija
Jacot, Michele (1952—)
Jahren, Anne
Jeriova, Kvetoslava (1956—)
Johansson, Irma
Jonsson, Magdalena (1969—)
Kajosmaa, Marjatta
Kania-Enke, Karin (1961—)
Kiehl, Marina (1965—)
Kinshofer, Christa (1961—)
Kirvesniemi, Marja-Liisa (1955—)
Kojevnikova, Elizaveta
Konzett, Ursula (1959—)
Koren, Katja (1975—)
Kostelic, Janica (1982—)
Kostner, Isolde (1975—)
Koznick, Kristina (1975—)
Krause, Sigrun
Kreiner, Kathy (1954—)
Kronberger, Petra (1969—)
Kuenzel, Claudia (1978—)
Kulakova, Galina (1942—)
Lalive, Caroline (1979—)
Lawrence, Andrea Mead (1932—)
Lawrence, Chiara (1975—)
Lazutina, Larissa (1965—)
Lee-Gartner, Kerrin (1966—)
Lehtonen, Mirja (1942—)
Leonardi Cortesi, Natascia (1971—)
Leu, Evelyne (1976—)
Lid, Hilde Synnove
Lignell, Kristen (c. 1965—)
Lindgren, Marie
Lindh, Hilary (1969—)
Lucas, Joy (1917—)
Lukkarinen, Marjut (1966—)
Määttä, Pirkko (1959—)
Magoni, Paoletta (1964—)
Mahringer, Erika (1924—)
Maier, Ulrike (1967–1994)
Marshall, Kirstie (1969—)
Martinod, Marie (c. 1984—)
Martinsen, Bente (1972—)
Martinsson, Barbro
Masnada, Florence (1968—)
Matikainen, Marjo (1965—)
McIntyre, Elizabeth (1965—)
McKenna, Lesley (1974—)
McKinney, Tamara (1962—)
McKnight, Kim
Meissnitzer, Alexandra (1973—)
Mekshilo, Eudokia
Mendes, Jonna (1979—)
Merle, Carole (1964—)
Messner, Pat (1954—)
Meyer, Antoinette
Mikkelsplass, Marit (1965—)
Mir, Isabelle (1949—)
Mitchell, Elyne (1913–2002)
Mittermaier, Rosi (1950—)
Mittermayer, Tatjana (1964—)
Moen-Guidon, Anita (1967—)
Montillet, Carole (1973—)
Mørdre, Berit
Morerod, Lise-Marie (1956—)
Moroder, Karin (1974—)
Mukhacheva, Lubov
Myrmael, Marit
Nadig, Marie-Thérése (1954—)
Nagejkina, Svetlana (1965—)
Nef, Sonja (1972—)
Nelson, Cindy (1955—)
Neumannova, Katerina (1973—)
Niemann, Gunda (1966—)
Nilsen, Elin (1968—)
Nybraaten, Inger-Helene (1960—)
Ochoa, Blanca Fernández (c. 1964—)
Oertli, Brigitte (1962—)
Olunina, Alevtina (1930—)
Paerson, Anja (1981—)
Pall, Olga (1947—)
Parisien, Julie (1971—)
Paruzzi, Gabriella (1969—)
Paulu, Blanka (1954—)
Pedersen, Hilde G. (1964—)
Pedersen, Solveig
Pelen, Perrine (1960—)
Pequegnot, Laure (1975—)
Percy, Karen (1966—)
Pettersen, Brit
Petzold, Barbara (1955—)
Pitou, Penny (1938—)
Polkunen, Sirkka (1927—)
Poysti, Toini K.
Proell-Moser, Annemarie (1953—)
Pusula, Senja (1941—)
Putzer, Karen (1978—)
Rantanen, Siiri (1924—)
Reichert, Ossi
Riihivuori, Hilkka (1952—)
Rochat, Laurence (1979—)
Rocheva, Nina
Roffe, Diann (1967—)
Rom, Dagmar (1928—)
Rostock, Marlies
Ruegg, Yvonne
Ruoppa, Eeva (1932—)
Sachenbacher, Evi (1980—)
Satoya, Tae (c. 1977—)
Saubert, Jean
Savolainen, Jaana (1964—)
Schleper, Sarah (1979—)
Schlunegger, Hedy (1923–2003)
Schmidt, Veronika
Schmitt, Sandra (c. 1982–2000)
Schneider, Vreni (1964—)
Schöpf, Regina
Schou Nilsen, Laila (1919–1998)
Scott, Beckie (1970—)
Seizinger, Katja (1972—)
Shaffer, Alexandra (1976—)
Sheehan, Patty (1956—)
Sherman-Kauf, Patti (1963—)
Sidorova, Evgenyia (c. 1935—)
Sikolova, Helena (1949—)
Smetanina, Raisa (1929—)
Snite, Betsy (1938–1984)
Stacey, Kim (1980—)
Stallmaier, Veronika (1966—)
Steggall, Zali (1974—)
Steurer, Florence (1949—)
Stone, Nikki (1971—)
Strandberg, Britt
Street, Picabo (1971—)
Suihkonen, Liisa (1943—)
Svet, Mateja (1968—)
Svobodova, Gabriela (1953—)
Svubova, Dagmar
Tae, Satoya (1976—)
Taggart, Michele (1970—)
Tagliabue, Elena (1977—)
Takalo, Helena (1947—)
Tchepalova, Julija (1976—)
Tikhonova, Tamara (1964—)
Tone, Lel (c. 1971—)
Totschnig, Brigitte (1954—)
Traa, Kari (1974—)
Tsuper, Alla (c. 1980—)
Välbe, Elena (1968—)
Vanzetta, Bice (1961—)
Venciené, Vida
Wachter, Anita (1967—)
Walliser, Maria (1963—)
Weinbrecht, Donna (1965—)
Wenzel, Hanni (1951—)
Wheeler, Lucile (1935—)
Wiberg, Pernilla (1970—)
Wideman, Lydia (1920—)
Wolf, Sigrid (1964—)
Xu Nannan (1979—)
Yeroshina, Radya
Zimmermann, Edith
Zimmermann, Heidi (1946—)

SKIING INSTRUCTOR
Golden, Diana (1963—)
Lucas, Joy (1917—)

SKYSURFER
Garcia-O'Brien, Tanya (c. 1973—)

SLALOM SKIER
See Skier.

SLAVE/SLAVE LABORER
See Serf/slave/slave laborer.

SLED-DOG RACER
Butcher, Susan (1954—)
Jonrowe, DeeDee (1953—)
Page, Dorothy G. (1921–1989)
Riddles, Libby (1956—)

SNOOKER PLAYER
Fisher, Allison (1968—)

SNOWBOARDER
Baker, Carlee (1978—)
Basich, Tina (1969—)
Beaman, Hana (1982—)
Blanc, Isabelle (1975—)
Bleiler, Gretchen (1981—)
Burnside, Cara-Beth (1968—)
Christy, Barrett (1971—)
Clark, Kelly (1983—)
Dakides, Tara (1975—)
Dixon, Tina (1976—)
Drouin, Candice (1976—)
Dunn, Shannon (1972—)
Jacobellis, Lindsey (1985—)
Jarvela, Satu
Kjeldaas, Stine Brun (1975—)
Koeck, Brigitte
Macleod, Jaime (1976—)
Matthews, Janet (1965—)
McKenna, Lesley (1974—)
Meyen, Janna (1977—)
Mills, Phoebe (1972—)
Molin-Kongsgard, Anne (1977—)
Oestvold, Line (1978—)
Olson, Leslee (1978—)
Poetzl, Ine (1976—)

Renoth, Heidi Maria (1978—)
Reuteler, Fabienne (1979—)
Ricker, Maelle (1978—)
Ruby, Karine (1978—)
Rudishauser, Corrie (1973—)
Sayres, Aurelie (1977—)
Simmons, Erin (1976—)
Stacey, Kim (1980—)
Teter, Hannah (1987—)
Thost, Nicola (1977—)
Trettel, Lidia (1973—)
Vano, Donna (c. 1955—)
Vidal, Doriane (1976—)
Voutilainen, Katrina (1975—)
Waara, Jennie (1975—)
Wehr-Häsler, Säbine (1967—)
Zurek, Natasza (1978—)
Zwink, Tara (1973—)

SOCCER PLAYER
Aarones, Ann Kristin (1973—)
Akers, Michelle (1966—)
Alves Lima, Daniela (1984—)
Angerer, Nadine (1978—)
Augustesen, Susanne (1956—)
Bachor, Isabell (1983—)
Bekkevold, Kristin (1977—)
Boxx, Shannon (1977—)
Brandebusemeyer, Nicole (1974—)
Carlsen, Agnete (1971—)
Chastain, Brandi (1968—)
Chen Yufeng
Costa, Renata (1986—)
de Belo, Roseli (1969—)
de Paula, Monica Angelica (1978—)
Donnelly, Geraldine (1965—)
dos Santos, Andreia (1977—)
dos Santos Augusto, Rosana (1982—)
Espeseth, Gro (1972—)
Estrela Moura, Elaine (1982—)
Fair, Lorrie (1978—)
Fan Yunjie (1972—)
Fawcett, Joy (1968—)
Fitschen, Doris (1968—)
Foudy, Julie (1971—)
French, Michelle (1977—)
Frustol, Tone Gunn (1975—)
Fuss, Sonja (1978—)
Gabarra, Carin (1965—)
Gao Hong (1967—)
Garefrekes, Kerstin (1979—)
Götte, Jeannette (1979—)
Gottschlich, Stefanie (1978—)
Grings, Inka (1978—)
Guenther, Sarah (1983—)
Gulbrandsen, Ragnhild (1977—)
Gulbrandsen, Solveig (1981—)
Hamm, Mia (1972—)
Harvey, Mary (1965—)
Haugen, Tone (1964—)
Haugenes, Margunn (1970—)
Heinrichs, April (1964—)
Hingst, Ariane (1979—)
Hoffmann, Melanie (1974—)
Hovland, Ingeborg (1969—)
Hucles, Angela (1978—)
Jensen, Christine Boe (1975—)
Jones, Steffi (1972—)
Jorgensen, Silje (1977—)
Katia (1977—)
Knudsen, Monica (1975—)
Kringen, Goril (1972—)
Kvitland, Bente (1974—)
Lehn, Unni (1977—)
Lilly, Kristine (1971—)
Lingor, Renate (1975—)
Liu Ailing (1967—)
Liu Ying (1974—)
Maciel Mota, Miraildes (1978—)
MacMillan, Shannon (1974—)
MacMillan, Shannon (1974—Medalen, Linda (1965—)
Meinert, Maren (1973—)
Mellgren, Dagny (1978—)
Milbrett, Tiffeny (1972—)
Minnert, Sandra (1973—)
Mitts, Heather (1978—)
Morace, Carolina (1964—)
Mueller, Claudia (1974—)
Mueller, Martina (1980—)
Mullinix, Siri (1978—)
Myklebust, Merete (1973—)
Nascimento Pinheiro, Graziele (1981—)
Nielsen, Lone Smidt (1961—)
Nordby, Bente (1974—)
Nymark Andersen, Nina (1972—)
Odebrecht, Viola (1983—)
Omilade, Navina (1981—)
O'Reilly, Heather (1985—)
Overbeck, Carla (1969—)
Parlow, Cindy (1978—)
Pearce, Christie (1975—)
Pellegrino, Aline (1982—)
Pereira da Silva, Kelly (1985—)
Pereira Ribeiro, Tania (1974—)
Pettersen, Marianne (1975—)
Pohlers, Conny (1978—)
Pretinha (1975—)
Prinz, Birgit (1977—)
Rapp, Anita (1977—)
Reddick, Cat (1982—)
Ribeiro Cabral, Juliana (1981—)
Riise, Hege (1969—)
Roberts, Tiffany (1977—)
Rottenberg, Silke (1972—)
Rozeira de Souza Silva, Cristiane (1985—)
Sandaune, Brit (1972—)
Scurry, Briana (1971—)
Serlenga, Nikki (1978—)
Seth, Reidun (1966—)
Shi Guihong
Shui Qingxia (1976—)
Sissi (1967—)
Slaton, Danielle (1980—)
Sobrero, Kate (1976—)
Stegemann, Kerstin (1977—)
Stoere, Heidi (1973—)
Sundhage, Pia (1960—)
Sun Qingmei
Suntaque, Andreia (1977—)
Sun Wen (1973—)
Svensson, Tina (1970—)
Tangeraas, Trine (1971—)
Tarpley, Lindsay (1983—)
Thun, Kjersti (1974—)
Venturini, Tisha (1973—)
Wagner, Aly (1980—)
Wambach, Abby (1980—)
Wang Liping (1973—)
Wei Haiying
Wen Lirong (1969—)
Whalen, Sara (1976—)
Wiegmann, Bettina (1971—)
Wilson, Staci (1976—)
Wimbersky, Petra (1982—)
Wunderlich, Pia (1975—)
Wunderlich, Tina (1977—)
Xie Huilin (1975—)
Yu Hongqi
Zhang Ouying (1975—)
Zhao Lihong (1972—)
Zhong Honglian

SOCIAL ACTIVIST/REFORMER
Aberdeen, Ishbel Maria Gordon, Lady (1857–1939)
Addams, Jane (1860–1935)
Allred, Gloria (1941—)
Alvarado, Elvia (1938—)
Ames, Fanny Baker (1840–1931)
Anderson, Maybanke (1845–1927)
Andrus, Ethel Percy (1884–1967)
Archer, Caroline Lilian (1922–1978)
Arnim, Bettine von (1785–1859)
Atkinson, Lily May (1866–1921)
Bambace, Angela (1898–1975)
Barnett, Henrietta (1851–1936)
Barry, Leonora M. (1849–1930)
Baughan, Blanche Edith (1870–1958)
Baume, Rosetta Lulah (1871–1934)
Belmont, Alva Smith (1853–1933)
Besant, Annie (1847–1933)
Bissell, Emily (1861–1948)
Blachford, Theodosia (1745–1817)
Blackwell, Alice Stone (1857–1950)
Blackwood, Hariot (c. 1845–1891)
Blair, Catherine (1872–1946)
Blake, Lillie Devereux (1833–1913)
Bloomer, Amelia Jenks (1818–1894)
Bonnevie, Margarete Ottilie (1884–1970)
Bonney, Mary Lucinda (1816–1900)
Booth, Evangeline (1865–1950)
Booth, Maud Ballington (1865–1948)
Bosshardt, Alida M. (1913—)
Bourgeoys, Marguerite (1620–1700)
Bowles, Eva del Vakia (1875–1943)
Brown, Martha McClellan (1838–1916)
Budzynska-Tylicka, Justyna (1876–1936)
Bullinger, Anna (c. 1504–1564)
Bullock, Margaret (1845–1903)
Bullowa, Emilie (1869–1942)
Burjan, Hildegard (1883–1933)
Butler, Josephine (1828–1906)
Cadbury, Geraldine Southall (1865–1941)
Callwood, June (1924—)
Cameron, Donaldina (1869–1968)
Carpenter, Mary (1807–1877)
Casgrain, Thérèse (1896–1981)
Cavendish, Lucy Caroline (1841–1925)
Charteris, Catherine Morice (1835–1918)
Cilento, Phyllis (1894–1987)
Claflin, Tennessee (1846–1923)
Colclough, Mary Ann (1836–1885)
Coman, Katharine (1857–1915)
Coman, Otilia (1942—)
Comstock, Elizabeth Leslie (1815–1891)
Cook, Freda Mary (1896–1990)
Cowie, Bessie Lee (1860–1950)
Crowdy, Rachel (1884–1964)
Cunnington, Eveline Willert (1849–1916)
Cusack, Margaret Anne (1832–1899)
Dall, Caroline Wells (1822–1912)
Darton, Patience (1911–1996)
David, Caroline Edgeworth (1856–1951)
Davis, Paulina Wright (1813–1876)
Decker, Sarah Platt (1852–1912)
de Mille, Agnes (1905–1993)
Denny, Arbella (1707–1792)
Diggs, Annie LePorte (1848–1916)
Dix, Dorothea Lynde (1802–1887)
Dornemann, Luise (1901–1992)
Dransfeld, Hedwig (1871–1925)
Dreier, Katherine Sophie (1877–1952)
Dreier, Margaret (1868–1945)
Dreier, Mary Elisabeth (1875–1963)
Dreier Sisters
Dunham, Katherine (1909–2006)
Edson, Katherine Philips (1870–1933)
Einstein, Hannah Bachman (1862–1929)

Evans, Elizabeth Glendower (1856–1937)
Felton, Rebecca Latimer (1835–1930)
Fenwick, Ethel Gordon (1857–1947)
Fernando, Sylvia (1904–1983)
Ferner, Ellen Elizabeth (1869–1930)
Ferrin, Mary Upton (1810–1881)
Field, Ethel Maude (1882–1967)
Foltz, Clara (1849–1934)
Fonda, Jane (1937—)
Franklin, Jane (1792–1875)
Franklin, Miles (1879–1954)
Fraser, Annie Isabel (1868–1939)
Fraser, Janet (1883–1945)
Freeman, Alice (1857–1936)
French, Marilyn (1929—)
Friedan, Betty (1921–2006)
Fry, Elizabeth (1780–1845)
Fuller, Minnie Rutherford (1868–1946)
Gaines, Irene McCoy (1892–1964)
Gardner, Mary Sewall (1871–1961)
Gellhorn, Edna (1878–1970)
Gérin-Lajoie, Marie (1867–1945)
Gilbert, Ronnie (1926—)
Gilman, Elisabeth (1867–1950)
Gilmer, Elizabeth May (1880–1960)
Gilmore, Mary (1865–1962)
Glen, Esther (1881–1940)
Goldman, Emma (1869–1940)
Goldmark, Josephine (1877–1950)
Gonne, Maud (1866–1953)
Gordon, Anna Adams (1853–1931)
Gordon, Doris Clifton (1890–1956)
Gordon, Jean Margaret (1865–1931)
Gordon, Kate M. (1861–1932)
Gordon, Laura de Force (1838–1907)
Griffin, Elsie Mary (1884–1968)
Griffing, Josephine White (1814–1872)
Hale, Clara (1905–1992)
Hamilton, Alice (1869–1970)
Hansberry, Lorraine (1930–1965)
Harriman, Florence Jaffray (1870–1967)
Hart, Alice (fl. late-19th c.)
Hasbrouck, Lydia Sayer (1827–1910)
Hatcher, Orie Latham (1868–1946)
Hay, Mary Garrett (1857–1928)
Hayden, Mary (1862–1942)
Henry, Alice (1857–1943)
Hill, Octavia (1838–1912)
Hoge, Jane (1811–1890)
Holtby, Winifred (1898–1935)
Hoodless, Adelaide (1857–1910)
Hopkins, Ellice (1836–1904)
Howe, Julia Ward (1819–1910)
Howland, Emily (1827–1929)
How-Martyn, Edith (1875–1954)
Hurst, Fannie (1889–1968)
Hutchins, Grace (1885–1969)
Hutchinson, Amy May (1888–1985)
Iams, Lucy (1855–1924)
Ichikawa Fusae (1893–1981)
Ickes, Anna Thompson (1873–1935)
Ighodaro, Irene (1916–1995)
Ingham, Mary Hall (1866–1937)
Ireland, Patricia (1945—)
Jackson, Sarah Elizabeth (1858–1946)
Jacobs, Aletta (1854–1929)
Jacobs, Pattie Ruffner (1875–1935)
Kaur, Rajkumari Amrit (1889–1964)
Kehew, Mary Morton (1859–1918)
Keller, Nettie Florence (1875–1974)
Kennedy, Kate (1827–1890)
Kingsbury, Susan (1870–1949)
Labotsibeni Gwamile laMdluli (c. 1858–1925)
La Follette, Belle Case (1859–1931)
Lathrop, Julia Clifford (1858–1932)
Laws, Annie (1855–1927)
Lawson, Roberta Campbell (1878–1940)
Leichter, Käthe (1895–1942)
Levine, Lena (1903–1965)
Lewis, Graceanna (1821–1912)
Livermore, Mary A. (1820–1905)
Low, Caroline Sarah (1876–1934)
Lowell, Josephine Shaw (1843–1905)
Lozier, Clemence S. (1813–1888)
Lucas, Margaret Bright (1818–1890)
Lyttelton, Edith (1865–1948)
Martin, Emma (1812–1851)
Martin, Georgia (1866–1946)
Masaryk, Alice Garrigue (1879–1966)
Mason, Lucy Randolph (1882–1959)
May, Abby W. (1829–1888)
McCracken, Mary Ann (1770–1866)
McDowell, Mary Eliza (1854–1936)
McMillan, Margaret (1860–1931)
McMillan, Rachel (1859–1917)
Mead, Lucia Ames (1856–1936)
Menuhin, Hephzibah (1920–1981)
Metcalfe, Alexandra (1903–1995)
Metcalfe, Augusta Corson (1881–1971)
Meyer, Agnes (1887–1970)
Meyer, Lucy (1849–1922)
Miller, Annie Jenness (b. 1859)
Miller, Elizabeth Smith (1822–1911)
Mistral, Gabriela (1889–1957)
Montemayor, Alice Dickerson (1902–1989)
Montgomery, Helen Barrett (1861–1934)
Montseny, Federica (1905–1994)
Morgenstern, Lina B. (1830–1909)
Moskowitz, Belle (1877–1933)
Mumford, Mary Bassett (1842–1935)
Murphy, Emily (1868–1933)
Myrdal, Alva (1902–1986)
Nathan, Maud (1862–1946)
Nation, Carry (1846–1911)
Neill, Elizabeth Grace (1846–1926)
Newman, Angelia L. (1837–1910)
Niboyet, Eugénie (1797–1883)
Nichols, Mary Gove (1810–1884)
Norton, Eleanor Holmes (1937—)
Ocloo, Esther (1919–2002)
O'Hair, Madalyn Murray (1919–1995)
O'Hare, Kate Richards (1876–1948)
Onians, Edith (1866–1955)
O'Reilly, Leonora (1870–1927)
Orelli, Susanna (1845–1939)
Ottenberg, Nettie Podell (1887–1982)
Ottesen-Jensen, Elise (1886–1973)
Ovington, Mary White (1865–1951)
Pacari, Nina (1961—)
Packard, Elizabeth (1816–1897)
Paget, Rosalind (1855–1948)
Palmer, Helen (1917–1979)
Pankhurst, Emmeline (1858–1928)
Parlby, Irene (1868–1965)
Peabody, Elizabeth Palmer (1804–1894)
Pechey-Phipson, Edith (1845–1908)
Perkins, Frances (1880–1965)
Perón, Eva (1919–1952)
Petersen, Alicia O'Shea (1862–1923)
Pettit, Katherine (1868–1936)
Pintasilgo, Maria de Lurdes (1930–2004)
Pizzey, Erin (1939—)
Popp, Adelheid (1869–1939)
Pyke, Margaret (1893–1966)
Ramabai, Pandita (1858–1922)
Rathbone, Eleanor (1872–1946)
Ravera, Camilla (1889–1988)
Reeves, Magdalene Stuart (1865–1953)
Regan, Agnes (1869–1943)
Ricard, Marthe (1889–1982)
Ricker, Marilla (1840–1920)
Roche, Josephine (1886–1976)
Rodríguez, Evangelina (1879–1947)
Roosevelt, Eleanor (1884–1962)
Rose, Ernestine (1810–1892)
Rout, Ettie Annie (1877–1936)
Ruffin, Josephine St. Pierre (1842–1924)
Rumsey, Mary Harriman (1881–1934)
Runciman, Jane Elizabeth (1873–1950)
Rye, Maria Susan (1829–1903)
Sabin, Pauline Morton (1887–1955)
Safford, Mary Jane (1834–1891)
Salomon, Alice (1872–1948)
Sanders, Elizabeth Elkins (1762–1851)
Sanger, Margaret (1879–1966)
Sarandon, Susan (1946—)
Schlesinger, Therese (1863–1940)
Schoff, Hannah Kent (1853–1940)
Schuyler, Louisa Lee (1837–1926)
Schwerin, Jeanette (1852–1899)
Scudder, Vida (1861–1954)
Shaw, Anna Howard (1847–1919)
Sheehy-Skeffington, Hanna (1877–1946)
Signoret, Simone (1921–1985)
Simcox, Edith (1844–1901)
Simkhovitch, Mary (1867–1951)
Simms, Florence (1873–1923)
Slagle, Eleanor Clarke (1871–1942)
Smith, Abby (1797–1878)
Smith, Bathsheba (1822–1910)
Smith, Julia (1792–1886)
Smith, Mary Ellen (1861–1933)
Somerset, Isabella (1851–1921)
Spence, Catherine (1825–1910)
Spencer, Anna (1851–1931)
Stanton, Elizabeth Cady (1815–1902)
Starr, Ellen Gates (1859–1940)
Steinem, Gloria (1934—)
Stewart, Frances Ann (1840–1916)
Stocks, Mary Danvers (1891–1975)
Stoecker, Helene (1869–1943)
Storni, Alfonsina (1892–1938)
Stout, Anna Paterson (1858–1931)
Talbot, Marion (1858–1948)
Taylor, Ann (1782–1866)
Taylor, Elizabeth Best (1868–1941)
Taylor, Helen (1831–1907)
Taylor, Jane (1783–1824)
Templeton, Rini (1935–1986)
Theodoropoulou, Avra (1880–1963)
Thompson, Blanche Edith (1874–1963)
Thompson, Louise (1901–1999)
Tree, Marietta (1917–1991)
Tristan, Flora (1803–1844)
Trollope, Frances Milton (1779–1863)
Tusap, Srbuhi (1841–1901)
Twining, Louisa (1820–1912)
Tyabji, Kamila (1918–2004)
Ueland, Clara Hampson (1860–1927)
Van Kleeck, Mary Abby (1883–1972)
Van Vorst, Marie Louise (1867–1936)
Vasey, Jessie (1897–1966)
von Richthofen, Else (1874–1973)
Wald, Lillian D. (1867–1940)
Ward, Elizabeth Stuart Phelps (1844–1911)
Way, Amanda M. (1828–1914)
Webb, Beatrice (1858–1943)
Wells, Kate Gannett (1838–1911)
Wheeler, Anna Doyle (1785–c. 1850)
Willard, Frances E. (1839–1898)
Willing, Jennie Fowler (1834–1916)
Winkworth, Susanna (1820–1884)
Winter, Alice Ames (1865–1944)
Woerishoffer, Carola (1885–1911)
Wollstonecraft, Mary (1759–1797)
Woolson, Abba Goold (1838–1921)
Wordsworth, Elizabeth (1840–1932)
Wright, Frances (1795–1852)

Yamada, Waka (1879–1956)
Yu Manzhen (fl. 1900)

SOCIALIST
Meer, Fatima (1928—)

SOCIALITE/SOCIETY LEADER
Abrantès, Laure d' (1784–1838)
Aikin, Lucy (1781–1864)
Astor, Caroline Schermerhorn (1830–1908)
Astor, Madeleine Talmadge (c. 1893–1940)
Ayer, Harriet Hubbard (1849–1903)
Bagnold, Enid (1889–1981)
Belmont, Alva Smith (1853–1933)
Bethell, Thyra Talvase (1882–1972)
Bibesco, Marthe Lucie (1887–1973)
Bingham, Anne Willing (1764–1801)
Bingham, Henrietta (1901–1968)
Bonaparte, Elizabeth Patterson (1785–1879)
Breckinridge, Mary (1881–1965)
Chesnut, Mary Boykin (1823–1886)
Clark, Kate Emma (1847–1926)
Clay, Virginia Tunstall (1825–1915)
Cole, Anna Russell (1846–1926)
Cowles, Anna Roosevelt (1855–1931)
Crowe, Ellen (c. 1845–1930)
Cunard, Maud (1872–1948)
Cushing Sisters
Douglas, Adèle Cutts (1835–1899)
Emerson, Faye (1917–1983)
Fish, Marian (1853–1915)
Fosburgh, Minnie Astor (1906–1978)
Franks, Rebecca (c. 1760–1823)
Gardner, Isabella Stewart (1840–1924)
Gibbs, Mary Elizabeth (1836–1920)
Greenhow, Rose O'Neal (c. 1817–1864)
Guest, C.Z. (1920–2003)
Hampton, Hope (1897–1982)
Harkness, Rebekah (1915–1982)
Harriman, Florence Jaffray (1870–1967)
Harriman, Pamela (1920–1997)
Hearst, Catherine Campbell (1917–1998)
Hearst, Millicent (1882–1974)
Henrotin, Ellen Martin (1847–1922)
Herz, Henriette (1764–1847)
Howe, Julia Ward (1819–1910)
Hoyt, Julia (c. 1897–1955)
James, Alice Gibbens (1849–1922)
James, Mary Walsh (1810–1882)
Jones, Jennifer (1919—)
Kehew, Mary Morton (1859–1918)
Kelso, Elizabeth (1889–1967)
Kennedy, Joan (1936—)
Kennedy, Kathleen (1920–1948)
Kingsley, Dorothy (1909–1997)
Lancaster, Nancy (1897–1994)
Lawford, Patricia Kennedy (1924—)
Leslie, Miriam Folline Squier (1836–1914)
Le Vert, Octavia Walton (1811–1877)
Lincoln, Mary Todd (1818–1882)
Longworth, Alice Roosevelt (1884–1980)
Luhan, Mabel Dodge (1879–1962)
MacLeish, Martha Hillard (1856–1947)
Madison, Dolley Payne (1768–1849)
Mansel, Lucy (c. 1830–1915)
Marron, Eugenie (1899–1999)
McCormick, Edith Rockefeller (1872–1932)
McCormick, Katherine Medill (d. 1932)
McLean, Evalyn Walsh (1886–1947)
Mendelssohn, Henriette (1768–1831)
Mesta, Perle (1889–1975)
Mitford, Deborah (1920—)
Mitford, Diana (1910–2003)
Mitford, Unity (1914–1948)
Monckton, Mary (1746–1840)
Montagu, Elizabeth (1720–1800)
Morgan, Frances Louisa (1845–1924)
Morgan, Jane Norton Grew (1868–1925)
Mosley, Cynthia (1898–1933)
Nichols, Ruth (1901–1960)
Paget, Mary (1865–1919)
Paley, Babe (1915–1978)
Palmer, Bertha Honoré (1849–1918)
Parish, Sister (1910–1994)
Parnis, Mollie (1905–1992)
Paston, Agnes (c. 1405–1479)
Pickens, Lucy (1832–1899)
Reid, Helen Rogers (1882–1970)
Reynolds, Rachel Selina (1838–1928)
Rockefeller, Laura Spelman (1839–1915)
Rockefeller, Margaretta (1926—)
Rockefeller, Mary Todhunter (1907–1999)
Roosevelt, Alice Lee (1861–1884)
Roosevelt, Anna Hall (1863–1892)
Roosevelt, Sara Delano (1854–1941)
Sage, Kay (1898–1963)
Sears, Eleanora (1881–1968)
Seton, Elizabeth Ann (1774–1821)
Shippen, Peggy (1760–1804)
Song Meiling (b. 1897)
Speyer, Ellin Prince (1849–1921)
Sprague, Kate Chase (1840–1899)
Swetchine, Anne Sophie (1782–1857)
Tencin, Claudine Alexandrine Guérin de (1685–1749)
Vanderbilt, Alice Gwynne (1845–1934)
Vanderbilt, Gladys Moore (1886–1965)
Vanderbilt, Maria (1821–1896)
Vanderbilt, Sophia Johnson (1797–1868)
Waldegrave, Frances (1821–1879)
Watts Russell, Elizabeth Rose Rebecca (1833/34–1905)
Werlein, Elizebeth Thomas (1883–1946)
Whitney, Betsey Cushing Roosevelt (1908–1998)
Whitney, Gertrude Vanderbilt (1875–1942)
Wilson, Helen Ann (1793/94–1871)
Wister, Sarah Butler (1835–1908)
Wylie, Elinor (1885–1928)

SOCIAL LEADER
Dawson, Mary Elizabeth (1833–1924)
Deans, Jane (1823–1911)
Dougherty, Sarah (c. 1817–1898)

SOCIAL REFORMER
Caro, Margaret (1848–1938)
Cons, Emma (1838–1912)
Daldy, Amey (c. 1829–1920)
Fulton, Catherine (1829–1919)
Phule, Savitribai (1831–1897)
Pickersgill, Mary (1776–1857)
Prejean, Helen (1939—)
Roy, Julie (c. 1938—)
Ruzicka, Marla (1976–2005)
Wolf, Hazel (1898–2000)

SOCIAL-WELFARE ORGANIZATION FOUNDER
Addams, Jane (1860–1935)
Adivar, Halide Edib (c. 1884–1964)
Ames, Fanny Baker (1840–1931)
Anthony, Susan B., II (1916–1991)
Arenal, Concepción (1820–1893)
Awolowo, Hannah (1915—)
Baker, Augusta (1911–1998)
Baker, S. Josephine (1873–1945)
Ballinger, Margaret (1894–1980)
Barnett, Henrietta (1851–1936)
Belmont, Eleanor Robson (1879–1979)
Blachford, Theodosia (1745–1817)
Booth, Maud Ballington (1865–1948)
Bré, Ruth (1862–1911)
Breckinridge, Sophonisba Preston (1866–1948)
Bremer, Edith (1885–1964)
Brunschvicg, Cécile (1877–1946)
Buck, Pearl S. (1892–1973)
Burjan, Hildegard (1883–1933)
Carlén, Emilia (1807–1892)
Coachman, Alice (1923—)
Cobb, Jewell Plummer (1924—)
Cobbe, Frances Power (1822–1904)
Cooper, Whina (1895–1994)
Crothers, Rachel (1878–1958)
Denny, Arbella (1707–1792)
Dick, Gladys (1881–1963)
Dreier, Katherine Sophie (1877–1952)
Dreier, Margaret (1868–1945)
Dreier, Mary Elisabeth (1875–1963)
Duchêne, Gabrielle (1870–1954)
Einstein, Hannah Bachman (1862–1929)
Élizabeth of Ranfaing (d. 1649)
Elizabeth of Wied (1843–1916)
Eustis, Dorothy (1886–1946)
Fabiola (d. 399)
Fedde, Sister Elizabeth (1850–1921)
Felton, Rebecca Latimer (1835–1930)
Gladney, Edna (1886–1961)
Glaser, Elizabeth (1947–1994)
Graf, Steffi (1969—)
Graham, Isabella (1742–1814)
Gratz, Rebecca (1781–1869)
Greville, Frances Evelyn (1861–1938)
Hale, Clara (1905–1992)
Harand, Irene (1900–1975)
Hill, Octavia (1838–1912)
Hopkins, Ellice (1836–1904)
Hunt, Marsha (1917—)
Hurd-Mead, Kate Campbell (1867–1941)
Hurst, Margery (1913–1989)
Idar, Jovita (1885–1946)
Ingraham, Mary Shotwell (1887–1981)
Jackson, Marjorie (1931—)
Jebb, Eglantyne (1876–1928)
Joyner, Florence Griffith (1959–1998)
Juchacz, Marie (1879–1956)
Kossak, Zofia (1890–1968)
Lane, Harriet (1830–1903)
Lazarus, Emma (1849–1887)
Léo, André (1832–1900)
Lewisohn, Alice (1883–1972)
Lewisohn, Irene (1892–1944)
Livermore, Mary A. (1820–1905)
Loeb, Sophie Irene (1876–1929)
Lowell, Josephine Shaw (1843–1905)
Lynn, Kathleen (1874–1955)
Maria I of Braganza (1734–1816)
Martin, Lillien Jane (1851–1943)
Marzouk, Zahia (1906–1988)
McCracken, Mary Ann (1770–1866)
McLean, Alice (1886–1968)
Meredith, Louisa Anne (1812–1895)
Miramion, Madame de (1629–1696)
Monnier, Adrienne (c. 1892–1955)
Morgan, Anne (1873–1952)
Osborne, Susan M. (1858–1918)
Ottendorfer, Anna Uhl (1815–1884)
Paget, Muriel (1876–1938)
Palm, Etta Aelders (1743–1799)
Pankhurst, Sylvia (1882–1960)
Pappenheim, Bertha (1859–1936)
Petre, Maude (1863–1942)
Phuc, Kim (c. 1963—)
Rippin, Jane Deeter (1882–1953)
Rutherford, Mildred (1851–1928)
Sabin, Florence (1871–1953)
Shaw, Pauline Agassiz (1841–1917)
Smith, Emma Hale (1804–1879)

Somerset, Isabella (1851–1921)
Speyer, Ellin Prince (1849–1921)
Stapleton, Ruth Carter (1929–1983)
Stern, Frances (1873–1947)
Tarry, Ellen (b. 1906)
Teresa, Mother (1910–1997)
Theodoropoulou, Avra (1880–1963)
Thompson, Elizabeth Rowell (1821–1899)
Tingley, Katherine (1847–1929)
Trubnikova, Mariia (1835–1897)
Valentine, Lila (1865–1921)
Vejjabul, Pierra (b. 1909)
Von Trapp, Maria (1905–1987)
Waddles, Charleszetta (1912–2001)
Wald, Lillian D. (1867–1940)
Werlein, Elizebeth Thomas (1883–1946)
Weston, Agnes (1840–1918)
Williams, Elizabeth Sprague (1869–1922)
Wise, Louise Waterman (1874–1947)
Wolfe, Catharine L. (1828–1887)
Wood, Edith Elmer (1871–1945)
Wright, Laura Maria (1809–1886)
Youville, Marie Marguerite d' (1701–1771)

SOCIAL-WELFARE REFORMER

Hill, Emily (1847–1930)
Player, Mary Josephine (c. 1857–1924)

SOCIAL-WELFARE WORKER

Abbott, Edith (1876–1957)
Abbott, Grace (1878–1939)
Abegg, Elisabeth (1882–1974)
Abraham, Constance Palgrave (1864–1942)
Aitken, Jessie (1867–1934)
Alden, Cynthia Westover (1862–1931)
Allen, Viola (1867–1948)
Annabella (1909–1996)
Aquash, Anna Mae (1945–1976)
Armitage, Rachelina Hepburn (1873–1955)
Astor, Brooke (b. 1902)
Aubert, Mary Joseph (1835–1926)
Balch, Emily Greene (1867–1961)
Barnum, Gertrude (1866–1948)
Barot, Madeleine (1909–1995)
Barrett, Janie Porter (1865–1948)
Barrett, Kate Waller (1857–1925)
Barton, Clara (1821–1912)
Bateson, Mary (1865–1906)
Batten, Mollie (1905–1985)
Bayer, Adèle (1814–1892)
Bernays, Marie (1883–1939)
Bethune, Mary McLeod (1875–1955)
Birney, Alice McLellan (1858–1907)
Bishop, Isabella (1831–1904)
Bissell, Emily (1861–1948)
Bodichon, Barbara (1827–1891)
Booth, Evangeline (1865–1950)
Booth, Maud Ballington (1865–1948)
Bottomley, Virginia (1948—)
Bowen, Louise (1859–1953)
Bradford, Cornelia Foster (1847–1935)
Bramwell-Booth, Catherine (1883–1987)
Branch, Anna Hempstead (1875–1937)
Breckinridge, Madeline McDowell (1872–1920)
Breckinridge, Sophonisba Preston (1866–1948)
Bremer, Edith (1885–1964)
Bremer, Fredrika (1801–1865)
Brooks, Charlotte (1918—)
Brooks, Gwendolyn (1917–2000)
Brophy, Brigid (1929–1995)
Brown, Minnijean (b. 1942)
Brownson, Josephine (1880–1942)
Bullowa, Emilie (1869–1942)
Burdett-Coutts, Angela (1814–1906)
Byers, Margaret (1832–1912)
Cabrini, Frances Xavier (1850–1917)
Calisher, Hortense (b. 1911)
Cannon, Ida (1877–1960)
Caradus, Elizabeth (1832–1912)
Cardale, Effie (1873–1960)
Carey, Miriam E. (1858–1937)
Carse, Matilda Bradley (1835–1917)
Cartland, Barbara (1901–2000)
Casilda (d. about 1007)
Chapman, Sylvia (1896–1995)
Churchill, Clementine (1885–1977)
Clark, Hilda (1881–1955)
Coffey, Ann (1946—)
Colcord, Joanna Carver (1882–1960)
Collins, Ellen (1828–1912)
Collins, Jennie (1828–1887)
Cousins, Margaret (1878–1954)
Cowie, Eliza Jane (1835–1902)
Coyle, Grace Longwell (1892–1962)
Cratty, Mabel (1868–1928)
Crothers, Rachel (1878–1958)
Cushman, Vera (1876–1946)
Davis, Katharine Bement (1860–1935)
de Burgos, Julia (1914–1953)
Deland, Margaret (1857–1945)
Despard, Charlotte (1844–1939)
Devi, Maitreyi (1914–1990)
Diana (1961–1997)
Dinwiddie, Emily (1879–1949)
Dodge, Grace Hoadley (1856–1914)
Don, Rachel (1866–1941)
Doremus, Sarah Platt (1802–1877)
Draper, Helen (1871–1951)
Drexel, Constance (1894–1956)
Dulles, Eleanor Lansing (1895–1996)
Duncan, Isadora (1878–1927)
Duncan, Sheena (1932—)
Dunn, Loula Friend (1896–1977)
Earhart, Amelia (1897–1937)
Einstein, Hannah Bachman (1862–1929)
Elliott, Maxine (1868–1940)
Falconer, Martha Platt (1862–1941)
Farnham, Eliza W. (1815–1864)
Fedde, Sister Elizabeth (1850–1921)
Fields, Annie Adams (1834–1915)
Figner, Vera (1852–1942)
Fingerin, Agnes (d. 1515)
Fischer, Greta (1909–1988)
Fischer, Ruth (1895–1961)
Flower, Lucy (1837–1921)
Follett, Mary Parker (1868–1933)
Foltz, Clara (1849–1934)
Franklin, Jane (1792–1875)
Friedman, Esther Pauline (1918–2002)
Friedman, Pauline Esther (1918—)
Fukuda Hideko (1865–1927)
Gabrielli, Caterina (1730–1796)
Gaidinliu, Rani (1915–1993)
Gaskell, Elizabeth (1810–1865)
Gasteazoro, Ana (1950–1993)
Geddes, Annabella Mary (1864–1955)
Gilbert, Linda (1847–1895)
Gleason, Kate (1865–1933)
Glenn, Mary Willcox (1869–1940)
Gordon, Annie Elizabeth (1873–1951)
Gordon, Eliza (1877–1938)
Graham, Isabella (1742–1814)
Gredal, Eva (1927–1995)
Greenwood, Ellen Sarah (1837–1917)
Hainisch, Marianne (1839–1936)
Haldane, Elizabeth S. (1862–1937)
Hale, Lucretia Peabody (1820–1900)
Hallowell, Anna (1831–1905)
Hamilton, Gordon (1892–1967)
Hanan, Susanna (1870–1970)
Harari, Manya (1905–1969)
Harris, Barbara (1930—)
Harrison, Hazel (1883–1969)
Haslam, Anna (1829–1922)
Hassan, Margaret (1944–2004)
Haviland, Laura S. (1808–1898)
Hayes, Lucy Webb (1831–1889)
Haynes, Elizabeth Ross (1883–1953)
Height, Dorothy (1912—)
Hesselgren, Kerstin (1872–1962)
Hill, Betty (1919–2004)
Hill, Octavia (1838–1912)
Hobhouse, Emily (1860–1926)
Hobson, Elizabeth Christophers (1831–1912)
Hoey, Jane M. (1892–1968)
Hoge, Jane (1811–1890)
Hooper, Kate Challis (1894–1982)
Hoover, Lou Henry (1874–1944)
Hunt, Marsha (1917—)
Huntington, Emily (1841–1909)
Hurst, Fannie (1889–1968)
Iams, Lucy (1855–1924)
Jacobs, Frances Wisebart (1843–1892)
Jacobs, Harriet A. (1813–1897)
Jameson, Anna Brownell (1794–1860)
Jansen, Elly (1929—)
Jarrett, Mary Cromwell (1877–1961)
Juchacz, Marie (1879–1956)
Kander, Lizzie Black (1858–1940)
Kennedy, Ethel (1928—)
Kingsley, Mary H. (1862–1900)
Kirk, Cybele Ethel (1870–1957)
Köstler, Marie (1879–1965)
Koszutska, Maria (1876–1939)
Krupskaya, Nadezhda (1869–1939)
Kübler-Ross, Elisabeth (1926–2004)
Kuzwayo, Ellen (1914–2006)
Lacey, Janet (1903–1988)
Lagerlöf, Selma (1858–1940)
Lathrop, Julia Clifford (1858–1932)
Lefaucheux, Marie-Helene (1904–1964)
Le Mair, H. Willebeek (1889–1966)
Loeb, Sophie Irene (1876–1929)
Loebinger, Lotte (1905–1999)
Longueville, Anne Geneviève, Duchesse de (1619–1679)
Lothrop, Alice (1870–1920)
Lovejoy, Esther Pohl (1869–1967)
Lowry, Edith (1897–1970)
Lundberg, Emma (1881–1954)
Lyons, Sophie (1848–1924)
Macfarlane, Edith Mary (1871–1948)
Macphail, Agnes (1890–1954)
Maher, Mary Cecilia (1799–1878)
Marie of Rumania (1875–1938)
Marzouk, Zahia (1906–1988)
Maude, Sibylla Emily (1862–1935)
Maxtone Graham, Joyce (1901–1953)
May, Geraldine (1895–1997)
Mbogo, Jael (1939—)
McCombs, Elizabeth Reid (1873–1935)
McMillan, Rachel (1859–1917)
McQueen, Mary (1860–1945)
McVicar, Annie (1862–1954)
Merrill, Mary (1853–1924)
Metcalfe, Augusta Corson (1881–1971)
Michel, Louise (1830–1905)
Minor, Virginia L. (1824–1894)
Morgan, Anne (1873–1952)
Mosher, Eliza Maria (1846–1928)
Mountbatten, Edwina Ashley (1901–1960)
Newman, Angelia L. (1837–1910)
Nichols, Lee Ann (c. 1956–1994)
Nienhuys, Janna
Oddon, Yvonne (1902–1982)
O'Hair, Madalyn Murray (1919–1995)
Ostenso, Martha (1900–1963)
Ottenberg, Nettie Podell (1887–1982)

Ovington, Mary White (1865–1951)
Paget, Muriel (1876–1938)
Palmer, Bertha Honoré (1849–1918)
Palmer, Phoebe Worrall (1807–1874)
Pankhurst, Sylvia (1882–1960)
Pappenheim, Bertha (1859–1936)
Patti, Adelina (1843–1919)
Paul, Alice (1885–1977)
Paul, Annette (1863–1952)
Perkins, Frances (1880–1965)
Peter, Sarah Worthington (1800–1877)
Pethick-Lawrence, Emmeline (1867–1954)
Player, Mary Josephine (c. 1857–1924)
Porter, Eliza Chappell (1807–1888)
Pratt, Anna Beach (1867–1932)
Prior, Margaret (1773–1842)
Rama Rau, Dhanvanthi (1893–1987)
Randolph, Virginia (1874–1958)
Rankin, Annabelle (1908–1986)
Rankin, Jeannette (1880–1973)
Rapoport, Lydia (1923–1971)
Reynolds, Rachel Selina (1838–1928)
Richmond, Mary E. (1861–1928)
Ricker, Marilla (1840–1920)
Rippin, Jane Deeter (1882–1953)
Robertson, Alice Mary (1854–1931)
Robinson, Mary (1944—)
Rohde, Ruth Bryan Owen (1885–1954)
Royden, A. Maude (1876–1956)
Rudman, Annie (1844–1928)
Ryder, Sue (1923–2000)
Salm-Salm, Agnes, Princess (1840–1912)
Salomon, Alice (1872–1948)
Sampson, Edith S. (1901–1979)
Saunders, Cicely (1918–2005)
Schlösinger, Rose (1907–1943)
Schnackenberg, Annie Jane (1835–1905)
Schoff, Hannah Kent (1853–1940)
Schroeder, Bertha (1872–1953)
Schuyler, Philippa Duke (1931–1967)
Scudéry, Madeleine de (1607–1701)
Sendler, Irena (b. 1910)
Shaw, Anna Howard (1847–1919)
Sheehy-Skeffington, Hanna (1877–1946)
Sherwood, Mary Elizabeth (1826–1903)
Sieveking, Amalie (1794–1859)
Sikakane, Joyce Nomafa (1943—)
Smith, Frances Hagell (1877–1948)
Smith, Virginia Thrall (1836–1903)
Smith, Zilpha Drew (1851–1926)
Smythe, Emily Anne (c. 1845–1887)
Snow, Sarah Ellen Oliver (1864–1939)
Solomon, Hannah Greenebaum (1858–1942)
Sonja (1937—)
Spafford, Belle Smith (1895–1982)
Stern, Frances (1873–1947)
Stewart, Catherine Campbell (1881–1957)
Stewart, Mary Downie (1876–1957)
Street, Jessie (1889–1970)
Streeter, Ruth Cheney (1895–1990)
Strong, Anna Louise (1885–1970)
Stuart, Miranda (c. 1795–1865)
Sutherland, Selina Murray McDonald (1839–1909)
Taft, Jessie (1882–1960)
Tarry, Ellen (b. 1906)
Taylor, Elizabeth (1932—)
ten Boom, Corrie (1892–1983)
Tennant, Margaret Mary (1869–1946)
Tennent, Madge Cook (1889–1972)
Tillion, Germaine (b. 1907)
Tingley, Katherine (1847–1929)
Tod, Isabella (1836–1896)
Tolstoy, Alexandra (1884–1979)
Towle, Charlotte (1896–1966)
Truth, Sojourner (c. 1797–1883)
Tsahai Haile Selassie (1919–1942)
Van Lew, Elizabeth (1818–1900)
Van Vorst, Marie Louise (1867–1936)
Van Waters, Miriam (1887–1974)
Volkonskaya, Maria (1805–1863)
Wald, Florence (1917—)
Waldo, Ruth Fanshaw (1885–1975)
Ward, Anne (c. 1825–1896)
Weber, Helene (1881–1962)
West, Dorothy (1907–1998)
Wharton, Edith (1862–1937)
White, Eartha M. (1876–1974)
Whitney, Charlotte Anita (1867–1955)
Whitney, Dorothy Payne (1887–1968)
Whitty, May (1865–1948)
Williams, Elizabeth Sprague (1869–1922)
Williamson, Jessie Marguerite (c. 1855–1937)
Williamson, Sarah Eileen (1974—)
Wilson, Charlotte (1854–1944)
Winnemucca, Sarah (1844–1891)
Wise, Louise Waterman (1874–1947)
Wittenmyer, Annie Turner (1827–1900)
Wittpenn, Caroline Stevens Alexander (1859–1932)
Woodhouse, Margaret Chase Going (1890–1984)
Woolsey, Abby Howland (1828–1893)
Woolsey, Georgeanna Muirson (1833–1906)
Woolsey, Jane Stuart (1830–1891)
Woolsey, Sarah Chauncey (1835–1905)
Wormeley, Katharine Prescott (1830–1908)
Wrede, Mathilda (1864–1928)
Wright, Helena (1887–1982)
Wright, Sophie Bell (1866–1912)
Younghusband, Eileen Louise (1902–1981)
Zell, Katharina Schütz (c. 1497–1562)

SOCIOLINGUIST

Bébel-Gisler, Dany (1935–2003)

SOCIOLOGIST

Aptheker, Bettina (1944—)
Bernard, Jessie (1903–1996)
Blackstone, Tessa (1942—)
Brodber, Erna (1936—)
Campbell, Helen Stuart (1839–1918)
Delphy, Christine (1941—)
Duby-Blom, Gertrude (1901–1993)
First, Ruth (1925–1982)
George, Zelma Watson (1904–1994)
Gorbacheva, Raisa (1932–1999)
Hagood, Margaret (1907–1963)
Hart, Judith (1924—)
Haynes, Elizabeth Ross (1883–1953)
Johnson, Virginia E. (1925—)
Kellor, Frances Alice (1873–1952)
Kirkwood, Julieta (1936–1985)
Komarovsky, Mirra (1906–1999)
Lee, Rose Hum (1904–1964)
Masaryk, Alice Garrigue (1879–1966)
Mayreder, Rosa (1858–1938)
McKenney, Ruth (1911–1972)
Mernissi, Fatima (1940—)
Myrdal, Alva (1902–1986)
Oakley, Ann (1944—)
Parsons, Elsie Clews (1875–1941)
Starovoitova, Galina (1946–1998)
Sullerot, Evelyne (1924—)
Takenishi, Hiroko (1929—)
Thiam, Awa (1936—)
Van Brempt, Kathleen (1969—)
Van Lancker, Anne E.M. (1954—)
Vargas, Virginia (1945—)
Wunderlich, Frieda (1884–1965)
Zaslavskaya, Tatyana (1924—)

SOFTBALL COACH

Fernandez, Lisa (1971—)
Joyce, Joan (1940—)

SOFTBALL PLAYER

Allen, Sandra (1978—)
Ambrosie, Christie (1976—)
Amico, Leah (1974—)
Ando, Misako (1971—)
An Zhongxin (Fl. 1996)
Berg, Laura (1975—)
Bonn, Gillian (1973—)
Brown, Joanne (1972—)
Brundage, Jennifer (1973—)
Bustos, Crystl (1977—)
Carpadios, Marissa (1977—)
Chen Hong
Cooper, Kim (1965—)
Cornell, Sheila (1962—)
Crawford, Fiona (1977—)
Crudgington, Carolyn (1968—)
Dienelt, Kerry (1969—)
Doman, Amanda (1977—)
Edebone, Peta (1969—)
Fairhurst, Sue
Fernandez, Lisa (c. 1971—)
Finch, Jennie (1980—)
Flowers, Tairia (1981—)
Follas, Selina
Freed, Amanda (1979—)
Fujii, Yumiko (c. 1972—)
Granger, Michele (1970—)
Grayson, Betty Evans (1925–1979)
Hardie, Kelly (1969—)
Harding, Tanya (1972—)
Harrigan, Lori (1970—)
Harris, Dionna (1968—)
He Liping
Henderson, Danielle (1977—)
Hodgskin, Natalie (1976—)
Holliday, Jenny (1964—)
Inui, Emi (1983—)
Ishikawa, Taeko (c. 1976—)
Ito, Kazue (1977—)
Iwabuchi, Yumi (1979—)
Joyce, Joan (1940—)
Jung, Lovieanne (1980—)
Kobayashi, Yoshimi (c. 1968—)
Koseki, Shiori (c. 1972—)
Kretschman, Kelly (1979—)
Lei Li
Lester, Joyce (1958—)
Liu Xuqing (1968—)
Liu Yaju
Maher, Kim (1971—)
Masubuchi, Mariko (1980—)
Matsumoto, Naomi (1968—)
Ma Ying
McDermid, Sally (1965—)
McFalls, Jennifer (1971—)
McRae, Francine (1969—)
Mendoza, Jessica (1980—)
Mishina, Masumi (1982—)
Morrow, Simmone (1976—)
Mosley, Tracey (1973—)
Naito, Emi (1979—)
Nelson, Marjorie (1937—)
Nuveman, Stacey (1978—)
Osterman, Catherine (1983—)
Ou Jingbai
Petrie, Haylea (1969—)
Porter, Stacey (1982—)
Richardson, Dot (1961—)
Richardson, Nicole (1970—)
Roche, Melanie (1970—)
Saito, Haruka (1970—)
Sakai, Hiroko (1978—)
Sakamoto, Naoko (1985—)
Sato, Rie (1980—)
Sato, Yuki (1980—)

Smith, Julie (1968—)
Smith, Michele (1967—)
Stokes, Shelly (1967—)
Takayama, Juri (1976—)
Tamoto, Hiroko (c. 1974—)
Tao Hua
Tickey, Bertha (1925—)
Titcume, Natalie (1975—)
Topping, Jenny (1980—)
Tyler, Danielle (1974—)
Ueno, Yukiko (1982—)
Utsugi, Reika (1963—)
Venturella, Michelle (1973—)
Wang Lihong (1970—)
Wang Ying
Ward, Natalie (1975—)
Watley, Natasha (1981—)
Wei Qiang
Wilkins, Brooke (1974—)
Williams, Christa (1978—)
Wilson, Ruth (1919–2001)
Wyborn, Kerry (1977—)
Xu Jian
Yamada, Eri (1984—)
Yamada, Miyo (c. 1976—)
Yamaji, Noriko (1970—)
Yan Fang
Zaharias, Babe Didrikson (1911–1956)
Zhang Chunfang

SOLDIER/WARRIOR

Adivar, Halide Edib (c. 1884–1964)
Agostina (1788–1857)
Amazon Army of Dahomey (1818–1892)
A Nong (c. 1005–1055)
Awashonks (fl. mid-late 17th c.)
Barnwell, Barbara Olive (c. 1919–c. 1977)
Bates, Vietta M. (1922–1972)
Ba Trieu (225–248)
Blanche of Rossi (d. 1237)
Bonney, Anne (1700–?)
Botchkareva, Maria (1889–?)
Bouboulina, Laskarina (1771–1825)
Boudica (26/30–60)
Brant, Molly (c. 1736–1796)
Brewer, Lucy (fl. 1812)
Brownell, Kady (b. 1842)
Cammermeyer, Margarethe (1942—)
Carney, Winifred (1887–1943)
Caulier, Madeleine (d. 1712)
Cavanagh, Kit (1667–1739)
Christie, Susan (c. 1969—)
Chrodielde (fl. 590)
Clarke, Mary (1924—)
Claude des Armoises (fl. 1400s)
Corbin, Margaret Cochran (1751–c. 1800)
Durgawati (d. 1564)
Durova, Nadezhda (1783–1866)
Edmonds, Emma (1841–1898)
England, Lynndie (1982—)
Erauso, Catalina de (1592–1635)
Fernig, Félicité de (c. 1776–after 1831)
Fernig, Théophile de (c. 1779–c. 1818)
Figueur, Thérèse (1774–1861)
Flynn, Jeannie
Foix, Janine-Marie de (fl. 1377)
Fu Hao (fl. 1040 BCE)
Gaboimilla
Garibaldi, Anita (c. 1821–1849)
Grabowski, Halina (1928–2003)
Guirande de Lavaur (d. 1211)
Gwenllian of Wales (fl. 1137)
Harley, Brilliana (c. 1600–1643)
Haye, Nicolaa de la (1160–1218)
Hetha (fl. 10th c.)
Hoskins, Olive (1882–1975)
Hua Mu-Lan (fl. 5th c.)
Jagiello, Appolonia (1825–1866)
Jeanne de Belleville (fl. 1343)
Jeanne des Armoises (fl. 1438)
Joan of Arc (c. 1412–1431)
Johnson, Opha Mae (c. 1899—)
Kang Keqing (1911–1992)
Kosmodemyanskaya, Zoya (1923–1941)
Lakshmibai (c. 1835–1858)
Libussa (c. 680–738)
Litvyak, Lidiya (1921–1943)
Lloyd-Davies, Vanessa (1960–2005)
Longabarba, Bona (fl. 15th c.)
Ludington, Sybil (1761–1839)
Madeleine de Saint-Nectaire (fl. 1575)
Magnus (d. 1676)
Marguerite de Bressieux (d. 1450)
McCauley, Mary Ludwig Hays
Medici, Eleonora de (1522–1562)
Michel, Louise (1830–1905)
Mmanthatisi (c. 1780–c. 1836)
Modthryth (fl. 520)
Nandi (c. 1760s–1827)
Nanny (fl. 1730s)
Nanye'hi (1738–1822)
Njinga (c. 1580s–1663)
Pieronne of Brittany (d. 1430)
Piestewa, Lori Ann (1980–2003)
Plater, Emilja (1806–1831)
Read, Mary (1680–1721)
Rodiani, Onorata (d. 1452)
Roxane (c. 345–310 BCE)
Sampson, Deborah (1760–1827)
Sandes, Flora (1876–1956)
Senesh, Hannah (1921–1944)
Sforza, Caterina (c. 1462–1509)
Sichelgaita of Salerno (1040–1090)
Siege Warfare and Women (8th c.–17th c.)
Silang, Gabriela (1731–1763)
Smirnow, Zoya (fl. 1914)
Snell, Hannah (1723–1792)
Stanley, Charlotte (1599–1664)
Statira II (c. 360–331 BCE)
Stuart, Miranda (c. 1795–1865)
Talbot, Mary Anne (1778–1808)
Tamiris (fl. 550–530 BCE)
Tattersall, Philippa (c. 1975—)
Taytu (c. 1850–1918)
Te Kiri Karamu, Heni (1840–1933)
Thalestris (fl. 334 BCE)
Thusnelda (fl. 1st c.)
Tomoe Gozen (fl. c. 12th c.)
Travers, Susan (1909–2003)
Trung Sisters (d. 43)
Vaught, Wilma L. (1930—)
Velásquez, Loreta (1842–1897)
Walsh, Loretta (1898–c. 1988)
Wa Shi (1498–1560)
Wetamoo (c. 1650–1676)
Zenobia (r. 267–272)

SONGWRITER

Agnesi, Maria Teresa (1720–1795)
Alexander, Cecil Frances (1818–1895)
Aluli, Irmgard (c. 1912–2001)
Amos, Tori (1963—)
Amphlett, Christina (c. 1960—)
Armen, Kay (1920—)
Axton, Mae Boren (1914–1997)
Baillie, Grizel (1665–1746)
Bates, Katherine Lee (1859–1929)
Bean, Janet Beveridge (1964—)
Benatar, Pat (1953—)
Berberian, Cathy (1925–1983)
Bergman, Marilyn (1929—)
Bjork (1965—)
Blamire, Susanna (1747–1794)
Bonoff, Karla (1952—)
Bryant, Felice (1925–2003)
Bush, Kate (1958—)
Carey, Mariah (1970—)
Carnes, Kim (1945—)
Carpenter, Mary Chapin (1958—)
Carter, Anita (b. 1933)
Carter, Carlene (1955—)
Carter, Helen (b. 1927)
Cash, June Carter (1929—)
Cash, June Carter (1929–2003)
Cole, Paula (1968—)
Colvin, Shawn (1956—)
Comden, Betty (1915—)
Coolidge, Priscilla
Crawford, Louise Macartney (1790–1858)
Cunningham, Agnes (1909–2004)
DeMent, Iris (1961—)
Denny, Sandy (1947–1978)
DeShannon, Jackie (1944—)
Dickson, Barbara (1947—)
DiFranco, Ani (1970—)
Duncan, Rosetta (1890–1959)
Duncan, Vivian (1902–1986)
Elliott, Missy (1971—)
Enya (1961—)
Exene (1956—)
Fields, Dorothy (1904–1974)
Fisher, Doris (1915–2003)
Fordham, Julia (1962—)
Harvey, P.J. (1969—)
Hendryx, Nona (1945—)
Howie, Fanny Rose (1868–1916)
Hynde, Chrissie (1951—)
Ian, Janis (1951—)
Iyall, Debora (1954—)
King, Carole (1942—)
Lang, K.D. (1961—)
Larson, Nicolette (1952–1997)
Lauper, Cyndi (1953—)
Lee, Peggy (1920–2002)
Leigh, Carolyn (1926–1983)
Lil' Kim (1975—)
Lincoln, Abbey (1930—)
Lopes, Lisa (1971–2002)
Lulu (1948—)
Lynn, Barbara (1942—)
Lynn, Loretta (1935—)
MacColl, Kirsty (1959–2000)
Madonna (1958—)
Manchester, Melissa (1951—)
Mangeshkar, Lata (1929—)
Mann, Aimee (1960—)
McKee, Maria (1964—)
McLachlan, Sarah (1968—)
McVie, Christine (1943—)
Merchant, Natalie (1963—)
Mira Bai (1498–1547)
Mitchell, Joni (1943—)
Monnot, Marguerite (1903–1961)
Morissette, Alanis (1974—)
Nairne, Carolina (1766–1845)
Near, Holly (1949—)
Nicks, Stevie (1948—)
Nyro, Laura (1947–1997)
Ono, Yoko (1933—)
Osborne, Joan (1962—)
Oslin, K.T. (1941—)
Parton, Dolly (1946—)
Praxilla (fl. 450 BCE)
Quatro, Suzi (1950—)
Rexach, Sylvia (1922–1961)
Reynolds, Malvina (1900–1978)
Roche, Maggie (1951—)
Sade (1959—)

Occupational Index

Sainte-Marie, Buffy (1941—)
Schekeryk, Melanie (1947—)
Scott, Sherry (c. 1948—)
Seeger, Peggy (1935—)
Simon, Carly (1945—)
Simone, Nina (1933—)
Simone, Nina (1933–2003)
Simpson, Valerie (1946—)
Smith, Patti (1946—)
Spivey, Victoria (1906–1976)
Streisand, Barbra (1942—)
Sunshine, Marion (1894–1963)
Vega, Suzanne (1959—)
Velazquez, Consuelo (1916–2005)
Warnes, Jennifer (1947—)
West, Dottie (1932–1991)
White, Karyn (1965—)
White, Maude Valerie (1855–1937)
Williams, Lucinda (1953—)
Williams, Victoria (1958—)
Wright, Betty (1953—)
Wright, Syreeta (1946–2004)

SORCERER/SOOTHSAYER
See Prophet/sibyl/visionary.

SPANISH DANCER
Cobos, Antonia (c. 1920—)
Doering, Jane (c. 1922—)
Lopez, Encarnación (1898–1945)
Maracci, Carmelita (b. 1911)
Mercé, Antonia (c. 1886–1936)
Otero, Caroline (1868–1965)
Ricarda, Ana (c. 1925—)

SPECIAL-EDUCATION EXPERT
Davey, Constance (1882–1963)
Dunlop, Florence (c. 1896–1963)
Faggs, Mae (1932—)
Koontz, Elizabeth (1919–1989)
Rogers, Harriet B. (1834–1919)
Stern, Catherine Brieger (1894–1973)
Vachetta, Roseline (1951—)

SPEECH/READING SPECIALIST
Gardner, Maria Louisa (1879–1968)
Kahn, Madeline (1942–1999)
Lewis, Elma (1921—)
McAllister, Anne Hunter (1892–1983)
Wood, Evelyn (1909–1995)

SPEECHWRITER
Noonan, Peggy (1950—)

SPEEDSKATER
An Sang-Mi
Auch, Susan (1966—)
Averina, Tatiana (1950–2001)
Baier, Anke (1972—)
Bazhanova, Svetlana (1972—)
Börner, Jacqueline (1965—)
Boudrias, Christine (1972—)
Klein, Kit (1910–1985)

SPIRITUALIST
Blavatsky, Helena (1831–1891)
Brown, Rosemary (1916–2001)
Claflin, Tennessee (1846–1923)
Cottrell, Violet May (1887–1971)
Davis, Mary Fenn (1824–1886)
Davis, Paulina Wright (1813–1876)
DeMorgan, Evelyn (1850–1919)
Fox, Kate (c. 1839–1892)
Fox, Leah (c. 1818–1890)
Fox, Margaret (c. 1833–1893)
Glyn, Elinor (1864–1943)
Harris, Jane Elizabeth (c. 1852–1942)
Marion, Frances (1888–1973)
Nichols, Mary Gove (1810–1884)
Palladino, Eusapia (1854–1918)
Piper, Leonora E. (1859–1950)
Rambova, Natacha (1897–1966)
Woodhull, Victoria (1838–1927)

SPIRITUAL LEADER
See Religious/spiritual leader.

SPIRITUAL WRITER
See Religious/spiritual writer.

SPORTS ADMINISTRATOR
Bell, Elizabeth Viola (1897–1990)

SPORTS/ATHLETICS EDUCATOR
See Athletic coach/instructor.
See Physical-education instructor.

SPORTSCASTER
George, Phyllis (1949—)

SPORTS-TEAM OWNER
Manley, Effa (1900–1981)
Payson, Joan Whitney (1903–1975)

SPORTSWEAR DESIGNER
Jacobs, Helen Hull (1908–1997)
Maxwell, Vera (1901–1995)
McCardell, Claire (1905–1958)
Neumann, Vera (1907–1993)
Reid, Rose Marie (1906–1978)
Stewart, Ellen (c. 1920—)

SPORTS WRITER
Bland, Lilian (1878–1971)
Pollard, Marjorie (1899–1982)
Rosenfeld, Fanny (1905–1969)
Rosenfeld, Fanny "Bobbie" (1903–1969)
St. Johns, Adela Rogers (1894–1988)

SPRINTER
See Runner.

SPY
Aaronsohn, Sarah (1890–1917)
Atkins, Vera (c. 1908–2000)
Bailey, Ann (1742–1825)
Behn, Aphra (1640?–1689)
Bell, Gertrude (1868–1926)
Benario, Olga (1908–1942)
Bentley, Elizabeth Turrill (1908–1963)
Boom, Christel (1927–2004)
Borrel, Andrée (1919–1944)
Boyd, Belle (1844–1900)
Brousse, Amy (1910–1963)
Brunner, Josefine (1909–1943)
Bunke, Tamara (1937–1967)
Carré, Mathilde (1908–c. 1970)
Chisholm, Janet (1929–2004)
Cohen, Lona (1913–1993)
Cohen, Shula (fl. 1960s)
Coppi, Hilde (1909–1943)
Cornescou, Irina Soltanovna (1916—)
Cushman, Pauline (1833–1893)
de Bettignies, Louise (d. 1918)
Dorn, Erna (1912–1953)
Eberhardt, Isabelle (1877–1904)
Edmonds, Emma (1841–1898)
Falkenhayn, Benita von (d. 1935)
Fénelon, Fania (1918–1983)
Granville, Christine (1915–1952)
Greenhow, Rose O'Neal (c. 1817–1864)
Harnack, Mildred (1902–1943)
Harrison, Marguerite (1879–1967)
Hart, Nancy (c. 1846–1902)
Herrmann, Liselotte (1909–1938)
Honecker, Margot (1927—)
Ingalls, Laura H. (c. 1900–c. 1988)
Kawashima, Yoshiko (1906–1947)
Khan, Noor Inayat (1914–1944)
Knuth, Maria (d. 1954)
Kuckhoff, Greta (1902–1981)
Kuczinski, Ruth (1907–2000)
Makaryeva, Nadiezhda (1925—)
Malinovska, Valentina
Marble, Alice (1913–1990)
McKenna, Marthe (1893–1969)
Oddon, Yvonne (1902–1982)
O'Hare, Kate Richards (1876–1948)
Palm, Etta Aelders (1743–1799)
Perez, Maria (fl. 13th c.)
Pierce, Joanne E. (c. 1941—)
Plessis, Alphonsine (1824–1847)
Poyntz, Juliet Stuart (1886–c. 1937)
Radyonska, Tanya (1924—)
Rafael, Sylvia (1938–2005)
Reik, Haviva (1914–1944)
Reisner, Larissa (1895–1926)
Ricard, Marthe (1889–1982)
Rimington, Stella (1935—)
Rinaldi, Angela (c. 1916—)
Roley, Susan Lynn (c. 1947—)
Rosenberg, Ethel (1915–1953)
Salavarrieta, Pola (1795–1817)
Sansom, Odette (1912–1995)
Schultz, Sigrid (1893–1980)
Schulze-Boysen, Libertas (1913–1942)
Schumacher, Elisabeth (1904–1942)
Senesh, Hannah (1921–1944)
Stöbe, Ilse (1911–1942)
Szabo, Violette (1921–1945)
Théroigne de Méricourt, Anne-Josèphe (1762–1817)
Tillion, Germaine (b. 1907)
Tubman, Harriet (1821–1913)
Van Lew, Elizabeth (1818–1900)
Velásquez, Loreta (1842–1897)
Vicario, Leona (1789–1842)
Villameur, Lise (1905–2004)
Walkinshaw, Clementina (c. 1726–1802)
Walter, Lucy (c. 1630–1658)
Witherington, Pearl (1914—)
Yurina, Esfir (1923—)
Zelle, Margaretha (1876–1917)

SQUASH PLAYER
Devoy, Susan (1964—)
McKay, Heather (1941—)
Sears, Eleanora (1881–1968)

STADHOLDER
Maria Christina (1742–1798)
Maria Elisabeth (1680–1741)

STAGECOACH DRIVER
Field, Mary (1896–c. 1968)
Orchard, Sadie (c. 1853–1943)
Parkhurst, Charlotte (d. 1879)

STAGECOACH ROBBER
Hart, Pearl (c. 1875–c. 1924)

STAINED-GLASS ARTIST/DESIGNER
Barker, Cicely Mary (1895–1973)
Fortesque-Brickdale, Eleanor (1872–1945)
Geddes, Wilhelmina (1887–1955)
Hone, Evie (1894–1955)
Mackintosh, Margaret (1865–1933)
Oakley, Violet (1874–1961)
O'Brien, Catherine (1881–1963)
Purser, Sarah (1848–1943)

Rhind, Ethel (c. 1879–1952)
Tauber-Arp, Sophie (1889–1943)

STATISTICIAN
Chadwick, Florence (1918–1995)
Cox, Gertrude Mary (1900–1978)
Cunliffe, Stella (1917—)
Geiringer, Hilda (1893–1973)
Gutteridge, Helena Rose (1879–1960)
Hagood, Margaret (1907–1963)
Kipling, Charlotte (1919–1992)
Kock, Karin (1891–1976)
Steel, Dawn (1946–1997)
Wright, Judith (1915–2000)

STENOGRAPHER
Rout, Ettie Annie (1877–1936)

STEWARDESS
Hicks, Adelaide (1845–1930)

STILL-LIFE PAINTER
Content, Marjorie (1895–1984)
Galizia, Fede (1578–1630)
Hamnett, Nina (1890–1956)
Hartigan, Grace (1922—)
Hodgkins, Frances (1869–1947)
Jones, Loïs Mailou (1905–1998)
Lempicka, Tamara de (1898–1980)
Lundeberg, Helen (1908–1999)
Modersohn-Becker, Paula (1876–1907)
Moillon, Louise (1610–1696)
Münter, Gabriele (1877–1962)
Neel, Alice (1900–1984)
Nourse, Elizabeth (1859–1938)
Oosterwyck, Maria van (1630–1693)
Peale, Anna Claypoole (1791–1878)
Peale, Margaretta Angelica (1795–1882)
Peale, Sarah Miriam (1800–1885)
Peeters, Clara (1594–after 1657)
Preston, Margaret Rose (c. 1875–1963)
Redpath, Anne (1895–1965)
Ruysch, Rachel (1664–1750)
Sandel, Cora (1880–1974)
Stern, Irma (1894–1966)
Valadon, Suzanne (1865–1938)
Vallayer-Coster, Anne (1744–1818)
Wyeth, Henriette (1907–1997)

STORYTELLER
Arnow, Harriette Simpson (1908–1986)
Bailey, Carolyn Sherwin (1875–1961)
Baker, Augusta (1911–1998)
Brown, Marcia (1918—)
Crosby, Fanny (1820–1915)
Cusack, Dymphna (1902–1981)
Dinesen, Isak (1885–1962)
Düringsfeld, Ida von (1815–1876)
Ewing, Juliana Horatia (1841–1885)
Goethe, Elisabeth (1730–1808)
Hurston, Zora Neale (c. 1891–1960)
Johnston, Mary (1870–1936)
Lagerlöf, Selma (1858–1940)
Lindgren, Astrid (1907–2002)
Macdonald, Flora (1722–1790)
Park, Ruth (1923—)
Porter, Anna Maria (1780–1832)
Potter, Beatrix (1866–1943)
Prince, Lucy Terry (c. 1730–1821)
Richardson, Henry Handel (1870–1946)
Sawyer, Ruth (1880–1970)
Sayers, Peig (1873–1958)
Skram, Amalie (1846–1905)
Thérèse of Lisieux (1873–1897)
Thompson, Flora (1876–1947)
Wiggin, Kate Douglas (1856–1923)
Wilson, Nancy (1937—)

STRIPTEASE ARTIST
See Exotic dancer.

STUNT PERFORMER
Barnes, Pancho (1901–1975)
Gibson, Helen (1892–1977)
Holm, Eleanor (1913—)
Holmes, Helen (1892–1950)
Omlie, Phoebe Fairgrave (1902–1975)
O'Neil, Kitty (1947—)

SUFFRAGIST
Adam, Juliette la Messine (1836–1936)
Addams, Jane (1860–1935)
Allen, Florence Ellinwood (1884–1966)
Allen, Mary Sophia (1878–1964)
Ames, Blanche (1878–1969)
Ames, Jessie Daniel (1883–1972)
Anderson, Elizabeth Garrett (1836–1917)
Anneke, Mathilde Franziska (1817–1884)
Anthony, Katharine Susan (1877–1965)
Anthony, Susan B. (1820–1906)
Auclert, Hubertine (1848–1914)
Augspurg, Anita (1857–1943)
Austin, Mary Hunter (1868–1934)
Avery, Rachel G. (1858–1919)
Ayrton, Hertha Marks (1854–1923)
Bailey, Hannah Johnston (1839–1923)
Bajer, Matilde (1840–1934)
Baker, Isabel Noeline (1878–1958)
Baker, S. Josephine (1873–1945)
Balfour, Betty (1867–1942)
Balfour, Frances (1858–1931)
Barns, Cornelia Baxter (1888–1941)
Barrett, Kate Waller (1857–1925)
Barron, Jennie Loitman (1891–1969)
Barry, Leonora M. (1849–1930)
Barton, Clara (1821–1912)
Bateson, Mary (1865–1906)
Bayly, Ada Ellen (1857–1903)
Beale, Dorothea (1831–1906)
Bear-Crawford, Annette (1853–1899)
Beard, Mary Ritter (1876–1958)
Becker, Lydia (1827–1890)
Belmont, Alva Smith (1853–1933)
Bennett, Louie (1870–1956)
Benson, Stella (1892–1933)
Bernardino, Minerva (1907–1998)
Berry, Harriet Morehead (1877–1940)
Besant, Annie (1847–1933)
Billington-Greig, Teresa (1877–1964)
Bishop, Harriet E. (1817–1883)
Bittenbender, Ada Matilda (1848–1925)
Black, Clementina (1854–1922)
Blackburn, Helen (1842–1903)
Blackwell, Alice Stone (1857–1950)
Blair, Catherine (1872–1946)
Blake, Lillie Devereux (1833–1913)
Blankenburg, Lucretia L. (1845–1937)
Blatch, Harriot Stanton (1856–1940)
Bloomer, Amelia Jenks (1818–1894)
Bloor, Ella Reeve (1862–1951)
Bohm-Schuch, Clara (1879–1936)
Boissevain, Inez M. (1886–1916)
Boissevain, Mia (1878–1959)
Bondfield, Margaret (1873–1953)
Booth, Evangeline (1865–1950)
Botchkareva, Maria (1889–?)
Boucherett, Jessie (1825–1905)
Bradwell, Myra (1831–1894)
Breckinridge, Madeline McDowell (1872–1920)
Breckinridge, Sophonisba Preston (1866–1948)
Brion, Hélène (1882–1962)
Brown, Hallie Quinn (c. 1845–1949)
Brown, Olympia (1835–1926)
Brown, Rosemary (1930—)
Brown Blackwell, Antoinette (1825–1921)
Brunschvicg, Cécile (1877–1946)
Bryant, Louise (1885–1936)
Bugbee, Emma (1888–1981)
Burleigh, Celia C. (1826–1875)
Burns, Lucy (1879–1966)
Burroughs, Nannie Helen (c. 1878–1961)
Butler, Josephine (1828–1906)
Cadilla de Martínez, Maria (1886–1951)
Calkins, Mary Whiton (1863–1930)
Campoamor, Clara (1888–1972)
Cannon, Annie Jump (1863–1941)
Caradus, Elizabeth (1832–1912)
Carney, Winifred (1887–1943)
Carpenter, Mary (1807–1877)
Carroll, Anna Ella (1815–1894)
Cary, Mary Ann Shadd (1823–1893)
Cary, Phoebe (1824–1871)
Casgrain, Thérèse (1896–1981)
Catt, Carrie Chapman (1859–1947)
Cauer, Minna (1841–1922)
Chace, Elizabeth Buffum (1806–1899)
Chapin, Augusta (1836–1905)
Charlotte (1896–1985)
Chase, Agnes Meara (1869–1963)
Chauvin, Jeanne (1862–1926)
Cheney, Ednah Dow (1824–1904)
Chevenix, Helen (1886–1963)
Claflin, Tennessee (1846–1923)
Clark, Hilda (1881–1955)
Clarke, Grace Julian (1865–1938)
Clarke, Mary Goulden (d. 1910)
Clay, Laura (1849–1941)
Clay, Virginia Tunstall (1825–1915)
Cobbe, Frances Power (1822–1904)
Colby, Clara Bewick (1846–1916)
Collett, Camilla (1813–1895)
Colton, Mary (1822–1898)
Cons, Emma (1838–1912)
Corbett, Marie (1859–1932)
Corbett-Ashby, Margery (1882–1981)
Courtney, Kathleen (1878–1974)
Cousins, Margaret (1878–1954)
Couzins, Phoebe Wilson (1842–1913)
Crane, Caroline Bartlett (1858–1935)
Cunningham, Minnie Fisher (1882–1964)
Dalrymple, Learmonth White (1827–1906)
Daniels, Mabel Wheeler (1878–1971)
Dark, Eleanor (1901–1985)
David, Caroline Edgeworth (1856–1951)
Davies, Emily (1830–1921)
Davies, Margaret Llewelyn (1861–1944)
Davis, Paulina Wright (1813–1876)
Davison, Emily (1872–1913)
Day, Dorothy (1897–1980)
Demorest, Ellen Curtis (1824–1898)
Denison, Flora MacDonald (1867–1921)
Dennett, Mary Ware (1872–1947)
Deroin, Jeanne-Françoise (1805–1894)
Despard, Charlotte (1844–1939)
DeVoe, Emma Smith (1848–1927)
Diggs, Annie LePorte (1848–1916)
Dilke, Emily (1840–1904)
Dorr, Rheta Childe (1866–1948)
Douglas, Marjory Stoneman (1890–1998)
Dransfeld, Hedwig (1871–1925)
Dreier, Katherine Sophie (1877–1952)
Dreier, Margaret (1868–1945)
Dreier, Mary Elisabeth (1875–1963)
Drexel, Constance (1894–1956)
Drummond, Flora (1869–1949)
Dulac, Germaine (1882–1942)
Dunbar-Nelson, Alice (1875–1935)
Duniway, Abigail Scott (1834–1915)
Durand, Marguerite (1864–1936)
Dyk, Ruth (1901–2000)

Earle, Alice Morse (1851–1911)
Eastman, Annis Ford (1852–1910)
Eastman, Crystal (1881–1928)
Eberle, Abastenia St. Leger (1878–1942)
Edger, Kate (1857–1935)
Edwards, Henrietta Muir (1849–1933)
Elliott, Sarah Barnwell (1848–1928)
Evans, Elizabeth Glendower (1856–1937)
Evans, Mary Anne (1819–1880)
Fawcett, Millicent Garrett (1847–1929)
Felton, Rebecca Latimer (1835–1930)
Fern, Fanny (1811–1872)
Ferrin, Mary Upton (1810–1881)
Fickert, Auguste (1855–1910)
Field, Sara Bard (b. 1882)
Fisher, Cicely Corbett (1885–1959)
Fisher, Margaret (c. 1874–1958)
Fleming, Williamina Paton (1857–1911)
Florence, Mary Sargant (1857–1954)
Flynn, Elizabeth Gurley (1890–1964)
Foltz, Clara (1849–1934)
Ford, Isabella O. (1855–1924)
Franklin, Miles (1879–1954)
Freundlich, Emmy (1878–1948)
Fukuda Hideko (1865–1927)
Fuller, Minnie Rutherford (1868–1946)
Fullerton, Mary Eliza (1868–1946)
Furuhjelm, Annie (1854–1937)
Gage, Matilda Joslyn (1826–1898)
Gale, Zona (1874–1938)
Galindo de Topete, Hermila (1896–1954)
Gardener, Helen Hamilton (1853–1925)
Gardiner, Muriel (1901–1985)
Garrett, Mary Elizabeth (1854–1915)
Gellhorn, Edna (1878–1970)
Gellhorn, Martha (1908–1998)
Gérin-Lajoie, Marie (1867–1945)
Gilman, Charlotte Perkins (1860–1935)
Goldstein, Vida (1869–1949)
Gordon, Jean Margaret (1865–1931)
Gordon, Kate M. (1861–1932)
Gordon, Laura de Force (1838–1907)
Gore-Booth, Eva (1870–1926)
Gougar, Helen (1843–1907)
Gourd, Emilie (1879–1946)
Grant, Julia (1826–1902)
Grew, Mary A. (1813–1896)
Grimké, Sarah Moore (1792–1873)
Guilbert, Yvette (1865–1944)
Gutteridge, Helena Rose (1879–1960)
Gwynne-Vaughan, Helen (1879–1967)
Hagan, Ellen (1873–1958)
Hainisch, Marianne (1839–1936)
Hamilton, Cicely (1872–1952)
Hamilton, Mary (1882–1966)
Hanaford, Phebe Ann (1829–1921)
Harper, Ida Husted (1851–1931)
Harraden, Beatrice (1864–1936)
Harriman, Florence Jaffray (1870–1967)
Hasbrouck, Lydia Sayer (1827–1910)
Haslam, Anna (1829–1922)
Hatton, Marion (1835–1905)
Haviland, Laura S. (1808–1898)
Hay, Mary Garrett (1857–1928)
Hayden, Mary (1862–1942)
Hebard, Grace Raymond (1861–1936)
Henderson, Christina Kirk (1861–1953)
Henry, Alice (1857–1943)
Heymann, Lida (1867–1943)
Hill, Emily (1847–1930)
Hollingworth, Leta Stetter (1886–1939)
Holmes, Julia Archibald (1838–1887)
Hooker, Isabella Beecher (1822–1907)
Hooper, Jessie Jack (1865–1935)
Hopkins, Ellice (1836–1904)
Horne, Alice Merrill (1868–1948)
Hosmer, Harriet (1830–1908)
Houston, Lucy (1858–1936)
Howe, Julia Ward (1819–1910)
Howland, Emily (1827–1929)
Huck, Winnifred Sprague Mason (1882–1936)
Hull, Hannah (1872–1958)
Hunt, Violet (1866–1942)
Hunton, Addie D. Waites (1875–1943)
Ichikawa, Fusae (1893–1981)
Ichikawa Fusae (1893–1981)
Ingham, Mary Hall (1866–1937)
Inglis, Elsie Maud (1864–1917)
Irwin, Inez Haynes (1873–1970)
Jacob, Rosamund (1888–1960)
Jacobs, Aletta (1854–1929)
Jacobs, Pattie Ruffner (1875–1935)
Johnson, Adelaide (1859–1955)
Johnston, Mary (1870–1936)
Jones, Jane Elizabeth (1813–1896)
Jordan, Elizabeth Garver (1865–1947)
Juchacz, Marie (1879–1956)
Kearney, Belle (1863–1939)
Keller, Helen (1880–1968)
Kelley, Florence (1859–1932)
Kendall, Marie Hartig (1854–1943)
Kenney, Annie (1879–1953)
Kenyon, Dorothy (1888–1972)
Kirchwey, Freda (1893–1976)
Krog, Gina (1847–1916)
Kuliscioff, Anna (c. 1854–1925)
La Follette, Belle Case (1859–1931)
Lagerlöf, Selma (1858–1940)
Laidlaw, Harriet Burton (1873–1949)
Lampkin, Daisy (1883–1965)
La Rochefoucauld, Edmée, Duchesse de (1895–1991)
Lathrop, Julia Clifford (1858–1932)
Laughlin, Gail (1868–1952)
Lawson, Louisa (1848–1920)
Lease, Mary Elizabeth (1853–1933)
Lee, Mary (1821–1909)
Lemlich, Clara (1888–1982)
Leslie, Miriam Folline Squier (1836–1914)
Lewald, Fanny (1811–1889)
Lewis, Graceanna (1821–1912)
Livermore, Mary A. (1820–1905)
Lockrey, Sarah Hunt (1863–1929)
Lockwood, Belva Ann (1830–1917)
Longshore, Hannah E. (1819–1901)
Lovejoy, Esther Pohl (1869–1967)
Lozier, Clemence S. (1813–1888)
Lucas, Margaret Bright (1818–1890)
Luce, Clare Boothe (1903–1987)
Lutz, Berta (1894–1976)
Lynn, Kathleen (1874–1955)
Lytton, Constance (1869–1923)
MacFall, Frances E. (1854–1943)
Macmillan, Chrystal (1871–1937)
Macurdy, Grace Harriet (1866–1946)
Madison, Cleo (1883–1964)
Mahoney, Mary Eliza (1845–1926)
Mangakahia, Meri Te Tai (1868–1920)
Manning, Marie (c. 1873–1945)
Mansfield, Arabella (1846–1911)
Manus, Rosa (1881–1942)
Markievicz, Constance (1868–1927)
Martin, Anne Henrietta (1875–1951)
Martin, Lillien Jane (1851–1943)
Masaryk, Charlotte Garrigue (1850–1923)
Mason, Lucy Randolph (1882–1959)
May, Abby W. (1829–1888)
May, Isabella (1850–1926)
McClung, Nellie L. (1873–1951)
McCormick, Katharine Dexter (1875–1967)
McCormick, Ruth Hanna (1880–1944)
McCoubrey, Margaret (1880–1955)
McCracken, Elizabeth (c. 1865–1944)
McCreery, Maria (1883–1938)
McCulloch, Catharine (1862–1945)
McKane, Alice Woodby (1865–1948)
McKinney, Louise (1868–1931)
McMillan, Rachel (1859–1917)
McNeill, Florence Marian (1885–1973)
Mead, Lucia Ames (1856–1936)
Merrick, Caroline (1825–1908)
Meynell, Alice (1847–1922)
Miller, Emma Guffey (1874–1970)
Miller, Florence Fenwick (1854–1935)
Minor, Virginia L. (1824–1894)
Misme, Jane (1865–1935)
Mitchell, Hannah (1871–1956)
Monod, Sarah (1836–1912)
Moreau de Justo, Alicia (1885–1986)
Morris, Esther Hobart (1814–1902)
Mott, Lucretia (1793–1880)
Mundt, Klara Müller (1814–1873)
Murphy, Emily (1868–1933)
Murray, Margaret (1863–1963)
Mussey, Ellen Spencer (1850–1936)
Nathan, Maud (1862–1946)
Niboyet, Eugénie (1797–1883)
Nichols, Clarina (1810–1885)
Nicol, Helen Lyster (1854–1932)
Noailles, Anna de (1876–1933)
Nolan, Mae Ella (1886–1973)
Norris, Kathleen (1880–1966)
Nutting, Mary Adelaide (1858–1948)
O'Day, Caroline (1869–1943)
O'Hare, Kate Richards (1876–1948)
O'Neill, Rose Cecil (1874–1944)
O'Reilly, Leonora (1870–1927)
Osburn, Lucy (1835–1891)
Ostler, Emma Brignell (c. 1848–1922)
O'Sullivan, Mary Kenney (1864–1943)
Ottenberg, Nettie Podell (1887–1982)
Ottesen-Jensen, Elise (1886–1973)
Owens-Adair, Bethenia (1840–1926)
Palencia, Isabel de (1878–c. 1950)
Pankhurst, Adela (1885–1961)
Pankhurst, Christabel (1880–1958)
Pankhurst, Emmeline (1858–1928)
Pankhurst, Sylvia (1882–1960)
Park, Maud Wood (1871–1955)
Parlby, Irene (1868–1965)
Paterson, Emma (1848–1886)
Patterson, Hannah (1879–1937)
Paul, Alice (1885–1977)
Peabody, Elizabeth Palmer (1778–1853)
Pechey-Phipson, Edith (1845–1908)
Peck, Annie Smith (1850–1935)
Pelletier, Madeleine (1874–1939)
Perón, Eva (1919–1952)
Petersen, Alicia O'Shea (1862–1923)
Pethick-Lawrence, Emmeline (1867–1954)
Pinchot, Cornelia (1881–1960)
Pollitzer, Anita (1894–1975)
Popp, Adelheid (1869–1939)
Potonié-Pierre, Eugénie (1844–1898)
Powell, Mary Sadler (1854/55?–1946)
Preston, May Wilson (1873–1949)
Pugh, Sarah (1800–1884)
Putnam, Helen (1857–1951)
Rankin, Jeannette (1880–1973)
Rathbone, Eleanor (1872–1946)
Rattray, Lizzie Frost (1855–1931)
Ray, Charlotte E. (1850–1911)
Reeves, Magdalene Stuart (1865–1953)
Reid, Helen Rogers (1882–1970)
Remond, Sarah Parker (1826–1894)
Reynolds, Rachel Selina (1838–1928)
Rhondda, Margaret (1883–1958)
Richards, Shelah (1903–1985)

Ricker, Marilla (1840–1920)
Rinehart, Mary Roberts (1876–1958)
Ripley, Martha Rogers (1843–1912)
Rives, Amélie (1863–1945)
Robins, Elizabeth (1862–1952)
Robinson, Harriet Hanson (1825–1911)
Rodríguez, Evangelina (1879–1947)
Rose, Ernestine (1810–1892)
Roussel, Nelly (1878–1922)
Royden, A. Maude (1876–1956)
Ruffin, Josephine St. Pierre (1842–1924)
Russell, Lillian (1861–1922)
Sabin, Florence (1871–1953)
Safford, Mary Jane (1834–1891)
Sage, Margaret Olivia (1828–1918)
Salmon, Lucy Maynard (1853–1927)
Sanford, Maria Louise (1836–1920)
Schlesinger, Therese (1863–1940)
Schmahl, Jeanne (1846–1916)
Schnackenberg, Annie Jane (1835–1905)
Schneiderman, Rose (1882–1972)
Schreiber, Adele (1872–1957)
Schreiner, Olive (1855–1920)
Schwimmer, Rosika (1877–1948)
Scott, Rose (1847–1925)
Scott-Maxwell, Florida (1883–1979)
Scudder, Janet (1869–1940)
Seaman, Elizabeth Cochrane (1864–1922)
Seidel, Amalie (1876–1952)
Seton, Grace Gallatin (1872–1959)
Severance, Caroline M. (1820–1914)
Sewall, May Wright (1844–1920)
Seymour, Mary F. (1846–1893)
Shaarawi, Huda (1879–1947)
Shafik, Doria (1908–1975)
Shaw, Anna Howard (1847–1919)
Shaw, Mary G. (1854–1929)
Shaw, Pauline Agassiz (1841–1917)
Sheehy-Skeffington, Hanna (1877–1946)
Sheppard, Kate (1847–1934)
Sherwin, Belle (1868–1955)
Sherwood, Katharine Margaret (1841–1914)
Sherwood, Mary (1856–1935)
Shuler, Nettie Rogers (1862–1939)
Sidgwick, Eleonora Mildred (1845–1936)
Simkhovitch, Mary (1867–1951)
Sinclair, May (1863–1946)
Smith, Abby (1797–1878)
Smith, Julia (1792–1886)
Smith, Zilpha Drew (1851–1926)
Smyth, Ethel (1858–1944)
Snyder, Alice D. (1887–1943)
Somerville, Nellie Nugent (1863–1952)
Southworth, E.D.E.N. (1819–1899)
Spence, Catherine (1825–1910)
Spencer, Anna (1851–1931)
St. Denis, Ruth (1877–1968)
Stanton, Elizabeth Cady (1815–1902)
Stevens, Lillian (1844–1914)
Stewart, Eliza Daniel (1816–1908)
Stewart, Isabel Maitland (1878–1963)
Stocks, Mary Danvers (1891–1975)
Stone, Constance (1856–1902)
Stone, Lucy (1818–1893)
Stopes, Marie (1880–1958)
Storni, Alfonsina (1892–1938)
Stowe, Emily Howard (1831–1903)
Strachey, Pippa (1872–1968)
Strachey, Ray (1887–1940)
Strange, Michael (1890–1950)
Stritt, Marie (1856–1928)
Swanwick, Helena (1864–1939)
Swisshelm, Jane Grey (1815–1884)
Taylor, Helen (1831–1907)
Taylor, Lucy Hobbs (1833–1910)
Taylor, Sophia Louisa (1847–1903)
Terrell, Mary Church (1863–1954)
Thomas, Lillian Beynon (1874–1961)
Thomas, M. Carey (1857–1935)
Thomas, Mary Myers (1816–1888)
Thompson, Dorothy (1893–1961)
Thompson, Elizabeth Rowell (1821–1899)
Thorpe, Rose Hartwick (1850–1939)
Tod, Isabella (1836–1896)
Todd, Marion Marsh (1841–post 1913)
Troup, Augusta Lewis (c. 1848–1920)
Tubman, Harriet (1821–1913)
Turner, Eliza Sproat (1826–1903)
Ueland, Clara Hampson (1860–1927)
Upton, Harriet Taylor (1853–1945)
Uttley, Alison (1884–1976)
Uzès, Anne, Duchesse d' (1847–1933)
Valentine, Lila (1865–1921)
Vanderbilt, Consuelo (1877–1964)
Vernon, Mabel (1883–1975)
Vérone, Maria (1874–1938)
Villard, Fanny Garrison (1844–1928)
Waite, Catherine (1829–1913)
Wald, Lillian D. (1867–1940)
Walker, Mary Edwards (1832–1919)
Wallace, Zerelda G. (1817–1901)
Ward, Elizabeth Stuart Phelps (1844–1911)
Ward, Hortense (1872–1944)
Way, Amanda M. (1828–1914)
Webb, Beatrice (1858–1943)
Weber, Helene (1881–1962)
Webster, Augusta (1837–1894)
Weed, Ethel (1906–1975)
Weiss, Louise (1893–1983)
Wells, Emmeline B. (1828–1921)
Wells, Marguerite Milton (1872–1959)
Wells-Barnett, Ida (1862–1931)
Welsh, Lilian (1858–1938)
West, Rebecca (1892–1983)
Wheeler, Anna Doyle (1785–c. 1850)
White, Anna (1831–1910)
White, Sue Shelton (1887–1943)
Whiting, Lilian (1847–1942)
Whitman, Sarah Helen (1803–1878)
Whitney, Charlotte Anita (1867–1955)
Whitney, Dorothy Payne (1887–1968)
Wilkinson, Ellen (1891–1947)
Willard, Frances E. (1839–1898)
Willing, Jennie Fowler (1834–1916)
Windeyer, Mary (1836–1912)
Wittenmyer, Annie Turner (1827–1900)
Woerishoffer, Carola (1885–1911)
Wolstenholme-Elmy, Elizabeth (1834–1913)
Woodbury, Helen Sumner (1876–1933)
Woodhull, Victoria (1838–1927)
Woolf, Virginia (1882–1941)
Woolley, Helen (1874–1947)
Workman, Fanny (1859–1925)
Wright, Martha Coffin (1806–1875)
Wylie, Ida A.R. (1885–1959)
Wyse Power, Jennie (1858–1941)
Yamada Waka (1879–1956)
Yevonde (1893–1975)
Yosano Akiko (1878–1942)
Younger, Maud (1870–1936)

SULTANA
de Rivery, Aimee Dubucq (c. 1762–1817)
Gülabahar (fl. 1521)
Hadice Turhan (1627–1683)
Hafsa (d. 1534)
Hatice (fl. 1500–1536)
Kösem (1589–1651)
Nurbanu (1525–1583)
Razia (1211–1240)
Reign of Women (1520–1683)
Roxelana (c. 1504–1558)
Safiye (d. 1603)
Sah Sultana (fl. 1500s)
Shajar al-Durr (d. 1259)

SUPREME COURT JUSTICE
See Justice of the U.S. Supreme Court.

SURFER
Andersen, Lisa (1969—)
Benson, Linda (c. 1944—)
Botha, Wendy (1965—)
Burridge, Pam (1965—)
Calhoun, Marge (fl. 1950s)
Ching, Laura Blears (c. 1951—)
Hawkins, Mary Ann (1919–1993)
Hoffman, Joyce (c. 1948—)
Kennelly, Keala (1978—)
Kohner, Kathy (1941—)
Letham, Isobel (1899–1995)
Mearig, Kim (1963—)
Menczer, Pauline (1970—)
Munro, Mimi (1952—)
Nelson, Jodie (1976—)
O'Donnell, Phyllis (1937—)
Poppler, Jericho (1951—)
Sunn, Rell (1951–1998)
Zamba, Frieda (1965—)

SURGEON
Albright, Tenley (1935—)
Aldrich-Blake, Louisa (1865–1925)
André, Valerie (1922—)
Barringer, Emily Dunning (1876–1961)
Barrows, Isabel Hayes (1845–1913)
Brown, Charlotte (1846–1904)
Brown, Dorothy (1919—)
Bryant, Alice Gertrude (c. 1862–1942)
Cleveland, Emeline Horton (1829–1878)
Cust, Aleen (1868–1937)
Dickens, Helen Octavia (1909–2001)
Dimock, Susan (1847–1875)
Frantz, Virginia Kneeland (1896–1967)
Guillemete du Luys (fl. 1479)
Hersende of France (fl. 1250)
Inglis, Elsie Maud (1864–1917)
Joshua, Joan O. (1912–1993)
Keller, Nettie Florence (1875–1974)
Lin, Hazel (1913–1986)
Margaret of Ypres (fl. 1322)
Maxwell, Constantia (1886–1962)
McLean, Mary Hancock (1861–1930)
Mergler, Marie Josepha (1851–1901)
Morani, Alma Dea (1907–2001)
Murray, Lilian (1871–1960)
Pattison, Dorothy W. (1832–1878)
Richardson, Dot (1961—)
Romano, Francesca (fl. 1321)
Scharlieb, Mary Ann (1845–1930)
Scudder, Ida (1870–1960)
Stuart, Miranda (c. 1795–1865)
Summerskill, Edith (1901–1980)
Thomas, Debi (1967—)
Thompson, Mary Harris (1829–1895)
Travell, Janet G. (1901–1997)
Van Hoosen, Bertha (1863–1952)
Virdimura of Sicily (fl. 1376)
Walker, Mary Edwards (1832–1919)

SURGEON GENERAL (U.S.)
Elders, Joycelyn (1933—)
Novello, Antonia (1944—)
Petry, Lucile (1902–1999)

SUSPENSE-FICTION WRITER
See Mystery/Suspense-fiction writer.

SWIMMER

Abdo, Reema (1963—)
Abernethy, Moira (1939—)
Adler, Margarete (1896–?)
Ahmann-Leighton, Crissy (1970—)
Alexander, Lisa (1968—)
Alshammar, Therese (1977—)
Amundrud, Gail (1957—)
Andersen, Greta (1927—)
Andrew, Janice (1943—)
Andrews, Theresa (1962—)
Anke, Hannelore (1957—)
Antonova, Elena (1974–)
Aoki, Mayumi (1953—)
Arendt, Gisela (1918–1969)
Arsenault, Samantha (1981—)
Atwood, Susan (1953—)
Azarova, Elena (1973—)
Babanina, Svetlana (1943—)
Babashoff, Shirley (1957—)
Babb-Sprague, Kristen (1968—)
Ball, Catherine (1951—)
Bardach, Georgina (1983—)
Barker, Florence (b. 1908)
Barkman, Jane (1951—)
Baron, Mietje (1908–1948)
Barr, Beth (1971—)
Bartosik, Alison (1983—)
Bauer, Sybil (1903–1927)
Bauerschmidt, Maritta (1950—)
Beachley, Layne (1972—)
Beard, Amanda (1981—)
Beaumont, Lyne (1978—)
Becker-Pinkston, Elizabeth (1903–1989)
Beckmann, Gudrun (1955—)
Bedford, B.J. (1972—)
Bedford, Marie (1907—)
Beier, Roswitha (1956—)
Bell, Lynette (1947—)
Bell, Marilyn (1937—)
Belote, Melissa (1956—)
Benko, Lindsay (1976—)
Bennett, Brooke (1980—)
Bentum, Cornelia van (1965—)
Berg, Aina (b. 1902)
Beumer, Catharina (1947—)
Beyermann, Ina (1967—)
Bianco, Suzannah (1973—)
Bimolt, Klena (1945—)
Bjedov, Djurdica (1947—)
Bleibtrey, Ethelda M. (1902–1978)
Bogdanova, Yuliya (1964—)
Boglioli, Wendy (1955—)
Botsford, Beth (1981—)
Braun, Maria-Johanna (1911–1982)
Bremner, Janice (1974—)
Brendel, Daniela (1973—)
Bridges, Alice (1916—)
Brienese, Karin (1969—)
Brigitha, Enith Salle (1955—)
Brunner, Ursula (1941—)
Brusnikina, Olga (1978—)
Burke, Lynn (1943—)
Buschschulte, Antje (1978—)
Cai Huijue
Calligaris, Novella (1954—)
Calub, Dyana (1975—)
Cameron, Michelle (1962—)
Campbell, Jeannette (1916–2003)
Caron, Christine (1948—)
Carr, Catherine (1954—)
Carson, Gladys (b. 1903)
Carstensen-Nathansen, Fritze (1925—)
Carver-Dias, Claire (1977—)
Caslaru, Beatrice (1975—)
Caulkins, Tracy (1963—)
Cederqvist, Jane (1945—)
Chadwick, Florence (1918–1995)
Chan, Erin (1979—)
Chao Na
Chen Yan (1981—)
Clark, Barbara Lynne (1958—)
Clark, Karen (1972—)
Cleland, Tammy (1975—)
Cliff, Leslie (1955—)
Cohen, Tiffany (1966—)
Colella, Lynn (1950—)
Colqhoun, Alva (1942—)
Cone, Carin (1940—)
Cooper, Margaret Joyce (b. 1909)
Corridon, Marie (1930—)
Corson, Marilyn (1954—)
Costie, Candace (1963—)
Coughlan, Angela (1952—)
Coughlin, Natalie (1982—)
Coventry, Kirsty (1983—)
Cox, Lynne (1957—)
Crapp, Lorraine J. (1938—)
Croft, June (1963—)
Crow, Tamara (1977—)
Curtis, Ann (1926—)
Czopek, Agnieszka (1964—)
Dahne, Heike (1961—)
Dallmann, Petra (1978—)
Dangalakova-Bogomilova, Tanya (1964—)
Daniel, Ellie (1950—)
Davies, Elizabeth Valerie (b. 1912)
Davies, Judy Joy (1928—)
Davies, Sharron (1962—)
Davydova, Anastasia (1983—)
Deardurff, Deena (1957—)
de Bruijn, Inge (1973—)
Dedieu, Virginie (1979—)
de Jong, Reggie (1964—)
Dekker, Inge (1985—)
Dendeberova, Yelena (1969—)
Dennis, Clare (1916–1971)
de Rover, Jolanda (1963—)
de Varona, Donna (1947—)
Devyatova, Tatyana (1949—)
Dewar, Phyllis (1915–1961)
Diers, Ines (1963—)
Dobratz, Erin (1982—)
Doerries, Jana (1975—)
Donnelly, Euphrasia (b. 1906)
Draves, Victoria (1924—)
Dressel, Vally (1893—)
Duenkel, Ginny (1947—)
Duenkel, Jenny (b. 1947)
Duggan, Keltie (1970—)
Durack, Fanny (1889–1956)
Dyroen-Lancer, Becky (1971—)
Eberle, Verena (1950—)
Ederle, Gertrude (1905–2003)
Edwards, Margaret (1939—)
Egami, Ayano
Egerszegi, Krisztina (1974—)
Eife, Andrea (1956—)
Ellis, Kathleen (1946—)
Ender, Kornelia (1958–)
Engel-Kramer, Ingrid (1943—)
Epstein, Charlotte (1884–1938)
Eriksson, Agneta (1965—)
Ermakova, Anastasia (1983—)
Evans, Janet (1971—)
Everlund, Gurli (1902–1985)
Ferguson, Cathy Jean (1948—)
Figues de Saint Marie, Solenne (1979—)
Finneran, Sharon (1946—)
Fletcher, Jennie (1890–1968)
Fonteyn, Karen (1969—)
Ford, Michelle Jan (1962—)
Fox, Catherine (1977—)
Frankeva, Antoaneta (1971—)
Fraser, Dawn (1937—)
Frechette, Sylvie (1967—)
Freeman, Mavis (1918—)
Friedrich, Heike (1970—)
Frommater, Uta (1948—)
Fuhrmann, Barbel (1940—)
Fujii, Raika (1974—)
Fujiki, Mayuko (1975—)
Fujimaru, Michiyo (1979—)
Gabriel-Koether, Rosemarie (1956—)
Garapick, Nancy (1961—)
Garatti-Saville, Eleanor (1909—)
Garceau, Catherine (1978—)
Geissler, Ines (1963—)
Genenger, Martha (1911—)
Geraghty, Agnes (1906–1974)
Geweniger, Ute (1964—)
Gibson, Catherine (1931—)
Gibson, Cheryl (1959—)
Goebel, Barbara (1943—)
Goetz, Janina (1981—)
Gordon, Helen (1934—)
Gotz, Daniela (1987—)
Gould, Shane (1956—)
Goyette, Cynthia (1946—)
Greville, Julia (1979—)
Grishchenkova, Alla (1961—)
Gromova, Maria (1984—)
Groot, Chantal (1982—)
Grunert, Martina (1949—)
Guest, Irene (1900–1979)
Gurr, Donna Marie (1955—)
Gustafsson, Tina (1962—)
Gustavson, Linda (1949—)
Gyarmati, Andrea (1954—)
Gyenge, Valeria (1933—)
Gylling, Jane (1902–1961)
Hadding, Annette (1975—)
Haislett, Nicole (1972—)
Halbsguth, Ruth (1916—)
Hall, Kaye (1951—)
Hambrook, Sharon (1963—)
Hanson, Brooke (1978—)
Han Xue (1981—)
Happe-Krey, Ursula (1926—)
Harada, Saho (1982—)
Hardcastle, Sarah (1969—)
Harding, Phyllis (b. 1907)
Harrison, Joan (1935—)
Harstick, Sara (1981—)
Harup, Karen-Margrete (1924—)
Hase, Dagmar (1969—)
Hasse, Ute (1963—)
Hedgepeth, Whitney L. (1971—)
Heemskerk, Marianne (1944—)
Heijting-Schuhmacher, Irma (1925—)
Helser, Brenda (1926—)
Hempel, Claudia (1958—)
Henke, Jana (1973—)
Henne, Jan (1947—)
Henneken, Thamar (1979—)
Henry, Jodie (1983—)
Herbst, Christine (1957—)
Heyns, Penny (1974—)
Higson, Allison (1973—)
Hogg, Wendy (1956—)
Hogshead, Nancy (1962—)
Holm, Eleanor (1913–2004)
Hörner, Silke (1965—)
Hould-Marchand, Valérie (1980—)
Huang Xiaomin (1970—)
Huelsenbeck, Sarina (1962—)
Hughes, Edna (1916—)

Hunger, Daniela (1972—)
Hustede, Heike (1946—)
Hveger, Ragnhild (1920—)
Hyman, Misty (1979—)
Ichtchenko, Natalia (1986—)
Isoda, Yoko
Iwasaki, Kyoko (1978—)
Jackson, Trina (1977—)
Jacobsen, Else (1911–1965)
James, Hilda (b. 1904)
Jameson, Helen (1963—)
Jardin, Anne (1959—)
Jasontek, Rebecca (1975—)
Jeans, Constance (b. 1899)
Jedrzejczak, Otylia (1983—)
Jeffrey, Rhi (1986—)
Jezek, Linda (1960—)
Jimbo, Rei
Jöhncke, Louise (1976—)
Johns, Helen (1914—)
Johnson, Emma (1980—)
Johnson, Jenna (1967—)
Jones, Leisel (1985—)
Jorgensen, Janel (1971—)
Josephson, Karen (1964—)
Josephson, Sarah (1964—)
Joyce, Kara Lynn (1985—)
Kaciusyte, Lina (1963—)
Kalama, Thelma (1931–1999)
Kammerling, Anna-Karin (1980—)
Kawabe, Miho (1974—)
Kawamoto, Evelyn (1933—)
Kawase, Akiko (1971—)
Kawashima, Naoko (1981—)
Keith, Vicki (1959—)
Kellerman, Annette (1886–1975)
Kelly, Margaret (1956—)
Kemp, Jennifer (1955—)
Kempner, Patty (1942—)
Kerr, Jane (1968—)
Khasyanova, Elvira (1981—)
Kielgass, Kerstin (1969—)
Kight-Wingard, Lenore (1911–2000)
Kimura, Saeko (1963—)
King, Ellen (b. 1909)
Kint, Cor (d. 2002)
Kirichenko, Olga (1976—)
Kisseleva, Maria (1974—)
Kitao, Kanako (1982—)
Kleber, Ina (1964—)
Kleine, Megan (1974—)
Klochkova, Yana (1982—)
Knacke, Christiane (1962—)
Kok, Ada (1947—)
Kolb, Claudia (1949—)
Komarova, Stanislava (1986—)
Komisarz, Rachel (1976—)
Konetzni, Hilde (1905–1980)
Konrads, Ilsa (1944—)
Koshevaya, Marina (1960—)
Kotani, Mikako (1966—)
Koujela, Olga (1985—)
Kovacs, Agnes (1981—)
Kowal, Kristy (1978—)
Kozlova, Anna (1972—)
Kraus, Angelika (1950—)
Krause, Barbara (1959—)
Krause, Roswitha (1949—)
Kremer, Mitzi (1968—)
Kriel, Marianne
Kruglova, Yelena (1962—)
Kruse, Pamela (1950—)
Kryczka, Kelly (1961—)
Kueper, Ursula (1937—)
Kulesza, Kasia (1976—)
Lackie, Ethel (1907–1979)
Ladde, Cornelia (1915—)
Lagerberg, Catherina (1941—)
Lambert, Adelaide (1907–1996)
Landells, Suzanne (1964—)
Lapp, Bernice (1917—)
Larsen, Christine (1967—)
Lassig, Rosemary (1941—)
LaVine, Jacqueline (1929—)
Lay, Marion (1948—)
Leech, Faith (1941—)
Le Jingyi (1975—)
Lempereur, Ingrid (1969—)
Lenton, Lisbeth (1985—)
LeSueur, Emily Porter (1972—)
Letourneau, Fanny (1979—)
Lewis, Hayley (1974—)
Lignot, Myriam (1975—)
Li Ji (1986—)
Limpert, Marianne (1972—)
Lindner, Helga (1951—)
Lin Li (1970—)
Linssen-Vaessen, Marie-Louise (1928–1993)
Liu Limin (1976—)
Ljungdahl, Carina (1960—)
Lohmar, Leni (1914—)
Lonsbrough, Anita (1941—)
Loveless, Lea (1971—)
Lowe, Sara (1984—)
Lu Bin (1977—)
Lung, Noemi Ildiko (1968—)
Luo Xuejuan (1984—)
Lyons, Beatrice (1930—)
Maakal, Jenny (1913—)
Maas, Annelies (1960—)
Machnow, Emy (1897–1974)
MacPherson, Michelle (1966—)
Madison, Helene (1913–1970)
Maehata, Hideko (1914–1995)
Manaudou, Laure (1986—)
Mann, Shelley (1937—)
Maracineanu, Roxana (1975—)
Maroney, Susan Jean (1974—)
Marsman, Margot (1932—)
Martensson, Agneta (1961—)
Martino, Angel (1967—)
Mastenbroek, Rie (1919—)
Mastenbroek, Rie (1919–2003)
Mayer, Helene (1910–1953)
McClements, Lyn (1951—)
McCormick, Kelly (1960—)
McCormick, Patricia (1930—)
McDonald, Julie (1970—)
McFall, Lauren (1980—)
McFarlane, Tracey (1966—)
McGill, Linda (1945—)
McKean, Olive (1915—)
McKenzie, Grace (b. 1903)
McKim, Josephine (1910—)
Meagher, Mary T. (1964—)
Mealing, Philomena (1912–2002)
Meany, Helen (1904–1991)
Meissner, Katrin (1973—)
Melien, Lori (1972—)
Meshcheryakova, Natalya (1972—)
Metella, Malia (1982—)
Metschuck, Caren (1963—)
Meyer, Debbie (1952—)
Milch, Klara (1891—)
Mills, Alice (1986—)
Minamoto, Sumika (1979—)
Mitchell, Elizabeth (1966—)
Mocanu, Diana (1984—)
Moe, Karen (1952—)
Moehring, Anke (1969—)
Moore, Isabella (1894–1975)
Moras, Karen (1954—)
Moravcova, Martina (1976—)
Morgan, Sandra (1942—)
Morton, Lucy (1898–1980)
Motoyoshi, Miwako (1960—)
Muehe, Lotte (1910–1981)
Muis, Marianne (1968—)
Muis, Mildred (1968—)
Munz, Diana (1982—)
Murphy, Janice (1942—)
Myburgh, Jeanette (1940—)
Myburgh, Natalie (1940—)
Nakajima, Riho (1978—)
Nakamura, Mai (1979—)
Nakamura, Reiko (1982—)
Nakanishi, Yuko (1981—)
Nakao, Miki (1978—)
Nall, Anita (1976—)
Neall, Gail (1955—)
Nehua, Katerina (1903–1948)
Neilson, Sandy (1956—)
Nesbitt, Stephanie (1985—)
Newby-Fraser, Paula (1962—)
Nian Yun (c. 1983—)
Nielsson, Susanne (1960—)
Nilsson, Karin (b. 1904)
Noall, Patricia (1970—)
Nord, Kathleen (1965—)
Norelius, Martha (1908–1955)
Normand, Kirstin (1974—)
Nott, Andrea (1982—)
Novak, Eva (1930—)
Novak, Ilona (1925—)
Novokshchenova, Olga (1974—)
Nugent, Andrea (1968—)
Nyad, Diana (1949—)
Okuno, Fumiko (1972—)
O'Neill, Susie (1973—)
Onishi, Junko (1974—)
Osgerby, Ann (1963—)
Osipowich, Albina (1911–1964)
Osygus, Simone (1968—)
Ottenbrite, Anne (1966—)
Otto, Kristin (1966—)
Otto, Louise (1896—)
Ouden, Willemijntje den (1918–1997)
Ovchinnikova, Elena (1982—)
Oversloot, Maria (1914—)
Pang Jiaying (1985—)
Patrascoiu, Aneta (1957—)
Pearson, Michele (1962—)
Pease, Heather (1975—)
Pechstein, Heidi (1944—)
Pedersen, Susan (1953—)
Pellegrini, Federica (1988—)
Perchina, Irina (1978—)
Pettersson, Wivan (1904–1976)
Peyton, Kim (1957–1986)
Phillips, Karen (1966—)
Pielen, Silke (1955—)
Pielke, Christiane (1963—)
Piper, Carly (1983—)
Playfair, Judy (1953—)
Plewinski, Catherine (1968—)
Poewe, Sarah (1983—)
Poirot, Catherine (1963—)
Poleska, Anne (1980—)
Polit, Cornelia (1963—)
Poll, Claudia (1972—)
Poll, Sylvia (1970—)
Pollack, Andrea (1961—)
Potec, Camelia Alina (1982—)
Priemer, Petra (1961—)
Primrose-Smith, Elizabeth (c. 1948—)
Prozumenshchykova, Galina (1948—)
Qian Hong (1971—)
Quance, Kristine (1975—)

Quann, Megan (1984—)
Radcliffe, Charlotte (b. 1903)
Rai, Pamela (1966—)
Ramenofsky, Marilyn (1946—)
Ramey, Nancy (1940—)
Ramirez, Maria Teresa (1953—)
Randall, Martha (1948—)
Rapp, Susan (1965—)
Rawls, Katherine (1918–1982)
Read, Cari (1970—)
Reineck, Heidemarie (1952—)
Reinisch, Rica (1965—)
Rennie, Rhoda
Richardson, Michelle (1969—)
Richter, Ulrike (1959—)
Riedel, Petra (1964—)
Riggin, Aileen (1906–2002)
Riise-Arndt, Eva (1919—)
Riley, Samantha (1972—)
Roberts, Susan (1939—)
Rooney, Giaan (1982—)
Rosazza, Joan (1935—)
Rosenberg, Grete (1896–1979)
Rothhammer, Keena (1957—)
Rudkovskaya, Yelena (1973—)
Ruiz, Tracie (1963—)
Rund, Cathleen (1977—)
Rusanova, Lyubov (1954—)
Russell, Kathleen
Ruuska, Sylvia (1942—)
Ryan, Sarah (1977—)
Sandeno, Kaitlin (1983—)
Sanders, Summer (1972—)
Savelyeva, Tatyana (1947—)
Savery, Jill (1972—)
Schileru, Dacia W.
Schlicht, Svenja (1967—)
Schmidt, Carmela (1962—)
Schmidt, Ingrid (1945—)
Schmitz, Ingeborg (1922—)
Schmuck, Uta (1949—)
Schneider, Petra (1963—)
Schneyder, Nathalie (1968—)
Schoenfield, Dana (1953—)
Schoenrock, Sybille (1964—)
Scholz, Anke (1978—)
Schrader, Hilde (1910–1966)
Schroth, Frances (b. 1893)
Schuler, Carolyn (1943—)
Schulze, Sabina (1972—)
Schuster, Susanne (1963—)
Sears, Eleanora (1881–1968)
Sears, Mary (1939—)
Sedakova, Olga (c. 1972—)
Sehmisch, Elke (1955—)
Seick, Karin (1961—)
Selbach, Johanna (1918—)
Senff, Dina (1920—)
Shan Ying (1978—)
Shealey, Courtney (c. 1978—)
Shibata, Ai (1982—)
Shields, Susan (1952—)
Shorina, Anna (1982—)
Shubina, Yelena (1974—)
Siering, Lauri (1957—)
Simmons-Carrasco, Heather (1970—)
Simons, Nancy (1938—)
Sirch, Cornelia (1966—)
Sjöberg, Johanna (1978—)
Sloan, Susan (1958—)
Smith, Michelle (1969—)
Smith, Rebecca (1959—)
Smith, Shannon (1961—)
Soia, Elena (1981—)
Sorensen, Inge (1924—)
Speirs, Annie (1889–1926)
Spillane, Joan (1943—)
Steer, Irene (1889–1947)
Steffin, Christel (1940—)
Steinbach, Angela (1955—)
Steinbach, Sabine (1952—)
Steinbeck, Janet (1951—)
Steinseifer, Carrie (1968—)
Stellmach, Manuela (1970—)
Stepan, Mary Louise (1935—)
Sterkel, Jill (1961—)
Stevenson, Nicole (1971—)
Steward, Natalie (1943—)
Stewart, Jean (1930—)
Stewart, Sarah (1911—)
Sticker, Josephine (1894—)
Stickles, Terri Lee (1946—)
Stindt, Hermine (1888–1974)
Stobs, Shirley (1942—)
Stockbauer, Hannah (1982—)
Stouder, Sharon (1948—)
Strauss, Astrid (1968—)
Streeter, Alison (1964—)
Strunnikova, Natalya (1964—)
Sudduth, Jill (1971—)
Suzuki, Emiko (1981—)
Swagerty, Jane (1951—)
Szabo, Tünde (1974—)
Szekely, Eva (1927—)
Szoke, Katalin (1935—)
Tachibana, Miya (1974—)
Taillon, Jacinthe (1977—)
Tajima, Yasuko (1981—)
Takahashi, Kaori (1974—)
Takayama, Aki (1970—)
Takeda, Miho (1976—)
Tanaka, Junko (1973—)
Tanaka, Masami (1979—)
Tanaka, Miyako (1967—)
Tanaka, Satoko (1942—)
Tanner, Elaine (1951—)
Tanner, Vera (b. 1906)
Taormina, Sheila (1969—)
Tappin, Ashley T. (1974—)
Tatham, Reidun (1978—)
Tatsumi, Juri (1979—)
Tauber, Ulrike (1958—)
Taylor, Stella (1929–2003)
Taylor-Smith, Shelley (1961—)
Temes, Judit (1930—)
ten Elsen, Eva-Maria (1937—)
Termeulen, Johanna (1929–2001)
Terpstra, Erica (1943—)
Teuscher, Cristina (1978—)
Thien, Margot (1971—)
Thomas, Petria (1975—)
Thompson, Jenny (1973—)
Thomson, Kirsten (1983—)
Thorn, Robyn (1945—)
Thuemer, Petra (1961—)
Tolkacheva, Irina (1982—)
Torres, Dara (1967—)
Treiber, Birgit (1960—)
Urselmann, Wiltrud (1942—)
Ustinova, Natalya (1944—)
Ustrowski, Betina (1976—)
Van Almsick, Franziska (1978—)
Vanderburg, Helen (1959—)
van der Goes, Frederica
van der Plaats, Adriana (1971—)
van der Wildt, Paulina (1944—)
Van Dyken, Amy (1973—)
van Rijn, Wilma (1971—)
van Rooijen, Manon (1982—)
van Staveren, Petra (1966—)
van Velsen, Wilma (1964—)
van Vliet, Petronella (1926—)
van Voorn, Koosje (1935—)
van Weerdenburg, Wilhelmina (1946—)
Varcoe, Helen (b. 1907)
Vare, Glenna Collett (1903–1989)
Varganova, Svetlana (1964—)
Vasilieva, Yulia (1978—)
Vasilkova, Elvira (1962—)
Vassioukova, Olga (1980—)
Veldhuis, Marleen (1979—)
Verstappen, Annemarie (1965—)
Vidali, Lynn (1952—)
Vierdag, Maria (b. 1905)
Vilagos, Penny (1963—)
Vilagos, Vicky (1963—)
Vlieghuis, Kirsten (1976—)
Vogel, Renate (1955—)
Völker, Sandra (1974—)
Vollmer, Dana (1987—)
von Saltza, Chris (1944—)
Voorbij, Aartje (1940—)
Voskes, Elles (1964—)
Wagner, Allison (1977—)
Wagner, Catherina (1919—)
Wagstaff, Elizabeth (1974—)
Wainwright, Helen (1906—)
Waldo, Carolyn (1964—)
Walker, Laura (1970—)
Wang Xiaohong (1968—)
Watson, Lynette (1952—)
Watson, Pokey (1950—)
Wayte, Mary (1965—)
Weber, Jutta (1954—)
Wegner, Gudrun (1955—)
Wehselau, Mariechen (1906—)
Wehselau, Mariechen (1906–1992)
Weigang, Birte (1968—)
Weinberg, Wendy (1958—)
Weir, Amanda (1986—)
Weiss, Gisela (1943—)
Wells, Melissa Foelsch (1932—)
Wetzko, Gabriele (1954—)
White, Amy (1968—)
Whitfield, Beverly (1954–1996)
Wichman, Sharon (1952—)
Wielema, Geertje (1934—)
Williams, Esther (1923—)
Wilson, Marilyn (1943—)
Winkel, Kornelia (1944—)
Wood, Carolyn (1945—)
Woodbridge, Margaret (1902—)
Woodhead, Cynthia (1964—)
Woodley, Erin (1972—)
Wright, Camille (1955—)
Wylie, Wilhelmina (1892–1984)
Xu Yanwei (1984—)
Yang Wenyi (1972—)
Yang Yu (1985—)
Yoneda, Yuko (1979—)
Yurchenya, Marina (1959—)
Zahourek, Berta (1896–1967)
Zanotto, Kendra (1981—)
Zemina, Kathryn (1968—)
Zhao Kun (1973—)
Zhivanevskaya, Nina (1977—)
Zhuang Yong (1972—)
Zhu Yingwen (1981—)
Zimmerman, Suzanne (1925—)
Zimmermann, Kathrin (1966—)
Zindler, Petra (1966—)
Zscherpe, Iris (1967—)

SWIMMING COACH/INSTRUCTOR

Andersen, Greta (1927—)
Bell, Marilyn (1937—)
Chadwick, Florence (1918–1995)
Ederle, Gertrude (1906—)

Ferguson, Cathy Jean (1948—)
Fraser, Gretchen (1919–1994)
Shiley, Jean (1911–1998)

SWINDLER
See Confidence artist (accused).

SYNCRONIZED SWIMMER
Buzonas, Gail Johnson (1954—)

TABLE-TENNIS PLAYER
Aarons, Ruth Hughes (1918–1980)
Chen Jing (1968—)
Chen Zihe (1968—)
Deng Yaping (1973—)
Fazlic, Jasna (1970—)
Feng, Amy (1969—)
Gao Jun (1969—)
Guo Yue (1988—)
Hong Ch-Ok (1970—)
Hyun Jung-Hwa (1969—)
Jiao Zhimin (1963—)
Kim Hyang-Mi (1979—)
Kim Kyung-Ah (1977—)
Kim Moo Kyo
Lee Eun-Sil (1976—)
Li Bun-Hui (1968—)
Li Huifen (1963—)
Li Ju (1976—)
Liu Wei
Niu Jianfeng (1981—)
Park Hae-Jung
Perkucin, Gordana (1962—)
Qiao Hong (1968—)
Qiao Yunping
Rozeanu, Angelica (1921–2006)
Ryu Ji-Hae (1976—)
Segun, Mabel (1930—)
Suk Eun-Mi (1976—)
Sun Jin (1980—)
Wang Nan (1978—)
Yang Ying (1977—)
Yang Young-Ja (1964—)
Yu Sun-Bok (1970—)
Zhang Yining (1981—)

TAEKWONDO PLAYER
Abdallah, Nia (1984—)
Baverel, Myriam (1981—)
Bikcin, Hamide (1978—)
Boorapolchai, Yaowapa (1984—)
Bosshart, Dominique (1977—)
Burns, Lauren (1974—)
Carmona, Adriana (1972—)
Chen Shih Hsin (1978—)
Chen Zhong (1982—)
Chi Shu-Ju (c. 1983—)
Gundersen, Trude (1977—)
Hwang Kyung-Sun (1978—)
Ivanova, Natalia (c. 1971—)
Jang Ji-Won (1979—)
Jung Jae-Eun (c. 1981—)
Labrada Diaz, Yanelis Yuliet (1981—)
Lee Sun-Hee
Luo Wei (1983—)
Melendez Rodriguez, Urbia
Mystakidou, Elisavet (1977—)
Okamoto, Yoriko (1971—)
Salazar Blanco, Iridia (1982—)
Tran Hieu Ngan (1974—)

TALENT AGENT/SCOUT
Alexander, Florence (1904–1993)
Bergere, Ouida (1885–1974)
Broder, Jane (d. 1977)
Caldwell, Sarah (1924—)
Carol, Sue (1906–1982)
Fernandez, Mrs. E.L. (1852–1909)
Gibson, Wynne (1903–1987)
Houghton, Edith (1912—)
Knopf, Blanche (1894–1966)
Marr, Sally (1906–1997)
Nelson, Maud (1881–1944)
Roberts, Flora (c. 1921–1998)
Safier, Gloria (d. 1985)
Van Cleve, Edith (1894–1985)
Wood, Audrey (1905–1985)

TANBUR PLAYER
Osmanoglu, Gevheri (1904–1980)

TAP DANCER
Astaire, Adele (1898–1981)
Brown, Mary Jane (1917–1997)
Bruce, Betty (1920–1974)
Bufalino, Brenda (1937—)
Cline, Patsy (1932–1963)
Ebsen, Vilma (1911—)
Etting, Ruth (1896–1978)
Keeler, Ruby (1909–1993)
Langford, Bonnie (1964—)
LeGon, Jeni (1916—)
McKinney, Nina Mae (c. 1912–1967)
Miller, Ann (1919–2004)
Nealy, Frances (1918–1997)
Picon, Molly (1898–1992)
Powell, Eleanor (1910–1982)
Vera-Ellen (1920–1981)
Verdon, Gwen (1925–2000)
Whitney, Eleanore (1917—)

TAPESTRY DESIGNER
Zorach, Marguerite Thompson (1887–1968)

TEJANO SINGER
Mendoza, Lydia (1916—)
Selena (1971–1995)

TELEGRAPH OPERATOR
Stuart, Wilhelmina Magdalene (1895–1985)

TELEVISION EXECUTIVE
Laybourne, Geraldine (1947—)

TELEVISION/RADIO ADMINISTRATOR
Bolen, Lin (1941—)
Cooney, Joan Ganz (1929—)
Sanders, Marlene (1931—)
Waller, Judith Cary (1889–1973)
Winant, Ethel (1922–2003)

TELEVISION/RADIO COMMENTATOR
Amanpour, Christiane (1958—)
Ashrawi, Hanan (1946—)
Beatty, Bessie (1886–1947)
Caldicott, Helen (1938—)
Cilento, Phyllis (1894–1987)
Coates, Gloria (1938—)
Cooper, Christin (1961—)
Davenport, Marcia (1903–1996)
de Varona, Donna (1947—)
Farrar, Geraldine (1882–1967)
Ferraro, Geraldine (1935—)
Fleming, Peggy (1948—)
Foudy, Julie (1971—)
Hawkes, Sharlene (c. 1964—)
Heldman, Julie (1945—)
Houter, Marleen (1961—)
King, Billie Jean (1943—)
Luxford, Nola (1895–1994)
Mannes, Marya (1904–1990)
Morton, Katherine E. (1885–1968)
Myers, Dee Dee (1961—)
Parsons, Harriet (1906–1983)
Payne, Ethel (1911–1991)
Peacocke, Isabel Maud (1881–1973)
Retton, Mary Lou (1968—)
Roberts, Robin (1960—)
Saarinen, Aline (1914–1972)
Scanlan, Nelle (1882–1968)
Shane, Mary Driscoll (c. 1949—)
Sierens, Gayle (1954—)
Smeal, Eleanor (1939—)
Taylor, Melanie Smith (1949—)
Thompson, Dorothy (1893–1961)
Tufty, Esther Van Wagoner (1896–1986)
Witt, Katarina (1965—)

TELEVISION/RADIO DIRECTOR
Adams, Mary Grace (1898–1984)
Dzerzhinska, Sofia (1882–1968)
Foster, Dianne (1928—)
Hobby, Oveta Culp (1905–1995)
Huston, Anjelica (1951—)
Keaton, Diane (1946—)
Mack, Nila (1891–1953)
Marshall, Penny (1942—)
Miró, Pilar (1940–1997)
O'Hair, Madalyn Murray (1919–1995)
Poston, Elizabeth (1905–1987)
Rosay, Françoise (1891–1974)
Sanders, Marlene (1931—)
Shearer, Moira (1926—)
Walker, Nancy (1922–1992)
Waller, Judith Cary (1889–1973)
Warner, Deborah (1959—)

TELEVISION/RADIO JOURNALIST
Abbott, Diane (1953—)
Adams, Mary Grace (1898–1984)
Adie, Kate (1945—)
Barrett, Rona (1934—)
Breckinridge, Mary Martin (b. 1905)
Chung, Connie (1946—)
Clwyd, Ann (1937—)
Couric, Katie (1957—)
Craig, May (1888–1975)
Dando, Jill (1961–1999)
Dickerson, Nancy (1927–1997)
Ellerbee, Linda (1944—)
Frederick, Pauline (1908–1990)
Furness, Betty (1916–1994)
George, Phyllis (1949—)
Huebner, Robin (1961—)
Hunter-Gault, Charlayne (1942—)
Ifill, Gwen (1955—)
Mackin, Catherine (1939–1982)
McAleese, Mary (1951—)
Molinari, Susan (1958—)
Ortiz, Letizia (1972—)
Pauley, Jane (1950—)
Perkins, Susan (c. 1954—)
Ries, Frédérique (1959—)
Roberts, Cokie (1943—)
Savitch, Jessica (1947–1983)
Shriver, Maria (1955—)
Simpson, Carole (1940—)
Stahl, Lesley (1941—)
Vincent, Marjorie (c. 1965—)
Walters, Barbara (1929—)
Winfrey, Oprah (1954—)

TELEVISION/RADIO PRODUCER
Adams, Mary Grace (1898–1984)
Aubry, Cécile (1928—)
Ayling, Sue (1945–2003)
Babbin, Jacqueline (1921–2001)
Bazin, Janine (1923–2003)
Bentley, Helen Delich (1923—)
Berg, Gertrude (1899–1966)

Carlin, Cynthia (d. 1973)
Dale, Margaret (1922—)
Dennison, Jo-Carroll (c. 1924—)
de Passe, Suzanne (1946—)
Dunn, Barbara (c. 1910—)
Goldberg, Whoopi (1949—)
Gordon, Dorothy (1889–1970)
Granville, Bonita (1923–1988)
Heywood, Joan (1923—)
Jarvis, Lucy (1919—)
Kirkbride, Julie (1960—)
La Plante, Lynda (1946—)
Lupino, Ida (1914–1995)
Mack, Nila (1891–1953)
Marshall, Penny (1942—)
McKnight, Marian (c. 1937—)
McLaughlin-Gill, Frances (1919—)
Myles, Lynda (1947—)
Parks, Hildy (1926–2004)
Patrick, Gail (1911–1980)
Pearce, Philippa (1920—)
Reisenberg, Nadia (1904–1983)
Richards, Shelah (1903–1985)
Roseanne (1952—)
Rountree, Martha (1911–1999)
Sanders, Marlene (1931—)
Saralegui, Cristina (1948—)
Saunders, Doris (1921—)
Schneider, Claudine (1947—)
Steele, Alison (c. 1937–1995)
Steele, Barbara (1937—)
Sweet, Rachel (1963—)
Thomas, Marlo (1937—)
Trilling, Diana (1905–1996)
van Praagh, Peggy (1910–1990)
Warren, Elinor Remick (1900–1991)
Weinstein, Hannah (1911–1984)
Winfrey, Oprah (1954—)
Yorkin, Nicole (1958—)

TELEVISION/RADIO-PROGRAM HOST

Allan, Elizabeth (1908–1990)
Allen, Rosalie (1924–2003)
Allison, Fran (1907–1989)
Angelica, Mother (1923—)
Arthur, Jean (1900–1991)
Baclanova, Olga (1899–1974)
Bailey, Pearl (1918–1990)
Bankhead, Tallulah (1902–1968)
Barrie, Wendy (1912–1978)
Basham, Maud Ruby (1879–1963)
Bell, Margaret Brenda (1891–1979)
Bergen, Polly (1929—)
Black, Cilla (1943—)
Brown, Ruth (1928—)
Bunke, Tamara (1937–1967)
Burnett, Carol (1933—)
Buttrose, Ita (1942—)
Carlson, Gretchen (c. 1966—)
Chen, Joyce (1918–1994)
Child, Julia (1912–2004)
Claster, Nancy (1915–1997)
Clooney, Rosemary (1928–2002)
Coca, Imogene (1909–2001)
Cornett, Leanza (1971—)
Couric, Katie (1957—)
Crawford, Cindy (1966—)
Cumming, Adelaide Hawley (1905–1998)
Day, Doris (1924—)
DeGeneres, Ellen (1958—)
Ellerbee, Linda (1944—)
Farmer, Frances (1913–1970)
Finnbogadóttir, Vigdís (1930—)
Fleming, Nancy (c. 1941—)
Francis, Arlene (1908–2001)
Frederick, Pauline (1908–1990)
Gabor, Eva (1919–1995)
Garland, Judy (1922–1969)
Gordon, Dorothy (1889–1970)
Green, Grace Winifred (1907–1976)
Hay, Jean Emily (1903–1984)
Horwich, Frances (1908–2001)
Hutton, Betty (1921—)
Jackson, Mahalia (1911–1972)
Jenner, Andrea (1891–1985)
Kennedy, Helena (1950—)
Kilgallen, Dorothy (1913–1965)
Kuroyanagi, Tetsuko (1933—)
La Barbara, Joan (1947—)
Lane, Priscilla (1917–1995)
Laverty, Maura (1907–1966)
Lewis, Shari (1933–1998)
Little, Tawny (c. 1957—)
Lopes, Lisa (1971–2002)
MacGregor, Sue (1941—)
Maffett, Debra Sue (c. 1957—)
Markova, Alicia (1910–2004)
Mason, Pamela (1918–1996)
Maura, Carmen (1945—)
Maxwell, Elsa (1883–1963)
Meeuwsen, Terry (1949—)
Meyner, Helen Stevenson (1929–1997)
Moffo, Anna (1932—)
Murray, Kathryn (1906–1999)
Myers, Carmel (1899–1980)
Myerson, Bess (1924—)
O'Donnell, Rosie (1962—)
Osmond, Marie (1959—)
O'Sullivan, Maureen (1911–1998)
Palmer, Lilli (1914–1986)
Parkhurst, Helen (1887–1973)
Paterson, Jennifer (1928–1999)
Pauley, Jane (1950—)
Payne, Freda (1945—)
Powell, Susan (c. 1959—)
Quatro, Suzi (1950—)
Raye, Martha (1916–1994)
Reagan, Maureen (1941–2001)
Ritter, Erika (1948—)
Roberts, Robin (1960—)
Sanders, Marlene (1931—)
Sapp, Carolyn (1967—)
Saralegui, Cristina (1948—)
Schiffer, Claudia (1970—)
Schneider, Claudine (1947—)
Scott, Hazel (1920–1981)
Scott, Martha (1914–2003)
Sharman, Helen (1963—)
Shore, Dinah (1917–1994)
Sills, Beverly (1929—)
Singleton, Penny (1908–2003)
Smith, Delia (1941—)
Smith, Kate (1907–1986)
Stafford, Jo (1920—)
Stahl, Lesley (1941—)
Stanwyck, Barbara (1907–1990)
Stewart, Martha (1941—)
Swanson, Gloria (1897–1983)
Taylor, Eva (1895–1977)
Tennant, Veronica (1946—)
Travers, Mary (1936—)
Trudeau, Margaret (1948—)
Turner, Debbye (1966—)
Vanderbilt, Amy (1908–1974)
Vernon, Barbara (1916–1978)
Walker, Barbara Jo (1926–2000)
Walters, Barbara (1929—)
Warwick, Dionne (1940—)
Wells, Kitty (1919—)
Wilson, Carnie (1968—)
Wilson, Nancy (1937—)
Winfrey, Oprah (1954—)
Wolf, Kate (1942–1986)
Wyman, Jane (1914—)
Young, Loretta (1913–2000)

TELEVISION/RADIO-SERIES ACTRESS

Ace, Jane (1905–1974)
Allen, Gracie (1902–1964)
Allyson, June (1917—)
Anderson, Judith (1898–1992)
Arden, Eve (1907–1990)
Audley, Maxine (1923–1992)
Baddeley, Angela (1904–1976)
Baddeley, Hermione (1906–1986)
Ball, Lucille (1911–1989)
Baxter, Anne (1923–1985)
Beavers, Louise (1902–1962)
Bel Geddes, Barbara (1922—)
Benaderet, Bea (1906–1968)
Bennett, Joan (1910–1990)
Berg, Gertrude (1899–1966)
Black, Shirley Temple (1928—)
Booth, Shirley (1907–1992)
Brian, Mary (1906–2002)
Byington, Spring (1886–1971)
Compton, Fay (1894–1978)
Darvas, Lili (1902–1974)
Davis, Joan (1907–1961)
Dors, Diana (1931–1984)
Fontaine, Joan (1917—)
Gabor, Eva (1919–1995)
Gardner, Ava (1922–1990)
Gaynor, Janet (1906–1984)
Gersten, Berta (c. 1896–1972)
Goldberg, Whoopi (1949—)
Gordon, Hannah (1941—)
Hamilton, Margaret (1902–1985)
Hickson, Joan (1906–1998)
Hilliard, Harriet (1909–1994)
Holm, Celeste (1919—)
Hoppe, Marianne (1911—)
Horney, Brigitte (1911–1988)
Hudson, Rochelle (1916–1972)
Jones, Shirley (1934—)
Kahn, Madeline (1942–1999)
Karioka, Tahiya (c. 1921–1999)
Kitt, Eartha (1928—)
Lanchester, Elsa (1902–1986)
Lister, Moira (1923—)
Lockwood, Margaret (1916–1990)
Lollobrigida, Gina (1927—)
Lupino, Ida (1914–1995)
Malone, Dorothy (1925—)
Manchester, Melissa (1951—)
Mansfield, Jayne (1933–1967)
Masina, Giulietta (1920–1994)
Matthews, Jessie (1907–1981)
McCambridge, Mercedes (1916–2004)
McCormack, Patty (1945—)
McDaniel, Hattie (1895–1952)
Meadows, Audrey (1922–1996)
Meadows, Jayne (1920—)
Montgomery, Elizabeth (1933–1995)
Moorehead, Agnes (1900–1974)
Moran, Lois (1907–1990)
Muir, Jean (1928–1995)
Natwick, Mildred (1908–1994)
Newmar, Julie (1935—)
Nolan, Kathleen (1933—)
Oliver, Edith (1913–1998)
Payne, Virginia (1908–1977)
Perón, Eva (1919–1952)
Pitts, ZaSu (1898–1963)
Powell, Jane (1929—)
Prowse, Juliet (1936–1996)
Quatro, Suzi (1950—)
Queen Latifah (1970—)

Ralston, Esther (1902–1994)
Reed, Donna (1921–1986)
Revere, Anne (1903–1990)
Roberts, Rachel (1927–1980)
Rogers, Dale Evans (1912–2001)
Saint, Eva Marie (1924—)
Scott, Martha (1914–2003)
Singleton, Penny (1908–2003)
Smith, Alexis (1921–1993)
Smith, Samantha (1972–1985)
Sondergaard, Gale (1899–1985)
Sothern, Ann (1909–2001)
Stanwyck, Barbara (1907–1990)
Stapleton, Maureen (1925—)
Thompson, Sada (1929—)
Turner, Lana (1921–1995)
Vail, Myrtle (1888–1978)
Vance, Vivian (1909–1979)
Walker, Nancy (1922–1992)
Washington, Fredi (1903–1994)
Waters, Ethel (1896–1977)
Weld, Tuesday (1943—)
Werner, Ilse (1918—)
Wiley, Lee (1915–1975)
Winters, Shelley (1920–2005)
Withers, Jane (1926—)
Wood, Peggy (1892–1978)
Worth, Irene (1916–2002)
Wyatt, Jane (1911—)
Wyman, Jane (1914—)
Yearwood, Trisha (1964—)
Young, Loretta (1913–2000)

TELEVISION/RADIO WRITER

Angelou, Maya (1928—)
Armen, Margaret (1921–2003)
Avedon, Barbara Hammer (1930–1994)
Backhouse, Elizabeth (b. 1917)
Baker, Dorothy (1907–1968)
Benson, Sally (1900–1972)
Bentley, Helen Delich (1923—)
Berg, Gertrude (1899–1966)
Bombeck, Erma (1927–1996)
Boyd, Susan (1949–2004)
Bron, Eleanor (1934—)
Cunard, Grace (c. 1891–1967)
Diamond, Selma (1920–1985)
Gordon, Dorothy (1889–1970)
Hummert, Anne (1905–1996)
Jefferis, Barbara (1917–2004)
Kallen, Lucille (1922–1999)
Kennedy, Helena (1950—)
La Plante, Lynda (1946—)
Laverty, Maura (1907–1966)
Lochhead, Liz (1947—)
Løveid, Cecilie (1951—)
Mack, Nila (1891–1953)
Meredith, Gwen (b. 1907)
Myles, Lynda (1947—)
Nixon, Agnes (1927—)
Phillips, Irna (1901–1973)
Phipson, Joan (1912–2003)
Price, Eugenia (1916–1996)
Ritter, Erika (1948—)
Roseanne (1952—)
Saunders, Jennifer (1958—)
Vollmer, Lula (d. 1955)
Yorkin, Nicole (1958—)

TEMPERANCE REFORMER

Anthony, Susan B. (1820–1906)
Bailey, Hannah Johnston (1839–1923)
Barry, Leonora M. (1849–1930)
Bateham, Josephine (1829–1901)
Batson, Flora (1864–1906)
Baylis, Lilian (1874–1937)
Beecher, Catharine (1800–1878)
Bickerdyke, Mary Ann (1817–1901)
Bittenbender, Ada Matilda (1848–1925)
Bloomer, Amelia Jenks (1818–1894)
Bloor, Ella Reeve (1862–1951)
Boole, Ella (1858–1952)
Booth, Catherine (1829–1890)
Borden, Lizzie (1860–1927)
Brehm, Marie Caroline (1859–1926)
Brown, Hallie Quinn (c. 1845–1949)
Brown, Martha McClellan (1838–1916)
Brown Blackwell, Antoinette (1825–1921)
Byers, Margaret (1832–1912)
Carse, Matilda Bradley (1835–1917)
Catt, Carrie Chapman (1859–1947)
Chapin, Sallie F. (c. 1830–1896)
Colman, Julia (1828–1909)
Cowie, Bessie Lee (1860–1950)
Crandall, Prudence (1803–1890)
Dalrymple, Learmonth White (1827–1906)
Davis, Paulina Wright (1813–1876)
Diggs, Annie LePorte (1848–1916)
Dobson, Emily (1842–1934)
Edger, Kate (1857–1935)
Felton, Rebecca Latimer (1835–1930)
Fletcher, Alice Cunningham (1838–1923)
Foster, J. Ellen (1840–1910)
Fowler, Lydia Folger (1822–1879)
Fuller, Loïe (1862–1928)
Fuller, Minnie Rutherford (1868–1946)
Gage, Frances D. (1808–1884)
Gage, Matilda Joslyn (1826–1898)
Gilman, Charlotte Perkins (1860–1935)
Gougar, Helen (1843–1907)
Grimké, Sarah Moore (1792–1873)
Hall, Anna Maria (1800–1881)
Hanaford, Phebe Ann (1829–1921)
Harper, Frances E.W. (1825–1911)
Harsant, Florence Marie (1891–1994)
Haviland, Laura S. (1808–1898)
Hay, Mary Garrett (1857–1928)
Hayes, Lucy Webb (1831–1889)
Henmyer, Annie W. (1827–1900)
Hill, Emily (1847–1930)
Hobhouse, Emily (1860–1926)
Holley, Marietta (1836–1926)
Holmes, Mary Jane (1825–1907)
Howard, Rosalind Frances (1845–1921)
Howland, Emily (1827–1929)
Hunt, Mary Hanchett (1830–1906)
Johnson, Ellen Cheney (1829–1899)
Kearney, Belle (1863–1939)
Kelley, Abby (1810–1887)
Kendall, Marie Hartig (1854–1943)
King, Henrietta Chamberlain (1832–1925)
Kirk, Cybele Ethel (1870–1957)
Lease, Mary Elizabeth (1853–1933)
Lee, Mary (1821–1909)
Lewis, Graceanna (1821–1912)
Livermore, Mary A. (1820–1905)
Lockwood, Belva Ann (1830–1917)
Lozier, Clemence S. (1813–1888)
Lucas, Margaret Bright (1818–1890)
May, Isabella (1850–1926)
McCarthy, Mary Ann Recknall (1866–1933)
McClung, Nellie L. (1873–1951)
McCracken, Mary Ann (1770–1866)
McCulloch, Catharine (1862–1945)
McDowell, Mary Eliza (1854–1936)
McKinney, Louise (1868–1931)
Merrick, Caroline (1825–1908)
Moskowitz, Belle (1877–1933)
Mussey, Ellen Spencer (1850–1936)
Myrdal, Alva (1902–1986)
Nation, Carry (1846–1911)
Newman, Angelia L. (1837–1910)
Nichols, Clarina (1810–1885)
Nicol, Helen Lyster (1854–1932)
Orelli, Susanna (1845–1939)
Osburn, Lucy (1835–1891)
Ostler, Emma Brignell (c. 1848–1922)
Owens-Adair, Bethenia (1840–1926)
Parsons, Betty Pierson (1900–1982)
Petersen, Alicia O'Shea (1862–1923)
Pettit, Katherine (1868–1936)
Powell, Mary Sadler (1854/55?–1946)
Preston, Ann (1813–1872)
Richards, Ellen Swallow (1842–1911)
Sage, Margaret Olivia (1828–1918)
Salter, Susanna Medora (1860–1961)
Schnackenberg, Annie Jane (1835–1905)
Sewell, Anna (1820–1878)
Shaw, Anna Howard (1847–1919)
Sheppard, Kate (1847–1934)
Smith, Amanda Berry (1837–1915)
Smith, Lucy Masey (1861–1936)
Smith, Zilpha Drew (1851–1926)
Somerset, Isabella (1851–1921)
Somerville, Nellie Nugent (1863–1952)
Soule, Caroline White (1824–1903)
Spencer, Anna (1851–1931)
Spencer, Lilly Martin (1822–1902)
Stanton, Elizabeth Cady (1815–1902)
Stevens, Lillian (1844–1914)
Stevenson, Sarah Hackett (1841–1909)
Stewart, Eliza Daniel (1816–1908)
Stoddard, Cora Frances (1872–1936)
Stokes, Caroline Phelps (1854–1909)
Stokes, Olivia Phelps (1847–1927)
Stone, Lucy (1818–1893)
Tarbell, Ida (1857–1944)
Taylor, Elizabeth Best (1868–1941)
Thomas, Mary Myers (1816–1888)
Thompson, Eliza (1816–1905)
Thompson, Elizabeth Rowell (1821–1899)
Tod, Isabella (1836–1896)
Todd, Marion Marsh (1841–post 1913)
Towne, Laura Matilda (1825–1901)
Tutwiler, Julia Strudwick (1841–1916)
Upton, Harriet Taylor (1853–1945)
Van Grippenberg, Alexandra (1859–1913)
Van Rensselaer, Martha (1864–1932)
Wallace, Zerelda G. (1817–1901)
Ward, Anne (c. 1825–1896)
Washington, Margaret Murray (c. 1861–1925)
Way, Amanda M. (1828–1914)
Wells-Barnett, Ida (1862–1931)
Weston, Agnes (1840–1918)
Whitney, Anne (1821–1915)
Willard, Frances E. (1839–1898)
Willing, Jennie Fowler (1834–1916)
Windeyer, Mary (1836–1912)
Wittenmyer, Annie Turner (1827–1900)
Wright, Laura Maria (1809–1886)

TENNIS COACH/INSTRUCTOR

Gibson, Althea (1927—)
Richards, Renée (1934—)
Sukova, Vera (1931–1982)
Tennant, Eleanor (1895–1974)
Tennant, Eleanor (fl. 1920–1940)

TENNIS PLAYER

Abraham, Constance Palgrave (1864–1942)
Adlerstrahle, Maertha (1868–1956)
Aitchison, Helen (1881–?)
Akhurst, Daphne (1903–1933)
Alvarez, Lili de (1905—)
Atkinson, Juliette P. (1873–1944)
Aussem, Cilly (1909–1963)
Austin, Tracy (1962—)
Bartkowicz, Peaches (1949—)

Bearnish, Geraldine (1885–1972)
Betz, Pauline (1919—)
Boogert, Kristie (1973—)
Boothby, Dora (1881–1970)
Bouman, Kea (1903–1998)
Broquedis, Marguerite (1893–1983)
Brough, Louise (1923—)
Browne, Mary K. (1891–1971)
Bueno, Maria (1939—)
Cahill, Mabel E. (1863–?)
Callens, Els (1970—)
Capriati, Jennifer (1976—)
Casals, Rosemary (1948—)
Castenschiold, Thora (1882–1979)
Chambers, Dorothea Lambert (1878–1960)
Cheney, Dorothy Bundy (1916—)
Clijsters, Kim (1983—)
Coetzer, Amanda (1971—)
Colyer, Evelyn (1902–1930)
Connolly, Maureen (1934–1969)
Cooper, Charlotte (1871–1966)
Court, Margaret Smith (1942—)
Covell, Phyllis (1895–1982)
Curtis, Harriot (1881–1974)
Curtis, Peggy (1883–1965)
Dalton, Judy Tegart (fl. 1960s–1970s)
Davenport, Lindsay (1976—)
Dementieva, Elena (1981—)
Dod, Charlotte (1871–1960)
Dokic, Jelena (1983—)
Durr, Françoise (1942—)
Eastlake-Smith, Gladys (1883–1941)
Evert, Chris (1954—)
Fernandez, Gigi (1964—)
Fernandez, Mary Joe (1971—)
Fick, Sigrid (1887–1979)
Fry, Shirley (1927—)
Garrison, Zina (1963—)
Gibson, Althea (1927–2003)
Goolagong Cawley, Evonne (1951—)
Graf, Steffi (1969—)
Greene, Angela (1879—)
Hannam, Edith (1878–1951)
Hard, Darlene (1936—)
Hart, Doris (1925—)
Heldman, Julie (1945—)
Henin-Hardenne, Justine (1982—)
Hillyard, Blanche Bingley (1864–1938)
Hingis, Martina (1980—)
Holman, Dorothy (1883–?)
Jacobs, Helen Hull (1908–1997)
Jessup, Marion (b. 1897)
Jones, Ann Haydon (1938—)
Jones, Marion (1879–1965)
King, Billie Jean (1943—)
Koering, Dorothea (1880–1945)
Kohde-Kilsch, Claudia (1963—)
Kournikova, Anna (1981—)
Kuznetsova, Svetlana (1985—)
Leeming, Marjorie (1903–1987)
Lehane, Jan (1941—)
Lenglen, Suzanne (1899–1938)
Li Ting (1980—)
Lucic, Mirjana (1982—)
Majoli, Iva (1977—)
Maleeva, Magdalena (1975—)
Maleeva, Manuela (1967—)
Mallory, Molla (1884–1959)
Marble, Alice (1913–1990)
Martinez, Conchita (1972—)
Mathieu, Simone (1908–1980)
Mauresmo, Amelie (1979—)
McKane, Kitty (1896–1992)
McNair, Winifred (1877–1954)
McQuillan, Rachel (1971—)
Meskhi, Leila (1968—)
Molik, Alicia (1981—)
Moore, Elisabeth H. (1876–1959)
Moran, Gussie (1923—)
Mortimer, Angela (1932—)
Myskina, Anastasia (1981—)
Navratilova, Martina (1956—)
Niederkirchner, Käte (1909–1944)
Novotna, Jana (1968—)
Nunneley, Kathleen Mary (1872–1956)
Nuthall, Betty (1911–1983)
Oremans, Miriam (1972—)
Osborne, Margaret (1918—)
Palfrey, Sarah (1912–1996)
Parton, Mabel (b. 1881)
Peters, Roumania (1917–2003)
Pierce, Mary (1975—)
Pound, Louise (1872–1958)
Prevost, Hélène
Provis, Nicole (1969—)
Raymond, Lisa (1973—)
Richards, Renée (1934—)
Ride, Sally (b. 1951)
Rosenbaum, Hedwig
Round, Dorothy (1908–1982)
Ruano Pascual, Virginia (1973—)
Rubin, Chandra (1976—)
Ryan, Elizabeth (1891–1979)
Sabatini, Gabriela (1970—)
Sanchez Vicario, Arantxa (1971—)
Sears, Eleanora (1881–1968)
Seizinger, Katja (1972—)
Seles, Monica (1973—)
Sharapova, Maria (1987—)
Shepherd-Barron, Dorothy (1897–1953)
Shriver, Pam (1962—)
Skrbkova, Milada (1897–1965)
Slowe, Lucy Diggs (1885–1937)
Smylie, Elizabeth (1963—)
Sperling, Hilde (1908–1981)
Stammers, Kay (1914–2005)
Stove, Betty (1945—)
Suarez, Paola (1976—)
Sukova, Helena (1965—)
Sukova, Vera (1931–1982)
Sun Tian Tian (1981—)
Sutton, May (1887–1975)
Tarabini, Patricia (1968—)
Tennant, Eleanor (fl. 1920–1940)
Turnbull, Wendy (1952—)
Turner, Lesley (1942—)
van Roost, Dominique (1973—)
Vlasto, Didi (1903–1985)
Wade, Virginia (1945—)
Washington, Ora (1899–1971)
Watson, Maud (b. 1864)
Wightman, Hazel Hotchkiss (1886–1974)
Williams, Serena (1981—)
Williams, Venus (1980—)
Wills, Helen Newington (1905–1998)
Winch, Joan
Zvereva, Natasha (1971—)

TERRORIST
See Political terrorist.

TEST PILOT
See Experimental aviator.

TEXTBOOK WRITER
Abbott, Berenice (1898–1991)
Adams, Maude (1872–1953)
Andrews, Eliza Frances (1840–1931)
Arbuthnot, May Hill (1884–1969)
Ayrton, Hertha Marks (1854–1923)
Bates, Katherine Lee (1859–1929)
Beale, Dorothea (1831–1906)
Beard, Mary Ritter (1876–1958)
Botta, Anne C.L. (1815–1891)
Burnett, Hallie Southgate (1908–1991)
Cadilla de Martínez, Maria (1886–1951)
Carabillo, Toni (1926–1997)
Châtelet, Émilie du (1706–1749)
Clarke, Edith (1883–1959)
Corson, Juliet (1841–1897)
Coyle, Grace Longwell (1892–1962)
Delano, Jane Arminda (1862–1919)
Deutsch, Helene (1884–1982)
Diller, Angela (1877–1968)
Eddy, Mary Baker (1821–1910)
Esau, Katherine (1898–1997)
Frederick, Christine (1883–1970)
Gardner, Mary Sewall (1871–1961)
Goldring, Winifred (1888–1971)
Gray, Nicolete (1911–1997)
Gruenberg, Sidonie (1881–1974)
Gwynne-Vaughan, Helen (1879–1967)
Hagood, Margaret (1907–1963)
Haines, Helen (1872–1961)
Hamilton, Gordon (1892–1967)
Hoffman, Malvina (1885–1966)
Hyde, Ida (1857–1945)
Hyslop, Beatrice Fry (1899–1973)
Immerwahr, Clara (1870–1915)
Jackson, Nell (1929–1988)
Johnson, Eleanor Murdoch (1892–1987)
Johnson, Virginia E. (1925—)
Knopf, Eleanora Bliss (1883–1974)
Kyrk, Hazel (1886–1957)
Lee, Rose Hum (1904–1964)
Mayer, Maria Goeppert (1906–1972)
Meyer, Lucy (1849–1922)
Morgan, Ann Haven (1882–1966)
Phelps, Almira Lincoln (1793–1884)
Post, Emily (1872–1960)
Richards, Ellen Swallow (1842–1911)
Richman, Julia (1855–1912)
Rickert, Edith (1871–1938)
Robb, Isabel Hampton (1860–1910)
Roland, Pauline (1805–1852)
Rowson, Susanna (1762–1824)
Rutherford, Mildred (1851–1928)
Scharrer, Berta (1906–1995)
Scott, Charlotte Angas (1858–1931)
Semple, Ellen Churchill (1863–1932)
Sewell, Elizabeth Missing (1815–1906)
Sharman, Helen (1963—)
Spence, Catherine (1825–1910)
Stead, Christina (1902–1983)
Stevenson, Sarah Hackett (1841–1909)
Stewart, Cora Wilson (1875–1958)
Sullivan, Mary Quinn (1877–1939)
Taussig, Helen Brooke (1898–1986)
Taylor, Eva (1895–1977)
Valette, Aline (1850–1899)
Van Blarcom, Carolyn (1879–1960)
Waller, Judith Cary (1889–1973)
Whitney, Phyllis A. (b. 1903)
Willard, Emma Hart (1787–1870)
Williams, Anna Wessels (1863–1954)
Woodbury, Helen Sumner (1876–1933)
Wright, Muriel Hazel (1889–1975)
Wu, Chien-Shiung (1912–1997)
Yurka, Blanche (1887–1974)

TEXTILE ARTIST/DESIGNER
Albers, Anni (1899–1994)
Ashley, Laura (1925–1985)
Brandt, Marianne (1893–1983)
Bright, Mary (1954–2002)
Bryk, Rut (1916–1999)
Conboy, Sara McLaughlin (1870–1928)

Conran, Shirley (1932—)
Delaunay, Sonia (1885–1979)
Ditzel, Nana (1923–2005)
Eames, Ray (1912–1988)
Furtseva, Ekaterina (1910–1974)
Grizodubova, Valentina (1910–1993)
Haraszty, Eszter (c. 1910–1994)
Hepworth, Barbara (1903–1975)
Höch, Hannah (1889–1978)
Jones, Loïs Mailou (1905–1998)
King, Jessie Marion (1875–1949)
Liebes, Dorothy (1897–1972)
Maas-Fjetterstrom, Marta (1873–1941)
Mackintosh, Margaret (1865–1933)
Mairet, Ethel (1872–1952)
Morris, May (1862–1938)
Nessim, Barbara (1939—)
Quant, Mary (1934—)
Reich, Lilly (1885–1947)
Reinhild (fl. 8th c.)
Saarinen, Loja (1879–1968)
Schary, Hope Skillman (1908–1981)
Stepanova, Varvara (1894–1958)
Strengell, Marianne (1909–1998)
Swanson, Pipsan Saarinen (1905–1979)
Tauber-Arp, Sophie (1889–1943)
Telalkowska, Wanda (1905–1986)
Wheeler, Candace (1827–1923)

TEXTILE MANUFACTURER
Beale, Mary (1632–1699)
Biryukova, Alexandra (1929—)
Schary, Hope Skillman (1908–1981)

TEXTILE MERCHANT
Fingerin, Agnes (d. 1515)
Fugger, Barbara Baesinger (d. 1497)

THANATOLOGIST
Kübler-Ross, Elisabeth (1926–2004)

THEATER CRITIC
Becker, May Lamberton (1873–1958)
Blue, Rita Hassan (c. 1905–1973)
Coates, Gloria (1938—)
Crist, Judith (1922—)
Cross, Zora (1890–1964)
Deutsch, Helen (1906–1992)
Flanner, Janet (1892–1978)
Gibbons, Stella (1902–1989)
Harrison, Marguerite (1879–1967)
Helburn, Theresa (1887–1959)
Isaacs, Edith (1878–1956)
Leslie, Amy (1855–1939)
Macardle, Dorothy (1889–1958)
Malpede, Karen (1945—)
Misme, Jane (1865–1935)
Moholy, Lucia (1894–1989)
Oliver, Edith (1913–1998)
Paoli, Betty (1814–1894)
Parker, Dorothy (1893–1967)
Quimby, Harriet (1875–1912)
Skinner, Constance Lindsay (1877–1939)
Solano, Solita (1888–1975)
Travers, P.L. (1906–1996)
Waldorf, Wilella (c. 1900–1946)
Walters, Barbara (1929—)
White, Antonia (1899–1980)

THEATER DIRECTOR
Abady, Josephine (c. 1950–2002)
Bradley, Lillian Trimble (1875–?)
Caldwell, Zoë (1933—)
Cárdenas, Nancy (1934–1994)
Carroll, Vinnette (1922–2002)
Church, Esmé (1893–1972)
De Reyes, Consuelo (1893–1948)
Foster, Frances (1924–1997)
Helliwell, Ethel (c. 1905—)
Lynne, Gillian (1926—)
Mnouchkine, Ariane (1938—)
Piscator, Maria Ley (1899–1999)
Pollock, Sharon (1936—)
Strasberg, Paula (1911–1966)
Suzman, Janet (1939—)
Taymor, Julie (1952—)
Tharp, Twyla (1941—)
Vaughan, Gladys (d. 1987)
Victor, Lucia (1912–1986)

THEATER MANAGER
Andreeva, Maria Fedorovna (1868–1953)
Baker, Sarah (1736–1816)
Bancroft, Lady (1839–1921)
Baylis, Lilian (1874–1937)
Bellew, Kyrle (1887–1948)
Bonstelle, Jessie (1871–1932)
Bowers, Elizabeth Crocker (1830–1895)
Carte, Bridget D'Oyly (1908–1985)
Celeste, Madame (1811–1882)
Cooper, Gladys (1888–1971)
Davenport, Fanny (1850–1898)
Drew, Louisa Lane (1820–1897)
Geistinger, Marie (1833–1903)
Horniman, Annie (1860–1937)
Jenner, Caryl (1917—)
Keene, Laura (c. 1826–1873)
Komissarzhevskaya, Vera (1864–1910)
Marbury, Elisabeth (1856–1933)
Montansier, Marguerite (1730–1820)
Neilson, Julia Emilie (1868–1957)
Neuber, Caroline (1697–1760)
Richards, Shelah (1903–1985)
Stewart, Ellen (c. 1920—)
Vestris, Lucia (1797–1856)
Wood, Matilda (1831–1915)

THEATER OR THEATRICAL COMPANY/ TROUPE FOUNDER
Adler, Stella (1902–1993)
Anderson, Regina M. (1900–1993)
Andjaparidze, Veriko (1900–1987)
Andreeva, Maria Fedorovna (1868–1953)
Ashcroft, Peggy (1907–1991)
Ashwell, Lena (1872–1957)
Baker, Sarah (1736–1816)
Balkanska, Mimi (b. 1902)
Baylis, Lilian (1874–1937)
Brand, Phoebe (1907–2004)
Christina of Sweden (1626–1689)
Cons, Emma (1838–1912)
Crawford, Cheryl (1902–1986)
Cunningham, Sarah (1918–1986)
de Mille, Agnes (1905–1993)
Dukakis, Olympia (1931—)
Dunham, Katherine (1909–2006)
Egyptian Singers and Entrepreneurs (fl. 1920s)
Ehre, Ida (1900–1989)
Ehrlich, Ida Lublenski (d. 1986)
Fichandler, Zelda (1924—)
Fitzgerald, Geraldine (1913–2005)
Foster, Frances (1924–1997)
Fox, Carol (1926–1981)
Gregory, Augusta (1852–1932)
Humphrey, Doris (1895–1958)
Jeans, Isabel (1891–1985)
Jones, Margo (1911–1955)
Kaminska, Ida (1899–1980)
Komissarzhevskaya, Vera (1864–1910)
Kotopoúli, Maríka (1887–1954)
Latimer, Sally (1910—)
Leontovich, Eugénie (1894–1993)
Lewisohn, Alice (1883–1972)
Lewisohn, Irene (1892–1944)
Lindfors, Viveca (1920–1995)
Littlewood, Joan (1914–2002)
Mahdiyya, Munira al- (c. 1895–1965)
Major, Clare Tree (d. 1954)
Mikey, Fanny (1931—)
Raucourt, Mlle (1756–1815)
Richards, Beah (1920–2000)
Robins, Elizabeth (1862–1952)
Sagan, Leontine (1889–1974)
Sarton, May (1912–1995)
Serreau, Geneviève (1915–1981)
Sokolow, Anna (1910–2000)
Stern, Edith Rosenwald (1895–1980)
Stewart, Ellen (c. 1920—)
Sulka, Elaine (1933–1994)
Teer, Barbara Ann (1937—)
Thompson, Louise (1901–1999)
Vance, Nina (1914–1980)
Viertel, Salka (1889–1978)
Ward, Winifred Louise (1884–1975)

THEATRICAL DESIGNER
Adams, Maude (1872–1953)
Baylis, Nadine (1940—)
Benois, Nadia (1896–1975)
Bernstein, Aline (1882–1955)
Bjornson, Maria (1949–2002)
Calthrop, Gladys E. (1894–1980)
Craig, Edith (1869–1947)
Duff Gordon, Lucy (1862–1935)
Dunham, Katherine (1909–2006)
Eckart, Jean (1921–1993)
Exter, Alexandra (1882–1949)
Fedorovitch, Sophie (1893–1953)
Fini, Leonor (1908–1996)
Goncharova, Natalia (1881–1962)
Graham, Martha (1894–1991)
Graves, Nancy (1940–1995)
Herbert, Jocelyn (1917–2003)
Laurencin, Marie (1883–1956)
Lermontova, Nadezhda Vladimirovna (1885–1921)
Mahony, Marion (1871–1961)
Moiseiwitsch, Tanya (1914–2003)
Oman, Julia Trevelyan (1930–2003)
Rambova, Natacha (1897–1966)
Raverat, Gwen (1885–1957)
Stepanova, Varvara (1894–1958)
Wertmüller, Lina (1928—)

THEATRICAL DIRECTOR
Adler, Sara (1858–1953)
Adler, Stella (1902–1993)
Archer, Robyn (1948—)
Berghaus, Ruth (1927–1996)
Bonstelle, Jessie (1871–1932)
Caldwell, Sarah (1924—)
Carte, Bridget D'Oyly (1908–1985)
Chabrillan, Céleste de (1824–1909)
Crawford, Cheryl (1902–1986)
Cunard, Grace (c. 1891–1967)
Dalrymple, Jean (1910–1998)
Davis, Judy (1955—)
Ehre, Ida (1900–1989)
Espert, Nuria (1935—)
Fichandler, Zelda (1924—)
Fitton, Doris (1897–1985)
Flanagan, Hallie (1889–1969)
Fox, Carol (1926–1981)
Franken, Rose (c. 1895–1988)
Glaspell, Susan (1876–1948)
Goodbody, Buzz (1946–1975)
Gregory, Augusta (1852–1932)
Heiberg, Johanne Luise (1812–1890)
Helburn, Theresa (1887–1959)

Hoppe, Marianne (1911—)
Hull, Josephine (1886–1957)
Jones, Margo (1911–1955)
Kaminska, Ida (1899–1980)
Kemp-Welch, Joan (1906–1999)
Lacis, Asja (1891–1979)
Le Gallienne, Eva (1899–1991)
Lehmann, Beatrix (1903–1979)
Leontovich, Eugénie (1894–1993)
Lewis, Elma (1921—)
Lewisohn, Alice (1883–1972)
Lewisohn, Irene (1892–1944)
Littlewood, Joan (1914–2002)
Loebinger, Lotte (1905–1999)
Major, Clare Tree (d. 1954)
Malina, Judith (1926—)
Malpede, Karen (1945—)
Marsh, Ngaio (1895–1982)
McKenna, Siobhan (1922–1986)
McKenzie, Julia (1941—)
Perry, Antoinette (1888–1946)
Resnik, Regina (1922—)
Scott, Martha (1914–2003)
Smith, Dodie (1896–1990)
Stewart, Ellen (c. 1920—)
Sutherland, Efua (1924–1996)
Vance, Nina (1914–1980)
Walker, Nancy (1922–1992)
Warner, Deborah (1959—)
Webster, Margaret (1905–1972)
Weigel, Helene (1900–1971)

THEATRICAL MANAGER
Carpenter, Maud (d. 1967)
Church, Esmé (1893–1972)
Compton, Virginia (1853–1940)
Melnotte, Violet (1856–1935)
Melville, June (1915–1970)
Millard, Evelyn (1869–1941)
Price, Nancy (1880–1970)
Waller, Florence (1862–1912)
Wiman, Anna Deere (1924–1963)

THEATRICAL PERFORMER
Palmer, Elizabeth Mary (1832–1897)

THEATRICAL PRODUCER
Abrahams, Doris Cole (1925—)
Albertson, Lillian (1881–1962)
Allen, Rita (d. 1968)
arsh, Ngaio (1895–1982)
Babbin, Jacqueline (1921–2001)
Blue, Rita Hassan (c. 1905–1973)
Bonfils, Helen (c. 1890–1972)
Bryant, Hazel (1939–1983)
Crawford, Cheryl (1902–1986)
Dalrymple, Jean (1910–1998)
Dronke, Minnie Maria (1904–1987)
Fichandler, Zelda (1924—)
Fitton, Doris (1897–1985)
Flanagan, Hallie (1889–1969)
Frank, Mary K. (1911–1988)
Franken, Rose (c. 1895–1988)
Goldberg, Whoopi (1949—)
Harris, Renee (1885–1969)
Harris, Sylvia (d. 1966)
Helburn, Theresa (1887–1959)
Herscher, Sylvia (1913–2004)
Holden, Joan (1939—)
Holt, Stella (d. 1967)
Jacobson, Helen (d. 1974)
Jones, Margo (1911–1955)
Karatza, Rallou (1778–1830)
Lee, Auriol (1880–1941)
Le Gallienne, Eva (1899–1991)
Lehmann, Beatrix (1903–1979)
LeNoire, Rosetta (1911–2002)
Lortel, Lucille (1902–1999)
Lupino, Ida (1914–1995)
Macy, Gertrude (1904–1983)
Malpede, Karen (1945—)
Marbury, Elisabeth (1856–1933)
McIntosh, Madge (1875–1950)
Montagu, Helen (1928–2004)
Mooney, Ria (1904–1973)
Nicholls, Marjory Lydia (1890–1930)
Nichtern, Claire (c. 1921–1994)
Perry, Antoinette (1888–1946)
Perry, Elaine (1921–1986)
Rees, Rosemary (c. 1876–1963)
Reiner, Ethel Linder (d. 1971)
Robinson, Kathleen (1901–1983)
Rye, Daphne (1916—)
Selznick, Irene Mayer (1910–1990)
Stewart, Ellen (c. 1920—)
Stone, Paula (1912–1997)
Vance, Nina (1914–1980)
Victor, Lucia (1912–1986)
Wiman, Anna Deere (1924–1963)
Yorkin, Nicole (b. 1958)
Yorkin, Peg (1927—)

THEATRICAL PROMOTER
Palmer, Elizabeth Mary (1832–1897)

THEOLOGIAN
Daly, Mary (1928—)
Fiorenza, Elisabeth Schuessler (1938—)
Gebara, Ivone (1944—)
Harkness, Georgia (1891–1974)
Henderlite, Rachel (1905–1991)
Julian of Norwich (c. 1342–c. 1416)
Lyman, Mary Ely (1887–1975)
Ruether, Rosemary (1936—)
van Schurmann, Anna Maria (1607–1678)

THEORIST
Akselrod, Liubo (1868–1946)
Arendt, Hannah (1906–1975)
Baker, Ella (1903–1986)
Baum, Marie (1874–1964)
Crowe, Sylvia (1901–1997)
de Cleyre, Voltairine (1866–1912)
Dembo, Tamara (1902–1993)
Deutsch, Helene (1884–1982)
Dittmar, Louise (1807–1884)
Dohm, Hedwig (1831–1919)
Dulac, Germaine (1882–1942)
Dulles, Eleanor Lansing (1895–1996)
Épinay, Louise-Florence-Pétronille, Madame la Live d' (1726–1783)
Follett, Mary Parker (1868–1933)
Freud, Anna (1895–1982)
Fuller, Margaret (1810–1850)
Gilman, Charlotte Perkins (1860–1935)
Horney, Karen (1885–1952)
Kollontai, Alexandra (1872–1952)
Lacore, Suzanne (1875–1975)
Luxemburg, Rosa (1870–1919)
Meitner, Lise (1878–1968)
Nin, Anais (1903–1977)
Noether, Emmy (1882–1935)
Pellerier, Madeleine (1874–1939)
Rand, Ayn (1905–1982)
Rich, Adrienne (1929—)
Stepanova, Varvara (1894–1958)
Svilova, Elizaveta (1900–1975)
Wu, Chien-Shiung (1912–1997)
Young, Ella Flagg (1845–1918)

THEOSOPHIST
Besant, Annie (1847–1933)
Blavatsky, Helena (1831–1891)
Cousins, Margaret (1878–1954)
Denison, Flora MacDonald (1867–1921)
Helmrich, Dorothy (1889–1984)
Horniman, Annie (1860–1937)
Kingsford, Anna (1846–1888)
Lytton, Emily (1874–1964)
Rambova, Natacha (1897–1966)
Tingley, Katherine (1847–1929)
von Wiegand, Charmion (1899–1993)
Whiting, Lilian (1847–1942)
Young, Ella (1867–1951)

THEREMIN PLAYER
Rockmore, Clara (1911–1998)

THIEF (ACCUSED)
Adams, Mary (d. 1702)
Baker, Mary Ann (1834–1905)
Barker, Ma (1872–1935)
Bassett, Ann (1878–1956)
Bonner, Antoinette (1892–1920)
Bryant, Mary (1765–?)
Catchpole, Margaret (1762–1819)
Chadwick, Cassie L. (1859–1907)
Churchill, Deborah (1677–1708)
Dagoe, Hannah (d. 1763)
Diver, Jenny (1700–1740)
Fisher, Margaret (b. 1689)
Frith, Mary (c. 1584–1659)
Giriat, Madame (b. 1866)
Hanau, Marthe (c. 1884–1935)
Hart, Pearl (c. 1875–c. 1924)
Hearst, Patricia Campbell (1954—)
Henrys, Catherine (c. 1805–1855)
Kelly, Kathryn Thorne (1904–1998?)
Lyons, Sophie (1848–1924)
McLeod, Mrs. (d. 1727)
Moders, Mary (1643–1673)
Newman, Julia St. Clair (1818–?)
Parker, Bonnie (1910–1934)
Peck, Ellen (1829–1915)
Pfeiffer, Anna Ursula (1813–1863)
Starr, Belle (1848–1889)
Watson, Ellen (1861–1889)
Webster, Kate (1849–1879)
Wilson, Sarah (1750–?)

TIGHTROPE DANCER
Whiteside, Jane (1855–1875)

TOOL/TOOLING MANUFACTURER
Gleason, Kate (1865–1933)
Spain, Jayne (1927—)

TOTEM PAINTER
Carr, Emily (1871–1945)

TRACK-AND-FIELD ATHLETE
Ackermann, Rosemarie (1952—)
Afolabi, Bisi
Ahrens, Marlene (1933—)
Ajunwa, Chioma (1970—)
Aksyonova-Shapovalova, Lyudmila (1947—)
Alfeyeva, Lidiya (1946—)
Alozie, Glory (1977—)
Amoore, Judith Pollock (1940—)
Anders, Beth (1951—)
Andersen, Roxanne (1912–2002)
Andersen-Scheiss, Gabriela (1945—)
Anderson, Jodi (1957—)
Anisimova, Tatyana (1949—)
Anisimova, Vera (1952—)
Antyukh, Natalia (1981—)
Applebee, Constance (1873–1981)
Arden, Daphne (1941—)
Arimori, Yuko (1966—)
Armitage, Heather (1933—)

Arron, Christine (1973—)
Ashford, Evelyn (1957—)
Astafei, Galina (1968—)
Auerswald, Ingrid (1957—)
Babakova, Inga (1967—)
Bagryantseva, Yelizaveta (1920—)
Baikauskaite, Laimute (1956—)
Bailes, Margaret Johnson (1951—)
Bailey, Aleen (1980—)
Bailey, Angela (1962—)
Bakogianni, Niki (1968—)
Balas, Iolanda (1936—)
Balzer, Karin (1938—)
Barron, Gayle (c. 1947—)
Batten, Kim (1969—)
Bauma, Herma (1915–2003)
Beames, Adrienne
Becker-Steiner, Marion (1950—)
Beclea-Szekely, Violeta (1965—)
Beglyakova, Irina (1933—)
Behrendt, Kerstin (1967—)
Bell, Florence (1909—)
Belova, Irina (1968—)
Benhassi, Hasna (1978—)
Benida, Nouria (1970—)
Bergqvist, Kajsa (1976—)
Berman, Sara Mae (1936—)
Besfamilnaya, Nadezhda (1950—)
Besson, Colette (1946—)
Bidiouane, Nouzha (1969—)
Biechi, Anni (1940—)
Black, Marilyn (1944—)
Blagoeva, Yordanka (1947—)
Bland, Harriet (1915–1991)
Blankers-Koen, Fanny (1918–2004)
Board, Lillian (1948–1970)
Bochina, Natalya (1962—)
Bodendorf, Carla (1953—)
Boedding-Eckhoff, Inge (1947—)
Bogoslovskaya, Olga (1964—)
Bolden, Jeanette (1960—)
Bondarenko, Olga (1960—)
Bonds, Rosie (1944—)
Bonner, Beth (1952–1998)
Boulmerka, Hassiba (1968—)
Boyle, Raelene (1951—)
Bragina, Lyudmila (1943—)
Brand, Esther (1924—)
Braumueller, Ellen (1910—)
Braun, Sabine (1965—)
Breuer, Grit (1972—)
Brill, Debbie (1953—)
Brisco-Hooks, Valerie (1960—)
Brookshaw, Dorothy (1912—)
Brouwer, Bertha (1930—)
Brown, Alice Regina (1960—)
Brown, Audrey (b. 1913)
Brown, Earlene Dennis (1935—)
Brown, Judi (1961—)
Brunet, Roberta (1965—)
Bryant, Rosalyn (1956—)
Bryzgina, Olga (1963—)
Budd, Zola (1966—)
Bufanu, Valeria (1946—)
Buford-Bailey, Tonja (1970—)
Bukharina, Galina (1945—)
Bukovec, Brigita (1970—)
Burgher, Michelle (1977—)
Burke, Barbara (1917—)
Busch, Sabine (1962—)
Bussman, Gabriele (1959—)
Bykova, Tamara (1958—)
Cacchi, Paola (1945—)
Caird, Maureen (1951—)
Callender, Beverley (1956—)
Cameron, Hilda (b. 1912)
Campbell, Juliet (1970—)
Campbell, Veronica (1982—)
Carew, Mary (1913–2002)
Carlstedt, Lily (1926—)
Catherwood, Ethel (1910–1987)
Catuna, Anuta (1968—)
Cawley, Shirley (1932—)
Ceplak, Jolanda (1976—)
Chalmers, Angela (1963—)
Chamberlain, Ann Marie (1935—)
Chardonnet, Michele (1956—)
Cheeseborough, Chandra (1959—)
Cheeseman, Sylvia (1929—)
Chenchik, Taisiya (1936—)
Chen Yueling (1968—)
Chepchumba, Joyce (1970—)
Chivás, Silvia (1954—)
Chizhova, Nadezhda (1945—)
Chudina, Alexandra (1923–1990)
Cieply-Wieczorkowna, Teresa (1937—)
Cioncan, Maria (1977—)
Cistjakova, Galina (1962—)
Clark, Marjorie (b. 1909)
Clarke, Eldece (1965—)
Claus, Hildrun (1939—)
Cloete, Hestrie (1978—)
Coachman, Alice (1923—)
Cobian, Miguelina (1941—)
Cojocaru, Christiana (1962—)
Colander-Richardson, LaTasha (1976—)
Colon, Maria (1958—)
Cook, Myrtle (1902–1985)
Copeland, Lillian (1904–1964)
Costian, Daniela (1965—)
Cox, Crystal (1979—)
Craciunescu, Florenta (1955—)
Crawford Rogert, Yunaika (1982—)
Croker, Norma (1934—)
Crooks, Charmaine (1961—)
Cross, Jessica (b. 1909)
Csák, Ibolya (b. 1915)
Cumba Jay, Yumileidi (1975—)
Cuthbert, Betty (1938—)
Cuthbert, Juliet (1964—)
Dafovska, Ekaterina (c. 1976—)
Daniels, Isabelle Frances (1937—)
Davis-Thompson, Pauline (1966—)
Davy, Nadia (1980—)
Dawes, Eva (1912—)
Defar, Meseret (1983—)
Deniz, Leslie (1962—)
De Reuck, Colleen (1964—)
Desforges, Jean Catherine (1929—)
Devers, Gail (1966—)
Devetzi, Hrysopiyi (1975—)
Dibaba, Ejigayehu (1982—)
Dibaba, Tirunesh (1985—)
Dixon, Diane (1964—)
dMelpomene (fl. 1896)
Dod, Charlotte (1871–1960)
Dolson, Mildred (1918—)
Donath, Ursula (1931—)
Donkova, Yordanka (1961—)
Dorio, Gabriella (1957—)
Dörre, Katrin (1961—)
Douglas, Sandra (1967—)
Dragila, Stacy (1971—)
Drechsler, Heike (1964—)
Driscoll, Jean (1966—)
Driscoll, Jean (1967—)
Dumbadze, Nina (1919–1983)
Dupureur, Maryvonne (1937—)
Dzhigalova, Lyudmila (1962—)
Echols, Sheila Ann (1964—)
Edwards, Torri (1977—)
Ehrhardt, Anneliese (1950—)
Elejarde, Marlene (1950–1989)
El Moutawakel, Nawal (1962—)
Emmelmann-Siemon, Kirsten (1961—)
Engquist, Ludmila (1964—)
Faggs, Mae (1932—)
Falck, Hildegard (1949—)
Farmer-Patrick, Sandra (1962—)
Favor, Suzy (1968—)
Felix, Allyson (1985—)
Felix, Sylviane (1977—)
Felke, Petra (1959—)
Feofanova, Svetlana (1980—)
Fergerson, Mable (1955—)
Ferguson, Debbie (1976—)
Fernandez, Adriana (1971—)
Ferrell, Barbara (1947—)
Fiacconi, Franca (1965—)
Fibingerova, Helena (1949—)
Fiedler, Ellen (1958—)
Fikotová, Olga (1932—)
Finn-Burrell, Michelle (1965—)
Fireva, Tatyana (1982—)
Fitzgerald, Benita (1961—)
Fleischer, Ottilie (1911—)
Flintoff, Debra (1960—)
Flosadottir, Vala (1978—)
Forkel, Karen (1970—)
Foster, Diane (1928—)
Freeman, Cathy (1973—)
Freeman, Michele
Frizzell, Mary (1913–1972)
Frizzell, Mildred (1911—)
Fuchs, Ruth (1946—)
Furtsch, Evelyn (1911—)
Fynes, Sevatheda (1974—)
Fyodorova, Olga (1983—)
Gaines, Chryste (1970—)
Gallagher, Kim (1964–2002)
Gansky-Sachse, Diana (1963—)
Gardner, Maureen (1928–1974)
Gareau, France (1967—)
Gareau, Jacqueline (1953—)
Garisch-Culmberger, Renate (1939—)
Gaugel, Heide-Elke (1959—)
Gentile-Cordiale, Edera (1920–1993)
Gentzel, Inga (1908–1991)
Gibb, Roberta (1942—)
Girard, Patricia (1968—)
Gisolf, Carolina (1910—)
Göhr, Marlies (1958—)
Golubnichaya, Mariya (1924—)
Gommers, Maria (1939—)
Goncharenko, Svetlana (1971—)
Gorchakova, Yelena (1933—)
Gorecka, Halina (1938—)
Gorman, Miki (1935—)
Govorova, Olena (1973—)
Goyshchik-Nasanova, Tatyana (1952—)
Graf, Stephanie (1973—)
Graham, Kim (1971—)
Graham-Fenton, Lorraine (1973—)
Grigorieva, Tatiana (1975—)
Guevara, Ana (1977—)
Guidry, Carlette (1969—)
Gummel-Helmboldt, Margitte (1941—)
Gunda, Saida (1959—)
Gunnell, Sally (1966—)
Gusenbauer, Ilona (1947—)
Gyarmati, Olga (1924—)
Halkia, Fani (1979—)
Hall, Evelyne (1909–1993)
Halstead, Nellie (1910–1991)
Hammond, Kathleen (1951—)
Hannan, Cora (c. 1912—)
Hansen, Jacqueline A. (c. 1949—)
Hardy, Catherine (1930—)

Hartley, Donna-Marie (1955—)
Hasenjager-Robb, Daphne (1929—)
Hattestad, Trine (1966—)
Hayes, Joanna (1976—)
Hearnshaw, Susan (1961—)
Heine, Jutta (1940—)
Heinrich, Christina (1949—)
Hellmann-Opitz, Martina (1960—)
Helten, Inge (1950—)
Hemmings, Deon (1968—)
Henderson, Monique (1983—)
Hendrix, Brunhilde (1938—)
Henkel-Redetzky, Heike (1964—)
Hennagan, Monique (1976—)
Heritage, Doris Brown (1942—)
Herschmann, Nicole (1975—)
Hickman, Libbie (1965—)
Hinzmann, Gabriele (1947—)
Hiscock, Eileen (1909—)
Hitomi, Kinue (1908–1931)
Hitomi Kinue (1908–1931)
Hoffman, Abby (1947—)
Hoffmeister, Gunhild (1944—)
Holdmann, Anni (1900–1960)
Holmes, Kelly (1970—)
Hommola, Ute (1952—)
Hopkins, Thelma (1936—)
Hopper, Grace Murray (1906–1992)
Howard, Denean (1964—)
Howard, Sherri (1962—)
Hoyte-Smith, Joslyn Y. (1954—)
Huang Zhihong (1965—)
Hudson, Martha (1939—)
Hunte, Heather (1959—)
Huntley, Joni (1956—)
Hurtis, Muriel (1979—)
Hyman, Dorothy (1941—)
Idehen, Faith (1973—)
Ilyina-Kolesnikova, Nadezhda (1949—)
Ingram, Sheila Rena (1957—)
Ionescu, Valeria (1960—)
Isinbayeva, Yelena (1982—)
Itkina, Maria (1932—)
Ivan, Paula (1963—)
Ivanova, Natalya (1981—)
Ivanova, Olimpiada (1970—)
Jackson, Grace (1961—)
Jackson, Marjorie (1931—)
Jackson, Nell (1929–1988)
Jacobs, Simmone (1966—)
Jahl, Evelin (1956—)
Janiszewska, Barbara (1936—)
Janko, Eva (1945—)
Jaunzeme, Ineze (1932—)
Jayasinghe, Susanthika (1975—)
Jennings, Lynn (1960—)
Jesionowska, Celina (1933—)
Jiles, Pamela (1955—)
Jones, Barbara (1937—)
Jones, Brenda (1936—)
Jones, Esther (1969—)
Jones, Marion (1975—)
Jones, Patricia (1930—)
Joyner, Florence Griffith (1959–1998)
Joyner-Kersee, Jackie (1962—)
Jozwiakowska, Jaroslawa (1937—)
Junker, Helen (1905—)
Kaesling, Dagmar (1947—)
Kaiser, Natasha (1967—)
Kalediene, Birute (1934—)
Kasparkova, Sarka (1971—)
Kastor, Deena (1973—)
Kaufer, Evelyn (1953—)
Kaun, Elfriede (1914—)
Kazankina, Tatyana (1951—)
Kelesidou, Anastasia (1972—)
Kellner, Rosa (1910—)
Khabarova, Irina (1966—)
Khnykina, Nadezhda (1933–1994)
Khristova, Ivanka (1941—)
Khristova, Tsvetanka (1962—)
Khudorozhkina, Irina (1968—)
Kielan, Urszula (1960—)
Kiesl, Theresia (1963—)
Kilborn, Pam (1939—)
Killingbeck, Molly (1959—)
King, Joyce (1921—)
Kiplagat, Lornah (1974—)
Kirst, Jutta (1954—)
Kisabaka, Linda (1969—)
Klapezynski, Ulrike (1953—)
Kleiberne-Kontsek, Jolan (1939—)
Klein, Helga (1931—)
Kleinert, Nadine (1975—)
Klier-Schaller, Johanna (1952—)
Klimovica-Drevina, Inta (1951—)
Klobukowska, Ewa (1946—)
Kluft, Carolina (1983—)
Knab, Ursula (1929–1989)
Koch, Beate (1967—)
Koch, Marita (1957—)
Koehler, Gisela (1931—)
Kolpakova, Tatyana (1959—)
Komisova, Vera (1953—)
Kondratyeva, Lyudmila (1958—)
Konga, Pauline (c. 1971—)
Konopacka, Halina (1900–1989)
Konyayeva, Nadezhda (1931—)
Korolchik, Yanina (1976—)
Kostadinova, Stefka (1965—)
Kotlyarova, Olga (1976—)
Kotova, Tatyana (1976—)
Kozyr, Valentina (1950—)
Krachevskaya-Dolzhenko, Svetlana (1944—)
Krasnomovets, Olesya (1979—)
Krasovska, Olena (1976—)
Kratochvilova, Jarmila (1951—)
Krause, Christiane (1950—)
Krauss, Kathe (1906–1970)
Kravets, Inessa (1966—)
Krepkina, Vera (1933—)
Kristiansen, Ingrid (1956—)
Krivelyova, Svetlana (1969—)
Kroniger, Annegret (1952—)
Krueger, Luise (1915—)
Krug, Barbara (1956—)
Kruglova, Larisa (1972—)
Krzesinska, Elzbieta (1934—)
Kuehne, Rita (1947—)
Kumbernuss, Astrid (1970—)
Kuscsik, Nina (c. 1940—)
Kuzenkova, Olga (1970—)
Kwadzniewska, Maria (1913—)
Lambert, Margaret Bergmann (1914—)
Lamy, Jennifer (1949—)
Langbein, Martha (1941—)
Lange, Marita (1943—)
Langer, Lucyna (1956—)
Lannaman, Sonia M. (1956—)
Larrieu, Francie (1952—)
Lasovskaya, Inna (1969—)
Lathan-Brehmer, Christina (1958—)
Lawrence, Tayna (1975—)
Leatherwood, Lillie (1964—)
Lebedeva, Natalya (1949—)
Lebedeva, Tatyana (1976—)
Ledovskaya, Tatyana (1966—)
Leistenschneider, Nicole (1967—)
Leone, Giuseppina (1934—)
Lerwill, Sheila (1928—)
Lesovaya, Tatyana (1956—)
Leyman, Ann-Britt (1922—)
Li Chunxiu (1969—)
Lillak, Tiina (1961—)
Li Meisu (1959—)
Lisovskaya, Natalya (1962—)
Loewe, Gabriele (1958—)
Loghin, Mihaela (1952—)
Loroupe, Tegla (1973—)
Losch, Claudia (1960—)
Lotz, Ingrid (1934—)
Lovin, Fita (1951—)
Luettge, Johanna (1936—)
Macdonald, Linsey (1964—)
Mackay, Nancy (1929—)
Maillart, Ella (1903–1997)
Malchugina-Mikheyeva, Galina (1962—)
Maletzki, Doris (1952—)
Malone, Maicel (1969—)
Mang, Veronique (1984—)
Manjani, Miréla (1976—)
Manley, Dorothy (1927—)
Manning, Madeline (1948—)
Manoliu, Lia (1932–1998)
Marinova, Tereza (1977—)
Markova, Olga (c. 1969—)
Marten Garcia, Maritza (1963—)
Martin, Gael (1956—)
Martin, LaVonna (1966—)
Maslakova-Zharkova, Lyudmila (1952—)
Mason-Brown, Michele (1939—)
Masterkova, Svetlana (1968—)
Maston, June (1928—)
Mathews, Marlene (1934—)
Matthews, Margaret (1935—)
Mauermayer, Gisela (1913–1995)
May, Fiona (1969—)
Mazeas, Jacqueline (1920—)
Mbango Etone, Françoise (1976—)
McColgan-Lynch, Elizabeth (1964—)
McDaniel, Mildred (1933–2004)
McDonald, Beverly (1970—)
McGuire, Edith (1944—)
McKay, Heather (1941—)
McKiernan, Catherina (1969—)
McKinnon, Betty (1924—)
McMillan, Kathy (1957—)
McNeil, Loretta T. (1907–1988)
McPaul, Louise (1969—)
Meagher, Aileen (1910–1987)
Melinte, Doina (1956—)
Mellor, Fleur (1936—)
Melnik, Faina (1945—)
Menendez, Osleidys (1979—)
Menis, Argentina (1948—)
Merrill, Jan (1956—)
Merritt, Kim (c. 1955—)
Merry, Katharine (1974—)
Meyer, Elana (1966—)
Meyers, Ann (1955—)
Meyfarth, Ulrike (1956—)
Mickler, Ingrid (1942—)
Miles, Jearl (1966—)
Miller, Inger (1972—)
Mineyeva, Olga (1952—)
Mitchell, Nikole
Moeller-Gladisch, Silke (1964—)
Mollenhauer, Paula (1908–1988)
Moller, Lorraine (1955—)
Moreau, Janet (1927—)
Moreno, Yipsi (1980—)
Morrison, Melissa (1971—)
Mota, Rosa (1958—)
Mueller, Petra (1965—)
Mueller, Romy (1958—)
Mullins, Aimee (c. 1973—)
Münchow, Kirsten (1977—)
Murray, Yvonne (1964—)

Mutola, Maria (1972—)
Myers, Viola (1928—)
Nazarova, Natalya (1979—)
Nazarova, Olga (1955—)
Nazarova-Bagryantseva, Irina (1957—)
Ndereba, Catherine (1972—)
Neimke, Kathrin (1966—)
Nemeth, Angela (1946—)
Nerius, Steffi (1972—)
Nesterenko, Yuliya (1979—)
Netter, Mildrette (1948—)
Neubauer-Ruebsam, Dagmar (1962—)
Newby-Fraser, Paula (1962—)
Nicholas, Cindy (1957—)
Nikolayeva, Yelena (1966—)
Noguchi, Mizuki (1978—)
Norman, Decima (1909–1983)
Nurutdinova, Liliya (1963—)
Ochichi, Isabella (1979—)
Ogunkoya, Falilat (1969—)
Okayo, Margaret (1976—)
Okorokova, Antonina (1941—)
Olizarenko, Nadezhda (1953—)
Olney, Violet (1911—)
Ondieki, Lisa (1960—)
Onyali, Mary (1968—)
Opara, Charity (1972—)
Opara-Thompson, Christy (1971—)
Osburn, Ruth (1912–1994)
Ostermeyer, Micheline (1922–2001)
O'Sullivan, Sonia (1969—)
Ottey, Merlene (1960—)
Ottey-Page, Merlene (1960—)
Ozolina, Elvira (1939—)
Packer, Ann E. (1942—)
Palmer, Lillian (b. 1913)
Panfil, Wanda (1959—)
Pantelimon, Oana (1972—)
Parlby, Irene (1868–1965)
Parviainen, Katri (1914–2002)
Pashley, Anne (1935—)
Patoulidou, Paraskevi (1965—)
Patterson, Audrey (1926–1996)
Patterson-Tyler, Audrey (1926–1996)
Paul-Foulds, June (1934—)
Payne, Marita (1960—)
Pearce, Caroline (1925—)
Pearce, Jean (1921—)
Pearce, May (1915–1981)
Pearce, Morna (1932—)
Pearce Sisters (fl. 1936–1956)
Pechenkina, Natalya (1946—)
Peleshenko, Larisa (1964—)
Penes, Mihaela (1947—)
Perec, Marie-Jose (1968—)
Peris-Kneebone, Nova (1971—)
Perrone, Elisabetta (1968—)
Perry, Nanceen (1977—)
Peters, Mary (1939—)
Petersen-Kallensee, Marga (1919—)
Petkova-Vergova, Mariya (1950—)
Petrova, Ludmila (1968—)
Piccinini, Amelia (1917–1979)
Pinigina-Kulchunova, Mariya (1958—)
Pippig, Uta (1965—)
Pisareva, Mariya (1934—)
Plaetzer, Kjersti (1972—)
Pollard, Marjorie (1899–1982)
Pomoshchnikova, Natalya (1965—)
Ponomareva-Romashkova, Nina (1929—)
Popkova, Vera (1943—)
Porter, Gwendoline (c. 1909—)
Possekel, Elvira (1953—)
Press, Irina (1939—)
Press, Tamara (1939—)
Privalova, Irina (1968—)
Probert, Michelle (1960—)
Prorochenko-Burakova, Tatyana (1952—)
Providokhina-Fyodorenko, Tatyana (1953—)
Pufe, Margitta (1952—)
Puica, Maricica (1950—)
Quesada, Violetta (1947—)
Quintero Alvarez, Ioamnet (1972—)
Quinton, Carol (1936—)
Quirot, Ana (1963—)
Qu Yunxia (1972—)
Radcliffe, Paula (1973—)
Radke, Lina (1903–1983)
Rand, Mary (1940—)
Rantanen, Heli Orvokki (1970—)
Reel, Chi Cheng (1944—)
Renk, Silke (1967—)
Restrepo, Ximena (1969—)
Rezkova, Miloslava (1950—)
Ribeiro, Fernanda (1969—)
Richards, Sandie (1968—)
Richards, Sanya (1985—)
Richardson, Jillian (1965—)
Richter, Annegret (1950—)
Ritter, Louise (1958—)
Roba, Fatuma (1973—)
Robinson, Betty (1911–1997)
Robinson, Moushaumi (1981—)
Rochat-Moser, Franziska (1966–2002)
Roe, Allison (1957—)
Rogachyova, Lyudmila (1966—)
Rogers, Annette (b. 1913)
Rogowska, Anna (1981—)
Rohde, Brigitte (1954—)
Rohländer, Uta (1969—)
Romanova, Yelena (1963—)
Romay, Fulgencia (1944—)
Rosendahl, Heidemarie (1947—)
Rosenfeld, Fanny (1905–1969)
Rosenfeld, Fanny "Bobbie" (1903–1969)
Rücker, Anja (1972—)
Rudasne-Antal, Marta (1937—)
Rudolph, Wilma (1940–1994)
Rueckes, Anette (1951—)
Ruzina, Yelena (1964—)
Sabaite, Nijole (1950—)
Sadova, Natalya (1972—)
Samolenko, Tatyana (1961—)
Samotesova, Lyudmila (1939—)
Samuelson, Joan Benoit (1957—)
Sander, Maria (1924—)
Sanderson, Tessa (1956—)
Sapenter, Debra (1952—)
Saville, Jane (1974—)
Schaffer, Ine (1923—)
Schmidt, Helene (1906–1985)
Schmidt, Kathryn (1953—)
Schulter-Mattler, Heike (1958—)
Scott-Pomales, Catherine
Scrivens, Jean (1935—)
Sears, Eleanora (1881–1968)
Seidler, Helga (1949—)
Shchelkanova, Tatyana (1937—)
Sherwood, Sheila (1945—)
Shevtsova, Lyudmila (1934—)
Shikolenko, Natalya (1964—)
Shiley, Jean (1911–1998)
Shirley, Dorothy (1939—)
Shishigina, Olga (1968—)
Shmonina, Marina (1965—)
Shtereva, Nikolina (1955—)
Siebert, Gloria (1964—)
Silai, Ileana (1941—)
Simagina, Irina (1982—)
Simeoni, Sara (1953—)
Simon, Lidia (1973—)
Simonetto de Portela, Noemi (1926—)
Simpson, Janet (1944—)
Simpson, Sherone (1984—)
Skachko-Pakhovskaya, Tatyana (1954—)
Skolimowska, Kamila (1982—)
Skujyte, Austra (1979—)
Slaney, Mary Decker (1958—)
Slesarenko, Yelena (1982—)
Slupianek, Ilona (1956—)
Sly, Wendy (1959—)
Smallwood-Cook, Kathryn (1960—)
Smith, Ethel (1907–1979)
Smith, Phylis (1965—)
Smith, Ronetta (1980—)
Sokolova-Kulichkova, Natalya (1949—)
Sotherton, Kelly (1976—)
Sotnikova, Yuliya (1970—)
Stad-de Jong, Xenia (1922—)
Stalman, Ria (1951—)
Stanciu, Anisoara (1962—)
Stecher, Renate (1950—)
Stephens, Helen (1918–1994)
Steuer, Anni (b. 1913)
Stevens, Rochelle (1966—)
Stoeva, Vasilka (1940—)
Stoute, Jennifer (1965—)
Streidt, Ellen (1952—)
Strickland, Shirley (1925–2004)
Strike, Hilda (1910–1989)
Stringer, C. Vivian (1948—)
Strong, Shirley (1958—)
Struppert, Barbel (1950—)
Stubnick, Christa (1933—)
Sturrup, Chandra (1971—)
Styopina, Viktoriya (1976—)
Sui Xinmei
Suranova-Kucmanova, Eva (1946—)
Sussiek, Christine (1960—)
Svedberg, Ruth (1903–2004)
Switzer, Kathy (1947—)
Szabo, Gabriela (1975—)
Szewinska, Irena (1946—)
Tabakova, Yuliya (1980—)
Takahashi, Naoko (1972—)
Talysheva-Tregub, Tatyana (1937—)
Taylor, Angella (1958—)
Taylor, Betty (1916–1977)
Tereshchuk-Antipova, Tetiana (1969—)
Teske, Charlotte (1949—)
Thánou, Ekateríni (1975—)
Thimm-Finger, Ute (1958—)
Thrower, Norma (1936—)
Tirlea-Manolache, Ionela (1976—)
Tochenova, Klavdiya (1921—)
Todten, Jaqueline (1954—)
Tomashova, Tatyana (1975—)
Tordasi Schwarczenberger, Ildiko (1951—)
Torrence, Gwen (1965—)
Toussaint, Cheryl (1952—)
Trandenkova-Krivosheva, Marina (1967—)
Trotter, Deedee (1982—)
Tsoumeleka, Athanasia (1982—)
Tulu, Derartu (1969—)
Turner, Kim (1961—)
Tyler, Dorothy J. (1920—)
Tyshkevich, Tamara (1931—)
Tyus, Wyomia (1945—)
Utondu, Beatrice (1969—)
Valdes, Carmen (1954—)
Valla, Trebisonda (1916—)
van der Kade-Koudijs, Gerda (1923—)
van Langen, Ellen (1966—)
Vasco, María (1975—)
Vickers, Janeene (1968—)
Viscopoleanu, Viorica (1939—)
Voigt, Angela (1951—)
Von Bremen, Wilhelmina (1909–1976)

Voronina, Zinaida (1947—)
Voros, Zsuzsanna (1977—)
Wachtel, Christine (1965—)
Waitz, Grete (1953—)
Wajs, Jadwiga (1912–1990)
Walsh, Stella (1911–1980)
Wami, Gete (1974—)
Wang Junxia (1973—)
Wang Liping (1976—)
Wang Yan (1971—)
Wartenberg, Christiane (1956—)
Washburn, Mary (1907–1994)
Webb, Violet (1915—)
Weidenbach, Lisa Larsen (c. 1962—)
Welch, Priscilla (1944—)
Werner, Marianne (1924—)
Westermann, Liesel (1944—)
Whitbread, Fatima (1961—)
White, Marilyn Elaine (1944—)
White, Willye B. (1939—)
Wilden, Rita (1947—)
Wiley, Mildred (1901–2000)
Williams, Lauryn (1983—)
Williams, Lucinda (1937—)
Williams, Lynn (1960—)
Williams, Novlene (1982—)
Williams, Tonique (1976—)
Williams, Yvette (1929—)
Williamson, Audrey (1926—)
Winter, Liane (1942—)
Witziers-Timmer, Jeanette (1923–2005)
Wöckel-Eckert, Bärbel (1955—)
Wodars, Sigrun (1965—)
Wright, Dana (1959—)
Wujak, Brigitte (1955—)
Wyludda, Ilke (1969—)
Xing Huina (1984—)
Yatchenko, Irina (1965—)
Yegorova, Valentina (1964—)
Yelesina, Yelena (1970—)
Yorgova, Diana (1942—)
Young, Dannette (1964—)
Yusuf, Fatima (1971—)
Zaczkiewicz, Claudia (1962—)
Zaharias, Babe Didrikson (1911–1956)
Zakharova, Svetlana (1970—)
Zatopek, Dana (1922—)
Zehrt, Monika (1952—)
Zhirova, Marina (1963—)
Zhupiyeva, Yelena (1960—)
Zinn, Elfi (1953—)
Zvereva, Ellina (1960—)
Zybina, Galina (1931—)
Zykina, Olesya (1980—)
Zyuskova, Nina (1952—)

TRACK-AND-FIELD COACH

Jackson, Nell (1929–1988)

TRADER

See Fur trader.
See Merchant/Trader.
See Securities broker.

TRAMPOLINIST

Cockburn, Karen (1980—)
Dogonadze, Anna (1973—)
Ford, Judith (c. 1950—)
Huang Shanshan (1986—)
Karavaeva, Irina (1975—)
Tsyhuleva, Oksana

TRANSLATOR/INTERPRETER

Adler, Valentine (1898–1942)
Akhmadulina, Bella (1937—)
Akhmatova, Anna (1889–1966)
Aliye, Fatima (1862–1936)
Andreeva, Maria Fedorovna (1868–1953)
Aníchkova, Anna (1868–1935)
Anna Ivanovna (1693–1740)
Anscombe, G.E.M. (1919–2001)
Anstei, Olga Nikolaevna (1912–1985)
Armand, Inessa (1874–1920)
Arnim, Bettine von (1785–1859)
Ascarelli, Devora (fl. 1601)
Aubin, Penelope (c. 1685–1731)
Aury, Dominique (1907–1998)
Austin, Sarah (1793–1867)
Ayscough, Florence (1875/78–1942)
Bacinetti-Florenzi, Marianna (1802–1870)
Balabanoff, Angelica (1878–1965)
Barney, Natalie Clifford (1876–1972)
Barnicoat, Constance Alice (1872–1922)
Baron, Devorah (1887–1956)
Barr, Margaret Scolari (1901–1987)
Barykova, Anna Pavlovna (1839–1893)
Basset, Mary Roper (fl. 1544–1572)
Beach, Sylvia (1887–1962)
Beauchamp, Margaret (d. 1482)
Becher, Lilly (1901–1976)
Bell, Gertrude (1868–1926)
Belloc, Louise (1796–1881)
Belot, Madame (1719–1804)
Bentley, Catherine (fl. 1635)
Bianco, Margery Williams (1881–1944)
Biehl, Charlotta Dorothea (1731–1788)
Bins, Patrícia (1930—)
Bishop, Elizabeth (1911–1979)
Blackwell, Alice Stone (1857–1950)
Blanc, Marie-Thérèse (1840–1907)
Blind, Mathilde (1841–1896)
Booth, Mary Louise (1831–1889)
Bosco, María Angélica (1917—)
Boye, Karin (1900–1941)
Braunschweig-Lüneburg, Sibylle Ursula von (1629–1671)
Briet, Marguerite de (c. 1510–c. 1550)
Brooke, Charlotte (1740–1793)
Brooks, Louise (1906–1985)
Brown, Margaret Wise (1910–1952)
Buber-Neumann, Margarete (1901–1989)
Buck, Pearl S. (1892–1973)
Budberg, Moura (1892–1974)
Bunke, Tamara (1937–1967)
Burgess, Renate (1910–1988)
Cabrini, Frances Xavier (1850–1917)
Caldwell, Sarah (1924—)
Campoamor, Clara (1888–1972)
Carter, Elizabeth (1717–1806)
Cary, Elizabeth (1586–1639)
Cassian, Nina (1924—)
Cecchi D'Amico, Suso (1914—)
Cecil, Mildred Cooke (1526–1589)
César, Ana Cristina (1952–1983)
Chang, Eileen (1920–1995)
Chanler, Margaret (b. 1862)
Chen Jingrong (1917–1989)
Chesnut, Mary Boykin (1823–1886)
Chiumina, Olga Nikolaevna (1865–1909)
Churchill, Fanny (d. 1899)
Cialente, Fausta (1898–1994)
Clark, Eleanor (1913–1996)
Clemence of Barking (fl. 12th c.)
Clerke, Ellen Mary (1840–1906)
Colenso, Elizabeth (1821–1904)
Coleridge, Sara (1802–1852)
Collyer, Mary (d. 1763)
Conant, Hannah Chaplin (1809–1865)
Coutinho, Sônia (1939—)
Dabrowska, Maria (1889–1965)
Dacier, Anne (1654–1720)
Dacre, Barbarina (1768–1854)
d'Arconville, Geneviève (1720–1805)
Dean, Vera Micheles (1903–1972)
Deledda, Grazia (1871–1936)
Deutsch, Babette (1895–1982)
Duff-Gordon, Lucie (1821–1869)
Dutt, Toru (1856–1877)
Eastlake, Elizabeth (1809–1893)
Edinger, Tilly (1897–1967)
Eisner, Lotte (1896–1983)
Elizabeth of Wied (1843–1916)
Elizabeth Petrovna (1709–1762)
Espín de Castro, Vilma (1934—)
Evans, Mary Anne (1819–1880)
Ewing, Juliana Horatia (1841–1885)
Fabian, Dora (1901–1935)
Favre, Julie Velten (1834–1896)
Feinstein, Elaine (1930—)
Ferguson, Elizabeth Graeme (1737–1801)
Fielding, Sarah (1710–1768)
Figes, Eva (1932—)
Fisher, Dorothy Canfield (1879–1958)
Fox, Caroline (1819–1871)
Freer, Agnes Rand (1878–1972)
Frischmuth, Barbara (1941—)
Gág, Wanda (1893–1946)
Garnett, Constance (1862–1946)
Gerhardt, Ida (1905–1997)
Ginsburg, Mirra (1909–2000)
Ginzburg, Natalia (1916–1991)
Godden, Rumer (1907–1998)
Goldberg, Lea (1911–1970)
Gottsched, Luise Adelgunde (1713–1762)
Gournay, Marie le Jars de (1565–1645)
Grossman, Edith (1936—)
Guest, Lady Charlotte (1812–1895)
Haldane, Charlotte (1894–1969)
Hale, Sarah Preston (1796–1866)
Hamilton, Emma (1765–1815)
Hapgood, Isabel (1850–1928)
Harari, Manya (1905–1969)
Harnack, Mildred (1902–1943)
Harrison, Constance Cary (1843–1920)
Hartwig, Julia (1921—)
Herbert, Mary (1561–1621)
Hobhouse, Emily (1860–1926)
Howitt, Mary (1799–1888)
Huber, Therese (1764–1829)
Hull, Eleanor (fl. 15th c.)
Hume, Anna (fl. 1644)
Hutchinson, Lucy (1620–post 1675)
Issaia, Nana (1934—)
Jacobs, Aletta (1854–1929)
Jameson, Anna Brownell (1794–1860)
Jameson, Storm (1891–1986)
Janés, Clara (1940—)
Jesenská, Milena (1896–1945)
Jolas, Maria (1893–1987)
Jonker, Ingrid (1933–1965)
Judson, Sarah Boardman (1803–1845)
Kairi, Evanthia (1797–1866)
Kaminska, Ida (1899–1980)
Karatza, Rallou (1778–1830)
Klimova, Rita (1931–1993)
Kohut, Rebekah (1864–1951)
Kolmar, Gertrud (1894–1943)
Konopnicka, Maria (1842–1910)
Kulman, Elisabeth (1808–1825)
Lafite, Marie-Elisabeth Bouée de (c. 1750–1794)
La Flesche, Susette (1854–1902)
Lang, Leonora (1851–1933)
Latimer, Elizabeth W. (1822–1904)
Lavoisier, Marie (1758–1836)
Lazarus, Emma (1849–1887)
Lee, Muna (1895–1965)
Lehmann, Rosamond (1901–1990)
Lemoine-Luccioni, Eugénie (1912—)
Lennox, Charlotte (1720–1804)

León, Maria Teresa (1903–1988)
Leontias, Sappho (1832–1900)
Levertov, Denise (1923–1997)
Levi, Natalia (1901–1972)
Lochhead, Liz (1947—)
Locke, Anne Vaughan (c. 1530–c. 1590)
Longhi, Lucia Lopresti (1895–1985)
Lord, Lucy Takiora (c. 1842–1893)
Lowe-Porter, Helen (1876–1963)
Lowney, Shannon (1969–1994)
Lumley, Joanna (c. 1537–1576)
Lutz, Berta (1894–1976)
Lyell, Mary Horner (1808–1873)
MacEwen, Gwendolyn (1941–1987)
MacInnes, Helen (1907–1985)
Maksimovic, Desanka (1898–1993)
Malinche (c. 1500–1531)
Malraux, Clara (c. 1897–1982)
Man, Judith (fl. 1640s)
Mandelstam, Nadezhda (1899–1980)
Manner, Eeva-Liisa (1921–1995)
Mansfield, Katherine (1888–1923)
Marshall, Joyce (1913—)
Martin, Claire (1914—)
Massee, May (1881–1966)
McKenna, Rollie (1918–2003)
McKenna, Siobhan (1922–1986)
Melissanthi (c. 1907–c. 1991)
Merril, Judith (1923–1997)
Modotti, Tina (1896–1942)
Montgomery, Helen Barrett (1861–1934)
Montolieu, Pauline (1751–1832)
Montour, Isabelle (1667–c. 1750)
Moore, Aubertine Woodward (1841–1929)
Moore, Marianne (1887–1972)
Morath, Inge (1923–2002)
More, Agnes (1591–1656)
Moutza-Martinengou, Elisavet (1801–1832)
Muir, Willa (1890–1970)
Musgrove, Mary (c. 1690–c. 1763)
Naheed, Kishwar (1940—)
Nanye'hi (1738–1822)
Nathan, Maud (1862–1946)
Naubert, Christiane Benedikte (1756–1819)
Necker de Saussure, Albertine (1766–1841)
Nesbitt, Cathleen (1888–1982)
Neufvic, Madame de (fl. 17th c.)
Newlin, Dika (1923—)
Newman, Frances (1883–1928)
Nice, Margaret Morse (1883–1974)
Orbell, Margaret (1934—)
Paoli, Betty (1814–1894)
Pappenheim, Bertha (1859–1936)
Parsons, Eliza (c. 1748–1811)
Parthenay, Catherine de (1554–1631)
Pavlova, Karolina (1807–1893)
Paxinou, Katina (1900–1973)
Penfold, Merimeri (1924—)
Peri Rossi, Cristina (1941—)
Peter, Sarah Worthington (1800–1877)
Petrovýkh, Mariia (1908–1979)
Pierangeli, Rina Faccio (1876–1960)
Pizarnik, Alejandra (1936–1972)
Ploennies, Luise von (1803–1872)
Polier, Marie-Elizabeth (1742–1817)
Przybyszewska, Dagny Juel (1867–1901)
Pukui, Mary Kawena (1895–1986)
Putnam, Mary T.S. (1810–1898)
Raine, Kathleen (1908–2003)
Raverat, Gwen (1885–1957)
Reeve, Clara (1729–1807)
Reiche, Maria (1903–1998)
Richards, Ellen Swallow (1842–1911)
Richardson, Dorothy (1873–1957)
Richardson, Henry Handel (1870–1946)
Ridler, Anne (1912–2001)
Robert-Kéralio, Louise (1758–1821)
Robinson, Therese Albertine Louise von Jakob (1797–1870)
Rothmann, Maria Elisabeth (1875–1975)
Royde-Smith, Naomi Gwladys (c. 1880–1964)
Royer, Clémence (1830–1902)
Russell, Elizabeth (1540–1609)
Sacajawea (c. 1787–c. 1812 or 1884)
Sachs, Nelly (1891–1970)
Sampter, Jessie (1883–1938)
Sandel, Cora (1880–1974)
Sansom, Odette (1912–1995)
Sauvé, Jeanne (1922–1993)
Sayers, Dorothy L. (1893–1957)
Schlegel-Schelling, Caroline (1763–1809)
Schultz, Sigrid (1893–1980)
Senesh, Hannah (1921–1944)
Shchepkina-Kupernik, Tatiana (1874–1952)
Silvia Sommerlath (1943—)
Sinclair, May (1863–1946)
Singer, Winnaretta (1865–1943)
Sirota, Beate (1923—)
Smith, Abby (1797–1878)
Smith, Julia (1792–1886)
Solano, Solita (1888–1975)
Spivak, Gayatri Chakravorty (1942—)
Stade, Richardis von (d. 1152)
Stein, Edith (1891–1942)
Stokes, Rose Pastor (1879–1933)
Swanwick, Anna (1813–1899)
Szold, Henrietta (1860–1945)
Szymborska, Wislawa (1923—)
Tappan, Eva March (1854–1930)
Tastu, Amable (1798–1885)
Tautari, Mary (d. 1906)
Te Kiri Karamu, Heni (1840–1933)
Thomas, Edith Matilda (1854–1925)
Toguri, Iva (1916—)
Travers, P.L. (1906–1996)
Truganini (1812–1876)
Tsebrikova, M.K. (1835–1917)
Tsvetaeva, Marina (1892–1941)
Tyler, Margaret (d. 1595)
Ukrainka, Lesya (1871–1913)
Utley, Freda (1898–1977)
Vaa, Aslaug (1889–1965)
Vakalo, Eleni (1921—)
van Stockum, Hilda (b. 1908)
Vardill, Anna Jane (1781–1852)
Vengerova, Zinaida (1867–1941)
Vesaas, Halldis Moren (1907–1995)
Veselitskaia, Lidiia Ivanovna (1857–1936)
Victoria Adelaide (1840–1901)
Vivien, Renée (1877–1909)
von Richthofen, Else (1874–1973)
Voynich, Ethel (1864–1960)
Wauneka, Annie Dodge (1910–1997)
Wedgwood, C.V. (1910–1997)
Weil, Simone (1909–1943)
Wen Jieruo (1927—)
Wheelock, Lucy (1857–1946)
White, Antonia (1899–1980)
White, Maude Valerie (1855–1937)
Wilde, Jane (1821–1896)
Wilson, Charlotte (1854–1944)
Winkworth, Catherine (1827–1878)
Winkworth, Susanna (1820–1884)
Winnemucca, Sarah (1844–1891)
Wise, Louise Waterman (1874–1947)
Wollstonecraft, Mary (1759–1797)
Wormeley, Katharine Prescott (1830–1908)
Wright, Laura Maria (1809–1886)
Yamada Waka (1879–1956)
Yang Jiang (b. 1911)
Yezierska, Anzia (c. 1881–1970)
Yourcenar, Marguerite (1903–1987)
Zardoya, Concha (1914–2004)
Zasulich, Vera (1849–1919)
Zetkin, Clara (1857–1933)
Zhao Luorui (b. 1912)
Zimetbaum, Mala (1920–1944)
Ziyada, Mayy (1886–1941)
Zrinska, Ana Katarina (1625–1673)
Zur Mühlen, Hermynia (1883–1951)

TRAVELER
See Explorer/Traveler.

TRAVEL WRITER
Anderson, Erica (1914–1976)
Audouard, Olympe (1830–1890)
Bacheracht, Therese von (1804–1852)
Baden-Powell, Olave (1889–1977)
Beloff, Nora (1919–1997)
Benson, Stella (1892–1933)
Berlepsch, Emilie von (1755–1830)
Betham-Edwards, Matilda (1836–1919)
Bishop, Isabella (1831–1904)
Brassey, Anna (1839–1887)
Bremer, Fredrika (1801–1865)
Briche, Adelaide de la (1755–1844)
Bunge de Gálvez, Delfina (1881–1952)
Bögli, Lina (1858–1941)
Chevalier, Caroline (c. 1832–1917)
Clark, Eleanor (1913–1996)
Cockburn, Patricia (1914–1989)
Costello, Louisa Stuart (1799–1870)
Davidson, Robyn (1950—)
Dieulafoy, Jane (1851–1916)
Duff-Gordon, Lucie (1821–1869)
Duncan, Sara Jeanette (1861–1922)
Eberhardt, Isabelle (1877–1904)
Fiennes, Celia (1662–1741)
Fraser, Mary Crawford (1851–1922)
Glümer, Claire von (1825–1906)
Gordon-Cumming, Eka (1837–1924)
Hill, Ernestine (1899–1972)
Jacobs, Aletta (1854–1929)
Kennett, Margaret Brett (fl. 1723–1725)
Kingsley, Mary H. (1862–1900)
Kinzie, Juliette Magill (1806–1870)
La Roche, Sophie von (1730–1807)
Leslie, Miriam Folline Squier (1836–1914)
Le Vert, Octavia Walton (1811–1877)
Lewis, Agnes Smith (1843–1926)
Lichnowsky, Mechthilde (1879–1958)
Lindgren, Astrid (1907–2002)
Macaulay, Rose (1881–1958)
Maillart, Ella (1903–1997)
Malraux, Clara (c. 1897–1982)
Mannin, Ethel (1900–1984)
Martineau, Harriet (1802–1876)
McCarthy, Mary (1912–1989)
Meredith, Louisa Anne (1812–1895)
Miller, Anna Riggs (1741–1781)
Monroe, Harriet (1860–1936)
More, Hannah (1745–1833)
Morris, Jan (1926—)
Murphy, Dervla (1931—)
Naudé, Adèle (1910–1981)
Niles, Blair (1880–1959)
O'Brien, Kate (1897–1974)
Packer, Joy (1905–1977)
Paget, Violet (1856–1935)
Pardoe, Julia (1804–1862)
Parker, Mary Ann (fl. 1795)
Pfeiffer, Ida (1797–1858)
Piozzi, Hester Lynch (1741–1821)
Rama Rau, Santha (1923—)
Ross, Violet Florence (1862–1915)
Rubinstein, Renate (1929–1990)
Rüegg, Annelise (1879–1934)

Schaw, Janet (d. around 1801)
Schopenhauer, Johanna (1766–1838)
Schwarzenbach, Annemarie (1908–1942)
Scidmore, Eliza Ruhamah (1856–1928)
Shaw, Elizabeth (1920–1992)
Sheridan, Clare (1885–1970)
Simon, Kate (1912–1990)
Somerville, E. (1858–1949)
Spofford, Harriet Prescott (1835–1921)
Stark, Freya (1893–1993)
Strong, Anna Louise (1885–1970)
Stuart-Wortley, Emmeline (1806–1855)
Tarsouli, Athena (1884–1974)
Tennant, Kylie (1912–1988)
Terhune, Mary Virginia (1830–1922)
Thompson, Era Bell (1906–1986)
Todd, Mabel Loomis (1858–1932)
Tracy, Honor (1913–1989)
Trollope, Frances Milton (c. 1779–1863)
Vivanti, Annie (1868–1942)
Wakefield, Priscilla (1751–1832)
West, Rebecca (1892–1983)
Wollstonecraft, Mary (1759–1797)
Wood, Edith Elmer (1871–1945)
Woolson, Constance Fenimore (1840–1894)
Wordsworth, Dorothy (1771–1855)

TREASURER (GOVERNMENT)
Anderson, Bette B. (c. 1929—)
Clark, Georgia Neese (1900–1995)
Morton, Azie Taylor (c. 1936–2003)
Pfost, Gracie (1906–1965)
Priest, Ivy Baker (1905–1975)
Richards, Ann Willis (1933—)

TRIATHLETE
Allen, Katherine (1970—)
Bartholomew, Susan (1969—)
Flannery, Judy (1939–1997)
Harrop, Loretta (1975—)
Hedrick, Heather (c. 1972—)
Jones, Michellie (1969—)
McMahon, Brigitte (1967—)
Messmer, Magali (1971—)
Newby-Fraser, Paula (1962—)
Taormina, Sheila (1969—)

TRIBAL LEADER
Afua Koba (fl. 1834–1884)
Akers, Dolly Smith (1901–1986)
Amohau, Merekotia (1898–1978)
Awashonks (fl. mid-late 17th c.)
Brant, Molly (c. 1736–1796)
Carroll, Heni Materoa (1852/56?–1930)
Cherrington, Te Paea (c. 1877–1937)
Faulkner, Ruawahine Irihapeti (?–1855)
Hei, Akenehi (1877/78?–1910)
Herangi, Te Kirihaehae Te Puea (1883–1952)
Hine-i-paketia (fl. 1850–1870)
Hine-i-turama (c. 1818–1864)
Hinematioro (d. 1823)
Hinerangi, Sophia (c. 1830–1911)
Kaaro, Ani (fl. 1885–1901)
Kahutia, Riperata (c. 1838–1887)
Kokoro-Barrett, Hiria (1870–1943)
Love, Ripeka Wharawhara (1882–1953)
Maihi, Rehutai (1895–1967)
Mangakahia, Meri Te Tai (1868–1920)
Mankiller, Wilma (1945—)
Matenga, Huria (1840/42–1909)
Mmanthatisi (c. 1780–c. 1836)
Morete, Maraea (1844–1907)
Nanye'hi (1738–1822)
Nga-kahu-whero (fl. 1800–1836)
Ngata, Arihia Kane (1879–1929)
Niniwa-i-te-rangi (1854–1929)
Papakura, Makereti (1873–1930)
Parata, Katherine Te Rongokahira (1873–1939)
Pinepine Te Rika (1857/58–1954)
Pitini-Morera, Hariata Whakatau (1871/72?–1938)
Puhiwahine Te Rangi-hirawea, Rihi (d. 1906)
Rere-o-maki (d. 1868)
Riley, Mary Velasquez (1908–1987)
Riwai, Kiti Karaka (1870–1927)
Rongonui, Kahupake (1868/69?–1947)
Stirling, Mihi Kotukutuku (1870–1956)
Taiaroa, Tini Kerei (c. 1846–1934)
Tamairangi (fl. 1820–1828)
Tapsell, Ngatai Tohi Te Ururangi (1844–1928)
Te Kahuhiapo, Rahera (1820s?–1910)
Te Kakapi, Ripeka Wharawhara-i-te-rangi (?–1880)
Te Kiri Karamu, Heni (1840–1933)
Tenetahi, Rahui Te Kiri (d. 1913)
Te Paea Tiaho (1820s?–1875)
Te Pikinga (c. 1800–after 1868)
Te Rangi-i-paia II (fl. 1818–1829)
Te Rangimarie, Puna Himene (fl. 1908–1911)
Te Rau-o-te-rangi, Kahe (?–c. 1871)
Te Rohu (fl. 1820–1850)
Te Taiawatea Rangitukehu, Maata (1848/49?–1929)
Te Whaiti, Kaihau Te Rangikakapi Maikara (1863–1937)
Te Wherowhero, Piupiu (1886/87?–1937)
Topeora, Rangi Kuini Wikitoria (?–1865/73)
Turikatuku (d. 1827)
Waitaoro (c. 1848–1929)
Waitohi (?–1839)
Wauneka, Annie Dodge (1910–1997)
Wetamoo (c. 1650–1676)
Wyllie, Kate (d. 1913)
Yates, Ngawini (1852/53?–1910)

TRIBAL REPRESENTATIVE
Pomare, Hariata (fl. 1863–1864)

TROMBONIST
Boswell, Connee (1907–1976)
Liston, Melba (1926—)

TROUBADOUR
Alais (fl. 12th c.)
Alamanda of France (fl. late 12th c.)
de Dia, Beatrice (c. 1160–1212)
Garsenda (1170–c. 1257)
Guillelma de Rosers (fl. 1240–1260)
Isabella (b. 1180)
Iselda, Lady (fl. 12th c.)
Iseut de Capio (1140–?)
Lombarda (b. 1190)
Tibors (b. around 1130)

TRUMPETER
Kendall, Kay (1926–1959)
King, Coretta Scott (1927—)
Robinson, Cynthia (1946—)
Scott, Hazel (1920–1981)
Snow, Valaida (c. 1903–1956)
Zwilich, Ellen Taaffe (1939—)

TSARINA
Dessilava (fl. 1197–1207)
Elizabeth of Baden (1779–1826)
Eudoxia Lopukhina (1669–1731)
Godunova, Irene (d. 1603)
Irene Lascaris (d. around 1270)
Irene Paleologina (fl. 1279–1280)
Maria Paleologina (fl. 1271–1279)
Maria Skuratova (d. 1605)

TUNBUR PLAYER
Ubaida (fl. c. 830)

UGUBHU PLAYER
Magogo ka Dinizulu, Constance (1900–1984)

UNION LEADER/ACTIVIST/ORGANIZER
See Labor activist.

UNITED NATIONS DELEGATE/ REPRESENTATIVE
Anderson, Eugenie Moore (1909–1997)
Anttila, S. Inkeri (1916—)
Armstrong, Anne L. (1927—)
Astorga, Nora (1949–1988)
Bailey, Pearl (1918–1990)
Balch, Emily Greene (1867–1961)
Barrow, Nita (1916–1995)
Begtrup, Bodil (1903–1987)
Bernardino, Minerva (1907–1998)
Black, Shirley Temple (1928—)
Bolton, Frances Payne (1885–1977)
Brooks, Angie (1928—)
Brunschvicg, Cécile (1877–1946)
Bruntland, Gro Harlem (1939—)
Bunker, Carol Laise (1918–1991)
Castle, Barbara (1910–2002)
Cisse, Jeanne-Martin (1926—)
Clouzot, Vera (1921–1960)
Darton, Patience (1911–1996)
Douglas, Helen Gahagan (1900–1980)
Dunne, Irene (1898–1990)
El Saadawi, Nawal (1931—)
Fenwick, Millicent (1910–1992)
Figueroa, Ana (1907–1970)
Freundlich, Emmy (1878–1948)
George, Zelma Watson (1904–1994)
Gildersleeve, Virginia Crocheron (1877–1965)
Hawkes, Jacquetta (1910–1996)
Horsbrugh, Florence (1889–1969)
Hulme, Kathryn (1900–1981)
Jagan, Janet (1920—)
Kasilag, Lucrecia R. (1918—)
Khan, Begum Liaquat Ali (1905–1990)
Kirkpatrick, Jeane (1926—)
Lefaucheux, Marie-Helene (1904–1964)
Makeba, Miriam (1932—)
McCormick, Anne O'Hare (1880–1954)
Menchú, Rigoberta (1959—)
Miller, Frieda S. (1889–1973)
Mongella, Gertrude (1945—)
Myrdal, Alva (1902–1986)
Ogot, Grace (1930—)
Pandit, Vijaya Lakshmi (1900–1990)
Pintasilgo, Maria de Lurdes (1930–2004)
Rapoport, Lydia (1923–1971)
Rohde, Ruth Bryan Owen (1885–1954)
Roosevelt, Eleanor (1884–1962)
Salt, Barbara (1904–1975)
Sampson, Edith S. (1901–1979)
Sipilä, Helvi (1915—)
Street, Jessie (1889–1970)
Tree, Marietta (1917–1991)
Wells, Melissa Foelsch (1932—)
Wilson, Cairine (1885–1962)

URBAN DESIGNER
Moody, Deborah (c. 1583–c. 1659)
Schütte-Lihotzky, Margarete (1897–2000)
Smith, Chloethiel Woodard (1910–1992)

VAUDEVILLE/BURLESQUE/VARIETY PERFORMER
Adelaide (c. 1884–1959)
Adler, Stella (1902–1993)
Allen, Gracie (1902–1964)

Andrews, Laverne (1911–1967)
Astaire, Adele (1898–1981)
Bacon, Faith (1909–1956)
Bailey, Frankie (1859–1953)
Baker, Belle (1893–1957)
Baker, Josephine (1906–1975)
Ball, Lucille (1911–1989)
Barrett, Minnette (1880–1964)
Barrymore, Diana (1921–1960)
Bartet, Jeanne Julia (1854–1941)
Batson, Flora (1864–1906)
Bayes, Nora (1880–1928)
Bayne, Beverly (1894–1982)
Bergere, Valerie (1872–1938)
Blaine, Vivian (1921–1995)
Blanche, Ada (1862–1953)
Blondell, Joan (1906–1979)
Bordoni, Irene (1895–1953)
Bow, Clara (1904–1965)
Bowman, Patricia (1904–1999)
Brent, Evelyn (1899–1975)
Brice, Fanny (1891–1951)
Burrows-Fontaine, Evan (1898–1984)
Busch, Mae (1891–1946)
Cameron, Dorothy (d. 1958)
Campbell, Mrs. Patrick (1865–1940)
Canova, Judy (1916–1983)
Carlson, Violet (d. 1997)
Carus, Emma (1879–1927)
Castle, Irene (c. 1893–1969)
Caswell, Maude (c. 1880–?)
Cherry, Addie (c. 1859–1942)
Cherry, Effie (d. 1944)
Claire, Ina (1892–1985)
Clayton, Bessie (c. 1878–1948)
Cline, Maggie (1857–1934)
Coca, Imogene (1909–2001)
Cohen, Myra (1892–1959)
Coles, Joyce (b. around 1904)
Collins, Janet (1917–2003)
Collins, José (1887–1958)
Crabtree, Lotta (1847–1924)
Critchfield, Lee (c. 1909—)
Cushman, Pauline (1833–1893)
Dalrymple, Jean (1910–1998)
Dandridge, Dorothy (1923–1965)
Dare, Phyllis (1890–1975)
Dare, Zena (1887–1975)
Davis, Joan (1907–1961)
Dean, Dora (c. 1872–1950)
Déjazet, Pauline-Virginie (1797–1875)
Delf, Juliet (d. 1962)
Delroy, Irene (1898–?)
Deslys, Gaby (1884–1920)
Dolly, Jenny (1892–1941)
Dolly, Rosie (1892–1970)
Doner, Kitty (1895–1988)
Dorziat, Gabrielle (1886–1979)
Douglas, Lizzie (1897–1973)
Dressler, Marie (1869–1934)
Duncan, Rosetta (1890–1959)
Elseeta (1883–1903)
Etting, Ruth (1896–1978)
Fatima, Djemille (c. 1890–1921)
Flowerton, Consuelo (1900–1965)
Foy, Madeline (1903–1988)
Foy, Mary (1901–1987)
Froman, Jane (1907–1980)
Fuller, Loïe (1862–1928)
Garland, Judy (1922–1969)
Gaxton, Madeline (1897–1990)
George, Gladys (1900–1954)
Gitana, Gertie (1887–1957)
Glaser, Lulu (1874–1958)
Glyn, Elinor (1864–1943)
Grable, Betty (1916–1973)
Guinan, Texas (1884–1933)
Hackett, Jeanette (c. 1898–1979)
Hading, Jane (1859–1941)
Havoc, June (b. 1916)
Hilliard, Harriet (1909–1994)
Hoffmann, Gertrude (1871–1966)
Holliday, Judy (1921–1965)
Horne, Lena (1917—)
Irwin, May (1862–1938)
Janis, Elsie (1889–1956)
Johnson, Julie (1903–1973)
Johnson, Osa (1894–1953)
Jones, Sissieretta (1869–1933)
Joyce, Peggy Hopkins (1893–1957)
Kane, Helen (1904–1966)
Keller, Helen (1880–1968)
Kellerman, Annette (1886–1975)
La Belle Marie (c. 1882–1935)
Lane, Lola (1909–1981)
La Roy, Rita (1907–1993)
La Rue, Grace (1880–1956)
Lawrence, Gertrude (1898–1952)
Lee, Gypsy Rose (1914–1970)
Lee, Jane (c. 1912–1957)
Leitzel, Lillian (1892–1931)
Lillie, Beatrice (1894–1989)
Loftus, Cissie (1876–1943)
Loftus, Marie (1857–1940)
Logan, Ella (1913–1969)
Lokelani, Princess Lei (c. 1898–1921)
Lopokova, Lydia (c. 1892–1981)
Lord, Pauline (1890–1950)
Love, Mabel (1874–1953)
Mabley, Jackie (1894–1975)
MacDonald, Jeanette (1903–1965)
Mack, Nila (1891–1953)
Macy, Anne Sullivan (1866–1936)
Madison, Cleo (1883–1964)
Marmein, Irene (1894–1972)
Marmein, Miriam (1897–1970)
Marmein, Phyllis (1908–1994)
Martin, Sara (1884–1955)
Mathis, June (1892–1927)
Maxwell, Elsa (1883–1963)
Maxwell, Vera (c. 1892–1950)
McDaniel, Hattie (1895–1952)
McKinney, Nina Mae (c. 1912–1967)
McPartland, Marian (1920—)
Menzelli, Lola (c. 1898–1951)
Mercer, Mabel (1900–1983)
Merman, Ethel (1912–1984)
Miles, Lizzie (1895–1963)
Miller, Marilyn (1898–1936)
Millman, Bird (1895–1940)
Mitchell, Abbie (1884–1960)
Moore, Grace (1898–1947)
Moran, Polly (1884–1952)
Morgan, Helen (1900–1941)
Morgan, Marion (c. 1887–1971)
Morris, Clara (1847–1925)
Musidora (1884–1957)
Orkin, Ruth (1921–1985)
Pavlova, Anna (1881–1931)
Pickford, Mary (1893–1979)
Picon, Molly (1898–1992)
Ponselle, Rosa (1897–1981)
Porter, Katherine Anne (1890–1980)
Potter, Maureen (1925–2004)
Primus, Pearl (1919–1994)
Printemps, Yvonne (1894–1977)
Puck, Eva (1892–1979)
Rainey, Ma (1886–1939)
Ralston, Esther (1902–1994)
Raye, Martha (1916–1994)
Réjane, Gabrielle (1857–1920)
Riggs, Katherine Witchie (d. 1967)
Rogers, Ginger (1911–1995)
Roth, Lillian (1910–1980)
Russell, Lillian (1861–1922)
Scheff, Fritzi (1879–1954)
Schumann-Heink, Ernestine (1861–1936)
Scott, Esther Mae (1893–1979)
Sedgwick, Josie (1898–1973)
Seeley, Blossom (1891–1974)
Shields, Ella (1879–1952)
Shipman, Nell (1892–1970)
Simon, Simone (1910–2005)
Simpson, Adele (1903–1995)
Smith, Bessie (1894–1937)
Smith, Clara (1894–1935)
Smith, Kate (1907–1986)
Smith, Mamie (1883–1946)
Smith, Trixie (1895–1943)
Spivey, Victoria (1906–1976)
St. Denis, Ruth (1877–1968)
Stonehouse, Ruth (1892–1941)
Sunshine, Marion (1894–1963)
Sweet, Blanche (1895–1986)
Tanguay, Eva (1878–1947)
Taylor, Eva (1895–1977)
Taylor, Laurette (1884–1946)
Tempest, Florence (c. 1891–?)
Templeton, Fay (1865–1939)
Terriss, Ellaline (1871–1971)
Thomas, Edna (1885–1974)
Tucker, Sophie (1884–1966)
Turner, Florence E. (c. 1888–1946)
Vail, Myrtle (1888–1978)
Vaughan, Sarah (1924–1990)
Walker, Nancy (1922–1992)
Warren, Lavinia (1841–1919)
Waters, Ethel (1896–1977)
Weeks, Ada May (1898–1978)
West, Mae (1893–1980)
Westley, Helen (1875–1942)
White, Frances (1896–1969)
Whitty, May (1865–1948)
Wiesenthal, Grete (1885–1970)
Williams, Mary Lou (1910–1981)
Wilson, Edith (1896–1981)
Withers, Jane (1926—)
Wood, Matilda (1831–1915)
Young, Clara Kimball (1890–1960)

VENTRILOQUIST

See Puppeteer.

VETERINARIAN

Hinson, Lois E. (1926—)
Kennedy, Suzanne (c. 1955—)
Kilbourn, Annelisa (1967–2002)
Turner, Debbye (1966—)
Uvarov, Olga (1910–2001)

VICEREINE

Curzon, Mary Leiter (1870–1906)
Mountbatten, Edwina Ashley (1901–1960)

VICOMTESS

See Viscountess.

VINTNER

Clicquot, Mme (1777–1866)

VIOLINIST

Alda, Frances (1879–1952)
Apgar, Virginia (1909–1974)
Aranyi, Jelly d' (1895–1966)
Bacewicz, Grazyna (1909–1969)
Bach, Maria (1896–1978)
Barbi, Alice (1862–1948)
Bowen, Catherine Drinker (1897–1973)
Brown, Iona (1941–2004)

Butler, Helen May (1867–1957)
Caldwell, Sarah (1924—)
Carlson, Gretchen (c. 1966—)
Chambers, Norah (1905–1989)
Chung, Kyung-Wha (1948—)
Clarke, Rebecca (1886–1979)
Comberti, Micaela (1952–2003)
Davies, Gwendoline (1882–1951)
DeLay, Dorothy (1917–2002)
De Vito, Gioconda (1907–1994)
Eckhardt-Gramatté, S.C. (1899–1974)
Fachiri, Adila (1886–1962)
Harrison, May (1891–1959)
Honeyman, Susie
Krauss, Alison (1971—)
La Palme, Béatrice (1878–1921)
Macnaghten, Anne (1908–2002)
Magnes, Frances (1919—)
Menuhin, Hephzibah (1920–1981)
Midori (1971—)
Morini, Erica (1904–1995)
Myrtil, Odette (1898–1978)
Neruda, Wilma (c. 1838–1911)
Neveu, Ginette (1919–1949)
Nilsson, Christine (1843–1921)
Parlow, Kathleen (1890–1963)
Pejacevic, Dora (1885–1923)
Powell, Maud (1867–1920)
Rockmore, Clara (1911–1998)
Rosé, Alma (1906–1944)
Rowell, Mary (1958—)
Salerno-Sonnenberg, Nadja (1961—)
Sembrich, Marcella (1858–1935)
Speyer, Leonora (1872–1956)
Thompson, Helen (1908–1974)
Urso, Camilla (1842–1902)

VIROLOGIST
Horstmann, Dorothy M. (1911–2001)
Krim, Mathilde (1926—)

VISCOUNTESS
Alford, Marianne Margaret (1817–1888)
Astor, Nancy Witcher (1879–1964)
Cary, Elizabeth (1586–1639)
Churchill, Anne (1684–1716)
Constance (fl. 1100)
Disraeli, Mary Anne (1792–1872)
Eccles, Mary Hyde (1912–2003)
Elphinstone, Hester Maria (1764–1857)
Elphinstone, Margaret Mercer (1788–1867)
Ermengarde of Narbonne (c. 1120–c. 1194)
Finch, Anne (1631–1679)
Fitzclarence, Amelia (1807–1858)
Fitzhugh, Anne (fl. 1466)
Grandval, Marie Felicia (1830–1907)
Howard, Muriel (d. 1512)
Josephine (1763–1814)
Lamb, Emily (d. 1869)
Margaret de Rohan (1397–1428)
Melbourne, Elizabeth (d. 1818)
Messenger, Margaret (1948—)
Nelson, Frances Herbert (1761–1831)
Noailles, Marie-Laure de (1902–1970)
Rhondda, Margaret (1883–1958)
Saint Mars, Gabrielle de (1804–1872)
Smythe, Emily Anne (c. 1845–1887)
Spencer, Henrietta Frances (1761–1821)
Spencer, Sarah (1955—)
Stephanie de Beauharnais (1789–1860)
Villiers, Barbara (d. 1708)

VISIONARY
See Prophet/sibyl/visionary.

VOCALIST
See Singer.

VOICE TEACHER
Cappiani, Luisa (b. 1835)
Cigna, Gina (b. 1900)
DeGaetani, Jan (1933–1989)
Liebling, Estelle (1880–1970)
Marchesi, Mathilde (1821–1913)
Novello-Davies, Clara (1861–1943)
Palmer, Elizabeth Mary (1832–1897)
Williams, Camilla (1922—)

VOLLEYBALL PLAYER
Abramova, Nelli (1940—)
Aguero, Taimaris (1977—)
Akhaminova, Yelena (1961—)
Alvares, Ana (1965—)
Andreyuk, Yelena (1958—)
Arakida, Yuko (1954—)
Artamonova, Evguenia (1975—)
Aszkielowiczowna, Halina (1947—)
Badulina, Svetlana (1960—)
Baik Myung-Sun (1956—)
Barros, Leila (1971—)
Barros, Zoila (1976—)
Beauprey, Jeanne (1961—)
Becker, Carolyn (1958—)
Bede, Shelda (1973—)
Behar, Adriana (1969—)
Belikova, Anastasia (1979—)
Bell, Regla (1971—)
Bergen, Larisa (1949—)
Biltauere, Astra (1944—)
Bodziak, Ericleia (1969—)
Borisova, Verka (1955—)
Borozna, Lyudmila (1954—)
Bozhurina, Tsvetana (1952—)
Buldakova, Lyudmila (1938—)
Bullin, Katharina (1959—)
Byon Kyung-Ja (1956—)
Caldeira, Hilma (1972—)
Calderon Diaz, Rosir (1984—)
Calderon Martinez, Mercedes (1965—)
Carrillo de la Paz, Nancy (1986—)
Carvajal Rivera, Magaly Esther (1968—)
Cervera, Luisa (1964—)
Chachkova, Lioubov (1977—)
Chang Hee-Sook (1955—)
Chebukina, Yelena (1965—)
Chen Jing (1975—)
Chernyshova, Lyudmila (1952—)
Chisholm, Linda (1957—)
Chmielnicka, Lidia (1939—)
Chukanova, Olga (1980—)
Cobbs, Janet (1967—)
Coimbra, Erika (1980—)
Conceicao, Janina (1972—)
Connelly, Ana Paula (1972—)
Cook, Natalie (1975—)
Costa, Marlenis (1973—)
Crockett, Rita Louise (1957—)
Cross-Battle, Tara (1968—)
Cui Yongmei (1969—)
Cunha, Marcia Regina (1969—)
Czajkowska, Krystyna (1936—)
Czekalla, Barbara (1951—)
De La Guerra, Alejandra (1968—)
Dias, Virna (1971—)
Dimitrova, Rositsa (1955—)
Dimitrova, Tanya (1957—)
Egami, Yumi (1957—)
Endicott, Lori (1967—)
Fajardo, Demisse (1964—)
Feng Kun (1978—)
Fernandez, Ana Ivis (1973—)
Fetzer, Brigitte (1956—)
Flachmeier, Laurie (1959—)
Fraga, Kely (1974—)
Francia, Mirka (1975—)
Fujimoto, Yuko (1943—)
Fukunaka, Sachiko (1946—)
Furukawa, Makiko (1947—)
Gallardo, Miriam (1968—)
Galushka, Vera (1945—)
Gamova, Ekaterina (1980—)
Garcia, Rosa (1964—)
Gato, Idalmis (1971—)
Georgieva, Maya (1955—)
Godina, Elena (1977—)
Gogova, Tanya (1950—)
Golimowska, Maria (1932—)
Gonobobleva, Tatyana Pavlovna (1948—)
Gratcheva, Tatiana (1973—)
Green, Debbie (1958—)
Gureyeva, Lyudmila (1943—)
Hama, Keiko (1947—)
Handa, Yuriko (1940—)
Heim, Andrea (1961—)
He Qi (1973—)
Heredia, Isabel (1963—)
Hiro, Norie (1965—)
Hirose, Miyoko (1959—)
Horny, Katherine (1969—)
Hou Yuzhu (1963—)
Hwang He-Suk (1945—)
Hyman, Flo (1954–1986)
Iida, Takako (1946—)
Ilieva, Valentina (1962—)
Inoue, Setsuko (1946—)
Ishida, Kyoko (1960—)
Isobe, Sata (1944—)
Iwahara, Toyoko (1945—)
Izquierdo, Lilia (1967—)
Jakubowska, Krystyna (1942—)
Jang Ok-Rim (1948—)
Jiang Ying (1963—)
Jo Hea-Jung (1953—)
Jung Soo-Nok (1955—)
Kagabu, Yoko (1960—)
Kaisheva, Rumyana (1955—)
Kanesaka, Katsuko (1954—)
Kang Ok-Sun (1946—)
Kasai, Masae (1933—)
Kato, Kiyomi (1953—)
Katusheva, Marita (1938—)
Kemner, Caren (1965—)
Kim Myong-Suk (1947—)
Kim Su-Dae (1942—)
Kim Yeun-Ja (1943—)
Kim Zung-Bok (1945—)
Kojima, Yukiyo (1945—)
Kondo, Masako (1941—)
Kordaczukowna, Danuta (1939–1988)
Korukovets, Alexandra (1976—)
Korytova, Svetlana (1968—)
Kostrzewa, Ute (1961—)
Kozakova, Olga (1951—)
Kozyreva, Lyubov (1956—)
Kraynova, Tatyana (1967—)
Kristolova, Anka (1955—)
Krivosheyeva, Olga (1961—)
Krupowa, Krystyna (1939—)
Kudreva, Natalya (1942—)
Kumysh, Marina (1964—)
Kushner, Natalya (1954—)
Lai Yawen (1970—)
Lang Ping (1960—)
Lantratov, Vera (1947—)
Latamblet Daudinot, Norka (1962—)
Lawanson, Ruth (1963—)
Ledwigowa, Jozefa (1935—)
Lee Soon-Bok (1950—)
Lee Soo-Nok (1955—)
Lehmann, Heike (1962—)

Leontyeva, Galina (1941—)
Liang Yan (1961—)
Li Guojun (1966—)
Liley, Tammy (1965—)
Lima, Ricarda (1979—)
Li Shan (1980—)
Liu Xiaoning (1975—)
Liu Yanan (1980—)
Li Yan (1976—)
Li Yanjun (1963—)
Li Yueming (1968—)
Loginova, Lidiya (1951—)
Lopes, Katia (1973—)
Luis, Alejandrina (1967—)
Lukanina, Ninel (1937—)
Maeda, Echiko (1952—)
Magers, Rose (1960—)
Makogonova, Irina (1959—)
Ma Kum-Ja (1955—)
Malaga, Natalia (1964—)
Marko, Jadwiga (1939—)
Martinez Adlun, Maybelis (1977—)
Masakayan, Liz (1964—)
Matsuda, Noriko (1952—)
Matsumura, Katsumi (1944—)
Matsumura, Yoshiko (1941—)
May, Misty (1977—)
McPeak, Holly (1969—)
Mesa Luaces, Liana (1977—)
Mikhaylovskaya, Lyudmila (1937—)
Mishak, Valentina (1942—)
Mitsuya, Yuko (1958—)
Miyajima, Keiko (1965—)
Miyamoto, Emiko (1937—)
Morita, Kimie (1958—)
Morozova, Natalia (1973—)
Moser, Ana (1968—)
Mummhardt, Christine (1951—)
Munoz Carrazana, Aniara (1980—)
Muradyan, Nina (1954—)
Nakada, Kumi (1965—)
Niemczykowa, Barbara (1943—)
Nikishina, Svetlana (1958—)
Nikolaeva, Olga (1972—)
Nikulina, Marina (1963—)
Odaka, Emiko (1962—)
Oden, Elaina (1967—)
Oden, Kimberley (1964—)
O'Farrill, Raisa (1972—)
Ogiyenko, Valentina (1965—)
Oinuma, Sumie (1946—)
Okamoto, Mariko (1951—)
Oliveira, Elisangela (1978—)
Oliveira, Walewska (1979—)
Ortiz Calvo, Tania (1965—)
Ortiz Charro, Yahima (1981—)
Osadchaya, Liliya (1953—)
Ostromecka, Krystyna (1948—)
Otani, Sachiko (1965—)
Paek Myong-Suk (1954—)
Pan Wenli (1969—)
Parkhomchuk, Irina (1965—)
Park Mi-Kum (1955—)
Peppler, Mary Jo (1944—)
Perez del Solar, Gabriela (1968—)
Petrunova, Silva (1956—)
Pires Tavares, Sandra (1973—)
Plotnikova, Elena (1978—)
Ponyaeva, Tatyana (1946—)
Porzecowna, Elzbieta (1945—)
Potachova, Olga (1976—)
Pottharst, Kerri-Ann (1965—)
Pueschel, Karin (1958—)
Radzevich, Nadezhda (1953—)
Ramirez Hechevarria, Daymi (1983—)
Razumova, Natalya (1961—)
Reece, Gabrielle (1970—)
Ri Chun-Ok (1947—)
Rodrigues, Karin (1971—)
Rodrigues, Monica (1967—)
Roffeis, Karla (1958—)
Roshchina, Tatyana (1941—)
Rostova, Anna (1950—)
Ruddins, Kimberly (1963—)
Rudovskaya, Lyubov (1950—)
Ruiz, Yumilka (1978—)
Rutkowska, Jadwiga (1934—)
Ryom Chun-Ja (1942—)
Ryskal, Inna (1944—)
Ryzhova, Antonina (1934—)
Safronova, Natalia (1979—)
Salikhova, Roza (1944—)
Samuel Ramos, Adriana (1966—)
Sanchez Salfran, Marta (1973—)
Sanders, Tonya (1968—)
Sanglard, Ana Flavia (1970—)
Sargsian, Inessa (1972—)
Sarycheva, Tatyana (1949—)
Sasaki, Setsuko (1944—)
Sato, Liane (1964—)
Schmidt, Martina (1960—)
Schultz, Annette (1957—)
Shchetinina, Lyudmila (1951—)
Sheshenina, Marina (1985—)
Shibuki, Ayano (1941—)
Shimakage, Seiko (1949—)
Shinozaki, Yoko (1945—)
Shiokawa, Michiko (1951—)
Shirai, Takako (1952—)
Shishikura, Kunie (1946—)
Shkurnova, Olga (1962—)
Sidorenko, Tatyana (1966—)
Silva, Jackie (1962—)
Silva, Raquel (1978—)
Sliwkowa, Maria (1935—)
Smirnova, Irina (1968—)
Smoleyeva, Nina (1948—)
Solovova, Olga (1953—)
Song Nina (1980—)
Souza, Helia (1970—)
Sugiyama, Kayoko (1961—)
Su Huijuan (1964—)
Sun Yue (1973—)
Suruagy, Sandra (1963—)
Szczesniewska, Zofia (1943–1988)
Takayama, Suzue (1946—)
Takayanagi, Shoko (1954—)
Tanida, Kuniko (1939—)
Tebenikhina, Irina (1978—)
Tellez Palacio, Dulce M. (1983—)
Tichtchenko, Elizaveta (1975—)
Tiit, Cecilia (1962—)
Tikhonina, Tamara (1934—)
Tiourina, Elena (1971—)
Torrealva, Gina (1961—)
Torres, Regla (1975—)
Tyurina, Lyubov (1943—)
Uribe, Cenaida (1964—)
Vasilevskaia, Elena (1978—)
Venturini, Fernanda (1970—)
Volkova, Yelena (1960—)
Vollertsen, Julie (1959—)
Walsh, Kerri (1978—)
Wang Lina (1978—)
Wang Yajun (1962—)
Wang Yi (1973—)
Wang Ziling (1972—)
Weishoff, Paula (1962—)
Westendorf, Anke (1954—)
Wiechowna, Wanda (1946—)
Williams, Natalie (1970—)
Woodstra, Susan (1957—)
Wu Dan (1968—)
Wu Yongmei (1975—)
Yamamoto, Noriko (1945—)
Yamazaki, Yaeko (1950—)
Yang Hao (1980—)
Yang Xiaojun (1963—)
Yang Xilan (1961—)
Yano, Hiromi (1955—)
Yokoyama, Juri (1955—)
Yoshida, Mariko (1954—)
Yoshida, Setsuko (1942—)
Youngs, Elaine (1970—)
Yu Jung-Hye (1954—)
Yu Kyung-Hwa (1953—)
Yun Young-Nae (1952—)
Yusova, Zoya (1948—)
Zetterlund, Yoko (1969—)
Zhang Na (1980—)
Zhang Ping (1982—)
Zhang Rongfang (1957—)
Zhang Yuehong (1975—)
Zhao Ruirui (1981—)
Zheng Meizhu (1962—)
Zhou Suhong (1979—)
Zhou Xiaolan (1957—)
Zhu Ling (1957—)
Zhu Yunying (1978—)

VOODOOIST
Jackson, Julia (fl. 19th c.)

WAKEBOARDER
Copeland-Durham, Emily (1984—)
Friday, Dallas J. (1986—)
Gaytan, Andrea
Hamilton, Tara (1982—)
Hammarberg, Gretchen
Kent, Leslie (1981—)
Major, Maeghan (1984—)
Marquardt, Melissa (1983—)

WALKER (DISTANCE)
James, Esther Marion Pretoria (1900–1990)
Sears, Eleanora (1881–1968)

WAR CRIMINAL
Dorn, Erna (1912–1953)
Grese, Irma (1923–1945)
Koch, Ilse (1906–1967)
Mandel, Maria (1912–1948)
Oberheuser, Herta (1911–1978)
Plavsic, Biljana (1930—)

WAR PHOTOGRAPHER
See Combat photographer.

WAR-RELIEF WORKER
Abegg, Elisabeth (1882–1974)
Allen, Viola (1867–1948)
Barton, Clara (1821–1912)
Bethune, Mary McLeod (1875–1955)
Bullowa, Emilie (1869–1942)
Churchill, Clementine (1885–1977)
Crothers, Rachel (1878–1958)
Deland, Margaret (1857–1945)
Drexel, Constance (1894–1956)
Dulles, Eleanor Lansing (1895–1996)
Duncan, Isadora (1878–1927)
Elliott, Maxine (1868–1940)
Fowle, Elida Rumsey (1842–1919)
Hainisch, Marianne (1839–1936)
Hallowell, Anna (1831–1905)
Harrison, Hazel (1883–1969)
Haslam, Anna (1829–1922)
Hobhouse, Emily (1860–1926)
Hoge, Jane (1811–1890)
Hoover, Lou Henry (1874–1944)

Hurst, Fannie (1889–1968)
Jacobs, Harriet A. (1813–1897)
Köstler, Marie (1879–1965)
Kübler-Ross, Elisabeth (1926–2004)
Lovejoy, Esther Pohl (1869–1967)
Marie of Rumania (1875–1938)
Maxtone Graham, Joyce (1901–1953)
Minor, Virginia L. (1824–1894)
Mountbatten, Edwina Ashley (1901–1960)
Paget, Muriel (1876–1938)
Pankhurst, Sylvia (1882–1960)
Porter, Eliza Chappell (1807–1888)
Rohde, Ruth Bryan Owen (1885–1954)
Ryder, Sue (1923–2000)
Salm-Salm, Agnes, Princess (1840–1912)
Smythe, Emily Anne (c. 1845–1887)
Street, Jessie (1889–1970)
Strong, Anna Louise (1885–1970)
Tingley, Katherine (1847–1929)
Truth, Sojourner (c. 1797–1883)
Van Vorst, Marie Louise (1867–1936)
Wharton, Edith (1862–1937)
Whitty, May (1865–1948)
Wise, Louise Waterman (1874–1947)
Wittenmyer, Annie Turner (1827–1900)
Woolsey, Sarah Chauncey (1835–1905)
Wormeley, Katharine Prescott (1830–1908)
Wrede, Mathilda (1864–1928)

WARRIOR
See Soldier/warrior.

WATERCOLORIST
Airy, Anna (1882–1964)
Allingham, Helen Patterson (1848–1926)
Anderson, Anne (1874–1930)
Andrews, Doris (1920–2003)
Basseporte, Magdalene (?–c. 1780)
Beale, Mary (1632–1699)
Bennett, Gwendolyn B. (1902–1981)
Bianco, Pamela (1906–1994)
Bodichon, Barbara (1827–1891)
Bonacci Brunamonti, Maria Alinda (1841–1903)
Bonheur, Rosa (1822–1899)
Bridges, Fidelia (1834–1923)
Butler, Elizabeth Thompson (1846–1933)
Cam, Helen M. (1885–1968)
Cameron, Kate (1874–1965)
Carrington, Leonora (1917—)
Cassatt, Mary (1844–1926)
Cavell, Edith (1865–1915)
Corbaux, Fanny (1812–1883)
de Kooning, Elaine Fried (1918–1989)
Eakins, Susan Hannah (1851–1938)
Fanshawe, Catherine Maria (1765–1834)
Fassett, Cornelia (1831–1898)
Fletcher, Alice Cunningham (1838–1923)
Gág, Wanda (1893–1946)
Garzoni, Giovanna (1600–1670)
Gibbs, May (1877–1969)
Goodridge, Sarah (1788–1853)
Graves, Nancy (1940–1995)
Green, Elizabeth Shippen (1871–1954)
Greenaway, Kate (1846–1901)
Hall, Anne (1792–1863)
Hamnett, Nina (1890–1956)
Harrison, Caroline Scott (1832–1892)
Hartigan, Grace (1922—)
Hepworth, Barbara (1903–1975)
Hodgkins, Frances (1869–1947)
Hoffman, Malvina (1885–1966)
Hokinson, Helen E. (1893–1949)
Holden, Evelyn (1877–c. 1969)
Jekyll, Gertrude (1843–1932)
John, Gwen (1876–1939)
King, Jessie Marion (1875–1949)
Lehmann, Lotte (1888–1976)
Lemmon, Sarah Plummer (1836–1923)
Lewis, Graceanna (1821–1912)
Mackintosh, Margaret (1865–1933)
Martin, Maria (1796–1863)
Mee, Margaret (1909–1988)
Mirabal de González, Patria (1924–1960)
Mirabal de Guzmán, María Teresa (1936–1960)
Mirabal de Tavárez, Minerva (1927–1960)
Moran, Mary Nimmo (1842–1899)
Morgan, Barbara (1900–1992)
Morgan, Maud (1903–1999)
Morisot, Berthe (1841–1895)
Münter, Gabriele (1877–1962)
Neel, Alice (1900–1984)
Nicholls, Rhoda Holmes (1854–1930)
Outhwaite, Ida Rentoul (1888–1960)
Palmer, Frances Flora (1812–1876)
Parsons, Betty Pierson (1900–1982)
Peale, Anna Claypoole (1791–1878)
Peale, Margaretta Angelica (1795–1882)
Peale, Sarah Miriam (1800–1885)
Peña, Tonita (1893–1949)
Pinney, Eunice Griswold (1770–1849)
Popova, Liubov (1889–1924)
Potter, Beatrix (1866–1943)
Redpath, Anne (1895–1965)
Rentoul, Annie Isobel (c. 1855–1928)
Rey, Margret (1906–1996)
Sachs, Nelly (1891–1970)
Siddal, Elizabeth (1829–1862)
Sofronova, Antonina (1892–1966)
Sowerby, Millicent (1878–1967)
Stephens, Alice Barber (1858–1932)
Tallien, Thérésa (1773–1835)
Tarrant, Margaret (1888–1959)
Tauber-Arp, Sophie (1889–1943)
Walcott, Mary Morris (1860–1940)
Welty, Eudora (1909–2001)
Zhukova, Maria (1804–1855)

WATER-POLO PLAYER
Akobia, Marina (1975—)
Allucci, Carmela (1970—)
Anikeeva, Ekaterina (1965—)
Araujo, Alexandra (1972—)
Asilian, Dimitra (1972—)
Beauregard, Robin (1979—)
Bosurgi, Silvia (1979—)
Castle, Naomi (1974—)
Conti, Francesca (1972—)
di Mario, Tania (1979—)
Dingeldein, Margaret (1980—)
Ellinaki, Georgia (1974—)
Estes, Ellen (1978—)
Fox, Joanne (1979—)
Frank, Jacqueline (1980—)
Gigli, Elena (1985—)
Golda, Natalie (1981—)
Grego, Melania (1973—)
Gusterson, Bridgette (1973—)
Hankin, Simone
Higgins, Yvette (1978—)
Hooper, Kate
Johnson, Courtney (1974—)
Karagianni, Eftychia (1973—)
Konoukh, Sofia (1980—)
Koroleva, Maria (1974—)
Koutouzova, Natalia (1975—)
Kouzina, Svetlana (1975—)
Kozompoli, Stavroula (1974—)
Lara, Georgia (1980—)
Liosi, Kyriaki (1979—)
Lorenz, Ericka (1981—)
Malato, Giusy (1971—)
Mayer, Bronwyn
Melidoni, Aniopi (1977—)
Miller, Gail
Mills, Melissa (1973—)
Moody, Heather (1973—)
Munro, Thalia (1982—)
Musumeci, Maddalena (1976—)
Mylonaki, Anthoula (1984—)
Oikonomopoulou, Aikaterini (1978—)
Orwig, Bernice (1976—)
O'Toole, Maureen (1961—)
Payne, Nicolle (1976—)
Petri, Heather (1978—)
Petrova, Ioulia (1979—)
Petrova, Tatiana (1973—)
Ragusa, Cinzia (1977—)
Roumpesi, Antigoni (1983—)
Rulon, Kelly (1984—)
Rytova, Galina (1975—)
Sciolti, Gabriella (1974—)
Sheehy, Kathy (1970—)
Simmons, Coralie (1977—)
Smurova, Elena (1973—)
Stachowski, Amber (1983—)
Swail, Julie (1972—)
Tokoun, Elena (1974—)
Tolkounova, Irina (1971—)
Toth, Noemi (1976—)
Vassilieva, Ekaterina (1976—)
Villa, Brenda (1980—)
Watson, Debbie (1965—)
Weekes, Liz (1971—)
Woodhouse, Danielle
Woods, Taryn (1975—)
Zanchi, Manuela (1977—)

WEAVER
Albers, Anni (1899–1994)
Conboy, Sara McLaughlin (1870–1928)
Eriksen, Gunn (1956—)
Furtseva, Ekaterina (1910–1974)
Grizodubova, Valentina (1910–1993)
Hicks, Sheila (1934—)
Hutchinson, Amy Hadfield (1874–1971)
Liebes, Dorothy (1897–1972)
Mairet, Ethel (1872–1952)
Mulvany, Josephine (1901–1967)
Mulvany, Sybil Mary (1899–1983)
Pitini-Morera, Hariata Whakatau (1871/72?–1938)
Saarinen, Loja (1879–1968)
Strengell, Marianne (1909–1998)
Tauber-Arp, Sophie (1889–1943)

WEIGHTLIFTER
Batsiushka, Hanna (1981—)
Chatziioannou, Ioanna (1973—)
Chen Xiaomin (1977—)
Chen Yanqing (1979—)
Ding Meiyuan (1979—)
Haworth, Cheryl (1983—)
Jang Mi-Ran (1983—)
Jimenez Mendivil, Soraya (1977—)
Kameaim, Wandee (1978—)
Kasaeva, Zarema (1987—)
Krutzler, Eszter (1981—)
Kuo Yi-Hang (1975—)
Li Feng-Ying (1975—)
Lin Weining (1979—)
Liu Chunhong (1985—)
Li Zhuo (1981—)
Malleswari, Karnam (1975—)
Markus, Erzsebet (1969—)
Mosquera Mena, Mabel (1969—)
Nott, Tara (1972—)
Ogbeifo, Ruth (1967—)

Polsak, Udomporn (1981—)
Popova, Valentina (1972—)
Ri Song Hui (1978—)
Rumbewas, Raema Lisa (1980—)
Skakun, Nataliya (1981—)
Slamet, Winarni Binti (1975—)
Sri, Indriyani (1978—)
Stukalava, Tatsiana (1975—)
Suta, Khassaraporn (1971—)
Tang Gonghong (1979—)
Taylan, Nurcan (1983—)
Thongsuk, Pawina (1979—)
Urrutia, Maria Isabel (1965—)
Wiratthaworn, Aree (1980—)
Wrobel, Agata (1981—)
Yang Xia (1977—)
Zabolotnaia, Natalia (1985—)

WELFARE WORKER
See Social-welfare worker.

WHEELCHAIR MARATHONER
Driscoll, Jean (1967—)

WHISTLEBLOWER
Coughlin, Paula A. (c. 1961—)
Ragghianti, Marie (1942—)
Silkwood, Karen (1946–1974)

WINDSURFER
Cochran, Angela (1965—)

WIRELESS OPERATOR
Khan, Noor Inayat (1914–1944)

WITCH (ACCUSED)
Balfour, Alison (d. 1596)
Bathory, Elizabeth (1560–1614)
Bavent, Madeleine (fl. 1642)
Bernauer, Agnes (d. 1435)
Boleyn, Anne (c. 1507–1536)
Bowen, Elizabeth (1899–1973)
Brinvilliers, Marie de (1630–1676)
Cadière, Catherine (b. 1709)
David, Catherine (fl. 15th c.)
Demandols de la Palud, Madeleine (fl. 17th century)
Deshayes, Catherine (d. 1680)
Droiturière, Marion la (d. 1390)
Fontanges, Duchesse de (1661–1681)
French "Witches" (14th–16th centuries)
Galigaï, Leonora (c. 1570–1617)
Hicks, Elizabeth (1705–1716)
Hicks, Mary (d. 1716)
Horne, Janet (d. 1727)
Joanna of Navarre (c. 1370–1437)
Joan of Arc (c. 1412–1431)
Judith of Bavaria (802–843)
Kyteler, Alice (fl. 1324)
Lemp, Rebecca (d. 1590)
Murray, Elizabeth (1626–1698)
Nurse, Rebecca (1621–1692)
Pieronne of Brittany (d. 1430)
Saenger von Mossau, Renata (1680–1749)
Sampson, Agnes (d. 1591)
Shipton, Mother (1488–1561)
Shore, Jane (c. 1445–c. 1527)
Trapnel, Anna (fl. 1642–1661)
Wenham, Jane (d. 1730)
Willums, Sigbrit (fl. 1507–1523)

WOMEN'S-RIGHTS ACTIVIST

Abaijah, Josephine (1942—)
Abayomi, Oyinkansola (1897–1990)
Aberdeen, Ishbel Maria Gordon, Lady (1857–1939)
Abiertas, Josepha (1894–1929)
Abzug, Bella (1920–1998)
Achurch, Janet (1864–1916)
Adam, Juliette la Messine (1836–1936)
Adams, Abigail (1744–1818)
Addams, Jane (1860–1935)
Adler, Emma (1858–1935)
Aidoo, Ama Ata (1942—)
Aikin, Lucy (1781–1864)
Akhmatova, Anna (1889–1966)
Allart, Hortense (1801–1879)
Allen, Florence Ellinwood (1884–1966)
Allen, Mary Sophia (1878–1964)
Ames, Blanche (1878–1969)
Ames, Jessie Daniel (1883–1972)
Anderson, Elizabeth Garrett (1836–1917)
Andree, Elfrida (1841–1929)
Angelou, Maya (1928—)
Anneke, Mathilde Franziska (1817–1884)
Anselmi, Tina (1927—)
Anthony, Katharine Susan (1877–1965)
Anthony, Susan B. (1820–1906)
Anthony, Susan B., II (1916–1991)
Anttila, S. Inkeri (1916—)
Aptheker, Bettina (1944—)
Arceo, Liwayway (1924—)
Archambault, Mademoiselle (c. 1724–?)
Armand, Inessa (1874–1920)
Astell, Mary (1666–1731)
Aston, Luise (1814–1871)
Astorga, Nora (1949–1988)
Atkinson, Ti-Grace (1939—)
Auclert, Hubertine (1848–1914)
Audouard, Olympe (1830–1890)
Augspurg, Anita (1857–1943)
Austin, Mary Hunter (1868–1934)
Aves, Isabel Annie (1887–1938)
Ayrton, Hertha Marks (1854–1923)
Babcock, Maud May (1867–1954)
Bagley, Sarah (b. 1806)
Bailey, Hannah Johnston (1839–1923)
Bajer, Matilde (1840–1934)
Baker, S. Josephine (1873–1945)
Balfour, Frances (1858–1931)
Barakat, Hidiya Afifi (1898–1969)
Barnes, Djuna (1892–1982)
Barney, Natalie Clifford (1876–1972)
Barney, Nora (1883–1971)
Barns, Cornelia Baxter (1888–1941)
Barot, Madeleine (1909–1995)
Barreno, Maria Isabel (1938—)
Barrett, Kate Waller (1857–1925)
Barry, Leonora M. (1849–1930)
Barton, Clara (1821–1912)
Bass, Mary Elizabeth (1876–1956)
Bateson, Mary (1865–1906)
Bäumer, Gertrud (1873–1954)
Bayly, Ada Ellen (1857–1903)
Beale, Dorothea (1831–1906)
Bear-Crawford, Annette (1853–1899)
Beard, Mary Ritter (1876–1958)
Beauvoir, Simone de (1908–1986)
Becker, Lydia (1827–1890)
Beere, Thekla (1901–1991)
Begtrup, Bodil (1903–1987)
Bellamy, Madge (1899–1990)
Bellil, Samira (1972–2004)
Belmont, Alva Smith (1853–1933)
Bemberg, Maria Luisa (1922–1995)
Benedict, Ruth (1887–1948)
Bennett, Louie (1870–1956)
Benson, Stella (1892–1933)
Bernardino, Minerva (1907–1998)
Besant, Annie (1847–1933)
Besnyö, Eva (1910–2003)
Bethune, Louise Blanchard (1856–1913)
Beynon, Francis Marion (1884–1951)
Billington-Greig, Teresa (1877–1964)
Black, Clementina (1854–1922)
Blackburn, Helen (1842–1903)
Blackwell, Alice Stone (1857–1950)
Blake, Lillie Devereux (1833–1913)
Blatch, Harriot Stanton (1856–1940)
Bloomer, Amelia Jenks (1818–1894)
Bloor, Ella Reeve (1862–1951)
Bodichon, Barbara (1827–1891)
Bohm-Schuch, Clara (1879–1936)
Boissevain, Inez M. (1886–1916)
Boissevain, Mia (1878–1959)
Bol Poel, Martha (1877–1956)
Bondfield, Margaret (1873–1953)
Bonnevie, Margarete Ottilie (1884–1970)
Booth, Evangeline (1865–1950)
Botchkareva, Maria (1889–?)
Boucherett, Jessie (1825–1905)
Bradwell, Myra (1831–1894)
Braun, Lily (1865–1916)
Bré, Ruth (1862–1911)
Breckinridge, Sophonisba Preston (1866–1948)
Bremer, Fredrika (1801–1865)
Brennan, Anna Teresa (1879–1962)
Brinvilliers, Marie de (1630–1676)
Brion, Hélène (1882–1962)
Brittain, Vera (1893–1970)
Brooks, Romaine (1874–1970)
Brown, Hallie Quinn (c. 1845–1949)
Brown, Olympia (1835–1926)
Brown, Rosemary (1930—)
Brown Blackwell, Antoinette (1825–1921)
Brunschvicg, Cécile (1877–1946)
Bryant, Louise (1885–1936)
Bryant, Sophie (1850–1922)
Büchner, Luise (1821–1877)
Budzynska-Tylicka, Justyna (1876–1936)
Bugbee, Emma (1888–1981)
Burns, Lucy (1879–1966)
Burroughs, Nannie Helen (c. 1878–1961)
Butler, Josephine (1828–1906)
Cadilla de Martínez, Maria (1886–1951)
Calkins, Mary Whiton (1863–1930)
Cambridge, Ada (1844–1926)
Campoamor, Clara (1888–1972)
Cannon, Annie Jump (1863–1941)
Canth, Minna (1844–1897)
Carabillo, Toni (1926–1997)
Carlén, Emilia (1807–1892)
Carney, Winifred (1887–1943)
Carpenter, Mary (1807–1877)
Carroll, Anna Ella (1815–1894)
Carter, Angela (1940–1992)
Carter, Eunice Hunton (1899–1970)
Cary, Mary Ann Shadd (1823–1893)
Cary, Phoebe (1824–1871)
Casgrain, Thérèse (1896–1981)
Castellanos, Rosario (1925–1974)
Catt, Carrie Chapman (1859–1947)
Cauer, Minna (1841–1922)
Chapin, Augusta (1836–1905)
Charlotte (1896–1985)
Charteris, Catherine Morice (1835–1918)
Chase, Agnes Meara (1869–1963)
Châtelet, Émilie du (1706–1749)
Chattopadhyaya, Kamaladevi (1903–1988)
Chauvin, Jeanne (1862–1926)
Cheney, Ednah Dow (1824–1904)
Chevenix, Helen (1886–1963)
Child, Lydia Maria (1802–1880)
Christine de Pizan (c. 1363–c. 1431)
Cilento, Phyllis (1894–1987)
Claflin, Tennessee (1846–1923)
Clarke, Mary Goulden (d. 1910)
Clisby, Harriet (1830–1931)

Cobbe, Frances Power (1822–1904)
Collett, Camilla (1813–1895)
Cooper, Anna J. (c. 1858–1964)
Corbett, Marie (1859–1932)
Corbett-Ashby, Margery (1882–1981)
Costa, Maria Velho de (b. 1938)
Cousins, Margaret (1878–1954)
Cowan, Edith (1861–1932)
Craik, Dinah Maria Mulock (1826–1887)
Crandall, Prudence (1803–1890)
Crane, Caroline Bartlett (1858–1935)
Cullis, Winifred Clara (1875–1956)
Cunningham, Minnie Fisher (1882–1964)
Curzon, Irene (1896–1966)
Cutler, Hannah Conant (1815–1896)
Dall, Caroline Wells (1822–1912)
Dalrymple, Learmonth White (1827–1906)
Daniels, Mabel Wheeler (1878–1971)
Dark, Eleanor (1901–1985)
Davey, Constance (1882–1963)
David, Caroline Edgeworth (1856–1951)
Davies, Emily (1830–1921)
Davies, Margaret Llewelyn (1861–1944)
Davis, Dorothy Hilliard (1917–1994)
Davis, Paulina Wright (1813–1876)
Davison, Emily (1872–1913)
Day, Dorothy (1897–1980)
Debo, Angie (1890–1988)
de Cleyre, Voltairine (1866–1912)
De Costa, Maria Velho (b. 1938)
Demorest, Ellen Curtis (1824–1898)
Deng Yingchao (1903–1992)
Deng Yuzhi (b. 1900)
Denison, Flora MacDonald (1867–1921)
Dennett, Mary Ware (1872–1947)
Deraismes, Maria (1828–1894)
Deroin, Jeanne-Françoise (1805–1894)
Despard, Charlotte (1844–1939)
Deutsch, Helene (1884–1982)
Devanny, Jean (1894–1962)
Dexter, Caroline (1819–1884)
Dickinson, Anna E. (1842–1932)
Diggs, Annie LePorte (1848–1916)
Dilke, Emily (1840–1904)
Dirie, Waris (1967—)
Di Robilant, Daisy, Countess (fl. 1922–1933)
Dittmar, Louise (1807–1884)
Dixie, Lady Florence (1857–1905)
Dohm, Hedwig (1831–1919)
Doolittle, Hilda (1886–1961)
Doremus, Sarah Platt (1802–1877)
Dornemann, Luise (1901–1992)
Dorr, Rheta Childe (1866–1948)
Douglas, Marjory Stoneman (1890–1998)
Dransfeld, Hedwig (1871–1925)
Dreier, Katherine Sophie (1877–1952)
Dreier, Margaret (1868–1945)
Dreier, Mary Elisabeth (1875–1963)
Drew, Jane (1911–1996)
Drexel, Constance (1894–1956)
Drummond, Flora (1869–1949)
Duchêne, Gabrielle (1870–1954)
Duff Gordon, Lucy (1862–1935)
Dulac, Germaine (1882–1942)
Dunbar-Nelson, Alice (1875–1935)
Duniway, Abigail Scott (1834–1915)
Durack, Fanny (1889–1956)
Durand, Marguerite (1864–1936)
Dworkin, Andrea (1946–2005)
Earhart, Amelia (1897–1937)
Earle, Alice Morse (1851–1911)
Eastman, Crystal (1881–1928)
Ebadi, Shirin (1947—)
Eberle, Abastenia St. Leger (1878–1942)
Edwards, Henrietta Muir (1849–1933)
Efflatoun, Inji (1923–1989)
Efflatoun, Inji
Egyptian Feminism (1800–1980)
Elizabeth von Habsburg (1883–1963)
Elliott, Harriet Wiseman (1884–1947)
El Saadawi, Nawal (1931—)
Espín de Castro, Vilma (1934—)
Evans, Elizabeth Glendower (1856–1937)
Evans, Mary Anne (1819–1880)
Faithfull, Emily (1835–1895)
Farrokhzad, Forugh (1935–1967)
Fawcett, Millicent Garrett (1847–1929)
Felton, Rebecca Latimer (1835–1930)
Ferber, Edna (1885–1968)
Fern, Fanny (1811–1872)
Ferrin, Mary Upton (1810–1881)
Fickert, Auguste (1855–1910)
Fiedler, Bobbi (1937—)
Figes, Eva (1932—)
Figueroa, Ana (1907–1970)
Firestone, Shulamith (1945—)
First, Ruth (1925–1982)
Fisher, Cicely Corbett (1885–1959)
Fisher, Dorothy Canfield (1879–1958)
Flanagan, Hallie (1889–1969)
Fleeson, Doris (1901–1970)
Fleming, Williamina Paton (1857–1911)
Fletcher, Alice Cunningham (1838–1923)
Florence, Mary Sargant (1857–1954)
Flynn, Elizabeth Gurley (1890–1964)
Foltz, Clara (1849–1934)
Ford, Betty (1918—)
Ford, Isabella O. (1855–1924)
Fowler, Lydia Folger (1822–1879)
Franklin, Miles (1879–1954)
Freeman, Alice (1857–1936)
Freundlich, Emmy (1878–1948)
Friedan, Betty (1921–2006)
Fukuda Hideko (1865–1927)
Fuller, Margaret (1810–1850)
Fullerton, Mary Eliza (1868–1946)
Gage, Frances D. (1808–1884)
Gage, Matilda Joslyn (1826–1898)
Gale, Zona (1874–1938)
Galindo de Topete, Hermila (1896–1954)
Gardener, Helen Hamilton (1853–1925)
Gardiner, Muriel (1901–1985)
Garfield, Lucretia (1832–1918)
Garrett, Mary Elizabeth (1854–1915)
Garvey, Amy Jacques (1896–1973)
Gayatri Devi (1919—)
Gellhorn, Martha (1908–1998)
Gérin-Lajoie, Marie (1867–1945)
Gilman, Charlotte Perkins (1860–1935)
Gilmore, Mary (1865–1962)
Ginsburg, Ruth Bader (1933—)
Goldman, Emma (1869–1940)
Goldstein, Vida (1869–1949)
Goldthwaite, Anne Wilson (1869–1944)
Gomez, Sara (1943–1974)
Gonne, Maud (1866–1953)
Goodbody, Buzz (1946–1975)
Gordon, Laura de Force (1838–1907)
Gore-Booth, Eva (1870–1926)
Gouges, Olympe de (1748–1793)
Gourd, Emilie (1879–1946)
Grant, Julia (1826–1902)
Gray, Hanna Holborn (1930—)
Grey, Maria Georgina (1816–1906)
Griffing, Josephine White (1814–1872)
Grimké, Angelina E. (1805–1879)
Grimké, Charlotte L. Forten (1837–1914)
Grimké, Sarah Moore (1792–1873)
Guilbert, Yvette (1865–1944)
Gutiérrez de Mendoza, Juana Belén (1875–1942)
Gutteridge, Helena Rose (1879–1960)
Gwynne-Vaughan, Helen (1879–1967)
Hackett, Joan (1942–1983)
Hagan, Ellen (1873–1958)
Hagman, Lucina (1853–1946)
Hainisch, Marianne (1839–1936)
Haldane, Charlotte (1894–1969)
Hale, Ruth (1886–1934)
Hale, Sarah Josepha (1788–1879)
Halimi, Gisèle (1927—)
Hall, Anna Maria (1800–1881)
Hall, Radclyffe (1880–1943)
Hamilton, Cicely (1872–1952)
Hamilton, Mary (1882–1966)
Hanaford, Phebe Ann (1829–1921)
Hanim, Latife (1898–1975)
Hansteen, Aasta (1824–1908)
Harding, Florence K. (1860–1924)
Harper, Frances E.W. (1825–1911)
Harper, Ida Husted (1851–1931)
Harraden, Beatrice (1864–1936)
Harriman, Florence Jaffray (1870–1967)
Harris, Barbara (1930—)
Hasbrouck, Lydia Sayer (1827–1910)
Haslam, Anna (1829–1922)
Hatcher, Orie Latham (1868–1946)
Havemeyer, Louisine (1855–1929)
Haviland, Laura S. (1808–1898)
Hay, Mary Garrett (1857–1928)
Hayden, Mary (1862–1942)
Hays, Mary (1760–1843)
Hebard, Grace Raymond (1861–1936)
Height, Dorothy (1912—)
Henrotin, Ellen Martin (1847–1922)
Henry, Alice (1857–1943)
Hepburn, Katharine (1907—)
Héricourt, Jenny Poinsard d' (1809–1875)
Hesselgren, Kerstin (1872–1962)
Heymann, Lida (1867–1943)
Hidari Sachiko (1930—)
Hillman, Bessie (1889–1970)
Hiratsuka Raichō (1886–1971)
Hirsch, Rachel (1870–1953)
Holley, Marietta (1836–1926)
Hollingworth, Leta Stetter (1886–1939)
Hollins, Marion B. (1892–1944)
Holm, Jeanne (1921—)
Holmes, Julia Archibald (1838–1887)
Holt, Winifred (1870–1945)
Holtby, Winifred (1898–1935)
Homaira (1916–2002)
Hooker, Isabella Beecher (1822–1907)
Hopkins, Ellice (1836–1904)
Horne, Alice Merrill (1868–1948)
Horney, Karen (1885–1952)
Horta, Maria Teresa (1938—)
Hosmer, Harriet (1830–1908)
Hossain, Rokeya Sakhawat (1880–1932)
Houston, Lucy (1858–1936)
Howard, Rosalind Frances (1845–1921)
Howe, Julia Ward (1819–1910)
Howland, Emily (1827–1929)
How-Martyn, Edith (1875–1954)
Hrotsvitha of Gandersheim (c. 935–1001)
Huck, Winnifred Sprague Mason (1882–1936)
Hughes, Sarah T. (1896–1985)
Hunt, Harriot Kezia (1805–1875)
Hunt, Violet (1866–1942)
Hunton, Addie D. Waites (1875–1943)
Hurst, Fannie (1889–1968)
Ibarbourou, Juana de (1895–1979)
Ichikawa Fusae (1893–1981)
Idar, Jovita (1885–1946)
Ihrer, Emma (1857–1911)
Inglis, Elsie Maud (1864–1917)
Inyama, Rosemary (b. 1903)

Ireland, Patricia (1945—)
Irwin, Inez Haynes (1873–1970)
Jaburkova, Jozka (d. 1944)
Jacob, Rosamund (1888–1960)
Jacobs, Aletta (1854–1929)
Jacobs, Harriet A. (1813–1897)
Jagan, Janet (1920—)
Jambrišak, Marija (1847–1937)
Jameson, Storm (1891–1986)
Janeway, Elizabeth (1913–2005)
Jesenská, Milena (1896–1945)
Jesse, Fryniwyd Tennyson (1888–1958)
Jewett, Sarah Orne (1849–1909)
Jewsbury, Geraldine (1812–1880)
Jiagge, Annie (1918–1996)
Johnson, Adelaide (1859–1955)
Johnston, Mary (1870–1936)
Jordan, Elizabeth Garver (1865–1947)
Juana Inés de la Cruz (1651–1695)
Juchacz, Marie (1879–1956)
Kairi, Evanthia (1797–1866)
Kamal, Sufia (1911–1999)
Kang Keqing (1911–1992)
Kartini (1879–1904)
Kautsky, Luise (1864–1944)
Kehajia, Kalliopi (1839–1905)
Kéita, Aoua (1912–1979)
Keller, Helen (1880–1968)
Kelley, Abby (1810–1887)
Kelley, Florence (1859–1932)
Kelly, Petra (1947–1992)
Kendall, Marie Hartig (1854–1943)
Kennedy, Florynce (1916–2000)
Kenney, Annie (1879–1953)
Kenyon, Dorothy (1888–1972)
Kéthly, Anna (1889–1976)
Key, Ellen (1849–1926)
Khan, Begum Liaquat Ali (1905–1990)
King, Billie Jean (1943—)
Kirchwey, Freda (1893–1976)
Kishida Toshiko (1863–1901)
Kitzinger, Sheila (1929—)
Kobrynska, Natalia Ivanovna (1855–1920)
Kollontai, Alexandra (1872–1952)
Kollwitz, Käthe (1867–1945)
Kolstad, Eva (1918–1998)
Konopnicka, Maria (1842–1910)
Kovalskaia, Elizaveta (1851–1943)
Kreps, Juanita (1921—)
Krog, Gina (1847–1916)
Kuhn, Maggie (1905–1995)
Kuliscioff, Anna (c. 1854–1925)
Kushida Fuki (1899–2001)
Labé, Louise (c. 1523–1566)
Lacombe, Claire (1765–?)
La Follette, Belle Case (1859–1931)
La Follette, Fola (1882–1970)
Lagerlöf, Selma (1858–1940)
Lampkin, Daisy (1883–1965)
Landeta, Matilde (1913—)
Lang, Marie (1858–1934)
Lange, Helene (1848–1930)
La Rochefoucauld, Edmée, Duchesse de (1895–1991)
Laskaridou, Aikaterini (1842–1916)
Lathrop, Julia Clifford (1858–1932)
Lawrence, Susan (1871–1947)
Lawson, Louisa (1848–1920)
Lear, Frances (1923–1996)
Lease, Mary Elizabeth (1853–1933)
Lee, Mary (1821–1909)
Lefaucheux, Marie-Helene (1904–1964)
Le Gallienne, Eva (1899–1991)
Leginska, Ethel (1886–1970)
Lehmann, Rosamond (1901–1990)
Lemel, Nathalie (1827–1921)
Lemlich, Clara (1888–1982)
Léo, André (1832–1900)
Léon, Pauline (1758–?)
Leontias, Sappho (1832–1900)
Lerner, Gerda (1920—)
Leslie, Miriam Folline Squier (1836–1914)
Le Sueur, Meridel (1900–1996)
Levison, Mary (1923—)
Lewald, Fanny (1811–1889)
Lewis, Graceanna (1821–1912)
Livermore, Mary A. (1820–1905)
Lockwood, Belva Ann (1830–1917)
Longshore, Hannah E. (1819–1901)
Lorde, Audre (1934–1992)
Lovejoy, Esther Pohl (1869–1967)
Lowney, Shannon (1969–1994)
Lozier, Clemence S. (1813–1888)
Lucas, Margaret Bright (1818–1890)
Luce, Clare Boothe (1903–1987)
Lutz, Berta (1894–1976)
Lynn, Kathleen (1874–1955)
Lyons, Enid (1897–1981)
Lytton, Constance (1869–1923)
MacFall, Frances E. (1854–1943)
MacGill, Elsie (d. 1980)
MacGill, Helen Gregory (1871–1947)
Mackinnon, Catherine A. (1946—)
Macmillan, Chrystal (1871–1937)
Macphail, Agnes (1890–1954)
Macurdy, Grace Harriet (1866–1946)
Madison, Cleo (1883–1964)
Mahoney, Mary Eliza (1845–1926)
Majerová, Marie (1882–1967)
Malaika, Nazik al- (1923–1992)
Manning, Marie (c. 1873–1945)
Mansfield, Arabella (1846–1911)
Manus, Rosa (1881–1942)
Markievicz, Constance (1868–1927)
Martin, Anne Henrietta (1875–1951)
Martin, Lillien Jane (1851–1943)
Martineau, Harriet (1802–1876)
Martinson, Moa (1890–1964)
Marzouk, Zahia (1906–1988)
Masaryk, Charlotte Garrigue (1850–1923)
Masiotene, Ona (1883–1949)
Mason, Lucy Randolph (1882–1959)
Matsui, Yayori (1934–2002)
Mayreder, Rosa (1858–1938)
McClung, Nellie L. (1873–1951)
McCormick, Katharine Dexter (1875–1967)
McCormick, Ruth Hanna (1880–1944)
McCoubrey, Margaret (1880–1955)
McCracken, Elizabeth (c. 1865–1944)
McCracken, Mary Ann (1770–1866)
McCulloch, Catharine (1862–1945)
McDowell, Anne E. (1826–1901)
McKane, Alice Woodby (1865–1948)
McKinney, Louise (1868–1931)
Mead, Lucia Ames (1856–1936)
Meena (1956–1987)
Mehta, Hansa (1897–1995)
Mesta, Perle (1889–1975)
Mészáros, Márta (1931—)
Meyer, Annie Nathan (1867–1951)
Meyers, Jan (1928—)
Meynell, Alice (1847–1922)
Michaëlis, Karin (1872–1950)
Michel, Louise (1830–1905)
Millay, Edna St. Vincent (1892–1950)
Miller, Alice Duer (1874–1942)
Millett, Kate (1934—)
Mink, Paule (1839–1901)
Minor, Virginia L. (1824–1894)
Mirabal de González, Patria (1924–1960)
Mirabal de Guzmán, María Teresa (1936–1960)
Mirabal de Tavárez, Minerva (1927–1960)
Miró, Pilar (1940–1997)
Misme, Jane (1865–1935)
Mitchell, Hannah (1871–1956)
Mitchell, Juliet (1934—)
Mitchell, Roma (1913–2000)
Monod, Sarah (1836–1912)
Montreal Massacre (1989)
Montseny, Federica (1905–1994)
Moore, Audley (1898–1997)
Moreau de Justo, Alicia (1885–1986)
Morris, Esther Hobart (1814–1902)
Mott, Lucretia (1793–1880)
Mozzoni, Anna Maria (1837–1920)
M'rabet, Fadéla (1935—)
Mundt, Klara Müller (1814–1873)
Murnaghan, Sheelagh (1924–1993)
Murphy, Emily (1868–1933)
Murray, Judith Sargent (1751–1820)
Murray, Margaret (1863–1963)
Murray, Pauli (1910–1985)
Mussey, Ellen Spencer (1850–1936)
Nasser, Tahia (1923—)
Nassif, Malak Hifni (1886–1918)
Nathan, Maud (1862–1946)
Navratilova, Martina (1956—)
Negri, Ada (1870–1945)
Nelken, Margarita (1896–1968)
Newman, Pauline (1887–1986)
Nguyen Thi Dinh (1920–1992)
Niboyet, Eugénie (1797–1883)
Nichols, Clarina (1810–1885)
Nikolaeva, Klavdiia (1893–1944)
Nin, Anais (1903–1977)
Noailles, Anna de (1876–1933)
Noce, Teresa (1900–1980)
Nolan, Mae Ella (1886–1973)
Noor al-Hussein (1951—)
Noronha, Joana de (fl. c. 1850)
Norris, Kathleen (1880–1966)
Norton, Caroline (1808–1877)
Nováková, Teréza (1853–1912)
Nutting, Mary Adelaide (1858–1948)
Nyad, Diana (1949—)
O'Brien, Kate (1897–1974)
Ocampo, Victoria (1890–1979)
O'Day, Caroline (1869–1943)
O'Hare, Kate Richards (1876–1948)
Olberg, Oda (1872–1955)
O'Neill, Rose Cecil (1874–1944)
O'Reilly, Leonora (1870–1927)
Orzeszkowa, Eliza (1841–1910)
Osburn, Lucy (1835–1891)
O'Sullivan, Mary Kenney (1864–1943)
Ottenberg, Nettie Podell (1887–1982)
Ottesen-Jensen, Elise (1886–1973)
Otto-Peters, Luise (1819–1895)
Ovington, Mary White (1865–1951)
Owens-Adair, Bethenia (1840–1926)
Pahlavi, Ashraf (1919—)
Palencia, Isabel de (1878–c. 1950)
Palm, Etta Aelders (1743–1799)
Palmer, Bertha Honoré (1849–1918)
Pankhurst, Adela (1885–1961)
Pankhurst, Christabel (1880–1958)
Pankhurst, Emmeline (1858–1928)
Pankhurst, Sylvia (1882–1960)
Pappenheim, Bertha (1859–1936)
Pardo Bazán, Emilia (1852–1921)
Park, Maud Wood (1871–1955)
Parkes, Bessie Rayner (1829–1925)
Parlby, Irene (1868–1965)
Parren, Kalliroe (1861–1940)
Parturier, Françoise (1919—)
Paterson, Emma (1848–1886)
Paul, Alice (1885–1977)

Peabody, Elizabeth Palmer (1778–1853)
Pechey-Phipson, Edith (1845–1908)
Peck, Annie Smith (1850–1935)
Pelham, Mary Singleton Copley (c. 1710–1789)
Pelletier, Madeleine (1874–1939)
Perón, Eva (1919–1952)
Perovskaya, Sonia (1853–1881)
Perry, Eleanor (1915–1981)
Petersen, Alicia O'Shea (1862–1923)
Pethick-Lawrence, Emmeline (1867–1954)
Phillips, Lena Madesin (1881–1955)
Pierangeli, Rina Faccio (1876–1960)
Pinkham, Lydia E. (1819–1883)
Pollitzer, Anita (1894–1975)
Polson, Florence Ada Mary Lamb (1877–1941)
Popp, Adelheid (1869–1939)
Potonié-Pierre, Eugénie (1844–1898)
Pound, Louise (1872–1958)
Preston, May Wilson (1873–1949)
Procter, Adelaide (1825–1864)
Prou, Suzanne (1920–1995)
Ptaschkina, Nelly (1903–1920)
Pugh, Sarah (1800–1884)
Qiu Jin (c. 1875–1907)
Ramirez, Sara Estela (1881–1910)
Rankin, Jeannette (1880–1973)
Ransome-Kuti, Funmilayo (1900–1978)
Rathbone, Eleanor (1872–1946)
Ray, Charlotte E. (1850–1911)
Reagan, Maureen (1941–2001)
Reddy, Helen (1942—)
Reid, Helen Rogers (1882–1970)
Reinig, Christa (1926—)
Remond, Sarah Parker (1826–1894)
Reuter, Gabriele (1859–1941)
Rhondda, Margaret (1883–1958)
Ricard, Marthe (1889–1982)
Rich, Adrienne (1929—)
Richards, Shelah (1903–1985)
Ricker, Marilla (1840–1920)
Rinehart, Mary Roberts (1876–1958)
Ripley, Martha Rogers (1843–1912)
Rives, Amélie (1863–1945)
Robins, Elizabeth (1862–1952)
Robinson, Harriet Hanson (1825–1911)
Robinson, Mary (1944—)
Rochefort, Christiane (1917–1998)
Rodríguez, Evangelina (1879–1947)
Rodríguez de Tió, Lola (1843–1924)
Rohde, Ruth Bryan Owen (1885–1954)
Roland, Pauline (1805–1852)
Rome, Esther (1945–1995)
Rosa Manus (1881–1942)
Rose, Ernestine (1810–1892)
Roussel, Nelly (1878–1922)
Rowson, Susanna (1762–1824)
Royden, A. Maude (1876–1956)
Royer, Clémence (1830–1902)
Ruffin, Josephine St. Pierre (1842–1924)
Russell, Dora (1894–1986)
Russell, Lillian (1861–1922)
Rye, Maria Susan (1829–1903)
Sabin, Florence (1871–1953)
Sackville-West, Vita (1892–1962)
Sadat, Jehan (1933—)
Safford, Mary Jane (1834–1891)
Sage, Margaret Olivia (1828–1918)
Salmon, Lucy Maynard (1853–1927)
Salomon, Alice (1872–1948)
Samoilova, Konkordiya (1876–1921)
Sanford, Maria Louise (1836–1920)
Sanger, Margaret (1879–1966)
Sangster, Margaret (1838–1912)
Sarfatti, Margherita (1880–1961)
Sauvé, Jeanne (1922–1993)
Schacherer-Elek, Ilona (1907–1988)
Schary, Hope Skillman (1908–1981)
Schlesinger, Therese (1863–1940)
Schmahl, Jeanne (1846–1916)
Schneiderman, Rose (1882–1972)
Schreiber, Adele (1872–1957)
Schreiner, Olive (1855–1920)
Schroeder, Patricia (1940—)
Schwimmer, Rosika (1877–1948)
Scott, Ann London (1929–1975)
Scott, Rose (1847–1925)
Scudder, Janet (1869–1940)
Seaman, Elizabeth Cochrane (1864–1922)
Seidel, Amalie (1876–1952)
Selbert, Elisabeth (1896–1986)
Seton, Grace Gallatin (1872–1959)
Severance, Caroline M. (1820–1914)
Séverine (1855–1929)
Sewall, Lucy Ellen (1837–1890)
Sewall, May Wright (1844–1920)
Seymour, Mary F. (1846–1893)
Seyrig, Delphine (1932–1990)
Shaarawi, Huda (1879–1947)
Shafik, Doria (1908–1975)
Shapiro, Betty Kronman (1907–1989)
Shaver, Dorothy (1897–1959)
Shaw, Anna Howard (1847–1919)
Shaw, Mary G. (1854–1929)
Shaw, Pauline Agassiz (1841–1917)
Sheehy-Skeffington, Hanna (1877–1946)
Shelley, Mary (1797–1851)
Sheppard, Kate (1847–1934)
Sherwin, Belle (1868–1955)
Sherwood, Katharine Margaret (1841–1914)
Sherwood, Mary (1856–1935)
Shirreff, Emily (1814–1897)
Sidgwick, Eleonora Mildred (1845–1936)
Silang, Gabriela (1731–1763)
Silinga, Annie (1910–1983)
Simcox, Edith (1844–1901)
Simkhovitch, Mary (1867–1951)
Sinclair, May (1863–1946)
Sipilä, Helvi (1915—)
Sirota, Beate (1923—)
Smeal, Eleanor (1939—)
Smedley, Agnes (1892–1950)
Smith, Abby (1797–1878)
Smith, Elizabeth Oakes (1806–1893)
Smith, Julia (1792–1886)
Smith, Margaret Chase (1897–1995)
Smith, Mary Louise (1914–1997)
Smith, Zilpha Drew (1851–1926)
Smyth, Ethel (1858–1944)
Snyder, Alice D. (1887–1943)
Somerville, Nellie Nugent (1863–1952)
Southworth, E.D.E.N. (1819–1899)
Spain, Jayne (1927—)
Spence, Catherine (1825–1910)
Spencer, Anne (1882–1975)
St. Denis, Ruth (1877–1968)
Staël, Germaine de (1766–1817)
Stanton, Elizabeth Cady (1815–1902)
Stasova, Nadezhda (1822–1895)
Stead, Christina (1902–1983)
Steel, Dawn (1946–1997)
Steinem, Gloria (1934—)
Stephens, Kate (1853–1938)
Stevens, Lillian (1844–1914)
Stevenson, Sarah Hackett (1841–1909)
Stewart, Alice (1906–2002)
Stewart, Eliza Daniel (1816–1908)
Stewart, Isabel Maitland (1878–1963)
Stewart, Maria W. (1803–1879)
Stocks, Mary Danvers (1891–1975)
Stoecker, Helene (1869–1943)
Stone, Constance (1856–1902)
Stone, Lucinda Hinsdale (1814–1900)
Stone, Lucy (1818–1893)
Stopes, Marie (1880–1958)
Storni, Alfonsina (1892–1938)
Stowe, Emily Howard (1831–1903)
Strange, Michael (1890–1950)
Street, Jessie (1889–1970)
Stritt, Marie (1856–1928)
Strong, Harriet (1844–1929)
Strossen, Nadine (1950—)
Sullerot, Evelyne (1924—)
Summerskill, Edith (1901–1980)
Suzman, Helen (1917—)
Svetla, Caroline (1830–1899)
Svolou, Maria (d. 1976)
Swanwick, Anna (1813–1899)
Swisshelm, Jane Grey (1815–1884)
Tabouis, Geneviève (1892–1985)
Taggard, Genevieve (1894–1948)
Taylor, Harriet (1807–1858)
Taylor, Helen (1831–1907)
Taylor, Lucy Hobbs (1833–1910)
Taymuriyya, 'A'isha 'Ismat al- (1840–1902)
Tereshkova, Valentina (1937—)
Terrell, Mary Church (1863–1954)
Theodoropoulou, Avra (1880–1963)
Théroigne de Méricourt, Anne-Josèphe (1762–1817)
Thomas, M. Carey (1857–1935)
Thomas, Mary Myers (1816–1888)
Thompson, Clara (1893–1958)
Thompson, Dorothy (1893–1961)
Thompson, Elizabeth Rowell (1821–1899)
Thoresen, Cecilie (1858–1911)
Thorpe, Rose Hartwick (1850–1939)
Three Marias, The
Thygeson, Sylvie Thompson (1868–1975)
Tinayre, Marcelle (c. 1870–1948)
Tito, Jovanka Broz (1924—)
Tod, Isabella (1836–1896)
Todd, Marion Marsh (1841–post 1913)
Tomaszewicz-Dobrska, Anna (1854–1918)
Toyen (1902–1980)
Traba, Marta (1930–1983)
Tristan, Flora (1803–1844)
Troll-Borostyani, Irma von (1847–1912)
Troup, Augusta Lewis (c. 1848–1920)
Trubnikova, Mariia (1835–1897)
Truth, Sojourner (c. 1797–1883)
Tubman, Harriet (1821–1913)
Tucker, C. DeLores (1927–2005)
Tuqan, Fadwa (1917–2003)
Tusap, Srbuhi (1841–1901)
Tweedy, Hilda (b. 1911)
Tyabji, Kamila (1918–2004)
Upton, Harriet Taylor (1853–1945)
Uttley, Alison (1884–1976)
Uzès, Anne, Duchesse d' (1847–1933)
Vaa, Aslaug (1889–1965)
Valentine, Lila (1865–1921)
Valette, Aline (1850–1899)
Vanderbilt, Consuelo (1877–1964)
Van Grippenberg, Alexandra (1859–1913)
Van Kleeck, Mary Abby (1883–1972)
Van Lew, Elizabeth (1818–1900)
van Schurmann, Anna Maria (1607–1678)
Van Vorst, Marie Louise (1867–1936)
Varda, Agnes (1928—)
Vasconcellos, Karoline Michaëlis de (1851–1925)
Veil, Simone (1927—)
Vejjabul, Pierra (b. 1909)
Velho da Costa, Maria (1938—)
Vengerova, Zinaida (1867–1941)
Vernon, Mabel (1883–1975)
Vérone, Maria (1874–1938)
Villard, Fanny Garrison (1844–1928)
Voilquin, Suzanne (1801–1877)

Wägner, Elin (1882–1949)
Waite, Catherine (1829–1913)
Wald, Lillian D. (1867–1940)
Walker, Maggie Lena (1867–1934)
Walker, Mary Edwards (1832–1919)
Wallace, Zerelda G. (1817–1901)
Ward, Elizabeth Stuart Phelps (1844–1911)
Ward, Hortense (1872–1944)
Ward, Irene (1895–1980)
Warren, Mercy Otis (1728–1814)
Wattleton, Faye (1943—)
Way, Amanda M. (1828–1914)
Webb, Beatrice (1858–1943)
Weber, Helene (1881–1962)
Weber, Helene Marie (b. 1824)
Webster, Augusta (1837–1894)
Weddington, Sarah R. (1945—)
Weed, Ethel (1906–1975)
Weiss, Louise (1893–1983)
Wells, Emmeline B. (1828–1921)
Wells, Marguerite Milton (1872–1959)
Wells-Barnett, Ida (1862–1931)
Welsh, Lilian (1858–1938)
West, Rebecca (1892–1983)
Wheeler, Anna Doyle (1785–c. 1850)
White, Anna (1831–1910)
White, Sue Shelton (1887–1943)
Whiting, Lilian (1847–1942)
Whitman, Sarah Helen (1803–1878)
Whitney, Anne (1821–1915)
Whitney, Charlotte Anita (1867–1955)
Whitney, Dorothy Payne (1887–1968)
Whitton, Charlotte (1896–1975)
Wickham, Anna (1883–1947)
Wieland, Joyce (1931–1998)
Wilde, Jane (1821–1896)
Wilhelmine of Darmstadt (1765–1796)
Wilkinson, Ellen (1891–1947)
Willard, Emma Hart (1787–1870)
Willard, Frances E. (1839–1898)
Williams, Mary Wilhelmine (1878–1944)
Willing, Jennie Fowler (1834–1916)
Wilson, Charlotte (1854–1944)
Wilson, Margaret W. (1882–1973)
Windeyer, Mary (1836–1912)
Winfrey, Oprah (1954—)
Wittenmyer, Annie Turner (1827–1900)
Woerishoffer, Carola (1885–1911)
Wolf, Christa (1929—)
Wollstonecraft, Mary (1759–1797)
Wolstenholme-Elmy, Elizabeth (1834–1913)
Woodbury, Helen Sumner (1876–1933)
Woodhull, Victoria (1838–1927)
Woodward, Joanne (1930—)
Woolf, Virginia (1882–1941)
Woolley, Helen (1874–1947)
Woolley, Mary E. (1863–1947)
Woolson, Abba Goold (1838–1921)
Wootton, Barbara (1897–1988)
Workman, Fanny (1859–1925)
Wright, Frances (1795–1852)
Wright, Helena (1887–1982)
Wright, Martha Coffin (1806–1875)
Wu, Chien-Shiung (1912–1997)
Wunderlich, Frieda (1884–1965)
Wu Zetian (624–705)
Wylie, Ida A.R. (1885–1959)
Wyse Power, Jennie (1858–1941)
Xiang Jingyu (1895–1928)
Xiao Hong (1911–1942)
Yamada, Mitsuye (1923—)
Yamada Waka (1879–1956)
Yard, Molly (1912–2005)
Yevonde (1893–1975)
Yorkin, Peg (1927—)
Yosano Akiko (1878–1942)
Younger, Maud (1870–1936)
Zagorka (1873–1957)
Zayas y Sotomayor, María de (1590–c. 1650)
Zayyat, Latifa al- (1923—)
Zetkin, Clara (1857–1933)
Zetterling, Mai (1925–1994)
Ziyada, Mayy (1886–1941)

WOOL MERCHANT

Ponten, Clare van der (fl. 14th c.)
Rose of Burford (fl. 15th c.)
Wollerin, Cecilie (d. 1341)

WRESTLER

Gomis, Anna (1973—)
Hamaguchi, Kyoko (1978—)
Icho, Chiharu (1981—)
Icho, Kaori (1984—)
Legrand, Lise (1976—)
Maniourova, Gouzel (1978—)
McMann, Sara (1980—)
Merleni, Irini (1982—)
Miranda, Patricia (1979—)
Verbeek, Tonya (1977—)
Wang Xu (1985—)
Yoshida, Saori (1982—)

WRITER

See also Biographer.
See also Book reviewer.
See also Children's writer.
See also Columnist.
See also Combat correspondent.
See also Crime/Detective-fiction writer.
See also Culinary-arts writer.
See also Diarist.
See also Essayist.
See also Etiquette writer.
See also Fantasy/Science-fiction writer.
See also Foreign correspondent.
See also Gothic-fiction writer.
See also Historical-fiction writer.
See also Horror fiction writer.
See also Hymn writer.
See also Letter writer.
See also Medical writer.
See also Memoirist.
See also Mystery/Suspense fiction writer.
See also Nature writer.
See also Nonfiction writer.
See also Novelist.
See also Playwright.
See also Poet.
See also Regional writer.
See also Religious/spiritual writer.
See also Romance-fiction writer.
See also Satirist.
See also Scenarist.
See also Screenwriter.
See also Scriptwriter.
See also Short-fiction writer.
See also Sports writer.
See also Television/Radio writer.
See also Textbook writer.
See also Travel writer.
See also Young-adult writer.
Agate, May (1892–1960)
Alberti, Sophie (1826–1892)
Alfon, Estrella (1917–1982)
Ames, Eleanor Maria (1830–1908)
Andersen, Catherine Ann (1870–1957)
Anderson, Ethel Mason (1883–1958)
Atkins, Evelyn (c. 1910–1997)
Aubert, Mary Joseph (1835–1926)
Bain, Wilhelmina Sherriff (1848–1944)
Baker McLaglan, Eleanor Southey (1879–1969)
Basham, Maud Ruby (1879–1963)
Baughan, Blanche Edith (1870–1958)
Bergen, Polly (1929—)
Blackwell, Ellen Wright (1864–1952)
Blair, Emily Newell (1877–1951)
Bolton, Sarah Knowles (1841–1916)
Brown, Vanessa (1928–1999)
Bryant, Dorothy (1930—)
Burnett, Carol (1933—)
Campbell, Lady Colin (1949—)
Carroll, Gladys Hasty (1904–1999)
Cartagena, Teresa de (c. 1420–1470)
Cellier, Elizabeth (fl. 1679)
Clark, Kate Emma (1847–1926)
Cleobulina of Rhodes (fl. 570 BCE)
Cleopatra (fl. 1st c. BCE)
Coad, Nellie (1883–1974)
Cole, Edith (1870–1927)
Cottrell, Violet May (1887–1971)
Cowie, Bessie Lee (1860–1950)
Cunnington, Eveline Willert (1849–1916)
Denis, Louise (c. 1710–1790)
Dhuoda of Septimania (fl. 820–843)
Dorsey, Sarah Anne (1829–1879)
Drower, E.S. (1879–1972)
Du Faur, Emmeline Freda (1882–1935)
Duggan, Eileen May (1894–1972)
Edwards, Edna Park (c. 1895–1967)
Fitzgerald, Frances Scott (1921–1986)
Fraser, Shelagh (1922–2000)
Gaughin, Lorraine (1924–1974)
Gibson, Emily Patricia (1863/64?–1947)
Gillmore, Margalo (1897–1986)
Glinka, Avdotia Pavlovna (1795–1863)
Gunning, Elizabeth (1769–1823)
Halkett, Anne (1622–1699)
Hampshire, Susan (1938—)
Harris, Jane Elizabeth (c. 1852–1942)
Harsant, Florence Marie (1891–1994)
Hay, Mary (1901–1957)
Hetherington, Jessie Isabel (1882–1971)
Hewett, Ellen Anne (1843–1926)
Hickey, Mary St. Domitille (1882–1958)
Higgins, Sarah (1830–1923)
Innes, Catherine Lucy (1839/40–1900)
Irvine-Smith, Fanny Louise (1878–1948)
Ivan, Rosalind (1880–1959)
Knef, Hildegard (1925–2002)
Lawson, Joan (1907–2002)
Low, Caroline Sarah (1876–1934)
Maclean, Hester (1859–1932)
Macpherson, Margaret Louisa (1895–1974)
Macy, Gertrude (1904–1983)
Malcolm, Emilie Monson (1829/30–1905)
Marly, Florence (1918–1978)
Martin, Emma (1812–1851)
Martin, Hannah (1830–1903)
Martin, Mary Ann (1817–1884)
Mason, Pamela (1918–1996)
Meiser, Edith (1898–1993)
Miller, Patsy Ruth (1904–1995)
Moncrieff, Pérrine (1893–1979)
Morete, Maraea (1844–1907)
Morton, Katherine E. (1885–1968)
Mostel, Kate (1918–1986)
Myers, Phoebe (1866–1947)
Papakura, Makereti (1873–1930)
Polson, Florence Ada Mary Lamb (1877–1941)
Porter, Sarah (1791–1862)
Powell, Mary Sadler (1854/55?–1946)
Rees, Annie Lee (1864–1949)
Reeves, Magdalene Stuart (1865–1953)
Richmond, Mary Elizabeth (1853–1949)
Rollett, Hilda (1873–1970)
Ross, Forrestina Elizabeth (1860–1936)

Occupational Index

Rout, Ettie Annie (1877–1936)
Shayle George, Frances (c. 1827–1890)
Soper, Eileen Louise (1900–1989)
Suisted, Laura Jane (1840–1903)
White, Emily Louisa Merielina (1839–1936)
Wilson, Helen Mary (1869–1957)
Wilson, Margery (1896–1986)
Wood, Susan (1836–1880)

XOSA SINGER
Makeba, Miriam (1932—)

YIDDISH-THEATER ACTRESS
Adler, Celia (1890–1979)
Adler, Julia (1897–1995)
Adler, Sara (1858–1953)
Adler, Stella (1902–1993)
Appel, Anna (1888–1963)
Bozyk, Reizl (1914–1993)
Gersten, Berta (c. 1896–1972)
Goldberg, Rose (d. 1966)
Goldstein, Jennie (1896–1960)
Held, Anna (c. 1865–1918)
Jacobson, Henrietta (1906–1988)
Kalich, Bertha (1874–1939)
Kaminska, Ida (1899–1980)
Noemi, Lea (1883–1973)
Picon, Molly (1898–1992)
Schnitzer, Henriette (1891–1979)
Weissman, Dora (1881–1974)

YOUNG-ADULT WRITER
Enright, Elizabeth (1909–1968)
Mantle, Winifred Langford (1911–1983)
Sutcliff, Rosemary (1920–1992)

ZOO ADMINISTRATOR
Benchley, Belle (1882–1973)

ZOOLOGIST
Abercrombie, M.L.J. (1909–1984)
Anable, Gloria Hollister (1903–1988)
Bailey, Florence (1863–1948)
Bidder, Anna McClean (1903–2001)
Bonnevie, Kristine (1872–1948)
Boring, Alice Middleton (1883–1955)
Carothers, E. Eleanor (1882–1957)
Clapp, Cornelia Maria (1849–1934)
Colborn, Theodora (1927—)
Eales, Nellie B. (1889–1989)
Fossey, Dian (1932–1985)
Fretter, Vera (1905–1992)
Gordon, Isabella (1901–1988)
Guthrie, Mary Jane (1895–1975)
Hanson, Jean (1919–1973)
Harvey, Ethel Browne (1885–1965)
Hibbard, Hope (1893–1988)
Hyman, Libbie Henrietta (1888–1969)
Jenkin, Penelope M. (1902–1994)
Kirkaldy, Jane Willis (c. 1869–1932)
Manton, Sidnie (1902–1979)
McLaren, Anne Laura (1927—)
Mellanby, Helen (1911–2001)
Merian, Maria Sybilla (1647–1717)
Moody, Agnes Claypole (1870–1954)
Morgan, Ann Haven (1882–1966)
Moss, Cynthia (1940—)
Murtfeldt, Mary (1848–1913)
Nice, Margaret Morse (1883–1974)
Oppenheimer, Jane Marion (1911–1996)
Ormerod, Eleanor A. (1828–1901)
Patch, Edith (1876–1954)
Payne, Katy (1937—)
Rathbun, Mary Jane (1860–1943)
Ray, Dixy Lee (1914–1994)
Rees, Gwendolen (1906–1994)
Robertson, Muriel (1883–1973)
Rothschild, Miriam (1908–2005)
Sexton, Elsie Wilkins (1868–1959)
Shorten, Monica (1923–1993)
Slosson, Annie Trumbull (1838–1926)
Stanwood, Cordelia (1865–1958)
Tizard, Catherine (1931—)